COLLINS
FRENCH★ENGLISH
ENGLISH★FRENCH
DICTIONARY

Collins Dual Language Dictionaries
Published by Berkley Books

FRENCH/ENGLISH	ENGLISH/FRENCH DICTIONARY
GERMAN/ENGLISH	ENGLISH/GERMAN DICTIONARY
ITALIAN/ENGLISH	ENGLISH/ITALIAN DICTIONARY
SPANISH/ENGLISH	ENGLISH/SPANISH DICTIONARY

COLLINS

FRENCH★ENGLISH
ENGLISH★FRENCH
DICTIONARY

PIERRE-HENRI COUSIN

BERKLEY BOOKS, NEW YORK

General Editor
R. H. Thomas

The text of this dictionary has been
adapted from the Collins Gem
French-English, English-French
Dictionary

First published in this edition 1982

Contributors
Claude Nimmo, Lorna Sinclair, Philippe Patry,
Hélène Lewis, Elizabeth Campbell, Renée Birks

Editorial Staff
Catherine Love, Lesley Robertson

This Berkley book contains the complete
text of the original edition.
It has been completely reset in a typeface
designed for easy reading and was printed
from new film.

COLLINS FRENCH/ENGLISH · ENGLISH/FRENCH
DICTIONARY

A Berkley Book / published by arrangement with
Collins Publishers

PRINTING HISTORY
Collins Gem edition published 1979
Berkley edition / August 1982
Ninth printing / November 1986

ISBN: 0-425-10270-X

A BERKLEY BOOK ® TM 757,375
Berkley Books are published by The Berkley Publishing Group,
200 Madison Avenue, New York, New York 10016.
The name "BERKLEY" and the stylized "B" with design
are trademarks belonging to Berkley Publishing Corporation.

PRINTED IN THE UNITED STATES OF AMERICA

INTRODUCTION

L'usager qui désire comprendre l'anglais - qui déchiffre - trouvera dans ce dictionnaire un vocabulaire moderne et très complet, comprenant de nombreux composés et locutions appartenant à la langue contemporaine. Il trouvera aussi dans l'ordre alphabétique les principales formes irrégulières, avec un renvoi à la forme de base où figure la traduction, ainsi qu'abréviations, sigles et noms géographiques choisis parmi les plus courants.

L'usager qui veut s'exprimer - communiquer - dans la langue étrangère trouvera un traitement détaillé du vocabulaire fondamental, avec de nombreuses indications le guidant vers la traduction juste, et lui montrant comment l'utiliser correctement.

The user whose aim is to read and understand French will find in this dictionary a comprehensive and up-to-date wordlist including numerous phrases in current use. He will also find listed alphabetically the main irregular forms with a cross-reference to the basic form where a translation is given, as well as some of the most common abbreviations, acronyms and geographical names.

The user who wishes to communicate and to express himself in the foreign language will find clear and detailed treatment of all the basic words, with numerous indications pointing to the appropriate translation, and helping him to use it correctly.

abréviations	vi	abbreviations
symboles phonétiques	viii	phonetic symbols
FRANÇAIS - ANGLAIS	1	FRENCH - ENGLISH
ANGLAIS - FRANÇAIS	273	ENGLISH - FRENCH
le verbe français	492	French verb forms
les nombres et l'heure	494	numbers and time

ABRÉVIATIONS

ABBREVIATIONS

ABBREVIATIONS

adjectif, locution adjective	**a**	adjective, adjectival phrase
abréviation	**ab(b)r**	abbreviation
adverbe, locution adverbiale	**ad**	adverb, adverbial phrase
administration	**ADMIN**	administration
agriculture	**AGR**	agriculture
anatomie	**ANAT**	anatomy
architecture	**ARCHIT**	architecture
l'automobile	**AUT(O)**	the motor car and motoring
aviation, voyages aériens	**AVIAT**	flying, air travel
biologie	**BIO(L)**	biology
botanique	**BOT**	botany
anglais de Grande-Bretagne	**Brit**	British English
conjonction	**cj**	conjunction
langue familière (! emploi vulgaire)	**col (!)**	colloquial usage (! particularly offensive)
commerce, finance, banque	**COMM**	commerce, finance, banking
construction	**CONSTR**	building
nom utilisé comme adjectif, ne peut s'employer ni comme attribut, ni après le nom qualifié	**cpd**	compound element: noun used as an adjective and which cannot follow the noun it qualifies
cuisine, art culinaire	**CULIN**	cookery
déterminant: article, adjectif démonstratif ou indéfini etc	**dét, det**	determiner: article, demonstrative etc.
économie	**ECON**	economics
électricité, électronique	**ELEC**	electricity, electronics
exclamation, interjection	**excl**	exclamation, interjection
féminin	**f**	feminine
langue familière (! emploi vulgaire)	**fam (!)**	colloquial usage (! particularly offensive)
emploi figuré	**fig**	figurative use
(verbe anglais) dont la particule est inséparable du verbe	**fus**	(phrasal verb) where the particle cannot be separated from main verb
dans la plupart des sens; généralement	**gén, gen**	in most or all senses; generally
géographie, géologie	**GEO**	geography, geology
géométrie	**GEOM**	geometry
invariable	**inv**	invariable
irrégulier	**irg**	irregular
domaine juridique	**JUR**	law
grammaire, linguistique	**LING**	grammar, linguistics
masculin	**m**	masculine
mathématiques, algèbre	**MATH**	mathematics, calculus
médecine	**MED**	medical term, medicine
masculin ou féminin, suivant le sexe	**m/f**	either masculine or feminine depending on sex
domaine militaire, armée	**MIL**	military matters
musique	**MUS**	music
nom	**n**	noun
navigation, nautisme	**NAVIG, NAUT**	sailing, navigation
adjectif ou nom numérique	**num**	numeral adjective or noun
	o.s.	oneself
péjoratif	**péj, pej**	derogatory, pejorative
photographie	**PHOT(O)**	photography
physiologie	**PHYSIOL**	physiology
pluriel	**pl**	plural
politique	**POL**	politics
participe passé	**pp**	past participle
préposition	**prép, prep**	preposition
psychologie, psychiatrie	**PSYCH**	psychology, psychiatry

temps du passé	**pt**	past tense
nom non comptable: ne peut s'utiliser au pluriel	**q**	collective (uncountable) noun: is not used in the plural
quelque chose	**qch**	
quelqu'un	**qn**	
religions, domaine ecclésiastique	**REL**	religions, church service
	sb	somebody
enseignement, système scolaire et universitaire	**SCOL**	schooling, schools and universities
singulier	**sg**	singular
	sth	something
subjonctif	**sub**	subjunctive
sujet (grammatical)	**su(b)j**	(grammatical) subject
techniques, technologie	**TECH**	technical term, technology
télécommunications	**TEL**	telecommunications
télévision	**TV**	television
typographie	**TYP(O)**	typography, printing
anglais des USA	**US**	American English
verbe	**vb**	verb
verbe ou groupe verbal à fonction intransitive	**vi**	verb or phrasal verb used intransitively
verbe ou groupe verbal à fonction transitive	**vt**	verb or phrasal verb used transitively
zoologie	**ZOOL**	zoology
marque déposée	®	registered trademark
indique une équivalence culturelle	≈	introduces a cultural equivalent

TRANSCRIPTION PHONÉTIQUE   PHONETIC TRANSCRIPTION

CONSONNES   CONSONANTS

NB. **p, b, t, d, k, g** sont suivis d'une aspiration en anglais / are not aspirated in French.

poupée poupe	**p**	puppy pope
bombe	**b**	baby cab
tente thermal	**t**	tent strut
dinde	**d**	daddy mended
coq qui képi sac pastèque	**k**	cork kiss chord lock
gag gare bague gringalet	**g**	gag guess
sale ce ça dessous nation tous	**s**	so rice struts kiss crescent
zéro maison rose	**z**	cousin pods buzz zero
tache chat	**ʃ**	sheep sugar crash masher
gilet juge	**ʒ**	pleasure beige
	tʃ	church
	dʒ	judge general veg
fer phare gaffe paraphe	**f**	farm raffle
valve	**v**	very brave rev
	θ	thin sloth maths
	ð	that other loathe clothes
lent salle sol	**l**	little place ball
rare venir rentrer	**R**	
	r	rat rare stirring strut
maman femme	**m**	mummy ram bomber comb
non nonne	**n**	no ran running
gnôle agneau vigne	**ɲ**	
	ŋ	singing rang bank
hop ! (avec h aspiré)	**h**	hat reheat
yeux paille pied hier	**j**	yet
nouer oui	**w**	wall bewail
huile lui	**ɥ**	
	x	loch

DIVERS   MISCELLANEOUS

dans la transcription de l'anglais: le r final se prononce en liaison devant une voyelle	**∗**	in French wordlist: no liaison
dans la transcription de l'anglais: précède la syllabe accentuée	**'**	in French transcription: no liaison

VOYELLES VOWELS

NB. La mise en équivalence de certains sons n'indique qu'une ressemblance approximative.
The pairing of some vowel sounds only indicates approximate equivalence.

ici vie lyre	**i i:**	heel bead
	ɪ	hit pity
jouer été fermée	e	
lait jouet merci	ɛ	set tent
patte plat amour	a æ	bat apple
bas pâte	ɑ ɑ:	after car calm
	ʌ	fun cousin
le premier	ə	over above
beurre peur	œ	
peu deux	ø ə:	urn fern work
mort or homme	ɔ	wash pot
geôle mot dôme eau gauche	o ɔ:	born cork
genou roue	u	full soot
	u:	boon lewd
rue vêtu urne	y	

DIPHTONGUES DIPHTHONGS

ɪə	beer tier
ɛə	tear fair there
eɪ	date plaice day
aɪ	life buy cry
au	owl foul now
əu	low no
ɔɪ	boil boy oily
uə	poor tour

VOYELLES NASALES NASAL VOWELS

matin plein	ɛ̃
brun	œ̃
vent sang an dans	ɑ̃
non pont	ɔ̃

ix

COLLINS

FRENCH·ENGLISH
ENGLISH·FRENCH

DICTIONARY

FRANÇAIS-ANGLAIS
FRENCH-ENGLISH

A

a *vb voir* **avoir.**

à (*à* + *le* = **au**, *à* + *les* = **aux**) [a, o] *prép* (*situation*) at, in ; (*direction, attribution*) to ; (*provenance*) from ; (*moyen*) with, by ; **payé au mois** paid by the month ; **100 km/unités à l'heure** 100 km/units per hour ; **à 3 heures/minuit** at 3 o'clock/midnight ; **au mois de juin** in the month of June ; **se chauffer au gaz** to heat one's house with gas ; **à bicyclette** by bicycle *ou* on a bicycle ; **l'homme aux yeux bleus** the man with the blue eyes ; **à la semaine prochaine!** see you next week! ; **à la russe** the Russian way, in the Russian fashion.

abaisser [abese] *vt* to lower, bring down ; (*manette*) to pull down ; (*fig*) to debase ; to humiliate ; **s'~** *vi* to go down ; (*fig*) to demean o.s. ; **s'~ à qch** to stoop *ou* descend to doing/to sth.

abandon [abɑ̃dɔ̃] *nm* abandoning ; deserting ; giving up ; relinquishing ; (*SPORT*) withdrawal ; (*fig*) lack of constraint ; relaxed pose *ou* mood ; **être à l'~** to be in a state of neglect.

abandonné, e [abɑ̃dɔne] *a* (*solitaire*) deserted.

abandonner [abɑ̃dɔne] *vt* to leave, abandon, desert ; (*projet, activité*) to abandon, give up ; (*SPORT*) to retire *ou* withdraw from ; (*céder*) to surrender, relinquish ; **s'~** *vi* to let o.s. go ; **s'~ à** (*paresse, plaisirs*) to give o.s. up to.

abasourdir [abazuʀdiʀ] *vt* to stun, stagger.

abat-jour [abaʒuʀ] *nm inv* lampshade.

abats [aba] *nmpl* (*de bœuf, porc*) offal *sg* ; (*de volaille*) giblets.

abattage [abataʒ] *nm* cutting down, felling ; (*entrain*) go, dynamism.

abattement [abatmɑ̃] *nm* enfeeblement ; dejection, despondency ; (*déduction*) reduction ; **~ fiscal** ≈ tax allowance.

abattis [abati] *nmpl* giblets.

abattoir [abatwaʀ] *nm* abattoir, slaughterhouse.

abattre [abatʀ(ə)] *vt* (*arbre*) to cut down, fell ; (*mur, maison*) to pull down ; (*avion, personne*) to shoot down ; (*animal*) to shoot, kill ; (*fig*) to wear out, tire out ; to demoralize ; **s'~** *vi* to crash down ; **s'~ sur** to beat down on ; to rain down on.

abbaye [abei] *nf* abbey.

abbé [abe] *nm* priest ; (*d'une abbaye*) abbot ; **M. l'~** Father.

abc, ABC [abese] *nm* alphabet primer ; (*fig*) rudiments *pl*.

abcès [apsɛ] *nm* abscess.

abdication [abdikɑsjɔ̃] *nf* abdication.

abdiquer [abdike] *vi* to abdicate // *vt* to renounce, give up.

abdomen [abdomɛn] *nm* abdomen ; **abdominal, e, aux** *a* abdominal // *nmpl*: **faire des abdominaux** to do exercises for the stomach muscles.

abécédaire [abesedɛʀ] *nm* alphabet primer.

abeille [abɛj] *nf* bee.

aberrant, e [abɛʀɑ̃, -ɑ̃t] *a* absurd.

abêtir [abetiʀ] *vt* to turn into a half-wit.

abhorrer [abɔʀe] *vt* to abhor, loathe.

abîme [abim] *nm* abyss, gulf.

abîmer [abime] *vt* to spoil, damage ; **s'~** *vi* to get spoilt *ou* damaged ; (*tomber*) to sink, founder.

abject, e [abʒɛkt] *a* abject, despicable.

abjurer [abʒyʀe] *vt* to abjure, renounce.

ablation [ablɑsjɔ̃] *nf* removal.

ablutions [ablysjɔ̃] *nfpl*: **faire ses ~** to perform one's ablutions.

abnégation [abnegɑsjɔ̃] *nf* (self-)abnegation.

aboiement [abwamɑ̃] *nm* bark, barking *q*.

abois [abwa] *nmpl*: **aux ~** at bay.

abolir [abɔliʀ] *vt* to abolish ; **abolition** *nf* abolition.

abominable [abɔminabl(ə)] *a* abominable.

abondance [abɔ̃dɑ̃s] *nf* abundance ; (*richesse*) affluence.

abondant, e [abɔ̃dɑ̃, -ɑ̃t] *a* plentiful, abundant, copious.

abonder [abɔ̃de] *vi* to abound, be plentiful ; **~ en** to be full of, abound in ; **~ dans le sens de qn** to concur with sb.

abonné, e [abɔne] *nm/f* subscriber ; season ticket holder.

abonnement [abɔnmɑ̃] *nm* subscription ; (*pour transports en commun, concerts*) season ticket.

abonner [abɔne] *vt*: **s'~ à** to subscribe to, take out a subscription to.

abord [abɔʀ] *nm*: **être d'un ~ facile** to be approachable ; **~s** *nmpl* surroundings ; **au premier ~** at first sight, initially ; **d'~** *ad* first.

abordable [abɔʀdabl(ə)] *a* approachable ; reasonably priced.

abordage [abɔʀdaʒ] *nm* boarding.

aborder [abɔʀde] *vi* to land // *vt* (*sujet, difficulté*) to tackle ; (*personne*) to approach ; (*rivage etc*) to reach ; (*NAVIG: attaquer*) to board ; (: *heurter*) to collide with.

aborigène [abɔʀiʒɛn] *nm* aborigine, native.

aboulique [abulik] *a* totally lacking in willpower.

aboutir [abutiʀ] *vi* (*négociations etc*) to succeed ; **~ à/dans/sur** to end up at/in/on ; **aboutissants** *nmpl voir* **tenants.**

aboyer [abwaje] *vi* to bark.

abracadabrant, e [abʀakadabʀɑ̃, -ɑ̃t] *a* incredible, preposterous.

abrasif, ive [abʀazif, -iv] *a, nm* abrasive.

abrégé [abʀeʒe] *nm* summary.

abréger [abʀeʒe] *vt* (*texte*) to shorten, abridge ; (*mot*) to shorten, abbreviate ; (*réunion, voyage*) to cut short, shorten.

abreuver [abʀœve] *vt* to water; (*fig*): ~ qn de to shower *ou* swamp sb with; **s'~** *vi* to drink; **abreuvoir** *nm* watering place.

abréviation [abʀevjasjɔ̃] *nf* abbreviation.

abri [abʀi] *nm* shelter; **à l'~** under cover; **à l'~ de** sheltered from; (*fig*) safe from.

abricot [abʀiko] *nm* apricot; **abricotier** *nm* apricot tree.

abriter [abʀite] *vt* to shelter; (*loger*) to accommodate; **s'~** to shelter, take cover.

abroger [abʀɔʒe] *vt* to repeal, abrogate.

abrupt, e [abʀypt] *a* sheer, steep; (*ton*) abrupt.

abruti, e [abʀyti] *nm/f* (*fam*) idiot, moron.

abrutir [abʀytiʀ] *vt* to daze; to exhaust; to stupefy.

abscisse [apsis] *nf* abscissa, X axis.

absence [apsɑ̃s] *nf* absence; (*MÉD*) blackout; mental blank.

absent, e [apsɑ̃, -ɑ̃t] *a* absent; (*chose*) missing, lacking; (*distrait: air*) vacant, faraway // *nm/f* absentee; **absentéisme** *nm* absenteeism; **s'absenter** *vi* to take time off work; (*sortir*) to leave, go out.

absinthe [apsɛ̃t] *nf* (*boisson*) absinth(e); (*BOT*) wormwood, absinth(e).

absolu, e [apsɔly] *a* absolute; (*caractère*) rigid, uncompromising; **~ment** *ad* absolutely.

absolution [apsɔlysjɔ̃] *nf* absolution.

absolutisme [apsɔlytism(ə)] *nm* absolutism.

absolve etc *vb voir* **absoudre.**

absorbant, e [apsɔʀbɑ̃, -ɑ̃t] *a* absorbent.

absorbé, e [apsɔʀbe] *a* engrossed, absorbed.

absorber [apsɔʀbe] *vt* to absorb; (*gén MÉD: manger, boire*) to take.

absoudre [apsudʀ(ə)] *vt* to absolve.

abstenir [apstəniʀ]: **s'~** *vi* (*POL*) to abstain; **s'~ de qch/de faire** to refrain from sth/from doing; **abstention** *nf* abstention; **abstentionnisme** *nm* abstentionism.

abstinence [apstinɑ̃s] *nf* abstinence.

abstraction [apstʀaksjɔ̃] *nf* abstraction; **faire ~ de** to set *ou* leave aside.

abstraire [apstʀɛʀ] *vt* to abstract; **abstrait, e** *a* abstract.

absurde [apsyʀd(ə)] *a* absurd // *nm* absurdity; absurd; **par l'~** *ad* absurdio; **absurdité** *nf* absurdity.

abus [aby] *nm* (*excès*) abuse, misuse; (*injustice*) abuse; **~ de confiance** breach of trust; embezzlement.

abuser [abyze] *vi* to go too far, overstep the mark // *vt* to deceive, mislead; **~ de** *vt* (*force, droit*) to misuse; (*alcool*) to take to excess; (*violer, duper*) to take advantage of; **s'~** (*se méprendre*) to be mistaken; **abusif, ive** *a* exorbitant; excessive; improper.

acabit [akabi] *nm*: **de cet ~** of that type.

académicien, ne [akademisjɛ̃, -jɛn] *nm/f* academician.

académie [akademi] *nf* (*société*) learned society; (*école: d'art, de danse*) academy; (*ART: nu*) nude; (*SCOL: circonscription*) ≈ regional education authority; **l'A~ (française)** the French Academy; **académique** *a* academic.

acajou [akaʒu] *nm* mahogany.

acariâtre [akaʀjɑtʀ(ə)] *a* sour(-tempered).

accablement [akabləmɑ̃] *nm* despondency, depression.

accabler [akable] *vt* to overwhelm, overcome; (*suj: témoignage*) to condemn, damn; **~ qn d'injures** to heap *ou* shower abuse on sb; **~ qn de travail** to overburden sb with work; **accablé de dettes/soucis** weighed down with debts/cares.

accalmie [akalmi] *nf* lull.

accaparer [akapaʀe] *vt* to monopolize; (*sujet: travail etc*) to take up (all) the time *ou* attention of.

accéder [aksede]: **~ à** *vt* (*lieu*) to reach; (*fig: pouvoir*) to accede to; (: *poste*) to attain; (*accorder: requête*) to grant, accede to.

accélérateur [akseleʀatœʀ] *nm* accelerator.

accélération [akseleʀasjɔ̃] *nf* speeding up; acceleration.

accélérer [akseleʀe] *vt* (*mouvement, travaux*) to speed up // *vi* (*AUTO*) to accelerate.

accent [aksɑ̃] *nm* accent; (*inflexions expressives*) tone (of voice); (*PHONÉTIQUE, fig*) stress; **aux ~s de** (*musique*) to the strains of; **mettre l'~ sur** (*fig*) to stress; **~ aigu/grave** acute/grave accent.

accentuation [aksɑ̃tɥasjɔ̃] *nf* accenting; stressing.

accentuer [aksɑ̃tɥe] *vt* (*LING: orthographe*) to accent; (: *phonétique*) to stress, accent; (*fig*) to accentuate, emphasize; to increase; **s'~** *vi* to become more marked *ou* pronounced.

acceptable [aksɛptabl(ə)] *a* satisfactory, acceptable.

acceptation [aksɛptasjɔ̃] *nf* acceptance.

accepter [aksɛpte] *vt* to accept; **~ de faire** to agree to do; (*tolérer*): **~ que qn fasse** to agree to sb doing, let sb do.

acception [aksɛpsjɔ̃] *nf* meaning, sense.

accès [aksɛ] *nm* (*à un lieu*) access; (*MÉD*) attack; fit, bout; outbreak // *nmpl* (*routes etc*) means of access, approaches; **d'~ facile** easily accessible; **~ de colère** fit of anger; **~ de joie** burst of joy; **donner ~ à** (*lieu*) to give access to; (*carrière*) to open the door to; **avoir ~ auprès de qn** to have access to sb.

accessible [aksesibl(ə)] *a* accessible; (*livre, sujet*): **~ à qn** within the reach of sb; (*sensible*): **~ à la pitié/l'amour** open to pity/love.

accession [aksɛsjɔ̃] *nf*: **~ à** accession to; attainment of.

accessit [aksesit] *nm* (*SCOL*) ≈ certificate of merit.

accessoire [akseswaʀ] *a* secondary, of secondary importance; incidental // *nm* accessory; (*THÉÂTRE*) prop; **accessoiriste** *nm/f* (*TV, CINÉMA*) property man/girl.

accident [aksidɑ̃] *nm* accident; **par ~** by chance; **~ de la route** road accident; **accidenté e** *a* damaged *ou* injured (in an accident); (*relief, terrain*) uneven; hilly; **accidentel, le** *a* accidental.

acclamation [aklamasjɔ̃] *nf*: **par ~**

(*vote*) by acclamation ; —s *nfpl* cheers, cheering *sg*.

acclamer [aklame] *vt* to cheer, acclaim.

acclimatation [aklimatasjɔ̃] *nf* acclimatization.

acclimater [aklimate] *vt* to acclimatize ; **s'—** *vi* to become acclimatized.

accointances [akwɛ̃tɑ̃s] *nfpl*: **avoir des ~ avec** to have contacts with.

accolade [akɔlad] *nf* (*amicale*) embrace ; (*signe*) brace ; **donner l'~ à qn** to embrace sb.

accoler [akɔle] *vt* to place side by side.

accommodant, e [akɔmɔdɑ̃, -ɑ̃t] *a* accommodating.

accommodement [akɔmɔdmɑ̃] *nm* compromise.

accommoder [akɔmɔde] *vt* (*CULIN*) to prepare ; (*points de vue*) to reconcile ; **s'~ de** to put up with ; to make do with.

accompagnateur, trice [akɔ̃paɲatœr, -tris] *nm/f* (*MUS*) accompanist ; (*de voyage: guide*) guide ; (: *d'enfants*) accompanying adult ; (: *de voyage organisé*) courier.

accompagnement [akɔ̃paɲmɑ̃] *nm* (*MUS*) accompaniment.

accompagner [akɔ̃paɲe] *vt* to accompany, be ou go ou come with ; (*MUS*) to accompany.

accompli, e [akɔ̃pli] *a* accomplished.

accomplir [akɔ̃plir] *vt* (*tâche, projet*) to carry out ; (*souhait*) to fulfil ; **s'~** *vi* to be fulfilled ; **accomplissement** *nm* carrying out ; fulfilment.

accord [akɔr] *nm* (*entente, convention, LING*) agreement ; (*entre des styles, tons etc*) harmony ; (*consentement*) agreement, consent ; (*MUS*) chord ; **se mettre d'~** to come to an agreement (with each other) ; **être d'~** to agree ; **~ parfait** (*MUS*) tonic chord.

accordéon [akɔrdeɔ̃] *nm* (*MUS*) accordion ; **accordéoniste** *nm/f* accordionist.

accorder [akɔrde] *vt* (*faveur, délai*) to grant ; (*harmoniser*) to match ; (*MUS*) to tune ; **s'~** to get on together ; to agree ; (*LING*) to agree ; **accordeur** *nm* (*MUS*) tuner.

accoster [akɔste] *vt* (*NAVIG*) to draw alongside ; (*personne*) to accost // *vi* (*NAVIG*) to berth.

accotement [akɔtmɑ̃] *nm* (*de route*) verge, shoulder ; **—s non stabilisés** soft verges.

accoter [akɔte] *vt*: **~ qch contre/à** to lean ou rest sth against/on ; **s'~ contre/à** to lean against/on.

accouchement [akuʃmɑ̃] *nm* delivery, (child)birth ; labour.

accoucher [akuʃe] *vi* to give birth, have a baby ; (*être en travail*) to be in labour // *vi* to deliver ; **~ d'un garçon** to give birth to a boy ; **accoucheur** *nm*: (**médecin**) **accoucheur** obstetrician ; **accoucheuse** *nf* midwife.

accouder [akude]: **s'~** *vi*: **s'~ à/contre** to rest one's elbows on/against ; **accoudoir** *nm* armrest.

accouplement [akupləmɑ̃] *nm* mating ; coupling.

accoupler [akuple] *vt* to couple ; (*pour la reproduction*) to mate ; **s'~** to mate.

accourir [akurir] *vi* to rush ou run up.

accoutrement [akutrəmɑ̃] *nm* (*péj*) getup, rig-out.

accoutumance [akutymɑ̃s] *nf* (*gén*) adaptation ; (*MÉD*) addiction.

accoutumé, e [akutyme] *a* (*habituel*) customary, usual.

accoutumer [akutyme] *vt*: **~ qn à qch/faire** to accustom sb to sth/to doing ; **s'~ à** to get accustomed *ou* used to.

accréditer [akredite] *vt* (*nouvelle*) to substantiate ; **~ qn (auprès de)** to accredit sb (to).

accroc [akro] *nm* (*déchirure*) tear ; (*fig*) hitch, snag.

accrochage [akrɔʃaʒ] *nm* hanging (up) ; hitching (up) ; (*AUTO*) (minor) collision, bump ; (*MIL*) encounter, engagement ; (*dispute*) clash, brush.

accroche-cœur [akrɔʃkœr] *nm* kiss-curl.

accrocher [akrɔʃe] *vt* (*suspendre*): **~ qch à** to hang sth (up) on ; (*attacher: remorque*): **~ qch à** to hitch sth (up) to ; (*heurter*) to catch ; to catch on ; to hit ; (*déchirer*): **~ qch (à)** to catch (on) ; (*MIL*) to engage ; (*fig*) to catch, attract ; **s'~** (*se disputer*) to have a clash *ou* brush ; **s'~ à** (*rester pris à*) to catch on ; (*agripper, fig*) to hang on *ou* cling to.

accroissement [akrwasmɑ̃] *nm* increase.

accroître [akrwatr(ə)] *vt* to increase ; **s'~** *vi* to increase.

accroupi, e [akrupi] *a* squatting, crouching (down).

accroupir [akrupir]: **s'~** *vi* to squat, crouch (down).

accru, e [akry] *pp* de **accroître**.

accu [aky] *nm abr de* **accumulateur**.

accueil [akœj] *nm* welcome ; **comité d'~** reception committee.

accueillir [akœjir] *vt* to welcome ; (*loger*) to accommodate.

acculer [akyle] *vt*: **~ qn à ou contre** to drive sb back against ; **~ qn dans** to corner sb in ; **~ qn à** (*faillite*) to drive sb to the brink of.

accumulateur [akymylatœr] *nm* accumulator.

accumulation [akymylasjɔ̃] *nf* accumulation ; **chauffage/radiateur à ~** (night-)storage heating/heater.

accumuler [akymyle] *vt* to accumulate, amass ; **s'~** *vi* to accumulate ; to pile up.

accusateur, trice [akyzatœr, -tris] *nm/f* accuser // *a* accusing ; (*document, preuve*) incriminating.

accusatif [akyzatif] *nm* (*LING*) accusative.

accusation [akyzasjɔ̃] *nf* (*gén*) accusation ; (*JUR*) charge ; (*partie*): **l'~** the prosecution ; **mettre en ~** to indict.

accusé, e [akyze] *nm/f* accused ; defendant ; **~ de réception** acknowledgement of receipt.

accuser [akyze] *vt* to accuse ; (*fig*) to emphasize, bring out ; to show ; **~ qn de** to accuse sb of ; (*JUR*) to charge sb with ; **qch de** (*rendre responsable*) to blame sth for ; **~ réception de** to acknowledge receipt of.

acerbe [asɛrb(ə)] *a* caustic, acid.

acéré, e [aseʀe] a sharp.

achalandé, e [aʃalɑ̃de] a: **bien ~** well-stocked ; well-patronized.

acharné, e [aʃaʀne] a (lutte, adversaire) fierce, bitter ; (travail) relentless, unremitting.

acharnement [aʃaʀnəmɑ̃] nm fierceness ; relentlessness.

acharner [aʃaʀne]: **s'~** vi: **s'~ sur** to go at fiercely, hound ; **s'~ contre** to set o.s. against ; to dog, pursue ; **s'~ à faire** to try doggedly to do ; to persist in doing.

achat [aʃa] nm buying q ; purchase ; **faire l'~ de** to buy, purchase ; **faire des ~s** to do some shopping, buy a few things.

acheminer [aʃmine] vt (courrier) to forward, dispatch ; (troupes) to convey, transport ; (train) to route ; **s'~ vers** to head for.

acheter [aʃte] vt to buy, purchase ; (soudoyer) to buy ; **~ qch à** (marchand) to buy ou purchase sth from ; (ami etc: offrir) to buy sth for ; **acheteur, euse** nm/f buyer ; shopper ; (COMM) buyer ; (JUR) vendee, purchaser.

achevé, e [aʃve] a: **d'un ridicule ~** thoroughly ou absolutely ridiculous.

achèvement [aʃɛvmɑ̃] nm completion ; finishing.

achever [aʃve] vt to complete, finish ; to end ; (blessé) to finish off ; **s'~** vi to end.

achoppement [aʃɔpmɑ̃] nm: **pierre d'~** stumbling block.

acide [asid] a acid, sharp ; (CHIMIE) acid(ic) // nm (CHIMIE) acid ; **acidifier** vt to acidify ; **acidité** nf acidity ; sharpness ; **acidulé, e** a slightly acid ; **bonbons acidulés** acid drops.

acier [asje] nm steel ; **aciérie** nf steelworks sg.

acné [akne] nf acne.

acolyte [akɔlit] nm (péj) confederate.

acompte [akɔ̃t] nm deposit ; (versement régulier) instalment ; (sur somme due) payment on account ; **un ~ de 100 F** 100 F on account.

acoquiner [akɔkine]: **s'~ avec** vt (péj) to team up with.

à-côté [akote] nm side-issue ; (argent) extra.

à-coup [aku] nm (du moteur) (hic)cough ; (fig) jolt ; **sans ~s** smoothly ; **par ~s** by fits and starts.

acoustique [akustik] nf (d'une salle) acoustics pl ; (science) acoustics sg // a acoustic.

acquéreur [akeʀœʀ] nm buyer, purchaser.

acquérir [akeʀiʀ] vt to acquire ; (par achat) to purchase, acquire ; (valeur) to gain ; **ce que ses efforts lui ont acquis** what his efforts have won ou gained (for) him.

acquiescer [akjese] vi (opiner) to agree ; (consentir) : **~ (à qch)** to acquiesce ou assent (to sth).

acquis, e [aki, -iz] pp de **acquérir** // nm (accumulated) experience ; **être ~ à** (plan, idée) to fully agree with ; **son aide nous est ~e** we can count on ou be sure of her help.

acquisition [akizizjɔ̃] nf acquisition ; purchase ; **faire l'~ de** to acquire ; to purchase.

acquit [aki] vb voir **acquérir** // nm (quittance) receipt ; **pour ~** received ; **par ~ de conscience** to set one's mind at rest.

acquittement [akitmɑ̃] nm acquittal ; payment, settlement.

acquitter [akite] vt (JUR) to acquit ; (facture) to pay, settle ; **s'~ de** to discharge ; to fulfil, carry out.

âcre [ɑkʀ(ə)] a acrid, pungent.

acrobate [akʀɔbat] nm/f acrobat.

acrobatie [akʀɔbasi] nf (art) acrobatics sg ; (exercice) acrobatic feat ; **~ aérienne** aerobatics sg ; **acrobatique** a acrobatic.

acte [akt(ə)] nm act, action ; (THÉÂTRE) act ; **~s** nmpl (compterendu) proceedings ; **prendre ~ de** to note, take note of ; **faire ~ de présence** to put in an appearance ; **l'~ d'accusation** the charges ; the bill of indictment ; **~ de naissance** birth certificate.

acteur, trice [aktœʀ, -tʀis] nm/f actor/actress.

actif, ive [aktif, -iv] a active // nm (COMM) assets pl ; (fig): **avoir à son ~** to have to one's credit ; **mettre à son ~** to add to one's list of achievements.

action [aksjɔ̃] nf (gén) action ; (COMM) share ; **une bonne ~** a good deed ; **~ en diffamation** libel action ; **actionnaire** nm/f shareholder ; **actionner** vt to work ; to activate.

active [aktiv] a voir **actif** ; **~ment** ad actively.

activer [aktive] vt to speed up ; **s'~** vi bustle about ; to hurry up.

activiste [aktivist(ə)] nm/f activist.

activité [aktivite] nf activity ; **volcan en ~** active volcano.

actrice [aktʀis] nf voir **acteur**.

actualiser [aktualize] vt to actualize ; to bring up to date.

actualité [aktualite] nf (d'un problème) topicality ; (évènements): **l'~** current events ; **les ~s** (CINÉMA, TV) the news.

actuel, le [aktuɛl] a (présent) present ; (d'actualité) topical ; (non virtuel) actual ; **~lement** ad at present ; at the present time.

acuité [akɥite] nf acuteness.

acuponcteur, acupuncteur [akypɔ̃ktœʀ] nm acupuncturist.

acuponcture, acupuncture [akypɔ̃ktyʀ] nf acupuncture.

adage [adaʒ] nm adage.

adagio [adadʒjo] nm adagio.

adaptateur, trice [adaptatœʀ, -tʀis] nm/f adapter // nm (ÉLEC) adapter.

adaptation [adaptɑsjɔ̃] nf adaptation.

adapter [adapte] vt to adapt ; **~ qch à** (approprier) to adapt sth to (fit) ; **~ qch sur/dans/à** (fixer) to fit sth on/into/to ; **s'~ (à)** (suj: personne) to adapt (to).

additif [aditif] nm additional clause ; (CHIMIE) additive.

addition [adisjɔ̃] nf addition ; (au café) bill ; **additionnel, le** a additional.

additionner [adisjɔne] vt to add (up) ; **~**

un produit d'eau to add water to a product.

adepte [adɛpt(ə)] *nm/f* follower.

adéquat, e [adekwa, -at] *a* appropriate, suitable.

adhérence [adeRɑ̃s] *nf* adhesion.

adhérent, e [adeRɑ̃, -ɑ̃t] *nm/f* (*de club*) member.

adhérer [adeRe] *vi* (*coller*) to adhere, stick ; **~ à** *vt* (*coller*) to adhere *ou* stick to ; (*se rallier à: parti, club*) to join ; to be a member of ; (: *opinion, mouvement*) to support ; **adhésif, ive** *a* adhesive, sticky // *nm* adhesive ; **adhésion** *nf* joining ; membership ; support.

ad hoc [adɔk] *a* ad hoc.

adieu, x [adjø] *excl* goodbye // *nm* farewell ; **dire ~ à qn** to say goodbye *ou* farewell to sb.

adipeux, euse [adipø, -øz] *a* bloated, fat ; (*ANAT*) adipose.

adjacent, e [adʒasɑ̃, -ɑ̃t] *a* adjacent.

adjectif [adʒɛktif] *nm* adjective ; **~ attribut** adjectival complement ; **~ épithète** attributive adjective.

adjoindre [adʒwɛ̃dR(ə)] *vt* : **~ qch à** to attach sth to ; to add sth to ; **~ qn à** (*personne*) to appoint sb as an assistant to ; (*comité*) to appoint sb to, attach sb to ; **s'~** (*collaborateur etc*) to take on, appoint ; **adjoint, e** *nm/f* assistant ; **adjoint au maire** deputy mayor ; **directeur adjoint** assistant manager ; **adjonction** *nf* attaching ; addition ; appointment.

adjudant [adʒydɑ̃] *nm* (*MIL*) warrant officer.

adjudicataire [adʒydikatɛR] *nm/f* successful bidder, purchaser ; successful tenderer.

adjudication [adʒydikasjɔ̃] *nf* sale by auction ; (*pour travaux*) invitation to tender.

adjuger [adʒyʒe] *vt* (*prix, récompense*) to award ; (*lors d'une vente*) to auction (off) ; **s'~** *vt* to take for o.s.

adjurer [adʒyRe] *vt* : **~ qn de faire** to implore *ou* beg sb to do.

adjuvant [adʒyvɑ̃] *nm* adjuvant ; additive ; stimulant.

admettre [admɛtR(ə)] *vt* (*visiteur, nouveau-venu*) to admit, let in ; (*candidat: SCOL*) to pass ; (*TECH: gaz, eau, air*) to admit ; (*tolérer*) to allow, accept ; (*reconnaître*) to admit, acknowledge.

administrateur, trice [administRatœR, -tRis] *nm/f* (*COMM*) director ; (*ADMIN*) administrator.

administratif, ive [administRatif, -iv] *a* administrative.

administration [administRasjɔ̃] *nf* administration ; **l'A~** ≈ the Civil Service.

administré, e [administRe] *nm/f*: **ses ~s** the citizens in his care.

administrer [administRe] *vt* (*firme*) to manage, run ; (*biens, remède, sacrement etc*) to administer.

admirable [admiRabl(ə)] *a* admirable, wonderful.

admirateur, trice [admiRatœR, -tRis] *nm/f* admirer.

admiratif, ive [admiRatif, -iv] *a* admiring.

admiration [admiRɑsjɔ̃] *nf* admiration.

admirer [admiRe] *vt* to admire.

admis, e *pp de* **admettre**.

admissible [admisibl(ə)] *a* (*candidat*) eligible ; (*comportement*) admissible, acceptable.

admission [admisjɔ̃] *nf* admission ; acknowledgement ; **tuyau d'~** intake pipe ; **demande d'~** application for membership.

admonester [admɔnɛste] *vt* to admonish.

adolescence [adɔlesɑ̃s] *nf* adolescence.

adolescent, e [adɔlesɑ̃, -ɑ̃t] *nm/f* adolescent.

adonner [adɔne]: **s'~ à** *vt* (*sport*) to devote o.s. to ; (*boisson*) to give o.s. over to.

adopter [adɔpte] *vt* to adopt ; (*projet de loi etc*) to pass ; **adoptif, ive** *a* (*parents*) adoptive ; (*fils, patrie*) adopted ; **adoption** *nf* adoption.

adoration [adɔRɑsjɔ̃] *nf* adoration ; worship.

adorer [adɔRe] *vt* to adore ; (*REL*) to worship, adore.

adosser [adose] *vt*: **~ qch à ou contre** to stand sth against ; **s'~ à ou contre** to lean with one's back against.

adoucir [adusiR] *vt* (*goût, température*) to make milder ; (*avec du sucre*) to sweeten ; (*peau, voix*) to soften ; (*caractère, personne*) to mellow ; (*peine*) to soothe, allay ; **s'~** *vi* to become milder ; to soften ; to mellow.

adresse [adRɛs] *nf* (*voir adroit*) skill, dexterity ; (*domicile*) address ; **à l'~ de** (*pour*) for the benefit of.

adresser [adRese] *vt* (*lettre: expédier*) to send ; (: *écrire l'adresse sur*) to address ; (*injure, compliments*) to address ; **~ qn à un docteur/bureau** to refer *ou* send sb to a doctor/an office ; **~ la parole à qn** to speak to *ou* address sb ; **s'~ à** (*parler à*) to speak to, address ; (*s'informer auprès de*) to go and see, go and speak to ; (: *bureau*) to enquire at ; (*suj: livre, conseil*) to be aimed at.

Adriatique [adRiatik] *nf*: **l'~** the Adriatic.

adroit, e [adRwa, -wat] *a* (*joueur, mécanicien*) skilful, dext(e)rous ; (*politicien etc*) shrewd, skilled ; **adroitement** *ad* skilfully ; dext(e)rously.

aduler [adyle] *vt* to adulate.

adulte [adylt(ə)] *nm/f* adult, grown-up // *a* (*chien, arbre*) fully-grown, mature ; (*attitude*) adult, grown-up ; **l'âge ~** adulthood.

adultère [adyltɛR] *a* adulterous // *nm/f* adulterer/adulteress // *nm* (*acte*) adultery ; **adultérin, e** *a* born of adultery.

advenir [advəniR] *vi* to happen ; **qu'est-il advenu de** what has become of.

adverbe [advɛRb(ə)] *nm* adverb.

adversaire [advɛRsɛR] *nm/f* (*SPORT, gén*) opponent, adversary ; (*MIL*) adversary, enemy ; (*non partisan*): **~ de** opponent of.

adverse [advɛRs(ə)] *a* opposing.

adversité [advɛRsite] *nf* adversity.

aérateur [aeRatœR] *nm* ventilator.

aération [aeRɑsjɔ̃] *nf* airing ; ventilation ;

conduit d'~ ventilation shaft; **bouche d'~** air-vent.

aéré, e [aeʀe] a (*pièce, local*) airy, well-ventilated; (*tissu*) loose-woven.

aérer [aeʀe] vt to air; (*fig*) to lighten; **s'~** vi to get some (fresh) air.

aérien, ne [aeʀjɛ̃ -jɛn] a (*AVIAT*) air cpd, aerial; (*câble, métro*) overhead; (*fig*) light.

aéro... [aeʀɔ] préfixe: **~-club** nm flying club; **~-drome** nm aerodrome; **~dynamique** a aerodynamic, streamlined // nf aerodynamics sg; **~gare** nf airport (buildings); (*en ville*) air terminal; **~glisseur** nm hovercraft; **~nautique** a aeronautical // nf aeronautics sg; **~naval, e** a air and sea cpd // nf the Fleet Air Arm; **~phagie** nf aerophagy; **~port** nm airport; **~porté, e** a airborne, air-lifted; **~sol** nm aerosol; **~spatial, e, aux** a aerospace; **~train** nm hovertrain.

affable [afabl(ə)] a affable.

affadir [afadiʀ] vt to make insipid ou tasteless.

affaiblir [afebliʀ] vt to weaken; **s'~** vi to weaken, grow weaker; **affaiblissement** nm weakening.

affaire [afɛʀ] nf (*problème, question*) matter; (*criminelle, judiciaire*) case; (*scandaleuse etc*) affair; (*entreprise*) business; (*marché, transaction*) (business) deal; (*pièce of*) business q; (*occasion intéressante*) good deal, bargain; **~s** nfpl affairs; (*activité commerciale*) business sg; (*effets personnels*) things, belongings; **ce sont mes ~s** (*cela me concerne*) that's my business; **ceci fera l'~** this will do (nicely); **avoir ~ à** to be faced with; to be dealing with; **les A~s étrangères** (*POL*) Foreign Affairs; **s'affairer** vi to busy o.s., bustle about; **affairisme** nm (political) racketeering.

affaisser [afese]: **s'~** vi (*terrain, immeuble*) to subside, sink; (*personne*) to collapse.

affaler [afale] vi: **s'~ dans/sur** to collapse ou slump into/onto.

affamer [afame] vt to starve.

affectation [afɛktɑsjɔ̃] nf allotment; appointment; posting; (*voir affecté*) affectedness.

affecté, e [afɛkte] a affected.

affecter [afɛkte] vt (*émouvoir*) to affect, move; (*feindre*) to affect, feign; (*telle ou telle forme etc*) to take on, assume; **~ qch à** to allocate ou allot sth to; **~ qn à** to appoint sb to; (*diplomate*) to post sb to; **~ qch d'un coefficient etc** to modify sth by a coefficient etc, tag a coefficient etc onto sth.

affectif, ive [afɛktif, -iv] a emotional, affective.

affection [afɛksjɔ̃] nf affection; (*mal*) ailment; **affectionner** vt to be fond of.

affectueux, euse [afɛktɥø, -øz] a affectionate.

afférent, e [afeʀɑ̃ -ɑ̃t] a: **~ à** pertaining ou relating to.

affermir [afɛʀmiʀ] vt to consolidate, strengthen.

affichage [afiʃaʒ] nm billposting; (*électronique*) display; **~ numérique** ou **digital** digital display.

affiche [afiʃ] nf poster; (*officielle*) (public) notice; (*THÉÂTRE*) bill.

afficher [afiʃe] vt (*affiche*) to put up, post up; (*réunion*) to announce by (means of) posters ou public notices; (*électroniquement*) to display; (*fig*) to exhibit, display; **s'~** (*péj*) to flaunt o.s.

affilée [afile]: **d'~** ad at a stretch.

affiler [afile] vt to sharpen.

affilier [afilje] vt: **s'~ à** to become affiliated to.

affiner [afine] vt to refine; **s'~** vi to become (more) refined.

affinité [afinite] nf affinity.

affirmatif, ive [afiʀmatif, -iv] a affirmative // nf: **répondre par l'affirmative** to reply yes ou in the affirmative; **dans l'affirmative** if (the answer) is yes, if he does (ou you do etc).

affirmation [afiʀmɑsjɔ̃] nf assertion.

affirmer [afiʀme] vt (*prétendre*) to maintain, assert; (*autorité etc*) to assert.

affleurer [aflœʀe] vi to show on the surface.

affliction [afliksjɔ̃] nf affliction.

affligé, e [afliʒe] a distressed, grieved; **~ de** (*maladie, tare*) afflicted with.

affliger [afliʒe] vt (*peiner*) to distress, grieve.

affluence [aflyɑ̃s] nf crowds pl; **heures d'~** rush hours; **jours d'~** busiest days.

affluent [aflyɑ̃] nm tributary.

affluer [aflye] vi (*secours, biens*) to flood in, pour in; (*sang*) to rush, flow; **afflux** nm flood, influx; rush.

affoler [afɔle] vt to throw into a panic; **s'~** vi to panic.

affranchir [afʀɑ̃ʃiʀ] vt to put a stamp ou stamps on; (*à la machine*) to frank; (*esclave*) to enfranchise, emancipate; (*fig*) to free, liberate; **affranchissement** nm franking; freeing; **tarifs d'affranchissement** postal rates; **affranchissement insuffisant** insufficient postage.

affres [afʀ(ə)] nfpl: **dans les ~ de** in the throes of.

affréter [afʀete] vt to charter.

affreux, euse [afʀø, -øz] a (*laid*) hideous, ghastly; (*épouvantable*) dreadful, awful.

affriolant, e [afʀijɔlɑ̃, -ɑ̃t] a tempting, arousing.

affront [afʀɔ̃] nm affront.

affronter [afʀɔ̃te] vt to confront, face.

affubler [afyble] vt (*péj*): **~ qn de** to rig ou deck sb out in; (*surnom*) to attach to sb.

affût [afy] nm (*de canon*) gun carriage; **à l'~ (de)** (*gibier*) lying in wait (for); (*fig*) on the look-out (for).

affûter [afyte] vt to sharpen, grind.

afin [afɛ̃]: **~ que** cj so that, in order that; **~ de faire** in order to do, so as to do.

a fortiori [afɔʀsjɔʀi] ad all the more, a fortiori.

A.F.P. sigle f = Agence France Presse.

africain, e [afʀikɛ̃, -ɛn] a, nm/f African.

Afrique [afʀik] nf: **l'~** Africa; **l'~ du Sud** South Africa.

agacer [agase] vt to pester, tease; (*involontairement*) to irritate, aggravate; (*aguicher*) to excite, lead on.

âge [ɑʒ] *nm* age; **quel ~ as-tu?** how old are you?; **prendre de l'~** to be getting on (in years), grow older; **l'~ ingrat** the awkward *ou* difficult age; **l'~ mûr** maturity, middle age; **âgé, e** a old, elderly; **âgé de 10 ans** 10 years old.

agence [aʒɑ̃s] *nf* agency, office; (*succursale*) branch; ~ **immobilière** estate agent's (office); ~ **matrimoniale** marriage bureau; ~ **de voyages** travel agency.

agencer [aʒɑ̃se] *vt* to put together; to arrange, lay out.

agenda [aʒɛ̃da] *nm* diary.

agenouiller [aʒnuje]: **s'~** *vi* to kneel (down).

agent [aʒɑ̃] *nm* (*aussi:* ~ **de police**) policeman; (ADMIN) official, officer; (*fig: élément, facteur*) agent; ~ **d'assurances** insurance broker; ~ **de change** stockbroker; ~ (**secret**) (secret) agent.

agglomération [aglɔmeʁasjɔ̃] *nf* town; built-up area; **l'~ parisienne** the urban area of Paris.

aggloméré [aglɔmeʁe] *nm* (*bois*) chipboard; (*pierre*) conglomerate.

agglomérer [aglɔmeʁe] *vt* to pile up; (TECH: *bois, pierre*) to compress.

agglutiner [aglytine] *vt* to stick together; **s'~** *vi* to congregate.

aggraver [agʁave] *vt* to worsen, aggravate; (JUR: *peine*) to increase; **s'~** *vi* to worsen.

agile [aʒil] *a* agile, nimble; **agilité** *nf* agility, nimbleness.

agir [aʒiʁ] *vi* (*se comporter*) to behave, act; (*faire quelque chose*) to act, take action; (*avoir de l'effet*) to act; **il s'agit de** it's a matter *ou* question of; it is about; (*il importe que*): **il s'agit de faire** we (*ou* you *etc*) must do; **agissements** *nmpl* (*gén péj*) schemes, intrigues.

agitateur, trice [aʒitatœʁ, -tʁis] *nm/f* agitator.

agitation [aʒitɑsjɔ̃] *nf* (hustle and) bustle; agitation, excitement; (*politique*) unrest, agitation.

agité, e [aʒite] *a* fidgety, restless; agitated, perturbed; (*journée*) hectic; **une mer ~e** a rough *ou* choppy sea; **un sommeil ~** a disturbed *ou* broken sleep.

agiter [aʒite] *vt* (*bouteille, chiffon*) to shake; (*bras, mains*) to wave; (*préoccuper, exciter*) to trouble, perturb; **s'~** *vi* to bustle about; (*dormeur*) to toss and turn; (*enfant*) to fidget; (POL) to grow restless.

agneau, x [aɲo] *nm* lamb.

agonie [agɔni] *nf* mortal agony, pangs *pl* of death; (*fig*) death throes *pl*.

agonir [agɔniʁ] *vt*: ~ **qn d'injures** to hurl abuse at sb.

agoniser [agɔnize] *vi* to be dying.

agrafe [agʁaf] *nf* (*de vêtement*) hook, fastener; (*de bureau*) staple; **agrafer** *vt* to fasten; to staple; **agrafeuse** *nf* stapler.

agraire [agʁɛʁ] *a* agrarian; (*mesure, surface*) land *cpd*.

agrandir [agʁɑ̃diʁ] *vt* (*magasin, domaine*) to extend, enlarge; (*trou*) to enlarge, make bigger; (PHOTO) to enlarge, blow up; **s'~** *vi* to be extended; to be enlarged; **agrandissement** *nm* extension; enlarge-

ment; **agrandisseur** *nm* (PHOTO) enlarger.

agréable [agʁeabl(ə)] *a* pleasant, nice.

agréé, e [agʁee] *a*: **concessionnaire ~** registered dealer.

agréer [agʁee] *vt* (*requête*) to accept; ~ **à** *vt* to please, suit; **veuillez ~ ...** (*formule épistolaire*) yours faithfully.

agrégation [agʁegɑsjɔ̃] *nf* highest teaching diploma in France (*competitive examination*); **agrégé, e** *nm/f* holder of the *agrégation*.

agréger [agʁeʒe]: **s'~** *vi* to aggregate.

agrément [agʁemɑ̃] *nm* (*accord*) consent, approval; (*attraits*) charm, attractiveness; (*plaisir*) pleasure.

agrémenter [agʁemɑ̃te] *vt* to embellish, adorn.

agrès [agʁɛ] *nmpl* (gymnastics) apparatus *sg*.

agresser [agʁese] *vt* to attack.

agresseur [agʁesœʁ] *nm* aggressor, attacker; (POL, MIL) aggressor.

agressif, ive [agʁesif, -iv] *a* aggressive.

agression [agʁesjɔ̃] *nf* attack; (POL, MIL, PSYCH) aggression.

agressivité [agʁesivite] *nf* aggressiveness.

agreste [agʁɛst(ə)] *a* rustic.

agricole [agʁikɔl] *a* agricultural, farm *cpd*.

agriculteur [agʁikyltœʁ] *nm* farmer.

agriculture [agʁikyltyʁ] *nf* agriculture, farming.

agripper [agʁipe] *vt* to grab, clutch; (*pour arracher*) to snatch, grab; **s'~ à** to cling (on) to, clutch, grip.

agronome [agʁɔnɔm] *nm/f* agronomist.

agronomie [agʁɔnɔmi] *nf* agronomy, agronomics *sg*.

agrumes [agʁym] *nmpl* citrus fruit(s).

aguerrir [ageʁiʁ] *vt* to harden.

aguets [agɛ]: **aux ~** *ad*: **être aux ~** to be on the look-out.

aguicher [agiʃe] *vt* to entice.

ahurissement [ayʁismɑ̃] *nm* stupefaction.

ai *vb voir* **avoir**.

aide [ɛd] *nm/f* assistant // *nf* assistance, help; (*secours financier*) aid; **à l'~ de** (*avec*) with the help *ou* aid of; **aller à l'~ de qn** to go to sb's aid *ou* to help sb; **venir en ~ à qn** to help sb, come to sb's assistance; **appeler (qn) à l'~** to call for help (from sb); ~ **comptable** *nm* accountant's assistant; ~ **électricien** *nm* electrician's mate; ~ **familiale** *nf* mother's help, home help; ~ **de laboratoire** *nm/f* laboratory assistant; ~ **sociale** *nf* (*assistance*) ≈ social security; ~ **soignant, e** *nm/f* auxiliary nurse; ~ **mémoire** *nm inv* memoranda pages *pl*; (*key facts*) handbook.

aider [ede] *vt* to help; ~ **à qch** (*faciliter*) to help (towards) sth; **s'~ de** (*se servir de*) to use, make use of.

aie *etc vb voir* **avoir**.

aïe [aj] *excl* ouch.

aïeul, e [ajœl] *nm/f* grandparent, grandfather/grandmother; forbear.

aïeux [ajø] *nmpl* grandparents; forbears, forefathers.

aigle [ɛgl(ə)] nm eagle.

aigre [ɛgr(ə)] a sour, sharp; (fig) sharp, cutting; **~-doux, douce** a bitter-sweet; **~let, te** a sourish, sharpish; **aigreur** nf sourness; sharpness; **aigreurs d'estomac** heartburn sg; **aigrir** vt (personne) to embitter; (caractère) to sour; **s'aigrir** vi to become embittered; to sour; (lait etc) to turn sour.

aigu, ë [egy] a (objet, arête) sharp, pointed; (son, voix) high-pitched, shrill; (note) high(-pitched); (douleur, intelligence) acute, sharp.

aigue-marine [ɛgmaʀin] nf aquamarine.

aiguillage [eguijaʒ] nm (RAIL) points pl.

aiguille [eguij] nf needle; (de montre) hand; **~ à tricoter** knitting needle.

aiguiller [eguije] vt (orienter) to direct; (RAIL) to shunt; **aiguilleur** nm (RAIL) pointsman; **aiguilleur du ciel** air traffic controller.

aiguillon [eguijɔ̃] nm (d'abeille) sting; (fig) spur, stimulus; **aiguillonner** vt to spur ou goad on.

aiguiser [egize] vt to sharpen, grind; (fig) to stimulate; to sharpen; to excite.

ail [aj] nm garlic.

aile [ɛl] nf wing; **ailé, e** a winged; **aileron** nm (de requin) fin; (d'avion) aileron; (de voiture) aerofoil; **ailette** nf (TECH) fin; blade; wing; **ailier** nm winger.

aille etc vb voir **aller**.

ailleurs [ajœʀ] ad elsewhere, somewhere else; **partout/nulle part ~** everywhere/nowhere else; **d'~** ad (du reste) moreover, besides; **par ~** ad (d'autre part) moreover, furthermore.

aimable [ɛmabl(ə)] a kind, nice; **~ment** ad kindly.

aimant [ɛmɑ̃] nm magnet.

aimant, e [ɛmɑ̃, -ɑ̃t] a loving, affectionate.

aimanter [ɛmɑ̃te] vt to magnetize.

aimer [eme] vt to love; (d'amitié, affection, par goût) to like; (souhait): **j'aimerais...** I would like...; **bien ~ qn/qch** to quite like sb/sth; **j'aime mieux** ou **autant vous dire que** I may as well tell you that; **j'aimerais autant y aller** ou **j'aimerais mieux y aller maintenant** I'd sooner ou rather go now; **j'aimerais mieux y aller maintenant** I'd much rather go now.

aine [ɛn] nf groin.

aîné, e [ene] a elder, older; (le plus âgé) eldest, oldest // nm/f eldest child ou one, oldest boy ou son/girl ou daughter; **il est mon ~ (de 2 ans)** (rapports non familiaux) he's (2 years) older than me, he's 2 years my senior; **~s** nmpl (fig: anciens) elders; **aînesse** nf: **droit d'aînesse** birthright.

ainsi [ɛ̃si] ad (de cette façon) like this, in this way, thus; (ce faisant) thus // cj thus, so; **~ que** (comme) (just) as; (et aussi) as well as; **pour ~ dire** so to speak, as it were; **et ~ de suite** and so on (and so forth).

air [ɛʀ] nm air; (mélodie) tune; (expression) look, air; **en l'~** (up) into the air; **tirer en l'~** to fire shots in the air; **prendre l'~** to get some (fresh) air; (avion) to take off; **avoir l'~** (sembler) to look, appear; **avoir l'~ de** to look like; **avoir l'~ de faire** to look as though one is doing, appear to be doing.

---

aire [ɛʀ] nf (zone, fig, MATH) area; (nid) eyrie; **~ d'atterrissage** landing strip; landing patch; **~ de jeu** play area; **~ de lancement** launching site; **~ de stationnement** parking area; (d'autoroute) lay-by.

aisance [ɛzɑ̃s] nf ease; (richesse) affluence; **être dans l'~** to be well-off, be affluent.

aise [ɛz] nf comfort // a: **être bien ~ que** to be delighted that; **~s** nfpl: **aimer ses ~s** to like one's (creature) comforts; **prendre ses ~s** to make o.s. comfortable; **frémir d'~** to shudder with pleasure; **être à l'~** ou **à son ~** to be comfortable; (pas embarrassé) to be at ease; (financièrement) to be comfortably off; **se mettre à l'~** to make o.s. comfortable; **être mal à l'~** ou **à son ~** to be uncomfortable; to be ill at ease; **mettre qn mal à l'~** to make sb feel ill at ease; **à votre ~** please yourself, just as you like; **en faire à son ~** to do as one likes; **aisé, e** a easy; (assez riche) well-to-do, well-off; **aisément** ad easily.

aisselle [ɛsɛl] nf armpit.

ait vb voir **avoir**.

ajonc [aʒɔ̃] nm gorse q.

ajouré, e [aʒuʀe] a openwork cpd.

ajournement [aʒuʀnəmɑ̃] nm adjournment; deferment; postponement.

ajourner [aʒuʀne] vt (réunion) to adjourn; (décision) to defer, postpone; (candidat) to refer; (conscrit) to defer.

ajout [aʒu] nm addition.

ajouter [aʒute] vt to add; **~ à** vt (accroître) to add to; **s'~ à** to add to; **~ foi à** to lend ou give credence to.

ajustage [aʒystaʒ] nm fitting.

ajusté, e [aʒyste] a: **bien ~** (robe etc) close-fitting.

ajustement [aʒystəmɑ̃] nm adjustment.

ajuster [aʒyste] vt (régler) to adjust; (vêtement) to alter; (coup de fusil) to aim; (cible) to aim at; (TECH, gén: adapter): **~ qch à** to fit sth to; **ajusteur** nm metal worker.

alambic [alɑ̃bik] nm still.

alanguir [alɑ̃giʀ]: **s'~** vi to grow languid.

alarme [alaʀm(ə)] nf alarm; **donner l'~** to give ou raise the alarm; **alarmer** vt to alarm; **s'alarmer** vi to become alarmed.

Albanie [albani] nf: **l'~** Albania.

albâtre [albɑtʀ(ə)] nm alabaster.

albatros [albatʀos] nm albatross.

albinos [albinos] nm/f albino.

album [albɔm] nm album.

albumen [albymɛn] nm albumen.

albumine [albymin] nf albumin; **avoir** ou **faire de l'~** to suffer from albuminuria.

alcalin, e [alkalɛ̃, -in] a alkaline.

alchimie [alʃimi] nf alchemy; **alchimiste** nm alchemist.

alcool [alkɔl] nm: **l'~** alcohol; **un ~** a spirit, a brandy; **~ à brûler** methylated spirits; **~ à 90°** surgical spirit; **~ique** a, nm/f alcoholic; **~isé, e** a alcoholic; **~isme** nm alcoholism; **alco(o)test** ® nm breathalyser; (test) breath-test.

alcôve [alkov] nf alcove, recess.

aléas [alea] *nmpl* hazards ; **aléatoire** *a* uncertain.

alentour [alɑ̃tuʀ] *ad* around (about) ; **~s** *nmpl* surroundings ; **aux ~s de** in the vicinity *ou* neighbourhood of, around about ; (*temps*) (*a*)round about.

alerte [alɛʀt(ə)] *a* agile, nimble ; brisk, lively // *nf* alert ; warning ; **donner l'~** to give the alert ; **alerter** *vt* to alert.

alèse [alɛz] *nf* (*drap*) undersheet, drawsheet.

alèser [aleze] *vt* to ream.

alevin [alvɛ̃] *nm* alevin, young fish.

algarade [algaʀad] *nf* row, dispute.

algèbre [alʒɛbʀ(ə)] *nf* algebra ; **algébrique** *a* algebraic.

Alger [alʒe] *n* Algiers.

Algérie [alʒeʀi] *nf* Algeria ; **algérien, ne** *a, nm/f* Algerian.

Algérois, e [alʒeʀwa, -waz] *nm/f* inhabitant *ou* native of Algiers // *nm*: **l'~** the Algiers region.

algorithme [algɔʀitm(ə)] *nm* algorithm.

algue [alg(ə)] *nf* (*gén*) seaweed *q* ; (*BOT*) alga (*pl* algae).

alibi [alibi] *nm* alibi.

aliénation [aljenɑsjɔ̃] *nf* alienation.

aliéné, e [aljene] *nm/f* insane person, lunatic (*péj*).

aliéner [aljene] *vt* to alienate ; (*bien, liberté*) to give up ; **s'~** *vt* to alienate.

alignement [aliɲmɑ̃] *nm* alignment ; lining up ; **à l'~** in line.

aligner [aliɲe] *vt* to align, line up ; (*idées, chiffres*) to string together ; (*adapter*): **~ qch sur** to bring sth into alignment with ; **s'~** (*soldats etc*) to line up ; **s'~ sur** (*POL*) to align o.s. on.

aliment [alimɑ̃] *nm* food ; **alimentaire** *a* food *cpd* ; (*péj*: *besogne*) done merely to earn a living, done as a potboiler ; **produits alimentaires** foodstuffs, foods.

alimentation [alimɑ̃tɑsjɔ̃] *nf* feeding ; supplying ; (*commerce*) food trade ; (*produits*) groceries *pl* ; (*régime*) diet.

alimenter [alimɑ̃te] *vt* to feed ; (*TECH*): **~ (en)** to supply (with) ; to feed (with) ; (*fig*) to sustain, keep going.

alinéa [alinea] *nm* paragraph ; **'nouvel ~'** new line.

aliter [alite] : **s'~** *vi* to take to one's bed.

alizé [alize] *a, nm*: (**vent**) **~** trade wind.

allaiter [alete] *vt* to (breast-)feed, nurse ; (*suj*: *animal*) to suckle.

allant [alɑ̃] *nm* drive, go.

allécher [aleʃe] *vt*: **~ qn** to make sb's mouth water ; to tempt sb, entice sb.

allée [ale] *nf* (*de jardin*) path ; (*en ville*) avenue, drive. **~s et venues** *nfpl* comings and goings.

allégation [alegɑsjɔ̃] *nf* allegation.

alléger [aleʒe] *vt* (*voiture*) to make lighter ; (*chargement*) to lighten ; (*souffrance*) to alleviate, soothe.

allégorie [alegɔʀi] *nf* allegory.

allègre [alɛgʀ(ə)] *a* lively, jaunty ; gay, cheerful.

allégresse [alegʀɛs] *nf* (*joie*) elation, gaiety.

alléguer [alege] *vt* to put forward (as proof *ou* an excuse).

Allemagne [almaɲ] *nf*: **l'~** Germany ; **l'~ de l'Est/Ouest** East/West Germany ; **allemand, e** *a, nm/f, nm* (*langue*) German.

aller [ale] *nm* (*trajet*) outward journey ; (*billet*) single *ou* one-way ticket // *vi* (*gén*) to go ; **~ à** (*convenir*) to suit ; (*suj*: *forme, pointure etc*) to fit ; **~ avec** (*couleurs, style etc*) to go (well) with ; **je vais y aller/me fâcher** I'm going to go/to get angry ; **~ voir** to go and see, go to see ; **comment allez-vous** *ou* **ça va?** how are you? ; **comment ça va?** (*affaires etc*) how are things? ; **il va bien/mal** he's well/not well, he's fine/ill ; **ça va bien/mal** (*affaires etc*) it's going well/not going well ; **il y a de leur vie** their lives are at stake ; **s'en ~** *vi* (*partir*) to be off, go, leave ; (*disparaître*) to go away ; **~ et retour** *nm* (*trajet*) return trip *ou* journey ; (*billet*) return (ticket).

allergie [alɛʀʒi] *nf* allergy ; **allergique** *a* allergic ; **allergique à** allergic to.

alliage [aljaʒ] *nm* alloy.

alliance [aljɑ̃s] *nf* (*MIL, POL*) alliance ; (*mariage*) marriage ; (*bague*) wedding ring ; **neveu par ~** nephew by marriage.

allié, e [alje] *nm/f* ally ; **parents et ~s** relatives and relatives by marriage.

allier [alje] *vt* (*métaux*) to alloy ; (*POL, gén*) to ally ; (*fig*) to combine ; **s'~** to become allies ; (*éléments, caractéristiques*) to combine ; **s'~ à** to become allied to *ou* with.

allô [alo] *excl* hullo, hallo.

allocataire [alɔkatɛʀ] *nm/f* beneficiary.

allocation [alɔkɑsjɔ̃] *nf* allowance ; **~ (de) chômage** unemployment benefit ; **~ (de) logement** rent allowance *ou* subsidy ; **~s familiales** family allowance(s).

allocution [alɔkysjɔ̃] *nf* short speech.

allonger [alɔ̃ʒe] *vt* to lengthen, make longer ; (*étendre*: *bras, jambe*) to stretch (out) ; **s'~** *vi* to get longer ; (*se coucher*) to lie down, stretch out ; **~ le pas** to hasten one's step(s).

allouer [alwe] *vt*: **~ qch à** to allocate sth to, allot sth to.

allumage [alymaʒ] *nm* (*AUTO*) ignition.

allume... [alym] *préfixe*: **~-cigare** *nm inv* cigar lighter ; **~-gaz** *nm inv* gas lighter.

allumer [alyme] *vt* (*lampe, phare, radio*) to put *ou* switch on ; (*pièce*) to put *ou* switch the light(s) on in ; (*feu*) to light ; **s'~** *vi* (*lumière, lampe*) to come *ou* go on.

allumette [alymɛt] *nf* match.

allumeuse [alymøz] *nf* (*péj*) teaser, vamp.

allure [alyʀ] *nf* (*vitesse*) speed ; pace ; (*démarche*) walk ; (*maintien*) bearing ; (*aspect, air*) look ; **avoir de l'~** to have style *ou* a certain elegance ; **à toute ~** at top *ou* full speed.

allusion [alyzjɔ̃] *nf* allusion ; (*sous-entendu*) hint ; **faire ~ à** to allude *ou* refer to ; to hint at.

alluvions [alyvjɔ̃] *nfpl* alluvial deposits, alluvium *sg*.

almanach [almana] *nm* almanac.

aloi [alwa] *nm*: **de bon ~** of genuine worth *ou* quality.

alors [alɔʀ] *ad* then, at that time // *cj* then, so ; **~ que** *cj* (*au moment où*) when, as ; (*pendant que*) while, when ; (*tandis que*) whereas, while.

alouette [alwɛt] *nf* (sky)lark.

alourdir [aluʀdiʀ] *vt* to weigh down, make heavy.

aloyau [alwajo] *nm* sirloin.

alpage [alpaʒ] *nm* high mountain pasture.

Alpes [alp(ə)] *nfpl*: **les ~** the Alps; **alpestre** *a* alpine.

alphabet [alfabɛ] *nm* alphabet; (*livre*) ABC (book), primer; **alphabétique** *a* alphabetic(al); **alphabétiser** *vt* to teach to read and write; to eliminate illiteracy in.

alpin, e [alpɛ̃, -in] *a* alpine; **alpinisme** *nm* mountaineering, climbing; **alpiniste** *nm/f* mountaineer, climber.

Alsace [alzas] *nf* Alsace; **alsacien, ne** *a*, *nm/f* Alsatian.

altérer [alteʀe] *vt* to falsify; to distort; to debase; to impair; (*donner soif à*) to make thirsty; **s'~** *vi* to deteriorate; to spoil.

alternance [altɛʀnɑ̃s] *nf* alternation; **en ~** alternately.

alternateur [altɛʀnatœʀ] *nm* alternator.

alternatif, ive [altɛʀnatif, -iv] *a* alternating // *nf* (*choix*) alternative; **alternativement** *ad* alternately.

alterner [altɛʀne] *vt* to alternate // *vi*: **~ (avec)** to alternate (with); **(faire) ~ qch avec qch** to alternate sth with sth.

Altesse [altɛs] *nf* Highness.

altier, ière [altje, -jɛʀ] *a* haughty.

altimètre [altimɛtʀ(ə)] *nm* altimeter.

altiste [altist(ə)] *nm/f* viola player, violist.

altitude [altityd] *nf* altitude, height; **à 1000 m d'~** at a height ou an altitude of 1000 m; **en ~** at high altitudes.

alto [alto] *nm* (*instrument*) viola // *nf* (*contr*)alto.

altruisme [altʀɥism(ə)] *nm* altruism.

aluminium [alyminjɔm] *nm* aluminium.

alunir [alyniʀ] *vi* to land on the moon.

alvéole [alveɔl] *nf* (*de ruche*) alveolus; **alvéolé, e** *a* honeycombed.

amabilité [amabilite] *nf* kindness, amiability; **il a eu l'~ de** he was kind ou good enough to.

amadou [amadu] *nm* touchwood, amadou.

amadouer [amadwe] *vt* to coax, cajole; to mollify, soothe.

amaigrir [amegʀiʀ] *vt* to make thin ou thinner; **régime amaigrissant** slimming diet.

amalgamer [amalgame] *vt* to amalgamate.

amande [amɑ̃d] *nf* (*de l'amandier*) almond; (*de noyau de fruit*) kernel; **amandier** *nm* almond (tree).

amant [amɑ̃] *nm* lover.

amarre [amaʀ] *nf* (NAVIG) (mooring) rope ou line; **~s** moorings; **amarrer** *vt* (NAVIG) to moor; (*gén*) to make fast.

amas [amɑ] *nm* heap, pile.

amasser [amɑse] *vt* to amass; **s'~** *vi* to pile up; to accumulate; to gather.

amateur [amatœʀ] *nm* amateur; **en ~** (*péj*) amateurishly; **musicien/sportif ~** amateur musician/sportsman; **~ de musique/sport** *etc* music/sport *etc* lover; **~isme** *nm* amateurism; (*péj*) amateurishness.

amazone [amazon] *nf*: **en ~** sidesaddle.

ambages [ɑ̃baʒ]: **sans ~** *ad* without beating about the bush, plainly.

ambassade [ɑ̃basad] *nf* embassy; (*mission*): **en ~** on a mission; **ambassadeur, drice** *nm/f* ambassador/ambassadress.

ambiance [ɑ̃bjɑ̃s] *nf* atmosphere.

ambiant, e [ɑ̃bjɑ̃, -ɑ̃t] *a* (*air, milieu*) surrounding; (*température*) ambient.

ambidextre [ɑ̃bidɛkstʀ(ə)] *a* ambidextrous.

ambigu, ë [ɑ̃bigy] *a* ambiguous; **ambiguïté** *nf* ambiguousness *q*, ambiguity.

ambitieux, euse [ɑ̃bisjø, -øz] *a* ambitious.

ambition [ɑ̃bisjɔ̃] *nf* ambition; **ambitionner** *vt* to have as one's aim ou ambition.

ambivalent, e [ɑ̃bivalɑ̃, -ɑ̃t] *a* ambivalent.

ambre [ɑ̃bʀ(ə)] *nm*: **~ (jaune)** amber; **~ gris** ambergris.

ambulance [ɑ̃bylɑ̃s] *nf* ambulance; **ambulancier, ière** *nm/f* ambulance man/woman.

ambulant, e [ɑ̃bylɑ̃, -ɑ̃t] *a* travelling, itinerant.

âme [ɑm] *nf* soul; **~ sœur** kindred spirit.

améliorer [ameljɔʀe] *vt* to improve; **s'~** *vi* to improve, get better.

aménagement [amenaʒmɑ̃] *nm* fitting out; laying out; developing; **~s** *nmpl* developments; **l'~ du territoire** ≈ town and country planning; **~s fiscaux** tax adjustments.

aménager [amenaʒe] *vt* (*agencer, transformer*) to fit out; to lay out; (: *quartier, territoire*) to develop; (*installer*) to fix up, put in; **ferme aménagée** converted farmhouse.

amende [amɑ̃d] *nf* fine; **mettre à l'~** to penalize; **faire ~ honorable** to make amends.

amender [amɑ̃de] *vt* (*loi*) to amend; (*terre*) to enrich; **s'~** *vi* to mend one's ways.

amène [amɛn] *a* affable; **peu ~** unkind.

amener [amne] *vt* to bring; (*causer*) to bring about; (*baisser: drapeau, voiles*) to strike; **s'~** *vi* (*fam*) to show up, turn up.

amenuiser [amənɥize]: **s'~** *vi* to grow slimmer, lessen; to dwindle.

amer, amère [amɛʀ] *a* bitter.

américain, e [ameʀikɛ̃, -ɛn] *a*, *nm/f* American.

Amérique [ameʀik] *nf* America; **l'~ centrale** Central America; **l'~ latine** Latin America; **l'~ du Nord** North America; **l'~ du Sud** South America.

amerrir [ameʀiʀ] *vi* to land (on the sea).

amertume [amɛʀtym] *nf* bitterness.

améthyste [ametist(ə)] *nf* amethyst.

ameublement [amœbləmɑ̃] *nm* furnishing; (*meubles*) furniture; **articles d'~** furnishings; **tissus d'~** soft furnishings, fabrics.

ameuter [amøte] *vt* (*badauds*) to draw a crowd of; (*peuple*) to rouse, stir up.

ami, e [ami] *nm/f* friend; (*amant/maîtresse*) boyfriend/girlfriend // *a*: **pays/groupe ~** friendly country/group; **être (très) ~ avec qn** to be (very) good friends with sb ; **être ~ de l'ordre** to be a lover of order ; **un ~ des arts** a patron of the arts ; **un ~ des chiens** a dog lover.

amiable [amjabl(ə)]: **à l'~** *ad* (*JUR*) out of court ; (*gén*) amicably.

amiante [amjɑ̃t] *nm* asbestos.

amibe [amib] *nf* amoeba (*pl* ae).

amical, e, aux [amikal, -o] *a* friendly // *nf* (*club*) association.

amidon [amidɔ̃] *nm* starch ; **amidonner** *vt* to starch.

amincir [amɛ̃siʀ] *vt* (*objet*) to thin (down) ; **~ qn** to make sb thinner *ou* slimmer ; **s'~** *vi* to get thinner ; to get slimmer.

amiral, aux [amiʀal, -o] *nm* admiral ; **amirauté** *nf* admiralty.

amitié [amitje] *nf* friendship ; **prendre en ~** to take a liking to, befriend ; **faire** *ou* **présenter ses ~s à qn** to send sb one's best wishes *ou* kind regards.

ammoniac [amɔnjak] *nm*: **(gaz) ~** ammonia.

ammoniaque [amɔnjak] *nf* ammonia (water).

amnésie [amnezi] *nf* amnesia ; **amnésique** *a* amnesic.

amnistie [amnisti] *nf* amnesty ; **amnistier** *vt* to amnesty.

amoindrir [amwɛ̃dʀiʀ] *vt* to reduce.

amollir [amɔliʀ] *vt* to soften.

amonceler [amɔ̃sle] *vt*, **s'~** *vi* to pile *ou* heap up ; (*fig*) to accumulate.

amont [amɔ̃]: **en ~** *ad* upstream ; (*sur une pente*) uphill ; **en ~ de** *prép* upstream from ; uphill from, above.

amorce [amɔʀs(ə)] *nf* (*sur un hameçon*) bait ; (*explosif*) cap ; primer ; priming ; (*fig*: *début*) beginning(s), start ; **amorcer** *vt* to bait ; to prime ; to begin, start.

amorphe [amɔʀf(ə)] *a* passive, lifeless.

amortir [amɔʀtiʀ] *vt* (*atténuer*: *choc*) to absorb, cushion ; (*bruit, douleur*) to deaden ; (*COMM*: *dette*) to pay off, amortize ; (: *mise de fonds*) to write off ; (: *matériel*) to write off, depreciate ; **~ un abonnement** to make a season ticket pay (for itself).

amour [amuʀ] *nm* love ; (*liaison*) love affair, love ; (*statuette etc*) cupid ; **faire l'~** to make love ; **s'~acher de** (*péj*) to become infatuated with ; **~ette** *nf* passing fancy ; **~eux, euse** *a* (*regard, tempérament*) amorous ; (*vie, problèmes*) love *cpd* ; (*personne*): **~eux (de qn)** in love (with sb) // *nm/f* lover // *nmpl* courting couple(s) ; **être ~eux de qch** to be passionately fond of sth ; **un ~eux de la nature** a nature lover ; **~-propre** *nm* self-esteem, pride.

amovible [amɔvibl(ə)] *a* removable, detachable.

ampère [ɑ̃pɛʀ] *nm* amp(ere) ; **~mètre** *nm* ammeter.

amphibie [ɑ̃fibi] *a* amphibious.

amphithéâtre [ɑ̃fiteɑtʀ(ə)] *nm* amphitheatre ; (*d'université*) lecture hall *ou* theatre.

amphore [ɑ̃fɔʀ] *nf* amphora.

ample [ɑ̃pl(ə)] *a* (*vêtement*) roomy, ample ; (*gestes, mouvement*) broad ; (*ressources*) ample ; **~ment** *ad* amply ; **~ment**

suffisant ample, more than enough ; **ampleur** *nf* (*importance*) scale, size ; extent, magnitude.

amplificateur [ɑ̃plifikatœʀ] *nm* amplifier.

amplifier [ɑ̃plifje] *vt* (*son, oscillation*) to amplify ; (*fig*) to expand, increase.

amplitude [ɑ̃plityd] *nf* amplitude ; (*des températures*) range.

ampoule [ɑ̃pul] *nf* (*électrique*) bulb ; (*de médicament*) phial ; (*aux mains, pieds*) blister.

ampoulé, e [ɑ̃pule] *a* (*péj*) turgid, pompous.

amputation [ɑ̃pytasjɔ̃] *nf* amputation.

amputer [ɑ̃pyte] *vt* (*MÉD*) to amputate ; (*fig*) to cut *ou* reduce drastically ; **~ qn d'un bras/pied** to amputate sb's arm/foot.

amulette [amylɛt] *nf* amulet.

amusant, e [amyzɑ̃, -ɑ̃t] *a* (*divertissant, spirituel*) entertaining, amusing ; (*comique*) funny, amusing.

amusé, e [amyze] *a* amused.

amuse-gueule [amyzgœl] *nm inv* appetizer, snack.

amusement [amyzmɑ̃] *nm* (*voir amusé*) amusement ; (*voir amuser*) entertaining, amusing ; (*jeu etc*) amusement, diversion.

amuser [amyze] *vt* (*divertir*) to entertain, amuse ; (*égayer, faire rire*) to amuse ; (*détourner l'attention de*) to distract ; **s'~** *vi* (*jouer*) to amuse o.s., play ; (*se divertir*) to enjoy o.s., have fun ; (*fig*) to mess about ; **s'~ de qch** (*trouver comique*) to find sth amusing ; **s'~ avec** *ou* **de qn** (*duper*) to make a fool of sb ; **amusette** *nf* idle pleasure, trivial pastime ; **amuseur** *nm* entertainer ; (*péj*) clown.

amygdale [amidal] *nf* tonsil ; **opérer qn des ~s** to take sb's tonsils out.

an [ɑ̃] *nm* year.

anachronique [anakʀɔnik] *a* anachronistic ; **anachronisme** *nm* anachronism.

anagramme [anagʀam] *nf* anagram.

anal, e, aux [anal, -o] *a* anal.

analgésique [analʒezik] *nm* analgesic.

analogie [analɔʒi] *nf* analogy.

analogue [analɔg] *a*: **~ (à)** analogous (to), similar (to).

analphabète [analfabɛt] *nm/f* illiterate.

analyse [analiz] *nf* (*gén*) analysis ; (*MÉD*) test ; **faire l'~ de** to analyse ; **~ grammaticale** grammatical analysis, parsing (*SCOL*) ; **analyser** *vt* to analyse ; (*MÉD*) to test ; **analyste** *nm/f* analyst ; (*psychanalyste*) (psycho)analyst ; **analytique** *a* analytical.

ananas [anana] *nm* pineapple.

anarchie [anaʀʃi] *nf* (*gén, POL*) anarchy ; **anarchisme** *nm* anarchism ; **anarchiste** *a* anarchistic // *nm/f* anarchist.

anathème [anatɛm] *nm*: **jeter l'~ sur, lancer l'~ contre** to anathematize, curse.

anatomie [anatɔmi] *nf* anatomy ; **anatomique** *a* anatomical.

ancestral, e, aux [ɑ̃sɛstʀal, -o] *a* ancestral.

ancêtre [ɑ̃sɛtʀ(ə)] *nm/f* ancestor ; (*fig*): **l'~ de** the forerunner of ; **~s** *nmpl* (*aïeux*) ancestors, forefathers.

anche [ɑ̃ʃ] *nf* reed.

anchois [ɑ̃ʃwa] *nm* anchovy.

ancien, ne [ɑ̃sjɛ̃, -jɛn] *a* old ; (*de jadis, de l'antiquité*) ancient ; (*précédent, ex-*) former, old // *nm/f* (*dans une tribu*) elder ; **un ~ ministre** a former minister ; **être plus ~ que qn dans une maison** to have been in a firm longer than sb ; to be senior to sb (in a firm) ; **anciennement** *ad* formerly ; **ancienneté** *nf* oldness ; antiquity ; (ADMIN: *length of*) service ; seniority.

ancrage [ɑ̃kʀaʒ] *nm* anchoring ; (NAVIG) anchorage ; (CONSTR) cramp(-iron), anchor.

ancre [ɑ̃kʀ(ə)] *nf* anchor ; **jeter/lever l'~** to cast/weigh anchor ; **à l'~** at anchor.

ancrer [ɑ̃kʀe] *vt* (CONSTR: *câble etc*) to anchor ; (*fig*) to fix firmly ; **s'~** *vi* (NAVIG) to (cast) anchor.

Andorre [ɑ̃dɔʀ] *n* Andorra.

andouille [ɑ̃duj] *nf* (CULIN) *sausage made of chitterlings* ; (*fam*) clot, nit.

âne [ɑn] *nm* donkey, ass ; (*péj*) dunce, fool.

anéantir [aneɑ̃tiʀ] *vt* to annihilate, wipe out ; (*fig*) to obliterate, destroy ; to overwhelm.

anecdote [anɛkdɔt] *nf* anecdote ; **anecdotique** *a* anecdotal.

anémie [anemi] *nf* anaemia ; **anémié, e** *a* anaemic ; (*fig*) enfeebled ; **anémique** *a* anaemic.

anémone [anemɔn] *nf* anemone ; **~ de mer** sea anemone.

ânerie [ɑnʀi] *nf* stupidity ; stupid *ou* idiotic comment *etc*.

ânesse [ɑnɛs] *nf* she-ass.

anesthésie [anɛstezi] *nf* anaesthesia ; **faire une ~ locale à qn** to give sb a local anaesthetic ; **anesthésier** *vt* to anaesthetize ; **anesthésique** *a* anaesthetic ; **anesthésiste** *nm/f* anaesthetist.

anfractuosité [ɑ̃fʀaktɥozite] *nf* crevice.

ange [ɑ̃ʒ] *nm* angel ; **être aux ~s** to be over the moon ; **~ gardien** guardian angel ; **angélique** *a* angelic(al).

angélus [ɑ̃ʒelys] *nm* angelus.

angine [ɑ̃ʒin] *nf* sore throat, throat infection (*tonsillitis or pharyngitis*) ; **~ de poitrine** angina (pectoris).

anglais, e [ɑ̃glɛ, -ɛz] *a* English // *nm/f* : **A~, e** Englishman/woman // *nm* (*langue*) English ; **les A~** the English ; **~es** *nfpl* (*cheveux*) ringlets ; **filer à l'~e** to take French leave.

angle [ɑ̃gl(ə)] *nm* angle ; (*coin*) corner ; **~ droit/obtus/aigu** right/obtuse/acute angle.

Angleterre [ɑ̃glətɛʀ] *nf* : **l'~** England.

anglican, e [ɑ̃glikɑ̃, -an] *a* Anglican.

anglicisme [ɑ̃glisism(ə)] *nm* anglicism.

angliciste [ɑ̃glisist(ə)] *nm/f* English scholar ; student of English.

anglo... [ɑ̃glɔ] *préfixe* Anglo-, anglo(-) ; **~phile** *a* anglophilic ; **~phobe** *a* anglophobic ; **~phone** *a* English-speaking ; **~saxon, ne** *a* Anglo-Saxon.

angoisse [ɑ̃gwas] *nf* : **l'~** anguish *q* ; **angoisser** *vt* to harrow, cause anguish to.

anguille [ɑ̃gij] *nf* eel ; **~ de mer** conger (eel).

angulaire [ɑ̃gylɛʀ] *a* angular.

anguleux, euse [ɑ̃gylø, -øz] *a* angular.

anicroche [anikʀɔʃ] *nf* hitch, snag.

animal, e, aux [animal, -o] *a, nm* animal ; **~ier** *a*: **peintre ~ier** animal painter.

animateur, trice [animatœʀ, -tʀis] *nm/f* (*de télévision, music-hall*) compère ; (*de maison de jeunes*) leader, organizer.

animation [animasjɔ̃] *nf* (*voir animé*) business ['bɪznɪs] ; liveliness ; (CINÉMA: *technique*) animation.

animé, e [anime] *a* (*rue, lieu*) busy, lively ; (*conversation, réunion*) lively, animated ; (*opposé à inanimé, aussi* LING) animate.

animer [anime] *vt* (*ville, soirée*) to liven up, enliven ; (*mettre en mouvement*) to drive ; (*stimuler*) to drive, impel ; **s'~** *vi* to liven up, come to life.

animosité [animozite] *nf* animosity.

anis [ani] *nm* (CULIN) aniseed ; (BOT) anise.

ankyloser [ɑ̃kiloze] : **s'~** *vi* to get stiff, to ankylose.

annales [anal] *nfpl* annals.

anneau, x [ano] *nm* (*de rideau, bague*) ring ; (*de chaîne*) link.

année [ane] *nf* year ; **l'~ scolaire/fiscale** the school/tax year ; **~-lumière** *nf* light year.

annexe [anɛks(ə)] *a* (*problème*) related ; (*document*) appended ; (*salle*) adjoining // *nf* (*bâtiment*) annex(e) ; (*de document, ouvrage*) annex, appendix ; (*jointe à une lettre, un dossier*) enclosure.

annexer [anɛkse] *vt* (*pays, biens*) to annex ; **~ qch à** (*joindre*) to append sth to ; **annexion** *nf* annexation.

annihiler [aniile] *vt* to annihilate.

anniversaire [anivɛʀsɛʀ] *nm* birthday ; (*d'un événement, bâtiment*) anniversary // *a*: **jour ~** anniversary.

annonce [anɔ̃s] *nf* announcement ; (*signe, indice*) sign ; (*aussi*: **~ publicitaire**) advertisement ; (CARTES) declaration ; **les petites ~s** the classified advertisements, the small ads.

annoncer [anɔ̃se] *vt* to announce ; (*être le signe de*) to herald ; **s'~ bien/difficile** to look promising/difficult ; **annonceur, euse** *nm/f* (TV, RADIO: *speaker*) announcer ; (*publicitaire*) advertiser ; **l'Annonciation** *nf* the Annunciation.

annotation [anɔtasjɔ̃] *nf* annotation.

annoter [anɔte] *vt* to annotate.

annuaire [anɥɛʀ] *nm* yearbook, annual ; **~ téléphonique** (telephone) directory, phone book.

annuel, le [anɥɛl] *a* annual, yearly ; **~lement** *ad* annually, yearly.

annuité [anɥite] *nf* annual instalment.

annulaire [anɥlɛʀ] *nm* ring *ou* third finger.

annulation [anɥlasjɔ̃] *nf* cancellation ; annulment ; quashing.

annuler [anɥle] *vt* (*rendez-vous, voyage*) to cancel, call off ; (*mariage*) to annul ; (*jugement*) to quash ; (*résultats*) to declare void ; (MATH, PHYSIQUE) to cancel out.

anoblir [anɔbliʀ] *vt* to ennoble.

anode [anɔd] *nf* anode.

anodin, e [anɔdɛ̃, -in] *a* harmless ; insignificant, trivial.

anomalie [anɔmali] *nf* anomaly.

ânonner [ɑnɔne] *vi*, *vt* to read in a drone ; to read in a fumbling manner.
anonymat [anɔnima] *nm* anonymity.
anonyme [anɔnim] *a* anonymous ; (*fig*) impersonal.
anorak [anɔʀak] *nm* anorak.
anormal, e, aux [anɔʀmal, -o] *a* abnormal ; (*insolite*) unusual, abnormal.
anse [ɑ̃s] *nf* (*de panier, tasse*) handle ; (*GÉO*) cove.
antagoniste [ɑ̃tagɔnist(ə)] *a* antagonistic // *nm* antagonist.
antan [ɑ̃tɑ̃]: **d'~** *a* of yesteryear, of long ago.
antarctique [ɑ̃taʀktik] *a* Antarctic // *nm*: **l'A~** the Antarctic.
antécédent [ɑ̃tesedɑ̃] *nm* (*LING*) antecedent ; **~s** *nmpl* (*MÉD etc*) past history *sg*.
antédiluvien, ne [ɑ̃tedilyvjɛ̃, -jɛn] *a* (*fig*) ancient, antediluvian.
antenne [ɑ̃tɛn] *nf* (*de radio, télévision*) aerial ; (*d'insecte*) antenna (*pl* ae), feeler ; (*poste avancé*) outpost ; (*petite succursale*) sub-branch ; **passer à l'~** to go on the air ; **prendre l'~** to tune in ; **2 heures d'~** 2 hours' broadcasting time.
antépénultième [ɑ̃tepenyltjɛm] *a* antepenultimate, last but two.
antérieur, e [ɑ̃teʀjœʀ] *a* (*d'avant*) previous, earlier ; (*de devant*) front ; **~ à** prior *ou* previous to ; **passé/futur ~** (*LING*) past/future anterior ; **~ement** *ad* earlier ; previously ; **~ement à** prior *ou* previous to ; **antériorité** *nf* precedence (*in time*).
anthologie [ɑ̃tɔlɔʒi] *nf* anthology.
anthracite [ɑ̃tʀasit] *nm* anthracite.
anthropo... [ɑ̃tʀɔpɔ] *préfixe*: **~centrisme** *nm* anthropocentrism ; **~logie** *nf* anthropology ; **~logue** *nm/f* anthropologist ; **~métrie** *nf* anthropometry ; **~morphisme** *nm* anthropomorphism ; **~phage** *a* cannibalistic, anthropophagous.
anti... [ɑ̃ti] *préfixe* anti...; **~aérien, ne** *a* anti-aircraft ; **abri ~aérien** air-raid shelter ; **~alcoolique** *a* against alcohol ; **ligue ~alcoolique** temperance league ; **~atomique** *a*: **abri ~atomique** fallout shelter ; **~biotique** *nm* antibiotic ; **~brouillard** *a*: **phare ~brouillard** fog lamp ; **~cancéreux, euse** *a* cancer *cpd*.
antichambre [ɑ̃tiʃɑ̃bʀ(ə)] *nf* antechamber, anteroom ; **faire ~** to wait (for an audience).
antichar [ɑ̃tiʃaʀ] *a* anti-tank.
anticipation [ɑ̃tisipasjɔ̃] *nf* anticipation ; payment in advance ; **livre/film d'~** science fiction book/film.
anticipé, e [ɑ̃tisipe] *a* (*règlement, paiement*) early, in advance ; (*joie etc*) anticipated, early ; **avec mes remerciements ~s** thanking you in advance *ou* anticipation.
anticiper [ɑ̃tisipe] *vt* (*événement, coup*) to anticipate, foresee ; (*paiement*) to pay *ou* make in advance // *vi* to look *ou* think ahead ; to jump ahead ; to anticipate ; **~ sur** to anticipate.
anticlérical, e, aux [ɑ̃tikleʀikal, -o] *a* anticlerical.
anticonceptionnel, le [ɑ̃tikɔ̃sɛpsjɔnɛl] *a* contraceptive.

anticorps [ɑ̃tikɔʀ] *nm* antibody.
anticyclone [ɑ̃tisiklon] *nm* anticyclone.
antidater [ɑ̃tidate] *vt* to backdate, predate.
antidérapant, e [ɑ̃tideʀapɑ̃, -ɑ̃t] *a* non-skid.
antidote [ɑ̃tidɔt] *nm* antidote.
antienne [ɑ̃tjɛn] *nf* (*fig*) chant, refrain.
antigel [ɑ̃tiʒɛl] *nm* antifreeze.
Antilles [ɑ̃tij] *nfpl*: **les ~** the West Indies.
antilope [ɑ̃tilɔp] *nf* antelope.
antimilitariste [ɑ̃timilitaʀist(ə)] *a* antimilitarist.
antimite(s) [ɑ̃timit] *a, nm*: **(produit) ~** mothproofer ; moth repellent.
antiparasite [ɑ̃tipaʀazit] *a* (*RADIO, TV*) anti-interference ; **dispositif ~** suppressor.
antipathie [ɑ̃tipati] *nf* antipathy ; **antipathique** *a* unpleasant, disagreeable.
antiphrase [ɑ̃tifʀaz] *nf*: **par ~** ironically.
antipodes [ɑ̃tipɔd] *nmpl* (*GÉO*): **les ~** the antipodes ; (*fig*): **être aux ~ de** to be the opposite extreme of.
antiquaire [ɑ̃tikɛʀ] *nm/f* antique dealer.
antique [ɑ̃tik] *a* antique ; (*très vieux*) ancient, antiquated.
antiquité [ɑ̃tikite] *nf* (*objet*) antique ; **l'A~** Antiquity ; **magasin d'~s** antique shop.
antirabique [ɑ̃tiʀabik] *a* rabies *cpd*.
antiraciste [ɑ̃tiʀasist(ə)] *a* antiracist, antiracialist.
antirides [ɑ̃tiʀid] *a* (*crème*) anti-wrinkle.
antirouille [ɑ̃tiʀuj] *a inv*: **peinture ~** antirust paint ; **traitement ~** rustproofing.
antisémite [ɑ̃tisemit] *a* anti-semitic ; **antisémitisme** *nm* anti-semitism.
antiseptique [ɑ̃tisɛptik] *a, nm* antiseptic.
antitétanique [ɑ̃titetanik] *a* tetanus *cpd*.
antithèse [ɑ̃titɛz] *nf* antithesis.
antituberculeux, euse [ɑ̃titybɛʀkylø, -øz] *a* tuberculosis *cpd*.
antivol [ɑ̃tivɔl] *a, nm*: **(dispositif) ~** anti-theft device.
antre [ɑ̃tʀ(ə)] *nm* den, lair.
anus [anys] *nm* anus.
anxiété [ɑ̃ksjete] *nf* anxiety.
anxieux, euse [ɑ̃ksjø, -øz] *a* anxious, worried.
aorte [aɔʀt(ə)] *nf* aorta.
août [u] *nm* August.
apaisement [apɛzmɑ̃] *nm* calming ; soothing ; appeasement ; **~s** *nmpl* soothing reassurances ; pacifying words.
apaiser [apeze] *vt* (*colère*) to calm, quell, soothe ; (*faim*) to appease, assuage ; (*douleur*) to soothe ; (*personne*) to calm (down), pacify ; **s'~** *vi* (*tempête, bruit*) to die down, subside.
apanage [apanaʒ] *nm*: **être l'~ de** to be the privilege *ou* prerogative of.
aparté [apaʀte] *nm* (*THÉÂTRE*) aside ; (*entretien*) private conversation ; **en ~** *ad* in an aside ; in private.
apathie [apati] *nf* apathy ; **apathique** *a* apathetic.
apatride [apatʀid] *nm/f* stateless person.
apercevoir [apɛʀsəvwaʀ] *vt* to see ; **s'~ de** *vt* to notice ; **s'~ que** to notice that.

aperçu [apɛʀsy] *nm* (*vue d'ensemble*) general survey ; (*intuition*) insight.

apéritif, ive [apeʀitif, -iv] *nm* (*boisson*) aperitif ; (*réunion*) pre-lunch (*ou* -dinner) drinks *pl* // *a* which stimulates the appetite ; **prendre l'~** to have drinks (before lunch *ou* dinner) *ou* an aperitif.

apesanteur [apəzɑ̃tœʀ] *nf* weightlessness.

à-peu-près [apøpʀɛ] *nm inv* (*péj*) vague approximation.

apeuré, e [apœʀe] *a* frightened, scared.

aphone [afɔn] *a* voiceless.

aphrodisiaque [afʀɔdizjak] *a, nm* aphrodisiac.

aphte [aft(ə)] *nm* mouth ulcer.

aphteuse [aftøz] *af*: **fièvre ~** foot-and-mouth disease.

apiculteur [apikyltœʀ] *nm* beekeeper.

apiculture [apikyltyʀ] *nf* beekeeping, apiculture.

apitoyer [apitwaje] *vt* to move to pity ; **~ qn sur** to move sb to pity for, make sb feel sorry for ; **s'~ (sur)** to feel pity *ou* compassion (for).

aplanir [aplaniʀ] *vt* to level ; (*fig*) to smooth away, iron out.

aplati, e [aplati] *a* flat, flattened.

aplatir [aplatiʀ] *vt* to flatten ; **s'~** *vi* to become flatter ; to be flattened ; (*fig*) to lie flat on the ground ; (: *fam*) to fall flat on one's face ; (: *péj*) to grovel.

aplomb [aplɔ̃] *nm* (*équilibre*) balance, equilibrium ; (*fig*) self-assurance ; nerve ; **d'~** *ad* steady ; (*CONSTR*) plumb.

apocalypse [apɔkalips(ə)] *nf* apocalypse.

apogée [apɔʒe] *nm* (*fig*) peak, apogee.

apolitique [apɔlitik] *a* apolitical.

apologie [apɔlɔʒi] *nf* vindication, praise.

apoplexie [apɔplɛksi] *nf* apoplexy.

a posteriori [aposteʀjɔʀi] *ad* after the event, with hindsight, a posteriori.

apostolat [apɔstɔla] *nm* (*REL*) apostolate, discipleship ; (*gén*) proselytism, preaching ; **apostolique** *a* apostolic.

apostrophe [apɔstʀɔf] *nf* (*signe*) apostrophe ; (*appel*) interpellation.

apostropher [apɔstʀɔfe] *vt* (*interpeller*) to shout at, address sharply.

apothéose [apɔteoz] *nf* pinnacle (of achievement) ; grand finale.

apôtre [apotʀ(ə)] *nm* apostle, disciple.

apparaître [apaʀɛtʀ(ə)] *vi* to appear // *vb avec attribut* to appear, seem ; **il apparaît que** it appears that.

apparat [apaʀa] *nm*: **tenue/dîner d'~** ceremonial dress/dinner ; **~ critique** (*d'un texte*) critical apparatus.

appareil [apaʀɛj] *nm* piece of apparatus, device ; appliance ; (*politique, syndical*) machinery ; (*avion*) (aero)plane, aircraft *inv* ; (*téléphonique*) phone ; (*dentier*) brace ; **~ digestif/reproducteur** digestive/reproductive system *ou* apparatus ; **qui est à l'~?** who's speaking? ; **dans le plus simple ~** in one's birthday suit ; **~ de photographie, ~-(photo)** *nm* camera ; **~ 24 x 36 ou petit format** 35mm. camera.

appareillage [apaʀɛjaʒ] *nm* (*appareils*) equipment ; (*NAVIG*) casting off, getting under way.

appareiller [apaʀeje] *vi* (*NAVIG*) to cast off, get under way // *vt* (*assortir*) to match up.

apparemment [apaʀamɑ̃] *ad* apparently.

apparence [apaʀɑ̃s] *nf* appearance ; **en ~** apparently, seemingly.

apparent, e [apaʀɑ̃, -ɑ̃t] *a* visible ; obvious ; (*superficiel*) apparent ; **coutures ~es** topstitched seams ; **poutres ~es** exposed beams.

apparenté, e [apaʀɑ̃te] *a*: **~ à** related to ; (*fig*) similar to.

appariteur [apaʀitœʀ] *nm* attendant, porter (*in French universities*).

apparition [apaʀisjɔ̃] *nf* appearance ; (*surnaturelle*) apparition.

appartement [apaʀtəmɑ̃] *nm* flat.

appartenance [apaʀtənɑ̃s] *nf*: **~ à** belonging to, membership of.

appartenir [apaʀtəniʀ]: **~ à** *vt* to belong to ; (*faire partie de*) to belong to, be a member of ; **il lui appartient de** it is up to him to, it is his duty to.

apparu, e *pp de* **apparaître**.

appas [apɑ] *nmpl* (*d'une femme*) charms.

appât [apɑ] *nm* (*PÊCHE*) bait ; (*fig*) lure, bait ; **appâter** *vt* (*hameçon*) to bait ; (*poisson, fig*) to lure, entice.

appauvrir [apovʀiʀ] *vt* to impoverish ; **s'~** *vi* to grow poorer, become impoverished.

appel [apɛl] *nm* call ; (*nominal*) roll call ; (: *SCOL*) register ; (*MIL*: *recrutement*) call up ; (*JUR*) appeal ; **faire ~ à** (*invoquer*) to appeal to ; (*avoir recours à*) to call on ; (*nécessiter*) to call for, require ; **faire ou interjeter ~** (*JUR*) to appeal, lodge an appeal ; **faire l'~** to call the roll ; to call the register ; **sans ~** (*fig*) final, irrevocable ; **~ d'air** in-draught ; **~ d'offres** (*COMM*) invitation to tender ; **faire un ~ de phares** to flash one's headlights ; **~ (téléphonique)** (tele)phone call.

appelé [aple] *nm* (*MIL*) conscript.

appeler [aple] *vt* to call ; (*faire venir*: *médecin etc*) to call, send for ; (*fig*: *nécessiter*) to call for, demand ; **être appelé à** (*fig*) to be destined to ; **~ qn à comparaître** (*JUR*) to summon sb to appear ; **en ~ à** to appeal to ; **s'~**: **elle s'appelle Gabrielle** her name is Gabrielle, she's called Gabrielle ; **comment ça s'appelle?** what is it called?

appellation [apelasjɔ̃] *nf* designation, appellation.

appendice [apɛ̃dis] *nm* appendix ; **appendicite** *nf* appendicitis.

appentis [apɑ̃ti] *nm* lean-to.

appesantir [apzɑ̃tiʀ]: **s'~** *vi* to grow heavier ; **s'~ sur** (*fig*) to dwell at length on.

appétissant, e [apetisɑ̃, -ɑ̃t] *a* appetizing, mouth-watering.

appétit [apeti] *nm* appetite ; **avoir un gros/petit ~** to have a big/small appetite ; **bon ~!** enjoy your meal!

applaudir [aplodiʀ] *vt* to applaud // *vi* to applaud, clap ; **~ à** *vt* (*décision*) to applaud, commend ; **applaudissements** *nmpl* applause *sg*, clapping *sg*.

application [aplikasjɔ̃] *nf* application.

applique [aplik] nf wall lamp.

appliqué, e [aplike] a (élève etc) industrious, assiduous; (science) applied.

appliquer [aplike] vt to apply; (loi) to enforce; **s'~** vi (élève etc) to apply o.s.; **s'~ à faire qch** to apply o.s. to doing sth, take pains to do sth.

appoint [apwɛ̃] nm (extra) contribution ou help; **avoir/faire l'~** (en payant) to have/give the right change ou money; **chauffage d'~** extra heating.

appointments [apwɛ̃tmɑ̃] nmpl salary sg.

appontement [apɔ̃tmɑ̃] nm landing stage, wharf.

apport [apɔʀ] nm supply; contribution.

apporter [apɔʀte] vt to bring.

apposer [apoze] vt to append; to affix.

apposition [apozisjɔ̃] nf appending; affixing; (LING): **en ~** in apposition.

appréciable [apʀesjabl(ə)] a (important) appreciable, significant.

appréciation [apʀesjasjɔ̃] nf appreciation; estimation, assessment; **~s** (avis) assessment sg, appraisal sg.

apprécier [apʀesje] vt to appreciate; (évaluer) to estimate, assess.

appréhender [apʀeɑ̃de] vt (craindre) to dread; (arrêter) to apprehend; **~ que** to fear that; **~ de faire** to dread doing.

appréhension [apʀeɑ̃sjɔ̃] nf apprehension.

apprendre [apʀɑ̃dʀ(ə)] vt to learn; (événement, résultats) to learn of, hear of; **~ qch à qn** (informer) to tell sb (of) sth; (enseigner) to teach sb sth; **~ à faire qch** to learn to do sth; **~ à qn à faire qch** to teach sb to do sth; **apprenti, e** nm/f apprentice; (fig) novice, beginner; **apprentissage** nm learning; (COMM, SCOL: période) apprenticeship.

apprêt [apʀɛ] nm (sur un cuir, une étoffe) dressing; (sur un mur) size; (sur un papier) finish.

apprêté, e [apʀɛte] a (fig) affected.

apprêter [apʀɛte] vt to dress, finish.

appris, e pp de **apprendre**.

apprivoiser [apʀivwaze] vt to tame.

approbateur, trice [apʀɔbatœʀ, -tʀis] a approving.

approbation [apʀɔbasjɔ̃] nf approval.

approche [apʀɔʃ] nf approaching; approach; **à l'~ du bateau/de l'ennemi** as the ship/enemy approached ou drew near.

approché, e [apʀɔʃe] a approximate.

approcher [apʀɔʃe] vi to approach, come near // vt (vedette, artiste) to come close to, approach; (rapprocher): **~ qch (de qch)** to bring ou put ou move sth near (to sth); **~ de** vt to draw near to; (quantité, moment) to approach; **s'~ de** vt to approach, go ou come ou move near to.

approfondi, e [apʀɔfɔ̃di] a thorough, detailed.

approfondir [apʀɔfɔ̃diʀ] vt to deepen, make deeper; (fig) to go (deeper ou further) into.

approprié, e [apʀɔpʀije] a: **~ (à)** appropriate (to), suited to.

approprier [apʀɔpʀije]: **s'~** vt to appropriate, take over.

approuver [apʀuve] vt to agree with; (autoriser: loi, projet) to approve, pass; (trouver louable) to approve of.

approvisionnement [apʀɔvizjɔnmɑ̃] nm supplying; (provisions) supply, stock.

approvisionner [apʀɔvizjɔne] vt to supply; (compte bancaire) to pay funds into; **~ qn en** to supply sb with; **s'~ en** to stock up with.

approximatif, ive [apʀɔksimatif, -iv] a approximate, rough; vague; **approximativement** ad approximately, roughly, vaguely.

Appt abr de **appartement**.

appui [apɥi] nm support; **prendre ~ sur** to lean on; to rest on; **à l'~ de** (pour prouver) in support of; **~ de la fenêtre** the windowsill, the window ledge; **appui-tête** nm, **appuie-tête** nm inv headrest.

appuyer [apɥije] vt (poser): **~ qch sur/contre** to lean ou rest sth on/against; (soutenir: personne, demande) to support, back (up); **~ sur** (bouton) to press, push; (frein) to press on, push down; (mot, détail) to stress, emphasize; (suj: chose: peser sur) to rest (heavily) on, press against; **s'~ sur** vt to lean on; to rely on; **~ à droite** to bear (to the) right.

âpre [ɑpʀ(ə)] a acrid, pungent; (fig) harsh, bitter; **~ au gain** grasping, greedy.

après [apʀɛ] prép after // ad afterwards; **2 heures ~** 2 hours later; **~ qu'il est ou soit parti/avoir fait** after he left/having done; **d'~** prép (selon) according to; **~ coup** ad after the event, afterwards; **~ tout** ad (au fond) after all; **et (puis) ~?** so what?; **~-demain** ad the day after tomorrow; **~-guerre** nm postwar years pl; **~-midi** nm ou nf inv afternoon; **~-ski** nm inv (chaussure) snow boot; (moment) après-ski.

à-propos [apʀopo] nm (d'une remarque) aptness; **faire preuve d'~** to show presence of mind, do the right thing.

apte [apt(ə)] a: **~ à qch/faire qch** capable of sth/doing sth; **~ (au service)** (MIL) fit (for service); **aptitude** nf ability, aptitude.

aquarelle [akwaʀɛl] nf (tableau) watercolour; (genre) watercolours pl, aquarelle.

aquarium [akwaʀjɔm] nm aquarium.

aquatique [akwatik] a aquatic, water cpd.

aqueduc [akdyk] nm aqueduct.

aqueux, euse [akø, -øz] a aqueous.

arabe [aʀab] a Arabic; (désert, cheval) Arabian; (nation, peuple) Arab // nm/f: **A~** Arab // nm (langue) Arabic.

arabesque [aʀabɛsk(ə)] nf arabesque.

Arabie [aʀabi] nf: **l'~ (Séoudite)** Saudi Arabia.

arable [aʀabl(ə)] a arable.

arachide [aʀaʃid] nf (plante) groundnut (plant); (graine) peanut, groundnut.

araignée [aʀeɲe] nf spider; **~ de mer** spider crab.

araser [aʀaze] vt to level; to plane (down).

aratoire [aʀatwaʀ] a: **instrument ~** ploughing implement.

arbalète [aʀbalɛt] nf crossbow.

arbitrage [aʀbitʀaʒ] nm refereeing; umpiring; arbitration.

arbitraire [aʀbitʀɛʀ] a arbitrary.

arbitre [aʀbitʀ(ə)] nm (SPORT) referee ; (: TENNIS, CRICKET) umpire ; (fig) arbiter, judge ; (JUR) arbitrator ; **arbitrer** vt to referee ; to umpire ; to arbitrate.

arborer [aʀbɔʀe] vt to bear, display ; to sport.

arboriculture [aʀbɔʀikyltyʀ] nf arboriculture.

arbre [aʀbʀ(ə)] nm tree ; (TECH) shaft ; ~ **généalogique** family tree ; ~ **de transmission** (AUTO) driveshaft ; **arbrisseau, x** nm shrub.

arbuste [aʀbyst(ə)] nm small shrub, bush.

arc [aʀk] nm (arme) bow ; (GÉOM) arc ; (ARCHIT) arch ; ~ **de cercle** arc of a circle ; **en** ~ **de cercle** a semi-circular ; **A**~ **de triomphe** Triumphal Arch.

arcade [aʀkad] nf arch(way) ; ~**s** arcade sg, arches ; ~ **sourcilière** arch of the eyebrows.

arcanes [aʀkan] nmpl mysteries.

arc-boutant [aʀkbutɑ̃] nm flying buttress.

arc-bouter [aʀkbute]: **s'**~ vi: **s'**~ **contre** to lean ou press against.

arceau, x [aʀso] nm (métallique etc) hoop.

arc-en-ciel [aʀkɑ̃sjɛl] nm rainbow.

archaïque [aʀkaik] a archaic ; **archaïsme** nm archaism.

arche [aʀʃ(ə)] nf arch ; ~ **de Noé** Noah's Ark.

archéologie [aʀkeɔlɔʒi] nf archeology ; **archéologique** a archeological ; **archéologue** nm/f archeologist.

archer [aʀʃe] nm archer.

archet [aʀʃɛ] nm bow.

archevêché [aʀʃəveʃe] nm archbishopric ; archbishop's palace.

archevêque [aʀʃəvɛk] nm archbishop.

archi... [aʀʃi] préfixe (très) dead, extra ; ~**simple** dead simple ; ~**bondé** chock-a-block, packed solid.

archipel [aʀʃipɛl] nm archipelago.

architecte [aʀʃitɛkt(ə)] nm architect.

architecture [aʀʃitɛktyʀ] nf architecture.

archives [aʀʃiv] nfpl archives ; **archiviste** nm/f archivist.

arçon [aʀsɔ̃] nm voir **cheval**.

arctique [aʀktik] a Arctic // nm: **l'A**~ the Arctic ; **l'océan A**~ the Arctic Ocean.

ardemment [aʀdamɑ̃] ad ardently, fervently.

ardent, e [aʀdɑ̃, -ɑ̃t] a (soleil) blazing ; (fièvre) raging ; (amour) ardent, passionate ; (prière) fervent ; **ardeur** nf blazing heat ; fervour, ardour.

ardoise [aʀdwaz] nf slate.

Ardt abr de **arrondissement**.

ardu, e [aʀdy] a arduous, difficult.

are [aʀ] nm are, 100 square metres.

arène [aʀɛn] nf arena ; ~**s** nfpl bull-ring sg.

arête [aʀɛt] nf (de poisson) bone ; (d'une montagne) ridge ; (GÉOM, gén) edge (where two faces meet).

argent [aʀʒɑ̃] nm (métal) silver ; (monnaie) money ; ~ **liquide** ready money, (ready) cash ; ~ **de poche** pocket money ; **argenté, e** a silver(y) ; (métal) silverplated ; **argenter** vt to silver(-plate) ; **argenterie** nf silverware ; silver plate.

argentin, e [aʀʒɑ̃tɛ̃, -in] a (son) silvery ; (d'Argentine) Argentinian, Argentine // nm/f Argentinian, Argentine.

Argentine [aʀʒɑ̃tin] nf: **l'**~ Argentina, the Argentine.

argile [aʀʒil] nf clay ; **argileux, euse** a clayey.

argot [aʀgo] nm slang ; **argotique** a slang cpd; slangy.

arguer [aʀgɥe] : ~ **de** vt to put forward as a pretext ou reason.

argument [aʀgymɑ̃] nm argument.

argumenter [aʀgymɑ̃te] vi to argue.

argus [aʀgys] nm guide to second-hand car prices.

arguties [aʀgysi] nfpl pettifoggery sg, quibbles.

aride [aʀid] a arid.

aristocrate [aʀistɔkʀat] nm/f aristocrat.

aristocratie [aʀistɔkʀasi] nf aristocracy ; **aristocratique** a aristocratic.

arithmétique [aʀitmetik] a arithmetic(al) // nf arithmetic.

armateur [aʀmatœʀ] nm shipowner.

armature [aʀmatyʀ] nf framework ; (de tente etc) frame ; (de soutien-gorge) bone, wiring.

arme [aʀm(ə)] nf weapon ; (section de l'armée) arm ; ~**s** nfpl (blason) (coat of) arms ; **les** ~**s** (profession) soldiering sg ; **passer par les** ~**s** to execute (by firing squad) ; **en** ~**s** up in arms ; **prendre/présenter les** ~**s** to take up/present arms ; **se battre à l'**~ **blanche** to fight with blades ; ~ **à feu** firearm.

armée [aʀme] nf army ; ~ **de l'air** Air Force ; **l'**~ **du Salut** the Salvation Army ; ~ **de terre** Army.

armement [aʀməmɑ̃] nm (matériel) arms pl, weapons pl ; (: d'un pays) arms pl, armament.

armer [aʀme] vt to arm ; (arme à feu) to cock ; (appareil-photo) to wind on ; ~ **qch de** to fit sth with ; to reinforce sth with ; ~ **qn de** to arm ou equip sb with.

armistice [aʀmistis] nm armistice.

armoire [aʀmwaʀ] nf (tall) cupboard ; (penderie) wardrobe.

armoiries [aʀmwaʀi] nfpl coat sg of arms.

armure [aʀmyʀ] nf armour q, suit of armour.

armurier [aʀmyʀje] nm gunsmith ; armourer.

aromates [aʀɔmat] nmpl seasoning sg, herbs (and spices).

aromatisé, e [aʀɔmatize] a flavoured.

arôme [aʀom] nm aroma ; fragrance.

arpège [aʀpɛʒ] nm arpeggio.

arpentage [aʀpɑ̃taʒ] nm (land) surveying.

arpenter [aʀpɑ̃te] vt (salle, couloir) to pace up and down.

arpenteur [aʀpɑ̃tœʀ] nm land surveyor.

arqué, e [aʀke] a bow, bandy ; arched.

arrachage [aʀaʃaʒ] nm: ~ **des mauvaises herbes** weeding.

arrache-pied [aʀaʃpje]: **d'**~ ad relentlessly.

arracher [aʀaʃe] vt to pull out ; (page etc) to tear off, tear out ; (déplanter: légume) to lift ; (: herbe, souche) to pull up ; (bras etc: par explosion) to blow off ; (: par accident) to tear off; ~ qch à qn to snatch sth from sb; (fig) to wring sth out of sb, wrest sth from sb; ~ qn à (solitude, rêverie) to drag sb out of; (famille etc) to tear ou wrench sb away from; s'~ vt (article très recherché) to fight over.

arraisonner [aʀɛzɔne] vt (bateau) to board and search.

arrangeant, e [aʀɑ̃ʒɑ̃, -ɑ̃t] a accommodating, obliging.

arrangement [aʀɑ̃ʒmɑ̃] nm arrangement.

arranger [aʀɑ̃ʒe] vt (gén) to arrange; (réparer) to fix, put right; (régler) to settle, sort out; (convenir à) to suit, be convenient for; s'~ (se mettre d'accord) to come to an agreement ou arrangement; je vais m'~ I'll try and manage; ça va s'~ it'll sort itself out; s'~ pour faire to manage so that one can do; **arrangeur** nm (MUS) arranger.

arrestation [aʀɛstɑsjɔ̃] nf arrest.

arrêt [aʀɛ] nm stopping; (de bus etc) stop; (JUR) judgment, decision; (FOOTBALL) save; ~s nmpl (MIL) arrest sg; être à l'~ to be stopped, have come to a halt; rester ou tomber en ~ devant to stop short in front of; sans ~ without stopping, non-stop; continually; ~ de travail stoppage (of work).

arrêté [aʀete] nm order, decree.

arrêter [aʀete] vt to stop; (chauffage etc) to turn off, switch off; (fixer: date etc) to appoint, decide on; (criminel, suspect) to arrest; ~ de faire to stop doing; s'~ vi to stop.

arrhes [aʀ] nfpl deposit sg.

arrière [aʀjɛʀ] nm back; (SPORT) fullback // a inv: siège/roue ~ back ou rear seat/wheel; à l'~ ad behind, at the back; en ~ ad behind; (regarder) back, behind; (tomber, aller) backwards; en ~ de prép behind; arriéré, e a (péj) backward // nm (d'argent) arrears pl; ~boutique nf back shop; ~garde nf rearguard; ~goût nm aftertaste; ~grand-mère nf great-grandmother; nm great-grandfather; ~pays nm inv hinterland; ~pensée nf ulterior motive; mental reservation; ~petits-enfants nmpl great-grandchildren; ~plan nm background; ~saison nf late autumn; ~train nm hindquarters pl.

arrimer [aʀime] vt to stow; to secure, fasten securely.

arrivage [aʀivaʒ] nm arrival.

arrivée [aʀive] nf arrival; (ligne d'arrivée) finish; ~ d'air/de gaz air/gas inlet; à mon ~ when I arrived.

arriver [aʀive] vi to arrive; (survenir) to happen, occur; il arrive à Paris à 8h he gets to ou arrives at Paris at 8; ~ à (atteindre) to reach; ~ à faire qch to succeed in doing sth; il arrive que it happens that; il lui arrive de faire he sometimes does; arriviste nm/f go-getter.

arrogance [aʀɔgɑ̃s] nf arrogance.

arrogant, e [aʀɔgɑ̃, -ɑ̃t] a arrogant.

arroger [aʀɔʒe]: s'~ vt to assume (without right).

arrondi, e [aʀɔ̃di] a round // nm roundness.

arrondir [aʀɔ̃diʀ] vt (forme, objet) to

round; (somme) to round off; s'~ vi to become round(ed).

arrondissement [aʀɔ̃dismɑ̃] nm (ADMIN) ≈ district.

arrosage [aʀozaʒ] nm watering; tuyau d'~ hose(pipe).

arroser [aʀoze] vt to water; (victoire) to celebrate (over a drink); (CULIN) to baste; **arroseuse** nf water cart; **arrosoir** nm watering can.

arsenal, aux [aʀsənal, -o] nm (NAVIG) naval dockyard; (MIL) arsenal; (fig) gear, paraphernalia.

arsenic [aʀsənik] nm arsenic.

art [aʀ] nm art; ~s et métiers applied arts and crafts; ~s ménagers homecraft sg, domestic science sg.

artère [aʀtɛʀ] nf (ANAT) artery; (rue) main road; **artériel, le** a arterial; **artériosclérose** nf arteriosclerosis.

arthrite [aʀtʀit] nf arthritis.

arthrose [aʀtʀoz] nf (degenerative) osteoarthritis.

artichaut [aʀtiʃo] nm artichoke.

article [aʀtikl(ə)] nm article; (COMM) item, article; à l'~ de la mort be at the point of death; ~ de fond (PRESSE) feature article.

articulaire [aʀtikylɛʀ] a of the joints, articular.

articulation [aʀtikylɑsjɔ̃] nf articulation; (ANAT) joint.

articuler [aʀtikyle] vt to articulate; s'~ (sur) (ANAT, TECH) to articulate (to).

artifice [aʀtifis] nm device, trick.

artificiel, le [aʀtifisjɛl] a artificial; ~lement ad artificially.

artificier [aʀtifisje] nm pyrotechnist.

artificieux, euse [aʀtifisjø, -øz] a guileless, deceitless.

artillerie [aʀtijʀi] nf artillery, ordnance; **artilleur** nm artilleryman, gunner.

artisan [aʀtizɑ̃] nm artisan, (self-employed) craftsman; l'~ de la victoire the architect of victory; **artisanal, e, aux** a of ou made by craftsmen; (péj) cottage industry cpd, unsophisticated; **artisanat** nm arts and crafts pl.

artiste [aʀtist(ə)] nm/f artist; (de variétés) entertainer; performer; singer; actor/actress; **artistique** a artistic.

aryen, ne [aʀjɛ, -jɛn] a Aryan.

as vb [a] voir avoir // nm [ɑs] ace.

ascendance [asɑ̃dɑ̃s] nf (origine) ancestry.

ascendant, e [asɑ̃dɑ̃, -ɑ̃t] a upward // nm ascendancy; ~s nmpl ascendants.

ascenseur [asɑ̃sœʀ] nm lift.

ascension [asɑ̃sjɔ̃] nf ascent; climb; l'A~ (REL) the Ascension.

ascète [asɛt] nm/f ascetic; **ascétique** a ascetic.

asepsie [asɛpsi] nf asepsis; **aseptique** a aseptic; **aseptiser** vt to sterilize; to disinfect.

asiatique [azjatik] a, nm/f Asiatic, Asian.
Asie [azi] nf Asia.

asile [azil] nm (refuge) refuge, sanctuary; (POL): droit d'~ (political) asylum; (pour malades mentaux) home, asylum; (pour vieillards) home.

aspect [aspɛ] *nm* appearance, look ; (*fig*) aspect, side ; (*LING*) aspect ; **à l'~ de** at the sight of.

asperge [aspɛrʒ(ə)] *nf* asparagus *q*.

asperger [aspɛrʒe] *vt* to spray, sprinkle.

aspérité [asperite] *nf* excrescence, protruding bit (of rock *etc*).

aspersion [aspɛrsjɔ̃] *nf* spraying, sprinkling.

asphalte [asfalt(ə)] *nm* asphalt ; **asphalter** *vt* to asphalt.

asphyxie [asfiksi] *nf* suffocation, asphyxia, asphyxiation ; **asphyxier** *vt* to suffocate, asphyxiate ; (*fig*) to stifle.

aspic [aspik] *nm* (*ZOOL*) asp ; (*CULIN*) aspic.

aspirant, e [aspirā, -āt] *a:* **pompe ~e** suction pump // *nm* (*NAVIG*) midshipman.

aspirateur [aspiRatœr] *nm* vacuum cleaner, hoover.·

aspiration [aspirɑsjɔ̃] *nf* inhalation ; sucking (up) ; drawing up ; **~s** *nf* (*ambitions*) aspirations.

aspirer [aspire] *vt* (*air*) to inhale ; (*liquide*) to suck (up) ; (*suj: appareil*) to suck *ou* draw up ; **~ à** *vt* to aspire to.

aspirine [aspirin] *nf* aspirin.

assagir [asaʒir] *vt*, **s'~** *vi* to quieten down, sober down.

assaillant, e [asajɑ̃, -ɑ̃t] *nm/f* assailant, attacker.

assaillir [asajir] *vt* to assail, attack ; **~ qn de** (*questions*) to assail *ou* bombard sb with.

assainir [asenir] *vt* to clean up ; to purify.

assaisonnement [asɛzɔnmɑ̃] *nm* seasoning.

assaisonner [asɛzɔne] *vt* to season.

assassin [asasɛ̃] *nm* murderer ; assassin.

assassinat [asasina] *nm* murder ; assassination.

assassiner [asasine] *vt* to murder ; to assassinate.

assaut [aso] *nm* assault, attack ; **prendre d'~** to (take by) storm, assault ; **donner l'~** to attack ; **faire ~ de** (*rivaliser*) to vie with *ou* rival each other in.

assécher [aseʃe] *vt* to drain.

assemblage [asɑ̃blaʒ] *nm* assembling ; (*MENUISERIE*) joint ; **un ~ de** (*fig*) a collection of.

assemblée [asɑ̃ble] *nf* (*réunion*) meeting ; (*public, assistance*) gathering ; assembled people ; (*POL*) assembly ; **l'A~ Nationale** the (French) National Assembly.

assembler [asɑ̃ble] *vt* (*joindre, monter*) to assemble, put together ; (*amasser*) to gather (together), collect (together) ; **s'~** *vi* to gather, collect.

assener, asséner [asene] *vt:* **~ un coup à qn** to deal sb a blow.

assentiment [asɑ̃timɑ̃] *nm* assent, consent ; approval.

asseoir [aswar] *vt* (*malade, bébé*) to sit up ; to sit down ; (*autorité, réputation*) to establish ; **~ qch sur** to build sth on ; to base sth on ; **s'~** *vi* to sit (o.s.) down.

assermenté, e [asɛrmɑ̃te] *a* sworn, on oath.

asservir [asɛrvir] *vt* to subjugate, enslave.

assesseur [asesœr] *nm* (*JUR*) assessor.

asseye *etc vb voir* **asseoir.**

assez [ase] *ad* (*suffisamment*) enough, sufficiently ; (*passablement*) rather, quite, fairly ; **est-il ~ fort/rapide?** is he strong/fast enough *ou* sufficiently strong/fast? ; **il est passé ~ vite** he went past rather *ou* quite *ou* fairly fast ; **~ de pain/livres** enough *ou* sufficient bread/books ; **travailler ~** to work sufficiently (hard), work (hard) enough.

assidu, e [asidy] *a* assiduous, painstaking ; regular ; **assiduités** *nfpl* assiduous attentions.

assied *etc vb voir* **asseoir.**

assiéger [asjeʒe] *vt* to besiege, lay siege to ; (*suj: foule, touristes*) to mob, besiege.

assiérai *etc vb voir* **asseoir.**

assiette [asjɛt] *nf* plate ; (*contenu*) plate(ful) ; (*équilibre*) seat ; seating ; trim ; **~ anglaise** assorted cold meats ; **~ creuse** (soup) dish, soup plate ; **~ à dessert** dessert plate ; **~ de l'impôt** basis of (tax) assessment ; **~ plate** (dinner) plate.

assigner [asiɲe] *vt:* **~ qch à** (*poste, part, travail*) to assign *ou* allot sth to ; (*limites*) to set *ou* fix sth to ; (*cause, effet*) to ascribe *ou* attribute sth to ; **~ qn à** (*affecter*) to assign sb to ; **~ qn à résidence** (*JUR*) to assign a forced residence to sb.

assimiler [asimile] *vt* to assimilate, absorb ; (*comparer*): **~ qch/qn à** to liken *ou* compare sth/sb to ; **ils sont assimilés aux infirmières** (*ADMIN*) they are classed as nurses ; **s'~** *vi* (*s'intégrer*) to be assimilated *ou* absorbed.

assis, e [asi, -iz] *pp de* **asseoir** // *a* sitting (down), seated // *nf* (*CONSTR*) course ; (*GÉO*) stratum (*pl* a) ; (*fig*) basis (*pl* bases), foundation ; **~es** *nfpl* (*JUR*) assizes ; (*congrès*) (annual) conference.

assistance [asistɑ̃s] *nf* (*public*) audience ; (*aide*) assistance ; **porter ~ à qn** to give sb assistance ; **l'A~ (publique)** (*-1953*) ≈ National Assistance ; Child Care.

assistant, e [asistɑ̃, -ɑ̃t] *nm/f* assistant ; (*d'université*) probationary lecturer ; **les ~s** *nmpl* (*auditeurs etc*) those present ; **~e sociale** social worker.

assisté, e [asiste] *a* (*AUTO*) power assisted.

assister [asiste] *vt* to assist ; **~ à** *vt* (*scène, événement*) to witness ; (*conférence, séminaire*) to attend, be (present) at ; (*spectacle, match*) to be at, see.

association [asɔsjasjɔ̃] *nf* association.

associé, e [asɔsje] *nm/f* associate ; partner.

associer [asɔsje] *vt* to associate ; **~ qn à** (*profits*) to give sb a share of ; (*affaire*) to make sb a partner in ; (*joie, triomphe*) to include sb in ; **~ qch à** (*joindre, allier*) to combine sth with ; **s'~** (*suj pl*) to join together ; (*COMM*) to form a partnership ; **s'~** *vt* (*collaborateur*) to take on (as a partner) ; **s'~ à qn pour faire** to join (forces) *ou* join together with sb to do ; **s'~ à** to be combined with ; (*opinions, joie de qn*) to share in.

assoiffé, e [aswafe] *a* thirsty.

assolement [asɔlmɑ̃] *nm* (systematic) rotation of crops.

assombrir [asɔ̃bRiR] *vt* to darken ; (*fig*) to fill with gloom ; **s'~** *vi* to darken ; to cloud over ; to become gloomy.

assommer [asɔme] *vt* to batter to death ; (*étourdir, abrutir*) to knock out ; to stun ; (*fam: ennuyer*) to bore stiff.

Assomption [asɔ̃psjɔ̃] *nf*: **l'~** the Assumption.

assorti, e [asɔRti] *a* matched, matching ; **fromages/légumes ~s** assorted cheeses/vegetables ; **~ à** matching.

assortiment [asɔRtimɑ̃] *nm* assortment, selection.

assortir [asɔRtiR] *vt* to match ; **~ qch à** to match sth with ; **~ qch de** to accompany sth with ; **s'~ de** to be accompanied by.

assoupi, e [asupi] *a* a dozing, sleeping ; (*fig*) (be)numbed ; dulled ; stilled.

assoupir [asupiR]: **s'~** *vi* to doze off.

assouplir [asupliR] *vt* to make supple ; (*fig*) to relax.

assourdir [asuRdiR] *vt* (*bruit*) to deaden, muffle ; (*suj: bruit*) to deafen.

assouvir [asuviR] *vt* to satisfy, appease.

assujettir [asyʒetiR] *vt* to subject, subjugate ; **~ qn à** (*règle, impôt*) to subject sb to.

assumer [asyme] *vt* (*fonction, emploi*) to assume, take on.

assurance [asyRɑ̃s] *nf* (*certitude*) assurance ; (*confiance en soi*) (self-)confidence ; (*contrat*) insurance (policy) ; (*secteur commercial*) insurance ; **~ maladie** health insurance ; **~ tous risques** (AUTO) comprehensive insurance ; **~s sociales** ≈ National Insurance ; **~-vie** *nf* life assurance *ou* insurance.

assuré, e [asyRe] *a* (*victoire etc*) certain, sure ; (*démarche, voix*) assured, (self-)confident ; (*certain*): **~ de** confident of // *nm/f* insured (person) ; **~ social** ≈ member of the National Insurance scheme ; **~ment** *ad* assuredly, most certainly.

assurer [asyRe] *vt* (COMM) to insure ; (*stabiliser*) to steady ; to stabilize ; (*victoire etc*) to ensure, make certain ; (*frontières, pouvoir*) to make secure ; (*service, garde*) to provide ; to operate ; (*garantir*): **~ qch à qn** to secure *ou* guarantee sth for sb ; (*certifier*) to assure sb that ; **~ à qn que** to assure sb that ; **~ qn de** to assure sb of ; **s'~** (contre) (COMM) to insure o.s. (against) ; **s'~ de/que** (*vérifier*) to make sure of/that ; **s'~ (de)** (*aide de qn*) to secure (for o.s.) ; **assureur** *nm* insurance agent ; insurers *pl*.

astérisque [asteRisk(ə)] *nm* asterisk.

asthmatique [asmatik] *a* asthmatic.

asthme [asm(ə)] *nm* asthma.

asticot [astiko] *nm* maggot.

astiquer [astike] *vt* to polish, shine.

astre [astR(ə)] *nm* star.

astreignant, e [astReɲɑ̃, -ɑ̃t] *a* demanding.

astreindre [astRɛ̃dR(ə)] *vt*: **~ qn à qch** to force sth upon sb ; **~ qn à faire** to compel *ou* force sb to do.

astringent, e [astRɛ̃ʒɑ̃, -ɑ̃t] · *a* astringent.

astrologie [astRɔlɔʒi] · *nf* astrology ; **astrologue** *nm/f* astrologer.

astronaute [astRɔnot] *nm/f* astronaut.

astronautique [astRɔnotik] *nf* astronautics *sg*.

astronome [astRɔnɔm] *nm/f* astronomer.

astronomie [astRɔnɔmi] *nf* astronomy ; **astronomique** *a* astronomic(al).

astuce [astys] *nf* shrewdness, astuteness ; (*truc*) trick, clever way ; (*plaisanterie*) wisecrack ; **astucieux, euse** *a* shrewd, clever, astute.

asymétrique [asimetRik] *a* asymmetric(al).

atelier [atəlje] *nm* workshop ; (*de peintre*) studio.

athée [ate] *a* atheistic // *nm/f* atheist.

Athènes [atɛn] *n* Athens.

athlète [atlɛt] *nm/f* (SPORT) athlete ; (*costaud*) muscleman ; **athlétique** *a* athletic ; **athlétisme** *nm* athletics *sg*.

atlantique [atlɑ̃tik] *a* Atlantic // *nm*: **l'(océan) A~** the Atlantic (Ocean).

atlas [atlɑs] *nm* atlas.

atmosphère [atmɔsfɛR] *nf* atmosphere ; **atmosphérique** *a* atmospheric.

atome [atom] *nm* atom ; **atomique** *a* (*bombe, pile*) atomic, nuclear ; (*usine*) nuclear ; (*nombre, masse*) atomic.

atomiseur [atɔmizœR] *nm* atomiser.

atone [atɔn] *a* lifeless.

atours [atuR] *nmpl* attire *sg*, finery *sg*.

atout [atu] *nm* trump ; (*fig*) asset ; trump card ; '**~ pique/trèfle'** spades/clubs are trumps.

âtre [ɑtR(ə)] *nm* hearth.

atroce [atRɔs] *a* atrocious ; dreadful ; **atrocité** *nf* atrocity.

atrophie [atRɔfi] *nf* atrophy.

atrophier [atRɔfje]: **s'~** *vi* to atrophy.

attabler [atable]: **s'~** *vi* to sit down at (the) table.

attachant, e [ataʃɑ̃, -ɑ̃t] *a* engaging, lovable, likeable.

attache [ataʃ] *nf* clip, fastener ; (*fig*) tie ; **à l'~** (*chien*) tied up.

attaché, e [ataʃe] *a*: **être ~ à** (*aimer*) to be attached to // *nm* (ADMIN) attaché ; **~-case** *nm inv* attaché case.

attachement [ataʃmɑ̃] *nm* attachment.

attacher [ataʃe] *vt* to tie up ; (*étiquette*) to attach, tie on ; (*souliers*) to do up // *vi* (*poêle, riz*) to stick ; **s'~ à** (*par affection*) to become attached to ; **s'~ à faire qch** to endeavour to do sth ; **~ qch à** to tie *ou* fasten *ou* attach sth to.

attaquant [atakɑ̃] *nm* (MIL) attacker ; (SPORT) striker, forward.

attaque [atak] *nf* attack ; (*cérébrale*) stroke ; (*d'épilepsie*) fit.

attaquer [atake] *vt* to attack ; (*en justice*) to bring an action against, sue ; (*travail*) to tackle, set about // *vi* to attack ; **s'~ à** to attack ; (*épidémie, misère*) to tackle, attack.

attardé, e [ataRde] *a* (*passants*) late ; (*enfant*) backward ; (*conceptions*) old-fashioned.

attarder [ataRde]: **s'~** *vi* to linger ; to stay on.

atteindre [atɛ̃dʀ(ə)] vt to reach; (blesser) to hit; (contacter) to reach, contact, get in touch with; (émouvoir) to affect.

atteint, e [atɛ̃, -ɛ̃t] a (MÉD): **être ~ de** to be suffering from // nf attack; **hors d'~** out of reach; **porter ~e à** to strike a blow at; to undermine.

attelage [atlaʒ] nm (de remorque etc) coupling; (animaux) team; (harnachement) harness; yoke.

atteler [atle] vt (cheval, bœufs) to hitch up; (wagons) to couple; **s'~ à** (travail) to buckle down to.

attelle [atɛl] nf splint.

attenant, e [atnɑ̃, -ɑ̃t] a: ~ (à) adjoining.

attendre [atɑ̃dʀ(ə)] vt (gén) to wait for; (être destiné ou réservé à) to await, be in store for // vi to wait; **s'~ à (ce que)** (escompter) to expect (that); **~ un enfant** to be expecting (a baby); **~ de faire/d'être** to wait until one does/is; **~ que** to wait until; **~ qch de** to expect sth of; **en attendant** ad meanwhile, in the meantime; be that as it may.

attendri, e [atɑ̃dʀi] a tender.

attendrir [atɑ̃dʀiʀ] vt to move (to pity); (viande) to tenderize; **s'~ (sur)** to be moved ou touched (by); **attendrissant, e** a moving, touching; **attendrissement** nm emotion; pity.

attendu [atɑ̃dy] nm: ~s reasons adduced for a judgment; ~ **que** cj considering that, since.

attentat [atɑ̃ta] nm assassination attempt; ~ **à la bombe** bomb attack; ~ **à la pudeur** indecent exposure q; indecent assault q.

attente [atɑ̃t] nf wait; (espérance) expectation.

attenter [atɑ̃te]: ~ **à** vt (liberté) to violate; ~ **à la vie de qn** to make an attempt on sb's life.

attentif, ive [atɑ̃tif, -iv] a (auditeur) attentive; (travail) scrupulous; careful; ~ **à** paying attention to; mindful of; careful to.

attention [atɑ̃sjɔ̃] nf attention; (prévenance) attention, thoughtfulness q; **à l'~ de** for the attention of; **faire ~ (à)** to be careful (of); **faire ~ (à ce) que** to be ou make sure that; **~!** careful!, watch ou mind (out)!; **attentionné, e** a thoughtful, considerate.

attentisme [atɑ̃tism(ə)] nm wait-and-see policy.

attentivement [atɑ̃tivmɑ̃] ad attentively.

atténuer [atenɥe] vt to alleviate, ease; to lessen; to mitigate the effects of; **s'~** vi to ease; to abate.

atterrer [ateʀe] vt to dismay, appal.

atterrir [ateʀiʀ] vi to land; **atterrissage** nm landing; **atterrissage sur le ventre** belly landing.

attestation [atɛstasjɔ̃] nf certificate; ~ **médicale** doctor's certificate.

attester [atɛste] vt to testify to, vouch for; (démontrer) to attest, testify to; ~ **que** to testify that.

attiédir [atjedir]: **s'~** vi to become luke-warm; (fig) to cool down.

attifé, e [atife] a (fam) got up, rigged out.

attique [atik] nm: **appartement en ~** penthouse (flat).

attirail [atiʀaj] nm gear; (péj) paraphernalia.

attirance [atiʀɑ̃s] nf attraction; (séduction) lure.

attirant, e [atiʀɑ̃, -ɑ̃t] a attractive, appealing.

attirer [atiʀe] vt to attract; (appâter) to lure, entice; ~ **qn dans un coin/vers soi** to draw sb into a corner/towards one; ~ **l'attention de qn (sur)** to attract sb's attention (to); to draw sb's attention (to); **s'~ des ennuis** to bring trouble upon o.s., get into trouble.

attiser [atize] vt (feu) to poke (up), stir up; (fig) to fan the flame of, stir up.

attitré, e [atitʀe] a qualified; accredited; appointed.

attitude [atityd] nf attitude; (position du corps) bearing.

attouchements [atuʃmɑ̃] nmpl touching sg; (sexuels) fondling sg, stroking sg.

attraction [atʀaksjɔ̃] nf (gén) attraction; (de cabaret, cirque) number.

attrait [atʀɛ] nm appeal, attraction; lure; **éprouver de l'~ pour** to be attracted to; ~s nmpl attractions.

attrape [atʀap] nf voir **farce** // préfixe: **~-nigaud** nm con.

attraper [atʀape] vt (gén) to catch; (habitude, amende) to get, pick up; (fam: duper) to take in.

attrayant, e [atʀɛjɑ̃, -ɑ̃t] a attractive.

attribuer [atʀibɥe] vt (prix) to award; (rôle, tâche) to allocate, assign; (imputer): ~ **qch à** to attribute sth to, ascribe sth to, put sth down to; **s'~** vt (s'approprier) to claim for o.s.

attribut [atʀiby] nm attribute; (LING) complement.

attribution [atʀibysjɔ̃] nf awarding; allocation, assignment; attribution; ~s nfpl (compétence) attributions.

attrister [atʀiste] vt to sadden.

attroupement [atʀupmɑ̃] nm crowd, mob.

attrouper [atʀupe]: **s'~** vi to gather.

au [o] prép + dét voir **à**.

aubade [obad] nf dawn serenade.

aubaine [obɛn] nf godsend; (financière) windfall.

aube [ob] nf dawn, daybreak; **à l'~** at dawn ou daybreak; **à l'~ de** (fig) at the dawn of.

aubépine [obepin] nf hawthorn.

auberge [obɛʀʒ(ə)] nf inn; ~ **de jeunesse** youth hostel.

aubergine [obɛʀʒin] nf aubergine.

aubergiste [obɛʀʒist(ə)] nm/f inn-keeper, hotel-keeper.

aucun, e [okœ̃, -yn] dét no, tournure négative + any; (positif) any // pronom none, tournure négative + any; any(one); **il n'y a ~ livre** there isn't any book, there is no book; **je n'en vois ~ qui** I can't see any which, I (can) see none which; **sans ~ doute** without any doubt; **plus qu'~ autre** more than any other; ~ **des deux** neither of the two; ~ **d'entre eux** none of them; **d'~s** (certains) some;

aucunement ad in no way, not in the least.
audace [odas] nf daring, boldness; (péj) audacity; **audacieux, euse** a daring, bold.
au-delà [odla] ad beyond // nm: l'~ the beyond; ~ **de** prép beyond.
au-dessous [odsu] ad underneath; below; ~ **de** prép under(neath), below; (limite, somme etc) below, under; (dignité, condition) below.
au-dessus [odsy] ad above; ~ **de** prép above.
au-devant [odvɑ̃]: ~ **de** prép: **aller** ~ **de** (personne, danger) to go (out) and meet; (souhaits de qn) to anticipate.
audience [odjɑ̃s] nf audience; (JUR: séance) hearing; **trouver** ~ **auprès de** to arouse much interest among, get the (interested) attention of.
audio-visuel, le [odjɔvizɥɛl] a audiovisual.
auditeur, trice [oditœʀ, -tʀis] nm/f (à la radio) listener; (à une conférence) member of the audience, listener; ~ **libre** unregistered student (attending lectures).
audition [odisjɔ̃] nf (ouïe, écoute) hearing; (JUR: de témoins) examination; (MUS, THÉÂTRE: épreuve) audition; **auditionner** vt, vi to audition.
auditoire [oditwaʀ] nm audience.
auditorium [oditɔʀjɔm] nm (public) studio.
auge [oʒ] nf trough.
augmentation [ɔgmɑ̃tasjɔ̃] nf increasing; raising; increase; ~ **(de salaire)** rise (in salary).
augmenter [ɔgmɑ̃te] vt (gén) to increase; (salaire, prix) to increase, raise, put up; (employé) to increase the salary of, give a (salary) rise to // vi to increase.
augure [ɔgyʀ] nm soothsayer, oracle; **de bon/mauvais** ~ of good/ill omen.
augurer [ɔgyʀe] vt: ~ **qch de** to foresee sth (coming) out of; ~ **bien de** to augur well for.
auguste [ɔgyst(ə)] a august, noble, majestic.
aujourd'hui [oʒuʀdɥi] ad today.
aumône [omon] nf alms sg (pl inv); **faire l'~ (à qn)** to give alms (to sb); **faire l'~ de qch à qn** (fig) to favour sb with sth.
aumônerie [omonʀi] nf chaplaincy.
aumônier [omonje] nm chaplain.
auparavant [oparavɑ̃] ad before(hand).
auprès [opʀɛ]: ~ **de** prép next to, close to; (recourir, s'adresser) to; (en comparaison de) compared with, next to.
auquel [okɛl] prép + pronom voir **lequel**.
aurai etc vb voir **avoir**.
auréole [oʀeɔl] nf halo; (tache) ring.
auriculaire [oʀikylɛʀ] nm little finger.
aurons etc vb voir **avoir**.
aurore [ɔʀɔʀ] nf dawn, daybreak; ~ **boréale** northern lights pl.
ausculter [oskylte] vt to auscultate.
auspices [ɔspis] nmpl: **sous les** ~ **de** under the patronage ou auspices of; **sous de bons/mauvais** ~ under favourable/unfavourable auspices.
aussi [osi] ad (également) also, too; (de comparaison) as // cj therefore, consequently; ~ **fort que** as strong as; **moi**

~ me too, so do I; ~ **bien que** (de même que) as well as.
aussitôt [osito] ad straight away, immediately; ~ **que** as soon as; ~ **envoyé** as soon as it is (ou was) sent.
austère [ostɛʀ] a austere; **austérité** nf austerity.
austral, e [ɔstʀal] a southern.
Australie [ɔstʀali] nf Australia; **australien, ne** a, nm/f Australian.
autant [otɑ̃] ad so much; (comparatif): ~ **(que)** as much (as); (nombre) as many (as); ~ **(de)** so much (ou many); as much (ou many); ~ **partir** we (ou you etc) had better leave; **y en a-t-il** ~ **(qu'avant)?** are there as many (as before)?; **is there as much (as before)?; **il n'est pas découragé pour** ~ he isn't discouraged for all that; **pour** ~ **que** cj assuming, as long as; **d'**~ **plus/mieux (que)** all the more/the better (since).
autarcie [otaʀsi] nf autarchy.
autel [otɛl] nm altar.
auteur [otœʀ] nm author; l'~ **de cette remarque** the person who said that; ~-**compositeur** nm composer-songwriter.
authentifier [otɑ̃tifje] vt to authenticate.
authentique [otɑ̃tik] a authentic, genuine.
auto [oto] nf car.
auto... [oto] préfixe auto..., self-; ~**biographie** nf autobiography.
autobus [otobys] nm bus.
autocar [otokaʀ] nm coach.
autochtone [otɔktɔn] nm/f native.
auto-collant, e [otɔkɔlɑ̃, -ɑ̃t] a self-adhesive; (enveloppe) self-seal // nm sticker.
auto-couchettes [otɔkuʃɛt] a: **train** ~ car sleeper train.
autocratique [otɔkʀatik] a autocratic.
autocritique [otɔkʀitik] nf self-criticism.
autodéfense [otodefɑ̃s] nf self-defence; **groupe d'**~ vigilance committee.
autodidacte [otodidakt(ə)] nm/f self-taught person.
auto-école [otɔekɔl] nf driving school.
autofinancement [otofinɑ̃smɑ̃] nm self-financing.
autogestion [otoʒɛstjɔ̃] nf self-management.
autographe [otogʀaf] nm autograph.
automate [otomat] nm automaton.
automatique [otomatik] a automatic // nm: l'~ ≈ subscriber trunk dialling; ~**ment** ad automatically; **automatiser** vt to automate; **automatisme** nm automatism.
automne [otɔn] nm autumn.
automobile [otomɔbil] a motor cpd // nf (motor) car; l'~ motoring; the car industry; **automobiliste** nm/f motorist.
autonome [otonɔm] a autonomous; **autonomie** nf autonomy; (POL) self-government, autonomy; **autonomie de vol range**.
autopsie [otɔpsi] nf post mortem (examination), autopsy.
autorisation [otoʀizasjɔ̃] nf permission, authorization; (papiers) permit; **avoir l'**~ **de faire** to be allowed ou have permission to do, be authorized to do.

autorisé, e [ɔtɔrize] a (*opinion, sources*) authoritative.

autoriser [ɔtɔrize] vt to give permission for, authorize ; (*fig*) to allow (of), sanction ; ~ **qn à faire** to give permission to sb to do, authorize sb to do.

autoritaire [ɔtɔritɛr] a authoritarian.

autorité [ɔtɔrite] nf authority ; **faire** ~ to be authoritative.

autoroute [ɔtɔrut] nf motorway.

auto-stop [ɔtɔstɔp] nm: **l'**~ hitch-hiking ; **faire de l'**~ to hitch-hike ; **prendre qn en** ~ to give sb a lift ; **~peur, euse** nm/f hitch-hiker, hitcher.

autour [otur] ad around ; ~ **de** prép around ; (*environ*) around, about ; **tout** ~ ad all around.

autre [otr(ə)] a other ; **un** ~ **verre** (*supplémentaire*) one more glass, another glass ; (*différent*) another glass, a different glass ; **un** ~ another (one) ; **l'**~ the other (one) ; **les** ~**s** (*autrui*) others ; **l'un et l'**~ both (of them) ; **se détester** etc **l'un l'**~/**les uns les** ~**s** to hate etc each other/one another ; **se sentir** ~ to feel different ; **d'une semaine à l'**~ from one week to the next ; (*incessamment*) any week now ; ~ **chose** something else ; ~ **part** ad somewhere else ; **d'**~ **part** ad on the other hand ; **entre** ~**s** among others ; **nous/vous** ~**s** us/you (lot).

autrefois [otrəfwa] ad in the past.

autrement [otrəmã] ad differently ; in another way ; (*sinon*) otherwise ; ~ **dit** in other words.

Autriche [otriʃ] nf Austria ; **autrichien, ne** a, nm/f Austrian.

autruche [otryʃ] nf ostrich.

autrui [otrui] pronom others.

auvent [ovã] nm canopy.

aux [o] prép + dét voir **à**.

auxiliaire [ɔksiljɛr] a, nm, nf auxiliary.

auxquels, auxquelles [okɛl] prép + pronom voir **lequel**.

av. abr de **avenue**.

avachi, e [avaʃi] a limp, flabby.

aval [aval] nm (*accord*) endorsement, backing ; (*GÉO*) **en** ~ downstream, downriver ; (*sur une pente*) downhill ; **en** ~ **de** downstream ou downriver from ; downhill from.

avalanche [avalãʃ] nf avalanche ; ~ **poudreuse** powder snow avalanche.

avaler [avale] vt to swallow.

avance [avãs] nf (*de troupes* etc) advance ; progress ; (*d'argent*) advance ; (*opposé à retard*) lead ; being ahead of schedule ; ~**s** nfpl overtures ; (*amoureuses*) advances ; **une** ~ **de 300 m/4 h** (*SPORT*) a 300 m/4 hour lead ; (**être**) **en** ~ (to be) early ; (*sur un programme*) (to be) ahead of schedule ; **payer d'**~ to pay in advance ; **à l'**~ in advance, beforehand.

avancé, e [avãse] a advanced ; well on ou under way // nf projection ; overhang ; jutting part.

avancement [avãsmã] nm (*professionnel*) promotion.

avancer [avãse] vt to move forward, advance ; (*projet, travail*) to make progress ; (*être en saillie*) to overhang ; to project ; to jut out ; (*montre, réveil*) to be fast ; to gain // vt to move forward, advance ; (*argent*) to advance ; **s'**~ vi to move forward, advance ; (*fig*) to commit o.s. ; to overhang ; to project ; to jut out ; **j'avance (d'une heure)** I'm (an hour) fast.

avanies [avani] nfpl snubs.

avant [avã] prép before // ad: **trop/plus** ~ too far/further forward // a inv: **siège/roue** ~ front seat/wheel // nm (*d'un véhicule, bâtiment*) front ; (*SPORT: joueur*) forward ; ~ **qu'il parte/de faire** before he leaves/doing ; ~ **tout** (*surtout*) above all ; **à l'**~ (*dans un véhicule*) in (the) front ; **en** ~ ad forward(s) ; **en** ~ **de** prép in front of.

avantage [avãtaʒ] nm advantage ; (*TENNIS*): ~ **service/dehors** advantage ou van in/out ; ~**s sociaux** fringe benefits ; **avantager** vt (*favoriser*) to favour ; (*embellir*) to flatter ; **avantageux, euse** a attractive ; attractively priced.

avant-bras [avãbra] nm inv forearm.

avant-centre [avãsãtr(ə)] nm centre-forward.

avant-coureur [avãkurœr] a: **signe** ~ forerunner.

avant-dernier, ère [avãdɛrnje, -jɛr] a, nm/f next to last, last but one.

avant-garde [avãgard(ə)] nf (*MIL*) vanguard ; (*fig*) avant-garde.

avant-goût [avãgu] nm foretaste.

avant-hier [avãtjɛr] ad the day before yesterday.

avant-poste [avãpɔst(ə)] nm outpost.

avant-première [avãprəmjɛr] nf (*de film*) preview.

avant-projet [avãprɔʒɛ] nm pilot study.

avant-propos [avãprɔpo] nm foreword.

avant-veille [avãvɛj] nf: **l'**~ two days before.

avare [avar] a miserly, avaricious // nm/f miser ; ~ **de** (*compliments* etc) sparing of ; **avarice** nf avarice, miserliness ; **avaricieux, euse** a miserly, niggardly.

avarié, e [avarje] a rotting, going off.

avaries [avari] nfpl (*NAVIG*) damage sg.

avatar [avatar] nm misadventure ; metamorphosis (*pl* phoses).

avec [avɛk] prép with ; (*à l'égard de*) to(wards), with.

avenant, e [avnã, -ãt] a pleasant ; **à l'**~ ad in keeping.

avènement [avɛnmã] nm (*d'un roi*) accession, succession ; (*d'un changement*) advent, coming.

avenir [avnir] nm future ; **à l'**~ in future ; **politicien d'**~ politician with prospects ou a future.

Avent [avã] nm: **l'**~ Advent.

aventure [avãtyr] nf adventure ; (*amoureuse*) affair ; **s'aventurer** vi to venture ; **aventureux, euse** a adventurous, venturesome ; (*projet*) risky, chancy ; **aventurier, ère** nm/f adventurer // nf (*péj*) adventuress.

avenu, e [avny] a: **nul et non** ~ null and void.

avenue [avny] nf avenue.

avérer [avere] : **s'**~ vb avec attribut to prove (to be).

averse [avɛʀs(ə)] nf shower.

aversion [avɛʀsjɔ̃] nf aversion, loathing.

averti, e [avɛʀti] a (well-)informed.

avertir [avɛʀtiʀ] vt: ~ qn (de qch/que) to warn sb (of sth/that); (renseigner) to inform sb (of sth/that); **avertissement** nm warning; **avertisseur** nm horn, hooter.

aveu, x [avø] nm confession.

aveugle [avœgl(ə)] a blind; **~ment** nm blindness; **aveuglément** ad blindly; **aveugler** vt to blind; **à l'aveuglette** ad groping one's way along; (fig) in the dark, blindly.

aviateur, trice [avjatœʀ, -tʀis] nm/f aviator, pilot.

aviation [avjɑsjɔ̃] nf aviation; (sport) flying; (MIL) air force.

avide [avid] a eager; (péj) greedy, grasping; **avidité** nf eagerness; greed.

avilir [aviliʀ] vt to debase.

aviné, e [avine] a intoxicated, drunken.

avion [avjɔ̃] nm aeroplane; **aller (quelque part) en** ~ to go (somewhere) by plane, fly (somewhere); **par** ~ by airmail; ~ **à réaction** jet (aeroplane).

aviron [aviʀɔ̃] nm oar; (sport): l'~ rowing.

avis [avi] nm opinion; (notification) notice; **être d'~ que** to be of the opinion that; **changer d'~** to change one's mind; **jusqu'à nouvel** ~ until further notice.

avisé, e [avize] a sensible, wise; **être bien/mal** ~ **de faire** to be well-/ill-advised to do.

aviser [avize] vt (voir) to notice, catch sight of; (informer): ~ qn de/que to advise ou inform sb of/that // vi to think about things, assess the situation; **s'~ de qch/que** to become suddenly aware of sth/that; **s'~ de faire** to take it into one's head to do.

avocat, e [avɔka, -at] nm/f (JUR) barrister; (fig) advocate, champion // nm (CULIN) avocado (pear); l'~ **de la défense/partie civile** the counsel for the defence/plaintiff; ~ **d'affaires** business lawyer; ~ **général** assistant public prosecutor; **~-stagiaire** nm ~ barrister doing his articles.

avoine [avwan] nf oats pl.

avoir [avwaʀ] nm assets pl, resources pl // vt (gén) to have; (fam: duper) to do // vb auxiliaire to have; ~ **à faire qch** to have to do sth; **il a 3 ans** he is 3 (years old); **voir faim, peur** etc; ~ **3 mètres de haut** to be 3 metres high; **il y a there is** + sg, there are + pl; (temporel): **il y a 10 ans** 10 years ago; **il y a 10 ans/longtemps que je le sais** I've known it for 10 years/a long time; **il y a 10 ans qu'il est arrivé** it's 10 years since he arrived; **il ne peut y en** ~ **qu'un** there can only be one; **il n'y a qu'à** we (ou you etc) will just have to; **qu'est-ce qu'il y a?** what's the matter?, what is it?; **en** ~ **à** ou **contre qn** to have a down on sb.

avoisinant, e [avwazinɑ̃, -ɑ̃t] a neighbouring.

avoisiner [avwazine] vt to be near ou close to; (fig) to border ou verge on.

avortement [avɔʀtəmɑ̃] nm abortion.

avorter [avɔʀte] vi (MÉD) to have an abortion; (fig) to fail.

avorton [avɔʀtɔ̃] nm (péj) little runt.

avoué, e [avwe] a avowed // nm (JUR) ≈ solicitor.

avouer [avwe] vt (crime, défaut) to confess (to); ~ **avoir fait/que** to admit ou confess to having done/that.

avril [avʀil] nm April.

axe [aks(ə)] nm axis (pl axes); (de roue etc) axle; (fig) main line; ~ **routier** trunk road, main road; ~ **de symétrie** symmetry axis; **axer** vt: **axer qch sur** to centre sth on.

ayant droit [ɛjɑ̃dʀwa] nm assignee; ~ **à** (pension etc) person eligible for ou entitled to.

ayons etc vb voir **avoir**.

azalée [azale] nf azalea.

azimut [azimyt] nm azimuth; **tous ~s** (fig) omnidirectional.

azote [azɔt] nm nitrogen; **azoté, e** a nitrogenous.

azur [azyʀ] nm (couleur) azure, sky blue; (ciel) sky, skies pl.

azyme [azim] a: **pain** ~ unleavened bread.

B

B.A. sigle f (= bonne action) good deed (for the day).

babiller [babije] vi to prattle, chatter; (bébé) to babble.

babines [babin] nfpl chops.

babiole [babjɔl] nf (bibelot) trinket; (vétille) trifle.

bâbord [babɔʀ] nm: **à** ou **par** ~ to port, on the port side.

babouin [babwɛ̃] nm baboon.

bac [bak] nm (SCOL) abr de **baccalauréat**; (bateau) ferry; (récipient) tub; tray; tank; ~ **à glace** ice-tray.

baccalauréat [bakalɔʀea] nm ≈ GCE A-levels.

bâche [baʃ] nf tarpaulin, canvas sheet.

bachelier, ère [baʃəlje, -ljɛʀ] nm/f holder of the baccalauréat.

bâcher [baʃe] vt to cover (with a canvas sheet ou a tarpaulin).

bachot [baʃo] nm abr de **baccalauréat**.

bacille [basil] nm bacillus (pl i).

bâcler [bakle] vt to botch (up).

bactérie [bakteʀi] nf bacterium (pl ia); **bactériologie** nf bacteriology.

badaud, e [bado, -od] nm/f idle onlooker, stroller.

baderne [badɛʀn(ə)] nf (péj): **(vieille)** ~ old fossil.

badigeon [badiʒɔ̃] nm distemper; colour-wash; **badigeonner** vt to distemper; to colourwash; (barbouiller) to daub.

badin, e [badɛ̃, -in] a light-hearted, playful.

badinage [badinaʒ] nm banter.

badine [badin] nf switch (stick).

badiner [badine] vi: ~ **avec qch** to treat sth lightly.

badminton [badmintɔn] nm badminton.

baffe [baf] nf (fam) slap, clout.

bafouer [bafwe] vt to deride, ridicule.

bafouiller [bafuje] vi, vt to stammer.

bâfrer [bɑfʀe] *vi, vt (fam)* to guzzle, gobble,

bagage [bagaʒ] *nm:* ∼s luggage *sg;* ∼ littéraire (stock of) literary knowledge; ∼s à main hand-luggage.

bagarre [bagaʀ] *nf* fight, brawl; **il aime la** ∼ he loves a fight, he likes fighting; **se bagarrer** *vi* to have a fight *ou* scuffle, fight.

bagatelle [bagatɛl] *nf* trifle, trifling sum *ou* matter.

bagnard [baɲaʀ] *nm* convict.

bagne [baɲ] *nm* penal colony.

bagnole [baɲɔl] *nf (fam)* car, motor.

bagout [bagu] *nm* glibness; **avoir du** ∼ to have the gift of the gab.

bague [bag] *nf* ring; ∼ **de fiançailles** engagement ring; ∼ **de serrage** clip.

baguenauder [bagnode]: **se** ∼ *vi* to trail around, loaf around.

baguer [bage] *vt* to ring.

baguette [bagɛt] *nf* stick; *(cuisine chinoise)* chopstick; *(de chef d'orchestre)* baton; *(pain)* stick of (French) bread; ∼ **magique** magic wand; ∼ **de tambour** drumstick.

bahut [bay] *nm* chest.

baie [bɛ] *nf (GÉO)* bay; *(fruit)* berry; ∼ *(vitrée)* picture window.

baignade [bɛɲad] *nf* bathing.

baigné, e [beɲe] *a:* ∼ **de** bathed in; soaked with; flooded with.

baigner [beɲe] *vt (bébé)* to bath // *vi:* ∼ **dans son sang** to lie in a pool of blood; ∼ **dans la brume** to be shrouded in mist; **se** ∼ *vi* to have a swim, go swimming *ou* bathing; **baigneur, euse** *nm/f* bather; **baignoire** *nf* bath(tub).

bail, baux [baj, bo] *nm* lease.

bâillement [bɑjmɑ̃] *nm* yawn.

bâiller [bɑje] *vi* to yawn; *(être ouvert)* to gape.

bailleur [bɑjœʀ] *nm:* ∼ **de fonds** sponsor, backer.

bâillon [bɑjɔ̃] *nm* gag; **bâillonner** *vt* to gag.

bain [bɛ̃] *nm* bath; **prendre un** ∼ to have a bath; ∼ **de foule** walkabout; ∼ **de soleil** sunbathing *q;* **prendre un** ∼ **de soleil** to sunbathe; ∼s **de mer** sea bathing *sg;* ∼-**marie** *nm* double boiler; **faire chauffer au** ∼-**marie** *(boîte etc)* to immerse in boiling water.

baïonnette [bajɔnɛt] *nf* bayonet.

baisemain [bɛzmɛ̃] *nm* kissing a lady's hand.

baiser [beze] *nm* kiss // *vt (main, front)* to kiss; *(fam!)* to screw (!).

baisse [bɛs] *nf* fall, drop; '∼ **sur la viande** 'meat prices down'.

baisser [bese] *vt* to lower; *(radio, chauffage)* to turn down; *(AUTO: phares)* to dip // *vi* to fall, drop, go down; **se** ∼ *vi* to bend down.

bajoues [baʒu] *nfpl* chaps, chops.

bal [bal] *nm* dance; *(grande soirée)* ball; ∼ **costumé** fancy-dress ball; ∼ **musette** dance *(with accordion accompaniment)*.

balade [balad] *nf* walk, stroll; *(en voiture)* drive.

balader [balade] *vt (traîner)* to trail round; **se** ∼ *vi* to go for a walk *ou* stroll; to go for a drive.

baladeuse [baladøz] *nf* inspection lamp.

baladin [baladɛ̃] *nm* wandering entertainer.

balafre [balafʀ(ə)] *nf* gash, slash; *(cicatrice)* scar; **balafrer** *vt* to gash, slash.

balai [balɛ] *nm* broom, brush; ∼-**brosse** *nm* deck scrubber.

balance [balɑ̃s] *nf* scales *pl;* *(de précision)* balance; *(signe):* **la B**∼ Libra, the Scales; **être de la B**∼ to be Libra; ∼ **des comptes/forces** balance of payments/power; ∼ **romaine** steelyard.

balancer [balɑ̃se] *vt* to swing; *(lancer)* to fling, chuck; *(renvoyer, jeter)* to chuck out // *vi* to swing; **se** ∼ *vi* to swing; to rock; to sway; **se** ∼ **de** *(fam)* not to care about; **balancier** *nm (de pendule)* pendulum; *(de montre)* balance wheel; *(perche)* (balancing) pole; **balançoire** *nf* swing; *(sur pivot)* seesaw.

balayer [baleje] *vt (feuilles etc)* to sweep up, brush up; *(pièce)* to sweep; *(chasser)* to sweep away; to sweep aside; *(suj: radar)* to scan; *(: phares)* to sweep across; **balayeur, euse** *nm/f* roadsweeper // *nf (engin)* roadsweeper; **balayures** *nfpl* sweepings.

balbutier [balbysje] *vi, vt* to stammer.

balcon [balkɔ̃] *nm* balcony; *(THÉÂTRE)* dress circle.

baldaquin [baldakɛ̃] *nm* canopy.

baleine [balɛn] *nf* whale; *(de parapluie, corset)* rib; **baleinière** *nf* whaleboat.

balise [baliz] *nf (NAVIG)* beacon; *(marker)* buoy; *(AVIAT)* runway light, beacon; *(AUTO, SKI)* sign, marker; **baliser** *vt* to mark out (with beacons *ou* lights *etc).*

balistique [balistik] *nf* ballistics *sg.*

balivernes [balivɛʀn(ə)] *nfpl* twaddle *sg,* nonsense *sg.*

ballade [balad] *nf* ballad.

ballant, e [balɑ̃, -ɑ̃t] *a* dangling.

ballast [balast] *nm* ballast.

balle [bal] *nf (de fusil)* bullet; *(de sport)* ball; *(du blé)* chaff; *(paquet)* bale; ∼ **perdue** stray bullet.

ballerine [balʀin] *nf* ballet dancer; ballet shoe.

ballet [balɛ] *nm* ballet.

ballon [balɔ̃] *nm (de sport)* ball; *(jouet, AVIAT)* balloon; *(de vin)* glass; ∼ **de football** football.

ballonner [balɔne] *vt:* **j'ai le ventre ballonné** I feel bloated.

ballon-sonde [balɔ̃sɔ̃d] *nm* sounding balloon.

ballot [balo] *nm* bundle; *(péj)* nitwit.

ballottage [balɔtaʒ] *nm (POL)* second ballot.

ballotter [balɔte] *vi* to roll around; to toss // *vt* to shake *ou* throw about; to toss.

balluchon [balyʃɔ̃] *nm* bundle (of clothes).

balnéaire [balneɛʀ] *a* seaside *cpd.*

balourd, e [baluʀ, -uʀd(ə)] *a* clumsy, doltish; **balourdise** *nf* clumsiness, doltishness; blunder.

balte [balt] *a* Baltic.

Baltique [baltik] *nf*: **la (mer)** ～ the Baltic (Sea).

baluchon [balyʃ5] *nm* = **balluchon.**

balustrade [balystʀad] *nf* railings *pl*, handrail.

bambin [bɑ̃bɛ̃] *nm* little child.

bambou [bɑ̃bu] *nm* bamboo.

ban [bɑ̃] *nm* round of applause, cheer; ～**s** *nmpl* (*de mariage*) banns; **être/mettre au** ～ **de** to be outlawed/to outlaw from; **le** ～ **et l'arrière-**～ **de sa famille** every last one of his relatives.

banal, e [banal] *a* banal, commonplace; (*péj*) trite; **four/moulin** ～ village oven/mill; ～**ité** *nf* banality; truism, trite remark.

banane [banan] *nf* banana; ～**raie** *nf* banana plantation; **bananier** *nm* banana tree; banana boat.

banc [bɑ̃] *nm* seat, bench; (*de poissons*) shoal; ～ **des accusés** dock; ～ **d'essai** (*fig*) testing ground; ～ **de sable** sandbank; ～ **des témoins** witness box.

bancaire [bɑ̃kɛʀ] *a* banking, bank *cpd*.

bancal, e [bɑ̃kal] *a* wobbly; bandy-legged.

bandage [bɑ̃daʒ] *nm* bandaging; bandage; ～ **herniaire** truss.

bande [bɑ̃d] *nf* (*de tissu etc*) strip; (*MÉD*) bandage; (*motif*) stripe; (*magnétique etc*) tape; (*groupe*) band; (*péj*): ～ **de bunch** *ou* crowd of; **par la** ～ in a roundabout way; **donner de la** ～ to list; **faire** ～ **à part** to keep to o.s.; ～ **dessinée** strip cartoon; ～ **perforée** punched tape; ～ **de roulement** (*de pneu*) tread; ～ **sonore** sound track.

bandeau, x [bɑ̃do] *nm* headband; (*sur les yeux*) blindfold; (*MÉD*) head bandage.

bander [bɑ̃de] *vt* (*blessure*) to bandage; (*muscle*) to tense; ～ **les yeux à qn** to blindfold sb.

banderole [bɑ̃dʀɔl] *nf* banner, streamer.

bandit [bɑ̃di] *nm* bandit; **banditisme** *nm* violent crime, armed robberies *pl*.

bandoulière [bɑ̃duljɛʀ] *nf*: **en** ～ (slung *ou* worn) across the shoulder.

banjo [bɑ̃(d)ʒo] *nm* banjo.

banlieue [bɑ̃ljø] *nf* suburbs *pl*; **lignes/quartiers de** ～ suburban lines/areas; **trains de** ～ commuter trains.

bannière [banjɛʀ] *nf* banner.

bannir [baniʀ] *vt* to banish.

banque [bɑ̃k] *nf* bank; (*activités*) banking; ～ **d'affaires** merchant bank.

banqueroute [bɑ̃kʀut] *nf* bankruptcy.

banquet [bɑ̃kɛ] *nm* dinner; (*d'apparat*) banquet.

banquette [bɑ̃kɛt] *nf* seat.

banquier [bɑ̃kje] *nm* banker.

banquise [bɑ̃kiz] *nf* ice field.

baptême [batɛm] *nm* christening; baptism; ～ **de l'air** first flight; **baptiser** *vt* to christen.

baquet [bakɛ] *nm* tub, bucket.

bar [baʀ] *nm* bar.

baragouin [baʀagwɛ̃] *nm* gibberish.

baraque [baʀak] *nf* shed; (*fam*) house; ～ **foraine** fairground stand.

baraqué, e [baʀake] *a* well-built, hefty.

baraquements [baʀakmɑ̃] *nmpl* huts (*for refugees, workers etc*).

baratin [baʀatɛ̃] *nm* (*fam*) smooth talk, patter; **baratiner** *vt* to chat up.

barbare [baʀbaʀ] *a* barbaric // *nm/f* barbarian.

barbe [baʀb(ə)] *nf* beard; **quelle** ～ (*fam*) what a drag *ou* bore; ～ **à papa** candy-floss.

barbelé [baʀbəle] *nm* barbed wire *q*.

barbiche [baʀbiʃ] *nf* goatee.

barbiturique [baʀbityʀik] *nm* barbiturate.

barboter [baʀbɔte] *vi* to paddle, dabble // *vt* (*fam*) to filch.

barboteuse [baʀbɔtøz] *nf* rompers *pl*.

barbouiller [baʀbuje] *vt* to daub; **avoir l'estomac barbouillé** to feel queasy *ou* sick.

barbu, e [baʀby] *a* bearded.

barda [baʀda] *nm* (*fam*) kit, gear.

barde [baʀd(ə)] *nf* (*CULIN*) sliver of fat bacon.

bardé, e [baʀde] *a*: ～ **de médailles** *etc* bedecked with medals *etc*.

barder [baʀde] *vi* (*fam*): **ça va** ～ sparks will fly, things are going to get hot.

barème [baʀɛm] *nm* scale; table; ～ **des salaires** salary scale.

barguigner [baʀgiɲe] *vi*: **sans** ～ without (any) humming and hawing *ou* shilly-shallying.

baril [baʀil] *nm* barrel; keg.

barillet [baʀijɛ] *nm* (*de revolver*) cylinder.

bariolé, e [baʀjole] *a* many-coloured, rainbow-coloured.

baromètre [baʀɔmɛtʀ(ə)] *nm* barometer.

baron [baʀ5] *nm* baron; **baronne** *nf* baroness.

baroque [baʀɔk] *a* (*ART*) baroque; (*fig*) weird.

baroud [baʀud] *nm*: ～ **d'honneur** gallant last stand.

barque [baʀk(ə)] *nf* small boat.

barrage [baʀaʒ] *nm* dam; (*sur route*) road-block, barricade.

barre [baʀ] *nf* bar; (*NAVIG*) helm; (*écrite*) line, stroke; (*JUR*): **comparaître à la** ～ to appear as a witness; ～ **fixe** (*GYM*) horizontal bar; ～ **à mine** crowbar; ～**s parallèles** (*GYM*) parallel bars.

barreau, x [baʀo] *nm* bar; (*JUR*): **le** ～ the Bar.

barrer [baʀe] *vt* (*route etc*) to block; (*mot*) to cross out; (*chèque*) to cross; (*NAVIG*) to steer; **se** ～ *vi* (*fam*) to clear off.

barrette [baʀɛt] *nf* (*pour cheveux*) (hair) slide.

barreur [baʀœʀ] *nm* helmsman; (*aviron*) coxswain.

barricade [baʀikad] *nf* barricade; **barricader** *vt* to barricade; **se barricader chez soi** (*fig*) to lock o.s. in.

barrière [baʀjɛʀ] *nf* fence; (*obstacle*) barrier.

barrique [baʀik] *nf* barrel, cask.

baryton [baʀit5] *nm* baritone.

bas, basse [bɑ, bɑs] *a* low // *nm* bottom, lower part; (*chaussette*) stocking // *nf* (*MUS*) bass // *ad* low; **plus** ～ lower down; (*dans un texte*) further on, below; (*parler*) more softly; **au** ～ **mot** at the lowest estimate; **enfant en** ～ **âge** infant, young child; **en** ~ down below; at (*ou* to) the bottom; (*dans une maison*) downstairs; **en** ~ **de** at the bottom of; **mettre** ~ *vi* to give birth; **à** ~ ...! 'down with ...!'; ~ **morceaux** *nmpl* (*viande*) cheap cuts.

basalte [bazalt(ə)] *nm* basalt.

basané, e [bazane] *a* tanned, bronzed.

bas-côté [bakote] *nm* (*de route*) verge; (*d'église*) (side) aisle.

bascule [baskyl] *nf*: (**jeu de**) ~ seesaw; (**balance à**) ~ scales *pl*; **fauteuil à** ~ rocking chair; **système à** ~ tip-over device; rocker device.

basculer [baskyle] *vi* to fall over, topple (over); (*benne*) to tip up // *vt* (*gén*: **faire** ~) to topple over; to tip out, tip up.

base [baz] *nf* base; (*POL*) rank and file; (*fondement, principe*) basis (*pl* bases); **de** ~ basic; **à** ~ **de café** *etc* coffee *etc* -based; **baser** *vt* to base; **se baser sur** (*données, preuves*) to base one's argument on.

bas-fond [bafɔ̃] *nm* (*NAVIG*) shallow; ~**s** (*fig*) dregs.

basilic [bazilik] *nm* (*CULIN*) basil.

basilique [bazilik] *nf* basilica.

basket(-ball) [baskɛt(bol)] *nm* basketball.

basque [bask(ə)] *a*, *nm/f* Basque.

bas-relief [bəʀəljɛf] *nm* bas relief.

basse [bɑs] *a*, *nf voir* **bas**; ~**-cour** *nf* farmyard.

bassin [basɛ̃] *nm* (*cuvette*) bowl; (*pièce d'eau*) pond, pool; (*de fontaine*, *GÉO*) basin; (*ANAT*) pelvis; (*portuaire*) dock.

bassiste [basist(ə)] *nm/f* (double) bass player.

bastingage [bastɛ̃gaʒ] *nm* (ship's) rail.

bastion [bastjɔ̃] *nm* bastion.

bas-ventre [bɑvɑ̃tʀ(ə)] *nm* (lower part of the) stomach.

bat *vb voir* **battre**.

bât [bɑ] *nm* packsaddle.

bataille [batɑj] *nf* battle; fight.

bataillon [batɑjɔ̃] *nm* battalion.

bâtard, e [bɑtɑʀ, -aʀd(ə)] *nm/f* illegitimate child, bastard (*péj*).

bateau, x [bato] *nm* boat, ship.

batelier, -ière [batəlje, -jɛʀ] *nm/f* (*de bac*) ferryman.

bat-flanc [baflɑ̃] *nm inv* raised boards for sleeping, in cells, army huts *etc*.

bâti, e [bɑti] *a*: **bien** ~ well-built // *nm* (*armature*) frame.

batifoler [batifɔle] *vi* to frolic *ou* lark about.

bâtiment [bɑtimɑ̃] *nm* building; (*NAVIG*) ship, vessel; (*industrie*) building trade.

bâtir [bɑtiʀ] *vt* to build.

bâtisse [bɑtis] *nf* building.

bâton [bɑtɔ̃] *nm* stick; **à** ~**s rompus** informally.

bâtonnier [bɑtɔnje] *nm* ≈ president of the Bar.

batraciens [batʀasjɛ̃] *nmpl* amphibians.

bats *vb voir* **battre**.

battage [bataʒ] *nm* (*publicité*) (hard) plugging.

battant [batɑ̃] *nm* (*de cloche*) clapper; (*de volets*) shutter, flap; (*de porte*) side; **porte à double** ~ double door.

battement [batmɑ̃] *nm* (*de cœur*) beat; (*intervalle*) interval (*between classes, trains etc*); ~ **de paupières** blinking *q* (of eyelids); **10 minutes de** ~ 10 minutes to spare.

batterie [batʀi] *nf* (*MIL*, *ÉLEC*) battery; (*MUS*) drums *pl*, drum kit; ~ **de cuisine** pots and pans *pl*, kitchen utensils *pl*.

batteur [batœʀ] *nm* (*MUS*) drummer; (*appareil*) whisk; **batteuse** *nf* (*AGR*) threshing machine.

battre [batʀ(ə)] *vt* to beat; (*suj*: *pluie, vagues*) to beat *ou* lash against; (*œufs etc*) to beat up, whisk; (*blé*) to thresh; (*passer au peigne fin*) to scour // *vi* (*cœur*) to beat; (*volets etc*) to bang, rattle; **se** ~ *vi* to fight; ~ **la mesure** to beat time; ~ **en brèche** to demolish; ~ **son plein** to be at its height, be going full swing; ~ **pavillon britannique** to fly the British flag; ~ **des mains** to clap one's hands; ~ **des ailes** to flap its wings; ~ **en retraite** to beat a retreat.

battue [baty] *nf* (*chasse*) beat; (*policière etc*) search, hunt.

baume [bom] *nm* balm.

bauxite [boksit] *nf* bauxite.

bavard, e [bavaʀ, -aʀd(ə)] *a* (very) talkative; gossipy; **bavardage** *nm* chatter *q*; gossip *q*; **bavarder** *vi* to chatter; (*indiscrètement*) to gossip; to blab.

bave [bav] *nf* dribble; (*de chien etc*) slobber, slaver; (*d'escargot*) slime; **baver** *vi* to dribble; to slobber, slaver; **bavette** *nf* bib; **baveux, euse** *a* dribbling; (*omelette*) runny.

bavure [bavyʀ] *nf* smudge; (*fig*) hitch, flaw.

bayer [baje] *vi*: ~ **aux corneilles** to stand gaping.

bazar [bazaʀ] *nm* general store; (*fam*) jumble; **bazarder** *vt* (*fam*) to chuck out.

B.C.G. *sigle m* (= *bacille Calmette-Guérin*) BCG.

bd. *abr de* **boulevard**.

B.D. *sigle f* = **bande dessinée**.

béant, e [beɑ̃, -ɑ̃t] *a* gaping.

béat, e [bea, -at] *a* showing open-eyed wonder; blissful; **béatitude** *nf* bliss.

beau(bel), belle, beaux [bo, bɛl] *a* beautiful, fine, lovely; (*homme*) handsome // *nf* (*SPORT*) decider // *ad*: **il fait** ~ the weather's fine *ou* fair; **un** ~ **jour** one (fine) day; **de plus belle** more than ever, even more; **on a** ~ **essayer** however hard *ou* no matter how hard we try; **faire le** ~ (*chien*) to sit up and beg.

beaucoup [boku] *ad* a lot; much (*gén en tournure négative*); **il ne boit pas** ~ he doesn't drink much *ou* a lot; ~ **de** (*nombre*) many, a lot of; (*quantité*) a lot of, much; ~ **plus/trop** *etc* far *ou* much more/too much; **de** ~ by far.

beau-fils [bofis] *nm* son-in-law; (*remariage*) stepson.

beau-frère [bofʀɛʀ] *nm* brother-in-law.

beau-père [bopɛʀ] *nm* father-in-law; stepfather.

beauté [bote] *nf* beauty; **de toute** ~ beautiful; **en** ~ with a flourish, brilliantly.

beaux-arts [bozaʀ] *nmpl* fine arts.

beaux-parents [boparɑ̃] *nmpl* wife's/husband's family *sg ou pl*, in-laws.

bébé [bebe] *nm* baby.

bec [bɛk] *nm* beak, bill; (*de plume*) nib; (*de récipient*) spout; lip; (*fam*) mouth; ~ **de gaz** (street) gaslamp; ~ **verseur** pouring lip.

bécane [bekan] *nf* bike.

bécasse [bekas] *nf* (*ZOOL*) woodcock; (*fam*) silly goose.

bec-de-lièvre [bɛkdəljɛvR(ə)] *nm* harelip.

bêche [bɛʃ] *nf* spade; **bêcher** *vt* to dig.

bécoter [bekɔte]: **se** ~ *vi* to smooch.

becquée [beke] *nf*: **donner la** ~ **à** to feed.

becqueter [bɛkte] *vt* to peck (at).

bedaine [bədɛn] *nf* paunch.

bedeau, x [bədo] *nm* beadle.

bedonnant, e [bədɔnɑ̃, -ɑ̃t] *a* paunchy, potbellied.

bée [be] *a*: **bouche** ~ gaping.

beffroi [befRwa] *nm* belfry.

bégayer [begeje] *vt, vi* to stammer.

bègue [bɛg] *nm/f*: **être** ~ to have a stammer.

bégueule [begœl] *a* prudish.

béguin [begɛ̃] *nm*: **avoir le** ~ **de** *ou* **pour** to have a crush on.

beige [bɛʒ] *a* beige.

beignet [bɛɲɛ] *nm* fritter.

bel [bɛl] *a voir* **beau**.

bêler [bele] *vi* to bleat.

belette [bəlɛt] *nf* weasel.

belge [bɛlʒ(ə)] *a, nm/f* Belgian.

Belgique [bɛlʒik] *nf* Belgium.

bélier [belje] *nm* ram; (*engin*) (battering) ram; (*signe*): **le B**~ Aries, the Ram; **être du B**~ to be Aries.

belle [bɛl] *af, nf voir* **beau**; ~-**fille** *nf* daughter-in-law; (*remariage*) stepdaughter; ~-**mère** *nf* mother-in-law; stepmother; ~-**sœur** *nf* sister-in-law.

belligérant, e [beliʒeRɑ̃, -ɑ̃t] *a* belligerent.

belliqueux, euse [belikø, -øz] *a* aggressive, warlike.

belvédère [bɛlvedɛR] *nm* panoramic viewpoint (*or small building at such a place*).

bémol [bemɔl] *nm* (*MUS*) flat.

bénédiction [benediksjɔ̃] *nf* blessing.

bénéfice [benefis] *nm* (*COMM*) profit; (*avantage*) benefit; **bénéficiaire** *nm/f* beneficiary; **bénéficier de** *vt* to enjoy; to benefit by *ou* from; to get, be given; **bénéfique** *a* beneficial.

benêt [bənɛ] *nm* simpleton.

bénévole [benevɔl] *a* voluntary, unpaid.

bénin, igne [benɛ̃, -iɲ] *a* minor, mild; (*tumeur*) benign.

bénir [beniR] *vt* to bless; **bénit, e** *a* consecrated; **eau bénite** holy water; **bénitier** *nm* stoup, font (*for holy water*).

benjamin, e [bɛ̃ʒamɛ̃, -in] *nm/f* youngest child.

benne [bɛn] *nf* skip; (*de téléphérique*) (cable) car; ~ **basculante** tipper.

benzine [bɛzin] *nf* benzine.

béotien, ne [beɔsjɛ̃, -jɛn] *nm/f* philistine.

B.E.P.C. *sigle m voir* **brevet**.

béquille [bekij] *nf* crutch; (*de bicyclette*) stand.

bercail [bɛRkaj] *nm* fold.

berceau, x [bɛRso] *nm* cradle, crib.

bercer [bɛRse] *vt* to rock, cradle; (*suj: musique etc*) to lull; ~ **qn** (*promesses etc*) to delude sb with; **berceuse** *nf* lullaby.

béret (basque) [beRɛ(bask(ə))] *nm* beret.

berge [bɛRʒ(ə)] *nf* bank.

berger, ère [bɛRʒe, -ɛR] *nm/f* shepherd/shepherdess; **bergerie** *nf* sheep pen.

berline [bɛRlin] *nf* (*AUTO*) saloon (car).

berlingot [bɛRlɛ̃go] *nm* (*emballage*) carton (*pyramid shaped*).

berlue [bɛRly] *nf*: **j'ai la** ~ I must be seeing things.

berne [bɛRn(ə)] *nf*: **en** ~ at half-mast.

berner [bɛRne] *vt* to fool.

besogne [bəzɔɲ] *nf* work *q*, job; **besogneux, euse** *a* hard-working.

besoin [bəzwɛ̃] *nm* need; (*pauvreté*): **le** ~ need, want; ~**s** (**naturels**) nature's needs; **faire ses** ~**s** to relieve o.s.; **avoir** ~ **de qch/faire qch** to need sth/to do sth; **au** ~ if need be; **pour les** ~**s de la cause** for the purpose in hand.

bestial, e, aux [bɛstjal, -o] *a* bestial, brutish.

bestiaux [bɛstjo] *nmpl* cattle.

bestiole [bɛstjɔl] *nf* (tiny) creature.

bétail [betaj] *nm* livestock, cattle *pl*.

bête [bɛt] *nf* animal; (*bestiole*) insect, creature // a stupid, silly; **il cherche la petite** ~ he's being pernickety *ou* overfussy; ~ **noire** pet hate, bugbear; ~ **sauvage** wild beast; ~ **de somme** beast of burden.

bêtise [betiz] *nf* stupidity; stupid thing (to say *ou* do).

béton [betɔ̃] *nm* concrete; ~ **armé** reinforced concrete; **bétonner** *vt* to concrete (over); **bétonnière** *nf* cement mixer.

betterave [bɛtRav] *nf* (*rouge*) beetroot; ~ **fourragère** mangel-wurzel; ~ **sucrière** sugar beet.

beugler [bøgle] *vi* to low; (*radio etc*) to blare // *vt* (*chanson etc*) to bawl out.

beurre [bœR] *nm* butter; **beurrer** *vt* to butter; **beurrier** *nm* butter dish.

beuverie [bœvRi] *nf* drinking session.

bévue [bevy] *nf* blunder.

bi... [bi] *préfixe* bi... , two-.

biais [bjɛ] *nm* (*moyen*) device, expedient; (*aspect*) angle; **en** ~, **de** ~ (*obliquement*) at an angle; (*fig*) indirectly; **biaiser** *vi* (*fig*) to sidestep the issue.

bibelot [biblo] *nm* trinket, curio.

biberon [bibRɔ̃] *nm* (feeding) bottle; **nourrir au** ~ to bottle-feed.

bible [bibl(ə)] *nf* bible.

biblio... [biblijo] *préfixe*: ~**bus** *nm* mobile library van; ~**graphie** *nf* bibliography; ~**phile** *nm/f* booklover; ~**thécaire** *nm/f* librarian; ~**thèque** *nf* library; (*meuble*) bookcase.

biblique [biblik] *a* biblical.

bicarbonate [bikaRbɔnat] *nm*: ~ (**de soude**) bicarbonate of soda.

biceps [bisɛps] *nm* biceps.

biche [biʃ] *nf* doe.

bichonner [biʃɔne] vt to groom.
bicolore [bikɔlɔR] a two-coloured.
bicoque [bikɔk] nf (péj) shack.
bicorne [bikɔRn(ə)] nm cocked hat.
bicyclette [bisiklɛt] nf bicycle.
bide [bid] nm (fam: ventre) belly ; (THÉÂTRE) flop.
bidet [bidɛ] nm bidet.
bidon [bidɔ̃] nm can // a inv (fam) phoney.
bidonville [bidɔ̃vil] nm shanty town.
bielle [bjɛl] nf connecting rod.
bien [bjɛ̃] nm good ; (patrimoine) property q ; **faire du ~ à qn** to do sb good ; **dire du ~ de** to speak well of ; **changer en ~** to turn to the good ; **~s de consommation** consumer goods // ad (travailler) well ; ~ **jeune** rather young ; ~ **assez** quite enough ; ~ **mieux** very much better ; ~ **du temps/ des gens** quite a time/a number of people ; **j'espère ~ y aller** 1 do hope to go ; **je veux ~ le faire** (concession) I'm (quite) willing to do it ; **il faut ~ le faire** it has to be done ; ~ **sûr** certainly ; **c'est ~ fait** (mérité) it serves him (ou her etc) right ; **croyant ~ faire** thinking he was doing the right thing // a inv (à l'aise): **être ~** to be fine ; **ce n'est pas ~ de** it's not right to ; **cette maison est ~** this house is (very) good ; **elle est ~** (jolie) she's good-looking ; **des gens ~** (parfois péj) respectable people ; **être ~ avec qn** to be on good terms with sb ; ~ **que** cj although ; **~-aimé, e** a (chose) beloved ; **~-être** nm well-being ; **~faisance** nf charity ; **~faisant, e** a (chose) beneficial ; **~fait** nm. act of generosity, benefaction ; (de la science etc) benefit ; **~faiteur, trice** nm/f benefactor/benefactress ; **~-fondé** nm soundness ; **~-fonds** nm property ; **~heureux, euse** a happy ; (REL) blessed, blest.
biennal, e, aux [bjenal, -o] a biennial.
bienséance [bjɛ̃seɑ̃s] nf propriety, decorum q.
bienséant, e [bjɛ̃seɑ̃, -ɑ̃t] a proper, seemly.
bientôt [bjɛ̃to] ad soon ; **à ~** see you soon.
bienveillance [bjɛ̃vejɑ̃s] nf kindness.
bienveillant, e [bjɛ̃vejɑ̃, -ɑ̃t] a kindly.
bienvenu, e [bjɛ̃vny] a welcome // nm/f: **être le ~/la ~e** to be welcome // nf: **souhaiter la ~e à** to welcome ; **~e à** welcome to.
bière [bjɛR] nf (boisson) beer ; (cercueil) bier ; ~ **blonde** lager ; ~ **brune** brown ale ; ~ **(à la) pression** draught beer.
biffer [bife] vt to cross out.
bifteck [biftɛk] nm steak.
bifurcation [bifyRkasjɔ̃] nf fork (in road).
bifurquer [bifyRke] vi (route) to fork ; (véhicule) to turn off.
bigame [bigam] a bigamous ; **bigamie** nf bigamy.
bigarré, e [bigaRe] a multicoloured ; (disparate) motley.
bigorneau, x [bigɔRno] nm winkle.
bigot, e [bigo, -ɔt] (péj) a churchy // nm/f church fiend.
bigoudi [bigudi] nm curler.
bijou, x [biʒu] nm jewel ; **~terie** nf jeweller's (shop) ; jewellery ; **~tier, ière** nm/f jeweller.
bikini [bikini] nm bikini.
bilan [bilɑ̃] nm (COMM) balance sheet(s) ; end of year statement ; (fig) (net) outcome ; (: de victimes) toll ; **faire le ~ de** to assess ; to review ; **déposer son ~** to file a bankruptcy statement.
bilatéral, e, aux [bilateRal, -o] a bilateral.
bile [bil] nf bile ; **se faire de la ~** (fam) to worry o.s. sick.
biliaire [biljɛR] a biliary.
bilieux, euse [biljø, -jøz] a bilious ; (fig: colérique) testy.
bilingue [bilɛ̃g] a bilingual.
billard [bijaR] nm billiards sg ; billiard table.
bille [bij] nf (gén) ball ; (du jeu de billes) marble ; (de bois) log.
billet [bijɛ] nm (aussi: ~ **de banque**) (bank)note ; (de cinéma, de bus etc) ticket ; (courte lettre) note ; ~ **circulaire** round-trip ticket ; ~ **de faveur** complimentary ticket ; ~ **de loterie** lottery ticket ; ~ **de quai** platform ticket.
billion [biljɔ̃] nm billion.
billot [bijo] nm block.
bimensuel, le [bimɑ̃sɥɛl] a bimonthly, two-monthly.
bimoteur [bimɔtœR] a twin-engined.
binaire [binɛR] a binary.
binocle [binɔkl(ə)] nm pince-nez.
binôme [binom] nm binomial.
bio... [bjɔ] préfixe bio... ; **~-dégradable** a biodegradable ; **~graphe** nm/f biographer ; **~graphie** nf biography ; **~graphique** a biographical ; **~logie** nf biology ; **~logique** a biological ; **~logiste** nm/f biologist.
bipède [bipɛd] nm biped, two-footed creature.
biplan [biplɑ̃] nm biplane.
biréacteur [biReaktœR] nm twin- engined jet.
bis, e [bi, biz] a (couleur) greyish brown // ad [bis]: **12 ~ 12a** ou A // excl, nm [bis] encore // nf (baiser) kiss ; (vent) North wind.
bisannuel, le [bizanɥɛl] a biennial.
bisbille [bisbij] nf: **être en ~ avec qn** to be at loggerheads with sb.
biscornu, e [biskɔRny] a crooked, weird(-looking).
biscotte [biskɔt] nf rusk.
biscuit [biskɥi] nm biscuit ; sponge cake.
bise [biz] a, nf voir **bis**.
biseau, x [bizo] nm bevelled edge ; **en ~** bevelled ; **~ter** vt to bevel.
bison [bizɔ̃] nm bison.
bisque [bisk(ə)] nf: ~ **d'écrevisses** shrimp bisque.
bissectrice [bisɛktRis] nf bisector.
bisser [bise] vt to encore.
bissextile [bisɛkstil] a: **année ~** leap year.
bissexué, e [bisɛksɥe] a bisexual.
bistouri [bisturi] nm lancet.
bistre [bistR(ə)] a bistre.
bistro(t) [bistRo] nm bistrot, café.

bitte [bit] *nf*: ~ **d'amarrage** bollard (*NAUT*).
bitume [bitym] *nm* asphalt.
bivouac [bivwak] *nm* bivouac;
bivouaquer *vi* to bivouac.
bizarre [bizaʀ] *a* strange, odd.
blafard, e [blafaʀ, -aʀd(ə)] *a* wan.
blague [blag] *nf* (*propos*) joke; (*farce*) trick; **sans ~!** no kidding!; ~ **à tabac** tobacco pouch.
blaguer [blage] *vi* to joke // *vt* to tease; **blagueur, euse** *a* teasing // *nm/f* joker.
blaireau, x [blɛʀo] *nm* (*ZOOL*) badger; (*brosse*) shaving brush.
blâmable [blɑmabl(ə)] *a* blameworthy.
blâme [blɑm] *nm* blame; (*sanction*) reprimand.
blâmer [blɑme] *vt* to blame.
blanc, blanche [blɑ̃, blɑ̃ʃ] *a* white; (*non imprimé*) blank; (*innocent*) pure // *nm/f* white, white man/woman // *nm* (*couleur*) white; (*linge*): **le** ~ whites *pl*; (*espace non écrit*) blank; (*aussi*: ~ **d'œuf**) (egg-)white; (*aussi*: ~ **de poulet**) breast, white meat; (*aussi*: ~ **de** white wine // *nf* (*MUS*) minim; **chèque en** ~ blank cheque; **à** ~ *ad* (*chauffer*) white-hot; (*tirer, charger*) with blanks; ~-**bec** *nm* greenhorn; **blancheur** *nf* whiteness.
blanchir [blɑ̃ʃiʀ] *vt* (*gén*) to whiten; (*linge*) to launder; (*CULIN*) to blanch; (*fig: disculper*) to clear // *vi* to grow white; (*cheveux*) to go white; **blanchissage** *nm* (*du linge*) laundering; **blanchisserie** *nf* laundry; **blanchisseur, euse** *nm/f* launderer.
blanc-seing [blɑ̃sɛ̃] *nm* signed blank paper.
blaser [blɑze] *vt* to make blasé.
blason [blazɔ̃] *nm* coat of arms.
blasphème [blasfɛm] *nm* blasphemy; **blasphémer** *vi* to blaspheme // *vt* to blaspheme against.
blatte [blat] *nf* cockroach.
blazer [blazɛʀ] *nm* blazer.
blé [ble] *nm* wheat; ~ **en herbe** wheat on the ear.
bled [blɛd] *nm* (*péj*) hole; (*en Afrique du nord*): **le** ~ the interior.
blême [blɛm] *a* pale.
blennorragie [blenɔʀaʒi] *nf* blennorrhoea.
blessant, e [blɛsɑ̃, -ɑ̃t] *a* hurtful.
blessé, e [blese] *a* injured // *nm/f* injured person; casualty.
blesser [blese] *vt* to injure; (*délibérément: MIL etc*) to wound; (*suj: souliers etc, offenser*) to hurt; **se** ~ to injure o.s.; **se** ~ **au pied** etc to injure one's foot etc.
blessure [blesyʀ] *nf* injury; wound.
blet, te [blɛ, blɛt] *a* overripe.
bleu [blø] *a* blue; (*bifteck*) very rare // *nm* (*couleur*) blue; (*novice*) greenhorn; (*contusion*) bruise; (*vêtement: aussi*: ~**s**) overalls *pl*; **au** ~ (*CULIN*) au bleu.
bleuet [bløɛ] *nm* cornflower.
bleuir [bløiʀ] *vt*, *vi* to turn blue.
bleuté, e [bløte] *a* blue-shaded.
blindage [blɛ̃daʒ] *nm* armour-plating.
blinder [blɛ̃de] *vt* to armour; (*fig*) to harden.
blizzard [blizaʀ] *nm* blizzard.

bloc [blɔk] *nm* (*de pierre etc*) block; (*de papier à lettres*) pad; (*ensemble*) group, block; **serré à** ~ tightened right down; **en** ~ as a whole; wholesale; ~ **opératoire** operating theatre suite.
blocage [blɔkaʒ] *nm* blocking; jamming; freezing; (*PSYCH*) hang-up.
bloc-moteur [blɔkmɔtœʀ] *nm* engine block.
bloc-notes [blɔknɔt] *nm* note pad.
blocus [blɔkys] *nm* blockade.
blond, e [blɔ̃, -ɔ̃d] *a* fair, blond; (*sable, blés*) golden // *nm/f* fair-haired *ou* blond man/woman; ~ **cendré** ash blond; **blondeur** *nf* fairness.
bloquer [blɔke] *vt* (*passage*) to block; (*pièce mobile*) to jam; (*crédits, compte*) to freeze; (*regrouper*) to group; ~ **les freins** to jam on the brakes.
blottir [blɔtiʀ]: **se** ~ *vi* to huddle up.
blouse [bluz] *nf* overall.
blouson [bluzɔ̃] *nm* lumber jacket; ~ **noir** (*fig*) ≈ teddy boy.
blues [bluz] *nm* blues *pl*.
bluet [blyɛ] *nm* = **bleuet.**
bluff [blœf] *nm* bluff; ~**er** *vi*, *vt* to bluff.
boa [bɔa] *nm* boa.
bobard [bɔbaʀ] *nm* (*fam*) tall story.
bobèche [bɔbɛʃ] *nf* candle-ring.
bobine [bɔbin] *nf* reel; (*machine à coudre*) spool; (*ELEC*) coil.
bocage [bɔkaʒ] *nm* grove, copse.
bocal, aux [bɔkal, -o] *nm* jar.
bock [bɔk] *nm* (beer) glass; glass of beer.
bœuf [bœf, *pl* bø] *nm* ox (*pl* oxen), steer; (*CULIN*) beef.
bohème [bɔɛm] *a* happy-go-lucky, unconventional.
bohémien, ne [bɔemjɛ̃, -jɛn] *nm/f* gipsy.
boire [bwaʀ] *vt* to drink; (*s'imprégner de*) to soak up; ~ **un verre** to have a drink.
bois [bwa] *nm* wood; **de** ~, **en** ~ wooden; ~ **de lit** bedstead.
boisé, e [bwaze] *a* wooded.
boiser [bwaze] *vt* (*galerie de mine*) to timber; (*chambre*) to panel; (*terrain*) to plant with trees.
boiseries [bwazʀi] *nfpl* panelling *sg*.
boisson [bwasɔ̃] *nf* drink; **pris de** ~ drunk, intoxicated; ~**s alcoolisées** alcoholic beverages *ou* drinks; ~**s gazeuses** fizzy drinks.
boîte [bwat] *nf* box; **aliments en** ~ canned *ou* tinned foods; ~ **de sardines/petits pois** can *ou* tin of sardines/peas; ~ **d'allumettes** box of matches; (*vide*) matchbox; ~ **de conserves** can *ou* tin (of food); ~ **crânienne** cranium, brainpan; ~ **à gants** glove compartment; ~ **aux lettres** letterbox; ~ **de nuit** night club; ~ **postale (B.P.)** P.O. Box; ~ **de vitesses** gear box.
boiter [bwate] *vi* to limp; (*fig*) to wobble; to be shaky; **boiteux, euse** *a* lame; wobbly; shaky.
boîtier [bwatje] *nm* case; ~ **de montre** watch case.
boive etc *vb voir* **boire.**
bol [bɔl] *nm* bowl; **un** ~ **d'air** a dose of fresh air.

bolet [bɔlɛ] *nm* boletus (mushroom).

bolide [bɔlid] *nm* racing car; **comme un ~** at top speed, like a rocket.

bombance [bɔ̃bɑ̃s] *nf*: **faire ~** to have a feast, revel.

bombardement [bɔ̃baʀdəmɑ̃] *nm* bombing.

bombarder [bɔ̃baʀde] *vt* to bomb; **~ qn de** (*cailloux, lettres*) to bombard sb with; **~ qn directeur** to thrust sb into the director's seat; **bombardier** *nm* bomber.

bombe [bɔ̃b] *nf* bomb; (*atomiseur*) (aerosol) spray; **faire la ~** (*fam*) to go on a binge.

bombé, e [bɔ̃be] *a* rounded; bulging; cambered.

bomber [bɔ̃be] *vi* to bulge; to camber // *vt*: **~ le torse** to swell out one's chest.

bon, bonne [bɔ̃, bɔn] *a* good; (*charitable*): **~ (envers)** good (to), kind (to); (*juste*): **le ~ numéro/moment** the right number/moment; (*approprié*): **à/pour ~** fit to/for // *nm* (*billet*) voucher; (*aussi*: **~ cadeau**) gift coupon *ou* voucher // *nf* (*domestique*) maid // *ad*: **il fait ~** it's *ou* the weather's fine; **sentir ~** to smell good; **tenir ~** to stand firm, hold out; **pour de ~** for good; **de bonne heure** early; **~ anniversaire!** happy birthday!; **~ voyage!** have a good journey!, enjoy your trip!; **bonne chance!** good luck!; **bonne année!** happy New Year!; **bonne nuit!** good night!; **~ enfant** *a inv* accommodating, easy-going; **~ d'essence** *nm* petrol coupon; **~ marché** *a inv, ad* cheap; **~ mot** *nm* witticism; **~ sens** *nm* common sense; **~ à tirer** *nm* pass for press; **~ du Trésor** *nm* Treasury bond; **~ vivant** *nm* jovial chap; **bonne d'enfant** *nf* nanny; **bonne femme** *nf* (*péj*) woman; female; **bonne à tout faire** *nf* general help; **bonnes œuvres** *nfpl* charitable works; charities.

bonasse [bɔnas] *a* soft, meek.

bonbon [bɔ̃bɔ̃] *nm* (boiled) sweet.

bonbonne [bɔ̃bɔn] *nf* demijohn; carboy.

bonbonnière [bɔ̃bɔnjɛʀ] *nf* sweet box, bonbonnière.

bond [bɔ̃] *nm* leap; **faire un ~** to leap in the air.

bonde [bɔ̃d] *nf* (*d'évier etc*) plug; (: *trou*) plughole; (*de tonneau*) bung; bunghole.

bondé, e [bɔ̃de] *a* packed (full).

bondir [bɔ̃diʀ] *vi* to leap.

bonheur [bɔnœʀ] *nm* happiness; **porter ~ (à qn)** to bring (sb) luck; **au petit ~** haphazardly; **par ~** fortunately.

bonhomie [bɔnɔmi] *nf* goodnaturedness.

bonhomme [bɔnɔm] *nm* (*pl* **bonshommes** [bɔ̃zɔm]) fellow // *a* goodnatured; **aller son ~ de chemin** to carry on in one's own sweet way; **~ de neige** snowman.

boni [bɔni] *nm* profit.

bonification [bɔnifikasjɔ̃] *nf* bonus.

bonifier [bɔnifje] *vt* to improve.

boniment [bɔnimɑ̃] *nm* patter *q*.

bonjour [bɔ̃ʒuʀ] *excl, nm* good morning (*ou* afternoon); hello; **dire ~ à qn** to say hello *ou* good morning/afternoon to sb.

bonne [bɔn] *a, nf voir* **bon**; **~ment** *ad*: **tout ~ment** quite simply.

bonnet [bɔnɛ] *nm* bonnet, hat; (*de soutiengorge*) cup; **~ d'âne** dunce's cap; **~ de bain** bathing cap; **~ de nuit** nightcap.

bonneterie [bɔnɛtʀi] *nf* hosiery.

bon-papa [bɔ̃papa] *nm* grandpa, grandad.

bonsoir [bɔ̃swaʀ] *excl* good evening.

bonté [bɔ̃te] *nf* kindness *q*; **avoir la ~ de** to be kind *ou* good enough to.

borborygme [bɔʀbɔʀigm] *nm* rumbling noise.

bord [bɔʀ] *nm* (*de table, verre, falaise*) edge; (*de rivière, lac*) bank; (*de route*) side; (*monter*) **à ~** (to go) on board; **jeter par-dessus ~** to throw overboard; **le commandant/les hommes du ~** the ship's master/crew; **au ~ de la mer** at the seaside; **être au ~ des larmes** to be on the verge of tears.

bordage [bɔʀdaʒ] *nm* planking *q*, plating *q*.

bordeaux [bɔʀdo] *nm* Bordeaux (wine) // *a inv* maroon.

bordée [bɔʀde] *nf* broadside; **une ~ d'injures** a volley of abuse.

bordel [bɔʀdɛl] *nm* brothel.

border [bɔʀde] *vt* (*être le long de*) to border; to line; (*garnir*): **~ qch de** to line sth with; to trim sth with; (*qn dans son lit*) to tuck up.

bordereau, x [bɔʀdəʀo] *nm* docket; slip; statement, invoice.

bordure [bɔʀdyʀ] *nf* border; (*sur un vêtement*) trim(ming), border; **en ~ de** on the edge of.

borgne [bɔʀɲ(ə)] *a* one-eyed; **hôtel ~** shady hotel.

borne [bɔʀn(ə)] *nf* boundary stone; (*gén*: **~ kilométrique**) kilometre-marker, ≈ milestone; **~s** *nfpl* (*fig*) limits; **dépasser les ~s** to go too far; **sans ~(s)** boundless.

borné, e [bɔʀne] *a* narrow; narrowminded.

borner [bɔʀne] *vt* to limit; to confine; **se ~ à faire** to content o.s. with doing; to limit o.s. to doing.

bosquet [bɔskɛ] *nm* copse, grove.

bosse [bɔs] *nf* (*de terrain etc*) bump; (*enflure*) lump; (*du bossu, du chameau*) hump; **avoir la ~ des maths** *etc* to have a gift for maths *etc*; **il a roulé sa ~** he's been around.

bosseler [bɔsle] *vt* (*ouvrer*) to emboss; (*abîmer*) to dent.

bosser [bɔse] *vi* (*fam*) to work; to slog (hard).

bossu, e [bɔsy] *nm/f* hunchback.

bot [bo] *am*: **pied ~** club foot.

botanique [bɔtanik] *nf*: **la ~** botany // *a* botanic(al).

botaniste [bɔtanist(ə)] *nm/f* botanist.

botte [bɔt] *nf* (*soulier*) (high) boot; (*ESCRIME*) thrust; (*gerbe*): **~ de paille** bundle of straw; **~ de radis/d'asperges** bunch of radishes/asparagus; **~s de caoutchouc** wellington boots.

botter [bɔte] *vt* to put boots on; to kick; (*fam*): **ça me botte** I fancy that.

bottier [bɔtje] *nm* bootmaker.

bottin [bɔtɛ̃] *nm* directory.

bottine [bɔtin] *nf* ankle boot, bootee.

bouc [buk] *nm* goat ; (*barbe*) goatee ; ~ **émissaire** scapegoat.

boucan [bukɑ̃] *nm* din, racket.

bouche [buʃ] *nf* mouth ; **faire le** ~ **à** ~ **à qn** to give sb the kiss of life, to practise mouth-to-mouth resuscitation on sb ; ~ **de chaleur** hot air vent ; ~ **d'égout** manhole ; ~ **d'incendie** fire hydrant ; ~ **de métro** métro entrance.

bouché, e [buʃe] *a* (*temps, ciel*) overcast ; (*péj: personne*) thick ; (*JAZZ: trompette*) muted ; **avoir le nez** ~ to have a blocked (-up) nose.

bouchée [buʃe] *nf* mouthful ; ~**s à la reine** chicken vol-au-vents.

boucher [buʃe] *nm* butcher // *vt* (*pour colmater*) to stop up ; to fill up ; (*obstruer*) to block (up) ; **se** ~ **le nez** to hold one's nose ; **se** ~ (*tuyau etc*) to block up, get blocked up.

bouchère [buʃɛʀ] *nf* (*woman*) butcher ; butcher's wife.

boucherie [buʃʀi] *nf* butcher's (shop) ; butchery ; (*fig*) slaughter.

bouche-trou [buʃtʀu] *nm* (*fig*) stop-gap.

bouchon [buʃɔ̃] *nm* (*en liège*) cork ; (*autre matière*) stopper ; (*fig: embouteillage*) holdup ; (*PÊCHE*) float ; ~ **doseur** measuring cap.

bouchonner [buʃɔne] *vt* to rub down.

boucle [bukl(ə)] *nf* (*forme, figure*) loop ; (*objet*) buckle ; ~ (**de cheveux**) curl ; ~ **d'oreilles** earring.

bouclé, e [bukle] *a* (*cheveux*) curly ; (*tapis*) uncut.

boucler [bukle] *vt* (*fermer: ceinture etc*) to fasten up ; (: *magasin*) to shut ; (*terminer*) to finish off ; to complete ; (: *budget*) to balance ; (*enfermer*) to shut away ; to lock up ; (: *quartier*) to seal off // *vi* to curl.

bouclier [buklije] *nm* shield.

bouddhiste [budist(ə)] *nm/f* Buddhist.

bouder [bude] *vi* to sulk // *vt* to turn one's nose up at ; to refuse to have anything to do with ; **bouderie** *nf* sulking *q* ; **boudeur, euse** *a* sullen, sulky.

boudin [budɛ̃] *nm* (*CULIN*) black pudding ; (*TECH*) roll.

boudoir [budwaʀ] *nm* boudoir.

boue [bu] *nf* mud.

bouée [bwe] *nf* buoy ; ~ (**de sauvetage**) lifebuoy.

boueux, euse [bwø, -øz] *a* muddy // *nm* refuse collector.

bouffe [buf] *nf* (*fam*) grub, food.

bouffée [bufe] *nf* puff ; ~ **de fièvre/de honte** flush of fever/shame ; ~ **d'orgueil** fit of pride.

bouffer [bufe] *vi* (*fam*) to eat ; (*COUTURE*) to puff out // *vt* (*fam*) to eat.

bouffi, e [bufi] *a* swollen.

bouffon, ne [bufɔ̃, -ɔn] *a* farcical, comical // *nm* jester.

bouge [buʒ] *nm* (*low*) dive ; hovel.

bougeoir [buʒwaʀ] *nm* candlestick.

bougeotte [buʒɔt] *nf:* **avoir la** ~ to have the fidgets.

bouger [buʒe] *vi* to move ; (*dent etc*) to

be loose ; (*changer*) to alter ; (*agir*) to stir // *vt* to move.

bougie [buʒi] *nf* candle ; (*AUTO*) sparking plug.

bougon, ne [bugɔ̃, -ɔn] *a* grumpy.

bougonner [bugɔne] *vi, vt* to grumble.

bougre [bugʀ(ə)] *nm* chap ; (*fam*): **ce** ~ **de** that confounded.

bouillabaisse [bujabɛs] *nf* bouillabaisse.

bouillant, e [bujɑ̃, -ɑ̃t] *a* (*qui bout*) boiling ; (*très chaud*) boiling (hot) ; (*fig: ardent*) hot-headed.

bouilleur de cru [bujœʀdəkʀy] *nm* (*home*) distiller.

bouillie [buji] *nf* gruel ; (*de bébé*) cereal ; **en** ~ (*fig*) crushed.

bouillir [bujiʀ] *vi, vt* to boil ; ~ **de colère** *etc* to seethe with anger *etc*.

bouilloire [bujwaʀ] *nf* kettle.

bouillon [bujɔ̃] *nm* (*CULIN*) stock *q* ; (*bulles, écume*) bubble ; ~ **de culture** culture medium.

bouillonner [bujɔne] *vi* to bubble ; (*fig*) to bubble up ; to foam.

bouillotte [bujɔt] *nf* hot-water bottle.

boulanger, ère [bulɑ̃ʒe, -ɛʀ] *nm/f* baker // *nf* (*woman*) baker ; baker's wife.

boulangerie [bulɑ̃ʒʀi] *nf* bakery, baker's (shop) ; (*commerce*) bakery ; ~ **industrielle** bakery ; ~**-pâtisserie** *nf* baker's and confectioner's (shop).

boule [bul] *nf* (*gén*) ball ; (*pour jouer*) bowl ; ~ **de neige** snowball ; **faire** ~ **de neige** to snowball.

bouleau, x [bulo] *nm* (silver) birch.

bouledogue [buldɔg] *nm* bulldog.

boulet [bulɛ] *nm* (*aussi* : ~ **de canon**) cannonball ; (*de bagnard*) ball and chain ; (*charbon*) (coal) nut.

boulette [bulɛt] *nf* ball.

boulevard [bulvaʀ] *nm* boulevard.

bouleversement [bulvɛʀsəmɑ̃] *nm* (*politique, social*) upheaval.

bouleverser [bulvɛʀse] *vt* (*émouvoir*) to overwhelm ; (*causer du chagrin*) to distress ; (*pays, vie*) to disrupt ; (*papiers, objets*) to turn upside down, upset.

boulier [bulje] *nm* abacus ; (*de jeu*) scoring board.

boulimie [bulimi] *nf* compulsive eating, bulimia.

boulon [bulɔ̃] *nm* bolt ; **boulonner** *vt* to bolt.

boulot [bulo] *nm* (*fam: travail*) work.

boulot, te [bulo, -ɔt] *a* plump, tubby.

bouquet [bukɛ] *nm* (*de fleurs*) bunch (of flowers), bouquet ; (*de persil etc*) bunch ; (*parfum*) bouquet ; (*fig*) crowning piece.

bouquetin [buktɛ̃] *nm* ibex.

bouquin [bukɛ̃] *nm* book ; **bouquiner** *vi* to read ; to browse around (in a bookshop) ; **bouquiniste** *nm/f* bookseller.

bourbeux, euse [buʀbø, -øz] *a* muddy.

bourbier [buʀbje] *nm* (quag)mire.

bourde [buʀd(ə)] *nf* (*erreur*) howler ; (*gaffe*) blunder.

bourdon [buʀdɔ̃] *nm* bumblebee.

bourdonnement [buʀdɔnmɑ̃] *nm* buzzing.

bourdonner [buʀdɔne] vi to buzz.
bourg [buʀ] nm town.
bourgade [buʀgad] nf township.
bourgeois, e [buʀʒwa, -waz] a (souvent péj) ≈ (upper) middle class ; bourgeois // nm/f (autrefois) burgher.
bourgeoisie [buʀʒwazi] nf ≈ upper middle classes pl ; bourgeoisie ; **petite ~** middle classes.
bourgeon [buʀʒɔ̃] nm bud ; **bourgeonner** vi to bud.
Bourgogne [buʀgɔɲ] nf: **la ~** Burgundy // nm: **b~** burgundy (wine).
bourguignon, ne [buʀgiɲɔ̃, -ɔn] a of ou from Burgundy, Burgundian ; **bœuf ~** bœuf bourguignon.
bourlinguer [buʀlɛ̃ge] vi to knock about a lot, get around a lot.
bourrade [buʀad] nf shove, thump.
bourrage [buʀaʒ] nm: **~ de crâne** brain-washing ; (SCOL) cramming.
bourrasque [buʀask(ə)] nf squall.
bourratif, ive [buʀatif, -iv] a filling, stodgy.
bourreau, x [buʀo] nm executioner ; (fig) torturer ; **~ de travail** glutton for work.
bourreler [buʀle] vt: **être bourrelé de remords** to be racked by remorse.
bourrelet [buʀlɛ] nm draught excluder ; (de peau) fold ou roll (of flesh).
bourrer [buʀe] vt (pipe) to fill ; (poêle) to pack ; (valise) to cram (full) ; ~ **de** to cram (full) with ; to stuff with ; **~ de coups** to hammer blows on, pummel.
bourrique [buʀik] nf (âne) ass.
bourru, e [buʀy] a surly, gruff.
bourse [buʀs(ə)] nf (subvention) grant ; (porte-monnaie) purse ; **la B~** the Stock Exchange ; **boursier, ière** a (COMM) Stock Market cpd // nm/f (SCOL) grant-holder.
boursouflé, e [buʀsufle] a swollen, puffy ; (fig) bombastic, turgid.
boursoufler [buʀsufle] vt to puff up, bloat ; **se ~** vi (visage) to swell ou puff up ; (peinture) to blister.
bous vb voir **bouillir**.
bousculade [buskylad] nf rush ; crush.
bousculer [buskyle] vt to knock over ; to knock into ; (fig) to push, rush.
bouse [buz] nf: **~ (de vache)** (cow) dung q.
bousiller [buzije] vt (fam) to wreck.
boussole [busɔl] nf compass.
bout [bu] vb voir **bouillir** // nm bit ; (extrémité: d'un bâton etc) tip ; (: d'une ficelle, table, rue, période) end ; **au ~ de** (après) at the end of, after ; **pousser qn à ~** to push sb to the limit (of his patience) ; **venir à ~ de** to manage to overcome ou finish sth ; **à ~ portant** at point-blank range ; **~ filtre** filter tip.
boutade [butad] nf quip, sally.
boute-en-train [butɑ̃tʀɛ̃] nm inv live wire.
bouteille [butɛj] nf bottle ; (de gaz butane) cylinder.
boutique [butik] nf shop ; **boutiquier, ière** nm/f shopkeeper.
bouton [butɔ̃] nm (BOT) bud ; (MÉD) spot ; (électrique etc) button ; (de porte) knob ; **~ de manchette** cuff-link ; **~ d'or** butter-

cup ; **boutonner** vt to button up, do up ; **boutonneux, euse** a spotty ; **boutonnière** nf buttonhole ; **~-pression** nm press stud, snap fastener.
bouture [butyʀ] nf cutting.
bouvreuil [buvʀœj] nm bullfinch.
bovidé [bɔvide] nm bovine.
bovin, e [bɔvɛ̃, -in] a bovine ; **~s** nmpl cattle.
bowling [bɔliŋ] nm (tenpin) bowling ; (salle) bowling alley.
box [bɔks] nm lock-up (garage) ; cubicle ; (d'écurie) loose-box ; **le ~ des accusés** the dock.
boxe [bɔks(ə)] nf boxing ; **boxer** vi to box ; **boxeur** nm boxer.
boyau, x [bwajo] nm (corde de raquette etc) (cat) gut ; (galerie) passage(way) ; (narrow) gallery ; (pneu de bicyclette) tubeless tyre // nmpl (viscères) entrails, guts.
boycotter [bɔjkɔte] vt to boycott.
B.P. sigle de **boîte postale.**
bracelet [bʀaslɛ] nm bracelet ; **~-montre** nm wristwatch.
braconner [bʀakɔne] vi to poach ; **braconnier** nm poacher.
brader [bʀade] vt to sell off, sell cheaply.
braguette [bʀagɛt] nf fly, flies pl.
brailler [bʀaje] vi to bawl, yell // vt to bawl out, yell out.
braire [bʀɛʀ] vi to bray.
braise [bʀɛz] nf embers pl.
braiser [bʀeze] vt to braise.
bramer [bʀame] vi to bell ; (fig) to wail.
brancard [bʀɑ̃kaʀ] nm (civière) stretcher ; (bras, perche) shaft ; **brancardier** nm stretcher-bearer.
branchages [bʀɑ̃ʃaʒ] nmpl branches, boughs.
branche [bʀɑ̃ʃ] nf branch ; (de lunettes) side-piece.
brancher [bʀɑ̃ʃe] vt to connect (up) ; (en mettant la prise) to plug in.
branchies [bʀɑ̃ʃi] nfpl gills.
brandir [bʀɑ̃diʀ] vt to brandish, wield.
brandon [bʀɑ̃dɔ̃] nm firebrand.
branle [bʀɑ̃l] nm: **donner le ~ à** to set in motion.
branle-bas [bʀɑ̃lba] nm inv commotion.
branler [bʀɑ̃le] vi to be shaky, be loose // vt: **la tête** to shake one's head.
braquage [bʀakaʒ] nm (fam) stick-up ; (AUTO): **rayon de ~** turning circle.
braquer [bʀake] vi (AUTO) to turn (the wheel) // vt (revolver etc): **~ qch sur** to aim sth at, point sth at ; (mettre en colère): **~ qn** to antagonize sb, put sb's back up.
bras [bʀa] nm arm // nmpl (fig: travailleurs) labour sg, hands ; **saisir qn à ~-le-corps** to take hold of sb (a)round the waist ; **à ~ raccourcis** with fists flying ; **~ droit** (fig) right-hand man ; **~ de levier** lever arm ; **~ de mer** arm of the sea, sound.
brasero [bʀazeʀo] nm brazier.
brasier [bʀazje] nm blaze, (blazing) inferno.
brassage [bʀasaʒ] nm mixing.
brassard [bʀasaʀ] nm armband.
brasse [bʀas] nf (nage) breast-stroke ;

(*mesure*) fathom ; ~ **papillon** butterfly (-stroke).

brassée [bʀase] *nf* armful.

brasser [bʀase] *vt* to mix ; ~ **l'argent/les affaires** to handle a lot of money/business.

brasserie [bʀasʀi] *nf* (*restaurant*) brasserie ; (*usine*) brewery.

brasseur [bʀasœʀ] *nm* (*de bière*) brewer ; ~ **d'affaires** big businessman.

brassière [bʀasjɛʀ] *nf* (baby's) vest.

bravache [bʀavaʃ] *nm* blusterer, braggart.

bravade [bʀavad] *nf*: **par** ~ out of bravado.

brave [bʀav] *a* (*courageux*) brave ; (*bon, gentil*) good, kind.

braver [bʀave] *vt* to defy.

bravo [bʀavo] *excl* bravo // *nm* cheer.

bravoure [bʀavuʀ] *nf* bravery.

break [bʀɛk] *nm* (AUTO) estate car.

brebis [bʀəbi] *nf* ewe ; ~ **galeuse** black sheep.

brèche [bʀɛʃ] *nf* breach, gap ; **être sur la** ~ (*fig*) to be on the go.

bredouille [bʀəduj] *a* empty-handed.

bredouiller [bʀəduje] *vi, vt* to mumble, stammer.

bref, brève [bʀɛf, bʀɛv] *a* short, brief // *ad* in short // *nf*: **(voyelle) brève** short vowel ; **d'un ton** ~ sharply, curtly ; **en** ~ in short, in brief.

brelan [bʀəlɑ̃] *nm* three of a kind ; ~ **d'as** three aces.

brème [bʀɛm] *nf* bream.

Brésil [bʀezil] *nm* Brazil ; **b~ien, ne** *a, nm/f* Brazilian.

Bretagne [bʀətaɲ] *nf* Brittany.

bretelle [bʀətɛl] *nf* (*de fusil etc*) sling ; (*de combinaison, soutien-gorge*) strap ; (*autoroute*) slip road ; **~s** *nfpl* (*pour pantalon*) braces.

breton, ne [bʀətɔ̃, -ɔn] *a, nm/f* Breton.

breuvage [bʀœvaʒ] *nm* beverage, drink.

brève [bʀɛv] *a, nf voir* **bref**.

brevet [bʀəvɛ] *nm* diploma, certificate ; ~ **(d'invention)** patent ; ~ **d'apprentissage** certificate of apprenticeship ; ~ **d'études du premier cycle (B.E.P.C.)** ≈ O levels ; **breveté, e** *a* patented ; (*diplômé*) qualified ; **breveter** *vt* to patent.

bréviaire [bʀevjɛʀ] *nm* breviary.

bribes [bʀib] *nfpl* bits, scraps ; snatches ; **par** ~ piecemeal.

bric-à-brac [bʀikabʀak] *nm inv* bric-a-brac, jumble.

bricolage [bʀikɔlaʒ] *nm*: **le** ~ do-it-yourself (jobs).

bricole [bʀikɔl] *nf* trifle ; small job.

bricoler [bʀikɔle] *vi* to do D.I.Y. jobs ; to potter about ; to do odd jobs // *vt* to fix up ; to tinker with ; **bricoleur, euse** *nm/f* handyman, D.I.Y. enthusiast.

bride [bʀid] *nf* bridle ; (*d'un bonnet*) string, tie ; **à** ~ **abattue** flat out, hell for leather ; **tenir en** ~ to keep in check ; **lâcher la** ~ **à, laisser la** ~ **sur le cou à** to give free rein to.

bridé, e [bʀide] *a*: **yeux** ~**s** slit eyes.

brider [bʀide] *vt* (*réprimer*) to keep in check ; (*cheval*) to bridle ; (CULIN: *volaille*) to truss.

bridge [bʀidʒ(ə)] *nm* bridge.

brièvement [bʀijɛvmɑ̃] *ad* briefly.

brièveté [bʀijɛvte] *nf* brevity.

brigade [bʀigad] *nf* (POLICE) squad ; (MIL) brigade ; (*gén*) team.

brigand [bʀigɑ̃] *nm* brigand.

brigandage [bʀigɑ̃daʒ] *nm* robbery.

briguer [bʀige] *vt* to aspire to.

brillamment [bʀijamɑ̃] *ad* brilliantly.

brillant, e [bʀijɑ̃, -ɑ̃t] *a* brilliant ; bright ; (*luisant*) shiny, shining // *nm* (*diamant*) brilliant.

briller [bʀije] *vi* to shine.

brimade [bʀimad] *nf* vexation, harassment *q* ; bullying *q*.

brimbaler [bʀɛ̃bale] *vb* = **bringuebaler.**

brimer [bʀime] *vt* to harass ; to bully.

brin [bʀɛ̃] *nm* (*de laine, ficelle etc*) strand ; (*fig*): **un** ~ **de** a bit of ; ~ **d'herbe** blade of grass ; ~ **de muguet** sprig of lily of the valley ; ~ **de paille** wisp of straw.

brindille [bʀɛ̃dij] *nf* twig.

bringuebaler [bʀɛ̃gbale] *vi* to shake (about) // *vt* to cart about.

brio [bʀijo] *nm* brilliance ; (MUS) brio ; **avec** ~ brilliantly, with panache.

brioche [bʀijɔʃ] *nf* brioche (bun) ; (*fam: ventre*) paunch.

brique [bʀik] *nf* brick // *a inv* brick red.

briquer [bʀike] *vt* to polish up.

briquet [bʀikɛ] *nm* (*cigarette*) lighter.

brisant [bʀizɑ̃] *nm* reef ; (*vague*) breaker.

brise [bʀiz] *nf* breeze.

brise-glace [bʀizglas] *nm inv* icebreaker.

brise-jet [bʀizʒɛt] *nm inv* tap swirl.

brise-lames [bʀizlam] *nm inv* breakwater.

briser [bʀize] *vt* to break ; **se** ~ *vi* to break ; **briseur, euse de grève** *nm/f* strike-breaker.

britannique [bʀitanik] *a* British // *nm/f* British person ; **les B~s** the British.

broc [bʀo] *nm* pitcher.

brocanteur, euse [bʀɔkɑ̃tœʀ, -øz] *nm/f* junkshop owner ; junk dealer.

broche [bʀɔʃ] *nf* brooch ; (CULIN) spit ; (*fiche*) spike, peg ; **à la** ~ spit-roast, roasted on a spit.

broché, e [bʀɔʃe] *a* (*livre*) paper-backed.

brochet [bʀɔʃɛ] *nm* pike *inv*.

brochette [bʀɔʃɛt] *nf* skewer ; ~ **de décorations** row of medals.

brochure [bʀɔʃyʀ] *nf* pamphlet, brochure, booklet.

broder [bʀɔde] *vt* to embroider // *vi* to embroider the facts ; **broderie** *nf* embroidery.

bromure [bʀɔmyʀ] *nm* bromide.

broncher [bʀɔ̃ʃe] *vi*: **sans** ~ without flinching ; without turning a hair.

bronches [bʀɔ̃ʃ] *nfpl* bronchial tubes ; **bronchite** *nf* bronchitis ; **broncho-pneumonie** [bʀɔ̃kɔ-] *nf* broncho-pneumonia *q*.

bronze [bʀɔ̃z] *nm* bronze.

bronzé, e [bʀɔ̃ze] *a* tanned.

bronzer [bʀɔ̃ze] *vt* to tan // *vi* to get a tan ; **se** ~ to sunbathe.

brosse [bʀɔs] *nf* brush ; **donner un coup de** ~ **à qch** to give sth a brush ; **coiffé**

en ~ with a crewcut ; ~ **à cheveux** hairbrush ; ~ **à dents** toothbrush ; ~ **à habits** clothesbrush ; **brosser** vt (nettoyer) to brush ; (fig: tableau etc) to paint ; to draw.

brouette [bʀuɛt] nf wheelbarrow.

brouhaha [bʀuaa] nm hubbub.

brouillard [bʀujaʀ] nm fog.

brouille [bʀuj] nf quarrel.

brouiller [bʀuje] vt to mix up ; to confuse ; (RADIO) to cause interference to ; to jam ; (rendre trouble) to cloud ; (désunir: amis) to set at odds ; **se** ~ vi (ciel, vue) to cloud over ; (détails) to become confused ; **se** ~ **(avec)** to fall out (with).

brouillon, ne [bʀujɔ̃, -ɔn] a disorganised ; unmethodical // nm draft.

broussailles [bʀusaj] nfpl undergrowth sg ; **broussailleux, euse** a bushy.

brousse [bʀus] nf: **la** ~ the bush.

brouter [bʀute] vt to graze on // vi to graze ; (AUTO) to judder.

broutille [bʀutij] nf trifle.

broyer [bʀwaje] vt to crush ; ~ **du noir** to be down in the dumps.

bru [bʀy] nf daughter-in-law.

brucelles [bʀysɛl] nfpl: **(pinces)** ~ tweezers.

bruine [bʀɥin] nf drizzle.

bruiner [bʀɥine] vb impersonnel: **il bruine** it's drizzling, there's a drizzle.

bruire [bʀɥiʀ] vi to murmur ; to rustle.

bruit [bʀɥi] nm: **un** ~ a noise, a sound ; (fig: rumeur) a rumour ; **le** ~ noise ; **pas/trop de** ~ no/too much noise ; **sans** ~ without a sound, noiselessly ; ~ **de fond** background noise.

bruitage [bʀɥitaʒ] nm sound effects pl ; **bruiteur, euse** nf sound-effects engineer.

brûlant, e [bʀylɑ̃, -ɑ̃t] a burning (hot) ; (liquide) boiling (hot) ; (regard) fiery ; (sujet) red-hot.

brûlé, e [bʀyle] a (fig: démasqué) blown // nm: **odeur de** ~ smell of burning.

brûle-pourpoint [bʀylpuʀpwɛ̃]: **à** ~ ad point-blank.

brûler [bʀyle] vt to burn ; (suj: eau bouillante) to scald ; (consommer: électricité, essence) to use ; (feu rouge, signal) to go through (without stopping) // vi to burn ; (jeu) to be warm ; **se** ~ to burn o.s. ; to scald o.s. ; **se** ~ **la cervelle** to blow one's brains out ; ~ **(d'impatience) de faire qch** to burn with impatience ou be dying to do sth.

brûleur [bʀylœʀ] nm burner.

brûlure [bʀylyʀ] nf (lésion) burn ; (sensation) burning (sensation) ; ~**s d'estomac** heartburn sg.

brume [bʀym] nf mist ; **brumeux, euse** a misty ; (fig) hazy.

brun, e [bʀœ̃, -yn] a brown ; (cheveux, personne) dark // nm (couleur) brown ; **brunir** vi to get a tan // vt to tan.

brusque [bʀysk(ə)] a (soudain) abrupt, sudden ; (rude) abrupt, brusque ; ~**ment** ad (soudainement) abruptly ; suddenly ; **brusquer** vt to rush ; **brusquerie** nf abruptness, brusqueness.

brut, e [bʀyt] a raw, crude, rough ; (COMM) gross // nf brute ; **(champagne)** ~ brut

champagne ; **(pétrole)** ~ crude (oil).

brutal, e, aux [bʀytal, -o] a brutal ; ~**iser** vt to handle roughly, manhandle ; ~**ité** nf brutality q.

brute [bʀyt] a, nf voir **brut**.

Bruxelles [bʀysɛl] n Brussels.

bruyamment [bʀɥijamɑ̃] ad noisily.

bruyant, e [bʀɥijɑ̃, -ɑ̃t] a noisy.

bruyère [bʀɥijɛʀ] nf heather.

bu, e pp de **boire**.

buanderie [bɥɑ̃dʀi] nf laundry.

buccal, e, aux [bykal, -o] a: **par voie** ~**e** orally.

bûche [byʃ] nf log ; **prendre une** ~ (fig) to come a cropper ; ~ **de Noël** Yule log.

bûcher [byʃe] nm pyre ; bonfire // vb (fam) vi to swot, slog away // vt to swot up.

bûcheron [byʃʀɔ̃] nm woodcutter.

bucolique [bykɔlik] a bucolic, pastoral.

budget [bydʒɛ] nm budget ; **budgétaire** [bydʒetɛʀ] a budgetary, budget cpd.

buée [bɥe] nf (sur une vitre) mist ; (de l'haleine) steam.

buffet [byfɛ] nm (meuble) sideboard ; (de réception) buffet ; ~ **(de gare)** station buffet.

buffle [byfl(ə)] nm buffalo.

buis [bɥi] nm box tree ; (bois) box(wood).

buisson [bɥisɔ̃] nm bush.

buissonnière [bɥisɔnjɛʀ] af: **faire l'école** ~ to play truant.

bulbe [bylb(ə)] nm (BOT, ANAT) bulb ; (coupole) onion-shaped dome.

bulgare [bylgaʀ] a, nm/f Bulgarian.

Bulgarie [bylgaʀi] nf Bulgaria.

bulldozer [buldozɛʀ] nm bulldozer.

bulle [byl] nf bubble ; (papale) bull ; ~ **de savon** soap bubble.

bulletin [byltɛ̃] nm (communiqué, journal) bulletin ; (papier) form ; ticket ; (SCOL) report ; ~ **d'informations** news bulletin ; ~ **météorologique** weather report ; ~ **de santé** medical bulletin ; ~ **(de vote)** ballot paper.

buraliste [byʀalist(ə)] nm/f tobacconist ; clerk.

bure [byʀ] nf homespun ; frock.

bureau, x [byʀo] nm (meuble) desk ; (pièce, service) office ; ~ **de change** (foreign) exchange office ou bureau ; ~ **de location** box office ; ~ **de poste** post office ; ~ **de tabac** tobacconist's (shop) ; ~ **de vote** polling station ; **~crate** nm bureaucrat ; **~cratie** [-kʀasi] nf bureaucracy ; **~cratique** a bureaucratic.

burette [byʀɛt] nf (de mécanicien) oilcan ; (de chimiste) burette.

burin [byʀɛ̃] nm cold chisel ; (ART) burin.

buriné, e [byʀine] a (fig: visage) craggy, seamed.

burlesque [byʀlɛsk(ə)] a ridiculous ; (LITTÉRATURE) burlesque.

burnous [byʀnu(s)] nm burnous.

bus vb [by] voir **boire** // nm [bys] bus.

buse [byz] nf buzzard.

busqué, e [byske] a: **nez** ~ hook(ed) nose.

buste [byst(ə)] nm (ANAT) chest ; bust ; (sculpture) bust.

but [by] vb voir **boire** // nm [parfois byt] (cible) target ; (fig) goal ; aim ; (FOOTBALL etc) goal ; **de ~ en blanc** point-blank ; **avoir pour ~ de faire** to aim to do ; **dans le ~ de** with the intention of.

butane [bytan] nm butane ; calor gas.

buté, e [byte] a stubborn, obstinate // nf (TECH) stop ; (ARCHIT) abutment.

buter [byte] vi : **~ contre/sur** to bump into ; to stumble against // vt to antagonize ; **se ~** vi to get obstinate ; to dig in one's heels.

buteur [bytœR] nm striker.

butin [bytɛ̃] nm booty, spoils pl ; (d'un vol) loot.

butiner [bytine] vi to gather nectar.

butor [bytɔR] nm (fig) lout.

butte [byt] nf mound, hillock ; **être en ~ à** to be exposed to.

buvais etc vb voir **boire**.

buvard [byvaR] nm blotter.

buvette [byvɛt] nf refreshment room ; refreshment stall.

buveur, euse [byvœR, -øz] nm/f drinker.

byzantin, e [bizɑ̃tɛ̃, -in] a Byzantine.

C

c' [s] dét voir **ce**.

ça [sa] pronom (pour désigner) this ; (: plus loin) that ; (comme sujet indéfini) it ; **~ m'étonne que** it surprises me that ; **~ va?** how are you? ; how are things? ; (d'accord?) OK?, all right? ; **c'est ~** that's right.

çà [sa] ad : **~ et là** here and there.

caban [kabɑ̃] nm reefer jacket, donkey jacket.

cabane [kaban] nf hut, cabin.

cabanon [kabanɔ̃] nm chalet ; (country) cottage.

cabaret [kabaRɛ] nm night club.

cabas [kabɑ] nm shopping bag.

cabestan [kabɛstɑ̃] nm capstan.

cabillaud [kabijo] nm cod inv.

cabine [kabin] nf (de bateau) cabin ; (de plage) (beach) hut ; (de piscine etc) cubicle ; (de camion, train) cab ; (d'avion) cockpit ; **~ (d'ascenseur)** lift cage ; **~ d'essayage** fitting room ; **~ spatiale** space capsule ; **~ (téléphonique)** call ou (tele)phone box, (tele)phone booth.

cabinet [kabinɛ] nm (petite pièce) closet ; (de médecin) surgery ; (de notaire etc) office ; (: clientèle) practice ; (POL) Cabinet ; (d'un ministre) advisers pl ; **~s** nmpl (w.-c.) toilet sg, loo sg ; **~ d'affaires** business consultants' (bureau), business partnership ; **~ de toilette** toilet ; **~ de travail** study.

câble [kɑbl(ə)] nm cable.

câbler [kɑble] vt to cable.

cabosser [kabɔse] vt to dent.

cabotage [kabɔtaʒ] nm coastal navigation ; **caboteur** nm coaster.

cabotinage [kabɔtinaʒ] nm playacting ; third-rate acting, ham acting.

cabrer [kabRe] : **se ~** vi (cheval) to rear up ; (avion) to nose up ; (fig) to revolt, rebel ; to jib.

cabri [kabRi] nm kid.

cabriole [kabRijɔl] nf caper ; somersault.

cabriolet [kabRijɔlɛ] nm convertible.

cacahuète [kakaɥɛt] nf peanut.

cacao [kakao] nm cocoa (powder) ; (boisson) cocoa.

cachalot [kaʃalo] nm sperm whale.

cache [kaʃ] nm mask, card (for masking) // nf hiding place.

cache-cache [kaʃkaʃ] nm : **jouer à ~** to play hide-and-seek.

cachemire [kaʃmiR] nm cashmere // a : **dessin ~** paisley pattern.

cache-nez [kaʃne] nm inv scarf, muffler.

cache-pot [kaʃpo] nm inv flower-pot holder.

cacher [kaʃe] vt to hide, conceal ; **~ qch à qn** to hide ou conceal sth from sb ; **se ~** to hide ; to be hidden ou concealed ; **il ne s'en cache pas** he makes no secret of it.

cachet [kaʃɛ] nm (comprimé) tablet ; (sceau : du roi) seal ; (: de la poste) postmark ; (rétribution) fee ; (fig) style, character ; **cacheter** vt to seal.

cachette [kaʃɛt] nf hiding place ; **en ~** on the sly, secretly.

cachot [kaʃo] nm dungeon.

cachotterie [kaʃɔtRi] nf mystery ; **faire des ~s** to be secretive.

cactus [kaktys] nm cactus.

cadastre [kadastR(ə)] nm cadastre, land register.

cadavérique [kadaveRik] a deathly (pale), deadly pale.

cadavre [kadavR(ə)] nm corpse, (dead) body.

cadeau, x [kado] nm present, gift ; **faire un ~ à qn** to give sb a present ou gift ; **faire ~ de qch à qn** to make a present of sth to sb, give sb sth as a present.

cadenas [kadnɑ] nm padlock ; **cadenasser** vt to padlock.

cadence [kadɑ̃s] nf (MUS) cadence ; rhythm ; (de travail etc) rate ; **~s** nfpl (en usine) production rate sg ; **en ~** rhythmically ; in time ; **cadencé, e** a rhythmic(al).

cadet, te [kadɛ, -ɛt] a younger ; (le plus jeune) youngest // nm/f youngest child ou one, youngest boy ou son/girl ou daughter ; **il est mon ~ (de deux ans)** (rapports non familiaux) he's (2 years) younger than me, he's 2 years my junior ; **les ~s** (SPORT) the minors (15 - 17 years).

cadran [kadRɑ̃] nm dial ; **~ solaire** sundial.

cadre [kadR(ə)] nm frame ; (environnement) surroundings pl ; (limites) scope // nm/f (ADMIN) managerial employee, executive // a : **loi ~** outline ou blueprint law ; **~ moyen/supérieur** (ADMIN) middle/senior management employee, junior/senior executive ; **rayer qn des ~s** to discharge sb ; to dismiss sb ; **dans le ~ de** (fig) within the framework ou context of.

cadrer [kadRe] vi : **~ avec** to tally ou correspond with // vt (CINÉMA) to centre.

caduc, uque [kadyk] a obsolete ; (BOT) deciduous.

cafard [kafaʀ] nm cockroach; **avoir le ~** to be down in the dumps, be feeling low.
café [kafe] nm coffee; (bistro) café // inv coffee-coloured; **~ au lait** white coffee; **~ noir** black coffee; **~ tabac** tobacconist's or newsagent's also serving coffee and spirits; **~ine** nf caffeine; **cafetier, ière** nm/f café-owner // nf (pot) coffee-pot.
cafouiller [kafuje] vi to get in a shambles; to work in fits and starts.
cage [kaʒ] nf cage; **~ (des buts)** goal; **en ~** in a cage, caged up ou in; **~ d'ascenseur** lift shaft; **~ d'escalier** (stair)well; **~ thoracique** rib cage.
cageot [kaʒo] nm crate.
cagibi [kaʒibi] nm shed.
cagneux, euse [kaɲø, -øz] a knock-kneed.
cagnotte [kaɲɔt] nf kitty.
cagoule [kagul] nf cowl; hood; (ski etc) cagoule.
cahier [kaje] nm notebook; (TYPO) signature; **~ de revendications/doléances** list of claims/grievances; **~ de brouillons** roughbook, jotter; **~ des charges** schedule (of conditions); **~ d'exercices** exercise book.
cahin-caha [kaɛ̃kaa] ad: **aller ~** to jog along; (fig) to be so-so.
cahot [kao] nm jolt, bump; **cahoter** vi to bump along, jog along.
cahute [kayt] nf shack, hut.
caïd [kaid] nm big chief, boss.
caille [kaj] nf quail.
caillé, e [kaje] a: **lait ~** curdled milk, curds pl.
cailler [kaje] vi (lait) to curdle; (sang) to clot.
caillot [kajo] nm (blood) clot.
caillou, x [kaju] nm (little) stone; **~ter** vt (chemin) to metal; **~teux, euse** a stony; pebbly.
Caire [kɛʀ] nm: **le ~** Cairo.
caisse [kɛs] nf box; (où l'on met la recette) cashbox; till; (où l'on paye) cash desk; check-out; (de banque) cashier's desk; teller's desk; (TECH) case, casing; **~ enregistreuse** cash register; **~ d'épargne** savings bank; **~ de retraite** pension fund; **caissier, ière** nm/f cashier.
caisson [kɛsɔ̃] nm box, case.
cajoler [kaʒɔle] vt to wheedle, coax; to surround with love and care, make a fuss of.
cake [kɛk] nm fruit cake.
calaminé, e [kalamine] a (AUTO) coked up.
calamité [kalamite] nf calamity, disaster.
calandre [kalɑ̃dʀ(ə)] nf radiator grill; (machine) calender, mangle.
calanque [kalɑ̃k] nf rocky inlet.
calcaire [kalkɛʀ] nm limestone // a (eau) hard; (GÉO) limestone cpd.
calciné, e [kalsine] a burnt to ashes.
calcium [kalsjɔm] nm calcium.
calcul [kalkyl] nm calculation; **le ~** (SCOL) arithmetic; **~ différentiel/intégral** differential/integral calculus; **~ (biliaire)** (gall)stone; **~ (rénal)** (kidney) stone; **~ateur** nm, **~atrice** nf calculator.
calculer [kalkyle] vt to calculate, work out, reckon; (combiner) to calculate.

cale [kal] nf (de bateau) hold; (en bois) wedge, chock; **~ sèche** dry dock.
calé, e [kale] a (fam) clever, bright.
calebasse [kalbas] nf calabash, gourd.
caleçon [kalsɔ̃] nm pair of underpants, trunks pl; **~ de bain** bathing trunks pl.
calembour [kalɑ̃buʀ] nm pun.
calendes [kalɑ̃d] nfpl: **renvoyer aux ~ grecques** to postpone indefinitely.
calendrier [kalɑ̃dʀije] nm calendar; (fig) timetable.
cale-pied [kalpje] nm inv toe clip.
calepin [kalpɛ̃] nm notebook.
caler [kale] vt to wedge, chock up; **~ (son moteur/véhicule)** to stall (one's engine/vehicle).
calfater [kalfate] vt to caulk.
calfeutrer [kalføtʀe] vt to (make) draughtproof; **se ~** to make o.s. snug and comfortable.
calibre [kalibʀ(ə)] nm (d'un fruit) grade; (d'une arme) bore, calibre; (fig) calibre; **calibrer** vt to grade.
calice [kalis] nm (REL) chalice; (BOT) calyx.
califourchon [kalifuʀʃɔ̃]: **à ~** ad astride; **à ~ sur** astride, straddling.
câlin, e [kalɛ̃, -in] a cuddly, cuddlesome; tender.
câliner [kaline] vt to fondle, cuddle.
calleux, euse [kalø, -øz] a horny, callous.
calligraphie [kaligʀafi] nf calligraphy.
calmant [kalmɑ̃] nm tranquillizer, sedative; painkiller.
calme [kalm(ə)] a calm, quiet // nm calm(ness), quietness; **~ plat** (NAVIG) dead calm.
calmer [kalme] vt to calm (down); (douleur, inquiétude) to ease, soothe; **se ~** to calm down.
calomnie [kalɔmni] nf slander; (écrite) libel; **calomnier** vt to slander; to libel; **calomnieux, euse** a slanderous; libellous.
calorie [kalɔʀi] nf calorie.
calorifère [kalɔʀifɛʀ] nm stove.
calorifique [kalɔʀifik] a calorific.
calorifuge [kalɔʀifyʒ] a (heat-) insulating, heat-retaining.
calot [kalo] nm forage cap.
calotte [kalɔt] nf (coiffure) skullcap; (gifle) slap; **~ glaciaire** icecap.
calque [kalk(ə)] nm (dessin) tracing; (fig) carbon copy.
calquer [kalke] vt to trace; (fig) to copy exactly.
calvaire [kalvɛʀ] nm (croix) wayside cross, calvary; (souffrances) suffering, martyrdom.
calvitie [kalvisi] nf baldness.
camaïeu [kamajø] nm: **(motif en) ~** monochrome motif.
camarade [kamaʀad] nm/f friend, pal; (POL) comrade; **~rie** nf friendship.
cambouis [kɑ̃bwi] nm engine oil.
cambrer [kɑ̃bʀe] vt to arch; **se ~** to arch one's back; **pied très cambré** foot with high arches ou insteps.
cambriolage [kɑ̃bʀijolaʒ] nm burglary.
cambrioler [kɑ̃bʀijole] vt to burgle; **cambrioleur, euse** nm/f burglar.

cambrure [kɑ̃bʀyʀ] *nf* (*de la route*) camber.

cambuse [kɑ̃byz] *nf* storeroom.

came [kam] *nf*: **arbre à ~s** camshaft; **arbre à ~s en tête** overhead camshaft.

camée [kame] *nm* cameo.

caméléon [kamele5] *nm* chameleon.

camelot [kamlo] *nm* street pedlar.

camelote [kamlɔt] *nf* rubbish, trash, junk.

caméra [kameʀa] *nf* camera; (*d'amateur*) cine-camera.

camion [kamjɔ̃] *nm* lorry, truck; (*plus petit, fermé*) van; **~-citerne** *nm* tanker; **camionnage** *nm* haulage; **camionnette** *nf* (small) van; **camionneur** *nm* (*entrepreneur*) haulage contractor; (*chauffeur*) lorry *ou* truck driver; van driver.

camisole [kamizɔl] *nf*: **~ (de force)** strait jacket.

camomille [kamɔmij] *nf* camomile; (*boisson*) camomile tea.

camouflage [kamuflaʒ] *nm* camouflage.

camoufler [kamufle] *vt* to camouflage; (*fig*) to conceal, cover up.

camouflet [kamufle] *nm* snub.

camp [kɑ̃] *nm* camp; (*fig*) side; **~ de nudistes/vacances** nudist/holiday camp; **~ de concentration** concentration camp.

campagnard, e [kɑ̃paɲaʀ, -aʀd(ə)] *a* country *cpd* // *nm/f* countryman/woman.

campagne [kɑ̃paɲ] *nf* country, countryside; (*MIL, POL, COMM*) campaign; **à la ~** in the country; **faire ~ pour** to campaign for.

campement [kɑ̃pmɑ̃] *nm* camp, encampment.

camper [kɑ̃pe] *vi* to camp // *vt* to pull *ou* put on firmly; to sketch; **se ~ devant** to plant o.s. in front of; **campeur, euse** *nm/f* camper.

camphre [kɑ̃fʀ(ə)] *nm* camphor.

camping [kɑ̃piŋ] *nm* camping; (**terrain de) ~** campsite, camping site; **faire du ~** to go camping.

camus, e [kamy, -yz] *a*: **nez ~** pug nose.

Canada [kanada] *nm*: **le ~** Canada; **canadien, ne** *a, nm/f* Canadian // *nf* (*veste*) fur-lined jacket.

canaille [kanɑj] *nf* (*péj*) scoundrel // *a* raffish, rakish.

canal, aux [kanal, -o] *nm* canal; (*naturel*) channel; (*ADMIN*): **par le ~ de** through (the medium of), via.

canalisation [kanalizɑsjɔ̃] *nf* (*tuyau*) pipe.

canaliser [kanalize] *vt* to canalize; (*fig*) to channel.

canapé [kanape] *nm* settee, sofa; (*CULIN*) canapé, open sandwich.

canard [kanaʀ] *nm* duck.

canari [kanaʀi] *nm* canary.

cancans [kɑ̃kɑ̃] *nmpl* (malicious) gossip *sg*.

cancer [kɑ̃sɛʀ] *nm* cancer; (*signe*): **le C~** Cancer, the Crab; **être du C~** to be Cancer; **cancéreux, euse** *a* cancerous; suffering from cancer; **cancérigène** *a* carcinogenic.

cancre [kɑ̃kʀ(ə)] *nm* dunce.

cancrelat [kɑ̃kʀəla] *nm* cockroach.

candélabre [kɑ̃delabʀ(ə)] *nm* candelabrum; street lamp, lamppost.

candeur [kɑ̃dœʀ] *nf* ingenuousness, guilelessness.

candi [kɑ̃di] *a inv*: **sucre ~** (sugar-)candy.

candidat, e [kɑ̃dida, -at] *nm/f* candidate; (*à un poste*) applicant, candidate; **candidature** *nf* candidature; application; **poser sa candidature** to submit an application, apply.

candide [kɑ̃did] *a* ingenuous, guileless, naïve.

cane [kan] *nf* (female) duck.

caneton [kant5] *nm* duckling.

canette [kanɛt] *nf* (*de bière*) (flip-top) bottle; (*de machine à coudre*) spool.

canevas [kanva] *nm* (*COUTURE*) canvas (for tapestry work); (*fig*) framework, structure.

caniche [kaniʃ] *nm* poodle.

canicule [kanikyl] *nf* scorching heat; midsummer heat, dog days *pl*.

canif [kanif] *nm* penknife, pocket knife.

canin, e [kanɛ̃, -in] *a* canine // *nf* canine (tooth), eye tooth; **exposition ~e** dog show.

caniveau, x [kanivo] *nm* gutter.

canne [kan] *nf* (walking) stick; **~ à pêche** fishing rod; **~ à sucre** sugar cane.

canné, e [kane] *a* (*chaise*) cane *cpd*.

cannelle [kanɛl] *nf* cinnamon.

cannelure [kanlyʀ] *nf* flute, fluting *q*.

cannibale [kanibal] *nm/f* cannibal.

canoë [kanɔe] *nm* canoe; (*sport*) canoeing.

canon [kanɔ̃] *nm* (*arme*) gun; (*d'une arme: tube*) barrel; (*fig*) model; **canon à: droit ~** canon law; **~ rayé** rifled barrel.

cañon [kanɔ̃] *nm* canyon.

canoniser [kanɔnize] *vt* to canonize.

canonnade [kanɔnad] *nf* cannonade.

canonnier [kanɔnje] *nm* gunner.

canonnière [kanɔnjɛʀ] *nf* gunboat.

canot [kano] *nm* boat, ding(h)y; **~ pneumatique** rubber *ou* inflatable ding(h)y; **~ de sauvetage** lifeboat; **canoter** *vi* to go rowing.

canotier [kanɔtje] *nm* boater.

cantate [kɑ̃tat] *nf* cantata.

cantatrice [kɑ̃tatʀis] *nf* (*opera*) singer.

cantine [kɑ̃tin] *nf* canteen.

cantique [kɑ̃tik] *nm* hymn.

canton [kɑ̃tɔ̃] *nm* district regrouping *several communes*; (*en Suisse*) canton.

cantonade [kɑ̃tɔnad]: **à la ~** *ad* to everyone in general; from the rooftops.

cantonner [kɑ̃tɔne] *vt* (*MIL*) to billet; to station; **se ~ dans** to confine o.s. to.

cantonnier [kɑ̃tɔnje] *nm* roadmender, roadman.

canular [kanylaʀ] *nm* hoax.

caoutchouc [kautʃu] *nm* rubber; **~ mousse** foam rubber; **caoutchouté, e** *a* rubberized; **caoutchouteux, euse** *a* rubbery.

cap [kap] *nm* (*GÉO*) cape; headland; (*fig*) hurdle; watershed; (*NAVIG*): **changer de ~** to change course; **mettre le ~ sur** to head *ou* steer for.

C.A.P. sigle m = Certificat d'aptitude professionnelle (obtained after trade apprenticeship).

capable [kapabl(ə)] a able, capable ; ~ **de qch/faire** capable of sth/doing ; **livre** ~ **d'intéresser** book liable ou likely to be of interest.

capacité [kapasite] nf (compétence) ability ; (JUR, contenance) capacity ; ~ **(en droit)** basic legal qualification.

cape [kap] nf cape, cloak ; **rire sous** ~ to laugh up one's sleeve.

C.A.P.E.S. [kapɛs] sigle m = Certificat d'aptitude au professorat de l'enseignement du second degré.

capharnaüm [kafaʀnaɔm] nm shambles sg.

capillaire [kapilɛʀ] a (soins, lotion) hair cpd ; (vaisseau etc) capillary ; **capillarité** nf capillarity.

capilotade [kapilɔtad] : **en** ~ ad crushed to a pulp ; smashed to pieces.

capitaine [kapitɛn] nm captain ; ~ **des pompiers** fire chief, firemaster ; ~**rie** nf (du port) harbour master's (office).

capital, e, aux [kapital -o] a major ; of paramount importance ; fundamental ; (JUR) capital // nm capital ; (fig) stock ; asset // nf (ville) capital ; (lettre) capital (letter) ; // nmpl (fonds) capital sg, money sg ; ~ **(social)** authorized capital ; ~**iser** vt to amass, build up ; (COMM) to capitalize ; ~**isme** nm capitalism ; ~**iste** a, nm/f capitalist.

capiteux, euse [kapitø, -øz] a heady ; sensuous, alluring.

capitonner [kapitɔne] vt to pad.

capitulation [kapitylɑsjɔ̃] nf capitulation.

capituler [kapityle] vi to capitulate.

caporal, aux [kapɔʀal, -o] nm lance corporal.

capot [kapo] nm (AUTO) bonnet.

capote [kapɔt] nf (de voiture) hood ; (de soldat) greatcoat.

capoter [kapɔte] vi to overturn.

câpre [kɑpʀ(ə)] nf caper.

caprice [kapʀis] nm whim, caprice ; passing fancy ; ~**s** (de la mode etc) vagaries ; **capricieux, euse** a capricious ; whimsical ; temperamental.

Capricorne [kapʀikɔʀn] nm: **le** ~ Capricorn, the Goat ; **être du** ~ to be Capricorn.

capsule [kapsyl] nf (de bouteille) cap ; (amorce) primer ; cap ; (BOT etc, spatiale) capsule.

capter [kapte] vt (ondes radio) to pick up ; (eau) to harness ; (fig) to win, capture.

captieux, euse [kapsjø, -øz] a specious.

captif, ive [kaptif, -iv] a captive // nm/f captive, prisoner.

captiver [kaptive] vt to captivate.

captivité [kaptivite] nf captivity ; **en** ~ in captivity.

capture [kaptyʀ] nf capture, catching q ; catch.

capturer [kaptyʀe] vt to capture, catch.

capuche [kapyʃ] nf hood.

capuchon [kapyʃɔ̃] nm hood ; (de stylo) cap, top.

capucin [kapysɛ̃] nm Capuchin monk.

capucine [kapysin] nf (BOT) nasturtium.

caquet [kakɛ] nm: **rabattre le** ~ **à qn** to bring sb down a peg or two.

caqueter [kakte] vi (poule) to cackle ; (fig) to prattle, blether.

car [kaʀ] nm coach // cj because, for ; ~ **de reportage** broadcasting ou radio van.

carabine [kaʀabin] nf carbine, rifle.

caracoler [kaʀakɔle] vi to caracole, prance.

caractère [kaʀaktɛʀ] nm (gén) character ; **en** ~**s gras** in bold type ; **en petits** ~**s** in small print ; **avoir du** ~ to have character ; **avoir bon/mauvais** ~ to be good-/ill-natured ou -tempered ; **caractériel, le** a (of) character // nm/f emotionally disturbed child.

caractérisé, e [kaʀakteʀize] a: **c'est une grippe/de l'insubordination** ~**e** it is a clear(-cut) case of flu/insubordination.

caractériser [kaʀakteʀize] vt to characterize ; **se** ~ **par** to be characterized ou distinguished by.

caractéristique [kaʀakteʀistik] a, nf characteristic.

carafe [kaʀaf] nf decanter ; carafe.

carambolage [kaʀɑ̃bɔlaʒ] nm multiple crash, pileup.

caramel [kaʀamɛl] nm (bonbon) caramel, toffee ; (substance) caramel ; **caraméliser** vt to caramelize.

carapace [kaʀapas] nf shell.

carat [kaʀa] nm carat ; **or à 18** ~**s** 18-carat gold.

caravane [kaʀavan] nf caravan ; **caravanier** nm caravanner ; **caravaning** nm caravanning ; (emplacement) caravan site.

carbone [kaʀbɔn] nm carbon ; (feuille) carbon, sheet of carbon paper ; (double) carbon (copy).

carbonique [kaʀbɔnik] a: **gaz** ~ carbonic acid gas ; **neige** ~ dry ice.

carbonisé, e [kaʀbɔnize] a charred.

carboniser [kaʀbɔnize] vt to carbonize ; to burn down, reduce to ashes.

carburant [kaʀbyʀɑ̃] nm (motor) fuel.

carburateur [kaʀbyʀatœʀ] nm carburettor.

carburation [kaʀbyʀɑsjɔ̃] nf carburation.

carcan [kaʀkɑ̃] nm (fig) yoke, shackles pl.

carcasse [kaʀkas] nf carcass ; (de véhicule etc) shell.

carder [kaʀde] vt to card.

cardiaque [kaʀdjak] a cardiac, heart cpd // nm/f heart patient.

cardigan [kaʀdigɑ̃] nm cardigan.

cardinal, e, aux [kaʀdinal, -o] a cardinal // nm (REL) cardinal.

cardiologie [kaʀdjɔlɔʒi] nf cardiology ; **cardiologue** nm/f cardiologist, heart specialist.

carême [kaʀɛm] nm: **le C**~ Lent.

carence [kaʀɑ̃s] nf incompetence, inadequacy ; (manque) deficiency ; ~ **vitaminique** vitamin deficiency.

carène [kaʀɛn] nf hull.

caréner [kaʀene] vt (NAVIG) to careen ; (carrosserie) to streamline.

caressant, e [kaʀɛsɑ̃, -ɑ̃t] *a* affectionate; caressing, tender.

caresse [kaʀɛs] *nf* caress.

caresser [kaʀese] *vt* to caress, stroke, fondle; (*fig: projet, espoir*) to toy with.

cargaison [kaʀgɛzɔ̃] *nf* cargo, freight.

cargo [kaʀgo] *nm* cargo boat, freighter.

caricatural, e, aux [kaʀikatyʀal, -o] *a* caricatural, caricature-like.

caricature [kaʀikatyʀ] *nf* caricature; (*politique etc*) (satirical) cartoon; **caricaturiste** *nm/f* caricaturist; (satirical) cartoonist.

carie [kaʀi] *nf:* **la ~ (dentaire)** tooth decay; **une ~** a hole (in a tooth); **carié, e** *a:* **dent cariée** bad *ou* decayed tooth.

carillon [kaʀijɔ̃] *nm* (*d'église*) bells *pl*; (*pendule*) chimes *pl*; (*de porte*): **~ (électrique)** (electric) door chime *ou* bell; **carillonner** *vi* to ring, chime, peal.

carlingue [kaʀlɛ̃g] *nf* cabin.

carnage [kaʀnaʒ] *nm* carnage, slaughter.

carnassier, ière [kaʀnasje, -jɛʀ] *a* carnivorous // *nm* carnivore.

carnation [kaʀnasjɔ̃] *nf* complexion; **~s** (*PEINTURE*) flesh tones.

carnaval [kaʀnaval] *nm* carnival.

carné, e [kaʀne] *a* meat *cpd*, meat-based.

carnet [kaʀnɛ] *nm* (*calepin*) notebook; (*de tickets, timbres etc*) book; (*d'école*) school report; (*journal intime*) diary; **~ de chèques** cheque book; **~ de commandes** order book; **~ à souches** counterfoil book.

carnier [kaʀnje] *nm* gamebag.

carnivore [kaʀnivɔʀ] *a* a carnivorous // *nm* carnivore.

carotide [kaʀɔtid] *nf* carotid (artery).

carotte [kaʀɔt] *nf* carrot.

carpe [kaʀp(ə)] *nf* carp.

carpette [kaʀpɛt] *nf* rug.

carquois [kaʀkwa] *nm* quiver.

carre [kaʀ] *nf* (*de ski*) edge.

carré, e [kaʀe] *a* square; (*fig: franc*) straightforward // *nm* (*de terrain, jardin*) patch, plot; (*NAVIG: salle*) wardroom; (*MATH*) square; **élever un nombre au ~** to square a number; **mètre/kilomètre ~** square metre/kilometre; (*CARTES*): **~ d'as/de rois** four aces/kings.

carreau, x [kaʀo] *nm* (*en faïence etc*) (floor) tile; (*wall*) tile; (*de fenêtre*) (window) pane; (*motif*) check, square; (*CARTES: couleur*) diamonds *pl*; (*: carte*) diamond; **tissu à ~x** checked fabric.

carrefour [kaʀfuʀ] *nm* crossroads *sg*.

carrelage [kaʀlaʒ] *nm* tiling.

carreler [kaʀle] *vt* to tile.

carrelet [kaʀlɛ] *nm* (*poisson*) plaice.

carreleur [kaʀlœʀ] *nm* (floor) tiler.

carrément [kaʀemɑ̃] *ad* straight out, bluntly; straight; definitely.

carrer [kaʀe]: **se ~** *vi:* **se ~ dans un fauteuil** to settle o.s. comfortably *ou* ensconce o.s. in an armchair.

carrier [kaʀje] *nm:* **(ouvrier) ~** quarryman, quarrier.

carrière [kaʀjɛʀ] *nf* (*de roches*) quarry; (*métier*) career; **militaire de ~** professional soldier; **faire ~ dans** to make one's career in.

carriole [kaʀjɔl] *nf* (*péj*) old cart.

carrossable [kaʀɔsabl(ə)] *a* suitable for (motor) vehicles.

carrosse [kaʀɔs] *nm* (horse-drawn) coach.

carrosserie [kaʀɔsʀi] *nf* body, coachwork q; (*activité, commerce*) coachbuilding; **atelier de ~** coachbuilder's workshop; (*pour réparations*) body repairs shop, panel beaters' (yard); **carrossier** *nm* coachbuilder; (*dessinateur*) car designer.

carrousel [kaʀuzɛl] *nm* (*ÉQUITATION*) carousel; (*fig*) merry-go-round.

carrure [kaʀyʀ] *nf* build; (*fig*) stature, calibre.

cartable [kaʀtabl(ə)] *nm* (*d'écolier*) satchel, (school)bag.

carte [kaʀt(ə)] *nf* (*de géographie*) map; (*marine, du ciel*) chart; (*de fichier, d'abonnement etc, à jouer*) card; (*au restaurant*) menu; (*aussi:* **~ postale**) (post)card; (*aussi:* **~ de visite**) (visiting) card; **avoir/donner ~ blanche** to have/give carte blanche *ou* a free hand; **à la ~** (*au restaurant*) à la carte; **~ de crédit** credit card; **~ d'état-major** ≈ Ordnance Survey map; **la ~ grise** (*AUTO*) the (car) registration card; **~ d'identité** identity card; **~ perforée** punch(ed) card; **la ~ verte** (*AUTO*) the green card; **la ~ des vins** the wine list; **~-lettre** *nf* letter-card.

carter [kaʀtɛʀ] *nm* (*AUTO: d'huile*) sump; (*: de la boîte de vitesses*) casing; (*de bicyclette*) chain guard.

cartilage [kaʀtilaʒ] *nm* (*ANAT*) cartilage.

cartographe [kaʀtɔgʀaf] *nm/f* cartographer.

cartographie [kaʀtɔgʀafi] *nf* cartography, map-making.

cartomancien, ne [kaʀtɔmɑ̃sjɛ̃, -ɛn] *nm/f* fortune-teller (*with cards*).

carton [kaʀtɔ̃] *nm* (*matériau*) cardboard; (*boîte*) (cardboard) box; (*d'invitation*) invitation card; (*ART*) sketch; cartoon; **faire un ~** (*au tir*) to have a go at the rifle range; to score a hit; **~ (à dessin)** portfolio; **cartonnage** *nm* cardboard (packing); **cartonné, e** *a* (*livre*) hardback, cased; **~-pâte** *nm* pasteboard; **de ~-pâte** (*fig*) cardboard *cpd*.

cartouche [kaʀtuʃ] *nf* cartridge; (*de cigarettes*) carton; **cartouchière** *nf* cartridge belt.

cas [kɑ] *nm* case; **faire peu de ~/grand ~ de** to attach little/great importance to; **en aucun ~** on no account, under no circumstances (whatsoever); **au ~ où** in case; **en ~ de** in case of, in the event of; **en ~ de besoin** if need be; **en tout ~** in any case, at any rate; **~ de conscience** matter of conscience.

casanier, ière [kazanje, -jɛʀ] *a* stay-at-home.

casaque [kazak] *nf* (*de jockey*) blouse.

cascade [kaskad] *nf* waterfall, cascade; (*fig*) stream, torrent.

cascadeur, euse [kaskadœʀ, -øz] *nm/f* stuntman/girl.

case [kɑz] *nf* (*hutte*) hut; (*compartiment*) compartment; (*pour le courrier*) pigeonhole; (*sur un formulaire, de mots croisés, d'échiquier*) square.

casemate [kazmat] *nf* blockhouse.

caser [kɑze] *vt* to put; to tuck; to put up; (*péj*) to find a job for; to find a husband for.

caserne [kazɛʀn(ə)] *nf* barracks *sg ou pl*; ~ment *nm* barrack buildings *pl*.

cash [kaʃ] *ad*: **payer** ~ to pay cash down.

casier [kɑzje] *nm* (*à journaux etc*) rack; (*de bureau*) filing cabinet; (: *à cases*) set of pigeonholes; (*case*) compartment; pigeonhole; (: *à clef*) locker; (*PÊCHE*) lobster pot; ~ **à bouteilles** bottle rack; ~ **judiciaire** police record.

casino [kazino] *nm* casino.

casque [kask(ə)] *nm* helmet; (*chez le coiffeur*) (hair-)drier; (*pour audition*) (head-)phones *pl*, headset.

casquette [kaskɛt] *nf* cap.

cassant, e [kɑsɑ̃, -ɑ̃t] *a* brittle; (*fig*) brusque, abrupt.

cassate [kasat] *nf*: **(glace)** ~ cassata.

cassation [kasɑsjɔ̃] *nf*: **recours en** ~ appeal to the Supreme Court.

casse [kas] *nf* (*pour voitures*): **mettre à la** ~ to scrap, send to the breakers (*dégâts*): **il y a eu de la** ~ there were a lot of breakages.

casse... [kas] *préfixe*: ~-**cou** *a inv* daredevil, reckless; **crier** ~-**cou à qn** to warn sb (*against a risky undertaking*); ~-**croûte** *nm inv* snack; ~-**noisette(s)**, ~-**noix** *nm inv* nutcrackers *pl*; ~-**pieds** *a, nm/f inv* (*fam*): **il est** ~-**pieds, c'est un** ~-**pieds** he's a pain (in the neck).

casser [kɑse] *vt* to break; (*ADMIN: gradé*) to demote; (*JUR*) to quash // *vi*, **se** ~ to break.

casserole [kasʀɔl] *nf* saucepan; **à la** ~ (*CULIN*) braised.

casse-tête [kɑstɛt] *nm inv* (*fig*) brain teaser; headache (*fig*).

cassette [kasɛt] *nf* (*bande magnétique*) cassette; (*coffret*) casket.

cassis [kasis] *nm* blackcurrant; (*de la route*) dip, bump.

cassonade [kasɔnad] *nf* brown sugar.

cassoulet [kasulɛ] *nm* cassoulet.

cassure [kɑsyʀ] *nf* break, crack.

castagnettes [kastaɲɛt] *nfpl* castanets.

caste [kast(ə)] *nf* caste.

castor [kastɔʀ] *nm* beaver.

castrer [kastʀe] *vt* to castrate; to geld; to doctor.

cataclysme [kataklism(ə)] *nm* cataclysm.

catacombes [katakɔ̃b] *nfpl* catacombs.

catadioptre [katadjɔptʀ(ə)] *nm* = **cataphote**.

catafalque [katafalk(ə)] *nm* catafalque.

catalogue [katalɔg] *nm* catalogue.

cataloguer [katalɔge] *vt* to catalogue, to list; (*péj*) to put a label on.

catalyse [kataliz] *nf* catalysis; **catalyseur** *nm* catalyst.

cataphote [katafɔt] *nm* reflector.

cataplasme [kataplasm(ə)] *nm* poultice.

catapulte [katapylt(ə)] *nf* catapult; **catapulter** *vt* to catapult.

cataracte [kataʀakt(ə)] *nf* cataract;

opérer qn de la ~ to operate on sb for (a) cataract.

catarrhe [kataʀ] *nm* catarrh.

catastrophe [katastʀɔf] *nf* catastrophe, disaster; **catastrophique** *a* catastrophic, disastrous.

catch [katʃ] *nm* (all-in) wrestling; ~**eur, euse** *nm/f* (all-in) wrestler.

catéchiser [kateʃize] *vt* to catechize; to indoctrinate; to lecture; **catéchisme** *nm* catechism; **catéchumène** [katekymɛn] *nm/f* catechumen (*trainee convert*).

catégorie [kategɔʀi] *nf* category.

catégorique [kategɔʀik] *a* categorical.

cathédrale [katedʀal] *nf* cathedral.

cathode [katɔd] *nf* cathode.

catholicisme [katɔlisism(ə)] *nm* (Roman) Catholicism.

catholique [katɔlik] *a, nm/f* (Roman) Catholic; **pas très** ~ a bit shady ou fishy.

catimini [katimini]: **en** ~ *ad* on the sly, on the quiet.

cauchemar [koʃmaʀ] *nm* nightmare; ~**desque** *a* nightmarish.

caudal, e, aux [kodal, -o] *a* caudal, tail *cpd*.

causal, e [kozal] *a* causal; ~**ité** *nf* causality.

cause [koz] *nf* cause; (*JUR*) lawsuit, case; brief; **à** ~ **de** because of, owing to; **pour** ~ **de** on account of; owing to; **(et) pour** ~ and for a (very) good reason; **être en** ~ to be at stake; to be involved; to be in question; **mettre en** ~ to implicate; to call into question; **remettre en** ~ to challenge, call into question.

causer [koze] *vt* to cause // *vi* to chat, talk.

causerie [kozʀi] *nf* talk.

caustique [kostik] *a* caustic.

cauteleux, euse [kotlø, -øz] *a* wily.

cautériser [koteʀize] *vt* to cauterize.

caution [kosjɔ̃] *nf* guarantee, security; (*JUR*) bail (bond); (*fig*) backing, support; **payer la** ~ **de qn** to stand bail for sb; **libéré sous** ~ released on bail.

cautionnement [kosjɔnmɑ̃] *nm* (*somme*) guarantee, security.

cautionner [kosjɔne] *vt* to guarantee; (*soutenir*) to support.

cavalcade [kavalkad] *nf* (*fig*) stampede.

cavalerie [kavalʀi] *nf* cavalry.

cavalier, ière [kavalje, -jɛʀ] *a* (*désinvolte*) offhand // *nm/f* rider; (*au bal*) partner // *nm* (*ÉCHECS*) knight; **faire** ~ **seul** to go it alone.

cave [kav] *nf* cellar; (*cabaret*) (cellar) nightclub // *a*: **yeux** ~s sunken eyes.

caveau, x [kavo] *nm* vault.

caverne [kavɛʀn(ə)] *nf* cave.

caverneux, euse [kavɛʀnø, -øz] *a* cavernous.

caviar [kavjaʀ] *nm* caviar(e).

cavité [kavite] *nf* cavity.

CC *sigle voir* **corps**.

C.C.P. *sigle m voir* **compte**.

CD *sigle voir* **corps**.

ce(c'), cet, cette, ces [sə, sɛt, se] *dét* (*gén*) this; these *pl*; (*non-proximité*) that; those *pl*; **cette nuit** (*qui vient*) tonight; (*passée*) last night // *pronom*: ~ **qui,** ~

que what; (*chose qui ...*): **il est bête, ~ qui me chagrine** he's stupid, which saddens me; **tout ~ qui bouge** everything that ou which moves; **tout ~ que je sais** all I know; **~ dont j'ai parlé** what I talked about; **ce que c'est grand** how big it is!, what a size it is!; **c'est petit/grand** it's ou it is small/big; **c'est un peintre, ce sont des peintres** he's ou he is a painter, they are painters; **c'est le facteur** etc (*à la porte*) it's the postman etc; **c'est une voiture** it's a car; **qui est-ce?** who is it?; (*en désignant*) who is he/she?; **qu'est-ce?** what is it?; *voir aussi* **-ci, est-ce que, n'est-ce pas, c'est-à-dire.**

ceci [səsi] *pronom* this.

cécité [sesite] *nf* blindness.

céder [sede] *vt* to give up // *vi* (*pont, barrage*) to give way; (*personne*) to give in; **~ à** to yield to, give in to.

cédille [sedij] *nf* cedilla.

cèdre [sɛdR(ə)] *nm* cedar.

C.E.E. *sigle f* (= *Communauté économique européenne*) EEC (European Economic Community).

ceindre [sɛ̃dR(ə)] *vt* (*mettre*) to put on, don; (*entourer*): **~ qch de qch** to put sth round sth.

ceinture [sɛ̃tyR] *nf* belt; (*taille*) waist; (*fig*) ring; belt; circle; **~ de sécurité** safety ou seat belt; **~ (de sécurité) à enrouleur** inertia reel seat belt; **ceinturer** *vt* (*saisir*) to grasp (round the waist); (*entourer*) to surround; **ceinturon** *nm* belt.

cela [səla] *pronom* that; (*comme sujet indéfini*) it; **~ m'étonne que** it surprises me that; **quand/où ~?** when/where (was that)?

célèbre [selɛbR(ə)] *a* famous.

célébrer [selebRe] *vt* to celebrate; (*louer*) to extol.

célébrité [selebRite] *nf* fame; (*star*) celebrity.

céleri [sɛlRi] *nm*: **~(-rave)** celeriac; **~ (en branche)** celery.

célérité [seleRite] *nf* speed, swiftness.

céleste [selɛst(ə)] *a* celestial; heavenly.

célibat [seliba] *nm* celibacy; bachelor/spinsterhood.

célibataire [selibatɛR] *a* single, unmarried // *nm/f* bachelor/unmarried ou single woman.

celle, celles [sɛl] *pronom voir* celui.

cellier [selje] *nm* storeroom.

cellophane [selɔfan] *nf* cellophane.

cellulaire [selylɛR] *a* (*BIO*) cell *cpd*, cellular; **voiture ou fourgon ~** prison ou police van.

cellule [selyl] *nf* (*gén*) cell.

cellulite [selylit] *nf* excess fat, cellulitis.

cellulose [selyloz] *nf* cellulose.

celui, celle, ceux, celles [səlɥi, sɛl, sø] *pronom* the one; **~ qui bouge** the one which ou that moves; (*personne*) the one who moves; **~ que je vois** the one (which ou that) I see; the one (whom) I see; **~ dont je parle** the one I'm talking about; **~ qui veut** (*valeur indéfinie*) whoever wants, the man ou person who wants; **~ du salon/du dessous** the one in (ou from) the lounge/below; **~ de mon frère** my

brother's; **celui-ci/-là, celle-ci/-là** this/that one; **ceux-ci, celles-ci** these ones; **ceux-là, celles-là** those (ones).

cénacle [senakl(ə)] *nm* (*literary*) coterie ou set.

cendre [sɑ̃dR(ə)] *nf* ash; **~s** (*d'un foyer*) ash(es), cinders; (*volcaniques*) ash *sg*; (*d'un défunt*) ashes; **sous la ~** (*CULIN*) in (the) embers; **cendré, e** *a* (*couleur*) ashen; (*piste*) **cendrée** cinder track; **cendrier** *nm* ashtray.

cène [sɛn] *nf*: **la ~** (Holy) Communion; (*ART*) the Last Supper.

censé, e [sɑ̃se] *a*: **être ~ faire** to be supposed to do.

censeur [sɑ̃sœR] *nm* (*SCOL*) vice-principal, deputy-head; (*CINÉMA, POL*) censor.

censure [sɑ̃syR] *nf* censorship.

censurer [sɑ̃syRe] *vt* (*CINÉMA, PRESSE*) to censor; (*POL*) to censure.

cent [sɑ̃] *num* a hundred, one hundred; **centaine** *nf*: **une centaine (de)** about a hundred, a hundred or so; (*COMM*) a hundred; **plusieurs centaines (de)** several hundred; **des centaines (de)** hundreds (of); **centenaire** *a* hundred-year-old // *nm/f* centenarian // *nm* (*anniversaire*) centenary; **centième** *num* hundredth; **centigrade** *nm* centigrade; **centigramme** *nm* centigramme; **centilitre** *nm* centilitre; **centime** *nm* centime; **centimètre** *nm* centimetre; (*ruban*) tape measure, measuring tape.

central, e, aux [sɑ̃tRal, -o] *a* central // *nm*: **~ (téléphonique)** (telephone) exchange // *nf*: **~e électrique/nucléaire** electric/nuclear power-station; **~e syndicale** group of affiliated trade unions.

centraliser [sɑ̃tRalize] *vt* to centralize.

centre [sɑ̃tR(ə)] *nm* centre; **~ de gravité** centre of gravity; **~ de tri** (*POSTES*) sorting office; **le ~-ville** the town centre; **centrer** *vt* to centre // *vi* (*FOOTBALL*) to centre the ball.

centrifuge [sɑ̃tRifyʒ] *a*: **force ~** centrifugal force; **centrifuger** *vt* to centrifuge.

centripète [sɑ̃tRipɛt] *a*: **force ~** centripetal force.

centuple [sɑ̃typl(ə)] *nm*: **le ~ de qch** a hundred times sth; **au ~** a hundredfold; **centupler** *vi, vt* to increase a hundredfold.

cep [sɛp] *nm* (vine) stock; **cépage** *nm* (type of) vine.

cèpe [sɛp] *nm* (edible) boletus.

cependant [səpɑ̃dɑ̃] *ad* however, nevertheless.

céramique [seRamik] *nf* ceramic; (*art*) ceramics *sg*.

cercle [sɛRkl(ə)] *nm* circle; (*objet*) band, hoop; **~ vicieux** vicious circle.

cercueil [sɛRkœj] *nm* coffin.

céréale [seReal] *nf* cereal.

cérébral, e, aux [seRebRal, -o] *a* (*ANAT*) cerebral, brain *cpd*; (*fig*) mental, cerebral.

cérémonial [seRemɔnjal] *nm* ceremonial.

cérémonie [seRemɔni] *nf* ceremony; **~s** (*péj*) fuss *sg*, to-do *sg*; **cérémonieux, euse** *a* ceremonious, formal.

cerf [sɛR] *nm* stag.

cerfeuil [sɛʀfœj] nm chervil.
cerf-volant [sɛʀvɔlɑ̃] nm kite.
cerise [səʀiz] nf cherry; **cerisier** nm cherry (tree).
cerné, e [sɛʀne] a: **les yeux** ~s with dark rings ou shadows under the eyes.
cerner [sɛʀne] vt (MIL etc) to surround; (fig: problème) to delimit, define.
cernes [sɛʀn(ə)] nfpl (dark) rings, shadows (under the eyes).
certain, e [sɛʀtɛ̃, -ɛn] a certain; (sûr): ~ **(de/que)** certain ou sure (of/ that) // dét certain; **d'un** ~ **âge** past one's prime, not so young; **un** ~ **temps** (quite) some time; ~s pronom some; **certainement** ad (probablement) most probably ou likely; (bien sûr) certainly, of course.
certes [sɛʀt(ə)] ad admittedly; of course; indeed (yes).
certificat [sɛʀtifika] nm certificate; **le** ~ **d'études** the school leaving certificate.
certifié, e [sɛʀtifje] a: **professeur** ~ qualified teacher.
certifier [sɛʀtifje] vt to certify, guarantee; ~ **à qn que** to assure sb that, guarantee to sb that.
certitude [sɛʀtityd] nf certainty.
cerveau, x [sɛʀvo] nm brain.
cervelas [sɛʀvəla] nm saveloy.
cervelle [sɛʀvɛl] nf (ANAT) brain; (CULIN) brain(s).
cervical, e, aux [sɛʀvikal, -o] a cervical.
ces [se] dét voir **ce**.
césarienne [sezaʀjɛn] nf caesarean (section), section.
cessantes [sɛsɑ̃t] afpl: **toutes affaires** ~ forthwith.
cessation [sɛsɑsjɔ̃] nf: ~ **des hostilités** cessation of hostilities; ~ **de paiements/commerce** suspension of payments/trading.
cesse [sɛs]: **sans** ~ ad continually, constantly; continuously; **il n'avait de** ~ **que** he would not rest until.
cesser [sese] vt to stop // vi to stop, cease; ~ **de faire** to stop doing.
cessez-le-feu [seselfø] nm inv ceasefire.
cession [sɛsjɔ̃] nf transfer.
c'est-à-dire [sɛtadiʀ] ad that is (to say).
cet [sɛt] dét voir **ce**.
cétacé [setase] nm cetacean.
cette [sɛt] dét voir **ce**.
ceux [sø] pronom voir **celui**.
C.F.D.T. sigle f = Confédération française et démocratique du travail (a major association of French trade unions).
C.G.C. sigle f = Confédération générale des cadres (union of managerial employees).
C.G.T. sigle f = Confédération générale du travail (a major association of French trade unions).
chacal [ʃakal] nm jackal.
chacun, e [ʃakœ̃, -yn] pronom each; (indéfini) everyone, everybody.
chagrin, e [ʃagʀɛ̃, -gʀin] a ill-humoured, morose // nm grief, sorrow; **avoir du** ~ to be grieved ou sorrowful; **chagriner** vt to grieve, distress; (contrarier) to bother, worry.
chahut [ʃay] nm uproar; **chahuter** vt to

rag, bait // vi to make an uproar; **chahuteur, euse** nm/f rowdy.
chai [ʃɛ] nm wine and spirit store(house).
chaîne [ʃɛn] nf chain; (RADIO, TV: stations) channel; **travail à la** ~ production line work; **faire la** ~ to form a (human) chain; ~ **(haute-fidélité ou hi-fi)** hi-fi system; ~ **(de montage ou de fabrication)** production ou assembly line; ~ **(de montagnes)** (mountain) range; **chaînette** nf (small) chain; **chaînon** nm link.
chair [ʃɛʀ] nf flesh // a: **(couleur)** ~ flesh-coloured; **avoir la** ~ **de poule** to have goosepimples ou gooseflesh; **bien en** ~ plump, well-padded; ~ **à saucisses** sausage meat.
chaire [ʃɛʀ] nf (d'église) pulpit; (d'université) chair.
chaise [ʃɛz] nf chair; ~ **de bébé** high chair; ~ **longue** deckchair.
chaland [ʃalɑ̃] nm (bateau) barge.
châle [ʃɑl] nm shawl.
chalet [ʃalɛ] nm chalet.
chaleur [ʃalœʀ] nf heat; (fig) warmth; fire, fervour; heat.
chaleureux, euse [ʃalœʀø, -øz] a warm.
challenge [ʃalɑ̃ʒ] nm contest, tournament.
chaloupe [ʃalup] nf launch; (de sauvetage) lifeboat.
chalumeau, x [ʃalymo] nm blowlamp, blowtorch.
chalut [ʃaly] nm trawl (net); **chalutier** nm trawler; (pêcheur) trawlerman.
chamailler [ʃamaje]: **se** ~ vi to squabble, bicker.
chamarré, e [ʃamaʀe] a richly coloured ou brocaded.
chambarder [ʃɑ̃baʀde] vt to turn upside down, upset.
chambranle [ʃɑ̃bʀɑl] nm (door) frame.
chambre [ʃɑ̃bʀ(ə)] nf bedroom; (TECH) chamber; (POL) chamber, house; (JUR) court; (COMM) chamber; federation; **faire** ~ **à part** to sleep in separate rooms; **stratège en** ~ armchair strategist; ~ **à un lit/deux lits** (à l'hôtel) single-/double-ou twin-bedded room; ~ **d'accusation** court of criminal appeal; ~ **à air** (de pneu) (inner) tube; ~ **d'amis** spare ou guest room; ~ **à coucher** bedroom; **la C~ des députés** the Chamber of Deputies, ≈ the House (of Commons); ~ **forte** strongroom; ~ **froide ou frigorifique** cold room; ~ **des machines** engine-room; ~ **meublée** bed-sitter, furnished room; ~ **noire** (PHOTO) dark room.
chambrée [ʃɑ̃bʀe] nf room.
chambrer [ʃɑ̃bʀe] vt (vin) to bring to room temperature.
chameau, x [ʃamo] nm camel.
chamois [ʃamwa] nm chamois // a: (couleur) ~ fawn, buff (-coloured).
champ [ʃɑ̃] nm field; (PHOTO): **dans le** ~ in the picture; **prendre du** ~ to draw back; ~ **de bataille** battlefield; ~ **de courses** racecourse; ~ **de mines** minefield.
champagne [ʃɑ̃paɲ] nm champagne.
champêtre [ʃɑ̃pɛtʀ(ə)] a country cpd, rural.

champignon [ʃɑ̃piɲɔ̃] *nm* mushroom; (*terme générique*) fungus (*pl* i); **~ de couche** *ou* **de Paris** cultivated mushroom; **~ vénéneux** toadstool, poisonous mushroom.

champion, ne [ʃɑ̃pjɔ̃, -jɔn] *a*, *nm/f* champion; **championnat** *nm* championship.

chance [ʃɑ̃s] *nf*: **la ~** luck; **une ~** a stroke *ou* piece of luck *ou* good fortune; (*occasion*) a lucky break; **~s** *nfpl* (*probabilités*) chances; **avoir de la ~** to be lucky; **il a des ~s de gagner** he has a chance of winning.

chanceler [ʃɑ̃sle] *vi* to totter.

chancelier [ʃɑ̃səlje] *nm* (*allemand*) chancellor; (*d'ambassade*) secretary.

chanceux, euse [ʃɑ̃sø, -øz] *a* lucky, fortunate.

chancre [ʃɑ̃kR(ə)] *nm* canker.

chandail [ʃɑ̃daj] *nm* (thick) jumper *ou* sweater.

Chandeleur [ʃɑ̃dlœR] *nf*: **la ~** Candlemas.

chandelier [ʃɑ̃dəlje] *nm* candlestick; (*à plusieurs branches*) candelabra, candlestick.

chandelle [ʃɑ̃dɛl] *nf* (tallow) candle; **dîner aux ~s** candlelight dinner.

change [ʃɑ̃ʒ] *nm* (COMM) exchange; **opérations de ~** (foreign) exchange transactions; **contrôle des ~s** exchange control.

changeant, e [ʃɑ̃ʒɑ̃, -ɑ̃t] *a* changeable, fickle.

changement [ʃɑ̃ʒmɑ̃] *nm* change; **~ de vitesses** gears; gear change.

changer [ʃɑ̃ʒe] *vt* (*modifier*) to change, alter; (*remplacer*, COMM, *rhabiller*) to change // *vi* to change, alter; **se ~** to change (o.s.); **~ de** (*remplacer*: *adresse*, *nom*, *voiture etc*) to change one's; (*échanger*, *alterner*: *côté*, *place*, *train etc*) to change + *npl*; **~ de couleur/direction** to change colour/direction; **~ d'idée** to change one's mind; **~ de place avec qn** to change places with sb; **~ (de train etc)** to change (trains *etc*); **~ qch en** to change sth into.

changeur [ʃɑ̃ʒœR] *nm* (*personne*) moneychanger; **~ automatique** change machine; **~ de disques** record changer, autochange.

chanoine [ʃanwan] *nm* canon.

chanson [ʃɑ̃sɔ̃] *nf* song.

chansonnier [ʃɑ̃sɔnje] *nm* cabaret artist (*specializing in political satire*); song book.

chant [ʃɑ̃] *nm* song; (*art vocal*) singing; (*d'église*) hymn; (*de poème*) canto; (TECH): **de ~** on edge.

chantage [ʃɑ̃taʒ] *nm* blackmail; **faire du ~** to use blackmail; **soumettre qn à un ~** to blackmail sb.

chanter [ʃɑ̃te] *vt*, *vi* to sing; **si cela lui chante** (*fam*) if he feels like it *ou* fancies it.

chanterelle [ʃɑ̃tRɛl] *nf* chanterelle (*edible mushroom*).

chanteur, euse [ʃɑ̃tœr, -øz] *nm/f* singer.

chantier [ʃɑ̃tje] *nm* (building) site; (*sur une route*) roadworks *pl*; **mettre en ~** to put in hand, start work on; **~ naval** shipyard.

chantonner [ʃɑ̃tɔne] *vi*, *vt* to sing to oneself, hum.

chanvre [ʃɑ̃vR(ə)] *nm* hemp.

chaos [kao] *nm* chaos; **chaotique** *a* chaotic.

chaparder [ʃapaRde] *vt* to pinch, pilfer.

chapeau, x [ʃapo] *nm* hat; **~ mou** trilby; **~x de roues** hub caps.

chapeauter [ʃapote] *vt* (ADMIN) to head, oversee.

chapelet [ʃaplɛ] *nm* (REL) rosary; (*fig*): **un ~ de** a string of; **dire son ~** to tell one's beads.

chapelle [ʃapɛl] *nf* chapel; **~ ardente** chapel of rest.

chapelure [ʃaplyR] *nf* (dried) bread-crumbs *pl*.

chaperon [ʃapRɔ̃] *nm* chaperon; **chaperonner** *vt* to chaperon.

chapiteau, x [ʃapito] *nm* (ARCHIT) capital; (*de cirque*) marquee, big top.

chapitre [ʃapitR(ə)] *nm* chapter; (*fig*) subject, matter; **avoir voix au ~** to have a say in the matter.

chapitrer [ʃapitre] *vt* to lecture.

chaque [ʃak] *dét* each, every; (*indéfini*) every.

char [ʃaR] *nm* (*à foin etc*) cart, waggon; (*de carnaval*) float; **~ (d'assaut)** tank.

charabia [ʃaRabja] *nm* (*péj*) gibberish, gobbledygook.

charade [ʃaRad] *nf* riddle; (*mimée*) charade.

charbon [ʃaRbɔ̃] *nm* coal; **~ de bois** charcoal; **charbonnage** *nm*: **les charbonnages de France** the (French) Coal Board *sg*; **charbonnier** *nm* coalman.

charcuterie [ʃaRkytRi] *nf* (*magasin*) pork butcher's shop and delicatessen; (*produits*) cooked pork meats *pl*; **charcutier, ière** *nm/f* pork butcher.

chardon [ʃaRdɔ̃] *nm* thistle.

charge [ʃaRʒ(ə)] *nf* (*fardeau*) load, burden; (*explosif*, ÉLEC, MIL, JUR) charge; (*rôle, mission*) responsibility; **~s** *nfpl* (*du loyer*) service charges; **à la ~ de** (*dépendant de*) dependent upon, supported by; (*aux frais de*) chargeable to, payable by; **j'accepte, à ~ de revanche** I accept, provided I can do the same for you (in return) one day; (*suj: véhicule*) to take on; **prendre en ~** to take charge of; (*dépenses*) to take care of; **~ utile** (AUTO) live load; **~s sociales** social security con-tributions.

chargé [ʃaRʒe] *nm*: **~ d'affaires** chargé d'affaires; **~ de cours** ≈ senior lecturer.

chargement [ʃaRʒəmɑ̃] *nm* (*action*) loading, charging; (*objets*) load.

charger [ʃaRʒe] *vt* (*voiture, fusil, caméra*) to load; (*batterie*) to charge // *vi* (MIL *etc*) to charge; **se ~** to see *ou* take charge *ou* charge of; **~ qn de qch/faire qch** to give sb the responsibility for sth/of doing sth; to put sb in charge of sth/doing sth.

chariot [ʃaRjo] *nm* trolley; (*charrette*) waggon; (*de machine à écrire*) carriage; **~ élévateur** fork-lift truck.

charitable [ʃaRitabl(ə)] *a* charitable; kind.

charité [ʃaRite] *nf* charity; **faire la ~ à** to

give to charity ; to do charitable works ;
faire la ~ à to give (something) to.
charlatan [ʃaʀlatɑ̃] nm charlatan.
charmant, e [ʃaʀmɑ̃, -ɑ̃t] a charming.
charme [ʃaʀm(ə)] nm charm ; **charmer** vt
to charm ; **je suis charmé de** I'm delighted
to ; **charmeur, euse** nm/f charmer ;
charmeur de serpents snake charmer.
charnel, le [ʃaʀnɛl] a carnal.
charnier [ʃaʀnje] nm mass grave.
charnière [ʃaʀnjɛʀ] nf hinge ; (fig)
turning-point.
charnu, e [ʃaʀny] a fleshy.
charogne [ʃaʀɔɲ] nf carrion q ; (fam!)
bastard (!).
charpente [ʃaʀpɑ̃t] nf frame(work) ; (fig)
structure, framework ; build, frame ; **charpentier** nm carpenter.
charpie [ʃaʀpi] nf: **en ~** (fig) in shreds
ou ribbons.
charretier [ʃaʀtje] nm carter.
charrette [ʃaʀɛt] nf cart.
charrier [ʃaʀje] vt to carry (along) ; to
cart, carry.
charrue [ʃaʀy] nf plough.
charte [ʃaʀt(ə)] nf charter.
chas [ʃa] nm eye (of needle).
chasse [ʃas] nf hunting ; (au fusil)
shooting ; (poursuite) chase ; (aussi: ~
d'eau) flush ; **la ~ est ouverte** the
hunting season is open ; **~ gardée** private
hunting grounds pl ; **prendre en ~,
donner la ~ à** to give chase to ; **tirer la
~ (d'eau)** to flush the toilet, pull the
chain ; **~ à courre** hunting ; **~ à l'homme**
manhunt ; **~ sous-marine** underwater
fishing.
châsse [ʃas] nf reliquary, shrine.
chassé-croisé [ʃasekwaze] nm (DANSE)
chassé-croisé ; (fig) mix-up where people
miss each other in turn.
chasse-neige [ʃasnɛʒ] nm inv
snowplough.
chasser [ʃase] vt to hunt ; (expulser) to
chase away ou out, drive away ou out ;
(dissiper) to chase ou sweep away ; to
dispel, drive away ; **chasseur, euse** nm/f
hunter // nm (avion) fighter ; (domestique)
page (boy), messenger (boy) ; **chasseurs
alpins** mountain infantry sg ou pl.
chassieux, ieuse [ʃasjø, -øz] a sticky,
gummy.
châssis [ʃasi] nm (AUTO) chassis ; (cadre)
frame ; (de jardin) cold frame.
chaste [ʃast(ə)] a chaste ; **~té** nf chastity.
chasuble [ʃazybl(ə)] nf chasuble.
chat [ʃa] nm cat ; **~ sauvage** wildcat.
châtaigne [ʃatɛɲ] nf chestnut ;
châtaignier nm chestnut (tree).
châtain [ʃatɛ̃] a inv chestnut (brown) ;
chestnut-haired.
château, x [ʃato] nm castle ; **~ d'eau**
water tower ; **~ fort** stronghold, fortified
castle ; **~ de sable** sandcastle.
châtier [ʃatje] vt to punish, castigate ;
(fig: style) to polish, refine ; **châtiment** nm
punishment, castigation.
chatoiement [ʃatwamɑ̃] nm
shimmer(ing).
chaton [ʃatɔ̃] nm (ZOOL) kitten ; (BOT)
catkin ; (de bague) bezel ; stone.

chatouiller [ʃatuje] vt to tickle ; (l'odorat,
le palais) to titillate ; **chatouilleux, euse**
a ticklish ; (fig) touchy, over-sensitive.
chatoyer [ʃatwaje] vi to shimmer.
châtrer [ʃatʀe] vt to castrate ; to geld ; to
doctor.
chatte [ʃat] nf (she-)cat.
chaud, e [ʃo, -od] a (gén) warm ; (très
chaud) hot ; (fig) hearty ; keen ; heated ; **il
fait ~** it's warm ; it's hot ; **manger ~** to
have something hot to eat ; **avoir ~** to
be warm ; to be hot ; **ça me tient ~** it
keeps me warm ; **rester au ~** to stay in
the warmth ; **chaudement** ad warmly ;
(fig) hotly.
chaudière [ʃodjɛʀ] nf boiler.
chaudron [ʃodʀɔ̃] nm cauldron.
chaudronnerie [ʃodʀɔnʀi] nf (usine)
boilerworks ; (activité) boilermaking ;
(boutique) coppersmith's workshop.
chauffage [ʃofaʒ] nm heating ; **~ central**
central heating.
chauffant, e [ʃofɑ̃, -ɑ̃t] a: **couverture ~e**
electric blanket ; **plaque ~e** hotplate.
chauffard [ʃofaʀ] nm (péj) reckless
driver ; roadhog ; hit-and-run driver.
chauffe-bain [ʃofbɛ̃] nm, **chauffe-eau**
[ʃofo] nm inv water-heater.
chauffer [ʃofe] vt to heat // vi to heat
up, warm up ; (trop chauffer: moteur) to
overheat ; **se ~** (se mettre en train) to
warm up ; (au soleil) to warm o.s.
chaufferie [ʃofʀi] nf boiler room.
chauffeur [ʃofœʀ] nm driver ; (privé)
chauffeur.
chaume [ʃom] nm (du toit) thatch ; (tiges)
stubble.
chaumière [ʃomjɛʀ] nf (thatched)
cottage.
chaussée [ʃose] nf road(way) ; (digue)
causeway.
chausse-pied [ʃospje] nm shoe-horn.
chausser [ʃose] vt (bottes, skis) to put on ;
(enfant) to put shoes on ; (suj: soulier) to
fit ; **~ du 38/42** to take size 38/42 ; **~
grand/bien** to be big-/well-fitting ; **se ~**
to put one's shoes on.
chaussette [ʃosɛt] nf sock.
chausseur [ʃosœʀ] nm (marchand)
footwear specialist, shoemaker.
chausson [ʃosɔ̃] nm slipper ; **~ (aux
pommes)** (apple) turnover.
chaussure [ʃosyʀ] nf shoe ; (commerce)
shoe industry ou trade ; **~s montantes**
ankle boots ; **~s de ski** ski boots.
chaut [ʃo] vb: **peu me ~** it matters little
to me.
chauve [ʃov] a bald.
chauve-souris [ʃovsuʀi] nf bat.
chauvin, e [ʃovɛ̃, -in] a chauvinistic,
jingoistic ; **chauvinisme** nm chauvinism ;
jingoism.
chaux [ʃo] nf lime ; **blanchi à la ~**
whitewashed.
chavirer [ʃaviʀe] vi to capsize, overturn.
chef [ʃɛf] nm head, leader ; (de cuisine)
chef ; **en ~** (MIL etc) in chief ; **~
d'accusation** charge, count (of
indictment) ; **~ d'atelier** (shop) foreman ;
~ de bureau head clerk ; **~ de clinique**
senior hospital lecturer ; **~ d'entreprise**

company head ; ~ **d'équipe** team leader ;
~ **d'état** head of state ; ~ **de famille** head
of the family ; ~ **de file** (*de parti etc*)
leader ; ~ **de gare** station master ; ~
d'orchestre conductor ; ~ **de rayon**
department(al) supervisor ; ~ **de service**
departmental head.

chef-d'œuvre [ʃɛdœvʀ(ə)] *nm* master-
piece.

chef-lieu [ʃɛfljø] *nm* county town.

cheftaine [ʃɛftɛn] *nf* (guide) captain.

cheik [ʃɛk] *nm* sheik.

chemin [ʃəmɛ̃] *nm* path ; (*itinéraire,
direction, trajet*) way ; **en** ~ on the way ;
~ **de fer** railway ; **par** ~ **de fer** by rail ;
les ~**s de fer** the railways.

cheminée [ʃəmine] *nf* chimney ; (*à
l'intérieur*) chimney piece, fireplace ; (*de
bateau*) funnel.

cheminement [ʃəminmɑ̃] *nm* progress ;
course.

cheminer [ʃəmine] *vi* to walk (along).

cheminot [ʃəmino] *nm* railwayman.

chemise [ʃəmiz] *nf* shirt ; (*dossier*) folder ;
~ **de nuit** nightdress ; ~**rie** *nf*
(gentlemen's) outfitters' ; **chemisette** *nf*
short-sleeved shirt.

chemisier [ʃəmizje] *nm* blouse.

chenal, aux [ʃənal, -o] *nm* channel.

chêne [ʃɛn] *nm* oak (tree) ; (*bois*) oak.

chenet [ʃənɛ] *nm* fire-dog, andiron.

chenil [ʃənil] *nm* kennels *pl*.

chenille [ʃənij] *nf* (*ZOOL*) caterpillar ;
(*AUTO*) caterpillar track ; **véhicule à** ~**s**
tracked vehicle, caterpillar ; **chenillette** *nf*
tracked vehicle.

cheptel [ʃɛptɛl] *nm* livestock.

chèque [ʃɛk] *nm* cheque ; ~ **barré/sans
provision** crossed/bad cheque ; ~ **au
porteur** cheque to bearer ; **chéquier** *nm*
cheque book.

cher, ère [ʃɛʀ] *a* (*aimé*) dear ; (*coûteux*)
expensive, dear // *ad* : **cela coûte** ~ it's
expensive, it costs a lot of money // *nf* :
la bonne chère good food ; **mon** ~, **ma
chère** my dear.

chercher [ʃɛʀʃe] *vt* to look for ; (*gloire etc*)
to seek ; **aller** ~ to go for, go and fetch ;
~ **à faire** to try to do.

chercheur, euse [ʃɛʀʃœʀ, -øz] *nm/f*
researcher, research worker ; ~ **de** seeker
of ; hunter of ; ~ **d'or** gold digger.

chère [ʃɛʀ] *a,nf voir* **cher**.

chéri, e [ʃeʀi] *a* beloved, dear ; (**mon**) ~
darling.

chérir [ʃeʀiʀ] *vt* to cherish.

cherté [ʃɛʀte] *nf* : **la** ~ **de la vie** the high
cost of living.

chérubin [ʃeʀybɛ̃] *nm* cherub.

chétif, ive [ʃetif, -iv] *a* puny, stunted.

cheval, aux [ʃəval, -o] *nm* horse ; (*AUTO*) :
~ (**vapeur**) (C.V.) horsepower *q* ; **50
chevaux (au frein)** 50 brake horsepower,
50 b.h.p. ; **10 chevaux (fiscaux)** 10
horsepower (*for tax purposes*) ; **faire du** ~
to ride ; **à** ~ on horseback ; **à** ~ **sur**
astride, straddling ; (*fig*) overlapping ; ~
d'arçons vaulting horse.

chevaleresque [ʃəvalʀɛsk(ə)] *a*
chivalrous.

chevalerie [ʃəvalʀi] *nf* chivalry ;
knighthood.

chevalet [ʃəvalɛ] *nm* easel.

chevalier [ʃəvalje] *nm* knight ; ~ **servant**
escort.

chevalière [ʃəvaljɛʀ] *nf* signet ring.

chevalin, e [ʃəvalɛ̃, -in] *a* of horses,
equine ; (*péj*) horsy ; **boucherie** ~**e** horse-
meat butcher's.

cheval-vapeur [ʃəvalvapœʀ] *nm voir*
cheval.

chevauchée [ʃəvoʃe] *nf* ride ; cavalcade.

chevaucher [ʃəvoʃe] *vi* (*aussi* : **se** ~) to
overlap (each other) // *vt* to be astride,
straddle.

chevelu, e [ʃəvly] *a* with a good head of
hair, hairy (*péj*).

chevelure [ʃəvlyʀ] *nf* hair *q*.

chevet [ʃəvɛ] *nm* : **au** ~ **de qn** at sb's
bedside ; **lampe de** ~ bedside lamp.

cheveu, x [ʃəvø] *nm* hair ; // *nmpl*
(*chevelure*) hair *sg* ; **avoir les** ~**x courts**
to have short hair.

cheville [ʃəvij] *nf* (*ANAT*) ankle ; (*de bois*)
peg ; (*pour enfoncer un clou*) plug ; ~
ouvrière (*fig*) kingpin.

chèvre [ʃɛvʀ(ə)] *nf* (she-)goat.

chevreau, x [ʃəvʀo] *nm* kid.

chèvrefeuille [ʃɛvʀəfœj] *nm*
honeysuckle.

chevreuil [ʃəvʀœj] *nm* roe deer *inv* ;
(*CULIN*) venison.

chevron [ʃəvʀɔ̃] *nm* (*poutre*) rafter ;
(*motif*) chevron, v(-shape) ; **à** ~**s** chevron-
patterned ; herringbone.

chevronné, e [ʃəvʀɔne] *a* seasoned,
experienced.

chevrotant, e [ʃəvʀɔtɑ̃, -ɑ̃t] *a* quavering.

chevrotine [ʃəvʀɔtin] *nf* buckshot *q*.

chewing-gum [ʃwiŋɡɔm] *nm* chewing
gum.

chez [ʃe] *prép* (*à la demeure de*) : ~ **qn** at
(*ou* to) sb's house *ou* place ; (*parmi*)
among ; ~ **moi** at home ; (*avec direction*)
home ; ~ **le boulanger** (*à la boulangerie*)
at the baker's ; ~ **ce musicien** (*dans ses
œuvres*) in this musician ; ~**-soi** *nm inv*
home.

chic [ʃik] *a inv* chic, smart ; (*généreux*)
nice, decent // *nm* stylishness ; **avoir le**
~ **de** to have the knack of ; **de** ~ *ad* off
the cuff ; ~! great!, terrific!

chicane [ʃikan] *nf* (*obstacle*) zigzag ;
(*querelle*) squabble.

chiche [ʃiʃ] *a* niggardly, mean // *excl* (*à
un défi*) you're on!

chicorée [ʃikɔʀe] *nf* (*café*) chicory ;
(*salade*) endive.

chicot [ʃiko] *nm* stump.

chien [ʃjɛ̃] *nm* dog ; (*de pistolet*) hammer ;
en ~ **de fusil** curled up ; ~ **de garde**
guard dog.

chiendent [ʃjɛ̃dɑ̃] *nm* couch grass.

chien-loup [ʃjɛ̃lu] *nm* wolfhound.

chienne [ʃjɛn] *nf* dog, bitch.

chier [ʃje] *vi* (*fam!*) to crap (!).

chiffe [ʃif] *nf* : **il est mou comme une** ~,
c'est une ~ **molle** he's spineless *ou* wet.

chiffon [ʃifɔ̃] *nm* (*de ménage*) (piece of)
rag.

chiffonner [ʃifɔne] vt to crumple, crease.
chiffonnier [ʃifɔnje] nm ragman, rag-and-bone man ; (meuble) chiffonier.
chiffre [ʃifʀ(ə)] nm (représentant un nombre) figure ; numeral ; (montant, total) total, sum ; (d'un code) code, cipher ; ~s **romains/arabes** roman/arabic figures ou numerals ; **en ~s ronds** in round figures ; **écrire un nombre en ~s** to write a number in figures ; ~ **d'affaires** turnover ; **chiffrer** vt (dépense) to put a figure to, assess ; (message) to (en)code, cipher.
chignole [ʃiɲɔl] nf drill.
chignon [ʃiɲɔ̃] nm chignon, bun.
Chili [ʃili] nm: **le ~** Chile ; **chilien, ne** a, nm/f Chilean.
chimère [ʃimɛʀ] nf (wild) dream, chimera ; pipe dream, idle fancy.
chimie [ʃimi] nf: **la ~** chemistry ; **chimique** a chemical ; **produits chimiques** chemicals ; **chimiste** nm/f chemist.
Chine [ʃin] nf: **la ~** China.
chiné, e [ʃine] a flecked.
chinois, e [ʃinwa, -waz] a Chinese ; (fig: péj) pernickety, fussy // nm/f Chinese // nm (langue): **le ~** Chinese.
chiot [ʃjo] nm pup(py).
chipoter [ʃipote] vi to nibble ; to quibble ; to haggle.
chips [ʃips] nfpl (aussi: **pommes ~**) crisps.
chique [ʃik] nf quid, chew.
chiquenaude [ʃiknod] nf flick, flip.
chiquer [ʃike] vi to chew tobacco.
chiromancien, ne [kiʀɔmɑ̃sjɛ̃, -ɛn] nm/f palmist.
chirurgical, e, aux [ʃiʀyʀʒikal, -o] a surgical.
chirurgie [ʃiʀyʀʒi] nf surgery ; ~ **esthétique** plastic surgery ; **chirurgien, ne** nm/f surgeon.
chiure [ʃjyʀ] nf: ~s **de mouche** fly specks.
chlore [klɔʀ] nm chlorine.
chloroforme [klɔʀɔfɔʀm(ə)] nm chloroform.
chlorophylle [klɔʀɔfil] nf chlorophyll.
choc [ʃɔk] nm impact ; shock ; crash ; (moral) shock ; (affrontement) clash ; **opératoire/nerveux** post-operative/(nervous) shock.
chocolat [ʃɔkɔla] nm chocolate ; (boisson) (hot) chocolate ; ~ **à croquer** plain chocolate ; ~ **au lait** milk chocolate.
chœur [kœʀ] nm (chorale) choir ; (OPÉRA, THÉÂTRE) chorus ; (ARCHIT) choir, chancel ; **en ~** in chorus.
choir [ʃwaʀ] vi to fall.
choisi, e [ʃwazi] a (de premier choix) carefully chosen ; select ; **textes ~s** selected writings.
choisir [ʃwaziʀ] vt to choose, select.
choix [ʃwa] nm choice ; selection ; **avoir le ~** to have the choice ; **premier ~** (COMM) class ou grade one ; **de ~** choice, selected ; **au ~** as you wish ou prefer.
choléra [kɔleʀa] nm cholera.
chômage [ʃomaʒ] nm unemployment ; **mettre au ~** to make redundant, put out of work ; **être au ~** to be unemployed ou

out of work ; ~ **partiel** short-time working ; ~ **technique** lay-offs pl; **chômer** vi to be unemployed, be idle ; **jour chômé** public holiday ; **chômeur, euse** nm/f unemployed person, person out of work.
chope [ʃɔp] nf tankard.
choquer [ʃɔke] vt (offenser) to shock ; (commotionner) to shake (up).
choral, e [kɔʀal] a choral // nf choral society, choir.
chorégraphe [kɔʀegʀaf] nm/f choreographer.
chorégraphie [kɔʀegʀafi] nf choreography.
choriste [kɔʀist(ə)] nm/f choir member ; (OPÉRA) chorus member.
chorus [kɔʀys] nm: **faire ~ (avec)** to voice one's agreement (with).
chose [ʃoz] nf thing ; **c'est peu de ~** it's nothing (really) ; it's not much.
chou, x [ʃu] nm cabbage // a inv cute ; **mon petit ~** (my) sweetheart ; ~ **à la crème** cream bun (made of choux pastry).
choucas [ʃuka] nm jackdaw.
chouchou, te [ʃuʃu, -ut] nm/f (SCOL) teacher's pet.
choucroute [ʃukʀut] nf sauerkraut.
chouette [ʃwɛt] nf owl // a (fam) great, smashing.
chou-fleur [ʃuflœʀ] nm cauliflower.
chou-rave [ʃuʀav] nm kohlrabi.
choyer [ʃwaje] vt to cherish ; to pamper.
chrétien, ne [kʀetjɛ̃, -ɛn] a, nm/f Christian ; **chrétiennement** ad in a Christian way ou spirit ; **chrétienté** nf Christendom.
Christ [kʀist] nm: **le ~** Christ ; **c~** (crucifix etc) figure of Christ ; **christianiser** vt to convert to Christianity ; **christianisme** nm Christianity.
chromatique [kʀɔmatik] a chromatic.
chrome [kʀom] nm chromium ; **chromé, e** a chromium-plated.
chromosome [kʀɔmozom] nm chromosome.
chronique [kʀɔnik] a chronic // nf (de journal) column, page ; (historique) chronicle ; (RADIO, TV): **la ~ sportive/théâtrale** the sports/theatre review ; **la ~ locale** local news and gossip ; **chroniqueur** nm columnist ; chronicler.
chronologie [kʀɔnɔlɔʒi] nf chronology ; **chronologique** a chronological.
chronomètre [kʀɔnɔmɛtʀ(ə)] nm stopwatch ; **chronométrer** vt to time.
chrysalide [kʀizalid] nf chrysalis.
chrysanthème [kʀizɑ̃tɛm] nm chrysanthemum.
chu, e [ʃy] pp de **choir**.
chuchoter [ʃyʃɔte] vt, vi to whisper.
chuinter [ʃɥɛte] vi to hiss.
chut [ʃyt] excl sh!
chute [ʃyt] nf fall ; (de bois, papier: déchet) scrap ; **la ~ des cheveux** hair loss ; **faire une ~ (de 10 m)** to fall (10 m) ; ~ **de pluie/neige** rain/snowfalls ; ~ **(d'eau)** waterfall ; ~ **libre** free fall.

Chypre [ʃipʀ] *n* Cyprus ; **chypriote** *a*, *nm/f* = **cypriote**.

-ci, ci- [si] *ad voir* **par, ci-contre, ci-joint** *etc* // *dét*: **ce garçon-ci/-là** this/that boy ; **ces femmes-ci/-là** these/those women.

ci-après [siapʀɛ] *ad* hereafter.

cible [sibl(ə)] *nf* target.

ciboire [sibwaʀ] *nm* ciborium (*vessel*).

ciboule [sibul] *nf* (large) chive ; **ciboulette** *nf* (smaller) chive.

cicatrice [sikatʀis] *nf* scar.

cicatriser [sikatʀize] *vt* to heal ; **se ~** to heal (up), form a scar.

ci-contre [sikɔ̃tʀ(ə)] *ad* opposite.

ci-dessous [sidəsu] *ad* below.

ci-dessus [sidəsy] *ad* above.

ci-devant [sidvɑ̃] *nm/f* aristocrat who lost his/her title in the French Revolution.

cidre [sidʀ(ə)] *nm* cider.

Cie *abr de* **compagnie.**

ciel [sjɛl] *nm* sky ; (*REL*) heaven ; **~s** *nmpl* (*PEINTURE etc*) skies ; **cieux** *nmpl* sky *sg*, skies ; (*REL*) heaven *sg* ; **à ~ ouvert** open-air ; (*mine*) opencast ; **~ de lit** canopy.

cierge [sjɛʀʒ(ə)] *nm* candle.

cigale [sigal] *nf* cicada.

cigare [sigaʀ] *nm* cigar.

cigarette [sigaʀɛt] *nf* cigarette.

ci-gît [siʒi] *ad* + *vb* here lies.

cigogne [sigɔɲ] *nf* stork.

ciguë [sigy] *nf* hemlock.

ci-inclus, e [siɛ̃kly, -yz] *a, ad* enclosed.

ci-joint, e [siʒwɛ̃, -ɛt] *a, ad* enclosed.

cil [sil] *nm* (eye)lash.

ciller [sije] *vi* to blink.

cimaise [simɛz] *nf* picture rail.

cime [sim] *nf* top ; (*montagne*) peak.

ciment [simɑ̃] *nm* cement ; **~ armé** reinforced concrete ; **cimenter** *vt* to cement ; **cimenterie** *nf* cement works *sg*.

cimetière [simtjɛʀ] *nm* cemetery ; (*d'église*) churchyard ; **~ de voitures** scrapyard.

cinéaste [sineast(ə)] *nm/f* film-maker.

ciné-club [sineklœb] *nm* film club ; film society.

cinéma [sinema] *nm* cinema ; **~scope** *nm* cinemascope ; **~thèque** *nf* film archives *pl ou* library ; **~tographique** *a* film *cpd*, cinema *cpd*.

cinéphile [sinefil] *nm/f* film *ou* cinema enthusiast.

cinétique [sinetik] *a* kinetic.

cinglé, e [sɛ̃gle] *a* (*fam*) barmy.

cingler [sɛ̃gle] *vt* to lash ; (*fig*) to sting // *vi* (*NAVIG*): **~ vers** to make *ou* head for.

cinq [sɛ̃k] *num* five.

cinquantaine [sɛ̃kɑ̃ten] *nf*: **une ~** (de) about fifty.

cinquante [sɛ̃kɑ̃t] *num* fifty ; **~naire** *a, nm/f* fifty-year-old ; **cinquantième** *num* fiftieth.

cinquième [sɛ̃kjɛm] *num* fifth.

cintre [sɛ̃tʀ(ə)] *nm* coat-hanger ; (*ARCHIT*) arch ; **~s** *nmpl* (*THÉÂTRE*) flies.

cintré, e [sɛ̃tʀe] *a* curved ; (*chemise*) fitted, slim-fitting.

cirage [siʀaʒ] *nm* (shoe) polish.

circoncision [siʀkɔ̃sizjɔ̃] *nf* circumcision.

circonférence [siʀkɔ̃feʀɑ̃s] *nf* circumference.

circonflexe [siʀkɔ̃flɛks(ə)] *a*: **accent ~** circumflex accent.

circonscription [siʀkɔ̃skʀipsjɔ̃] *nf* district ; **~ électorale** (*d'un député*) constituency.

circonscrire [siʀkɔ̃skʀiʀ] *vt* to define, delimit ; (*incendie*) to contain.

circonspect, e [siʀkɔ̃spɛkt] *a* circumspect, cautious.

circonstance [siʀkɔ̃stɑ̃s] *nf* circumstance ; (*occasion*) occasion ; **~s atténuantes** attenuating circumstances.

circonstancié, e [siʀkɔ̃stɑ̃sje] *a* detailed.

circonstanciel, le [siʀkɔ̃stɑ̃sjɛl] *a*: **complément/proposition ~(le)** adverbial phrase/clause.

circonvenir [siʀkɔ̃vniʀ] *vt* to circumvent.

circonvolutions [siʀkɔ̃vɔlysjɔ̃] *nfpl* twists, convolutions.

circuit [siʀkɥi] *nm* (*trajet*) tour, (round) trip ; (*ÉLEC, TECH*) circuit ; **~ automobile** motor circuit ; **~ de distribution** distribution network.

circulaire [siʀkylɛʀ] *a, nf* circular.

circulation [siʀkylɑsjɔ̃] *nf* circulation ; (*AUTO*): **la ~** (the) traffic ; **mettre en ~** to put into circulation.

circuler [siʀkyle] *vi* to drive (along) ; to walk along ; (*train etc*) to run ; (*sang, devises*) to circulate ; **faire ~** (*nouvelle*) to spread (about), circulate ; (*badauds*) to move on.

cire [siʀ] *nf* wax.

ciré [siʀe] *nm* oilskin.

cirer [siʀe] *vt* to wax, polish ; **cireur** *nm* shoeshine-boy ; **cireuse** *nf* floor polisher.

cirque [siʀk(ə)] *nm* circus ; (*arène*) amphitheatre ; (*GÉO*) cirque ; (*fig*) chaos, bedlam ; carry-on.

cirrhose [siʀoz] *nf*: **~ du foie** cirrhosis of the liver.

cisaille(s) [sizaj] *nf(pl)* (gardening) shears *pl* ; **cisailler** *vt* to clip.

ciseau, x [sizo] *nm*: **~ (à bois)** chisel ; // *nmpl* (pair of) scissors ; **sauter en ~x** to do a scissors jump ; **~ à froid** cold chisel.

ciseler [sizle] *vt* to chisel, carve.

citadelle [sitadɛl] *nf* citadel.

citadin, e [sitadɛ̃, -in] *nm/f* city dweller // *a* town *cpd*, city *cpd*, urban.

citation [sitɑsjɔ̃] *nf* (*d'auteur*) quotation ; (*JUR*) summons *sg* ; (*MIL*: *récompense*) mention.

cité [site] *nf* town ; (*plus grande*) city ; **~ ouvrière** (workers') housing estate ; **~ universitaire** students' residences *pl*.

citer [site] *vt* (*un auteur*) to quote (from) ; (*nommer*) to name ; (*JUR*) to summon.

citerne [sitɛʀn(ə)] *nf* tank.

cithare [sitaʀ] *nf* zither.

citoyen, ne [sitwajɛ̃, -ɛn] *nm/f* citizen ; **citoyenneté** *nf* citizenship.

citron [sitʀɔ̃] *nm* lemon ; **~ vert** lime ; **citronnade** *nf* lemonade ; **citronnier** *nm* lemon tree.

citrouille [sitʀuj] *nf* pumpkin.

civet [sivɛ] *nm* stew ; **~ de lièvre** jugged hare.

civette [sivɛt] nf (BOT) chives pl; (ZOOL) civet (cat).

civière [sivjɛR] nf stretcher.

civil, e [sivil] a (JUR, ADMIN, poli) civil; (non militaire) civilian // nm civilian; **en ~** in civilian clothes; **dans le ~** in civilian life.

civilisation [sivilizɑsjɔ̃] nf civilization.

civiliser [sivilize] vt to civilize.

civique [sivik] a civic.

civisme [sivism(ə)] nm public-spiritedness.

claie [klɛ] nf grid, riddle.

clair, e [klɛR] a light; (chambre) light, bright; (eau, son, fig) clear // ad: **voir ~** to see clearly; **bleu ~** light blue; **tirer qch au ~** to clear sth up, clarify sth; **mettre au ~** (notes etc) to tidy up; **le plus ~ de son temps/argent** the better part of his time/money; **en ~** (non codé) in clear; **~ de lune** moonlight; **~ement** ad clearly.

claire-voie [klɛRvwa]: **à ~** ad letting the light through; openwork cpd.

clairière [klɛRjɛR] nf clearing.

clairon [klɛRɔ̃] nm bugle; **claironner** vt (fig) to trumpet, shout from the rooftops.

clairsemé, e [klɛRsəme] a sparse.

clairvoyant, e [klɛRvwajɑ̃, -ɑ̃t] a perceptive, clear-sighted.

clameur [klamœR] nf clamour.

clandestin, e [klɑ̃dɛstɛ̃, -in] a clandestine; (POL) underground, clandestine.

clapier [klapje] nm (rabbit) hutch.

clapoter [klapɔte] vi to lap; **clapotis** nm lap(ping).

claquage [klakaʒ] nm pulled ou strained muscle.

claque [klak] nf (gifle) slap.

claquer [klake] vi (drapeau) to flap; (porte) to bang, slam; (coup de feu) to ring out // vt (porte) to slam, bang; (doigts) to snap; **se ~ un muscle** to pull ou strain a muscle.

claquettes [klakɛt] nfpl tap-dancing sg.

clarifier [klaRifje] vt (gifle) to clarify.

clarinette [klaRinɛt] nf clarinet.

clarté [klaRte] nf lightness; brightness; (d'un son, de l'eau) clearness; (d'une explication) clarity.

classe [klɑs] nf class; (SCOL: local) class(room); (: leçon) class; (: élèves) class, form; **~ touriste** economy class; **faire ses ~s** (MIL) to do one's (recruit's) training; **faire la ~** (SCOL) to be ou the teacher; to teach; **aller en ~** to go to school.

classement [klɑsmɑ̃] nm classifying; filing; grading; closing; (rang: SCOL) place; (: SPORT) placing; (liste: SCOL) class list (in order of merit); (: SPORT) placings pl; **premier au ~ général** (SPORT) first overall.

classer [klɑse] vt (idées, livres) to classify; (papiers) to file; (candidat, concurrent) to grade; (JUR: affaire) to close; **se ~ premier/dernier** to come first/last; (SPORT) to finish first/last.

classeur [klɑsœR] nm (cahier) file; (meuble) filing cabinet.

classification [klasifikɑsjɔ̃] nf classification.

classifier [klɑsifje] vt to classify.

classique [klɑsik] a classical; (sobre: coupe etc) classic(al); (habituel) standard, classic // nm classic; classical author.

claudication [klodikɑsjɔ̃] nf limp.

clause [kloz] nf clause.

claustrer [klostRe] vt to confine.

claustrophobie [klostRɔfɔbi] nf claustrophobia.

clavecin [klavsɛ̃] nm harpsichord.

clavicule [klavikyl] nf clavicle, collarbone.

clavier [klavje] nm keyboard.

clé ou **clef** [kle] nf key; (MUS) clef; (de mécanicien) spanner // a: **problème ~** key problem; **~ de sol/de la** treble/bass clef; **~ anglaise** (monkey) wrench; **~ de contact** ignition key; **~ à molette** adjustable spanner; **~ de voûte** keystone.

clémence [klemɑ̃s] nf mildness; leniency.

clément, e [klemɑ̃, -ɑ̃t] a (temps) mild; (indulgent) lenient.

cleptomane [klɛptɔman] nm/f = **kleptomane**.

clerc [klɛR] nm: **~ de notaire** solicitor's clerk.

clergé [klɛRʒe] nm clergy.

clérical, e, aux [kleRikal, -o] a clerical.

cliché [kliʃe] nm (PHOTO) negative; print; (TYPO) (printing) plate; (LING) cliché.

client, e [klijɑ̃, -ɑ̃t] nm/f (acheteur) customer, client; (d'hôtel) guest, patron; (du docteur) patient; (de l'avocat) client; **clientèle** nf (du magasin) customers pl, clientèle; (du docteur, de l'avocat) practice; **accorder sa clientèle à** to give one's custom to.

cligner [kliɲe] vi: **~ des yeux** to blink (one's eyes); **~ de l'œil** to wink.

clignotant [kliɲɔtɑ̃] nm (AUTO) indicator.

clignoter [kliɲɔte] vi (étoiles etc) to twinkle; (lumière: à intervalles réguliers) to flash; (: vaciller) to flicker.

climat [klima] nm climate; **climatique** a climatic.

climatisation [klimatizɑsjɔ̃] nf air conditioning; **climatisé, e** a air-conditioned.

clin d'œil [klɛ̃dœj] nm wink; **en un ~** in a flash.

clinique [klinik] a clinical // nf nursing home, (private) clinic.

clinquant, e [klɛ̃kɑ̃, -ɑ̃t] a flashy.

cliqueter [klikte] vi to clash; to jangle, jingle; to chink.

clitoris [klitɔRis] nm clitoris.

clivage [klivaʒ] nm cleavage.

clochard, e [klɔʃaR, -aRd(ə)] nm/f tramp.

cloche [klɔʃ] nf (d'église) bell; (fam) clot; **~ à fromage** cheese-cover.

cloche-pied [klɔʃpje]: **à ~** ad on one leg, hopping (along).

clocher [klɔʃe] nm church tower; (en pointe) steeple // vi (fam) to be ou go wrong; **de ~** (péj) parochial.

clocheton [klɔʃtɔ̃] nm pinnacle.

clochette [klɔʃɛt] nf bell.

cloison [klwazɔ̃] nf partition (wall); **cloisonner** vt to partition (off); to divide up; (fig) to compartmentalize.

cloître [klwatʀ(ə)] nm cloister.
cloîtrer [klwatʀe] vt: **se ~** to shut o.s. up ou away; (REL) to enter a convent ou monastery.
clopin-clopant [klɔpɛ̃klɔpɑ̃] ad hobbling along; (fig) so-so.
cloporte [klɔpɔʀt(ə)] nm woodlouse (pl lice).
cloque [klɔk] nf blister.
clore [klɔʀ] vt to close; **clos, e** a voir **maison, huis, vase** // nm (enclosed) field.
clôture [klotyʀ] nf closure, closing; (barrière) enclosure, fence; **clôturer** vt (terrain) to enclose, close off; (festival, débats) to close.
clou [klu] nm nail; (MÉD) boil; **~s** nmpl = **passage clouté**; **pneus à ~s** studded tyres; **le ~ du spectacle** the highlight of the show; **~ de girofle** clove; **~er** vt to nail down ou up; (fig): **~er sur/contre** to pin to/against; **~té, e** a studded.
clown [klun] nm clown; **faire le ~** (fig) to clown (about), play the fool.
club [klœb] nm club.
C.N.R.S. sigle m = Centre national de la recherche scientifique.
coaguler [kɔagyle] vi, vt, **se ~** to coagulate.
coaliser [kɔalize]: **se ~** vi to unite, join forces.
coalition [kɔalisjɔ̃] nf coalition.
coasser [kɔase] vi to croak.
cobaye [kɔbaj] nm guinea-pig.
cocagne [kɔkaɲ] nf: **pays de ~** land of plenty; **mât de ~** greasy pole (fig).
cocaïne [kɔkain] nf cocaine.
cocarde [kɔkaʀd(ə)] nf rosette.
cocardier, ère [kɔkaʀdje, -ɛʀ] a jingoistic, chauvinistic.
cocasse [kɔkas] a comical, funny.
coccinelle [kɔksinɛl] nf ladybird.
coccyx [kɔksis] nm coccyx.
cocher [kɔʃe] nm coachman // vt to tick off; (entailler) to notch.
cochère [kɔʃɛʀ] af: **porte ~** carriage entrance.
cochon, ne [kɔʃɔ̃, -ɔn] nm pig // nm/f (péj) (filthy) pig; beast; swine // a (fam) dirty, smutty; **cochonnerie** nf (fam) filth; rubbish, trash.
cochonnet [kɔʃɔnɛ] nm (BOULES) jack.
cocktail [kɔktɛl] nm cocktail; (réception) cocktail party.
coco [kɔko] nm voir **noix**; (fam) bloke, geezer.
cocon [kɔkɔ̃] nm cocoon.
cocorico [kɔkɔʀiko] excl, nm cock-a-doodle-do.
cocotier [kɔkɔtje] nm coconut palm.
cocotte [kɔkɔt] nf (en fonte) casserole; **~ (minute)** pressure cooker; **~ en papier** paper shape; **ma ~** (fam) sweetie (pie).
cocu [kɔky] nm cuckold.
code [kɔd] nm code // a: **éclairage ~, phares ~s** dipped lights; **se mettre en ~(s)** to dip one's (head)lights; **~ civil** Common Law; **~ pénal** penal code; **~ postal** (numéro) postal code; **~ de la route** highway code; **coder** vt to (en)code; **codifier** vt to codify.

coefficient [kɔefisjɑ̃] nm coefficient.
coercition [kɔɛʀsisjɔ̃] nf coercion.
cœur [kœʀ] nm heart; (CARTES: couleur) hearts pl; (: carte) heart; **avoir bon ~** to be kind-hearted; **avoir mal au ~** to feel sick; **~ de laitue/d'artichaut** lettuce/artichoke heart; **de tout son ~** with all one's heart; **en avoir le ~ net** to be clear in one's own mind (about it); **par ~** by heart; **de bon ~** willingly; **avoir à ~ de faire** to make a point of doing; **cela lui tient à ~** that's (very) close to his heart.
coffrage [kɔfʀaʒ] nm (CONSTR: action) coffering; (: dispositif) form(work).
coffre [kɔfʀ(ə)] nm (meuble) chest; (d'auto) boot; **avoir du ~** (fam) to have a lot of puff; **~(-fort)** nm safe.
coffrer [kɔfʀe] vt (fam) to put inside, lock up.
coffret [kɔfʀɛ] nm casket; **~ à bijoux** jewel box.
cogner [kɔɲe] vi to knock.
cohabiter [kɔabite] vi to live together.
cohérent, e [kɔeʀɑ̃, -ɑ̃t] a coherent, consistent.
cohésion [kɔezjɔ̃] nf cohesion.
cohorte [kɔɔʀt(ə)] nf troop.
cohue [kɔy] nf crowd.
coi, coite [kwa, kwat] a: **rester ~** to remain silent.
coiffe [kwaf] nf headdress.
coiffé, e [kwafe] a: **bien/mal ~** with tidy/untidy hair; **~ d'un béret** wearing a beret; **~ en arrière** with one's hair brushed ou combed back.
coiffer [kwafe] vt (fig) to cover, top; **~ qn** to do sb's hair; **~ qn d'un béret** to put a beret on sb; **se ~** to do one's hair; to put on a ou one's hat.
coiffeur, euse [kwafœʀ, -øz] nm/f hairdresser // nf (table) dressing table.
coiffure [kwafyʀ] nf (cheveux) hairstyle, hairdo; (chapeau) hat, headgear q; (art): **la ~** hairdressing.
coin [kwɛ̃] nm corner; (pour graver) die; (pour coincer) wedge; (poinçon) hallmark; **l'épicerie du ~** the local grocer; **dans le ~** (les alentours) in the area, around about; locally; **au ~ du feu** by the fireside; **regard en ~** side(ways) glance.
coincer [kwɛ̃se] vt to jam; (fam) to catch (out); to nab.
coïncidence [kɔɛ̃sidɑ̃s] nf coincidence.
coïncider [kɔɛ̃side] vi: **~ (avec)** to coincide (with).
coing [kwɛ̃] nm quince.
coït [kɔit] nm coitus.
coite [kwat] af voir **coi**.
coke [kɔk] nm coke.
col [kɔl] nm (de chemise) collar; (encolure, cou) neck; (de montagne) pass; **~ du fémur** neck of the thighbone; **~ roulé** polo-neck; **~ de l'utérus** cervix.
coléoptère [kɔleɔptɛʀ] nm beetle.
colère [kɔlɛʀ] nf anger; **une ~** a fit of anger; **coléreux, euse** a, **colérique** a quick-tempered, irascible.
colifichet [kɔlifiʃɛ] nm trinket.
colimaçon [kɔlimasɔ̃] nm: **escalier en ~** spiral staircase.

colin [kɔlɛ̃] nm hake.
colique [kɔlik] nf diarrhoea ; colic (pains).
colis [kɔli] nm parcel.
collaborateur, trice [kɔlabɔRatœR, -tRis] nm/f (aussi POL) collaborator ; (d'une revue) contributor.
collaboration [kɔlabɔRɑsjɔ̃] nf collaboration.
collaborer [kɔlabɔRe] vi to collaborate ; ~ à to collaborate on ; (revue) to contribute to.
collant, e [kɔlɑ̃, -ɑ̃t] a sticky ; (robe etc) clinging, skintight ; (péj) clinging // nm (bas) tights pl ; (de danseur) leotard.
collation [kɔlɑsjɔ̃] nf light meal.
colle [kɔl] nf glue ; (à papiers peints) (wallpaper) paste ; (devinette) teaser, poser.
collecte [kɔlɛkt(ə)] nf collection.
collecter [kɔlɛkte] vt to collect ; **collecteur** nm (égout) main sewer.
collectif, ive [kɔlɛktif, -iv] a collective ; (visite, billet etc) group cpd.
collection [kɔlɛksjɔ̃] nf collection ; (ÉDITION) series ; **pièce de** ~ collector's item ; **faire (la)** ~ **de** to collect ; **collectionner** vt (tableaux, timbres) to collect ; **collectionneur, euse** nm/f collector.
collectivité [kɔlɛktivite] nf group ; **la** ~ the community, the collectivity ; **les** ~**s locales** local communities.
collège [kɔlɛʒ] nm (école) (secondary) school ; (assemblée) body ; **collégial, e, aux** a collegiate ; **collégien, ne** nm/f schoolboy/girl.
collègue [kɔlɛg] nm/f colleague.
coller [kɔle] vt (papier, timbre) to stick (on) ; (affiche) to stick up ; (enveloppe) to stick down ; (morceaux) to stick ou glue together ; (fam: mettre, fourrer) to stick, shove ; (SCOL: fam) to keep in, give detention to // vi (être collant) to be sticky ; (adhérer) to stick ; ~ **qch sur** to stick (ou paste ou glue) sth on(to) ; ~ **à** to stick to ; (fig) to cling to.
collerette [kɔlRɛt] nf ruff ; (TECH) flange.
collet [kɔlɛ] nm (piège) snare, noose ; (cou): **prendre qn au** ~ to grab sb by the throat ; ~ **monté a** inv straight-laced.
collier [kɔlje] nm (bijou) necklace ; (de chien, TECH) collar ; ~ **(de barbe), barbe en** ~ narrow beard along the line of the jaw.
colline [kɔlin] nf hill.
collision [kɔlizjɔ̃] nf collision, crash ; **entrer en** ~ **(avec)** to collide (with).
colloque [kɔlɔk] nm colloquium, symposium.
colmater [kɔlmate] vt (fuite) to seal off ; (brèche) to plug, fill in.
colombe [kɔlɔ̃b] nf dove.
colon [kɔlɔ̃] nm settler ; (enfant) boarder (in children's holiday camp).
côlon [kolɔ̃] nm colon.
colonel [kɔlɔnɛl] nm colonel ; (armée de l'air) group captain.
colonial, e, aux [kɔlɔnjal, -o] a colonial ; ~**isme** nm colonialism.
colonie [kɔlɔni] nf colony ; ~ **(de vacances)** holiday camp (for children).

colonisation [kɔlɔnizɑsjɔ̃] nf colonization.
coloniser [kɔlɔnize] vt to colonize.
colonne [kɔlɔn] nf column ; **se mettre en** ~ **par deux/quatre** to get into twos/fours ; **en** ~ **par deux** in double file ; ~ **de secours** rescue party ; ~ **(vertébrale)** spine, spinal column.
colophane [kɔlɔfan] nf rosin.
colorant [kɔlɔRɑ̃] nm colouring.
coloration [kɔlɔRɑsjɔ̃] nf colour(ing).
colorer [kɔlɔRe] vt to colour.
colorier [kɔlɔRje] vt to colour (in) ; **album à** ~ colouring book.
coloris [kɔlɔRi] nm colour, shade.
colossal, e, aux [kɔlɔsal, -o] a colossal, huge.
colporter [kɔlpɔRte] vt to hawk, peddle ; **colporteur, euse** nm/f hawker, pedlar.
colza [kɔlza] nm rape(seed).
coma [kɔma] nm coma ; **être dans le** ~ to be in a coma ; ~**teux, euse** a comatose.
combat [kɔ̃ba] nm fight ; fighting q ; ~ **de boxe** boxing match ; ~ **de rues** street fighting q.
combatif, ive [kɔ̃batif, -iv] a of a fighting spirit.
combattant [kɔ̃batɑ̃] nm combatant ; (d'une rixe) brawler ; **ancien** ~ war veteran.
combattre [kɔ̃batR(ə)] vt to fight ; (épidémie, ignorance) to combat, fight against.
combien [kɔ̃bjɛ̃] ad (quantité) how much ; (nombre) how many ; (exclamatif) how ; ~ **de much ; how many ; ~ de temps** how long, how much time ; ~ **coûte/pèse ceci?** how much does this cost/weigh?
combinaison [kɔ̃binɛzɔ̃] nf combination ; (astuce) device, scheme ; (de femme) slip ; (d'aviateur) flying suit ; (d'homme-grenouille) wetsuit ; (bleu de travail) boilersuit.
combine [kɔ̃bin] nf trick ; (péj) scheme, fiddle.
combiné [kɔ̃bine] nm (aussi: téléphonique) receiver.
combiner [kɔ̃bine] vt to combine ; (plan, horaire) to work out, devise.
comble [kɔ̃bl(ə)] a (salle) packed (full) // nm (du bonheur, plaisir) height ; ~**s** nmpl (CONSTR) attic sg, loft sg ; **c'est le** ~ **!** that beats everything!, that takes the biscuit!
combler [kɔ̃ble] vt (trou) to fill in ; (besoin, lacune) to fill ; (déficit) to make good ; (satisfaire) to gratify, fulfil ; ~ **qn de joie** to fill sb with joy ; ~ **qn d'honneurs** to shower sb with honours.
combustible [kɔ̃bystibl(ə)] a combustible // nm fuel.
combustion [kɔ̃bystjɔ̃] nf combustion.
comédie [kɔmedi] nf comedy ; (fig) playacting q ; ~ **musicale** musical ; **comédien, ne** nm/f actor/actress ; (comique) comedy actor/actress, comedian/comedienne ; (fig) sham.
comestible [kɔmɛstibl(ə)] a edible.
comète [kɔmɛt] nf comet.
comique [kɔmik] a (drôle) comical ; (THÉÂTRE) comic // nm (artiste) comic,

comedian ; **le ~ de qch** the funny *ou* comical side of sth.
comité [kɔmite] *nm* committee ; **~ d'entreprise** work's council.
commandant [kɔmɑ̃dɑ̃] *nm* (*gén*) commander, commandant ; (*MIL: grade*) major ; (*armée de l'air*) squadron leader ; (*NAVIG, AVIAT*) captain.
commande [kɔmɑ̃d] *nf* (*COMM*) order ; **~s** *nfpl* (*AVIAT etc*) controls ; **passer une ~ (de)** to put in an order (for) ; **sur ~** to order ; **~ à distance** remote control.
commandement [kɔmɑ̃dmɑ̃] *nm* command ; (*ordre*) command, order ; (*REL*) commandment.
commander [kɔmɑ̃de] *vt* (*COMM*) to order ; (*diriger, ordonner*) to command ; **~ à** (*MIL*) to command ; (*contrôler, maîtriser*) to have control over ; **~ à qn de faire** to command *ou* order sb to do.
commanditaire [kɔmɑ̃ditɛʀ] *nm* sleeping partner.
commandite [kɔmɑ̃dit] *nf*: (**société en**) **~** limited partnership.
commando [kɔmɑ̃do] *nm* commando (squad).
comme [kɔm] *prép* like ; (*en tant que*) as // *cj* as ; (*parce que, puisque*) as, since // *ad*: **~ il est fort/c'est bon!** how strong he is/good it is! ; **faites-le ~ cela** *ou* **ça** do it like this *ou* this way ; **~ ci ~ ça** so-so, middling ; **joli ~ tout** ever so pretty.
commémoration [kɔmemɔʀɑsjɔ̃] *nf* commemoration.
commémorer [kɔmemɔʀe] *vt* to commemorate.
commencement [kɔmɑ̃smɑ̃] *nm* beginning ; start ; commencement ; **~s** (*débuts*) beginnings.
commencer [kɔmɑ̃se] *vt* to begin, start, commence ; (*être placé au début de*) to begin // *vi* to begin, start, commence ; **~ à** *ou* **de faire** to begin *ou* start doing.
commensal, e, aux [kɔmɑ̃sal, -o] *nm/f* companion at table.
comment [kɔmɑ̃] *ad* how ; **~?** (*que dites-vous*) (I beg your) pardon?
commentaire [kɔmɑ̃tɛʀ] *nm* comment ; remark ; **~ (de texte)** (*SCOL*) commentary.
commentateur, trice [kɔmɑ̃tatœʀ, -tʀis] *nm/f* commentator.
commenter [kɔmɑ̃te] *vt* (*jugement, événement*) to comment (up)on ; (*RADIO, TV: match, manifestation*) to cover, give a commentary on.
commérages [kɔmeʀaʒ] *nmpl* gossip *sg*.
commerçant, e [kɔmɛʀsɑ̃, -ɑ̃t] *a* commercial ; shopping ; trading ; commercially shrewd // *nm/f* shopkeeper, trader.
commerce [kɔmɛʀs(ə)] *nm* (*activité*) trade, commerce ; (*boutique*) business ; **le petit ~** small shopowners *pl*, small traders *pl* ; **faire ~ de** to trade in ; (*fig: péj*) to trade on ; **vendu dans le ~** sold in the shops ; **vendu hors-~** sold directly to the public ; **commercial, e, aux** *a* commercial, trading ; (*péj*) commercial ; **commercialiser** *vt* to market.
commère [kɔmɛʀ] *nf* gossip.
commettre [kɔmɛtʀ(ə)] *vt* to commit.

commis [kɔmi] *nm* (*de magasin*) (shop) assistant ; (*de banque*) clerk ; **~ voyageur** commercial traveller.
commisération [kɔmizeʀɑsjɔ̃] *nf* commiseration.
commissaire [kɔmisɛʀ] *nm* (*de police*) ≈ (police) superintendent ; (*de rencontre sportive etc*) steward ; **~-priseur** *nm* auctioneer.
commissariat [kɔmisaʀja] *nm* police station ; (*ADMIN*) commissionership.
commission [kɔmisjɔ̃] *nf* (*comité, pourcentage*) commission ; (*message*) message ; (*course*) errand ; **~s** *nfpl* (*achats*) shopping *sg* ; **commissionnaire** *nm* delivery boy (*ou* man) ; messenger.
commissure [kɔmisyʀ] *nf*: **les ~s des lèvres** the corners of the mouth.
commode [kɔmɔd] *a* (*pratique*) convenient, handy ; (*facile*) easy ; (*air, personne*) easy-going ; (*personne*): **pas ~** awkward (to deal with) // *nf* chest of drawers ; **commodité** *nf* convenience.
commotion [kɔmosjɔ̃] *nf*: **~ (cérébrale)** concussion ; **commotionné, e** *a* shocked, shaken.
commuer [kɔmɥe] *vt* to commute.
commun, e [kɔmœ̃, -yn] *a* common ; (*pièce*) communal, shared ; (*réunion, effort*) joint // *nf* (*ADMIN*) commune, ≈ district ; (*: urbaine*) ≈ borough ; **~s** *nmpl* (*bâtiments*) outbuildings ; **cela sort du ~** it's out of the ordinary ; **le ~ des mortels** the common run of people ; **en ~** (*faire*) jointly ; **mettre en ~** to pool, share ; **communal, e, aux** *a* (*ADMIN*) of the commune, ≈ (district *ou* borough) council *cpd*.
communauté [kɔmynote] *nf* community ; (*JUR*): **régime de la ~** communal estate settlement.
commune [kɔmyn] *a, nf voir* **commun**.
communiant, e [kɔmynjɑ̃, -ɑ̃t] *nm/f* communicant ; **premier ~** child taking his first communion.
communicatif, ive [kɔmynikatif, -iv] *a* (*personne*) communicative ; (*rire*) infectious.
communication [kɔmynikɑsjɔ̃] *nf* communication ; **~ (téléphonique)** (telephone) call ; **vous avez la ~** this is your call, you're through ; **donnez-moi la ~ avec** put me through to ; **~ interurbaine** trunk call ; **~ en PCV** reverse charge call.
communier [kɔmynje] *vi* (*REL*) to receive communion ; (*fig*) to be united.
communion [kɔmynjɔ̃] *nf* communion.
communiqué [kɔmynike] *nm* communiqué.
communiquer [kɔmynike] *vt* (*nouvelle, dossier*) to pass on, convey ; (*maladie*) to pass on ; (*peur etc*) to communicate ; (*chaleur, mouvement*) to transmit // *vi* to communicate ; **se ~ à** (*se propager*) to spread to.
communisme [kɔmynism(ə)] *nm* communism ; **communiste** *a, nm/f* communist.
commutateur [kɔmytatœʀ] *nm* (*ÉLEC*) (change-over) switch, commutator.

compact, e [kɔ̃pakt] *a* dense ; compact.
compagne [kɔ̃paɲ] *nf* companion.
compagnie [kɔ̃paɲi] *nf* (*firme*, MIL)
company ; (*groupe*) gathering ; (*présence*):
la ~ de qn sb's company ; **tenir ~ à qn**
to keep sb company ; **fausser ~ à qn** to give
sb the slip, slip ou sneak away from sb ;
en ~ de in the company of ; **Dupont et
~, Dupont et Cie** Dupont and Company,
Dupont and Co.
compagnon [kɔ̃paɲɔ̃] *nm* companion ;
(*autrefois: ouvrier*) craftsman ; journeyman.
comparable [kɔ̃paRabl(ə)] *a*: **~ (à)**
comparable (to).
comparaison [kɔ̃paRɛzɔ̃] *nf* comparison ;
(*métaphore*) simile.
comparaître [kɔ̃paRɛtR(ə)] *vi*: **~
(devant)** to appear (before).
comparatif, ive [kɔ̃paRatif, -iv] *a*
comparative.
comparé, e [kɔ̃paRe] *a*: **littérature** *etc*
~e comparative literature *etc*.
comparer [kɔ̃paRe] *vt* to compare ; **~
qch/qn à** *a* ou **et** (*pour choisir*) to compare
sth/sb with ou and ; (*pour établir une
similitude*) to compare sth/sb to.
comparse [kɔ̃paRs(ə)] *nm/f* (*péj*)
associate, stooge.
compartiment [kɔ̃paRtimɑ̃] *nm*
compartment ; **compartimenté, e** *a*
partitioned ; (*fig*) compartmentalized.
comparution [kɔ̃paRysjɔ̃] *nf* appearance.
compas [kɔ̃pa] *nm* (GÉOM) (pair of)
compasses *pl* ; (NAVIG) compass.
compassé, e [kɔ̃pɑse] *a* starchy, formal.
compassion [kɔ̃pasjɔ̃] *nf* compassion.
compatible [kɔ̃patibl(ə)] *a* compatible.
compatir [kɔ̃patiR] *vi*: **~ (à)** to
sympathize (with).
compatriote [kɔ̃patRijɔt] *nm/f*
compatriot.
compensation [kɔ̃pɑ̃sɑsjɔ̃] *nf*
compensation ; (BANQUE) clearing.
compenser [kɔ̃pɑ̃se] *vt* to compensate
for, make up for.
compère [kɔ̃pɛR] *nm* accomplice.
compétence [kɔ̃petɑ̃s] *nf* competence.
compétent, e [kɔ̃petɑ̃, -ɑ̃t] *a* (*apte*)
competent, capable ; (JUR) competent.
compétition [kɔ̃petisjɔ̃] *nf* (*gén*)
competition ; (SPORT: *épreuve*) event ; **la ~**
competitive sport ; **la ~ automobile**
motor racing.
compiler [kɔ̃pile] *vt* to compile.
complainte [kɔ̃plɛ̃t] *nf* lament.
complaire [kɔ̃plɛR]: **se ~** *vi*: **se ~
dans/parmi** to take pleasure in being
among.
complaisance [kɔ̃plɛzɑ̃s] *nf* kindness ;
(*péj*) indulgence ; **attestation de ~**
certificate produced to oblige a patient etc ;
pavillon de ~ flag of convenience.
complaisant, e [kɔ̃plɛzɑ̃, -ɑ̃t] *a* (*aimable*)
kind, obliging ; (*péj*) over-obliging,
indulgent.
complément [kɔ̃plemɑ̃] *nm* complement ;
supplement ; **~** remainder ; (LING)
complement ; **~ d'information** (ADMIN)
supplementary ou further information ; **~
d'agent** agent ; **~** (**d'objet**)
direct/indirect direct/indirect object ; **~**

(circonstanciel) de lieu/temps adverbial
phrase of place/time ; **~ de nom**
possessive phrase ; **complémentaire** *a*
complementary ; (*additionnel*)
supplementary.
complet, ète [kɔ̃plɛ, -ɛt] *a* complete ;
(*plein: hôtel etc*) full // *nm* (*aussi*: **~-
veston**) suit ; **compléter** *vt* (*porter à la
quantité voulue*) to complete ; (*augmenter*)
to complement, supplement ; to add to ; **se
compléter** *vt réciproque* (*personnes*) to
complement one another // *vi* (*collection
etc*) to be building up.
complexe [kɔ̃plɛks(ə)] *a* complex // *nm*
(PSYCH) complex, hang-up ; (*bâtiments*): **~
hospitalier** hospital complex ; **complexé,
e** *a* mixed-up, hung-up ; **complexité** *nf*
complexity.
complication [kɔ̃plikɑsjɔ̃] *nf* complexity,
intricacy ; (*difficulté, ennui*) complication.
complice [kɔ̃plis] *nm* accomplice ;
complicité *nf* complicity.
compliment [kɔ̃plimɑ̃] *nm* (*louange*) compliment ; **~s** *nmpl* (*félicitations*) congratulations ; **complimenter qn (sur** ou **de)** to
congratulate ou compliment sb (on).
compliqué, e [kɔ̃plike] *a* complicated,
complex, intricate ; (*personne*) complicated.
compliquer [kɔ̃plike] *vt* to complicate ; **se
~** *vi* (*situation*) to become complicated ; **se
~ la vie** to make life difficult ou complicated for o.s.
complot [kɔ̃plo] *nm* plot ; **comploter** *vi*,
vt to plot.
comportement [kɔ̃pɔRtəmɑ̃] *nm* behaviour ; (TECH: *d'une pièce, d'un véhicule*)
behaviour, performance.
comporter [kɔ̃pɔRte] *vt* to be composed
of, consist of, comprise ; (*être équipé de*)
to have ; (*impliquer*) to entail, involve ; **se
~** *vi* to behave ; (TECH) to behave, perform.
composant [kɔ̃pozɑ̃] *nm* component, constituent.
composante [kɔ̃pozɑ̃t] *nf* component.
composé, e [kɔ̃poze] *a* (*visage, air*)
studied ; (BIO, CHIMIE, LING) compound // *nm*
(CHIMIE, LING) compound.
composer [kɔ̃poze] *vt* (*musique, texte*) to
compose ; (*mélange, équipe*) to make up ;
(*faire partie de*) to make up, form ; (TYPO)
to set // *vi* (SCOL) to sit ou do a test ;
(*transiger*) to come to terms ; **se ~ de** to
be composed of, be made up of ; **~ un
numéro** (*au téléphone*) to dial a number.
composite [kɔ̃pozit] *a* heterogeneous.
compositeur, trice [kɔ̃pozitœR, -tRis]
nm/f (MUS) composer ; (TYPO) compositor,
typesetter.
composition [kɔ̃pozisjɔ̃] *nf* composition ;
(SCOL) test ; (TYPO) typesetting, composition ; **de bonne ~** (*accommodant*) easy to
deal with ; **amener qn à ~** to get sb to
come to terms.
composter [kɔ̃pɔste] *vt* to date stamp ; to
punch ; **composteur** *nm* date stamp ;
punch ; (TYPO) composing stick.
compote [kɔ̃pɔt] *nf* stewed fruit *q* ; **~ de
pommes** stewed apples ; **compotier** *nm*
fruit dish ou bowl.
compréhensible [kɔ̃pReɑ̃sibl(ə)] *a* com-
prehensible ; (*attitude*) understandable.

compréhensif, ive [kɔ̃pʀeɑ̃sif, -iv] *a* understanding.

compréhension [kɔ̃pʀeɑ̃sjɔ̃] *nf* understanding ; comprehension.

comprendre [kɔ̃pʀɑ̃dʀ(ə)] *vt to* understand ; (*se composer de*) to comprise, consist of.

compresse [kɔ̃pʀɛs] *nf* compress.

compresseur [kɔ̃pʀɛsœʀ] *am voir* **rouleau.**

compression [kɔ̃pʀɛsjɔ̃] *nf* compression ; reduction.

comprimé, e [kɔ̃pʀime] *a:* **air ~** compressed air // *nm* tablet.

comprimer [kɔ̃pʀime] *vt* to compress ; (*fig: crédit etc*) to reduce, cut down.

compris, e [kɔ̃pʀi, -iz] *pp de* **comprendre** // *a* (*inclus*) included ; **~ entre** (*situé*) contained between ; **la maison ~e/non ~e, y/non ~ la maison** including/excluding the house ; **service ~** service (charge) included ; **100 F tout ~** 100 F all inclusive *ou* all-in.

compromettre [kɔ̃pʀɔmɛtʀ(ə)] *vt to* compromise.

compromis [kɔ̃pʀɔmi] *nm* compromise.

compromission [kɔ̃pʀɔmisjɔ̃] *nf* compromise, deal.

comptabilité [kɔ̃tabilite] *nf* (*activité, technique*) accounting, accountancy ; (*d'une société: comptes*) accounts *pl*, books *pl* ; (: *service*) accounts office *ou* department.

comptable [kɔ̃tabl(ə)] *nm/f* accountant // *a* accounts *cpd*, accounting.

comptant [kɔ̃tɑ̃] *ad:* **payer ~** to pay cash ; **acheter ~** to buy for cash.

compte [kɔ̃t] *nm* count, counting ; (*total, montant*) count, (right) number ; (*bancaire, facture*) account ; **~s** *nmpl* accounts, books ; (*fig*) explanation *sg* ; **faire le ~ de** to count up, make a count of ; **en fin de ~** (*fig*) all things considered, weighing it all up ; **à bon ~** at a favourable price ; (*fig*) lightly ; **avoir son ~** (*fig: fam*) to have had it ; **pour le ~ de** on behalf of ; **travailler à son ~** to work for oneself ; **rendre ~ (à qn) de qch** to give (sb) an account of sth ; **~s chèques postaux (C.C.P.)** ≈ (Post Office) Giro account ; **~ courant** current account ; **~ de dépôt** deposit account ; **~ à rebours** countdown.

compte-gouttes [kɔ̃tgut] *nm inv* dropper.

compter [kɔ̃te] *vt* to count ; (*facturer*) to charge for ; (*avoir à son actif, comporter*) to have ; (*prévoir*) to allow, reckon ; (*espérer*): **~ réussir/revenir** to expect to succeed/return // *vi* to count ; (*être économe*) to economize ; (*être non négligeable*) to count, matter ; (*valoir*): **~ pour** to count for ; (*figurer*): **~ parmi** to be *ou* rank among ; **~ sur** *vt* to count (up)on ; **~ avec qch/qn** to reckon with *ou* take account of sth/sb ; **sans ~ que** besides which ; **à ~ du 10 janvier** (*COMM*) (as) from 10th January.

compte-rendu [kɔ̃tʀɑ̃dy] *nm* account, report ; (*de film, livre*) review.

compte-tours [kɔ̃ttuʀ] *nm inv* rev(olution) counter.

compteur [kɔ̃tœʀ] *nm* meter ; **~ de vitesse** speedometer.

comptine [kɔ̃tin] *nf* nursery rhyme.

comptoir [kɔ̃twaʀ] *nm* (*de magasin*) counter ; (*de café*) counter, bar ; (*colonial*) trading post.

compulser [kɔ̃pylse] *vt* to consult.

comte, comtesse [kɔ̃t, kɔ̃tɛs] *nm/f* count/countess.

con, ne [kɔ̃, kɔn] *a* (*fam!*) bloody stupid (!).

concave [kɔ̃kav] *a* concave.

concéder [kɔ̃sede] *vt* to grant ; (*défaite, point*) to concede ; **~ que** to concede that.

concentration [kɔ̃sɑ̃tʀɑsjɔ̃] *nf* concentration.

concentrationnaire [kɔ̃sɑ̃tʀɑsjɔnɛʀ] *a* of *ou* in concentration camps.

concentré [kɔ̃sɑ̃tʀe] *nm* concentrate.

concentrer [kɔ̃sɑ̃tʀe] *vt* to concentrate ; **se ~** to concentrate.

concentrique [kɔ̃sɑ̃tʀik] *a* concentric.

concept [kɔ̃sɛpt] *nm* concept.

conception [kɔ̃sɛpsjɔ̃] *nf* conception.

concerner [kɔ̃sɛʀne] *vt* to concern ; **en ce qui me concerne** as far as I am concerned ; **en ce qui concerne ceci** as far as this is concerned, with regard to this.

concert [kɔ̃sɛʀ] *nm* concert ; **de ~** *ad* in unison ; together.

concerter [kɔ̃sɛʀte] *vt* to devise ; **se ~** (*collaborateurs etc*) to put one's heads together, consult (each other).

concertiste [kɔ̃sɛʀtist(ə)] *nm/f* concert artist.

concerto [kɔ̃sɛʀto] *nm* concerto.

concession [kɔ̃sesjɔ̃] *nf* concession.

concessionnaire [kɔ̃sesjɔnɛʀ] *nm/f* agent, dealer.

concevoir [kɔ̃svwaʀ] *vt* (*idée, projet*) to conceive (of) ; (*méthode, plan d'appartement, décoration etc*) to plan, devise ; (*enfant*) to conceive ; **appartement bien/mal conçu** well-/badly-designed *ou* -planned flat.

concierge [kɔ̃sjɛʀʒ(ə)] *nm/f* caretaker.

concile [kɔ̃sil] *nm* council, synod.

conciliabules [kɔ̃siljabyl] *nmpl* (private) discussions, confabulations.

conciliation [kɔ̃siljɑsjɔ̃] *nf* conciliation.

concilier [kɔ̃silje] *vt* to reconcile ; **se ~ qn/l'appui de qn** to win sb over/sb's support.

concis, e [kɔ̃si, -iz] *a* concise ; **concision** *nf* concision, conciseness.

concitoyen, ne [kɔ̃sitwajɛ̃, -jɛn] *nm/f* fellow citizen.

conclave [kɔ̃klav] *nm* conclave.

concluant, e [kɔ̃klyɑ̃, -ɑ̃t] *a* conclusive.

conclure [kɔ̃klyʀ] *vt* to conclude ; **~ à l'acquittement** to decide in favour of an acquittal ; **~ au suicide** to come to the conclusion (*ou JUR*) to pronounce) that it is a case of suicide.

conclusion [kɔ̃klyzjɔ̃] *nf* conclusion ; **~s** *nfpl* (*JUR*) submissions ; findings.

conçois *etc vb voir* **concevoir.**

concombre [kɔ̃kɔ̃bʀ(ə)] *nm* cucumber.

concordance [kɔ̃kɔʀdɑs] *nf* concordance ; **la ~ des temps** (*LING*) the sequence of tenses.

concorde [kɔ̃kɔʀd(ə)] *nf* concord.

concorder [kɔkɔʀde] *vi* to tally, agree.
concourir [kɔkuʀiʀ] *vi* (SPORT) to compete; **~ à** *vt* (effet etc) to work towards.
concours [kɔkuʀ] *nm* competition; (SCOL) competitive examination; (assistance) aid, help; **recrutement par voie de ~** recruitment by (competitive) examination; **~ de circonstances** combination of circumstances; **~ hippique** horse show.
concret, ète [kɔkʀɛ, -ɛt] *a* concrete.
concrétiser [kɔkʀetize] *vt* (plan, projet) to put in concrete form; **se ~** *vi* to materialize.
conçu, e [kɔsy] *pp de* **concevoir.**
concubinage [kɔkybinaʒ] *nm* (JUR) cohabitation.
concupiscence [kɔkypisɑ̃s] *nf* concupiscence.
concurremment [kɔkyʀamɑ̃] *ad* concurrently; jointly.
concurrence [kɔkyʀɑ̃s] *nf* competition; **jusqu'à ~ de** up to; **~ déloyale** unfair competition.
concurrent, e [kɔkyʀɑ̃, -ɑ̃t] *a* competing // *nm/f* (SPORT, ÉCON etc) competitor; (SCOL) candidate.
condamnation [kɔdɑnasjɔ̃] *nf* condemnation; sentencing; sentence; conviction; **~ à mort** death sentence.
condamner [kɔdane] *vt* (blâmer) to condemn; (JUR) to sentence; (porte, ouverture) to fill in, block up; (obliger): **~ qn à qch/faire** to condemn sb to sth/to do; **~ qn à 2 ans de prison** to sentence sb to 2 years' imprisonment; **~ qn à une amende** to impose a fine on sb, request sb to pay a fine.
condensateur [kɔdɑ̃satœʀ] *nm* condenser.
condensation [kɔdɑ̃sasjɔ̃] *nf* condensation.
condensé [kɔdɑ̃se] *nm* digest.
condenser [kɔdɑ̃se] *vt*, **se ~** *vi* to condense.
condescendre [kɔdesɑ̃dʀ(ə)] *vi*: **~ à** to condescend to.
condiment [kɔdimɑ̃] *nm* condiment.
condisciple [kɔdisipl(ə)] *nm/f* school fellow, fellow student.
condition [kɔdisjɔ̃] *nf* condition; **~s** *nfpl* (tarif, prix) terms; (circonstances) conditions; **sans ~** *a* unconditional // *ad* unconditionally; **sous ~ que** on condition that; **à ~ de/que** provided that; **conditionnel, le** *a* conditional // *nm* conditional (tense); **conditionner** *vt* (déterminer) to determine; (COMM: produit) to package; (fig: personne) to condition; **air conditionné** air conditioning; **réflexe conditionné** conditioned reflex.
condoléances [kɔdɔleɑ̃s] *nfpl* condolences.
conducteur, trice [kɔdyktœʀ, -tʀis] *a* (ÉLEC) conducting // *nm/f* driver // *nm* (ÉLEC etc) conductor.
conduire [kɔdɥiʀ] *vt* (véhicule, passager) to drive; (délégation, troupeau) to lead; **se ~** *vi* to behave; **~ vers/à** to lead towards/to; **~ qn quelque part** to take sb somewhere; to drive sb somewhere.

conduit [kɔdɥi] *nm* (TECH) conduit, pipe; (ANAT) duct, canal.
conduite [kɔdɥit] *nf* (en auto) driving; (comportement) behaviour; (d'eau, de gaz) pipe; **sous la ~ de** led by; **~ forcée** pressure pipe; **~ à gauche** left-hand drive; **~ intérieure** saloon (car).
cône [kon] *nm* cone.
confection [kɔfɛksjɔ̃] *nf* (fabrication) making; (COUTURE): **la ~** the clothing industry, the rag trade; **vêtement de ~** ready-to-wear ou off-the-peg garment.
confectionner [kɔfɛksjɔne] *vt* to make.
confédération [kɔfedeʀasjɔ̃] *nf* confederation.
conférence [kɔfeʀɑ̃s] *nf* (exposé) lecture; (pourparlers) conference; **~ de presse** press conference; **conférencier, ère** *nm/f* lecturer.
conférer [kɔfeʀe] *vt*: **~ à qn** (titre, grade) to confer on sb; **~ à qch/qn** (aspect etc) to endow sth/sb with, give (to) sth/sb.
confesser [kɔfese] *vt* to confess; **se ~** (REL) to go to confession; **confesseur** *nm* confessor.
confession [kɔfɛsjɔ̃] *nf* confession; (culte: catholique etc) denomination; **confessionnal, aux** *nm* confessional; **confessionnel, le** *a* denominational.
confetti [kɔfeti] *nm* confetti *q*.
confiance [kɔfjɑ̃s] *nf* confidence, trust; faith; **avoir ~ en** to have confidence ou faith in, trust; **mettre qn en ~** to win sb's trust; **~ en soi** self-confidence.
confiant, e [kɔfjɑ̃, -ɑ̃t] *a* confident; trusting.
confidence [kɔfidɑ̃s] *nf* confidence.
confident, e [kɔfidɑ̃, -ɑ̃t] *nm/f* confidant/confidante.
confidentiel, le [kɔfidɑ̃sjɛl] *a* confidential.
confier [kɔfje] *vt*: **~ à qn** (objet en dépôt, travail etc) to entrust to sb; (secret, pensée) to confide to sb; **se ~ à qn** to confide in sb.
configuration [kɔfigyʀasjɔ̃] *nf* configuration, layout.
confiné, e [kɔfine] *a* enclosed; stale.
confiner [kɔfine] *vt*: **se ~ dans** ou **à** to confine o.s. to; **~ à** *vt* to confine to.
confins [kɔfɛ̃] *nmpl*: **aux ~ de** on the borders of.
confirmation [kɔfiʀmasjɔ̃] *nf* confirmation.
confirmer [kɔfiʀme] *vt* to confirm.
confiscation [kɔfiskasjɔ̃] *nf* confiscation.
confiserie [kɔfizʀi] *nf* (magasin) confectioner's ou sweet shop; **~s** *nfpl* (bonbons) confectionery *sg*, sweets; **confiseur, euse** *nm/f* confectioner.
confisquer [kɔfiske] *vt* to confiscate.
confit, e [kɔfi, -it] *a*: **fruits ~s** crystallized fruits // *nm*: **~ d'oie** conserve of goose.
confiture [kɔfityʀ] *nf* jam; **~ d'oranges** (orange) marmalade.
conflit [kɔfli] *nm* conflict.
confluent [kɔflyɑ̃] *nm* confluence.
confondre [kɔfɔdʀ(ə)] *vt* (jumeaux, faits) to confuse, mix up; (témoin, menteur) to confound; **se ~** *vi* to merge; **se ~ en**

excuses to offer profuse apologies, apologize profusely.

confondu, e [kɔ̃fɔ̃dy] *a* (*stupéfait*) speechless, overcome.

conformation [kɔ̃fɔrmasjɔ̃] *nf* conformation.

conforme [kɔ̃fɔrm(ə)] *a*: ~ à in accordance with ; in keeping with ; true to.

conformé, e [kɔ̃fɔrme] *a*: **bien** ~ well-formed.

conformer [kɔ̃fɔrme] *vt*: ~ **qch à** to model sth on ; **se** ~ **à** to conform to ; **conformisme** *nm* conformity ; **conformiste** *a, nm/f* conformist.

conformité [kɔ̃fɔrmite] *nf* conformity ; agreement ; **en** ~ **avec** in accordance with ; in keeping with.

confort [kɔ̃fɔr] *nm* comfort ; **tout** ~ (*COMM*) with all mod cons ; **confortable** *a* comfortable.

confrère [kɔ̃frɛr] *nm* colleague ; fellow member ; **confrérie** *nf* brotherhood.

confrontation [kɔ̃frɔ̃tasjɔ̃] *nf* confrontation.

confronté, e [kɔ̃frɔ̃te] *a*: ~ **à** confronted by, facing.

confronter [kɔ̃frɔ̃te] *vt* to confront ; (*textes*) to compare, collate.

confus, e [kɔ̃fy, -yz] *a* (*vague*) confused ; (*embarrassé*) embarrassed.

confusion [kɔ̃fyzjɔ̃] *nf* (*voir confus*) confusion ; embarrassement ; (*voir confondre*) confusion ; mixing up ; (*erreur*) confusion.

congé [kɔ̃ʒe] *nm* (*vacances*) holiday ; (*arrêt de travail*) time off *q* ; leave *q* ; (*MIL*) leave *q* ; (*avis de départ*) notice ; **en** ~ on holiday ; off (work) ; on leave ; **semaine/jour de** ~ week/day off ; **prendre** ~ **de qn** to take one's leave of sb ; **donner son** ~ **à** to hand *ou* give in one's notice to ; ~ **de maladie** sick leave ; ~**s payés** paid holiday.

congédier [kɔ̃ʒedje] *vt* to dismiss.

congélateur [kɔ̃ʒelatœr] *nm* freezer, deep freeze.

congeler [kɔ̃ʒle] *vt* to freeze.

congénère [kɔ̃ʒenɛr] *nm/f* fellow (bear *ou* lion *etc*), fellow creature.

congénital, e, aux [kɔ̃ʒenital, -o] *a* congenital.

congère [kɔ̃ʒɛr] *nf* snowdrift.

congestion [kɔ̃ʒɛstjɔ̃] *nf* congestion ; ~ **cérébrale** stroke ; ~ **pulmonaire** congestion of the lungs.

congestionner [kɔ̃ʒɛstjɔne] *vt* to congest ; (*MÉD*) to flush.

congratuler [kɔ̃gratyle] *vt* to congratulate.

congre [kɔ̃gr(ə)] *nm* conger (eel).

congrégation [kɔ̃gregasjɔ̃] *nf* (*REL*) congregation ; (*gén*) assembly ; gathering.

congrès [kɔ̃grɛ] *nm* congress.

congru, e [kɔ̃gry] *a*: **la portion** ~**e** the smallest *ou* meanest share.

conifère [kɔnifɛr] *nm* conifer.

conique [kɔnik] *a* conical.

conjecture [kɔ̃ʒɛktyr] *nf* conjecture, speculation *q*.

conjecturer [kɔ̃ʒɛktyre] *vt, vi* to conjecture.

conjoint, e [kɔ̃ʒwɛ̃, -wɛ̃t] *a* joint // *nm/f* spouse.

conjonctif, ive [kɔ̃ʒɔ̃ktif, -iv] *a*: **tissu** ~ connective tissue.

conjonction [kɔ̃ʒɔ̃ksjɔ̃] *nf* (*LING*) conjunction.

conjonctivite [kɔ̃ʒɔ̃ktivit] *nf* conjunctivitis.

conjoncture [kɔ̃ʒɔ̃ktyr] *nf* circumstances *pl* ; **la** ~ (**économique**) the economic climate *ou* circumstances.

conjugaison [kɔ̃ʒygɛzɔ̃] *nf* (*LING*) conjugation.

conjugal, e, aux [kɔ̃ʒygal, -o] *a* conjugal ; married.

conjuguer [kɔ̃ʒyge] *vt* (*LING*) to conjugate ; (*efforts etc*) to combine.

conjuration [kɔ̃ʒyrasjɔ̃] *nf* conspiracy.

conjuré, e [kɔ̃ʒyre] *nm/f* conspirator.

conjurer [kɔ̃ʒyre] *vt* (*sort, maladie*) to avert ; ~ **qn de faire qch** to beseech *ou* entreat sb to do sth.

connaissance [kɔnɛsɑ̃s] *nf* (*savoir*) knowledge *q* ; (*personne connue*) acquaintance ; (*conscience, perception*) consciousness ; **être sans** ~ to be unconscious ; **perdre** ~ to lose consciousness ; **à ma/sa** ~ to (the best of) my/his knowledge ; **avoir** ~ **de** to be aware of ; **prendre** ~ **de** (*document etc*) to peruse ; **en** ~ **de cause** with full knowledge of the facts.

connaisseur, euse [kɔnɛsœr, -øz] *nm/f* connoisseur // *a* expert.

connaître [kɔnɛtr(ə)] *vt* to know ; (*éprouver*) to experience ; (*avoir*) to have ; to enjoy ; ~ **de nom/vue** to know by name/sight ; **ils se sont connus à Genève** they (first) met in Geneva.

connecter [kɔnɛkte] *vt* to connect.

connexe [kɔnɛks(ə)] *a* closely related.

connexion [kɔnɛksjɔ̃] *nf* connection.

connu, e [kɔny] *a* (*célèbre*) well-known.

conquérant, e [kɔ̃kerɑ̃, -ɑ̃t] *nm/f* conqueror.

conquérir [kɔ̃kerir] *vt* to conquer, win ; **conquête** *nf* conquest.

consacrer [kɔ̃sakre] *vt* (*REL*) : ~ **qch (à)** to consecrate sth (to) ; (*fig: usage etc*) to sanction, establish ; (*employer*) : ~ **qch à** to devote *ou* dedicate sth to ; **se** ~ **à qch/faire** to dedicate *ou* devote o.s. to/to doing.

consanguin, e [kɔ̃sɑ̃gɛ̃, -in] *a* between blood relations.

conscience [kɔ̃sjɑ̃s] *nf* conscience ; (*perception*) consciousness ; **avoir/prendre** ~ **de** to be/become aware of ; **perdre** ~ to lose consciousness ; **avoir bonne/mauvaise** ~ to have a clear/guilty conscience ; ~ **professionnelle** professional conscience ; **consciencieux, euse** *a* conscientious ; **conscient, e** *a* conscious ; **conscient de** aware *ou* conscious of.

conscription [kɔ̃skripsjɔ̃] *nf* conscription.

conscrit [kɔ̃skri] *nm* conscript.

consécration [kɔ̃sekrasjɔ̃] *nf* consecration.

consécutif, ive [kɔ̃sekytif, -iv] *a* consecutive ; ~ **à** following upon.

conseil [kɔ̃sɛj] *nm* (*avis*) piece of advice, advice *q* ; (*assemblée*) council ; (*expert*): ~ **en recrutement** recruitment consultant // *a*: **ingénieur-~** consulting engineer, engineering consultant ; **tenir** ~ to hold a meeting ; to deliberate ; **prendre** ~ (**auprès de qn**) to take advice (from sb) ; ~ **d'administration** board (of directors) ; ~ **de discipline** disciplinary committee ; ~ **de guerre** court-martial ; **le** ~ **des ministres** ≈ the Cabinet ; ~ **municipal** town council.

conseiller [kɔ̃seje] *vt* (*personne*) to advise ; (*méthode, action*) to recommend, advise.

conseiller, ère [kɔ̃seje, kɔ̃sɛjɛʀ] *nm/f* adviser ; ~ **matrimonial** marriage guidance counsellor ; ~ **municipal** town councillor.

consentement [kɔ̃sɑ̃tmɑ̃] *nm* consent.

consentir [kɔ̃sɑ̃tiʀ] *vt*: ~ (**à qch/faire**) to agree *ou* consent (to sth/to doing) ; ~ **qch à qn** to grant sb sth.

conséquence [kɔ̃sekɑ̃s] *nf* consequence, outcome ; ~**s** *nfpl* consequences, repercussions ; **en** ~ (*donc*) consequently ; (*de façon appropriée*) accordingly ; **ne pas tirer à** ~ to be unlikely to have any repercussions.

conséquent, e [kɔ̃sekɑ̃, -ɑ̃t] *a* logical, rational ; **par** ~ consequently.

conservateur, trice [kɔ̃sɛʀvatœʀ, -tʀis] *a* conservative // *nm/f* (*POL*) conservative ; (*de musée*) curator.

conservation [kɔ̃sɛʀvɑsjɔ̃] *nf* preserving ; preservation ; retention ; keeping.

conservatoire [kɔ̃sɛʀvatwaʀ] *nm* academy.

conserve [kɔ̃sɛʀv(ə)] *nf* (*gén pl*) canned *ou* tinned food ; ~**s de poisson** canned *ou* tinned fish ; **en** ~ canned, tinned ; **de** ~ (*ensemble*) in convoy ; in concert.

conserver [kɔ̃sɛʀve] *vt* (*faculté*) to retain, keep ; (*amis, livres*) to keep ; (*maintenir en bon état, aussi CULIN*) to preserve ; **conserverie** *nf* canning factory.

considérable [kɔ̃sideʀabl(ə)] *a* considerable, significant, extensive.

considération [kɔ̃sideʀɑsjɔ̃] *nf* consideration ; (*estime*) esteem, respect ; ~**s** *nfpl* (*remarques*) reflections ; **prendre en** ~ to take into consideration *ou* account ; **en** ~ **de** given, because of.

considéré, e [kɔ̃sideʀe] *a* respected.

considérer [kɔ̃sideʀe] *vt* to consider ; (*regarder*) to consider, study ; ~ **qch comme** to regard sth as.

consigne [kɔ̃siɲ] *nf* (*COMM*) deposit ; (*de gare*) left luggage (office) ; (*punition: SCOL*) detention ; (: *MIL*) confinement to barracks ; (*ordre, instruction*) orders *pl*.

consigner [kɔ̃siɲe] *vt* (*note, pensée*) to record ; (*punir*) to confine to barracks ; to put in detention ; (*COMM*) to put a deposit on.

consistance [kɔ̃sistɑ̃s] *nf* consistency.

consistant, e [kɔ̃sistɑ̃, -ɑ̃t] *a* thick ; solid.

consister [kɔ̃siste] *vi*: ~ **en/dans/à faire** to consist of/in/in doing.

consœur [kɔ̃sœʀ] *nf* (*lady*) colleague ; fellow member.

consolation [kɔ̃sɔlɑsjɔ̃] *nf* consolation *q*, comfort *q*.

console [kɔ̃sɔl] *nf* console.

consoler [kɔ̃sɔle] *vt* to console ; **se** ~ (**de qch**) to console o.s. (for sth).

consolider [kɔ̃sɔlide] *vt* to strengthen, reinforce ; (*fig*) to consolidate.

consommateur, trice [kɔ̃sɔmatœʀ, -tʀis] *nm/f* (*ÉCON*) consumer ; (*dans un café*) customer.

consommation [kɔ̃sɔmɑsjɔ̃] *nf* consumption ; (*JUR*) consummation ; (*boisson*) drink ; ~ **aux 100 km** (*AUTO*) (fuel) consumption per 100 km, ≈ miles per gallon (m.p.g.).

consommé, e [kɔ̃sɔme] *a* consummate // *nm* consommé.

consommer [kɔ̃sɔme] *vt* (*suj: personne*) to eat *ou* drink, consume ; (*suj: voiture, usine, poêle*) to use (up), consume ; (*JUR*) to consummate // *vi* (*dans un café*) to (have a) drink.

consonance [kɔ̃sɔnɑ̃s] *nf* consonance ; **nom à** ~ **étrangère** foreign-sounding name.

consonne [kɔ̃sɔn] *nf* consonant.

consorts [kɔ̃sɔʀ] *nmpl*: **et** ~ (*péj*) and company, and his bunch *ou* like.

conspirateur, trice [kɔ̃spiʀatœʀ, -tʀis] *nm/f* conspirator, plotter.

conspiration [kɔ̃spiʀɑsjɔ̃] *nf* conspiracy.

conspirer [kɔ̃spiʀe] *vi* to conspire, plot.

conspuer [kɔ̃spɥe] *vt* to boo, shout down.

constamment [kɔ̃stamɑ̃] *ad* constantly.

constant, e [kɔ̃stɑ̃, -ɑ̃t] *a* constant ; (*personne*) steadfast.

constat [kɔ̃sta] *nm* (*d'huissier*) certified report (*by bailiff*) ; (*de police*) report.

constatation [kɔ̃statɑsjɔ̃] *nf* noticing ; certifying ; (*remarque*) observation.

constater [kɔ̃state] *vt* (*remarquer*) to note, notice ; (*ADMIN, JUR*: *attester*) to certify ; (*dégâts*) to note ; ~ **que** (*dire*) to state that.

constellation [kɔ̃stelɑsjɔ̃] *nf* constellation.

constellé, e [kɔ̃stele] *a*: ~ **de** studded *ou* spangled with ; spotted with.

consternation [kɔ̃stɛʀnɑsjɔ̃] *nf* consternation, dismay.

constipation [kɔ̃stipɑsjɔ̃] *nf* constipation.

constipé, e [kɔ̃stipe] *a* constipated ; (*fig*) stiff.

constitué, e [kɔ̃stitɥe] *a*: ~ **de** made up *ou* composed of ; **bien** ~ of sound constitution ; well-formed.

constituer [kɔ̃stitɥe] *vt* (*comité, équipe*) to set up, form ; (*dossier, collection*) to put together, build up ; (*suj: éléments, parties: composer*) to make up, constitute ; (*représenter, être*) to constitute ; **se** ~ **prisonnier** to give o.s. up.

constitution [kɔ̃stitysjɔ̃] *nf* setting up ; building up ; (*composition*) composition, make-up ; (*santé, POL*) constitution ; **constitutionnel, le** *a* constitutional.

constructeur [kɔ̃stʀyktœʀ] *nm* manufacturer, builder.

construction [kɔ̃stʀyksjɔ̃] *nf* construction, building.

construire [kɔ̃stʀɥiʀ] *vt* to build, construct.

consul [kɔ̃syl] *nm* consul; **~aire** *a* consular; **~at** *nm* consulate.

consultation [kɔ̃syltɑsjɔ̃] *nf* consultation; **~s** *nfpl* (POL) talks; **aller à la ~** (MÉD) to go to the surgery; **heures de ~** (MÉD) surgery hours.

consulter [kɔ̃sylte] *vt* to consult // *vi* (*médecin*) to hold surgery.

consumer [kɔ̃syme] *vt* to consume; **se ~** *vi* to burn; **se ~ de chagrin/douleur** to be consumed with sorrow/grief.

contact [kɔ̃takt] *nm* contact; **au ~ de** (*air, peau*) on contact with; (*gens*) through contact with; **mettre/couper le ~** (AUTO) to switch on/off the ignition; **entrer en ~** (*fils, objets*) to come into contact, make contact; **se mettre en ~ avec** (RADIO) to make contact with; **prendre ~ avec** (*relation d'affaires, connaissance*) to get in touch ou contact with; **~er** *vt* to contact, get in touch with.

contagieux, euse [kɔ̃taʒjø, -øz] *a* contagious, infectious.

contagion [kɔ̃taʒjɔ̃] *nf* contagion.

container [kɔ̃tɛnɛʀ] *nm* container.

contaminer [kɔ̃tamine] *vt* to contaminate.

conte [kɔ̃t] *nm* tale; **~ de fées** fairy tale.

contempler [kɔ̃tɑ̃ple] *vt* to contemplate, gaze at.

contemporain, e [kɔ̃tɑ̃pɔʀɛ̃, -ɛn] *a, nm/f* contemporary.

contenance [kɔ̃tnɑ̃s] *nf* (*d'un récipient*) capacity; (*attitude*) bearing, attitude; **perdre ~** to lose one's composure; **se donner une ~** to give the impression of composure.

contenir [kɔ̃tniʀ] *vt* to contain; (*avoir une capacité de*) to hold.

content, e [kɔ̃tɑ̃, -ɑ̃t] *a* pleased, glad; **~ de** pleased with; **contentement** *nm* contentment, satisfaction; **contenter** *vt* to satisfy, please; (*envie*) to satisfy; **se contenter de** to content o.s. with.

contentieux [kɔ̃tɑ̃sjø] *nm* (COMM) litigation; litigation department; (POL etc) contentious issues *pl*.

contenu [kɔ̃tny] *nm* (*d'un bol*) contents *pl*; (*d'un texte*) content.

conter [kɔ̃te] *vt* to recount, relate.

contestable [kɔ̃tɛstabl(ə)] *a* questionable.

contestation [kɔ̃tɛstɑsjɔ̃] *nf* questioning, contesting; (POL): **la ~** anti-establishment activity, protest.

conteste [kɔ̃tɛst(ə)]: **sans ~** *ad* unquestionably, indisputably.

contester [kɔ̃tɛste] *vt* to question, contest // *vi* (POL, gén) to protest, rebel (against established authority).

conteur, euse [kɔ̃tœʀ, -øz] *nm/f* storyteller.

contexte [kɔ̃tɛkst(ə)] *nm* context.

contigu, ë [kɔ̃tigy] *a*: **~ (à)** adjacent (to).

continent [kɔ̃tinɑ̃] *nm* continent; **continental, e, aux** *a* continental.

contingences [kɔ̃tɛ̃ʒɑ̃s] *nfpl* contingencies.

contingent [kɔ̃tɛ̃ʒɑ̃] *nm* (MIL) contingent; (COMM) quota; **contingenter** *vt* (COMM) to fix a quota on.

continu, e [kɔ̃tiny] *a* continuous; (*courant*) **~** direct current, DC.

continuation [kɔ̃tinɥasjɔ̃] *nf* continuation.

continuel, le [kɔ̃tinɥɛl] *a* (*qui se répète*) constant, continual; (*continu*) continuous.

continuer [kɔ̃tinɥe] *vt* (*travail, voyage etc*) to continue (with), carry on (with), go on (with); (*prolonger: alignement, rue*) to continue // *vi* (*pluie, vie, bruit*) to continue, go on; (*voyageur*) to go on; **~ à ou de faire** to go on ou continue doing.

continuité [kɔ̃tinɥite] *nf* continuity, continuation.

contorsion [kɔ̃tɔʀsjɔ̃] *nf* contortion; **se contorsionner** *vi* to contort o.s., writhe about.

contour [kɔ̃tuʀ] *nm* outline, contour; **~s** *nmpl* (*d'une rivière etc*) windings.

contourner [kɔ̃tuʀne] *vt* to bypass, walk (*ou* drive) round.

contraceptif, ive [kɔ̃tʀasɛptif, -iv] *a, nm* contraceptive.

contraception [kɔ̃tʀasɛpsjɔ̃] *nf* contraception.

contracté, e [kɔ̃tʀakte] *a* (*muscle*) tense, contracted; (*personne: tendu*) tense, tensed up.

contracter [kɔ̃tʀakte] *vt* (*muscle etc*) to tense, contract; (*maladie, dette, obligation*) to contract; (*assurance*) to take out; **se ~** *vi* (*métal, muscles*) to contract; **contraction** *nf* contraction.

contractuel, le [kɔ̃tʀaktɥɛl] *a* contractual // *nm/f* (*agent*) traffic warden; (*employé*) contract employee.

contradiction [kɔ̃tʀadiksjɔ̃] *nf* contradiction; **contradictoire** *a* contradictory, conflicting; **débat contradictoire** (open) debate.

contraignant, e [kɔ̃tʀɛɲɑ̃, -ɑ̃t] *a* restricting.

contraindre [kɔ̃tʀɛ̃dʀ(ə)] *vt*: **~ qn à faire** to force ou compel sb to do.

contraint, e [kɔ̃tʀɛ̃, -ɛ̃t] *a* (*mine, air*) constrained, forced // *nf* constraint; **sans ~e** unrestrainedly, unconstrainedly.

contraire [kɔ̃tʀɛʀ] *a, nm* opposite; **~ à** contrary to; **au ~** on the contrary.

contrarier [kɔ̃tʀaʀje] *vt* (*personne*) to annoy, bother; (*fig*) to impede; to thwart, frustrate; **contrariété** *nf* annoyance.

contraste [kɔ̃tʀast(ə)] *nm* contrast; **contraster** *vi* to contrast.

contrat [kɔ̃tʀa] *nm* contract.

contravention [kɔ̃tʀavɑ̃sjɔ̃] *nf* (*infraction*): **~ à** contravention of; (*amende*) fine; (*P.V. pour stationnement interdit*) parking ticket; **dresser ~ à** (*automobiliste*) to book; to write out a parking ticket for.

contre [kɔ̃tʀ(ə)] *prép* against; (*en échange*) (in exchange) for // *préfixe*: **~-amiral, aux** *nm* rear admiral; **~-attaque** *nf* counter-attack; **~-attaquer** *vi* to counter-attack; **~-balancer** *vt* to counter-balance; (*fig*) to offset.

contrebande [kɔ̃tʀabɑ̃d] *nf* (*trafic*) contraband, smuggling; (*marchandise*) contraband, smuggled goods *pl*; **faire la ~ de** to smuggle; **contrebandier** *nm* smuggler.

contrebas [kɔ̃tʀəbɑ]: **en ~ ad** (down) below.

contrebasse [kɔ̃tʀəbas] nf (double) bass; **contrebassiste** nm/f (double) bass player.

contrecarrer [kɔ̃tʀəkaʀe] vt to thwart.

contrecœur [kɔ̃tʀəkœʀ]: **à ~ ad** (be)grudgingly, reluctantly.

contrecoup [kɔ̃tʀəku] nm repercussions pl.

contre-courant [kɔ̃tʀəkuʀɑ̃]: **à ~ ad** against the current.

contredire [kɔ̃tʀədiʀ] vt (personne) to contradict; (témoignage, assertion, faits) to refute.

contrée [kɔ̃tʀe] nf region; land.

contre-écrou [kɔ̃tʀekʀu] nm lock nut.

contre-espionnage [kɔ̃tʀɛspjɔnaʒ] nm counter-espionage.

contre-expertise [kɔ̃tʀɛkspɛʀtiz] nf second (expert) assessment.

contrefaçon [kɔ̃tʀəfasɔ̃] nf forgery.

contrefaire [kɔ̃tʀəfɛʀ] vt (document, signature) to forge, counterfeit; (personne, démarche) to mimic; (dénaturer: sa voix etc) to disguise.

contrefait, e [kɔ̃tʀəfɛ, -ɛt] a misshapen, deformed.

contreforts [kɔ̃tʀəfɔʀ] nmpl foothills.

contre-indication [kɔ̃tʀɛ̃dikasjɔ̃] nf contra-indication.

contre-jour [kɔ̃tʀəʒuʀ]: **à ~ ad** against the sunlight.

contremaître [kɔ̃tʀəmɛtʀ(ə)] nm foreman.

contre-manifestation [kɔ̃tʀəmanifɛstasjɔ̃] nf counter-demonstration.

contremarque [kɔ̃tʀəmaʀk(ə)] nf (ticket) pass-out ticket.

contre-offensive [kɔ̃tʀɔfɑ̃siv] nf counter-offensive.

contrepartie [kɔ̃tʀəpaʀti] nf compensation; **en ~ in** compensation; in return.

contre-performance [kɔ̃tʀəpɛʀfɔʀmɑ̃s] nf below-average performance.

contrepèterie [kɔ̃tʀəpetʀi] nf spoonerism.

contre-pied [kɔ̃tʀəpje] nm: **prendre le ~ de** to take the opposing view of; to take the opposite course to; **prendre qn à ~** (SPORT) to wrong-foot sb.

contre-plaqué [kɔ̃tʀəplake] nm plywood.

contre-plongée [kɔ̃tʀəplɔ̃ʒe] nf low-angle shot.

contrepoids [kɔ̃tʀəpwa] nm counterweight, counterbalance; **faire ~** to act as a counterbalance.

contrepoint [kɔ̃tʀəpwɛ̃] nm counter point.

contrer [kɔ̃tʀe] vt to counter.

contresens [kɔ̃tʀəsɑ̃s] nm misinterpretation; mistranslation; nonsense q; **à ~ ad** the wrong way.

contresigner [kɔ̃tʀəsiɲe] vt to countersign.

contretemps [kɔ̃tʀətɑ̃] nm hitch, contretemps; **à ~ ad** (MUS) out of time; (fig) at an inopportune moment.

contre-terrorisme [kɔ̃tʀətɛʀɔʀism(ə)] nm counter-terrorism.

contre-torpilleur [kɔ̃tʀətɔʀpijœʀ] nm destroyer.

contrevenir [kɔ̃tʀəvniʀ]: **~ à** vt to contravene.

contribuable [kɔ̃tʀibɥabl(ə)] nm/f taxpayer.

contribuer [kɔ̃tʀibɥe]: **~ à** vt to contribute towards; **contribution** nf contribution; **les contributions** (bureaux) ≈ the Tax Office, the Inland Revenue; **contributions directes/indirectes** (impôts) direct/indirect taxation; **mettre à contribution** to call upon.

contrit, e [kɔ̃tʀi, -it] a contrite.

contrôle [kɔ̃tʀol] nm checking q, check; supervision; monitoring; **perdre le ~ de son véhicule** to lose control of one's vehicle; **~ d'identité** identity check; **~ des naissances** birth control.

contrôler [kɔ̃tʀole] vt (vérifier) to check; (surveiller) to supervise; to monitor, control; (maîtriser, COMM: firme) to control; **contrôleur, euse** nm/f (de train) (ticket) inspector; (de bus) (bus) conductor/tress.

contrordre [kɔ̃tʀɔʀdʀ(ə)] nm counter-order, countermand; **sauf ~ unless** otherwise directed.

controverse [kɔ̃tʀɔvɛʀs(ə)] nf controversy; **controversé, e** a much debated.

contumace [kɔ̃tymas]: **par ~ ad** in absentia.

contusion [kɔ̃tyzjɔ̃] nf bruise, contusion.

convaincre [kɔ̃vɛ̃kʀ(ə)] vt: **~ qn (de qch)** to convince sb (of sth); **~ qn (de faire)** to persuade sb (to do); **~ qn de** (JUR: délit) to convict sb of.

convalescence [kɔ̃valesɑ̃s] nf convalescence; **maison de ~** convalescent home.

convalescent, e [kɔ̃valesɑ̃, -ɑ̃t] a, nm/f convalescent.

convenable [kɔ̃vnabl(ə)] a (décent) acceptable, proper; (assez bon) decent, acceptable; adequate, passable.

convenance [kɔ̃vnɑ̃s] nf: **à ma/votre ~** to my/your liking; **~s** nfpl proprieties.

convenir [kɔ̃vniʀ] vi to be suitable; **~ à** to suit; **il convient de** it is advisable to; (bienséant) it is right ou proper to; **~ de** vt (bien-fondé de qch) to admit (to), acknowledge; (date, somme etc) to agree upon; **~ que** (admettre) to admit that, acknowledge the fact that; **~ de faire qch** to agree to do sth; **il a été convenu que** it has been agreed that; **comme convenu** as agreed.

convention [kɔ̃vɑ̃sjɔ̃] nf convention; **~s** nfpl (convenances) convention sg, social conventions; **de ~ conventional**; **~ collective** (ÉCON) collective agreement; **conventionné, e** a (ADMIN) ≈ National Health cpd; **conventionnel, le** a conventional.

conventuel, le [kɔ̃vɑ̃tɥɛl] a monastic; monastery cpd; conventual, convent cpd.

convenu, e pp de **convenir**.

convergent, e [kɔ̃vɛʀʒɑ̃, -ɑ̃t] a convergent.

converger [kɔ̃vɛʀʒe] vi to converge.

conversation [kɔ̃vɛʀsasjɔ̃] nf conversation; **avoir de la ~** to be a good conversationalist.

converser [kɔ̃vɛʀse] *vi* to converse.
conversion [kɔ̃vɛʀsjɔ̃] *nf* conversion; (*SKI*) kick turn.
convertir [kɔ̃vɛʀtiʀ] *vt*: ~ **qn (à)** to convert sb (to); ~ **qch en** to convert sth into; **se** ~ **(à)** to be converted (to).
convexe [kɔ̃vɛks(ə)] *a* convex.
conviction [kɔ̃viksjɔ̃] *nf* conviction.
convienne *etc vb voir* **convenir**.
convier [kɔ̃vje] ,*vt*: ~ **qn à** (*dîner etc*) to (cordially) invite sb to; ~ **qn à faire** to urge sb to do.
convive [kɔ̃viv] *nm/f* guest (*at table*).
convocation [kɔ̃vɔkasjɔ̃] *nf* convening, convoking; invitation; summoning; (*document*) notification to attend; summons *sg*.
convoi [kɔ̃vwa] *nm* (*de voitures, prisonniers*) convoy; (*train*) train; ~ (**funèbre**) funeral procession.
convoiter [kɔ̃vwate] *vt* to covet; **convoitise** *nf* covetousness; (*sexuelle*) lust, desire.
convoler [kɔ̃vɔle] *vi*: ~ (**en justes noces**) to be wed.
convoquer [kɔ̃vɔke] *vt* (*assemblée*) to convene, convoke; (*subordonné, témoin*) to summon; ~ **qn (à)** (*réunion*) to invite sb (to attend).
convoyer [kɔ̃vwaje] *vt* to escort; **convoyeur** *nm* (*NAVIG*) escort ship; **convoyeur de fonds** security guard.
convulsions [kɔ̃vylsjɔ̃] *nfpl* convulsions.
coopératif, ive [kɔɔpeʀatif, -iv] *a*, *nf* co-operative.
coopération [kɔɔpeʀasjɔ̃] *nf* co-operation; (*ADMIN*): **la C**~ ≈ Voluntary Service Overseas (*sometimes done in place of Military Service*).
coopérer [kɔɔpeʀe] *vi*: ~ (**à**) to cooperate (in).
coordination [kɔɔʀdinasjɔ̃] *nf* co-ordination.
coordonné, e [kɔɔʀdɔne] *a* coordinated // *nf* (*LING*) coordinate clause; ~**s** *nmpl* (*vêtements*) coordinates; ~**es** *nfpl* (*MATH*) coordinates.
coordonner [kɔɔʀdɔne] *vt* to coordinate.
copain, copine [kɔpɛ̃, kɔpin] *nm/f* mate, pal // *a*: **être** ~ **avec** to be pally with.
copeau, x [kɔpo] *nm* shaving; (*de métal*) turning.
copie [kɔpi] *nf* copy; (*SCOL*) script, paper; exercise.
copier [kɔpje] *vt* to copy; **copieuse** *nf* photo-copier.
copieux, euse [kɔpjø, -øz] *a* copious, hearty.
copilote [kɔpilɔt] *nm* (*AVIAT*) co-pilot; (*AUTO*) co-driver, navigator.
copine [kɔpin] *nf voir* **copain**.
copiste [kɔpist(ə)] *nm/f* copyist, transcriber.
coproduction [kɔpʀɔdyksjɔ̃] *nf* coproduction, joint production.
copropriété [kɔpʀɔpʀijete] *nf* co-ownership, joint ownership; **acheter en** ~ to buy on a co-ownership basis.
copulation [kɔpylasjɔ̃] *nf* copulation.
coq [kɔk] *nm* cock; rooster.

coq-à-l'âne [kɔkalɑn] *nm inv* abrupt change of subject.
coque [kɔk] *nf* (*de noix, mollusque*) shell; (*de bateau*) hull; **à la** ~ (*CULIN*) boiled.
coquelicot [kɔkliko] *nm* poppy.
coqueluche [kɔklyʃ] *nf* whooping-cough.
coquet, te [kɔkɛ, -ɛt] *a* flirtatious; appearance-conscious; pretty.
coquetier [kɔktje] *nm* egg-cup.
coquillage [kɔkijaʒ] *nm* (*mollusque*) shellfish *inv*; (*coquille*) shell.
coquille [kɔkij] *nf* shell; (*TYPO*) misprint; ~ **de beurre** shell of butter; ~ **de noix** nutshell; ~ **St Jacques** scallop.
coquin, e [kɔkɛ̃, -in] *a* mischievous, roguish; (*polisson*) naughty // *nm/f* (*péj*) rascal.
cor [kɔʀ] *nm* (*MUS*) horn; (*MÉD*): **(au pied)** corn; **réclamer à** ~ **et à cri** (*fig*) to clamour for; ~ **anglais** cor anglais; ~ **de chasse** hunting horn.
corail, aux [kɔʀaj, -o] *nm* coral *q*.
Coran [kɔʀɑ̃] *nm*: **le** ~ the Koran.
corbeau, x [kɔʀbo] *nm* crow.
corbeille [kɔʀbɛj] *nf* basket; (*à la Bourse*): **la** ~ the stockbrokers' central enclosure; ~ **de mariage** (*fig*) wedding presents *pl*; ~ **à ouvrage** work-basket; ~ **à pain** bread-basket; ~ **à papier** waste paper basket *ou* bin.
corbillard [kɔʀbijaʀ] *nm* hearse.
cordage [kɔʀdaʒ] *nm* rope; ~**s** *nmpl* (*de voilure*) rigging *sg*.
corde [kɔʀd(ə)] *nf* rope; (*de violon, raquette, d'arc*) string; (*trame*): **la** ~ the thread; (*ATHLÉTISME, AUTO*): **la** ~ the rails *pl*; **semelles de** ~ rope soies; ~ **à linge** washing *ou* clothes line; ~ **à lisse** (*climbing*) rope; ~ **à nœuds** knotted climbing rope; ~ **raide** tight-rope; ~ **à sauter** skipping rope; ~**s vocales** vocal cords.
cordeau, x [kɔʀdo] *nm* string, line; **tracé au** ~ as straight as a die.
cordée [kɔʀde] *nf* (*d'alpinistes*) rope, roped party.
cordial, e, aux [kɔʀdjal, -jo] *a* warm, cordial; ~**ité** *nf* warmth, cordiality.
cordon [kɔʀdɔ̃] *nm* cord, string; ~ **sanitaire/de police** sanitary/police cordon; ~ **bleu** cordon bleu; ~ **ombilical** umbilical cord.
cordonnerie [kɔʀdɔnʀi] *nf* shoe repairer's *ou* mender's (shop).
cordonnier [kɔʀdɔnje] *nm* shoe repairer *ou* mender, cobbler.
coreligionnaire [kɔʀeliʒjɔnɛʀ] *nm/f* (*d'un musulman, juif etc*) fellow Mahometan/Jew *etc*.
coriace [kɔʀjas] *a* tough.
cormoran [kɔʀmɔʀɑ̃] *nm* cormorant.
cornac [kɔʀnak] *nm* elephant driver.
corne [kɔʀn(ə)] *nf* horn; (*de cerf*) antler; ~ **d'abondance** horn of plenty; ~ **de brume** (*NAVIG*) foghorn.
cornée [kɔʀne] *nf* cornea.
corneille [kɔʀnɛj] *nf* crow.
cornélien, ne [kɔʀneljɛ̃, -jɛn] *a* (*débat etc*) where love and duty conflict.
cornemuse [kɔʀnəmyz] *nf* bagpipes *pl*.

corner nm [kɔʀnɛʀ] (FOOTBALL) corner (kick) // vb [kɔʀne] vt (pages) to make dog-eared // vi (klaxonner) to blare out.

cornet [kɔʀnɛ] nm (paper) cone ; (de glace) cornet, cone ; ~ à piston cornet.

cornette [kɔʀnɛt] nf cornet (headgear).

corniaud [kɔʀnjo] nm (chien) mongrel ; (péj) twit, clot.

corniche [kɔʀniʃ] nf cornice.

cornichon [kɔʀniʃɔ̃] nm gherkin.

cornue [kɔʀny] nf retort.

corollaire [kɔʀɔlɛʀ] nm corollary.

corolle [kɔʀɔl] nf corolla.

coron [kɔʀɔ̃] nm mining cottage ; mining village.

coronaire [kɔʀɔnɛʀ] a coronary.

corporation [kɔʀpɔʀɑsjɔ̃] nf corporate body ; (au moyen-âge) guild.

corporel, le [kɔʀpɔʀɛl] a bodily ; (punition) corporal ; **soins** ~**s** care sg of the body.

corps [kɔʀ] nm (gén) body ; (cadavre) (dead) body ; à son ~ **défendant** against one's will ; à ~ **perdu** headlong ; **perdu** ~ **et biens** lost with all hands ; **prendre** ~ to take shape ; **faire** ~ **avec** to be joined to ; to form one body with ; **d'armée** army corps ; ~ **de ballet** corps de ballet ; **le** ~ **consulaire (CC)** the consular corps ; ~ **à** ~ ad hand-to-hand // nm clinch ; **le** ~ **du délit** (JUR) corpus delicti ; **le** ~ **diplomatique (CD)** the diplomatic corps ; **le** ~ **électoral** the electorate // nm ~ **enseignant** the teaching profession ; ~ **étranger** (MÉD) foreign body ; ~ **de garde** guardroom.

corpulent, e [kɔʀpylɑ̃, -ɑ̃t] a stout, corpulent.

correct, e [kɔʀɛkt] a (exact) accurate, correct ; (bienséant, honnête) correct ; (passable) adequate ; ~**ement** ad accurately ; correctly.

correcteur, trice [kɔʀɛktœʀ, -tʀis] nm/f (SCOL) examiner, marker ; (TYPO) proof-reader.

correction [kɔʀɛksjɔ̃] nf (voir corriger) correction ; (voir correct) correctness ; (rature, surcharge) correction, emendation ; (coups) thrashing ; ~ (des épreuves) proofreading.

correctionnel, le [kɔʀɛksjɔnɛl] a (JUR): **chambre** ~**le** ≈ police magistrate's court.

corrélation [kɔʀelɑsjɔ̃] nf correlation.

correspondance [kɔʀɛspɔ̃dɑ̃s] nf correspondence ; (de train, d'avion) connection ; **ce train assure la** ~ **avec l'avion de 10 heures** this train connects with the 10 o'clock plane ; **cours par** ~ correspondence course ; **vente par** ~ mail-order business ; **correspondancier, ère** nm/f correspondence clerk.

correspondant, e [kɔʀɛspɔ̃dɑ̃, -ɑ̃t] nm/f correspondent.

correspondre [kɔʀɛspɔ̃dʀ(ə)] vi (données, témoignages) to correspond, tally ; (chambres) to communicate ; ~ **à** to correspond to ; ~ **avec qn** to correspond with sb.

corrida [kɔʀidɑ] nf bullfight.

corridor [kɔʀidɔʀ] nm corridor, passage.

corrigé [kɔʀiʒe] nm (SCOL) correct version ; fair copy.

corriger [kɔʀiʒe] vt (devoir) to correct, mark ; (texte) to correct, emend ; (erreur, défaut) to correct, put right ; (punir) to thrash ; ~ **qn de** (défaut) to cure sb of.

corroborer [kɔʀɔbɔʀe] vt to corroborate.

corroder [kɔʀɔde] vt to corrode.

corrompre [kɔʀɔ̃pʀ(ə)] vt (soudoyer) to bribe ; (dépraver) to corrupt.

corrosion [kɔʀozjɔ̃] nf corrosion.

corruption [kɔʀypsjɔ̃] nf bribery ; corruption.

corsage [kɔʀsɑʒ] nm bodice ; blouse.

corsaire [kɔʀsɛʀ] nm pirate, corsair ; privateer.

corse [kɔʀs(ə)] a, nm/f Corsican // nf: **la** **C**~ Corsica.

corsé, e [kɔʀse] a vigorous ; full-flavoured ; (fig) spicy ; tricky.

corselet [kɔʀsəlɛ] nm corselet.

corset [kɔʀsɛ] nm corset ; bodice.

corso [kɔʀso] nm: ~ **fleuri** procession of floral floats.

cortège [kɔʀtɛʒ] nm procession.

corvée [kɔʀve] nf chore, drudgery q ; (MIL) fatigue (duty).

cosmétique [kɔsmetik] nm hair-oil ; beauty care product.

cosmique [kɔsmik] a cosmic.

cosmonaute [kɔsmɔnot] nm/f cosmonaut, astronaut.

cosmopolite [kɔsmɔpɔlit] a cosmopolitan.

cosmos [kɔsmɔs] nm outer space ; cosmos.

cosse [kɔs] nf (BOT) pod, hull.

cossu, e [kɔsy] a opulent-looking, well-to-do.

costaud, e [kɔsto, -od] a strong, sturdy.

costume [kɔstym] nm (d'homme) suit ; (de théâtre) costume ; **costumé, e** a dressed up.

cote [kɔt] nf (en Bourse etc) quotation ; quoted value ; (d'un cheval): **la** ~ **de** the odds pl on ; (d'un candidat etc) rating ; (mesure: sur une carte) spot height ; (: sur un croquis) dimension ; (de classement) (classification) mark ; reference number ; **inscrit à la** ~ quoted on the Stock Exchange ; ~ **d'alerte** danger ou flood level.

côte [kot] nf (rivage) coast(line) ; (pente) slope ; (: sur une route) hill ; (ANAT) rib ; (d'un tricot, tissu) rib, ribbing q ; ~ **à** ~ ad side by side ; **la** **C**~ **(d'Azur)** the (French) Riviera.

côté [kote] nm (gén) side ; (direction) way, direction ; **de tous les** ~**s** from all directions ; **de quel** ~ **est-il parti?** which way ou in which direction did he go? ; **de ce/de l'autre** ~ this/the other way ; **du** ~ **de** (provenance) from ; (direction) towards ; **du** ~ **de Lyon** (proximité) the Lyons way, near Lyons ; **de** ~ ad sideways ; on one side ; to one side ; aside ; **laisser de** ~ to leave on one side ; **mettre de** ~ to put on one side, put aside ; **à** ~ ad (right) nearby ; beside ; next door ; (d'autre part) besides ; **à** ~ beside, next to ; (fig) in comparison to ; **à** ~ **(de la cible)** off target, wide (of the mark) ; **être aux** ~**s de** to be by the side of.

coteau, x [kɔto] *nm* hill.
côtelé, e [kotle] *a* ribbed ; **pantalon en velours** ~ corduroy trousers *pl*.
côtelette [kotlɛt] *nf* chop.
coter [kɔte] *vt* (*en Bourse*) to quote.
coterie [kɔtʀi] *nf* set.
côtier, ière [kotje, -jɛʀ] *a* coastal.
cotisation [kɔtizasjɔ̃] *nf* subscription, dues *pl* ; (*pour une pension*) contributions *pl*.
cotiser [kɔtize] *vi* : ~ (à) to pay contributions (to) ; **se** ~ to club together.
coton [kɔtɔ̃] *nm* cotton ; ~ **hydrophile** (absorbent) cotton-wool.
côtoyer [kotwaje] *vt* to be close to ; to rub shoulders with ; to run alongside ; to be bordering *ou* verging on.
cotte [kɔt] *nf* : ~ **de mailles** coat of mail.
cou [ku] *nm* neck.
couard, e [kwaʀ, -aʀd] *a* cowardly.
couchage [kuʃaʒ] *nm voir* **sac**.
couchant [kuʃɑ̃] *a* : **soleil** ~ setting sun.
couche [kuʃ] *nf* (*strate: gén, GÉO*) layer, stratum (*pl* a) ; (*de peinture, vernis*) coat ; (*de poussière, crème*) layer ; (*de bébé*) nappy, napkin ; ~**s** *nfpl*, (*MÉD*) confinement *sg* ; ~**s sociales** social levels *ou* strata ; ~-**culotte** *nf* disposable nappy and waterproof pants in one.
coucher [kuʃe] *nm* (*du soleil*) setting // *vt* (*personne*) to put to bed ; (: *loger*) to put up ; (*objet*) to lay on its side ; (*écrire*) to inscribe, couch // *vi* (*dormir*) to sleep, spend the night ; (*fam*): ~ **avec qn** to sleep with sb, go to bed with sb ; **se** ~ *vi* (*pour dormir*) to go to bed ; (*pour se reposer*) to lie down ; (*soleil*) to set, go down ; **à prendre avant le** ~ (*MÉD*) take at night *ou* before going to bed ; ~ **de soleil** sunset.
couchette [kuʃɛt] *nf* couchette ; (*de marin*) bunk.
coucou [kuku] *nm* cuckoo // *excl* peek-a-boo.
coude [kud] *nm* (*ANAT*) elbow ; (*de tuyau, de la route*) bend ; ~ **à** ~ *ad* shoulder to shoulder, side by side.
cou-de-pied [kudpje] *nm* instep.
coudre [kudʀ(ə)] *vt* (*bouton*) to sew on ; (*robe*) to sew (up) /-/ *vi* to sew.
couenne [kwan] *nf* (*de lard*) rind.
couettes [kwɛt] *nfpl* bunches.
couffin [kufɛ̃] *nm* Moses basket ; (straw) basket.
couiner [kwine] *vi* to squeal.
coulant, e [kulɑ̃, -ɑ̃t] *a* (*indulgent*) easygoing ; (*fromage etc*) runny.
coulée [kule] *nf* (*de lave, métal en fusion*) flow ; ~ **de neige** snowslide.
couler [kule] *vi* to flow, run ; (*fuir: stylo, récipient*) to leak ; (*sombrer: bateau*) to sink // *vt* (*cloche, sculpture*) to cast ; (*bateau*) to sink ; (*fig*) to ruin, bring down ; **se** ~ **dans** (*interstice etc*) to slip into ; **il a coulé une bielle** (*AUTO*) his big-end went.
couleur [kulœʀ] *nf* colour ; (*CARTES*) suit.
couleuvre [kulœvʀ(ə)] *nf* grass snake.
coulisse [kulis] *nf* (*TECH*) runner ; ~**s** *nfpl* (*THÉÂTRE*) wings ; (*fig*): **dans les** ~**s** behind the scenes ; **porte à** ~ sliding door ; **coulisser** *vi* to slide, run.

couloir [kulwaʀ] *nm* corridor, passage ; (*de bus*) gangway ; (*SPORT: de piste*) lane ; (*GÉO*) gully ; ~ **de navigation** shipping lane.
coulpe [kulp(ə)] *nf* : **battre sa** ~ to repent openly.
coup [ku] *nm* (*heurt, choc*) knock ; (*affectif*) blow, shock ; (*agressif*) blow ; (*avec arme à feu*) shot ; (*de l'horloge*) chime ; stroke ; (*SPORT*) stroke ; shot ; blow ; (*ÉCHECS*) move ; ~ **de coude/genou** nudge (with the elbow)/with the knee ; **à** ~**s de hache/marteau** (hitting) with an axe/a hammer ; ~ **de tonnerre** clap of thunder ; ~ **de sonnette** ring of the bell ; ~ **de crayon/pinceau** stroke of the pencil/brush ; **donner un** ~ **de balai** to sweep up, give the floor a sweep ; **donner un** ~ **de chiffon** to go round with the duster ; **avoir le** ~ (*fig*) to have the knack ; **boire un** ~ to have a drink ; **d'un seul** ~ (*subitement*) suddenly ; (*à la fois*) at one go ; in one blow ; **du premier** ~ first time *ou* go, at the first attempt ; **du même** ~ at the same time ; **à** ~ **sûr** definitely, without fail ; **sur le** ~ outright ; **sous le** ~ **de** (*surprise etc*) under the influence of ; **tomber sous le** ~ **de la loi** to constitute a statutory offence ; ~ **de chance** stroke of luck ; ~ **de couteau** stab (of a knife) ; ~ **dur** hard blow ; ~ **d'envoi** kick-off ; ~ **d'essai** first attempt ; ~ **d'état** coup d'état ; ~ **de feu** shot ; ~ **de filet** (*POLICE*) haul ; ~ **franc** free kick ; ~ **de frein** (sharp) braking *q* ; ~ **de fusil** rifle shot ; ~ **de grâce** coup de grâce ; ~ **de main** : **donner un** ~ **de main à qn** to give sb a (helping) hand ; ~ **d'œil** glance ; ~ **de pied** kick ; ~ **de poing** punch ; ~ **de soleil** sunburn ; ~ **de téléphone** phone call ; ~ **de tête** (*fig*) (sudden) impulse ; ~ **de théâtre** (*fig*) dramatic turn of events ; ~ **de vent** gust of wind.
coupable [kupabl(ə)] *a* guilty ; (*pensée*) guilty, culpable // *nm/f* (*gén*) culprit ; (*JUR*) guilty party ; ~ **de** guilty of.
coupe [kup] *nf* (*verre*) goblet ; (*à fruits*) dish ; (*SPORT*) cup ; (*de cheveux, de vêtement*) cut ; (*graphique, plan*) (cross) section ; **être sous la** ~ **de** to be under the control of ; **faire des** ~**s sombres dans** to make drastic cuts in.
coupé [kupe] *nm* (*AUTO*) coupé.
coupe-circuit [kupsiʀkɥi] *nm inv* cutout, circuit breaker.
coupée [kupe] *nf* (*NAVIG*) gangway.
coupe-papier [kuppapje] *nm inv* paper knife.
couper [kupe] *vt* to cut ; (*retrancher*) to cut (out), take out ; (*route, courant*) to cut off ; (*appétit*) to take away ; (*fièvre*) to take down, reduce ; (*vin, cidre*) to blend ; (: *à table*) to dilute (with water) // *vi* to cut ; (*prendre un raccourci*) to take a short-cut ; (*CARTES: diviser le paquet*) to cut ; (: *avec l'atout*) to trump ; **se** ~ (*se blesser*) to cut o.s. ; (*en témoignant etc*) to give o.s. away ; ~ **la parole à qn** to cut sb short.
couperet [kupʀɛ] *nm* cleaver, chopper.
couperosé, e [kupʀoze] *a* blotchy.
couple [kupl(ə)] *nm* couple ; ~ **de torsion** torque.

coupler [kuple] *vt* to couple (together).

couplet [kuplɛ] *nm* verse.

coupole [kupɔl] *nf* dome ; cupola.

coupon [kupɔ̃] *nm* (*ticket*) coupon ; (*de tissu*) remnant ; roll ; ~-**réponse international** international reply coupon.

coupure [kupyʀ] *nf* cut ; (*billet de banque*) note ; (*de journal*) cutting ; ~ **de courant** power cut.

cour [kuʀ] *nf* (*de ferme, jardin*) (court)yard ; (*d'immeuble*) back yard ; (JUR, *royale*) court ; **faire la** ~ **à qn** to court sb ; ~ **d'assises** court of assizes, ≈ Crown Court ; ~ **de cassation** Court of Cassation ; ~ **martiale** court-martial.

courage [kuʀaʒ] *nm* courage, bravery ; **courageux, euse** *a* brave, courageous.

couramment [kuʀamɑ̃] *ad* commonly ; (*avec aisance: parler*) fluently.

courant, e [kuʀɑ̃, -ɑ̃t] *a* (*fréquent*) common ; (COMM, *gén: normal*) standard ; (*en cours*) current // *nm* current ; (*fig*) movement ; trend ; **être au** ~ (**de**) (*fait, nouvelle*) to know (about) ; **mettre qn au** ~ (**de**) (*fait, nouvelle*) to tell sb (about) ; (*nouveau travail etc*) to teach sb the basics (of) ; **se tenir au** ~ (**de**) (*techniques etc*) to keep o.s. up-to-date (on) ; **dans le** ~ **de** (*pendant*) in the course of ; **le 10** ~ (COMM) the 10th inst ; ~ **d'air** draught ; ~ **électrique** (electric) current, power.

courbature [kuʀbatyʀ] *nf* ache ; **courbaturé, e** *a* aching.

courbe [kuʀb(ə)] *a* curved // *nf* curve ; ~ **de niveau** contour line.

courber [kuʀbe] *vt* to bend ; ~ **la tête** to bow one's head ; **se** ~ *vi* (*branche etc*) to bend, curve ; (*personne*) to bend (down).

courbette [kuʀbɛt] *nf* low bow.

coureur, euse [kuʀœʀ, -øz] *nm/f* (SPORT) runner (*ou* driver) ; (*péj*) womaniser/ manhunter ; ~ **cycliste/automobile** racing cyclist/driver.

courge [kuʀʒ(ə)] *nf* (BOT) gourd ; (CULIN) marrow.

courgette [kuʀʒɛt] *nf* courgette, zucchini.

courir [kuʀiʀ] *vi* (*gen*) to run ; (*se dépêcher*) to rush ; (*fig: rumeurs*) to go round ; (COMM: *intérêt*) to accrue // *vt* (SPORT: *épreuve*) to compete in ; (*risque*) to run ; (*danger*) to face ; ~ **les cafés/bals** to do the rounds of the cafés/dances ; **le bruit court que** the rumour is going round that ; ~ **après qn** to run after sb, chase (after) sb.

couronne [kuʀɔn] *nf* crown ; (*de fleurs*) wreath, circlet.

couronnement [kuʀɔnmɑ̃] *nm* coronation, crowning ; (*fig*) crowning achievement.

couronner [kuʀɔne] *vt* to crown.

courons *etc vb voir* **courir**.

courre [kuʀ] *vb voir* **chasse**.

courrier [kuʀje] *nm* mail, post ; (*lettres à écrire*) letters *pl* ; (*rubrique*) column ; **long/moyen** ~ *a* (AVIAT) long-/medium-haul ; ~ **du cœur** problem page.

courroie [kuʀwa] *nf* strap ; (TECH) belt ; ~ **de transmission/de ventilateur** driving/fan belt.

courrons *etc vb voir* **courir**.

courroucé, e [kuʀuse] *a* wrathful.

cours [kuʀ] *nm* (*leçon*) lesson ; class ; (*série de leçons*) course ; (*cheminement*) course ; (*écoulement*) flow ; (*avenue*) walk ; (COMM) rate ; price ; **donner libre** ~ **à** to give free expression to ; **avoir** ~ (*monnaie*) to be legal tender ; (*fig*) to be current ; (SCOL) to have a class *ou* lecture ; **en** (*année*) current ; (*travaux*) in progress ; **en** ~ **de route** on the way ; **au** ~ **de** in the course of, during ; **le** ~ **du change** the exchange rate ; ~ **d'eau** water course, generic term for streams, rivers ; ~ **du soir** night school.

course [kuʀs(ə)] *nf* running ; (SPORT: *épreuve*) race ; (*trajet: du soleil*) course ; (: *d'un projectile*) flight ; (: *d'une pièce mécanique*) travel ; (*excursion*) outing ; climb ; (*d'un taxi, autocar*) journey, trip ; (*petite mission*) errand ; ~**s** *nfpl* (*achats*) shopping *sg* ; (HIPPISME) races.

court, e [kuʀ, kuʀt(ə)] *a* short // *ad* short // *nm:* ~ (**de tennis**) (tennis) court ; **tourner** ~ to come to a sudden end ; **à** ~ **de** short of ; **prendre qn de** ~ to catch sb unawares ; **tirer à la** ~**e paille** to draw lots ; ~-**bouillon** *nm* court-bouillon ; ~-**circuit** *nm* short-circuit.

courtier, ère [kuʀtje, -jɛʀ] *nm/f* broker.

courtisan [kuʀtizɑ̃] *nm* courtier.

courtisane [kuʀtizan] *nf* courtesan.

courtiser [kuʀtize] *vt* to court, woo.

courtois, e [kuʀtwa, -waz] *a* courteous ; **courtoisie** *nf* courtesy.

couru, e *pp de* **courir**.

cousais *etc vb voir* **coudre**.

cousin, e [kuzɛ̃, -in] *nm/f* cousin.

coussin [kusɛ̃] *nm* cushion.

cousu, e [kuzy] *pp de* **coudre** // *a:* ~ **d'or** rolling in riches.

coût [ku] *nm* cost ; **le** ~ **de la vie** the cost of living.

coûtant [kutɑ̃] *am:* **au prix** ~ at cost price.

couteau, x [kuto] *nm* knife ; ~ **à cran d'arrêt** flick-knife ; ~ **de poche** pocket knife ; ~-**scie** *nm* serrated-edged knife.

coutellerie [kutɛlʀi] *nf* cutlery shop ; cutlery.

coûter [kute] *vt, vi* to cost ; **combien ça coûte?** how much is it?, what does it cost? ; **coûte que coûte** at all costs ; **coûteux, euse** *a* costly, expensive.

coutume [kutym] *nf* custom ; **coutumier, ère** *a* customary.

couture [kutyʀ] *nf* sewing ; dress-making ; (*points*) seam.

couturier [kutyʀje] *nm* fashion designer, couturier.

couturière [kutyʀjɛʀ] *nf* dressmaker.

couvée [kuve] *nf* brood, clutch.

couvent [kuvɑ̃] *nm* (*de sœurs*) convent ; (*de frères*) monastery ; (*établissement scolaire*) convent (school).

couver [kuve] *vt* to hatch ; (*maladie*) to be sickening for // *vi* (*feu*) to smoulder ; (*révolte*) to be brewing ; ~ **qn/qch des yeux** to look lovingly at ; to look longingly at.

couvercle [kuvɛʀkl(ə)] *nm* lid ; (*de bombe aérosol etc, qui se visse*) cap, top.

couvert, e [kuvɛʀ, -ɛʀt(ə)] pp de **couvrir** // a (ciel) overcast ; (coiffé d'un chapeau) wearing a hat // a (table) place setting ; (place à table) place ; (au restaurant) cover charge ; ~s nmpl place settings ; cutlery sg ; ~ **de** covered with ou in ; **bien ~** (habillé) well wrapped up ; **mettre le ~** to lay the table ; **à ~** under cover ; **sous le ~ de** under the shelter of ; (fig) under cover of.

couverture [kuvɛʀtyʀ] nf (de lit) blanket ; (de bâtiment) roofing ; (de livre, fig: d'un espion etc) cover.

couveuse [kuvøz] nf (à poules) sitter, brooder ; (de maternité) incubator.

couvre... [kuvʀ(ə)] préfixe: **~-chef** nm hat ; **~-feu** nm curfew ; **~-lit** nm bedspread.

couvreur [kuvʀœʀ] nm roofer.

couvrir [kuvʀiʀ] vt to cover ; **se ~** (ciel) to cloud over ; (s'habiller) to cover up, wrap up ; (se coiffer) to put on one's hat ; (par une assurance) to cover o.s. ; **se ~ de** (fleurs, boutons) to become covered in.

crabe [kʀɑb] nm crab.

crachat [kʀaʃa] nm spittle q, spit q.

cracher [kʀaʃe] vi to spit // vt to spit out ; (fig: lave etc) to belch (out) ; **~ du sang** to spit blood.

crachin [kʀaʃɛ̃] nm drizzle.

crachoir [kʀaʃwaʀ] nm spittoon ; (de dentiste) bowl.

craie [kʀɛ] nf chalk.

craindre [kʀɛ̃dʀ(ə)] vt to fear, be afraid of ; (être sensible à: chaleur, froid) to be easily damaged by ; **~ de/que** to be afraid of/that.

crainte [kʀɛ̃t] nf fear ; **de ~ de/que** for fear of/that ; **craintif, ive** a timid.

cramoisi, e [kʀamwazi] a crimson.

crampe [kʀɑ̃p] nf cramp ; **~ d'estomac** stomach cramp.

crampon [kʀɑ̃pɔ̃] nm (de semelle) stud ; (ALPINISME) crampon.

cramponner [kʀɑ̃pɔne]: **se ~** vi: **se ~ (à)** to hang ou cling on (to).

cran [kʀɑ̃] nm (entaille) notch ; (de courroie) hole ; (courage) guts pl ; **~ d'arrêt** safety catch ; **~ de mire** bead.

crâne [kʀɑn] nm skull.

crâner [kʀɑne] vi (fam) to swank, show off.

crânien, ne [kʀɑnjɛ̃, -jɛn] a cranial, skull cpd, brain cpd.

crapaud [kʀapo] nm toad.

crapule [kʀapyl] nf villain.

craquelure [kʀaklyʀ] nf crack ; crackle q.

craquement [kʀakmɑ̃] nm crack, snap ; (du plancher) creak, creaking q.

craquer [kʀake] vi (bois, plancher) to creak ; (fil, branche) to snap ; (couture) to come apart, burst ; (fig) to break down // vt: **~ une allumette** to strike a match.

crasse [kʀas] nf grime, filth.

crassier [kʀasje] nm slag heap.

cratère [kʀatɛʀ] nm crater.

cravache [kʀavaʃ] nf (riding) crop ; **cravacher** vt to use the crop on.

cravate [kʀavat] nf tie ; **cravater** vt to put a tie on ; (fig) to grab round the neck.

crawl [kʀol] nm crawl ; **dos crawlé** backstroke.

crayeux, euse [kʀɛjø, -øz] a chalky.

crayon [kʀɛjɔ̃] nm pencil ; (de rouge à lèvres etc) stick, pencil ; **écrire au ~** to write in pencil ; **~ à bille** ball-point pen ; **~ de couleur** crayon, colouring pencil.

créance [kʀeɑ̃s] nf (COMM) (financial) claim, (recoverable) debt ; **créancier, ière** nm/f creditor.

créateur, trice [kʀeatœʀ, -tʀis] a creative // nm/f creator.

création [kʀeasjɔ̃] nf creation.

créature [kʀeatyʀ] nf creature.

crécelle [kʀesɛl] nf rattle.

crèche [kʀɛʃ] nf (de Noël) crib ; (garderie) crèche, day nursery.

crédence [kʀedɑ̃s] nf (small) sideboard.

crédit [kʀedi] nm (gén) credit ; **~s** nmpl funds ; **payer/acheter à ~** to pay/buy on credit ou on easy terms ; **faire ~ à qn** to give sb credit ; **créditer** vt: **créditer un compte (de)** to credit an account (with) ; **créditeur, trice** a in credit, credit cpd // nm/f customer in credit.

crédule [kʀedyl] a credulous, gullible ; **crédulité** nf credulity, gullibility.

créer [kʀee] vt to create ; (THÉÂTRE) to produce (for the first time).

crémaillère [kʀemajɛʀ] nf (RAIL) rack ; (tige crantée) trammel ; **direction à ~** (AUTO) rack and pinion steering ; **pendre la ~** to have a house-warming party.

crémation [kʀemasjɔ̃] nf cremation.

crématoire [kʀematwaʀ] a: **four ~** crematorium.

crème [kʀɛm] nf cream ; (entremets) cream dessert // a inv cream(-coloured) ; **un (café) ~** ≈ a white coffee ; **~ fouettée** whipped cream ; **~ à raser** shaving cream ; **crémerie** nf dairy ; (tearoom) teashop ; **crémeux, euse** a creamy ; **crémier, ière** nm/f dairy-man/woman.

créneau, x [kʀeno] nm (de fortification) crenel(le) ; (fig) gap ; slot ; (AUTO): **faire un ~** to reverse into a parking space (between cars alongside the kerb).

créole [kʀeɔl] a, nm, nf Creole.

crêpe [kʀɛp] nf (galette) pancake // nm (tissu) crêpe ; (de deuil) black mourning crêpe ; black armband (ou hatband ou ribbon) ; **semelle (de) ~** crêpe sole ; **crêpé, e** a (cheveux) backcombed ; **~rie** nf pancake shop ou restaurant.

crépi [kʀepi] nm roughcast ; **crépir** vt to roughcast.

crépiter [kʀepite] vi to sputter ; splutter ; to crackle ; to rattle out ; to patter.

crépon [kʀepɔ̃] nm seersucker.

crépu, e [kʀepy] a frizzy, fuzzy.

crépuscule [kʀepyskyl] nm twilight, dusk.

crescendo [kʀeʃendo] nm, ad (MUS) crescendo ; **aller ~** (fig) to rise higher and higher, grow ever greater.

cresson [kʀesɔ̃] nm watercress.

crête [kʀɛt] nf (de coq) comb ; (de vague, montagne) crest.

crétin, e [kʀetɛ̃, -in] nm/f cretin.

cretonne [kʀatɔn] nf cretonne.

creuser [kRøze] vt (trou, tunnel) to dig; (sol) to dig a hole in; (bois) to hollow out; (fig) to go (deeply) into; **cela creuse (l'estomac)** that gives you a real appetite; **se ~ (la cervelle)** to rack one's brains.

creuset [kRøzε] nm crucible; (fig) melting pot; (severe) test.

creux, euse [kRø, -øz] a hollow // nm hollow; (fig: sur graphique etc) trough; **heures creuses** slack periods; off-peak periods; **le ~ de l'estomac** the pit of the stomach.

crevaison [kRəvεzɔ̃] nf puncture.

crevasse [kRəvas] nf (dans le sol) crack, fissure; (de glacier) crevasse; (de la peau) crack.

crevé, e [kRəve] a (fatigué) fagged out, worn out.

crève-cœur [kRεvkœR] nm inv heartbreak.

crever [kRəve] vt (papier) to tear, break; (tambour, ballon) to burst // vi (pneu) to burst; (automobiliste) to have a puncture; (abcès, outre, nuage) to burst (open); (fam) to die; **cela lui a crevé un œil** it blinded him in one eye.

crevette [kRəvεt] nf: ~ **(rose)** prawn; ~ **grise** shrimp.

cri [kRi] nm cry, shout; (d'animal: spécifique) cry, call; **c'est le dernier ~** (fig) it's the latest fashion.

criant, e [kRijɑ̃, -ɑ̃t] a (injustice) glaring.

criard, e [kRijaR, -aRd(ə)] a (couleur) garish, loud; (voix) yelling.

crible [kRibl(ə)] nm riddle; (mécanique) screen, jig; **passer qch au ~** to put sth through a riddle; (fig) to go over sth with a fine-tooth comb.

criblé, e [kRible] a: ~ **de** riddled with.

cric [kRik] nm (AUTO) jack.

crier [kRije] vi (pour appeler) to shout, cry (out); (de peur, de douleur etc) to scream, yell; (fig: grincer) to squeal, screech // vt (ordre, injure) to shout (out), yell (out); **crieur de journaux** nm newspaper seller.

crime [kRim] nm crime; (meurtre) murder; **criminaliste** nm/f specialist in criminal law; **criminalité** nf criminality, crime; **criminel, le** a criminal // nm/f criminal; murderer; **criminel de guerre** war criminal; **criminologiste** nm/f criminologist.

crin [kRε̃] nm hair q; (fibre) horsehair; **à tous ~s, à tout ~** diehard, out-and-out.

crinière [kRinjεR] nf mane.

crique [kRik] nf creek, inlet.

criquet [kRikε] nm locust; grasshopper.

crise [kRiz] nf crisis (pl crises); (MÉD) attack; fit; ~ **cardiaque** heart attack; ~ **de foi** crisis of belief; ~ **de foie** bilious attack; ~ **de nerfs** attack of nerves.

crispation [kRispɑsjɔ̃] nf twitch; contraction; tenseness.

crisper [kRispe] vt to tense; (poings) to clench; **se ~** to tense; to clench; (personne) to get tense.

crisser [kRise] vi (neige) to crunch; (tissu) to rustle; (pneu) to screech.

cristal, aux [kRistal, -o] nm crystal // nmpl (objets) crystal(ware) sg; ~ **de plomb** (lead) crystal; ~ **de roche** rock-

crystal; **cristaux de soude** washing soda sg.

cristallin, e [kRistalε̃, -in] a a crystal-clear // nm (ANAT) crystalline lens.

cristalliser [kRistalize] vi, vt, se ~ vi to crystallize.

critère [kRitεR] nm criterion (pl ia).

critique [kRitik] a a critical // nm/f (de théâtre, musique) critic // nf criticism; (THÉÂTRE etc: article) review; **la ~** (activité) criticism; (personnes) the critics pl.

critiquer [kRitike] vt (dénigrer) to criticize; (évaluer, juger) to assess, examine (critically).

croasser [kRɔase] vi to caw.

croc [kRo] nm (dent) fang; (de boucher) hook.

croc-en-jambe [kRɔkɑ̃ʒɑ̃b] nm: **faire un ~ à qn** to trip sb up.

croche [kRɔʃ] nf (MUS) quaver; **double ~** semiquaver.

crochet [kRɔʃε] nm hook; (clef) picklock; (détour) detour; (BOXE): ~ **du gauche** left hook; (TRICOT): aiguille) crochet-hook; (: technique) crochet; ~**s** nmpl (TYPO) square brackets; **vivre aux ~s de qn** to live ou sponge off sb; **crocheter** vt (serrure) to pick.

crochu, e [kRɔʃy] a hooked; claw-like.

crocodile [kRɔkɔdil] nm crocodile.

crocus [kRɔkys] nm crocus.

croire [kRwaR] vt to believe; ~ **qn honnête** to believe sb (to be) honest; **se ~ fort** to think one is strong; ~ **que** to believe ou think that; ~ **à, ~ en** to believe in.

crois vb voir **croître.**

croisade [kRwazad] nf crusade.

croisé, e [kRwaze] a (veston) double-breasted // nm (guerrier) crusader // nf (fenêtre) window, casement; ~**e d'ogives** intersecting ribs; **à la ~e des chemins** at the crossroads.

croisement [kRwazmɑ̃] nm (carrefour) crossroads sg; (BIO) crossing; crossbreed.

croiser [kRwaze] vt (personne, voiture) to pass; (route) to cross, cut across; (BIO) to cross // vi (NAVIG) to cruise; ~ **les jambes/bras** to cross one's legs/fold one's arms; **se ~** (personnes, véhicules) to pass each other; (routes) to cross, intersect; (lettres) to cross (in the post); (regards) to meet.

croiseur [kRwazœR] nm cruiser (warship).

croisière [kRwazjεR] nf cruise; **vitesse de ~** (AUTO etc) cruising speed.

croisillon [kRwazijɔ̃] nm: **motif/fenêtre à ~s** lattice pattern/window.

croissance [kRwasɑ̃s] nf growing, growth; **maladie de ~** growth disease; ~ **économique** economic growth.

croissant, e [kRwasɑ̃, -ɑ̃t] a growing; rising // nm (à manger) croissant; (motif) crescent.

croître [kRwɑtR(ə)] vi to grow; (lune) to wax.

croix [kRwa] nf cross; **en ~** a, ad in the form of a cross; **la C~ Rouge** the Red Cross.

croquant, e [kRɔkɑ̃, -ɑ̃t] a a crisp, crunchy // nm/f (péj) yokel, (country) bumpkin.

croque... [kRɔk] *préfixe:* ~-**mitaine** *nm* bog(e)y-man ; ~-**monsieur** *nm inv* toasted ham and cheese sandwich ; ~-**mort** *nm* (*péj*) pallbearer.

croquer [kRɔke] *vt* (*manger*) to crunch ; to munch ; (*dessiner*) to sketch // *vi* to be crisp *ou* crunchy.

croquet [kRɔkɛ] *nm* croquet.

croquette [kRɔkɛt] *nf* croquette.

croquis [kRɔki] *nm* sketch.

cross(-country) [kRɔs(kuntRi)] *nm* cross-country race *ou* run ; cross-country racing *ou* running.

crosse [kRɔs] *nf* (*de fusil*) butt ; (*de revolver*) grip ; (*d'évêque*) crook, crosier ; (*de hockey*) hockey stick.

crotte [kRɔt] *nf* droppings *pl*.

crotté, e [kRɔte] *a* muddy, mucky.

crottin [kRɔtɛ̃] *nm:* ~ (**de cheval**) (horse) dung *ou* manure.

crouler [kRule] *vi* (*s'effondrer*) to collapse ; (*être délabré*) to be crumbling.

croupe [kRup] *nf* croup, rump ; **en** ~ pillion.

croupier [kRupje] *nm* croupier.

croupir [kRupiR] *vi* to stagnate.

croustillant, e [kRustijɑ̃, -ɑ̃t] *a* crisp ; (*fig*) spicy.

croustiller [kRustije] *vi* to be crisp *ou* crusty.

croûte [kRut] *nf* crust ; (*du fromage*) rind ; (*de vol-au-vent*) case ; (*MÉD*) scab ; **en** ~ (*CULIN*) in pastry, in a pie ; ~ **aux champignons** mushrooms on toast ; ~ **au fromage** cheese on toast *q* ; ~ **de pain** (*morceau*) crust (of bread) ; ~ **terrestre** earth's crust.

croûton [kRutɔ̃] *nm* (*CULIN*) crouton ; (*bout du pain*) crust, heel.

croyance [kRwajɑ̃s] *nf* belief.

croyant, e [kRwajɑ̃, -ɑ̃t] *nm/f* believer.

C.R.S. *sigle fpl* = *Compagnies républicaines de sécurité (a state security police force)* // *sigle m* member of the C.R.S.

cru, e [kRy] *pp de* **croire** // *a* (*non cuit*) raw ; (*lumière, couleur*) harsh ; (*paroles, description*) crude // *nm* (*vignoble*) vineyard ; (*vin*) wine // *nf* (*d'un cours d'eau*) swelling, rising ; **de son (propre)** ~ (*fig*) of his own devising ; **du** ~ local ; **en** ~**e** in spate.

crû *pp de* **croître**.

cruauté [kRyote] *nf* cruelty.

cruche [kRyʃ] *nf* pitcher, (earthenware) jug.

crucial, e, aux [kRysjal, -o] *a* crucial.

crucifier [kRysifje] *vt* to crucify.

crucifix [kRysifi] *nm* crucifix.

cruciforme [kRysifɔRm(ə)] *a* cruciform, cross-shaped.

cruciverbiste [kRysiveRbist(ə)] *nm/f* crossword puzzle enthusiast.

crudité [kRydite] *nf* crudeness *q* ; harshness *q* ; ~**s** *nfpl* (*CULIN*) salads.

crue [kRy] *nf voir* **cru**.

cruel, le [kRyɛl] *a* cruel.

crus *etc*, **crûs** *etc vb voir* **croire**, **croître**.

crustacés [kRystase] *nmpl* shellfish.

crypte [kRipt(ə)] *nf* crypt.

cubage [kybaʒ] *nm* cubage, cubic content.

cube [kyb] *nm* cube ; (*jouet*) brick, building block ; **mètre** ~ cubic metre ; **2 au** ~ = **8 2** cubed is 8 ; **élever au** ~ to cube ; **cubique** *a* cubic.

cueillette [kœjɛt] *nf* picking, gathering ; harvest *ou* crop (of fruit).

cueillir [kœjiR] *vt* (*fruits, fleurs*) to pick, gather ; (*fig*) to catch.

cuiller *ou* **cuillère** [kɥijɛR] *nf* spoon ; ~ **à café** coffee spoon ; (*CULIN*) ≈ teaspoonful ; ~ **à soupe** soup-spoon ; (*CULIN*) ≈ tablespoonful ; **cuillerée** *nf* spoonful.

cuir [kɥiR] *nm* leather ; (*avant tannage*) hide ; ~ **chevelu** scalp.

cuirasse [kɥiRas] *nf* breastplate ; **cuirassé** *nm* (*NAVIG*) battleship.

cuire [kɥiR] *vt* (*aliments*) to cook ; (*poterie*) to fire // *vi* to cook ; (*picoter*) to smart, sting, burn ; **bien cuit** (*viande*) well done ; **trop cuit** overdone.

cuisine [kɥizin] *nf* (*pièce*) kitchen ; (*art culinaire*) cookery, cooking ; (*nourriture*) cooking, food ; **faire la** ~ to cook, make a *ou* the meal ; **cuisiner** *vt* to cook ; (*fam*) to grill // *vi* to cook ; **cuisinier, ière** *nm/f* cook // *nf* (*poêle*) cooker.

cuisse [kɥis] *nf* (*ANAT*) thigh ; (*CULIN*) leg.

cuisson [kɥisɔ̃] *nf* cooking ; firing.

cuistre [kɥistR(ə)] *nm* prig.

cuit, e *pp de* **cuire**.

cuivre [kɥivR(ə)] *nm* copper ; **les** ~**s** (*MUS*) the brass ; **cuivré, e** a coppery ; bronzed.

cul [ky] *nm* (*fam!*) arse (!), bum ; ~ **de bouteille** bottom of a bottle.

culasse [kylas] *nf* (*AUTO*) cylinder-head ; (*de fusil*) breech.

culbute [kylbyt] *nf* somersault ; (*accidentelle*) tumble, fall ; **culbuter** *vi* to (take a) tumble, fall (head over heels) ; **culbuteur** *nm* (*AUTO*) rocker arm.

cul-de-jatte [kydʒat] *nm/f* legless cripple.

cul-de-sac [kydsak] *nm* cul-de-sac.

culinaire [kylinɛR] *a* culinary.

culminant, e [kylminɑ̃, -ɑ̃t] a: **point** ~ highest point.

culminer [kylmine] *vi* to reach its highest point ; to tower.

culot [kylo] *nm* (*d'ampoule*) cap ; (*effronterie*) cheek, nerve.

culotte [kylɔt] *nf* (*pantalon*) pants *pl*, trousers *pl* ; (*de femme*): (**petite**) ~ knickers *pl* ; ~ **de cheval** riding breeches *pl*.

culotté, e [kylɔte] a (*pipe*) seasoned ; (*cuir*) mellowed ; (*effronté*) cheeky.

culpabilité [kylpabilite] *nf* guilt.

culte [kylt(ə)] *nm* (*religion*) religion ; (*hommage, vénération*) worship ; (*protestant*) service.

cultivateur, trice [kyltivatœR, -tRis] *nm/f* farmer.

cultivé, e [kyltive] a (*personne*) cultured, cultivated.

cultiver [kyltive] *vt* to cultivate ; (*légumes*) to grow, cultivate.

culture [kyltyR] *nf* cultivation ; growing ; (*connaissances etc*) culture ; (**champs de**) ~**s** land(s) under cultivation ; ~ **physique** physical training ; **culturel, le** *a* cultural ; **culturisme** *nm* body-building.

cumin [kymɛ̃] nm (CULIN) caraway seeds pl, cumin.

cumul [kymyl] nm (voir cumuler) holding (ou drawing) concurrently ; ~ **de peines** sentences to run consecutively.

cumuler [kymyle] vt (emplois, honneurs) to hold concurrently ; (salaires) to draw concurrently ; (JUR: droits) to accumulate.

cupide [kypid] a greedy, grasping.

curatif, ive [kyratif, -iv] a curative.

cure [kyR] nf (MÉD) course of treatment ; (REL) cure, living ; presbytery, ≈ vicarage ; **faire une ~ de fruits** to go on a fruit cure ou diet ; **n'avoir ~ de** to pay no attention to ; ~ **de sommeil** sleep therapy q.

curé [kyRe] nm parish priest ; **M. le ~** ≈ Vicar.

cure-dent [kyRdɑ̃] nm toothpick.

cure-pipe [kyRpip] nm pipe cleaner.

curer [kyRe] vt to clean out.

curieux, euse [kyRjø, -øz] a (étrange) strange, curious ; (indiscret) curious, inquisitive ; (intéressé) inquiring, curious // nmpl (badauds) onlookers, bystanders ; **curiosité** nf curiosity, inquisitiveness ; (objet) curio(sity) ; (site) unusual feature ou sight.

curiste [kyRist(ə)] nm/f person taking the waters at a spa.

curriculum vitae [kyRikylɔmvite] nm inv (abr **C.V.**) curriculum vitae.

curry [kyRi] nm curry ; **poulet au ~** curried chicken, chicken curry.

curseur [kyRsœR] nm (de règle) slide ; (de fermeture-éclair) slider.

cursif, ive [kyRsif, -iv] a: **écriture cursive** cursive script.

cutané, e [kytane] a cutaneous, skin cpd.

cuti-réaction [kytiReaksjɔ̃] nf (MÉD) skin-test.

cuve [kyv] nf vat ; (à mazout etc) tank.

cuvée [kyve] nf vintage.

cuvette [kyvɛt] nf (récipient) bowl, basin ; (du lavabo) (wash)basin ; (des w.-c.) pan ; (GÉO) basin.

C.V. sigle m (AUTO) voir **cheval** ; (COMM) = curriculum vitae.

cyanure [sjanyR] nm cyanide.

cybernétique [sibɛRnetik] nf cybernetics sg.

cyclable [siklabl(ə)] a: **piste ~ cycle** track.

cyclamen [siklamɛn] nm cyclamen.

cycle [sikl(ə)] nm cycle.

cyclique [siklik] a cyclic(al).

cyclisme [siklism] nm cycling.

cycliste [siklist(ə)] nm/f cyclist // a cycle cpd.

cyclomoteur [siklɔmɔtœR] nm moped ; **cyclomotoriste** nm/f moped-rider.

cyclone [siklon] nm hurricane.

cygne [siɲ] nm swan.

cylindre [silɛ̃dR(ə)] nm cylinder ; **moteur à 4 ~s en ligne** straight-4 engine ; **cylindrée** nf (AUTO) (cubic) capacity ; **une (voiture de) grosse cylindrée** a big-engined car ; **cylindrique** a cylindrical.

cymbale [sɛ̃bal] nf cymbal.

cynique [sinik] a cynical ; **cynisme** nm cynicism.

cyprès [sipRɛ] nm cypress.

cypriote [sipRjɔt] a, nm/f Cypriot.

cyrillique [siRilik] a Cyrillic.

cystite [sistit] nf cystitis.

cytise [sitiz] nm laburnum.

D

d' prép, dét voir **de**.

dactylo [daktilo] nf (aussi: ~**graphe**) typist ; (aussi: ~**graphie**) typing, typewriting ; ~**graphier** vt to type (out).

dada [dada] nm hobby-horse.

daigner [deɲe] vt to deign.

daim [dɛ̃] nm (fallow) deer inv ; (peau) buckskin ; (imitation) suede.

dallage [dalaʒ] nm paving.

dalle [dal] nf paving stone, flag(stone) ; slab.

daltonien, ne [daltɔnjɛ̃, -jɛn] a colour-blind.

dam [dam] nm: **au grand ~ de** much to the detriment ou annoyance of.

dame [dam] nf lady ; (CARTES, ÉCHECS) queen ; ~**s** nfpl (jeu) draughts sg.

damer [dame] vt to ram ou pack down ; ~ **le pion à** (fig) to get the better of.

damier [damje] nm draughtboard ; (dessin) check (pattern).

damner [dane] vt to damn.

dancing [dɑ̃siŋ] nm dance hall.

dandiner [dɑ̃dine]: **se ~** vi to sway about ; to waddle along.

Danemark [danmaRk] nm Denmark.

danger [dɑ̃ʒe] nm danger ; **mettre en ~** to endanger, put in danger ; **dangereux, euse** a dangerous.

danois, e [danwa, -waz] a Danish // nm/f: **D~, e** Dane // nm (langue) Danish.

dans [dɑ̃] prép in ; (direction) into, to ; (à l'intérieur de) in, inside ; **je l'ai pris ~ le tiroir/salon** I took it out of ou from the drawer/lounge ; **boire ~ un verre** to drink out of ou from a glass ; ~ **2 mois** in 2 months, in 2 months' time, 2 months from now ; ~ **les 20 F** about 20 F.

dansant, e [dɑ̃sɑ̃, -ɑ̃t] a: **soirée ~e** evening of dancing ; dinner dance.

danse [dɑ̃s] nf: **la ~** dancing ; (classique) (ballet) dancing ; **une ~** a dance ; **danser** vi, vt to dance ; **danseur, euse** nm/f ballet dancer/ballerina ; (au bal etc) dancer ; partner ; **en danseuse** (à vélo) standing on the pedals.

dard [daR] nm (organ).

darder [daRde] vt to shoot, send forth.

date [dat] nf date ; **faire ~** to mark a milestone ; ~ **de naissance** date of birth ; **dater** vt, vi to date ; **dater de** to date from, go back to ; **à dater de** (as) from.

datif [datif] nm dative.

datte [dat] nf date ; **dattier** nm date palm.

dauphin [dofɛ̃] nm (ZOOL) dolphin ; (du roi) dauphin ; (fig) heir apparent.

daurade [dɔRad] nf gilt-head.

davantage [davɑ̃taʒ] ad more ; (plus longtemps) longer ; ~ **de** more.

DCA [desea] sigle f (= défense contre avions): **la ~** anti-aircraft defence.

de (*de* + *le* = **du**, *de* + *les* = **des**) [də, dy, de] *prép* of; (*provenance*) from; (*moyen*) with; **la voiture d'Élisabeth/de mes parents** Elizabeth's/my parents' car; **un mur de brique/bureau d'acajou** a brick wall/mahogany desk; **augmenter** *etc* **de 10F** to increase by 10F; **une pièce de 2 m de large** *ou* **large de 2 m** a room 2 m wide *ou* in width, a 2 m wide room; **un bébé de 10 mois** a 10-month-old baby; **un séjour de 2 ans** a 2-year stay; **12 mois de crédit/travail** 12 months' credit/work // *dét*: **du vin, de l'eau, des pommes** (some) wine, (some) water, (some) apples; **des enfants sont venus** some children came; **a-t-il du vin?** has he got any wine?; **il ne veut pas de pommes** he doesn't want any apples; **il n'a pas d'enfants** he has no children, he hasn't got any children; **pendant des mois** for months.

dé [de] *nm* (à jouer) die *ou* dice (*pl* dice); (*aussi*: **~ à coudre**) thimble; **~s** *nmpl* (*jeu*) (game of) dice; **un coup de ~s** a throw of the dice.

déambuler [deɑ̃byle] *vi* to stroll about.

débâcle [debɑkl(ə)] *nf* rout.

déballer [debale] *vt* to unpack.

débandade [debɑ̃dad] *nf* rout; scattering.

débarbouiller [debaʀbuje] *vt* to wash; **se ~** to wash (one's face).

débarcadère [debaʀkadɛʀ] *nm* landing stage.

débardeur [debaʀdœʀ] *nm* docker, stevedore; (*maillot*) slipover, tank top.

débarquement [debaʀkəmɑ̃] *nm* unloading; landing; disembarcation; (MIL) landing.

débarquer [debaʀke] *vt* to unload, land // *vi* to disembark; (*fig*) to turn up.

débarras [debaʀa] *nm* lumber room; junk cupboard; outhouse; **bon ~!** good riddance!

débarrasser [debaʀase] *vt* to clear; **~ qn de** (*vêtements, paquets*) to relieve sb of; (*habitude, ennemi*) to rid sb of; **~ qch de** (*fouillis etc*) to clear sth of; **se ~ de** *vt* to get rid of; to rid o.s. of.

débat [deba] *nm* discussion, debate; **~s** (POL) proceedings, debates.

débattre [debatʀ(ə)] *vt* to discuss, debate; **se ~** *vi* to struggle.

débauche [deboʃ] *nf* debauchery; **une ~ de** (*fig*) a profusion of; a riot of.

débaucher [deboʃe] *vt* (*licencier*) to lay off, dismiss; (*entraîner*) to lead astray, debauch.

débile [debil] *a* weak, feeble; **~ mental, e** *nm/f* mental defective.

débit [debi] *nm* (*d'un liquide, fleuve*) (rate of) flow; (*d'un magasin*) turnover (of goods); (*élocution*) delivery; (*bancaire*) debit; **avoir un ~ de 10 F** to be 10 F in debit; **~ de boissons** drinking establishment; **~ de tabac** tobacconist's (shop); **débiter** *vt* (*compte*) to debit; (*liquide, gaz*) to yield, produce, give out; (*couper: bois, viande*) to cut up; (*vendre*) to retail; (*péj: paroles etc*) to come out with, churn out; **débiteur, trice** *nm/f* debtor // *a* in debit.

déblai [deblɛ] *nm* earth (*moved*).

déblaiement [deblɛmɑ̃] *nm* clearing; **travaux de ~** earth moving *sg*.

déblayer [debleje] *vt* to clear.

débloquer [debloke] *vt* (*frein*) to release; (*prix, crédits*) to free.

déboires [debwaʀ] *nmpl* setbacks.

déboiser [debwaze] *vt* to clear of trees; to deforest.

déboîter [debwate] *vt* (AUTO) to pull out; **se ~ le genou** *etc* to dislocate one's knee *etc*.

débonnaire [debonɛʀ] *a* easy-going, good-natured.

débordé, e [debɔʀde] *a*: **être ~ de** (*travail, demandes*) to be snowed under with.

débordement [debɔʀdəmɑ̃] *nm* overflowing.

déborder [debɔʀde] *vi* to overflow; (*lait etc*) to boil over // *vt* (MIL, SPORT) to outflank; **~ (de) qch** (*dépasser*) to extend beyond sth; **~ de** (*joie, zèle*) to be brimming over with *ou* bursting with.

débouché [debuʃe] *nm* (*pour vendre*) outlet; (*perspective d'emploi*) opening; (*sortie*): **au ~ de la vallée** where the valley opens out (onto the plain); **au ~ de la rue Dupont** (*sur le boulevard*) where the rue Dupont meets the boulevard.

déboucher [debuʃe] *vt* (*évier, tuyau etc*) to unblock; (*bouteille*) to uncork, open // *vi*: **~ de** to emerge from, come out of; **~ sur** to come out onto; to open out onto; (*fig*) to arrive at, lead up to.

débourser [debuʀse] *vt* to pay out, lay out.

debout [dəbu] *ad*: **être ~** (*personne*) to be standing, stand; (: *levé, éveillé*) to be up (and about); (*chose*) to be upright; **être encore ~** (*fig: en état*) to be still going; to be still standing; **se mettre ~** to get up (on one's feet); **se tenir ~** to stand; **~!** stand up!; (*du lit*) get up!; **cette histoire ne tient pas ~** this story doesn't hold water.

déboutonner [debutone] *vt* to undo, unbutton; **se ~** *vi* to come undone *ou* unbuttoned.

débraillé, e [debʀɑje] *a* slovenly, untidy.

débrayage [debʀɛjaʒ] *nm* (AUTO) clutch; (: *action*) disengaging the clutch; (*grève*) stoppage; **faire un double ~** to double-declutch.

débrayer [debʀɛje] *vi* (AUTO) to declutch, disengage the clutch; (*cesser le travail*) to stop work.

débridé, e [debʀide] *a* unbridled, unrestrained.

débris [debʀi] *nm* (*fragment*) fragment // *nmpl* (*déchets*) pieces; rubbish *sg*; debris *sg*.

débrouillard, e [debʀujaʀ, -aʀd(ə)] *a* smart, resourceful.

débrouiller [debʀuje] *vt* to disentangle, untangle; (*fig*) to sort out, unravel; **se ~** *vi* to manage.

débroussailler [debʀusaje] *vt* to clear (of brushwood).

débusquer [debyske] *vt* to drive out (from cover).

début [deby] *nm* beginning, start; ~s *nmpl* beginnings; début *sg*.

débutant, e [debytɑ̃, -ɑ̃t] *nm/f* beginner, novice.

débuter [debyte] *vi* to begin, start; (*faire ses débuts*) to start out.

deçà [dəsa]: **en ~ de** *prép* this side of.

décacheter [dekaʃte] *vt* to unseal, open.

décade [dekad] *nf* (*10 jours*) (period of) ten days; (*10 ans*) decade.

décadence [dekadɑ̃s] *nf* decadence; decline.

décaféiné, e [dekafeine] *a* decaffeinated, caffeine-free.

décalage [dekalaʒ] *nm* gap; discrepancy; move forward *ou* back; shift forward *ou* back; ~ **horaire** time difference (between time zones); time-lag.

décalcomanie [dekalkɔmani] *nf* transfer.

décaler [dekale] *vt* (*dans le temps: avancer*) to bring forward; (: *retarder*) to put back; (*changer de position*) to shift forward *ou* back; ~ **de 2 h** to bring *ou* move forward 2 hours; to put back 2 hours.

décalquer [dekalke] *vt* to trace; (*par pression*) to transfer.

décamper [dekɑ̃pe] *vi* to clear out *ou* off.

décanter [dekɑ̃te] *vt* to (allow to) settle (and decant); **se ~** to settle.

décapant [dekapɑ̃] *nm* acid solution; scouring agent; paint stripper.

décaper [dekape] *vt* to clean; (*avec abrasif*) to scour; (*avec papier de verre*) to sand.

décapiter [dekapite] *vt* to behead; (*par accident*) to decapitate; (*fig*) to cut the top off; to remove the top men from.

décapotable [dekapɔtabl(ə)] *a* convertible.

décapoter [dekapɔte] *vt* to put down the top of.

décapsuler [dekapsyle] *vt* to take the cap *ou* top off; **décapsuleur** *nm* bottle-opener.

décathlon [dekatlɔ̃] *nm* decathlon.

décédé, e [desede] *a* deceased.

décéder [desede] *vi* to die.

déceler [desle] *vt* to discover, detect; to indicate, reveal.

décélération [deseleɾɑsjɔ̃] *nf* deceleration.

décembre [desɑ̃bɾ(ə)] *nm* December.

décemment [desamɑ̃] *ad* decently.

décence [desɑ̃s] *nf* decency.

décennie [desni] *nf* decade.

décent, e [desɑ̃, -ɑ̃t] *a* decent.

décentraliser [desɑ̃tɾalize] *vt* to decentralize.

décentrer [desɑ̃tɾe] *vt* to decentre; **se ~** to move off-centre.

déception [desɛpsjɔ̃] *nf* disappointment.

décerner [desɛɾne] *vt* to award.

décès [desɛ] *nm* death, decease.

décevoir [desvwaɾ] *vt* to disappoint.

déchaîner [deʃene] *vt* (*passions, colère*) to unleash; (*rires etc*) to give rise to, arouse; **se ~** *vi* to rage; to burst out, explode; (*se mettre en colère*) to fly into a rage, loose one's fury.

déchanter [deʃɑ̃te] *vi* to become disillusioned.

décharge [deʃaɾʒ(ə)] *nf* (*dépôt d'ordures*) rubbish tip *ou* dump; (*électrique*) electrical discharge; (*salve*) volley of shots; **à la ~ de** in defence of.

déchargement [deʃaɾʒəmɑ̃] *nm* unloading.

décharger [deʃaɾʒe] *vt* (*marchandise, véhicule*) to unload; (*ELEC*) to discharge; (*arme: neutraliser*) to unload; (: *faire feu*) to discharge, fire; ~ **qn de** (*responsabilité*) to relieve sb of, release sb from.

décharné, e [deʃaɾne] *a* bony, emaciated, fleshless.

déchausser [deʃose] *vt* (*personne*) to take the shoes off; (*skis*) to take off; **se ~** to take off one's shoes; (*dent*) to come *ou* work loose.

déchéance [deʃeɑ̃s] *nf* degeneration; decay, decline; fall.

déchet [deʃɛ] *nm* (*de bois, tissu etc*) scrap; (*perte: gén COMM*) wastage, waste; ~**s** *nmpl* (*ordures*) refuse *sg*, rubbish *sg*.

déchiffrer [deʃifɾe] *vt* to decipher.

déchiqueter [deʃikte] *vt* to tear *ou* pull to pieces.

déchirant, e [deʃiɾɑ̃, -ɑ̃t] *a* heart-breaking, heart-rending.

déchirement [deʃiɾmɑ̃] *nm* (*chagrin*) wrench, heartbreak; (*gén pl: conflit*) rift, split.

déchirer [deʃiɾe] *vt* to tear; (*mettre en morceaux*) to tear up; (*pour ouvrir*) to tear off; (*arracher*) to tear out; (*fig*) to rack; to tear; to tear apart; **se ~** *vi* to tear, rip; **se ~ un muscle** to tear a muscle.

déchirure [deʃiɾyɾ] *nf* (*accroc*) tear, rip; ~ **musculaire** torn muscle.

déchoir [deʃwaɾ] *vi* (*personne*) to lower o.s., demean o.s.

déchu, e [deʃy] *a* fallen; deposed.

décibel [desibɛl] *nm* decibel.

décidé, e [deside] *a* (*personne, air*) determined; **c'est ~** it's decided; **être ~ à faire** to be determined to do.

décidément [desidemɑ̃] *ad* undoubtedly; really.

décider [deside] *vt*: ~ **qch** to decide on sth; ~ **de faire/que** to decide to do/that; ~ **qn (à faire qch)** to persuade *ou* induce sb (to do sth); ~ **de qch** to decide upon sth; (*suj: chose*) to determine sth; **se ~ (à faire)** to decide (to do), make up one's mind (to do); **se ~ pour** to decide on *ou* in favour of.

décilitre [desilitɾ(ə)] *nm* decilitre.

décimal, e, aux [desimal, -o] *a, nf* decimal.

décimer [desime] *vt* to decimate.

décimètre [desimɛtɾ(ə)] *nm* decimetre; **double ~** (20 cm) ruler.

décisif, ive [desizif, -iv] *a* decisive; (*qui l'emporte*): **le facteur/ l'argument ~** the deciding factor/ argument.

décision [desizjɔ̃] *nf* decision; (*fermeté*) decisiveness, decision; **emporter** *ou* **faire la ~** to be decisive.

déclamation [deklamɑsjɔ̃] *nf* declamation; (*péj*) ranting, spouting.

déclaration [deklaɾɑsjɔ̃] *nf* declaration; registration; (*discours: POL etc*) statement; ~ **(d'amour)** declaration; ~ **de décès**

registration of death; ~ **de guerre** declaration of war; ~ **(d'impôts)** statement of income, tax declaration, ≈ tax return; ~ **(de sinistre)** (insurance) claim.

déclarer [deklaʀe] vt to declare, announce; (revenus, marchandises) to declare; (décès, naissance) to register; **se** ~ (feu, maladie) to break out; ~ **que** to declare that.

déclassement [deklɑsmɑ̃] nm (RAIL etc) change of class.

déclasser [deklɑse] vt to relegate; to downgrade; to lower in status.

déclenchement [deklɑ̃ʃmɑ̃] nm release; setting off.

déclencher [deklɑ̃ʃe] vt (mécanisme etc) to release; (sonnerie) to set off, activate; (attaque, grève) to launch; (provoquer) to trigger off; **se** ~ to release itself; to go off.

déclic [deklik] nm trigger mechanism; (bruit) click.

déclin [deklɛ̃] nm decline.

déclinaison [deklinɛzɔ̃] nf declension.

décliner [dekline] vi to decline // vt (invitation) to decline, refuse; (responsabilité) to refuse to accept; (nom, adresse) to state; (LING) to decline.

déclivité [deklivite] nf slope, incline; **en** ~ sloping, on the incline.

décocher [dekɔʃe] vt to throw; to shoot.

décoder [dekɔde] vt to decipher, decode.

décoiffer [dekwafe] vt: ~ **qn** to disarrange ou mess up sb's hair; to take sb's hat off; **se** ~ to take off one's hat.

décoincer [dekwɛ̃se] vt to unjam, loosen.

déçois etc vb voir **décevoir**.

décolère [dekɔlɛʀe] vi: **il ne décolère pas** he's still angry, he hasn't calmed down.

décollage [dekɔlaʒ] nm (AVIAT) takeoff.

décoller [dekɔle] vt to unstick // vi (avion) to take off; **se** ~ to come unstuck.

décolletage [dekɔltaʒ] nm (TECH) cutting.

décolleté, e [dekɔlte] a low-necked, low-cut; wearing a low-cut dress // nm low neck(line); (bare) neck and shoulders; (plongeant) cleavage.

décolorant [dekɔlɔʀɑ̃] nm decolorant, bleaching agent.

décoloration [dekɔlɔʀasjɔ̃] nf: **se faire une** ~ (chez le coiffeur) to have one's hair bleached ou lightened.

décolorer [dekɔlɔʀe] vt (tissu) to fade; (cheveux) to bleach, lighten; **se** ~ vi to fade.

décombres [dekɔ̃bʀ(ə)] nmpl rubble sg, debris sg.

décommander [dekɔmɑ̃de] vt to cancel; (invités) to put off; **se** ~ to cancel one's appointment etc, cry off.

décomposé, e [dekɔ̃poze] a (visage) haggard, distorted.

décomposer [dekɔ̃poze] vt to break up; (CHIMIE) to decompose; (MATH) to factorize; **se** ~ vi (pourrir) to decompose; **décomposition** nf breaking up; decomposition; factorization; **en décomposition** (organisme) in a state of decay, decomposing.

décompression [dekɔ̃pʀɛsjɔ̃] nf decompression.

décompte [dekɔ̃t] nm deduction; (facture) breakdown (of an account), detailed account.

déconcentration [dekɔ̃sɑ̃tʀasjɔ̃] nf (des industries etc) dispersal.

déconcentré, e [dekɔ̃sɑ̃tʀe] a (sportif etc) who has lost (his/her) concentration.

déconcerter [dekɔ̃sɛʀte] vt to disconcert, confound.

déconfit, e [dekɔ̃fi, -it] a crestfallen, downcast.

déconfiture [dekɔ̃fityʀ] nf failure, defeat; collapse, ruin.

décongeler [dekɔ̃ʒle] vt to thaw (out).

décongestionner [dekɔ̃ʒɛstjɔne] vt (MÉD) to decongest; (rues) to relieve congestion in.

déconnecter [dekɔnɛkte] vt to disconnect.

déconseiller [dekɔ̃seje] vt: ~ **qch (à qn)** to advise (sb) against sth; ~ **à qn de faire** to advise sb against doing.

déconsidérer [dekɔ̃sideʀe] vt to discredit.

déconsigner [dekɔ̃siɲe] vt (valise) to collect (from left luggage); (bouteille) to return the deposit on.

décontenancer [dekɔ̃tnɑ̃se] vt to disconcert, discountenance.

décontracter [dekɔ̃tʀakte] vt, **se** ~ to relax.

déconvenue [dekɔ̃vny] nf disappointment.

décor [dekɔʀ] nm décor; (paysage) scenery; ~s nmpl (THÉÂTRE) scenery sg, décor sg; (CINÉMA) set sg.

décorateur [dekɔʀatœʀ] nm (interior) decorator; (CINÉMA) set designer.

décoratif, ive [dekɔʀatif, -iv] a decorative.

décoration [dekɔʀasjɔ̃] nf decoration.

décorer [dekɔʀe] vt to decorate.

décortiquer [dekɔʀtike] vt to shell; (riz) to hull; (fig) to dissect.

décorum [dekɔʀɔm] nm decorum, etiquette.

découcher [dekuʃe] vi to spend the night away from home.

découdre [dekudʀ(ə)] vt to unpick, take the stitching out of; **se** ~ to come unstitched; **en** ~ (fig) to fight, do battle.

découler [dekule] vi: ~ **de** to ensue ou follow from.

découpage [dekupaʒ] nm cutting up; carving; (image) cut-out (figure); ~ **électoral** division into constituencies.

découper [dekupe] vt (papier, tissu etc) to cut up; (volaille, viande) to carve; (détacher: manche, article) to cut out; **se** ~ **sur** (ciel, fond) to stand out against.

découplé, e [dekuple] a: **bien** ~ well-built, well-proportioned.

découpure [dekupyʀ] nf: ~s (morceaux) cut-out bits; (d'une côte, arête) indentations, jagged outline sg.

découragement [dekuʀaʒmɑ̃] nm discouragement, despondency.

décourager [dekuʀaʒe] vt to discourage, dishearten; (dissuader) to discourage, put off; **se** ~ to lose heart, become discouraged; ~ **qn de faire/de qch** to discourage sb from doing/from sth, put sb off doing/sth.

décousu, e [dekuzy] *a* unstitched; (*fig*) disjointed, disconnected.

découvert, e [dekuvɛʀ, -ɛʀt(ə)] *a* (*tête*) bare, uncovered; (*lieu*) open, exposed // *nm* (*bancaire*) overdraft // *nf* discovery; **a** ~ *ad* (MIL) exposed, without cover; (*fig*) openly // *a* (COMM) overdrawn; **aller à la** ~ **e de** to go in search of.

découvrir [dekuvʀiʀ] *vt* to discover; (*apercevoir*) to see; (*enlever ce qui couvre ou protège*) to uncover; (*montrer, dévoiler*) to reveal; **se** ~ to take off one's hat; to take off some clothes; (*au lit*) to uncover o.s.; (*ciel*) to clear; ~ **que** to discover that, find out that.

décrasser [dekʀase] *vt* to clean.

décrépi, e [dekʀepi] *a* peeling; with roughcast rendering removed.

décrépit, e [dekʀepi, -it] *a* decrepit; **décrépitude** *nf* decrepitude; decay.

decrescendo [dekʀeʃɛndo] *nm* (MUS) decrescendo; **aller** ~ (*fig*) to decline, be on the wane.

décret [dekʀe] *nm* decree; **décréter** *vt* to decree; to order; to declare; ~**-loi** *nm* statutory order.

décrié, e [dekʀije] *a* disparaged.

décrire [dekʀiʀ] *vt* to describe; (*courbe, cercle*) to follow, describe.

décrochement [dekʀɔʃmɑ̃] *nm* (*d'un mur etc*) recess.

décrocher [dekʀɔʃe] *vt* (*dépendre*) to take down; (*téléphone*) to take off the hook; (: *pour répondre*): ~ **(le téléphone)** to pick up *ou* lift the receiver; (*fig: contrat etc*) to get, land // *vi* to drop out; to switch off.

décroître [dekʀwatʀ(ə)] *vi* to decrease, decline, diminish.

décrue [dekʀy] *nf* drop in level (of the waters).

décrypter [dekʀipte] *vt* to decipher.

déçu, e [desy] *pp de* **décevoir**.

déculotter [dekylɔte] *vt*: ~ **qn** to take off *ou* down sb's trousers.

décuple [dekypl(ə)] *nm*: **le** ~ **de** ten times; **au** ~ tenfold; **décupler** *vt, vi* to increase tenfold.

dédaigner [dedeɲe] *vt* to despise, scorn; (*négliger*) to disregard, spurn; ~ **de faire** to consider it beneath one to do; not to deign to do; **dédaigneux, euse** *a* scornful, disdainful.

dédain [dedɛ̃] *nm* scorn, disdain.

dédale [dedal] *nm* maze.

dedans [dədɑ̃] *ad* inside; (*pas en plein air*) indoors, inside // *nm* inside; **au** ~ on the inside; inside; **en** ~ (*vers l'intérieur*) inwards; *voir aussi* **là.**

dédicace [dedikas] *nf* dedication; (*manuscrite, sur une photo etc*) inscription; **dédicacer** [dedikase] *vt*: ~ **(à qn)** to sign (for sb), autograph (for sb), inscribe (to sb).

dédier [dedje] *vt* to dedicate.

dédire [dediʀ]: **se** ~ *vi* to go back on one's word; to retract, recant.

dédit [dedi] *nm* (COMM) forfeit, penalty.

dédommagement [dedɔmaʒmɑ̃] *nm* compensation.

dédommager [dedɔmaʒe] *vt*: ~ **qn (de)** to compensate sb (for); (*fig*) to repay sb (for).

dédouaner [dedwane] *vt* to clear through customs.

dédoublement [dedubləmɑ̃] *nm* splitting; (PSYCH): ~ **de la personnalité** split *ou* dual personality.

dédoubler [deduble] *vt* (*classe, effectifs*) to split (into two); (*couverture etc*) to unfold; (*manteau*) to remove the lining of; ~ **un train/les trains** to run a relief train/additional trains.

déduction [dedyksjɔ̃] *nf* (*d'argent*) deduction; (*raisonnement*) deduction, inference.

déduire [deduiʀ] *vt*: ~ **qch (de)** (*ôter*) to deduct sth (from); (*conclure*) to deduce *ou* infer sth (from).

déesse [deɛs] *nf* goddess.

défaillance [defajɑ̃s] *nf* (*syncope*) blackout; (*fatigue*) (sudden) weakness *q*; (*technique*) fault, failure; (*morale etc*) weakness; ~ **cardiaque** heart failure.

défaillant, e [defajɑ̃, -ɑ̃t] *a* (JUR: *témoin*) defaulting.

défaillir [defajiʀ] *vi* to faint; to feel faint; (*mémoire etc*) to fail.

défaire [defɛʀ] *vt* (*installation, échafaudage*) to take down, dismantle; (*paquet etc, nœud, vêtement*) to undo; **se** ~ *vi* to come undone; **se** ~ **de** *vt* (*se débarrasser de*) to get rid of; (*se séparer de*) to part with.

défait, e [defɛ, -ɛt] *a* (*visage*) haggard, ravaged // *nf* defeat.

défaitiste [defetist(ə)] *a*, *nm/f* defeatist.

défalquer [defalke] *vt* to deduct.

défaut [defo] *nm* (*moral*) fault, failing, defect; (*d'étoffe, métal*) fault, flaw, defect; (*manque, carence*): ~ **de** lack of; shortage of; **en** ~ at fault; in the wrong; **faire** ~ (*manquer*) to be lacking; **à** ~ **de** failing that; **à** ~ for lack *ou* want of; **par** ~ (JUR) in his (*ou* her *etc*) absence.

défaveur [defavœʀ] *nf* disfavour.

défavorable [defavɔʀabl(ə)] *a* unfavourable.

défavoriser [defavɔʀize] *vt* to put at a disadvantage.

défectif, ive [defɛktif, -iv] *a*: **verbe** ~ defective verb.

défection [defɛksjɔ̃] *nf* defection, failure to give support *ou* assistance; failure to appear; **faire** ~ (*d'un parti etc*) to withdraw one's support, leave.

défectueux, euse [defɛktɥø, -øz] *a* faulty, defective; **défectuosité** *nf* defectiveness *q*; defect, fault.

défendre [defɑ̃dʀ(ə)] *vt* to defend; (*interdire*) to forbid; ~ **à qn qch/de faire** to forbid sb sth/to do; **se** ~ to defend o.s.; **il se défend** (*fig*) he can hold his own; **ça se défend** (*fig*) it holds together; **se** ~ **de/contre** (*se protéger*) to protect o.s. from/against; **se** ~ **de** (*se garder de*) to refrain from; (*nier*): **se** ~ **de vouloir** to deny wanting.

défense [defɑ̃s] *nf* defence; (*d'éléphant etc*) tusk; '~ **de fumer/cracher**' 'no smoking/ spitting', 'smoking/spitting prohibited'; **défenseur** *nm* defender; (*JUR*) counsel for the defence; **défensif, ive** *a*, *nf* defensive.

déférent, e [defeʀɑ̃, -ɑ̃t] *a* (*poli*) deferential, deferent.

déférer [defeʀe] *vt* (*JUR*) to refer; ~ **à** *vt* (*requête, décision*) to defer to; ~ **qn à la justice** to hand sb over to justice.

déferlement [defɛʀləmɑ̃] *nm* breaking; surge.

déferler [defɛʀle] *vi* (*vagues*) to break; (*fig*) to surge.

défi [defi] *nm* (*provocation*) challenge; (*bravade*) defiance.

défiance [defjɑ̃s] *nf* mistrust, distrust.

déficience [defisjɑ̃s] *nf* deficiency.

déficit [defisit] *nm* (*COMM*) deficit; (*PSYCH etc: manque*) defect; **être en** ~ to be in deficit, be in the red.

défier [defje] *vt* (*provoquer*) to challenge; (*fig*) to defy, brave; **se** ~ **de** (*se méfier de*) to distrust, mistrust; ~ **qn de faire** to challenge *ou* defy sb to do; ~ **qn à** (*jeu etc*) to challenge sb to.

défigurer [defigyʀe] *vt* to disfigure; (*suj: boutons etc*) to mar *ou* spoil (the looks of); (*fig: œuvre*) to mutilate, deface.

défilé [defile] *nm* (*GÉO*) (narrow) gorge *ou* pass; (*soldats*) parade; (*manifestants*) procession, march; **un** ~ **de** (*voitures, visiteurs etc*) a stream of.

défiler [defile] *vi* (*troupes*) to march past; (*sportifs*) to parade; (*manifestants*) to march; (*visiteurs*) to pour, stream; **se** ~ *vi* (*se dérober*) to slip away, sneak off.

défini, e [defini] *a* definite.

définir [definiʀ] *vt* to define.

définitif, ive [definitif, -iv] *a* (*final*) final, definitive; (*pour longtemps*) permanent, definitive; (*sans appel*) final, definite // *nf:* **en définitive** eventually; (*somme toute*) when all is said and done.

définition [definisjɔ̃] *nf* definition; (*de mots croisés*) clue; (*TV*) (picture) resolution.

définitivement [definitivmɑ̃] *ad* definitively; permanently; definitely.

déflagration [deflagʀɑsjɔ̃] *nf* explosion.

déflation [deflɑsjɔ̃] *nf* deflation; **déflationniste** *a* deflationist, deflationary.

déflecteur [deflɛktœʀ] *nm* (*AUTO*) quarter-light.

déflorer [deflɔʀe] *vt* (*jeune fille*) to deflower; (*fig*) to spoil the charm of.

défoncer [defɔ̃se] *vt* (*caisse*) to stave in; (*porte*) to smash in *ou* down; (*lit, fauteuil*) to burst (the springs of); (*terrain, route*) to rip *ou* plough up.

déformant, e [defɔʀmɑ̃, -ɑ̃t] *a:* **glace** *ou* **miroir** ~(**e**) distorting mirror.

déformation [defɔʀmɑsjɔ̃] *nf* loss of shape; deformation; distortion; ~ **professionnelle** conditioning by one's job.

déformer [defɔʀme] *vt* to put *ou* of shape; (*corps*) to deform; (*pensée, fait*) to distort; **se** ~ *vi* to lose its shape.

défouler [defule]: **se** ~ *vi* (*PSYCH*) to work off one's tensions, release one's pent-up feelings; (*gén*) to unwind, let off steam.

défraîchir [defʀeʃiʀ]: **se** ~ *vi* to fade; to become worn.

défrayer [defʀeje] *vt:* ~ **qn** to pay sb's expenses; ~ **la chronique** to be in the news, be the main topic of conversation.

défricher [defʀiʃe] *vt* to clear (for cultivation).

défroquer [defʀɔke] *vi* (*gén:* **se** ~) to give up the cloth, renounce one's vows.

défunt, e [defœ̃, -œ̃t] *a:* **son** ~ **père** his late father // *nm/f* deceased.

dégagé, e [degaʒe] *a* clear; (*ton, air*) casual, jaunty.

dégagement [degaʒmɑ̃] *nm* emission; freeing; clearing; (*espace libre*) clearing; passage; clearance; (*FOOTBALL*) clearance; **voie de** ~ slip road; **itinéraire de** ~ alternative route (*to relieve traffic congestion*).

dégager [degaʒe] *vt* (*exhaler*) to give off, emit; (*délivrer*) to free, extricate; (*MIL: troupes*) to relieve; (*désencombrer*) to clear; (*isoler: idée, aspect*) to bring out; ~ **qn de** (*engagement, parole etc*) to release *ou* free sb from; **se** ~ *vi* (*odeur*) to emanate, be given off; (*passage, ciel*) to clear; **se** ~ **de** (*fig: engagement etc*) to get out of; to go back on.

dégaîner [degene] *vt* to draw.

dégarnir [degaʀniʀ] *vt* (*vider*) to empty, clear; **se** ~ *vi* to empty; to be cleaned out *ou* cleared; (*tempes, crâne*) to go bald.

dégâts [degɑ] *nmpl* damage *sg*.

dégazer [degaze] *vi* (*pétrolier*) to clean its tanks.

dégel [deʒɛl] *nm* thaw.

dégeler [deʒle] *vt* to thaw (out); (*fig*) to unfreeze // *vi* to thaw (out).

dégénéré, e [deʒeneʀe] *a, nm/f* degenerate.

dégénérer [deʒeneʀe] *vi* to degenerate; (*empirer*) to go from bad to worse.

dégingandé, e [deʒɛ̃gɑ̃de] *a* gangling, lanky.

dégivrage [deʒivʀaʒ] *nm* defrosting; de-icing.

dégivrer [deʒivʀe] *vt* (*frigo*) to defrost; (*vitres*) to de-ice; **dégivreur** *nm* defroster; de-icer.

déglutir [deglytiʀ] *vt* to swallow.

dégonflé, e [degɔ̃fle] *a* (*pneu*) flat.

dégonfler [degɔ̃fle] *vt* (*pneu, ballon*) to let down, deflate; **se** ~ *vi* (*fam*) to chicken out.

dégouliner [deguline] *vi* to trickle, drip; ~ **de** to be dripping with.

dégoupiller [degupije] *vt* (*grenade*) to take the pin out of.

dégourdi, e [deguʀdi] *a* smart, resourceful.

dégourdir [deguʀdiʀ] *vt* to warm (up); **se** ~ (**les jambes**) to stretch one's legs (*fig*).

dégoût [degu] *nm* disgust, distaste.

dégoûtant, e [degutɑ̃, -ɑ̃t] *a* disgusting.

dégoûter [degute] *vt* to disgust; **cela me dégoûte** I find this disgusting *ou* revolting; ~ **qn de qch** to put sb off sth.

dégoutter [degute] *vi* to drip; ~ **de** to be dripping with.

dégradé, e [degʀade] *a* (*couleur*) shaded off // *nm* (*PEINTURE*) gradation.

dégrader [degʀade] *vt* (*MIL: officier*) to degrade; (*abîmer*) to damage, deface;

(*avilir*) to degrade, debase ; **se ~** (*relations, situation*) to deteriorate.
dégrafer [degʀafe] *vt* to unclip, unhook, unfasten.
dégraissage [degʀɛsaʒ] *nm*: **~ et nettoyage à sec** dry cleaning.
dégraisser [degʀese] *vt* (*soupe*) to skim ; (*vêtement*) to take the grease marks out of.
degré [dəgʀe] *nm* degree ; (*d'escalier*) step ; **brûlure au 1er/2ème ~** 1st/2nd degree burn ; **équation du 1er/2ème ~** linear/quadratic equation ; **alcool à 90 ~s** 90% proof alcohol (*on Gay-Lussac scale*) ; **vin de 10 ~s** 10° wine (*on Gay-Lussac scale*) ; **par ~(s)** *ad* by degrees, gradually.
dégressif, ive [degʀesif, -iv] *a* on a decreasing sliding scale, degressive.
dégrever [degʀəve] *vt* to grant tax relief to ; to reduce the tax burden on.
dégringoler [degʀɛ̃gɔle] *vi* to tumble (down).
dégriser [degʀize] *vt* to sober up.
dégrossir [degʀosiʀ] *vt* (*bois*) to trim ; (*fig*) to work out roughly ; to knock the rough edges off.
déguenillé, e [dɛgnije] *a* ragged, tattered.
déguerpir [degɛʀpiʀ] *vi* to clear off, scarper.
déguisement [degizmɑ̃] *nm* disguise.
déguiser [degize] *vt* to disguise ; **se ~** (*se costumer*) to dress up ; (*pour tromper*) to disguise o.s.
dégustation [degystasjɔ̃] *nf* tasting ; sampling ; savouring ; (*séance*): **~ de vin(s)** wine-tasting session.
déguster [degyste] *vt* (*vins*) to taste ; (*fromages etc*) to sample ; (*savourer*) to enjoy, savour.
déhancher [deɑ̃ʃe]: **se ~** *vi* to sway one's hips ; to lean (one's weight) on one hip.
dehors [dəɔʀ] *ad* outside ; (*en plein air*) outdoors, outside // *nm* outside // *nmpl* (*apparences*) appearances, exterior *sg* ; **mettre** *ou* **jeter ~** (*expulser*) to throw out ; **au ~** outside ; outwardly ; **au ~ de** outside ; **en ~** (*vers l'extérieur*) outside ; outwards ; **en ~ de** (*hormis*) apart from.
déjà [deʒa] *ad* already ; (*auparavant*) before, already ; **quel nom, ~?** what was the name again?
déjanter [deʒɑ̃te]: **se ~** *vi* (*pneu*) to come off the rim.
déjeté, e [deʒte] *a* lop-sided, crooked.
déjeuner [deʒœne] *vi* to (have) lunch ; (*le matin*) to have breakfast // *nm* lunch ; (*petit déjeuner*) breakfast.
déjouer [deʒwe] *vt* to elude ; to foil, thwart.
delà [dəla] *ad*: **par ~, en ~ (de), au ~ (de)** beyond.
délabrer [delabʀe]: **se ~** *vi* to fall into decay, become dilapidated.
délacer [delase] *vt* to unlace, undo.
délai [delɛ] *nm* (*attente*) waiting period ; (*sursis*) extension (of time) ; (*temps accordé*) time limit ; **sans ~** without delay ; **à bref ~** shortly, very soon ; at short notice ; **dans les ~s** within the time limit ; **comptez un ~ de livraison de 10 jours** allow 10 days for delivery.

délaisser [delese] *vt* to abandon, desert.
délasser [delɑse] *vt* (*reposer*) to relax ; (*divertir*) to divert, entertain ; **se ~** to relax.
délateur, trice [delatœʀ, -tʀis] *nm/f* informer.
délation [delɑsjɔ̃] *nf* denouncement, informing.
délavé, e [delave] *a* faded.
délayer [deleje] *vt* (*CULIN*) to mix (with water *etc*) ; (*peinture*) to thin down ; (*fig*) to pad out, spin out.
delco [dɛlko] *nm* (*AUTO*) distributor.
délecter [delɛkte]: **se ~** *vi*: **se ~ de** to revel *ou* delight in.
délégation [delegɑsjɔ̃] *nf* delegation.
délégué, e [delege] *a* delegated // *nm/f* delegate ; representative.
déléguer [delege] *vt* to delegate.
délester [delɛste] *vt* (*navire*) to unballast.
délibération [deliberɑsjɔ̃] *nf* deliberation.
délibéré, e [delibere] *a* (*conscient*) deliberate ; (*déterminé*) determined, resolute.
délibérément [deliberemɑ̃] *ad* deliberately.
délibérer [delibere] *vi* to deliberate.
délicat, e [delika, -at] *a* delicate ; (*plein de tact*) tactful ; (*attentionné*) thoughtful ; (*exigeant*) fussy, particular ; **procédés peu ~s** unscrupulous methods ; **délicatement** *ad* delicately ; (*avec douceur*) gently ; **délicatesse** *nf* delicacy, delicate nature ; tactfulness ; thoughtfulness ; **délicatesses** *nfpl* attentions, consideration *sg*.
délice [delis] *nm* delight.
délicieux, euse [delisjø, -jøz] *a* (*au goût*) delicious ; (*sensation, impression*) delightful.
délictueux, euse [deliktɥø, -ɥøz] *a* criminal.
délié, e [delje] *a* nimble, agile ; slender, fine // *nm*: **les ~s** the upstrokes (*in handwriting*).
délier [delje] *vt* to untie ; **~ qn de** (*serment etc*) to free *ou* release sb from.
délimitation [delimitɑsjɔ̃] *nf* delimitation, demarcation.
délimiter [delimite] *vt* to delimit, demarcate ; to determine ; to define.
délinquance [delɛ̃kɑ̃s] *nf* criminality ; **~ juvénile** juvenile delinquency.
délinquant, e [delɛ̃kɑ̃, -ɑ̃t] *a, nm/f* delinquent.
déliquescence [delikesɑ̃s] *nf*: **en ~** in a state of decay.
délire [deliʀ] *nm* (*fièvre*) delirium ; (*fig*) frenzy ; lunacy.
délirer [deliʀe] *vi* to be delirious ; (*fig*) to be raving, be going wild.
délit [deli] *nm* (criminal) offence ; **~ de droit commun** violation of common law ; **~ politique** political offence ; **~ de presse** violation of the press laws.
délivrance [delivʀɑ̃s] *nf* freeing, release ; (*sentiment*) relief.
délivrer [delivʀe] *vt* (*prisonnier*) to (set) free, release ; (*passeport, certificat*) to issue ; **~ qn de** (*ennemis*) to set sb free from, deliver *ou* free sb from ; (*fig*) to relieve sb of ; to rid sb of.
déloger [deloʒe] *vt* (*locataire*) to turn out ; (*objet coincé, ennemi*) to dislodge.

déloyal, e, aux [delwajal, -o] a disloyal; unfair.

delta [dɛlta] nm (GÉO) delta.

déluge [delyʒ] nm (biblique) Flood, Deluge; (grosse pluie) downpour, deluge; (grand nombre): ∼ **de** flood of.

déluré, e [delyʀe] a smart, resourceful; (péj) forward, pert.

démagnétiser [demaɲetize] vt to demagnetize.

démagogie [demagɔʒi] nf demagogy, demagoguery; **démagogique** a demagogic, popularity-seeking; votecatching; **démagogue** a demagogic // nm demagogue.

démaillé, e [demaje] a (bas) laddered, with a run, with runs.

demain [dəmɛ̃] ad tomorrow.

demande [dəmɑ̃d] nf (requête) request; (revendication) demand; (ADMIN, formulaire) application; (ÉCON): **la** ∼ demand; '∼s **d'emploi'** situations wanted; ∼ **en mariage** (marriage) proposal; ∼ **de naturalisation** application for naturalization; ∼ **de poste** job application.

demandé, e [dəmɑ̃de] a (article etc): **très** ∼ (very) much in demand.

demander [dəmɑ̃de] vt to ask for; (question: date, heure etc) to ask; (requérir, nécessiter) to require, demand; ∼ **qch à qn** to ask sb for sth; to ask sb sth; ∼ **à qn de faire** to ask sb to do; ∼ **que/pourquoi** to ask that/why; **se** ∼ **si/pourquoi** etc to wonder if/why etc; (sens purement réfléchi) to ask o.s. if/why etc; **on vous demande au téléphone** you're wanted on the phone, someone's asking for you on the phone.

demandeur, euse [dəmɑ̃dœʀ, -øz] nm/f: ∼ **d'emploi** job-seeker; (job) applicant.

démangeaison [demɑ̃ʒɛzɔ̃] nf itching.

démanger [demɑ̃ʒe] vi to itch; **la main me démange** my hand is itching; **l'envie me démange de** I'm itching to.

démanteler [demɑ̃tle] vt to break up; to demolish.

démaquillant [demakijɑ̃] nm make-up remover.

démaquiller [demakije] vt: **se** ∼ to remove one's make-up.

démarcage [demaʀkaʒ] nm = **démarquage**.

démarcation [demaʀkɑsjɔ̃] nf demarcation.

démarchage [demaʀʃaʒ] nm (COMM) door-to-door selling.

démarche [demaʀʃ(ə)] nf (allure) gait, walk; (intervention) step; approach; (fig: intellectuelle) thought processes pl; approach; **faire des** ∼**s auprès de qn** to approach sb.

démarcheur, euse [demaʀʃœʀ, -øz] nm/f (COMM) door-to-door salesman/woman.

démarquage [demaʀkaʒ] nm mark-down.

démarqué, e [demaʀke] a (FOOTBALL) unmarked.

démarquer [demaʀke] vt (prix) to mark down; (joueur) to stop marking.

démarrage [demaʀaʒ] nm starting q, start; ∼ **en côte** hill start.

démarrer [demaʀe] vi (conducteur) to start (up); (véhicule) to move off; (travaux) to get moving; (coureur: accélérer) to pull away; **démarreur** nm (AUTO) starter.

démasquer [demaske] vt to unmask.

démâter [demate] vt to dismast // vi to be dismasted.

démêler [demele] vt to untangle, disentangle.

démêlés [demele] nmpl problems.

démembrer [demɑ̃bʀe] vt to slice up, tear apart.

déménagement [demenaʒmɑ̃] nm (du point de vue du locataire) move; (: du déménageur) removal; **entreprise/camion de** ∼ removal firm/van.

déménager [demenaʒe] vt (meubles) to (re)move // vi to move (house); **déménageur** nm removal man; (entrepreneur) furniture remover.

démence [demɑ̃s] nf dementia; madness, insanity.

démener [demne]: **se** ∼ vi to thrash about; (fig) to exert o.s.

démenti [demɑ̃ti] nm denial, refutation.

démentiel, le [demɑ̃sjɛl] a insane.

démentir [demɑ̃tiʀ] vt (nouvelle) to refute; (suj: faits etc) to belie, refute; ∼ **que** to deny that; **ne pas se** ∼ not to fail; to keep up.

démériter [demerite] vi: ∼ **auprès de qn** to come down in sb's esteem.

démesure [deməzyʀ] nf immoderation, immoderateness; **démesuré, e** a immoderate, disproportionate.

démettre [demɛtʀ(ə)] vt: ∼ **qn de** (fonction, poste) to dismiss sb from; **se** ∼ **(de ses fonctions)** to resign (from) one's duties; **se** ∼ **l'épaule** etc to dislocate one's shoulder etc.

demeurant [dəmœʀɑ̃]: **au** ∼ ad for all that.

demeure [dəmœʀ] nf residence; **mettre qn en** ∼ **de faire** to enjoin ou order sb to do; **à** ∼ ad permanently.

demeurer [dəmœʀe] vi (habiter) to live; (séjourner) to stay; (rester) to remain.

demi, e [dəmi] a: **et** ∼: **trois heures/bouteilles et** ∼**es** three and a half hours/bottles, three hours/bottles and a half; **il est 2 heures/midi et** ∼**e** it's half past 2/12 // nm (bière) ≈ half-pint (.25 litre); (FOOTBALL) half-back; **à** ∼ ad half-; **ouvrir à** ∼ to half-open; **à** ∼ **fini** half-completed; **à la** ∼**e** (heure) on the half-hour.

demi... [dəmi] préfixe half-, semi..., demi-; ∼-**cercle** nm semicircle; **en** ∼-**cercle** a semicircular // ad in a half circle; ∼-**douzaine** nf half-dozen, half a dozen; ∼-**finale** nf semifinal; ∼-**fond** nm (SPORT) medium-distance running; ∼-**frère** nm half-brother; ∼-**gros** nm wholesale trade; ∼-**heure** nf half-hour, half an hour; ∼-**jour** nm half-light; ∼-**journée** nf half-day, half a day.

démilitariser [demilitaʀize] vt to demilitarize.

demi-litre [dəmilitʀ(ə)] nm half-litre, half a litre.

demi-livre [dəmilivʀ(ə)] *nf* half-pound, half a pound.
demi-longueur [dəmilɔ̃gœʀ] *nf* (*SPORT*) half-length, half a length.
demi-lune [dəmilyn] *ad*: **en ~** semicircular.
demi-mesure [dəmimzyʀ] *nf* half-measure.
demi-mot [dəmimo]: **à ~** *ad* without having to spell things out.
déminer [demine] *vt* to clear of mines; **démineur** *nm* bomb disposal expert.
demi-pension [dəmipɑ̃sjɔ̃] *nf* (*à l'hôtel*) half-board.
demi-pensionnaire [dəmipɑ̃sjɔnɛʀ] *nm/f* (*au lycée*) half-boarder.
demi-place [dəmiplas] *nf* half-fare.
démis, e [demi, -iz] *a* (*épaule etc*) dislocated.
demi-saison [dəmisɛzɔ̃] *nf*: **vêtements de ~** spring *ou* autumn clothing.
demi-sel [dəmisɛl] *a inv* (*beurre, fromage*) slightly salted.
demi-sœur [dəmisœʀ] *nf* half-sister.
démission [demisjɔ̃] *nf* resignation; **donner sa ~** to give *ou* hand in one's notice, hand in one's resignation; **démissionner** *vi* (*de son poste*) to resign, give *ou* hand in one's notice.
demi-tarif [dəmitaʀif] *nm* half-price; (*TRANSPORTS*) half-fare.
demi-tour [dəmituʀ] *nm* about-turn; **faire un ~** (*MIL etc*) to make an about-turn; **faire ~** to turn (and go) back; (*AUTO*) to do a U-turn.
démobilisation [demɔbilizasjɔ̃] *nf* demobilization.
démocrate [demɔkʀat] *a* democratic // *nm/f* democrat.
démocratie [demɔkʀasi] *nf* democracy; **~ populaire/libérale** people's/liberal democracy.
démocratique [demɔkʀatik] *a* democratic.
démocratiser [demɔkʀatize] *vt* to democratize.
démodé, e [demɔde] *a* old-fashioned.
démographie [demɔgʀafi] *nf* demography.
démographique [demɔgʀafik] *a* demographic; **poussée ~** increase in population.
demoiselle [dəmwazɛl] *nf* (*jeune fille*) young lady; (*célibataire*) single lady, maiden lady; **~ d'honneur** bridesmaid.
démolir [demɔliʀ] *vt* to demolish.
démolisseur [demɔlisœʀ] *nm* demolition worker.
démolition [demɔlisjɔ̃] *nf* demolition.
démon [demɔ̃] *nm* demon, fiend; evil spirit; (*enfant turbulent*) devil, demon; **le D~** the Devil.
démoniaque [demɔnjak] *a* fiendish.
démonstrateur, trice [demɔ̃stʀatœʀ, -tʀis] *nm/f* demonstrator.
démonstratif, ive [demɔ̃stʀatif, -iv] *a* (*aussi LING*) demonstrative.
démonstration [demɔ̃stʀasjɔ̃] *nf* demonstration; (*aérienne, navale*) display.
démonté, e [demɔ̃te] *a* (*fig*) raging, wild.

démonter [demɔ̃te] *vt* (*machine etc*) to take down, dismantle; (*fig: personne*) to disconcert; **se ~** *vi* (*personne*) to lose countenance.
démontrer [demɔ̃tʀe] *vt* to demonstrate, show.
démoraliser [demɔʀalize] *vt* to demoralize.
démordre [demɔʀdʀ(ə)] *vi*: **ne pas ~ de** to refuse to give up, stick to.
démouler [demule] *vt* (*gâteau*) to turn out.
démoustiquer [demustike] *vt* to clear of mosquitoes.
démultiplication [demyltiplikasjɔ̃] *nf* reduction; reduction ratio.
démuni, e [demyni] *a* (*sans argent*) impoverished; **~ de** without, lacking in.
démunir [demyniʀ] *vt*: **~ qn de** to deprive sb of; **se ~ de** to part with, give up.
dénatalité [denatalite] *nf* fall in the birth rate.
dénaturer [denatyʀe] *vt* (*goût*) to alter (completely); (*pensée, fait*) to distort, misrepresent.
dénégations [denegasjɔ̃] *nfpl* denials.
dénicher [deniʃe] *vt* to unearth; to track *ou* hunt down.
dénier [denje] *vt* to deny.
dénigrer [denigʀe] *vt* to denigrate, run down.
dénivellation [denivɛlasjɔ̃] *nf*, **dénivellement** [denivɛlmɑ̃] *nm* ramp; dip; difference in level.
dénombrer [denɔ̃bʀe] *vt* (*compter*) to count; (*énumérer*) to enumerate, list.
dénominateur [denɔminatœʀ] *nm* denominator; **~ commun** common denominator.
dénomination [denɔminasjɔ̃] *nf* designation, appellation.
dénommer [denɔme] *vt* to name.
dénoncer [denɔ̃se] *vt* to denounce; **se ~** to give o.s. up, come forward; **dénonciation** *nf* denunciation.
dénoter [denɔte] *vt* to denote.
dénouement [denumɑ̃] *nm* outcome, conclusion; (*THÉÂTRE*) dénouement.
dénouer [denwe] *vt* to unknot, undo.
dénoyauter [denwajɔte] *vt* to stone; **appareil à ~, dénoyauteur** *nm* stoner.
denrée [dɑ̃ʀe] *nf* food(stuff); **~s alimentaires** foodstuffs.
dense [dɑ̃s] *a* dense.
densité [dɑ̃site] *nf* denseness; density; (*PHYSIQUE*) density.
dent [dɑ̃] *nf* tooth (*pl* teeth); **faire ses ~s** to teethe, cut (one's) teeth; **en ~s de scie** serrated; jagged; **~ de lait/sagesse** milk/wisdom tooth; **dentaire** *a* dental; **denté, e** *a*: **roue dentée** cog wheel.
dentelé, e [dɑ̃tle] *a* jagged, indented.
dentelle [dɑ̃tɛl] *nf* lace *q*.
dentier [dɑ̃tje] *nm* denture.
dentifrice [dɑ̃tifʀis] *nm, a*: **(pâte) ~** toothpaste.
dentiste [dɑ̃tist(ə)] *nm/f* dentist.
dentition [dɑ̃tisjɔ̃] *nf* teeth *pl*; dentition.
dénudé, e [denyde] *a* bare.
dénuder [denyde] *vt* to bare.

dénué, e [denɥe] a: ~ **de** devoid of ; lacking in.

dénuement [denymã] nm destitution.

déodorant [deɔdɔʀã] nm deodorant.

dépannage [depanaʒ] nm: **service de ~** (AUTO) breakdown service.

dépanner [depane] vt (véhicule, télévision) to fix, repair ; (fig) to bail out, help out ; **dépanneuse** nf breakdown lorry.

déparer [depaʀe] vt to spoil, mar.

départ [depaʀ] nm leaving q, departure ; (SPORT) start ; (sur un horaire) departure ; **à son ~** when he left.

départager [depaʀtaʒe] vt to decide between.

département [depaʀtəmã] nm department.

départir [depaʀtiʀ]: **se ~ de** vt to abandon, depart from.

dépassé, e [depɑse] a superseded, outmoded.

dépassement [depɑsmã] nm (AUTO) overtaking q.

dépasser [depɑse] vt (véhicule, concurrent) to overtake ; (endroit) to pass, go past ; (somme, limite) to exceed ; (fig: en beauté etc) to surpass, outshine ; (être en saillie sur) to jut out above (ou in front of) // vi (AUTO) to overtake ; (jupon) to show.

dépaysement [depeizmã] nm disorientation ; change of scenery.

dépayser [depeize] vt to disorientate.

dépecer [depase] vt to joint, cut up ; to dismember.

dépêche [depɛʃ] nf dispatch ; ~ (télégraphique) wire.

dépêcher [depeʃe] vt to dispatch ; **se ~** vi to hurry.

dépeindre [depɛ̃dʀ(ə)] vt to depict.

dépendance [depãdãs] nf dependence, dependency.

dépendre [depãdʀ(ə)] vt (tableau) to take down ; ~ **de** vt to depend on ; (financièrement etc) to be dependent on.

dépens [depã] nmpl: **aux ~ de** at the expense of.

dépense [depãs] nf spending q, expense, expenditure q ; (fig) consumption ; expenditure ; **une ~ de 100 F** an outlay ou expenditure of 100 F ; ~ **physique** (physical) exertion ; ~s **publiques** public expenditure.

dépenser [depãse] vt to spend ; (gaz, eau) to use ; (fig) to expend, use up ; **se ~** (se fatiguer) to exert o.s.

dépensier, ière [depãsje, -jɛʀ] a: **il est** ~ he's a spendthrift.

déperdition [depɛʀdisjɔ̃] nf loss.

dépérir [depeʀiʀ] vi to waste away ; to wither.

dépêtrer [depetʀe] vt: **se ~ de** to extricate o.s. from.

dépeupler [depœple] vt to depopulate ; **se ~** to be depopulated ; (rivière, forêt) to empty of wildlife etc.

déphasé, e [defaze] a (ÉLEC) out of phase ; (fig) out of touch.

dépilatoire [depilatwaʀ] a depilatory, hair removing.

dépistage [depistaʒ] nm (MÉD) detection.

dépister [depiste] vt to detect ; (voleur) to track down ; (poursuivants) to throw off the scent.

dépit [depi] nm vexation, frustration ; **en ~ de** prép in spite of ; **en ~ du bon sens** contrary to all good sense ; **dépité, e** a vexed, frustrated.

déplacé, e [deplase] a (propos) out of place, uncalled-for.

déplacement [deplasmã] nm moving ; shifting ; transfer ; trip, travelling q ; ~ **d'air** displacement of air ; ~ **de vertèbre** slipped disc.

déplacer [deplase] vt (table, voiture) to move, shift ; (employé) to transfer, move ; **se ~** vi to move ; (organe) to be displaced ; (voyager) to travel // vt (vertèbre etc) to displace.

déplaire [deplɛʀ] vt: **ceci me déplaît** I don't like this, I dislike this ; **il cherche à nous ~** he's trying to displease us ou be disagreeable to us ; **se ~ quelque part** to dislike it somewhere ; **déplaisant, e** a disagreeable, unpleasant.

déplaisir [depleziʀ] nm displeasure, annoyance.

dépliant [deplijã] nm leaflet.

déplier [deplije] vt to unfold.

déplisser [deplise] vt to smooth out.

déploiement [deplwamã] nm deployment ; display.

déplorer [deplɔʀe] vt to deplore ; to lament.

déployer [deplwaje] vt to open out, spread ; to deploy ; to display, exhibit.

dépoli, e [depɔli] a: **verre ~** frosted glass.

déportation [depɔʀtasjɔ̃] nf deportation.

déporté, e [depɔʀte] nm/f deportee ; (39-45) concentration camp prisoner.

déporter [depɔʀte] vt (POL) to deport ; (dévier) to carry off course.

déposant, e [depozã, -ãt] nm/f (épargnant) depositor.

dépose [depoz] nf taking out ; taking down.

déposer [depoze] vt (gén: mettre, poser) to lay down, put down, set down ; (à la banque, à la consigne) to deposit ; (passager) to drop (off), set down ; (démonter: serrure, moteur) to take out ; (: rideau) to take down ; (roi) to depose ; (ADMIN: faire enregistrer) to file ; to lodge ; to submit ; to register // vi to form a sediment ou deposit ; (JUR): ~ (contre) to testify ou give evidence (against) ; **se ~** vi to settle ; **dépositaire** nm/f (JUR) depository ; (COMM) agent ; **déposition** nf (JUR) deposition.

déposséder [deposede] vt to dispossess.

dépôt [depo] nm (à la banque, sédiment) deposit ; (entrepôt, réserve) warehouse, store ; (gare) depot ; (prison) cells pl ; ~ **légal** registration of copyright.

dépotoir [depɔtwaʀ] nm dumping ground, rubbish dump.

dépouille [depuj] nf (d'animal) skin, hide ; (humaine): ~ (**mortelle**) mortal remains pl.

dépouillé, e [depuje] a (fig) bare, bald ; ~ **de** stripped of ; lacking in.

dépouiller [depuje] vt (animal) to skin ; (spolier) to deprive of one's possessions ; (documents) to go through, peruse ; ~

qn/qch de to strip sb/sth of ; ~ **le scrutin** to count the votes.

dépourvu, e [depuʀvy] a : ~ **de** lacking in, without ; **au** ~ ad unprepared.

dépoussiérer [depusjeʀe] vt to remove dust from.

dépravation [depʀavɑsjɔ̃] nf depravity.

dépraver [depʀave] vt to deprave.

dépréciation [depʀesjɑsjɔ̃] nf depreciation.

déprécier [depʀesje] vt, **se** ~ vi to depreciate.

déprédations [depʀedɑsjɔ̃] nfpl damage sg.

dépression [depʀɛsjɔ̃] nf depression ; ~ **(nerveuse)** (nervous) breakdown.

déprimer [depʀime] vt to depress.

dépuceler [depysle] vt (fam) to take the virginity of.

depuis [dəpɥi] prép (temps: date) since ; (: période) for ; (espace) since, from ; (quantité, rang: à partir de) from // ad (ever) since ; ~ **que** (ever) since ; **quand le connaissez-vous?** how long have you known him? ; **je le connais** ~ **3 ans** I've known him for 3 years ; ~ **lors** since then.

députation [depytɑsjɔ̃] nf deputation ; (fonction) position of deputy, ≈ Parliamentary seat.

député, e [depyte] nm/f (POL) deputy, ≈ Member of Parliament.

députer [depyte] vt to delegate ; ~ **qn auprès de** to send sb (as a representative) to.

déraciner [deʀasine] vt to uproot.

déraillement [deʀɑjmɑ̃] nm derailment.

dérailler [deʀaje] vi (train) to be derailed ; **faire** ~ to derail.

dérailleur [deʀɑjœʀ] nm (de vélo) dérailleur gears pl.

déraisonnable [deʀɛzɔnabl(ə)] a unreasonable.

déraisonner [deʀɛzɔne] vi to talk nonsense, rave.

dérangement [deʀɑ̃ʒmɑ̃] nm (gêne) trouble ; (gastrique etc) disorder ; (mécanique) breakdown ; **en** ~ (téléphone) out of order.

déranger [deʀɑ̃ʒe] vt (personne) to trouble, bother ; to disturb ; (projets) to disrupt, upset ; (objets, vêtements) to disarrange ; **se** ~ to put o.s. out ; (to take the trouble to) come ou go out ; **est-ce que cela vous dérange si** do you mind if.

dérapage [deʀapaʒ] nm skid, skidding q.

déraper [deʀape] vi (voiture) to skid ; (personne, semelles, couteau) to slip ; (fig) to go out of control.

dératiser [deʀatize] vt to rid of rats.

déréglé, e [deʀegle] a (mœurs) dissolute.

dérégler [deʀegle] vt (mécanisme) to put out of order, cause to break down ; (estomac) to upset ; **se** ~ vi to break down, go wrong.

dérider [deʀide] vt, **se** ~ vi to brighten up.

dérision [deʀizjɔ̃] nf: **tourner en** ~ to deride.

dérisoire [deʀizwaʀ] a derisory.

dérivatif [deʀivatif] nm distraction.

dérivation [deʀivɑsjɔ̃] nf derivation ; diversion.

dérive [deʀiv] nf (de dériveur) centre-board ; **aller à la** ~ (NAVIG, fig) to drift.

dérivé, e [deʀive] a derived // nm (LING) derivative ; (TECH) by-product // nf (MATH) derivative.

dériver [deʀive] vt (MATH) to derive ; (cours d'eau etc) to divert // vi (bateau) to drift ; ~ **de** to derive from ; **dériveur** nm sailing dinghy.

dermatologie [dɛʀmatɔlɔʒi] nf dermatology ; **dermatologue** nm/f dermatologist.

dernier, ière [dɛʀnje, -jɛʀ] a last ; (le plus récent) latest, last ; **lundi/le mois** ~ last Monday/month ; **du** ~ **chic** extremely smart ; **les** ~**s honneurs** the last tribute ; **en** ~ ad last ; **ce** ~ the latter ; **dernièrement** ad recently ; ~~-**né**, **dernière-née** nm/f (enfant) last-born.

dérobade [deʀɔbad] nf side-stepping q.

dérobé, e [deʀɔbe] a (porte) secret, hidden ; **à la** ~-**e** surreptitiously.

dérober [deʀɔbe] vt to steal ; ~ **qch à (la vue de) qn** to conceal ou hide sth from sb('s view) ; **se** ~ vi (s'esquiver) to slip away ; to shy away ; **se** ~ **sous** (s'effondrer) to give way beneath ; **se** ~ **à** (justice, regards) to hide from ; (obligation) to shirk.

dérogation [deʀɔgɑsjɔ̃] nf (special) dispensation.

déroger [deʀɔʒe]: ~ **à** vt to go against, depart from.

dérouiller [deʀuje] vt: **se** ~ **les jambes** to stretch one's legs (fig).

déroulement [deʀulmɑ̃] nm (d'une opération etc) progress.

dérouler [deʀule] vt (ficelle) to unwind ; (papier) to unroll ; **se** ~ vi to unwind ; to unroll, come unrolled ; (avoir lieu) to take place ; (se passer) to go on ; to go (off) ; to unfold.

déroute [deʀut] nf rout ; total collapse ; **mettre en** ~ to rout.

dérouter [deʀute] vt (avion, train) to reroute, divert ; (étonner) to disconcert, throw (out).

derrière [dɛʀjɛʀ] ad behind // prép behind // nm (d'une maison) back ; (postérieur) behind, bottom ; **les pattes de** ~ the back legs, the hind legs ; **par** ~ from behind ; (fig) in an underhand way, behind one's back.

des [de] dét, prép + dét voir **de**.

dès [dɛ] prép from ; ~ **que** cj as soon as ; ~ **son retour** as soon as he was (ou is) back ; ~ **lors** ad from then on ; ~ **lors que** cj from the moment (that).

D.E.S. sigle m = diplôme d'études supérieures.

désabusé, e [dezabyze] a disillusioned.

désaccord [dezakɔʀ] nm disagreement.

désaccordé, e [dezakɔʀde] a (MUS) out of tune.

désaffecté, e [dezafɛkte] a disused.

désaffection [dezafɛksjɔ̃] nf: ~ **pour** estrangement from.

désagréable [dezagʀeable(ə)] *a* unpleasant, disagreeable.

désagréger [dezagʀeʒe]: **se ~** *vi* to disintegrate, break up.

désagrément [dezagʀemɑ̃] *nm* annoyance, trouble *q*.

désaltérer [dezalteʀe] *vt*: **se ~** to quench one's thirst ; **ça désaltère** it's thirst-quenching, it takes your thirst away.

désamorcer [dezamɔʀse] *vt* to remove the primer from ; (*fig*) to defuse ; to forestall.

désappointé, e [dezapwɛ̃te] *a* disappointed.

désapprobation [dezapʀɔbɑsjɔ̃] *nf* disapproval.

désapprouver [dezapʀuve] *vt* to disapprove of.

désarçonner [dezaʀsɔne] *vt* to unseat, throw ; (*fig*) to throw, nonplus.

désarmement [dezaʀməmɑ̃] *nm* disarmament.

désarmer [dezaʀme] *vt* (*MIL, aussi fig*) to disarm ; (*NAVIG*) to lay up.

désarroi [dezaʀwa] *nm* helplessness, disarray.

désarticulé, e [dezaʀtikyle] *a* (*pantin, corps*) dislocated.

désarticuler [dezaʀtikyle] *vt*: **se ~** (*acrobate*) to contort (o.s.).

désassorti, e [dezasɔʀti] *a* unmatching, unmatched.

désastre [dezastʀ(ə)] *nm* disaster ; **désastreux, euse** *a* disastrous.

désavantage [dezavɑ̃taʒ] *nm* disadvantage ; (*inconvénient*) drawback, disadvantage ; **désavantager** *vt* to put at a disadvantage ; **désavantageux, euse** *a* unfavourable, disadvantageous.

désavouer [dezavwe] *vt* to disown, repudiate, disclaim.

désaxé, e [dezakse] *a* (*fig*) unbalanced.

désaxer [dezakse] *vt* (*roue*) to put out of true.

desceller [desele] *vt* (*pierre*) to pull free.

descendance [desɑ̃dɑ̃s] *nf* (*famille*) descendants *pl*, issue ; (*origine*) descent.

descendant, e [desɑ̃dɑ̃, -ɑ̃t] *nm/f* descendant.

descendre [desɑ̃dʀ(ə)] *vt* (*escalier, montagne*) to go (*ou* come) down ; (*valise, paquet*) to take *ou* get down ; (*étagère etc*) to lower ; (*fam: abattre*) to shoot down // *vi* to go (*ou* come) down ; (*chemin*) to go down ; (*passager: s'arrêter*) to get out, alight ; (*niveau, température*) to go *ou* come down, fall, drop ; **~ à pied/en voiture** to walk/drive down, to go down on foot/by car ; **~ de** (*famille*) to be descended from ; **~ du train** to get out of *ou* off the train ; **~ d'un arbre** to climb down from a tree ; **~ de cheval** to dismount, get off one's horse.

descente [desɑ̃t] *nf* descent, going down ; (*chemin*) way down ; (*SKI*) downhill (race) ; **au milieu de la ~** halfway down ; **freinez dans les ~s** use the brakes going downhill ; **~ de lit** bedside rug ; **~ (de police)** (police) raid.

description [dɛskʀipsjɔ̃] *nf* description.

désembuer [dezɑ̃bɥe] *vt* to demist.

désemparé, e [dezɑ̃paʀe] *a* bewildered, distraught ; (*véhicule*) crippled.

désemparer [dezɑ̃paʀe] *vi*: **sans ~** without stopping.

désemplir [dezɑ̃pliʀ] *vi*: **ne pas ~** to be always full.

désenchantement [dezɑ̃ʃɑ̃tmɑ̃] *nm* disenchantment ; disillusion.

désenfler [dezɑ̃fle] *vi* to become less swollen.

désengagement [dezɑ̃gaʒmɑ̃] *nm* (*POL*) disengagement.

désensibiliser [desɑ̃sibilize] *vt* (*MÉD*) to desensitize.

déséquilibre [dezekilibʀ(ə)] *nm* (*position*): **être en ~** to be unsteady ; (*fig: des forces, du budget*) imbalance ; (*PSYCH*) unbalance.

déséquilibré, e [dezekilibʀe] *nm/f* (*PSYCH*) unbalanced person.

déséquilibrer [dezekilibʀe] *vt* to throw off balance.

désert, e [dezɛʀ, -ɛʀt(ə)] *a* deserted // *nm* desert.

déserter [dezɛʀte] *vi, vt* to desert ; **déserteur** *nm* deserter ; **désertion** *nf* desertion.

désertique [dezɛʀtik] *a* desert *cpd* ; barren, empty.

désescalade [dezɛskalad] *nf* (*MIL*) de-escalation.

désespéré, e [dezɛspeʀe] *a* desperate ; **~ment** *ad* desperately.

désespérer [dezɛspeʀe] *vt* to drive to despair // *vi*, **se ~** *vi* to despair ; **~ de** to despair of.

désespoir [dezɛspwaʀ] *nm* despair ; **faire le ~ de qn** to be the despair of sb ; **en ~ de cause** in desperation.

déshabillé, e [dezabije] *a* undressed // *nm* négligée.

déshabiller [dezabije] *vt* to undress ; **se ~** to undress (o.s.).

déshabituer [dezabitɥe] *vt*: **se ~ de** to get out of the habit of.

désherbant [dezɛʀbɑ̃] *nm* weed-killer.

déshériter [dezeʀite] *vt* to disinherit.

déshérités [dezeʀite] *nmpl*: **les ~** the underprivileged.

déshonneur [dezɔnœʀ] *nm* dishonour, disgrace.

déshonorer [dezɔnɔʀe] *vt* to dishonour, bring disgrace upon.

déshydraté, e [dezidʀate] *a* dehydrated.

désidérata [dezideʀata] *nmpl* requirements.

désignation [dezinɑsjɔ̃] *nf* naming, appointment ; (*signe, mot*) name, designation.

désigner [dezine] *vt* (*montrer*) to point out, indicate ; (*dénommer*) to denote, refer to ; (*nommer: candidat etc*) to name, appoint.

désillusion [dezilyzjɔ̃] *nf* disillusion(ment).

désinence [dezinɑ̃s] *nf* ending, inflexion.

désinfectant, e [dezɛ̃fɛktɑ̃, -ɑ̃t] *a, nm* disinfectant.

désinfecter [dezɛ̃fɛkte] *vt* to disinfect.

désinfection [dezɛ̃fɛksjɔ̃] *nf* disinfection.
désintégrer [dezɛ̃tegʀe] *vt*, **se ~** *vi* to disintegrate.
désintéressé, e [dezɛ̃teʀese] *a* disinterested, unselfish.
désintéresser [dezɛ̃teʀese] *vt*: **se ~ (de)** to lose interest (in).
désintoxication [dezɛ̃tɔksikɑsjɔ̃] *nf* treatment for alcoholism.
désinvolte [dezɛ̃vɔlt(ə)] *a* casual, off-hand; **désinvolture** *nf* casualness.
désir [deziʀ] *nm* wish; (*fort, sensuel*) desire.
désirer [deziʀe] *vt* to want, wish for; (*sexuellement*) to desire; **je désire ...** (*formule de politesse*) I would like ...; **il désire que tu l'aides** he wants you to help him; **~ faire** to want *ou* wish to do.
désireux, euse [deziʀø, -øz] *a*: **~ de faire** anxious to do.
désistement [dezistəmɑ̃] *nm* withdrawal.
désister [deziste]: **se ~** *vi* to stand down, withdraw.
désobéir [dezɔbeiʀ] *vi*: **~ (à qn/qch)** to disobey (sb/sth); **désobéissance** *nf* disobedience; **désobéissant, e** *a* disobedient.
désobligeant, e [dezɔbliʒɑ̃, -ɑ̃t] *a* disagreeable, unpleasant.
désodorisant [dezɔdɔʀizɑ̃] *nm* air freshener, deodorizer.
désœuvré, e [dezœvʀe] *a* idle; **désœuvrement** *nm* idleness.
désolation [dezɔlɑsjɔ̃] *nf* distress, grief; desolation, devastation.
désolé, e [dezɔle] *a* (*paysage*) desolate; **je suis ~** I'm sorry.
désoler [dezɔle] *vt* to distress, grieve.
désolidariser [desɔlidaʀize] *vt*: **se ~ de** *ou* **d'avec** to dissociate o.s. from.
désopilant, e [dezɔpilɑ̃, -ɑ̃t] *a* screamingly funny, hilarious.
désordonné, e [dezɔʀdɔne] *a* untidy, disorderly.
désordre [dezɔʀdʀ(ə)] *nm* disorder(liness), untidiness; (*anarchie*) disorder; **~s** *nmpl* (*POL*) disturbances, disorder *sg*; **en ~** in a mess, untidy.
désorganiser [dezɔʀganize] *vt* to disorganize.
désorienté, e [dezɔʀjɑ̃te] *a* disorientated; (*fig*) bewildered.
désormais [dezɔʀmɛ] *ad* in future, from now on.
désosser [dezose] *vt* to bone.
despote [dɛspɔt] *nm* despot, tyrant; **despotisme** *nm* despotism.
desquels, desquelles [dekɛl] *prép* + *pronom voir* **lequel**.
dessaisir [deseziʀ]: **se ~ de** *vt* to give up, part with.
dessaler [desale] *vt* (*eau de mer*) to desalinate; (*CULIN*) to soak.
desséché, e [desefe] *a* dried up.
dessécher [desefe] *vt* to dry out, parch; **se ~** *vi* to dry out.
dessein [desɛ̃] *nm* design; **dans le ~ de** with the intention of; **à ~** intentionally, deliberately.
desserrer [deseʀe] *vt* to loosen; (*frein*) to

release; (*poing, dents*) to unclench; (*objets alignés*) to space out.
dessert [desɛʀ] *nm* dessert, pudding.
desserte [desɛʀt(ə)] *nf* (*table*) sideboard table; (*transport*): **la ~ du village est assurée par autocar** there is a coach service to the village.
desservir [desɛʀviʀ] *vt* (*ville, quartier*) to serve; (*nuire à*) to go against, put at a disadvantage; **~ (la table)** to clear the table.
dessin [desɛ̃] *nm* (*œuvre, art*) drawing; (*motif*) pattern, design; (*contour*) (out)line; **~ animé** cartoon (film); **~ humoristique** cartoon.
dessinateur, trice [desinatœʀ, -tʀis] *nm/f* drawer; (*de bandes dessinées*) cartoonist; (*industriel*) draughtsman.
dessiner [desine] *vt* to draw; (*concevoir: carrosserie, maison*) to design.
dessoûler [desule] *vt*, *vi* to sober up.
dessous [dəsu] *ad* underneath, beneath // *nm* underside // *nmpl* (*sous-vêtements*) underwear *sg*; **en ~, par ~** underneath; below; **au-~** below; **de ~ le lit** from under the bed; **au-~ de** below; (*peu digne de*) beneath; **avoir le ~** to get the worst of it; **~-de-plat** *nm inv* tablemat.
dessus [dəsy] *ad* on top; (*collé, écrit*) on it // *nm* top; **en ~** above; **par ~** *ad* over it // *prép* over; **au-~** above; **au-~ de** above; **avoir le ~** to get the upper hand; **~-de-lit** *nm inv* bedspread.
destin [destɛ̃] *nm* fate; (*avenir*) destiny.
destinataire [destinatɛʀ] *nm/f* (*POSTES*) addressee; (*d'un colis*) consignee.
destination [destinɑsjɔ̃] *nf* (*lieu*) destination; (*usage*) purpose; **à ~ de** bound for, travelling to.
destinée [destine] *nf* fate; (*existence, avenir*) destiny.
destiner [destine] *vt*: **~ qn à** (*poste, sort*) to destine sb for, intend sb to + *verbe*; **~ qn/qch à** (*prédestiner*) to mark sb/sth out for, destine sb/sth to + *verbe*; **~ qch à** (*envisager d'affecter*) to intend to use sth for; **~ qch à qn** (*envisager de donner*) to intend to give sth to sb, intend sb to have sth; (*adresser*) to intend sth for sb; to aim sth at sb; **se ~ à l'enseignement** to intend to become a teacher; **être destiné à** (*sort*) to be destined to + *verbe*; (*usage*) to be intended *ou* meant for; (*suj: sort*) to be in store for.
destituer [destitɥe] *vt* to depose.
destructeur, trice [destʀyktœʀ, -tʀis] *a* destructive.
destruction [destʀyksjɔ̃] *nf* destruction.
désuet, ète [desɥɛ, -ɛt] *a* outdated, outmoded; **désuétude** *nf*: **tomber en désuétude** to fall into disuse, become obsolete.
désuni, e [dezyni] *a* divided, disunited.
détachant [detaʃɑ̃] *nm* stain remover.
détachement [detaʃmɑ̃] *nm* detachment.
détacher [detaʃe] *vt* (*enlever*) to detach, remove; (*défaire*) to untie; (*ADMIN*): **~ qn (auprès de/à)** to send sb on secondment (to); (*MIL*) to detail; **se ~** *vi* (*tomber*) to come off; to come out; (*se défaire*) to come undone; (*SPORT*) to pull *ou* break away; **se**

~ **sur** to stand out against; **se ~ de** (*se désintéresser*) to grow away from.

détail [detaj] *nm* detail; (*COMM*): **le ~** retail; **au ~** *ad* (*COMM*) retail; separately; **donner le ~ de** to give a detailed account of; (*compte*) to give a breakdown of; **en ~** in detail.

détaillant [detajã] *nm* retailer.

détaillé, e [detaje] *a* (*récit*) detailed.

détailler [detaje] *vt* (*COMM*) to sell retail; to sell separately; (*expliquer*) to explain in detail; to detail; (*examiner*) to look over, examine.

détartrant [detartrã] *nm* descaling agent.

détaxer [detakse] *vt* to reduce the tax on; to remove the tax from.

détecter [detɛkte] *vt* to detect; **détecteur** *nm* detector; **détection** *nf* detection.

détective [detɛktiv] *nm* (*Brit: policier*) detective; ~ (**privé**) private detective *ou* investigator.

déteindre [detɛ̃dʀ(ə)] *vi* (*tissu*) to lose its colour; (*fig*): ~ **sur** to rub off on.

dételer [detle] *vt* to unharness; to unhitch.

détendre [detɑ̃dʀ(ə)] *vt* (*fil*) to slacken, loosen; (*relaxer*) to relax; **se ~** to lose its tension; to relax.

détenir [detniʀ] *vt* (*fortune, objet, secret*) to be in possession of, have (in one's possession); (*prisonnier*) to detain, hold; (*record*) to hold; ~ **le pouvoir** to be in power.

détente [detɑ̃t] *nf* relaxation; (*POL*) détente; (*d'une arme*) trigger; (*d'un athlète qui saute*) spring.

détenteur, trice [detɑ̃tœʀ, -tʀis] *nm/f* holder.

détention [detɑ̃sjɔ̃] *nf* possession; detention; holding; ~ **préventive** (pretrial) custody.

détenu, e [detny] *nm/f* prisoner.

détergent [detɛʀʒɑ̃] *nm* detergent.

détérioration [deteʀjɔʀasjɔ̃] *nf* damaging; deterioration, worsening.

détériorer [deteʀjɔʀe] *vt* to damage; **se ~ vi** to deteriorate.

déterminant [detɛʀminɑ̃] *nm* (*LING*) determiner.

détermination [detɛʀminasjɔ̃] *nf* determining; (*résolution*) resolution.

déterminé, e [detɛʀmine] *a* (*résolu*) determined; (*précis*) specific, definite.

déterminer [detɛʀmine] *vt* (*fixer*) to determine; (*décider*): ~ **qn à faire** to decide sb to do; **se ~ à faire** to make up one's mind to do.

déterrer [detɛʀe] *vt* to dig up.

détersif [detɛʀsif] *nm* detergent.

détestable [detɛstabl(ə)] *a* foul, ghastly; detestable, odious.

détester [detɛste] *vt* to hate, detest.

détonant, e [detɔnɑ̃, -ɑ̃t] *a*: **mélange ~** explosive mixture.

détonateur [detɔnatœʀ] *nm* detonator.

détonation [detɔnasjɔ̃] *nf* detonation, bang, report (of a gun).

détoner [detɔne] *vi* to detonate, explode.

détonner [detɔne] *vi* (*MUS*) to go out of tune; (*fig*) to clash.

détour [detuʀ] *nm* detour; (*tournant*) bend, curve; **sans ~** (*fig*) without beating

about the bush, in a straightforward manner.

détourné, e [detuʀne] *a* (*moyen*) roundabout.

détournement [detuʀnəmɑ̃] *nm* diversion, rerouting; ~ **d'avion** hijacking; ~ (**de fonds**) embezzlement *ou* misappropriation (of funds); ~ **de mineur** corruption of a minor.

détourner [detuʀne] *vt* to divert; (*avion*) to divert, reroute; (: *par la force*) to hijack; (*yeux, tête*) to turn away; (*de l'argent*) to embezzle, misappropriate; **se ~** to turn away.

détracteur, trice [detʀaktœʀ, -tʀis] *nm/f* disparager, critic.

détraquer [detʀake] *vt* to put out of order; (*estomac*) to upset; **se ~ vi** to go wrong.

détrempe [detʀɑ̃p] *nf* (*ART*) tempera.

détrempé, e [detʀɑ̃pe] *a* (*sol*) sodden, waterlogged.

détresse [detʀɛs] *nf* distress.

détriment [detʀimɑ̃] *nm*: **au ~ de** to the detriment of.

détritus [detʀitys] *nmpl* rubbish *sg*, refuse *sg*.

détroit [detʀwa] *nm* strait.

détromper [detʀɔ̃pe] *vt* to disabuse.

détrôner [detʀone] *vt* to dethrone, depose; (*fig*) to oust, dethrone.

détrousser [detʀuse] *vt* to rob.

détruire [detʀɥiʀ] *vt* to destroy.

dette [dɛt] *nf* debt.

D.E.U.G. [dœg] *sigle m* = *diplôme d'études universitaires générales.*

deuil [dœj] *nm* (*perte*) bereavement; (*période*) mourning; (*chagrin*) grief; **porter le/être en ~** to wear/be in mourning.

deux [dø] *num* two; **les ~** both; **ses ~ mains** both his hands, his two hands; **les ~ points** the colon *sg*; **deuxième** *num* second; **~-pièces** *nm inv* (*tailleur*) two-piece suit; (*de bain*) two-piece (swimsuit); (*appartement*) two-roomed flat; **~-roues** *nm inv* two-wheeled vehicle; **~-temps** a two-stroke.

devais *etc vb voir* **devoir.**

dévaler [devale] *vt* to hurtle down.

dévaliser [devalize] *vt* to rob, burgle.

dévaloriser [devalɔʀize] *vt*, **se ~ vi** to depreciate.

dévaluation [devalɥasjɔ̃] *nf* depreciation; (*ECON: mesure*) devaluation.

dévaluer [devalɥe] *vt* to devalue.

devancer [dəvɑ̃se] *vt* to be ahead of; to get ahead of; to arrive before; (*prévenir*) to anticipate; ~ **l'appel** (*MIL*) to enlist before call-up; **devancier, ière** *nm/f* precursor.

devant [dəvɑ̃] *ad* in front; (*à distance: en avant*) ahead // *prép* in front of; ahead of; (*avec mouvement: passer*) past; (*fig*) before, in front of; faced with, in the face of; in view of // *nm* front; **prendre les ~s** to make the first move; **les pattes de ~** the front legs, the forelegs; **par ~** (*boutonner*) at the front; (*entrer*) the front way; **aller au-~ de qn** to go out to meet sb ; **aller au-~ de** (*désirs de qn*) to anticipate.

devanture [dəvɑ̃tyʀ] *nf* (*façade*) (shop) front ; (*étalage*) display ; (shop) window.

dévastation [devastɑsjɔ̃] *nf* devastation.

dévaster [devaste] *vt* to devastate.

déveine [devɛn] *nf* rotten luck *q*.

développement [devlɔpmɑ̃] *nm* development.

développer [devlɔpe] *vt* to develop ; **se ~** *vi* to develop.

devenir [dəvniʀ] *vb avec attribut* to become ; **~ instituteur** to become a teacher ; **que sont-ils devenus?** what has become of them?

dévergondé, e [devɛʀgɔ̃de] *a* wild, shameless.

devers [dəvɛʀ] *ad*: **par ~ soi** to oneself.

déverser [devɛʀse] *vt* (*liquide*) to pour (out) ; (*ordures*) to tip (out) ; **se ~ dans** (*fleuve, mer*) to flow into ; **déversoir** *nm* overflow.

dévêtir [devetiʀ] *vt*, **se ~** to undress.

devez *etc vb voir* **devoir**.

déviation [devjɑsjɔ̃] *nf* (*aussi AUTO*) diversion ; **~ de la colonne (vertébrale)** curvature of the spine.

dévider [devide] *vt* to unwind ; **dévidoir** *nm* reel.

devienne *etc vb voir* **devenir**.

dévier [devje] *vt* (*fleuve, circulation*) to divert ; (*coup*) to deflect // *vi* to veer (off course) ; (*faire*) **~** (*projectile*) to deflect ; (*véhicule*) to push off course.

devin [dəvɛ̃] *nm* soothsayer, seer.

deviner [dəvine] *vt* to guess ; (*prévoir*) to foretell ; to foresee ; (*apercevoir*) to distinguish.

devinette [dəvinɛt] *nf* riddle.

devins *etc vb voir* **devenir**.

devis [dəvi] *nm* estimate, quotation.

dévisager [deviʒaʒe] *vt* to stare at.

devise [dəviz] *nf* (*formule*) motto, watchword ; (*ÉCON*: *monnaie*) currency ; **~s** *nfpl* (*argent*) currency *sg*.

deviser [dəvize] *vi* to converse.

dévisser [devise] *vt* to unscrew, undo ; **se ~** *vi* to come unscrewed.

dévoiler [devwale] *vt* to unveil.

devoir [dəvwaʀ] *nm* duty ; (*SCOL*) piece of homework, homework *q* ; (: *en classe*) exercise // *vt* (*argent, respect*): **~ qch (à qn)** to owe (sb) sth ; (*suivi de l'infinitif*: *obligation*): **il doit le faire** he has to do it, he must do it ; (: *intention*): **il doit partir demain** he is (due) to leave tomorrow ; (: *probabilité*): **il doit être tard** it must be late.

dévolu, e [devɔly] *a*: **~ à** allotted to // *nm*: **jeter son ~ sur** to fix one's choice on.

dévorant, e [devɔʀɑ̃, -ɑ̃t] *a* (*faim, passion*) raging.

dévorer [devɔʀe] *vt* to devour ; (*suj: feu, soucis*) to consume.

dévot, e [devo, -ɔt] *a* devout, pious.

dévotion [devosjɔ̃] *nf* devoutness ; **être à la ~ de qn** to be totally devoted to sb.

dévoué, e [devwe] *a* devoted.

dévouement [devumɑ̃] *nm* devotion, dedication.

dévouer [devwe]: **se ~** *vi* (*se sacrifier*): **se ~ (pour)** to sacrifice o.s. (for) ; (*se consacrer*): **se ~ à** to devote *ou* dedicate o.s. to.

dévoyé, e [devwaje] *a* delinquent.

devrai *etc vb voir* **devoir**.

dextérité [dɛksteʀite] *nf* skill, dexterity.

diabète [djabɛt] *nm* diabetes *sg* ; **diabétique** *nm/f* diabetic.

diable [djɑbl(ə)] *nm* devil ; **diabolique** *a* diabolical.

diabolo [djabɔlo] *nm* (*boisson*) lemonade and fruit (*ou mint etc*) cordial.

diacre [djakʀ(ə)] *nm* deacon.

diadème [djadɛm] *nm* diadem.

diagnostic [djagnɔstik] *nm* diagnosis *sg* ; **diagnostiquer** *vt* to diagnose.

diagonal, e aux [djagɔnal, -o] *a*, *nf* diagonal ; **en ~e** diagonally ; **lire en ~é** to skim through.

diagramme [djagʀam] *nm* chart, graph.

dialecte [djalɛkt(ə)] *nm* dialect.

dialogue [djalɔg] *nm* dialogue ; **dialoguer** *vi* to converse ; (*POL*) to have a dialogue.

diamant [djamɑ̃] *nm* diamond ; **diamantaire** *nm* diamond dealer.

diamètre [djamɛtʀ(ə)] *nm* diameter.

diapason [djapazɔ̃] *nm* tuning fork.

diaphragme [djafʀagm] *nm* (*ANAT, PHOTO*) diaphragm ; (*contraceptif*) diaphragm, cap ; **ouverture du ~** (*PHOTO*) aperture.

diapositive [djapozitiv] *nf* transparency, slide.

diapré, e [djapʀe] *a* many-coloured.

diarrhée [djaʀe] *nf* diarrhoea.

diatribe [djatʀib] *nf* diatribe.

dictaphone [diktafɔn] *nm* Dictaphone.

dictateur [diktatœʀ] *nm* dictator ; **dictatorial, e, aux** *a* dictatorial ; **dictature** *nf* dictatorship.

dictée [dikte] *nf* dictation ; **prendre sous ~** to take down (*sth dictated*).

dicter [dikte] *vt* to dictate.

diction [diksjɔ̃] *nf* diction, delivery ; **cours de ~** speech production lesson.

dictionnaire [diksjɔnɛʀ] *nm* dictionary ; **~ bilingue/encyclopédique** bilingual/encyclopaedic dictionary.

dicton [diktɔ̃] *nm* saying, dictum.

didactique [didaktik] *a* technical ; didactic.

dièse [djɛz] *nm* sharp.

diesel [djezɛl] *nm*, *a inv* diesel.

diète [djɛt] *nf* (*jeûne*) starvation diet ; (*régime*) diet ; **être à la ~** to be on a starvation diet.

diététicien, ne [djetetisjɛ̃, -jɛn] *nm/f* dietician.

diététique [djetetik] *nf* dietetics *sg* ; **magasin ~** health food shop.

dieu, x [djø] *nm* god ; **D~** God ; **le bon D~** the good Lord.

diffamation [difamɑsjɔ̃] *nf* slander ; (*écrite*) libel ; **attaquer qn en ~** to sue sb for libel (*ou* slander).

diffamer [difame] *vt* to slander, defame ; to libel.

différé [difeʀe] *nm* (*TV*): **en ~** (pre-)recorded.

différence [difeʀɑ̃s] nf difference ; **à la ~ de** unlike.

différencier [difeʀɑ̃sje] vt to differentiate ; **se ~** vi (organisme) to become differentiated ; **se ~ de** to differentiate o.s. from ; to differ from.

différend [difeʀɑ̃] nm difference (of opinion), disagreement.

différent, e [difeʀɑ̃, -ɑ̃t] a: **~ (de)** different (from) ; **~s objets** different ou various objects.

différentiel, le [difeʀɑ̃sjɛl] a, nm differential.

différer [difeʀe] vt to postpone, put off // vi: **~ (de)** to differ (from) ; **~ de faire** to delay doing.

difficile [difisil] a difficult ; (exigeant) hard to please, difficult (to please) ; **~ment** ad with difficulty ; **~ment lisible** difficult ou hard to read.

difficulté [difikylte] nf difficulty ; **en ~** (bateau, alpiniste) in trouble ou difficulties ; **avoir de la ~ à faire** to have difficulty (in) doing.

difforme [difɔʀm(ə)] a deformed, misshapen ; **difformité** nf deformity.

diffracter [difʀakte] vt to diffract.

diffus, e [dify, -yz] a diffuse.

diffuser [difyze] vt (chaleur, bruit) to diffuse ; (émission, musique) to broadcast ; (nouvelle, idée) to circulate ; (COMM) to distribute ; **diffuseur** nm diffuser ; distributor ; **diffusion** nf diffusion ; broadcast(ing) ; circulation ; distribution.

digérer [diʒeʀe] vt to digest ; (fig: accepter) to stomach, put up with ; **digestible** a digestible ; **digestif, ive** a digestive // nm (after-dinner) liqueur ; **digestion** nf digestion.

digital, e, aux [diʒital, -o] a digital.

digne [diɲ] a dignified ; **~ de** worthy of ; **~ de foi** trustworthy.

dignitaire [diɲitɛʀ] nm dignitary.

dignité [diɲite] nf dignity.

digue [dig] nf dike, dyke.

dilapider [dilapide] vt to squander, waste.

dilater [dilate] vt to dilate ; (gaz, métal) to cause to expand ; (ballon) to distend ; **se ~** vi to expand.

dilemme [dilɛm] nm dilemma.

diligence [diliʒɑ̃s] nf stagecoach, diligence ; (empressement) despatch.

diligent, e [diliʒɑ̃, -ɑ̃t] a prompt and efficient, diligent.

diluer [dilɥe] vt to dilute.

diluvien, ne [dilyvjɛ̃, -jɛn] a: **pluie ~ne** torrential rain.

dimanche [dimɑ̃ʃ] nm Sunday.

dimension [dimɑ̃sjɔ̃] nf (grandeur) size ; (cote, de l'espace) dimension.

diminuer [diminɥe] vt to reduce, decrease ; (ardeur etc) to lessen ; (personne: physiquement) to undermine ; (dénigrer) to belittle // vi to decrease, diminish ; **diminutif** nm (LING) diminutive ; (surnom) pet name ; **diminution** nf decreasing, diminishing.

dinde [dɛ̃d] nf turkey.

dindon [dɛ̃dɔ̃] nm turkey.

dîner [dine] nm dinner // vi to have dinner.

dingue [dɛ̃g] a (fam) crazy.

diode [djɔd] nf diode.

diphtérie [difteʀi] nf diphtheria.

diphtongue [diftɔ̃g] nf diphthong.

diplomate [diplɔmat] a diplomatic // nm diplomat ; (fig) diplomatist.

diplomatie [diplɔmasi] nf diplomacy ; **diplomatique** a diplomatic.

diplôme [diplom] nm diploma, certificate ; (diploma) examination ; **diplômé, e** a qualified.

dire [diʀ] nm: **au ~ de** according to ; **leur ~s** what they say // vt to say ; (secret, mensonge) to tell ; **~ l'heure/la vérité** to tell the time/the truth ; **~ qch à qn** to tell sb sth ; **~ que** to say that ; **~ à qn que** to tell sb that ; **~ à qn qu'il fasse** ou **de faire** to tell sb to do ; **on dit que** they say that ; **si cela lui dit** (plaire) if he fancies it ; **que dites-vous de** (penser) what do you think of ; **on dirait que** it looks (ou sounds etc) as though.

direct, e [diʀɛkt] a direct // nm (TV): **en ~** live ; **~ement** ad directly.

directeur, trice [diʀɛktœʀ, -tʀis] nm/f (d'entreprise) director ; (de service) manager/eress ; (d'école) headmaster/mistress ; **~ de thèse** (SCOL) supervisor.

direction [diʀɛksjɔ̃] nf management ; conducting ; supervision ; (AUTO) steering ; (sens) direction ; **sous la ~ de** (MUS) conducted by.

directive [diʀɛktiv] nf directive, instruction.

dirent vb voir **dire**.

dirigeable [diʀiʒabl(ə)] a, nm: **(ballon) ~** dirigible.

dirigeant, e [diʀiʒɑ̃, -ɑ̃t] a managerial ; ruling // nm/f (d'un parti etc) leader ; (d'entreprise) manager, member of the management.

diriger [diʀiʒe] vt (entreprise) to manage, run ; (véhicule) to steer ; (orchestre) to conduct ; (recherches, travaux) to supervise, be in charge of ; (braquer: regard, arme): **~ sur** to point ou level ou aim at ; (fig: critiques): **~ contre** to aim at ; **se ~** (s'orienter) to find one's way ; **se ~ vers** ou **sur** to make ou head for.

dirigisme [diʀiʒism(ə)] nm (ÉCON) state intervention, interventionism.

dis etc vb voir **dire**.

discernement [disɛʀnəmɑ̃] nm discernment, judgment.

discerner [disɛʀne] vt to discern, make out.

disciple [disipl(ə)] nm/f disciple.

disciplinaire [disiplinɛʀ] a disciplinary.

discipline [disiplin] nf discipline ; **discipliné, e** a (well-)disciplined ; **discipliner** vt to discipline ; to control.

discontinu, e [diskɔ̃tiny] a intermittent.

discontinuer [diskɔ̃tinɥe] vi: **sans ~** without stopping, without a break.

disconvenir [diskɔ̃vniʀ] vi: **ne pas ~ de qch/que** not to deny sth/that.

discordance [diskɔʀdɑ̃s] nf discordance ; conflict.

discordant, e [diskɔʀdɑ̃, -ɑ̃t] a discordant ; conflicting.

discorde [diskɔʀd(ə)] *nf* discord, dissension.

discothèque [diskɔtɛk] *nf* (*disques*) record collection ; (: *dans une bibliothèque*) record library ; (*boîte de nuit*) disco(thèque).

discourir [diskuʀiʀ] *vi* to discourse, hold forth.

discours [diskuʀ] *nm* speech.

discréditer [diskʀedite] *vt* to discredit.

discret, ète [diskʀɛ, -ɛt] *a* discreet ; (*fig*) unobtrusive ; quiet ; **discrètement** *ad* discreetly.

discrétion [diskʀesjɔ̃] *nf* discretion ; **être à la ~ de qn** to be in sb's hands ; **à ~** unlimited ; as much as one wants.

discrimination [diskʀiminɑsjɔ̃] *nf* discrimination ; **sans ~** indiscriminately ; **discriminatoire** *a* discriminatory.

disculper [diskylpe] *vt* to exonerate.

discussion [diskysjɔ̃] *nf* discussion.

discuté, e [diskyte] *a* controversial.

discuter [diskyte] *vt* (*contester*) to question, dispute ; (*débattre: prix*) to discuss // *vi* to talk ; (*ergoter*) to argue ; **~ de** to discuss.

dise *etc vb voir* **dire**.

disert, e [dizɛʀ, -ɛʀt(ə)] *a* loquacious.

disette [dizɛt] *nf* food shortage.

diseuse [dizøz] *nf:* **~ de bonne aventure** fortuneteller.

disgrâce [disgʀɑs] *nf* disgrace.

disgracieux, euse [disgʀasjø, -jøz] *a* ungainly, awkward.

disjoindre [disʒwɛ̃dʀ(ə)] *vt* to take apart ; **se ~** *vi* to come apart.

disjoncteur [disʒɔ̃ktœʀ] *nm* (*ÉLEC*) circuit breaker, cutout.

dislocation [dislɔkɑsjɔ̃] *nf* dislocation.

disloquer [dislɔke] *vt* (*membre*) to dislocate ; (*chaise*) to dismantle ; (*troupe*) to disperse ; **se ~** *vi* (*parti, empire*) to break up ; **se ~ l'épaule** to dislocate one's shoulder.

disons *vb voir* **dire**.

disparaître [dispaʀɛtʀ(ə)] *vi* to disappear ; (*à la vue*) to vanish, disappear ; to be hidden *ou* concealed ; (*être manquant*) to go missing, disappear ; (*se perdre: traditions etc*) to die out ; **faire ~** to remove ; to get rid of.

disparate [dispaʀat] *a* disparate ; ill-assorted.

disparité [dispaʀite] *nf* disparity.

disparition [dispaʀisjɔ̃] *nf* disappearance.

disparu, e [dispaʀy] *nm/f* missing person ; (*défunt*) departed.

dispendieux, euse [dispɑ̃djø, -jøz] *a* extravagant, expensive.

dispensaire [dispɑ̃sɛʀ] *nm* community clinic.

dispense [dispɑ̃s] *nf* exemption ; **~ d'âge** special exemption from age limit.

dispenser [dispɑ̃se] *vt* (*donner*) to lavish, bestow ; (*exempter*): **~ qn de** to exempt sb from ; **se ~ de** to avoid ; to get out of.

disperser [dispɛʀse] *vt* to scatter ; (*fig: son attention*) to dissipate ; **se ~** *vi* to scatter ; (*fig*) to dissipate one's efforts.

disponibilité [disponibilite] *nf* availability ; (*ADMIN*): **être en ~** to be on leave of absence.

disponible [disponibl(ə)] *a* available.

dispos [dispo] *am:* (**frais et**) **~** fresh (as a daisy).

disposé, e [dispoze] *a* (*d'une certaine manière*) arranged, laid-out ; **bien/mal ~** (*humeur*) in a good/bad mood ; **~ à** (*prêt à*) willing *ou* prepared to.

disposer [dispoze] *vt* (*arranger, placer*) to arrange ; (*inciter*): **~ qn à qch/faire qch** to dispose *ou* incline sb towards sth/to do sth // *vi:* **vous pouvez ~** you may leave ; **~ de** *vt* to have (at one's disposal) ; to use ; **se ~ à faire** to prepare to do, be about to do.

dispositif [dispozitif] *nm* device ; (*fig*) system, plan of action ; set-up.

disposition [dispozisjɔ̃] *nf* (*arrangement*) arrangement, layout ; (*humeur*) mood ; (*tendance*) tendency ; **~s** *nfpl* (*mesures*) steps, measures ; (*préparatifs*) arrangements ; (*testamentaires*) provisions ; (*aptitudes*) bent *sg*, aptitude *sg* ; **à la ~ de qn** at sb's disposal.

disproportion [dispʀopɔʀsjɔ̃] *nf* disproportion ; **disproportionné, e** *a* disproportionate, out of all proportion.

dispute [dispyt] *nf* quarrel, argument.

disputer [dispyte] *vt* (*match*) to play ; (*combat*) to fight ; (*course*) to run, fight ; **se ~** *vi* to quarrel, have a quarrel ; **~ qch à qn** to fight with sb for *ou* over sth.

disquaire [diskɛʀ] *nm/f* record dealer.

disqualification [diskalifikɑsjɔ̃] *nf* disqualification.

disqualifier [diskalifje] *vt* to disqualify.

disque [disk(ə)] *nm* (*MUS*) record ; (*forme, pièce*) disc ; (*SPORT*) discus ; **~ d'embrayage** (*AUTO*) clutch plate.

dissection [disɛksjɔ̃] *nf* dissection.

dissemblable [disɑ̃blabl(ə)] *a* dissimilar.

disséminer [disemine] *vt* to scatter.

disséquer [diseke] *vt* to dissect.

dissertation [disɛʀtɑsjɔ̃] *nf* (*SCOL*) essay.

disserter [disɛʀte] *vi:* **~ sur** to discourse upon.

dissident, e [disidɑ̃, -ɑ̃t] *a, nm/f* dissident.

dissimulation [disimylɑsjɔ̃] *nf* concealing ; (*duplicité*) dissimulation.

dissimuler [disimyle] *vt* to conceal ; **se ~** to conceal o.s. ; to be concealed.

dissipation [disipɑsjɔ̃] *nf* squandering ; unruliness ; (*débauche*) dissipation.

dissiper [disipe] *vt* to dissipate ; (*fortune*) to squander, fritter away ; **se ~** *vi* (*brouillard*) to clear, disperse ; (*doutes*) to disappear, melt away ; (*élève*) to become undisciplined *ou* unruly.

dissolu, e [disɔly] *a* dissolute.

dissolution [disɔlysjɔ̃] *nf* dissolving ; (*POL, JUR*) dissolution.

dissolvant, e [disɔlvɑ̃, -ɑ̃t] *a* (*fig*) debilitating // *nm* (*CHIMIE*) solvent ; **~ (gras)** nail varnish remover.

dissonant, e [disɔnɑ̃, -ɑ̃t] *a* discordant.

dissoudre [disudʀ(ə)] *vt* to dissolve ; **se ~** *vi* to dissolve.

dissuader [disɥade] *vt:* **~ qn de faire/de qch** to dissuade sb from doing/from sth.

dissuasion [disɥazjɔ̃] *nf* dissuasion ; **force de ~** deterrent power.

dissymétrique [disimetʀik] *a* dissymmetrical.

distance [distɑ̃s] *nf* distance ; *(fig: écart)* gap ; **à ~** at *ou* from a distance ; **à une ~ de 10 km, à 10 km de ~** 10 km away, at a distance of 10 km ; **à 2 ans de ~** with a gap of 2 years ; **garder ses ~s** to keep one's distance ; **tenir la ~** *(SPORT)* to cover the distance, last the course ; **distancer** *vt* to outdistance, leave behind.

distant, e [distɑ̃, -ɑ̃t] *a* *(réservé)* distant, aloof ; *(éloigné)* distant, far away ; **~ de** *(lieu)* far away ou a long way from ; **~ de 5 km (d'un lieu)** 5 km away (from a place).

distendre [distɑ̃dʀ(ə)] *vt*, **se ~** *vi* to distend.

distillation [distilasjɔ̃] *nf* distillation, distilling.

distillé, e [distile] *a*: **eau ~e** distilled water.

distiller [distile] *vt* to distil ; *(fig)* to exude ; to elaborate ; **distillerie** *nf* distillery.

distinct, e [distɛ̃(kt), distɛ̃kt(ə)] *a* distinct ; **distinctement** *ad* distinctly ; **distinctif, ive** *a* distinctive.

distinction [distɛ̃ksjɔ̃] *nf* distinction.

distingué, e [distɛ̃ge] *a* distinguished.

distinguer [distɛ̃ge] *vt* to distinguish.

distraction [distʀaksjɔ̃] *nf* *(manque d'attention)* absent-mindedness ; *(oubli)* lapse (in concentration *ou* attention) ; *(détente)* diversion, recreation ; *(passe-temps)* distraction, entertainment.

distraire [distʀɛʀ] *vt* *(déranger)* to distract ; *(divertir)* to entertain, divert ; *(détourner: somme d'argent)* to divert, misappropriate ; **se ~** to amuse ou enjoy o.s.

distrait, e [distʀɛ, -ɛt] *a* absent-minded.

distribuer [distʀibɥe] *vt* to distribute ; to hand out ; *(CARTES)* to deal (out) ; *(courrier)* to deliver ; **distributeur** *nm* *(COMM)* distributor ; *(automatique)* (vending *ou* slot) machine ; **distribution** *nf* distribution ; *(postale)* delivery ; *(choix d'acteurs)* casting, cast ; **distribution des prix** *(SCOL)* prize giving.

district [distʀik(t)] *nm* district.

dites [dit] *voir* **dire**.

dit, e [di, dit] *pp de* **dire** // *a* *(fixé)*: **le jour ~** the arranged day ; *(surnommé)*: **X, ~ Pierrot** X, known as *ou* called Pierrot.

dithyrambique [ditiʀɑ̃bik] *a* eulogistic.

diurétique [djyʀetik] *a* a diuretic.

diurne [djyʀn(ə)] *a* diurnal, daytime *cpd*.

divagations [divagasjɔ̃] *nfpl* wanderings, ramblings ; ravings.

divaguer [divage] *vi* to ramble ; to rave.

divan [divɑ̃] *nm* divan ; **~-lit** *nm* divan (bed).

divergence [divɛʀʒɑ̃s] *nf* divergence.

divergent, e [divɛʀʒɑ̃, -ɑ̃] *a* divergent.

diverger [divɛʀʒe] *vi* to diverge.

divers, e [divɛʀ, -ɛʀs(ə)] *a* *(varié)* diverse, varied ; *(différent)* different, various, // *dét* *(plusieurs)* various, several ; **(frais) ~** sundries, miscellaneous (expenses) ;

diversement *ad* in various *ou* diverse ways ; **diversifier** *vt* to diversify.

diversion [divɛʀsjɔ̃] *nf* diversion ; **faire ~** to create a diversion.

diversité [divɛʀsite] *nf* diversity ; variety.

divertir [divɛʀtiʀ] *vt* to amuse, entertain ; **se ~** to amuse *ou* enjoy o.s. ; **divertissement** *nm* entertainment ; *(MUS)* divertimento, divertissement.

dividende [dividɑ̃d] *nm* *(MATH, COMM)* dividend.

divin, e [divɛ̃, -in] *a* divine ; **diviniser** *vt* to deify ; **divinité** *nf* divinity.

diviser [divize] *vt* *(gén, MATH)* to divide ; *(morceler, subdiviser)* to divide (up), split (up) ; **diviseur** *nm* *(MATH)* divisor ; **division** *nf* *(gén)* division.

divorce [divɔʀs(ə)] *nm* divorce ; **divorcé, e** *nm/f* divorcee ; **divorcer** *vi* to get a divorce, get divorced ; **divorcer de** *ou* **d'avec qn** to divorce sb.

divulgation [divylgasjɔ̃] *nf* disclosure.

divulguer [divylge] *vt* to divulge, disclose.

dix [dis] *num* ten ; **dixième** *num* tenth.

dizaine [dizɛn] *nf* (10) ten ; *(environ 10)*: **une ~ (de)** about ten, ten or so.

do [do] *nm* *(note)* C ; *(en chantant la gamme)* do(h).

docile [dɔsil] *a* docile ; **docilité** *nf* docility.

dock [dɔk] *nm* dock.

docker [dɔkɛʀ] *nm* docker.

docte [dɔkt(ə)] *a* learned.

docteur [dɔktœʀ] *nm* doctor.

doctoral, e, aux [dɔktɔʀal, -o] *a* pompous, bombastic.

doctorat [dɔktɔʀa] *nm*: **~ d'Université** ≈ Ph.D. ; **~ d'état** ≈ Higher Doctorate.

doctoresse [dɔktɔʀɛs] *nf* lady doctor.

doctrinaire [dɔktʀinɛʀ] *a* doctrinaire ; pompous, sententious.

doctrine [dɔktʀin] *nf* doctrine.

document [dɔkymɑ̃] *nm* document.

documentaire [dɔkymɑ̃tɛʀ] *a*, *nm* documentary.

documentaliste [dɔkymɑ̃talist(ə)] *nm/f* archivist ; researcher.

documentation [dɔkymɑ̃tasjɔ̃] *nf* documentation, literature ; *(PRESSE, TV: service)* research.

documenté, e [dɔkymɑ̃te] *a* well-informed, well-documented ; well-researched.

documenter [dɔkymɑ̃te] *vt*: **se ~ (sur)** to gather information *ou* material (on *ou* about).

dodeliner [dɔdline] *vi*: **~ de la tête** to nod one's head gently.

dodo [dɔdo] *nm*: **aller faire ~** to go to bye-byes.

dodu, e [dɔdy] *a* plump.

dogmatique [dɔgmatik] *a* dogmatic.

dogme [dɔgm(ə)] *nm* dogma.

dogue [dɔg] *nm* mastiff.

doigt [dwa] *nm* finger ; **à deux ~s de** within an ace *ou* an inch of ; **un ~ de lait/whisky** a drop of milk/whisky ; **~ de pied** toe.

doigté [dwate] *nm* *(MUS)* fingering ; fingering technique ; *(fig: habileté)* diplomacy, tact.

doigtier [dwatje] *nm* fingerstall.
doit *etc vb voir* **devoir**.
doléances [dɔleɑs] *nfpl* complaints; grievances.
dolent, e [dɔlɑ̃, -ɑ̃t] *a* doleful, mournful.
dollar [dɔlaʀ] *nm* dollar.
D.O.M. [*parfois* dɔm] *sigle m ou mpl* = *département(s) d'outre-mer.*
domaine [dɔmɛn] *nm* estate, property; (*fig*) domain, field; **tomber dans le** ~ **public** (*JUR*) to be out of copyright.
domanial, e, aux [dɔmanjal, -jo] *a* (*forêt, biens*) national, state *cpd*.
dôme [dom] *nm* dome.
domesticité [dɔmɛstisite] *nf* (domestic) staff.
domestique [dɔmɛstik] *a* domestic // *nm/f* servant, domestic.
domestiquer [dɔmɛstike] *vt* to domesticate.
domicile [dɔmisil] *nm* home, place of residence; **à** ~ at home; **domicilié, e** *a*: **être domicilié à** to have one's home in *ou* at.
dominant, e [dɔminɑ̃, -ɑ̃t] *a* dominant; predominant.
dominateur, trice [dɔminatœʀ, -tʀis] *a* dominating; domineering.
domination [dɔminasjɔ̃] *nf* domination.
dominer [dɔmine] *vt* to dominate; (*passions etc*) to control, master; (*surpasser*) to outclass, surpass; (*surplomber*) to tower above, dominate // *vi* to be in the dominant position; **se** ~ to control o.s.
dominical, e, aux [dɔminikal, -o] *a* Sunday *cpd*, dominical.
domino [dɔmino] *nm* domino; ~**s** *nmpl* (*jeu*) dominoes *sg.*
dommage [dɔmaʒ] *nm* (*préjudice*) harm, injury; (*dégâts, pertes*) damage *q*; **c'est** ~ **de faire/que** it's a shame *ou* pity to do/that; ~**s-intérêts** *nmpl* damages.
dompter [dɔ̃te] *vt* to tame; **dompteur, euse** *nm/f* trainer; liontamer.
don [dɔ̃] *nm* (*cadeau*) gift; (*charité*) donation; (*aptitude*) gift, talent; **avoir des** ~**s pour** to have a gift *ou* talent for.
donateur, trice [dɔnatœʀ, -tʀis] *nm/f* donor.
donation [dɔnasjɔ̃] *nf* donation.
donc [dɔ̃k] *cj* therefore, so; (*après une digression*) so, then.
donjon [dɔ̃ʒɔ̃] *nm* keep, donjon.
donné, e [dɔne] *a* (*convenu*) given // *nf* (*MATH, gén*) datum (*pl* data); **étant** ~ ... given ... .
donner [dɔne] *vt* to give; (*vieux habits etc*) to give away; (*spectacle*) to show; to put on; ~ **qch à qn** to give sb sth, give sth to sb; ~ **sur** (*suj: fenêtre, chambre*) to look (out) onto; ~ **dans** (*piège etc*) to fall into; **se** ~ **à fond (à son travail)** to give one's all (to one's work); **s'en** ~ **à cœur joie** (*fam*) to have a great time (of it).
donneur, euse [dɔnœʀ, -øz] *nm/f* (*MÉD*) donor; (*CARTES*) dealer; ~ **de sang** blood donor.
dont [dɔ̃] *pronom relatif:* **la maison** ~ **je vois le toit** the house whose roof I can see, the house I can see the roof of; **la**

maison ~ **le toit est rouge** the house whose roof is red *ou* the roof of which is red; **l'homme** ~ **je connais la sœur** the man whose sister I know; **10 blessés,** ~ **2 grièvement** 10 injured, 2 of them seriously; **2 livres,** ~ **l'un est 2 books,** one of which is; **il y avait plusieurs personnes,** ~ **Gabrielle** there were several people, among whom was Gabrielle; **le fils** ~ **il est si fier** the son he's so proud of; **ce** ~ **je parle** what I'm talking about; *voir adjectifs et verbes à complément prépositionnel:* **responsable de, souffrir de** *etc.*
dorade [dɔʀad] *nf* = **daurade.**
doré, e [dɔʀe] *a* golden; (*avec dorure*) gilt, gilded.
dorénavant [dɔʀenavɑ̃] *ad* from now on, henceforth.
dorer [dɔʀe] *vt* (*cadre*) to gild; (*faire*) ~ (*CULIN*) to brown (in the oven).
dorloter [dɔʀlɔte] *vt* to pamper, cosset.
dormant, e [dɔʀmɑ̃, -ɑ̃t] *a*: **eau** ~**e** still water.
dormeur, euse [dɔʀmœʀ, -øz] *nm/f* sleeper.
dormir [dɔʀmiʀ] *vi* to sleep; (*être endormi*) to be asleep.
dorsal, e, aux [dɔʀsal, -o] *a* dorsal.
dortoir [dɔʀtwaʀ] *nm* dormitory.
dorure [dɔʀyʀ] *nf* gilding.
doryphore [dɔʀifɔʀ] *nm* Colorado beetle.
dos [do] *nm* back; (*de livre*) spine; '**voir au** ~' 'see over'; **de** ~ from the back, from behind; **à** ~ **de chameau** riding on a camel.
dosage [dozaʒ] *nm* mixture.
dos-d'âne [dodɑn] *nm* humpback.
dose [doz] *nf* dose.
doser [doze] *vt* to measure out; to mix in the correct proportions; (*fig*) to expend in the right amounts *ou* proportion; to strike a balance between; **doseur** *nm* measure.
dossard [dosaʀ] *nm* number (*worn by competitor*).
dossier [dosje] *nm* (*renseignements, fichier*) file; (*enveloppe*) folder, file; (*de chaise*) back.
dot [dɔt] *nf* dowry.
doter [dɔte] *vt:* ~ **qn/qch de** to equip sb/sth with.
douairière [dwɛʀjɛʀ] *nf* dowager.
douane [dwan] *nf* (*poste, bureau*) customs *pl*; (*taxes*) (customs) duty; **passer la** ~ to go through customs; **douanier, ière** *a* customs *cpd* // *nm* customs officer.
doublage [dublaʒ] *nm* (*CINÉMA*) dubbing.
double [dubl(ə)] *a, ad* double // *nm* (*2 fois plus*): **le** ~ **(de)** twice as much (*ou* many) (as), double the amount (*ou* number) (of); (*autre exemplaire*) duplicate, copy; (*sosie*) double; **en** ~ **(exemplaire)** in duplicate; **faire** ~ **emploi** to be redundant; ~ **carburateur** twin carburettor; **à** ~**s commandes** dual-control; ~ **messieurs/mixte** men's/mixed doubles *sg*; ~ **toit** (*de tente*) fly sheet.
doublé, e [duble] *a* (*vêtement*): ~ **(de)** lined (with).
doublement [dubləmɑ̃] *nm* doubling;

twofold increase // ad doubly; in two ways, on two counts.

doubler [duble] vt (multiplier par 2) to double; (vêtement) to line; (dépasser) to overtake, pass; (film) to dub; (acteur) to stand in for // vi to double, increase twofold; ~ **(la classe)** (SCOL) to repeat a year.

doublure [dublyʀ] nf lining; (CINÉMA) stand-in.

douce [dus] a voir **doux**; ~**âtre** a sickly sweet; ~**ment** ad gently; slowly; ~**reux, euse** a (péj) sugary, suave; **douceur** nf mildness; gentleness; softness; sweetness; **douceurs** nfpl (friandises) sweets.

douche [duʃ] nf shower; ~**s** nfpl (salle) shower room sg; **se doucher** to have ou take a shower.

doué, e [dwe] a gifted, talented; ~ **de** endowed with.

douille [duj] nf (ÉLEC) socket; (de projectile) case.

douillet, te [dujɛ, -ɛt] a cosy; (péj) soft.

douleur [dulœʀ] nf pain; (chagrin) grief, distress; **il a eu la** ~ **de perdre son père** he suffered the grief of losing his father; **douloureux, euse** a painful.

doute [dut] nm doubt; **sans** ~ ad no doubt.

douter [dute] vt to doubt; ~ **de** vt (allié) to doubt, have (one's) doubts about; (résultat) to be doubtful of; **se** ~ **de qch/que** to suspect sth/that; **je m'en doutais** I suspected as much.

douteux, euse [dutø, -øz] a (incertain) doubtful; (discutable) dubious, questionable; (péj) dubious-looking.

douve [duv] nf (de château) moat; (de tonneau) stave.

Douvres [duvʀ(ə)] n Dover.

doux, douce [du, dus] a (lisse, moelleux, pas vif: couleur, non calcaire: eau) soft; (sucré, agréable) sweet; (peu fort: moutarde etc, clément: climat) mild; (pas brusque) gentle.

douzaine [duzɛn] nf (12) dozen; (environ 12): **une** ~ **(de)** a dozen or so, twelve or so.

douze [duz] num twelve; **douzième** num twelfth.

doyen, ne [dwajɛ̃, -ɛn] nm/f (en âge, ancienneté) most senior member; (de faculté) dean.

draconien, ne [dʀakɔnjɛ̃, -jɛn] a draconian; stringent.

dragage [dʀagaʒ] nm dredging.

dragée [dʀaʒe] nf sugared almond; (MÉD) (sugar-coated) pill.

dragon [dʀagɔ̃] nm dragon.

drague [dʀag] nf (filet) dragnet; (bateau) dredger; **draguer** vt (rivière) to dredge; to drag // vi (fam) to try and pick up girls; to chat up birds; **dragueur de mines** nm minesweeper.

drainage [dʀɛnaʒ] nm drainage.

drainer [dʀene] vt to drain.

dramatique [dʀamatik] a dramatic; (tragique) tragic // nf (TV) (television) drama.

dramatiser [dʀamatize] vt to dramatize.

dramaturge [dʀamatyʀʒ(ə)] nm dramatist, playwright.

drame [dʀam] nm (THÉÂTRE) drama; (catastrophe) drama, tragedy.

drap [dʀa] nm (de lit) sheet; (tissu) woollen fabric.

drapeau, x [dʀapo] nm flag; **sous les** ~**x** with the colours, in the army.

draper [dʀape] vt to drape.

draperies [dʀapʀi] nfpl hangings.

drapier [dʀapje] nm (woollen) cloth manufacturer; (marchand) clothier.

dresser [dʀese] vt (mettre vertical, monter: tente) to put up, erect; (fig: liste, bilan, contrat) to draw up; (animal) to train; **se** ~ vi (falaise, obstacle) to stand; to tower (up); (personne) to draw o.s. up; ~ **qn contre qn d'autre** to set sb against sb else.

dresseur, euse [dʀesœʀ, -øz] nm/f trainer.

dressoir [dʀeswaʀ] nm dresser.

dribbler [dʀible] vt, vi (SPORT) to dribble.

drogue [dʀɔg] nf drug; **la** ~ drugs pl.

drogué, e [dʀɔge] nm/f drug addict.

droguer [dʀɔge] vt (victime) to drug; (malade) to give drugs to; **se** ~ (aux stupéfiants) to take drugs; (péj: de médicaments) to dose o.s. up.

droguerie [dʀɔgʀi] nf hardware shop.

droguiste [dʀɔgist(ə)] nm keeper (ou owner) of a hardware shop.

droit, e [dʀwa, dʀwat] a (non courbe) straight; (vertical) upright, straight; (fig: loyal, franc) upright, straight(forward); (opposé à gauche) right, right-hand // ad straight // nm (prérogative) right; (taxe) duty, tax; (: d'inscription) fee; (lois, branche): **le** ~ law // nf (ligne) straight line; **avoir le** ~ **de** to be allowed to; **avoir** ~ **à** to be entitled to; **être en** ~ **de** to have a ou the right to; **faire** ~ **à** to grant, accede to; **être dans son** ~ to be within one's rights; **à** ~ **e on the right**; (direction) (to the) right; **de** ~**e** (POL) right-wing; ~ **d'auteur** copyright; ~**s d'auteur** royalties; **le** ~ **de vote** the right (to) vote.

droitier, ière [dʀwatje, -jɛʀ] nm/f right-handed person.

droiture [dʀwatyʀ] nf uprightness, straightness.

drôle [dʀol] a (amusant) funny, amusing; (bizarre) funny, peculiar.

dromadaire [dʀɔmadɛʀ] nm dromedary.

dru, e [dʀy] a (cheveux) thick, bushy; (pluie) heavy.

drugstore [dʀœgstɔʀ] nm drugstore.

D.S.T. sigle f = direction de la surveillance du territoire (the French internal security service).

du [dy] prép + dét, dét voir **de**.

dû, due [dy] vb voir **devoir** // a (somme) owing, owed; (: venant à échéance) due; (causé par): ~ **à** due to // nm due; (somme) dues pl.

dubitatif, ive [dybitatif, -iv] a doubtful, dubious.

duc [dyk] nm duke; **duché** nm dukedom; **duchesse** nf duchess.

duel [dɥɛl] nm duel.

dûment [dymɑ̃] ad duly.

dune [dyn] nf dune.
Dunkerque [dœkɛʀk] n Dunkirk.
duo [dɥo] nm (MUS) duet ; (fig: couple) duo, pair.
dupe [dyp] nf dupe // a: **(ne pas) être ~ de** (not) to be taken in by.
duper [dype] vt to dupe, deceive.
duperie [dypʀi] nf deception, dupery.
duplex [dyplɛks] nm (appartement) split-level appartment, duplex.
duplicata [dyplikata] nm duplicate.
duplicateur [dyplikatœʀ] nm duplicator.
duplicité [dyplisite] nf duplicity.
duquel [dykɛl] prép + pronom voir **lequel**.
dur, e [dyʀ] a (pierre, siège, travail, problème) hard ; (lumière, voix, climat) harsh ; (sévère) hard, harsh ; (cruel) hard(-hearted) ; (porte, col) stiff ; (viande) tough // ad hard ; ~ **d'oreille** hard of hearing.
durable [dyʀabl(ə)] a lasting.
durant [dyʀɑ̃] prép (au cours de) during ; (pendant) for ; ~ **des mois, des mois ~** for months.
durcir [dyʀsiʀ] vt, vi, **se ~** vi to harden.
durcissement [dyʀsismɑ̃] nm hardening.
durée [dyʀe] nf length ; (d'une pile etc) life ; (déroulement: des opérations etc) duration ; **pour une ~ illimitée** for an unlimited length of time.
durement [dyʀmɑ̃] ad harshly.
durer [dyʀe] vi to last.
dureté [dyʀte] nf hardness ; harshness ; stiffness ; toughness.
durit [dyʀit] nf ® (radiator) hose (for car).
dus etc vb voir **devoir**.
duvet [dyvɛ] nm down ; **(sac de couchage en) ~** down-filled sleeping bag.
dynamique [dinamik] a dynamic.
dynamisme [dinamism(ə)] nm dynamism.
dynamite [dinamit] nf dynamite.
dynamiter [dinamite] vt to (blow up with) dynamite.
dynamo [dinamo] nf dynamo.
dynastie [dinasti] nf dynasty.
dysenterie [disɑ̃tʀi] nf dysentery.
dyslexie [dislɛksi] nf dyslexia, word-blindness.
dyspepsie [dispɛpsi] nf dyspepsia.

E

eau, x [o] nf water // nfpl waters ; **prendre l'~** to leak, let in water ; **faire ~** to leak ; **tomber à l'~** (fig) to fall through ; **~ de Cologne** Eau de Cologne ; **~ courante** running water ; **~ douce** fresh water ; **~ de Javel** bleach ; **~ minérale** mineral water ; **~ salée** salt water ; **~ de toilette** toilet water ; **les E~x et Forêts** (ADMIN) ≈ the National Forestry Commission ; **~-de-vie** nf brandy ; **~-forte** nf etching.
ébahi, e [ebai] a dumbfounded, flabbergasted.
ébats [eba] nmpl frolics, gambols.
ébattre [ebatʀ(ə)]: **s'~** vi to frolic.
ébauche [eboʃ] nf (rough) outline, sketch.
ébaucher [eboʃe] vt to sketch out, outline ; **s'~** vi to take shape.

ébène [ebɛn] nf ebony.
ébéniste [ebenist(ə)] nm cabinetmaker ; **ébénisterie** nf cabinetmaking ; (bâti) cabinetwork.
éberlué, e [ebɛʀlɥe] a astounded, flabbergasted.
éblouir [ebluiʀ] vt to dazzle.
éblouissement [ebluismɑ̃] nm dazzle ; (faiblesse) dizzy turn.
éborgner [ebɔʀɲe] vt: ~ **qn** to blind sb in one eye.
éboueur [ebwœʀ] nm dustman.
ébouillanter [ebujɑ̃te] vt to scald ; (CULIN) to blanch.
éboulement [ebulmɑ̃] nm falling rocks pl, rock fall.
ébouler [ebule]: **s'~** vi to crumble, collapse.
éboulis [ebuli] nmpl fallen rocks.
ébouriffé, e [ebuʀife] a tousled, ruffled.
ébranler [ebʀɑ̃le] vt to shake ; (rendre instable: mur) to weaken ; **s'~** vi (partir) to move off.
ébrécher [ebʀeʃe] vt to chip.
ébriété [ebʀijete] nf: **en état d'~** in a state of intoxication.
ébrouer [ebʀue]: **s'~** vi to shake o.s. ; to snort.
ébruiter [ebʀɥite] vt to spread, disclose.
ébullition [ebylisjɔ̃] nf boiling point ; **en ~** boiling ; (fig) in an uproar.
écaille [ekaj] nf (de poisson) scale ; (de coquillage) shell ; (matière) tortoiseshell ; (de roc etc) flake.
écailler [ekaje] vt (poisson) to scale ; (huître) to open ; **s'~** vi to flake ou peel (off).
écarlate [ekaʀlat] a scarlet.
écarquiller [ekaʀkije] vt: ~ **les yeux** to stare wide-eyed.
écart [ekaʀ] nm gap ; (embardée) swerve ; sideways leap ; (fig) departure, deviation ; **à l'~** ad out of the way ; **à l'~ de** prép away from ; (fig) out of ; **~ de conduite** misdemeanour.
écarté, e [ekaʀte] a (maison, route) out-of-the-way, remote ; (ouvert): **les jambes ~es** legs apart ; **les bras ~s** arms outstretched.
écarteler [ekaʀtəle] vt to quarter ; (fig) to tear.
écartement [ekaʀtəmɑ̃] nm space, gap ; (RAIL) gauge.
écarter [ekaʀte] vt (séparer) to move apart, separate ; (éloigner) to push back, move away ; (ouvrir: bras, jambes) to spread, open ; (: rideau) to draw (back) ; (éliminer: candidat, possibilité) to dismiss ; **s'~** vi to part ; to move away ; **s'~ de** to wander from.
ecchymose [ekimoz] nf bruise.
ecclésiastique [eklezjastik] a ecclesiastical // nm ecclesiastic.
écervelé, e [esɛʀvəle] a scatterbrained, featherbrained.
échafaud [eʃafo] nm scaffold.
échafaudage [eʃafodaʒ] nm scaffolding ; (fig) heap, pile.
échafauder [eʃafode] vt (plan) to construct.

échalas [eʃala] nm stake, pole.

échalote [eʃalɔt] nf shallot.

échancrure [eʃɑ̃kRyR] nf (de robe) scoop neckline ; (de côte, arête rocheuse) indentation.

échange [eʃɑ̃ʒ] nm exchange ; **en ~ de** in exchange ou return for.

échanger [eʃɑ̃ʒe] vt: **~ qch (contre)** to exchange sth (for) ; **échangeur** nm (AUTO) interchange.

échantillon [eʃɑ̃tijɔ̃] nm sample ; **échantillonnage** nm selection of samples.

échappatoire [eʃapatwaR] nf way out.

échappée [eʃape] nf (vue) vista ; (CYCLISME) breakaway.

échappement [eʃapmɑ̃] nm (AUTO) exhaust.

échapper [eʃape]: **~ à** vt (gardien) to escape (from) ; (punition, péril) to escape ; **~ à qn** (détail, sens) to escape sb ; (objet qu'on tient) to slip out of sb's hands ; **s'~** vi to escape ; **l'~ belle** to have a narrow escape.

écharde [eʃaRd(ə)] nf splinter (of wood).

écharpe [eʃaRp(ə)] nf scarf (pl scarves) ; (de maire) sash ; **avoir un bras en ~** to have one's arm in a sling ; **prendre en ~** (dans une collision) to hit sideways on.

écharper [eʃaRpe] vt to tear to pieces.

échasse [eʃas] nf stilt.

échassier [eʃasje] nm wader.

échauffement [eʃofmɑ̃] nm overheating.

échauffer [eʃofe] vt (métal, moteur) to overheat ; (fig: exciter) to fire, excite ; **s'~** (SPORT) to warm up ; (dans la discussion) to become heated.

échauffourée [eʃofuRe] nf clash, brawl.

échéance [eʃeɑ̃s] nf (d'un paiement: date) settlement date ; (: somme due) financial commitment(s) ; (fig) deadline ; **à brève/longue ~** a short-/long-term // ad in the short/long run.

échéant [eʃeɑ̃]: **le cas ~** ad if the case arises.

échec [eʃɛk] nm failure ; (ÉCHECS): **~ et mat/au roi** checkmate/check ; **~s** nmpl (jeu) chess sg ; **tenir en ~** to hold in check ; **faire ~ à** to foil ou thwart.

échelle [eʃɛl] nf ladder ; (fig, d'une carte) scale ; **à l'~ de** on the scale of ; **sur une grande ~** on a large scale ; **faire la courte ~ à qn** to give sb a leg up.

échelon [eʃlɔ̃] nm (d'échelle) rung ; (ADMIN) grade.

échelonner [eʃlɔne] vt to space out, spread out.

écheveau, x [eʃvo] nm skein, hank.

échevelé, e [eʃəvle] a tousled, dishevelled ; wild, frenzied.

échine [eʃin] nf backbone, spine.

échiquier [eʃikje] nm chessboard.

écho [eko] nm echo ; **~s** nmpl (potins) gossip sg, rumours.

échoir [eʃwaR] vi (dette) to fall due ; (délais) to expire ; **~ à** vt to fall to.

échoppe [eʃɔp] nf stall, booth.

échouer [eʃwe] vi to fail // vt (bateau) to ground ; **s'~** vi to run aground.

échu, e [eʃy] pp voir **échoir**.

éclabousser [eklabuse] vt to splash.

éclair [eklɛR] nm (d'orage) flash of lightning, lightning q ; (fig) flash, spark ; (gâteau) éclair.

éclairage [eklɛRaʒ] nm lighting.

éclaircie [eklɛRsi] nf bright ou sunny interval.

éclaircir [eklɛRsiR] vt to lighten ; (fig) to clear up ; to clarify ; (CULIN) to thin (down) ; **s'~ la voix** to clear one's throat ; **éclaircissement** nm clearing up ; clarification.

éclairer [eklɛRe] vt (lieu) to light (up) ; (personne: avec une lampe de poche etc) to light the way for ; (fig) to enlighten ; to shed light on // vi: **~ mal/bien** to give a poor/good light ; **s'~ à la bougie/l'électricité** to use candlelight/have electric lighting.

éclaireur, euse [eklɛRœR, -øz] nm/f (scout) (boy) scout/(girl) guide // nm (MIL) scout ; **partir en ~** to go off to reconnoitre.

éclat [ekla] nm (de bombe, de verre) fragment ; (du soleil, d'une couleur etc) brightness, brilliance ; (d'une cérémonie) splendour ; (scandale): **faire un ~** to cause a commotion ; **des ~s de verre** broken glass ; flying glass ; **~ de rire** burst ou roar of laughter ; **~ de voix** shout.

éclatant, e [eklatɑ̃, -ɑ̃t] a brilliant, bright.

éclater [eklate] vi (pneu) to burst ; (bombe) to explode ; (guerre, épidémie) to break out ; (groupe, parti) to break up ; **~ de rire** to burst out laughing.

éclipse [eklips(ə)] nf eclipse.

éclipser [eklipse] vt to eclipse ; **s'~** vi to slip away.

éclopé, e [eklɔpe] a lame.

éclore [eklɔR] vi (œuf) to hatch ; (fleur) to open (out).

écluse [eklyz] nf lock ; **éclusier** nm lock keeper.

écœurer [ekœRe] vt: **~ qn** to make sb feel sick.

école [ekɔl] nf school ; **aller à l'~** to go to school ; **faire ~** to collect a following ; **~ de dessin/danse** art/dancing school ; **~ hôtelière** catering college ; **~ normale (d'instituteurs)** teachers' training college ; **~ de secrétariat** secretarial college ; **écolier, ière** nm/f schoolboy/girl.

écologie [ekɔlɔʒi] nf ecology ; environmental studies pl ; **écologique** a ecological ; environmental ; **écologiste** nm/f ecologist ; environmentalist.

éconduire [ekɔ̃dɥiR] vt to dismiss.

économat [ekɔnɔma] nm bursar's office.

économe [ekɔnɔm] a thrifty // nm/f (de lycée etc) bursar.

économie [ekɔnɔmi] nf (vertu) economy, thrift ; (gain: d'argent, de temps etc) saving ; (science) economics sg ; (situation économique) economy ; **~s** nfpl (pécule) savings ; **économique** a (avantageux) economical ; (ÉCON) economic.

économiser [ekɔnɔmize] vt, vi to save.

économiste [ekɔnɔmist(ə)] nm/f economist.

écoper [ekɔpe] vi to bale out ; (fig) to cop it ; **~ (de)** vt to get.

écorce [ekɔRs(ə)] nf bark ; (de fruit) peel ; **écorcer** vt to bark.

écorché [ekɔʀʃe] *nm* cut-away drawing.
écorcher [ekɔʀʃe] *vt* (*animal*) to skin; (*égratigner*) to graze; **écorchure** *nf* graze.
écossais, e [ekɔsɛ, -ɛz] *a* Scottish // *nm/f*: **E~, e** Scot.
Écosse [ekɔs] *nf* Scotland.
écosser [ekɔse] *vt* to shell.
écot [eko] *nm*: **payer son ~** to pay one's share.
écouler [ekule] *vt* to sell; to dispose of; **s'~** *vi* (*eau*) to flow (out); (*jours, temps*) to pass (by).
écourter [ekuʀte] *vt* to curtail, cut short.
écoute [ekut] *nf* (*RADIO, TV*): **temps/heure d'~** listening (*ou* viewing) time/hour; **prendre l'~** to tune in; **rester à l'~ (de)** to stay listening (to) *ou* tuned in (to); **~s téléphoniques** phone tapping *sg*.
écouter [ekute] *vt* to listen to; **écouteur** *nm* (*TÉL*) receiver; (*RADIO*) headphones *pl*, headset.
écoutille [ekutij] *nf* hatch.
écran [ekʀɑ̃] *nm* screen.
écrasant, e [ekʀɑzɑ̃, -ɑ̃t] *a* overwhelming.
écraser [ekʀɑze] *vt* to crush; (*piéton*) to run over; **s'~ (au sol)** to crash; **s'~ contre** to crash into.
écrémer [ekʀeme] *vt* to skim.
écrevisse [ekʀəvis] *nf* crayfish *inv*.
écrier [ekʀije]: **s'~** *vi* to exclaim.
écrin [ekʀɛ̃] *nm* case, box.
écrire [ekʀiʀ] *vt* to write; **ça s'écrit comment?** how is it spelt?, how do you write that?; **écrit** *nm* document; (*examen*) written paper; **par écrit** in writing.
écriteau, x [ekʀito] *nm* notice, sign.
écritoire [ekʀitwaʀ] *nf* writing case.
écriture [ekʀityʀ] *nf* writing; (*COMM*) entry; **~s** *nfpl* (*COMM*) accounts, books; **l'É~ (sainte), les É~s** the Scriptures.
écrivain [ekʀivɛ̃] *nm* writer.
écrou [ekʀu] *nm* nut.
écrouer [ekʀue] *vt* to imprison; to remand in custody.
écrouler [ekʀule]: **s'~** *vi* to collapse.
écru, e [ekʀy] *a* (*toile*) raw, unbleached.
écueil [ekœj] *nm* reef; (*fig*) pitfall; stumbling block.
écuelle [ekɥɛl] *nf* bowl.
éculé, e [ekyle] *a* (*chaussure*) down-at-heel; (*fig: péj*) hackneyed.
écume [ekym] *nf* foam; (*CULIN*) scum; **écumer** *vt* (*CULIN*) to skim; (*fig*) to plunder // *vi* (*mer*) to foam; (*fig*) to boil with rage; **écumoire** *nf* skimmer.
écureuil [ekyʀœj] *nm* squirrel.
écurie [ekyʀi] *nf* stable.
écusson [ekysɔ̃] *nm* badge.
écuyer, ère [ekɥije, -ɛʀ] *nm/f* rider.
eczéma [ɛgzema] *nm* eczema.
édenté, e [edɑ̃te] *a* toothless.
E.D.F. *sigle f* = Électricité de France, ≈ Electricity Board.
édifice [edifis] *nm* building, edifice.
édifier [edifje] *vt* to build, erect; (*fig*) to edify.
édiles [edil] *nmpl* city fathers.
édit [edi] *nm* edict.
éditer [edite] *vt* (*publier*) to publish; (: *disque*) to produce; (*préparer: texte*) to

edit; **éditeur, trice** *nm/f* editor; publisher; **édition** *nf* editing *q*; edition; (*industrie du livre*) publishing.
éditorial, aux [editɔʀjal, -o] *nm* editorial, leader; **~iste** *nm/f* editorial *ou* leader writer.
édredon [edʀədɔ̃] *nm* eiderdown.
éducatif, ive [edykatif, -iv] *a* educational.
éducation [edykasjɔ̃] *nf* education; (*familiale*) upbringing; (*manières*) (good) manners *pl*; **l'É~ (Nationale)** ≈ The Department of Education; **~ physique** physical education.
édulcorer [edylkɔʀe] *vt* to sweeten; (*fig*) to tone down.
éduquer [edyke] *vt* to educate; (*élever*) to bring up; (*faculté*) to train.
effacer [efase] *vt* to erase, rub out; **s'~** *vi* (*inscription etc*) to wear off; (*pour laisser passer*) to step aside; **~ le ventre** to pull one's stomach in.
effarement [efaʀmɑ̃] *nm* alarm.
effarer [efaʀe] *vt* to alarm.
effaroucher [efaʀuʃe] *vt* to frighten *ou* scare away; to alarm.
effectif, ive [efɛktif, -iv] *a* real; effective // *nm* (*MIL*) strength; (*SCOL*) total number of pupils, size; **~s** *nmpl* numbers, strength *sg*; **effectivement** *ad* effectively; (*réellement*) actually, really; (*en effet*) indeed.
effectuer [efɛktɥe] *vt* (*opération, mission*) to carry out; (*déplacement, trajet*) to make, complete; (*mouvement*) to execute, make.
efféminé, e [efemine] *a* effeminate.
effervescent, e [efɛʀvesɑ̃, -ɑ̃t] *a* (*cachet, boisson*) effervescent; (*fig*) agitated, in a turmoil.
effet [efɛ] *nm* (*résultat, artifice*) effect; (*impression*) impression; **~s** *nmpl* (*vêtements etc*) things; **faire de l'~** (*médicament, menace*) to have an effect, be effective; **en ~** *ad* indeed.
effeuiller [efœje] *vt* to remove the leaves (*ou* petals) from.
efficace [efikas] *a* (*personne*) efficient; (*action, médicament*) effective; **efficacité** *nf* efficiency; effectiveness.
effigie [efiʒi] *nf* effigy.
effilé, e [efile] *a* slender; sharp; streamlined.
effiler [efile] *vt* (*cheveux*) to thin (out); (*tissu*) to fray.
effilocher [efilɔʃe]: **s'~** *vi* to fray.
efflanqué, e [eflɑ̃ke] *a* emaciated.
effleurer [eflœʀe] *vt* to brush (against); (*sujet, idée*) to touch upon; (*suj: idée, pensée*): **~ qn** to cross sb's mind.
effluves [eflyv] *nmpl* exhalation(s).
effondrement [efɔ̃dʀəmɑ̃] *nm* collapse.
effondrer [efɔ̃dʀe]: **s'~** *vi* to collapse.
efforcer [efɔʀse]: **s'~ de** *vt*: **s'~ de faire** to try hard to do.
effort [efɔʀ] *nm* effort; **faire un ~** to make an effort.
effraction [efʀaksjɔ̃] *nf* breaking-in; **s'introduire par ~ dans** to break into.
effrangé, e [efʀɑ̃ʒe] *a* fringed; (*effiloché*) frayed.
effrayant, e [efʀɛjɑ̃, -ɑ̃t] *a* frightening, fearsome; (*sens affaibli*) dreadful.

effrayer [efʀeje] *vt* to frighten, scare; (*rebuter*) to put off; **s'~ (de)** to be frightened *ou* scared (by).

effréné, e [efʀene] *a* wild.

effriter [efʀite]: **s'~** *vi* to crumble.

effroi [efʀwa] *nm* terror, dread *q*.

effronté, e [efʀɔ̃te] *a* insolent, brazen.

effroyable [efʀwajabl(ə)] *a* horrifying, appalling.

effusion [efyzjɔ̃] *nf* effusion; **sans ~ de sang** without bloodshed.

égailler [egaje]: **s'~** *vi* to scatter, disperse.

égal, e, aux [egal, -o] *a* (*identique, ayant les mêmes droits*) equal; (*plan: surface*) even, level; (*constant: vitesse*) steady; (*équitable*) even // *nm/f* equal; **être ~ à** (*prix, nombre*) to be equal to; **ça lui est ~** it's all the same to him, it doesn't matter to him; he doesn't mind; **sans ~** matchless, unequalled; **à l'~ de** (*comme*) just like; **d'~ à ~** as equals; **~ement** *ad* equally; evenly; (*aussi*) too, as well; **~er** *vt* to equal; **~iser** *vt* (*sol, salaires*) to level -(out); (*chances*) to equalize // *vi* (*SPORT*) to equalize; **~itaire** *a* egalitarian; **~ité** *nf* equality; evenness; steadiness; (*MATH*) identity; **être à ~ité (de points)** to be level; **~ité de droits** equality of rights; **~ité d'humeur** evenness of temper.

égard [egaʀ] *nm*: **~s** *nmpl* consideration *sg*; **à cet ~** in this respect; **eu ~ à** in view of; **par ~ pour** out of consideration for; **sans ~ pour** without regard for; **à l'~ de** *prép* towards; concerning.

égarement [egaʀmɑ̃] *nm* distraction; aberration.

égarer [egaʀe] *vt* (*objet*) to mislay; (*moralement*) to lead astray; **s'~** *vi* to get lost, lose one's way; (*objet*) to go astray; (*fig: dans une discussion*) to wander.

égayer [egeje] *vt* (*personne*) to amuse; to cheer up; (*récit, endroit*) to brighten up, liven up.

égide [eʒid] *nf*: **sous l'~ de** under the aegis of.

églantier [eglɑ̃tje] *nm* wild *ou* dog rose(-bush).

églantine [eglɑ̃tin] *nf* wild *ou* dog rose.

églefin [egləfɛ̃] *nm* haddock.

église [egliz] *nf* church; **aller à l'~** (*être pratiquant*) to go to church, be a churchgoer.

égocentrique [egɔsɑ̃tʀik] *a* egocentric, self-centred.

égoïsme [egɔism(ə)] *nm* selfishness, egoism; **égoïste** *a* selfish, egoistic // *nm/f* egoist.

égorger [egɔʀʒe] *vt* to cut the throat of.

égosiller [egozije]: **s'~** *vi* to shout o.s. hoarse.

égout [egu] *nm* sewer; **égoutier** *nm* sewer worker.

égoutter [egute] *vt* (*linge*) to wring out; (*vaisselle*) to drain // *vi*, **s'~** *vi* to drip; **égouttoir** *nm* draining board; (*mobile*) draining rack.

égratigner [egʀatiɲe] *vt* to scratch; **égratignure** *nf* scratch.

égrener [egʀəne] *vt*: **~ une grappe, ~ des raisins** to pick grapes off a bunch.

égrillard, e [egʀijaʀ, -aʀd(ə)] *a* ribald, bawdy.

Égypte [eʒipt(ə)] *nf* Egypt; **égyptien, ne** *a*, *nm/f* Egyptian; **égyptologie** *nf* Egyptology.

eh [e] *excl* hey!; **~ bien** well.

éhonté, e [eɔ̃te] *a* shameless, brazen.

éjaculation [eʒakylasjɔ̃] *nf* ejaculation.

éjaculer [eʒakyle] *vi* to ejaculate.

éjectable [eʒɛktabl(ə)] *a*: **siège ~** ejector seat.

éjecter [eʒɛkte] *vt* (*TECH*) to eject; (*fam*) to kick *ou* chuck out.

élaboration [elabɔʀasjɔ̃] *nf* elaboration.

élaborer [elabɔʀe] *vt* to elaborate.

élaguer [elage] *vt* to prune.

élan [elɑ̃] *nm* (*ZOOL*) elk, moose; (*SPORT: avant le saut*) run up; (*de véhicule ou objet en mouvement*) momentum; (*fig: de tendresse etc*) surge; **prendre son ~/de l'~** to take a run up/gather speed.

élancé, e [elɑ̃se] *a* slender.

élancement [elɑ̃smɑ̃] *nm* shooting pain.

élancer [elɑ̃se]: **s'~** *vi* to dash, hurl o.s.; (*fig: arbre, clocher*) to soar (upwards).

élargir [elaʀʒiʀ] *vt* to widen; (*vêtement*) to let out; (*JUR*) to release; **s'~** *vi* to widen; (*vêtement*) to stretch.

élasticité [elastisite] *nf* (*aussi ÉCON*) elasticity.

élastique [elastik] *a* elastic // *nm* (*de bureau*) rubber band; (*pour la couture*) elastic *q*.

électeur, trice [elɛktœʀ, -tʀis] *nm/f* elector, voter.

élection [elɛksjɔ̃] *nf* election; **~s** *nfpl* (*POL*) election(s); **~ partielle** ≈ by-election.

électoral, e, aux [elɛktɔʀal, -o] *a* electoral, election *cpd*.

électorat [elɛktɔʀa] *nm* electorate.

électricien, ne [elɛktʀisjɛ̃, -jɛn] *nm/f* electrician.

électricité [elɛktʀisite] *nf* electricity; **allumer/éteindre l'~** to put on/off the light; **~ statique** static electricity.

électrifier [elɛktʀifje] *vt* (*RAIL*) to electrify.

électrique [elɛktʀik] *a* electric.

électriser [elɛktʀize] *vt* to electrify.

électro... [elɛktʀo] *préfixe*: **~-aimant** *nm* electromagnet; **~cardiogramme** *nm* electrocardiogram; **~choc** *nm* electric shock treatment; **~cuter** *vt* to electrocute; **~cution** *nf* electrocution; **~de** *nf* electrode; **~encéphalogramme** *nm* electroencephalogram; **~gène** *a*: **groupe ~gène** generating set; **~lyse** *nf* electrolysis *sg*; **~magnétique** *a* electromagnetic; **~ménager** *a*: **appareils ~ménagers** domestic (electrical) appliances.

électron [elɛktʀɔ̃] *nm* electron.

électronicien, ne [elɛktʀɔnisjɛ̃, -jɛn] *nm/f* electronics engineer.

électronique [elɛktʀɔnik] *a* electronic // *nf* electronics *sg*.

électrophone [elɛktʀɔfɔn] *nm* record player.

élégance [elegɑ̃s] *nf* elegance.

élégant, e [elegɑ̃, -ɑ̃t] *a* elegant; (*solution*)

neat, elegant; (*attitude*, *procédé*) courteous, civilized.

élément [elemɑ̃] *nm* element; (*pièce*) component, part; **~s** *nmpl* (*aussi: rudiments*) elements; **élémentaire** *a* elementary; (CHIMIE) elemental.

éléphant [elefɑ̃] *nm* elephant.

élevage [ɛlvaʒ] *nm* breeding; (*de bovins*) cattle breeding *ou* rearing.

élévateur [elevatœʀ] *nm* elevator.

élévation [elevasjɔ̃] *nf* (*gén*) elevation; (*voir élever*) raising; (*voir s'élever*) rise.

élève [elɛv] *nm/f* pupil; **~ infirmière** *nf* student nurse.

élevé, e [ɛlve] *a* (*prix, sommet*) high; (*fig: noble*) elevated; **bien/mal ~** well-/ill-mannered.

élever [ɛlve] *vt* (*enfant*) to bring up, raise; (*bétail, volaille*) to breed; (*abeilles*) to keep; (*hausser: immeuble, taux, niveau*) to raise; (*fig: âme, esprit*) to elevate; (*édifier: monument*) to put up, erect; **s'~** *vi* (*avion, alpiniste*) to go up; (*niveau, température, aussi: cri etc*) to rise; *survenir: difficultés*) to arise; **s'~ à** (*suj: frais, dégâts*) to amount to, add up to; **s'~ contre qch** to rise up against sth; **~ une protestation/critique** to raise a protest/make a criticism; **~ la voix** to raise one's voice; **~ qn au rang de** to raise *ou* elevate sb to the rank of; **éleveur, euse** *nm/f* cattle breeder.

élidé, e [elide] *a* elided.

éligible [eliʒibl(ə)] *a* eligible.

élimé, e [elime] *a* worn (thin), threadbare.

élimination [eliminasjɔ̃] *nf* elimination.

éliminatoire [eliminatwaʀ] *a* eliminatory; disqualifying // *nf* (SPORT) heat.

éliminer [elimine] *vt* to eliminate.

élire [eliʀ] *vt* to elect; **~ domicile à** to take up residence in *ou* at.

élision [elizjɔ̃] *nf* elision.

élite [elit] *nf* elite.

elle [ɛl] *pronom* (*sujet*) she; (: *chose*) it; (*complément*) her; it; **~s** (*sujet*) they; (*complément*) them; **~-même** herself; itself; **~-s-mêmes** themselves; *voir note sous* **il**.

ellipse [elips(ə)] *nf* ellipse; (LING) ellipsis *sg*; **elliptique** *a* elliptical.

élocution [elɔkysjɔ̃] *nf* delivery; **défaut d'~** speech impediment.

éloge [elɔʒ] *nm* praise (*gén q*); **faire l'~ de** to praise; **élogieux, euse** *a* laudatory, full of praise.

éloigné, e [elwaɲe] *a* distant, far-off.

éloignement [elwaɲmɑ̃] *nm* removal; putting off; estrangement; distance.

éloigner [elwaɲe] *vt* (*objet*): **~ qch (de)** to move *ou* take sth away (from); (*personne*): **~ qn (de)** to take sb away *ou* remove sb (from); (*échéance*) to put off, postpone; (*soupçons, danger*) to ward off; **s'~ (de)** (*personne*) to go away (from); (*véhicule*) to move away (from); (*affectivement*) to become estranged (from).

élongation [elɔ̃gasjɔ̃] *nf* strained muscle.

éloquence [elɔkɑ̃s] *nf* eloquence.

éloquent, e [elɔkɑ̃, -ɑ̃t] *a* eloquent.

élu, e [ely] *pp de* **élire** // *nm/f* (POL) elected representative.

élucider [elyside] *vt* to elucidate.

élucubrations [elykybʀasjɔ̃] *nfpl* wild imaginings.

éluder [elyde] *vt* to evade.

émacié, e [emasje] *a* emaciated.

émail, aux [emaj, -o] *nm* enamel.

émaillé, e [emaje] *a* enamelled; (*fig*): **~ de** dotted with.

émanation [emanasjɔ̃] *nf* emanation, exhalation.

émanciper [emɑ̃sipe] *vt* to emancipate; **s'~** (*fig*) to become emancipated *ou* liberated.

émaner [emane]: **~ de** *vt* to come from; (ADMIN) to proceed from.

émarger [emaʀʒe] *vt* to sign; **~ de 1000 F à un budget** to receive 1000 F out of a budget.

émasculer [emaskyle] *vt* to emasculate.

emballage [ɑ̃balaʒ] *nm* wrapping; packaging.

emballer [ɑ̃bale] *vt* to wrap (up); (*dans un carton*) to pack (up); (*fig: fam*) to thrill (to bits); **s'~** *vi* (*moteur*) to race; (*cheval*) to bolt; (*fig: personne*) to get carried away.

embarcadère [ɑ̃baʀkadɛʀ] *nm* landing stage, pier.

embarcation [ɑ̃baʀkasjɔ̃] *nf* (small) boat, (small) craft *inv*.

embardée [ɑ̃baʀde] *nf* swerve; **faire une ~** to swerve.

embargo [ɑ̃baʀgo] *nm* embargo; **mettre l'~ sur** to put an embargo on, embargo.

embarquement [ɑ̃baʀkɑ̃mɑ̃] *nm* embarkation; loading; boarding.

embarquer [ɑ̃baʀke] *vt* (*personne*) to embark; (*marchandise*) to load; (*fam*) to cart off; to nick // *vi* (*passager*) to board; (NAVIG) to ship water; **s'~** *vi* to embark; **s'~ dans** (*affaire, aventure*) to embark upon.

embarras [ɑ̃baʀa] *nm* (*obstacle*) hindrance; (*confusion*) embarrassment; (*ennuis*): **être dans l'~** to be in a predicament *ou* an awkward position; **~ gastrique** stomach upset.

embarrasser [ɑ̃baʀase] *vt* (*encombrer*) to clutter (up); (*gêner*) to hinder, hamper; (*fig*) to cause embarrassment to; to put in an awkward position; **s'~ de** to burden o.s. with.

embauche [ɑ̃boʃ] *nf* hiring; **bureau d'~** labour office.

embaucher [ɑ̃boʃe] *vt* to take on, hire; **s'~** to get o.s. hired.

embauchoir [ɑ̃boʃwaʀ] *nm* shoetree.

embaumer [ɑ̃bome] *vt* to embalm; to fill with its fragrance; **~ la lavande** to be fragrant with (the scent of) lavender.

embellir [ɑ̃beliʀ] *vt* to make more attractive; (*une histoire*) to embellish // *vi* to grow lovelier *ou* more attractive.

embêtements [ɑ̃bɛtmɑ̃] *nmpl* trouble *sg*.

embêter [ɑ̃bete] *vt* to bother; **s'~** *vi* (*s'ennuyer*) to be bored; **il ne s'embête pas!** (*ironique*) he does all right for himself!

emblée [ɑ̃ble]: **d'~** *ad* straightaway.

emblème [ãblɛm] *nm* emblem.

emboîter [ãbwate] *vt* to fit together; **s'~ dans** to fit into; **s'~ (l'un dans l'autre)** to fit together; **~ le pas à qn** to follow in sb's footsteps.

embolie [ãbɔli] *nf* embolism.

embonpoint [ãbɔpwɛ̃] *nm* stoutness.

embouché, e [ãbuʃe] *a*: **mal ~** foul-mouthed.

embouchure [ãbuʃyR] *nf* (GÉO) mouth; (MUS) mouthpiece.

embourber [ãbuRbe]: **s'~** *vi* to get stuck in the mud.

embourgeoiser [ãbuR3waze]: **s'~** *vi* to adopt a middle-class outlook.

embout [ãbu] *nm* (de canne) tip; (de tuyau) nozzle.

embouteillage [ãbutɛjaʒ] *nm* traffic jam, (traffic) holdup.

emboutir [ãbutiR] *vt* (TECH) to stamp; (heurter) to crash into, ram.

embranchement [ãbRãʃmã] *nm* (routier) junction; (classification) branch.

embraser [ãbRaze]: **s'~** *vi* to flare up.

embrassades [ãbRasad] *nfpl* hugging and kissing *sg*.

embrasser [ãbRase] *vt* to kiss; (sujet, période) to embrace, encompass; (carrière, métier) to take up, enter upon.

embrasure [ãbRazyR] *nf*: **dans l'~ de la porte** in the door(way).

embrayage [ãbRɛjaʒ] *nm* (mécanisme) clutch.

embrayer [ãbReje] *vi* (AUTO) to let in the clutch.

embrigader [ãbRigade] *vt* to recruit.

embrocher [ãbRɔʃe] *vt* to (put on a) spit.

embrouillamini [ãbRujamini] *nm* (fam) muddle.

embrouiller [ãbRuje] *vt* (fils) to tangle (up); (fiches, idées, personne) to muddle up; **s'~** *vi* (personne) to get in a muddle.

embroussaillé, e [ãbRusaje] *a* overgrown, bushy.

embruns [ãbRœ̃] *nmpl* sea spray *sg*.

embryon [ãbRijɔ̃] *nm* embryo; **embryonnaire** *a* embryonic.

embûches [ãbyʃ] *nfpl* pitfalls, traps.

embué, e [ãbɥe] *a* misted up.

embuscade [ãbyskad] *nf* ambush; **tendre une ~ à** to lay an ambush for.

embusquer [ãbyske] *vt* to put in ambush; **s'~** *vi* to take up position (for an ambush).

éméché, e [emeʃe] *a* tipsy, merry.

émeraude [ɛmRod] *nf* emerald // *a inv* emerald-green.

émerger [emɛRʒe] *vi* to emerge; (faire saillie, aussi fig) to stand out.

émeri [ɛmRi] *nm*: **toile** *ou* **papier ~** emery paper.

émérite [emeRit] *a* highly skilled.

émerveiller [emɛRveje] *vt* to fill with wonder; **s'~ de** to marvel at.

émetteur, trice [emetœR, -tRis] *a* transmitting; (poste) ~ transmitter.

émettre [emɛtR(ə)] *vt* (son, lumière) to give out, emit; (message etc: RADIO) to transmit; (billet, timbre, emprunt) to issue; (hypothèse, avis) to voice, put forward //

vi: **~ sur ondes courtes** to broadcast on short wave.

émeus etc *vb voir* **émouvoir**.

émeute [emøt] *nf* riot; **émeutier, ère** *nm/f* rioter.

émietter [emjete] *vt* to crumble; (fig) to split up, to disperse.

émigrant, e [emigRã, -ãt] *nm/f* emigrant.

émigré, e [emigRe] *nm/f* expatriate.

émigrer [emigRe] *vi* to emigrate.

éminemment [eminamã] *ad* eminently.

éminence [eminãs] *nf* distinction; (colline) knoll, hill; **Son É~** his (ou her) Eminence.

éminent, e [eminã, -ãt] *a* distinguished.

émir [emiR] *nm* emir; **~at** *nm* emirate.

émissaire [emisɛR] *nm* emissary.

émission [emisjɔ̃] *nf* emission; transmission; issue; (RADIO, TV) programme, broadcast.

emmagasiner [ãmagazine] *vt* to (put into) store; (fig) to store up.

emmailloter [ãmajɔte] *vt* to wrap up.

emmanchure [ãmãʃyR] *nf* armhole.

emmêler [ãmele] *vt* to tangle (up); (fig) to muddle up; **s'~** to get into a tangle.

emménager [ãmenaʒe] *vi* to move in; **~ dans** to move into.

emmener [ãmne] *vt* to take (with one); (comme otage, capture) to take away; (SPORT, MIL: joueurs, soldats) to lead; **~ qn au cinéma** to take sb to the cinema.

emmerder [ãmɛRde] (fam!) *vt* to bug, bother; **s'~** (s'ennuyer) to be bored stiff.

emmitoufler [ãmitufle] *vt* to wrap up (warmly).

emmurer [ãmyRe] *vt* to wall up, immure.

émoi [emwa] *nm* (agitation, effervescence) commotion; (trouble) agitation.

émoluments [emɔlymã] *nmpl* remuneration *sg*, fee *sg*.

émonder [emɔ̃de] *vt* to prune.

émotif, ive [emɔtif, -iv] *a* emotional.

émotion [emɔsjɔ̃] *nf* emotion; **avoir des ~s** (fig) to get a fright; **émotionnel, le** *a* emotional.

émoulu, e [emuly] *a*: **frais ~ de** fresh from, just out of.

émousser [emuse] *vt* to blunt; (fig) to dull.

émouvoir [emuvwaR] *vt* (troubler) to stir, affect; (toucher, attendrir) to move; (indigner) to rouse; (effrayer) to disturb, worry; **s'~** *vi* to be affected; to be moved; to be roused; to be disturbed ou worried.

empailler [ãpaje] *vt* to stuff.

empaler [ãpale] *vt* to impale.

empaqueter [ãpakte] *vt* to pack up.

emparer [ãpaRe]: **s'~ de** *vt* (objet) to seize, grab; (comme otage, MIL) to seize; (suj: peur, doute) to take hold of.

empâter [ãpate]: **s'~** *vi* to thicken out.

empattement [ãpatmã] *nm* (AUTO) wheelbase; (TYPO) serif.

empêchement [ãpɛʃmã] *nm* (unexpected) obstacle, hitch.

empêcher [ãpeʃe] *vt* to prevent; **~ qn de faire** to prevent ou stop sb (from) doing; **~ que qch (n')arrive/qn (ne)**

fasse to prevent sth from happening/sb from doing; **il n'empêche que** nevertheless, be that as it may; **il n'a pas pu s'~ de rire** he couldn't help laughing.

empêcheur [ɑ̃pɛʃœʀ] *nm*: **~ de danser en rond** spoilsport, killjoy.

empeigne [ɑ̃pɛɲ] *nf* upper(s).

empereur [ɑ̃pʀœʀ] *nm* emperor.

empesé, e [ɑ̃pəze] *a* (*fig*) stiff, starchy.

empeser [ɑ̃pəze] *vt* to starch.

empester [ɑ̃pɛste] *vt* (*lieu*) to stink out // *vi* to stink, reek; **~ le tabac/le vin** to stink *ou* reek of tobacco/wine.

empêtrer [ɑ̃petʀe] *vt*: **s'~ dans** (*fils etc*) to get tangled up in.

emphase [ɑ̃faz] *nf* pomposity, bombast.

empierrer [ɑ̃pjeʀe] *vt* (*route*) to metal.

empiéter [ɑ̃pjete]: **~ sur** *vt* to encroach upon.

empiffrer [ɑ̃pifʀe]: **s'~** *vi* (*péj*) to stuff o.s.

empiler [ɑ̃pile] *vt* to pile (up), stack (up).

empire [ɑ̃piʀ] *nm* empire; (*fig*) influence.

empirer [ɑ̃piʀe] *vi* to worsen, deteriorate.

empirique [ɑ̃piʀik] *a* empirical.

emplacement [ɑ̃plasmɑ̃] *nm* site.

emplâtre [ɑ̃plɑtʀ(ə)] *nm* plaster; (*fam*) twit.

emplette [ɑ̃plɛt] *nf*: **faire l'~ de** to purchase; **~s** *nfpl* shopping *sg*.

emplir [ɑ̃pliʀ] *vt* to fill; **s'~ (de)** to fill (with).

emploi [ɑ̃plwa] *nm* use; (*COMM, ÉCON*) employment; (*poste*) job, situation; **d'~ facile** easy to use; **~ du temps** timetable, schedule.

employé, e [ɑ̃plwaje] *nm/f* employee; **~ de bureau/banque** office/bank employee *ou* clerk.

employer [ɑ̃plwaje] *vt* (*outil, moyen, méthode, mot*) to use; (*ouvrier, main-d'œuvre*) to employ; **s'~ à faire** to apply *ou* devote o.s. to doing; **employeur, euse** *nm/f* employer.

empocher [ɑ̃pɔʃe] *vt* to pocket.

empoignade [ɑ̃pwaɲad] *nf* row, set-to.

empoigne [ɑ̃pwaɲ] *nf*: **foire d'~** free-for-all.

empoigner [ɑ̃pwaɲe] *vt* to grab; **s'~** (*fig*) to have a row *ou* set-to.

empoisonnement [ɑ̃pwazɔnmɑ̃] *nm* poisoning.

empoisonner [ɑ̃pwazɔne] *vt* to poison; (*empester: air, pièce*) to stink out; (*fam*): **~ qn** to drive sb mad.

emportement [ɑ̃pɔʀtəmɑ̃] *nm* fit of rage, anger *q*.

emporte-pièce [ɑ̃pɔʀtəpjɛs] *nm inv* (*TECH*) punch; **à l'~** *a* (*fig*) incisive.

emporter [ɑ̃pɔʀte] *vt* to take (with one); (*en dérobant ou enlevant, emmener: blessés, voyageurs*) to take away; (*entraîner*) to carry away *ou* along; (*arracher*) to tear off; to carry away; (*MIL: position*) to take; (*avantage, approbation*) to win; **s'~** *vi* (*de colère*) to fly into a rage, lose one's temper; **l'~ (sur)** to get the upper hand (of); (*méthode etc*) to prevail (over); **boissons à l'~** take-away drinks.

empourpré, e [ɑ̃puʀpʀe] *a* crimson.

empreint, e [ɑ̃pʀɛ̃, -ɛ̃t] *a*: **~ de** marked with; tinged with // *nf* (*de pied, main*) print; (*fig*) stamp, mark; **~e (digitale)** fingerprint.

empressé, e [ɑ̃pʀese] *a* attentive; (*péj*) overanxious to please, overattentive.

empressement [ɑ̃pʀɛsmɑ̃] *nm* (*hâte*) eagerness.

empresser [ɑ̃pʀese]: **s'~** *vi* to bustle about; **s'~ auprès de qn** to surround sb with attentions; **s'~ de faire** (*se hâter*) to hasten to do.

emprise [ɑ̃pʀiz] *nf* hold, ascendancy; **sous l'~ de** under the influence of.

emprisonnement [ɑ̃pʀizɔnmɑ̃] *nm* imprisonment.

emprisonner [ɑ̃pʀizɔne] *vt* to imprison, jail.

emprunt [ɑ̃pʀœ̃] *nm* borrowing *q*, loan (*from debtor's point of view*); (*LING etc*) borrowing; **~ public à 5%** 5% public loan.

emprunté, e [ɑ̃pʀœ̃te] *a* (*fig*) ill-at-ease, awkward.

emprunter [ɑ̃pʀœ̃te] *vt* to borrow; (*itinéraire*) to take, follow; (*style, manière*) to adopt, assume; **emprunteur, euse** *nm/f* borrower.

empuantir [ɑ̃pyɑ̃tiʀ] *vt* to stink out.

ému, e [emy] *pp de* **émouvoir** // *a* excited; touched; moved.

émulation [emylasjɔ̃] *nf* emulation.

émule [emyl] *nm/f* imitator.

émulsion [emylsjɔ̃] *nf* emulsion.

en [ɑ̃] *prép in*; (*avec direction*) to; (*moyen*): **~ avion/taxi** by plane/taxi; (*composition*): **~ verre** made of glass, glass *cpd*; **se casser ~ plusieurs morceaux** to break into several pieces; **~ dormant** while sleeping, as one sleeps; **~ sortant** on going out, as he went out; **~ réparation** being repaired, under repair; **~ T/étoile** T-/star-shaped; **~ chemise/chaussettes** in one's shirt/socks; **peindre qch ~ rouge** to paint sth red; **~ soldat** as a soldier; **le même ~ plus grand** the same only *ou* but bigger // *pronom* (*provenance*): **j'~ viens** I've come from there; (*cause*): **j'~ suis malade** he's ill because of it; (*complément de nom*): **j'~ connais les dangers** I know its dangers; (*indéfini*): **j'~ ai/veux** I have/want some; **~ as-tu?** have you got any?; **je n'~ veux pas** I don't want any; **j'~ ai assez** I've got enough (of it *ou* them); (*fig*) I've had enough; **j'~ ai 2** I've got 2 (of them); **combien y ~ a-t-il?** how many (of them) are there?; **j'~ suis fier/ai besoin** I am proud of it/need it: *voir le verbe ou l'adjectif lorsque 'en' correspond à 'de' introduisant un complément prépositionnel.*

E.N.A. [ena] *sigle f* = École Nationale d'Administration: *one of the* **Grandes Écoles**; **énarque** *nm/f* former E.N.A. student.

encablure [ɑ̃kablyʀ] *nf* (*NAVIG*) cable's length.

encadrement [ɑ̃kadʀəmɑ̃] *nm* framing; training; (*de porte*) frame.

encadrer [ɑ̃kadʀe] *vt* (*tableau, image*) to frame; (*fig: entourer*) to surround; to

flank; (*personnel*, *soldats etc*) to train;
encadreur nm (picture) framer.

encaisse [ãkɛs] nf cash in hand; ~
or/métallique gold/gold and silver
reserves.

encaissé, e [ãkese] a steep-sided; with
steep banks.

encaisser [ãkese] vt (*chèque*) to cash;
(*argent*) to collect; (*fig: coup, défaite*) to
take; **encaisseur** nm collector (*of debts
etc*).

encan [ãkã]: à l'~ ad by auction.

encanailler [ãkanaje]: s'~ vi to become
vulgar ou common; to mix with the riffraff.

encart [ãkaʀ] nm insert.

encastrer [ãkastʀe] vt: ~ **qch dans** (*mur*)
to embed sth in(to); (*boîtier*) to fit sth into;
s'~ dans to fit into; (*heurter*) to crash into.

encaustique [ãkostik] nf polish, wax;
encaustiquer vt to polish, wax.

enceinte [ãsɛ̃t] af: ~ (**de 6 mois**) (6
months) pregnant // nf (*mur*) wall;
(*espace*) enclosure; ~ (**acoustique**)
speaker system.

encens [ãsã] nm incense; **encenser** vt to
(in)cense; (*fig*) to praise to the skies;
encensoir nm thurible.

encercler [ãsɛʀkle] vt to surround.

enchaîner [ãʃene] vt to chain up;
(*mouvements, séquences*) to link (together)
// vi to carry on.

enchanté, e [ãʃãte] a delighted;
enchanted; ~ (**de faire votre
connaissance**) pleased to meet you, how
do you do?.

enchantement [ãʃãtmã] nm delight;
(*magie*) enchantment; **comme par** ~ as
if by magic.

enchanter [ãʃãte] vt to delight.

enchâsser [ãʃase] vt: ~ **qch (dans)** to
set sth (in).

enchère [ãʃɛʀ] nf bid; **faire une** ~ to
(make a) bid; **mettre/vendre aux** ~**s** to
put up for (sale by)/sell by auction.

enchevêtrer [ãʃvetʀe] vt to tangle (up).

enclave [ãklav] nf enclave; **enclaver** vt
to enclose, hem in.

enclencher [ãklãʃe] vt (*mécanisme*) to
engage; **s'~** vi to engage.

enclin, e [ãklɛ̃, -in] a: ~ **à** inclined ou
prone to.

enclore [ãklɔʀ] vt to enclose.

enclos [ãklo] nm enclosure.

enclume [ãklym] nf anvil.

encoche [ãkɔʃ] nf notch.

encoignure [ãkɔɲyʀ] nf corner.

encoller [ãkɔle] vt to paste.

encolure [ãkɔlyʀ] nf (*tour de cou*) collar
size; (*col, cou*) neck.

encombrant, e [ãkɔ̃bʀã, -ãt] a
cumbersome, bulky.

encombre [ãkɔ̃bʀ(ə)]: **sans** ~ ad without
mishap ou incident.

encombrement [ãkɔ̃bʀəmã] nm (*d'un
lieu*) cluttering (up); (*d'un objet:
dimensions*) bulk.

encombrer [ãkɔ̃bʀe] vt to clutter (up);
(*gêner*) to hamper; **s'~ de** (*bagages etc*)
to load ou burden o.s. with; ~ **le passage**
to block ou obstruct the way.

encontre [ãkɔ̃tʀ(ə)]: **à l'~ de** prép
against, counter to.

encorbellement [ãkɔʀbɛlmã] nm
corbelled construction; **fenêtre en**~ oriel
window.

encore [ãkɔʀ] ad (*continuation*) still; (*de
nouveau*) again; (*restriction*) even then ou
so; (*intensif*): ~ **plus fort/mieux** even
louder/better; **pas** ~ not yet; ~ **une fois**
(once) again; ~ **deux jours** still two days,
two more days; **si** ~ if only.

encouragement [ãkuʀaʒmã] nm
encouragement.

encourager [ãkuʀaʒe] vt to encourage.

encourir [ãkuʀiʀ] vt to incur.

encrasser [ãkʀase] vt to foul up; to soot
up.

encre [ãkʀ(ə)] nf ink; ~ **de Chine** Indian
ink; ~ **sympathique** invisible ink;
encrer vt to ink; **encreur** am: **rouleau
encreur** inking roller; **encrier** nm inkwell.

encroûter [ãkʀute]: **s'~** vi (*fig*) to get
into a rut, get set in one's ways.

encyclique [ãsiklik] nf encyclical.

encyclopédie [ãsiklɔpedi] nf
encyclopaedia; **encyclopédique** a
encyclopaedic.

endémique [ãdemik] a endemic.

endetter [ãdete] vt, s'~ vi to get into debt.

endeuiller [ãdœje] vt to plunge into
mourning; **manifestation endeuillée par**
event over which a tragic shadow was cast
by.

endiablé, e [ãdjable] a furious;
boisterous.

endiguer [ãdige] vt to dyke (up); (*fig*) to
check, hold back.

endimancher [ãdimãʃe] vt: **s'~** to put
on one's Sunday best.

endive [ãdiv] nf chicory q.

endocrine [ãdɔkʀin] af: **glande** ~
endocrine (gland).

endoctriner [ãdɔktʀine] vt to
indoctrinate.

endommager [ãdɔmaʒe] vt to damage.

endormi, e [ãdɔʀmi] a asleep; (*fig*)
sleepy, drowsy; sluggish.

endormir [ãdɔʀmiʀ] vt to put to sleep;
(*MÉD*: *dent, nerf*) to anaesthetize; (*fig:
soupçons*) to allay; **s'~** vi to fall asleep,
go to sleep.

endosser [ãdose] vt (*responsabilité*) to
take, shoulder; (*chèque*) to endorse;
(*uniforme, tenue*) to put on, don.

endroit [ãdʀwa] nm place; (*opposé à
l'envers*) right side; **à l'**~ right side out;
the right way up; (*vêtement*) the right way
out; **à l'**~ **de** prép regarding, with regard
to.

enduire [ãdɥiʀ] vt to coat; ~ **qch de** to
coat sth with; **enduit** nm coating.

endurance [ãdyʀãs] nf endurance.

endurant, e [ãdyʀã, -ãt] a tough, hardy.

endurcir [ãdyʀsiʀ] vt (*physiquement*) to
toughen; (*moralement*) to harden; **s'~** vi
to become tougher; to become hardened.

endurer [ãdyʀe] vt to endure, bear.

énergétique [enɛʀʒetik] a (*ressources etc*)
energy cpd.

énergie [enɛʀʒi] nf (*PHYSIQUE*) energy;
(*TECH*) power; (*fig: physique*) energy;

énergumène [enɛʁgymɛn] *nm* rowdy character *ou* customer.

énerver [enɛʁve] *vt* to irritate, annoy ; **s'~** *vi* to get excited, get worked up.

enfance [ɑ̃fɑ̃s] *nf* (*âge*) childhood ; (*fig*) infancy ; (*enfants*) children *pl* ; **petite ~** infancy.

enfant [ɑ̃fɑ̃] *nm/f* child (*pl* children) ; **~ de chœur** *nm* (*REL*) altar boy ; **~ prodige** child prodigy ; **enfanter** *vi* to give birth // *vt* to give birth to ; **enfantillage** *nm* (*péj*) childish behaviour *q* ; **enfantin, e** *a* childlike ; child *cpd*.

enfer [ɑ̃fɛʁ] *nm* hell.

enfermer [ɑ̃fɛʁme] *vt* to shut up ; (*à clef, interner*) to lock up.

enferrer [ɑ̃feʁe]: **s'~** *vi* : **s'~ dans** to tangle o.s. up in.

enfiévré, e [ɑ̃fjevʁe] *a* (*fig*) feverish.

enfilade [ɑ̃filad] *nf* : **une ~ de** a series *ou* line of (interconnecting).

enfiler [ɑ̃file] *vt* (*vêtement*) : **~ qch** to slip sth on, slip into sth ; (*insérer*) : **~ qch dans** to stick into ; (*rue, couloir*) to take ; (*perles*) to string ; (*aiguille*) to thread ; **s'~ dans** to disappear into.

enfin [ɑ̃fɛ̃] *ad* at last ; (*en énumérant*) lastly ; (*de restriction, résignation*) still ; well ; (*pour conclure*) in a word.

enflammer [ɑ̃flame] *vt* to set fire to ; (*MÉD*) to inflame ; **s'~** to catch fire ; to become inflamed.

enflé, e [ɑ̃fle] *a* swollen ; (*péj: style*) bombastic, turgid.

enfler [ɑ̃fle] *vi* to swell (up) ; **s'~** *vi* to swell ; **enflure** *nf* swelling.

enfoncer [ɑ̃fɔ̃se] *vt* (*clou*) to drive in ; (*faire pénétrer*) : **~ qch dans** to push *ou* knock *ou* drive sth into ; (*forcer: porte*) to break open ; (*plancher*) to cause to cave in ; (*fam: surpasser*) to lick // *vi* (*dans la vase etc*) to sink in ; (*sol, surface porteuse*) to give way ; **s'~** *vi* to sink ; **s'~ dans** to sink into ; (*forêt, ville*) to disappear into.

enfouir [ɑ̃fwiʁ] *vt* (*dans le sol*) to bury ; (*dans un tiroir etc*) to tuck away ; **s'~ dans/sous** to bury o.s. in/under.

enfourcher [ɑ̃fuʁʃe] *vt* to mount.

enfourner [ɑ̃fuʁne] *vt* : **~ qch dans** to shove *ou* stuff sth into.

enfreindre [ɑ̃fʁɛ̃dʁ(ə)] *vt* to infringe, break.

enfuir [ɑ̃fɥiʁ]: **s'~** *vi* to run away *ou* off.

enfumer [ɑ̃fyme] *vt* to smoke out.

engagé, e [ɑ̃gaʒe] *a* (*littérature etc*) engagé, committed.

engageant, e [ɑ̃gaʒɑ̃, -ɑ̃t] *a* attractive, appealing.

engagement [ɑ̃gaʒmɑ̃] *nm* taking on, engaging ; starting ; investing ; (*d'un écrivain etc, professionnel, financier*) commitment ; (*pro-messe*) agreement, promise ; (*MIL: combat*) engagement ; **prendre l'~ de faire** to undertake to do ; **sans ~** (*COMM*) without obligation.

engager [ɑ̃gaʒe] *vt* (*embaucher*) to take on, engage ; (*commencer*) to start ; (*lier*) to bind, commit ; (*impliquer, entraîner*) to involve ; (*investir*) to invest, lay out ; (*faire intervenir*) to engage ; (*inciter*) : **~ qn à faire** to urge sb to do ; (*faire pénétrer*) : **~ qch dans** to insert sth into ; **s'~** (*s'embaucher*) to hire o.s., get taken on ; (*MIL*) to enlist ; (*promettre, politiquement*) to commit o.s. ; (*débuter*) to start (up) ; **s'~ à faire** to undertake to do ; **s'~ dans** (*rue, passage*) to enter, turn into ; (*s'emboîter*) to engage *ou* fit into ; (*fig: affaire, discussion*) to enter into, embark on.

engelures [ɑ̃ʒlyʁ] *nfpl* chilblains.

engendrer [ɑ̃ʒɑ̃dʁe] *vt* to father ; (*fig*) to create, breed.

engin [ɑ̃ʒɛ̃] *nm* machine ; instrument ; vehicle ; (*AVIAT*) aircraft *inv* ; missile ; **~ (explosif)** (explosive) device.

englober [ɑ̃glɔbe] *vt* to include.

engloutir [ɑ̃glutiʁ] *vt* to swallow up ; **s'~** to be engulfed.

engoncé, e [ɑ̃gɔ̃se] *a* : **~ dans** cramped in.

engorger [ɑ̃gɔʁʒe] *vt* to obstruct, block ; **s'~** *vi* to become blocked.

engouement [ɑ̃gumɑ̃] *nm* (sudden) passion.

engouffrer [ɑ̃gufʁe] *vt* to swallow up, devour ; **s'~ dans** to rush into.

engourdi, e [ɑ̃guʁdi] *a* numb.

engourdir [ɑ̃guʁdiʁ] *vt* to numb ; (*fig*) to dull, blunt ; **s'~** to go numb.

engrais [ɑ̃gʁɛ] *nm* manure ; **~ (chimique)** (chemical) fertilizer.

engraisser [ɑ̃gʁese] *vt* to fatten (up) // *vi* (*péj*) to get fat(ter).

engrenage [ɑ̃gʁənaʒ] *nm* gears *pl*, gearing ; (*fig*) chain.

engueuler [ɑ̃gœle] *vt* (*fam*) to bawl out.

enhardir [ɑ̃aʁdiʁ]: **s'~** *vi* to grow bolder.

énigmatique [enigmatik] *a* enigmatic.

énigme [enigm(ə)] *nf* riddle.

enivrer [ɑ̃nivʁe] *vt* : **s'~** to get drunk ; **s'~ de** (*fig*) to become intoxicated with.

enjambée [ɑ̃ʒɑ̃be] *nf* stride.

enjamber [ɑ̃ʒɑ̃be] *vt* to stride over ; (*suj: pont etc*) to span, straddle.

enjeu, x [ɑ̃ʒø] *nm* stakes *pl*.

enjoindre [ɑ̃ʒwɛ̃dʁ(ə)] *vt* : **~ à qn de faire** to enjoin *ou* order sb to do.

enjôler [ɑ̃ʒole] *vt* to coax, wheedle.

enjoliver [ɑ̃ʒɔlive] *vt* to embellish ; **enjoliveur** *nm* (*AUTO*) hub cap.

enjoué, e [ɑ̃ʒwe] *a* playful.

enlacer [ɑ̃lase] *vt* (*étreindre*) to embrace, hug ; (*suj: lianes*) to wind round, entwine.

enlaidir [ɑ̃lediʁ] *vt* to make ugly // *vi* to become ugly.

enlèvement [ɑ̃lɛvmɑ̃] *nm* removal ; abduction, kidnapping ; **l'~ des ordures ménagères** refuse collection.

enlever [ɑ̃lve] *vt* (*ôter: gén*) to remove ; (*: vêtement, lunettes*) to take off ; (*: MÉD: organe*) to remove, take out ; (*emporter: ordures etc*) to collect, take away ; (*prendre*) : **~ qch à qn** to take sth (away) from sb ; (*kidnapper*) to abduct, kidnap ; (*obtenir: prix, contrat*) to win ; (*MIL: position*) to take ; (*morceau de piano etc*) to execute with spirit *ou* brio.

enliser [ɑ̃lize]: **s'~** *vi* to sink, get stuck.

enluminure [ɑ̃lyminyʀ] *nf* illumination.

enneigé, e [ɑ̃neʒe] *a* snowy; snowed-up.

enneigement [ɑ̃nɛʒmɑ̃] *nm* depth of snow, snowfall; **bulletin d'~** snow report.

ennemi, e [ɛnmi] *a* hostile; (*MIL*) enemy *cpd* // *nm, nf* enemy; **être ~ de** to be strongly averse *ou* opposed to.

ennoblir [ɑ̃nɔbliʀ] *vt* to ennoble.

ennui [ɑ̃nɥi] *nm* (*lassitude*) boredom; (*difficulté*) trouble *q*; **avoir des ~s** to be in trouble; **ennuyer** *vt* to bother; (*lasser*) to bore; **s'ennuyer** to be bored; **s'ennuyer de** (*regretter*) to miss; **ennuyeux, euse** *a* boring, tedious; annoying.

énoncé [enɔse] *nm* terms *pl*; wording; (*LING*) utterance.

énoncer [enɔse] *vt* to say, express; (*conditions*) to set out, state.

enorgueillir [ɑ̃nɔʀɡœjiʀ]: **s'~ de** *vt* to pride o.s. on; to boast.

énorme [enɔʀm(ə)] *a* enormous, huge; **énormément** *ad* enormously, tremendously; **énormément de neige/gens** an enormous amount of snow/number of people; **énormité** *nf* enormity, hugeness; outrageous remark.

enquérir [ɑ̃keʀiʀ]: **s'~ de** *vt* to inquire about.

enquête [ɑ̃kɛt] *nf* (*de journaliste, de police*) investigation; (*judiciaire, administrative*) inquiry; (*sondage d'opinion*) survey; **enquêter** *vi* to investigate; to hold an inquiry; to conduct a survey; **enquêteur, euse** *ou* **trice** *nm/f* officer in charge of the investigation; person conducting a survey.

enquiers *etc vb voir* **enquérir**.

enraciné, e [ɑ̃ʀasine] *a* deep-rooted.

enragé, e [ɑ̃ʀaʒe] *a* (*MÉD*) rabid, with rabies; (*fig*) fanatical.

enrageant, e [ɑ̃ʀaʒɑ̃, -ɑ̃t] *a* infuriating.

enrager [ɑ̃ʀaʒe] *vi* to be furious, be in a rage.

enrayer [ɑ̃ʀeje] *vt* to check, stop; **s'~** *vi* (*arme à feu*) to jam.

enregistrement [ɑ̃ʀʒistʀəmɑ̃] *nm* recording; (*ADMIN*) registration; **~ des bagages** (*à l'aéroport*) luggage check-in.

enregistrer [ɑ̃ʀʒistʀe] *vt* (*MUS etc*) to record; (*remarquer, noter*) to note, record; (*fig: mémoriser*) to make a mental note of; (*ADMIN*) to register; (*bagages: par train*) to register; (: *à l'aéroport*) to check in.

enrhumer [ɑ̃ʀyme]: **s'~** *vi* to catch a cold.

enrichir [ɑ̃ʀiʃiʀ] *vt* to make rich(er); (*fig*) to enrich; **s'~** to get rich(er).

enrober [ɑ̃ʀɔbe] *vt*: **~ qch de** to coat sth with; (*fig*) to wrap sth up in.

enrôler [ɑ̃ʀole] *vt* to enlist; **s'~ (dans)** to enlist (in).

enrouer [ɑ̃ʀwe]: **s'~** *vi* to go hoarse.

enrouler [ɑ̃ʀule] *vt* (*fil, corde*) to wind (up); **~ qch autour de** to wind sth (a)round; **s'~** to coil up; to wind; **enrouleur** *nm voir* **ceinture**.

enrubanné, e [ɑ̃ʀybane] *a* trimmed with ribbon.

ensabler [ɑ̃sɑble] *vt* (*port, canal*) to silt up, sand up; (*embarcation*) to strand (on a sandbank); **s'~** *vi* to silt up; to get stranded.

ensanglanté, e [ɑ̃sɑ̃ɡlɑ̃te] *a* covered with blood.

enseignant, e [ɑ̃sɛɲɑ̃, -ɑ̃t] *a* teaching // *nm/f* teacher.

enseigne [ɑ̃sɛɲ] *nf* sign // *nm*: **~ de vaisseau** lieutenant; **à telle ~ que** so much so that; **~ lumineuse** neon sign.

enseignement [ɑ̃sɛɲmɑ̃] *nm* teaching; (*ADMIN*): **~ primaire/ secondaire** primary/secondary education.

enseigner [ɑ̃sɛɲe] *vt, vi* to teach; **~ qch à qn/à qn que** to teach sb sth/sb that.

ensemble [ɑ̃sɑ̃bl(ə)] *ad* together // *nm* (*assemblage, MATH*) set; (*totalité*): **l'~ du/de la** the whole *ou* entire; (*vêtement féminin*) ensemble, suit; (*unité, harmonie*) unity; (*résidentiel*) housing development; **impression/idée d'~** overall *ou* general impression/ idea; **dans l'~** (*en gros*) on the whole; **~ vocal/musical** vocal/musical ensemble.

ensemblier [ɑ̃sɑ̃blije] *nm* interior designer.

ensemencer [ɑ̃sməse] *vt* to sow.

enserrer [ɑ̃seʀe] *vt* to hug (tightly).

ensevelir [ɑ̃səvliʀ] *vt* to bury.

ensoleillé, e [ɑ̃sɔleje] *a* sunny.

ensoleillement [ɑ̃sɔlɛjmɑ̃] *nm* period *ou* hours of sunshine.

ensommeillé, e [ɑ̃sɔmeje] *a* sleepy, drowsy.

ensorceler [ɑ̃sɔʀsəle] *vt* to enchant, bewitch.

ensuite [ɑ̃sɥit] *ad* then, next; (*plus tard*) afterwards, later; **~ de quoi** after which.

ensuivre [ɑ̃sɥivʀ(ə)]: **s'~** *vi* to follow, ensue.

entaille [ɑ̃tɑj] *nf* (*encoche*) notch; (*blessure*) cut.

entailler [ɑ̃tɑje] *vt* to notch; to cut; **s'~ le doigt** to cut one's finger.

entamer [ɑ̃tɑme] *vt* (*pain, bouteille*) to start; (*hostilités, pourparlers*) to open; (*fig: altérer*) to make a dent in; to shake; to damage.

entartrer [ɑ̃taʀtʀe]: **s'~** *vi* to fur up; (*dents*) to scale.

entassement [ɑ̃tɑsmɑ̃] *nm* (*tas*) pile, heap.

entasser [ɑ̃tɑse] *vt* (*empiler*) to pile up, heap up; (*tenir à l'étroit*) to cram together; **s'~** *vi* to pile up; to cram.

entendement [ɑ̃tɑ̃dmɑ̃] *nm* understanding.

entendre [ɑ̃tɑ̃dʀ(ə)] *vt* to hear; (*comprendre*) to understand; (*vouloir dire*) to mean; (*vouloir*): **~ être obéi/que** to intend *ou* mean to be obeyed/that; **j'ai entendu dire que** I've heard (it said) that; **~ raison** to see sense; **s'~** *vi* (*sympathiser*) to get on; (*se mettre d'accord*) to agree; **s'~ à qch/à faire** (*être compétent*) to be good at sth/doing.

entendu, e [ɑ̃tɑ̃dy] *a* (*réglé*) agreed; (*au courant: air*) knowing; (*c'est*) **~!** all right, agreed; **c'est ~** (*concession*) all right, granted; **bien ~!** of course!

entente [ɑ̃tɑ̃t] *nf* (*entre amis, pays*) understanding, harmony; (*accord, traité*) agreement, understanding; **à double ~** (*sens*) with a double meaning.

entériner [ɑ̃teʀine] *vt* to ratify, confirm.

entérite [ɑ̃teʀit] *nf* enteritis *q*.

enterrement [ɑ̃tɛʀmɑ̃] *nm* burying ; (*cérémonie*) funeral, burial.

enterrer [ɑ̃teʀe] *vt* to bury.

entêtant, e [ɑ̃tɛtɑ̃, -ɑ̃t] *a* heady.

en-tête [ɑ̃tɛt] *nm* heading ; **papier à ~** headed notepaper.

entêté, e [ɑ̃tete] *a* stubborn.

entêter [ɑ̃tete]: **s'~** *vi*: **s'~ (à faire)** to persist (in doing).

enthousiasme [ɑ̃tuzjasm(ə)] *nm* enthusiasm ; **enthousiasmer** *vt* to fill with enthusiasm ; **s'enthousiasmer (pour qch)** to get enthusiastic (about sth) ; **enthousiaste** *a* enthusiastic.

enticher [ɑ̃tiʃe]: **s'~ de** *vt* to become infatuated with.

entier, ère [ɑ̃tje, -jɛʀ] *a* (*non entamé, en totalité*) whole ; (*total, complet*) complete ; (*fig: caractère*) unbending, averse to compromise // *nm* (MATH) whole ; **en ~** totally ; in its entirety ; **lait ~** full-cream milk ; **pain ~** wholemeal bread ; **entièrement** *ad* entirely, completely, wholly.

entité [ɑ̃tite] *nf* entity.

entonner [ɑ̃tɔne] *vt* (*chanson*) to strike up.

entonnoir [ɑ̃tɔnwaʀ] *nm* (*ustensile*) funnel ; (*trou*) shell-hole, crater.

entorse [ɑ̃tɔʀs(ə)] *nf* (MÉD) sprain ; (*fig*): **~ à la loi/au règlement** infringement of the law/rule.

entortiller [ɑ̃tɔʀtije] *vt* (*envelopper*): **~ qch dans/avec** to wrap sth in/with ; (*enrouler*): **~ qch autour de** to twist ou wind sth (a)round ; (*fam*): **~ qn** to get round sb ; to hoodwink sb.

entourage [ɑ̃tuʀaʒ] *nm* circle ; family (circle) ; entourage ; (*ce qui enclôt*) surround.

entourer [ɑ̃tuʀe] *vt* to surround ; (*apporter son soutien à*) to rally round ; **~ de** to surround with ; (*trait*) to encircle with.

entourloupettes [ɑ̃tuʀlupɛt] *nfpl* mean tricks.

entracte [ɑ̃tʀakt(ə)] *nm* interval.

entraide [ɑ̃tʀɛd] *nf* mutual aid ou assistance ; **s'entraider** to help each other.

entrailles [ɑ̃tʀaj] *nfpl* entrails ; bowels.

entrain [ɑ̃tʀɛ̃] *nm* spirit ; **avec/sans ~** spiritedly/half-heartedly.

entraînant, e [ɑ̃tʀɛnɑ̃, -ɑ̃t] *a* (*musique*) stirring, rousing.

entraînement [ɑ̃tʀɛnmɑ̃] *nm* training ; (TECH): **~ à chaîne/galet** chain/wheel drive.

entraîner [ɑ̃tʀene] *vt* (*tirer: wagons*) to pull ; (*charrier*) to carry ou drag along ; (TECH) to drive ; (*emmener: personne*) to take (off) ; (*mener à l'assaut, influencer*) to lead ; (SPORT) to train ; (*impliquer*) to entail ; (*causer*) to lead to, bring about ; **~ qn à faire** (*inciter*) to lead sb to do ; **s'~** (SPORT) to train ; **s'~ à qch/à faire** to train o.s. for sth/to do ; **entraîneur, euse** *nm/f* (SPORT) coach, trainer // *nm* (HIPPISME) trainer // *nf* (*de bar*) hostess.

entrave [ɑ̃tʀav] *nf* hindrance.

entraver [ɑ̃tʀave] *vt* (*circulation*) to hold up ; (*action, progrès*) to hinder, hamper.

entre [ɑ̃tʀ(ə)] *prép* between ; (*parmi*) among(st) ; **l'un d'~ eux/nous** one of them/us ; **ils se battent ~ eux** they are fighting among(st) themselves.

entrebâillé, e [ɑ̃tʀəbɑje] *a* half-open, ajar.

entrechoquer [ɑ̃tʀəʃɔke]: **s'~** *vi* to knock ou bang together.

entrecôte [ɑ̃tʀəkot] *nf* entrecôte ou rib steak.

entrecouper [ɑ̃tʀəkupe] *vt*: **~ qch de** to intersperse sth with.

entrecroiser [ɑ̃tʀəkʀwaze] *vt*, **s'~** *vi* intertwine.

entrée [ɑ̃tʀe] *nf* entrance ; (*accès: au cinéma etc*) admission ; (*billet*) (admission) ticket ; (CULIN) first course ; **d'~** *ad* from the outset ; **'~ interdite'** 'no admittance ou entry' ; **'~ libre'** 'admission free' ; **~ des artistes** stage door ; **~ en matière** introduction ; **~ de service** service entrance.

entrefaites [ɑ̃tʀəfɛt]: **sur ces ~** *ad* at this juncture.

entrefilet [ɑ̃tʀəfilɛ] *nm* paragraph (*short article*).

entregent [ɑ̃tʀəʒɑ̃] *nm*: **avoir de l'~** to have an easy manner.

entrejambes [ɑ̃tʀəʒɑ̃b] *nm* crotch.

entrelacer [ɑ̃tʀəlase] *vt*, **s'~** *vi* to intertwine.

entrelarder [ɑ̃tʀəlaʀde] *vt* to lard.

entremêler [ɑ̃tʀəmele] *vt*: **~ qch de** to (inter)mingle sth with.

entremets [ɑ̃tʀəmɛ] *nm* cream dessert.

entremetteur, euse [ɑ̃tʀəmɛtœʀ, -øz] *nm/f* go-between.

entremettre [ɑ̃tʀəmɛtʀ(ə)]: **s'~** *vi* to intervene.

entremise [ɑ̃tʀəmiz] *nf* intervention ; **par l'~ de** through.

entrepont [ɑ̃tʀəpɔ̃] *nm* steerage.

entreposer [ɑ̃tʀəpoze] *vt* to store, put into storage.

entrepôt [ɑ̃tʀəpo] *nm* warehouse.

entreprenant, e [ɑ̃tʀəpʀənɑ̃, -ɑ̃t] *a* (*actif*) enterprising ; (*trop galant*) forward.

entreprendre [ɑ̃tʀəpʀɑ̃dʀ(ə)] *vt* (*se lancer dans*) to undertake ; (*commencer*) to begin ou start (upon) ; (*personne*) to buttonhole ; to tackle ; **~ de faire** to undertake to do.

entrepreneur [ɑ̃tʀəpʀənœʀ] *nm*: **~ (en bâtiment)** (building) contractor ; **~ de pompes funèbres** (funeral) undertaker.

entreprise [ɑ̃tʀəpʀiz] *nf* (*société*) firm, concern ; (*action*) undertaking, venture.

entrer [ɑ̃tʀe] *vi* to go (ou come) in, enter ; (*faire*): **~ qch dans** to get sth into ; **~ dans** (*gén*) to enter ; (*pièce*) to go (ou come) into, enter ; (*club*) to join ; (*heurter*) to run into ; (*partager: vues, craintes de qn*) to share ; (*être une composante de*) to go into ; to form part of ; **~ à l'hôpital** to go into hospital ; **laisser ~ qn/qch** to let sb/sth in ; **faire ~** (*visiteur*) to show in.

entresol [ɑ̃tʀəsɔl] *nm* entresol, mezzanine.

entre-temps [ɑ̃tʀətɑ̃] *ad* meanwhile, (in the) meantime.

entretenir [ɑ̃tʀətniʀ] *vt* to maintain ; (*amitié*) to keep alive ; (*famille, maîtresse*) to support, keep ; **~ qn (de)** to speak to sb (about) ; **s'~ (de)** to converse (about).

entretien [ɑ̃tRətjɛ̃] *nm* maintenance ; (*discussion*) discussion, talk ; (*audience*) interview.
entrevoir [ɑ̃tRəvwaR] *vt* (*à peine*) to make out ; (*brièvement*) to catch a glimpse of.
entrevue [ɑ̃tRəvy] *nf* meeting ; (*audience*) interview.
entr'ouvert, e [ɑ̃tRuvɛR, -ɛRt(ə)] *a* half-open.
énumérer [enymeRe] *vt* to list, enumerate.
envahir [ɑ̃vaiR] *vt* to invade ; (*suj: inquiétude, peur*) to come over ; **envahissant, e** *a* (*péj: personne*) interfering, intrusive ; **envahisseur** *nm* (*MIL*) invader.
enveloppe [ɑ̃vlɔp] *nf* (*de lettre*) envelope ; (*TECH*) casing ; outer layer ; **mettre sous ~** to put in an envelope.
envelopper [ɑ̃vlɔpe] *vt* to wrap ; (*fig*) to envelop, shroud.
envenimer [ɑ̃vnime] *vt* to aggravate.
envergure [ɑ̃vɛRgyR] *nf* (*d'un oiseau, avion*) wingspan ; (*fig*) scope ; calibre.
enverrai *etc vb voir* **envoyer**.
envers [ɑ̃vɛR] *prép* towards, to // *nm* other side ; (*d'une étoffe*) wrong side ; **à l'~** upside down ; back to front ; (*vêtement*) inside out.
envie [ɑ̃vi] *nf* (*sentiment*) envy ; (*souhait*) desire, wish ; (*tache sur la peau*) birthmark ; (*filet de peau*) hangnail ; **avoir ~ de** to feel like ; (*désir plus fort*) to want ; **avoir ~ de** to feel like doing ; to want to do ; **avoir ~ que** to wish that ; **donner à qn l'~ de faire** to make sb want to do ; **ça lui fait ~** he would like that ; **envier** *vt* to envy ; **envieux, euse** *a* envious.
environ [ɑ̃viRɔ̃] *ad*: **~ 3 h/2 km, 3 h/2 km ~** (around) about 3 o'clock/2 km, 3 o'clock/2 km or so ; **~s** *nmpl* surroundings ; **aux ~s de** around.
environnement [ɑ̃viRɔnmɑ̃] *nm* environment.
environner [ɑ̃viRɔne] *vt* to surround.
envisager [ɑ̃vizaʒe] *vt* (*examiner, considérer*) to view, contemplate ; (*avoir en vue*) to envisage ; **~ de faire** to consider *ou* contemplate doing.
envoi [ɑ̃vwa] *nm* sending ; (*paquet*) parcel, consignment.
envol [ɑ̃vɔl] *nm* takeoff.
envolée [ɑ̃vɔle] *nf* (*fig*) flight.
envoler [ɑ̃vɔle]: **s'~** *vi* (*oiseau*) to fly away *ou* off ; (*avion*) to take off ; (*papier, feuille*) to blow away ; (*fig*) to vanish (into thin air).
envoûter [ɑ̃vute] *vt* to bewitch.
envoyé, e [ɑ̃vwaje] *nm/f* (*POL*) envoy ; (*PRESSE*) correspondent.
envoyer [ɑ̃vwaje] *vt* to send ; (*lancer*) to hurl, throw ; **~ chercher** to send for ; **envoyeur, euse** *nm/f* sender.
éolien, ne [eɔljɛ̃, -jɛn] *a* wind *cpd*.
épagneul, e [epaɲœl] *nm/f* spaniel.
épais, se [epɛ, -ɛs] *a* thick ; **épaisseur** *nf* thickness ; **épaissir** *vt*, **s'épaissir** *vi* to thicken.
épanchement [epɑ̃ʃmɑ̃] *nm*: **un ~ de sinovie** water on the knee ; **~s** *nmpl* (*fig*) (sentimental) outpourings.

épancher [epɑ̃ʃe] *vt* to give vent to ; **s'~** *vi* to open one's heart ; (*liquide*) to pour out.
épandage [epɑ̃daʒ] *nm* manure spreading.
épanouir [epanwiR]: **s'~** *vi* (*fleur*) to bloom, open out ; (*visage*) to light up ; (*fig*) to blossom (out), bloom ; to open up ; **épanouissement** *nm* blossoming ; opening up.
épargnant, e [epaRɲɑ̃, -ɑ̃t] *nm/f* saver, investor.
épargne [epaRɲ(ə)] *nf* saving.
épargner [epaRɲe] *vt* to save ; (*ne pas tuer ou endommager*) to spare // *vi* to save ; **~ qch à qn** to spare sb sth.
éparpiller [epaRpije] *vt* to scatter ; (*pour répartir*) to disperse ; (*fig: efforts*) to dissipate ; **s'~** *vi* to scatter ; (*fig*) to dissipate one's efforts.
épars, e [epaR, -aRs(ə)] *a* scattered.
épatant, e [epatɑ̃, -ɑ̃t] *a* (*fam*) super, splendid.
épaté, e [epate] *a*: **nez ~** flat nose (with wide nostrils).
épater [epate] *vt* to amaze ; to impress.
épaule [epol] *nf* shoulder.
épaulement [epolmɑ̃] *nm* escarpment ; retaining wall.
épauler [epole] *vt* (*aider*) to back up, support ; (*arme*) to raise (to one's shoulder) // *vi* to (take) aim.
épaulette [epolɛt] *nf* (*MIL*) epaulette ; (*de combinaison*) shoulder strap.
épave [epav] *nf* wreck.
épée [epe] *nf* sword.
épeler [eple] *vt* to spell.
éperdu, e [epɛRdy] *a* distraught, overcome ; passionate ; frantic.
éperon [epRɔ̃] *nm* spur ; **éperonner** *vt* to spur (on) ; (*navire*) to ram.
épervier [epɛRvje] *nm* (*ZOOL*) sparrowhawk ; (*PÊCHE*) casting net.
éphèbe [efɛb] *nm* beautiful young man.
éphémère [efemɛR] *a* ephemeral, fleeting.
éphéméride [efemeRid] *nf* block *ou* tear-off calendar.
épi [epi] *nm* (*de blé, d'orge*) ear ; **stationnement en ~** angled parking.
épice [epis] *nf* spice ; **épicé, e** *a* highly spiced, spicy ; (*fig*) spicy.
épicéa [episea] *nm* spruce.
épicer [epise] *vt* to spice ; (*fig*) to add spice to.
épicerie [episRi] *nf* (*magasin*) grocer's shop ; (*denrées*) groceries *pl* ; **~ fine** delicatessen (shop) ; **épicier, ière** *nm/f* grocer.
épidémie [epidemi] *nf* epidemic.
épiderme [epidɛRm(ə)] *nm* skin, epidermis ; **épidermique** *a* skin *cpd*, epidermic.
épier [epje] *vt* to spy on, watch closely ; (*occasion*) to look out for.
épieu, x [epjø] *nm* (hunting-)spear.
épilatoire [epilatwaR] *a* depilatory, hair-removing.
épilepsie [epilɛpsi] *nf* epilepsy ; **épileptique** *a*, *nm/f* epileptic.
épiler [epile] *vt* (*jambes*) to remove the hair from ; (*sourcils*) to pluck ; **se faire ~** to get unwanted hair removed.

épilogue [epilɔg] nm (fig) conclusion, dénouement.

épiloguer [epilɔge] vi: ~ **sur** to hold forth on.

épinard [epinaʀ] nm spinach q.

épine [epin] nf thorn, prickle ; (d'oursin etc) spine, prickle ; ~ **dorsale** backbone ; **épineux, euse** a thorny, prickly.

épingle [epɛ̃gl(ə)] nf pin ; **virage en ~ à cheveux** hairpin bend ; ~ **de cravate** tie pin ; ~ **de nourrice** ou **de sûreté** ou **double** safety pin.

épingler [epɛ̃gle] vt (badge, décoration): ~ **qch sur** to pin sth on(to) ; (fam) to catch, nick.

épinière [epinjɛʀ] af voir **moelle**.

Épiphanie [epifani] nf Epiphany.

épique [epik] a epic.

épiscopal, e, aux [episkɔpal, -o] a episcopal.

épiscopat [episkɔpa] nm bishopric, episcopate.

épisode [epizɔd] nm episode ; **film/roman à ~s** serialized film/novel, serial ; **épisodique** a occasional.

épissure [episyʀ] nf splice.

épistolaire [epistɔlɛʀ] a epistolary.

épitaphe [epitaf] nf epitaph.

épithète [epitɛt] nf (nom, surnom) epithet ; **adjectif ~** attributive adjective.

épître [epitʀ(ə)] nf epistle.

éploré, e [eplɔʀe] a in tears, tearful.

épluche-légumes [eplyʃlegym] nm inv potato peeler.

éplucher [eplyʃe] vt (fruit, légumes) to peel ; (comptes, dossier) to go over with a fine-tooth comb ; **éplucheur** nm (automatic) peeler ; **épluchures** nfpl peelings.

épointer [epwɛ̃te] vt to blunt.

éponge [epɔ̃ʒ] nf sponge ; **éponger** vt (liquide) to mop ou sponge up ; (surface) to sponge ; (fig: déficit) to soak up, absorb ; **s' éponger le front** to mop one's brow.

épopée [epɔpe] nf epic.

époque [epɔk] nf (de l'histoire) age, era ; (de l'année, la vie) time ; **d'~** a (meuble) period cpd.

épouiller [epuje] vt to pick lice off ; to delouse.

époumoner [epumɔne] : **s'~** vi to shout o.s. hoarse.

épouse [epuz] nf wife (pl wives).

épouser [epuze] vt to marry ; (fig: idées) to espouse ; (: forme) to fit.

épousseter [epuste] vt to dust.

époustouflant, e [epustuflɑ̃, -ɑ̃t] a staggering, mind-boggling.

épouvantable [epuvɑ̃tabl(ə)] a appalling, dreadful.

épouvantail [epuvɑ̃taj] nm (à moineaux) scarecrow ; (fig) bog(e)y ; bugbear.

épouvante [epuvɑ̃t] nf terror ; **film d'~** horror film ; **épouvanter** vt to terrify.

époux [epu] nm husband // nmpl (married) couple.

éprendre [epʀɑ̃dʀ(ə)]: **s'~ de** vt to fall in love with.

épreuve [epʀœv] nf (d'examen) test ; (malheur, difficulté) trial, ordeal ; (PHOTO) print ; (d'imprimerie) proof ; (SPORT) event ;

à l'~ **des balles** bulletproof ; **à toute ~** unfailing ; **mettre à l'~** to put to the test.

épris, e [epʀi, -iz] vb voir **éprendre**.

éprouver [epʀuve] vt (tester) to test ; (mettre à l'épreuve) to put to the test ; (marquer, faire souffrir) to afflict, distress ; (ressentir) to feel.

éprouvette [epʀuvɛt] nf test tube.

épuisé, e [epɥize] a exhausted ; (livre) out of print.

épuisement [epɥizmɑ̃] nm exhaustion ; **jusqu'à ~ des stocks** while stocks last.

épuiser [epɥize] vt (fatiguer) to exhaust, wear ou tire out ; (stock, sujet) to exhaust ; **s'~** vi to wear ou tire o.s. out, exhaust o.s. (stock) to run out.

épuisette [epɥizɛt] nf landing net ; shrimping net.

épurer [epyʀe] vt (liquide) to purify ; (parti, administration) to purge ; (langue, texte) to refine.

équarrir [ekaʀiʀ] vt (pierre, arbre) to square (off) ; (animal) to quarter.

équateur [ekwatœʀ] nm equator ; **(la république de) l'É~** Ecuador.

équation [ekwasjɔ̃] nf equation ; **mettre en ~** to equate.

équatorial, e, aux [ekwatɔʀjal, -o] a equatorial.

équerre [ekɛʀ] nf (à dessin) (set) square ; (pour fixer) brace ; **en ~** at right angles ; **à l'~, d'~** straight.

équestre [ekɛstʀ(ə)] a equestrian.

équidistant, e [ekɥidistɑ̃, -ɑ̃t] a: ~ **(de)** equidistant (from).

équilatéral, e, aux [ekɥilateʀal, -o] a equilateral.

équilibrage [ekilibʀaʒ] nm (AUTO): ~ **des roues** wheel balancing.

équilibre [ekilibʀ(ə)] nm balance ; (d'une balance) equilibrium ; **garder/perdre l'~** to keep/lose one's balance ; **être en ~** to be balanced ; **équilibré, e** a (fig) well-balanced, stable ; **équilibrer** vt to balance ; **s'équilibrer** (poids) to balance ; (fig: défauts etc) to balance each other out ; **équilibriste** nm/f tightrope walker.

équinoxe [ekinɔks] nm equinox.

équipage [ekipaʒ] nm crew.

équipe [ekip] nf team ; (bande: parfois péj) bunch.

équipée [ekipe] nf escapade.

équipement [ekipmɑ̃] nm equipment ; ~s nmpl amenities, facilities ; installations.

équiper [ekipe] vt to equip ; (voiture, cuisine) to equip, fit out ; ~ **qn/qch de** to equip sb/sth with ; **s'~** (sportif) to equip o.s., kit o.s. out.

équipier, ière [ekipje, -jɛʀ] nm/f team member.

équitable [ekitabl(ə)] a fair.

équitation [ekitɑsjɔ̃] nf (horse-)riding.

équité [ekite] nf equity.

équivalence [ekivalɑ̃s] nf equivalence.

équivalent, e [ekivalɑ̃, -ɑ̃t] a, nm equivalent.

équivaloir [ekivalwaʀ]: ~ **à** vt to be equivalent to ; (représenter) to amount to.

équivoque [ekivɔk] a equivocal, ambiguous ; (louche) dubious // nf ambiguity.

érable [eRabl(ə)] nm maple.
érafler [eRafle] vt to scratch; **éraflure** nf scratch.
éraillé, e [eRɑje] a (voix) rasping, hoarse.
ère [ɛR] nf era; **en l'an 1050 de notre ~** in the year 1050 A.D.
érection [eRɛksjɔ̃] nf erection.
éreinter [eRɛ̃te] vt to exhaust, wear out; (fig: critiquer) to slate.
ergot [ɛRgo] nm (de coq) spur; (TECH) lug.
ériger [eRiʒe] vt (monument) to erect; **s'~ en critique** to set o.s. up as a critic.
ermitage [ɛRmitaʒ] nm retreat.
ermite [ɛRmit] nm hermit.
éroder [eRɔde] vt to erode; **érosion** nf erosion.
érotique [eRɔtik] a erotic; **érotisme** nm eroticism.
erratum, a [ɛRatɔm, -a] nm erratum (pl a).
errer [ɛRe] vi to wander.
erreur [ɛRœR] nf mistake, error; (morale) error; **être dans l'~** to be mistaken; **par ~** by mistake; ~ **judiciaire** miscarriage of justice; ~ **de jugement** error of judgment.
erroné, e [ɛRɔne] a wrong, erroneous.
éructer [eRykte] vt belch, eructate.
érudit, e [eRydi, -it] a erudite, learned // nm/f scholar; **érudition** nf erudition, scholarship.
éruptif, ive [eRyptif, -iv] a eruptive.
éruption [eRypsjɔ̃] nf eruption; (cutanée) outbreak.
es vb voir **être**.
ès [ɛs] prép: **licencié ~ lettres/sciences** ≈ Bachelor of Arts/Science.
escabeau, x [ɛskabo] nm (tabouret) stool; (échelle) stepladder.
escadre [ɛskadR(ə)] nf (NAVIG) squadron; (AVIAT) wing.
escadrille [ɛskadRij] nf (AVIAT) flight.
escadron [ɛskadRɔ̃] nm squadron.
escalade [ɛskalad] nf climbing q; (POL etc) escalation.
escalader [ɛskalade] vt to climb, scale.
escale [ɛskal] nf (NAVIG) call; port of call; (AVIAT) stop(over); **faire ~ à** to put in at, call in at; to stop over at.
escalier [ɛskalje] nm stairs pl; **dans l'~ ou les ~s** on the stairs; ~ **roulant** escalator; ~ **de service** backstairs.
escalope [ɛskalɔp] nf escalope.
escamotable [ɛskamɔtabl(ə)] a retractable; fold-away.
escamoter [ɛskamɔte] vt (esquiver) to get round, evade; (faire disparaître) to conjure away.
escapade [ɛskapad] nf: **faire une ~** to go on a jaunt; to run away ou off.
escargot [ɛskaRgo] nm snail.
escarmouche [ɛskaRmuʃ] nf skirmish.
escarpé, e [ɛskaRpe] a steep.
escarpement [ɛskaRpəmɑ̃] nm steep slope.
escarpin [ɛskaRpɛ̃] nm flat(-heeled) shoe.
escarre [ɛskaR] nf bedsore.
escient [ɛsjɑ̃] nm: **à bon ~** advisedly.
esclaffer [ɛsklafe]: **s'~** vi to guffaw.

esclandre [ɛsklɑ̃dR(ə)] nm scene, fracas.
esclavage [ɛsklavaʒ] nm slavery.
esclave [ɛsklav] nm/f slave; **être ~ de** (fig) to be a slave of.
escompte [ɛskɔ̃t] nm discount.
escompter [ɛskɔ̃te] vt (COMM) to discount; (espérer) to expect, reckon upon; ~ **que** to reckon ou expect that.
escorte [ɛskɔRt(ə)] nf escort; **escorter** vt to escort; **escorteur** nm (NAVIG) escort (ship).
escouade [ɛskwad] nf squad.
escrime [ɛskRim] nf fencing; **escrimeur, euse** nm/f fencer.
escrimer [ɛskRime]: **s'~** vi: **s'~ à faire** to wear o.s. out doing.
escroc [ɛskRo] nm swindler, conman.
escroquer [ɛskRɔke] vt: ~ **qn (de qch)/qch (à qn)** to swindle sb (out of sth)/sth (out of sb); **escroquerie** nf swindle.
espace [ɛspas] nm space; ~ **vital** living space.
espacer [ɛspase] vt to space out; **s'~** vi (visites etc) to become less frequent.
espadon [ɛspadɔ̃] nm swordfish inv.
espadrille [ɛspadRij] nf rope-soled sandal.
Espagne [ɛspaɲ(ə)] nf: **l'~** Spain; **espagnol, e** a Spanish // nm/f: **Espagnol, e** Spaniard // nm (langue) Spanish.
espagnolette [ɛspaɲɔlɛt] nf (window) catch; **fermé à l'~** resting on the catch.
espèce [ɛspɛs] nf (BIO, BOT, ZOOL) species inv; (gén: sorte) sort, kind, type; (péj): ~ **de maladroit/de brute!** you clumsy oaf/brute!; ~**s** nfpl (COMM) cash sg; (REL) species; **en l'~** ad in the case in point.
espérance [ɛspeRɑ̃s] nf hope; ~ **de vie** (DÉMOGRAPHIE) life expectancy.
espérer [ɛspeRe] vt to hope for; **j'espère (bien)** I hope so; ~ **que/faire** to hope that/to do; ~ **en** to trust in.
espiègle [ɛspjɛgl(ə)] a mischievous; ~**rie** nf mischievousness; piece of mischief.
espion, ne [ɛspjɔ̃, -ɔn] nm/f spy; **avion ~** spy plane.
espionnage [ɛspjɔnaʒ] nm espionage, spying.
espionner [ɛspjɔne] vt to spy (up)on.
esplanade [ɛsplanad] nf esplanade.
espoir [ɛspwaR] nm hope.
esprit [ɛspRi] nm (pensée, intellect) mind; (humour, ironie) wit; (mentalité, d'une loi etc, fantôme etc) spirit; **l'~ d'équipe/de compétition** team/competitive spirit; **faire de l'~** to try to be witty; **reprendre ses ~s** to come to; **perdre l'~** to lose one's mind; ~**s chagrins** faultfinders.
esquif [ɛskif] nm skiff.
esquimau, de, x [ɛskimo, -od] a, nm/f Eskimo.
esquinter [ɛskɛ̃te] vt (fam) to mess up.
esquisse [ɛskis] nf sketch; **l'~ d'un sourire/changement** the suggestion of a smile/of change.
esquisser [ɛskise] vt to sketch; **s'~** vi (amélioration) to begin to be detectable; ~ **un sourire** to give a vague smile.
esquive [ɛskiv] nf (BOXE) dodging; (fig) side-stepping.

esquiver [ɛskive] vt to dodge ; **s'~** vi to slip away.

essai [esɛ] nm testing ; trying ; (tentative) attempt, try, (RUGBY) try ; (LITTÉRATURE) essay ; **~s** (AUTO) trials ; **~ gratuit** (COMM) free trial ; **à l'~** on a trial basis.

essaim [esɛ̃] nm swarm ; **essaimer** vi to swarm ; (fig) to spread, expand.

essayage [esɛjaʒ] nm (d'un vêtement) trying on, fitting.

essayer [eseje] vt (gén) to try ; (vêtement, chaussures) to try (on) ; (tester: ski, voiture) to test ; (restaurant, méthode) to try (out) // vi to try ; **~ de faire** to try ou attempt to do ; **s'~ à faire** to try one's hand at doing.

essence [esɑ̃s] nf (de voiture) petrol ; (extrait de plante, PHILOSOPHIE) essence ; (espèce: d'arbre) species inv ; **prendre de l'~** to get petrol ; **~ de citron/rose** lemon/rose oil.

essentiel, le [esɑ̃sjɛl] a essential ; **emporter l'~** to take the essentials ; **c'est l'~** (ce qui importe) that's the main thing ; **l'~ de** (la majeure partie) the main part of.

esseulé, e [esœle] a forlorn.

essieu, x [esjø] nm axle.

essor [esɔʀ] nm (de l'économie etc) rapid expansion ; **prendre son ~** (oiseau) to fly off.

essorer [esɔʀe] vt (en tordant) to wring (out) ; (par la force centrifuge) to spin-dry ; **essoreuse** nf mangle, wringer ; spin-dryer.

essouffler [esufle] vt to make breathless ; **s'~** vi to get out of breath.

essuie-glace [esɥiglas] nm inv windscreen wiper.

essuie-mains [esɥimɛ̃] nm inv hand towel.

essuyer [esɥije] vt to wipe ; (fig: subir) to suffer ; **s'~** (après le bain) to dry o.s. ; **~ la vaisselle** to dry up, dry the dishes.

est [ɛst] vb [ɛ] voir **être** // nm: **l'~** the east // a east ; (côte) east(ern) ; **à l'~** in the east ; (direction) to the east, east(wards) ; **à l'~ de** (to the) east of.

estafette [ɛstafɛt] nf (MIL) dispatch rider.

estafilade [ɛstafilad] nf gash, slash.

est-allemand, e [ɛstalmɑ̃, -ɑ̃d] a East German.

estaminet [ɛstaminɛ] nm tavern.

estampe [ɛstɑ̃p] nf print, engraving.

estampille [ɛstɑ̃pij] nf stamp.

est-ce que [ɛskə] ad: **~ c'est cher/c'était bon?** is it expensive/was it good? ; **quand est-ce qu'il part?** when does he leave?, when is he leaving? ; **qui est-ce qui le connaît/a fait ça?** who knows him/did that? ; voir aussi **que**.

esthète [ɛstɛt] nm/f aesthete.

esthéticienne [ɛstetisjɛn] nf beautician.

esthétique [ɛstetik] a attractive ; aesthetically pleasing // nf aesthetics sg.

estimation [ɛstimɑsjɔ̃] nf valuation ; assessment.

estime [ɛstim] nf esteem, regard.

estimer [ɛstime] vt (respecter) to esteem, hold in high regard ; (expertiser) to value ; (évaluer) to assess, estimate ; (penser): **~ que/être** to consider that/o.s. to be ;

j'estime la distance à 10 km I reckon the distance to be 10 km.

estival, e, aux [ɛstival, -o] a summer cpd.

estivant, e [ɛstivɑ̃, -ɑ̃t] nm/f (summer) holiday-maker.

estocade [ɛstɔkad] nf death-blow.

estomac [ɛstɔma] nm stomach.

estomaqué, e [ɛstɔmake] a flabbergasted.

estompe [ɛstɔ̃p] nf stump ; stump-drawing.

estomper [ɛstɔ̃pe] vt (ART) to shade off ; (fig) to blur, dim ; **s'~** vi to soften ; to become blurred.

estrade [ɛstʀad] nf platform, rostrum.

estragon [ɛstʀagɔ̃] nm tarragon.

estropié, e [ɛstʀɔpje] nm/f cripple.

estropier [ɛstʀɔpje] vt to cripple, maim ; (fig) to twist, distort.

estuaire [ɛstɥɛʀ] nm estuary.

estudiantin, e [ɛstydjɑ̃tɛ̃, -in] a student cpd.

esturgeon [ɛstyʀʒɔ̃] nm sturgeon.

et [e] cj and ; **~ lui?** what about him? ; **~ alors!** so what!

étable [etabl(ə)] nf cowshed.

établi [etabli] nm (work)bench.

établir [etabliʀ] vt (papiers d'identité, facture) to make out ; (liste, programme) to draw up ; (gouvernement, artisan etc: aider à s'installer) to set up, establish ; (entreprise, atelier, camp) to set up ; (réputation, usage, fait, culpabilité) to establish ; **s'~** vi (se faire: entente etc) to be established ; **s'~** (à son compte) to set up one's own business ; **s'~ à/près de** to settle in/near.

établissement [etablismɑ̃] nm making out ; drawing up ; setting up, establishing ; (entreprise, institution) establishment ; **~ de crédit** credit institution ; **~ industriel** industrial plant, factory ; **~ scolaire** school, educational establishment.

étage [etaʒ] nm (d'immeuble) storey, floor ; (de fusée) stage ; (GÉO: de culture, végétation) level ; **au 2ème ~** on the 2nd floor ; **de bas ~** a low ; **étager** vt (cultures) to lay out in tiers ; **s'étager** vi (prix) to range ; (zones, cultures) to lie on different levels.

étagère [etaʒɛʀ] nf (rayon) shelf ; (meuble) shelves pl, set of shelves.

étai [etɛ] nm stay, prop.

étain [etɛ̃] nm tin ; (ORFÈVRERIE) pewter q.

étais etc vb voir **être**.

étal [etal] nm stall.

étalage [etalaʒ] nm display ; display window ; **faire ~ de** to show off, parade ; **étalagiste** nm/f window-dresser.

étale [etal] a (mer) slack.

étalement [etalmɑ̃] nm spreading, staggering.

étaler [etale] vt (carte, nappe) to spread (out) ; (peinture, liquide) to spread ; (échelonner: paiements, dates, vacances) to spread, stagger ; (exposer: marchandises) to display ; (richesses, connaissances) to parade ; **s'~** vi (liquide) to spread out ; (fam) to come a cropper ; **s'~ sur** (suj: paiements etc) to be spread out over.

étalon [etalɔ̃] nm (mesure) standard ; (cheval) stallion ; **étalonner** vt to calibrate.

étamer [etame] *vt* (*casserole*) to tin(plate) ; (*glace*) to silver.

étamine [etamin] *nf* (*BOT*) stamen ; (*tissu*) butter muslin.

étanche [etɑ̃ʃ] *a* (*récipient*) watertight ; (*montre, vêtement*) waterproof.

étancher [etɑ̃ʃe] *vt* (*liquide*) to stop (flowing) ; ~ **sa soif** to quench *ou* slake one's thirst.

étang [etɑ̃] *nm* pond.

étant [etɑ̃] *vb voir* **être, donné.**

étape [etap] *nf* stage ; (*lieu d'arrivée*) stopping place ; (: *CYCLISME*) staging point ; **faire** ~ **à** to stop off at.

état [eta] *nm* (*POL, condition*) state ; (*d'un article d'occasion*) condition, state ; (*liste*) inventory, statement ; (*condition professionnelle*) profession, trade ; (: *sociale*) status ; **en mauvais** ~ in poor condition ; **en** ~ **(de marche)** in (working) order ; **remettre en** ~ to repair ; **hors d'**~ out of order ; **être en** ~/**hors d'**~ **de faire** to be in a/in no fit state to do ; **en tout** ~ **de cause** in any event ; **être dans tous ses** ~**s** to be in a state ; **faire** ~ **de** (*alléguer*) to put forward ; **en** ~ **d'arrestation** under arrest ; **en** ~ **de grâce** (*REL*) in a state of grace ; (*fig*) inspired ; ~ **civil** civil status ; ~ **des lieux** inventory of fixtures ; ~ **de santé** state of health ; ~ **de siège/d'urgence** state of siege/emergency ; ~**s d'âme** moods ; ~**s de service** service record *sg* ; **étatiser** *vt* to bring under state control.

état-major [etamaʒɔʀ] *nm* (*MIL*) staff ; (*d'un parti etc*) top advisers *pl* ; top management.

États-Unis [etazyni] *nmpl*: **les** ~ **(d'Amérique)** the United States (of America).

étau, x [eto] *nm* vice.

étayer [eteje] *vt* to prop *ou* shore up ; (*fig*) to back up.

et c(a)etera [ɛtsetera], **etc.** *ad* et cetera, and so on, etc.

été [ete] *pp de* **être** // *nm* summer.

éteignoir [etɛɲwaʀ] *nm* (*candle*) extinguisher ; (*péj*) killjoy, wet blanket.

éteindre [etɛ̃dʀ(ə)] *vt* (*lampe, lumière, radio*) to turn *ou* switch off ; (*cigarette, incendie, bougie*) to put out, extinguish ; (*JUR: dette*) to extinguish ; **s'**~ *vi* to go out ; to go off ; (*mourir*) to pass away ; **éteint, e** *a* (*fig*) lacklustre, dull ; (*volcan*) extinct.

étendard [etɑ̃daʀ] *nm* standard.

étendre [etɑ̃dʀ(ə)] *vt* (*appliquer: pâte, liquide*) to spread ; (*déployer: carte etc*) to spread out ; (*sur un fil: lessive, linge*) to hang up *ou* out ; (*bras, jambes, par terre: blessé*) to stretch out ; (*diluer*) to dilute, thin ; (*fig: agrandir*) to extend ; (*fam: adversaire*) to floor ; **s'**~ *vi* (*augmenter, se propager*) to spread ; (*terrain, forêt etc*): **s'**~ **jusqu'à/de ... à** to stretch as far as/from ... to ; **s'**~ **(sur)** (*s'allonger*) to stretch out (upon) ; (*se reposer*) to lie down (on) ; (*fig: expliquer*) to elaborate *ou* enlarge (upon).

étendu, e [etɑ̃dy] *a* extensive // *nf* (*d'eau, de sable*) stretch, expanse ; (*importance*) extent.

éternel, le [etɛʀnɛl] *a* eternal ; **les neiges** ~**les** perpetual snow.

éterniser [etɛʀnize]: **s'**~ *vi* to last for ages ; to stay for ages.

éternité [etɛʀnite] *nf* eternity ; **de toute** ~ from time immemorial.

éternuer [etɛʀnɥe] *vi* to sneeze.

êtes *vb voir* **être.**

étêter [etete] *vt* (*arbre*) to poll(ard) ; (*clou, poisson*) to cut the head off.

éther [etɛʀ] *nm* ether.

éthique [etik] *a* ethical // *nf* ethics *sg*.

ethnie [ɛtni] *nf* ethnic group.

ethnographie [ɛtnɔgʀafi] *nf* ethnography.

ethnologie [ɛtnɔlɔʒi] *nf* ethnology ; **ethnologue** *nm/f* ethnologist.

éthylisme [etilism(ə)] *nm* alcoholism.

étiage [etjaʒ] *nm* low water.

étiez *vb voir* **être.**

étinceler [etɛ̃sle] *vi* to sparkle.

étincelle [etɛ̃sɛl] *nf* spark.

étioler [etjole]: **s'**~ *vi* to wilt.

étique [etik] *a* skinny, bony.

étiqueter [etikte] *vt* to label.

étiquette [etikɛt] *nf* label ; (*protocole*): **l'**~ etiquette.

étirer [etiʀe] *vt* to stretch ; (*ressort*) to stretch out ; **s'**~ *vi* (*personne*) to stretch ; (*convoi, route*) to stretch ; **s'**~ **sur** to stretch out over.

étoffe [etɔf] *nf* material, fabric.

étoffer [etɔfe] *vt, s'*~ *vi* to fill out.

étoile [etwal] *nf* star ; **à la belle** ~ in the open ; ~ **filante** shooting star ; ~ **de mer** starfish ; **étoilé, e** *a* starry.

étole [etɔl] *nf* stole.

étonnant, e [etɔnɑ̃, -ɑ̃t] *a* amazing.

étonnement [etɔnmɑ̃] *nm* surprise, amazement.

étonner [etɔne] *vt* to surprise, amaze ; **s'**~ **que/de** to be amazed that/at ; **cela m'étonnerait (que)** (*j'en doute*) I'd be very surprised (if).

étouffant, e [etufɑ̃, -ɑ̃t] *a* stifling.

étouffée [etufe]: **à l'**~ *ad* (*CULIN*) steamed ; braised.

étouffer [etufe] *vt* to suffocate ; (*bruit*) to muffle ; (*scandale*) to hush up // *vi* to suffocate ; (*avoir trop chaud*) to feel stifled ; **s'**~ *vi* (*en mangeant etc*) to choke.

étourderie [etuʀdəʀi] *nf* heedlessness ; thoughtless blunder.

étourdi, e [etuʀdi] *a* (*distrait*) scatterbrained, heedless.

étourdir [etuʀdiʀ] *vt* (*assommer*) to stun, daze ; (*griser*) to make dizzy *ou* giddy ; **étourdissant, e** *a* staggering ; **étourdissement** *nm* dizzy spell.

étourneau, x [etuʀno] *nm* starling.

étrange [etʀɑ̃ʒ] *a* strange.

étranger, ère [etʀɑ̃ʒe, -ɛʀ] *a* foreign ; (*pas de la famille, non familier*) strange // *nm/f* foreigner ; stranger // *nm*: **à l'**~ abroad ; **de l'**~ from abroad ; ~ **à** (*fig*) unfamiliar to ; irrelevant to.

étranglement [etʀɑ̃gləmɑ̃] *nm* (*d'une vallée etc*) constriction, narrow passage.

étrangler [etʀɑ̃gle] *vt* to strangle ; **s'**~ *vi* (*en mangeant etc*) to choke ; (*se resserrer*) to make a bottleneck.

étrave [etʀav] nf stem.

être [ɛtʀ(ə)] nm being // vb avec attribut, vi to be // vb auxiliaire to have (ou parfois be); **il est instituteur** he is a teacher; ~ **à qn** (appartenir) to be sb's, to belong to sb; **c'est à moi/eux** it is ou it's mine/theirs; **c'est à lui de le faire** it's up to him to do it; ~ **de** (provenance, origine) to be from; (appartenance) to belong to; **nous sommes le 10 janvier** it's the 10th of January (today); **il est 10 heures, c'est 10 heures** it is ou it's 10 o'clock; **c'est à réparer** it needs repairing; **c'est à essayer** it should be tried; ~ **humain** human being; voir aussi **est-ce que, n'est-ce pas, c'est-à-dire, ce.**

étreindre [etʀɛ̃dʀ(ə)] vt to clutch, grip; (amoureusement, amicalement) to embrace; **s'~** to embrace; **étreinte** nf clutch, grip; embrace.

étrenner [etʀene] vt to use (ou wear) for the first time.

étrennes [etʀɛn] nfpl Christmas box sg (fig).

étrier [etʀije] nm stirrup.

étriller [etʀije] vt (cheval) to curry; (fam: battre) to trounce.

étriper [etʀipe] vt to gut; (fam): ~ **qn** to tear sb's guts out.

étriqué, e [etʀike] a skimpy.

étroit, e [etʀwa, -wat] a narrow; (vêtement) tight; (fig: serré) close, tight; **à l'~** ad cramped; ~ **d'esprit** narrow-minded; **étroitesse** nf narrowness.

étude [etyd] nf studying; (ouvrage, rapport) study; (de notaire: bureau) office; (: charge) practice; (SCOL: salle de travail) study room; ~**s** nfpl (SCOL) studies; **être à l'~** (projet etc) to be under consideration; **faires des ~s de droit/médecine** to study ou read law/medicine.

étudiant, e [etydjɑ̃, -ɑ̃t] nm/f student.

étudié, e [etydje] a (démarche) studied; (système) carefully designed.

étudier [etydje] vt, vi to study.

étui [etɥi] nm case.

étuve [etyv] nf steamroom; (appareil) sterilizer.

étuvée [etyve]: **à l'~** ad braised.

étymologie [etimɔlɔʒi] nf etymology; **étymologique** a etymological.

eu, eue [y] pp voir **avoir.**

eucalyptus [økaliptys] nm eucalyptus.

eugénique [øʒenik] a eugenic // nf eugenics sg.

euh [ø] excl er.

eunuque [ønyk] nm eunuch.

euphémisme [øfemism(ə)] nm euphemism.

euphonie [øfɔni] nf euphony.

euphorie [øfɔʀi] nf euphoria; **euphorique** a euphoric.

eurasien, ne [øʀazjɛ̃, -ɛn] a, nm/f Eurasian.

Europe [øʀɔp] nf Europe; **européen, ne** a, nm/f European.

eus etc vb voir **avoir.**

euthanasie [øtanazi] nf euthanasia.

eux [ø] pronom (sujet) they; (objet) them.

évacuation [evakɥasjɔ̃] nf evacuation.

évacuer [evakɥe] vt (salle, région) to evacuate, clear; (occupants, population) to evacuate; (toxine etc) to evacuate, discharge.

évadé, e [evade] a escaped // nm/f escapee.

évader [evade]: **s'~** vi to escape.

évaluation [evalɥasjɔ̃] nf assessment, evaluation.

évaluer [evalɥe] vt to assess, evaluate.

évangélique [evɑ̃ʒelik] a evangelical.

évangéliser [evɑ̃ʒelize] vt to evangelize.

évangile [evɑ̃ʒil] nm gospel.

évanouir [evanwiʀ]: **s'~** vi to faint, pass out; (disparaître) to vanish, disappear.

évanouissement [evanwismɑ̃] nm (syncope) fainting fit; (dans un accident) loss of consciousness.

évaporation [evapɔʀasjɔ̃] nf evaporation.

évaporé, e [evapɔʀe] a giddy, scatterbrained.

évaporer [evapɔʀe]: **s'~** vi to evaporate.

évaser [evɑze] vt (tuyau) to widen, open out; (jupe, pantalon) to flare; **s'~** vi to widen, open out.

évasif, ive [evazif, -iv] a evasive.

évasion [evazjɔ̃] nf escape; **littérature d'~** escapist literature.

évêché [eveʃe] nm bishopric; bishop's palace.

éveil [evɛj] nm awakening; **être en ~** to be alert.

éveillé, e [eveje] a awake; (vif) alert, sharp.

éveiller [eveje] vt to (a)waken; **s'~** vi to (a)waken; (fig) to be aroused.

événement [evɛnmɑ̃] nm event.

éventail [evɑ̃taj] nm fan; (choix) range; **en ~** fanned out; fan-shaped.

éventaire [evɑ̃tɛʀ] nm stall, stand.

éventer [evɑ̃te] vt (secret) to discover, lay open; (avec un éventail) to fan; **s'~** vi (parfum) to go stale.

éventrer [evɑ̃tʀe] vt to disembowel; (fig) to tear ou rip open.

éventualité [evɑ̃tɥalite] nf eventuality; possibility; **dans l'~ de** in the event of.

éventuel, le [evɑ̃tɥɛl] a possible; ~**lement** ad possibly.

évêque [evɛk] nm bishop.

évertuer [evɛʀtɥe]: **s'~** vi: **s'~ à faire** to try very hard to do.

éviction [eviksjɔ̃] nf ousting, supplanting; (de locataire) eviction.

évidemment [evidamɑ̃] ad obviously.

évidence [evidɑ̃s] nf obviousness; obvious fact; **de toute ~** quite obviously ou evidently; **en ~** conspicuous; **mettre en ~** to highlight; to bring to the fore.

évident, e [evidɑ̃, -ɑ̃t] a obvious, evident.

évider [evide] vt to scoop out.

évier [evje] nm (kitchen) sink.

évincer [evɛ̃se] vt to oust, supplant.

évitement [evitmɑ̃] nm: **place d'~** (AUTO) passing place.

éviter [evite] vt to avoid; ~ **de faire/que qch ne se passe** to avoid doing/sth happening; ~ **qch à qn** to spare sb sth.

évocateur, trice [evɔkatœʀ, -tʀis] a evocative, suggestive.

évocation [evɔkɑsjɔ̃] nf evocation.

évolué, e [evɔlɥe] a advanced.

évoluer [evɔlɥe] vi (enfant, maladie) to develop; (situation, moralement) to evolve, develop; (aller et venir: danseur etc) to move about, circle; **évolution** nf development; evolution; **évolutions** nfpl movements.

évoquer [evɔke] vt to call to mind, evoke; (mentionner) to mention.

ex... [εks] préfixe ex-.

exacerber [εgzasεʀbe] vt to exacerbate.

exact, e [εgzakt] a (précis) exact, accurate, precise; (correct) correct; (ponctuel) punctual; **l'heure ~e** the right ou exact time; **~ement** ad exactly, accurately, precisely; correctly; (c'est cela même) exactly.

exactions [εgzaksjɔ̃] nfpl exactions.

exactitude [εgzaktityd] nf exactitude, accurateness, precision.

ex aequo [εgzeko] a equally placed; **classé 1er ~** placed equal first.

exagération [εgzaʒeʀɑsjɔ̃] nf exaggeration.

exagéré, e [εgzaʒeʀe] a (prix etc) excessive.

exagérer [εgzaʒeʀe] vt to exaggerate // vi (abuser) to go too far; overstep the mark; (déformer les faits) to exaggerate.

exaltation [εgzaltɑsjɔ̃] nf exaltation.

exalté, e [εgzalte] a (over)excited // nm/f (péj) fanatic.

exalter [εgzalte] vt (enthousiasmer) to excite, elate; (glorifier) to exalt.

examen [εgzamε̃] nm examination; (SCOL) exam, examination; **à l'~** under consideration; (COMM) on approval; **~ blanc** mock exam(ination); **~ de la vue** sight test.

examinateur, trice [εgzaminatœʀ, -tʀis] nm/f examiner.

examiner [εgzamine] vt to examine.

exaspération [εgzaspeʀɑsjɔ̃] nf exasperation.

exaspérer [εgzaspeʀe] vt to exasperate; to exacerbate.

exaucer [εgzose] vt (vœu) to grant, fulfil; **~ qn** to grant sb's wishes.

excavateur [εkskavatœʀ] nm excavator, mechanical digger.

excavation [εkskavɑsjɔ̃] nf excavation.

excavatrice [εkskavatʀis] nf = **excavateur.**

excédent [εksedɑ̃] nm surplus; **en ~** surplus; **~ de bagages** excess luggage; **excédentaire** a surplus, excess.

excéder [εksede] vt (dépasser) to exceed; (agacer) to exasperate.

excellence [εksεlɑ̃s] nf excellence; (titre) Excellency.

excellent, e [εksεlɑ̃, -ɑ̃t] a excellent.

exceller [εksele] vi: **~ (dans)** to excel (in).

excentricité [εksɑ̃tʀisite] nf eccentricity; **excentrique** a eccentric; (quartier) outlying.

excepté, e [εksεpte] a, prép: **les élèves ~s**, **les élèves excepté** except for ou apart from the pupils; **~ si** except if.

excepter [εksεpte] vt to except.

exception [εksεpsjɔ̃] nf exception; **à l'~ de** except for, with the exception of; **d'~** (mesure, loi) special, exceptional; **exceptionnel, le** a exceptional.

excès [εksε] nm surplus // nmpl excesses; **à l'~** (méticuleux, généreux) to excess; **~ de vitesse** speeding q, exceeding the speed limit; **~ de zèle** overzealousness q; **excessif, ive** a excessive.

exciper [εksipe]: **~ de** vt to plead.

excitant [εksitɑ̃] nm stimulant.

excitation [εksitɑsjɔ̃] nf (état) excitement.

exciter [εksite] vt to excite; (suj: café etc) to stimulate; **s'~** vi to get excited; **~ qn à** (révolte etc) to incite sb to.

exclamation [εksklamɑsjɔ̃] nf exclamation.

exclamer [εksklame]: **s'~** vi to exclaim.

exclure [εskklyʀ] vt (faire sortir) to expel; (ne pas compter) to exclude, leave out; (rendre impossible) to exclude, rule out; **exclusif, ive** a exclusive; **exclusion** nf expulsion; **à l'exclusion de** with the exclusion ou exception of; **exclusivement** ad exclusively; **exclusivité** nf exclusiveness; (COMM) exclusive rights pl; **film passant en exclusivité à** film showing only at.

excommunier [εkskɔmynje] vt to excommunicate.

excréments [εkskʀemɑ̃] nmpl excrement sg, faeces.

excroissance [εkskʀwasɑ̃s] nf excrescence, outgrowth.

excursion [εkskyʀsjɔ̃] nf (en autocar) excursion, trip; (à pied) walk, hike; **faire une ~** to go on an excursion ou a trip; to go on a walk ou hike; **excursionniste** nm/f tripper; hiker.

excuse [εkskyz] nf excuse; **~s** nfpl apology sg, apologies.

excuser [εkskyze] vt to excuse; **s'~ (de)** to apologize (for); **'excusez-moi'** 'I'm sorry'; (pour attirer l'attention) 'excuse me'.

exécrable [εgzekʀɑbl(ə)] a atrocious.

exécrer [εgzekʀe] vt to loathe, abhor.

exécutant, e [εgzekytɑ̃, -ɑ̃t] nm/f performer.

exécuter [εgzekyte] vt (prisonnier) to execute; (tâche etc) to execute, carry out; (MUS: jouer) to perform, execute; **s'~** vi to comply; **exécuteur, trice** nm/f (testamentaire) executor // nm (bourreau) executioner; **exécutif, ive** a, nm (POL) executive; **exécution** nf execution; carrying out; **mettre à exécution** to carry out.

exégèse [εgzeʒεz] nf exegesis.

exemplaire [εgzɑ̃plεʀ] a exemplary // nm copy.

exemple [εgzɑ̃pl(ə)] nm example; **par ~** for instance, for example; **donner l'~** to set an example; **prendre ~ sur** to take as a model; **à l'~ de** just like.

exempt, e [εgzɑ̃, -ɑ̃t] a: **~ de** (dispensé de) exempt from; (ne comportant pas de) free from.

exempter [εgzɑ̃te] vt: **~ de** to exempt from.

exercé, e [ɛgzɛʀse] a trained.

exercer [ɛgzɛʀse] vt (pratiquer) to exercise, practise; (faire usage de: prérogative) to exercise; (effectuer: influence, contrôle, pression) to exert; (former) to exercise, train // vi (médecin) to be in practice; **s'~** (sportif, musicien) to practise; (se faire sentir: pression etc) to be exerted.

exercice [ɛgzɛʀsis] nm practice; exercising; (tâche, travail) exercise; (activité, sportive, physique): **l'~** exercise; (MIL): **l'~** drill; (COMM, ADMIN: période) accounting period; **en ~** (juge) in office; (médecin) practising; **dans l'~ de ses fonctions** in the discharge of his duties.

exhaler [ɛgzale] vt to exhale; to utter, breathe; **s'~** vi to rise (up).

exhaustif, ive [ɛgzostif, -iv] a exhaustive.

exhiber [ɛgzibe] vt (montrer: papiers, certificat) to present, produce; (péj) to display, flaunt **s'~** to parade; (suj: exhibitionniste) to expose o.s; **exhibitionnisme** nm exhibitionism.

exhorter [ɛgzɔʀte] vt: **~ qn à faire** to urge sb to do.

exhumer [ɛgzyme] vt to exhume.

exigeant, e [ɛgziʒɑ̃, -ɑ̃t] a demanding; (péj) hard to please.

exigence [ɛgziʒɑ̃s] nf demand, requirement.

exiger [ɛgziʒe] vt to demand, require.

exigu, ë [ɛgzigy] a (lieu) cramped, tiny.

exil [ɛgzil] nm exile; **en ~** in exile; **~é, e** nm/f exile; **~er** vt to exile; **s'~er** to go into exile.

existence [ɛgzistɑ̃s] nf existence.

exister [ɛgziste] vi to exist; **il existe un/des** there is a/are (some).

exode [ɛgzɔd] nm exodus.

exonérer [ɛgzɔneʀe] vt: **~ de** to exempt from.

exorbitant, e [ɛgzɔʀbitɑ̃, -ɑ̃t] a exorbitant.

exorbité, e [ɛgzɔʀbite] a: **yeux ~s** bulging eyes.

exorciser [ɛgzɔʀsize] vt to exorcize.

exotique [ɛgzɔtik] a exotic; **exotisme** nm exoticism; exotic flavour ou atmosphere.

expansif, ive [ɛkspɑ̃sif, -iv] a expansive, communicative.

expansion [ɛkspɑ̃sjɔ̃] nf expansion.

expatrier [ɛkspatʀije] vt: **s'~** to leave one's country, expatriate o.s.

expectative [ɛkspɛktativ] nf: **être dans l'~** to be still waiting.

expectorer [ɛkspɛktɔʀe] vi to expectorate.

expédient [ɛkspedjɑ̃] nm (péj) expedient; **vivre d'~s** to live by one's wits.

expédier [ɛkspedje] vt (lettre, paquet) to send; (troupes) to dispatch; (péj: travail etc) to dispose of, dispatch; **expéditeur, trice** nm/f sender.

expéditif, ive [ɛkspeditif, -iv] a quick, expeditious.

expédition [ɛkspedisjɔ̃] nf sending; (scientifique, sportive, MIL) expedition.

expéditionnaire [ɛkspedisjɔnɛʀ] a: **corps ~** task force.

expérience [ɛkspeʀjɑ̃s] nf (de la vie) experience; (scientifique) experiment; **avoir de l'~** to have experience, be experienced; **avoir l'~ de** to have experience of.

expérimental, e, aux [ɛkspeʀimɑ̃tal, -o] a experimental.

expérimenté, e [ɛkspeʀimɑ̃te] a experienced.

expérimenter [ɛkspeʀimɑ̃te] vt (technique) to test out, experiment with.

expert, e [ɛkspɛʀ, -ɛʀt(ə)] a, nm expert; **~ en assurances** insurance valuer; **~-comptable** nm ≈ chartered accountant.

expertise [ɛkspɛʀtiz] nf valuation; assessment; valuer's (ou assessor's) report; (JUR) (forensic) examination.

expertiser [ɛkspɛʀtize] vt (objet de valeur) to value; (voiture accidentée etc) to assess damage to.

expier [ɛkspje] vt to expiate, atone for.

expiration [ɛkspiʀasjɔ̃] nf expiry; breathing out q.

expirer [ɛkspiʀe] vi (venir à échéance, mourir) to expire; (respirer) to breathe out.

explétif, ive [ɛkspletif, -iv] a expletive.

explicatif, ive [ɛksplikatif, -iv] a explanatory.

explication [ɛksplikasjɔ̃] nf explanation; (discussion) discussion; argument; **~ de texte** (SCOL) critical analysis (of a text).

explicite [ɛksplisit] a explicit; **expliciter** vt to make explicit.

expliquer [ɛksplike] vt to explain; **s'~** (discuter) to discuss things; to have it out; **son erreur s'explique** one can understand his mistake.

exploit [ɛksplwa] nm exploit, feat.

exploitant [ɛksplwatɑ̃] nm farmer.

exploitation [ɛksplwatasjɔ̃] nf exploitation; running; **~ agricole** farming concern.

exploiter [ɛksplwate] vt (mine) to exploit, work; (entreprise, ferme) to run, operate; (clients, ouvriers, erreur, don) to exploit; **exploiteur, euse** nm/f exploiter.

explorateur, trice [ɛksplɔʀatœʀ, -tʀis] nm/f explorer.

exploration [ɛksplɔʀasjɔ̃] nf exploration.

explorer [ɛksplɔʀe] vt to explore.

exploser [ɛksploze] vi to explode, blow up; (engin explosif) to go off; (fig: joie, colère) to burst out, explode; (personne: de colère) to explode, flare up; **explosif, ive** a, nm explosive; **explosion** nf explosion.

exportateur, trice [ɛkspɔʀtatœʀ, -tʀis] a export cpd, exporting // nm exporter.

exportation [ɛkspɔʀtasjɔ̃] nf exportation; export.

exporter [ɛkspɔʀte] vt to export.

exposant [ɛkspozɑ̃] nm exhibitor; (MATH) exponent.

exposé, e [ɛkspoze] nm talk // a: **~ au sud** facing south, with a southern aspect; **bien ~** well situated; **très ~** very exposed.

exposer [ɛkspoze] vt (marchandise) to display; (peinture) to exhibit, show; (parler de: problème, situation) to explain, set out; (mettre en danger, orienter, PHOTO) to expose; **~ qn/qch à** to expose sb/sth to ; **exposition** nf displaying ; exhibiting ; setting out ; (voir exposé) aspect, situation ; (manifestation) exhibition ; (PHOTO) exposure.

exprès [εkspRε] ad (délibérément) on purpose ; (spécialement) specially ; **faire ~ de faire qch** to do sth on purpose.

exprès, esse [εkspRεs] a (ordre, défense) express, formal // a inv, ad (PTT) express.

express [εkspRεs] a, nm: (café) ~ espresso ; (train) ~ fast train.

expressément [εkspRεsemɑ̃] ad expressly ; specifically.

expressif, ive [εkspResif, -iv] a expressive.

expression [εkspResjɔ̃] nf expression.

exprimer [εkspRime] vt (sentiment, idée) to express ; (jus, liquide) to press out ; **s'~ vi** (personne) to express o.s.

expropriation [εkspRɔpRijɑsjɔ̃] nf expropriation ; **frapper d'~** to put a compulsory purchase order on.

exproprier [εkspRɔpRije] vt to buy up (ou buy the property of) by compulsory purchase, expropriate.

expulser [εkspylse] vt to expel ; (locataire) to evict ; (FOOTBALL) to send off ; **expulsion** nf expulsion ; eviction ; sending off.

expurger [εkspyRʒe] vt to expurgate, bowdlerize.

exquis, e [εkski, -iz] a exquisite ; delightful.

exsangue [εksɑ̃g] a bloodless, drained of blood.

extase [εkstɑz] nf ecstasy ; **s'extasier sur** to go into ecstasies ou raptures over.

extenseur [εkstɑ̃sœR] nm (SPORT) chest expander.

extensible [εkstɑ̃sibl(ə)] a extensible.

extensif, ive [εkstɑ̃sif, -iv] a extensive.

extension [εkstɑ̃sjɔ̃] nf (d'un muscle, ressort) stretching ; (MÉD) ; **à l'~** in traction ; (fig) extension ; expansion.

exténuer [εkstenɥe] vt to exhaust.

extérieur, e [εksteRjœR] a (porte, mur etc) outer, outside ; (au dehors: escalier, w.-c.) outside ; (commerce) foreign ; (influences) external ; (apparent: calme, gaieté etc) surface cpd // nm (d'une maison, d'un récipient etc) outside, exterior ; (d'une personne: apparence) exterior ; (d'un groupe social): **l'~** the outside world ; **à l'~** outside ; (à l'étranger) abroad ; **~ement** ad on the outside ; (en apparence) on the surface ; **extérioriser** vt to show ; to exteriorize.

exterminer [εkstεRmine] vt to exterminate, wipe out.

externat [εkstεRna] nm day school.

externe [εkstεRn(ə)] a external, outer // nm/f (MÉD) non-resident medical student ; (SCOL) day pupil.

extincteur [εkstε̃ktœR] nm (fire) extinguisher.

extinction [εkstε̃ksjɔ̃] nf extinction ; (JUR: d'une dette) extinguishment ; **~ de voix** loss of voice.

extirper [εkstiRpe] vt (tumeur) to extirpate ; (plante) to root out, pull up.

extorquer [εkstɔRke] vt: **~ qch à qn** to extort sth from sb.

extra [εkstRa] a inv first-rate ; top-quality // nm inv extra help.

extraction [εkstRaksjɔ̃] nf extraction.

extrader [εkstRade] vt to extradite ; **extradition** nf extradition.

extraire [εkstRεR] vt to extract ; **extrait** nm (de plante) extract ; (de film, livre) extract, excerpt.

extra-lucide [εkstRalysid] a: **voyante ~** clairvoyant.

extraordinaire [εkstRaɔRdinεR] a extraordinary ; (POL: mesures) special ; **ambassadeur ~** ambassador extraordinary.

extravagance [εkstRavagɑ̃s] nf extravagance q ; extravagant behaviour q.

extravagant, e [εkstRavagɑ̃, -ɑ̃t] a extravagant ; wild.

extraverti, e [εkstRavεRti] a extrovert.

extrême [εkstRεm] a, nm extreme ; **~ment** ad extremely ; **~-onction** nf last rites pl, Extreme Unction ; **E~-Orient** nm Far East ; **extrémiste** a, nm/f extremist.

extrémité [εkstRemite] nf end ; (situation) straits pl, plight ; (geste désespéré) extreme action ; **~s** nfpl (pieds et mains) extremities ; **à la dernière ~** (à l'agonie) on the point of death.

exubérant, e [εgzybeRɑ̃, -ɑ̃t] a exuberant.

exulter [εgzylte] vi to exult.

exutoire [εgzytwaR] nm outlet, release.

ex-voto [εksvɔto] nm inv ex-voto.

F

F abr de **franc.**

fa [fa] nm inv (MUS) F ; (en chantant la gamme) fa.

fable [fabl(ə)] nf fable ; (mensonge) story, tale.

fabricant [fabRikɑ̃] nm manufacturer, maker.

fabrication [fabRikɑsjɔ̃] nf manufacture, making.

fabrique [fabRik] nf factory.

fabriquer [fabRike] vt to make ; (industriellement) to manufacture, make ; (fig): **qu'est-ce qu'il fabrique?** what is he doing?

fabulation [fabylɑsjɔ̃] nf fantasizing.

fabuleux, euse [fabylø, -øz] a fabulous, fantastic.

façade [fasad] nf front, façade ; (fig) façade.

face [fas] nf face ; (fig: aspect) side // a: **le côté ~** heads ; **perdre la ~** to lose face ; **en ~ de** prép opposite ; (fig) in front of ; **de ~** ad from the front ; face on ; **~ à** prép facing ; (fig) faced with, in the face of ; **faire ~ à** to face ; **~ à ~** ad facing each other // nm inv encounter ; **~-à-main** nm lorgnette.

facéties [fasesi] nfpl jokes, pranks.

facétieux, euse [fasesjø, -øz] a mischievous.

facette [fasεt] nf facet.

fâché, e [faʃe] a angry ; (désolé) sorry.

fâcher [faʃe] vt to anger ; **se ~ vi** to get angry ; **se ~ avec** (se brouiller) to fall out with.

fâcheux, euse [fɑʃø, -øz] a unfortunate, regrettable.

facial, e, aux [fasjal, -o] a facial.

faciès [fasjɛs] nm features pl, facies.

facile [fasil] a easy; (accommodant) easy-going; ~**ment** ad easily; **facilité** nf easiness; (disposition, don) aptitude; **facilités** nfpl facilities; **facilités de paiement** easy terms; **faciliter** vt to make easier.

façon [fasɔ̃] nf (manière) way; (d'une robe etc) making-up; cut; ~s nfpl (péj) fuss sg; **de quelle** ~? (in) what way?; **de** ~ **à** so as to; **de** ~ **à ce que** so that; **de toute** ~ anyway, in any case.

faconde [fakɔ̃d] nf loquaciousness, volubility.

façonner [fasɔne] vt (fabriquer) to manufacture; (travailler: matière) to shape, fashion; (fig) to mould, shape.

fac-similé [faksimile] nm facsimile.

facteur, trice [faktœʀ, -tʀis] nm/f postman/woman // nm (MATH, fig: élément) factor; ~ **d'orgues** organ builder; ~ **de pianos** piano maker.

factice [faktis] a artificial.

faction [faksjɔ̃] nf (groupe) faction; (surveillance) guard ou sentry (duty) watch; **en** ~ on guard; standing watch; **factionnaire** nm guard, sentry.

factoriel, le [faktɔʀjɛl] a factorial.

factotum [faktɔtɔm] nm odd-job man, dogsbody.

facture [faktyʀ] nf (à payer: gén) bill; (: COMM) invoice; (d'un artisan, artiste) technique, workmanship; **facturer** vt to invoice.

facultatif, ive [fakyltatif, -iv] a optional; (arrêt de bus) request cpd.

faculté [fakylte] nf (intellectuelle, d'université) faculty; (pouvoir, possibilité) power.

fadaises [fadɛz] nfpl twaddle sg.

fade [fad] a insipid.

fading [fadiŋ] nm (RADIO) fading.

fagot [fago] nm (de bois) bundle of sticks.

fagoté, e [fagɔte] a (fam): **drôlement** ~ in a peculiar getup.

faible [fɛbl(ə)] a weak; (voix, lumière, vent) faint; (rendement, intensité, revenu etc) low // nm weak point; weakness, soft spot; ~ **d'esprit** feeble-minded; **faiblesse** nf weakness; **faiblir** vi to weaken; (lumière) to dim; (vent) to drop.

faïence [fajɑ̃s] nf earthenware q; piece of earthenware.

faignant, e [fɛɲɑ̃, -ɑ̃t] nm/f = **fainéant, e.**

faille [faj] vb voir **faillir** // nf (GÉO) fault; (fig) flaw, weakness.

faillible [fajibl(ə)] a fallible.

faim [fɛ̃] nf hunger; **avoir** ~ to be hungry; **rester sur sa** ~ (aussi fig) to be left wanting more.

fainéant, e [fɛneɑ̃, -ɑ̃t] nm/f idler, loafer.

faire [fɛʀ] vt to make; (effectuer: travail, opération) to do; **vraiment? fit-il** really? he said; **fait à la main/machine** hand-/machine-made; ~ **du bruit/des taches** to make a noise/marks; ~ **du rugby/piano** to play rugby/play the piano; ~ **le malade/l'ignorant** to act the invalid/the fool; ~ **de qn un frustré/avocat** to make sb a frustrated person/a lawyer; **cela ne me fait rien** (m'est égal) I don't care ou mind; (me laisse froid) it has no effect on me; **cela ne fait rien** it doesn't matter; **je vous le fais 10 F** (j'en demande 10 F) I'll let you have it for 10 F; **que faites-vous?** (quel métier etc) what do you do?; (quelle activité: au moment de la question) what are you doing?; **comment a-t-il fait pour** how did he manage to; **qu'a-t-il fait de sa valise?** what has he done with his case?; **2 et 2 font 4** 2 and 2 are ou make 4 // vb attribut: **ça fait 10 m/15 F** it's 10 m/15 F // vb substitut: **ne le casse pas comme je l'ai fait** don't break it as I did // vb impersonnel voir **jour, froid** etc; **ça fait 2 ans qu'il est parti** it's 2 years since he left; **ça fait 2 ans qu'il y est** he's been there for 2 years; **faites! please do!; il ne fait que critiquer** (sans cesse) all he (ever) does is criticize; (seulement) he's only criticizing; ~ **vieux/démodé** to look old/old-fashioned // ~ **faire:** ~ **réparer qch** to get ou have sth repaired; ~ **tomber/bouger qch** to make sth fall/move; **cela fait dormir** it makes you sleep; ~ **travailler les enfants** to make the children work, get the children to work; ~ **punir les enfants** to have the children punished; ~ **démarrer un moteur/chauffer de l'eau** to start up an engine/heat some water; **se** ~ **examiner la vue/opérer** to have one's eyes tested/have an operation; **il s'est fait aider (par qn)** he got sb to help him; **il va se** ~ **tuer/punir** he's going to get himself killed/get (himself) punished; **se** ~ **faire un vêtement** to get a garment made for o.s. // **se** ~ vi (fromage, vin) to mature; **se** ~ **à** (s'habituer) to get used to; **cela se fait beaucoup/ne se fait pas** it's done a lot/not done; **comment se fait-il/faisait-il que** how is it/was it that; **se** ~ **vieux** to be getting old; **se** ~ **des amis** to make friends; **il ne s'en fait pas** he doesn't worry.

faisable [fəzabl(ə)] a feasible.

faisan, e [fəzɑ̃, -an] nm/f pheasant.

faisandé, e [fəzɑ̃de] a high.

faisceau, x [fɛso] nm (de lumière etc) beam; (de branches etc) bundle.

faiseur, euse [fəzœʀ, -øz] nm/f (gén:péj): ~ **de** maker of // nm (bespoke) tailor.

faisons vb voir **faire.**

fait [fɛ] nm (événement) event, occurrence; (réalité, donnée: s'oppose à hypothèse) fact; **le** ~ **que/de manger** the fact that/of eating; **être le** ~ **de** (causé par) to be the work of; **être au** ~ **(de)** to be informed (of); **au** ~ (à propos) by the way; **en venir au** ~ to get to the point; **de** ~ a (opposé à: de droit) de facto // ad in fact; **du** ~ **de ceci/qu'il a menti** because of ou on account of this/his having lied; **de ce** ~ therefore, for this reason; **en** ~ in fact; **en** ~ **de repas** by way of a meal; **prendre** ~ **et cause pour qn** to support sb, side with sb; **prendre qn sur le** ~ to catch sb in the act; ~ **d'armes** feat of arms; ~ **divers** (short) news item; **les** ~**s et gestes de qn** sb's actions ou doings.

fait, e [fɛ, fɛt] a (mûr: fromage, melon) ripe ; **un homme ~** a grown man ; **c'en est ~ de notre tranquillité** that's the end of our peace.

faîte [fɛt] nm top ; (fig) pinnacle, height.

faites vb voir **faire**.

faîtière [fɛtjɛʀ] nf (de tente) ridge pole.

fait-tout nm inv, **faitout** nm [fɛtu] stewpot.

fakir [fakiʀ] nm wizard.

falaise [falɛz] nf cliff.

fallacieux, euse [falasjø, -øz] a fallacious ; deceptive ; illusory.

falloir [falwaʀ] vb impersonnel: **il va ~ 100 F** we'll (ou I'll) need 100 F ; **il doit ~ du temps** that must take time ; **il me faudrait 100 F** I would need 100 F ; **il vous faut tourner à gauche après l'église** you have to ou want to turn left past the church ; **nous avons ce qu'il (nous) faut** we have what we need ; **il faut qu'il parte/a fallu qu'il parte** (obligation) he has to ou must leave/had to leave ; **il a fallu le faire** it had to be done // **s'en ~: il s'en est fallu de 100 F/5 minutes** we (ou they) were 100 F short/5 minutes late (ou early) ; **il s'en faut de beaucoup qu'il soit** he is far from being ; **il s'en est fallu de peu que cela n'arrive** it very nearly happened.

falot, e [falo, -ɔt] a dreary, colourless // nm lantern.

falsifier [falsifje] vt to falsify ; to doctor.

famé, e [fame] a: **mal ~** disreputable, of ill repute.

famélique [famelik] a half-starved.

fameux, euse [famø, -øz] a (illustre) famous ; (bon: repas, plat etc) first-rate, first-class.

familial, e, aux [familjal, -o] a family cpd // nf (AUTO) estate car.

familiariser [familjaʀize] vt: **~ qn avec** to familiarize sb with.

familiarité [familjaʀite] nf informality ; familiarity ; **~ avec** (sujet, science) familiarity with ; **~s** nfpl familiarities.

familier, ière [familje, -jɛʀ] a (connu, impertinent) familiar ; (dénotant une certaine intimité) informal, friendly ; (LING) informal, colloquial // nm regular (visitor).

famille [famij] nf family ; **il a de la ~ à Paris** he has relatives in Paris.

famine [famin] nf famine.

fan [fan] nm/f fan.

fanal, aux [fanal, -o] nm beacon ; lantern.

fanatique [fanatik] a fanatical // nm/f fanatic ; **fanatisme** nm fanaticism.

faner [fane]: **se ~** vi to fade.

faneur, euse [fanœʀ, -øz] nm/f hay-maker.

fanfare [fɑ̃faʀ] nf (orchestre) brass band ; (musique) fanfare.

fanfaron, ne [fɑ̃faʀɔ̃, -ɔn] nm/f braggart.

fange [fɑ̃ʒ] nf mire.

fanion [fanjɔ̃] nm pennant.

fanon [fanɔ̃] nm (de baleine) plate of baleen ; (repli de peau) dewlap, wattle.

fantaisie [fɑ̃tezi] nf (spontanéité) fancy, imagination ; (caprice) whim ; extravagance ; (MUS) fantasia // a: **bijou/pain ~** fancy jewellery/bread ;

fantaisiste a (péj) unorthodox, eccentric // nm/f (de music-hall) variety artist ou entertainer.

fantasme [fɑ̃tasm(ə)] nm fantasy.

fantasque [fɑ̃task(ə)] a whimsical, capricious ; fantastic.

fantassin [fɑ̃tasɛ̃] nm infantryman.

fantastique [fɑ̃tastik] a fantastic.

fantoche [fɑ̃tɔʃ] nm (péj) puppet.

fantomatique [fɑ̃tɔmatik] a ghostly.

fantôme [fɑ̃tom] nm ghost, phantom.

faon [fɑ̃] nm fawn.

farce [faʀs(ə)] nf (viande) stuffing ; (blague) (practical) joke ; (THÉÂTRE) farce ; **~s et attrapes** jokes and novelties ; **farceur, euse** nm/f practical joker ; **farcir** vt (viande) to stuff ; (fig): **farcir qch de** to stuff sth with.

fard [faʀ] nm make-up.

fardeau, x [faʀdo] nm burden.

farder [faʀde] vt to make up.

farfelu, e [faʀfəly] a cranky, hare-brained.

farfouiller [faʀfuje] vi (péj) to rummage around.

farine [faʀin] nf flour ; **farineux, euse** a (sauce, pomme) floury // nmpl (aliments) starchy foods.

farouche [faʀuʃ] a shy, timid ; savage, wild ; fierce.

fart [faʀ(t)] nm (ski) wax ; **farter** vt to wax.

fascicule [fasikyl] nm volume.

fascination [fasinasjɔ̃] nf fascination.

fasciner [fasine] vt to fascinate.

fascisme [faʃism(ə)] nm fascism ; **fasciste** a, nm/f fascist.

fasse etc vb voir **faire**.

faste [fast(ə)] nm splendour // a: **c'est un jour ~** it's his (ou our) lucky day.

fastidieux, euse [fastidjø, -øz] a tedious, tiresome.

fastueux, euse [fastɥø, -øz] a sumptuous, luxurious.

fat [fa] am conceited, smug.

fatal, e [fatal] a fatal ; (inévitable) inevitable ; **~isme** nm fatalism ; fatalistic outlook ; **~ité** nf fate ; fateful coincidence ; inevitability.

fatidique [fatidik] a fateful.

fatigant, e [fatigɑ̃, -ɑ̃t] a tiring ; (agaçant) tiresome.

fatigue [fatig] nf tiredness, fatigue.

fatiguer [fatige] vt to tire, make tired ; (TECH) to put a strain on, strain ; (fig: importuner) to wear out // vi (moteur) to labour, strain ; **se ~** to get tired ; to tire o.s. (out).

fatras [fatʀa] nm jumble, hotchpotch.

fatuité [fatɥite] nf conceitedness, smug-ness.

faubourg [fobuʀ] nm suburb.

fauché, e [foʃe] a (fam) broke.

faucher [foʃe] vt (herbe) to cut ; (champs, blés) to reap ; (fig) to cut down ; to mow down ; **faucheur, euse** nm/f, nf (machine) reaper, mower.

faucille [fosij] nf sickle.

faucon [fokɔ̃] nm falcon, hawk.

faudra vb voir **falloir**.

faufiler [fofile] vt to tack, baste ; **se ~** vi: **se ~ dans** to edge one's way into ; **se ~**

parmi/entre to thread one's way among/between.

faune [fon] *nf* (*ZOOL*) wildlife, fauna // *nm* faun.

faussaire [fosɛʀ] *nm* forger.

fausse [fos] *a voir* **faux.**

faussement [fosmɑ̃] *ad* (*accuser*) wrongly, wrongfully; (*croire*) falsely, erroneously.

fausser [fose] *vt* (*objet*) to bend, buckle; (*fig*) to distort.

fausset [fosɛ] *nm*: **voix de ~** falsetto voice.

faussete [foste] *nf* wrongness; falseness.

faut *vb voir* **falloir.**

faute [fot] *nf* (*erreur*) mistake, error; (*péché, manquement*) misdemeanour; (*FOOTBALL etc*) offence; (*TENNIS*) fault; (*responsabilité*): **par la ~ de** through the fault of, because of; **c'est de sa/ma ~** it's his/my fault; **être en ~** to be in the wrong; **~ de** (*temps, argent*) for ou through lack of; **sans ~** *ad* without fail; **~ de frappe** typing error; **~ d'orthographe** spelling mistake; **~ professionnelle** professional misconduct *q*.

fauteuil [fotœj] *nm* armchair; **~ club** (*big*) easy chair; **~ d'orchestre** seat in the front stalls; **~ roulant** wheelchair.

fauteur [fotœʀ] *nm*: **~ de troubles** trouble-maker.

fautif, ive [fotif, -iv] *a* (*incorrect*) incorrect, inaccurate; (*responsable*) at fault, in the wrong; guilty // *nm/f* culprit.

fauve [fov] *nm* wildcat // *a* (*couleur*) fawn.

faux [fo] *nf* scythe.

faux, fausse [fo, fos] *a* (*inexact*) wrong; (*falsifié*) fake; forged; (*sournois, postiche*) false // *ad* (*MUS*) out of tune // *nm* (*copie*) fake, forgery; (*opposé au vrai*): **le ~** falsehood; **le ~ numéro/la fausse clef** the wrong number/key; **faire ~ bond à qn** to stand sb up; **~ col** detachable collar; **~ frais** *nmpl* extras, incidental expenses; **~ mouvement** awkward movement; **~ nez** funny nose; **~ pas** tripping *q*; (*fig*) faux pas; **~ témoignage** (*délit*) perjury; **fausse alerte** false alarm; **fausse couche** miscarriage; **~-filet** *nm* sirloin; **~-fuyant** *nm* equivocation; **~-monnayeur** *nm* counterfeiter, forger.

faveur [favœʀ] *nf* favour; (*ruban*) ribbon; **traitement de ~** preferential treatment; **à la ~ de** under cover of; thanks to; **en ~ de** in favour of.

favorable [favɔʀabl(ə)] *a* favourable.

favori, te [favɔʀi, -it] *a, nm/f* favourite; **~s** *nmpl* (*barbe*) sideboards, sideburns.

favoriser [favɔʀize] *vt* to favour.

favoritisme [favɔʀitism(ə)] *nm* (*péj*) favouritism.

FB *sigle* = *franc belge.*

fébrile [febʀil] *a* feverish, febrile.

fécal, e, aux [fekal, -o] *a voir* **matière.**

fécond, e [fekɔ̃, -ɔ̃d] *a* fertile; **féconder** *vt* to fertilize; **fécondité** *nf* fertility.

fécule [fekyl] *nf* potato flour.

fédéral, e, aux [fedeʀal, -o] *a* federal; **fédéralisme** *nm* federalism.

fédération [fedeʀɑsjɔ̃] *nf* federation.

fée [fe] *nf* fairy; **~rie** *nf* enchantment; **~rique** *a* magical, fairytale *cpd.*

feignant, e [fɛɲɑ̃, -ɑ̃t] *nm/f* = **fainéant, e.**

feindre [fɛ̃dʀ(ə)] *vt* to feign // *vi* to dissemble; **~ de faire** to pretend to do.

feinte [fɛ̃t] *nf* (*SPORT*) dummy.

fêler [fele] *vt* to crack.

félicitations [felisitɑsjɔ̃] *nfpl* congratulations.

félicité [felisite] *nf* bliss.

féliciter [felisite] *vt*: **~ qn (de)** to congratulate sb (on).

félin, e [felɛ̃, -iːn] *a* feline // *nm* (big) cat.

félon, ne [felɔ̃, -ɔn] *a* perfidious, treacherous.

fêlure [felyʀ] *nf* crack.

femelle [fəmɛl] *a* (*aussi ELEC, TECH*) female // *nf* female; **souris ~** female mouse, she-mouse.

féminin, e [feminɛ̃, -in] *a* feminine; (*sexe*) female; (*équipe, vêtements etc*) women's // *nm* feminine; **féministe** *a* feminist; **féminité** *nf* femininity.

femme [fam] *nf* woman; (*épouse*) wife (*pl* wives); **devenir ~** to attain womanhood; **~ de chambre** cleaning lady; **~ de ménage** domestic help, cleaning lady.

fémur [femyʀ] *nm* femur, thighbone.

fenaison [fənɛzɔ̃] *nf* haymaking.

fendre [fɑ̃dʀ(ə)] *vt* (*couper en deux*) to split; (*fissurer*) to crack; (*fig: traverser*) to cut through; to cleave through; **se ~** *vi* to crack; **fendu, e** *a* (*sol, mur*) cracked; (*jupe*) slit.

fenêtre [fənɛtʀ(ə)] *nf* window.

fenouil [fənuj] *nm* fennel.

fente [fɑ̃t] *nf* (*fissure*) crack; (*de boîte à lettres etc*) slit.

féodal, e, aux [feɔdal, -o] *a* feudal; **féodalité** *nf* feudality.

fer [fɛʀ] *nm* iron; (*de cheval*) shoe; **au ~ rouge** with a red-hot iron; **~ à cheval** horseshoe; **~ forgé** wrought iron; **~ de lance** spearhead; **~ (à repasser)** iron; **~ à souder** soldering iron.

ferai *etc vb voir* **faire.**

fer-blanc [fɛʀblɑ̃] *nm* tin(plate); **ferblanterie** *nf* tinplate making; tinware; **ferblantier** *nm* tinsmith.

férié, e [feʀje] *a*: **jour ~** public holiday.

ferions *etc vb voir* **faire.**

férir [feʀiʀ]: **sans coup ~** *ad* without meeting any opposition.

ferme [fɛʀm(ə)] *a* firm // *ad* (*travailler etc*) hard // *nf* (*exploitation*) farm; (*maison*) farmhouse.

fermé, e [fɛʀme] *a* closed, shut; (*gaz, eau etc*) off; (*fig: personne*) uncommunicative; (: *milieu*) exclusive.

ferment [fɛʀmɑ̃] *nm* ferment.

fermentation [fɛʀmɑ̃tɑsjɔ̃] *nf* fermentation.

fermenter [fɛʀmɑ̃te] *vi* to ferment.

fermer [fɛʀme] *vt* to close, shut; (*cesser l'exploitation de*) to close down, shut down; (*eau, lumière, électricité, robinet*) to put off, turn off; (*aéroport, route*) to close // *vi* to close, shut; to close down, shut down; **se**

~ *vi* (*yeux*) to close, shut ; (*fleur, blessure*) to close up.

fermeté [fɛʀməte] *nf* firmness.

fermeture [fɛʀmətyʀ] *nf* closing ; shutting ; closing *ou* shutting down ; putting *ou* turning off ; (*dispositif*) catch ; fastening, fastener ; **heure de ~** (COMM) closing time ; **jour de ~** (COMM) day on which the shop (*etc*) is closed ; **~ éclair** ® *ou* **à glissière** zip (fastener), zipper.

fermier, ière [fɛʀmje, -jɛʀ] *nm* farmer // *nf* woman farmer ; farmer's wife // *a*: **beurre/cidre ~** farm butter/cider.

fermoir [fɛʀmwaʀ] *nm* clasp.

féroce [feʀɔs] *a* ferocious, fierce.

ferons *vb voir* **faire.**

ferraille [feʀɑj] *nf* scrap iron ; **mettre à la ~** to scrap ; **ferrailleur** *nm* scrap merchant.

ferré, e [feʀe] *a* hobnailed ; steel-tipped ; (*fam*): **~ en** well up on, hot at.

ferrer [feʀe] *vt* (*cheval*) to shoe ; (*chaussure*) to nail ; (*canne*) to tip ; (*poisson*) to strike.

ferreux, euse [feʀø, -øz] *a* ferrous.

ferronnerie [feʀɔnʀi] *nf* ironwork ; **~ d'art** wrought iron work ; **ferronnier** *nm* craftsman in wrought iron ; ironware merchant.

ferroviaire [feʀɔvjɛʀ] *a* rail(way) *cpd.*

ferrure [feʀyʀ] *nf* (ornamental) hinge.

ferry-boat [feʀebot] *nm* ferry.

fertile [fɛʀtil] *a* fertile ; **~ en incidents** eventful, packed with incidents ; **fertiliser** *vt* to fertilize ; **fertilité** *nf* fertility.

féru, e [feʀy] *a*: **~ de** with a keen interest in.

férule [feʀyl] *nf*: **être sous la ~ de qn** to be under sb's (iron) rule.

fervent, e [fɛʀvɑ̃, -ɑ̃t] *a* fervent.

ferveur [fɛʀvœʀ] *nf* fervour.

fesse [fɛs] *nf* buttock ; **fessée** *nf* spanking.

festin [fɛstɛ̃] *nm* feast.

festival [fɛstival] *nm* festival ; **~ier** *nm* festival-goer.

festivités [fɛstivite] *nfpl* festivities, merry-making *sg.*

feston [fɛstɔ̃] *nm* (ARCHIT) festoon ; (COUTURE) scallop.

festoyer [fɛstwaje] *vi* to feast.

fêtard [fɛtaʀ] *nm* (*péj*) high liver, merry-maker.

fête [fɛt] *nf* (*religieuse*) feast ; (*publique*) holiday ; (*en famille etc*) celebration ; (*kermesse*) fête, fair, festival ; (*du nom*) feast day, name day ; **faire la ~** to live it up ; **faire ~ à qn** to give sb a warm welcome ; **les ~s (de fin d'année)** the Christmas and New Year holidays, the festive season ; **la salle/le comité des ~s** the village hall/ festival committee ; **~ foraine** (fun) fair ; **~ mobile** movable feast (day) ; **la F~ Nationale** the national holiday ; **la Fête-Dieu** Corpus Christi ; **fêter** *vt* to celebrate ; (*personne*) to have a celebration for.

fétiche [fetiʃ] *nm* fetish ; **fétichisme** *nm* fetishism.

fétide [fetid] *a* fetid.

fétu [fety] *nm*: **~ de paille** wisp of straw.

feu [fø] *a inv*: **~ son père** his late father.

feu, x [fø] *nm* (*gén*) fire ; (*signal lumineux*) light ; (*de cuisinière*) ring ; (*sensation de brûlure*) burning (sensation) // *nmpl* (*éclat, lumière*) fire *sg* ; (AUTO) (traffic) lights ; **à ~ doux/vif** over a slow/brisk heat ; **à petit ~** (CULIN) over a gentle heat ; **faire ~** to fire ; **tué au ~** killed in action ; **mettre à ~** (*fusée*) to fire off ; **prendre ~** to catch fire ; **mettre le ~ à** to set fire to, set on fire ; **faire du ~** to make a fire ; **avez-vous du ~?** (*pour cigarette*) have you (got) a light? ; **~ rouge/vert/orange** red/green/ amber light ; **~ arrière** rear light ; **~ d'artifice** firework ; (*spectacle*) fireworks *pl* ; **~ de camp** campfire ; **~ de cheminée** chimney fire ; **~ de joie** bonfire ; **~ de paille** (*fig*) flash in the pan ; **~x de brouillard** fog-lamps ; **~x de croisement** dipped headlights ; **~x de position** sidelights ; **~x de route** headlights, headlamps.

feuillage [fœjaʒ] *nm* foliage, leaves *pl.*

feuille [fœj] *nf* (*d'arbre*) leaf (*pl* leaves) ; **~ (de papier)** sheet (of paper) ; **~ d'or/de métal** gold/metal leaf ; **~ d'impôts** tax form ; **~ morte** dead leaf ; **~ de température** temperature chart ; **~ de vigne** (BOT) vine leaf ; (*sur statue*) fig leaf ; **~ volante** loose sheet.

feuillet [fœjɛ] *nm* leaf (*pl* leaves), page.

feuilleté, e [fœjte] *a* (CULIN) flaky.

feuilleter [fœjte] *vt* (*livre*) to leaf through.

feuilleton [fœjtɔ̃] *nm* serial.

feuillu, e [fœjy] *a* leafy ; **~s** *nmpl* (BOT) broad-leaved trees.

feulement [følmɑ̃] *nm* growl.

feutre [føtʀ(ə)] *nm* felt ; (*chapeau*) felt hat ; **feutré, e** *a* feltlike ; (*pas, voix*) muffled ; **feutrer** *vt* to felt ; (*fig*) to muffle // *vi*, **se feutrer** *vi* to felt ; **feutrine** *nf* (lightweight) felt.

fève [fɛv] *nf* broad bean.

février [fevʀije] *nm* February.

FF *sigle* = **franc français.**

F.F.I. *sigle fpl* = **Forces françaises de l'intérieur** (1942-45) // *sigle m* **member of the F.F.I.**

fi [fi] *excl*: **faire ~ de** to snap one's fingers at.

fiacre [fjakʀ(ə)] *nm* (hackney) cab *ou* carriage.

fiançailles [fjɑ̃sɑj] *nfpl* engagement *sg.*

fiancé, e [fjɑ̃se] *nm/f* fiancé/fiancée // *a*: **être ~ (à)** to be engaged (to).

fiancer [fjɑ̃se] : **se ~** *vi*: **se ~ (avec)** to become engaged (to).

fibre [fibʀ(ə)] *nf* fibre ; **~ de verre** fibreglass, glass fibre ; **fibreux, euse** *a* fibrous ; (*viande*) stringy.

ficeler [fisle] *vt* to tie up.

ficelle [fisɛl] *nf* string *g* ; piece *ou* length of string.

fiche [fiʃ] *nf* (*pour fichier*) (index) card ; (*formulaire*) form ; (ÉLEC) plug.

ficher [fiʃe] *vt* (*pour un fichier*) to file ; (POLICE) to put on file ; (*planter*): **~ qch dans** to stick *ou* drive sth into ; (*fam*) to do ; to give ; to stick *ou* shove ; **fiche(-moi) le camp** (*fam*) clear off ; **fiche-moi la paix** (*fam*) leave me alone ; **se ~ dans** (*s'enfoncer*) to get stuck in, embed itself in ; **se ∼ de** (*fam*) to make fun of ; not to care about.

fichier [fiʃje] *nm* file ; card index.

fichu, e [fiʃy] *pp de* **ficher** (*fam*) // *a* (*fam*: *fini, inutilisable*) bust, done for ; (: *intensif*) wretched, darned // *nm* (*foulard*) (head)scarf (*pl* scarves) ; **mal ∼** (*fam*) feeling lousy ; useless.

fictif, ive [fiktif, -iv] *a* fictitious.

fiction [fiksjɔ̃] *nf* fiction ; (*fait imaginé*) invention.

fidèle [fidɛl] *a*: **∼ (à)** faithful (to) // *nm/f* (*REL*): **les ∼s** the faithful ; (*à l'église*) the congregation ; **fidélité** *nf* faithfulness ; **fidélité conjugale** marital fidelity.

fief [fjɛf] *nm* fief ; (*fig*) preserve ; stronghold.

fiel [fjɛl] *nm* gall.

fiente [fjɑ̃t] *nf* (*bird*) droppings *pl*.

fier [fje]: **se ∼ à** *vt* to trust.

fier, fière [fjɛʀ] *a* proud ; **∼ de** proud of ; **avoir fière allure** to cut a fine figure ; **∼té** *nf* pride.

fièvre [fjɛvʀ(ə)] *nf* fever ; **avoir de la ∼/39 de ∼** to have a high temperature/a temperature of 39°C ; **∼ typhoïde** typhoid fever ; **fiévreux, euse** *a* feverish.

fifre [fifʀ(ə)] *nm* fife ; fife-player.

figer [fiʒe] *vt* to congeal ; (*fig*: *personne*) to freeze, root to the spot ; **se ∼** *vi* to congeal ; to freeze ; (*institutions etc*) to become set, stop evolving.

figue [fig] *nf* fig ; **figuier** *nm* fig tree.

figurant, e [figyʀɑ̃, -ɑ̃t] *nm/f* ; (*THÉÂTRE*) walk-on ; (*CINÉMA*) extra.

figuratif, ive [figyʀatif, -iv] *a* representational, figurative.

figuration [figyʀɑsjɔ̃] *nf* walk-on parts *pl* ; extras *pl*.

figure [figyʀ] *nf* (*visage*) face ; (*image, tracé, forme, personnage*) figure ; (*illustration*) picture, diagram ; **faire ∼** to look like.

figuré, e [figyʀe] *a* (*sens*) figurative.

figurer [figyʀe] *vi* to appear // *vt* to represent ; **se ∼ que** to imagine that.

figurine [figyʀin] *nf* figurine.

fil [fil] *nm* (*brin, fig*: *d'une histoire*) thread ; (*du téléphone*) cable, wire ; (*textile de lin*) linen ; (*d'un couteau*: *tranchant*) edge ; **au ∼ des années** with the passing of the years ; **au ∼ de l'eau** with the stream *ou* current ; **donner/recevoir un coup de ∼** to make/get a phone call ; **∼ à coudre** (sewing) thread *ou* yarn ; **∼ électrique** electric wire ; **∼ de fer** wire ; **∼ de fer barbelé** barbed wire ; **∼ à pêche** fishing line ; **∼ à plomb** plumbline ; **∼ à souder** soldering wire.

filament [filamɑ̃] *nm* (*ÉLEC*) filament ; (*de liquide*) trickle, thread.

filandreux, euse [filɑ̃dʀø, -øz] *a* stringy.

filasse [filas] *a inv* white blond.

filature [filatyʀ] *nf* (*fabrique*) mill ; (*policière*) shadowing *q*, tailing *q*.

file [fil] *nf* line ; **∼ (d'attente)** queue ; **prendre la ∼** to join the (end of the) queue ; **prendre la ∼ de droite** (*AUTO*) to move into the right-hand lane ; **se mettre en ∼** to form a line ; (*AUTO*) to get into

lane ; **en ∼ indienne** in single file ; **à la ∼** *ad* (*d'affilée*) in succession.

filer [file] *vt* (*tissu, toile, verre*) to spin ; (*dérouler*: *câble etc*) to pay ou let out ; to veer out ; (*prendre en filature*) to shadow, tail ; (*fam*: *donner*): **∼ qch à qn** to slip sb sth // *vi* (*bas, maille, liquide, pâte*) to run ; (*aller vite*) to fly past *ou* by ; (*fam*: *partir*) to make off ; **∼ doux** to behave o.s., toe the line.

filet [filɛ] *nm* net ; (*CULIN*) fillet ; (*d'eau, de sang*) trickle ; **∼ (à provisions)** string bag.

filetage [filtaʒ] *nm* threading ; thread.

fileter [filte] *vt* to thread.

filial, e, aux [filjal, -o] *a* filial // *nf* (*COMM*) subsidiary.

filiation [filjɑsjɔ̃] *nf* filiation.

filière [filjɛʀ] *nf*: **passer par la ∼** to go through the (administrative) channels ; **suivre la ∼** (*dans sa carrière*) to work one's way up (through the hierarchy).

filiforme [filifɔʀm(ə)] *a* spindly ; thread-like.

filigrane [filigʀan] *nm* (*d'un billet, timbre*) watermark ; **en ∼** (*fig*) showing just beneath the surface.

filin [filɛ̃] *nm* rope.

fille [fij] *nf* girl ; (*opposé à fils*) daughter ; **∼ de joie** prostitute ; **∼ de salle** waitress ; **∼-mère** (*péj*) unmarried mother ; **fillette** *nf* (little) girl.

filleul, e [fijœl] *nm/f* godchild, godson/daughter.

film [film] *nm* (*pour photo*) (roll of) film ; (*œuvre*) film, picture, movie ; (*couche*) film ; **∼ muet/parlant** silent/talking picture *ou* movie ; **∼ d'animation** animated film ; **filmer** *vt* to film.

filon [filɔ̃] *nm* vein, lode ; (*fig*) lucrative line, money spinner.

fils [fis] *nm* son ; **∼ de famille** moneyed young man.

filtre [filtʀ(ə)] *nm* filter ; '**∼ ou sans ∼?**' 'tipped or plain?' ; **à air** (*AUTO*) air filter ; **filtrer** *vt* to filter ; (*fig*: *candidats, visiteurs*) to screen // *vi* to filter (through).

fin [fɛ̃] *nf* end ; **∼s** *nfpl* (*but*) ends ; **à (la) ∼ mai** at the end of May ; **en ∼ de semaine** at the end of the week ; **prendre ∼** to come to an end ; **mettre ∼ à** to put an end to ; **à la ∼** *ad* in the end, eventually ; **sans ∼** *a* endless // *ad* endlessly.

fin, e [fɛ̃, fin] *a* (*papier, couche, fil*) thin ; (*cheveux, poudre, pointe, visage*) fine ; (*taille*) neat, slim ; (*esprit, remarque*) subtle ; shrewd // *ad* (*moudre, couper*) finely // *nf* (*alcool*) liqueur brandy ; **∼ prêt/soûl** quite ready/drunk ; **un ∼ tireur** a crack shot ; **avoir la vue/l'ouïe ∼e** to have sharp eyes/ears, have keen eyesight/hearing ; **or/linge/vin ∼** fine gold/linen/wine ; **repas ∼** gourmet meal ; **une ∼e mouche** (*fig*) a sharp customer ; **∼es herbes** mixed herbs.

final, e [final] *a, nf* final ; **quarts de ∼e** quarter finals ; **8èmes/16èmes de ∼e** 2nd/1st round (*in 5 round knock-out competition*) ; **∼ement** *ad* finally, in the end ; (*après tout*) after all ; **∼iste** *nm/f* finalist.

finance [finɑ̃s] *nf* finance;~s *nfpl* (*situation financière*) finances; (*activités financières*) finance *sg*; **moyennant** ~ for a fee *ou* consideration; **financer** *vt* to finance; **financier, ière** *a* financial // *nm* financier.

finaud, e [fino, -od] *a* wily.

finesse [fines] *nf* thinness; fineness; neatness; slimness; subtlety; shrewdness; ~s *nfpl* (*subtilités*) niceties; finer points.

fini, e [fini] *a* finished; (*MATH*) finite; (*intensif*): **un égoïste** ~ an egotist through and through // *nm* (*d'un objet manufacturé*) finish.

finir [finir] *vt* to finish // *vi* to finish, end; ~ **quelque part** to end *ou* finish up somewhere; ~ **de faire** to finish doing; (*cesser*) to stop doing; ~ **par faire** to end *ou* finish up doing; **il finit par m'agacer** he's beginning to get on my nerves; ~ **en pointe/tragédie** to end in a point/in tragedy; **en** ~ **avec** to be *ou* have done with; **il va mal** ~ he will come to a bad end.

finish [finiʃ] *nm* (*SPORT*) finish.

finissage [finisaʒ] *nm* finishing.

finition [finisjɔ̃] *nf* finishing; finish.

finlandais, e [fɛ̃lɑ̃dɛ, -ɛz] *a* Finnish // *nm/f* Finn.

Finlande [fɛ̃lɑ̃d] *nf*: **la** ~ Finland; **finnois** *nm* Finnish.

fiole [fjɔl] *nf* phial.

fiord [fjɔʀ(d)] *nm* = **fjord**.

fioriture [fjɔʀityʀ] *nf* embellishment, flourish.

firmament [fiʀmamɑ̃] *nm* firmament, skies *pl*.

firme [fiʀm(ə)] *nf* firm.

fis *vb voir* **faire.**

fisc [fisk] *nm* tax authorities *pl*, ≈ Inland Revenue; ~**al, e, aux** *a* tax *cpd*, fiscal; ~**alité** *nf* tax system; (*charges*) taxation.

fission [fisjɔ̃] *nf* fission.

fissure [fisyʀ] *nf* crack.

fissurer [fisyʀe] *vt*, **se** ~ *vi* to crack.

fiston [fistɔ̃] *nm* (*fam*) son, lad.

fit *vb voir* **faire.**

fixateur [fiksatœʀ] *nm* (*PHOTO*) fixer; (*pour cheveux*) hair cream.

fixatif [fiksatif] *nm* fixative.

fixation [fiksɑsjɔ̃] *nf* fixing; fastening; setting; (*de ski*) binding; (*PSYCH*) fixation.

fixe [fiks(ə)] *a* fixed; (*emploi*) steady, regular // *nm* (*salaire*) basic salary; **à heure** ~ at a set time; **menu à prix** ~ set menu.

fixé, e [fikse] *a*: **être** ~ (**sur**) (*savoir à quoi s'en tenir*) to have made up one's mind (about); to know for certain (about).

fixement [fiksəmɑ̃] *ad* (*regarder*) fixedly, steadily.

fixer [fikse] *vt* (*attacher*): ~ **qch** (**à/sur**) to fix *ou* fasten sth (to/onto); (*déterminer*) to fix, set; (*CHIMIE, PHOTO*) to fix; (*poser son regard sur*) to look hard at, stare at; **se** ~ (*s'établir*) to settle down; **se** ~ **sur** (*suj*: *attention*) to focus on.

fjord [fjɔʀ(d)] *nm* fjord, fiord.

flacon [flakɔ̃] *nm* bottle.

flageller [flaʒele] *vt* to flog, scourge.

flageoler [flaʒɔle] *vi* (*jambes*) to sag.

flageolet [flaʒɔlɛ] *nm* (*MUS*) flageolet; (*CULIN*) dwarf kidney bean.

flagorneur, euse [flagɔʀnœʀ, -øz] *nm/f* toady, fawner.

flagrant, e [flagʀɑ̃, -ɑ̃t] *a* flagrant, blatant; **en** ~ **délit** in the act, in flagrante delicto.

flair [flɛʀ] *nm* sense of smell; (*fig*) intuition; **flairer** *vt* (*humer*) to sniff (at); (*détecter*) to scent.

flamand, e [flamɑ̃, -ɑ̃d] *a, nm* (*langue*) Flemish // *nm/f* Fleming; **les F**~**s** the Flemish.

flamant [flamɑ̃] *nm* flamingo.

flambant [flɑ̃bɑ̃] *ad*: ~ **neuf** brand new.

flambé, e [flɑ̃be] *a* (*CULIN*) flambé // *nf* blaze; (*fig*) flaring-up, explosion.

flambeau, x [flɑ̃bo] *nm* (flaming) torch.

flamber [flɑ̃be] *vi* to blaze (up) // *vt* (*poulet*) to singe; (*aiguille*) to sterilize.

flamboyant, e [flɑ̃bwajɑ̃, -ɑ̃t] *a* flashing, blazing; flaming.

flamboyer [flɑ̃bwaje] *vi* to blaze (up); to flame.

flamingant, e [flamɛ̃gɑ̃, -ɑ̃t] *a* Flemish-speaking.

flamme [flam] *nf* flame; (*fig*) fire, fervour; **en** ~**s** on fire, ablaze.

flammèche [flamɛʃ] *nf* (flying) spark.

flan [flɑ̃] *nm* (*CULIN*) custard tart *ou* pie.

flanc [flɑ̃] *nm* side; (*MIL*) flank; **à** ~ **de colline** on the hillside; **prêter le** ~ **à** (*fig*) to lay o.s. open to.

flancher [flɑ̃ʃe] *vi* to fail, pack up.

flanelle [flanɛl] *nf* flannel.

flâner [flɑne] *vi* to stroll; **flânerie** *nf* stroll.

flanquer [flɑ̃ke] *vt* to flank; (*fam*: *mettre*): ~ **qch sur/dans** to bung *ou* shove sth on/into; (: *jeter*): ~ **par terre/à la porte** to fling to the ground/chuck out.

flapi, e [flapi] *a* dog-tired.

flaque [flak] *nf* (*d'eau*) puddle; (*d'huile, de sang etc*) pool.

flash, pl flashes [flaʃ] *nm* (*PHOTO*) flash; ~ (**d'information**) newsflash.

flasque [flask(ə)] *a* flabby.

flatter [flate] *vt* to flatter; (*caresser*) to stroke; **se** ~ **de qch** to pride o.s. on sth; **flatterie** *nf* flattery *q*; **flatteur, euse** *a* flattering // *nm/f* flatterer.

fléau, x [fleo] *nm* scourge, curse; (*de balance*) beam; (*pour le blé*) flail.

flèche [flɛʃ] *nf* arrow; (*de clocher*) spire; (*de grue*) jib; **monter en** ~ (*fig*) to soar, rocket; **flécher** *vt* to arrow, mark with arrows; **flèchette** *nf* dart; **flèchettes** *nfpl* (*jeu*) darts *sg*.

fléchir [fleʃiʀ] *vt* (*corps, genou*) to bend; (*fig*) to sway, weaken // *vi* (*poutre*) to sag, bend; (*fig*) to weaken, flag; **fléchissement** *nm* bending; sagging; flagging.

flegmatique [flɛgmatik] *a* phlegmatic.

flegme [flɛgm(ə)] *nm* composure.

flemmard, e [flemaʀ, -aʀd(ə)] *nm/f* lazy-bones *sg*, loafer.

flétrir [fletʀiʀ] *vt* to wither; (*stigmatiser*) to condemn (in the most severe terms); **se** ~ *vi* to wither.

fleur [flœʀ] *nf* flower; (*d'un arbre*) blossom, bloom; **être en ~** (*arbre*) to be in blossom *ou* bloom; **tissu à ~s** flowered *ou* flowery fabric; **à ~ de terre** just above the ground; **~ de lis** fleur-de-lis.

fleurer [flœʀe] *vt:* **~ la lavande** to be fragrant with the scent of lavender.

fleuret [flœʀɛ] *nm* (*arme*) foil; (*sport*) fencing.

fleuri, e [flœʀi] *a* in flower *ou* bloom; surrounded by flowers; (*fig*) flowery; florid.

fleurir [flœʀiʀ] *vi* (*rose*) to flower; (*arbre*) to blossom; (*fig*) to flourish // *vt* (*tombe*) to put flowers on; (*chambre*) to decorate with flowers.

fleuriste [flœʀist(ə)] *nm/f* florist.

fleuron [flœʀɔ̃] *nm* jewel (*fig*).

fleuve [flœv] *nm* river.

flexible [flɛksibl(ə)] *a* flexible.

flexion [flɛksjɔ̃] *nf* flexing, bending; (*LING*) inflection.

flibustier [flibystje] *nm* buccaneer.

flic [flik] *nm* (*fam: péj*) cop.

flirter [flœʀte] *vi* to flirt.

F.L.N. *sigle m = Front de libération nationale* (*during the Algerian war*).

flocon [flɔkɔ̃] *nm* flake; (*de laine etc: boulette*) flock; **~s d'avoine** oatflakes.

flonflons [flɔ̃flɔ̃] *nmpl* blare *sg.*

floraison [flɔʀɛzɔ̃] *nf* flowering; blossoming; flourishing.

floral, e, aux [flɔʀal, -o] *a* floral, flower *cpd.*

floralies [flɔʀali] *nfpl* flower show *sg.*

flore [flɔʀ] *nf* flora.

florissant, e [flɔʀisɑ̃, -ɑ̃t] *vb voir* **fleurir** // *a* flourishing.

flot [flo] *nm* flood, stream; (*marée*) flood tide; **~s** *nmpl* (*de la mer*) waves; **être à ~** (*NAVIG*) to be afloat; (*fig*) to be on an even keel; **entrer à ~s** to be streaming *ou* pouring in.

flottage [flɔtaʒ] *nm* (*du bois*) floating.

flottaison [flɔtɛzɔ̃] *nf:* **ligne de ~** waterline.

flottant, e [flɔtɑ̃, -ɑ̃t] *a* (*vêtement*) loose (-fitting); (*cours, barème*) floating.

flotte [flɔt] *nf* (*NAVIG*) fleet; (*fam*) water; rain.

flottement [flɔtmɑ̃] *nm* (*fig*) wavering, hesitation.

flotter [flɔte] *vi* to float; (*nuage, odeur*) to drift; (*drapeau*) to fly; (*vêtements*) to hang loose; (*monnaie*) to float // *vt* to float; **faire ~** to float; **flotteur** *nm* float.

flottille [flɔtij] *nf* flotilla.

flou, e [flu] *a* fuzzy, blurred; (*fig*) woolly, vague.

flouer [flue] *vt* to swindle.

fluctuation [flyktɥasjɔ̃] *nf* fluctuation.

fluet, te [flyɛ, -ɛt] *a* thin, slight.

fluide [flɥid] *a* a fluid; (*circulation etc*) flowing freely // *nm* fluid; (*force*) (mysterious) power; **fluidité** *nf* fluidity; free flow.

fluor [flyɔʀ] *nm* fluorine.

fluorescent, e [flyɔʀesɑ̃, -ɑ̃t] *a* fluorescent.

flûte [flyt] *nf* flute; (*verre*) flute glass; (*pain*) long loaf (*pl* loaves); **~!** drat it!;

petite ~ piccolo (*pl s*); **~ à bec** recorder; **~ de Pan** panpipes *pl*; **flûtiste** *nm/f* flautist, flute player.

fluvial, e, aux [flyvjal, -o] *a* river *cpd*, fluvial.

flux [fly] *nm* incoming tide; (*écoulement*) flow; **le ~ et le reflux** the ebb and flow.

fluxion [flyksjɔ̃] *nf:* **~ de poitrine** pneumonia.

FM *sigle voir* **modulation**.

F.M.I. *sigle m voir* **fonds**.

foc [fɔk] *nm* jib.

focal, e, aux [fɔkal, -o] *a* focal // *nf* focal length.

fœtal, e, aux [fetal, -o] *a* foetal, fetal.

fœtus [fetys] *nm* foetus, fetus.

foi [fwa] *nf* faith; **sous la ~ du serment** under *ou* on oath; **ajouter ~ à** to lend credence to; **digne de ~** reliable; **sur la ~ de** on the word *ou* strength of; **être de bonne/mauvaise ~** to be sincere/insincere.

foie [fwa] *nm* liver; **~ gras** foie gras.

foin [fwɛ̃] *nm* hay; **faire les ~s** to make hay; **faire du ~** (*fig: fam*) to kick up a row.

foire [fwaʀ] *nf* fair; (*fête foraine*) (fun) fair; **faire la ~** (*fig: fam*) to whoop it up; **~ (exposition)** trade fair.

fois [fwa] *nf:* **une/deux ~** once/twice; **trois/vingt ~** three/twenty times; **2 ~ 2** twice 2, 2 times 2; **deux/quatre ~ plus grand (que)** twice/four times as large (as); **une ~** (*dans le passé*) once; (*dans le futur*) sometime; **une ~ pour toutes** once and for all; **une ~ que c'est fait** once it's done; **une ~ parti** once he had left; **des ~** (*parfois*) sometimes; **cette ~** this (*ou* that) time; **à la ~** (*ensemble*) (all) at once; **à la ~ grand et beau** both tall and handsome.

foison [fwazɔ̃] *nf:* **une ~ de** an abundance of; **à ~** ad in plenty.

foisonner [fwazɔne] *vi* to abound; **~ en** *ou* **de** to abound in.

fol [fɔl] *a voir* **fou**.

folâtre [fɔlɑtʀ(ə)] *a* playful.

folâtrer [fɔlɑtʀe] *vi* to frolic (about).

folie [fɔli] *nf* (*d'une décision, d'un acte*) madness, folly; (*état*) madness, insanity; (*acte*) folly; **la ~ des grandeurs** delusions of grandeur; **faire des ~s** (*en dépenses*) to be extravagant.

folklore [fɔlklɔʀ] *nm* folklore; **folklorique** *a* folk *cpd*; (*fam*) weird.

folle [fɔl] *a, nf voir* **fou**; **~ment** *ad* (*très*) madly, wildly.

follet [fɔlɛ] *am:* **feu ~** will-o'-the-wisp.

fomenter [fɔmɑ̃te] *vt* to stir up, foment.

foncé, e [fɔ̃se] *a* dark; **bleu ~** dark blue.

foncer [fɔ̃se] *vt* to make darker // *vi* to go darker; (*fam: aller vite*) to tear *ou* belt along; **~ sur** to charge at.

foncier, ière [fɔ̃sje, -jɛʀ] *a* (*honnêteté etc*) basic, fundamental; (*malhonnêteté*) deeprooted, (*COMM*) real estate *cpd*; **foncièrement** *ad* basically; thoroughly.

fonction [fɔ̃ksjɔ̃] *nf* (*rôle, MATH, LING*) function; (*emploi, poste*) post, position; **~s** (*professionnelles*) duties; **entrer en ~s** to take up one's post *ou* duties; to take up office ; **voiture de** ~ car provided with the post ; **être** ~ **de** (*dépendre de*) to depend on ; **en** ~ **de** (*par rapport à*) according to ; **faire** ~ **de** to serve as ; **la** ~ **publique** the public *ou* state service.

fonctionnaire [fɔ̃ksjɔnɛʀ] *nm/f* state employee, local authority employee ; (*dans l'administration*) ≈ civil servant.

fonctionnel, le [fɔ̃ksjɔnɛl] *a* functional.

fonctionnement [fɔ̃ksjɔnmɑ̃] *nm* functioning.

fonctionner [fɔ̃ksjɔne] *vi* to work, function ; (*entreprise*) to operate, function ; **faire** ~ to work, operate.

fond [fɔ̃] *nm voir aussi* **fonds** ; (*d'un récipient, trou*) bottom ; (*d'une salle, scène*) back ; (*d'un tableau, décor*) background ; (*opposé à la forme*) content ; (*SPORT*): **le** ~ long distance (running) ; **au** ~ **de** at the bottom of ; **at the back of** ; **à** ~ *ad* (*connaître, soutenir*) thoroughly ; (*appuyer, visser*) right down *ou* home ; **à** ~ (**de train**) *ad* (*fam*) full tilt ; **dans le** ~, **au** ~ *ad* (*en somme*) basically, really ; **de** ~ **en comble** *ad* from top to bottom ; ~ **sonore** background noise ; ~ **de teint** make-up base.

fondamental, e, aux [fɔ̃damɑ̃tal, -o] *a* fundamental.

fondant, e [fɔ̃dɑ̃, -ɑ̃t] *a* (*neige*) melting ; (*poire*) that melts in the mouth ; (*chocolat*) fondant.

fondateur, trice [fɔ̃datœʀ, -tʀis] *nm/f* founder ; **membre** ~ founder member.

fondation [fɔ̃dasjɔ̃] *nf* founding ; (*établissement*) foundation ; ~**s** *nfpl* (*d'une maison*) foundations ; **travaux de** ~ foundation works.

fondé, e [fɔ̃de] *a* (*accusation etc*) well-founded ; **mal** ~ unfounded ; **être** ~ **à croire** to have grounds for believing *ou* good reason to believe ; ~ **de pouvoir** *nm* authorized representative ; (*banking*) executive (*having the signature*).

fondement [fɔ̃dmɑ̃] *nm* (*derrière*) behind ; ~**s** *nmpl* foundations ; **sans** ~ *a* (*rumeur etc*) groundless, unfounded.

fonder [fɔ̃de] *vt* to found ; ~ **qch sur** to base sth on ; **se** ~ **sur** (*suj: personne*) to base o.s. on.

fonderie [fɔ̃dʀi] *nf* smelting works *sg*.

fondeur [fɔ̃dœʀ] *nm*: (**ouvrier**) ~ caster.

fondre [fɔ̃dʀ(ə)] *vt* to melt ; (*dans l'eau: sucre, sel*) to dissolve ; (*fig: mélanger*) to merge, blend // *vi* to melt ; to dissolve ; (*fig*) to melt away ; (*se précipiter*): ~ **sur** to swoop down on ; **faire** ~ to melt ; to dissolve ; ~ **en larmes** to burst into tears.

fondrière [fɔ̃dʀijɛʀ] *nf* rut.

fonds [fɔ̃] *nm* (*de bibliothèque*) collection ; (*COMM*): ~ (**de commerce**) business ; (*fig*): ~ **de probité** *etc* fund of integrity *etc* // *nmpl* (*argent*) funds ; **à** ~ **perdus** *ad* with little or no hope of getting the money back ; **F**~ **Monétaire International** (**FMI**) International Monetary Fund (IMF) ; ~ **de roulement** *nm* float.

fondu, e [fɔ̃dy] *a* (*beurre, neige*) melted ; (*métal*) molten // *nm* (*CINÉMA*): ~ (**enchaîné**) dissolve // *nf* (*CULIN*) fondue.

font *vb voir* **faire**.

fontaine [fɔ̃tɛn] *nf* fountain ; (*source*) spring.

fonte [fɔ̃t] *nf* melting ; (*métal*) cast iron ; **la** ~ **des neiges** the (spring) thaw.

fonts baptismaux [fɔ̃batismo] *nmpl* (baptismal) font *sg*.

football [futbol] *nm* football, soccer ; ~ **de table** table football ; ~**eur** *nm* footballer, football *ou* soccer player.

footing [futiŋ] *nm* jogging.

for [fɔʀ] *nm*: **dans son** ~ **intérieur** in one's heart of hearts.

forage [fɔʀaʒ] *nm* drilling, boring.

forain, e [fɔʀɛ̃, -ɛn] *a* fairground *cpd* // *nm* stallholder ; fairground entertainer.

forçat [fɔʀsa] *nm* convict.

force [fɔʀ(ə)] *nf* strength ; (*puissance: surnaturelle etc*) power ; (*PHYSIQUE, MÉCANIQUE*) force ; ~**s** *nfpl* (*physiques*) strength *sg* ; (*MIL*) forces ; (*effectifs*): **d'importantes** ~**s de police** big contingents of police ; **à** ~ **d'insister** by dint of insisting ; as he (*ou* I) kept on insisting ; **de** ~ **ad** forcibly, by force ; **par la** ~ using force ; **faire** ~ **de rames/voiles** to ply the oars/cram on sail ; **être de** ~ **à faire** to be up to doing ; **de première** ~ first class ; ~ **d'âme** fortitude ; ~ **de frappe** strike force ; ~ **d'inertie** force of inertia ; **la** ~ **publique** the authorities responsible for public order ; ~**s d'intervention** peace-keeping force *sg* ; **les** ~**s de l'ordre** the police.

forcé, e [fɔʀse] *a* forced ; unintended ; inevitable.

forcément [fɔʀsemɑ̃] *ad* necessarily ; inevitably ; (*bien sûr*) of course.

forcené, e [fɔʀsəne] *a* frenzied // *nm/f* maniac.

forceps [fɔʀsɛps] *nm* forceps *pl*.

forcer [fɔʀse] *vt* (*contraindre*): ~ **qn à faire** to force sb to do ; (*porte, serrure, plante*) to force ; (*moteur, voix*) to strain // *vi* (*SPORT*) to overtax o.s. ; ~ **la dose/l'allure** to overdo it/increase the pace ; ~ **l'attention/le respect** to command attention/respect.

forcing [fɔʀsiŋ] *nm*: **faire le** ~ to pile on the pressure.

forcir [fɔʀsiʀ] *vi* (*grossir*) to broaden out ; (*vent*) to freshen.

forer [fɔʀe] *vt* to drill, bore.

forestier, ière [fɔʀɛstje, -jɛʀ] *a* forest *cpd*.

foret [fɔʀɛ] *nm* drill.

forêt [fɔʀɛ] *nf* forest.

foreuse [fɔʀøz] *nf* (electric) drill.

forfait [fɔʀfɛ] *nm* (*COMM*) fixed *ou* set price ; all-in deal *ou* price ; (*crime*) infamy ; **déclarer** ~ to withdraw ; **gagner par** ~ to win by a walkover ; **travailler à** ~ to work for a lump sum ; **forfaitaire** *a* inclusive ; set ; ~-**vacances** *nm* (all-inclusive) holiday package.

forfanterie [fɔʀfɑ̃tʀi] *nf* boastfulness *q*.

forge [fɔʀʒ(ə)] *nf* forge, smithy.

forger [fɔʀʒe] *vt* to forge ; (*fig: personnalité*) to form ; (: *prétexte*) to contrive, make up ; **être forgé de toutes pièces** to be a complete fabrication.

forgeron [fɔʀʒəʀɔ̃] *nm* (black)smith.

formaliser [fɔʀmalize]: **se ~** vi: **se ~ (de)** to take offence (at).

formalité [fɔʀmalite] nf formality.

format [fɔʀma] nm size; **petit ~** small size; (PHOTO) 35 mm (film).

formation [fɔʀmasjɔ̃] nf forming; training; (MUS) group; (MIL, AVIAT, GÉO) formation; **la ~ professionnelle** professional training.

forme [fɔʀm(ə)] nf (gén) form; (d'un objet) shape, form; **~s** nfpl (bonnes manières) proprieties; (d'une femme) figure sg; **en ~ de poire** pear-shaped, in the shape of a pear; **être en ~** (SPORT etc) to be on form; **en bonne et due ~** in due form; **prendre ~** to take shape.

formel, le [fɔʀmɛl] a (preuve, décision) definite, positive; (logique) formal; **~lement** ad (absolument) positively.

former [fɔʀme] vt (gén) to form; (éduquer: soldat, ingénieur etc) to train; **se ~** vi to form.

formidable [fɔʀmidabl(ə)] a tremendous.

formol [fɔʀmɔl] nm formalin, formol.

formulaire [fɔʀmylɛʀ] nm form.

formule [fɔʀmyl] nf (gén) formula; (formulaire) form; **~ de politesse** polite phrase; letter ending.

formuler [fɔʀmyle] vt (émettre: réponse, vœux) to formulate; (expliciter: sa pensée) to express.

fort, e [fɔʀ, fɔʀt(ə)] a strong; (intensité, rendement) high, great; (corpulent) stout // ad (serrer, frapper) hard; (sonner) loud(ly); (beaucoup) greatly, very much; (très) most // nm (édifice) fort; (point fort) strong point, forte; **c'est un peu ~!** it's a bit much!; **avoir ~ à faire pour faire** to have a hard job doing; **se faire ~ de ...** to claim one can ...; **~ bien/peu** very well/few; **au plus ~ de** (au milieu de) in the thick of, at the height of.

forteresse [fɔʀtəʀɛs] nf fortress.

fortifiant [fɔʀtifjɑ̃] nm tonic.

fortifications [fɔʀtifikasjɔ̃] nfpl fortifications.

fortifier [fɔʀtifje] vt to strengthen, fortify; (MIL) to fortify.

fortin [fɔʀtɛ̃] nm (small) fort.

fortiori [fɔʀtjɔʀi]: **à ~** ad all the more so.

fortuit, e [fɔʀtɥi, -it] a fortuitous, chance cpd.

fortune [fɔʀtyn] nf fortune; **faire ~** to make one's fortune; **de ~** a makeshift; chance cpd.

fortuné, e [fɔʀtyne] a wealthy, well-off.

forum [fɔʀɔm] nm forum.

fosse [fos] nf (grand trou) pit; (tombe) grave; **la ~ aux lions/ours** the lions' den/bear pit; **~ commune** common ou communal grave; **~ (d'orchestre)** (orchestra) pit; **~ à purin** cesspit; **~s nasales** nasal fossae pl.

fossé [fose] nm ditch; (fig) gulf, gap.

fossette [fosɛt] nf dimple.

fossile [fosil] nm fossil // a fossilized, fossil.

fossoyeur [foswajœʀ] nm gravedigger.

fou(fol), folle [fu, fɔl] a mad; (déréglé etc) wild, erratic; (fam: extrême, très grand) terrific, tremendous // nm/f mad-

man/woman // nm (du roi) jester, fool; (ÉCHECS) bishop; **être ~ de** to be mad ou crazy about; **faire le ~** (enfant etc) to play ou act the fool; **avoir le ~ rire** to have the giggles.

foudre [fudʀ(ə)] nf lightning; **~s** nfpl (colère) wrath sg.

foudroyant, e [fudʀwajɑ̃, -ɑ̃t] a lightning cpd, stunning.

foudroyer [fudʀwaje] vt to strike down; **il a été foudroyé** he was struck by lightning.

fouet [fwɛ] nm whip; (CULIN) whisk; **de plein ~** ad (se heurter) head on; **~ter** vt to whip; to whisk.

fougère [fuʒɛʀ] nf fern.

fougue [fug] nf ardour, spirit; **fougueux, euse** a fiery, ardent.

fouille [fuj] nf search; **~s** nfpl (archéologiques) excavations; **passer à la ~** to be searched.

fouiller [fuje] vt to search; (creuser) to dig // vi: **~ dans/parmi** to rummage in/among.

fouillis [fuji] nm jumble, muddle.

fouine [fwin] nf stone marten.

fouiner [fwine] vi (péj): **~ dans** to nose around ou about in.

fouisseur, euse [fwisœʀ, -øz] a burrowing.

foulante [fulɑ̃t] af: **pompe ~** force pump.

foulard [fulaʀ] nm scarf (pl scarves).

foule [ful] nf crowd; **la ~** crowds pl; **les ~s** the masses; **une ~ de** masses of.

foulée [fule] nf stride.

fouler [fule] vt to press; (sol) to tread upon; **se ~** (fam) to overexert o.s.; **se ~ la cheville** to sprain one's ankle; **~ aux pieds** to trample underfoot.

foulure [fulyʀ] nf sprain.

four [fuʀ] nm oven; (de potier) kiln; (THÉÂTRE: échec) flop.

fourbe [fuʀb(ə)] a deceitful; **~rie** nf deceitfulness; deceit.

fourbi [fuʀbi] nm (fam) gear, clobber.

fourbir [fuʀbiʀ] vt: **~ ses armes** (fig) to get ready for the fray.

fourbu, e [fuʀby] a exhausted.

fourche [fuʀʃ(ə)] nf pitchfork; (de bicyclette) fork.

fourchette [fuʀʃɛt] nf fork; (STATISTIQUE) bracket, margin.

fourchu, e [fuʀʃy] a split; forked.

fourgon [fuʀgɔ̃] nm van; (RAIL) wag(g)on; **~ mortuaire** hearse.

fourgonnette [fuʀgɔnɛt] nf (delivery) van.

fourmi [fuʀmi] nf ant; **~s** nfpl (fig) pins and needles; **avoir des ~s** to have pins and needles.

fourmilière [fuʀmiljɛʀ] nf ant-hill.

fourmiller [fuʀmije] vi to swarm; **~ de** to be teeming with; to be swarming with.

fournaise [fuʀnɛz] nf blaze; (fig) furnace, oven.

fourneau, x [fuʀno] nm stove.

fournée [fuʀne] nf batch.

fourni, e [fuʀni] a (barbe, cheveux) thick; (magasin): **bien ~ (en)** well stocked (with).

fournir [fuʀniʀ] vt to supply; (preuve, exemple) to provide, supply; (effort) to put in; **~ qch à qn** to supply sth to sb, to supply ou provide sb with sth; **~ qn en**

(COMM) to supply sb with; **fournisseur, euse** nm/f supplier.

fourniture [fuʀnityʀ] nf supply(ing); **~s** nfpl supplies; **~s de bureau** office supplies, stationery; **~s scolaires** school stationery.

fourrage [fuʀaʒ] nm fodder, forage.

fourrager [fuʀaʒe] vi: **~ dans/ parmi** to rummage through/among.

fourrager, ère [fuʀaʒe, -ɛʀ] a fodder cpd.

fourré, e [fuʀe] a (bonbon, chocolat) filled; (manteau, botte) fur-lined // nm thicket.

fourreau, x [fuʀo] nm sheath; (de parapluie) cover.

fourrer [fuʀe] vt (fam): **~ qch dans** to stick ou shove sth into; **se ~ dans/sous** to get into/under.

fourre-tout [fuʀtu] nm inv (sac) holdall; (péj) junk room ou cupboard; (fig) rag-bag.

fourreur [fuʀœʀ] nm furrier.

fourrière [fuʀjɛʀ] nf pound.

fourrure [fuʀyʀ] nf fur; (sur l'animal) coat; **manteau/col de ~** fur coat/collar.

fourvoyer [fuʀvwaje]: **se ~** vi to go astray, stray; **se ~ dans** to stray into.

foutre [futʀ] vt (fam!) = **ficher** (fam!); **foutu, e** a (fam!) = **fichu, e** a.

foyer [fwaje] nm (de cheminée) hearth; (fig) seat, centre; family; home; (social) club; hostel; (salon) foyer; (OPTIQUE, PHOTO) focus sg; **lunettes à double ~** bi-focal glasses.

fracas [fʀaka] nm din; crash; roar.

fracassant, e [fʀakasɑ̃, -ɑ̃t] a sensational, staggering.

fracasser [fʀakase] vt to smash.

fraction [fʀaksjɔ̃] nf fraction; **fractionner** vt to divide (up), split (up).

fracture [fʀaktyʀ] nf fracture; **~ du crâne** fractured skull; **~ de la jambe** broken leg.

fracturer [fʀaktyʀe] vt (coffre, serrure) to break open; (os, membre) to fracture.

fragile [fʀaʒil] a fragile, delicate; (fig) frail; **fragilité** nf fragility.

fragment [fʀagmɑ̃] nm (d'un objet) fragment, piece; (d'un texte) passage, extract; **fragmentaire** a sketchy; **fragmenter** vt to split up.

frai [fʀɛ] nm spawn; spawning.

fraîche [fʀɛʃ] a voir frais; **~ment** ad coolly; freshly, newly; **fraîcheur** nf coolness; freshness; **fraîchir** vi to get cooler; (vent) to freshen.

frais, fraîche [fʀɛ, fʀɛʃ] a (air, eau, accueil) cool; (petit pois, œufs, souvenir, couleur, troupes) fresh // ad (récemment) newly, fresh(ly); **il fait ~** it's cool; **servir ~** chill before serving, serve chilled // nm: **mettre au ~** to put in a cool place; **prendre le ~** to take a breath of cool air // nmpl (débours) expenses; (COMM) costs; charges; **faire des ~** to spend; to go to a lot of expense; **~ de déplacement** travel(ling) expenses; **~généraux** overheads; **~ de scolarité** school fees.

fraise [fʀɛz] nf strawberry; (TECH) countersink (bit); (de dentiste) drill; **~ des bois** wild strawberry; **fraiser** vt to countersink; **fraisier** nm strawberry plant.

framboise [fʀɑ̃bwaz] nf raspberry; **framboisier** nm raspberry bush.

franc, franche [fʀɑ̃, fʀɑ̃ʃ] a (personne) frank, straightforward; (visage, rire) open; (net: refus, couleur) clear; (: coupure) clean; (intensif) downright; (exempt): **~ de port** post free, postage paid, carriage paid // ad: **parler ~** to be frank ou candid // nm franc.

français, e [fʀɑ̃sɛ, -ɛz] a French // nm/f: **F~, e** Frenchman/woman // nm (langue) French; **les F~** the French.

France [fʀɑ̃s] nf: **la ~** France.

franche [fʀɑ̃ʃ] a voir franc; **~ment** ad frankly; clearly; (tout à fait) downright.

franchir [fʀɑ̃ʃiʀ] vt (obstacle) to clear, get over; (seuil, ligne, rivière) to cross; (distance) to cover.

franchise [fʀɑ̃ʃiz] nf frankness; (douanière, d'impôt) exemption; (ASSURANCES) excess.

franciser [fʀɑ̃size] vt to gallicize, Frenchify.

franc-maçon [fʀɑ̃masɔ̃] nm freemason; **franc-maçonnerie** nf freemasonry.

franco [fʀɑ̃ko] ad (COMM) carriage paid, postage paid.

franco... [fʀɑ̃ko] préfixe: **~phile** a francophile; **~phone** a French-speaking // nm/f French speaker; **~phonie** nf French-speaking communities.

franc-parler [fʀɑ̃paʀle] nm inv outspokenness.

franc-tireur [fʀɑ̃tiʀœʀ] nm (MIL) irregular; (fig) freelance.

frange [fʀɑ̃ʒ] nf fringe.

frangipane [fʀɑ̃ʒipan] nf almond paste.

franquette [fʀɑ̃kɛt]: **à la bonne ~** ad without (any) fuss.

frappe [fʀap] nf (d'une dactylo, pianiste, machine à écrire) touch; (BOXE) punch; (péj) hood, thug.

frappé, e [fʀape] a iced.

frapper [fʀape] vt to hit, strike; (étonner) to strike; (monnaie) to strike, stamp; **se ~** (s'inquiéter) to get worked up; **~ à la porte** to knock (at) the door; **~ dans ses mains** to clap one's hands; **~ du poing sur** to bang one's fist on; **frappé de stupeur** dumbfounded.

frasques [fʀask(ə)] nfpl escapades.

fraternel, le [fʀatɛʀnɛl] a brotherly, fraternal.

fraterniser [fʀatɛʀnize] vi to fraternize.

fraternité [fʀatɛʀnite] nf brotherhood.

fratricide [fʀatʀisid] a fratricidal.

fraude [fʀod] nf fraud; (SCOL) cheating; **passer qch en ~** to smuggle sth in (ou out); **~ fiscale** tax evasion; **frauder** vi, vt to cheat; **fraudeur, euse** nm/f person guilty of fraud; candidate who cheats; tax evader; **frauduleux, euse** a fraudulent.

frayer [fʀeje] vt to open up, clear // vi to spawn; (fréquenter): **~ avec** to mix ou associate with; **se ~ un passage dans** to clear o.s. a path through, force one's way through.

frayeur [fʀejœʀ] nf fright.

fredaines [fʀədɛn] nfpl mischief sg, escapades.

fredonner [fʀədɔne] vt to hum.
freezer [fʀizœʀ] nm freezing compartment.
frégate [fʀegat] nf frigate.
frein [fʀɛ̃] nm brake ; **mettre un ~ à** (fig) to put a brake on, check ; **~ à main** handbrake ; **~ moteur** engine braking ; **~s à disques** disc brakes ; **~s à tambour** drum brakes.
freinage [fʀɛnaʒ] nm braking ; **distance de ~** braking distance ; **traces de ~** tyre marks.
freiner [fʀene] vi to brake // vt (progrès etc) to check.
frelaté, e [fʀəlate] a adulterated ; (fig) tainted.
frêle [fʀɛl] a frail, fragile.
frelon [fʀəlɔ̃] nm hornet.
frémir [fʀemiʀ] vi to tremble, shudder ; to shiver ; to quiver.
frêne [fʀɛn] nm ash.
frénésie [fʀenezi] nf frenzy ; **frénétique** a frenzied, frenetic.
fréquemment [fʀekamɑ̃] ad frequently.
fréquence [fʀekɑ̃s] nf frequency.
fréquent, e [fʀekɑ̃, -ɑ̃t] a frequent.
fréquentation [fʀekɑ̃tasjɔ̃] nf frequenting ; seeing ; **~s** nfpl company sg.
fréquenté, e [fʀekɑ̃te] a: **très ~** (very) busy ; **mal ~** patronized by disreputable elements.
fréquenter [fʀekɑ̃te] vt (lieu) to frequent ; (personne) to see (frequently).
frère [fʀɛʀ] nm brother.
fresque [fʀɛsk(ə)] nf (ART) fresco.
fret [fʀɛ] nm freight.
fréter [fʀete] vt to charter.
frétiller [fʀetije] vi to wriggle.
fretin [fʀətɛ̃] nm: **le menu ~** the small fry.
friable [fʀijabl(ə)] a crumbly, friable.
friand, e [fʀijɑ̃, -ɑ̃d] a: **~ de** very fond of.
friandise [fʀijɑ̃diz] nf sweet.
fric [fʀik] nm (fam) cash.
fric-frac [fʀikfʀak] nm break-in.
friche [fʀiʃ]: **en ~** a, ad (lying) fallow.
friction [fʀiksjɔ̃] nf (massage) rub, rub-down ; (chez le coiffeur) scalp massage ; (TECH, fig) friction ; **frictionner** vt to rub (down) ; to massage.
frigidaire [fʀiʒidɛʀ] nm ® refrigerator.
frigide [fʀiʒid] a frigid ; **frigidité** nf frigidity.
frigo [fʀigo] nm fridge.
frigorifier [fʀigɔʀifje] vt to refrigerate ; **frigorifique** a refrigerating.
frileux, euse [fʀilø, -øz] a sensitive to (the) cold.
frimas [fʀima] nmpl wintry weather sg.
frimousse [fʀimus] nf (sweet) little face.
fringale [fʀɛgal] nf: **avoir la ~** to be ravenous.
fringant, e [fʀɛgɑ̃, -ɑ̃t] a dashing.
fripé, e [fʀipe] a crumpled.
fripier, ère [fʀipje, -jɛʀ] nm/f secondhand clothes dealer.
fripon, ne [fʀipɔ̃, -ɔn] a roguish, mischievous // nm/f rascal, rogue.

fripouille [fʀipuj] nf scoundrel.
frire [fʀiʀ] vt, vi, **faire ~** to fry.
frise [fʀiz] nf frieze.
frisé, e [fʀize] a curly, curly-haired ; (chicorée) **~e** curly endive.
friser [fʀize] vt, vi to curl ; **se faire ~** to have one's hair curled.
frisson [fʀisɔ̃] nm shudder, shiver ; quiver ; **frissonner** vi to shudder, shiver ; to quiver.
frit, e [fʀi, fʀit] pp de **frire** // a fried // nf: (**pommes**) **~es** chips, French fried potatoes ; **friteuse** nf chip pan ; **friture** nf (huile) (deep) fat ; (plat): **friture (de poissons)** fried fish ; (RADIO) crackle, crackling q.
frivole [fʀivɔl] a frivolous.
froid, e [fʀwa, fʀwad] a, nm cold ; **il fait ~** it's cold ; **avoir ~** to be cold ; **prendre ~** to catch a chill ou cold ; **jeter un ~** (fig) to cast a chill ; **être en ~ avec** to be on bad terms with ; **froidement** ad (accueillir) coldly ; (décider) coolly.
froisser [fʀwase] vt to crumple (up), crease ; (fig) to hurt, offend ; **se ~** vi to crumple, crease ; to take offence ou umbrage ; **se ~ un muscle** to strain a muscle.
frôler [fʀole] vt to brush against ; (suj: projectile) to skim past ; (fig) to come within a hair's breadth of ; to come very close to.
fromage [fʀɔmaʒ] nm cheese ; **~ blanc** soft white cheese ; **~ de tête** pork brawn ; **fromager, ère** nm/f cheesemonger ; **fromagerie** nf cheese dairy.
froment [fʀɔmɑ̃] nm wheat.
froncer [fʀɔ̃se] vt to gather ; **~ les sourcils** to frown.
frondaisons [fʀɔ̃dɛzɔ̃] nfpl foliage sg.
fronde [fʀɔ̃d] nf sling ; (fig) rebellion, rebelliousness.
front [fʀɔ̃] nm forehead, brow ; (MIL) front ; **avoir le ~ de faire** to have the effrontery ou front to do ; **de ~** ad (se heurter) head-on ; (rouler) together (i.e. 2 or 3 abreast) ; (simultanément) at once ; **faire ~ à** to face up to ; **~ de mer** (sea) front ; **frontal, e, aux** a frontal.
frontalier, ière [fʀɔ̃talje, -jɛʀ] a border cpd, frontier cpd // nm/f: (**travailleurs**) **~s** workers who cross the border to go to work, commuters from across the border.
frontière [fʀɔ̃tjɛʀ] nf (GÉO, POL) frontier, border ; (fig) frontier, boundary.
frontispice [fʀɔ̃tispis] nm frontispiece.
fronton [fʀɔ̃tɔ̃] nm pediment ; (de pelote basque) (front) wall.
frottement [fʀɔtmɑ̃] nm rubbing, scraping ; rubbing ou scraping noise.
frotter [fʀɔte] vi to rub, scrape // vt to rub ; (pour nettoyer) to rub (up) ; to scrub ; **~ une allumette** to strike a match.
frottoir [fʀɔtwaʀ] nm (d'allumettes) friction strip ; (pour encaustiquer) (long-handled) brush.
fructifier [fʀyktifje] vi to yield a profit ; **faire ~** to turn to good account.
fructueux, euse [fʀyktyø, -øz] a fruitful ; profitable.

frugal, e, aux [fʀygal, -o] a frugal.

fruit [fʀɥi] nm fruit (gén q); **~s de mer** seafood(s); **~s secs** dried fruit sg; **fruité, e** a fruity; **fruitier, ière** a: **arbre fruitier** fruit tree // nm/f fruiterer, greengrocer.

fruste [fʀyst(ə)] a unpolished. uncultivated.

frustration [fʀystʀɑsjɔ̃] nf frustration.

frustrer [fʀystʀe] vt to frustrate.

FS sigle = franc suisse.

fugace [fygas] a fleeting.

fugitif, ive [fyʒitif, -iv] a (lueur, amour) fleeting; (prisonnier etc) fugitive, runaway // nm/f fugitive.

fugue [fyg] nf (d'un enfant) running away q; (MUS) fugue; **faire une ~** to run away, abscond.

fuir [fɥiʀ] vt to flee from; (éviter) to shun // vi to run away; (gaz, robinet) to leak.

fuite [fɥit] nf flight; (écoulement) leak, leakage; (divulgation) leak; **être en ~** to be on the run; **mettre en ~** to put to flight; **prendre la ~** to take flight.

fulgurant, e [fylgyʀɑ̃, -ɑ̃t] a lightning cpd, dazzling.

fulminer [fylmine] vi: **~ (contre)** to thunder forth (against).

fume-cigarette [fymsigaʀɛt] nm inv cigarette holder.

fumé, e [fyme] a (CULIN) smoked; (verres) (grey-)tinted // nf smoke.

fumer [fyme] vi to smoke; (soupe) to steam // vt to smoke; (terre, champ) to manure.

fumerie [fymʀi] nf: **~ d'opium** opium den.

fumerolles [fymʀɔl] nfpl gas and smoke (from volcano).

fûmes vb voir **être**.

fumet [fymɛ] nm aroma.

fumeur, euse [fymœʀ, -øz] nm/f smoker.

fumeux, euse [fymø, -øz] a (péj) woolly.

fumier [fymje] nm manure.

fumigation [fymigasjɔ̃] nf fumigation.

fumigène [fymiʒɛn] a smoke cpd.

fumiste [fymist(ə)] nm (ramoneur) chimney sweep // nm/f (péj) shirker; phoney.

fumisterie [fymistəʀi] nf (péj) fraud, con.

fumoir [fymwaʀ] nm smoking room.

funambule [fynɑ̃byl] nm tightrope walker.

funèbre [fynɛbʀ(ə)] a funeral cpd; (fig) doleful; funereal.

funérailles [fyneʀɑj] nfpl funeral sg.

funéraire [fyneʀɛʀ] a funeral cpd, funerary.

funeste [fynɛst(ə)] a disastrous; deathly.

funiculaire [fynikylɛʀ] nm funicular (railway).

fur [fyʀ]: **au ~ et à mesure** ad as one goes along; **au ~ et à mesure que** as, as soon as; **au ~ et à mesure de leur progression** as they advance (ou advanced).

furet [fyʀɛ] nm ferret.

fureter [fyʀte] vi (péj) to nose about.

fureur [fyʀœʀ] nf fury; (passion): **~ de** passion for; **faire ~** to be all the rage.

furibond, e [fyʀibɔ̃, -ɔ̃d] a furious.

furie [fyʀi] nf fury; (femme) shrew, vixen; **en ~** (mer) raging; **furieux, euse** a furious.

furoncle [fyʀɔ̃kl(ə)] nm boil, furuncle.

furtif, ive [fyʀtif, -iv] a furtive.

fus vb voir **être**.

fusain [fyzɛ̃] nm (BOT) spindle-tree; (ART) charcoal.

fuseau, x [fyzo] nm (pour filer) spindle; **~ horaire** time zone.

fusée [fyze] nf rocket; **~ éclairante** flare.

fuselage [fyzlaʒ] nm fuselage.

fuselé, e [fyzle] a slender; tapering.

fuser [fyze] vi (rires etc) to burst forth.

fusible [fyzibl(ə)] nm (ÉLEC: fil) fuse wire; (: fiche) fuse.

fusil [fyzi] nm (de guerre, à canon rayé) rifle, gun; (de chasse, à canon lisse) shotgun, gun; **fusilier** [-lje] nm rifleman; **fusillade** [-jad] nf gunfire q, shooting q; shooting battle; **fusiller** vt to shoot; **~-mitrailleur** nm machine gun.

fusion [fyzjɔ̃] nf fusion, melting; (fig) merging; (COMM) merger; **en ~** (métal, roches) molten; **fusionner** vi to merge.

fustiger [fystiʒe] vt to denounce.

fut vb voir **être**.

fût [fy] nm (tonneau) barrel, cask; (de canon) stock; (d'arbre) bole, trunk; (de colonne) shaft.

futaie [fytɛ] nf forest, plantation.

futile [fytil] a futile; frivolous.

futur, e [fytyʀ] a, nm future; **au ~** (LING) in the future; **~iste** a futuristic.

fuyant, e [fɥijɑ̃, -ɑ̃t] vb voir **fuir** // a (regard etc) evasive; (lignes etc) receding; (perspective) vanishing.

fuyard, e [fɥijaʀ, -aʀd(ə)] nm/f runaway.

G

gabardine [gabaʀdin] nf gabardine.

gabarit [gabaʀi] nm (fig) size; calibre; (TECH) template.

gabegie [gabʒi] nf (péj) chaos.

gâcher [gɑʃe] vt (gâter) to spoil, ruin; (gaspiller) to waste; (plâtre) to temper; (mortier) to mix.

gâchette [gɑʃɛt] nf trigger.

gâchis [gɑʃi] nm waste q.

gadoue [gadu] nf sludge.

gaffe [gaf] nf (instrument) boat hook; (erreur) blunder; **faire ~** (fam) to be careful; **gaffer** vi to blunder.

gag [gag] nm gag.

gage [gaʒ] nm (dans un jeu) forfeit; (fig: de fidélité) token; **~s** nmpl (salaire) wages; (garantie) guarantee sg; **mettre en ~** to pawn; **laisser en ~** to leave as a security.

gager [gaʒe] vt: **~ que** to bet ou wager that.

gageure [gaʒyʀ] nf: **c'est une ~** it's attempting the impossible.

gagnant, e [gɑɲɑ̃, -ɑ̃t] a: **billet/ numéro ~** winning ticket/number // nm/f winner.

gagne-pain [gɑɲpɛ̃] nm inv job.

gagner [gɑɲe] vt to win; (somme d'argent, revenu) to earn; (aller vers, atteindre) to reach // vi to win; (fig) to gain; ~ **du temps/de la place** to gain time/save space; ~ **sa vie** to earn one's living; ~ **du terrain** to gain ground; ~ **à faire** (s'en trouver bien) to be better off doing.

gai, e [ge] a gay, cheerful; (un peu ivre) merry.

gaieté [gete] nf cheerfulness; ~**s** nfpl (souvent ironique) delights; **de ~ de cœur** with a light heart.

gaillard, e [gajaR, -aRd(ə)] a (robuste) sprightly; (grivois) bawdy, ribald // nm/f (strapping) fellow/wench.

gain [gɛ̃] nm (revenu) earnings pl; (bénéfice: gén pl) profits pl; (au jeu: gén pl) winnings pl; (fig: de temps, place) saving; **avoir ~ de cause** to win the case; (fig) to be proved right.

gaine [gɛn] nf (corset) girdle; (fourreau) sheath; (de fil électrique etc) outer covering; ~**-culotte** nf pantie girdle; **gainer** vt to cover.

gala [gala] nm official reception; **soirée de ~** gala evening.

galant, e [galɑ̃, -ɑ̃t] a (courtois) courteous, gentlemanly; (entreprenant) flirtatious, gallant; (aventure, poésie) amorous; **en ~e compagnie** with a lady friend/gentleman friend.

galaxie [galaksi] nf galaxy.

galbe [galb(ə)] nm curve(s); shapeliness.

gale [gal] nf scabies sg.

galéjade [galeʒad] nf tall story.

galère [galɛR] nf galley.

galerie [galRi] nf gallery; (THÉÂTRE) circle; (de voiture) roof rack; (fig: spectateurs) audience; ~ **marchande** shopping arcade; ~ **de peinture** (private) art gallery.

galérien [galeRjɛ̃] nm galley slave.

galet [galɛ] nm pebble; (TECH) wheel; ~**s** nmpl pebbles, shingle sg.

galette [galɛt] nf flat cake.

galeux, euse [galø, -øz] a: **un chien ~** a mangy dog.

galimatias [galimatja] nm (péj) gibberish.

Galles [gal] n: **le pays de ~** Wales.

gallicisme [galisism(ə)] nm French idiom; (tournure fautive) gallicism.

gallois, e [galwa, -waz] a, nm (langue) Welsh // nm/f: **G~, e** Welshman/woman.

galon [galɔ̃] nm (MIL) stripe; (décoratif) piece of braid.

galop [galo] nm gallop; **au ~** at a gallop.

galopade [galɔpad] nf stampede.

galoper [galɔpe] vi to gallop.

galopin [galɔpɛ̃] nm urchin, ragamuffin.

galvaniser [galvanize] vt to galvanize.

galvauder [galvode] vt to debase.

gambader [gɑ̃bade] vi (animal, enfant) to leap about.

gamelle [gamɛl] nf mess tin; billy can; (fam): **ramasser une ~** to come a cropper.

gamin, e [gamɛ̃, -in] nm/f kid // a mischievous, playful.

gamme [gam] nf (MUS) scale; (fig) range.

gammé, e [game] a: **croix ~e** swastika.

gang [gɑ̃g] nm gang.

ganglion [gɑ̃glijɔ̃] nm ganglion.

gangrène [gɑ̃gRɛn] nf gangrene.

gangue [gɑ̃g] nf coating.

ganse [gɑ̃s] nf braid.

gant [gɑ̃] nm glove; ~ **de toilette** (face) flannel; ~**s de boxe** boxing gloves; **ganté, e** a: **ganté de blanc** wearing white gloves; **ganterie** nf glove trade; glove shop.

garage [gaRaʒ] nm garage; ~ **à vélos** bicycle shed; **garagiste** nm/f garage owner; garage mechanic ou man.

garant, e [gaRɑ̃, -ɑ̃t] nm/f guarantor // nm guarantee; **se porter ~ de** to vouch for; to be answerable for.

garantie [gaRɑ̃ti] nf guarantee; (gage) security, surety; **(bon de) ~** guarantee ou warranty slip.

garantir [gaRɑ̃tiR] vt to guarantee; (protéger): ~ **de** to protect from; **je vous garantis que** I can assure you that; **garanti 2 ans/pure laine** guaranteed for 2 years/pure wool.

garçon [gaRsɔ̃] nm boy; (célibataire) bachelor; (jeune homme) boy, lad; ~ **boucher/coiffeur** butcher's/hairdresser's assistant; ~ **de courses** messenger; ~ **d'écurie** stable lad; **garçonnet** nm small boy; **garçonnière** nf bachelor flat.

garde [gaRd(ə)] nm (de prisonnier) guard; (de domaine etc) warden; (soldat, sentinelle) guardsman // nf guarding; looking after; (soldats, BOXE, ESCRIME) guard; (faction) watch; (d'une arme) hilt; (TYPO): **(page de) ~** endpaper; flyleaf; **de ~** a, ad on duty; **monter la ~** to stand guard; **être sur ses ~s** to be on one's guard; **mettre en ~** to warn; **prendre ~ (à)** to be careful (of); ~ **champêtre** nm rural policeman; ~ **du corps** nm bodyguard; ~ **d'enfants** nf child minder; ~ **des enfants** nf (après divorce) custody of the children; ~ **forestier** nm forest warden; ~ **mobile** nm, nf mobile guard; ~ **des Sceaux** nm ≈ Lord Chancellor; ~ **à vue** nf (JUR) ≈ police custody; ~**-à-vous** nm inv: **être/se mettre au ~-à-vous** to be at/stand to attention.

garde... [gaRd(ə)] préfixe: ~**-barrière** nm/f level-crossing keeper; ~**-boue** inv mudguard; ~**-chasse** nm gamekeeper; ~**-fou** nm railing, parapet; ~**-malade** nf home nurse; ~**-manger** nm inv meat safe; pantry, larder; ~**-meuble** nm furniture depository; ~**-pêche** nm inv water bailiff; fisheries protection ship.

garder [gaRde] vt (conserver) to keep; (surveiller: prisonnier, enfants) to look after; (: immeuble, lieu) to guard; ~ **le lit/la chambre** to stay in bed/indoors; **se ~ vt** (aliment: se conserver) to keep; **se ~ de faire** to be careful not to do; **pêche/chasse gardée** private fishing/hunting (ground).

garderie [gaRdəRi] nf day nursery, crèche.

garde-robe [gaRdəRɔb] nf wardrobe.

gardeur, euse [gaRdœR, -øz] nm/f (d'animaux) cowherd; goatherd.

gardien, ne [gaRdjɛ̃, -jɛn] nm/f (garde) guard; (de prison) warder; (de domaine, réserve) warden; (de musée etc) attendant; (de phare, cimetière) keeper; (d'immeuble) caretaker; (fig) guardian; ~ **de but**

goalkeeper ; ~ **de nuit** night watchman ; ~ **de la paix** policeman.
gare [gaʀ] *nf* (railway) station // *excl* watch out! ; ~ **à ne pas ...** mind you don't ... ; ~ **maritime** harbour station ; ~ **routière** coach station.
garenne [gaʀɛn] *nf voir* **lapin**.
garer [gaʀe] *vt* to park ; **se** ~ to park ; (*pour laisser passer*) to draw into the side.
gargariser [gaʀgaʀize]: **se** ~ *vi* to gargle ; **gargarisme** *nm* gargling *q* ; gargle.
gargote [gaʀgɔt] *nf* cheap restaurant.
gargouille [gaʀguj] *nf* gargoyle.
gargouiller [gaʀguje] *vi* to gurgle.
garnement [gaʀnəmɑ̃] *nm* tearaway, scallywag.
garni, e [gaʀni] *a* (*plat*) served with vegetables (and chips or pasta or rice) // *nm* furnished accommodation *q*.
garnir [gaʀniʀ] *vt* to decorate ; to fill ; to cover ; ~ **qch de** (*orner*) to decorate sth with ; to trim sth with ; (*approvisionner*) to fill *ou* stock sth with ; (*protéger*) to fit sth with ; (CULIN) to garnish sth with.
garnison [gaʀnizɔ̃] *nf* garrison.
garniture [gaʀnityʀ] *nf* (CULIN) vegetables *pl* ; trimmings *pl* ; filling ; (*décoration*) trimming ; (*protection*) fittings *pl* ; ~ **de frein** brake lining ; ~ **intérieure** (AUTO) interior trim.
garrot [gaʀo] *nm* (MÉD) tourniquet ; (*torture*) garrotte.
garrotter [gaʀɔte] *vt* to tie up ; (*fig*) to muzzle.
gars [gɑ] *nm* lad ; guy.
gas-oil [gazɔjl] *nm* diesel oil.
gaspillage [gaspijaʒ] *nm* waste.
gaspiller [gaspije] *vt* to waste.
gastrique [gastʀik] *a* gastric, stomach *cpd*.
gastronome [gastʀɔnɔm] *nm/f* gourmet.
gastronomie [gastʀɔnɔmi] *nf* gastronomy.
gâteau, x [gɑto] *nm* cake ; ~ **sec** biscuit.
gâter [gɑte] *vt* to spoil ; **se** ~ *vi* (*dent, fruit*) to go bad ; (*temps, situation*) to change for the worse.
gâterie [gɑtʀi] *nf* little treat.
gâteux, euse [gɑtø, -øz] *a* senile.
gauche [goʃ] *a* left, left-hand ; (*maladroit*) awkward, clumsy // *nf* (POL) left (wing) ; **à** ~ on the left ; (*direction*) (to the) left ; **à** ~ **de** (on *ou* to the) left of ; **à la** ~ **de** to the left of ; **gaucher, ère** a left-handed ; ~**rie** *nf* awkwardness, clumsiness ; **gauchir** *vt* to warp ; **gauchisant, e** a left-wing tendencies ; **gauchiste** *nm/f* leftist.
gaufre [gofʀ(ə)] *nf* waffle.
gaufrer [gofʀe] *vt* (*papier*) to emboss ; (*tissu*) to goffer.
gaufrette [gofʀɛt] *nf* wafer.
gaule [gol] *nf* (long) pole.
gaulois, e [golwa, -waz] a Gallic ; (*grivois*) bawdy // *nf*: **G~**, e Gaul.
gausser [gose]: **se** ~ **de** *vt* to deride.
gaver [gave] *vt* to force-feed ; (*fig*): ~ **de** to cram with, fill up with.
gaz [gɑz] *nm inv* gas ; **mettre les** ~ (AUTO) to put one's foot down ; ~ **lacrymogène** tear gas ; ~ **de ville** town gas.

gaze [gɑz] *nf* gauze.
gazéifié, e [gazeifje] a aerated.
gazelle [gazɛl] *nf* gazelle.
gazer [gɑze] *vt* to gas // *vi* (*fam*) to be going *ou* working well.
gazette [gazɛt] *nf* news sheet.
gazeux, euse [gazø, -øz] a gaseous ; **eau gazeuse** soda water.
gazoduc [gɑzɔdyk] *nm* gas pipeline.
gazomètre [gazɔmɛtʀ(ə)] *nm* gasometer.
gazon [gɑzɔ̃] *nm* (*herbe*) turf ; grass ; (*pelouse*) lawn.
gazouiller [gazuje] *vi* to chirp ; (*enfant*) to babble.
geai [ʒɛ] *nm* jay.
géant, e [ʒeɑ̃, -ɑ̃t] a gigantic, giant ; (COMM) giant-size // *nm/f* giant.
geindre [ʒɛ̃dʀ(ə)] *vi* to groan, moan.
gel [ʒɛl] *nm* frost ; freezing.
gélatine [ʒelatin] *nf* gelatine ; **gélatineux, euse** a jelly-like, gelatinous.
gelé, e [ʒəle] a frozen.
gelée [ʒəle] *nf* jelly ; (*gel*) frost ; ~ **blanche** hoarfrost, white frost.
geler [ʒəle] *vt, vi* to freeze ; **il gèle** it's freezing ; **gelures** *nfpl* frostbite *sg.*
Gémeaux [ʒemo] *nmpl*: **les** ~ Gemini, the Twins ; **être des** ~ to be Gemini.
gémir [ʒemiʀ] *vi* to groan, moan ; **gémissement** *nm* groan, moan.
gemme [ʒɛm] *nf* gem(stone).
gênant, e [ʒɛnɑ̃, -ɑ̃t] a annoying ; embarrassing.
gencive [ʒɑ̃siv] *nf* gum.
gendarme [ʒɑ̃daʀm(ə)] *nm* gendarme ; ~**rie** *nf* military police force in countryside and small towns ; their police station or barracks.
gendre [ʒɑ̃dʀ(ə)] *nm* son-in-law.
gêne [ʒɛn] *nf* (*à respirer, bouger*) discomfort, difficulty ; (*dérangement*) bother, trouble ; (*manque d'argent*) financial difficulties *pl ou* straits *pl* ; (*confusion*) embarrassment.
gêné, e [ʒene] a embarrassed.
généalogie [ʒenealɔʒi] *nf* genealogy ; **généalogique** a genealogical.
gêner [ʒene] *vt* (*incommoder*) to bother ; (*encombrer*) to hamper ; to be in the way ; (*déranger*) to bother ; (*embarrasser*): ~ **qn** to make sb feel ill-at-ease ; **se** ~ to put o.s. out.
général, e, aux [ʒeneʀal, -o] a, *nm* general // *nf*: (*répétition*) ~**e** final dress rehearsal ; **en** ~ usually, in general ; ~**ement** ad generally.
généralisation [ʒeneʀalizɑsjɔ̃] *nf* generalization.
généralisé, e [ʒeneʀalize] a general.
généraliser [ʒeneʀalize] *vt, vi* to generalize ; **se** ~ *vi* to become widespread.
généraliste [ʒeneʀalist(ə)] *nm/f* general practitioner, G.P.
généralités [ʒeneʀalite] *nfpl* generalities ; (*introduction*) general points.
générateur, trice [ʒeneʀatœʀ, -tʀis] a: ~ **de** which causes *ou* brings about // *nf* generator.
génération [ʒeneʀɑsjɔ̃] *nf* generation.

génèreusement [ʒeneRøzmã] *ad* generously.

généreux, euse [ʒeneRø, -øz] *a* generous.

générique [ʒeneRik] *a* generic // *nm* (CINÉMA) credits *pl*, credit titles *pl*.

générosité [ʒeneRozite] *nf* generosity.

genèse [ʒənɛz] *nf* genesis.

genêt [ʒənɛ] *nm* broom *q*.

génétique [ʒenetik] *a* genetic // *nf* genetics *sg*.

Genève [ʒənɛv] *n* Geneva ; **genevois, e** *a, nm/f* Genevan.

génial, e, aux [ʒenjal, -o] *a* of genius.

génie [ʒeni] *nm* genius ; (MIL): **le ~** the Engineers *pl* ; **~ civil** civil engineering.

genièvre [ʒənjɛvR(ə)] *nm* juniper (tree) ; (*boisson*) geneva ; **grain de ~** juniper berry.

génisse [ʒenis] *nf* heifer.

génital, e, aux [ʒenital, -o] *a* genital.

génitif [ʒenitif] *nm* genitive.

genou, x [ʒnu] *nm* knee ; **à ~x** on one's knees ; **se mettre à ~x** to kneel down ; **genouillère** *nf* (SPORT) kneepad.

genre [ʒɑ̃R] *nm* kind, type, sort ; (*allure*) manner ; (LING) gender ; (ART) genre ; (ZOOL *etc*) genus.

gens [ʒɑ̃] *nmpl* (*f in some phrases*) people *pl*.

gentil, le [ʒɑ̃ti, -ij] *a* kind ; (*enfant: sage*) good ; (*sympa: endroit etc*) nice ; **gentillesse** *nf* kindness ; **gentiment** *ad* kindly.

génuflexion [ʒenyflɛksjɔ̃] *nf* genuflexion.

géographe [ʒeɔgRaf] *nm/f* geographer.

géographie [ʒeɔgRafi] *nf* geography ; **géographique** *a* geographical.

geôlier [ʒolje] *nm* jailer.

géologie [ʒeɔlɔʒi] *nf* geology ; **géologique** *a* geological ; **géologue** *nm/f* geologist.

géomètre [ʒeɔmɛtR(ə)] *nm/f*: **(arpenteur-)~** (land) surveyor.

géométrie [ʒeɔmetRi] *nf* geometry ; **à ~ variable** (AVIAT) swing-wing ; **géométrique** *a* geometric.

gérance [ʒeRɑ̃s] *nf* management ; **mettre en ~** to appoint a manager for.

géranium [ʒeRanjɔm] *nm* geranium.

gérant, e [ʒeRɑ̃, -ɑ̃t] *nm/f* manager/manageress ; **~ d'immeuble** managing agent.

gerbe [ʒɛRb(ə)] *nf* (*de fleurs*) spray ; (*de blé*) sheaf (*pl* sheaves) ; (*fig*) shower, burst.

gercé, e [ʒɛRse] *a* chapped.

gerçure [ʒɛRsyR] *nf* crack.

gérer [ʒeRe] *vt* to manage.

gériatrie [ʒeRjatRi] *nf* geriatrics *sg* ; **gériatrique** *a* geriatric.

germain, e [ʒɛRmɛ̃, -ɛn] *a*: **cousin ~** first cousin.

germanique [ʒɛRmanik] *a* Germanic.

germe [ʒɛRm(ə)] *nm* germ.

germer [ʒɛRme] *vi* to sprout ; to germinate.

gésier [ʒezje] *nm* gizzard.

gésir [ʒeziR] *vi* to be lying (down) ; *voir aussi* **ci-gît**.

gestation [ʒɛstasjɔ̃] *nf* gestation.

geste [ʒɛst(ə)] *nm* gesture ; move ; motion.

gesticuler [ʒɛstikyle] *vi* to gesticulate.

gestion [ʒɛstjɔ̃] *nf* management.

gibecière [ʒibsjɛR] *nf* gamebag.

gibet [ʒibɛ] *nm* gallows *pl*.

gibier [ʒibje] *nm* (*animaux*) game ; (*fig*) prey.

giboulée [ʒibule] *nf* sudden shower.

giboyeux, euse [ʒibwajø, -øz] *a* well-stocked with game.

gicler [ʒikle] *vi* to spurt, squirt.

gicleur [ʒiklœR] *nm* (AUTO) jet.

gifle [ʒifl(ə)] *nf* slap (in the face) ; **gifler** *vt* to slap (in the face).

gigantesque [ʒigɑ̃tɛsk(ə)] *a* gigantic.

gigogne [ʒigɔɲ] *a*: **lits ~s** pull-out *ou* stowaway beds ; **tables/poupées ~s** nest of tables/dolls.

gigot [ʒigo] *nm* leg (of mutton *ou* lamb).

gigoter [ʒigɔte] *vi* to wriggle (about).

gilet [ʒilɛ] *nm* waistcoat ; (*pull*) cardigan ; (*de corps*) vest ; **~ pare-balles** bulletproof jacket ; **~ de sauvetage** life jacket.

gin [dʒin] *nm* gin.

gingembre [ʒɛ̃ʒɑ̃bR(ə)] *nm* ginger.

girafe [ʒiRaf] *nf* giraffe.

giratoire [ʒiRatwaR] *a*: **sens ~** roundabout.

girofle [ʒiRɔfl(ə)] *nm*: **clou de ~** clove.

girouette [ʒiRwɛt] *nf* weather vane *ou* cock.

gisait *etc vb voir* **gésir**.

gisement [ʒizmɑ̃] *nm* deposit.

gît *vb voir* **gésir**.

gitan, e [ʒitɑ̃, -an] *nm/f* gipsy.

gîte [ʒit] *nm* home ; shelter ; **~ rural** farmhouse accommodation *q* (for tourists).

givrage [ʒivRaʒ] *nm* icing.

givre [ʒivR(ə)] *nm* (hoar) frost.

glabre [glabR(ə)] *a* hairless ; clean-shaven.

glace [glas] *nf* ice ; (*crème glacée*) ice cream ; (*verre*) sheet of glass ; (*miroir*) mirror ; (*de voiture*) window ; **~s** *nfpl* (GÉO) ice sheets, ice *sg*.

glacé, e [glase] *a* icy ; (*boisson*) iced.

glacer [glase] *vt* to freeze ; (*boisson*) to chill, ice ; (*gâteau*) to ice ; (*papier, tissu*) to glaze ; (*fig*): **~ qn** to chill sb ; to make sb's blood run cold.

glaciaire [glasjɛR] *a* ice *cpd* ; glacial.

glacial, e [glasjal] *a* icy.

glacier [glasje] *nm* (GÉO) glacier ; (*marchand*) ice-cream maker.

glacière [glasjɛR] *nf* icebox.

glaçon [glasɔ̃] *nm* icicle ; (*pour boisson*) ice cube.

glaïeul [glajœl] *nm* gladiola.

glaire [glɛR] *nf* (MÉD) phlegm *q*.

glaise [glɛz] *nf* clay.

gland [glɑ̃] *nm* acorn ; (*décoration*) tassel ; (ANAT) glans.

glande [glɑ̃d] *nf* gland.

glaner [glane] *vt, vi* to glean.

glapir [glapiR] *vi* to yelp.

glas [glɑ] *nm* knell, toll.

glauque [glok] *a* dull blue-green.

glissade [glisad] *nf* (*par jeu*) slide ; (*chute*) slip ; (*dérapage*) skid.

glissant, e [glisɑ̃, -ɑ̃t] *a* slippery.

glissement [glismɑ̃] *nm* sliding ; (*fig*) shift ; **~ de terrain** landslide.

glisser [glise] *vi* (*avancer*) to glide *ou* slide along; (*coulisser, tomber*) to slide; (*déraper*) to slip; (*être glissant*) to be slippery // *vt*: ~ **qch sous/dans/à** to slip sth under/into/to; ~ **sur** (*fig: détail etc*) to skate over; **se ~ dans/entre** to slip into/between; **glissière** *nf* slide channel; **à glissière** sliding; **glissoire** *nf* slide.

global, e, aux [glɔbal, -o] *a* overall.

globe [glɔb] *nm* globe; **sous ~** under glass; ~ **oculaire** eyeball; **le ~ terrestre** the globe.

globule [glɔbyl] *nm* (*du sang*): ~ **blanc/rouge** white/red corpuscle.

globuleux, euse [glɔbylø, -øz] *a*: **yeux ~** protruding eyes.

gloire [glwaʀ] *nf* glory; (*mérite*) distinction, credit; (*personne*) celebrity; **glorieux, euse** *a* glorious; **glorifier** *vt* to glorify, extol.

glossaire [glɔsɛʀ] *nm* glossary.

glousser [gluse] *vi* to cluck; (*rire*) to chuckle.

glouton, ne [glutɔ̃, -ɔn] *a* gluttonous, greedy.

glu [gly] *nf* birdlime.

gluant, e [glyɑ̃, -ɑ̃t] *a* sticky, gummy.

glycine [glisin] *nf* wisteria.

go [go]: **tout de ~** *ad* straight out.

G.O. *sigle* = **grandes ondes**.

gobelet [gɔblɛ] *nm* tumbler; beaker; (*à dés*) cup.

gober [gɔbe] *vt* to swallow.

godet [gɔdɛ] *nm* pot.

godiller [gɔdije] *vi* to scull.

goéland [gɔelɑ̃] *nm* (sea)gull.

goélette [gɔelɛt] *nf* schooner.

goémon [gɔemɔ̃] *nm* wrack.

gogo [gɔgo] *nm* (*péj*) mug, sucker; **à ~** *ad* galore.

goguenard, e [gɔgnaʀ, -aʀd(ə)] *a* mocking.

goguette [gɔgɛt] *nf*: **en ~** on the binge.

goinfre [gwɛ̃fʀ(ə)] *nm* glutton; **se goinfrer** *vi* to make a pig of o.s.; **se goinfrer de** to guzzle.

goitre [gwatʀ(ə)] *nm* goitre.

golf [gɔlf] *nm* golf; golf course; ~ **miniature** crazy *ou* miniature golf.

golfe [gɔlf(ə)] *nm* gulf; bay.

gomme [gɔm] *nf* (*à effacer*) rubber, eraser; (*résine*) gum; **gommer** *vt* to erase; to gum.

gond [gɔ̃] *nm* hinge; **sortir de ses ~s** (*fig*) to fly off the handle.

gondole [gɔ̃dɔl] *nf* gondola.

gondoler [gɔ̃dɔle] *vi*, **se ~** *vi* to warp; to buckle.

gondolier [gɔ̃dɔlje] *nm* gondolier.

gonflage [gɔ̃flaʒ] *nm* inflating, blowing up.

gonflé, e [gɔ̃fle] *a* swollen; bloated.

gonfler [gɔ̃fle] *vt* (*pneu, ballon*) to inflate, blow up; (*nombre, importance*) to inflate // *vi* to swell (up); (*CULIN*: *pâte*) to rise; **gonfleur** *nm* air pump.

gong [gɔ̃g] *nm* gong.

goret [gɔʀɛ] *nm* piglet.

gorge [gɔʀʒ(ə)] *nf* (*ANAT*) throat; (*poitrine*) breast; (*GÉO*) gorge; (*rainure*) groove.

gorgé, e [gɔʀʒe] *a*: ~ **de** filled with; (*eau*) saturated with // *nf* mouthful; sip; gulp.

gorille [gɔʀij] *nm* gorilla; (*fam*) bodyguard.

gosier [gozje] *nm* throat.

gosse [gɔs] *nm/f* kid.

gothique [gɔtik] *a* gothic.

goudron [gudʀɔ̃] *nm* tar; **goudronner** *vt* to tarmac.

gouffre [gufʀ(ə)] *nm* abyss, gulf.

goujat [guʒa] *nm* boor.

goujon [guʒɔ̃] *nm* gudgeon.

goulée [gule] *nf* gulp.

goulet [gulɛ] *nm* bottleneck.

goulot [gulo] *nm* neck; **boire au ~** to drink from the bottle.

goulu, e [guly] *a* greedy.

goupillon [gupijɔ̃] *nm* (*REL*) sprinkler.

gourd, e [guʀ, guʀd(ə)] *a* numb (with cold).

gourde [guʀd(ə)] *nf* (*récipient*) flask.

gourdin [guʀdɛ̃] *nm* club, bludgeon.

gourmand, e [guʀmɑ̃, -ɑ̃d] *a* greedy; **gourmandise** *nf* greed; (*bonbon*) sweet.

gourmet [guʀmɛ] *nm* epicure.

gourmette [guʀmɛt] *nf* chain bracelet.

gousse [gus] *nf*: ~ **d'ail** clove of garlic.

gousset [gusɛ] *nm* (*de gilet*) fob.

goût [gu] *nm* taste; **prendre ~ à** to develop a taste *ou* a liking for.

goûter [gute] *vt* (*essayer*) to taste; (*apprécier*) to enjoy // *vi* to have (afternoon) tea // *nm* (afternoon) tea; ~ **à** to taste, sample; ~ **de** to have a taste of.

goutte [gut] *nf* drop; (*MÉD*) gout; (*alcool*) brandy; ~**s** *nfpl* (*MÉD*) (nose) drops.

goutte-à-goutte [gutagut] *nm* (*MÉD*) drip; **alimenter au ~** to drip-feed.

gouttelette [gutlɛt] *nf* droplet.

gouttière [gutjɛʀ] *nf* gutter.

gouvernail [guvɛʀnaj] *nm* rudder; (*barre*) helm, tiller.

gouvernante [guvɛʀnɑ̃t] *nf* governess.

gouverne [guvɛʀn(ə)] *nf*: **pour sa ~** for his guidance.

gouvernement [guvɛʀnəmɑ̃] *nm* government; **membre du ~** Cabinet member; **gouvernemental, e, aux** *a* government *cpd*; pro-government.

gouverner [guvɛʀne] *vt* to govern; **gouverneur** *nm* governor; commanding officer.

grâce [gʀɑs] *nf* grace; favour; (*JUR*) pardon; ~**s** *nfpl* (*REL*) grace *sg*; **dans les bonnes ~s de qn** in favour with sb; **faire ~ à qn de qch** to spare sb sth; **rendre ~(s) à** to give thanks to; **demander ~** to beg for mercy; **droit de ~** right of reprieve; ~ **à** *prép* thanks to; **gracier** *vt* to pardon; **gracieux, euse** *a* graceful.

gracile [gʀasil] *a* slender.

gradation [gʀadasjɔ̃] *nf* gradation.

grade [gʀad] *nm* rank; **monter en ~** to be promoted.

gradé [gʀade] *nm* officer.

gradin [gʀadɛ̃] *nm* tier; step; ~**s** *nmpl* (*de stade*) terracing *sg*.

graduation [gʀaduasjɔ̃] *nf* graduation.

graduel, le [gʀaduɛl] *a* gradual; progressive.

graduer [gradɥe] vt (effort etc) to increase gradually ; (règle, verre) to graduate ; **exercices gradués** exercises graded for difficulty.

graffiti [grafiti] nmpl graffiti.

grain [grɛ̃] nm (gén) grain ; (NAVIG) squall ; ~ **de beauté** beauty spot ; ~ **de café** coffee bean ; ~ **de poivre** peppercorn ; ~ **de poussière** speck of dust ; ~ **de raisin** grape.

graine [grɛn] nf seed ; ~**tier** nm seed merchant.

graissage [grɛsaʒ] nm lubrication, greasing.

graisse [grɛs] nf fat ; (lubrifiant) grease ; **graisser** vt to lubricate, grease ; (tacher) to make greasy ; **graisseux, euse** a greasy ; (ANAT) fatty.

grammaire [gramɛr] nf grammar ; **grammatical, e, aux** a grammatical.

gramme [gram] nm gramme.

grand, e [grɑ̃, grɑ̃d] a (haut) tall ; (gros, vaste, large) big, large ; (long) long ; (sens abstraits) great // ad: ~ **ouvert** wide open ; **son** ~ **frère** his older brother ; **il est assez** ~ **pour** he's old enough to ; **au** ~ **air** in the open (air) ; ~**s blessés/brûlés** casualties with severe injuries/burns ; ~ **angle** nm (PHOTO) wide-angle lens sg ; ~ **écart** splits pl ; ~ **ensemble** housing scheme ; ~ **magasin** department store ; ~**e personne** grown-up ; ~**es écoles** prestige schools of university level, with competitive entrance examination ; ~**es lignes** (RAIL) main lines ; ~**es vacances** summer holidays ; **grand-chose** nm/f inv: **pas grand-chose** not much ; **Grande-Bretagne** nf: **la Grande-Bretagne** (Great) Britain ; **grandeur** nf (dimension) size ; magnitude ; (fig) greatness ; **grandeur nature** life-size ; **grandir** vi (enfant, arbre) to grow ; (bruit, hostilité) to increase, grow // vt: **grandir qn** (suj: vêtement, chaussure) to make sb look taller ; (fig) to make sb grow in stature ; ~**-mère** nf grandmother ; ~**-messe** nf high mass ; ~**-père** nm grandfather ; ~**-route** nf main road ; ~**-rue** nf high street ; ~**s-parents** nmpl grandparents.

grange [grɑ̃ʒ] nf barn.

granit [granit] nm granite.

granule [granyle] nm granule.

granuleux, euse [granylø, -øz] a granular.

graphie [grafi] nf written form.

graphique [grafik] a graphic // nm graph.

graphisme [grafism(ə)] nm graphic arts pl ; graphics sg.

graphologie [grafɔlɔʒi] nf graphology ; **graphologue** nm/f graphologist.

grappe [grap] nf cluster ; ~ **de raisin** bunch of grapes.

grappiller [grapije] vt to glean.

grappin [grapɛ̃] nm grapnel ; **mettre le** ~ **sur** (fig) to get one's claws on.

gras, se [grɑ, grɑs] a (viande, soupe) fatty ; (personne) fat ; (surface, main) greasy ; (toux) loose, phlegmy ; (rire) throaty ; (plaisanterie) coarse ; (crayon) soft-lead ; (TYPO) bold // nm (CULIN) fat ; **faire la** ~**se matinée** to have a lie-in ;

~**sement** ad: ~**sement payé** handsomely paid ; ~**souillet, te** a podgy, plump.

gratification [gratifikasjɔ̃] nf bonus.

gratifier [gratifje] vt: ~ **qn de** to favour sb with, reward sb with ; (sourire etc) to favour sb with.

gratin [gratɛ̃] nm (CULIN) cheese-topped dish ; cheese topping.

gratiné, e [gratine] a (CULIN) au gratin ; (fam) hellish.

gratis [gratis] ad free.

gratitude [gratityd] nf gratitude.

gratte-ciel [gratsjɛl] nm inv skyscraper.

grattement [gratmɑ̃] nm (bruit) scratching (noise).

gratte-papier [gratpapje] nm inv (péj) penpusher.

gratter [grate] vt (frotter) to scrape ; (enlever) to scrape off ; (bras, bouton) to scratch ; **grattoir** nm scraper.

gratuit, e [gratɥi, -ɥit] a (entrée, billet) free ; (fig) gratuitous.

gratuitement [gratɥitmɑ̃] ad free.

gravats [grava] nmpl rubble sg.

grave [grav] a (maladie, accident) serious, bad ; (sujet, problème) serious, grave ; (air) grave, solemn ; (voix, son) deep, low-pitched // nm (MUS) low register ; **blessé** ~ seriously injured person ; ~**ment** ad seriously ; gravely.

graver [grave] vt to engrave ; **graveur** nm engraver.

gravier [gravje] nm gravel q ; **gravillons** nmpl gravel sg, loose chippings ou gravel.

gravir [gravir] vt to climb (up).

gravitation [gravitasjɔ̃] nf gravitation.

gravité [gravite] nf seriousness ; gravity ; (PHYSIQUE) gravity.

graviter [gravite] vi: ~ **autour de** to revolve around.

gravure [gravyr] nf engraving ; (reproduction) print ; plate.

gré [gre] nm: **à son** ~ to his liking ; as he pleases ; **au** ~ **de** according to, following ; **contre le** ~ **de** qn against sb's will ; **de son (plein)** ~ of one's own free will ; **de** ~ **ou de force** whether one likes it or not ; **de bon** ~ willingly ; **de** ~ **à** ~ (COMM) by mutual agreement ; **savoir** ~ **à qn de qch** to be grateful to sb for sth.

grec, grecque [grɛk] a Greek ; (classique: vase etc) Grecian // nm/f Greek.

Grèce [grɛs] nf: **la** ~ Greece.

gréement [gremɑ̃] nm rigging.

greffe [grɛf] nf grafting q, graft ; transplanting q, transplant // nm (JUR) office.

greffer [grefe] vt (BOT, MÉD: tissu) to graft ; (MÉD: organe) to transplant.

greffier [grefje] nm clerk of the court.

grégaire [gregɛr] a gregarious.

grège [grɛʒ] a: **soie** ~ raw silk.

grêle [grɛl] a (very) thin // nf hail.

grêlé, e [grele] a pockmarked.

grêler [grele] vb impersonnel: **il grêle** it's hailing.

grêlon [grelɔ̃] nm hailstone.

grelot [grəlo] nm little bell.

grelotter [grəlɔte] vi (trembler) to shiver.

grenade [grənad] *nf* (*explosive*) grenade ; (*BOT*) pomegranate ; ~ **lacrymogène** teargas grenade.

grenadier [grənadje] *nm* (*MIL*) grenadier ; (*BOT*) pomegranate tree.

grenat [grəna] *a inv* dark red.

grenier [grənje] *nm* attic ; (*de ferme*) loft.

grenouille [grənuj] *nf* frog.

grenu, e [grəny] *a* grainy, grained.

grès [grɛ] *nm* sandstone ; (*poterie*) stoneware.

grésiller [grezije] *vi* to sizzle ; (*RADIO*) to crackle.

grève [grɛv] *nf* (*d'ouvriers*) strike ; (*plage*) shore ; **se mettre en/faire** ~ to go on/be on strike ; ~ **de la faim** hunger strike ; ~ **sauvage** wildcat strike ; ~ **sur le tas** sit down strike ; ~ **tournante** strike by rota ; ~ **du zèle** work-to-rule *q*.

grever [grəve] *vt* to put a strain on ; **grevé d'impôts** crippled by taxes.

gréviste [grevist(ə)] *nm/f* striker.

gribouiller [gribuje] *vt* to scribble, scrawl // *vi* to doodle.

grief [grijɛf] *nm* grievance ; **faire** ~ **à qn de** to reproach sb for.

grièvement [grijɛvmɑ̃] *ad* seriously.

griffe [grif] *nf* claw ; (*fig*) signature.

griffer [grife] *vt* to scratch.

griffonner [grifɔne] *vt* to scribble.

grignoter [griɲɔte] *vt* to nibble *ou* gnaw at.

gril [gril] *nm* steak *ou* grill pan.

grillade [grijad] *nf* grill.

grillage [grijaʒ] *nm* (*treillis*) wire netting ; wire fencing.

grille [grij] *nf* (*portail*) (metal) gate ; (*d'égout*) (metal) grate ; (*fig*) grid.

grille-pain [grijpɛ̃] *nm inv* toaster.

griller [grije] *vt* (*aussi* : **faire** ~: *pain*) to toast ; (: *viande*) to grill ; (*fig* : *ampoule etc*) to burn out, blow.

grillon [grijɔ̃] *nm* cricket.

grimace [grimas] *nf* grimace ; (*pour faire rire*) : **faire des** ~**s** to pull *ou* make faces.

grimer [grime] *vt* to make up.

grimper [grɛ̃pe] *vi, vt* to climb.

grincement [grɛ̃smɑ̃] *nm* grating (noise) ; creaking (noise).

grincer [grɛ̃se] *vi* (*porte, roue*) to grate ; (*plancher*) to creak ; ~ **des dents** to grind one's teeth.

grincheux, euse [grɛ̃ʃø, -øz] *a* grumpy.

grippe [grip] *nf* flu, influenza ; **grippé, e** *a* : **être grippé** to have flu.

gripper [gripe] *vt, vi* to jam.

gris, e [gri, griz] *a* grey ; (*ivre*) tipsy.

grisaille [grizaj] *nf* greyness, dullness.

grisant, e [grizɑ̃, -ɑ̃t] *a* intoxicating, exhilarating.

griser [grize] *vt* to intoxicate.

grisonner [grizɔne] *vi* to be going grey.

grisou [grizu] *nm* firedamp.

grive [griv] *nf* thrush.

grivois, e [grivwa, -waz] *a* saucy.

grog [grɔg] *nm* grog.

grogner [grɔɲe] *vi* to growl ; (*fig*) to grumble.

groin [grwɛ̃] *nm* snout.

grommeler [grɔmle] *vi* to mutter to o.s.

grondement [grɔ̃dmɑ̃] *nm* rumble.

gronder [grɔ̃de] *vi* to rumble ; (*fig* : *révolte*) to be brewing // *vt* to scold.

gros, se [gro, gros] *a* big, large ; (*obèse*) fat ; (*travaux, dégâts*) extensive ; (*large* : *trait, fil*) thick, heavy // *ad* : **risquer/gagner** ~ to risk/win a lot // *nm* (*COMM*) : **le** ~ the wholesale business ; **prix de** ~ wholesale price ; **par** ~ **temps** / ~ **se mer** in rough weather/heavy seas ; **le** ~ **de** the main body of ; the bulk of ; **en** ~ roughly ; (*COMM*) wholesale ; ~ **intestin** large intestine ; ~ **lot** jackpot ; ~ **mot** coarse word, vulgarity ; ~ **plan** (*PHOTO*) close-up ; ~ **sel** cooking salt ; ~ **se caisse** big drum.

groseille [grozɛj] *nf* : ~ (**rouge**) / (**blanche**) red/white currant ; ~ **à maquereau** gooseberry ; **groseillier** *nm* red *ou* white currant bush ; gooseberry bush.

grosse [gros] *a voir* **gros**.

grossesse [grosɛs] *nf* pregnancy.

grosseur [grosœr] *nf* size ; fatness ; (*tumeur*) lump.

grossier, ière [grosje, -jɛr] *a* coarse ; (*travail*) rough ; crude ; (*évident* : *erreur*) gross ; **grossièrement** *ad* coarsely ; roughly, crudely ; (*en gros*) roughly.

grossir [grosir] *vi* (*personne*) to put on weight ; (*fig*) to grow, get bigger ; (*rivière*) to swell // *vt* to increase ; to exaggerate ; (*au microscope*) to magnify ; (*suj* : *vêtement*) : ~ **qn** to make sb look fatter ; **grossissement** *nm* (*optique*) magnification.

grossiste [grosist(ə)] *nm/f* wholesaler.

grosso modo [grosomɔdo] *ad* roughly.

grotte [grɔt] *nf* cave.

grouiller [gruje] *vi* to mill about ; to swarm about ; ~ **de** to be swarming with.

groupe [grup] *nm* group ; ~ **sanguin** blood group.

groupement [grupmɑ̃] *nm* grouping ; group.

grouper [grupe] *vt* to group ; **se** ~ to get together.

gruau [gryo] *nm* : **pain de** ~ wheaten bread.

grue [gry] *nf* crane.

grumeaux [grymo] *nmpl* lumps.

grutier [grytje] *nm* crane driver.

Guadeloupe [gwadlup] *nf* : **la** ~ Guadeloupe.

gué [ge] *nm* ford ; **passer à** ~ to ford.

guenilles [gənij] *nfpl* rags.

guenon [gənɔ̃] *nf* female monkey.

guépard [gepar] *nm* cheetah.

guêpe [gɛp] *nf* wasp.

guêpier [gepje] *nm* (*fig*) trap.

guère [gɛr] *ad* (*avec adjectif, adverbe*) : **ne ...** ~ hardly ; (*avec verbe*) : **ne ...** ~ *tournure négative* + much ; hardly ever ; *tournure négative* + (very) long ; **il n'y a** ~ **que/de** there's hardly anybody (*ou* anything) but/hardly any.

guéridon [geridɔ̃] *nm* pedestal table.

guérilla [gerija] *nf* guerrilla warfare.

guérillero [gerijero] *nm* guerrilla.

guérir [gerir] *vt* (*personne, maladie*) to cure ; (*membre, plaie*) to heal // *vi* (*personne*) to recover, be cured ; (*plaie, chagrin*) to heal ; ~ **de** to be cured of, recover from ; ~ **qn de** to cure sb of ; **guérison** *nf* curing ; healing ; recovery ; **guérissable** *a* curable ; **guérisseur, euse** *nm/f* healer.

guérite [geʀit] *nf* sentry box.

guerre [gɛʀ] *nf* war ; (*méthode*) : ~ **atomique/de tranchées** atomic/ trench warfare *q* ; **en** ~ at war ; **faire la** ~ **à** to wage war against ; **de** ~ **lasse** finally ; ~ **civile/ mondiale** civil/world war ; ~ **d'usure** war of attrition ; **guerrier, ière** *a* warlike // *nm/f* warrior ; **guerroyer** *vi* to wage war.

guet [gɛ] *nm*: **faire le** ~ to be on the watch *ou* look-out.

guet-apens [gɛtapɑ̃] *nm* ambush.

guêtre [gɛtʀ(ə)] *nf* gaiter.

guetter [gete] *vt* (*épier*) to watch (intently) ; (*attendre*) to watch (out) for ; to be lying in wait for ; **guetteur** *nm* look-out.

gueule [gœl] *nf* mouth ; (*fam*) face ; mouth ; ~ **de bois** (*fam*) hangover.

gueuler [gœle] *vi* (*fam*) to bawl.

gueux [gø] *nm* beggar ; rogue.

gui [gi] *nm* mistletoe.

guichet [giʃɛ] *nm* (*de bureau, banque*) counter, window ; (*d'une porte*) wicket, hatch ; **les** ~**s** (*à la gare, au théâtre*) the ticket office ; **guichetier, ière** *nm/f* counter clerk.

guide [gid] *nm* guide.

guider [gide] *vt* to guide.

guidon [gidɔ̃] *nm* handlebars *pl*.

guignol [giɲɔl] *nm* ≈ Punch and Judy show ; (*fig*) clown.

guillemets [gijmɛ] *nmpl*: **entre** ~ in inverted commas *ou* quotation marks ; ~ **de répétition** ditto marks.

guilleret, te [gijʀɛ, -ɛt] *a* perky, bright.

guillotine [gijɔtin] *nf* guillotine ; **guillotiner** *vt* to guillotine.

guindé, e [gɛ̃de] *a* stiff, starchy.

guirlande [giʀlɑ̃d] *nf* garland ; (*de papier*) paper chain.

guise [giz] *nf*: **à votre** ~ as you wish *ou* please ; **en** ~ **de** by way of.

guitare [gitaʀ] *nf* guitar ; **guitariste** *nm/f* guitarist, guitar player.

gustatif, ive [gystatif, -iv] *a* gustatory ; *voir* **papille**.

guttural, e, aux [gytyʀal, -o] *a* guttural.

Guyane [gɥijan] *n*: **la** ~ Guiana.

gymkhana [ʒimkana] *nm* rally.

gymnase [ʒimnɑz] *nm* gym(nasium).

gymnaste [ʒimnast(ə)] *nm/f* gymnast.

gymnastique [ʒimnastik] *nf* gymnastics *sg* ; (*au réveil etc*) keep fit exercises *pl*.

gynécologie [ʒinekɔlɔʒi] *nf* gynaecology ; **gynécologue** *nm/f* gynaecologist.

gypse [ʒips(ə)] *nm* gypsum.

H

h. *abr de* **heure.**

habile [abil] *a* skilful ; (*malin*) clever ; ~**té** *nf* skill, skilfulness ; cleverness.

habilité, e [abilite] *a*: ~ **à faire** entitled to do, empowered to do.

habillé, e [abije] *a* dressed ; (*chic*) dressy ; (*TECH*): ~ **de** covered with ; encased in.

habillement [abijmɑ̃] *nm* clothes *pl* ; (*profession*) clothing industry.

habiller [abije] *vt* to dress ; (*fournir en vêtements*) to clothe ; **s'**~ to dress (o.s.) ; (*se déguiser, mettre des vêtements chic*) to dress up ; **s'**~ **de/en** to dress in/dress up as ; **s'**~ **chez/à** to buy one's clothes from/at.

habit [abi] *nm* outfit ; ~**s** *nmpl* (*vêtements*) clothes ; ~ **(de soirée)** tails *pl* ; evening dress.

habitable [abitabl(ə)] *a* (in)habitable.

habitacle [abitakl(ə)] *nm* cockpit ; (*AUTO*) passenger cell.

habitant, e [abitɑ̃, -ɑ̃t] *nm/f* inhabitant ; (*d'une maison*) occupant, occupier ; **loger chez l'**~ to stay with the locals.

habitat [abita] *nm* housing conditions *pl* ; (*BOT, ZOOL*) habitat.

habitation [abitasjɔ̃] *nf* living ; residence, home ; house ; ~**s à loyer modéré (HLM)** low-rent housing *sg*, ≈ council flats.

habité, e [abite] *a* inhabited ; lived in.

habiter [abite] *vt* to live in ; (*suj: sentiment*) to dwell in // *vi*: ~ **à/dans** to live in *ou* at/in.

habitude [abityd] *nf* habit ; **avoir l'**~ **de faire** to be in the habit of doing ; (*expérience*) to be used to doing ; **d'**~ usually ; **comme d'**~ as usual.

habitué, e [abitɥe] *a*: **être** ~ **à** to be used *ou* accustomed to // *nm/f* regular visitor ; regular (customer).

habituel, le [abitɥɛl] *a* usual.

habituer [abitɥe] *vt*: ~ **qn à** to get sb used to ; **s'**~ **à** to get used to.

*hâbleur, euse [ˈɑblœʀ, -øz] *a* boastful.

*hache [ˈaʃ] *nf* axe.

*haché, e [ˈaʃe] *a* minced ; (*fig*) jerky.

*hacher [ˈaʃe] *vt* (*viande*) to mince ; (*persil*) to chop.

*hachis [ˈaʃi] *nm* mince *q*.

*hachisch [ˈaʃiʃ] *nm* hashish.

*hachoir [ˈaʃwaʀ] *nm* chopper ; (*meat*) mincer ; chopping board.

*hachures [ˈaʃyʀ] *nfpl* hatching *sg*.

*hagard, e [ˈagaʀ, -aʀd(ə)] *a* wild, distraught.

*haie [ˈɛ] *nf* hedge ; (*SPORT*) hurdle ; (*fig: rang*) line, row ; **200 m** ~**s** 200 m hurdles ; ~ **d'honneur** guard of honour.

*haillons [ˈajɔ̃] *nmpl* rags.

*haine [ˈɛn] *nf* hatred ; **haineux, euse** *a* full of hatred.

*haïr [ˈaiʀ] *vt* to detest, hate.

*halage [ˈalaʒ] *nm*: **chemin de** ~ towpath.

*hâle [ˈɑl] *nm* (sun)tan ; ***hâlé, e** *a* (sun)tanned, sunburnt.

haleine [alɛn] *nf* breath ; **hors d'**~ out of breath ; **tenir en** ~ to hold spellbound ; to keep in suspense ; **de longue** ~ *a* long-term.

*haleter [ˈalte] *vt* to pant.

*hall [ˈol] *nm* hall.

hallali [alali] *nm* kill.

*halle [ˈal] *nf* (covered) market ; ~**s** *nfpl* central food market *sg*.

hallucinant, e [alysinɑ̃, -ɑ̃t] *a* staggering.
hallucination [alysinɑsjɔ̃] *nf* hallucination.
halluciné, e [alysine] *nm/f* person suffering from hallucinations; (*raving*) lunatic.
*halo ['alo] *nm* halo.
*halte ['alt(ə)] *nf* stop, break; stopping place; (*RAIL*) halt // *excl* stop!; faire ~ to stop.
haltère [altɛR] *nm* dumbbell, barbell; ~s *nmpl* (*activité*) weight lifting *sg*; haltérophile *nm/f* weight lifter.
*hamac ['amak] *nm* hammock.
*hameau, x ['amo] *nm* hamlet.
hameçon [amsɔ̃] *nm* (fish) hook.
*hampe ['ɑ̃p] *nf* shaft.
*hamster ['amstɛR] *nm* hamster.
*hanche ['ɑ̃ʃ] *nf* hip.
*hand-ball ['ɑdbal] *nm* handball.
*handicap ['ɑ̃dikap] *nm* handicap; *~é, e a* handicapped // *nm/f* physically (*ou* mentally) handicapped person; ~é moteur spastic; *~er vt* to handicap.
*hangar ['ɑ̃gaR] *nm* shed.
*hanneton ['antɔ̃] *nm* cockchafer.
*hanter ['ɑ̃te] *vt* to haunt.
*hantise ['ɑ̃tiz] *nf* obsessive fear.
*happer ['ape] *vt* to snatch; (*suj: train etc*) to hit.
*haranguer ['aRɑ̃ge] *vt* to harangue.
*haras ['aRɑ] *nm* stud farm.
harassant, e ['aRasɑ̃, -ɑ̃t] *a* exhausting.
*harceler ['aRsəle] *vt* (*MIL, CHASSE*) to harass, harry; (*importuner*) to plague.
*hardes ['aRd(ə)] *nfpl* rags.
*hardi, e ['aRdi] *a* bold, daring.
*hareng ['aRɑ̃] *nm* herring.
*hargne ['aRɲ(ə)] *nf* aggressiveness.
*haricot ['aRiko] *nm* bean; ~ vert/blanc French/haricot bean.
harmonica [aRmɔnika] *nm* mouth organ.
harmonie [aRmɔni] *nf* harmony; harmonieux, euse *a* harmonious; harmonique *nm ou nf* harmonic; harmoniser *vt* to harmonize.
*harnaché, e ['aRnaʃe] *a* (*fig*) rigged out.
*harnacher ['aRnaʃe] *vt* to harness.
*harnais ['aRnɛ] *nm* harness.
*harpe ['aRp(ə)] *nf* harp; *harpiste *nm/f* harpist.
*harpon ['aRpɔ̃] *nm* harpoon; *harponner *vt* to harpoon; (*fam*) to collar.
*hasard ['azaR] *nm*: le ~ chance, fate; un ~ a coincidence; a stroke of luck; au ~ aimlessly; at random; haphazardly; par ~ by chance; à tout ~ just in case; on the off chance.
*hasarder ['azaRde] *vt* (*mot*) to venture; (*fortune*) to risk; se ~ à faire to risk doing, venture to do.
*hasardeux, euse ['azaRdǿ, -ǿz] *a* hazardous, risky; (*hypothèse*) rash.
*haschisch ['aʃiʃ] *nm* hashish.
*hâte ['ɑt] *nf* haste; à la ~ hurriedly, hastily; en ~ posthaste, with all possible speed; avoir ~ de to be eager *ou* anxious to; *hâter *vt* to hasten; se hâter to hurry; se hâter de to hurry *ou* hasten to.

*hâtif, ive ['ɑtif, -iv] *a* hurried; hasty; (*légume*) early.
*hausse ['os] *nf* rise, increase; (*de fusil*) backsight adjuster; en ~ rising.
*hausser ['ose] *vt* to raise; ~ les épaules to shrug (one's shoulders).
*haut, e ['o, 'ot] *a* high; (*grand*) tall; (*son, voix*) high(-pitched) // *ad* high // *nm* top (part); de 3 m de ~ 3 m high, 3 m in height; des ~s et des bas ups and downs; en ~ lieu in high places; à ~e voix aloud, out loud; du ~ de from the top of; de ~ en bas up and down; downwards; plus ~ higher up, further up; (*dans un texte*) above; (*parler*) louder; en ~ up above; at (*ou* to) the top; (*dans une maison*) upstairs; en ~ de at the top of; la ~e couture/coiffure haute couture/coiffure; ~e fidélité hi-fi, high fidelity.
*hautain, e ['otɛ̃, -ɛn] *a* (*personne, regard*) haughty.
*hautbois ['obwɑ] *nm* oboe.
*haut-de-forme ['odfɔRm(ə)] *nm* top hat.
*hautement ['otmɑ̃] *ad* highly.
*hauteur ['otœR] *nf* height; (*GÉO*) height, hill; (*fig*) loftiness; haughtiness; à ~ des yeux at eye level; à la ~ de (*sur la même ligne*) level with; by; (*fig*) equal to; à la ~ (*fig*) up to it, equal to the task.
*haut-fond ['ofɔ̃] *nm* shallow, shoal.
*haut-fourneau ['ofuRno] *nm* blast *ou* smelting furnace.
*haut-le-cœur ['olkœR] *nm inv* retch, heave.
*haut-parleur ['opaRlœR] *nm* (loud)speaker.
*hâve ['ɑv] *a* gaunt.
*havre ['ɑvR(ə)] *nm* haven.
*Haye ['ɛ] *n*: la ~ the Hague.
*hayon ['ɛjɔ̃] *nm* tailgate.
hebdomadaire [ɛdbɔmadɛR] *a, nm* weekly.
héberger [ebɛRʒe] *vt* to accommodate, lodge; (*réfugiés*) to take in.
hébété, e [ebete] *a* dazed.
hébraïque [ebRaik] *a* Hebrew, Hebraic.
hébreu, x [ebRø] *am, nm* Hebrew.
H.E.C. *sigle fpl* = Hautes études commerciales.
hécatombe [ekatɔ̃b] *nf* slaughter.
hectare [ɛktaR] *nm* hectare, 10,000 square metres.
hectolitre [ɛktolitR] *nm* hectolitre.
hégémonie [eʒemɔni] *nf* hegemony.
*hein ['ɛ̃] *excl* eh?
*hélas ['elɑs] *excl* alas! // *ad* unfortunately.
*héler ['ele] *vt* to hail.
hélice [elis] *nf* propeller.
hélicoïdal, e, aux [elikɔidal, -o] *a* helical; helicoid.
hélicoptère [elikɔptɛR] *nm* helicopter.
héliogravure [eljogRavyR] *nf* heliogravure.
héliport [elipɔR] *nm* heliport.
héliporté, e [elipɔRte] *a* transported by helicopter.
hellénique [elenik] *a* Hellenic.
helvétique [ɛlvetik] *a* Swiss.

hématome [ematom] nm haematoma.
hémicycle [emisikl(ə)] nm semicircle ; (POL): l'~ ≈ the benches (of the Commons).
hémiplégie [emipleʒi] nf paralysis of one side, hemiplegia.
hémisphère [emisfɛʀ] nf: ~ nord/sud northern/southern hemisphere.
hémophile [emɔfil] a haemophiliac.
hémorragie [emɔʀaʒi] nf bleeding q, haemorrhage.
hémorroïdes [emɔʀɔid] nfpl piles, haemorrhoids.
*__hennir__ ['eniʀ] vi to neigh, whinny.
hépatite [epatit] nf hepatitis, liver infection.
herbe [ɛʀb(ə)] nf grass ; (CULIN, MÉD) herb ; en ~ unripe ; (fig) budding ; **herbeux, euse** a grassy ; **herbicide** nm weed-killer ; **herbier** nm herbarium ; **herboriser** vi to collect plants, botanize ; **herboriste** nm/f herbalist ; **herboristerie** nf herbalist's shop ; herb trade.
*__hère__ ['ɛʀ] nm: pauvre ~ poor wretch.
héréditaire [eʀeditɛʀ] a hereditary.
hérédité [eʀedite] nf heredity.
hérésie [eʀezi] nf heresy ; **hérétique** nm/f heretic.
*__hérissé, e__ ['eʀise] a bristling ; ~ de spiked with ; (fig) bristling with.
*__hérisser__ ['eʀise] vt: ~ qn (fig) to ruffle sb ; se ~ vi to bristle, bristle up.
*__hérisson__ ['eʀisɔ] nm hedgehog.
héritage [eʀitaʒ] nm inheritance ; (fig) heritage ; legacy ; **faire un (petit)** ~ to come into (a little) money.
hériter [eʀite] vi: ~ de qch (de qn) to inherit sth (from sb) ; ~ de qn to inherit sb's property ; **héritier, ière** nm/f heir/heiress.
hermétique [ɛʀmetik] a airtight ; watertight ; (fig) abstruse ; impenetrable ; ~ment ad tightly, hermetically.
hermine [ɛʀmin] nf ermine.
*__hernie__ ['ɛʀni] nf hernia.
héroïne [eʀɔin] nf heroine ; (drogue) heroin.
héroïque [eʀɔik] a heroic.
héroïsme [eʀɔism(ə)] nm heroism.
*__héron__ ['eʀɔ̃] nm heron.
*__héros__ ['eʀo] nm hero.
*__herse__ ['ɛʀs(ə)] nf harrow ; (de château) portcullis.
hésitant, e [ezitɑ̃, -ɑ̃t] a hesitant.
hésitation [ezitɑsjɔ̃] nf hesitation.
hésiter [ezite] vi: ~ (à faire) to hesitate (to do).
hétéroclite [eteʀɔklit] a heterogeneous ; (objets) sundry.
*__hêtre__ ['ɛtʀ(ə)] nm beech.
heure [œʀ] nf hour ; (SCOL) period ; (moment, moment fixé) time ; **c'est l'~** it's time ; **quelle ~ est-il?** what time is it? ; **être à l'~** to be on time ; (montre) to be right ; **mettre à l'~** to set right ; **à toute ~** at any time ; **24** ~s **sur 24** round the clock, 24 hours a day ; **à l'~ qu'il est** at this time (of day) ; by now ; **sur l'~** at once ; **locale/d'été** local/summer time ; ~s **de bureau** office hours ; ~s **supplémentaires** overtime sg.

heureusement [œʀøzmɑ̃] ad (par bonheur) fortunately, luckily.
heureux, euse [œʀø, -øz] a happy ; (chanceux) lucky, fortunate ; (judicieux) felicitous, fortunate.
*__heurt__ ['œʀ] nm (choc) collision ; ~s nmpl (fig) clashes.
*__heurté, e__ ['œʀte] a (fig) jerky, uneven.
*__heurter__ ['œʀte] vt (mur) to strike, hit ; (personne) to collide with ; (fig) to go against, upset ; se ~ à vt to collide with ; (fig) to come up against ; **heurtoir** nm door knocker.
hexagone [ɛgzagɔn] nm hexagon.
*__hiatus__ ['jatys] nm hiatus.
hiberner [ibɛʀne] vi to hibernate.
*__hibou, x__ ['ibu] nm owl.
*__hideux, euse__ ['idø, -øz] a hideous.
hier [jɛʀ] ad yesterday ; ~ **matin/soir** yesterday morning/ evening ; **toute la journée d'**~ all day yesterday ; **toute la matinée d'**~ all yesterday morning.
*__hiérarchie__ ['jeʀaʀʃi] nf hierarchy ; *__hiérarchique__ a hierarchic ; *__hiérarchiser__ vt to' organize into a hierarchy.
hiéroglyphe [jeʀɔglif] nm hieroglyphic.
hilare [ilaʀ] a mirthful ; **hilarité** nf hilarity, mirth.
hindou, e [ɛ̃du] a, nm/f Hindu ; Indian.
hippique [ipik] a equestrian, horse cpd.
hippisme [ipism(ə)] nm (horse) riding.
hippodrome [ipɔdʀom] nm racecourse.
hippopotame [ipɔpɔtam] nm hippopotamus.
hirondelle [iʀɔ̃dɛl] nf swallow.
hirsute [iʀsyt] a hairy ; shaggy ; tousled.
hispanique [ispanik] a Hispanic.
*__hisser__ ['ise] vt to hoist, haul up ; se ~ sur to haul o.s. up onto.
histoire [istwaʀ] nf (science, événements) history ; (anecdote, récit, mensonge) story ; (affaire) business q ; (chichis: gén pl) fuss q ; ~s nfpl (ennuis) trouble sg ; **historien, ne** nm/f historian ; **historique** a historic.
hiver [ivɛʀ] nm winter ; ~nal, e, aux a winter cpd ; wintry ; ~ner vi to winter.
H.L.M. sigle m ou f voir **habitation**.
*__hocher__ ['ɔʃe] vt: ~ **la tête** to nod ; (signe négatif ou dubitatif) to shake one's head.
*__hochet__ ['ɔʃɛ] nm rattle.
*__hockey__ ['ɔkɛ] nm: ~ **(sur glace/gazon)** (ice/field) hockey ; *__hockeyeur__ nm hockey player.
holding ['ɔldiŋ] nm holding company.
hold-up ['ɔldœp] nm inv hold-up.
*__hollandais, e__ ['ɔlɑdɛ, -ɛz] a, nm (langue) Dutch // nm/f: **H**~, e Dutchman/ woman ; **les H**~ the Dutch.
*__Hollande__ ['ɔlɑd] nf Holland.
*__homard__ ['ɔmaʀ] nm lobster.
homéopathie [ɔmeɔpati] nf homoeopathy ; **homéopathique** a homoeopathic.
homérique [ɔmeʀik] a Homeric.
homicide [ɔmisid] nm murder // nm/f murderer/eress ; ~ **involontaire** manslaughter.
hommage [ɔmaʒ] nm tribute ; ~s nmpl: **présenter ses** ~s to pay one's respects ;

rendre ~ à to pay tribute *ou* homage to;
faire ~ de qch à qn to present sb with
sth.

homme [ɔm] *nm* man; ~ d'affaires
businessman; ~ d'État statesman; ~ de
main hired man; ~ de paille stooge; ~-
grenouille *nm* frogman; ~-orchestre *nm*
one-man band.

homogène [ɔmɔʒɛn] *a* homogeneous;
homogénéité *nf* homogeneity.

homologue [ɔmɔlɔg] *nm/f* counterpart,
opposite number.

homologué, e [ɔmɔlɔge] *a* (SPORT)
officially recognized, ratified; (*tarif*)
authorized.

homonyme [ɔmɔnim] *nm* (LING)
homonym; (*d'une personne*) namesake.

homosexualité [ɔmɔsɛksɥalite] *nf*
homosexuality.

homosexuel, le [ɔmɔsɛksɥɛl] *a*
homosexual.

*****Hongrie** [ɔ̃gʀi] *nf*: la ~ Hungary;
*****hongrois, e** *a*, *nm/f*, *nm* (*langue*)
Hungarian.

honnête [ɔnɛt] *a* (*intègre*) honest; (*juste,
satisfaisant*) fair; ~ment *ad* honestly;
~té *nf* honesty.

honneur [ɔnœʀ] *nm* honour; (*mérite*): l'~
lui revient the credit is his; en l'~ de
in honour of; (*événement*) on the occasion
of; faire ~ à (*engagements*) to honour;
(*famille*) to be a credit to; (*fig: repas etc*)
to do justice to; être à l'~ to be in the
place of honour; être en ~ to be in
favour; membre d'~ honorary member;
table d'~ top table.

honorable [ɔnɔʀabl(ə)] *a* worthy,
honourable; (*suffisant*) decent; ~ment *ad*
honorably; decently.

honoraire [ɔnɔʀɛʀ] *a* honorary; ~s *nmpl*
fees *pl*; professeur ~ professor emeritus.

honorer [ɔnɔʀe] *vt* to honour; (*estimer*) to
hold in high regard; (*faire honneur à*) to
do credit to; s'~ de to pride o.s. upon;
honorifique *a* honorary.

*****honte** [ɔ̃t] *nf* shame; avoir ~ de to be
ashamed of; faire ~ à qn to make sb
(feel) ashamed; *****honteux, euse** *a*
ashamed; (*conduite, acte*) shameful,
disgraceful.

hôpital, aux [ɔpital, -o] *nm* hospital.

*****hoquet** [ɔkɛ] *nm* hiccough; avoir le ~
to have (the) hiccoughs; **hoqueter** *vi* to
hiccough.

horaire [ɔʀɛʀ] *a* hourly // *nm* timetable,
schedule.

*****horions** [ɔʀjɔ̃] *nmpl* blows.

horizon [ɔʀizɔ̃] *nm* horizon; (*paysage*)
landscape, view; sur l'~ on the skyline
ou horizon.

horizontal, e, aux [ɔʀizɔ̃tal, -o] *a*
horizontal; ~ement *ad* horizontally.

horloge [ɔʀlɔʒ] *nf* clock; l'~ parlante the
speaking clock; **horloger, ère** *nm/f*
watchmaker; clockmaker; ~rie *nf* watch-
making; watchmaker's (shop);
clockmaker's (shop); pièces d'~rie
watch parts *ou* components.

*****hormis** [ɔʀmi] *prép* save.

hormonal, e, aux [ɔʀmɔnal, -o] *a*
hormonal.

hormone [ɔʀmɔn] *nf* hormone.

horoscope [ɔʀɔskɔp] *nm* horoscope.

horreur [ɔʀœʀ] *nf* horror; avoir ~ de to
loathe *ou* detest; **horrible** *a* horrible;
horrifier *vt* to horrify.

horripiler [ɔʀipile] *vt* to exasperate.

*****hors** [ɔʀ] *prép* except (for); ~ de out of;
~ pair outstanding; ~ de propos
inopportune; être ~ de soi to be beside
o.s.; ~-bord *nm inv* speedboat (with
outboard motor); ~-concours *a* ineligible
to compete; (*fig*) in a class of one's own;
~-d'œuvre *nm inv* hors d'œuvre; ~-jeu
nm inv offside; ~-la-loi *nm inv* outlaw;
~-taxe *a* duty-free; ~-texte *nm inv* plate.

hortensia [ɔʀtɑ̃sja] *nm* hydrangea.

horticulteur, trice [ɔʀtikyltœʀ, -tʀis]
nm/f horticulturalist.

horticulture [ɔʀtikyltyʀ] *nf* horticulture.

hospice [ɔspis] *nm* (*de vieillards*) home.

hospitalier, ière [ɔspitalje, -jɛʀ] *a*
(*accueillant*) hospitable; (MÉD: *service,
centre*) hospital *cpd*.

hospitaliser [ɔspitalize] *vt* to take (*ou*
send) to hospital, hospitalize.

hospitalité [ɔspitalite] *nf* hospitality.

hostie [ɔsti] *nf* host.

hostile [ɔstil] *a* hostile; **hostilité** *nf*
hostility; **hostilités** *nfpl* hostilities.

hôte [ot] *nm* (*maître de maison*) host;
(*invité*) guest; (*client*) patron; (*fig*)
inhabitant, occupant.

hôtel [otɛl] *nm* hotel; aller à l'~ to stay
in a hotel; ~ (*particulier*) (*private*)
mansion; ~ de ville town hall; **hôtelier,
ière** *a* hotel *cpd* // *nm/f* hotelier, hotel-
keeper; ~lerie *nf* hotel business;
(*auberge*) inn.

hôtesse [otɛs] *nf* hostess; ~ de l'air air
hostess *ou* stewardess.

*****hotte** [ɔt] *nf* (*panier*) basket (*carried on
the back*); (*de cheminée*) hood; ~
aspirante cooker hood.

*****houblon** [ublɔ̃] *nm* (BOT) hop; (*pour la
bière*) hops *pl*.

*****houille** [uj] *nf* coal; ~ blanche
hydroelectric power; *****houiller, ère** *a* coal
cpd; coal-bearing.

*****houle** [ul] *nf* swell.

*****houlette** [ulɛt] *nf*: sous la ~ de under
the guidance of.

*****houleux, euse** [ulø, -øz] *a* heavy,
swelling; (*fig*) stormy, turbulent.

*****houppe** [up] *nf*, *****houppette** [upɛt] *nf*
powder puff.

*****hourra** [uʀa] *nm* cheer // *excl* hurrah!

*****houspiller** [uspije] *vt* to scold.

*****housse** [us] *nf* cover; dust cover; loose
ou stretch cover; ~ (*penderie*) hanging
wardrobe.

*****houx** [u] *nm* holly.

*****hublot** [yblo] *nm* porthole.

*****huche** [yʃ] *nf*: ~ à pain bread bin.

*****huées** [ɥe] *nfpl* boos.

*****huer** [ɥe] *vt* to boo.

huile [ɥil] *nf* oil; (ART) oil painting; (*fam*)
bigwig; ~ de foie de morue cod-liver oil;
~ de table salad oil; **huiler** *vt* to oil;
huileux, euse *a* oily.

huis [ɥi] *nm*: à ~ clos in camera.

huissier [ɥisje] *nm* usher ; (*JUR*) ≈ bailiff.
*****huit** [ɥit] *num* eight ; **samedi en ~** a week on Saturday ; **dans ~ jours** in a week('s time) ; **une huitaine de jours** a week or so ; *****huitième** *num* eighth.
huître [ɥitʀ(ə)] *nf* oyster.

humain, e [ymɛ̃, -ɛn] *a* human ; (*compatissant*) humane // *nm* human (being) ; **humaniser** *vt* to humanize ; **humanitaire** *a* humanitarian ; **humanité** *nf* humanity.
humble [œ̃bl(ə)] *a* humble.
humecter [ymɛkte] *vt* to dampen ; **s'~ les lèvres** to moisten one's lips.
*****humer** ['yme] *vt* to smell ; to inhale.
humeur [ymœʀ] *nf* mood ; (*tempérament*) temper ; (*irritation*) bad temper ; **de bonne/mauvaise ~** in a good/bad mood.
humide [ymid] *a* damp ; (*main, yeux*) moist ; (*climat, chaleur*) humid ; (*route*) wet ; **humidificateur** *nm* humidifier ; **humidifier** *vt* to humidify ; **humidité** *nf* humidity ; dampness ; **traces d'humidité** traces of moisture *ou* damp.
humiliation [ymiljasjɔ̃] *nf* humiliation.
humilier [ymilje] *vt* to humiliate.
humilité [ymilite] *nf* humility, humbleness.
humoriste [ymɔʀist(ə)] *nm/f* humorist.
humoristique [ymɔʀistik] *a* humorous ; humoristic.
humour [ymuʀ] *nm* humour ; **avoir de l'~** to have a sense of humour ; **~ noir** sick humour.
*****huppé, e** ['ype] *a* crested ; (*fam*) posh.
*****hurlement** ['yʀləmɑ̃] *nm* howling *q*, howl, yelling *q*, yell.
*****hurler** ['yʀle] *vi* to howl, yell.
hurluberlu [yʀlybɛʀly] *nm* (*péj*) crank.
*****hutte** ['yt] *nf* hut.
hybride [ibʀid] *a* hybrid.
hydratant, e [idʀatɑ̃, -ɑ̃t] *a* (*crème*) moisturizing.
hydrate [idʀat] *nm*: **~s de carbone** carbohydrates.
hydraulique [idʀolik] *a* hydraulic.
hydravion [idʀavjɔ̃] *nm* seaplane, hydroplane.
hydro... [idʀo] *préfixe*: **~carbures** *nmpl* hydrocarbon oils ; **~cution** *nf* immersion syncope ; **~-électrique** *a* hydroelectric ; **~gène** *nm* hydrogen ; **~glisseur** *nm* hydroplane ; **~graphie** *nf* (*fleuves*) hydrography ; **~phile** *a voir* **coton**.
hyène [jɛn] *nf* hyena.
hygiène [iʒjɛn] *nf* hygiene ; **~ intime** personal hygiene ; **hygiénique** *a* hygienic.
hymne [imn(ə)] *nm* hymn ; **~ national** national anthem.
hypermarché [ipɛʀmaʀʃe] *nm* hypermarket.
hypermétrope [ipɛʀmetʀɔp] *a* longsighted, hypermetropic.
hypertension [ipɛʀtɑ̃sjɔ̃] *nf* high blood pressure, hypertension.
hypnose [ipnoz] *nf* hypnosis ; **hypnotique** *a* hypnotic ; **hypnotiser** *vt* to hypnotize.
hypocrisie [ipɔkʀizi] *nf* hypocrisy.
hypocrite [ipɔkʀit] *a* hypocritical // *nm/f* hypocrite.

hypotension [ipotɑ̃sjɔ̃] *nf* low blood pressure, hypotension.
hypothécaire [ipotekɛʀ] *a* hypothecary ; **garantie/prêt ~** mortgage security/loan.
hypothèque [ipotɛk] *nf* mortgage ; **hypothéquer** *vt* to mortgage.
hypothèse [ipotez] *nf* hypothesis ; **hypothétique** *a* hypothetical.
hystérie [isteʀi] *nf* hysteria ; **hystérique** *a* hysterical.

I

ibérique [ibeʀik] *a*: **la péninsule ~** the Iberian peninsula.
iceberg [isbɛʀg] *nm* iceberg.
ici [isi] *ad* here ; **jusqu'~** as far as this ; until now ; **d'~ là** by then ; in the meantime ; **d'~ peu** before long.
icône [ikon] *nf* icon.
iconographie [ikɔnɔgʀafi] *nf* iconography ; (collection of) illustrations.
idéal, e, aux [ideal, -o] *a* ideal // *nm* ideal ; ideals *pl* ; **~iser** *vt* to idealize ; **~iste** a idealistic // *nm/f* idealist.
idée [ide] *nf* idea ; **avoir dans l'~ que** to have an idea that ; **~ fixe** idée fixe, obsession ; **~s noires** black *ou* dark thoughts ; **~s reçues** accepted ideas.
identification [idɑ̃tifikasjɔ̃] *nf* identification.
identifier [idɑ̃tifje] *vt* to identify ; **~ qch/qn à** to identify sth/sb with ; **s'~ à** (*héros etc*) to identify with.
identique [idɑ̃tik] *a*: **~ (à)** identical (to).
identité [idɑ̃tite] *nf* identity.
idéologie [ideɔlɔʒi] *nf* ideology.
idiomatique [idjɔmatik] *a*: **expression ~** idiom, idiomatic expression.
idiot, e [idjo, idjɔt] *a* idiotic // *nm/f* idiot ; **idiotie** [-si] *nf* idiocy ; idiotic remark *etc*.
idiotisme [idjɔtism(ə)] *nm* idiom, idiomatic phrase.
idolâtrer [idolatʀe] *vt* to idolize.
idole [idɔl] *nf* idol.
idylle [idil] *nf* idyll ; **idyllique** *a* idyllic.
if [if] *nm* yew.
I.F.O.P. [ifɔp] *sigle m* = *Institut français d'opinion publique*.
igloo [iglu] *nm* igloo.
ignare [iɲaʀ] *a* ignorant.
ignifugé, e [iɲifyʒe] *a* fireproof(ed).
ignoble [iɲɔbl(ə)] *a* vile.
ignominie [iɲɔmini] *nf* ignominy ; ignominious *ou* base act.
ignorance [iɲɔʀɑ̃s] *nf* ignorance.
ignorant, e [iɲɔʀɑ̃, -ɑ̃t] *a* ignorant.
ignorer [iɲɔʀe] *vt* (*ne pas connaître*) not to know, be unaware *ou* ignorant of ; (*être sans expérience de: plaisir, guerre etc*) not to know about, have no experience of ; (*bouder: personne*) to ignore ; **j'ignore comment/si** I do not know how/if ; **~ que** to be unaware that, not to know that.
il [il] *pronom* he ; (*animal, chose, en tournure impersonnelle*) it ; NB: *en anglais les navires et les pays sont en général assimilés aux femelles, et les bébés aux choses, si le sexe n'est pas spécifié ;* **~s** they ; **il neige** it's snowing ; *voir aussi* **avoir**.

île [il] *nf* island ; **les ~s anglo-normandes** the Channel Islands ; **les ~s Britanniques** the British Isles.

illégal, e, aux [ilegal, -o] *a* illegal, unlawful ; **~ité** *nf* illegality, unlawfulness ; **être dans l'~ité** to be outside the law.

illégitime [ileʒitim] *a* illegitimate ; (*optimisme, sévérité*) unjustified ; unwarranted ; **illégitimité** *nf* illegitimacy ; **gouverner dans l'illégitimité** to rule illegally.

illettré, e [iletʀe] *a, nm/f* illiterate.

illicite [ilisit] *a* illicit.

illimité, e [ilimite] *a* (*immense*) boundless, unlimited ; (*congé, durée*) indefinite, unlimited.

illisible [ilizibl(ə)] *a* illegible ; (*roman*) unreadable.

illogique [iloʒik] *a* illogical.

illumination [ilyminɑsjɔ̃] *nf* illumination, floodlighting ; flash of inspiration ; **~s** *nfpl* illuminations, lights.

illuminer [ilymine] *vt* to light up ; (*monument, rue: pour une fête*) to illuminate, floodlight ; **s'~** *vi* to light up.

illusion [ilyzjɔ̃] *nf* illusion ; **se faire des ~s** to delude o.s. ; **faire ~** to delude *ou* fool people ; **~ d'optique** optical illusion ; **illusionniste** *nm/f* conjuror ; **illusoire** *a* illusory, illusive.

illustrateur [ilystʀatœʀ] *nm* illustrator.

illustration [ilystʀɑsjɔ̃] *nf* illustration ; (*d'un ouvrage: photos*) illustrations *pl*.

illustre [ilystʀ(ə)] *a* illustrious, renowned.

illustré, e [ilystʀe] *a* illustrated // *nm* illustrated magazine ; comic.

illustrer [ilystʀe] *vt* to illustrate ; **s'~** to become famous, win fame.

îlot [ilo] *nm* small island, islet ; (*de maisons*) block.

image [imaʒ] *nf* (*gén*) picture ; (*comparaison, ressemblance, OPTIQUE*) image ; **~ de marque** brand image ; (*d'un politicien*) public image ; **~ pieuse** holy picture ; **imagé, e** *a* full of imagery.

imaginaire [imaʒinɛʀ] *a* imaginary.

imagination [imaʒinɑsjɔ̃] *nf* imagination ; (*chimère*) fancy ; **avoir de l'~** to be imaginative, have a good imagination.

imaginer [imaʒine] *vt* to imagine ; (*inventer: expédient, mesure*) to devise, think up ; **s'~** *vt* (*se figurer: scène etc*) to imagine, picture ; **s'~ que** to imagine that ; **~ de faire** (*se mettre dans l'idée de*) to dream up the idea of doing.

imbattable [ɛ̃batabl(ə)] *a* unbeatable.

imbécile [ɛ̃besil] *a* idiotic // *nm/f* idiot ; (*MÉD*) imbecile ; **imbécillité** *nf* idiocy ; imbecility ; idiotic action (*ou* remark *etc*).

imberbe [ɛ̃bɛʀb(ə)] *a* beardless.

imbiber [ɛ̃bibe] *vt:* **~ qch de** to moisten *ou* wet sth with ; **s'~ de** to become saturated with.

imbriquer [ɛ̃bʀike] **s'~** *vi* to overlap (each other) ; (*fig*) to become interlinked *ou* interwoven.

imbu, e [ɛ̃by] *a:* **~ de** full of.

imbuvable [ɛ̃byvabl(ə)] *a* undrinkable.

imitateur, trice [imitatœʀ, -tʀis] *nm/f* (*gén*) imitator ; (*MUSIC-HALL:* d'une *personnalité*) impersonator.

imitation [imitɑsjɔ̃] *nf* imitation ; (*sketch*) imitation, impression ; impersonation ; **sac ~ cuir** bag in imitation *ou* simulated leather.

imiter [imite] *vt* to imitate ; (*contrefaire: signature, document*) to forge, copy ; (*avoir l'aspect de*) to look like ; **il se leva et je l'imitai** he got up and I did likewise.

immaculé, e [imakyle] *a* spotless ; immaculate.

immangeable [ɛ̃mɑ̃ʒabl(ə)] *a* inedible, uneatable.

immanquable [ɛ̃mɑ̃kabl(ə)] *a* (*cible*) impossible to miss.

immatriculation [imatʀikylɑsjɔ̃] *nf* registration.

immatriculer [imatʀikyle] *vt* to register ; **faire/se faire ~** to register ; **voiture immatriculée dans la Seine** car with a Seine registration (number).

immédiat, e [imedja, -at] *a* immediate // *nm:* **dans l'~** for the time being ; **immédiatement** *ad* immediately.

immense [imɑ̃s] *a* immense.

immergé, e [imɛʀʒe] *a* submerged.

immerger [imɛʀʒe] *vt* to immerse, submerge ; to lay under water ; **s'~** *vi* (*sous-marin*) to dive, submerge.

immérité, e [imeʀite] *a* undeserved.

immeuble [imœbl(ə)] *nm* building // *a* (*JUR*) immovable, real ; **~ locatif** block of rented flats.

immigrant, e [imigʀɑ̃, -ɑ̃t] *nm/f* immigrant.

immigration [imigʀɑsjɔ̃] *nf* immigration.

immigré, e [imigʀe] *nm/f* immigrant.

immigrer [imigʀe] *vi* to immigrate.

imminent, e [iminɑ̃, -ɑ̃t] *a* imminent, impending.

immiscer [imise] **s'~** *vi:* **s'~ dans** to interfere in *ou* with.

immobile [imɔbil] *a* still, motionless ; (*pièce de machine*) fixed ; (*fig*) unchanging.

immobilier, ière [imɔbilje, -jɛʀ] *a* property *cpd*, in real property // *nm:* **l'~** the property *ou* the real estate business.

immobilisation [imɔbilizɑsjɔ̃] *nf* immobilization ; **~s** *nfpl* (*COMM*) fixed assets.

immobiliser [imɔbilize] *vt* (*gén*) to immobilize ; (*circulation, véhicule, affaires*) to bring to a standstill ; **s'~** (*personne*) to stand still ; (*machine, véhicule*) to come to a halt *ou* standstill.

immobilité [imɔbilite] *nf* stillness ; immobility.

immodéré, e [imɔdeʀe] *a* immoderate, inordinate.

immoler [imɔle] *vt* to immolate, sacrifice.

immonde [imɔ̃d] *a* foul.

immondices [imɔ̃dis] *nmpl* refuse *sg* ; filth *sg*.

immoral, e, aux [imɔʀal, -o] *a* immoral.

immortaliser [imɔʀtalize] *vt* to immortalize.

immortel, le [imɔʀtɛl] *a* immortal.

immuable [imɥabl(ə)] *a* immutable ; unchanging.

immunisé 130 imposture

immunisé, e [imynize] *a*: ~ **contre** immune to.
immuniser [imynize] *vt* to immunize.
immunité [imynite] *nf* immunity; ~ **diplomatique** diplomatic immunity; ~ **parlementaire** parliamentary privilege.
impact [ɛpakt] *nm* impact.
impair, e [ɛpɛʀ] *a* odd // *nm* faux pas, blunder.
imparable [ɛpaʀabl(ə)] *a* unstoppable.
impardonnable [ɛpaʀdɔnabl(ə)] *a* unpardonable, unforgivable.
imparfait, e [ɛpaʀfɛ, -ɛt] *a* imperfect // *nm* imperfect (tense).
impartial, e, aux [ɛpaʀsjal, -o] *a* impartial, unbiased; ~**ité** *nf* impartiality.
impartir [ɛpaʀtiʀ] *vt*: ~ **qch à qn** to assign sth to sb; to bestow sth upon sb.
impasse [ɛpɑs] *nf* dead-end, cul-de-sac; *(fig)* deadlock.
impassible [ɛpasibl(ə)] *a* impassive.
impatience [ɛpasjɑs] *nf* impatience.
impatient, e [ɛpasjɑ, -ɑt] *a* impatient; **impatienter** *vt* to irritate, annoy; **s'impatienter** to get impatient; **s'impatienter de/contre** to lose patience at/with, grow impatient at/with.
impayable [ɛpɛjabl(ə)] *a* (*drôle*) priceless.
impayé, e [ɛpeje] *a* unpaid.
impeccable [ɛpekabl(ə)] *a* faultless, impeccable; spotlessly clean; impeccably dressed; *(fam)* smashing.
impénétrable [ɛpenetʀabl(ə)] *a* impenetrable.
impénitent, e [ɛpenitɑ, -ɑt] *a* unrepentant.
impensable [ɛpɑsabl(ə)] *a* unthinkable; unbelievable.
impératif, ive [ɛpeʀatif, -iv] *a* imperative; *(JUR)* mandatory // *nm* (*LING*) imperative; ~**s** *nmpl* requirements; demands.
impératrice [ɛpeʀatʀis] *nf* empress.
imperceptible [ɛpɛʀsɛptibl(ə)] *a* imperceptible.
imperfection [ɛpɛʀfɛksjɔ] *nf* imperfection.
impérial, e, aux [ɛpeʀjal, -o] *a* imperial // *nf* upper deck; **autobus à** ~**e** double-decker bus.
impérialiste [ɛpeʀjalist(ə)] *a* imperialist.
impérieux, euse [ɛpeʀjø, -øz] *a* (*caractère, ton*) imperious; (*obligation, besoin*) pressing, urgent.
impérissable [ɛpeʀisabl(ə)] *a* undying; imperishable.
imperméabiliser [ɛpɛʀmeabilize] *vt* to waterproof.
imperméable [ɛpɛʀmeabl(ə)] *a* waterproof; (*GÉO*) impermeable; *(fig)*: ~ **à** impervious to // *nm* raincoat; ~ **à l'air** airtight.
impersonnel, le [ɛpɛʀsɔnɛl] *a* impersonal.
impertinence [ɛpɛʀtinɑs] *nf* impertinence.
impertinent, e [ɛpɛʀtinɑ, -ɑt] *a* impertinent.
imperturbable [ɛpɛʀtyʀbabl(ə)] *a* imperturbable; unruffled; unshakeable.

impétrant, e [ɛpetʀɑ, -ɑt] *nm/f* *(JUR)* applicant.
impétueux, euse [ɛpetɥø, -øz] *a* fiery.
impie [ɛpi] *a* impious, ungodly; **impiété** *nf* impiety.
impitoyable [ɛpitwajabl(ə)] *a* pitiless, merciless.
implacable [ɛplakabl(ə)] *a* implacable.
implanter [ɛplɑte] *vt* (*usine, industrie, usage*) to establish; (*colons etc*) to settle; (*idée, préjugé*) to implant; **s'** ~ **dans** to be established in; to settle in; to become implanted in.
implication [ɛplikasjɔ] *nf* implication.
implicite [ɛplisit] *a* implicit.
impliquer [ɛplike] *vt* to imply; ~ **qn (dans)** to implicate sb (in).
implorer [ɛplɔʀe] *vt* to implore.
implosion [ɛplozjɔ] *nf* implosion.
impoli, e [ɛpɔli] *a* impolite, rude; ~**tesse** *nf* impoliteness, rudeness; impolite *ou* rude remark.
impondérable [ɛpɔdeʀabl(ə)] *nm* imponderable.
impopulaire [ɛpɔpylɛʀ] *a* unpopular.
importance [ɛpɔʀtɑs] *nf* importance; **avoir de l'** ~ to be important; **sans** ~ unimportant.
important, e [ɛpɔʀtɑ, -ɑt] *a* important; (*en quantité*) considerable, sizeable; extensive; (*péj: airs, ton*) self-important // *nm*: **l'** ~ the important thing.
importateur, trice [ɛpɔʀtatœʀ, -tʀis] *a* importing // *nm* importer; **pays** ~ **de blé** wheat-importing country.
importation [ɛpɔʀtasjɔ] *nf* importation; introduction; (*produit*) import.
importer [ɛpɔʀte] *vt* (*COMM*) to import; (*maladies, plantes*) to introduce // *vi* (*être important*) to matter; ~ **à qn** to matter to sb; **il importe qu'il fasse** he must do, it is important that he should do; **peu m'importe** I don't mind; I don't care; **peu importe (que)** it doesn't matter (if); *voir aussi* **n'importe.**
import-export [ɛpɔʀɛkspɔʀ] *nm* import-export business.
importun, e [ɛpɔʀtœ, -yn] *a* irksome, importunate; (*arrivée, visite*) inopportune, ill-timed // *nm* intruder; **importuner** *vt* to bother.
imposable [ɛpozabl(ə)] *a* taxable.
imposant, e [ɛpozɑ, -ɑt] *a* imposing.
imposer [ɛpoze] *vt* (*taxer*) to tax; ~ **qch à qn** to impose sth on sb; **s'** ~ (*être nécessaire*) to be imperative; (*montrer sa prominence*) to stand out, emerge; (*artiste: se faire connaître*) to win recognition, come to the fore; **en** ~ **à** to impress.
imposition [ɛpozisjɔ] *nf* (*ADMIN*) taxation.
impossibilité [ɛpɔsibilite] *nf* impossibility; **être dans l'** ~ **de faire** to be unable to do, find it impossible to do.
impossible [ɛpɔsibl(ə)] *a* impossible; **il m'est** ~ **de le faire** it is impossible for me to do it, I can't possibly do it; **faire l'** ~ **(pour que)** to do one's utmost (so that).
imposteur [ɛpɔstœʀ] *nm* impostor.
imposture [ɛpɔstyʀ] *nf* imposture, deception.

impôt [ɛ̃po] *nm* tax ; (*taxes*) taxation ;
taxes *pl* ; **~s** *nmpl* (*contributions*) (income)
tax *sg* ; **payer 1000 F d'~s** to pay 1,000
F in tax ; **~ sur le chiffre d'affaires**
corporation tax ; **~ foncier** land tax ; **~
sur les plus-values** capital gains tax ; **~
sur le revenu** income tax.

impotent, e [ɛ̃pɔtɑ̃, -ɑ̃t] *a* disabled.

impraticable [ɛ̃pRatikabl(ə)] *a* (*projet*)
impracticable,   unworkable ;   (*piste*)
impassable.

imprécation [ɛ̃pRekɑsjɔ̃] *nf* imprecation.

imprécis, e [ɛ̃pResi, -iz] *a* (*contours,
souvenir*)   imprecise,   vague ;   (*tir*)
inaccurate, imprecise.

imprégner [ɛ̃pReɲe] *vt* (*tissu, tampon*): **~
(de)** to soak *ou* impregnate (with) ; (*lieu,
air*): **~ (de)** to fill (with) ; (*suj: amertume,
ironie*) to pervade ; **s'~ de** to become
impregnated with ; to be filled with ; (*fig*)
to absorb.

imprenable [ɛ̃pRənabl(ə)] *a* (*forteresse*)
impregnable ; **vue ~** unimpeded outlook.

impresario [ɛ̃pResaRjo] *nm* manager,
impresario.

impression [ɛ̃pResjɔ̃] *nf* impression ;
(*d'un ouvrage, tissu*) printing ; (*PHOTO*)
exposure ; **faire bonne ~** to make a good
impression.

impressionnant, e [ɛ̃pResjɔnɑ̃, -ɑ̃t] *a*
impressive ; upsetting.

impressionner [ɛ̃pResjɔne] *vt* (*frapper*)
to impress ; (*troubler*) to upset ; (*PHOTO*) to
expose.

impressionnisme [ɛ̃pResjɔnism(ə)] *nm*
impressionism.

imprévisible [ɛ̃pRevizibl(ə)]   *a*
unforeseeable.

imprévoyant, e [ɛ̃pRevwajɑ̃, -ɑ̃t] *a*
lacking in foresight ; (*en matière d'argent*)
improvident.

imprévu, e [ɛ̃pRevy] *a* unforeseen,
unexpected // *nm* unexpected incident ;
en cas d'~ if anything unexpected
happens.

imprimé [ɛ̃pRime] *nm* (*formulaire*) printed
form ; (*POSTES*) printed matter *q* ; (*tissu*)
printed fabric.

imprimer [ɛ̃pRime] *vt* to print ; (*apposer:
visa, cachet*) to stamp ; (*empreinte etc*) to
imprint ; (*publier*) to publish ; (*communiquer: mouvement, impulsion*) to impart,
transmit ; **imprimerie** *nf* printing ;
(*établissement*) printing works *sg* ; (*atelier*)
printing house, printery ; **imprimeur** *nm*
printer ; **imprimeur-éditeur/-libraire**
printer and publisher/bookseller.

improbable [ɛ̃pRɔbabl(ə)] *a* unlikely,
improbable.

improductif, ive [ɛ̃pRɔdyktif, -iv] *a*
unproductive.

impromptu, e [ɛ̃pRɔ̃pty] *a* impromptu ;
sudden.

impropre [ɛ̃pRɔpR(ə)] *a* inappropriate ; **~
à** unsuitable for ; **impropriété** *nf* (*de
langage*) incorrect usage *q*.

improvisé, e [ɛ̃pRɔvize] *a* makeshift,
improvised ; (*jeu etc*) scratch, improvised.

improviser [ɛ̃pRɔvize] *vt, vi* to improvise ;
s'~ (*secours, réunion*) to be improvised ;
s'~ cuisinier to (decide to) act as cook.

improviste [ɛ̃pRɔvist(ə)]: **à l'~** *ad*
unexpectedly, without warning.

imprudemment [ɛ̃pRydamɑ̃]   *ad*
carelessly ; unwisely, imprudently.

imprudence [ɛ̃pRydɑ̃s] *nf* carelessness ;
imprudence ; act of carelessness ; foolish
ou unwise action.

imprudent, e [ɛ̃pRydɑ̃, -ɑ̃t] *a* (*conducteur,
geste, action*) careless ; (*remarque*) unwise,
imprudent ; (*projet*) foolhardy.

impubère [ɛ̃pybɛR] *a* below the age of
puberty.

impudent, e [ɛ̃pydɑ̃, -ɑ̃t] *a* impudent ;
brazen.

impudique [ɛ̃pydik] *a* shameless.

impuissance [ɛ̃pɥisɑ̃s] *nf* helplessness ;
ineffectiveness ; impotence.

impuissant, e [ɛ̃pɥisɑ̃, -ɑ̃t] *a* helpless ;
(*sans effet*) ineffectual ; (*sexuellement*)
impotent // *nm* impotent man ; **~ à faire**
powerless to do.

impulsif, ive [ɛ̃pylsif, -iv] *a* impulsive.

impulsion [ɛ̃pylsjɔ̃] *nf* (*ELEC, instinct*)
impulse ; (*élan, influence*) impetus.

impunément [ɛ̃pynemɑ̃]   *ad* with
impunity.

impur, e [ɛ̃pyR] *a* impure ; **~eté** *nf*
impurity.

imputation [ɛ̃pytɑsjɔ̃] *nf* imputation,
charge.

imputer [ɛ̃pyte] *vt* (*attribuer*): **~ qch à** to
ascribe *ou* impute sth to ; (*COMM*): **~ à ou
sur** to charge to.

imputrescible [ɛ̃pytResibl(ə)] *a* which
does not rot.

inabordable [inabɔRdabl(ə)] *a* (*lieu*)
inaccessible ; (*cher*) prohibitive.

inaccentué, e [inaksɑ̃tɥe] *a* (*LING*)
unstressed.

inacceptable [inaksɛptabl(ə)]   *a*
unacceptable ; inadmissible.

inaccessible [inaksesibl(ə)]   *a*
inaccessible ; unattainable ; (*insensible*): **~
à** impervious to.

inaccoutumé, e [inakutyme]   *a*
unaccustomed.

inachevé, e [inaʃve] *a* unfinished.

inactif, ive [inaktif, -iv] *a* inactive, idle.

inaction [inaksjɔ̃] *nf* inactivity.

inactivité [inaktivite] *nf* (*ADMIN*): **en ~** out
of active service.

inadapté, e [inadapte] *a* (*gén*): **~ à** not
adapted to, unsuited to ; (*PSYCH*)
maladjusted.

inadmissible [inadmisibl(ə)]   *a*
inadmissible.

inadvertance [inadvɛRtɑ̃s]: **par ~** *ad*
inadvertently.

inaliénable [inaljenabl(ə)] *a* inalienable.

inaltérable [inalteRabl(ə)] *a* (*matière*)
stable ; (*fig*) unchanging ; **~ à** unaffected
by ; **couleur ~** (**au lavage/à la lumière**)
fast colour/fade-resistant colour.

inamovible [inamɔvibl(ə)] *a* fixed ; (*JUR*)
irremovable.

inanimé, e [inanime] *a* (*matière*)
inanimate ; (*évanoui*) unconscious ; (*sans
vie*) lifeless.

inanité [inanite] *nf* futility.

inanition [inanisjɔ̃] *nf*: **tomber d'~** to
faint with hunger (and exhaustion).

inaperçu, e [inapɛʀsy] a: **passer ~** to go unnoticed.

inappliqué, e [inaplike] a lacking in application.

inappréciable [inapʀesjabl(ə)] a (service) invaluable ; (différence, nuance) inappreciable.

inapte [inapt(ə)] a: **~ à** incapable of ; (MIL) unfit for.

inattaquable [inatakabl(ə)] a (MIL) unassailable ; (texte, preuve) irrefutable.

inattendu, e [inatɑ̃dy] a unexpected.

inattentif, ive [inatɑ̃tif, -iv] a inattentive ; **~ à** (dangers, détails) heedless of ; **inattention** nf inattention ; **faute d'inattention** careless mistake.

inaugural, e, aux [inɔgyʀal, -o] a (cérémonie) inaugural, opening ; (vol, voyage) maiden.

inauguration [inɔgyʀasjɔ̃] nf opening ; unveiling.

inaugurer [inɔgyʀe] vt (monument) to unveil ; (exposition, usine) to open ; (fig) to inaugurate.

inavouable [inavwabl(ə)] a a shameful ; undisclosable.

inavoué, e [inavwe] a unavowed.

incalculable [ɛ̃kalkylabl(ə)] a incalculable.

incandescence [ɛ̃kɑ̃desɑ̃s] nf incandescence ; **porter à ~** to heat white-hot.

incantation [ɛ̃kɑ̃tasjɔ̃] nf incantation.

incapable [ɛ̃kapabl(ə)] a incapable ; **~ de faire** incapable of doing ; (empêché) unable to do.

incapacité [ɛ̃kapasite] nf incapability ; (JUR) incapacity ; **être dans l'~ de faire** to be unable to do ; **~ permanente/de travail** permanent/industrial disablement ; **~ électorale** ineligibility to vote.

incarcérer [ɛ̃kaʀseʀe] vt to incarcerate.

incarnation [ɛ̃kaʀnasjɔ̃] nf incarnation.

incarné, e [ɛ̃kaʀne] a incarnate ; (ongle) ingrown.

incarner [ɛ̃kaʀne] vt to embody, personify ; (THÉÂTRE) to play ; (REL) to incarnate.

incartade [ɛ̃kaʀtad] nf prank, escapade.

incassable [ɛ̃kasabl(ə)] a unbreakable.

incendiaire [ɛ̃sɑ̃djɛʀ] a incendiary ; (fig: discours) inflammatory // nm/f fire-raiser, arsonist.

incendie [ɛ̃sɑ̃di] nm fire ; **~ criminel** arson q ; **~ de forêt** forest fire.

incendier [ɛ̃sɑ̃dje] vt (mettre le feu à) to set fire to, set alight ; (brûler complètement) to burn down.

incertain, e [ɛ̃sɛʀtɛ̃, -ɛn] a uncertain ; (temps) uncertain, unsettled ; (imprécis: contours) indistinct, blurred ; **incertitude** nf uncertainty.

incessamment [ɛ̃sesamɑ̃] ad very shortly.

incessant, e [ɛ̃sesɑ̃, -ɑ̃t] a incessant, unceasing.

inceste [ɛ̃sɛst(ə)] nm incest.

inchangé, e [ɛ̃ʃɑ̃ʒe] a unchanged, unaltered.

incidemment [ɛ̃sidamɑ̃] ad in passing.

incidence [ɛ̃sidɑ̃s] nf (effet, influence) effect ; (PHYSIQUE) incidence.

incident [ɛ̃sidɑ̃] nm incident ; **~ de parcours** minor hitch ou setback ; **~ technique** technical difficulties pl.

incinérateur [ɛ̃sineʀatœʀ] nm incinerator.

incinérer [ɛ̃sineʀe] vt (ordures) to incinerate ; (mort) to cremate.

incise [ɛ̃siz] nf (LING) interpolated clause.

incisif, ive [ɛ̃sizif, -iv] a incisive, cutting // nf incisor.

incision [ɛ̃sizjɔ̃] nf incision ; (d'un abcès) lancing.

inciter [ɛ̃site] vt: **~ qn à faire** to incite ou prompt sb to do.

inclinaison [ɛ̃klinɛzɔ̃] nf (déclivité: d'une route etc) incline ; (: d'un toit) slope ; (état penché: d'un mur) lean ; (: de la tête) tilt ; (: d'un navire) list.

inclination [ɛ̃klinasjɔ̃] nf (penchant) inclination, tendency ; **~ de (la) tête** nod (of the head) ; **~ (de buste)** bow.

incliner [ɛ̃kline] vt (tête, bouteille) to tilt ; (inciter): **~ qn à qch/à faire** to encourage sb towards sth/to do // vi: **~ à qch/à faire** to incline towards sth/doing ; to tend towards sth/to do ; **s'~** (route) to slope ; **s'~ (devant)** to bow (before) ; (céder) to give in ou yield (to) ; **~ la tête** ou **le front** to give a slight bow.

inclure [ɛ̃klyʀ] vt to include ; (joindre à un envoi) to enclose ; **jusqu'au 10 mars inclus** until 10th March inclusive.

incoercible [ɛ̃kɔɛʀsibl(ə)] a uncontrollable.

incognito [ɛ̃kɔɲito] ad incognito.

incohérence [ɛ̃kɔeʀɑ̃s] nf inconsistency.

incohérent, e [ɛ̃kɔeʀɑ̃, -ɑ̃t] a inconsistant ; incoherent.

incollable [ɛ̃kɔlabl(ə)] a: **il est ~** he's got all the answers.

incolore [ɛ̃kɔlɔʀ] a colourless.

incomber [ɛ̃kɔ̃be]: **~ à** vt (suj: devoirs, responsabilité) to rest ou be incumbent upon ; (: frais, travail) to be the responsibility of.

incombustible [ɛ̃kɔ̃bystibl(ə)] a incombustible.

incommensurable [ɛ̃kɔmɑ̃syʀabl(ə)] a immeasurable.

incommode [ɛ̃kɔmɔd] a inconvenient ; (posture, siège) uncomfortable.

incommoder [ɛ̃kɔmɔde] vt: **~ qn** to bother ou inconvenience sb ; (embarrasser) to make sb feel uncomfortable ou ill at ease.

incomparable [ɛ̃kɔ̃paʀabl(ə)] a not comparable ; (inégalable) incomparable, matchless.

incompatibilité [ɛ̃kɔ̃patibilite] nf incompatibility ; **~ d'humeur** (mutual) incompatibility.

incompatible [ɛ̃kɔ̃patibl(ə)] a incompatible.

incompétent, e [ɛ̃kɔ̃petɑ̃, -ɑ̃t] a (ignorant) inexpert ; (JUR) incompetent, not competent.

incomplet, ète [ɛ̃kɔ̃plɛ, -ɛt] a incomplete.

incompréhensible [ɛ̃kɔ̃pʀeɑ̃sibl(ə)] a incomprehensible.

incompréhensif, ive [ɛ̃kɔ̃pʀeɑ̃sif, -iv] *a* lacking in understanding; unsympathetic.

incompris, e [ɛ̃kɔ̃pʀi, -iz] *a* misunderstood.

inconcevable [ɛ̃kɔ̃svabl(ə)] *a* inconceivable.

inconciliable [ɛ̃kɔ̃siljabl(ə)] *a* irreconcilable.

inconditionnel, le [ɛ̃kɔ̃disjɔnɛl] *a* unconditional; (*partisan*) unquestioning.

inconduite [ɛ̃kɔ̃dɥit] *nf* wild behaviour *q*.

inconfortable [ɛ̃kɔ̃fɔʀtabl(ə)] *a* uncomfortable.

incongru, e [ɛ̃kɔ̃gʀy] *a* unseemly.

inconnu, e [ɛ̃kɔny] *a* unknown; new, strange // *nm/f* stranger; unknown person (*ou* artist *etc*) // *nm*: **l'~** the unknown // *nf* (MATH) unknown; (*fig*) unknown factor.

inconsciemment [ɛ̃kɔ̃sjamɑ̃] *ad* unconsciously; thoughtlessly.

inconscience [ɛ̃kɔ̃sjɑ̃s] *nf* unconsciousness; thoughtlessness, recklessness.

inconscient, e [ɛ̃kɔ̃sjɑ̃, -ɑ̃t] *a* unconscious; (*irréfléchi*) thoughtless, reckless // *nm* (PSYCH): **l'~** the subconscious, the unconscious; **~ de** unaware of.

inconsidéré, e [ɛ̃kɔ̃sideʀe] *a* ill-considered.

inconsistant, e [ɛ̃kɔ̃sistɑ̃, -ɑ̃t] *a* flimsy, weak; runny.

inconstant, e [ɛ̃kɔ̃stɑ̃, -ɑ̃t] *a* inconstant, fickle.

incontestable [ɛ̃kɔ̃tɛstabl(ə)] *a* indisputable.

incontesté, e [ɛ̃kɔ̃tɛste] *a* undisputed.

incontinence [ɛ̃kɔ̃tinɑ̃s] *nf* incontinence.

incontinent, e [ɛ̃kɔ̃tinɑ̃, -ɑ̃t] *a* incontinent // *ad* forthwith.

incontrôlable [ɛ̃kɔ̃tʀolabl(ə)] *a* unverifiable.

inconvenant, e [ɛ̃kɔ̃vnɑ̃, -ɑ̃t] *a* unseemly, improper.

inconvénient [ɛ̃kɔ̃venjɑ̃] *nm* (*d'une situation, d'un projet*) disadvantage, drawback; (*d'un remède, changement etc*) risk, inconvenience; **si vous n'y voyez pas d'~** if you have no objections.

incorporation [ɛ̃kɔʀpɔʀɑsjɔ̃] *nf* (MIL) call-up.

incorporer [ɛ̃kɔʀpɔʀe] *vt* ~ **(à)** to mix in (with); (*paragraphe etc*): ~ **(dans)** to incorporate (in); (*territoire, immigrants*): ~ **(à)** to incorporate (into); (MIL: *appeler*) to recruit, call up; (: *affecter*): ~ **qn dans** to enlist sb into.

incorrect, e [ɛ̃kɔʀɛkt] *a* (*impropre, inconvenant*) improper; (*défectueux*) faulty; (*inexact*) incorrect; (*impoli*) impolite; (*déloyal*) underhand.

incorrigible [ɛ̃kɔʀiʒibl(ə)] *a* incorrigible.

incorruptible [ɛ̃kɔʀyptibl(ə)] *a* incorruptible.

incrédule [ɛ̃kʀedyl] *a* incredulous; (REL) unbelieving.

increvable [ɛ̃kʀəvabl(ə)] *a* (*pneu*) puncture-proof; (*fam*) tireless.

incriminer [ɛ̃kʀimine] *vt* (*personne*) to incriminate; (*action, conduite*) to bring

under attack; (*bonne foi, honnêteté*) to call into question.

incroyable [ɛ̃kʀwajabl(ə)] *a* incredible; unbelievable.

incroyant, e [ɛ̃kʀwajɑ̃, -ɑ̃t] *nm/f* nonbeliever.

incrustation [ɛ̃kʀystɑsjɔ̃] *nf* inlaying *q*; inlay; (*dans une chaudière etc*) fur *q*, scale *q*.

incruster [ɛ̃kʀyste] *vt* (ART): ~ **qch dans/qch de** to inlay sth into/sth with; (*radiateur etc*) to coat with scale *ou* fur; **s'~** *vi* (*invité*) to take root; (*radiateur etc*) **to** become coated with fur *ou* scale; **s'~ dans** (*suj: corps étranger, caillou*) to become embedded in.

incubateur [ɛ̃kybatœʀ] *nm* incubator.

incubation [ɛ̃kybɑsjɔ̃] *nf* incubation.

inculpation [ɛ̃kylpɑsjɔ̃] *nf* charging *q*; charge.

inculpé, e [ɛ̃kylpe] *nm/f* accused.

inculper [ɛ̃kylpe] *vt*: ~ **(de)** to charge (with).

inculquer [ɛ̃kylke] *vt*: ~ **qch à** to inculcate sth in *ou* instil sth into.

inculte [ɛ̃kylt(ə)] *a* uncultivated; (*esprit, peuple*) uncultured; (*barbe*) unkempt.

incurable [ɛ̃kyʀabl(ə)] *a* incurable.

incurie [ɛ̃kyʀi] *nf* carelessness.

incursion [ɛ̃kyʀsjɔ̃] *nf* incursion, foray.

incurvé, e [ɛ̃kyʀve] *a* curved.

Inde [ɛ̃d] *nf*: **l'~** India.

indécence [ɛ̃desɑ̃s] *nf* indecency; indecent remark (*ou* act *etc*).

indécent, e [ɛ̃desɑ̃, -ɑ̃t] *a* indecent.

indéchiffrable [ɛ̃deʃifʀabl(ə)] *a* indecipherable.

indécis, e [ɛ̃desi, -iz] *a* indecisive; (*perplexe*) undecided; **indécision** *nf* indecision; indecisiveness.

indéfendable [ɛ̃defɑ̃dabl(ə)] *a* indefensible.

indéfini, e [ɛ̃defini] *a* (*imprécis, incertain*) undefined; (*illimité, LING*) indefinite; **~ment** *ad* indefinitely; **~ssable** *a* indefinable.

indéformable [ɛ̃defɔʀmabl(ə)] *a* that keeps its shape.

indélébile [ɛ̃delebil] *a* indelible.

indélicat, e [ɛ̃delika, -at] *a* tactless; dishonest.

indémaillable [ɛ̃demɑjabl(ə)] *a* run-resist.

indemne [ɛ̃dɛmn(ə)] *a* unharmed.

indemniser [ɛ̃dɛmnize] *vt*: ~ **qn (de)** to compensate sb (for).

indemnité [ɛ̃dɛmnite] *nf* (*dédommagement*) compensation *q*; (*allocation*) allowance; ~ **de licenciement** redundancy payment; ~ **de logement** housing allowance; ~ **parlementaire** ≈ M.P.'s salary.

indéniable [ɛ̃denjabl(ə)] *a* undeniable, indisputable.

indépendamment [ɛ̃depɑ̃damɑ̃] *ad* independently; ~ **de** (*abstraction faite de*) irrespective of; (*en plus de*) over and above.

indépendance [ɛ̃depɑ̃dɑ̃s] *nf* independence.

indépendant, e [ɛ̃depɑ̃dɑ̃, -ɑ̃t] *a* independent; ~ **de** independent of;

chambre ~e room with private entrance.
indescriptible [ɛ̃dɛskʀiptibl(ə)] a indescribable.

indésirable [ɛ̃deziʀabl(ə)] a undesirable.

indestructible [ɛ̃dɛstʀyktibl(ə)] a indestructible ; (marque, impression) indelible.

indétermination [ɛ̃detɛʀminɑsjɔ̃] nf indecision ; indecisiveness.

indéterminé, e [ɛ̃detɛʀmine] a unspecified ; indeterminate ; indeterminable.

index [ɛ̃dɛks] nm (doigt) index finger ; (d'un livre etc) index ; **mettre à l'~** to blacklist.

indexé, e [ɛ̃dɛkse] a (ÉCON): ~ (sur) index-linked (to).

indicateur [ɛ̃dikatœʀ] nm (POLICE) informer ; (livre) guide ; directory ; (TECH) gauge ; indicator ; ~ **des chemins de fer** railway timetable ; ~ **de direction** (AUTO) indicator ; ~ **immobilier** property gazette ; ~ **de rues** street directory ; ~ **de vitesse** speedometer.

indicatif, ive [ɛ̃dikatif, -iv] a: **à titre** ~ for (your) information // nm (LING) indicative ; (d'une émission) theme ou signature tune ; (téléphonique) dialling code ; ~ **d'appel** (RADIO) call sign.

indication [ɛ̃dikasjɔ̃] nf indication ; (renseignement) information q ; ~s nfpl (directives) instructions.

indice [ɛ̃dis] nm (marque, signe) indication, sign ; (POLICE: lors d'une enquête) clue ; (JUR: présomption) piece of evidence ; (SCIENCE, TECH) index ; (ADMIN) grading ; rating ; ~ **d'octane** octane rating ; ~ **des prix** price index ; ~ **de traitement** salary grading.

indicible [ɛ̃disibl(ə)] a inexpressible.

indien, ne [ɛ̃djɛ̃, -jɛn] a Indian // nm/f: **I~, ne** (d'Amérique) Red Indian ; (d'Inde) Indian.

indifféremment [ɛ̃diferamɑ̃] ad (sans distinction) equally (well) ; indiscriminately.

indifférence [ɛ̃diferɑ̃s] nf indifference.

indifférent, e [ɛ̃diferɑ̃, -ɑ̃t] a (peu intéressé) indifferent ; ~ **à** (insensible à) indifferent to, unconcerned about ; (peu intéressant pour) indifferent to ; immaterial to.

indigence [ɛ̃diʒɑ̃s] nf poverty.

indigène [ɛ̃diʒɛn] a native, indigenous ; local // nm/f native.

indigent, e [ɛ̃diʒɑ̃, -ɑ̃t] a destitute, poverty-stricken ; (fig) poor.

indigeste [ɛ̃diʒɛst(ə)] a indigestible.

indigestion [ɛ̃diʒɛstjɔ̃] nf indigestion q.

indignation [ɛ̃diɲasjɔ̃] nf indignation.

indigne [ɛ̃diɲ] a unworthy.

indigner [ɛ̃diɲe] vt to make indignant ; **s'~ (de/contre)** to be (ou become) indignant (at).

indignité [ɛ̃diɲite] nf unworthiness q ; shameful act.

indiqué, e [ɛ̃dike] a (adéquat) appropriate, suitable ; (conseillé) suitable, advisable.

indiquer [ɛ̃dike] vt (désigner): ~ **qch/qn à qn** to point sth/sb out to sb ; (suj: pendule, aiguille) to show ; (suj: étiquette, plan) to show, indicate ; (faire connaître:

médecin, restaurant): ~ **qch/qn à qn** to tell sb of sth/sb ; (renseigner sur) to point out, tell ; (déterminer: date, lieu) to give, state ; (dénoter) to indicate, point to ; **pourriez-vous m'~ les toilettes/l'heure?** could you direct me to the toilets/tell me the time?

indirect, e [ɛ̃diʀɛkt] a indirect.

indiscipline [ɛ̃disiplin] nf lack of discipline ; **indiscipliné, e** a undisciplined ; (fig) unmanageable.

indiscret, ète [ɛ̃diskʀɛ, -ɛt] a indiscreet ; **indiscrétion** nf indiscretion.

indiscutable [ɛ̃diskytabl(ə)] a indisputable.

indispensable [ɛ̃dispɑ̃sabl(ə)] a indispensable ; essential.

indisponible [ɛ̃dispɔnibl(ə)] a unavailable.

indisposé, e [ɛ̃dispoze] a indisposed, unwell.

indisposer [ɛ̃dispoze] vt (incommoder) to upset ; (déplaire à) to antagonize.

indistinct, e [ɛ̃distɛ̃, -ɛ̃kt(ə)] a indistinct ; **indistinctement** ad (voir, prononcer) indistinctly ; (sans distinction) without distinction, indiscriminately.

individu [ɛ̃dividy] nm individual ; **~aliser** vt to individualize ; (personnaliser) to tailor to individual requirements ; **~aliste** nm/f individualist.

individuel, le [ɛ̃dividɥɛl] a (gén) individual ; (opinion, livret, contrôle, avantages) personal ; **chambre ~le** single room ; **maison ~le** detached house ; **propriété ~le** personal ou private property.

indocile [ɛ̃dɔsil] a unruly.

indolent, e [ɛ̃dɔlɑ̃, -ɑ̃t] a indolent.

indolore [ɛ̃dɔlɔʀ] a painless.

indomptable [ɛ̃dɔ̃tabl(ə)] a untameable ; (fig) invincible, indomitable.

Indonésie [ɛ̃donezi] nf Indonesia ; **indonésien, ne** a, nm/f Indonesian.

indu, e [ɛ̃dy] a: **à des heures ~es** at some ungodly hour.

indubitable [ɛ̃dybitabl(ə)] a indubitable.

induire [ɛ̃dɥiʀ] vt: ~ **qch de** to induce sth from ; ~ **qn en erreur** to lead sb astray, mislead sb.

indulgence [ɛ̃dylʒɑ̃s] nf indulgence ; leniency.

indulgent, e [ɛ̃dylʒɑ̃, -ɑ̃t] a (parent, regard) indulgent ; (juge, examinateur) lenient.

indûment [ɛ̃dymɑ̃] ad wrongfully ; without due cause.

industrialiser [ɛ̃dystʀijalize] vt to industrialize ; **s'~** to become industrialized.

industrie [ɛ̃dystʀi] nf industry ; ~ **du spectacle** entertainment business ; **industriel, le** a industrial // nm industrialist ; manufacturer.

industrieux, euse [ɛ̃dystʀijø, -øz] a industrious.

inébranlable [inebʀɑ̃labl(ə)] a (masse, colonne) solid ; (personne, certitude, foi) steadfast, unwavering.

inédit, e [inedi, -it] a (correspondance etc)

hitherto unpublished; (*spectacle, moyen*) novel, original.

ineffable [inefabl(ə)] a inexpressible, ineffable.

ineffaçable [inefasabl(ə)] a indelible.

inefficace [inefikas] a (*remède, moyen*) ineffective; (*machine, employé*) inefficient; **inefficacité** nf ineffectiveness; inefficiency.

inégal, e, aux [inegal, -o] a unequal; uneven.

inégalable [inegalabl(e)] a matchless.

inégalé, e [inegale] a unmatched, unequalled.

inégalité [inegalite] nf inequality; unevenness q; ~ **de 2 hauteurs** difference *ou* disparity between 2 heights.

inélégant, e [inelegā, -āt] a inelegant; (*indélicat*) discourteous.

inéligible [inelizibl(ə)] a ineligible.

inéluctable [inelyktabl(ə)] a inescapable, ineluctable.

inemployé, e [inɑ̃plwaje] a unused.

inénarrable [inenaRabl(ə)] a hilarious.

inepte [inɛpt(ə)] a inept; **ineptie** [-si] nf ineptitude; nonsense q.

inépuisable [inepɥizabl(ə)] a inexhaustible.

inerte [inɛrt(ə)] a lifeless; (*apathique*) passive, inert; (*PHYSIQUE, CHIMIE*) inert.

inertie [inɛrsi] nf inertia.

inespéré, e [inɛspere] a unhoped-for.

inesthétique [inɛstetik] a unsightly.

inestimable [inɛstimabl(e)] a priceless; (*fig: bienfait*) invaluable.

inévitable [inevitabl(ə)] a unavoidable; (*fatal, habituel*) inevitable.

inexact, e [inɛgzakt] a inaccurate, inexact; unpunctual; **~itude** nf inaccuracy.

inexcusable [inɛkskyzabl(ə)] a inexcusable, unforgivable.

inexécutable [inɛgzekytabl(ə)] a impracticable, unworkable; (*MUS*) unplayable.

inexistant, e [inɛgzistā, -āt] a nonexistent.

inexorable [inɛgzɔRabl(ə)] a inexorable.

inexpérience [inɛksperjās] nf inexperience, lack of experience.

inexplicable [inɛksplikabl(ə) a inexplicable.

inexpliqué, e [inɛksplike] a unexplained.

inexploité, e [inɛksplwate] a unexploited, untapped.

inexpressif, ive [inɛkspresif, -iv] a inexpressive; expressionless.

inexprimable [inɛksprimabl(ə)] a inexpressible.

inexprimé, e [inɛksprime] a unspoken, unexpressed.

inextensible [inɛkstɑ̃sibl(ə)] a (*tissu*) nonstretch.

in extenso [inɛkstɛ̃so] ad in full.

inextricable [inɛkstrikabl(ə)] a inextricable.

in extremis [inɛkstremis] ad at the last minute // a last-minute; (*testament*) death bed cpd.

infaillibilité [ɛ̃fajibilite] nf infallibility.

infaillible [ɛ̃fajibl(ə)] a infallible; (*instinct*) infallible, unerring.

infâme [ɛ̃fam] a vile.

infanterie [ɛ̃fɑ̃tRi] nf infantry.

infanticide [ɛ̃fɑ̃tisid] nm/f child-murderer/eress // nm (*meurtre*) infanticide.

infantile [ɛ̃fɑ̃til] a (*MÉD*) infantile, child cpd; (*ton, réaction, péj*) infantile, childish.

infarctus [ɛ̃faRktys] nm: ~ **(du myocarde)** coronary (thrombosis).

infatigable [ɛ̃fatigabl(ə)] a tireless, indefatigable.

infatué, e [ɛ̃fatɥe] a conceited; ~ **de** full of.

infécond, e [ɛ̃fekɔ̃, -ɔ̃d] a infertile, barren.

infect, e [ɛ̃fɛkt] a vile, foul; (*repas, vin*) revolting, foul.

infecter [ɛ̃fɛkte] vt (*atmosphère, eau*) to contaminate; (*MÉD*) to infect; **s'~** to become infected *ou* septic; **infectieux, euse** [-sjø, -øz] a infectious; **infection** [-sjɔ̃] nf infection.

inféoder [ɛ̃feɔde] vt: **s'~ à** to pledge allegiance to.

inférer [ɛ̃fere] vt: ~ **qch de** to infer sth from.

inférieur, e [ɛ̃feRjœR] a lower; (*en qualité, intelligence*) inferior // nm/f inferior; ~ **à** (*somme, quantité*) less *ou* smaller than; (*moins bon que*) inferior to; (*tâche: pas à la hauteur de*) unequal to; **infériorité** nf inferiority.

infernal, e, aux [ɛ̃fɛRnal, -o] a (*chaleur, rythme*) infernal; (*méchanceté, complot*) diabolical.

infester [ɛ̃fɛste] vt to infest; **infesté de moustiques** infested with mosquitoes, mosquito-ridden.

infidèle [ɛ̃fidɛl] a unfaithful; (*REL*) infidel; **infidélité** nf unfaithfulness q.

infiltration [ɛ̃filtRasjɔ̃] nf infiltration.

infiltrer [ɛ̃filtRe]: **s'~** vi: **s'~ dans** to penetrate into; (*liquide*) to seep into; (*fig: noyauter*) to infiltrate.

infime [ɛ̃fim] a minute, tiny; (*inférieur*) lowly.

infini, e [ɛ̃fini] a infinite // nm infinity; **à l'~** (*MATH*) to infinity; (*discourir*) ad infinitum, endlessly; (*agrandir, varier*) infinitely; (*à perte de vue*) endlessly (into the distance); **~ment** ad infinitely; **infinité** nf: **une infinité de** an infinite number of.

infinitif, ive [ɛ̃finitif, -iv] a, nm infinitive.

infirme [ɛ̃fiRm(ə)] a disabled // nm/f disabled person; ~ **de guerre** war cripple; ~ **du travail** industrially disabled person.

infirmer [ɛ̃fiRme] vt to invalidate.

infirmerie [ɛ̃fiRmaRi] nf sick bay.

infirmier, ière [ɛ̃fiRmje, -jɛR] nm/f nurse; **infirmière chef** sister; **infirmière diplômée** registered nurse; **infirmière visiteuse** ≈ district nurse.

infirmité [ɛ̃fiRmite] nf disability.

inflammable [ɛ̃flamabl(ə)] a (in)flammable.

inflammation [ɛ̃flamasjɔ̃] nf inflammation.

inflation [ɛ̃flɑsjɔ̃] *nf* inflation ;
inflationniste *a* inflationist.
infléchir [ɛ̃fleʃiʀ] *vt* (*fig: politique*) to
reorientate, redirect.
inflexible [ɛ̃flɛksibl(ə)] *a* inflexible.
inflexion [ɛ̃flɛksjɔ̃] *nf* inflexion ; ~ **de la
tête** slight nod (of the head).
infliger [ɛ̃fliʒe] *vt:* ~ **qch (à qn)** to inflict
sth (on sb) ; (*amende, sanction*) to impose
sth (on sb).
influençable [ɛ̃flyɑ̃sabl(ə)] *a* easily
influenced.
influence [ɛ̃flyɑ̃s] *nf* influence ; (*d'un
médicament*) effect ; **influencer** *vt* to
influence ; **influent, e** *a* influential.
influer [ɛ̃flye] : ~ **sur** *vt* to have an
influence upon.
influx [ɛ̃fly] *nm:* ~ **nerveux** (nervous)
impulse.
informaticien, ne [ɛ̃fɔʀmatisjɛ̃, -jɛn]
nm/f computer scientist.
information [ɛ̃fɔʀmɑsjɔ̃] *nf*
(*renseignement*) piece of information ;
(*PRESSE, TV: nouvelle*) news *sg* ; (*diffusion de
renseignements, INFORMATIQUE*) information ;
(*JUR*) inquiry, investigation ; **voyage d'~**
fact-finding trip ; **agence d'~** news
agency ; **journal d'~** quality newspaper.
informatique [ɛ̃fɔʀmatik] *nf* (*techniques*)
data processing ; (*science*) computer
science ; **informatiser** *vt* to computerize.
informe [ɛ̃fɔʀm(ə)] *a* shapeless.
informer [ɛ̃fɔʀme] *vt:* ~ **qn (de)** to
inform sb (of) // *vi* (*JUR*): ~ **contre/sur**
to initiate inquiries about ; **s'~** (**sur**) to
inform o.s. (about) ; **s'~ (de/si)** to inquire
ou find out (about/whether *ou* if).
infortune [ɛ̃fɔʀtyn] *nf* misfortune.
infraction [ɛ̃fʀaksjɔ̃] *nf* offence ; ~ **à**
violation *ou* breach of ; **être en** ~ **to** be
in breach of the law.
infranchissable [ɛ̃fʀɑ̃ʃisabl(ə)] *a*
impassable ; (*fig*) insuperable.
infrarouge [ɛ̃fʀaʀuʒ] *a, nm* infrared.
infrastructure [ɛ̃fʀastʀyktyʀ] *nf* (*d'une
route etc*) substructure ; (*AVIAT, MIL*) ground
installations *pl* ; (*ÉCON: touristique etc*)
infrastructure.
infroissable [ɛ̃fʀwasabl(ə)] *a* crease-
resistant.
infructueux, euse [ɛ̃fʀyktɥø, -øz] *a*
fruitless, unfruitful.
infus, e [ɛ̃fy, -yz] *a:* **avoir la science ~e**
to have innate knowledge.
infuser [ɛ̃fyze] *vt* (*thé*) to brew ; (*tisane*)
to infuse // *vi* to brew ; to infuse ; **infusion**
nf (*tisane*) infusion, herb tea.
ingambe [ɛ̃gɑ̃b] *a* spry, nimble.
ingénier [ɛ̃ʒenje] : **s'~** *vi:* **s'~ à faire** to
strive to do.
ingénieur [ɛ̃ʒenjœʀ] *nm* engineer ; ~
agronome/chimiste agricultural/chemi-
cal engineer ; ~ **du son** sound engineer.
ingénieux, euse [ɛ̃ʒenjø, -øz] *a*
ingenious, clever ; **ingéniosité** *nf*
ingenuity.
ingénu, e [ɛ̃ʒeny] *a* ingenuous, artless //
nf (*THÉÂTRE*) ingénue.
ingérer [ɛ̃ʒeʀe] : **s'~** *vi:* **s'~ dans** to
interfere in.

ingrat, e [ɛ̃gʀa, -at] *a* (*personne*)
ungrateful ; (*sol*) barren, arid ; (*travail,
sujet*) arid, thankless ; (*visage*)
unprepossessing ; **ingratitude** *nf*
ingratitude.
ingrédient [ɛ̃gʀedjɑ̃] *nm* ingredient.
inguérissable [ɛ̃geʀisabl(ə)] *a* incurable.
ingurgiter [ɛ̃gyʀʒite] *vt* to swallow.
inhabile [inabil] *a* clumsy ; (*fig*) inept.
inhabitable [inabitabl(ə)] *a* uninhabitable.
inhabité, e [inabite] *a* (*régions*)
uninhabited ; (*maison*) unoccupied.
inhabituel, le [inabitɥɛl] *a* unusual.
inhalateur [inalatœʀ] *nm* inhaler ; ~
d'oxygène oxygen mask.
inhalation [inalɑsjɔ̃] *nf* (*MÉD*) inhalation ;
faire des ~s to use an inhalation bath.
inhérent, e [ineʀɑ̃, -ɑ̃t] *a:* ~ **à** inherent
in.
inhibition [inibisjɔ̃] *nf* inhibition.
inhospitalier, ière [inɔspitalje, -jɛʀ] *a*
inhospitable.
inhumain, e [inymɛ̃, -ɛn] *a* inhuman.
inhumation [inymɑsjɔ̃] *nf* interment,
burial.
inhumer [inyme] *vt* to inter, bury.
inimaginable [inimaʒinabl(ə)] *a*
unimaginable.
inimitable [inimitabl(ə)] *a* inimitable.
inimitié [inimitje] *nf* enmity.
ininflammable [inɛ̃flamabl(ə)] *a* non-
flammable.
inintelligent, e [inɛ̃teliʒɑ̃, -ɑ̃t] *a*
unintelligent.
inintelligible [inɛ̃teliʒibl(ə)] *a* unintelli-
gible.
inintéressant, e [inɛ̃teʀesɑ̃, -ɑ̃t] *a*
uninteresting.
ininterrompu, e [inɛ̃teʀɔ̃py] *a* (*file, série*)
unbroken ; (*flot, vacarme*) uninterrupted,
non-stop ; (*effort*) unremitting, continuous.
iniquité [inikite] *nf* iniquity.
initial, e, aux [inisjal, -o] *a, nf* initial.
initiateur, trice [inisjatœʀ, -tʀis] *nm/f*
initiator ; (*d'une mode, technique*)
innovator, pioneer.
initiative [inisjativ] *nf* initiative ; **prendre
l'~ de qch/de faire** to take the initiative
for sth/of *ou* in doing ; **avoir de l'~** to
have initiative, show enterprise.
initier [inisje] *vt:* ~ **qn à** to initiate sb
into ; (*faire découvrir: art, jeu*) to introduce
sb to.
injecté, e [ɛ̃ʒɛkte] *a:* **yeux ~s de sang**
bloodshot eyes.
injecter [ɛ̃ʒɛkte] *vt* to inject ; **injection**
[-sjɔ̃] *nf* injection ; **à injection** *a* (*AUTO*) fuel
injection *cpd*.
injonction [ɛ̃ʒɔ̃ksjɔ̃] *nf* injunction, order.
injure [ɛ̃ʒyʀ] *nf* insult, abuse *q*.
injurier [ɛ̃ʒyʀje] *vt* to insult, abuse ;
injurieux, euse *a* abusive, insulting.
injuste [ɛ̃ʒyst(ə)] *a* unjust, unfair ;
injustice *nf* injustice.
inlassable [ɛ̃lɑsabl(ə)] *a* tireless,
indefatigable.
inné, e [ine] *a* innate, inborn.
innocence [inɔsɑ̃s] *nf* innocence.
innocent, e [inɔsɑ̃, -ɑ̃t] *a* innocent // *nm/f*

innocent person ; **innocenter** vt to clear, prove innocent.

innombrable [inɔ̃bʀabl(ə)] a innumerable.

innommable [inɔmabl(ə)] a unspeakable.

innover [inɔve] vi to break new ground.

inobservation [inɔpsɛʀvasjɔ̃] nf non-observation, inobservance.

inoccupé, e [inɔkype] a unoccupied.

inoculer [inɔkyle] vt: ~ qch à qn (volontairement) to inoculate sb with sth ; (accidentellement) to infect sb with sth ; ~ qn contre to inoculate sb against.

inodore [inɔdɔʀ] a (gaz) odourless ; (fleur) scentless.

inoffensif, ive [inɔfɑ̃sif, -iv] a harmless, innocuous.

inondation [inɔ̃dasjɔ̃] nf flooding q ; flood.

inonder [inɔ̃de] vt to flood ; (fig) to inundate, overrun ; ~ de (fig) to flood ou swamp with.

inopérable [inɔpeʀabl(ə)] a inoperable.

inopérant, e [inɔpeʀɑ̃, -ɑ̃t] a inoperative, ineffective.

inopiné, e [inɔpine] a unexpected, sudden.

inopportun, e [inɔpɔʀtœ̃, -yn] a ill-timed, untimely ; inappropriate ; (moment) inopportune.

inoubliable [inublijabl(ə)] a unforgettable.

inouï, e [inwi] a unheard-of, extraordinary.

inoxydable [inɔksidabl(ə)] a stainless ; (couverts) stainless steel cpd.

inqualifiable [ɛ̃kalifjabl(ə)] a unspeakable.

inquiet, ète [ɛ̃kjɛ, -ɛt] a (par nature) anxious ; (momen-tanément) worried.

inquiétant, e [ɛ̃kjetɑ̃, -ɑ̃t] a worrying, disturbing.

inquiéter [ɛ̃kjete] vt to worry, disturb ; (harceler) to harass ; s'~ to worry, become anxious ; s'~ de to worry about ; (s'enquérir de) to inquire about.

inquiétude [ɛ̃kjetyd] nf anxiety ; donner de l'~ ou des ~s à to worry ; avoir de l'~ ou des ~s au sujet de to feel anxious ou worried about.

inquisition [ɛ̃kizisjɔ̃] nf inquisition.

insaisissable [ɛ̃sezisabl(ə)] a elusive.

insalubre [ɛ̃salybʀ(ə)] a insalubrious, unhealthy.

insanité [ɛ̃sanite] nf madness q, insanity q.

insatiable [ɛ̃sasjabl(ə)] a insatiable.

insatisfait, e [ɛ̃satisfɛ, -ɛt] a (non comblé) unsatisfied ; unfulfilled ; (mécontent) dissatisfied.

inscription [ɛ̃skʀipsjɔ̃] nf (sur un mur, écriteau etc) inscription ; (à une institution: voir s'inscrire) enrolment ; registration.

inscrire [ɛ̃skʀiʀ] vt (marquer: sur son calepin etc) to note ou write down ; (: sur un mur, une affiche etc) to write ; (: dans la pierre, le métal) to inscribe ; (mettre: sur une liste, un budget etc) to put down ; ~ qn à (club, école etc) to enrol sb at ; s'~ (pour une excursion etc) to put one's name down ; s'~ (à) (club, parti) to join ; (université) to register ou enrol (at) ; (examen, concours) to register ou enter (for) ; s'~ en faux contre to challenge.

insecte [ɛ̃sɛkt(ə)] nm insect ; **insecticide** nm insecticide.

insécurité [ɛ̃sekyʀite] nf insecurity, lack of security.

I.N.S.E.E. [inse] sigle m = Institut national de la statistique et des études économiques.

insémination [ɛ̃seminasjɔ̃] nf insemination.

insensé, e [ɛ̃sɑ̃se] a insane.

insensibiliser [ɛ̃sɑ̃sibilize] vt to anaesthetize.

insensible [ɛ̃sɑ̃sibl(ə)] a (nerf, membre) numb ; (dur, indifférent) insensitive ; (imperceptible) imperceptible.

inséparable [ɛ̃sepaʀabl(ə)] a inseparable.

insérer [ɛ̃seʀe] vt to insert ; s'~ dans to fit into ; to come within.

insidieux, euse [ɛ̃sidjø, -øz] a insidious.

insigne [ɛ̃siɲ] nm (d'un parti, club) badge // a distinguished ; ~s nmpl (d'une fonction) insignia pl.

insignifiant, e [ɛ̃siɲifjɑ̃, -ɑ̃t] a insignificant ; trivial.

insinuation [ɛ̃sinɥasjɔ̃] nf innuendo, insinuation.

insinuer [ɛ̃sinɥe] vt to insinuate, imply ; s'~ dans to seep into ; (fig) to worm one's way into ; to creep into.

insipide [ɛ̃sipid] a insipid.

insistance [ɛ̃sistɑ̃s] nf insistence ; avec ~ insistently.

insister [ɛ̃siste] vi to insist ; (s'obstiner) to keep trying ; ~ sur (détail, note) to stress.

insociable [ɛ̃sɔsjabl(ə)] a unsociable.

insolation [ɛ̃sɔlasjɔ̃] nf (MED) sunstroke q ; (ensoleillement) period of sunshine.

insolence [ɛ̃sɔlɑ̃s] nf insolence q.

insolent, e [ɛ̃sɔlɑ̃, -ɑ̃t] a insolent.

insolite [ɛ̃sɔlit] a strange, unusual.

insoluble [ɛ̃sɔlybl(ə)] a insoluble.

insolvable [ɛ̃sɔlvabl(ə)] a insolvent.

insomnie [ɛ̃sɔmni] nf insomnia q, sleeplessness q.

insondable [ɛ̃sɔ̃dabl(ə)] a unfathomable.

insonore [ɛ̃sɔnɔʀ] a soundproof ; **insonoriser** vt to soundproof.

insouciance [ɛ̃susjɑ̃s] nf carefree attitude ; heedless attitude.

insouciant, e [ɛ̃susjɑ̃, -ɑ̃t] a carefree ; (imprévoyant) heedless.

insoumis, e [ɛ̃sumi, -iz] a (caractère, enfant) rebellious, refractory ; (contrée, tribu) unsubdued.

insoumission [ɛ̃sumisjɔ̃] nf rebelliousness ; (MIL) absence without leave.

insoupçonnable [ɛ̃supsɔnabl(ə)] a above suspicion.

insoupçonné, e [ɛ̃supsɔne] a unsuspected.

insoutenable [ɛ̃sutnabl(ə)] a (argument) untenable ; (chaleur) unbearable.

inspecter [ɛ̃spɛkte] vt to inspect.

inspecteur, trice [ɛ̃spɛktœʀ, -tʀis] nm/f inspector ; ~ d'Académie ≈ Chief Education Officer ; ~ des finances ≈ Treasury Inspector.

inspection [ɛ̃spɛksjɔ̃] nf inspection.

inspiration [ɛ̃spiʀasjɔ̃] nf inspiration ; breathing in q ; sous l'~ de prompted by.

inspirer [ɛ̃spiʀe] vt (gén) to inspire // vi (aspirer) to breathe in ; **s'~ de** (suj: artiste) to draw one's inspiration from ; (suj: tableau) to be inspired by ; **~ à qn** (œuvre, action) to inspire sb with ; (dégoût, crainte) to fill sb with ; **ça ne m'inspire pas** I'm not keen on the idea.

instable [ɛ̃stabl(ə)] a (meuble, équilibre) unsteady ; (population, temps) unsettled ; (paix, régime, caractère) unstable.

installation [ɛ̃stalasjɔ̃] nf installation ; putting in ou up ; fitting out ; settling in ; (appareils etc) fittings pl, installations pl ; **~s** nfpl installations, plant sg ; facilities.

installer [ɛ̃stale] vt (loger): **~ qn** to get sb settled, install sb ; (placer) to put, place ; (meuble) to put in ; (rideau, étagère, tente) to put up ; (gaz, électricité etc) to put in, install ; (appartement) to fit out ; **s'~** (s'établir: artisan, dentiste etc) to set o.s. up ; (se loger) to settle (o.s.) ; (emménager) to settle in ; (sur un siège, à un emplacement) to settle (down) ; (fig: maladie, grève) to take a firm hold ou grip.

instamment [ɛ̃stamɑ̃] ad urgently.

instance [ɛ̃stɑ̃s] nf (JUR: procédure) (legal) proceedings pl ; (ADMIN: autorité) authority ; **~s** nfpl (prières) entreaties ; **affaire en ~** matter pending ; **être en ~ de divorce** to be awaiting a divorce ; **en seconde ~** on appeal.

instant [ɛ̃stɑ̃] nm moment, instant ; **dans un ~** in a moment ; **à l'~** this instant ; **à tout ~** at any moment ; constantly ; **pour l'~** for the moment, for the time being ; **par ~s** at times ; **de tous les ~s** perpetual.

instantané, e [ɛ̃stɑ̃tane] a (lait, café) instant ; (explosion, mort) instantaneous // nm snapshot.

instar [ɛ̃staʀ]: **à l'~ de** prép following the example of, like.

instaurer [ɛ̃stɔʀe] vt to institute.

instigateur, trice [ɛ̃stigatœʀ, -tʀis] nm/f instigator.

instigation [ɛ̃stigasjɔ̃] nf: **à l'~ de qn** at sb's instigation.

instinct [ɛ̃stɛ̃] nm instinct ; **~ de conservation** instinct of self-preservation ; **instinctif, ive** a instinctive.

instituer [ɛ̃stitɥe] vt to institute, set up.

institut [ɛ̃stity] nm institute ; **~ de beauté** beauty salon ; **I~ Universitaire de Technologie (IUT)** ≈ Polytechnic.

instituteur, trice [ɛ̃stitytœʀ, -tʀis] nm/f (primary school) teacher.

institution [ɛ̃stitysjɔ̃] nf institution ; (collège) private school.

instructeur, trice [ɛ̃stʀyktœʀ, -tʀis] a (MIL): **sergent ~** drill sergeant ; (JUR): **juge ~** examining magistrate // nm/f instructor.

instructif, ive [ɛ̃stʀyktif, -iv] a instructive.

instruction [ɛ̃stʀyksjɔ̃] nf (enseignement, savoir) education ; (JUR) (preliminary) investigation and hearing ; (directive) instruction ; **~s** nfpl (mode d'emploi) directions, instructions ; **~ civique** civics sg ; **~ religieuse** religious instruction ; **~ professionnelle** vocational training.

instruire [ɛ̃stʀɥiʀ] vt (élèves) to teach ; (recrues) to train ; (JUR: affaire) to conduct the investigation for ; **s'~** to educate o.s. ; **~ qn de qch** (informer) to inform ou advise sb of sth ; **instruit, e** a educated.

instrument [ɛ̃stʀymɑ̃] nm instrument ; **~ à cordes/vent** stringed/wind instrument ; **~ de mesure** measuring instrument ; **~ de musique** musical instrument ; **~ de travail** (working) tool.

insu [ɛ̃sy] nm: **à l'~ de qn** without sb knowing (it).

insubmersible [ɛ̃sybmɛʀsibl(ə)] a unsinkable.

insubordination [ɛ̃sybɔʀdinasjɔ̃] nf rebelliousness ; (MIL) insubordination.

insuccès [ɛ̃syksɛ] nm failure.

insuffisance [ɛ̃syfizɑ̃s] nf insufficiency ; inadequacy ; **~s** nfpl (lacunes) inadequacies ; **~ cardiaque** cardiac insufficiency q.

insuffisant, e [ɛ̃syfizɑ̃, -ɑ̃t] a insufficient ; (élève, travail) inadequate.

insuffler [ɛ̃syfle] vt: **~ qch dans** to blow sth into ; **~ qch à qn** to inspire sb with sth.

insulaire [ɛ̃sylɛʀ] a island cpd ; (attitude) insular.

insulte [ɛ̃sylt(ə)] nf insult ; **insulter** vt to insult.

insupportable [ɛ̃sypɔʀtabl(ə)] a unbearable.

insurgé, e [ɛ̃syʀʒe] a, nm/f insurgent, rebel.

insurger [ɛ̃syʀʒe]: **s'~** vi: **s'~ (contre)** to rise up ou rebel (against).

insurmontable [ɛ̃syʀmɔ̃tabl(ə)] a (difficulté) insuperable ; (aversion) unconquerable.

insurrection [ɛ̃syʀɛksjɔ̃] nf insurrection, revolt.

intact, e [ɛ̃takt] a intact.

intangible [ɛ̃tɑ̃ʒibl(ə)] a intangible ; (principe) inviolable.

intarissable [ɛ̃taʀisabl(ə)] a inexhaustible.

intégral, e, aux [ɛ̃tegʀal, -o] a complete // nf (MATH) integral ; **~ement** ad in full.

intégrant, e [ɛ̃tegʀɑ̃, -ɑ̃t] a: **faire partie ~e de** to be an integral part of, be part and parcel of.

intègre [ɛ̃tɛgʀ(ə)] a upright.

intégrer [ɛ̃tegʀe] vt: **~ qch à/dans** to integrate sth into ; **s'~ à/dans** to become integrated into.

intégrité [ɛ̃tegʀite] nf integrity.

intellect [ɛ̃telɛkt] nm intellect.

intellectuel, le [ɛ̃telɛktɥɛl] a intellectual // nm/f intellectual ; (péj) highbrow.

intelligence [ɛ̃teliʒɑ̃s] nf intelligence ; (compréhension): **l'~ de** the understanding of ; (complicité): **regard d'~** glance of complicity ; (accord): **vivre en bonne ~ avec qn** to be on good terms with sb ; **~s** nfpl (MIL, fig) secret contacts.

intelligent, e [ɛ̃teliʒɑ̃, -ɑ̃t] a intelligent.

intelligible [ɛ̃teliʒibl(ə)] a intelligible.

intempérance [ɛ̃tɑ̃peʀɑ̃s] nf intemperance q ; overindulgence q.

intempéries [ɛ̃tɑ̃peʀi] nfpl bad weather sg.

intempestif, ive [ε̃tɑ̃pεstif, -iv] *a* untimely.

intenable [ε̃tnabl(ə)] *a* (*chaleur*) unbearable.

intendance [ε̃tɑ̃dɑ̃s] *nf* (MIL) supply corps; supplies office; (SCOL: *bureau*) bursar's office.

intendant, e [ε̃tɑ̃dɑ̃, -ɑ̃t] *nm/f* (MIL) quartermaster; (SCOL) bursar; (*d'une propriété*) steward.

intense [ε̃tɑ̃s] *a* intense; **intensif, ive** *a* intensive; **intensifier** *vt*, **s'intensifier** to intensify; **intensité** *nf* intensity.

intenter [ε̃tɑ̃te] *vt*: ~ **un procès contre** *ou* **à** to start proceedings against.

intention [ε̃tɑ̃sjɔ̃] *nf* intention; (JUR) intent; **avoir l'~ de faire** to intend to do, have the intention of doing; **à l'~ de** *prép* for; (*renseignement*) for the benefit *ou* information of; (*film, ouvrage*) aimed at; **à cette ~** with this aim in view; **intentionné, e** *a*: **bien intentionné** well-meaning *ou* -intentioned; **mal intentionné** ill-intentioned; **intentionnel, le** *a* intentional, deliberate.

inter [ε̃tεr] *nm* (TEL) *abr de* **interurbain**; (SPORT): ~-**gauche**/ -**droit** inside-left/-right.

intercalaire [ε̃tεrkalεr] *a*: **feuillet** ~ insert; **fiche** ~ divider.

intercaler [ε̃tεrkale] *vt* to insert; **s'~ entre** to come in between; to slip in between.

intercéder [ε̃tεrsede] *vi*: ~ (**pour qn**) to intercede (on behalf of sb).

intercepter [ε̃tεrsεpte] *vt* to intercept; (*lumière, chaleur*) to cut off; **interception** [-sjɔ̃] *nf* interception; **avion d'interception** interceptor.

interchangeable [ε̃tεrʃɑ̃ʒabl(ə)] *a* interchangeable.

interclasse [ε̃tεrklɑs] *nm* (SCOL) break (between classes).

interdiction [ε̃tεrdiksjɔ̃] *nf* ban; ~ **de séjour** (JUR) order banning ex-prisoner from frequenting specified places.

interdire [ε̃tεrdir] *vt* to forbid; (ADMIN: *stationnement, meeting, passage*) to ban, prohibit; (: *journal, livre*) to ban; ~ **qch à qn** to forbid sb sth; ~ **à qn de faire** to forbid sb to do, prohibit sb from doing; (*suj: empêchement*) to prevent *ou* preclude sb from doing.

interdit, e [ε̃tεrdi, -it] *a* (*stupéfait*) taken aback // *nm* interdict, prohibition.

intéressant, e [ε̃tεresɑ̃, -ɑ̃t] *a* interesting.

intéressé, e [ε̃tεrese] *a* (*parties*) involved, concerned; (*amitié, motifs*) self-interested; **les** ~**s** those concerned *ou* involved.

intéressement [ε̃tεrεsmɑ̃] *nm* (COMM) profit-sharing.

intéresser [ε̃tεrese] *vt* (*captiver*) to interest; (*toucher*) to be of interest *ou* concern to; (ADMIN: *concerner*) to affect, concern; (COMM: *travailleur*) to give a share in the profits to; (: *partenaire*) to interest (in the business); **s'~ à** to take an interest in, be interested in.

intérêt [ε̃tεrε] *nm* (*gén, aussi* COMM) interest; (*égoïsme*) self-interest; **avoir des** ~**s dans** (COMM) to have a financial

interest *ou* a stake in; **avoir ~ à faire** to be well-advised to do.

interférer [ε̃tεrfere] *vi*: ~ (**avec**) to interfere (with).

intérieur, e [ε̃terjœr] *a* (*mur, escalier, poche*) inside; (*commerce, politique*) domestic; (*cour, calme, vie*) inner; (*navigation*) inland // *nm* (*d'une maison, d'un récipient etc*) inside; (*d'un pays, aussi: décor, mobilier*) interior; (POL): **l'I~** the Interior, ≈ the Home Office; **à l'~ (de)** inside; (*fig*) within; **en** ~ (CINÉMA) in the studio; **vêtement d'~** indoor garment.

intérim [ε̃terim] *nm* interim period; **assurer l'~ (de)** to deputize (for); **par** ~ *a* interim // *ad* in a temporary capacity; ~**aire** *a* temporary, interim.

intérioriser [ε̃terjɔrize] *vt* to internalize.

interjection [ε̃tεrʒεksjɔ̃] *nf* interjection.

interligne [ε̃tεrliɲ] *nm* space between the lines // *nf* lead; **simple/double** ~ single/double spacing.

interlocuteur, trice [ε̃tεrlɔkytœr, -tris] *nm/f* speaker; **son** ~ the person he was speaking to.

interlope [ε̃tεrlɔp] *a* shady.

interloquer [ε̃tεrlɔke] *vt* to take aback.

interlude [ε̃tεrlyd] *nm* interlude.

intermède [ε̃tεrmεd] *nm* interlude.

intermédiaire [ε̃tεrmedjεr] *a* intermediate; middle; half-way // *nm/f* intermediary; (COMM) middleman; **sans** ~ directly; **par l'~ de** through.

interminable [ε̃tεrminabl(ə)] *a* never-ending.

intermittence [ε̃tεrmitɑ̃s] *nf*: **par** ~ sporadically, intermittently.

intermittent, e [ε̃tεrmitɑ̃, -ɑ̃t] *a* intermittent.

internat [ε̃tεrna] *nm* (SCOL) boarding school.

international, e, aux [ε̃tεrnasjɔnal, -o] *a* international // *nm/f* (SPORT) international player.

interne [ε̃tεrn(ə)] *a* internal // *nm/f* (SCOL) boarder; (MÉD) houseman.

interner [ε̃tεrne] *vt* (POL) to intern; (MÉD) to confine to a mental institution.

interpellation [ε̃tεrpelɑsjɔ̃] *nf* interpellation; (POL) question.

interpeller [ε̃tεrpele] *vt* (*appeler*) to call out to; (*apostropher*) to shout at; (POLICE) to take in for questioning; (POL) to question.

interphone [ε̃tεrfɔn] *nm* intercom.

interposer [ε̃tεrpoze] *vt* to interpose; **s'~** *vi* to intervene; **par personnes interposées** through a third party.

interprétariat [ε̃tεrpretarja] *nm* interpreting.

interprétation [ε̃tεrpretɑsjɔ̃] *nf* interpretation.

interprète [ε̃tεrprεt] *nm/f* interpreter; (*porte-parole*) spokes-man.

interpréter [ε̃tεrprete] *vt* to interpret.

interrogateur, trice [ε̃tεrɔgatœr, -tris] *a* questioning, inquiring // *nm/f* (SCOL) (oral) examiner.

interrogatif, ive [ε̃terɔgatif, -iv] *a* (LING) interrogative.

interrogation [ɛteRɔgɑsjɔ̃] *nf* question ; (*SCOL*) (written *ou* oral) test.

interrogatoire [ɛteRɔgatwaR] *nm* (*POLICE*) questioning *q* ; (*JUR*) cross-examination.

interroger [ɛteRɔʒe] *vt* to question ; (*données, ordinateur*) to consult ; (*SCOL*) to test.

interrompre [ɛteRɔ̃pR(ə)] *vt* (*gén*) to interrupt ; (*travail, voyage*) to break off, interrupt ; **s'~** to break off.

interrupteur [ɛteRyptœR] *nm* switch.

interruption [ɛteRypsjɔ̃] *nf* interruption ; **sans ~** without a break ; **~ de grossesse** termination of pregnancy.

intersection [ɛteRsɛksjɔ̃] *nf* intersection.

interstice [ɛteRstis] *nm* crack ; slit.

interurbain [ɛteRyRbɛ̃] *nm* (*TÉL*) trunk call service.

intervalle [ɛteRval] *nm* (*espace*) space ; (*de temps*) interval ; **dans l'~** in the meantime.

intervenir [ɛteRvəniR] *vi* (*gén*) to intervene ; (*survenir*) to take place ; **~ auprès de** to intervene with ; **la police a dû ~** police had to be called in ; **les médecins ont dû ~** the doctors had to operate.

intervention [ɛteRvɑ̃sjɔ̃] *nf* intervention ; **~ chirurgicale** (surgical) operation.

intervertir [ɛteRvɛRtiR] *vt* to invert (the order of), reverse.

interview [ɛteRvju] *nf* interview ; **interviewer** *vt* [-ve] to interview.

intestin, e [ɛtɛstɛ̃, -in] *a* internal // *nm* intestine ; **~ grêle** small intestine ; **intestinal, e, aux** *a* intestinal.

intime [ɛtim] *a* intimate ; (*vie, journal*) private ; (*conviction*) inmost ; (*dîner, cérémonie*) held among friends, quiet // *nm/f* close friend.

intimer [ɛtime] *vt* (*JUR*) to notify ; **~ à qn l'ordre de faire** to order sb to do.

intimider [ɛtimide] *vt* to intimidate.

intimité [ɛtimite] *nf* intimacy ; privacy ; private life ; **dans l'~** in private ; (*sans formalités*) with only a few friends, quietly.

intitulé [ɛtityle] *nm* title.

intituler [ɛtityle] *vt*: **comment a-t-il intitulé son livre?** what title did he give his book? ; **s'~** to be entitled ; (*personne*) to call o.s.

intolérable [ɛtɔleRabl(ə)] *a* intolerable.

intolérance [ɛtɔleRɑ̃s] *nf* intolerance.

intolérant, e [ɛtɔleRɑ̃, -ɑ̃t] *a* intolerant.

intonation [ɛtɔnɑsjɔ̃] *nf* intonation.

intouchable [ɛtuʃabl(ə)] *a* (*fig*) above the law, sacrosanct ; (*REL*) untouchable.

intoxication [ɛtɔksikasjɔ̃] *nf* poisoning *q* ; (*fig*) brainwashing ; **~ alimentaire** food poisoning.

intoxiquer [ɛtɔksike] *vt* to poison ; (*fig*) to brainwash.

intraduisible [ɛtRaduizibl(ə)] *a* untranslatable ; (*fig*) impossible to render.

intraitable [ɛtRɛtabl(ə)] *a* inflexible, uncompromising.

intransigeance [ɛtRɑ̃ziʒɑ̃s] *nf* intransigence.

intransigeant, e [ɛtRɑ̃ziʒɑ̃, -ɑ̃t] *a* intransigent ; (*morale, passion*) uncompromising.

intransitif, ive [ɛtRɑ̃zitif, -iv] *a* (*LING*) intransitive.

intransportable [ɛtRɑ̃spɔRtabl(ə)] *a* (*blessé*) unable to travel.

intraveineux, euse [ɛtRavɛnø, -øz] *a* intravenous.

intrépide [ɛtRepid] *a* dauntless.

intrigant, e [ɛtRigɑ̃, -ɑ̃t] *nm/f* schemer.

intrigue [ɛtRig] *nf* intrigue.

intriguer [ɛtRige] *vi* to scheme // *vt* to puzzle, intrigue.

intrinsèque [ɛtRɛ̃sɛk] *a* intrinsic.

introduction [ɛtRɔdyksjɔ̃] *nf* introduction.

introduire [ɛtRɔduiR] *vt* to introduce ; (*visiteur*) to show in ; (*aiguille, clef*): **~ qch dans** to insert *ou* introduce sth into ; **s'~** (*techniques, usages*) to be introduced ; **s'~ dans** to gain entry into ; to get o.s. accepted into ; (*eau, fumée*) to get into.

introniser [ɛtRɔnize] *vt* to enthrone.

introspection [ɛtRɔspɛksjɔ̃] *nf* introspection.

introuvable [ɛtRuvabl(ə)] *a* which cannot be found ; (*COMM*) unobtainable.

introverti, e [ɛtRɔvɛRti] *nm/f* introvert.

intrus, e [ɛtRy, -yz] *nm/f* intruder.

intrusion [ɛtRyzjɔ̃] *nf* intrusion ; interference.

intuitif, ive [ɛtuitif, -iv] *a* intuitive.

intuition [ɛtuisjɔ̃] *nf* intuition.

inusable [inyzabl(ə)] *a* hard-wearing.

inusité, e [inyzite] *a* not in common use ; unaccustomed.

inutile [inytil] *a* useless ; (*superflu*) unnecessary ; **inutilisable** *a* unusable ; **inutilité** *nf* uselessness.

invaincu, e [ɛ̃vɛ̃ky] *a* unbeaten ; unconquered.

invalide [ɛ̃valid] *a* disabled ; **~ de guerre** disabled ex-serviceman ; **~ du travail** industrially disabled person.

invalider [ɛ̃valide] *vt* to invalidate.

invalidité [ɛ̃validite] *nf* disability.

invariable [ɛ̃vaRjabl(ə)] *a* in-variable.

invasion [ɛ̃vɑzjɔ̃] *nf* invasion.

invectiver [ɛ̃vɛktive] *vt* to hurl abuse at // *vi*: **~ contre** to rail against.

invendable [ɛ̃vɑ̃dabl(ə)] *a* unsaleable ; unmarketable ; **invendus** *nmpl* unsold goods.

inventaire [ɛ̃vɑ̃tɛR] *nm* inventory ; (*COMM*: *liste*) stocklist ; (: *opéra-tion*) stocktaking *q* ; (*fig*) survey.

inventer [ɛ̃vɑ̃te] *vt* to invent ; (*subterfuge*) to devise, invent ; (*histoire, excuse*) to make up, invent ; **~ de faire** to hit on the idea of doing ; **inventeur** *nm* inventor ; **inventif, ive** *a* inventive ; **invention** [-sjɔ̃] *nf* invention.

inventorier [ɛ̃vɑ̃tɔRje] *vt* to make an inventory of.

inverse [ɛ̃vɛRs(ə)] *a* reverse ; opposite ; inverse // *nm* inverse, reverse ; **en proportion ~** in inverse proportion ; **dans l'ordre ~** in the reverse order ; **en sens ~** in (*ou* from) the opposite direction ; **~ment** *ad* conversely ; **inverser** *vt* to invert, reverse ; (*ELEC*) to reverse ; **inversion** *nf* inversion ; reversal.

inverti, e [ɛ̃vɛʀti] nm/f homosexual.
investigation [ɛ̃vɛstigɑsjɔ̃] nf investigation, inquiry.
investir [ɛ̃vɛstiʀ] vt to invest; **investissement** nm investment; **investiture** nf investiture; (à une élection) nomination.
invétéré, e [ɛ̃veteʀe] a (habitude) ingrained; (bavard, buveur) inveterate.
invincible [ɛ̃vɛ̃sibl(ə)] a invincible, unconquerable.
invisible [ɛ̃vizibl(ə)] a invisible.
invitation [ɛ̃vitɑsjɔ̃] nf invitation.
invité, e [ɛ̃vite] nm/f guest.
inviter [ɛ̃vite] vt to invite; ~ qn à faire to invite sb to do; (suj: chose) to induce ou tempt sb to do.
involontaire [ɛ̃vɔlɔ̃tɛʀ] a (mouvement) involuntary; (insulte) unintentional; (complice) unwitting.
invoquer [ɛ̃vɔke] vt (Dieu, muse) to call upon, invoke; (prétexte) to put forward (as an excuse); (témoignage) to call upon; (loi, texte) to refer to; ~ **la clémence de qn** to beg sb ou appeal to sb for clemency.
invraisemblable [ɛ̃vʀɛsɑ̃blabl(ə)] a unlikely, improbable; incredible.
invulnérable [ɛ̃vylneʀabl(ə)] a invulnerable.
iode [jɔd] nm iodine.
ion [jɔ̃] nm ion.
ionique [jɔnik] a (ARCHIT) Ionic; (SCIENCE) ionic.
irai etc vb voir **aller.**
Irak [iʀɑk] nm Iraq; **irakien, ne** a, nm/f Iraqi.
Iran [iʀɑ̃] nm Iran; **Iranien, ne** nm/f Iranian.
irascible [iʀasibl(ə)] a short-tempered, irascible.
irions etc vb voir **aller.**
iris [iʀis] nm iris.
irisé, e [iʀize] a iridescent.
irlandais, e [iʀlɑdɛ, -ɛz] a, nm (langue) Irish // nm/f: I~, e Irishman/woman; **les** I~ the Irish.
Irlande [iʀlɑ̃d] nf Ireland; ~ **du Nord** Northern Ireland.
ironie [iʀɔni] nf irony; **ironique** a ironical; **ironiser** vi to be ironical.
irons etc vb voir **aller.**
irradier [iʀadje] vi to radiate // vt to irradiate.
irraisonné, e [iʀɛzɔne] a irrational, unreasoned.
irrationnel, le [iʀasjɔnɛl] a irrational.
irréalisable [iʀealizabl(ə)] a unrealizable; impracticable.
irréconciliable [iʀekɔ̃siljabl(ə)] a unreconcilable.
irrécupérable [iʀekypeʀabl(ə)] a unreclaimable, beyond repair; (personne) beyond redemption ou recall.
irrécusable [iʀekyzabl(ə)] a unimpeachable.
irréductible [iʀedyktibl(ə)] a indomitable, implacable; (MATH) irreducible.
irréel, le [iʀeɛl] a unreal.
irréfléchi, e [iʀeflefi] a thoughtless.

irréfutable [iʀefytabl(ə)] a irrefutable.
irrégularité [iʀegylaʀite] nf irregularity; unevenness q.
irrégulier, ière [iʀegylje, -jɛʀ] a irregular; uneven; (élève, athlète) erratic.
irrémédiable [iʀemedjabl(ə)] a irreparable.
irremplaçable [iʀɑ̃plasabl(ə)] a irreplaceable.
irréparable [iʀepaʀabl(ə)] a beyond repair; (fig) irreparable.
irrépressible [iʀepʀesibl(ə)] a irrepressible, uncontrollable.
irréprochable [iʀepʀɔʃabl(ə)] a irreproachable, beyond reproach; (tenue, toilette) impeccable.
irrésistible [iʀezistibl(ə)] a irresistible; (preuve, logique) compelling.
irrésolu, e [iʀezɔly] a irresolute.
irrespectueux, euse [iʀɛspɛktɥø, -øz] a disrespectful.
irrespirable [iʀɛspiʀabl(ə)] a unbreathable; (fig) oppressive, stifling.
irresponsable [iʀɛspɔ̃sabl(ə)] a irresponsible.
irrévérencieux, euse [iʀeveʀɑ̃sjø, -øz] a irreverent.
irréversible [iʀevɛʀsibl(ə)] a irreversible.
irrévocable [iʀevɔkabl(ə)] a irrevocable.
irrigation [iʀigɑsjɔ̃] nf irrigation.
irriguer [iʀige] vt to irrigate.
irritable [iʀitabl(ə)] a irritable.
irritation [iʀitɑsjɔ̃] nf irritation.
irriter [iʀite] vt (agacer) to irritate, annoy; (MÉD: enflammer) to irritate; **s'**~ **contre/de** to get annoyed ou irritated at/with.
irruption [iʀypsjɔ̃] nf irruption q; **faire** ~ **dans** to burst into.
Islam [islam] nm Islam; **islamique** a Islamic.
islandais, e [islɑ̃dɛ, -ɛz] a, nm (langue) Icelandic // nm/f Icelander.
Islande [islɑ̃d] nf Iceland.
isocèle [izɔsɛl] a isoceles.
isolant, e [izɔlɑ̃, -ɑ̃t] a insulating; (insonorisant) soundproofing.
isolation [izɔlɑsjɔ̃] nf insulation.
isolé, e [izɔle] a isolated; insulated.
isolement [izɔlmɑ̃] nm isolation; solitary confinement.
isoler [izɔle] vt to isolate; (prisonnier) to put in solitary confinement; (ville) to cut off, isolate; (ÉLEC) to insulate; **isoloir** nm polling booth.
Israël [isʀaɛl] nm Israel; **israélien, ne** a, nm/f Israeli; **israélite** a Jewish // nm/f Jew/Jewess.
issu, e [isy] a: ~ **de** descended from; (fig) stemming from // nf (ouverture, sortie) exit; (solution) way out, solution; (dénouement) outcome; **à l'**~**e de** at the conclusion ou close of; **rue sans** ~**e** dead end, no through road.
isthme [ism(ə)] nm isthmus.
Italie [itali] nf Italy; **Italien, ne** a, nm, nf Italian.
italique [italik] nm: **en** ~ in italics.
itinéraire [itineʀɛʀ] nm itinerary, route.

itinérant, e [itineʀɑ̃, -ɑ̃t] *a* itinerant, travelling.

I.U.T. *sigle m voir* **institut.**

ivoire [ivwaʀ] *nm* ivory.

ivre [ivʀ(ə)] *a* drunk; ~ **de** (*colère, bonheur*) wild with; **ivresse** *nf* drunkenness; **ivrogne** *nm/f* drunkard.

J

j' [ʒ] *pronom voir* **je.**

jabot [ʒabo] *nm* (ZOOL) crop; (*de vêtement*) jabot.

jacasser [ʒakase] *vi* to chatter.

jachère [ʒaʃɛʀ] *nf*: (être) en ~ (to lie) fallow.

jacinthe [ʒasɛ̃t] *nf* hyacinth.

jade [ʒad] *nm* jade.

jadis [ʒadis] *ad* in times past, formerly.

jaillir [ʒajiʀ] *vi* (*liquide*) to spurt out, gush out; (*fig*) to rear up; to burst out; to flood out.

jais [ʒɛ] *nm* jet; (**d'un noir) de** ~ jet-black.

jalon [ʒalɔ̃] *nm* range pole; (*fig*) milestone; **jalonner** *vt* to mark out; (*fig*) to mark, punctuate.

jalouser [ʒaluze] *vt* to be jealous of.

jalousie [ʒaluzi] *nf* jealousy; (*store*) (venetian) blind.

jaloux, se [ʒalu, -uz] *a* jealous.

jamais [ʒamɛ] *ad* never; (*sans négation*) ever; **ne ... ~** never.

jambage [ʒɑ̃baʒ] *nm* (*de lettre*) downstroke; (*de porte*) jamb.

jambe [ʒɑ̃b] *nf* leg; **jambières** *nfpl* leggings; (SPORT) shin pads.

jambon [ʒɑ̃bɔ̃] *nm* ham.

jante [ʒɑ̃t] *nf* (wheel) rim.

janvier [ʒɑ̃vje] *nm* January.

Japon [ʒapɔ̃] *nm* Japan; **japonais, e** *a, nm, nf* Japanese.

japper [ʒape] *vi* to yap, yelp.

jaquette [ʒakɛt] *nf* (*de cérémonie*) morning coat; (*de livre*) dust cover, dust jacket.

jardin [ʒaʀdɛ̃] *nm* garden; ~ **d'acclimatation** zoological gardens *pl*; ~ **d'enfants** nursery school; ~ **public** (public) park, public gardens *pl*; **jardinage** *nm* gardening; **jardinier, ière** *nm/f* gardener // *nf* (*de fenêtre*) window box; **jardinière d'enfants** nursery school teacher.

jargon [ʒaʀgɔ̃] *nm* jargon.

jarre [ʒaʀ] *nf* (earthenware) jar.

jarret [ʒaʀɛ] *nm* back of knee, ham; (CULIN) knuckle, shin.

jarretelle [ʒaʀtɛl] *nf* suspender.

jarretière [ʒaʀtjɛʀ] *nf* garter.

jaser [ʒaze] *vi* to chatter, prattle; (*indiscrètement*) to gossip.

jasmin [ʒasmɛ̃] *nm* jasmin.

jaspe [ʒasp(ə)] *nm* jasper.

jatte [ʒat] *nf* basin, bowl.

jauge [ʒoʒ] *nf* (*capacité*) capacity, tonnage; (*instrument*) gauge; **jauger** *vt* to gauge the capacity of; (*fig*) to size up; **jauger 3000 tonneaux** to measure 3,000 tons.

jaune [ʒon] *a, nm* yellow // *nm/f* Asiatic // *ad* (*fam*): **rire** ~ to laugh on the other side of one's face; ~ **d'œuf** (egg) yolk; **jaunir** *vi, vt* to turn yellow.

jaunisse [ʒonis] *nf* jaundice.

javel [ʒavɛl] *nf voir* **eau.**

javelot [ʒavlo] *nm* javelin.

jazz [dʒaz] *nm* jazz.

J.-C. *sigle voir* **Jésus-Christ.**

je, j' [ʒ(ə)] *pronom* I.

jean [dʒin] *nm* jeans *pl.*

jérémiades [ʒeʀemjad] *nfpl* moaning *sg.*

jerrycan [ʒeʀikan] *nm* jerrycan.

jersey [ʒɛʀze] *nm* jersey.

Jésus-Christ [ʒezykʀi(st)] *n* Jesus Christ; **600 avant/après** ~ *ou* **J.-C.** 600 B.C./A.D.

jet [ʒɛ] *nm* (*lancer*) throwing q, throw; (*jaillissement*) jet; spurt; (*de tuyau*) nozzle; (*avion*) [dʒɛt] jet; **arroser au** ~ to hose; **du premier** ~ at the first attempt or shot; ~ **d'eau** fountain; spray.

jetée [ʒəte] *nf* jetty; pier.

jeter [ʒəte] *vt* (*gén*) to throw; (*se défaire de*) to throw away *ou* out; (*son, lueur etc*) to give out; ~ **qch à qn** to throw sth to sb; (*de façon agressive*) to throw *ou* hurl sth at sb; ~ **un coup d'œil (à)** to take a look (at); ~ **l'effroi parmi** to spread fear among; ~ **un sort à qn** to cast a spell on sb; **se** ~ **dans** (*fleuve*) to flow into.

jeton [ʒətɔ̃] *nm* (*au jeu*) counter; (*de téléphone*) token; ~**s de présence** (director's) fees.

jette *etc vb voir* **jeter.**

jeu, x [ʒø] *nm* (*divertissement*, TECH: *d'une pièce*) play; (*défini par des règles*, TENNIS: *partie*, FOOTBALL *etc*: *façon de jouer*) game; (THÉÂTRE *etc*) acting; (*au casino*): **le** ~ gambling; (*fonctionnement*) working, interplay; (*série d'objets, jouet*) set; (CARTES) hand; **en** ~ at stake; at work; (FOOTBALL) in play; **remettre en** ~ to throw in; **entrer/mettre en** ~ to come/bring into play; ~ **de boules** game of bowls; (*endroit*) bowling pitch; (*boules*) set of bowls; ~ **de cartes** card game; (*paquet*) pack of cards; ~ **de construction** building set; ~ **d'échecs** chess set; ~ **de hasard** game of chance; ~ **de mots** pun; **le** ~ **de l'oie** snakes and ladders *sg*; ~ **d'orgue(s)** organ stop; ~ **de société** parlour game; **J** ~ **x olympiques (J.O.)** Olympic Games.

jeudi [ʒødi] *nm* Thursday.

jeûn [ʒœ̃]: **à** ~ *ad* on an empty stomach.

jeune [ʒœn] *a* young; **les** ~**s** young people, the young; ~ **fille** *nf* girl; ~ **homme** *nm* young man; ~ **premier** leading man; ~**s gens** *nmpl* young people.

jeûne [ʒøn] *nm* fast.

jeunesse [ʒœnɛs] *nf* youth; (*aspect*) youthfulness; youngness; (*jeunes*) young people *pl*, youth.

J. O. *sigle voir* **jeu.**

joaillerie [ʒɔajʀi] *nf* jewel trade; jewellery; **joaillier, ière** *nm/f* jeweller.

jobard [ʒɔbaʀ] *nm* (*péj*) sucker, mug.

jockey [ʒɔkɛ] *nm* jockey.

joie [ʒwa] *nf* joy.

joindre [ʒwɛdʀ(ə)] *vt* to join; (*à une lettre*): ~ **qch à** to enclose sth with; (*contacter*) to contact, get in touch with; ~ **les mains/talons** to put one's hands/heels together; **se** ~ **à** to join.

joint [ʒwɛ] *nm* joint; (*ligne*) join; (*de ciment etc*) pointing *q*; ~ **de cardan** cardan joint; ~ **de culasse** cylinder head gasket; ~ **de robinet** washer.

joli [ʒɔli] *a* pretty, attractive; **c'est du** ~! (*ironique*) that's very nice!; ~**ment** *ad* prettily, attractively; (*fam: très*) pretty.

jonc [ʒɔ̃] *nm* (bul)rush.

joncher [ʒɔ̃ʃe] *vt* (*suj: choses*) to be strewed on; **jonché de** strewn with.

jonction [ʒɔ̃ksjɔ̃] *nf* joining; (**point de**) ~ junction; **opérer une** ~ (MIL *etc*) to rendez-vous.

jongler [ʒɔ̃gle] *vi* to juggle; **jongleur, euse** *nm/f* juggler.

jonquille [ʒɔ̃kij] *nf* daffodil.

Jordanie [ʒɔʀdani] *nf*: **la** ~ Jordan.

joue [ʒu] *nf* cheek; **mettre en** ~ to take aim at.

jouer [ʒwe] *vt* (*partie, carte, coup,* MUS: *morceau*) to play; (*somme d'argent, réputation*) to stake, wager; (*pièce, rôle*) to perform; (*film*) to show; (*simuler: sentiment*) to affect, feign // *vi* to play; (THÉÂTRE, CINÉMA) to act, perform; (*bois, porte: se voiler*) to warp; (*clef, pièce: avoir du jeu*) to be loose; ~ **sur** (*miser*) to gamble on; ~ **de** (MUS) to play; ~ **du couteau/des coudes** to use knives/one's elbows; ~ **à** (*jeu, sport, roulette*) to play; ~ **au héros** to play the hero; ~ **avec** (*risquer*) to gamble with; **se** ~ **de** (*difficultés*) to make light of; **se** ~ **de qn** to deceive *ou* dupe sb; ~ **un tour à qn** to play a trick on sb; ~ **serré** to play a close game; ~ **de malchance** to be dogged with ill-luck.

jouet [ʒwe] *nm* toy; **être le** ~ **de** (*illusion etc*) to be the victim of.

joueur, euse [ʒwœʀ, -øz] *nm/f* player; **être beau/mauvais** ~ to be a good/bad loser.

joufflu, e [ʒufly] *a* chubby-cheeked, chubby.

joug [ʒu] *nm* yoke.

jouir [ʒwiʀ]: ~ **de** *vt* to enjoy; **jouissance** *nf* pleasure; (JUR) use; **jouisseur, euse** *nm/f* sensualist.

joujou [ʒuʒu] *nm* (*fam*) toy.

jour [ʒuʀ] *nm* day; (*opposé à la nuit*) day, daytime; (*clarté*) daylight; (*fig: aspect*) light; (*ouverture*) opening; openwork *q*; **au** ~ **le** ~ from day to day; **de nos** ~**s** these days, nowadays; **il fait** ~ it's daylight; **au** ~ in daylight; **au grand** ~ (*fig*) in the open; **mettre au** ~ to uncover, disclose; **mettre à** ~ to bring up to date, update; **donner le** ~ **à** to give birth to; **voir le** ~ to be born; **se faire** ~ to become clear.

journal, aux [ʒuʀnal, -o] *nm* (news)paper; (*personnel*) journal, diary; ~ **parlé/télévisé** radio/ television news *sg*; ~ **de bord** log.

journalier, ière [ʒuʀnalje, -jɛʀ] *a* daily; (*banal*) everyday // *nm* day labourer.

journalisme [ʒuʀnalism(ə)] *nm* journalism; **journaliste** *nm/f* journalist.

journée [ʒuʀne] *nf* day; **la** ~ **continue** the 9 to 5 working day (with short lunch break).

journellement [ʒuʀnɛlmã] *ad* daily.

joute [ʒut] *nf* duel.

jouvence [ʒuvãs] *nf*: **bain de** ~ rejuvenating experience.

jovial [ʒɔvjal] *a* jovial, jolly.

joyau, x [ʒwajo] *nm* gem, jewel.

joyeux, euse [ʒwajø, -øz] *a* joyful, merry; ~ **Noël!** merry *ou* happy Christmas!; ~ **anniversaire!** many happy returns!

jubilé [ʒybile] *nm* jubilee.

jubiler [ʒybile] *vi* to be jubilant, exult.

jucher [ʒyʃe] *vt*: ~ **qch sur** to perch sth (up)on // *vi* (*oiseau*): ~ **sur** to perch (up)on; **se** ~ **sur** to perch o.s. (up)on.

judaïque [ʒydaik] *a* (*loi*) Judaic; (*religion*) Jewish.

judaïsme [ʒydaism(ə)] *nm* Judaism.

judas [ʒyda] *nm* (*trou*) spy-hole.

judiciaire [ʒydisjɛʀ] *a* judicial.

judicieux, euse [ʒydisjø, -øz] *a* judicious.

judo [ʒydo] *nm* judo; ~**ka** *nm/f* judoka.

juge [ʒyʒ] *nm* judge; ~ **d'instruction** examining magis-trate; ~ **de paix** justice of the peace; ~ **de touche** linesman.

jugé [ʒyʒe]: **au** ~ *ad* by guesswork.

jugement [ʒyʒmã] *nm* judgment; (JUR: *au criminel*) sentence; (: *au civil*) decision; ~ **de valeur** value judgment.

jugeote [ʒyʒɔt] *nf* (*fam*) gumption.

juger [ʒyʒe] *vt* to judge; ~ **qn/qch satisfaisant** to consider sb/sth (to be) satisfactory; ~ **que** to think *ou* consider that; ~ **bon de faire** to consider it a good idea to do, see fit to do; ~ **de** *vt* to appreciate.

jugulaire [ʒygylɛʀ] *a* jugular // *nf* (MIL) chinstrap.

juif, ive [ʒɥif, -iv] *a* Jewish // *nm/f* Jew/Jewess.

juillet [ʒɥijɛ] *nm* July.

juin [ʒɥɛ̃] *nm* June.

jumeau, elle, x [ʒymo, -ɛl] *a, nm/f* twin; **jumelles** *nfpl* binoculars.

jumeler [ʒymle] *vt* to twin; **roues jumelées** double wheels.

jumelle [ʒymɛl] *a, nf voir* **jumeau**.

jument [ʒymã] *nf* mare.

jungle [ʒɔ̃gl(ə)] *nf* jungle.

jupe [ʒyp] *nf* skirt; ~**-culotte** *nf* divided skirt, culotte(s).

jupon [ʒypɔ̃] *nm* waist slip *ou* petticoat.

juré, e [ʒyʀe] *nm/f* juror, juryman/wo-man // *a*: **ennemi** ~ sworn enemy.

jurer [ʒyʀe] *vt* (*obéissance etc*) to swear, vow // *vi* (*dire des jurons*) to swear, curse; (*dissoner*): ~ **(avec)** to clash (with); (*s'engager*): ~ **de faire/que** to swear *ou* vow to do/that; (*affirmer*): ~ **que** to swear *ou* vouch that; ~ **de qch** (*s'en porter garant*) to swear to sth.

juridiction [ʒyʀidiksjɔ̃] *nf* jurisdiction; court(s) of law.

juridique [ʒyʀidik] *a* legal.

juriste [ʒyRist(ə)] *nm/f* jurist ; lawyer.
juron [ʒyRɔ̃] *nm* curse, swearword.
jury [ʒyRi] *nm* (*JUR*) jury ; (*SCOL*) board (of examiners), jury.
jus [ʒy] *nm* juice ; (*de viande*) gravy, (meat) juice ; ~ **de fruits** fruit juice ; ~ **de raisin/tomates** grape/tomato juice.
jusant [ʒyzɑ̃] *nm* ebb (tide).
jusque [ʒysk(ə)]: **jusqu'à** *prép* (*endroit*) as far as, (up) to ; (*moment*) until, till ; (*limite*) up to ; ~ **sur/dans** up to, as far as ; (*y compris*) even on/in ; **jusqu'à présent** until now, so far.
juste [ʒyst(ə)] *a* (*équitable*) just, fair ; (*légitime*) just, justified ; (*exact, vrai*) right ; (*étroit, insuffisant*) tight // *ad* right ; tight ; (*chanter*) in tune ; (*seulement*) just ; ~ **assez/au-dessus** just enough/above ; **pouvoir tout ~ faire** to be only just able to do ; **au** ~ exactly, actually ; **le ~ milieu** the happy medium ; ~**ment** *ad* rightly ; justly ; (*précisément*): **c'est** ~**ment ce que** that's just *ou* precisely what ; **justesse** *nf* (*précision*) accuracy ; (*d'une remarque*) aptness ; (*d'une opinion*) soundness ; **de justesse** just, by a narrow margin.
justice [ʒystis] *nf* (*équité*) fairness, justice ; (*ADMIN*) justice ; **rendre la** ~ to dispense justice ; **obtenir** ~ to obtain justice ; **rendre** ~ **à qn** to do sb justice ; **se faire** ~ to take the law into one's own hands ; (*se suicider*) to take one's life.
justiciable [ʒystisjabl(ə)] *a*: ~ **de** (*JUR*) answerable to.
justicier, ière [ʒystisje, -jɛR] *nm/f* judge, righter of wrongs.
justifiable [ʒystifjabl(ə)] *a* justifiable.
justification [ʒystifikɑsjɔ̃] *nf* justification.
justifier [ʒystifje] *vt* to justify ; ~ **de** *vt* to prove.
jute [ʒyt] *nm* jute.
juteux, euse [ʒytø, -øz] *a* juicy.
juvénile [ʒyvenil] *a* young, youthful.
juxtaposer [ʒykstapoze] *vt* to juxtapose.

K

kaki [kaki] *a inv* khaki.
kaléidoscope [kaleidɔskɔp] *nm* kaleidoscope.
kangourou [kɑ̃guRu] *nm* kangaroo.
karaté [kaRate] *nm* karate.
karting [kaRtiŋ] *nm* go-carting, karting.
kayac, kayak [kajak] *nm* kayak.
képi [kepi] *nm* kepi.
kermesse [kɛRmɛs] *nf* bazaar, (charity) fête ; village fair.
kérosène [keRozɛn] *nm* jet fuel ; rocket fuel.
kibboutz [kibuts] *nm* kibbutz.
kidnapper [kidnape] *vt* to kidnap.
kilogramme [kilɔgRam] *nm*, **kilo** *nm* kilogramme.
kilométrage [kilɔmetRaʒ] *nm* number of kilometres travelled, ≈ mileage.
kilomètre [kilɔmɛtR(ə)] *nm* kilometre.
kilométrique [kilɔmetRik] *a* (*distance*) in kilometres ; **compteur** ~ ≈ mileage indicator.

kilowatt [kilɔwat] *nm* kilowatt.
kinésithérapeute [kineziteRapøt] *nm/f* physiotherapist.
kiosque [kjɔsk(ə)] *nm* kiosk, stall.
kirsch [kiRʃ] *nm* kirsch.
klaxon [klaksɔn] *nm* horn ; **klaxonner** *vi*, *vt* to hoot.
kleptomane [klɛptɔman] *nm/f* kleptomaniac.
km. *abr de* **kilomètre** ; **km./h** (= *kilomètres-heure*) ≈ m.p.h. (miles per hour).
knock-out [nɔkawt] *nm* knock-out.
K.-O. [kao] *a inv* (knocked) out, out for the count.
kolkhoze [kɔlkoz] *nm* kolkhoz.
kyrielle [kiRjɛl] *nf*: **une** ~ **de** a stream of.
kyste [kist(ə)] *nm* cyst.

L

l' [l] *dét voir* **le**.
la [la] *nm* (*MUS*) A ; (*en chantant la gamme*) la.
la [la] *dét voir* **le**.
là [la] (*voir aussi* **-ci, celui**) *ad* there ; (*ici*) here ; (*dans le temps*) then ; **est-ce que Catherine est** ~? is Catherine there *ou* in? ; **elle n'est pas** ~ she isn't in *ou* here ; **c'est** ~ **que** this is where ; ~ **où** where ; **de** ~ (*fig*) hence ; **par** ~ (*fig*) by that ; **tout est** ~ (*fig*) that's what it's all about ; ~**-bas** *ad* there.
label [labɛl] *nm* stamp, seal.
labeur [labœR] *nm* toil *q*, toiling *q*.
labo [labo] *nm* (*abr de* **laboratoire**) lab.
laborantin, e [labɔRɑ̃tɛ̃, -in] *nm/f* laboratory assistant.
laboratoire [labɔRatwaR] *nm* laboratory ; ~ **de langues/** **d'analyses** language/(medical) analysis laboratory.
laborieux, euse [labɔRjø, -øz] *a* (*tâche*) laborious ; (*personne*) hard-working, industrious.
labour [labuR] *nm* ploughing *q* ; ~**s** *nmpl* ploughed fields ; **cheval de** ~ plough- *ou* cart-horse ; **bœuf de** ~ ox (*pl* oxen).
labourer [labuRe] *vt* to plough ; (*fig*) to make deep gashes *ou* furrows in ; **laboureur** *nm* ploughman.
labyrinthe [labiRɛ̃t] *nm* labyrinth, maze.
lac [lak] *nm* lake.
lacer [lase] *vt* to lace *ou* do up.
lacérer [laseRe] *vt* to tear to shreds, lacerate.
lacet [lasɛ] *nm* (*de chaussure*) lace ; (*route*) sharp bend ; (*piège*) snare.
lâche [lɑʃ] *a* (*poltron*) cowardly ; (*desserré*) loose, slack // *nm/f* coward.
lâcher [lɑʃe] *nm* (*de ballons, oiseaux*) release // *vt* to let go of ; (*ce qui tombe, abandonner*) to drop ; (*oiseau, animal: libérer*) to release, set free ; (*fig: mot, remarque*) to let slip, come out with ; (*SPORT: distancer*) to leave behind // *vi* (*fil, amarres*) to break, give way ; (*freins*) to fail ; ~ **les amarres** (*NAVIG*) to cast off (the moorings) ; ~ **les chiens** to unleash the dogs ; ~ **prise** to let go.

lâcheté [lɑʃte] *nf* cowardice ; lowness.
lacis [lɑsi] *nm* maze.
laconique [lakɔnik] *a* laconic.
lacrymogène [lakʀimɔʒɛn] *a voir* **gaz**, **grenade**.
lacté, e [lakte] *a* (*produit, régime*) milk *cpd*.
lacune [lakyn] *nf* gap.
lacustre [lakystʀ(ə)] *a* lake *cpd*, lakeside *cpd*.
lad [lad] *nm* stable-lad.
là-dedans [ladədɑ̃] *ad* inside (there), in it ; (*fig*) in that ; **là-dehors** *ad* out there ; **là-derrière** *ad* behind there ; (*fig*) behind that ; **là-dessous** *ad* underneath, under there ; (*fig*) behind that ; **là-dessus** *ad* on there ; (*fig*) at that point ; about that ; **là-devant** *ad* there (in front).
ladite [ladit] *dét voir* **ledit**.
ladre [ladʀ(ə)] *a* miserly.
lagon [lagɔ̃] *nm* lagoon.
lagune [lagyn] *nf* lagoon.
là-haut [la'o] *ad* up there.
laïc [laik] *a, nm/f* = **laïque**.
laïciser [laisize] *vt* to secularize.
laid, e [lɛ, lɛd] *a* ugly ; (*fig: acte*) mean, cheap ; **laideron** *nm* ugly girl ; **laideur** *nf* ugliness *q* ; meanness *q*.
laie [lɛ] *nf* wild sow.
lainage [lɛnaʒ] *nm* woollen garment ; woollen material.
laine [lɛn] *nf* wool ; ~ **de verre** glass wool ; **laineux, euse** *a* woolly.
laïque [laik] *a* lay, civil ; (*SCOL*) state *cpd* (*as opposed to private and Roman Catholic*) // *nm/f* layman/woman.
laisse [lɛs] *nf* (*de chien*) lead, leash ; **tenir en ~** to keep on a lead.
laisser [lese] *vt* to leave // *vb auxiliaire*: ~ **qn faire** to let sb do ; **se ~ exploiter** to let o.s. be exploited ; **se ~ aller** to let o.s. go ; **laisse-toi faire** let me (*ou* him) do it ; **cela ne laisse pas de surprendre** nonetheless it is surprising ; **~- aller** *nm* carelessness, slovenliness ; **laissez-passer** *nm inv* pass.
lait [lɛ] *nm* milk ; **frère/sœur de ~** foster brother/sister ; **~ écrémé/ concentré** skimmed/evaporated milk ; **~ démaquillant/de beauté** cleansing/beauty lotion ; **laitage** *nm* milk food ; **laiterie** *nf* dairy ; **laiteux, euse** *a* milky ; **laitier, ière** *a* milk *cpd* // *nm/f* milkman/dairywoman.
laiton [lɛtɔ̃] *nm* brass.
laitue [lety] *nf* lettuce.
laïus [lajys] *nm* (*péj*) spiel.
lambeau, x [lɑ̃bo] *nm* scrap ; **en ~x** in tatters, tattered.
lambin, e [lɑ̃bɛ̃, -in] *a* (*péj*) slow.
lambris [lɑ̃bʀi] *nm* panelling *q* ; **lambrissé, e** *a* panelled.
lame [lam] *nf* blade ; (*vague*) wave ; (*lamelle*) strip ; ~ **de fond** ground swell *q* ; ~ **de rasoir** razor blade.
lamé [lame] *nm* lamé.
lamelle [lamɛl] *nf* thin strip *ou* blade ; (*de champignon*) gill.
lamentable [lamɑ̃tabl(ə)] *a* appalling ; pitiful.
lamentation [lamɑ̃tɑsjɔ̃] *nf* wailing *q*, lamentation ; moaning *q*.
lamenter [lamɑ̃te]: **se ~** *vi*: **se ~ (sur)** to moan (over).
laminer [lamine] *vt* to laminate ; **laminoir** *nm* rolling mill.
lampadaire [lɑ̃padɛʀ] *nm* (*de salon*) standard lamp.
lampe [lɑ̃p(ə)] *nf* lamp ; (*TECH*) valve ; ~ **à pétrole** paraffin lamp ; ~ **de poche** torch ; ~ **à souder** blowlamp.
lampée [lɑ̃pe] *nf* gulp, swig.
lampe-tempête [lɑ̃ptɑ̃pɛt] *nf* storm lantern.
lampion [lɑ̃pjɔ̃] *nm* Chinese lantern.
lampiste [lɑ̃pist(ə)] *nm* light (maintenance) man ; (*fig*) underling.
lance [lɑ̃s] *nf* spear ; ~ **d'incendie** fire hose.
lancée [lɑ̃se] *nf*: **être/continuer sur sa ~** to be under way/keep going.
lance-flammes [lɑ̃sflam] *nm inv* flamethrower.
lance-grenades [lɑ̃sgʀənad] *nm inv* grenade launcher.
lancement [lɑ̃smɑ̃] *nm* launching.
lance-pierres [lɑ̃spjɛʀ] *nm inv* catapult
lancer [lɑ̃se] *nm* (*SPORT*) throwing *q*, throw ; (*PÊCHE*) rod and reel fishing // *vt* to throw ; (*émettre, projeter*) to throw out, send out ; (*produit, fusée, bateau, artiste*) to launch ; (*injure*) to hurl, fling ; (*proclamation, mandat d'arrêt*) to issue ; (*moteur*) to send roaring away ; ~ **qch à qn** to throw sth to sb ; (*de façon aggressive*) to throw *ou* hurl sth at sb ; **se ~** *vi* (*prendre de l'élan*) to build up speed ; (*se précipiter*): **se ~ sur/contre** to rush at ; **se ~ dans** (*discussion*) to launch into ; (*aventure*) to embark on ; **au poids** *nm* putting the shot ; **lance-roquettes** *nm inv* rocket launcher ; **lance-torpilles** *nm inv* torpedo tube.
lancinant, e [lɑ̃sinɑ̃, -ɑ̃t] *a* (*regrets etc*) haunting ; (*douleur*) shooting, throbbing.
landau [lɑ̃do] *nm* pram.
lande [lɑ̃d] *nf* moor.
langage [lɑ̃gaʒ] *nm* language.
lange [lɑ̃ʒ] *nm* flannel blanket ; **~s** swaddling clothes.
langer [lɑ̃ʒe] *vt* to change (the nappy of) ; **table à ~** changing table.
langoureux, euse [lɑ̃guʀø, -øz] *a* languorous.
langouste [lɑ̃gust(ə)] *nf* crayfish *inv* ; **langoustine** *nf* Dublin Bay prawn.
langue [lɑ̃g] *nf* (*ANAT, CULIN*) tongue ; (*LING*) language ; (*bande*): ~ **de terre** spit of land ; **tirer la ~ (à)** to stick out one's tongue (at) ; **de ~ française** French-speaking ; ~ **maternelle** native language ; **mother tongue** ; ~ **verte** slang ; ~ **vivante** living language ; **~-de-chat** *nf* finger biscuit, sponge finger.
languette [lɑ̃gɛt] *nf* tongue.
langueur [lɑ̃gœʀ] *nf* languidness.
languir [lɑ̃giʀ] *vi* to languish, (*conversation*) to flag: **faire ~ qn** to keep sb waiting.
lanière [lanjɛʀ] *nf* (*de fouet*) lash ; (*de valise, bretelle*) strap.
lanterne [lɑ̃tɛʀn(ə)] *nf* (*portable*) lantern ;

(*électrique*) light, lamp; (*de voiture*) (side)light; ~ **rouge** (*fig*) tail-ender.
lapalissade [lapalisad] *nf* statement of the obvious.
laper [lape] *vt* to lap up.
lapereau, x [lapro] *nm* young rabbit.
lapidaire [lapidɛr] *a* (*fig*) terse.
lapider [lapide] *vt* to stone.
lapin [lapɛ̃] *nm* rabbit; (*peau*) rabbitskin; ~ **de garenne** wild rabbit.
laps [laps] *nm:* ~ **de temps** space of time, time *q*.
lapsus [lapsys] *nm* slip.
laquais [lakɛ] *nm* lackey.
laque [lak] *nf* lacquer; (*brute*) lac, shellac // *nm* lacquer; piece of lacquer ware; **laqué, e** *a* lacquered; with lacquer finish.
laquelle [lakɛl] *pronom voir* **lequel.**
larbin [larbɛ̃] *nm* (*péj*) flunkey.
larcin [larsɛ̃] *nm* theft.
lard [lar] *nm* (*graisse*) fat; (*bacon*) (streaky) bacon.
larder [larde] *vt* (*CULIN*) to lard.
lardon [lardɔ̃] *nm* (*CULIN*) lardon.
large [larʒ(ə)] *a* wide; broad; (*fig*) generous // *ad*: **calculer/voir** ~ to allow extra/think big // *nm* (*largeur*): **5 m de** ~ 5 m wide *ou* in width; (*mer*): **le** ~ the open sea; **en** ~ *ad* sideways; **au** ~ **de** off; ~ **d'esprit** broad-minded; ~**ment** *ad* widely; greatly; easily; amply; generously; **largesse** *nf* generosity; **largesses** liberalities; **largeur** *nf* (*qu'on mesure*) width; (*impression visuelle*) wideness, width; breadth; broadness.
larguer [large] *vt* to drop: ~ **les amarres** to cast off (the moorings).
larme [larm(ə)] *nf* tear; (*fig*): **une** ~ **de** a drop of; **en** ~**s** in tears; **larmoyant, e** *a* tearful; **larmoyer** *vi* (*yeux*) to water; (*se plaindre*) to whimper.
larron [larɔ̃] *nm* thief (*pl* thieves).
larve [larv(ə)] *nf* (*ZOOL*) larva (*pl* ae); (*fig*) worm.
larvé, e [larve] *a* (*fig*) latent.
laryngite [larɛ̃ʒit] *nf* laryngitis.
laryngologiste [larɛ̃gɔlɔʒist(ə)] *nm/f* throat specialist.
larynx [larɛ̃ks] *nm* larynx.
las, lasse [lɑ, lɑs] *a* weary.
lascar [laskar] *nm* character; rogue.
lascif, ive [lasif, -iv] *a* lascivious.
laser [lazɛr] *a, nm*: (**rayon**) ~ laser (beam).
lasse [lɑs] *af voir* **las.**
lasser [lɑse] *vt* to weary, tire; **se** ~ **de** to grow weary *ou* tired of.
lassitude [lɑsityd] *nf* lassitude, weariness.
lasso [laso] *nm* lasso.
latent, e [latɑ̃, -ɑ̃t] *a* latent.
latéral, e, aux [lateral, -o] *a* side *cpd*, lateral.
latex [latɛks] *nm* latex.
latin, e [latɛ̃, -in] *a, nm, nf* Latin; **latiniste** *nm/f* Latin scholar (*ou* student); **latino-américain, e** *a* Latin-American.
latitude [latityd] *nf* latitude; (*fig*): **avoir la** ~ **de faire** to be left free *ou* be at liberty to do; **à 48° de** ~ **Nord** at latitude 48° North.

latrines [latrin] *nfpl* latrines.
latte [lat] *nf* lath, slat; (*de plancher*) board.
lattis [lati] *nm* lathwork.
lauréat, e [lɔrea, -at] *nm/f* winner.
laurier [lɔrje] *nm* (*BOT*) laurel; (*CULIN*) bay leaves *pl*; ~**s** *nmpl* (*fig*) laurels.
lavable [lavabl(ə)] *a* washable.
lavabo [lavabo] *nm* (*de salle de bains*) washbasin; ~**s** *nmpl* toilet *sg*.
lavage [lavaʒ] *nm* washing *q*, wash; ~ **d'estomac/d'intestin** stomach/intestinal wash; ~ **de cerveau** brainwashing *q*.
lavande [lavɑ̃d] *nf* lavender.
lavandière [lavɑ̃djɛr] *nf* washerwoman.
lave [lav] *nf* lava *q*.
lave-glace [lavglas] *nm* (*AUTO*) windscreen washer.
lavement [lavmɑ̃] *nm* (*MÉD*) enema.
laver [lave] *vt* to wash; (*tache*) to wash off; (*fig: affront*) to avenge; **se** ~ to have a wash, wash; **se** ~ **les mains/dents** to wash one's hands/clean one's teeth; ~ **qn de** (*accusation*) to clear sb of; **laverie** *nf:* **laverie (automatique)** launderette.
lavette [lavɛt] *nf* dish cloth.
laveur, euse [lavœr, -øz] *nm/f* cleaner.
lave-vaisselle [lavvɛsɛl] *nm inv* dishwasher.
lavis [lavi] *nm* (*technique*) washing; (*dessin*) wash drawing.
lavoir [lavwar] *nm* wash house; washtub.
laxatif, ive [laksatif, -iv] *a, nm* laxative.
laxisme [laksism(ə)] *nm* laxity.
layette [lɛjɛt] *nf* layette.
le(l'), la, les [l(ə), la, le] *dét* the // *pronom* (*personne: mâle*) him; (: *femelle*) her; (*animal, chose*) it; (*remplaçant une phrase*) it *ou non traduit*; (*indique une possession*): **se casser la jambe** *etc* to break one's leg *etc*; *voir note sous* **il**; **les** them; **je ne le savais pas** I didn't know (about it); **il était riche et ne l'est plus** he was once rich but no longer is; **levez la main** put your hand up; **avoir les yeux gris/le nez rouge** to have grey eyes/a red nose; **le jeudi** *etc ad* (*d'habitude*) on Thursdays *etc*; (*ce jeudi-là*) on the Thursday *etc*; **le matin/soir** *ad* in the morning/evening; mornings/evenings; **10 F le mètre/kilo** 10 F a *ou* per metre/kilo; **le tiers/quart de** a third/quarter of.
lécher [leʃe] *vt* to lick; (*laper: lait, eau*) to lick *ou* lap up; ~ **les vitrines** to go window-shopping.
leçon [ləsɔ̃] *nf* lesson; **faire la** ~ to teach; **faire la** ~ **à** (*fig*) to give a lecture to; ~**s de conduite** driving lessons; ~**s particulières** private lessons *ou* tuition *sg*.
lecteur, trice [lɛktœr, -tris] *nm/f* reader; (*d'université*) foreign language assistant // *nm* (*TECH*): ~ **de cassettes** cassette player.
lecture [lɛktyr] *nf* reading.
ledit [lədi], **ladite** [ladit], *mpl* **lesdits** [ledi], *fpl* **lesdites** [ledit] *dét* the aforesaid.
légal, e, aux [legal, -o] *a* legal; ~**ement** *ad* legally; ~**iser** *vt* to legalize; ~**ité** *nf* legality, lawfulness; **être dans/sortir de la** ~**ité** to be within/step outside the law.
légataire [legatɛr] *nm:* ~ **universel** sole legatee.

légation [legɑsjɔ̃] nf legation.
légendaire [leʒɑ̃dɛʀ] a legendary.
légende [leʒɑ̃d] nf (mythe) legend; (de carte, plan) key, legend; (de dessin) caption, legend.
léger, ère [leʒe, -ɛʀ] a light; (bruit, retard) slight; (superficiel) thoughtless; (volage) free and easy; flighty; **blessé ~** slightly injured person; **à la légère** ad (parler, agir) rashly, thoughtlessly; **légèrement** ad lightly; thoughtlessly, rashly; **légèrement plus grand** slightly bigger; **légèreté** nf lightness; thoughtlessness.
légiférer [leʒifeʀe] vi to legislate.
légion [leʒjɔ̃] nf legion; **~ étrangère** foreign legion; **~ d'honneur** Legion of Honour; **légionnaire** nm legionnaire.
législateur [leʒislatœʀ] nm legislator, lawmaker.
législatif, ive [leʒislatif, -iv] a legislative.
législation [leʒislɑsjɔ̃] nf legislation.
législature [leʒislɑtyʀ] nf legislature; term (of office).
légiste [leʒist(ə)] a: **médecin ~** forensic surgeon.
légitime [leʒitim] a (JUR) lawful, legitimate; (fig) justified, rightful, legitimate; **en état de ~ défense** in self-defence; **~ment** ad justifiably, rightfully; **légitimité** nf (JUR) legitimacy.
legs [lɛg] nm legacy.
léguer [lege] vt: **~ qch à qn** (JUR) to bequeath sth to sb; (fig) to hand sth down ou pass sth on to sb.
légume [legym] nm vegetable.
lendemain [lɑ̃dmɛ̃] nm: **le ~** the next ou following day; **le ~ matin/soir** the next ou following morning/evening; **le ~ de** the day after; **au ~ de** in the days following; in the wake of; **penser au ~** to think of the future; **sans ~** short-lived; **de beaux ~s** bright prospects.
lénifiant, e [lenifjɑ̃, -ɑ̃t] a soothing.
lent, e [lɑ̃, lɑ̃t] a slow; **lentement** ad slowly; **lenteur** nf slowness q.
lentille [lɑ̃tij] nf (OPTIQUE) lens sg; (BOT) lentil.
léopard [leɔpaʀ] nm leopard.
lèpre [lɛpʀ(ə)] nf leprosy; **lépreux, euse** nm/f leper // a (fig) flaking, peeling.
lequel [ləkɛl], **laquelle** [lakɛl], mpl **lesquels**, fpl **lesquelles** [lekɛl] (avec à, de: **auquel, duquel** etc) pronom (interrogatif) which, which one; (relatif: personne: sujet) who; (: objet, après préposition) whom; (: chose) which // a: **auquel cas** in which case.
les [le] dét voir **le**.
lesbienne [lɛsbjɛn] nf lesbian.
lesdits [ledi], **lesdites** [ledit] dét voir **ledit**.
léser [leze] vt to wrong.
lésiner [lezine] vt: **~ (sur)** to skimp (on).
lésion [lezjɔ̃] nf lesion, damage q; **~s cérébrales** brain damage.
lesquels, lesquelles [lekɛl] pronom voir **lequel**.
lessive [lesiv] nf (poudre) washing powder; (linge) washing q, wash; (opération) washing q; **faire la ~** to do the washing.

lessivé, e [lesive] a (fam) washed out; cleaned out.
lessiver [lesive] vt to wash.
lessiveuse [lesivøz] nf (récipient) (laundry) boiler.
lest [lɛst] nm ballast.
leste [lɛst(ə)] a sprightly, nimble.
lester [lɛste] vt to ballast.
léthargie [letaʀʒi] nf lethargy.
léthargique [letaʀʒik] a lethargic.
lettre [lɛtʀ(ə)] nf letter; **~s** nfpl literature sg; (SCOL) arts (subjects); **à la ~** literally; **en toutes ~s** in words, in full; **~ de change** bill of exchange.
lettré, e [letʀe] a well-read, scholarly.
leu [lø] voir **queue**.
leucémie [løsemi] nf leukaemia.
leur [lœʀ] dét their // pronom them; **le(la) ~, les ~s** theirs; **à ~ approche** as they came near; **à ~ vue** at the sight of them.
leurre [lœʀ] nm (appât) lure; (fig) delusion; snare.
leurrer [lœʀe] vt to delude, deceive.
levain [ləvɛ̃] nm leaven.
levant, e [ləvɑ̃, -ɑ̃t] a: **soleil ~** rising sun // nm: **le L~** the Levant.
levé, e [ləve] a: **être ~** to be up.
levée [ləve] nf (POSTES) collection; (CARTES) trick; **~ de boucliers** general outcry; **~ du corps** collection of the body from house of the deceased, before funeral; **~ d'écrou** release from custody; **~ de terre** levee; **~ de troupes** levy.
lever [ləve] vt (vitre, bras etc) to raise; (soulever de terre, supprimer: interdiction, siège) to lift; (séance) to close; (impôts, armée) to levy; (CHASSE) to start; to flush; (fam: fille) to pick up // vi (CULIN) to rise // nm: **au ~** on getting up; **se ~** vi to get up; (soleil) to rise; (jour) to break; (brouillard) to lift; **ça va se ~** the weather will clear; **~ du jour** daybreak; **~ du rideau** curtain; **~ de rideau** curtain raiser; **~ de soleil** sunrise.
levier [ləvje] nm lever; **faire ~ sur** to lever up (ou off); **~ de changement de vitesse** gear lever.
lèvre [lɛvʀ(ə)] nf lip; **petites/grandes ~s** (ANAT) labia minora/majora.
lévrier [levʀije] nm greyhound.
levure [ləvyʀ] nf yeast.
lexicographie [lɛksikɔgʀafi] nf lexicography, dictionary writing.
lexique [lɛksik] nm vocabulary; lexicon.
lézard [lezaʀ] nm lizard.
lézarde [lezaʀd(ə)] nf crack; **lézarder: se lézarder** vi to crack.
liaison [ljɛzɔ̃] nf (rapport) connection, link; (RAIL, AVIAT etc) link; (amoureuse) affair; (PHONÉTIQUE) liaison; **entrer/être en ~ avec** to get/be in contact with; **~ radio** radio contact.
liane [ljan] nf creeper.
liant, e [ljɑ̃, -ɑ̃t] a sociable.
liasse [ljas] nf wad, bundle.
Liban [libɑ̃] nm: **le ~** (the) Lebanon; **libanais, e a, nm/f** Lebanese.
libations [libasjɔ̃] nfpl libations.
libelle [libɛl] nm lampoon.
libeller [libele] vt (chèque, mandat): **~ (au nom de)** to make out (to); (lettre) to word.

libellule [libelyl] *nf* dragonfly.
libéral, e, aux [liberal, -o] *a, nm/f* liberal ; **~iser** *vt* to liberalize ; **~isme** *nm* liberalism.
libéralité [liberalite] *nf* liberality *q,* generosity *q.*
libérateur, trice [liberatœr, -tris] *a* liberating // *nm/f* liberator.
libération [liberɑsjɔ̃] *nf* liberation, freeing ; release ; discharge.
libérer [libere] *vt* (*délivrer*) to free, liberate ; (: *moralement, PSYCH*) to liberate ; (*relâcher*) to release ; to discharge ; (*dégager: gaz, cran d'arrêt*) to release ; **se ~** (*de rendez-vous*) to try and be free, get out of previous engagements ; **~ qn de** to free sb from ; (*promesse*) to release sb from.
libertaire [liberter] *a* libertarian.
liberté [liberte] *nf* freedom ; (*loisir*) free time ; **~s** *nfpl* (*privautés*) liberties ; **mettre/être en ~** to set/be free ; **en ~ provisoire/surveillée/conditionnelle** on bail/ probation/parole ; **~ d'esprit** independence of mind ; **~ d'opinion** freedom of thought ; **~ de réunion** right to hold meetings ; **~s individuelles** personal freedom *sg.*
libertin, e [libertɛ̃, -in] *a* libertine, licentious ; **libertinage** *nm* licentiousness.
libidineux, euse [libidinø, -øz] *a* libidinous, lustful.
libido [libido] *nf* libido.
libraire [librer] *nm/f* bookseller.
librairie [libreri] *nf* bookshop.
libre [libr(ə)] *a* free ; (*route*) clear ; (*pas pris ou occupé: place etc*) vacant ; empty ; not engaged ; not taken ; (*SCOL*) private and Roman Catholic (*as opposed to 'laïque'*) ; **~ de qch/de faire** free from sth/ to do ; **~-échange** *nm* free trade ; **~-ment** *ad* freely ; **~-service** *nm* self-service store.
librettiste [libretist(ə)] *nm/f* librettist.
Libye [libi] *nf*: **la ~** Libya ; **libyen, ne** *a, nm/f* Libyan.
licence [lisɑ̃s] *nf* (*permis*) permit ; (*diplôme*) (first) degree ; (*liberté*) liberty ; licence ; licentiousness ; **licencié, e** *nm/f* (*SCOL*): **licencié ès lettres/en droit** ≈ Bachelor of Arts/Law ; (*SPORT*) member of a·sports federation.
licenciement [lisɑ̃simɑ̃] *nm* dismissal ; laying off *q* ; redundancy.
licencier [lisɑ̃sje] *vt* (*renvoyer*) to dismiss ; (*débaucher*) to make redundant ; to lay off.
licencieux, euse [lisɑ̃sjø, -øz] *a* licentious.
lichen [likɛn] *nm* lichen.
licite [lisit] *a* lawful.
licorne [likɔrn(ə)] *nf* unicorn.
licou [liku] *nm* halter.
lie [li] *nf* dregs *pl,* sediment.
lié, e [lje] *a*: **très ~ avec** very friendly with ou close to ; **~ par** (*serment*) bound by.
liège [ljɛʒ] *nm* cork.
lien [ljɛ̃] *nm* (*corde, fig: affectif*) bond ; (*rapport*) link, connection ; **~ de parenté** family tie.
lier [lje] *vt* (*attacher*) to tie up ; (*joindre*) to link up ; (*fig: unir, engager*) to bind ; (*CULIN*) to thicken ; **~ qch à** to tie sth to ;

to link sth to ; **~ conversation avec** to strike up a conversation with ; **se ~ avec** to make friends with.
lierre [ljɛr] *nm* ivy.
liesse [ljɛs] *nf*: **être en ~** to be celebrating ou jubilant.
lieu, x [ljø] *nm* place // *nmpl* (*habitation*) premises ; (*endroit: d'un accident etc*) scene *sg* ; **en ~ sûr** in a safe place ; **en premier ~** in the first place ; **en dernier ~** lastly ; **avoir ~** to take place ; **avoir ~ de faire** to have grounds ou good reason for doing ; **tenir ~ de** to take the place of ; to serve as ; **donner ~ à** to give rise to, give cause for ; **au ~ de** instead of ; **au ~ qu'il y aille** instead of him going ; **~ commun** commonplace ; **~ géométrique** locus.
lieu-dit *nm, pl* **lieux-dits** [ljødi] locality.
lieue [ljø] *nf* league.
lieutenant [ljøtnɑ̃] *nm* lieutenant.
lièvre [ljɛvr(ə)] *nm* hare.
liftier [liftje] *nm* lift boy.
ligament [ligamɑ̃] *nm* ligament.
ligature [ligatyr] *nf* ligature ; **ligaturer** *vt* to ligature.
lige [liʒ] *a*: **homme ~** (*péj*) henchman.
ligne [liɲ] *nf* (*gén*) line ; (*TRANSPORTS: liaison*) service ; (: *trajet*) route ; (*silhouette féminine*): **garder la ~** to keep one's figure ; **'à la ~'** 'new paragraph' ; **entrer en ~ de compte** to be taken into account ; to come into it ; **~ de but/médiane** goal/halfway line ; **~ d'horizon** skyline.
lignée [liɲe] *nf* line ; lineage ; descendants *pl.*
ligneux, euse [liɲø, -øz] *a* ligneous, woody.
lignite [liɲit] *nm* lignite.
ligoter [ligɔte] *vt* to tie up.
ligue [lig] *nf* league ; **liguer: se liguer** *vi* to form a league ; **se liguer contre** (*fig*) to combine against.
lilas [lila] *nm* lilac.
limace [limas] *nf* slug.
limaille [limaj] *nf*: **~ de fer** iron filings *pl.*
limande [limɑ̃d] *nf* dab.
lime [lim] *nf* file ; **~ à ongles** nail file ; **limer** *vt* to file (down) ; (*ongles*) to file ; (*fig: prix*) to pare down, trim.
limier [limje] *nm* bloodhound ; (*détective*) sleuth.
liminaire [liminɛr] *a* (*propos*) introductory.
limitation [limitɑsjɔ̃] *nf* limitation, restriction.
limite [limit] *nf* (*de terrain*) boundary ; (*partie ou point extrême*) limit ; **charge/vitesse ~** maximum speed/load ; **cas ~** borderline case ; **date ~** deadline.
limiter [limite] *vt* (*restreindre*) to limit, restrict ; (*délimiter*) to border, form the boundary of.
limitrophe [limitrɔf] *a* border *cpd* ; **~ de** bordering on.
limoger [limɔʒe] *vt* to dismiss.
limon [limɔ̃] *nm* silt.
limonade [limɔnad] *nf* (fizzy) lemonade.
limpide [lɛ̃pid] *a* limpid.
lin [lɛ̃] *nm* flax.

linceul [lɛ̃sœl] *nm* shroud.
linéaire [lineɛʀ] *a* linear.
linge [lɛ̃ʒ] *nm* (*serviettes etc*) linen ; (*pièce de tissu*) cloth ; (*aussi*: ∼ **de corps**) underwear ; (*aussi*: ∼ **de toilette**) towel ; (*lessive*) washing ; ∼ **sale** dirty linen.
lingerie [lɛ̃ʒʀi] *nf* lingerie, underwear.
lingot [lɛ̃go] *nm* ingot.
linguiste [lɛ̃gɥist(ə)] *nm/f* linguist.
linguistique [lɛ̃gɥistik] *a* linguistic // *nf* linguistics *sg*.
lino(léum) [lino(leɔm)] *nm* lino(leum).
lion, ne [ljɔ̃, ljɔn] *nm/f* lion/lioness ; (*signe*): **le L**∼ Leo, the Lion ; **être du L**∼ to be Leo ; **lionceau, x** *nm* lion cub.
lippu, e [lipy] *a* thick-lipped.
liquéfier [likefje] *vt*, **se** ∼ *vi* to liquefy.
liqueur [likœʀ] *nf* liqueur.
liquidation [likidasjɔ̃] *nf* liquidation ; (*COMM*) clearance (sale).
liquide [likid] *a* liquid // *nm* liquid ; (*COMM*): **en** ∼ in ready money *ou* cash.
liquider [likide] *vt* (*société, biens, témoin gênant*) to liquidate ; (*compte, problème*) to settle ; (*COMM*: *articles*) to clear, sell off.
liquidités [likidite] *nfpl* (*COMM*) liquid assets.
liquoreux, euse [likɔʀø, -øz] *a* syrupy.
lire [liʀ] *nf* (*monnaie*) lira // *vt*, *vi* to read ; ∼ **qch à qn** to read sth (out) to sb.
lis *vb* [li] *voir* **lire** // *nm* [lis] = **lys**.
liseré [lizʀe] *nm* border, edging.
liseron [lizʀɔ̃] *nm* bindweed.
liseuse [lizøz] *nf* book-cover.
lisible [lizibl(ə)] *a* legible.
lisière [lizjɛʀ] *nf* (*de forêt*) edge ; (*de tissu*) selvage.
lisons *vb voir* **lire**.
lisse [lis] *a* smooth ; **lisser** *vt* to smooth.
liste [list(ə)] *nf* list ; **faire la** ∼ **de** to list, make out a list of ; ∼ **électorale** electoral roll.
lit [li] *nm* (*gén*) bed ; **faire son** ∼ to make one's bed ; **aller/se mettre au** ∼ to go to/get into bed ; **prendre le** ∼ to take to one's bed ; **d'un premier** ∼ (*JUR*) of a first marriage ; ∼ **de camp** campbed.
litanie [litani] *nf* litany.
literie [litʀi] *nf* bedding ; bedclothes *pl*.
lithographie [litɔgʀafi] *nf* lithography ; (*épreuve*) lithograph.
litière [litjɛʀ] *nf* litter.
litige [litiʒ] *nm* dispute ; **litigieux, euse** *a* litigious, contentious.
litre [litʀ(ə)] *nm* litre ; (*récipient*) litre measure.
littéraire [liteʀɛʀ] *a* literary.
littéral, e, aux [liteʀal, -o] *a* literal.
littérature [liteʀatyʀ] *nf* literature.
littoral, e, aux [litɔʀal, -o] *a* coastal // *nm* coast.
liturgie [lityʀʒi] *nf* liturgy ; **liturgique** *a* liturgical.
livide [livid] *a* livid, pallid.
livraison [livʀɛzɔ̃] *nf* delivery.
livre [livʀ(ə)] *nm* book // *nf* (*poids, monnaie*) pound ; ∼ **de bord** logbook ; ∼ **d'or** visitors' book ; ∼ **de poche** paperback (*cheap and pocket size*).

livré, e [livʀe] *a*: ∼ **à soi-même** left to o.s. *ou* one's own devices // *nf* livery.
livrer [livʀe] *vt* (*COMM*) to deliver ; (*otage, coupable*) to hand over ; (*secret, information*) to give away ; **se** ∼ **à** (*se confier*) to confide in ; (*se rendre*) to give o.s. up to ; (*s'abandonner à: débauche etc*) to give o.s. up *ou* over to ; (*faire: pratiques, actes*) to indulge in ; (: *travail*) to be engaged in, engage in ; (: *sport*) to practise ; (: *enquête*) to carry out ; ∼ **bataille** to give battle.
livresque [livʀɛsk(ə)] *a* bookish.
livret [livʀɛ] *nm* booklet ; (*d'opéra*) libretto (*pl s*) ; ∼ **de caisse d'épargne** (savings) bank-book ; ∼ **de famille** (official) family record book ; ∼ **scolaire** (school) report book.
livreur, euse [livʀœʀ, -øz] *nm/f* delivery boy *ou* man/girl *ou* woman.
lobe [lɔb] *nm*: ∼ **de l'oreille** ear lobe.
lobé, e [lɔbe] *a* (*ARCHIT*) foiled.
lober [lɔbe] *vt* to lob.
local, e, aux [lɔkal, -o] *a* local // *nm* (*salle*) premises *pl* // *nmpl* premises.
localiser [lɔkalize] *vt* (*repérer*) to locate, place ; (*limiter*) to localize, confine.
localité [lɔkalite] *nf* locality.
locataire [lɔkatɛʀ] *nm/f* tenant ; (*de chambre*) lodger.
locatif, ive [lɔkatif, -iv] *a* (*charges, réparations*) incumbent upon the tenant ; (*valeur*) rental ; (*immeuble*) with rented flats, used as a letting concern.
location [lɔkasjɔ̃] *nf* (*par le locataire*) renting ; (*par l'usager: de voiture etc*) hiring ; (*par le propriétaire*) renting out, letting ; hiring out ; (*COMM*): '∼ **de voitures**' 'car hire *ou* rental' ; ∼**-vente** *nf* form of hire purchase for housing.
lock-out [lɔkawt] *nm inv* lockout.
locomotion [lɔkɔmosjɔ̃] *nf* locomotion.
locomotive [lɔkɔmɔtiv] *nf* locomotive, engine ; (*fig*) pacesetter, pacemaker.
locution [lɔkysjɔ̃] *nf* phrase, locution.
logarithme [lɔgaʀitm(ə)] *nm* logarithm.
loge [lɔʒ] *nf* (*THÉÂTRE: d'artiste*) dressing room ; (: *de spectateurs*) box ; (*de concierge, franc-maçon*) lodge.
logement [lɔʒmɑ̃] *nm* accommodation *q*, flat ; housing *q* ; **chercher un** ∼ to look for a flat *ou* for accommodation ; **construire des** ∼**s bon marché** to build cheap housing *sg ou* flats ; **crise du** ∼ housing shortage.
loger [lɔʒe] *vt* to accommodate // *vi* to live ; **se** ∼: **trouver à se** ∼ to find accommodation ; **se** ∼ **dans** (*suj: balle, flèche*) to lodge itself in ; **logeur, euse** *nm/f* landlord/landlady.
loggia [lɔdʒja] *nf* loggia.
logiciel [lɔʒisjɛl] *nm* software.
logique [lɔʒik] *a* logical // *nf* logic ; ∼**ment** *ad* logically.
logis [lɔʒi] *nm* home ; abode, dwelling.
logistique [lɔʒistik] *nf* logistics *sg*.
loi [lwa] *nf* law ; **faire la** ∼ to lay down the law.
loin [lwɛ̃] *ad* far ; (*dans le temps*) a long way off ; a long time ago ; **plus** ∼ further ; **moins** ∼ (**que**) not as far (as) ; ∼ **de far**

from ; **pas ~ de 1000 F** not far off a 1000 F ; **au ~** far off ; **de ~** *ad* from a distance ; *(fig: de beaucoup)* by far ; **il vient de ~** he's come a long way ; he comes from a long way away.

lointain, e [lwɛ̃tɛ̃, -ɛn] *a* faraway, distant ; *(dans le futur, passé)* distant, far-off ; *(cause, parent)* remote, distant // *nm:* **dans le ~** in the distance.

loir [lwaʀ] *nm* dormouse *(pl mice)*.

loisir [lwaziʀ] *nm:* **heures de ~** spare time ; **~s** *nmpl* leisure *sg* ; leisure activities ; **avoir le ~ de faire** to have the time *ou* opportunity to do ; **à ~** at leisure ; at one's pleasure.

londonien, ne [lɔ̃dɔnjɛ̃, -jɛn] *a* London *cpd*, of London // *nm/f:* **L~, ne** Londoner.

Londres [lɔ̃dʀ(ə)] *n* London.

long, longue [lɔ̃, lɔ̃g] *a* long // *ad:* **en savoir ~** to know a great deal // *nm:* **de 3 m de ~** 3 m long, 3 m in length // *nf:* **à la longue** in the end ; **faire ~ feu** to fizzle out ; **ne pas faire ~ feu** not to last long ; **du ~ cours** (NAVIG) ocean *cpd*, oceangoing ; **être ~ à faire** to take a long time to do ; **en ~** *ad* lengthwise ; **(tout) le ~ de** (all) along ; **tout au ~ de** *(année, vie)* throughout ; **de ~ en large** *(marcher)* to and fro, up and down.

longanimité [lɔ̃ganimite] *nf* forbearance.

longe [lɔ̃ʒ] *nf* *(corde)* tether ; lead ; *(CULIN)* loin.

longer [lɔ̃ʒe] *vt* to go *(ou* walk *ou* drive) along(side) ; *(suj: mur, route)* to border.

longévité [lɔ̃ʒevite] *nf* longevity.

longiligne [lɔ̃ʒiliɲ] *a* long-limbed.

longitude [lɔ̃ʒityd] *nf* longitude ; **à 45° de ~ ouest** at 45° longitude west.

longitudinal, e, aux [lɔ̃ʒitydinal, -o] *a* longitudinal, lengthways ; running lengthways.

longtemps [lɔ̃tɑ̃] *ad* (for) a long time, (for) long ; **avant ~** before long ; **pour/pendant ~** for a long time/long ; **mettre ~ à faire** to take a long time to do.

longue [lɔ̃g] *af voir* **long** ; **~ment** *ad* for a long time, at length.

longueur [lɔ̃gœʀ] *nf* length ; **~s** *nfpl* *(fig: d'un film etc)* lengthy *ou* drawn-out parts ; **sur une ~ de 10 km** for *ou* over 10 km ; **en ~** *ad* lengthwise ; **tirer en ~** to drag on ; **à ~ de journée** all day long ; **~ d'onde** wavelength.

longue-vue [lɔ̃gvy] *nf* telescope.

lopin [lɔpɛ̃] *nm:* **~ de terre** patch of land.

loquace [lɔkas] *a* loquacious, talkative.

loque [lɔk] *nf* *(personne)* wreck ; **~s** *nfpl* *(habits)* rags.

loquet [lɔkɛ] *nm* latch.

lorgner [lɔʀɲe] *vt* to eye ; to have one's eye on.

lorgnon [lɔʀɲɔ̃] *nm* lorgnette.

loriot [lɔʀjo] *nm* (golden) oriole.

lors [lɔʀ]: **~ de** *prép* at the time of ; during ; **~ même que** even though.

lorsque [lɔʀsk(ə)] *cj* when, as.

losange [lɔzɑ̃ʒ] *nm* diamond ; *(GÉOM)* lozenge ; **en ~** diamond-shaped.

lot [lo] *nm* *(part)* share ; *(de loterie)* prize ; *(fig: destin)* fate, lot.

loterie [lɔtʀi] *nf* lottery ; raffle.

loti, e [lɔti] *a:* **bien/mal ~** well-/badly off *(as regards luck, circumstances)*.

lotion [losjɔ̃] *nf* lotion.

lotir [lɔtiʀ] *vt* *(terrain)* to divide into plots ; to sell by lots ; **lotissement** *nm* housing development ; plot, lot.

loto [lɔto] *nm* lotto ; numerical lottery.

louable [lwabl(ə)] *a* praiseworthy, commendable.

louage [lwaʒ] *nm:* **voiture de ~** hired car ; hire car.

louange [lwɑ̃ʒ] *nf:* **à la ~ de** in praise of ; **~s** *nfpl* praise *sg*.

louche [luʃ] *a* shady, fishy, dubious // *nf* ladle.

loucher [luʃe] *vi* to squint ; *(fig):* **~ sur** to have one's eye on.

louer [lwe] *vt* *(maison: suj: propriétaire)* to let, rent (out) ; *(: locataire)* to rent ; *(voiture etc)* to hire out, rent (out) ; to hire, rent ; *(réserver)* to book ; *(faire l'éloge de)* to praise ; **'à louer'** 'to let' ; **~ qn de** to praise sb for ; **se ~ de** to congratulate o.s. on.

loufoque [lufɔk] *a* crazy, zany.

loulou [lulu] *nm* *(chien)* spitz.

loup [lu] *nm* wolf *(pl* wolves) ; **~ de mer** *(marin)* old seadog.

loupe [lup] *nf* magnifying glass ; **~ de noyer** burr walnut.

louper [lupe] *vt* *(manquer)* to miss ; *(gâcher)* to mess up, bungle.

lourd, e [luʀ, luʀd(ə)] *a, ad* heavy ; **~ de** *(conséquences, menaces)* charged *ou* fraught with ; **lourdaud, e** *a* *(péj)* clumsy ; oafish ; **lourdement** *ad* heavily ; **lourdeur** *nf* heaviness ; **lourdeur d'estomac** indigestion *q*.

loutre [lutʀ(ə)] *nf* otter.

louve [luv] *nf* she-wolf.

louveteau, x [luvto] *nm* wolf-cub ; *(scout)* cub.

louvoyer [luvwaje] *vi* (NAVIG) to tack ; *(fig)* to hedge, evade the issue.

lover [lɔve]: **se ~** *vi* to coil up.

loyal, e, aux [lwajal, -o] *a* *(fidèle)* loyal, faithful ; *(fair-play)* fair ; **loyauté** *nf* loyalty, faithfulness ; fairness.

loyer [lwaje] *nm* rent.

lu, e [ly] *pp de* **lire**.

lubie [lybi] *nf* whim, craze.

lubrifiant [lybʀifjɑ̃] *nm* lubricant.

lubrifier [lybʀifje] *vt* to lubricate.

lubrique [lybʀik] *a* lecherous.

lucarne [lykaʀn(ə)] *nf* skylight.

lucide [lysid] *a* *(conscient)* lucid, conscious ; *(perspicace)* clear-headed ; lucid ; **lucidité** *nf* lucidity.

luciole [lysjɔl] *nf* firefly.

lucratif, ive [lykʀatif, -iv] *a* lucrative ; profitable ; **à but non ~** non profit-making.

luette [lɥɛt] *nf* uvula.

lueur [lɥœʀ] *nf* *(chatoyante)* glimmer *q* ; *(métallique, mouillée)* gleam *q* ; *(rougeoyante, chaude)* glow *q* ; *(pâle)* (faint) light ; *(fig)* glimmer ; gleam.

luge [lyʒ] *nf* sledge.

lugubre [lygybʀ(ə)] *a* gloomy ; dismal.

lui [lɥi] *pronom* (*chose, animal*) it ; (*personne: mâle*) him ; (: *en sujet*) he ; (: *femelle*) her ; *voir note sous* **il** ; ~**-même** himself ; itself.

luire [lɥiʀ] *vi* to shine ; to glow ; to gleam.

lumbago [lɔbago] *nm* lumbago.

lumière [lymjɛʀ] *nf* light ; ~**s** *nfpl* (*d'une personne*) knowledge *sg*, wisdom *sg* ; **à la ~ de** by the light of ; (*fig*) in the light of ; **fais de la ~** let's have some light, give us some light ; **mettre en ~** (*fig*) to bring out *ou* to light ; ~ **du jour/soleil** day/sunlight.

luminaire [lyminɛʀ] *nm* lamp, light.

lumineux, euse [lyminø, -øz] *a* (*émettant de la lumière*) luminous ; (*éclairé*) illuminated ; (*ciel, journée, couleur*) bright ; (*relatif à la lumière: rayon etc*) of light, light *cpd* ; (*fig: regard*) radiant ; **luminosité** *nf* (*TECH*) luminosity.

lunaire [lynɛʀ] *a* lunar, moon *cpd*.

lunatique [lynatik] *a* whimsical, temperamental.

lunch [lœntʃ] *nm* (*réception*) buffet lunch.

lundi [lœdi] *nm* Monday ; ~ **de Pâques** Easter Monday.

lune [lyn] *nf* moon ; ~ **de miel** honeymoon.

luné, e [lyne] *a*: **bien/mal ~** in a good/bad mood.

lunette [lynɛt] *nf*: **il y a belle ~** ages ago. ~**s** *nfpl* glasses, spectacles ; (*protectrices*) goggles ; ~ **d'approche** telescope ; ~ **arrière** (*AUTO*) rear window ; ~**s noires** dark glasses ; ~**s de soleil** sunglasses.

lurette [lyʀɛt] *nf*: **il y a belle ~** ages ago.

luron, ne [lyʀɔ̃, -ɔn] *nm/f* lad/lass ; **joyeux** *ou* **gai ~** gay dog.

lus *etc vb voir* **lire**.

lustre [lystʀ(ə)] *nm* (*de plafond*) chandelier ; (*fig: éclat*) lustre.

lustrer [lystʀe] *vt* (*faire briller*) to lustre ; (*poil d'un animal*) to put a sheen on ; (*user*) to make shiny.

lut *vb voir* **lire**.

luth [lyt] *nm* lute ; **luthier** *nm* (stringed-)instrument maker.

lutin [lytɛ̃] *nm* imp, goblin.

lutrin [lytʀɛ̃] *nm* lectern.

lutte [lyt] *nf* (*conflit*) struggle ; (*sport*) wrestling ; **lutter** *vi* to fight, struggle ; to wrestle ; **lutteur** *nm* wrestler ; (*fig*) battler, fighter.

luxation [lyksɑsjɔ̃] *nf* dislocation.

luxe [lyks(ə)] *nm* luxury ; **de ~** a luxury *cpd*.

Luxembourg [lyksɑ̃buʀ] *nm*: **le ~** Luxemburg.

luxer [lykse] *vt*: **se ~ l'épaule** to dislocate one's shoulder.

luxueux, euse [lyksɥø, -øz] *a* luxurious.

luxure [lyksyʀ] *nf* lust.

luxuriant, e [lyksyʀjɑ̃, -ɑ̃t] *a* luxuriant, lush.

luzerne [lyzɛʀn(ə)] *nf* lucerne, alfalfa.

lycée [lise] *nm* (*state*) secondary school ; **lycéen, ne** *nm/f* secondary school pupil.

lymphatique [lɛ̃fatik] *a* (*fig*) lethargic, sluggish.

lymphe [lɛ̃f] *nf* lymph.

lyncher [lɛ̃ʃe] *vt* to lynch.

lynx [lɛks] *nm* lynx.

lyophilisé, e [ljɔfilize] *a* freeze-dried.

lyre [liʀ] *nf* lyre.

lyrique [liʀik] *a* lyrical ; (*OPÉRA*) lyric ; **comédie ~** comic opera ; **théâtre ~** opera house (*for light opera*) ; **lyrisme** *nm* lyricism.

lys [lis] *nm* lily.

M

m' [m] *pronom voir* **me**.

M. [ɛm] *abr de* **Monsieur**.

ma [ma] *dét voir* **mon**.

maboul, e [mabul] *a* (*fam*) loony.

macabre [makɑbʀ(ə)] *a* macabre, gruesome.

macadam [makadam] *nm* tarmac.

macaron [makaʀɔ̃] *nm* (*gâteau*) macaroon ; (*insigne*) (round) badge.

macaronis [makaʀɔni] *nmpl* macaroni *sg*.

macédoine [masedwan] *nf*: ~ **de fruits** fruit salad.

macérer [maseʀe] *vi, vt* to macerate ; (*dans du vinaigre*) to pickle.

mâchefer [maʃfɛʀ] *nm* clinker, cinders *pl*.

mâcher [maʃe] *vt* to chew ; **ne pas ~ ses mots** not to mince one's words.

machin [maʃɛ̃] *nm* (*fam*) thingummy, whatsit ; contraption, thing.

machinal, e, aux [maʃinal, -o] *a* mechanical, automatic.

machination [maʃinɑsjɔ̃] *nf* scheming, frame-up.

machine [maʃin] *nf* machine ; (*locomotive*) engine ; (*fig: rouages*) machinery ; **faire ~ arrière** (*NAVIG*) to go astern ; ~ **à laver/coudre/ tricoter** washing/sewing/knitting machine ; ~ **à écrire** typewriter ; ~ **à sous** fruit machine ; ~ **à vapeur** steam engine ; ~**-outil** *nf* machine tool ; ~**rie** *nf* machinery, plant ; (*d'un navire*) engine room ; **machinisme** *nm* mechanization ; **machiniste** *nm* (*THÉÂTRE*) scene shifter ; (*de bus, métro*) driver.

mâchoire [maʃwaʀ] *nf* jaw ; ~ **de frein** brake shoe.

mâchonner [maʃɔne] *vt* to chew (at).

maçon [masɔ̃] *nm* bricklayer ; builder.

maçonner [masɔne] *vt* (*revêtir*) to face, render (with cement) ; (*boucher*) to brick up.

maçonnerie [masɔnʀi] *nf* (*murs*) brickwork ; masonry, stonework ; (*activité*) bricklaying ; building.

maçonnique [masɔnik] *a* masonic.

maculer [makyle] *vt* to stain ; (*TYPO*) to mackle.

Madame [madam], *pl* **Mesdames** [medam] *nf*: ~ **X** Mrs [ˈmɪsɪz] X ; **occupez-vous de ~/Monsieur/ Mademoiselle** please serve this lady/gentleman/(young) lady ; **bonjour ~/Monsieur/Mademoiselle** good morning ; (*ton déférent*) good morning Madam/Sir/Madam ; (*le nom est connu*) good morning Mrs/Mr/Miss X ; ~**/Monsieur/ Mademoiselle!** (*pour appeler*) Madam/Sir/Miss! ; ~**/Monsieur/Mademoiselle** (*sur lettre*) Dear Madam/Sir/Madam, **chère ~/cher**

Monsieur/chère Mademoiselle Dear Mrs/Mr/Miss X.

Mademoiselle [madmwazɛl], *pl* **Mesdemoiselles** [medmwazɛl] *nf* Miss ; *voir aussi* **Madame.**

madère [madɛʀ] *nm* Madeira (wine).

madone [madɔn] *nf* madonna.

madré, e [madʀe] *a* crafty, wily.

madrier [madʀije] *nm* beam.

madrilène [madʀilɛn] *a* of *ou* from Madrid.

maestria [maɛstʀija] *nf* (masterly) skill.

maf(f)ia [mafja] *nf* Maf(f)ia.

magasin [magazɛ̃] *nm* (*boutique*) shop ; (*entrepôt*) warehouse ; (*d'une arme*) magazine ; **en ~** (*COMM*) in stock ; **magasinier** *nm* warehouseman.

magazine [magazin] *nm* magazine.

mage [maʒ] *nm*: **les Rois M~s** the Magi, the (Three) Wise Men.

magicien, ne [maʒisjɛ̃, -jɛn] *nm/f* magician.

magie [maʒi] *nf* magic ; **magique** *a* magic ; (*enchanteur*) magical.

magistral, e, aux [maʒistʀal, -o] *a* (*œuvre, adresse*) masterly ; (*ton*) authoritative ; (*gifle etc*) sound, resounding ; (*ex cathedra*): **enseignement ~** lecturing, lectures *pl*.

magistrat [maʒistʀa] *nm* magistrate.

magistrature [maʒistʀatyʀ] *nf* magistracy, magistrature.

magma [magma] *nm* (*GÉO*) magma ; (*fig*) jumble.

magnanerie [maɲanʀi] *nf* silk farm.

magnanime [maɲanim] *a* magnanimous.

magnat [magna] *nm* tycoon, magnate.

magnésie [maɲezi] *nf* magnesia.

magnésium [maɲezjɔm] *nm* magnesium.

magnétique [maɲetik] *a* magnetic.

magnétiser [maɲetize] *vt* to magnetize ; (*fig*) to mesmerize, hypnotize.

magnétisme [maɲetism(ə)] *nm* magnetism.

magnéto [maɲeto] *nf* (*ÉLEC*) magneto.

magnétophone [maɲetɔfɔn] *nm* tape recorder ; **~ à cassettes** cassette recorder.

magnétoscope [maɲetɔskɔp] *nm* video-tape recorder.

magnificence [maɲifisɑ̃s] *nf* (*faste*) magnificence, splendour.

magnifique [maɲifik] *a* magnificent.

magnolia [maɲɔlja] *nm* magnolia.

magnum [magnɔm] *nm* magnum.

magot [mago] *nm* (*argent*) pile (of money) ; nest egg.

mahométan, e [maɔmetɑ̃, -an] *a* Mohammedan, Mahometan.

mai [mɛ] *nm* May.

maigre [mɛgʀ(ə)] *a* (very) thin, skinny ; (*viande*) lean ; (*fromage*) low-fat ; (*végétation*) thin, sparse ; (*fig*) poor, meagre, skimpy // *ad*: **faire ~** not to eat meat ; **jours ~s** days of abstinence, fish days ; **maigreur** *nf* thinness ; **maigrir** *vi* to get thinner, lose weight.

maille [maj] *nf* stitch ; **avoir ~ à partir avec qn** to have a brush with sb.

maillet [majɛ] *nm* mallet.

maillon [majɔ̃] *nm* link.

maillot [majo] *nm* (*aussi*: **~ de corps**) vest ; (*de danseur*) leotard ; (*de sportif*) jersey ; **~ de bain** bathing costume, swimsuit ; (*d'homme*) bathing trunks *pl*.

main [mɛ̃] *nf* hand ; **à la ~** in one's hand ; **se donner la ~** to hold hands ; **donner ou tendre la ~ à qn** to hold out one's hand to sb ; **se serrer la ~** to shake hands ; **serrer la ~ à qn** to shake hands with sb ; **sous la ~** to ou at hand ; **à ~ levée** (*ART*) freehand ; **à ~s levées** (*voter*) with a show of hands ; **attaque à ~ armée** armed attack ; **à ~ droite/gauche** to the right/left ; **à remettre en ~s propres** to be delivered personally ; **de première ~** (*renseignement*) first-hand ; (*COMM: voiture etc*) second-hand with only one previous owner ; **faire ~ basse sur** to help o.s. with ; **mettre la dernière ~ à** to put the finishing touches to ; **se faire/perdre la ~** to get one's hand in/lose one's touch ; **~ courante** handrail.

mainate [mɛnat] *nm* myna(h) bird.

main-d'œuvre [mɛ̃dœvʀ(ə)] *nf* manpower, labour.

main-forte [mɛ̃fɔʀt(ə)] *nf*: **prêter ~ à qn** to come to sb's assistance.

mainmise [mɛ̃miz] *nf* seizure ; (*fig*): **~ sur** complete hold on.

maint, e [mɛ̃, mɛ̃t] *a* many a ; **~s** many ; **à ~es reprises** time and (time) again.

maintenant [mɛ̃tnɑ̃] *ad* now ; (*actuellement*) nowadays.

maintenir [mɛ̃tniʀ] *vt* (*retenir, soutenir*) to support ; (*contenir: foule etc*) to keep in check, hold back ; (*conserver*) to maintain, uphold ; (*affirmer*) to maintain ; **se ~** *vi* to hold ; to keep steady ; to persist.

maintien [mɛ̃tjɛ̃] *nm* maintaining, upholding ; (*attitude*) bearing.

maire [mɛʀ] *nm* mayor.

mairie [meʀi] *nf* (*résidence*) town hall ; (*administration*) town council.

mais [mɛ] *cj* but ; **~ non!** of course not! ; **~ enfin** but after all ; (*indignation*) look here!

maïs [mais] *nm* maize.

maison [mɛzɔ̃] *nf* house ; (*chez-soi*) home ; (*COMM*) firm // *a inv* (*CULIN*) home-made ; made by the chef ; (*fig*) in-house, own ; (*fam*) first-rate ; **à la ~** at home ; (*direction*) home ; **~ d'arrêt** remand home ; **~ close** brothel ; **~ de correction** reformatory ; **~ des jeunes** youth club ; **~ mère** parent company ; **~ de repos** convalescent home ; **~ de retraite** old people's home ; **~ de santé** mental home ; **maisonnée** *nf* household, family ; **maisonnette** *nf* small house, cottage.

maître, esse [mɛtʀ(ə), mɛtʀɛs] *nm/f* master/mistress ; (*SCOL*) teacher, schoolmaster/mistress // *nm* (*peintre etc*) master ; (*titre*): **M~ (Me) Maître**, term of address gen for a barrister // *nf* (*amante*) mistress // *a* (*principal, essentiel*) main ; **être ~ de** (*soi-même, situation*) to be in control of ; **se rendre ~ de** (*pays, ville*) to gain control of ; (*situation, incendie*) to bring under control ; **une maîtresse femme** a managing woman ; **~ d'armes** fencing master ; **~ chanteur** blackmailer ;

~ de chapelle choirmaster; ~ de conférences ≈ senior lecturer; ~/maîtresse d'école teacher, schoolmaster/ mistress; ~ d'hôtel (domestique) butler; (d'hôtel) head waiter; ~ de maison host; ~ nageur lifeguard; ~ à penser intellectual leader; ~ queux chef; maîtresse de maison hostess; housewife (pl wives); ~-autel nm high altar.

maîtrise [metʀiz] nf (aussi: ~ de soi) self-control, self-possession; (habileté) skill, mastery; (suprématie) mastery, command; (diplôme) ≈ master's degree.

maîtriser [metʀize] vt (cheval, incendie) to (bring under) control; (sujet) to master; (émotion) to control, master; se ~ vt réfléchi to control o.s.

majesté [maʒɛste] nf majesty.

majestueux, euse [maʒɛstɥø, -øz] a majestic.

majeur, e [maʒœʀ] a (important) major; (JUR) of age; (fig) adult // nm/f person who has come of age ou attained his/her majority // nm (doigt) middle finger; en ~e partie for the most part.

major [maʒɔʀ] nm (SCOL): ~ de la promotion first of one's year.

majordome [maʒɔʀdɔm] nm majordomo.

majorer [maʒɔʀe] vt to increase.

majorette [maʒɔʀɛt] nf majorette.

majoritaire [maʒɔʀitɛʀ] a majority cpd: système/scrutin ~ majority system/ballot.

majorité [maʒɔʀite] nf (gén) majority; (parti) party in power; en ~ mainly.

majuscule [maʒyskyl] a, nf: (lettre) ~ capital (letter).

mal, maux [mal, mo] nm (opposé au bien) evil; (tort, dommage) harm; (douleur physique) pain, ache; (maladie) illness, sickness q // ad badly // a: c'est ~ (de faire) it's bad ou wrong (to do); être ~ to be uncomfortable; être ~ avec qn to be on bad terms with sb; il comprend ~ he has difficulty in understanding; il a ~ compris he misunderstood; dire du ~ de to speak ill of; ne voir aucun ~ à to see no harm in, see nothing wrong in; craignant ~ faire fearing he was doing the wrong thing; faire du ~ à qn to hurt sb; to harm sb; se faire ~ to hurt o.s.; se faire ~ au pied to hurt one's foot; ça fait ~ it hurts (fig); j'ai ~ (ici) it hurts (here); j'ai ~ au dos my back aches, I've got a pain in my back; avoir ~ à la tête/aux dents/au cœur to have a headache/have toothache/feel sick; avoir le ~ de l'air to be airsick; avoir le ~ du pays to be homesick; prendre ~ to be taken ill, feel unwell; ~ de mer seasickness; ~ en point a inv in a bad state; maux de ventre stomach ache sg.

malade [malad] a ill, sick; (poitrine, jambe) bad; (plante) diseased // nm/f invalid, sick person; (à l'hôpital etc) patient; tomber ~ to fall ill; être ~ du cœur to have heart trouble ou a bad heart; ~ mental mentally sick ou ill person.

maladie [maladi] nf (spécifique) disease, illness; (mauvaise santé) illness, sickness; (fig: manie) mania; ~ de peau skin

disease; maladif, ive a sickly; (curiosité, besoin) pathological.

maladresse [maladʀɛs] nf clumsiness q; (gaffe) blunder.

maladroit, e [maladʀwa, -wat] a clumsy.

malaise [malɛz] nm (MÉD) feeling of faintness; feeling of discomfort; (fig) uneasiness, malaise.

malaisé, e [maleze] a difficult.

malappris, e [malapʀi, -iz] nm/f ill-mannered ou boorish person.

malaria [malaʀja] nf malaria.

malavisé, e [malavize] a ill-advised, unwise.

malaxer [malakse] vt to knead; to mix.

malchance [malʃɑs] nf misfortune, ill luck q; par ~ unfortunately; malchanceux, euse a unlucky.

malcommode [malkɔmɔd] a impractical, inconvenient.

maldonne [maldɔn] nf (CARTES) misdeal; il y a ~ (fig) there's been a misunderstanding.

mâle [mal] a (aussi ÉLEC, TECH) male; (viril: voix, traits) manly // nm male; souris ~ male mouse, he-mouse.

malédiction [malediksjɔ̃] nf curse.

maléfice [malefis] nm evil spell.

maléfique [malefik] a evil, baleful.

malencontreux, euse [malɑ̃kɔ̃tʀø, -øz] a unfortunate, untoward.

malentendu [malɑ̃tɑ̃dy] nm misunderstanding.

malfaçon [malfasɔ̃] nf fault.

malfaisant, e [malfəzɑ̃, -ɑ̃t] a evil, harmful.

malfaiteur [malfɛtœʀ] nm lawbreaker, criminal; burglar, thief (pl thieves).

malfamé, e [malfame] a disreputable, of ill repute.

malformation [malfɔʀmɑsjɔ̃] nf malformation.

malfrat [malfʀa] nm villain, crook.

malgache [malgaʃ] a, nm/f Madagascan, Malagasy // nm (langue) Malagasy.

malgré [malgʀe] prép in spite of, despite; ~ tout ad all the same.

malhabile [malabil] a clumsy.

malheur [malœʀ] nm (situation) adversity, misfortune; (événement) misfortune; disaster, tragedy; malheureux, euse a (triste) unhappy, miserable; (infortuné, regrettable) unfortunate; (malchanceux) unlucky; (insignifiant) wretched // nm/f poor soul; unfortunate creature; les malheureux the destitute.

malhonnête [malɔnɛt] a dishonest; (impoli) rude; ~té nf dishonesty; rudeness q.

malice [malis] nf mischievousness; (méchanceté): par ~ out of malice ou spite; sans ~ guileless; malicieux, euse a mischievous.

malin, igne [malɛ̃, -iɲ] a (futé: f gén: maline) smart, shrewd; (MÉD) malignant; faire le ~ to show off; éprouver un ~ plaisir à to take malicious pleasure in.

malingre [malɛ̃gʀ(ə)] a puny.

malle [mal] nf trunk.

malléable [maleabl(ə)] a malleable.

malle-poste [malpɔst(ə)] nf mail coach.
mallette [malɛt] nf (small) suitcase ;
overnight case ; attaché case.
malmener [malmǝne] vt to manhandle ;
(fig) to give a rough handling to.
malodorant, e [malɔdɔRɑ̃, -ɑ̃t] a foul- ou
ill-smelling.
malotru [malɔtRy] nm lout, boor.
malpoli, e [malpɔli] nm/f rude individual.
malpropre [malpRɔpR(ə)] a dirty.
malsain, e [malsɛ̃, -ɛn] a unhealthy.
malséant, e [malseɑ̃, -ɑ̃t] a unseemly,
unbecoming.
malsonnant, e [malsɔnɑ̃, -ɑ̃t] a offensive.
malt [malt] nm malt.
maltais, e [maltɛ, -ɛz] a, nm/f Maltese.
Malte [malt(ə)] nf Malta.
maltraiter [maltRete] vt (brutaliser) to
manhandle, ill-treat.
malveillance [malvɛjɑ̃s] nf (animosité) ill
will ; (intention de nuire) malevolence ; (JUR)
malicious intent q.
malveillant, e [malvɛjɑ̃, -ɑ̃t] a
malevolent, malicious.
malversation [malvɛRsɑsjɔ̃] nf
embezzlement, misappropriation (of
funds).
maman [mamɑ̃] nf mum, mother.
mamelle [mamɛl] nf teat.
mamelon [mamlɔ̃] nm (ANAT) nipple ;
(colline) knoll, hillock.
mammifère [mamifɛR] nm mammal.
mammouth [mamut] nm mammoth.
manche [mɑ̃ʃ] nf (de vêtement) sleeve ;
(d'un jeu, tournoi) round ; (GÉO): **la M —**
the Channel // nm (d'outil, casserole)
handle ; (de pelle, pioche etc) shaft ; (de
violon, guitare) neck ; (fam) clumsy oaf ; ~
à air nf (AVIAT) wind-sock ; ~ **à balai** nm
broomstick ; (AVIAT) joystick.
manchette [mɑ̃ʃɛt] nf (de chemise) cuff ;
(coup) forearm blow ; (titre) headline.
manchon [mɑ̃ʃɔ̃] nm (de fourrure) muff ;
~ **à incandescence** incandescent (gas)
mantle.
manchot [mɑ̃ʃo] nm one-armed man ;
armless man ; (ZOOL) penguin.
mandarine [mɑ̃daRin] nf mandarin
(orange), tangerine.
mandat [mɑ̃da] nm (postal) postal ou
money order ; (d'un député etc) mandate ;
(procuration) power of attorney, proxy ;
(POLICE) warrant ; ~ **d'amener** summons
sg ; ~ **d'arrêt** warrant for arrest ; ~ **de
dépôt** committal order ; **mandataire** nm/f
representative ; proxy.
mander [mɑ̃de] vt to summon.
mandibule [mɑ̃dibyl] nf mandible.
mandoline [mɑ̃dɔlin] nf mandolin(e).
manège [manɛʒ] nm riding school ; (à la
foire) roundabout, merry-go-round ; (fig)
game, ploy.
manette [manɛt] nf lever, tap.
manganèse [mɑ̃ganɛz] nm manganese.
mangeable [mɑ̃ʒabl(ə)] a edible, eatable.
mangeaille [mɑ̃ʒaj] nf (péj) grub.
mangeoire [mɑ̃ʒwaR] nf trough, manger.
manger [mɑ̃ʒe] vt to eat ; (ronger: suj:
rouille etc) to eat into ou away // vi to
eat ; **mangeur, euse** nm/f eater.

mangouste [mɑ̃gust(ə)] nf mongoose.
mangue [mɑ̃g] nf mango.
maniable [manjabl(ə)] a (outil) handy ;
(voiture, voilier) easy to handle.
maniaque [manjak] a finicky, fussy ;
suffering from a mania // nm/f maniac.
manie [mani] nf mania ; (tic) odd habit.
maniement [manimɑ̃] nm handling ; ~
d'armes arms drill.
manier [manje] vt to handle.
manière [manjɛR] nf (façon) way,
manner ; ~**s** nfpl (attitude) manners ;
(chichis) fuss sg ; **de** ~ **à so as to** ; **de telle**
~ **que** in such a way that ; **de cette** ~
in this way ou manner ; **d'une** ~ **générale**
generally speaking, as a general rule ; **de
toute** ~ in any case ; **adverbe de** ~
adverb of manner.
maniéré, e [manjeRe] a affected.
manif [manif] nf demo (pl s).
manifestant, e [manifɛstɑ̃, -ɑ̃t] nm/f
demonstrator.
manifestation [manifɛstɑsjɔ̃] nf (de joie,
mécontentement) expression, demonstration ; (symptôme) outward sign ; (fête etc)
event ; (POL) demonstration.
manifeste [manifɛst(ə)] a obvious,
evident // nm manifesto (pl s).
manifester [manifɛste] vt (volonté,
intentions) to show, indicate ; (joie, peur)
to express, show // vi to demonstrate ; **se**
~ vi (émotion) to show ou express itself ;
(difficultés) to arise ; (symptômes) to
appear ; (témoin etc) to come forward.
manigance [manigɑ̃s] nf scheme.
manigancer [manigɑ̃se] vt to plot, devise.
manioc [manjɔk] nm cassava, manioc.
manipuler [manipyle] vt to handle ; (fig)
to manipulate.
manivelle [manivɛl] nf crank.
manne [man] nf (REL) manna ; (fig)
godsend.
mannequin [manikɛ̃] nm (COUTURE)
dummy ; (MODE) model.
manœuvre [manœvR(ə)] nf (gén)
manœuvre // nm labourer.
manœuvrer [manœvRe] vt to manœuvre ;
(levier, machine) to operate // vi to
manœuvre.
manoir [manwaR] nm manor ou country
house.
manomètre [manɔmɛtR(ə)] nm gauge,
manometer.
manquant, e [mɑ̃kɑ̃, -ɑ̃t] a missing.
manque [mɑ̃k] nm (insuffisance): ~ **de**
lack of ; (vide) emptiness, gap ; (MÉD)
withdrawal ; ~**s** nmpl (lacunes) faults,
defects ; ~ **à gagner** loss of profit ou
earnings.
manqué, e [mɑ̃ke] a failed ; **garçon** ~
tomboy.
manquement [mɑ̃kmɑ̃] nm: ~ **à**
(discipline, règle) breach of.
manquer [mɑ̃ke] vi (faire défaut) to be
lacking ; (être absent) to be missing ;
(échouer) to fail // vt to miss // vb
impersonnel: **il (nous) manque encore 100
F** we are still 100 F short ; **il manque des
pages (au livre)** there are some pages
missing ou some pages are missing (from
the book) ; **l'argent qui leur manque** the

money they need *ou* are short of; **le pied/la voix lui manqua** he missed his footing/his voice failed him; ~ **à qn** (*absent etc*): **il/cela me manque** I miss him/this; ~ **à** *vt* (*règles etc*) to be in breach of, fail to observe; ~ **de** *vt* to lack; **ne pas ~ de faire: il n'a pas manqué de le dire** he sure enough said it, he didn't fail to say it; ~ **(de) faire: il a manqué (de) se tuer** he very nearly got killed.

mansarde [mɑ̃saʀd(ə)] *nf* attic; **mansardé, e** *a* attic *cpd*.

mansuétude [mɑ̃sɥetyd] *nf* leniency.

mante [mɑ̃t] *nf*: ~ **religieuse** praying mantis.

manteau, x [mɑ̃to] *nm* coat; ~ **de cheminée** mantelpiece.

mantille [mɑ̃tij] *nf* mantilla.

manucure [manykyʀ] *nf* manicurist.

manuel, le [manɥɛl] *a* manual // *nm/f* manually gifted pupil *etc* (*as opposed to intellectually gifted*) // *nm* (*ouvrage*) manual, handbook.

manufacture [manyfaktyʀ] *nf* factory.

manufacturé, e [manyfaktyʀe] *a* manufactured.

manuscrit, e [manyskʀi, -it] *a* handwritten // *nm* manuscript.

manutention [manytɑ̃sjɔ̃] *nf* (*COMM*) handling; **manutentionnaire** *nm/f* warehouseman/woman, packer.

mappemonde [mapmɔ̃d] *nf* (*plane*) map of the world; (*sphère*) globe.

maquereau, x [makʀo] *nm* (*ZOOL*) mackerel *inv*; (*fam*) pimp.

maquerelle [makʀɛl] *nf* (*fam*) madam.

maquette [makɛt] *nf* (*d'un décor, bâtiment, véhicule*) (scale) model; (*d'une page illustrée*) paste-up.

maquignon [makiɲɔ̃] *nm* horse-dealer.

maquillage [makijaʒ] *nm* making up; faking; (*crème etc*) make-up.

maquiller [makije] *vt* (*personne, visage*) to make up; (*truquer: passeport, statistique*) to fake; (*: voiture volée*) to do over (*respray etc*); **se** ~ to make up (one's face).

maquis [maki] *nm* (*GÉO*) scrub; (*fig*) tangle; (*MIL*) maquis, underground fighting *q*.

marabout [maʀabu] *nm* (*ZOOL*) marabou(t).

maraîcher, ère [maʀɛʃe, maʀɛʃɛʀ] *a*: **cultures maraîchères** market gardening *sg* // *nm/f* market gardener.

marais [maʀɛ] *nm* marsh, swamp; ~ **salant** salt pen, saltern.

marasme [maʀasm(ə)] *nm* stagnation, slump.

marathon [maʀatɔ̃] *nm* marathon.

marâtre [maʀɑtʀ(ə)] *nf* cruel mother.

maraude [maʀod] *nf* pilfering, thieving (*of poultry, crops*); (*dans un verger*) scrumping; (*vagabondage*) prowling; **en** ~ on the prowl; (*taxi*) cruising.

marbre [maʀbʀ(ə)] *nm* (*pierre, statue*) marble; (*d'une table, commode*) marble top; (*TYPO*) stone, bed; **rester de** ~ to remain stonily indifferent; **marbrer** *vt* to mottle, blotch; (*TECH: papier*) to marble; ~**rie** *nf* monumental mason's yard; **marbrier** *nm* monumental mason.

marc [maʀ] *nm* (*de raisin, pommes*) marc; ~ **de café** coffee grounds *pl ou* dregs *pl*.

marcassin [maʀkasɛ̃] *nm* young wild boar.

marchand, e [maʀʃɑ̃, -ɑ̃d] *nm/f* shopkeeper, tradesman/woman; (*au marché*) stallholder; (*spécifique*): ~ **de cycles/tapis** bicycle/carpet dealer; ~ **de charbon/vins** coal/wine merchant // *a*: **prix/valeur** ~**(e)** market price/value; ~ **de biens** real estate agent; ~ **de couleurs** ironmonger; ~**/e de fruits** fruiterer, fruit merchant; ~**/e de journaux** newsagent; ~**/e de légumes** greengrocer; ~**/e de poisson** fishmonger, fish merchant; ~**e de quatre saisons** costermonger; ~ **de tableaux** art dealer.

marchander [maʀʃɑ̃de] *vt* (*article*) to bargain *ou* haggle over; (*éloges*) to be sparing with // *vi* to bargain, haggle.

marchandise [maʀʃɑ̃diz] *nf* goods *pl*, merchandise *q*.

marche [maʀʃ(ə)] *nf* (*d'escalier*) step; (*activité*) walking; (*promenade, trajet, allure*) walk; (*démarche*) walk, gait; (*MIL etc, MUS*) march; (*fonctionnement*) running; (*progression*) progress; course; **ouvrir/fermer la** ~ to lead the way/bring up the rear; **dans le sens de la** ~ (*RAIL*) facing the engine; **en** ~ (*monter etc*) while the vehicle is moving *ou* in motion; **mettre en** ~ to start; **remettre qch en** ~ to set *ou* start sth going again; **se mettre en** ~ (*personne*) to get moving; (*machine*) to start; ~ **arrière** reverse (gear); **faire** ~ **arrière** to reverse; (*fig*) to backtrack, back-pedal; ~ **à suivre** (correct) procedure; (*sur notice*) (step by step) instructions *pl*.

marché [maʀʃe] *nm* (*lieu, COMM, ÉCON*) market; (*ville*) trading centre; (*transaction*) bargain, deal; **M~ commun** Common Market; ~ **aux fleurs** flower market; ~ **noir** black market; **faire du** ~ **noir** to buy and sell on the black market; ~ **aux puces** flea market.

marchepied [maʀʃəpje] *nm* (*RAIL*) step; (*AUTO*) running board; (*fig*) stepping stone.

marcher [maʀʃe] *vi* to walk; (*MIL*) to march; (*aller: voiture, train, affaires*) to go; (*prospérer*) to go well; (*fonctionner*) to work, run; (*fam*) to go along, agree; to be taken in; ~ **sur** to walk on; (*mettre le pied sur*) to step on *ou* in; (*MIL*) to march upon; ~ **dans** (*herbe etc*) to walk in *ou* on; (*flaque*) to step in; **faire** ~ **qn** to pull sb's leg; to lead sb up the garden path; **marcheur, euse** *nm/f* walker.

mardi [maʀdi] *nm* Tuesday; **M~ gras** Shrove Tuesday.

mare [maʀ] *nf* pond; ~ **de sang** pool of blood.

marécage [maʀekaʒ] *nm* marsh, swamp; **marécageux, euse** *a* marshy, swampy.

maréchal, aux [maʀeʃal, -o] *nm* marshal; ~ **des logis** (*MIL*) sergeant.

maréchal-ferrant [maʀeʃalfɛʀɑ̃] *nm* blacksmith, farrier.

maréchaussée [maʀeʃose] *nf* constabulary.

marée [maʀe] *nf* tide; (*poissons*) fresh (sea) fish; ~ **haute/basse** high/low tide;

~ **montante/ descendante** rising/ebb tide.

marelle [maʀɛl] nf: **(jouer à) la** ~ (to play) hopscotch.

marémotrice [maʀemɔtʀis] af tidal.

mareyeur, euse [maʀɛjœʀ, -øz] nm/f wholesale (sea) fish merchant.

margarine [maʀgaʀin] nf margarine.

marge [maʀʒ] nf margin; **en** ~ in the margin; **en** ~ **de** (fig) on the fringe of; cut off from; connected with; ~ **bénéficiaire** profit margin.

margelle [maʀʒɛl] nf coping.

margeur [maʀʒœʀ] nm margin stop.

marginal, e, aux [maʀʒinal, -o] a marginal.

marguerite [maʀgəʀit] nf marguerite, (oxeye) daisy.

marguillier [maʀgije] nm churchwarden.

mari [maʀi] nm husband.

mariage [maʀjaʒ] nm (union, état, fig) marriage; (noce) wedding; ~ **civil/religieux** civil ou registry office/church wedding; **un** ~ **de raison/d'amour** a marriage of convenience/love match; ~ **en blanc** unconsummated marriage; ~ **en blanc** white wedding.

marié, e [maʀje] a married // nm/f (bride)groom/bride; **les** ~**s** the bride and groom; **les (jeunes)** ~**s** the newly-weds.

marier [maʀje] vt to marry; (fig) to blend; **se** ~ **(avec)** to marry, get married (to) (fig) to blend (with).

marin, e [maʀɛ̃, -in] a sea cpd, marine // nm sailor // nf navy; (ART) seascape; ~**e de guerre** navy; ~**e marchande** merchant navy; ~**e à voiles** sailing ships pl.

marinade [maʀinad] nf marinade.

marine [maʀin] af, nf voir **marin** // a inv navy (blue) // nm (MIL) marine.

mariner [maʀine] vi, vt to marinate, marinade.

marinier [maʀinje] nm bargee.

marinière [maʀinjɛʀ] nf smock // a inv: **moules** ~ mussels in white wine.

marionnette [maʀjɔnɛt] nf puppet.

marital, e, aux [maʀital, -o] a marital, husband's; ~**ement** ad as husband and wife.

maritime [maʀitim] a sea cpd, maritime.

marjolaine [maʀʒɔlɛn] nf marjoram.

mark [maʀk] nm mark.

marmaille [maʀmaj] nf (péj) (gang of) brats pl.

marmelade [maʀməlad] nf stewed fruit, compote; **en** ~ (fig) crushed (to a pulp).

marmite [maʀmit] nf (cooking-)pot.

marmiton [maʀmitɔ̃] nm kitchen boy.

marmonner [maʀmɔne] vt, vi to mumble, mutter.

marmot [maʀmo] nm brat.

marmotte [maʀmɔt] nf marmot.

marmotter [maʀmɔte] vt (prière) to mumble, mutter.

marne [maʀn(ə)] nf marl.

Maroc [maʀɔk] nm: **le** ~ Morocco; **marocain, e** a, nm/f Moroccan.

maroquin [maʀɔkɛ̃] nm morocco (leather); (fig) (minister's) portfolio.

maroquinerie [maʀɔkinʀi] nf leather craft; fine leather goods pl.

marotte [maʀɔt] nf fad.

marquant, e [maʀkɑ̃, -ɑ̃t] a outstanding.

marque [maʀk(ə)] nf mark; (SPORT, JEU: décompte des points) score; (COMM: de produits) brand; make; (: de disques) label; **à vos** ~**s!** (SPORT) on your marks!; **de** ~ a (COMM) brand-name cpd; proprietary; (fig) high-class; distinguished; ~ **déposée** registered trademark; ~ **de fabrique** trademark.

marqué, e [maʀke] a marked.

marquer [maʀke] vt to mark; (inscrire) to write down; (bétail) to brand; (SPORT: but etc) to score; (: joueur) to mark; (accentuer: taille etc) to emphasize; (manifester: refus, intérêt) to show // vi (événement, personnalité) to stand out, be outstanding; (SPORT) to score; ~ **les points** (tenir la marque) to keep the score.

marqueterie [maʀkətʀi] nf inlaid work, marquetry.

marquis, e [maʀki, -iz] nm/f marquis ou marquess/marchioness // nf (auvent) glass canopy ou awning.

marraine [maʀɛn] nf godmother.

marrant, e [maʀɑ̃, -ɑ̃t] a (fam) funny.

marre [maʀ] ad (fam): **en avoir** ~ **de** to be fed up with.

marrer [maʀe]: **se** ~ vi (fam) to have a (good) laugh.

marron [maʀɔ̃] nm (fruit) chestnut // a inv brown // am (péj) crooked; bogus; ~**s glacés** marrons glacés; **marronnier** nm chestnut (tree).

mars [maʀs] nm March.

Mars [maʀs] nf ou m Mars.

marsouin [maʀswɛ̃] nm porpoise.

marsupiaux [maʀsypjo] nmpl marsupials.

marteau, x [maʀto] nm hammer; (de porte) knocker; ~**-piqueur** nm pneumatic drill.

martel [maʀtɛl] nm: **se mettre** ~ **en tête** to worry o.s.

marteler [maʀtəle] vt to hammer.

martial, e, aux [maʀsjal, -o] a martial.

martien, ne [maʀsjɛ̃, -jɛn] a Martian, of ou from Mars.

martinet [maʀtinɛ] nm (fouet) small whip; (ZOOL) swift.

martingale [maʀtɛ̃gal] nf (COUTURE) half-belt; (JEU) winning formula.

Martinique [maʀtinik] nf: **la** ~ Martinique.

martin-pêcheur [maʀtɛ̃pɛʃœʀ] nm kingfisher.

martre [maʀtʀ(ə)] nf marten.

martyr, e [maʀtiʀ] nm/f martyr // a martyred; **enfants** ~**s** battered children.

martyre [maʀtiʀ] nm martyrdom; (fig: sens affaibli) agony, torture.

martyriser [maʀtiʀize] vt (REL) to martyr; (fig) to bully; to batter.

marxisme [maʀksism(ə)] nm Marxism.

mascarade [maskaʀad] nf masquerade.

mascotte [maskɔt] nf mascot.

masculin, e [maskylɛ̃, -in] a masculine; (sexe, population) male; (équipe, vêtements) men's; (viril) manly // nm masculine.

masochisme [mazɔʃism(ə)] *nm* masochism.

masque [mask(ə)] *nm* mask ; ~ **à gaz** gas mask.

masqué, e [maske] *a* masked.

masquer [maske] *vt* (*cacher: paysage, porte*) to hide, conceal ; (*dissimuler: vérité, projet*) to mask, obscure.

massacrant, e [masakʀɑ̃, -ɑ̃t] *a*: **humeur** ~**e** foul temper.

massacre [masakʀ(ə)] *nm* massacre, slaughter.

massacrer [masakʀe] *vt* to massacre, slaughter ; (*fig: texte etc*) to murder.

massage [masaʒ] *nm* massage.

masse [mas] *nf* mass ; (*péj*): **la** ~ the masses *pl* ; (*ÉLEC*) earth ; (*maillet*) sledgehammer ; ~**s** *nfpl* masses ; **une** ~ **de, des** ~**s de** (*fam*) masses *ou* loads of ; **en** ~ *ad* (*en bloc*) in bulk ; (*en foule*) en masse // *a* (*exécutions, production*) mass *cpd* ; ~ **salariale** aggregate remuneration (of employees).

massepain [maspɛ̃] *nm* marzipan.

masser [mase] *vt* (*assembler*) to gather ; (*pétrir*) to massage ; **se** ~ *vi* to gather ; **masseur, euse** *nm/f* masseur/masseuse.

massicot [masiko] *nm* guillotine.

massif, ive [masif, -iv] *a* (*porte*) solid, massive ; (*visage*) heavy, large ; (*bois, or*) solid ; (*dose*) massive ; (*déportations etc*) mass *cpd* // *nm* (*montagneux*) massif ; (*de fleurs*) clump, bank.

massue [masy] *nf* club, bludgeon.

mastic [mastik] *nm* (*pour vitres*) putty ; (*pour fentes*) filler.

mastiquer [mastike] *vt* (*aliment*) to chew, masticate ; (*fente*) to fill ; (*vitre*) to putty.

masturbation [mastyʀbasjɔ̃] *nf* masturbation.

masure [mazyʀ] *nf* tumbledown cottage.

mat, e [mat] *a* (*couleur, métal*) mat(t) ; (*bruit, son*) dull // *a inv* (*ÉCHECS*): **être** ~ to be checkmate.

mât [mɑ] *nm* (*NAVIG*) mast ; (*poteau*) pole, post.

match [matʃ] *nm* match ; ~ **nul** draw ; **faire** ~ **nul** to draw.

matelas [matla] *nm* mattress ; ~ **pneumatique** air bed *ou* mattress ; ~ **à ressorts** spring *ou* interior-sprung mattress.

matelasser [matlase] *vt* to pad ; to quilt.

matelot [matlo] *nm* sailor, seaman.

mater [mate] *vt* (*personne*) to bring to heel, subdue ; (*révolte*) to put down.

matérialiser [mateʀjalize] : **se** ~ *vi* to materialize.

matérialiste [mateʀjalist(ə)] *a* materialistic.

matériau, x [mateʀjo] *nm* material // *nmpl* material(s).

matériel, le [mateʀjɛl] *a* material // *nm* equipment *q* ; (*de camping etc*) gear *q* ; ~ **d'exploitation** (*COMM*) plant.

maternel, le [matɛʀnɛl] *a* (*amour, geste*) motherly, maternal ; (*grand-père, oncle*) maternal // *nf* (*aussi*: **école** ~**le**) (state) nursery school.

maternité [matɛʀnite] *nf* (*établissement*) maternity hospital ; (*état de mère*) motherhood, maternity ; (*grossesse*) pregnancy.

mathématicien, ne [matematisjɛ̃, -jɛn] *nm/f* mathematician.

mathématique [matematik] *a* mathematical ; ~**s** *nfpl* (*science*) mathematics *sg*.

matière [matjɛʀ] *nf* (*PHYSIQUE*) matter ; (*COMM, TECH*) material, matter *q* ; (*fig: d'un livre etc*) subject matter, material ; (*SCOL*) subject ; **en** ~ **de** as regards ; **donner** ~ **à** to give cause to ; ~ **plastique** plastic ; ~**s fécales** faeces ; ~**s grasses** fat content *sg* ; ~**s premières** raw materials.

matin [matɛ̃] *nm, ad* morning ; **matinal, e, aux** *a* (*toilette, gymnastique*) morning *cpd* ; (*de bonne heure*) early ; **être matinal** (*personne*) to be up early ; to be an early riser.

matinée [matine] *nf* morning ; (*spectacle*) matinée, afternoon performance.

mâtiner [mɑtine] *vt* to cross.

matois, e [matwa, -waz] *a* wily.

matou [matu] *nm* tom(cat).

matraque [matʀak] *nf* cosh ; (*de policier*) truncheon ; **matraquer** *vt* to beat up (with a truncheon) ; to cosh ; (*fig: disque*) to plug.

matriarcal, e, aux [matʀijaʀkal, -o] *a* matriarchal.

matrice [matʀis] *nf* (*ANAT*) womb ; (*TECH*) mould ; (*MATH etc*) matrix.

matricule [matʀikyl] *nf* (*aussi*: **registre** ~) roll, register // *nm* (*aussi*: **numéro** ~) (*MIL*) regimental number ; (*ADMIN*) reference number.

matrimonial, e, aux [matʀimɔnjal, -o] *a* marital, marriage *cpd*.

mâture [mɑtyʀ] *nf* masts *pl*.

maturité [matyʀite] *nf* maturity ; (*d'un fruit*) ripeness, maturity.

maudire [modiʀ] *vt* to curse.

maudit, e [modi, -it] *a* (*fam: satané*) blasted, confounded.

maugréer [mogʀee] *vi* to grumble.

Mauresque [mɔʀɛsk] *a* Moorish.

mausolée [mozɔle] *nm* mausoleum.

maussade [mosad] *a* sullen.

mauvais, e [mɔvɛ, -ɛz] *a* bad ; (*faux*): **le** ~ **numéro/moment** the wrong number/moment ; (*méchant, malveillant*) malicious, spiteful // *ad*: **il fait** ~ the weather is bad ; **sentir** ~ to have a nasty smell, smell bad *ou* nasty ; **la mer est** ~**e** the sea is rough ; ~ **coup** (*fig*) criminal venture ; ~ **garçon** tough ; ~ **plaisant** hoaxer ; ~ **traitements** ill treatment *sg* ; ~**e herbe** weed ; ~**e langue** gossip, scandalmonger ; ~**e passe** difficult situation ; bad patch ; ~**e tête** rebellious *ou* headstrong customer.

mauve [mov] *a* mauve // *nf* mallow.

mauviette [movjɛt] *nf* (*péj*) weakling.

maux [mo] *nmpl voir* **mal.**

maximal, e, aux [maksimal, -o] *a* maximal.

maxime [maksim] *nf* maxim.

maximum [maksimɔm] *a, nm* maximum ; **au** ~ *ad* (*le plus possible*) to the full ; as much as one can ; (*tout au plus*) at the (very) most *ou* maximum.

mayonnaise [majɔnɛz] nf mayonnaise.

mazout [mazut] nm (fuel) oil.

me, m' [m(ə)] pronom me ; (réfléchi) myself.

Me abr de **Maître**.

méandres [meɑ̃dR(ə)] nmpl meanderings.

mec [mɛk] nm (fam) bloke.

mécanicien, ne [mekanisjɛ̃, -jɛn] nm/f mechanic ; (RAIL) (train ou engine) driver ; ~-**dentiste** nm/f dental technician.

mécanique [mekanik] a mechanical // nf (science) mechanics sg ; (technologie) mechanical engineering ; (AUTO): **s'y connaître en** ~ to be mechanically minded ; (mécanisme) mechanism ; engineering ; works pl ; **ennui** ~ engine trouble q ; **mécaniser** vt to mechanize.

mécanisme [mekanism(ə)] nm mechanism.

mécanographie [mekanɔgRafi] nf (mechanical) data processing.

mécène [mesɛn] nm patron.

méchanceté [meʃɑ̃ste] nf nastiness, maliciousness ; nasty ou spiteful ou malicious remark (ou action).

méchant, e [meʃɑ̃, -ɑ̃t] a nasty, malicious, spiteful ; (enfant: pas sage) naughty ; (animal) vicious ; (avant le nom: valeur péjorative) nasty ; miserable ; (: intensive) terrific.

mèche [mɛʃ] nf (de lampe, bougie) wick ; (d'un explosif) fuse ; (de vilebrequin, perceuse) bit ; (de fouet) lash ; (de cheveux) lock ; **vendre la** ~ to give the game away ; **de** ~ **avec** in league with.

méchoui [meʃwi] nm whole sheep barbecue.

mécompte [mekɔ̃t] nm miscalculation ; (déception) disappointment.

méconnaissable [mekɔnɛsabl(ə)] a unrecognizable.

méconnaissance [mekɔnɛsɑ̃s] nf ignorance.

méconnaître [mekɔnɛtR(ə)] vt (ignorer) to be unaware of ; (mésestimer) to misjudge.

mécontent, e [mekɔ̃tɑ̃, -ɑ̃t] a: ~ (de) discontented ou dissatisfied ou displeased (with) ; (contrarié) annoyed (at) ; **mécontentement** nm dissatisfaction, discontent, displeasure ; annoyance ; **mécontenter** vt to displease.

médaille [medaj] nf medal ; **médaillé, e** nm/f (SPORT) medal-holder.

médaillon [medajɔ̃] nm (portrait) medallion ; (bijou) locket ; (CULIN) médaillon ; **en** ~ a (carte etc) inset.

médecin [medsɛ̃] nm doctor ; **généraliste** general practitioner, G.P.

médecine [medsin] nf medicine ; ~ **légale** forensic medicine ; ~ **du travail** occupational ou industrial medicine.

médian, e [medjɑ̃, -an] a (MATH) median.

médiateur, trice [medjatœr, -tRis] nm/f mediator ; arbitrator.

médiation [medjasjɔ̃] nf mediation ; (dans conflit social etc) arbitration.

médical, e, aux [medikal, -o] a medical.

médicament [medikamɑ̃] nm medicine, drug.

médicinal, e, aux [medisinal, -o] a medicinal.

médico-légal, e, aux [medikɔlegal, -o] a forensic.

médiéval, e, aux [medjeval, -o] a medieval.

médiocre [medjɔkR(ə)] a mediocre, poor ; **médiocrité** nf mediocrity.

médire [mediR] vi: ~ **de** to speak ill of ; **médisance** nf scandalmongering ; piece of scandal ou of malicious gossip.

méditatif, ive [meditatif, -iv] a thoughtful.

méditation [meditasjɔ̃] nf meditation.

méditer [medite] vt (approfondir) to meditate on, ponder (over) ; (combiner) to meditate // vi to meditate ; ~ **de faire** to contemplate doing, plan to do.

Méditerranée [mediteRane] nf: **la (mer)** ~ the Mediterranean (Sea) ; **méditerranéen, ne** a, nm/f Mediterranean.

médium [medjɔm] nm medium (person).

médius [medjys] nm middle finger.

méduse [medyz] nf jellyfish.

méduser [medyze] vt to dumbfound.

meeting [mitiŋ] nm (POL, SPORT) rally ; ~ **d'aviation** air show.

méfait [mefɛ] nm (faute) misdemeanour, wrongdoing ; ~**s** nmpl (ravages) ravages, damage sg.

méfiance [mefjɑ̃s] nf mistrust, distrust.

méfiant, e [mefjɑ̃, -ɑ̃t] a mistrustful, distrustful.

méfier [mefje]: **se** ~ vi to be wary ; to be careful ; **se** ~ **de** vt to mistrust, distrust, be wary of ; (faire attention) to be careful about.

mégarde [megaRd(ə)] nf: **par** ~ accidentally ; by mistake.

mégère [meʒɛR] nf shrew.

mégot [mego] nm cigarette end.

meilleur, e [mɛjœR] a, ad better ; (valeur superlative) best // nm: **le** ~ (celui qui ...) the best (one) ; (ce qui ...) the best // nf: **la** ~**e** the best (one) ; **le** ~ **des deux** the better of the two ; ~ **marché** cheaper.

mélancolie [melɑ̃kɔli] nf melancholy, gloom ; **mélancolique** a melancholic, melancholy.

mélange [melɑ̃ʒ] nm mixture.

mélanger [melɑ̃ʒe] vt (substances) to mix ; (vins, couleurs) to blend ; (mettre en désordre) to mix up, muddle (up).

mélasse [melas] nf treacle, molasses sg.

mêlée [mele] nf mêlée, scramble ; (RUGBY) scrum(mage).

mêler [mele] vt (substances, odeurs, races) to mix ; (embrouiller) to muddle (up), mix up ; **se** ~ to mix ; to mingle ; **se** ~ **à** (suj: personne) to join ; to mix with ; (: odeurs etc) to mingle with ; **se** ~ **de** (suj: personne) to meddle with, interfere in ; ~ **qn à** (affaire) to get sb mixed up ou involved in.

mélodie [melɔdi] nf melody ; **mélodieux, euse** a melodious, tuneful ; **mélodique** a melodic.

mélodrame [melɔdRam] nm melodrama.

mélomane [melɔman] nm/f music lover.

melon [məlɔ̃] nm (BOT) (honeydew) melon ; (aussi: **chapeau** ~) bowler (hat) ; ~ **d'eau** watermelon.

mélopée [melɔpe] nf monotonous chant.
membrane [mɑ̃bʀan] nf membrane.
membre [mɑ̃bʀ(ə)] nm (ANAT) limb;
(personne, pays, élément) member // a
member; ~ (viril) (male) organ.
même [mɛm] a same // pronom: le(la) ~
the same (one) // ad even; en ~ temps
at the same time; **ce sont ses
paroles/celles-là** ~s they are his very
words/the very ones; **il n'a** ~ **pas pleuré**
he didn't even cry; **ici** ~ at this very
place; **à** ~ **la bouteille** straight from the
bottle; **à** ~ **la peau** next to the skin; **être
à** ~ **de faire** to be in a position ou be
able to do; **mettre qn à** ~ **de faire** to
enable sb to do; **faire de** ~ to do likewise;
lui de ~ so does (ou did ou is) he; **de**
~ **que** just as; **il en va/est allé de** ~
pour the same goes/happened for.
mémento [meméto] nm (agenda)
engagement diary; (ouvrage) summary.
mémoire [memwaʀ] nf memory // nm
(ADMIN, JUR) memorandum (pl à); (SCOL)
dissertation, paper; ~s nmpl memoirs;
avoir la ~ **des chiffres** to have a good
memory for figures; **à la** ~ **de** to the ou
in memory of; **pour** ~ ad for the record;
de ~ **d'homme** in living memory; **de** ~
ad from memory.
mémorable [memɔʀabl(ə)] a memorable.
mémorandum [memɔʀɑ̃dɔm] nm
memorandum (pl à).
mémorial, aux [memɔʀjal, -o] nm
memorial.
menaçant, e [mənasɑ̃, -ɑ̃t] a threatening,
menacing.
menace [mənas] nf threat.
menacer [mənase] vt to threaten.
ménage [menaʒ] nm (travail)
housekeeping, housework; (couple)
(married) couple; (famille, ADMIN)
household; **faire le** ~ to do the
housework; **faire des** ~s to go out
charring; **monter son** ~ to set up house;
se mettre en ~ **(avec)** to set up house
(with); **heureux en** ~ happily married;
faire bon ~ **avec** to get on well with;
~ **de poupée** doll's kitchen set; **à trois**
love triangle.
ménagement [menaʒmɑ̃] nm care and
attention; ~s nmpl (égards) consideration
sg, attention sg.
ménager [menaʒe] vt (traiter) to handle
with tact ou treat considerately; (utiliser)
to use sparingly; to use with care;
(prendre soin de) to take (great) care of,
look after; (organiser) to arrange;
(installer) to put in; to make; ~ **qch à
qn** (réserver) to have sth in store for sb.
ménager, ère [menaʒe, -ɛʀ] a household
cpd, domestic // nf housewife (pl wives).
ménagerie [menaʒʀi] nf menagerie.
mendiant, e [mɑ̃djɑ̃, -ɑ̃t] nm/f beggar.
mendicité [mɑ̃disite] nf begging.
mendier [mɑ̃dje] vi to beg // vt to beg
(for).
menées [məne] nfpl intrigues, manœuvres.
mener [məne] vt to lead; (enquête) to
conduct; (affaires) to manage // vi: ~ (à
la marque) to lead, be in the lead; ~
à/dans (emmener) to take to/into; ~ qch
à terme ou à bien to see sth through (to

a successful conclusion), complete sth
successfully.
meneur, euse [mənœʀ, -øz] nm/f leader;
(péj) agitator; ~ **d'hommes** born leader;
~ **de jeu** compère; quizmaster.
méningite [menɛ̃ʒit] nf meningitis q.
ménopause [menɔpoz] nf menopause.
menotte [mənɔt] nf (main) mitt, tiny
hand; ~s nfpl handcuffs; **passer les** ~s
à to handcuff.
mensonge [mɑ̃sɔ̃ʒ] nm lie; lying q;
mensonger, ère a false.
mensualité [mɑ̃syalite] nf monthly
payment; monthly salary.
mensuel, le [mɑ̃syɛl] a monthly.
mensurations [mɑ̃syʀasjɔ̃] nfpl
measurements.
mental, e, aux [mɑ̃tal, -o] a mental.
mentalité [mɑ̃talite] nf mentality.
menteur, euse [mɑ̃tœʀ, -øz] nm/f liar.
menthe [mɑ̃t] nf mint; ~ (à l'eau)
peppermint cordial.
mention [mɑ̃sjɔ̃] nf (note) note, comment;
(SCOL): ~ **bien** etc ≈ grade B etc (ou upper
2nd class etc) pass; **faire** ~ **de** to
mention; **mentionner** vt to mention.
mentir [mɑ̃tiʀ] vi to lie; to be lying.
menton [mɑ̃tɔ̃] nm chin.
menu, e [məny] a slim, slight; tiny; (frais,
difficulté) minor // ad (couper, hacher) very
fine // nm menu; **par le** ~ (raconter) in
minute detail; ~e **monnaie** small change.
menuet [mənyɛ] nm minuet.
menuiserie [mənyizʀi] nf (travail)
joinery, carpentry; woodwork; (local)
joiner's workshop; (ouvrage) woodwork q.
menuisier [mənyizje] nm joiner,
carpenter.
méprendre [mepʀɑ̃dʀ(ə)]: **se** ~ vi: **se** ~
sur to be mistaken (about).
mépris [mepʀi] nm (dédain) contempt,
scorn; (indifférence): **le** ~ **de** contempt ou
disregard for; **au** ~ **de** regardless of, in
defiance of.
méprisable [mepʀizabl(ə)] a
contemptible, despicable.
méprisant, e [mepʀizɑ̃, -ɑ̃t] a
contemptuous, scornful.
méprise [mepʀiz] nf mistake, error;
misunderstanding.
mépriser [mepʀize] vt to scorn, despise;
(gloire, danger) to scorn, spurn.
mer [mɛʀ] nf sea; (marée) tide; **en** ~ at
sea; **prendre la** ~ to put out to sea; **en
haute** ~ off shore, on the open sea; **la**
~ **du Nord/Rouge** the North/Red Sea.
mercantile [mɛʀkɑ̃til] a (péj) mercenary.
mercenaire [mɛʀsənɛʀ] nm mercenary,
hired soldier.
mercerie [mɛʀsəʀi] nf haberdashery;
haberdasher's shop.
merci [mɛʀsi] excl thank you // nf: **à la**
~ **de qn/qch** at sb's mercy/the mercy of
sth; ~ **beaucoup** thank you very much;
~ **de** thank you for; **sans** ~ merciless.
mercier, ière [mɛʀsje, -jɛʀ] nm/f
haberdasher.
mercredi [mɛʀkʀədi] nm Wednesday; ~
des Cendres Ash Wednesday.
mercure [mɛʀkyʀ] nm mercury.

merde [mɛʀd(ə)] (*fam!*) *nf* shit (!) // *excl* bloody hell (!).

mère [mɛʀ] *nf* mother; ~ **célibataire** unmarried mother.

méridien [meʀidjɛ̃] *nm* meridian.

méridional, e, aux [meʀidjɔnal, -o] *a* southern ~ *nm/f* Southerner.

meringue [məʀɛ̃g] *nf* meringue.

merisier [məʀizje] *nm* wild cherry (tree).

méritant, e [meʀitɑ̃, -ɑ̃t] *a* deserving.

mérite [meʀit] *nm* merit; le ~ **(de ceci) lui revient** the credit (for this) is his.

mériter [meʀite] *vt* to deserve.

méritoire [meʀitwaʀ] *a* praiseworthy, commendable.

merlan [mɛʀlɑ̃] *nm* whiting.

merle [mɛʀl(ə)] *nm* blackbird.

merveille [mɛʀvɛj] *nf* marvel, wonder; **faire** ~ to work wonders; **à** ~ perfectly, wonderfully.

merveilleux, euse [mɛʀvɛjø, -øz] *a* marvellous, wonderful.

mes [me] *dét voir* **mon**.

mésalliance [mezaljɑ̃s] *nf* misalliance, mismatch.

mésange [mezɑ̃ʒ] *nf* tit(mouse) (*pl* mice); ~ **bleue** blue tit.

mésaventure [mezavɑ̃tyʀ] *nf* misadventure, misfortune.

Mesdames [medam] *nfpl voir* **Madame**.

Mesdemoiselles [medmwazɛl] *nfpl voir* **Mademoiselle**.

mésentente [mezɑ̃tɑ̃t] *nf* dissension, disagreement.

mésestimer [mezɛstime] *vt* to underestimate, underrate; to have low regard for.

mesquin, e [mɛskɛ̃, -in] *a* mean, petty; **mesquinerie** *nf* pettiness *q*, meanness *q*.

mess [mɛs] *nm* mess.

message [mesaʒ] *nm* message; ~ **téléphoné** telegram dictated by telephone; **messager, ère** *nm/f* messenger; **messageries** *nfpl* parcels service *sg*; distribution service *sg*.

messe [mɛs] *nf* mass; **aller à la** ~ to go to mass; ~ **de minuit** midnight mass.

messie [mesi] *nm*: **le M**~ the Messiah.

Messieurs [mesjø] *nmpl* (*abr* **Messrs**) *voir* **Monsieur**.

mesure [məzyʀ] *nf* (*évaluation, dimension*) measurement; (*étalon, récipient, contenu*) measure; (*MUS: cadence*) time, tempo; (: *division*) bar; (*retenue*) moderation; (*disposition*) measure, step; **sur** ~ (*costume*) made-to-measure; **à la** ~ **de** (*fig*) worthy of; on the same scale as; **dans la** ~ **où** insofar as, inasmuch as; **à** ~ **que** as; **en** ~ (*MUS*) in time *ou* tempo; **être en** ~ **de** to be in a position to; **dépasser la** ~ (*fig*) to overstep the mark.

mesurer [məzyʀe] *vt* to measure; (*juger*) to weigh up, assess; (*limiter*) to limit, ration; (*modérer*) to moderate; (*proportionner*): ~ **qch à** to match sth to, gear sth to; **se** ~ **avec** to have a confrontation with; to tackle; **il mesure 1 m 80** he's 1 m 80 tall.

met *vb voir* **mettre**.

métairie [meteʀi] *nf* smallholding.

métal, aux [metal, -o] *nm* metal; ~**lique** *a* metallic; ~**lisé, e** *a* (*peinture*) metallic; ~**lurgie** *nf* metallurgy; ~**lurgiste** *nm/f* steel *ou* metal worker; metallurgist.

métamorphose [metamɔʀfoz] *nf* metamorphosis (*pl* oses).

métaphore [metafɔʀ] *nf* metaphor.

métaphysique [metafizik] *nf* metaphysics *sg* // *a* metaphysical.

métayer, ère [meteje, metejɛʀ] *nm/f* (tenant) farmer.

météo [meteo] *nf* weather report; ≈ Met Office.

météore [meteɔʀ] *nm* meteor.

météorologie [meteɔʀɔlɔʒi] *nf* meteorology; **météorologique** *a* meteorological, weather *cpd*.

métèque [metɛk] *nm* (*péj*) wop.

méthode [metɔd] *nf* method; (*livre, ouvrage*) manual, tutor; **méthodique** *a* methodical.

méticuleux, euse [metikylø, -øz] *a* meticulous.

métier [metje] *nm* (*profession: gén*) job; (: *manuel*) trade; (: *artisanal*) craft; (*technique, expérience*) (acquired) skill *ou* technique; (*aussi*: ~ **à tisser**) (weaving) loom; **être du** ~ to be in the trade *ou* profession.

métis, se [metis] *a, nm/f* half-caste, half-breed.

métisser [metise] *vt* to cross.

métrage [metʀaʒ] *nm* (*de tissu*) length, ≈ yardage; (*CINÉMA*) footage, length; **long/moyen/court** ~ full-length/medium-length/short film.

mètre [mɛtʀ(ə)] *nm* metre; (*règle*) (metre) rule; (*ruban*) tape measure; **métrique** *a* metric // *nf* metrics *sg*.

métro [metʀo] *nm* underground, subway.

métropole [metʀɔpɔl] *nf* (*capitale*) metropolis; (*pays*) home country; **métropolitain, e** *a* metropolitan.

mets [mɛ] *nm* dish.

metteur [metœʀ] *nm*: ~ **en scène** (*THÉÂTRE*) producer; (*CINÉMA*) director; ~ **en ondes** producer.

mettre [mɛtʀ(ə)] *vt* (*placer*) to put; (*vêtement: revêtir*) to put on; (: *porter*) to wear; (*installer: gaz, l'électricité*) to put in; (*faire fonctionner: chauffage, électricité*) to put on; (*noter, écrire*) to say, put down; **mettons que** let's suppose *ou* say that; ~ **en bouteille/en sac** to bottle/put in bags *ou* sacks; **y** ~ **du sien** to pull one's weight; ~ **du temps/2 heures à faire** to take time/2 hours doing; **se** ~: **n'avoir rien à se** ~ to have nothing to wear; **se** ~ **de l'encre sur les doigts** to get ink on one's fingers; **se** ~ **au lit** to get into bed; **se** ~ **au piano** (*s'asseoir*) to sit down at the piano; (*apprendre*) to start learning the piano; **se** ~ **à faire** to begin *ou* start doing *ou* to do; **se** ~ **au travail/à l'étude** to get down to work/one's studies.

meublant, e [mœblɑ̃, -ɑ̃t] *a* (*tissus etc*) effective (in the room), decorative.

meuble [mœbl(ə)] *nm* piece of furniture; furniture *q* // *a* (*terre*) loose, friable *q*; (*JUR*): **biens** ~**s** movables; **meublé** *nm* furnished room (*ou* flatlet); **meubler** *vt* to furnish;

(fig): **meubler qch (de)** to fill sth (with); **se meubler** to furnish one's house.

meugler [møgle] *vi* to low, moo.

meule [møl] *nf (à broyer)* millstone; *(à aiguiser)* grindstone; *(à polir)* buffwheel; *(de foin, blé)* stack; *(de fromage)* round.

meunerie [mønʀi] *nf* flour trade; milling; **meunier, ière** *nm* miller // *nf* miller's wife // *af inv (CULIN)* meunière.

meure *etc vb voir* **mourir.**

meurtre [mœʀtʀ(ə)] *nm* murder; **meurtrier, ière** *a (arme etc)* deadly; *(fureur, instincts)* murderous // *nm/f* murderer/eress // *nf (ouverture)* loophole.

meurtrir [mœʀtʀiʀ] *vt* to bruise; *(fig)* to wound; **meurtrissure** *nf* bruise; *(fig)* scar.

meus *etc vb voir* **mouvoir.**

meute [møt] *nf* pack.

mexicain, e [mɛksikɛ̃, -ɛn] *a, nm/f* Mexican.

Mexico [mɛksiko] *n* Mexico City.

Mexique [mɛksik] *nm:* **le ~** Mexico.

MF *sigle f voir* **modulation.**

Mgr *abr de* **Monseigneur.**

mi [mi] *nm (MUS)* E; *(en chantant la gamme)* mi.

mi... [mi] *préfixe* half(-); mid-; **à la ~-janvier** in mid-January; **~-bureau, ~-chambre** half office, half bedroom; **à ~-jambes/-corps** (up *ou* down) to the knees/waist; **à ~-hauteur/-pente** halfway up *ou* down/up *ou* down the hill.

miauler [mjole] *vi* to mew.

mica [mika] *nm* mica.

mi-carême [mikaʀɛm] *nf:* **la ~** the third Thursday in Lent.

miche [miʃ] *nf* round *ou* cob loaf.

mi-chemin [miʃmɛ̃]: **à ~** *ad* halfway, midway.

mi-clos, e [miklo, -kloz] *a* half-closed.

micmac [mikmak] *nm (péj)* carry-on.

micro [mikʀo] *nm* mike, microphone.

microbe [mikʀɔb] *nm* germ, microbe.

microfiche [mikʀɔfiʃ] *nf* microfiche.

microfilm [mikʀɔfilm] *nm* microfilm.

microphone [mikʀɔfɔn] *nm* microphone.

microscope [mikʀɔskɔp] *nm* microscope; **au ~** under *ou* through the microscope.

midi [midi] *nm* midday, noon; *(moment du déjeuner)* lunchtime; **à ~** at 12 (o'clock) *ou* midday *ou* noon; *(sud)* south; **en plein ~** (right) in the middle of the day; facing south.

mie [mi] *nf* crumb (of the loaf).

miel [mjɛl] *nm* honey.

mielleux, euse [mjɛlø, -øz] *a (péj)* sugary, honeyed.

mien, ne [mjɛ̃, mjɛn] *pronom:* **le(la) ~(ne), les ~s** mine; **les ~s** my family.

miette [mjɛt] *nf (de pain, gâteau)* crumb; *(fig: de la conversation etc)* scrap; **en ~s** *(fig)* in pieces *ou* bits.

mieux [mjø] *ad* better // *a* better; *(plus joli)* better-looking // *nm (progrès)* improvement; **le ~** the best (thing); **le(la) ~, les ~** the best; **le ~ des deux** the better of the two; **les livres les ~ faits** the best made books; **de mon/ton ~** as best I/you can *(ou* could); **de ~ en ~** better and better; **pour le ~** for the best;

au ~ at best; **au ~ avec** on the best of terms with.

mièvre [mjɛvʀ(ə)] *a* mawkish, sickly sentimental.

mignon, ne [miɲɔ̃, -ɔn] *a* sweet, cute.

migraine [migʀɛn] *nf* headache; migraine.

migrateur, trice [migʀatœʀ, -tʀis] *a* migratory.

migration [migʀasjɔ̃] *nf* migration.

mijaurée [miʒɔʀe] *nf* pretentious girl.

mijoter [miʒɔte] *vt* to simmer; *(préparer avec soin)* to cook lovingly; *(affaire, projet)* to plot, cook up // *vi* to simmer.

mil [mil] *num* = **mille.**

mildiou [mildju] *nm* mildew.

milice [milis] *nf* militia; **milicien, ne** *nm/f* militia man/woman.

milieu, x [miljø] *nm (centre)* middle; *(fig)* middle course *ou* way; happy medium; *(BIO, GÉO)* environment; *(entourage social)* milieu; background; circle; *(pègre):* **le ~** the underworld; **au ~ de** in the middle of.

militaire [militɛʀ] *a* military, army *cpd* // *nm* serviceman.

militant, e [militɑ̃, -ɑ̃t] *a, nm/f* militant.

militer [milite] *vi* to be a militant; **~ pour/contre** *(suj: faits, raisons etc)* to militate in favour of/against.

mille [mil] *num a ou* one thousand // *nm (mesure):* **~** **(marin)** nautical mile; **mettre dans le ~** to hit the bull's-eye; to be bang on target; **~feuille** *nm* cream *ou* vanilla slice; **millénaire** *nm* millennium // *a* a thousand-year-old; *(fig)* ancient; **~-pattes** *nm inv* centipede.

millésime [milezim] *nm* year; **millésimé, e** *a* vintage *cpd*.

millet [mijɛ] *nm* millet.

milliard [miljaʀ] *nm* milliard, thousand million; **milliardaire** *nm/f* multi-millionaire.

millier [milje] *nm* thousand; **un ~ (de)** a thousand or so, about a thousand; **par ~s** in (their) thousands, by the thousand.

milligramme [miligʀam] *nm* milligramme.

millimètre [milimɛtʀ(ə)] *nm* millimetre; **millimétré, e** *a:* **papier millimétré** graph paper.

million [miljɔ̃] *nm* million; **deux ~s de** two million; **toucher cinq ~s** to get five million; **riche à ~s** worth millions; **millionnaire** *nm/f* millionaire.

mime [mim] *nm/f (acteur)* mime(r) // *nm (art)* mime, miming.

mimer [mime] *vt* to mime; *(singer)* to mimic, take off.

mimétisme [mimetism(ə)] *nm (BIO)* mimicry.

mimique [mimik] *nf (funny)* face; *(signes)* gesticulations *pl*, sign language *q*.

mimosa [mimoza] *nm* mimosa.

minable [minabl(ə)] *a* shabby (-looking); pathetic.

minauder [minode] *vi* to mince, simper.

mince [mɛ̃s] *a* thin; *(personne, taille)* slim, slender; *(fig: profit, connaissances)* slight, small // *excl* drat it!; **minceur** *nf* thinness; slimness, slenderness.

mine [min] *nf* (*physionomie*) expression, look; (*extérieur*) exterior, appearance; (*de crayon*) lead; (*gisement, exploitation, explosif*) mine; ~s *nfpl* (*péj*) simpering airs; **avoir bonne** ~ (*personne*) to look well; (*ironique*) to look an utter idiot; **avoir mauvaise** ~ to look unwell *ou* poorly; **faire** ~ **de faire** to make a pretence of doing; to make as if to do; ~ **de rien** *ad* with a casual air; although you wouldn't think so; ~ **de charbon** coalmine; ~ **à ciel ouvert** opencast mine.

miner [mine] *vt* (*saper*) to undermine, erode; (*MIL*) to mine.

minerai [minʀɛ] *nm* ore.

minéral, e, aux [mineʀal, -o] *a* mineral; (*CHIMIE*) inorganic // *nm* mineral.

minéralogie [mineʀalɔʒi] *nf* mineralogy.

minéralogique [mineʀalɔʒik] *a* mineralogical; **plaque** ~ number plate; **numéro** ~ registration number.

minet, te [minɛ, -ɛt] *nm/f* (*chat*) pussycat; (*péj*) young trendy/dollybird.

mineur, e [minœʀ] *a* minor // *nm/f* (*JUR*) minor, person under age // *nm* (*travailleur*) miner; ~ **de fond** face worker.

miniature [minjatyʀ] *a, nf* miniature; **miniaturiser** *vt* to miniaturize.

minibus [minibys] *nm* minibus.

mini-cassette [minikasɛt] *nf* cassette (recorder).

minier, ière [minje, -jɛʀ] *a* mining.

mini-jupe [miniʒyp] *nf* mini-skirt.

minimal, e, aux [minimal, -o] *a* minimum.

minime [minim] *a* minor, minimal // *nm/f* (*SPORT*) junior.

minimiser [minimize] *vt* to minimize; (*fig*) to play down.

minimum [minimɔm] *a, nm* minimum; **au** ~ (*AL moins*) at the very least; ~ **vital** living wage; subsistence level.

ministère [ministɛʀ] *nm* (*aussi REL*) ministry; (*cabinet*) government; ~ **public** (*JUR*) Prosecution, State Prosecutor; **ministériel, le** *a* cabinet *cpd*; ministerial.

ministre [ministʀ(ə)] *nm* (*aussi REL*) minister; ~ **d'État** senior minister (*of the Interior or of Justice*).

minium [minjɔm] *nm* red lead paint.

minois [minwa] *nm* little face.

minoritaire [minɔʀitɛʀ] *a* minority *cpd*.

minorité [minɔʀite] *nf* minority; **être en** ~ to be in the *ou* a minority; **mettre en** ~ (*POL*) to defeat.

minoterie [minɔtʀi] *nf* flour-mill.

minuit [minɥi] *nm* midnight.

minuscule [minyskyl] *a* minute, tiny // *nf*: (**lettre**) ~ small letter.

minute [minyt] *nf* minute; (*JUR*: *original*) minute, draft; **à la** ~ (just) this instant; there and then; ~ **steak** ~ minute steak; **minuter** *vt* to time; **minuterie** *nf* time switch.

minutieux, euse [minysjø, -øz] *a* meticulous; minutely detailed; requiring painstaking attention to detail.

mioche [mjɔʃ] *nm* (*fam*) nipper, brat.

mirabelle [miʀabɛl] *nf* (cherry) plum; (*eau-de-vie*) plum brandy.

miracle [miʀakl(ə)] *nm* miracle; **miraculé, e** *a* who has been miraculously cured (*ou* rescued); **miraculeux, euse** *a* miraculous.

mirador [miʀadɔʀ] *nm* (*MIL*) watchtower.

mirage [miʀaʒ] *nm* mirage.

mire [miʀ] *nf*: **point de** ~ target; (*fig*) focal point; **ligne de** ~ line of sight.

mirer [miʀe] *vt* (*œufs*) to candle; **se** ~ *vi*: **se** ~ **dans** to gaze at one's reflection in; to be mirrored in.

mirifique [miʀifik] *a* wonderful.

mirobolant, e [miʀɔbɔlɑ̃, -ɑ̃t] *a* fantastic.

miroir [miʀwaʀ] *nm* mirror.

miroiter [miʀwate] *vi* to sparkle, shimmer; **faire** ~ **qch à qn** to paint sth in glowing colours for sb, dangle sth in front of sb's eyes.

miroiterie [miʀwatʀi] *nf* mirror factory; mirror dealer's (shop).

mis, e [mi, miz] *pp de* **mettre** // *a*: **bien** ~ well dressed // *nf* (*argent: au jeu*) stake; (*tenue*) clothing; attire; **être de** ~e to be acceptable *ou* in season; ~**e de fonds** capital outlay; ~**e à mort** kill; ~**e en plis** set; ~**e au point** (*fig*) clarification (*voir aussi* **point**); ~**e en scène** production.

misaine [mizɛn] *nf*: **mât de** ~ foremast.

misanthrope [mizɑ̃tʀɔp] *nm/f* misanthropist.

mise [miz] *a, nf voir* **mis**.

miser [mize] *vt* (*enjeu*) to stake, bet; ~ **sur** *vt* (*cheval, numéro*) to bet on; (*fig*) to bank *ou* count on.

misérable [mizeʀabl(ə)] *a* (*lamentable, malheureux*) pitiful, wretched; (*pauvre*) poverty-stricken; (*insignifiant, mesquin*) miserable // *nm/f* wretch; (*miséreux*) poor wretch.

misère [mizɛʀ] *nf* (extreme) poverty, destitution; ~**s** *nfpl* woes, miseries; little troubles; **être dans la** ~ to be destitute *ou* poverty-stricken; **salaire de** ~ starvation wage; **miséreux, euse** *nm/f* down-and-out.

miséricorde [mizeʀikɔʀd(ə)] *nf* mercy, forgiveness; **miséricordieux, euse** *a* merciful, forgiving.

misogyne [mizɔʒin] *a* misogynous // *nm/f* misogynist.

missel [misɛl] *nm* missal.

missile [misil] *nm* missile.

mission [misjɔ̃] *nf* mission; **partir en** ~ (*ADMIN, POL*) to go on an assignment; **missionnaire** *nm/f* missionary.

missive [misiv] *nf* missive.

mit *vb voir* **mettre**.

mitaine [mitɛn] *nf* mitt(en).

mite [mit] *nf* clothes moth; **mité, e** *a* moth-eaten.

mi-temps [mitɑ̃] *nf inv* (*SPORT*: *période*) half (*pl* halves); (: *pause*) half-time; **à** ~ *a, ad* part-time.

miteux, euse [mitø, -øz] *a* seedy, shabby.

mitigé, e [mitiʒe] *a* lukewarm; mixed.

mitonner [mitɔne] *vt* to cook with loving care; (*fig*) to cook up quietly.

mitoyen, ne [mitwajɛ̃, -ɛn] *a* common, party *cpd*; **maisons** ~**nes** semi-detached houses; (*plus de deux*) terraced houses.

mitraille [mitʀɑj] *nf* grapeshot ; shellfire.
mitrailler [mitʀɑje] *vt* to machine-gun ;
(*fig: photographier*) to take shot after shot
of ; ~ **qn de** to pelt sb with, bombard sb
with ; **mitraillette** *nf* submachine gun ;
mitrailleur *nm* machine gunner ;
mitrailleuse *nf* machine gun.
mitre [mitʀ(ə)] *nf* mitre.
mitron [mitʀɔ̃] *nm* baker's boy.
mi-voix [mivwa]: **à** ~ *ad* in a low *ou*
hushed voice.
mixage [miksaʒ] *nm* (CINÉMA) (sound)
mixing.
mixer [miksœʀ] *nm* (food) mixer.
mixité [miksite] *nf* (SCOL) coeducation.
mixte [mikst(ə)] *a* (*gén*) mixed ; (SCOL)
mixed, coeducational ; **à usage** ~ dual-
purpose ; **cuisinière** ~ gas and electric
cooker ; **équipe** ~ combined team.
mixture [mikstyʀ] *nf* mixture ; (*fig*)
concoction.
M.L.F. *sigle m* = *mouvement de libération
de la femme*, ≈ Women's Lib.
Mlle, *pl* **Mlles** *abr de* **Mademoiselle**.
MM *abr de* **Messieurs**.
Mme, *pl* **Mmes** *abr de* **Madame**.
mnémotechnique [mnemɔtɛknik] *a*
mnemonic.
Mo *abr de* **métro**.
mobile [mɔbil] *a* mobile ; (*pièce de
machine*) moving ; (*élément de meuble etc*)
movable // *nm* (*motif*) motive ; (*œuvre
d'art*) mobile ; (PHYSIQUE) moving object *ou*
body.
mobilier, ière [mɔbilje, -jɛʀ] *a* (JUR)
personal // *nm* furniture ; **valeurs
mobilières** transferable securities ; **vente
mobilière** sale of personal property *ou*
chattels.
mobilisation [mɔbilizasjɔ̃] *nf*
mobilization.
mobiliser [mɔbilize] *vt* (MIL, *gén*) to
mobilize.
mobilité [mɔbilite] *nf* mobility.
mocassin [mɔkasɛ̃] *nm* moccasin.
moche [mɔʃ] *a* (*fam*) ugly ; rotten.
modalité [mɔdalite] *nf* form, mode ; ~**s**
nfpl (*d'un accord etc*) clauses, terms.
mode [mɔd] *nf* fashion ; (*commerce*)
fashion trade *ou* industry // *nm* (*manière*)
form, mode ; (LING) mood ; (MUS) mode ; **à
la** ~ fashionable, in fashion ; ~ **d'emploi**
directions *pl* (for use) ; ~ **de vie** way of
life.
modèle [mɔdɛl] *a*, *nm* model ; (*qui pose:
de peintre*) sitter ; ~ **déposé** registered
design ; ~ **réduit** small-scale model ; ~
de série production model.
modelé [mɔdle] *nm* relief ; contours *pl*.
modeler [mɔdle] *vt* (ART) to model, mould ;
(*suj: vêtement, érosion*) to mould, shape ;
~ **qch sur/d'après** to model sth on.
modérateur, trice [mɔdeʀatœʀ, -tʀis] *a*
moderating // *nm/f* moderator.
modération [mɔdeʀasjɔ̃] *nf* moderation.
modéré, e [mɔdeʀe] *a*, *nm/f* moderate.
modérer [mɔdeʀe] *vt* to moderate ; **se** ~
vi to restrain o.s.
moderne [mɔdɛʀn(ə)] *a* modern // *nm*
modern style ; modern furniture ;
moderniser *vt* to modernize.

modeste [mɔdɛst(ə)] *a* modest ; **modestie**
nf modesty.
modicité [mɔdisite] *nf*: **la** ~ **des prix** *etc*
the low prices *etc*.
modification [mɔdifikasjɔ̃] *nf*
modification.
modifier [mɔdifje] *vt* to modify, alter ;
(LING) to modify ; **se** ~ *vi* to alter.
modique [mɔdik] *a* modest.
modiste [mɔdist(ə)] *nf* milliner.
modulation [mɔdylasjɔ̃] *nf* modulation ;
~ **de fréquence (FM** *ou* **MF)** frequency
modulation.
module [mɔdyl] *nm* module.
moduler [mɔdyle] *vt* to modulate ; (*air*) to
warble.
moelle [mwal] *nf* marrow ; (*fig*) pith, core ;
~ **épinière** spinal chord.
moelleux, euse [mwalø, -øz] *a* soft ; (*au
goût, à l'ouïe*) mellow.
moellon [mwalɔ̃] *nm* rubble stone.
mœurs [mœʀ] *nfpl* (*conduite*) morals ;
(*manières*) manners ; (*pratiques sociales,
mode de vie*) habits ; **passer dans les** ~
to become the custom ; **contraire aux
bonnes** ~ contrary to proprieties.
mohair [mɔɛʀ] *nm* mohair.
moi [mwa] *pronom* me ; (*emphatique*): ~,
je for my part, I, I myself.
moignon [mwaɲɔ̃] *nm* stump.
moi-même [mwamɛm] *pronom* myself ;
(*emphatique*) I myself.
moindre [mwɛ̃dʀ(ə)] *a* lesser ; lower ;
le(la) ~, **les** ~**s** the least, the slightest.
moine [mwan] *nm* monk, friar.
moineau, x [mwano] *nm* sparrow.
moins [mwɛ̃] *ad* less // *cj*: ~ **2** minus 2 ;
~ **je travaille, mieux je me porte** the less
I work the better I feel ; ~ **grand que** not
as tall as, less tall than ; **le(la)** ~ **doué(e)**
the least gifted ; **le** ~ the least ; ~ **de**
(*sable, eau*) less ; (*livres, gens*) fewer ; ~
de 2 ans/100 F less than 2 years/100 F ;
~ **de midi** not yet midday ; **100 F/3 jours
de** ~ 100 F/3 days less ; **3 livres en** ~
3 books fewer ; **3 books too few** ; ~ **de
l'argent en** ~ less money ; **le soleil en**
~ but for the sun, minus the sun ; **à** ~
que *cj* unless ; **à** ~ **de faire** unless we do
(*ou* he does) ; **à** ~ **de** (*imprévu, accident*)
barring any ; **au** ~ at least ; **de** ~ **en** ~
less and less ; **pour le** ~ at the very least ;
du ~ at least ; **il est** ~ **cinq** it's five to ;
il fait ~ **cinq** it's five below (freezing) *ou*
minus five.
moiré, e [mwaʀe] *a* (*tissu, papier*) moiré,
watered ; (*reflets*) shimmering.
mois [mwa] *nm* month ; ~ **double** (COMM)
extra month's salary.
moïse [mɔiz] *nm* Moses basket.
moisi, e [mwazi] *a* mouldy, mildewed //
nm mould, mildew ; **odeur de** ~ musty
smell.
moisir [mwaziʀ] *vi* to go mouldy ; (*fig*) to
rot ; to hang about.
moisissure [mwazisyʀ] *nf* mould *q.*
moisson [mwasɔ̃] *nf* harvest ; (*fig*): **faire
une** ~ **de** to gather a wealth of ;
moissonner *vt* to harvest, reap ; (*fig*) to
collect ; **moissonneur, euse** *nm/f*
harvester, reaper // *nf* (*machine*)

harvester; **moissonneuse-batteuse** *nf* combine harvester.

moite [mwat] *a* sweaty, sticky.

moitié [mwatje] *nf* half (*pl* halves); (*épouse*): **sa ~** his loving wife, his better half; **la ~** half; **la ~ de** half (of), half the amount (*ou* number) of; **la ~ du temps/des gens** half the time/the people; **à la ~ de** halfway through; **~ moins grand** half as tall; **~ plus long** half as long again, longer by half; **à ~** half (*avant le verbe*); half- (*avant l'adjectif*); **de ~** by half; **~ ~** half-and-half.

moka [mɔka] *nm* mocha coffee; mocha cake.

mol [mɔl] *a voir* **mou.**

molaire [mɔlɛʀ] *nf* molar.

molécule [mɔlekyl] *nf* molecule.

moleskine [mɔlɛskin] *nf* imitation leather.

molester [mɔlɛste] *vt* to manhandle, maul (about).

molette [mɔlɛt] *nf* toothed *ou* cutting wheel.

molle [mɔl] *af voir* **mou;** **~ment** *ad* softly; (*péj*) sluggishly; (*protester*) feebly; **mollesse** *nf* softness; flabbiness; limpness; sluggishness.

mollet [mɔlɛ] *nm* calf (*pl* calves) // *am*: **œuf ~** soft-boiled egg; **molletière** *af*: **bande molletière** puttee.

molletonné, e [mɔltɔne] *a* fleece-lined, flannelette-lined.

mollir [mɔliʀ] *vi* to give way; to relent; to go soft.

mollusque [mɔlysk(ə)] *nm* (ZOOL) mollusc.

molosse [mɔlɔs] *nm* big ferocious dog.

môme [mom] *nm/f* (*fam*: *enfant*) brat; (: *fille*) bird.

moment [mɔmɑ̃] *nm* moment; **ce n'est pas le ~** this is not the (right) time; **à un certain ~** at some point; **pour un bon ~** for a good while; **pour le ~** for the moment, for the time being; **au ~ de** at the time of; **au ~ où** as; at a time when; **à tout ~** at any time *ou* moment; constantly, continually; **en ce ~** at the moment; at present; **sur le ~** at the time; **par ~s** now and then, at times; **du ~ où** *ou* **que** seeing that, since; **momentané, e** *a* temporary, momentary.

momie [mɔmi] *nf* mummy.

mon [mɔ̃], **ma** [ma], *pl* **mes** [me] *dét* my.

monacal, e, aux [mɔnakal, -o] *a* monastic.

monarchie [mɔnaʀʃi] *nf* monarchy; **monarchiste** *a*, *nm/f* monarchist.

monarque [mɔnaʀk(ə)] *nm* monarch.

monastère [mɔnastɛʀ] *nm* monastery.

monastique [mɔnastik] *a* monastic.

monceau, x [mɔ̃so] *nm* heap.

mondain, e [mɔ̃dɛ̃, -ɛn] *a* society *cpd*; social; fashionable // *nm/f* society man/woman, socialite // *nf*: **la M~e, la police ~e ≈** the vice squad; **mondanités** *nfpl* society life *sg*; (*society*) small talk *sg*; (*society*) gossip column *sg*.

monde [mɔ̃d] *nm* world; (*haute société*): **le ~** (high) society; (*milieu*): **être du même ~** to move in the same circles; (*gens*): **il y a du ~** (*beaucoup de gens*) there are many people; (*quelques personnes*) there are some people; **y a-t-il du ~ dans le salon?** is there anybody in the lounge?; **beaucoup/peu de ~** many/few people; **le meilleur** *etc* **du ~** the best *etc* in the world *ou* on earth; **mettre au ~** to bring into the world; **pas le moins du ~** not in the least; **se faire un ~ de qch** to make a great deal of fuss about sth; **mondial, e, aux** *a* (*population*) world *cpd*; (*influence*) world-wide; **mondialement** *ad* throughout the world; **mondovision** *nf* world coverage by satellite.

monégasque [mɔnegask(ə)] *a* Monegasque, of *ou* from Monaco.

monétaire [mɔnetɛʀ] *a* monetary.

mongolien, ne [mɔ̃gɔljɛ̃, -jɛn] *a*, *nm/f* mongol.

mongolisme [mɔ̃gɔlism(ə)] *nm* mongolism.

moniteur, trice [mɔnitœʀ, -tʀis] *nm/f* (SPORT) instructor/instructress; (*de colonie de vacances*) supervisor // *nm*: **~ cardiaque** cardiac monitor; **~ d'auto-école** driving instructor.

monnaie [mɔnɛ] *nf* (*pièce*) coin; (ÉCON, *gén*: *moyen d'échange*) currency; (*petites pièces*): **avoir de la ~** to have (some) change; **faire de la ~** to get (some) change; **avoir/faire la ~ de 20 F** to have change of/get change for 20 F; **faire à qn la ~ de 20 F** to give sb change for 20 F, change 20 F for sb; **rendre à qn la ~ (sur 20 F)** to give sb the change (out of *ou* from 20 F); **c'est ~ courante** it's a common occurrence; **monnayer** *vt* to convert into cash; (*talent*) to capitalize on; **monnayeur** *nm voir* **faux.**

monocle [mɔnɔkl(ə)] *nm* monocle, eyeglass.

monocorde [mɔnɔkɔʀd(ə)] *a* monotonous.

monoculture [mɔnɔkyltyʀ] *nf* single-crop farming, monoculture.

monogramme [mɔnɔgʀam] *nm* monogram.

monolingue [mɔnɔlɛ̃g] *a* monolingual.

monologue [mɔnɔlɔg] *nm* monologue, soliloquy; **monologuer** *vi* to soliloquize.

monôme [mɔnom] *nm* (MATH) monomial; (*d'étudiants*) students' rag procession.

monoplace [mɔnɔplas] *a*, *nm*, *nf* single-seater, one-seater.

monopole [mɔnɔpɔl] *nm* monopoly; **monopoliser** *vt* to monopolize.

monorail [mɔnɔʀaj] *nm* monorail, monorail train.

monosyllabe [mɔnɔsilab] *nm* monosyllable, word of one syllable.

monotone [mɔnɔtɔn] *a* monotonous; **monotonie** *nf* monotony.

monseigneur [mɔ̃sɛɲœʀ] *nm* (*archevêque, évêque*) Your (*ou* His) Grace; (*cardinal*) Your (*ou* His) Eminence; **Mgr Thomas** Bishop Thomas; Cardinal Thomas.

Monsieur [məsjø], *pl* **Messieurs** [mesjø] *titre* Mr ['mɪstə*] // *nm* (*homme quelconque*): **un/le m~** a/the gentleman; *voir aussi* **Madame.**

monstre [mɔ̃stʀ(ə)] *nm* monster // *a*: **un travail ~** a fantastic amount of work; an enormous job; **monstrueux, euse** *a* monstrous; **monstruosité** *nf* monstrosity.

mont [mɔ̃] nm: par ∼s et par vaux up hill and down dale; le M∼ Blanc Mont Blanc; le ∼ de Vénus mons veneris.

montage [mɔ̃taʒ] nm putting up; mounting, setting; assembly; (PHOTO) photomontage; (CINÉMA) editing; ∼ sonore sound editing.

montagnard, e [mɔ̃taɲaʀ, -aʀd(ə)] a mountain cpd // nm/f mountain-dweller.

montagne [mɔ̃taɲ] nf (cime) mountain; (région): la ∼ the mountains pl; ∼s russes big dipper sg, switchback sg.

montant, e [mɔ̃tɑ̃, -ɑ̃t] a rising; (robe, corsage) high-necked // nm (somme, total), (sum) total, (total) amount; (de fenêtre) upright; (de lit) post.

mont-de-piété [mɔ̃dpjete] nm pawnshop.

monte-charge [mɔ̃tʃaʀʒ(ə)] nm inv goods lift, hoist.

montée [mɔ̃te] nf rising, rise; ascent, climb; (chemin) way up; (côte) hill; au milieu de la ∼ halfway up; le moteur chauffe dans les ∼s the engine overheats going uphill.

monte-plats [mɔ̃tpla] nm inv service lift.

monter [mɔ̃te] vt (escalier, côte) to go (ou come) up; (valise, paquet) to take (ou bring) up; (cheval) to mount; (femelle) to cover, serve; (étagère) to raise; (tente, échafaudage) to put up; (machine) to assemble; (bijou) to mount, set; (COUTURE) to set in; to sew on; (CINÉMA) to edit; (THÉÂTRE) to put on, stage; (société etc) to set up // vi to go (ou come) up; (avion etc) to climb, go up; (chemin, niveau, température) to go up, rise; (passager) to get on; (à cheval): ∼ bien/mal to ride well/badly; ∼ à pied/en voiture to walk/drive up, go up on foot/by car; ∼ dans le train/l'avion to get into the train/plane, board the train/plane; ∼ sur to climb up onto; ∼ à cheval to get on ou mount a horse; se ∼ (s'équiper) to equip o.s., get kitted up; se ∼ à (frais etc) to add up to, come to; ∼ qn contre qn to set sb against sb; ∼ la tête à qn to give sb ideas; monteur, euse nm/f (TECH) fitter; (CINÉMA) (film) editor.

monticule [mɔ̃tikyl] nm mound.

montre [mɔ̃tʀ(ə)] nf watch; (ostentation): pour la ∼ for show; faire ∼ de to show, display; contre la ∼ (SPORT) against the clock; ∼-bracelet nf wrist watch.

montrer [mɔ̃tʀe] vt to show; ∼ qch à qn to show sb sth; montreur de marionnettes nm puppeteer.

monture [mɔ̃tyʀ] nf (bête) mount; (d'une bague) setting; (de lunettes) frame.

monument [mɔnymɑ̃] nm monument; ∼ aux morts war memorial; monumental, e, aux a monumental.

moquer [mɔke]: se ∼ de vt to make fun of, laugh at; (fam: se désintéresser de) not to care about; (tromper): se ∼ de qn to take sb for a ride.

moquerie [mɔkʀi] nf mockery q.

moquette [mɔkɛt] nf fitted carpet, wall-to-wall carpeting q.

moqueur, euse [mɔkœʀ, -øz] a mocking.

moral, e, aux [mɔʀal, -o] a moral // nm morale // nf (conduite) morals pl; (règles) moral code, ethic; (valeurs) moral standards pl, morality; (science) ethics sg, moral philosophy; (conclusion: d'une fable etc) moral; au ∼, sur le plan ∼ morally; faire la ∼e à to lecture, preach at; ∼isateur, trice a moralizing, sanctimonious; ∼iser vt (sermonner) to lecture, preach at; ∼iste nm/f moralist // a moralistic; ∼ité nf morality; (conduite) morals pl; (conclusion, enseignement) moral.

morbide [mɔʀbid] a morbid.

morceau, x [mɔʀso] nm piece, bit; (d'une œuvre) passage, extract; (MUS) piece; (CULIN: de viande) cut; mettre en ∼x to pull to pieces ou bits.

morceler [mɔʀsəle] vt to break up, divide up.

mordant, e [mɔʀdɑ̃, -ɑ̃t] a scathing, cutting; biting // nm spirit; bite, punch.

mordicus [mɔʀdikys] ad (affirmer etc) obstinately, stubbornly.

mordiller [mɔʀdije] vt to nibble at, chew at.

mordoré, e [mɔʀdɔʀe] a lustrous bronze.

mordre [mɔʀdʀ(ə)] vt to bite; (suj: lime, vis) to bite into // vi (poisson) to bite; ∼ dans (fruit) to bite into; ∼ sur (fig) to go over into, overlap into; ∼ à l'hameçon to bite, rise to the bait.

mordu, e [mɔʀdy] pp de mordre // a (amoureux) smitten // nm/f: un ∼ du jazz/de la voile a jazz/sailing fanatic ou buff.

morfondre [mɔʀfɔ̃dʀ(ə)]: se ∼ vi to fret.

morgue [mɔʀg(ə)] nf (arrogance) haughtiness; (lieu: de la police) morgue; (: à l'hôpital) mortuary.

moribond, e [mɔʀibɔ̃, -ɔ̃d] a dying, moribound.

morille [mɔʀij] nf morel.

morne [mɔʀn(ə)] a dismal, dreary.

morose [mɔʀoz] a sullen, morose.

morphine [mɔʀfin] nf morphine; morphinomane nm/f morphine addict.

morphologie [mɔʀfɔlɔʒi] nf morphology.

mors [mɔʀ] nm bit.

morse [mɔʀs(ə)] nm (ZOOL) walrus; (TÉL) Morse (code).

morsure [mɔʀsyʀ] nf bite.

mort [mɔʀ] nf death; se donner la ∼ to take one's life.

mort, e [mɔʀ, mɔʀt(ə)] pp de mourir // a dead // nm/f (défunt) dead man/woman; (victime): il y a eu plusieurs ∼s several people were killed, there were several killed // nm (CARTES) dummy; ∼ ou vif dead or alive; ∼ de peur/fatigue frightened to death/dead tired.

mortadelle [mɔʀtadɛl] nf mortadella (type of luncheon meat).

mortalité [mɔʀtalite] nf mortality, death rate.

mortel, le [mɔʀtɛl] a (poison etc) deadly, lethal; (accident, blessure) fatal; (REL) mortal; (fig) deathly; deadly boring // nm/f mortal.

morte-saison [mɔʀtəsɛzɔ̃] nf slack ou off season.

mortier [mɔʀtje] nm (gén) mortar.

mortifier [mɔrtifje] *vt* to mortify.

mort-né, e [mɔrne] *a* (*enfant*) stillborn ;
(*fig*) abortive.

mortuaire [mɔrtɥɛr] *a* funeral *cpd* ; **avis**
~s death announcements, intimations ;
chapelle ~ mortuary chapel ; **couronne**
~ (funeral) wreath ; **domicile ~** house of
the deceased ; **drap ~** pall.

morue [mɔry] *nf* (*ZOOL*) cod *inv* ; (*CULIN:*
salée) salt-cod ; **morutier** *nm* cod
fisherman ; cod fishing boat.

morveux, euse [mɔrvø, -øz] *a* (*fam*)
snotty-nosed.

mosaïque [mɔzaik] *nf* (*ART*) mosaic ; (*fig*)
patchwork.

Moscou [mɔsku] *n* Moscow ; **moscovite**
a of *ou* from Moscow // *nm/f* Moscovite.

mosquée [mɔske] *nf* mosque.

mot [mo] *nm* word ; (*message*) line, note ;
(*bon mot etc*) saying ; sally ; **~ à ~** *a, ad*
word for word ; **~ pour ~** word for word,
verbatim ; **prendre qn au ~** to take sb
at his word ; **avoir son ~ à dire** to have
a say ; **~s croisés** crossword (puzzle) *sg* ;
~ d'ordre watchword ; **~ de passe**
password.

motard [mɔtar] *nm* motorcycle cop.

motel [mɔtɛl] *nm* motel.

moteur, trice [mɔtœr, -tris] *a* (*ANAT,*
PHYSIOL) motor ; (*troubles*) motory ; (*TECH*)
driving ; (*AUTO*): **à 4 roues motrices**
4-wheel drive // *nm* engine, motor ; (*fig*)
mover, mainspring ; **à ~** power-driven,
motor *cpd* ; **~ à deux temps** two-stroke
engine ; **~ à explosion** internal
combustion engine.

motif [mɔtif] *nm* (*cause*) motive ;
(*décoratif*) design, pattern, motif ; (*d'un*
tableau) subject, motif ; (*MUS*) figure,
motif ; **~s** *nmpl* (*JUR*) grounds *pl* ; **sans ~**
a groundless.

motion [mɔsjɔ̃] *nf* motion ; **~ de censure**
motion of censure, vote of no confidence.

motivation [mɔtivasjɔ̃] *nf* motivation.

motivé, e [mɔtive] *a* (*acte*) justified ;
(*personne*) motivated.

motiver [mɔtive] *vt* (*justifier*) to justify,
account for ; (*ADMIN, JUR, PSYCH*) to motivate.

moto [mɔto] *nf* (*motor*)bike ; **~-cross** *nm*
motocross ; **~cyclette** *nf* motorbike,
motorcycle ; **~cyclisme** *nm* motorcycle
racing ; **~cycliste** *nm/f* motorcyclist.

motorisé, e [mɔtɔrize] *a* (*troupe*)
motorized ; (*personne*) having transport *ou*
a car.

motrice [mɔtris] *a* *voir* **moteur** ;
motricité *nf* motor functions.

motte [mɔt] *nf:* **~ de terre** lump of earth,
clod (of earth) ; **~ de gazon** turf, sod ; **~**
de beurre lump of butter.

motus [mɔtys] *excl:* **~ (et bouche**
cousue)! mum's the word!

mou(mol), molle [mu, mɔl] *a* soft ; (*péj*)
flabby ; limp ; sluggish ; feeble // *nm*
(*abats*) lights *pl*, lungs *pl* ; (*de la corde*):
avoir du ~ to be slack.

mouchard [muʃar] *nm* (*ESCRIME*) grass
// *nm* (*appareil*) control device.

mouche [muʃ] *nf* fly ; (*ESCRIME*) button ; (*de*
taffetas) patch ; **prendre la ~** to take the
huff ; **faire ~** to score a bull's-eye.

moucher [muʃe] *vt* (*enfant*) to blow the
nose of ; (*chandelle*) to snuff (out) ; **se ~**
vi to blow one's nose.

moucheron [muʃrɔ̃] *nm* midge.

moucheté, e [muʃte] *a* dappled ; flecked ;
(*ESCRIME*) buttoned.

mouchoir [muʃwar] *nm* handkerchief,
hanky ; **~ en papier** tissue, paper hanky.

moudre [mudr(ə)] *vt* to grind.

moue [mu] *nf* pout ; **faire la ~** to pout ;
(*fig*) to pull a face.

mouette [mwɛt] *nf* (sea)gull.

moufle [mufl(ə)] *nf* (*gant*) mitt(en) ; (*TECH*)
pulley block.

mouflon [muflɔ̃] *nm* mouf(f)lon.

mouillage [mujaʒ] *nm* (*NAVIG: lieu*)
anchorage, moorings *pl*.

mouillé, e [muje] *a* wet.

mouiller [muje] *vt* (*humecter*) to wet,
moisten ; (*tremper*): **~ qn/qch** to make
sb/sth wet ; (*couper, diluer*) to water
down ; (*mine etc*) to lay // *vi* (*NAVIG*) to
lie *ou* be at anchor ; **se ~** to get wet ; (*fam*)
to commit o.s. ; to get o.s. involved ; **~**
l'ancre to drop *ou* cast anchor ; **mouillure**
nf wet q ; wet patch.

moulage [mulaʒ] *nm* moulding ; casting ;
(*objet*) cast.

moule [mul] *nf* mussel // *nm* (*creux, CULIN*)
mould ; (*modèle plein*) cast ; **~ à gâteaux**
nm cake tin.

moulent *vb voir* **moudre**.

mouler [mule] *vt* (*brique*) to mould ;
(*statue*) to cast ; (*visage, bas-relief*) to make
a cast of ; (*lettre*) to shape with care ; (*suj:*
vêtement) to hug, fit closely round ; **~ qch**
sur (*fig*) to model sth on.

moulin [mulɛ̃] *nm* mill ; (*fam*) engine ; **~**
à café/à poivre coffee/pepper mill ; **~ à**
légumes (vegetable) shredder ; **~ à**
paroles (*fig*) chatterbox ; **~ à prières**
prayer wheel ; **~ à vent** windmill.

moulinet [mulinɛ] *nm* (*de treuil*) winch ;
(*de canne à pêche*) reel ; (*mouvement*): **faire**
des ~s avec qch to whirl sth around.

moulinette [mulinɛt] *nf* (vegetable)
shredder.

moulu, e [muly] *pp de* **moudre**.

moulure [mulyr] *nf* (*ornement*) moulding.

mourant, e [murɑ̃, -ɑ̃t] *a* dying // *nm/f*
dying man/woman.

mourir [murir] *vi* to die ; (*civilisation*) to
die out ; **~ de froid/faim** to die of
exposure/hunger ; **~ de faim/d'ennui**
(*fig*) to be starving/be bored to death ; **~**
d'envie de faire to be dying to do.

mousquetaire [muskətɛr] *nm* musketeer.

mousqueton [muskətɔ̃] *nm* (*fusil*)
carbine ; (*anneau*) snap-link, karabiner.

mousse [mus] *nf* (*BOT*) moss ; (*écume: sur*
eau, bière) froth, foam ; (: *shampooing*)
lather ; (*CULIN*) mousse // *nm* (*NAVIG*) ship's
boy ; **bain de ~** bubble bath ; **bas ~**
stretch stockings ; **balle ~** rubber ball ; **~**
carbonique (fire-fighting) foam ; **~ de**
nylon stretch nylon ; foam ; **~ à raser**
shaving foam.

mousseline [muslin] *nf* muslin ; chiffon ;
pommes ~ creamed potatoes.

mousser [muse] *vi* to foam ; to lather.

mousseux, euse [musǿ, -ǿz] *a* frothy // *nm*: (vin) ~ sparkling wine.
mousson [musɔ̃] *nf* monsoon.
moussu, e [musy] *a* mossy.
moustache [mustaʃ] *nf* moustache; ~s *nfpl* (du chat) whiskers *pl*; **moustachu, e** *a* wearing a moustache.
moustiquaire [mustikɛʀ] *nf* mosquito net (ou screen).
moustique [mustik] *nm* mosquito.
moutarde [mutaʀd(ə)] *nf* mustard.
mouton [mutɔ̃] *nm* (ZOOL, péj) sheep *inv*; (peau) sheepskin; (CULIN) mutton; ~s *nmpl* (fig) white horses; fluffy *ou* fleecy clouds; bits of fluff.
mouture [mutyʀ] *nf* grinding; (péj) rehash.
mouvant, e [muvɑ̃, -ɑ̃t] *a* unsettled; changing; shifting.
mouvement [muvmɑ̃] *nm* (gén, aussi: mécanisme) movement; (fig) activity; impulse; reaction; gesture; (MUS: rythme) tempo (pl s); **en** ~ in motion; on the move; **mettre qch en** ~ to set sth in motion, set sth going; ~ **d'humeur** fit *ou* burst of temper; ~ **d'opinion** trend of (public) opinion; **le** ~ **perpétuel** perpetual, motion; **mouvementé, e** *a* (vie, poursuite) eventful; (réunion) turbulent.
mouvoir [muvwaʀ] *vt* (levier, membre) to move; (machine) to drive; **se** ~ to move.
moyen, ne [mwajɛ̃, -ɛn] *a* average; (tailles, prix) medium; (de grandeur moyenne) medium-sized // *nm* (façon) means *sg*, way // *nf* average; (MATH) mean; (SCOL: à l'examen) pass mark; (AUTO) average speed; ~s *nmpl* (capacités) means; **au** ~ **de** by means of; **y a-t-il** ~ **de ...?** is it possible to ...?, can one ...?; **par quel** ~? how?, which way?, by which means?; **par tous les** ~s by every possible means, every possible way; **employer les grands** ~s to resort to drastic measures; **par ses propres** ~s all by oneself; **en** ~**ne** on (an) average; ~ **de locomotion/d'expression** means of transport/expression; ~ **âge** Middle Ages; ~ **ne d'âge** average age.
moyennant [mwajɛnɑ̃] *prép* (somme) for; (service, conditions) in return for; (travail, effort) with.
Moyen-Orient [mwajɛnɔʀjɑ̃] *nm*: **le** ~ the Middle East.
moyeu, x [mwajǿ] *nm* hub.
mû, mue [my] *pp de* **mouvoir**.
mucosité [mykozite] *nf* mucus *q*.
mucus [mykys] *nm* mucus *q*.
mue [my] *pp voir* **mouvoir** // *nf* moulting; sloughing; breaking of the voice.
muer [mɥe] *vi* (oiseau, mammifère) to moult; (serpent) to slough; (jeune garçon): **il mue** his voice is breaking; **se** ~ **en** to transform into.
muet, te [mɥɛ, -ɛt] *a* dumb; (fig): ~ **d'admiration** *etc* speechless with admiration *etc*; (joie, douleur, CINEMA) silent; (LING: lettre) silent, mute; (carte) blank // *nm/f* mute.
mufle [myfl(ə)] *nm* muzzle; (goujat) boor // *a* boorish.
mugir [myʒiʀ] *vi* to bellow; to low; (fig) to howl.

muguet [mygɛ] *nm* lily of the valley.
mulâtre, tresse [mylɑtʀ(ə), -tʀɛs] *nm/f* mulatto.
mule [myl] *nf* (ZOOL) (she-)mule; ~s *nfpl* (pantoufles) mules.
mulet [mylɛ] *nm* (ZOOL) (he-)mule; **muletier, ière** *a*: **chemin muletier** mule track.
mulot [mylo] *nm* field mouse (*pl* mice).
multicolore [myltikɔlɔʀ] *a* multicoloured.
multinational, e, aux [myltinasjɔnal, -o] *a* multinational.
multiple [myltipl(ə)] *a* multiple, numerous; (varié) many, manifold // *nm* (MATH) multiple.
multiplicateur [myltiplikatœʀ] *nm* multiplier.
multiplication [myltiplikasjɔ̃] *nf* multiplication.
multiplicité [myltiplisite] *nf* multiplicity.
multiplier [myltiplije] *vt* to multiply; **se** ~ *vi* to multiply; to increase in number.
multitude [myltityd] *nf* multitude; mass; **une** ~ **de** a vast number of, a multitude of.
municipal, e, aux [mynisipal, -o] *a* municipal; town *cpd*, ≈ borough *cpd*.
municipalité [mynisipalite] *nf* (corps municipal) town council, corporation; (commune) town, municipality.
munir [myniʀ] *vt*: ~ **qn/qch de** to equip sb/sth with.
munitions [mynisjɔ̃] *nfpl* ammunition *sg*.
muqueuse [mykǿz] *nf* mucous membrane.
mur [myʀ] *nm* wall; ~ **du son** sound barrier.
mûr, e [myʀ] *a* ripe; (personne) mature // *nf* blackberry; mulberry.
muraille [myʀɑj] *nf* (high) wall.
mural, e, aux [myʀal, -o] *a* wall *cpd*; mural.
mûrement [myʀmɑ̃] *ad*: **ayant** ~ **réfléchi** having given the matter much thought.
murène [myʀɛn] *nf* moray (eel).
murer [myʀe] *vt* (enclos) to wall (in); (porte, issue) to wall up; (personne) to wall up *ou* in.
muret [myʀɛ] *nm* low wall.
mûrier [myʀje] *nm* blackberry bush; mulberry tree.
mûrir [myʀiʀ] *vi* (fruit, blé) to ripen; (abcès, furoncle) to come to a head; (fig: idée, personne) to mature // *vt* to ripen; to (make) mature.
murmure [myʀmyʀ] *nm* murmur; ~s *nmpl* (plaintes) murmurings, mutterings; **murmurer** *vi* to murmur; (se plaindre) to mutter, grumble.
musaraigne [myzaʀɛɲ] *nf* shrew.
musarder [myzaʀde] *vi* to dawdle (along); to idle (about).
musc [mysk] *nm* musk.
muscade [myskad] *nf* nutmeg.
muscat [myska] *nm* muscat grape; muscatel (wine).
muscle [myskl(ə)] *nm* muscle; **musclé, e** *a* muscular; **musculation** *nf*: **exercices de musculation** muscle-developing exercises; **musculature** *nf* muscle structure, muscles *pl*.

museau, x [myzo] *nm* muzzle.
musée [myze] *nm* museum ; art gallery.
museler [myzle] *vt* to muzzle ; **muselière** *nf* muzzle.
musette [myzɛt] *nf* (*sac*) lunchbag // à *inv* (*orchestre etc*) accordion *cpd*.
muséum [myzeɔm] *nm* museum.
musical, e, aux [myzikal, -o] *a* musical.
music-hall [myzikol] *nm* variety theatre ; (*genre*) variety.
musicien, ne [myzisjɛ̃, -jɛn] *nm/f* musician.
musique [myzik] *nf* music ; (*fanfare*) band ; **faire de la ~** to make some music ; to play an instrument ; **~ de chambre** chamber music ; **~ de fond** background music.
musqué, e [myske] *a* musky.
musulman, e [myzylmɑ̃, -an] *a, nm/f* Moslem, Muslim.
mutation [mytasjɔ̃] *nf* (ADMIN) transfer ; (BIO) mutation.
muter [myte] *vt* (ADMIN) to transfer.
mutilation [mytilɑsjɔ̃] *nf* mutilation.
mutilé, e [mytile] *nm/f* disabled person (*through loss of limbs*).
mutiler [mytile] *vt* to mutilate, maim ; (*fig*) to mutilate, deface.
mutin, e [mytɛ̃, -in] *a* (*air, ton*) mischievous, impish // *nm/f* (MIL, NAVIG) mutineer.
mutiner [mytine]: **se ~** *vi* to mutiny ; **mutinerie** *nf* mutiny.
mutisme [mytism(ə)] *nm* silence.
mutuel, le [mytɥɛl] *a* mutual // *nf* mutual benefit society.
myocarde [mjɔkaRd(ə)] *nm* voir **infarctus**.
myope [mjɔp] *a* short-sighted ; **myopie** *nf* short-sightedness, myopia.
myosotis [mjozɔtis] *nm* forget-me-not.
myriade [miRjad] *nf* myriad.
myrtille [miRtij] *nf* bilberry, whortleberry.
mystère [mistɛR] *nm* mystery ; **mystérieux, euse** *a* mysterious.
mysticisme [mistisism(ə)] *nm* mysticism.
mystification [mistifikɑsjɔ̃] *nf* hoax ; mystification.
mystifier [mistifje] *vt* to fool ; to mystify.
mystique [mistik] *a* mystic, mystical // *nm/f* mystic.
mythe [mit] *nm* myth ; **mythique** *a* mythical.
mythologie [mitɔlɔʒi] *nf* mythology ; **mythologique** *a* mythological.
mythomane [mitɔman] *nm/f* mythomaniac.

N

n' [n] *ad* voir **ne**.
nacelle [nasɛl] *nf* (*de ballon*) basket.
nacre [nakR(ə)] *nf* mother of pearl ; **nacré, ~e** *a* pearly.
nage [naʒ] *nf* swimming ; style of swimming, stroke ; **tra-verser/s'éloigner à la ~** to swim across/away ; **en ~** bathed in perspiration.
nageoire [naʒwaR] *nf* fin.

nager [naʒe] *vi* to swim ; **nageur, euse** *nm/f* swimmer.
naguère [nagɛR] *ad* formerly.
naïf, ïve [naif, naiv] *a* naive.
nain, e [nɛ̃, nɛn] *nm/f* dwarf.
naissance [nɛsɑ̃s] *nf* birth ; **donner ~ à** to give birth to ; (*fig*) to give rise to ; **aveugle de ~** born blind ; **Français de ~** French by birth ; **à la ~ des cheveux** at the roots of the hair.
naissant, e [nɛsɑ̃, -ɑ̃t] *a* budding, incipient ; dawning.
naître [nɛtR(ə)] *vi* to be born ; (*conflit, complications*): **~ de** to arise from, be born out of ; **~ à** (*amour, poésie*) to awaken to ; **il est né en 1960** he was born in 1960 ; **il naît plus de filles que de garçons** there are more girls born than boys ; **faire ~** (*fig*) to give rise to, arouse.
naïveté [naivte] *nf* naïvety.
nantir [nɑ̃tiR] *vt*: **~ qn de** to provide sb with ; **les nantis** (*péj*) the well-to-do.
napalm [napalm] *nm* napalm.
nappe [nap] *nf* tablecloth ; (*fig*) sheet ; layer ; **~ron** *nm* table-mat.
naquit *etc vb voir* **naître**.
narcisse [naRsis] *nm* narcissus.
narcissisme [naRsisism(ə)] *nm* narcissism.
narcotique [naRkɔtik] *a, nm* narcotic.
narguer [naRge] *vt* to taunt.
narine [naRin] *nf* nostril.
narquois, e [naRkwa, -waz] *a* derisive, mocking.
narrateur, trice [naRatœR, -tRis] *nm/f* narrator.
narrer [naRe] *vt* to tell the story of, recount.
nasal, e, aux [nazal, -o] *a* nasal.
naseau, x [nazo] *nm* nostril.
nasiller [nazije] *vi* to speak with a (nasal) twang.
nasse [nas] *nf* fish-trap.
natal, e [natal] *a* native.
nataliste [natalist(ə)] *a* supporting a rising birth rate.
natalité [natalite] *nf* birth rate.
natation [natasjɔ̃] *nf* swimming.
natif, ive [natif, -iv] *a* native.
nation [nɑsjɔ̃] *nf* nation ; **les N~s Unies** the United Nations.
national, e, aux [nasjɔnal, -o] *a* national // *nf*: (*route*) **~e** trunk road, ≈ A road ; **obsèques ~es** state funeral ; **~iser** *vt* to nationalize ; **~isme** *nm* nationalism ; **~ité** *nf* nationality.
natte [nat] *nf* (*tapis*) mat ; (*cheveux*) plait.
naturaliser [natyRalize] *vt* to naturalize.
naturaliste [natyRalist(ə)] *nm/f* naturalist.
nature [natyR] *nf* nature // *a, ad* (CULIN) plain, without seasoning or sweetening ; (*café, thé*) black, without sugar ; **payer en ~** to pay in kind ; **peint d'après ~** painted from life ; **~ morte** still-life ; **naturel, le** *a* (*gén, aussi: enfant*) natural // *nm* naturalness ; disposition, nature ; (*autochtone*) native ; **naturellement** *ad* naturally ; (*bien sûr*) of course ; **naturisme** *nm* naturism ; **naturiste** *nm/f* naturist.
naufrage [nofRaʒ] *nm* (ship)wreck ; (*fig*) wreck ; **faire ~** to be shipwrecked ;

naufragé, e nm/f shipwreck victim, castaway.

nauséabond, e [nozeabɔ̃, -ɔ̃d] a foul, nauseous.

nausée [noze] nf nausea.

nautique [notik] a nautical, water cpd.

nautisme [notism] nm water sports.

naval, e [naval] a naval.

navet [navɛ] nm turnip ; (péj) third-rate film.

navette [navɛt] nf shuttle ; (en car etc) shuttle (service) ; **faire la ~ (entre)** to go to and fro ou shuttle (between).

navigable [navigabl(ə)] a navigable.

navigateur [navigatœr] nm (NAVIG) seafarer, sailor ; (AVIAT) navigator.

navigation [navigasjɔ̃] nf navigation, sailing ; shipping.

naviguer [navige] vi to navigate, sail.

navire [navir] nm ship.

navrer [navre] vt to upset, distress ; **je suis navré** I'm so sorry.

N.B. sigle (= nota bene) NB.

ne, n' [n(ə)] ad voir **pas, plus, jamais** etc ; (explétif) non traduit.

né, e [ne] pp (voir **naître**): **~ en 1960** born in 1960 ; **~e Scott** née Scott // a: **un comédien ~** a born comedian.

néanmoins [neɑ̃mwɛ̃] ad nevertheless, yet.

néant [neɑ̃] nm nothingness ; **réduire à ~** to bring to nought ; to deny.

nébuleux, euse [nebylø, -øz] a nebulous.

nébulosité [nebylozite] nf cloud cover ; **~ variable** cloudy ou some cloud in places.

nécessaire [nesesɛr] a necessary // nm necessary ; (sac) kit ; **~ de couture** sewing kit ; **~ de toilette** toilet bag ; **nécessité** nf necessity ; **nécessiter** vt to require ; **nécessiteux, euse** a needy.

nec plus ultra [nɛkplysyltra] nm: **le ~ de** the last word in.

nécrologique [nekrɔlɔʒik] a: **article ~** obituary ; **rubrique ~** obituary column.

nécromancien, ne [nekrɔmɑ̃sjɛ̃, -jɛn] nm/f necromancer.

nécrose [nekroz] nf necrosis.

néerlandais, e [neɛrlɑ̃dɛ, -ɛz] a Dutch.

nef [nɛf] nf (d'église) nave.

néfaste [nefast(ə)] a baneful ; ill-fated.

négatif, ive [negatif, iv] a negative // nm (PHOTO) negative.

négligé, e [negliʒe] a (en désordre) slovenly // nm (tenue) negligee.

négligence [negliʒɑ̃s] nf carelessness q ; careless omission.

négligent, e [negliʒɑ̃, -ɑ̃t] a careless.

négliger [negliʒe] vt (épouse, jardin) to neglect ; (tenue) to be careless about ; (avis, précautions) to disregard ; **~ de faire** to fail to do, not bother to do ; **se ~ to** neglect o.s.

négoce [negɔs] nm trade.

négociant [negɔsjɑ̃] nm merchant.

négociateur [negɔsjatœr] nm negotiator.

négociation [negɔsjasjɔ̃] nf negotiation.

négocier [negɔsje] vi, vt to negotiate.

nègre [nɛgr(ə)] nm Negro ; hack(writer) // a Negro.

négresse [negrɛs] nf Negro woman.

neige [nɛʒ] nf snow ; **~ carbonique** dry ice ; **neiger** vi to snow ; **neigeux, euse** a snowy, snow-covered.

nénuphar [nenyfar] nm water-lily.

néologisme [neɔlɔʒism(ə)] nm neologism.

néon [neɔ̃] nm neon.

néophyte [neɔfit] nm/f novice.

néo-zélandais, e [eɔzelɑ̃dɛ, -ɛz] a New Zealand cpd // nm/f New Zealander.

nerf [nɛr] nm nerve ; (fig) vim, stamina ; **nerveux, euse** a nervous ; (voiture) nippy, responsive ; (tendineux) sinewy ; **nervosité** nf excitability ; state of agitation ; nervousness.

nervure [nɛrvyr] nf vein ; (ARCHIT, TECH) rib.

n'est-ce pas [nɛspɑ] ad isn't it?, won't you? etc, selon le verbe qui précède ; **~ que c'est bon?** it's good, don't you think?

net, nette [nɛt] a (sans équivoque, distinct) clear ; (évident) definite ; (propre) neat, clean ; (COMM: prix, salaire) net // ad (refuser) flatly ; **s'arrêter ~** to stop dead ; **la lame a cassé ~** the blade snapped clean through ; **mettre au ~** to copy out, tidy up ; **~teté** nf clearness.

nettoyage [nɛtwajaʒ] nm cleaning ; **~ à sec** dry cleaning.

nettoyer [nɛtwaje] vi to clean ; (fig) to clean out.

neuf [nœf] num nine.

neuf, neuve [nœf, nœv] a new // nm: **repeindre à ~** to redecorate ; **remettre à ~** to do up (as good as new), refurbish.

neurasthénique [nørastenik] a neurasthenic.

neurologie [nørɔlɔʒi] nf neurology.

neutraliser [nøtralize] vt to neutralize.

neutralité [nøtralite] nf neutrality.

neutre [nøtr(ə)] a neutral ; (LING) neuter // nm (LING) neuter.

neutron [nøtrɔ̃] nm neutron.

neuve [nœv] a voir **neuf**.

neuvième [nœvjɛm] num ninth.

névé [neve] nm permanent snowpatch.

neveu, x [nəvø] nm nephew.

névralgie [nevralʒi] nf neuralgia.

névrite [nevrit] nf neuritis.

névrose [nevroz] nf neurosis ; **névrosé, e** a, nm/f neurotic.

nez [ne] nm nose ; **~ à ~ avec** face to face with.

ni [ni] cj: **~ l'un ~ l'autre ne sont** neither one nor the other are ; **il n'a rien dit ~ fait** he hasn't said or done anything.

niais, e [njɛ, -ɛz] a silly, thick.

niche [niʃ] nf (du chien) kennel ; (de mur) recess, niche.

nichée [niʃe] nf brood, nest.

nicher [niʃe] vi to nest ; **se ~ dans** to lodge o.s. in ; to hide in.

nickel [nikɛl] nm nickel.

nicotine [nikɔtin] nf nicotine.

nid [ni] nm nest ; **~ de poule** pothole.

nièce [njɛs] nf niece.

nième [ɛnjɛm] num: **à la ~ fois** the nth time.

nier [nje] vt to deny.

nigaud, e [nigo, -od] nm/f booby, fool.

n'importe [nɛ̃pɔʀt(ə)] ad: ~ **qui/quoi/où** anybody/anything/ anywhere ; ~ **quand** any time ; ~ **quel** any ; ~ **lequel/laquelle** any (one) ; ~ **comment** (sans soin) carelessly.

nippes [nip] nfpl togs.

nippon, e [nipɔ̃, -ɔn] a Japanese.

nique [nik] nf: **faire la ~ à** to thumb one's nose at (fig).

nitouche [nituʃ] nf (péj): **c'est une sainte ~** she looks as if butter wouldn't melt in her mouth, she's a little hypocrite.

nitrate [nitʀat] nm nitrate.

nitroglycérine [nitʀogliseʀin] nf nitroglycérin(e).

niveau, x [nivo] nm level ; (des élèves, études) standard ; **de ~** (avec) level (with) ; ~ **(à bulle)** spirit level ; **le ~ de la mer** sea level ; ~ **de vie** standard of living.

niveler [nivle] vt to level ; **nivellement** nm levelling.

nobiliaire [nɔbiljɛʀ] a voir **particule.**

noble [nɔbl(ə)] a noble // nm/f noble (man/woman) ; **noblesse** nf nobility ; (d'une action etc) nobleness.

noce [nɔs] nf wedding ; (gens) wedding party (ou guests pl) ; **faire la ~** (fam) to go on a binge ; ~**s d'or/d'argent** golden/silver wedding.

nocif, ive [nɔsif, -iv] a harmful, noxious.

noctambule [nɔktãbyl] nm night-bird, late-nighter.

nocturne [nɔktyʀn(ə)] a nocturnal // nf (SPORT) floodlit fixture.

Noël [nɔɛl] nm Christmas.

nœud [nø] nm (de corde, du bois, NAVIG) knot ; (ruban) bow ; (fig: liens) bond, tie ; ~ **coulant** noose ; ~ **papillon** bow tie.

noir, e [nwaʀ] a black ; (obscur, sombre) dark // nm/f black man/woman, Negro/Negro woman // nm: **dans le ~** in the dark // nf (MUS) crotchet ; ~**ceur** nf blackness ; darkness ; ~**cir** vt, vi to blacken.

noise [nwaz] nf: **chercher ~ à** to try and pick a quarrel with.

noisetier [nwaztje] nm hazel.

noisette [nwazɛt] nf hazelnut.

noix [nwa] nf walnut ; (fam) twit ; (CULIN): **une ~ de beurre** a knob of butter ; **à la ~** (fam) worthless ; ~ **de cajou** cashew nut ; ~ **de coco** coconut ; ~ **muscade** nutmeg.

nom [nɔ̃] nm name ; (LING) noun ; ~ **commun/propre** common/proper noun ; ~ **d'emprunt** assumed name ; ~ **de famille** surname ; ~ **de jeune fille** maiden name.

nomade [nɔmad] a nomadic // nm/f nomad.

nombre [nɔ̃bʀ(ə)] nm number ; **venir en ~** to come in large numbers ; **depuis ~ d'années** for many years ; **ils sont au ~ de 3** there are 3 of them ; **au ~ de mes amis** among my friends ; ~ **premier/entier** prime/whole number.

nombreux, euse [nɔ̃bʀø, -øz] a many, numerous ; (avec nom sg: foule etc) large ; **peu ~** few ; small.

nombril [nɔ̃bʀi] nm navel.

nomenclature [nɔmãklatyʀ] nf wordlist ; list of items.

nominal, e, aux [nɔminal, -o] a nominal.

nominatif [nɔminatif] nm nominative.

nomination [nɔminasjɔ̃] nf nominative.

nommément [nɔmemã] ad (désigner) by name.

nommer [nɔme] vt (baptiser) to name, give a name to ; (qualifier) to call ; (mentionner) to name, give the name of ; (élire) to appoint, nominate ; **se ~ : il se nomme Pascal** his name's Pascal, he's called Pascal.

non [nɔ̃] ad (réponse) no ; (avec loin, sans, seulement) not ; ~ **que** not that ; ~ **plus : moi ~ plus** neither do I, I don't either.

nonagénaire [nɔnaʒenɛʀ] nm/f man/woman in their nineties.

non-alcoolisé, e [nɔnalkɔlize] a non-alcoholic.

nonchalance [nɔ̃ʃalãs] nf nonchalance, casualness.

non-fumeur [nɔ̃fymœʀ] nm non-smoker.

non-lieu [nɔ̃ljø] nm: **il y a eu ~** the case was dismissed.

nonne [nɔn] nf nun.

nonobstant [nɔnɔpstã] prép notwithstanding.

non-sens [nɔ̃sãs] nm absurdity.

nord [nɔʀ] nm North // a northern ; north ; ~**-africain, e** a, nm/f North-African ; ~**-est** nm North-East ; **nordique** a nordic, northern European ; ~**-ouest** nm North-West.

normal, e, aux [nɔʀmal, -o] a normal // nf: **la ~e** the norm, the average ; ~**ement** ad normally ; ~**iser** vi (COMM, TECH) to standardize ; (POL) to normalize.

normand, e [nɔʀmã, -ãd] a of Normandy.

Normandie [nɔʀmãdi] nf Normandy.

norme [nɔʀm(ə)] nf norm ; (TECH) standard.

Norvège [nɔʀvɛʒ] nf Norway ; **norvégien, ne** a, nm, nf Norwegian.

nos [no] dét voir **notre.**

nostalgie [nɔstalʒi] nf nostalgia.

notable [nɔtabl(ə)] a notable, noteworthy ; (marqué) noticeable, marked // nm prominent citizen.

notaire [nɔtɛʀ] nm notary ; solicitor.

notamment [nɔtamã] ad in particular, among others.

notarié, e [nɔtaʀje] a: **acte ~** deed drawn up by a notary.

note [nɔt] nf (écrite, MUS) note ; (SCOL) mark ; (facture) bill ; **prendre ~ de** to write down ; to note ; ~ **de service** memorandum.

noté, e [nɔte] a: **être bien/mal ~** (employé etc) to have a good/bad record.

noter [nɔte] vt (écrire) to write down ; (remarquer) to note, notice.

notice [nɔtis] nf summary, short article ; (brochure) leaflet, instruction book.

notifier [nɔtifje] vt: ~ **qch à qn** to notify sb of sth, notify sth to sb.

notion [nɔsjɔ̃] nf notion, idea.

notoire [nɔtwaʀ] a widely known ; (en mal) notorious ; **le fait est ~ ou de notoriété publique** the fact is common knowledge.

notre, nos [nɔtʀ(ə), no] *dét* our.
nôtre [notʀ(ə)] *pronom*: **le/la ~** ours ; **les ~s** ours ; *(alliés etc)* our own people ; **soyez des ~s** join us // à ours.
nouer [nwe] *vt* to tie, knot ; *(fig: alliance etc)* to strike up ; **sa gorge se noua** a lump came to her throat.
noueux, euse [nwø, -øz] *a* gnarled.
nougat [nuga] *nm* nougat.
nouilles [nuj] *nfpl* noodles ; pasta *sg*.
nourri, e [nuʀi] *a (feu etc)* sustained.
nourrice [nuʀis] *nf* wet-nurse.
nourrir [nuʀiʀ] *vt* to feed ; *(fig: espoir)* to harbour, nurse ; **logé nourri** with board and lodging ; **~ au sein** to breast-feed ; **nourrissant, e** a nourishing, nutritious.
nourrisson [nuʀisɔ̃] *nm* (unweaned) infant.
nourriture [nuʀityʀ] *nf* food.
nous [nu] *pronom (sujet)* we ; *(objet)* us ; **~-mêmes** ourselves.
nouveau(nouvel), elle, x [nuvo, -εl] *a* new // *nm/f* new pupil *ou* (employee) // *nf* (piece of) news *sg* ; *(LITTÉRATURE)* short story ; **de ~, à ~** again ; **je suis sans nouvelles de lui** I haven't heard from him ; **~ venu, nouvelle venue** *nm/f* newcomer ; **Nouvel An** New Year ; **~-né, e** *nm/f* newborn baby ; **Nouvelle-Zélande** *nf* New Zealand ; **~té** *nf* novelty ; *(COMM)* new film *(ou book ou* creation *etc)*.
nouvel *am*; **nouvelle** *af, nf* [nuvεl] *voir* **nouveau**.
novateur, trice [nɔvatœʀ, -tʀis] *nm/f* innovator.
novembre [nɔvɑ̃bʀ(ə)] *nm* November.
novice [nɔvis] *a* inexperienced // *nm/f* novice.
noyade [nwajad] *nf* drowning *q*.
noyau, x [nwajo] *nm (de fruit)* stone ; *(BIO, PHYSIQUE)* nucleus ; *(ÉLEC, GÉO, fig: centre)* core ; **~ter** *vt (POL)* to infiltrate
noyé, e [nwaje] *nm/f* drowning *(ou* drowned) man/woman.
noyer [nwaje] *nm* walnut (tree) ; *(bois)* walnut // *vt* to drown ; *(fig)* to flood ; to submerge ; **se ~** to be drowned, drown ; *(suicide)* to drown o.s.
nu, e [ny] *a* naked ; *(membres)* naked, bare ; *(chambre, fil, plaine)* bare // *nm (ART)* nude ; **le ~ intégral** total nudity ; **~-pieds** barefoot ; **~-tête**, bareheaded ; **à mains ~es** with one's bare hands ; **se mettre ~** to strip ; **mettre à ~** to bare.
nuage [nɥaʒ] *nm* cloud ; **nuageux, euse** *a* cloudy.
nuance [nɥɑ̃s] *nf (de couleur, sens)* shade ; **il y a une ~ (entre)** there's a slight difference (between) ; **une ~ de tristesse** a tinge of sadness ; **nuancer** *vt (opinion)* to bring some reservations *ou* qualifications to.
nubile [nybil] *a* nubile.
nucléaire [nykleεʀ] *a* nuclear.
nudisme [nydism] *nm* nudism ; **nudiste** *nm/f* nudist.
nudité [nydite] *nf* nudity, nakedness ; bareness.
nues [ny] *nfpl*: **tomber des ~** to be taken aback ; **porter qn aux ~** to praise sb to the skies.

nuée [nɥe] *nf*: **une ~ de** a cloud *ou* host *ou* swarm of.
nuire [nɥiʀ] *vi* to be harmful ; **~ à** to harm, do damage to ; **nuisible** *a* harmful ; **animal nuisible** pest.
nuit [nɥi] *nf* night ; **il fait ~** it's dark ; **cette ~** last night ; tonight ; **~ blanche** sleepless night ; **~ de noces** wedding night ; **nuitamment** *ad* by night ; **nuitées** *nfpl* overnight stays, beds occupied *(in statistics)*.
nul, nulle [nyl] *a (aucun)* no ; *(minime)* nil, non-existent ; *(non valable)* null ; *(péj)* useless, hopeless // *pronom* none, no one ; **résultat ~, match ~** draw ; **~ le part** *ad* nowhere ; **~lement** *ad* by no means ; **~lité** *nf* nullity ; hopelessness ; hopeless individual, nonentity.
numéraire [nymeʀεʀ] *nm* cash ; metal currency.
numération [nymeʀɑsjɔ̃] *nf*: **~ décimale/binaire** decimal/binary notation.
numérique [nymeʀik] *a* numerical.
numéro [nymeʀo] *nm* number ; *(spectacle)* act, turn ; **~ter** *vt* to number.
numismate [nymismat] *nm/f* numismatist, coin collector.
nuptial, e, aux [nypsjal, -o] *a* nuptial ; wedding *cpd*.
nuque [nyk] *nf* nape of the neck.
nutritif, ive [nytʀitif, -iv] *a* nutritional ; *(aliment)* nutritious.
nylon [nilɔ̃] *nm* nylon.
nymphomane [nɛ̃fɔman] *nf* nymphomaniac.

O

oasis [ɔazis] *nf* oasis *(pl* oases).
obédience [ɔbedjɑ̃s] *nf* allegiance.
obéir [ɔbeiʀ] *vi* to obey ; **~ à** to obey ; *(suj: moteur, véhicule)* to respond to ; **obéissance** *nf* obedience ; **obéissant, e** *a* obedient.
obélisque [ɔbelisk(ə)] *nm* obelisk.
obèse [ɔbεz] *a* obese ; **obésité** *nf* obesity.
objecter [ɔbʒεkte] *vt (prétexter)* to plead, put forward as an excuse ; **~ qch à** *(argument)* to put forward sth against ; **~ (à qn) que** to object (to sb) that.
objecteur [ɔbʒεktœʀ] *nm*: **~ de conscience** conscientious objector.
objectif, ive [ɔbʒεktif, -iv] *a* objective // *nm (OPTIQUE, PHOTO)* lens *sg*, objective ; *(MIL, fig)* objective ; **~ à focale variable** zoom lens.
objection [ɔbʒεksjɔ̃] *nf* objection ; **~ de conscience** conscientious objection.
objectivité [ɔbʒεktivite] *nf* objectivity.
objet [ɔbʒε] *nm* object ; *(d'une discussion, recherche)* subject ; **être *ou* faire l'~ de** *(discussion)* to be the subject of ; *(soins)* to be given *ou* shown ; **sans ~** a purposeless ; groundless ; **~ d'art** objet d'art ; **~s personnels** personal items ; **~s de toilette** toilet requisites ; **~s trouvés** lost property *sg*.
objurgations [ɔbʒyʀgɑsjɔ̃] *nfpl* objurgations ; entreaties.
obligation [ɔbligɑsjɔ̃] *nf* obligation ; *(COMM)* bond, debenture ; **être dans l'~ de**

faire to be obliged to do; **avoir l'~ de faire** to be under an obligation to do; **obligatoire** a compulsory, obligatory.

obligé, e [ɔbliʒe] a (redevable): **être très ~ à qn** to be most obliged to sb; **obligeance** nf: **avoir l'obligeance de** to be kind ou good enough to; **obligeant, e** a obliging; kind.

obliger [ɔbliʒe] vt (contraindre): **~ qn à faire** to force ou oblige sb to do; (JUR: engager) to bind; (rendre service à) to oblige; **je suis bien obligé** I have to.

oblique [ɔblik] a oblique; **regard ~** sidelong glance; **en ~** ad diagonally; **obliquer** vi: **obliquer vers** to turn off towards.

oblitération [ɔbliterɑsjɔ̃] nf cancelling q, cancellation.

oblitérer [ɔblitere] vt (timbre-poste) to cancel.

oblong, oblongue [ɔblɔ̃, -ɔ̃g] a oblong.

obnubiler [ɔbnybile] vt to obsess.

obole [ɔbɔl] nf offering.

obscène [ɔpsɛn] a obscene; **obscénité** nf obscenity.

obscur, e [ɔpskyR] a dark; (fig) obscure; vague; humble, lowly; **~cir** vt to darken; (fig) to obscure; **s'~cir** vi to grow dark; **~ité** nf darkness; **dans l'~ité** in the dark, in darkness.

obsédé, e [ɔpsede] nm/f: **~(e) sexuel(le)** sex maniac.

obséder [ɔpsede] vt to obsess, haunt.

obsèques [ɔpsɛk] nfpl funeral sg.

obséquieux, euse [ɔpsekjø, -øz] a obsequious.

observateur, trice [ɔpsɛRvatœR, -tRis] a observant, perceptive // nm/f observer.

observation [ɔpsɛRvɑsjɔ̃] nf observation; (d'un règlement etc) observance; (commentaire) observation, remark; (reproche) reproof; **en ~** (MÉD) under observation.

observatoire [ɔpsɛRvatwaR] nm observatory; (lieu élevé) observation post, vantage point.

observer [ɔpsɛRve] vt (regarder) to observe, watch; (examiner) to examine; (scientifiquement, aussi: règlement, jeûne etc) to observe; (surveiller) to watch; (remarquer) to observe, notice; **faire ~ qch à qn** (dire) to point out sth to sb.

obsession [ɔpsesjɔ̃] nf obsession; **avoir l'~ de** to have an obsession with.

obstacle [ɔpstakl(ə)] nm obstacle; (ÉQUITATION) jump, hurdle; **faire ~ à** (lumière) to block out; (projet) to hinder, put obstacles in the path of; **~s antichars** tank defences.

obstétrique [ɔpstetRik] nf obstetrics sg.

obstination [ɔpstinɑsjɔ̃] nf obstinacy.

obstiné, e [ɔpstine] a obstinate.

obstiner [ɔpstine]: **s'~** vi to insist, dig one's heels in; **s'~ à faire** to persist (obstinately) in doing; **s'~ sur qch** to keep working at sth, labour away at sth.

obstruction [ɔpstRyksjɔ̃] nf obstruction, blockage; (SPORT) obstruction; **faire de l'~** (fig) to be obstructive.

obstruer [ɔpstRye] vt to block, obstruct; **s'~** vi to become blocked.

obtempérer [ɔptɑ̃peRe] vi to obey; **~ à** to obey, comply with.

obtenir [ɔptəniR] vt to obtain, get; (total, résultat) to arrive at, reach; to achieve, obtain; **~ de pouvoir faire** to obtain permission to do; **~ de qn qu'il fasse** to get sb to agree to do; **obtention** nf obtaining.

obturateur [ɔptyRatœR] nm (PHOTO) shutter; **~ à rideau** focal plane shutter.

obturation [ɔptyRɑsjɔ̃] nf closing (up); **~ (dentaire)** filling; **vitesse d'~** (PHOTO) shutter speed.

obturer [ɔptyRe] vt to close (up); (dent) to fill.

obtus, e [ɔpty, -yz] a obtuse.

obus [ɔby] nm shell.

obvier [ɔbvje]: **~ à** vt to obviate.

O.C. sigle voir **onde**.

occasion [ɔkazjɔ̃] nf (aubaine, possibilité) opportunity; (circonstance) occasion; (COMM: article non neuf) secondhand buy; (: acquisition avantageuse) bargain; **à plusieurs ~s** on several occasions; **avoir l'~ de faire** to have the opportunity to do; **être l'~ de** to occasion, give rise to; **à l'~** ad sometimes, on occasions; some time; **d'~** a, ad secondhand.

occasionnel, le a (fortuit) chance cpd: (non régulier) occasional; casual.

occasionner [ɔkazjɔne] vt to cause, bring about; **~ qch à qn** to cause sb sth.

occident [ɔksidɑ̃] nm: **l'~** the west; **occidental, e, aux** western; (POL) Western // nm/f Westerner.

occiput [ɔksipyt] nm back of the head, occiput.

occire [ɔksiR] vt to slay.

occitan, e [ɔksitɑ̃, -an] a of the langue d'oc, of Provençal French.

occlusion [ɔklyzjɔ̃] nf: **~ intestinale** obstruction of the bowels.

occulte [ɔkylt(ə)] a occult, supernatural.

occulter [ɔkylte] vt (fig) to overshadow.

occupant, e [ɔkypɑ̃, -ɑ̃t] a occupying // nm/f (d'un appartement) occupier, occupant // nm (MIL) occupying forces pl; (POL: d'usine etc) occupier.

occupation [ɔkypɑsjɔ̃] nf occupation.

occupé, e [ɔkype] a (MIL, POL) occupied; (personne: affairé, pris) busy; (place, sièges) taken; (toilettes, ligne) engaged.

occuper [ɔkype] vt to occupy; (main-d'œuvre) to employ; **s'~** to occupy o.s., keep o.s. busy; **s'~ de** (être responsable de) to be in charge of; (se charger de: affaire) to take charge of, deal with; (: clients etc) to attend to; (s'intéresser à, pratiquer) to be involved in; **ça occupe trop de place** it takes up too much room.

occurrence [ɔkyRɑ̃s] nf: **en l'~** in this case.

océan [ɔseɑ̃] nm ocean; **l'~ Indien** the Indian Ocean; **l'Océanie** nf Oceania; **océanique** a oceanic; **océanographie** nf oceanography.

ocelot [ɔslo] nm ocelot; (fourrure) ocelot fur.

ocre [ɔkR(ə)] a inv ochre.

octane [ɔktan] nm octane.

octave [ɔktav] *nf* octave.
octobre [ɔktɔbR(ə)] *nm* October.
octogénaire [ɔktɔʒenɛR] *a. nm/f* octogenarian.
octogone [ɔktɔgɔn] *nm* octagon.
octroi [ɔktRwa] *nm* granting.
octroyer [ɔktRwaje] *vt*: ~ **qch à qn** to grant sth to sb, grant sb sth.
oculaire [ɔkylɛR] *a* ocular, eye *cpd* // *nm* (de microscope) eyepiece.
oculiste [ɔkylist(ə)] *nm/f* eye specialist, oculist.
ode [ɔd] *nf* ode.
odeur [ɔdœR] *nf* smell.
odieux, euse [ɔdjø, -øz] *a* odious, hateful.
odorant, e [ɔdɔRɑ̃, -ɑ̃t] *a* sweet-smelling, fragrant.
odorat [ɔdɔRa] *nm* (sense of) smell.
odoriférant, e [ɔdɔRifeRɑ̃, -ɑ̃t] *a* sweet-smelling, fragrant.
odyssée [ɔdise] *nf* odyssey.
œcuménique [ekymenik] *a* oecumenical.
œil [œj], *pl* **yeux** [jø] *nm* eye; **à l'~** (*fam*) for free; **à l'~ nu** with the naked eye; **tenir qn à l'~** to keep an eye *ou* a watch on sb; **avoir l'~ à** to keep an eye on; **faire de l'~ à qn** to make eyes at sb; **à l'~ vif** with a lively expression; **fermer les yeux (sur)** (*fig*) to turn a blind eye (to); **fermer l'~** to get a moment's sleep; ~ **de verre** glass eye.
œillade [œjad] *nf*: **lancer une ~ à qn** to wink at sb, give sb a wink; **faire des ~s à** to make eyes at.
œillères [œjɛR] *nfpl* blinkers.
œillet [œjɛ] *nm* (BOT) carnation; (trou) eyelet.
œnologue [enɔlɔg] *nm/f* oenologist, wine expert.
œsophage [enɔfaʒ] *nm* oesophagus.
œuf [œf, *pl* ø] *nm* egg; **étouffer dans l'~** to nip in the bud; ~ **à la coque/dur** boiled/hard-boiled egg; ~ **au plat** fried egg; ~**s brouillés** scrambled eggs; ~ **de Pâques** Easter egg; ~ **à repriser** darning egg.
œuvre [œvR(ə)] *nf* (tâche) task, undertaking; (ouvrage achevé, livre, tableau etc) work; (ensemble de la production artistique) works *pl*; (organisation charitable) charity // *nm* (d'un artiste) works *pl*; (CONSTR): **le gros ~** the shell; **être à l'~** to be at work; **mettre en ~** (moyens) to make use of; ~ **d'art** work of art.
offense [ɔfɑ̃s] *nf* insult; (REL) péché; transgression, trespass.
offenser [ɔfɑ̃se] *vt* to offend, hurt; (principes, Dieu) to offend against; **s'~ de** to take offence at.
offensif, ive [ɔfɑ̃sif, -iv] *a*, nf offensive; **passer à l'offensive** to go into the attack *ou* offensive.
offert, e [ɔfɛR, -ɛRt(ə)] *pp* de **offrir**.
offertoire [ɔfɛRtwaR] *nm* offertory.
office [ɔfis] *nm* (charge) office; (agence) bureau, agency; (REL) service // *nm ou nf* (pièce) pantry; **faire ~ de** to act as; to do duty as; **d'~** *ad* automatically; **bons ~s** (POL) good offices; ~ **du tourisme** tourist bureau.

officialiser [ɔfisjalize] *vt* to make official.
officiel, le [ɔfisjɛl] *a*, nm/f official.
officier [ɔfisje] *nm* officer // *vi* to officiate; ~ **de l'état-civil** registrar; ~ **ministériel** member of the legal profession; ~ **de police** ≈ police officer.
officieux, euse [ɔfisjø, -øz] *a* unofficial.
officinal, e, aux [ɔfisinal, -o] *a*: **plantes ~es** medicinal plants.
officine [ɔfisin] *nf* (de pharmacie) dispensary; (pharmacie) pharmacy; (gén péj: bureau) agency, office.
offrande [ɔfRɑ̃d] *nf* offering.
offrant [ɔfRɑ̃] *nm*: **au plus ~** to the highest bidder.
offre [ɔfR(ə)] *nf* offer; (aux enchères) bid; (ADMIN: soumission) tender; (ECON): **l'~** supply; ~ **d'emploi** job advertised; **'~s d'emploi'** situations vacant; ~ **publique d'achat (O.P.A.)** takeover bid; ~**s de service** offer of service.
offrir [ɔfRiR] *vt* to offer; (faire cadeau de): ~ **(à qn)** to give (to sb); **s'~** *vi* (occasion, paysage) to present itself // *vt* (vacances, voiture) to treat o.s. to; ~ **(à qn) de faire qch** to offer to do sth (for sb); ~ **à boire à qn** to offer sb a drink; **s'~ comme guide/en otage** to offer one's services as (a) guide/offer o.s. as hostage; **s'~ aux regards** (suj: personne) to expose o.s. to the public gaze.
offset [ɔfsɛt] *nm* offset (printing).
offusquer [ɔfyske] *vt* to offend; **s'~ de** to take offence at, be offended by.
ogive [ɔʒiv] *nf* (ARCHIT) diagonal rib; (d'obus, de missile) nose cone; **voûte en ~** rib vault; **arc en ~** lancet arch; ~ **nucléaire** nuclear warhead.
ogre [ɔgR(ə)] *nm* ogre.
oie [wa] *nf* (ZOOL) goose (pl geese).
oignon [ɔɲɔ̃] *nm* (BOT, CULIN) onion; (de tulipe etc: bulbe) bulb; (MÉD) bunion; **petits ~s** pickling onions.
oindre [wɛ̃dR(ə)] *vt* to anoint.
oiseau, x [wazo] *nm* bird; ~ **de proie** bird of prey; ~**-mouche** *nm* hummingbird.
oisellerie [wazɛlRi] *nf* bird shop.
oiseux, euse [wazø, -øz] *a* pointless; trivial.
oisif, ive [wazif, -iv] *a* idle // *nm/f* (péj) man/woman of leisure; **oisiveté** *nf* idleness.
O.K. [ɔkɛ] *excl* O.K., all right.
oléagineux, euse [ɔleaʒinø, -øz] *a* oleaginous, oil-producing.
oléoduc [ɔleɔdyk] *nm* (oil) pipeline.
olfactif, ive [ɔlfaktif, -iv] *a* olfactory.
oligarchie [ɔligaRʃi] *nf* oligarchy.
olivâtre [ɔlivɑtR(ə)] *a* olive-greenish; (teint) sallow.
olive [ɔliv] *nf* (BOT) olive // *a inv* olive(-green); ~**raie** *nf* olive grove; **olivier** *nm* olive tree; (bois) olive wood.
olympiade [ɔlɛ̃pjad] *nf* (période) Olympiad; **les ~s** (jeux) the Olympiad *sg*.
olympien, ne [ɔlɛ̃pjɛ̃, -jɛn] *a* Olympian, of Olympian aloofness.
olympique [ɔlɛ̃pik] *a* Olympic.
ombilical, e, aux [ɔ̃bilikal, -o] *a* umbilical.

ombrage [ɔ̃bʀaʒ] nm (ombre) (leafy) shade ; (fig): **prendre ~ de** to take umbrage ou offence at ; **ombragé, e** a shaded, shady ; **ombrageux, euse** a (cheval) skittish, nervous ; (personne) touchy, easily offended.

ombre [ɔ̃bʀ(ə)] nf (espace non ensoleillé) shade ; (ombre portée, tache) shadow ; **à l'~** in the shade ; (fam) behind bars ; **à l'~ de** in the shade of ; (tout près de, fig) in the shadow of ; **tu me fais de l'~** you're in my light ; **ça nous donne de l'~** it gives us (some) shade ; **vivre dans l'~** (fig) to live in obscurity ; **laisser dans l'~** (fig) to leave in the dark ; **~ à paupières** eyeshadow ; **~ portée** shadow ; **~s chinoises** (spectacle) shadow show sg.

ombrelle [ɔ̃bʀɛl] nf parasol, sunshade.

omelette [ɔmlɛt] nf omelette ; **~ au fromage/au jambon** cheese/ham omelette ; **~ aux herbes** omelette with herbs.

omettre [ɔmɛtʀ(ə)] vt to omit, leave out ; **~ de faire** to fail ou omit to do ; **omission** nf omission.

omni... [ɔmni] préfixe: **~bus** nm slow ou stopping train ; **~potent, e** a omnipotent ; **~scient, e** a omniscient ; **~vore** a omnivorous.

omoplate [ɔmɔplat] nf shoulder blade.

O.M.S. sigle f voir **organisation**.

on [ɔ̃] pronom (indéterminé): **~ peut le faire ainsi** you one can do it like this, it can be done like this ; (quelqu'un): **~ les a attaqués** they were attacked ; (nous): **~ va y aller demain** we're going tomorrow ; (les gens): **autrefois, ~ croyait aux fantômes** they used to believe in ghosts years ago ; **~ vous demande au téléphone** there's a phone call for you, there's somebody on the phone for you ; **~ ne peut plus** ad: **~ ne peut plus stupide** as stupid as can be.

oncle [ɔ̃kl(ə)] nm uncle.

onctueux, euse [ɔ̃ktɥø, -øz] a creamy, smooth ; (fig) smooth, unctuous.

onde [ɔ̃d] nf (PHYSIQUE) wave ; **sur l'~** on the waters ; **sur les ~s** on the radio ; **mettre en ~s** to produce for the radio ; **sur ~s courtes (o.c.)** on short wave sg ; **moyennes/ longues ~s** medium/long wave sg.

ondée [ɔ̃de] nf shower.

on-dit [ɔ̃di] nm inv rumour.

ondoyer [ɔ̃dwaje] vi to ripple, wave.

ondulant, e [ɔ̃dylɑ̃, -ɑ̃t] a swaying ; undulating.

ondulation [ɔ̃dylɑsjɔ̃] nf undulation.

onduler [ɔ̃dyle] vi to undulate ; (cheveux) to wave.

onéreux, euse [ɔneʀø, -øz] a costly ; **à titre ~** in return for payment.

ongle [ɔ̃gl(ə)] nm (ANAT) nail ; **se faire les ~s** to do one's nails.

onglet [ɔ̃glɛ] nm (rainure) (thumbnail) groove ; (bande de papier) tab.

onguent [ɔ̃gɑ̃] nm ointment.

onomatopée [ɔnɔmatɔpe] nf onomatopoeia.

ont vb voir **avoir**.

O.N.U. [ɔny] sigle f voir **organisation**.

onyx [ɔniks] nm onyx.

onze [ɔ̃z] num eleven ; **onzième** num eleventh.

O.P.A. sigle f voir **offre**.

opacité [ɔpasite] nf opaqueness.

opale [ɔpal] nf opal.

opalin, e [ɔpalɛ̃, -in] a, nf opaline.

opaque [ɔpak] a opaque.

O.P.E.P. [ɔpɛp] sigle f (= organisation des pays exportateurs de pétrole) O.P.E.C. (organization of petroleum exporting countries).

opéra [ɔpeʀa] nm opera ; (édifice) opera house ; **~-comique** nm light opera, opéra comique.

opérateur, trice [ɔpeʀatœʀ, -tʀis] nm/f operator ; **~ (de prise de vues)** cameraman.

opération [ɔpeʀɑsjɔ̃] nf operation ; (COMM) dealing.

opératoire [ɔpeʀatwaʀ] a operating ; (choc etc) post-operative.

opéré, e [ɔpeʀe] nm/f patient (having undergone an operation).

opérer [ɔpeʀe] vt (MÉD) to operate on ; (faire, exécuter) to carry out, make // vi (remède: faire effet) to act, work ; (procéder) to proceed ; (MÉD) to operate ; **s'~** vi (avoir lieu) to occur, take place ; **se faire ~** to have an operation ; **se faire ~ des amygdales/du cœur** to have one's tonsils out/have a heart operation.

opérette [ɔpeʀɛt] nf operetta, light opera.

ophtalmologie [ɔftalmɔlɔʒi] nf ophthalmology ; **ophtalmologue** nm/f ophthalmologist.

opiner [ɔpine] vi: **~ de la tête** to nod assent.

opiniâtre [ɔpinjɑtʀ(ə)] a stubborn.

opinion [ɔpinjɔ̃] nf opinion ; **l'~ (publique)** public opinion.

opium [ɔpjɔm] nm opium.

opportun, e [ɔpɔʀtœ̃, -yn] a timely, opportune ; **en temps ~** at the appropriate time ; **opportunisme** nm opportunism ; **opportuniste** a, nm/f opportunist ; **opportunité** nf timeliness, opportuneness.

opposant, e [ɔpozɑ̃, -ɑ̃t] a opposing ; **~s** nmpl opponents.

opposé, e [ɔpoze] a (direction, rive) opposite ; (faction) opposing ; (couleurs) contrasting ; (opinions, intérêts) conflicting ; (contre): **~ à** opposed to, against // nm: **l'~** the other ou opposite side (ou direction) ; (contraire) the opposite ; **à l'~** (fig) on the other hand ; **à l'~ de** on the other ou opposite side from ; (fig) contrary to, unlike.

opposer [ɔpoze] vt (meubles, objets) to place opposite each other ; (personnes, armées, équipes) to oppose ; (couleurs, termes, tons) to contrast ; **~ qch à** (comme obstacle, défense) to set sth against ; (comme objection) to put sth forward against ; to put up sth to ; (en contraste) to set sth opposite ; to match sth with ; **s'~** (sens réciproque) to conflict ; to clash ; to face each other ; to contrast ; **s'~ à** (interdire, empêcher) to oppose ; (tenir tête à) to rebel against ; **sa religion s'y oppose**

it's against his religion; **s'~ à ce que qn
fasse** to be opposed to sb's doing.

opposition [ɔpozisjɔ̃] *nf* opposition; **par
~ à** as opposed to, in contrast with;
entrer en ~ avec to come into conflict
with; **être en ~ avec** (*idées, conduite*) to
be at variance with; **faire ~ à un chèque**
to stop a cheque.

oppresser [ɔpRese] *vt* to oppress;
oppresseur *nm* oppressor; **oppressif, ive**
a oppressive; **oppression** *nf* oppression;
(*malaise*) feeling of suffocation.

opprimer [ɔpRime] *vt* to oppress; (*liberté,
opinion*) to suppress, stifle; (*suj: chaleur
etc*) to suffocate, oppress.

opprobre [ɔpRɔbR(ə)] *nm* disgrace.

opter [ɔpte] *vi*: **~ pour** to opt for; **~
entre** to choose between.

opticien, ne [ɔptisjɛ̃, -ɛn] *nm/f* optician.

optimal, e, aux [ɔptimal, -o] *a* optimal.

optimisme [ɔptimism(ə)] *nm* optimism;
optimiste *nm/f* optimist.

optimum [ɔptimɔm] *a* optimum.

option [ɔpsjɔ̃] *nf* option; **matière à ~**
(*SCOL*) optional subject; **prendre une ~
sur** to take (out) an option on.

optique [ɔptik] *a* (*nerf*) optic; (*verres*)
optical // *nf* (*PHOTO: lentilles etc*) optics *pl*;
(*science, industrie*) optics *sg*; (*fig: manière
de voir*) perspective.

opulence [ɔpylɑ̃s] *nf* wealth, opulence.

opulent, e [ɔpylɑ̃, -ɑ̃t] *a* wealthy, opulent;
(*formes, poitrine*) ample, generous.

or [ɔR] *nm* gold // *cj* now, but; **en ~** gold
cpd; (*fig*) golden, marvellous; **d'~** (*fig*)
golden.

oracle [ɔRakl(ə)] *nm* oracle.

orage [ɔRaʒ] *nm* (thunder)storm;
orageux, euse *a* stormy.

oraison [ɔRɛzɔ̃] *nf* orison, prayer; **~
funèbre** funeral oration.

oral, e, aux [ɔRal, -o] *a, nm* oral; **~ement**
ad orally.

orange [ɔRɑ̃ʒ] *nf, a inv* orange; **orangé,
e** *a* orangey, orange-coloured; **orangeade**
nf orangeade; **oranger** *nm* orange tree;
~raie *nf* orange grove; **~rie** *nf* orangery.

orateur [ɔRatœR] *nm* speaker; orator.

oratoire [ɔRatwaR] *nm* oratory; wayside
shrine // *a* oratorical.

orbital, e, aux [ɔRbital, -o] *a* orbital.

orbite [ɔRbit] *nf* (*ANAT*) (eye-)socket;
(*PHYSIQUE*) orbit; **mettre sur ~** to put into
orbit; (*fig*) to launch; **dans l'~ de** (*fig*)
within the sphere of influence of.

orchestration [ɔRkɛstRasjɔ̃] *nf*
orchestration.

orchestre [ɔRkɛstR(ə)] *nm* orchestra; (*de
jazz, danse*) band; (*places*) stalls *pl*;
orchestrer *vt* (*MUS*) to orchestrate; (*fig*) to
mount, stage-manage.

orchidée [ɔRkide] *nf* orchid.

ordinaire [ɔRdinɛR] *a* ordinary;
everyday; standard // *nm* ordinary;
(*menus*) everyday fare // *nf* (*essence*) ≈
two-star (petrol); **d'~** usually, ordinarily;
à l'~ usually, ordinarily.

ordinal, e, aux [ɔRdinal, -o] *a* ordinal.

ordinateur [ɔRdinatœR] *nm* computer.

ordination [ɔRdinasjɔ̃] *nf* ordination.

ordonnance [ɔRdɔnɑ̃s] *nf* organization;
layout; (*MÉD*) prescription; (*JUR*) order;
(*MIL*) orderly, batman; **d'~** (*MIL*)
regulation *cpd*.

ordonné, e [ɔRdɔne] *a* tidy, orderly;
(*MATH*) ordered // *nf* (*MATH*) ordinate,
Y-axis.

ordonner [ɔRdɔne] *vt* (*agencer*) to
organize, arrange; (: *meubles,
appartement*) to lay out, arrange; (*donner
un ordre*): **~ à qn de faire** to order sb to
do; (*MATH*) to (arrange in) order; (*REL*) to
ordain; (*MÉD*) to prescribe; (*JUR*) to order.

ordre [ɔRdR(ə)] *nm* (*gén*) order; (*propreté
et soin*) orderliness, tidiness; (*nature*): **d'~
pratique** of a practical nature; **~s** *nmpl*
(*REL*) holy orders; **mettre en ~** to tidy
(up), put in order; **avoir de l'~** to be tidy
ou orderly; **mettre bon ~ à** to put to
rights, sort out; **être aux ~s de qn/sous
les ~s de qn** to be at sb's disposal/under
sb's command; **jusqu'à nouvel ~** until
further notice; **dans le même ~ d'idées**
in this connection; **donnez-nous un ~ de
grandeur** give us some idea as regards
size (*ou* the amount); **de premier ~** first-
rate; **~ du jour** (*d'une réunion*) agenda;
(*MIL*) order of the day; **à l'~ du jour** on
the agenda; (*fig*) topical; (*MIL: citer*) in
dispatches; **~ de route** marching orders
pl.

ordure [ɔRdyR] *nf* filth *q*; **~s** (*balayures,
déchets*) rubbish *sg*, refuse *sg*; **~s
ménagères** household refuse; **ordurier,
ière** *a* lewd, filthy.

oreille [ɔRɛj] *nf* (*ANAT*) ear; (*de marmite,
tasse*) handle; **avoir de l'~** to have a good
ear (for music).

oreiller [ɔReje] *nm* pillow.

oreillette [ɔRɛjɛt] *nf* (*ANAT*) auricle.

oreillons [ɔRɛjɔ̃] *nmpl* mumps *sg*.

ores [ɔR]: **d'~ et déjà** *ad* already.

orfèvre [ɔRfɛvR(ə)] *nm* goldsmith;
silversmith; **orfèvrerie** *nf* goldsmith's (*ou*
silversmith's) trade; (*ouvrage*) gold (*ou*
silver) plate.

orfraie [ɔRfRɛ] *nm* white-tailed eagle;
pousser des cris d'~ to yell at the top
of one's voice.

organe [ɔRgan] *nm* organ; (*porte-parole*)
representative, mouthpiece; **~s de
commande** (*TECH*) controls; **~s de
transmission** (*TECH*) transmission system
sg.

organigramme [ɔRganigRam] *nm*
organization chart; flow chart.

organique [ɔRganik] *a* organic.

organisateur, trice [ɔRganizatœR, -tRis]
nm/f organizer.

organisation [ɔRganizasjɔ̃] *nf*
organization; **O~ des Nations Unies
(O.N.U.)** United Nations (Organization)
(U.N., U.N.O.); **O~ mondiale de la santé
(O.M.S.)** World Health Organization
(W.H.O.); **O~ du traité de l'Atlantique
Nord (O.T.A.N.)** North Atlantic Treaty
Organization (N.A.T.O.).

organiser [ɔRganize] *vt* to organize;
(*mettre sur pied: service etc*) to set up; **s'~**
to get organized.

organisme [ɔRganism(ə)] *nm* (*BIO*)

organism ; (*corps humain*) body ; (ADMIN, POL *etc*) body, organism.

organiste [ɔʀɡanist(ə)] *nm/f* organist.

orgasme [ɔʀɡasm(ə)] *nm* orgasm, climax.

orge [ɔʀʒ(ə)] *nf* barley.

orgelet [ɔʀʒalɛ] *nm* sty(e).

orgie [ɔʀʒi] *nf* orgy.

orgue [ɔʀɡ(ə)] *nm* organ ; ~**s** *nfpl* organ *sg* ; ~ **de Barbarie** barrel *ou* street organ.

orgueil [ɔʀɡœj] *nm* pride ; **orgueilleux, euse** *a* proud.

Orient [ɔʀjɑ̃] *nm*: **l'~** the East, the Orient.

orientable [ɔʀjɑ̃tabl(ə)] *a* adjustable.

oriental, e, aux [ɔʀjɑ̃tal, -o] *a* oriental, eastern ; (*frontière*) eastern // *nm/f*: **O~, e** Oriental.

orientation [ɔʀjɑ̃tasjɔ̃] *nf* positioning ; adjustment ; orientation ; direction ; (*d'un journal*) leanings *pl* ; **avoir le sens de l'~** to have a (good) sense of direction ; ~ **professionnelle** careers advising ; careers advisory service.

orienté, e [ɔʀjɑ̃te] *a* (*fig: article, journal*) slanted ; **bien/mal ~** (*appartement*) well/badly positioned ; ~ **au sud** facing south *ou* with a southern aspect.

orienter [ɔʀjɑ̃te] *vt* (*situer*) to position ; (*placer, disposer: pièce mobile*) to adjust, position ; (*tourner*) to direct, turn ; (*voyageur, touriste, recherches*) to direct ; (*fig: élève*) to orientate ; **s'~** (*se repérer*) to find one's bearings ; **s'~ vers** (*fig*) to turn towards ; **orienteur** *nm* (SCOL) careers adviser.

orifice [ɔʀifis] *nm* opening, orifice.

oriflamme [ɔʀiflam] *nf* banner, standard.

origan [ɔʀiɡɑ̃] *nm* (CULIN) oregano.

originaire [ɔʀiʒinɛʀ] *a* original ; **être ~ de** to be a native of ; (*provenir de*) to originate from ; to be native to.

original, e, aux [ɔʀiʒinal, -o] *a* original ; (*bizarre*) eccentric // *nm/f* eccentric // *nm* (*document etc, ART*) original ; (*dactylographie*) top copy ; ~**ité** *nf* originality *q* ; eccentricity.

origine [ɔʀiʒin] *nf* origin ; **d'~** of origin ; (*pneus etc*) original ; (*bureau postal*) dispatching ; **dès l'~** at *ou* from the outset ; **à l'~** originally ; **avoir son ~ dans** to have its origins in, originate in ; **originel, le** *a* original.

oripeaux [ɔʀipo] *nmpl* rags.

O.R.L. *nm/f ou titre* = **oto-rhino-laryngologiste**.

orme [ɔʀm(ə)] *nm* elm.

orné, e [ɔʀne] *a* ornate.

ornement [ɔʀnəmɑ̃] *nm* ornament ; (*fig*) embellishment, adornment ; ~**s sacerdotaux** vestments ; **ornemental, e, aux** *a* ornamental ; **ornementer** *vt* to ornament.

orner [ɔʀne] *vt* to decorate, adorn ; ~ **qch de** to decorate sth with.

ornière [ɔʀnjɛʀ] *nf* rut.

ornithologie [ɔʀnitɔlɔʒi] *nf* ornithology.

orphelin, e [ɔʀfəlɛ̃, -in] *a* orphan(ed) // *nm/f* orphan ; ~ **de père/mère** fatherless/motherless ; **orphelinat** *nm* orphanage.

O.R.S.E.C. [ɔʀsɛk] *sigle* (= *organisation des secours*): **le plan ~** disaster contingency plan.

orteil [ɔʀtɛj] *nm* toe ; **gros ~** big toe.

O.R.T.F. *sigle m* = *Office de la radiodiffusion et télévision française* (*the French broadcasting corporation*).

orthodoxe [ɔʀtɔdɔks(ə)] *a* orthodox ; **orthodoxie** *nf* orthodoxy.

orthographe [ɔʀtɔɡʀaf] *nf* spelling ; **orthographier** *vt* to spell ; **mal orthographié** misspelt.

orthopédie [ɔʀtɔpedi] *nf* orthopaedics *sg* ; **orthopédique** *a* orthopaedic ; **orthopédiste** *nm/f* orthopaedic specialist.

ortie [ɔʀti] *nf* (stinging) nettle.

os [ɔs, *pl* o] *nm* bone ; **sans ~** (BOUCHERIE) off the bone, boned ; ~ **à moelle** marrowbone.

O.S. *sigle m voir* **ouvrier.**

oscillation [ɔsilɑsjɔ̃] *nf* oscillation ; ~**s** *nfpl* (*fig*) fluctuations.

osciller [ɔsile] *vi* (*pendule*) to swing ; (*au vent etc*) to rock ; (TECH) to oscillate ; (*fig*): ~ **entre** to waver *ou* fluctuate between.

osé, e [oze] *a* daring, bold.

oseille [ozɛj] *nf* sorrel.

oser [oze] *vi, vt* to dare ; ~ **faire** to dare (to) do.

osier [ozje] *nm* willow ; **d'~, en ~** wicker(work).

ossature [ɔsatyʀ] *nf* (ANAT) frame, skeletal structure ; (: *du visage*) bone structure ; (*fig*) framework.

osselet [ɔslɛ] *nm* (ANAT) ossicle ; **jouer aux ~s** to play knucklebones.

ossements [ɔsmɑ̃] *nmpl* bones.

osseux, euse [ɔsø, -øz] *a* bony ; (*tissu, maladie, greffe*) bone *cpd.*

ossifier [ɔsifje]: **s'~** *vi* to ossify.

ossuaire [ɔsɥɛʀ] *nm* ossuary.

ostensible [ɔstɑ̃sibl(ə)] *a* conspicuous.

ostensoir [ɔstɑ̃swaʀ] *nm* monstrance.

ostentation [ɔstɑ̃tasjɔ̃] *nf* ostentation ; **faire ~ de** to parade, make a display of.

ostracisme [ɔstʀasism(ə)] *nm* ostracism ; **frapper d'~** to ostracize.

ostréiculture [ɔstʀeikyltyʀ] *nf* oyster-farming.

otage [ɔtaʒ] *nm* hostage ; **prendre qn comme ~** to take sb hostage.

O.T.A.N. [ɔtɑ̃] *sigle f voir* **organisation.**

otarie [ɔtaʀi] *nf* sea-lion.

ôter [ote] *vt* to remove ; (*soustraire*) to take away ; ~ **qch à qn** to take sth (away) from sb ; ~ **qch de** to remove sth from.

otite [ɔtit] *nf* ear infection.

oto-rhino(-laryngologiste) [ɔtɔʀino-(laʀɛ̃ɡɔlɔʒist(ə)] *nm/f* ear nose and throat specialist.

ou [u] *cj* or ; ~ **...** ~ either ... or ; ~ **bien** or (else).

où [u] *ad, pronom* where ; (*dans lequel*) in which, into which ; from which, out of which ; (*sur lequel*) on which ; (*sens de 'que'*): **au train** ~ **ça va/prix** ~ **c'est** at the rate it's going/price it is ; **le jour** ~ **il est parti the day (that) he left ; **par** ~ **passer?** which way should we go? ; **les villes par** ~ **il est passé** the towns he went through ; **le village d'~ je viens** the village I come from ; **la chambre** ~ **il était**

the room he was in; **d'~ vient qu'il est parti?** how come he left?

ouate [wat] *nf* cotton wool; *(bourre)* padding, wadding; **ouaté, e** a cotton-wool; *(doublé)* quilted; *(fig)* cocoon-like; muffled.

oubli [ubli] *nm (acte)*: **l'~ de** forgetting; *(étourderie)* forgetfulness *q*; *(négligence)* omission, oversight; *(absence de souvenirs)* oblivion; **~ de soi** self-effacement, self-negation.

oublier [ublije] *vt (gén)* to forget; *(ne pas voir: erreurs etc)* to miss; *(ne pas mettre: virgule, nom)* to leave out; *(laisser quelque part: chapeau etc)* to leave behind; **s'~** to forget o.s.

oubliettes [ublijɛt] *nfpl* dungeon *sg*.

oublieux, euse [ublij∅, -∅z] *a* forgetful.

oued [wɛd] *nm* wadi.

ouest [wɛst] *nm* west // *a inv* west; *(région)* western; **à l'~** in the west; *(to the)* west, westwards; **à l'~ de** (to the) west of; **vent d'~** westerly wind; **~-allemand, e** a, *nm/f* West German.

ouf [uf] *excl* phew!

oui [wi] *ad* yes; **répondre (par) ~** to answer yes.

ouï-dire [widiʀ] *nm inv*: **par ~** by hearsay.

ouïe [wi] *nf* hearing; **~s** *nfpl (de poisson)* gills; *(de violon)* sound-hole.

ouïr [wiʀ] *vt* to hear; **avoir ouï dire que** to have heard it said that.

ouistiti [wistiti] *nm* marmoset.

ouragan [uʀagɑ̃] *nm* hurricane; *(fig)* storm.

ourlé, e [uʀle] *a* hemmed; *(fig)* rimmed.

ourler [uʀle] *vt* to hem.

ourlet [uʀlɛ] *nm* hem; *(de l'oreille)* rim.

ours [uʀs] *nm* bear; **~ brun/blanc** brown/polar bear; **~ mal léché** uncouth fellow; **~ (en peluche)** teddy (bear).

ourse [uʀs(ə)] *nf (ZOOL)* she-bear; **la Grande/Petite O~** the Great/Little Bear, Ursa Major/ Minor.

oursin [uʀsɛ̃] *nm* sea urchin.

ourson [uʀsɔ̃] *nm* (bear-)cub.

ouste [ust(ə)] *excl* hop it!

outil [uti] *nm* tool.

outillage [utijaʒ] *nm* set of tools; *(d'atelier)* equipment *q*.

outiller [utije] *vt (ouvrier, usine)* to equip.

outrage [utʀaʒ] *nm* insult; **faire subir les derniers ~s à** *(femme)* to ravish; **~ aux bonnes mœurs** outrage to public decency; **~ à magistrat** contempt of court; **~ à la pudeur** indecent behaviour *q*.

outrageant, e [utʀaʒɑ̃, -ɑ̃t] *a* offensive.

outrager [utʀaʒe] *vt* to offend gravely; *(fig: contrevenir à)* to outrage, insult.

outrance [utʀɑ̃s] *nf* excessiveness *q*, excess; **à ~** *ad* excessively, to excess; **outrancier, ière** *a* extreme.

outre [utʀ(ə)] *nf* goatskin, water skin // *prép* besides // *ad*: **passer ~ à** to disregard, take no notice of; **en ~** besides, moreover; **~ que** apart from the fact that; **~ mesure** immoderately; unduly.

outré, e [utʀe] *a* excessive, exaggerated; outraged.

outre-Atlantique [utʀəatlɑ̃tik] *ad* across the Atlantic.

outrecuidance [utʀəkɥidɑ̃s] *nf* presumptuousness *q*.

outre-Manche [utʀəmɑ̃ʃ] *ad* across the Channel.

outremer [utʀəmɛʀ] *a* ultramarine.

outre-mer [utʀəmɛʀ] *ad* overseas.

outrepasser [utʀəpɑse] *vt* to go beyond, exceed.

outrer [utʀe] *vt* to exaggerate; to outrage.

outsider [awtsajdœʀ] *nm* outsider.

ouvert, e [uvɛʀ, -ɛʀt(ə)] *pp de* **ouvrir** // *a* open; *(robinet, gaz etc)* on; **ouvertement** *ad* openly.

ouverture [uvɛʀtyʀ] *nf* opening; *(MUS)* overture; *(POL)*: **l'~** the widening of the political spectrum; *(PHOTO)*: **~ (du diaphragme)** aperture; **~s** *nfpl (propositions)* overtures; **~ d'esprit** open-mindedness; **heures d'~** *(COMM)* opening hours; **jours d'~** *(COMM)* days of opening.

ouvrable [uvʀabl(ə)] *a*: **jour ~** working day, weekday.

ouvrage [uvʀaʒ] *nm (tâche, de tricot etc, MIL)* work *q*; *(texte, livre)* work; **corbeille à ~** work basket; **~ d'art** *(GÉNIE CIVIL)* bridge or tunnel etc.

ouvragé, e [uvʀaʒe] *a* finely embroidered *(ou* worked *ou* carved).

ouvrant, e [uvʀɑ̃, -ɑ̃t] *a*: **toit ~** *(AUTO)* sunshine roof.

ouvre-boîte(s) [uvʀəbwat] *nm inv* tin *ou* can opener.

ouvre-bouteille(s) [uvʀəbutɛj] *nm inv* bottle-opener.

ouvreuse [uvʀ∅z] *nf* usherette.

ouvrier, ière [uvʀje, -jɛʀ] *nm/f* worker // *nf (ZOOL)* worker (bee) // *a* working-class; industrial; labour *cpd*; workers'; **classe ouvrière** working class; **~ qualifié** skilled worker; **~ spécialisé (O.S.)** semiskilled worker; **~ d'usine** factory worker.

ouvrir [uvʀiʀ] *vt (gén)* to open; *(brèche, passage)* to open up; *(commencer l'exploitation de, créer)* to open (up); *(eau, électricité, chauffage, robinet)* to turn on; *(MÉD: abcès)* to open up, cut open // *vi* to open; to open up; **s'~** *vi* to open; **s'~ à** *(art etc)* to open one's mind to; **s'~ à qn (de qch)** to open one's heart to sb *(about sth)*; **s'~ les veines** to slash *ou* cut one's wrists; **~ l'appétit à qn** to whet sb's appetite.

ouvroir [uvʀwaʀ] *nm* workroom; sewing room.

ovaire [ovɛʀ] *nm* ovary.

ovale [oval] *a* oval.

ovation [ovasjɔ̃] *nf* ovation; **ovationner** *vt*: **ovationner qn** to give sb an ovation.

O.V.N.I. [ovni] *sigle m (= objet volant non identifié)* U.F.O. (unidentified flying object).

ovule [ovyl] *nm (PHYSIOL)* ovum *(pl ova)*; *(MÉD)* pessary.

oxydable [oksidabl(ə)] *a* liable to rust.

oxyde [oksid] *nm* oxide; **~ de carbone** carbon monoxide.

oxyder [okside]: **s'~** *vi* to become oxidized.

oxygène [ɔksiʒɛn] *nm* oxygen ; *(fig)*: **cure d'~** fresh air cure.

oxygéné, e [ɔksiʒene] *a*: **eau ~e** hydrogen peroxide.

ozone [ozɔn] *nm* ozone.

P

pacage [pakaʒ] *nm* grazing, pasture.

pachyderme [paʃidɛʀm(ə)] *nm* pachyderm ; elephant.

pacifier [pasifje] *vt* to pacify.

pacifique [pasifik] *a (personne)* peaceable ; *(intentions, coexistence)* peaceful // *nm*: **le P~, l'océan P~** the Pacific (Ocean).

pacotille [pakɔtij] *nf (péj)* cheap goods *pl* ; **de ~** cheap.

pacte [pakt(ə)] *nm* pact, treaty.

pactiser [paktize] *vi*: **~ avec** to come to terms with.

pagaie [pagɛ] *nf* paddle.

pagaille [pagaj] *nf* mess, shambles *sg*.

pagayer [pageje] *vi* to paddle.

page [paʒ] *nf* page // *nm* page ; **mettre en ~s** to make up (into pages) ; **à la ~** *(fig)* up-to-date.

pagne [paɲ] *nm* loincloth.

pagode [pagɔd] *nf* pagoda.

paie [pɛ] *nf* = **paye**.

paiement [pɛmɑ̃] *nm* = **payement**.

païen, ne [pajɛ̃, -jɛn] *a, nm/f* pagan, heathen.

paillard, e [pajaʀ, -aʀd(ə)] *a* bawdy.

paillasse [pajas] *nf* straw mattress.

paillasson [pajasɔ̃] *nm* doormat.

paille [paj] *nf* straw ; *(défaut)* flaw ; **~ de fer** steel wool.

pailleté, e [pajte] *a* sequined.

paillette [pajɛt] *nf* speck, flake ; **~s** *nfpl (décoratives)* sequins, spangles ; **lessive en ~s** soapflakes *pl*.

pain [pɛ̃] *nm (substance)* bread ; *(unité)* loaf *(pl* loaves) (of bread) ; *(morceau)*: **~ de cire** *etc* bar of wax *etc* ; **~ bis/complet** brown/ wholemeal bread ; **~ d'épice** gingerbread ; **~ grillé** toast ; **~ de mie** sandwich loaf ; **~ de seigle** rye bread ; **~ de sucre** sugar loaf.

pair, e [pɛʀ] *a (nombre)* even // *nm* peer ; **aller de ~ (avec)** to go hand in hand *ou* together (with) ; **au ~** *(FINANCE)* at par ; **jeune fille au ~** au pair girl.

paire [pɛʀ] *nf* pair ; **une ~ de lunettes/tenailles** a pair of glasses/pincers.

paisible [pezibl(ə)] *a* peaceful, quiet.

paître [pɛtʀ(ə)] *vi* to graze.

paix [pɛ] *nf* peace ; *(fig)* peacefulness ; peace ; **faire la ~ avec** to make peace with ; **avoir la ~** to have peace (and quiet).

palabrer [palabʀe] *vi* to argue endlessly.

palace [palas] *nm* luxury hotel.

palais [palɛ] *nm* palace ; *(ANAT)* palate ; **le P~ Bourbon** the National Assembly *buildings* ; **~ des expositions** exhibition hall ; **le P~ de Justice** the Law Courts *pl*.

palan [palɑ̃] *nm* hoist.

pale [pal] *nf (d'hélice, de rame)* blade ; *(de roue)* paddle.

pâle [pɑl] *a* pale ; **bleu ~** pale blue.

paléontologie [paleɔ̃tɔlɔʒi] *nf* paleontology.

Palestine [palɛstin] *nf*: **la ~** Palestine ; **palestinien, ne** *a, nm/f* Palestinian.

palet [palɛ] *nm* disc ; *(HOCKEY)* puck.

paletot [palto] *nm* (short) coat.

palette [palɛt] *nf (de peintre)* palette.

palétuvier [paletyvje] *nm* mangrove.

pâleur [pɑlœʀ] *nf* paleness.

palier [palje] *nm (d'escalier)* landing ; *(fig)* level, plateau ; *(TECH)* bearing ; **nos voisins de ~** our neighbours across the landing ; **en ~** *ad* level ; **par ~s** in stages ; **pallère** *af* landing *cpd*.

pâlir [pɑliʀ] *vi* to turn *ou* go pale ; *(couleur)* to fade.

palissade [palisad] *nf* fence.

palissandre [palisɑ̃dʀ(ə)] *nm* rosewood.

palliatif [paljatif] *nm* palliative ; *(expédient)* stopgap measure.

pallier [palje] *vt*, **~ à** *vt* to offset, make up for.

palmarès [palmaʀɛs] *nm* record of achievements ; *(SCOL)* prize list ; *(SPORT)* list of winners.

palme [palm(ə)] *nf (BOT)* palm leaf *(pl* leaves) ; *(symbole)* palm ; *(en caoutchouc)* flipper ; **~s (académiques)** decoration for services to education ; **palmé, e** *a (pattes)* webbed.

palmeraie [palməʀɛ] *nf* palm grove.

palmier [palmje] *nm* palm tree.

palmipède [palmipɛd] *nm* palmiped, webfooted bird.

palombe [palɔ̃b] *nf* woodpigeon, ringdove.

pâlot, te [pɑlo, -ɔt] *a* pale, peaky.

palourde [paluʀd(ə)] *nf* clam.

palper [palpe] *vt* to feel, finger.

palpitant, e [palpitɑ̃, -ɑ̃t] *a* thrilling.

palpitation [palpitasjɔ̃] *nf* palpitation.

palpiter [palpite] *vi (cœur, pouls)* to beat ; *(: plus fort)* to pound, throb ; *(narines, chair)* to quiver.

paludisme [palydism(ə)] *nm* paludism, malaria.

pâmer [pɑme]: **se ~** *vi* to swoon ; *(fig)*: **se ~ devant** to go into raptures over ; **pâmoison** *nf*: **tomber en pâmoison** to swoon.

pampa [pɑ̃pa] *nf* pampas *pl*.

pamphlet [pɑ̃flɛ] *nm* lampoon, satirical tract.

pamplemousse [pɑ̃pləmus] *nm* grapefruit.

pan [pɑ̃] *nm* section, piece // *excl* bang! ; **~ de chemise** shirt tail.

panacée [panase] *nf* panacea.

panachage [panaʃaʒ] *nm* blend, mix.

panache [panaʃ] *nm* plume ; *(fig)* spirit, panache.

panaché, e [panaʃe] *a*: **œillet ~** variegated carnation ; **glace ~e** mixed-flavour ice cream ; **salade ~e** mixed salad ; **bière ~e** shandy.

panaris [panaʀi] *nm* whitlow.

pancarte [pɑ̃kaʀt(ə)] *nf* sign, notice ; *(dans un défilé)* placard.

pancréas [pɑ̃kʀeɑs] nm pancreas.

pané, e [pane] a fried in breadcrumbs.

panier [panje] nm basket; **mettre au ~** to chuck away; **~ à provisions** shopping basket; **~ à salade** Black Maria, police van; **~-repas** nm packed lunch.

panification [panifikɑsjɔ̃] nf bread-making.

panique [panik] nf, a panic; **paniquer** vi to panic.

panne [pan] nf (d'un mécanisme, moteur) breakdown; **être/tomber en ~** to have broken down/break down; **être en ~ d'essence** ou **sèche** to have run out of petrol; **~ d'électricité** ou **de courant** power ou electrical failure.

panneau, x [pano] nm (écriteau) sign, notice; (de boiserie, de tapisserie etc) panel; **tomber dans le ~** (fig) to walk into the trap; **~ d'affichage** notice board; **~ de signalisation** roadsign; **~-réclame** nm hoarding.

panonceau, x [panɔ̃so] nm sign.

panoplie [panɔpli] nf (jouet) outfit; (d'armes) display; (fig) array.

panorama [panɔʀama] nm panorama; **panoramique** a panoramic; (carrosserie) with panoramic windows.

panse [pɑ̃s] nf paunch.

pansement [pɑ̃smɑ̃] nm dressing, bandage; **~ adhésif** sticking plaster.

panser [pɑ̃se] vt (plaie) to dress, bandage; (bras) to put a dressing on, bandage; (cheval) to groom.

pantalon [pɑ̃talɔ̃] nm (aussi: **~s, paire de ~s**) trousers pl, pair of trousers; **~ de ski** ski pants pl.

pantelant, e [pɑ̃tlɑ̃, -ɑ̃t] a gasping for breath, panting.

panthère [pɑ̃tɛʀ] nf panther.

pantin [pɑ̃tɛ̃] nm jumping jack; (péj) puppet.

pantois [pɑ̃twa] am: **rester ~** to be flabbergasted.

pantomime [pɑ̃tɔmim] nf mime; (pièce) mime show.

pantouflard, e [pɑ̃tuflaʀ, -aʀd(ə)] a (péj) stay-at-home.

pantoufle [pɑ̃tufl(ə)] nf slipper.

panure [panyʀ] nf breadcrumbs pl.

paon [pɑ̃] nm peacock.

papa [papa] nm dad(dy).

papauté [papote] nf papacy.

pape [pap] nm pope.

paperasse [papʀas] nf (péj) bumf q, papers pl; forms pl; **~rie** nf (péj) red tape q; paperwork q.

papeterie [papetʀi] nf (usine) paper mill; (magasin) stationer's (shop).

papetier, ière [paptje, -jɛʀ] nm/f paper-maker; stationer; **~-libraire** nm bookseller and stationer.

papier [papje] nm paper; (article) article; **~s** nmpl (aussi: **~s d'identité**) (identity) papers; **~ couché/glacé** art/glazed paper; **~ (d')aluminium** aluminium foil, tinfoil; **~ d'Arménie** incense paper; **~ bible** India ou bible paper; **~ buvard** blotting paper; **~ calque** tracing paper; **~ carbone** carbon paper; **~ collant** sellotape ®, sticky tape; **~ hygiénique**

toilet paper; **~ journal** newsprint; (pour emballer) newspaper; **~ à lettres** writing paper, notepaper; **~ mâché** papier-mâché; **~ machine** typing paper; **~ peint** wallpaper; **~ pelure** India paper; **~ de soie** tissue paper; **~ de tournesol** litmus paper; **~ de verre** sandpaper.

papille [papij] nf: **~s gustatives** taste buds.

papillon [papijɔ̃] nm butterfly; (fam: contravention) (parking) ticket; (TECH: écrou) wing ou butterfly nut; **~ de nuit** moth.

papillote [papijɔt] nf curlpaper.

papilloter [papijɔte] vi to blink, flicker.

papoter [papɔte] vi to chatter.

paprika [papʀika] nm paprika.

paquebot [pakbo] nm liner.

pâquerette [pɑkʀɛt] nf daisy.

Pâques [pak] nm, nfpl Easter; **faire ses ~** to do one's Easter duties.

paquet [pakɛ] nm packet; (colis) parcel; (fig: tas): **~ de pile** ou **heap of**; **mettre le ~** (fam) to give one's all; **~ de mer** big wave; **paquetage** nm (MIL) kit, pack; **~-cadeau** nm gift-wrapped parcel.

par [paʀ] prép by; **finir** etc **~** to end etc with; **~ amour** out of love; **passer ~ Lyon/la côte** to go via ou through Lyons/along by the coast; **~ la fenêtre** (jeter, regarder) out of the window; **3 ~ jour/personne** 3 a ou per day/head; **2 ~ 2** two at a time; in twos; **~ où?** which way?; **~ ici** this way; (dans le coin) round here; **~-ci, ~-là** here and there.

para [paʀa] nm (abr de **parachutiste**) para.

parabole [paʀabɔl] nf (REL) parable; (GÉOM) parabola; **parabolique** a parabolic.

parachever [paʀaʃve] vt to perfect.

parachute [paʀaʃyt] nm parachute.

parachutiste [paʀaʃytist(ə)] nm/f parachutist; (MIL) paratrooper.

parade [paʀad] nf (spectacle, défilé) parade; (ESCRIME, BOXE) parry; (ostentation): **faire ~ de** to display, show off.

paradis [paʀadi] nm heaven, paradise.

paradoxal, e, aux [paʀadɔksal, -o] a paradoxical.

paradoxe [paʀadɔks(ə)] nm paradox.

parafe [paʀaf] nm, **parafer** vt voir **paraphe, parapher**.

paraffine [paʀafin] nf paraffin; paraffin wax.

parages [paʀaʒ] nmpl: **dans les ~ (de)** in the area ou vicinity (of).

paragraphe [paʀagʀaf] nm paragraph.

paraître [paʀɛtʀ(ə)] vb avec attribut to seem, look, appear // vi to appear; (être visible) to show; (PRESSE, ÉDITION) to be published, come out, appear; (briller) to show off // vb impersonnel: **il paraît que** it seems ou appears that, they say that; **il me paraît que** it seems to me that.

parallèle [paʀalɛl] a parallel; (police, marché) unofficial // nm (comparaison): **faire un ~ entre** to draw a parallel between; (GÉO) parallel // nf parallel (line); **parallélisme** nm parallelism; (AUTO) wheel alignment; **parallélogramme** nm parallelogram.

paralyser [paʀalize] vt to paralyze.
paralysie [paʀalizi] nf paralysis.
paralytique [paʀalitik] a, nm/f paralytic.
paramédical, e, aux [paʀamedikal, -o] a paramedical.
paranoïaque [paʀanɔjak] nm/f paranoiac.
parapet [paʀapɛ] nm parapet.
paraphe [paʀaf] nm flourish; initials pl; signature; **parapher** vt to initial; to sign.
paraphrase [paʀafʀɑz] nf paraphrase.
parapluie [paʀaplɥi] nm umbrella; ~ **pliant** telescopic umbrella.
parasite [paʀazit] nm parasite // a (BOT, BIO) parasitic(al); ~**s** (TÉL) interference sg.
parasol [paʀasɔl] nm parasol, sunshade.
paratonnerre [paʀatɔnɛʀ] nm lightning conductor.
paravent [paʀavɑ̃] nm folding screen.
parc [paʀk] nm (public) park, gardens pl; (de château etc) grounds pl; (pour le bétail) pen, enclosure; (d'enfant) playpen; (MIL: entrepôt) depot; (ensemble d'unités) stock; fleet; ~ **'automobile** (d'un pays) number of cars on the roads; (d'une société) car fleet; ~ **à huîtres** oyster bed; ~ **national** national park; ~ **de stationnement** car park.
parcelle [paʀsɛl] nf fragment, scrap; (de terrain) plot, parcel.
parce que [paʀsk(ə)] cj because.
parchemin [paʀʃəmɛ̃] nm parchment.
parcimonie [paʀsimɔni] nf parsimony, parsimoniousness.
parc(o)mètre [paʀk(ɔ)mɛtʀ(ə)] nm parking meter.
parcourir [paʀkuʀiʀ] vt (trajet, distance) to cover; (article, livre) to skim ou glance through; (lieu) to go all over, travel up and down; (suj: frisson, vibration) to run through; ~ **des yeux** to run one's eye over.
parcours [paʀkuʀ] nm (trajet) journey; (itinéraire) route; (SPORT: de golf etc) course; (: accompli par un concurrent) round; run; lap.
par-delà [paʀdəla] prép beyond.
par-dessous [paʀdəsu] prép, ad under(neath).
pardessus [paʀdəsy] nm overcoat.
par-dessus [paʀdəsy] prép over (the top of) // ad over (the top); ~ **le marché** on top of all that.
par-devant [paʀdəvɑ̃] prép in the presence of, before // ad at the front; round the front.
pardon [paʀdɔ̃] nm forgiveness q // excl sorry; (pour interpeller etc) excuse me; **demander** ~ **à qn (de)** to apologize to sb (for); **je vous demande** ~ I'm sorry; excuse me.
pardonner [paʀdɔne] vt to forgive; ~ **qch à qn** to forgive sb for sth.
paré, e [paʀe] a ready, prepared.
pare-balles [paʀbal] a inv bulletproof.
pare-boue [paʀbu] nm inv mudguard.
pare-brise [paʀbʀiz] nm inv windscreen.
pare-chocs [paʀʃɔk] nm inv bumper.
pareil, le [paʀɛj] a (identique) the same, alike; (similaire) similar; (tel): **un courage/livre** ~ such courage/a book,

courage/a book like this; **de** ~**s livres** such books; **j'en veux un** ~ I'd like one just like it; **rien de** ~ no (ou any) such thing, nothing (ou anything) like it; **ses** ~**s** one's fellow men; one's peers; **ne pas avoir son(sa)** ~**(le)** to be second to none; ~ **à** the same as; similar to; **sans** ~ unparalleled, unequalled; ~**lement** ad the same, alike; in such a way; (également) likewise.
parement [paʀmɑ̃] nm (CONSTR) facing; (REL): ~ **d'autel** antependium.
parent, e [paʀɑ̃, -ɑ̃t] nm/f: **un/une** ~/**e** a relative ou relation // a: **être** ~ **de** to be related to; ~**s** nmpl (père et mère) parents; **parenté** nf (lien) relationship; (personnes) relatives pl, relations pl.
parenthèse [paʀɑ̃tɛz] nf (ponctuation) bracket, parenthesis; (MATH) bracket; (digression) parenthesis, digression; **ouvrir/ fermer la** ~ to open/close the brackets; **entre** ~**s** in brackets; (fig) incidentally.
parer [paʀe] vt to adorn; (CULIN) to dress, trim; (éviter) to ward off; ~ **à** (danger) to ward off; (inconvénient) to deal with; ~ **au plus pressé** to attend to what's most urgent.
pare-soleil [paʀsɔlɛj] nm inv sun visor.
paresse [paʀɛs] nf laziness; **paresser** vi to laze around; **paresseux, euse** a lazy; (fig) slow, sluggish // nm (ZOOL) sloth.
parfaire [paʀfɛʀ] vt to perfect; to complete.
parfait, e [paʀfɛ, -ɛt] a perfect // nm (LING) perfect (tense); (CULIN) parfait // excl fine, excellent; **parfaitement** ad perfectly // excl (most) certainly.
parfois [paʀfwa] ad sometimes.
parfum [paʀfœ̃] nm (produit) perfume, scent; (odeur: de fleur) scent, fragrance; (: de tabac, vin) aroma; (à choisir: de glace, milk-shake) flavour; **parfumé, e** a (fleur, fruit) fragrant; (papier à lettres etc) scented; (femme) wearing perfume ou scent, perfumed; **parfumé au café** coffee-flavoured, flavoured with coffee; **parfumer** vt (suj: odeur, bouquet) to perfume; (mouchoir) to put scent ou perfume on; (crème, gâteau) to flavour; **se parfumer** to put on (some) perfume ou scent; to use perfume ou scent; **parfumerie** nf (commerce) perfumery; (produits) perfumes pl; (boutique) perfume shop.
pari [paʀi] nm bet, wager; (SPORT) bet; **P~ Mutuel urbain (P.M.U.)** (State-controlled) organisation for forecast betting on horse-racing.
paria [paʀja] nm outcast.
parier [paʀje] vt to bet; **parieur** nm (turfiste etc) punter.
Paris [paʀi] n Paris; **parisien, ne** a Parisian; (GÉO, ADMIN) Paris cpd // nm/f: **Parisien, ne** Parisian.
paritaire [paʀitɛʀ] a: **commission** ~ joint commission.
parité [paʀite] nf parity.
parjure [paʀʒyʀ] nm (acte) false oath, perjury; breach of oath, perjury // nm/f perjurer; **se parjurer** to forswear ou perjure o.s

parking [parkiŋ] nm (lieu) car park.

parlant, e [parlã, -ãt] a (fig) graphic, vivid; eloquent; (CINÉMA) talking // ad: **généralement ~** generally speaking.

parlement [parləmã] nm parliament; **parlementaire** a parliamentary // nm/f member of parliament; parliamentarian; negotiator, mediator.

parlementer [parləmãte] vi to negotiate, parley.

parler [parle] nm speech; dialect // vi to speak, talk; (avouer) to talk; **~ (à qn) de** to talk ou speak (to sb) about; **~ pour qn** (intercéder) to speak for sb; **~ le/en français** to speak French/in French; **~ affaires** to talk business; **~ en dormant/du nez** to talk in one's sleep/through one's nose; **sans ~ de** (fig) not to mention, to say nothing of; **tu parles!** you must be joking!

parloir [parlwar] nm (d'une prison, d'un hôpital) visiting room; (REL) parlour.

parmi [parmi] prép among(st).

parodie [parɔdi] nf parody; **parodier** vt (œuvre, auteur) to parody.

paroi [parwa] nf wall; (cloison) partition; **~ rocheuse** rock face.

paroisse [parwas] nf parish; **paroissial, e, aux** a parish cpd; **paroissien, ne** nm/f parishioner // nm prayer book.

parole [parɔl] nf (faculté): **la ~** speech; (mot, promesse) word; **~s** nfpl (MUS) words, lyrics; **tenir ~** to keep one's word; **prendre la ~** to speak; **demander la ~** to ask for permission to speak; **je le crois sur ~** I'll take his word for it.

paroxysme [parɔksism(ə)] nm height, paroxysm.

parpaing [parpɛ̃] nm bond-stone, parpen.

parquer [parke] vt (voiture, matériel) to park; (bestiaux) to pen (in ou up); (prisonniers) to pack in.

parquet [parkɛ] nm (parquet) floor; (JUR): **le ~** the Public Prosecutor's department; **parqueter** vt to lay a parquet floor.

parrain [parɛ̃] nm godfather; (d'un nouvel adhérent) sponsor, proposer; **parrainer** vt (nouvel adhérent) to sponsor, propose; (entreprise) to promote, sponsor.

parricide [parisid] nm, nf parricide.

pars vb voir **partir**.

parsemer [parsəme] vt (suj: feuilles, papiers) to be scattered over; **~ qch de** to scatter sth with.

part [par] nf (qui revient à qn) share; (fraction, partie) part; (FINANCE) (non-voting) share; **prendre ~ à** (débat etc) to take part in; (soucis, douleur de qn) to share in; **faire ~ de qch à qn** to announce sth to sb, inform sb of sth; **pour ma ~** as for me, as far as I'm concerned; **à ~ entière** a full; **de la ~ de** (au nom de) on behalf of; (donné par) from; **de toute(s) ~(s)** from all sides ou quarters; **de ~ et d'autre** on both sides, on either side; **de ~ en ~** right through; **d'une ~ ... d'autre** on the one hand ... on the other hand; **à ~** separately; (de côté) aside // prép apart from, except for // a exceptional, special; **faire la ~ des choses** to make allowances.

partage [partaʒ] nm dividing up; sharing (out) q, share-out; sharing; **recevoir qch en ~** to receive sth as one's share (ou lot); **sans ~** undivided.

partagé, e [partaʒe] a (opinions etc) divided.

partager [partaʒe] vt to share; (distribuer, répartir) to share (out); (morceler, diviser) to divide (up); **se ~** vt (héritage etc) to share between themselves (ou ourselves).

partance [partãs]: **en ~** ad outbound, due to leave; **en ~ pour** (bound) for.

partant [partã] vb voir **partir** // nm (SPORT) starter; (HIPPISME) runner.

partenaire [partənɛr] nm/f partner.

parterre [partɛr] nm (de fleurs) (flower) bed, border; (THÉÂTRE) stalls pl.

parti [parti] nm (POL) party; (décision) course of action; (personne à marier) match; **tirer ~ de** to take advantage of, turn to good account; **prendre le ~ de faire** to make up one's mind to do, resolve to do; **prendre le ~ de qn** to stand up for sb, side with sb; **prendre ~ (pour/contre)** to take sides ou a stand (for/against); **prendre son ~ de** to come to terms with; **~ pris** bias.

partial, e, aux [parsjal, -o] a biased, partial.

participant, e [partisipã, -ãt] nm/f participant; (à un concours) entrant; (d'une société) member.

participation [partisipasjɔ̃] nf participation; sharing; (COMM) interest; **la ~ aux bénéfices** profit-sharing; **la ~ ouvrière** worker participation.

participe [partisip] nm participle; **~ passé/présent** past/present participle.

participer [partisipe]: **~ à** vt (course, réunion) to take part in; (profits etc) to share in; (frais etc) to contribute to; (entreprise: financièrement) to cooperate in; (chagrin, succès de qn) to share (in); **~ de** vt to partake of.

particularisme [partikylarism(ə)] nm sense of identity; specific characteristic.

particularité [partikylarite] nf particularity; (distinctive) characteristic, feature.

particule [partikyl] nf particle; **~ (nobiliaire)** nobiliary particle.

particulier, ière [partikylje, -jɛr] a (personnel, privé) private; (spécial) special, particular; (caractéristique) characteristic, distinctive; (spécifique) particular // nm (individu: ADMIN) private individual; **'~ vend ...'** (COMM) 'for sale privately ...'; **~ à** peculiar to; **en ~** ad (surtout) in particular, particularly; (en privé) in private; **particulièrement** ad particularly.

partie [parti] nf (gén) part; (profession, spécialité) field, subject; (JUR etc: protagonistes) party; (de cartes, tennis etc) game; **une ~ de campagne/de pêche** an outing in the country/a fishing party ou trip; **en ~** ad partly, in part; **faire ~ de** to belong to; (suj: chose) to be part of; **prendre qn à ~** to take sb to task; (malmener) to set on sb; **en grande ~** largely, in the main; **~ civile** (JUR) private *party associating in action with public prosecutor.*

partiel, le [parsjɛl] *a* partial // *nm* (SCOL) class exam.

partir [partiʀ] *vi* (*gén*) to go; (*quitter*) to go, leave; (*s'éloigner*) to go (*ou* drive *etc*) away *ou* off; (*moteur*) to start; (*pétard*) to go off; **~ de** (*lieu: quitter*) to leave; (: *commencer à*) to start from; (*date*) to run *ou* start from; **à ~ de** from.

partisan, e [partizɑ̃, -an] *nm/f* partisan // *a*: **être ~ de qch/faire** to be in favour of sth/doing.

partitif, ive [partitif, -iv] *a*: **article ~** article used in the partitive genitive.

partition [partisjɔ̃] *nf* (MUS) score.

partout [partu] *ad* everywhere; **~ où il allait** everywhere *ou* wherever he went; **trente ~** (TENNIS) thirty all.

paru, e *pp* de **paraître**.

parure [paryʀ] *nf* (*toilette, bijoux*) finery *q*; jewellery *q*; (*assortiment*) set.

parution [parysjɔ̃] *nf* publication, appearance.

parvenir [parvəniʀ]: **~ à** *vt* (*atteindre*) to reach; (*réussir*): **~ à faire** to manage to do, succeed in doing; **faire ~ qch à qn** to have sth sent to sb.

parvenu, e [parvəny] *nm/f* (*péj*) parvenu, upstart.

parvis [parvi] *nm* square (*in front of a church*).

pas [pɑ] *nm voir le mot suivant* // *ad* not; **~ de** no; **ne ... ~**: **il ne le voit ~/ne l'a ~ vu/ne le verra ~** he doesn't see it/hasn't seen it *ou* didn't see it/won't see it; **ils n'ont ~ de voiture/d'enfants** they haven't got a car/any children, they have no car/children; **il m'a dit de ne ~ le faire** he told me not to do it; **il n'est ~ plus grand** he isn't bigger, he's no bigger; **... lui ~ ou** lui he doesn't (*ou* isn't *etc*); **non ~ que ...** not that ...; **une pomme ~ mûre** an apple which isn't ripe; **~ du tout** not at all; **~ plus tard qu'hier** only yesterday; **~ mal** a not bad, quite good (*ou* pretty *ou* nice) // *ad* quite well; (*beaucoup*) quite a lot; **~ mal de** quite a lot of.

pas [pɑ] *ad voir le mot précédent* // *nm* (*allure, mesure*) pace; (*démarche*) tread; (*enjambée, DANSE*) step; (*bruit*) (foot)step; (*trace*) footprint; (*TECH: de vis, d'écrou*) thread; **~ à ~** step by step; **au ~** at walking pace; **mettre qn au ~** to bring sb to heel; **au ~ de gymnastique/de course** at a jog trot/at a run; **à ~ de loup** stealthily; **faire les cent ~** to pace up and down; **faire les premiers ~** to make the first move; **sur le ~ de la porte** on the doorstep; **le ~ de Calais** (*détroit*) the Straits of Dover; **~ de porte** (COMM) key money.

pascal, e, aux [paskal, -o] *a* Easter *cpd*.

passable [pɑsabl(ə)] *a* (*travail*) passable, tolerable.

passage [pɑsaʒ] *nm* (*fait de passer*) *voir* **passer**; (*lieu, prix de la traversée, extrait de livre etc*) passage; (*chemin*) way; **de ~** (*touristes*) passing through; (*amants etc*) casual; **~ clouté** pedestrian crossing; **'~ interdit'** 'no entry'; **~ à niveau** level

crossing; **'~ protégé'** right of way over secondary road(s) on your right; **~ souterrain** subway, underground passage; **~ à tabac** beating-up.

passager, ère [pɑsaʒe, -ɛʀ] *a* a passing // *nm/f* passenger; **~ clandestin** stowaway.

passant, e [pɑsɑ̃, -ɑ̃t] *a* (*rue, endroit*) busy // *nm/f* passer-by // *nm* (*pour ceinture etc*) loop.

passe [pɑs] *nf* (SPORT, *magnétique*, NAVIG) pass // *nm* (*passe-partout*) master *ou* skeleton key; **être en ~ de faire** to be on the way to doing.

passé, e [pɑse] *a* (*événement, temps*) past; (*couleur, tapisserie*) faded // *prép* after // *nm* past; (LING) past (tense); **il est ~ midi** *ou* **midi ~** it's gone twelve; **~ de mode** out of fashion; **~ composé** perfect (tense); **~ simple** past historic.

passe-droit [pɑsdʀwa] *nm* special privilege.

passéiste [pɑseist] *a* a backward-looking.

passementerie [pɑsmɑ̃tʀi] *nf* trimmings *pl*.

passe-montagne [pɑsmɔ̃taɲ] *nm* balaclava.

passe-partout [pɑspartu] *nm inv* master *ou* skeleton key // *a inv* all-purpose.

passe-passe [pɑspɑs] *nm*: **tour de ~** trick, sleight of hand *q*.

passe-plats [pɑspla] *nm inv* serving hatch.

passeport [pɑspɔʀ] *nm* passport.

passer [pɑse] *vi* (*se rendre, aller*) to go; (*voiture, piétons: défiler*) to pass (by), go by; (*faire une halte rapide: facteur, laitier etc*) to come, call; (: *pour rendre visite*) to call *ou* drop in; (*courant, air, lumière, franchir un obstacle etc*) to get through; (*accusé, projet de loi*): **~ devant** to come before; (*film, émission*) to be on; (*temps, jours*) to pass, go by; (*couleur, papier*) to fade; (*douleur*) to pass, go away; (CARTES) to pass; (SCOL) to go up (to the next class) // *vt* (*frontière, rivière etc*) to cross; (*douane*) to go through; (*examen*) to sit, take; (*visite médicale etc*) to have; (*journée, temps*) to spend; (*donner*): **~ qch à qn** to pass sth to sb; to give sb sth; (*transmettre*): **~ qch à qn** to pass sth on to sb; (*enfiler: vêtement*) to slip on; (*faire entrer, mettre*): **(faire) ~ qch dans/par** to get sth into/through; (*café*) to pour the water on; (*thé, soupe*) to strain; (*film, pièce*) to show, put on; (*disque*) to play, put on; (*marché, accord*) to agree on; (*tolérer*): **~ qch à qn** to let sb get away with sth; **se ~** *vi* (*avoir lieu: scène, action*) to take place; (*se dérouler: entretien etc*) to go; (*arriver*): **que s'est-il passé?** what happened?; (*s'écouler: semaine etc*) to pass, go by; **se ~ de** *vt* to go *ou* do without; **se ~ les mains sous l'eau/de l'eau sur le visage** to put one's hands under the tap/run water over one's face; **~ par** to go through; **passe devant/par ici** go in front/this way; **~ sur** *vt* (*faute, détail inutile*) to pass over; **~ avant qch/qn** (*fig*) to come before sth/sb; **laisser ~** (*air, lumière, personne*) to let through; (*occasion*) to let slip, miss; (*erreur*) to overlook; **~ à la radio/fouille** to be

X-rayed/searched ; ~ **à la radio/télévision** to be on the radio/on television ; ~ **pour riche** to be taken for a rich man ; **il passait pour avoir** he was said to have ; ~ **à l'opposition** to go over to the opposition ; **passons!** let's say no more (about it) ; ~ **en seconde,** ~ **la seconde** (AUTO) to change into second ; ~ **qch en fraude** to smuggle sth in (ou out) ; ~ **la main par la portière** to stick one's hand out of the door ; ~ **le balai/l'aspirateur** to sweep up/hoover ; **je vous passe M. X** (je vous mets en communication avec lui) I'm putting you through to Mr X ; (je lui passe l'appareil) here is Mr X, I'll hand you over to Mr X.

passerelle [pɑsʀɛl] nf footbridge ; (de navire, avion) gangway.

passe-temps [pɑstɑ̃] nm inv pastime.

passeur, euse [pɑsœʀ, -øz] nm/f smuggler.

passible [pasibl(ə)] a: ~ **de** liable to.

passif, ive [pasif, -iv] a passive // nm (LING) passive ; (COMM) liabilities pl.

passion [pɑsjɔ̃] nf passion ; **avoir la ~ de** to have a passion for ; **passionné, e** a passionate ; impassioned ; **passionnel, le** a of passion ; **passionner** vt (personne) to fascinate, grip ; **se passionner pour** to take an avid interest in ; to have a passion for.

passoire [pɑswaʀ] nf sieve ; (à légumes) colander ; (à thé) strainer.

pastel [pastɛl] nm, a inv (ART) pastel.

pastèque [pastɛk] nf watermelon.

pasteur [pastœʀ] nm (protestant) minister, pastor.

pasteuriser [pastœʀize] vt to pasteurize.

pastiche [pastiʃ] nf pastiche.

pastille [pastij] nf (à sucer) lozenge, pastille ; (de papier etc) (small) disc ; ~**s pour la toux** throat lozenges.

pastis [pastis] nm pastis.

patate [patat] nf spud ; ~ **douce** sweet potato.

patauger [patoʒe] vi (pour s'amuser) to splash about ; (avec effort) to wade about ; ~ **dans** (en marchant) to wade through.

pâte [pɑt] nf (à tarte) pastry ; (à pain) dough ; (à frire) batter ; (substance molle) paste ; cream ; ~**s** nfpl (macaroni etc) pasta sg ; **fromage à ~ dure/molle** hard/soft cheese ; ~ **d'amandes** almond paste ; ~ **brisée** shortcrust pastry ; ~ **de fruits** crystallized fruit q ; ~ **à modeler** modelling clay, Plasticine ® ; ~ **à papier** paper pulp.

pâté [pɑte] nm (charcuterie) pâté ; (tache) ink blot ; (de sable) sandcastle, sandpie ; ~ **en croûte** ≈ pork pie ; ~ **de maisons** block (of houses).

pâtée [pɑte] nf mash, feed.

patente [patɑ̃t] nf (COMM) trading licence.

patère [pateʀ] nf (coat-)peg.

paternel, le [patɛʀnɛl] a (amour, soins) fatherly ; (ligne, autorité) paternal.

paternité [patɛʀnite] nf paternity, fatherhood.

pâteux, euse [pɑtø, -øz] a thick ; pasty.

pathétique [patetik] a moving, pathetic.

pathologie [patɔlɔʒi] nf pathology.

patibulaire [patibylɛʀ] a sinister.

patience [pasjɑ̃s] nf patience.

patient, e [pasjɑ̃, -ɑ̃t] a, nm/f patient.

patienter [pasjɑ̃te] vi to wait.

patin [patɛ̃] nm skate ; (sport) skating ; (de traineau, luge) runner ; (pièce de tissu) cloth pad (used as slippers to protect polished floor) ; ~**s (à glace)** (ice) skates ; ~**s à roulettes** roller skates.

patinage [patinaʒ] nm skating ; ~ **artistique/de vitesse** figure/speed skating.

patine [patin] nf sheen.

patiner [patine] vi to skate ; (embrayage) to slip ; (roue, voiture) to spin ; **se ~** vi (meuble, cuir) to acquire a sheen, become polished ; **patineur, euse** nm/f skater ; **patinoire** nf skating rink, (ice) rink.

pâtir [pɑtiʀ]: ~ **de** vt to suffer because of.

pâtisserie [pɑtisʀi] nf (boutique) cake shop ; (métier) confectionery ; (à la maison) pastry- ou cake-making, baking ; ~**s** nfpl (gâteaux) pastries, cakes ; **pâtissier, ière** nm/f pastrycook ; confectioner.

patois [patwa] nm dialect, patois.

patriarche [patʀijaʀʃ(ə)] nm patriarch.

patrie [patʀi] nf homeland.

patrimoine [patʀimwan] nm inheritance, patrimony.

patriote [patʀijɔt] a patriotic // nm/f patriot ; **patriotique** a patriotic.

patron, ne [patʀɔ̃, -ɔn] nm/f (chef) boss, manager/eress ; (propriétaire) owner, proprietor/tress ; (employeur) employer ; (MED) ≈ senior consultant ; (REL) patron saint // nm (COUTURE) pattern ; ~ **de thèse** supervisor (of postgraduate thesis) ; **patronal, e, aux** a (syndicat, intérêts) employers'.

patronage [patʀɔnaʒ] nm patronage ; (paroisse) youth club.

patronat [patʀɔna] nm employers pl.

patronner [patʀɔne] vt to sponsor, support.

patrouille [patʀuj] nf patrol ; **patrouiller** vi to patrol, be on patrol.

patte [pat] nf (jambe) leg ; (pied: de chien, chat) paw ; (: d'oiseau) foot ; (languette) strap ; (: de poche) flap ; **à ~s d'éléphant** a bell-bottomed ; ~**s d'oie** (fig) crow's feet.

pattemouille [patmuj] nf damp cloth (for ironing).

pâturage [pɑtyʀaʒ] nm pasture.

pâture [pɑtyʀ] nf food.

paume [pom] nf palm.

paumer [pome] vt (fam) to lose.

paupière [popjɛʀ] nf eyelid.

paupiette [popjɛt] nf: ~**s de veau** veal olives.

pause [poz] nf (arrêt) break ; (en parlant, MUS) pause.

pauvre [povʀ(ə)] a poor // nm/f poor man/woman ; **les ~s** the poor ; ~ **en calcium** with a low calcium content ; ~**té** nf (état) poverty.

pavaner [pavane]: **se ~** vi to strut about.

pavé, e [pave] a paved ; cobbled // nm (bloc) paving stone ; cobblestone ; (pavage) paving.

pavillon [pavijɔ̃] nm (de banlieue) small (detached) house; (kiosque) lodge; pavilion; (d'hôpital) ward; (MUS: de cor etc) bell; (ANAT: de l'oreille) pavilion, pinna; (drapeau) flag; ~ **de complaisance** flag of convenience.

pavoiser [pavwaze] vt to deck with flags // vi to put out flags; (fig) to rejoice, exult.

pavot [pavo] nm poppy.

payant, e [pɛjɑ̃, -ɑ̃t] a (spectateurs etc) paying; (fig: entreprise) profitable; **c'est** ~ you have to pay, there is a charge.

paye [pɛj] nf pay, wages pl.

payement [pɛjmɑ̃] nm payment.

payer [peje] vt (créancier, employé, loyer) to pay; (achat, réparations, fig: faute) to pay for // vi to pay; (métier) to be well-paid; (tactique etc) to pay off; **il me l'a fait ~ 10 F** he charged me 10 F for it; ~ **qch à qn** to buy sth for sb, buy sb sth; **ils nous ont payé le voyage** they paid for our trip; ~ **de sa personne** to give of o.s.; ~ **d'audace** to act with great daring; **cela ne paie pas de mine** it doesn't look much; **se ~ la tête de qn** to take the mickey out of sb; to take sb for a ride.

pays [pei] nm country; land; region; village; **du ~** a local.

paysage [peizaʒ] nm landscape; **paysagiste** nm/f landscape gardener; landscape painter.

paysan, ne [peizɑ̃, -an] nm/f countryman/woman; farmer; (péj) peasant // a country cpd; farming, farmers'.

Pays-Bas [peiba] nmpl: **les** ~ the Netherlands.

P.C.V. sigle voir **communication**.

P.D.G. sigle m voir **président**.

péage [peaʒ] nm toll; (endroit) tollgate; **pont à** ~ toll bridge.

peau, x [po] nf skin; **gants de** ~ fine leather gloves; ~ **de chamois** (chiffon) chamois leather, shammy; **P~-Rouge** nm/f Red Indian, redskin.

peccadille [pekadij] nf trifle; peccadillo.

pêche [pɛʃ] nf (sport, activité) fishing; (poissons pêchés) catch; (fruit) peach; ~ **à la ligne** (en rivière) angling.

péché [peʃe] nm sin; ~ **mignon** weakness.

pêche-abricot [pɛʃabriko] nf yellow peach.

pécher [peʃe] vi (REL) to sin; (fig) to err; to be flawed.

pêcher [peʃe] nm peach tree // vi to go fishing; (en rivière) to go angling // vt to catch, land; to fish for; ~ **au chalut** to trawl.

pêcheur, eresse [peʃœr, peʃrɛs] nm/f sinner.

pêcheur [pɛʃœr] nm fisherman; angler; ~ **de perles** pearl diver.

pectoraux [pɛktɔro] nmpl pectoral muscles.

pécule [pekyl] nm savings pl, nest egg; (d'un détenu) earnings pl (paid on release).

pécuniaire [pekynjɛr] a financial.

pédagogie [pedagɔʒi] nf educational methods pl, pedagogy; **pédagogique** a educational; **formation pédagogique**

teacher training; **pédagogue** nm/f teacher; educationalist.

pédale [pedal] nf pedal; **pédaler** vi to pedal; **pédalier** nm pedal and gear mechanism.

pédalo [pedalo] nm pedalo, pedal-boat.

pédant, e [pedɑ̃, -ɑ̃t] a (péj) pedantic.

pédéraste [pederast(ə)] nm homosexual, pederast.

pédestre [pedɛstr(ə)] a: **tourisme** ~ hiking.

pédiatre [pedjatr(ə)] nm/f paediatrician, child specialist.

pédiatrie [pedjatri] nf paediatrics sg.

pédicure [pedikyr] nm/f chiropodist.

pègre [pɛgr(ə)] nf underworld.

peignais etc vb voir **peindre**.

peigne [pɛɲ] nm comb.

peigné, e [peɲe] a: **laine** ~**e** wool worsted; combed wool.

peigner [peɲe] vt to comb (the hair of); **se** ~ to comb one's hair.

peignis etc vb voir **peindre**.

peignoir [peɲwar] nm dressing gown; ~ **de bain** bathrobe.

peindre [pɛ̃dr(ə)] vt to paint; (fig) to portray, depict.

peine [pɛn] nf (affliction) sorrow, sadness q; (mal, effort) trouble q, effort; (difficulté) difficulty; (punition, châtiment) punishment; (JUR) sentence; **faire de la** ~ **à qn** to distress ou upset sb; **prendre la** ~ **de faire** to go to the trouble of doing; **se donner de la** ~ to make an effort; **ce n'est pas la** ~ **de faire** there's no point in doing, it's not worth doing; **avoir de la** ~ **à faire** to have difficulty doing; **à** ~ ad scarcely, hardly, barely; **à** ~ ... **que** hardly ... than; **sous** ~: **sous** ~ **d'être puni** for fear of being punished; **défense d'afficher sous** ~ **d'amende** billposters will be fined; **peiner** vi to work hard; to struggle; (moteur, voiture) to labour // vt to grieve, sadden.

peintre [pɛ̃tr(ə)] nm painter; ~ **en bâtiment** house painter, painter and decorator; ~ **d'enseignes** signwriter.

peinture [pɛ̃tyr] nf painting; (couche de couleur, couleur) paint; (surfaces peintes: aussi: ~**s**) paintwork; ~ **mate/brillante** matt/gloss paint; '~ **fraîche**' 'wet paint'.

péjoratif, ive [peʒɔratif, -iv] a pejorative, derogatory.

pelage [pəlaʒ] nm coat, fur.

pêle-mêle [pɛlmɛl] ad higgledy-piggledy.

peler [pəle] vt, vi to peel.

pèlerin [pɛlrɛ̃] nm pilgrim; **pèlerinage** nm pilgrimage; place of pilgrimage, shrine.

pélican [pelikɑ̃] nm pelican.

pelle [pɛl] nf shovel; (d'enfant, de terrassier) spade; ~ **à gâteau** cake slice; ~ **mécanique** mechanical digger; ~**ter** vt to shovel (up).

pelletier [pɛltje] nm furrier.

pellicule [pelikyl] nf film; ~**s** nfpl (MÉD) dandruff sg.

pelote [pəlɔt] nf (de fil, laine) ball; (d'épingles) pin cushion; ~ **basque** pelota.

peloter [pəlɔte] vt (fam) to feel (up); **se** ~ to pet.

peloton [pəlɔtɔ̃] *nm* group, squad; (*CYCLISME*) pack; ~ **d'exécution** firing squad.

pelotonner [pəlɔtɔne]: **se** ~ *vi* to curl (o.s.) up.

pelouse [pəluz] *nf* lawn.

peluche [pəlyʃ] *nf*: **animal en** ~ fluffy animal, soft toy; **pelucher** *vi* to become fluffy, fluff up.

pelure [pəlyʀ] *nf* peeling, peel *q*; ~ **d'oignon** onion skin.

pénal, e, aux [penal, -o] *a* penal.

pénaliser [penalize] *vt* to penalize.

pénalité [penalite] *nf* penalty.

penalty, ies [penalti, -z] *nm* (*SPORT*) penalty (kick).

penaud, e [pəno, -od] *a* sheepish, contrite.

penchant [pɑ̃ʃɑ̃] *nm* tendency, propensity; liking, fondness.

penché, e [pɑ̃ʃe] *a* slanting.

pencher [pɑ̃ʃe] *vi* to tilt, lean over // *vt* to tilt; **se** ~ *vi* to lean over; (*se baisser*) to bend down; **se** ~ **sur** to bend over; (*fig: problème*) to look into; **se** ~ **au dehors** to lean out; ~ **pour** to be inclined to favour.

pendaison [pɑ̃dɛzɔ̃] *nf* hanging.

pendant, e [pɑ̃dɑ̃, -ɑ̃t] *a* hanging (out); (*ADMIN, JUR*) pending // *nm* counterpart; matching piece // *prép* during; **faire** ~ **à** to match; to be the counterpart of; ~**s d'oreilles** drop *ou* pendant earrings.

pendeloque [pɑ̃dlɔk] *nf* pendant.

pendentif [pɑ̃dɑ̃tif] *nm* pendant.

penderie [pɑ̃dʀi] *nf* wardrobe; (*placard*) walk-in cupboard.

pendre [pɑ̃dʀ(ə)] *vt, vi* to hang; **se** ~ **(à)** (*se suicider*) to hang o.s. (on); **se** ~ **à** (*se suspendre*) to hang from; ~ **à** to hang (down) from; ~ **qch à** (*mur*) to hang sth (up) on; (*plafond*) to hang sth (up) from.

pendule [pɑ̃dyl] *nf* clock // *nm* pendulum.

pendulette [pɑ̃dylɛt] *nf* small clock.

pêne [pɛn] *nm* bolt.

pénétrer [penetʀe] *vi* to come *ou* get in // *vt* to penetrate; ~ **dans** to enter; (*suj: projectile*) to penetrate; (: *air, eau*) to come into, get into; **se** ~ **de qch** to get sth firmly set in one's mind.

pénible [penibl(ə)] *a* (*astreignant*) hard; (*affligeant*) painful; (*personne, caractère*) tiresome; ~**ment** *ad* with difficulty.

péniche [peniʃ] *nf* barge; ~ **de débarquement** landing craft *inv*.

pénicilline [penisilin] *nf* penicillin.

péninsule [penɛ̃syl] *nf* peninsula.

pénis [penis] *nm* penis.

pénitence [penitɑ̃s] *nf* (*repentir*) penitence; (*peine*) penance.

pénitencier [penitɑ̃sje] *nm* penitentiary.

pénombre [penɔ̃bʀ(ə)] *nf* half-light, darkness.

pense-bête [pɑ̃sbɛt] *nm* aide-mémoire.

pensée [pɑ̃se] *nf* thought; (*démarche, doctrine*) thinking *q*; (*BOT*) pansy; **en** ~ in one's mind.

penser [pɑ̃se] *vi* to think // *vt* to think; (*concevoir: problème, machine*) to think out; ~ **à** to think of; (*songer à: ami, vacances*) to think of *ou* about; (*réfléchir à: problème, offre*) ~ **à qch** to think about

sth *ou* sth over; ~ **à faire qch** to think of doing sth; ~ **faire qch** to be thinking of doing sth, intend to do sth; **penseur** *nm* thinker; **pensif, ive** *a* pensive, thoughtful.

pension [pɑ̃sjɔ̃] *nf* (*allocation*) pension; (*prix du logement*) board and lodgings, bed and board; (*maison particulière*) boarding house; (*hôtel*) guesthouse, hotel; (*école*) boarding school; **prendre** ~ **chez** to take board and lodging at; **prendre qn en** ~ to take sb (in) as a lodger; **mettre en** ~ to send to boarding school; ~ **alimentaire** (*d'étudiant*) living allowance; (*de divorcée*) maintenance allowance; alimony; ~ **complète** full board; ~ **de famille** boarding house, guesthouse; **pensionnaire** *nm/f* boarder; guest; **pensionnat** *nm* boarding school.

pentagone [pɛ̃tagɔn] *nm* pentagon.

pente [pɑ̃t] *nf* slope; **en** ~ a sloping.

Pentecôte [pɑ̃tkot] *nf*: **la** ~ Whitsun; (*dimanche*) Whitsunday; **lundi de** ~ Whit Monday.

pénurie [penyʀi] *nf* shortage.

pépier [pepje] *vi* to chirp, tweet.

pépin [pepɛ̃] *nm* (*BOT: graine*) pip; (*ennui*) snag, hitch; (*fam*) brolly.

pépinière [pepinjɛʀ] *nf* tree nursery; (*fig*) nest, breeding-ground.

pépite [pepit] *nf* nugget.

perçant, e [pɛʀsɑ̃, -ɑ̃t] *a* sharp, keen; piercing, shrill.

percée [pɛʀse] *nf* (*trouée*) opening; (*MIL*) breakthrough; (*SPORT*) break.

perce-neige [pɛʀsanɛʒ] *nf inv* snowdrop.

percepteur [pɛʀsɛptœʀ] *nm* tax collector.

perceptible [pɛʀsɛptibl(ə)] *a* perceptible.

perception [pɛʀsɛpsjɔ̃] *nf* perception; (*d'impôts etc*) collection.

percer [pɛʀse] *vt* to pierce; (*ouverture etc*) to make; (*mystère, énigme*) to penetrate // *vi* to come through; to break through; ~ **une dent** to cut a tooth.

perceuse [pɛʀsøz] *nf* drill.

percevoir [pɛʀsəvwaʀ] *vt* (*distinguer*) to perceive, detect; (*taxe, impôt*) to collect; (*revenu, indemnité*) to receive.

perche [pɛʀʃ(ə)] *nf* (*ZOOL*) perch; (*bâton*) pole.

percher [pɛʀʃe] *vt*: ~ **qch sur** to perch sth on // *vi*, **se** ~ *vi* (*oiseau*) to perch; **perchoir** *nm* perch.

perclus, e [pɛʀkly, -yz] *a*: ~ **de** (*rhumatismes*) crippled with.

perçois *etc vb voir* **percevoir.**

percolateur [pɛʀkɔlatœʀ] *nm* percolator.

perçu, e *pp de* **percevoir.**

percussion [pɛʀkysjɔ̃] *nf* percussion.

percuter [pɛʀkyte] *vt* to strike; (*suj: véhicule*) to crash into.

perdant, e [pɛʀdɑ̃, -ɑ̃t] *nm/f* loser.

perdition [pɛʀdisjɔ̃] *nf*: **en** ~ (*NAVIG*) in distress; **lieu de** ~ den of vice.

perdre [pɛʀdʀ(ə)] *vt* to lose; (*gaspiller: temps, argent*) to waste; (*personne: moralement etc*) to ruin // *vi* to lose; (*sur une vente etc*) to lose out; (*récipient*) to leak; **se** ~ *vi* (*s'égarer*) to get lost, lose one's way; (*fig*) to go to waste; to disappear, vanish.

perdreau, x [pɛʀdʀo] *nm* (young) partridge.

perdrix [pɛʀdʀi] *nf* partridge.

perdu, e [pɛʀdy] *pp de* **perdre** // *a* (*isolé*) out-of-the-way, godforsaken; (*COMM*: *emballage*) non-returnable; (*malade*): **il est ~** there's no hope left for him; **à vos moments ~s** in your spare time.

père [pɛʀ] *nm* father; **~s** *nmpl* (*ancêtres*) forefathers; **de ~ en fils** from father to son; **~ de famille** man with a family; family man; **le ~ Noël** Father Christmas.

péremptoire [peʀãptwaʀ] *a* peremptory.

perfection [pɛʀfɛksjɔ̃] *nf* perfection.

perfectionné, e [pɛʀfɛksjɔne] *a* sophisticated.

perfectionnement [pɛʀfɛksjɔnmã] *nm* improvement.

perfectionner [pɛʀfɛksjɔne] *vt* to improve, perfect; **se ~ en anglais** to improve one's English.

perfide [pɛʀfid] *a* perfidious, treacherous.

perforant, e [pɛʀfɔʀã, -ãt] *a* (*balle*) armour-piercing.

perforateur, trice [pɛʀfɔʀatœʀ, -tʀis] *nm/f* punch-card operator // *nm* (*perceuse*) borer; drill // *nf* (*perceuse*) borer; drill; (*pour cartes*) card-punch; (*de bureau*) punch.

perforation [pɛʀfɔʀasjɔ̃] *nf* perforation; punching; (*trou*) hole.

perforatrice [pɛʀfɔʀatʀis] *nf voir* **perforateur.**

perforer [pɛʀfɔʀe] *vt* to perforate; to punch a hole (*ou* holes) in; (*ticket, bande, carte*) to punch.

performance [pɛʀfɔʀmãs] *nf* performance.

perfusion [pɛʀfyzjɔ̃] *nf* perfusion; **faire une ~ à qn** to put sb on a drip.

péricliter [peʀiklite] *vi* to go downhill.

péril [peʀil] *nm* peril; **périlleux, euse** [-jø, -øz] *a* perilous.

périmé, e [peʀime] *a* (out)dated; (*ADMIN*) out-of-date, expired.

périmètre [peʀimɛtʀ(ə)] *nm* perimeter.

période [peʀjɔd] *nf* period; **périodique** *a* (*phases*) periodic; (*publication*) periodical; (*MATH*: *fraction*) recurring // *nm* periodical; **garniture** *ou* **serviette périodique** sanitary towel.

péripéties [peʀipesi] *nfpl* events, episodes.

périphérie [peʀifeʀi] *nf* periphery; (*d'une ville*) outskirts *pl*; **périphérique** *a* (*quartiers*) outlying; (*ANAT, TECH*) peripheral; (*station de radio*) operating from outside France // *nm* (*AUTO*) ring road.

périphrase [peʀifʀaz] *nf* circumlocution.

périple [peʀipl(ə)] *nm* journey.

périr [peʀiʀ] *vi* to die, perish.

périscope [peʀiskɔp] *nm* periscope.

périssable [peʀisabl(ə)] *a* perishable.

péritonite [peʀitɔnit] *nf* peritonitis.

perle [pɛʀl(ə)] *nf* pearl; (*de plastique, métal, sueur*) bead.

perlé, e [pɛʀle] *a*: **grève ~e** go-slow.

perler [pɛʀle] *vi* to form in droplets.

perlier, ière [pɛʀlje, -jɛʀ] *a* pearl *cpd*.

permanence [pɛʀmanãs] *nf* permanence; (*local*) (duty) office; **strike**

headquarters; emergency service; **assurer une ~** (*service public, bureaux*) to operate *ou* maintain a basic service; **être de ~** to be on call *ou* duty; **en ~** *ad* permanently; continuously.

permanent, e [pɛʀmanã, -ãt] *a* permanent; (*spectacle*) continuous // *nf* perm, permanent wave.

perméable [pɛʀmeabl(ə)] *a* (*terrain*) permeable; **~ à** (*fig*) receptive *ou* open to.

permettre [pɛʀmɛtʀ(ə)] *vt* to allow, permit; **~ à qn de faire/qch** to allow sb to do/sth.

permis [pɛʀmi] *nm* permit, licence; **~ de chasse** hunting permit; **~ (de conduire)** (driving) licence; **~ de construire** planning permission; **~ d'inhumer** burial certificate; **~ poids lourds** HGV (driving) licence; **~ de séjour** residence permit.

permission [pɛʀmisjɔ̃] *nf* permission; (*MIL*) leave; (: *papier*) pass; **en ~** on leave; **avoir la ~ de faire** to have permission to do, be allowed to do; **permissionnaire** *nm* soldier on leave.

permuter [pɛʀmyte] *vt* to change around, permutate // *vi* to change, swap.

pernicieux, euse [pɛʀnisjø, -øz] *a* pernicious.

pérorer [peʀɔʀe] *vi* to hold forth.

perpendiculaire [pɛʀpãdikylɛʀ] *a, nf* perpendicular.

perpétrer [pɛʀpetʀe] *vt* to perpetrate.

perpétuel, le [pɛʀpetɥɛl] *a* perpetual; (*ADMIN etc*) permanent; for life.

perpétuer [pɛʀpetɥe] *vt* to perpetuate.

perpétuité [pɛʀpetɥite] *nf*: **à ~** *a, ad* for life; **être condamné à ~** to be sentenced to life imprisonment, receive a life sentence.

perplexe [pɛʀplɛks(ə)] *a* perplexed, puzzled.

perquisition [pɛʀkizisjɔ̃] *nf* (police) search; **perquisitionner** *vi* to carry out a search.

perron [pɛʀɔ̃] *nm* steps *pl* (in front of mansion *etc*).

perroquet [pɛʀɔkɛ] *nm* parrot.

perruche [peʀyʃ] *nf* budgerigar, budgie.

perruque [peʀyk] *nf* wig.

persan, e [pɛʀsã, -an] *a* Persian.

persécuter [pɛʀsekyte] *vt* to persecute; **persécution** *nf* persecution.

persévérant, e [pɛʀseveʀã, -ãt] *a* persevering.

persévérer [pɛʀseveʀe] *vi* to persevere.

persiennes [pɛʀsjɛn] *nfpl* (metal) shutters.

persiflage [pɛʀsiflaʒ] *nm* mockery *q*.

persil [pɛʀsi] *nm* parsley.

Persique [pɛʀsik] *a*: **le golfe ~** the (Persian) Gulf.

persistant, e [pɛʀsistã, -ãt] *a* persistent; (*feuilles*) evergreen; **à feuillage ~** evergreen.

persister [pɛʀsiste] *vi* to persist; **~ à faire qch** to persist in doing sth.

personnage [pɛʀsɔnaʒ] *nm* (*notable*) personality; figure; (*individu*) character, individual; (*THÉÂTRE*) character; (*PEINTURE*) figure.

personnaliser [pɛrsɔnalize] *vt* to personalize.

personnalité [pɛrsɔnalite] *nf* personality.

personne [pɛrsɔn] *nf* person // *pronom* nobody, no one ; (*quelqu'un*) anybody, anyone ; ~s people *pl*; **il n'y a** ~ there's nobody in, there isn't anybody in ; **10 F par** ~ 10 F per person *ou* a head ; ~ **âgée** elderly person ; **personnel, le** *a* personal // *nm* staff ; personnel ; **personnellement** *ad* personally ; **personnifier** *vt* to personify ; to typify.

perspective [pɛrspɛktiv] *nf* (*ART*) perspective ; (*vue, coup d'œil*) view ; (*point de vue*) viewpoint, angle ; (*chose escomptée, envisagée*) prospect ; **en** ~ in prospect ; in the offing.

perspicace [pɛrspikas] *a* clear-sighted, gifted with (*ou* showing) insight.

persuader [pɛrsɥade] *vt*: ~ **qn (de/de faire)** to persuade sb (of/to do) ; **persuasif, ive** *a* persuasive ; **persuasion** *nf* persuasion.

perte [pɛrt(ə)] *nf* loss ; (*de temps*) waste ; (*fig: morale*) ruin ; **à** ~ (*COMM*) at a loss ; **à** ~ **de vue** as far as the eye can (*ou* could) see ; (*fig*) interminably ; ~ **sèche** dead loss ; ~ **s blanches** (vaginal) discharge *sg*.

pertinent, e [pɛrtinɑ̃, -ɑ̃t] *a* apt, pertinent ; discerning, judicious.

perturbation [pɛrtyrbasjɔ̃] *nf* disruption ; perturbation ; ~ **(atmosphérique)** atmospheric disturbance.

perturber [pɛrtyrbe] *vt* to disrupt ; (*PSYCH*) to perturb, disturb.

pervenche [pɛrvɑ̃ʃ] *nf* periwinkle.

pervers, e [pɛrvɛr, -ɛrs(ə)] *a* perverted, depraved ; perverse.

perversion [pɛrvɛrsjɔ̃] *nf* perversion.

perverti, e [pɛrvɛrti] *nm/f* pervert.

pervertir [pɛrvɛrtir] *vt* to pervert.

pesage [pəzaʒ] *nm* weighing ; (*HIPPISME*) weigh-in ; weighing room ; enclosure.

pesamment [pəzamɑ̃] *ad* heavily.

pesant, e [pəzɑ̃, -ɑ̃t] *a* heavy ; (*fig*) burdensome // *nm*: **valoir son** ~ **de** to be worth one's weight in.

pesanteur [pəzɑ̃tœr] *nf* gravity.

pèse-bébé [pɛzbebe] *nm* (baby) scales *pl*.

pesée [pəze] *nf* weighing ; (*BOXE*) weigh-in ; (*pression*) pressure.

pèse-lettre [pɛzlɛtr(ə)] *nm* letter scales *pl*.

pèse-personne [pɛzpɛrsɔn] *nm* (bathroom) scales *pl*.

peser [pəze] *vt, vb avec attribut* to weigh // *vi* to be heavy ; (*fig*) to carry weight ; ~ **sur** (*levier, bouton*) to press, push ; (*fig*) to lie heavy on ; to influence ; ~ **à qn** to weigh heavy on sb.

pessaire [pesɛr] *nm* pessary.

pessimisme [pesimism(ə)] *nm* pessimism ; **pessimiste** *a* pessimistic // *nm/f* pessimist.

peste [pɛst(ə)] *nf* plague.

pester [pɛste] *vi*: ~ **contre** to curse.

pestiféré, e [pɛstifere] *nm/f* plague victim.

pestilentiel, le [pɛstilɑ̃sjɛl] *a* foul.

pet [pɛ] *nm* (fam!) fart (!).

pétale [petal] *nm* petal.

pétanque [petɑ̃k] *nf* petanque (bowls).

pétarader [petarade] *vi* to backfire.

pétard [petar] *nm* banger ; cracker ; (*RAIL*) detonator.

péter [pete] *vi* (fam: *casser, sauter*) to burst ; to bust ; (fam!) to fart (!).

pétiller [petije] *vi* (*flamme, bois*) to crackle ; (*mousse, champagne*) to bubble ; (*yeux*) to sparkle.

petit, e [pəti, -it] *a* (*gén*) small ; (*main, objet, colline, en âge: enfant*) small, little (*avant le nom*) ; (*voyage*) short, little ; (*bruit etc*) faint, slight ; (*mesquin*) mean ; **nm** (*d'un animal*) young *pl*; **faire des** ~s to have kittens (*ou* puppies *etc*) ; **en** ~ in miniature ; **mon** ~ **son** ; little one ; **ma** ~**e** dear ; little one ; **pauvre** ~ poor little thing ; **la classe des** ~s the infant class ; **pour** ~s **et grands** for children and adults ; **les tout-petits** the little ones, the tiny tots ; **à** ~ **à** ~ bit by bit, gradually ; ~**/e ami/e** boyfriend/girlfriend ; ~ **déjeuner** breakfast ; ~ **doigt** little finger, pinkie ; ~ **four** petit four ; ~**e vérole** smallpox ; ~**s pois** petit pois *pl*, garden pea(s) ; ~**-bourgeois**, ~**e-bourgeoise** *a* (*péj*) petit-bourgeois(e), middle-class ; ~**e-fille** *nf* granddaughter ; ~**-fils** *nm* grandson.

pétition [petisjɔ̃] *nf* petition.

petit-lait [pətilɛ] *nm* whey.

petit-nègre [pətinɛgr(ə)] *nm* (*péj*) pidgin French.

petits-enfants [pətizɑ̃fɑ̃] *nmpl* grandchildren.

pétrifier [petrifje] *vt* to petrify ; (*fig*) to paralyze, transfix.

pétrin [petrɛ̃] *nm* kneading-trough ; (*fig*): **dans le** ~ in a jam *ou* fix.

pétrir [petrir] *vt* to knead.

pétrole [petrɔl] *nm* oil ; (*pour lampe, réchaud etc*) paraffin (oil) ; **pétrolier, ière** *a* oil *cpd* // *nm* oil tanker ; **pétrolifère** *a* oil(-bearing).

peu [pø] *ad* (*tournure négative* + much ; (*avec adjectif*) *tournure négative* + very // *pronom* few // *nm* little ; ~ **avant/après** shortly before/afterwards ; ~ **de** (*nombre*) few, *négation* + (very) many ; (*quantité*) little, *négation* + (very) much ; **pour** ~ **de temps** for (only) a short while ; **le** ~ **de gens qui** the few people who ; **le** ~ **de sable qui** what little sand, the little sand which ; **un (petit)** ~ a little (bit) ; **un** ~ **de** a little ; **un** ~ **plus/moins de** slightly more/less (*ou* fewer) ; **de** ~ (only) just ; ~ **à** ~ little by little ; **à** ~ **près** just about, more or less ; **à** ~ **près 10 kg/10 F** approximately 10 kg/10 F ; **avant** ~ before long.

peuplade [pœplad] *nf* (*horde, tribu*) tribe, people.

peuple [pœpl(ə)] *nm* people.

peupler [pœple] *vt* (*pays, région*) to populate ; (*étang*) to stock ; (*suj: hommes, poissons*) to inhabit ; (*fig: imagination, rêves*) to fill.

peuplier [pøplije] *nm* poplar (tree).

peur [pœr] *nf* fear ; **avoir** ~ **(de/de faire/que)** to be frightened *ou* afraid (of/of doing/that) ; **faire** ~ **à** to frighten ;

de ~ de/que for fear of/that ; ~eux,
euse a fearful, timorous.
peut vb voir pouvoir.
peut-être [pøtɛtʀ(ə)] ad perhaps, maybe ;
~ que perhaps, maybe ; ~ bien qu'il
fera/est he may well do/be.
peux etc vb voir pouvoir.
phalange [falɑ̃ʒ] nf (ANAT) phalanx (pl
phalanges) ; (MIL) phalanx (pl es).
phallocrate [falɔkʀat] nm male
chauvinist.
phallus [falys] nm phallus.
phare [faʀ] nm (en mer) lighthouse ;
(d'aéroport) beacon ; (de véhicule)
headlamp ; mettre ses ~s to put on the
full beam ; ~s de recul reversing lights.
pharmaceutique [faʀmasøtik] a
pharmaceutic(al).
pharmacie [faʀmasi] nf (science)
pharmacology ; (magasin) chemist's,
pharmacy ; (officine) dispensary ;
(produits) pharmaceuticals pl ;
pharmacien, ne nm/f pharmacist,
chemist.
pharyngite [faʀɛ̃ʒit] nf pharyngitis q.
pharynx [faʀɛ̃ks] nm pharynx.
phase [fɑz] nf phase.
phénomène [fenɔmɛn] nm phenomenon
(pl a) ; (monstre) freak.
philanthrope [filɑ̃tʀɔp] nm/f
philanthropist.
philanthropie [filɑ̃tʀɔpi] nf philanthropy.
philatélie [filateli] nf philately, stamp
collecting ; philatéliste nm/f philatelist,
stamp collector.
philharmonique [filaʀmɔnik] a
philharmonic.
philo [filo] nf abr de philosophie.
philosophe [filɔzɔf] nm/f philosopher //
a philosophical.
philosophie [filɔzɔfi] nf philosophy ;
philosophique a philosophical.
phobie [fɔbi] nf phobia.
phonétique [fɔnetik] a phonetic // nf
phonetics sg.
phonographe [fɔnɔgʀaf] nm (wind-up)
gramophone.
phoque [fɔk] nm seal ; (fourrure) sealskin.
phosphate [fɔsfat] nm phosphate.
phosphore [fɔsfɔʀ] nm phosphorus.
phosphorescent, e [fɔsfɔʀesɑ̃, -ɑ̃t] a
luminous.
photo [fɔto] nf photo(graph) ; en ~ in ou
on a photograph ; prendre en ~ to take
a photo of ; aimer la/faire de la ~ to like
taking/take photos ; ~ d'identité
passport photograph.
photo... [fɔto] préfixe : ~copie nf
photocopying, photostatting ; photocopy,
photostat (copy) ; ~copier vt to
photocopy, photostat ; ~électrique a
photoelectric ; ~génique a photogenic ;
~graphe nm/f photographer ; ~graphie
nf (procédé, technique) photography ;
(cliché) photograph ; faire de la ~graphie
to have photography as a hobby ; to be
a photographer ; ~graphier vt to
photograph, take ; ~graphique a
photographic ; ~maton nm photo-booth,
photomat ; ~-robot nf identikit (picture).

phrase [fʀɑz] nf (LING) sentence ; (propos,
MUS) phrase ; ~s (péj) flowery language sg.
phtisie [ftizi] nf consumption.
physicien, ne [fizisjɛ̃, -ɛn] nm/f physicist.
physiologie [fizjɔlɔʒi] nf physiology ;
physiologique a physiological.
physionomie [fizjɔnɔmi] nf face ;
physionomiste nm/f good judge of faces ;
person who has a good memory for faces.
physique [fizik] a physical // nf
physique // a physics sg ; au ~
physically ; ~ment ad physically.
piaffer [pjafe] vi to stamp.
piailler [pjaje] vi to squawk.
pianiste [pjanist(ə)] nm/f pianist.
piano [pjano] nm piano.
pianoter [pjanɔte] vi to tinkle away (at
the piano) ; (tapoter) : ~ sur to drum one's
fingers on.
piaule [pjol] nf (fam) pad.
piauler [pjole] vi to whimper ; to cheep.
pic [pik] nm (instrument) pick(axe) ;
(montagne) peak ; (ZOOL) woodpecker ; à ~
ad vertically ; (fig) just at the right time.
pichenette [piʃnɛt] nf flick.
pichet [piʃe] nm jug.
pickpocket [pikpɔkɛt] nm pickpocket.
pick-up [pikœp] nm record player.
picorer [pikɔʀe] vt to peck.
picotement [pikɔtmɑ̃] nm tickle q ;
smarting q ; prickling q.
picoter [pikɔte] vt (suj : oiseau) to peck //
vi (irriter) to smart, prickle.
pie [pi] nf magpie ; (fig) chatterbox.
pièce [pjɛs] nf (d'un logement) room ;
(THÉÂTRE) play ; (de mécanisme, machine)
part ; (de monnaie) coin ; (COUTURE) patch ;
(document) document ; (de drap, fragment,
de bétail, de collection) piece ; dix francs
~ ten francs each ; vendre à la ~ to sell
separately ou individually ;
travailler/payer à la ~ to do
piecework/pay piece rate ; un maillot une
~ a one-piece swimsuit ; un deux-~s
cuisine a two-room(ed) flat with kitchen ;
~ à conviction exhibit ; ~ d'eau
ornamental lake ou pond ; ~ d'identité :
avez-vous une ~ d'identité? have you
got any (means of) identification? ; ~
montée tiered cake ; ~s détachées
spares, (spare) parts ; en ~s détachées
(à monter) in kit form.
pied [pje] nm foot (pl feet) ; (de verre)
stem ; (de table) leg ; (de lampe) base ; ~
nus barefoot ; à ~ on foot ; à ~ sec
without getting one's feet wet ; au ~ de
la lettre literally ; au ~ levé at a
moment's notice ; de ~ en cap from head
to foot ; en ~ (portrait) full-length ; avoir
~ to be able to touch the bottom, not to
be out of one's depth ; avoir le ~ marin
to be a good sailor ; perdre ~ to lose one's
footing ; sur ~ (AGR) on the stalk, uncut ;
(debout, rétabli) up and about ; mettre sur
~ (entreprise) to set up ; mettre à ~ to
dismiss ; to lay off ; sur le ~ de guerre
ready for action ; sur ~ d'intervention on
stand-by ; faire du ~ à qn to give sb a
(warning) kick ; to play footsy with sb ;
~ de lit footboard ; ~ de nez : faire un
~ de nez à to thumb one's nose at ; ~
de salade lettuce plant ; ~ de vigne vine ;

~-à-terre *nm* *inv* pied-à-terre ; **~- de-biche** *nm* claw ; (*COUTURE*) presser foot ; **~-de-poule** *a* *inv* hound's-tooth.

piédestal, aux [pjedɛstal, -o] *nm* pedestal.

pied-noir [pjenwaʀ] *nm* Algerian-born Frenchman.

piège [pjɛʒ] *nm* trap ; **prendre au ~** to trap ; **piéger** *vt* (*avec une mine*) to booby-trap ; **lettre-/voiture piégée** letter-/car-bomb.

pierraille [pjɛʀɑj] *nf* loose stones *pl*.

pierre [pjɛʀ] *nf* stone ; **~ à briquet** flint ; **~ fine** semiprecious stone ; **~ de taille** freestone *q* ; **~ de touche** touchstone ; **mur de ~s sèches** drystone wall.

pierreries [pjɛʀʀi] *nfpl* gems, precious stones.

piété [pjete] *nf* piety.

piétiner [pjetine] *vi* (*trépigner*) to stamp (one's foot) ; (*marquer le pas*) to stand about ; (*fig*) to be at a standstill // *vt* to trample on.

piéton, ne [pjetɔ̃, -ɔn] *nm/f* pedestrian ; **piétonnier, ière** *a* pedestrian *cpd*.

piètre [pjɛtʀ(ə)] *a* poor, mediocre.

pieu, x [pjø] *nm* post ; (*pointu*) stake.

pieuvre [pjœvʀ(ə)] *nf* octopus.

pieux, euse [pjø, -øz] *a* pious.

pigeon [piʒɔ̃] *nm* pigeon ; **~ voyageur** homing pigeon ; **pigeonnier** *nm* pigeon house.

piger [piʒe] *vi, vt* (*fam*) to understand.

pigment [pigmɑ̃] *nm* pigment.

pignon [piɲɔ̃] *nm* (*de mur*) gable ; (*d'engrenage*) cog(wheel), gearwheel ; (*graine*) pine kernel ; **avoir ~ sur rue** (*fig*) to have a prosperous business.

pile [pil] *nf* (*tas*) pile ; (*ÉLEC*) battery // *a*: **le côté ~** tails // *ad* (*s'arrêter etc*) dead ; **à deux heures ~** at two on the dot ; **jouer à ~ ou face** to toss up (for it) ; **~ ou face?** heads or tails?

piler [pile] *vt* to crush, pound.

pileux, euse [pilø, -øz] *a*: **système ~** (body) hair.

pilier [pilje] *nm* pillar.

pillard, e [pijaʀ, -aʀd(ə)] *nm/f* looter, plunderer.

piller [pije] *vt* to pillage, plunder, loot.

pilon [pilɔ̃] *nm* pestle.

pilonner [pilɔne] *vt* to pound.

pilori [pilɔʀi] *nm*: **mettre** *ou* **clouer au ~** to pillory.

pilotage [pilɔtaʒ] *nm* piloting ; flying ; **~ sans visibilité** blind flying.

pilote [pilɔt] *nm* pilot ; (*de char, voiture*) driver // *a* pilot *cpd* ; **~ de ligne/d'essai/de chasse** airline/test/fighter pilot.

piloter [pilɔte] *vt* to pilot ; to fly ; to drive ; (*fig*): **~ qn** to guide sb round.

pilotis [pilɔti] *nm* pile ; stilt.

pilule [pilyl] *nf* pill ; **prendre la ~** to be on the pill.

pimbêche [pɛ̃bɛʃ] *nf* (*péj*) stuck-up girl.

piment [pimɑ̃] *nm* (*BOT*) pepper, capsicum ; (*fig*) spice, piquancy ; **~ rouge** (*CULIN*) chilli.

pimpant, e [pɛ̃pɑ̃, -ɑ̃t] *a* trim and fresh-looking.

pin [pɛ̃] *nm* pine (tree) ; (*bois*) pine(wood).

pince [pɛ̃s] *nf* (*outil*) pliers *pl* ; (*de homard, crabe*) pincer, claw ; (*COUTURE*: *pli*) dart ; **~ à sucre/glace** sugar/ice tongs *pl* ; **~ à épiler** tweezers *pl* ; **~ à linge** clothes peg ; **~s de cycliste** bicycle clips.

pinceau, x [pɛ̃so] *nm* (paint)brush.

pincé, e [pɛ̃se] *a* (*air*) stiff // *nf*: **une ~e de** a pinch of.

pincer [pɛ̃se] *vt* to pinch ; (*MUS: cordes*) to pluck ; (*COUTURE*) to dart, put darts in ; (*fam*) to nab ; **se ~ le nez** to hold one's nose.

pince-sans-rire [pɛ̃ssɑ̃ʀiʀ] *a inv* deadpan.

pincettes [pɛ̃sɛt] *nfpl* (*pour le feu*) (fire) tongs.

pinède [pinɛd] *nf* pinewood, pine forest.

pingouin [pɛ̃gwɛ̃] *nm* penguin.

ping-pong [piŋpɔ̃g] *nm* table tennis.

pingre [pɛ̃gʀ(ə)] *a* niggardly.

pinson [pɛ̃sɔ̃] *nm* chaffinch.

pintade [pɛ̃tad] *nf* guinea-fowl.

pin-up [pinœp] *nf inv* pinup (girl).

pioche [pjɔʃ] *nf* pickaxe ; **piocher** *vt* to dig up (with a pickaxe) ; (*fam*) to swot at ; **piocher dans** to dig into.

piolet [pjɔlɛ] *nm* ice axe.

pion, ne [pjɔ̃, pjɔn] *nm/f* (*SCOL*: *péj*) student paid to supervise schoolchildren // *nm* (*ÉCHECS*) pawn ; (*DAMES*) piece, draught.

pionnier [pjɔnje] *nm* pioneer.

pipe [pip] *nf* pipe ; **~ de bruyère** briar pipe.

pipeau, x [pipo] *nm* (reed-)pipe.

pipe-line [pajplajn] *nm* pipeline.

pipi [pipi] *nm* (*fam*): **faire ~** to have a wee.

piquant, e [pikɑ̃, -ɑ̃t] *a* (*barbe, rosier etc*) prickly ; (*saveur, sauce*) hot, pungent ; (*fig*) racy, biting // *nm* (*épine*) thorn, prickle ; (*de hérisson*) quill, spine ; (*fig*) spiciness, spice.

pique [pik] *nf* pike ; (*fig*) cutting remark // *nm* (*CARTES*: *couleur*) spades *pl* ; (*: carte*) spade.

piqué, e [pike] *a* (*COUTURE*) (machine-)stitched ; quilted ; (*fam*) barmy // *nm* (*AVIAT*) dive ; (*TEXTILE*) piqué.

pique-assiette [pikasjɛt] *nm/f inv* (*péj*) scrounger, sponger.

pique-nique [piknik] *nm* picnic.

piquer [pike] *vt* (*percer*) to prick ; (*planter*): **~ qch dans** to stick sth into ; (*fixer*): **~ qch à/sur** to pin sth onto ; (*MÉD*) to give a jab to ; (*: animal blessé*) to put to sleep ; (*suj: insecte, fumée, ortie*) to sting ; (*suj: poivre*) to burn ; (*: froid*) to bite ; (*COUTURE*) to machine (stitch) ; (*intérêt etc*) to arouse ; (*fam*) to pick up ; to pinch ; to nab // *vi* (*avion*) to go into a dive ; (*saveur*) to be pungent ; to be sour ; **~ sur** to swoop down on ; to head straight for ; **se ~ de faire** to pride o.s. on one's ability to do ; **~ du nez** (*avion*) to go into a nose-dive ; **~ un galop/un cent mètres** to break into a gallop/put on a sprint ; **~ une crise** to throw a fit.

piquet [pikɛ] *nm* (*pieu*) post, stake ; (*de tente*) peg ; **mettre un élève au ~** to make a pupil stand in the corner ; **~ de grève** (strike-)picket ; **~ d'incendie** fire-fighting squad.

piqueté, e [pikte] a: ~ **de** dotted with.

piqûre [pikyʀ] nf (d'épingle) prick; (d'ortie) sting; (de moustique) bite; (MÉD) injection; (COUTURE) (straight) stitch; straight stitching; **faire une** ~ **à qn** to give sb an injection.

pirate [piʀat] nm, a pirate; ~ **de l'air** hijacker.

pire [piʀ] a worse; (superlatif): **le(la)** ~ ... the worst ... // nm: **le** ~ **(de)** the worst (of).

pirogue [piʀɔg] nf dugout canoe.

pirouette [piʀwɛt] nf pirouette.

pis [pi] nm (de vache) udder; (pire): **le** ~ the worst // a, ad worse; **pis-aller** nm inv stopgap.

pisciculture [pisikyltyʀ] nf fish farming.

piscine [pisin] nf (swimming) pool; ~ **couverte** indoor (swimming) pool.

pissenlit [pisɑ̃li] nm dandelion.

pisser [pise] vi (fam!) to pee (!); **pissotière** nf (fam) public urinal.

pistache [pistaʃ] nf pistachio (nut).

piste [pist(ə)] nf (d'un animal, sentier) track, trail; (indice) lead; (de stade, de magnétophone) track; (de cirque) ring; (de danse) floor; (de patinage) rink; (de ski) run; (AVIAT) runway.

pistil [pistil] nm pistil.

pistolet [pistɔlɛ] nm (arme) pistol, gun; (à peinture) spray gun; ~ **à bouchon/air comprimé** popgun/ airgun; ~-**mitrailleur** nm submachine gun.

piston [pistɔ̃] nm (TECH) piston; (MUS) valve; (fig) string-pulling; **pistonner** vt (candidat) to pull strings for.

pitance [pitɑ̃s] nf (péj) (means of) sustenance.

piteux, euse [pitø, -øz] a pitiful, sorry (avant le nom).

pitié [pitje] nf pity; **sans** ~ a pitiless, merciless; **faire** ~ to inspire pity; **il me fait** ~ I pity him, I feel sorry for him; **avoir** ~ **de** (compassion) to pity, feel sorry for; (merci) to have pity ou mercy on.

piton [pitɔ̃] nm (clou) peg, bolt; ~ **rocheux** rocky outcrop.

pitoyable [pitwajabl(ə)] a pitiful.

pitre [pitʀ(ə)] nm clown; **pitrerie** nf tomfoolery q.

pittoresque [pitɔʀɛsk(ə)] a picturesque.

pivot [pivo] nm pivot; **pivoter** vi to swivel; to revolve.

pizza [pidza] nf pizza.

P.J. sigle f voir **police**.

Pl. abr de **place**.

placage [plakaʒ] nm (bois) veneer.

placard [plakaʀ] nm (armoire) cupboard; (affiche) poster, notice; (TYPO) galley; ~ **publicitaire** display advertisement; **placarder** vt (affiche) to put up.

place [plas] nf (emplacement, situation, classement) place; (de ville, village) square; (espace libre) room, space; (de parking) space; (siège: de train, cinéma, voiture) seat; (emploi) job; **en** ~ (mettre) in its place; **sur** ~ on the spot; **faire** ~ **à** to give way to; **faire de la** ~ to make room for; **ça prend de la** ~ it takes up a lot of room ou space; **à la** ~ **de** in place of, instead of; **une quatre** ~**s** (AUTO) a four-

seater; **il y a 20** ~**s assises/debout** there are 20 seats/is standing room for 20; ~ **forte** fortified town.

placé, e [plase] a (HIPPISME) placed; **haut** ~ (fig) high-ranking.

placement [plasmɑ̃] nm placing; investment; **bureau de** ~ employment agency.

placenta [plasɑ̃ta] nm placenta.

placer [plase] vt to place; (convive, spectateur) to seat; (capital, argent) to place, invest; (dans la conversation) to put ou get in; ~ **qn chez** to get sb a job at (ou with); **se** ~ **au premier rang** to go and stand (ou sit) in the first row.

placide [plasid] a placid.

plafond [plafɔ̃] nm ceiling.

plafonner [plafɔne] vi to reach one's (ou a) ceiling.

plage [plaʒ] nf beach; (station) (seaside) resort; (fig) band, bracket; (de disque) track, band; ~ **arrière** (AUTO) parcel ou back shelf.

plagiat [plaʒja] nm plagiarism.

plagier [plaʒje] vt to plagiarize.

plaider [plede] vi (avocat) to plead; (plaignant) to go to court, litigate // vt to plead; ~ **pour** (fig) to speak for; **plaideur, euse** nm/f litigant; **plaidoirie** nf (JUR) speech for the defence; **plaidoyer** nm (JUR) speech for the defence; (fig) plea.

plaie [plɛ] nf wound.

plaignant, e [plɛɲɑ̃, -ɑ̃t] nm/f plaintiff.

plaindre [plɛ̃dʀ(ə)] vt to pity, feel sorry for; **se** ~ (gémir) to moan; (protester, rouspéter): **se** ~ **(à qn) (de)** to complain (to sb) (about); (souffrir): **se** ~ **de** to complain of.

plaine [plɛn] nf plain.

plain-pied [plɛ̃pje]: **de** ~ ad at street-level; (fig) straight; **de** ~ **avec** on the same level as.

plainte [plɛ̃t] nf (gémissement) moan, groan; (doléance) complaint; **porter** ~ to lodge a complaint; **plaintif, ive** a plaintive.

plaire [plɛʀ] vi to be a success, be successful; to please; ~ **à:** **cela me plaît** I like it; **essayer de** ~ **à qn** (en étant serviable etc) to try and please sb; **elle plaît aux hommes** she's a success with men, men like her; **se** ~ **quelque part** to like being somewhere ou like it somewhere; **se** ~ **à faire** to take pleasure in doing; **ce qu'il vous plaira** what(ever) you like ou wish; **s'il vous plaît** please.

plaisamment [plɛzamɑ̃] ad pleasantly.

plaisance [plɛzɑ̃s] nf (aussi: **navigation de** ~) (pleasure) sailing, yachting; **plaisancier** nm amateur sailor, yachting enthusiast.

plaisant, e [plɛzɑ̃, -ɑ̃t] a pleasant; (histoire, anecdote) amusing.

plaisanter [plɛzɑ̃te] vi to joke; **pour** ~ for a joke; **on ne plaisante pas avec cela** that's no joking matter; **plaisanterie** nf joke; joking q; **plaisantin** nm joker.

plaise etc vb voir **plaire**.

plaisir [plɛziʀ] nm pleasure; **faire** ~ **à qn** (délibérément) to be nice to sb, please sb; (suj: cadeau, nouvelle etc): **ceci me fait** ~ I'm delighted ou very pleased with this; **prendre** ~ **à/faire** to take pleasure in/in doing; **à ~** freely; for the sake of it; **au ~ (de vous revoir)** (I hope to) see you again; **pour le ou par ~** for pleasure.

plan, e [plã, -an] *a* flat // *nm* plan; (GÉOM) plane; (*fig*) level, plane; (CINÉMA) shot; **au premier/second ~** in the foreground/middle distance; **à l'arrière ~** in the background; **mettre qch au premier ~** (*fig*) to consider sth to be of primary importance; **sur le ~ sexuel** sexually, as far as sex is concerned; **~ d'eau** stretch of water; **~ de travail** work programme *ou* schedule.

planche [plãʃ] *nf* (*pièce de bois*) plank, (wooden) board; (*illustration*) plate; **les ~s** (THÉÂTRE) the stage *sg*, the boards; **faire la ~** (*dans l'eau*) to float on one's back; **~ à dessin** drawing board; **~ à pain** breadboard; **~ à repasser** ironing board; **~ de salut** (*fig*) sheet anchor.

plancher [plãʃe] *nm* floor; floorboards *pl*; (*fig*) minimum level.

plancton [plãktɔ̃] *nm* plankton.

planer [plane] *vi* to glide; **~ sur** (*fig*) to hang over; to hover above.

planétaire [planetɛʀ] *a* planetary.

planète [planɛt] *nf* planet.

planeur [planœʀ] *nm* glider.

planification [planifikasjɔ̃] *nf* (economic) planning.

planifier [planifje] *vt* to plan.

planning [planiŋ] *nm* programme, schedule; **~ familial** family planning.

planque [plãk] *nf* (*fam*) cushy number; hideout; stash.

plant [plã] *nm* seedling, young plant.

plantaire [plãtɛʀ] *a voir* **voûte**.

plantation [plãtasjɔ̃] *nf* plantation.

plante [plãt] *nf* plant; **~ d'appartement** house *ou* pot plant; **~ du pied** sole (of the foot).

planter [plãte] *vt* (*plante*) to plant; (*enfoncer*) to hammer *ou* drive in; (*tente*) to put up, pitch; (*fam*) to dump; to ditch; **~ qch dans** to hammer *ou* drive sth into; to stick sth into; **se ~ dans** to stick into; to get stuck in; **se ~ devant** to plant o.s. in front of; **planteur** *nm* planter.

planton [plãtɔ̃] *nm* orderly.

plantureux, euse [plãtyʀø, -øz] *a* copious, lavish; buxom.

plaquage [plakaʒ] *nm* (RUGBY) tackle.

plaque [plak] *nf* plate; (*de verglas, d'eczéma*) patch; (*avec inscription*) plaque; **~s (minéralogiques ou de police ou d'immatriculation)** number plates; **~ de beurre** tablet of butter; **~ chauffante** hotplate; **~ de chocolat** bar of chocolate; **~ d'identité** identity disc; **~ tournante** (*fig*) centre.

plaqué, e [plake] *a*: **~ or/argent** gold-/silver-plated; **~ acajou** veneered in mahogany.

plaquer [plake] *vt* (*bijou*) to plate; (*bois*) to veneer; (*aplatir*): **~ qch sur/contre** to make sth stick *ou* cling to; (RUGBY) to bring down; (*fam*) to ditch; **se ~ contre** to flatten o.s. against; **~ qn contre** to pin sb to.

plaquette [plakɛt] *nf* tablet; bar; (*livre*) small volume.

plasma [plasma] *nm* plasma.

plastic [plastik] *nm* plastic explosive.

plastifié, e [plastifje] *a* plastic-coated.

plastique [plastik] *a* plastic // *nm* plastic // *nf* plastic arts *pl*; modelling.

plastiquer [plastike] *vt* to blow up (*with a plastic bomb*).

plastron [plastʀɔ̃] *nm* shirt front.

plastronner [plastʀɔne] *vi* to swagger.

plat, e [pla, -at] *a* flat; (*cheveux*) straight; (*personne, livre*) dull // *nm* (*récipient*, CULIN) dish; (*d'un repas*): **le premier ~** the first course; (*partie plate*): **le ~ de la main** the flat of the hand; **à ~ ventre** *ad* face down; (*tomber*) flat on one's face; **à ~** *ad*, *a* (*aussi*: *pneu, batterie*) flat; **~ du jour** day's special (menu); **~ de résistance** main course.

platane [platan] *nm* plane tree.

plateau, x [plato] *nm* (*support*) tray; (GÉO) plateau; (*de tourne-disques*) turntable; (CINÉMA) set; **~ à fromages** cheeseboard.

plate-bande [platbãd] *nf* flower bed.

platée [plate] *nf* dish(ful).

plate-forme [platfɔʀm(ə)] *nf* platform; **~ de forage/pétrolière** drilling/oil rig.

platine [platin] *nm* platinum // *nf* (*d'un tourne-disque*) turntable.

plâtras [plɑtʀa] *nm* rubble *q.*

plâtre [plɑtʀ(ə)] *nm* (*matériau*) plaster; (*statue*) plaster statue; (MÉD) (plaster) cast; **avoir un bras dans le ~** to have an arm in plaster; **plâtrer** *vt* to plaster; (MÉD) to set *ou* put in a (plaster) cast.

plausible [plozibl(ə)] *a* plausible.

plébiscite [plebisit] *nm* plebiscite.

plein, e [plɛ̃, -ɛn] *a* full; (*porte, roue*) solid; (*chienne, jument*) big (with young) // *nm*: **faire le ~ (d'essence)** to fill up (with petrol); **les ~s** the downstrokes (*in handwriting*); **~ de** full of; **à ~es mains** (*ramasser*) in handfuls; (*empoigner*) firmly; **à ~ régime** at maximum revs; (*fig*) full steam; **à ~ temps** full-time; **en ~ air/~ mer** in the open air/on the open sea; **en ~ soleil** right out in the sun; **en ~e nuit/rue** in the middle of the night/street; **en ~ milieu** right in the middle; **en ~ jour** in broad daylight; **en ~ sur** right on; **~-emploi** *nm* full employment.

plénière [plenjɛʀ] *af*: **assemblée ~** plenary assembly.

plénitude [plenityd] *nf* fullness.

pléthore [pletɔʀ] *nf*: **~ de** overabundance *ou* plethora of.

pleurer [plœʀe] *vi* to cry; (*yeux*) to water // *vt* to mourn (for); **~ sur** *vt* to lament (over), to bemoan.

pleurésie [plœʀezi] *nf* pleurisy.

pleurnicher [plœʀniʃe] *vi* to grizzle, whine.

pleurs [plœʀ] *nmpl*: **en ~** in tears.

pleutre [pløtʀ(ə)] *a* cowardly.

pleuvoir [pløvwaʀ] *vb impersonnel* to rain // *vi* (*fig*): **~ (sur)** to shower down (upon); to be showered upon.

plexiglas [plɛksiglas] *nm* plexiglass.

pli [pli] *nm* fold; (*de jupe*) pleat; (*de pantalon*) crease; (*aussi*: **faux ~**) crease; (*enveloppe*) envelope; (*lettre*) letter;

(CARTES) trick ; **prendre le ~ de faire** to get into the habit of doing ; **~ d'aisance** inverted pleat.

pliage [plijaʒ] nm folding ; (ART) origami.

pliant, e [plijɑ̃, -ɑ̃t] a folding // nm folding stool, campstool.

plier [plije] vt to fold ; (pour ranger) to fold up ; (table pliante) to fold down ; (genou, bras) to bend // vi to bend ; (fig) to yield ; **se ~ à** to submit to ; **~ bagages** to pack up (and go).

plinthe [plɛ̃t] nf skirting board.

plissé, e [plise] a (GÉO) folded // nm (COUTURE) pleats pl.

plissement [plismɑ̃] nm (GÉO) fold.

plisser [plise] vt (rider, chiffonner) to crease ; (jupe) to put pleats in.

plomb [plɔ̃] nm (métal) lead ; (d'une cartouche) (lead) shot ; (PÊCHE) sinker ; (sceau) (lead) seal ; (ÉLEC) fuse ; **mettre à ~** to plumb.

plombage [plɔ̃baʒ] nm (de dent) filling.

plomber [plɔ̃be] vt (canne, ligne) to weight (with lead) ; (colis, wagon) to put a lead seal on ; (dent) to fill.

plomberie [plɔ̃bʀi] nf plumbing.

plombier [plɔ̃bje] nm plumber.

plonge [plɔ̃ʒ] nf: **faire la ~** to be a washer-up.

plongeant, e [plɔ̃ʒɑ̃, -ɑ̃t] a (vue) from above ; (tir, décolleté) plunging.

plongée [plɔ̃ʒe] nf diving q ; (de sous-marin) submersion, dive ; **en ~** (sous-marin) submerged ; (prise de vue) high angle.

plongeoir [plɔ̃ʒwaʀ] nm diving board.

plongeon [plɔ̃ʒɔ̃] nm dive.

plonger [plɔ̃ʒe] vi to dive // vt: **~ qch dans** (immerger) to plunge ou dip sth into ; (planter) to thrust sth into ; (fig) to plunge sth into ; **plongeur, euse** nm/f diver ; (de café) washer-up.

ployer [plwaje] vt to bend // vi to sag ; to bend.

plu pp de **plaire, pleuvoir**.

pluie [plɥi] nf rain ; (fig): **~ de** shower of ; **retomber en ~** to shower down ; **sous la ~** in the rain.

plume [plym] nf feather ; (pour écrire) (pen) nib ; (fig) pen.

plumeau, x [plymo] nm feather duster.

plumer [plyme] vt to pluck.

plumet [plymɛ] nm plume.

plumier [plymje] nm pencil box.

plupart [plypaʀ]: **la ~** pronom the majority, most (of them) ; **la ~ des** most, the majority of ; **la ~ du temps/d'entre nous** most of the time/of us ; **pour la ~** ad for the most part, mostly.

pluriel [plyʀjɛl] nm plural ; **au ~** in the plural.

plus vb [ply] voir **plaire** // ad [ply, plyz + voyelle] (comparatif) more, adjectif court + ...er ; (davantage) [plys] more ; (négatif): **ne ... ~** no more, tournure négative + any more ; no longer // cj [plys]: **~ 2 plus 2** ; **~ que** more than ; **~ grand que** bigger than ; **~ de 10 personnes** more than 10 people, over 10 people ; **~ de pain** more bread ; **~ il travaille, ~ il est heureux** the more he works, the happier he is ; **le**

~ intelligent/grand the most intelligent/biggest ; **3 heures/kilos de ~ que** 3 hours/kilos more than ; **~ de** what's more, moreover ; **3 kilos en ~** 3 kilos more, 3 extra kilos ; **en ~ de** in addition to ; **de ~ en ~** more and more ; (tout) **au ~** at the (very) most ; **~ ou moins** more or less ; **ni ~ ni moins** no more, no less.

plusieurs [plyzjœʀ] dét, pronom several ; **ils sont ~** there are several of them.

plus-que-parfait [plyskəpaʀfɛ] nm pluperfect, past perfect.

plus-value [plyvaly] nf appreciation ; capital gain ; surplus.

plut vb voir **plaire**.

plûtot [plyto] ad rather ; **je ferais ~ ceci** I'd rather ou sooner do this ; **fais ~ comme ça** try this way instead, you'd better try this way ; **~ que (de) faire** rather than ou instead of doing.

pluvieux, euse [plyvjø, -øz] a rainy, wet.

P.M.U. sigle m voir **pari**.

pneu, x [pnø] nm tyre ; letter sent by pneumatic tube.

pneumatique [pnømatik] a pneumatic ; rubber cpd // nm tyre.

pneumonie [pnømɔni] nf pneumonia.

P.O. sigle = petites ondes.

poche [pɔʃ] nf pocket ; (déformation): **faire une/des ~(s)** to bag ; (sous les yeux) bag, pouch // nm (abr de livre de ~) (pocket-size) paperback ; **de ~** pocket cpd.

poché, e [pɔʃe] a: **œuf ~** poached egg ; **œil ~** black eye.

poche-revolver [pɔʃʀevɔlvɛʀ] nf hip pocket.

pochette [pɔʃɛt] nf (de timbres) wallet, envelope ; (d'aiguilles etc) case ; (sur veston) breast pocket ; (mouchoir) breast pocket handkerchief ; **~ d'allumettes** book of matches ; **~ de disque** record sleeve.

pochoir [pɔʃwaʀ] nm (ART) stencil ; transfer.

podium [pɔdjɔm] nm podium (pl ia).

poêle [pwal] nm stove // nf: **~ (à frire)** frying pan.

poêlon [pwalɔ̃] nm casserole.

poème [pɔɛm] nm poem.

poésie [pɔezi] nf (poème) poem ; (art): **la ~** poetry.

poète [pɔɛt] nm poet.

poétique [pɔetik] a poetic.

pognon [pɔɲɔ̃] nm (fam) dough.

poids [pwa] nm weight ; (SPORT) shot ; **vendre au ~** to sell by weight ; **prendre du ~** to put on weight ; **~ plume/mouche/coq/** moyen (BOXE) feather/fly/bantam/ middleweight ; **~ et haltères** weight lifting sg ; **~ lourd** (BOXE) heavyweight ; (camion) (big) lorry ; (: ADMIN) heavy goods vehicle (HGV) ; **~ mort** dead load.

poignant, e [pwaɲɑ̃, -ɑ̃t] a poignant, harrowing.

poignard [pwaɲaʀ] nm dagger ; **poignarder** vt to stab, knife.

poigne [pwaɲ] nf grip ; (fig) firm-handedness.

poignée [pwaɲe] *nf* (*de sel etc, fig*) handful; (*de couvercle, porte*) handle; ~ **de main** handshake.

poignet [pwaɲɛ] *nm* (ANAT) wrist; (*de chemise*) cuff.

poil [pwal] *nm* (ANAT) hair; (*de pinceau, brosse*) bristle; (*de tapis*) strand; (*pelage*) coat; (*ensemble des poils*): **avoir du ~ sur la poitrine** to have hair(s) on one's chest, have a hairy chest; **à ~** a (*fam*) starkers; **au ~** a (*fam*) hunky-dory; **poilu, e** a hairy.

poinçon [pwɛ̃sɔ̃] *nm* awl; bodkin; style; die; (*marque*) hallmark; **poinçonner** *vt* to stamp; to hallmark; (*billet, ticket*) to clip, punch; **poinçonneuse** *nf* (*outil*) punch.

poing [pwɛ̃] *nm* fist.

point [pwɛ̃] *nm* (*marque, signe*) dot; (: *de ponctuation*) full stop; (*moment, de score etc, fig: question*) point; (*endroit*) spot; (COUTURE, TRICOT) stitch // **ad = pas**; **faire le ~** (NAVIG) to take a bearing; (*fig*) to take stock (of the situation); **en tout ~** in every respect; **sur le ~ de faire** (just) about to do; **à tel ~ que** so much so that; **mettre au ~** (*mécanisme, procédé*) to perfect; (*appareil-photo*) to focus; (*affaire*) to settle; **à ~** (CULIN) medium; just right; **à ~** (*nommé*) just at the right time; ~ (*de côté*) stitch (*pain*); ~ **culminant** summit; (*fig*) height, climax; ~ **d'eau** spring; water point; ~ **d'exclamation** exclamation mark; ~ **faible** weak point; ~ **final** full stop, period; ~ **d'interrogation** question mark; ~ **mort** (AUTO): **au ~ mort** in neutral; ~ **noir** (*sur le visage*) blackhead; (AUTO) accident spot; ~ **de repère** landmark; (*dans le temps*) point of reference; ~ **de vente** retail outlet; ~ **de vue** viewpoint; (*fig: opinion*) point of view; **du ~ de vue de** from the point of view of; ~**s cardinaux** points of the compass, cardinal points; ~**s de suspension** suspension points.

pointe [pwɛ̃t] *nf* point; (*d'une île*) headland; (*allusion*) dig; sally; (*fig*): **une ~ d'ail/d'accent** a touch ou hint of garlic/of an accent; **être à la ~ de** (*fig*) to be in the forefront of; **sur la ~ des pieds** on tip-toe; **en ~** ad (*tailler*) into a point // a pointed, tapered; **de ~** a (*technique etc*) leading; **heures/jours de ~** peak hours/days; **faire du 180 en ~** (AUTO) to have a top ou maximum speed of 180; **faire des ~s** (DANSE) to dance on points; ~ **de vitesse** burst of speed.

pointer [pwɛ̃te] *vt* (*cocher*) to tick off; (*employés etc*) to check in (ou out); (*diriger: canon, longue-vue, doigt*): ~ **vers qch** to point at sth // *vi* (*employé*) to clock in (ou out); **pointeuse** *nf* timeclock.

pointillé [pwɛ̃tije] *nm* (*trait*) dotted line; (ART) stippling q.

pointilleux, euse [pwɛ̃tijø, -øz] a particular, pernickety.

pointu, e [pwɛ̃ty] a pointed; (*clou*) sharp; (*voix*) shrill.

pointure [pwɛ̃tyr] *nf* size.

point-virgule [pwɛ̃virgyl] *nm* semi-colon.

poire [pwar] *nf* pear; (*fam: péj*) mug; ~ **à injections** syringe.

poireau, x [pwaro] *nm* leek.

poirier [pwarje] *nm* pear tree.

pois [pwa] *nm* (BOT) pea; (*sur une étoffe*) dot, spot; **à ~** (*cravate etc*) dotted, polka-dot *cpd*; ~ **chiche** chickpea; ~ **de senteur** sweet pea.

poison [pwazɔ̃] *nm* poison.

poisse [pwas] *nf* rotten luck.

poisseux, euse [pwasø, -øz] a sticky.

poisson [pwasɔ̃] *nm* fish *gén inv*; **les P~s** (*signe*) Pisces, the Fishes; **être des P~s** to be Pisces; ~ **d'avril!** April fool!; **poissonnerie** *nf* fish-shop; **poissonneux, euse** a abounding in fish; **poissonnier, ière** *nm/f* fishmonger.

poitrail [pwatraj] *nm* breast.

poitrine [pwatrin] *nf* chest; (*seins*) bust, bosom; (CULIN) breast; ~ **de bœuf** brisket.

poivre [pwavr(ə)] *nm* pepper; ~ **en grains/moulu** whole/ground pepper; **poivré, e** a peppery; **poivrier** *nm* (BOT) pepper plant; (*ustensile*) pepperpot.

poivron [pwavrɔ̃] *nm* pepper, capsicum; ~ **vert/rouge** green/red pepper.

poker [pɔkɛr] *nm*: **le ~** poker; ~ **d'as** four aces.

polaire [pɔlɛr] a polar.

polariser [pɔlarize] *vt* to polarize; (*fig*) to attract; to focus.

pôle [pol] *nm* (GÉO, ÉLEC) pole; **le ~ Nord/Sud** the North/South Pole.

polémique [pɔlemik] a controversial, polemic(al) // *nf* controversy; **polémiste** *nm/f* polemist, polemicist.

poli, e [pɔli] a polite; (*lisse*) smooth; polished.

police [pɔlis] *nf* police; (*discipline*): **assurer la ~ de** ou **dans** to keep order in; **peine de simple ~** sentence imposed by a magistrate ou police court; ~ **d'assurance** insurance policy; ~ **judiciaire, P.J.** ≈ Criminal Investigation Department, C.I.D.; ~ **des mœurs** ≈ vice squad; ~ **secours** ≈ emergency services *pl*.

polichinelle [pɔliʃinɛl] *nm* Punch; (*péj*) buffoon.

policier, ière [pɔlisje, -jɛr] a police *cpd* // *nm* policeman; (*aussi:* **roman ~**) detective novel.

policlinique [pɔliklinik] *nf* ≈ outpatients (department).

polio(myélite) [pɔljɔ(mjelit)] *nf* polio(myelitis); **poliomyélitique** *nm/f* polio patient ou case.

polir [pɔlir] *vt* to polish.

polisson, ne [pɔlisɔ̃, -ɔn] a naughty.

politesse [pɔlitɛs] *nf* politeness; ~**s** (*exchange of*) courtesies, polite gestures; **rendre une ~ à qn** to return sb's favour.

politicien, ne [pɔlitisjɛ̃, -ɛn] *nm/f* politician.

politique [pɔlitik] a political // *nf* (*science, pratique, activité*) politics *sg*; (*mesures, méthode*) policies *pl*; **politiser** *vt* to politicize; **politiser qn** to make sb politically aware.

pollen [pɔlɛn] *nm* pollen.

polluer [pɔlɥe] *vt* to pollute; **pollution** *nf* pollution.

polo [pɔlo] *nm* (*sport*) polo; (*tricot*) sweat shirt.

Pologne [pɔlɔɲ] *nf*: **la ~** Poland; **polonais, e** *a*, *nm* (*langue*) Polish // *nm/f* Pole.

poltron, ne [pɔltRɔ̃, -ɔn] *a* cowardly.

poly... [pɔli] *préfixe*: **~clinique** *nf* polyclinic; **~copier** *vt* to duplicate; **~gamie** *nf* polygamy; **~glotte** *a* polyglot; **~gone** *nm* polygon.

Polynésie [pɔlinezi] *nf*: **la ~** Polynesia.

polytechnicien, ne [pɔlitɛknisjɛ̃, -ɛn] *nm/f* student (or former student) *of the École Polytechnique*.

polyvalent, e [pɔlivalɑ̃, -ɑ̃t] *a* polyvalent; versatile, multi-purpose // *nm* ≈ tax inspector.

pommade [pɔmad] *nf* ointment, cream.

pomme [pɔm] *nf* (*BOT*) apple; (*boule décorative*) knob; (*pomme de terre*): **steak ~s (frites)** steak and chips; **tomber dans les ~s** (*fam*) to pass out; **~ d'Adam** Adam's apple; **~ d'arrosoir** (*sprinkler*) rose; **~ de pin** pine *ou* fir cone; **~ de terre** potato; **~s vapeur** boiled potatoes.

pommé, e [pɔme] *a* (*chou etc*) firm, with a good heart.

pommeau, x [pɔmo] *nm* (*boule*) knob; (*de selle*) pommel.

pommette [pɔmɛt] *nf* cheekbone.

pommier [pɔmje] *nm* apple tree.

pompe [pɔ̃p] *nf* pump; (*faste*) pomp (and ceremony); **~ à bicyclette** bicycle pump; **~ à essence** petrol pump; **~ à incendie** fire engine (*apparatus*); **~s funèbres** funeral parlour *sg*, undertaker's *sg*.

pomper [pɔ̃pe] *vt* to pump; (*évacuer*) to pump out; (*aspirer*) to pump up; (*absorber*) to soak up // *vi* to pump.

pompeux, euse [pɔ̃pø, -øz] *a* pompous.

pompier [pɔ̃pje] *nm* fireman // *am* (*style*) pretentious, pompous.

pompon [pɔ̃pɔ̃] *nm* pompom, bobble.

pomponner [pɔ̃pɔne] *vt* to titivate, dress up.

ponce [pɔ̃s] *nf*: **pierre ~** pumice stone.

poncer [pɔ̃se] *vt* to sand (down); **ponceuse** *nf* sander.

poncif [pɔ̃sif] *nm* cliché.

ponction [pɔ̃ksjɔ̃] *nf*: **~ lombaire** lumbar puncture.

ponctualité [pɔ̃ktɥalite] *nf* punctuality.

ponctuation [pɔ̃ktɥasjɔ̃] *nf* punctuation.

ponctuel, le [pɔ̃ktɥɛl] *a* (*à l'heure, aussi TECH*) punctual; (*fig: opération etc*) one-off, single; (*scrupuleux*) punctilious, meticulous.

ponctuer [pɔ̃ktɥe] *vt* to punctuate; (*MUS*) to phrase.

pondéré, e [pɔ̃dere] *a* level-headed, composed.

pondre [pɔ̃dR(ə)] *vt* to lay; (*fig*) to produce // *vi* to lay.

poney [pɔnɛ] *nm* pony.

pongiste [pɔ̃ʒist] *nm/f* table tennis player.

pont [pɔ̃] *nm* bridge; (*AUTO*): **~ arrière/avant** rear/front axle; (*NAVIG*) deck; **faire le ~** to take the extra day off; **~ aérien** airlift; **~ d'envol** flight deck; **~ de graissage** ramp (*in garage*); **~ roulant** travelling crane; **~ suspendu** suspension bridge; **~ tournant** swing bridge; **P~s et Chaussées** highways department.

ponte [pɔ̃t] *nf* laying // *nm* (*fam*) big shot.

pontife [pɔ̃tif] *nm* pontiff.

pontifier [pɔ̃tifje] *vi* to pontificate.

pont-levis [pɔ̃lvi] *nm* drawbridge.

pop [pɔp] *a inv* pop.

populace [pɔpylas] *nf* (*péj*) rabble.

populaire [pɔpylɛʀ] *a* popular; (*manifestation*) mass *cpd, of the people*; (*milieux, clientèle*) working-class; **populariser** *vt* to popularize; **popularité** *nf* popularity.

population [pɔpylasjɔ̃] *nf* population.

populeux, euse [pɔpylø, -øz] *a* densely populated.

porc [pɔR] *nm* (*ZOOL*) pig; (*CULIN*) pork; (*peau*) pigskin.

porcelaine [pɔRsəlɛn] *nf* porcelain, china; piece of china(ware).

porcelet [pɔRsəlɛ] *nm* piglet.

porc-épic [pɔRkepik] *nm* porcupine.

porche [pɔRʃ(ə)] *nm* porch.

porcherie [pɔRʃəʀi] *nf* pigsty.

porcin, e [pɔRsɛ̃, -in] *a* porcine; (*fig*) piglike.

pore [pɔR] *nm* pore; **poreux, euse** *a* porous.

pornographie [pɔRnɔgʀafi] *nf* pornography; **pornographique** *a* (*abr* **porno**) pornographic.

port [pɔR] *nm* (*NAVIG*) harbour, port; (*ville*) port; (*de l'uniforme etc*) wearing; (*pour lettre*) postage; (*pour colis, aussi: posture*) carriage; **~ d'arme** (*JUR*) carrying of a firearm; **~ d'attache** (*NAVIG*) port of registry; **~ franc** free port.

portail [pɔRtaj] *nm* gate; (*de cathédrale*) portal.

portant, e [pɔRtɑ̃, -ɑ̃t] *a* (*murs*) structural, weight-bearing; **bien/mal ~** in good/poor health.

portatif, ive [pɔRtatif, -iv] *a* portable.

porte [pɔRt(ə)] *nf* door; (*de ville, forteresse, SKI*) gate; **mettre à la ~** to throw out; **~ d'entrée** front door; **~ à ~** *nm* door-to-door selling.

porte... [pɔRt(ə)] *préfixe*: **~-à-faux** *nm*: **en ~-à-faux** cantilevered; precariously balanced; **~-avions** *nm inv* aircraft carrier; **~-bagages** *nm inv* luggage rack; **~-bonheur** *nm inv* lucky charm; **~-cartes** *nm inv* card holder; map wallet; **~-cigarettes** *nm inv* cigarette case; **~-clefs** *nm inv* keyring; **~-crayon** *nm* pencil holder; **~-documents** *nm inv* attaché *ou* document case.

portée [pɔRte] *nf* (*d'une arme*) range; (*fig*) impact, import; scope, capability; (*de chatte etc*) litter; (*MUS*) stave, staff (*pl* staves); **à/hors de ~** (*de*) within/out of reach (of); **à ~ de (la) main** within (arm's) reach; **à ~ de voix** within earshot; **à la ~ de qn** (*fig*) at sb's level, within sb's capabilities.

porte-fenêtre [pɔRtfənɛtR(ə)] *nf* French window.

portefeuille [pɔRtəfœj] *nm* wallet; (*POL, BOURSE*) portfolio.

porte-jarretelles [pɔRtʒaRtɛl] *nm inv* suspender belt.

portemanteau, x [pɔrtmɑ̃to] *nm* coat hanger ; coat rack.

porte-mine [pɔrtəmin] *nm* propelling pencil.

porte-monnaie [pɔrtmɔnɛ] *nm inv* purse.

porte-parole [pɔrtparɔl] *nm inv* spokesman.

porte-plume [pɔrtəplym] *nm inv* penholder.

porter [pɔrte] *vt* (*charge ou sac etc, aussi: fœtus*) to carry ; (*sur soi: vêtement, barbe, bague*) to wear ; (*fig: responsabilité etc*) to bear, carry ; (*inscription, marque, titre, patronyme, suj: arbre: fruits, fleurs*) to bear ; (*apporter*): ~ **qch quelque part/à qn** to take sth somewhere/to sb ; (*inscrire*): ~ **qch sur** to put sth down on ; to enter sth in // *vi* (*voix, regard, canon*) to carry ; (*coup, argument*) to hit home ; ~ **sur** (*peser*) to rest on ; (*accent*) to fall on ; (*conférence etc*) to concern ; (*heurter*) to strike ; **se ~** *vi* (*se sentir*): **se ~ bien/mal** to be well/unwell ; (*aller*): **se ~ vers** to go towards ; **être porté à faire** to be apt *ou* inclined to do ; **elle portait le nom de Rosalie** she was called Rosalie ; ~ **qn au pouvoir** to bring sb to power ; ~ **son âge** to look one's age ; **se faire ~ malade** to report sick ; ~ **la main à son chapeau** to raise one's hand to one's hat ; ~ **son effort sur** to direct one's efforts towards.

porte-savon [pɔrtsavɔ̃] *nm* soapdish.

porte-serviettes [pɔrtsɛrvjɛt] *nm inv* towel rail.

porteur, euse [pɔrtœr, -øz] *a*: **être ~ de** (*nouvelle*) to be the bearer of // *nm* (*de bagages*) porter ; (*comm: de chèque*) bearer.

porte-voix [pɔrtəvwa] *nm inv* loudhailer.

portier [pɔrtje] *nm* commissionnaire, porter.

portière [pɔrtjɛr] *nf* door.

portillon [pɔrtijɔ̃] *nm* gate.

portion [pɔrsjɔ̃] *nf* (*part*) portion, share ; (*partie*) portion, section.

portique [pɔrtik] *nm* (*gym*) crossbar ; (*archit*) portico ; (*rail*) gantry.

porto [pɔrto] *nm* port (wine).

portrait [pɔrtrɛ] *nm* portrait ; photograph ; **portraitiste** *nm/f* portrait painter ; ~**-robot** *nm* Identikit *ou* photo-fit picture.

portuaire [pɔrtɥɛr] *a* port *cpd*, harbour *cpd*.

portugais, e [pɔrtygɛ, -ɛz] *a, nm, nf* Portuguese.

Portugal [pɔrtygal] *nm*: **le ~** Portugal.

pose [poz] *nf* laying ; hanging ; (*attitude, d'un modèle*) pose ; (*photo*) exposure.

posé, e [poze] *a* serious.

posemètre [pozmɛtr(ə)] *nm* exposure meter.

poser [poze] *vt* (*déposer*): ~ **qch (sur)/qn à** to put sth down (on)/drop sb at ; (*placer*): ~ **qch sur/quelque part** to put sth on/somewhere ; (*installer: moquette, carrelage*) to lay ; (: *rideaux, papier peint*) to hang ; (*question*) to ask ; (*principe, conditions*) to lay *ou* set down ; (*problème*) to formulate ; (*difficulté*) to pose // *vi* (*modèle*) to pose ; to sit ; **se ~** (*oiseau, avion*) to land ; (*question*) to arise.

poseur, euse [pozœr, -øz] *nm/f* (*péj*) show-off, poseur ; ~ **de parquets/ carrelages** floor/tile layer.

positif, ive [pozitif, -iv] *a* positive.

position [pozisjɔ̃] *nf* position ; **prendre ~** (*fig*) to take a stand.

posologie [pozɔlɔʒi] *nf* directions *pl* for use, dosage.

posséder [pɔsede] *vt* to own, possess ; (*qualité, talent*) to have, possess ; (*bien connaître: métier, langue*) to master, have a thorough knowledge of ; (*sexuellement, aussi: suj: colère etc*) to possess ; (*fam: duper*) to take in ; **possesseur** *nm* owner ; **possessif, ive** *a, nm* possessive ; **possession** *nf* ownership *q*; possession ; **être/entrer en possession de qch** to be in/take possession of sth.

possibilité [pɔsibilite] *nf* possibility ; ~**s** *nfpl* (*moyens*) means ; (*potentiel*) potential *sg* ; **avoir la ~ de faire** to be in a position to do ; to have the opportunity to do.

possible [pɔsibl(ə)] *a* possible ; (*projet, entreprise*) feasible // *nm*: **faire son ~** to do all one can, do one's utmost ; **le plus/moins de livres** ~ as many/few books as possible ; **le plus/moins d'eau** ~ as much/little water as possible ; **dès que** ~ as soon as possible ; **gentil** *etc* **au** ~ as nice *etc* as it is possible to be.

postal, e, aux [pɔstal, -o] *a* postal, post office *cpd* ; **sac** ~ mailbag, postbag.

poste [pɔst(ə)] *nf* (*service*) post, postal service ; (*administration, bureau*) post office // *nm* (*fonction, mil*) post ; (*de radio etc*) set ; (*de budget*) item ; ~**s** *nfpl* post office *sg* ; **P~s et Télécommunications (P.T.T.:** *abr de* **P**ostes, **T**élégraphes, **T**éléphones) = General Post Office (G.P.O.) ; ~ (**de radio/télévision**) *nm* (radio/television) set ; ~ **émetteur** *nm* transmitting set ; ~ **d'essence** *nm* petrol *ou* filling station ; ~ **d'incendie** *nm* fire point ; ~ **de péage** *nm* tollgate ; ~ **de pilotage** *nm* cockpit ; ~ (**de police**) *nm* police station ; ~ **restante** *nf* poste restante ; ~ **de secours** *nm* first-aid post.

poster *vt* [pɔste] to post // *nm* [pɔstɛr] poster.

postérieur, e [pɔsterjœr] *a* (*date*) later ; (*partie*) back // *nm* (*fam*) behind.

posteriori [pɔsterjɔri]: **a** ~ *ad* with hindsight, a posteriori.

postérité [pɔsterite] *nf* posterity.

posthume [pɔstym] *a* posthumous.

postiche [pɔstiʃ] *a* false // *nm* hairpiece.

postillonner [pɔstijɔne] *vi* to sp(l)utter.

post-scriptum [pɔstskriptɔm] *nm inv* postscript.

postulant, e [pɔstylɑ̃, -ɑ̃t] *nm/f* applicant.

postulat [pɔstyla] *nm* postulate.

postuler [pɔstyle] *vt* (*emploi*) to apply for, put in for.

posture [pɔstyr] *nf* posture, position ; (*fig*) position.

pot [po] *nm* jar, pot ; carton ; (*en métal*) tin ; **boire un ~** (*fam*) to have a drink ; ~ (**de chambre**) (chamber)pot ; ~ **d'échappement** exhaust pipe ; ~ **de fleurs** plant pot, flowerpot ; (*fleurs*) pot plant ; ~ **à tabac** tobacco jar.

potable [pɔtabl(ə)] *a* (*fig*) drinkable ; decent ; **eau** ~ drinking water.

potache [pɔtaʃ] *nm* schoolboy.

potage [pɔtaʒ] *nm* soup ; soup course.

potager, ère [pɔtaʒe, -ɛʀ] *a* (*plante*) edible, vegetable *cpd* ; (**jardin**) ~ kitchen *ou* vegetable garden.

potasse [pɔtas] *nf* potassium hydroxide ; (*engrais*) potash.

potasser [pɔtase] *vt* (*fam*) to swot up.

pot-au-feu [pɔtofø] *nm inv* (beef) stew ; (*viande*) stewing beef.

pot-de-vin [pɔdvɛ̃] *nm* bribe.

poteau, x [pɔto] *nm* post ; ~ (**d'exécution**) execution post, stake ; ~ **indicateur** signpost ; ~ **télégraphique** telegraph pole ; ~**x** (**de but**) goal-posts.

potelé, e [pɔtle] *a* plump, chubby.

potence [pɔtɑ̃s] *nf* gallows *sg*.

potentiel, le [pɔtɑ̃sjɛl] *a, nm* potential.

poterie [pɔtʀi] *nf* pottery ; piece of pottery.

potiche [pɔtiʃ] *nf* large vase.

potier [pɔtje] *nm* potter.

potins [pɔtɛ̃] *nmpl* gossip *sg*.

potion [posjɔ̃] *nf* potion.

potiron [pɔtiʀɔ̃] *nm* pumpkin.

pot-pourri [popuʀi] *nm* potpourri, medley.

pou, x [pu] *nm* louse (*pl* lice).

poubelle [pubɛl] *nf* (dust)bin.

pouce [pus] *nm* thumb.

poudre [pudʀ(ə)] *nf* powder ; (*fard*) (face) powder ; (*explosif*) gunpowder ; **en** ~: **café en** ~ instant coffee ; **savon en** ~ soap powder ; **lait en** ~ dried *ou* powdered milk ; **poudrer** *vt* to powder ; ~**rie** *nf* gunpowder factory ; **poudreux, euse** *a* dusty ; powdery ; **neige poudreuse** powder snow ; **poudrier** *nm* (powder) compact ; **poudrière** *nf* powder magazine ; (*fig*) powder keg.

poudroyer [pudʀwaje] *vi* to rise in clouds *ou* a flurry.

pouf [puf] *nm* pouffe.

pouffer [pufe] *vi* : ~ (**de rire**) to snigger ; to giggle.

pouilleux, euse [pujø, -øz] *a* flea-ridden ; (*fig*) grubby ; seedy.

poulailler [pulaje] *nm* henhouse ; (*THÉÂTRE*) **le** ~ the gods *sg*.

poulain [pulɛ̃] *nm* foal ; (*fig*) protégé.

poularde [pulaʀd(ə)] *nf* fatted chicken.

poule [pul] *nf* (*ZOOL*) hen ; (*CULIN*) (boiling) fowl ; (*fam*) tart ; broad ; ~ **d'eau** moorhen ; ~ **mouillée** coward ; ~ **pondeuse** layer ; ~ **au riz** chicken and rice.

poulet [pulɛ] *nm* chicken ; (*fam*) cop.

pouliche [puliʃ] *nf* filly.

poulie [puli] *nf* pulley ; block.

poulpe [pulp(ə)] *nm* octopus.

pouls [pu] *nm* pulse ; **prendre le** ~ **de qn** to feel sb's pulse.

poumon [pumɔ̃] *nm* lung ; ~ **d'acier** iron lung.

poupe [pup] *nf* stern ; **en** ~ astern.

poupée [pupe] *nf* doll ; **jouer à la** ~ to play with one's doll *ou* dolls.

poupon [pupɔ̃] *nm* babe-in-arms ; **pouponnière** *nf* crèche, day nursery.

pour [puʀ] *prép* for ; ~ **faire** (so as) to do, in order to do ; ~ **avoir fait** for having done ; ~ **que** so that, in order that ; ~ **riche qu'il soit** rich though he may be ; ~ **10 F d'essence** 10 francs' worth of petrol ; ~ **cent** per cent ; ~ **ce qui est de** as for ; **le** ~ **et le contre** the pros and cons.

pourboire [puʀbwaʀ] *nm* tip.

pourcentage [puʀsɑ̃taʒ] *nm* percentage.

pourchasser [puʀʃase] *vt* to pursue.

pourlécher [puʀleʃe]: **se** ~ *vi* to lick one's lips.

pourparlers [puʀpaʀle] *nmpl* talks, negotiations ; **être en** ~ **avec** to be having talks with.

pourpre [puʀpʀ(ə)] *a* crimson.

pourquoi [puʀkwa] *ad, cj* why // *nm inv*: **le** ~ (**de**) the reason (for).

pourrai *etc vb voir* **pouvoir**.

pourri, e [puʀi] *a* rotten.

pourrir [puʀiʀ] *vi* to rot ; (*fruit*) to go rotten *ou* bad // *vt* to rot ; (*fig*) to corrupt ; to spoil thoroughly ; **pourriture** *nf* rot.

pourrons *etc vb voir* **pouvoir**.

poursuite [puʀsɥit] *nf* pursuit, chase ; ~**s** *nfpl* (*JUR*) legal proceedings ; (**course**) ~ track race ; (*fig*) chase.

poursuivant, e [puʀsɥivɑ̃, -ɑ̃t] *nm/f* pursuer.

poursuivre [puʀsɥivʀ(ə)] *vt* to pursue, chase (after) ; (*relancer*) to hound, harry ; (*obséder*) to haunt ; (*JUR*) to bring proceedings against, prosecute ; (: *au civil*) to sue ; (*but*) to strive towards ; (*voyage, études*) to carry on with, continue // *vi* to carry on, go on ; **se** ~ *vi* to go on, continue.

pourtant [puʀtɑ̃] *ad* yet ; **c'est** ~ **facile** (and) yet it's easy.

pourtour [puʀtuʀ] *nm* perimeter.

pourvoi [puʀvwa] *nm* appeal.

pourvoir [puʀvwaʀ] *vt*: ~ **qch/qn de** to equip sth/sb with // *vi*: ~ **à** to provide for ; (*emploi*) to fill ; **se** ~ (*JUR*): **se** ~ **en cassation** to take one's case to the Court of Appeal.

pourvu, e [puʀvy] *a*: ~ **de** equipped with ; ~ **que** *cj* (*si*) provided that, so long as ; (*espérons que*) let's hope (that).

pousse [pus] *nf* growth ; (*bourgeon*) shoot.

poussé, e [puse] *a* sophisticated, advanced ; (*moteur*) souped-up.

pousse-café [puskafe] *nm inv* (after-dinner) liqueur.

poussée [puse] *nf* thrust ; (*coup*) push ; (*MÉD*) eruption ; (*fig*) upsurge.

pousse-pousse [puspus] *nm inv* rickshaw.

pousser [puse] *vt* to push ; (*inciter*): ~ **qn à** to urge *ou* press sb to + *infinitif*; (*acculer*): ~ **qn à** to drive sb to ; (*émettre*: *cri etc*) to give ; (*stimuler*) to urge on ; to drive hard ; (*poursuivre*) to carry on (further) // *vi* to push ; (*croître*) to grow ; (*aller*): ~ **plus loin** to push on a bit further ; **se** ~ *vi* to move over ; **faire** ~ (*plante*) to grow.

poussette [pusɛt] *nf* (*voiture d'enfant*) push chair.

poussière [pusjɛʀ] *nf* dust ; (*grain*) speck of dust ; **et des ~s** (*fig*) and a bit ; **~ de charbon** coaldust ; **poussiéreux, euse** *a* dusty.

poussif, ive [pusif, -iv] *a* wheezy, wheezing.

poussin [pusɛ̃] *nm* chick.

poutre [putʀ(ə)] *nf* beam ; (*en fer, ciment armé*) girder ; **poutrelle** *nf* girder.

pouvoir [puvwaʀ] *nm* power ; (POL: *dirigeants*): **le ~** those in power, the government // *vb* + *infinitif* can ; (*suj: personne*) can, to be able to ; (*permission*) can, may ; (*probabilité, hypothèse*) may ; **il peut arriver que** it may happen that ; **il pourrait pleuvoir** it might rain ; **déçu de ne pas ~ le faire** disappointed not to be able to do it *ou* that he couldn't do it ; **il aurait pu le dire!** he could *ou* might have said! ; **il se peut que** it may be that ; **je n'en peux plus** I'm exhausted ; I can't take any more ; **~ d'achat** purchasing power ; **les ~s publics** the authorities.

prairie [pʀeʀi] *nf* meadow.

praliné, e [pʀaline] *a* sugared ; praline-flavoured.

praticable [pʀatikabl(ə)] *a* passable, practicable.

praticien, ne [pʀatisjɛ̃, -jɛn] *nm/f* practitioner.

pratiquant, e [pʀatikɑ̃, -ɑ̃t] *a* practising.

pratique [pʀatik] *nf* practice // *a* practical ; **dans la ~** in (actual) practice ; **mettre en ~** to put into practice.

pratiquement [pʀatikmɑ̃] *ad* (*pour ainsi dire*) practically, virtually.

pratiquer [pʀatike] *vt* to practise ; (*intervention, opération*) to carry out ; (*ouverture, abri*) to make // *vi* (REL) to be a churchgoer.

pré [pʀe] *nm* meadow.

préalable [pʀealabl(ə)] *a* preliminary ; **condition ~ (de)** precondition (for), prerequisite (for) ; **sans avis ~** without prior *ou* previous notice ; **au ~** first, beforehand.

préambule [pʀeɑ̃byl] *nm* preamble ; (*fig*) prelude ; **sans ~** straight away.

préau, x [pʀeo] *nm* playground ; inner courtyard.

préavis [pʀeavi] *nm* notice ; **~ de congé** notice ; **communication avec ~** (TÉL) personal *ou* person to person call.

précaire [pʀekɛʀ] *a* precarious.

précaution [pʀekosjɔ̃] *nf* precaution ; **avec ~** cautiously ; **par ~** as a precaution.

précédemment [pʀesedamɑ̃] *ad* before, previously.

précédent, e [pʀesedɑ̃, -ɑ̃t] *a* previous // *nm* precedent ; **sans ~** unprecedented ; **le jour ~** the day before, the previous day.

précéder [pʀesede] *vt* to precede ; (*marcher ou rouler devant*) to be in front of ; (*arriver avant*) to get ahead of.

précepte [pʀesɛpt(ə)] *nm* precept.

précepteur, trice [pʀesɛptœʀ, tʀis] *nm/f* (private) tutor.

prêcher [pʀeʃe] *vt* to preach.

précieux, euse [pʀesjø, -øz] *a* precious ; invaluable ; (*style, écrivain*) précieux, precious.

précipice [pʀesipis] *nm* drop, chasm ; (*fig*) abyss ; **au bord du ~** at the edge of the precipice.

précipitamment [pʀesipitamɑ̃] *ad* hurriedly, hastily.

précipitation [pʀesipitɑsjɔ̃] *nf* (*hâte*) haste ; **~s (atmosphériques)** (atmospheric) precipitation *sg*.

précipité, e [pʀesipite] *a* fast ; hurried ; hasty.

précipiter [pʀesipite] *vt* (*faire tomber*): **~ qn/qch du haut de** to throw *or* hurl sb/sth off *ou* from ; (*hâter: marche*) to quicken ; (: *départ (événements)*) to move faster ; **se ~ sur/vers** to rush at/towards.

précis, e [pʀesi, -iz] *a* precise ; (*tir, mesures*) accurate, precise // *nm* handbook ; **précisément** *ad* precisely ; **préciser** *vt* (*expliquer*) to be more specific about, clarify ; (*spécifier*) to state, specify ; **se préciser** *vi* to become clear(er) ; **précision** *nf* precision ; accuracy ; point *ou* detail (*made clear or to be clarified*) ; **précisions** *nfpl* further details.

précoce [pʀekɔs] *a* early ; (*enfant*) precocious ; (*calvitie*) premature.

préconçu, e [pʀekɔ̃sy] *a* preconceived.

préconiser [pʀekɔnize] *vt* to advocate.

précurseur [pʀekyʀsœʀ] *am* precursory // *nm* forerunner, precursor.

prédécesseur [pʀedesesœʀ] *nm* predecessor.

prédestiner [pʀedɛstine] *vt*: **~ qn à qch/faire** to predestine sb for sth/to do.

prédicateur [pʀedikatœʀ] *nm* preacher.

prédiction [pʀediksjɔ̃] *nf* prediction.

prédilection [pʀedilɛksjɔ̃] *nf*: **avoir une ~ pour** to be partial to ; **de ~** favourite.

prédire [pʀediʀ] *vt* to predict.

prédisposer [pʀedispoze] *vt*: **~ qn à qch/faire** to predispose sb to sth/to do.

prédominer [pʀedɔmine] *vi* to predominate ; (*avis*) to prevail.

préfabriqué, e [pʀefabʀike] *a* prefabricated // *nm* prefabricated material.

préface [pʀefas] *nf* preface ; **préfacer** *vt* to write a preface for.

préfectoral, e, aux [pʀefɛktɔʀal, -o] *a* prefectoral.

préfecture [pʀefɛktyʀ] *nf* prefecture ; **~ de police** police headquarters.

préférable [pʀefeʀabl(ə)] *a* preferable.

préféré, e [pʀefeʀe] *a, nm/f* favourite.

préférence [pʀefeʀɑ̃s] *nf* preference ; **de ~** preferably ; **de ~ à** in preference to, rather than ; **obtenir la ~ sur** to have preference over ; **préférentiel, le** *a* preferential.

préférer [pʀefeʀe] *vt*: **~ qn/qch (à)** to prefer sb/sth (to), like sb/sth better (than) ; **~ faire** to prefer to do ; **je préférerais du thé** I would rather have tea, I'd prefer tea.

préfet [pʀefɛ] *nm* prefect ; **~ de police** prefect of police, ≈ Metropolitan Commissioner.

préfixe [pʀefiks(ə)] *nm* prefix.

préhistoire [pʀeistwaʀ] *nf* prehistory ; **préhistorique** *a* prehistoric.

préjudice [pʀeʒydis] nm (matériel) loss; (moral) harm q; **porter** ~ **à** to harm, be detrimental to; **au** ~ **de** at the expense of.

préjugé [pʀeʒyʒe] nm prejudice; **avoir un** ~ **contre** to be prejudiced ou biased against.

préjuger [pʀeʒyʒe]: ~ **de** vt to prejudge.

prélasser [pʀelɑse]: **se** ~ vi to lounge.

prélat [pʀela] nm prelate.

prélavage [pʀelavaʒ] nm pre-wash.

prélèvement [pʀelɛvmɑ̃] nm deduction; withdrawal; **faire un** ~ **de sang** to take a blood sample.

prélever [pʀelve] vt (échantillon) to take; (argent): ~ **(sur)** to deduct (from); (: sur son compte): ~ **(sur)** to withdraw (from).

préliminaire [pʀeliminɛʀ] a preliminary; ~**s** nmpl preliminary talks; preliminaries.

prélude [pʀelyd] nm prelude; (avant le concert) warm-up.

prématuré, e [pʀematyʀe] a premature; (retraite) early // nm premature baby.

préméditation [pʀemeditɑsjɔ̃] nf: **avec** ~ **a** premeditated // ad with intent; **préméditer** vt to premeditate, plan.

premier, ière [pʀəmje, -jɛʀ] a first; (branche, marche, grade) bottom; (fig) basic; prime; initial // nf (THÉÂTRE) first night; (CINÉMA) première; (exploit) first; **le** ~ **venu** the first person to come along; **P— Ministre** Prime Minister; **premièrement** ad firstly.

prémisse [pʀemis] nf premise.

prémonition [pʀemɔnisjɔ̃] nf premonition; **prémonitoire** a premonitory.

prémunir [pʀemyniʀ]: **se** ~ vi: **se** ~ **contre** to protect o.s. from, guard o.s. against.

prénatal, e [pʀenatal] a (MÉD) antenatal.

prendre [pʀɑ̃dʀ(ə)] vt to take; (ôter): ~ **qch à** to take sth from; (aller chercher) to get, fetch; (se procurer) to get; (malfaiteur, poisson) to catch; (passager) to pick up; (personnel, aussi: couleur, goût) to take on; (locataire) to take in; (élève etc: traiter) to handle; (voix, ton) to put on; (coincer): **se** ~ **les doigts dans** to get one's fingers caught in // vi (liquide, ciment) to set; (greffe, vaccin) to take; (mensonge) to be successful; (feu: foyer) to go; (: incendie) to start; (allumette) to light; (se diriger): ~ **à gauche** to turn (to the) left; ~ **qn pour** to take sb for; **se** ~ **pour** to think one is; **s'en** ~ **à** (agresser) to set about; (critiquer) to attack; **se** ~ **d'amitié/d'affection pour** to befriend/become fond of; **s'y** ~ (procéder) to set about it; **s'y** ~ **à l'avance** to see to it in advance; **s'y** ~ **à deux fois** to try twice, make two attemps.

preneur [pʀənœʀ] nm: **être/trouver** ~ to be willing to buy/find a buyer.

preniez, prenne etc vb voir **prendre**.

prénom [pʀenɔ̃] nm first ou Christian name; **prénommer** vt: **elle se prénomme Claude** her (first) name is Claude.

prénuptial, e, aux [pʀenypsjal, -o] a premarital.

préoccupation [pʀeɔkypɑsjɔ̃] nf (souci) worry, anxiety; (idée fixe) preoccupation.

préoccuper [pʀeɔkype] vt to worry; to preoccupy; **se** ~ **de qch** to be concerned about sth; to show concern about sth.

préparatifs [pʀepaʀatif] nmpl preparations.

préparation [pʀepaʀɑsjɔ̃] nf preparation; (SCOL) piece of homework.

préparatoire [pʀepaʀatwaʀ] a preparatory.

préparer [pʀepaʀe] vt to prepare; (café) to make; (examen) to prepare for; (voyage, entreprise) to plan; **se** ~ vi (orage, tragédie) to brew, be in the air; **se** ~ **(à qch/faire)** to prepare (o.s.) ou get ready (for sth/to do); ~ **qch à qn** (surprise etc) to have sth in store for sb.

prépondérant, e [pʀepɔ̃deʀɑ̃, -ɑ̃t] a major, dominating.

préposé, e [pʀepoze] a: ~ **à** in charge of // nm/f employee; official; attendant; postman/woman.

préposition [pʀepozisjɔ̃] nf preposition.

prérogative [pʀeʀɔgativ] nf prerogative.

près [pʀɛ] ad near, close; ~ **de** prép near (to), close to; (environ) nearly, almost; **de** ~ ad closely; **à 5 kg** ~ to within about 5 kg; **à cela** ~ **que** apart from the fact that.

présage [pʀezaʒ] nm omen.

présager [pʀezaʒe] vt to foresee.

presbyte [pʀɛsbit] a long-sighted.

presbytère [pʀɛsbitɛʀ] nm presbytery.

presbytérien, ne [pʀɛsbiteʀjɛ̃, -jɛn] a, nm/f Presbyterian.

prescription [pʀɛskʀipsjɔ̃] nf (instruction) order, instruction; (MÉD, JUR) prescription.

prescrire [pʀɛskʀiʀ] vt to prescribe; **se** ~ vi (JUR) to lapse; **prescrit, e** a (date etc) stipulated.

préséance [pʀeseɑ̃s] nf precedence q.

présence [pʀezɑ̃s] nf presence; (au bureau etc) attendance; **en** ~ **de** in (the) presence of; (fig) in the face of; ~ **d'esprit** presence of mind.

présent, e [pʀezɑ̃, -ɑ̃t] a, nm present; **à** ~ **(que)** now (that).

présentateur, trice [pʀezɑ̃tatœʀ, -tʀis] nm/f presenter.

présentation [pʀezɑ̃tɑsjɔ̃] nf introduction; presentation; (allure) appearance.

présenter [pʀezɑ̃te] vt to present; (soumettre) to submit; (invité, conférencier): ~ **qn (à)** to introduce sb (to) // vi: ~ **mal/bien** to have an unattractive/a pleasing appearance; **se** ~ vi (sur convocation) to report, come; (à une élection) to stand; (occasion) to arise; **se** ~ **bien/mal** to look good/not too good; **présentoir** nm display shelf (pl shelves).

préservatif [pʀezɛʀvatif] nm sheath, condom.

préserver [pʀezɛʀve] vt: ~ **de** to protect from; to save from.

présidence [pʀezidɑ̃s] nf presidency; office of President; chairmanship.

président [pʀezidɑ̃] nm (POL) president; (d'une assemblée, COMM) chairman; ~ **directeur général (P.D.G.)** chairman and managing director; ~ **du jury** (JUR) foreman of the jury; (*d'examen*) chief examiner; **présidente** *nf* president; president's wife; chairwoman; **présidentiel, le** [-sjɛl] *a* presidential.

présider [pʀezide] *vt* to preside over; (*dîner*) to be the guest of honour at; ~ à *vt* to direct; to govern.

présomption [pʀezɔ̃psjɔ̃] *nf* presumption.

présomptueux, euse [pʀezɔ̃ptɥø, -øz] *a* presumptuous.

presque [pʀɛsk(ə)] *ad* almost, nearly; ~ **rien** hardly anything; ~ **pas** hardly (at all).

presqu'île [pʀɛskil] *nf* peninsula.

pressant, e [pʀɛsɑ̃, -ɑ̃t] *a* urgent.

presse [pʀɛs] *nf* press; (*affluence*): **heures de** ~ busy times; **sous** ~ a in press, being printed; ~ **féminine** women's magazines *pl*; ~ **d'information** quality newspapers *pl*.

pressé, e [pʀese] *a* in a hurry; (*air*) hurried; (*besogne*) urgent; **orange** ~**e** fresh orange juice.

presse-citron [pʀɛssitʀɔ̃] *nm inv* lemon squeezer.

pressentiment [pʀesɑ̃timɑ̃] *nm* foreboding, premonition.

pressentir [pʀesɑ̃tiʀ] *vt* to sense; (*prendre contact avec*) to approach.

presse-papiers [pʀɛspapje] *nm inv* paperweight.

presser [pʀese] *vt* (*fruit, éponge*) to squeeze; (*interrupteur, bouton*) to press, push; (*allure, affaire*) to speed up; (*débiteur etc*) to press; (*inciter*): ~ **qn de faire** to urge *ou* press sb to do // *vi* to be urgent; **rien ne presse** there's no hurry; **se** ~ (*se hâter*) to hurry (up); (*se grouper*) to crowd; **se** ~ **contre qn** to squeeze up against sb; ~ **qn entre ses bras** to hug sb (tight).

pressing [pʀesiŋ] *nm* steam-pressing; (*magasin*) dry-cleaner's.

pression [pʀesjɔ̃] *nf* pressure; **faire** ~ **sur** to put pressure on; **sous** ~ pressurized, under pressure; (*fig*) keyed up; ~ **artérielle** blood pressure.

pressoir [pʀeswaʀ] *nm* (wine *ou* oil *etc*) press.

pressurer [pʀesyʀe] *vt* (*fig*) to squeeze.

pressurisé, e [pʀesyʀize] *a* pressurized.

prestance [pʀɛstɑ̃s] *nf* presence, imposing bearing.

prestataire [pʀɛstatɛʀ] *nm/f* person receiving benefits.

prestation [pʀɛstasjɔ̃] *nf* (*allocation*) benefit; (*d'une assurance*) cover *q*; (*d'une entreprise*) service provided; (*d'un joueur, artiste*) performance; ~ **de serment** taking the oath; ~ **de service** provision of a service.

preste [pʀɛst(ə)] *a* nimble; swift; ~**ment** *ad* swiftly.

prestidigitateur, trice [pʀɛstidiʒitatœʀ, -tʀis] *nm/f* conjurer.

prestidigitation [pʀɛstidiʒitasjɔ̃] *nf* conjuring.

prestige [pʀɛstiʒ] *nm* prestige; **prestigieux, euse** *a* prestigious.

présumer [pʀezyme] *vt*: ~ **que** to presume *ou* assume that; ~ **de** to

overrate; ~ **qn coupable** to presume sb guilty.

prêt, e [pʀɛ, pʀɛt] *a* ready // *nm* lending *q*; loan; ~ **sur gages** pawnbroking *q*; **prêt-à-porter** *nm* ready-to-wear *ou* off-the-peg clothes *pl*.

prétendant [pʀetɑ̃dɑ̃] *nm* pretender; (*d'une femme*) suitor.

prétendre [pʀetɑ̃dʀ(ə)] *vt* (*affirmer*): ~ **que** to claim that; (*avoir l'intention de*): ~ **faire qch** to mean *ou* intend to do sth; ~ **à** *vt* (*droit, titre*) to lay claim to; **prétendu, e** *a* (*supposé*) so-called.

prête-nom [pʀɛtnɔ̃] *nm* (*péj*) figurehead.

prétentieux, euse [pʀetɑ̃sjø, -øz] *a* pretentious.

prétention [pʀetɑ̃sjɔ̃] *nf* claim; pretentiousness.

prêter [pʀete] *vt* (*livres, argent*): ~ **qch (à)** to lend sth (to); (*supposer*): ~ **à qn** (*caractère, propos*) to attribute to sb // *vi* (*aussi*: **se** ~: *tissu, cuir*) to give; ~ **à** (*commentaires etc*) to be open to, give rise to; **se** ~ **à** to lend o.s. (*ou* itself) to; (*manigances etc*) to go along with; ~ **assistance à** to give help to; ~ **serment** to take the oath; ~ **l'oreille** to listen; **prêteur** *nm* moneylender; **prêteur sur gages** pawnbroker.

prétexte [pʀetɛkst(ə)] *nm* pretext, excuse; **sous aucun** ~ on no account; **prétexter** *vt* to give as a pretext *ou* an excuse.

prêtre [pʀɛtʀ(ə)] *nm* priest; **prêtrise** *nf* priesthood.

preuve [pʀœv] *nf* proof; (*indice*) proof, evidence *q*; **faire** ~ **de** to show; **faire ses** ~**s** to prove o.s. (*ou* itself).

prévaloir [pʀevalwaʀ] *vi* to prevail; **se** ~ **de** *vt* to take advantage of; to pride o.s. on.

prévenances [pʀevnɑ̃s] *nfpl* thoughtfulness *sg*, kindness *sg*.

prévenant, e [pʀevnɑ̃, -ɑ̃t] *a* thoughtful, kind.

prévenir [pʀevniʀ] *vt* (*avertir*): ~ **qn (de)** to warn sb (about); (*informer*): ~ **qn (de)** to tell *ou* inform sb (about); (*éviter*) to avoid, prevent; (*anticiper*) to forestall; to anticipate; (*influencer*): ~ **qn contre** to prejudice sb against.

préventif, ive [pʀevɑ̃tif, -iv] *a* preventive.

prévention [pʀevɑ̃sjɔ̃] *nf* prevention; ~ **routière** road safety.

prévenu, e [pʀevny] *nm/f* (*JUR*) defendant, accused.

prévision [pʀevizjɔ̃] *nf*: ~**s** predictions forecast *sg*; **en** ~ **de** in anticipation of; ~**s météorologiques** *ou* **du temps** weather forecast *sg*.

prévoir [pʀevwaʀ] *vt* (*deviner*) to foresee; (*s'attendre à*) to expect, reckon on; (*prévenir*) to anticipate; (*organiser*) to plan; (*préparer, réserver*) to allow; **prévu pour 4 personnes** designed for 4 people; **prévu pour 10h** scheduled for 10 o'clock.

prévoyance [pʀevwajɑ̃s] *nf* foresight; **une société/caisse de** ~ a provident society/contingency fund.

prévoyant, e [pʀevwajɑ̃, -ɑ̃t] *a* gifted with (*ou* showing) foresight.

prier [pʀije] *vi* to pray // *vt* (*Dieu*) to pray to ; (*implorer*) to beg ; (*demander*): ~ **qn de faire** to ask sb to do ; **se faire** ~ to need coaxing *ou* persuading ; **je vous en prie** please do ; don't mention it.

prière [pʀijɛʀ] *nf* prayer ; '~ **de faire ...**' 'please do ...'.

primaire [pʀimɛʀ] *a* primary ; (*péj*) simple-minded ; simplistic // *nm* (*SCOL*) primary education.

primauté [pʀimote] *nf* (*fig*) primacy.

prime [pʀim] *nf* (*bonification*) bonus ; (*subside*) premium ; allowance ; (*COMM*: *cadeau*) free gift ; (*ASSURANCES, BOURSE*) premium // *a*: **de** ~ **abord** at first glance ; ~ **de risque** danger money *q*.

primer [pʀime] *vt* (*l'emporter sur*) to prevail over ; (*récompenser*) to award a prize to // *vi* to dominate ; to prevail.

primesautier, ère [pʀimsotje, -jɛʀ] *a* impulsive.

primeur [pʀimœʀ] *nf*: **avoir la** ~ **de** to be the first to hear (*ou* see *etc*) ; ~**s** *nfpl* (*fruits, légumes*) early fruits and vegetables ; **marchand de** ~**s** greengrocer.

primevère [pʀimvɛʀ] *nf* primrose.

primitif, ive [pʀimitif, -iv] *a* primitive ; (*originel*) original // *nm/f* primitive.

primordial, e, aux [pʀimɔʀdjal, -o] *a* essential, primordial.

prince, esse [pʀɛ̃s, pʀɛ̃sɛs] *nm/f* prince/princess ; ~ **de Galles** *nm inv* check cloth ; ~ **héritier** crown prince ; **princier, ière** *a* princely.

principal, e, aux [pʀɛ̃sipal, -o] *a* principal, main // *nm* (*SCOL*) principal, head(master) // *nf*: (**proposition**) ~**e** main clause.

principauté [pʀɛ̃sipote] *nf* Principality.

principe [pʀɛ̃sip] *nm* principle ; **partir du** ~ **que** to work on the principle *ou* assumption that ; **pour le** ~ on principle, for the sake of it ; **de** ~ *a* (*accord, hostilité*) automatic ; **par** ~ on principle ; **en** ~ (*habituellement*) as a rule ; (*théoriquement*) in principle.

printanier, ère [pʀɛ̃tanje, -jɛʀ] *a* spring *cpd* ; spring-like.

printemps [pʀɛ̃tɑ̃] *nm* spring.

priori [pʀijɔʀi]: **a** ~ *ad* without the benefit of hindsight ; a priori ; initially.

prioritaire [pʀijɔʀitɛʀ] *a* having priority ; (*AUTO*) having right of way.

priorité [pʀijɔʀite] *nf* (*AUTO*): **avoir la** ~ (**sur**) to have right of way (over) ; ~ **à droite** right of way to vehicles coming from the right ; **en** ~ as a (matter of) priority.

pris, e [pʀi, pʀiz] *pp de* **prendre** // *a* (*place*) taken ; (*journée, mains*) full ; (*billets*) sold ; (*personne*) busy ; (*MÉD*: *enflammé*): **avoir le nez/la gorge** ~(**e**) to have a stuffy nose/a hoarse throat ; (*saisi*): **être** ~ **de peur/de fatigue** to be stricken with fear/overcome with fatigue.

prise [pʀiz] *nf* (*d'une ville*) capture ; (*PÊCHE, CHASSE*) catch ; (*de judo ou catch, point d'appui ou pour empoigner*) hold ; (*ÉLEC*: *fiche*) plug ; (: *femelle*) socket ; (: *au mur*) point ; **en** ~ (*AUTO*) in gear ; **être aux** ~**s avec** to be grappling with ; to be battling

with ; **lâcher** ~ to let go ; ~ **en charge** (*taxe*) pick-up charge ; ~ **de courant** power point ; ~ **d'eau** water (supply) point ; tap ; ~ **multiple** adaptor ; ~ **de sang** blood test ; ~ **de son** sound recording ; ~ **de tabac** pinch of snuff ; ~ **de terre** earth ; ~ **de vue(s)** filming, shooting.

priser [pʀize] *vt* (*tabac, héroïne*) to take ; (*estimer*) to prize, value // *vi* to take snuff.

prisme [pʀism(ə)] *nm* prism.

prison [pʀizɔ̃] *nf* prison ; **aller/être en** ~ to go to/be in prison *ou* jail ; **faire de la** ~ to serve time ; **prisonnier, ière** *nm/f* prisoner // *a* captive ; **faire qn prisonnier** to take sb prisoner.

prit *vb voir* **prendre**.

privations [pʀivasjɔ̃] *nfpl* privations, hardships.

privé, e [pʀive] *a* private ; (*dépourvu*): ~ **de** without, lacking ; **en** ~ in private.

priver [pʀive] *vt*: ~ **qn de** to deprive sb of ; **se** ~ **de** to go *ou* do without ; **ne pas se** ~ **de faire** not to refrain from doing.

privilège [pʀivilɛʒ] *nm* privilege ; **privilégié, e** *a* privileged.

prix [pʀi] *nm* (*valeur*) price ; (*récompense, SCOL*) prize ; **hors de** ~ exorbitantly priced ; **à aucun** ~ not at any price ; **à tout** ~ at all costs ; ~ **d'achat/de vente** purchasing/selling price.

probabilité [pʀɔbabilite] *nf* probability.

probable [pʀɔbabl(ə)] *a* likely, probable ; ~**ment** *ad* probably.

probant, e [pʀɔbɑ̃, -ɑ̃t] *a* convincing.

probité [pʀɔbite] *nf* integrity, probity.

problème [pʀɔblɛm] *nm* problem.

procédé [pʀɔsede] *nm* (*méthode*) process ; (*comportement*) behaviour *q*.

procéder [pʀɔsede] *vi* to proceed ; to behave ; ~ **à** *vt* to carry out.

procédure [pʀɔsedyʀ] *nf* (*ADMIN, JUR*) procedure.

procès [pʀɔsɛ] *nm* trial ; (*poursuites*) proceedings *pl* ; **être en** ~ **avec** to be involved in a lawsuit with.

procession [pʀɔsesjɔ̃] *nf* procession.

processus [pʀɔsesys] *nm* process.

procès-verbal, aux [pʀɔsɛvɛʀbal, -o] *nm* (*constat*) statement ; (*aussi*: **P.V.**): **avoir un** ~ to get a parking ticket ; to be booked ; (*de réunion*) minutes *pl*.

prochain, e [pʀɔʃɛ̃, -ɛn] *a* next ; (*proche*) impending ; near // *nm* fellow man ; **la** ~**e fois/semaine** ~**e** next time/week ; **prochainement** *ad* soon, shortly.

proche [pʀɔʃ] *a* nearby ; (*dans le temps*) imminent ; close at hand ; (*parent, ami*) close ; ~**s** *nmpl* close relatives, next of kin ; **être** ~ (**de**) to be near, be close (to) ; **de** ~ **en** ~ gradually ; **le P**— **Orient** the Middle East, the Near East.

proclamation [pʀɔklamɑsjɔ̃] *nf* proclamation.

proclamer [pʀɔklame] *vt* to proclaim.

procréer [pʀɔkʀee] *vt* to procreate.

procuration [pʀɔkyʀɑsjɔ̃] *nf* proxy ; power of attorney.

procurer [pʀɔkyʀe] *vt* (*fournir*): ~ **qch à qn** to get *ou* obtain sth for sb ; (*causer*:

plaisir etc): ~ **qch à qn** to bring *ou* give sb sth; **se** ~ *vt* to get.

procureur [pʀɔkyʀœʀ] *nm* public prosecutor.

prodige [pʀɔdiʒ] *nm* marvel, wonder; *(personne)* prodigy; **prodigieux, euse** *a* prodigious; phenomenal.

prodigue [pʀɔdig] *a* generous; extravagant, wasteful; **fils** ~ prodigal son.

prodiguer [pʀɔdige] *vt (argent, biens)* to be lavish with; *(soins, attentions):* ~ **qch à qn** to give sb sth; to lavish sth on sb.

producteur, trice [pʀɔdyktœʀ, -tʀis] *a:* ~ **de blé** wheat-producing // *nm/f* producer.

productif, ive [pʀɔdyktif, -iv] *a* productive.

production [pʀɔdyksjɔ̃] *nf (gén)* production; *(rendement)* output; *(produits)* products *pl*, goods *pl*.

productivité [pʀɔdyktivite] *nf* productivity.

produire [pʀɔdɥiʀ] *vt* to produce; **se** ~ *vi (acteur)* to perform, appear; *(événement)* to happen, occur.

produit [pʀɔdɥi] *nm (gén)* product; ~**s agricoles** farm produce *sg*; ~ **d'entretien** cleaning product.

proéminent, e [pʀɔeminɑ̃, -ɑ̃t] *a* prominent.

profane [pʀɔfan] *a (REL)* secular // *nm/f* layman.

profaner [pʀɔfane] *vt* to desecrate.

proférer [pʀɔfeʀe] *vt* to utter.

professer [pʀɔfese] *vt (déclarer)* to profess // *vi* to teach.

professeur [pʀɔfesœʀ] *nm* teacher; *(titulaire d'une chaire)* professor; ~ **(de faculté)** (university) lecturer.

profession [pʀɔfesjɔ̃] *nf* profession; **sans** ~ unemployed; **professionnel, le** *a, nm/f* professional.

professorat [pʀɔfesɔʀa] *nm:* **le** ~ **the** teaching profession.

profil [pʀɔfil] *nm* profile; *(d'une voiture)* line, contour; **de** ~ in profile; ~**er** *vt* to streamline; **se** ~**er** *vi (arbre, tour)* to stand out, be silhouetted.

profit [pʀɔfi] *nm (avantage)* benefit, advantage; *(COMM, FINANCE)* profit; **au** ~ **de** in aid of; **tirer** ~ **de** to profit from; **mettre à** ~ to take advantage of; to turn to good account.

profitable [pʀɔfitabl(ə)] *a* beneficial; profitable.

profiter [pʀɔfite] *vi:* ~ **de** to take advantage of; to make the most of; ~ **à** to be of benefit to, benefit; to be profitable to.

profond, e [pʀɔfɔ̃, -ɔ̃d] *a* deep; *(méditation, mépris)* profound; **profondeur** *nf* depth.

profusion [pʀɔfyzjɔ̃] *nf* profusion; **à** ~ in plenty.

progéniture [pʀɔʒenityʀ] *nf* offspring *inv.*

programmation [pʀɔgʀamasjɔ̃] *nf* programming.

programme [pʀɔgʀam] *nm* programme; *(TV, RADIO)* programmes *pl*; *(SCOL)* syllabus, curriculum; *(INFORMATIQUE)* program; **au** ~ **de ce soir** *(TV)* among tonight's

programmes; **programmer** *vt (TV, RADIO)* to put on, show; *(INFORMATIQUE)* to program; **programmeur, euse** *nm/f* computer programmer.

progrès [pʀɔgʀɛ] *nm* progress *q*; **faire des/être en** ~ to make/be making progress.

progresser [pʀɔgʀese] *vi* to progress; *(troupes etc)* to make headway *ou* progress; **progressif, ive** *a* progressive; **progression** *nf* progression; *(d'une troupe etc)* advance, progress.

prohiber [pʀɔibe] *vt* to prohibit, ban.

proie [pʀwa] *nf* prey *q*; **être la** ~ **de** to fall prey to; **être en** ~ **à** to be prey to; to be suffering.

projecteur [pʀɔʒɛktœʀ] *nm* projector; *(de théâtre, cirque)* spotlight.

projectile [pʀɔʒɛktil] *nm* missile; *(d'arme)* projectile, bullet *(ou shell etc).*

projection [pʀɔʒɛksjɔ̃] *nf* projection; showing; **conférence avec** ~**s** lecture with slides *(ou a film).*

projet [pʀɔʒɛ] *nm* plan; *(ébauche)* draft; **faire des** ~**s** to make plans; ~ **de loi** bill.

projeter [pʀɔʒte] *vt (envisager)* to plan; *(film, photos)* to project; *(: passer)* to show; *(ombre, lueur)* to throw, cast, project; *(jeter)* to throw up *(ou off ou out).*

prolétaire [pʀɔletɛʀ] *nm* proletarian; **prolétariat** *nm* proletariat.

proliférer [pʀɔlifeʀe] *vi* to proliferate.

prolifique [pʀɔlifik] *a* prolific.

prolixe [pʀɔliks(ə)] *a* verbose.

prologue [pʀɔlɔg] *nm* prologue.

prolongation [pʀɔlɔ̃gasjɔ̃] *nf* prolongation; extension; ~**s** *nfpl (FOOTBALL)* extra time *sg.*

prolongement [pʀɔlɔ̃ʒmɑ̃] *nm* extension; ~**s** *nmpl (fig)* repercussions, effects; **dans le** ~ **de** running on from.

prolonger [pʀɔlɔ̃ʒe] *vt (débat, séjour)* to prolong; *(délai, billet, rue)* to extend; *(suj: chose)* to be a continuation an extension of; **se** ~ *vi* to go on.

promenade [pʀɔmnad] *nf* walk *(ou drive ou ride)*; **faire une** ~ to go for a walk; **une** ~ **en voiture/à vélo** a drive/(bicycle) ride.

promener [pʀɔmne] *vt (chien)* to take out for a walk, *(fig)* to carry around; to trail round; *(doigts, regard):* ~ **qch sur** to run sth over; **se** ~ *vi* to go for *(ou be out for)* a walk, *(fig):* **se** ~ **sur** to wander over; **promeneur, euse** *nm/f* walker, stroller.

promesse [pʀɔmɛs] *nf* promise; ~ **d'achat** commitment to buy.

prometteur, euse [pʀɔmetœʀ, -øz] *a* promising.

promettre [pʀɔmɛtʀ(ə)] *vt* to promise // *vi* to be *ou* look promising; **se** ~ **de faire** to resolve *ou* mean to do; ~ **à qn de faire** to promise sb that one will do.

promiscuité [pʀɔmiskɥite] *nf* crowding; lack of privacy.

promontoire [pʀɔmɔ̃twaʀ] *nm* headland.

promoteur, trice [pʀɔmɔtœʀ, -tʀis] *nm/f (instigateur)* instigator, promoter; ~ **(immobilier)** property developer.

promotion [pʀɔmosjɔ̃] nf promotion.
promouvoir [pʀɔmuvwaʀ] vt to promote.
prompt, e [pʀɔ̃, pʀɔ̃t] a swift, rapid.
promulguer [pʀɔmylge] vt to promulgate.
prôner [pʀone] vt (louer) to laud, extol ; (préconiser) to advocate, commend.
pronom [pʀɔnɔ̃] nm pronoun ; **pronominal, e, aux** a pronominal ; reflexive.
prononcé, e [pʀɔnɔ̃se] a pronounced, marked.
prononcer [pʀɔnɔ̃se] vt (son, mot, jugement) to pronounce ; (dire) to utter ; (allocution) to deliver // vi : ~ **bien/mal** to have a good/poor pronunciation ; se ~ vi to reach a decision, give a verdict ; se ~ **sur** to give an opinion on ; se ~ **contre** to come down against ; **prononciation** nf pronunciation.
pronostic [pʀɔnɔstik] nm (MÉD) prognosis (pl oses) ; (fig: aussi: ~s) forecast.
propagande [pʀɔpagɑ̃d] nf propaganda.
propager [pʀɔpaʒe] vt to spread ; se ~ vi to spread ; (PHYSIQUE) to be propagated.
prophète [pʀɔfɛt] nm prophet.
prophétie [pʀɔfesi] nf prophecy ; **prophétiser** vt to prophesy.
propice [pʀɔpis] a favourable.
proportion [pʀɔpɔʀsjɔ̃] nf proportion ; **en** ~ **de** in proportion to ; **toute(s)** ~**(s) gardée(s)** making due allowance(s) ; **proportionnel, le** a proportional ; **proportionner** vt: **proportionner qch à** to proportion ou adjust sth to.
propos [pʀɔpo] nm (paroles) talk q, remark ; (intention) intention, aim ; (sujet): **à quel** ~? what about? ; **à** ~ **de** about, regarding ; **à tout** ~ for no reason at all ; **à** ~ ad by the way ; (opportunément) (just) at the right moment.
proposer [pʀɔpoze] vt (suggérer): ~ **qch (à qn)/de faire** to suggest sth (to sb)/doing, propose to do ; (offrir): ~ **qch à qn/de faire** to offer sb sth/to do ; (candidat) to nominate, put forward ; (loi, motion) to propose ; se ~ **(pour faire)** to offer one's services (to do) ; se ~ **de faire** to intend ou propose to do ; **proposition** nf suggestion ; proposal ; offer ; (LING) clause.
propre [pʀɔpʀ(ə)] a (net) clean, tidy ; (possessif) own ; (sens) literal ; (particulier): ~ **à** peculiar to, characteristic of ; (approprié): ~ **à** suitable ou appropriate for ; (de nature à): ~ **à faire** likely to do, that will do // nm: **recopier au** ~ to make a fair copy of ; ~**ment** ad cleanly ; neatly, tidily ; **à** ~**ment parler** strictly speaking ; ~**té** nf cleanliness, cleanness ; neatness ; tidiness.
propriétaire [pʀɔpʀijetɛʀ] nm/f owner ; (d'hôtel etc) proprietor/ tress, owner ; (pour le locataire) landlord/lady ; ~ **(immobilier)** house-owner ; householder ; ~ **récoltant** grower ; ~ **(terrien)** landowner.
propriété [pʀɔpʀijete] nf (droit) ownership ; (objet, immeuble etc) property gén q ; (villa) residence, property ; (terres) property gén q, land gén q ; (qualité, CHIMIE, MATH) property ; (correction) appropriateness, suitability.

propulser [pʀɔpylse] vt (missile) to propel ; (projeter) to hurl, fling.
prorata [pʀɔʀata] nm inv: **au** ~ **de** in proportion to, on the basis of.
proroger [pʀɔʀɔʒe] vt to put back, defer ; (assemblée) to adjourn, prorogue.
prosaïque [pʀozaik] a mundane, prosaic.
proscrire [pʀɔskʀiʀ] vt (bannir) to banish ; (interdire) to ban, prohibit.
prose [pʀoz] nf prose (style).
prospecter [pʀɔspɛkte] vt to prospect ; (COMM) to canvass.
prospectus [pʀɔspɛktys] nm (feuille) leaflet ; (dépliant) brochure, leaflet.
prospère [pʀɔspɛʀ] a prosperous ; (entreprise) thriving, flourishing ; **prospérer** vi to thrive ; **prospérité** nf prosperity.
prosterner [pʀɔstɛʀne]: se ~ vi to bow low, prostrate o.s.
prostituée [pʀɔstitɥe] nf prostitute.
prostitution [pʀɔstitysjɔ̃] nf prostitution.
prostré, e [pʀɔstʀe] a prostrate.
protagoniste [pʀɔtagɔnist(ə)] nm protagonist.
protecteur, trice [pʀɔtɛktœʀ, -tʀis] a protective ; (air, ton: péj) patronizing // nm/f protector.
protection [pʀɔtɛksjɔ̃] nf protection ; (d'un personnage influent: aide) patronage.
protégé, e [pʀɔteʒe] nm/f protégé/e.
protège-cahier [pʀɔtɛʒkaje] nm exercise-book cover.
protéger [pʀɔteʒe] vt to protect ; se ~ **de/contre** to protect o.s. from.
protéine [pʀɔtein] nf protein.
protestant, e [pʀɔtɛstɑ̃, -ɑ̃t] a, nm/f Protestant ; **protestantisme** nm Protestantism.
protestation [pʀɔtɛstasjɔ̃] nf (plainte) protest ; (déclaration) protestation, profession.
protester [pʀɔtɛste] vi: ~ **(contre)** to protest (against ou about) ; ~ **de** (son innocence, sa loyauté) to protest.
prothèse [pʀɔtɛz] nf artificial limb, prosthesis ; ~ **dentaire** denture ; dental engineering.
protocolaire [pʀɔtɔkɔlɛʀ] a formal ; of protocol.
protocole [pʀɔtɔkɔl] nm protocol ; (fig) etiquette ; ~ **d'accord** draft treaty.
prototype [pʀɔtɔtip] nm prototype.
protubérance [pʀɔtybeʀɑ̃s] nf bulge, protuberance ; **protubérant, e** a protruding, bulging, protuberant.
proue [pʀu] nf bow(s pl), prow.
prouesse [pʀuɛs] nf feat.
prouver [pʀuve] vt to prove.
provenance [pʀɔvnɑ̃s] nf origin ; (de mot, coutume) source ; **avion en** ~ **de** plane (arriving) from.
provenir [pʀɔvniʀ]: ~ **de** vt to come from ; (résulter de) to be due to, be the result of.
proverbe [pʀɔvɛʀb(ə)] nm proverb ; **proverbial, e, aux** a proverbial.
providence [pʀɔvidɑ̃s] nf: **la** ~ providence ; **providentiel, le** a providential.

province [pʀɔvɛ̃s] *nf* province; **provincial, e, aux** *a* provincial.
proviseur [pʀɔvizœʀ] *nm* ≈ head(master).
provision [pʀɔvizjɔ̃] *nf* (*réserve*) stock, supply; (*avance: à un avocat, avoué*) retainer, retaining fee; (*COMM*) funds *pl* (in account); reserve; ~**s** *nfpl* (*vivres*) provisions, food *q*; **faire** ~ **de** to stock up with; **armoire à** ~**s** food cupboard.
provisoire [pʀɔvizwaʀ] *a* temporary; (*JUR*) provisional; ~**ment** *ad* temporarily, for the time being.
provocant, e [pʀɔvɔkɑ̃, -ɑ̃t] *a* provocative.
provocation [pʀɔvɔkɑsjɔ̃] *nf* provocation.
provoquer [pʀɔvɔke] *vt* (*défier*) to provoke; (*causer*) to cause, bring about; (: *curiosité*) to arouse, give rise to; (: *aveux*) to prompt, elicit.
proxénète [pʀɔksenɛt] *nm* procurer.
proximité [pʀɔksimite] *nf* nearness, closeness, proximity; (*dans le temps*) imminence, closeness; **à** ~ near *ou* close by; **à** ~ **de** near (to), close to.
prude [pʀyd] *a* prudish.
prudence [pʀydɑ̃s] *nf* carefulness; caution; prudence; **avec** ~ carefully; cautiously; wisely; **par (mesure de)** ~ as a precaution.
prudent, e [pʀydɑ̃, -ɑ̃t] *a* (*pas téméraire*) careful, cautious, prudent; (: *en général*) safety-conscious; (*sage, conseillé*) wise, sensible; (*réservé*) cautious; **ce n'est pas** ~ it's risky; it's not sensible; **soyez** ~ take care, be careful.
prune [pʀyn] *nf* plum.
pruneau, x [pʀyno] *nm* prune.
prunelle [pʀynɛl] *nf* pupil; eye.
prunier [pʀynje] *nm* plum tree.
psalmodier [psalmɔdje] *vt* to chant; (*fig*) to drone out.
psaume [psom] *nm* psalm.
pseudonyme [psedɔnim] *nm* (*gén*) fictitious name; (*d'écrivain*) pseudonym, pen name; (*de comédien*) stage name.
psychanalyse [psikanaliz] *nf* psychoanalysis; **psychanalyser** *vt* to psychoanalyze; **se faire psychanalyser** to undergo (psycho)analysis; **psychanalyste** *nm/f* psychoanalyst.
psychiatre [psikjatʀ(ə)] *nm/f* psychiatrist.
psychiatrie [psikjatʀi] *nf* psychiatry; **psychiatrique** *a* psychiatric; (*hôpital*) mental, psychiatric.
psychique [psiʃik] *a* psychological.
psychologie [psikɔlɔʒi] *nf* psychology; **psychologique** *a* psychological; **psychologue** *nm/f* psychologist; **être psychologue** (*fig*) to be a good psychologist.
psychose [psikoz] *nf* psychosis; obsessive fear.
Pte *abr de* **porte**.
P.T.T. *sigle fpl voir* **poste**.
pu *pp de* **pouvoir**.
puanteur [pɥɑ̃tœʀ] *nf* stink, stench.
pubère [pybɛʀ] *a* pubescent; **puberté** *nf* puberty.

pubis [pybis] *nm* (*bas-ventre*) pubes *pl*; (*os*) pubis.
public, ique [pyblik] *a* public; (*école, instruction*) state *cpd* // *nm* public; (*assistance*) audience; **en** ~ in public.
publication [pyblikɑsjɔ̃] *nf* publication.
publiciste [pyblisist(ə)] *nm/f* adman.
publicitaire [pyblisitɛʀ] *a* advertising *cpd*; (*film, voiture*) publicity *cpd*.
publicité [pyblisite] *nf* (*méthode, profession*) advertising; (*annonce*) advertisement; (*révélations*) publicity.
publier [pyblije] *vt* to publish.
publique [pyblik] *af voir* **public**.
puce [pys] *nf* flea; ~**s** *nfpl* (*marché*) flea market *sg*.
puceau, x [pyso] *am*: **être** ~ to be a virgin.
pucelle [pysɛl] *af*: **être** ~ to be a virgin.
pudeur [pydœʀ] *nf* modesty.
pudibond, e [pydibɔ̃, -ɔ̃d] *a* prudish.
pudique [pydik] *a* (*chaste*) modest; (*discret*) discreet.
puer [pɥe] (*péj*) *vi* to stink // *vt* to stink of, reek of.
puéricultrice [pɥeʀikyltʀis] *nf* paediatric nurse.
puériculture [pɥeʀikyltyʀ] *nf* paediatric nursing; infant care.
puéril, e [pɥeʀil] *a* childish.
pugilat [pyʒila] *nm* (fist) fight.
puis [pɥi] *vb voir* **pouvoir** // *ad* then; **et** ~ **and** (then).
puiser [pɥize] *vt* (*eau*): ~ (**dans**) to draw (from); ~ **dans qch** to dip into sth.
puisque [pɥisk(ə)] *cj* since.
puissance [pɥisɑ̃s] *nf* power; **en** ~ *a* potential; **2 (à la)** ~ **5** 2 to the power of 5.
puissant, e [pɥisɑ̃, -ɑ̃t] *a* powerful.
puisse *etc vb voir* **pouvoir**.
puits [pɥi] *nm* well; ~ **de mine** mine shaft.
pull(-over) [pul(ɔvœʀ)] *nm* sweater, jumper.
pulluler [pylyle] *vi* to swarm.
pulmonaire [pylmɔnɛʀ] *a* lung *cpd*; (*artère*) pulmonary.
pulpe [pylp(ə)] *nf* pulp.
pulsation [pylsɑsjɔ̃] *nf* beat.
pulsion [pylsjɔ̃] *nf* drive, urge.
pulvérisateur [pylveʀizatœʀ] *nm* spray.
pulvériser [pylveʀize] *vt* (*solide*) to pulverize; (*liquide*) to spray; (*fig*) to pulverize; to smash.
punaise [pynɛz] *nf* (*ZOOL*) bug; (*clou*) drawing pin.
punch [pɔ̃ʃ] *nm* (*boisson*) punch; [pœnʃ] (*BOXE*) punching ability; (*fig*) punch; **punching-ball** *nm* punchball.
punir [pyniʀ] *vt* to punish; **punition** *nf* punishment.
pupille [pypij] *nf* (*ANAT*) pupil // *nm/f* (*enfant*) ward; ~ **de l'État** child in care; ~ **de la Nation** war orphan.
pupitre [pypitʀ(ə)] *nm* (*SCOL*) desk; (*REL*) lectern; (*de chef d'orchestre*) rostrum; ~ **de commande** panel.
pur, e [pyʀ] *a* pure; (*vin*) undiluted; (*whisky*) neat; **en** ~**e perte** fruitlessly, to no avail.

purée [pyʀe] nf: ~ (de pommes de terre) mashed potatoes pl; ~ de marrons chestnut purée.

pureté [pyʀte] nf purity.

purgatif, ive [pyʀgatif] nm purgative, purge.

purgatoire [pyʀgatwaʀ] nm purgatory.

purge [pyʀʒ(ə)] nf (POL) purge; (MÉD) purging q; purge.

purger [pyʀʒe] vt (radiateur) to flush (out), drain; (circuit hydraulique) to bleed; (MÉD, POL) to purge; (JUR: peine) to serve.

purifier [pyʀifje] vt to purify; (TECH: métal) to refine.

purin [pyʀɛ̃] nm liquid manure.

puritain, e [pyʀitɛ̃, -ɛn] a, nm/f Puritan; **puritanisme** nm Puritanism.

pur-sang [pyʀsɑ̃] nm inv thoroughbred, purebred.

purulent, e [pyʀylɑ̃, -ɑ̃t] a purulent.

pus [py] nm pus.

pusillanime [pyzilanim] a fainthearted.

putain [pytɛ̃] nf (fam!) whore(!); ce/cette ~ de ... this bloody ...(!).

putréfier [pytʀefje] vt, se ~ vi to putrefy, rot.

puzzle [pœzl(ə)] nm jigsaw (puzzle).

P.V. sigle m = **procès-verbal**.

pygmée [pigme] a pygmy.

pyjama [piʒama] nm pyjamas pl, pair of pyjamas.

pylône [pilon] nm pylon.

pyramide [piʀamid] nf pyramid.

pyromane [piʀɔman] nm/f fire bug, arsonist.

python [pitɔ̃] nm python.

Q

QG [kyʒe] voir **quartier**.

QI [kyi] voir **quotient**.

quadragénaire [kadʀaʒenɛʀ] nm/f man/woman in his/her forties.

quadrangulaire [kwadʀɑ̃gylɛʀ] a quadrangular.

quadrilatère [k(w)adʀilatɛʀ] nm quadrilateral; four-sided area.

quadrillage [kadʀijaʒ] nm (lignes etc) square pattern, criss-cross pattern.

quadrillé, e [kadʀije] a (papier) squared.

quadriller [kadʀije] vt (papier) to mark out in squares; (POLICE) to keep under tight control, be positioned throughout.

quadrimoteur [k(w)adʀimɔtœʀ] nm four-engined plane.

quadripartite [kwadʀipaʀtit] a four-power; four-party.

quadriphonie [kadʀifɔni] nf quadriphony.

quadriréacteur [k(w)adʀiʀeaktœʀ] nm four-engined jet.

quadrupède [k(w)adʀypɛd] nm quadruped.

quadruple [k(w)adʀypl(ə)] nm: le ~ de four times as much as; **quadrupler** vt, vi to increase fourfold; **quadruplés, ées** nm/fpl quadruplets, quads.

quai [ke] nm (de port) quay; (de gare) platform; (de cours d'eau, canal) embankment; **être à** ~ (navire) to be alongside; (train) to be in the station.

qualificatif, ive [kalifikatif, -iv] a (LING) qualifying // nm (terme) term; (LING) qualifier.

qualification [kalifikasjɔ̃] nf qualification.

qualifier [kalifje] vt to qualify; (appeler): ~ qch/qn de to describe sth/sb as; se ~ vi (SPORT) to qualify; **être qualifié pour** to be qualified for.

qualité [kalite] nf quality; (titre, fonction) position; en ~ de in one's capacity as; avoir ~ pour to have authority to.

quand [kɑ̃] cj, ad when; ~ **je serai riche** when I'm rich; ~ **même** nevertheless; all the same; really; ~ **bien même** even though.

quant [kɑ̃]: ~ à prép as for, as to; regarding.

quant-à-soi [kɑ̃taswa] nm: **rester sur son** ~ to remain aloof.

quantième [kɑ̃tjɛm] nm day (of the month).

quantifier [kɑ̃tifje] vt to quantify.

quantitatif, ive [kɑ̃titatif, -iv] a quantitative.

quantité [kɑ̃tite] nf quantity, amount; (SCIENCE) quantity; (grand nombre): une ou des ~(s) de a great deal of; a lot of; en grande ~ in large quantities; du travail en ~ a great deal of work; ~ de many.

quarantaine [kaʀɑ̃tɛn] nf (MÉD) quarantine; la ~ forty, the forty mark; (âge) forty, the forties pl; une ~ (de) forty or so, about forty; **mettre en** ~ to put into quarantine; (fig) to send to Coventry.

quarante [kaʀɑ̃t] num forty.

quart [kaʀ] nm (fraction) quarter; (surveillance) watch; (partie): un ~ de poulet/fromage a chicken quarter/a quarter of a cheese; un ~ de beurre a quarter kilo of butter, ≈ a half pound of butter; un ~ de vin a quarter litre of wine; une livre un ~ ou et ~ one and a quarter pounds; le ~ de a quarter of; ~ d'heure quarter of an hour; être de/prendre le ~ to keep/take the watch; ~ de tour quarter turn.

quarteron [kaʀtəʀɔ̃] nm (péj) small bunch, handful.

quartette [kwaʀtɛt] nm quartet(te).

quartier [kaʀtje] nm (de ville) district, area; (de bœuf) quarter; (de fruit, fromage) piece; ~s nmpl (MIL, BLASON) quarters; **cinéma de** ~ local cinema; **avoir** ~ (MIL) to have leave from barracks; **ne pas faire de** ~ to spare no-one, give no quarter; ~ **général (QG)** headquarters (HQ).

quartier-maître [kaʀtjemɛtʀ(ə)] nm ≈ leading seaman.

quartz [kwaʀts] nm quartz.

quasi [kazi] ad almost, nearly // préfixe: ~-certitude near certainty; ~ment ad almost, nearly.

quatorze [katɔʀz(ə)] num fourteen.

quatrain [katʀɛ̃] nm quatrain.

quatre [katʀ(ə)] num four; à ~ **pattes** on all fours; **tiré à** ~ **épingles** dressed up to the nines; **faire les** ~ **cent coups** to get a bit wild; **se mettre en** ~ **pour qn** to go out of one's way for sb; ~ **à** ~ (monter, descendre) four at a time; ~-

vingt-dix *num* ninety; **~-vingts** *num* eighty; **quatrième** *num* fourth.

quatuor [kwatɥɔʀ] *nm* quartet(te).

que [kə] *cj* (*gén*) that; (*après comparatif*) than; as: *voir* **plus, autant** *etc*; **il sait ~ tu es là** he knows (that) you're here; **je veux ~ tu acceptes** I want you to accept; **il a dit ~ oui** he said he would (*ou* it was *etc, suivant le contexte*); **si vous y allez ou ~ vous lui téléphoniez** if you go there or (if you) phone him; **quand il rentrera et qu'il aura mangé** when he gets back and (when he) has eaten; **qu'il le veuille ou non** whether he likes it or not; **tenez-le qu'il ne tombe pas** hold it so (that) it doesn't fall; **qu'il fasse ce qu'il voudra** let him do as he pleases; *voir* **avant, pour, tel** *etc* // *ad*: **qu'il ou qu'est-ce qu'il est bête/court vite** he is so silly/runs so fast; **~ de** what a lot of // *pronom*: **l'homme ~ je vois** the man (whom) I see; **le livre ~ tu vois** the book (that *ou* which) you see; **un jour ~ j'étais** a day when I was; **c'est une erreur ~ de croire** it's a mistake to believe; **~ fais-tu?, qu'est-ce que tu fais?** what are you doing?; **~ préfères-tu, celui-ci ou celui-là?** which do you prefer, this one or that one?

Québec [kebɛk] *nm*: **le ~** Quebec.

quel, quelle [kɛl] *a*: **~ livre/ homme?** what book/man?; (*parmi un certain choix*) which book/man?; **~ est cet homme/ce livre?** who/what is this man/ book?; **~ est le plus grand?** which is the tallest (*ou* biggest *etc*)?; **~s acteurs préférez-vous?** which actors do you prefer?; **dans ~s pays êtes-vous allé?** which *ou* what countries did you go to?; **~le surprise!** what a surprise!; **~ que soit le coupable** whoever is guilty; **~ que soit votre avis** whatever your opinion; whichever is your opinion.

quelconque [kɛlkɔ̃k] *a* (*médiocre*) indifferent, poor; (*sans attrait*) ordinary, plain; (*indéfini*) **un ami/ prétexte ~** some friend/pretext or other; **un livre ~ suffira** any book will do.

quelque [kɛlk(ə)] *dét* some; **~s** a few, some, *tournure interrogative* + any; **les ~s livres qui** the few books which // *ad* (*environ*): **~ 100 mètres** some 100 metres; **~ livre qu'il choisisse** whatever (*ou* whichever) book he chooses; **20 kg et ~(s)** a bit over 20 kg; **~ chose** something, *tournure interrogative* + anything; **~ chose d'autre** something else; anything else; **~ part** somewhere; **~ peu** rather, somewhat; **en ~ sorte** as it were; **quelquefois** *ad* sometimes; **quelques-uns, -unes** [-zœ̃] *pronom* some, a few.

quelqu'un, une [kɛlkœ̃, -yn] *pronom* someone, somebody, *tournure interrogative* + anyone *ou* anybody; **~ d'autre** someone *ou* somebody else; anybody else.

quémander [kemɑ̃de] *vt* to beg for.

qu'en dira-t-on [kɑ̃diʀatɔ̃] *nm inv*: **le ~** gossip, what people say.

quenelle [kənɛl] *nf* quenelle.

quenouille [kənuj] *nf* distaff.

querelle [kəʀɛl] *nf* quarrel.

quereller [kəʀele]: **se ~** *vi* to quarrel; **querelleur, euse** *a* quarrelsome.

qu'est-ce que (*ou* **qui**) [kɛskə(ki)] *voir* **que, qui.**

question [kɛstjɔ̃] *nf* (*gén*) question; (*fig*) matter; issue; **il a été ~ de we** (*ou* they) spoke about; **il est ~ de les emprisonner** there's talk of them being jailed; **de quoi est-il ~?** what is it about?; **il n'en est pas ~** there's no question of it; **en ~** in question; **hors de ~** out of the question; **remettre en ~** to question; **poser la ~ de confiance** (*POL*) to ask for a vote of confidence.

questionnaire [kɛstjɔnɛʀ] *nm* questionnaire; **questionner** *vt* to question.

quête [kɛt] *nf* collection; (*recherche*) quest, search; **faire la ~** (*à l'église*) to take the collection; (*artiste*) to pass the hat round; **en ~ de qch** in search of sth; **quêter** *vi* (*à l'église*) to take the collection; (*dans la rue*) to collect money (for charity) // *vt* to seek.

quetsche [kwɛtʃ(ə)] *nf* damson.

queue [kø] *nf* tail; (*fig*: *du classement*) bottom; (: *de poêle*) handle; (: *de fruit, feuille*) stalk; (: *de train, colonne, file*) rear; **en ~** (*de train*) at the rear (of the train); **faire la ~** to queue (up); **se mettre à la ~** to join the queue; **à la ~ leu leu** in single file; (*fig*) one after the other; **~ de cheval** ponytail; **~ de poisson:** **faire une ~ de poisson à qn** (*AUTO*) to cut in front of sb; **~-de-pie** *nf* (*habit*) tails *pl*, tail coat.

queux [kø] *am voir* **maître.**

qui [ki] *pronom* (*personne*) who, *prép* + whom; (*chose, animal*) which, that; **qu'est-ce ~ est sur la table?** what is on the table?; **à ~ est ce sac?** whose bag is this?; **à ~ parlais-tu?** who were you talking to?, to whom were you talking?; **amenez ~ vous voulez** bring who you like; **~ que ce soit** whoever it may be.

quiche [kiʃ] *nf*: **~ lorraine** quiche Lorraine.

quiconque [kikɔ̃k] *pronom* (*celui qui*) whoever, anyone who; (*personne*) anyone, anybody.

quidam [kɥidam] *nm* fellow.

quiétude [kjetyd] *nf* (*d'un lieu*) quiet, tranquillity; **en toute ~** in complete peace; (*mentale*) with complete peace of mind.

quignon [kiɲɔ̃] *nm*: **~ de pain** crust of bread; hunk of bread.

quille [kij] *nf* skittle; (*jeu de*) **~s** ninepins *sg*, skittles *sg*.

quincaillerie [kɛ̃kɑjʀi] *nf* (*ustensiles*) hardware, ironmongery; (*magasin*) hardware shop, ironmonger's; **quincaillier, ère** *nm/f* ironmonger.

quinconce [kɛ̃kɔ̃s] *nm*: **en ~** in staggered rows.

quinine [kinin] *nf* quinine.

quinquagénaire [kɛ̃kazenɛʀ] *nm/f* man/woman in his/her fifties.

quinquennal, e, aux [kɛ̃kenal, -o] *a* five-year, quinquennial.

quintal, aux [kɛ̃tal, -o] *nm* quintal (*100 kg*).

quinte [kɛ̃t] *nf*: **~ (de toux)** coughing fit.

quintette [kɛ̃tɛt] nm quintet(te).

quintuple [kɛ̃typl(ə)] nm: **le ~ de** five times as much as; **quintupler** vt, vi to increase fivefold; **quintuplés, ées** nm/fpl quintuplets, quins.

quinzaine [kɛ̃zɛn] nf: **une ~ (de)** about fifteen, fifteen or so; **une ~ (de jours)** a fortnight, two weeks.

quinze [kɛ̃z] num fifteen; **demain en ~** a fortnight ou two weeks tomorrow; **dans ~ jours** in a fortnight('s time), in two weeks(' time).

quiproquo [kipRɔko] nm misunderstanding; (THÉÂTRE) (case of) mistaken identity.

quittance [kitɑ̃s] nf (reçu) receipt; (facture) bill.

quitte [kit] a: **être ~ envers qn** to be no longer in sb's debt; (fig) to be quits with sb; **être ~ de** (obligation) to be clear of; **en être ~ à bon compte** to get off lightly; **~ à faire** even if it means doing; **~ ou double** (jeu) double your money.

quitter [kite] vt to leave (espoir, illusion) to give up; (vêtement) to take off; **se ~** (couples, interlocuteurs) to part; **ne quittez pas** (au téléphone) hold the line.

qui-vive [kiviv] nm: **être sur le ~** to be on the alert.

quoi [kwa] pronom (interrogatif) what; **~ de neuf?** what's the news?; **as-tu de ~ écrire?** have you anything to write with?; **il n'a pas de ~ se l'acheter** he can't afford it, he hasn't got the money to buy it; **~ qu'il arrive** whatever happens; **~ qu'il en soit** be that as it may; **~ que ce soit** anything at all; **il n'y a pas de ~ '** (please) don't mention it'; **en ~ puis-je vous aider?** how can I help you?

quoique [kwak(ə)] cj (al)though.

quolibet [kɔlibɛ] nm gibe, jeer.

quorum [kɔrɔm] nm quorum.

quota [kwɔta] nm quota.

quote-part [kɔtpaR] nf share.

quotidien, ne [kɔtidjɛ̃, -ɛn] a daily; (banal) everyday // nm (journal) daily (paper).

quotient [kɔsjɑ̃] nm (MATH) quotient; **~ intellectuel (QI)** intelligence quotient (IQ).

quotité [kɔtite] nf (FINANCE) quota.

R

r. abr de **route, rue.**

rabâcher [Rabɑʃe] vt to harp on, keep on repeating.

rabais [Rabɛ] nm reduction, discount; **au ~** at a reduction ou discount.

rabaisser [Rabese] vt (rabattre) to reduce; (dénigrer) to belittle.

rabat [Raba] nm flap.

rabat-joie [Rabaʒwa] nm/f inv killjoy, spoilsport.

rabatteur, euse [RabatœR, -øz] nm/f (de gibier) beater; (péj) tout.

rabattre [Rabatʀ(ə)] vt (couvercle, siège) to pull ou close down; (col) to turn down; (gibier) to drive; (somme d'un prix) to deduct, take off; **se ~** vi (bords, couvercle) to fall shut; (véhicule, coureur) to cut in; **se ~ sur** vt to fall back on.

rabbin [Rabɛ̃] nm rabbi.

rabique [Rabik] a rabies cpd.

râble [Rɑbl(ə)] nm back; (CULIN) saddle.

râblé, e [Rɑble] a broad-backed, stocky.

rabot [Rabo] nm plane; **raboter** vt to plane (down).

raboteux, euse [Rabotø, -øz] a uneven, rough.

rabougri, e [Rabugri] a stunted.

rabrouer [Rabrue] vt to snub, rebuff.

racaille [Rakaj] nf (péj) rabble, riffraff.

raccommodage [Rakɔmɔdaʒ] nm mending q, repairing q; darning q.

raccommoder [Rakɔmɔde] vt to mend, repair; (chaussette) to darn.

raccompagner [Rakɔpaɲe] vt to take ou see back.

raccord [RakɔR] nm link; **~ de maçonnerie** pointing q; **~ de peinture** join; touch up.

raccordement [RakɔRdəmɑ̃] nm joining up.

raccorder [RakɔRde] vt to join (up), link up; (suj: pont etc) to connect, link; **~ au réseau du téléphone** to connect to the telephone service.

raccourci [Rakursi] nm short cut.

raccourcir [RakursiR] vt to shorten // vi (vêtement) to shrink.

raccroc [RakRo] nm: **par ~** ad by chance.

raccrocher [RakRoʃe] vt (tableau, vêtement) to hang back up; (récepteur) to put down // vi (TÉL) to hang up, ring off; **se ~ à** vt to cling to, hang on to.

race [Ras] nf race; (d'animaux, fig: espèce) breed; (ascendance, origine) stock, race; **de ~ a** purebred, pedigree; **racé, e** a thoroughbred.

rachat [Raʃa] nm buying; buying back; redemption; atonement.

racheter [Raʃte] vt (article perdu) to buy another; (davantage): **~ du lait/3 œufs** to buy more milk/another 3 eggs ou 3 more eggs; (après avoir vendu) to buy back; (d'occasion) to buy; (COMM: part, firme) to buy up; (: pension, rente) to redeem; (REL: pécheur) to redeem; (: péché) to atone for, expiate; (mauvaise conduite, oubli, défaut) to make up for; **se ~** (REL) to redeem o.s.; (gén) to make amends, make up for it.

rachitique [Raʃitik] a suffering from rickets; (fig) scraggy, scrawny.

racial, e, aux [Rasjal, -o] a racial.

racine [Rasin] nf root; **~ carrée/cubique** square/cube root; **prendre ~** (fig) to take root; to put down roots.

racisme [Rasism(ə)] nm racism, racialism; **raciste** a, nm/f racist, racialist.

racket [Rakɛt] nm racketeering q.

raclée [Rɑkle] nf (fam) hiding, thrashing.

racler [Rɑkle] vt (os, plat) to scrape; (tache, boue) to scrape off; (suj: chose: frotter contre) to scrape (against).

raclette [Rɑklɛt] nf (CULIN) raclette (Swiss cheese dish).

racoler [Rakɔle] vt (attirer: suj: prostituée) to solicit; (: parti, marchand) to tout for; (attraper) to pick up; **racoleur, euse** a (péj: publicité) cheap and alluring // nf streetwalker.

racontars [ʀakɔ̃taʀ] *nmpl* stories, gossip *sg.*

raconter [ʀakɔ̃te] *vt*: ~ (à qn) (*décrire*) to relate (to sb), tell (sb) about ; (*dire*) to tell (sb).

racorni, e [ʀakɔʀni] *a* hard(ened).

radar [ʀadaʀ] *nm* radar.

rade [ʀad] *nf* (natural) harbour ; **en ~ de Toulon** in Toulon harbour ; **rester en ~** (*fig*) to be left stranded.

radeau, x [ʀado] *nm* raft.

radial, e, aux [ʀadjal, -o] *a* radial ; **pneu à carcasse ~e** radial tyre.

radiateur [ʀadjatœʀ] *nm* radiator, heater ; (*AUTO*) radiator ; **~ électrique/à gaz** electric/gas heater *ou* fire.

radiation [ʀadjasjɔ̃] *nf* (*voir radier*) striking off *q* ; (*PHYSIQUE*) radiation.

radical, e, aux [ʀadikal, -o] *a* radical // *nm* (*LING*) stem.

radier [ʀadje] *vt* to strike off.

radieux, euse [ʀadjø, -øz] *a* radiant ; brilliant, glorious.

radin, e [ʀadɛ̃, -in] *a* (*fam*) stingy.

radio [ʀadjo] *nf* radio ; (*MÉD*) X-ray // *nm* radiogram, radiotelegram ; radio operator ; **à la ~** on the radio ; **se faire faire une ~ (des poumons)** to have an X-ray taken (of one's lungs).

radio... [ʀadjo] *préfixe*: **~actif, ive** *a* radio-active ; **~activité** *nf* radioactivity ; **radio-diffuser** *vt* to broadcast (by radio) ; **~graphie** *nf* radiography ; (*photo*) X-ray photograph, radiograph ; **~graphier** *vt* to X-ray ; **~logue** *nm/f* radiologist ; **~phonique** *a* radio *cpd* ; **~reportage** *nm* radio report ; **~scopie** *nf* radioscopy ; **~télégraphie** *nf* radiotelegraphy ; **~télévisé, e** *a* broadcast on radio and television.

radis [ʀadi] *nm* radish ; **~ noir** horseradish *q.*

radium [ʀadjɔm] *nm* radium.

radoter [ʀadɔte] *vi* to ramble on.

radoub [ʀadu] *nm*: **bassin de ~** dry dock.

radoucir [ʀadusiʀ]: **se ~** *vi* (*se réchauffer*) to become milder ; (*se calmer*) to calm down ; to soften.

rafale [ʀafal] *nf* (*vent*) gust (of wind) ; (*tir*) burst of gunfire ; **~ de mitrailleuse** burst of machine-gun fire.

raffermir [ʀafɛʀmiʀ] *vt*, **se ~** *vi* (*tissus, muscle*) to firm up ; (*fig*) to strengthen.

raffinage [ʀafinaʒ] *nm* refining.

raffiné, e [ʀafine] *a* refined.

raffinement [ʀafinmɑ̃] *nm* refinement.

raffiner [ʀafine] *vt* to refine ; **raffinerie** *nf* refinery.

raffoler [ʀafɔle]: **~ de** *vt* to be very keen on.

raffut [ʀafy] *nm* (*fam*) row, racket.

rafistoler [ʀafistɔle] *vt* (*fam*) to patch up.

rafle [ʀɑfl(ə)] *nf* (*de police*) roundup, raid.

rafler [ʀɑfle] *vt* (*fam*) to swipe, run off with.

rafraîchir [ʀafʀeʃiʀ] *vt* (*atmosphère, température*) to cool (down) ; (*aussi*: **mettre à ~**) to chill ; (*suj*: *air, eau*) to freshen up ; (: *boisson*) to refresh ; (*fig*: *rénover*) to brighten up ; **se ~** to grow cooler ; to freshen up ; to refresh o.s. ;

rafraîchissant, e *a* refreshing ; **rafraîchissement** *nm* cooling ; (*boisson etc*) cool drink, refreshment.

ragaillardir [ʀagajaʀdiʀ] *vt* (*fam*) to perk *ou* buck up.

rage [ʀaʒ] *nf* (*MÉD*): **la ~** rabies ; (*fureur*) rage, fury ; **faire ~** to rage ; **~ de dents** (raging) toothache ; **rager** *vi* to fume (with rage) ; **rageur, euse** *a* snarling ; ill-tempered.

raglan [ʀaglɑ̃] *a inv* raglan.

ragot [ʀago] *nm* (*fam*) malicious gossip *q.*

ragoût [ʀagu] *nm* (*plat*) stew.

rai [ʀɛ] *nm*: **un ~ de soleil/lumière** a sunray/ray of light.

raid [ʀɛd] *nm* (*MIL*) raid ; (*SPORT*) long-distance trek.

raide [ʀɛd] *a* (*tendu*) taut, tight ; (*escarpé*) steep ; (*droit*: *cheveux*) straight ; (*ankylosé, dur, guindé*) stiff ; (*fam*) steep, stiff ; stony broke // *ad* (*en pente*) steeply ; **~ mort** stone dead ; **raideur** *nf* steepness ; stiffness ; **raidir** *vt* (*muscles*) to stiffen ; (*câble*) to pull taut, tighten ; **se raidir** *vi* to stiffen ; to become taut ; (*personne*) to tense up ; to brace o.s. ; to harden.

raie [ʀɛ] *nf* (*ZOOL*) skate, ray ; (*rayure*) stripe ; (*des cheveux*) parting.

raifort [ʀɛfɔʀ] *nm* horseradish.

rail [ʀɑj] *nm* (*barre d'acier*) rail ; (*chemins de fer*) railways *pl* ; **les ~s** (*la voie ferrée*) the rails, the track *sg* ; **par ~** by rail ; **~ conducteur** live *ou* conductor rail.

railler [ʀɑje] *vt* to scoff at, jeer at.

rainure [ʀenyʀ] *nf* groove ; slot.

rais [ʀɛ] *nm* = **rai**.

raisin [ʀezɛ̃] *nm* (*aussi*: **~s**) grapes *pl* ; (*variété*): **~ muscat** muscat grape ; **~s secs** raisins, currants.

raison [ʀezɔ̃] *nf* reason ; **avoir ~** to be right ; **donner ~ à qn** to agree with sb ; to prove sb right ; **avoir ~ de qn/qch** to get the better of sb/sth ; **se faire une ~** to learn to live with it ; **perdre la ~** to become insane ; to take leave of one's senses ; **demander ~ à qn de** (*affront etc*) to demand satisfaction from sb for ; **~ de plus** all the more reason ; **à plus forte ~** all the more so ; **en ~ de** because of ; according to ; in proportion to ; **à ~ de** at the rate of ; **~ sociale** corporate name ; **raisonnable** *a* reasonable, sensible.

raisonnement [ʀezɔnmɑ̃] *nm* reasoning ; arguing ; argument.

raisonner [ʀezɔne] *vi* (*penser*) to reason ; (*argumenter, discuter*) to argue // *vt* (*personne*) to reason with ; (*attitude*: *justifier*) to reason out.

rajeunir [ʀaʒœniʀ] *vt* (*suj*: *coiffure, robe*): **~ qn** to make sb look younger ; (*suj*: *cure etc*) to rejuvenate ; (*fig*) to brighten up ; to give a new look to ; to inject new blood into // *vi* to become (*ou* look) younger.

rajouter [ʀaʒute] *vt*: **~ du sel/un œuf** to add some more salt/another egg ; **~ que** to add that.

rajuster [ʀaʒyste] *vt* (*vêtement*) to straighten, tidy ; (*salaires*) to adjust ; (*machine*) to readjust ; **se ~** to tidy *ou* straighten o.s. up.

râle [ʀɑl] *nm* groan ; **~ d'agonie** death rattle.

ralenti [Ralɑ̃ti] nm: au ~ (AUTO): **tourner au** ~ to tick over, idle; (CINÉMA) in slow motion; (fig) at a slower pace.

ralentir [Ralɑ̃tiʀ] vt, vi, **se** ~ vi to slow down.

râler [Rɑle] vi to groan; (fam) to grouse, moan (and groan).

ralliement [Ralimɑ̃] nm rallying.

rallier [Ralje] vt (rassembler) to rally; (rejoindre) to rejoin; (gagner à sa cause) to win over; **se** ~ **à** (avis) to come over ou round to.

rallonge [Ralɔ̃ʒ] nf (de table) (extra) leaf (pl leaves); (de vêtement etc) extra piece.

rallonger [Ralɔ̃ʒe] vt to lengthen.

rallumer [Ralyme] vt to light up again; (fig) to revive; **se** ~ vi (lumière) to come on again.

rallye [Rali] nm rally; (POL) march.

ramages [Ramaʒ] nmpl leaf pattern sg; songs.

ramassage [Ramɑsaʒ] nm: ~ **scolaire** school bus service.

ramassé, e [Ramɑse] a (trapu) squat, stocky.

ramasse-miettes [Ramɑsmjɛt] nm inv table-tidy.

ramasse-monnaie [Ramɑsmɔnɛ] nm inv change-tray.

ramasser [Ramɑse] vt (objet tombé ou par terre, fam) to pick up; (recueillir) to collect; (récolter) to gather; (: pommes de terre) to lift; **se** ~ vi (sur soi-même) to huddle up; to crouch; **ramasseur, euse de balles** nm/f ballboy/girl; **ramassis** nm (péj) bunch; jumble.

rambarde [Rɑ̃baʀd(ə)] nf guardrail.

rame [Ram] nf (aviron) oar; (de métro) train; (de papier) ream; ~ **de haricots** bean support.

rameau, x [Ramo] nm (small) branch; **les R~x** (REL) Palm Sunday sg.

ramener [Ramne] vt to bring back; (reconduire) to take back; (rabattre: couverture, visière): ~ **qch sur** to pull sth back over; ~ **qch à** (réduire à, aussi MATH) to reduce sth to; **se** ~ vi (fam) to roll ou turn up; **se** ~ **à** (se réduire à) to come ou boil down to.

ramer [Rame] vi to row; **rameur, euse** nm/f rower.

ramier [Ramje] nm: (**pigeon**) ~ woodpigeon.

ramification [Ramifikasjɔ̃] nf ramification.

ramifier [Ramifje]: **se** ~ vi (tige, secte, réseau): **se** ~ (**en**) to branch out (into); (veines, nerfs) to ramify.

ramollir [Ramɔliʀ] vt to soften; **se** ~ vi to go soft.

ramoner [Ramɔne] vt to sweep; **ramoneur** nm (chimney) sweep.

rampe [Rɑ̃p] nf (d'escalier) banister(s pl); (dans un garage, d'un terrain) ramp; (THÉÂTRE): **la** ~ **the** footlights pl; ~ **de lancement** launching pad.

ramper [Rɑ̃pe] vi to crawl.

rancard [Rɑ̃kaʀ] nm (fam) date; tip.

rancart [Rɑ̃kaʀ] nm: **mettre au** ~ to scrap.

rance [Rɑ̃s] a rancid.

rancœur [Rɑ̃kœʀ] nf rancour, resentment.

rançon [Rɑ̃sɔ̃] nf ransom; (fig) price.

rancune [Rɑ̃kyn] nf grudge, rancour; **garder** ~ **à qn** (**de qch**) to bear sb a grudge (for sth); **sans** ~! no hard feelings!; **rancunier, ière** a vindictive, spiteful.

randonnée [Rɑ̃dɔne] nf ride; (à pied) walk, ramble; hike, hiking q.

rang [Rɑ̃] nm (rangée) row; (grade, condition sociale, classement) rank; ~**s** (MIL) ranks; **se mettre en** ~**s/sur un** ~ to get into ou form rows/a line; **sur 3** ~**s** (lined up) 3 deep; **se mettre en** ~**s par 4** to form fours ou rows of 4; **se mettre sur les** ~**s** (fig) to get into the running; **au premier** ~ in the first row; (fig) ranking first; **avoir** ~ **de** to hold the rank of.

rangé, e [Rɑ̃ʒe] a (sérieux) orderly, steady.

rangée [Rɑ̃ʒe] nf row.

ranger [Rɑ̃ʒe] vt (classer, grouper) to order, arrange; (mettre à sa place) to put away; (mettre de l'ordre dans) to tidy up; (arranger, disposer: en cercle etc) to arrange; (fig: classer): ~ **qn/qch parmi** to rank sb/sth among; **se** ~ vi (véhicule, conducteur: s'écarter) to pull over; (: s'arrêter) to pull in; (piéton) to step aside; (s'assagir) to settle down; **se** ~ **à** (avis) to come round to, fall in with.

ranimer [Ranime] vt (personne évanouie) to bring round; (revigorer: forces, courage) to restore; (réconforter: troupes etc) to kindle new life in; (douleur, souvenir) to revive; (feu) to rekindle.

rapace [Rapas] nm bird of prey // a (péj) rapacious, grasping.

rapatrier [Rapatʀije] vt to repatriate; (capitaux) to bring (back) home.

râpe [Rɑp] nf (CULIN) grater; (à bois) rasp.

râpé, e [Rɑpe] a (tissu) threadbare; (CULIN) grated.

râper [Rɑpe] vt (CULIN) to grate; (gratter, râcler) to rasp.

rapetasser [Raptase] vt (fam) to patch up.

rapetisser [Raptise] vt: ~ **qch** to shorten sth; to make sth look smaller // vi, **se** ~ vi to shrink.

rapide [Rapid] a fast; (prompt) quick // nm express (train); (de cours d'eau) rapid; ~**ment** ad fast; quickly; **rapidité** nf speed; quickness.

rapiécer [Rapjese] vt to patch.

rappel [Rapɛl] nm (d'un ambassadeur, MIL) recall; (THÉÂTRE) curtain call; (MÉD: vaccination) booster; (ADMIN: de salaire) back pay q; (d'une aventure, d'un nom) reminder; (TECH) return; (NAVIG) sitting out; (ALPINISME: aussi: ~ **de corde**) abseiling q, roping down q, abseil; ~ **à l'ordre** call to order.

rappeler [Raple] vt (pour faire revenir, retéléphoner) to call back; (ambassadeur, MIL) to recall; (faire se souvenir): ~ **qch à qn** to remind sb of sth; **se** ~ vt (se souvenir de) to remember, recall; ~ **qn à la vie** to bring sb back to life; **ça rappelle la Provence** it's reminiscent of Provence, it reminds you of Provence.

rappliquer [Raplike] vi (fam) to turn up.

rapport [RapɔR] *nm* (*compte rendu*) report ; (*profit*) yield, return ; revenue ; (*lien, analogie*) relationship ; (*proportion*: MATH, TECH) ratio (*pl* s) ; ~**s** *nmpl* (*entre personnes, pays*) relations ; **avoir ~ à** to have something to do with, concern ; **être en ~ avec** (*idée de corrélation*) to be in keeping with ; **être/se mettre en ~ avec qn** to have dealings with sb/get in touch with sb ; **par ~ à** in relation to ; with regard to ; **sous le ~ de** from the point of view of ; ~**s** **(sexuels)** (sexual) intercourse *sg*.

rapporter [RapɔRte] *vt* (*rendre, ramener*) to bring back ; (*apporter davantage*) to bring more ; (*COUTURE*) to sew on ; (*suj*: *investissement*) to yield ; (: *activité*) to bring in ; (*relater*) to report ; (*JUR*: *annuler*) to revoke // *vi* (*investissement*) to give a good return *ou* yield ; (: *activité*) to be very profitable ; ~ **qch à** (*fig*: *rattacher*) to relate sth to ; **se ~ à** (*correspondre à*) to relate to ; **s'en ~ à** to rely on ; **rapporteur, euse** *nm/f* (*de procès, commission*) reporter ; (*péj*) telltale // *nm* (GÉOM) protractor.

rapproché, e [RapRɔʃe] *a* (*proche*) near, close at hand ; ~**s** (*l'un de l'autre*) at close intervals.

rapprochement [RapRɔʃmɑ̃] *nm* (*reconciliation*: *de nations, familles*) reconciliation ; (*analogie, rapport*) parallel.

rapprocher [RapRɔʃe] *vt* (*chaise d'une table*): ~ **qch (de)** to bring sth closer (to) ; (*deux tuyaux*) to bring closer together ; (*réunir*) to bring together ; (*établir une analogie entre*) to establish a parallel between ; **se ~** *vi* to draw closer *ou* nearer ; (*fig*: *familles, pays*) to come together ; to come closer together ; **se ~ de** to come closer to ; (*présenter une analogie avec*) to be close to.

rapt [Rapt] *nm* abduction.

raquette [Rakɛt] *nf* (*de tennis*) racket ; (*de ping-pong*) bat ; (*à neige*) snowshoe.

rare [RaR] *a* rare ; (*main-d'œuvre, denrées*) scarce ; (*cheveux, herbe*) sparse.

raréfier [RaRefje]: **se ~** *vi* to grow scarce ; (*air*) to rarefy.

rarement [RaRmɑ̃] *ad* rarely, seldom.

rareté [RaRte] *nf* rarity ; scarcity.

ras, e [Rɑ, Rɑz] *a* (*tête, cheveux*) close-cropped ; (*poil, herbe*) short // *ad* short ; **en ~e campagne** in open country ; **à ~ bords** to the brim ; **au ~ de** level with ; **en avoir ~ le bol** (*fam*) to be fed up ; ~ **du cou** (*pull, robe*) crew-neck.

rasade [Razad] *nf* glassful.

rasé, e [Raze] *a*: ~ **de frais** freshly shaven ; ~ **de près** close-shaven.

rase-mottes [Razmɔt] *nm inv*: **faire du ~** to hedgehop.

raser [Raze] *vt* (*barbe, cheveux*) to shave off ; (*menton, personne*) to shave ; (*fam*: *ennuyer*) to bore ; (*démolir*) to raze (to the ground) ; (*frôler*) to graze ; to skim ; **se ~** to shave ; (*fam*) to be bored (to tears) ; **rasoir** *nm* razor ; **rasoir électrique** electric shaver *ou* razor ; **rasoir de sûreté** safety razor.

rassasier [Rasazje] *vt* to satisfy ; **être rassasié** (*dégoûté*) to be sated ; to have had more than enough.

rassemblement [Rasɑ̃bləmɑ̃] *nm* (*groupe*) gathering ; (POL) union ; association ; (MIL): **le ~ parade**.

rassembler [Rasɑ̃ble] *vt* (*réunir*) to assemble, gather ; (*regrouper, amasser*) to gather together, collect ; **se ~** *vi* to gather.

rasseoir [RaswaR]: **se ~** *vi* to sit down again.

rasséréner [RaseRene]: **se ~** *vi* to recover one's serenity.

rassis, e [Rasi, -iz] *a* (*pain*) stale.

rassurer [RasyRe] *vt* to reassure ; **se ~** to feel reassured ; **rassure-toi** put your mind at rest *ou* at ease.

rat [Ra] *nm* rat ; ~ **d'hôtel** hotel thief (*pl* thieves) ; ~ **musqué** muskrat.

ratatiné, e [Ratatine] *a* shrivelled (up), wrinkled.

rate [Rat] *nf* spleen.

raté, e [Rate] *a* (*tentative*) unsuccessful, failed // *nm/f* failure // *nm* misfiring *q*.

râteau, x [Rɑto] *nm* rake.

râtelier [Rɑtəlje] *nm* rack ; (*fam*) false teeth *pl*.

rater [Rate] *vi* (*affaire, projet etc*) to go wrong, fail / / *vt* (*cible, train, occasion*) to miss ; (*démonstration, plat*) to spoil ; (*examen*) to fail.

ratifier [Ratifje] *vt* to ratify.

ration [Rasjɔ̃] *nf* ration ; (*fig*) share.

rationnel, le [Rasjɔnɛl] *a* rational.

rationnement [Rasjɔnmɑ̃] *nm* rationing ; **ticket de ~** ration coupon.

rationner [Rasjɔne] *vt* to ration.

ratisser [Ratise] *vt* (*allée*) to rake ; (*feuilles*) to rake up ; (*suj*: *armée, police*) to comb.

raton [Ratɔ̃] *nm*: ~ **laveur** raccoon.

R.A.T.P. *sigle f* (= *Régie autonome des transports parisiens*) Paris transport authority.

rattacher [Rataʃe] *vt* (*animal, cheveux*) to tie up again ; (*incorporer*: ADMIN *etc*): ~ **qch à** to join sth to, unite sth with ; (*fig*: *relier*): ~ **qch à** to link sth with, relate sth to ; (: *lier*): ~ **qn à** to bind *ou* tie sb to.

rattrapage [RatRapaʒ] *nm* (SCOL) remedial classes *pl*.

rattraper [RatRape] *vt* (*fugitif*) to recapture ; (*retenir, empêcher de tomber*) to catch (hold of) ; (*atteindre, rejoindre*) to catch up with ; (*réparer*: *imprudence, erreur*) to make up for ; **se ~** *vi* to make up for lost time ; to make good one's losses ; to make up for it ; **se ~ (à)** (*se raccrocher*) to stop o.s. falling (by catching hold of).

rature [RatyR] *nf* deletion, erasure ; **raturer** *vt* to cross out, delete, erase.

rauque [Rok] *a* raucous ; hoarse.

ravagé, e [Ravaʒe] *a* (*visage*) harrowed.

ravager [Ravaʒe] *vt* to devastate, ravage.

ravages [Ravaʒ] *nmpl* ravages ; **faire des ~** to wreak havoc.

ravaler [Ravale] *vt* (*mur, façade*) to restore ; (*déprécier*) to lower ; ~ **sa colère/son dégoût** to stifle one's anger/distaste.

ravauder [Ravode] *vt* to repair, mend.

rave [Rav] *nf* (BOT) rape.

ravi, e [Ravi] *a* delighted ; **être ~ de/que** to be delighted with/that.

ravier [Ravje] *nm* hors d'œuvre dish.
ravigote [Ravigɔt] *a:* **sauce ~** oil and vinegar dressing with shallots.
ravigoter [Ravigɔte] *vt (fam)* to buck up.
ravin [Ravɛ̃] *nm* gully, ravine.
raviner [Ravine] *vt* to furrow, gully.
ravir [Ravir] *vt (enchanter)* to delight; *(enlever):* **~ qch à qn** to rob sb of sth; **à ~** *ad* beautifully.
raviser [Ravize]: **se ~** *vi* to change one's mind.
ravissant, e [Ravisɑ̃, -ɑ̃t] *a* a delightful; ravishing.
ravisseur, euse [Ravisœr, -øz] *nm/f* abductor.
ravitaillement [Ravitɑjmɑ̃] *nm* resupplying; refuelling; *(provisions)* supplies *pl;* **aller au ~** to go for fresh supplies.
ravitailler [Ravitɑje] *vt* to resupply; *(véhicule)* to refuel; **se ~** *vi* to get fresh supplies.
raviver [Ravive] *vt (feu, douleur)* to revive; *(couleurs)* to brighten up.
ravoir [Ravwar] *vt* to get back.
rayé, e [Reje] *a (à rayures)* striped; *(éraflé)* scratched.
rayer [Reje] *vt (érafler)* to scratch; *(barrer)* to cross ou score out; *(d'une liste: radier)* to cross ou strike off.
rayon [Rɛjɔ̃] *nm (de soleil etc)* ray; *(GÉOM)* radius; *(de roue)* spoke; *(étagère)* shelf *(pl* shelves); *(de grand magasin)* department; *(de ruche)* (honey)comb; **dans un ~ de** within a radius of; **~ d'action** range; **~ de soleil** sunbeam, ray of sunlight; **~s X** X-rays.
rayonnage [Rɛjɔnaʒ] *nm* set of shelves.
rayonnement [Rɛjɔnmɑ̃] *nm* radiation; *(fig)* radiance; influence.
rayonner [Rɛjɔne] *vi (chaleur, énergie)* to radiate; *(fig)* to shine forth; to be radiant; *(avenues, axes etc)* to radiate; *(touriste)* to go touring *(from one base).*
rayure [Rɛjyr] *nf (motif)* stripe; *(éraflure)* scratch; *(rainure, d'un fusil)* groove; **à ~s** striped.
raz-de-marée [Rɑdmare] *nm inv* tidal wave.
razzia [Razja] *nf* raid, foray.
ré [Re] *nm (MUS)* D; *(en chantant la gamme)* re.
réacteur [Reaktœr] *nm* jet engine.
réaction [Reaksjɔ̃] *nf* reaction; **moteur à ~** jet engine; **~ en chaîne** chain reaction; **réactionnaire** *a* reactionary.
réadapter [Readapte] *vt* to readjust; *(MÉD)* to rehabilitate; **se ~ (à)** to readjust (to).
réaffirmer [Reafirme] *vt* to reaffirm, reassert.
réagir [Reaʒir] *vi* to react.
réalisateur, trice [Realizatœr, -tris] *nm/f (TV, CINÉMA)* director.
réalisation [Realizasjɔ̃] *nf* carrying out; realization; fulfilment; achievement; production; *(œuvre)* production; creation; work.
réaliser [Realize] *vt (projet, opération)* to carry out, realize; *(rêve, souhait)* to realize, fulfil; *(exploit)* to achieve; *(achat, vente)* to make; *(film)* to produce; *(se rendre compte de, COMM: bien, capital)* to realize; **se ~** *vi* to be realized.
réaliste [Realist(ə)] *a* a realistic; *(peintre, roman)* realist // *nm/f* realist.
réalité [Realite] *nf* reality; **en ~** in *(actual)* fact; **dans la ~** in reality.
réanimation [Reanimasjɔ̃] *nf* resuscitation; **service de ~** intensive care unit.
réarmer [Rearme] *vt (arme)* to reload // *vi (état)* to rearm.
réassurance [Reasyrɑ̃s] *nf* reinsurance.
rébarbatif, ive [Rebarbatif, -iv] *a* forbidding, off-putting.
rebattre [Rəbatr(ə)] *vt:* **~ les oreilles à qn de qch** to keep harping on to sb about sth; **rebattu, e** *a* hackneyed.
rebelle [Rəbɛl] *nm/f* rebel // *a (troupes)* rebel; *(enfant)* rebellious; *(mèche etc)* unruly; **~ à** unamenable to; unwilling to + *verbe.*
rebeller [Rəbele]: **se ~** *vi* to rebel.
rébellion [Rebeljɔ̃] *nf* rebellion; *(rebelles)* rebel forces *pl.*
reboiser [Rəbwaze] *vt* to replant with trees, reafforest.
rebondi, e [Rəbɔ̃di] *a* a rounded; chubby, well-rounded.
rebondir [Rəbɔ̃dir] *vi (ballon: au sol)* to bounce; (: *contre un mur)* to rebound; *(fig: procès, action, conversation)* to get moving again, be suddenly revived; **rebondissements** *nmpl (fig)* twists and turns, sudden revivals.
rebord [Rəbɔr] *nm* edge.
rebours [Rəbur]: **à ~** *ad* the wrong way.
rebouteux, euse [Rəbutø, -øz] *nm/f (péj)* bonesetter.
rebrousse-poil [Rəbruspwal]: **à ~** *ad* the wrong way.
rebrousser [Rəbruse] *vt:* **~ chemin** to turn back.
rebuffade [Rəbyfad] *nf* rebuff.
rébus [Rebys] *nm inv* rebus.
rebut [Rəby] *nm:* **mettre au ~** to scrap, discard.
rebuter [Rəbyte] *vt* to put off.
récalcitrant, e [Rekalsitrɑ̃, -ɑ̃t] *a* refractory.
recaler [Rəkale] *vt (SCOL)* to fail.
récapituler [Rekapityle] *vt* to recapitulate; to sum up.
recel [Rəsɛl] *nm* receiving (stolen goods).
receler [Rəsəle] *vt (produit d'un vol)* to receive; *(malfaiteur)* to harbour; *(fig)* to conceal; **receleur, euse** *nm/f* receiver.
récemment [Resamɑ̃] *ad* recently.
recensement [Rəsɑ̃smɑ̃] *nm* census; inventory.
recenser [Rəsɑ̃se] *vt (population)* to take a census of; *(inventorier)* to make an inventory of; *(dénombrer)* to list.
récent, e [Resɑ̃, -ɑ̃t] *a* recent.
récépissé [Resepise] *nm* receipt.
récepteur, trice [Reseptœr, -tris] *a* receiving // *nm* receiver; **~ (de radio)** radio set *ou* receiver.
réception [Resepsjɔ̃] *nf* receiving *q;* *(accueil)* reception, welcome; *(bureau)* reception desk; *(réunion mondaine)*

reception, party; (*pièces*) reception rooms *pl*; (SPORT: *après un saut*) landing; (: *du ballon*) catching *q*; **jour/heures de ~** day/hours for receiving visitors (*ou* students *etc*); (MÉD) surgery day/hours; **réceptionnaire** *nm/f* receiving clerk; **réceptionner** *vt* (COMM) to take delivery of; (SPORT: *ballon*) to catch (and control); **réceptionniste** *nm/f* receptionist.

récession [Resesjɔ̃] *nf* recession.

recette [Rəsɛt] *nf* (CULIN) recipe; (*fig*) formula, recipe; (COMM) takings *pl*; (ADMIN: *bureau*) tax *ou* revenue office; **~s** *nfpl* (COMM: *rentrées*) receipts.

receveur, euse [RəsvœR, -øz] *nm/f* (*des contributions*) tax collector; (*des postes*) postmaster/mistress; (*d'autobus*) conductor/conductress.

recevoir [RəsvwaR] *vt* to receive; (*lettre, prime*) to receive, get; (*client, patient, représentant*) to see; (SCOL: *candidat*) to pass // *vi* to receive visitors; to give parties; to see patients *etc*; **se ~** *vi* (*athlète*) to land; **être reçu** (*à un examen*) to pass.

rechange [Rəʃɑ̃ʒ]: **de ~ a** (*pièces, roue*) spare; (*fig*: *plan*) alternative; **des vêtements de ~** a change of clothes.

rechaper [Rəʃape] *vt* to remould, retread.

réchapper [Reʃape]: **~ de** *ou* **à** *vt* (*accident, maladie*) to come through.

recharge [RəʃaRʒ(ə)] *nf* refill.

recharger [RəʃaRʒe] *vt* (*camion, fusil, appareil-photo*) to reload; (*briquet, stylo*) to refill; (*batterie*) to recharge.

réchaud [Reʃo] *nm* (*portable*) stove; plate-warmer.

réchauffer [Reʃofe] *vt* (*plat*) to reheat; (*mains, personne*) to warm; **se ~** *vi* (*température*) to get warmer.

rèche [Rɛʃ] *a* rough.

recherche [RəʃɛRʃ(ə)] *nf* (*action*): **la ~ de** the search for; (*raffinement*) affectedness, studied elegance; (*scientifique etc*): **la ~** research; **~s** *nfpl* (*de la police*) investigations; (*scientifiques*) research *sg*; **être/se mettre à la ~ de** to be/go in search of.

recherché, e [RəʃɛRʃe] *a* (*rare, demandé*) much sought-after; (*raffiné*) studied, affected.

rechercher [RəʃɛRʃe] *vt* (*objet égaré, fugitif*) to look for, search for; (*témoins, main-d'œuvre*) to look for; (*causes d'un phénomène, nouveau procédé*) to try to find; (*bonheur etc, l'amitié de qn*) to seek.

rechigner [Rəʃiɲe] *vi*: **~ (à)** to balk (at).

rechute [Rəʃyt] *nf* (MÉD) relapse; (*dans le péché, le vice*) lapse; **faire une ~** to have a relapse.

récidiver [Residive] *vi* to commit a second (*ou* subsequent) offence; (*fig*) to do it again; **récidiviste** *nm/f* second (*ou* habitual) offender, recidivist.

récif [Resif] *nm* reef.

récipient [Resipjɑ̃] *nm* container.

réciproque [ResipRɔk] *a* reciprocal; **~ment** *ad* reciprocally; **et ~ment** and vice versa.

récit [Resi] *nm* story.

récital [Resital] *nm* recital.

récitation [Resitasjɔ̃] *nf* recitation.

réciter [Resite] *vt* to recite.

réclamation [Reklamasjɔ̃] *nf* complaint; **~s** (*bureau*) complaints department *sg*.

réclame [Reklam] *nf*: **la ~** advertising; **une ~** an advert(isement); **article en ~** special offer.

réclamer [Reklame] *vt* (*aide, nourriture etc*) to ask for; (*revendiquer: dû, part, indemnité*) to claim, demand; (*nécessiter*) to demand, require // *vi* to complain; **se ~ de** to give as one's authority; to claim filiation with.

reclasser [Rəklɑse] *vt* (*fig: fonctionnaire etc*) to regrade.

reclus, e [Rəkly, -yz] *nm/f* recluse.

réclusion [Reklyzjɔ̃] *nf* imprisonment.

recoin [Rəkwɛ̃] *nm* nook, corner; (*fig*) hidden recess.

reçois *etc vb voir* **recevoir**.

récolte [Rekɔlt(ə)] *nf* harvesting; gathering; (*produits*) harvest, crop; (*fig*) crop, collection.

récolter [Rekɔlte] *vt* to harvest, gather (in); (*fig*) to collect; to get.

recommandable [Rəkɔmɑ̃dabl(ə)] *a* commendable.

recommandation [Rəkɔmɑ̃dasjɔ̃] *nf* recommendation.

recommandé [Rəkɔmɑ̃de] *nm* (POSTES): **en ~** by registered mail.

recommander [Rəkɔmɑ̃de] *vt* to recommend; (*suj: qualités etc*) to commend; (POSTES) to register; **~ à qn de faire** to recommend sb to do; **se ~ à qn** to commend o.s. to sb; **se ~ de qn** to give sb's name as a reference.

recommencer [Rəkɔmɑ̃se] *vt* (*reprendre: lutte, séance*) to resume, start again; (*refaire: travail, explications*) to start afresh, start (over) again; (*récidiver: erreur*) to make again // *vi* to start again; (*récidiver*) to do it again.

récompense [Rekɔ̃pɑ̃s] *nf* reward; (*prix*) award; **récompenser** *vt*: **récompenser qn (de** *ou* **pour)** to reward sb for.

réconciliation [Rekɔ̃siljasjɔ̃] *nf* reconciliation.

réconcilier [Rekɔ̃silje] *vt* to reconcile; **~ qn avec qch** to reconcile sb to sth; **se ~ (avec)** to be reconciled (with).

reconduction [Rəkɔ̃dyksjɔ̃] *nf* renewal.

reconduire [Rəkɔ̃dɥiR] *vt* (*raccompagner*) to take *ou* see back; (JUR, POL: *renouveler*) to renew.

réconfort [Rekɔ̃fɔR] *nm* comfort.

réconforter [Rekɔ̃fɔRte] *vt* (*consoler*) to comfort; (*revigorer*) to fortify.

reconnaissance [Rəkɔnɛsɑ̃s] *nf* recognition; acknowledgement; (*gratitude*) gratitude, gratefulness; (MIL) reconnaissance, recce; **~ de dette** acknowledgement of a debt, IOU.

reconnaissant, e [Rəkɔnɛsɑ̃, -ɑ̃t] *a* grateful; **je vous serais ~ de bien vouloir** I should be most grateful if you would (kindly).

reconnaître [RəkɔnɛtR(ə)] *vt* to recognize; (MIL: *lieu*) to reconnoitre; (JUR: *enfant, dette, droit*) to acknowledge; **~ que** to admit *ou* acknowledge that; **~ qn/qch**

à (*l'identifier grâce à*) to recognize sb/sth by.

reconstituant, e [Rǝkɔ̃stituɑ̃, -ɑ̃t] a (*régime*) strength-building // *nm* tonic, pick-me-up.

reconstituer [Rǝkɔ̃stitɥe] *vt* (*monument ancien*) to recreate, build a replica of; (*fresque, vase brisé*) to piece together, reconstitute; (*événement, accident*) to reconstruct; (*fortune, patrimoine*) to rebuild; (BIO: *tissus etc*) to regenerate; **reconstitution** *nf* (JUR: *d'accident etc*) reconstruction.

reconstruire [Rǝkɔ̃stRɥiR] *vt* to rebuild.

record [RǝkɔR] *nm, a* record.

recoupement [Rǝkupmɑ̃] *nm*: **par ~** by cross-checking.

recouper [Rǝkupe]: **se ~** *vi* (*témoignages*) to tie *ou* match up.

recourbé, e [RǝkuRbe] *a* curved; hooked; bent.

recourir [RǝkuRiR]: **~ à** *vt* (*ami, agence*) to turn *ou* appeal to; (*force, ruse, emprunt*) to resort *ou* have recourse to.

recours [RǝkuR] *nm* (JUR) appeal; **avoir ~ à** = **recourir à**; **en dernier ~** as a last resort; **sans ~** final; with no way out; **~ en grâce** plea for clemency (*ou* pardon).

recouvrer [RǝkuvRe] *vt* (*vue, santé etc*) to recover, regain; (*impôts*) to collect; (*créance*) to recover.

recouvrir [RǝkuvRiR] *vt* (*couvrir à nouveau*) to re-cover; (*couvrir entièrement, aussi fig*) to cover; (*cacher, masquer*) to conceal, hide; **se ~** (*se superposer*) to overlap.

recracher [RǝkRaʃe[*vt* to spit out.

récréatif, ive [RekReatif, -iv] *a* of entertainment; recreational.

récréation [RekReɑsjɔ̃] *nf* recreation, entertainment; (SCOL) break.

récrier [RekRije]: **se ~** *vi* to exclaim.

récriminations [RekRiminɑsjɔ̃] *nfpl* remonstrations, complaints.

recroqueviller [RǝkRɔkvije]: **se ~** *vi* (*feuilles*) to curl *ou* shrivel up; (*personne*) to huddle up.

recru, e [RǝkRy] *a*: **~ de fatigue** exhausted // *nf* recruit.

recrudescence [RǝkRydesɑ̃s] *nf* fresh outbreak.

recrue [RǝkRy] *a, nf voir* **recru**.

recruter [RǝkRyte] *vt* to recruit.

rectal, e, aux [Rɛktal, -o] *a*: **par voie ~e** rectally.

rectangle [Rɛktɑ̃gl(ǝ)] *nm* rectangle; **rectangulaire** *a* rectangular.

recteur [Rɛktœʀ] *nm* ≈ (regional) director of education.

rectificatif, ive [Rɛktifikatif, -iv] *a* corrected // *nm* correction.

rectification [Rɛktifikɑsjɔ̃] *nf* correction.

rectifier [Rɛktifje] *vt* (*tracé, virage*) to straighten; (*calcul, adresse*) to correct; (*erreur, faute*) to rectify, put right.

rectiligne [Rɛktiliɲ] *a* straight; (GÉOM) rectilinear.

rectitude [Rɛktityd] *nf* rectitude, uprightness.

reçu, e [Rǝsy] *pp de* **recevoir** // *a* (*admis, consacré*) accepted // *nm* (COMM) receipt.

recueil [Rǝkœj] *nm* collection.

recueillement [Rǝkœjmɑ̃] *nm* meditation, contemplation.

recueillir [RǝkœjiR] *vt* to collect; (*voix, suffrages*) to win; (*accueillir: réfugiés, chat*) to take in; **se ~** *vi* to gather one's thoughts; to meditate.

recul [Rǝkyl] *nm* retreat; recession; decline; (*d'arme à feu*) recoil, kick; **avoir un mouvement de ~** to recoil, start back; **prendre du ~** to stand back; **avec le ~** with the passing of time, in retrospect.

reculade [Rǝkylad] *nf* (*péj*) climb-down.

reculé, e [Rǝkyle] *a* remote.

reculer [Rǝkyle] *vi* to move back, back away; (AUTO) to reverse, back (up); (*fig*) to (be on the) decline; to be losing ground; (: *se dérober*) to shrink back // *vt* to move back; to reverse, back (up); (fig: *possibilités, limites*) to extend; (: *date, décision*) to postpone.

reculons [Rǝkylɔ̃]: **à ~** *ad* backwards.

récupérer [RekypeRe] *vt* (*rentrer en possession de*) to recover, get back; (*recueillir: ferraille etc*) to salvage (for reprocessing); (*délinquant etc*) to rehabilitate // *vi* to recover.

récurer [RekyRe] *vt* to scour.

récuser [Rekyze] *vt* to challenge; **se ~** to decline to give an opinion.

reçut *vb voir* **recevoir**.

recycler [Rǝsikle] *vt* (SCOL) to reorientate; (*employés*) to retrain.

rédacteur, trice [RedaktœR, -tRis] *nm/f* (*journaliste*) writer; subeditor; (*d'ouvrage de référence*) editor, compiler; **~ en chef** chief editor; **~ publicitaire** copywriter.

rédaction [Redaksjɔ̃] *nf* writing; (*rédacteurs*) editorial staff; (*bureau*) editorial office(s); (SCOL: *devoir*) essay, composition.

reddition [Redisjɔ̃] *nf* surrender.

rédemption [Redɑpsjɔ̃] *nf* redemption.

redescendre [Rǝdesɑ̃dR(ǝ)] *vi* (*à nouveau*) to go back down; (*après la montée*) to go down (again) // *vt* (*pente etc*) to go down.

redevable [Rǝdvabl(ǝ)] *a*: **être ~ de qch à qn** (*somme*) to owe sb sth; (*fig*) to be indebted to sb for sth.

redevance [Rǝdvɑ̃s] *nf* (*téléphonique*) rental charge; (*radiophonique*) licence fee.

rédhibitoire [RedibitwaR] *a*: **vice ~** (*fig*) irretrievable flaw.

rédiger [Redize] *vt* to write; (*contrat*) to draw up.

redire [RǝdiR] *vt* to repeat; **trouver à ~ à** to find fault with; **redite** *nf* (*needless*) repetition.

redondance [Rǝdɔ̃dɑ̃s] *nf* redundancy.

redoublé, e [Rǝduble] *a*: **à coups ~s** even harder, twice as hard.

redoubler [Rǝduble] *vi* (*tempête, violence*) to intensify, get even stronger *ou* fiercer etc; (SCOL) to repeat a year; **~ de** *vt* to be twice as + *adjectif*; **le vent redouble de violence** the wind is blowing twice as hard.

redoutable [ʀədutabl(ə)] a formidable, fearsome.

redouter [ʀədute] vt to fear; (appréhender) to dread.

redressement [ʀədʀɛsmɑ̃] nm: **maison de ~** reformatory.

redresser [ʀədʀese] vt (arbre, mât) to set upright, right; (pièce tordue) to straighten out; (AVIAT, AUTO) to straighten up; (situation, économie) to put right; **se ~** vi (objet penché) to right itself; to straighten up; (personne) to sit (ou stand) up; to sit (ou stand) up straight.

redresseur [ʀədʀɛsœʀ] nm: **~ de torts** righter of wrongs.

réduction [ʀedyksjɔ̃] nf reduction.

réduire [ʀedɥiʀ] vt (gén, aussi CULIN, MATH) to reduce; (prix, dépenses) to cut, reduce; (carte) to scale down, reduce; (MÉD: fracture) to set; (rebelles) to put down; **se ~ à** (revenir à) to boil down to; **~ en** (se transformer en) to be reduced to.

réduit [ʀedɥi] nm tiny room, recess.

rééducation [ʀeedykasjɔ̃] nf (d'un membre) re-education; (de délinquants, d'un blessé) rehabilitation; **~ de la parole** speech therapy.

réel, le [ʀeɛl] a real // nm: **le ~** reality.

réélection [ʀeelɛksjɔ̃] nf re-election.

réélire [ʀeeliʀ] vt to re-elect.

réellement [ʀeɛlmɑ̃] ad really.

réemploi [ʀeɑ̃plwa] nm = **remploi**.

réescompte [ʀeɛskɔ̃t] nm rediscount.

réévaluation [ʀeevalɥasjɔ̃] nf revaluation.

réévaluer [ʀeevalɥe] vt to revalue.

réexpédier [ʀeɛkspedje] vt (à l'envoyeur) to return, send back; (au destinataire) to send on, forward.

ref. abr de **référence**.

refaire [ʀəfɛʀ] vt (faire de nouveau, recommencer) to do again; (réparer, restaurer) to do up; **se ~** vi (en santé) to recover; (en argent) to make up one's losses; **être refait** (fam: dupé) to be had.

réfection [ʀefɛksjɔ̃] nf repair.

réfectoire [ʀefɛktwaʀ] nm (de collège, couvent, caserne) refectory.

référence [ʀefeʀɑ̃s] nf reference; **~s** nfpl (recommandations) reference sg; **faire ~ à** to refer to; **ouvrage de ~** reference work.

référendum [ʀefeʀɑ̃dɔm] nm referendum.

référer [ʀefeʀe]: **se ~ à** vt to refer to; **en ~ à qn** to refer the matter to sb.

refiler [ʀəfile] vt (fam): **~ qch à qn** to palm sth off on sb; to pass sth on to sb.

réfléchi, e [ʀefleʃi] a (caractère) thoughtful; (action) well-thought-out; (LING) reflexive.

réfléchir [ʀefleʃiʀ] vt to reflect // vi to think; **~ à** ou **sur** to think about.

reflet [ʀəflɛ] nm reflection; (sur l'eau etc) sheen q, glint.

refléter [ʀəflete] vt to reflect; **se ~** vi to be reflected.

réflex [ʀeflɛks] a inv (PHOTO) reflex.

réflexe [ʀeflɛks(ə)] nm, a reflex; **avoir de bons ~s** to have good reactions ou reflexes.

réflexion [ʀeflɛksjɔ̃] nf (de la lumière etc, pensée) reflection; (fait de penser) thought; (remarque) remark; **~s** nfpl (méditations) thought sg, reflection sg; **sans ~** without thinking; **~ faite, à la ~** on reflection.

refluer [ʀəflye] vi to flow back; (foule) to surge back.

reflux [ʀəfly] nm (de la mer) ebb.

refondre [ʀəfɔ̃dʀ(ə)] vt (texte) to recast.

réformateur, trice [ʀefɔʀmatœʀ, -tʀis] nm/f reformer.

Réformation [ʀefɔʀmasjɔ̃] nf: **la ~** the Reformation.

réforme [ʀefɔʀm(ə)] nf reform; (MIL) declaration of unfitness for service; discharge (on health grounds); (REL): **la R~** the Reformation.

réformé, e [ʀefɔʀme] a, nm/f (REL) Protestant.

réformer [ʀefɔʀme] vt to reform; (MIL: recrue) to declare unfit for service; (: soldat) to discharge, invalid out.

réformisme [ʀefɔʀmism(ə)] nm reformism, policy of reform.

refoulé, e [ʀəfule] a (PSYCH) frustrated, repressed.

refoulement [ʀəfulmɑ̃] nm (PSYCH) repression.

refouler [ʀəfule] vt (envahisseurs) to drive back, repulse; (liquide) to force back; (fig) to suppress; (PSYCH) to repress.

réfractaire [ʀefʀaktɛʀ] a (minerai) refractory; (brique) fire cpd; (prêtre) non-juring; **soldat ~** draft evader; **être ~ à** to resist.

réfracter [ʀefʀakte] vt to refract.

refrain [ʀəfʀɛ̃] nm (MUS) refrain, chorus; (air, fig) tune.

réfréner, refréner [ʀəfʀene, ʀefʀene] vt to curb, check.

réfrigérant, e [ʀefʀiʒeʀɑ̃, -ɑ̃t] a refrigerant, cooling.

réfrigérer [ʀefʀiʒeʀe] vt to refrigerate.

refroidir [ʀəfʀwadiʀ] vt to cool; (fig) to have a cooling effect on // vi to cool (down); **se ~** vi (prendre froid) to catch a chill; (temps) to get cooler ou colder; (fig) to cool (off); **refroidissement** nm cooling; (grippe etc) chill.

refuge [ʀəfyʒ] nm refuge; (pour piétons) (traffic) island.

réfugié, e [ʀefyʒje] a, nm/f refugee.

réfugier [ʀefyʒje]: **se ~** vi to take refuge.

refus [ʀəfy] nm refusal; **ce n'est pas de ~** I won't say no, it's welcome.

refuser [ʀəfyze] vt to refuse; (SCOL: candidat) to fail; **~ qch à qn/de faire** to refuse sb sth/to do; **~ du monde** to have to turn customers away; **se ~ à qch/à faire** to refuse to do.

réfuter [ʀefyte] vt to refute.

regagner [ʀəɡaɲe] vt (argent, faveur) to win back; (lieu) to get back to; **~ le temps perdu** to make up (for) lost time; **~ du terrain** to regain ground.

regain [ʀəɡɛ̃] nm (herbe) second crop of hay; (renouveau): **un ~ de** renewed + nom.

régal [ʀeɡal] nm treat.

régalade [ʀeɡalad] ad: **à la ~** from the bottle (held away from the lips).

régaler [ʀegale] vt: ~ qn to treat sb to a delicious meal ; ~ qn de to treat sb to ; se ~ vi to have a delicious meal ; (fig) to enjoy o.s.

regard [ʀəgaʀ] nm (coup d'œil) look, glance ; (expression) look (in one's eye) ; **parcourir/menacer du** ~ to cast an eye over/look threateningly at ; **au** ~ **de** (loi, morale) from the point of view of ; **en** ~ (vis à vis) opposite ; **en** ~ **de** in comparison with.

regardant, e [ʀəgaʀdã, -ãt] a: très/peu ~ **(sur)** quite fussy/very free (about) ; (économe) very tight-fisted/quite generous (with).

regarder [ʀəgaʀde] vt (examiner, observer, lire) to look at ; (film, télévision, match) to watch ; (envisager: situation, avenir) to view ; (considérer: son intérêt etc) to be concerned with ; (être orienté vers): ~ **(vers)** to face ; (concerner) to concern // vi to look, see ; ~ **à** vt (dépense qualité, détails) to be fussy with ou over ; ~ **à faire** to hesitate doing ; **dépenser sans** ~ to spend freely ; ~ **qn/qch comme** ~ to regard sb/sth as ; ~ **(qch) dans le dictionnaire/l'annuaire** to look (sth up) in the dictionary/directory ; **cela me regarde** it concerns me, it's my business.

régate(s) [ʀegat] nf(pl) regatta.

régénérer [ʀeʒeneʀe] vt to regenerate ; (fig) to revive.

régent [ʀeʒã] nm regent.

régenter [ʀeʒãte] vt to rule over ; to dictate to.

régie [ʀeʒi] nf (COMM, INDUSTRIE) state-owned company ; (THÉÂTRE, CINÉMA) production ; **la** ~ **de l'État** state control.

regimber [ʀəʒɛ̃be] vi to balk, jib.

régime [ʀeʒim] nm (POL) régime ; (ADMIN: des prisons, fiscal etc) system ; (MÉD) diet ; (GÉO) régime ; (TECH) (engine) speed ; (fig) rate, pace ; (de bananes, dattes) bunch ; **se mettre au/suivre un** ~ to go on/be on a diet ; ~ **sans sel** salt-free diet ; **à bas/haut** ~ (AUTO) at low/high revs ; ~ **matrimonial** marriage settlement.

régiment [ʀeʒimã] nm (MIL: unité) regiment ; (fig: fam): **un** ~ **de** an army of ; **un copain de** ~ a pal from military service ou (one's) army days.

région [ʀeʒjõ] nf region ; **la** ~ **parisienne** the Paris area ; **régional, e, aux** a regional ; **régionalisme** nm regionalism.

régir [ʀeʒiʀ] vt to govern.

régisseur [ʀeʒisœʀ] nm (d'un domaine) steward ; (CINÉMA, TV) assistant director ; (THÉÂTRE) stage manager.

registre [ʀəʒistʀ(ə)] nm (livre) register ; logbook ; ledger ; (MUS, LING) register ; (d'orgue) stop.

réglage [ʀeglaʒ] nm adjustment ; tuning.

règle [ʀɛgl(ə)] nf (instrument) ruler ; (loi, prescription) rule ; ~s nfpl (PHYSIOL) period sg ; **en** ~ (papiers d'identité) in order ; **être/se mettre en** ~ to be/put o.s. straight with the authorities ; **en** ~ **générale** as a (general) rule ; ~ **à calcul** slide rule.

réglé, e [ʀegle] a well-ordered ; stable, steady ; (papier) ruled ; (femme): **bien** ~s whose periods are regular.

règlement [ʀɛgləmã] nm settling ; (arrêté) regulation ; (règles, statuts) regulations pl, rules pl ; ~ **de compte(s)** settling of scores ; **réglementaire** a conforming to the regulations ; (tenue, uniforme) regulation cpd.

règlementation [ʀɛgləmãtɑsjõ] nf regulation, control ; regulations pl.

réglementer [ʀɛgləmãte] vt to regulate, control.

régler [ʀegle] vt (mécanisme, machine) to regulate, adjust ; (moteur) to tune ; (thermostat etc) to set, adjust ; (emploi du temps etc) to organize, plan ; (question, conflit, facture, dette) to settle ; (fournisseur) to settle up with, pay ; (papier) to rule ; ~ **son compte à qn** to sort sb out, settle sb ; ~ **un compte avec qn** to settle a score with sb.

réglisse [ʀeglis] nf liquorice.

règne [ʀɛɲ] nm (d'un roi etc, fig) reign ; (BIO): **le** ~ **végétal/animal** the vegetable/animal kingdom.

régner [ʀeɲe] vi (roi) to rule, reign ; (fig) to reign.

regorger [ʀəgɔʀʒe] vi to overflow ; ~ **de** to overflow with, be bursting with.

régression [ʀegʀesjõ] nf regression, decline.

regret [ʀəgʀɛ] nm regret ; **à** ~ with regret ; **avec** ~ regretfully ; **être au** ~ **de devoir faire** to regret having to do.

regrettable [ʀəgʀɛtabl(ə)] a regrettable.

regretter [ʀəgʀete] vt to regret ; (personne) to miss ; ~ **que** to regret that, be sorry that ; **je regrette** I'm sorry.

regrouper [ʀəgʀupe] vt (grouper) to group together ; (contenir) to include, comprise ; **se** ~ vi to gather (together).

régulariser [ʀegylaʀize] vt (fonctionnement, trafic) to regulate ; (passeport, papiers) to put in order ; (sa situation) to straighten out, regularize.

régularité [ʀegylaʀite] nf regularity.

régulateur, trice [ʀegylatœʀ, -tʀis] a regulating.

régulier, ière [ʀegylje, -jɛʀ] a (gén) regular ; (vitesse, qualité) steady ; (répartition, pression, paysage) even ; (TRANSPORTS: ligne, service) scheduled, regular ; (légal, réglementaire) lawful, in order ; (fam: correct) straight, on the level ; **régulièrement** ad regularly ; steadily ; evenly ; normally.

réhabiliter [ʀeabilite] vt to rehabilitate ; (fig) to restore to favour.

rehausser [ʀəose] vt to heighten, raise ; (fig) to set off, enhance.

rein [ʀɛ̃] nm kidney ; ~s nmpl (dos) back sg ; **avoir mal aux** ~s to have backache.

reine [ʀɛn] nf queen.

reine-claude [ʀɛnklod] nf greengage.

reinette [ʀɛnɛt] nf rennet, pippin.

réintégrer [ʀeɛ̃tegʀe] vt (lieu) to return to ; (fonctionnaire) to reinstate.

réitérer [ʀeiteʀe] vt to repeat, reiterate.

rejaillir [ʀəʒajiʀ] vi to splash up ; ~ **sur** to splash up onto ; (fig) to rebound on ; to fall upon.

rejet [ʀəʒɛ] nm (action, aussi MÉD)

rejection ; (*POÉSIE*) enjambement, rejet ; (*BOT*) shoot.

rejeter [Rɜ3te] vt (*relancer*) to throw back ; (*vomir*) to bring *ou* throw up ; (*écarter*) to reject ; (*déverser*) to throw out, discharge ; ~ **la tête/les épaules en arrière** to throw one's head/pull one's shoulders back ; ~ **la responsabilité de qch sur qn** to lay the responsibility for sth at sb's door.

rejeton [Rɜ3tɔ̃] nm offspring.

rejoindre [Rɜ3wɛ̃dR(ə)] vt (*famille, régiment*) to rejoin, return to ; (*lieu*) to get (back) to ; (*suj: route*) to meet, join ; (*rattraper*) to catch up (with) ; **se** ~ vi to meet ; **je te rejoins au café** I'll see *ou* meet you at the café.

réjoui, e [Rɜ3wi] a (*mine*) joyous.

réjouir [Rɜ3wiR] vt to delight ; **se** ~ vi to be delighted ; to rejoice ; **se** ~ **de qch/faire** to be delighted about sth/to do ; **réjouissances** nfpl (*joie*) rejoicing sg ; (*fête*) festivities, merry-making sg.

relâche [Rəlɑʃ] : **faire** ~ vi (*navire*) to put into port ; (*CINÉMA*) to be closed ; **sans** ~ ad without respite *ou* a break.

relâché, e [Rəlɑʃe] a loose, lax.

relâcher [Rəlɑʃe] vt (*ressort, prisonnier*) to release ; (*étreinte, cordes*) to loosen // vi (*NAVIG*) to put into port ; **se** ~ vi to loosen ; (*discipline*) to become slack *ou* lax ; (*élève etc*) to slacken off.

relais [Rəlɛ] nm (*SPORT*): (**course de**) ~ relay (race) ; (*RADIO, TV*) relay ; **équipe de** ~ shift team ; relay team ; **prendre le** ~ (**de**) to take over (from) ; ~ **de poste** post house, coaching inn ; ~ **routier** ≈ transport café.

relance [Rəlɑ̃s] nf boosting, revival.

relancer [Rəlɑ̃se] vt (*balle*) to throw back (again) ; (*moteur*) to restart ; (*fig*) to boost, revive ; (*personne*): ~ **qn** to pester sb ; to get on to sb again.

relater [Rəlate] vt to relate, recount.

relatif, ive [Rəlatif, -iv] a relative.

relation [Rəlasjɔ̃] nf (*récit*) account, report ; (*rapport*) relation(ship) ; ~**s** nfpl (*rapports*) relation ; relationship sg ; (*connaissances*) connections ; **être/entrer en** ~(**s**) **avec** to be in contact *ou* be dealing/get in contact with ; ~**s publiques** public relations.

relativement [Rəlativmɑ̃] ad relatively ; ~ **à** in relation to.

relativité [Rəlativite] nf relativity.

relax [Rəlaks] a inv, **relaxe** [Rəlaks(ə)] a informal, casual ; easy-going.

relaxer [Rəlakse] vt to relax ; (*JUR*) to discharge ; **se** ~ vi to relax.

relayer [Rəleje] vt (*collaborateur, coureur etc*) to relieve, take over from ; (*RADIO, TV*) to relay ; **se** ~ (*dans une activité*) to take it in turns.

relégation [Rəlegasjɔ̃] nf (*SPORT*) relegation.

reléguer [Rəlege] vt to relegate.

relent(s) [Rəlɑ̃] nm(pl) (foul) smell.

relève [Rəlɛv] nf relief ; relief team (*ou* troops pl) ; **prendre la** ~ to take over.

relevé, e [Rəlve] a (*bord de chapeau*) turned-up ; (*manches*) rolled-up ; (*virage*) banked ; (*fig: style*) elevated ; (: *sauce*) highly-seasoned // nm (*lecture*) reading ;

(*de cotes*) plotting ; (*liste*) statement ; list ; (*facture*) account ; ~ **de compte** bank statement.

relever [Rəlve] vt (*statue, meuble*) to stand up again ; (*personne tombée*) to help up ; (*vitre, plafond, niveau de vie*) to raise ; (*col*) to turn up ; (*style, conversation*) to elevate ; (*plat, sauce*) to season ; (*sentinelle, équipe*) to relieve ; (*souligner: fautes, points*) to pick out ; (*constater: traces etc*) to find, pick up ; (: *défi*) to accept, take up ; (*noter: adresse etc*) to take down, note ; (: *plan*) to sketch ; (: *cotes etc*) to plot ; (*compteur*) to read ; (*ramasser: cahiers, copies*) to collect, take in ; ~ **de** vt (*maladie*) to be recovering from ; (*être du ressort de*) to be a matter for ; (*ADMIN: dépendre de*) to come under ; (*fig*) to pertain to ; **se** ~ vi (*se remettre debout*) to get up ; ~ **qn de** (*vœux*) to release sb from ; (*fonctions*) to relieve sb of ; ~ **la tête** to look up ; to hold up one's head.

relief [Rəljɛf] nm relief ; (*de pneu*) tread pattern ; ~**s** nmpl (*restes*) remains ; **en** ~ in relief ; (*photographie*) three-dimensional ; **mettre en** ~ (*fig*) to bring out, highlight.

relier [Rəlje] vt to link up ; (*livre*) to bind ; ~ **qch à** to link sth to ; **livre relié cuir** leather-bound book ; **relieur, euse** nm/f (book)binder.

religieux, euse [Rəliʒjø, -øz] a religious // nm monk // nf nun ; (*gâteau*) cream bun.

religion [Rəliʒjɔ̃] nf religion ; (*piété, dévotion*) faith ; **entrer en** ~ to take one's vows.

reliquaire [RəlikɛR] nm reliquary.

reliquat [Rəlika] nm balance ; remainder.

relique [Rəlik] nf relic.

relire [RəliR] vt (*à nouveau*) to reread, read again ; (*vérifier*) to read over.

reliure [RəljyR] nf binding.

reluire [RəluiR] vi to gleam ; **reluisant, e** a gleaming ; **peu reluisant** (*fig*) unattractive ; unsavoury.

remâcher [Rəmɑʃe] vt to chew or ruminate over.

remailler [Rəmɑje] vt to darn ; to mend.

remaniement [Rəmanimɑ̃] nm: ~ **ministériel** Cabinet reshuffle.

remanier [Rəmanje] vt to reshape, recast ; (*POL*) to reshuffle.

remarquable [RəmaRkabl(ə)] a remarkable.

remarque [RəmaRk(ə)] nf remark ; (*écrite*) note.

remarquer [RəmaRke] vt (*voir*) to notice ; (*dire*): ~ **que** to remark that ; **se** ~ to be noticeable ; **se faire** ~ to draw attention to o.s. ; **faire** ~ (**à qn**) **que** to point out (to sb) that ; **faire** ~ **qch (à qn)** to point sth out (to sb) ; **remarquez que** mark you, mind you.

rembarrer [Rɑ̃baRe] vt: ~ **qn** to rebuff sb ; to put sb in his/her place.

remblai [Rɑ̃blɛ] nm embankment.

remblayer [Rɑ̃bleje] vt to bank up ; (*fossé*) to fill in.

rembourrage [Rɑ̃buRaʒ] nm stuffing ; padding.

rembourré, e [ʀɑ̃buʀe] a padded.
rembourrer [ʀɑ̃buʀe] vt to stuff ; (*dossier, vêtement, souliers*) to pad.
remboursement [ʀɑ̃buʀsəmɑ̃] nm repayment ; **envoi contre ~** cash on delivery.
rembourser [ʀɑ̃buʀse] vt to pay back, repay.
rembrunir [ʀɑ̃bʀyniʀ]: **se ~** vi to darken ; to grow sombre.
remède [ʀəmɛd] nm (*médicament*) medicine ; (*traitement, fig*) remedy, cure.
remédier [ʀəmedje]: **~ à** vt to remedy.
remembrement [ʀəmɑ̃bʀəmɑ̃] nm (AGR) regrouping of lands.
remémorer [ʀəmemɔʀe]: **se ~** vt to recall, recollect.
remerciements [ʀəmɛʀsimɑ̃] nmpl thanks.
remercier [ʀəmɛʀsje] vt to thank ; (*congédier*) to dismiss ; **~ qn de/d'avoir fait** to thank sb for/for having done ; **non, je vous remercie** no thank you.
remettre [ʀəmɛtʀ(ə)] vt (*vêtement*): **~ qch** to put sth back on, put sth on again ; (*replacer*): **~ qch quelque part** to put sth back somewhere ; (*ajouter*): **~ du sel/un sucre** to add more salt/another lump of sugar ; (*rétablir: personne*): **~ qn** to set sb back on his/her feet ; (*rendre, restituer*): **~ qch à qn** to give sth back to sb, return sth to sb ; (*donner, confier: paquet, argent*): **~ qch à qn** to hand over sth to sb, deliver sth to sb ; (*prix, décoration*): **~ qch à qn** to present sb with sth ; (*ajourner*): **~ qch (à)** to postpone sth *ou* put sth off (until) ; **se ~** vi to get better, recover ; **se ~ de** to recover from, get over ; **s'en ~ à** to leave it (up) to.
remise [ʀəmiz] nf delivery ; presentation ; (*rabais*) discount ; (*local*) shed ; **~ en jeu** (FOOTBALL) throw-in ; **~ de peine** reduction of sentence.
rémission [ʀemisjɔ̃]: **sans ~** a irremediable *ou* unremittingly.
remontant [ʀəmɔ̃tɑ̃] nm tonic, pick-me-up.
remontée [ʀəmɔ̃te] nf rising ; ascent ; **~s mécaniques** (SKI) towing equipment sg *ou* facilities.
remonte-pente [ʀəmɔ̃tpɑ̃t] nm skilift, (ski) tow.
remonter [ʀəmɔ̃te] vi (*à nouveau*) to go back up ; (*après une descente*) to go up (again) ; (*jupe*) to pull *ou* ride up // vt (*pente*) to go up ; (*fleuve*) to sail (*ou* swim *etc*) up ; (*manches, pantalon*) to roll up ; (*col*) to turn up ; (*rayon, limite*) to raise ; (*fig: personne*) to buck up ; (*moteur, meuble*) to put back together, reassemble ; (*garde-robe etc*) to renew, replenish ; (*montre, mécanisme*) to wind up ; **~ à** (*dater de*) to date *ou* go back to ; **~ en voiture** to get back into the car.
remontoir [ʀəmɔ̃twaʀ] nm winding mechanism, winder.
remontrance [ʀəmɔ̃tʀɑ̃s] nf reproof, reprimand.
remontrer [ʀəmɔ̃tʀe] vt (*fig*): **en ~ à** to prove one's superiority over.
remords [ʀəmɔʀ] nm remorse q ; **avoir des ~** to feel remorse, be conscience-stricken.

remorque [ʀəmɔʀk(ə)] nf trailer ; **prendre/être en ~** to tow/be on tow ; **remorquer** vt to tow ; **remorqueur** nm tug(boat).
rémoulade [ʀemulad] nf dressing with mustard and herbs.
rémouleur [ʀemulœʀ] nm (knife- *ou* scissor-)grinder.
remous [ʀəmu] nm (*d'un navire*) (back)wash q ; (*de rivière*) swirl, eddy // nmpl (*fig*) stir sg.
rempailler [ʀɑ̃paje] vt to reseat (with straw).
remparts [ʀɑ̃paʀ] nmpl walls, ramparts.
rempiler [ʀɑ̃pile] vi (MIL: fam) to join up again.
remplaçant, e [ʀɑ̃plasɑ̃, -ɑ̃t] nm/f replacement, substitute, stand-in ; (THÉÂTRE) understudy ; (SCOL) supply teacher.
remplacement [ʀɑ̃plasmɑ̃] nm replacement ; (*job*) replacement work q ; **assurer le ~ de qn** (*suj: remplaçant*) to stand in *ou* substitute for sb.
remplacer [ʀɑ̃plase] vt to replace ; (*prendre temporairement la place de*) to stand in for ; (*tenir lieu de*) to take the place of, act as a substitute for ; **~ qch/qn par** to replace sth/sb with.
rempli, e [ʀɑ̃pli] a (*emploi du temps*) full, busy ; **~ de** full of, filled with.
remplir [ʀɑ̃pliʀ] vt to fill (up) ; (*questionnaire*) to fill out *ou* up ; (*obligations, fonction, condition*) to fulfil ; **se ~** vi to fill up.
remplissage [ʀɑ̃plisaʒ] nm (*fig: péj*) padding.
remploi [ʀɑ̃plwa] nm re-use.
remporter [ʀɑ̃pɔʀte] vt (*marchandise*) to take away ; (*fig*) to win, achieve.
remuant, e [ʀəmɥɑ̃, -ɑ̃t] a restless.
remue-ménage [ʀəmymenaʒ] nm inv commotion.
remuer [ʀəmɥe] vt to move ; (*café, sauce*) to stir // vi to move ; (*fig: opposants*) to show signs of unrest ; **se ~** vi to move ; (*se démener*) to stir o.s. ; (*fam*) to get a move on.
rémunération [ʀemyneʀɑsjɔ̃] nf remuneration.
rémunérer [ʀemyneʀe] vt to remunerate, pay.
renâcler [ʀənɑkle] vi to snort ; (*fig*) to grumble, balk.
renaissance [ʀənɛsɑ̃s] nf rebirth, revival ; **la R~** the Renaissance.
renaître [ʀənɛtʀ(ə)] vi to be revived.
rénal, e, aux [ʀenal, -o] a renal, kidney cpd.
renard [ʀənaʀ] nm fox.
rencard [ʀɑ̃kaʀ] nm = **rancard**.
rencart [ʀɑ̃kaʀ] nm = **rancart**.
renchérir [ʀɑ̃ʃeʀiʀ] vi to become more expensive ; (*fig*): **~ (sur)** to add something (to).
rencontre [ʀɑ̃kɔ̃tʀ(ə)] nf (*entrevue, congrès, match etc*) meeting ; (*imprévue*) encounter ; **faire la ~ de qn** to meet sb ;

aller à la ~ de qn to go and meet sb ; **amours de ~** casual love affairs.

rencontrer [ʀɑ̃kɔ̃tʀe] vt to meet ; (mot, expression) to come across ; (difficultés) to meet with ; **se ~** vi to meet ; (véhicules) to collide.

rendement [ʀɑ̃dmɑ̃] nm (d'un travailleur, d'une machine) output ; (d'une culture) yield ; (d'un investissement) return ; **à plein ~** at full capacity.

rendez-vous [ʀɑ̃devu] nm (rencontre) appointment ; (: d'amoureux) date ; (lieu) meeting place ; **donner ~ à qn** to arrange to meet sb ; **fixer un ~ à qn** to give sb an appointment ; **avoir/prendre ~ (avec)** to have/make an appointment (with).

rendre [ʀɑ̃dʀ(ə)] vt (livre, argent etc) to give back, return ; (otages, visite etc) to return ; (sang, aliments) to bring up ; (sons: suj: instrument) to produce, make ; (exprimer, traduire) to render ; (faire devenir): **~ qn célèbre/qch possible** to make sb famous/sth possible ; **se ~** vi (capituler) to surrender, give o.s. up ; (aller): **se ~ quelque part** to go somewhere ; **se ~ à** (arguments etc) to bow to ; (ordres) to comply with ; **~ la vue/la santé à qn** to restore sb's sight/health ; **~ la liberté à qn** to set sb free.

renégat, e [ʀənega, -at] nm/f renegade.

rênes [ʀɛn] nfpl reins.

renfermé, e [ʀɑ̃fɛʀme] a (fig) withdrawn // nm: **sentir le ~** to smell stuffy.

renfermer [ʀɑ̃fɛʀme] vt to contain ; **se ~ (sur soi-même)** to withdraw into o.s.

renflé, e [ʀɑ̃fle] a bulging, bulbous.

renflement [ʀɑ̃fləmɑ̃] nm bulge.

renflouer [ʀɑ̃flue] vt to refloat ; (fig) to set back on its (ou his/her) feet (again).

renfoncement [ʀɑ̃fɔ̃smɑ̃] nm recess.

renforcer [ʀɑ̃fɔʀse] vt to reinforce.

renfort [ʀɑ̃fɔʀ]: **~s** nmpl reinforcements ; **en ~** as a back-up ; **à grand ~ de** with a great deal of.

renfrogner [ʀɑ̃fʀɔɲe]: **se ~** vi to scowl.

rengaine [ʀɑ̃gɛn] nf (péj) old tune.

rengainer [ʀɑ̃gɛne] vt (revolver) to put back in its holster.

rengorger [ʀɑ̃gɔʀʒe]: **se ~** vi (fig) to puff o.s. up.

renier [ʀənje] vt (parents) to disown, repudiate ; (foi) to renounce.

renifler [ʀənifle] vi to sniff // vt (tabac) to sniff up ; (odeur) to sniff.

renne [ʀɛn] nm reindeer inv.

renom [ʀənɔ̃] nm reputation ; renown ; **renommé, e** a celebrated, renowned // nf fame.

renoncement [ʀənɔ̃smɑ̃] nm abnegation, renunciation.

renoncer [ʀənɔ̃se] vi: **~ à** vt to give up ; **~ à faire** to give up all idea of doing ; to give up trying to do.

renouer [ʀənwe] vt (cravate etc) to retie ; **~ avec** (tradition) to revive ; (habitude) to take up again ; **~ avec qn** to take up with sb again.

renouveau, x [ʀənuvo] nm: **~ de succès** renewed success ; **le ~ printanier** springtide.

renouveler [ʀənuvle] vt to renew ; (exploit, méfait) to repeat ; **se ~** vi (incident) to recur, happen again, be repeated ; (cellules etc) to be renewed ou replaced ; **renouvellement** nm renewal ; recurrence.

rénovation [ʀenɔvasjɔ̃] nf renovation ; restoration.

rénover [ʀenɔve] vt (immeuble) to renovate, do up ; (meuble) to restore ; (enseignement) to reform.

renseignement [ʀɑ̃sɛɲmɑ̃] nm information q, piece of information ; **prendre des ~s sur** to make inquiries about, ask for information about ; **(guichet des) ~s** information desk.

renseigner [ʀɑ̃sɛɲe] vt: **~ qn (sur)** to give information to sb (about) ; **se ~** vi to ask for information, make inquiries.

rentable [ʀɑ̃tabl(ə)] a profitable.

rente [ʀɑ̃t] nf income ; pension ; government stock ou bond ; **~ viagère** life annuity ; **rentier, ière** nm/f person of private means.

rentrée [ʀɑ̃tʀe] nf: **~ (d'argent)** cash q coming in ; **la ~ (des classes)** the start of the new school year ; **la ~ (parlementaire)** the reopening ou reassembly of parliament ; **faire sa ~** (artiste, acteur) to make a comeback.

rentrer [ʀɑ̃tʀe] vi (entrer de nouveau) to go (ou come) back in ; (entrer) to go (ou come) in ; (revenir chez soi) to go (ou come) (back) home ; (air, clou: pénétrer) to go in ; (revenu, argent) to come in // vt (foins) to bring in ; (véhicule) to put away ; (chemise dans pantalon etc) to tuck in ; (griffes) to draw in ; (train d'atterrissage) to raise ; (fig: larmes, colère etc) to hold back ; **~ le ventre** to pull in one's stomach ; **~ dans** to go (ou come) back into ; to go back (ou come) into ; (famille, patrie) to go back ou return to ; (heurter) to crash into ; **~ dans l'ordre** to be back to normal ; **~ dans ses frais** to recover one's expenses (ou initial outlay).

renversant, e [ʀɑ̃vɛʀsɑ̃, -ɑ̃t] a amazing.

renverse [ʀɑ̃vɛʀs(ə)]: **à la ~** ad backwards.

renverser [ʀɑ̃vɛʀse] vt (faire tomber: chaise, verre) to knock over, overturn ; (piéton) to knock down ; (liquide, contenu) to spill, upset ; (retourner: verre, image) to turn upside down, invert ; (: ordre des mots etc) to reverse ; (fig: gouvernement etc) to overthrow ; (stupéfier) to bowl over, stagger ; **se ~** vi to fall over ; to overturn ; to spill ; **~ la tête/le corps (en arrière)** to tip one's head back/throw one's body back.

renvoi [ʀɑ̃vwa] nm dismissal ; return ; reflection ; postponement ; (référence) cross-reference ; (éructation) belch.

renvoyer [ʀɑ̃vwaje] vt to send back ; (congédier) to dismiss ; (lumière) to reflect ; (son) to echo ; (ajourner): **~ qch (à)** to put sth off ou postpone sth (until) ; **~ qn à** (fig) to refer sb to.

réorganiser [ʀeɔʀganize] vt to reorganize.

réouverture [ʀeuvɛʀtyʀ] nf reopening.

repaire [Rəpɛʀ] nm den.

repaître [Rəpɛtʀ(ə)] vt (rabattre) to fold down ou over; **se ~ de** vt to feed on; to wallow ou revel in.

répandre [Repɑ̃dʀ(ə)] vt (renverser) to spill; (étaler, diffuser) to spread; (lumière) to shed; (chaleur, odeur) to give off; **se ~** vi to spill; to spread; **se ~ en** (injures etc) to pour out; **répandu, e** a (opinion, usage) widespread.

réparation [Repaʀasjɔ̃] nf repairing q, repair.

réparer [Repaʀe] vt to repair; (fig: offense) to make up for, atone for; (: oubli, erreur) to put right.

repartie [Rəpaʀti] nf retort; **avoir de la ~** to be quick at repartee.

repartir [Rəpaʀtiʀ] vi to set off again; to leave again; (fig) to get going again, pick up again; **~ à zéro** to start from scratch (again).

répartir [Repaʀtiʀ] vt (pour attribuer) to share out; (pour disperser, disposer) to divide up; (poids, chaleur) to distribute; **se ~** vt (travail, rôles) to share out between themselves; **répartition** nf sharing out; dividing up, distribution.

repas [Rəpɑ] nm meal.

repasser [Rəpase] vi to come (ou go) back // vt (vêtement, tissu) to iron; to retake, resit; to show again; (leçon, rôle: revoir) to go over (again).

repêchage [Rəpeʃaʒ] nm (SCOL): **question de ~** question to give candidates a second chance.

repêcher [Rəpeʃe] vt (noyé) to recover the body of, fish out.

repentir [Rəpɑ̃tiʀ] nm repentance; **se ~** vi to repent; **se ~ de** to repent (of).

répercussions [RepɛRkysjɔ̃] nfpl repercussions.

répercuter [RepɛRkyte]: **se ~** vi (bruit) to reverberate; (fig): **se ~ sur** to have repercussions on.

repère [Rəpɛʀ] nm mark; (monument etc) landmark.

repérer [Rəpeʀe] vt (erreur, connaissance) to spot; (abri, ennemi) to locate; **se ~** vi to find one's way about; **se faire ~** to be spotted.

répertoire [RepɛRtwaR] nm (liste) (alphabetical) list; (carnet) index notebook; (de carnet) thumb index; (indicateur) directory, index; (d'un théâtre, artiste) repertoire; **répertorier** vt to itemize, list.

répéter [Repete] vt to repeat; (préparer: leçon: aussi vi) to learn, go over; (THÉÂTRE) to rehearse; **se ~** (redire) to repeat o.s.; (se reproduire) to be repeated, recur.

répétition [Repetisjɔ̃] nf repetition; rehearsal; **~s** nfpl (leçons) private coaching sg; **armes à ~** repeater weapons; **~ générale** final dress rehearsal.

repeupler [Rəpœple] vt to repopulate; to restock.

répit [Repi] nm respite; **sans ~** without letting up.

replet, ète [Rəplɛ, -ɛt] a a chubby, fat.

repli [Rəpli] nm (d'une étoffe) fold; (MIL, fig) withdrawal.

replier [Rəplije] vt (rabattre) to fold down ou over; **se ~** vi (troupes, armée) to withdraw, fall back.

réplique [Replik] nf (repartie, fig) reply; (THÉÂTRE) line; (copie) replica; **donner la ~ à** to play opposite; to match; **sans ~** no-nonsense; irrefutable.

répliquer [Replike] vi to reply; (riposter) to retaliate.

répondre [Repɔ̃dʀ(ə)] vi to answer, reply; (freins, mécanisme) to respond; **~ à** vt to reply to, answer; (avec impertinence): **~ à qn** to answer sb back; (invitation, convocation) to reply to; (affection, salut) to return; (provocation, suj: mécanisme etc) to respond to; (correspondre à: besoin) to answer; (: conditions) to meet; (: description) to match; **~ que** to answer ou reply that; **~ de** to answer for.

réponse [Repɔ̃s] nf answer, reply; **avec ~ payée** (POSTES) reply-paid; **en ~ à** in reply to.

report [RəpɔR] nm transfer; postponement.

reportage [RəpɔRtaʒ] nm (bref) report; (écrit: documentaire) story; article; (en direct) commentary; (genre, activité): **le ~** reporting.

reporter nm [RəpɔRtɛʀ] reporter // vt [RəpɔRte] (total): **~ qch sur** to carry sth forward ou over to; (ajourner): **~ qch (à)** to postpone sth (until); (transférer): **~ qch sur** to transfer sth to; **se ~ à** (époque) to think back to; (document) to refer to.

repos [Rəpo] nm rest; (fig) peace (and quiet); peace of mind; (MIL): **~!** stand at ease!; **en ~** at rest; **de tout ~** safe.

repose [Rəpoz] nf refitting.

reposé, e [Rəpoze] a fresh, rested.

reposer [Rəpoze] vt (verre, livre) to put down; (délasser) to rest; (problème) to reformulate // vi (liquide, pâte) to settle, rest; **~ sur** to be built on; (fig) to rest on; **se ~** vi to rest; **se ~ sur qn** to rely on sb.

repoussant, e [Rəpusɑ̃, -ɑ̃t] a repulsive.

repoussé, e [Rəpuse] a (cuir) embossed (by hand).

repousser [Rəpuse] vi to grow again // vt to repel, repulse; (offre) to turn down, reject; (tiroir, personne) to push back; (différer) to put back.

répréhensible [Repreɑ̃sibl(ə)] a reprehensible.

reprendre [RəpʀɑdR(ə)] vt (prisonnier, ville) to recapture; (objet prêté, donné) to take back; (chercher): **je viendrai te ~ à 4h** I'll come and fetch you ou I'll come back for you at 4; (se resservir de): **~ du pain/un œuf** to take (ou eat) more bread/another egg; (COMM: article usagé) to take back; to take in part exchange; (firme, entreprise) to take over; (travail, promenade) to resume; (emprunter: argument, idée) to take up, use; (refaire: article etc) to go over again; (jupe etc) to alter; to take in (ou up); to let out (ou down); (émission, pièce) to put on again; (réprimander) to tell off; (corriger) to correct // vi (classes, pluie) to start (up) again; (activités, travaux, combats) to resume, start (up) again; (affaires, *industrie)* to pick up; *(dire)*: **reprit-il** he went on; ~ *(se ressaisir)* to recover, pull o.s. together; **s'y** ~ to make another attempt; ~ **des forces** to recover one's strength; ~ **courage** to take new heart; ~ **ses habitudes/sa liberté** to get back into one's old habits/regain one's freedom; ~ **la route** to resume one's journey, set off again; ~ **haleine** *ou* **son souffle** to get one's breath back.

représailles [Rəprezaj] *nfpl* reprisals, retaliation *sg.*

représentant, e [Rəprezɑ̃tɑ̃, -ɑ̃t] *nm/f* representative.

représentatif, ive [Rəprezɑ̃tatif, -iv] *a* representative.

représentation [Rəprezɑ̃tɑsjɔ̃] *nf* representation; performing; *(symbole, image)* representation; *(spectacle)* performance; *(COMM):* **la** ~ commercial travelling; sales representation; **frais de** ~ *(d'un diplomate)* entertainment allowance.

représenter [Rəprezɑ̃te] *vt* to represent; *(donner: pièce, opéra)* to perform; **se** ~ *vt (se figurer)* to imagine; to visualize.

répression [Represjɔ̃] *nf* suppression; repression; *(POL):* **la** ~ repression.

réprimande [Reprimɑ̃d] *nf* reprimand, rebuke; **réprimander** *vt* to reprimand, rebuke.

réprimer [Reprime] *vt* to suppress, repress.

repris [Rəpri] *nm:* ~ **de justice** ex-prisoner, ex-convict.

reprise [Rəpriz] *nf (TV)* repeat; *(CINÉMA)* rerun; *(AUTO)* acceleration *q;* *(COMM)* trade-in, part exchange; *(de location)* sum asked for any extras or improvements made to the property; *(raccommodage)* darn; mend; **à plusieurs** ~**s** on several occasions, several times.

repriser [Rəprize] *vt* to darn; to mend.

réprobateur, trice [RepRɔbatœR, -tRis] *a* reproving.

réprobation [Reprɔbɑsjɔ̃] *nf* reprobation.

reproche [Rəprɔʃ] *nm (remontrance)* reproach; **faire des** ~**s à qn** to reproach sb; **sans** ~**(s)** beyond *ou* above reproach.

reprocher [Rəprɔʃe] *vt:* ~ **qch à qn** to reproach *ou* blame sb for sth; ~ **qch à** *(machine, théorie)* to have sth against.

reproducteur, trice [RəprɔdyktœR, -tRis] *a* reproductive.

reproduction [Rəprɔdyksjɔ̃] *nf* reproduction; ~ **interdite** all rights (of reproduction) reserved.

reproduire [RəprɔduiR] *vt* to reproduce; **se** ~ *vi (BIO)* to reproduce; *(recommencer)* to recur, re-occur.

réprouvé, e [Repruve] *nm/f* reprobate.

réprouver [Repruve] *vt* to reprove.

reptation [Reptɑsjɔ̃] *nf* crawling.

reptile [Reptil] *nm* reptile.

repu, e [Rəpy] *a* satisfied, sated.

républicain, e [Repyblikɛ̃, -ɛn] *a, nm/f* republican.

république [Repyblik] *nf* republic; **la R~ fédérale allemande** the Federal Republic of Germany.

répudier [Repydje] *vt (femme)* to repudiate; *(doctrine)* to renounce.

répugnance [Repyɲɑ̃s] *nf* repugnance, loathing.

répugnant, e [Repyɲɑ̃, -ɑ̃t] *a* repulsive; loathsome.

répugner [Repyɲe]: ~ **à** *vt:* ~ **à qn** to repel *ou* disgust sb; ~ **à faire** to be loath *ou* reluctant to do.

répulsion [Repylsjɔ̃] *nf* repulsion.

réputation [Repytɑsjɔ̃] *nf* reputation; **réputé, e** *a* renowned.

requérir [RəkeRiR] *vt (nécessiter)* to require, call for; *(au nom de la loi)* to call upon; *(JUR: peine)* to call for, demand.

requête [Rəkɛt] *nf* request, petition; *(JUR)* petition.

requiem [Rekɥijɛm] *nm* requiem.

requin [Rəkɛ̃] *nm* shark.

requis, e [Rəki, -iz] *pp de* **requérir**.// *a* required.

réquisition [Rekizisjɔ̃] *nf* requisition; **réquisitionner** *vt* to requisition.

réquisitoire [RekizitwaR] *nm (JUR)* closing speech for the prosecution; *(fig):* ~ **contre** indictment of.

R.E.R. *sigle m* (= *réseau express régional*) Greater Paris high speed commuter train.

rescapé, e [Rɛskape] *nm/f* survivor.

rescousse [Rɛskus] *nf:* **aller à la** ~ **de qn** to go to sb's aid *ou* rescue; **appeler qn à la** ~ to call on sb for help.

réseau, x [Rezo] *nm* network.

réservation [Rezɛrvɑsjɔ̃] *nf* booking, reservation.

réserve [Rezɛrv(ə)] *nf (gén)* reserve; *(entrepôt)* storeroom; *(restriction, aussi: d'Indiens)* reservation; *(de pêche, chasse)* preserve; **sous** ~ **de** subject to; **sans** ~ **ad** unreservedly; **de** ~ *(provisions etc)* in reserve.

réservé, e [Rezɛrve] *a (discret)* reserved; *(chasse, pêche)* private; ~ **à/pour** reserved for.

réserver [Rezɛrve] *vt (gén)* to reserve; *(retenir: par une agence, au guichet)* to book, reserve; *(mettre de côté, garder):* ~ **qch pour/à** to keep *ou* save sth for; ~ **qch à qn** to reserve *(ou* book) sth for sb; *(fig: destiner)* to have sth in store for sb; **se** ~ **le droit de faire** to reserve the right to do.

réserviste [Rezɛrvist(ə)] *nm* reservist.

réservoir [RezɛrvwaR] *nm* tank; *(plan d'eau)* reservoir.

résidence [Rezidɑ̃s] *nf* residence; ~ **secondaire** second home; **(en)** ~ **surveillée** (under) house arrest; **résidentiel, le** *a* residential.

résider [Rezide] *vi:* ~ **à/dans/en** to reside in; ~ **dans** *(fig)* to lie in.

résidu [Rezidy] *nm* residue *q.*

résignation [Reziɲɑsjɔ̃] *nf* resignation.

résigner [Reziɲe] *vt* to relinquish, resign; **se** ~ *vi:* **se** ~ **(à qch/faire)** to resign o.s. (to sth/to doing).

résilier [Rezilje] *vt* to terminate.

résille [Rezij] *nf* (hair)net.

résine [Rezin] *nf* resin; **résiné, e** *a:* **vin résiné** retsina; **résineux, euse** *a* resinous // *nm* coniferous tree.

résistance [Rezistɑ̃s] nf resistance; (de réchaud, bouilloire: fil) element.

résistant, e [Rezistɑ̃, -ɑ̃t] a (personne) robust, tough; (matériau) strong, hard-wearing // nm/f (patriote) Resistance worker ou fighter.

résister [Reziste] vi to resist; ~ à vt (assaut, tentation) to resist; (effort, souffrance) to withstand; (suj: matériau, plante) to stand up to, withstand; (personne: désobéir à) to stand up to, oppose.

résolu, e [Rezɔly] pp de **résoudre** // a (ferme) resolute; **être ~ à qch/faire** to be set upon sth/doing.

résolution [Rezɔlysjɔ̃] nf solving; (fermeté, décision) resolution.

résolve etc vb voir **résoudre**.

résonance [Rezɔnɑ̃s] nf resonance.

résonner [Rezɔne] vi (cloche, pas) to reverberate, resound; (salle) to be resonant; ~ **de** to resound with.

résorber [RezɔRbe]: **se ~** vi (MÉD) to be resorbed; (fig) to be reduced; to be absorbed.

résoudre [RezudR(ə)] vt to solve; ~ **de faire** to resolve to do; **se ~ à faire** to bring o.s. to do.

respect [Rɛspɛ] nm respect; **tenir en ~** to keep at bay.

respectable [Rɛspɛktabl(ə)] a respectable.

respecter [Rɛspɛkte] vt to respect; **le lexicographe qui se respecte** (fig) any self-respecting lexicographer.

respectif, ive [Rɛspɛktif, -iv] a respective; **respectivement** ad respectively.

respectueux, euse [Rɛspɛktɥø, -øz] a respectful; ~ **de** respectful of.

respiration [RɛspiRasjɔ̃] nf breathing q; **faire une ~ complète** to breathe in and out; ~ **artificielle** artificial respiration.

respirer [RɛspiRe] vi to breathe; (fig) to get one's breath, have a break; to breathe again // vt to breathe (in), inhale; (manifester: santé, calme etc) to exude.

resplendir [Rɛsplɑ̃diR] vi to shine; (fig): ~ (**de**) to be radiant (with).

responsabilité [Rɛspɔ̃sabilite] nf responsibility; (légale) liability; **refuser la ~ de** to deny responsibility (ou liability) for; **prendre ses ~s** to assume responsibility for one's actions.

responsable [Rɛspɔ̃sabl(ə)] a responsible // nm/f (du ravitaillement etc) person in charge; (de parti, syndicat) official; ~ **de** responsible for; (légalement: de dégâts etc) liable for; (chargé de) in charge of, responsible for.

resquiller [Rɛskije] vi (au cinéma, au stade) to get in on the sly; (dans le train) to fiddle a free ride; **resquilleur, euse** nm/f gatecrasher; fare dodger.

ressac [Rəsak] nm backwash.

ressaisir [RəseziR]: **se ~** vi to regain one's self-control; (équipe sportive) to rally.

ressasser [Rəsɑse] vt (remâcher) to keep turning over; (redire) to keep trotting out.

ressemblance [Rəsɑ̃blɑ̃s] nf (visuelle) resemblance, similarity, likeness; (: ART) likeness; (analogie, trait commun) similarity.

ressemblant, e [Rəsɑ̃blɑ̃, -ɑ̃t] a (portrait) lifelike, true to life.

ressembler [Rəsɑ̃ble]: ~ **à** vt to be like; to resemble; (visuellement) to look like; **se ~** to be (ou look) alike.

ressemeler [Rəsəmle] vt to (re)sole.

ressentiment [Rəsɑ̃timɑ̃] nm resentment.

ressentir [Rəsɑ̃tiR] vt to feel; **se ~ de** to feel (ou show) the effects of.

resserre [RəseR] nf shed.

resserrer [RəseRe] vt (pores) to close; (nœud, boulon) to tighten (up); (fig: liens) to strengthen; **se ~** vi (route, vallée) to narrow; (liens) to strengthen; **se ~ (autour de)** to draw closer (around); to close in (on).

resservir [RəseRviR] vi to do ou serve again // vt: ~ **qch (à qn)** to serve sth up again (to sb); ~ **de qch (à qn)** to give (sb) a second helping of sth; ~ **qn (d'un plat)** to give sb a second helping (of a dish).

ressort [RəsɔR] nm (pièce) spring; (force morale) spirit; (recours): **en dernier ~** as a last resort; (compétence): **être du ~ de** to fall within the competence of.

ressortir [RəsɔRtiR] vi to go (ou come) out (again); (contraster) to stand out; ~ **de** (résulter de): **il ressort de ceci que** it emerges from this that; ~ **à** (JUR) to come under the jurisdiction of; (ADMIN) to be the concern of; **faire ~** (fig: souligner) to bring out.

ressortissant, e [RəsɔRtisɑ̃, -ɑ̃t] nm/f national.

ressource [RəsuRs(ə)] nf: **avoir la ~ de** to have the possibility of; **leur seule ~ était de** the only course open to them was to; ~**s** nfpl resources; (fig) possibilities.

ressusciter [Resysite] vt to resuscitate, restore to life; (fig) to revive, bring back // vi to rise (from the dead).

restant, e [Rɛstɑ̃, -ɑ̃t] a remaining // nm: **le ~ (de)** the remainder (of); **un ~ de** (de trop) some left-over; (fig: vestige) a remnant ou last trace of.

restaurant [RɛstɔRɑ̃] nm restaurant; **manger au ~** to eat out; ~ **d'entreprise** staff canteen; ~ **universitaire** university refectory.

restaurateur, trice [RɛstɔRatœR, -tris] nm/f restaurant owner, restaurateur; (de tableaux) restorer.

restauration [RɛstɔRasjɔ̃] nf restoration; (hôtellerie) catering.

restaurer [RɛstɔRe] vt to restore; **se ~** vi to have something to eat.

restauroute [RɛstɔRut] nm = **restoroute**.

reste [Rɛst(ə)] nm (restant): **le ~ (de)** the rest (of); (de trop): **un ~ (de)** some left-over; (vestige): **un ~ de** a remnant ou last trace of; ~**s** nmpl left-overs; (d'une cité etc, dépouille mortelle) remains; **avoir du temps de ~** to have time to spare; **ne voulant pas être en ~** not wishing to be outdone; **sans demander son ~** without waiting to hear more; **du ~, au ~** ad besides, moreover.

rester [Rɛste] vi (dans un lieu, un état, une position) to stay, remain; (subsister) to remain, be left; (durer) to last, live on //

vb impersonnel: **il reste du pain/2 œufs** there's some bread/there are 2 eggs left (over); **il reste du temps/10 minutes** there's some time/there are 10 minutes left; **il me reste assez de temps** I have enough time left; **ce qui reste à faire** what remains to be done; **ce qui me reste à faire** what remains for me to do; **en ~ à** (*stade, menaces*) to go no further than, only go as far as; **restons-en là** let's leave it at that; **y ~: il a failli y ~** he nearly met his end.

restituer [Rɛstitue] *vt* (*objet, somme*): **~ qch (à qn)** to return sth (to sb); (*TECH*) to release; to reproduce.

restoroute [Rɛstɔʀut] *nm* motorway restaurant.

restreindre [Rɛstʀɛ̃dʀ(ə)] *vt* to restrict, limit; **se ~** *vi* (*champ de recherches*) to narrow.

restriction [Rɛstʀiksjɔ̃] *nf* restriction; **~s** (*mentales*) reservations.

résultat [Rezylta] *nm* result; (*conséquence*) outcome *q*, result; (*d'élection etc*) results *pl*; **~s sportifs** sports results.

résulter [Rezylte]: **~ de** *vt* to result from, be the result of.

résumé [Rezyme] *nm* summary, résumé; **en ~** *ad* in brief; to sum up.

résumer [Rezyme] *vt* (*texte*) to summarize; (*récapituler*) to sum up; (*fig*) to epitomize, typify; **se ~ à** to come down to.

résurrection [RezyRɛksjɔ̃] *nf* resurrection; (*fig*) revival.

rétablir [RetabliR] *vt* to restore, re-establish; (*personne: suj: traitement*): **~ qn** to restore sb to health, help sb recover; (*ADMIN*): **~ qn dans son emploi** to reinstate sb in his post; **se ~** *vi* (*guérir*) to recover; (*silence, calme*) to return, be restored; (*GYM etc*): **se ~ (sur)** to pull o.s. up (onto); **rétablissement** *nm* restoring; recovery; pull-up.

rétamer [Retame] *vt* to re-coat, re-tin.

retaper [Rətape] *vt* (*maison, voiture etc*) to do up; (*fam: revigorer*) to buck up; (*redactylographier*) to retype.

retard [RətaR] *nm* (*d'une personne attendue*) lateness *q*; (*sur l'horaire, un programme, une échéance*) delay; (*fig: scolaire, mental etc*) backwardness; **en ~ (de 2 heures)** (2 hours) late; **avoir un ~ de 2 km** (*SPORT*) to be 2 km behind; **avoir du ~** to be late; (*sur un programme*) to be behind (schedule); **prendre du ~** (*train, avion*) to be delayed; (*montre*) to lose (time); **sans ~** *ad* without delay; **~ à l'allumage** (*AUTO*) retarded spark.

retardataire [RətaRdatɛR] *nm/f* latecomer.

retardement [RətaRdəmɑ̃]: **à ~** *a* delayed action *cpd*; **bombe à ~** time bomb.

retarder [RətaRde] *vt* (*sur un horaire*): **~ qn (d'une heure)** to delay sb (an hour); (*sur un programme*): **~ qn (de 3 mois)** to set sb back *ou* delay sb (3 months); (*départ, date*): **~ qch (de 2 jours)** to put sth back (2 days), delay sth (for *ou* by 2 days) // *vi* (*montre*) to be slow; to lose (time); **je retarde (d'une heure)** I'm (an hour) slow.

retenir [RətniR] *vt* (*garder, retarder*) to keep, detain; (*maintenir: objet qui glisse, fig: colère, larmes*) to hold back; (: *objet suspendu*) to hold; (: *chaleur, odeur*) to retain; (*fig: empêcher d'agir*): **~ qn (de faire)** to hold sb back (from doing); (*se rappeler*) to remember; (*réserver*) to reserve; (*accepter*) to accept; (*prélever*): **~ qch (sur)** to deduct sth (from); **se ~** (*se raccrocher*): **se ~ à** to hold onto; (*se contenir*): **se ~ de faire** to restrain o.s. from doing; **~ son souffle** *ou* **haleine** to hold one's breath; **je pose 3 et je retiens 2** put down 3 and carry 2.

retentir [Rətɑ̃tiR] *vi* to ring out; (*salle*): **de ~** to ring *ou* resound with; **~ sur** *vt* (*fig*) to have an effect upon.

retentissant, e [Rətɑ̃tisɑ̃, -ɑ̃t] *a* resounding; (*fig*) impact-making.

retentissement [Rətɑ̃tismɑ̃] *nm* repercussion; effect, impact; stir.

retenue [Rətny] *nf* (*prélèvement*) deduction; (*SCOL*) detention; (*modération*) (self-)restraint; (*réserve*) reserve, reticence.

réticence [Retisɑ̃s] *nf* hesitation, reluctance *q*.

rétif, ive [Retif, -iv] *a* restive.

rétine [Retin] *nf* retina.

retiré, e [RətiRe] *a* secluded.

retirer [RətiRe] *vt* to withdraw; (*vêtement, lunettes*) to take off, remove; (*extraire*): **~ qch de** to take sth out of, remove sth from; (*reprendre: bagages, billets*) to collect, pick up; **~ des avantages de** to derive advantages from; **se ~** *vi* (*partir, reculer*) to withdraw; (*prendre sa retraite*) to retire; **se ~ de** to withdraw from; to retire from.

retombées [Rətɔ̃be] *nfpl* (*radioactives*) fallout *sg*; (*fig*) fallout; spin-offs.

retomber [Rətɔ̃be] *vi* (*à nouveau*) to fall again; (*atterrir: après un saut etc*) to land; (*tomber, redescendre*) to fall back; (*pendre*) to fall, hang (down); (*échoir*): **~ sur qn** to fall on sb.

rétorquer [RetɔRke] *vt*: **~ (à qn) que** to retort (to sb) that.

retors, e [RətɔR, -ɔRs(ə)] *a* wily.

rétorsion [RetɔRsjɔ̃] *nf*: **mesures de ~** reprisals.

retouche [Rətuʃ] *nf* touching up *q*; alteration.

retoucher [Rətuʃe] *vt* (*photographie, tableau*) to touch up; (*texte, vêtement*) to alter.

retour [RətuR] *nm* return; **au ~** when we (*ou* they *etc*) get (*ou* got) back; **on the way back**; **être de ~ (de)** to be back (from); **par ~ du courrier** by return of post; **~ en arrière** (*CINÉMA*) flashback; (*mesure*) backward step; **~ offensif** renewed attack.

retourner [RətuRne] *vt* (*dans l'autre sens: matelas, crêpe*) to turn over; (: *caisse*) to turn upside down; (: *sac, vêtement*) to turn inside out; (*fig: argument*) to turn back; (*e remuant: terre, sol, foin*) to turn over; (*émouvoir: personne*) to shake; (*renvoyer, restituer*): **~ qch à qn** to return sth to sb // *vi* (*aller, revenir*): **~ quelque part/à** to go back *ou* return somewhere/to; **~ à**

(*état, activité*) to return to, go back to ; **se ~** *vi* to turn over ; (*tourner la tête*) to turn round ; **se ~ contre** (*fig*) to turn against ; **savoir de quoi il retourne** to know what it is all about ; **~ en arrière** *ou* **sur ses pas** to turn back, retrace one's steps.

retracer [ʀətʀase] *vt* to relate, recount.

rétracter [ʀetʀakte] *vt*, **se ~** *vi* to retract.

retraduire [ʀətʀadɥiʀ] *vt* to translate again ; (*dans la langue de départ*) to translate back.

retrait [ʀətʀɛ] *nm* (*voir retirer*) withdrawal ; collection ; redemption ; (*voir se retirer*) withdrawal ; (*rétrécissement*) shrinkage ; **en ~** a set back ; **~ du permis (de conduire)** disqualification from driving.

retraite [ʀətʀɛt] *nf* (*d'une armée, REL, refuge*) retreat ; (*d'un employé*) retirement ; (*retirement*) pension ; **être/mettre à la ~** to be retired *ou* in retirement/pension off *ou* retire ; **prendre sa ~** to retire ; **~ anticipée** early retirement ; **~ aux flambeaux** torchlight tattoo ; **retraité, e** *a* retired // *nm/f* (*old age*) pensioner.

retranchement [ʀətʀɑ̃ʃmɑ̃] *nm* entrenchment.

retrancher [ʀətʀɑ̃ʃe] *vt* (*passage, détails*) to take out, remove ; (*nombre, somme*): **~ qch de** to take *ou* deduct sth from ; (*couper*) to cut off ; **se ~ derrière/dans** to entrench o.s. behind/in ; (*fig*) to take refuge behind/in.

retransmettre [ʀətʀɑ̃smɛtʀ(ə)] *vt* (*RADIO*) to broadcast, relay ; (*TV*) to show ; **retransmission** *nf* broadcast ; showing.

retraverser [ʀətʀavɛʀse] *vt* (*dans l'autre sens*) to cross back over.

rétrécir [ʀetʀesiʀ] *vt* (*vêtement*) to take in // *vi* to shrink ; **se ~** *vi* to narrow.

retremper [ʀətʀɑ̃pe] *vt*: **se ~ dans** (*fig*) to reimmerse o.s. in.

rétribuer [ʀetʀibɥe] *vt* (*travail*) to pay for ; (*personne*) to pay ; **rétribution** *nf* payment.

rétro [ʀetʀo] *a inv*: **la mode ~** the nostalgia vogue.

rétroactif, ive [ʀetʀoaktif, -iv] *a* retroactive.

rétrograde [ʀetʀogʀad] *a* reactionary, backward-looking.

rétrograder [ʀetʀogʀade] *vi* (*élève*) to fall back ; (*économie*) to regress ; (*AUTO*) to change down.

rétrospective [ʀetʀospɛktiv] *nf* retrospective exhibition ; season showing old films ; **~ment** *ad* in retrospect.

retrousser [ʀətʀuse] *vt* to roll up.

retrouvailles [ʀətʀuvɑj] *nfpl* reunion *sg*.

retrouver [ʀətʀuve] *vt* (*fugitif, objet perdu*) to find ; (*occasion*) to find again ; (*calme, santé*) to regain ; (*revoir*) to see again ; (*rejoindre*) to meet (again), join ; **se ~** *vi* to meet ; (*s'orienter*) to find one's way ; **se ~ quelque part** to find o.s. somewhere ; to end up somewhere ; **s'y ~** (*rentrer dans ses frais*) to break even.

rétroviseur [ʀetʀovizœʀ] *nm* (rear-view *ou* driving) mirror.

réunion [ʀeynjɔ̃] *nf* bringing together ; joining ; (*séance*) meeting ; **l'île de la R~, la R~** Réunion.

réunir [ʀeyniʀ] *vt* (*convoquer*) to call together ; (*rassembler*) to gather together ; (*cumuler*) to combine ; (*rapprocher*) to bring together (again), reunite ; (*rattacher*) to join (together) ; **se ~** *vi* (*se rencontrer*) to meet ; (*s'allier*) to unite.

réussi, e [ʀeysi] *a* successful.

réussir [ʀeysiʀ] *vi* to succeed, be successful ; (*à un examen*) to pass ; (*plante, culture*) to thrive, do well // *vi* to make a success of ; to bring off ; **~ à faire** to succeed in doing ; **~ à qn** to go right for sb ; to agree with sb.

réussite [ʀeysit] *nf* success ; (*CARTES*) patience.

revaloir [ʀəvalwaʀ] *vt*: **je vous revaudrai cela** I'll repay you some day ; (*en mal*) I'll pay you back for this.

revaloriser [ʀəvaloʀize] *vt* (*monnaie*) to revalue ; (*salaires, pensions*) to raise the level of ; (*institution, tradition*) to reassert the value of.

revanche [ʀəvɑ̃ʃ] *nf* revenge ; **prendre sa ~ (sur)** to take one's revenge (on) ; **en ~** on the other hand.

rêvasser [ʀɛvase] *vi* to daydream.

rêve [ʀɛv] *nm* dream ; (*activité psychique*): **le ~** dreaming ; **~ éveillé** daydreaming *q*, daydream.

revêche [ʀəvɛʃ] *a* surly, sour-tempered.

réveil [ʀevɛj] *nm* (*d'un dormeur*) waking up *q* ; (*fig*) awakening ; (*pendule*) alarm (clock) ; **au ~** when I (*ou* he) woke up, on waking (up) ; **sonner le ~** (*MIL*) to sound the reveille.

réveille-matin [ʀevɛjmatɛ̃] *nm inv* alarm clock.

réveiller [ʀeveje] *vt* (*personne*) to wake up ; (*fig*) to awaken, revive ; **se ~** *vi* to wake up ; (*fig*) to be revived, reawaken.

réveillon [ʀevɛjɔ̃] *nm* Christmas Eve ; (*de la Saint-Sylvestre*) New Year's Eve ; Christmas Eve (*ou* New Year's Eve) party *ou* dinner ; **réveillonner** *vi* to celebrate Christmas Eve (*ou* New Year's Eve).

révélateur, trice [ʀevelatœʀ, -tʀis] *a*: **~ (de qch)** revealing (sth) // *nm* (*PHOTO*) developer.

révélation [ʀevelasjɔ̃] *nf* revelation.

révéler [ʀevele] *vt* (*gén*) to reveal ; (*divulguer*) to disclose, reveal ; (*dénoter*) to reveal, show ; (*faire connaître au public*): **~ qn/qch** to make sb/ sth widely known, bring sb/sth to the public's notice ; **se ~** *vi* to be revealed, reveal itself // *vb avec attribut* to prove (to be).

revenant, e [ʀəvnɑ̃, -ɑ̃t] *nm/f* ghost.

revendeur, euse [ʀəvɑ̃dœʀ, -øz] *nm/f* (*détaillant*) retailer ; (*d'occasions*) secondhand dealer.

revendication [ʀəvɑ̃dikasjɔ̃] *nf* claim, demand ; **journée de ~** day of action (in support of one's claims).

revendiquer [ʀəvɑ̃dike] *vt* to claim, demand ; (*responsabilité*) to claim // *vi* to agitate in favour of one's claims.

revendre [ʀəvɑ̃dʀ(ə)] *vt* (*d'occasion*) to resell ; (*vendre davantage de*): **~ du sucre/un foulard/deux bagues** to sell more sugar/another scarf/ another two rings ; **à ~** *ad* (*en abondance*) to spare, aplenty.

revenir [Rəvniʀ] vi to come back; (CULIN):
faire ~ to brown; (coûter): ~ **cher/à 100
F** (à qn) to cost (sb) a lot/100 F; ~ **à**
(études, projet) to return to, go back to;
(équivaloir à) to amount to; ~ **à qn**
(rumeur, nouvelle) to get back to sb, reach
sb's ears; (part, honneur) to go to sb, be
sb's; (souvenir, nom) to come back to sb;
~ **de** (fig: maladie, étonnement) to recover
from; ~ **sur** (question, sujet) to go back
over; (engagement) to go back on; ~ **à
la charge** to return to the attack; ~ **à
soi** to come round; **n'en pas ~: je n'en
reviens pas** I can't get over it; ~ **sur ses
pas** to retrace one's steps; **cela revient
à dire que** it amounts to saying that.
revente [Rəvɑ̃t] nf resale.
revenu [Rəvny] nm income; (de l'État)
revenue; (d'un capital) yield; ~**s** nmpl
income sg.
rêver [Reve] vi, vt to dream; ~ **de
qch/faire** to dream of sth/doing; ~ **à** to
dream of.
réverbération [Reveʀbeʀɑsj5] nf
reflection.
réverbère [Reveʀbeʀ] nm street lamp ou
light.
réverbérer [Reveʀbere] vt to reflect.
révérence [ReveʀɑS] nf (vénération)
reverence; (salut) bow; curtsey.
révérend, e [Reveʀɑ̃, -ɑ̃d] a: **le ~ père
Pascal** the Reverend Father Pascal.
révérer [Revere] vt to revere.
rêverie [Rɛvʀi] nf daydreaming q,
daydream.
revers [RəvɛR] nm (de feuille, main) back;
(d'étoffe) wrong side; (de pièce, médaille)
back, reverse; (TENNIS, PING-PONG)
backhand; (de veston) lapel; (de pantalon)
turn-up; (fig: échec) setback; **le ~ de la
médaille** the other side of the coin;
prendre à ~ (MIL) to take from the rear.
réversible [Reveʀsibl(ə)] a reversible.
revêtement [Rəvɛtmɑ̃] nm (de paroi)
facing; (des sols) flooring; (de chaussée)
surface; (de tuyau etc) enduit) coating.
revêtir [Rəvɛtiʀ] vt (habit) to don, put on;
(fig) to take on; ~ **qn de** to dress sb in;
(fig) to endow ou invest sb with; ~ **qch
de** to cover sth with; (fig) to cloak sth
in; ~ **d'un visa** to append a visa to.
rêveur, euse [RɛvœR, -øz] a dreamy //
nm/f dreamer.
revient [Rəvjɛ̃] vb voir **revenir** // nm: **prix
de ~** cost price.
revigorer [Rəvigore] vt to invigorate,
brace up; to revive, buck up.
revirement [RəviʀmA] nm change of
mind; (d'une situation) reversal.
réviser [Revize] vt (texte, SCOL: matière) to
revise; (comptes) to audit; (machine,
installation, moteur) to overhaul, service;
(JUR: procès) to review.
révision [Revizj5] nf revision; auditing q;
overhaul; servicing q; review; **conseil de
~** (MIL) recruiting board; **faire ses ~s**
(SCOL) to do one's revision, revise; **la ~
des 10000 km** (AUTO) the 10,000 km
service.
revisser [Rəvise] vt to screw back again.
revivifier [Rəvivifje] vt to revitalize.

revivre [RəvivR(ə)] vi (reprendre des forces)
to come alive again; (traditions) to be
revived // vt (épreuve, moment) to relive.
révocation [Revokasj5] nf dismissal;
revocation.
revoir [RəvwaR] vt to see again; (réviser)
to revise // nm: **au ~** goodbye; **dire au
~ à qn** to say goodbye to sb.
révolte [Revolt(ə)] nf rebellion, revolt.
révolter [Revolte] vt to revolt; to outrage,
appal; **se ~** vi: **se ~ (contre)** to rebel
(against); **se ~ (à)** to be outraged (by).
révolu, e [Revoly] a past; (ADMIN): **âgé de
18 ans ~s** over 18 years of age; **après
3 ans ~s** when 3 full years have passed.
révolution [Revolysj5] nf revolution;
révolutionnaire a, nm/f revolutionary;
révolutionner vt to revolutionize; (fig) to
stir up.
revolver [RevolvɛR] nm gun; (à barillet)
revolver.
révoquer [Revoke] vt (fonctionnaire) to
dismiss, remove from office; (arrêt,
contrat) to revoke.
revue [Rəvy] nf (inventaire, examen)
review; (MIL: défilé) review, march-past;
(: inspection) inspection, review;
(périodique) review, magazine; (pièce
satirique) revue; (de music-hall) variety
show; **passer en ~** to review, inspect;
(fig) to review, survey; to go through.
révulsé, e [Revylse] a (yeux) rolled
upwards; (visage) contorted.
rez-de-chaussée [Redʃose] nm inv
ground floor.
RF sigle = République Française.
rhabiller [Rabije] vt: **se ~** to get dressed
again, put one's clothes on again.
rhapsodie [Rapsodi] nf rhapsody.
rhénan, e [Renɑ̃, -an] a Rhine cpd.
Rhénanie [Renani] nf: **la ~** the Rhineland.
rhésus [Rezys] a, nm rhesus.
rhétorique [Retoʀik] nf rhetoric.
rhéto-roman, e [Retoʀomɑ̃, -an] a
Rhaeto-Romanic.
Rhin [Rɛ̃] nm: **le ~** the Rhine.
rhinocéros [Rinoseʀos] nm rhinoceros.
rhodanien, ne [Rodanjɛ̃, -jɛn] a Rhone
cpd.
Rhodésie [Rodezi] nf: **la ~** Rhodesia;
rhodésien, ne a Rhodesian.
rhododendron [RododɛdR5] nm
rhododendron.
Rhône [Ron] nm: **le ~** the Rhone.
rhubarbe [Rybaʀb(ə)] nf rhubarb.
rhum [Rom] nm rum.
rhumatisant, e [Rymatizɑ̃, -ɑ̃t] nm/f
rheumatic.
rhumatismal, e, aux [Rymatismal, -o] a
rheumatic.
rhumatisme [Rymatism(ə)] nm
rheumatism q.
rhume [Rym] nm cold; ~ **de cerveau**
head cold; **le ~ des foins** hay fever.
ri [Ri] pp de **rire**.
riant, e [Rjɑ̃, -ɑ̃t] a smiling, cheerful.
ribambelle [Ribɑbɛl] nf: **une ~ de** a herd
ou swarm of.
ricaner [Rikane] vi (avec méchanceté) to
snigger; (bêtement, avec gêne) to giggle.

riche [ʀiʃ] a (gén) rich; (personne, pays) rich, wealthy; ~ **en** rich in; ~ **de** full of; rich in; **richesse** nf wealth; (fig) richness; **richesses** nfpl wealth sg; treasures; **richesse en vitamines** high vitamin content.

ricin [ʀisɛ̃] nm: **huile de** ~ castor oil.

ricocher [ʀikɔʃe] vi: ~ **(sur)** to rebound (off); (sur l'eau) to bounce (on ou off); **faire** ~ (galet) to skim.

ricochet [ʀikɔʃɛ] nm rebound; bounce; **faire des** ~**s** to skim pebbles; **par** ~ ad on the rebound; (fig) as an indirect result.

rictus [ʀiktys] nm grin; (snarling) grimace.

ride [ʀid] nf wrinkle; (fig) ripple.

ridé, e [ʀide] a wrinkled.

rideau, x [ʀido] nm curtain; ~ **de fer** metal shutter; (POL): **le** ~ **de fer** the Iron Curtain.

ridelle [ʀidɛl] nf slatted side.

rider [ʀide] vt to wrinkle; (fig) to ripple; to ruffle the surface of; **se** ~ vi (avec l'âge) to become wrinkled; (de contrariété) to wrinkle.

ridicule [ʀidikyl] a ridiculous // nm ridiculousness q; **le** ~ ridicule; **tourner en** ~ to ridicule; **ridiculiser** vt to ridicule; **se ridiculiser** to make a fool of o.s.

rie vb voir **rire**.

rien [ʀjɛ̃] pronom nothing; (quelque chose) anything; **ne** ... ~ nothing, tournure négative + anything // nm nothing; ~ **d'autre** nothing else; ~ **du tout** nothing at all; ~ **que** just, only; nothing but; **il n'a** ~ (n'est pas blessé) he's all right; **un petit** ~ (cadeau) a little something; **des** ~**s** trivia pl.

rieur, euse [ʀjœʀ, -øz] a cheerful, merry.

rigide [ʀiʒid] a stiff; (fig) rigid; strict; **rigidité** nf rigidity; **la rigidité cadavérique** rigor mortis.

rigolade [ʀigɔlad] nf: **la** ~ fun; (fig): **c'est de la** ~ it's a cinch; it's a big farce.

rigole [ʀigɔl] nf (conduit) channel; (filet d'eau) rivulet.

rigoler [ʀigɔle] vi (rire) to laugh; (s'amuser) to have (some) fun; (plaisanter) to be joking ou kidding.

rigolo, ote [ʀigɔlo, -ɔt] a (fam) funny // nm/f comic; (péj) fraud, phoney.

rigoureux, euse [ʀiguʀø, -øz] a (morale) rigorous, strict; (personne) stern, strict; (climat, châtiment) rigorous, harsh, severe; (interdiction, neutralité) strict; (preuves, analyse, méthode) rigorous.

rigueur [ʀigœʀ] nf rigour; strictness; harshness; **'tenue de soirée de** ~**'** 'evening dress (to be worn)'; **être de** ~ to be the usual thing ou be the rule; **à la** ~ at a pinch; possibly; **tenir** ~ **à qn de qch** to hold sth against sb.

rillettes [ʀijɛt] nfpl potted meat sg.

rime [ʀim] nf rhyme; **rimer** vi: **rimer (avec)** to rhyme (with); **ne rimer à rien** not to make sense.

rinçage [ʀɛ̃saʒ] nm rinsing (out); (opération) rinse.

rince-doigts [ʀɛ̃sdwa] nm inv finger-bowl.

rincer [ʀɛ̃se] vt to rinse; (récipient) to rinse out.

ring [ʀiŋ] nm (boxing) ring.

rions vb voir **rire**.

ripaille [ʀipaj] nf: **faire** ~ to feast.

ripoliné, e [ʀipɔline] a enamel-painted.

riposte [ʀipɔst(ə)] nf retort, riposte; (fig) counter-attack, reprisal.

riposter [ʀipɔste] vi to retaliate // vt: ~ **que** to retort that; ~ **à** vt to counter; to reply to.

rire [ʀiʀ] vi to laugh; (se divertir) to have fun // nm laugh; **le** ~ laughter; ~ **de** vt to laugh at; **se** ~ **de** to make light of; **pour** ~ (pas sérieusement) for a joke ou a laugh.

ris [ʀi] vb voir **rire** // nm: ~ **de veau** (calf) sweetbread.

risée [ʀize] nf: **être la** ~ **de** to be the laughing stock of.

risette [ʀizɛt] nf: **faire** ~ **(à)** to give a nice little smile (to).

risible [ʀizibl(ə)] a laughable, ridiculous.

risque [ʀisk(ə)] nm risk; **le** ~ danger; **prendre des** ~**s** to take risks; **à ses** ~**s et périls** at his own risk; **au** ~ **de** at the risk of.

risqué, e [ʀiske] a risky; (plaisanterie) risqué, daring.

risquer [ʀiske] vt to risk; (allusion, question) to venture, hazard; **tu risques qu'on te renvoie** you risk being dismissed; **ça ne risque rien** it's quite safe; ~ **de: il risque de se tuer** he could get ou risks getting himself killed; **il a risqué de se tuer** he almost got himself killed; **ce qui risque de se produire** what might ou could well happen; **il ne risque pas de recommencer** there's no chance of him doing that again; **se** ~ **dans** (s'aventurer) to venture into; **se** ~ **à faire** (tenter) to venture ou dare to do; **risque-tout** nm/f inv daredevil.

rissoler [ʀisɔle] vi, vt: **(faire)** ~ to brown.

ristourne [ʀistuʀn(ə)] nf rebate.

rite [ʀit] nm rite; (fig) ritual.

ritournelle [ʀituʀnɛl] nf (fig) tune.

rituel, le [ʀityɛl] a, nm ritual.

rivage [ʀivaʒ] nm shore.

rival, e, aux [ʀival, -o] a, nm/f rival.

rivaliser [ʀivalize] vi: ~ **avec** to rival, vie with; (être comparable) to hold its own against, compare with; ~ **avec qn de** (élégance etc) to vie with ou rival sb in.

rivalité [ʀivalite] nf rivalry.

rive [ʀiv] nf shore; (de fleuve) bank.

river [ʀive] vt (clou, pointe) to clinch; (plaques) to rivet together; **être rivé sur/à** to be riveted on/to.

riverain, e [ʀivʀɛ̃, -ɛn] a riverside cpd; lakeside cpd; roadside cpd // nm/f riverside (ou lakeside) resident; local ou roadside resident.

rivet [ʀivɛ] nm rivet; **riveter** vt to rivet (together).

rivière [ʀivjɛʀ] nf river; ~ **de diamants** diamond rivière.

rixe [ʀiks(ə)] nf brawl, scuffle.

riz [ʀi] nm rice; ~ **au lait** rice pudding; **rizière** nf paddy-field.

R.N. sigle f = **route nationale**, voir **national**.

robe [ʀɔb] nf dress; (de juge, d'ecclésiastique) robe; (de professeur) gown; (pelage) coat; ~ **de soirée/de mariée** evening/ wedding dress; ~ **de baptême** christening robe; ~ **de chambre** dressing gown; ~ **de grossesse** maternity dress.

robinet [ʀɔbinɛ] nm tap; ~ **du gaz** gas tap; ~ **mélangeur** mixer tap; **robinetterie** nf taps pl, plumbing.

roboratif, ive [ʀɔbɔʀatif, -iv] a bracing, invigorating.

robot [ʀɔbo] nm robot.

robuste [ʀɔbyst(ə)] a robust, sturdy.

roc [ʀɔk] nm rock.

rocade [ʀɔkad] nf (AUTO) by-road, bypass.

rocaille [ʀɔkaj] nf loose stones pl; rocky ou stony ground; (jardin) rockery, rock garden // a (style) rocaille; **rocailleux, euse** a rocky, stony; (voix) harsh.

rocambolesque [ʀɔkɑ̃bɔlɛsk(ə)] a fantastic, incredible.

roche [ʀɔʃ] nf rock.

rocher [ʀɔʃe] nm rock; (ANAT) petrosal bone.

rochet [ʀɔʃɛ] nm: **roue à** ~ **rachet** wheel.

rocheux, euse [ʀɔʃø, -øz] a rocky.

rock (and roll) [ʀɔk(ɛnʀɔl)] nm (musique) rock(-'n'-roll); (danse) jive.

rodage [ʀɔdaʒ] nm running in; **en** ~ (AUTO) running in.

rodéo [ʀɔdeo] nm rodeo (pl s).

roder [ʀɔde] vt (moteur, voiture) to run in.

rôder [ʀode] vi to roam ou wander about; (de façon suspecte) to lurk ou loiter (about ou around); **rôdeur, euse** nm/f prowler.

rodomontades [ʀɔdɔmɔ̃tad] nfpl bragging; sabre rattling sg.

rogatoire [ʀɔgatwaʀ] a: **commisson** ~ letters rogatory.

rogne [ʀɔɲ] nf: **être en** ~ to be ratty ou in a temper.

rogner [ʀɔɲe] vt to trim; to clip; (fig) to whittle down; ~ **sur** (fig) to cut down ou back on.

rognons [ʀɔɲɔ̃] nmpl kidneys.

rognures [ʀɔɲyʀ] nfpl trimmings; clippings.

rogue [ʀɔg] a arrogant.

roi [ʀwa] nm king; **le jour** ou **la fête des R~s, les ~s** Twelfth Night.

roitelet [ʀwatlɛ] nm wren; (péj) kinglet.

rôle [ʀol] nm role; (contribution) part.

rollmops [ʀɔlmɔps] nm rollmop.

romain, e [ʀɔmɛ̃, -ɛn] a, nm/f Roman // nf (BOT) cos (lettuce).

roman, e [ʀɔmɑ̃, -an] a (ARCHIT) Romanesque; (LING) Romance, Romanic // nm novel; ~ **d'espionnage** spy novel ou story; ~ **photo** romantic picture story.

romance [ʀɔmɑ̃s] nf ballad.

romancer [ʀɔmɑ̃se] vt to make into a novel; to romanticize.

romanche [ʀɔmɑ̃ʃ] a, nm Romansh.

romancier, ière [ʀɔmɑ̃sje, -jɛʀ] nm/f novelist.

romand, e [ʀɔmɑ̃, -ɑ̃d] a of ou from French-speaking Switzerland.

romanesque [ʀɔmanɛsk(ə)] a (fantastique) fantastic; storybook cpd; (sentimental) romantic; (LITTÉRATURE) novelistic.

roman-feuilleton [ʀɔmɑ̃fœjtɔ̃] nm serialized novel.

romanichel, le [ʀɔmaniʃɛl] nm/f gipsy.

romantique [ʀɔmɑ̃tik] a romantic.

romantisme [ʀɔmɑ̃tism(ə)] nm romanticism.

romarin [ʀɔmaʀɛ̃] nm rosemary.

Rome [ʀɔm] nf Rome.

rompre [ʀɔ̃pʀ(ə)] vt to break; (entretien, fiançailles) to break off // vi (fiancés) to break it off; **se** ~ vi to break; (MÉD) to burst, rupture; **se** ~ **les os** ou **le cou** to break one's neck; ~ **avec** to break with; **rompez (les rangs)!** (MIL) dismiss!, fall out!

rompu, e [ʀɔ̃py] a (fourbu) exhausted, worn out; ~ **à** with wide experience of; inured to.

romsteak [ʀɔmstɛk] nm rumpsteak q.

ronce [ʀɔ̃s] nf (BOT) bramble branch; (MENUISERIE): ~ **de noyer** burr walnut; ~**s** nfpl brambles, thorns.

ronchonner [ʀɔ̃ʃɔne] vi (fam) to grouse, grouch.

rond, e [ʀɔ̃, ʀɔ̃d] a round; (joues, mollets) well-rounded; (fam: ivre) tight // nm (cercle) ring; (fam: sou) **je n'ai plus un** ~ I haven't a penny left // nf (gén: de surveillance) rounds pl, patrol; (danse) round (dance); (MUS) semibreve; **en** ~ (s'asseoir, danser) in a ring; **à la** ~**e** (alentour): **à 10 km à la** ~**e** for 10 km round; (à chacun son tour): **passer qch à la** ~**e** to pass sth (a)round; **faire des** ~**s de jambe** to bow and scrape; ~ **de serviette** serviette ring; ~**-de-cuir** nm (péj) penpusher; **rondelet, e** a plump.

rondelle [ʀɔ̃dɛl] nf (TECH) washer; (tranche) slice, round.

rondement [ʀɔ̃dmɑ̃] ad briskly; frankly.

rondeur [ʀɔ̃dœʀ] nf (d'un bras, des formes) plumpness; (bonhomie) friendly straightforwardness; ~**s** nfpl (d'une femme) curves.

rondin [ʀɔ̃dɛ̃] nm log.

rond-point [ʀɔ̃pwɛ̃] nm roundabout.

ronéotyper [ʀɔneotipe] vt to duplicate, roneo.

ronflant, e [ʀɔ̃flɑ̃, -ɑ̃t] a (péj) high-flown, grand.

ronflement [ʀɔ̃flɑmɑ̃] nm snore, snoring q.

ronfler [ʀɔ̃fle] vi to snore; (moteur, poêle) to hum; to roar.

ronger [ʀɔ̃ʒe] vt to gnaw (at); (suj: vers, rouille) to eat into; ~ **son frein** to champ (at) the bit; **se** ~ **de souci, se** ~ **les sangs** to worry o.s. sick, fret; **se** ~ **les ongles** to bite one's nails; **rongeur, euse** nm/f rodent.

ronronner [ʀɔ̃ʀɔne] vi to purr.

roque [ʀɔk] nm (ÉCHECS) castling; **roquer** vi to castle.

roquet [ʀɔkɛ] nm nasty little lap-dog.

roquette [ʀɔkɛt] nf rocket.

rosace [ʀozas] nf (vitrail) rose window, rosace; (motif: de plafond etc) rose.

rosaire [ʀozɛʀ] nm rosary.

rosbif [ʀɔsbif] nm: **du** ~ roasting beef; (cuit) roast beef; **un** ~ a joint of beef.

rose [Roz] *nf* rose ; (*vitrail*) rose window // *a* pink ; ~ **bonbon** *a inv* candy pink ; ~ **des vents** compass card.

rosé, e [Roze] *a* a pinkish ; (**vin**) ~ rosé (wine).

roseau, x [Rozo] *nm* reed.

rosée [Roze] *nf* dew ; **goutte de ~** dewdrop.

roseraie [RozRɛ] *nf* rose garden ; (*plantation*) rose nursery.

rosette [Rozɛt] *nf* rosette (*gen of the Légion d'honneur*).

rosier [Rozje] *nm* rosebush, rose tree.

rosir [RoziR] *vi* to go pink.

rosse [Rɔs] *nf* (*péj: cheval*) nag // *a* nasty, vicious.

rosser [Rɔse] *vt* (*fam*) to thrash.

rossignol [Rɔsiɲɔl] *nm* (*ZOOL*) nightingale ; (*crochet*) picklock.

rot [Ro] *nm* belch ; (*de bébé*) burp.

rotatif, ive [Rɔtatif, -iv] *a* rotary // *nf* rotary press.

rotation [Rɔtasjɔ̃] *nf* rotation ; (*fig*) rotation, swap-around ; turnover ; **par ~** on a rota basis ; ~ **des cultures** rotation of crops ; ~ **des stocks** stock turnover.

roter [Rɔte] *vi* (*fam*) to burp, belch.

rôti [Roti] *nm:* **du ~** roasting meat ; (*cuit*) roast meat ; **un ~ de bœuf/porc** a joint of beef/pork.

rotin [Rɔtɛ̃] *nm* rattan (cane) ; **fauteuil en ~ cane** (arm)chair.

rôtir [RotiR] *vt* (*aussi:* **faire ~**) to roast // *vi* to roast ; **se ~ au soleil** to bask in the sun ; **rôtisserie** *nf* steakhouse ; roast meat counter (*ou* shop) ; **rôtissoire** *nf* (roasting) spit.

rotonde [Rɔtɔ̃d] *nf* (*ARCHIT*) rotunda ; (*RAIL*) engine shed.

rotondité [Rɔtɔ̃dite] *nf* roundness.

rotor [Rɔtɔʀ] *nm* rotor.

rotule [Rɔtyl] *nf* kneecap, patella.

roturier, ière [Rɔtyʀje, -jɛʀ] *nm/f* commoner.

rouage [Rwaʒ] *nm* cog(wheel), gearwheel ; (*de montre*) part ; (*fig*) cog ; ~**s** *fig*) internal structure *sg*.

roublard, e [RublaR, -aRd(ə)] *a* (*péj*) crafty, wily.

rouble [Rubl(ə)] *nm* rouble.

roucouler [Rukule] *vi* to coo ; (*fig: péj*) to warble.

roue [Ru] *nf* wheel ; **faire la ~** (*paon*) to spread *ou* fan its tail ; (*GYM*) to do a cartwheel ; **descendre en ~ libre** to freewheel *ou* coast down ; ~ **à aubes** paddle wheel ; ~ **dentée** cogwheel ; ~ **de secours** spare wheel.

roué, e [Rwe] *a* wily.

rouer [Rwe] *vt:* ~ **qn de coups** to give sb a thrashing.

rouet [Rwɛ] *nm* spinning wheel.

rouge [Ruʒ] *a, nm/f* red // *nm* red ; (*fard*) rouge ; (**vin**) ~ red wine ; **passer au ~** (*signal*) to go red ; (*automobiliste*) to go through the red lights ; **porter au ~** (*métal*) to bring to red heat ; ~ **(à lèvres)** lipstick ; **rougeâtre** *a* reddish ; ~**-gorge** *nm* robin (redbreast).

rougeole [Ruʒɔl] *nf* measles *sg*.

rougeoyer [Ruʒwaje] *vi* to glow red.

rouget [Ruʒɛ] *nm* mullet.

rougeur [RuʒœR] *nf* redness ; (*du visage*) red face ; ~**s** *nfpl* (*MÉD*) red blotches.

rougir [RuʒiR] *vi* (*de honte, timidité*) to blush, flush ; (*de plaisir, colère*) to flush ; (*fraise, tomate*) to go turn red ; (*ciel*) to redden.

rouille [Ruj] *nf* rust // *a inv* rust-coloured, rusty.

rouillé, e [Ruje] *a* rusty.

rouiller [Ruje] *vt* to rust // *vi* to rust, go rusty ; **se ~** *vi* to rust ; (*fig*) to become rusty ; to grow stiff.

roulade [Rulad] *nf* (*GYM*) roll ; (*CULIN*) rolled meat *q* ; (*MUS*) roulade, run.

roulant, e [Rulɑ̃, -ɑ̃t] *a* (*meuble*) on wheels ; (*surface, trottoir*) moving ; **matériel ~** (*RAIL*) rolling stock ; **personnel ~** (*RAIL*) train crews *pl*.

rouleau, x [Rulo] *nm* (*de papier, tissu, pièces de monnaie, SPORT*) roll ; (*de machine à écrire*) roller, platen ; (*à mise en plis, à peinture, vague*) roller ; ~ **compresseur** steamroller ; ~ **à pâtisserie** rolling pin ; ~ **de pellicule** roll of film.

roulement [Rulmɑ̃] *nm* (*bruit*) rumbling *q*, rumble ; (*rotation*) rotation ; turnover ; **par ~** on a rota basis ; ~ **(à billes)** ball bearings *pl* ; ~ **de tambour** drum roll.

rouler [Rule] *vt* to roll ; (*papier, tapis*) to roll up ; (*CULIN: pâte*) to roll out ; (*fam*) to do, con // *vi* (*bille, boule*) to roll ; (*voiture, train*) to go, run ; (*automobiliste*) to drive ; (*cycliste*) to ride ; (*bateau*) to roll ; (*tonnerre*) to rumble, roll ; (*dégringoler*): ~ **en bas de** to roll down ; ~ **sur** (*suj: conversation*) to turn on ; **se ~ dans** (*boue*) to roll in ; (*couverture*) to roll o.s. (up) in ; ~ **les épaules/hanches** to sway one's shoulders/wiggle one's hips.

roulette [Rulɛt] *nf* (*de table, fauteuil*) castor ; (*de pâtissier*) pastry wheel ; (*jeu*): **la ~** roulette ; **à ~s** on castors.

roulis [Ruli] *nm* roll(ing).

roulotte [Rulɔt] *nf* caravan.

roumain, e [Rumɛ̃, -ɛn] *a, nm/f* Romanian.

Roumanie [Rumani] *nf* Romania.

roupiller [Rupije] *vi* (*fam*) to sleep.

rouquin, e [Rukɛ̃, -in] *nm/f* (*péj*) redhead.

rouspéter [Ruspete] *vi* (*fam*) to moan, grouse.

rousse [Rus] *a voir* **roux**.

rousseur [RusœR] *nf:* **tache de ~** freckle.

roussi [Rusi] *nm:* **ça sent le ~** there's a smell of burning ; (*fig*) I can smell trouble.

roussir [RusiR] *vt* to scorch // *vi* (*feuilles*) to go *ou* turn brown ; (*CULIN*): **faire ~** to brown.

route [Rut] *nf* road ; (*fig: chemin*) way ; (*itinéraire, parcours*) route ; (*fig: voie*) road, path ; **par (la)** ~ by road ; **il y a 3h de ~** it's a 3-hour ride *ou* journey ; **en ~** *ad* on the way ; **mettre en ~** to start up ; **se mettre en ~** to set off ; **faire ~ vers** to head towards ; **routier, ière** *a* road *cpd* // *nm* (*camionneur*) (long-distance) lorry *ou* truck driver ; (*restaurant*) ≈ transport café ; (*scout*) ≈ rover // *nf* (*voiture*) touring car.

routine [Rutin] nf routine ; **routinier, ière** a (péj) humdrum ; addicted to routine.

rouvrir [RuvRiR] vt, vi to reopen, open again ; **se ~** vi (blessure) to open up again.

roux, rousse [Ru, Rus] a red ; (personne) red-haired // nm/f redhead // nm (CULIN) roux.

royal, e, aux [Rwajal, -o] a royal ; (fig) fit for a king, princely ; blissful ; thorough.

royaliste [Rwajalist(ə)] a, nm/f royalist.

royaume [Rwajom] nm kingdom ; (fig) realm ; **le R~ Uni** the United Kingdom.

royauté [Rwajote] nf (dignité) kingship ; (régime) monarchy.

R.S.V.P. sigle (= répondez s'il vous plaît) R.S.V.P.

Rte abr de **route**.

ruade [Ryad] nf kick.

ruban [Rybã] nm (gén) ribbon ; (pour ourlet, couture) binding ; (de téléscripteur etc) tape ; (d'acier) strip ; **~ adhésif** adhesive tape.

rubéole [Rybeɔl] nf German measles sg, rubella.

rubicond, e [Rybikɔ̃, -ɔ̃d] a rubicund, ruddy.

rubis [Rybi] nm ruby ; (HORLOGERIE) jewel.

rubrique [RybRik] nf (titre, catégorie) heading, rubric ; (PRESSE: article) column.

ruche [Ryʃ] nf hive.

rude [Ryd] a (barbe, toile) rough ; (métier, tâche) hard, tough ; (climat) severe, harsh ; (bourru) harsh, rough ; (fruste) rugged, tough ; (fam) jolly good ; **~ment** ad (tomber, frapper) hard ; (traiter, reprocher) harshly ; (fam: très) terribly, jolly ; (: beaucoup) jolly hard.

rudimentaire [RydimãtɛR] a rudimentary, basic.

rudiments [Rydimã] nmpl rudiments ; basic knowledge sg ; basic principles.

rudoyer [Rydwaje] vt to treat harshly.

rue [Ry] nf street.

ruée [Rɥe] nf rush.

ruelle [Rɥɛl] nf alley(-way).

ruer [Rɥe] vi (cheval) to kick out ; **se ~** vi: **se ~ sur** to pounce on ; **se ~ vers/dans/hors de** to rush ou dash towards/into/out of ; **~ dans les brancards** to become rebellious.

rugby [Rygbi] nm Rugby (football) ; **~ à treize/quinze** Rugby League/Union.

rugir [RyʒiR] vi to roar ; **rugissement** nm roar, roaring q.

rugosité [Rygozite] nf roughness ; (aspérité) rough patch.

rugueux, euse [Rygø, -øz] a rough.

ruine [Rɥin] nf ruin ; **~s** nfpl ruins.

ruiner [Rɥine] vt to ruin ; **ruineux, euse** a terribly expensive to buy (ou run), ruinous ; extravagant.

ruisseau, x [Rɥiso] nm stream, brook ; (caniveau) gutter ; (fig): **~x de** floods of, streams of.

ruisseler [Rɥisle] vi to stream ; **~ (d'eau)** to be streaming (with water).

rumeur [RymœR] nf (bruit confus) rumbling ; hubbub q ; murmur(ing) ; (nouvelle) rumour.

ruminer [Rymine] vt (herbe) to ruminate ; (fig) to ruminate on ou over, chew over

// vi (vache) to chew the cud, ruminate.

rumsteak [Rɔ̃mstɛk] nm = **romsteak.**

rupture [RyptyR] nf (de câble, digue) breaking ; (de tendon) rupture, tearing ; (de négociations etc) breakdown ; (de contrat) breach ; (séparation, désunion) break-up, split ; **en ~ de ban** at odds with authority.

rural, e, aux [RyRal, -o] a rural, country cpd // nmpl: **les ruraux** country people.

ruse [Ryz] nf: **la ~** cunning, craftiness ; trickery ; **une ~** a trick, a ruse ; **rusé, e** a cunning, crafty.

russe [Rys] a, nm, nf Russian.

Russie [Rysi] nf: **la ~** Russia.

rustique [Rystik] a rustic.

rustre [RystR(ə)] nm boor.

rut [Ryt] nm: **être en ~** to be in ou on heat, be rutting.

rutabaga [Rytabaga] nm swede.

rutilant, e [Rytilã, -ãt] a gleaming.

rythme [Ritm(ə)] nm rhythm ; (vitesse) rate ; (: de la vie) pace, tempo ; **au ~ de 10 par jour** at the rate of 10 a day ; **rythmé, e** a rhythmic(al) ; **rythmique** a rhythmic(al) // nf rhythmics sg.

S

s' [s] pronom voir **se.**

sa [sa] dét voir **son.**

S.A. sigle voir **société.**

sable [sabl(ə)] nm sand ; **~s mouvants** quicksand(s).

sablé [sable] nm shortbread biscuit.

sabler [sable] vt to sand ; (contre le verglas) to grit ; **~ le champagne** to drink champagne.

sableux, euse [sablø, -øz] a sandy.

sablier [sablije] nm hourglass ; (de cuisine) egg timer.

sablière [sablijɛR] nf sand quarry.

sablonneux, euse [sablɔnø, -øz] a sandy.

saborder [sabɔRde] vt (navire) to scuttle ; (fig) to wind up, shut down.

sabot [sabo] nm clog ; (de cheval, bœuf) hoof ; **~ de frein** brake shoe.

sabotage [sabotaʒ] nm sabotage.

saboter [sabote] vt to sabotage ; **saboteur, euse** nm/f saboteur.

sabre [sabR(ə)] nm sabre.

sac [sak] nm bag ; (à charbon etc) sack ; (pillage) sack(ing) ; **mettre à ~** to sack ; **~ à provisions/de voyage** shopping/travelling bag ; **~ de couchage** sleeping bag ; **~ à dos** rucksack ; **~ à main** handbag.

saccade [sakad] nf jerk ; **par ~s** jerkily ; haltingly.

saccager [sakaʒe] vt (piller) to sack, lay waste ; (dévaster) to create havoc in, wreck.

saccharine [sakaRin] nf saccharin(e).

sacerdoce [sasɛRdɔs] nm priesthood ; (fig) calling, vocation ; **sacerdotal, e, aux** a priestly, sacerdotal.

sache etc vb voir **savoir.**

sachet [saʃɛ] nm (small) bag ; (de lavande, poudre, shampooing) sachet ; **~ de thé** tea bag.

sacoche [sakɔʃ] nf (gén) bag; (de bicyclette) saddlebag; (du facteur) (post-)bag; (d'outils) toolbag.

sacre [sakR(ə)] nm coronation; consecration.

sacré, e [sakRe] a sacred; (fam: satané) blasted; (: fameux): **un ~ ...** a heck of a ...; (ANAT) sacral.

sacrement [sakRəmɑ̃] nm sacrament; **les derniers ~s** the last rites.

sacrer [sakRe] vt (roi) to crown; (évêque) to consecrate // vi to curse, swear.

sacrifice [sakRifis] nm sacrifice.

sacrifier [sakRifje] vt to sacrifice; **~ à** vt to conform to; **articles sacrifiés** (COMM) items given away at knock-down prices.

sacrilège [sakRilɛʒ] nm sacrilege // a sacrilegious.

sacristain [sakRistɛ̃] nm sexton; sacristan.

sacristie [sakRisti] nf sacristy; (culte protestant) vestry.

sacro-saint, e [sakRɔsɛ̃, -sɛ̃t] a sacrosanct.

sadique [sadik] a sadistic // nm/f sadist.

sadisme [sadism(ə)] nm sadism.

safari [safaRi] nm safari; **faire un ~** to go on safari; **~-photo** nm photographic safari.

safran [safRɑ̃] nm saffron.

sagace [sagas] a sagacious, shrewd.

sagaie [sagɛ] nf assegai.

sage [saʒ] a wise; (enfant) good // nm wise man; sage.

sage-femme [saʒfam] nf midwife (pl wives).

sagesse [saʒɛs] nf wisdom.

Sagittaire [saʒitɛR] nm: **le ~** Sagittarius, the Archer; **être du ~** to be Sagittarius.

Sahara [saaRa] nm: **le ~** the Sahara (desert).

saharienne [saaRjɛn] nf safari jacket.

saignant, e [sɛɲɑ̃, -ɑ̃t] a (viande) rare; (blessure, plaie) bleeding.

saignée [seɲe] nf (MÉD) bleeding q, bloodletting q; (ANAT): **la ~ du bras** the bend of the arm; (fig) heavy losses pl; savage cut.

saignement [sɛɲmɑ̃] nm bleeding; **~ de nez** nosebleed.

saigner [seɲe] vi to bleed // vt to bleed; (animal) to kill (by bleeding); **~ du nez** to have a nosebleed.

saillant, e [sajɑ̃, -ɑ̃t] a (pommettes, menton) prominent; (corniche etc) projecting; (fig) salient, outstanding.

saillie [saji] nf (sur un mur etc) projection; (trait d'esprit) witticism; (accouplement) covering, serving; **faire ~** to project, stick out.

saillir [sajiR] vi to project, stick out; (veine, muscle) to bulge // vt (ÉLEVAGE) to cover, serve.

sain, e [sɛ̃, sɛn] a healthy; (dents, constitution) healthy, sound; (lectures) wholesome; **~ et sauf** safe and sound, unharmed; **~ d'esprit** sound in mind, sane.

saindoux [sɛ̃du] nm lard.

saint, e [sɛ̃, sɛ̃t] a holy; (fig) saintly // nm/f saint; **le S~ Esprit** the Holy Spirit ou Ghost; **la S~e Vierge** the Blessed Vir-

gin; **sainteté** nf holiness; **le S~-Père** the Holy Father, the Pontiff; **le S~-Siège** the Holy See; **la S~-Sylvestre** New Year's Eve.

sais etc vb voir **savoir**.

saisie [sezi] nf seizure.

saisir [seziR] vt to take hold of, grab; (fig: occasion) to seize; (comprendre) to grasp; (entendre) to get, catch; (suj: émotions) to take hold of, come over; (CULIN) to fry quickly; (JUR: biens, publication) to seize; (: juridiction): **~ un tribunal d'une affaire** to submit ou refer a case to a court; **se ~ de** vt to seize; **saisissant, e** a startling, striking; **saisissement** nm emotion.

saison [sɛzɔ̃] nf season; **la belle ~** the summer months; **en/hors ~** in/out of season; **haute/morte ~** high/slack season; **la ~ des pluies/des amours** the rainy/ mating season; **saisonnier, ière** a seasonal // nm (travailleur) seasonal worker.

sait vb voir **savoir**.

salace [salas] a salacious.

salade [salad] nf (BOT) lettuce etc (generic term); (CULIN) (green) salad; (fam) tangle, muddle; **haricots en ~** bean salad; **~ de concombres** cucumber salad; **~ de fruits** fruit salad; **~ russe** Russian salad; **saladier** nm salad bowl.

salaire [salɛR] nm (annuel, mensuel) salary; (hebdomadaire, journalier) pay, wages pl; (fig) reward; **~ de base** basic salary/wage; **~ minimum interprofessionnel garanti (SMIG)/de croissance (SMIC)** index-linked guaranteed minimum wage.

salaison [salɛzɔ̃] nf salting; **~s** nfpl salt meat sg.

salami [salami] nm salami q, salami sausage.

salant [salɑ̃] am: **marais ~** salt pan.

salarial, e, aux [salaRjal, -o] a salary cpd, wage(s) cpd.

salarié, e [salaRje] a salaried; wage-earning // nm/f salaried employee; wage-earner.

salaud [salo] nm (fam!) sod (!), bastard (!).

sale [sal] a dirty, filthy.

salé, e [sale] a (liquide, saveur) salty; (CULIN) salted, salt cpd; (fig) spicy, juicy; steep, stiff.

saler [sale] vt to salt.

saleté [salte] nf (état) dirtiness; (crasse) dirt, filth; (tache etc) dirt q, something dirty; (fig) filthy trick; rubbish q; filth q; infection, bug.

salière [saljɛR] nf saltcellar.

saligaud [saligo] nm (fam!) sod (!).

salin, e [salɛ̃, -in] a saline // nf saltworks sg; salt marsh.

salinité [salinite] nf salinity, salt-content.

salir [saliR] vt to (make) dirty; (fig) to soil the reputation of; **se ~** to get dirty; **salissant, e** a (tissu) which shows the dirt; (métier) dirty, messy.

salive [saliv] nf saliva; **saliver** vi to salivate.

salle [sal] nf room; (d'hôpital) ward; (de restaurant) dining room; (d'un cinéma) auditorium; (: public) audience; **faire ~**

comble to have a full house; ~ **d'attente** waiting room; ~ **de bain(s)** bathroom; ~ **de bal** ballroom; ~ **de cinéma** cinema; ~ **de classe** classroom; ~ **commune** (*d'hôpital*) ward; ~ **de concert** concert hall; ~ **de douches** shower-room; ~ **d'eau** shower-room; ~ **d'embarquement** (*à l'aéroport*) departure lounge; ~ **des machines** engine room; ~ **à manger** dining room; ~ **d'opération** (*d'hôpital*) operating theatre; ~ **de projection** film theatre; ~ **de séjour** living room; ~ **de spectacle** theatre; cinema; ~ **des ventes** saleroom.

salon [salɔ̃] *nm* lounge, sitting room; (*mobilier*) lounge suite; (*exposition*) exhibition, show; (*mondain, littéraire*) salon; ~ **de coiffure** hairdressing salon; ~ **de thé** tearoom.

salopard [salɔpaʀ] *nm* (*fam!*) bastard (!).

salope [salɔp] *nf* (*fam!*) bitch(!).

saloperie [salɔpʀi] *nf* (*fam!*) filth *q*; dirty trick; rubbish *q*.

salopette [salɔpɛt] *nf* overall(s).

salpêtre [salpɛtʀ(ə)] *nm* saltpetre.

salsifis [salsifi] *nm* salsify, oyster-plant.

saltimbanque [saltɛ̃bɑ̃k] *nm/f* (travelling) acrobat.

salubre [salybʀ(ə)] *a* healthy, salubrious; **salubrité** *nf* healthiness, salubrity; **salubrité publique** public health.

saluer [salɥe] *vt* (*pour dire bonjour, fig*) to greet; (*pour dire au revoir*) to take one's leave; (*MIL*) to salute.

salut [saly] *nm* (*sauvegarde*) safety; (*REL*) salvation; (*geste*) wave; (*parole*) greeting; (*MIL*) salute // *excl* (*fam*) hi (there); (*style relevé*) (all) hail.

salutaire [salytɛʀ] *a* beneficial; salutary.

salutations [salytɑsjɔ̃] *nfpl* greetings; **recevez mes ~ distinguées** ou **respectueuses** yours faithfully.

salutiste [salytist(ə)] *nm/f* Salvationist.

salve [salv(ə)] *nf* salvo; volley of shots.

samaritain [samaʀitɛ̃] *nm*: **le bon S~** the Good Samaritan.

samedi [samdi] *nm* Saturday.

sanatorium [sanatɔʀjɔm] *nm* sanatorium (*pl* a).

sanctifier [sɑ̃ktifje] *vt* to sanctify.

sanction [sɑ̃ksjɔ̃] *nf* sanction; (*fig*) penalty; **prendre des ~s contre** to impose sanctions on; **sanctionner** *vt* (*loi, usage*) to sanction; (*punir*) to punish.

sanctuaire [sɑ̃ktɥɛʀ] *nm* sanctuary.

sandale [sɑ̃dal] *nf* sandal.

sandalette [sɑ̃dalɛt] *nf* sandal.

sandwich [sɑ̃dwitʃ] *nm* sandwich; **pris en ~** sandwiched.

sang [sɑ̃] *nm* blood; **en ~** covered in blood; **se faire du mauvais ~** to fret, get in a state.

sang-froid [sɑ̃fʀwa] *nm* calm, sangfroid; **de ~** in cold blood.

sanglant, e [sɑ̃glɑ̃, -ɑ̃t] *a* a bloody, covered in blood; (*combat*) bloody.

sangle [sɑ̃gl(ə)] *nf* strap; ~**s** (*pour lit etc*) webbing *sg*; **sangler** *vt* to strap up; (*animal*) to girth.

sanglier [sɑ̃glije] *nm* (wild) boar.

sanglot [sɑ̃glo] *nm* sob; **sangloter** *vi* to sob.

sangsue [sɑ̃sy] *nf* leech.

sanguin, e [sɑ̃gɛ̃, -in] *a* blood *cpd*; (*fig*) fiery // *nf* blood orange; (*ART*) red pencil drawing.

sanguinaire [sɑ̃ginɛʀ] *a* bloodthirsty; bloody.

sanguinolent, e [sɑ̃ginɔlɑ̃, -ɑ̃t] *a* streaked with blood.

sanitaire [sanitɛʀ] *a* health *cpd*; **installation/appareil ~** bathroom plumbing/appliance; ~**s** *nmpl* (*salle de bain et w.-c.*) bathroom *sg*.

sans [sɑ̃] *prép* without; ~ **qu'il s'en aperçoive** without him ou his noticing; ~-**scrupules** unscrupulous; ~ **manches** sleeveless; ~-**abri** *nmpl* homeless (*after a flood etc*); ~-**emploi** *nmpl* jobless; ~-**façon** *a inv* fuss-free; free and easy; ~-**gêne** *a inv* inconsiderate; ~-**logis** *nmpl* homeless (*through poverty*); ~-**travail** *nmpl* unemployed, jobless.

santal [sɑ̃tal] *nm* sandal(wood).

santé [sɑ̃te] *nf* health; **en bonne ~** in good health; **boire à la ~ de qn** to drink (to) sb's health; **'à la ~ de'** 'here's to'; **à ta/votre ~!** cheers!

santon [sɑ̃tɔ̃] *nm* ornamental figure at a Christmas crib.

saoul, e [su, sul] *a* = **soûl, e.**

sape [sap] *nf*: **travail de ~** (*MIL*) sap; (*fig*) insidious undermining process ou work.

saper [sape] *vt* to undermine, sap.

sapeur [sapœʀ] *nm* sapper; ~-**pompier** *nm* fireman.

saphir [safiʀ] *nm* sapphire.

sapin [sapɛ̃] *nm* fir (tree); (*bois*) fir; ~ **de Noël** Christmas tree; **sapinière** *nf* fir plantation ou forest.

sarabande [saʀabɑ̃d] *nf* saraband; (*fig*) hullabaloo; whirl.

sarbacane [saʀbakan] *nf* blowpipe, blowgun; (*jouet*) peashooter.

sarcasme [saʀkasm(ə)] *nm* sarcasm *q*; piece of sarcasm; **sarcastique** *a* sarcastic.

sarcler [saʀkle] *vt* to weed; **sarcloir** *nm* (weeding) hoe, spud.

sarcophage [saʀkɔfaʒ] *nm* sarcophagus (*pl* i).

Sardaigne [saʀdɛɲ] *nf*: **la ~** Sardinia; **sarde** *a*, *nm/f* Sardinian.

sardine [saʀdin] *nf* sardine; ~**s à l'huile** sardines in oil.

sardonique [saʀdɔnik] *a* sardonic.

S.A.R.L. *sigle voir* **société.**

sarment [saʀmɑ̃] *nm*: ~ **(de vigne)** vine shoot.

sarrasin [saʀazɛ̃] *nm* buckwheat.

sarrau [saʀo] *nm* smock.

Sarre [saʀ] *nf*: **la ~** the Saar.

sarriette [saʀjɛt] *nf* savory.

sarrois, e [saʀwa, -waz] *a* Saar *cpd* // *nm/f*: **S~, e** an inhabitant ou native of the Saar.

sas [sɑ] *nm* (*de sous-marin, d'engin spatial*) airlock; (*d'écluse*) lock.

satané, e [satane] *a* confounded.

satanique [satanik] *a* satanic, fiendish.

satelliser [satelize] *vt* (*fusée*) to put into orbit; (*fig: pays*) to make into a satellite.

satellite [satelit] *nm* satellite ; **pays ~ satellite** country ; **~-espion** *nm* spy satellite.

satiété [sasjete]: **à ~** *ad* to satiety *ou* satiation ; (*répéter*) *ad* nauseam.

satin [satẽ] *nm* satin ; **satiné, e** *a* satiny ; (*peau*) satin-smooth.

satire [satiʀ] *nf* satire ; **satirique** *a* satirical ; **satiriser** *vt* to satirize.

satisfaction [satisfaksjɔ̃] *nf* satisfaction.

satisfaire [satisfɛʀ] *vt* to satisfy ; **~ à** *vt* (*engagement*) to fulfil ; (*revendications, conditions*) to satisfy, meet ; to comply with ; **satisfaisant, e** *a* satisfactory ; (*qui fait plaisir*) satisfying ; **satisfait, e** *a* satisfied ; **satisfait de** happy *ou* satisfied with ; pleased with.

saturation [satyʀɑsjɔ̃] *nf* saturation.

saturer [satyʀe] *vt* to saturate.

satyre [satiʀ] *nm* satyr ; (*péj*) lecher.

sauce [sos] *nf* sauce ; (*avec un rôti*) gravy ; **~ tomate** tomato sauce ; **saucière** *nf* sauceboat ; gravy boat.

saucisse [sosis] *nf* sausage.

saucisson [sosisɔ̃] *nm* (slicing) sausage ; **~ à l'ail** garlic sausage.

sauf [sof] *prép* except ; **~ si** (*à moins que*) unless ; **~ erreur** if I'm not mistaken ; **~ avis contraire** unless you hear to the contrary.

sauf, sauve [sof, sov] *a* unharmed, unhurt ; (*fig: honneur*) intact, saved ; **laisser la vie sauve à qn** to spare sb's life.

sauf-conduit [sofkɔ̃dɥi] *nm* safe-conduct.

sauge [soʒ] *nf* sage.

saugrenu, e [sogʀəny] *a* preposterous, ludicrous.

saule [sol] *nm* willow (tree) ; **~ pleureur** weeping willow.

saumâtre [somɑtʀ(ə)] *a* briny.

saumon [somɔ̃] *nm* salmon *inv* // *a inv* salmon (pink) ; **saumoné, e** *a*: **truite saumonée** salmon trout.

saumure [somyʀ] *nf* brine.

sauna [sona] *nm* sauna.

saupoudrer [sopudʀe] *vt*: **~ qch de** to sprinkle sth with.

saur [sɔʀ] *am*: **hareng ~** smoked *ou* red herring, kipper.

saurai *etc vb voir* **savoir**.

saut [so] *nm* jump ; (*discipline sportive*) jumping ; **faire un ~** to (make a) jump *ou* leap ; **faire un ~ chez qn** to pop over to sb's (place) ; **au ~ du lit** on getting out of bed ; **~ en hauteur/longueur** high/long jump ; **~ à la corde** skipping ; **~ à la perche** pole vaulting ; **~ périlleux** somersault.

saute [sot] *nf*: **~ de vent/température** sudden change of wind direction/in the temperature.

sauté, e [sote] *a* (*CULIN*) sauté // *nm*: **~ de veau** sauté of veal.

saute-mouton [sotmutɔ̃] *nm*: **jouer à ~** to play leapfrog.

sauter [sote] *vi* to jump, leap ; (*exploser*) to blow up, explode ; (: *fusibles*) to blow ; (*se rompre*) to snap, burst ; (*se détacher*) to pop out (*ou* off) // *vt* to jump (over), leap (over) ; (*fig: omettre*) to skip, miss

(out) ; **faire ~** to blow up ; to burst open ; (*CULIN*) to sauté ; **~ à pieds joints** to make a standing jump ; **~ en parachute** to make a parachute jump ; **~ au cou de qn** to fly into sb's arms ; **~ aux yeux** to be quite obvious.

sauterelle [sotʀɛl] *nf* grasshopper.

sauteur, euse [sotœʀ, -øz] *nm/f* (*athlète*) jumper // *nf* (*casserole*) shallow casserole ; **~ à la perche** pole vaulter ; **~ à skis** skijumper.

sautiller [sotije] *vi* to hop ; to skip.

sautoir [sotwaʀ] *nm* chain ; **~ (de perles)** string of pearls.

sauvage [sovaʒ] *a* (*gén*) wild ; (*peuplade*) savage ; (*farouche*) unsociable ; (*barbare*) wild, savage ; (*non officiel*) unauthorized, unofficial // *nm/f* savage ; (*timide*) unsociable type, recluse ; **~rie** *nf* wildness ; savagery ; unsociability.

sauve [sov] *af voir* **sauf**.

sauvegarde [sovgaʀd(ə)] *nf* safeguard ; **sous la ~ de** under the protection of ; **sauvegarder** *vt* to safeguard.

sauve-qui-peut [sovkipø] *nm inv* stampede, mad rush // *excl* run for your life!

sauver [sove] *vt* to save ; (*porter secours à*) to rescue ; (*récupérer*) to salvage, rescue ; (*fig: racheter*) to save, redeem ; **se ~** *vi* (*s'enfuir*) to run away ; (*fam: partir*) to be off ; **~ la vie à qn** to save sb's life ; **sauvetage** *nm* rescue ; **sauveteur** *nm* rescuer ; **sauvette: à la sauvette** *ad* (*vendre*) without authorization ; (*se marier etc*) hastily, hurriedly ; **sauveur** *nm* saviour.

savais *etc vb voir* **savoir**.

savamment [savamɑ̃] *ad* (*avec érudition*) learnedly ; (*habilement*) skilfully, cleverly.

savane [savan] *nf* savannah.

savant, e [savɑ̃, -ɑ̃t] *a* a scholarly, learned ; (*calé*) clever // *nm* scientist.

saveur [savœʀ] *nf* flavour ; (*fig*) savour.

savoir [savwaʀ] *vt* to know ; (*être capable de*): **il sait nager** he knows how to swim, he can swim // *nm* knowledge ; **se ~** (*être connu*) to be known ; **à ~** *ad* that is, namely ; **faire ~ qch à qn** to inform sb about sth, to let sb know sth ; **pas que je sache** not as far as I know ; **~-faire** *nm inv* savoir-faire, know-how.

savon [savɔ̃] *nm* (*produit*) soap ; (*morceau*) bar *ou* tablet of soap ; (*fam*): **passer un ~ à qn** to give sb a good dressing-down ; **savonner** *vt* to soap ; **savonnette** *nf* bar *ou* tablet of soap ; **savonneux, euse** *a* soapy.

savons *vb voir* **savoir**.

savourer [savuʀe] *vt* to savour.

savoureux, euse [savuʀø, -øz] *a* tasty ; (*fig*) spicy, juicy.

saxo(phone) [saksɔ(fɔn)] *nm* sax(ophone) ; **saxophoniste** *nm/f* saxophonist, sax(ophone) player.

saynète [sɛnɛt] *nf* playlet.

sbire [sbiʀ] *nm* (*péj*) henchman.

scabreux, euse [skabʀø, -øz] *a* risky ; (*indécent*) improper, shocking.

scalpel [skalpɛl] *nm* scalpel.

scalper [skalpe] *vt* to scalp.

scandale [skɑ̃dal] *nm* scandal; (*tapage*): **faire du** ~ to make a scene, create a disturbance; **faire** ~ to scandalize people; **scandaleux, euse** *a* scandalous, outrageous; **scandaliser** *vt* to scandalize; **se scandaliser (de)** to be scandalized (by).

scander [skɑ̃de] *vt* (*vers*) to scan; (*slogans*) to chant; **en scandant les mots** stressing each word.

scandinave [skɑ̃dinav] *a*, ~ *nm/f* Scandinavian.

Scandinavie [skɑ̃dinavi] *nf* Scandinavia.

scaphandre [skafɑ̃dʀ(ə)] *nm* (*de plongeur*) diving suit; (*de cosmonaute*) space-suit; ~ **autonome** aqualung.

scarabée [skaʀabe] *nm* beetle.

scarlatine [skaʀlatin] *nf* scarlet fever.

scarole [skaʀɔl] *nf* endive.

scatologique [skatɔlɔʒik] *a* scatological, lavatorial.

sceau, x [so] *nm* seal; (*fig*) stamp, mark.

scélérat, e [selera, -at] *nm/f* villain, blackguard.

sceller [sele] *vt* to seal.

scellés [sele] *nmpl* seals.

scénario [senaʀjo] *nm* (*CINÉMA*) scenario; screenplay, script; (*fig*) pattern; scenario; **scénariste** *nm/f* scriptwriter.

scène [sɛn] *nf* (*gén*) scene; (*estrade, fig: théâtre*) stage; **entrer en** ~ to come on stage; **mettre en** ~ (*THÉÂTRE*) to stage; (*CINÉMA*) to direct; (*fig*) to present, introduce; **porter à la** ~ to adapt for the stage; **faire une** ~ **(à qn)** to make a scene (with sb); ~ **de ménage** domestic fight *ou* scene; **scénique** *a* theatrical; scenic.

scepticisme [sɛptisism(ə)] *nm* scepticism.

sceptique [sɛptik] *a* sceptical // *nm/f* sceptic.

sceptre [sɛptʀ(ə)] *nm* sceptre.

schéma [ʃema] *nm* (*diagramme*) diagram, sketch; (*fig*) outline; pattern; **schématique** *a* diagrammatic(al), schematic; (*fig*) oversimplified.

schisme [ʃism(ə)] *nm* schism; rift, split.

schiste [ʃist(ə)] *nm* schist.

schizophrène [skizɔfʀɛn] *nm/f* schizophrenic.

schizophrénie [skizɔfʀeni] *nf* schizophrenia.

sciatique [sjatik] *a*: **nerf** ~ sciatic nerve // *nf* sciatica.

scie [si] *nf* saw; (*fam*) catch-tune; ~ **à bois** wood saw; ~ **circulaire** circular saw; ~ **à découper** fretsaw; ~ **à métaux** hacksaw.

sciemment [sjamɑ̃] *ad* knowingly, wittingly.

science [sjɑ̃s] *nf* science; (*savoir*) knowledge; (*savoir-faire*) art, skill; ~**s naturelles** (*SCOL*) natural science *sg*, biology *sg*; ~**-fiction** *nf* science fiction; **scientifique** *a* scientific // *nm/f* scientist; science student.

scier [sje] *vt* to saw; (*retrancher*) to saw off; **scierie** *nf* sawmill; **scieur de long** *nm* pit sawyer.

scinder [sɛ̃de] *vt*, **se** ~ *vi* to split (up).

scintillement [sɛ̃tijmɑ̃] *nm* sparkling *q*.

scintiller [sɛ̃tije] *vi* to sparkle.

scission [sisjɔ̃] *nf* split.

sciure [sjyʀ] *nf*: ~ **(de bois)** sawdust.

sclérose [skleʀoz] *nf* sclerosis; (*fig*) ossification; ~ **en plaques** multiple sclerosis; **sclérosé, e** *a* sclerosed, sclerotic; ossified.

scolaire [skɔlɛʀ] *a* school *cpd*; (*péj*) schoolish; **scolariser** *vt* to provide with schooling (*ou* schools); **scolarité** *nf* schooling; **frais de scolarité** school fees.

scooter [skutœʀ] *nm* (motor) scooter.

scorbut [skɔʀbyt] *nm* scurvy.

score [skɔʀ] *nm* score.

scories [skɔʀi] *nfpl* scoria *pl*.

scorpion [skɔʀpjɔ̃] *nm* (*signe*): **le S**— Scorpio, the Scorpion; **être du S**— to be Scorpio.

scout, e [skut] *a*, *nm* scout; **scoutisme** *nm* (*boy*) scout movement; (*activités*) scouting.

scribe [skʀib] *nm* scribe; (*péj*) penpusher.

script [skʀipt] *nm* printing; (*CINÉMA*) (*shooting*) script; ~**-girl** [-gœʀl] *nf* continuity girl.

scrupule [skʀypyl] *nm* scruple; **scrupuleux, euse** *a* scrupulous.

scrutateur, trice [skʀytatœʀ, -tʀis] *a* searching.

scruter [skʀyte] *vt* to search, scrutinize; (*l'obscurité*) to peer into; (*motifs, comportement*) to examine, scrutinize.

scrutin [skʀytɛ̃] *nm* (*vote*) ballot; (*ensemble des opérations*) poll; ~ **à deux tours** poll with two ballots *ou* rounds; ~ **de liste** list system.

sculpter [skylte] *vt* to sculpt; (*suj: érosion*) to carve; **sculpteur** *nm* sculptor.

sculptural, e, aux [skyltyʀal, -o] *a* sculptural; (*fig*) statuesque.

sculpture [skyltyʀ] *nf* sculpture; ~ **sur bois** wood carving.

S.D.E.C.E. [zdɛk] *sigle m* = *service de documentation extérieure et de contre-espionnage*, ≈ Intelligence Service.

se, s' [s(ə)] *pronom* (*emploi réfléchi*) oneself, *m* himself, *f* herself, *sujet non humain* itself; *pl* themselves; (: *réciproque*) one another, each other; (: *passif*): **cela se répare facilement** it is easily repaired; (: *possessif*): ~ **casser la jambe/laver les mains** to break one's leg/wash one's hands; *autres emplois pronominaux: voir le verbe en question*.

séance [seɑ̃s] *nf* (*d'assemblée, récréative*) meeting, session; (*de tribunal*) sitting, session; (*musicale, CINÉMA, THÉÂTRE*) performance; ~ **tenante** forthwith.

séant, e [seɑ̃, -ɑ̃t] *a* seemly, fitting // *nm* posterior.

seau, x [so] *nm* bucket, pail; ~ **à glace** ice-bucket.

sec, sèche [sɛk, sɛʃ] *a* dry; (*raisins, figues*) dried; (*cœur, personne: insensible*) hard, cold // *nm*: **tenir au** ~ to keep in a dry place // *ad* hard; **je le bois** ~ I drink it straight *ou* neat; **à** ~ *a* dried up.

sécateur [sekatœʀ] *nm* secateurs *pl*, shears *pl*, pair of shears *ou* secateurs.

sécession [sesesjɔ̃] *nf*: **faire** ~ to secede; **la guerre de S**~ the American Civil War.

séchage [seʃaʒ] *nm* drying; seasoning.
sèche [sɛʃ] *af voir* **sec**.
sèche-cheveux [sɛʃʃəvø] *nm inv* hairdrier.
sécher [seʃe] *vt* to dry; (*dessécher: peau, blé*) to dry (out); (: *étang*) to dry up; (*bois*) to season; (*fam: classe, cours*) to skip // *vi* to dry; to dry out; to dry up; (*fam: candidat*) to be stumped; **se ~** (*après le bain*) to dry o.s.
sécheresse [seʃRɛs] *nf* dryness; (*absence de pluie*) drought.
séchoir [seʃwaR] *nm* drier.
second, e [səgɔ̃, -ɔ̃d] *a* a second // *nm* (*assistant*) second in command; (NAVIG) first mate // *nf* second-class; **voyager en ~** to travel second-class; **de ~e main** second-hand; **secondaire** *a* secondary; **seconder** *vt* to assist.
secouer [səkwe] *vt* to shake; (*passagers*) to rock; (*traumatiser*) to shake (up); **se ~** (*chien*) to shake itself; (*fam: se démener*) to shake o.s. up; **~ la poussière d'un tapis** to shake off the dust from a carpet.
secourable [səkuRabl(ə)] *a* helpful.
secourir [səkuRiR] *vt* (*aller sauver*) to (go and) rescue; (*prodiguer des soins à*) to help, assist; (*venir en aide à*) to assist, aid; **secourisme** *nm* first aid; life saving; **secouriste** *nm/f* first-aid worker.
secours [səkuR] *nm* help, aid, assistance // *nmpl* aid *sg*; **cela lui a été d'un grand ~** this was a great help to him; **au ~!** help! **appeler au ~** to shout ou call for help; **appeler qn à son ~** to call sb to one's assistance; **porter ~ à qn** to give sb assistance, help sb; **les premiers ~** first aid *sg*; **le ~ en montagne** mountain rescue.
secousse [səkus] *nf* jolt, bump; (*électrique*) shock; (*fig: psychologique*) jolt, shock; **~ sismique ou tellurique** earth tremor.
secret, ète [səkRɛ, -ɛt] *a* secret; (*fig: renfermé*) reticent, reserved // *nm* secret; (*discrétion absolue*): **le ~** secrecy; **en ~** in secret, secretly; **au ~** in solitary confinement; **~ de fabrication** trade secret; **~ professionnel** professional secrecy.
secrétaire [səkReteR] *nm/f* secretary // *nm* (*meuble*) writing desk, secretaire; **~ d'ambassade** embassy secretary; **~ de direction** private ou personal secretary; **~ d'État** Secretary of State; **~ général** Secretary-General; **~ de mairie** town clerk; **~ de rédaction** sub-editor; **secrétariat** *nm* (*profession*) secretarial work; (*bureau: d'entreprise, d'école*) (secretary's) office; (: *d'organisation internationale*) secretariat; (POL *etc: fonction*) secretaryship, office of Secretary.
sécréter [sekRete] *vt* to secrete; **sécrétion** [-sjɔ̃] *nf* secretion.
sectaire [sɛktɛR] *a* sectarian, bigoted.
secte [sɛkt(ə)] *nf* sect.
secteur [sɛktœR] *nm* sector; (ADMIN) district; (ÉLEC): **branché sur le ~** plugged into the mains (supply); **fonctionne sur pile et ~** battery or mains operated; **le ~ privé** the private sector; **le ~**

primaire/tertiaire primary/tertiary industry.
section [sɛksjɔ̃] *nf* section; (*de parcours d'autobus*) fare stage; (MIL: *unité*) platoon; **tube de ~ 6,5 mm** tube with a 6.5 mm bore; **~ rythmique** rhythm section; **sectionner** *vt* to sever.
sectoriel, le [sɛktɔRjɛl] *a* sector-based.
séculaire [sekylɛR] *a* secular; (*très vieux*) age-old.
séculier, ière [sekylje, -jɛR] *a* secular.
sécuriser [sekyRize] *vt* to give (a feeling of) security to.
sécurité [sekyRite] *nf* safety; security; **impression de ~** sense of security; **la ~ internationale** international security; **système de ~** safety system; **être en ~** to be safe; **la ~ de l'emploi** job security; **la ~ routière** road safety; **la ~ sociale** ≈ (the) Social Security.
sédatif, ive [sedatif, -iv] *a, nm* sedative.
sédentaire [sedɑ̃tɛR] *a* sedentary.
sédiment [sedimɑ̃] *nm* sediment; **~s** *nmpl* (*alluvions*) sediment *sg*.
séditieux, euse [sedisjø, -øz] *a* insurgent; seditious.
sédition [sedisjɔ̃] *nf* insurrection; sedition.
séducteur, trice [sedyktœR, -tRis] *a* seductive // *nm/f* seducer/seductress.
séduction [sedyksjɔ̃] *nf* seduction; (*charme, attrait*) appeal, charm.
séduire [sedɥiR] *vt* to charm; (*femme: abuser de*) to seduce; **séduisant, e** *a* (*femme*) seductive; (*homme, offre*) very attractive.
segment [sɛgmɑ̃] *nm* segment; (AUTO): **~ (de piston)** piston ring; **segmenter** *vt* to segment.
ségrégation [segRegasjɔ̃] *nf* segregation.
seiche [sɛʃ] *nf* cuttlefish.
séide [seid] *nm* (*péj*) henchman.
seigle [sɛgl(ə)] *nm* rye.
seigneur [sɛɲœR] *nm* lord; **le S~** the Lord; **~ial, e, aux** *a* lordly, stately.
sein [sɛ̃] *nm* breast; (*entrailles*) womb; **au ~ de** *prép* (*équipe, institution*) within; (*flots, bonheur*) in the midst of; **donner le ~ à** (*bébé*) to feed (at the breast); to breast-feed.
séisme [seism(ə)] *nm* earthquake.
séismique [seismik] *etc voir* **sismique** *etc*.
seize [sɛz] *num* sixteen; **seizième** *num* sixteenth.
séjour [seʒuR] *nm* stay; (*pièce*) living room; **~ner** *vi* to stay.
sel [sɛl] *nm* salt; (*fig*) wit; spice; **~ de cuisine/de table** cooking/table salt; **~ gemme** rock salt.
sélection [selɛksjɔ̃] *nf* selection; **~ professionnelle** professional recruitment; **sélectionner** *vt* to select.
self-service [sɛlfsɛRvis] *a, nm* self-service.
selle [sɛl] *nf* saddle; **~s** *nfpl* (MÉD) stools; **aller à la ~** (MÉD) to pass a motion; **se mettre en ~** to mount, get into the saddle; **seller** *vt* to saddle.
sellette [sɛlɛt] *nf*: **être sur la ~** to be on the carpet.
sellier [selje] *nm* saddler.

selon [səlɔ̃] *prép* according to ; (*en se conformant à*) in accordance with.

semailles [səmɑj] *nfpl* sowing *sg*.

semaine [səmɛn] *nf* week ; **en ~** during the week, on weekdays.

sémantique [semɑ̃tik] *a* semantic // *nf* semantics *sg*.

sémaphore [semafɔʀ] *nm* semaphore signal.

semblable [sɑ̃blabl(ə)] *a* similar ; (*de ce genre*): **de ~s mésaventures** such mishaps // *nm* fellow creature *ou* man ; **~ à** similar to, like.

semblant [sɑ̃blɑ̃] *nm*: **un ~ de vérité** a semblance of truth ; **faire ~ (de faire)** to pretend (to do).

sembler [sɑ̃ble] *vb avec attribut* to seem // *vb impersonnel*: **il semble que/inutile de** it seems *ou* appears that/useless to ; **il me semble que** it seems to me that ; I think (that) ; **~ être** to seem to be ; **comme bon lui semble** as he sees fit.

semelle [səmɛl] *nf* sole ; (*intérieure*) insole, inner sole ; **~s compensées** platform soles.

semence [səmɑ̃s] *nf* (*graine*) seed ; (*clou*) tack.

semer [səme] *vt* to sow ; (*fig: éparpiller*) to scatter ; (: *poursuivants*) to lose, shake off ; **semé de** (*difficultés*) riddled with.

semestre [səmɛstʀ(ə)] *nm* half-year ; (*SCOL*) semester ; **semestriel, le** *a* half-yearly ; semestral.

semeur, euse [səmœʀ, -øz] *nm/f* sower.

sémillant, e [semijɑ̃, -ɑ̃t] *a* vivacious ; dashing.

séminaire [seminɛʀ] *nm* seminar ; (*REL*) seminary ; **séminariste** *nm* seminarist.

semi-remorque [səmiʀəmɔʀk(ə)] *nf* trailer // *nm* articulated lorry.

semis [səmi] *nm* (*terrain*) seedbed, seed plot ; (*plante*) seedling.

sémite [semit] *a* Semitic.

sémitique [semitik] *a* Semitic.

semoir [səmwaʀ] *nm* seed-bag ; seeder.

semonce [səmɔ̃s] *nf* reprimand ; **coup de ~** warning shot across the bows.

semoule [səmul] *nf* semolina.

sempiternel, le [sɑ̃pitɛʀnɛl] *a* eternal, never-ending.

sénat [sena] *nm* Senate ; **sénateur** *nm* Senator.

sénile [senil] *a* senile ; **sénilité** *nf* senility.

sens [sɑ̃s] *nm* (*PHYSIOL, instinct*) sense ; (*signification*) meaning, sense ; (*direction*) direction // *nmpl* (*sensualité*) senses ; **reprendre ses ~** to regain consciousness, **avoir le ~ des affaires/la mesure** to have business sense/a sense of moderation ; **ça n'a pas de ~** that doesn't make (any) sense ; **dans le ~ des aiguilles d'une montre** clockwise ; **~ commun** common sense ; **~ dessus dessous** upside down ; **~ interdit, ~ unique** one-way street.

sensation [sɑ̃sasjɔ̃] *nf* sensation ; **faire ~** to cause a sensation, create a stir ; **à ~** (*péj*) sensational ; **sensationnel, le** *a* sensational ; (*fig*) terrific.

sensé, e [sɑ̃se] *a* sensible.

sensibiliser [sɑ̃sibilize] *vt*: **~ qn à** to make sb sensitive to.

sensibilité [sɑ̃sibilite] *nf* sensitivity ; (*affectivité, émotivité*) sensitivity, sensibility.

sensible [sɑ̃sibl(ə)] *a* a sensitive ; (*aux sens*) perceptible ; (*appréciable*: *différence, progrès*) appreciable, noticeable ; **~ à** sensitive to ; **~ment** *ad* (*notablement*) appreciably, noticeably ; (*à peu près*): **ils ont ~ment le même poids** they weigh approximately the same ; **~rie** *nf* sentimentality, mawkishness ; squeamishness.

sensitif, ive [sɑ̃sitif, -iv] *a* (*nerf*) sensory ; (*personne*) oversensitive.

sensoriel, le [sɑ̃sɔʀjɛl] *a* sensory, sensorial.

sensualité [sɑ̃sɥalite] *nf* sensuality ; sensuousness.

sensuel, le [sɑ̃sɥɛl] *a* sensual ; sensuous.

sente [sɑ̃t] *nf* path.

sentence [sɑ̃tɑ̃s] *nf* (*jugement*) sentence ; (*adage*) maxim ; **sentencieux, euse** *a* sententious.

senteur [sɑ̃tœʀ] *nf* scent, perfume.

sentier [sɑ̃tje] *nm* path.

sentiment [sɑ̃timɑ̃] *nm* feeling ; **recevez mes ~s respectueux** yours faithfully ; **faire du ~** (*péj*) to be sentimental ; **sentimental, e, aux** *a* sentimental ; (*vie, aventure*) love *cpd*.

sentinelle [sɑ̃tinɛl] *nf* sentry ; **en ~** on sentry duty ; standing guard.

sentir [sɑ̃tiʀ] *vt* (*par l'odorat*) to smell ; (*par le goût*) to taste ; (*au toucher, fig*) to feel ; (*répandre une odeur de*) to smell of ; (: *ressemblance*) to smell like ; (*avoir la saveur de*) to taste of ; to taste like ; (*fig: dénoter, annoncer*) to be indicative of ; to smack of ; to foreshadow // *vi* to smell ; **~ mauvais** to smell bad ; **se ~ bien** to feel good ; **se ~ mal** (*être indisposé*) to feel unwell *ou* ill ; **se ~ le courage/la force de faire** to feel brave/strong enough to do ; **ne plus se ~ de joie** to be beside o.s. with joy ; **il ne peut pas le ~** (*fam*) he can't stand him.

seoir [swaʀ] : **~ à** *vt* to become.

séparation [separasjɔ̃] *nf* separation ; (*cloison*) division, partition ; **~ de biens** division of property (*in marriage settlement*) ; **~ de corps** legal separation.

séparatisme [separatism(ə)] *nm* separatism.

séparé, e [separe] *a* (*appartements, pouvoirs*) separate ; (*époux*) separated ; **~ de** separate from ; separated from ; **~ment** *ad* separately.

séparer [separe] *vt* (*gén*) to separate ; (*suj: divergences etc*) to divide ; to drive apart ; (: *différences, obstacles*) to stand between ; (*détacher*): **~ qch de** to pull sth (off) from ; (*dissocier*) to distinguish between ; (*diviser*): **~ qch par** to divide sth (up) with ; **~ une pièce en deux** to divide a room into two ; **se ~** (*époux*) to separate, part ; (*prendre congé: amis etc*) to part, leave each other ; (*adversaires*) to separate ; **se diviser: route, tige etc**) to divide ; (*se détacher*): **se ~ (de)** to split off (from) ; to come off ; **se ~ de** (*époux*) to separate *ou* part from; (*employé, objet personnel*) to part with.

sept [sɛt] *num* seven.

septembre [sɛptɑ̃bR(ə)] *nm* September.

septennat [sɛptena] *nm* seven-year term (of office); seven-year reign.

septentrional, e, aux [sɛptɑ̃tRijɔnal, -o] *a* northern.

septicémie [sɛptisemi] *nf* blood poisoning, septicaemia.

septième [sɛtjɛm] *num* seventh.

septique [sɛptik] *a*: **fosse ~** septic tank.

septuagénaire [sɛptɥaʒenɛR] *a, nm/f* septuagenarian.

sépulcre [sepylkR(ə)] *nm* sepulchre.

sépulture [sepyltyR] *nf* burial; burial place, grave.

séquelles [sekɛl] *nfpl* after-effects; (*fig*) aftermath *sg*; consequences.

séquence [sekɑ̃s] *nf* sequence.

séquestre [sekɛstR(ə)] *nm* impoundment; **mettre sous ~** to impound.

séquestrer [sekɛstRe] *vt* (*personne*) to confine illegally; (*biens*) to impound.

serai *etc vb voir* **être.**

serein, e [səRɛ̃, -ɛn] *a* serene; (*jugement*) dispassionate.

sérénade [seRenad] *nf* serenade; (*fam*) hullabaloo.

sérénité [seRenite] *nf* serenity.

serez *vb voir* **être.**

serf, serve [sɛR, sɛRv(ə)] *nm/f* serf.

serge [sɛRʒ(ə)] *nf* serge.

sergent [sɛRʒɑ̃] *nm* sergeant; **~-chef** *nm* staff sergeant; **~-major** *nm* ≈ quartermaster sergeant.

sériciculture [seRisikyltyR] *nf* silkworm breeding, sericulture.

série [seRi] *nf* (*de questions, d'accidents*) series *inv*; (*de clés, casseroles, outils*) set; (*catégorie: SPORT*) rank; class; **en ~** in quick succession; (*COMM*) mass *cpd*; **de ~** a standard; **hors ~** (*COMM*) custom-built; (*fig*) outstanding; **~ noire** *nm* (*crime*) thriller; **sérier** *vt* to classify, sort out.

sérieusement [seRjøzmɑ̃] *ad* seriously; reliably; responsibly; **~?** do you mean it?, are you talking in earnest?

sérieux, euse [seRjø, -øz] *a* serious; (*élève, employé*) reliable, responsible; (*client, maison*) reliable, dependable; (*offre, proposition*) genuine, serious; (*grave, sévère*) serious, solemn; (*maladie, situation*) serious, grave // *nm* seriousness; reliability; **garder son ~** to keep a straight face; **manquer de ~** not to be very responsible (*ou* reliable); **prendre qch/qn au ~** to take sth/sb seriously.

serin [səRɛ̃] *nm* canary.

seriner [səRine] *vt*: **~ qch à qn** to drum sth into sb.

seringue [səRɛ̃g] *nf* syringe.

serions *vb voir* **être.**

serment [sɛRmɑ̃] *nm* (*juré*) oath; (*promesse*) pledge, vow; **faire le ~ de** to take a vow to, swear to; **sous ~** on *ou* under oath.

sermon [sɛRmɔ̃] *nm* sermon; (*péj*) sermon, lecture.

serpe [sɛRp(ə)] *nf* billhook.

serpent [sɛRpɑ̃] *nm* snake; **~ à sonnettes** rattlesnake.

serpenter [sɛRpɑ̃te] *vi* to wind.

serpentin [sɛRpɑ̃tɛ̃] *nm* (*tube*) coil; (*ruban*) streamer.

serpillière [sɛRpijɛR] *nf* floorcloth.

serrage [sɛRaʒ] *nm* tightening; **collier de ~** clamp.

serre [sɛR] *nf* (*AGR*) greenhouse; **~s** *nfpl* (*griffes*) claws, talons; **~ chaude** hothouse.

serré, e [seRe] *a* (*tissu*) closely woven; (*réseau*) dense; (*écriture*) close; (*habits*) tight; (*fig: lutte, match*) tight, close-fought; (*passagers etc*) (tightly) packed.

serre-livres [sɛRlivR(ə)] *nm inv* book ends *pl*.

serrement [sɛRmɑ̃] *nm*: **~ de main** handshake; **~ de cœur** pang of anguish.

serrer [seRe] *vt* (*tenir*) to grip *ou* hold tight; (*comprimer, coincer*) to squeeze; (*poings, mâchoires*) to clench; (*suj: vêtement*) to be too tight for; to fit tightly; (*rapprocher*) to close up, move closer together; (*ceinture, nœud, frein, vis*) to tighten // *vi*: **~ à droite** to keep to the right; to move into the right-hand lane; **se ~** (*se rapprocher*) to squeeze up; **se ~ contre qn** to huddle up to sb; **se ~ les coudes** to stick together, back one another up; **~ la main à qn** to shake sb's hand; **~ qn dans ses bras** to hug sb, clasp sb in one's arms; **~ la gorge à qn** (*suj: chagrin*) to bring a lump to sb's throat; **~ qn de près** to follow close behind sb; **~ le trottoir** to hug the kerb; **~ sa droite** to keep well to the right; **~ la vis à qn** to crack down harder on sb.

serre-tête [sɛRtɛt] *nm inv* (*bandeau*) headband; (*bonnet*) skullcap.

serrure [seRyR] *nf* lock.

serrurerie [seRyRRi] *nf* (*métier*) locksmith's trade; **~ d'art** ornamental ironwork.

serrurier [seRyRje] *nm* locksmith.

sert *etc vb voir* **servir.**

sertir [sɛRtiR] *vt* (*pierre*) to set; (*pièces métalliques*) to crimp.

sérum [seRɔm] *nm* serum; **~ antivenimeux** snakebite serum; **~ sanguin** (blood) serum; **~ de vérité** truth drug.

servage [sɛRvaʒ] *nm* serfdom.

servant [sɛRvɑ̃] *nm* server.

servante [sɛRvɑ̃t] *nf* (maid)servant.

serve [sɛRv] *nf voir* **serf.**

serveur, euse [sɛRvœR, -øz] *nm/f* waiter/waitress.

serviable [sɛRvjabl(ə)] *a* obliging, willing to help.

service [sɛRvis] *nm* (*gén*) service; (*série de repas*): **premier ~** first sitting; (*pourboire*) service (charge); (*assortiment de vaisselle*) set, service; (*bureau: de la vente etc*) department, section; (*travail*): **pendant le ~** on duty; **~s** *nmpl* (*travail, ÉCON*) services; **faire le ~** to serve; **être en ~ chez qn** (*domestique*) to be in sb's service; **être au ~ de** (*patron, patrie*) to be in the service of; **être au ~ de qn** (*collaborateur, voiture*) to be at sb's service; **rendre ~**

à to help; **il aime rendre ~** he likes to help; **rendre un ~ à qn** to do sb a favour; **heures de ~** hours of duty; **être de ~** to be on duty; **avoir 25 ans de ~** to have completed 25 years' service; **être/mettre en ~** to be in/put into service ou operation; **~ à thé/café** tea/coffee set ou service; **~ après vente** after-sales service; **en ~ commandé** on an official assignment; **~ funèbre** funeral service; **~ militaire** military service; **~ d'ordre** police (ou stewards) in charge of maintaining order; **~s secrets** secret service sg.

serviette [sɛRvjɛt] nf (de table) (table) napkin, serviette; (de toilette) towel; (porte-documents) briefcase; **~ hygiénique** sanitary towel ou pad; **~-éponge** nf terry towel.

servile [sɛRvil] a servile.

servir [sɛRviR] vt (gén) to serve; (dîneur: au restaurant) to wait on; (client: au magasin) to serve, attend to; (fig: aider): **~ qn** to aid sb; to serve sb's interests; to stand sb in good stead; (COMM: rente) to pay // vi (TENNIS) to serve; (CARTES) to deal; **se ~** (prendre d'un plat) to help o.s.; **se ~ de** (plat) to help o.s. to; (voiture, outil, relations) to use; **~ à qn** (diplôme, livre) to be of use to sb; **ça m'a servi pour faire** it was useful to me when I did; I used it to do; **~ à qch/faire** (outil etc) to be used for sth/doing; **ça peut ~** it may come in handy; **ça peut encore ~** it can still be used (ou of use); **à quoi cela sert-il (de faire)?** what's the use (of doing)?; **cela ne sert à rien** it's no use; **~ (à qn) de** to serve as (for sb); **~ la messe** to serve Mass; **~ à dîner (à qn)** to serve dinner (to sb).

serviteur [sɛRvitœR] nm servant.

servitude [sɛRvityd] nf servitude; (fig) constraint; (JUR) easement.

servo... [sɛRvo] préfixe: **~frein** servo (-assisted) brake.

ses [se] dét voir **son**.

session [sesjɔ̃] nf session.

set [sɛt] nm set.

seuil [sœj] nm doorstep; (fig) threshold; **sur le ~ de sa maison** in the doorway of his house, on his doorstep; **au ~ de** (fig) on the threshold ou brink ou edge of.

seul, e [sœl] a (sans compagnie, en isolation) alone; (avec nuance affective: isolé) lonely; (unique): **un ~ livre** only one book, a single book; **le ~ livre** the only book; **ce livre, ce livre ~** this book alone, only this book // ad (vivre) alone, on one's own; **parler tout ~** to talk to oneself; **faire qch (tout) ~** to do sth (all) on one's own ou (all) by oneself // nm, nf **il en reste un(e) ~(e)** there's only one left; **à lui (tout) ~** single-handed, on his own.

seulement [sœlmɑ̃] ad (pas davantage): **~ 5, 5 ~** only 5; (exclusivement): **~ eux** only them, them alone; (pas avant): **~ hier/à 10h** only yesterday/at 10 o'clock; **non ~... mais aussi ou encore** not only ... but also.

sève [sɛv] nf sap.

sévère [sevɛR] a severe; **sévérité** nf severity.

sévices [sevis] nmpl (physical) cruelty sg, ill treatment sg.

sévir [seviR] vi (punir) to use harsh measures, crack down on; (suj: fléau) to rage, be rampant; **~ contre** (abus) to deal ruthlessly with, crack down on.

sevrer [səvRe] vt to wean; (fig): **~ qn de** to deprive sb of.

sexagénaire [sɛgzaʒenɛR] a, nm/f sexagenarian.

sexe [sɛks(ə)] nm sex; (organe mâle) member; **sexologue** nm/f sexologist, sex specialist.

sextant [sɛkstɑ̃] nm sextant.

sexualité [sɛksyalite] nf sexuality.

sexué, e [sɛksye] a sexual.

sexuel, le [sɛksyɛl] a sexual; **acte ~** sex act.

seyait vb voir **seoir**.

seyant, e [sɛjɑ̃, -ɑ̃t] a becoming.

shampooing [ʃɑ̃pwɛ̃] nm shampoo; **se faire un ~** to shampoo one's hair; **~ colorant** (colour) rinse.

short [ʃɔRt] nm (pair of) shorts pl.

si [si] nm (MUS) B; (en chantant la gamme) si, se // ad (oui) yes; (tellement) so // cj if; **~ seulement** if only; **(tant et) ~ bien que** so much so that; **~ rapide qu'il soit** however fast he may be, fast though he is; **je me demande ~** I wonder if ou whether.

siamois, e [sjamwa, -waz] a Siamese; **frères/sœurs siamois/es** Siamese twins.

Sicile [sisil] nf: **la ~** Sicily; **sicilien, ne** a Sicilian.

sidéré, e [sideRe] a staggered.

sidérurgie [sideRyRʒi] nf iron and steel industry.

siècle [sjɛkl(ə)] nm century; (époque) age; (REL): **le ~** the world.

sied [sje] vb voir **seoir**.

siège [sjɛʒ] nm seat; (d'entreprise) head office; (d'organisation) headquarters pl; (MIL) siege; **mettre le ~ devant** to besiege; **présentation par le ~** (MÉD) breech presentation; **~ baquet** bucket seat; **~ social** registered office.

siéger [sjeʒe] vi to sit.

sien, ne [sjɛ̃, sjɛn] pronom: **le(la) ~(ne), les ~s(~nes)** his; hers; its; **faire des ~nes** (fam) to be up to one's (usual) tricks; **les ~s** (sa famille) one's family.

siérait etc vb voir **seoir**.

sieste [sjɛst(ə)] nf (afternoon) snooze ou nap, siesta; **faire la ~** to have a snooze ou nap.

sieur [sjœR] nm: **le ~ Thomas** Mr Thomas; (en plaisantant) Master Thomas.

sifflant, e [siflɑ̃, -ɑ̃t] a (bruit) whistling; (toux) wheezing; (consonne) **~e** sibilant.

sifflement [sifləmɑ̃] nm whistle, whistling q; hissing noise; whistling noise.

siffler [sifle] vi (gén) to whistle; (avec un sifflet) to blow (on) one's whistle; (en parlant, dormant) to wheeze; (serpent, vapeur) to hiss // vt (chanson) to whistle; (chien etc) to whistle for; (fille) to whistle at; (pièce, orateur) to hiss, boo; (faute) to blow one's whistle at; (fin du match, départ) to blow one's whistle for; (fam: verre, bouteille) to guzzle, knock back.

sifflet [siflɛ] *nm* whistle ; ~**s** *nmpl* (*de mécontentement*) whistles, boos ; **coup de** ~ whistle.

siffloter [siflɔte] *vi, vt* to whistle.

sigle [sigl(ə)] *nm* acronym, (set of) initials *pl.*

signal, aux [siɲal, -o] *nm* (*signe convenu, appareil*) signal ; (*indice, écriteau*) sign ; **donner le** ~ **de** to give the signal for ; ~ **d'alarme** alarm signal ; ~ **horaire** time signal ; **signaux (lumineux)** (*AUTO*) traffic signals.

signalement [siɲalmɑ̃] *nm* description, particulars *pl.*

signaler [siɲale] *vt* to indicate ; to announce ; to report ; (*faire remarquer*): ~ **qch à qn/à qn que** to point out sth to sb/to sb that ; **se** ~ **par** to distinguish o.s. by ; **se** ~ **à l'attention de qn** to attract sb's attention.

signalétique [siɲaletik] *a:* **fiche** ~ identification sheet.

signalisation [siɲalizasjɔ̃] *nf* signalling, signposting ; signals *pl*, roadsigns *pl* ; **panneau de** ~ roadsign.

signaliser [siɲalize] *vt* to put up roadsigns on ; to put signals on.

signataire [siɲatɛʀ] *nm/f* signatory.

signature [siɲatyʀ] *nf* signing ; signature.

signe [siɲ] *nm* sign ; (*TYPO*) mark ; **c'est bon** ~ it's a good sign ; **faire un** ~ **de la main** to give a sign with one's hand ; **faire** ~ **à qn** (*fig*) to get in touch with sb ; **faire** ~ **à qn d'entrer** to motion (to) sb to come in ; **en** ~ **de** as a sign *ou* mark of ; **le** ~ **de la croix** the sign of the Cross ; ~ **de ponctuation** punctuation mark ; ~ **du zodiaque** sign of the zodiac.

signer [siɲe] *vt* to sign ; **se** ~ *vi* to cross o.s.

signet [siɲɛ] *nm* bookmark.

significatif, ive [siɲifikatif, -iv] *a* significant.

signification [siɲifikasjɔ̃] *nf* meaning.

signifier [siɲifje] *vt* (*vouloir dire*) to mean, signify ; (*faire connaître*): ~ **qch (à qn)** to make sth known (to sb) ; (*JUR*): ~ **qch à qn** to serve notice of sth on sb.

silence [silɑ̃s] *nm* silence ; (*MUS*) rest ; **garder le** ~ to keep silent, say nothing ; **passer sous** ~ to pass over (in silence) ; **réduire au** ~ to silence ; **silencieux, euse** *a* quiet, silent // *nm* silencer.

silex [silɛks] *nm* flint.

silhouette [silwɛt] *nf* outline, silhouette ; (*lignes, contour*) outline ; (*figure*) figure.

silicium [silisjɔm] *nm* silicon.

silicone [silikɔn] *nf* silicone.

silicose [silikoz] *nf* silicosis, dust disease.

sillage [sijaʒ] *nm* wake ; (*fig*) trail.

sillon [sijɔ̃] *nm* furrow ; (*de disque*) groove ; **sillonner** *vt* to furrow ; to cross, criss-cross.

silo [silo] *nm* silo.

simagrées [simagʀe] *nfpl* fuss *sg* ; airs and graces.

simiesque [simjɛsk(ə)] *a* monkey-like, ape-like.

similaire [similɛʀ] *a* similar ; **similarité** *nf* similarity ; **simili...** *préfixe* imitation *cpd*,

artificial ; **similicuir** *nm* imitation leather ; **similitude** *nf* similarity.

simple [sɛ̃pl(ə)] *a* (*gén*) simple ; (*non multiple*) single ; ~**s** *nmpl* (*MÉD*) medicinal plants ; ~ **messieurs** (*TENNIS*) men's singles *sg* ; **un** ~ **particulier** an ordinary citizen ; **cela varie du** ~ **au double** it can double, it can be double the price *etc* ; ~ **course** a single ; ~ **d'esprit** *nm/f* simpleton ; ~ **soldat** private ; **simplicité** *nf* simplicity ; **simplifier** *vt* to simplify ; **simpliste** *a* simplistic.

simulacre [simylakʀ(ə)] *nm* enactement ; (*péj*): **un** ~ **de** a pretence of, a sham.

simulateur, trice [simylatœʀ, -tʀis] *nm/f* shammer, pretender ; (*qui se prétend malade*) malingerer // *nm:* ~ **de vol** flight simulator.

simulation [simylasjɔ̃] *nf* shamming, simulation ; malingering.

simuler [simyle] *vt* to sham, simulate ; (*suj: substance, revêtement*) to simulate.

simultané, e [simyltane] *a* simultaneous ; ~**ment** *ad* simultaneously.

sincère [sɛ̃sɛʀ] *a* sincere ; genuine ; heartfelt ; **sincérité** *nf* sincerity.

sinécure [sinekyʀ] *nf* sinecure.

sine die [sinedje] *ad* sine die, indefinitely.

sine qua non [sinekwanɔ̃] *a:* **condition** ~ indispensable condition.

singe [sɛ̃ʒ] *nm* monkey ; (*de grande taille*) ape.

singer [sɛ̃ʒe] *vt* to ape, mimic.

singeries [sɛ̃ʒʀi] *nfpl* antics ; (*simagrées*) airs and graces.

singulariser [sɛ̃gylaʀize] *vt* to mark out ; **se** ~ to call attention to o.s.

singularité [sɛ̃gylaʀite] *nf* peculiarity.

singulier, ière [sɛ̃gylje, -jɛʀ] *a* remarkable, singular ; (*LING*) singular // *nm* singular.

sinistre [sinistʀ(ə)] *a* sinister // *nm* (*incendie*) blaze ; (*catastrophe*) disaster ; (*ASSURANCES*) accident (*giving rise to a claim*) ; **sinistré, e** *a* disaster-stricken // *nm/f* disaster victim.

sino... [sino] *préfixe:* ~**-indien** Sino-Indian, Chinese-Indian.

sinon [sinɔ̃] *cj* (*autrement, sans quoi*) otherwise, or else ; (*sauf*) except, other than ; (*si ce n'est*) if not.

sinueux, euse [sinɥø, -øz] *a* winding ; (*fig*) tortuous ; **sinuosités** *nfpl* winding *sg*, curves.

sinus [sinys] *nm* (*ANAT*) sinus ; (*GÉOM*) sine ; **sinusite** *nf* sinusitis, sinus infection.

sionisme [sjɔnism(ə)] *nm* Zionism.

siphon [sifɔ̃] *nm* (*tube, d'eau gazeuse*) siphon ; (*d'évier etc*) U-bend ; **siphonner** *vt* to siphon.

sire [siʀ] *nm* (*titre*): **S**~ Sire ; **un triste** ~ an unsavoury individual.

sirène [siʀɛn] *nf* siren ; ~ **d'alarme** air-raid siren ; fire alarm.

sirop [siʀo] *nm* (*à diluer: de fruit etc*) syrup, cordial ; (*boisson*) cordial ; (*pharmaceutique*) syrup, mixture ; ~ **de menthe** mint syrup *ou* cordial ; ~ **contre la toux** cough syrup *ou* mixture.

siroter [siʀɔte] *vt* to sip.

sis, e [si, siz] *a:* ~ **rue de la Paix** located in the rue de la Paix.

sismique [sismik] *a* seismic.

sismographe [sismɔgRaf] *nm* seismograph.

sismologie [sismɔlɔʒi] *nf* seismology.

site [sit] *nm* (*paysage, environnement*) setting; (*d'une ville etc: emplacement*) site; ~ (**pittoresque**) beauty spot; ~**s touristiques** places of interest; ~**s naturels/historiques** natural/ historic sites.

sitôt [sito] *ad:* ~ **parti** as soon as he had left; **pas de** ~ not for a long time.

situation [sitɥasjɔ̃] *nf* (*gén*) situation; (*d'un édifice, d'une ville*) situation, position; location.

situé, e [sitɥe] *a:* **bien** ~ well situated, in a good location; ~ **à/près de** situated at/near.

situer [sitɥe] *vt* to site, situate; (*en pensée*) to set, place; **se** ~ *vi:* **se** ~ **à/près de** to be situated at/near.

six [sis] *num* six; **sixième** *num* sixth.

sketch [skɛtʃ] *nm* (*variety*) sketch.

ski [ski] *nm* (*objet*) ski; (*sport*) skiing; **faire du** ~ to ski; ~ **de fond** lang-lauf; ~ **nautique** water-skiing; ~ **de piste** downhill skiing; ~ **de randonnée** cross-country skiing; **skier** *vi* to ski; **skieur, euse** *nm/f* skier.

slalom [slalɔm] *nm* slalom; **faire du** ~ **entre** to slalom between; ~ **géant/spécial** giant/special slalom.

slave [slav] *a* Slav(onic), Slavic.

slip [slip] *nm* (*sous-vêtement*) pants *pl*, briefs *pl*; (*de bain: d'homme*) (bathing ou swimming) trunks *pl*; (: *du bikini*) (bikini) briefs *pl*.

slogan [slɔgɑ̃] *nm* slogan.

S.M.I.C., S.M.I.G. [smik, smig] *sigle m voir* **salaire**.

smoking [smɔkiŋ] *nm* dinner ou evening suit.

snack [snak] *nm* snack bar.

S.N.C.F. *sigle f = société nationale des chemins de fer français,* ≈ British Rail.

snob [snɔb] *a* snobbish // *nm/f* snob; ~**isme** *nm* snobbery.

sobre [sɔbR(ə)] *a* temperate, abstemious; (*élégance, style*) sober; ~ **de** (*gestes, compliments*) sparing of; **sobriété** *nf* temperance, abstémiousness; sobriety.

sobriquet [sɔbRikɛ] *nm* nickname.

soc [sɔk] *nm* ploughshare.

sociable [sɔsjabl(ə)] *a* sociable.

social, e, aux [sɔsjal, -o] *a* social.

socialisme [sɔsjalism(ə)] *nm* socialism; **socialiste** *nm/f* socialist.

sociétaire [sɔsjetɛR] *nm/f* member.

société [sɔsjete] *nf* society; (*sportive*) club; (*COMM*) company; **la bonne** ~ polite society; **la** ~ **d'abondance/de consommation** the affluent/consumer society; ~ **anonyme (S.A.)** ≈ limited company; ~ **à responsabilité limitée (S.A.R.L.)** type of limited liability company (*with non negotiable shares*).

sociologie [sɔsjɔlɔʒi] *nf* sociology; **sociologue** *nm/f* sociologist.

socle [sɔkl(ə)] *nm* (*de colonne, statue*) plinth, pedestal; (*de lampe*) base.

socquette [sɔkɛt] *nf* ankle sock.

sodium [sɔdjɔm] *nm* sodium.

sœur [sœR] *nf* sister; (*religieuse*) nun, sister; ~ **Élisabeth** (*REL*) Sister Elizabeth.

soi [swa] *pronom* oneself; **cela va de** ~ that ou it goes without saying, it stands to reason; ~**-disant** *a inv* so-called // *ad* supposedly.

soie [swa] *nf* silk; (*de porc, sanglier: poil*) bristle; ~**rie** *nf* (*industrie*) silk trade; (*tissu*) silk.

soif [swaf] *nf* thirst; (*fig*): ~ **de** thirst ou craving for; **avoir** ~ to be thirsty; **donner** ~ **à qn** to make sb thirsty.

soigné, e [swaɲe] *a* (*tenue*) well-groomed, neat; (*travail*) careful, meticulous; (*fam*) whopping; stiff.

soigner [swaɲe] *vt* (*malade, maladie: suj: docteur*) to treat; (*suj: infirmière, mère*) to nurse, look after; (*blessé*) to tend; (*travail, détails*) to take care over; (*jardin, chevelure, invités*) to look after; **soigneur** *nm* (*CYCLISME, FOOTBALL*) trainer; (*BOXE*) second.

soigneusement [swaɲøzmɑ̃] *ad* carefully.

soigneux, euse [swaɲø, -øz] *a* (*propre*) tidy, neat; (*méticuleux*) painstaking, careful; ~ **de** careful with.

soi-même [swamɛm] *pronom* oneself.

soin [swɛ̃] *nm* (*application*) care; (*propreté, ordre*) tidiness, neatness; (*responsabilité*): **le** ~ **de qch** the care of sth; ~**s** *nmpl* (*à un malade, blessé*) treatment *sg*, medical attention *sg*; (*attentions, prévenance*) care and attention *sg*; (*hygiène*) care *sg*; ~**s de la chevelure/de beauté** hair-/beauty care; **les** ~**s du ménage** the care of the home; **avoir** ou **prendre** ~ **de** to take care of, look after; **avoir** ou **prendre** ~ **de faire** to take care to do; **sans** ~ *a* careless; untidy; **les premiers** ~**s** first aid *sg*; **aux bons** ~**s de** c/o, care of.

soir [swaR] *nm, ad* evening; **ce** ~ this evening, tonight; **demain** ~ tomorrow evening, tomorrow night.

soirée [swaRe] *nf* evening; (*réception*) party; (*film, pièce*) to give an evening performance of.

soit [swa] *vb voir* **être**: ~ **un triangle ABC** let ABC be a triangle // *cj* (*à savoir*) namely, to wit; (*ou*): ~ ... ~ ... either ... or // *ad* so be it; very well; ~ **que** ... ~ **que** ou **que** whether ... or whether.

soixantaine [swasɑ̃tɛn] *nf:* **une** ~ (**de**) sixty or so, about sixty.

soixante [swasɑ̃t] *num* sixty.

soja [sɔʒa] *nm* soya; (*graines*) soya beans *pl*; **germes de** ~ beansprouts.

sol [sɔl] *nm* ground; (*de logement*) floor; (*revêtement*) flooring *q*; (*territoire, AGR, GÉO*) soil; (*MUS*) G; (*en chantant la gamme*) so(h).

solaire [sɔlɛR] *a* solar, sun *cpd*.

solarium [sɔlaRjɔm] *nm* solarium.

soldat [sɔlda] *nm* soldier; **S**— **inconnu** Unknown Warrior ou Soldier; ~ **de plomb** tin ou toy soldier.

solde [sɔld(ə)] *nf* pay // *nm* (*COMM*) balance; ~**s** *nmpl* ou *nfpl* (*COMM*) sale goods; sales; **à la** ~ **de qn** (*péj*) in sb's

pay; ~ **à payer** balance outstanding; **en ~ at** sale price; **aux ~s** at the sales.
solder [sɔlde] vt (compte) to settle; (marchandise) to sell at sale price, sell off; **se ~ par** (fig) to end in; **article soldé (à) 10 F** item reduced to 10 F.
sole [sɔl] nf sole inv.
soleil [sɔlɛj] nm sun; (lumière) sun(light); (temps ensoleillé) sun(shine); (feu d'artifice) Catherine wheel; (acrobatie) grand circle; (BOT) sunflower; **il y a** ou **il fait du ~** it's sunny; **au ~** in the sun; **le ~ de minuit** the midnight sun.
solennel, le [sɔlanɛl] a solemn; ceremonial; **solenniser** vt to solemnize; **solennité** nf (d'une fête) solemnity; (fête) grand occasion.
solfège [sɔlfɛʒ] nm rudiments pl of music.
soli [sɔli] pl de **solo.**
solidaire [sɔlidɛR] a (personnes) who stand together, who show solidarity; (pièces mécaniques) interdependent; **être ~ de** (collègues) to stand by; (mécanisme) to be bound up with, be dependent on; **se solidariser avec** to show solidarity with; **solidarité** nf solidarity; interdependence; **par solidarité (avec)** (cesser le travail etc) in sympathy (with).
solide [sɔlid] a solid; (mur, maison, meuble) solid, sturdy; (connaissances, argument) sound; (personne, estomac) robust, sturdy // nm solid; **solidifier** vt, **se solidifier** vi to solidify; **solidité** nf solidity; sturdiness.
soliloque [sɔlilɔk] nm soliloquy.
soliste [sɔlist(ə)] nm/f soloist.
solitaire [sɔlitɛR] a (sans compagnie) solitary, lonely; (isolé) solitary, isolated, lone; (désert) lonely // nm/f recluse; loner // nm (diamant, jeu) solitaire.
solitude [sɔlityd] nf loneliness; (paix) solitude.
solive [sɔliv] nf joist.
sollicitations [sɔlisitɑsjɔ̃] nfpl entreaties, appeals; enticements; promptings.
solliciter [sɔlisite] vt (personne) to appeal to; (emploi, faveur) to seek; (moteur) to prompt; (suj: occupations, attractions etc): **~ qn** to appeal to sb's curiosity etc; to entice sb; to make demands on sb's time; **~ qn de faire** to appeal to ou request sb to do.
sollicitude [sɔlisityd] nf concern.
solo [sɔlo] nm, pl **soli** [sɔli] (MUS) solo (pl s or soli).
solstice [sɔlstis] nm solstice.
soluble [sɔlybl(ə)] a soluble.
solution [sɔlysjɔ̃] nf solution; **~ de continuité** solution of continuity, gap; **~ de facilité** easy way out.
solvabilité [sɔlvabilite] nf solvency.
solvable [sɔlvabl(ə)] a solvent.
solvant [sɔlvɑ̃] nm solvent.
sombre [sɔ̃bR(ə)] a dark; (fig) sombre, gloomy.
sombrer [sɔ̃bRe] vi (bateau) to sink, go down; **~ dans** (misère, désespoir) to sink into.
sommaire [sɔmɛR] a (simple) basic; (expéditif) summary // nm summary.
sommation [sɔmɑsjɔ̃] nf (JUR) summons sg; (avant de faire feu) warning.

somme [sɔm] nf (MATH) sum; (fig) amount; (argent) sum, amount // nm: **faire un ~** to have a (short) nap; **faire la ~ de** to add up; **en ~** ad all in all; **~ toute** ad when all's said and done.
sommeil [sɔmɛj] nm sleep; **avoir ~** to be sleepy; **avoir le ~ léger** to be a light sleeper; **en ~** (fig) dormant; **sommeiller** vi to doze; (fig) to lie dormant.
sommelier [sɔmǝlje] nm wine waiter.
sommer [sɔme] vt: **~ qn de faire** to command ou order sb to do; (JUR) to summon sb to do.
sommes vb voir aussi **être.**
sommet [sɔmɛ] nm top; (d'une montagne) summit, top; (fig: de la perfection, gloire) height; (GÉOM: d'angle) vertex (pl vertices).
sommier [sɔmje] nm: **~ (à ressorts)** springing q; (interior-sprung) divan base; **~ métallique** mesh-springing; mesh-sprung divan base.
sommité [sɔmite] nf prominent person, leading light.
somnambule [sɔmnɑ̃byl] nm/f sleepwalker.
somnifère [sɔmnifɛR] nm sleeping drug (ou pill).
somnolent, e [sɔmnɔlɑ̃, -ɑ̃t] a sleepy, drowsy.
somnoler [sɔmnɔle] vi to doze.
somptuaire [sɔ̃ptɥɛR] a: **lois ~s** sumptuary laws; **dépenses ~s** extravagant expenditure sg.
somptueux, euse [sɔ̃ptɥø, -øz] a sumptuous; lavish.
son [sɔ̃], **sa** [sa], pl **ses** [se] dét (antécédent humain mâle) his; (: femelle) her; (: valeur indéfinie) one's, his/her; (: non humain) its; voir note sous **il.**
son [sɔ̃] nm sound; (résidu) bran.
sonate [sɔnat] nf sonata.
sondage [sɔ̃daʒ] nm (de terrain) boring, drilling; (mer, atmosphère) sounding; probe; (enquête) survey, sounding out of opinion; **~ (d'opinion)** (opinion) poll.
sonde [sɔ̃d] nf (NAVIG) lead ou sounding line; (MÉTÉOROLOGIE) sonde; (MÉD) probe; catheter; feeding tube; (TECH) borer, driller; (pour fouiller etc) probe; **~ à avalanche** pole (for probing snow and locating victims); **~ spatiale** probe.
sonder [sɔ̃de] vt (NAVIG) to sound; (atmosphère, plaie, bagages etc) to probe; (TECH) to bore, drill; (fig) to sound out; to probe.
songe [sɔ̃ʒ] nm dream.
songer [sɔ̃ʒe] vi to dream; **~ à** (rêver à) to muse over, think over; (penser à) to think of; (envisager) to contemplate, think of; to consider; **~ que** to consider that; to think that; **songerie** nf reverie; **songeur, euse** a pensive.
sonnailles [sɔnɑj] nfpl jingle of bells.
sonnant, e [sɔnɑ̃, -ɑ̃t] a: **en espèces ~es et trébuchantes** in coin of the realm; **à 8 heures ~es** on the stroke of 8.
sonné, e [sɔne] a (fam) cracked; **il est midi ~** it's gone twelve; **il a quarante ans bien ~s** he's well into his forties.
sonner [sɔne] vi to ring // vt (cloche) to ring; (glas, tocsin) to sound; (portier,

infirmière) to ring for ; (messe) to ring the bell for ; (fam: suj: choc, coup) to knock out ; ~ **du clairon** to sound the bugle ; ~ **faux** (instrument) to sound out of tune ; (rire) to ring false ; ~ **les heures** to strike the hours ; **minuit vient de** ~ midnight has just struck ; ~ **chez qn** to ring sb's doorbell, ring at sb's door.

sonnerie [sɔnʀi] nf (son) ringing ; (sonnette) bell ; (mécanisme d'horloge) striking mechanism ; ~ **d'alarme** alarm bell ; ~ **de clairon** bugle call.

sonnet [sɔnɛ] nm sonnet.

sonnette [sɔnɛt] nf bell ; ~ **d'alarme** alarm bell ; ~ **de nuit** night-bell.

sono [sɔno] nf abr de **sonorisation**.

sonore [sɔnɔʀ] a (voix) sonorous, ringing ; (salle, métal) resonant ; (ondes, film, signal) sound cpd ; (LING) voiced.

sonorisation [sɔnɔʀizasjɔ̃] nf (installations) public address system, P.A. system.

sonoriser [sɔnɔʀize] vt (film, spectacle) to add the sound track to ; (salle) to fit with a public address system.

sonorité [sɔnɔʀite] nf (de piano, violon) tone ; (de voix, mot) sonority ; (d'une salle) resonance ; acoustics pl.

sont vb voir **être**.

sophistiqué, e [sɔfistike] a sophisticated.

soporifique [sɔpɔʀifik] a soporific.

sorbet [sɔʀbɛ] nm water ice, sorbet.

sorcellerie [sɔʀsɛlʀi] nf witchcraft q, sorcery q.

sorcier, ière [sɔʀsje, -jɛʀ] nm/f sorcerer/witch ou sorceress.

sordide [sɔʀdid] a sordid ; squalid.

sornettes [sɔʀnɛt] nfpl twaddle sg.

sort [sɔʀ] nm (fortune, destinée) fate ; (condition, situation) lot ; (magique) curse, spell ; **le** ~ **en est jeté** the die is cast ; **tirer au** ~ to draw lots ; **tirer qch au** ~ to draw lots for sth.

sorte [sɔʀt(ə)] nf sort, kind ; **de la** ~ ad in that way ; **de** ~ **à** so as to, in order to ; **de (telle)** ~ **que, en** ~ **que** so that ; so much so that.

sortie [sɔʀti] nf (issue) way out, exit ; (MIL) sortie ; (fig: verbale) outburst ; sally ; (promenade) outing ; (le soir: au restaurant etc) night out ; (COMM: somme) : ~**s** items of expenditure ; outgoings sans sg ; **à sa** ~ **as he went out** ou left ; **à la** ~ **de l'école/l'usine** (moment) after school/work ; when school/the factory comes out ; (lieu) at the school/factory gates ; **à la** ~ **de ce nouveau modèle** when this new model comes out, when they bring out this new model ; ~ **de bain** (vêtement) bathrobe ; '~ **de camions'** 'vehicle exit', 'lorries turning' ; ~ **de secours** emergency exit.

sortilège [sɔʀtilɛʒ] nm (magic) spell.

sortir [sɔʀtiʀ] vi (gén) to come out ; (partir, se promener, aller au spectacle etc) to go out ; (numéro gagnant) to come up // vt (gén) to take out ; (produit, ouvrage, modèle) to bring out ; (boniments, incongruités) to come out with ; (fam: expulser) to throw out ; ~ **qch de** to take sth out of ; ~ **de** (gén) to leave ; (endroit) to go (ou come) out of, leave ; (rainure etc)

to come out of ; (cadre, compétence) to be outside ; (provenir de: famille etc) to come from ; **se** ~ **de** (affaire, situation) to get out of ; **s'en** ~ (malade) to pull through ; (d'une difficulté etc) to come through all right ; to get through, be able to manage.

S.O.S. sigle m mayday, SOS.

sosie [sɔzi] nm double.

sot, sotte [so, sɔt] a silly, foolish // nm/f fool ; **sottise** nf silliness, foolishness ; silly ou foolish thing (to do ou say).

sou [su] nm: **près de ses** ~**s** tight-fisted ; **sans le** ~ penniless ; **pas un** ~ **de bon sens** not a scrap ou an ounce of good sense.

soubassement [subasmɑ̃] nm base.

soubresaut [subʀəso] nm start ; jolt.

soubrette [subʀɛt] nf soubrette, maidservant.

souche [suʃ] nf (d'arbre) stump ; (de carnet) counterfoil, stub ; **de vieille** ~ of old stock.

souci [susi] nm (inquiétude) worry ; (préoccupation) concern ; (BOT) marigold ; **se faire du** ~ to worry ; **avoir (le)** ~ **de** to have concern for.

soucier [susje]: **se** ~ **de** vt to care about.

soucieux, euse [susjø, -øz] a concerned, worried ; ~ **de** concerned about ; **peu** ~ **de/que** caring little about/whether.

soucoupe [sukup] nf saucer ; ~ **volante** flying saucer.

soudain, e [sudɛ̃, -ɛn] a (douleur, mort) sudden // ad suddenly, all of a sudden ; **soudainement** ad suddenly ; **soudaineté** nf suddenness.

soude [sud] nf soda.

soudé, e [sude] a (fig: pétales, organes) joined (together).

souder [sude] vt (avec fil à souder) to solder ; (par soudure autogène) to weld ; (fig) to bind ou knit together ; to fuse (together).

soudoyer [sudwaje] vt (péj) to bribe, buy over.

soudure [sudyʀ] nf soldering ; welding ; (joint) soldered joint ; weld.

souffert, e [sufɛʀ, -ɛʀt(ə)] pp de **souffrir**.

souffle [sufl(ə)] nm (en expirant) breath ; (en soufflant) puff, blow ; (respiration) breathing ; (d'explosion, de ventilateur) blast ; (du vent) blowing ; (fig) inspiration ; **avoir du/manquer de** ~ to have a lot of/be short of breath ; **être à bout de** ~ to be out of breath ; **avoir le** ~ **court** to be short-winded ; **un** ~ **d'air** ou **de vent** a breath of air, a puff of wind.

soufflé, e [sufle] a (CULIN) soufflé ; (fam: ahuri, stupéfié) staggered // nm (CULIN) soufflé.

souffler [sufle] vi (gén) to blow ; (haleter) to puff (and blow) // vt (feu, bougie) to blow out ; (chasser: poussière etc) to blow away ; (TECH: verre) to blow ; (suj: explosion) to destroy (with its blast) ; (dire) : ~ **qch à qn** to whisper sth to sb ; (fam: voler) : ~ **qch à qn** to nick sth from sb ; ~ **son rôle à qn** to prompt sb ; **laisser** ~ **qn** (fig) to give sb a breather.

soufflet [suflɛ] nm (instrument) bellows pl ; (entre wagons) vestibule ; (gifle) slap (in the face).

souffleur, euse [suflœʀ, -øz] *nm/f* (*THÉÂTRE*) prompter.

souffrance [sufʀɑ̃s] *nf* suffering ; **en ~** (*marchandise*) awaiting delivery ; (*affaire*) pending.

souffrant, e [sufʀɑ̃, -ɑ̃t] *a* unwell.

souffre-douleur [sufʀədulœʀ] *nm inv* whipping boy, underdog.

souffreteux, euse [sufʀətø, -øz] *a* sickly.

souffrir [sufʀiʀ] *vi* to suffer ; to be in pain // *vt* to suffer, endure ; (*supporter*) to bear, stand ; (*admettre: exception etc*) to allow *ou* admit of ; **~ de** (*maladie, froid*) to suffer from ; **~ des dents** to have trouble with one's teeth ; **faire ~ qn** (*suj: personne*) to make sb suffer ; (: *dents, blessure etc*) to hurt sb.

soufre [sufʀ(ə)] *nm* sulphur.

souhait [swɛ] *nm* wish ; **tous nos ~s de** good wishes *ou* our best wishes for ; **riche etc à ~** as rich *etc* as one could wish ; **à vos ~s!** bless you!

souhaitable [swɛtabl(ə)] *a* desirable.

souhaiter [swete] *vt* to wish for ; **~ le bonjour à qn** to bid sb good day ; **~ la bonne année à qn** to wish sb a happy New Year.

souiller [suje] *vt* to dirty, soil ; (*fig*) to sully, tarnish ; **souillure** *nf* stain.

soûl, e [su, sul] *a* drunk // *nm*: **boire tout son ~** to drink one's fill.

soulagement [sulaʒmɑ̃] *nm* relief.

soulager [sulaʒe] *vt* to relieve.

soûler [sule] *vt*: **~ qn** to get sb drunk ; (*suj: boisson*) to make sb drunk ; (*fig*) to make sb's head spin *ou* reel ; **se ~** to get drunk ; **se ~ de** (*fig*) to intoxicate o.s. with ; **soûlerie** *nf* (*péj*) drunken binge.

soulèvement [sulɛvmɑ̃] *nm* uprising ; (*GÉO*) upthrust.

soulever [sulve] *vt* to lift ; (*vagues, poussière*) to send up ; (*peuple*) to stir up (to revolt) ; (*enthousiasme*) to arouse ; (*question, débat*) to raise ; **se ~** *vi* (*peuple*) to rise up ; (*personne couchée*) to lift o.s. up ; **cela me soulève le cœur** it makes me feel sick.

soulier [sulje] *nm* shoe ; **~s plats/à talons** flat/heeled shoes.

souligner [suliɲe] *vt* to underline ; (*fig*) to emphasize ; to stress.

soumettre [sumɛtʀ] *vt* (*pays*) to subject, subjugate ; (*rebelle*) to put down, subdue ; **~ qn/qch à** to subject sb/sth to ; **~ qch à qn** (*projet etc*) to submit sth to sb ; **se ~ (à)** (*se rendre, obéir*) to submit (to) ; **se ~ à** (*formalités etc*) to submit to ; (*régime etc*) to submit o.s. to.

soumis, e [sumi, -iz] *a* submissive ; **revenus ~ à l'impôt** taxable income.

soumission [sumisjɔ̃] *nf* (*voir se soumettre*) submission ; (*docilité*) submissiveness ; (*COMM*) tender.

soupape [supap] *nf* valve ; **~ de sûreté** safety valve.

soupçon [supsɔ̃] *nm* suspicion ; (*petite quantité*): **un ~ de** a hint *ou* touch of ; **soupçonner** *vt* to suspect ; **soupçonneux, euse** *a* suspicious.

soupe [sup] *nf* soup ; **~ au lait** *a inv* quick-tempered ; **~ à l'oignon/de poisson**

soupente [supɑ̃t] *nf* cupboard under the stairs.

souper [supe] *vi* to have supper // *nm* supper ; **avoir soupé de** (*fam*) to be sick and tired of.

soupeser [supəze] *vt* to weigh in one's hand(s), feel the weight of ; (*fig*) to weigh up.

soupière [supjɛʀ] *nf* (soup) tureen.

soupir [supiʀ] *nm* sigh ; (*MUS*) crotchet rest ; **rendre le dernier ~** to breathe one's last.

soupirail, aux [supiʀaj, -o] *nm* (small) basement window.

soupirant [supiʀɑ̃] *nm* (*péj*) suitor, wooer.

soupirer [supiʀe] *vi* to sigh ; **~ après qch** to yearn for sth.

souple [supl(ə)] *a* supple ; (*fig: règlement, caractère*) flexible ; (: *démarche, taille*) lithe, supple ; **souplesse** *nf* suppleness ; flexibility.

source [suʀs(ə)] *nf* (*point d'eau*) spring ; (*d'un cours d'eau, fig*) source ; **prendre sa ~ à/dans** (*suj: cours d'eau*) to have its source at/in ; **tenir qch de bonne ~/de ~ sûre** to have sth on good authority/from a reliable source ; **thermale/d'eau minérale** hot *ou* thermal/mineral spring.

sourcier [suʀsje] *nm* water diviner.

sourcil [suʀsij] *nm* (eye)brow ; **sourcilière** *af voir* arcade.

sourciller [suʀsije] *vi*: **sans ~** without turning a hair *ou* batting an eyelid.

sourcilleux, euse [suʀsijø, -øz] *a* pernickety.

sourd, e [suʀ, suʀd(ə)] *a* deaf ; (*bruit, voix*) muffled ; (*couleur*) muted ; (*douleur*) dull ; (*lutte*) silent, hidden ; (*LING*) voiceless // *nm/f* deaf person.

sourdait *etc vb voir* **sourdre.**

sourdine [suʀdin] *nf* (*MUS*) mute ; **en ~** *ad* softly, quietly ; **mettre une ~ à** (*fig*) to tone down.

sourd-muet, sourde-muette [suʀmyɛ, suʀdmyɛt] *a* deaf-and-dumb // *nm/f* deaf-mute.

sourdre [suʀdʀ(ə)] *vi* to rise.

souriant, e [suʀjɑ̃, -ɑ̃t] *a* cheerful.

souricière [suʀisjɛʀ] *nf* mousetrap ; (*fig*) trap.

sourire [suʀiʀ] *nm* smile // *vi* to smile ; **~ à qn** to smile at sb ; (*fig*) to appeal to sb ; to smile on sb ; **faire un ~ à qn** to give sb a smile ; **garder le ~** to keep smiling.

souris [suʀi] *nf* mouse (*pl* mice).

sournois, e [suʀnwa, -waz] *a* deceitful, underhand.

sous [su] *prép* (*gén*) under ; **~ la pluie/le soleil** in the rain/sunshine ; **~ terre** *a, ad* underground ; **~ peu** *ad* shortly, before long.

sous... [su, suz + *vowel*] *préfixe* sub- ; under... ; **~-catégorie** sub-category ; **~-alimenté/-équipé/-développé** under-nourished/equipped/developed.

sous-bois [subwa] *nm inv* undergrowth.

sous-chef [suʃɛf] *nm* deputy chief clerk.

souscription [suskripsjɔ̃] *nf* subscription; **offert en ~** available on subscription.

souscrire [suskrir]: **~ à** *vt* to subscribe to.

sous-directeur, trice [sudirɛktœr, -tris] *nm/f* assistant manager/ manageress, sub-manager/ manageress.

sous-emploi [suzɑ̃plwa] *nm* underemployment.

sous-entendre [suzɑ̃tɑ̃dr(ə)] *vt* to imply, infer; **sous-entendu, e** *a* implied; (*verbe, complément*) understood // *nm* innuendo, insinuation.

sous-estimer [suzɛstime] *vt* to underestimate.

sous-exposer [suzɛkspoze] *vt* to underexpose.

sous-fifre [sufifr] *nm* (*péj*) underling.

sous-jacent, e [suʒasɑ̃, -ɑ̃t] *a* underlying.

sous-lieutenant [suljøtnɑ̃] *nm* sublieutenant.

sous-locataire [sulɔkatɛr] *nm/f* subtenant.

sous-louer [sulwe] *vt* to sublet.

sous-main [sumɛ̃] *nm inv* desk blotter; **en ~** *ad* secretly.

sous-marin, e [sumarɛ̃, -in] *a* (*flore, volcan*) submarine; (*navigation, pêche, explosif*) underwater // *nm* submarine.

sous-officier [suzɔfisje] *nm* ≈ non-comissioned officer (N.C.O.).

sous-préfecture [suprefɛktyr] *nf* subprefecture.

sous-préfet [suprefɛ] *nm* sub-prefect.

sous-produit [suprɔdɥi] *nm* by-product; (*fig: péj*) pale imitation.

sous-secrétaire [susəkretɛr] *nm*: **~ d'État** Under-Secretary of State.

soussigné, e [susiɲe] *a*: **je ~** I the undersigned.

sous-sol [susɔl] *nm* basement; (*GÉO*) subsoil.

sous-titre [sutitr(ə)] *nm* subtitle; **sous-titré, e** *a* with subtitles.

soustraction [sustraksjɔ̃] *nf* subtraction.

soustraire [sustrɛr] *vt* to subtract, take away; (*dérober*): **~ qch à qn** to remove sth from sb; **~ qn à** (*danger*) to shield sb from; **se ~ à** (*autorité etc*) to elude, escape from.

sous-traitance [sutrɛtɑ̃s(ə)] *nf* subcontracting.

sous-verre [suvɛr] *nm inv* glass mount.

sous-vêtement [suvɛtmɑ̃] *nm* undergarment, item of underwear; **~s** *nmpl* underwear *sg*.

soutane [sutan] *nf* cassock, soutane.

soute [sut] *nf* hold; **~ à bagages** baggage hold.

soutenable [sutnabl(ə)] *a* (*opinion*) tenable, defensible.

soutenance [sutnɑ̃s] *nf*: **~ de thèse** ≈ viva voce (examination).

soutènement [sutɛnmɑ̃] *nm*: **mur de ~** retaining wall.

souteneur [sutnœr] *nm* procurer.

soutenir [sutnir] *vt* to support; (*assaut, choc*) to stand up to, withstand; (*intérêt, effort*) to keep up; (*assurer*): **~ que** to

maintain that; **se ~** (*dans l'eau etc*) to hold o.s. up; **~ la comparaison avec** to bear *ou* stand comparison with; **soutenu, e** *a* (*efforts*) sustained, unflagging; (*style*) elevated.

souterrain, e [sutɛrɛ̃, -ɛn] *a* underground // *nm* underground passage.

soutien [sutjɛ̃] *nm* support; **~ de famille** breadwinner.

soutien-gorge [sutjɛ̃gɔrʒ(ə)] *nm* bra.

soutirer [sutire] *vt*: **~ qch à qn** to squeeze *ou* get sth out of sb.

souvenance [suvnɑ̃s] *nf*: **avoir ~ de** to recollect.

souvenir [suvnir] *nm* (*réminiscence*) memory; (*cadeau*) souvenir, keepsake; (*de voyage*) souvenir // *vb*: **se ~ de** *vt* to remember; **se ~ que** to remember that; **en ~ de** in memory *ou* remembrance of.

souvent [suvɑ̃] *ad* often; **peu ~** seldom, infrequently.

souverain, e [suvrɛ̃, -ɛn] *a* sovereign; (*fig: mépris*) supreme // *nm/f* sovereign, monarch; **souveraineté** *nf* sovereignty.

soviétique [sovjetik] *a* Soviet // *nm/f*: **S~** Soviet citizen.

soyeux, euse [swajø, øz] *a* silky.

soyons *etc vb voir* **être**.

S.P.A. *sigle f* (= *société protectrice des animaux*) ≈ R.S.P.C.A.

spacieux, euse [spasjø, -øz] *a* spacious; roomy.

spaghettis [spageti] *nmpl* spaghetti *sg*.

sparadrap [sparadra] *nm* adhesive *ou* sticking plaster.

spartiate [sparsjat] *a* Spartan; **~s** *nfpl* (*sandales*) Roman sandals.

spasme [spazm(ə)] *nm* spasm.

spasmodique [spazmɔdik] *a* spasmodic.

spatial, e, aux [spasjal, -o] *a* (*AVIAT*) space *cpd*; (*PSYCH*) spatial.

spatule [spatyl] *nf* (*ustensile*) slice; spatula; (*bout*) tip.

speaker, ine [spikœr, -krin] *nm/f* announcer.

spécial, e, aux [spesjal, -o] *a* special; (*bizarre*) peculiar; **~ement** *ad* especially, particularly; (*tout exprès*) specially.

spécialisé, e [spesjalize] *a* specialised.

spécialiser [spesjalize] *vt*: **se ~** to specialize.

spécialiste [spesjalist(ə)] *nm/f* specialist.

spécialité [spesjalite] *nf* speciality; (*SCOL*) special field; **~ pharmaceutique** patent medicine.

spécieux, euse [spesjø, -øz] *a* specious.

spécification [spesifikasjɔ̃] *nf* specification.

spécifier [spesifje] *vt* to specify, state.

spécifique [spesifik] *a* specific.

spécimen [spesimɛn] *nm* specimen; (*revue etc*) specimen *ou* sample copy.

spectacle [spɛktakl(ə)] *nm* (*tableau, scène*) sight; (*représentation*) show; (*industrie*) show business, entertainment; **se donner en ~** (*péj*) to make a spectacle *ou* an exhibition of o.s.; **spectaculaire** *a* spectacular.

spectateur, trice [spɛktatœr, -tris] *nm/f* (*CINÉMA etc*) member of the audience;

(*SPORT*) spectator; (*d'un évènement*) onlooker, witness.

spectre [spɛktʀ(ə)] *nm* (*fantôme, fig*) spectre; (*PHYSIQUE*) spectrum (*pl* a); ~ **solaire** solar spectrum.

spéculateur, trice [spekylatœʀ, -tʀis] *nm/f* speculator.

spéculation [spekylɑsjɔ̃] *nf* speculation.

spéculer [spekyle] *vi* to speculate; ~ **sur** (*COMM*) to speculate in; (*réfléchir*) to speculate on; (*tabler sur*) to bank ou rely on.

spéléologie [speleɔlɔʒi] *nf* (*étude*) speleology; (*activité*) potholing; **spéléologue** *nm/f* speleologist; potholer.

spermatozoïde [spɛʀmatozɔid] *nm* sperm, spermatozoon (*pl* zoa).

sperme [spɛʀm(ə)] *nm* semen, sperm.

sphère [sfɛʀ] *nf* sphere; **sphérique** *a* spherical.

sphincter [sfɛ̃ktɛʀ] *nm* sphincter.

spiral, aux [spiʀal, -o] *nm* hairspring.

spirale [spiʀal] *nf* spiral; **en ~** in a spiral.

spire [spiʀ] *nm* (single) turn; whorl.

spiritisme [spiʀitism(ə)] *nm* spiritualism, spiritism.

spirituel, le [spiʀitɥɛl] *a* spiritual; (*fin, piquant*) witty; **musique ~le** sacred music; **concert ~** concert of sacred music.

spiritueux [spiʀitɥø] *nm* spirit.

splendeur [splɑ̃dœʀ] *nf* splendour.

splendide [splɑ̃did] *a* splendid; magnificent.

spolier [spɔlje] *vt*: ~ **qn (de)** to despoil sb (of).

spongieux, euse [spɔ̃ʒjø, -øz] *a* spongy.

spontané, e [spɔ̃tane] *a* spontaneous.

sporadique [spɔʀadik] *a* sporadic.

sport [spɔʀ] *nm* sport // *a inv* (*vêtement*) casual; **faire du ~** to do sport; ~**s d'équipe/d'hiver** team/winter sports; **sportif, ive** *a* (*journal, association, épreuve*) sports *cpd*; (*allure, démarche*) athletic; (*attitude, esprit*) sporting.

spot [spɔt] *nm* (*lampe*) spot(light); (*annonce*): ~ (**publicitaire**) commercial (break).

sprint [spʀint] *nm* sprint.

square [skwaʀ] *nm* public garden(s).

squelette [skəlɛt] *nm* skeleton; **squelettique** *a* scrawny; (*fig*) skimpy.

stabilisateur, trice [stabilizatœʀ, -tʀis] *a* stabilizing // *nm* stabilizer; anti-roll device; tailplane.

stabiliser [stabilize] *vt* to stabilize; (*terrain*) to consolidate.

stabilité [stabilite] *nf* stability.

stable [stabl(ə)] *a* stable, steady.

stade [stad] *nm* (*SPORT*) stadium; (*phase, niveau*) stage.

stage [staʒ] *nm* training period; training course; (*d'avocat stagiaire*) articles *pl*; **stagiaire** *nm/f, a* trainee.

stagnant, e [stagnɑ̃, -ɑ̃t] *a* stagnant.

stalactite [stalaktit] *nf* stalactite.

stalagmite [stalagmit] *nf* stalagmite.

stalle [stal] *nf* stall, box.

stand [stɑ̃d] *nm* (*d'exposition*) stand; (*de foire*) stall; ~ **de tir** (*MIL*) firing range;

(*à la foire, SPORT*) shooting range; ~ **de ravitaillement** pit.

standard [stɑ̃daʀ] *a inv* standard // *nm* switchboard; **standardiser** *vt* to standardize; **standardiste** *nm/f* switchboard operator.

standing [stɑ̃diŋ] *nm* standing; **immeuble de grand ~** block of luxury flats.

star [staʀ] *nf* star.

starter [staʀtɛʀ] *nm* (*AUTO*) choke.

station [stɑsjɔ̃] *nf* station; (*de bus*) stop; (*de villégiature*) resort; (*posture*): **la ~ debout** standing, an upright posture; ~ **de ski** ski resort; ~ **de taxis** taxi rank.

stationnaire [stɑsjɔnɛʀ] *a* stationary.

stationnement [stɑsjɔnmɑ̃] *nm* parking; **zone de ~ interdit** no parking area; ~ **alterné** parking on alternate sides.

stationner [stɑsjɔne] *vi* to park.

station-service [stɑsjɔ̃sɛʀvis] *nf* service station.

statique [statik] *a* static.

statisticien, ne [statistisjɛ̃, -jɛn] *nm/f* statistician.

statistique [statistik] *nf* (*science*) statistics *sg*; (*rapport, étude*) statistic // *a* statistical; ~**s** (*données*) statistics *pl*.

statue [staty] *nf* statue.

statuer [statɥe] *vi*: ~ **sur** to rule on, give a ruling on.

statuette [statɥɛt] *nf* statuette.

statu quo [statykwo] *nm* status quo.

stature [statyʀ] *nf* stature.

statut [staty] *nm* status; ~**s** *nmpl* (*JUR, ADMIN*) statutes; **statutaire** *a* statutory.

Sté *abr de* **société**.

steak [stɛk] *nm* steak.

stèle [stɛl] *nf* stela, stele.

stellaire [stelɛʀ] *a* stellar.

stencil [stɛnsil] *nm* stencil.

sténo... [steno] *préfixe*: ~(**dactylo**) *nf* shorthand typist; ~(**graphie**) *nf* shorthand; ~**graphier** *vt* to take down in shorthand.

stentor [stɑ̃tɔʀ] *nm*: **voix de ~** stentorian voice.

steppe [stɛp] *nf* steppe.

stère [stɛʀ] *nm* stere.

stéréo(phonie) [steʀeo(fɔni)] *nf* stereo(phony); **stéréo(phonique)** *a* stereo(phonic).

stéréotype [steʀeotip] *nm* stereotype; **stéréotypé, e** *a* stereotyped.

stérile [steʀil] *a* sterile; (*terre*) barren; (*fig*) fruitless, futile.

stérilet [steʀilɛ] *nm* coil, loop.

stériliser [steʀilize] *vt* to sterilize.

stérilité [steʀilite] *nf* sterility.

sternum [stɛʀnɔm] *nm* breastbone, sternum.

stéthoscope [stetɔskɔp] *nm* stethoscope.

stigmates [stigmat] *nmpl* scars, marks; (*REL*) stigmata *pl*.

stigmatiser [stigmatize] *vt* to denounce, stigmatize.

stimulant, e [stimylɑ̃, -ɑ̃t] *a* stimulating // *nm* (*MÉD*) stimulant; (*fig*) stimulus (*pl* i), incentive.

stimulation [stimylɑsjɔ̃] *nf* stimulation.
stimuler [stimyle] *vt* to stimulate.
stimulus, i [stimylys, -i] *nm* stimulus (*pl* i).
stipulation [stipylɑsjɔ̃] *nf* stipulation.
stipuler [stipyle] *vt* to stipulate, specify.
stock [stɔk] *nm* stock; ~ **d'or** (*FINANCE*) gold reserves *pl*; ~**er** *vt* to stock; ~**iste** *nm* stockist.
stoïque [stɔik] *a* stoic, stoical.
stomacal, e, aux [stɔmakal, -o] *a* gastric, stomach *cpd*.
stop [stɔp] *nm* (*AUTO*: écriteau) stop sign; (: signal) brake-light; (dans un télégramme) stop // *excl* stop.
stoppage [stɔpaʒ] *nm* invisible mending.
stopper [stɔpe] *vt* to stop, halt; (*COUTURE*) to mend // *vi* to stop, halt.
store [stɔʀ] *nm* blind; (de magasin) shade, awning.
strabisme [stʀabism(ə)] *nm* squinting.
strangulation [stʀɑ̃gylɑsjɔ̃] *nf* strangulation.
strapontin [stʀapɔ̃tɛ̃] *nm* jump *ou* foldaway seat.
strass [stʀas] *nm* paste, strass.
stratagème [stʀataʒɛm] *nm* stratagem.
stratège [stʀatɛʒ] *nm* strategist.
stratégie [stʀateʒi] *nf* strategy; **stratégique** *a* strategic.
stratifié, e [stʀatifje] *a* (*GÉO*) stratified; (*TECH*) laminated.
stratosphère [stʀatɔsfɛʀ] *nf* stratosphere.
strict, e [stʀikt(ə)] *a* strict; (tenue, décor) severe, plain; **son droit le plus** ~ his most basic right; **dans la plus** ~**e intimité** strictly in private; **le** ~ **nécessaire/minimum** the bare essentials/minimum.
strident, e [stʀidɑ̃, -ɑ̃t] *a* shrill, strident.
stridulations [stʀidylɑsjɔ̃] *nfpl* stridulations, chirrings.
strie [stʀi] *nf* streak; (*ANAT*, *GÉO*) stria (*pl* ae).
strier [stʀije] *vt* to streak; to striate.
strip-tease [stʀiptiz] *nm* striptease; **strip-teaseuse** *nf* stripper, striptease artist.
striures [stʀijyʀ] *nfpl* streaking *sg*.
strophe [stʀɔf] *nf* verse, stanza.
structure [stʀyktyʀ] *nf* structure; ~**s d'accueil/touristiques** reception/tourist facilities; **structurer** *vt* to structure.
stuc [styk] *nm* stucco.
studieux, euse [stydjø, -øz] *a* studious; devoted to study.
studio [stydjo] *nm* (logement) (one-roomed) flatlet; (d'artiste, *TV* etc) studio (*pl* s).
stupéfaction [stypefaksjɔ̃] *nf* stupefaction, amazement.
stupéfait, e [stypefɛ, -ɛt] *a* amazed.
stupéfiant, e [stypefjɑ̃, -ɑ̃t] *a* stunning, astounding // *nm* (*MÉD*) drug, narcotic.
stupéfier [stypefje] *vt* to stupefy; (étonner) to stun, astonish.
stupeur [stypœʀ] *nf* (inertie, insensibilité) stupor; (étonnement) astonishment, amazement.

stupide [stypid] *a* stupid; **stupidité** *nf* stupidity; stupid thing (to do *ou* say).
style [stil] *nm* style; **meuble de** ~ period piece of furniture.
stylé, e [stile] *a* well-trained.
stylet [stile] *nm* stiletto, stylet.
stylisé, e [stilize] *a* stylized.
styliste [stilist(ə)] *nm/f* designer; stylist.
stylistique [stilistik] *nf* stylistics *sg*.
stylo [stilo] *nm*: ~ **(à encre)** (fountain) pen; ~ **(à) bille** ball-point pen; ~**-feutre** *nm* felt-tip pen.
su, e [sy] *pp* **de savoir** // *nm*: **au** ~ **de** with the knowledge of.
suaire [sɥɛʀ] *nm* shroud.
suave [sɥav] *a* sweet; suave, smooth; mellow.
subalterne [sybaltɛʀn(ə)] *a* (employé, officier) junior; (rôle) subordinate, subsidiary // *nm/f* subordinate, inferior.
subconscient [sypkɔ̃sjɑ̃] *nm* subconscious.
subdiviser [sybdivize] *vt* to subdivide; **subdivision** *nf* subdivision.
subir [sybiʀ] *vt* (affront, dégâts, mauvais traitements) to suffer; (influence, charme) to be under, be subjected to; (traitement, opération, châtiment) to undergo.
subit, e [sybi, -it] *a* sudden; **subitement** *ad* suddenly, all of a sudden.
subjectif, ive [sybʒɛktif, -iv] *a* subjective.
subjonctif [sybʒɔ̃ktif] *nm* subjunctive.
subjuguer [sybʒyge] *vt* to subjugate.
sublime [syblim] *a* sublime.
sublimer [syblime] *vt* to sublimate.
submergé, e [sybmɛʀʒe] *a* submerged; (fig): ~ **de** snowed under with; overwhelmed with.
submerger [sybmɛʀʒe] *vt* to submerge; (suj: foule) to engulf; (fig) to overwhelm.
submersible [sybmɛʀsibl(ə)] *nm* submarine.
subordination [sybɔʀdinɑsjɔ̃] *nf* subordination.
subordonné, e [sybɔʀdɔne] *a, nm/f* subordinate; ~ **à** subordinate to; subject to, depending on.
subordonner [sybɔʀdɔne] *vt*: ~ **qn/qch à** to subordinate sb/sth to.
subornation [sybɔʀnɑsjɔ̃] *nf* bribing.
subrepticement [sybʀɛptismɑ̃] *ad* surreptitiously.
subside [sypsid] *nm* grant.
subsidiaire [sypsidjɛʀ] *a*: **question** ~ deciding question.
subsistance [sybzistɑ̃s] *nf* subsistence; **pourvoir à la** ~ **de qn** to keep sb, provide for sb's subsistence *ou* keep.
subsister [sybziste] *vi* (rester) to remain, subsist; (vivre) to live; (survivre) to live on.
substance [sypstɑ̃s] *nf* substance.
substantiel, le [sypstɑ̃sjɛl] *a* substantial.
substantif [sypstɑ̃tif] *nm* noun, substantive; **substantiver** *vt* to nominalize.
substituer [sypstitɥe] *vt*: ~ **qn/qch à** to substitute sb/sth for; **se** ~ **à qn** (représenter) to substitute for sb; (évincer) to substitute o.s. for sb.

substitut [sypstity] nm (JUR) deputy public prosecutor ; (succédané) substitute.

substitution [sypstitysjɔ̃] nf substitution.

subterfuge [sypterfyʒ] nm subterfuge.

subtil, e [syptil] a subtle.

subtiliser [syptilize] vt : ~ **qch (à qn)** to spirit sth away (from sb).

subtilité [syptilite] nf subtlety.

subvenir [sybvəniʀ] : ~ **à** vt to meet.

subvention [sybvɑ̃sjɔ̃] nf subsidy, grant ; **subventionner** vt to subsidize.

subversif, ive [sybvɛʀsif, -iv] a subversive ; **subversion** nf subversion.

suc [syk] nm (BOT) sap ; (de viande, fruit) juice ; ~s **gastriques** gastric ou stomach juices.

succédané [syksedane] nm substitute.

succéder [syksede] : ~ **à** vt (directeur, roi etc) to succeed ; (venir après: dans une série) to follow, succeed ; **se** ~ vi (accidents, années) to follow one another.

succès [syksɛ] nm success ; **avoir du** ~ to be a success, be successful ; ~ **de librairie** bestseller ; ~ (féminins) conquests.

successeur [syksesœʀ] nm successor.

successif, ive [syksesif, -iv] a successive.

succession [syksesjɔ̃] nf (série, POL) succession ; (JUR: patrimoine) estate, inheritance ; **prendre la** ~ **de** (directeur) to succeed, take over from ; (entreprise) to take over.

succinct, e [syksɛ̃, -ɛ̃t] a succinct.

succion [syksjɔ̃] nf: **bruit de** ~ sucking noise.

succomber [sykɔ̃be] vi to die, succumb ; (fig): ~ **à** to give way to, succumb to.

succulent, e [sykylɑ̃, -ɑ̃t] a succulent.

succursale [sykyʀsal] nf branch ; **magasin à** ~s **multiples** chain ou multiple store.

sucer [syse] vt to suck.

sucette [sysɛt] nf (bonbon) lollipop.

sucre [sykʀ(ə)] nm (substance) sugar ; (morceau) lump of sugar, sugar lump ou cube ; ~ **de canne/betterave** cane/beet sugar ; ~ **en morceaux/cristallisé/en poudre** lump/coarse-grained/ granulated sugar ; ~ **d'orge** barley sugar ; **sucré, e** a (produit alimentaire) sweetened ; (au goût) sweet ; (péj) sugary, honeyed ; **sucrer** vt (thé, café) to sweeten, put sugar in ; **sucrer qn** to put sugar in sb's tea (ou coffee etc) ; **se sucrer** to help o.s. to sugar, have some sugar ; (fam) to line one's pocket(s) ; **sucrerie** nf (usine) sugar refinery ; **sucreries** nfpl (bonbons) sweets, sweet things ; **sucrier, ière** a sugar cpd ; sugar-producing // nm (fabricant) sugar producer ; (récipient) sugar bowl ou basin.

sud [syd] nm: **le** ~ **the** south // a inv south ; (côte) south, southern ; **au** ~ (situation) in the south ; (direction) to the south ; **au** ~ **de** (to the) south of ; ~-**africain, e** a, nm/f South African ; ~-**américain, e** a, nm/f South American.

sudation [sydasjɔ̃] nf sweating, sudation.

sud-est [sydɛst] nm, a inv south-east.

sud-ouest [sydwɛst] nm, a inv south-west.

Suède [sɥɛd] nf: **la** ~ Sweden ; **suédois,**

e a Swedish // nm/f: **Suédois, e** Swede // nm (langue) Swedish.

suer [sɥe] vi to sweat ; (suinter) to ooze // vt (fig) to exude ; ~ **à grosses gouttes** to sweat profusely.

sueur [sɥœʀ] nf sweat ; **en** ~ sweating, in a sweat ; **avoir des** ~s **froides** to be in a cold sweat.

suffire [syfiʀ] vi (être assez): ~ (**à qn/pour qch/pour faire**) to be enough ou sufficient (for sb/for sth/to do) ; (satisfaire): **cela lui suffit** he's content with this, this is enough for him ; **se** ~ to be self-sufficient ; **cela suffit pour les irriter/qu'ils se fâchent** it's enough to annoy them/for them to get angry ; **il suffit d'une négligence/qu'on oublie pour que ...** it only takes one act of carelessness/one only needs to forget for

suffisamment [syfizamɑ̃] ad sufficiently, enough ; ~ **de** sufficient, enough.

suffisance [syfizɑ̃s] nf (vanité) self-importance, bumptiousness ; (quantité): **en** ~ in plenty.

suffisant, e [syfizɑ̃, -ɑ̃t] a (temps, ressources) sufficient ; (résultats) satisfactory ; (vaniteux) self-important, bumptious.

suffixe [syfiks(ə)] nm suffix.

suffocation [syfɔkasjɔ̃] nf suffocation.

suffoquer [syfɔke] vt to choke, suffocate ; (stupéfier) to stagger, astound // vi to choke, suffocate.

suffrage [syfʀaʒ] nm (POL: voix) vote ; (: méthode): ~ **indirect** indirect suffrage ; (du public etc) approval q ; ~s **exprimés** valid votes.

suggérer [syɡʒeʀe] vt to suggest ; **suggestif, ive** a suggestive ; **suggestion** nf suggestion.

suicidaire [sɥisidɛʀ] a suicidal.

suicide [sɥisid] nm suicide.

suicidé, e [sɥiside] nm/f suicide.

suicider [sɥiside] : **se** ~ vi to commit suicide.

suie [sɥi] nf soot.

suif [sɥif] nm tallow.

suinter [sɥɛ̃te] vi to ooze.

suis vb voir **être**.

suisse [sɥis] a, nm/f Swiss // nm (bedeau) ≈ verger // nf: **la S**— Switzerland ; **la S**—**romande/allemande** French-speaking/ German-speaking Switzerland ~ **romand, e** a, nm/f Swiss French ; ~-**alle-mand, e** a, nm/f Swiss German ; **Suisse-se** nf Swiss (woman ou girl).

suite [sɥit] nf (continuation: d'énumération etc) rest, remainder ; (: de feuilleton) continuation ; (: second film etc sur le même thème) sequel ; (série: de maisons, rooms) suite ; **une** ~ **de** a series ou succession of ; (MATH) series sg ; (conséquence) result ; (ordre, liaison logique) coherence ; (appartement, MUS) suite ; (escorte) retinue, suite ; ~s nfpl (d'une maladie etc) effects ; **prendre la** ~ **de** (directeur etc) to succeed, take over from ; **donner** ~ **à** (requête, projet) to follow up ; **faire** ~ **à** to follow ; (faisant) ~ **à votre lettre** du further to your letter of the ; **de** ~ ad (d'affilée) in succession ; (immédiatement) at once ; **par la** ~

afterwards, subsequently ; **à la** ~ *ad* one after the other ; **à la** ~ **de** (*derrière*) behind ; (*en conséquence de*) following ; **par** ~ **de** owing to, as a result of ; **avoir de la** ~ **dans les idées** to show great singleness of purpose ; **attendre la** ~ to wait and see what comes next.

suivant, e [sɥivɑ̃, -ɑ̃t] *a* next, following ; (*ci-après*): **l'exercice** ~ the following exercise // *prép* (*selon*) according to ; **au** ~! next!

suiveur [sɥivœR] *nm* (*CYCLISME*) (official) follower.

suivi, e [sɥivi] *a* (*régulier*) regular ; (*COMM: article*) in general production ; (*cohérent*) consistent ; coherent ; **très/peu** ~ (*cours*) well-/poorly-attended ; (*feuilleton etc*) widely/not widely followed.

suivre [sɥivR(ə)] *vt* (*gén*) to follow ; (*SCOL: cours*) to attend ; (: *leçon*) to follow, attend to ; (: *programme*) to keep up with ; (*COMM: article*) to continue to stock // *vi* to follow ; (*élève*) to attend, pay attention ; to keep up, follow ; **se** ~ (*accidents etc*) to follow one after the other ; (*raisonnement*) to be coherent ; **faire** ~ (*lettre*) to forward ; ~ **son cours** (*enquête etc*) to run ou take its course ; '**à** ~' 'to be continued'.

sujet, te [syʒɛ, -ɛt] *a*: **être** ~ **à** (*vertige etc*) to be liable *ou* subject to // *nm/f* (*d'un souverain*) subject // *nm* subject ; (*raison: d'une dispute etc*) cause ; **avoir** ~ **de se plaindre** to have cause for complaint ; **au** ~ **de** *prép* about ; ~ **à caution** *a* questionable ; ~ **de conversation** topic *ou* subject of conversation ; ~ **d'examen** (*SCOL*) examination question ; examination paper ; ~ **d'expérience** (*BIO etc*) experimental subject.

sujétion [syʒesjɔ̃] *nf* subjection ; (*fig*) constraint.

sulfater [sylfate] *vt* to spray with copper sulphate.

sulfureux, euse [sylfyRø, -øz] *a* sulphurous.

sulfurique [sylfyRik] *a*: **acide** ~ sulphuric acid.

summum [sɔmɔm] *nm*: **le** ~ **de** the height of.

superbe [sypɛRb(ə)] *a* magnificent, superb.

super(carburant) [sypɛR(kaRbyRɑ̃)] *nm* high-octane petrol.

supercherie [sypɛRʃəRi] *nf* trick.

superfétatoire [sypɛRfetatwaR] *a* superfluous.

superficie [sypɛRfisi] *nf* (*surface*) area ; (*fig*) surface.

superficiel, le [sypɛRfisjɛl] *a* superficial.

superflu, e [sypɛRfly] *a* superfluous.

supérieur, e [sypeRjœR] *a* (*lèvre, étages, classes*) upper ; (*plus élevé: température, niveau*): ~ **(à)** higher (than) ; (*meilleur: qualité, produit*): ~ **(à)** superior (to) ; (*excellent, hautain*) superior // *nm, nf* superior ; **Mère** ~**e** Mother Superior ; **à l'étage** ~ on the next floor up ; ~ **en nombre** superior in number ; **supériorité** *nf* superiority.

superlatif [sypɛRlatif] *nm* superlative.

supermarché [sypɛRmaRʃe] *nm* supermarket.

superposer [sypɛRpoze] *vt* to superpose ; (*faire chevaucher*) to superimpose ; **se** ~ *vi* (*images, souvenirs*) to be superimposed ; **lits superposés** bunk beds.

superpréfet [sypɛRpRefɛ] *nm* prefect in charge of a region.

superproduction [sypɛRpRodyksjɔ̃] *nf* (*film*) spectacular.

superpuissance [sypɛRpɥisɑ̃s] *nf* superpower.

supersonique [sypɛRsɔnik] *a* supersonic.

superstitieux, euse [sypɛRstisjø, -øz] *a* superstitious.

superstition [sypɛRstisjɔ̃] *nf* superstition.

superstructure [sypɛRstRyktyR] *nf* superstructure.

superviser [sypɛRvize] *vt* to supervise.

supplanter [syplɑ̃te] *vt* to supplant.

suppléance [sypleɑ̃s] *nf* supply post.

suppléant, e [sypleɑ̃, -ɑ̃t] *a* (*juge, fonctionnaire*) deputy *cpd* ; (*professeur*) supply *cpd* // *nm/f* deputy ; supply teacher ; **médecin** ~ locum.

suppléer [syplee] *vt* (*ajouter: mot manquant etc*) to supply, provide ; (*compenser: lacune*) to fill in ; (: *défaut*) to make up for ; (*remplacer: professeur*) to stand in for ; (: *juge*) to deputize for ; ~ **à** *vt* to make up for ; to substitute for.

supplément [syplemɑ̃] *nm* supplement ; **un** ~ **de travail** extra *ou* additional work ; **un** ~ **de frites** etc an extra portion of chips etc ; **un** ~ **de 100 F** a supplement of 100 F, an extra *ou* additional 100 F ; **ceci est en** ~ (*au menu etc*) this is extra, there is an extra charge for this ; **supplémentaire** *a* additional, further ; (*train, bus*) relief *cpd*, extra.

supplétif, ive [sypletif, -iv] *a* (*MIL*) auxiliary.

supplication [syplikɑsjɔ̃] *nf* (*REL*) supplication ; ~**s** *nfpl* (*adjurations*) pleas, entreaties.

supplice [syplis] *nm* (*peine corporelle*) torture *q* ; form of torture ; (*douleur physique, morale*) torture, agony.

supplier [syplije] *vt* to implore, beseech.

supplique [syplik] *nf* petition.

support [sypɔR] *nm* support ; (*pour livre, outils*) stand ; ~ **audio-visuel** audio-visual aid ; ~ **publicitaire** advertising medium.

supportable [sypɔRtabl(ə)] *a* (*douleur*) bearable.

supporter *nm* [sypɔRtɛR] supporter, fan // *vt* [sypɔRte] (*poids, poussée*) to support ; (*conséquences, épreuve*) to bear, endure ; (*défauts, personne*) to tolerate, put up with ; (*suj: chose: chaleur etc*) to withstand ; (*suj: personne: chaleur, vin*) to take.

supposé, e [sypoze] *a* (*nombre*) estimated ; (*auteur*) supposed.

supposer [sypoze] *vt* to suppose ; (*impliquer*) to presuppose ; **à** ~ **que** supposing (that) ; **supposition** *nf* supposition.

suppositoire [sypozitwaR] *nm* suppository.

suppôt [sypo] *nm* (*péj*) henchman.

suppression [sypRɛsjɔ̃] *nf* removal ; deletion ; cancellation ; suppression.

supprimer [sypʀime] *vt* (*cloison, cause, anxiété*) to remove ; (*clause, mot*) to delete ; (*congés, service d'autobus etc*) to cancel ; (*publication, article*) to suppress ; (*emplois, privilèges, témoin gênant*) to do away with.

suppurer [sypyʀe] *vi* to suppurate.

supputations [sypytɑsjɔ̃] *nfpl* calculations, reckonings.

supputer [sypyte] *vt* to calculate, reckon.

suprématie [sypʀemasi] *nf* supremacy.

suprême [sypʀɛm] *a* supreme.

sur [syʀ] *prép* (*gén*) on ; (*par-dessus*) over ; (*au-dessus*) above ; (*direction*) towards ; (*à propos de*) about, on ; **un ~ 10** one out of 10 ; **4m ~ 2** 4m by 2 ; **je n'ai pas d'argent ~ moi** I haven't got any money with ou on me ; **~ ce** *ad* hereupon.

sur, e [syʀ] *a* sour.

sûr, e [syʀ] *a* sure, certain ; (*digne de confiance*) reliable ; (*sans danger*) safe ; **peu ~** unreliable ; **~ de qch** sure ou certain of sth ; **être ~ de qn** to be sure of sb ; **~ de soi** self-assured, self-confident ; **le plus ~ est de** the safest thing is to.

surabonder [syʀabɔ̃de] *vi* to be overabundant.

suraigu, uë [syʀegy] *a* very shrill.

surajouter [syʀaʒute] *vt:* **~ qch à** to add sth to.

suralimenté, e [syʀalimɑ̃te] *a* overfed.

suranné, e [syʀane] *a* outdated, outmoded.

surbaissé, e [syʀbese] *a* lowered, low.

surcharge [syʀʃaʀʒ(ə)] *nf* (*de passagers, marchandises*) excess load ; (*correction*) alteration ; (*PHILATÉLIE*) surcharge ; **prendre des passagers en ~** to take on excess ou extra passengers ; **~ de bagages** excess luggage ; **~ de travail** extra work.

surcharger [syʀʃaʀʒe] *vt* to overload ; (*timbre-poste*) to surcharge.

surchauffé, e [syʀʃofe] *a* overheated.

surchoix [syʀʃwa] *a inv* top-quality.

surclasser [syʀklɑse] *vt* to outclass.

surcouper [syʀkupe] *vt* to overtrump.

surcroît [syʀkʀwa] *nm:* **un ~ de** additional + *nom* ; **par** ou **de ~** moreover ; **en ~** in addition.

surdi-mutité [syʀdimytite] *nf:* **atteint de ~** deaf and dumb.

surdité [syʀdite] *nf* deafness.

sureau, x [syʀo] *nm* elder (tree).

surélever [syʀelve] *vt* to raise, heighten.

sûrement [syʀmɑ̃] *ad* reliably ; safely, securely ; (*certainement*) certainly.

surenchère [syʀɑ̃ʃɛʀ] *nf* (*aux enchères*) higher bid ; (*sur prix fixe*) overbid ; (*fig*) overstatement ; outbidding tactics *pl* ; **surenchérir** *vi* to bid higher ; to raise one's bid ; (*fig*) to try and outbid each other.

surent *vb voir* **savoir**.

surestimer [syʀɛstime] *vt* to overestimate.

sûreté [syʀte] *nf* (*voir* **sûr**) reliability ; safety ; (*JUR*) guaranty ; surety ; **mettre en ~** to put in a safe place ; **pour plus de ~** as an extra precaution ; to be on the safe side ; **la S~ (nationale)** division of the Ministère de l'Intérieur heading all police forces except the gendarmerie and the Paris préfecture de police.

surexcité, e [syʀɛksite] *a* overexcited.

surexposer [syʀɛkspoze] *vt* to overexpose.

surf [syʀf] *nm* surfing.

surface [syʀfas] *nf* surface ; (*superficie*) surface area ; **faire ~** to surface ; **en ~** *ad* near the surface ; (*fig*) superficially ; **la pièce fait 100m² de ~** the room has a surface area of 100m² ; **~ de réparation** penalty area.

surfait, e [syʀfɛ, -ɛt] *a* overrated.

surfin, e [syʀfɛ̃, -in] *a* superfine.

surgelé, e [syʀʒəle] *a* (deep-)frozen.

surgir [syʀʒiʀ] *vi* (*personne, véhicule*) to appear suddenly ; (*geyser etc: de terre*) to shoot up ; (*fig: problème, conflit*) to arise.

surhomme [syʀɔm] *nm* superman.

surhumain, e [syʀymɛ̃, -ɛn] *a* superhuman.

surimposer [syʀɛ̃poze] *vt* to overtax.

surimpression [syʀɛ̃pʀesjɔ̃] *nf* (*PHOTO*) double exposure ; **en ~** superimposed.

sur-le-champ [syʀləʃɑ̃] *ad* immediately.

surlendemain [syʀlɑ̃dmɛ̃] *nm:* **le ~ (soir)** two days later (in the evening) ; **le ~ de** two days after.

surmenage [syʀmønaʒ] *nm* overwork ; **le ~ intellectuel** mental fatigue.

surmené, e [syʀmøne] *a* overworked.

surmener [syʀmøne] *vt*, **se ~** *vi* to overwork.

surmonter [syʀmɔ̃te] *vt* (*suj: coupole etc*) to surmount, top ; (*vaincre*) to overcome, surmount.

surmultipliée, e [syʀmyltiplije] *a, nf:* **(vitesse) ~e** overdrive.

surnager [syʀnaʒe] *vi* to float.

surnaturel, le [syʀnatyʀɛl] *a, nm* supernatural.

surnom [syʀnɔ̃] *nm* nickname.

surnombre [syʀnɔ̃bʀ(ə)] *nm:* **être en ~** to be too many (ou one too many).

surnommer [syʀnɔme] *vt* to nickname.

surnuméraire [syʀnymeʀɛʀ] *nm/f* supernumerary.

suroît [syʀwa] *nm* sou'wester.

surpasser [syʀpɑse] *vt* to surpass.

surpeuplé, e [syʀpœple] *a* overpopulated.

surplis [syʀpli] *nm* surplice.

surplomb [syʀplɔ̃] *nm* overhang ; **en ~** overhanging.

surplomber [syʀplɔ̃be] *vi* to be overhanging // *vt* to overhang ; to tower above.

surplus [syʀply] *nm* (*COMM*) surplus ; (*reste*) : **~ de bois** wood left over ; **~ américains** American army surplus *sg*.

surprenant, e [syʀpʀənɑ̃, -ɑ̃t] *a* surprising.

surprendre [syʀpʀɑ̃dʀ(ə)] *vt* (*étonner, prendre à l'improviste*) to surprise ; (*tomber sur: intrus etc*) to catch ; (*fig*) to detect ; to chance ou happen upon ; to intercept ; to overhear ; **~ la vigilance/bonne foi de qn** to catch sb out/betray sb's good faith ; **se ~ à faire** to catch ou find o.s. doing.

surprime [syʀpʀim] *nf* additional premium.

surpris, e [syʀpʀi, -iz] a: ~ **(de/que)** surprised (at/that).

surprise [syʀpʀiz] nf surprise; **faire une** ~ **à qn** to give sb a surprise; **par** ~ ad by surprise.

surprise-partie [syʀpʀizpaʀti] nf party.

surproduction [syʀpʀɔdyksjɔ̃] nf overproduction.

surréaliste [syʀʀealist(ə)] a surrealist.

sursaut [syʀso] nm start, jump; ~ **de** (énergie, indignation) sudden fit ou burst of; **en** ~ ad with a start; **sursauter** vi to (give a) start, jump.

surseoir [syʀswaʀ]: ~ **à** vt to defer; (JUR) to stay.

sursis [syʀsi] nm (JUR: gén) suspended sentence; (à l'exécution capitale, aussi fig) reprieve; (MIL): ~ **(d'appel ou d'incorporation)** deferment; **condamné à 5 mois (de prison) avec** ~ given a 5-month suspended (prison) sentence; **sursitaire** nm (MIL) deferred conscript.

sursois etc vb voir **surseoir**.

surtaxe [syʀtaks(ə)] nf surcharge.

surtout [syʀtu] ad (avant tout, d'abord) above all; (spécialement, particulièrement) especially; **il aime le sport,** ~ **le football** he likes sport, especially football; **cet été, il a** ~ **fait de la pêche** this summer he went fishing more than anything (else); ~, **ne dites rien!** whatever you do — don't say anything!; ~ **pas!** certainly ou definitely not!; ~ **que...** especially as ...

surveillance [syʀvɛjɑ̃s] nf watch; (POLICE, MIL) surveillance; **sous** ~ **médicale** under medical supervision; **la** ~ **du territoire** internal security (voir aussi **D.S.T.**).

surveillant, e [syʀvɛjɑ̃, -ɑ̃t] nm/f (de prison) warder; (SCOL) monitor; (de travaux) supervisor, overseer.

surveiller [syʀveje] vt (enfant, élèves, bagages) to watch, keep an eye on; (malade) to watch over; (prisonnier, suspect) to keep (a) watch on; (territoire, bâtiment) to (keep) watch over; (travaux, cuisson) to supervise; (SCOL: examen) to invigilate; ~ **se** ~ to keep a check ou watch on o.s.; ~ **son langage/sa ligne** to watch one's language/figure.

survenir [syʀvəniʀ] vi (incident, retards) to occur, arise; (événement) to take place; (personne) to appear, arrive.

survêtement [syʀvɛtmɑ̃] nm tracksuit.

survie [syʀvi] nf survival; (REL) afterlife; **une** ~ **de quelques mois** a few more months of life.

survivant, e [syʀvivɑ̃, -ɑ̃t] nm/f survivor.

survivre [syʀvivʀ(ə)] vi to survive; ~ **à** vt (accident etc) to survive; (personne) to outlive.

survol [syʀvɔl] nm flying over.

survoler [syʀvɔle] vt to fly over; (fig: livre) to skim through.

survolté, e [syʀvɔlte] a (ÉLEC) stepped up, boosted; (fig) worked up.

sus [sy(s)]: **en** ~ **de** prép in addition to, over and above; **en** ~ ad in addition; ~ **à** excl: ~ **au tyran!** at the tyrant!

susceptibilité [sysɛptibilite] nf sensitiveness q.

susceptible [sysɛptibl(ə)] a touchy, sensitive; ~ **d'amélioration** ou **d'être amélioré** that can be improved, open to improvement; ~ **de faire** able to do; liable to do.

susciter [sysite] vt (admiration) to arouse; (obstacles, ennuis): ~ **(à qn)** to create (for sb).

susdit, e [sysdi, -dit] a foresaid.

susmentionnè, e [sysmɑ̃sjɔne] a abovementioned.

suspect, e [syspɛ(kt), -ɛkt(ə)] a suspicious; (témoignage, opinions) suspect // nm/f suspect; **peu** ~ **de** most unlikely to be suspected of.

suspecter [syspɛkte] vt to suspect; (honnêteté de qn) to question, have one's suspicions about; ~ **qn d'être** to suspect sb of being.

suspendre [syspɑ̃dʀ(ə)] vt (accrocher: vêtement): ~ **qch (à)** to hang sth up (on); (fixer: lustre etc): ~ **qch à** to hang sth from; (interrompre, demettre) to suspend; (remettre) to defer; **se** ~ **à** to hang from.

suspendu, e [syspɑ̃dy] pp de **suspendre** // a (accroché): ~ **à** hanging on (ou from); (perché): ~ **au-dessus de** suspended over; (AUTO): **bien/mal** ~ with good/poor suspension.

suspens [syspɑ̃]: **en** ~ ad (affaire) in abeyance; **tenir en** ~ to keep in suspense.

suspense [syspɑ̃s] nm suspense.

suspension [syspɑ̃sjɔ̃] nf suspension; deferment; (AUTO) suspension; (lustre) pendent light fitting; **en** ~ in suspension, suspended; ~ **d'audience** adjournment.

suspicion [syspisjɔ̃] nf suspicion.

sustenter [systɑ̃te]: **se** ~ vi to take sustenance.

susurrer [sysyʀe] vt to whisper.

sut vb voir **savoir**.

suture [sytyʀ] nf: **point de** ~ stitch; **suturer** vt to stitch up, suture.

svelte [svɛlt(ə)] a slender, svelte.

S.V.P. sigle (= s'il vous plaît) please.

syllabe [silab] nf syllable.

sylvestre [silvɛstʀ(ə)] a: **pin** ~ Scots pine, Scotch fir.

sylviculture [silvikyltyʀ] nf forestry, sylviculture.

symbole [sɛ̃bɔl] nm symbol; **symbolique** a symbolic(al); (geste, offrande) token cpd; (salaire, dommage-intérêts) nominal; **symboliser** vt to symbolize.

symétrie [simetʀi] nf symmetry; **symétrique** a symmetrical.

sympa [sɛ̃pa] a abr de **sympathique**.

sympathie [sɛ̃pati] nf (inclination) liking; (affinité) fellow feeling; (condoléances) sympathy; **accueillir avec** ~ (projet) to receive favourably; **avoir de la** ~ **pour qn** to like sb, have a liking for sb; **témoignages de** ~ expressions of sympathy; **croyez à toute ma** ~ you have my deepest sympathy.

sympathique [sɛ̃patik] a nice, friendly; likeable; pleasant.

sympathisant, e [sɛ̃patizɑ̃, -ɑ̃t] nm/f sympathizer.

sympathiser [sɛ̃patize] vi (voisins etc: s'entendre) to get on (well); (: se fréquenter) to socialize, see each other ; ~ **avec** to get on (well) with ; to see, socialize with.

symphonie [sɛ̃fɔni] *nf* symphony ; **symphonique** *a* (*orchestre*, *concert*) symphony *cpd* ; (*musique*) symphonic.

symptomatique [sɛ̃ptɔmatik] *a* symptomatic.

symptôme [sɛ̃ptom] *nm* symptom.

synagogue [sinagɔg] *nf* synagogue.

synchronique [sɛ̃kʀɔnik] *a*: **tableau** ~ synchronic table of events.

synchroniser [sɛ̃kʀɔnize] *vt* to synchronize.

syncope [sɛ̃kɔp] *nf* (*MÉD*) blackout ; (*MUS*) syncopation ; **tomber en** ~ to faint, pass out ; **syncopé, e** *a* syncopated.

syndic [sɛ̃dik] *nm* managing agent.

syndical, e, aux [sɛ̃dikal, -o] *a* (trade-)union *cpd* ; ~**isme** *nm* trade unionism ; union(ist) activities *pl* ; ~**iste** *nm/f* trade unionist.

syndicat [sɛ̃dika] *nm* (*d'ouvriers*, *employés*) (trade) union ; (*autre association d'intérêts*) union, association ; ~ **d'initiative** tourist office *ou* bureau ; ~ **patronal** employers' syndicate, federation of employers ; ~ **de propriétaires** association of property owners.

syndiqué, e [sɛ̃dike] *a* belonging to a (trade) union ; **non** ~ non-union.

syndiquer [sɛ̃dike]: **se** ~ *vi* to form a trade union ; (*adhérer*) to join a trade union.

syndrome [sɛ̃dʀom] *nm* syndrome.

synode [sinɔd] *nm* synod.

synonyme [sinɔnim] *a* synonymous // *nm* synonym ; ~ **de** synonymous with.

synoptique [sinɔptik] *a*: **tableau** ~ synoptic table.

synovie [sinɔvi] *nf* synovia.

syntaxe [sɛ̃taks(ə)] *nf* syntax.

synthèse [sɛ̃tɛz] *nf* synthesis (*pl* es) ; **faire la** ~ **de** to synthesize.

synthétique [sɛ̃tetik] *a* synthetic.

synthétiseur [sɛ̃tetizœʀ] *nm* (*MUS*) synthesizer.

syphilis [sifilis] *nf* syphilis.

Syrie [siʀi] *nf*: **la** ~ Syria ; **syrien, ne** *a*, *nm/f* Syrian.

systématique [sistematik] *a* systematic.

systématiser [sistematize] *vt* to systematize.

système [sistɛm] *nm* system ; **le** ~ **D** resourcefulness ; **le** ~ **solaire** the solar system.

T

t' [t(ə)] *pronom voir* **te**.

ta [ta] *dét voir* **ton**.

tabac [taba] *nm* tobacco ; tobacconist's (shop) // *a inv*: (**couleur**) ~ buff(-coloured) ; **passer qn à** ~ to beat sb up ; ~ **blond/brun** light/dark tobacco ; ~ **gris** shag ; ~ **à priser** snuff ; **tabagie** *nf* smoke den ; **tabatière** *nf* snuffbox.

tabernacle [tabɛʀnakl(ə)] *nm* tabernacle.

table [tabl(ə)] *nf* table ; **à** ~! dinner *etc* is ready! ; **se mettre à** ~ to sit down to eat ; (*fig*: *fam*) to come clean ; **mettre la** ~ to lay the table ; **faire** ~ **rase de** to make a clean sweep of ; ~ **basse** coffee table ;

~ **d'écoute** wire-tapping set ; ~ **d'harmonie** sounding board ; ~ **des matières** (table of) contents *pl* ; ~ **de multiplication** multiplication table ; ~ **de nuit** *ou* **de chevet** bedside table ; ~ **ronde** (*débat*) round table ; ~ **de toilette** washstand.

tableau, x [tablo] *nm* painting ; (*reproduction*, *fig*) picture ; (*panneau*) board ; (*schéma*) table, chart ; ~ **d'affichage** notice board ; ~ **de bord** dashboard ; (*AVIAT*) instrument panel ; ~ **de chasse** tally ; ~ **noir** blackboard.

tabler [table] *vi*: ~ **sur** to count *ou* bank on.

tablette [tablɛt] *nf* (*planche*) shelf (*pl* shelves) ; ~ **de chocolat** bar of chocolate.

tablier [tablije] *nm* apron ; (*de pont*) roadway.

tabou [tabu] *nm*, *a* taboo.

tabouret [tabuʀɛ] *nm* stool.

tabulateur [tabylatœʀ] *nm* tabulator.

tac [tak] *nm*: **du** ~ **au** ~ tit for tat.

tache [taʃ] *nf* (*saleté*) stain, mark ; (*ART*, *de couleur*, *lumière*) spot ; splash, patch ; **faire** ~ **d'huile** to spread, gain ground.

tâche [taʃ] *nf* task ; **travailler à la** ~ to do general jobbing, work as a jobbing gardener/builder *etc*.

tacher [taʃe] *vt* to stain, mark ; (*fig*) to sully, stain.

tâcher [taʃe] *vi*: ~ **de faire** to try *ou* endeavour to do.

tâcheron [taʃʀɔ̃] *nm* (*fig*) drudge.

tacite [tasit] *a* tacit.

taciturne [tasityʀn(ə)] *a* taciturn.

tacot [tako] *nm* (*péj*) banger.

tact [takt] *nm* tact ; **avoir du** ~ to be tactful, have tact.

tactile [taktil] *a* tactile.

tactique [taktik] *a* tactical // *nf* (*technique*) tactics *sg* ; (*plan*) tactic.

taie [tɛ] *nf*: ~ (**d'oreiller**) pillowslip, pillowcase.

taille [taj] *nf* cutting ; pruning ; (*milieu du corps*) waist ; (*hauteur*) height ; (*grandeur*) size ; **de** ~ **à faire** capable of doing ; **de** ~ a sizeable.

taille-crayon(s) [tajkʀɛjɔ̃] *nm* pencil sharpener.

tailler [taje] *vt* (*pierre*, *diamant*) to cut ; (*arbre*, *plante*) to prune ; (*vêtement*) to cut out ; (*crayon*) to sharpen ; **se** ~ *vt* (*ongles*, *barbe*) to trim, cut ; (*fig*: *réputation*) to gain, win // *vi* (*fam*) to beat it ; ~ **dans** (*chair*, *bois*) to cut into.

tailleur [tajœʀ] *nm* (*couturier*) tailor ; (*vêtement*) suit, costume ; **en** ~ (*assis*) cross-legged ; ~ **de diamants** diamond-cutter.

taillis [taji] *nm* copse.

tain [tɛ̃] *nm* silvering ; **glace sans** ~ two-way mirror.

taire [tɛʀ] *vt* to keep to o.s., conceal // *vi*: **faire** ~ **qn** to make sb be quiet ; (*fig*) to silence sb ; **se** ~ *vi* (*s'arrêter de parler*) to fall silent, stop talking ; (*ne pas parler*) to be silent *ou* quiet ; to keep quiet ; **tais-toi!, taisez-vous!** be quiet!

talc [talk] *nm* talcum powder.

talé, e [tale] a (*fruit*) bruised.

talent [talɑ̃] nm talent ; **talentueux, euse** a talented.

talion [taljɔ̃] nm: **la loi du ~** an eye for an eye.

talisman [talismɑ̃] nm talisman.

talon [talɔ̃] nm heel ; (*de chèque, billet*) stub, counterfoil ; **~s plats/aiguilles** flat/stiletto heels.

talonner [talɔne] vt to follow hard behind ; (*fig*) to hound.

talonnette [talɔnɛt] nf heelpiece.

talquer [talke] vt to put talcum powder on.

talus [taly] nm embankment.

tambour [tɑ̃buR] nm (MUS, aussi TECH) drum ; (*musicien*) drummer ; (*porte*) revolving door(s pl).

tambourin [tɑ̃buRɛ̃] nm tambourine.

tambouriner [tɑ̃buRine] vi: ~ **contre** to drum against ou on.

tambour-major [tɑ̃buRmaʒɔR] nm drum major.

tamis [tami] nm sieve.

Tamise [tamiz] nf: **la ~** the Thames.

tamisé, e [tamize] a (*fig*) subdued, soft.

tamiser [tamize] vt to sieve, sift.

tampon [tɑ̃pɔ̃] nm (*de coton, d'ouate*) wad, pad ; (*amortisseur*) buffer ; (*bouchon*) plug, stopper ; (*cachet, timbre*) stamp ; ~ **(hygiénique)** tampon ; **tamponner** vt (*timbres*) to stamp ; (*heurter*) to crash ou ram into ; **tamponneuse** a: **autos tamponneuses** dodgems.

tam-tam [tamtam] nm tomtom.

tandem [tɑ̃dɛm] nm tandem ; (*fig*) duo, pair.

tandis [tɑ̃di]: ~ **que** cj while.

tangage [tɑ̃gaʒ] nm pitching (and tossing).

tangent, e [tɑ̃ʒɑ̃, -ɑ̃t] a (MATH): ~ **à** tangential to ; (*fam*) close // nf (MATH) tangent.

tangible [tɑ̃ʒibl(ə)] a tangible, concrete.

tango [tɑ̃go] nm tango.

tanguer [tɑ̃ge] vi to pitch (and toss).

tanière [tanjɛR] nf lair, den.

tanin [tanɛ̃] nm tannin.

tank [tɑ̃k] nm tank.

tanné, e [tane] a weather-beaten.

tanner [tane] vt to tan.

tannerie [tanRi] nf tannery.

tanneur [tanœR] nm tanner.

tant [tɑ̃] ad so much ; ~ **de** (*sable, eau*) so much ; (*gens, livres*) so many ; ~ **que** cj as long as ; ~ **que** (*comparatif*) as much as ; ~ **mieux** that's great ; so much the better ; ~ **pis** never mind ; too bad ; ~ **pis pour lui** too bad for him ; ~ **soit peu** a little bit ; (*even*) remotely.

tante [tɑ̃t] nf aunt.

tantinet [tɑ̃tinɛ]: **un ~** ad a tiny bit.

tantôt [tɑ̃to] ad (*parfois*): ~ ... ~ now ... now ; (*cet après-midi*) this afternoon.

taon [tɑ̃] nm horsefly, gadfly.

tapage [tapaʒ] nm uproar, din ; ~ **nocturne** (JUR) disturbance of the peace (at night).

tapageur, euse [tapaʒœR, -øz] a loud, flashy ; noisy.

tape [tap] nf slap.

tape-à-l'œil [tapalœj] a inv flashy, showy.

taper [tape] vt (*porte*) to bang, slam ; (*dactylographier*) to type (out) ; (*fam: emprunter*): ~ **qn de 10 F** to touch sb for 10 F, cadge 10 F off sb // vi (*soleil*) to beat down ; ~ **sur qn** to thump sb ; (*fig*) to run sb down ; ~ **sur qch** to hit sth ; to bang on sth ; ~ **à** (*porte etc*) to knock on ; ~ **dans** vt (*se servir*) to dig into ; ~ **des mains/pieds** to clap one's hands/stamp one's feet ; ~ **à (la machine)** to type.

tapi, e [tapi] a: ~ **dans/derrière** crouching ou cowering in/behind ; hidden away in/behind.

tapioca [tapjɔka] nm tapioca.

tapis [tapi] nm carpet ; (*de table*) cloth ; **mettre sur le ~** (*fig*) to bring up for discussion ; ~ **roulant** conveyor belt ; ~ **de sol** (*de tente*) groundsheet ; **~-brosse** nm doormat.

tapisser [tapise] vt (*avec du papier peint*) to paper ; (*recouvrir*): ~ **qch (de)** to cover sth (with).

tapisserie [tapisRi] nf (*tenture, broderie*) tapestry ; (*: travail*) tapestry-making ; tapestry work ; (*papier peint*) wallpaper ; **faire ~** to sit out, be a wallflower.

tapissier, ière [tapisje, -jɛR] nm/f: **~-(-décorateur)** upholsterer (and decorator).

tapoter [tapɔte] vt to pat, tap.

taquet [takɛ] nm wedge ; peg.

taquin, e [takɛ̃, -in] a teasing.

taquiner [takine] vt to tease.

tarabiscoté, e [taRabiskɔte] a over-ornate, fussy.

tarabuster [taRabyste] vt to bother, worry.

tarauder [taRode] vt (TECH) to tap ; to thread ; (*fig*) to pierce.

tard [taR] ad late ; **au plus ~** at the latest ; **plus ~** later (on) ; **sur le ~** late in life.

tarder [taRde] vi (*chose*) to be a long time coming ; (*personne*): ~ **à faire** to delay doing ; **il me tarde d'être** I am longing to be ; **sans (plus) ~** without (further) delay.

tardif, ive [taRdif, -iv] a late ; **tardivement** ad late.

tare [taR] nf (COMM) tare ; (*fig*) defect ; taint, blemish.

targuer [taRge]: **se ~ de** vt to boast about.

tarif [taRif] nm (*liste*) price list ; tariff ; (*barème*) rates pl ; fares pl ; tariff ; (*prix*) rate ; fare ; **~-aire** a tariff cpd ; **~er** vt to fix the price ou rate for ; **~é 10 F** priced 10 F.

tarir [taRiR] vi to dry up, run dry // vt to dry up.

tarot(s) [taRo] nm(pl) tarot cards.

tartare [taRtaR] a (CULIN) tartar(e).

tarte [taRt(ə)] nf tart ; ~ **aux pommes/à la crème** apple/custard tart ; **~lette** nf tartlet.

tartine [taRtin] nf slice of bread and butter (*ou jam*) ; ~ **au miel** slice of bread and honey ; **tartiner** vt to spread ; **fromage à tartiner** cheese spread.

tartre [taRtR(ə)] nm (*des dents*) tartar ; (*de chaudière*) fur, scale.

tas [tɑ] *nm* heap, pile ; (*fig*): **un ~ de** heaps of, lots of ; **en ~** in a heap *ou* pile ; **dans le ~** (*fig*) in the crowd ; among them ; **formé sur le ~** trained on the job.

tasse [tɑs] *nf* cup.

tassé, e [tɑse] *a*: **bien ~** (*café etc*) strong.

tasser [tɑse] *vt* (*terre, neige*) to pack down ; (*entasser*): **~ qch dans** to cram sth into ; **se ~** *vi* (*terrain*) to settle ; (*fig*) to sort itself out, settle down.

tâter [tɑte] *vt* to feel ; (*fig*) to try out ; to test out ; **~ de** (*prison etc*) to have a taste of ; **se ~** (*hésiter*) to be in two minds ; **~ le terrain** (*fig*) to test the ground.

tatillon, ne [tatijɔ̃, -ɔn] *a* pernickety.

tâtonnement [tɑtɔnmɑ̃] *nm*: **par ~s** (*fig*) by trial and error.

tâtonner [tɑtɔne] *vi* to grope one's way along.

tâtons [tɑtɔ̃]: **à ~** *ad*: **chercher/avancer à ~** to grope around for/grope one's way forward.

tatouage [tatwaʒ] *nm* tattooing ; (*dessin*) tattoo.

tatouer [tatwe] *vt* to tattoo.

taudis [todi] *nm* hovel, slum.

taupe [top] *nf* mole ; **taupinière** *nf* molehill.

taureau, x [tɔro] *nm* bull ; (*signe*): **le T~** Taurus, the Bull ; **être du T~** to be Taurus.

tauromachie [tɔrɔmaʃi] *nf* bullfighting.

taux [to] *nm* rate ; (*d'alcool*) level ; **~ d'intérêt** interest rate.

tavelé, e [tavle] *a* marbled.

taverne [tavɛrn(ə)] *nf* inn, tavern.

taxe [taks] *nf* tax ; (*douanière*) duty ; **~ de séjour** tourist tax ; **~ à la valeur ajoutée (T.V.A.)** value added tax (V.A.T.).

taxer [takse] *vt* (*personne*) to tax ; (*produit*) to put a tax on, tax ; (*fig*): **~ qn de** to call sb + *attribut* ; to accuse sb of, tax sb with.

taxi [taksi] *nm* taxi.

taximètre [taksimɛtr(ə)] *nm* (taxi)meter.

taxiphone [taksifɔn] *nm* pay phone.

T.C.F. *sigle m* = *Touring Club de France,* ≈ AA *ou* RAC.

Tchécoslovaquie [tʃekɔslɔvaki] *nf* Czechoslovakia ; **tchèque** *a, nm, nf* Czech.

te, t' [t(ə)] *pronom* you ; (*réfléchi*) yourself.

té [te] *nm* T-square.

technicien, ne [tɛknisjɛ̃, -jɛn] *nm/f* technician.

technique [tɛknik] *a* technical // *nf* technique ; **~ment** *ad* technically.

technocrate [tɛknɔkrat] *nm/f* technocrat.

technocratie [tɛknɔkrasi] *nf* technocracy.

technologie [tɛknɔlɔʒi] *nf* technology ; **technologique** *a* technological.

teck [tɛk] *nm* teak.

teckel [tekɛl] *nm* dachshund.

teignais *etc vb voir* **teindre**.

teigne [tɛɲ] *nf* (*ZOOL*) moth ; (*MÉD*) ringworm.

teigneux, euse [tɛɲø, -øz] *a* (*péj*) nasty, scabby.

teindre [tɛ̃dr(ə)] *vt* to dye.

teint, e [tɛ̃, tɛ̃t] *a* dyed // *nm* (*du visage*)

complexion, colouring ; colour // *nf* shade, colour ; **grand ~** *a inv* colourfast.

teinté, e [tɛ̃te] *a* (*verres*) tinted ; (*bois*) stained ; **~ acajou** mahogany-stained ; **~ de** (*fig*) tinged with.

teinter [tɛ̃te] *vt* to tint ; (*bois*) to stain ; **teinture** *nf* dyeing ; (*substance*) dye ; (*MÉD*): **teinture d'iode** tincture of iodine.

teinturerie [tɛ̃tyrri] *nf* dry cleaner's.

teinturier [tɛ̃tyrje] *nm* dry cleaner.

tel, telle [tɛl] *a* (*pareil*) such ; (*comme*): **~ un/des ...** like a/ like... ; (*indéfini*) such-and-such a, a given ; (*intensif*): **un ~/de ~s ...** such (a)/such ... ; **rien de ~** nothing like it, no such thing ; **~ que** *cj* like, such as ; **~ quel** as it is *ou* stands (*ou* was *etc*).

tél. *abr de* **téléphone**.

télé [tele] *nf* (*abr de* **télévision**) (*poste*) T.V. (set) ; **à la ~** on the telly, on T.V.

télé... [tele] *préfixe*: **~benne** *nf* (*benne*) telecabine, gondola // *nm* telecabine ; **~cabine** *nf* (*benne*) telecabine, gondola // *nm* telecabine ; **~commande** *nf* remote control ; **~commander** *vt* to operate by remote control ; **~communications** *nfpl* telecommunications ; **~férique** *nm* = **~phérique** ; **~gramme** *nm* telegram.

télégraphe [telegraf] *nm* telegraph ; **télégraphie** *nf* telegraphy ; **télégraphier** *vt* to telegraph, cable ; **télégraphique** *a* telegraph *cpd*, telegraphic ; (*fig*) telegraphic ; **télégraphiste** *nm/f* telegraphist.

téléguider [telegide] *vt* to operate by remote control, radio-control.

téléobjectif [teleɔbʒɛktif] *nm* telephoto lens *sg*.

télépathie [telepati] *nf* telepathy.

téléphérique [teleferik] *nm* cable-car.

téléphone [telefɔn] *nm* telephone ; (*appel*) (telephone) call ; telephone conversation ; **avoir le ~** to be on the (tele)phone ; **au ~** on the phone ; **les T~s** ≈ Post Office Telecommunications ; **~ arabe** bush telephone ; **~ manuel** manually-operated telephone system ; **téléphoner** *vt* to telephone // *vi* to telephone, ring ; to make a phone call ; **téléphoner à** to phone up, ring up, call up ; **téléphonique** *a* telephone *cpd*, phone *cpd* ; **téléphoniste** *nm/f* telephonist, telephone operator ; (*d'entreprise*) switchboard operator.

télescope [telɛskɔp] *nm* telescope.

télescoper [telɛskɔpe] *vt* to smash up ; **se ~** (*véhicules*) to concertina.

télescopique [telɛskɔpik] *a* telescopic.

téléscripteur [teleskriptœr] *nm* teleprinter.

télésiège [telesjɛʒ] *nm* chairlift.

téléski [teleski] *nm* ski-tow ; **~ à archets** T-bar tow ; **~ à perche** button lift.

téléspectateur, trice [telespɛktatœr, -tris] *nm/f* (television) viewer.

téléviser [televize] *vt* to televise.

téléviseur [televizœr] *nm* television set.

télévision [televizjɔ̃] *nf* television ; **avoir la ~** to have a television ; **à la ~** on television.

télex [telɛks] *nm* telex.

telle [tɛl] *a voir* **tel**.

tellement [tɛlmɑ̃] *ad* (*tant*) so much ; (*si*) so ; ~ **plus grand (que)** so much bigger (than) ; ~ **de** (*sable, eau*) so much ; (*gens, livres*) so many ; **il s'est endormi** ~ **il était fatigué** he was so tired (that) he fell asleep ; **pas** ~ not (all) that much ; not (all) that + *adjectif*.

tellurique [telyʀik] *a*: **secousse** ~ earth tremor.

téméraire [temeʀɛʀ] *a* reckless, rash ; **témérité** *nf* recklessness, rashness.

témoignage [temwaɲaʒ] *nm* (*JUR: déclaration*) testimony *q*, evidence *q* ; (: *faits*) evidence *q* ; (*rapport, récit*) account ; (*fig: d'affection etc*) token, mark ; expression.

témoigner [temwaɲe] *vt* (*intérêt, gratitude*) to show // *vi* (*JUR*) to testify, give evidence ; ~ **que** to testify that ; (*fig*) to reveal that, testify to the fact that ; ~ **de** *vt* to bear witness to, testify to.

témoin [temwɛ̃] *nm* witness ; (*SPORT*) baton ; (*CONSTR*) telltale // *a* control *cpd*, test *cpd* ; **appartement** ~ show flat ; **être** ~ **de** to witness ; to vouch for ; **prendre à** ~ to call to witness ; ~ **de moralité** character reference ; ~ **oculaire** eyewitness.

tempe [tɑ̃p] *nf* temple.

tempérament [tɑ̃peʀamɑ̃] *nm* temperament, disposition ; (*santé*) constitution ; **à** ~ (*vente*) on deferred (payment) terms ; (*achat*) by instalments, hire purchase *cpd* ; **avoir du** ~ to be hot-blooded.

tempérance [tɑ̃peʀɑ̃s] *nf* temperance.

température [tɑ̃peʀatyʀ] *nf* temperature ; **prendre la** ~ **de** to take the temperature of ; (*fig*) to gauge the feeling of ; **avoir ou faire de la** ~ to have *ou* be running a temperature.

tempéré, e [tɑ̃peʀe] *a* temperate.

tempérer [tɑ̃peʀe] *vt* to temper.

tempête [tɑ̃pɛt] *nf* storm ; ~ **de sable/neige** sand/snowstorm.

tempêter [tɑ̃pɛte] *vi* to rant and rave.

temple [tɑ̃pl(ə)] *nm* temple ; (*protestant*) church.

tempo [tɛmpo] *nm* tempo (*pl* s).

temporaire [tɑ̃pɔʀɛʀ] *a* temporary ; ~**ment** *ad* temporarily.

temporel, le [tɑ̃pɔʀɛl] *a* temporal.

temporiser [tɑ̃pɔʀize] *vi* to temporize, play for time.

temps [tɑ̃] *nm* (*atmosphérique*) weather ; (*durée*) time ; (*époque*) time, times *pl* ; (*LING*) tense ; (*MUS*) beat ; (*TECH*) stroke ; **il fait beau/mauvais** ~ the weather is fine/bad ; **avoir le** ~**/tout le** ~**/juste le** ~ to have time/plenty of time/just enough time ; **avoir fait son** ~ (*fig*) to have had its (*ou* his *etc*) day ; **en** ~ **de paix/guerre** in peacetime/wartime ; **en** ~ **utile** *ou* **voulu** in due time *ou* course ; **de** ~ **en** ~, **de** ~ **à autre** from time to time, now and again ; **à** ~ (*partir, arriver*) in time ; **à** ~ **partiel** *ad*, *a* part-time ; **dans le** ~ at one time ; **de tout** ~ always ; **du** ~ **que** at the time when, in the days when ; ~ **d'arrêt** pause, halt ; ~ **mort** (*COMM*) slack period.

tenable [tənabl(ə)] *a* bearable.

tenace [tənas] *a* tenacious, persistent ; **ténacité** *nf* tenacity, persistence.

tenailler [tənɑje] (*fig*) *vt* to torment, torture.

tenailles [tənɑj] *nfpl* pincers.

tenais *etc vb voir* **tenir**.

tenancier, ière [tənɑ̃sje, -jɛʀ] *nm/f* manager/manageress.

tenant, e [tənɑ̃, -ɑ̃t] *a voir* **séance** // *nm/f* (*SPORT*): ~ **du titre** title-holder // *nm*: **d'un seul** ~ in one piece ; **les** ~**s et les aboutissants** the ins and outs.

tendance [tɑ̃dɑ̃s] *nf* (*opinions*) leanings *pl*, sympathies *pl* ; (*inclination*) tendency ; (*évolution*) trend ; **à la hausse** upward trend ; **avoir** ~ **à** to have a tendency to, tend to ; **tendancieux, euse** *a* tendentious.

tendeur [tɑ̃dœʀ] *nm* (*de vélo*) chain-adjuster ; (*de câble*) wire-strainer ; (*de tente*) runner ; (*attache*) sandow, elastic strap.

tendon [tɑ̃dɔ̃] *nm* tendon, sinew ; ~ **d'Achille** Achilles' tendon.

tendre [tɑ̃dʀ(ə)] *a* (*viande, légumes*) tender ; (*bois, roche, couleur*) soft ; (*affectueux*) tender, loving // *vt* (*élastique, peau*) to stretch, draw tight ; (*muscle*) to tense ; (*donner*): ~ **qch à qn** to hold sth out to sb ; to offer sb sth ; (*fig: piège*) to set, lay ; (*tapisserie*): **tendu de soie** hung with silk, with silk hangings ; **se** ~ *vi* (*corde*) to tighten ; (*relations*) to become strained ; ~ **à qch/à faire** to tend towards sth/to do ; ~ **l'oreille** to prick up one's ears ; ~ **la main/le bras** to hold out one's hand/stretch out one's arm ; ~**ment** *ad* tenderly, lovingly ; **tendresse** *nf* tenderness.

tendu, e [tɑ̃dy] *pp de* **tendre** // *a* tight ; tensed ; strained.

ténèbres [tenɛbʀ(ə)] *nfpl* darkness *sg* ; **ténébreux, euse** *a* obscure, mysterious ; (*personne*) saturnine.

teneur [tənœʀ] *nf* content, substance ; (*d'une lettre*) terms *pl*, content ; ~ **en cuivre** copper content.

ténia [tenja] *nm* tapeworm.

tenir [təniʀ] *vt* to hold ; (*magasin, hôtel*) to run ; (*promesse*) to keep // *vi* to hold ; (*neige, gel*) to last ; **se** ~ *vi* (*avoir lieu*) to be held, take place ; (*être: personne*) to stand ; **se** ~ **droit** to stand up (*ou* sit up) straight ; **bien se** ~ to behave well ; **se** ~ **à qch** to hold on to sth ; **s'en** ~ **à qch** to confine o.s. to sth ; to stick to sth ; ~ **à** *vt* to be attached to ; to care about ; to depend on ; to stem from ; ~ **à faire** to want to do, be keen to do ; ~ **de** *vt* to partake of ; to take after ; **ça ne tient qu'à lui** it is entirely up to him ; ~ **qn pour** to take sb for ; ~ **qch de qn** (*histoire*) to have heard *ou* learnt sth from sb ; (*qualité, défaut*) to have inherited *ou* got sth from sb ; ~ **les comptes** to keep the books ; ~ **un rôle** to play a part ; ~ **l'alcool** to be able to hold a drink ; ~ **le coup** to hold out ; ~ **3 jours/2 mois** (*résister*) to hold out *ou* last 3 days/2 months ; ~ **au chaud/à l'abri** to keep hot/under shelter *ou* cover ; **tiens/tenez, voilà le stylo!**

there's the pen! ; **tiens, Alain!** look, here's Alain! ; **tiens?** (*surprise*) really?

tennis [tenis] *nm* tennis ; (*aussi:* **court de** ~) tennis court // *nm ou fpl* (*aussi:* **chaussures de** ~) tennis *ou* gym shoes ; ~ **de table** table tennis ; ~**man** *nm* tennis player.

ténor [tenɔʀ] *nm* tenor.

tension [tɑ̃sjɔ̃] *nf* tension ; (*fig*) tension ; strain ; (MÉD) blood pressure ; **faire** *ou* **avoir de la** ~ to have high blood pressure.

tentaculaire [tɑ̃takylɛʀ] *a* (*fig*) sprawling.

tentacule [tɑ̃takyl] *nm* tentacle.

tentant, e [tɑ̃tɑ̃, -ɑ̃t] *a* tempting.

tentateur, trice [tɑ̃tatœʀ, -tʀis] *a* tempting // *nm* (REL) tempter.

tentation [tɑ̃tasjɔ̃] *nf* temptation.

tentative [tɑ̃tativ] *nf* attempt, bid ; ~ **d'évasion** escape bid.

tente [tɑ̃t] *nf* tent ; ~ **à oxygène** oxygen tent.

tenter [tɑ̃te] *vt* (*éprouver, attirer*) to tempt ; (*essayer*): ~ **qch/de faire** to attempt *ou* try sth/to do ; **être tenté de** to be tempted to ; ~ **sa chance** to try one's luck.

tenture [tɑ̃tyʀ] *nf* hanging.

tenu, e [təny] *pp de* **tenir** // *a* (*maison, comptes*): **bien** ~ well-kept ; (*obligé*): ~ **de faire** under an obligation to do // *nf* (*action de tenir*) running ; keeping ; holding ; (*vêtements*) clothes *pl*, gear ; (*allure*) dress *q*, appearance ; (*comportement*) manners *pl*, behaviour ; **en grande** ~**e** in full dress ; **en petite** ~**e** scantily dressed *ou* clad ; **avoir de la** ~**e** to have good manners ; (*journal*) to have a high standard ; **une** ~**e de voyage/sport** travelling/sports clothes *pl ou* gear *q* ; ~**e de combat** combat gear *ou* dress ; ~**e de route** road-holding ; ~**e de soirée** evening dress.

ténu, e [teny] *a* (*indice, nuance*) tenuous, subtle ; (*fil, objet*) fine ; (*voix*) thin.

ter [tɛʀ] *a*: **16** ~ 16b *ou* B.

térébenthine [teʀebɑ̃tin] *nf*: (**essence de**) ~ (oil of) turpentine.

tergiverser [tɛʀʒivɛʀse] *vi* to shilly-shally.

terme [tɛʀm(ə)] *nm* term ; (*fin*) end ; **vente/achat à** ~ (COMM) forward sale/purchase ; **à court/long** ~ *a* short-/long-term *ou* -range // *ad* in the short/long term ; **à** ~ (MÉD) a full-term // *ad* at term ; **avant** ~ (MÉD) *a* premature // *ad* prematurely ; **mettre un** ~ **à** to put an end *ou* a stop to.

terminaison [tɛʀminɛzɔ̃] *nf* (LING) ending.

terminal, e, aux [tɛʀminal, -o] *a* final // *nm* terminal // *nf* (SCOL) ≈ Upper Sixth.

terminer [tɛʀmine] *vt* to end ; (*nourriture, repas*) to finish ; **se** ~ *vi* to end ; **se** ~ **par** to end with.

terminologie [tɛʀminɔlɔʒi] *nf* terminology.

terminus [tɛʀminys] *nm* terminus (*pl* i).

termite [tɛʀmit] *nm* termite, white ant.

terne [tɛʀn(ə)] *a* dull.

ternir [tɛʀniʀ] *vt* to dull ; (*fig*) to sully, tarnish ; **se** ~ *vi* to become dull.

terrain [teʀɛ̃] *nm* (*sol, fig*) ground ; (COMM) land *q*, plot (of land) ; site ; **sur le** ~ (*fig*) on the field ; ~ **de football/rugby**

football/rugby pitch ; ~ **d'aviation** airfield ; ~ **de camping** camping site ; **un** ~ **d'entente** an area of agreement ; ~ **de golf** golf course ; ~ **de jeu** games field ; playground ; ~ **de sport** sports ground ; ~ **vague** waste ground *q*.

terrasse [teʀas] *nf* terrace ; (*de café*) pavement area, terrasse ; **à la** ~ (*café*) outside.

terrassement [teʀasmɑ̃] *nm* earth-moving, earthworks *pl* ; embankment.

terrasser [teʀase] *vt* (*adversaire*) to floor, bring down ; (*suj: maladie etc*) to lay low.

terrassier [teʀasje] *nm* navvy, roadworker.

terre [tɛʀ] *nf* (*gén, aussi* ÉLEC) earth ; (*substance*) soil, earth ; (*opposé à mer*) land *q* ; (*contrée*) land ; ~**s** *nfpl* (*terrains*) lands, land *sg* ; **le travail de la** ~ work on the land ; **en** ~ (*pipe, poterie*) clay *cpd* ; **à** ~ *ou* **par** ~ (*mettre, être*) on the ground (*ou* floor) ; (*jeter, tomber*) to the ground, down ; ~ **cuite** earthenware ; terracotta ; **la** ~ **ferme** dry land, terra firma ; ~ **glaise** clay ; **la T**~ **Sainte** the Holy Land ; ~ **à** ~ *inv* down-to-earth, matter-of-fact.

terreau [teʀo] *nm* compost.

terre-plein [tɛʀplɛ̃] *nm* platform.

terrer [teʀe] : **se** ~ *vi* to hide away ; to go to ground.

terrestre [teʀɛstʀ(ə)] *a* (*surface*) earth's, of the earth ; (BOT, ZOOL, MIL) land *cpd* ; (REL) earthly, worldly.

terreur [teʀœʀ] *nf* terror *q*, fear.

terrible [teʀibl(ə)] *a* terrible, dreadful ; (*fam*) terrific ; ~**ment** *ad* (*très*) terribly, awfully.

terrien, ne [teʀjɛ̃, -jɛn] *nm/f* countryman/woman, man/woman of the soil ; (*non martien etc*) earthling.

terrier [teʀje] *nm* burrow, hole ; (*chien*) terrier.

terrifier [teʀifje] *vt* to terrify.

terril [teʀil] *nm* slag heap.

terrine [teʀin] *nf* (*récipient*) terrine ; (CULIN) pâté.

territoire [teʀitwaʀ] *nm* territory ; **territorial, e, aux** *a* territorial.

terroir [teʀwaʀ] *nm* (AGR) soil ; **accent du** ~ country *ou* rural accent.

terroriser [teʀɔʀize] *vt* to terrorize ; **terrorisme** *nm* terrorism ; **terroriste** *nm/f* terrorist.

tertiaire [tɛʀsjɛʀ] *a* tertiary // *nm* (ÉCON) tertiary sector, service industries *pl*.

tertre [tɛʀtʀ(ə)] *nm* hillock, mound.

tes [te] *dét voir* **ton**.

tesson [tesɔ̃] *nm*: ~ **de bouteille** piece of broken bottle.

test [tɛst] *nm* test.

testament [tɛstamɑ̃] *nm* (JUR) will ; (REL) Testament ; **faire son** ~ to make out one's will ; **testamentaire** *a* of a will.

tester [tɛste] *vt* to test.

testicule [tɛstikyl] *nm* testicle.

tétanos [tetanos] *nm* tetanus, lockjaw.

têtard [tɛtaʀ] *nm* tadpole.

tête [tɛt] *nf* head ; (*cheveux*) hair *q* ; (*visage*) face ; (FOOTBALL) header ; **de** ~ *a* (*wagon etc*) front *cpd* // *ad* (*calculer*) in one's head, mentally ; **perdre la** ~ (*fig*) to lose one's head ; to go off one's head ; **tenir** ~ **à qn** to stand up to *ou* defy sb ; **la** ~ **en bas** with one's head down ; **la** ~ **la première** (*tomber*) headfirst ; **faire une** ~ (*FOOTBALL*) to head the ball ; **faire la** ~ (*fig*) to sulk ; **en** ~ (*SPORT*) in the lead ; at the front *ou* head ; **en** ~ **à** ~ in private, alone together ; **de la** ~ **aux pieds** from head to toe ; ~ **d'affiche** (*THÉÂTRE etc*) top of the bill ; ~ **de bétail** head *inv* of cattle ; ~ **chercheuse** homing device ; ~ **de lecture** pickup head ; ~ **de liste** (*POL*) chief candidate ; ~ **de mort** skull and crossbones ; ~ **de série** (*TENNIS*) seeded player, seed ; ~ **de Turc** (*fig*) whipping boy ; ~ **de veau** (*CULIN*) calf's head ; ~**-à-queue** *nm inv:* **faire un** ~**-à-queue** to spin round ; ~**-à-** ~ *nm inv* tête-à-tête ; ~**-bêche** *ad* head to tail.

tétée [tete] *nf* (*action*) sucking ; (*repas*) feed.

téter [tete] *vt:* ~ (**sa mère**) to suck at one's mother's breast, feed.

tétine [tetin] *nf* teat ; (*sucette*) dummy.

téton [tet3] *nm* (*fam*) breast.

têtu, e [tety] *a* stubborn, pigheaded.

texte [tɛkst(ə)] *nm* text ; **apprendre son** ~ (*THÉÂTRE*) to learn one's lines.

textile [tɛkstil] *a* textile *cpd* // *nm* textile ; textile industry.

textuel, le [tɛkstɥɛl] *a* literal, word for word.

texture [tɛkstyR] *nf* texture.

thé [te] *nm* tea ; **prendre le** ~ to have tea ; **faire le** ~ to make the tea.

théâtral, e, aux [teɑtRal, -o] *a* theatrical.

théâtre [teɑtR(ə)] *nm* theatre ; (*techniques, genre*) drama, theatre ; (*activité*) stage, theatre ; (*œuvres*) plays *pl,* dramatic works *pl* ; (*fig: lieu*): **le** ~ **de** the scene of ; (*péj*) histrionics *pl,* playacting ; **faire du** ~ to be on the stage ; to do some acting ; ~ **filmé** filmed stage productions *pl.*

théière [tejɛR] *nf* teapot.

thème [tɛm] *nm* theme ; (*SCOL: traduction*) prose (composition).

théologie [teɔlɔʒi] *nf* theology ; **théologien** *nm* theologian ; **théologique** *a* theological.

théorème [teɔRɛm] *nm* theorem.

théoricien, ne [teɔRisjɛ̃, -jɛn] *nm/f* theoretician, theorist.

théorie [teɔRi] *nf* theory ; **théorique** *a* theoretical.

thérapeutique [teRapøtik] *a* therapeutic // *nf* therapeutics *sg.*

thérapie [teRapi] *nf* therapy.

thermal, e, aux [tɛRmal, -o] *a* thermal ; **station** ~**e** spa ; **cure** ~**e** water cure.

thermes [tɛRm(ə)] *nmpl* thermal baths ; (*romains*) thermae *pl.*

thermique [tɛRmik] *a* (*énergie*) thermic ; (*unité*) thermal.

thermomètre [tɛRmɔmɛtR(ə)] *nm* thermometer.

thermonucléaire [tɛRmɔnykleɛR] *a* thermonuclear.

thermos ® [tɛRmos] *nm ou nf:* (**bouteille**) ~ vacuum *ou* Thermos ® flask.

thermostat [tɛRmɔsta] *nm* thermostat.

thésauriser [tezɔRize] *vi* to hoard money.

thèse [tɛz] *nf* thesis (*pl* theses).

thon [t3] *nm* tuna (fish).

thoracique [tɔRasik] *a* thoracic.

thorax [tɔRaks] *nm* thorax.

thrombose [tR3boz] *nf* thrombosis.

thym [tɛ̃] *nm* thyme.

thyroïde [tiRɔid] *nf* thyroid (gland).

tiare [tjaR] *nf* tiara.

tibia [tibja] *nm* shinbone, tibia ; shin.

tic [tik] *nm* tic, (nervous) twitch ; (*de langage etc*) mannerism.

ticket [tikɛ] *nm* ticket ; ~ **de quai** platform ticket.

tic-tac [tiktak] *nm inv* tick-tock ; **tictaquer** *vi* to tick (away).

tiède [tjɛd] *a* lukewarm ; tepid ; (*vent, air*) mild, warm ; **tiédir** *vi* to cool ; to grow warmer.

tien, tienne [tjɛ̃, tjɛn] *pronom:* **le** ~ (**la tienne**), **les** ~**s** (**tiennes**) yours ; **à la tienne!** cheers!

tiens [tjɛ̃] *vb, excl voir* **tenir.**

tierce [tjɛRs(ə)] *a, nf voir* **tiers.**

tiercé [tjɛRse] *nm system of forecast betting giving first 3 horses.*

tiers, tierce [tjɛR, tjɛRs(ə)] *a* a third // *nm* (*JUR*) third party ; (*fraction*) third // *nf* (*MUS*) third ; (*CARTES*) tierce ; **une tierce personne** a third party ; ~ **provisionnel** interim payment of tax.

tige [tiʒ] *nf* stem ; (*baguette*) rod.

tignasse [tiɲas] *nf* (*péj*) shock *ou* mop of hair.

tigre [tigR(ə)] *nm* tiger.

tigré, e [tigRe] *a* striped ; spotted.

tigresse [tigRɛs] *nf* tigress.

tilleul [tijœl] *nm* lime (tree), linden (tree) ; (*boisson*) lime(-blossom) tea.

timbale [tɛ̃bal] *nf* (*metal*) tumbler ; ~**s** *nfpl* (*MUS*) timpani, kettledrums.

timbre [tɛ̃bR(ə)] *nm* (*tampon*) stamp ; (*aussi:* ~**-poste**) (postage) stamp ; (*cachet de la poste*) postmark ; (*sonnette*) bell ; (*MUS: de voix, instrument*) timbre, tone.

timbrer [tɛ̃bRe] *vt* to stamp.

timide [timid] *a* shy ; timid ; (*timoré*) timid, timorous ; **timidité** *nf* shyness, timidity.

timonerie [timɔnRi] *nf* wheelhouse.

timoré, e [timɔRe] *a* timorous.

tins *etc vb voir* **tenir.**

tintamarre [tɛ̃tamaR] *nm* din, uproar.

tinter [tɛ̃te] *vi* to ring, chime ; (*argent, clefs*) to jingle.

tir [tiR] *nm* (*sport*) shooting ; (*fait ou manière de tirer*) firing *q* ; (*FOOTBALL*) shot ; (*stand*) shooting gallery ; ~ **d'obus-de mitraillette** shell/machine gun fire ; ~ **à l'arc** archery ; ~ **au pigeon** clay pigeon shooting.

tirade [tiRad] *nf* tirade.

tirage [tiRaʒ] *nm* (*action*) printing ; (*de journal*) circulation ; (*de livre*) (print-)run ; edition ; (*de cheminée*) draught ; (*de loterie*) draw ; (*désaccord*) friction ; ~ **au sort** drawing lots.

tirailler [tiRɑje] *vt* to pull at, tug at // *vi* to fire at random ; **tirailleur** *nm* skirmisher.

tirant [tiʀɑ̃] *nm*: ~ **d'eau** draught.
tire [tiʀ] *nf*: **vol à la** ~ pickpocketing.
tiré [tiʀe] *nm* (COMM) drawee ; ~ **à part** off-print.
tire-au-flanc [tiʀoflɑ̃] *nm inv* (*péj*) skiver.
tire-bouchon [tiʀbuʃɔ̃] *nm* corkscrew.
tire-d'aile [tiʀdɛl]: **à** ~ *ad* swiftly.
tire-fesses [tiʀfɛs] *nm inv* ski-tow.
tirelire [tiʀliʀ] *nf* moneybox.
tirer [tiʀe] *vt* (*gén*) to pull ; (*extraire*): ~ **qch de** to take *ou* pull sth out of ; to get sth out of ; to extract sth from ; (*tracer*: *ligne, trait*) to draw, trace ; (*fermer*: *volet, rideau*) to draw, close ; (*choisir*: *carte, conclusion, aussi* COMM: *chèque*) to draw ; (*en faisant feu*: *balle, coup*) to fire ; (: *animal*) to shoot ; (*journal, livre, photo*) to print ; (FOOTBALL: *corner etc*) to take // *vi* (*faire feu*) to fire ; (*faire du tir*, FOOTBALL) to shoot ; (*cheminée*) to draw ; **se** ~ *vi* (*fam*) to push off ; **s'en** ~ to pull through, get off ; ~ **sur** to pull on *ou* at ; to shoot *ou* fire at ; (*pipe*) to draw on ; (*fig*: *avoisiner*) to verge *ou* border on ; ~ **son nom de** to take *ou* get its name from ; ~ **qn de** (*embarras etc*) to help *ou* get sb out of ; ~ **à l'arc/la carabine** to shoot with a bow and arrow/with a rifle.
tiret [tiʀe] *nm* dash.
tireur, euse [tiʀœʀ, -øz] *nm/f* gunman ; (COMM) drawer ; **bon** ~ good shot ; ~ **d'élite** marksman ; ~**s débutants** beginners at shooting.
tiroir [tiʀwaʀ] *nm* drawer ; ~**-caisse** *nm* till.
tisane [tizan] *nf* herb tea.
tison [tizɔ̃] *nm* brand ; **tisonner** *vt* to poke ; **tisonnier** *nm* poker.
tissage [tisaʒ] *nm* weaving *q*.
tisser [tise] *vt* to weave ; **tisserand** *nm* weaver.
tissu [tisy] *nm* fabric, material, cloth *q* ; (ANAT, BIO) tissue ; ~ **de mensonges** web of lies.
tissu, e [tisy] *a*: ~ **de** woven through with.
tissu-éponge [tisyepɔ̃ʒ] *nm* (terry) towelling *q*.
titane [titan] *nm* titanium.
titanesque [titanɛsk(ə)] *a* titanic.
titre [titʀ(ə)] *nm* (*gén*) title ; (*de journal*) headline ; (*diplôme*) qualification ; (COMM) security ; (CHIMIE) titre ; **en** ~ (*champion, responsable*) official, recognised ; **à juste** ~ with just cause, rightly ; **à quel** ~? on what grounds? ; **à aucun** ~ on no account ; **au même** ~ **(que)** in the same way (as) ; **à** ~ **d'exemple** as an *ou* by way of an example ; **à** ~ **d'information** for (your) information ; **à** ~ **gracieux** free of charge ; **à** ~ **d'essai** on a trial basis ; **à** ~ **privé** in a private capacity ; ~ **de propriété** title deed ; ~ **de transport** ticket.
titré, e [titʀe] *a* titled.
titrer [titʀe] *vt* (CHIMIE) to titrate ; to assay ; (PRESSE) to run as a headline ; (*suj*: *vin*): ~ **10°** to be 10° proof.
tituber [titybe] *vi* to stagger *ou* reel (along).
titulaire [titylɛʀ] *a* (ADMIN) appointed, with tenure // *nm* (ADMIN) incumbent ; **être**

~ **de** (*poste*) to hold ; (*permis*) to be the holder of.
toast [tost] *nm* slice *ou* piece of toast ; (*de bienvenue*) (welcoming) toast ; **porter un** ~ **à qn** to propose *ou* drink a toast to sb.
toboggan [tɔbɔgɑ̃] *nm* toboggan.
toc [tɔk] *nm*: **en** ~ imitation *cpd*.
tocsin [tɔksɛ̃] *nm* alarm (bell).
toge [tɔʒ] *nf* toga ; (*de juge*) gown.
tohu-bohu [tɔybɔy] *nm* confusion ; commotion.
toi [twa] *pronom* you.
toile [twal] *nf* (*matériau*) cloth *q* ; (*bâche*) piece of canvas ; (*tableau*) canvas ; **grosse** ~ canvas ; **tisser sa** ~ (*araignée*) to spin its web ; ~ **d'araignée** cobweb ; ~ **cirée** oilcloth ; ~ **de fond** (*fig*) backdrop ; ~ **de jute** hessian ; ~ **de lin** linen.
toilette [twalɛt] *nf* wash ; (*s'habiller et se préparer*) getting ready, washing and dressing ; (*habits*) outfit ; dress *q* ; ~**s** *nfpl* (w.-c.) toilet *sg* ; **les** ~**s des dames/messieurs** the ladies'/gents' (toilets) ; **faire sa** ~ to have a wash, get washed ; **articles de** ~ toiletries ; ~ **intime** personal hygiene.
toi-même [twamɛm] *pronom* yourself.
toise [twaz] *nf*: **passer à la** ~ to have one's height measured.
toiser [twaze] *vt* to eye up and down.
toison [twazɔ̃] *nf* (*de mouton*) fleece ; (*cheveux*) mane.
toit [twa] *nm* roof.
toiture [twatyʀ] *nf* roof.
tôle [tol] *nf* sheet metal *q* ; (*plaque*) steel *ou* iron sheet ; ~**s** (*carrosserie*) bodywork *sg* ; panels ; ~ **d'acier** sheet steel *q* ; ~ **ondulée** corrugated iron.
tolérable [tɔleʀabl(ə)] *a* tolerable, bearable.
tolérance [tɔleʀɑ̃s] *nf* tolerance ; (*hors taxe*) allowance.
tolérant, e [tɔleʀɑ̃, -ɑ̃t] *a* tolerant.
tolérer [tɔleʀe] *vt* to tolerate ; (ADMIN: *hors taxe etc*) to allow.
tôlerie [tolʀi] *nf* sheet metal manufacture ; sheet metal workshop.
tollé [tɔle] *nm*: **un** ~ (**de protestations**) a general outcry.
T.O.M. [*parfois*: tɔm] *sigle m(pl)* = *territoire(s) d'outre-mer*.
tomate [tɔmat] *nf* tomato.
tombal, e [tɔ̃bal] *a*: **pierre** ~**e** tombstone, gravestone.
tombant, e [tɔ̃bɑ̃, -ɑ̃t] *a* (*fig*) drooping, sloping.
tombe [tɔ̃b] *nf* (*sépulture*) grave ; (*avec monument*) tomb.
tombeau, x [tɔ̃bo] *nm* tomb.
tombée [tɔ̃be] *nf*: **à la** ~ **du jour** *ou* **de la nuit** at the close of day, at nightfall.
tomber [tɔ̃be] *vi* to fall // *vt*: **la veste** to slip off one's jacket ; **laisser** ~ to drop ; ~ **sur** *vt* (*rencontrer*) to come across ; (*attaquer*) to set about ; ~ **de fatigue/sommeil** to drop from exhaustion/be falling asleep on one's feet ; **ça tombe bien** it comes at the right time ; **il est bien tombé** he's been lucky.
tombereau, x [tɔ̃bʀo] *nm* tipcart.

tombeur [tɔ̃bœʀ] *nm (péj)* Casanova.
tombola [tɔ̃bɔla] *nf* tombola.
tome [tɔm] *nm* volume.
tommette [tɔmɛt] *nf* hexagonal floor tile.
ton, ta, *pl* **tes** [tɔ̃, ta, te] *dét* your.
ton [tɔ̃] *nm (gén)* tone ; *(MUS)* key ; *(couleur)* shade, tone ; **de bon ~** in good taste.
tonal, e [tɔnal] *a* tonal.
tonalité [tɔnalite] *nf (au téléphone)* dialling tone ; *(MUS)* tonality ; key ; *(fig)* tone.
tondeuse [tɔ̃døz] *nf (à gazon)* (lawn)-mower ; *(du coiffeur)* clippers *pl* ; *(pour la tonte)* shears *pl*.
tondre [tɔ̃dʀ(ə)] *vt (pelouse, herbe)* to mow ; *(haie)* to cut, clip ; *(mouton, toison)* to shear ; *(cheveux)* to crop.
tonifiant, e [tɔnifjɑ̃, -ɑ̃t] *a* invigorating, revivifying.
tonifier [tɔnifje] *vt (peau, organisme)* to tone up.
tonique [tɔnik] *a* fortifying *// nm, nf* tonic.
tonitruant, e [tɔnitʀyɑ̃, -ɑ̃t] *a:* **voix ~e** thundering voice.
tonnage [tɔnaʒ] *nm* tonnage.
tonne [tɔn] *nf* metric ton, tonne.
tonneau, x [tɔno] *nm (à vin, cidre)* barrel ; *(NAVIG)* ton ; **faire des ~x** *(voiture, avion)* to roll over.
tonnelier [tɔnəlje] *nm* cooper.
tonnelle [tɔnɛl] *nf* bower, arbour.
tonner [tɔne] *vi* to thunder ; **il tonne** it is thundering, there's some thunder.
tonnerre [tɔnɛʀ] *nm* thunder ; **~ d'applaudissements** thunderous applause ; **du ~** *a (fam)* terrific.
tonsure [tɔ̃syʀ] *nf* tonsure ; bald patch.
tonte [tɔ̃t] *nf* shearing.
tonus [tɔnys] *nm* tone.
top [tɔp] *nm:* **au 3ème ~** at the 3rd stroke *// a:* **~ secret** top secret.
topaze [tɔpaz] *nf* topaz.
toper [tɔpe] *vi:* **tope-/topez-là!** it's a deal!, you're on!
topinambour [tɔpinɑ̃buʀ] *nm* Jerusalem artichoke.
topographie [tɔpɔgʀafi] *nf* topography ; **topographique** *a* topographical.
toponymie [tɔpɔnimi] *nf* study of place-names, toponymy.
toque [tɔk] *nf (de fourrure)* fur hat ; **~ de jockey/juge** jockey's/judge's cap ; **~ de cuisinier** chef's hat.
toqué, e [tɔke] *a (fam)* touched, cracked.
torche [tɔʀʃ(ə)] *nf* torch ; **se mettre en ~** *(parachute)* to candle.
torcher [tɔʀʃe] *vt (fam)* to wipe.
torchère [tɔʀʃɛʀ] *nf* flare.
torchon [tɔʀʃɔ̃] *nm* cloth, duster ; *(à vaisselle)* tea towel, dish towel.
tordre [tɔʀdʀ(ə)] *vt (chiffon)* to wring ; *(barre, fig: visage)* to twist ; **se ~** *vi (barre)* to bend ; *(roue)* to twist, buckle ; *(ver, serpent)* to writhe ; **se ~ le pied/bras** to twist *ou* sprain one's foot/arm ; **se ~ de douleur/rire** to writhe in pain/be doubled up with laughter.
tordu, e [tɔʀdy] *a (fig)* warped, twisted.
torero [tɔʀeʀo] *nm* bullfighter.
tornade [tɔʀnad] *nf* tornado.

torpeur [tɔʀpœʀ] *nf* torpor, drowsiness.
torpille [tɔʀpij] *nf* torpedo ; **torpiller** *vt* to torpedo.
torréfier [tɔʀefje] *vt* to roast.
torrent [tɔʀɑ̃] *nm* torrent, mountain stream ; *(fig):* **~ de** torrent *ou* flood of ; **il pleut à ~s** the rain is lashing down ; **torrentiel, le** *a* torrential.
torride [tɔʀid] *a* torrid.
torsade [tɔʀsad] *nf* twist ; *(ARCHIT)* cable moulding ; **torsader** *vt* to twist.
torse [tɔʀs(ə)] *nm (ANAT)* torso ; chest.
torsion [tɔʀsjɔ̃] *nf* twisting ; torsion.
tort [tɔʀ] *nm (défaut)* fault ; *(préjudice)* wrong *q* ; **~s** *nmpl (JUR)* fault *sg* ; **avoir ~** to be wrong ; **être dans son ~** to be in the wrong ; **donner ~ à qn** to lay the blame on sb ; *(fig)* to prove sb wrong ; **causer du ~ à** to harm ; to be harmful *ou* detrimental to ; **en ~** in the wrong, at fault ; **à ~** wrongly ; **à ~ et à travers** wildly.
torticolis [tɔʀtikɔli] *nm* stiff neck.
tortiller [tɔʀtije] *vt* to twist ; to twiddle ; **se ~** *vi* to wriggle, squirm.
tortionnaire [tɔʀsjɔnɛʀ] *nm* torturer.
tortue [tɔʀty] *nf* tortoise.
tortueux, euse [tɔʀtɥø, -øz] *a (rue)* twisting ; *(fig)* tortuous.
torture [tɔʀtyʀ] *nf* torture ; **torturer** *vt* to torture ; *(fig)* to torment.
torve [tɔʀv(ə)] *a:* **regard ~** menacing *ou* grim look.
tôt [to] *ad* early ; **~ ou tard** sooner or later ; **si ~** so early ; *(déjà)* so soon ; **au plus ~** at the earliest, as soon as possible ; **plus ~** earlier ; **il eut ~ fait de faire** he soon did.
total, e, aux [tɔtal, -o] *a, nm* total ; **au ~** in total *ou* all ; **faire le ~** to work out the total, add up ; **~ement** *ad* totally, completely ; **~iser** *vt* total (up).
totalitaire [tɔtalitɛʀ] *a* totalitarian.
totalité [tɔtalite] *nf:* **la ~ de** all of, the total amount *(ou* number) of ; the whole + *sg* ; **en ~** entirely.
totem [tɔtɛm] *nm* totem.
toubib [tubib] *nm (fam)* doctor.
touchant, e [tuʃɑ̃, -ɑ̃t] *a* touching.
touche [tuʃ] *nf (de piano, de machine à écrire)* key ; *(PEINTURE etc)* stroke, touch ; *(fig: de nostalgie)* touch, hint ; *(RUGBY)* line-out ; *(FOOTBALL: aussi:* **remise en ~)** throw-in ; *(: ligne de ~)* touch-line ; *(ESCRIME)* hit ; **en ~** in *(ou* into) touch ; **avoir une drôle de ~** to look a sight.
touche-à-tout [tuʃatu] *nm/f inv (péj)* meddler ; dabbler.
toucher [tuʃe] *nm* touch *// vt* to touch ; *(palper)* to feel ; *(atteindre: d'un coup de feu etc)* to hit ; *(affecter)* to touch, affect ; *(concerner)* to concern, affect ; *(contacter)* to reach, contact ; *(recevoir: récompense)* to receive, get ; *(: salaire)* to draw, get ; **au ~** to the touch ; **se ~** *(être en contact)* to touch ; **~ à** to touch ; *(modifier)* to touch, tamper *ou* meddle with ; *(traiter de, concerner)* to touch on ; to have to do with, concern ; **je vais lui en ~ un mot** I'll have a word with him about it ; **~ à sa fin** to be drawing to a close.

touffe [tuf] *nf* tuft.

touffu, e [tufy] *a* thick, dense; *(fig)* complex, involved.

toujours [tuʒuʀ] *ad* always; *(encore)* still; *(constamment)* forever; ~ **plus** more and more; **pour** ~ forever; ~ **est-il que** the fact remains that; **essaie** ~ (you can) try anyway.

toupie [tupi] *nf* (spinning) top.

tour [tuʀ] *nf* tower; *(immeuble)* high-rise block, tower block; *(ÉCHECS)* castle, rook // *nm (excursion)* stroll, walk; run, ride; trip; *(SPORT: aussi:* ~ **de piste)** lap; *(d'être servi ou de jouer etc, tournure, de vis ou clef)* turn; *(de roue etc)* revolution; *(circonférence):* **de 3 m de** ~ 3 m round, with a circumference *ou* girth of 3 m; *(POL: aussi:* ~ **de scrutin)** ballot; *(ruse, de prestidigitation)* trick; *(de potier)* wheel; *(à bois, métaux)* lathe; **faire le** ~ **de** to go round; *(à pied)* to walk round; **faire un** ~ to go for a walk; *(en voiture etc)* to go for a ride; **faire 2** ~**s** to go round twice; *(hélice etc)* to turn *ou* revolve twice; **fermer à double** ~ *vi* to double-lock the door; **c'est au** ~ **de Renée** it's Renée's turn; **à** ~ **de rôle,** **à** ~ **in** turn; ~ **de taille/tête** waist/head measurement; ~ **de chant** song recital; ~ **de contrôle** *nf* control tower; ~ **de garde** spell of duty; ~ **d'horizon** *(fig)* general survey; ~ **de lit** valance; ~ **de reins** sprained back.

tourbe [tuʀb(ə)] *nf* peat; **tourbière** *nf* peat-bog.

tourbillon [tuʀbijɔ̃] *nm* whirlwind; *(d'eau)* whirlpool; *(fig)* whirl, swirl; **tourbillonner** *vi* to whirl, swirl; to whirl *ou* swirl round.

tourelle [tuʀɛl] *nf* turret.

tourisme [tuʀism(ə)] *nm* tourism; tourist industry; **agence de** ~ tourist agency; **faire du** ~ to do some sightseeing, go touring; **touriste** *nm/f* tourist; **touristique** *à* tourist *cpd*; *(région)* touristic, with tourist appeal.

tourment [tuʀmã] *nm* torment.

tourmente [tuʀmãt] *nf* storm.

tourmenté, e [tuʀmãte] *a* tormented, tortured.

tourmenter [tuʀmãte] *vt* to torment; **se** ~ *vi* to fret, worry o.s.

tournage [tuʀnaʒ] *nm (d'un film)* shooting.

tournant, e [tuʀnã, -ãt] *a: voir* **plaque, grève** // *nm (de route)* bend; *(fig)* turning point.

tournebroche [tuʀnəbʀɔʃ] *nm* roasting spit.

tourne-disque [tuʀnədisk(ə)] *nm* record player.

tournée [tuʀne] *nf (du facteur etc)* round; *(d'artiste, politicien)* tour; *(au café)* round (of drinks); ~ **musicale** concert tour.

tourner [tuʀne] *vt* to turn; *(contourner)* to get round; *(CINÉMA)* to shoot; to make // *vi* to turn; *(moteur)* to run; *(compteur)* to tick away; *(lait etc)* to turn (sour); **se** ~ *vi* to turn round; **se** ~ **vers** to turn to; to turn towards; **bien** ~ to turn out well; ~ **autour de** to go round; to revolve round; *(péj)* to hang round; ~ **à/en** to turn into; ~ **à la pluie/au rouge** to turn

rainy/red; ~ **le dos à** to turn one's back on; to have one's back to; **se** ~ **les pouces** to twiddle one's thumbs; ~ **la tête** to look away; ~ **la tête à qn** *(fig)* to go to sb's head; ~ **de l'œil** to pass out.

tournesol [tuʀnəsɔl] *nm* sunflower.

tourneur [tuʀnœʀ] *nm* turner; lathe-operator.

tournevis [tuʀnəvis] *nm* screwdriver.

tourniquet [tuʀnikɛ] *nm (pour arroser)* sprinkler; *(portillon)* turnstile; *(présentoir)* revolving stand.

tournoi [tuʀnwa] *nm* tournament.

tournoyer [tuʀnwaje] *vi* to whirl round; to swirl round.

tournure [tuʀnyʀ] *nf (LING)* turn of phrase; form; phrasing; *(évolution):* **la** ~ **de qch** the way sth is developing; *(aspect):* **la** ~ **de** the look of; ~ **d'esprit** turn *ou* cast of mind; **la** ~ **des évènements** the turn of events.

tourte [tuʀt(ə)] *nf* pie.

tourteau, x [tuʀto] *nm (AGR)* oilcake, cattle-cake; *(ZOOL)* edible crab.

tourterelle [tuʀtəʀɛl] *nf* turtledove.

tous *dét* [tu], *pronom* [tus] *voir* **tout.**

Toussaint [tusɛ̃] *nf:* **la** ~ All Saints' Day.

tousser [tuse] *vi* to cough; **toussoter** *vi* to have a slight cough; to cough a little; *(pour avertir)* to give a slight cough.

tout, e, *pl* **tous, toutes** [tu, tus, tut] *dét* **all;** ~ **le lait** all the milk, the whole of the milk; ~**e la nuit** all night, the whole night; ~ **le livre** the whole book; ~ **un pain** a whole loaf; **tous les livres** all the books; **toutes les nuits** every night; **à** ~ **âge** at any age; **toutes les fois** every time; **toutes les 3/2 semaines** every third/other *ou* second week; **tous les 2** both *ou* each of us (*ou* them); **toutes les 3** all 3 of us (*ou* them); ~ **le temps** all the time; the whole time; **c'est** ~ **le contraire** it's quite the opposite; **il avait pour** ~**e nourriture** his only food was // *pronom* everything, all; **tous, toutes** all (of them); **je les vois tous** I can see them all *ou* all of them; **nous y sommes tous allés** all of us went, we all went; **en** ~ in all // *ad* quite; very; ~ **en haut** right at the top; **le** ~ **premier** the very first; **le livre** ~ **entier** the whole book; ~ **seul** all alone; ~ **droit** straight ahead; ~ **en travaillant** while working, as *ou* while he *etc* works // *nm* whole; **le** ~ all of it (*ou* them), the whole lot; ~ **d'abord** first of all; ~ **à coup** suddenly; ~ **à fait** absolutely; ~ **à l'heure** a short while ago; in a short while, shortly; ~ **de même** all the same; ~ **le monde** everybody; ~ **de suite** immediately, straight away; ~ **terrain** *ou* **tous terrains** *a inv* general-purpose; ~**-à-l'égout** *nm inv* mains drainage.

toutefois [tutfwa] *ad* however.

toutou [tutu] *nm (fam)* doggie.

toux [tu] *nf* cough.

toxicomane [tɔksikɔman] *nm/f* drug addict.

toxine [tɔksin] *nf* toxin.

toxique [tɔksik] *a* toxic, poisonous.

trac [tʀak] *nm* nerves *pl*; *(THÉÂTRE)* stage

fright; **avoir le ~** to get an attack of nerves; to have stage fright.

tracas [tRaka] *nm* bother *q*, worry *q*; **tracasser** *vt* to worry, bother; to harass; **se tracasser** *vi* to worry o.s., fret; **tracasserie** *nf* annoyance *q*; harassment *q*; **tracassier, ière** *a* irksome.

trace [tRas] *nf* (*empreintes*) tracks *pl*; (*marques, aussi fig*) mark; (*restes, vestige*) trace; (*indice*) sign; **~s de pas** footprints.

tracé [tRase] *nm* line; layout.

tracer [tRase] *vt* to draw; (*mot*) to trace; (*piste*) to open up.

trachée(-artère) [tRaʃe(aRtɛR)] *nf* windpipe, trachea; **trachéite** [tRakeit] *nf* tracheitis.

tract [tRakt] *nm* tract, pamphlet.

tractations [tRaktɑsjɔ̃] *nfpl* dealings, bargaining *sg*.

tracteur [tRaktœR] *nm* tractor.

traction [tRaksjɔ̃] *nf* traction; (*GYM*) pull-up; **~ avant/arrière** front-wheel/rear-wheel drive; **~ électrique** electric(al) traction *ou* haulage.

tradition [tRadisjɔ̃] *nf* tradition; **traditionnel, le** *a* traditional.

traducteur, trice [tRadyktœR, -tRis] *nm/f* translator.

traduction [tRadyksjɔ̃] *nf* translation.

traduire [tRaduiR] *vt* to translate; (*exprimer*) to render, convey; **~ en français** to translate into French; **~ en justice** to bring before the courts.

trafic [tRafik] *nm* traffic; **~ d'armes** arms dealing; **trafiquant, e** *nm/f* trafficker; dealer; **trafiquer** *vt* (*péj*) to doctor, tamper with // *vi* to traffic, be engaged in trafficking.

tragédie [tRaʒedi] *nf* tragedy; **tragédien, ne** *nm/f* tragedian/tragedienne.

tragique [tRaʒik] *a* tragic; **~ment** *ad* tragically.

trahir [tRaiR] *vt* to betray; (*fig*) to give away, reveal; **trahison** *nf* betrayal; (*MIL*) treason.

train [tRɛ̃] *nm* (*RAIL*) train; (*allure*) pace; (*fig: ensemble*) set; **mettre qch en ~** to get sth under way; **mettre qn en ~** to put sb in good spirits; **se mettre en ~** to get started; to warm up; **se sentir en ~** to feel in good form; **~ avant/arrière** front-wheel/rear-wheel axle unit; **~ d'atterrissage** undercarriage; **~ autos-couchettes** car-sleeper train; **~ électrique** (*jouet*) (electric) train set; **~ de pneus** set of tyres; **~ de vie** style of living.

traînant, e [tRɛnɑ̃, -ɑ̃t] *a* (*voix, ton*) drawling.

traînard, e [tRɛnaR, -aRd(ə)] *nm/f* (*péj*) slowcoach.

traîne [tRɛn] *nf* (*de robe*) train; **être à la ~** to be in tow; to lag behind.

traîneau, x [tRɛno] *nm* sleigh, sledge.

traînée [tRɛne] *nf* streak, trail; (*péj*) slut.

traîner [tRɛne] *vt* (*remorque*) to pull; (*enfant, chien*) to drag ou trail along // *vi* (*être en désordre*) to lie around; (*marcher lentement*) to dawdle (along); (*vagabonder*) to hang about; (*agir lentement*) to idle about; (*durer*) to drag on; **se ~** *vi* to crawl

along; to drag o.s. along; (*durer*) to drag on; **~ les pieds** to drag one's feet.

train-train [tRɛ̃tRɛ̃] *nm* humdrum routine.

traire [tRɛR] *vt* to milk.

trait [tRɛ] *nm* (*ligne*) line; (*de dessin*) stroke; (*caractéristique*) feature, trait; (*flèche*) dart, arrow; shaft; **~s** *nmpl* (*du visage*) features; **d'un ~** (*boire*) in one gulp; **de ~** *a* (*animal*) draught; **avoir ~ à** to concern; **~ de caractère** characteristic, trait; **~ d'esprit** flash of wit; **~ d'union** hyphen; (*fig*) link.

traitant [tRɛtɑ̃] *am*: **votre médecin ~** your usual *ou* family doctor; **shampooing ~** medicated shampoo.

traite [tRɛt] *nf* (*COMM*) draft; (*AGR*) milking; (*trajet*) stretch; **d'une (seule) ~** without stopping (once); **la ~ des noirs** the slave trade.

traité [tRete] *nm* treaty.

traitement [tRɛtmɑ̃] *nm* treatment; processing; (*salaire*) salary.

traiter [tRete] *vt* (*gén*) to treat; (*TECH: matériaux*) to process, treat; (*affaire*) to deal with, handle; (*qualifier*): **~ qn d'idiot** to call sb a fool // *vi* to deal; **~ de** *vt* to deal with; **bien/mal ~** to treat well/ill-treat.

traiteur [tRɛtœR] *nm* caterer.

traître, esse [tRɛtR(ə), -tRɛs] *a* (*dangereux*) treacherous // *nm* traitor; **prendre qn en ~** to make an insidious attack on sb; **traîtrise** *nf* treachery, treacherousness.

trajectoire [tRaʒɛktwaR] *nf* trajectory, path.

trajet [tRaʒɛ] *nm* journey; (*itinéraire*) route; (*fig*) path, course.

tralala [tRalala] *nm* (*péj*) fuss.

tram [tRam] *nm abr de* **tramway**.

trame [tRam] *nf* (*de tissu*) weft; (*fig*) framework; texture; (*TYPO*) screen.

tramer [tRame] *vt* to plot, hatch.

tramway [tRamwɛ] *nm* tram(way); tram(car).

tranchant, e [tRɑ̃ʃɑ̃, -ɑ̃t] *a* sharp; (*fig*) peremptory // *nm* (*d'un couteau*) cutting edge; (*de la main*) edge.

tranche [tRɑ̃ʃ] *nf* (*morceau*) slice; (*arête*) edge; (*partie*) section; (*série*) block; issue; bracket.

tranché, e [tRɑ̃ʃe] *a* (*couleurs*) distinct, sharply contrasted; (*opinions*) clear-cut, definite // *nf* trench.

trancher [tRɑ̃ʃe] *vt* to cut, sever; (*fig: résoudre*) to settle // *vi*: **~ avec** to contrast sharply with.

tranchet [tRɑ̃ʃɛ] *nm* knife.

tranchoir [tRɑ̃ʃwaR] *nm* chopper.

tranquille [tRɑ̃kil] *a* calm, quiet; (*enfant, élève*) quiet; (*rassuré*) easy in one's mind, with one's mind at rest; **se tenir ~** (*enfant*) to be quiet; **avoir la conscience ~** to have an easy conscience; **laisse-moi/laisse-ça ~** leave me/it alone; **~ment** *ad* calmly; **tranquillisant** *nm* tranquillizer; **tranquilliser** *vt* to reassure; **tranquillité** *nf* quietness; peace (and quiet); **tranquillité (d'esprit)** peace of mind.

transaction [tʀɑ̃zaksjɔ̃] *nf* (COMM) transaction, deal.

transat [tʀɑ̃zat] *nm* deckchair.

transatlantique [tʀɑ̃zatlɑ̃tik] *a* transatlantic // *nm* transatlantic liner.

transborder [tʀɑ̃sbɔʀde] *vt* to tran(s)ship.

transcendant, e [tʀɑ̃sɑ̃dɑ̃, -ɑ̃t] *a* transcendent(al).

transcription [tʀɑ̃skʀipsjɔ̃] *nf* transcription.

transcrire [tʀɑ̃skʀiʀ] *vt* to transcribe.

transe [tʀɑ̃s] *nf*: **entrer en ~** to go into a trance ; **~s** agony *sg*.

transférer [tʀɑ̃sfeʀe] *vt* to transfer ; **transfert** *nm* transfer.

transfigurer [tʀɑ̃sfiɡyʀe] *vt* to transform.

transformateur [tʀɑ̃sfɔʀmatœʀ] *nm* transformer.

transformation [tʀɑ̃sfɔʀmasjɔ̃] *nf* transformation ; (RUGBY) conversion.

transformer [tʀɑ̃sfɔʀme] *vt* to transform, alter ('alter' *implique un changement moins radical*) ; (*matière première, appartement*, RUGBY) to convert ; **~ en** to transform into ; to turn into ; to convert into ; **se ~** *vi* to be transformed ; to alter.

transfuge [tʀɑ̃sfyʒ] *nm* renegade.

transfusion [tʀɑ̃sfyzjɔ̃] *nf*: **~ sanguine** blood transfusion.

transgresser [tʀɑ̃sɡʀese] *vt* to contravene, disobey.

transhumance [tʀɑ̃zymɑ̃s] *nf* transhumance, seasonal move to new pastures.

transi, e [tʀɑ̃zi] *a* numb (with cold), chilled to the bone.

transiger [tʀɑ̃ziʒe] *vi* to compromise, come to an agreement.

transistor [tʀɑ̃zistɔʀ] *nm* transistor.

transit [tʀɑ̃zit] *nm* transit ; **~er** *vi* to pass in transit.

transitif, ive [tʀɑ̃zitif, -iv] *a* transitive.

transition [tʀɑ̃zisjɔ̃] *nf* transition ; **de ~** transitional ; **transitoire** *a* transitional, provisional ; transient.

translucide [tʀɑ̃slysid] *a* translucent.

transmetteur [tʀɑ̃smetœʀ] *nm* transmitter.

transmettre [tʀɑ̃smetʀ(ə)] *vt* (*passer*): **~ qch à qn** to pass sth on to sb ; (TECH, TÉL, MÉD) to transmit ; (TV, RADIO: *retransmettre*) to broadcast ; **transmissible** *a* transmissible.

transmission [tʀɑ̃smisjɔ̃] *nf* transmission, passing on ; (AUTO) transmission ; **~s** *nfpl* (MIL) ≈ signals corps ; **~ de pensée** telepathy.

transparaître [tʀɑ̃spaʀɛtʀ(ə)] *vi* to show (through).

transparence [tʀɑ̃spaʀɑ̃s] *nf* transparence ; **par ~** (*regarder*) against a source of light ; (*voir*) showing through.

transparent, e [tʀɑ̃spaʀɑ̃, -ɑ̃t] *a* transparent.

transpercer [tʀɑ̃spɛʀse] *vt* to go through, pierce.

transpiration [tʀɑ̃spiʀasjɔ̃] *nf* perspiration.

transpirer [tʀɑ̃spiʀe] *vi* to perspire.

transplanter [tʀɑ̃splɑ̃te] *vt* (MÉD, BOT) to transplant ; (*personne*) to uproot, move.

transport [tʀɑ̃spɔʀ] *nm* transport ; **~s en commun** public transport *sg*.

transporter [tʀɑ̃spɔʀte] *vt* to carry, move ; (COMM) to transport, convey ; (*fig*) to send into raptures ; **~ qn à l'hôpital** to take sb to hospital ; **transporteur** *nm* haulier, haulage contractor.

transposer [tʀɑ̃spoze] *vt* to transpose ; **transposition** *nf* transposition.

transvaser [tʀɑ̃svaze] *vt* to decant.

transversal, e, aux [tʀɑ̃svɛʀsal, -o] *a* transverse, cross(-) ; cross-country ; running at right angles.

trapèze [tʀapɛz] *nm* (GÉOM) trapezium ; (*au cirque*) trapeze ; **trapéziste** *nm/f* trapeze artist.

trappe [tʀap] *nf* trap door.

trappeur [tʀapœʀ] *nm* trapper, fur trader.

trapu, e [tʀapy] *a* squat, stocky.

traquenard [tʀaknaʀ] *nm* trap.

traquer [tʀake] *vt* to track down ; (*harceler*) to hound.

traumatiser [tʀomatize] *vt* to traumatize.

traumatisme [tʀomatism(ə)] *nm* traumatism.

travail, aux [tʀavaj, -o] *nm* (*gén*) work ; (*tâche, métier*) work *q*, job ; (ÉCON, MÉD) labour // *nmpl* (*de réparation, agricoles etc*) work *sg* ; (*sur route*) roadworks *pl* ; (*de construction*) building (work) ; **être/entrer en ~** (MÉD) to be in/start labour ; **être sans ~** (*employé*) to be out of work *ou* unemployed ; **~ noir** moonlighting ; **travaux des champs** farmwork *sg* ; **travaux dirigés** (SCOL) supervised practical work *sg* ; **travaux forcés** hard labour *sg* ; **travaux manuels** (SCOL) handicrafts ; **travaux ménagers** housework *sg* ; **travaux publics** ≈ public works *sg*.

travaillé, e [tʀavaje] *a* (*style*) polished.

travailler [tʀavaje] *vi* to work ; (*bois*) to warp // *vt* (*bois, métal*) to work ; (*objet d'art, discipline, fig: influencer*) to work on ; **cela le travaille** it is on his mind ; **~ la terre** to till the land ; **~ son piano** to do one's piano practice ; **~ à** to work on ; (*fig: contribuer à*) to work towards ; **travailleur, euse** *a* hard-working // *nm/f* worker ; **travailleur de force** labourer ; **travailliste** *a* Labour.

travée [tʀave] *nf* row ; (ARCHIT) bay ; span.

travelling [tʀavliŋ] *nm* (*chariot*) dolly ; (*technique*) tracking ; **~ optique** zoom shots *pl*.

travers [tʀavɛʀ] *nm* fault, failing ; **en ~ (de)** across ; **au ~ (de)** through ; **de ~** *a* askew // *ad* sideways ; (*fig*) the wrong way ; **à ~** through ; **regarder de ~** (*fig*) to look askance at.

traverse [tʀavɛʀs(ə)] *nf* (RAIL) sleeper ; **chemin de ~** shortcut.

traversée [tʀavɛʀse] *nf* crossing.

traverser [tʀavɛʀse] *vt* (*gén*) to cross ; (*ville, tunnel, aussi: percer, fig*) to go through ; (*suj: ligne, trait*) to run across.

traversin [tʀavɛʀsɛ̃] *nm* bolster.

travesti [tʀavɛsti] nm (costume) fancy dress ; (artiste de cabaret) female impersonator, drag artist ; (pervers) transvestite.

travestir [tʀavɛstiʀ] vt (vérité) to misrepresent ; **se** ~ to dress up ; to put on drag ; to dress as a woman.

trébucher [tʀebyʃe] vi: ~ **(sur)** to stumble (over), trip (against).

trèfle [tʀɛfl(ə)] nm (BOT) clover ; (CARTES: couleur) clubs pl ; (: carte) club ; ~ **à quatre feuilles** four-leaf clover.

treillage [tʀɛjaʒ] nm lattice work.

treille [tʀɛj] nf vine arbour ; climbing vine.

treillis [tʀɛji] nm (métallique) wire-mesh ; (toile) canvas ; (uniforme) battle-dress.

treize [tʀɛz] num thirteen ; **treizième** num thirteenth.

tréma [tʀema] nm diaeresis.

tremble [tʀɑ̃bl(ə)] nm (BOT) aspen.

tremblement [tʀɑ̃bləmɑ̃] nm trembling q, shaking q, shivering q ; ~ **de terre** earthquake.

trembler [tʀɑ̃ble] vi to tremble, shake ; ~ **de** (froid, fièvre) to shiver ou tremble with ; (peur) to shake ou tremble with ; ~ **pour qn** to fear for sb ; **trembloter** vi to tremble ou shake slightly.

trémolo [tʀemɔlo] nm (instrument) tremolo ; (voix) quaver.

trémousser [tʀemuse]: **se** ~ vi to jig about, wriggle about.

trempe [tʀɑ̃p] nf (fig): **de cette/sa** ~ **of** this/his calibre.

trempé, e [tʀɑ̃pe] a a soaking (wet), drenched ; (TECH) tempered.

tremper [tʀɑ̃pe] vt to soak, drench ; (aussi: **faire** ~, **mettre à** ~) to soak ; (plonger): ~ **qch dans** to dip sth in(to) // vi to soak ; (fig): ~ **dans** to be involved ou have a hand in ; **se** ~ vi to have a quick dip ; **se faire** ~ to get soaked ou drenched ; **trempette** nf: **faire trempette** to have a quick dip.

tremplin [tʀɑ̃plɛ̃] nm springboard ; (SKI) ski-jump.

trentaine [tʀɑ̃tɛn] nf: **une** ~ **(de)** thirty or so, about thirty.

trente [tʀɑ̃t] num thirty ; **trentième** num thirtieth.

trépaner [tʀepane] vt to trepan, trephine.

trépasser [tʀepase] vi to pass away.

trépider [tʀepide] vi to vibrate.

trépied [tʀepje] nm (d'appareil) tripod ; (meuble) trivet.

trépigner [tʀepiɲe] vi to stamp (one's feet).

très [tʀɛ] ad very ; much + pp, highly + pp ; ~ **critique** much criticized ; ~ **industrialisé** highly industrialized ; **j'ai** ~ **faim** I'm very hungry.

trésor [tʀezɔʀ] nm treasure ; (ADMIN) finances pl ; funds pl ; **T~** **(public)** public revenue.

trésorerie [tʀezɔʀʀi] nf (fonds) funds pl ; (gestion) accounts pl ; (bureaux) accounts department ; (poste) treasurership ; **difficultés de** ~ cash problems, shortage of cash ou funds.

trésorier, ière [tʀezɔʀje, -jɛʀ] nm/f treasurer ; ~**-payeur** nm paymaster.

tressaillir [tʀesajiʀ] vi to shiver, shudder ; to quiver.

tressauter [tʀesote] vi to start, jump.

tresse [tʀɛs] nf braid, plait.

tresser [tʀese] vi (cheveux) to braid, plait ; (fil, jonc) to plait ; (corbeille) to weave ; (corde) to twist.

tréteau, x [tʀeto] nm trestle ; **les** ~**x** (fig) the stage.

treuil [tʀœj] nm winch ; **treuiller** vt to winch up.

trève [tʀɛv] nf (MIL, POL) truce ; (fig) respite ; ~ **de ...** enough of this... .

tri [tʀi] nm sorting out q ; selection ; (POSTES) sorting ; sorting office.

triage [tʀijaʒ] nm (RAIL) shunting ; (gare) marshalling yard.

triangle [tʀijɑ̃gl(ə)] nm triangle ; ~ **rectangle** right-angled triangle.

tribal, e, aux [tʀibal, -o] a tribal.

tribord [tʀibɔʀ] nm: **à** ~ to starboard, on the starboard side.

tribu [tʀiby] nf tribe.

tribulations [tʀibylɑsjɔ̃] nfpl tribulations, trials.

tribunal, aux [tʀibynal, -o] nm (JUR) court ; (MIL) tribunal ; ~ **de police/pour enfants** police/juvenile court ; ~ **d'instance** ≈ magistrates' court ; ~ **de grande instance** ≈ high court.

tribune [tʀibyn] nf (estrade) platform, rostrum ; (débat) forum ; (d'église, de tribunal) gallery ; (de stade) stand ; ~ **libre** (PRESSE) opinion column.

tribut [tʀiby] nm tribute.

tributaire [tʀibytɛʀ] a: **être** ~ **de** to be dependent on ; (GÉO) to be a tributary of.

tricher [tʀiʃe] vi to cheat ; **tricherie** nf cheating q ; **tricheur, euse** nm/f cheat.

tricolore [tʀikɔlɔʀ] a three-coloured ; (français) red, white and blue.

tricot [tʀiko] nm (technique, ouvrage) knitting q ; (tissu) knitted fabric ; (vêtement) jersey, sweater.

tricoter [tʀikɔte] vt to knit.

trictrac [tʀiktʀak] nm backgammon.

tricycle [tʀisikl(ə)] nm tricycle.

triennal, e, aux [tʀiɛnal, -o] a three-yearly ; three-year.

trier [tʀije] vt to sort out ; (POSTES, fruits) to sort.

trigonométrie [tʀigɔnɔmetʀi] nf trigonometry.

trimbaler [tʀɛ̃bale] vt to cart around, trail along.

trimer [tʀime] vi to slave away.

trimestre [tʀimɛstʀ(ə)] nm (SCOL) term ; (COMM) quarter ; **trimestriel, le** a quarterly ; (SCOL) end-of-term.

tringle [tʀɛ̃gl(ə)] nf rod.

Trinité [tʀinite] nf Trinity.

trinquer [tʀɛ̃ke] vi to clink glasses ; (fam) to cop it ; ~ **à qch/la santé de qn** to drink to sth/sb.

trio [tʀijo] nm trio.

triomphal, e, aux [tʀijɔ̃fal, -o] a triumphant, triumphal.

triomphant, e [tʀijɔ̃fɑ̃, -ɑ̃t] a triumphant.

triomphe [tʀijɔ̃f] nm triumph ; **être reçu/porté en** ~ to be given a triumphant welcome/be carried shoulder-high in triumph.

triompher [tʀijɔ̃fe] vi to triumph, win; ~ **de** to triumph over, overcome.

tripes [tʀip] nfpl (CULIN) tripe sg; (fam) guts.

triple [tʀipl(ə)] a triple; treble // nm: **le ~ (de)** (comparaison) three times as much (as); **en ~ exemplaire** in triplicate; **~ment** ad three times over; in three ways, on three counts // nm trebling, threefold increase; **tripler** vi, vt to triple, treble, increase threefold.

tripot [tʀipo] nm (péj) dive.

tripotage [tʀipɔtaʒ] nm (péj) jiggery-pokery.

tripoter [tʀipɔte] vt to fiddle with, finger.

trique [tʀik] nf cudgel.

triste [tʀist(ə)] a sad; (péj): **personnage/affaire** sorry individual/affair; **tristesse** nf sadness.

triturer [tʀityʀe] vt (pâte) to knead; (objets) to manipulate.

trivial, e, aux [tʀivjal, -o] a coarse, crude; (commun) mundane.

troc [tʀɔk] nm (ÉCON) barter; (transaction) exchange, swap.

troglodyte [tʀɔglɔdit] nm/f cave dweller, troglodyte.

trognon [tʀɔɲɔ̃] nm (de fruit) core; (de légume) stalk.

trois [tʀwɑ] num three; **troisième** num third; **troisièmement** ad thirdly; **~-quarts** nmpl: **les ~-quarts de** three-quarters of.

trolleybus [tʀɔlɛbys] nm trolley bus.

trombe [tʀɔ̃b] nf waterspout; **des ~s d'eau** a downpour; **en ~** (arriver, passer) like a whirlwind.

trombone [tʀɔ̃bɔn] nm (MUS) trombone; (de bureau) paper clip; **~ à coulisse** slide trombone; **tromboniste** nm/f trombonist.

trompe [tʀɔ̃p] nf (d'éléphant) trunk; (MUS) trumpet, horn; **~ d'Eustache** Eustachian tube; **~s utérines** Fallopian tubes.

trompe-l'œil [tʀɔ̃plœj] nm: **en ~** in trompe-l'œil style.

tromper [tʀɔ̃pe] vt to deceive; (vigilance, poursuivants) to elude; **se ~** vi to make a mistake, be mistaken; **se ~ de voiture/jour** to take the wrong car/get the day wrong; **se ~ de 3 cm/20 F** to be out by 3 cm/20 F; **tromperie** nf deception, trickery q.

trompette [tʀɔ̃pɛt] nf trumpet; **en ~** (nez) turned-up; **trompettiste** nm/f trumpet player.

trompeur, euse [tʀɔ̃pœʀ, -øz] a deceptive, misleading.

tronc [tʀɔ̃] nm (BOT, ANAT) trunk; (d'église) collection box; **~ d'arbre** tree trunk; **~ commun** (SCOL) common-core syllabus; **~ de cône** truncated cone.

tronche [tʀɔ̃ʃ] nf (fam) mug, face.

tronçon [tʀɔ̃sɔ̃] nm section.

tronçonner [tʀɔ̃sɔne] vt to saw up; **tronçonneuse** nf chain saw.

trône [tʀon] nm throne.

trôner [tʀone] vi (fig) to sit in the place of honour.

tronquer [tʀɔ̃ke] vt to truncate; (fig) to curtail.

trop [tʀo] ad vb + too much, too + adjectif, adverbe; **~ (nombreux)** too many; **~ peu (nombreux)** too few; **~ (souvent)** too often; **~ (longtemps)** (for) too long; **~ de** (nombre) too many; (quantité) too much; **de ~, en ~**: **des livres en ~** a few books too many, a few extra books; **du lait en ~** some milk over ou extra, too much milk; **3 livres/F de ~** 3 books too many/F too much.

trophée [tʀofe] nm trophy.

tropical, e, aux [tʀɔpikal, -o] a tropical.

tropique [tʀɔpik] nm tropic; **~s** nmpl tropics.

trop-plein [tʀɔplɛ̃] nm (tuyau) overflow ou outlet (pipe); (liquide) overflow.

troquer [tʀɔke] vt: **~ qch contre** to barter ou trade sth for; (fig) to swap sth for.

trot [tʀo] nm trot; **aller au ~** to trot along; **partir au ~** to set off at a trot.

trotter [tʀɔte] vi to trot; (fig) to scamper along (ou about).

trotteuse [tʀɔtøz] nf (de montre) second hand.

trottiner [tʀɔtine] vi (fig) to scamper along (ou about).

trottinette [tʀɔtinɛt] nf (child's) scooter.

trottoir [tʀɔtwaʀ] nm pavement; **faire le ~** (péj) to walk the streets; **~ roulant** moving walkway, travellator.

trou [tʀu] nm hole; (fig) gap; **~ d'air** air pocket; **~ de mémoire** blank, lapse of memory; **le ~ de la serrure** the keyhole.

troublant, e [tʀublɑ̃, -ɑ̃t] a disturbing.

trouble [tʀubl(ə)] a (liquide) cloudy; (image, mémoire) indistinct, hazy; (affaire) shady, murky // nm (désarroi) distress, agitation; (émoi sensuel) turmoil, agitation; (embarras) confusion; (zizanie) unrest, discord; **~s** nmpl (POL) disturbances, troubles, unrest sg; (MÉD) trouble sg, disorders.

trouble-fête [tʀubləfɛt] nm/f inv spoilsport.

troubler [tʀuble] vt (embarrasser) to confuse, disconcert; (émouvoir) to agitate; to disturb; to perturb; (perturber: ordre etc) to disrupt, disturb; (liquide) to make cloudy; **se ~** vi (personne) to become flustered ou confused; **~ l'ordre public** to cause a breach of the peace.

troué, e [tʀue] a with a hole (ou holes) in it // nf gap; (MIL) breach.

trouer [tʀue] vt to make a hole (ou holes) in; (fig) to pierce.

trouille [tʀuj] nf (fam): **avoir la ~** to have the jitters, be in a funk.

troupe [tʀup] nf (MIL) troop; (groupe) troop, group; **la ~** (MIL) the army; the troops pl; **~ (de théâtre)** (theatrical) company.

troupeau, x [tʀupo] nm (de moutons) flock; (de vaches) herd.

trousse [tʀus] nf case, kit; (d'écolier) pencil case; (de docteur) instrument case; **aux ~s de** (fig) on the heels ou tail of; **~ à outils** toolkit; **~ de toilette** toilet ou sponge bag.

trousseau, x [tʀuso] *nm (de jeune mariée)* trousseau ; ~ **de clefs** bunch of keys.

trouvaille [tʀuvaj] *nf* find.

trouver [tʀuve] *vt* to find ; *(rendre visite)*: **aller/venir** ~ **qn** to go/come and see sb ; **je trouve que** I find *ou* think that ; ~ **à boire/critiquer** to find something to drink/criticize ; **se** ~ *vi (être)* to be ; *(être soudain)* to find o.s. ; **se** ~ **être/avoir** to happen to be/have ; **il se trouve que** it happens that, it turns out that ; **se** ~ **bien** to feel well ; **se** ~ **mal** to pass out.

truand [tʀyɑ̃] *nm* villain, crook.

truc [tʀyk] *nm (astuce)* way, device ; *(de cinéma, prestidigitateur)* trick effect ; *(chose)* thing ; *(machin)* thingumajig, whatsit ; **avoir le** ~ to have the knack.

truchement [tʀyʃmɑ̃] *nm*: **par le** ~ **de qn** through (the intervention of) sb.

truculent, e [tʀykylɑ̃, -ɑ̃t] *a* colourful.

truelle [tʀyɛl] *nf* trowel.

truffe [tʀyf] *nf* truffle ; *(nez)* nose.

truffer [tʀyfe] *vt (CULIN)* to garnish with truffles ; **truffé de** *(fig)* peppered with ; bristling with.

truie [tʀɥi] *nf* sow.

truite [tʀɥit] *nf* trout *inv*.

truquage [tʀyka3] *nm* fixing ; *(CINÉMA)* special effects *pl.*

truquer [tʀyke] *vt (élections, serrure, dés)* to fix ; *(CINÉMA)* to use special effects in.

trust [tʀœst] *nm (COMM)* trust.

tsar [dzaʀ] *nm* tsar.

T.S.F. [teɛsɛf] *sigle f (= télégraphie sans fil)* wireless.

tsigane [tsigan] *a, nm/f* = **tzigane**.

T.S.V.P. *sigle (= tournez s.v.p.)* P.T.O. (please turn over).

T.T.C. *sigle* = *toutes taxes comprises.*

tu [ty] *pronom* you // *nm*: **employer le** ~ to use the 'tu' form.

tu, e [ty] *pp de* **taire.**

tuba [tyba] *nm (MUS)* tuba ; *(SPORT)* snorkel.

tube [tyb] *nm* tube ; pipe ; *(chanson, disque)* hit song *ou* record ; ~ **digestif** alimentary canal, digestive tract.

tuberculeux, euse [tybɛʀkylø, -øz] *a* tubercular // *nm/f* tuberculosis *ou* TB patient.

tuberculose [tybɛʀkyloz] *nf* tuberculosis.

tubulaire [tybylɛʀ] *a* tubular.

tubulure [tybylyʀ] *nf* pipe ; piping *q* ; *(AUTO)* manifold.

tué, e [tɥe] *nm/f*: **5** ~**s 5** killed *ou* dead.

tuer [tɥe] *vt* to kill ; **se** ~ *vi* to be killed ; **se** ~ **au travail** *(fig)* to work o.s. to death ; **tuerie** *nf* slaughter *q.*

tue-tête [tytɛt]: **à** ~ *ad* at the top of one's voice.

tueur [tɥœʀ] *nm* killer ; ~ **à gages** hired killer.

tuile [tɥil] *nf* tile ; *(fam)* spot of bad luck, blow.

tulipe [tylip] *nf* tulip.

tuméfié, e [tymefje] *a* puffy, swollen.

tumeur [tymœʀ] *nf* growth, tumour.

tumulte [tymylt(ə)] *nm* commotion, hubbub.

tumultueux, euse [tymyltɥø, -øz] *a* stormy, turbulent.

tunique [tynik] *nf* tunic ; *(de femme)* smock, tunic.

Tunisie [tynizi] *nf*: **la** ~ Tunisia ; **tunisien, ne** *a, nm/f* Tunisian.

tunnel [tynɛl] *nm* tunnel.

turban [tyʀbɑ̃] *nm* turban.

turbin [tyʀbɛ̃] *nm (fam)* work *q.*

turbine [tyʀbin] *nf* turbine.

turboréacteur [tyʀbɔʀeaktœʀ] *nm* turbojet.

turbulences [tyʀbylɑ̃s] *nfpl (AVIAT)* turbulence *sg.*

turbulent, e [tyʀbylɑ̃, -ɑ̃t] *a* boisterous, unruly.

turc, turque [tyʀk(ə)] *a* Turkish // *nm/f*: **T~, Turque** Turk/Turkish woman // *nm (langue)* Turkish ; **à la turque** *ad* cross-legged // *a (w.-c.)* seatless.

turf [tyʀf] *nm* racing ; ~**iste** *nm/f* racegoer.

turpitude [tyʀpityd] *nf* base act, baseness *q.*

turque [tyʀk(ə)] *a, nf voir* **turc.**

Turquie [tyʀki] *nf*: **la** ~ Turkey.

turquoise [tyʀkwaz] *nf, a inv* turquoise.

tus *etc vb voir* **taire.**

tutelle [tytɛl] *nf (JUR)* guardianship ; *(POL)* trusteeship ; **sous la** ~ **de** *(fig)* under the supervision of.

tuteur [tytœʀ] *nm (JUR)* guardian ; *(de plante)* stake, support.

tutoyer [tytwaje] *vt*: ~ **qn** to address sb as 'tu'.

tuyau, x [tɥijo] *nm* pipe ; *(flexible)* tube ; *(fam)* tip ; gen *q* ; ~ **d'arrosage** hosepipe ; ~ **d'échappement** exhaust pipe ; ~**té, e** a fluted ; ~**terie** *nf* piping *q.*

tuyère [tɥijɛʀ] *nf* nozzle.

T.V.A. *sigle f voir* **taxe.**

tympan [tɛ̃pɑ̃] *nm (ANAT)* eardrum.

type [tip] *nm* type ; *(fam)* chap, bloke // *a* typical, standard ; **avoir le** ~ **nordique** to be Nordic-looking.

typhoïde [tifɔid] *nf* typhoid (fever).

typhon [tifɔ̃] *nm* typhoon.

typhus [tifys] *nm* typhus (fever).

typique [tipik] *a* typical.

typographe [tipɔgʀaf] *nm/f* typographer.

typographie [tipɔgʀafi] *nf* typography ; *(procédé)* letterpress (printing) ; **typographique** *a* typographical ; letterpress *cpd.*

tyran [tiʀɑ̃] *nm* tyrant ; **tyrannie** *nf* tyranny ; **tyrannique** *a* tyrannical ; **tyranniser** *vt* to tyrannize.

tzigane [dzigan] *a* gipsy, tzigane // *nm/f* (Hungarian) gipsy, Tzigane.

U

ubiquité [ybikɥite] *nf*: **avoir le don d'** ~ to be everywhere at once *ou* be ubiquitous.

ulcère [ylsɛʀ] *nm* ulcer ; ~ **à l'estomac** stomach ulcer.

ulcérer [ylseʀe] *vt (MÉD)* to ulcerate ; *(fig)* to sicken, appal.

ultérieur, e [ylteʀjœʀ] *a* later, subsequent ; **remis à une date** ~**e** postponed to a later date ; ~**ement** *ad* later.

ultimatum [yltimatɔm] *nm* ultimatum.
ultime [yltim] *a* final.
ultra... [yltʀa] *préfixe*: ~**moderne**/
-**rapide** ultra-modern/-fast; ~-**sensible** *a*
(PHOTO) high-speed; ~-**sons** *nmpl*
ultrasonics; ~-**violet, te** *a* ultraviolet.
un, une [œ̃, yn] *dét* a, an + *voyelle //*
pronom, num, a one; **l'un l'autre, les ~s**
les autres each other, one another; **l'~**
..., l'autre (the) one ..., the other; **les ~s**
..., les autres some ..., others; **l'~ et**
l'autre (of them); **l'~ ou l'autre**
either (of them); **l'~ des meilleurs** one
of the best.
unanime [ynanim] *a* unanimous;
unanimité *nf* unanimity; **à l'unanimité**
unanimously.
uni, e [yni] *a* (*ton, tissu*) plain; (*surface*)
smooth, even; (*famille*) close(-knit); (*pays*)
united.
unification [ynifikasjɔ̃] *nf* uniting;
unification; standardization.
unifier [ynifje] *vt* to unite, unify;
(*systèmes*) to standardize, unify.
uniforme [ynifɔʀm(ə)] *a* (*mouvement*)
regular, uniform; (*surface, ton*) even;
(*objets, maisons*) uniform // *nm* uniform;
être sous l'~ (MIL) to be serving;
uniformiser *vt* to make uniform;
(*systèmes*) to standardize; **uniformité** *nf*
regularity; uniformity; evenness.
unijambiste [yniʒɑ̃bist(ə)] *nm/f* one-
legged man/woman.
unilatéral, e, aux [ynilateʀal, -o] *a*
unilateral; **stationnement ~** parking on
one side only.
union [ynjɔ̃] *nf* union; ~ **conjugale** union
of marriage; ~ **de consommateurs**
consumers' association; **l'U~ soviétique**
the Soviet Union.
unique [ynik] *a* (*seul*) only; (*le même*): **un**
prix/système ~ a single price/system;
(*exceptionnel*) unique; **ménage à salaire**
~ one-salary family; **route à voie** ~
single-lane road; **fils/fille** ~ only
son/daughter; ~ **en France** the only one
of its kind in France; ~**ment** *ad* only,
solely; (*juste*) only, merely.
unir [yniʀ] *vt* (*nations*) to unite; (*éléments,*
couleurs) to combine; (*en mariage*) to
unite, join together; ~ **qch à** to unite sth
with; to combine sth with; **s'~** to unite;
(*en mariage*) to be joined together.
unisson [ynisɔ̃]: **à l'~** in unison.
unitaire [yniteʀ] *a* unitary; **prix** ~ price
per unit.
unité [ynite] *nf* (*harmonie, cohésion*) unity;
(COMM, MIL, *de mesure*, MATH) unit.
univers [ynivɛʀ] *nm* universe.
universel, le [ynivɛʀsɛl] *a* universal;
(*esprit*) all-embracing.
universitaire [ynivɛʀsitɛʀ] *a* university
cpd; (*diplôme, études*) academic, university
cpd // nm/f academic.
université [ynivɛʀsite] *nf* university.
uranium [yʀanjɔm] *nm* uranium.
urbain, e [yʀbɛ̃, -ɛn] *a* urban, city *cpd*,
town *cpd*; (*poli*) urbane; **urbaniser** *vt* to
urbanize; **urbanisme** *nm* town planning;
urbaniste *nm/f* town planner.
urgence [yʀʒɑ̃s] *nf* urgency; (MÉD *etc*)

emergency; **d'~** *a* emergency *cpd //* *ad*
as a matter of urgency.
urgent, e [yʀʒɑ̃, -ɑ̃t] *a* urgent.
urinal, aux [yʀinal, -o] *nm* (bed) urinal.
urine [yʀin] *nf* urine; **uriner** *vi* to urinate;
urinoir *nm* (public) urinal.
urne [yʀn(ə)] *nf* (*électorale*) ballot box;
(*vase*) urn; **aller aux ~s** (*voter*) to go to
the polls.
URSS [*parfois*: yʀs] *sigle f*: **l'~** the USSR.
urticaire [yʀtikɛʀ] *nf* nettle rash.
us [ys] *nmpl*: ~ **et coutumes** (habits and)
customs.
U.S.A. *sigle mpl*: **les ~** the U.S.A.
usage [yzaʒ] *nm* (*emploi, utilisation*) use;
(*coutume*) custom; (LING): **l'~** usage; **faire**
~ **de** (*pouvoir, droit*) to exercise; **avoir**
l'~ de to have the use of; **à l'~** *ad* with
use; **à l'~ de** (*pour*) for (use of); **en** ~
in use; **hors d'~** out of service; wrecked;
à ~ interne to be taken; **à ~ externe**
for external use only.
usagé, e [yzaʒe] *a* (*usé*) worn; (*d'occasion*)
used.
usager, ère [yzaʒe, -ɛʀ] *nm/f* user.
usé, e [yze] *a* worn; (*banal*) hackneyed.
user [yze] *vt* (*outil*) to wear down;
(*vêtement*) to wear out; (*matière*) to wear
away; (*consommer: charbon etc*) to use;
s'~ *vi* to wear; to wear out; (*fig*) to
decline; **s'~ à la tâche** to wear o.s. out
with work; ~ **de** *vt* (*moyen, procédé*) to
use, employ; (*droit*) to exercise.
usine [yzin] *nf* factory; ~ **à gaz** gasworks
sg; ~ **marémotrice** tidal power station.
usiner [yzine] *vt* (TECH) to machine.
usité, e [yzite] *a* in common use,
common; **peu** ~ rarely used.
ustensile [ystɑ̃sil] *nm* implement; ~ **de**
cuisine kitchen utensil.
usuel, le [yzɥɛl] *a* everyday, common.
usufruit [yzyfʀɥi] *nm* usufruct.
usuraire [yzyʀɛʀ] *a* usurious.
usure [yzyʀ] *nf* wear; worn state; (*de*
l'usurier) usury; **avoir qn à l'~** to wear
sb down; **usurier, ière** *nm/f* usurer.
usurper [yzyʀpe] *vt* to usurp.
ut [yt] *nm* (MUS) C.
utérin, e [yteʀɛ̃, -in] *a* uterine.
utérus [yteʀys] *nm* uterus, womb.
utile [ytil] *a* useful.
utilisation [ytilizasjɔ̃] *nf* use.
utiliser [ytilize] *vt* to use.
utilitaire [ytilitɛʀ] *a* utilitarian; (*objets*)
practical.
utilité [ytilite] *nf* usefulness *q*; use; **jouer**
les ~s (THÉÂTRE) to play bit parts;
reconnu d'~ publique state-approved;
c'est d'une grande ~ it's of great use.
utopie [ytɔpi] *nf* utopian idea *ou* view;
utopia; **utopiste** *nm/f* utopian.
uvule [yvyl] *nf* uvula.

V

va *vb voir* **aller**.
vacance [vakɑ̃s] *nf* (ADMIN) vacancy; ~**s**
nfpl holiday(s *pl*), vacation *sg*; **prendre**
des/ses ~s to take a holiday/one's
holiday(s); **aller en ~s** to go on holiday;

vacancier, ière nm/f holiday-maker.
vacant, e [vakɑ̃, -ɑ̃t] a vacant.
vacarme [vakaʀm(ə)] nm row, din.
vaccin [vaksɛ̃] nm vaccine; (opération) vaccination; **vaccination** nf vaccination; **vacciner** vt to vaccinate; (fig) to make immune.
vache [vaʃ] nf (ZOOL) cow; (cuir) cowhide // a (fam) rotten, mean; ~ **à eau** (canvas) water bag; ~ **à lait** (péj) mug, sucker; ~ **laitière** dairy cow; **vachement** ad (fam) damned, hellish; **vacher, ère** nm/f cowherd; **vacherie** nf (fam) meanness q; dirty trick; nasty remark.
vaciller [vasije] vi to sway, wobble; (bougie, lumière) to flicker; (fig) to be failing, falter.
vacuité [vakɥite] nf emptiness, vacuity.
vade-mecum [vademekɔm] nm inv pocketbook.
vadrouiller [vadʀuje] vi to rove around ou about.
va-et-vient [vaevjɛ̃] nm inv (de pièce mobile) to and fro (ou up and down) movement; (de personnes, véhicules) comings and goings pl, to-ings and fro-ings pl.
vagabond, e [vagabɔ̃, -ɔ̃d] a wandering; (imagination) roaming, roving // nm (rôdeur) tramp, vagrant; (voyageur) wanderer.
vagabondage [vagabɔ̃daʒ] nm roaming, wandering; (JUR) vagrancy.
vagabonder [vagabɔ̃de] vi to roam, wander.
vagin [vaʒɛ̃] nm vagina.
vagissement [vaʒismɑ̃] nm cry (of newborn baby).
vague [vag] nf wave // a vague; (regard) faraway; (manteau, robe) loose(-fitting); (quelconque) **un ~ bureau/cousin** some office/cousin or other // nm: **rester dans le ~** to keep things rather vague; **regarder dans le ~** to gaze into space; ~ **à l'âme** nm vague melancholy; ~ **d'assaut** nf (MIL) wave of assault; ~ **de chaleur** nf heatwave; ~ **de fond** nf ground swell; ~ **de froid** nf cold spell; ~**ment** ad vaguely.
vaillant, e [vajɑ̃, -ɑ̃t] a (courageux) brave, gallant; (robuste) vigorous, hale and hearty; **n'avoir plus un sou** ~ to be penniless.
vaille vb voir **valoir**.
vain, e [vɛ̃, vɛn] a vain; **en ~** ad in vain.
vaincre [vɛ̃kʀ(ə)] vt to defeat; (fig) to conquer, overcome; **vaincu, e** nm/f defeated party; **vainqueur** nm victor; (SPORT) winner // am victorious.
vais vb voir **aller**.
vaisseau, x [vɛso] nm (ANAT) vessel; (NAVIG) ship, vessel; ~ **spatial** spaceship.
vaisselier [vɛsəlje] nm dresser.
vaisselle [vɛsɛl] nf (service) crockery; (plats etc à laver) (dirty) dishes pl; (lavage) washing-up; **faire la ~** to do the washing-up ou the dishes.
val, vaux ou **vals** [val, vo] nm valley.
valable [valabl(ə)] a valid; (acceptable) decent, worthwhile.

valent etc vb voir **valoir**.
valet [valɛ] nm valet; (CARTES) jack, knave; ~ **de chambre** manservant, valet; ~ **de ferme** farmhand; ~ **de pied** footman.
valeur [valœʀ] nf (gén) value; (mérite) worth, merit; (COMM: titre) security; **mettre en ~** (bien) to exploit; (terrain, région) to develop; (fig) to highlight; to show off to advantage; **avoir de la ~** to be valuable; **prendre de la ~** to go up ou gain in value.
valeureux, euse [valœrø, -øz] a valorous.
valide [valid] a (en bonne santé) fit, well; (indemne) able-bodied, fit; (valable) valid; **valider** vt to validate; **validité** nf validity.
valions vb voir **valoir**.
valise [valiz] nf (suit)case; **la ~ (diplomatique)** the diplomatic bag.
vallée [vale] nf valley.
vallon [valɔ̃] nm small valley.
vallonné, e [valɔne] n undulating.
valoir [valwaʀ] vi (être valable) to hold, apply // vt (prix, valeur, effort) to be worth; (causer): ~ **qch à qn** to earn sb sth; **se** ~ to be of equal merit; (péj) to be two of a kind; **faire** ~ (droits, prérogatives) to assert; (domaine, capitaux) to exploit; **faire ~ que** to point out that; **à ~ on account; à ~ sur** to be deducted from; **vaille que vaille** somehow or other; **cela ne me dit rien qui vaille** I don't like the look of it at all; **ce climat ne me vaut rien** this climate doesn't suit me; ~ **la peine** to be worth the trouble ou worth it; ~ **mieux: il vaut mieux se taire** it's better to say nothing; **ça ne vaut rien** it's worthless; **que vaut ce candidat?** how good is this applicant?
valoriser [valɔʀize] vt (ÉCON) to develop (the economy of); (PSYCH) to increase the standing of.
valse [vals(ə)] nf waltz; **valser** vi to waltz; (fig): **aller valser** to go flying.
valu, e [valy] pp de **valoir**.
valve [valv(ə)] nf valve.
vandale [vɑ̃dal] nm/f vandal; **vandalisme** nm vandalism.
vanille [vanij] nf vanilla.
vanité [vanite] nf vanity; **vaniteux, euse** a vain, conceited.
vanne [van] nf gate.
vanner [vane] vt to winnow.
vannerie [vanʀi] nf basketwork.
vantail, aux [vɑ̃taj, -o] nm door, leaf (pl leaves).
vantard, e [vɑ̃taʀ, -aʀd(ə)] a boastful; **vantardise** nf boastfulness q; boast.
vanter [vɑ̃te] vt to speak highly of, vaunt; **se** ~ vi to boast, brag; **se** ~ **de** to boast of.
va-nu-pieds [vanypje] nm/f inv tramp, beggar.
vapeur [vapœʀ] nf steam; (émanation) vapour, fumes pl; ~**s** nfpl (bouffées) vapours; **à** ~ steam-powered, steam cpd; **à toute** ~ full steam ahead; (fig) at full tilt; **renverser la** ~ to reverse engines; (fig) to backtrack, backpedal; **cuit à la** ~ steamed.

vaporeux, euse [vapɔʁø, -øz] a (flou) hazy, misty; (léger) filmy, gossamer cpd.

vaporisateur [vapɔʁizatœʁ] nm spray.

vaporiser [vapɔʁize] vt (CHIMIE) to vaporize; (parfum etc) to spray.

vaquer [vake] vi: ~ à ses occupations to attend to one's affairs, go about one's business.

varappe [vaʁap] nf rock climbing; **varappeur, euse** nm/f (rock) climber.

varech [vaʁɛk] nm wrack, varec.

vareuse [vaʁøz] nf (blouson) pea jacket; (d'uniforme) tunic.

variable [vaʁjabl(ə)] a variable; (temps, humeur) changeable, variable; (TECH: à plusieurs positions etc) adaptable; (LING) inflectional; (divers: résultats) varied, various // nf (MATH) variable.

variante [vaʁjɑ̃t] nf variant.

variation [vaʁjasjɔ̃] nf variation; changing q, change.

varice [vaʁis] nf varicose vein.

varicelle [vaʁisɛl] nf chickenpox.

varié, e [vaʁje] a varied; (divers) various; **hors-d'œuvre** ~s selection of hors d'œuvres.

varier [vaʁje] vi to vary; (temps, humeur) to vary, change // vt to vary.

variété [vaʁjete] nf variety; **spectacle de** ~s variety show.

variole [vaʁjɔl] nf smallpox.

variqueux, euse [vaʁikø, -øz] a varicose.

vas vb voir **aller**.

vase [vɑz] nm vase // nf silt, mud; **en** ~ **clos** in isolation; ~ **de nuit** chamberpot; ~s **communicants** communicating vessels.

vaseline [vazlin] nf vaseline.

vaseux, euse [vazø, -øz] a silty, muddy; (fig: confus) woolly, hazy; (: fatigué) peaky; woozy.

vasistas [vazistɑs] nm fanlight.

vaste [vast(ə)] a vast, immense.

Vatican [vatikɑ̃] nm: **le** ~ the Vatican.

vaticiner [vatisine] vi (péj) to make pompous predictions.

va-tout [vatu] nm: **jouer son** ~ to stake one's all.

vaudeville [vodvil] nm vaudeville, light comedy.

vaudrai etc vb voir **valoir**.

vau-l'eau [volo]: **à** ~ ad with the current; (fig) adrift.

vaurien, ne [voʁjɛ̃, -ɛn] nm/f good-for-nothing, guttersnipe.

vautour [votuʁ] nm vulture.

vautrer [votʁe]: **se** ~ vi: **se** ~ **dans/sur** to wallow in/sprawl on.

vaux [vo] pl de **val** // vb voir **valoir**.

veau, x [vo] nm (ZOOL) calf (pl calves); (CULIN) veal; (peau) calfskin.

vecteur [vɛktœʁ] nm vector; (MIL) carrier.

vécu, e [veky] pp de **vivre** // a (aventure) real(-life).

vedette [vədɛt] nf (artiste etc) star; (canot) patrol boat; launch; **avoir la** ~ to top the bill, get star billing.

végétal, e, aux [veʒetal, -o] a vegetable // nm vegetable, plant.

végétarien, ne [veʒetaʁjɛ̃, -ɛn] a, nm/f vegetarian.

végétarisme [veʒetaʁism(ə)] nm vegetarianism.

végétation [veʒetasjɔ̃] nf vegetation; ~s nfpl (MÉD) adenoids.

végéter [veʒete] vi (fig) to vegetate; to stagnate.

véhément, e [veemɑ̃, -ɑ̃t] a vehement.

véhicule [veikyl] nm vehicle; ~ **utilitaire** commercial vehicle.

veille [vɛj] nf (garde) watch; (PSYCH) wakefulness; (jour): **la** ~ the day before, the previous day; **la** ~ **au soir** the previous evening; **la** ~ **de** the day before; **à la** ~ **de** on the eve of.

veillée [veje] nf (soirée) evening; (réunion) evening gathering; ~ **d'armes** night before combat; ~ (**mortuaire**) watch.

veiller [veje] vi to stay ou sit up; to be awake; to be on watch; to be watchful // vt (malade, mort) to watch over, sit up with; ~ **à** vt to attend to, see to; ~ **à ce que** to make sure that, see to it that; ~ **sur** vt to keep a watch ou an eye on; **veilleur de nuit** nm night watchman.

veilleuse [vɛjøz] nf (lampe) night light; (AUTO) sidelight; (flamme) pilot light; **en** ~ a, ad (lampe) dimmed.

veinard, e [vɛnaʁ, -aʁd(ə)] nm/f (fam) lucky devil.

veine [vɛn] nf (ANAT, du bois etc) vein; (filon) vein, seam; (fam: chance): **avoir de la** ~ to be lucky; (inspiration) inspiration; **veiné, e** a veined; (bois) grained; **veineux, euse** a venous.

vêler [vele] vi to calve.

vélin [velɛ̃] nm vellum (paper).

velléitaire [veleitɛʁ] a irresolute, indecisive.

velléités [veleite] nfpl vague impulses.

vélo [velo] nm bike, cycle; **faire du** ~ to go cycling.

véloce [velɔs] a swift.

vélodrome [velodʁɔm] nm velodrome.

vélomoteur [velomotœʁ] nm light motorcycle.

velours [vəluʁ] nm velvet; ~ **côtelé** corduroy.

velouté, e [vəlute] a (au toucher) velvety; (à la vue) soft, mellow; (au goût) smooth, mellow // nm: ~ **d'asperges/de tomates** cream of asparagus/tomato (soup).

velu, e [vəly] a hairy.

venais etc vb voir **venir**.

venaison [vənɛzɔ̃] nf venison.

vénal, e, aux [venal, -o] venal; ~**ité** nf venality.

venant [vənɑ̃]: **à tout** ~ ad to all and sundry.

vendange [vɑ̃dɑʒ] nf (opération, période: aussi: ~s) grape harvest; (raisins) grape crop, grapes pl.

vendanger [vɑ̃dɑʒe] vi to harvest the grapes; **vendangeur, euse** nm/f grape-picker.

vendeur, euse [vɑ̃dœʁ, -øz] nm/f (de magasin) shop assistant; sales assistant; (COMM) salesman/woman // nm (JUR) vendor, seller; ~ **de journaux** newspaper seller.

vendre [vɑ̃dR(ə)] *vt* to sell; ~ **qch à qn** to sell sb sth; **cela se vend à la douzaine** these are sold by the dozen; **cela se vend bien** it's selling well; **'à** ~**'** 'for sale.'

vendredi [vɑ̃dRədi] *nm* Friday; **V**~ **saint** Good Friday.

vénéneux, euse [venenø, -øz] *a* poisonous.

vénérable [veneRabl(ə)] *a* venerable.

vénération [veneRɑsjɔ̃] *nf* veneration.

vénérer [veneRe] *vt* to venerate.

vénérien, ne [veneRjɛ̃, -ɛn] *a* venereal.

vengeance [vɑ̃ʒɑ̃s] *nf* vengeance *q*, revenge *q*; act of vengeance *ou* revenge

venger [vɑ̃ʒe] *vt* to avenge; **se** ~ *vi* to avenge o.s.; *(par rancune)* to take revenge; **se** ~ **de qch** to avenge o.s. for sth; to take one's revenge for sth; **se** ~ **de qn** to take revenge on sb; **se** ~ **sur** to wreak vengeance upon; to take revenge on *ou* through; to take it out on; **vengeur, eresse** *a* vengeful // *nm/f* avenger.

véniel, le [venjɛl] *a* venial.

venimeux, euse [vənimø, -øz] *a* poisonous, venomous; *(fig: haineux)* venomous, vicious.

venin [vənɛ̃] *nm* venom, poison.

venir [vəniR] *vi* to come; ~ **de** to come from; ~ **de faire: je viens d'y aller/de le voir** I've just been there/seen him; **s'il vient à pleuvoir** if it should rain, if it happens to rain; **j'en viens à croire que** I have come to believe that; **il en est venu à mendier** he has been reduced to begging; **faire** ~ *(docteur, plombier)* to call (out).

vent [vɑ̃] *nm* wind; **il y a du** ~ it's windy; **c'est du** ~ it's all hot air; **au** ~ to windward; **sous le** ~ to leeward; **avoir le** ~ **debout/arrière** to head into the wind/have the wind astern; **dans le** ~ *(fam)* trendy, with it; **prendre le** ~ *(fig)* to see which way the wind blows; **avoir** ~ **de** to get wind of.

vente [vɑ̃t] *nf* sale; **la** ~ *(activité)* selling; *(secteur)* sales *pl*; **mettre en** ~ to put on sale; *(objets personnels)* to put up for sale; ~ **de charité** sale in aid of charity; ~ **aux enchères** auction sale.

venter [vɑ̃te] *vb impersonnel*: **il vente** the wind is blowing; **venteux, euse** *a* windswept, windy.

ventilateur [vɑ̃tilatœR] *nm* fan.

ventilation [vɑ̃tilɑsjɔ̃] *nf* ventilation.

ventiler [vɑ̃tile] *vt* to ventilate; *(total, statistiques)* to break down.

ventouse [vɑ̃tuz] *nf (ampoule)* cupping glass; *(de caoutchouc)* suction pad; *(ZOOL)* sucker.

ventre [vɑ̃tR(ə)] *nm (ANAT)* stomach; *(fig)* belly; **prendre du** ~ to be getting a paunch; **avoir mal au** ~ to have stomach ache.

ventricule [vɑ̃tRikyl] *nm* ventricle.

ventriloque [vɑ̃tRilɔk] *nm/f* ventriloquist.

ventripotent, e [vɑ̃tRipotɑ̃, -ɑ̃t] *a* potbellied.

ventru, e [vɑ̃tRy] *a* potbellied.

venu, e [vəny] *pp* de **venir** // *a*: **être mal** ~ **à** *ou* **de faire** to have no grounds for doing, be in no position to do // *nf* coming.

vêpres [vɛpR(ə)] *nfpl* vespers.

ver [vɛR] *nm voir aussi* **vers**; worm; *(des fruits etc)* maggot; *(du bois)* woodworm *q*; ~ **luisant** glow-worm; ~ **à soie** silkworm; ~ **solitaire** tapeworm; ~ **de terre** earthworm.

véracité [veRasite] *nf* veracity.

véranda [veRɑ̃da] *nf* veranda(h).

verbal, e, aux [vɛRbal, -o] *a* verbal.

verbaliser [vɛRbalize] *vi (POLICE)* to book *ou* report an offender.

verbe [vɛRb(ə)] *nm (LING)* verb; *(voix)*: **avoir le** ~ **sonore** to have a sonorous tone (of voice); *(expression)*: **la magie du** ~ the magic of language *ou* the word; *(REL)*: **le V**~ the Word.

verbeux, euse [vɛRbø, -øz] *a* verbose, wordy.

verdâtre [vɛRdɑtR(ə)] *a* greenish.

verdeur [vɛRdœR] *nf (vigueur)* vigour, vitality; *(crudité)* forthrightness; *(défaut de maturité)* tartness, sharpness.

verdict [vɛRdik(t)] *nm* verdict.

verdir [vɛRdiR] *vi, vt* to turn green.

verdoyant, e [vɛRdwajɑ̃, -ɑ̃t] *a* green, verdant.

verdure [vɛRdyR] *nf* greenery, verdure.

véreux, euse [veRø, -øz] *a* worm-eaten; *(malhonnête)* shady, corrupt.

verge [vɛRʒ(ə)] *nf (ANAT)* penis; *(baguette)* stick, cane.

verger [vɛRʒe] *nm* orchard.

verglacé, e [vɛRglase] *a* icy, iced-over.

verglas [vɛRgla] *nm* (black) ice.

vergogne [vɛRgɔɲ]: **sans** ~ *ad* shamelessly.

véridique [veRidik] *a* truthful, veracious.

vérification [veRifikɑsjɔ̃] *nf* checking *q*, check.

vérifier [veRifje] *vt* to check; *(corroborer)* to confirm, bear out.

vérin [veRɛ̃] *nm* jack.

véritable [veRitabl(ə)] *a* real; *(ami, amour)* true; **un** ~ **désastre** an absolute disaster.

vérité [veRite] *nf* truth; *(d'un portrait romanesque)* lifelikeness; *(sincérité)* truthfulness, sincerity.

vermeil, le [vɛRmɛj] *a* bright red, ruby-red // *nm (substance)* vermeil.

vermicelles [vɛRmisɛl] *nmpl* vermicelli *sg*.

vermillon [vɛRmijɔ̃] *a inv* vermilion, scarlet.

vermine [vɛRmin] *nf* vermin *pl*.

vermoulu, e [vɛRmuly] *a* worm-eaten, with woodworm.

vermout(h) [vɛRmut] *nm* vermouth.

verni, e [vɛRni] *a (fam)* lucky; **cuir** ~ patent leather.

vernir [vɛRniR] *vt (bois, tableau, ongles)* to varnish; *(poterie)* to glaze.

vernis [vɛRni] *nm (enduit)* varnish; glaze; *(fig)* veneer; ~ **à ongles** nail polish *ou* varnish.

vernissage [vɛRnisaʒ] *nm* varnishing, glazing; *(d'une exposition)* preview.

vérole [veRɔl] *nf (variole)* smallpox; *(fam: syphilis)* pox.

verrai *etc vb voir* **voir**.

verre [vɛR] *nm* glass; *(de lunettes)* lens *sg*; **boire** *ou* **prendre un** ~ to have a drink;

~ **à vin/à liqueur** wine/liqueur glass; ~ **à dents** tooth mug; ~ **dépoli** frosted glass; ~ **de lampe** lamp glass *ou* chimney; ~ **de montre** watch glass; ~ **à pied** stemmed glass; ~**s de contact** contact lenses.

verrerie [vɛʀʀi] *nf (fabrique)* glassworks *sg*; *(activité)* glass-making; glass-working; *(objets)* glassware.

verrière [vɛʀjɛʀ] *nf (grand vitrage)* window; *(toit vitré)* glass roof.

verrons *etc vb voir* **voir**.

verroterie [vɛʀɔtʀi] *nf* glass beads *pl ou* jewellery.

verrou [vɛʀu] *nm (targette)* bolt; *(fig)* constriction; **mettre le** ~ **to bolt the door**; **mettre qn sous les** ~**s** to put sb behind bars; **verrouiller** *vt* to bolt; *(MIL: brèche)* to close.

verrue [vɛʀy] *nf* wart; *(fig)* eyesore.

vers [vɛʀ] *nm* line // *nmpl (poésie)* verse *sg* // *prép (en direction de)* toward(s); *(près de)* around (about); *(temporel)* about, around.

versant [vɛʀsɑ̃] *nm* slopes *pl*, side.

versatile [vɛʀsatil] *a* fickle, changeable.

verse [vɛʀs(ə)]: ~ *a ad*: **il pleut à** ~ it's pouring (with rain).

versé, e [vɛʀse] *a*: **être** ~ **dans** *(science)* to be (well-)versed in.

Verseau [vɛʀso] *nm*: **le** ~ Aquarius, the water-carrier; **être du** ~ to be Aquarius.

versement [vɛʀsəmɑ̃] *nm* payment; **en 3** ~**s** in 3 instalments.

verser [vɛʀse] *vt (liquide, grains)* to pour; *(larmes, sang)* to shed; *(argent)* to pay; *(soldat: affecter)*: ~ **qn dans** to assign sb to // *vi (véhicule)* to overturn; *(fig)*: ~ **dans** to lapse into.

verset [vɛʀsɛ] *nm* verse; versicle.

verseur [vɛʀsœʀ] *am voir* **bec**.

versifier [vɛʀsifje] *vt* to put into verse // *vi* to versify, write verse.

version [vɛʀsjɔ̃] *nf* version; *(SCOL)* translation *(into the mother tongue)*.

verso [vɛʀso] *nm* back; **voir au** ~ see over(leaf).

vert, e [vɛʀ, vɛʀt(ə)] *a* green; *(vin)* young; *(vigoureux)* sprightly; *(cru)* forthright // *nm* green; ~ **d'eau** *a inv* sea-green; ~ **pomme** *a inv* apple-green; ~**-de-gris** *nm* verdigris // *a inv* grey(ish)-green.

vertébral, e, aux [vɛʀtebʀal, -o] *a voir* **colonne**.

vertèbre [vɛʀtɛbʀ(ə)] *nf* vertebra *(pl ae)*; **vertébré, e** *a, nm/f* vertebrate.

vertement [vɛʀtəmɑ̃] *ad (réprimander)* sharply.

vertical, e, aux [vɛʀtikal, -o] *a, nf* vertical; **à la** ~**e** *ad*, ~**ement** *ad* vertically; ~**ité** *nf* verticalness, verticality.

vertige [vɛʀtiʒ] *nm (peur du vide)* vertigo; *(étourdissement)* dizzy spell; *(fig)* fever; **vertigineux, euse** *a* breathtaking; breathtakingly high *(ou* deep).

vertu [vɛʀty] *nf* virtue; **en** ~ **de** *prép* in accordance with; ~**eux, euse** *a* virtuous.

verve [vɛʀv(ə)] *nf* witty eloquence; **être en** ~ to be in brilliant form.

verveine [vɛʀvɛn] *nf (BOT)* verbena, vervain; *(infusion)* verbena tea.

vésicule [vezikyl] *nf* vesicle; ~ **biliaire** gall-bladder.

vespasienne [vɛspazjɛn] *nf* urinal.

vespéral, e, aux [vɛspeʀal, -o] *a* vespertine, evening *cpd*.

vessie [vesi] *nf* bladder.

veste [vɛst(ə)] *nf* jacket; ~ **droite/croisée** single-/double-breasted jacket.

vestiaire [vɛstjɛʀ] *nm (au théâtre etc)* cloakroom; *(de stade etc)* changing-room.

vestibule [vɛstibyl] *nm* hall.

vestige [vɛstiʒ] *nm* relic; trace; *(fig)* remnant, vestige; ~**s** *nmpl* remains; remnants, relics.

vestimentaire [vɛstimɑ̃tɛʀ] *a (dépenses)* clothing; *(détail)* of dress; *(élégance)* sartorial.

veston [vɛstɔ̃] *nm* jacket.

vêtement [vɛtmɑ̃] *nm* garment, item of clothing; *(comm)*: **le** ~ the clothing industry; ~**s** *nmpl* clothes; ~**s de sport** sportswear *sg*, sports clothes.

vétéran [veteʀɑ̃] *nm* veteran.

vétérinaire [veteʀinɛʀ] *a* veterinary // *nm/f* vet, veterinary surgeon.

vétille [vetij] *nf* trifle, triviality.

vétilleux, euse [vetijø, -øz] *a* punctilious.

vêtir [vetiʀ] *vt* to clothe, dress.

veto [veto] *nm* veto; **opposer un** ~ **à** to veto.

vêtu, e [vety] *pp de* **vêtir** // *a*: ~ **de** dressed in, wearing; **chaudement** ~ warmly dressed.

vétuste [vetyst(ə)] *a* ancient, timeworn.

veuf, veuve [vœf, vœv] *a* widowed // *nm* widower // *nf* widow.

veuille *etc vb voir* **vouloir**.

veule [vøl] *a* spineless.

veuvage [vœvaʒ] *nm* widowhood.

veuve [vœv] *a, nf voir* **veuf**.

veux *vb voir* **vouloir**.

vexations [vɛksasjɔ̃] *nfpl* humiliations.

vexatoire [vɛksatwaʀ] *a*: **mesures** ~**s** harassment *sg*.

vexer [vɛkse] *vt* to hurt, upset; **se** ~ *vi* to be hurt, get upset.

viabiliser [vjabilize] *vt* to provide with services *(water etc)*.

viabilité [vjabilite] *nf* viability; *(d'un chemin)* practicability.

viable [vjabl(ə)] *a* viable.

viaduc [vjadyk] *nm* viaduct.

viager, ère [vjaʒe, -ɛʀ] *a*: **rente viagère** life annuity // *nm*: **mettre en** ~ to sell in return for a life annuity.

viande [vjɑ̃d] *nf* meat.

viatique [vjatik] *nm (REL)* viaticum; *(fig)* provisions *pl (ou* money) for the journey.

vibraphone [vibʀafɔn] *nm* vibraphone, vibes *pl*.

vibration [vibʀasjɔ̃] *nf* vibration.

vibrer [vibʀe] *vi* to vibrate; *(son, voix)* to be vibrant; *(fig)* to be stirred; **faire** ~ to (cause to) vibrate; to stir, thrill; **vibro-masseur** *nm* vibrator.

vicaire [vikɛʀ] *nm* curate.

vice [vis] *nm* vice; *(défaut)* fault; ~ **de forme** legal flaw *ou* irregularity.

vice... [vis] *préfixe*: ~**-consul** *nm* vice-consul; ~**-président, e** *nm/f* vice-president; vice-chairman; ~**-roi** *nm* viceroy.

vice-versa [visevɛʀsa] *ad* vice versa.

vichy [viʃi] *nm* (*toile*) gingham; (*eau*) Vichy water.

vicié, e [visje] *a* (*air*) polluted, tainted; (*JUR*) invalidated.

vicieux, euse [visjø, -øz] *a* (*pervers*) dirty(-minded); nasty; (*fautif*) incorrect, wrong.

vicinal, e, aux [visinal, -o] *a*: **chemin** ~ by-road, byway.

vicissitudes [visisityd] *nfpl* (trials and) tribulations.

vicomte [vikɔ̃t] *nm* viscount.

victime [viktim] *nf* victim; (*d'accident*) casualty; **être (la)** ~ **de** to be the victim of; **être** ~ **d'une attaque/d'un accident** to suffer a stroke/be involved in an accident.

victoire [viktwaʀ] *nf* victory; **victorieux, euse** *a* victorious; (*sourire, attitude*) triumphant.

victuailles [viktɥaj] *nfpl* provisions.

vidange [vidãʒ] *nf* (*d'un fossé, réservoir*) emptying; (*AUTO*) oil change; (*de lavabo: bonde*) waste outlet; ~**s** *nfpl* (*matières*) sewage *sg*; **faire la** ~ (*AUTO*) to change the oil, do an oil change; **vidanger** *vt* to empty.

vide [vid] *a* empty // *nm* (*PHYSIQUE*) vacuum; (*solution de continuité*) (empty) space, gap; (*sous soi: dans une falaise etc*) drop; (*futilité, néant*) void; **sous** ~ *ad* in a vacuum; **emballé sous** ~ vacuum packed; **à** ~ *ad* (*sans occupants*) empty; (*sans charge*) unladen; (*TECH*) without gripping *ou* being in gear.

vide-ordures [vidɔʀdyʀ] *nm inv* (rubbish) chute.

vide-poches [vidpɔʃ] *nm inv* tidy; (*AUTO*) glove compartment.

vider [vide] *vt* to empty; (*CULIN: volaille, poisson*) to gut, clean out; (*régler: querelle*) to settle; (*fatiguer*) to wear out; (*fam: expulser*) to throw out, chuck out; **se** ~ *vi* to empty; ~ **les lieux** to quit *ou* vacate the premises; **videur** *nm* (*de boîte de nuit*) bouncer.

vie [vi] *nf* life (*pl* lives); **être en** ~ to be alive; **sans** ~ lifeless; **à** ~ for life; **avoir la** ~ **dure** to have nine lives; to die hard; **mener la** ~ **dure à qn** to make life a misery for sb.

vieil [vjɛj] *am voir* **vieux**.

vieillard [vjɛjaʀ] *nm* old man; **les** ~**s** old people, the elderly.

vieille [vjɛj] *a, nf voir* **vieux**.

vieilleries [vjɛjʀi] *nfpl* old things *ou* stuff *sg*.

vieillesse [vjɛjɛs] *nf* old age; (*vieillards*): **la** ~ the old *pl*, the elderly *pl*.

vieillir [vjejiʀ] *vi* (*prendre de l'âge*) to grow old; (*population, vin*) to age; (*doctrine, auteur*) to become dated // *vt* to age; **il a beaucoup vieilli** he has aged a lot; **vieillissement** *nm* growing old; ageing.

vieillot, te [vjejo, -ɔt] *a* antiquated, quaint.

vielle [vjɛl] *nf* hurdy-gurdy.

vienne, viens *etc vb voir* **venir**.

vierge [vjɛʀʒ(ə)] *a* (*jeune fille*): **être** ~ to be a virgin // *nf* virgin; (*signe*): **la V**~ Virgo, the Virgin; **être de la V**~ to be Virgo; ~ **de** (*sans*) free from, unsullied by.

vieux(vieil), vieille [vjø, vjɛj] *a* old // *nm/f* old man/woman // *nmpl* old people; **un petit** ~ a little old man; **mon/ma vieille** (*fam*) old man/girl; **prendre un coup de** ~ to put years on; **un** ~ **de la vieille** one of the old brigade; ~ **garçon** *nm* bachelor; ~ **jeu** *a inv* old-fashioned; ~ **rose** *a inv* old rose; **vieil or** *a inv* old gold; **vieille fille** *nf* spinster.

vif, vive [vif, viv] *a* (*animé*) lively; (*alerte*) sharp, quick; (*brusque*) sharp, brusque; (*aigu*) sharp; (*lumière, couleur*) brilliant; (*air*) crisp; (*vent*) keen; (*émotion*) keen, sharp; (*fort: regret, déception*) great, deep; (*vivant*): **brûlé** ~ burnt alive; **de vive voix** personally; **piquer qn au** ~ to cut sb to the quick; **tailler dans le** ~ to cut into the living flesh; **à** ~ (*plaie*) open; **avoir les nerfs à** ~ to be on edge; **sur le** ~ (*ART*) from life; **entrer dans le** ~ **du sujet** to get to the very heart of the matter.

vif-argent [vifaʀʒã] *nm inv* quicksilver.

vigie [viʒi] *nf* look-out; look-out post, crow's nest.

vigilance [viʒilɑ̃s] *nf* vigilance.

vigilant, e [viʒilã, -ãt] *a* vigilant.

vigne [viɲ] *nf* (*plante*) vine; (*plantation*) vineyard; ~ **vierge** Virginia creeper.

vigneron [viɲʀɔ̃] *nm* wine grower.

vignette [viɲɛt] *nf* (*motif*) vignette; (*de marque*) manufacturer's label *ou* seal; (*ADMIN*) ≈ (road) tax disc; price label (*on medicines for reimbursement by Social Security*).

vignoble [viɲɔbl(ə)] *nm* (*plantation*) vineyard; (*vignes d'une région*) vineyards *pl*.

vigoureux, euse [viguʀø, -øz] *a* vigorous, strong, robust.

vigueur [vigœʀ] *nf* vigour; **être/entrer en** ~ to be in/come into force; **en** ~ current.

vil, e [vil] *a* vile, base; **à** ~ **prix** at a very low price.

vilain, e [vilɛ̃, -ɛn] *a* (*laid*) ugly; (*affaire, blessure*) nasty; (*pas sage: enfant*) naughty // *nm* (*paysan*) villein, villain; **ça va tourner au** ~ it's going to turn nasty.

vilebrequin [vilbʀəkɛ̃] *nm* (*outil*) (bit-)brace; (*AUTO*) crankshaft.

vilenie [vilni] *nf* vileness *q*, baseness *q*.

vilipender [vilipãde] *vt* to revile, vilify.

villa [vila] *nf* (detached) house.

village [vilaʒ] *nm* village; ~ **de toile** tent village; **villageois, e** *a* village *cpd* // *nm/f* villager.

ville [vil] *nf* town; (*importante*) city; (*administration*): **la** ~ ≈ the Corporation; ≈ the (town) council.

villégiature [vileʒiatyʀ] *nf* holiday; (holiday) resort.

vin [vɛ̃] *nm* wine; **avoir le** ~ **gai** to get happy after a few drinks; ~ **d'honneur** reception (*with wine and snacks*); ~ **de**

messe mass wine ; ~ **ordinaire** table wine ; ~ **de pays** local wine.

vinaigre [vinɛgʀ(ə)] nm vinegar ; **tourner au** ~ (fig) to turn sour ; ~ **de vin/d'alcool** wine/spirit vinegar ; **vinaigrette** nf vinaigrette, French dressing ; **vinaigrier** nm (fabricant) vinegar-maker ; (flacon) vinegar cruet ou bottle.

vinasse [vinas] nf (péj) cheap wine.

vindicatif, ive [vɛ̃dikatif, -iv] a vindictive.

vindicte [vɛ̃dikt(ə)] nf: **désigner qn à la** ~ **publique** to expose sb to public condemnation.

vineux, euse [vinø, -øz] a win(e)y.

vingt [vɛ̃, vɛ̃t + vowel and in 22 etc] num twenty ; **vingtaine** nf: **une vingtaine (de)** around twenty, twenty or so ; **vingtième** num twentieth.

vinicole [vinikɔl] a wine cpd, wine-growing.

vins etc vb voir **venir**.

viol [vjɔl] nm (d'une femme) rape ; (d'un lieu sacré) violation.

violacé, e [vjɔlase] a purplish, mauvish.

violation [vjɔlasjɔ̃] nf desecration ; violation.

violemment [vjɔlamɑ̃] ad violently.

violence [vjɔlɑ̃s] nf violence ; ~**s** nfpl acts of violence ; **faire** ~ **à qn** to do violence to sb.

violent, e [vjɔlɑ̃, -ɑ̃t] a violent ; (remède) drastic ; (besoin, désir) intense, urgent.

violenter [vjɔlɑ̃te] vt to assault (sexually).

violer [vjɔle] vt (femme) to rape ; (sépulture) to desecrate, violate ; (règlement, traité) to violate.

violet, te [vjɔlɛ, -ɛt] a, nm purple, mauve // nf (fleur) violet.

violon [vjɔlɔ̃] nm violin ; (fam: prison) lock-up ; **premier** ~ (MUS) first violin ou fiddle ; ~ **d'Ingres** (artistic) hobby.

violoncelle [vjɔlɔ̃sɛl] nm cello ; **violoncelliste** nm/f cellist.

violoniste [vjɔlɔnist(ə)] nm/f violinist, violin-player.

vipère [vipɛʀ] nf viper, adder.

virage [viʀaʒ] nm (d'un véhicule) turn ; (d'une route, piste) bend ; (CHIMIE) change in colour ; (de cuti-réaction) positive reaction ; (PHOTO) toning ; (fig: POL) change in policy ; **prendre un** ~ to go into a bend, take a bend ; ~ **sans visibilité** blind bend.

viral, e, aux [viʀal, -o] a viral.

virée [viʀe] nf (courte) run ; (: à pied) walk ; (longue) trip ; hike, walking tour.

virement [viʀmɑ̃] nm (COMM) transfer ; ~ **bancaire/postal** (bank) credit/(National) Giro transfer.

virent vb voir aussi **voir**.

virer [viʀe] vt (COMM): ~ **qch (sur)** to transfer sth (into) ; (PHOTO) to tone // vi to turn ; (CHIMIE) to change colour ; (cuti-réaction) to come up positive ; (PHOTO) to tone ; ~ **au bleu** to turn blue ; ~ **de bord** to tack ; ~ **sur l'aile** to bank.

virevolte [viʀvɔlt(ə)] nf twirl ; **virevolter** vi to twirl around.

virginité [viʀʒinite] nf virginity.

virgule [viʀgyl] nf comma ; (MATH) point ;

4 ~ 2 4 point 2 ; ~ **flottante** floating decimal.

viril, e [viʀil] a (propre à l'homme) masculine ; (énergique, courageux) manly, virile ; ~**ité** nf masculinity ; manliness ; (sexuelle) virility.

virtualité [viʀtɥalite] nf virtuality ; potentiality.

virtuel, le [viʀtɥɛl] a potential ; (théorique) virtual ; ~**lement** a potentially ; (presque) virtually.

virtuose [viʀtɥoz] nm/f (MUS) virtuoso ; (gén) master ; **virtuosité** nf virtuosity ; masterliness, masterful skills pl.

virulent, e [viʀylɑ̃, -ɑ̃t] a virulent.

virus [viʀys] nm virus.

vis vb [vi] voir **voir, vivre** // nf [vis] screw ; ~ **sans fin** worm, endless screw.

visa [viza] nm (sceau) stamp ; (validation de passeport) visa ; ~ **de censure** (censor's) certificate.

visage [vizaʒ] nm face ; **visagiste** nm/f beautician.

vis-à-vis [vizavi] ad face to face // nm person opposite ; face etc opposite ; ~ **de** prép opposite ; (fig) towards, vis-à-vis ; **en** ~ facing ou opposite each other, **sans** ~ (immeuble) with an open outlook.

viscéral, e, aux [viseʀal, -o] a (fig) deep-seated, deep-rooted.

viscères [visɛʀ] nmpl intestines, entrails.

viscosité [viskozite] nf viscosity.

visée [vize] nf (avec une arme) aiming ; (ARPENTAGE) sighting ; ~**s** nfpl (intentions) designs.

viser [vize] vi to aim // vt to aim at ; (concerner) to be aimed ou directed at ; (apposer un visa sur) to stamp, visa ; ~ **à qch/faire** to aim at sth/at doing ou to do.

viseur [vizœʀ] nm (d'arme) sights pl ; (PHOTO) viewfinder.

visibilité [vizibilite] nf visibility.

visible [vizibl(ə)] a visible ; (disponible): **est-il** ~? can he see me?, will he see visitors?

visière [vizjɛʀ] nf (de casquette) peak ; (qui s'attache) eyeshade.

vision [vizjɔ̃] nf vision ; (sens) (eye)sight, vision ; (fait de voir): **la** ~ **de** the sight of ; **première** ~ (CINEMA) first showing ; **visionnaire** a, nm/f visionary ; **visionner** vt to view ; **visionneuse** nf viewer.

visite [vizit] nf visit ; (personne qui rend visite) visitor ; (médicale, à domicile) visit, call ; **la** ~ (MÉD) (medical) consultations pl, surgery ; (MIL): **d'entrée** medicals pl ; (: quotidienne) sick parade ; **faire une** ~ **à qn** to call on sb, pay sb a visit ; **rendre** ~ **à qn** to visit sb, pay sb a visit ; **être en** ~ **(chez qn)** to be visiting (sb) ; **heures de** ~ (hôpital, prison) visiting hours ; **le droit de** ~ (JUR: aux enfants) right of access, access ; ~ **de douane** customs inspection ou examination.

visiter [vizite] vt to visit ; (musée, ville) to visit, go round ; **visiteur, euse** nm/f visitor ; **visiteur des douanes** customs inspector.

vison [vizɔ̃] nm mink.

visqueux, euse [viskø, -øz] a viscous ; (péj) gooey ; slimy.

visser [vise] vt: ~ qch (fixer, serrer) to screw sth on.

visu [vizy]: de ~ ad with one's own eyes.

visuel, le [vizyɛl] a visual // nm (visual) display.

vit vb voir **voir, vivre**.

vital, e, aux [vital, -o] a vital.

vitalité [vitalite] nf vitality.

vitamine [vitamin] nf vitamin; **vitaminique** a vitamin cpd.

vite [vit] ad (rapidement) quickly, fast; (sans délai) quickly; soon; **faire** ~ to act quickly; to be quick; **viens** ~ come quick(ly).

vitesse [vitɛs] nf speed; (AUTO: dispositif) gear; **faire de la** ~ to drive fast ou at speed; **prendre qn de** ~ to outstrip sb; get ahead of sb; **prendre de la** ~ to pick up ou gather speed; **à toute** ~ at full ou top speed; ~ **acquise** momentum; ~ **du son** speed of sound.

viticole [vitikol] a wine cpd, wine-growing.

viticulteur [vitikyltœr] nm wine grower.

viticulture [vitikyltyr] nf wine growing.

vitrage [vitraʒ] nm (cloison) glass partition; (toit) glass roof; (rideau) net curtain.

vitrail, aux [vitraj, -o] nm stained-glass window.

vitre [vitr(ə)] nf (window) pane; (de portière, voiture) window.

vitré, e [vitre] a glass cpd.

vitrer [vitre] vt to glaze.

vitreux, euse [vitrø, -øz] a vitreous; (terne) glassy.

vitrier [vitrije] nm glazier.

vitrifier [vitrifje] vt to vitrify; (parquet) to glaze.

vitrine [vitrin] nf (devanture) (shop) window; (étalage) display; (petite armoire) display cabinet; **en** ~ in the window, on display; ~ **publicitaire** display case, showcase.

vitriol [vitrijɔl] nm vitriol; **au** ~ (fig) vitriolic.

vitupérer [vitypere] vi to rant and rave; ~ **contre** to rail against.

vivable [vivabl(ə)] a (personne) livable-with; (endroit) fit to live in.

vivace a [vivas] (arbre, plante) hardy; (fig) indestructible, inveterate // ad [vivatʃe] (MUS) vivace.

vivacité [vivasite] nf liveliness, vivacity; sharpness; brilliance.

vivant, e [vivã, -ãt] a (qui vit) living, alive; (animé) lively; (preuve, exemple) living // nm: **du** ~ **de qn** in sb's lifetime; **les** ~**s et les morts** the living and the dead.

vivats [viva] nmpl cheers.

vive [viv] af voir **vif** // vb voir **vivre** // excl: ~ **le roi!** long live the king!; ~ **les vacances!** hurrah for the holidays!; ~**ment** ad vivaciously; sharply // excl: ~**ment les vacances!** I can't wait for the holidays!, roll on the holidays!

viveur [vivœr] nm (péj) high liver, pleasure-seeker.

vivier [vivje] nm fish tank; fishpond.

vivifiant, e [vivifjã, -ãt] a invigorating.

vivions vb voir **vivre**.

vivisection [vivisɛksjɔ̃] nf vivisection.

vivoter [vivote] vi to rub along, struggle along.

vivre [vivr(ə)] vi, vt to live // nm: **le** ~ **et le logement** board and lodging; ~**s** nmpl provisions, food supplies; **il vit encore** he is still alive; **se laisser** ~ to take life as it comes; **ne plus** ~ (être anxieux) to live on one's nerves; **il a vécu** (eu une vie aventureuse) he has seen life; **ce régime a vécu** this regime has had its day; **être facile à** ~ to be easy to get on with; **faire** ~ **qn** (pourvoir à sa subsistance) to provide (a living) for sb; ~ **mal** (chichement) to have a meagre existence; ~ **de** (salaire etc) to live on.

vlan [vlɑ̃] excl wham!, bang!

vocable [vɔkabl(ə)] nm term.

vocabulaire [vɔkabylɛr] nm vocabulary.

vocal, e, aux [vɔkal, -o] a vocal.

vocalique [vɔkalik] a vocalic, vowel cpd.

vocalise [vɔkaliz] nf singing exercise.

vocation [vɔkasjɔ̃] nf vocation, calling.

vociférations [vɔsiferasjɔ̃] nfpl cries of rage, screams.

vociférer [vɔsifere] vi, vt to scream.

vodka [vɔdka] nf vodka.

vœu, x [vø] nm wish; (à Dieu) vow; **faire** ~ **de** to take a vow of; ~**x de bonne année** best wishes for the New Year; **avec tous nos** ~**x** with every good wish ou our best wishes.

vogue [vɔg] nf fashion, vogue.

voguer [vɔge] vi to sail.

voici [vwasi] prép (pour introduire, désigner) here is + sg, here are + pl; **et** ~ **que...** and now it (ou he)...; voir aussi **voilà**.

voie [vwa] nf way; (RAIL) track, line; (AUTO) lane; **suivre la** ~ **hiérarchique** to go through official channels; **être en bonne** ~ to be shaping ou going well; **mettre qn sur la** ~ to put sb on the right track; **être en** ~ **d'achèvement/de rénovation** to be nearing completion/in the process of renovation; **à** ~ **étroite** narrow-gauge; **route à 2/3** ~**s** 2-/3-lane road; **par la** ~ **aérienne/maritime** by air/sea; ~ **d'eau** (NAVIG) leak; ~ **ferrée** track; railway line; **par** ~ **ferrée** by rail; ~ **de garage** (RAIL) siding; **la** ~ **lactée** the Milky Way; ~ **navigable** waterway; ~ **privée** private road; **la** ~ **publique** the public highway.

voilà [vwala] prép (en désignant) there is + sg, there are + pl; **les** ~ ou **voici** here ou there they are; **en** ~ ou **voici un** here's one, there's one; ~ ou **voici deux ans** two years ago; ~ ou **voici deux ans que** it's two years since; **et** ~! there we are!; ~ **tout** that's all; '~ ou **voici**' (en offrant etc) 'there ou here you are'.

voile [vwal] nm veil; (tissu léger) net // nf sail; (sport) sailing; **prendre le** ~ to take the veil; **mettre à la** ~ to make way under sail; ~ **du palais** nm soft palate, velum; ~ **au poumon** nm shadow on the lung.

voiler [vwale] vt to veil; (fausser: roue) to buckle; (: bois) to warp; **se** ~ vi (lune, regard) to mist over; (ciel) to grow hazy; (voix) to become husky; (roue, disque) to buckle; (*planche*) to warp; **se ~ la face** to hide one's face.

voilette [vwalɛt] *nf* (hat) veil.

voilier [vwalje] *nm* sailing ship; (*de plaisance*) sailing boat.

voilure [vwalyʀ] *nf* (*de voilier*) sails *pl*; (*d'avion*) aerofoils *pl*; (*de parachute*) canopy.

voir [vwaʀ] *vi*, *vt* to see; **se ~**; **se ~ critiquer/transformer** to be criticized/transformed; **cela se voit** (*cela arrive*) it happens; (*c'est visible*) that's obvious, it shows; **~ venir** (*fig*) to wait and see; **faire ~ qch à qn** to show sb sth; **en faire ~ à qn** (*fig*) to give sb a hard time; **ne pas pouvoir ~ qn** (*fig*) not to be able to stand sb; **regardez ~** just look; **dites-~** tell me; **voyons!** let's see now; (*indignation etc*) come (along) now!; **avoir quelque chose à ~ avec** to have something to do with.

voire [vwaʀ] *ad* indeed; nay.

voirie [vwaʀi] *nf* highway maintenance; (*administration*) highways department; (*enlèvement des ordures*) refuse collection.

voisin, e [vwazɛ̃, -in] *a* (*proche*) neighbouring; (*contigu*) next; (*ressemblant*) connected // *nm/f* neighbour; **voisinage** *nm* (*proximité*) proximity; (*environs*) vicinity; (*quartier, voisins*) neighbourhood; **relations de bon voisinage** neighbourly terms; **voisiner** *vi*: **voisiner avec** to be side by side with.

voiture [vwatyʀ] *nf* car; (*wagon*) coach, carriage; **~ d'enfant** pram; **~ d'infirme** invalid carriage; **~ de sport** sports car; **~-lit** *nf* sleeper.

voix [vwa] *nf* voice; (*POL*) vote; **à haute ~** aloud; **à ~ basse** in a low voice; **à 2/4 ~** (*MUS*) in 2/4 parts; **avoir ~ au chapitre** to have a say in the matter; **mettre aux ~** to put to the vote.

vol [vɔl] *nm* (*mode de locomotion*) flying; (*trajet, voyage, groupe d'oiseaux*) flight; (*mode d'appropriation*) theft, stealing; (*larcin*) theft; **à ~ d'oiseau** as the crow flies; **au ~: attraper qch au ~** to catch sth as it flies past; **prendre son ~** to take flight; **en ~** in flight; **~ avec effraction** breaking and entering *q*, break-in; **~ libre** *ou* **sur aile delta** hang-gliding; **~ à main armée** armed robbery; **~ de nuit** night flight; **~ à voile** gliding.

volage [vɔlaʒ] *a* fickle.

volaille [vɔlɑj] *nf* (*oiseaux*) poultry *pl*; (*viande*) poultry *q*; (*oiseau*) fowl; **volailler** *nm* poulterer.

volant, e [vɔlɑ̃, -ɑ̃t] *a* voir **feuille** etc // *nm* (*d'automobile*) (steering) wheel; (*de commande*) wheel; (*objet lancé*) shuttlecock; (*jeu*) battledore and shuttlecock; (*bande de tissu*) flounce; (*feuillet détachable*) tear-off portion; **les ~s** (*AVIAT*) the flight staff.

volatil, e [vɔlatil] *a* volatile.

volatile [vɔlatil] *nm* (*volaille*) bird; (*tout oiseau*) winged creature.

volatiliser [vɔlatilize]: **se ~** *vi* (*CHIMIE*) to volatize; (*fig*) to vanish into thin air.

vol-au-vent [vɔlovɑ̃] *nm inv* vol-au-vent.

volcan [vɔlkɑ̃] *nm* volcano; **volcanique** *a*

volcanic; **volcanologue** *nm/f* vulcanologist.

volée [vɔle] *nf* (*groupe d'oiseaux*) flight, flock; (*TENNIS*) volley; **~ de coups/de flèches** volley of blows/arrows; **à la ~:** **rattraper à la ~** to catch in mid air; **lancer à la ~** to fling about; **à toute ~** (*sonner les cloches*) vigorously; (*lancer un projectile*) with full force.

voler [vɔle] *vi* (*avion, oiseau, fig*) to fly; (*voleur*) to steal // *vt* (*objet*) to steal; (*personne*) to rob; **~ qch à qn** to steal sth from sb.

volet [vɔlɛ] *nm* (*de fenêtre*) shutter; (*AVIAT*) flap; (*de feuillet, document*) section; **trié sur le ~** hand-picked.

voleter [vɔlte] *vi* to flutter (about).

voleur, euse [vɔlœʀ, -øz] *nm/f* thief (*pl* thieves) // *a* thieving.

volière [vɔljɛʀ] *nf* aviary.

volontaire [vɔlɔ̃tɛʀ] *a* voluntary; (*caractère, personne*: *décidé*) self-willed // *nm/f* volunteer; **volontariat** *nm* voluntary service.

volonté [vɔlɔ̃te] *nf* (*faculté de vouloir*) will; (*énergie, fermeté*) will(power); (*souhait, désir*) wish; **se servir/boire à ~** to take/drink as much as one likes; **bonne ~** goodwill, willingness; **mauvaise ~** lack of goodwill, unwillingness.

volontiers [vɔlɔ̃tje] *ad* (*de bonne grâce*) willingly; (*avec plaisir*) willingly, gladly; (*habituellement, souvent*) readily, willingly; **'~'** 'with pleasure', 'I'd be glad to'.

volt [vɔlt] *nm* volt; **~age** *nm* voltage.

volte-face [vɔltafas] *nf inv* about-turn.

voltige [vɔltiʒ] *nf* (*ÉQUITATION*) trick riding; (*au cirque*) acrobatic feat; (*AVIAT*) (aerial) acrobatics *sg*; **numéro de haute ~** acrobatic act.

voltiger [vɔltiʒe] *vi* to flutter (about).

voltigeur, euse [vɔltiʒœʀ, -øz] *nm/f* (*au cirque*) acrobat.

voltmètre [vɔltmɛtʀ(ə)] *nm* voltmeter.

volubile [vɔlybil] *a* voluble.

volume [vɔlym] *nm* volume; (*GÉOM*: *solide*) solid; **volumineux, euse** *a* voluminous, bulky.

volupté [vɔlypte] *nf* sensual delight *ou* pleasure; **voluptueux, euse** *a* voluptuous.

volute [vɔlyt] *nf* (*ARCHIT*) volute; **~ de fumée** curl of smoke.

vomi [vɔmi] *nm* vomit.

vomir [vɔmiʀ] *vi* to vomit, be sick // *vt* to vomit, bring up; (*fig*) to belch out, spew out; (*exécrer*) to loathe, abhor; **vomissement** *nm* vomiting *q*; **vomissure** *nf* vomit *q*; **vomitif** *nm* emetic.

vont [vɔ̃] *vb* voir **aller.**

vorace [vɔʀas] *a* voracious.

vos [vo] *dét* voir **votre.**

votant, e [vɔtɑ̃, -ɑ̃t] *nm/f* voter.

vote [vɔt] *nm* vote; **~ par correspondance/procuration** postal/proxy vote.

voter [vɔte] *vi* to vote // *vt* (*loi, décision*) to vote for.

votre [vɔtʀ(ə)], *pl* **vos** [vo] *dét* your.

vôtre [votʀ(ə)] *pronom*: **le ~, la ~, les ~s** yours; **les ~s** (*fig*) your family *ou* folks; **à la ~** (*toast*) your (good) health!

voudrai etc vb voir **vouloir**.

voué, e [vwe] a: ~ à doomed to, destined for.

vouer [vwe] vt: ~ qch à (Dieu/un saint) to dedicate sth to; ~ **sa vie/son temps à** (étude, cause etc) to devote one's life/time to; ~ **une haine/amitié éternelle à qn** to vow undying hatred/love to sb.

vouloir [vulwaʀ] vi to show will, have willpower // vt to want // nm: **le bon** ~ **de qn** sb's goodwill; sb's pleasure; ~ **que qn fasse** to want sb to do; **je voudrais ceci** I would like this; **veuillez attendre** please wait; **je veux bien** (bonne volonté) I'll be happy to; (concession) fair enough, that's fine; **si on veut** (en quelque sorte) if you like; **que me veut-il?** what does he want with me?; ~ **dire (que)** (signifier) to mean (that); **sans le** ~ (involontairement) without meaning to, unintentionally; **en** ~ **à qn** to bear sb a grudge; **en** ~ **à qch** (avoir des visées sur) to be after sth; **s'en** ~ **de** to be annoyed with o.s. for; ~ **de qch/qn** (accepter) to want sth/sb.

voulu, e [vuly] a (requis) required, requisite; (délibéré) deliberate, intentional.

vous [vu] pronom you; (objet indirect) (to) you; (réfléchi) yourself, pl yourselves; (réciproque) each other // nm: **employer le** ~ (vouvoyer) to use the 'vous' form; ~**-même** yourself; ~**-mêmes** yourselves.

voûte [vut] nf vault; ~ **du palais** (ANAT) roof of the mouth; ~ **plantaire** arch (of the foot).

voûté, e [vute] a a vaulted, arched; (dos, personne) bent, stooped.

voûter [vute] vt (ARCHIT) to arch, vault; **se**~ vi (dos, personne) to become stooped.

vouvoyer [vuvwaje] vt: ~ **qn** to address sb as 'vous'.

voyage [vwajaʒ] nm journey, trip; (fait de voyager): **le** ~ travel(ling); **partir/être en** ~ to go off/be away on a journey ou trip; **faire un** ~ to go on ou make a trip ou journey; **faire bon** ~ to have a good journey; ~ **d'agrément/d'affaires** pleasure/business trip; ~ **de noces** honeymoon; ~ **organisé** package tour.

voyager [vwajaʒe] vi to travel; **voyageur, euse** nm/f traveller; (passager) passenger; **voyageur (de commerce)** commercial traveller.

voyant, e [vwajɑ̃, -ɑ̃t] a (couleur) loud, gaudy // nm (signal) (warning) light // nf clairvoyant.

voyelle [vwajɛl] nf vowel.

voyeur, euse [vwajœʀ, -øz] nm/f voyeur; peeping Tom.

voyou [vwaju] nm lout, hoodlum; (enfant) guttersnipe // a loutish.

vrac [vʀak]: **en** ~ ad higgledy-piggledy; (COMM) in bulk.

vrai, e [vʀɛ] a (véridique: récit, faits) true; (non factice, authentique) real; **à** ~ **dire** to tell the truth; **être dans le** ~ to be right.

vraiment [vʀɛmɑ̃] ad really.

vraisemblable [vʀɛsɑ̃blabl(ə)] a (plausible) likely, plausible; (probable) likely, probable; ~**ment** ad in all likelihood, very likely.

vraisemblance [vʀɛsɑ̃blɑ̃s] nf likelihood, plausibility; (romanesque) verisimilitude.

vrille [vʀij] nf (de plante) tendril; (outil) gimlet; (spirale) spiral; (AVIAT) spin.

vriller [vʀije] vt to bore into, pierce.

vrombir [vʀɔ̃biʀ] vi to hum.

vu [vy] prép (en raison de) in view of; ~ **que** in view of the fact that.

vu, e [vy] pp de **voir** // a: **bien/mal** ~ (fig) well/poorly thought of; good/bad form // nm: **au** ~ **et au su de tous** openly and publicly.

vue [vy] nf (fait de voir): **la** ~ **de** the sight of; (sens, faculté) (eye)sight; (panorama, image, photo) view; (spectacle) sight; ~**s** nfpl (idées) views; (dessein) designs; **perdre la** ~ to lose one's (eye)sight; **perdre de** ~ to lose sight of; **à la** ~ **de tous** in full view of everybody; **hors de** ~ out of sight; **à première** ~ at first sight; **connaître de** ~ to know by sight; **à** ~ (COMM) at sight; **tirer à** ~ to shoot on sight; **à** ~ **d'œil** visibly; at a quick glance; **en** ~ (visible) in sight; (COMM) in the public eye; **avoir qch en** ~ (intentions) to have one's sights on sth; **en** ~ **de** (arriver, être) within sight of; **en** ~ **de faire** with the intention of doing, with a view to doing; ~ **de l'esprit** theoretical view.

vulcaniser [vylkanize] vt to vulcanize.

vulgaire [vylgɛʀ] a (grossier) vulgar, coarse; (trivial) commonplace, mundane; (péj: quelconque): **de** ~**s touristes/chaises de cuisine** common tourists/kitchen chairs; (BOT, ZOOL: non latin) common; (communément) commonly; ~**ment** ad vulgarly, coarsely; (communément) commonly; **vulgarisation** nf: **ouvrage de vulgarisation** popularizing work, popularization; **vulgariser** vt to popularize; to coarsen; **vulgarité** nf vulgarity, coarseness.

vulnérable [vylneʀabl(ə)] a vulnerable.

vulve [vylv(ə)] nf vulva.

W X Y Z

wagon [vagɔ̃] nm (de voyageurs) carriage; (de marchandises) truck, wagon; ~**-citerne** nm tanker; ~**-lit** nm sleeper, sleeping car; ~**-poste** nm mail van; ~**-restaurant** nm restaurant ou dining car.

wallon, ne [valɔ̃, -ɔn] a Walloon.

waters [watɛʀ] nmpl toilet sg, loo sg.

watt [wat] nm watt.

w.-c. [vese] nmpl toilet sg, lavatory sg.

week-end [wikɛnd] nm weekend.

western [wɛstɛʀn] nm western.

whisky, pl whiskies [wiski] nm whisky.

x [iks] nm: **plainte contre X** (JUR) action against person or persons unknown; **l'X** the École Polytechnique.

xénophobe [ksenɔfɔb] nm/f xenophobe.

xérès [gzeʀɛs] nm sherry.

xylographie [ksilɔgʀafi] nf xylography; (image) xylograph.

xylophone [ksilɔfɔn] nm xylophone.

y [i] *ad* (*à cet endroit*) there ; (*dessus*) on it (*ou* them) ; (*dedans*) in it (*ou* them) // *pronom* (about *ou* on *ou* of) it: *vérifier la syntaxe du verbe employé* ; **j'~ pense** I'm thinking about it ; *voir aussi* **aller, avoir.**

yacht [jɔt] *nm* yacht.

yaourt [jauʀt] *nm* yoghourt.

yeux [jø] *pl de* **œil.**

yoga [jɔga] *nm* yoga.

yoghourt [jɔguʀt] *nm* = **yaourt.**

yole [jɔl] *nf* skiff.

yougoslave [jugɔslav] *a, nm/f* Yugoslav(ian).

Yougoslavie [jugɔslavi] *nf* Yugoslavia.

youyou [juju] *nm* dinghy.

yo-yo [jojo] *nm inv* yo-yo.

zèbre [zɛbʀ(ə)] *nm* (*ZOOL*) zebra.

zébré, e [zebʀe] *a* striped, streaked ; **zébrure** *nf* stripe, streak.

zélateur, trice [zelatœʀ, -tʀis] *nm/f* partisan, zealot.

zèle [zɛl] *nm* zeal ; **faire du ~** (*péj*) to be over-zealous ; **zélé, e** *a* zealous.

zénith [zenit] *nm* zenith.

zéro [zeʀo] *nm* zero, nought ; **au-dessous de ~** below zero (Centigrade) *ou* freezing ; **partir de ~** to start from scratch ; **trois (buts) à ~ 3** (goals to) nil.

zeste [zɛst(ə)] *nm* peel, zest ; **un ~ de citron** a piece of lemon peel.

zézayer [zezeje] *vi* to have a lisp.

zibeline [ziblin] *nf* sable.

zigzag [zigzag] *nm* zigzag ; **zigzaguer** *vi* to zigzag (along).

zinc [zɛ̃g] *nm* (*CHIMIE*) zinc ; (*comptoir*) bar, counter.

zizanie [zizani] *nf*: **semer la ~** to stir up ill-feeling.

zizi [zizi] *nm* (*fam*) willy.

zodiaque [zɔdjak] *nm* zodiac.

zona [zɔna] *nm* shingles *sg.*

zone [zon] *nf* zone, area ; (*quartiers*): **la ~** the slum belt ; **~ bleue** ≈ restricted parking area.

zoo [zoo] *nm* zoo.

zoologie [zɔɔlɔʒi] *nf* zoology ; **zoologique** *a* zoological ; **zoologiste** *nm/f* zoologist.

Z.U.P. [zyp] *sigle f* = **zone à urbaniser en priorité,** ≈ (planned) housing scheme.

zut [zyt] *excl* dash (it)!

ENGLISH-FRENCH
ANGLAIS-FRANÇAIS

A

a, an [eɪ, ə, æn, ən, n] *det* un(e) ; **3 a day/week** 3 par jour/semaine ; **10 km an hour** 10 km à l'heure.

A [eɪ] *n* (MUS) la *m*.

A.A. *n abbr of Automobile Association* ; *Alcoholics Anonymous*.

aback [ə'bæk] *ad*: **to be taken ~** être stupéfait(e).

abacus, pl abaci ['æbəkəs, -saɪ] *n* boulier *m*.

abandon [ə'bændən] *vt* abandonner // *n* abandon *m*.

abashed [ə'bæʃt] *a* confus(e), embarrassé(e).

abate [ə'beɪt] *vi* s'apaiser, se calmer.

abattoir ['æbətwɑ:*] *n* abattoir *m*.

abbey ['æbɪ] *n* abbaye *f*.

abbot ['æbət] *n* père supérieur.

abbreviate [ə'bri:vɪeɪt] *vt* abréger ; **abbreviation** [-'eɪʃən] *n* abréviation *f*.

abdicate ['æbdɪkeɪt] *vt,vi* abdiquer ; **abdication** [-'keɪʃən] *n* abdication *f*.

abdomen ['æbdəmən] *n* abdomen *m*; **abdominal** [æb'dɔmɪnl] *a* abdominal(e).

abduct [æb'dʌkt] *vt* enlever ; **abduction** [-ʃən] *n* enlèvement *m*.

abet [ə'bɛt] *vt* encourager ; aider.

abeyance [ə'beɪəns] *n*: **in ~** (*law*) en désuétude ; (*matter*) en suspens.

abhor [əb'hɔ:*] *vt* abhorrer, exécrer ; **~rent** *a* odieux(euse), exécrable.

abide [ə'baɪd], *pt,pp* **abode** *or* **abided** [ə'baɪd, ə'bəud] *vt* souffrir, supporter ; **to ~ by** *vt fus* observer, respecter.

ability [ə'bɪlɪtɪ] *n* compétence *f*; capacité *f*; talent *m*.

ablaze [ə'bleɪz] *a* en feu, en flammes ; **~ with light** resplendissant de lumière.

able ['eɪbl] *a* compétent(e) ; **to be ~ to do sth** pouvoir faire qch, être capable de faire qch ; **~-bodied** *a* robuste ; **ably** *ad* avec compétence *or* talent, habilement.

abnormal [æb'nɔ:məl] *a* anormal(e) ; **~ity** [-'mælɪtɪ] *n* anomalie *f*.

aboard [ə'bɔ:d] *ad* à bord // *prep* à bord de.

abode [ə'bəud] *pt,pp* of **abide**.

abolish [ə'bɔlɪʃ] *vt* abolir.

abolition [æbəu'lɪʃən] *n* abolition *f*.

abominable [ə'bɔmɪnəbl] *a* abominable.

aborigine [æbə'rɪdʒɪnɪ] *n* aborigène *m/f*.

abort [ə'bɔ:t] *vt* faire avorter ; **~ion** [ə'bɔ:ʃən] *n* avortement *m*; **~ive** *a* manqué(e).

abound [ə'baund] *vi* abonder ; **to ~ in** abonder en, regorger de.

about [ə'baut] *prep* au sujet de, à propos de // *ad* environ ; (*here and there*) de côté et d'autre, çà et là ; **it takes ~ 10 hours** ça prend environ or à peu près 10 heures ; **at ~ 2 o'clock** vers 2 heures ; **it's ~ here** c'est par ici, c'est dans les parages ; **to walk ~ the town** se promener dans or à travers la ville ; **to be ~ to**: he was

~ to cry il allait pleurer, il était sur le point de pleurer ; **what *or* how ~ doing this?** et si nous faisions ceci? ; **~ turn** *n* demi-tour *m*.

above [ə'bʌv] *ad* au-dessus // *prep* au-dessus de ; **mentioned ~** mentionné ci-dessus ; **costing ~ £10** coûtant plus de 10 livres ; **~ all** par-dessus tout, surtout ; **~board** *a* franc(franche), loyal(e), honnête.

abrasion [ə'breɪʒən] *n* frottement *m*; (*on skin*) écorchure *f*.

abrasive [ə'breɪzɪv] *a* abrasif(ive) ; (*fig*) caustique, agressif(ive).

abreast [ə'brɛst] *ad* de front ; **to keep ~ of** se tenir au courant de.

abridge [ə'brɪdʒ] *vt* abréger.

abroad [ə'brɔ:d] *ad* à l'étranger.

abrupt [ə'brʌpt] *a* (*steep, blunt*) abrupt(e) ; (*sudden, gruff*) brusque.

abscess ['æbsɪs] *n* abcès *m*.

abscond [əb'skɔnd] *vi* disparaître, s'enfuir.

absence ['æbsəns] *n* absence *f*.

absent ['æbsənt] *a* absent(e) ; **~ee** [-'ti:] *n* absent/e ; **~eeism** [-'ti:ɪzəm] *n* absentéisme *m*; **~-minded** *a* distrait(e) ; **~mindedness** *n* distraction *f*.

absolute ['æbsəlu:t] *a* absolu(e) ; **~ly** [-'lu:tlɪ] *ad* absolument.

absolve [əb'zɔlv] *vt*: **to ~ sb (from)** (*sin etc*) absoudre qn (de) ; **to ~ sb from** (*oath*) délier qn de.

absorb [əb'zɔ:b] *vt* absorber ; **to be ~ed in a book** être plongé dans un livre ; **~ent** *a* absorbant(e) ; **~ent cotton** *n* (*US*) coton *m* hydrophile ; **~ing** *a* absorbant(e).

abstain [əb'steɪn] *vi*: **to ~ (from)** s'abstenir (de).

abstemious [æb'sti:mɪəs] *a* sobre, frugal(e).

abstention [əb'stɛnʃən] *n* abstention *f*.

abstinence ['æbstɪnəns] *n* abstinence *f*.

abstract *a and n* ['æbstrækt] *a* abstrait(e) // *n* (*summary*) résumé *m* // *vt* [æb'strækt] extraire.

absurd [əb'sə:d] *a* absurde ; **~ity** *n* absurdité *f*.

abundance [ə'bʌndəns] *n* abondance *f*; **abundant** *a* abondant(e).

abuse *n* [ə'bju:s] abus *m*; insultes *fpl*, injures *fpl* // *vt* [ə'bju:z] abuser de ; **abusive** *a* grossier(ère), injurieux(euse).

abysmal [ə'bɪzməl] *a* exécrable ; (*ignorance etc*) sans bornes.

abyss [ə'bɪs] *n* abîme *m*, gouffre *m*.

academic [ækə'dɛmɪk] *a* universitaire ; (*pej: issue*) oiseux(euse), purement théorique // *n* universitaire *m/f*; **~ freedom** *n* liberté *f* académique.

academy [ə'kædəmɪ] *n* (*learned body*) académie *f*; (*school*) collège *m*; **military/naval ~** école militaire/navale ; **~ of music** conservatoire *m*.

accede [æk'siːd] *vi*: **to ~ to** (*request, throne*) accéder à.

accelerate [æk'sɛləreɪt] *vt,vi* accélérer ; **acceleration** [-'reɪʃən] *n* accélération *f*; **accelerator** *n* accélérateur *m*.

accent ['æksənt] *n* accent *m*.

accept [ək'sɛpt] *vt* accepter ; **~able** *a* acceptable ; **~ance** *n* acceptation *f*.

access ['æksɛs] *n* accès *m* ; **to have ~ to** (*information, library etc*) avoir accès à, pouvoir utiliser or consulter ; (*person*) avoir accès auprès de ; **~ible** [æk'sɛsəbl] *a* accessible ; **~ion** [æk'sɛʃən] *n* accession *f*.

accessory [æk'sɛsəri] *n* accessoire *m* ; **toilet accessories** *npl* articles *mpl* de toilette.

accident ['æksɪdənt] *n* accident *m* ; (*chance*) hasard *m* ; **by ~** par hasard ; accidentellement ; **~al** [-'dɛntl] *a* accidentel(le) ; **~ally** [-'dɛntəlɪ] *ad* accidentellement ; **~-prone** *a* sujet(te) aux accidents.

acclaim [ə'kleɪm] *vt* acclamer // *n* acclamation *f*.

acclimatize [ə'klaɪmətaɪz] *vt*: **to become ~d** s'acclimater.

accommodate [ə'kɔmədeɪt] *vt* loger, recevoir ; (*oblige, help*) obliger ; (*adapt*): **to ~ one's plans to** adapter ses projets à.

accommodating [ə'kɔmədeɪtɪŋ] *a* obligeant(e), arrangeant(e).

accommodation [əkɔmə'deɪʃən] *n* logement *m* ; **he's found ~** il a trouvé à se loger ; **they have ~ for 500** ils peuvent recevoir 500 personnes, il y a de la place pour 500 personnes.

accompaniment [ə'kʌmpənɪmənt] *n* accompagnement *m*.

accompanist [ə'kʌmpənɪst] *n* accompagnateur/trice.

accompany [ə'kʌmpənɪ] *vt* accompagner.

accomplice [ə'kʌmplɪs] *n* complice *m/f*.

accomplish [ə'kʌmplɪʃ] *vt* accomplir ; **~ed** *a* accompli(e) ; **~ment** *n* accomplissement *m* ; réussite *f*, résultat *m* ; **~ments** *npl* talents *mpl*.

accord [ə'kɔːd] *n* accord *m* // *vt* accorder ; **of his own ~** de son plein gré ; **~ance** *n*: **in ~ance with** conformément à ; **~ing to** selon ; **~ingly** *ad* en conséquence.

accordion [ə'kɔːdɪən] *n* accordéon *m*.

accost [ə'kɔst] *vt* accoster, aborder.

account [ə'kaunt] *n* (*COMM*) compte *m* ; (*report*) compte rendu ; récit *m* ; **by all ~s** au dire de tous ; **of little ~** de peu d'importance ; **on ~** en acompte ; **on no ~** en aucun cas ; **on ~ of** à cause de ; **to take into ~, take ~ of** tenir compte de ; **to ~ for** expliquer, rendre compte de ; **~able** *a* responsable.

accountancy [ə'kauntənsɪ] *n* comptabilité *f*.

accountant [ə'kauntənt] *n* comptable *m/f*.

accredited [ə'krɛdɪtɪd] *a* accrédité(e), admis(e).

accretion [ə'kriːʃən] *n* accroissement *m*.

accrue [ə'kruː] *vi* s'accroître ; **~d interest** intérêt couru.

accumulate [ə'kjuːmjuleɪt] *vt* accumuler, amasser // *vi* s'accumuler, s'amasser ; **accumulation** [-'leɪʃən] *n* accumulation *f*.

accuracy ['ækjurəsɪ] *n* exactitude *f*, précision *f*.

accurate ['ækjurɪt] *a* exact(e), précis(e) ; **~ly** *ad* avec précision.

accusation [ækju'zeɪʃən] *n* accusation *f*.

accusative [ə'kjuːzətɪv] *n* (*LING*) accusatif *m*.

accuse [ə'kjuːz] *vt* accuser ; **~d** *n* accusé/e.

accustom [ə'kʌstəm] *vt* accoutumer, habituer ; **~ed** *a* (*usual*) habituel(le) ; **~ed to** habitué or accoutumé à.

ace [eɪs] *n* as *m* ; **within an ~ of** à deux doigts or un cheveu de.

ache [eɪk] *n* mal *m*, douleur *f* // *vi* (*be sore*) faire mal, être douloureux(euse) ; **my head ~s** j'ai mal à la tête ; **I'm aching all over** j'ai mal partout.

achieve [ə'tʃiːv] *vt* (*aim*) atteindre ; (*victory, success*) remporter, obtenir ; (*task*) accomplir ; **~ment** *n* exploit *m*, réussite *f*.

acid ['æsɪd] *a,n* acide (*m*) ; **~ity** [ə'sɪdɪtɪ] *n* acidité *f*.

acknowledge [ək'nɔlɪdʒ] *vt* (*letter*) accuser réception de ; (*fact*) reconnaître ; **~ment** *n* accusé *m* de réception.

acne ['æknɪ] *n* acné *m*.

acorn ['eɪkɔːn] *n* gland *m*.

acoustic [ə'kuːstɪk] *a* acoustique ; **~s** *n,npl* acoustique *f*.

acquaint [ə'kweɪnt] *vt*: **to ~ sb with sth** mettre qn au courant de qch ; **to be ~ed with** (*person*) connaître ; **~ance** *n* connaissance *f*.

acquire [ə'kwaɪə*] *vt* acquérir.

acquisition [ækwɪ'zɪʃən] *n* acquisition *f*.

acquisitive [ə'kwɪzɪtɪv] *a* qui a l'instinct de possession or le goût de la propriété.

acquit [ə'kwɪt] *vt* acquitter ; **to ~ o.s. well** bien se comporter, s'en tirer très honorablement ; **~tal** *n* acquittement *m*.

acre ['eɪkə*] *n* acre *f* (= 4047 *m²*) ; **~age** *n* superficie *f*.

acrimonious [ækrɪ'məunɪəs] *a* acrimonieux(euse), aigre.

acrobat ['ækrəbæt] *n* acrobate *m/f*.

acrobatics [ækrəu'bætɪks] *n,npl* acrobatie *f*.

across [ə'krɔs] *prep* (*on the other side*) de l'autre côté de ; (*crosswise*) en travers de // *ad* de l'autre côté ; en travers ; **to walk ~** (*the road*) traverser (la route) ; **to take sb ~ the road** faire traverser la route à qn ; **a road ~ the wood** une route qui traverse le bois ; **~ from** en face de.

act [ækt] *n* acte *m*, action *f* ; (*THEATRE*) acte ; (*in music-hall etc*) numéro *m* ; (*LAW*) loi *f* // *vi* agir ; (*THEATRE*) jouer ; (*pretend*) jouer la comédie // *vt* (*role*) jouer ; **to ~ Hamlet** tenir or jouer le rôle d'Hamlet ; **to ~ the fool** faire l'idiot ; **to ~ as** servir de ; **~ing** *a* suppléant(e), par intérim // *n* (*of actor*) jeu *m* ; (*activity*): **to do some ~ing** faire du théâtre or du cinéma.

action ['ækʃən] *n* action *f* ; (*MIL*) combat(s) *m(pl)* ; (*LAW*) procès *m*, action en justice ; **out of ~** hors de combat ; hors d'usage ; **to take ~** agir, prendre des mesures.

activate ['æktɪveɪt] *vt* (*mechanism*)

actionner, faire fonctionner; (CHEM, PHYSICS) activer.
active ['æktɪv] a actif(ive); (volcano) en activité; ~ly ad activement.
activity [æk'tɪvɪtɪ] n activité f.
actor ['æktə*] n acteur m.
actress ['æktrɪs] n actrice f.
actual ['æktjuəl] a réel(le), véritable; ~ly ad réellement, véritablement; en fait.
acumen ['ækjumən] n perspicacité f.
acupuncture ['ækjupʌŋktʃə*] n acupuncture f.
acute [ə'kju:t] a aigu(ë); (mind, observer) pénétrant(e).
ad [æd] n abbr of **advertisement**.
A.D. ad (abbr of Anno Domini) ap. J.-C.
Adam ['ædəm] n Adam m; ~'s apple n pomme f d'Adam.
adamant ['ædəmənt] a inflexible.
adapt [ə'dæpt] vt adapter // vi: to ~ (to) s'adapter (à); ~able a (device) adaptable; (person) qui s'adapte facilement; ~ation [ædæp'teɪʃən] n adaptation f; ~er n (ELEC) adapteur m.
add [æd] vt ajouter; (figures: also: to ~ up) additionner // vi: to ~ to (increase) ajouter, accroître.
adder ['ædə*] n vipère f.
addict ['ædɪkt] n intoxiqué m; (fig) fanatique m/f; ~ed [ə'dɪktɪd] a: to be ~ed to (drink etc) être adonné à; (fig: football etc) être un fanatique de; ~ion [ə'dɪkʃən] n (MED) dépendance f.
adding machine ['ædɪŋməʃi:n] n machine f à calculer.
addition [ə'dɪʃən] n addition f; in ~ de plus; de surcroît; in ~ to en plus de; ~al a supplémentaire.
additive ['ædɪtɪv] n additif m.
addled ['ædld] a (egg) pourri(e).
address [ə'drɛs] n adresse f; (talk) discours m, allocution f //vt adresser; (speak to) s'adresser à.
adenoids ['ædɪnɔɪdz] npl végétations fpl.
adept ['ædɛpt] a: ~ at expert(e) à or en.
adequate ['ædɪkwɪt] a adéquat(e); suffisant(e); compétent(e); ~ly ad de façon adéquate.
adhere [əd'hɪə*] vi: to ~ to adhérer à; (fig: rule, decision) se tenir à.
adhesion [əd'hi:ʒən] n adhésion f.
adhesive [əd'hi:zɪv] a adhésif(ive) // n adhésif m.
adjacent [ə'dʒeɪsənt] a adjacent(e); ~ to adjacent à.
adjective ['ædʒɛktɪv] n adjectif m.
adjoining [ə'dʒɔɪnɪŋ] a voisin(e), adjacent(e), attenant(e) // prep voisin de, adjacent à.
adjourn [ə'dʒə:n] vt ajourner // vi suspendre la séance; lever la séance; clore la session; (go) se retirer.
adjust [ə'dʒʌst] vt ajuster, régler; rajuster // vi: to ~ (to) s'adapter (à); ~able a réglable; ~ment n ajustage m, réglage m; (of prices, wages) rajustement m; (of person) adaptation f.
adjutant ['ædʒətənt] n adjudant m.
ad-lib [æd'lɪb] vt,vi improviser // n improvisation f // ad: **ad lib** à volonté, à discrétion.

administer [əd'mɪnɪstə*] vt administrer; (justice) rendre.
administration [ədmɪnɪs'treɪʃən] n administration f.
administrative [əd'mɪnɪstrətɪv] a administratif(ive).
administrator [əd'mɪnɪstreɪtə*] n administrateur/trice.
admirable ['ædmərəbl] a admirable.
admiral ['ædmərəl] n amiral m; A~ty n amirauté f; ministère m de la Marine.
admiration [ædmə'reɪʃən] n admiration f.
admire [əd'maɪə*] vt admirer; ~r n admirateur/trice.
admission [əd'mɪʃən] n admission f; (to exhibition, night club etc) entrée f; (confession) aveu m.
admit [əd'mɪt] vt laisser entrer; admettre; (agree) reconnaître, admettre; to ~ of admettre, permettre; to ~ to reconnaître, avouer; ~tance n admission f, (droit m d')entrée f; ~tedly ad il faut en convenir.
admonish [əd'mɔnɪʃ] vt donner un avertissement à; réprimander.
ado [ə'du:] n: without (any) more ~ sans plus de cérémonies.
adolescence [ædəu'lɛsns] n adolescence f.
adolescent [ædəu'lɛsnt] a,n adolescent(e).
adopt [ə'dɔpt] vt adopter; ~ed a adoptif(ive), adopté(e); ~ion [ə'dɔpʃən] n adoption f.
adore [ə'dɔ:*] vt adorer; **adoringly** ad avec adoration.
adorn [ə'dɔ:n] vt orner; ~ment n ornement m.
adrenalin [ə'drɛnəlɪn] n adrénaline f.
Adriatic (Sea) [eɪdrɪ'ætɪk(si:)] n Adriatique f.
adrift [ə'drɪft] ad à la dérive.
adroit [ə'drɔɪt] a adroit(e), habile.
adult ['ædʌlt] n adulte m/f.
adulterate [ə'dʌltəreɪt] vt frelater, falsifier.
adultery [ə'dʌltərɪ] n adultère m.
advance [əd'vɑ:ns] n avance f // vt avancer // vi s'avancer; in ~ en avance, d'avance; ~d a avancé(e); (SCOL: studies) supérieur(e); ~ment n avancement m.
advantage [əd'vɑ:ntɪdʒ] n (also TENNIS) avantage m; to take ~ of profiter de; ~ous [ædvən'teɪdʒəs] a avantageux(euse).
advent ['ædvənt] n avènement m, venue f; A~ Avent m.
adventure [əd'vɛntʃə*] n aventure f; **adventurous** [-tʃərəs] a aventureux(euse).
adverb ['ædvə:b] n adverbe m.
adversary ['ædvəsərɪ] n adversaire m/f.
adverse ['ædvə:s] a contraire, adverse; in ~ circumstances dans l'adversité; ~ to hostile à.
adversity [əd'və:sɪtɪ] n adversité f.
advert ['ædvə:t] n abbr of **advertisement**.
advertise ['ædvətaɪz] vi(vt) faire de la publicité or de la réclame (pour); mettre une annonce (pour vendre).
advertisement [əd'və:tɪsmənt] n (COMM) réclame f, publicité f; (in classified ads) annonce f.

advertising ['ædvətaɪzɪŋ] n publicité f, réclame f.

advice [əd'vaɪs] n conseils mpl; (notification) avis m; **piece of ~** conseil.

advisable [əd'vaɪzəbl] a recommandable, indiqué(e).

advise [əd'vaɪz] vt conseiller; **to ~ sb of sth** aviser or informer qn de qch; **~r** n conseiller/ère; **advisory** [-əɪ] a consultatif(ive).

advocate vt ['ædvəkeɪt] recommander, prôner.

aegis ['iːdʒɪs] n: **under the ~ of** sous l'égide de.

aerial ['ɛərɪəl] n antenne f // a aérien(ne).

aeroplane ['ɛərəpleɪn] n avion m.

aerosol ['ɛərəsɔl] n aérosol m.

aesthetic [iːs'θetɪk] a esthétique.

afar [ə'fɑː*] ad: **from ~** de loin.

affable ['æfəbl] a affable.

affair [ə'fɛə*] n affaire f; (also: **love ~**) liaison f; aventure f.

affect [ə'fɛkt] vt affecter; **~ation** [æfɛk'teɪʃən] n affectation f; **~ed** a affecté(e).

affection [ə'fɛkʃən] n affection f; **~ate** a affectueux(euse); **~ately** ad affectueusement.

affiliated [ə'fɪlieɪtɪd] a affilié(e).

affinity [ə'fɪnɪtɪ] n affinité f.

affirmation [æfə'meɪʃən] n affirmation f, assertion f.

affirmative [ə'fəːmətɪv] a affirmatif(ive) // n: **in the ~** dans or par l'affirmative.

affix [ə'fɪks] vt apposer, ajouter.

afflict [ə'flɪkt] vt affliger; **~ion** [ə'flɪkʃən] n affliction f, détresse f.

affluence ['æfluəns] n abondance f, opulence f.

affluent ['æfluənt] a abondant(e); opulent(e); (person) dans l'aisance, riche.

afford [ə'fɔːd] vt se permettre; avoir les moyens d'acheter or d'entretenir; (provide) fournir, procurer; **I can't ~ the time** je n'ai vraiment pas le temps.

affray [ə'freɪ] n échauffourée f.

affront [ə'frʌnt] n affront m; **~ed** a insulté(e).

afield [ə'fiːld] ad: **far ~** loin.

afloat [ə'fləut] a à flot // ad: **to stay ~** surnager; **to keep/get a business ~** maintenir à flot/lancer une affaire.

afoot [ə'fut] ad: **there is something ~** il se prépare quelque chose.

aforesaid [ə'fɔːsɛd] a susdit(e), susmentionné(e).

afraid [ə'freɪd] a effrayé(e); **to be ~ of** or **to** avoir peur de; **I am ~ that** je crains que + sub.

afresh [ə'frɛʃ] ad de nouveau.

Africa ['æfrɪkə] n Afrique f; **~n** a africain(e) // n Africain/e.

aft [ɑːft] ad à l'arrière, vers l'arrière.

after ['ɑːftə*] prep,ad après // cj après que, après avoir or être + pp; **what/who are you ~?** que/qui cherchez-vous?; **ask ~ him** demandez de ses nouvelles; **~ all** après tout; **~-effects** npl répercussions fpl; (of illness) séquelles fpl, suites fpl; **~life** n vie future; **~math** n conséquences fpl; **in the ~math of** dans

les mois or années etc qui suivirent, au lendemain de; **~noon** n après-midi m or f; **~-shave (lotion)** n after-shave m; **~thought** n: **I had an ~thought** il m'est venu une idée après coup; **~wards** ad après.

again [ə'gɛn] ad de nouveau; **to begin/see ~** recommencer/revoir; **not ... ~** ne ... plus; **~ and ~** à plusieurs reprises; **he's opened it ~** il l'a rouvert, il l'a de nouveau or l'a encore ouvert.

against [ə'gɛnst] prep contre; **~ a blue background** sur un fond bleu.

age [eɪdʒ] n âge m // vt,vi vieillir; **it's been ~s since** ça fait une éternité que; **to come of ~** atteindre sa majorité; **~d a** âgé(e); **~d 10** âgé de 10 ans; **the ~d** ['eɪdʒɪd] les personnes âgées; **~ group** n tranche f d'âge; **~less** a sans âge; **~ limit** n limite f d'âge.

agency ['eɪdʒənsɪ] n agence f; **through** or **by the ~ of** par l'entremise or l'action de.

agenda [ə'dʒɛndə] n ordre m du jour.

agent ['eɪdʒənt] n agent m.

aggravate ['ægrəveɪt] vt aggraver; (annoy) exaspérer.

aggravation [ægrə'veɪʃən] n (of quarrel) envenimement m.

aggregate ['ægrɪgeɪt] n ensemble m, total m; **on ~** (SPORT) au goal average.

aggression [ə'grɛʃən] n agression f.

aggressive [ə'grɛsɪv] a agressif(ive); **~ness** n agressivité f.

aggrieved [ə'griːvd] a chagriné(e), affligé(e).

aghast [ə'gɑːst] a consterné(e), atterré(e).

agile ['ædʒaɪl] a agile.

agitate ['ædʒɪteɪt] vt rendre inquiet(ète) or agité(e); agiter // vi faire de l'agitation (politique); **to ~ for** faire campagne pour; **agitator** n agitateur/trice (politique).

ago [ə'gəu] ad: **2 days ~** il y a deux jours; **not long ~** il n'y a pas longtemps.

agonizing ['ægənaɪzɪŋ] a angoissant(e); déchirant(e).

agony ['ægənɪ] n grande souffrance or angoisse; **to be in ~** souffrir le martyre.

agree [ə'griː] vt (price) convenir de // vi: **to ~ (with)** (person) être d'accord (avec); (statements etc) concorder (avec); (LING) s'accorder (avec); **to ~ to do** accepter de or consentir à faire; **to ~ to sth** consentir à qch; **to ~ that** (admit) convenir or reconnaître que; **they ~ on this** ils sont d'accord sur ce point; **they ~d on going/a price** ils se mirent d'accord pour y aller/sur un prix; **garlic doesn't ~ with me** je ne supporte pas l'ail; **~able** a agréable; (willing) consentant(e), d'accord; **are you ~able to this?** est-ce que cela vous va or convient?; **~d** a (time, place) convenu(e); **to be ~d** être d'accord; **~ment** n accord m; **in ~ment** d'accord.

agricultural [ægrɪ'kʌltʃərəl] a agricole.

agriculture ['ægrɪkʌltʃə*] n agriculture f.

aground [ə'graund] ad: **to run ~** s'échouer.

ahead [ə'hɛd] ad en avant; devant; **~ of** devant; (fig: schedule etc) en avance sur; **~ of time** en avance; **go right** or **straight ~** allez tout droit; **they were (right) ~**

of us ils nous précédaient (de peu), ils étaient (juste) devant nous.

aid [eɪd] n aide f // vt aider ; **to ~ and abet** (LAW) se faire le complice de.

aide [eɪd] n (person) collaborateur/trice, assistant/e.

ailment ['eɪlmənt] n petite maladie, affection f.

aim [eɪm] vt: **to ~ sth at** (such as gun, camera) braquer or pointer qch sur, diriger qch contre ; (missile) lancer qch à or contre or en direction de ; (remark, blow) destiner or adresser qch à // vi (also: **to take ~**) viser // n but m; **to ~ at** viser ; (fig) viser (à) ; avoir pour but or ambition ; **to ~ to do** avoir l'intention de faire ; **~less** a sans but ; **~lessly** ad sans but, à l'aventure.

air [ɛə*] n air m // vt aérer ; (grievances, ideas) exposer (librement) // cpd (currents, attack etc) aérien(ne) ; (remark, blow) destiner pneumatique ; **~borne** a en vol; aeroporté(e) ; **~-conditioned** a climatisé(e), à air conditionné ; **~-conditioning** n climatisation f; **~-cooled** a à refroidissement à air ; **~craft** n,pl inv avion m; **~craft carrier** n porte-avions m inv; **~ cushion** n coussin m d'air; **A~ Force** n Armée f de l'air; **~gun** n fusil m à air comprimé ; **~ hostess** n hôtesse f de l'air; **~ily** ad d'un air dégagé ; **~ letter** n aérogramme m; **~lift** n pont aérien ; **~line** n ligne aérienne ; compagnie f d'aviation ; **~liner** n avion m de ligne ; **~lock** n sas m; **by ~mail** par avion; **~port** n aéroport m; **~ raid** n attaque aérienne ; **~sick** a qui a le mal de l'air; **~strip** n terrain m d'atterrissage ; **~tight** a hermétique ; **~y** a bien aéré(e) ; (manners) dégagé(e).

aisle [aɪl] n (of church) allée centrale ; nef latérale.

ajar [ə'dʒɑː*] a entrouvert(e).

alarm [ə'lɑːm] n alarme f // vt alarmer ; **~ clock** n réveille-matin m, réveil m; **~ist** n alarmiste m/f.

Albania [æl'beɪnɪə] n Albanie f.

album ['ælbəm] n album m; (L.P.) 33 tours m inv.

albumen ['ælbjumɪn] n albumine f; (of egg) albumen m.

alchemy ['ælkɪmɪ] n alchimie f.

alcohol ['ælkəhɔl] n alcool m; **~ic** [-'hɔlɪk] a,n alcoolique (m/f); **~ism** n alcoolisme m.

alcove ['ælkəuv] n alcôve f.

alderman ['ɔːldəmən] n conseiller municipal (en Angleterre).

ale [eɪl] n bière f.

alert [ə'ləːt] a alerte, vif(vive) ; vigilant(e) // n alerte f; **on the ~** sur le qui-vive ; (MIL) en état d'alerte.

algebra ['ældʒɪbrə] n algèbre m.

Algeria [æl'dʒɪərɪə] n Algérie f; **~n** a algérien(ne) // n Algérien/ne.

Algiers [æl'dʒɪəz] n Alger.

alias ['eɪlɪæs] ad alias // n faux nom, nom d'emprunt.

alibi ['ælɪbaɪ] n alibi m.

alien ['eɪlɪən] n étranger/ère // a: ~ **(to/from)** étranger(ère) (à) ; **~ate** vt aliéner ; s'aliéner ; **~ation** [-'neɪʃən] n aliénation f.

alight [ə'laɪt] a,ad en feu // vi mettre pied à terre ; (passenger) descendre ; (bird) se poser.

align [ə'laɪn] vt aligner ; **~ment** n alignement m.

alike [ə'laɪk] a semblable, pareil(le) // ad de même ; **to look ~** se ressembler.

alimony ['ælɪmənɪ] n (payment) pension f alimentaire.

alive [ə'laɪv] a vivant(e) ; (active) plein(e) de vie ; ~ **with** grouillant(e) de ; ~ **to** sensible à.

alkali ['ælkəlaɪ] n alcali m.

all [ɔːl] a tout(e), tous(toutes) pl // pronoun tout m; (pl) tous(toutes) // ad tout ; ~ **wrong/alone** tout faux/seul ; ~ **the time/his life** tout le temps/toute sa vie ; ~ **five** (tous) les cinq ; ~ **of them** tous, toutes ; ~ **of it** tout ; ~ **of us went** nous y sommes tous allés ; **not as hard** etc as ~ **that** pas si dur etc que ça ; ~ **in ~** à tout prendre, l'un dans l'autre.

allay [ə'leɪ] vt (fears) apaiser, calmer.

allegation [æli'geɪʃən] n allégation f.

allege [ə'lɛdʒ] vt alléguer, prétendre ; **~dly** [ə'lɛdʒɪdlɪ] ad à ce que l'on prétend, paraît-il.

allegiance [ə'liːdʒəns] n fidélité f, obéissance f.

allegory ['ælɪgərɪ] n allégorie f.

all-embracing ['ɔːlɪm'breɪsɪŋ] a universel(le).

allergic [ə'ləːdʒɪk] a: ~ **to** allergique à.

allergy ['ælədʒɪ] n allergie f.

alleviate [ə'liːvɪeɪt] vt soulager, adoucir.

alley ['ælɪ] n ruelle f; (in garden) allée f.

alliance [ə'laɪəns] n alliance f.

allied ['ælaɪd] a allié(e).

alligator ['ælɪgeɪtə*] n alligator m.

all-important ['ɔːlɪm'pɔːtənt] a capital(e), crucial(e).

all-in ['ɔːlɪn] a (also ad: charge) tout compris ; ~ **wrestling** n catch m.

alliteration [əlɪtə'reɪʃən] n allitération f.

all-night ['ɔːl'naɪt] a ouvert(e) or qui dure toute la nuit.

allocate ['æləkeɪt] vt (share out) répartir, distribuer ; (duties): **to ~ sth to** assigner or attribuer qch à ; (sum, time): **to ~ sth to allouer** qch à ; **to ~ sth for** affecter qch à.

allocation [æləu'keɪʃən] n: ~ **(of money)** crédit(s) m(pl), somme(s) allouée(s).

allot [ə'lɔt] vt (share out) répartir, distribuer ; (time): **to ~ sth to** allouer qch à ; (duties): **to ~ sth to** assigner qch à ; **~ment** n (share) part f; (garden) lopin m de terre (loué à la municipalité).

all-out ['ɔːl'aut] a (effort etc) total(e) // ad: **all out** à fond.

allow [ə'lau] vt (practice, behaviour) permettre, autoriser ; (sum to spend etc) accorder, allouer ; (sum, time estimated) compter, prévoir ; (concede): **to ~ that** convenir que ; **to ~ sb to do** permettre à qn de faire, autoriser qn à faire ; **to ~ for** vt fus tenir compte de ; **~ance** n (money received) allocation f; subside m; indemnité f; (TAX) somme f déductible du revenu imposable, abattement m; **to make ~ances for** tenir compte de.

alloy ['ælɔɪ] *n* alliage *m*.

all right ['ɔːl'raɪt] *ad* (feel, work) bien ; (as answer) d'accord.

all-round ['ɔːl'raund] *a* compétent(e) dans tous les domaines ; (athlete etc) complet(ète).

all-time ['ɔːl'taɪm] *a* (record) sans précédent, absolu(e).

allude [ə'luːd] *vi*: **to ~ to** faire allusion à.

alluring [ə'ljuərɪŋ] *a* séduisant(e), alléchant(e).

allusion [ə'luːʒən] *n* allusion *f*.

alluvium [ə'luːvɪəm] *n* alluvions *fpl*.

ally ['ælaɪ] *n* allié *m*.

almighty [ɔːl'maɪtɪ] *a* tout-puissant.

almond ['ɑːmənd] *n* amande *f*.

almost ['ɔːlməust] *ad* presque.

alms [ɑːmz] *n* aumône(s) *f(pl)*.

alone [ə'ləun] *a* seul(e) ; **to leave sb ~** laisser qn tranquille ; **to leave sth ~** ne pas toucher à qch.

along [ə'lɔŋ] *prep* le long de // *ad*: **is he coming ~?** vient-il avec nous? ; **he was hopping/limping ~** il venait or avançait en sautillant/boitant ; **~ with** en compagnie de ; avec, en plus de ; **~side** *prep* le long de ; au côté de // *ad* bord à bord ; côte à côte.

aloof [ə'luːf] *a,ad* à distance, à l'écart ; **~ness** réserve (hautaine), attitude distante.

aloud [ə'laud] *ad* à haute voix.

alphabet ['ælfəbɛt] *n* alphabet *m* ; **~ical** [-'bɛtɪkəl] *a* alphabétique.

alpine ['ælpaɪn] *a* alpin(e), alpestre.

Alps [ælps] *npl*: **the ~** les Alpes *fpl*.

already [ɔːl'rɛdɪ] *ad* déjà.

alright [ɔːl'raɪt] *ad* = **all right**.

also ['ɔːlsəu] *ad* aussi.

altar ['ɔltə*] *n* autel *m*.

alter ['ɔltə*] *vt,vi* changer, modifier ; **~ation** [ɔltə'reɪʃən] *n* changement *m*, modification *f*.

alternate [ɔl'tɜːnɪt] *a* alterné(e), alternant(e), alternatif(ive) // *vi* ['ɔltəːneɪt] alterner ; **on ~ days** un jour sur deux, tous les deux jours ; **~ly** *ad* alternativement, en alternant ; **alternating** *a* (current) alternatif(ive).

alternative [ɔl'tɜːnətɪv] *a* (solutions) interchangeable, possible ; (solution) autre, de remplacement // *n* (choice) alternative *f* ; (other possibility) solution *f* de remplacement or de rechange, autre possibilité *f* ; **~ly** *ad*: **~ly one could** une autre or l'autre solution serait de.

alternator ['ɔltəːneɪtə*] *n* (AUT) alternateur *m*.

although [ɔːl'ðəu] *cj* bien que + *sub*.

altitude ['æltɪtjuːd] *n* altitude *f*.

alto ['æltəu] *n* (female) contralto *m* ; (male) haute-contre *f*.

altogether [ɔːltə'gɛðə*] *ad* entièrement, tout à fait ; (on the whole) tout compte fait ; (in all) en tout.

altruistic [æltru'ɪstɪk] *a* altruiste.

aluminium [ælju'mɪnɪəm], **aluminum** [ə'luːmɪnəm] (US) *n* aluminium *m*.

always ['ɔːlweɪz] *ad* toujours.

am [æm] *vb see* **be**.

a.m. *ad* (abbr of ante meridiem) du matin.

amalgamate [ə'mælgəmeɪt] *vt,vi* fusionner ; **amalgamation** [-'meɪʃən] *n* fusion *f* ; (COMM) fusionnement *m* ; amalgame *m*.

amass [ə'mæs] *vt* amasser.

amateur ['æmətə*] *n* amateur *m* // *a* (SPORT) amateur *inv* ; **~ish** *a* (pej) d'amateur.

amaze [ə'meɪz] *vt* stupéfier ; **~ment** *n* stupéfaction *f*, stupeur *f*.

ambassador [æm'bæsədə*] *n* ambassadeur *m*.

amber ['æmbə*] *n* ambre *m* ; **at ~** (AUT) à l'orange.

ambidextrous [æmbɪ'dɛkstrəs] *a* ambidextre.

ambiguity [æmbɪ'gjuɪtɪ] *n* ambiguïté *f*.

ambiguous [æm'bɪgjuəs] *a* ambigu(ë).

ambition [æm'bɪʃən] *n* ambition *f*.

ambitious [æm'bɪʃəs] *a* ambitieux(euse).

ambivalent [æm'bɪvələnt] *a* (attitude) ambivalent(e).

amble ['æmbl] *vi* (gen: **to ~ along**) aller d'un pas tranquille.

ambulance ['æmbjuləns] *n* ambulance *f*.

ambush ['æmbuʃ] *n* embuscade *f* // *vt* tendre une embuscade à.

ameliorate [ə'miːlɪəreɪt] *vt* améliorer.

amenable [ə'miːnəbl] *a*: **~ to** (advice etc) disposé(e) à écouter or suivre ; **~ to the law** responsable devant la loi.

amend [ə'mɛnd] *vt* (law) amender ; (text) corriger ; (habits) réformer // *vi* s'amender, se corriger ; **to make ~s** réparer ses torts, faire amende honorable ; **~ment** *n* (to law) amendement *m* ; (to text) correction *f*.

amenities [ə'miːnɪtɪz] *npl* aménagements *mpl* (prévus pour le loisir des habitants).

amenity [ə'miːnɪtɪ] *n* charme *m*, agrément *m*.

America [ə'mɛrɪkə] *n* Amérique *f* ; **~n** *a* américain(e) // *n* Américain/e ; **a~nize** *vt* américaniser.

amethyst ['æmɪθɪst] *n* améthyste *f*.

amiable ['eɪmɪəbl] *a* aimable, affable.

amicable ['æmɪkəbl] *a* amical(e).

amid(st) [ə'mɪd(st)] *prep* parmi, au milieu de.

amiss [ə'mɪs] *a,ad*: **there's something ~** il y a quelque chose qui ne va pas or qui cloche ; **to take sth ~** prendre qch mal or de travers.

ammunition [æmju'nɪʃən] *n* munitions *fpl*.

amnesia [æm'niːzɪə] *n* amnésie *f*.

amnesty ['æmnɪstɪ] *n* amnistie *f*.

amok [ə'mɔk] *ad*: **to run ~** être pris(e) d'un accès de folie furieuse.

among(st) [ə'mʌŋ(st)] *prep* parmi, entre.

amoral [æ'mɔrəl] *a* amoral(e).

amorous ['æmərəs] *a* amoureux(euse).

amorphous [ə'mɔːfəs] *a* amorphe.

amount [ə'maunt] *n* somme *f* ; montant *m* ; quantité *f* ; nombre *m* // *vi*: **to ~ to** (total) s'élever à ; (be same as) équivaloir à, revenir à.

amp(ère) ['æmp(ɛə*)] n ampère m.
amphibian [æm'fɪbɪən] n batracien m.
amphibious [æm'fɪbɪəs] a amphibie.
amphitheatre ['æmfɪθɪətə*] n amphithéâtre m.
ample ['æmpl] a ample; spacieux(euse); (enough): **this is** ~ c'est largement suffisant; **to have** ~ **time/room** avoir bien assez de temps/place, avoir largement le temps/la place.
amplifier ['æmplɪfaɪə*] n amplificateur m.
amplify ['æmplɪfaɪ] vt amplifier.
amply ['æmplɪ] ad amplement, largement.
amputate ['æmpjuteɪt] vt amputer.
amuck [ə'mʌk] ad = amok.
amuse [ə'mju:z] vt amuser; ~ment n amusement m.
an [æn, ən, n] det see **a**.
anaemia [ə'ni:mɪə] n anémie f.
anaemic [ə'ni:mɪk] a anémique.
anaesthetic [ænɪs'θetɪk] a,n anesthésique (m); **under the** ~ sous anesthésie.
anaesthetist [æ'ni:sθɪtɪst] n anesthésiste m/f.
anagram ['ænəgræm] n anagramme m.
analgesic [ænæl'dʒi:sɪk] a,n analgésique (m).
analogy [ə'nælədʒɪ] n analogie f.
analyse ['ænəlaɪz] vt analyser.
analysis, pl **analyses** [ə'næləsɪs, -si:z] n analyse f.
analyst ['ænəlɪst] n (US) psychanalyste m/f.
analytic(al) [ænə'lɪtɪk(əl)] a analytique.
analyze ['ænəlaɪz] vt (US) = **analyse**.
anarchist ['ænəkɪst] a,n anarchiste (m/f).
anarchy ['ænəkɪ] n anarchie f.
anathema [ə'næθɪmə] n: **it is** ~ **to him** il a cela en abomination.
anatomical [ænə'tɒmɪkəl] a anatomique.
anatomy [ə'nætəmɪ] n anatomie f.
ancestor ['ænsɪstə*] n ancêtre m, aïeul m.
ancestral [æn'sɛstrəl] a ancestral(e).
ancestry ['ænsɪstrɪ] n ancêtres mpl; ascendance f.
anchor ['æŋkə*] n ancre f // vi (also: **to drop** ~) jeter l'ancre, mouiller // vt mettre à l'ancre; ~**age** n mouillage m, ancrage m.
anchovy ['æntʃəvɪ] n anchois m.
ancient ['eɪnʃənt] a ancien(ne), antique; (fig) d'un âge vénérable, antique.
and [ænd] cj et; ~ **so on** et ainsi de suite; **try** ~ **come** tâchez de venir; **come** ~ **sit here** viens t'asseoir ici; **better** ~ **better** de mieux en mieux; **more** ~ **more** de plus en plus.
Andes ['ændi:z] npl: **the** ~ les Andes fpl.
anecdote ['ænɪkdəʊt] n anecdote f.
anemia [ə'ni:mɪə] n = **anaemia**.
anemic [ə'ni:mɪk] a = **anaemic**.
anesthetic [ænɪs'θetɪk] a,n = **anaesthetic**.
anesthetist [æ'ni:sθɪtɪst] n = **anaesthetist**.
anew [ə'nju:] ad à nouveau.
angel ['eɪndʒəl] n ange m.
anger ['æŋgə*] n colère f // vt mettre en colère, irriter.

angina [æn'dʒaɪnə] n angine f de poitrine.
angle ['æŋgl] n angle m; **from their** ~ de leur point de vue // vi: **to** ~ **for** (trout) pêcher; (compliments) chercher, quêter; ~**r** n pêcheur/euse à la ligne.
Anglican ['æŋglɪkən] a,n anglican(e).
anglicize ['æŋglɪsaɪz] vt angliciser.
angling ['æŋglɪŋ] n pêche f à la ligne.
Anglo- ['æŋgləʊ] prefix anglo(-); ~**Saxon** a,n anglo-saxon(ne).
angrily ['æŋgrɪlɪ] ad avec colère.
angry ['æŋgrɪ] a en colère, furieux(euse); **to be** ~ **with sb/at sth** être furieux contre qn/de qch; **to get** ~ se fâcher, se mettre en colère; **to make sb** ~ mettre qn en colère.
anguish ['æŋgwɪʃ] n angoisse f.
angular ['æŋgjʊlə*] a anguleux(euse).
animal ['ænɪməl] n animal m // a animal(e); ~ **spirits** npl entrain m, vivacité f.
animate vt ['ænɪmeɪt] animer // a ['ænɪmɪt] animé(e), vivant(e); ~**d** a animé(e).
animosity [ænɪ'mɒsɪtɪ] n animosité f.
aniseed ['ænɪsi:d] n anis m.
ankle ['æŋkl] n cheville f.
annex n ['ænɛks] (also: **annexe**) annexe f // vt [ə'nɛks] annexer; ~**ation** [-'eɪʃən] n annexion f.
annihilate [ə'naɪəleɪt] vt annihiler, anéantir.
anniversary [ænɪ'vɜ:sərɪ] n anniversaire m; ~ **dinner** n dîner commémoratif or anniversaire.
annotate ['ænəʊteɪt] vt annoter.
announce [ə'naʊns] vt annoncer; (birth, death) faire part de; ~**ment** n annonce f; (for births etc: in newspaper) avis m de faire-part; (:letter, card) faire-part m; ~**r** n (RADIO, TV) (between programmes) speaker/ine; (in a programme) présentateur/trice.
annoy [ə'nɔɪ] vt agacer, ennuyer, contrarier; **don't get** ~**ed!** ne vous fâchez pas!; ~**ance** n mécontentement m, contrariété f; ~**ing** a ennuyeux(euse), agaçant(e), contrariant(e).
annual ['ænjʊəl] a annuel(le) // n (BOT) plante annuelle; (book) album m; ~**ly** ad annuellement.
annuity [ə'nju:ɪtɪ] n rente f; **life** ~ rente viagère.
annul [ə'nʌl] vt annuler; (law) abroger; ~**ment** n annulation f; abrogation f.
annum ['ænəm] n see **per**.
anoint [ə'nɔɪnt] vt oindre.
anomalous [ə'nɒmələs] a anormal(e).
anomaly [ə'nɒməlɪ] n anomalie f.
anonymity [ænə'nɪmɪtɪ] n anonymat m.
anonymous [ə'nɒnɪməs] a anonyme.
anorak ['ænəræk] n anorak m.
another [ə'nʌðə*] a: ~ **book** (one more) un autre livre, encore un livre, un livre de plus; (a different one) un autre livre // pronoun un(e) autre, encore un(e), un(e) de plus; see also **one**.
answer ['ɑ:nsə*] n réponse f; solution f // vi répondre // vt (reply to) répondre à; (problem) résoudre; (prayer) exaucer; **to** ~ **the phone** répondre (au téléphone);

in ~ to your letter suite à or en réponse à votre lettre ; **to ~ the bell** or **the door** aller or venir ouvrir (la porte) ; **to ~ back** vi répondre, répliquer ; **to ~ for** vt fus répondre de, se porter garant de ; être responsable de ; **to ~ to** vt fus (description) répondre or correspondre à ; **~able** a: **~able (to sb/for sth)** responsable (devant qn/de qch) ; **I am ~able to no-one** je n'ai de comptes à rendre à personne.

ant [ænt] n fourmi f.

antagonism [æn'tægənizəm] n antagonisme m.

antagonist [æn'tægənist] n antagoniste m/f, adversaire m/f ; **~ic** [æntægə'nistik] a opposé(e) ; antagoniste.

antagonize [æn'tægənaiz] vt éveiller l'hostilité de, contrarier.

Antarctic [ænt'a:ktik] n Antarctique m // a antarctique, austral(e).

anteater ['ænti:tə*] n fourmilier m, tamanoir m.

antecedent [ænti'si:dənt] n antécédent m.

antelope ['æntiləup] n antilope f.

antenatal ['ænti'neitl] a prénatal(e) ; **~ clinic** n service m de consultation prénatale.

antenna, pl **~e** [æn'tɛnə, -ni:] n antenne f.

anthem ['ænθəm] n motet m ; **national ~** hymne national.

ant-hill ['ænthil] n fourmilière f.

anthology [æn'θɔlədʒi] n anthologie f.

anthropologist [ænθrə'pɔlədʒist] n anthropologue m/f.

anthropology [ænθrə'pɔlədʒi] n anthropologie f.

anti- [ænti] prefix anti-.

anti-aircraft ['ænti'ɛəkrɑ:ft] a antiaérien(ne) ; **~ defence** n défense f contre avions, DCA f.

antibiotic ['æntibai'ɔtik] a,n antibiotique (m).

anticipate [æn'tisipeit] vt s'attendre à ; prévoir ; (wishes, request) aller au devant de, devancer.

anticipation [æntisi'peiʃən] n attente f ; **thanking you in ~** en vous remerciant d'avance, avec mes remerciements anticipés.

anticlimax ['ænti'klaimæks] n réalisation décevante d'un événement que l'on escomptait important, intéressant etc.

anticlockwise ['ænti'klɔkwaiz] a dans le sens inverse des aiguilles d'une montre.

antics ['æntiks] npl singeries fpl.

anticyclone ['ænti'saikləun] n anticyclone m.

antidote ['æntidəut] n antidote m, contrepoison m.

antifreeze ['ænti'fri:z] n antigel m.

antipathy [æn'tipəθi] n antipathie f.

antiquarian [ænti'kwɛəriən] a: **~ bookshop** librairie f d'ouvrages anciens // n expert m en objets or livres anciens ; amateur m d'antiquités.

antiquated ['æntikweitid] a vieilli(e), suranné(e), vieillot(te).

antique [æn'ti:k] n objet m d'art ancien, meuble ancien or d'époque, antiquité f //

a ancien(ne) ; (pre-mediaeval) antique ; **~ dealer** n antiquaire m/f ; **~ shop** n magasin m d'antiquités.

antiquity [æn'tikwiti] n antiquité f.

antiseptic [ænti'sɛptik] a,n antiseptique (m).

antisocial ['ænti'səuʃəl] a peu liant(e), sauvage, insociable ; (against society) anti-social(e).

antlers ['æntləz] npl bois mpl, ramure f.

anus ['einəs] n anus m.

anvil ['ænvil] n enclume f.

anxiety [æŋ'zaiəti] n anxiété f ; (keenness): **~ to do** grand désir or impatience f de faire.

anxious ['æŋkʃəs] a anxieux(euse), (très) inquiet(ète) ; (keen): **~ to do/that** qui tient beaucoup à faire/à ce que ; impatient(e) de faire/que ; **~ly** ad anxieusement.

any ['ɛni] a (in negative and interrogative sentences = some) de, d' ; du, de l', de la, des ; (no matter which) n'importe quel(le), quelconque ; (each and every) tout(e), chaque ; **I haven't ~ money/books** je n'ai pas d'argent/de livres ; **have you ~ butter/children?** avez-vous du beurre/des enfants? ; **without ~ difficulty** sans la moindre difficulté ; **come (at) ~ time** venez à n'importe quelle heure ; **at ~ moment** à tout moment, d'un instant à l'autre ; **in ~ case** de toute façon ; en tout cas ; **at ~ rate** de toute façon // pronoun n'importe lequel(laquelle) ; (anybody) n'importe qui ; (in negative and interrogative sentences): **I haven't ~** je n'en ai pas, je n'en ai aucun ; **have you got ~?** en avez-vous? ; **can ~ of you sing?** est-ce que l'un d'entre vous or quelqu'un parmi vous sait chanter? // ad (in negative sentences) nullement, aucunement ; (in interrogative and conditional constructions) un peu ; tant soit peu ; **I can't hear him ~ more** je ne l'entends plus ; **are you feeling ~ better?** vous sentez-vous un peu mieux? ; **do you want ~ more soup?** voulez-vous encore un peu de soupe? ; **~body** pronoun n'importe qui ; (in interrogative sentences) quelqu'un ; (in negative sentences) **I don't see ~body** je ne vois personne ; **how** ad quoi qu'il en soit ; **~one = ~body** ; **~thing** pronoun (see **anybody**) n'importe quoi ; quelque chose ; ne ... rien ; **~time** ad n'importe quand ; **~way** ad de toute façon ; **~where** ad (see **anybody**) n'importe où ; quelque part ; **I don't see him ~where** je ne le vois nulle part.

apart [ə'pɑ:t] ad (to one side) à part ; de côté ; à l'écart ; (separately) séparément ; **10 miles/a long way ~** à 10 miles/très éloignés l'un de l'autre ; **they are living ~** ils sont séparés ; **~ from** prep à part, excepté.

apartheid [ə'pɑ:teit] n apartheid m.

apartment [ə'pɑ:tmənt] n (US) appartement m, logement m ; **~s** npl appartement m.

apathetic [æpə'θetik] a apathique, indifférent(e).

apathy ['æpəθi] n apathie f, indifférence f.

ape [eɪp] n (grand) singe // vt singer.
aperitif [ə'pɛrɪtɪv] n apéritif m.
aperture ['æpətʃjuə*] n orifice m, ouverture f; (PHOT) ouverture (du diaphragme).
apex ['eɪpɛks] n sommet m.
aphrodisiac [æfrəʊ'dɪzɪæk] a,n aphrodisiaque (m).
apiece [ə'pi:s] ad (for each person) chacun(e), par tête; (for each item) chacun(e), (la) pièce.
aplomb [ə'plɔm] n sang-froid m, assurance f.
apocalypse [ə'pɔkəlɪps] n apocalypse f.
apolitical [eɪpə'lɪtɪkl] a apolitique.
apologetic [əpɔlə'dʒɛtɪk] a (tone, letter) d'excuse; **to be very ~ about** s'excuser vivement de.
apologize [ə'pɔlədʒaɪz] vi: **to ~ (for sth to sb)** s'excuser (de qch auprès de qn), présenter ses excuses (à qn pour qch).
apology [ə'pɔlədʒɪ] n excuses fpl; **to send one's apologies** envoyer une lettre or un mot d'excuse, s'excuser (de ne pas pouvoir venir).
apoplexy ['æpəplɛksɪ] n apoplexie f.
apostle [ə'pɔsl] n apôtre m.
apostrophe [ə'pɔstrəfɪ] n apostrophe f.
appal [ə'pɔ:l] vt consterner, atterrer; horrifier; **~ling** a épouvantable; (stupidity) consternant(e).
apparatus [æpə'reɪtəs] n appareil m, dispositif m.
apparent [ə'pærənt] a apparent(e); **~ly** ad apparemment.
apparition [æpə'rɪʃən] n apparition f.
appeal [ə'pi:l] vi (LAW) faire or interjeter appel // n (LAW) appel m; (request) prière f; appel m; (charm) attrait m, charme m; **to ~ for** demander (instamment); implorer; **to ~ to** (subj: person) faire appel à; (subj: thing) plaire à; **to ~ to sb for mercy** implorer la pitié de qn, prier or adjurer qn d'avoir pitié; **it doesn't ~ to me** cela ne m'attire pas; **~ing** a (nice) attrayant(e); (touching) attendrissant(e).
appear [ə'pɪə*] vi apparaître, se montrer; (LAW) comparaître; (publication) paraître, sortir, être publié(e); (seem) paraître, sembler; **it would ~ that** il semble que; **to ~ in Hamlet** jouer dans Hamlet; **to ~ on TV** passer à la télé; **~ance** n apparition f; parution f; (look, aspect) apparence f, aspect m; **to put in or make an ~ance** faire acte de présence; (THEATRE): **by order of ~ance** par ordre d'entrée en scène.
appease [ə'pi:z] vt apaiser, calmer.
appendage [ə'pɛndɪdʒ] n appendice m.
appendicitis [əpɛndɪ'saɪtɪs] n appendicite f.
appendix, pl **appendices** [ə'pɛndɪks, -si:z] n appendice m.
appetite ['æpɪtaɪt] n appétit m.
appetizing ['æpɪtaɪzɪŋ] a appétissant(e).
applaud [ə'plɔ:d] vt,vi applaudir.
applause [ə'plɔ:z] n applaudissements mpl.
apple ['æpl] n pomme f; **it's the ~ of my eye** j'y tiens comme à la prunelle de mes

yeux; **~ tree** n pommier m; **~ turnover** n chausson m aux pommes.
appliance [ə'plaɪəns] n appareil m.
applicable [ə'plɪkəbl] a applicable.
applicant ['æplɪkənt] n candidat/e (for a post à un poste).
application [æplɪ'keɪʃən] n application f; (for a job, a grant etc) demande f; candidature f; **on ~** sur demande.
applied [ə'plaɪd] a appliqué(e); **~ arts** npl arts décoratifs.
apply [ə'plaɪ] vt (paint, ointment): **to ~ (to)** appliquer (sur); (theory, technique): **to ~ (to)** appliquer (à) // vi: **to ~ to** (ask) s'adresser à; (be suitable for, relevant to) s'appliquer à; **to ~ (for)** (permit, grant) faire une demande (en vue d'obtenir); (job) poser sa candidature (pour), faire une demande d'emploi (concernant); **to ~ the brakes** actionner les freins, freiner; **to ~ o.s. to** s'appliquer à.
appoint [ə'pɔɪnt] vt nommer, engager; (date, place) fixer, désigner; **~ment** n nomination f; rendez-vous m; **to make an ~ment (with)** prendre rendez-vous (avec).
apportion [ə'pɔ:ʃən] vt (share out) répartir, distribuer; **to ~ sth to sb** attribuer or assigner or allouer qch à qn.
appraisal [ə'preɪzl] n évaluation f.
appreciable [ə'pri:ʃəbl] a appréciable.
appreciate [ə'pri:ʃieɪt] vt (like) apprécier, faire cas de; être reconnaissant(e) de; (assess) évaluer; (be aware of) comprendre; se rendre compte de // vi (FINANCE) prendre de la valeur.
appreciation [əpri:ʃɪ'eɪʃən] n appréciation f; reconnaissance f; (COMM) hausse f, valorisation f.
appreciative [ə'pri:ʃɪətɪv] a (person) sensible; (comment) élogieux(euse).
apprehend [æprɪ'hɛnd] vt appréhender, arrêter; (understand) comprendre.
apprehension [æprɪ'hɛnʃən] n appréhension f, inquiétude f.
apprehensive [æprɪ'hɛnsɪv] a inquiet(-ète), appréhensif(ive).
apprentice [ə'prɛntɪs] n apprenti m; **~ship** n apprentissage m.
approach [ə'prəʊtʃ] vi approcher // vt (come near) approcher de; (ask, apply to) s'adresser à; (subject, passer-by) aborder // n approche f; accès m, abord m; démarche f (auprès de qn); démarche (intellectuelle); **~able** a accessible.
approbation [æprə'beɪʃən] n approbation f.
appropriate a [ə'prəʊprɪət] (take) s'approprier; (allot): **to ~ sth for** affecter qch à // a [ə'prəʊprɪeɪt] opportun(e); qui convient, approprié(e); **~ly** ad pertinemment, avec à-propos.
approval [ə'pru:vəl] n approbation f; **on ~** (COMM) à l'examen.
approve [ə'pru:v] vt approuver; **to ~ of** vt fus approuver; **~d school** n centre m d'éducation surveillée; **approvingly** ad d'un air approbateur.
approximate a [ə'prɔksɪmɪt] approximatif(ive) // vt [ə'prɔksɪmeɪt] se rapprocher de; être proche de;

approximation [-'meɪʃən] n approximation f.

apricot ['eɪprɪkɔt] n abricot m.

April ['eɪprəl] n avril m ; ~ **fool!** poisson d'avril!

apron ['eɪprən] n tablier m.

apt [æpt] a (suitable) approprié(e) ; (able): ~ **(at)** doué(e) (pour) ; apte (à) ; (likely): ~ **to do** susceptible de faire ; ayant tendance à faire.

aptitude ['æptɪtjuːd] n aptitude f.

aqualung ['ækwəlʌŋ] n scaphandre m autonome.

aquarium [ə'kwɛərɪəm] n aquarium m.

Aquarius [ə'kwɛərɪəs] n le Verseau ; **to be** ~ être du Verseau.

aquatic [ə'kwætɪk] a aquatique ; (SPORT) nautique.

aqueduct ['ækwɪdʌkt] n aqueduc m.

Arab ['ærəb] n Arabe m/f.

Arabia [ə'reɪbɪə] n Arabie f ; ~**n** a arabe.

Arabic ['ærəbɪk] a,n arabe (m).

arable ['ærəbl] a arable.

arbiter ['ɑːbɪtə*] n arbitre m.

arbitrary ['ɑːbɪtrərɪ] a arbitraire.

arbitrate ['ɑːbɪtreɪt] vi arbitrer ; trancher ; **arbitration** [-'treɪʃən] n arbitrage m.

arbitrator ['ɑːbɪtreɪtə*] n arbitre m, médiateur/trice.

arc [ɑːk] n arc m.

arcade [ɑː'keɪd] n arcade f ; (passage with shops) passage m, galerie f.

arch [ɑːtʃ] n arche f ; (of foot) cambrure f, voûte f plantaire // vt arquer, cambrer // a malicieux(euse) // prefix: ~(-) achevé(e) ; par excellence ; **pointed** ~ n ogive f.

archaeologist [ɑːkɪ'ɔlədʒɪst] n archéologue m/f.

archaeology [ɑːkɪ'ɔlədʒɪ] n archéologie f.

archaic [ɑː'keɪɪk] a archaïque.

archbishop [ɑːtʃ'bɪʃəp] n archevêque m.

arch-enemy ['ɑːtʃ'ɛnɪmɪ] n ennemi m de toujours or par excellence.

archeologist [ɑːkɪ'ɔlədʒɪst] n (US) = **archaeologist**.

archeology [ɑːkɪ'ɔlədʒɪ] n (US) = **archaeology**.

archer ['ɑːtʃə*] n archer m ; ~**y** n tir m à l'arc.

archetype ['ɑːkɪtaɪp] n prototype m, archétype m.

archipelago [ɑːkɪ'pɛlɪgəu] n archipel m.

architect ['ɑːkɪtɛkt] n architecte m ; ~**ural** [ɑːkɪ'tɛktʃərəl] a architectural(e) ; ~**ure** ['ɑːkɪtɛktʃə*] n architecture f.

archives ['ɑːkaɪvz] npl archives fpl ; **archivist** ['ɑːkɪvɪst] n archiviste m/f.

archway ['ɑːtʃweɪ] n voûte f, porche voûté or cintré.

Arctic ['ɑːktɪk] a arctique // n: **the** ~ l'Arctique m.

ardent ['ɑːdənt] a fervent(e).

arduous ['ɑːdjuəs] a ardu(e).

are [ɑː*] vb see **be**.

area ['ɛərɪə] n (GEOM) superficie f ; (zone) région f ; (:smaller) secteur m ; **dining** ~ n coin m salle à manger.

arena [ə'riːnə] n arène f.

aren't [ɑːnt] = **are not**.

Argentina [ɑːdʒən'tiːnə] n Argentine f ; **Argentinian** [-'tɪnɪən] a argentin(e) // n Argentin/e.

arguable ['ɑːgjuəbl] a discutable.

argue ['ɑːgjuː] vi (quarrel) se disputer ; (reason) argumenter ; **to** ~ **that** objecter or alléguer que, donner comme argument que.

argument ['ɑːgjumənt] n (reasons) argument m ; (quarrel) dispute f, discussion f ; (debate) discussion f, controverse f ; ~**ative** [ɑːgju'mɛntətɪv] a ergoteur(euse), raisonneur(euse).

arid ['ærɪd] a aride ; ~**ity** [ə'rɪdɪtɪ] n aridité f.

Aries ['ɛərɪz] n le Bélier ; **to be** ~ être du Bélier.

arise, pt arose, pp arisen [ə'raɪz, -'rəuz, -'rɪzn] vi survenir, se présenter ; **to** ~ **from** résulter de.

aristocracy [ærɪs'tɔkrəsɪ] n aristocratie f.

aristocrat ['ærɪstəkræt] n aristocrate m/f ; ~**ic** [-'krætɪk] a aristocratique.

arithmetic [ə'rɪθmətɪk] n arithmétique f.

ark [ɑːk] n: **Noah's A**~ l'Arche f de Noé.

arm [ɑːm] n bras m ; (MIL: branch) arme f // vt armer ; ~**s** npl (weapons, HERALDRY) armes fpl ; ~ **in** ~ bras dessus bras dessous ; ~**band** n brassard m ; ~**chair** n fauteuil m ; ~**ed** a armé(e) ; ~**ed robbery** n vol m à main armée ; ~**ful** n brassée f.

armistice ['ɑːmɪstɪs] n armistice m.

armour ['ɑːmə*] n armure f ; (also: ~-**plating**) blindage m ; (MIL: tanks) blindés mpl ; ~**ed car** n véhicule blindé ; ~**y** n arsenal m.

armpit ['ɑːmpɪt] n aisselle f.

army ['ɑːmɪ] n armée f.

aroma [ə'rəumə] n arôme m ; ~**tic** [ærə'mætɪk] a aromatique.

arose [ə'rəuz] pt of **arise**.

around [ə'raund] ad (tout) autour ; dans les parages // prep autour de ; (fig: about) environ ; vers ; **is he** ~? est-il dans les parages or là?

arouse [ə'rauz] vt (sleeper) éveiller ; (curiosity, passions) éveiller, susciter, exciter.

arpeggio [ɑː'pɛdʒɪəu] n arpège m.

arrange [ə'reɪndʒ] vt arranger ; (programme) arrêter, convenir de ; ~**ment** n arrangement m ; (plans etc): ~**ments** dispositions fpl.

array [ə'reɪ] n: ~ **of** déploiement m or étalage m de.

arrears [ə'rɪəz] npl arriéré m ; **to be in** ~ **with one's rent** devoir un arriéré de loyer, être en retard pour le paiement de son loyer.

arrest [ə'rɛst] vt arrêter ; (sb's attention) retenir, attirer // n arrestation f ; **under** ~ en état d'arrestation.

arrival [ə'raɪvəl] n arrivée f ; (COMM) arrivage m ; (person) arrivant/e.

arrive [ə'raɪv] vi arriver ; **to** ~ **at** vt fus (fig) parvenir à.

arrogance ['ærəgəns] n arrogance f.

arrogant ['ærəgənt] a arrogant(e).

arrow ['ærəu] *n* flèche *f*.

arsenal ['ɑːsɪnl] *n* arsenal *m*.

arsenic ['ɑːsnɪk] *n* arsenic *m*.

arson ['ɑːsn] *n* incendie criminel.

art [ɑːt] *n* art *m*; (*craft*) métier *m*; **A~s** *npl* (*SCOL*) les lettres *fpl*; ~ **gallery** *n* musée *m* d'art; (*small and private*) galerie *f* de peinture.

artefact ['ɑːtɪfækt] *n* objet fabriqué.

artery ['ɑːtərɪ] *n* artère *f*.

artful ['ɑːtful] *a* rusé(e).

arthritis [ɑː'θraɪtɪs] *n* arthrite *f*.

artichoke ['ɑːtɪtʃəuk] *n* artichaut *m*.

article ['ɑːtɪkl] *n* article *m*; (*LAW: training*): ~**s** *npl* ≈ stage *m*.

articulate *a* [ɑː'tɪkjulɪt] (*person*) qui s'exprime clairement et aisément; (*speech*) bien articulé(e), prononcé(e) clairement // *vi* [ɑː'tɪkjuleɪt] articuler, parler distinctement; ~**d lorry** *n* (camion *m*) semi-remorque *m*.

artifice ['ɑːtɪfɪs] *n* ruse *f*.

artificial [ɑːtɪ'fɪʃəl] *a* artificiel(le); ~ **respiration** *n* respiration artificielle.

artillery [ɑː'tɪlərɪ] *n* artillerie *f*.

artisan ['ɑːtɪzæn] *n* artisan/e.

artist ['ɑːtɪst] *n* artiste *m/f*; ~**ic** [ɑː'tɪstɪk] *a* artistique; ~**ry** *n* art *m*, talent *m*.

artless ['ɑːtlɪs] *a* naïf(ïve), simple, ingénu(e).

as [æz, əz] *cj* (*cause*) comme, puisque; (*time: moment*) alors que, comme; (: *duration*) tandis que; (*manner*) comme; (*in the capacity of*) en tant que, en qualité de; ~ **big** ~ aussi grand que; **twice** ~ **big** ~ deux fois plus grand que; **big** ~ **it is** si grand que ce soit; ~ **she said** comme elle l'avait dit; ~ **if** *or* **though** comme si; ~ **for** *or* **to** en ce qui concerne, quant à; ~ *or* **so long** ~ *cj* à condition que; si; ~ **much/many** (~) autant (que); ~ **soon** ~ *cj* aussitôt que, dès que; ~ **such** *ad* en tant que tel(le); ~ **well** *ad* aussi; ~ **well** ~ *cj* en plus de, en même temps que; *see also* **so, such**.

asbestos [æz'bɛstəs] *n* asbeste *m*, amiante *m*.

ascend [ə'sɛnd] *vt* gravir; ~**ancy** *n* ascendant *m*.

ascent [ə'sɛnt] *n* ascension *f*.

ascertain [æsə'teɪn] *vt* s'assurer de, vérifier; établir.

ascetic [ə'sɛtɪk] *a* ascétique.

ascribe [ə'skraɪb] *vt*: **to** ~ **sth to** attribuer qch à; (*blame*) imputer qch à.

ash [æʃ] *n* (*dust*) cendre *f*; ~ (**tree**) frêne *m*.

ashamed [ə'ʃeɪmd] *a* honteux(euse), confus(e); **to be** ~ **of** avoir honte de; **to be** ~ (**of o.s.**) **for having done** avoir honte d'avoir fait.

ashen ['æʃn] *a* (*pale*) cendreux(euse), blême.

ashore [ə'ʃɔː*] *ad* à terre; **to go** ~ aller à terre, débarquer.

ashtray ['æʃtreɪ] *n* cendrier *m*.

Asia ['eɪʃə] *n* Asie *f*; ~ **Minor** *n* Asie Mineure; ~**n** *n* Asiatique *m/f* // *a* asiatique; ~**tic** [eɪsɪ'ætɪk] *a* asiatique.

aside [ə'saɪd] *ad* de côté; à l'écart // *n* aparté *m*.

ask [ɑːsk] *vt* demander; (*invite*) inviter; **to** ~ **sb sth/to do sth** demander à qn qch/de faire qch; **to** ~ **sb about sth** questionner qn au sujet de qch; **se renseigner auprès de qn au sujet de qch**; **to** ~ **about the price** s'informer du prix, se renseigner au sujet du prix; **to** ~ (**sb**) **a question** poser une question (à qn); **to** ~ **sb out to dinner** inviter qn au restaurant; **to** ~ **for** *vt fus* demander.

askance [ə'skɑːns] *ad*: **to look** ~ **at sb** regarder qn de travers *or* d'un œil désapprobateur.

askew [ə'skjuː] *ad* de travers, de guinguois.

asleep [ə'sliːp] *a* endormi(e); **to be** ~ dormir, être endormi; **to fall** ~ s'endormir.

asp [æsp] *n* aspic *m*.

asparagus [əs'pærəgəs] *n* asperges *fpl*; ~ **tips** *npl* pointes *fpl* d'asperges.

aspect ['æspɛkt] *n* aspect *m*; (*direction in which a building etc faces*) orientation *f*, exposition *f*.

aspersions [əs'pəːʃənz] *npl*: **to cast** ~ **on** dénigrer.

asphalt ['æsfælt] *n* asphalte *m*.

asphyxiate [æs'fɪksɪeɪt] *vt* asphyxier; **asphyxiation** [-'eɪʃən] *n* asphyxie *f*.

aspirate *vt* ['æspəreɪt] aspirer // *a* ['æspərɪt] aspiré(e).

aspiration [æspə'reɪʃən] *n* aspiration *f*.

aspire [əs'paɪə*] *vi*: **to** ~ **to** aspirer à.

aspirin ['æsprɪn] *n* aspirine *f*.

ass [æs] *n* âne *m*; (*col*) imbécile *m/f*.

assail [ə'seɪl] *vt* assaillir; ~**ant** *n* agresseur *m*; assaillant *m*.

assassin [ə'sæsɪn] *n* assassin *m*; ~**ate** *vt* assassiner; ~**ation** [əsæsɪ'neɪʃən] *n* assassinat *m*.

assault [ə'sɔːlt] *n* (*MIL*) assaut *m*; (*gen: attack*) agression *f*; (*LAW*): ~ (**and battery**) voies *fpl* de fait, coups *mpl* et blessures *fpl* // *vt* attaquer; (*sexually*) violenter.

assemble [ə'sɛmbl] *vt* assembler // *vi* s'assembler, se rassembler.

assembly [ə'sɛmblɪ] *n* (*meeting*) rassemblement *m*; (*construction*) assemblage *m*; ~ **line** *n* chaîne *f* de montage.

assent [ə'sɛnt] *n* assentiment *m*, consentement *m* // *vi* donner son assentiment, consentir.

assert [ə'səːt] *vt* affirmer, déclarer; établir; ~**ion** [ə'səːʃən] *n* assertion *f*, affirmation *f*; ~**ive** *a* assuré(e), péremptoire.

assess [ə'sɛs] *vt* évaluer, estimer; (*tax, damages*) établir *or* fixer le montant de; (*property etc: for tax*) calculer la valeur imposable de; ~**ment** *n* évaluation *f*, estimation *f*; ~**or** *n* expert *m* (*en matière d'impôt et d'assurance*).

asset ['æsɛt] *n* avantage *m*, atout *m*; ~**s** *npl* capital *m*; avoir(s) *m(pl)*; actif *m*.

assiduous [ə'sɪdjuəs] *a* assidu(e).

assign [ə'saɪn] *vt* (*date*) fixer, arrêter; (*task*): **to** ~ **sth to** assigner qch à; (*resources*): **to** ~ **sth to** affecter qch à; (*cause, meaning*): **to** ~ **sth to** attribuer qch à; ~**ment** *n* tâche *f*, mission *f*.

assimilate [ə'sımıleıt] vt assimiler;
assimilation [-'leıʃən] n assimilation f.
assist [ə'sıst] vt aider, assister; secourir;
~**ance** n aide f, assistance f; secours mpl;
~**ant** n assistant/e, adjoint/e; (also: **shop**
~**ant**) vendeur/euse.
assizes [ə'saızız] npl assises fpl.
associate a,n [ə'səuʃııt] associé(e) // vb
[ə'səuʃıeıt] vt associer // vi: **to ~ with**
sb fréquenter qn.
association [əsəusı'eıʃən] n association f;
~ **football** n football m.
assorted [ə'sɔ:tıd] a assorti(e).
assortment [ə'sɔ:tmənt] n assortiment m.
assume [ə'sju:m] vt supposer;
(responsibilities etc) assumer; (attitude,
name) prendre, adopter; ~**d name** n nom
m d'emprunt.
assumption [ə'sʌmpʃən] n supposition f,
hypothèse f.
assurance [ə'ʃuərəns] n assurance f.
assure [ə'ʃuə*] vt assurer.
asterisk ['æstərısk] n astérisque m.
astern [ə'stə:n] ad à l'arrière.
asthma ['æsmə] n asthme m; ~**tic**
[æs'mætık] a,n asthmatique (m/f).
astir [ə'stə:*] ad en émoi.
astonish [ə'stɔnıʃ] vt étonner, stupéfier;
~**ment** n étonnement m.
astound [ə'staund] vt stupéfier, sidérer.
astray [ə'streı] ad: **to go** ~ s'égarer; (fig)
quitter le droit chemin.
astride [ə'straıd] ad à cheval // prep à
cheval sur.
astringent [əs'trındʒənt] a astringent(e)
// n astringent m.
astrologer [əs'trɔlədʒə*] n astrologue m.
astrology [əs'trɔlədʒı] n astrologie f.
astronaut ['æstrənɔ:t] n astronaute m/f.
astronomer [əs'trɔnəmə*] n astronome m.
astronomical [æstrə'nɔmıkəl] a
astronomique.
astronomy [əs'trɔnəmı] n astronomie f.
astute [əs'tju:t] a astucieux(euse),
malin(igne).
asunder [ə'sʌndə*] ad: **to tear** ~ déchirer.
asylum [ə'saıləm] n asile m.
at [æt] prep à; (because of: following surprised, annoyed etc) de; par; ~ **Pierre's**
chez Pierre; ~ **the baker's** chez le
boulanger, à la boulangerie; ~ **times**
parfois.
ate [eıt] pt of **eat**.
atheism ['eıθıızəm] n athéisme m.
atheist ['eıθııst] n athée m/f.
Athens ['æθınz] n Athènes f.
athlete ['æθli:t] n athlète m/f.
athletic [æθ'letık] a athlétique; ~**s** n
athlétisme m.
Atlantic [ət'læntık] a atlantique // a: **the**
~ **(Ocean)** l'Atlantique m, l'océan m
Atlantique.
atlas ['ætləs] n atlas m.
atmosphere ['ætməsfıə*] n atmosphère f.
atmospheric [ætməs'ferık] a
atmosphérique; ~**s** n (RADIO) parasites
mpl.
atoll ['ætɔl] n atoll m.
atom ['ætəm] n atome m; ~**ic** [ə'tɔmık]
a atomique; ~**(ic) bomb** n bombe f

atomique; ~**izer** ['ætəmaızə*] n
atomiseur m.
atone [ə'təun] vi: **to** ~ **for** expier, racheter.
atrocious [ə'trəuʃəs] a (very bad) atroce,
exécrable.
atrocity [ə'trɔsıtı] n atrocité f.
atrophy ['ætrəfı] n atrophie f // vt
atrophier // vi s'atrophier.
attach [ə'tætʃ] vt (gen) attacher;
(document, letter) joindre; (MIL: troops)
affecter; **to be** ~**ed to sb/sth** (to like) être
attaché à qn/qch; ~**é** [ə'tæʃeı] n attaché
m; ~**é case** n mallette f, attaché-case m;
~**ment** n (tool) accessoire m; (love):
~**ment (to)** affection f (pour),
attachement m (à).
attack [ə'tæk] vt attaquer; (task etc)
s'attaquer à // n attaque f; (also: **heart**
~) crise f cardiaque; ~**er** n attaquant m;
agresseur m.
attain [ə'teın] vt (also: **to** ~ **to**) parvenir
à, atteindre; acquérir; ~**ments** npl
connaissances fpl, résultats mpl.
attempt [ə'tempt] n tentative f // vt
essayer, tenter; ~**ed theft** etc (LAW)
tentative de vol etc; **to make an** ~ **on**
sb's life attenter à la vie de qn.
attend [ə'tend] vt (course) suivre;
(meeting, talk) assister à; (school, church)
aller à, fréquenter; (patient) soigner,
s'occuper de; **to** ~ **(up)on** servir; être au
service de; **to** ~ **to** vt fus (needs, affairs
etc) s'occuper de; (customer) s'occuper de,
servir; ~**ance** n (being present) présence
f; (people present) assistance f; ~**ant** n
employé/e; gardien/ne // a
concomitant(e), qui accompagne ou
s'ensuit.
attention [ə'tenʃən] n attention f; ~**s**
attentions fpl, prévenances fpl; ~! (MIL)
garde-à-vous!; **at** ~ (MIL) au
garde-à-vous; **for the** ~ **of** (ADMIN) à
l'attention de.
attentive [ə'tentıv] a attentif(ive); (kind)
prévenant(e); ~**ly** ad attentivement, avec
attention.
attenuate [ə'tenjueıt] vt atténuer // vi
s'atténuer.
attest [ə'test] vi: **to** ~ **to** témoigner de,
attester (de).
attic ['ætık] n grenier m, combles mpl.
attire [ə'taıə*] n habit m, atours mpl.
attitude ['ætıtju:d] n attitude f, manière f;
pose f, maintien m.
attorney [ə'tə:nı] n (lawyer) avoué m;
(having proxy) mandataire m; **A~**
General n (Brit) ≈ procureur général;
(US) ≈ garde m des Sceaux, ministre m
de la Justice; **power of** ~ n procuration
f.
attract [ə'trækt] vt attirer; ~**ion**
[ə'trækʃən] n (gen pl: pleasant things)
attraction f, attrait m; (PHYSICS) attraction
f; (fig: towards sth) attirance f; ~**ive** a
séduisant(e), attrayant(e).
attribute n ['ætrıbju:t] attribut m // vt
[ə'trıbju:t]: **to** ~ **sth to** attribuer qch à.
attrition [ə'trıʃən] n: **war of** ~ guerre f
d'usure.
aubergine ['əubəʒi:n] n aubergine f.
auburn ['ɔ:bən] a auburn inv, châtain roux
inv.

auction [ˈɔːkʃən] n (also: **sale by ~**) vente f aux enchères // vt (also: **to sell by ~**) vendre aux enchères ; (also: **to put up for ~**) mettre aux enchères ; **~eer** [-ˈnɪə*] n commissaire-priseur m.

audacious [ɔːˈdeɪʃəs] a impudent(e) ; audacieux(euse), intrépide.

audacity [ɔːˈdæsɪtɪ] n impudence f ; audace f.

audible [ˈɔːdɪbl] a audible.

audience [ˈɔːdɪəns] n (people) assistance f, auditoire m ; auditeurs mpl ; spectateurs mpl ; (interview) audience f.

audio-visual [ˈɔːdɪəʊˈvɪzjuəl] a audio-visuel(le).

audit [ˈɔːdɪt] n vérification f des comptes, apurement m // vt vérifier, apurer.

audition [ɔːˈdɪʃən] n audition f.

auditor [ˈɔːdɪtə*] n vérificateur m des comptes.

auditorium [ɔːdɪˈtɔːrɪəm] n auditorium m, salle f de concert or de spectacle.

augment [ɔːgˈment] vt,vi augmenter.

augur [ˈɔːgə*] vt (be a sign of) présager, annoncer // vi: **it ~s well** c'est bon signe or de bon augure, cela s'annonce bien.

August [ˈɔːgəst] n août m.

august [ɔːˈgʌst] a majestueux(euse), imposant(e).

aunt [ɑːnt] n tante f ; **~ie**, **~y** n diminutive of **aunt**.

au pair [ˈəʊˈpɛə*] n (also: **~ girl**) jeune fille f au pair.

aura [ˈɔːrə] n atmosphère f.

auspices [ˈɔːspɪsɪz] npl: **under the ~ of** sous les auspices de.

auspicious [ɔːsˈpɪʃəs] a de bon augure, propice.

austere [ɔsˈtɪə*] a austère.

Australia [ɔsˈtreɪlɪə] n Australie f ; **~n** a australien(ne) // n Australien/ne.

Austria [ˈɔstrɪə] n Autriche f ; **~n** a autrichien(ne) // n Autrichien/ne.

authentic [ɔːˈθentɪk] a authentique ; **~ate** vt établir l'authenticité de.

author [ˈɔːθə*] n auteur m.

authoritarian [ɔːθɔrɪˈtɛərɪən] a autoritaire.

authoritative [ɔːˈθɔrɪtətɪv] a (account) digne de foi ; (study, treatise) qui fait autorité ; (manner) autoritaire.

authority [ɔːˈθɔrɪtɪ] n autorité f ; (permission) autorisation (formelle) ; **the authorities** npl les autorités fpl, l'administration f.

authorize [ˈɔːθəraɪz] vt autoriser.

authorship [ˈɔːθəʃɪp] n paternité f (littéraire etc).

autistic [ɔːˈtɪstɪk] a autistique.

auto [ˈɔːtəʊ] n (US) auto f, voiture f.

autobiography [ɔːtəbaɪˈɔgrəfɪ] n autobiographie f.

autocratic [ɔːtəˈkrætɪk] a autocratique.

autograph [ˈɔːtəgrɑːf] n autographe m // vt signer, dédicacer.

automatic [ɔːtəˈmætɪk] a automatique // n (gun) automatique m ; **~ally** ad automatiquement.

automation [ɔːtəˈmeɪʃən] n automatisation f.

automaton, pl automata [ɔːˈtɔmətən, -tə] n automate m.

automobile [ˈɔːtəməbiːl] n (US) automobile f.

autonomous [ɔːˈtɔnəməs] a autonome.

autonomy [ɔːˈtɔnəmɪ] n autonomie f.

autopsy [ˈɔːtɔpsɪ] n autopsie f.

autumn [ˈɔːtəm] n automne m.

auxiliary [ɔːgˈzɪlɪərɪ] a auxiliaire // n auxiliaire m/f.

Av. abbr of **avenue**.

avail [əˈveɪl] vt: **to ~ o.s. of** user de ; profiter de // n: **to no ~** sans résultat, en vain, en pure perte.

availability [əveɪləˈbɪlɪtɪ] n disponibilité f.

available [əˈveɪləbl] a disponible ; **every ~ means** tous les moyens possibles or à sa (or notre etc) disposition.

avalanche [ˈævəlɑːnʃ] n avalanche f.

avant-garde [ˈævɑŋˈgɑːd] a d'avant-garde.

avaricious [ævəˈrɪʃəs] a avare.

Ave. abbr of **avenue**.

avenge [əˈvendʒ] vt venger.

avenue [ˈævənjuː] n avenue f.

average [ˈævərɪdʒ] n moyenne f // a moyen(ne) // vt (a certain figure) atteindre or faire etc en moyenne ; **on ~** en moyenne ; **above/below (the) ~** au-dessus/en-dessous de la moyenne ; **to ~ out vi: to ~ out at** représenter une moyenne, donner une moyenne de.

averse [əˈvəːs] a: **to be ~ to sth/doing** éprouver une forte répugnance envers qch/à faire ; **I wouldn't be ~ to a drink** un petit verre ne serait pas de refus, je ne dirais pas non à un petit verre.

aversion [əˈvəːʃən] n aversion f, répugnance f.

avert [əˈvəːt] vt prévenir, écarter ; (one's eyes) détourner.

aviary [ˈeɪvɪərɪ] n volière f.

aviation [eɪvɪˈeɪʃən] n aviation f.

avid [ˈævɪd] a avide ; **~ly** ad avidement, avec avidité.

avocado [ævəˈkɑːdəʊ] n (also: **~ pear**) avocat m.

avoid [əˈvɔɪd] vt éviter ; **~able** a évitable ; **~ance** n le fait d'éviter.

await [əˈweɪt] vt attendre ; **~ing attention/delivery** (COMM) en souffrance.

awake [əˈweɪk] a éveillé(e) ; (fig) en éveil // vb (pt **awoke** [əˈwəʊk], pp **awoken** [əˈwəʊkən] or **awaked**) vt éveiller // vi s'éveiller ; **to ~ to** conscient de ; **he was still ~** il ne dormait pas encore ; **~ning** [əˈweɪknɪŋ] n réveil m.

award [əˈwɔːd] n récompense f, prix m // vt (prize) décerner ; (LAW: damages) accorder.

aware [əˈwɛə*] a: **~ of** (conscious) conscient(e) de ; (informed) au courant de ; **to become ~ of** avoir conscience de, prendre conscience de ; se rendre compte de ; **politically/socially ~** sensibilisé aux or ayant pris conscience des problèmes politiques/sociaux ; **~ness** n le fait d'être conscient, au courant etc.

awash [əˈwɔʃ] a recouvert(e) (d'eau) ; **~ with** inondé(e) de.

away [ə'weɪ] *a,ad* (au) loin ; absent(e) ;
two kilometres ~ à (une distance de)
deux kilomètres, à deux kilomètres de
distance ; **two hours** ~ **by car** à deux
heures de voiture *or* de route ; **the holiday
was two weeks** ~ il restait deux
semaines jusqu'aux vacances ; ~ **from**
loin de ; **he's** ~ **for a week** il est parti
(pour) une semaine ; **to take** ~ *vt*
emporter ; **to work/pedal/laugh** *etc* ~ la
particule indique la constance et l'énergie de
l'action : il pédalait *etc* tant qu'il pouvait ;
to fade/wither *etc* — la particule renforce
l'idée de la disparition, l'éloignement ; ~
match *n* (SPORT) match *m* à l'extérieur.

awe [ɔ:] *n* respect mêlé de crainte, effroi
mêlé d'admiration ; ~**inspiring,** ~**some**
a impressionnant(e) ; ~**struck** *a* frappé(e)
d'effroi.

awful ['ɔ:fəl] *a* affreux(euse) ; ~**ly** *ad*
(*very*) terriblement, vraiment.

awhile [ə'waɪl] *ad* un moment, quelque
temps.

awkward ['ɔ:kwəd] *a* (*clumsy*) gauche,
maladroit(e) ; (*inconvenient*) malaisé(e),
d'emploi malaisé, peu pratique ;
(*embarrassing*) gênant(e), délicat(e).

awl [ɔ:l] *n* alène *f.*

awning ['ɔ:nɪŋ] *n* (*of tent*) auvent *m* ; (*of
shop*) store *m* ;(*of hotel etc*) marquise *f* (de
toile).

awoke, awoken [ə'wəuk, -kən] *pt,pp of*
awake.

awry [ə'raɪ] *ad,a* de travers ; **to go** ~ mal
tourner.

axe, ax (*US*) [æks] *n* hache *f // vt*
(*employee*) renvoyer ; (*project etc*)
abandonner ; (*jobs*) supprimer.

axiom ['æksɪəm] *n* axiome *m.*

axis, pl axes ['æksɪs, -sɪːz] *n* axe *m.*

axle ['æksl] *n* (*also:* ~**-tree**) essieu *m.*

ay(e) [aɪ] *excl* (*yes*) oui ; **the ayes** *npl* les
oui.

azure ['eɪʒə*] *a* azuré(e).

B

B [bi:] *n* (MUS) si *m.*

B.A. *abbr see* **bachelor.**

babble ['bæbl] *vi* babiller // *n* babillage
m.

baboon [bə'bu:n] *n* babouin *m.*

baby ['beɪbɪ] *n* bébé *m* ; ~ **carriage** *n* (*US*)
voiture *f* d'enfant ; ~**hood** *n* petite
enfance ; ~**ish** *a* enfantin(e), de bébé ; ~-
sit *vi* garder les enfants ; ~**-sitter** *n* baby-
sitter *m/f.*

bachelor ['bætʃələ*] *n* célibataire *m* ; **B—
of Arts/Science (B.A./B.Sc.)** ≈
licencié/e ès or en lettres/sciences ; **B—
of Arts/Science degree (B.A./B.Sc.)** *n*
≈ licence *f* ès or en lettres/ sciences ;
~**hood** *n* célibat *m.*

back [bæk] *n* (*of person, horse*) dos *m* ; (*of
hand*) dos, revers *m* ; (*of house*) derrière *m* ;
(*of car, train*) arrière *m* ; (*of chair*) dossier
m ; (*of page*) verso *m* ; (FOOTBALL) arrière
m // vt (*candidate: also:* ~ **up**) soutenir,
appuyer ; (*horse: at races*) parier or miser
sur ; (*car*) (faire) reculer // *vi* reculer ; (*car
etc*) faire marche arrière // *a* (*in com-
pounds*) de derrière, à l'arrière ; ~

seats/wheels (AUT) sièges *mpl*/roues *fpl*
arrière ; ~ **payments/rent** arriéré *m* de
paiements/loyer // *ad* (*not forward*) en
arrière ; (*returned*): **he's** ~ il est rentré, il
est de retour ; **he ran** ~ il est revenu en
courant ; (*restitution*): **throw the ball** ~
renvoie la balle ; **can I have it** ~? puis-
je le ravoir?, peux-tu me le rendre? ;
(*again*): **he called** ~ il a rappelé ; **to** ~
down *vi* rabattre de ses prétentions ; **to**
~ **out** *vi* (*of promise*) se dédire ; ~**ache**
n maux *mpl* de reins ; ~**bencher** *n* membre
du parlement sans portefeuille ; ~**biting** *n*
médisance(s) *f(pl)* ; ~**bone** *n* colonne
vertébrale, épine dorsale ; ~**cloth** *n* toile
f de fond ; ~**date** *vt* (*letter*) antidater ;
~**dated pay rise** augmentation *f* avec
effet rétroactif ; ~**er** *n* partisan *m* ; (COMM)
commanditaire *m* ; ~**fire** *vi* (AUT)
pétarader ; (*plans*) mal tourner ;
~**gammon** *n* trictrac *m* ; ~**ground** *n*
arrière-plan *m* ; (*of events*) situation *f*, conjoncture *f* ; (*basic knowledge*) éléments *mpl*
de base ; (*experience*) formation *f* ; ~**family
~ground** milieu familial ; ~**ground noise**
n bruit *m* de fond ; ~**hand** *n* (TENNIS: *also:*
~**hand stroke**) revers *m* ; ~**handed** *a*
(*fig*) déloyal(e) ; équivoque ; ~**hander** *n*
(*bribe*) pot-de-vin *m* ; ~**ing** *n* (*fig*) soutien
m, appui *m* ; ~**lash** *n* contre-coup *m*,
répercussion *f* ; ~**log** *n*: ~**log of work**
travail *m* en retard ; ~**number** *n* (*of
magazine etc*) vieux numéro ; ~ **pay** *n*
rappel *m* de traitement ; ~**side** *n* (*col*)
derrière *m*, postérieur *m* ; ~**stroke** *n* nage
f sur le dos ; ~**ward** *a* (*movement*) en
arrière ; (*measure*) rétrograde ; (*person,
country*) arriéré(e) ; attardé(e) ; (*shy*)
hésitant(e) ; ~**ward and forward movement** mouvement de va-et-vient ;
~**wards** *ad* (*move, go*) en arrière ; (*read
a list*) à l'envers, à rebours ; (*fall*) à la
renverse ; (*walk*) à reculons ; (*in time*) en
arrière, vers le passé ; ~**water** *n* (*fig*) coin
reculé ; bled perdu ; ~**yard** *n* arrière-cour
f.

bacon ['beɪkən] *n* bacon *m*, lard *m.*

bacteria [bæk'tɪərɪə] *npl* bactéries *fpl.*

bad [bæd] *a* mauvais(e) ; (*child*) vilain(e) ;
(*meat, food*) gâté(e), avarié(e) ; **his** ~ **leg**
sa jambe malade.

bade [bæd] *pt of* **bid.**

badge [bædʒ] *n* insigne *m* ; (*of policemen*)
plaque *f.*

badger ['bædʒə*] *n* blaireau *m // vt*
harceler.

badly ['bædlɪ] *ad* (*work, dress etc*) mal ; ~
wounded grièvement blessé ; **he needs it**
~ il en a absolument besoin ; ~ **off** *a,ad*
dans la gêne.

badminton ['bædmɪntən] *n* badminton *m.*

bad-tempered ['bæd'tɛmpəd] *a* ayant
mauvais caractère ; de mauvaise humeur.

baffle ['bæfl] *vt* (*puzzle*) déconcerter.

bag [bæg] *n* sac *m* ; (*of hunter*) gibecière
f ; chasse *f // vt* (*col: take*) empocher ;
s'approprier ; (TECH) mettre en sacs ; ~**s
under the eyes** poches *fpl* sous les yeux ;
~**ful** *n* plein sac ; ~**gage** *n* bagages *mpl* ;
~**gy** *a* avachi(e), qui fait des poches ;
~**pipes** *npl* cornemuse *f.*

Bahamas [bə'hɑ:məz] *npl*: **the** ~ les
Bahamas *fpl.*

bail [beɪl] *n* caution *f* // *vt* (*prisoner: gen:* **to give ~ to**) mettre en liberté sous caution; (*boat: also:* **~ out**) écoper; *see* **bale**; **to ~ out** *vt* (*prisoner*) payer la caution de.

bailiff ['beɪlɪf] *n* huissier *m*.

bait [beɪt] *n* appât *m* // *vt* appâter; (*fig*) tourmenter.

bake [beɪk] *vt* (*faire*) cuire au four // *vi* cuire (au four); faire de la pâtisserie; **~d beans** *npl* haricots blancs à la sauce tomate; **~r** *n* boulanger *m*; **~ry** *n* boulangerie *f*; boulangerie industrielle; **baking** *n* cuisson *f*; **baking powder** *n* levure *f* (chimique).

balaclava [bælə'klɑːvə] *n* (*also:* **~ helmet**) passe-montagne *m*.

balance ['bæləns] *n* équilibre *m*; (*COMM: sum*) solde *m*; (*scales*) balance *f*; (*ECON: of trade etc*) balance // *vt* mettre or faire tenir en équilibre; (*pros and cons*) peser; (*budget*) équilibrer; (*account*) balancer; (*compensate*) compenser, contrebalancer; **~ of trade/payments** balance commerciale/des comptes or paiements; **~d** *a* (*personality, diet*) équilibré(e); **~ sheet** *n* bilan *m*; **~ wheel** *n* balancier *m*.

balcony ['bælkənɪ] *n* balcon *m*.

bald [bɔːld] *a* chauve; (*tree, hill*) dénudé(e); **~ness** *n* calvitie *f*.

bale [beɪl] *n* balle *f*, ballot *m*; **to ~ out** *vi* (*of a plane*) sauter en parachute.

baleful ['beɪful] *a* funeste, maléfique.

balk [bɔːk] *vi:* **to ~ (at)** regimber (contre); (*horse*) se dérober (devant).

ball [bɔːl] *n* boule *f*; (*football*) ballon *m*; (*for tennis, golf*) balle *f*; (*dance*) bal *m*.

ballad ['bæləd] *n* ballade *f*.

ballast ['bæləst] *n* lest *m*.

ballerina [bælə'riːnə] *n* ballerine *f*.

ballet ['bæleɪ] *n* ballet *m*; (*art*) danse *f* (classique).

ballistics [bə'lɪstɪks] *n* balistique *f*.

balloon [bə'luːn] *n* ballon *m*; (*in comic strip*) bulle *f*; **~ist** *n* aéronaute *m/f*.

ballot ['bælət] *n* scrutin *m*; **~ box** *n* urne (*électorale*); **~ paper** *n* bulletin *m* de vote.

ball-point pen ['bɔːlpɔɪnt'pɛn] *n* stylo *m* à bille.

ballroom ['bɔːlrum] *n* salle *f* de bal.

balmy ['bɑːmɪ] *a* (*breeze, air*) doux(douce); (*col*) = **barmy**.

balsam ['bɔːlsəm] *n* baume *m*.

Baltic ['bɔːltɪk] *a,n:* **the ~ (Sea)** la (mer) Baltique.

bamboo [bæm'buː] *n* bambou *m*.

bamboozle [bæm'buːzl] *vt* (*col*) embobiner.

ban [bæn] *n* interdiction *f* // *vt* interdire.

banal [bə'nɑːl] *a* banal(e).

banana [bə'nɑːnə] *n* banane *f*.

band [bænd] *n* bande *f*; (*at a dance*) orchestre *m*; (*MIL*) musique *f*, fanfare *f*; **to ~ together** *vi* se liguer.

bandage ['bændɪdʒ] *n* bandage *m*, pansement *m*.

bandit ['bændɪt] *n* bandit *m*.

bandwagon ['bændwægən] *n:* **to jump on the ~** (*fig*) monter dans or prendre le train en marche.

bandy ['bændɪ] *vt* (*jokes, insults*) échanger; **to ~ about** employer à tout bout de champ or à tort et à travers.

bandy-legged ['bændɪ'lɛgd] *a* aux jambes arquées.

bang [bæŋ] *n* détonation *f*; (*of door*) claquement *m*; (*blow*) coup (violent) // *vt* frapper (violemment); (*door*) claquer // *vi* détoner; claquer; **to ~ at the door** cogner à la porte.

banger ['bæŋə*] *n* (*car: gen: old ~*) (*vieux*) tacot.

bangle ['bæŋgl] *n* bracelet *m*.

banish ['bænɪʃ] *vt* bannir.

banister(s) ['bænɪstə(z)] *n(pl)* rampe *f* (*d'escalier*).

banjo, ~es *or* **~s** ['bændʒəu] *n* banjo *m*.

bank [bæŋk] *n* banque *f*; (*of river, lake*) bord *m*, rive *f*; (*of earth*) talus *m*, remblai *m* // *vi* (*AVIAT*) virer sur l'aile; (*COMM*): **they ~ with Pitt's** leur banque or banquier est Pitt's; **to ~ on** *vt fus* miser or tabler sur; **~ account** *n* compte *m* en banque; **~er** *n* banquier *m*; **B~ holiday** *n* jour férié (*où les banques sont fermées*); **~ing** *n* opérations *fpl* bancaires; profession *f* de banquier; **~ing hours** *npl* heures *fpl* d'ouverture des banques; **~note** *n* billet *m* de banque; **~ rate** *n* taux *m* de l'escompte.

bankrupt ['bæŋkrʌpt] *n* failli/e // *a* en faillite; **to go ~** faire faillite; **~cy** *n* faillite *f*.

banner ['bænə*] *n* bannière *f*.

bannister(s) ['bænɪstə(z)] *n(pl)* = **banister(s)**.

banns [bænz] *npl* bans *mpl* (de mariage).

banquet ['bæŋkwɪt] *n* banquet *m*, festin *m*.

bantam-weight ['bæntəmweɪt] *n* poids *m* coq inv.

banter ['bæntə*] *n* badinage *m*.

baptism ['bæptɪzəm] *n* baptême *m*.

Baptist ['bæptɪst] *n* baptiste *m/f*.

baptize [bæp'taɪz] *vt* baptiser.

bar [bɑː*] *n* barre *f*; (*of window etc*) barreau *m*; (*of chocolate*) tablette *f*, plaque *f*; (*fig*) obstacle *m*; mesure *f* d'exclusion; (*pub*) bar *m*; (*counter: in pub*) comptoir *m*, bar; (*MUS*) mesure *f* // *vt* (*road*) barrer; (*window*) munir de barreaux; (*person*) exclure; (*activity*) interdire; **~ of soap** savonnette *f*; **the B~** (*LAW*) le barreau; **~ none** sans exception.

Barbados [bɑː'beɪdɔs] *n* Barbade *f*.

barbaric [bɑː'bærɪk] *a* barbare.

barbarous ['bɑːbərəs] *a* barbare, cruel(le).

barbecue ['bɑːbɪkjuː] *n* barbecue *m*.

barbed wire ['bɑːbd'waɪə*] *n* fil *m* de fer barbelé.

barber ['bɑːbə*] *n* coiffeur *m* (pour hommes).

barbiturate [bɑː'bɪtjurɪt] *n* barbiturique *m*.

bare [bɛə*] *a* nu(e) // *vt* mettre à nu, dénuder; (*teeth*) montrer; **the ~ essentials** le strict nécessaire; **~back** *ad* à cru, sans selle; **~faced** *a* impudent(e), effronté(e); **~foot** *a,ad* nu-pieds, (les) pieds nus; **~headed** *a,ad* nu-tête, (la) tête nue; **~ly** *ad* à peine.

bargain ['bɑːgɪn] n (transaction) marché m; (good buy) affaire f, occasion f // vi (haggle) marchander; (trade) négocier, traiter; **into the ~** par-dessus le marché.

barge [bɑːdʒ] n péniche f; **to ~ in** vi (walk in) faire irruption; (interrupt talk) intervenir mal à propos; **to ~ into** vt fus rentrer dans.

baritone ['bærɪtəun] n baryton m.

bark [bɑːk] n (of tree) écorce f; (of dog) aboiement m // vi aboyer.

barley ['bɑːlɪ] n orge f.

barmaid ['bɑːmeɪd] n serveuse f (de bar), barmaid f.

barman ['bɑːmən] n serveur m (de bar), barman m.

barmy ['bɑːmɪ] a (col) timbré(e), cinglé(e).

barn [bɑːn] n grange f.

barnacle ['bɑːnəkl] n anatife m, bernache f.

barometer [bə'rɔmɪtə*] n baromètre m.

baron ['bærən] n baron m; **~ess** baronne f.

barracks ['bærəks] npl caserne f.

barrage [bɑːrɑːʒ] n (MIL) tir m de barrage; (dam) barrage m.

barrel ['bærəl] n tonneau m; (of gun) canon m; **~ organ** n orgue m de Barbarie.

barren ['bærən] a stérile; (hills) aride.

barricade [bærɪ'keɪd] n barricade f // vt barricader.

barrier ['bærɪə*] n barrière f.

barring ['bɑːrɪŋ] prep sauf.

barrister ['bærɪstə*] n avocat (plaidant).

barrow ['bærəu] n (cart) charrette f à bras.

bartender ['bɑːtɛndə*] n (US) barman m.

barter ['bɑːtə*] n échange m, troc m // vt: **to ~ sth for** échanger qch contre.

base [beɪs] n base f // vt: **to ~ sth on** baser or fonder qch sur // a vil(e), bas(se); **coffee-~d** base de café; **a Paris-~d firm** une maison opérant de Paris or dont le siège est à Paris; **~ball** n base-ball m; **~ment** n sous-sol m.

bases ['beɪsiːz] npl of **basis**; ['beɪsɪz] npl of **base**.

bash [bæʃ] vt (col) frapper, cogner; **~ed in** a enfoncé(e), défoncé(e).

bashful ['bæʃful] a timide; modeste.

bashing ['bæʃɪŋ] n (col) raclée f.

basic ['beɪsɪk] a fondamental(e), de base; réduit(e) au minimum, rudimentaire; **~ally** [-lɪ] ad fondamentalement, à la base; en fait, au fond.

basil ['bæzl] n basilic m.

basin ['beɪsn] n (vessel, also GEO) cuvette f, bassin m; (for food) bol m; (also: **wash~**) lavabo m.

basis, pl **bases** ['beɪsɪs, -siːz] n base f.

bask [bɑːsk] vi: **to ~ in the sun** se chauffer au soleil.

basket ['bɑːskɪt] n corbeille f; (with handle) panier m; **~ball** n basket-ball m.

bass [beɪs] n (MUS) basse f; **~ clef** n clé f de fa.

bassoon [bə'suːn] n basson m.

bastard ['bɑːstəd] n enfant naturel(le), bâtard/e; (col!) salaud m(!).

baste [beɪst] vt (CULIN) arroser; (SEWING) bâtir, faufiler.

bastion ['bæstɪən] n bastion m.

bat [bæt] n chauve-souris f; (for baseball etc) batte f; (for table tennis) raquette f; **off one's own ~** de sa propre initiative; **he didn't ~ an eyelid** il n'a pas sourcillé or bronché.

batch [bætʃ] n (of bread) fournée f; (of papers) liasse f.

bated ['beɪtɪd] a: **with ~ breath** en retenant son souffle.

bath [bɑːθ, pl bɑːðz] n see also **baths**; bain m; (bathtub) baignoire f // vt baigner, donner un bain à; **to have a ~** prendre un bain; **~chair** n fauteuil roulant.

bathe [beɪð] vi se baigner // vt baigner; **~r** n baigneur/euse.

bathing ['beɪðɪŋ] n baignade f; **~ cap** n bonnet m de bain; **~ costume** n maillot m (de bain).

bath: **~mat** n tapis m de bain; **~room** n salle f de bains; **~s** n pl établissement m de bains(-douches); **~ towel** n serviette f de bain.

batman ['bætmən] n (MIL) ordonnance f.

baton ['bætən] n bâton m; (MUS) baguette f; (club) matraque f.

battalion [bə'tælɪən] n bataillon m.

batter ['bætə*] vt battre // n pâte f à frire; **~ed** a (hat, pan) cabossé(e); **~ wife/child** épouse/enfant maltraité(e) or martyr(e); **~ing ram** n bélier m (fig).

battery ['bætərɪ] n batterie f; (of torch) pile f.

battle ['bætl] n bataille f, combat m // vi se battre, lutter; **~ dress** n tenue f de campagne or d'assaut; **~field** n champ m de bataille; **~ments** npl remparts mpl; **~ship** n cuirassé m.

baulk [bɔːlk] vi = **balk**.

bawdy ['bɔːdɪ] a paillard(e).

bawl [bɔːl] vi hurler, brailler.

bay [beɪ] n (of sea) baie f; **to hold sb at ~** tenir qn à distance or en échec.

bayonet ['beɪənɪt] n baïonnette f.

bay window ['beɪ'wɪndəu] n baie vitrée.

bazaar [bə'zɑː*] n bazar m; vente f de charité.

bazooka [bə'zuːkə] n bazooka m.

b. & b., B. & B. abbr see **bed**.

BBC n abbr of British Broadcasting Corporation (office de la radiodiffusion et télévision britannique).

B.C. ad (abbr of before Christ) av. J.-C.

BCG n (abbr of Bacillus Calmette-Guérin) BCG.

be, pt **was, were**, pp **been** [biː, wɔz, wə:*, biːn] vi être; **how are you?** comment allez-vous?; **I am warm** j'ai chaud; **it is cold** il fait froid; **how much is it?** combien ça coûte?; **he is four (years old)** il a quatre ans; **2 and 2 are 4** 2 et 2 font 4; **where have you been?** où êtes-vous allé(s)?; où étiez-vous?

beach [biːtʃ] n plage f // vt échouer; **~wear** n tenues fpl de plage.

beacon ['biːkən] n (lighthouse) fanal m; (marker) balise f.

bead [biːd] n perle f.

beak [biːk] n bec m.

beaker ['biːkə*] n gobelet m.

beam [bi:m] *n* poutre *f*; (*of light*) rayon *m* // *vi* rayonner; ~**ing** *a* (*sun, smile*) radieux(euse).

bean [bi:n] *n* haricot *m*; (*of coffee*) grain *m*.

bear [bɛə*] *n* ours *m* // *vb* (*pt* **bore**, *pp* **borne** [bɔ:*, bɔ:n]) *vt* porter; (*endure*) supporter // *vi*: **to ~ right/left** obliquer à droite/gauche, se diriger vers la droite/gauche; **to ~ the responsibility of** assumer la responsabilité de; **to ~ comparison with** soutenir la comparaison avec; ~**able** *a* supportable.

beard [biəd] *n* barbe *f*; ~**ed** *a* barbu(e).

bearer ['bɛərə*] *n* porteur *m*.

bearing ['bɛəriŋ] *n* maintien *m*, allure *f*; (*connection*) rapport *m*; (**ball**) ~**s** *npl* roulements *mpl* (à billes); **to take a ~** faire le point; **to find one's ~s** s'orienter.

beast [bi:st] *n* bête *f*; (*col*): **he's a ~** c'est une brute; ~**ly** *a* infect(e).

beat [bi:t] *n* battement *m*; (*MUS*) temps *m*, mesure *f*; (*of policeman*) ronde *f* // *vt* (*pt* **beat**, *pp* **beaten**) battre; **off the ~en track** hors des chemins *or* sentiers battus; **to ~ about the bush** tourner autour du pot; **to ~ time** battre la mesure; **to ~ off** *vt* repousser; **to ~ up** *vt* (*col: person*) tabasser; (*eggs*) battre; ~**er** *n* (*for eggs, cream*) fouet *m*, batteur *m*; ~**ing** *n* raclée *f*.

beautician [bju:'tiʃən] *n* esthéticien/ne.

beautiful ['bju:tiful] *a* beau(belle); ~**ly** *ad* admirablement.

beautify ['bju:tifai] *vt* embellir.

beauty ['bju:ti] *n* beauté *f*; ~ **salon** *n* institut *m* de beauté; ~ **spot** *n* grain *m* de beauté; (*TOURISM*) site naturel (d'une grande beauté).

beaver ['bi:və*] *n* castor *m*.

becalmed [bi'kɑ:md] *a* immobilisé(e) par le calme plat.

became [bi'keim] *pt of* **become**.

because [bi'kɔz] *cj* parce que; ~ **of** *prep* à cause de.

beckon ['bɛkən] *vt* (*also:* ~ **to**) faire signe (de venir) à.

become [bi'kʌm] *vt* (*irg: like* **come**) devenir; **to ~ fat/thin** grossir/maigrir; **what has ~ of him?** qu'est-il devenu?

becoming [bi'kʌmiŋ] *a* (*behaviour*) convenable, bienséant(e); (*clothes*) seyant(e).

bed [bɛd] *n* lit *m*; (*of flowers*) parterre *m*; (*of coal, clay*) couche *f*; **to go to ~** aller se coucher; ~ **and breakfast (b. & b.)** *n* (*terms*) chambre et petit déjeuner; ~**clothes** *npl* couvertures *fpl* et draps *mpl*; ~**cover** *n* couvre-lit *m*, dessus-de-lit *m*; ~**ding** *n* literie *f*.

bedlam ['bɛdləm] *n* chahut *m*, cirque *m*.

bedpost ['bɛdpəust] *n* colonne *f* de lit.

bedraggled [bi'drægld] *a* dépenaillé(e), les vêtements en désordre.

bed: ~**ridden** *a* cloué(e) au lit; ~**room** *n* chambre *f* (à coucher); ~**side** *n*: **at sb's ~side** au chevet de qn; ~**side book** *n* livre *m* de chevet; ~**sit(ter)** *n* chambre meublée, studio *m*; ~**spread** *n* couvre-lit *m*, dessus-de-lit *m*.

bee [bi:] *n* abeille *f*.

beech [bi:tʃ] *n* hêtre *m*.

beef [bi:f] *n* bœuf *m*.

beehive ['bi:haiv] *n* ruche *f*.

beeline ['bi:lain] *n*: **to make a ~ for** se diriger tout droit vers.

been [bi:n] *pp of* **be**.

beer [biə*] *n* bière *f*.

beetle ['bi:tl] *n* scarabée *m*; coléoptère *m*.

beetroot ['bi:tru:t] *n* betterave *f*.

befall [bi'fɔ:l] *vi(vt)* (*irg: like* **fall**) advenir (à).

befit [bi'fit] *vt* seoir à.

before [bi'fɔ:*] *prep* (*of time*) avant; (*of space*) devant // *cj* avant que + *sub*; avant de // *ad* avant; **the week ~** la semaine précédente *or* d'avant; **I've seen it ~** je l'ai déjà vu; **I've never seen it ~** c'est la première fois que je le vois; ~**hand** *ad* au préalable, à l'avance.

befriend [bi'frɛnd] *vt* venir en aide à; traiter en ami.

beg [bɛg] *vi* mendier // *vt* mendier; (*favour*) quémander, solliciter; (*entreat*) supplier.

began [bi'gæn] *pt of* **begin**.

beggar ['bɛgə*] *n* (*also:* ~**man**, ~**woman**) mendiant/e.

begin [bi'gin] *vt*, *vi* commencer; ~**ner** *n* débutant/e; ~**ning** *n* commencement *m*, début *m*.

begrudge [bi'grʌdʒ] *vt*: **to ~ sb sth** envier qch à qn; donner qch à contrecœur *or* à regret à qn; **I don't ~ doing it** je le fais volontiers.

begun [bi'gʌn] *pp of* **begin**.

behalf [bi'hɑ:f] *n*: **on ~ of** de la part de; au nom de; pour le compte de.

behave [bi'heiv] *vi* se conduire, se comporter; (*well: also:* ~ **o.s.**) se conduire bien *or* comme il faut.

behaviour, behavior (*US*) [bi'heivjə*] *n* comportement *m*, conduite *f* (*the latter often from a moral point of view, the former being more objective*).

beheld [bi'hɛld] *pt,pp of* **behold**.

behind [bi'haind] *prep* derrière; (*time*) en retard sur // *ad* derrière; en retard // *n* derrière *m*; ~ **the scenes** dans les coulisses.

behold [bi'həuld] *vt* (*irg: like* **hold**) apercevoir, voir.

beige [beiʒ] *a* beige.

being ['bi:iŋ] *n* être *m*; **to come into ~** prendre naissance.

belated [bi'leitid] *a* tardif(ive).

belch [bɛltʃ] *vi* avoir un renvoi, roter // *vt* (*gen:* ~ **out:** *smoke etc*) vomir, cracher.

belfry ['bɛlfri] *n* beffroi *m*.

Belgian ['bɛldʒən] *a* belge, de Belgique // *n* Belge *m/f*.

Belgium ['bɛldʒəm] *n* Belgique *f*.

belie [bi'lai] *vt* démentir.

belief [bi'li:f] *n* (*opinion*) conviction *f*; (*trust, faith*) foi *f*; (*acceptance as true*) croyance *f*.

believable [bi'li:vəbl] *a* croyable.

believe [bi'li:v] *vt*, *vi* croire; ~**r** *n* croyant/e.

belittle [bi'litl] *vt* déprécier, rabaisser.

bell [bɛl] n cloche f; (small) clochette f, grelot m; (on door) sonnette f; (electric) sonnerie f; **~-bottomed trousers** npl pantalon m à pattes d'éléphant.

belligerent [bɪ'lɪdʒərənt] a (at war) belligérant(e); (fig) agressif(ive).

bellow ['bɛləu] vi mugir // vt (orders) hurler.

bellows ['bɛləuz] npl soufflet m.

belly ['bɛlɪ] n ventre m; **to ~ache** vi (col) ronchonner; **~button** n nombril m.

belong [bɪ'lɔŋ] vi: **to ~ to** appartenir à; (club etc) faire partie de; **this book ~s here** ce livre va ici, la place de ce livre est ici; **~ings** npl affaires fpl, possessions fpl.

beloved [bɪ'lʌvɪd] a (bien-)aimé(e), chéri(e) // n bien-aimé/e.

below [bɪ'ləu] prep sous, au-dessous de // ad en dessous; en contre-bas; **see ~** voir plus bas or plus loin or ci-dessous.

belt [bɛlt] n ceinture f; (TECH) courroie f // vt (thrash) donner une raclée à // vi (col) filer (à toutes jambes).

bench [bɛntʃ] n banc m; (in workshop) établi m; **the B~** (LAW) la magistrature, la Cour.

bend [bɛnd] vb (pt,pp bent [bɛnt]) vt courber; (leg, arm) plier // vi se courber // n (in road) virage m, tournant m; (in pipe, river) coude m; **to ~ down** vi se baisser; **to ~ over** vi se pencher.

beneath [bɪ'ni:θ] prep sous, au-dessous de; (unworthy of) indigne de // ad dessous, au-dessous, en bas.

benefactor ['bɛnɪfæktə*] n bienfaiteur m.

benefactress ['bɛnɪfæktrɪs] n bienfaitrice f.

beneficial [bɛnɪ'fɪʃəl] a salutaire; avantageux(euse).

benefit ['bɛnɪfɪt] n avantage m, profit m; (allowance of money) allocation f // vt faire du bien à, profiter à // vi: **he'll ~ from it** cela lui fera du bien, il y gagnera or s'en trouvera bien; **~ performance** n représentation f or gala m de bienfaisance.

Benelux ['bɛnɪlʌks] n Bénélux m.

benevolent [bɪ'nɛvələnt] a bienveillant(e).

bent [bɛnt] pt,pp of bend // n inclination f, penchant m // a (dishonest) véreux(euse); **to be ~ on** être résolu(e) à.

bequeath [bɪ'kwi:ð] vt léguer.

bequest [bɪ'kwɛst] n legs m.

bereaved [bɪ'ri:vd] n: **the ~** la famille du disparu.

bereavement [bɪ'ri:vmənt] n deuil m.

beret ['bɛreɪ] n béret m.

Bermuda [bə:'mju:də] n Bermudes fpl.

berry ['bɛrɪ] n baie f.

berserk [bə'sə:k] a: **to go ~** être pris(e) d'une rage incontrôlable; se déchaîner.

berth [bə:θ] n (bed) couchette f; (for ship) poste m d'amarrage; mouillage m // vi (in harbour) venir à quai; (at anchor) mouiller.

beseech, pt,pp **besought** [bɪ'si:tʃ, -'sɔ:t] vt implorer, supplier.

beset, pt,pp **beset** [bɪ'sɛt] vt assaillir.

beside [bɪ'saɪd] prep à côté de; **to be ~ o.s. (with anger)** être hors de soi.

besides [bɪ'saɪdz] ad en outre, de plus // prep en plus de; excepté.

besiege [bɪ'si:dʒ] vt (town) assiéger; (fig) assaillir.

besought [bɪ'sɔ:t] pt,pp of **beseech**.

bespectacled [bɪ'spɛktɪkld] a à lunettes.

best [bɛst] a meilleur(e) // ad le mieux; **the ~ part of** (quantity) le plus clair de, la plus grande partie de; **at ~** au mieux; **to make the ~ of sth** s'accommoder de qch (du mieux que l'on peut); **to the ~ of my knowledge** pour autant que je sache; **to the ~ of my ability** du mieux que je pourrai; **~ man** n garçon m d'honneur.

bestow [bɪ'stəu] vt accorder; (title) conférer.

bestseller ['bɛst'sɛlə*] n bestseller m, succès m de librairie.

bet [bɛt] n pari m // vt,vi (pt,pp bet or betted) parier.

betray [bɪ'treɪ] vt trahir; **~al** n trahison f.

better ['bɛtə*] a meilleur(e) // ad mieux // vt améliorer // n: **to get the ~ of** triompher de, l'emporter sur; **you had ~ do it** vous feriez mieux de le faire; **he thought ~ of it** il s'est ravisé; **to get ~** aller mieux; s'améliorer; **~ off** a plus à l'aise financièrement; (fig): **you'd be ~ off this way** vous vous en trouveriez mieux ainsi, ce serait mieux or plus pratique ainsi.

betting ['bɛtɪŋ] n paris mpl; **~ shop** n bureau m de paris.

between [bɪ'twi:n] prep entre // ad au milieu; dans l'intervalle.

bevel ['bɛvəl] n (also: **~ edge**) biseau m.

beverage ['bɛvərɪdʒ] n boisson f (gén sans alcool).

bevy ['bɛvɪ] n: **a ~ of** un essaim or une volée de.

beware [bɪ'wɛə*] vt,vi: **to ~ (of)** prendre garde (à).

bewildered [bɪ'wɪldəd] a dérouté(e), ahuri(e).

bewitching [bɪ'wɪtʃɪŋ] a enchanteur-(teresse).

beyond [bɪ'jɔnd] prep (in space) au-delà de; (exceeding) au-dessus de // ad au-delà; **~ doubt** hors de doute; **~ repair** irréparable.

bias ['baɪəs] n (prejudice) préjugé m, parti pris; (preference) prévention f; **~(s)ed** a partial(e), montrant un parti pris.

bib [bɪb] n bavoir m, bavette f.

Bible ['baɪbl] n Bible f.

bibliography [bɪblɪ'ɔɡrəfɪ] n bibliographie f.

bicker ['bɪkə*] vi se chamailler.

bicycle ['baɪsɪkl] n bicyclette f.

bid [bɪd] n offre f; (at auction) enchère f; (attempt) tentative f // vb (pt bade [bæd] or bid, pp bidden ['bɪdn] or bid) vi faire une enchère or offre // vt faire une enchère or offre de; **to ~ sb good day** souhaiter le bonjour à qn; **~der** n: **the highest ~der** le plus offrant; **~ding** n enchères fpl.

bide [baɪd] vt: **to ~ one's time** attendre son heure.

bier [bɪə*] n bière f.
big [bɪg] a grand(e); gros(se).
bigamy ['bɪgəmɪ] n bigamie f.
bigheaded ['bɪg'hɛdɪd] a prétentieux(euse).
big-hearted ['bɪg'hɑːtɪd] a au grand cœur.
bigot ['bɪgət] n fanatique m/f, sectaire m/f; ~**ed** a fanatique, sectaire; ~**ry** n fanatisme m, sectarisme m.
bigwig ['bɪgwɪg] n (col) grosse légume, huile f.
bike [baɪk] n vélo m, bécane f.
bikini [bɪ'kiːnɪ] n bikini m.
bile [baɪl] n bile f.
bilingual [baɪ'lɪŋgwəl] a bilingue.
bilious ['bɪlɪəs] a bilieux(euse); (fig) maussade, irritable.
bill [bɪl] n note f, facture f; (POL) projet m de loi; (US: banknote) billet m (de banque); (of bird) bec m; **to fit** or **fill the ~** (fig) faire l'affaire.
billet ['bɪlɪt] n cantonnement m (chez l'habitant).
billfold ['bɪlfəʊld] n (US) portefeuille m.
billiards ['bɪlɪədz] n (jeu m de) billard m.
billion ['bɪlɪən] n (Brit) billion m (million de millions), (US) milliard m.
billy goat ['bɪlɪgəʊt] n bouc m.
bin [bɪn] n boîte f; (also: dust~) poubelle f; (for coal) coffre m; **bread~** n boîte f or huche f à pain.
bind, pt,pp **bound** [baɪnd, baʊnd] vt attacher; (book) relier; (oblige) obliger, contraindre; ~**ing** n (of book) reliure f // a (contract) constituant une obligation.
bingo ['bɪŋgəʊ] n sorte de jeu de loto pratiqué dans des établissements publics et connaissant une grande vogue en Grande-Bretagne.
binoculars [bɪ'nɔkjʊləz] npl jumelles fpl.
bio... [baɪə'...] prefix: ~**chemistry** n biochimie f; ~**graphic(al)** a biographique; ~**graphy** [baɪ'ɔgrəfɪ] n biographie f; ~**logical** a biologique; ~**logist** [baɪ'ɔlədʒɪst] n biologiste m/f; ~**logy** [baɪ'ɔlədʒɪ] n biologie f.
birch [bəːtʃ] n bouleau m.
bird [bəːd] n oiseau m; (col: girl) nana f; ~'**s-eye view** n vue f à vol d'oiseau; (fig) vue d'ensemble or générale; ~ **watcher** n ornithologue m/f amateur.
birth [bəːθ] n naissance f; ~ **certificate** n acte m de naissance; ~ **control** n limitation f des naissances; méthode(s) contraceptive(s); ~**day** n anniversaire m; ~**place** n lieu m de naissance; ~ **rate** n (taux m de) natalité f.
biscuit ['bɪskɪt] n biscuit m.
bisect [baɪ'sɛkt] vt couper or diviser en deux.
bishop ['bɪʃəp] n évêque m.
bit [bɪt] pt of **bite** // n morceau m; (of tool) mèche f; (of horse) mors m; **a** ~ **of** un peu de; **a** ~ **mad/dangerous** un peu fou/risqué.
bitch [bɪtʃ] n (dog) chienne f; (col!) salope f (!), garce f.
bite [baɪt] vt,vi (pt **bit** [bɪt], pp **bitten** ['bɪtn]) mordre // n morsure f; (insect ~) piqûre f; (mouthful) bouchée f; **let's have**

a ~ (**to eat**) mangeons un morceau; **to** ~ **one's nails** se ronger les ongles.
biting ['baɪtɪŋ] a mordant(e).
bitten ['bɪtn] pp of **bite**.
bitter ['bɪtə*] a amer(ère); (wind, criticism) cinglant(e) // n (beer) bière f (à forte teneur en houblon); **to the** ~ **end** jusqu'au bout; ~**ness** n amertume f; goût amer; ~**sweet** a aigre-doux(douce).
bivouac ['bɪvuæk] n bivouac m.
bizarre [bɪ'zɑː*] a bizarre.
blab [blæb] vi jaser, trop parler // vt (also: ~ **out**) laisser échapper, aller raconter.
black [blæk] a noir(e) // n noir m // vt (shoes) cirer; (INDUSTRY) boycotter; **to give sb a** ~ **eye** pocher l'œil à qn, faire un œil au beurre noir à qn; ~ **and blue** a couvert(e) de bleus; ~**berry** n mûre f; ~**bird** n merle m; ~**board** n tableau noir; ~**currant** n cassis m; ~**en** vt noircir; ~**leg** n briseur m de grève, jaune m; ~**list** n liste noire; ~**mail** n chantage m // vt faire chanter, soumettre au chantage; ~**mailer** n maître-chanteur m; ~ **market** n marché noir; ~**out** n panne f d'électricité; (fainting) syncope f; (in wartime) black-out m; **the B~ Sea** n la mer Noire; ~**sheep** n brebis galeuse; ~**smith** n forgeron m.
bladder ['blædə*] n vessie f.
blade [bleɪd] n lame f; (of oar) plat m; ~ **of grass** brin m d'herbe.
blame [bleɪm] n faute f, blâme m // vt: **to** ~ **sb/sth for sth** attribuer à qn/qch la responsabilité de qch; reprocher qch à qn/qch; **who's to** ~? qui est le fautif or coupable or responsable? ~**less** a irréprochable.
bland [blænd] a affable; (taste) doux(douce), fade.
blank [blæŋk] a blanc(blanche); (look) sans expression, dénué(e) d'expression // n espace m vide, blanc m; (cartridge) cartouche f à blanc.
blanket ['blæŋkɪt] n couverture f.
blare [blɛə*] vi (brass band, horns, radio) beugler.
blarney ['blɑːnɪ] n boniment m.
blasé ['blɑːzeɪ] a blasé(e).
blasphemous ['blæsfɪməs] a (words) blasphématoire; (person) blasphémateur(trice).
blasphemy ['blæsfɪmɪ] n blasphème m.
blast [blɑːst] n souffle m; explosion f // vt faire sauter or exploser; ~**-off** n (SPACE) lancement m.
blatant ['bleɪtənt] a flagrant(e), criant(e).
blaze [bleɪz] n (fire) incendie m; (fig) flamboiement m // vi (fire) flamber; (fig) flamboyer, resplendir // vt: **to** ~ **a trail** (fig) montrer la voie.
blazer ['bleɪzə*] n blazer m.
bleach [bliːtʃ] n (also: household ~) eau f de Javel // vt (linen) blanchir; ~**ed** a (hair) oxygéné(e), décoloré(e).
bleak [bliːk] a morne, désolé(e).
bleary-eyed ['blɪərɪ'aɪd] a aux yeux pleins de sommeil.
bleat [bliːt] n bêlement m // vi bêler.
bleed, pt,pp **bled** [bliːd, blɛd] vt, vi

saigner ; **my nose is** ~**ing** je saigne du nez.

blemish ['blɛmɪʃ] *n* défaut *m* ; (*on reputation*) tache *f*.

blend [blɛnd] *n* mélange *m* // *vt* mélanger // *vi* (*colours etc*) se mélanger, se fondre, s'allier.

bless, *pt*,*pp* **blessed** *or* **blest** [blɛs, blɛst] *vt* bénir ; **to be** ~**ed with** avoir le bonheur de jouir de *or* d'avoir ; ~**ing** *n* bénédiction *f* ; bienfait *m*.

blew [blu:] *pt of* **blow**.

blight [blaɪt] *n* (*of plants*) rouille *f* // *vt* (*hopes etc*) anéantir, briser.

blimey ['blaɪmɪ] *excl* (*col*) mince alors !

blind [blaɪnd] *a* aveugle // *n* (*for window*) store *m* // *vt* aveugler ; **to turn a** ~ **eye** (**on** *or* **to**) fermer les yeux (sur) ; ~ **alley** *n* impasse *f* ; ~ **corner** *n* virage *m* sans visibilité ; ~**fold** *n* bandeau *m* // *a*,*ad* les yeux bandés // *vt* bander les yeux à ; ~**ly** *ad* aveuglément ; ~**ness** *n* cécité *f* ; (*fig*) aveuglement *m* ; ~ **spot** *n* (*AUT etc*) angle *m* aveugle ; (*fig*) angle mort.

blink [blɪŋk] *vi* cligner des yeux ; (*light*) clignoter ; ~**ers** *npl* œillères *fpl*.

blinking ['blɪŋkɪŋ] *a* (*col*): **this** ~... ce fichu *or* sacré ... .

bliss [blɪs] *n* félicité *f*, bonheur *m* sans mélange.

blister ['blɪstə*] *n* (*on skin*) ampoule *f*, cloque *f* ; (*on paintwork*) boursouflure *f* // *vi* (*paint*) se boursoufler, se cloquer.

blithe [blaɪð] *a* joyeux(euse), allègre.

blithering ['blɪðərɪŋ] *a* (*col*): **this** ~ **idiot** cet espèce d'idiot.

blitz [blɪts] *n* bombardement (aérien).

blizzard ['blɪzəd] *n* blizzard *m*, tempête *f* de neige.

bloated ['bləʊtɪd] *a* (*face*) bouffi(e) ; (*stomach*) gonflé(e).

blob [blɒb] *n* (*drop*) goutte *f* ; (*stain*, *spot*) tache *f*.

block [blɒk] *n* bloc *m* ; (*in pipes*) obstruction *f* ; (*toy*) cube *m* ; (*of buildings*) pâté *m* (de maisons) // *vt* bloquer ; ~**ade** [-'keɪd] *n* blocus *m* // *vt* faire le blocus de ; ~**age** *n* obstruction *f* ; ~**head** *n* imbécile *m*/*f* ; ~ **of flats** *n* immeuble (locatif) ; ~ **letters** *npl* majuscules *fpl*.

bloke [bləʊk] *n* (*col*) type *m*.

blonde [blɒnd] *a*,*n* blond(e).

blood [blʌd] *n* sang *m* ; ~ **donor** *n* donneur/euse de sang ; ~ **group** *n* groupe sanguin ; ~**less** *a* (*victory*) sans effusion de sang ; (*pale*) anémié(e) ; ~ **poisoning** *n* empoisonnement *m* du sang ; ~ **pressure** *n* tension *f* (artérielle) ; ~**shed** *n* effusion *f* de sang, carnage *m* ; ~**shot** *a*: ~**shot eyes** yeux injectés de sang ; ~**stained** *a* taché(e) de sang ; ~**stream** *n* sang *m*, système sanguin ; ~**thirsty** *a* sanguinaire ; ~ **transfusion** *n* transfusion *f* de sang ; ~**y** *a* sanglant(e) ; (*col!*): **this** ~**y** ... ce foutu..., ce putain de... (!) ; ~**y strong**/**good** (*col!*) vachement *or* sacrément fort/bon ; ~**y-minded** *a* (*col*) contrariant(e), obstiné(e).

bloom [blu:m] *n* fleur *f* ; (*fig*) épanouissement *m* // *vi* être en fleur, (*fig*) s'épanouir ; être florissant ; ~**ing** *a* (*col*): **this** ~**ing**... ce fichu *or* sacré... .

blossom ['blɒsəm] *n* fleur(s) *f*(*pl*) // *vi* être en fleurs ; (*fig*) s'épanouir.

blot [blɒt] *n* tache *f* // *vt* tacher ; (*ink*) sécher ; **to** ~ **out** *vt* (*memories*) effacer ; (*view*) cacher, masquer ; (*nation*, *city*) annihiler.

blotchy ['blɒtʃɪ] *a* (*complexion*) couvert(e) de marbrures.

blotting paper ['blɒtɪŋpeɪpə*] *n* buvard *m*.

blouse [blauz] *n* (*feminine garment*) chemisier *m*, corsage *m*.

blow [bləʊ] *n* coup *m* // *vb* (*pt* **blew**, *pp* **blown** [blu:, bləun]) *vi* souffler // *vt* (*glass*) souffler ; (*fuse*) faire sauter ; **to** ~ **one's nose** se moucher ; **to** ~ **a whistle** siffler ; **to** ~ **away** *vt* chasser, faire s'envoler ; **to** ~ **down** *vt* faire tomber, renverser ; **to** ~ **off** *vt* emporter ; **to** ~ **off course** faire dévier ; **to** ~ **out** *vi* éclater, sauter ; **to** ~ **over** *vi* s'apaiser ; **to** ~ **up** *vi* exploser, sauter // *vt* faire sauter ; (*tyre*) gonfler ; (*PHOT*) agrandir ; ~**lamp** *n* chalumeau *m* ; ~**-out** *n* (*of tyre*) éclatement *m*.

blubber ['blʌbə*] *n* blanc *m* de baleine // *vi* (*pej*) pleurer comme un veau.

bludgeon ['blʌdʒən] *n* gourdin *m*, trique *f*.

blue [blu:] *a* bleu(e) ; ~ **film**/**joke** film *m*/histoire *f* pornographique ; **to have the** ~**s** avoir le cafard ; ~**bell** *n* jacinthe *f* des bois ; ~**bottle** *n* mouche *f* à viande ; ~**jeans** *npl* blue-jeans *mpl* ; ~**print** *n* (*fig*) projet *m*, plan directeur.

bluff [blʌf] *vi* bluffer // *n* bluff *m* // *a* (*person*) bourru(e), brusque ; **to call sb's** ~ mettre qn au défi d'exécuter ses menaces.

blunder ['blʌndə*] *n* gaffe *f*, bévue *f* // *vi* faire une gaffe *or* une bévue.

blunt [blʌnt] *a* émoussé(e), peu tranchant(e) ; (*person*) brusque, ne mâchant pas ses mots // *vt* émousser ; ~**ly** *ad* carrément, sans prendre de gants ; ~**ness** *n* (*of person*) brusquerie *f*, franchise brutale.

blur [blə:*] *n* tache *or* masse floue *or* confuse // *vt* brouiller, rendre flou.

blurt [blə:t]: **to** ~ **out** *vt* (*reveal*) lâcher ; (*say*) balbutier, dire d'une voix entrecoupée.

blush [blʌʃ] *vi* rougir // *n* rougeur *f*.

blustering ['blʌstərɪŋ] *a* fanfaron(ne).

blustery ['blʌstərɪ] *a* (*weather*) à bourrasques.

B.O. *n* (*abbr of body odour*) odeurs corporelles.

boar [bɔ:*] *n* sanglier *m*.

board [bɔ:d] *n* planche *f* ; (*on wall*) panneau *m* ; (*committee*) conseil *m*, comité *m* ; (*in firm*) conseil d'administration *m* // *vt* (*ship*) monter à bord de ; (*train*) monter dans ; ~ **and lodging** *n* chambre *f* avec pension ; **full** ~ pension complète ; **with** ~ **and lodging** (*job*) logé nourri ; **to go by the** ~ (*fig*) : **which goes by the** ~ (*fig*) qu'on laisse tomber, qu'on abandonne ; **to** ~ **up** *vt* (*door*) condamner (*au moyen de planches, de tôle*) ; ~**er** *n* pensionnaire *m*/*f* ; (*SCOL*) interne *m*/*f*, pensionnaire *m*/*f* ; ~**ing house** *n* pension *f* ; ~**ing school** *n* internat *m*, pensionnat *m* ; ~ **room** *n* salle *f* du conseil d'administration (*souvent symbole de pouvoir décisionnaire*).

boast [bəʊst] *vi* se vanter // *vt* s'enorgueillir de // *n* vantardise *f* ; sujet *m* d'orgueil *or* de fierté ; ~**ful** *a* vantard(e) ; ~**fulness** *n* vantardise *f*.

boat [bəʊt] *n* bateau *m* ; (*small*) canot *m* ; barque *f* ; **to be in the same** ~ (*fig*) être logé à la même enseigne ; ~**er** *n* (*hat*) canotier *m* ; ~**ing** *n* canotage *m* ; ~**swain** ['bəʊsn] *n* maître *m* d'équipage.

bob [bɔb] *vi* (*boat, cork on water: also:* ~ **up and down**) danser, se balancer // *n* (*col*) = **shilling** ; **to** ~ **up** *vi* surgir *or* apparaître brusquement.

bobbin ['bɔbɪn] *n* bobine *f* ; (*of sewing machine*) navette *f*.

bobby ['bɔbɪ] *n* (*col*) ≈ agent *m* (de police).

bobsleigh ['bɔbsleɪ] *n* bob *m*.

bodice ['bɔdɪs] *n* corsage *m*.

bodily ['bɔdɪlɪ] *a* corporel(le) // *ad* physiquement ; dans son entier *or* ensemble ; en personne.

body ['bɔdɪ] *n* corps *m* ; (*of car*) carrosserie *f* ; (*of plane*) fuselage *m* ; (*fig: society*) organe *m*, organisme *m* ; (*fig: quantity*) ensemble *m*, masse *f* ; (*of wine*) corps *m* ; **in a** ~ en masse, ensemble ; ~**guard** *n* garde *m* du corps ; ~ **repairs** *npl* travaux *mpl* de carrosserie ; ~**work** *n* carrosserie *f*.

bog [bɔg] *n* tourbière *f* // *vt*: **to get** ~**ged down** (*fig*) s'enliser.

boggle ['bɔgl] *vi*: **the mind** ~**s** c'est incroyable, on en reste sidéré.

bogie ['bəʊgɪ] *n* bogie *m*.

bogus ['bəʊgəs] *a* bidon *inv* ; fantôme.

boil [bɔɪl] *vt* (faire) bouillir // *vi* bouillir // *n* (*MED*) furoncle *m* ; **to come to the** ~ bouillir ; **to** ~ **down** *vi* (*fig*): **to** ~ **down to** se réduire *or* ramener à ; ~**er** *n* chaudière *f* ; ~**er suit** *n* bleu *m* de travail, combinaison *f* ; ~**ing hot** *a* brûlant(e), bouillant(e) ; ~**ing point** *n* point *m* d'ébullition.

boisterous ['bɔɪstərəs] *a* bruyant(e), tapageur(euse).

bold [bəʊld] *a* hardi(e), audacieux(euse) ; (*pej*) effronté(e) ; (*outline, colour*) franc(franche), tranché(e), marqué(e) ; ~**ness** *n* hardiesse *f*, audace *f* ; aplomb *m*, effronterie *f* ; ~ **type** *n* caractères *mpl* gras.

Bolivia [bə'lɪvɪə] *n* Bolivie *f*.

bollard ['bɔləd] *n* (*NAUT*) bitte *f* d'amarrage ; (*AUT*) borne lumineuse *or* de signalisation.

bolster ['bəʊlstə*] *n* traversin *m* ; **to** ~ **up** *vt* soutenir.

bolt [bəʊlt] *n* verrou *m* ; (*with nut*) boulon *m* // *vt* verrouiller ; (*food*) engloutir // *vi* se sauver, filer (comme une flèche) ; **a** ~ **from the blue** (*fig*) un coup de tonnerre dans un ciel bleu.

bomb [bɔm] *n* bombe *f* // *vt* bombarder ; ~**ard** [bɔm'bɑ:d] *vt* bombarder ; ~**ardment** [bɔm'bɑ:dmənt] *n* bombardement *m*.

bombastic [bɔm'bæstɪk] *a* grandiloquent(e), pompeux(euse).

bomb disposal ['bɔmdɪspəʊzl] *n*: ~ **unit** section *f* de déminage.

bomber ['bɔmə*] *n* caporal *m* d'artillerie ; (*AVIAT*) bombardier *m*.

bombing ['bɔmɪŋ] *n* bombardement *m*.

bombshell ['bɔmʃɛl] *n* obus *m* ; (*fig*) bombe *f*.

bona fide ['bəʊnə'faɪdɪ] *a* de bonne foi ; (*offer*) sérieux(euse).

bond [bɔnd] *n* lien *m* ; (*binding promise*) engagement *m*, obligation *f* ; (*FINANCE*) obligation *f*.

bone [bəʊn] *n* os *m* ; (*of fish*) arête *f* // *vt* désosser ; ôter les arêtes de ; ~**-dry** *a* absolument sec(sèche) ; ~**r** *n* (*US*) gaffe *f*, bourde *f*.

bonfire ['bɔnfaɪə*] *n* feu *m* (de joie) ; (*for rubbish*) feu *m*.

bonnet ['bɔnɪt] *n* bonnet *m* ; (*Brit: of car*) capot *m*.

bonus ['bəʊnəs] *n* prime *f*, gratification *f*.

bony ['bəʊnɪ] *a* (*arm, face,* MED: *tissue*) osseux(euse) ; (*meat*) plein(e) d'os ; (*fish*) plein d'arêtes.

boo [bu:] *excl* hou!, peuh! // *vt* huer // *n* huée *f*.

booby trap ['bu:bɪtræp] *n* engin piégé.

book [buk] *n* livre *m* ; (*of stamps etc*) carnet *m* ; (*COMM*): ~**s** comptes *mpl*, comptabilité *f* // *vt* (*ticket*) prendre ; (*seat, room*) réserver ; (*driver*) dresser un procès-verbal à ; (*football player*) prendre le nom de ; ~**able** *a*: **seats are** ~**able** on peut réserver ses places ; ~**case** *n* bibliothèque *f* (meuble) ; ~ **ends** *npl* serre-livres *m inv* ; ~**ing office** *n* bureau *m* de location ; ~**keeping** *n* comptabilité *f* ; ~**let** *n* brochure *f* ; ~**maker** *n* bookmaker *m* ; ~**seller** *n* libraire *m/f* ; ~**shop** *n* librairie *f* ; ~**stall** *n* kiosque *m* à journaux ; ~**store** *n* = ~**shop**.

boom [bu:m] *n* (*noise*) grondement *m* ; (*busy period*) boom *m*, vague *f* de prospérité // *vi* gronder ; prospérer.

boomerang ['bu:məræŋ] *n* boomerang *m*.

boon [bu:n] *n* bénédiction *f*, grand avantage.

boorish ['bʊərɪʃ] *a* grossier(ère), rustre.

boost [bu:st] *n* stimulant *m*, remontant *m* ; (*MED: vaccine*) rappel *m* // *vt* stimuler.

boot [bu:t] *n* botte *f* ; (*for hiking*) chaussure *f* (de marche) ; (*for football etc*) soulier *m* ; (*Brit: of car*) coffre *m* ; **to** ~ (*in addition*) par-dessus le marché, en plus.

booth [bu:ð] *n* (*at fair*) baraque (foraine) ; (*of cinema, telephone etc*) cabine *f* ; (*also: voting* ~) isoloir *m*.

booty ['bu:tɪ] *n* butin *m*.

booze [bu:z] (*col*) *n* boissons *fpl* alcooliques, alcool *m* // *vi* boire, picoler.

border ['bɔ:də*] *n* bordure *f* ; bord *m* ; (*of a country*) frontière *f* ; **the B~** *la frontière entre l'Écosse et l'Angleterre* ; **the B~s** *la région frontière entre l'Écosse et l'Angleterre* ; **to** ~ **on** *vt fus* être voisin(e) de, toucher à ; ~**line** *n* (*fig*) ligne *f* de démarcation ; ~**line case** *n* cas *m* limite.

bore [bɔ:*] *pt of* **bear** // *vt* (*hole*) percer ; (*person*) ennuyer, raser // *n* (*person*) raseur/euse ; (*of gun*) calibre *m* ; ~**dom** *n* ennui *m*.

boring ['bɔ:rɪŋ] a ennuyeux(euse).

born [bɔ:n] a: **to be ~** naître; **I was ~ in 1960** je suis né en 1960; **~ blind** aveugle de naissance; **a ~ comedian** un comédien-né.

borne [bɔ:n] pp of **bear**.

borough ['bʌrə] n municipalité f.

borrow ['bɔrəu] vt: **to ~ sth (from sb)** emprunter qch (à qn).

borstal ['bɔ:stl] n ≈ maison f de correction.

bosom ['buzəm] n poitrine f; (fig) sein m; **~ friend** n ami/e intime.

boss [bɔs] n patron/ne // vt commander; **~y** a autoritaire.

bosun ['bəusn] n maître m d'équipage.

botanical [bə'tænɪkl] a botanique.

botanist ['bɔtənɪst] n botaniste m/f.

botany ['bɔtənɪ] n botanique f.

botch [bɔtʃ] vt (also: **~ up**) saboter, bâcler.

both [bəuθ] a les deux, l'un(e) et l'autre // pronoun: **~ (of them)** les deux, tous(toutes) (les) deux, l'un(e) et l'autre; **~ of us went, we ~ went** nous y sommes allés (tous) les deux // ad: **they sell ~ the fabric and the finished curtains** ils vendent (et) le tissu et les rideaux (finis), ils vendent à la fois le tissu et les rideaux (finis).

bother ['bɔðə*] vt (worry) tracasser; (needle, bait) importuner, ennuyer; (disturb) déranger // vi (gen: **~ o.s.**) se tracasser, se faire du souci; **to ~ doing** prendre la peine de faire // n: **it is a ~ to have to do** c'est vraiment ennuyeux d'avoir à faire; **it was no ~ finding** il n'y a eu aucun problème pour or ç'a été très facile de trouver.

bottle ['bɔtl] n bouteille f; (baby's) biberon m // vt mettre en bouteille(s); **to ~ up** vt refouler, contenir; **~neck** n étranglement m; **~-opener** n ouvre-bouteille m.

bottom ['bɔtəm] n (of container, sea etc) fond m; (buttocks) derrière m; (of page, list) bas m; (of chair) siège m // à du fond; du bas; **~less** a sans fond, insondable.

bough [bau] n branche f, rameau m.

bought [bɔ:t] pt,pp of **buy**.

boulder ['bəuldə*] n gros rocher (gén lisse, arrondi).

bounce [bauns] vi (ball) rebondir; (cheque) être refusé (étant sans provision); (gen: **to ~ forward/out** etc) bondir, s'élancer // vt faire rebondir // n (rebound) rebond m.

bound [baund] pt,pp of **bind** // n (gen pl) limite f; (leap) bond m // vt (leap) bondir; (limit) borner // a: **to be ~ to do sth** (obliged) être obligé(e) or avoir obligation de faire qch; **out of ~s** dont l'accès est interdit; **he's ~ to fail** (likely) il est sûr d'échouer, son échec est inévitable or assuré; **~ for** à destination de.

boundary ['baundrɪ] n frontière f.

boundless ['baundlɪs] a illimité(e), sans bornes.

bout [baut] n période f; (of malaria etc) accès m, crise f, attaque f; (BOXING etc) combat m, match m.

bow n [bəu] nœud m; (weapon) arc m; (MUS) archet m; [bau] révérence f, inclination f (du buste or corps) // vi [bau] faire une révérence, s'incliner; (yield): **to ~ to or before** s'incliner devant, se soumettre à.

bowels [bauəlz] npl intestins mpl; (fig) entrailles fpl.

bowl [bəul] n (for eating) bol m; (for washing) cuvette f; (ball) boule f; (of pipe) fourneau m // vi (CRICKET) lancer (la balle); **~s** n (jeu m de) boules fpl; **to ~ over** vt (fig) renverser (fig).

bow-legged ['bəulɛgɪd] a aux jambes arquées.

bowler ['bəulə*] n joueur m de boules; (CRICKET) lanceur m (de la balle); (also: **~ hat**) (chapeau m) melon m.

bowling ['bəulɪŋ] n (game) jeu m de boules; **~ alley** n bowling m; jeu m de quilles; **~ green** n terrain m de boules (gazonné et carré).

bow tie ['bəu'taɪ] n nœud m papillon.

box [bɔks] n boîte f; (also: **cardboard ~**) carton m; (THEATRE) loge f // vt mettre en boîte; (SPORT) boxer avec // vi boxer, faire de la boxe; **~er** n (person) boxeur m; (dog) boxer m; **~ing** n (SPORT) boxe f; **B~ing Day** n le lendemain de Noël; **~ing gloves** npl gants mpl de boxe; **~ing ring** n ring m; **~ office** n bureau m de location; **~ room** n débarras m; chambrette f.

boy [bɔɪ] n garçon m; (servant) boy m.

boycott ['bɔɪkɔt] n boycottage m // vt boycotter.

boyfriend ['bɔɪfrɛnd] n (petit) ami.

boyish ['bɔɪʃ] a d'enfant, de garçon.

B.R. abbr of British Rail.

bra [brɑ:] n soutien-gorge m.

brace [breɪs] n attache f, agrafe f; (on teeth) appareil m (dentaire); (tool) vilbrequin m; (TYP: also: **~ bracket**) accolade f // vt consolider, soutenir; **~s** npl bretelles fpl; **to ~ o.s.** (fig) se préparer mentalement.

bracelet ['breɪslɪt] n bracelet m.

bracing ['breɪsɪŋ] a tonifiant(e), tonique.

bracken ['brækən] n fougère f.

bracket ['brækɪt] n (TECH) tasseau m, support m; (group) classe f, tranche f; (also: **brace ~**) accolade f; (also: **round ~**) parenthèse f; (gen: **square ~**) crochet m // vt mettre entre parenthèse(s).

brag [bræg] vi se vanter.

braid [breɪd] n (trimming) galon m; (of hair) tresse f, natte f.

Braille [breɪl] n braille m.

brain [breɪn] n cerveau m; **~s** npl cervelle f; **he's got ~s** il est intelligent; **~less** a sans cervelle, stupide; **~wash** vt faire subir un lavage de cerveau à; **~wave** n idée géniale; **~y** a intelligent(e), doué(e).

braise [breɪz] vt braiser.

brake [breɪk] n (on vehicle) frein m // vt,vi freiner.

bramble ['bræmbl] n ronces fpl.

bran [bræn] n son m.

branch [brɑ:ntʃ] n branche f; (COMM) succursale f // vi bifurquer.

brand [brænd] n marque (commerciale) // vt (cattle) marquer (au fer rouge); (fig:

pej): **to ~ sb a communist** *etc* traiter *or* qualifier qn de communiste *etc.*

brandish ['brændɪʃ] *vt* brandir.

brand-new ['brænd'nju:] *a* tout(e) neuf(neuve), flambant neuf(neuve).

brandy ['brændɪ] *n* cognac *m*, fine *f*.

brash [bræʃ] *a* effronté(e).

brass [brɑ:s] *n* cuivre *m* (jaune), laiton *m*; **the ~** (*MUS*) les cuivres; **~ band** *n* fanfare *f*.

brassière ['bræsɪə*] *n* soutien-gorge *m*.

brat [bræt] *n* (*pej*) mioche *m/f*, môme *m/f*.

bravado [brə'vɑ:dəu] *n* bravade *f*.

brave [breɪv] *a* courageux(euse), brave // *n* guerrier indien // *vt* braver, affronter; **~ry** *n* bravure *f*, courage *m*.

brawl [brɔ:l] *n* rixe *f*, bagarre *f* // *vi* se bagarrer.

brawn [brɔ:n] *n* muscle *m*; (*meat*) fromage *m* de tête; **~y** a musclé(e), costaud(e).

bray [breɪ] *n* braiement *m* // *vi* braire.

brazen ['breɪzn] *a* impudent(e), effronté(e) // *vt*: **to ~ it** out payer d'effronterie, crâner.

brazier ['breɪzɪə*] *n* brasero *m*.

Brazil [brə'zɪl] *n* Brésil *m*; **~ian** *a* brésilien(ne) // *n* Brésilien/ne; **~ nut** *n* noix *f* du Brésil.

breach [bri:tʃ] *vt* ouvrir une brèche dans // *n* (*gap*) brèche *f*; (*breaking*): **~ of confidence** abus *m* de confiance; **~ of contract** rupture *f* de contrat; **~ of the peace** attentat *m* à l'ordre public.

bread [brɛd] *n* pain *m*; **~ and butter** *n* tartines *fpl* (beurrées); (*fig*) subsistance *f*; **~crumbs** *npl* miettes *fpl* de pain; (*CULIN*) chapelure *f*, panure *f*; **~ line** *n*: **to be on the ~ line** être sans le sou *or* dans l'indigence.

breadth [brɛtθ] *n* largeur *f*.

breadwinner ['brɛdwɪnə*] *n* soutien *m* de famille.

break [breɪk] *vb* (*pt* **broke** [brəuk], *pp* **broken** ['brəukən]) *vt* casser, briser; (*promise*) rompre; (*law*) violer // *vi* (se) casser, se briser; (*weather*) tourner // *n* (*gap*) brèche *f*; (*fracture*) cassure *f*; (*rest*) interruption *f*, arrêt *m*; (*:short*) pause *f*; (*:at school*) récréation *f*; (*chance*) chance *f*, occasion *f* favorable; **to ~ one's leg** *etc* se casser la jambe *etc*; **to ~ a record** battre un record; **to ~ the news to sb** annoncer la nouvelle à qn; **to ~ down** *vt* (*figures, data*) décomposer, analyser // *vi* s'effondrer; (*MED*) faire une dépression (nerveuse); (*AUT*) tomber en panne; **to ~ even** *vi* rentrer dans ses frais; **to ~ free** *or* **loose** *vi* se dégager, s'échapper; **to ~ in** *vt* (*horse etc*) dresser // *vi* (*burglar*) entrer par effraction; **to ~ into** *vt fus* (*house*) s'introduire *or* pénétrer par effraction dans; **to ~ off** *vi* (*speaker*) s'interrompre; (*branch*) se rompre; **to ~ open** *vt* (*door etc*) forcer, fracturer; **to ~ out** *vi* éclater, se déclarer; **to ~ out in spots** se couvrir de boutons; **to ~ up** *vi* (*partnership*) cesser, prendre fin; (*friends*) se séparer // *vt* fracasser, casser; (*fight etc*) interrompre, faire cesser; **~able** *a* cassable, fragile; **~age** *n* casse *f*; **~down** *n* (*AUT*) panne *f*; (*in communications*) rupture *f*; (*MED: also*: **nervous ~down**)

dépression (nerveuse); **~down lorry** *n* dépanneuse *f*; **~down service** *n* service *m* de dépannage; **~er** *n* brisant *m*.

breakfast ['brɛkfəst] *n* petit déjeuner *m*.

breakthrough ['breɪkθru:] *n* percée *f*.

breakwater ['breɪkwɔ:tə*] *n* brise-lames *m inv*, digue *f*.

breast [brɛst] *n* (*of woman*) sein *m*; (*chest*) poitrine *f*; (*of animal*) poitrine *f*, brasse *f*.

breath [brɛθ] *n* haleine *f*, souffle *m*; **to go out for a ~ of air** sortir prendre l'air; **out of ~** à bout de souffle, essoufflé(e); **~alyser** *n* alcootest *m*.

breathe [bri:ð] *vt,vi* respirer; **~r** *n* moment *m* de repos *or* de répit.

breathless ['brɛθlɪs] *a* essoufflé(e), haletant(e); oppressé(e).

breath-taking ['brɛθteɪkɪŋ] *a* stupéfiant(e), à vous couper le souffle.

breed [bri:d] *vb* (*pt,pp* **bred** [brɛd]) *vt* élever, faire l'élevage de // *vi* se reproduire // *n* race *f*, variété *f*; (*person*) élever; **~er** *n* (*person*) éleveur *m*; **~ing** *n* reproduction *f*; élevage *m*.

breeze [bri:z] *n* brise *f*.

breezy ['bri:zɪ] *a* frais(fraiche); aéré(e); désinvolte, jovial(e).

brevity ['brɛvɪtɪ] *n* brièveté *f*.

brew [bru:] *vt* (*tea*) faire infuser; (*beer*) brasser; (*plot*) tramer, préparer // *vi* (*tea*) infuser; (*beer*) fermenter; (*fig*) se préparer, couver; **~er** *n* brasseur *m*; **~ery** *n* brasserie *f* (fabrique).

bribe [braɪb] *n* pot-de-vin *m* // *vt* acheter; soudoyer; **~ry** *n* corruption *f*.

brick [brɪk] *n* brique *f*; **~layer** *n* maçon *m*; **~work** *n* briquetage *m*, maçonnerie *f*; **~works** *n* briqueterie *f*.

bridal ['braɪdl] *a* nuptial(e); **~ party** *n* noce *f*.

bride [braɪd] *n* mariée *f*, épouse *f*; **~groom** *n* marié *m*, époux *m*; **~smaid** *n* demoiselle *f* d'honneur.

bridge [brɪdʒ] *n* pont *m*; (*NAUT*) passerelle *f* (de commandement); (*of nose*) arête *f*; (*CARDS, DENTISTRY*) bridge *m* // *vt* (*river*) construire un pont sur; (*gap*) combler; **bridging loan** *n* prêt *m* de raccord.

bridle ['braɪdl] *n* bride *f* // *vt* refréner, mettre la bride à; (*horse*) brider; **~ path** *n* piste *or* allée cavalière.

brief [bri:f] *a* bref(brève) // *n* (*LAW*) dossier *m*, cause *f* // *vt* donner des instructions à; **~s** *npl* slip *m*; **~case** *n* serviette *f*; porte-documents *m inv*; **~ing** *n* instructions *fpl*; **~ly** *ad* brièvement; **~ness** *n* brièveté *f*.

brigade [brɪ'geɪd] *n* (*MIL*) brigade *f*.

brigadier [brɪgə'dɪə*] *n* brigadier général.

bright [braɪt] *a* brillant(e); (*room, weather*) clair(e); (*person*) intelligent(e), doué(e); (*colour*) vif(vive); **~en** *vt* (*room*) éclaircir; égayer // *vi* s'éclaircir; (*person: gen:* **~en up**) retrouver un peu de sa gaieté; **~ly** *ad* brillamment.

brilliance ['brɪljəns] *n* éclat *m*.

brilliant ['brɪljənt] *a* brillant(e).

brim [brɪm] *n* bord *m*; **~ful** *a* plein(e) à ras bord; (*fig*) débordant(e).

brine [braɪn] *n* eau salée; (*CULIN*) saumure *f*.

bring, *pt,pp* **brought** [brɪŋ, brɔːt] *vt*
(*thing*) apporter ; (*person*) amener ; **to ~
about** *vt* provoquer, entraîner ; **to ~ back**
vt rapporter ; ramener ; **to ~ down** *vt*
abaisser ; faire s'effondrer ; **to ~ forward**
vt avancer ; **to ~ off** *vt* (*task, plan*) réussir,
mener à bien ; **to ~ out** *vt* (*meaning*) faire
ressortir, mettre en relief ; **to ~ round** *or*
to *vt* (*unconscious person*) ranimer ; **to ~
up** *vt* élever ; (*question*) soulever.

brink [brɪŋk] *n* bord *m*.

brisk [brɪsk] *a* vif(vive), alerte.

bristle ['brɪsl] *n* poil *m* // *vi* se hérisser ;
bristling with hérissé(e) de.

Britain ['brɪtən] *n* Grande-Bretagne *f*.

British ['brɪtɪʃ] *a* britannique ; **the ~** *npl*
les Britanniques *mpl* ; **the ~ Isles** *npl* les
Îles *fpl* Britanniques.

Briton ['brɪtən] *n* Britannique *m/f*.

Brittany ['brɪtənɪ] *n* Bretagne *f*.

brittle ['brɪtl] *a* cassant(e), fragile.

broach [brəʊtʃ] *vt* (*subject*) aborder.

broad [brɔːd] *a* large ; (*distinction*)
général(e) ; (*accent*) prononcé(e) ; **in ~
daylight** en plein jour ; **~ hint** allusion
transparente ; **~cast** *n* émission *f* // *vb*
(*pt,pp* **broadcast**) *vt* radiodiffuser ;
téléviser // *vi* émettre ; **~casting** *n*
radiodiffusion *f* ; télévision *f* ; **to ~**
élargir // *vi* s'élargir ; **~ly** *ad* en gros,
généralement ; **~-minded** *a* large d'esprit.

brochure ['brəʊʃjʊə*] *n* prospectus *m*,
dépliant *m*.

broil [brɔɪl] *vt* rôtir ; **~er** *n* (*fowl*) poulet
m (*à rôtir*).

broke [brəʊk] *pt of* **break** // *a* (*col*)
fauché(e) ; **~n** *pp of* **break** // *a:* **~n leg**
etc jambe *etc* cassée ; **in ~n
French/English** dans un français/anglais
approximatif *ou* hésitant ; **~n-hearted** *a*
(ayant) le cœur brisé.

broker ['brəʊkə*] *n* courtier *m*.

bronchitis [brɔŋ'kaɪtɪs] *n* bronchite *f*.

bronze [brɔnz] *n* bronze *m* ; **~d** *a*
bronzé(e), hâlé(e).

brooch [brəʊtʃ] *n* broche *f*.

brood [bruːd] *n* couvée *f* // *vi* (*hen, storm*)
couver ; (*person*) méditer (sombrement),
ruminer ; **~y** *a* (*fig*) taciturne,
mélancolique.

brook [brʊk] *n* ruisseau *m*.

broom [brum] *n* balai *m* ; **~stick** *n*
manche *m* à balai.

Bros. *abbr of* **Brothers.**

broth [brɔθ] *n* bouillon *m* de viande et de
légumes.

brothel ['brɔθl] *n* maison close, bordel *m*.

brother ['brʌðə*] *n* frère *m* ; **~hood** *n*
fraternité *f* ; **~-in-law** *n* beau-frère *m* ;
~ly *a* fraternel(le).

brought [brɔːt] *pt,pp of* **bring.**

brow [braʊ] *n* front *m* ; (*rare, gen:* **eye~**)
sourcil *m* ; (*of hill*) sommet *m* ; **~beat** *vt*
intimider, brusquer.

brown [braʊn] *a* brun(e) // *n* (*colour*) brun
m // *vt* brunir ; (*CULIN*) faire dorer, faire
roussir ; **~ie** *n* jeannette *f*, éclaireuse
(cadette).

browse [braʊz] *vi* (*among books*)
bouquiner, feuilleter les livres.

bruise [bruːz] *n* bleu *m*, ecchymose *f*,
contusion *f* // *vt* contusionner, meurtrir //
vi (*fruit*) se taler, se meurtrir ; **to ~ one's
arm** se faire un bleu au bras.

brunette [bruː'nɛt] *n* (femme) brune.

brunt [brʌnt] *n*: **the ~ of** (*attack, criticism
etc*) le plus gros de.

brush [brʌʃ] *n* brosse *f* ; (*quarrel*)
accrochage *m*, prise *f* de bec // *vt* brosser ;
(*gen:* **~ past, ~ against**) effleurer, frôler ;
to ~ aside *vt* écarter, balayer ; **to ~ up**
vt (*knowledge*) rafraîchir, réviser ; **~-off** *n*:
to give sb the ~-off envoyer qn
promener ; **~wood** *n* broussailles *fpl*,
taillis *m*.

Brussels ['brʌslz] *n* Bruxelles ; **~ sprout**
n chou *m* de Bruxelles.

brutal ['bruːtl] *a* brutal(e) ; **~ity**
[bruː'tælɪtɪ] *n* brutalité *f*.

brute [bruːt] *n* brute *f*.

brutish ['bruːtɪʃ] *a* grossier(ère), brutal(e).

B.Sc. *abbr see* **bachelor.**

bubble ['bʌbl] *n* bulle *f* // *vi* bouillonner,
faire des bulles ; (*sparkle, fig*) pétiller.

buck [bʌk] *n* mâle *m* (*d'un lapin, lièvre, daim
etc*) ; (*US: col*) dollar *m* // *vi* ruer, lancer
une ruade ; **to pass the ~** (**to sb**) se
décharger de la responsabilité (sur qn) ; **to
~ up** *vi* (*cheer up*) reprendre du poil de
la bête, se remonter.

bucket ['bʌkɪt] *n* seau *m*.

buckle ['bʌkl] *n* boucle *f* // *vt* boucler,
attacher ; (*warp*) tordre, gauchir ; (: *wheel*)
voiler.

bud [bʌd] *n* bourgeon *m* ; (*of flower*) bouton
m // *vi* bourgeonner ; (*flower*) éclore.

Buddha ['budə] *n* Bouddha *m* ; **Buddhism**
n bouddhisme *m* ; **Buddhist** *a* bouddhiste
// *n* Bouddhiste *m/f*.

budding ['bʌdɪŋ] *a* (*flower*) en bouton ;
(*poet etc*) en herbe ; (*passion etc*)
naissant(e).

buddy ['bʌdɪ] *n* (US) copain *m*.

budge [bʌdʒ] *vt* faire bouger // *vi* bouger.

budgerigar ['bʌdʒərɪgɑː*] *n* perruche *f*.

budget ['bʌdʒɪt] *n* budget *m* // *vi*: **to ~
for sth** inscrire qch au budget.

budgie ['bʌdʒɪ] *n* = **budgerigar.**

buff [bʌf] *a* (couleur *f*) chamois *m* // *n*
(*enthusiast*) mordu/e.

buffalo, *pl* **~** *or* **~es** ['bʌfələu] *n* buffle
m ; (US) bison *m*.

buffer ['bʌfə*] *n* tampon *m* ; **~ state** *n* état
m tampon.

buffet *n* ['bufeɪ] (*bar, food*) buffet *m* // *vt*
['bʌfɪt] gifler, frapper ; secouer, ébranler.

buffoon [bə'fuːn] *n* buffon *m*, pitre *m*.

bug [bʌg] *n* (*insect*) punaise *f* ; (: *gen*)
insecte *m*, bestiole *f* ; (: *fig: germ*) virus *m*,
microbe *m* ; (*spy device*) dispositif *m*
d'écoute (électronique), micro clandestin
// *vt* garnir de dispositifs d'écoute ;
~bear *n* cauchemar *m*, bête noire *m*.

bugle ['bjuːgl] *n* clairon *m*.

build [bɪld] *n* (*of person*) carrure *f*,
charpente *f* // *vt* (*pt,pp* **built** [bɪlt])
construire, bâtir ; **~er** *n* entrepreneur *m* ;
~ing *n* construction *f* ; bâtiment *m*, construction *f* ; (*habitation, offices*) immeuble
m ; **~ing society** *n* société *f* de crédit
immobilier ; **to ~ up** *vt* accumuler,

amasser ; accroître ; **~-up** n (of gas etc) accumulation f.

built [bɪlt] pt,pp of **build** ; **well-~** a (person) bien bâti(e) ; **~-in** a (cupboard) encastré(e) ; (device) incorporé(e) ; intégré(e) ; **~-up** area n agglomération (urbaine) ; zone urbanisée.

bulb [bʌlb] n (BOT) bulbe m, oignon m ; (ELEC) ampoule f ; **~ous** a bulbeux(euse).

Bulgaria [bʌlˈgɛərɪə] n Bulgarie f ; **~n** a bulgare // n Bulgare m/f ; (LING) bulgare m.

bulge [bʌldʒ] n renflement m, gonflement m // vi faire saillie ; présenter un renflement ; **to be bulging with** être plein(e) à craquer de.

bulk [bʌlk] n masse f, volume m ; **in ~** (COMM) en vrac ; **the ~ of** la plus grande or grosse partie de ; **~head** n cloison f (étanche) ; **~y** a volumineux(euse), encombrant(e).

bull [bul] n taureau m ; **~dog** n bouledogue m.

bulldoze [ˈbuldəuz] vt passer or raser au bulldozer ; **~r** n bulldozer m.

bullet [ˈbulɪt] n balle f (de fusil etc).

bulletin [ˈbulɪtɪn] n bulletin m, communiqué m.

bullfight [ˈbulfaɪt] n corrida f, course f de taureaux ; **~er** n torero m ; **~ing** n tauromachie f.

bullion [ˈbuljən] n or m or argent m en lingots.

bullock [ˈbulək] n bœuf m.

bull's-eye [ˈbulzaɪ] n centre m (de la cible).

bully [ˈbulɪ] n brute f, tyran m // vt tyranniser, rudoyer ; (frighten) intimider ; **~ing** n brimades fpl.

bum [bʌm] n (col: backside) derrière m ; (tramp) vagabond/e, traîne-savates m/f inv ; **to ~ around** vi vagabonder.

bumblebee [ˈbʌmblbiː] n (ZOOL) bourdon m.

bump [bʌmp] n (blow) coup m, choc m ; (jolt) cahot m ; (on road etc, on head) bosse f // vt heurter, cogner ; **to ~ along** vi avancer en cahotant ; **to ~ into** vt fus rentrer dans, tamponner ; **~er** n (Brit) pare-chocs m inv // a : **~er crop/harvest** récolte/moisson exceptionnelle.

bumptious [ˈbʌmpʃəs] a suffisant(e), prétentieux(euse).

bumpy [ˈbʌmpɪ] a cahoteux(euse).

bun [bʌn] n petit pain au lait ; (of hair) chignon m.

bunch [bʌntʃ] n (of flowers) bouquet m ; (of keys) trousseau m ; (of bananas) régime m ; (of people) groupe m ; **~ of grapes** grappe f de raisin.

bundle [ˈbʌndl] n paquet m // vt (also: **~ up**) faire un paquet de ; (put): **to ~ sth/sb into** fourrer or enfourner qch/qn dans ; **to ~ off** vt (person) faire sortir (en toute hâte) ; expédier ; **to ~ out** vt éjecter, sortir (sans ménagements).

bung [bʌŋ] n bonde f, bouchon m // vt (throw: gen: **~ into**) flanquer.

bungalow [ˈbʌŋgələu] n bungalow m.

bungle [ˈbʌŋgl] vt bâcler, gâcher.

bunion [ˈbʌnjən] n oignon m (au pied).

bunk [bʌŋk] n couchette f ; **~ beds** npl lits superposés.

bunker [ˈbʌŋkə*] n (coal store) soute f à charbon ; (MIL, GOLF) bunker m.

bunny [ˈbʌnɪ] n (also: **~ rabbit**) Jeannot m lapin ; **~ girl** n hôtesse de cabaret.

bunting [ˈbʌntɪŋ] n pavoisement m, drapeaux mpl.

buoy [bɔɪ] n bouée f ; **to ~ up** vt faire flotter ; (fig) soutenir, épauler ; **~ancy** n (of ship) flottabilité f ; **~ant** a gai(e), plein(e) d'entrain.

burden [ˈbəːdn] n fardeau m, charge f // vt charger ; (oppress) accabler, surcharger.

bureau, pl **~x** [bjuəˈrəu, -z] n (furniture) bureau m, secrétaire m ; (office) bureau m, office m.

bureaucracy [bjuəˈrɔkrəsɪ] n bureaucratie f.

bureaucrat [ˈbjuərəkræt] n bureaucrate m/f, rond-de-cuir m ; **~ic** [-ˈkrætɪk] a bureaucratique.

burglar [ˈbəːglə*] n cambrioleur m ; **~ alarm** n sonnerie f d'alarme ; **~ize** vt (US) cambrioler ; **~y** n cambriolage m.

burgle [ˈbəːgl] vt cambrioler.

Burgundy [ˈbəːgəndɪ] n Bourgogne f.

burial [ˈberɪəl] n enterrement m ; **~ ground** n cimetière m.

burlesque [bəːˈlɛsk] n caricature f, parodie f.

burly [ˈbəːlɪ] a de forte carrure, costaud(e).

Burma [ˈbəːmə] n Birmanie f ; **Burmese** [-ˈmiːz] a birman(e), de Birmanie // n, pl inv Birman/e ; (LING) birman m.

burn [bəːn] vt,vi (pt,pp **burned** or **burnt** [bəːnt]) brûler // n brûlure f ; **to ~ down** vt incendier, détruire par le feu ; **~er** n brûleur m ; **~ing question** n question brûlante.

burnish [ˈbəːnɪʃ] vt polir.

burnt [bəːnt] pt,pp of **burn** ; **~ sugar** n caramel m.

burp [bəːp] (col) n rot m // vi roter.

burrow [ˈbʌrəu] n terrier m // vt creuser.

bursar [ˈbəːsə*] n économe m/f ; (student) boursier/ère ; **~y** n bourse f (d'études).

burst [bəːst] vb (pt,pp **burst**) vt crever ; faire éclater // vi éclater ; (tyre) crever // n explosion f ; (also: **~ pipe**) rupture f ; fuite f ; **~ of energy** déploiement soudain d'énergie, activité soudaine ; **~ of laughter** éclat m de rire ; **~ blood vessel** rupture f de vaisseau sanguin ; **to ~ into flames** s'enflammer soudainement ; **to ~ into laughter** éclater de rire ; **to ~ into tears** fondre en larmes ; **to be ~ing with** être plein (à craquer) de ; regorger de ; **to ~ into** vt fus faire irruption dans ; **to ~ open** vi s'ouvrir violemment or soudainement ; **to ~ out of** vt fus sortir précipitamment de.

bury [ˈberɪ] vt enterrer ; **to ~ one's face in one's hands** se couvrir le visage de ses mains ; **to ~ one's head in the sand** (fig) pratiquer la politique de l'autruche ; **to ~ the hatchet** enterrer la hache de guerre.

bus, **~es** [bʌs, ˈbʌsɪz] n autobus m.

bush [buʃ] n buisson m ; (scrub land) brousse f.

bushel ['buʃl] n boisseau m.
bushy ['buʃɪ] a broussailleux(euse), touffu(e).
busily ['bɪzɪlɪ] ad activement.
business ['bɪznɪs] n (matter, firm) affaire f; (trading) affaires fpl; (job, duty) travail m; **to be away on** ~ être en déplacement d'affaires; **it's none of my** ~ cela ne me regarde pas, ce ne sont pas mes affaires; **he means** ~ il ne plaisante pas, il est sérieux; ~**like** a sérieux(euse); efficace; ~**man** n homme m d'affaires.
bus-stop ['bʌsstɔp] n arrêt m d'autobus.
bust [bʌst] n buste m // a (broken) fichu(e), fini(e); **to go** ~ faire faillite.
bustle ['bʌsl] n remue-ménage m, affairement m // vi s'affairer, se démener; **bustling** a (person) affairé(e); (town) très animé(e).
bust-up ['bʌstʌp] n (col) engueulade f.
busy ['bɪzɪ] a occupé(e); (shop, street) très fréquenté(e) // vt; **to** ~ **o.s.** s'occuper; ~**body** n mouche f du coche, âme f charitable.
but [bʌt] cj mais // prep excepté, sauf; **nothing** ~ rien d'autre que; ~ **for** sans, si ce n'était pour; **all** ~ **finished** pratiquement fini; **anything** ~ **finished** tout sauf fini, très loin d'être fini.
butane ['bju:teɪn] n butane m.
butcher ['butʃə*] n boucher m // vt massacrer; (cattle etc for meat) tuer.
butler ['bʌtlə*] n maître m d'hôtel.
butt [bʌt] n (cask) gros tonneau; (thick end) (gros) bout; (of gun) crosse f; (of cigarette) mégot m; (fig: target) cible f // vt donner un coup de tête à.
butter ['bʌtə*] n beurre m // vt beurrer; ~ **dish** n beurrier m.
butterfly ['bʌtəflaɪ] n papillon m.
buttocks ['bʌtəks] npl fesses fpl.
button ['bʌtn] n bouton m // vt boutonner // vi se boutonner; ~**hole** n boutonnière f // vt accrocher, arrêter, retenir.
buttress ['bʌtrɪs] n contrefort m.
buxom ['bʌksəm] a aux formes avantageuses or épanouies, bien galbé(e).
buy [baɪ] vb (pt,pp **bought** [bɔːt]) vt acheter; **to** ~ **sb sth/sth from sb** acheter qch à qn; **to** ~ **sb a drink** offrir un verre or à boire à qn; **to** ~ **up** vt acheter en bloc, rafler; ~**er** n acheteur/euse.
buzz [bʌz] n bourdonnement m; (col: phone call) coup m de fil // vi bourdonner.
buzzard ['bʌzəd] n buse f.
buzzer ['bʌzə*] n timbre m électrique.
by [baɪ] prep par; (beside) à côté de; au bord de; (before): ~ **4 o'clock** avant 4 heures, d'ici 4 heures // ad see pass, go etc; ~ **bus/car** en autobus/voiture; **paid** ~ **the hour** payé à l'heure; **to increase** etc ~ **the hour** augmenter etc d'heure en heure; (all) ~ **oneself** tout(e) seul(e); ~ **the way** à propos; ~ **and large** dans l'ensemble; ~ **and** ~ bientôt.
bye(-bye) ['baɪ('baɪ)] excl au revoir!, salut!
by(e)-law ['baɪlɔ:] n arrêté municipal.
by-election ['baɪɪlekʃən] n élection (législative) partielle.
bygone ['baɪgɔn] a passé(e) // n: **let** ~**s be** ~**s** passons l'éponge, oublions le passé.

bypass ['baɪpɑ:s] n (route f de) contournement m // vt éviter.
by-product ['baɪprɔdʌkt] n sous-produit m, dérivé m; (fig) conséquence f secondaire, retombée f.
byre ['baɪə*] n étable f (à vaches).
bystander ['baɪstændə*] n spectateur/-trice, badaud/e.
byword ['baɪwə:d] n: **to be a** ~ **for** être synonyme de (fig).

C

C [si:] n (MUS) do m.
C. abbr of **centigrade**.
C.A. abbr of **chartered accountant**.
cab [kæb] n taxi m; (of train, truck) cabine f; (horse-drawn) fiacre m.
cabaret ['kæbəreɪ] n attractions fpl, spectacle m de cabaret.
cabbage ['kæbɪdʒ] n chou m.
cabin ['kæbɪn] n cabane f, hutte f; (on ship) cabine f; ~ **cruiser** n yacht m (à moteur).
cabinet ['kæbɪnɪt] n (POL) cabinet m; (furniture) petit meuble à tiroirs et rayons; (also: **display** ~) vitrine f, petite armoire vitrée; **cocktail** ~ n meuble-bar m; **medicine** ~ n armoire f à pharmacie; ~**maker** n ébéniste m.
cable ['keɪbl] n câble m // vt câbler, télégraphier; ~**car** n téléphérique m; ~**gram** n câblogramme m; ~ **railway** n funiculaire m.
cache [kæʃ] n cachette f; **a** ~ **of food** etc un dépôt secret de provisions etc, une cachette contenant des provisions etc.
cackle ['kækl] vi caqueter.
cactus, pl **cacti** ['kæktəs, -taɪ] n cactus m.
caddie ['kædɪ] n caddie m.
cadet [kə'dɛt] n (MIL) élève m officier.
cadge [kædʒ] vt se faire donner; **to** ~ **a meal (off sb)** se faire inviter à manger (par qn); ~**r** n pique-assiette m/f inv, tapeur/euse.
Caesarean [si:'zɛərɪən] a: ~ (**section**) césarienne f.
café ['kæfeɪ] n ≈ café(-restaurant) m (sans alcool); **cafeteria** [kæfɪ'tɪərɪə] n cafeteria f.
caffein(e) ['kæfi:n] n caféine f.
cage [keɪdʒ] n cage f // vt mettre en cage.
cagey ['keɪdʒɪ] a (col) réticent(e); méfiant(e).
Cairo ['kaɪərəu] n le Caire.
cajole [kə'dʒəul] vt couvrir de flatteries or de gentillesses.
cake [keɪk] n gâteau m; ~ **of soap** savonnette f; ~**d** a: ~**d with** raidi(e) par, couvert(e) d'une croûte de.
calamitous [kə'læmɪtəs] a catastrophique, désastreux(euse).
calamity [kə'læmɪtɪ] n calamité f, désastre m.
calcium ['kælsɪəm] n calcium m.
calculate ['kælkjuleɪt] vt calculer; **calculating** a calculateur(trice); **calculation** [-'leɪʃən] n calcul m; **calculator** [-'leɪtə*] n machine f à calculer, calculatrice f.

calculus ['kælkjuləs] n analyse f (mathématique), calcul infinitésimal; **integral/differential** ~ calcul intégral/différentiel.

calendar ['kæləndə*] n calendrier m; ~ **month** n mois m (de calendrier); ~ **year** n année civile.

calf, calves [kɑːf, kɑːvz] n (of cow) veau m; (of other animals) petit m; (also: ~skin) veau m, vachette f; (ANAT) mollet m.

calibre, caliber (US) ['kælɪbə*] n calibre m.

call [kɔːl] vt (gen, also TEL) appeler // vi appeler; (visit: also: ~ **in**, ~ **round**): **to** ~ **(for)** passer (prendre) // n (shout) appel m, cri m; (visit) visite f; (also: **telephone** ~) coup m de téléphone; communication f; **she's** ~ed **Suzanne** elle s'appelle Suzanne; **to be on** ~ être de permanence; **to** ~ **for** vt fus demander; **to** ~ **off** vt annuler; **to** ~ **on** vt fus (visit) rendre visite à, passer voir; (request): **to** ~ **on sb to do** inviter qn à faire; **to** ~ **up** vt (MIL) appeler, mobiliser; ~ **box** n cabine f téléphonique; ~ **er** n personne f qui appelle; visiteur m; ~ **girl** n call-girl f; ~ **ing** n vocation f; (trade, occupation) état m; ~ **ing card** n (US) carte f de visite.

callous ['kæləs] a dur(e), insensible; ~ **ness** n dureté f, manque m de cœur, insensibilité f.

callow ['kæləu] a sans expérience (de la vie).

calm [kɑːm] n calme m // vt calmer, apaiser // a calme; ~ **ly** ad calmement, avec calme; ~ **ness** n calme m; **to** ~ **down** vi se calmer, s'apaiser // vt calmer, apaiser.

calorie ['kælərɪ] n calorie f.

calve [kɑːv] vi vêler, mettre bas.

calves [kɑːvz] npl of **calf**.

camber ['kæmbə*] n (of road) bombement m.

Cambodia [kæm'bəudjə] n Cambodge m.

came [keɪm] pt of **come**.

camel ['kæməl] n chameau m.

cameo ['kæmɪəu] n camée m.

camera ['kæmərə] n appareil-photo m; (also: cine~, movie ~) caméra f; **35mm** ~ appareil 24 × 36 or petit format; **in** ~ à huis clos, en privé; ~ **man** n caméraman m.

camouflage ['kæməflɑːʒ] n camouflage m // vt camoufler.

camp [kæmp] n camp m // vi camper.

campaign [kæm'peɪn] n (MIL, POL etc) campagne f // vi (also fig) faire campagne.

campbed ['kæmp'bɛd] n lit m de camp.

camper ['kæmpə*] n campeur/euse.

camping ['kæmpɪŋ] n camping m; ~ **site** n (terrain m de) camping.

campsite ['kæmpsaɪt] n campement m.

campus ['kæmpəs] n campus m.

can [kæn] auxiliary vb (gen) pouvoir; (know how to) savoir; **I** ~ **swim** etc je sais nager etc; **I** ~ **speak French** je parle français // n (of milk, oil, water) bidon m; (US: tin) boîte f (de conserve) // vt mettre en conserve.

Canada ['kænədə] n Canada m.

Canadian [kə'neɪdɪən] a canadien(ne) // n Canadien/ne.

canal [kə'næl] n canal m.

canary [kə'nɛərɪ] n canari m, serin m.

cancel ['kænsəl] vt annuler; (train) supprimer; (party, appointment) décommander; (cross out) barrer, rayer; (stamp) oblitérer; ~ **lation** [-'leɪʃən] n annulation f; suppression f; oblitération f; (TOURISM) réservation annulée, client etc qui s'est décommandé.

cancer ['kænsə*] n cancer m; **C**~ (sign) le Cancer; **to be C**~ être du Cancer.

candid ['kændɪd] a (très) franc(franche), sincère.

candidate ['kændɪdeɪt] n candidat/e.

candle ['kændl] n bougie f; (of tallow) chandelle f; (in church) cierge m; **by** ~ **light** à la lumière d'une bougie; (dinner) aux chandelles; ~ **stick** n (also: ~ **holder**) bougeoir m; (bigger, ornate) chandelier m.

candour ['kændə*] n (grande) franchise or sincérité.

candy ['kændɪ] n sucre candi; (US) bonbon m; ~ **-floss** n barbe f à papa.

cane [keɪn] n canne f // vt (SCOL) administrer des coups de bâton à.

canine ['kænaɪn] a canin(e).

canister ['kænɪstə*] n boîte f (gén en métal).

cannabis ['kænəbɪs] n (drug) cannabis m; (also: ~ **plant**) chanvre indien.

canned ['kænd] a (food) en boîte, en conserve.

cannibal ['kænɪbəl] n cannibale m/f, anthropophage m/f; ~ **ism** n cannibalisme m, anthropophagie f.

cannon, pl ~ **or** ~ **s** ['kænən] n (gun) canon m; ~ **ball** n boulet m de canon.

cannot ['kænɔt] = **can not**.

canny ['kænɪ] a madré(e), finaud(e).

canoe [kə'nuː] n pirogue f; (SPORT) canoë m; ~ **ing** n (SPORT) canoë m; ~ **ist** n canoëiste m/f.

canon ['kænən] n (clergyman) chanoine m; (standard) canon m.

canonize ['kænənaɪz] vt canoniser.

can opener ['kænəupnə*] n ouvre-boîte m.

canopy ['kænəpɪ] n baldaquin m; dais m.

cant [kænt] n jargon m // vt, vi pencher.

can't [kænt] = **can not**.

cantankerous [kæn'tæŋkərəs] a querelleur(euse), acariâtre.

canteen [kæn'tiːn] n cantine f; (of cutlery) ménagère f.

canter ['kæntə*] n petit galop // vi aller au petit galop.

cantilever ['kæntɪliːvə*] n porte-à-faux m inv.

canvas ['kænvəs] n (gen) toile f; **under** ~ (camping) sous la tente; (NAUT) toutes voiles dehors.

canvass ['kænvəs] vt: ~ **ing** (POL) prospection électorale, démarchage électoral; (COMM) démarchage, prospection.

canyon ['kænjən] n cañon m, gorge f (profonde).

cap [kæp] n casquette f; (of pen) capuchon m; (of bottle) capsule f; (also: **Dutch** ~)

diaphragme m; (FOOTBALL) sèlection f pour l'équipe nationale // vt capsuler; (outdo) surpasser; ~ped with coiffé(e) de.

capability [keipə'biliti] n aptitude f, capacité f.

capable ['keipəbl] a capable; ~ **of** capable de; susceptible de.

capacity [kə'pæsiti] n capacité f, contenance f; aptitude f; **in his ~ as** en sa qualité de; **to work at full ~** travailler à plein rendement.

cape [keip] n (garment) cape f; (GEO) cap m.

caper ['keipə*] n (CULIN: gen: ~s) câpre f.

capital ['kæpitl] n (also: ~ **city**) capitale f; (money) capital m; (also: ~ **letter**) majuscule f; ~ **gains** npl plus-values fpl; ~**ism** n capitalisme m; ~**ist** a capitaliste; ~ **punishment** n peine capitale.

capitulate [kə'pitjuleit] vi capituler; **capitulation** [-'leiʃən] n capitulation f.

capricious [kə'priʃəs] a capricieux(euse), fantasque.

Capricorn ['kæprikɔ:n] n le Capricorne; **to be ~** être du Capricorne.

capsize [kæp'saiz] vt faire chavirer // vi chavirer.

capstan ['kæpstən] n cabestan m.

capsule ['kæpsju:l] n capsule f.

captain ['kæptin] n capitaine m // vt commander, être le capitaine de.

caption ['kæpʃən] n légende f.

captivate ['kæptiveit] vt captiver, fasciner.

captive ['kæptiv] a, n captif(ive).

captivity [kæp'tiviti] n captivité f.

capture ['kæptʃə*] vt capturer, prendre; (attention) capter // n capture f.

car [ka:*] n voiture f, auto f.

carafe [kə'ræf] n carafe f; (in restaurant: ~ **wine**) ≈ vin ouvert.

caramel ['kærəml] n caramel m.

carat ['kærət] n carat m.

caravan ['kærəvæn] n caravane f.

caraway ['kærəwei] n: ~ **seed** graine f de cumin, cumin m.

carbohydrates [ka:bəu'haidreits] npl (foods) aliments mpl riches en hydrate de carbone.

carbon ['ka:bən] n carbone m; ~ **copy** n carbone m; ~ **paper** n papier m carbone.

carburettor [ka:bju'rɛtə*] n carburateur m.

carcass ['ka:kəs] n carcasse f.

card [ka:d] n carte f; ~**board** n carton m; ~ **game** n jeu m de cartes.

cardiac ['ka:diæk] a cardiaque.

cardigan ['ka:digən] n cardigan m.

cardinal ['ka:dinl] a cardinal(e) // n cardinal m.

card index ['ka:dindɛks] n fichier m (alphabétique).

care [kɛə*] n soin m, attention f; (worry) souci m // vi: **to ~ about** se soucier de, s'intéresser à; **would you ~ to/for . . .?** voulez-vous ...?; **I wouldn't ~ to do it** je n'aimerais pas le faire; **in sb's ~** à la garde de qn, confié à qn; **to take ~** faire attention, prendre garde; **to take ~ of** vt s'occuper de, prendre soin de; **to ~**

for vt fus s'occuper de; (like) aimer; **I don't ~** ça m'est bien égal, peu m'importe; **I couldn't ~ less** cela m'est complètement égal, je m'en fiche complètement.

career [kə'riə*] n carrière f // vi (also: ~ **along**) aller à toute allure.

carefree ['kɛəfri:] a sans souci, insouciant(e).

careful ['kɛəful] a soigneux(euse); (cautious) prudent(e); (**be**) ~**!** (fais) attention!; ~**ly** ad avec soin, soigneusement; prudemment.

careless ['kɛəlis] a négligent(e); (heedless) insouciant(e); ~**ly** ad négligemment; avec insouciance; ~**ness** n manque m de soin, négligence f; insouciance f.

caress [kə'rɛs] n caresse f // vt caresser.

caretaker ['kɛəteikə*] n gardien/ne, concierge m/f.

car-ferry ['ka:fɛri] n (on sea) ferry (-boat) m; (on river) bac m.

cargo, ~es ['ka:gəu] n cargaison f, chargement m.

Caribbean [kæri'bi:ən] a: the ~ (**Sea**) la mer des Antilles or Caraïbes.

caricature ['kærikətjuə*] n caricature f.

carnal ['ka:nl] a charnel(le).

carnation [ka:'neiʃən] n œillet m.

carnival ['ka:nivəl] n (public celebration) carnaval m.

carol ['kærəl] n: (**Christmas**) ~ chant m de Noël.

carp [ka:p] n (fish) carpe f; **to ~ at** vt fus critiquer.

car park ['ka:pa:k] n parking m, parc m de stationnement.

carpenter ['ka:pintə*] n charpentier m.

carpentry ['ka:pintri] n charpenterie f, métier m de charpentier; (woodwork: at school etc) menuiserie f.

carpet ['ka:pit] n tapis m // vt recouvrir (d'un tapis).

carriage ['kæridʒ] n voiture f; (of goods) transport m; (: taxe) port m; (of typewriter) chariot m; (bearing) maintien m, port m; ~**way** n (part of road) chaussée f.

carrier ['kæriə*] n transporteur m, camionneur m; ~ **bag** n sac m en papier or en plastique; ~ **pigeon** n pigeon voyageur.

carrot ['kærət] n carotte f.

carry ['kæri] vt (subj: person) porter; (: vehicle) transporter; (a motion, bill) voter, adopter; (involve: responsibilities etc) comporter, impliquer // vi (sound) porter; **to be carried away** (fig) s'emballer, s'enthousiasmer; **to ~ on** vi: **to ~ on with sth/doing** continuer qch/à faire // vt entretenir, poursuivre; **to ~ out** vt (orders) exécuter; (investigation) effectuer; ~**cot** n porte-bébé m.

cart [ka:t] n charrette f // vt transporter.

cartilage ['ka:tilidʒ] n cartilage m.

cartographer [ka:'tɔgrəfə*] n cartographe m/f.

carton ['ka:tən] n (box) carton m; (of yogurt) pot m (en carton); (of cigarettes) cartouche f.

cartoon [kɑː'tuːn] n (PRESS) dessin m (humoristique); (satirical) caricature f; (comic strip) bande dessinée; (CINEMA) dessin animé; **~ist** n dessinateur/trice humoristique; caricaturiste m/f; auteur m de dessins animés; auteur m de bandes dessinées.

cartridge ['kɑːtrɪdʒ] n (for gun, pen) cartouche f; (for camera) chargeur m; (music tape) cassette f; (of record player) cellule f.

carve [kɑːv] vt (meat) découper; (wood, stone) tailler, sculpter; **carving** n (in wood etc) sculpture f; **carving knife** n couteau m à découper.

car wash ['kɑːwɔʃ] n station f de lavage (de voitures).

cascade [kæs'keɪd] n cascade f // vi tomber en cascade.

case [keɪs] n cas m; (LAW) affaire f, procès m; (box) caisse f, boîte f, étui m; (also: suit~) valise f; he hasn't put forward his ~ very well ses arguments ne sont guère convaincants; in ~ of en cas de; in ~ he au cas où il; just in ~ à tout hasard.

cash [kæʃ] n argent m; (COMM) argent liquide, numéraire m; liquidités fpl; (COMM: in payment) argent comptant, espèces fpl // vt encaisser; **to pay (in) ~** payer (en argent) comptant; **~ with order/ on delivery** (COMM) payable or paiement à la commande/livraison; **~book** n livre m de caisse; **~desk** n caisse f.

cashew [kæ'ʃuː] n (also: ~ nut) noix f de cajou.

cashier [kæ'ʃɪə*] n caissier/ère.

cashmere [kæʃ'mɪə*] n cachemire m.

cash payment ['kæʃ'peɪmənt] n paiement comptant, versement m en espèces.

cash register ['kæʃredʒɪstə*] n caisse enregistreuse.

casing ['keɪsɪŋ] n revêtement (protecteur), enveloppe (protectrice).

casino [kə'siːnəu] n casino m.

cask [kɑːsk] n tonneau m.

casket ['kɑːskɪt] n coffret m; (US: coffin) cercueil m.

casserole ['kæsərəul] n cocotte f; (food) ragoût m (en cocotte).

cassette [kæ'sɛt] n cassette f, musi-cassette f; **~player** lecteur m de cassettes; **~recorder** magnétophone m à cassettes.

cast [kɑːst] vt (pt, pp cast) (throw) jeter; (shed) perdre; se dépouiller de; (metal) couler, fondre // n (THEATRE) distribution f; (mould) moule m; (also: plaster ~) plâtre m; (THEATRE): **to ~ sb as Hamlet** attribuer à qn le rôle d'Hamlet; **to ~ one's vote** voter, exprimer son suffrage; **to ~ off** vi (NAUT) larguer les amarres.

castanets [kæstə'nɛts] npl castagnettes fpl.

castaway [kɑː'stəwəɪ] n naufragé/e.

caste [kɑːst] n caste f, classe sociale.

casting ['kɑːstɪŋ] a: **~ vote** voix prépondérante (pour départager).

cast iron ['kɑːst'aɪən] n fonte f.

castle ['kɑːsl] n château-fort m; (manor) château m.

castor ['kɑːstə*] n (wheel) roulette f; **~ oil** n huile f de ricin; **~ sugar** n sucre m semoule.

castrate [kæs'treɪt] vt châtrer.

casual ['kæʒjul] a (by chance) de hasard, fait(e) au hasard, fortuit(e); (irregular: work etc) temporaire; (unconcerned) désinvolte; **~ wear** n vêtements mpl sport inv; **~ labour** n main-d'œuvre f temporaire; **~ly** ad avec désinvolture, négligemment; fortuitement.

casualty ['kæʒjultɪ] n accidenté/e, blessé/e; (dead) victime f, mort/e; **heavy casualties** npl lourdes pertes.

cat [kæt] n chat m.

catalogue, catalog (US) ['kætələg] n catalogue m // vt cataloguer.

catalyst ['kætəlɪst] n catalyseur m.

catapult ['kætəpʌlt] n lance-pierres m inv, fronde f; (AVIAT, HISTORY) catapulte f.

cataract ['kætərækt] n (also MED) cataracte f.

catarrh [kə'tɑː*] n rhume m chronique, catarrhe f.

catastrophe [kə'tæstrəfɪ] n catastrophe f; **catastrophic** [kætə'strɔfɪk] a catastrophique.

catch [kætʃ] vb (pt,pp caught [cɔːt]) vt (ball, train, thief, cold) attraper; (person: by surprise) prendre, surprendre; (understand) saisir; (get entangled) accrocher // vi (fire) prendre // n (fish etc caught) prise f; (thief etc caught) capture f; (trick) attrape f; (TECH) loquet m; cliquet m; **to ~ sb's attention** or **eye** attirer l'attention de qn; **to ~ fire** prendre feu; **to ~ sight of** apercevoir; **to ~ up** vi se rattraper, combler son retard // vt (also: ~ up with) rattraper.

catching ['kætʃɪŋ] a (MED) contagieux(euse).

catchment area ['kætʃmənt'ɛərɪə] n (SCOL) aire f de recrutement; (GEO) bassin m hydrographique.

catch phrase ['kætʃfreɪz] n slogan m; expression toute faite.

catchy ['kætʃɪ] a (tune) facile à retenir.

catechism ['kætɪkɪzəm] n (REL) catéchisme m.

categoric(al) [kætɪ'gɔrɪk(əl)] a catégorique.

categorize ['kætɪgəraɪz] vt classer par catégories.

category ['kætɪgərɪ] n catégorie f.

cater ['keɪtə*] vi (gen: ~ for sb) préparer des repas, se charger de la restauration; **to ~ for** vt fus (needs) satisfaire, pourvoir à; (readers, consumers) s'adresser à, pourvoir aux besoins de; **~er** n traiteur m; fournisseur m; **~ing** n restauration f; approvisionnement m, ravitaillement m; **~ing (trade)** restauration f.

caterpillar ['kætəpɪlə*] n chenille f; **~ track** n chenille f; **~ vehicle** n véhicule m à chenille.

cathedral [kə'θiːdrəl] n cathédrale f.

catholic ['kæθəlɪk] a éclectique; universel(le); libéral(e); **C~** a,n (REL) catholique (m/f).

cattle ['kætl] npl bétail m, bestiaux mpl.

catty ['kætɪ] a méchant(e).
Caucasus ['kɔːkəsəs] n Caucase m.
caught [kɔːt] pt,pp of **catch**.
cauliflower ['kɔlɪflauə*] n chou-fleur m.
cause [kɔːz] n cause f // vt causer ; **there is no ~ for concern** il n'y a pas lieu de s'inquiéter.
causeway ['kɔːzweɪ] n chaussée (surélevée).
caustic ['kɔːstɪk] a caustique.
caution ['kɔːʃən] n prudence f; (warning) avertissement m // vt avertir, donner un avertissement à.
cautious ['kɔːʃəs] a prudent(e) ; **~ly** ad prudemment, avec prudence ; **~ness** n prudence f.
cavalier [kævə'lɪə*] a cavalier(ère), désinvolte.
cavalry ['kævəlrɪ] n cavalerie f.
cave [keɪv] n caverne f, grotte f; **to ~ in** vi (roof etc) s'effondrer ; **~man** n homme m des cavernes.
cavern ['kævən] n caverne f.
caviar(e) ['kævɪɑː*] n caviar m.
cavity ['kævɪtɪ] n cavité f.
cavort [kə'vɔːt] vi cabrioler, faire des cabrioles.
CBI n abbr of Confederation of British Industries (groupement du patronat).
cc abbr of cubic centimetres; carbon copy.
cease [siːs] vt,vi cesser ; **~fire** n cessez-le-feu m; **~less** a incessant(e), continuel(le).
cedar ['siːdə*] n cèdre m.
cede [siːd] vt céder.
cedilla [sɪ'dɪlə] n cédille f.
ceiling ['siːlɪŋ] n plafond m.
celebrate ['sɛlɪbreɪt] vt,vi célébrer ; **~d** a célèbre ; **celebration** [-'breɪʃən] n célébration f.
celebrity [sɪ'lɛbrɪtɪ] n célébrité f.
celery ['sɛlərɪ] n céleri m (en branches).
celestial [sɪ'lɛstɪəl] a céleste.
celibacy ['sɛlɪbəsɪ] n célibat m.
cell [sɛl] n (gen) cellule f; (ELEC) élément m (de pile).
cellar ['sɛlə*] n cave f.
'cellist ['tʃɛlɪst] n violoncelliste m/f.
'cello ['tʃɛləu] n violoncelle m.
cellophane ['sɛləfeɪn] n ® cellophane f ®.
cellular ['sɛljulə*] a cellulaire.
cellulose ['sɛljuləus] n cellulose f.
Celtic ['kɛltɪk, 'sɛltɪk] a celte.
cement [sə'mɛnt] n ciment m // vt cimenter.
cemetery ['sɛmɪtrɪ] n cimetière m.
cenotaph ['sɛnətɑːf] n cénotaphe m.
censor ['sɛnsə*] n censeur m ; **~ship** n censure f.
censure ['sɛnʃə*] vt blâmer, critiquer.
census ['sɛnsəs] n recensement m.
cent [sɛnt] n (US: coin) cent m, = 1:100 du dollar ; see also **per**.
centenary [sɛn'tiːnərɪ] n centenaire m.
center ['sɛntə*] n (US) = **centre**.
centi... ['sɛntɪ] prefix: **~grade** a centigrade ; **~litre** n centilitre m ; **~metre** n centimètre m.
centipede ['sɛntɪpiːd] n mille-pattes m inv.

central ['sɛntrəl] a central(e) ; **~ heating** n chauffage central ; **~ize** vt centraliser.
centre ['sɛntə*] n centre m; **~-forward** n (SPORT) avant-centre m // vt centrer ; (PHOT) cadrer **~-half** n (SPORT) demi-centre m.
centrifugal [sɛn'trɪfjugəl] a centrifuge.
century ['sɛntjurɪ] n siècle m.
ceramic [sɪ'ræmɪk] a céramique.
cereal ['siːrɪəl] n céréale f.
ceremony ['sɛrɪmənɪ] n cérémonie f; **to stand on ~** faire des façons.
certain ['sɜːtən] a certain(e) ; **to make ~ of** s'assurer de ; **for ~** certainement, sûrement ; **~ly** ad certainement ; **~ty** n certitude f.
certificate [sə'tɪfɪkɪt] n certificat m.
certify ['sɜːtɪfaɪ] vt certifier // vi: **to ~ to** attester.
cervix ['sɜːvɪks] n col m de l'utérus.
cessation [sə'seɪʃən] n cessation f, arrêt m.
cesspool ['sɛspuːl] n fosse f d'aisance.
Ceylon [sɪ'lɒn] n Ceylan m.
cf. (abbr = compare) cf., voir.
chafe [tʃeɪf] vt irriter, frotter contre.
chaffinch ['tʃæfɪntʃ] n pinson m.
chagrin ['ʃægrɪn] n contrariété f, déception f.
chain [tʃeɪn] n (gen) chaîne f // vt (also: **~ up**) enchaîner, attacher (avec une chaîne) ; **~ reaction** n réaction f en chaîne ; **to ~ smoke** vi fumer cigarette sur cigarette ; **~ store** n magasin m à succursales multiples.
chair [tʃɛə*] n chaise f; (armchair) fauteuil m; (of university) chaire f // vt (meeting) présider ; **~lift** n télésiège m ; **~man** n président m.
chalet ['ʃæleɪ] n chalet m.
chalice ['tʃælɪs] n calice m.
chalk [tʃɔːk] n craie f.
challenge ['tʃælɪndʒ] n défi m // vt défier ; (statement, right) mettre en question, contester ; **to ~ sb to a fight/game** inviter qn à se battre/à jouer (sous forme d'un défi) ; **to ~ sb to do** mettre qn au défi de faire ; **~r** n (SPORT) challenger m ; **challenging** a de défi, provocateur(trice).
chamber ['tʃeɪmbə*] n chambre f; **~ of commerce** chambre f de commerce ; **~maid** n femme f de chambre ; **~ music** n musique f de chambre ; **~pot** n pot m de chambre.
chamois ['ʃæmwɑː] n chamois m ; **~ leather** ['ʃæmɪlɛðə*] n peau f de chamois.
champagne [ʃæm'peɪn] n champagne m.
champion ['tʃæmpɪən] n champion/ne ; **~ship** n championnat m.
chance [tʃɑːns] n hasard m ; (opportunity) occasion f, possibilité f; (hope, likelihood) chance f // vt: **to ~ it** risquer (le coup), essayer // a fortuit(e), de hasard ; **there is little ~ of his coming** il est peu probable or il y a peu de chances qu'il vienne ; **to take a ~** prendre un risque ; **by ~** par hasard.
chancel ['tʃɑːnsəl] n chœur m.
chancellor ['tʃɑːnsələ*] n chancelier m ;

C~ of the Exchequer n chancelier m de l'Échiquier.

chandelier [ʃændə'lɪə*] n lustre m.

change [tʃeɪndʒ] vt (alter, replace, COMM: money) changer ; (switch, substitute: gear, hands, trains, clothes, one's name etc) changer de ; (transform): **to ~ sb into** changer or transformer qn en // vi (gen) changer ; (change clothes) se changer ; (be transformed): **to ~ into** se changer or transformer en // n changement m ; (money) monnaie f ; **to ~ one's mind** changer d'avis ; **a ~ of clothes** des vêtements de rechange ; **for a ~** pour changer ; **small ~** petite monnaie ; **to give sb ~ for or of £10** faire à qn la monnaie de 10 livres ; **~able** a (weather) variable ; **~over** n (to new system) changement m, passage m.

changing ['tʃeɪndʒɪŋ] a changeant(e) ; **~room** n (in shop) salon m d'essayage ; (SPORT) vestiaire m.

channel ['tʃænl] n (TV) chaîne f ; (waveband, groove, fig: medium) canal m ; (of river, sea) chenal m // vt canaliser ; **through the usual ~s** en suivant la filière habituelle ; **the (English) C~** la Manche ; **the C~ Islands** les îles de la Manche, les îles anglo-normandes.

chant [tʃɑ:nt] n chant m ; mélopée f ; psalmodie f // vt chanter, scander ; psalmodier.

chaos ['keɪɔs] n chaos m.

chaotic [keɪ'ɔtɪk] a chaotique.

chap [tʃæp] n (col: man) type m // vt (skin) gercer, crevasser.

chapel ['tʃæpəl] n chapelle f.

chaperon ['ʃæpərəun] n chaperon m // vt chaperonner.

chaplain ['tʃæplɪn] n aumônier m.

chapter ['tʃæptə*] n chapitre m.

char [tʃɑ:*] vt (burn) carboniser // vi (cleaner) faire des ménages // n = **charlady**.

character ['kærɪktə*] n caractère m ; (in novel, film) personnage m ; (eccentric) numéro m, phénomène m ; **~istic** [-'rɪstɪk] a,n caractéristique (f) ; **~ize** vt caractériser.

charade [ʃə'rɑ:d] n charade f.

charcoal ['tʃɑ:kəul] n charbon m de bois.

charge [tʃɑ:dʒ] n accusation f ; (LAW) inculpation f ; (cost) prix (demandé) ; (of gun, battery, MIL: attack) charge f // vt (LAW): **to ~sb (with)** inculper qn (de) ; (gun, battery, MIL: enemy) charger ; (customer, sum) faire payer // vi (gen with: up, along etc) foncer ; **~s** npl: **bank/labour ~s** frais mpl de banque/main-d'œuvre ; **to ~ in/out** entrer/sortir en trombe ; **to ~ down/up** dévaler/grimper à toute allure ; **is there a ~?** doit-on payer? ; **there's no ~** c'est gratuit, on ne fait pas payer ; **to take ~ of** se charger de ; **to be in ~ of** être responsable de, s'occuper de ; **to have ~ of sb** avoir la charge de qn ; **they ~d us £10 for the meal** ils nous ont fait payer le repas 10 livres, ils nous ont compté 10 livres pour le repas ; **how much do you ~ for this repair?** combien demandez-vous pour cette réparation? ; **to ~ an**

expense (up) to sb mettre une dépense sur le compte de qn.

charitable ['tʃærɪtəbl] a charitable.

charity ['tʃærɪtɪ] n charité f ; institution f charitable or de bienfaisance, œuvre f (de charité).

charlady ['tʃɑ:leɪdɪ] n femme f de ménage.

charm [tʃɑ:m] n charme m // vt charmer, enchanter ; **~ing** a charmant(e).

chart [tʃɑ:t] n tableau m, diagramme m ; graphique m ; (map) carte marine // vt dresser or établir la carte de.

charter ['tʃɑ:tə*] vt (plane) affréter // n (document) charte f ; **~ed accountant** n expert-comptable m ; **~ flight** n charter m.

charwoman ['tʃɑ:wumən] n = **charlady**.

chase [tʃeɪs] vt poursuivre, pourchasser // n poursuite f, chasse f.

chasm ['kæzəm] n gouffre m, abîme m.

chassis ['ʃæsɪ] n châssis m.

chastity ['tʃæstɪtɪ] n chasteté f.

chat [tʃæt] vi (also: **have a ~**) bavarder, causer // n conversation f.

chatter ['tʃætə*] vi (person) bavarder, papoter // n bavardage m, papotage m ; **my teeth are ~ing** je claque des dents ; **~box** n moulin m à paroles, babillard/e.

chatty ['tʃætɪ] a (style) familier(ère) ; (person) enclin(e) à bavarder or au papotage.

chauffeur ['ʃəufə*] n chauffeur m (de maître).

cheap [tʃi:p] a à bon marché inv, pas cher(chère) ; (joke) facile, d'un goût douteux ; (poor quality) à bon marché, de qualité médiocre // ad à bon marché, pour pas cher ; **~en** vt rabaisser, déprécier ; **~ly** ad à bon marché, à bon compte.

cheat [tʃi:t] vi tricher // vt tromper, duper ; (rob) escroquer // n tricheur/euse ; escroc m ; (trick) duperie f, tromperie f ; **~ing** n tricherie f.

check [tʃɛk] vt vérifier ; (passport, ticket) contrôler ; (halt) enrayer ; (restrain) maîtriser // n vérification f ; contrôle m ; (curb) frein m ; (bill) addition f ; (pattern: gen pl) carreaux mpl ; (US) = **cheque** ; **to ~ in** vi (in hotel) remplir sa fiche (d'hôtel) ; (at airport) se présenter à l'enregistrement // vt (luggage) (faire) enregistrer ; **to ~ off** vt cocher ; **to ~ out** vi (in hotel) régler sa note // vt (luggage) retirer ; **to ~ up** vi: **to ~ up (on sth)** vérifier (qch) ; **to ~ up on sb** se renseigner sur le compte de qn ; **~ers** n (US) jeu m de dames ; **~mate** n échec et mat m ; **~point** n contrôle m ; **~up** n (MED) examen médical, check-up m.

cheek [tʃi:k] n joue f ; (impudence) toupet m, culot m ; **~bone** n pommette f ; **~y** a effronté(e), culotté(e).

cheer [tʃɪə*] vt acclamer, applaudir ; (gladden) réjouir, réconforter // vi applaudir // n (gen pl) acclamations fpl, applaudissements mpl ; bravos mpl, hourras mpl ; **~s!** (à votre) santé! ; **to ~ up** vi se dérider, reprendre courage // vt remonter le moral à or de, dérider, égayer ; **~ful** a gai(e), joyeux(euse) ; **~fulness** n gaieté f, bonne humeur ; **~io** excl salut!, au revoir! ; **~less** a sombre, triste.

cheese [tʃiːz] n fromage m; **~board** n plateau m à fromages.

chef [ʃɛf] n chef (cuisinier).

chemical [ˈkɛmɪkəl] a chimique // n produit m chimique.

chemist [ˈkɛmɪst] n pharmacien/ne; (scientist) chimiste m/f; **~ry** n chimie f; **~'s (shop)** n pharmacie f.

cheque [tʃɛk] n chèque m; **~book** n chéquier m, carnet m de chèques.

chequered [ˈtʃɛkəd] a (fig) varié(e).

cherish [ˈtʃɛrɪʃ] vt chérir; (hope etc) entretenir.

cheroot [ʃəˈruːt] n cigare m de Manille.

cherry [ˈtʃɛrɪ] n cerise f.

chess [tʃɛs] n échecs mpl; **~board** n échiquier m; **~man** n pièce f (de jeu d'échecs); **~player** n joueur/euse d'échecs.

chest [tʃɛst] n poitrine f; (box) coffre m, caisse f; **~ of drawers** n commode f.

chestnut [ˈtʃɛsnʌt] n châtaigne f; **~ (tree)** n châtaignier m.

chew [tʃuː] vt mâcher; **~ing gum** n chewing-gum m.

chic [ʃiːk] a chic inv, élégant(e).

chick [tʃɪk] n poussin m.

chicken [ˈtʃɪkɪn] n poulet m; **~ feed** n (fig) broutilles fpl, bagatelle f; **~ pox** n varicelle f.

chick pea [ˈtʃɪkpiː] n pois m chiche.

chicory [ˈtʃɪkərɪ] n (for coffee) chicorée f; (salad) endive f.

chief [tʃiːf] n chef m // a principal(e); **~ly** ad principalement, surtout.

chiffon [ˈʃɪfɔn] n mousseline f de soie.

chilblain [ˈtʃɪlbleɪn] n engelure f.

child, pl **~ren** [tʃaɪld, ˈtʃɪldrən] n enfant m/f; **~birth** n accouchement m; **~hood** n enfance f; **~ish** a puéril(e), enfantin(e); **~like** a innocent(e), pur(e); **~ minder** n garde f d'enfants.

Chile [ˈtʃɪlɪ] n Chili m; **~an** a chilien(ne) // n Chilien/ne.

chill [tʃɪl] n froid m; (MED) refroidissement m, coup m de froid // a froid(e), glacial(e) // vt faire frissonner; refroidir; (CULIN) mettre au frais, rafraîchir; **serve ~ed** à servir frais; **~y** a froid(e), glacé(e); (sensitive to cold) frileux(euse); **to feel ~y** avoir froid.

chime [tʃaɪm] n carillon m // vi carillonner, sonner.

chimney [ˈtʃɪmnɪ] n cheminée f.

chimpanzee [tʃɪmpænˈziː] n chimpanzé m.

chin [tʃɪn] n menton m.

china [ˈtʃaɪnə] n porcelaine f; (vaisselle f en) porcelaine.

China [ˈtʃaɪnə] n Chine f.

Chinese [tʃaɪˈniːz] a chinois(e) // n (pl inv) Chinois/e; (LING) chinois m.

chink [tʃɪŋk] n (opening) fente f, fissure f; (noise) tintement m.

chip [tʃɪp] n (gen pl: CULIN) frite f; (of wood) copeau m; (of glass, stone) éclat m // vt (cup, plate) ébrécher; **~board** n aggloméré m; **~pings** npl: **loose ~pings** gravillons mpl.

chiropodist [kɪˈrɔpədɪst] n pédicure m/f.

chirp [tʃəːp] n pépiement m, gazouillis m // vi pépier, gazouiller.

chisel [ˈtʃɪzl] n ciseau m.

chit [tʃɪt] n mot m, note f.

chitchat [ˈtʃɪttʃæt] n bavardage m, papotage m.

chivalrous [ˈʃɪvəlrəs] a chevaleresque.

chivalry [ˈʃɪvəlrɪ] n chevalerie f; esprit m chevaleresque.

chives [tʃaɪvz] npl ciboulette f, civette f.

chloride [ˈklɔːraɪd] n chlorure m.

chlorine [ˈklɔːriːn] n chlore m.

chock [tʃɔk] n cale f; **~-a-block, ~-full** a plein(e) à craquer.

chocolate [ˈtʃɔklɪt] n chocolat m.

choice [tʃɔɪs] n choix m // a de choix.

choir [ˈkwaɪə*] n chœur m, chorale f; **~boy** n jeune choriste m, petit chanteur.

choke [tʃəuk] vi étouffer // vt étrangler; étouffer; (block) boucher, obstruer // n (AUT) starter m.

cholera [ˈkɔlərə] n choléra m.

choose, pt **chose,** pp **chosen** [tʃuːz, tʃəuz, ˈtʃəuzn] vt choisir; **to ~ to do** décider de faire, juger bon de faire.

chop [tʃɔp] vt (wood) couper (à la hache); (CULIN: also: **~ up**) couper (fin), émincer, hacher (en morceaux) // n coup m (de hache, du tranchant de la main); (CULIN) côtelette f; **~s** npl (jaws) mâchoires fpl; babines fpl; **to ~ down** vt (tree) abattre; **~py** a (sea) un peu agité(e); **~sticks** npl baguettes fpl.

choral [ˈkɔːrəl] a choral(e), chanté(e) en chœur.

chord [kɔːd] n (MUS) accord m.

chore [tʃɔː*] n travail m de routine; **household ~s** travaux mpl du ménage.

choreographer [kɔrɪˈɔgrəfə*] n chorégraphe m/f.

chorister [ˈkɔrɪstə*] n choriste m/f.

chortle [ˈtʃɔːtl] vi glousser.

chorus [ˈkɔːrəs] n chœur m; (repeated part of song, also fig) refrain m.

chose [tʃəuz] pt of **choose.**

chosen [ˈtʃəuzn] pp of **choose.**

chow [tʃau] n (dog) chow-chow m.

Christ [kraɪst] n Christ m.

christen [ˈkrɪsn] vt baptiser; **~ing** n baptême m.

Christian [ˈkrɪstɪən] a,n chrétien(ne); **~ity** [-ˈænɪtɪ] n christianisme m; chrétienté f; **~ name** n prénom m.

Christmas [ˈkrɪsməs] n Noël m or f; **~ card** n carte f de Noël; **~ Eve** n la veille de Noël; la nuit de Noël; **~ tree** n arbre m de Noël.

chrome [krəum] n = **chromium.**

chromium [ˈkrəumɪəm] n chrome m; (also: **~ plating**) chromage m.

chromosome [ˈkrəuməsəum] n chromosome m.

chronic [ˈkrɔnɪk] a chronique.

chronicle [ˈkrɔnɪkl] n chronique f.

chronological [krɔnəˈlɔdʒɪkəl] a chronologique.

chrysanthemum [krɪˈsænθəməm] n chrysanthème m.

chubby [ˈtʃʌbɪ] a potelé(e), rondelet(te).

chuck [tʃʌk] vt lancer, jeter ; **to ~ out** vt flanquer dehors *or* à la porte ; **to ~ (up)** vt lâcher, plaquer.

chuckle ['tʃʌkl] vi glousser.

chum [tʃʌm] n copain/copine.

chunk [tʃʌŋk] n gros morceau ; (*of bread*) quignon m.

church [tʃə:tʃ] n église f ; **~yard** n cimetière m.

churlish ['tʃə:liʃ] a grossier(ère) ; hargneux(euse).

churn [tʃə:n] n (*for butter*) baratte f ; (*for transport:* **milk ~**) (grand) bidon à lait.

chute [ʃu:t] n glissoire f ; (*also:* **rubbish ~**) vide-ordures m inv ; (*children's slide*) toboggan m.

chutney ['tʃʌtni] n condiment m à base de fruits.

CID n (*abbr of Criminal Investigation Department*) ≈ Police f judiciaire (P.J.).

cider ['saidə*] n cidre m.

cigar [si'gɑ:*] n cigare m.

cigarette [sigə'rɛt] n cigarette f ; **~ case** n étui m à cigarettes ; **~ end** n mégot m ; **~ holder** n fume-cigarettes m inv.

cinch [sintʃ] n (*col*): **it's a ~** c'est du gâteau, c'est l'enfance de l'art.

cinder ['sində*] n cendre f.

cine ['sini]: **~-camera** n caméra f ; **~-film** n film m.

cinema ['sinəmə] n cinéma m.

cine-projector [siniprə'dʒɛktə*] n projecteur m de cinéma.

cinnamon ['sinəmən] n cannelle f.

cipher ['saifə*] n code secret ; (*fig: faceless employee etc*) numéro m.

circle ['sə:kl] n cercle m ; (*in cinema*) balcon m // vi faire *or* décrire des cercles // vt (*surround*) entourer, encercler ; (*move round*) faire le tour de, tourner autour de.

circuit ['sə:kit] n circuit m ; **~ous** [sə:'kjuitəs] a indirect(e), qui fait un détour.

circular ['sə:kjulə*] a circulaire // n circulaire f.

circulate ['sə:kjuleit] vi circuler // vt faire circuler ; **circulation** [-'leiʃən] n circulation f ; (*of newspaper*) tirage m.

circumcise ['sə:kəmsaiz] vt circoncire.

circumference [sə'kʌmfərəns] n circonférence f.

circumspect ['sə:kəmspɛkt] a circonspect(e).

circumstances ['sə:kəmstənsiz] npl circonstances fpl ; (*financial condition*) moyens mpl, situation financière.

circus ['sə:kəs] n cirque m.

cistern ['sistən] n réservoir m (d'eau) ; (*in toilet*) réservoir de la chasse d'eau.

cite [sait] vt citer.

citizen ['sitizn] n (*POL*) citoyen/ne ; (*resident*): **the ~s of this town** les habitants de cette ville ; **~ship** n citoyenneté f.

citrus fruit ['sitrəs'fru:t] n agrume m.

city ['siti] n ville f, cité f ; **the C~** la Cité de Londres (*centre des affaires*).

civic ['sivik] a civique.

civil ['sivil] a civil(e) ; poli(e), civil ; **~ engineer** n ingénieur civil ; **~ engineering** n génie civil, travaux publics ; **~ian** [si'viliən] a,n civil(e).

civilization [sivilai'zeiʃən] n civilisation f.

civilized ['sivilaizd] a civilisé(e) ; (*fig*) où règnent les bonnes manières, empreint(e) d'une courtoisie de bon ton.

civil: **~ law** n code civil ; (*study*) droit civil ; **~ servant** n fonctionnaire m/f ; **C~ Service** n fonction publique, administration f ; **~ war** n guerre civile.

claim [kleim] vt revendiquer ; demander, prétendre à ; déclarer, prétendre // vi (*for insurance*) faire une déclaration de sinistre // n revendication f ; demande f ; prétention f, déclaration f ; (*right*) droit m, titre m ; (*insurance*) **~** demande f d'indemnisation, déclaration f de sinistre ; **~ant** n (*ADMIN, LAW*) requérant/e.

clam [klæm] n palourde f.

clamber ['klæmbə*] vi grimper, se hisser.

clammy ['klæmi] a humide et froid(e) (au toucher), moite.

clamp [klæmp] n étau m à main ; agrafe f, crampon m // vt serrer ; cramponner ; **to ~ down on** vt fus sévir contre, prendre des mesures draconiennes à l'égard de.

clan [klæn] n clan m.

clang [klæŋ] vi applaudir // vt: bruit m *or* fracas m métallique.

clap [klæp] vi applaudir // vt: **to ~ (one's hands)** battre des mains // n claquement m ; tape f ; **~ping** n applaudissements mpl.

claret ['klærət] n (vin m de) bordeaux m (rouge).

clarification [klærifi'keiʃən] n (*fig*) clarification f, éclaircissement m.

clarify ['klærifai] vt clarifier.

clarinet [klæri'nɛt] n clarinette f.

clarity ['klæriti] n clarté f.

clash [klæʃ] n choc m ; (*fig*) conflit m // vi se heurter ; être *or* entrer en conflit.

clasp [klɑ:sp] n fermoir m // vt serrer, étreindre.

class [klɑ:s] n (*gen*) classe f // vt classer, classifier.

classic ['klæsik] a classique // n (*author*) classique m ; (*race etc*) classique f ; **~al** a classique.

classification [klæsifi'keiʃən] n classification f.

classified ['klæsifaid] a (*information*) secret(ète) ; **~ ads**, petites annonces.

classify ['klæsifai] vt classifier, classer.

classmate ['klɑ:smeit] n camarade m/f de classe.

classroom ['klɑ:srum] n (salle f de) classe f.

clatter ['klætə*] n cliquetis m ; caquetage m // vi cliqueter ; (*talk*) caqueter, jacasser.

clause [klɔ:z] n clause f ; (*LING*) proposition f.

claustrophobia [klɔ:strə'fəubiə] n claustrophobie f.

claw [klɔ:] n griffe f ; (*of bird of prey*) serre f ; (*of lobster*) pince f // vt griffer ; déchirer.

clay [klei] n argile f.

clean [kli:n] a propre ; (*clear, smooth*) net(te) // vt nettoyer ; **to ~ out** vt nettoyer (à fond) ; **to ~ up** vt nettoyer ; (*fig*) remettre de l'ordre dans ; **~er** n (*person*) nettoyeur/euse, femme f de ménage ; (*also:* **dry ~er**) teinturier/ière ; (*product*) détachant m ; **~ing** n nettoyage *m*; ~**liness** ['klɛnlɪnɪs] *n* propreté *f*; ~**ly** *ad* proprement; nettement.

cleanse [klɛnz] *vt* nettoyer; purifier; ~**r** *n* détergent *m*; (*for face*) démaquillant *m*; **cleansing department** *n* service *m* de voirie.

clean-shaven ['kli:n'ʃeɪvn] *a* rasé(e) de près.

clean-up ['kli:n'ʌp] *n* nettoyage *m*.

clear [klɪə*] *a* clair(e); (*road, way*) libre, dégagé(e) // *vt* dégager, déblayer, débarrasser; faire évacuer; (*COMM: goods*) liquider; (*LAW: suspect*) innocenter; (*obstacle*) franchir *or* sauter sans heurter // *vi* (*weather*) s'éclaircir; (*fog*) se dissiper // *ad*: ~ **of** à distance de, à l'écart de; **to** ~ **one's throat** s'éclaircir la gorge; **to** ~ **up** *vi* s'éclaircir, se dissiper // *vt* ranger, mettre en ordre; (*mystery*) éclaircir, résoudre; ~**ance** *n* (*removal*) déblayage *m*; (*free space*) dégagement *m*; (*permission*) autorisation *f*; ~**ance sale** *n* liquidation *f*; ~**-cut** *a* précise(e), nettement défini(e); ~**ing** *n* clairière *f*; (*BANKING*) compensation *f*, clearing *m*; ~**ly** *ad* clairement; de toute évidence; ~**way** *n* (*Brit*) route *f* à stationnement interdit.

cleavage ['kli:vɪdʒ] *n* (*of dress*) décolleté *m*.

clef [klɛf] *n* (*MUS*) clé *f*.

clench [klɛntʃ] *vt* serrer.

clergy ['klə:dʒɪ] *n* clergé *m*; ~**man** *n* ecclésiastique *m*.

clerical ['klɛrɪkəl] *a* de bureau, d'employé de bureau; (*REL*) clérical(e), du clergé.

clerk [klɑ:k, (*US*) klə:rk] *n* employé/e de bureau; (*US: salesman/woman*) vendeur/-euse.

clever ['klɛvə*] *a* (*mentally*) intelligent(e); (*deft, crafty*) habile, adroit(e); (*device, arrangement*) ingénieux(euse), astucieux(euse).

cliché ['kli:ʃeɪ] *n* cliché *m*.

click [klɪk] *vi* faire un bruit sec *or* un déclic.

client ['klaɪənt] *n* client/e; ~**ele** [kli:ɑ:n'tɛl] *n* clientèle *f*.

cliff [klɪf] *n* falaise *f*.

climate ['klaɪmɪt] *n* climat *m*.

climax ['klaɪmæks] *n* apogée *m*, point culminant; (*sexual*) orgasme *m*.

climb [klaɪm] *vi* grimper, monter // *vt* gravir, escalader, monter sur // *n* montée *f*, escalade *f*; **to** ~ **down** *vi* (re)descendre; ~**er** *n* (*also*: **rock** ~**er**) grimpeur/euse, varappeur/ euse; ~**ing** *n* (*also*: **rock** ~**ing**) escalade *f*, varappe *f*.

clinch [klɪntʃ] *vt* (*deal*) conclure, sceller.

cling, *pt, pp* **clung** [klɪŋ, klʌŋ] *vi*: **to** ~ (**to**) se cramponner (à), s'accrocher (à); (*of clothes*) coller (à).

clinic ['klɪnɪk] *n* centre médical; ~**al** *a* clinique.

clink [klɪŋk] *vi* tinter, cliqueter.

clip [klɪp] *n* (*for hair*) barrette *f*; (*also*: **paper** ~) trombone *m*; (*also*: **bulldog** ~) pince *f* de bureau; (*holding hose etc*) collier *m or* bague *f* (métallique) de serrage // *vt* (*also*: ~ **together**: *papers*) attacher; (*hair, nails*) couper; (*hedge*) tailler; ~**pers** *npl* tondeuse *f*; (*also*: **nail** ~**pers**) coupe-ongles *m inv*.

clique [kli:k] *n* clique *f*, coterie *f*.

cloak [kləuk] *n* grande cape; ~**room** *n* (*for coats etc*) vestiaire *m*; (*W.C.*) toilettes *fpl*.

clock [klɔk] *n* (*large*) horloge *f*; (*small*) pendule *f*; ~**wise** *ad* dans le sens des aiguilles d'une montre; ~**work** *n* mouvement *m* (d'horlogerie); rouages *mpl*, mécanisme *m*.

clog [klɔg] *n* sabot *m* // *vt* boucher, encrasser // *vi* se boucher, s'encrasser.

cloister ['klɔɪstə*] *n* cloître *m*.

close *a, ad and derivatives* [kləus] *a* près, proche; (*writing, texture*) serré(e); (*watch*) étroit(e), strict(e); (*examination*) attentif(ive), minutieux(euse); (*weather*) lourd(e), étouffant(e); (*room*) mal aéré(e) // *ad* près, à proximité; **a** ~ **friend** un ami intime; **to have a** ~ **shave** (*fig*) l'échapper belle // *vb and derivatives* [kləuz] *vt* fermer // *vi* (*shop etc*) fermer; (*lid, door etc*) se fermer; (*end*) se terminer, se conclure // *n* (*end*) conclusion *f*; **to** ~ **down** *vt,vi* fermer (définitivement); ~**d** *a* (*shop etc*) fermé(e); (*road*) fermé à la circulation; ~**d shop** *n* organisation *f* qui n'admet que des travailleurs syndiqués; ~**ly** *ad* (*examine, watch*) de près.

closet ['klɔzɪt] *n* (*cupboard*) placard *m*, réduit *m*.

close-up ['kləusʌp] *n* gros plan.

closure ['kləuʒə*] *n* fermeture *f*.

clot [klɔt] *n* (*gen: blood* ~) caillot *m* // *vi* (*blood*) former des caillots; (: *external bleeding*) se coaguler; ~**ted cream** *n* crème caillée.

cloth [klɔθ] *n* (*material*) tissu *m*, étoffe *f*; (*also*: **tea~**) torchon *m*; lavette *f*.

clothe [kləuð] *vt* habiller, vêtir; ~**s** *npl* vêtements *mpl*, habits *mpl*; ~**s brush** *n* brosse *f* à habits; ~**s line** *n* corde *f* (à linge); ~**s peg** *n* pince *f* à linge.

clothing ['kləuðɪŋ] *n* = **clothes**.

cloud [klaud] *n* nuage *m*; ~**burst** *n* violente averse; ~**y** *a* nuageux(euse), couvert(e); (*liquid*) trouble.

clout [klaut] *n* (*blow*) taloche *f* // *vt* flanquer une taloche à.

clove [kləuv] *n* clou *m* de girofle; ~ **of garlic** gousse *f* d'ail.

clover ['kləuvə*] *n* trèfle *m*; ~**leaf** *n* feuille *f* de trèfle; ~**leaf junction** (*AUT*) croisement *m* en trèfle.

clown [klaun] *n* clown *m* // *vi* (*also*: ~ **about**, ~ **around**) faire le clown.

club [klʌb] *n* (*society*) club *m*; (*weapon*) massue *f*, matraque *f*; (*also*: **golf** ~) club // *vt* matraquer // *vi*: **to** ~ **together** s'associer; ~**s** *npl* (*CARDS*) trèfle *m*; ~**house** *n* pavillon *m*.

cluck [klʌk] *vi* glousser.

clue [klu:] *n* indice *m*; (*in crosswords*) définition *f*; **I haven't a** ~ je n'en ai pas la moindre idée.

clump [klʌmp] *n*: ~ **of trees** bouquet *m* d'arbres.

clumsy ['klʌmzɪ] *a* (*person*) gauche, maladroit(e); (*object*) malcommode, peu maniable.

clung [klʌŋ] *pt, pp of* **cling**.

cluster ['klʌstə*] *n* (petit) groupe // *vi* se rassembler.

clutch [klʌtʃ] n (grip, grasp) étreinte f, prise f; (AUT) embrayage m // vt agripper, serrer fort; **to ~ at** se cramponner à.

clutter ['klʌtə*] vt encombrer.

Co. abbr of county; **company**.

c/o (abbr of care of) c/o, aux bons soins de.

coach [kəutʃ] n (bus) autocar m; (horse-drawn) diligence f; (of train) voiture f, wagon m; (SPORT: trainer) entraîneur/euse // (school: tutor) répétiteur/trice // vt entraîner; donner des leçons particulières à.

coagulate [kəu'ægjuleɪt] vt coaguler // vi se coaguler.

coal [kəul] n charbon m; **~ face** n front m de taille; (**~**) **face workers** npl mineurs mpl de fond; **~field** n bassin houiller.

coalition [kəuə'lɪʃən] n coalition f.

coalman, coal merchant ['kəulmən, 'kəulmə:tʃənt] n charbonnier m, marchand m de charbon.

coalmine ['kəulmaɪn] n mine f de charbon.

coarse [kɔ:s] a grossier(ère), rude.

coast [kəust] n côte f // vi (with cycle etc) descendre en roue libre; **~al** a côtier(ère); **~er** n caboteur m; **~guard** n garde-côte m; **~line** n côte f, littoral m.

coat [kəut] n manteau m; (of animal) pelage m, poil m; (of paint) couche f // vt couvrir, enduire; **~ of arms** n blason m, armoiries fpl; **~ hanger** n cintre m; **~ing** n couche f, enduit m.

coax [kəuks] vt persuader par des cajoleries.

cob [kɔb] n see **corn**.

cobbles, cobblestones ['kɔblz, 'kɔblstəunz] npl pavés (ronds).

cobra ['kəubrə] n cobra m.

cobweb ['kɔbwɛb] n toile f d'araignée.

cocaine [kə'keɪn] n cocaïne f.

cock [kɔk] n (rooster) coq m; (male bird) mâle m // vt (gun) armer; **to ~ one's ears** (fig) dresser l'oreille; **~erel** n jeune coq m; **~-eyed** a (fig) de travers; qui louche; qui ne tient pas debout (fig).

cockle ['kɔkl] n coque f.

cockney ['kɔknɪ] n cockney m/f (habitant des quartiers populaires de l'East End de Londres), ≈ faubourien/ne.

cockpit ['kɔkpɪt] n (in aircraft) poste m de pilotage, cockpit m.

cockroach ['kɔkrəutʃ] n cafard m, cancrelat m.

cocktail ['kɔkteɪl] n cocktail m; **~ cabinet** n (meuble-)bar m; **~ party** n cocktail m; **~ shaker** n shaker m.

cocoa ['kəukəu] n cacao m.

coconut ['kəukənʌt] n noix f de coco.

cocoon [kə'ku:n] n cocon m.

cod [kɔd] n morue (fraîche), cabillaud m.

code [kəud] n code m.

codify ['kəudɪfaɪ] vt codifier.

coeducational ['kəuɛdju'keɪʃənl] a mixte.

cerce [kəu'ə:s] vt contraindre; **coercion** [-'ə:ʃən] n contrainte f.

coexistence ['kəuɪg'zɪstəns] n coexistence f.

coffee ['kɔfɪ] n café m; **~ grounds** npl marc m de café; **~pot** n cafetière f; **~ table** n (petite) table basse.

coffin ['kɔfɪn] n cercueil m.

cog [kɔg] n dent f (d'engrenage); **~wheel** n roue dentée.

cogent ['kəudʒənt] a puissant(e), convaincant(e).

cognac ['kɔnjæk] n cognac m.

coherent [kəu'hɪərənt] a cohérent(e).

coil [kɔɪl] n rouleau m, bobine f; (one loop) anneau m, spire f; (contraceptive) stérilet m // vt enrouler.

coin [kɔɪn] n pièce f de monnaie // vt (word) inventer; **~age** n monnaie f, système m monétaire; **~-box** n cabine f téléphonique.

coincide [kəuɪn'saɪd] vi coïncider; **~nce** [kəu'ɪnsɪdəns] n coïncidence f.

coke [kəuk] n coke m.

colander ['kɔləndə*] n passoire f (à légumes).

cold [kəuld] a froid(e) // n froid m; (MED) rhume m; **it's ~** il fait froid; **to be ~** avoir froid; **to have ~ feet** avoir froid aux pieds; (fig) avoir la frousse or la trouille; **to give sb the ~ shoulder** battre froid à qn; **~ly** a froidement; **~ sore** n herpès m.

coleslaw ['kəulslɔ:] n sorte de salade de chou cru.

colic ['kɔlɪk] n colique(s) f(pl).

collaborate [kə'læbəreɪt] vi collaborer; **collaboration** [-'reɪʃən] n collaboration f; **collaborator** n collaborateur/trice.

collage [kɔ'lɑ:ʒ] n (ART) collage m.

collapse [kə'læps] vi s'effondrer, s'écrouler // n effondrement m, écroulement m.

collapsible [kə'læpsəbl] a pliant(e); télescopique.

collar ['kɔlə*] n (of coat, shirt) col m; **~bone** n clavicule f.

collate [kɔ'leɪt] vt collationner.

colleague ['kɔli:g] n collègue m/f.

collect [kə'lɛkt] vt rassembler; ramasser; (as a hobby) collectionner; (call and pick up) (passer) prendre; (mail) faire la levée de, ramasser; (money owed) encaisser; (donations, subscriptions) recueillir // vi se rassembler; s'amasser; **~ed** a: **~ed works** œuvres complètes; **~ion** [kə'lɛkʃən] n collection f; levée f; (for money) collecte f, quête f.

collective [kə'lɛktɪv] a collectif(ive).

collector [kə'lɛktə*] n collectionneur m; (of taxes) percepteur m; (of rent, cash) encaisseur m.

college ['kɔlɪdʒ] n collège m; **~ of education** ≈ école normale.

collide [kə'laɪd] vi: **to ~ (with)** entrer en collision (avec); (fig) entrer en conflit (avec), se heurter (à).

colliery ['kɔlɪərɪ] n mine f de charbon, houillère f.

collision [kə'lɪʒən] n collision f, heurt m; (fig) conflit m.

colloquial [kə'ləukwɪəl] a familier(ère).

colon ['kəulən] n (sign) deux-points mpl; (MED) côlon m.

colonel ['kə:nl] n colonel m.

colonial [kə'ləunɪəl] a colonial(e).

colonize ['kɔlənaɪz] vt coloniser.

colony ['kɔlənɪ] n colonie f.
color ['kʌlə*] n,vt (US) = colour.
Colorado [kɔlə'rɑːdəu]: ~ **beetle** n doryphore m.
colossal [kə'lɔsl] a colossal(e).
colour, color (US) ['kʌlə*] n couleur f // vt colorer; peindre; (with crayons) colorier; (news) fausser, exagérer; ~s npl (of party, club) couleurs fpl; ~ **bar** n discrimination raciale (dans un établissement etc); ~-**blind** a daltonien(ne); ~**ed** a coloré(e); (photo) en couleur // n: ~**eds** personnes fpl de couleur; ~ **film** n (for camera) pellicule f (en) couleur; ~**ful** a coloré(e), vif(vive); (personality) pittoresque, haut(e) en couleurs; ~ **scheme** n combinaison f de(s) couleurs; ~ **television** n télévision f en couleur.
colt [kəult] n poulain m.
column ['kɔləm] n colonne f; ~**ist** ['kɔləmnɪst] n rédacteur/trice d'une rubrique.
coma ['kəumə] n coma m.
comb [kəum] n peigne m // vt (hair) peigner; (area) ratisser, passer au peigne fin.
combat ['kɔmbæt] n combat m // vt combattre, lutter contre.
combination [kɔmbɪ'neɪʃən] n (gen) combinaison f.
combine vb [kəm'baɪn] vt combiner; (one quality with another) joindre (à), allier (à) // vi s'associer; (CHEM) se combiner // n ['kɔmbaɪn] association f; (ECON) trust m; ~ (**harvester**) n moissonneuse-batteuse(-lieuse) f.
combustible [kəm'bʌstɪbl] a combustible.
combustion [kəm'bʌstʃən] n combustion f.
come, pt **came**, pp **come** [kʌm, keɪm] vi venir; arriver; to ~ **into sight** or **view** apparaître; to ~ **to** (decision etc) parvenir or arriver à; to ~ **undone/loose** se défaire/desserrer; to ~ **about** vi se produire, arriver; to ~ **across** vt fus rencontrer par hasard, tomber sur; to ~ **along** vi = to **come on**; to ~ **apart** vi s'en aller en morceaux; se détacher; to ~ **away** vi partir, s'en aller; se détacher; to ~ **back** vi revenir; to ~ **by** vt fus (acquire) obtenir, se procurer; to ~ **down** vi descendre; (prices) baisser; (buildings) s'écrouler; être démoli(e); to ~ **forward** vi s'avancer; se présenter, s'annoncer; to ~ **from** vi être originaire de; venir de; to ~ **in** vi entrer; to ~ **in for** vt fus (criticism etc) être l'objet de; to ~ **into** vt fus (money) hériter de; to ~ **off** vi (button) se détacher; (stain) s'enlever; (attempt) réussir; to ~ **on** vi (pupil, undertaking) faire des progrès, avancer; ~ **on!** viens!; allons!, allez!; to ~ **out** vi sortir; (book) paraître; (strike) cesser le travail, se mettre en grève; to ~ **to** vi revenir à soi; to ~ **up** vi monter; to ~ **up against** vt fus (resistance, difficulties) rencontrer; to ~ **up with** vt fus: he came up with an idea il a eu une idée, il a proposé quelque chose; to ~ **upon** vt fus tomber sur; ~**back** n (THEATRE etc) rentrée f.

comedian [kə'miːdɪən] n (in music hall etc) comique m; (THEATRE) comédien m.
comedienne [kəmiːdi'ɛn] n comédienne f.
comedown ['kʌmdaun] n déchéance f.
comedy ['kɔmɪdɪ] n comédie f.
comet ['kɔmɪt] n comète f.
comfort ['kʌmfət] n confort m, bien-être m; (solace) consolation f, réconfort m // vt consoler, réconforter; ~**s** npl aises fpl; ~**able** a confortable; ~ **station** n (US) toilettes fpl.
comic ['kɔmɪk] a (also: ~**al**) comique // n comique m; (magazine) illustré m; ~ **strip** n(pl) bande dessinée.
coming ['kʌmɪŋ] n arrivée f; ~(**s**) **and going(s)** n(pl) va-et-vient m inv.
comma ['kɔmə] n virgule f.
command [kə'mɑːnd] n ordre m, commandement m; (MIL: authority) commandement m; (mastery) maîtrise f // vt (troops) commander; (be able to get) (pouvoir) disposer de, avoir à sa disposition; (deserve) avoir droit à; to ~ **sb to do** donner l'ordre or commander à qn de faire; ~**eer** [kɔmən'dɪə*] vt réquisitionner (par la force); ~**er** n chef m; (MIL) commandant m; ~**ing officer** n commandant m.
commando [kə'mɑːndəu] n commando m; membre m d'un commando.
commemorate [kə'mɛməreɪt] vt commémorer; **commemoration** [-'reɪʃən] n commémoration f.
commemorative [kə'mɛmərətɪv] a commémoratif(ive).
commence [kə'mɛns] vt,vi commencer.
commend [kə'mɛnd] vt louer; recommander; ~**able** a louable; ~**ation** [kɔmɛn'deɪʃən] n éloge m; recommandation f.
commensurate [kə'mɛnʃərɪt] a: ~ **with** en proportion de, proportionné(e) à.
comment ['kɔmɛnt] n commentaire m // vi faire des remarques or commentaires; ~**ary** ['kɔməntərɪ] n commentaire m; (SPORT) reportage m (en direct); ~**ator** ['kɔmənteɪtə*] n commentateur m; reporter m.
commerce ['kɔmɜːs] n commerce m.
commercial [kə'mɜːʃəl] a commercial(e) // n (TV: also: ~ **break**) annonce f publicitaire, spot m (publicitaire); ~ **college** n école f de commerce; ~**ize** vt commercialiser; ~ **television** n la publicité à la télévision, les chaînes indépendantes; ~ **traveller** n voyageur m de commerce; ~ **vehicle** n véhicule m utilitaire.
commiserate [kə'mɪzəreɪt] vi: to ~ **with** compatir à.
commission [kə'mɪʃən] n (committee, fee) commission f; (order for work of art etc) commande f // vt (MIL) nommer (à un commandement); (work of art) commander, charger un artiste de l'exécution de; **out of** ~ (NAUT) hors de service; ~**aire** [kəmɪʃə'nɛə*] n (at shop, cinema etc) portier m (en uniforme); ~**er** n membre m d'une commission; (POLICE) préfet m (de police).
commit [kə'mɪt] vt (act) commettre; (to sb's care) confier (à); to ~ **o.s. (to do)** s'engager (à faire); to ~ **suicide** se

suicider; **to ~ to writing** coucher par écrit; **~ment** n engagement m, responsabilité(s) f(pl).

committee [kə'mɪtɪ] n comité m.

commodity [kə'mɔdɪtɪ] n produit m, marchandise f, article m; (food) denrée f.

common ['kɔmən] a (gen, also pej) commun(e); (usual) courant(e) // n terrain communal; **the C~s** npl la chambre des Communes; **in ~** en commun; **it's ~ knowledge that** il est bien connu or notoire que; **to the ~ good** pour le bien de tous, dans l'intérêt général; **~er** n roturier/ière; **~ ground** n (fig) terrain m d'entente; **~ law** n droit coutumier; **~ly** ad communément, généralement; couramment; **C~ Market** n Marché commun; **~place** a banal(e), ordinaire; **~room** n salle commune; (SCOL) salle des professeurs; **~ sense** n bon sens; **the C~wealth** n le Commonwealth.

commotion [kə'məuʃən] n désordre m, tumulte m.

communal ['kɔmju:nl] a (life) communautaire; (for common use) commun(e).

commune n ['kɔmju:n] (group) communauté f // vi [kə'mju:n]: **to ~ with** converser intimement avec; communier avec.

communicate [kə'mju:nɪkeɪt] vt communiquer, transmettre // vi: **to ~ (with)** communiquer (avec).

communication [kəmju:nɪ'keɪʃən] n communication f; **~ cord** n sonnette f d'alarme.

communion [kə'mju:nɪən] n (also: **Holy C~**) communion f.

communiqué [kə'mju:nɪkeɪ] n communiqué m.

communism ['kɔmjunɪzəm] n communisme m; **communist** a,n communiste (m/f).

community [kə'mju:nɪtɪ] n communauté f; **~ centre** n foyer socio-éducatif, centre m de loisirs; **~ chest** n (US) fonds commun.

commutation ticket [kɔmju'teɪʃəntɪkɪt] n (US) carte f d'abonnement.

commute [kə'mju:t] vi faire le trajet journalier (de son domicile à un lieu de travail assez éloigné) // vt (LAW) commuer; (MATH: terms etc) opérer la commutation de; **~r** n banlieusard/e (qui ... see vi).

compact a [kəm'pækt] compact(e) // n ['kɔmpækt] contrat m, entente f; (also: **powder ~**) poudrier m.

companion [kəm'pænɪən] n compagnon/-compagne; **~ship** n camaraderie f.

company ['kʌmpənɪ] n (also COMM, MIL, THEATRE) compagnie f; **he's good ~** il est d'une compagnie agréable; **we have ~** nous avons de la visite; **to keep sb ~** tenir compagnie à qn; **to part ~ with** se séparer de; **~ secretary** n (COMM) secrétaire général (d'une société).

comparable ['kɔmpərəbl] a comparable.

comparative [kəm'pærətɪv] a comparatif(ive); (relative) relatif(ive).

compare [kəm'pεə*] vt: **to ~ sth/sb with/to** comparer qch/qn avec or et/à // vi: **to ~ (with)** se comparer (à); être comparable (à); **comparison** [-'pærɪsn] n comparaison f; **in comparison (with)** en comparaison (de).

compartment [kəm'pɑ:tmənt] n (also RAIL) compartiment m.

compass ['kʌmpəs] n boussole f; **~es** npl compas m.

compassion [kəm'pæʃən] n compassion f, humanité f; **~ate** a accessible à la compassion, au cœur charitable et bienveillant; **on ~ate grounds** pour raisons personnelles or de famille.

compatible [kəm'pætɪbl] a compatible.

compel [kəm'pεl] vt contraindre, obliger; **~ling** a (fig: argument) irrésistible.

compendium [kəm'pεndɪəm] n abrégé m.

compensate ['kɔmpənseɪt] vt indemniser, dédommager // vi: **to ~ for** compenser; **compensation** [-'seɪʃən] n compensation f; (money) dédommagement m, indemnité f.

compère ['kɔmpεə*] n présentateur/trice, animateur/trice.

compete [kəm'pi:t] vi (take part) concourir; (vie): **to ~ (with)** rivaliser (avec), faire concurrence (à).

competence ['kɔmpɪtəns] n compétence f, aptitude f.

competent ['kɔmpɪtənt] a compétent(e), capable.

competition [kɔmpɪ'tɪʃən] n compétition f, concours m; (ECON) concurrence f.

competitive [kəm'pεtɪtɪv] a (ECON) concurrentiel(le); **~ examination** n (SCOL) concours m.

competitor [kəm'pεtɪtə*] n concurrent/e.

compile [kəm'paɪl] vt compiler.

complacency [kəm'pleɪsnsɪ] n contentement m de soi, vaine complaisance.

complacent [kəm'pleɪsnt] a (trop) content(e) de soi; suffisant(e).

complain [kəm'pleɪn] vi: **to ~ (about)** se plaindre (de); (in shop etc) réclamer (au sujet de); **to ~ of** vt fus (MED) se plaindre de; **~t** n plainte f; réclamation f; (MED) affection f.

complement n ['kɔmplɪmənt] complément m; (especially of ship's crew etc) effectif complet; **~ary** [kɔmplɪ'mεntərɪ] a complémentaire.

complete [kəm'pli:t] a complet(ète) // vt achever, parachever; (a form) remplir; **~ly** ad complètement; **completion** n achèvement m.

complex ['kɔmplεks] a complexe // n (PSYCH, buildings etc) complexe m.

complexion [kəm'plεkʃən] n (of face) teint m; (of event etc) aspect m, caractère m.

complexity [kəm'plεksɪtɪ] n complexité f.

compliance [kəm'plaɪəns] n (see compliant) docilité f; (see comply): **~ with** le fait de se conformer à; **in ~ with** en conformité avec, conformément à.

compliant [kəm'plaɪənt] a docile, très accommodant(e).

complicate ['kɔmplɪkeɪt] vt compliquer;

~d *a* compliqué(e); **complication** [-'keɪʃən] *n* complication *f*.
compliment *n* ['kɔmplɪmənt] compliment *m* // *vt* ['kɔmplɪmɛnt] complimenter; **~s** *npl* compliments *mpl*, hommages *mpl*; **~** vœux *mpl*; **~ary** [-'mɛntərɪ] *a* flatteur(euse); (*free*) à titre gracieux; **~ary ticket** *n* billet *m* de faveur.
comply [kəm'plaɪ] *vi*: **to ~ with** se soumettre à, se conformer à.
component [kəm'pəunənt] *a* composant(e), constituant(e) // *n* composant *m*, élément *m*.
compose [kəm'pəuz] *vt* composer; **to ~ o.s.** se calmer, se maîtriser; prendre une contenance; **~d** *a* calme, posé(e); **~r** *n* (*MUS*) compositeur *m*.
composite ['kɔmpəzɪt] *a* composite; (*BOT*, *MATH*) composé(e).
composition [kɔmpə'zɪʃən] *n* composition *f*.
compost ['kɔmpɔst] *n* compost *m*.
composure [kəm'pəuʒə*] *n* calme *m*, maîtrise *f* de soi.
compound ['kɔmpaund] *n* (*CHEM*, *LING*) composé *m*; (*enclosure*) enclos *m*, enceinte *f* // *a* composé(e); **~** **fracture** *n* fracture compliquée; **~** **interest** *n* intérêt composé.
comprehend [kɔmprɪ'hɛnd] *vt* comprendre; **comprehension** [-'hɛnʃən] *n* compréhension *f*.
comprehensive [kɔmprɪ'hɛnsɪv] *a* (très) complet(ète); **~** **policy** *n* (*INSURANCE*) assurance *f* tous risques; **~** (**school**) *n* école secondaire non sélective, avec libre circulation d'une section à l'autre, ≈ C.E.S. *m*.
compress *vt* [kəm'prɛs] comprimer // *n* ['kɔmprɛs] (*MED*) compresse *f*; **~ion** [-'prɛʃən] *n* compression *f*.
comprise [kəm'praɪz] *vt* (*also:* **be ~d of**) comprendre.
compromise ['kɔmprəmaɪz] *n* compromis *m* // *vt* compromettre // *vi* transiger, accepter un compromis.
compulsion [kəm'pʌlʃən] *n* contrainte *f*, force *f*.
compulsive [kəm'pʌlsɪv] *a* (*reason*, *demand*) coercitif(ive); (*PSYCH*) compulsif(ive); **he's a ~ smoker** c'est un fumeur invétéré.
compulsory [kəm'pʌlsərɪ] *a* obligatoire.
computer [kəm'pjuːtə*] *n* ordinateur *m*; (*mechanical*) calculatrice *f*; **~ize** *vt* traiter or automatiser par ordinateur; **~ language** *n* langage *m* machine or de programmation; **~ programming** *n* programmation *f*; **~ science** *n* informatique *f*; **~ scientist** *n* informaticien/ne.
comrade ['kɔmrɪd] *n* camarade *m/f*; **~ship** *n* camaraderie *f*.
con [kɔn] *vt* duper; escroquer.
concave ['kɔn'keɪv] *a* concave.
conceal [kən'siːl] *vt* cacher, dissimuler.
concede [kən'siːd] *vt* concéder // *vi* céder.
conceit [kən'siːt] *n* vanité *f*, suffisance *f*, prétention *f*; **~ed** *a* vaniteux(euse), suffisant(e).
conceivable [kən'siːvəbl] *a* concevable, imaginable.

conceive [kən'siːv] *vt* concevoir.
concentrate ['kɔnsəntreɪt] *vi* se concentrer // *vt* concentrer.
concentration [kɔnsən'treɪʃən] *n* concentration *f*; **~ camp** *n* camp *m* de concentration.
concentric [kɔn'sɛntrɪk] *a* concentrique.
concept ['kɔnsɛpt] *n* concept *m*.
conception [kən'sɛpʃən] *n* conception *f*.
concern [kən'səːn] *n* affaire *f*; (*COMM*) entreprise *f*, firme *f*; (*anxiety*) inquiétude *f*, souci *m* // *vt* concerner; **to be ~ed** (**about**) s'inquiéter (de), être inquiet (au sujet de); **~ing** *prep* en ce qui concerne, à propos de.
concert ['kɔnsət] *n* concert *m*; **in ~** à l'unisson, en chœur; ensemble; **~ed** [kən'səːtɪd] *a* concerté(e); **~ hall** *n* salle *f* de concert.
concertina [kɔnsə'tiːnə] *n* concertina *m* // *vi* se télescoper, se caramboler.
concerto [kən'tʃəːtəu] *n* concerto *m*.
concession [kən'sɛʃən] *n* concession *f*.
conciliation [kənsɪlɪ'eɪʃən] *n* conciliation *f*, apaisement *m*.
conciliatory [kən'sɪlɪətrɪ] *a* conciliateur(trice); conciliant(e).
concise [kən'saɪs] *a* concis(e).
conclave ['kɔnkleɪv] *n* assemblée secrète; (*REL*) conclave *m*.
conclude [kən'kluːd] *vt* conclure; **conclusion** [-'kluːʒən] *n* conclusion *f*; **conclusive** [-'kluːsɪv] *a* concluant(e), définitif(ive).
concoct [kən'kɔkt] *vt* confectionner, composer.
concourse ['kɔnkɔːs] *n* (*hall*) hall *m*, salle *f* des pas perdus; (*crowd*) affluence *f*, multitude *f*.
concrete ['kɔnkriːt] *n* béton *m* // *a* concret(ète); en béton.
concur [kən'kəː*] *vi* être d'accord.
concurrently [kən'kʌrntlɪ] *ad* simultanément.
concussion [kən'kʌʃən] *n* ébranlement *m*, secousse *f*; (*MED*) commotion (cérébrale).
condemn [kən'dɛm] *vt* condamner; **~ation** [kɔndɛm'neɪʃən] *n* condamnation *f*.
condensation [kɔndɛn'seɪʃən] *n* condensation *f*.
condense [kən'dɛns] *vi* se condenser // *vt* condenser; **~d milk** *n* lait condensé (sucré).
condescend [kɔndɪ'sɛnd] *vi* condescendre, s'abaisser; **~ing** *a* condescendant(e).
condition [kən'dɪʃən] *n* condition *f* // *vt* déterminer, conditionner; **on ~ that** à condition que + *sub*, à condition de; **~al** *a* conditionnel(le); **to be ~al upon** dépendre de.
condolences [kən'dəulənsɪz] *npl* condoléances *fpl*.
condone [kən'dəun] *vt* fermer les yeux sur, approuver (tacitement).
conducive [kən'djuːsɪv] *a*: **~ to** favorable à, qui contribue à.
conduct *n* ['kɔndʌkt] conduite *f* // *vt* [kən'dʌkt] conduire; (*manage*) mener, diriger; (*MUS*) diriger; **to ~ o.s.** se

conduire, se comporter ; **∼ed tour** *n* voyage organisé, visite guidée ; **∼or** *n* (of *orchestra*) chef *m* d'orchestre ; (on *bus*) receveur *m* ; (ELEC) conducteur *m* ; **∼ress** *n* (on *bus*) receveuse *f*.

conduit ['kɔndɪt] *n* conduit *m*, tuyau *m* ; tube *m*.

cone [kəun] *n* cône *m* ; (for *ice-cream*) cornet *m* ; (BOT) pomme *f* de pin, cône.

confectioner [kən'fɛkʃənə*] *n* (of *cakes*) pâtissier/ière ; (of *sweets*) confiseur/euse ; **∼y** *n* pâtisserie *f* ; confiserie *f*.

confederation [kənfɛdə'reɪʃən] *n* confédération *f*.

confer [kən'fə:*] *vt*: to **∼ sth on** conférer qch à // *vi* conférer, s'entretenir.

conference ['kɔnfərns] *n* conférence *f*.

confess [kən'fɛs] *vt* confesser, avouer // *vi* se confesser ; **∼ion** [-'fɛʃən] *n* confession *f* ; **∼ional** [-'fɛʃənl] *n* confessional *m* ; **∼or** *n* confesseur *m*.

confetti [kən'fɛti] *n* confettis *mpl*.

confide [kən'faɪd] *vi*: to **∼ in** s'ouvrir à, se confier à.

confidence ['kɔnfɪdns] *n* confiance *f* ; (*also*: self-**∼**) assurance *f*, confiance en soi ; (*secret*) confidence *f* ; **∼ trick** *n* escroquerie *f* ; **confident** *a* sûr(e), assuré(e) ; **confidential** [kɔnfɪ'dɛnʃəl] *a* confidentiel(le).

confine [kən'faɪn] *vt* limiter, borner ; (*shut up*) confiner, enfermer ; **∼s** ['kɔnfaɪnz] *npl* confins *mpl*, bornes *fpl* ; **∼d** *a* (*space*) restreint(e), réduit(e) ; **∼ment** *n* emprisonnement *m*, détention *f* ; (MIL) consigne *f* (au quartier) ; (MED) accouchement *m*.

confirm [kən'fə:m] *vt* (*report*) confirmer ; (*appointment*) ratifier ; **∼ation** [kɔnfə'meɪʃən] *n* confirmation *f* ; **∼ed** *a* invétéré(e), incorrigible.

confiscate ['kɔnfɪskeɪt] *vt* confisquer ; **confiscation** [-'keɪʃən] *n* confiscation *f*.

conflagration [kɔnflə'greɪʃən] *n* incendie *m*.

conflict *n* ['kɔnflɪkt] conflit *m*, lutte *f* // *vi* [kən'flɪkt] être *or* entrer en conflit ; (*opinions*) s'opposer, se heurter ; **∼ing** *a* contradictoire.

conform [kən'fɔ:m] *vi*: to **∼** (to) se conformer (à) ; **∼ist** *n* conformiste *m/f*.

confound [kən'faund] *vt* confondre ; **∼ed** *a* maudit(e), sacré(e).

confront [kən'frʌnt] *vt* confronter, mettre en présence ; (*enemy*, *danger*) affronter, faire face à ; **∼ation** [kɔnfrən'teɪʃən] *n* confrontation *f*.

confuse [kən'fju:z] *vt* embrouiller ; (*one thing with another*) confondre ; **confusing** *a* peu clair(e), déroutant(e) ; **confusion** [-'fju:ʒən] *n* confusion *f*.

congeal [kən'dʒi:l] *vi* (*oil*) se figer ; (*blood*) se coaguler.

congenial [kən'dʒi:nɪəl] *a* sympathique, agréable.

congenital [kən'dʒɛnɪtl] *a* congénital(e).

conger eel ['kɔŋgəri:l] *n* congre *m*.

congested [kən'dʒɛstɪd] *a* (MED) congestionné(e) ; (*fig*) surpeuplé(e) ; congestionné ; bloqué(e).

congestion [kən'dʒɛstʃən] *n* congestion *f* ; (*fig*) encombrement *m*.

conglomeration [kənglɔmə'reɪʃən] *n* groupement *m* ; agglomération *f*.

congratulate [kən'grætjuleɪt] *vt*: to **∼ sb** (on) féliciter qn (de) ; **congratulations** [-'leɪʃənz] *npl* félicitations *fpl*.

congregate ['kɔŋgrɪgeɪt] *vi* se rassembler, se réunir.

congregation [kɔŋgrɪ'geɪʃən] *n* assemblée *f* (des fidèles).

congress ['kɔŋgrɛs] *n* congrès *m* ; **∼man** *n* (US) membre *m* du Congrès.

conical ['kɔnɪkl] *a* (de forme) conique.

conifer ['kɔnɪfə*] *n* conifère *m* ; **∼ous** [kə'nɪfərəs] *a* (*forest*) de conifères.

conjecture [kən'dʒɛktʃə*] *n* conjecture *f* // *vt*, *vi* conjecturer.

conjugal ['kɔndʒugl] *a* conjugal(e).

conjugate ['kɔndʒugeɪt] *vt* conjuguer ; **conjugation** [-'geɪʃən] *n* conjugaison *f*.

conjunction [kən'dʒʌŋkʃən] *n* conjonction *f*.

conjunctivitis [kəndʒʌŋktɪ'vaɪtɪs] *n* conjonctivite *f*.

conjure ['kʌndʒə*] *vt* faire apparaître (par la prestidigitation) ; [kən'dʒuə*] conjurer, supplier ; to **∼ up** *vt* (*ghost*, *spirit*) faire apparaître ; (*memories*) évoquer ; **∼r** *n* prestidigitateur *m*, illusionniste *m/f* ; **conjuring trick** *n* tour *m* de prestidigitation.

conk [kɔŋk]: to **∼ out** *vi* (*col*) tomber *or* rester en panne.

conman ['kɔnmæn] *n* escroc *m*.

connect [kə'nɛkt] *vt* joindre, relier ; (ELEC) connecter ; (*fig*) établir un rapport entre, faire un rapprochement entre // *vi* (*train*): to **∼ with** assurer la correspondance avec ; **to be ∼ed with** avoir un rapport avec ; avoir des rapports avec, être en relation avec ; **∼ion** [-ʃən] *n* relation *f*, lien *m* ; (ELEC) connexion *f* ; (TEL) communication *f* ; **in ∼ion with** à propos de.

connexion [kə'nɛkʃən] *n* = connection.

conning tower ['kɔnɪŋtauə*] *n* kiosque *m* (de *sous-marin*).

connive [kə'naɪv] *vi*: to **∼ at** se faire le complice de.

connoisseur [kɔnɪ'sə*] *n* connaisseur *m*.

connotation [kɔnə'teɪʃən] *n* connotation *f*, implication *f*.

connubial [kə'nju:bɪəl] *a* conjugal(e).

conquer ['kɔŋkə*] *vt* conquérir ; (*feelings*) vaincre, surmonter ; **∼or** *n* conquérant *m*, vainqueur *m*.

conquest ['kɔŋkwɛst] *n* conquête *f*.

cons [kɔnz] *npl* see **pro**, **convenience**.

conscience ['kɔnʃəns] *n* conscience *f*.

conscientious [kɔnʃɪ'ɛnʃəs] *a* consciencieux(euse) ; (*scruple*, *objection*) de conscience ; **∼ objector** *n* objecteur *m* de conscience.

conscious ['kɔnʃəs] *a* conscient(e) ; **∼ness** *n* conscience *f* ; (MED) connaissance *f* ; **to lose/regain ∼ness** perdre/reprendre connaissance.

conscript ['kɔnskrɪpt] *n* conscrit *m* ; **∼ion** [kən'skrɪpʃən] *n* conscription *f*.

consecrate ['kɔnsɪkreɪt] vt consacrer.
consecutive [kən'sɛkjutɪv] a consécutif(ive).
consensus [kən'sɛnsəs] n consensus m.
consent [kən'sɛnt] n consentement m // vi: **to ~ (to)** consentir (à) ; **age of ~** âge nubile (légal).
consequence ['kɔnsɪkwəns] n suites fpl, conséquence f ; importance f.
consequently ['kɔnsɪkwəntlɪ] ad par conséquent, donc.
conservation [kɔnsə:'veɪʃən] n préservation f, protection f.
conservative [kən'sə:vətɪv] a conservateur(trice) ; (cautious) prudent(e) ; **C~** a,n conservateur(trice).
conservatory [kən'sə:vətrɪ] n (greenhouse) serre f.
conserve [kən'sə:v] vt conserver, préserver.
consider [kən'sɪdə*] vt considérer, réfléchir à ; (take into account) penser à, prendre en considération ; (regard, judge) considérer, estimer.
considerable [kən'sɪdərəbl] a considérable.
considerate [kən'sɪdərɪt] a prévenant(e), plein(e) d'égards.
consideration [kənsɪdə'reɪʃən] n considération f ; (reward) rétribution f, rémunération f ; **out of ~ for** par égard pour ; **under ~** à l'étude.
considering [kən'sɪdərɪŋ] prep étant donné.
consign [kən'saɪn] vt expédier, livrer ; **~ment** n arrivage m, envoi m.
consist [kən'sɪst] vi: **to ~ of** consister en, se composer de.
consistency [kən'sɪstənsɪ] n consistance f ; (fig) cohérence f.
consistent [kən'sɪstənt] a logique, cohérent(e) ; **~ with** compatible avec, en accord avec.
consolation [kɔnsə'leɪʃən] n consolation f.
console vt [kən'səul] consoler // n ['kɔnsəul] console f.
consolidate [kən'sɔlɪdeɪt] vt consolider.
consommé [kən'sɔmeɪ] n consommé m.
consonant ['kɔnsənənt] n consonne f.
consortium [kən'sɔ:tɪəm] n consortium m, comptoir m.
conspicuous [kən'spɪkjuəs] a voyant(e), qui attire la vue or l'attention.
conspiracy [kən'spɪrəsɪ] n conspiration f, complot m.
conspire [kən'spaɪə*] vi conspirer, comploter.
constable ['kʌnstəbl] n ≈ agent m de police, gendarme m ; **chief ~** n ≈ préfet m de police.
constabulary [kən'stæbjulərɪ] n ≈ police f, gendarmerie f.
constant ['kɔnstənt] a constant(e) ; incessant(e) ; **~ly** ad constamment, sans cesse.
constellation [kɔnstə'leɪʃən] n constellation f.
consternation [kɔnstə'neɪʃən] n consternation f.

constipated ['kɔnstɪpeɪtəd] a constipé(e).
constipation [kɔnstɪ'peɪʃən] n constipation f.
constituency [kən'stɪtjuənsɪ] n circonscription électorale.
constituent [kən'stɪtjuənt] n électeur/trice ; (part) élément constitutif, composant m.
constitute ['kɔnstɪtju:t] vt constituer.
constitution [kɔnstɪ'tju:ʃən] n constitution f ; **~al** a constitutionnel(le).
constrain [kən'streɪn] vt contraindre, forcer ; **~ed** a contraint(e), gêné(e) ; **~t** n contrainte f.
constrict [kən'strɪkt] vt rétrécir, resserrer ; gêner, limiter.
construct [kən'strʌkt] vt construire ; **~ion** [-ʃən] n construction f ; **~ive** a constructif(ive).
construe [kən'stru:] vt analyser, expliquer.
consul ['kɔnsl] n consul m ; **~ate** ['kɔnsjulɪt] n consulat m.
consult [kən'sʌlt] vt consulter ; **~ancy** n: **~ancy fee** honoraires mpl d'expert ; **~ant** n (MED) médecin consultant ; (other specialist) consultant m, (expert-)conseil m // a: **~ant engineer** ingénieur-conseil m ; **legal/management ~ant** conseiller m juridique/en gestion ; **~ation** [kɔnsəl'teɪʃən] n consultation f ; **~ing room** n cabinet m de consultation.
consume [kən'sju:m] vt consommer ; **~r** n consommateur/ trice ; **consumerism** n mouvement m pour la protection des consommateurs ; **~r society** n société f de consommation.
consummate ['kɔnsʌmeɪt] vt consommer.
consumption [kən'sʌmpʃən] n consommation f ; (MED) consomption f (pulmonaire).
cont. abbr of continued.
contact ['kɔntækt] n contact m ; (person) connaissance f, relation f // vt se mettre en contact or en rapport avec ; **~ lenses** npl verres mpl de contact.
contagious [kən'teɪdʒəs] a contagieux(euse).
contain [kən'teɪn] vt contenir ; **to ~ o.s.** se contenir, se maîtriser ; **~er** n récipient m ; (for shipping etc) container m.
contaminate [kən'tæmɪneɪt] vt contaminer ; **contamination** [-'neɪʃən] n contamination f.
cont'd abbr of continued.
contemplate ['kɔntəmpleɪt] vt contempler ; (consider) envisager ; **contemplation** [-'pleɪʃən] n contemplation f.
contemporary [kən'tɛmpərərɪ] a contemporain(e) ; (design, wallpaper) moderne // n contemporain/e.
contempt [kən'tɛmpt] n mépris m, dédain m ; **~ible** a méprisable, vil(e) ; **~uous** a dédaigneux(euse), méprisant(e).
contend [kən'tɛnd] vt: **to ~ that** soutenir or prétendre que // vi: **to ~ with** rivaliser avec, lutter avec ; **~er** n prétendant/e ; adversaire m/f.
content [kən'tɛnt] a content(e), satisfait(e) // vt contenter, satisfaire // n ['kɔntɛnt] contenu m ; teneur f ; **~s** npl

contenu; (*of barrel etc: capacity*) contenance *f*; **(table of)** ~s table *f* des matières; **to be** ~ **with** se contenter de; ~**ed** *a* content(e), satisfait(e).

contention [kən'tenʃən] *n* dispute *f*, contestation *f*; (*argument*) assertion *f*, affirmation *f*; **contentious** *a* querelleur(euse); litigieux(euse).

contentment [kən'tɛntmənt] *n* contentement *m*, satisfaction *f*.

contest *n* ['kɔntɛst] combat *m*, lutte *f*; (*competition*) concours *m* // *vt* [kən'tɛst] contester, discuter; (*compete for*) disputer; ~**ant** [kən'tɛstənt] *n* concurrent/e; (*in fight*) adversaire *m/f*.

context ['kɔntɛkst] *n* contexte *m*.

continent ['kɔntɪnənt] *n* continent *m*; **the C—** l'Europe continentale; ~**al** [-'nɛntl] *a* continental(e) // *n* Européen/ne (continental(e)).

contingency [kən'tɪndʒənsɪ] *n* éventualité *f*, événement imprévu; ~ **plan** *n* plan *m* d'urgence.

contingent [kən'tɪndʒənt] *a* contingent(e) // *n* contingent *m*; **to be** ~ **upon** dépendre de.

continual [kən'tɪnjuəl] *a* continuel(le); ~**ly** *ad* continuellement, sans cesse.

continuation [kəntɪnju'eɪʃən] *n* continuation *f*; (*after interruption*) reprise *f*; (*of story*) suite *f*.

continue [kən'tɪnjuː] *vi* continuer // *vt* continuer; (*start again*) reprendre; **to be** ~**d** (*story*) à suivre.

continuity [kɔntɪ'njuːtɪ] *n* continuité *f*; ~ **girl** *n* (CINEMA) script-girl *f*.

continuous [kən'tɪnjuəs] *a* continu(e), permanent(e).

contort [kən'tɔːt] *vt* tordre, crisper; ~**ion** [-'tɔːʃən] *n* crispation *f*, torsion *f*; (*of acrobat*) contorsion *f*; ~**ionist** [-'tɔːʃənɪst] *n* contorsionniste *m/f*.

contour ['kɔntuə*] *n* contour *m*, profil *m*; (*also:* ~ **line**) courbe *f* de niveau.

contraband ['kɔntrəbænd] *n* contrebande *f*.

contraception [kɔntrə'sɛpʃən] *n* contraception *f*.

contraceptive [kɔntrə'sɛptɪv] *a* contraceptif(ive), anticonceptionnel(le) // *n* contraceptif *m*.

contract *n* ['kɔntrækt] contrat *m* // *vb* [kən'trækt] *vi* (COMM): **to** ~ **to do sth** s'engager (par contrat) à faire qch; (*become smaller*) se contracter, se resserrer // *vt* contracter; ~**ion** [-ʃən] *n* contraction *f*; (LING) forme contractée; ~**or** *n* entrepreneur *m*.

contradict [kɔntrə'dɪkt] *vt* contredire; (*be contrary to*) démentir, être en contradiction avec; ~**ion** [-ʃən] *n* contradiction *f*.

contralto [kən'træltəu] *n* contralto *m*.

contraption [kən'træpʃən] *n* (*pej*) machin *m*, truc *m*.

contrary ['kɔntrərɪ] *a* contraire, opposé(e); [kən'trɛərɪ] (*perverse*) contrariant(e), entêté(e) // *n* contraire *m*; **on the** ~ au contraire; **unless you hear to the** ~ sauf avis contraire.

contrast *n* ['kɔntrɑːst] contraste *m* // *vt* [kən'trɑːst] mettre en contraste,

contraster; ~**ing** *a* opposé(e), contrasté(e).

contravene [kɔntrə'viːn] *vt* enfreindre, violer, contrevenir à.

contribute [kən'trɪbjuːt] *vi* contribuer // *vt*: **to** ~ **£10/an article to** donner 10 livres/un article à; **to** ~ **to** (*gen*) contribuer à; (*newspaper*) collaborer à; **contribution** [kɔntrɪ'bjuːʃən] *n* contribution *f*; **contributor** *n* (*to newspaper*) collaborateur/trice.

contrite ['kɔntraɪt] *a* contrit(e).

contrivance [kən'traɪvəns] *n* invention *f*, combinaison *f*; mécanisme *m*, dispositif *m*.

contrive [kən'traɪv] *vt* combiner, inventer // *vi*: **to** ~ **to do** s'arranger pour faire, trouver le moyen de faire.

control [kən'trəul] *vt* maîtriser; (*check*) contrôler // *n* contrôle *m*, autorité *f*; maîtrise *f*; ~**s** *npl* commandes *fpl*; **to be in** ~ **of** être maître de, maîtriser; être responsable de; **circumstances beyond our** ~ circonstances indépendantes de notre volonté; ~ **point** *n* (poste *m* de) contrôle; ~ **tower** *n* (AVIAT) tour *f* de contrôle.

controversial [kɔntrə'vəːʃl] *a* discutable, controversé(e).

controversy ['kɔntrəvəːsɪ] *n* controverse *f*, polémique *f*.

convalesce [kɔnvə'lɛs] *vi* relever de maladie, se remettre (d'une maladie).

convalescence [kɔnvə'lɛsns] *n* convalescence *f*.

convalescent [kɔnvə'lɛsnt] *a*, *n* convalescent(e).

convector [kən'vɛktə*] *n* radiateur *m* à convection, appareil *m* de chauffage par convection.

convene [kən'viːn] *vt* convoquer, assembler // *vi* se réunir, s'assembler.

convenience [kən'viːnɪəns] *n* commodité *f*; **at your** ~ quand *or* comme cela vous convient; **all modern** ~**s, all mod cons** avec tout le confort moderne, tout confort.

convenient [kən'viːnɪənt] *a* commode.

convent ['kɔnvənt] *n* couvent *m*; ~ **school** *n* couvent *m*.

convention [kən'vɛnʃən] *n* convention *f*; ~**al** *a* conventionnel(le).

converge [kən'vəːdʒ] *vi* converger.

conversant [kən'vəːsnt] *a*: **to be** ~ **with** s'y connaître en; être au courant de.

conversation [kɔnvə'seɪʃən] *n* conversation *f*; ~**al** *a* de la conversation; ~**alist** *n* brillant/e causeur/euse.

converse *n* ['kɔnvəːs] contraire *m*, inverse *m*; ~**ly** [-'vəːslɪ] *ad* inversement, réciproquement.

conversion [kən'vəːʃən] *n* conversion *f*; ~ **table** *n* table *f* de conversion.

convert *vt* [kən'vəːt] (REL, COMM) convertir; (*alter*) transformer, aménager; (RUGBY) transformer // *n* ['kɔnvəːt] converti/e; ~**ible** *n* (voiture *f*) décapotable *f*.

convex ['kɔn'vɛks] *a* convexe.

convey [kən'veɪ] *vt* transporter; (*thanks*) transmettre; (*idea*) communiquer; ~**or belt** *n* convoyeur *m*, tapis roulant.

convict vt [kən'vɪkt] déclarer (or reconnaître) coupable // n ['kɔnvɪkt] forçat m, convict m; ~ion [-'ʃən] n condamnation f; (belief) conviction f.

convince [kən'vɪns] vt convaincre, persuader; **convincing** a persuasif(ive), convaincant(e).

convivial [kən'vɪvɪəl] a joyeux(euse), plein(e) d'entrain.

convoy ['kɔnvɔɪ] n convoi m.

convulse [kən'vʌls] vt ébranler; **to be ~d with laughter** se tordre de rire.

convulsion [kən'vʌlʃən] n convulsion f.

coo [ku:] vi roucouler.

cook [kuk] vt (faire) cuire // vi cuire; (person) faire la cuisine // n cuisinier/ière; ~book n = ~ery book; ~er n cuisinière f; ~ery n cuisine f; ~ery book n livre m de cuisine; ~ie n (US) biscuit m, petit gâteau sec; ~ing n cuisine f.

cool [ku:l] a frais(fraîche); (not afraid) calme; (unfriendly) froid(e); (impertinent) effronté(e) // vt, vi rafraîchir, refroidir; ~ing tower n refroidisseur m; ~ness n fraîcheur f; sang-froid m, calme m.

coop [ku:p] n poulailler m // vt: to ~ up (fig) cloîtrer, enfermer.

co-op ['kəuɔp] n abbr of Cooperative (Society).

cooperate [kəu'ɔpəreɪt] vi coopérer, collaborer; **cooperation** [-'reɪʃən] n coopération f, collaboration f.

cooperative [kəu'ɔpərətɪv] a coopératif(ive) // n coopérative f.

coordinate [kəu'ɔ:dɪneɪt] vt coordonner; **coordination** [-'neɪʃən] coordination f.

coot [ku:t] n foulque f.

cop [kɔp] n (col) flic m.

cope [kəup] vi se débrouiller; **to ~ with** faire face à; s'occuper de.

co-pilot ['kəu'paɪlət] n copilote m.

copious ['kəupɪəs] a copieux(euse), abondant(e).

copper ['kɔpə*] n cuivre m; (col: policeman) flic m; ~s npl petite monnaie.

coppice ['kɔpɪs] n taillis m.

copse [kɔps] n = **coppice.**

copulate ['kɔpjuleɪt] vi copuler.

copy ['kɔpɪ] n copie f; (book etc) exemplaire m // vt copier; ~cat n (pej) copieur/euse; ~right n droit m d'auteur, copyright m; ~right reserved tous droits (de reproduction) réservés; ~writer n rédacteur/trice publicitaire.

coral ['kɔrəl] n corail m; ~ reef n récif m de corail.

cord [kɔ:d] n corde f; (fabric) velours côtelé; whipcord m; corde f.

cordial ['kɔ:dɪəl] a cordial(e), chaleureux(euse) // n sirop m; cordial m.

cordon ['kɔ:dn] n cordon m; to ~ off vt boucler (par cordon de police).

corduroy ['kɔ:dərɔɪ] n velours côtelé.

core [kɔ:*] n (of fruit) trognon m, cœur m; (TECH) noyau m // vt enlever le trognon or le cœur de.

coriander [kɔrɪ'ændə*] n coriandre f.

cork [kɔ:k] n liège m; (of bottle) bouchon m; ~age n droit payé par le client qui apporte sa propre bouteille de vin; ~screw n tire-bouchon m.

corm [kɔ:m] n bulbe m.

cormorant ['kɔ:mərnt] n cormoran m.

corn [kɔ:n] n blé m; (US: maize) maïs m; (on foot) cor m; ~ on the cob (CULIN) épi m de maïs au naturel.

cornea ['kɔ:nɪə] n cornée f.

corned beef ['kɔ:nd'bi:f] n corned-beef m.

corner ['kɔ:nə*] n coin m; (AUT) tournant m, virage m // vt acculer, mettre au pied du mur; coincer; (COMM: market) accaparer // vi prendre un virage; ~ flag n (FOOTBALL) piquet m de coin; ~ kick n corner m; ~stone n pierre f angulaire.

cornet ['kɔ:nɪt] n (MUS) cornet m à pistons; (of ice-cream) cornet m (de glace).

cornflour ['kɔ:nflauə*] n farine f de maïs, maïzena f.

cornice ['kɔ:nɪs] n corniche f.

Cornish ['kɔ:nɪʃ] a de Cornouailles, cornouaillais(e).

cornucopia [kɔ:nju'kəupɪə] n corne f d'abondance.

Cornwall ['kɔ:nwəl] n Cornouailles f.

corny ['kɔ:nɪ] a (col) rebattu(e), galvaudé(e).

corollary [kə'rɔlərɪ] n corollaire m.

coronary ['kɔrənərɪ] n: ~ (thrombosis) infarctus m (du myocarde), thrombose f coronaire.

coronation [kɔrə'neɪʃən] n couronnement m.

coroner ['kɔrənə*] n coroner m.

coronet ['kɔrənɪt] n couronne f.

corporal ['kɔ:pərl] n caporal m, brigadier m // a: ~ punishment châtiment corporel.

corporate ['kɔ:pərɪt] a en commun; constitué(e) (en corporation).

corporation [kɔ:pə'reɪʃən] n (of town) municipalité f, conseil municipal; (COMM) société f; ~ tax n = impôt m sur les bénéfices.

corps [kɔ:*], pl corps [kɔ:z] n corps m.

corpse [kɔ:ps] n cadavre m.

corpuscle ['kɔ:pʌsl] n corpuscule m.

corral [kə'rɑ:l] n corral m.

correct [kə'rɛkt] a (accurate) correct(e), exact(e); (proper) correct(e), convenable // vt corriger; ~ion [-ʃən] n correction f.

correlate ['kɔrɪleɪt] vt mettre en corrélation.

correspond [kɔrɪs'pɔnd] vi correspondre; ~ence n correspondance f; ~ence course n cours m par correspondance; ~ent n correspondant/e.

corridor ['kɔrɪdɔ:*] n couloir m, corridor m.

corroborate [kə'rɔbəreɪt] vt corroborer, confirmer.

corrode [kə'rəud] vt corroder, ronger // vi se corroder; **corrosion** [-'rəuʒən] n corrosion f.

corrugated ['kɔrəgeɪtɪd] a plissé(e); cannelé(e); ondulé(e); ~ cardboard n carton ondulé; ~ iron n tôle ondulée.

corrupt [kə'rʌpt] a corrompu(e) // vt corrompre; ~ion [-ʃən] n corruption f.

corset ['kɔ:sɪt] *n* corset *m*.

Corsica ['kɔ:sɪkə] *n* Corse *f*.

cortège [kɔ:'tɛ:ʒ] *n* cortège *m* (*gén funèbre*).

coruscating ['kɔrəskeɪtɪŋ] *a* scintillant(e).

cosh [kɔʃ] *n* matraque *f*.

cosignatory ['kəu'sɪgnətərɪ] *n* cosignataire *m/f*.

cosiness ['kəuzɪnɪs] *n* atmosphère douillette, confort *m*.

cos lettuce [kɔs'lɛtɪs] *n* (laitue *f*) romaine *f*.

cosmetic [kɔz'mɛtɪk] *n* produit *m* de beauté, cosmétique *m*.

cosmic ['kɔzmɪk] *a* cosmique.

cosmonaut ['kɔzmənɔ:t] *n* cosmonaute *m/f*.

cosmopolitan [kɔzmə'pɔlɪtn] *a* cosmopolite.

cosmos ['kɔzmɔs] *n* cosmos *m*.

cosset ['kɔsɪt] *vt* choyer, dorloter.

cost [kɔst] *n* coût *m* // *vb* (*pt, pp* **cost**) *vi* coûter // *vt* établir *or* calculer le prix de revient de; **it — s £5/too much** cela coûte cinq livres/trop cher; **it — him his life/job** ça lui a coûté la vie/son emploi; **at all — s** coûte que coûte, à tout prix.

co-star ['kəustɑ:*] *n* partenaire *m/f*.

costly ['kɔstlɪ] *a* coûteux(euse).

cost price ['kɔst'praɪs] *n* prix coûtant *or* de revient.

costume ['kɔstju:m] *n* costume *m*; (*lady's suit*) tailleur *m*; (*also*: **swimming —**) maillot *m* (de bain); **— jewellery** *n* bijoux *mpl* de fantaisie.

cosy ['kəuzɪ] *a* douillet(te).

cot [kɔt] *n* (*child's*) lit *m* d'enfant, petit lit.

cottage ['kɔtɪdʒ] *n* petite maison (à la campagne), cottage *m*; **— cheese** *n* fromage blanc (*maigre*).

cotton ['kɔtn] *n* coton *m*; **— dress** *etc* robe *etc en or* de coton; **— wool** *n* ouate *f*, coton *m* hydrophile.

couch [kautʃ] *n* canapé *m*; divan *m* // *vt* formuler, exprimer.

cough [kɔf] *vi* tousser // *n* toux *f*; **— drop** *n* pastille *f* pour *or* contre la toux.

could [kud] *pt of* **can**; **—n't = could not.**

council ['kaunsl] *n* conseil *m*; **city** *or* **town —** conseil municipal; **— estate** *n* (*quartier m or* zone *f* de) logements loués à/par la municipalité; **— house** *n* maison *f* (à loyer modéré) louée par la municipalité; **—lor** *n* conseiller/ère.

counsel ['kaunsl] *n* avocat/e; consultation *f*, délibération *f*; **—lor** *n* conseiller/ère.

count [kaunt] *vt, vi* compter // *n* compte *m*; (*nobleman*) comte *m*; **to — on** *vt fus* compter sur; **to — up** *vt* compter, additionner; **—down** *n* compte *m* à rebours.

countenance ['kauntɪnəns] *n* expression *f* // *vt* approuver.

counter ['kauntə*] *n* comptoir *m*; (*machine*) compteur *m* // *vt* aller à l'encontre de, opposer; (*blow*) parer // *ad*: **— to** à l'encontre de; contrairement à; **—act** *vt* neutraliser, contrebalancer; **—attack** *n* contre-attaque *f* // *vi* contre-attaquer; **—balance** *vt* contrebalancer,

faire contrepoids à; **—-clockwise** *ad* en sens inverse des aiguilles d'une montre; **—-espionage** *n* contre-espionnage *m*.

counterfeit ['kauntəfɪt] *n* faux *m*, contrefaçon *f* // *vt* contrefaire // *a* faux(fausse).

counterfoil ['kauntəfɔɪl] *n* talon *m*, souche *f*.

counterpart ['kauntəpɑ:t] *n* (*of document etc*) double *m*; (*of person*) homologue *m/f*.

countersink ['kauntəsɪŋk] *vt* (*hole*) fraiser.

countess ['kauntɪs] *n* comtesse *f*.

countless ['kauntlɪs] *a* innombrable.

countrified ['kʌntrɪfaɪd] *a* rustique, à l'air campagnard.

country ['kʌntrɪ] *n* pays *m*; (*native land*) patrie *f*; (*as opposed to town*) campagne *f*; (*region*) région *f*, pays *m*; **— dancing** *n* danse *f* folklorique; **— house** *n* manoir *m*, (petit) château; **—man** *n* (*national*) compatriote *m*; (*rural*) habitant *m* de la campagne, campagnard *m*; **—side** *n* campagne *f*.

county ['kauntɪ] *n* comté *m*; **— town** *n* chef-lieu *m*.

coup, —s [ku:, -z] *n* beau coup *m*; (*also*: **— d'état**) coup d'État.

coupé [ku:'peɪ] *n* coupé *m*.

couple ['kʌpl] *n* couple *m* // *vt* (*carriages*) atteler; (*TECH*) coupler; (*ideas, names*) associer; **a — of** deux.

couplet ['kʌplɪt] *n* distique *m*.

coupling ['kʌplɪŋ] *n* (*RAIL*) attelage *m*.

coupon ['ku:pɔn] *n* coupon *m*, bon-prime *m*, bon-réclame; (*COMM*) coupon *m*.

courage ['kʌrɪdʒ] *n* courage *m*; **—ous** [kə'reɪdʒəs] *a* courageux (euse).

courier ['kurɪə*] *n* messager *m*, courrier *m*; (*for tourists*) accompagnateur/trice.

course [kɔ:s] *n* cours *m*; (*of ship*) route *f*; (*CONSTR*) assise *f*; (*for golf*) terrain *m*; (*part of meal*) plat *m*; **— first** — entrée *f*; **of —** *ad* bien sûr; **in due —** en temps utile *or* voulu; **— of action** parti *m*, ligne *f* de conduite; **— of lectures** série *f* de conférences; **— of treatment** (*MED*) traitement *m*.

court [kɔ:t] *n* cour *f*; (*LAW*) cour, tribunal *m*; (*TENNIS*) court *m* // *vt* (*woman*) courtiser, faire la cour à; **out of —** (*LAW: settle*) à l'amiable; **to take to —** actionner *or* poursuivre en justice.

courteous ['kɜ:tɪəs] *a* courtois(e), poli(e).

courtesan [kɔ:tɪ'zæn] *n* courtisane *f*.

courtesy ['kɜ:təsɪ] *n* courtoisie *f*, politesse *f*.

court-house ['kɔ:thaus] *n* (*US*) palais *m* de justice.

courtier ['kɔ:tɪə*] *n* courtisan *m*, dame *f* de cour.

court-martial, *pl* **courts-martial** ['kɔ:t'mɑ:ʃəl] *n* cour martiale, conseil *m* de guerre.

courtroom ['kɔ:trum] *n* salle *f* de tribunal.

courtyard ['kɔ:tjɑ:d] *n* cour *f*.

cousin ['kʌzn] *n* cousin/e.

cove [kəuv] *n* petite baie, anse *f*.

covenant ['kʌvənənt] *n* contrat *m*, engagement *m*.

cover [ˈkʌvəˈ*] vt couvrir // n (for bed, of book, COMM) couverture f; (of pan) couvercle m; (over furniture) housse f; (shelter) abri m; **under ~** à l'abri; **~age** n reportage m; (INSURANCE) couverture f; **~ charge** n couvert m (supplément à payer); **~ing** n couverture f, enveloppe f; **~ing letter** n lettre explicative.

covet [ˈkʌvɪt] vt convoiter.

cow [kau] n vache f // cpd femelle.

coward [ˈkauəd] n lâche m/f; **~ice** [-ɪs] n lâcheté f; **~ly** a lâche.

cowboy [ˈkaubɔɪ] n cow-boy m.

cower [ˈkauəˈ*] vi se recroqueviller; trembler.

cowshed [ˈkauʃɛd] n étable f.

coxswain [ˈkɔksn] n (abbr: **cox**) barreur m; (of ship) patron m.

coy [kɔɪ] a faussement effarouché(e) or timide.

coyote [kɔɪˈəutɪ] n coyote m.

crab [kræb] n crabe m; **~ apple** n pomme f sauvage.

crack [kræk] n fente f, fissure f; fêlure f; lézarde f; (noise) craquement m, coup (sec) // vt fendre, fissurer; fêler; lézarder; (whip) faire claquer; (nut) casser // a (athlete) de première classe, d'élite; **to ~ up** vi être au bout du son rouleau, flancher; **~ed** a (col) toqué(e), timbré(e); **~er** n pétard m; biscuit (salé), craquelin m.

crackle [ˈkrækl] vi crépiter, grésiller // n (of china) craquelure f; **crackling** n crépitement m, grésillement m; (of pork) couenne f.

cradle [ˈkreɪdl] n berceau m.

craft [krɑːft] n métier m (artisanal); (cunning) ruse f, astuce f; (boat) embarcation f, barque f; **~sman** n artisan m, ouvrier (qualifié); **~smanship** n métier m, habileté f; **~y** a rusé(e), malin(igne), astucieux(euse).

crag [kræg] n rocher escarpé; **~gy** a escarpé(e), rocheux(euse).

cram [kræm] vt (fill): **to ~ sth with** bourrer qch de; (put): **to ~ sth into** fourrer qch dans; **~ming** n (fig: pej) bachotage m.

cramp [kræmp] n crampe f // vt gêner, entraver; **~ed** a à l'étroit, très serré(e).

crampon [ˈkræmpən] n crampon m.

cranberry [ˈkrænbərɪ] n canneberge f.

crane [kreɪn] n grue f.

cranium, pl **crania** [ˈkreɪnɪəm, ˈkreɪnɪə] n boîte crânienne.

crank [kræŋk] n manivelle f; (person) excentrique m/f; **~shaft** n vilebrequin m.

cranky [ˈkræŋkɪ] a excentrique, loufoque; (bad-tempered) grincheux(euse), revêche.

cranny [ˈkrænɪ] n see **nook**.

crash [kræʃ] n fracas m; (of car, plane) collision f // vt (plane) écraser // vi (plane) s'écraser; (two cars) se percuter, s'emboutir; (fig) s'effondrer; **to ~ into** se jeter or se fracasser contre; **~ course** n cours intensif; **~ helmet** n casque (protecteur); **~ landing** n atterrissage forcé or en catastrophe.

crate [kreɪt] n cageot m.

crater [ˈkreɪtəˈ*] n cratère m.

cravat(e) [krəˈvæt] n foulard (noué autour du cou).

crave [kreɪv] vt: **to ~ for** désirer violemment, avoir un besoin physiologique de, avoir une envie irrésistible de.

crawl [krɔːl] vi ramper; (vehicle) avancer au pas // n (SWIMMING) crawl m.

crayfish [ˈkreɪfɪʃ] n, pl inv écrevisse f; langoustine f.

crayon [ˈkreɪən] n crayon m (de couleur).

craze [kreɪz] n engouement m.

crazy [ˈkreɪzɪ] a fou(folle); **~ paving** n dallage irrégulier (en pierres plates).

creak [kriːk] vi grincer; craquer.

cream [kriːm] n crème f // a (colour) crème inv; **~ cake** n (petit) gâteau à la crème; **~ cheese** n fromage m à la crème, fromage blanc; **~ery** n (shop) crèmerie f; (factory) laiterie f; **~y** a crémeux(euse).

crease [kriːs] n pli m // vt froisser, chiffonner // vi se froisser, se chiffonner.

create [kriːˈeɪt] vt créer; **creation** [-ʃən] n création f; **creative** a créateur(trice); **creator** n créateur/trice.

creature [ˈkriːtʃəˈ*] n créature f.

credence [ˈkriːdns] n croyance f, foi f.

crèche, creche [krɛʃ] n garderie f, crèche f.

credentials [krɪˈdɛnʃlz] npl (papers) références fpl.

credibility [krɛdɪˈbɪlɪtɪ] n crédibilité f.

credible [ˈkrɛdɪbl] a digne de foi, crédible.

credit [ˈkrɛdɪt] n crédit m // vt (COMM) créditer; (believe: also: **give ~ to**) ajouter foi à, croire; **~s** npl (CINEMA) générique m; **to ~ sb with** (fig) prêter or attribuer à qn; **to ~ £5 to sb** créditer (le compte de) qn de 5 livres; **to one's ~** à son honneur; à son actif; **to take the ~ for** s'attribuer le mérite de; **it does him ~** cela lui fait honneur; **~able** a honorable, estimable; **~ card** n carte f de crédit; **~or** n créancier/ière.

credulity [krɪˈdjuːlɪtɪ] n crédulité f.

creed [kriːd] n croyance f; credo m, principes mpl.

creek [kriːk] n crique f, anse f; (US) ruisseau m, petit cours d'eau.

creep, pt, pp **crept** [kriːp, krɛpt] vi ramper; (fig) se faufiler, se glisser; (plant) grimper; **~er** n plante grimpante; **~y** a (frightening) qui fait frissonner, qui donne la chair de poule.

cremate [krɪˈmeɪt] vt incinérer; **cremation** [-ʃən] n incinération f.

crematorium, pl **crematoria** [krɛməˈtɔːrɪəm, -ˈtɔːrɪə] n four m crématoire.

creosote [ˈkrɪəsəut] n créosote f.

crêpe [kreɪp] n crêpe m; **~ bandage** n bande f Velpeau ®.

crept [krɛpt] pt, pp of **creep**.

crescendo [krɪˈʃɛndəu] n crescendo m.

crescent [ˈkrɛsnt] n croissant m; rue f (en arc de cercle).

cress [krɛs] n cresson m.

crest [krɛst] n crête f; (of helmet) cimier m; (of coat of arms) timbre m; **~fallen** a déconfit(e), découragé(e).

Crete [kriːt] n Crète f.

crevasse [krɪ'væs] *n* crevasse *f.*

crevice ['krɛvɪs] *n* fissure *f*, lézarde *f*, fente *f.*

crew [kru:] *n* équipage *m*; **to have a ~-cut** avoir les cheveux en brosse; **~-neck** *n* col ras.

crib [krɪb] *n* lit *m* d'enfant // *vt* (*col*) copier.

cribbage ['krɪbɪdʒ] *n* sorte de jeu de cartes.

crick [krɪk] *n* crampe *f.*

cricket ['krɪkɪt] *n* (*insect*) grillon *m*, cri-cri *m inv*; (*game*) cricket *m*; **~er** *n* joueur *m* de cricket.

crime [kraɪm] *n* crime *m*; **criminal** ['krɪmɪnl] *a*, *n* criminel(le); **the Criminal Investigation Department (C.I.D.)** ≈ la police judiciaire (P.J.).

crimp [krɪmp] *vt* friser, frisotter.

crimson ['krɪmzn] *a* cramoisi(e).

cringe [krɪndʒ] *vi* avoir un mouvement de recul; (*fig*) s'humilier, ramper.

crinkle ['krɪŋkl] *vt* froisser, chiffonner.

cripple ['krɪpl] *n* boiteux/euse, infirme *m/f* // *vt* estropier, paralyser.

crisis, *pl* **crises** ['kraɪsɪs, -si:z] *n* crise *f.*

crisp [krɪsp] *a* croquant(e); (*fig*) vif(vive); brusque; **~s** *npl* (*pommes*) chips *fpl.*

criss-cross ['krɪskrɔs] *a* entrecroisé(e).

criterion, *pl* **criteria** [kraɪ'tɪərɪən, -'tɪərɪə] *n* critère *m.*

critic ['krɪtɪk] *n* critique *m/f*; **~al** *a* critique; **~ally** ad d'un œil critique; **~ally ill** gravement malade; **~ism** ['krɪtɪsɪzm] *n* critique *f*; **~ize** ['krɪtɪsaɪz] *vt* critiquer.

croak [krəʊk] *vi* (*frog*) coasser; (*raven*) croasser.

crochet ['krəʊʃeɪ] *n* travail *m* au crochet.

crockery ['krɔkərɪ] *n* vaisselle *f.*

crocodile ['krɔkədaɪl] *n* crocodile *m.*

crocus ['krəʊkəs] *n* crocus *m.*

croft [krɔft] *n* petite ferme; **~er** *n* fermier *m.*

crony ['krəʊnɪ] *n* copain/copine.

crook [kruk] *n* escroc *m*; (*of shepherd*) houlette *f*; **~ed** ['krukɪd] *a* courbé(e), tordu(e); (*action*) malhonnête.

crop [krɔp] *n* récolte *f*; culture *f*; **to ~ up** *vi* surgir, se présenter, survenir.

cropper ['krɔpə*] *n*: **to come a ~** (*col*) faire la culbute, s'étaler.

croquet ['krəʊkeɪ] *n* croquet *m.*

croquette [krə'kɛt] *n* croquette *f.*

cross [krɔs] *n* croix *f*; (BIOL) croisement *m* // *vt* (*street etc*) traverser; (*arms, legs,* BIOL) croiser; (*cheque*) barrer // *a* en colère, fâché(e); **to ~ out** *vt* barrer, biffer; **to ~ over** *vi* traverser; **~bar** *n* barre transversale; **~breed** *n* hybride *m*, métis/se; **~country (race)** *n* cross(-country) *m*; **~-examination** *n* examen *m* contradictoire (*d'un témoin*); **~-examine** *vt* (LAW) faire subir un examen contradictoire à; **~-eyed** *a* qui louche; **~ing** *n* croisement *m*, carrefour *m*; (*sea-passage*) traversée *f*; (*also*: **pedestrian ~ing**) passage clouté; **~-reference** *n* renvoi *m*, référence *f*; **~roads** *n* carrefour *m*; **~ section** *n* (BIOL) coupe transversale; (*in population*) échantillon *m*; **~wind** *n* vent *m* de travers; **~wise** *ad* en travers; **~word** *n* mots croisés *mpl.*

crotch [krɔtʃ] *n* (*of garment*) entre-jambes *m inv.*

crotchet ['krɔtʃɪt] *n* (MUS) noire *f.*

crotchety ['krɔtʃɪtɪ] *a* (*person*) grognon(ne), grincheux(euse).

crouch [krautʃ] *vi* s'accroupir; se tapir; se ramasser.

crouton ['kru:tɔn] *n* croûton *m.*

crow [krəʊ] *n* (*bird*) corneille *f*; (*of cock*) chant *m* du coq, cocorico *m* // *vi* (*cock*) chanter; (*fig*) pavoiser, chanter victoire.

crowbar ['krəʊba:*] *n* levier *m.*

crowd [kraud] *n* foule *f* // *vt* bourrer, remplir // *vi* affluer, s'attrouper, s'entasser; **~ed** *a* bondé(e), plein(e); **~ed with** plein(e) de.

crown [kraun] *n* couronne *f*; (*of head*) sommet *m* de la tête, calotte crânienne; (*of hat*) fond *m*; (*of hill*) sommet *m* // *vt* couronner; **C~ court** *n* ≈ Cour *f* d'assises; **~ jewels** *npl* joyaux *mpl* de la Couronne; **~ prince** *n* prince héritier.

crow's-nest ['krəʊznɛst] *n* (*on sailing-ship*) nid *m* de pie.

crucial ['kru:ʃl] *a* crucial(e), décisif(ive).

crucifix ['kru:sɪfɪks] *n* crucifix *m*; **~ion** [-'fɪkʃən] *n* crucifixion *f.*

crucify ['kru:sɪfaɪ] *vt* crucifier, mettre en croix.

crude [kru:d] *a* (*materials*) brut(e); non raffiné(e); (*fig*: *basic*) rudimentaire, sommaire; (: *vulgar*) cru(e), grossier(ère); **~ (oil)** *n* (*pétrole*) brut *m.*

cruel [kruəl] *a* cruel(le); **~ty** *n* cruauté *f.*

cruet ['kru:ɪt] *n* huilier *m*; vinaigrier *m.*

cruise [kru:z] *n* croisière *f* // *vi* (*ship*) croiser; (*car*) rouler; (*aircraft*) voler; (*taxi*) être en maraude; **~r** *n* croiseur *m*; **cruising speed** *n* vitesse *f* de croisière.

crumb [krʌm] *n* miette *f.*

crumble ['krʌmbl] *vt* émietter // *vi* s'émietter; (*plaster etc*) s'effriter; (*land, earth*) s'ébouler; (*building*) s'écrouler, crouler; (*fig*) s'effondrer; **crumbly** *a* friable.

crumpet ['krʌmpɪt] *n* petite crêpe (épaisse).

crumple ['krʌmpl] *vt* froisser, friper.

crunch [krʌntʃ] *vt* croquer; (*underfoot*) faire craquer, écraser; faire crisser // *n* (*fig*) instant *m* or moment *m* critique, moment de vérité; **~y** *a* croquant(e), croustillant(e).

crusade [kru:'seɪd] *n* croisade *f*; **~r** *n* croisé *m.*

crush [krʌʃ] *n* foule *f*, cohue *f*; (*love*): **to have a ~ on sb** avoir le béguin pour qn; (*drink*): **lemon ~** citron pressé // *vt* écraser; (*crumple*) froisser; **~ing** *a* écrasant(e).

crust [krʌst] *n* croûte *f.*

crutch [krʌtʃ] *n* béquille *f*; (TECH) support *m.*

crux [krʌks] *n* point crucial.

cry [kraɪ] *vi* pleurer; (*shout*) crier // *n* cri *m*; **to ~ off** *vi* se dédire; se décommander; **~ing** *a* (*fig*) criant(e), flagrant(e).

crypt [krɪpt] *n* crypte *f.*

cryptic ['krɪptɪk] a énigmatique.

crystal ['krɪstl] n cristal m; ~-**clear** a clair(e) comme de l'eau de roche ; **crystallize** vt cristalliser // vi (se) cristalliser.

cu. abbr: ~ **ft.** = cubic feet ; ~ **in.** = cubic inches.

cub [kʌb] n petit m (d'un animal).

Cuba ['kju:bə] n Cuba m; ~**n** a cubain(e) // n Cubain/e.

cubbyhole ['kʌbɪhəul] n cagibi m.

cube [kju:b] n cube m // vt (MATH) élever au cube ; ~ **root** n racine f cubique ; **cubic** a cubique ; **cubic metre** etc mètre m cube etc.

cubicle ['kju:bɪkl] n box m, cabine f.

cuckoo ['kuku:] n coucou m; ~ **clock** n (pendule f à) coucou m.

cucumber ['kju:kʌmbə*] n concombre m.

cud [kʌd] n: to **chew** the ~ ruminer.

cuddle ['kʌdl] vt câliner, caresser // vi se blottir l'un contre l'autre ; **cuddly** a câlin(e).

cudgel ['kʌdʒl] n gourdin m.

cue [kju:] n queue f de billard ; (THEATRE etc) signal m.

cuff [kʌf] n (of shirt, coat etc) poignet m, manchette f; (US) = **turn-up** ; **off the** ~ ad de chic, à l'improviste ; ~**link** n bouton m de manchette.

cuisine [kwɪ'zi:n] n cuisine f, art m culinaire.

cul-de-sac ['kʌldəsæk] n cul-de-sac m, impasse f.

culinary ['kʌlɪnərɪ] a culinaire.

cull [kʌl] vt sélectionner.

culminate ['kʌlmɪneɪt] vi culminer ; **culmination** [-'neɪʃən] n point culminant.

culpable ['kʌlpəbl] a coupable.

culprit ['kʌlprɪt] n coupable m/f.

cult [kʌlt] n culte m.

cultivate ['kʌltɪveɪt] vt (also fig) cultiver ; **cultivation** [-'veɪʃən] n culture f.

cultural ['kʌltʃərəl] a culturel(le).

culture ['kʌltʃə*] n (also fig) culture f; ~**d** a cultivé(e) (fig).

cumbersome ['kʌmbəsəm] a encombrant(e), embarrassant(e).

cumulative ['kju:mjulətɪv] a cumulatif(ive).

cunning ['kʌnɪŋ] n ruse f, astuce f // a rusé(e), malin(igne).

cup [kʌp] n tasse f; (prize, event) coupe f; (of bra) bonnet m.

cupboard ['kʌbəd] n placard m.

Cupid ['kju:pɪd] n Cupidon m; (figurine) amour m.

cupidity [kju:'pɪdɪtɪ] n cupidité f.

cupola ['kju:pələ] n coupole f.

cup-tie ['kʌptaɪ] n match m de coupe.

curable ['kjuərəbl] a guérissable, curable.

curate ['kjuərɪt] n vicaire m.

curator [kjuə'reɪtə*] n conservateur m (d'un musée etc).

curb [kə:b] vt refréner, mettre un frein à // n frein m (fig) ; (US) = **kerb.**

curdle ['kə:dl] vi (se) cailler.

curds [kə:ds] npl lait caillé.

cure [kjuə*] vt guérir ; (CULIN) saler ; fumer ; sécher // n remède m.

curfew ['kə:fju:] n couvre-feu m.

curio ['kjuərɪəu] n bibelot m, curiosité f.

curiosity [kjuərɪ'ɔsɪtɪ] n curiosité f.

curious ['kjuərɪəs] a curieux(euse) ; ~**ly** ad curieusement.

curl [kə:l] n boucle f (de cheveux) // vt, vi boucler ; (tightly) friser ; to ~ **up** vi s'enrouler ; se pelotonner ; ~**er** n bigoudi m, rouleau m; (SPORT) joueur/euse de curling.

curling ['kə:lɪŋ] n (SPORT) curling m.

curly ['kə:lɪ] a bouclé(e) ; frisé(e).

currant ['kʌrnt] n raisin m de Corinthe, raisin sec.

currency ['kʌrnsɪ] n monnaie f; **foreign** ~ devises étrangères, monnaie étrangère ; **to gain** ~ (fig) s'accréditer.

current ['kʌrnt] n courant m // a courant(e) ; ~ **account** n compte courant ; ~ **affairs** npl (questions fpl d')actualité f; ~**ly** ad actuellement.

curriculum, pl ~**s** or **curricula** [kə'rɪkjuləm, -lə] n programme m d'études ; ~ **vitae** n curriculum vitae (C.V.) m.

curry ['kʌrɪ] n curry m // vt: to ~ **favour with** chercher à gagner la faveur or à s'attirer les bonnes grâces de ; **chicken** ~ curry de poulet, poulet m au curry ; ~ **powder** n poudre f de curry.

curse [kə:s] vi jurer, blasphémer // vt maudire // n malédiction f; fléau m; (swearword) juron m.

cursory ['kə:sərɪ] a superficiel(le), hâtif(ive).

curt [kə:t] a brusque, sec(sèche).

curtail [kə:'teɪl] vt (visit etc) écourter ; (expenses etc) réduire.

curtain ['kə:tn] n rideau m.

curts(e)y ['kə:tsɪ] n révérence f // vi faire une révérence.

curve [kə:v] n courbe f; (in the road) tournant m, virage m // vt courber // vi se courber ; (road) faire une courbe.

cushion ['kuʃən] n coussin m // vt (seat) rembourrer ; (shock) amortir.

custard ['kʌstəd] n (for pouring) crème anglaise.

custodian [kʌs'təudɪən] n gardien/ne ; (of collection etc) conservateur/trice.

custody ['kʌstədɪ] n (of child) garde f; (for offenders) détention préventive.

custom ['kʌstəm] n coutume f, usage m; (LAW) droit coutumier, coutume ; (COMM) clientèle f; ~**ary** a habituel(le).

customer ['kʌstəmə*] n client/e.

custom-made ['kʌstəm'meɪd] a (clothes) fait(e) sur mesure ; (other goods) hors série, fait(e) sur commande.

customs ['kʌstəmz] npl douane f; ~ **duty** n droits mpl de douane ; ~ **officer** n douanier m.

cut [kʌt] vb (pt, pp cut) vt couper ; (meat) découper ; (shape, make) tailler ; couper ; creuser ; graver ; (reduce) réduire // vi couper ; (intersect) se couper // n (gen) coupure f; (of clothes) coupe f; (of jewel) taille f; (in salary etc) réduction f; (of meat) morceau m; **power** ~ coupure de courant ; to ~ **teeth** (baby) faire ses dents ; to ~ **a tooth** percer une dent ; to ~ **down (on)** vt fus réduire ; to ~ **off** vt couper; (fig) isoler; **to ~ out** vt ôter; découper; tailler; **~away** a, n: **~away (drawing)** écorché m; **~back** n réductions fpl.

cute [kju:t] a mignon(ne), adorable; (clever) rusé(e), astucieux(euse).

cut glass [kʌt'glɑːs] n cristal taillé.

cuticle ['kjuːtɪkl] n (on nail): **~ remover** n repousse-peaux m inv.

cutlery ['kʌtləri] n couverts mpl; (trade) coutellerie f.

cutlet ['kʌtlɪt] n côtelette f.

cut: ~off switch n interrupteur m; **~out** n coupe-circuit m inv; **~-price** a au rabais, à prix réduit; **~ throat** n assassin m.

cutting ['kʌtɪŋ] a tranchant(e), coupant(e); (fig) cinglant(e), mordant(e) // n (PRESS) coupure f (de journal); (RAIL) tranchée f.

cuttlefish ['kʌtlfɪʃ] n seiche f.

cut-up ['kʌtʌp] a affecté(e), démoralisé(e).

cwt abbr of **hundredweight(s)**.

cyanide ['saɪənaɪd] n cyanure m.

cybernetics [saɪbə'nɛtɪks] n cybernétique f.

cyclamen ['sɪkləmən] n cyclamen m.

cycle ['saɪkl] n cycle m // vi faire de la bicyclette.

cycling ['saɪklɪŋ] n cyclisme m.

cyclist ['saɪklɪst] n cycliste m/f.

cyclone ['saɪkləun] n cyclone m.

cygnet ['sɪgnɪt] n jeune cygne m.

cylinder ['sɪlɪndə*] n cylindre m; **~ block** n bloc-cylindres m; **~ capacity** n cylindrée f; **~ head** n culasse f; **~-head gasket** n joint m de culasse.

cymbals ['sɪmblz] npl cymbales fpl.

cynic ['sɪnɪk] n cynique m/f; **~al** a cynique; **~ism** ['sɪnɪsɪzəm] n cynisme m.

cypress ['saɪprɪs] n cyprès m.

Cypriot ['sɪprɪət] a cypriote, chypriote // n Cypriote m/f, Chypriote m/f.

Cyprus ['saɪprəs] n Chypre f.

cyst [sɪst] n kyste m.

cystitis [sɪs'taɪtɪs] n cystite f.

czar [zɑː*] n tsar m.

Czech [tʃɛk] a tchèque // n Tchèque m/f; (LING) tchèque m.

Czechoslovakia [tʃɛkəslə'vækɪə] n la Tchécoslovaquie; **~n** a tchécoslovaque // n Tchécoslovaque m/f.

D

D [diː] n (MUS) ré m; **~-day** n le jour J.

dab [dæb] vt (eyes, wound) tamponner; (paint, cream) appliquer (par petites touches or rapidement); **a ~ of paint** un petit coup de peinture.

dabble ['dæbl] vi: **to ~ in** faire ou se mêler or s'occuper un peu de.

dad, daddy ['dæd, 'dædɪ] n papa m; **daddy-long-legs** n tipule f; faucheux m.

daffodil ['dæfədɪl] n jonquille f.

daft [dɑːft] a idiot(e), stupide; **to be ~ about** être toqué or mordu de.

dagger ['dægə*] n poignard m; **to be at ~s drawn with sb** être à couteaux tirés

avec qn; **to look ~s at sb** foudroyer qn du regard.

daily ['deɪlɪ] a quotidien(ne), journalier-(ère) // n quotidien m // ad tous les jours.

dainty ['deɪntɪ] a délicat(e), mignon(ne).

dairy ['dɛərɪ] n (shop) crèmerie f, laiterie f; (on farm) laiterie // a laitier(ère).

daisy ['deɪzɪ] n pâquerette f.

dale [deɪl] n vallon m.

dally ['dælɪ] vi musarder, flâner.

dam [dæm] n barrage m // vt endiguer.

damage ['dæmɪdʒ] n dégâts mpl, dommages mpl; (fig) tort m // vt endommager, abimer; (fig) faire du tort à; **~s** npl (LAW) dommages-intérêts mpl.

damn [dæm] vt condamner; (curse) maudire // n (col): **I don't give a ~** je m'en fous // a (col): **this ~ ...** ce sacré or foutu ...; **~ (it)!** zut!; **~ing** a (evidence) accablant(e).

damp [dæmp] a humide // n humidité f // vt (also: **~en**) (cloth, rag) humecter; (enthusiasm etc) refroidir; **~ness** n humidité f.

damson ['dæmzən] n prune f de Damas.

dance [dɑːns] n danse f; (ball) bal m // vi danser; **~ hall** n salle f de bal, dancing m; **~r** n danseur/euse.

dancing ['dɑːnsɪŋ] n danse f.

dandelion ['dændɪlaɪən] n pissenlit m.

dandruff ['dændrəf] n pellicules fpl.

Dane [deɪn] n Danois/e.

danger ['deɪndʒə*] n danger m; **there is a ~ of fire** il y a (un) risque d'incendie; **in ~** en danger; **he was in ~ of falling** il risquait de tomber; **~ous** a dangereux(euse); **~ously** ad dangereusement.

dangle ['dæŋgl] vt balancer; (fig) faire miroiter // vi pendre, se balancer.

Danish ['deɪnɪʃ] a danois(e) // n (LING) danois m.

dapper ['dæpə*] a pimpant(e).

dare [dɛə*] vt: **to ~ sb to do** défier qn or mettre qn au défi de faire // vi: **to ~ (to) do sth** oser faire qch; **~devil** n casse-cou m inv; **daring** a hardi(e), audacieux(euse).

dark [dɑːk] a (night, room) obscur(e), sombre; (colour, complexion) foncé(e), sombre; (fig) sombre // n: **in the ~** dans le noir; **in the ~ about** (fig) ignorant tout de; **after ~** après la tombée de la nuit; **~en** vt obscurcir, assombrir // vi s'obscurcir, s'assombrir; **~ glasses** npl lunettes noires; **~ness** n obscurité f; **~ room** n chambre noire.

darling ['dɑːlɪŋ] a, n chéri(e).

darn [dɑːn] vt repriser.

dart [dɑːt] n flèchette f // vi: **to ~ towards** (also: **make a ~ towards**) se précipiter or s'élancer vers; **to ~ away/along** partir/passer comme une flèche; **~s** n jeu m de flèchettes; **~board** n cible f (de jeu de flèchettes).

dash [dæʃ] n (sign) tiret m // vt (missile) jeter or lancer violemment; (hopes) anéantir // vi: **to ~ towards** (also: **make a ~ towards**) se précipiter ou se ruer vers; **to ~ away** vi partir à toute allure;

~board n tableau m de bord; **~ing** a
fringant(e).
data ['deɪtə] npl .données fpl; **~
processing** n traitement m (électronique)
de l'information.
date [deɪt] n date f; rendez-vous m; (fruit)
datte f // vt dater; **to ~** ad à ce jour;
out of ~ périmé(e); **up to ~** à la page;
mis(e) à jour; moderne; **~d the 13th** daté
du 13; **~d** démodé(e); **~line** n ligne f
de changement de date.
daub [dɔːb] vt barbouiller.
daughter ['dɔːtə*] n fille f; **~-in-law** n
belle-fille f, bru f.
daunt [dɔːnt] vt intimider, décourager;
~less a intrépide.
dawdle ['dɔːdl] vi traîner, lambiner.
dawn [dɔːn] n aube f, aurore f // vi (day)
se lever, poindre; (fig) naître, se faire jour.
day [deɪ] n jour m; (as duration) journée
f; (period of time, age) époque f, temps m;
the ~ before la veille, le jour précédent;
the following ~ le lendemain, le jour
suivant; **by ~** de jour; **~ boy/girl** n
(SCOL) externe m/f; **~break** n point m du
jour; **~dream** n rêverie f // vi rêver (tout
éveillé); **~light** n (lumière f du) jour m;
~time n jour m, journée f.
daze [deɪz] vt (subject: drug) hébéter; (:
blow) étourdir // n: **in a ~** hébété(e);
étourdi(e).
dazzle ['dæzl] vt éblouir, aveugler.
dead [dɛd] a mort(e); (numb) engourdi(e),
insensible // ad absolument,
complètement; **he was shot ~** il a été
tué d'un coup de revolver; **~ on time** à
l'heure pile; **~ tired** éreinté,
complètement fourbu; **to stop ~** s'arrêter
pile or net; **the ~** les morts m; **~en** vt (blow,
sound) amortir; (make numb) endormir,
rendre insensible; **~ end** n impasse f;
~ heat n (SPORT): **to finish in a ~ heat**
terminer ex-aequo; **~line** n date f or heure
f limite; **~lock** n impasse f (fig); **~ly** a
mortel(le); (weapon) meurtrier(ère);
~pan a impassible; (humour) pince-sans-
rire inv.
deaf [dɛf] a sourd(e); **~-aid** n appareil
auditif; **~en** vt rendre sourd; (fig)
assourdir; **~ening** a assourdissant(e);
~ness n surdité f; **~-mute** n sourd/e-
muet/te.
deal [diːl] n affaire f, marché m // vt (pt,
pp **dealt** [dɛlt]) (blow) porter; (cards)
donner, distribuer; **a great ~ (of)**
beaucoup (de); **to ~ in** faire le commerce
de; **to ~ with** vt fus (COMM) traiter avec;
(handle) s'occuper or se charger de; (be
about: book etc) traiter de; **~er** n
marchand m; **~ings** npl (COMM)
transactions fpl; (relations) relations fpl,
rapports mpl.
dean [diːn] n (SCOL) doyen m.
dear [dɪə*] a cher(chère); (expensive) cher,
coûteux(euse) // n: **my ~** mon cher/ma
chère; **~ me!** mon Dieu!; **D~
Sir/Madam** (in letter) Monsieur/Mada-
me; **D~ Mr/Mrs X** Cher
Monsieur/Chère Madame X; **~ly** ad
(love) tendrement; (pay) cher.
dearth [dəːθ] n disette f, pénurie f.

death [dɛθ] n mort f; (ADMIN) décès m;
~bed n lit m de mort; **~ certificate** n
acte m de décès; **~ duties** npl (Brit) droits
mpl de succession; **~ly** a de mort; **~
penalty** n peine f de mort; **~ rate** n (taux
m de) mortalité f.
debar [dɪ'bɑː*] vt: **to ~ sb from a club**
etc exclure qn d'un club etc; **to ~ sb from
doing** interdire à qn de faire.
debase [dɪ'beɪs] vt (currency) déprécier,
dévaloriser; (person) abaisser, avilir.
debatable [dɪ'beɪtəbl] a discutable,
contestable.
debate [dɪ'beɪt] n discussion f, débat m //
vt discuter, débattre // vi (consider): **to ~
whether** se demander si.
debauchery [dɪ'bɔːtʃərɪ] n débauche f.
debit ['dɛbɪt] n débit m // vt: **to ~ a sum
to sb** or **to sb's account** porter une
somme au débit de qn, débiter qn d'une
somme.
debris ['dɛbriː] n débris mpl, décombres
mpl.
debt [dɛt] n dette f; **to be in ~** avoir des
dettes, être endetté(e); **~or** n
débiteur/trice.
début ['deɪbjuː] n début(s) m(pl).
decade ['dɛkeɪd] n décennie f, décade f.
decadence ['dɛkədəns] n décadence f.
decanter [dɪ'kæntə*] n carafe f.
decarbonize [diː'kɑːbənaɪz] vt (AUT)
décalaminer.
decay [dɪ'keɪ] n décomposition f,
pourrissement m; (fig) déclin m,
délabrement m; (also: **tooth ~**) carie f
(dentaire) // vi (rot) se décomposer,
pourrir; (fig) se délabrer; décliner; se
détériorer.
decease [dɪ'siːs] n décès m; **~d** n
défunt/e.
deceit [dɪ'siːt] n tromperie f, supercherie
f; **~ful** a trompeur(euse).
deceive [dɪ'siːv] vt tromper; **to ~ o.s.**
s'abuser.
decelerate [diː'sɛləreɪt] vt,vi ralentir.
December [dɪ'sɛmbə*] n décembre m.
decency ['diːsənsɪ] n décence f.
decent ['diːsənt] a décent(e), convenable;
they were very ~ about it ils se sont
montrés très chics.
decentralize [diː'sɛntrəlaɪz] vt
décentraliser.
deception [dɪ'sɛpʃən] n tromperie f.
deceptive [dɪ'sɛptɪv] a trompeur(euse).
decibel ['dɛsɪbɛl] n décibel m.
decide [dɪ'saɪd] vt (person) décider;
(question, argument) trancher, régler // vi
se décider, décider; **to ~ to do/that**
décider de faire/que; **to ~ on** décider, se
décider pour; **to ~ on doing** décider de
faire; **~d** a (resolute) résolu(e), décidé(e);
(clear, definite) net(te), marqué(e); **~dly**
[-dɪdlɪ] ad résolument; incontestablement,
nettement.
deciduous [dɪ'sɪdjuəs] a à feuilles
caduques.
decimal ['dɛsɪməl] a décimal(e) // n
décimale f; **~ point** n ≈ virgule f.
decimate ['dɛsɪmeɪt] vt décimer.
decipher [dɪ'saɪfə*] vt déchiffrer.

decision [dɪ'sɪʒən] *n* décision *f*.
decisive [dɪ'saɪsɪv] *a* décisif(ive).
deck [dɛk] *n* (*NAUT*) pont *m*; (*of bus*): **top ~** impériale *f*; (*of cards*) jeu *m*; **~chair** *n* chaise longue; **~ hand** *n* matelot *m*.
declaration [dɛklə'reɪʃən] *n* déclaration *f*.
declare [dɪ'klɛə*] *vt* déclarer.
decline [dɪ'klaɪn] *n* (*decay*) déclin *m*; (*lessening*) baisse *f* // *vt* refuser, décliner // *vi* décliner; être en baisse, baisser.
declutch ['di:'klʌtʃ] *vi* débrayer.
decode ['di:'kəud] *vt* décoder.
decompose [di:kəm'pəuz] *vi* se décomposer; **decomposition** [di:kɒmpə'zɪʃən] *n* décomposition *f*.
decontaminate [di:kən'tæmɪneɪt] *vt* décontaminer.
décor ['deɪkɔ:*] *n* décor *m*.
decorate ['dɛkəreɪt] *vt* (*adorn, give a medal to*) décorer; (*paint and paper*) peindre et tapisser; **decoration** [-'reɪʃən] *n* (*medal etc, adornment*) décoration *f*; **decorative** ['dɛkərətɪv] *a* décoratif(ive); **decorator** *n* peintre *m* en bâtiment.
decoy ['di:kɔɪ] *n* piège *m*; **they used him as a ~ for the enemy** ils se sont servis de lui pour attirer l'ennemi.
decrease *n* ['di:kri:s] diminution *f* // *vt*, *vi* [di:'kri:s] diminuer.
decree [dɪ'kri:] *n* (*POL, REL*) décret *m*; (*LAW: of tribunal*) arrêt *m*, jugement *m*; **~ nisi** *n* jugement provisoire de divorce.
decrepit [dɪ'krɛpɪt] *a* décrépit(e); délabré(e).
dedicate ['dɛdɪkeɪt] *vt* consacrer; (*book etc*) dédier.
dedication [dɛdɪ'keɪʃən] *n* (*devotion*) dévouement *m*.
deduce [dɪ'dju:s] *vt* déduire, conclure.
deduct [dɪ'dʌkt] *vt*: **to ~ sth (from)** déduire qch (de), retrancher qch (de); (*from wage etc*) retenir qch (sur); **~ion** [dɪ'dʌkʃən] *n* (*deducting*) déduction *f*; (*from wage etc*) prélèvement *m*, retenue *f*; (*deducing*) déduction, conclusion *f*.
deed [di:d] *n* action *f*, acte *m*; (*LAW*) acte notarié, contrat *m*.
deep [di:p] *a* (*water, sigh, sorrow, thoughts*) profond(e); (*voice*) grave; **he took a ~ breath** il respira profondément, il prit son souffle; **4 metres ~** de 4 mètres de profondeur // *ad*: **~ in snow** recouvert(e) d'une épaisse couche de neige; **spectators stood 20 ~** il y avait 20 rangs de spectateurs; **knee-~ in water** dans l'eau jusqu'aux genoux; **~en** *vt* (*hole*) approfondir // *vi* s'approfondir; (*darkness*) s'épaissir; **~-freeze** *n* congélateur *m* // *vt* surgeler; **~-fry** *vt* faire frire (en friteuse); **~-sea** *a*: **~-sea diving** *n* plongée sous-marine; **~-sea fishing** *n* pêche hauturière; **~-seated** *a* (*beliefs*) profondément enraciné(e); **~-set** *a* (*eyes*) enfoncé(e).
deer [dɪə*] *n*, *pl inv*: **the ~** les cervidés *mpl* (*ZOOL*): (**red**) **~** cerf *m*; (**fallow**) **~** daim *m*; (**roe**) **~** chevreuil *m*; **~skin** *n* peau *f* de daim.
deface [dɪ'feɪs] *vt* dégrader; barbouiller; rendre illisible.

defamation [dɛfə'meɪʃən] *n* diffamation *f*.
default [dɪ'fɔ:lt] *vi* (*LAW*) faire défaut; (*gen*) manquer à ses engagements // *n*: **by ~** (*LAW*) par défaut, par contumace; (*SPORT*) par forfait; **~er** *n* (*in debt*) débiteur défaillant.
defeat [dɪ'fi:t] *n* défaite *f* // *vt* (*team, opponents*) battre; (*fig: plans, efforts*) faire échouer; **~ist** *a,n* défaitiste (*m/f*).
defect *n* ['di:fɛkt] défaut *m* // *vi* [dɪ'fɛkt]: **to ~ to the enemy/the West** passer à l'ennemi/l'Ouest; **~ive** [dɪ'fɛktɪv] *a* défectueux(euse).
defence [dɪ'fɛns] *n* défense *f*; **in ~ of** pour défendre; **~less** *a* sans défense.
defend [dɪ'fɛnd] *vt* défendre; **~ant** *n* défendeur/deresse; (*in criminal case*) accusé/e, prévenu/e; **~er** *n* défenseur *m*.
defense [dɪ'fɛns] *n* (*US*) = **defence**.
defensive [dɪ'fɛnsɪv] *a* défensif(ive).
defer [dɪ'fə:*] *vt* (*postpone*) différer, ajourner.
deference ['dɛfərəns] *n* déférence *f*; égards *mpl*.
defiance [dɪ'faɪəns] *n* défi *m*; **in ~ of** au mépris de.
defiant [dɪ'faɪənt] *a* provocant(e), de défi.
deficiency [dɪ'fɪʃənsɪ] *n* insuffisance *f*, déficience *f*; carence *f*; **~ disease** *n* maladie *f* de carence.
deficient [dɪ'fɪʃənt] *a* insuffisant(e); défectueux(euse); déficient(e); **~ in** manquant de.
deficit ['dɛfɪsɪt] *n* déficit *m*.
defile *vb* [dɪ'faɪl] *vt* souiller // *vi* défiler // *n* ['di:faɪl] défilé *m*.
define [dɪ'faɪn] *vt* définir.
definite ['dɛfɪnɪt] *a* (*fixed*) défini(e), (bien) déterminé(e); (*clear, obvious*) net(te), manifeste; (*LING*) défini(e); **he was ~ about it** il a été catégorique; il était sûr de son fait; **~ly** *ad* sans aucun doute.
definition [dɛfɪ'nɪʃən] *n* définition *f*.
definitive [dɪ'fɪnɪtɪv] *a* définitif(ive).
deflate [di:'fleɪt] *vt* dégonfler.
deflation [di:'fleɪʃən] *n* (*COMM*) déflation *f*.
deflect [dɪ'flɛkt] *vt* détourner, faire dévier.
deform [dɪ'fɔ:m] *vt* déformer; **~ed** *a* difforme; **~ity** *n* difformité *f*.
defraud [dɪ'frɔ:d] *vt* frauder; **to ~ sb of sth** soutirer qch malhonnêtement à qn; escroquer qch à qn; frustrer qn de qch.
defray [dɪ'freɪ] *vt*: **to ~ sb's expenses** défrayer qn (de ses frais), rembourser or payer à qn ses frais.
defrost [di:'frɔst] *vt* (*fridge*) dégivrer.
deft [dɛft] *a* adroit(e), preste.
defunct [dɪ'fʌŋkt] *a* défunt(e).
defuse [di:'fju:z] *vt* désamorcer.
defy [dɪ'faɪ] *vt* défier; (*efforts etc*) résister à.
degenerate *vi* [dɪ'dʒɛnəreɪt] dégénérer // *a* [dɪ'dʒɛnərɪt] dégénéré(e).
degradation [dɛgrə'deɪʃən] *n* dégradation *f*.
degrading [dɪ'greɪdɪŋ] *a* dégradant(e).
degree [dɪ'gri:] *n* degré *m*; grade *m* (universitaire); **a (first) ~ in maths** une licence en maths.
dehydrated [di:haɪ'dreɪtɪd] *a* déshydraté(e); (*milk, eggs*) en poudre.

de-ice [di:'aɪs] vt (windscreen) dégivrer.

deign [deɪn] vi: **to ~ to do** daigner faire.

deity ['di:ɪtɪ] n divinité f; dieu m, déesse f.

dejected [dɪ'dʒɛktɪd] a abattu(e), déprimé(e).

dejection [dɪ'dʒɛkʃən] n abattement m, découragement m.

delay [dɪ'leɪ] vt (journey, operation) retarder, différer; (travellers, trains) retarder // n délai m, retard m; **without ~** sans délai; sans tarder; **~ed-action** a à retardement.

delegate n ['dɛlɪgɪt] délégué/e // vt ['dɛlɪgeɪt] déléguer.

delegation [dɛlɪ'geɪʃən] n délégation f.

delete [dɪ'li:t] vt rayer, supprimer.

deliberate a [dɪ'lɪbərɪt] (intentional) délibéré(e); (slow) mesuré(e) // vi [dɪ'lɪbəreɪt] délibérer, réfléchir; **~ly** ad (on purpose) exprès, délibérément.

delicacy ['dɛlɪkəsɪ] n délicatesse f; (choice food) mets fin or délicat, friandise f.

delicate ['dɛlɪkɪt] a délicat(e).

delicatessen [dɛlɪkə'tɛsn] n épicerie fine.

delicious [dɪ'lɪʃəs] a délicieux(euse), exquis(e).

delight [dɪ'laɪt] n (grande) joie, grand plaisir // vt enchanter; **a ~ to the eyes** un régal or plaisir pour les yeux; **to take ~ in** prendre grand plaisir à; **to be the ~ of** faire les délices or la joie de; **~ful** a adorable; merveilleux(euse); délicieux(euse).

delinquency [dɪ'lɪŋkwənsɪ] n délinquance f.

delinquent [dɪ'lɪŋkwənt] a,n délinquant(e).

delirium [dɪ'lɪrɪəm] n délire m.

deliver [dɪ'lɪvə*] vt (mail) distribuer; (goods) livrer; (message) remettre; (speech) prononcer; (warning, ultimatum) lancer; (free) délivrer; (MED) accoucher; **to ~ the goods** (fig) tenir ses promesses; **~y** n distribution f; livraison f; (of speaker) élocution f; (MED) accouchement m; **to take ~y** of prendre livraison de.

delouse ['di:'laus] vt épouiller, débarrasser de sa (or leur etc) vermine.

delta ['dɛltə] n delta m.

delude [dɪ'lu:d] vt tromper, leurrer; **to ~ o.s.** se leurrer, se faire des illusions.

deluge ['dɛljuːdʒ] n déluge m.

delusion [dɪ'luːʒən] n illusion f.

delve [dɛlv] vi: **to ~ into** fouiller dans.

demagogue ['dɛməgɔg] n démagogue m/f.

demand [dɪ'mɑːnd] vt réclamer, exiger // n exigence f; (claim) revendication f; (ECON) demande f; **in ~** demandé(e), recherché(e); **on ~** sur demande; **~ing** a (boss) exigeant(e); (work) astreignant(e).

demarcation [di:mɑː'keɪʃən] n démarcation f.

demean [dɪ'miːn] vt: **to ~ o.s.** s'abaisser.

demeanour [dɪ'miːnə*] n comportement m; maintien m.

demented [dɪ'mɛntɪd] a dément(e), fou(folle).

demise [dɪ'maɪz] n décès m.

demister [di:'mɪstə*] n (AUT) dispositif m anti-buée inv.

demobilize [di:'məubɪlaɪz] vt démobiliser.

democracy [dɪ'mɔkrəsɪ] n démocratie f.

democrat ['dɛməkræt] n démocrate m/f; **~ic** [dɛmə'krætɪk] a démocratique.

demography [dɪ'mɔgrəfɪ] n démographie f.

demolish [dɪ'mɔlɪʃ] vt démolir.

demolition [dɛmə'lɪʃən] n démolition f.

demonstrate ['dɛmənstreɪt] vt démontrer, prouver.

demonstration [dɛmən'streɪʃən] n démonstration f, manifestation f.

demonstrative [dɪ'mɔnstrətɪv] a démonstratif(ive).

demonstrator ['dɛmənstreɪtə*] n (POL) manifestant/e.

demoralize [dɪ'mɔrəlaɪz] vt démoraliser.

demote [dɪ'məut] vt rétrograder.

demur [dɪ'məː*] vi protester; hésiter.

demure [dɪ'mjuə*] a sage, réservé(e); d'une modestie affectée.

den [dɛn] n tanière f, antre m.

denial [dɪ'naɪəl] n démenti m; dénégation f.

denigrate ['dɛnɪgreɪt] vt dénigrer.

denim ['dɛnɪm] n coton émerisé; **~s** npl (blue-)jeans mpl.

Denmark ['dɛnmɑːk] n Danemark m.

denomination [dɪnɔmɪ'neɪʃən] n (money) valeur f; (REL) confession f; culte m.

denominator [dɪ'nɔmɪneɪtə*] n dénominateur m.

denote [dɪ'nəut] vt dénoter.

denounce [dɪ'nauns] vt dénoncer.

dense [dɛns] a dense; (stupid) obtus(e), dur(e) or lent(e) à la comprenette; **~ly** ad: **~ly wooded** couvert d'épaisses forêts; **~ly populated** à forte densité (de population), très peuplé.

density ['dɛnsɪtɪ] n densité f.

dent [dɛnt] n bosse f // vt (also: **make a ~ in**) cabosser; **to make a ~ in** (fig) entamer.

dental ['dɛntl] a dentaire; **~ surgeon** n (chirurgien-)dentiste m.

dentifrice ['dɛntɪfrɪs] n dentifrice m.

dentist ['dɛntɪst] n dentiste m/f; **~ry** n art m dentaire.

denture ['dɛntʃə*] n dentier m.

deny [dɪ'naɪ] vt nier; (refuse) refuser; (disown) renier.

deodorant [di:'əudərənt] n désodorisant m, déodorant m.

depart [dɪ'pɑːt] vi partir; **to ~ from** (leave) quitter, partir de; (fig: differ from) s'écarter de.

department [dɪ'pɑːtmənt] n (COMM) rayon m; (SCOL) section f; (POL) ministère m, département m; **~ store** n grand magasin.

departure [dɪ'pɑːtʃə*] n départ m; (fig): **~ from** écart m par rapport à.

depend [dɪ'pɛnd] vi: **to ~ on** dépendre de; (rely on) compter sur; **it ~s** cela dépend; **~able** a sûr(e), digne de confiance; **~ence** n dépendance f; **~ant, ~ent** n personne f à charge.

depict [dɪ'pɪkt] vt (in picture) représenter; (in words) (dé)peindre, décrire.

depleted [dɪ'pli:tɪd] a (considérablement) réduit(e) or diminué(e).

deplorable [dɪ'plɔːrəbl] a déplorable, lamentable.

deplore [dɪ'plɔː*] vt déplorer.

deploy [dɪ'plɔɪ] vt déployer.

depopulation [diːpɔpjuˈleɪʃən] n dépopulation f, dépeuplement m.

deport [dɪ'pɔːt] vt déporter ; expulser ; **~ation** [diːpɔːˈteɪʃən] n déportation f, expulsion f ; **~ment** n maintien m, tenue f.

depose [dɪ'pəuz] vt déposer.

deposit [dɪ'pɔzɪt] n (CHEM, COMM, GEO) dépôt m ; (of ore, oil) gisement m ; (part payment) arrhes fpl, acompte m ; (on bottle etc) consigne f ; (for hired goods etc) cautionnement m, garantie f // vt déposer ; mettre or laisser en dépôt ; fournir or donner en acompte ; laisser en garantie ; **~ account** n compte m de dépôt ; **~or** n déposant e.

depot ['dɛpəu] n dépôt m.

deprave [dɪ'preɪv] vt dépraver, corrompre, pervertir.

depravity [dɪ'prævɪtɪ] n dépravation f.

deprecate ['dɛprɪkeɪt] vt désapprouver.

depreciate [dɪ'priːʃɪeɪt] vt déprécier // vi se déprécier, se dévaloriser ; **depreciation** [-'eɪʃən] n dépréciation f.

depress [dɪ'prɛs] vt déprimer ; (press down) appuyer sur, abaisser ; **~ed** a (person) déprimé(e), abattu(e) ; (area) en déclin, touché(e) par le sous-emploi ; **~ing** a déprimant(e) ; **~ion** [dɪ'prɛʃən] n dépression f.

deprivation [dɛprɪ'veɪʃən] n privation f ; (loss) perte f.

deprive [dɪ'praɪv] vt: **to ~ sb of** priver qn de ; enlever à qn ; **~d** a déshérité(e).

depth [dɛpθ] n profondeur f ; **in the ~s of** au fond de ; au cœur de ; au plus profond de ; **~ charge** n grenade sous-marine.

deputation [dɛpjuˈteɪʃən] n députation f, délégation f.

deputize ['dɛpjutaɪz] vi: **to ~ for** assurer l'intérim de.

deputy ['dɛpjutɪ] a: **~ chairman** vice-président m ; **~ head** directeur adjoint, sous-directeur m // n (replacement) suppléant/e, intérimaire m/f ; (second in command) adjoint/e.

derail [dɪ'reɪl] vt faire dérailler ; **to be ~ed** dérailler ; **~ment** n déraillement m.

deranged [dɪ'reɪndʒd] a (machine) déréglé(e) ; **to be (mentally) ~** avoir le cerveau dérangé.

derelict ['dɛrɪlɪkt] a abandonné(e), à l'abandon.

deride [dɪ'raɪd] vt railler.

derision [dɪ'rɪʒən] n dérision f.

derisive [dɪ'raɪsɪv] a moqueur (euse), railleur(euse).

derisory [dɪ'raɪsərɪ] a (sum) dérisoire ; (smile, person) moqueur(euse), railleur(euse).

derivation [dɛrɪ'veɪʃən] n dérivation f.

derivative [dɪ'rɪvətɪv] n dérivé m // a (person) méritant(e) ; (action, cause) méritoire.

derive [dɪ'raɪv] vt: **to ~ sth from** tirer qch de ; trouver qch dans // vi: **to ~ from** provenir de, dériver de.

dermatology [dəːmə'tɔlədʒɪ] n dermatologie f.

derogatory [dɪ'rɔgətərɪ] a désobligeant(e) ; péjoratif(ive).

derrick ['dɛrɪk] n mât m de charge ; derrick m.

desalination [diːsalɪˈneɪʃən] n dessalement m, dessalage m.

descend [dɪ'sɛnd] vt, vi descendre ; **to ~ from** descendre de, être issu de ; **~ant** n descendant/e.

descent [dɪ'sɛnt] n descente f ; (origin) origine f.

describe [dɪs'kraɪb] vt décrire ; **description** [-'krɪpʃən] n description f ; (sort) sorte f, espèce f ; **descriptive** [-'krɪptɪv] a descriptif(ive).

desecrate ['dɛsɪkreɪt] vt profaner.

desert n ['dɛzət] désert m // vb [dɪ'zəːt] vt déserter, abandonner // vi (MIL) déserter ; **~er** n déserteur m ; **~ion** [dɪ'zəːʃən] n désertion f.

deserve [dɪ'zəːv] vt mériter ; **deserving** a (person) méritant(e) ; (action, cause) méritoire.

design [dɪ'zaɪn] n (sketch) plan m, dessin m ; (layout, shape) conception f, ligne f ; (pattern) dessin m, motif(s) m(pl) ; (COMM) esthétique industrielle ; (intention) dessein m // vt dessiner ; concevoir ; **to have ~s on** avoir des visées sur ; **well-~ed** a bien conçu(e).

designate vt ['dɛzɪgneɪt] désigner // a ['dɛzɪgnɪt] désigné(e) ; **designation** [-'neɪʃən] n désignation f.

designer [dɪ'zaɪnə*] n (ART, TECH) dessinateur/trice ; (fashion) modéliste m/f.

desirability [dɪzaɪərəˈbɪlɪtɪ] n avantage m ; attrait m.

desirable [dɪ'zaɪərəbl] a désirable.

desire [dɪ'zaɪə*] n désir m // vt désirer, vouloir.

desirous [dɪ'zaɪərəs] a: **~ of** désireux-(euse) de.

desk [dɛsk] n (in office) bureau m ; (for pupil) pupitre m ; (in shop, restaurant) caisse f ; (in hotel, at airport) réception f.

desolate ['dɛsəlɪt] a désolé(e).

desolation [dɛsə'leɪʃən] n désolation f.

despair [dɪs'pɛə*] n désespoir m // vi: **to ~ of** désespérer de.

despatch [dɪs'pætʃ] n, vt = **dispatch**.

desperate ['dɛspərɪt] a désespéré(e) ; (fugitive) prêt(e) à tout ; **~ly** ad désespérément ; (very) terriblement, extrêmement.

desperation [dɛspə'reɪʃən] n désespoir m ; **in ~** à bout de nerf ; en désespoir de cause.

despicable [dɪs'pɪkəbl] a méprisable.

despise [dɪs'paɪz] vt mépriser, dédaigner.

despite [dɪs'paɪt] prep malgré, en dépit de.

despondent [dɪs'pɔndənt] a découragé(e), abattu(e).

dessert [dɪ'zəːt] n dessert m ; **~spoon** n cuiller f à dessert.

destination [dɛstɪ'neɪʃən] n destination f.

destine ['dɛstɪn] vt destiner.

destiny ['dɛstɪnɪ] n destinée f, destin m.

destitute ['dɛstɪtjuːt] a indigent(e), dans

le dénuement ; ～ **of** dépourvu or dénué de.

destroy [dɪs'trɔɪ] vt détruire ; ～**er** n (NAUT) contre-torpilleur m.

destruction [dɪs'trʌkʃən] n destruction f.

destructive [dɪs'trʌktɪv] a destructeur(trice).

detach [dɪ'tætʃ] vt détacher ; ～**able** a amovible, détachable ; ～**ed** a (attitude) détaché(e) ; ～**ed house** n pavillon m, maison(nette) (individuelle) ; ～**ment** n (MIL) détachement m ; (fig) détachement m, indifférence f.

detail ['di:teɪl] n détail m // vt raconter en détail, énumérer ; (MIL): to ～ sb (for) affecter qn (à), détacher qn (pour) ; **in** ～ en détail ; ～**ed** a détaillé(e).

detain [dɪ'teɪn] vt retenir ; (in captivity) détenir ; (in hospital) hospitaliser.

detect [dɪ'tɛkt] vt déceler, percevoir ; (MED, POLICE) dépister ; (MIL, RADAR, TECH) détecter ; ～**ion** [dɪ'tɛkʃən] n découverte f ; dépistage m ; détection f ; **to escape** ～**ion** échapper aux recherches, éviter d'être découvert ; crime ～**ion** le dépistage des criminels ; ～**ive** n agent m de la sûreté, policier m ; **private** ～**ive** détective privé ; ～**ive story** n roman policier ; ～**or** n détecteur m.

detention [dɪ'tɛnʃən] n détention f ; (SCOL) retenue f, consigne f.

deter [dɪ'tə:*] vt dissuader.

detergent [dɪ'tə:dʒənt] n détersif m, détergent m.

deteriorate [dɪ'tɪərɪəreɪt] vi se détériorer, se dégrader ; **deterioration** [-'reɪʃən] n détérioration f.

determination [dɪtə:mɪ'neɪʃən] n détermination f.

determine [dɪ'tə:mɪn] vt déterminer ; **to** ～ **to do** résoudre de faire, se déterminer à faire ; ～**d** a (person) déterminé(e), décidé(e) ; (quantity) déterminé, établi(e).

deterrent [dɪ'tɛrənt] n effet m de dissuasion ; force f de dissuasion.

detest [dɪ'tɛst] vt détester, avoir horreur de ; ～**able** a détestable, odieux(euse).

detonate ['dɛtəneɪt] vi exploser ; détoner // vt faire exploser or détoner ; **detonator** n détonateur m.

detour ['di:tuə*] n détour m.

detract [dɪ'trækt] vt: **to** ～ **from** (quality, pleasure) diminuer ; (reputation) porter atteinte à.

detriment ['dɛtrɪmənt] n: **to the** ～ **of** au détriment de, au préjudice de ; ～**al** [dɛtrɪ'mɛntl] a: ～**al to** préjudiciable or nuisible à.

devaluation [dɪvælju'eɪʃən] n dévaluation f.

devalue ['di:'vælju:] vt dévaluer.

devastate ['dɛvəsteɪt] vt dévaster.

devastating ['dɛvəsteɪtɪŋ] a dévastateur(trice).

develop [dɪ'vɛləp] vt (gen) développer ; (habit) contracter ; (resources) mettre en valeur, exploiter // vi se développer ; (situation, disease: evolve) évoluer ; (facts, symptoms: appear) se manifester, se produire ; ～**er** n (PHOT) révélateur m ; (of land) promoteur m ; ～**ing country** pays m en voie de développement ; ～**ment** n développement m ; (of affair, case)

rebondissement m, fait(s) nouveau(x).

deviate ['di:vɪeɪt] vi dévier.

deviation [di:vɪ'eɪʃən] n déviation f.

device [dɪ'vaɪs] n (scheme) moyen m, expédient m ; (apparatus) engin m, dispositif m.

devil ['dɛvl] n diable m ; démon m ; ～**ish** a diabolique.

devious [dɪ'vɪəs] a (means) détourné(e) ; (person) sournois(e), dissimulé(e).

devise [dɪ'vaɪz] vt imaginer, concevoir.

devoid [dɪ'vɔɪd] a: ～ **of** dépourvu(e) de, dénué(e) de.

devote [dɪ'vəut] vt: **to** ～ **sth to** consacrer qch à ; ～**d** a dévoué(e) ; **to be** ～**d to** être dévoué or très attaché à ; ～**e** [dɛvəu'ti:] n (REL) adepte m/f ; (MUS, SPORT) fervent/e.

devotion [dɪ'vəuʃən] n dévouement m, attachement m ; (REL) dévotion f, piété f.

devour [dɪ'vauə*] vt dévorer.

devout [dɪ'vaut] a pieux(euse), dévot(e).

dew [dju:] n rosée f.

dexterity [dɛks'tɛrɪtɪ] n dextérité f, adresse f.

diabetes [daɪə'bi:ti:z] n diabète m ; **diabetic** [-'bɛtɪk] a, n diabétique (m/f).

diaeresis [daɪ'ɛrɪsɪs] n tréma m.

diagnose [daɪəg'nəuz] vt diagnostiquer.

diagnosis, pl **diagnoses** [daɪəg'nəusɪs, -si:z] n diagnostic m.

diagonal [daɪ'æɡənl] a diagonal(e) // n diagonale f.

diagram ['daɪəgræm] n diagramme m, schéma m ; graphique m.

dial ['daɪəl] n cadran m // vt (number) faire, composer ; ～**ling tone** n tonalité f.

dialect ['daɪəlɛkt] n dialecte m.

dialogue ['daɪələg] n dialogue m.

diameter [daɪ'æmɪtə*] n diamètre m.

diamond ['daɪəmənd] n diamant m ; (shape) losange m ; ～**s** npl (CARDS) carreau m.

diaper ['daɪəpə*] n (US) couche f.

diaphragm ['daɪəfræm] n diaphragme m.

diarrhoea, diarrhea (US) [daɪə'rɪ:ə] n diarrhée f.

diary ['daɪərɪ] n (daily account) journal m ; (book) agenda m.

dice [daɪs] n, pl inv dé m // vt (CULIN) couper en dés or en cubes.

dictate vt [dɪk'teɪt] dicter // n ['dɪkteɪt] injonction f.

dictation [dɪk'teɪʃən] n dictée f.

dictator [dɪk'teɪtə*] n dictateur m ; ～**ship** n dictature f.

diction ['dɪkʃən] n diction f, élocution f.

dictionary ['dɪkʃənrɪ] n dictionnaire m.

did [dɪd] pt of **do**.

die [daɪ] n (pl: **dice**) dé m ; (pl: **dies**) coin m ; matrice f ; étampe f // vi mourir ; **to** ～ **away** vi s'éteindre ; **to** ～ **down** vi se calmer, s'apaiser ; **to** ～ **out** vi disparaître, s'éteindre.

Diesel ['di:zəl]: ～ **engine** n moteur m diesel.

diet ['daɪət] n alimentation f ; (restricted food) régime m // vi (also: **be on a** ～) suivre un régime.

differ ['dɪfə*] vi: **to** ～ **from sth** être différent de ; différer de ; **to** ～ **from sb**

over sth ne pas être d'accord avec qn au sujet de qch ; **~ence** n différence f ; (*quarrel*) différend m, désaccord m ; **~ent** a différent(e) ; **~ential** [-'renʃəl] n (AUT, wages) différentiel m ; **~entiate** [-'renʃieit] vt différencier // vi se différencier ; **to ~entiate between** faire une différence entre ; **~ently** ad différemment.

difficult ['dɪfɪkəlt] a difficile ; **~y** n difficulté f.

diffidence ['dɪfɪdəns] n manque m de confiance en soi, manque d'assurance.

diffident ['dɪfɪdənt] a qui manque de confiance or d'assurance, peu sûr(e) de soi.

diffuse a [dɪ'fju:s] diffus(e) // vt [dɪ'fju:z] diffuser, répandre.

dig [dɪg] vt (pt, pp **dug** [dʌg]) (hole) creuser ; (garden) bêcher // n (prod) coup m de coude ; (fig) coup de griffe or de patte ; **to ~ into** (snow, soil) creuser ; **to ~ one's nails into** enfoncer ses ongles dans ; **to ~ up** vt déterrer.

digest vt [dai'dʒɛst] digérer // n ['daidʒɛst] sommaire m, résumé m ; **~ible** [di'dʒɛstəbl] a digestible ; **~ion** [di'dʒɛstʃən] n digestion f.

digit ['dɪdʒɪt] n chiffre m (de 0 à 9) ; (finger) doigt m ; **~al** a digital(e) ; à affichage numérique or digital.

dignified ['dɪgnɪfaɪd] a digne.

dignitary ['dɪgnɪtəri] n dignitaire m.

dignity ['dɪgnɪtɪ] n dignité f.

digress [dai'grɛs] vi : **to ~ from** s'écarter de, s'éloigner de ; **~ion** [dai'grɛʃən] n digression f.

digs [dɪgz] npl (Brit: col) piaule f, chambre meublée.

dilapidated [dɪ'læpɪdeɪtɪd] a délabré(e).

dilate [dai'leit] vt dilater // vi se dilater.

dilatory ['dɪlətəri] a dilatoire.

dilemma [dai'lɛmə] n dilemme m.

diligent ['dɪlɪdʒənt] a appliqué(e), assidu(e).

dilute [dai'lu:t] vt diluer // a dilué(e).

dim [dɪm] a (light, eyesight) faible ; (memory, outline) vague, indécis(e) ; (stupid) borné(e), obtus(e) // vt (light) réduire, baisser.

dime [daim] n (US) = 10 cents.

dimension [dɪ'mɛnʃən] n dimension f.

diminish [dɪ'mɪnɪʃ] vt,vi diminuer.

diminutive [dɪ'mɪnjutɪv] a minuscule, tout(e) petit(e) // n (LING) diminutif m.

dimly ['dɪmlɪ] ad faiblement ; vaguement.

dimple ['dɪmpl] n fossette f.

dim-witted ['dɪm'wɪtɪd] a (col) stupide, borné(e).

din [dɪn] n vacarme m.

dine [daɪn] vi dîner ; **~r** n (person) dîneur/euse f ; (RAIL) = dining car.

dinghy ['dɪŋgɪ] n youyou m ; canot m pneumatique ; (also: **sailing ~**) voilier m, dériveur m.

dingy ['dɪndʒɪ] a miteux(euse), minable.

dining ['daɪnɪŋ] cpd : **~ car** n wagon-restaurant m ; **~ room** n salle f à manger.

dinner ['dɪnə*] n dîner m ; (public) banquet m ; **~ jacket** n smoking m ; **~ party** n dîner m ; **~ time** n heure f du dîner.

diocese ['daɪəsɪs] n diocèse m.

dip [dɪp] n déclivité f ; (in sea) baignade f, bain m // vt tremper, plonger ; (AUT: lights) mettre en code, baisser // vi plonger.

diphtheria [dɪf'θɪərɪə] n diphtérie f.

diphthong ['dɪfθɔŋ] n diphtongue f.

diploma [dɪ'pləumə] n diplôme m.

diplomacy [dɪ'pləuməsɪ] n diplomatie f.

diplomat ['dɪpləmæt] n diplomate m ; **~ic** [dɪplə'mætɪk] a diplomatique ; **~ic corps** n corps m diplomatique.

dipstick ['dɪpstɪk] n (AUT) jauge f de niveau d'huile.

dire [daɪə*] a terrible, extrême, affreux(euse).

direct [dai'rɛkt] a direct(e) // vt diriger, orienter ; **can you ~ me to ...?** pouvez-vous m'indiquer le chemin de ...? ; **~ current** n courant continu ; **~ hit** n coup m au but, touché m.

direction [dɪ'rɛkʃən] n direction f ; **sense of ~** sens m de l'orientation ; **~s** npl (advice) indications fpl ; **~s for use** mode m d'emploi.

directly [dɪ'rɛktlɪ] ad (in straight line) directement, tout droit ; (at once) tout de suite, immédiatement.

director [dɪ'rɛktə*] n directeur m ; administrateur m ; (THEATRE) metteur m en scène ; (CINEMA, TV) réalisateur/trice.

directory [dɪ'rɛktəri] n annuaire m.

dirt [də:t] n saleté f ; crasse f ; **~-cheap** a (ne) coûtant presque rien ; **~ road** n (US) chemin non macadamisé or non revêtu ; **~y** a sale // vt salir ; **~y story** n histoire cochonne ; **~y trick** n coup tordu.

disability [dɪsə'bɪlɪtɪ] n invalidité f, infirmité f.

disabled [dɪs'eɪbld] a infirme, invalide ; (maimed) mutilé(e) ; (through illness, old age) impotent(e).

disadvantage [dɪsəd'vɑ:ntɪdʒ] n désavantage m, inconvénient m ; **~ous** [dɪsædvɑ:n'teɪdʒəs] a désavantageux(euse).

disagree [dɪsə'gri:] vi (differ) ne pas concorder ; (be against, think otherwise): **to ~ (with)** ne pas être d'accord (avec) ; **garlic ~s with me** l'ail ne me convient pas, je ne supporte pas l'ail ; **~able** a désagréable ; **~ment** n désaccord m, différend m.

disallow ['dɪsə'lau] vt rejeter, désavouer.

disappear [dɪsə'pɪə*] vi disparaître ; **~ance** n disparition f.

disappoint [dɪsə'pɔɪnt] vt décevoir ; **~ment** n déception f.

disapproval [dɪsə'pru:vəl] n désapprobation f.

disapprove [dɪsə'pru:v] vi : **to ~ of** désapprouver.

disarm [dɪs'ɑ:m] vt désarmer ; **~ament** n désarmement m.

disarray [dɪsə'reɪ] n désordre m, confusion f.

disaster [dɪ'zɑ:stə*] n catastrophe f, désastre m ; **disastrous** a désastreux(euse).

disband [dɪs'bænd] vt démobiliser ; disperser // vi se séparer ; se disperser.

disbelief ['dɪsbə'li:f] n incrédulité f.

disc [dɪsk] n disque m.

discard [dɪs'kɑ:d] vt (old things) se défaire de, mettre au rencart or au rebut ; (fig) écarter, renoncer à.

disc brake ['dɪskbreɪk] n frein m à disque.

discern [dɪ'sə:n] vt discerner, distinguer ; ~ing a judicieux(euse), perspicace.

discharge vt [dɪs'tʃɑ:dʒ] (duties) s'acquitter de ; (waste etc) déverser ; décharger ; (ELEC, MED) émettre ; (patient) renvoyer (chez lui) ; (employee, soldier) congédier, licencier ; (defendant) relaxer, élargir // n ['dɪstʃɑ:dʒ] (ELEC, MED) émission f ; (dismissal) renvoi m ; licenciement m ; élargissement m ; to ~ one's gun faire feu.

disciple [dɪ'saɪpl] n disciple m.

disciplinary ['dɪsɪplɪnərɪ] a disciplinaire.

discipline ['dɪsɪplɪn] n discipline f // vt discipliner ; (punish) punir.

disc jockey ['dɪskdʒɔkɪ] n disque-jockey m.

disclaim [dɪs'kleɪm] vt désavouer, dénier.

disclose [dɪs'kləuz] vt révéler, divulguer ; **disclosure** [-'kləuʒə*] n révélation f, divulgation f.

disco ['dɪskəu] n abbr of discothèque.

discoloured [dɪs'kʌləd] a décoloré(e) ; jauni(e).

discomfort [dɪs'kʌmfət] n malaise m, gêne f ; (lack of comfort) manque m de confort.

disconcert [dɪskən'sə:t] vt déconcerter, décontenancer.

disconnect [dɪskə'nɛkt] vt détacher ; (ELEC, RADIO) débrancher ; (gas, water) couper ; ~ed a (speech, thought) décousu(e), peu cohérent(e).

disconsolate [dɪs'kɔnsəlɪt] a inconsolable.

discontent [dɪskən'tɛnt] n mécontentement m ; ~ed a mécontent(e).

discontinue [dɪskən'tɪnju:] vt cesser, interrompre ; '~ed' (COMM) 'fin de série'.

discord ['dɪskɔ:d] n discorde f, dissension f ; (MUS) dissonance f ; ~ant [dɪs'kɔ:dənt] a discordant(e), dissonant(e).

discothèque ['dɪskəutɛk] n discothèque f.

discount n ['dɪskaunt] remise f, rabais m // vt [dɪs'kaunt] ne pas tenir compte de.

discourage [dɪs'kʌrɪdʒ] vt décourager ; **discouraging** a décourageant(e).

discourteous [dɪs'kə:tɪəs] a incivil(e), discourtois(e).

discover [dɪs'kʌvə*] vt découvrir ; ~y n découverte f.

discredit [dɪs'krɛdɪt] vt mettre en doute ; discréditer.

discreet [dɪ'skri:t] a discret(ète) ; ~ly ad discrètement.

discrepancy [dɪ'skrɛpənsɪ] n divergence f, contradiction f.

discretion [dɪ'skrɛʃən] n discrétion f.

discriminate [dɪ'skrɪmɪneɪt] vi: to ~ between établir une distinction entre, faire la différence entre ; to ~ against pratiquer une discrimination contre ; **discriminating** a qui a du discernement ;

discrimination [-'neɪʃən] n discrimination f ; (judgment) discernement m.

discus ['dɪskəs] n disque m.

discuss [dɪ'skʌs] vt discuter de ; (debate) discuter ; ~ion [dɪ'skʌʃən] n discussion f.

disdain [dɪs'deɪn] n dédain m.

disease [dɪ'zi:z] n maladie f.

disembark [dɪsɪm'bɑ:k] vt,vi débarquer.

disembodied [dɪsɪm'bɔdɪd] a désincarné(e).

disembowel [dɪsɪm'bauəl] vt éviscérer, étriper.

disenchanted [dɪsɪn'tʃɑ:ntɪd] a désenchanté(e), désabusé(e).

disengage [dɪsɪn'geɪdʒ] vt dégager ; (TECH) déclencher ; to ~ the clutch (AUT) débrayer ; ~ment (POL) désengagement m.

disentangle [dɪsɪn'tæŋgl] vt démêler.

disfavour [dɪs'feɪvə*] n défaveur f ; disgrâce f // vt voir d'un mauvais œil, désapprouver.

disfigure [dɪs'fɪgə*] vt défigurer.

disgorge [dɪs'gɔ:dʒ] vt déverser.

disgrace [dɪs'greɪs] n honte f ; (disfavour) disgrâce f // vt déshonorer, couvrir de honte ; ~ful a scandaleux(euse), honteux(euse).

disgruntled [dɪs'grʌntld] a mécontent(e).

disguise [dɪs'gaɪz] n déguisement m // vt déguiser ; in ~ déguisé(e).

disgust [dɪs'gʌst] n dégoût m, aversion f // vt dégoûter, écœurer ; ~ing a dégoûtant(e) ; révoltant(e).

dish [dɪʃ] n plat m ; to do or wash the ~es faire la vaisselle ; to ~ up servir ; (facts, statistics) sortir, débiter ; ~cloth n (for drying) torchon m ; (for washing) lavette f.

dishearten [dɪs'hɑ:tn] vt décourager.

dishevelled [dɪ'ʃevəld] a ébouriffé(e) ; décoiffé(e) ; débraillé(e).

dishonest [dɪs'ɔnɪst] a malhonnête ; ~y n malhonnêteté f.

dishonour [dɪs'ɔnə*] n déshonneur m ; ~able a déshonorant(e).

dishwasher ['dɪʃwɔʃə*] n lave-vaisselle m ; (person) plongeur/euse.

disillusion [dɪsɪ'lu:ʒən] vt désabuser, désenchanter // n désenchantement m.

disinfect [dɪsɪn'fɛkt] vt désinfecter ; ~ant n désinfectant m.

disintegrate [dɪs'ɪntɪgreɪt] vi se désintégrer.

disinterested [dɪs'ɪntrəstɪd] a désintéressé(e).

disjointed [dɪs'dʒɔɪntɪd] a décousu(e), incohérent(e).

disk [dɪsk] n = disc.

dislike [dɪs'laɪk] n aversion f, antipathie f // vt ne pas aimer.

dislocate ['dɪsləkeɪt] vt disloquer ; déboîter ; désorganiser.

dislodge [dɪs'lɔdʒ] vt déplacer, faire bouger ; (enemy) déloger.

disloyal [dɪs'lɔɪəl] a déloyal(e).

dismal ['dɪzml] a lugubre, maussade.

dismantle [dɪs'mæntl] vt démonter ; (fort, warship) démanteler.

dismast [dɪs'mɑ:st] vt démâter.

dismay [dɪs'meɪ] *n* consternation *f* // *vt* consterner.

dismiss [dɪs'mɪs] *vt* congédier, renvoyer ; (*idea*) écarter ; (*LAW*) rejeter ; **~al** *n* renvoi *m*.

dismount [dɪs'maunt] *vi* mettre pied à terre.

disobedience [dɪsə'bi:dɪəns] *n* désobéissance *f* ; insoumission *f*.

disobedient [dɪsə'bi:dɪənt] *a* désobéissant(e) ; (*soldier*) indiscipliné(e).

disobey [dɪsə'beɪ] *vt* désobéir à.

disorder [dɪs'ɔ:də*] *n* désordre *m* ; (*rioting*) désordres *mpl* ; (*MED*) troubles *mpl* ; **~ly** *a* en désordre ; désordonné(e).

disorganize [dɪs'ɔ:gənaɪz] *vt* désorganiser.

disorientate [dɪs'ɔ:rɪənteɪt] *vt* désorienter.

disown [dɪs'əun] *vt* renier.

disparaging [dɪs'pærɪdʒɪŋ] *a* désobligeant(e).

disparity [dɪs'pærɪtɪ] *n* disparité *f*.

dispassionate [dɪs'pæʃənət] *a* calme, froid(e) ; impartial(e), objectif(ive).

dispatch [dɪs'pætʃ] *vt* expédier, envoyer // *n* envoi *m*, expédition *f* ; (*MIL, PRESS*) dépêche *f*.

dispel [dɪs'pɛl] *vt* dissiper, chasser.

dispensary [dɪs'pɛnsərɪ] *n* pharmacie *f* ; (*in chemist's*) officine *f*.

dispense [dɪs'pɛns] *vt* distribuer, administrer ; **to ~ sb from** dispenser qn de ; **to ~ with** *vt fus* se passer de ; **~r** *n* (*container*) distributeur *m* ; **dispensing chemist** *n* pharmacie *f*.

dispersal [dɪs'pə:sl] *n* dispersion *f* ; (*ADMIN*) déconcentration *f*.

disperse [dɪs'pə:s] *vt* disperser ; (*knowledge*) disséminer // *vi* se disperser.

dispirited [dɪs'pɪrɪtɪd] *a* découragé(e), déprimé(e).

displace [dɪs'pleɪs] *vt* déplacer ; **~d person** *n* (*POL*) personne déplacée ; **~ment** *n* déplacement *m*.

display [dɪs'pleɪ] *n* étalage *m* ; déploiement *m* ; affichage *m* ; (*screen*) écran *m* de visualisation, visuel *m* ; (*of feeling*) manifestation *f* ; (*pej*) ostentation *f* // *vt* montrer ; (*goods*) mettre à l'étalage, exposer ; (*results, departure times*) afficher ; (*troops*) déployer ; (*pej*) faire étalage de.

displease [dɪs'pli:z] *vt* mécontenter contrarier ; **~d with** mécontent(e) de ; **displeasure** [-'plɛʒə*] *n* mécontentement *m*.

disposable [dɪs'pəuzəbl] *a* (*pack etc*) à jeter ; (*income*) disponible.

disposal [dɪs'pəuzl] *n* (*availability, arrangement*) disposition *f* ; (*of property*) disposition *f*, cession *f* ; (*of rubbish*) évacuation *f*, destruction *f* ; **at one's ~** à sa disposition.

dispose [dɪs'pəuz] *vt* disposer ; **to ~ of** *vt* (*time, money*) disposer de ; (*unwanted goods*) se débarrasser de, se défaire de ; (*problem*) expédier ; **~d** *a*: **~d to do** disposé(e) à faire ; **disposition** [-'zɪʃən] *n* disposition *f* ; (*temperament*) naturel *m*.

disproportionate [dɪsprə'pɔ:ʃənət] *a* disproportionné(e).

disprove [dɪs'pru:v] *vt* réfuter.

dispute [dɪs'pju:t] *n* discussion *f* ; (*also:* **industrial ~**) conflit *m* // *vt* contester ; (*matter*) discuter ; (*victory*) disputer.

disqualification [dɪskwɔlɪfɪ'keɪʃən] *n* disqualification *f* ; **~ (from driving)** retrait *m* du permis (de conduire).

disqualify [dɪs'kwɔlɪfaɪ] *vt* (*SPORT*) disqualifier ; **to ~ sb for sth/from doing** rendre qn inapte à qch/à faire ; signifier à qn l'interdiction de faire ; mettre qn dans l'impossibilité de faire ; **to ~ sb (from driving) for speeding** retirer à qn son permis (de conduire) pour excès de vitesse.

disquiet [dɪs'kwaɪət] *n* inquiétude *f*, trouble *m*.

disregard [dɪsrɪ'gɑ:d] *vt* ne pas tenir compte de.

disrepair [dɪsrɪ'pɛə*] *n* mauvais état.

disreputable [dɪs'rɛpjutəbl] *a* (*person*) de mauvaise réputation, peu recommandable ; (*behaviour*) déshonorant(e).

disrespectful [dɪsrɪ'spɛktful] *a* irrespectueux(euse).

disrupt [dɪs'rʌpt] *vt* (*plans*) déranger ; (*conversation*) interrompre ; **~ion** [-'rʌpʃən] *n* dérangement *m* ; interruption *f*.

dissatisfaction [dɪssætɪs'fækʃən] *n* mécontentement *m*, insatisfaction *f*.

dissatisfied [dɪs'sætɪsfaɪd] *a*: **~ (with)** mécontent(e) *or* insatisfait(e) (de).

dissect [dɪ'sɛkt] *vt* disséquer.

disseminate [dɪ'sɛmɪneɪt] *vt* disséminer.

dissent [dɪ'sɛnt] *n* dissentiment *m*, différence *f* d'opinion.

disservice [dɪs'sə:vɪs] *n*: **to do sb a ~** rendre un mauvais service à qn ; desservir qn.

dissident [dɪsɪdnt] *a* dissident(e).

dissimilar [dɪ'sɪmɪlə*] *a*: **~ (to)** dissemblable (à), différent(e) (de).

dissipate ['dɪsɪpeɪt] *vt* dissiper ; (*energy, efforts*) disperser ; **~d** *a* dissolu(e) ; débauché(e).

dissociate [dɪ'səuʃɪeɪt] *vt* dissocier.

dissolute ['dɪsəlu:t] *a* débauché(e), dissolu(e).

dissolve [dɪ'zɔlv] *vt* dissoudre // *vi* se dissoudre, fondre ; (*fig*) disparaître.

dissuade [dɪ'sweɪd] *vt*: **to ~ sb (from)** dissuader qn (de).

distance ['dɪstns] *n* distance *f* ; **in the ~** au loin.

distant ['dɪstnt] *a* lointain(e), éloigné(e) ; (*manner*) distant(e), froid(e).

distaste [dɪs'teɪst] *n* dégoût *m* ; **~ful** *a* déplaisant(e), désagréable.

distemper [dɪs'tɛmpə*] *n* (*paint*) détrempe *f*, badigeon *m*.

distend [dɪs'tɛnd] *vt* distendre // *vi* se distendre, se ballonner.

distil [dɪs'tɪl] *vt* distiller ; **~lery** *n* distillerie *f*.

distinct [dɪs'tɪŋkt] *a* distinct(e) ; (*preference, progress*) marqué(e) ; **~ion** [dɪs'tɪŋkʃən] *n* distinction *f* ; (*in exam*) mention *f* très bien ; **~ive** *a* distinctif(ive) ; **~ly** *ad* distinctement ; expressément.

distinguish [dɪs'tɪŋgwɪʃ] vt distinguer ; différencier ; ∼ed a (eminent) distingué(e) ; ∼ing a (feature) distinctif(ive), caractéristique.

distort [dɪs'tɔ:t] vt déformer ; ∼ion [dɪs'tɔ:ʃən] n déformation f.

distract [dɪs'trækt] vt distraire, déranger ; ∼ed a éperdu(e), égaré(e) ; ∼ion [dɪs'trækʃən] n distraction f; égarement m; to drive sb to ∼ion rendre qn fou(folle).

distraught [dɪs'trɔ:t] a éperdu(e).

distress [dɪs'trɛs] n détresse f; (pain) douleur f // vt affliger ; ∼ed area n zone sinistrée ; ∼ing a douloureux(euse), pénible ; ∼ signal n signal m de détresse.

distribute [dɪs'trɪbju:t] vt distribuer ; **distribution** [-'bju:ʃən] n distribution f; **distributor** n distributeur m.

district ['dɪstrɪkt] n (of country) région f; (of town) quartier m; (ADMIN) district m; ∼ attorney n (US) ≈ procureur m de la République ; ∼ nurse n (Brit) infirmière visiteuse.

distrust [dɪs'trʌst] n méfiance f, doute m // vt se méfier de.

disturb [dɪs'tə:b] vt troubler ; (inconvenience) déranger ; ∼ance n dérangement m; (political etc) troubles mpl; (by drunks etc) tapage m; ∼ing a troublant(e), inquiétant(e).

disuse [dɪs'ju:s] n: to fall into ∼ tomber en désuétude f.

disused [dɪs'ju:zd] a désaffecté(e).

ditch [dɪtʃ] n fossé m // vt (col) abandonner.

dither ['dɪðə*] vi hésiter.

ditto ['dɪtəu] ad idem.

divan [dɪ'væn] n divan m.

dive [daɪv] n plongeon m; (of submarine) plongée f; (AVIAT) piqué m; (pej) bouge m // vi plonger ; ∼r n plongeur m.

diverge [daɪ'və:dʒ] vi diverger.

diverse [daɪ'və:s] a divers(e).

diversify [daɪ'və:sɪfaɪ] vt diversifier.

diversion [daɪ'və:ʃən] n (AUT) déviation f; (distraction, MIL) diversion f.

diversity [daɪ'və:sɪtɪ] n diversité f, variété f.

divert [daɪ'və:t] vt (traffic) dévier ; (river) détourner ; (amuse) divertir.

divest [daɪ'vɛst] vt: to ∼ sb of dépouiller qn de.

divide [dɪ'vaɪd] vt diviser ; (separate) séparer // vi se diviser ; ∼d skirt n jupe-culotte f.

dividend ['dɪvɪdɛnd] n dividende m.

divine [dɪ'vaɪn] a divin(e).

diving ['daɪvɪŋ] n plongée (sous-marine) ; ∼ board n plongeoir m; ∼ suit n scaphandre m.

divinity [dɪ'vɪnɪtɪ] n divinité f; théologie f.

division [dɪ'vɪʒən] n division f; séparation f; (Brit POL) vote m.

divorce [dɪ'vɔ:s] n divorce m // vt divorcer d'avec ; ∼d a divorcé(e) ; ∼e [-'si:] n divorcé/e.

divulge [daɪ'vʌldʒ] vt divulguer, révéler.

D.I.Y. a,n abbr of **do-it-yourself**.

dizziness ['dɪzɪnɪs] n vertige m, étourdissement m.

dizzy ['dɪzɪ] a (height) vertigineux(euse) ; to make sb ∼ donner le vertige à qn ; to feel ∼ avoir la tête qui tourne.

DJ n abbr of **disc jockey**.

do, pt did, pp done [du:, dɪd, dʌn] vt, vi faire ; he didn't laugh il n'a pas ri ; ∼ you want any? en voulez-vous?, est-ce que vous en voulez? ; she swims better than I ∼ elle nage mieux que moi ; he laughed, didn't he? il a ri, n'est-ce pas? ; ∼ they? ah oui?, vraiment? ; who broke it? - I did qui l'a cassé? - (c'est) moi ; ∼ you agree? - I ∼ êtes-vous d'accord? - oui ; to ∼ one's nails/teeth se faire les ongles/brosser les dents ; will it ∼? est-ce que ça ira? ; to ∼ without sth se passer de qch ; what did he ∼ with the cat? qu'a-t-il fait du chat? ; to ∼ away with vt fus supprimer, abolir ; to ∼ up vt remettre à neuf.

docile ['dəusaɪl] a docile.

dock [dɔk] n dock m; (LAW) banc m des accusés // vi se mettre à quai ; ∼er n docker m.

docket ['dɔkɪt] n bordereau m.

dockyard ['dɔkjɑ:d] n chantier m de construction navale.

doctor ['dɔktə*] n médecin m, docteur m; (Ph.D. etc) docteur // vt (cat) couper ; (fig) falsifier.

doctrine ['dɔktrɪn] n doctrine f.

document ['dɔkjumənt] n document m; ∼ary [-'mɛntərɪ] a, n documentaire (m) ; ∼ation [-'teɪʃən] n documentation f.

doddering ['dɔdərɪŋ] a (senile) gâteux(euse).

dodge [dɔdʒ] n truc m; combine f // vt esquiver, éviter.

dodgems ['dɔdʒəmz] npl autos tamponneuses.

dog [dɔg] n chien/ne ; ∼ biscuits npl biscuits mpl pour chien ; ∼ collar n collier m de chien ; (fig) faux-col m d'ecclésiastique ; ∼-eared a corné(e).

dogged ['dɔgɪd] a obstiné(e), opiniâtre.

dogma ['dɔgmə] n dogme m; ∼tic [-'mætɪk] a dogmatique.

doings ['du:ɪŋz] npl activités fpl.

do-it-yourself [du:ɪtjɔ:'sɛlf] n bricolage m.

doldrums ['dɔldrəmz] npl: to be in the ∼ avoir le cafard ; être dans le marasme.

dole [dəul] n (Brit) allocation f de chômage ; on the ∼ au chômage ; to ∼ out vt donner au compte-goutte.

doleful ['dəulful] a triste, lugubre.

doll [dɔl] n poupée f; to ∼ o.s. up se faire beau(belle).

dollar ['dɔlə*] n dollar m.

dolphin ['dɔlfɪn] n dauphin m.

domain [də'meɪn] n domaine m.

dome [dəum] n dôme m.

domestic [də'mɛstɪk] a (duty, happiness) familial(e) ; (policy, affairs, flights) intérieur(e) ; (animal) domestique ; ∼ated a domestiqué(e) ; (pej) d'intérieur.

domicile ['dɔmɪsaɪl] n domicile m.

dominant ['dɔmɪnənt] a dominant(e).

dominate ['dɔmɪneɪt] vt dominer ; **domination** [-'neɪʃən] n domination f;

domineering [-'nıərıŋ] *a* dominateur(trice), autoritaire.

dominion [də'mınıən] *n* domination *f*; territoire *m*; dominion *m*.

domino, ~**es** ['dɒmınəu] *n* domino *m*; ~**es** *n* (*game*) dominos *mpl*.

don [dɒn] *n* professeur *m* d'université // *vt* revêtir.

donate [də'neıt] *vt* faire don de. donner; **donation** [də'neıʃən] *n* donation *f*, don *m*.

done [dʌn] *pp* of **do**.

donkey ['dɒŋkı] *n* âne *m*.

donor ['dəunə*] *n* (*of blood etc*) donneur/euse; (*to charity*) donateur/trice.

don't [dəunt] *vb* = **do not**.

doom [du:m] *n* destin *m*; ruine *f* // *vt*: **to be ~ed** (**to failure**) être voué(e) à l'échec; ~**sday** *n* le Jugement dernier.

door [dɔ:*] *n* porte *f*; ~**bell** *n* sonnette *f*; ~**handle** *n* poignée *f* de porte; ~**man** *n* (*in hotel*) portier *m*; (*in block of flats*) concierge *m*; ~**mat** *n* paillasson *m*; ~**post** *n* montant *m* de porte; ~**step** *n* pas *m* de (la) porte, seuil *m*.

dope [dəup] *n* (*col*) drogue *f* // *vt* (*horse etc*) doper.

dopey ['dəupı] *a* (*col*) à moitié endormi(e).

dormant ['dɔ:mənt] *a* assoupi(e), en veilleuse; (*rule, law*) inappliqué(e).

dormice ['dɔ:maıs] *npl* of **dormouse**.

dormitory ['dɔ:mıtrı] *n* dortoir *m*.

dormouse, *pl* **dormice** ['dɔ:maus, -maıs] *n* loir *m*.

dosage ['dəusıdʒ] *n* dose *f*; dosage *m*; (*on label*) posologie *f*.

dose [dəus] *n* dose *f*; (*bout*) attaque *f* // *vt*: **to ~ o.s.** se bourrer de médicaments.

doss house ['dɒshaus] *n* asile *m* de nuit.

dot [dɒt] *n* point *m* // *vt*: ~**ted with** parsemé(e) de; **on the ~** à l'heure tapante.

dote [dəut]: **to ~ on** *vt fus* être fou(folle) de.

dotted line [dɒtıd'laın] *n* ligne pointillée; (*AUT*) ligne discontinue.

double ['dʌbl] *a* double // *ad* (*fold*) en deux; (*twice*): **to cost ~** (**sth**) coûter le double (de qch) *or* deux fois plus (que qch) // *n* double *f*; (*CINEMA*) doublure *f* // *vt* doubler; (*fold*) plier en deux // *vi* doubler; **at the ~** au pas de course; ~**s** *n* (*TENNIS*) double *m*; ~ **bass** *n* contrebasse *f*; ~ **bed** *n* grand lit *m*; ~ **bend** *n* virage *m* en S; ~-**breasted** *a* croisé(e); ~**cross** *vt* doubler, trahir; ~**decker** *n* autobus *m* à impériale; ~ **declutch** *vi* faire un double débrayage; ~ **exposure** *n* surimpression *f*; ~ **parking** *n* stationnement *m* en double file; ~ **room** *n* chambre *f* pour deux; **doubly** *ad* doublement, deux fois plus.

doubt [daut] *n* doute *m* // *vt* douter de; **to ~ that** douter que; ~**ful** *a* douteux(euse); (*person*) incertain(e); ~**less** *ad* sans doute, sûrement.

dough [dəu] *n* pâte *f*; ~**nut** *n* beignet *m*.

dour [duə*] *a* austère.

dove [dʌv] *n* colombe *f*.

Dover ['dəuvə*] *n* Douvres.

dovetail ['dʌvteıl] *n*: ~ **joint** *n* assemblage *m* à queue d'aronde // *vi* (*fig*) concorder.

---

dowdy ['daudı] *a* démodé(e); mal fagoté(e).

down [daun] *n* (*fluff*) duvet *m* // *ad* en bas // *prep* en bas de // *vt* (*enemy*) abattre; (*col: drink*) vider; **the D~s** collines crayeuses du S.-E. de l'Angleterre; ~ **with X!** à bas X!; ~-**at-heel** *a* éculé(e); (*fig*) miteux(euse); ~**cast** *a* démoralisé(e); ~**fall** *n* chute *f*; ruine *f*; ~**hearted** *a* découragé(e); ~**hill** *ad*: **to go ~hill** descendre; ~ **payment** *n* acompte *m*; ~**pour** *n* pluie torrentielle, déluge *m*; ~**right** *a* franc(franche); (*refusal*) catégorique; ~**stairs** *ad* au rez-de-chaussée; à l'étage inférieur; ~**stream** *ad* en aval; ~-**to-earth** *a* terre à terre *inv*; ~**town** *ad* en ville *a* (*US*): ~**town Chicago** le centre commerçant de Chicago; ~**ward** ['daunwəd] *a,ad*, ~**wards** ['daunwədz] *ad* vers le bas.

dowry ['dauri] *n* dot *f*.

doz. *abbr* of **dozen**.

doze [dəuz] *vi* sommeiller; **to ~ off** *vi* s'assoupir.

dozen ['dʌzn] *n* douzaine *f*; **a ~ books** une douzaine de livres.

Dr. *abbr* of **doctor**; **drive** (*n*).

drab [dræb] *a* terne, morne.

draft [drɑ:ft] *n* brouillon *m*; (*COMM*) traite *f*; (*US: MIL*) contingent *m*; (: *call-up*) conscription *f* // *vt* faire le brouillon de; *see also* **draught**.

drag [dræg] *vt* traîner; (*river*) draguer // *vi* traîner // *n* (*col*) raseur/euse; corvée *f*; **to ~ on** *vi* s'éterniser.

dragonfly ['drægənflaı] *n* libellule *f*.

drain [dreın] *n* égout *m*; (*on resources*) saignée *f* // *vt* (*land, marshes*) drainer, assécher; (*vegetables*) égoutter; (*reservoir etc*) vider // *vi* (*water*) s'écouler; ~**age** *n* système *m* d'égouts; ~**ing board**, ~**board** (*US*) *n* égouttoir *m*; ~**pipe** *n* tuyau *m* d'écoulement.

dram [dræm] *n* petit verre.

drama ['drɑ:mə] *n* (*art*) théâtre *m*, art *m* dramatique; (*play*) pièce *f*; (*event*) drame *m*; ~**tic** [drə'mætık] *a* dramatique; spectaculaire; ~**tist** ['dræmətıst] *n* auteur *m* dramatique.

drank [dræŋk] *pt* of **drink**.

drape [dreıp] *vt* draper; ~**s** *npl* (*US*) rideaux *mpl*; ~**r** *n* marchand/e de nouveautés.

drastic ['dræstık] *a* sévère; énergique.

draught [drɑ:ft] *n* courant *m* d'air; (*of chimney*) tirage *m*; (*NAUT*) tirant *m* d'eau; ~**s** *n* (jeu *m* de) dames *fpl*; **on ~** (*beer*) à la pression; ~**board** *n* damier *m*.

draughtsman ['drɑ:ftsmən] *n* dessinateur/trice (industriel/le).

draw [drɔ:] *vb* (*pt* **drew**, *pp* **drawn** [dru:, drɔ:n]) *vt* tirer; (*attract*) attirer; (*picture*) dessiner; (*line, circle*) tracer; (*money*) retirer // *vi* (*SPORT*) faire match nul // *n* match nul; tirage *m* au sort; loterie *f*; **to ~ to a close** toucher à *or* tirer à sa fin; **to ~ near** *vi* s'approcher; approcher; **to ~ out** *vi* (*lengthen*) s'allonger // *vt* (*money*) retirer; **to ~ up** *vi* (*stop*) s'arrêter // *vt* (*document*) établir, dresser; ~**back** *n* inconvénient *m*, désavantage *m*; ~**bridge** *n* pont-levis *m*.

drawer [drɔ:*] n tiroir m.

drawing ['drɔ:ɪŋ] n dessin m; ~ **board** n planche f à dessin; ~ **pin** n punaise f; ~ **room** n salon m.

drawl [drɔ:l] n accent traînant.

drawn [drɔ:n] pp of **draw**.

dread [drɛd] n épouvante f, effroi m // vt redouter, appréhender; ~**ful** a épouvantable, affreux(euse).

dream [dri:m] n rêve m // vt, vi (pt, pp **dreamed** or **dreamt** [drɛmt]) rêver; ~**er** n rêveur/euse; ~ **world** n monde m imaginaire; ~**y** a rêveur(euse).

dreary ['drɪərɪ] a triste; monotone.

dredge [drɛdʒ] vt draguer; ~**r** n (ship) dragueur m; (machine) drague f; (also: **sugar** ~**r**) saupoudreuse f.

dregs [drɛgz] npl lie f.

drench [drɛntʃ] vt tremper.

dress [drɛs] n robe f; (clothing) habillement m, tenue f // vt habiller; (wound) panser; (food) préparer; **to** ~ **up** vi s'habiller; (in fancy dress) se déguiser; ~ **circle** n premier balcon; ~ **designer** n modéliste m/f; ~**er** n (THEATRE) habilleur/euse; (also: **window** ~**er**) étalagiste m/f; (furniture) buffet m; ~**ing** n (MED) pansement m; (CULIN) sauce f, assaisonnement m; ~**ing gown** n robe f de chambre; ~**ing room** n (THEATRE) loge f; (SPORT) vestiaire m; ~**ing table** n coiffeuse f; ~**maker** n couturière f; ~**making** n couture f; travaux mpl de couture; ~ **rehearsal** n (répétition) générale; ~ **shirt** n chemise f à plastron.

drew [dru:] pt of **draw**.

dribble ['drɪbl] vi tomber goutte à goutte; (baby) baver // vt (ball) dribbler.

dried [draɪd] a (fruit, beans) sec(sèche); (eggs, milk) en poudre.

drift [drɪft] n (of current etc) force f; direction f; (of sand etc) amoncellement m; (of snow) rafale f; coulée f; (: on ground) congère f; (general meaning) sens général // vi (boat) aller à la dérive, dériver; (sand, snow) s'amonceler, s'entasser; ~**wood** n bois flotté.

drill [drɪl] n perceuse f; (bit) foret m; (of dentist) roulette f, fraise f; (MIL) exercice m // vt percer // vi (for oil) faire un or des forage(s).

drink [drɪŋk] n boisson f // vt, vi (pt **drank**, pp **drunk** [dræŋk, drʌŋk]) boire; **to have a** ~ boire quelque chose, boire un verre; prendre l'apéritif; ~**er** n buveur/euse; ~**ing water** n eau f potable.

drip [drɪp] n bruit m d'égouttement; goutte f; (MED) goutte-à-goutte m inv; perfusion f // vi tomber goutte à goutte; (washing) s'égoutter; (wall) suinter; ~-**dry** a (shirt) sans repassage; ~-**feed** vt alimenter au goutte-à-goutte or par perfusion; ~**ping** n graisse f de rôti; ~**ping wet** a trempé(e).

drive [draɪv] n promenade f or trajet m en voiture; (also: ~**way**) allée f; (energy) dynamisme m, énergie f; (PSYCH) besoin m, pulsion f; (push) effort (concerté); campagne f; (SPORT) drive m; (TECH) entraînement m; traction f; transmission f // vb (pt **drove**, pp **driven** [drəuv, 'drɪvn]) vt conduire; (nail) enfoncer; (push) chasser, pousser; (TECH: motor)

actionner; entraîner // vi (AUT: at controls) conduire; (: travel) aller en voiture; **left-/right-hand** ~ conduite f à gauche/droite.

driver ['draɪvə*] n conducteur/trice; (of taxi, bus) chauffeur m; ~**'s license** n (US) permis m de conduire.

driving ['draɪvɪŋ] a: ~ **rain** n pluie battante // n conduite f; ~ **belt** n courroie f de transmission; ~ **instructor** n moniteur m d'auto-école; ~ **lesson** n leçon f de conduite; ~ **licence** n (Brit) permis m de conduire; ~ **school** n auto-école f; ~ **test** n examen m du permis de conduire.

drizzle ['drɪzl] n bruine f, crachin m // vi bruiner.

droll [drəul] a drôle.

dromedary ['drɔmədərɪ] n dromadaire m.

drone [drəun] n bourdonnement m; (male bee) faux-bourdon m.

drool [dru:l] vi baver.

droop [dru:p] vi s'affaisser; tomber.

drop [drɔp] n goutte f; (fall) baisse f; (also: **parachute** ~) saut m; (of cliff) dénivellation f; à-pic m // vt laisser tomber; (voice, eyes, price) baisser; (set down from car) déposer // vi tomber; **to** ~ **off** vi (sleep) s'assoupir; **to** ~ **out** vi (withdraw) se retirer; (student etc) abandonner, décrocher; ~**pings** npl crottes fpl.

dross [drɔs] n déchets mpl; rebut m.

drought [draut] n sécheresse f.

drove [drəuv] pt of **drive** // n: ~**s of people** une foule de gens.

drown [draun] vt noyer // vi se noyer.

drowsy ['drauzɪ] a somnolent(e).

drudge [drʌdʒ] n bête f de somme (fig); ~**ry** ['drʌdʒərɪ] n corvée f.

drug [drʌg] n médicament m; (narcotic) drogue f // vt droguer; ~ **addict** n toxicomane m/f; ~**gist** n (US) pharmacien/ne-droguiste; ~**store** n (US) pharmacie-droguerie f, drugstore m.

drum [drʌm] n tambour m; (for oil, petrol) bidon m; ~**mer** n (joueur m de) tambour m; ~ **roll** n roulement m de tambour; ~**stick** n (MUS) baguette f de tambour; (of chicken) pilon m.

drunk [drʌŋk] pp of **drink** // a ivre, soûl(e) // n soûlard/e; homme/femme soûl(e); ~**ard** ['drʌŋkəd] n ivrogne m/f; ~**en** a ivre, soûl(e); ivrogne, d'ivrogne; ~**enness** n ivresse f; ivrognerie f.

dry [draɪ] a sec(sèche); (day) sans pluie // vt sécher; (clothes) faire sécher // vi sécher; **to** ~ **up** vi se tarir; ~-**cleaner** n teinturier; ~-**cleaner's** n teinturerie f; ~-**cleaning** n nettoyage m à sec; ~**er** n séchoir m; ~**ness** n sécheresse f; ~ **rot** n pourriture sèche (du bois).

dual ['djuəl] a double; ~ **carriageway** n route f à quatre voies; ~-**control** a à doubles commandes; ~ **nationality** n double nationalité f; ~-**purpose** a à double emploi.

dubbed [dʌbd] a (CINEMA) doublé(e); (nicknamed) surnommé(e).

dubious ['dju:bɪəs] a hésitant(e), incertain(e); (reputation, company) douteux(euse).

duchess ['dʌtʃɪs] n duchesse f.

duck [dʌk] n canard m // vi se baisser vivement, baisser subitement la tête ; ~**ling** n caneton m.

duct [dʌkt] n conduite f, canalisation f ; (ANAT) conduit m.

dud [dʌd] n (shell) obus non éclaté ; (object, tool): **it's a** ~ c'est de la camelote, ça ne marche pas // a (cheque) sans provision ; (note, coin) faux(fausse).

due [djuː] a dû(due) ; (expected) attendu(e) ; (fitting) qui convient // n dû m // ad: ~ **north** droit vers le nord ; ~**s** npl (for club, union) cotisation f ; (in harbour) droits mpl (de port) ; **in** ~ **course** en temps utile or voulu ; finalement ; ~ **to** dû(due) à ; causé(e) par.

duel ['djuəl] n duel m.

duet [djuːˈɛt] n duo m.

dug [dʌg] pt, pp of **dig**.

duke [djuːk] n duc m.

dull [dʌl] a ennuyeux(euse) ; terne ; (sound, pain) sourd(e) ; (weather, day) gris(e), maussade ; (blade) émoussé(e) // vt (pain, grief) atténuer ; (mind, senses) engourdir.

duly ['djuːlɪ] ad (on time) en temps voulu ; (as expected) comme il se doit.

dumb [dʌm] a muet(te) ; (stupid) bête ; **dumbfounded** [dʌmˈfaundɪd] a sidéré(e).

dummy ['dʌmɪ] n (tailor's model) mannequin m ; (SPORT) feinte f ; (for baby) tétine f // a faux(fausse), factice.

dump [dʌmp] n tas m d'ordures ; (place) décharge (publique) ; (MIL) dépôt m // vt (put down) déposer ; dèverser ; (get rid of) se débarrasser de ; ~**ing** n (ECON) dumping m ; (of rubbish): **'no** ~**ing'** 'décharge interdite'.

dumpling ['dʌmplɪŋ] n boulette f (de pâte).

dunce [dʌns] n âne m, cancre m.

dune [djuːn] n dune f.

dung [dʌŋ] n fumier m.

dungarees [dʌŋɡəˈriːz] npl bleu(s) m(pl) ; salopette f.

dungeon ['dʌndʒən] n cachot m.

Dunkirk [dʌnˈkəːk] n Dunkerque f.

dupe [djuːp] n dupe f // vt duper, tromper.

duplicate n ['djuːplɪkət] double m, copie exacte f // vt ['djuːplɪkeɪt] faire un double de ; (on machine) polycopier ; **in** ~ en deux exemplaires, en double ; **duplicator** n duplicateur m.

durable ['djuərəbl] a durable ; (clothes, metal) résistant(e), solide.

duration [djuəˈreɪʃən] n durée f.

duress [djuəˈrɛs] n: **under** ~ sous la contrainte.

during ['djuərɪŋ] prep pendant, au cours de.

dusk [dʌsk] n crépuscule m ; ~**y** a sombre.

dust [dʌst] n poussière f // vt (furniture) essuyer, épousseter ; (cake etc): **to** ~ **with** saupoudrer de ; ~**bin** n (Brit) poubelle f ; ~**er** n chiffon m ; ~**jacket** n jaquette f ; ~**man** n (Brit) boueux m, éboueur m ; ~**y** a poussiéreux(euse).

Dutch [dʌtʃ] a hollandais(e), néerlandais(e) // n (LING) hollandais m ; **the** ~ les Hollandais ; ~**man/woman** n Hollandais/e.

dutiable ['djuːtɪəbl] a taxable ; soumis(e) à des droits de douane.

duty ['djuːtɪ] n devoir m ; (tax) droit m, taxe f ; **duties** fpl fonctions fpl ; **on** ~ de service ; (at night etc) de garde ; **off** ~ libre, pas de service or de garde ; ~**-free** a exempté(e) de douane, hors-taxe.

dwarf [dwoːf] n nain/e // vt écraser.

dwell, pt, pp **dwelt** [dwɛl, dwɛlt] vi demeurer ; **to** ~ **on** vt fus s'étendre sur ; ~**ing** n habitation f, demeure f.

dwindle ['dwɪndl] vi diminuer, décroître.

dye [daɪ] n teinture f // vt teindre ; ~**stuffs** npl colorants mpl.

dying ['daɪɪŋ] a mourant(e), agonisant(e).

dyke [daɪk] n digue f.

dynamic [daɪˈnæmɪk] a dynamique ; ~**s** n or npl dynamique f.

dynamite ['daɪnəmaɪt] n dynamite f.

dynamo ['daɪnəməu] n dynamo f.

dynasty ['dɪnəstɪ] n dynastie f.

dysentery ['dɪsntrɪ] n dysenterie f.

E

E [iː] n (MUS) mi m.

each [iːtʃ] det chaque // pronoun chacun(e) ; ~ **one** chacun(e) ; ~ **other** se (or nous etc) ; **they hate** ~ **other** ils se détestent (mutuellement) ; **you are jealous of** ~ **other** vous êtes jaloux l'un de l'autre.

eagle ['iːgl] n aigle m.

ear [ɪə*] n oreille f ; (of corn) épi m ; ~**ache** n douleurs fpl aux oreilles ; ~**drum** n tympan m ; ~ **nose and throat specialist** n oto-rhino-laryngologiste m/f.

earl [əːl] n comte m.

earlier ['əːljə] a (date etc) plus rapproché(e) ; (edition etc) plus ancien(ne), antérieur(e) // ad plus tôt.

early ['əːlɪ] ad tôt, de bonne heure ; (ahead of time) en avance // a précoce ; anticipé(e) ; qui se manifeste (or se fait) tôt or de bonne heure ; **have an** ~ **night/start** couchez-vous/partez tôt or de bonne heure ; **take the** ~ **train/plane** prenez le premier train/vol ; **in the** ~ **or** ~ **in the spring/19th century** au début or commencement du printemps/ 19ème siècle ; ~ **retirement** n retraite anticipée.

earmark ['ɪəmɑːk] vt: **to** ~ **sth for** réserver or destiner qch à qch.

earn [əːn] vt gagner ; (COMM: yield) rapporter ; **this** ~**ed him much praise, he** ~**ed much praise for this** ceci lui a valu de nombreux éloges ; **he's** ~**ed his rest/reward** il mérite or a bien mérité or a bien gagné son repos/sa récompense.

earnest ['əːnɪst] a sérieux(euse) ; **in** ~ ad sérieusement, pour de bon.

earnings ['əːnɪŋz] npl salaire m ; gains mpl.

earphones ['ɪəfəunz] npl écouteurs mpl.

earring ['ɪərɪŋ] n boucle f d'oreille.

earshot ['ɪəʃɔt] n: **out of/within** ~ hors de portée/à portée de la voix.

earth [ə:θ] *n* (*gen, also* ELEC) terre *f*; (*of fox etc*) terrier *m* // *vt* (ELEC) relier à la terre; **~enware** *n* poterie *f*; faïence *f* // *a de or* en faïence; **~quake** *n* tremblement *m* de terre, séisme *m*; **~ tremor** *n* secousse *f* sismique; **~works** *npl* travaux *mpl* de terrassement; **~y** *a* (*fig*) terre à terre *inv*; truculent(e).

earwax ['ɪəwæks] *n* cérumen *m*.

earwig ['ɪəwɪg] *n* perce-oreille *m*.

ease [i:z] *n* facilité *f*, aisance *f* // *vt* (*soothe*) calmer; (*loosen*) relâcher, détendre; (*help pass*); **to ~ sth in/out** faire pénétrer/sortir qch délicatement *or* avec douceur; faciliter la pénétration/la sortie de qch; **life of** *vie* oisive; **at ~** à l'aise; (MIL) au repos; **to ~ off** *or* **up** *vi* diminuer; ralentir; se détendre.

easel ['i:zl] *n* chevalet *m*.

easily ['i:zɪlɪ] *ad* facilement.

east [i:st] *n* est *m* // *a* d'est // *ad* à l'est, vers l'est; **the E~** l'Orient *m*.

Easter ['i:stə*] *n* Pâques *fpl*.

easterly ['i:stəlɪ] *a* d'est.

eastern ['i:stən] *a* de l'est, oriental(e).

East Germany [i:st'dʒə:mənɪ] *n* Allemagne *f* de l'Est.

eastward(s) ['i:stwəd(z)] *ad* vers l'est, à l'est.

easy ['i:zɪ] *a* facile; (*manner*) aisé(e) // *ad*: **to take it** *or* **things ~** ne pas se fatiguer; ne pas (trop) s'en faire; **~ chair** *n* fauteuil *m*; **~ going** *a* accommodant(e), facile à vivre.

eat, *pt* **ate,** *pp* **eaten** [i:t, eɪt, 'i:tn] *vt* manger; **to ~ into, to ~ away at** *vt fus* ronger, attaquer; **~able** *a* mangeable; (*safe to eat*) comestible.

eaves [i:vz] *npl* avant-toit *m*.

eavesdrop ['i:vzdrɔp] *vi*: **to ~ (on a conversation)** écouter (une conversation) de façon indiscrète.

ebb [ɛb] *n* reflux *m* // *vi* refluer; (*fig: also:* **~ away**) décliner.

ebony ['ɛbənɪ] *n* ébène *f*.

ebullient [ɪ'bʌlɪənt] *a* exubérant(e).

eccentric [ɪk'sɛntrɪk] *a,n* excentrique (*m/f*).

ecclesiastic [ɪkli:zɪ'æstɪk] *n* ecclésiastique *m*; **~al** *a* ecclésiastique.

echo, ~es ['ɛkəu] *n* écho *m* // *vt* répéter; faire chorus avec // *vi* résonner; faire écho.

eclipse [ɪ'klɪps] *n* éclipse *f* // *vt* éclipser.

ecology [ɪ'kɔlədʒɪ] *n* écologie *f*.

economic [i:kə'nɔmɪk] *a* économique; (*business etc*) rentable; **~al** *a* économique; (*person*) économe; **~s** *n* économie *f* politique.

economist [ɪ'kɔnəmɪst] *n* économiste *m/f*.

economize [ɪ'kɔnəmaɪz] *vi* économiser, faire des économies.

economy [ɪ'kɔnəmɪ] *n* économie *f*.

ecstasy ['ɛkstəsɪ] *n* extase *f*; **to go into ecstasies over** s'extasier sur; **ecstatic** [-'tætɪk] *a* extatique, en extase.

ecumenical [i:kju'mɛnɪkl] *a* œcuménique.

eczema ['ɛksɪmə] *n* eczéma *m*.

eddy ['ɛdɪ] *n* tourbillon *m*.

edge [ɛdʒ] *n* bord *m*; (*of knife etc*) tranchant *m*, fil *m* // *vt* border; **on ~** (*fig*)

= **edgy**; **to have the ~ on** l'emporter (de justesse) sur, être légèrement meilleur que; **to ~ away from** s'éloigner furtivement de; **~ways** *ad* latéralement; **he couldn't get a word in ~ways** il ne pouvait pas placer un mot; **edging** *n* bordure *f*.

edgy ['ɛdʒɪ] *a* crispé(e), tendu(e).

edible ['ɛdɪbl] *a* comestible; (*meal*) mangeable.

edict ['i:dɪkt] *n* décret *m*.

edifice ['ɛdɪfɪs] *n* édifice *m*.

edit ['ɛdɪt] *vt* éditer; **~ion** [ɪ'dɪʃən] *n* édition *f*; **~or** *n* (*in newspaper*) rédacteur/trice; rédacteur/trice en chef; (*of sb's work*) éditeur/trice; **~orial** [-'tɔ:rɪəl] *a* de la rédaction, éditorial(e) // *n* éditorial *m*.

educate ['ɛdjukeɪt] *vt* instruire; éduquer.

education [ɛdju'keɪʃən] *n* éducation *f*; (*schooling*) enseignement *m*, instruction *f*; **~al** *a* pédagogique; scolaire; instructif(ive).

EEC *n* (*abbr of* European Economic Community) C.E.E. (Communauté économique européenne).

eel [i:l] *n* anguille *f*.

eerie ['ɪərɪ] *a* inquiétant(e), spectral(e), surnaturel(le).

effect [ɪ'fɛkt] *n* effet *m* // *vt* effectuer; **~s** *npl* (THEATRE) effets *mpl*; **to take ~** (*law*) entrer en vigueur, prendre effet; (*drug*) agir, faire son effet; **in ~** en fait; **~ive** *a* efficace; **~iveness** *n* efficacité *f*.

effeminate [ɪ'fɛmɪnət] *a* efféminé(e).

effervescent [ɛfə'vɛsnt] *a* effervescent(e).

efficacy ['ɛfɪkəsɪ] *n* efficacité *f*.

efficiency [ɪ'fɪʃənsɪ] *n* efficacité *f*; rendement *m*.

efficient [ɪ'fɪʃənt] *a* efficace; **~ly** *ad* efficacement.

effigy ['ɛfɪdʒɪ] *n* effigie *f*.

effort ['ɛfət] *n* effort *m*; **~less** *a* sans effort, aisé(e).

effrontery [ɪ'frʌntərɪ] *n* effronterie *f*.

e.g. *ad* (*abbr of exempli gratia*) par exemple, p. ex.

egalitarian [ɪgælɪ'tɛərɪən] *a* égalitaire.

egg [ɛg] *n* œuf *m*; **to ~ on** *vt* pousser; **~cup** *n* coquetier *m*; **~plant** *n* aubergine *f*; **~shell** *n* coquille *f* d'œuf // *a* (*colour*) blanc cassé *inv*.

ego ['i:gəu] *n* moi *m*.

egoist ['ɛgəuɪst] *n* égoïste *m/f*.

egotist ['ɛgəutɪst] *n* égocentrique *m/f*.

Egypt ['i:dʒɪpt] *n* Égypte *f*; **~ian** [ɪ'dʒɪpʃən] *a* égyptien(ne) // *n* Égyptien/ne.

eiderdown ['aɪdədaun] *n* édredon *m*.

eight [eɪt] *num* huit; **~een** *num* dix-huit; **~h** *num* huitième; **~y** *num* quatre-vingt(s).

Eire ['ɛərə] *n* République *f* d'Irlande.

either ['aɪðə*] *det* l'un ou l'autre; (*both, each*) chaque; **on ~ side** de chaque côté // *pronoun*: **~ (of them)** l'un ou l'autre; **I don't like ~** je n'aime ni l'un ni l'autre // *ad non plus*; **no, I don't ~** moi non plus // *cj*: **~ good or bad** ou bon ou mauvais, soit bon soit mauvais; **I haven't**

seen ~ **one or the other** je n'ai vu ni l'un ni l'autre.

ejaculation [ıdʒækju'leıʃən] n (PHYSIOL) éjaculation f.

eject [ı'dʒɛkt] vt expulser; éjecter; ~**or seat** n siège m éjectable.

eke [iːk]: **to ~ out** vt faire durer; augmenter.

elaborate a [ı'læbərıt] compliqué(e), recherché(e), minutieux (euse) // vb [ı'læbəreıt] vt élaborer // vi entrer dans les détails.

elapse [ı'læps] vi s'écouler, passer.

elastic [ı'læstık] a, n élastique (m); ~ **band** n élastique m; ~**ity** [-'tısıtı] n élasticité f.

elated [ı'leıtıd] a transporté(e) de joie.

elation [ı'leıʃən] n (grande) joie, allégresse f.

elbow ['ɛlbəu] n coude m.

elder ['ɛldə*] a aîné(e) // n (tree) sureau m; one's ~s ses aînés; ~**ly** a âgé(e) // n: **the** ~**ly** les personnes âgées.

eldest ['ɛldıst] a,n: **the** ~ (**child**) l'aîné(e) (des enfants).

elect [ı'lɛkt] vt élire; **to** ~ **to do** choisir de faire // a: **the president** ~ le président désigné; ~**ion** [ı'lɛkʃən] n élection f; ~**ioneering** [ılɛkʃə'nıərıŋ] n propagande électorale, manœuvres électorales; ~**or** n électeur/trice; ~**oral** a électoral(e); ~**orate** n électorat m.

electric [ı'lɛktrık] a électrique; ~**al** a électrique; ~ **blanket** n couverture chauffante; ~ **chair** n chaise f électrique; ~ **cooker** n cuisinière f électrique; ~ **current** n courant m électrique; ~ **fire** n radiateur m électrique.

electrician [ılɛk'trıʃən] n électricien m.

electricity [ılɛk'trısıtı] n électricité f.

electrify [ı'lɛktrıfaı] vt (RAIL) électrifier; (audience) électriser.

electro... [ı'lɛktrəu] prefix: **electrocute** [-kjuːt] vt électrocuter; **electrode** [ı'lɛktrəud] n électrode f; **electrolysis** [ılɛk'trɔlısıs] n électrolyse f.

electron [ı'lɛktrɔn] n électron m.

electronic [ılɛk'trɔnık] a électronique; ~**s** n électronique f.

elegance ['ɛlıgəns] n élégance f.

elegant ['ɛlıgənt] a élégant(e).

element ['ɛlımənt] n (gen) élément m; (of heater, kettle etc) résistance f; ~**ary** ['-'mɛntərı] a élémentaire; (school, education) primaire.

elephant ['ɛlıfənt] n éléphant m.

elevate ['ɛlıveıt] vt élever; ~**d railway** n métro aérien.

elevation [ɛlı'veıʃən] n élévation f; (height) altitude f.

elevator ['ɛlıveıtə*] n élévateur m, monte-charge m inv; (US: lift) ascenseur m.

eleven [ı'lɛvn] num onze; ~**ses** npl ≈ pause-café f; ~**th** a onzième.

elf, elves [ɛlf, ɛlvz] n lutin m.

elicit [ı'lısıt] vt: **to** ~ (**from**) obtenir (de), arracher (à).

eligible ['ɛlıdʒəbl] a éligible; (for membership) admissible; ~ **for a pension** ayant droit à la retraite.

eliminate [ı'lımıneıt] vt éliminer; **elimination** n élimination f.

élite [eı'liːt] n élite f.

ellipse [ı'lıps] n ellipse f.

elliptical [ı'lıptıkl] a elliptique.

elm [ɛlm] n orme m.

elocution [ɛlə'kjuːʃən] n élocution f.

elongated ['iːlɔŋgeıtıd] a étiré(e), allongé(e).

elope [ı'ləup] vi (lovers) s'enfuir (ensemble); ~**ment** n fugue amoureuse.

eloquence ['ɛləkwəns] n éloquence f.

eloquent ['ɛləkwənt] a éloquent(e).

else [ɛls] ad d'autre; **something** ~ quelque chose d'autre, autre chose; **somewhere** ~ ailleurs, autre part; **everywhere** ~ partout ailleurs; **where** ~? à quel autre endroit?; **little** ~ pas grand-chose d'autre; ~**where** ad ailleurs, autre part.

elucidate [ı'luːsıdeıt] vt élucider.

elude [ı'luːd] vt échapper à; (question) éluder.

elusive [ı'luːsıv] a insaisissable; (answer) évasif(ive).

elves [ɛlvz] npl of **elf**.

emaciated [ı'meısıeıtıd] a émacié(e), décharné(e).

emanate ['ɛməneıt] vi: **to** ~ **from** émaner de.

emancipate [ı'mænsıpeıt] vt émanciper; **emancipation** [-'peıʃən] n émancipation f.

embalm [ım'bɑːm] vt embaumer.

embankment [ım'bæŋkmənt] n (of road, railway) remblai m, talus m; (riverside) berge f, quai m; (dyke) digue f.

embargo, ~**es** [ım'bɑːgəu] n embargo m // vt frapper d'embargo, mettre l'embargo sur.

embark [ım'bɑːk] vi: **to** ~ (**on**) (s')embarquer (à bord de or sur) // vt embarquer; **to** ~ **on** (fig) se lancer or s'embarquer dans; ~**ation** [ɛmbɑː'keıʃən] n embarquement m.

embarrass [ım'bærəs] vt embarrasser, gêner; ~**ing** a gênant(e), embarrassant(e); ~**ment** n embarras m, gêne f.

embassy ['ɛmbəsı] n ambassade f.

embed [ım'bɛd] vt enfoncer, ficher, sceller.

embellish [ım'bɛlıʃ] vt embellir; enjoliver.

embers ['ɛmbəz] npl braise f.

embezzle [ım'bɛzl] vt détourner; ~**ment** n détournement m (de fonds).

embitter [ım'bıtə*] vt aigrir; envenimer.

emblem ['ɛmbləm] n emblème m.

embodiment [ım'bɔdımənt] n personification f, incarnation f.

embody [ım'bɔdı] vt (features) réunir, comprendre; (ideas) formuler, exprimer.

embossed [ım'bɔst] a repoussé(e); gaufré(e); ~ **with** où figure(nt) en relief.

embrace [ım'breıs] vt embrasser, étreindre; (include) embrasser, couvrir // n étreinte f.

embroider [ım'brɔıdə*] vt broder; (fig: story) enjoliver; ~**y** n broderie f.

embryo ['ɛmbrıəu] n (also fig) embryon m.

emerald ['ɛmərəld] n émeraude f.

emerge [ɪ'mə:dʒ] vi apparaître, surgir.
emergence [ɪ'mə:dʒəns] n apparition f.
emergency [ɪ'mə:dʒənsɪ] n urgence f; **in an** ~ en cas d'urgence; **state of** ~ état m d'urgence; ~ **exit** n sortie f de secours.
emergent [ɪ'mə:dʒənt] a: ~ **nation** pays m en voie de développement.
emery ['eməɪ] n: ~ **board** n lime f à ongles (en carton émerisé); ~ **paper** n papier m (d')émeri.
emetic [ɪ'metɪk] n vomitif m, émétique m.
emigrant ['emɪgrənt] n émigrant/e.
emigrate ['emɪgreɪt] vi émigrer; **emigration**[-'greɪʃən] n émigration f.
eminence ['emɪnəns] n éminence f.
eminent ['emɪnənt] a éminent(e).
emission [ɪ'mɪʃən] n émission f.
emit [ɪ'mɪt] vt émettre.
emotion [ɪ'məuʃən] n émotion f; ~**al** a (person) émotif(ive), très sensible; (scene) émouvant(e); (tone, speech) qui fait appel aux sentiments; ~**ally** ad: ~**ally disturbed** qui souffre de troubles de l'affectivité.
emotive [ɪ'məutɪv] a émotif(ive); ~ **power** n capacité f d'émouvoir or de toucher.
emperor ['empərə*] n empereur m.
emphasis, pl **ases** ['emfəsɪs, -si:z] n accent m; force f, insistance f.
emphasize ['emfəsaɪz] vt (syllable, word, point) appuyer or insister sur; (feature) souligner, accentuer.
emphatic [em'fætɪk] a (strong) énergique, vigoureux(euse); (unambiguous, clear) catégorique; ~**ally** ad avec vigueur or énergie; catégoriquement.
empire ['empaɪə*] n empire m.
empirical [em'pɪrɪkl] a empirique.
employ [ɪm'plɔɪ] vt employer; ~**ee** [-'i:] n employé/e; ~**er** n employeur/euse; ~**ment** n emploi m; ~**ment agency** n agence f or bureau m de placement; ~**ment exchange** n bourse f du travail.
empower [ɪm'pauə*] vt: **to** ~ **sb to do** autoriser or habiliter qn à faire.
empress ['emprɪs] n impératrice f.
emptiness ['emptɪnɪs] n vide m.
empty ['emptɪ] a vide; (threat, promise) en l'air, vain(e) // vt vider // vi se vider; (liquid) s'écouler; **on an** ~ **stomach** à jeun; ~**-handed** a les mains vides.
emulate ['emjuleɪt] vt rivaliser avec, imiter.
emulsion [ɪ'mʌlʃən] n émulsion f; ~ (paint) n peinture mate.
enable [ɪ'neɪbl] vt: **to** ~ **sb to do** permettre à qn de faire, donner à qn la possibilité de faire.
enamel [ɪ'næməl] n émail m.
enamoured [ɪ'næməd] a: ~ **of** amoureux(euse) de; (idea) enchanté(e) par.
encased [ɪn'keɪst] a: ~ **in** enfermé(e) dans, recouvert(e) de.
enchant [ɪn'tʃɑ:nt] vt enchanter; (subject: magic spell) ensorceler; ~**ing** a ravissant(e), enchanteur(eresse).
encircle [ɪn'sə:kl] vt entourer, encercler.
encl. (abbr of enclosed) annexe(s).

enclose [ɪn'kləuz] vt (land) clôturer; (letter etc): **to** ~ (**with**) joindre (à); **please find** ~**d** veuillez trouver ci-joint.
enclosure [ɪn'kləuʒə*] n enceinte f; (COMM) annexe f.
encore [ɔŋ'kɔ:*] excl, n bis (m).
encounter [ɪn'kauntə*] n rencontre f // vt rencontrer.
encourage [ɪn'kʌrɪdʒ] vt encourager; ~**ment** n encouragement m.
encroach [ɪn'krəutʃ] vi: **to** ~ (**up**)**on** empiéter sur.
encyclop(a)edia [ensaɪkləu'pi:dɪə] n encyclopédie f.
end [end] n (gen, also: aim) fin f; (of table, street etc) bout m, extrémité f // vt terminer; (also: **bring to an** ~, **put an** ~ **to**) mettre fin à // vi se terminer, finir; **to come to an** ~ prendre fin; **in the** ~ finalement; ~ **on** (object) debout, dressé(e); **for 5 hours on** ~ durant 5 heures d'affilée or de suite; **for hours on** ~ pendant des heures (et des heures); **to** ~ **up** vi: **to** ~ **up in** finir or se terminer par; (place) finir or aboutir à.
endanger [ɪn'deɪndʒə*] vt mettre en danger.
endearing [ɪn'dɪərɪŋ] a attachant(e).
endeavour [ɪn'devə*] n tentative f, effort m // vi: **to** ~ **to do** tenter or s'efforcer de faire.
ending ['endɪŋ] n dénouement m, conclusion f; (LING) terminaison f.
endive ['endaɪv] n chicorée f.
endless ['endlɪs] a sans fin, interminable; (patience, resources) inépuisable, sans limites.
endorse [ɪn'dɔ:s] vt (cheque) endosser; (approve) appuyer, approuver, sanctionner; ~**ment** n (on driving licence) contravention portée au permis de conduire.
endow [ɪn'dau] vt (provide with money) faire une donation à, doter; (equip): **to** ~ **with** gratifier de, doter de.
end product ['endprɔdəkt] n produit fini; (fig) résultat m.
endurable [ɪn'djuərəbl] a supportable.
endurance [ɪn'djuərəns] n endurance f, résistance f; patience f.
endure [ɪn'djuə*] vt supporter, endurer // vi durer.
enemy ['enəmɪ] a,n ennemi(e).
energetic [enə'dʒetɪk] a énergique; actif(ive); **qui fait se dispenser** (physiquement).
energy ['enədʒɪ] n énergie f.
enervating ['enə:veɪtɪŋ] a débilitant(e), affaiblissant(e).
enforce [ɪn'fɔ:s] vt (LAW) appliquer, faire respecter; ~**d** a forcé(e).
engage [ɪn'geɪdʒ] vt engager; (MIL) engager le combat avec // vi (TECH) s'enclencher, s'engrener; **to** ~ **in se** lancer dans; ~**d** a (busy, in use) occupé(e); (betrothed) fiancé(e); **to get** ~**d** se fiancer; **he is** ~**d in research/a survey** il fait de la recherche/une enquête; ~**ment** n obligation f, engagement m; rendez-vous m inv; (to marry) fiançailles fpl; (MIL) combat m; ~**ment ring** n bague f de fiançailles.

engaging [ɪn'geɪdʒɪŋ] a engageant(e), attirant(e).

engender [ɪn'dʒɛndə*] vt produire, causer.

engine ['ɛndʒɪn] n (AUT) moteur m; (RAIL) locomotive f; ~ **failure** n panne f; ~ **trouble** n ennuis mpl mécaniques.

engineer [ɛndʒɪ'nɪə*] n ingénieur m; (US: RAIL) mécanicien m; ~**ing** n engineering m, ingénierie f; (of bridges, ships) génie m; (of machine) mécanique f.

England ['ɪŋglənd] n Angleterre f.

English ['ɪŋglɪʃ] a anglais(e) // n (LING) anglais m; **the** ~ les Anglais; ~**man/woman** n Anglais/e.

engrave [ɪn'greɪv] vt graver.

engraving [ɪn'greɪvɪŋ] n gravure f.

engrossed [ɪn'grəust] a: ~ **in** absorbé(e) par, plongé(e) dans.

engulf [ɪn'gʌlf] vt engloutir.

enhance [ɪn'hɑːns] vt rehausser, mettre en valeur.

enigma [ɪ'nɪgmə] n énigme f; ~**tic** [ɛnɪg'mætɪk] a énigmatique.

enjoy [ɪn'dʒɔɪ] vt aimer, prendre plaisir à; (have: health, fortune) jouir de; (: success) connaître; **to** ~ **oneself** s'amuser; ~**able** a agréable; ~**ment** n plaisir m.

enlarge [ɪn'lɑːdʒ] vt accroître; (PHOT) agrandir // vi: **to** ~ **on** (subject) s'étendre sur; ~**ment** n (PHOT) agrandissement m.

enlighten [ɪn'laɪtn] vt éclairer; ~**ed** a éclairé(e); ~**ment** n édification f; vues éclairées; éclaircissements mpl; (HISTORY): **the E**~**ment** ≈ le Siècle des lumières.

enlist [ɪn'lɪst] vt recruter; (support) s'assurer // vi s'engager.

enmity ['ɛnmɪtɪ] n inimitié f.

enormity [ɪ'nɔːmɪtɪ] n énormité f.

enormous [ɪ'nɔːməs] a énorme.

enough [ɪ'nʌf] a, n: ~ **time/books** assez or suffisamment de temps/livres; **have you got** ~? (en) avez-vous assez? // ad: **big** ~ assez or suffisamment grand; **he has not worked** ~ il n'a pas assez or suffisamment travaillé, il n'a pas travaillé assez or suffisamment; ~! assez!, ça suffit!; **it's hot** ~ **(as it is)!** il fait assez chaud comme ça! ; ... **which, funnily** ~ ... qui, chose curieuse.

enquire [ɪn'kwaɪə*] vt,vi = inquire.

enrich [ɪn'rɪtʃ] vt enrichir.

enrol [ɪn'rəul] vt inscrire // vi s'inscrire; ~**ment** n inscription f.

ensconced [ɪn'skɒnst] a: ~ **in** bien calé(e) dans; plongé(e) dans.

ensign n (NAUT) ['ɛnsən] enseigne f, pavillon m; (MIL) ['ɛnsaɪn] porte- étendard m.

enslave [ɪn'sleɪv] vt asservir.

ensue [ɪn'sjuː] vi s'ensuivre, résulter.

ensure [ɪn'ʃuə*] vt assurer; garantir; **to** ~ **that** s'assurer que.

entail [ɪn'teɪl] vt entraîner, nécessiter.

entangle [ɪn'tæŋgl] vt emmêler, embrouiller.

enter ['ɛntə*] vt (room) entrer dans, pénétrer dans; (club, army) entrer à; (competition) s'inscrire à or pour; (sb for a competition) (faire) inscrire; (write down) inscrire, noter; **to** ~ **for** vt fus s'inscrire à, se présenter pour or à; **to** ~ **into** vt

---

fus (exploration) se lancer dans; (debate) prendre part à; (agreement) conclure; **to** ~ **up** vt inscrire; **to** ~ **(up)on** vt fus commencer.

enterprise ['ɛntəpraɪz] n entreprise f; (esprit m d')initiative f.

enterprising ['ɛntəpraɪzɪŋ] a entreprenant(e), dynamique.

entertain [ɛntə'teɪn] vt amuser, distraire; (invite) recevoir (à dîner); (idea, plan) envisager; ~**er** n artiste m/f de variétés; ~**ing** a amusant(e), distrayant(e); ~**ment** n (amusement) distraction f, divertissement m, amusement m; (show) spectacle m.

enthralled [ɪn'θrɔːld] a captivé(e).

enthusiasm [ɪn'θuːzɪæzəm] n enthousiasme m.

enthusiast [ɪn'θuːzɪæst] n enthousiaste m/f; **a jazz** etc ~ un fervent or passionné du jazz etc; ~**ic** [-'æstɪk] a enthousiaste.

entice [ɪn'taɪs] vt attirer, séduire.

entire [ɪn'taɪə*] a (tout) entier(ère); ~**ly** ad entièrement, complètement; ~**ty** [ɪn'taɪərɪtɪ] n: **in its** ~**ty** dans sa totalité.

entitle [ɪn'taɪtl] vt (allow): **to** ~ **sb to do** donner (le) droit à qn de faire; **to** ~ **sb to sth** donner droit à qch à qn; ~**d** a (book) intitulé(e); **to be** ~**d to do** avoir le droit de or être habilité à faire.

entrance n ['ɛntrns] entrée f // vt [ɪn'trɑːns] enchanter, ravir; **to gain** ~ **to** (university etc) être admis à; ~ **examination** n examen m d'entrée; ~ **fee** n droit m d'inscription; (to museum etc) prix m d'entrée.

entrant ['ɛntrnt] n participant/e; concurrent/e.

entreat [ɛn'triːt] vt supplier; ~**y** n supplication f, prière f.

entrée ['ɔntreɪ] n (CULIN) entrée f.

entrenched [ɛn'trɛntʃd] a retranché(e).

entrust [ɪn'trʌst] vt: **to** ~ **sth to** confier qch à.

entry ['ɛntrɪ] n entrée f; (in register) inscription f; ~ **form** n feuille f d'inscription.

entwine [ɪn'twaɪn] vt entrelacer.

enumerate [ɪ'njuːməreɪt] vt énumérer.

enunciate [ɪ'nʌnsɪeɪt] vt énoncer; prononcer.

envelop [ɪn'vɛləp] vt envelopper.

envelope ['ɛnvələup] n enveloppe f.

envious ['ɛnvɪəs] a envieux(euse).

environment [ɪn'vaɪərnmənt] n milieu m; environnement m; ~**al** [-'mɛntl] a écologique; du milieu.

envisage [ɪn'vɪzɪdʒ] vt envisager; prévoir.

envoy ['ɛnvɔɪ] n envoyé/e.

envy ['ɛnvɪ] n envie f // vt envier.

enzyme ['ɛnzaɪm] n enzyme m.

ephemeral [ɪ'fɛmərl] a éphémère.

epic ['ɛpɪk] n épopée f // a épique.

epidemic [ɛpɪ'dɛmɪk] n épidémie f.

epilepsy ['ɛpɪlɛpsɪ] n épilepsie f; **epileptic** [-'lɛptɪk] a,n épileptique (m/f).

epilogue ['ɛpɪlɒg] n épilogue m.

episode ['ɛpɪsəud] n épisode m.

epistle [ɪ'pɪsl] n épître f.

epitaph ['ɛpɪtɑːf] n épitaphe f.

epitome [ɪ'pɪtəmɪ] n résumé m;

quintessence f, type m; **epitomize** vt résumer; illustrer, incarner.

epoch ['iːpɔk] n époque f, ère f; **~-making** a qui fait époque.

equable ['ɛkwəbl] a égal(e); de tempérament égal.

equal ['iːkwl] a égal(e) // n égal/e // vt égaler; **~ to** (task) à la hauteur de; **~ to doing** de taille à or capable de faire; **~ity** [iː'kwɔlɪti] n égalité f; **~ize** vt,vi égaliser; **~izer** n but égalisateur; **~ly** ad également; (just as) tout aussi; **~(s) sign** n signe m d'égalité.

equanimity [ɛkwə'nɪmɪti] n égalité f d'humeur.

equate [ɪ'kweɪt] vt: **to ~ sth with** comparer qch à; assimiler qch à; **to ~ sth to** mettre qch en équation avec; égaler qch à; **equation** [ɪ'kweɪʃən] n (MATH) équation f.

equator [ɪ'kweɪtə*] n équateur m; **~ial** [ɛkwə'tɔːrɪəl] a équatorial(e).

equilibrium [iːkwɪ'lɪbrɪəm] n équilibre m.

equinox ['iːkwɪnɔks] n équinoxe m.

equip [ɪ'kwɪp] vt équiper; **to ~ sb/sth with** équiper or munir qn/qch de; **~ment** n équipement m; (electrical etc) appareillage m, installation f.

equitable ['ɛkwɪtəbl] a équitable.

equity ['ɛkwɪti] n équité f; **equities** npl (COMM) actions cotées en Bourse.

equivalent [ɪ'kwɪvələnt] a équivalent(e) // n équivalent m.

equivocal [ɪ'kwɪvəkl] a équivoque; (open to suspicion) douteux(euse).

era ['ɪərə] n ère f, époque f.

eradicate [ɪ'rædɪkeɪt] vt éliminer.

erase [ɪ'reɪz] vt effacer; **~r** n gomme f.

erect [ɪ'rɛkt] a droit(e) // vt construire; (monument) ériger; élever; (tent etc) dresser.

erection [ɪ'rɛkʃən] n érection f.

ermine ['əːmɪn] n hermine f.

erode [ɪ'rəud] vt éroder; (metal) ronger; **erosion** [ɪ'rəuʒən] n érosion f.

erotic [ɪ'rɔtɪk] a érotique; **~ism** [ɪ'rɔtɪsɪzm] n érotisme m.

err [əː*] vi se tromper; (REL) pécher.

errand ['ɛrnd] n course f, commission f; **~ boy** n garçon m de courses.

erratic [ɪ'rætɪk] a irrégulier(ère); inconstant(e).

erroneous [ɪ'rəunɪəs] a erroné(e).

error ['ɛrə*] n erreur f.

erudite ['ɛrjudaɪt] a savant(e).

erupt [ɪ'rʌpt] vi entrer en éruption; (fig) éclater; **~ion** [ɪ'rʌpʃən] n éruption f.

escalate ['ɛskəleɪt] vi s'intensifier; **escalation** [-'leɪʃən] n escalade f.

escalator ['ɛskəleɪtə*] n escalier roulant.

escapade [ɛskə'peɪd] n fredaine f; équipée f.

escape [ɪ'skeɪp] n évasion f; fuite f; (of gas etc) échappement m; fuite f // vi s'échapper, fuir; (from jail) s'évader; (fig) s'en tirer; (leak) s'échapper; fuir // vt échapper à; **to ~ from sb** échapper à qn; **to ~ from** (place) s'échapper de; (fig) fuir; **escapism** n évasion f (fig).

escort n ['ɛskɔːt] escorte f // vt [ɪ'skɔːt]

escorter; **~ agency** n bureau m d'hôtesses.

Eskimo ['ɛskɪməu] n Esquimau/de.

especially [ɪ'spɛʃlɪ] ad particulièrement; surtout; exprès.

espionage ['ɛspɪənɑːʒ] n espionnage m.

esplanade [ɛsplə'neɪd] n esplanade f.

Esquire [ɪ'skwaɪə*] n (abbr Esq.): **J. Brown, ~** Monsieur J. Brown.

essay ['ɛseɪ] n (SCOL) dissertation f; (LITERATURE) essai m; (attempt) tentative f.

essence ['ɛsns] n essence f.

essential [ɪ'sɛnʃl] a essentiel(le); (basic) fondamental(e); **~ly** ad essentiellement.

establish [ɪ'stæblɪʃ] vt établir; (business) fonder, créer; (one's power etc) asseoir, affermir; **~ment** n établissement m; **the E~ment** les pouvoirs établis; l'ordre établi; les milieux dirigeants.

estate [ɪ'steɪt] n domaine m, propriété f; biens mpl, succession f; **~ agent** n agent immobilier; **~ car** n (Brit) break m.

esteem [ɪ'stiːm] n estime f.

esthetic [ɪs'θɛtɪk] a (US) = **aesthetic**.

estimate n ['ɛstɪmət] estimation f; (COMM) devis m // vt ['ɛstɪmeɪt] estimer; **estimation** [-'meɪʃən] n opinion f; estime f.

estuary ['ɛstjuərɪ] n estuaire m.

etching ['ɛtʃɪŋ] n eau-forte f.

eternal [ɪ'təːnl] a éternel(le).

eternity [ɪ'təːnɪti] n éternité f.

ether ['iːθə*] n éther m.

ethical ['ɛθɪkl] a moral(e).

ethics ['ɛθɪks] n éthique f // npl moralité f.

ethnic ['ɛθnɪk] a ethnique.

ethnology [ɛθ'nɔlədʒɪ] n ethnologie f.

etiquette ['ɛtɪkɛt] n convenances fpl, étiquette f.

etymology [ɛtɪ'mɔlədʒɪ] n étymologie f.

eulogy ['juːlədʒɪ] n éloge m.

euphemism ['juːfəmɪzm] n euphémisme m.

euphoria [juː'fɔːrɪə] n euphorie f.

Europe ['juərəp] n Europe f; **~an** [-'pɪən] a européen(ne) // n Européen/ne.

euthanasia [juːθə'neɪzɪə] n euthanasie f.

evacuate [ɪ'vækjueɪt] vt évacuer; **evacuation** [-'eɪʃən] n évacuation f.

evade [ɪ'veɪd] vt échapper à; (question etc) éluder; (duties) se dérober à.

evaluate [ɪ'væljueɪt] vt évaluer.

evangelist [ɪ'vændʒəlɪst] n évangéliste m.

evangelize [ɪ'vændʒəlaɪz] vt évangéliser, prêcher l'Évangile à.

evaporate [ɪ'væpəreɪt] vi s'évaporer // vt faire évaporer; **~d milk** n lait concentré; **evaporation** [-'reɪʃən] n évaporation f.

evasion [ɪ'veɪʒən] n dérobade f; faux-fuyant m.

evasive [ɪ'veɪsɪv] a évasif(ive).

eve [iːv] n: **on the ~ of** à la veille de.

even ['iːvn] a régulier(ère); égal(e); (number) pair(e) // ad même; **~ more** encore plus; **~ so** quand même; **to ~ out** vi s'égaliser; **to get ~ with sb** prendre sa revanche sur qn.

evening ['iːvnɪŋ] n soir m; (as duration, event) soirée f; **in the ~** le soir; **~ class**

n cours *m* du soir ; ~ **dress** *n* (*man's*) habit *m* de soirée, smoking *m* ; (*woman's*) robe *f* de soirée.

evensong ['iːvnsɔŋ] *n* office *m* du soir.

event [ɪ'vɛnt] *n* événement *m* ; (*SPORT*) épreuve *f* ; **in the** ~ **of** en cas de ; ~**ful** a mouvementé(e).

eventual [ɪ'vɛntjuəl] *a* final(e) ; ~**ity** [-'ælɪtɪ] *n* possibilité *f*, éventualité *f* ; ~**ly** *ad* finalement.

ever ['ɛvə*] *ad* jamais ; (*at all times*) toujours ; **the best** ~ le meilleur qu'on ait jamais vu ; **have you** ~ **seen it?** l'as-tu déjà vu?, as-tu eu l'occasion *or* t'est-il arrivé de le voir? ; **hardly** ~ ne ... presque jamais ; ~ **since** *ad* depuis // *cj* depuis que ; ~ **so pretty** si joli ; ~**green** *n* arbre *m* à feuilles persistantes ; ~**lasting** *a* éternel(le).

every ['ɛvrɪ] *det* chaque ; ~ **day** tous les jours, chaque jour ; ~ **other/third day** tous les deux/trois jours ; ~ **other car** une voiture sur deux ; ~ **now and then** de temps en temps ; ~**body** *pronoun* tout le monde, tous *pl* ; ~**day** a quotidien(ne) ; de tous les jours ; ~**one** = ~**body** ; ~**thing** *pronoun* tout ; ~**where** *ad* partout.

evict [ɪ'vɪkt] *vt* expulser ; ~**ion** [ɪ'vɪkʃən] *n* expulsion *f*.

evidence ['ɛvɪdns] *n* (*proof*) preuve(s) *f(pl)* ; (*of witness*) témoignage *m* ; (*sign*) to **show** ~ **of** donner des signes de ; **to give** ~ témoigner, déposer ; **in** ~ (*obvious*) en évidence ; en vue.

evident ['ɛvɪdnt] *a* évident(e) ; ~**ly** *ad* de toute évidence.

evil ['iːvl] *a* mauvais(e) // *n* mal *m*.

evocative [ɪ'vɔkətɪv] *a* évocateur(trice).

evoke [ɪ'vəuk] *vt* évoquer.

evolution [iːvə'luːʃən] *n* évolution *f*.

evolve [ɪ'vɔlv] *vt* élaborer // *vi* évoluer, se transformer.

ewe [juː] *n* brebis *f*.

ewer ['juːə*] *n* broc *m*.

ex- [ɛks] *prefix* ex-.

exact [ɪg'zækt] *a* exact(e) // *vt*: **to** ~ **sth** (**from**) extorquer qch (à) ; exiger qch (de) ; ~**ing** *a* exigeant(e) ; (*work*) fatigant(e) ; ~**itude** *n* exactitude *f*, précision *f* ; ~**ly** *ad* exactement.

exaggerate [ɪg'zædʒəreɪt] *vt,vi* exagérer ; **exaggeration** [-'reɪʃən] *n* exagération *f*.

exalt [ɪg'zɔːlt] *vt* exalter ; élever.

exam [ɪg'zæm] *n abbr of* **examination.**

examination [ɪgzæmɪ'neɪʃən] *n* (*SCOL, MED*) examen *m*.

examine [ɪg'zæmɪn] *vt* (*gen*) examiner ; (*SCOL, LAW: person*) interroger ; (*at customs: luggage*) inspecter ; ~**r** *n* examinateur/trice.

example [ɪg'zɑːmpl] *n* exemple *m* ; **for** ~ par exemple.

exasperate [ɪg'zɑːspəreɪt] *vt* exaspérer, agacer.

excavate ['ɛkskəveɪt] *vt* excaver ; (*object*) mettre au jour ; **excavation** [-'veɪʃən] *n* excavation *f* ; **excavator** *n* excavateur *m*, excavatrice *f*.

exceed [ɪk'siːd] *vt* dépasser ; (*one's powers*) outrepasser ; ~**ingly** *ad* excessivement.

excel [ɪk'sɛl] *vi* exceller // *vt* surpasser.

excellence ['ɛksələns] *n* excellence *f*.

Excellency ['ɛksələnsɪ] *n*: **His** ~ son Excellence *f*.

excellent ['ɛksələnt] *a* excellent(e).

except [ɪk'sɛpt] *prep* (*also*: ~ **for,** ~**ing**) sauf, excepté, à l'exception de // *vt* excepter ; ~ **if/when** sauf si/quand ; ~ **that** excepté que, si ce n'est que ; ~**ion** [ɪk'sɛpʃən] *n* exception *f* ; **to take** ~**ion to** s'offusquer de ; ~**ional** [ɪk'sɛpʃənl] *a* exceptionnel(le).

excerpt ['ɛksəːpt] *n* extrait *m*.

excess [ɪk'sɛs] *n* excès *m* ; ~ **fare** *n* supplément *m* ; ~ **baggage** *n* excédent *m* de bagages ; ~**ive** *a* excessif(ive).

exchange [ɪks'tʃeɪndʒ] *n* échange *m* ; (*also*: **telephone** ~) central *m* // *vt* échanger ; ~ **market** *n* marché *m* des changes.

exchequer [ɪks'tʃɛkə*] *n* Échiquier *m*, ≈ ministère *m* des Finances.

excisable [ɪk'saɪzəbl] *a* taxable.

excise *n* ['ɛksaɪz] taxe *f* // *vt* [ɛk'saɪz] exciser ; ~ **duties** *npl* impôts indirects.

excite [ɪk'saɪt] *vt* exciter ; **to get** ~**d** s'exciter ; ~**ment** *n* excitation *f* ; **exciting** *a* passionnant(e).

exclaim [ɪk'skleɪm] *vi* s'exclamer ; **exclamation** [ɛksklə'meɪʃən] *n* exclamation *f* ; **exclamation mark** *n* point *m* d'exclamation.

exclude [ɪk'skluːd] *vt* exclure ; **exclusion** [ɪk'skluːʒən] *n* exclusion *f*.

exclusive [ɪk'skluːsɪv] *a* exclusif(ive) ; (*club, district*) sélect(e) ; (*item of news*) en exclusivité // *ad* (*COMM*) exclusivement, non inclus ; ~ **of VAT** TVA non comprise ; ~**ly** *ad* exclusivement ; ~ **rights** *npl* (*COMM*) exclusivité *f*.

excommunicate [ɛkskə'mjuːnɪkeɪt] *vt* excommunier.

excrement ['ɛkskrəmənt] *n* excrément *m*.

excruciating [ɪk'skruːʃɪeɪtɪŋ] *a* atroce, déchirant(e).

excursion [ɪk'skəːʃən] *n* excursion *f*.

excusable [ɪk'skjuːzəbl] *a* excusable.

excuse *n* [ɪk'skjuːs] excuse *f* // *vt* [ɪk'skjuːz] excuser ; **to** ~ **sb from** (*activity*) dispenser qn de ; ~ **me!** excusez-moi!, pardon!

execute ['ɛksɪkjuːt] *vt* exécuter.

execution [ɛksɪ'kjuːʃən] *n* exécution *f* ; ~**er** *n* bourreau *m*.

executive [ɪg'zɛkjutɪv] *n* (*COMM*) cadre *m* ; (*POL*) exécutif *m* // *a* exécutif(ive).

executor [ɪg'zɛkjutə*] *n* exécuteur/trice testamentaire.

exemplary [ɪg'zɛmplərɪ] *a* exemplaire.

exemplify [ɪg'zɛmplɪfaɪ] *vt* illustrer.

exempt [ɪg'zɛmpt] *a*: ~ **from** exempté(e) *or* dispensé(e) de // *vt*: **to** ~ **sb from** exempter *or* dispenser qn de ; ~**ion** [ɪg'zɛmpʃən] *n* exemption *f*, dispense *f*.

exercise ['ɛksəsaɪz] *n* exercice *m* // *vt* exercer ; (*patience, clemency*) faire preuve de ; (*dog*) promener ; **to take** ~ prendre de l'exercice ; ~ **book** *n* cahier *m*.

exert [ɪg'zəːt] *vt* exercer, employer ; **to** ~ **o.s.** se dépenser.

exhaust [ɪg'zɔ:st] n (also: ~ **fumes**) gaz mpl d'échappement ; (also: ~ **pipe**) tuyau m d'échappement // vt épuiser ; ~**ed** a épuisé(e) ; ~**ion** [ɪg'zɔ:stʃən] n épuisement m ; ~**ive** a très complet(ète).

exhibit [ɪg'zɪbɪt] n (ART) pièce f or objet m exposé(e) ; (LAW) pièce à conviction // vt exposer ; (courage, skill) faire preuve de ; ~**ion** [ɛksɪ'bɪʃən] n exposition f ; ~**ion of temper** n manifestation f de colère ; ~**ionist** [ɛksɪ'bɪʃənɪst] n exhibitionniste m/f ; ~**or** n exposant/e.

exhilarating [ɪg'zɪləreɪtɪŋ] a grisant(e) ; stimulant(e).

exhort [ɪg'zɔ:t] vt exhorter.

exile ['ɛksaɪl] n exil m ; exilé/e // vt exiler ; **in** ~ en exil.

exist [ɪg'zɪst] vi exister ; ~**ence** n existence f ; **to be in** ~**ence** exister.

exit ['ɛksɪt] n sortie f.

exonerate [ɪg'zɔnəreɪt] vt: **to** ~ **from** disculper de ; (free) exempter de.

exorcize ['ɛksɔ:saɪz] vt exorciser.

exotic [ɪg'zɔtɪk] a exotique.

expand [ɪk'spænd] vt agrandir ; accroître, étendre // vi (trade etc) se développer, s'accroître ; s'étendre ; (gas, metal) se dilater.

expanse [ɪk'spæns] n étendue f.

expansion [ɪk'spænʃən] n développement m, accroissement m ; dilatation f.

expatriate n [ɛks'pætrɪət] expatrié/e // vt [ɛks'pætrɪeɪt] expatrier, exiler.

expect [ɪk'spɛkt] vt (anticipate) s'attendre à, s'attendre à ce que + sub ; (count on) compter sur, escompter ; (hope for) espérer ; (require) demander, exiger ; (suppose) supposer ; (await, also baby) attendre // vi: **to be** ~**ing** être enceinte ; **to** ~ **sb to do** s'attendre à ce que qn fasse ; attendre de qn qu'il fasse ; ~**ant** a qui attend (quelque chose) ; ~**ant mother** n future maman ; ~**ation** [ɛkspɛk'teɪʃən] n attente f, prévisions fpl ; espérance(s) f(pl).

expedience, expediency [ɛk'spi:dɪəns, ɛk'spi:dɪənsɪ] n: **for the sake of** ~ parce que c'est plus convenable.

expedient [ɪk'spi:dɪənt] a indiqué(e), opportun(e) ; commode // n expédient m.

expedite ['ɛkspədaɪt] vt hâter ; expédier.

expedition [ɛkspə'dɪʃən] n expédition f.

expeditious [ɛkspə'dɪʃəs] a expéditif(ive), prompt(e).

expel [ɪk'spɛl] vt chasser, expulser ; (SCOL) renvoyer, exclure.

expend [ɪk'spɛnd] vt consacrer ; (use up) dépenser ; ~**able** a remplaçable ; ~**iture** [ɪk'spɛndɪtʃə*] n dépense f ; dépenses fpl.

expense [ɪk'spɛns] n dépense f ; frais mpl ; (high cost) coût m ; ~**s** npl (COMM) frais mpl ; **at great/little** ~ à grands/peu de frais ; **at the** ~ **of** aux dépens de ; ~ **account** n (note f de) frais mpl.

expensive [ɪk'spɛnsɪv] a cher(chère), coûteux(euse) ; **to be** ~ coûter cher ; ~ **tastes** npl goûts mpl de luxe.

experience [ɪk'spɪərɪəns] n expérience f // vt connaître ; éprouver ; ~**d** a expérimenté(e).

experiment [ɪk'spɛrɪmənt] n expérience f // vi faire une expérience ; **to** ~ **with** expérimenter ; ~**al** [-'mɛntl] a expérimental(e).

expert ['ɛkspə:t] a expert(e) // n expert m ; ~**ise** [-'ti:z] n (grande) compétence.

expire [ɪk'spaɪə*] vi expirer ; **expiry** n expiration f.

explain [ɪk'spleɪn] vt expliquer ; **explanation** [ɛksplə'neɪʃən] n explication f ; **explanatory** [ɪk'splænətrɪ] a explicatif(ive).

explicit [ɪk'splɪsɪt] a explicite ; (definite) formel(le).

explode [ɪk'spləud] vi exploser // vt faire exploser.

exploit n ['ɛksplɔɪt] exploit m // vt [ɪk'splɔɪt] exploiter ; ~**ation** [-'teɪʃən] n exploitation f.

exploration [ɛksplɔ'reɪʃən] n exploration f.

exploratory [ɪk'splɔrətrɪ] a (fig: talks) préliminaire.

explore [ɪk'splɔ:*] vt explorer ; (possibilities) étudier, examiner ; ~**r** n explorateur/trice.

explosion [ɪk'spləuʒən] n explosion f.

explosive [ɪk'spləusɪv] a explosif(ive) // n explosif m.

exponent [ɪk'spəunənt] n (of school of thought etc) interprète m, représentant m ; (MATH) exposant m.

export vt [ɛk'spɔ:t] exporter // n ['ɛkspɔ:t] exportation f // cpd d'exportation ; ~**ation** [-'teɪʃən] n exportation f ; ~**er** n exportateur m.

expose [ɪk'spəuz] vt exposer ; (unmask) démasquer, dévoiler ; **to** ~ **o.s.** (LAW) commettre un outrage à la pudeur.

exposure [ɪk'spəuʒə*] n exposition f ; (PHOT) (temps m de) pose f ; (: shot) pose f ; **suffering from** ~ (MED) souffrant des effets du froid et de l'épuisement ; ~**meter** n posemètre m.

expound [ɪk'spaund] vt exposer, expliquer.

express [ɪk'sprɛs] a (definite) formel(le), exprès(esse) ; (letter etc) exprès inv // n (train) rapide m // ad (send) exprès // vt exprimer ; ~**ion** [ɪk'sprɛʃən] n expression f ; ~**ive** a expressif(ive) ; ~**ly** ad expressément, formellement.

expropriate [ɛks'prəuprɪeɪt] vt exproprier.

expulsion [ɪk'spʌlʃən] n expulsion f ; renvoi m.

exquisite [ɛk'skwɪzɪt] a exquis(e).

extend [ɪk'stɛnd] vt (visit, street) prolonger ; (building) agrandir ; (offer) présenter, offrir // vi (land) s'étendre.

extension [ɪk'stɛnʃən] n prolongation f ; agrandissement m ; (building) annexe f ; (to wire, table) rallonge f ; (telephone: in offices) poste m ; (: in private house) téléphone m supplémentaire.

extensive [ɪk'stɛnsɪv] a étendu(e), vaste ; (damage, alterations) considérable ; (inquiries) approfondi(e) ; (use) largement répandu(e) ; **he's travelled** ~**ly** il a beaucoup voyagé ; ~ **travelling** déplacements fréquents et prolongés.

extent [ɪk'stɛnt] *n* étendue *f*; **to some ~** dans une certaine mesure; **to what ~?** dans quelle mesure?, jusqu'à quel point?

exterior [ɛk'stɪərɪə*] *a* extérieur(e), du dehors // *n* extérieur *m*; dehors *m*.

exterminate [ɪk'stə:mɪneɪt] *vt* exterminer; **extermination** [-'neɪʃən] *n* extermination *f*.

external [ɛk'stə:nl] *a* externe; **~ly** *ad* extérieurement.

extinct [ɪk'stɪŋkt] *a* éteint(e); **~ion** [ɪk'stɪŋkʃən] *n* extinction *f*.

extinguish [ɪk'stɪŋgwɪʃ] *vt* éteindre; **~er** *n* extincteur *m*.

extol [ɪk'stəul] *vt* porter aux nues, chanter les louanges de.

extort [ɪk'stɔ:t] *vt*: **to ~ sth (from)** extorquer qch (à); **~ion** [ɪk'stɔ:ʃən] *n* extorsion *f*; **~ionate** [ɪk'stɔ:ʃnət] *a* exorbitant(e).

extra ['ɛkstrə] *a* supplémentaire, de plus // *ad* (*in addition*) en plus // *n* supplément *m*; (*THEATRE*) figurant/e.

extra... ['ɛkstrə] *prefix* extra... .

extract *vt* [ɪk'strækt] extraire, (*tooth*) arracher; (*money, promise*) soutirer // *n* ['ɛkstrækt] extrait *m*; **~ion** [ɪk'strækʃən] *n* (*also descent*) extraction *f*.

extradite ['ɛkstrədaɪt] *vt* extrader; **extradition** [-'dɪʃən] *n* extradition *f*.

extramarital [ɛkstrə'mærɪtl] *a* extra-conjugal(e).

extramural [ɛkstrə'mjuərl] *a* hors-faculté *inv*.

extraneous [ɛk'streɪnɪəs] *a*: **~ to** étranger(ère) à.

extraordinary [ɪk'strɔ:dnrɪ] *a* extraordinaire.

extra time [ɛkstrə'taɪm] *n* (*FOOTBALL*) prolongations *fpl*.

extravagant [ɪk'strævəgənt] *a* extravagant(e); (*in spending*) prodigue, dépensier(ère); dispendieux(euse).

extreme [ɪk'stri:m] *a,n* extrême (*m*); **~ly** *ad* extrêmement; **extremist** *a,n* extrémiste (*m/f*).

extremity [ɪk'strɛmətɪ] *n* extrémité *f*.

extricate ['ɛkstrɪkeɪt] *vt*: **to ~ sth (from)** dégager qch (de).

extrovert ['ɛkstrəvə:t] *n* extraverti/e.

exuberant [ɪg'zju:bərnt] *a* exubérant(e).

exude [ɪg'zju:d] *vt* exsuder; (*fig*) respirer; **the charm *etc* he ~s** le charme *etc* qui émane de lui.

exult [ɪg'zʌlt] *vi* exulter, jubiler.

eye [aɪ] *n* œil *m* (*pl* yeux); (*of needle*) trou *m*, chas *m* // *vt* examiner; **to keep an ~ on** surveiller; **in the public ~** en vue; **~ball** *n* globe *m* oculaire; **~bath** *n* œillère *f* (*pour bains d'œil*); **~brow** *n* sourcil *m*; **~-catching** *a* voyant(e), accrocheur(euse); **~drops** *npl* gouttes *fpl* pour les yeux; **~glass** *n* monocle *m*; **~lash** *n* cil *m*; **~let** ['aɪlɪt] *n* œillet *m*; **~lid** *n* paupière *f*; **~-opener** *n* révélation *f*; **~shadow** *n* ombre *f* à paupières; **~sight** *n* vue *f*; **~sore** *n* horreur *f*, chose *f* qui dépare or enlaidit; **~wash** *n* bain *m* d'œil; (*fig*) frime *f*; **~ witness** *n* témoin *m* oculaire.

eyrie ['ɪərɪ] *n* aire *f*.

F

F [ɛf] *n* (*MUS*) fa *m*.

F. *abbr of* Fahrenheit.

fable ['feɪbl] *n* fable *f*.

fabric ['fæbrɪk] *n* tissu *m*.

fabrication [fæbrɪ'keɪʃən] *n* invention(s) *f(pl)*, fabulation *f*; fait *m* (*or* preuve *f*) forgé(e) de toutes pièces.

fabulous ['fæbjuləs] *a* fabuleux(euse); (*col: super*) formidable, sensationnel(le).

façade [fə'sɑ:d] *n* façade *f*.

face [feɪs] *n* visage *m*, figure *f*; expression *f*; grimace *f*; (*of clock*) cadran *m*; (*of building*) façade *f*; (*side, surface*) face *f* // *vt* faire face à; **to lose ~** perdre la face; **to pull a ~** faire une grimace; **in the ~ of** (*difficulties etc*) face à, devant; **on the ~ of it** à première vue; **to ~ up to** *vt fus* faire face à, affronter; **~ cloth** *n* gant *m* de toilette; **~ cream** *n* crème *f* pour le visage; **~ lift** *n* lifting *m*; (*of façade etc*) ravalement *m*, retapage *m*; **~ powder** *n* poudre *f* (*pour le visage*).

facet ['fæsɪt] *n* facette *f*.

facetious [fə'si:ʃəs] *a* facétieux(euse).

face-to-face ['feɪstə'feɪs] *ad* face à face.

face value ['feɪs'vælju:] *n* (*of coin*) valeur nominale; **to take sth at ~** (*fig*) prendre qch pour argent comptant.

facia ['feɪʃə] *n* = **fascia**.

facial ['feɪʃəl] *a* facial(e).

facile ['fæsaɪl] *a* facile.

facilitate [fə'sɪlɪteɪt] *vt* faciliter.

facility [fə'sɪlɪtɪ] *n* facilité *f*; **facilities** *npl* installations *fpl*, équipement *m*.

facing ['feɪsɪŋ] *n* (*of wall etc*) revêtement *m*; (*SEWING*) revers *m*.

facsimile [fæk'sɪmɪlɪ] *n* fac-similé *m*.

fact [fækt] *n* fait *m*; **in ~** en fait.

faction ['fækʃən] *n* faction *f*.

factor ['fæktə*] *n* facteur *m*.

factory ['fæktərɪ] *n* usine *f*, fabrique *f*.

factual ['fæktjuəl] *a* basé(e) sur les faits.

faculty ['fækəltɪ] *n* faculté *f*; (*US: teaching staff*) corps enseignant.

fad [fæd] *n* manie *f*; engouement *m*.

fade [feɪd] *vi* se décolorer, passer; (*light, sound, hope*) s'affaiblir, disparaître; (*flower*) se faner.

fag [fæg] *n* (*col: cigarette*) sèche *f*; (: *chore*): **what a ~!** quelle corvée!; **~ end** *n* mégot *m*; **~ged out** *a* (*col*) crevé(e).

fail [feɪl] *vt* (*exam*) échouer à; (*candidate*) recaler; (*subj: courage, memory*) faire défaut à // *vi* échouer; (*supplies*) manquer; (*eyesight, health, light*) baisser, s'affaiblir; **to ~ to do sth** (*neglect*) négliger de faire qch; (*be unable*) ne pas arriver *or* parvenir à faire qch; **without ~** à coup sûr; sans faute; **~ing** *n* défaut *m* // *prep* faute de; **~ure** ['feɪljə*] *n* échec *m*; (*person*) raté/e; (*mechanical etc*) défaillance *f*.

faint [feɪnt] *a* faible; (*recollection*) vague; (*mark*) à peine visible // *n* évanouissement *m* // *vi* s'évanouir; **to feel ~** défaillir; **~-hearted** *a* pusillanime; **~ly** *ad* faiblement; vaguement; ~**ness** n faiblesse f.

fair [fɛə*] a blond(e); équitable, juste, impartial(e); (skin, complexion) pâle, blanc(blanche); (weather) beau(belle); (good enough) assez bon(ne); (sizeable) considérable // ad (play) franc-jeu // à foire f; ~ **copy** n copie f au propre; corrigé m; ~**ly** ad équitablement; (quite) assez; ~**ness** n justice f, équité f, impartialité f.

fairy ['fɛərɪ] n fée f; ~ **tale** n conte m de fées.

faith [feɪθ] n foi f; (trust) confiance f; (sect) culte m, religion f; ~**ful** a fidèle; ~**fully** ad fidèlement.

fake [feɪk] n (painting etc) faux m; (photo) trucage m; (person) imposteur m // a faux(fausse); simulé(e) // vt simuler; (photo) truquer; (story) fabriquer; **his illness is a** ~ sa maladie est une comédie or de la simulation.

falcon ['fɔːlkən] n faucon m.

fall [fɔːl] n chute f; (US: autumn) automne m // vi (pt **fell**, pp **fallen** [fɛl, 'fɔːlən]) tomber; ~**s** npl (waterfall) chute f d'eau, cascade f; **to** ~ **flat** vi (on one's face) tomber de tout son long, s'étaler; (joke) tomber à plat; (plan) échouer; **to** ~ **back on** vt fus se rabattre sur; **to** ~ **behind** vi prendre du retard; **to** ~ **down** vi (person) tomber; (building, hopes) s'effondrer, s'écrouler; **to** ~ **for** vt fus (trick) se laisser prendre à; (person) tomber amoureux . de; **to** ~ **in** vi s'effondrer; (MIL) se mettre en rangs; **to** ~ **off** vi tomber; (diminish) baisser, diminuer; **to** ~ **out** vi (friends etc) se brouiller; **to** ~ **through** vi (plan, project) tomber à l'eau.

fallacy ['fæləsɪ] n erreur f, illusion f.

fallen ['fɔːlən] pp of **fall**.

fallible ['fæləbl] a faillible.

fallout ['fɔːlaut] n retombées f (radioactives).

fallow ['fæləu] a en jachère; en friche.

false [fɔːls] a faux(fausse); **under** ~ **pretences** sous un faux prétexte; ~ **alarm** n fausse alerte; ~**hood** n mensonge m; ~**ly** ad (accuse) à tort; ~ **teeth** npl fausses dents.

falter ['fɔːltə*] vi chanceler, vaciller.

fame [feɪm] n renommée f, renom m.

familiar [fə'mɪlɪə*] a familier(ère); **to be** ~ **with** (subject) connaître; ~**ity** [fəmɪlɪ'ærɪtɪ] n familiarité f; ~**ize** [fə'mɪlɪəraɪz] vt familiariser.

family ['fæmɪlɪ] n famille f; ~ **allowance** n allocations familiales; ~ **business** n entreprise familiale; ~ **doctor** n médecin m de famille; ~ **life** n vie f de famille.

famine ['fæmɪn] n famine f.

famished ['fæmɪʃt] a affamé(e).

famous ['feɪməs] a célèbre; ~**ly** ad (get on) fameusement, à merveille.

fan [fæn] n (folding) éventail m; (ELEC) ventilateur m; (person) fan m, admirateur/trice; supporter m/f // vt éventer; (fire, quarrel) attiser; **to** ~ **out** vi se déployer (en éventail).

fanatic [fə'nætɪk] n fanatique m/f; ~**al** a fanatique.

fan belt ['fænbɛlt] n courroie f de ventilateur.

fancied ['fænsɪd] a imaginaire.

fanciful ['fænsɪful] a fantaisiste.

fancy ['fænsɪ] n fantaisie f, envie f; imagination f // cpd (de) fantaisie inv // vt (feel like, want) avoir envie de; **to take a** ~ **to** se prendre d'affection pour; s'enticher de; **it took** or **caught my** ~ ça m'a plu; **to** ~ **that ...** se figurer or s'imaginer que ...; **he fancies her** elle lui plaît; ~ **dress** n déguisement m, travesti m; ~-**dress ball** n bal masqué or costumé.

fang [fæŋ] n croc m; (of snake) crochet m.

fanlight ['fænlaɪt] n imposte f.

fantastic [fæn'tæstɪk] a fantastique.

fantasy ['fæntəzɪ] n imagination f, fantaisie f; fantasme m; chimère f.

far [fɑː*] a: **the** ~ **side/end** l'autre côté/bout // ad loin; ~ **away**, ~ **off** au loin, dans le lointain; ~ **better** beaucoup mieux; ~ **from** loin de; **by** ~ de loin, de beaucoup; **go as** ~ **as the farm** allez jusqu'à la ferme; **as** ~ **as I know** pour autant que je sache; **as** ~ **as possible** dans la mesure du possible; ~**away** a lointain(e).

farce [fɑːs] n farce f.

farcical ['fɑːsɪkəl] a grotesque.

fare [fɛə*] n (on trains, buses) prix m du billet; (in taxi) prix de la course; (passenger in taxi) client m; (food) table f, chère f // vi se débrouiller.

Far East [fɑːr'iːst] n: **the** ~ l'Extrême-Orient m.

farewell [fɛə'wɛl] excl, n adieu m; ~ **party** n soirée f d'adieux.

far-fetched ['fɑː'fɛtʃt] a exagéré(e), poussé(e).

farm [fɑːm] n ferme f // vt cultiver; ~**er** n fermier/ère; cultivateur/trice; ~**hand** n ouvrier/ère agricole; ~**house** n (maison f de) ferme f; ~**ing** n agriculture f; **intensive** ~**ing** culture intensive; ~**land** n terres cultivées or arables; ~ **worker** n = ~**hand**; ~**yard** n cour f de ferme.

far-reaching ['fɑː'riːtʃɪŋ] a d'une grande portée.

far-sighted ['fɑː'saɪtɪd] a presbyte; (fig) prévoyant(e), qui voit loin.

fart [fɑːt] (col!) n pet m // vi péter.

farther ['fɑːðə*] ad plus loin.

farthest ['fɑːðɪst] superlative of **far**.

fascia ['feɪʃə] n (AUT) (garniture f du) tableau m de bord.

fascinate ['fæsɪneɪt] vt fasciner, captiver; **fascination** [-'neɪʃən] n fascination f.

fascism ['fæʃɪzəm] n fascisme m.

fascist ['fæʃɪst] a,n fasciste (m/f).

fashion ['fæʃən] n mode f; (manner) façon f, manière f // vt façonner; **in** ~ à la mode; **out of** ~ démodé(e); ~**able** a à la mode; ~ **show** n défilé m de mannequins or de mode.

fast [fɑːst] a rapide; (clock): **to be** ~ avancer; (dye, colour) grand or bon teint inv // ad vite, rapidement; (stuck, held) solidement // n jeûne m // vi jeûner; ~ **asleep** profondément endormi.

fasten ['fɑːsn] vt attacher, fixer ; (coat) attacher, fermer // vi se fermer, s'attacher ; **~er**, **~ing** n fermeture f, attache f.

fastidious [fæs'tɪdɪəs] a exigeant(e), difficile.

fat [fæt] a gros(se) // n graisse f ; (on meat) gras m.

fatal ['feɪtl] a mortel(le) ; fatal(e) ; désastreux(euse) ; **~ism** n fatalisme m ; **~ity** [fə'tælɪtɪ] n (road death etc) victime f, décès m ; **~ly** ad mortellement.

fate [feɪt] n destin m ; (of person) sort m ; **to meet one's ~** trouver la mort ; **~ful** a fatidique.

father ['fɑːðə*] n père m ; **~-in-law** n beau-père m ; **~ly** a paternel(le).

fathom ['fæðəm] n brasse f (= 1828 mm) // vt (mystery) sonder, pénétrer.

fatigue [fə'tiːg] n fatigue f ; (MIL) corvée f.

fatness ['fætnɪs] n corpulence f, grosseur f.

fatten ['fætn] vt,vi engraisser.

fatty ['fætɪ] a (food) gras(se).

fatuous ['fætjuəs] a stupide.

faucet ['fɔːsɪt] n (US) robinet m.

fault [fɔːlt] n faute f ; (defect) défaut m ; (GEO) faille f // vt trouver des défauts à, prendre en défaut ; **it's my ~** c'est de ma faute ; **to find ~ with** trouver à redire or à critiquer à ; **at ~** fautif(ive), coupable ; **to a ~** à l'excès ; **~less** a sans fautes ; impeccable ; irréprochable ; **~y** a défectueux(euse).

fauna ['fɔːnə] n faune f.

favour, favor (US) ['feɪvə*] n faveur f ; (help) service m // vt (proposition) être en faveur de ; (pupil etc) favoriser ; (team, horse) donner gagnant ; **to do sb a ~** rendre un service à qn ; **in ~ of** en faveur de ; **~able** a favorable ; (price) avantageux(euse) ; **~ably** ad favorablement ; **~ite** [-rɪt] a,n favori(te) ; **~itism** n favoritisme m.

fawn [fɔːn] n faon m // a (also: **~-coloured**) fauve // vi: **to ~ (up)on** flatter servilement.

fear [fɪə*] n crainte f, peur f // vt craindre ; **for ~ of** de peur que + sub or de + infinitive ; **~ful** a craintif(ive) ; (sight, noise) affreux(euse), épouvantable ; **~less** a intrépide, sans peur.

feasibility [fiːzə'bɪlɪtɪ] n (of plan) possibilité f de réalisation.

feasible ['fiːzəbl] a faisable, réalisable.

feast [fiːst] n festin m, banquet m ; (REL: also: **~ day**) fête f // vi festoyer ; **to ~ on** se régaler de.

feat [fiːt] n exploit m, prouesse f.

feather ['feðə*] n plume f ; **~weight** n poids m plume inv.

feature ['fiːtʃə*] n caractéristique f ; (article) chronique f, rubrique f // vt (subj: film) avoir pour vedette(s) // vi figurer (en bonne place) ; **~s** npl (of face) traits mpl ; **~ film** n film principal ; **~less** a anonyme, sans traits distinctifs.

February ['fɛbruərɪ] n février m.

fed [fɛd] pt,pp of **feed** ; **to be ~ up** en avoir marre or plein le dos.

federal ['fɛdərəl] a fédéral(e).

federation [fɛdə'reɪʃən] n fédération f.

fee [fiː] n rémunération f ; (of doctor, lawyer) honoraires mpl ; (of school, college etc) frais mpl de scolarité ; (for examination) droits mpl.

feeble ['fiːbl] a faible ; **~-minded** a faible d'esprit.

feed [fiːd] n (of baby) tétée f // vt (pt, pp **fed** [fɛd]) nourrir ; (horse etc) donner à manger à ; (machine) alimenter ; (data, information): **to ~ into** fournir à ; **to ~ on** vt fus se nourrir de ; **~back** n feedback m ; **~ing bottle** n biberon m.

feel [fiːl] n sensation f // vt (pt, pp **felt** [fɛlt]) toucher ; tâter, palper ; (cold, pain) sentir ; (grief, anger) ressentir, éprouver ; (think, believe): **to ~ (that)** trouver que ; **to ~ hungry/cold** avoir faim/froid ; **to ~ lonely/better** se sentir seul/mieux ; **to ~ sorry for** avoir pitié de ; **it ~s soft** c'est doux au toucher ; **it ~s like velvet** on dirait du velours, ça ressemble au velours ; **to ~ like** (want) avoir envie de ; **to ~ about** or **around** fouiller, tâtonner ; **~er** n (of insect) antenne f ; **to put out a ~er** tâter le terrain ; **~ing** n sensation f ; sentiment m ; **my ~ing is that...** j'estime que... .

feet [fiːt] npl of **foot**.

feign [feɪn] vt feindre, simuler.

felicitous [fɪ'lɪsɪtəs] a heureux(euse).

fell [fɛl] pt of **fall** // vt (tree) abattre ; (person) assommer ; **~-walking** n randonnée f en montagne.

fellow ['fɛləu] n type m ; compagnon m ; (of learned society) membre m ; **their ~ prisoners/students** leurs camarades prisonniers/étudiants ; **~ citizen** n concitoyen/ne ; **~ countryman** n compatriote m ; **~ men** npl semblables mpl ; **~ship** n association f ; amitié f, camaraderie f ; sorte de bourse universitaire.

felony ['fɛlənɪ] n crime m, forfait m.

felt [fɛlt] pt,pp of **feel** // n feutre m ; **~-tip pen** n stylo-feutre m.

female ['fiːmeɪl] n (ZOOL) femelle f ; (pej: woman) bonne femme // a (BIOL, ELEC) femelle ; (sex, character) féminin(e) ; (vote etc) des femmes ; (child etc) du sexe féminin ; **male and ~ students** étudiants et étudiantes ; **~ impersonator** n travesti m.

feminine ['fɛmɪnɪn] a féminin(e) // n féminin m.

feminist ['fɛmɪnɪst] n féministe m/f.

fence [fɛns] n barrière f ; (col: person) receleur/euse // vt (also: **~ in**) clôturer // vi faire de l'escrime ; **fencing** n escrime m.

fend [fɛnd] vi: **to ~ for o.s.** se débrouiller (tout seul).

fender ['fɛndə*] n garde-feu m inv ; (US) garde-boue m inv ; pare-chocs m inv.

ferment vi [fə'mɛnt] fermenter // n ['fɜːmɛnt] agitation f, effervescence f ; **~ation** [-'teɪʃən] n fermentation f.

fern [fɜːn] n fougère f.

ferocious [fə'rəuʃəs] a féroce.

ferocity [fə'rɔsɪtɪ] n férocité f.

ferry ['fɛrɪ] n (small) bac m ; (large: also: **~boat**) ferry(-boat) m // vt transporter.

fertile ['fɜ:taɪl] a fertile ; (*BIOL*) fécond(e) ; **~ period** n période f de fécondité ; **fertility** [fə'tɪlɪtɪ] n fertilité f ; fécondité f ; **fertilize** ['fɜ:tɪlaɪz] vt fertiliser ; féconder ; **fertilizer** n engrais m.

fervent ['fɜ:vənt] a fervent(e), ardent(e).

fester ['fɛstə*] vi suppurer.

festival ['fɛstɪvəl] n (*REL*) fête f ; (*ART, MUS*) festival m.

festive ['fɛstɪv] a de fête ; **the ~ season** (*Christmas*) la période des fêtes.

festivities [fɛs'tɪvɪtɪz] npl réjouissances fpl.

fetch [fɛtʃ] vt aller chercher ; (*sell for*) se vendre.

fetching ['fɛtʃɪŋ] a charmant(e).

fête [feɪt] n fête f, kermesse f.

fetish ['fɛtɪʃ] n fétiche m.

fetters ['fɛtəz] npl chaînes fpl.

fetus ['fi:təs] n (*US*) = **foetus**.

feud [fju:d] n dispute f, dissension f // vi se disputer, se quereller ; **~al** a féodal(e) ; **~alism** n féodalité f.

fever ['fi:və*] n fièvre f ; **~ish** a fiévreux(euse), fébrile.

few [fju:] a peu de ; **they were ~** ils étaient peu (nombreux) ; **a ~** a quelques // pronoun quelques-uns ; **~er** a moins de ; moins (nombreux) ; **~est** a le moins nombreux.

fiancé [fɪ'ɑ̃:ŋseɪ] n fiancé m ; **~e** n fiancée f.

fiasco [fɪ'æskəu] n fiasco m.

fib [fɪb] n bobard m.

fibre, fiber (*US*) ['faɪbə*] n fibre f ; **~glass** n fibre de verre.

fickle ['fɪkl] a inconstant(e), volage, capricieux(euse).

fiction ['fɪkʃən] n romans mpl, littérature f romanesque ; fiction f ; **~al** a fictif(ive).

fictitious [fɪk'tɪʃəs] a fictif(ive), imaginaire.

fiddle ['fɪdl] n (*MUS*) violon m ; (*cheating*) combine f ; escroquerie f // vt (*accounts*) falsifier, maquiller ; **to ~ with** vt fus tripoter ; **~r** n violoniste m/f.

fidelity [fɪ'dɛlɪtɪ] n fidélité f.

fidget ['fɪdʒɪt] vi se trémousser, remuer ; **~y** a agité(e), qui a la bougeotte.

field [fi:ld] n champ m ; (*fig*) domaine m, champ m ; (*SPORT: ground*) terrain m ; **~glasses** npl jumelles fpl ; **~ marshal** n maréchal m ; **~work** n travaux mpl pratiques (sur le terrain).

fiend [fi:nd] n démon m ; **~ish** a diabolique.

fierce [fɪəs] a (*look*) féroce, sauvage ; (*wind, attack*) (très) violent(e) ; (*fighting, enemy*) acharné(e).

fiery ['faɪərɪ] a ardent(e), brûlant(e) ; fougueux(euse).

fifteen [fɪf'ti:n] num quinze.

fifth [fɪfθ] num cinquième.

fiftieth ['fɪftɪɪθ] num cinquantième.

fifty ['fɪftɪ] num cinquante.

fig [fɪg] n figue f.

fight [faɪt] n bagarre f ; (*MIL*) combat m ; (*against cancer etc*) lutte f // vb (pt, pp **fought** [fɔ:t]) vt se battre contre ; (*cancer, alcoholism*) combattre, lutter contre // vi se battre ; **~er** n lutteur m (*fig*) ; (*plane*) chasseur m ; **~ing** n combats mpl.

figment ['fɪgmənt] n: **a ~ of the imagination** une invention.

figurative ['fɪgjurətɪv] a figuré(e).

figure ['fɪgə*] n (*DRAWING, GEOM*) figure f ; (*number, cipher*) chiffre m ; (*body, outline*) silhouette f, ligne f, formes fpl // vt (*US*) supposer // vi (*appear*) figurer ; (*US: make sense*) s'expliquer ; **to ~ out** vt arriver à comprendre ; calculer ; **~head** n (*NAUT*) figure f de proue ; (*pej*) prête-nom m ; **figure skating** n figures imposées (*en patinage*).

filament ['fɪləmənt] n filament m.

file [faɪl] n (*tool*) lime f ; (*dossier*) dossier m ; (*folder*) classeur m ; (*row*) file f // vt (*nails, wood*) limer ; (*papers*) classer ; (*LAW: claim*) faire enregistrer ; déposer ; **to ~ in/out** vi entrer/sortir l'un derrière l'autre ; **to ~ past** vt fus défiler devant.

filing ['faɪlɪŋ] n (*travaux mpl de*) classement m ; **~s** npl limaille f ; **~ cabinet** n classeur m (*meuble*).

fill [fɪl] vt remplir // n: **to eat one's ~** manger à sa faim ; **to ~ in** vt (*hole*) boucher ; (*form*) remplir ; **to ~ up** vt remplir // vi (*AUT*) faire le plein ; **~ it up, please** (*AUT*) le plein, s'il vous plaît.

fillet ['fɪlɪt] n filet m // vt préparer en filets.

filling ['fɪlɪŋ] n (*CULIN*) garniture f, farce f ; (*for tooth*) plombage m ; **~ station** n station f d'essence.

fillip ['fɪlɪp] n coup m de fouet (*fig*).

film [fɪlm] n film m ; (*PHOT*) pellicule f, film m // vt (*scene*) filmer ; **~ star** n vedette f de cinéma ; **~strip** n (*film m pour*) projection f fixe.

filter ['fɪltə*] n filtre m // vt filtrer ; **~ lane** n (*AUT*) voie f de sortie ; **~ tip** n bout m filtre.

filth [fɪlθ] n saleté f ; **~y** a sale, dégoûtant(e) ; (*language*) ordurier (ère), grossier(ère).

fin [fɪn] n (*of fish*) nageoire f.

final ['faɪnl] a final(e), dernier(ère) ; définitif(ive) // n (*SPORT*) finale f ; **~s** npl (*SCOL*) examens mpl de dernière année ; **~e** [fɪ'nɑ:lɪ] n finale m ; **~ist** n (*SPORT*) finaliste m/f ; **~ize** vt mettre au point ; **~ly** ad (*lastly*) en dernier lieu ; (*eventually*) enfin, finalement ; (*irrevocably*) définitivement.

finance [faɪ'næns] n finance f ; **~s** npl finances fpl // vt financer.

financial [faɪ'nænʃəl] a financier (ère) ; **~ly** ad financièrement ; **~ year** n année f budgétaire.

financier [faɪ'nænsɪə*] n financier m.

find [faɪnd] vt (pt, pp **found** [faund]) trouver ; (*lost object*) retrouver // n trouvaille f, découverte f ; **to ~ sb guilty** (*LAW*) déclarer qn coupable ; **to ~ out** vt se renseigner sur ; (*truth, secret*) découvrir ; (*person*) démasquer ; **to ~ out about** se renseigner sur ; (*by chance*) apprendre ; **~ings** npl (*LAW*) conclusions fpl, verdict m ; (*of report*) constatations fpl.

fine [faɪn] n a beau(belle) ; excellent(e) ; fin(e) // ad (*well*) très bien ; (*small*) fin, finement // n (*LAW*) amende f ; contravention f // vt (*LAW*) condamner à

une amende ; donner une contravention à ;
~ **arts** npl beaux-arts mpl.
finery ['faɪnərɪ] n parure f.
finesse [fɪ'nɛs] n finesse f.
finger ['fɪŋgə*] n doigt m // vt palper,
toucher ; ~**nail** n ongle m (de la main) ;
~**print** n empreinte digitale ; ~**stall** n
doigtier m ; ~**tip** n bout m du doigt.
finicky ['fɪnɪkɪ] a tatillon(ne),
méticuleux(euse) ; minutieux(euse).
finish ['fɪnɪʃ] n fin f ; (SPORT) arrivée f ;
(polish etc) finition f // vt finir, terminer
// vi finir, se terminer ; (session)
s'achever ; **to ~ off** vt finir, terminer ;
(kill) achever ; **to ~ up** vi,vt finir ; ~**ing
line** n ligne f d'arrivée ; ~**ing school** n
institution privée (pour jeunes filles).
finite ['faɪnaɪt] a fini(e) ; (verb) conju-
gué(e).
Finland ['fɪnlənd] n Finlande f.
Finn [fɪn] n Finnois/e ; Finlandais/e ;
~**ish** a finnois(e) ; finlandais(e) // n (LING)
finnois m.
fiord [fjɔ:d] n fjord m.
fir [fə:*] n sapin m.
fire ['faɪə*] n feu m ; incendie m // vt
(discharge): **to ~ a gun** tirer un coup de
feu ; (fig) enflammer, animer ; (dismiss)
mettre à la porte, renvoyer // vi tirer, faire
feu ; **on ~** en feu ; ~ **alarm** n avertisseur
m d'incendie ; ~**arm** n arme f à feu ; ~
brigade n (régiment m de
sapeurs-)pompiers mpl ; ~ **engine** n
pompe f à incendie ; ~ **escape** n escalier
m de secours ; ~ **extinguisher** n
extincteur m ; ~**man** n pompier m ; ~
master n capitaine m des pompiers ;
~**place** n cheminée f ; ~**proof** a ignifuge ;
~**side** n foyer m, coin m du feu ; ~ **station**
n caserne f de pompiers ; ~**wood** n bois
m de chauffage ; ~**work** n feu m
d'artifice ; ~**works** npl (display) feu(x)
d'artifice.
firing ['faɪərɪŋ] n (MIL) feu m, tir m ; ~
squad n peloton m d'exécution.
firm [fə:m] a ferme // n compagnie f, firme
f ; ~**ly** ad fermement ; ~**ness** n fermeté
f.
first [fə:st] a premier(ère) // ad (before
others) le premier, la première ; (before
other things) en premier, d'abord ; (when
listing reasons etc) en premier lieu,
premièrement // n (person: in race)
premier/ère ; (SCOL) mention f très bien ;
(AUT) première f ; **at ~** au commencement,
au début ; ~ **of all** tout d'abord, pour
commencer ; ~ **aid** premiers secours or
soins ; ~**-aid kit** n trousse f à pharmacie ;
~**-class** a de première classe ; ~**-hand** a
de première main ; ~ **lady** n (US) femme
f du président ; ~**ly** ad premièrement, en
premier lieu ; ~ **name** n prénom m ; ~
night n (THEATRE) première f ; ~**-rate** a
excellent(e).
fir tree ['fə:tri:] n sapin m.
fiscal ['fɪskəl] a fiscal(e).
fish [fɪʃ] n,pl inv poisson m ; poissons mpl
// vt,vi pêcher ; **to ~ a river** pêcher dans
une rivière ; **to go ~ing** aller à la pêche ;
~**erman** n pêcheur m ; ~**ery** n pêcherie
f ; ~ **fingers** npl bâtonnets de poisson
(congelés) ; ~ **hook** n hameçon m ; ~**ing**

boat n barque f de pêche ; ~**ing line** n
ligne f (de pêche) ; ~**ing rod** n canne f
à pêche ; ~**ing tackle** n attirail m de
pêche ; ~ **market** n marché m au poisson ;
~**monger** n marchand m de poisson ; ~
slice n pelle f à poisson ; ~**y** a (fig)
suspect(e), louche.
fission ['fɪʃən] n fission f.
fissure ['fɪʃə*] n fissure f.
fist [fɪst] n poing m.
fit [fɪt] a (MED, SPORT) en (bonne) forme ;
(proper) convenable ; approprié(e) // vt
(subj: clothes) aller à ; (adjust) ajuster ;
(put in, attach) installer, poser ; adapter ;
(equip) équiper, garnir, munir // vi
(clothes) aller ; (parts) s'adapter ; (in space,
gap) entrer, s'adapter // n (MED) accès m,
crise f ; (of coughing) quinte f ; ~ **to en
état de** ; ~ **for** digne de ; apte à ; **this
dress is a tight/good ~** cette robe est
un peu juste/(me) va très bien ; **by ~s
and starts** par à-coups ; **to ~ in** vi
s'accorder ; s'adapter ; **to ~ out** (also: ~
up) vt équiper ; ~**ful** a intermittent(e) ;
~**ment** n meuble encastré, élément m ;
~**ness** n (MED) forme f physique ; (of
remark) à-propos m, justesse f ; ~**ter** n
monteur m ; (DRESSMAKING) essayeur/euse ;
~**ting** a approprié(e) // n (of dress)
essayage m ; (of piece of equipment) pose
f, installation f ; ~**tings** npl installations
fpl.
five [faɪv] num cinq ; ~**r** n (Brit: col) billet
m de cinq livres.
fix [fɪks] vt fixer ; arranger ; (mend) réparer
// n: **to be in a ~** être dans le pétrin ;
~**ed** [fɪkst] a (prices etc) fixe ; ~**ture**
['fɪkstʃə*] n installation f (fixée) ; (SPORT)
rencontre f (au programme).
fizz [fɪz] vi pétiller.
fizzle ['fɪzl] vi pétiller ; **to ~ out** vi rater.
fizzy ['fɪzɪ] a pétillant(e) ; gazeux(euse).
fjord [fjɔ:d] n = **fiord**.
flabbergasted ['flæbəgɑ:stɪd] a sidéré(e),
ahuri(e).
flabby ['flæbɪ] a mou(molle).
flag [flæg] n drapeau m ; (also: ~**stone**)
dalle f // vi faiblir ; fléchir ; **to ~ down**
vt héler, faire signe (de s'arrêter) à ; ~ **of
convenience** n pavillon m de
complaisance.
flagon ['flægən] n bonbonne f.
flagpole ['flægpəʊl] n mât m.
flagrant ['fleɪgrənt] a flagrant(e).
flair [flɛə*] n flair m.
flake [fleɪk] n (of rust, paint) écaille f ; (of
snow, soap powder) flocon m // vi (also:
~ **off**) s'écailler.
flamboyant [flæm'bɔɪənt] a
flamboyant(e), éclatant(e) ; (person)
haut(e) en couleur.
flame [fleɪm] n flamme f.
flamingo [flə'mɪŋgəʊ] n flamant m (rose).
flammable ['flæməbl] a inflammable.
flan [flæn] n tarte f.
Flanders ['flɑ:ndəz] n Flandre(s) f(pl).
flange [flændʒ] n boudin m ; collerette f.
flank [flæŋk] n flanc m ; vt flanquer.
flannel ['flænl] n (also: **face** ~) gant m
de toilette ; (fabric) flanelle f ; (col) baratin
m ; ~**s** npl pantalon m de flanelle.

flap [flæp] *n* (*of pocket, envelope*) rabat *m*
// *vt* (*wings*) battre (de) // *vi* (*sail, flag*)
claquer ; (*col: also:* **be in a ~**) paniquer.

flare [flɛə*] *n* fusée éclairante ; (*in skirt etc*)
évasement *m* ; **to ~ up** vi s'embraser ; (*fig:
person*) se mettre en colère, s'emporter ;
(: *revolt*) éclater ; **~d** *a* (*trousers*) à jambes
évasées.

flash [flæʃ] *n* éclair *m* ; (*also:* **news ~**)
flash *m* (d'information) ; (PHOT) flash *m* //
vt (*switch on*) allumer (brièvement) ;
(*direct*) braquer ; **to ~ sth at** braquer sur qch ;
(*display*) étaler, exhiber ; (*send: message*)
câbler // *vi* briller ; jeter des éclairs ; (*light
on ambulance etc*) clignoter ; **in a ~** en un
clin d'œil ; **to ~ one's headlights** faire un
appel de phares ; **he ~ed by** *or* **past** il
passa (devant nous) comme un éclair ;
~back *n* flashback *m*, retour *m* en arrière ;
~ bulb *n* ampoule *f* de flash ; **~er** *n* (AUT)
clignotant *m*.

flashy [ˈflæʃɪ] *a* (*pej*) tape-à-l'œil *inv*,
tapageur(euse).

flask [flɑːsk] *n* flacon *m*, bouteille *f* ; (CHEM)
ballon *m* ; (*also:* **vacuum ~**) bouteille *f*
thermos ®.

flat [flæt] *a* plat(e) ; (*tyre*) dégonflé(e), à
plat ; (*denial*) catégorique ; (MUS)
bémolisé(e) // *n* (*rooms*) appartement *m* ;
(MUS) bémol *m* ; (AUT) crevaison *f*, pneu
crevé ; **to be ~-footed** avoir les pieds
plats ; **~ly** *ad* catégoriquement ; **~ness** *n*
(*of land*) absence *f* de relief, aspect plat ;
~ten *vt* (*also:* **~ten out**) aplatir.

flatter [ˈflætə*] *vt* flatter ; **~er** *n* flatteur
m ; **~ing** *a* flatteur(euse) ; **~y** *n* flatterie
f.

flatulence [ˈflætjuləns] *n* flatulence *f*.

flaunt [flɔːnt] *vt* faire étalage de.

flavour, flavor (US) [ˈfleɪvə*] *n* goût *m*,
saveur *f* ; (*of ice cream etc*) parfum *m* //
vt parfumer, aromatiser ; **vanilla~-ed** à
l'arôme de vanille, vanillé(e) ; **to give** *or*
add ~ to donner du goût à, relever ; **~ing**
n arôme *m* (synthétique).

flaw [flɔː] *n* défaut *m* ; **~less** *a* sans défaut.

flax [flæks] *n* lin *m* ; **~en** *a* blond(e).

flea [fliː] *n* puce *f*.

fledg(e)ling [ˈfledʒlɪŋ] *n* oisillon *m*.

flee, *pt*, *pp* **fled** [fliː, fled] *vt* fuir, s'enfuir
de // *vi* fuir, s'enfuir.

fleece [fliːs] *n* toison *f* // *vt* (*col*) voler,
filouter.

fleet [fliːt] *n* flotte *f* ; (*of lorries etc*) parc
m ; convoi *m*.

fleeting [ˈfliːtɪŋ] *a* fugace, fugitif(ive) ;
(*visit*) très bref(brève).

Flemish [ˈflemɪʃ] *a* flamand(e) // *n* (LING)
flamand *m* ; **the ~** les Flamands.

flesh [fleʃ] *n* chair *f* ; **~ wound** *n* blessure
superficielle.

flew [fluː] *pt of* **fly**.

flex [fleks] *n* fil *m* *or* câble *m* électrique
(souple) // *vt* fléchir ; (*muscles*) tendre ;
~ibility [-ˈbɪlɪtɪ] *n* flexibilité *f* ; **~ible** *a*
flexible.

flick [flɪk] *n* petite tape ; chiquenaude *f* ;
sursaut *m* ; **~ knife** *n* couteau *m* à cran
d'arrêt ; **to ~ through** *vt fus* feuilleter.

flicker [ˈflɪkə*] *vi* vaciller // *n* vacillement
m ; **a ~ of light** une brève lueur.

flier [ˈflaɪə*] *n* aviateur *m*.

flight [flaɪt] *n* vol *m* ; (*escape*) fuite *f* ; (*also:
~ of steps*) escalier *m* ; **to take ~**
prendre la fuite ; **to put to ~** mettre en
fuite ; **~ deck** *n* (AVIAT) poste *m* de
pilotage ; (NAUT) pont *m* d'envol.

flimsy [ˈflɪmzɪ] *a* (*partition, fabric*) peu
solide, mince ; (*excuse*) pauvre, mince.

flinch [flɪntʃ] *vi* tressaillir ; **to ~ from** se
dérober à, reculer devant.

fling, *pt*, *pp* **flung** [flɪŋ, flʌŋ] *vt* jeter,
lancer.

flint [flɪnt] *n* silex *m* ; (*in lighter*) pierre *f*
(à briquet).

flip [flɪp] *n* chiquenaude *f*.

flippant [ˈflɪpənt] *a* désinvolte,
irrévérencieux(euse).

flirt [flɜːt] *vi* flirter // *n* flirteuse *f* ; **~ation**
[-ˈteɪʃən] *n* flirt *m*.

flit [flɪt] *vi* voleter.

float [fləut] *n* flotteur *m* ; (*in procession*)
char *m* // *vi* flotter // *vt* faire flotter ; (*loan,
business*) lancer ; **~ing** *a* flottant(e).

flock [flɒk] *n* troupeau *m* ; (*of people*) foule
f.

flog [flɒg] *vt* fouetter.

flood [flʌd] *n* inondation *f* ; (*of words, tears
etc*) flot *m*, torrent *m* // *vt* inonder ; **in ~**
en crue ; **~ing** *n* inondation *f* ; **~light** *n*
projecteur *m* // *vt* éclairer aux
projecteurs, illuminer.

floor [flɔː*] *n* sol *m* ; (*storey*) étage *m* ; (*fig:
at meeting*): **the ~** l'assemblée *f*, les
membres *mpl* de l'assemblée // *vt*
terrasser ; **on the ~** par terre ; **ground ~**
(*Brit*), **first ~** (*US*) rez-de-chaussée *m* ;
first ~ (*Brit*), **second ~** (*US*) premier
étage ; **~board** *n* planche *f* (de plancher) ;
~ show *n* spectacle *m* de variétés.

flop [flɒp] *n* fiasco *m* // *vi* (*fail*) faire fiasco.

floppy [ˈflɒpɪ] *a* lâche, flottant(e) ; **~ hat**
n chapeau *m* à bords flottants.

flora [ˈflɔːrə] *n* flore *f*.

floral [ˈflɔːrl] *a* floral(e).

florid [ˈflɒrɪd] *a* (*complexion*) fleuri(e) ;
(*style*) plein(e) de fioritures.

florist [ˈflɒrɪst] *n* fleuriste *m/f*.

flounce [flauns] *n* volant *m* ; **to ~ out** vi
sortir dans un mouvement d'humeur.

flounder [ˈflaundə*] *vi* patauger.

flour [ˈflauə*] *n* farine *f*.

flourish [ˈflʌrɪʃ] *vi* prospérer // *vt* brandir
// *n* fioriture *f* ; (*of trumpets*) fanfare *f* ;
~ing *a* prospère, florissant(e).

flout [flaut] *vt* se moquer de, faire fi de.

flow [fləu] *n* flot *m* ; courant *m* ; circulation
f ; (*tide*) flux *m* // *vi* couler ; (*traffic*)
s'écouler ; (*robes, hair*) flotter ; **~ chart** *n*
organigramme *m*.

flower [ˈflauə*] *n* fleur *f* // *vi* fleurir ; **~
bed** *n* plate-bande *f* ; **~pot** *n* pot *m* (à
fleurs) ; **~y** *a* fleuri(e).

flown [fləun] *pp of* **fly**.

flu [fluː] *n* grippe *f*.

fluctuate [ˈflʌktjueɪt] *vi* varier, fluctuer ;
fluctuation [-ˈeɪʃən] *n* fluctuation *f*,
variation *f*.

fluency [ˈfluːənsɪ] *n* facilité *f*, aisance *f*.

fluent [ˈfluːənt] *a* (*speech*) coulant(e),
aisé(e) ; **he speaks ~ French, he's ~ in
French** il parle le français couramment ;

~ly ad couramment; avec aisance or facilité.

fluff [flʌf] n duvet m; peluche f; ~y a duveteux(euse); pelucheux (euse); ~y toy n jouet m en peluche.

fluid ['flu:ɪd] a,n fluide (m); ~ **ounce** n = 0.028 l; 0.05 pints.

fluke [flu:k] n (col) coup m de veine or de chance.

flung [flʌŋ] pt,pp of **fling**.

fluorescent [fluə'rɛsnt] a fluorescent(e).

fluoride ['fluəraɪd] n fluor m.

fluorine ['fluəri:n] n fluor m.

flurry ['flʌrɪ] n (of snow) rafale f, bourrasque f; ~ **of activity/excitement** affairement m/excitation f soudain(e).

flush [flʌʃ] n rougeur f; excitation f // vt nettoyer à grande eau // vi rougir // a: ~ **with** au ras de, de niveau avec; ~ **against** tout contre; to ~ **the toilet** tirer la chasse (d'eau); ~ed a (tout(e)) rouge.

fluster ['flʌstə*] n agitation f, trouble m; ~ed a énervé(e).

flute [flu:t] n flûte f.

fluted ['flu:tɪd] a cannelé(e).

flutter ['flʌtə*] n agitation f; (of wings) battement m // vi battre des ailes, voleter; (person) aller et venir dans une grande agitation.

flux [flʌks] n: **in a state of** ~ fluctuant sans cesse.

fly [flaɪ] n (insect) mouche f; (on trousers: also: **flies**) braguette f // vb (pt **flew**, pp **flown** [flu:, fləun]) vt piloter; (passengers, cargo) transporter (par avion); (distances) parcourir // vi voler; (passengers) aller en avion; (escape) s'enfuir, fuir; (flag) se déployer; to ~ **open** vi s'ouvrir brusquement; ~**ing** n (activity) aviation f // a: ~**ing visit** visite f éclair inv; with ~**ing colours** haut la main; ~**ing buttress** n arc-boutant m; ~**ing saucer** n soucoupe volante; ~**ing start** n: to get off to a ~**ing start** faire un excellent départ; ~**over** n (Brit: bridge) saut-de-mouton m; ~**past** n défilé aérien; ~**sheet** n (for tent) double toit m; ~**wheel** n volant m (de commande).

F.M. (abbr of frequency modulation) F.M., M.F. (modulation f de fréquence).

foal [fəul] n poulain m.

foam [fəum] n écume f; (on beer) mousse f; (also: **plastic** ~) mousse cellulaire or de plastique // vi écumer; (soapy water) mousser; ~ **rubber** n caoutchouc m mousse.

fob [fɔb] vt: to ~ **sb off with** refiler à qn; se débarrasser de qn avec.

focal ['fəukəl] a focal(e).

focus ['fəukəs] n (pl: ~es) foyer m; (of interest) centre m // vt (field glasses etc) mettre au point; (light rays) faire converger; **in** ~ au point; **out of** ~ pas au point.

fodder ['fɔdə*] n fourrage m.

foe [fəu] n ennemi m.

foetus ['fi:təs] n fœtus m.

fog [fɔg] n brouillard m; ~**gy** a: **it's** ~**gy** il y a du brouillard.

foible ['fɔɪbl] n faiblesse f.

foil [fɔɪl] vt déjouer, contrecarrer // n feuille f de métal; (also: **kitchen** ~) papier m d'alu(minium); (FENCING) fleuret m; **to act as a** ~ **to** (fig) servir de repoussoir or de faire-valoir à.

fold [fəuld] n (bend, crease) pli m; (AGR) parc m à moutons; (fig) bercail m // vt plier; **to** ~ **up** vi (map etc) se plier, se replier; (business) fermer boutique // vt (map etc) plier, replier; ~**er** n (for papers) chemise f; classeur m; (brochure) dépliant m; ~**ing** a (chair, bed) pliant(e).

foliage ['fəulɪɪdʒ] n feuillage m.

folk [fəuk] npl gens mpl // a folklorique; ~**s** npl famille f, parents mpl; ~**lore** ['fəuklɔ:*] n folklore m; ~**song** n chanson f folklorique (gén de l'Ouest américain).

follow ['fɔləu] vt suivre // vi suivre; (result) s'ensuivre; **he** ~**ed suit** il fit de même; **to** ~ **up** vt (victory) tirer parti de; (letter, offer) donner suite à; (case) suivre; ~**er** n disciple m/f, partisan/e; ~**ing** a suivant(e) // n partisans mpl, disciples mpl.

folly ['fɔlɪ] n inconscience f; sottise f; (building) folie f.

fond [fɔnd] a (memory, look) tendre, affectueux(euse); **to be** ~ **of** aimer beaucoup.

fondle ['fɔndl] vt caresser.

fondness ['fɔndnɪs] n (for things) attachement m; (for people) sentiments affectueux; a **special** ~ **for** une prédilection pour.

font [fɔnt] n fonts baptismaux.

food [fu:d] n nourriture f; ~ **mixer** n mixeur m; ~ **poisoning** n intoxication f alimentaire; ~**stuffs** npl denrées fpl alimentaires.

fool [fu:l] n idiot/e; (HISTORY: of king) bouffon m, fou m; (CULIN) purée f de fruits à la crème // vt berner, duper // vi (gen: ~ **around**) faire l'idiot or l'imbécile; ~**hardy** a téméraire, imprudent(e); ~**ish** a idiot(e), stupide; imprudent(e); écervelé(e); ~**proof** a (plan etc) infaillible.

foot [fut] n (pl: **feet** [fi:t]) pied m; (measure) pied (= 304 mm; 12 inches); (of animal) patte f // vt (bill) casquer, payer; **on** ~ à pied; ~ **and mouth (disease)** n fièvre aphteuse; ~**ball** n ballon m (de football); (sport) football m; ~**baller** n footballeur m; ~**brake** n frein m à pied; ~**bridge** n passerelle f; ~**hills** npl contreforts mpl; ~**hold** n prise f (de pied); ~**ing** n (fig) position f; to lose one's ~**ing** perdre pied; **on an equal** ~**ing** sur pied d'égalité; ~**lights** npl rampe f; ~**man** n laquais m; ~**note** n note f (en bas de page); ~**path** n sentier m; (in street) trottoir m; ~**rest** n marchepied m; ~**sore** a aux pieds endoloris; ~**step** n pas m; ~**wear** n chaussure(s) f(pl) (terme générique en anglais).

for [fɔ:*] prep pour; (during) pendant; (in spite of) malgré // cj car; **I haven't seen him** ~ **a week** je ne l'ai pas vu depuis une semaine, cela fait une semaine que je ne l'ai pas vu; **he went down** ~ **the paper** il est descendu chercher le journal; ~ **sale** à vendre.

forage ['fɔrɪdʒ] n fourrage m // vi fourrager, fouiller; ~ **cap** n calot m.

foray ['fɔreɪ] *n* incursion *f*.

forbad(e) [fə'bæd] *pt of* **forbid**.

forbearing [fɔ:'bɛərɪŋ] *a* patient(e), tolérant(e).

forbid, *pt* **forbad(e)**, *pp* **forbidden** [fə'bɪd, -'bæd, -'bɪdn] *vt* défendre, interdire ; ~**den** *a* défendu(e) ; ~**ding** *a* d'aspect *or* d'allure sévère *or* sombre.

force [fɔ:s] *n* force *f* // *vt* forcer ; **the F~s** *npl* l'armée *f* ; **in** ~ en force ; **to come into** ~ entrer en vigueur ; ~**d** [fɔ:st] *a* forcé(e) ; ~**ful** *a* énergique, volontaire.

forceps [fɔ:sɛps] *npl* forceps *m*.

forcibly ['fɔ:səblɪ] *ad* par la force, de force ; (*vigorously*) énergiquement.

ford [fɔ:d] *n* gué *m* // *vt* passer à gué.

fore [fɔ:*] *n*: **to the** ~ en évidence.

forearm ['fɔ:rɑ:m] *n* avant-bras *m inv*.

foreboding [fɔ:'bəudɪŋ] *n* pressentiment *m* (néfaste).

forecast ['fɔ:kɑ:st] *n* prévision *f* // *vt* (*irg: like* **cast**) prévoir.

forecourt ['fɔ:kɔ:t] *n* (*of garage*) devant *m*.

forefathers ['fɔ:fɑ:ðəz] *npl* ancêtres *mpl*.

forefinger ['fɔ:fɪŋgə*] *n* index *m*.

forego, *pt* **forewent**, *pp* **foregone** [fɔ:'gəu, -'wɛnt, -'gɔn] *vt* = **forgo**.

foregone [fɔ:'gɔn] *a*: **it's a** ~ **conclusion** c'est à prévoir, c'est couru d'avance.

foreground ['fɔ:graund] *n* premier plan.

forehead ['fɔrɪd] *n* front *m*.

foreign ['fɔrɪn] *a* étranger(ère) ; (*trade*) extérieur(e) ; ~ **body** *n* corps étranger ; ~**er** *n* étranger/ère ; ~ **exchange market** *n* marché *m* des devises ; ~ **exchange rate** *n* cours *m* des devises ; ~ **minister** *n* ministre *m* des Affaires étrangères.

foreleg ['fɔ:lɛg] *n* patte *f* de devant ; jambe antérieure.

foreman ['fɔ:mən] *n* contremaître *m*.

foremost ['fɔ:məust] *a* le(la) plus en vue ; premier(ère).

forensic [fə'rɛnsɪk] *a*: ~ **medicine** médecine légale ; ~ **expert** expert *m* de la police, expert légiste.

forerunner ['fɔ:rʌnə*] *n* précurseur *m*.

foresee, *pt* **foresaw**, *pp* **foreseen** [fɔ:'si:, -'sɔ:, -'si:n] *vt* prévoir ; ~**able** *a* prévisible.

foresight ['fɔ:saɪt] *n* prévoyance *f*.

forest ['fɔrɪst] *n* forêt *f*.

forestall [fɔ:'stɔ:l] *vt* devancer.

forestry ['fɔrɪstrɪ] *n* sylviculture *f*.

foretaste ['fɔ:teɪst] *n* avant-goût *m*.

foretell, *pt,pp* **foretold** [fɔ:'tɛl, -'təuld] *vt* prédire.

forever [fə'rɛvə*] *ad* pour toujours ; (*fig*) continuellement.

forewent [fɔ:'wɛnt] *pt of* **forego**.

foreword ['fɔ:wə:d] *n* avant-propos *m inv*.

forfeit ['fɔ:fɪt] *n* prix *m*, rançon *f* // *vt* perdre ; (*one's life, health*) payer de.

forgave [fə'geɪv] *pt of* **forgive**.

forge [fɔ:dʒ] *n* forge *f* // *vt* (*signature*) contrefaire ; (*wrought iron*) forger ; **to** ~ **documents/a will** fabriquer des faux papiers/un faux testament ; **to** ~ **money** fabriquer de la fausse monnaie ; **to** ~ **ahead** *vi* pousser de l'avant, prendre de l'avance ; ~**r** *n* faussaire *m* ; ~**ry** *n* faux *m*, contrefaçon *f*.

forget, *pt* **forgot**, *pp* **forgotten** [fə'gɛt, -'gɔt, -'gɔtn] *vt,vi* oublier ; ~**ful** *a* distrait(e), étourdi(e) ; ~**ful** *of* oublieux(euse) de ; ~**fulness** *n* tendance *f* aux oublis ; (*oblivion*) oubli *m*.

forgive, *pt* **forgave**, *pp* **forgiven** [fə'gɪv, -'geɪv, -'gɪvn] *vt* pardonner ; ~**ness** *n* pardon *m*.

forgo, *pt* **forwent**, *pp* **forgone** [fɔ:'gəu, -'wɛnt, -'gɔn] *vt* renoncer à.

forgot [fə'gɔt] *pt of* **forget**.

forgotten [fə'gɔtn] *pp of* **forget**.

fork [fɔ:k] *n* (*for eating*) fourchette *f* ; (*for gardening*) fourche *f* ; (*of roads*) bifurcation *f* ; (*of railways*) embranchement *m* // *vi* (*road*) bifurquer ; **to** ~ **out** (*col: pay*) *vt* allonger, se fendre de // *vi* casquer ; ~**ed** [fɔ:kt] *a* (*lightning*) en zigzags, ramifié(e) ; ~**-lift truck** *n* chariot élévateur.

form [fɔ:m] *n* forme *f* ; (*scol*) classe *f* ; (*questionnaire*) formulaire *m* // *vt* former ; **in top** ~ en pleine forme.

formal ['fɔ:məl] *a* (*offer, receipt*) en bonne et due forme ; (*person*) cérémonieux(euse), à cheval sur les convenances ; (*occasion, dinner*) officiel(le) ; (*ART, PHILOSOPHY*) formel(le) ; ~**ly** *ad* officiellement ; formellement ; cérémonieusement.

format ['fɔ:mæt] *n* format *m*.

formation [fɔ:'meɪʃən] *n* formation *f*.

formative ['fɔ:mətɪv] *a*: ~ **years** années *fpl* d'apprentissage (*fig*) or de formation (*d'un enfant, d'un adolescent*).

former ['fɔ:mə*] *a* ancien(ne) (*before n*), précédent(e) ; **the** ~ ... **the latter** le premier ... le second, celui-là ... celui-ci ; ~**ly** *ad* autrefois.

formidable ['fɔ:mɪdəbl] *a* redoutable.

formula ['fɔ:mjulə] *n* formule *f*.

formulate ['fɔ:mjuleɪt] *vt* formuler.

forsake, *pt* **forsook**, *pp* **forsaken** [fə'seɪk, -'suk, -'seɪkən] *vt* abandonner.

fort [fɔ:t] *n* fort *m*.

forte ['fɔ:tɪ] *n* (*point*) fort *m*.

forth [fɔ:θ] *ad* en avant ; **to go back and** ~ aller et venir ; **and so** ~ et ainsi de suite ; ~**coming** *a* qui va paraître *or* avoir lieu prochainement ; (*character*) ouvert(e), communicatif(ive) ; ~**right** *a* franc(franche), direct(e).

fortieth ['fɔ:tɪɪθ] *num* quarantième.

fortification [fɔ:tɪfɪ'keɪʃən] *n* fortification *f*.

fortify ['fɔ:tɪfaɪ] *vt* fortifier ; **fortified wine** *n* vin liquoreux *or* de liqueur.

fortitude ['fɔ:tɪtju:d] *n* courage *m*, force *f* d'âme.

fortnight ['fɔ:tnaɪt] *n* quinzaine *f*, quinze jours *mpl* ; ~**ly** *a* bimensuel(le) // *ad* tous les quinze jours.

fortress ['fɔ:trɪs] *n* forteresse *f*.

fortuitous [fɔ:'tju:ɪtəs] *a* fortuit(e).

fortunate ['fɔ:tʃənɪt] *a*: **to be** ~ avoir de la chance ; **it is** ~ **that** c'est une chance que, il est heureux que ; ~**ly** *ad* heureusement, par bonheur.

fortune ['fɔ:tʃən] *n* chance *f* ; (*wealth*) fortune *f* ; ~**-teller** *n* diseuse *f* de bonne aventure.

forty ['fɔ:tɪ] *num* quarante.

forum ['fɔ:rəm] *n* forum *m*, tribune *f*.

forward ['fɔ:wəd] *a* (*ahead of schedule*) en avance; (*movement, position*) en avant, vers l'avant; (*not shy*) ouvert(e); direct(e); effronté(e) // *ad* en avant // *n* (*SPORT*) avant *m* // *vt* (*letter*) faire suivre; (*parcel, goods*) expédier; (*fig*) promouvoir, contribuer au développement *or* à l'avancement de; **to move ~** avancer; **~s** *ad* en avant.

forwent [fɔ:'went] *pt of* forgo.

fossil ['fɔsl] *a,n* fossile (*m*).

foster ['fɔstə*] *vt* encourager, favoriser; **~ brother** *n* frère adoptif; frère de lait; **~ child** *n* enfant adopté; **~ mother** *n* mère adoptive; mère nourricière.

fought [fɔ:t] *pt, pp of* fight.

foul [faul] *a* (*weather, smell, food*) infect(e); (*language*) ordurier(ère); (*deed*) infâme // *n* (*FOOTBALL*) faute *f* // *vt* salir, encrasser; (*football player*) commettre une faute sur; **~ play** *n* (*SPORT*) jeu déloyal; **~ play is not suspected** la mort (*or* l'incendie *etc*) n'a pas de causes suspectes, on écarte l'hypothèse d'un meurtre (*or* d'un acte criminel).

found [faund] *pt, pp of* find // *vt* (*establish*) fonder; **~ation** [-'deɪʃən] *n* (*act*) fondation *f*; (*base*) fondement *m*; (*also:* **~ation cream**) fond *m* de teint; **~ations** *npl* (*of building*) fondations *fpl*.

founder ['faundə*] *n* fondateur *m* // *vi* couler, sombrer.

foundry ['faundrɪ] *n* fonderie *f*.

fount [faunt] *n* source *f*; **~ain** ['fauntɪn] *n* fontaine *f*; **~ain pen** *n* stylo *m* (à encre).

four [fɔ:*] *num* quatre; **on all ~s** à quatre pattes; **~some** ['fɔ:səm] *n* partie *f* à quatre; sortie *f* à quatre; **~teen** *num* quatorze; **~teenth** *num* quatorzième; **~th** *num* quatrième.

fowl [faul] *n* volaille *f*.

fox [fɔks] *n* renard *m* // *vt* mystifier.

foyer ['fɔɪeɪ] *n* vestibule *m*; (*THEATRE*) foyer *m*.

fraction ['frækʃən] *n* fraction *f*.

fracture ['fræktʃə*] *n* fracture *f* // *vt* fracturer.

fragile ['frædʒaɪl] *a* fragile.

fragment ['frægmənt] *n* fragment *m*; **~ary** *a* fragmentaire.

fragrance ['freɪgrəns] *n* parfum *m*.

fragrant ['freɪgrənt] *a* parfumé(e), odorant(e).

frail [freɪl] *a* fragile, délicat(e).

frame [freɪm] *n* (*of building*) charpente *f*; (*of human, animal*) charpente *f*, ossature *f*; (*of picture*) cadre *m*; (*of door, window*) encadrement *m*, chambranle *m*; (*of spectacles: also:* **~s**) monture *f* // *vt* encadrer; (*theory, plan*) construire, élaborer; **~ of mind** *n* disposition *f* d'esprit; **~work** *n* structure *f*.

France [frɑ:ns] *n* France *f*.

franchise ['fræntʃaɪz] *n* (*POL*) droit *m* de vote.

frank [fræŋk] *a* franc(franche) // *vt* (*letter*) affranchir; **~ly** *ad* franchement; **~ness** *n* franchise *f*.

frantic ['fræntɪk] *a* frénétique; **~ally** *ad* frénétiquement.

fraternal [frə'tə:nl] *a* fraternel(le).

fraternity [frə'tə:nɪtɪ] *n* (*club*) communauté *f*, confrérie *f*; (*spirit*) fraternité *f*.

fraternize ['frætənaɪz] *vi* fraterniser.

fraud [frɔ:d] *n* supercherie *f*, fraude *f*, tromperie *f*; imposteur *m*.

fraudulent ['frɔ:djulənt] *a* frauduleux(euse).

fraught [frɔ:t] *a*: **~ with** chargé(e) de, plein(e) de.

fray [freɪ] *n* bagarre *f* // *vt* effilocher // *vi* s'effilocher; **tempers were ~ed** les gens commençaient à s'énerver *or* perdre patience; **her nerves were ~ed** elle était à bout de nerfs.

freak [fri:k] *n* (*also cpd*) phénomène *m*, créature ou événement exceptionnel par sa rareté, son caractère d'anomalie.

freckle ['frekl] *n* tache *f* de rousseur.

free [fri:] *a* libre; (*gratis*) gratuit(e); (*liberal*) généreux(euse), large // *vt* (*prisoner etc*) libérer; (*jammed object or person*) dégager; **~** (**of charge**) *ad* gratuitement; **~dom** ['fri:dəm] *n* liberté *f*; **~-for-all** *n* mêlée générale; **~ kick** *n* coup franc; **~lance** *a* indépendant(e); **~ly** *ad* librement; (*liberally*) libéralement; **~mason** *n* franc-maçon *m*; **~masonry** *n* franc-maçonnerie *f*; **~ trade** *n* libre-échange *m*; **~way** *n* (*US*) autoroute *f*; **~wheel** *vi* descendre en roue libre; **~will** *n* libre arbitre *m*; **of one's own ~will** de son plein gré.

freeze [fri:z] *vb* (*pt* froze, *pp* frozen [frəuz, 'frəuzn]) *vi* geler // *vt* geler; (*food*) congeler; (*prices, salaries*) bloquer, geler // *n* gel *m*; blocage *m*; **~-dried** *a* lyophilisé(e); **~r** *n* congélateur *m*.

freezing ['fri:zɪŋ] *a*: **~ cold** *a* glacial(e); **~ point** *n* point *m* de congélation; **3 degrees below ~** 3 degrés au-dessous de zéro.

freight [freɪt] *n* (*goods*) fret *m*, cargaison *f*; (*money charged*) fret, prix *m* du transport; **~ car** *n* (*US*) wagon *m* de marchandises; **~er** *n* (*NAUT*) cargo *m*.

French [frentʃ] *a* français(e) // *n* (*LING*) français *m*; **the ~** les Français *mpl*; **~ fried** (**potatoes**) *npl* (pommes de terre *fpl*) frites *fpl*; **~man** *n* Français *m*; **~ window** *n* porte-fenêtre *f*; **~woman** *n* Française *f*.

frenzy ['frenzɪ] *n* frénésie *f*.

frequency ['fri:kwənsɪ] *n* fréquence *f*.

frequent *a* ['fri:kwənt] fréquent(e) // *vt* [frɪ'kwent] fréquenter; **~ly** *ad* fréquemment.

fresco ['freskəu] *n* fresque *f*.

fresh [freʃ] *a* frais(fraîche); (*new*) nouveau(nouvelle); (*cheeky*) familier(ère), culotté(e); **~en** *vi* (*of wind, air*) fraîchir; **to ~en up** *vi* faire un brin de toilette; **~ly** *ad* nouvellement, récemment; **~ness** *n* fraîcheur *f*; **~water** *a* (*fish*) d'eau douce.

fret [fret] *vi* s'agiter, se tracasser.

friar ['fraɪə*] *n* moine *m*, frère *m*.

friction ['frɪkʃən] *n* friction *f*, frottement *m*.

Friday ['fraɪdɪ] *n* vendredi *m*.

fridge [frɪdʒ] n frigo m, frigidaire m ®.

fried [fraɪd] pt, pp of **fry** // a frit(e).

friend [frɛnd] n ami/e; **to make ~s with** se lier (d'amitié) avec; **~liness** n attitude amicale; **~ly** a amical(e); gentil(le); **to be ~ly with** être ami(e) avec; **~ship** n amitié f.

frieze [fri:z] n frise f, bordure f.

frigate ['frɪgɪt] n (NAUT: modern) frégate f.

fright [fraɪt] n peur f, effroi m; **she looks a ~** elle a l'air d'un épouvantail; **~en** vt effrayer, faire peur à; **~ened a: to be ~ened (of)** avoir peur (de); **~ening** a effrayant(e); **~ful** a affreux(euse); **~fully** ad affreusement.

frigid ['frɪdʒɪd] a (woman) frigide; **~ity** [frɪ'dʒɪdɪtɪ] n frigidité f.

frill [frɪl] n (of dress) volant m; (of shirt) jabot m.

fringe [frɪndʒ] n frange f; (edge: of forest etc) bordure f; (fig): **on the ~** en marge; **~ benefits** npl avantages sociaux or en nature.

frisk [frɪsk] vt fouiller.

frisky ['frɪskɪ] a vif(vive), sémillant(e).

fritter ['frɪtə*] n beignet m; **to ~ away** vt gaspiller.

frivolity [frɪ'vɔlɪtɪ] n frivolité f.

frivolous ['frɪvələs] a frivole.

frizzy ['frɪzɪ] a crépu(e).

fro [frəu] see **to**.

frock [frɔk] n robe f.

frog [frɔg] n grenouille f; **~man** n homme-grenouille m.

frolic ['frɔlɪk] n ébats mpl // vi folâtrer, batifoler.

from [frɔm] prep de; **~ a pound/January** à partir d'une livre/de janvier; **~ what he says** d'après ce qu'il dit.

front [frʌnt] n (of house, dress) devant m; (of coach, train) avant m; (of book) couverture f; (promenade: also: **sea ~**) bord m de mer; (MIL, POL, METEOROLOGY) front m; (fig: appearances) contenance f, façade f // a de devant; premier(ère); **in ~ (of)** devant; **~age** ['frʌntɪdʒ] n façade f; **~al** a frontal(e); **~ door** n porte f d'entrée; (of car) portière f avant; **~ier** ['frʌntɪə*] n frontière f; **~ page** n première page; **~ room** n (Brit) pièce f de devant, salon m; **~-wheel drive** n traction f avant.

frost [frɔst] n gel m, gelée f; **~bite** n gelures fpl; **~ed** a (glass) dépoli(e); **~y** a (window) couvert(e) de givre; (welcome) glacial(e).

froth ['frɔθ] n mousse f; écume f.

frown [fraun] n froncement m de sourcils // vi froncer les sourcils.

froze [frəuz] pt of **freeze**; **~n** pp of **freeze** // a (food) congelé(e).

frugal ['fru:gəl] a frugal(e).

fruit [fru:t] n, pl inv fruit m; **~erer** n fruitier m, marchand/e de fruits; **~ful** a fructueux(euse); (plant, soil) fécond(e); **~ion** [fru:'ɪʃən] n: **to come to ~ion** se réaliser; **~ machine** n machine f à sous; **~ salad** n salade f de fruits.

frustrate [frʌs'treɪt] vt frustrer; (plot, plans) faire échouer; **~d** a frustré(e); **frustration** [-'treɪʃən] n frustration f.

fry, pt, pp **fried** [fraɪ, -d] vt (faire) frire; **the small ~** le menu fretin; **~ing pan** n poêle f (à frire).

ft. abbr of **foot, feet**.

fuchsia ['fju:ʃə] n fuchsia m.

fuddy-duddy ['fʌdɪdʌdɪ] n (pej) vieux schnock.

fudge [fʌdʒ] n (CULIN) sorte de confiserie à base de sucre, de beurre et de lait.

fuel [fjuəl] n (for heating) combustible m; (for propelling) carburant m; **~ oil** n mazout m; **~ tank** n cuve f à mazout, citerne f; (on vehicle) réservoir m de or à carburant.

fugitive ['fju:dʒɪtɪv] n fugitif/ive.

fulfil [ful'fɪl] vt (function) remplir; (order) exécuter; (wish, desire) satisfaire, réaliser; **~ment** n (of wishes) réalisation f.

full [ful] a plein(e); (details, information) complet(ète); (skirt) ample, large // ad: **to know ~ well that** savoir fort bien que; **I'm ~** j'ai bien mangé; **~ employment/fare** plein emploi/tarif; **a ~ two hours** deux bonnes heures; **at ~ speed** à toute vitesse; **in ~** (reproduce, quote) intégralement; (write name etc) en toutes lettres; **~back** n (RUGBY, FOOTBALL) arrière m; **~-length** a (portrait) en pied; **~ moon** n pleine lune; **~-sized** a (portrait etc) grandeur nature inv; **~ stop** n point m; **~-time** a (work) à plein temps // n (SPORT) fin f du match; **~y** ad entièrement, complètement; **~y-fledged** a (teacher, barrister) diplômé(e); (citizen, member) à part entière.

fumble ['fʌmbl] vi fouiller, tâtonner // vt (ball) mal réceptionner, cafouiller; **to ~ with** vt fus tripoter.

fume [fju:m] vi rager; **~s** npl vapeurs fpl, émanations fpl, gaz mpl.

fumigate ['fju:mɪgeɪt] vt désinfecter (par fumigation).

fun [fʌn] n amusement m, divertissement m; **to have ~** s'amuser; **for ~** pour rire; **it's not much ~** ce n'est pas très drôle or amusant; **to make ~ of** vt fus se moquer de.

function ['fʌŋkʃən] n fonction f; cérémonie f, soirée officielle // vi fonctionner; **~al** a fonctionnel(le).

fund [fʌnd] n caisse f, fonds m; (source, store) source f, mine f; **~s** npl fonds mpl.

fundamental [fʌndə'mɛntl] a fondamental(e); **~s** npl principes mpl de base; **~ly** ad fondamentalement.

funeral ['fju:nərəl] n enterrement m, obsèques fpl (more formal occasion); **~ director** n entrepreneur m des pompes funèbres; **~ service** n service m funèbre.

funereal [fju:'nɪərɪəl] a lugubre, funèbre.

fun fair ['fʌnfɛə*] n fête (foraine).

fungus, pl **fungi** ['fʌŋgəs, -gaɪ] n champignon m; (mould) moisissure f.

funnel ['fʌnl] n entonnoir m; (of ship) cheminée f.

funnily ['fʌnɪlɪ] ad drôlement; curieusement.

funny ['fʌnɪ] a amusant(e), drôle; (strange) curieux(euse), bizarre.

fur [fə:*] n fourrure f; (in kettle etc) (dépôt m de) tartre m; **~ coat** n manteau m de fourrure.

furious ['fjuəriəs] a furieux(euse); (*effort*) acharné(e); ~**ly** *ad* furieusement; avec acharnement.

furl [fə:l] *vt* rouler; (NAUT) ferler.

furlong ['fə:lɒŋ] *n* = 201.17 m (*terme d'hippisme*).

furlough ['fə:ləu] *n* (US) permission *f*, congé *m*.

furnace ['fə:nis] *n* fourneau *m*.

furnish ['fə:niʃ] *vt* meubler; (*supply*) fournir; ~**ings** *npl* mobilier *m*, articles *mpl* d'ameublement.

furniture ['fə:nitʃə*] *n* meubles *mpl*, mobilier *m*; **piece of** ~ meuble *m*; ~ **polish** *n* encaustique *f*.

furrier ['fʌriə*] *n* fourreur *m*.

furrow ['fʌrəu] *n* sillon *m*.

furry ['fə:ri] a (*animal*) à fourrure; (*toy*) en peluche.

further ['fə:ðə*] a supplémentaire, autre; nouveau(nouvelle); plus loin // *ad* plus loin; (*more*) davantage; (*moreover*) de plus // *vt* faire avancer or progresser, promouvoir; **until** ~ **notice** jusqu'à nouvel ordre or avis; ~ **education** *n* enseignement *m* post-scolaire (*recyclage, formation professionnelle*); ~**more** [fə:ðə'mɔ:*] *ad* de plus, en outre.

furthest ['fə:ðist] *superlative of* **far**.

furtive ['fə:tiv] a furtif(ive); ~**ly** *ad* furtivement.

fury ['fjuəri] *n* fureur *f*.

fuse, fuze (US) [fju:z] *n* fusible *m*; (*for bomb etc*) amorce *f*, détonateur *m* // *vt, vi* (*metal*) fondre; (*fig*) fusionner; (ELEC): **to** ~ **the lights** faire sauter les fusibles or les plombs; ~ **box** *n* boîte *f* à fusibles.

fuselage ['fju:zəlɑ:ʒ] *n* fuselage *m*.

fusion ['fju:ʒən] *n* fusion *f*.

fuss [fʌs] *n* chichis *mpl*, façons *fpl*, embarras *mpl*; (*complaining*) histoire(s) *f(pl)*; **to make a** ~ faire des façons etc; ~**y** *a* (*person*) tatillon(ne), difficile; chichiteux(euse); (*dress, style*) tarabiscoté(e).

futile ['fju:tail] a futile.

futility [fju:'tiliti] *n* futilité *f*.

future ['fju:tʃə*] a futur(e) // *n* avenir *m*; (LING) futur *m*; **in (the)** ~ à l'avenir; **futuristic** [-'ristik] a futuriste.

fuze [fju:z] *n, vt, vi* (US) = **fuse**.

fuzzy ['fʌzi] a (PHOT) flou(e); (*hair*) crépu(e).

G

g. *abbr of* **gram(s)**.

G [dʒi:] *n* (MUS) sol *m*.

gabble ['gæbl] *vi* bredouiller; jacasser.

gable ['geibl] *n* pignon *m*.

gadget ['gædʒit] *n* gadget *m*.

Gaelic ['geilik] *n* (LING) gaélique *m*.

gag [gæg] *n* bâillon *m*; (*joke*) gag *m* // *vt* bâillonner.

gaiety ['geiəti] *n* gaieté *f*.

gaily ['geili] *ad* gaiement.

gain [gein] *n* gain *m*, profit *m* // *vt* gagner // *vi* (*watch*) avancer; **to** ~ **in/by** gagner en/à; **to** ~ **3lbs (in weight)** prendre 3 livres; ~**ful** a profitable, lucratif(ive).

gainsay [gein'sei] *vt irg* (*like* **say**) contredire; nier.

gait [geit] *n* démarche *f*.

gal. *abbr of* **gallon**.

gala ['gɑ:lə] *n* gala *m*.

galaxy ['gæləksi] *n* galaxie *f*.

gale [geil] *n* rafale *f* de vent; coup *m* de vent.

gallant ['gælənt] a vaillant(e), brave; (*towards ladies*) empressé(e), galant(e); ~**ry** *n* bravoure *f*, vaillance *f*; empressement *m*, galanterie *f*.

gall-bladder ['gɔ:lblædə*] *n* vésicule *f* biliaire.

gallery ['gæləri] *n* galerie *f*; (*also:* **art** ~) musée *m*; (: *private*) galerie.

galley ['gæli] *n* (*ship's kitchen*) cambuse *f*; (*ship*) galère *f*; (TYP) placard *m*, galée *f*.

gallon ['gælən] *n* gallon *m* (= 4.543 l; 8 pints).

gallop ['gæləp] *n* galop *m* // *vi* galoper.

gallows ['gæləuz] *n* potence *f*.

gallstone ['gɔ:lstəun] *n* calcul *m* (biliaire).

gambit ['gæmbit] *n* (*fig*): (**opening**) ~ manœuvre *f* stratégique.

gamble ['gæmbl] *n* pari *m*, risque calculé // *vt, vi* jouer; **to** ~ **on** (*fig*) miser sur; ~**r** *n* joueur *m*; **gambling** *n* jeu *m*.

game [geim] *n* jeu *m*; (*event*) match *m*; (HUNTING) gibier *m* // a brave; (*ready*): **to be** ~ (**for sth/to do**) être prêt(e) (à qch/à faire), se sentir de taille (à faire); **a** ~ **of football/tennis** une partie de football/tennis; **big** ~ gros gibier; ~**keeper** *n* garde-chasse *m*.

gammon ['gæmən] *n* (*bacon*) quartier *m* de lard fumé; (*ham*) jambon fumé.

gamut ['gæmət] *n* gamme *f*.

gang [gæŋ] *n* bande *f*, groupe *m* // *vi*: **to** ~ **up on sb** se liguer contre qn.

gangrene ['gæŋgri:n] *n* gangrène *f*.

gangster ['gæŋstə*] *n* gangster *m*, bandit *m*.

gangway ['gæŋwei] *n* passerelle *f*; (*of bus*) couloir central; (THEATRE, CINEMA) allée *f*.

gantry ['gæntri] *n* portique *m*.

gaol [dʒeil] *n, vt* = **jail**.

gap [gæp] *n* trou *m*; (*in time*) intervalle *f*; (*fig*) lacune *f*; vide *m*.

gape [geip] *vi* être *or* rester bouche bée; **gaping** a (*hole*) béant(e).

garage ['gærɑ:ʒ] *n* garage *m*.

garb [gɑ:b] *n* tenue *f*, costume *m*.

garbage ['gɑ:bidʒ] *n* ordures *fpl*, détritus *mpl*; ~ **can** *n* (US) poubelle *f*, boîte *f* à ordures.

garbled ['gɑ:bld] a déformé(e); faussé(e).

garden ['gɑ:dn] *n* jardin *m* // *vi* jardiner; ~**er** *n* jardinier *m*; ~**ing** jardinage *m*.

gargle ['gɑ:gl] *vi* se gargariser // *n* gargarisme *m*.

gargoyle ['gɑ:gɔil] *n* gargouille *f*.

garish ['gɛəriʃ] a criard(e), voyant(e).

garland ['gɑ:lənd] *n* guirlande *f*; couronne *f*.

garlic ['gɑ:lik] *n* ail *m*.

garment ['gɑ:mənt] *n* vêtement *m*.

garnish ['gɑ:niʃ] *vt* garnir.

garret ['gærit] *n* mansarde *f*.

garrison ['gærisn] *n* garnison *f* // *vt* mettre en garnison, stationner.

garrulous ['gærjuləs] *a* volubile, loquace.

garter ['gɑ:tə*] *n* jarretière *f*.

gas [gæs] *n* gaz *m*; (*used as anaesthetic*): **to be given** ~ se faire endormir; (*US: gasoline*) essence *f* // *vt* asphyxier; (*MIL*) gazer; ~ **cooker** *n* cuisinière *f* à gaz; ~ **cylinder** *n* bouteille *f* de gaz; ~ **fire** *n* radiateur *m* à gaz.

gash [gæʃ] *n* entaille *f*; (*on face*) balafre *f* // *vt* taillader; balafrer.

gasket ['gæskɪt] *n* (*AUT*) joint *m* de culasse.

gasmask ['gæsmɑ:sk] *n* masque *m* à gaz.

gas meter ['gæsmi:tə*] *n* compteur *m* à gaz.

gasoline ['gæsəli:n] *n* (*US*) essence *f*.

gasp [gɑ:sp] *vi* haleter; (*fig*) avoir le souffle coupé.

gas ring ['gæsrɪŋ] *n* brûleur *m*.

gas stove ['gæsstəuv] *n* réchaud *m* à gaz; (*cooker*) cuisinière *f* à gaz.

gassy ['gæsɪ] *a* gazeux(euse).

gastric ['gæstrɪk] *a* gastrique; ~ **ulcer** *n* ulcère *m* de l'estomac.

gastronomy [gæs'trɔnəmɪ] *n* gastronomie *f*.

gasworks ['gæswə:ks] *n* usine *f* à gaz.

gate [geɪt] *n* (*of garden*) portail *m*; (*of farm*) barrière *f*; (*of building*) porte *f*; (*of lock*) vanne *f*; ~**crash** *vt* s'introduire sans invitation dans; ~**way** *n* porte *f*.

gather ['gæðə*] *vt* (*flowers, fruit*) cueillir; (*pick up*) ramasser; (*assemble*) rassembler, réunir; recueillir; (*understand*) comprendre // *vi* (*assemble*) se rassembler; **to ~ speed** prendre de la vitesse; ~**ing** *n* rassemblement *m*.

gauche [gəuʃ] *a* gauche, maladroit(e).

gaudy ['gɔ:dɪ] *a* voyant(e).

gauge [geɪdʒ] *n* (*standard measure*) calibre *m*; (*RAIL*) écartement *m*; (*instrument*) jauge *f* // *vt* jauger.

gaunt [gɔ:nt] *a* décharné(e); (*grim, desolate*) désolé(e).

gauntlet ['gɔ:ntlɪt] *n* (*fig*): **to run the ~ through an angry crowd** se frayer un passage à travers une foule hostile ou entre deux haies de manifestants *etc* hostiles.

gauze [gɔ:z] *n* gaze *f*.

gave [geɪv] *pt of* **give**.

gavel ['gævl] *n* marteau *m*.

gawp [gɔ:p] *vi*: **to ~ at** regarder bouche bée.

gay [geɪ] *a* (*person*) gai(e), réjoui(e); (*colour*) gai, vif(vive); (*col*) homosexuel(le).

gaze [geɪz] *n* regard *m* fixe; **to ~ at** *vt* fixer du regard.

gazelle [gə'zɛl] *n* gazelle *f*.

gazetteer [gæzə'tɪə*] *n* dictionnaire *m* géographique.

gazumping [gə'zʌmpɪŋ] *n* le fait de revenir sur une promesse de vente pour accepter un prix plus élevé.

G.B. *abbr of* **Great Britain**.

G.C.E. *n* (*abbr of General Certificate of Education*) ≈ baccalauréat *m*.

Gdns. *abbr of* **gardens**.

gear [gɪə*] *n* matériel *m*, équipement *m*; attirail *m*; (*TECH*) engrenage *m*; (*AUT*) vitesse *f*; **top/low/bottom** ~ quatrième (*or* cinquième/deuxième/première vi-

tesse; **in** ~ en prise; **out of** ~ au point mort; ~ **box** *n* boîte *f* de vitesse; ~ **lever**, ~ **shift** (*US*) *n* levier *m* de vitesse.

geese [gi:s] *npl of* **goose**.

gelatin(e) ['dʒɛləti:n] *n* gélatine *f*.

gelignite ['dʒɛlɪgnaɪt] *n* plastic *m*.

gem [dʒɛm] *n* pierre précieuse.

Gemini ['dʒɛmɪnaɪ] *n* les Gémeaux *mpl*; **to be** ~ être des Gémeaux.

gender ['dʒɛndə*] *n* genre *m*.

general ['dʒɛnərl] *n* général *m* // *a* général(e); **in** ~ en général; ~ **election** *n* élection(s) législative(s); ~**ization** [-'zeɪʃən] *n* généralisation *f*; ~**ize** *vi* généraliser; ~**ly** *ad* généralement; **G~ Post Office (GPO)** *n* Postes et Télécommunications *fpl* (PTT); ~ **practitioner (G.P.)** *n* généraliste *m/f*; **who's your G.P.?** qui est votre médecin traitant?

generate ['dʒɛnəreɪt] *vt* engendrer; (*electricity*) produire.

generation [dʒɛnə'reɪʃən] *n* génération *f*.

generator ['dʒɛnəreɪtə*] *n* générateur *m*.

generosity [dʒɛnə'rɔsɪtɪ] *n* générosité *f*.

generous ['dʒɛnərəs] *a* généreux (euse); (*copious*) copieux(euse).

genetics [dʒɪ'nɛtɪks] *n* génétique *f*.

Geneva [dʒɪ'ni:və] *n* Genève.

genial ['dʒi:nɪəl] *a* cordial(e), chaleureux(euse); (*climate*) clément(e).

genitals ['dʒɛnɪtlz] *npl* organes génitaux.

genitive ['dʒɛnɪtɪv] *n* génitif *m*.

genius ['dʒi:nɪəs] *n* génie *m*.

gent [dʒɛnt] *n* *abbr of* **gentleman**.

genteel [dʒɛn'ti:l] *a* de bon ton, distingué(e).

gentle ['dʒɛntl] *a* doux(douce).

gentleman ['dʒɛntlmən] *n* monsieur *m*; (*well-bred man*) gentleman *m*.

gentleness ['dʒɛntlnɪs] *n* douceur *f*.

gently ['dʒɛntlɪ] *ad* doucement.

gentry ['dʒɛntrɪ] *n* petite noblesse.

gents [dʒɛnts] *n* W.-C. *mpl* (pour hommes).

genuine ['dʒɛnjuɪn] *a* véritable, authentique; sincère.

geographer [dʒɪ'ɔgrəfə*] *n* géographe *m/f*.

geographic(al) [dʒɪə'græfɪk(l)] *a* géographique.

geography [dʒɪ'ɔgrəfɪ] *n* géographie *f*.

geological [dʒɪə'lɔdʒɪkl] *a* géologique.

geologist [dʒɪ'ɔlədʒɪst] *n* géologue *m/f*.

geology [dʒɪ'ɔlədʒɪ] *n* géologie *f*.

geometric(al) [dʒɪə'mɛtrɪk(l)] *a* géométrique.

geometry [dʒɪ'ɔmətrɪ] *n* géométrie *f*.

geranium [dʒɪ'reɪnjəm] *n* géranium *m*.

germ [dʒə:m] *n* (*MED*) microbe *m*; (*BIO, fig*) germe *m*.

German ['dʒə:mən] *a* allemand(e) // *n* Allemand/e; (*LING*) allemand *m*; ~ **measles** *n* rubéole *f*.

Germany ['dʒə:mənɪ] *n* Allemagne *f*.

germination [dʒə:mɪ'neɪʃən] *n* germination *f*.

gerrymandering [dʒɛrɪmændərɪŋ] *n* tripotage *m* du découpage électoral.

gestation [dʒɛs'teɪʃən] *n* gestation *f*.

gesticulate [dʒɛs'tɪkjuleɪt] *vi* gesticuler.
gesture ['dʒɛstjə*] *n* geste *m*.
get, *pt*, *pp* **got**, *pp* **gotten** (*US*) [gɛt, gɔt, 'gɔtn] *vt* (*obtain*) avoir, obtenir; (*receive*) recevoir; (*find*) trouver, acheter; (*catch*) attraper; (*fetch*) aller chercher; (*understand*) comprendre, saisir; (*have*): to **have got** avoir; (*become*): to ~ **rich/old** s'enrichir/vieillir // *vi*: to ~ **to** (*place*) aller à; arriver à; parvenir à; **he got across the bridge/under the fence** il a traversé le pont/est passé par-dessous la barrière; to ~ **ready/washed/shaved** *etc* se préparer/laver/raser *etc*; to ~ **sb to do sth** faire faire qch à qn; to ~ **sth through/out of** faire passer qch par/sortir qch de; to ~ **about** *vi* se déplacer; (*news*) se répandre; to ~ **along** *vi* (*agree*) s'entendre; (*depart*) s'en aller; (*manage*) = to **get by**; to ~ **at** *vt fus* (*attack*) s'en prendre à; (*reach*) attraper, atteindre; to ~ **away** *vi* partir, s'en aller; (*escape*) s'échapper; to ~ **away with** *vt fus* en être quitte pour; se faire passer ou pardonner; to ~ **back** *vi* (*return*) rentrer // *vt* récupérer, recouvrer; to ~ **by** *vi* (*pass*) passer; (*manage*) se débrouiller; to ~ **down** *vi*, *vt fus* descendre // *vt* descendre; (*depress*) déprimer; to ~ **down to** *vt fus* (*work*) se mettre à (faire); to ~ **in** *vi* entrer; (*train*) arriver; (*arrive home*) rentrer; to ~ **into** *vt fus* entrer dans; to ~ **into bed/a rage** se mettre au lit/en colère; to ~ **off** *vi* (*from train etc*) descendre; (*depart: person, car*) s'en aller; (*escape*) s'en tirer // *vt* (*remove: clothes, stain*) enlever // *vt fus* (*train, bus*) descendre de; to ~ **on** *vi* (*at exam etc*) se débrouiller; (*agree*): to ~ **on (with)** s'entendre (avec) // *vt fus* monter dans; (*horse*) monter sur; to ~ **out** *vi* sortir; (*of vehicle*) descendre // *vt* sortir; to ~ **out of** *vt fus* sortir de; (*duty etc*) échapper à, se soustraire à; to ~ **over** *vt fus* (*illness*) se remettre de; (*fig: person*) entortiller; to ~ **through** *vi* (*TEL*) avoir la communication; to ~ **through to** *vt fus* (*TEL*) atteindre; to ~ **together** *vi* se réunir // *vt* assembler; to ~ **up** *vi* (*rise*) se lever // *vt fus* monter; to ~ **up to** *vt fus* (*reach*) arriver à; (*prank etc*) faire; ~**away** *n* fuite *f*.
geyser ['giːzə*] *n* chauffe-eau *m inv*; (*GEO*) geyser *m*.
Ghana ['gɑːnə] *n* Ghana *m*; ~**ian** [-'neɪən] *a* ghanéen(ne) // *n* Ghanéen/ne.
ghastly ['gɑːstlɪ] *a* atroce, horrible; (*pale*) livide, blême.
gherkin ['gɜːkɪn] *n* cornichon *m*.
ghetto ['gɛtəʊ] *n* ghetto *m*.
ghost [gəʊst] *n* fantôme *m*, revenant *m*; ~**ly** *a* fantomatique.
giant ['dʒaɪənt] *n* géant/e // *a* géant(e), énorme.
gibberish ['dʒɪbərɪʃ] *n* charabia *m*.
gibe [dʒaɪb] *n* sarcasme *m* // *vi*: to ~ **at** railler.
giblets ['dʒɪblɪts] *npl* abats *mpl*.
giddiness ['gɪdɪnɪs] *n* vertige *m*.
giddy ['gɪdɪ] *a* (*dizzy*): to **be** ~ avoir le

vertige; (*height*) vertigineux(euse); (*thoughtless*) sot(te), étourdi(e).
gift [gɪft] *n* cadeau *m*, présent *m*; (*donation, ability*) don *m*; ~**ed** *a* doué(e).
gigantic [dʒaɪ'gæntɪk] *a* gigantesque.
giggle ['gɪgl] *vi* pouffer, ricaner sottement // *n* petit rire sot, ricanement *m*.
gild [gɪld] *vt* dorer.
gill *n* [dʒɪl] (*measure*) = 0.14 l; 0.25 pints; ~**s** [gɪlz] *npl* (*of fish*) ouïes *fpl*, branchies *fpl*.
gilt [gɪlt] *n* dorure *f* // *a* doré(e).
gimlet ['gɪmlɪt] *n* vrille *f*.
gimmick ['gɪmɪk] *n* truc *m*.
gin [dʒɪn] *n* (*liquor*) gin *m*.
ginger ['dʒɪndʒə*] *n* gingembre *m*; to ~ **up** *vt* secouer; animer; ~ **ale**, ~ **beer** *n* boisson gazeuse au gingembre; ~**bread** *n* pain *m* d'épices; ~ **group** *n* groupe *m* de pression; ~**haired** *a* roux(rousse).
gingerly ['dʒɪndʒəlɪ] *ad* avec précaution.
gingham ['gɪŋəm] *n* vichy *m*.
gipsy ['dʒɪpsɪ] *n* gitan/e, bohémien/ne.
giraffe [dʒɪ'rɑːf] *n* girafe *f*.
girder ['gɜːdə*] *n* poutrelle *f*.
girdle ['gɜːdl] *n* (*corset*) gaine *f* // *vt* ceindre.
girl [gɜːl] *n* fille *f*, fillette *f*; (*young unmarried woman*) jeune fille; (*daughter*) fille; **an English** ~ une jeune Anglaise; **a little English** ~ une petite Anglaise; ~**friend** *n* (*of girl*) amie *f*; (*of boy*) petite amie; ~**ish** *a* de jeune fille.
Giro ['dʒaɪrəʊ] *n*: **the National** ~ ≈ les comptes chèques postaux.
girth [gɜːθ] *n* circonférence *f*; (*of horse*) sangle *f*.
gist [dʒɪst] *n* essentiel *m*.
give [gɪv] *n* (*of fabric*) élasticité *f* // *vb* (*pt* **gave**, *pp* **given**) [geɪv, 'gɪvn]) *vt* donner // *vi* (*break*) céder; (*stretch: fabric*) se prêter; to ~ **sb sth**, ~ **sth to sb** donner qch à qn; to ~ **a cry/sigh** pousser un cri/un soupir; to ~ **away** *vt* donner; (*give free*) faire cadeau de; (*betray*) donner, trahir; (*disclose*) révéler; (*bride*) conduire à l'autel; to ~ **back** *vt* rendre; to ~ **in** *vi* céder // *vt* donner; to ~ **off** *vt* dégager; to ~ **out** *vt* distribuer; annoncer; to ~ **up** *vi* renoncer // *vt* renoncer à; to ~ **up smoking** arrêter de fumer; to ~ **o.s. up** se rendre; to ~ **way** *vi* céder; (*AUT*) donner la priorité.
glacier ['glæsɪə*] *n* glacier *m*.
glad [glæd] *a* content(e); ~**den** *vt* réjouir.
gladioli [glædɪ'əʊlaɪ] *npl* glaïeuls *mpl*.
gladly ['glædlɪ] *ad* volontiers.
glamorous ['glæmərəs] *a* séduisant(e).
glamour ['glæmə*] *n* éclat *m*, prestige *m*.
glance [glɑːns] *n* coup *m* d'œil // *vi*: to ~ **at** jeter un coup d'œil à; to ~ **off** (*bullet*) ricocher sur; **glancing** *a* (*blow*) oblique.
gland [glænd] *n* glande *f*.
glandular ['glændjʊlə*] *a*: ~ **fever** *n* mononucléose infectieuse.
glare [glɛə*] *n* lumière éblouissante // *vi* briller d'un éclat aveuglant; to ~ **at** lancer un ou des regard(s) furieux à; **glaring** *a* (*mistake*) criant(e), qui saute aux yeux.

glass [gla:s] n verre m; (also: **looking ~**) miroir m; **~es** npl lunettes fpl; **~house** n serre f; **~ware** n verrerie f; **~y** a (eyes) vitreux(euse).

glaze [gleiz] vt (door) vitrer; (pottery) vernir // n vernis m; **~d** a (eye) vitreux(euse); (pottery) verni(e); (tiles) vitrifié(e).

glazier ['gleiziə*] n vitrier m.

gleam [gli:m] n lueur f; rayon m // vi luire, briller; **~ing** a luisant(e).

glee [gli:] n joie f; **~ful** a joyeux(euse).

glen [glɛn] n vallée f.

glib [glɪb] a qui a du bagou; facile.

glide [glaid] vi glisser; (AVIAT, birds) planer // n glissement m; vol plané; **~r** n (AVIAT) planeur m; **gliding** n (AVIAT) vol m à voile.

glimmer ['glɪmə*] vi luire // n lueur f.

glimpse [glɪmps] n vision passagère, aperçu m // vt entrevoir, apercevoir.

glint [glɪnt] n éclair m // vi étinceler.

glisten ['glɪsn] vi briller, luire.

glitter ['glɪtə*] vi scintiller, briller // n scintillement m.

gloat [gləut] vi: **to ~ (over)** jubiler (à propos de).

global ['gləubl] a mondial(e).

globe [gləub] n globe m.

gloom [glu:m] n obscurité f; (sadness) tristesse f, mélancolie f; **~y** a sombre, triste, mélancolique.

glorification [glɔ:rɪfɪˈkeɪʃən] n glorification f.

glorify ['glɔ:rɪfaɪ] vt glorifier.

glorious ['glɔ:rɪəs] a glorieux (euse); splendide.

glory ['glɔ:rɪ] n gloire f; splendeur f; **to ~ in** se glorifier de.

gloss [glɔs] n (shine) brillant m, vernis m; **to ~ over** vt fus glisser sur.

glossary ['glɔsərɪ] n glossaire m, lexique m.

gloss paint ['glɔspeɪnt] n peinture brillante.

glossy ['glɔsɪ] a brillant(e), luisant(e); **~ (magazine)** n revue f de luxe.

glove [glʌv] n gant m; **~ compartment** n (AUT) boîte f à gants, vide-poches m inv.

glow [gləu] vi rougeoyer; (face) rayonner // n rougeoiement m.

glower ['glauə*] vi lancer des regards mauvais.

glucose ['glu:kəus] n glucose m.

glue [glu:] n colle f // vt coller.

glum [glʌm] a maussade, morose.

glut [glʌt] n surabondance f // vt rassasier; (market) encombrer.

glutton ['glʌtn] n glouton/ne; **a ~ for work** un bourreau de travail; **~ous** a glouton(ne); **~y** n gloutonnerie f; (sin) gourmandise f.

glycerin(e) ['glɪsəriːn] n glycérine f.

gm, gms abbr of **gram(s)**.

gnarled [nɑ:ld] a noueux(euse).

gnat [næt] n moucheron m.

gnaw [nɔ:] vt ronger.

gnome [nəum] n gnome m, lutin m.

go [gəu] vb (pt **went**, pp **gone** [wɛnt, gɔn]) vi aller; (depart) partir, s'en aller; (work) marcher; (be sold): **to ~ for £10** se vendre 10 livres; (fit, suit): **to ~ with** aller avec; (become): **to ~ pale/mouldy** pâlir/moisir; (break etc) céder // n (pl: **~es**): **to have a ~ (at)** essayer (de faire); **to be on the ~** être en mouvement; **whose ~ is it?** à qui est-ce de jouer?; **he's going to do it** va faire, il est sur le point de faire; **to ~ for a walk** aller se promener; **to ~ dancing/shopping** aller danser/faire les courses; **how is it ~ing?** comment ça marche?; **how did it ~?** comment est-ce que ça s'est passé?; **to ~ round the back/by the shop** passer par derrière/devant le magasin; **to ~ about** vi (rumour) se répandre // vt fus: **how do I ~ about this?** comment dois-je m'y prendre (pour faire ceci)?; **to ~ ahead** vi (make progress) avancer; (get going) y aller; **to ~ along** vi aller, avancer // vt fus longer, parcourir; **as you ~ along (with your work)** au fur et à mesure (de votre travail); **to ~ away** vi partir, s'en aller; **to ~ back** vi rentrer; revenir; (go again) retourner; **to ~ back on** vt fus (promise) revenir sur; **to ~ by** vi (years, time) passer, s'écouler // vt fus tenir à; en croire; **to ~ down** vi descendre; (ship) couler; (sun) se coucher // vt fus descendre; **to ~ for** vt fus (fetch) aller chercher; (like) aimer; (attack) s'en prendre à; attaquer; **to ~ in** vi entrer; **to ~ in for** vt fus (competition) se présenter à; (like) aimer; **to ~ into** vt fus entrer dans; (investigate) étudier, examiner; (embark on) se lancer dans; **to ~ off** vi partir, s'en aller; (food) se gâter; (explode) sauter; (event) se dérouler // vt fus ne plus aimer, ne plus avoir envie de; **the gun went off** le coup est parti; **to ~ off to sleep** s'endormir; **to ~ on** vi continuer; (happen) se passer; **to ~ on doing** continuer à faire; **to ~ on with** vt fus poursuivre, continuer; **to ~ out** vi sortir; (fire, light) s'éteindre; **to ~ over** vi (ship) chavirer // vt fus (check) revoir, vérifier; **to ~ through** vt fus (town etc) traverser; **to ~ up** vi monter; (price) augmenter // vt fus gravir; **to ~ without** vt fus se passer de.

goad [gəud] vt aiguillonner.

go-ahead ['gəuəhɛd] a dynamique, entreprenant(e) // n feu vert.

goal [gəul] n but m; **~keeper** n gardien m de but; **~-post** n poteau m de but.

goat [gəut] n chèvre f.

gobble ['gɔbl] vt (also: **~ down, ~ up**) engloutir.

go-between ['gəubɪtwi:n] n médiateur m.

goblet ['gɔblɪt] n goblet m.

goblin ['gɔblɪn] n lutin m.

go-cart ['gəukɑ:t] n kart m; **~ racing** n karting m.

god [gɔd] n dieu m; **G~** n Dieu m; **~child** n filleul/e; **~dess** n déesse f; **~father** n parrain m; **~-forsaken** a maudit(e); **~mother** n marraine f; **~send** n aubaine f; **~son** n filleul m.

goggle ['gɔgl] vi: **to ~ at** regarder avec des yeux ronds; **~s** npl lunettes fpl (protectrices: de motocycliste etc).

going ['gəuɪŋ] n (conditions) état m du terrain // a: **the ~ rate** le tarif (en vigueur); **a ~ concern** une affaire prospère.

go-kart ['gəuka:t] n = **go-cart**.

gold [gəuld] n or m // a en or; **~en a** (made of gold) en or; (gold in colour) doré(e); **~en rule/age** règle/âge d'or; **~fish** n poisson m rouge; **~mine** n mine f d'or.

golf [gɔlf] n golf m; **~ club** n club m de golf; (stick) club m, crosse f de golf; **~ course** n terrain m de golf; **~er** n joueur/euse de golf.

gondola ['gɔndələ] n gondole f.

gone [gɔn] pp of **go** // a parti(e).

gong [gɔŋ] n gong m.

good [gud] a bon(ne); (kind) gentil(le); (child) sage // n bien m; **~s** npl marchandise f; articles mpl; **she is ~ with children/her hands** elle sait bien s'occuper des enfants/sait se servir de ses mains; **would you be ~ enough to ...?** auriez-vous la bonté or l'amabilité de ...?; **a ~ deal (of)** beaucoup (de); **a ~ many** beaucoup (de); **~ morning/afternoon!** bonjour!; **~ evening!** bonsoir!; **~ night!** bonsoir!; (on going to bed) bonne nuit!; **~bye!** au revoir!; **G~ Friday** n Vendredi saint; **~-looking a** bien inv; **~ness** n (of person) bonté f; **for ~ness sake!** je vous en prie!; **~ness gracious!** mon Dieu!; **~will** n bonne volonté f; (COMM) réputation f (auprès de la clientèle).

goose, pl **geese** [gu:s, gi:s] n oie f.

gooseberry ['guzbəri] n groseille f à maquereau; **to play ~** tenir la chandelle.

gooseflesh ['gu:sflɛʃ] n chair f de poule.

gore [gɔ:*] vt encorner // n sang m.

gorge [gɔ:dʒ] n gorge f // vt: **to ~ o.s. (on)** se gorger (de).

gorgeous ['gɔ:dʒəs] a splendide, superbe.

gorilla [gə'rilə] n gorille m.

gorse [gɔ:s] n ajoncs mpl.

gory ['gɔ:ri] a sanglant(e).

go-slow ['gəu'sləu] n grève perlée.

gospel ['gɔspl] n évangile m.

gossamer ['gɔsəmə*] n (cobweb) fils mpl de la vierge; (light fabric) étoffe très légère.

gossip ['gɔsip] n bavardages mpl; commérage m, cancans mpl; (person) commère f // vi bavarder; (maliciously) cancaner, faire des commérages.

got [gɔt] pt,pp of **get**; **~ten** (US) pp of **get**.

gout [gaut] n goutte f.

govern ['gʌvən] vt (gen, LING) gouverner.

governess ['gʌvənis] n gouvernante f.

government ['gʌvnmənt] n gouvernement m; (ministers) ministère m // cpd de l'État; **~al** [-'mɛntl] a gouvernemental(e).

governor ['gʌvənə*] n (of state, bank) gouverneur m; (of school, hospital) administrateur m.

Govt abbr of **government**.

gown [gaun] n robe f; (of teacher, judge) toge f.

G.P. n abbr see **general**.

GPO n abbr see **general**.

grab [græb] vt saisir, empoigner; (property, power) se saisir de.

grace [greis] n grâce f // vt honorer; **5 days' ~** répit m de 5 jours; **to say ~** dire le bénédicité; (after meal) dire les grâces; **~ful a** gracieux(euse), élégant(e); **gracious** ['greiʃəs] a bienveillant(e); de bonne grâce; miséricordieux(euse).

gradation [grə'deiʃən] n gradation f.

grade [greid] n (COMM) qualité f; calibre m; catégorie f; (in hierarchy) grade m, échelon m; (US: SCOL) note f; classe f // vt classer; calibrer; graduer; **~ crossing** n (US) passage m à niveau.

gradient ['greidiənt] n inclinaison f, pente f; (GEOM) gradient m.

gradual ['grædjuəl] a graduel(le), progressif(ive); **~ly** ad peu à peu, graduellement.

graduate n ['grædjuit] diplômé/e d'université // vi ['grædjueit] obtenir un diplôme d'université; **graduation** [-'eiʃən] n cérémonie f de remise des diplômes.

graft [gra:ft] n (AGR, MED) greffe f; (bribery) corruption f // vt greffer; **hard ~** n (col) boulot acharné.

grain [grein] n grain m; **it goes against the ~** cela va à l'encontre de sa (or ma) nature.

gram [græm] n gramme m.

grammar ['græmə*] n grammaire f.

grammatical [grə'mætikl] a grammatical(e).

gramme [græm] n = **gram**.

gramophone ['græməfəun] n gramophone m.

granary ['grænəri] n grenier m.

grand [grænd] a magnifique, splendide; noble; **~children** npl petits-enfants mpl; **~dad** n grand-papa m; **~daughter** n petite-fille f; **~eur** ['grændjə*] n grandeur f, noblesse f; **~father** n grand-père m; **~iose** ['grændiəuz] a grandiose; (pej) pompeux(euse); **~ma** n grand-maman f; **~mother** n grand-mère f; **~pa n = ~dad**; **~ piano** n piano m à queue; **~son** n petit-fils m; **~stand** n (SPORT) tribune f.

granite ['grænit] n granit m.

granny ['græni] n grand-maman f.

grant [gra:nt] vt accorder; (a request) accéder à; (admit) concéder // n (SCOL) bourse f; (ADMIN) subside m, subvention f; **to take sth for ~ed** considérer qch comme acquis or allant de soi.

granulated ['grænjuleitid] a: **~ sugar** n sucre m en poudre.

granule ['grænju:l] n granule m.

grape [greip] n raisin m.

grapefruit ['greipfru:t] n pamplemousse m.

graph [gra:f] n graphique m, courbe f; **~ic a** graphique; (vivid) vivant(e).

grapple ['græpl] vi: **to ~ with** être aux prises avec.

grasp [gra:sp] vt saisir, empoigner; (understand) saisir, comprendre // n (grip) prise f; (fig) emprise f, pouvoir m; compréhension f, connaissance f; **~ing a** avide.

grass [gra:s] n herbe f; gazon m; **~hopper** n sauterelle f; **~land** n prairie f; **~ snake** n couleuvre f; **~y a** herbeux(euse).

grate [greit] n grille f de cheminée // vi grincer // vt (CULIN) râper.

grateful ['greɪtful] a reconnaissant(e); **~ly** ad avec reconnaissance.

grater ['greɪtə*] n râpe f.

gratify ['grætɪfaɪ] vt faire plaisir à; (whim) satisfaire; **~ing** a agréable; satisfaisant(e).

grating ['greɪtɪŋ] n (iron bars) grille f // a (noise) grinçant(e).

gratitude ['grætɪtjuːd] n gratitude f.

gratuitous [grə'tjuːɪtəs] a gratuit(e).

gratuity [grə'tjuːɪtɪ] n pourboire m.

grave [greɪv] n tombe f // a grave, sérieux(euse); **~digger** n fossoyeur m.

gravel ['grævl] n gravier m.

gravestone ['greɪvstəun] n pierre tombale.

graveyard ['greɪvjɑːd] n cimetière m.

gravitate ['grævɪteɪt] vi graviter.

gravity ['grævɪtɪ] n (PHYSICS) gravité f; pesanteur f; (seriousness) gravité f, sérieux m.

gravy ['greɪvɪ] n jus m (de viande); sauce f.

gray [greɪ] a = **grey**.

graze [greɪz] vi paître, brouter // vt (touch lightly) frôler, effleurer; (scrape) écorcher // n (MED) écorchure f.

grease [griːs] n (fat) graisse f; (lubricant) lubrifiant m // vt graisser; lubrifier; **~gun** n graisseur m; **~proof paper** n papier sulfurisé; **greasy** a gras(se), graisseux(euse).

great [greɪt] a grand(e); (col) formidable; **G~ Britain** n Grande-Bretagne f; **~grandfather** n arrière-grand-père m; **~grandmother** n arrière-grand-mère f; **~ly** ad très, grandement; (with verbs) beaucoup; **~ness** n grandeur f.

Grecian ['griːʃən] a grec(grecque).

Greece [griːs] n Grèce f.

greed [griːd] n (also: **~iness**) avidité f; (for food) gourmandise f; **~ily** ad avidement; avec gourmandise; **~y** a avide; gourmand(e).

Greek [griːk] a grec(grecque) // n Grec/Grecque; (LING) grec m.

green [griːn] a vert(e); (inexperienced) (bien) jeune, naïf(ïve) // n vert m; (stretch of grass) pelouse f; (also: **village ~**) ≈ place f du village; **~s** npl légumes verts; **~gage** n reine-claude f; **~grocer** n marchand m de fruits et légumes; **~house** n serre f; **~ish** a verdâtre.

Greenland ['griːnlənd] n Groenland m.

greet [griːt] vt accueillir; **~ing** n salutation f; **Christmas/birthday ~ings** souhaits mpl de Noël/de bon anniversaire; **~ing(s) card** n carte f de vœux.

gregarious [grə'gɛərɪəs] a grégaire; sociable.

grenade [grə'neɪd] n grenade f.

grew [gruː] pt of **grow**.

grey [greɪ] a gris(e); (dismal) sombre; **~haired** a aux cheveux gris; **~hound** n lévrier m.

grid [grɪd] n grille f; (ELEC) réseau m; **~iron** n gril m.

grief [griːf] n chagrin m, douleur f.

grievance ['griːvəns] n doléance f, grief m.

grieve [griːv] vi avoir du chagrin; se désoler // vt faire de la peine à, affliger; **to ~ at** se désoler de; pleurer.

grievous ['griːvəs] a grave; cruel(le).

grill [grɪl] n (on cooker) gril m // vt griller; (question) interroger longuement, cuisiner.

grille [grɪl] n grillage m; (AUT) calandre f.

grill(room) ['grɪl(rum)] n rôtisserie f.

grim [grɪm] a sinistre, lugubre.

grimace [grɪ'meɪs] n grimace f // vi grimacer, faire une grimace.

grime [graɪm] n crasse f.

grimy ['graɪmɪ] a crasseux(euse).

grin [grɪn] n large sourire m // vi sourire.

grind [graɪnd] vt (pt, pp ground [graund]) écraser; (coffee, pepper etc) moudre; (make sharp) aiguiser // n (work) corvée f; **to ~ one's teeth** grincer des dents.

grip [grɪp] n étreinte f, poigne f; prise f; (handle) poignée f; (holdall) sac m de voyage // vt saisir, empoigner; étreindre; **to come to ~s with** en venir aux prises avec; **to ~ the road** (AUT) adhérer à la route.

gripe(s) [graɪp(s)] n(pl) coliques fpl.

gripping ['grɪpɪŋ] a prenant(e), palpitant(e).

grisly ['grɪzlɪ] a sinistre, macabre.

gristle ['grɪsl] n cartilage m (de poulet etc).

grit [grɪt] n gravillon m; (courage) cran m // vt (road) sabler; **to ~ one's teeth** serrer les dents.

grizzle ['grɪzl] vi pleurnicher.

groan [grəun] n gémissement m; grognement m // vi gémir; grogner.

grocer ['grəusə*] n épicier m; **at the ~'s** à l'épicerie, chez l'épicier; **~ies** npl provisions fpl.

grog [grɔg] n grog m.

groggy ['grɔgɪ] a groggy inv.

groin [grɔɪn] n aine f.

groom [gruːm] n palefrenier m; (also: **bride~**) marié m // vt (horse) panser; (fig): **to ~ sb for** former qn pour.

groove [gruːv] n sillon m, rainure f.

grope [grəup] vi tâtonner; **to ~ for** vt fus chercher à tâtons.

gross [grəus] a grossier(ère); (COMM) brut(e); **~ly** ad (greatly) très, grandement.

grotesque [grə'tɛsk] a grotesque.

grotto ['grɔtəu] n grotte f.

ground [graund] pt, pp of **grind** // n sol m, terre f; (land) terrain m, terres fpl; (SPORT) terrain; (reason: gen pl) raison f // vt (plane) empêcher de décoller, retenir au sol // vi (ship) s'échouer; **~s** npl (of coffee etc) marc m; (gardens etc) parc m, domaine m; **on the ~, to the ~** par terre; **~ floor** n rez-de-chaussée m; **~ing** n (in education) connaissances fpl de base; **~less** a sans fondement; **~sheet** n tapis m de sol; **~staff** n équipage m au sol; **~work** n préparation f.

group [gruːp] n groupe m // vt (also: **~ together**) grouper // vi (also: **~ together**) se grouper.

grouse [graus] n, pl inv (bird) grouse f (sorte de coq de bruyère) // vi (complain) rouspéter, râler.

grove [grəuv] n bosquet m.

grovel ['grɔvl] vi (fig): **to ~ (before)** ramper (devant).

grow, pt **grew**, pp **grown** [grəu, gru:, grəun] vi (plant) pousser, croître ; (person) grandir ; (increase) augmenter, se développer ; (become): **to ~ rich/weak** s'enrichir/s'affaiblir // vt cultiver, faire pousser ; **to ~ up** vi grandir ; **~er** n producteur m ; **~ing** a (fear, amount) croissant(e), grandissant(e).

growl [graul] vi grogner.

grown [grəun] pp of **grow** // a adulte ; **~-up** n adulte m/f, grande personne.

growth [grəuθ] n croissance f, développement m ; (what has grown) pousse f ; poussée f ; (MED) grosseur f, tumeur f.

grub [grʌb] n larve f ; (col: food) bouffe f.

grubby ['grʌbɪ] a crasseux(euse).

grudge [grʌdʒ] n rancune f // vt: **to ~ sb sth** donner qch à qn à contre-cœur ; reprocher qch à qn ; **to bear sb a ~ (for)** garder rancune or en vouloir à qn (de) ; **he ~s spending** il rechigne à dépenser ; **grudgingly** ad à contre-cœur, de mauvaise grâce.

gruelling ['gruəlɪŋ] a exténuant(e).

gruesome ['gru:səm] a horrible.

gruff [grʌf] a bourru(e).

grumble ['grʌmbl] vi rouspéter, ronchonner.

grumpy ['grʌmpɪ] a grincheux (euse).

grunt [grʌnt] vi grogner // n grognement m.

G-string ['dʒi:strɪŋ] n (garment) cache-sexe m inv.

guarantee [gærən'ti:] n garantie f // vt garantir.

guarantor [gærən'tɔ:*] n garant/e.

guard [gɑ:d] n garde f, surveillance f ; (squad, BOXING, FENCING) garde f ; (one man) garde m ; (RAIL) chef m de train // vt garder, surveiller ; **~ed** a (fig) prudent(e) ; **~ian** n gardien/ne ; (of minor) tuteur/trice ; **~'s van** n (RAIL) fourgon m.

guerrilla [gə'rɪlə] n guérillero m ; **~ warfare** n guérilla f.

guess [gɛs] vi deviner // vt (US) croire, penser // n supposition f, hypothèse f ; **to take/have a ~** essayer de deviner ; **~work** n hypothèse f.

guest [gɛst] n invité/e ; (in hotel) client/e ; **~-house** n pension f ; **~ room** n chambre f d'amis.

guffaw [gʌ'fɔ:] n gros rire // vi pouffer de rire.

guidance ['gaɪdəns] n conseils mpl ; **under the ~ of** conseillé(e) or encadré(e) par, sous la conduite de.

guide [gaɪd] n (person, book etc) guide m // vt guider ; **(girl) ~** n guide f ; **~book** n guide m ; **~d missile** n missile téléguidé ; **~ dog** n chien m d'aveugle ; **~lines** npl (fig) instructions générales, conseils mpl.

guild [gɪld] n corporation f ; cercle m, association f ; **~hall** n (Brit) hôtel m de ville.

guile [gaɪl] n astuce f ; **~less** a candide.

guillotine ['gɪlətiːn] n guillotine f ; (for paper) massicot m.

guilt [gɪlt] n culpabilité f ; **~y** a coupable.

guinea ['gɪnɪ] n (Brit) guinée f (= 21 shillings: cette monnaie de compte ne s'emploie plus).

guinea pig ['gɪnɪpɪg] n cobaye m.

guise [gaɪz] n aspect m, apparence f.

guitar [gɪ'tɑ:*] n guitare f ; **~ist** n guitariste m/f.

gulf [gʌlf] n golfe m ; (abyss) gouffre m.

gull [gʌl] n mouette f.

gullet ['gʌlɪt] n gosier m.

gullible ['gʌlɪbl] a crédule.

gully ['gʌlɪ] n ravin m ; ravine f ; couloir m.

gulp [gʌlp] vi avaler sa salive ; (from emotion) avoir la gorge serrée, s'étrangler // vt (also: **~ down**) avaler // n: **at one ~** d'un seul coup.

gum [gʌm] n (ANAT) gencive f ; (glue) colle f ; (sweet) boule f de gomme ; (also: chewing-~) chewing-gum m // vt coller ; **~boil** n abcès m dentaire ; **~boots** npl bottes fpl en caoutchouc.

gumption ['gʌmpʃən] n bon sens, jugeote f.

gun [gʌn] n (small) revolver m, pistolet m ; (rifle) fusil m, carabine f ; (cannon) canon m ; **~boat** n canonnière f ; **~fire** n fusillade f ; **~man** n bandit armé ; **~ner** n artilleur m ; **at ~point** sous la menace du pistolet (or fusil) ; **~powder** n poudre f à canon ; **~shot** n coup m de feu ; **within ~shot** à portée de fusil ; **~smith** n armurier m.

gurgle ['gə:gl] n gargouillis m // vi gargouiller.

gush [gʌʃ] n jaillissement m, jet m // vi jaillir ; (fig) se répandre en effusions.

gusset ['gʌsɪt] n gousset m, soufflet m.

gust [gʌst] n (of wind) rafale f ; (of smoke) bouffée f.

gusto ['gʌstəu] n enthousiasme m.

gut [gʌt] n intestin m, boyau m ; (MUS etc) boyau m ; **~s** npl (courage) cran m.

gutter ['gʌtə*] n (of roof) gouttière f ; (in street) caniveau m ; (fig) ruisseau m.

guttural ['gʌtərl] a guttural(e).

guy [gaɪ] n (also: **~rope**) corde f ; (col: man) type m ; (figure) effigie de Guy Fawkes.

guzzle ['gʌzl] vi s'empiffrer // vt avaler gloutonnement.

gym [dʒɪm] n (also: **gymnasium**) gymnase m ; (also: **gymnastics**) gym f ; **~ shoes** npl chaussures fpl de gym(nastique) ; **~ slip** n tunique f (d'écolière).

gymnast ['dʒɪmnæst] n gymnaste m/f ; **~ics** [-'næstɪks] n, npl gymnastique f.

gynaecologist, gynecologist (US) [gaɪnɪ'kɔlədʒɪst] n gynécologue m/f.

gynaecology, gynecology (US) [gaɪnə'kɔlədʒɪ] n gynécologie f.

gypsy ['dʒɪpsɪ] n = **gipsy**.

gyrate [dʒaɪ'reɪt] vi tournoyer.

H

haberdashery ['hæbə'dæʃərɪ] n mercerie f.

habit ['hæbɪt] n habitude f ; (costume) habit m, tenue f.

habitable ['hæbɪtəbl] a habitable.
habitation [hæbɪ'teɪʃən] n habitation f.
habitual [hə'bɪtjuəl] a habituel(le); (drinker, liar) invétéré(e); ~**ly** ad habituellement, d'habitude.
hack [hæk] vt hacher, tailler // n (cut) entaille f; (blow) coup m; (pej: writer) nègre m.
hackney cab ['hæknɪ'kæb] n fiacre m.
hackneyed ['hæknɪd] a usé(e), rebattu(e).
had [hæd] pt, pp of **have**.
haddock, pl ~ or ~**s** ['hædək] n églefin m; **smoked** ~ haddock m.
hadn't ['hædnt] = **had not**.
haemorrhage, **hemorrhage** (US) ['hɛmərɪdʒ] n hémorragie f.
haemorrhoids, **hemorrhoids** (US) ['hɛmərɔɪdz] npl hémorroïdes fpl.
haggard ['hægəd] a hagard(e), égaré(e).
haggle ['hægl] vi marchander; **to** ~ **over** chicaner sur; **haggling** n marchandage m.
Hague [heɪg] n: **The** ~ La Haye.
hail [heɪl] n grêle f // vt (call) héler; (greet) acclamer // vi grêler; ~**stone** n grêlon m.
hair [hɛə*] n cheveux mpl; (single hair: on head) cheveu m; (: on body) poil m; **to do one's** ~ se coiffer; ~**brush** n brosse f à cheveux; ~**cut** n coupe f (de cheveux); ~**do** ['hɛədu:] n coiffure f; ~**dresser** n coiffeur/euse; ~**-drier** n sèche-cheveux m; ~**net** n résille f; ~ **oil** n huile f capillaire; ~**piece** n postiche m; ~**pin** n épingle f à cheveux; ~**pin bend** n virage m en épingle à cheveux; ~**raising** a à (vous) faire dresser les cheveux sur la tête; ~ **remover** n dépilateur m; ~ **spray** n laque f (pour les cheveux); ~**style** n coiffure f; ~**y** a poilu(e); chevelu(e); (fig) effrayant(e).
hake [heɪk] n colin m, merlu m.
half [hɑːf] n (pl: **halves** [hɑːvz]) moitié f // a demi(e) // ad (à) moitié, à demi; ~**an-hour** une demi-heure; **two and a** ~ deux et demi; **a week and a** ~ une semaine et demie; ~ (of it) la moitié; ~ (of) la moitié de; ~ **the amount of** la moitié de; **to cut sth in** ~ couper qch en deux; ~**back** n (SPORT) demi m; ~**breed**, ~**caste** n métis/se; ~**hearted** a tiède, sans enthousiasme; ~**hour** n demi-heure f; ~**penny** ['heɪpnɪ] n demi-penny m; (at) ~**price** à moitié prix; ~**time** n mi-temps f; ~**way** ad à mi-chemin.
halibut ['hælɪbət] n, pl inv flétan m.
hall [hɔːl] n salle f; (entrance way) hall m, entrée f; (corridor) couloir m; (mansion) château m, manoir m; ~ **of residence** n pavillon m or résidence f universitaire.
hallmark ['hɔːlmɑːk] n poinçon m; (fig) marque f.
hallo [hə'ləu] excl = **hello**.
hallucination [həluːsɪ'neɪʃən] n hallucination f.
halo ['heɪləu] n (of saint etc) auréole f; (of sun) halo m.
halt [hɔːlt] n halte f, arrêt m // vt faire arrêter // vi faire halte, s'arrêter.
halve [hɑːv] vt (apple etc) partager or diviser en deux; (expense) réduire de moitié.

halves [hɑːvz] npl of **half**.
ham [hæm] n jambon m.
hamburger ['hæmbəːgə*] n hamburger m.
hamstring ['hæmstrɪŋ] n (ANAT) tendon m du jarret.
hamlet ['hæmlɪt] n hameau m.
hammer ['hæmə*] n marteau m // vt (fig) éreinter, démolir.
hammock ['hæmək] n hamac m.
hamper ['hæmpə*] vt gêner // n panier m (d'osier).
hand [hænd] n main f; (of clock) aiguille f; (handwriting) écriture f; (at cards) jeu m; (worker) ouvrier/ère // vt passer, donner; **to give sb a** ~ donner un coup de main à qn; **at** ~ à portée de la main; **in** ~ en main; (work) en cours; **on the one** ~ ..., **on the other** ~ d'une part ..., d'autre part; **to** ~ **in** vt remettre; **to** ~ **out** vt distribuer; **to** ~ **over** vt transmettre; céder; ~**bag** n sac m à main; ~**ball** n handball m; ~**basin** n lavabo m; ~**book** n manuel m; ~**brake** n frein m à main; ~**cream** n crème f pour les mains; ~**cuffs** npl menottes fpl; ~**ful** n poignée f.
handicap ['hændɪkæp] n handicap m // vt handicaper.
handicraft ['hændɪkrɑːft] n travail m d'artisanat, technique artisanale.
handkerchief ['hæŋkətʃɪf] n mouchoir m.
handle ['hændl] n (of door etc) poignée f; (of cup etc) anse f; (of knife etc) manche m; (of saucepan) queue f; (for winding) manivelle f // vt toucher, manier; (deal with) s'occuper de; (treat: people) prendre; '~ **with care**' 'fragile'; ~**bar(s)** n(pl) guidon m.
hand-luggage ['hændlʌgɪdʒ] n bagages mpl à main.
handmade ['hændmeɪd] a fait(e) à la main.
handout ['hændaut] n documentation f, prospectus m.
handshake ['hændʃeɪk] n poignée f de main.
handsome ['hænsəm] a beau(belle); généreux(euse); considérable.
handwriting ['hændraɪtɪŋ] n écriture f.
handwritten ['hændrɪtn] a manuscrit(e), écrit(e) à la main.
handy ['hændɪ] a (person) adroit(e); (close at hand) sous la main; (convenient) pratique; **handyman** n bricoleur m; (servant) homme m à tout faire.
hang, pt, pp **hung** [hæŋ, hʌŋ] vt accrocher; (criminal: pt,pp **hanged**) pendre // vi pendre; (hair, drapery) tomber; **to** ~ **about** vi flâner, traîner; **to** ~ **on** vi (wait) attendre; **to** ~ **up** vi (TEL) raccrocher // vt accrocher, suspendre.
hangar ['hæŋə*] n hangar m.
hanger ['hæŋə*] n cintre m, portemanteau m.
hanger-on [hæŋər'ɔn] n parasite m.
hang-gliding ['hæŋglaɪdɪŋ] n vol m libre or sur aile delta.
hangover ['hæŋəuvə*] n (after drinking) gueule f de bois.
hang-up ['hæŋʌp] n complexe m.

hank [hæŋk] *n* écheveau *m*.

hanker ['hæŋkə*] *vi*: **to ~ after** avoir envie de.

hankie, hanky ['hæŋkɪ] *n abbr of* **handkerchief.**

haphazard [hæp'hæzəd] *a* fait(e) au hasard, fait(e) au petit bonheur.

happen ['hæpən] *vi* arriver; se passer, se produire; **as it ~s** justement; **~ing** *n* événement *m*.

happily ['hæpɪlɪ] *ad* heureusement.

happiness ['hæpɪnɪs] *n* bonheur *m*.

happy ['hæpɪ] *a* heureux(euse); **~ with** (*arrangements etc*) satisfait(e) de; **~-go-lucky** *a* insouciant(e).

harass ['hærəs] *vt* accabler, tourmenter; **~ment** *n* tracasseries *fpl*.

harbour, harbor (*US*) ['hɑ:bə*] *n* port *m* // *vt* héberger, abriter; **~ master** *n* capitaine *m* du port.

hard [hɑ:d] *a* dur(e) // *ad* (*work*) dur; (*think, try*) sérieusement; **to drink ~** boire sec; **~ luck!** pas de veine!; **no ~ feelings!** sans rancune!; **to be ~ of hearing** être dur(e) d'oreille; **to be ~ done by** être traité(e) injustement; **~back** *n* livre relié; **~board** *n* Isorel *m* ®; **~-boiled egg** *n* œuf dur; **~ cash** *n* espèces *fpl*; **~en** *vt* durcir; (*fig*) endurcir // *vi* durcir; **~ening** *n* durcissement *m*; **~-headed** *a* réaliste; décidé(e); **~ labour** *n* travaux forcés.

hardly ['hɑ:dlɪ] *ad* (*scarcely*) à peine; **it's ~ the case** ce n'est guère le cas; **~ anywhere** presque nulle part.

hardness ['hɑ:dnɪs] *n* dureté *f*.

hard sell ['hɑ:d'sel] *n* (*COMM*) promotion de ventes agressive.

hardship ['hɑ:dʃɪp] *n* épreuves *fpl*; privations *fpl*.

hard-up [hɑ:d'ʌp] *a* (*col*) fauché(e).

hardware ['hɑ:dwɛə*] *n* quincaillerie *f*; (*COMPUTERS*) matériel *m*; **~ shop** *n* quincaillerie *f*.

hard-wearing [hɑ:d'wɛərɪŋ] *a* solide.

hard-working [hɑ:d'wə:kɪŋ] *a* travailleur(euse).

hardy ['hɑ:dɪ] *a* robuste; (*plant*) résistant(e) au gel.

hare [hɛə*] *n* lièvre *m*; **~-brained** *a* farfelu(e); écervelé(e); **~lip** *n* (*MED*) bec-de-lièvre *m*.

harem [hɑ:'ri:m] *n* harem *m*.

harm [hɑ:m] *n* mal *m*; (*wrong*) tort *m* // *vt* (*person*) faire du mal or du tort à; (*thing*) endommager; **to mean no ~** ne pas avoir de mauvaises intentions; **out of ~'s way** à l'abri du danger, en lieu sûr; **~ful** *a* nuisible; **~less** *a* inoffensif(ive); sans méchanceté.

harmonic [hɑ:'mɔnɪk] *a* harmonique.

harmonica [hɑ:'mɔnɪkə] *n* harmonica *m*.

harmonics [hɑ:'mɔnɪks] *npl* harmoniques *mpl* or *fpl*.

harmonious [hɑ:'məʊnɪəs] *a* harmonieux(euse).

harmonium [hɑ:'məʊnɪəm] *n* harmonium *m*.

harmonize ['hɑ:mənaɪz] *vt* harmoniser // *vi* s'harmoniser.

harmony ['hɑ:mənɪ] *n* harmonie *f*.

harness ['hɑ:nɪs] *n* harnais *m* // *vt* (*horse*) harnacher; (*resources*) exploiter.

harp [hɑ:p] *n* harpe *f* // *vi*: **to ~ on about** parler tout le temps de; **~ist** *n* harpiste *m/f*.

harpoon [hɑ:'pu:n] *n* harpon *m*.

harpsichord ['hɑ:psɪkɔ:d] *n* clavecin *m*.

harrow ['hærəʊ] *n* (*AGR*) herse *f*.

harrowing ['hærəʊɪŋ] *a* déchirant(e).

harsh [hɑ:ʃ] *a* (*hard*) dur(e); (*severe*) sévère; (*rough: surface*) rugueux(euse); (*unpleasant: sound*) discordant(e); (: *colour*) criard(e); cru(e); (: *wine*) âpre; **~ly** *ad* durement; sévèrement; **~ness** *n* dureté *f*; sévérité *f*.

harvest ['hɑ:vɪst] *n* (*of corn*) moisson *f*; (*of fruit*) récolte *f*; (*of grapes*) vendange *f* // *vi* moissonner; récolter; vendanger; **~er** *n* (*machine*) moissonneuse *f*.

has [hæz] *see* **have.**

hash [hæʃ] *n* (*CULIN*) hachis *m*; (*fig: mess*) gâchis *m*; *also abbr of* **hashish.**

hashish ['hæʃɪʃ] *n* haschisch *m*.

hassle ['hæsl] *n* chamaillerie *f*.

haste [heɪst] *n* hâte *f*; précipitation *f*; **~n** ['heɪsn] *vt* hâter, accélérer // *vi* se hâter, s'empresser; **hastily** *ad* à la hâte; précipitamment; **hasty** *a* hâtif(ive); précipité(e).

hat [hæt] *n* chapeau *m*; **~box** *n* carton *m* à chapeau.

hatch [hætʃ] *n* (*NAUT: also*: **~way**) écoutille *f*; (*also*: **service ~**) passe-plats *m inv* // *vi* éclore // *vt* faire éclore; (*plot*) tramer.

hatchback ['hætʃbæk] *n* (*AUT*) modèle *m* avec hayon arrière.

hatchet ['hætʃɪt] *n* hachette *f*.

hate [heɪt] *vt* haïr, détester // *n* haine *f*; **to ~ to do** *or* **doing** détester faire; **~ful** *a* odieux(euse), détestable.

hatred ['heɪtrɪd] *n* haine *f*.

hat trick ['hættrɪk] *n* (*SPORT, also fig*) triplé *m* (*3 buts réussis au cours du même match etc*).

haughty ['hɔ:tɪ] *a* hautain(e), arrogant(e).

haul [hɔ:l] *vt* traîner, tirer; (*by lorry*) camionner; (*NAUT*) haler // *n* (*of fish*) prise *f*; (*of stolen goods etc*) butin *m*; **~age** *n* halage *m*; camionnage *m*; **~ier** *n* transporteur (routier), camionneur *m*.

haunch [hɔ:ntʃ] *n* hanche *f*; **~ of venison** *n* cuissot *m* de chevreuil.

haunt [hɔ:nt] *vt* (*subj: ghost, fear*) hanter; (: *person*) fréquenter // *n* repaire *m*.

have *pt,pp* **had** [hæv, hæd] *vt* avoir; (*meal, shower*) prendre; **to ~ sth done** faire faire qch; **he had a suit made** il s'est fait faire un costume; **she has to do it** il faut qu'elle le fasse, elle doit le faire; **I had better leave** je ferais mieux de partir; **to ~ it out with sb** s'expliquer (franchement) avec qn; **I won't ~ it** cela ne se passera pas ainsi; **he's been had** (*col*) il s'est fait avoir *or* rouler.

haven ['heɪvn] *n* port *m*; (*fig*) havre *m*.

haversack ['hævəsæk] *n* sac *m* à dos.

havoc ['hævək] *n* ravages *mpl*; **to play with** (*fig*) désorganiser; détraquer.

hawk [hɔːk] *n* faucon *m*.

hawker ['hɔːkə*] *n* colporteur *m*.

hay [heɪ] *n* foin *m*; ~ **fever** *n* rhume *m* des foins ; ~**stack** *n* meule *f* de foin.

haywire ['heɪwaɪə*] *a* (*col*): **to go** ~ perdre la tête ; mal tourner.

hazard ['hæzəd] *n* hasard *m*, chance *f* ; danger *m*, risque *m* // *vt* risquer, hasarder ; ~**ous** *a* hasardeux(euse), risqué(e).

haze [heɪz] *n* brume *f*.

hazelnut ['heɪzlnʌt] *n* noisette *f*.

hazy ['heɪzɪ] *a* brumeux(euse) ; (*idea*) vague ; (*photograph*) flou(e).

he [hiː] *pronoun* il ; **it is** ~ **who ...** c'est lui qui ... ; **here** ~ **is** le voici ; ~**-bear** *n* ours *m* mâle.

head [hɛd] *n* tête *f* ; (*leader*) chef *m* // *vt* (*list*) être en tête de ; (*group*) être à la tête de ; ~**s** (*on coin*) (le côté) face ; ~**s or tails** pile ou face ; **to** ~ **the ball** faire une tête ; **to** ~ **for** *vt fus* se diriger vers ; ~**ache** *n* mal *m* de tête ; ~ **cold** *n* rhume *m* de cerveau ; ~**ing** *n* titre *m* ; rubrique *f* ; ~**lamp** *n* phare *m* ; ~**land** *n* promontoire *m*, cap *m* ; ~**light** = ~**lamp** ; ~**line** *n* titre *m* ; ~**long** *ad* (*fall*) la tête la première ; (*rush*) tête baissée ; ~**master** *n* directeur *m*, proviseur *m* ; ~**mistress** *n* directrice *f* ; ~ **office** *n* bureau central ; ~**-on** *a* (*collision*) de plein fouet ; ~**phones** *npl* casque *m* (à écouteurs) ; ~**quarters (HQ)** *npl* bureau or siège central ; (*MIL*) quartier général ; ~**-rest** *n* appui-tête *m* ; ~**room** *n* (*in car*) hauteur *f* de plafond ; (*under bridge*) hauteur limite ; dégagement *m* ; ~**scarf** *n* foulard *m* ; ~**strong** *a* têtu(e), entêté(e) ; ~ **waiter** *n* maître m d'hôtel ; ~**way** *n* avance *f*, progrès *m* ; ~**wind** *n* vent *m* contraire ; ~**y** *a* capiteux(euse), enivrant(e).

heal [hiːl] *vt,vi* guérir.

health [hɛlθ] *n* santé *f* ; ~ **food shop** *n* magasin *m* diététique ; **the H**~ **Service** ≈ la Sécurité Sociale ; ~**y** *a* (*person*) en bonne santé ; (*climate, food, attitude etc*) sain(e).

heap [hiːp] *n* tas *m*, monceau *m* // *vt* entasser, amonceler.

hear, *pt*, *pp* **heard** [hɪə*, həːd] *vt* entendre ; (*news*) apprendre ; (*lecture*) assister à, écouter // *vi* entendre ; **to** ~ **about** avoir des nouvelles de ; entendre parler de ; **did you** ~ **about the move?** tu es au courant du déménagement? ; **to** ~ **from sb** recevoir des nouvelles de qn ; ~**ing** *n* (*sense*) ouïe *f* ; (*of witnesses*) audition *f* ; (*of a case*) audience *f* ; (*of committee*) séance *f* ; ~**ing aid** *n* appareil *m* acoustique ; **by** ~**say** *ad* par ouï-dire *m*.

hearse [həːs] *n* corbillard *m*.

heart [hɑːt] *n* cœur *m* ; ~**s** *npl* (*CARDS*) cœur ; **at** ~ au fond ; **by** ~ (*learn, know*) par cœur ; **to lose** ~ perdre courage, se décourager ; ~ **attack** *n* crise *f* cardiaque ; ~**beat** *n* battement *m* de cœur ; ~**breaking** *a* navrant(e), déchirant(e) ; **to be** ~**broken** avoir beaucoup de chagrin ; ~**burn** *n* brûlures *fpl* d'estomac ; ~ **failure** *n* arrêt *m* du cœur ; ~**felt** *a* sincère.

hearth [hɑːθ] *n* foyer *m*, cheminée *f*.

heartily ['hɑːtɪlɪ] *ad* chaleureusement ; (*laugh*) de bon cœur ; (*eat*) de bon appétit ; **to agree** ~ être entièrement d'accord.

heartless ['hɑːtlɪs] *a* sans cœur, insensible ; cruel(le).

heartwarming ['hɑːtwɔːmɪŋ] *a* réconfortant(e).

hearty ['hɑːtɪ] *a* chaleureux(euse) ; robuste ; vigoureux(euse).

heat [hiːt] *n* chaleur *f* ; (*fig*) ardeur *f* ; feu *m* ; (*SPORT: also:* **qualifying** ~) éliminatoire *f* // *vt* chauffer ; **to** ~ **up** *vi* (*liquids*) chauffer ; (*room*) se réchauffer // *vt* réchauffer ; ~**ed** *a* chauffé(e) ; (*fig*) passionné(e) ; échauffé(e), excité(e) ; ~**er** *n* appareil *m* de chauffage ; radiateur *m*.

heath [hiːθ] *n* (*Brit*) lande *f*.

heathen ['hiːðn] *a, n* païen(ne).

heather ['hɛðə*] *n* bruyère *f*.

heating ['hiːtɪŋ] *n* chauffage *m*.

heatstroke ['hiːtstrəuk] *n* coup *m* de chaleur.

heatwave ['hiːtweɪv] *n* vague *f* de chaleur.

heave [hiːv] *vt* soulever (avec effort) // *vi* se soulever // *n* nausée *f*, haut-le-cœur *m* ; (*push*) poussée *f*.

heaven ['hɛvn] *n* ciel *m*, paradis *m* ; ~ **forbid!** surtout pas! ; ~**ly** *a* céleste, divin(e).

heavily ['hɛvɪlɪ] *ad* lourdement ; (*drink, smoke*) beaucoup ; (*sleep, sigh*) profondément.

heavy ['hɛvɪ] *a* lourd(e) ; (*work, sea, rain, eater*) gros(se) ; (*drinker, smoker*) grand(e) ; **it's** ~ **going** ça ne va pas tout seul, c'est pénible ; ~**weight** *n* (*SPORT*) poids lourd.

Hebrew ['hiːbruː] *a* hébraïque // *n* (*LING*) hébreu *m*.

heckle ['hɛkl] *vt* interpeller (*un orateur*).

hectare ['hɛktɑː*] *n* hectare *m*.

hectic ['hɛktɪk] *a* agité(e), trépidant(e).

he'd [hiːd] = **he would, he had**.

hedge [hɛdʒ] *n* haie *f* // *vi* se défiler ; **to** ~ **one's bets** (*fig*) se couvrir ; **to** ~ **in** *vt* entourer d'une haie.

hedgehog ['hɛdʒhɔg] *n* hérisson *m*.

heed [hiːd] *vt* (*also:* **take** ~ **of**) tenir compte de, prendre garde à ; ~**less** *a* insouciant(e).

heel [hiːl] *n* talon *m* // *vt* (*shoe*) retalonner ; **to bring sb to** ~ rappeler qn à l'ordre.

hefty ['hɛftɪ] *a* (*person*) costaud(e) ; (*parcel*) lourd(e) ; (*piece, price*) gros(se).

heifer ['hɛfə*] *n* génisse *f*.

height [haɪt] *n* (*of person*) taille *f*, grandeur *f* ; (*of object*) hauteur *f* ; (*of plane, mountain*) altitude *f* ; (*high ground*) hauteur, éminence *f* ; (*fig: of glory*) sommet *m* ; (*: of stupidity*) comble *m* ; ~**en** *vt* hausser, surélever ; (*fig*) augmenter.

heir [ɛə*] *n* héritier *m* ; ~**ess** *n* héritière *f* ; ~**loom** *n* meuble *m* or bijou *m* or tableau *m*) de famille.

held [hɛld] *pt, pp* of **hold**.

helicopter ['hɛlɪkɔptə*] *n* hélicoptère *m*.

helium ['hiːlɪəm] *n* hélium *m*.

hell [hɛl] *n* enfer *m* ; **a** ~ **of a...** (*col*) un(e) sacré(e)... .

he'll [hiːl] = **he will, he shall**.

hellish [ˈhɛlɪʃ] a infernal(e).

hello [həˈləu] excl bonjour! ; salut! (to sb one addresses as 'tu') ; (surprise) tiens!

helm [hɛlm] n (NAUT) barre f.

helmet [ˈhɛlmɪt] n casque m.

helmsman [ˈhɛlmzmən] n timonier m.

help [hɛlp] n aide f ; (charwoman) femme f de ménage ; (assistant etc) employé/e // vt aider ; ~! au secours! ; ~ **yourself** (to bread) servez-vous (de pain) ; I can't ~ saying je ne peux pas m'empêcher de dire ; he can't ~ it il n'y peut rien ; ~er n aide m/f, assistant/e ; ~ful a serviable, obligeant(e) ; (useful) utile ; ~ing n portion f ; ~less a impuissant(e) ; faible.

hem [hɛm] n ourlet m // vt ourler ; **to ~ in** vt cerner.

hemisphere [ˈhɛmɪsfɪə*] n hémisphère m.

hemorrhage [ˈhɛmərɪdʒ] n (US) = **haemorrhage**.

hemorrhoids [ˈhɛmərɔɪdz] npl (US) = **haemorrhoids**.

hemp [hɛmp] n chanvre m.

hen [hɛn] n poule f.

hence [hɛns] ad (therefore) d'où, de là ; **2 years ~** d'ici 2 ans ; ~**forth** ad dorénavant.

henchman [ˈhɛntʃmən] n (pej) acolyte m, séide m.

henpecked [ˈhɛnpɛkt] a dominé par sa femme.

her [hə:*] pronoun (direct) la, l' + vowel or h mute ; (indirect) lui ; (stressed, after prep) elle ; see note at **she** // a son(sa), ses pl ; I see ~ je la vois ; give ~ a book donne-lui un livre ; after ~ après elle.

herald [ˈhɛrəld] n héraut m // vt annoncer.

heraldry [ˈhɛrəldrɪ] n héraldique f.

herb [hə:b] n herbe f ; ~s npl (CULIN) fines herbes.

herd [hə:d] n troupeau m // vt: ~**ed together** parqués (comme du bétail).

here [hɪə*] ad ici // excl tiens!, tenez! ; ~! présent! ; ~'s my sister voici ma sœur ; ~ she is la voici ; ~ she comes la voici qui vient ; ~**after** ad après, plus tard ; ci-après // n: the ~**after** l'au-delà m ; ~**by** ad (in letter) par la présente.

hereditary [hɪˈrɛdɪtrɪ] a héréditaire.

heredity [hɪˈrɛdɪtɪ] n hérédité f.

heresy [ˈhɛrəsɪ] n hérésie f.

heretic [ˈhɛrətɪk] n hérétique m/f ; ~**al** [hɪˈrɛtɪkl] a hérétique.

herewith [hɪəˈwɪð] ad avec ceci, ci-joint.

heritage [ˈhɛrɪtɪdʒ] n héritage m.

hermetically [hə:ˈmɛtɪklɪ] ad hermétiquement.

hermit [ˈhə:mɪt] n ermite m.

hernia [ˈhə:nɪə] n hernie f.

hero, ~es [ˈhɪərəu] n héros m ; ~**ic** [hɪˈrəuɪk] a héroïque.

heroin [ˈhɛrəuɪn] n héroïne f.

heroine [ˈhɛrəuɪn] n héroïne f.

heroism [ˈhɛrəuɪzm] n héroïsme m.

heron [ˈhɛrən] n héron m.

herring [ˈhɛrɪŋ] n hareng m.

hers [hə:z] pronoun le(la) sien(ne), les siens(siennes).

herself [hə:ˈsɛlf] pronoun (reflexive) se ; (emphatic) elle-même ; (after prep) elle.

he's [hi:z] = **he is, he has**.

hesitant [ˈhɛzɪtənt] a hésitant(e), indécis(e).

hesitate [ˈhɛzɪteɪt] vi: **to ~** (about/to do) hésiter (sur/à faire) ; **hesitation** [-ˈteɪʃən] n hésitation f.

hessian [ˈhɛsɪən] n toile f de jute.

het up [hɛtˈʌp] a agité(e), excité(e).

hew [hju:] vt tailler (à la hache).

hexagon [ˈhɛksəgən] n hexagone m ; ~**al** [-ˈsægənl] a hexagonal(e).

heyday [ˈheɪdeɪ] n: the ~ of l'âge m d'or de, les beaux jours de.

hi [haɪ] excl salut!

hibernate [ˈhaɪbəneɪt] vi hiberner.

hiccough, hiccup [ˈhɪkʌp] vi hoqueter // n hoquet m ; **to have (the) ~s** avoir le hoquet.

hid [hɪd] pt of **hide**.

hidden [ˈhɪdn] pp of **hide**.

hide [haɪd] n (skin) peau f // vb (pt hid, pp hidden [hɪd, ˈhɪdn]) vt: **to ~ sth (from sb)** cacher qch (à qn) // vi: **to ~ (from sb)** se cacher de qn ; ~-**and-seek** n cache-cache m ; ~**away** n cachette f.

hideous [ˈhɪdɪəs] a hideux(euse) ; atroce.

hiding [ˈhaɪdɪŋ] n (beating) correction f, volée f de coups ; **to be in ~** (concealed) se tenir caché(e) ; ~ **place** n cachette f.

hierarchy [ˈhaɪərɑ:kɪ] n hiérarchie f.

high [haɪ] a haut(e) ; (speed, respect, number) grand(e) ; (price) élevé(e) ; (wind) fort(e), violent(e) ; (voice) aigu(aiguë) // ad haut, en haut ; **20 m** ~ haut(e) de 20 m ; ~**brow** a,n intellectuel(le) ; ~**chair** n chaise haute (pour enfant) ; ~**-flying** a (fig) ambitieux(euse) ; ~**-handed** a très autoritaire ; très cavalier(ère) ; ~**-heeled** a à hauts talons ; ~**jack** = **hijack** ; ~ **jump** n (SPORT) saut m en hauteur ; ~**light** n (fig: of event) point culminant // vt faire ressortir, souligner ; ~**ly** ad très, fort, hautement ; ~**ly strung** a nerveux(euse), toujours tendu(e) ; **H~ Mass** n grand-messe f ; ~**ness** n hauteur f ; **Her H~ness** son Altesse f ; ~**-pitched** a aigu(aiguë) ; ~**-rise block** n tour f (d'habitation).

high school [ˈhaɪsku:l] n lycée m ; (US) établissement m d'enseignement supérieur.

high street [ˈhaɪstri:t] n grand-rue f.

highway [ˈhaɪweɪ] n grand'route f, route nationale.

hijack [ˈhaɪdʒæk] vt détourner (par la force) ; ~**er** n auteur m d'un détournement d'avion, pirate m de l'air.

hike [haɪk] vi aller à pied // n excursion f à pied, randonnée f ; ~**r** n promeneur/euse, excursionniste m/f ; **hiking** n excursions fpl à pied, randonnée f.

hilarious [hɪˈlɛərɪəs] a (behaviour, event) désopilant(e).

hilarity [hɪˈlærɪtɪ] n hilarité f.

hill [hɪl] n colline f ; (fairly high) montagne f ; (on road) côte f ; ~**side** n (flanc m de) coteau m ; ~ **start** n (AUT) démarrage m en côte ; ~**y** a vallonné(e) ; montagneux (euse) ; (road) à fortes côtes.

hilt [hɪlt] n (of sword) garde f.

him [hɪm] pronoun (direct) le, l' + vowel or h mute ; (stressed, indirect, after prep) lui ;

I see ~ je le vois; **give** ~ **a book** donne-lui un livre; **after** ~ après lui; ~**self** *pronoun* (*reflexive*) se; (*emphatic*) lui-même; (*after prep*) lui.

hind [haɪnd] *a* de derrière // *n* biche f.

hinder ['hɪndə*] *vt* gêner; (*delay*) retarder; (*prevent*): **to** ~ **sb from doing** empêcher qn de faire; **hindrance** ['hɪndrəns] *n* gêne f, obstacle m.

Hindu ['hɪndu:] *n* Hindou/e.

hinge [hɪndʒ] *n* charnière f // *vi* (*fig*): **to** ~ **on** dépendre de.

hint [hɪnt] *n* allusion f; (*advice*) conseil m // *vt*: **to** ~ **that** insinuer que // *vi*: **to** ~ **at** faire une allusion à.

hip [hɪp] *n* hanche f; ~ **pocket** *n* poche f revolver.

hippopotamus, *pl* ~**es** *or* **hippopotami** [hɪpə'pɔtəməs, -'pɔtəmaɪ] *n* hippopotame m.

hire ['haɪə*] *vt* (*car*, *equipment*) louer; (*worker*) embaucher, engager // *n* location f; **for** ~ à louer; (*taxi*) libre; ~ **purchase** (**H.P.**) *n* achat m (*or* vente f) à tempérament *or* crédit.

his [hɪz] *pronoun* le(la) sien(ne), les siens(siennes) // *a* son(sa), ses *pl*.

hiss [hɪs] *vi* siffler // *n* sifflement m.

historian [hɪ'stɔ:rɪən] *n* historien/ne.

historic(al) [hɪ'stɔrɪk(l)] *a* historique.

history ['hɪstərɪ] *n* histoire f.

hit [hɪt] *vt* (*pt, pp* **hit**) frapper; (*knock against*) cogner; (*reach: target*) atteindre, toucher; (*collide with: car*) entrer en collision avec, heurter; (*fig: affect*) toucher; (*find*) tomber sur // *n* coup m; (*success*) coup réussi; succès m; (*song*) chanson f à succès, tube m; **to** ~ **it off with sb** bien s'entendre avec qn; ~-**and-run driver** *n* chauffard m; ~-**or-miss** *a* fait(e) au petit bonheur.

hitch [hɪtʃ] *vt* (*fasten*) accrocher, attacher; (*also:* ~ **up**) remonter d'une saccade // *n* (*knot*) nœud m; (*difficulty*) anicroche f, contretemps m; **to** ~ **a lift** faire du stop.

hitch-hike ['hɪtʃhaɪk] *vi* faire de l'auto-stop; ~**r** *n* auto-stoppeur/ euse.

hive [haɪv] *n* ruche f.

H.M.S. *abbr of His(Her) Majesty's Ship*.

hoard [hɔ:d] *n* (*of food*) provisions fpl, réserves fpl; (*of money*) trésor m // *vt* amasser.

hoarding ['hɔ:dɪŋ] *n* panneau m d'affichage *or* publicitaire.

hoarfrost ['hɔ:frɔst] *n* givre m.

hoarse [hɔ:s] *a* enroué(e).

hoax [həuks] *n* canular m.

hob [hɔb] *n* plaque chauffante.

hobble ['hɔbl] *vi* boitiller.

hobby ['hɔbɪ] *n* passe-temps favori; ~-**horse** *n* cheval m à bascule; (*fig*) dada m.

hobo ['həubəu] *n* (*US*) vagabond m.

hock [hɔk] *n* vin m du Rhin.

hockey ['hɔkɪ] *n* hockey m.

hoe [həu] *n* houe f, binette f // *vt* biner, sarcler.

hog [hɔg] *n* sanglier m // *vt* (*fig*) accaparer; **to go the whole** ~ aller jusqu'au bout.

hoist [hɔɪst] *n* palan m // *vt* hisser.

hold [həuld] *vb* (*pt, pp* **held** [held]) *vt* tenir; (*contain*) contenir; (*keep back*) retenir; (*believe*) maintenir; considérer; (*possess*) avoir; détenir // *vi* (*withstand pressure*) tenir (bon); (*be valid*) valoir // *n* prise f; (*fig*) influence f; (*NAUT*) cale f; ~ **the line!** (*TEL*) ne quittez pas!; **to** ~ **one's own** (*fig*) (bien) se défendre; **to catch** *or* **get (a)** ~ **of** saisir; **to get** ~ **of** (*fig*) trouver; **to get** ~ **of o.s.** se contrôler; **to** ~ **back** *vt* retenir; (*secret*) cacher; **to** ~ **down** *vt* (*person*) maintenir à terre; (*job*) occuper; **to** ~ **off** *vt* tenir à distance; **to** ~ **on** *vi* tenir bon; (*wait*) attendre; ~ **on!** (*TEL*) ne quittez pas!; **to** ~ **on to** *vt fus* se cramponner à; (*keep*) conserver, garder; **to** ~ **out** *vt* offrir // *vi* (*resist*) tenir bon; **to** ~ **up** *vt* (*raise*) lever; (*support*) soutenir; (*delay*) retarder; ~**all** *n* fourre-tout m *inv*; ~**er** *n* (*of ticket, record*) détenteur/trice; (*of office, title etc*) titulaire m/f; (*of share*) intérêts mpl; (*farm*) ferme f; ~**ing company** *n* holding m; ~**up** *n* (*robbery*) hold-up m; (*delay*) retard m; (*in traffic*) embouteillage m.

hole [həul] *n* trou m // *vt* trouer, faire un trou dans.

holiday ['hɔlədɪ] *n* vacances fpl; (*day off*) jour m de congé; (*public*) jour férié; ~-**maker** *n* vacancier/ère; ~ **resort** *n* centre m de villégiature *or* de vacances.

holiness ['həulɪnɪs] *n* sainteté f.

Holland ['hɔlənd] *n* Hollande f.

hollow ['hɔləu] *a* creux(euse); (*fig*) faux(fausse) // *n* creux m; (*in land*) dépression f (de terrain), cuvette f // *vt*: **to** ~ **out** creuser, évider.

holly ['hɔlɪ] *n* houx m; ~-**hock** *n* rose trémière.

holster ['həulstə*] *n* étui m de revolver.

holy ['həulɪ] *a* saint(e); (*bread, water*) bénit(e); (*ground*) sacré(e); **H**~ **Ghost** *or* **Spirit** *n* Saint-Esprit m; ~ **orders** npl ordres (majeurs).

homage ['hɔmɪdʒ] *n* hommage m; **to pay** ~ **to** rendre hommage à.

home [həum] *n* foyer m, maison f; (*country*) pays natal, patrie f; (*institution*) maison f // *a* de famille; (*ECON, POL*) national(e), intérieur(e) // *ad* chez soi, à la maison; au pays natal; (*right in: nail etc*) à fond; **at** ~ chez soi, à la maison; **to go** (*or* **come**) ~ rentrer (chez soi), rentrer à la maison (*or* au pays); **make yourself at** ~ faites comme chez vous; **near my** ~ près de chez moi; ~ **address** *n* domicile permanent; ~**land** *n* patrie f; ~**less** *a* sans foyer; sans abri; ~**ly** simple, sans prétention; accueillant(e); ~-**made** *a* fait(e) à la maison; ~ **rule** *n* autonomie f; **H**~ **Secretary** *n* (*Brit*) ministre m de l'Intérieur; ~**sick** *a*: **to be** ~**sick** avoir le mal du pays; s'ennuyer de sa famille; ~ **town** *n* ville natale f; ~**ward** ['həumwəd] *a* (*journey*) du retour; ~**work** *n* devoirs mpl.

homicide ['hɔmɪsaɪd] *n* (*US*) homicide m.

homoeopathy [həumɪ'ɔpəθɪ] *n* homéopathie f.

homogeneous [hɔməu'dʒi:nɪəs] *a* homogène.

homosexual [hɔməu'sɛksjuəl] a,n homosexuel(le).

hone [həun] n pierre f à aiguiser // vt affûter, aiguiser.

honest ['ɔnɪst] a honnête; (sincere) franc(franche); ~**ly** ad honnêtement; franchement; ~**y** n honnêteté f.

honey ['hʌnɪ] n miel m; ~**comb** n rayon m de miel; (pattern) nid m d'abeilles, motif alvéolé; ~**moon** n lune f de miel; (trip) voyage m de noces.

honk [hɔŋk] n (AUT) coup m de klaxon // vi klaxonner.

honorary ['ɔnərərɪ] a honoraire; (duty, title) honorifique.

honour, honor ['ɔnə*] (US) ['ɔnə*] vt honorer // n honneur m; ~**able** a honorable; ~**s degree** n (SCOL) licence avec mention.

hood [hud] n capuchon m; (Brit: AUT) capote f; (US: AUT) capot m; ~**wink** vt tromper.

hoof, ~**s** or **hooves** [hu:f, hu:vz] n sabot m.

hook [huk] n crochet m; (on dress) agrafe f; (for fishing) hameçon m // vt accrocher; (dress) agrafer.

hooligan ['hu:lɪgən] n voyou m.

hoop [hu:p] n cerceau m; (of barrel) cercle m.

hoot [hu:t] vi (AUT) klaxonner; (siren) mugir // vt (jeer at) huer // n huée f; coup m de klaxon; mugissement m; **to ~ with laughter** rire aux éclats; ~**er** n (AUT) klaxon m; (NAUT) sirène f.

hooves [hu:vz] npl of **hoof**.

hop [hɔp] vi sauter; (on one foot) sauter à cloche-pied // n saut m.

hope [həup] vt,vi espérer // n espoir m; **I ~ so** je l'espère; **I ~ not** j'espère que non; ~**ful** a (person) plein(e) d'espoir; (situation) prometteur(euse), encourageant(e); ~**fully** ad avec espoir, avec optimisme; ~**less** a désespéré(e); (useless) nul(le).

hops [hɔps] npl houblon m.

horde [hɔːd] n horde f.

horizon [hə'raɪzn] n horizon m; ~**tal** [hɔrɪ'zɔntl] a horizontal(e).

hormone ['hɔːməun] n hormone f.

horn [hɔːn] n corne f; (MUS) cor m; (AUT) klaxon m; ~**ed** a (animal) à cornes.

hornet ['hɔːnɪt] n frelon m.

horny ['hɔːnɪ] a corné(e); (hands) calleux(euse).

horoscope ['hɔrəskəup] n horoscope m.

horrible ['hɔrɪbl] a horrible, affreux(euse).

horrid ['hɔrɪd] a méchant(e), désagréable.

horrify ['hɔrɪfaɪ] vt horrifier.

horror ['hɔrə*] n horreur f; ~ **film** n film m d'épouvante.

hors d'oeuvre [ɔː'dəːvrə] n hors d'œuvre m.

horse [hɔːs] n cheval m; **on ~back** à cheval; ~ **chestnut** n marron m (d'Inde); ~**drawn** a tiré(e) par des chevaux; ~**man** n cavalier m; ~**power** (h.p.) n puissance f (en chevaux); ~**racing** n courses fpl de chevaux; ~**radish** n raifort m; ~**shoe** n fer m à cheval.

horsy ['hɔːsɪ] a féru(e) d'équitation or de cheval; chevalin(e).

horticulture ['hɔːtɪkʌltʃə*] n horticulture f.

hose [həuz] n (also: ~**pipe**) tuyau m; (also: **garden** ~) tuyau d'arrosage.

hosiery ['həuzɪərɪ] n (in shop) (rayon m des) bas mpl.

hospitable ['hɔspɪtəbl] a hospitalier(ère).

hospital ['hɔspɪtl] n hôpital m; **in** ~ à l'hôpital.

hospitality [hɔspɪ'tælɪtɪ] n hospitalité f.

host [həust] n hôte m; (in hotel etc) patron m; (large number): **a** ~ **of** une foule de; (REL) hostie f.

hostage ['hɔstɪdʒ] n otage m.

hostel ['hɔstl] n foyer m; (**youth**) ~ n auberge f de jeunesse.

hostess ['həustɪs] n hôtesse f.

hostile ['hɔstaɪl] a hostile.

hostility [hɔ'stɪlɪtɪ] n hostilité f.

hot [hɔt] a chaud(e); (as opposed to only warm) très chaud; (spicy) fort(e); (fig) acharné(e); brûlant(e); violent(e), passionné(e); ~ **dog** n hot-dog m.

hotel [həu'tɛl] n hôtel m; ~**ier** n hôtelier/ère.

hot: ~**headed** a impétueux(euse); ~**house** n serre chaude; ~**ly** ad passionnément, violemment; ~-**water bottle** n bouillotte f.

hound [haund] vt poursuivre avec acharnement // n chien courant; **the ~s** la meute.

hour ['auə*] n heure f; ~**ly** a toutes les heures; ~**ly paid** a payé(e) à l'heure.

house n [haus] (pl: ~**s** ['hauzɪz]) (also: firm) maison f; (POL) chambre f; (THEATRE) salle f; auditoire m // vt [hauz] (person) loger, héberger; **the H~** (of Commons) la Chambre des communes; **on the ~** (fig) aux frais de la maison; ~ **arrest** n assignation f à domicile; ~**boat** n bateau (aménagé en habitation); ~**breaking** n cambriolage m (avec effraction); ~**hold** n famille f, ma²sonnée f; ménage m; ~**keeper** n gouvernante f; ~**keeping** n (work) ménage m; ~-**warming party** n pendaison f de crémaillère; ~**wife** n ménagère f; ~**work** n (travaux mpl du) ménage m.

housing ['hauzɪŋ] n logement m; ~ **estate** n cité f, lotissement m; ~ **shortage** n crise f du logement.

hovel ['hɔvl] n taudis m.

hover ['hɔvə*] vi planer; **to ~ round sb** rôder or tourner autour de qn; ~**craft** n aéroglisseur m.

how [hau] ad comment; ~ **are you?** comment allez-vous?; ~ **long have you been here?** depuis combien de temps êtes-vous là?; ~ **lovely!** que or comme c'est joli!; ~ **many/much?** combien?; ~ **many people/much milk** combien de gens/lait; ~ **old are you?** quel âge avez-vous?; ~ **is it that ...?** comment se fait-il que ...? + sub; ~**ever** ad de quelque façon or manière que + sub; (+ adjective) quelque or si ... que + sub; (in questions) comment // cj pourtant, cependant.

howl ['haul] n hurlement m // vi hurler.

howler ['haulə*] n gaffe f, bourde f.

h.p., H.P. see **hire**; **horse**.

HQ abbr of **headquarters**.

hr(s) abbr of **hour(s)**.

hub [hʌb] n (of wheel) moyeu m ; (fig) centre m, foyer m.

hubbub [ˈhʌbʌb] n brouhaha m.

hub cap [ˈhʌbkæp] n enjoliveur m.

huddle [ˈhʌdl] vi: **to ~ together** se blottir les uns contre les autres.

hue [hju:] n teinte f, nuance f ; **~ and cry** n tollé (général), clameur f.

huff [hʌf] n: **in a ~** fâché(e) ; **to take the ~** prendre la mouche.

hug [hʌg] vt serrer dans ses bras ; (shore, kerb) serrer // n étreinte f ; **to give sb a ~** serrer qn dans ses bras.

huge [hju:dʒ] a énorme, immense.

hulk [hʌlk] n (ship) vieux rafiot ; (car etc) carcasse f ; **~ing** a balourd(e).

hull [hʌl] n (of ship, nuts) coque f ; (of peas) cosse f.

hullo [həˈləu] excl = **hello**.

hum [hʌm] vt (tune) fredonner // vi fredonner ; (insect) bourdonner ; (plane, tool) vrombir // n fredonnement m ; bourdonnement m ; vrombissement m.

human [ˈhju:mən] a humain(e) // n être humain.

humane [hju:ˈmeɪn] a humain(e), humanitaire.

humanity [hju:ˈmænɪtɪ] n humanité f.

humble [ˈhʌmbl] a humble, modeste // vt humilier ; **humbly** ad humblement, modestement.

humbug [ˈhʌmbʌg] n fumisterie f ; (sweet) sorte de bonbon à la menthe.

humdrum [ˈhʌmdrʌm] a monotone, routinier(ère).

humid [ˈhju:mɪd] a humide ; **~ity** [-ˈmɪdɪtɪ] n humidité f.

humiliate [hju:ˈmɪlɪeɪt] vt humilier ; **humil'ation** [-ˈeɪʃən] n humiliation f.

humility [hju:ˈmɪlɪtɪ] n humilité f.

humorist [ˈhju:mərɪst] n humoriste m/f.

humorous [ˈhju:mərəs] a humoristique ; (person) plein(e) d'humour.

humour, humor (US) [ˈhju:mə*] n humour m ; (mood) humeur f // vt (person) faire plaisir à ; se prêter aux caprices de.

hump [hʌmp] n bosse f ; **~back** n dos-d'âne m.

hunch [hʌntʃ] n bosse f ; (premonition) intuition f ; **~back** n bossu(e) ; **~ed** a arrondi(e), voûté(e).

hundred [ˈhʌndrəd] num cent ; **~weight** n (Brit) = 50.8 kg ; 112 lb ; (US) = 45.3 kg ; 100 lb.

hung [hʌŋ] pt, pp of **hang**.

Hungarian [hʌŋˈgɛərɪən] a hongrois(e) // n Hongrois/e ; (LING) hongrois m.

Hungary [ˈhʌŋgərɪ] n Hongrie f.

hunger [ˈhʌŋgə*] n faim f // vi: **to ~ for** avoir faim de, désirer ardemment.

hungrily [ˈhʌŋgrəlɪ] ad voracement ; (fig) avidement.

hungry [ˈhʌŋgrɪ] a affamé(e) ; **to be ~** avoir faim.

hunt [hʌnt] vt (seek) chercher // vi chasser // n chasse f ; **~er** n chasseur m ; **~ing** n chasse f.

hurdle [ˈhə:dl] n (for fences) claie f ; (SPORT) haie f ; (fig) obstacle m.

hurl [hə:l] vt lancer (avec violence).

hurrah, hurray [huˈrɑ:, huˈreɪ] n hourra m.

hurricane [ˈhʌrɪkən] n ouragan m.

hurried [ˈhʌrɪd] a pressé(e), précipité(e) ; (work) fait(e) à la hâte ; **~ly** ad précipitamment, à la hâte.

hurry [ˈhʌrɪ] n hâte f, précipitation f // vi se presser, se dépêcher // vt (person) faire presser, faire se dépêcher ; (work) presser ; **to be in a ~** être pressé(e) ; **to do sth in a ~** faire qch en vitesse ; **to ~ in/out** entrer/sortir précipitamment.

hurt [hə:t] vb (pt, pp hurt) vt (cause pain to) faire mal à ; (injure, fig) blesser // vi faire mal // a blessé(e) ; **~ful** a (remark) blessant(e).

hurtle [ˈhə:tl] vt lancer (de toutes ses forces) // vi: **to ~ past** passer en trombe ; **to ~ down** dégringoler.

husband [ˈhʌzbənd] n mari m.

hush [hʌʃ] n calme m, silence m // vt faire taire ; **~!** chut!

husk [hʌsk] n (of wheat) balle f ; (of rice, maize) enveloppe f ; (of peas) cosse f.

husky [ˈhʌskɪ] a rauque ; (burly) costaud(e) // n chien m esquimau or de traîneau.

hustle [ˈhʌsl] vt pousser, bousculer // n bousculade f ; **~ and bustle** n tourbillon m (d'activité).

hut [hʌt] n hutte f ; (shed) cabane f ; (MIL) baraquement m.

hutch [hʌtʃ] n clapier m.

hyacinth [ˈhaɪəsɪnθ] n jacinthe f.

hybrid [ˈhaɪbrɪd] a, n hybride (m).

hydrant [ˈhaɪdrənt] n prise f d'eau ; (also: fire ~) bouche f d'incendie.

hydraulic [haɪˈdrɔ:lɪk] a hydraulique.

hydroelectric [haɪdrəuˈlɛktrɪk] a hydro-électrique.

hydrogen [ˈhaɪdrədʒən] n hydrogène m.

hyena [haɪˈi:nə] n hyène f.

hygiene [ˈhaɪdʒi:n] n hygiène f.

hygienic [haɪˈdʒi:nɪk] a hygiénique.

hymn [hɪm] n hymne m ; cantique m.

hyphen [ˈhaɪfn] n trait m d'union.

hypnosis [hɪpˈnəusɪs] n hypnose f.

hypnotism [ˈhɪpnətɪzm] n hypnotisme m.

hypnotist [ˈhɪpnətɪst] n hypnotiseur/euse.

hypnotize [ˈhɪpnətaɪz] vt hypnotiser.

hypocrisy [hɪˈpɔkrɪsɪ] n hypocrisie f.

hypocrite [ˈhɪpəkrɪt] n hypocrite m/f ; **hypocritical** [-ˈkrɪtɪkl] a hypocrite.

hypothesis, pl hypotheses [haɪˈpɔθɪsɪs, -sɪ:z] n hypothèse f.

hypothetic(al) [haɪpəuˈθɛtɪk(l)] a hypothétique.

hysteria [hɪˈstɪərɪə] n hystérie f.

hysterical [hɪˈstɛrɪkl] a hystérique ; **to become ~** avoir une crise de nerfs.

hysterics [hɪˈstɛrɪks] npl (violente) crise de nerfs ; (laughter) crise de rire.

I

I [aɪ] pronoun je ; (before vowel) j' ; (stressed) moi.

ice [aɪs] n glace f ; (on road) verglas m // vt (cake) glacer ; (drink) faire rafraîchir //

vi (*also*: ~ **over**) geler ; (*also*: ~ **up**) se givrer ; ~ **axe** *n* piolet *m* ; ~**berg** *n* iceberg *m* ; ~**box** *n* (*US*) réfrigérateur *m* ; (*Brit*) compartiment *m* à glace ; (*insulated box*) glacière *f* ; ~**-cold** *a* glacé(e) ; ~ **cream** *n* glace *f* ; ~ **cube** *n* glaçon *m* ; ~ **hockey** *n* hockey *m* sur glace.

Iceland ['aɪslənd] *n* Islande *f* ; ~**er** *n* Islandais/e ; ~**ic** [-'lændɪk] *a* islandais(e) // *n* (*LING*) islandais *m*.

ice rink ['aɪsrɪŋk] *n* patinoire *f*.

icicle ['aɪsɪkl] *n* glaçon *m* (*naturel*).

icing ['aɪsɪŋ] *n* (*AVIAT etc*) givrage *m* ; (*CULIN*) glaçage *m* ; ~ **sugar** *n* sucre *m* glace.

icon ['aɪkɔn] *n* icône *f*.

icy ['aɪsɪ] *a* glacé(e) ; (*road*) verglacé(e) ; (*weather, temperature*) glacial(e).

I'd [aɪd] = **I would, I had.**

idea [aɪ'dɪə] *n* idée *f*.

ideal [aɪ'dɪəl] *n* idéal *m* // *a* idéal(e) ; ~**ist** *n* idéaliste *m/f*.

identical [aɪ'dɛntɪkl] *a* identique.

identification [aɪdɛntɪfɪ'keɪʃən] *n* identification *f* ; **means of ~** pièce *f* d'identité.

identify [aɪ'dɛntɪfaɪ] *vt* identifier.

identity [aɪ'dɛntɪtɪ] *n* identité *f*.

ideology [aɪdɪ'ɔlədʒɪ] *n* idéologie *f*.

idiocy ['ɪdɪəsɪ] *n* idiotie *f*, stupidité *f*.

idiom ['ɪdɪəm] *n* langue *f*, idiome *m* ; (*phrase*) expression *f* idiomatique.

idiosyncrasy [ɪdɪəu'sɪŋkrəsɪ] *n* particularité *f*, caractéristique *f*.

idiot ['ɪdɪət] *n* idiot/e, imbécile *m/f* ; ~**ic** [-'ɔtɪk] *a* idiot(e), bête, stupide.

idle ['aɪdl] *a* sans occupation, désœuvré(e) ; (*lazy*) oisif(ive), paresseux(euse) ; (*unemployed*) au chômage ; (*machinery*) au repos ; (*question, pleasures*) vain(e), futile ; **to lie ~** être arrêté, ne pas fonctionner ; ~**ness** *n* désœuvrement *m* ; oisiveté *f* ; ~**r** *n* désœuvré/e ; oisif/ive.

idol ['aɪdl] *n* idole *f* ; ~**ize** *vt* idolâtrer, adorer.

idyllic [ɪ'dɪlɪk] *a* idyllique.

i.e. *ad* (*abbr of id est*) c'est-à-dire.

if [ɪf] *cj* si.

igloo ['ɪglu:] *n* igloo *m*.

ignite [ɪg'naɪt] *vt* mettre le feu à, enflammer // *vi* s'enflammer.

ignition [ɪg'nɪʃən] *n* (*AUT*) allumage *m* ; **to switch on/off the ~** mettre/couper le contact ; ~ **key** *n* (*AUT*) clé *f* de contact.

ignoramus [ɪgnə'reɪməs] *n* personne *f* ignare.

ignorance ['ɪgnərəns] *n* ignorance *f*.

ignorant ['ɪgnərənt] *a* ignorant(e).

ignore [ɪg'nɔ:*] *vt* ne tenir aucun compte de, ne pas relever ; (*person*) faire semblant de ne pas reconnaître, ignorer ; (*fact*) méconnaître.

ikon ['aɪkɔn] *n* = **icon**.

I'll [aɪl] = **I will, I shall**.

ill [ɪl] *a* (*sick*) malade ; (*bad*) mauvais(e) // *n* mal *m* ; **to take** *or* **be taken ~** tomber malade ; ~**-advised** *a* (*decision*) peu judicieux(euse) ; (*person*) malavisé(e) ; ~**at-ease** *a* mal à l'aise.

illegal [ɪ'li:gl] *a* illégal(e) ; ~**ly** *ad* illégalement.

illegible [ɪ'lɛdʒɪbl] *a* illisible.

illegitimate [ɪlɪ'dʒɪtɪmət] *a* illégitime.

ill-fated [ɪl'feɪtɪd] *a* malheureux(euse) ; (*day*) néfaste.

ill feeling [ɪl'fi:lɪŋ] *n* ressentiment *m*, rancune *f*.

illicit [ɪ'lɪsɪt] *a* illicite.

illiterate [ɪ'lɪtərət] *a* illettré(e) ; (*letter*) plein(e) de fautes.

ill-mannered [ɪl'mænəd] *a* impoli(e), grossier(ère).

illness ['ɪlnɪs] *n* maladie *f*.

illogical [ɪ'lɔdʒɪkl] *a* illogique.

ill-treat [ɪl'tri:t] *vt* maltraiter.

illuminate [ɪ'lu:mɪneɪt] *vt* (*room, street*) éclairer ; (*building*) illuminer ; ~**d sign** *n* enseigne lumineuse ; **illumination** [-'neɪʃən] *n* éclairage *m* ; illumination *f*.

illusion [ɪ'lu:ʒən] *n* illusion *f* ; **to be under the ~ that** s'imaginer *or* croire que.

illusive, illusory [ɪ'lu:sɪv, ɪ'lu:sərɪ] *a* illusoire.

illustrate ['ɪləstreɪt] *vt* illustrer ; **illustration** [-'streɪʃən] *n* illustration *f*.

illustrious [ɪ'lʌstrɪəs] *a* illustre.

ill will [ɪl'wɪl] *n* malveillance *f*.

I'm [aɪm] = **I am**.

image ['ɪmɪdʒ] *n* image *f* ; (*public face*) image de marque ; ~**ry** *n* images *fpl*.

imaginary [ɪ'mædʒɪnərɪ] *a* imaginaire.

imagination [ɪmædʒɪ'neɪʃən] *n* imagination *f*.

imaginative [ɪ'mædʒɪnətɪv] *a* imaginatif(ive) ; plein(e) d'imagination.

imagine [ɪ'mædʒɪn] *vt* s'imaginer ; (*suppose*) imaginer, supposer.

imbalance [ɪm'bæləns] *n* déséquilibre *m*.

imbecile ['ɪmbəsi:l] *n* imbécile *m/f*.

imbue [ɪm'bju:] *vt*: **to ~ sth with** imprégner qch de.

imitate ['ɪmɪteɪt] *vt* imiter ; **imitation** [-'teɪʃən] *n* imitation *f* ; **imitator** *n* imitateur/trice.

immaculate [ɪ'mækjulət] *a* impeccable ; (*REL*) immaculé(e).

immaterial [ɪmə'tɪərɪəl] *a* sans importance, insignifiant(e).

immature [ɪmə'tjuə*] *a* (*fruit*) qui n'est pas mûr(e) ; (*person*) qui manque de maturité.

immediate [ɪ'mi:dɪət] *a* immédiat(e) ; ~**ly** *ad* (*at once*) immédiatement ; ~**ly next to** juste à côté de.

immense [ɪ'mɛns] *a* immense ; énorme.

immerse [ɪ'mə:s] *vt* immerger, plonger ; **to ~ sth in** plonger qch dans.

immersion heater [ɪ'mə:ʃnhi:tə*] *n* chauffe-eau *m* électrique.

immigrant ['ɪmɪgrənt] *n* immigrant/e ; immigré/e.

immigration [ɪmɪ'greɪʃən] *n* immigration *f*.

imminent ['ɪmɪnənt] *a* imminent(e).

immobilize [ɪ'məubɪlaɪz] *vt* immobiliser.

immoderate [ɪ'mɔdərət] *a* immodéré(e), démesuré(e).

immoral [ɪ'mɔrl] *a* immoral(e) ; ~**ity** [-'rælɪtɪ] *n* immoralité *f*.

immortal [ɪ'mɔ:tl] *a, n* immortel(le) ; ~**ize** *vt* immortaliser.

immune [ɪ'mjuːn] a: ~ **(to)** immunisé(e)
(contre).

immunization [ɪmjunaɪ'zeɪʃən] n
immunisation f.

immunize ['ɪmjunaɪz] vt immuniser.

impact ['ɪmpækt] n choc m, impact m;
(fig) impact.

impair [ɪm'pɛə*] vt détériorer, diminuer.

impale [ɪm'peɪl] vt empaler.

impartial [ɪm'pɑːʃl] a impartial(e); ~**ity**
[ɪmpɑːʃɪ'ælɪtɪ] n impartialité f.

impassable [ɪm'pɑːsəbl] a infranchissable; (road) impraticable.

impassioned [ɪm'pæʃənd] a passionné(e).

impatience [ɪm'peɪʃəns] n impatience f.

impatient [ɪm'peɪʃənt] a impatient(e).

impeach [ɪm'piːtʃ] vt accuser, attaquer;
(public official) mettre en accusation.

impeccable [ɪm'pɛkəbl] a impeccable,
parfait(e).

impede [ɪm'piːd] vt gêner.

impediment [ɪm'pɛdɪmənt] n obstacle m;
(also: **speech** ~) défaut m d'élocution.

impending [ɪm'pɛndɪŋ] a imminent(e).

impenetrable [ɪm'pɛnɪtrəbl] a impénétrable.

imperative [ɪm'pɛrətɪv] a nécessaire;
urgent(e), pressant(e); (voice)
impérieux(euse) // n (LING) impératif m.

imperceptible [ɪmpə'sɛptɪbl] a imperceptible.

imperfect [ɪm'pəːfɪkt] a imparfait(e);
(goods etc) défectueux(euse) // n (LING:
also: ~ **tense**) imparfait m; ~**ion**
[-'fɛkʃən] n imperfection f, défectuosité f.

imperial [ɪm'pɪərɪəl] a impérial(e);
(measure) légal(e); ~**ism** n impérialisme
m.

imperil [ɪm'pɛrɪl] vt mettre en péril.

impersonal [ɪm'pəːsənl] a imper-
sonnel(le).

impersonate [ɪm'pəːsəneɪt] vt se faire
passer pour; (THEATRE) imiter;
impersonation [-'neɪʃən] n (LAW)
usurpation f d'identité; (THEATRE) imitation
f.

impertinent [ɪm'pəːtɪnənt] a imper-
tinent(e), insolent(e).

impervious [ɪm'pəːvɪəs] a imperméable;
(fig): ~ **to** insensible à; inaccessible à.

impetuous [ɪm'pɛtjuəs] a impé-
tueux(euse), fougueux(euse).

impetus ['ɪmpətəs] n impulsion f; (of
runner) élan m.

impinge [ɪm'pɪndʒ]: **to** ~ **on** vt fus
(person) affecter, toucher; (rights)
empiéter sur.

implausible [ɪm'plɔːzɪbl] a peu plausible.

implement n ['ɪmplɪmənt] outil m,
instrument m; (for cooking) ustensile m //
vt ['ɪmplɪmɛnt] exécuter, mettre à effet.

implicate ['ɪmplɪkeɪt] vt impliquer,
compromettre; **implication** [-'keɪʃən] n
implication f.

implicit [ɪm'plɪsɪt] a implicite; (complete)
absolu(e), sans réserve.

implore [ɪm'plɔː*] vt implorer, supplier.

imply [ɪm'plaɪ] vt suggérer, laisser
entendre; indiquer, supposer.

impolite [ɪmpə'laɪt] a impoli(e).

imponderable [ɪm'pɒndərəbl] a
impondérable.

import vt [ɪm'pɔːt] importer // n ['ɪmpɔːt]
(COMM) importation f; (meaning) portée f,
signification f.

importance [ɪm'pɔːtns] n importance f.

important [ɪm'pɔːtnt] a important(e).

importation [ɪmpɔː'teɪʃən] n importation
f.

imported [ɪm'pɔːtɪd] a importé(e),
d'importation.

importer [ɪm'pɔːtə*] n importateur/trice.

impose [ɪm'pəuz] vt imposer // vi: **to** ~
on sb abuser de la gentillesse (or crédulité)
de qn.

imposing [ɪm'pəuzɪŋ] a imposant(e),
impressionnant(e).

impossibility [ɪmpɒsə'bɪlɪtɪ] n impossibilité f.

impossible [ɪm'pɒsɪbl] a impossible.

impostor [ɪm'pɒstə*] n imposteur m.

impotence ['ɪmpətns] n impuissance f.

impotent ['ɪmpətnt] a impuissant(e).

impound [ɪm'paund] vt confisquer, saisir.

impoverished [ɪm'pɒvərɪʃt] a pauvre,
appauvri(e).

impracticable [ɪm'præktɪkəbl] a impraticable.

impractical [ɪm'præktɪkl] a pas pratique;
(person) qui manque d'esprit pratique.

imprecise [ɪmprɪ'saɪs] a imprécis(e).

impregnable [ɪm'prɛgnəbl] a (fortress)
imprenable; (fig) inattaquable; irréfutable.

impregnate ['ɪmprɛgneɪt] vt imprégner;
(fertilize) féconder.

impresario [ɪmprɪ'sɑːrɪəu] n impresario m.

impress [ɪm'prɛs] vt impressionner, faire
impression sur; (mark) imprimer,
marquer; **to** ~ **sth on sb** faire bien
comprendre qch à qn.

impression [ɪm'prɛʃən] n impression f;
(of stamp, seal) empreinte f; **to be under
the** ~ **that** avoir l'impression que; ~**able**
a impressionable, sensible; ~**ist** n
impressionniste m/f.

impressive [ɪm'prɛsɪv] a impression-
nant(e).

imprinted [ɪm'prɪntɪd] a: ~ **on**
imprimé(e) sur; (fig) imprimé(e) or
gravé(e) dans.

imprison [ɪm'prɪzn] vt emprisonner,
mettre en prison; ~**ment** n
emprisonnement m.

improbable [ɪm'prɒbəbl] a improbable;
(excuse) peu plausible.

impromptu [ɪm'prɒmptjuː] a
impromptu(e).

improper [ɪm'prɒpə*] a incorrect(e);
(unsuitable) déplacé(e), de mauvais goût;
indécent(e); **impropriety** [ɪmprə'praɪətɪ] n
inconvenance f; (of expression) impropriété f.

improve [ɪm'pruːv] vt améliorer // vi
s'améliorer; (pupil etc) faire des progrès;
~**ment** n amélioration f, progrès m.

improvisation [ɪmprəvaɪ'zeɪʃən] n
improvisation f.

improvise ['ɪmprəvaɪz] vt,vi improviser.

imprudence [ɪm'pruːdns] n imprudence f.

imprudent [ɪm'pruːdnt] a imprudent(e).

impudent ['ɪmpjudnt] *a* impudent(e).
impulse ['ɪmpʌls] *n* impulsion *f*.
impulsive [ɪm'pʌlsɪv] *a* impulsif(ive).
impunity [ɪm'pjuːnɪtɪ] *n* impunité *f*.
impure [ɪm'pjuə*] *a* impur(e).
impurity [ɪm'pjuərɪtɪ] *n* impureté *f*.
in [ɪn] *prep* dans ; (*with time: during, within*):
~ **May/2 days** en mai/2 jours ; (: *after*):
~ **2 weeks** dans 2 semaines ; (*with substance*) en ; (*with town*) à ; (*with country*):
it's ~ **France/Portugal** c'est en
France/au Portugal // *ad* dedans, à
l'intérieur ; (*fashionable*) à la mode ; **is he**
~? est-il là? ; ~ **the country** à la
campagne ; ~ **town** en ville ; ~ **the sun**
au soleil ; ~ **the rain** sous la pluie ; ~
French en français ; **a man** ~ 10 un
homme sur 10 ; ~ **hundreds** par
centaines ; **the best pupil** ~ **the class** le
meilleur élève de la classe ; ~ **saying this**
en disant ceci ; **their party is** ~ leur parti
est au pouvoir ; **to ask sb** ~ inviter qn
à entrer ; **to run/limp** *etc* ~ entrer en
courant/boitant *etc* ; **the** ~**s and outs of**
les tenants et aboutissants de.
in., ins *abbr of* **inch(es)**.
inability [ɪnə'bɪlɪtɪ] *n* incapacité *f*.
inaccessible [ɪnæk'sɛsɪbl] *a* inaccessible.
inaccuracy [ɪn'ækjurəsɪ] *n* inexactitude
f ; manque *m* de précision.
inaccurate [ɪn'ækjurət] *a* inexact(e) ;
(*person*) qui manque de précision.
inaction [ɪn'ækʃən] *n* inaction *f*, inactivité
f.
inactivity [ɪnæk'tɪvɪtɪ] *n* inactivité *f*.
inadequacy [ɪn'ædɪkwəsɪ] *n* insuffisance
f.
inadequate [ɪn'ædɪkwət] *a* insuffisant(e),
inadéquat(e).
inadvertently [ɪnəd'vɜːtntlɪ] *ad* par
mégarde.
inadvisable [ɪnəd'vaɪzəbl] *a* à
déconseiller ; **it is** ~ **to** il est déconseillé
de.
inane [ɪ'neɪn] *a* inepte, stupide.
inanimate [ɪn'ænɪmət] *a* inanimé(e).
inappropriate [ɪnə'prəʊprɪət] *a*
inopportun(e), mal à propos ; (*word,*
expression) impropre.
inapt [ɪn'æpt] *a* inapte ; peu approprié(e) ;
~**itude** *n* inaptitude *f*.
inarticulate [ɪnɑː'tɪkjulət] *a* (*a person*) qui
s'exprime mal ; (*speech*) indistinct(e).
inasmuch as [ɪnəz'mʌtʃæz] *ad* dans la
mesure où ; (*seeing that*) attendu que.
inattention [ɪnə'tɛnʃən] *n* manque *m*
d'attention.
inattentive [ɪnə'tɛntɪv] *a* inattentif(ive),
distrait(e) ; négligent(e).
inaudible [ɪn'ɔːdɪbl] *a* inaudible.
inaugural [ɪ'nɔːgjurəl] *a* inaugural(e).
inaugurate [ɪ'nɔːgjureɪt] *vt* inaugurer ;
(*president, official*) investir de ses
fonctions ; **inauguration** [-'reɪʃən] *n*
inauguration *f* ; investiture *f*.
in-between [ɪnbɪ'twiːn] *a* entre les deux.
inborn [ɪn'bɔːn] *a* (*feeling*) inné(e) ; (*defect*)
congénital(e).
inbred [ɪn'brɛd] *a* inné(e), naturel(le) ;
(*family*) consanguin(e).

inbreeding [ɪn'briːdɪŋ] *n* croisement *m*
d'animaux de même souche ; unions
consanguines.
Inc. *abbr see* **incorporated**.
incalculable [ɪn'kælkjuləbl] *a*
incalculable.
incapability [ɪnkeɪpə'bɪlɪtɪ] *n* incapacité *f*.
incapable [ɪn'keɪpəbl] *a* incapable.
incapacitate [ɪnkə'pæsɪteɪt] *vt*: **to** ~ **sb**
from doing rendre qn incapable de faire ;
~**d** *a* (*LAW*) frappé(e) d'incapacité.
incapacity [ɪnkə'pæsɪtɪ] *n* incapacité *f*.
incarcerate [ɪn'kɑːsəreɪt] *vt* incarcérer.
incarnate *a* [ɪn'kɑːnɪt] incarné(e) // *vt*
['ɪnkɑːneɪt] incarner ; **incarnation**
[-'neɪʃən] *n* incarnation *f*.
incendiary [ɪn'sɛndɪərɪ] *a* incendiaire.
incense *n* ['ɪnsɛns] encens *m* // *vt* [ɪn'sɛns]
(*anger*) mettre en colère ; ~ **burner** *n*
encensoir *m*.
incentive [ɪn'sɛntɪv] *n* encouragement *m*,
raison *f* de se donner de la peine ; ~ **bonus**
n prime *f* d'encouragement.
incessant [ɪn'sɛsnt] *a* incessant(e) ; ~**ly**
ad sans cesse, constamment.
incest ['ɪnsɛst] *n* inceste *m*.
inch [ɪntʃ] *n* pouce *m* (= 25 *mm*; 12 *in a*
foot) ; **within an** ~ **of** à deux doigts de ;
~ **tape** *n* centimètre *m* (de couturière).
incidence ['ɪnsɪdns] *n* (*of crime, disease*)
fréquence *f*.
incident ['ɪnsɪdnt] *n* incident *m* ; (*in book*)
péripétie *f*.
incidental [ɪnsɪ'dɛntl] *a* accessoire ;
(*unplanned*) accidentel(le) ; ~ **to** qui
accompagne ; ~ **expenses** *npl* faux frais
mpl ; ~**ly** [-'dɛntlɪ] *ad* (*by the way*) à
propos.
incinerator [ɪn'sɪnəreɪtə*] *n* incinérateur
m.
incipient [ɪn'sɪpɪənt] *a* naissant(e).
incision [ɪn'sɪʒən] *n* incision *f*.
incisive [ɪn'saɪsɪv] *a* incisif(ive) ;
mordant(e).
incite [ɪn'saɪt] *vt* inciter, pousser.
inclement [ɪn'klɛmənt] *a* inclément(e),
rigoureux(euse).
inclination [ɪnklɪ'neɪʃən] *n* inclination *f*.
incline *n* ['ɪnklaɪn] pente *f*, plan incliné //
vb [ɪn'klaɪn] *vt* incliner // *vi*: **to** ~ **to** avoir
tendance à ; **to be** ~**d to do** être enclin(e)
à faire ; avoir tendance à faire ; **to be well**
~**d towards sb** être bien disposé(e) à
l'égard de qn.
include [ɪn'kluːd] *vt* inclure, comprendre ;
including *prep* y compris.
inclusion [ɪn'kluːʒən] *n* inclusion *f*.
inclusive [ɪn'kluːsɪv] *a* inclus(e),
compris(e) ; ~ **terms** *npl* prix tout
compris.
incognito [ɪnkɒg'niːtəʊ] *ad* incognito.
incoherent [ɪnkəʊ'hɪərənt] *a*
incohérent(e).
income ['ɪnkʌm] *n* revenu *m* ; ~ **tax** *n*
impôt *m* sur le revenu ; ~ **tax inspector** *n*
inspecteur *m* des contributions directes ;
~ **tax return** *n* déclaration *f* des revenus.
incoming ['ɪnkʌmɪŋ] *a*: ~ **tide** *n* marée
montante.
incompatible [ɪnkəm'pætɪbl] *a* incompatible.

incompetence [ɪnˈkɒmpɪtns] *n* incompétence *f*, incapacité *f*.
incompetent [ɪnˈkɒmpɪtnt] *a* incompétent(e), incapable.
incomplete [ɪnkəmˈpliːt] *a* incomplet(ète).
incomprehensible [ɪnkɒmprɪˈhɛnsɪbl] *a* incompréhensible.
inconclusive [ɪnkənˈkluːsɪv] *a* peu concluant(e); (*argument*) peu convaincant(e).
incongruous [ɪnˈkɒngruəs] *a* peu approprié(e); (*remark, act*) incongru(e), déplacé(e).
inconsequential [ɪnkɒnsɪˈkwɛnʃl] *a* sans importance.
inconsiderate [ɪnkənˈsɪdərət] *a* (*action*) inconsidéré(e); (*person*) qui manque d'égards.
inconsistent [ɪnkənˈsɪstnt] *a* sans cohérence; peu logique; qui présente des contradictions; ~ **with** en contradiction avec.
inconspicuous [ɪnkənˈspɪkjuəs] *a* qui passe inaperçu(e); (*colour, dress*) discret(ète); **to make o.s.** ~ ne pas se faire remarquer.
inconstant [ɪnˈkɒnstnt] *a* inconstant(e); variable.
incontinence [ɪnˈkɒntɪnəns] *n* incontinence *f*.
incontinent [ɪnˈkɒntɪnənt] *a* incontinent(e).
inconvenience [ɪnkənˈviːnjəns] *n* inconvénient *m*; (*trouble*) dérangement *m* // *vt* déranger.
inconvenient [ɪnkənˈviːnjənt] *a* malcommode; (*time, place*) mal choisi(e), qui ne convient pas.
incorporate [ɪnˈkɔːpəreɪt] *vt* incorporer; (*contain*) contenir // *vi* fusionner; (*two firms*) se constituer en société; ~**d** *a*: ~**d company** (*US, abbr* **Inc.**) société *f* anonyme (S.A.).
incorrect [ɪnkəˈrɛkt] *a* incorrect(e); (*opinion, statement*) inexact(e).
incorruptible [ɪnkəˈrʌptɪbl] *a* incorruptible.
increase *n* [ˈɪnkriːs] augmentation *f* // *vi, vt* [ɪnˈkriːs] augmenter.
increasing [ɪnˈkriːsɪŋ] *a* (*number*) croissant(e); ~**ly** *ad* de plus en plus.
incredible [ɪnˈkrɛdɪbl] *a* incroyable.
incredulous [ɪnˈkrɛdjuləs] *a* incrédule.
increment [ˈɪnkrɪmənt] *n* augmentation *f*.
incriminate [ɪnˈkrɪmɪneɪt] *vt* incriminer, compromettre.
incubation [ɪnkjuˈbeɪʃən] *n* incubation *f*.
incubator [ˈɪnkjubeɪtə*] *n* incubateur *m*; (*for babies*) couveuse *f*.
incur [ɪnˈkəː*] *vt* (*expenses*) encourir; (*anger, risk*) s'exposer à; (*debt*) contracter; (*loss*) subir.
incurable [ɪnˈkjuərəbl] *a* incurable.
incursion [ɪnˈkəːʃən] *n* incursion *f*.
indebted [ɪnˈdɛtɪd] *a*: **to be** ~ **to sb** (**for**) être redevable à qn (de).
indecent [ɪnˈdiːsnt] *a* indécent(e), inconvenant(e); ~ **assault** *n* attentat *m* à la pudeur; ~ **exposure** *n* outrage *m* (public) à la pudeur.
indecision [ɪndɪˈsɪʒən] *n* indécision *f*.

indecisive [ɪndɪˈsaɪsɪv] *a* indécis(e); (*discussion*) peu concluant(e).
indeed [ɪnˈdiːd] *ad* en effet; vraiment; **yes** ~! certainement!
indefinable [ɪndɪˈfaɪnəbl] *a* indéfinissable.
indefinite [ɪnˈdɛfɪnɪt] *a* indéfini(e); (*answer*) vague; (*period, number*) indéterminé(e); ~**ly** *ad* (*wait*) indéfiniment; (*speak*) vaguement, avec imprécision.
indelible [ɪnˈdɛlɪbl] *a* indélébile.
indemnify [ɪnˈdɛmnɪfaɪ] *vt* indemniser, dédommager.
indentation [ɪndɛnˈteɪʃən] *n* découpure *f*; (*TYP*) alinéa *m*; (*on metal*) bosse *f*.
independence [ɪndɪˈpɛndns] *n* indépendance *f*.
independent [ɪndɪˈpɛndnt] *a* indépendant(e); ~**ly** *ad* de façon indépendante; ~**ly of** indépendamment de.
indescribable [ɪndɪˈskraɪbəbl] *a* indescriptible.
index [ˈɪndɛks] *n* (*pl*: ~**es**: *in book*) index *m*; (: *in library etc*) catalogue *m*; (*pl*: **indices** [ˈɪndɪsiːz]: *ratio, sign*) indice *m*; ~ **card** *n* fiche *f*; ~ **finger** *n* index *m*; ~-**linked** *a* indexé(e) (sur le coût de la vie *etc*).
India [ˈɪndɪə] *n* Inde *f*; ~**n** *a* indien(ne) // *n* Indien/ne; ~**n ink** *n* encre *f* de Chine; ~**n Ocean** *n* océan Indien; ~ **paper** *n* papier *m* bible.
indicate [ˈɪndɪkeɪt] *vt* indiquer; **indication** [-ˈkeɪʃən] *n* indication *f*, signe *m*.
indicative [ɪnˈdɪkətɪv] *a* indicatif(ive) // *n* (*LING*) indicatif *m*.
indicator [ˈɪndɪkeɪtə*] *n* (*sign*) indicateur *m*; (*AUT*) clignotant *m*.
indices [ˈɪndɪsiːz] *npl of* **index**.
indict [ɪnˈdaɪt] *vt* accuser; ~**able** *a* (*person*) passible de poursuites; ~**able offence** *n* délit pénal; ~**ment** *n* accusation *f*.
indifference [ɪnˈdɪfrəns] *n* indifférence *f*.
indifferent [ɪnˈdɪfrənt] *a* indifférent(e); (*poor*) médiocre, quelconque.
indigenous [ɪnˈdɪdʒɪnəs] *a* indigène.
indigestible [ɪndɪˈdʒɛstɪbl] *a* indigeste.
indigestion [ɪndɪˈdʒɛstʃən] *n* indigestion *f*, mauvaise digestion.
indignant [ɪnˈdɪgnənt] *a*: ~ (**at sth/with sb**) indigné(e) (de qch/contre qn).
indignation [ɪndɪgˈneɪʃən] *n* indignation *f*.
indignity [ɪnˈdɪgnɪtɪ] *n* indignité *f*, affront *m*.
indigo [ˈɪndɪgəu] *a* indigo *inv* // *n* indigo *m*.
indirect [ɪndɪˈrɛkt] *a* indirect(e); ~**ly** *ad* indirectement. /
indiscreet [ɪndɪˈskriːt] *a* indiscret(ète); (*rash*) imprudent(e).
indiscretion [ɪndɪˈskrɛʃən] *n* indiscrétion *f*; imprudence *f*.
indiscriminate [ɪndɪˈskrɪmɪnət] *a* (*person*) qui manque de discernement; (*admiration*) aveugle; (*killings*) commis(e) au hasard.
indispensable [ɪndɪˈspɛnsəbl] *a* indispensable.
indisposed [ɪndɪˈspəuzd] *a* (*unwell*) indisposé(e), souffrant(e).

indisposition [ɪndɪspə'zɪʃən] *n* (*illness*) indisposition *f*, malaise *m*.
indisputable [ɪndɪ'spjuːtəbl] *a* incontestable, indiscutable.
indistinct [ɪndɪ'stɪŋkt] *a* indistinct(e); (*memory, noise*) vague.
individual [ɪndɪ'vɪdjuəl] *n* individu *m* // *a* individuel(le); (*characteristic*) particulier(ère), original(e); **~ist** *n* individualiste *m/f*; **~ity** [-'ælɪtɪ] *n* individualité *f*; **~ly** *ad* individuellement.
indoctrinate [ɪn'dɔktrɪneɪt] *vt* endoctriner; **indoctrination** [-'neɪʃən] *n* endoctrinement *m*.
indolent ['ɪndələnt] *a* indolent(e), nonchalant(e).
indoor ['ɪndɔː*] *a* d'intérieur; (*plant*) d'appartement; (*swimming-pool*) couvert(e); (*sport, games*) pratiqué(e) en salle; **~s** [ɪn'dɔːz] *ad* à l'intérieur; (*at home*) à la maison.
indubitable [ɪn'djuːbɪtəbl] *a* indubitable, incontestable.
induce [ɪn'djuːs] *vt* persuader; (*bring about*) provoquer; **~ment** *n* incitation *f*; (*incentive*) but *m*; (*pej: bribe*) pot-de-vin *m*.
induct [ɪn'dʌkt] *vt* établir dans ses fonctions; (*fig*) initier.
induction [ɪn'dʌkʃən] *n* (*MED: of birth*) accouchement provoqué; **~ course** *n* stage *m* de mise au courant.
indulge [ɪn'dʌldʒ] *vt* (*whim*) céder à, satisfaire; (*child*) gâter // *vi*: **to ~ in** sth s'offrir qch, se permettre qch; se livrer à qch; **~nce** *n* fantaisie *f* (que l'on s'offre); (*leniency*) indulgence *f*; **~nt** *a* indulgent(e).
industrial [ɪn'dʌstrɪəl] *a* industriel(le); (*injury*) du travail; (*dispute*) ouvrier(ère); **~ action** *n* action revendicative; **~ estate** *n* zone industrielle; **~ist** *n* industriel *m*; **~ize** *vt* industrialiser.
industrious [ɪn'dʌstrɪəs] *a* travailleur(euse).
industry ['ɪndəstrɪ] *n* industrie *f*; (*diligence*) zèle *m*, application *f*.
inebriated [ɪ'niːbrɪeɪtɪd] *a* ivre.
inedible [ɪn'ɛdɪbl] *a* immangeable; (*plant etc*) non comestible.
ineffective [ɪnɪ'fɛktɪv] *a* inefficace.
ineffectual [ɪnɪ'fɛktʃuəl] *a* inefficace; incompétent(e).
inefficiency [ɪnɪ'fɪʃənsɪ] *n* inefficacité *f*.
inefficient [ɪnɪ'fɪʃənt] *a* inefficace.
inelegant [ɪn'ɛlɪgənt] *a* peu élégant(e).
ineligible [ɪn'ɛlɪdʒɪbl] *a* (*candidate*) inéligible; **to be ~ for** sth ne pas avoir droit à qch.
inept [ɪ'nɛpt] *a* inepte.
inequality [ɪnɪ'kwɔlɪtɪ] *n* inégalité *f*.
ineradicable [ɪnɪ'rædɪkəbl] *a* indéracinable, tenace.
inert [ɪ'nəːt] *a* inerte.
inertia [ɪ'nəːʃə] *n* inertie *f*; **~ reel seat belt** *n* ceinture *f* de sécurité à enrouleur.
inescapable [ɪnɪ'skeɪpəbl] *a* inéluctable, inévitable.
inessential [ɪnɪ'sɛnʃl] *a* superflu(e).
inestimable [ɪn'ɛstɪməbl] *a* inestimable, incalculable.
inevitable [ɪn'ɛvɪtəbl] *a* inévitable.

inexact [ɪnɪg'zækt] *a* inexact(e).
inexhaustible [ɪnɪg'zɔːstɪbl] *a* inépuisable.
inexorable [ɪn'ɛksərəbl] *a* inexorable.
inexpensive [ɪnɪk'spɛnsɪv] *a* bon marché *inv*.
inexperience [ɪnɪk'spɪərɪəns] *n* inexpérience *f*, manque *m* d'expérience; **~d** *a* inexpérimenté(e).
inexplicable [ɪnɪk'splɪkəbl] *a* inexplicable.
inexpressible [ɪnɪk'sprɛsɪbl] *a* inexprimable.
inextricable [ɪnɪk'strɪkəbl] *a* inextricable.
infallibility [ɪnfælə'bɪlɪtɪ] *n* infaillibilité *f*.
infallible [ɪn'fælɪbl] *a* infaillible.
infamous ['ɪnfəməs] *a* infâme, abominable.
infamy ['ɪnfəmɪ] *n* infamie *f*.
infancy ['ɪnfənsɪ] *n* petite enfance, bas âge; (*fig*) enfance *f*, débuts *mpl*.
infant ['ɪnfənt] *n* (*baby*) nourrisson *m*; (*young child*) petit(e) enfant; **~ile** *a* infantile; **~ school** *n* classes *fpl* préparatoires (*entre 5 et 7 ans*).
infantry ['ɪnfəntrɪ] *n* infanterie *f*; **~man** *n* fantassin *m*.
infatuated [ɪn'fætjueɪtɪd] *a*: **~ with** entiché(e) de.
infatuation [ɪnfætju'eɪʃən] *n* toquade *f*; engouement *m*.
infect [ɪn'fɛkt] *vt* infecter, contaminer; (*fig: pej*) corrompre; **~ed with** (*illness*) atteint(e) de; **~ion** [ɪn'fɛkʃən] *n* infection *f*; contagion *f*; **~ious** [ɪn'fɛkʃəs] *a* infectieux(euse); (*also: fig*) contagieux(euse).
infer [ɪn'fəː*] *vt* conclure, déduire; **~ence** ['ɪnfərəns] *n* conclusion *f*; déduction *f*.
inferior [ɪn'fɪərɪə*] *a* inférieur(e); (*goods*) de qualité inférieure // *n* inférieur/e; (*in rank*) subalterne *m/f*; **~ity** [ɪnfɪərɪ'ɔrɪtɪ] *n* infériorité *f*; **~ity complex** *n* complexe *m* d'infériorité.
infernal [ɪn'fəːnl] *a* infernal(e); **~ly** *ad* abominablement.
inferno [ɪn'fəːnəu] *n* enfer *m*; brasier *m*.
infertile [ɪn'fəːtaɪl] *a* stérile; **infertility** [-'tɪlɪtɪ] *n* infertilité *f*, stérilité *f*.
infested [ɪn'fɛstɪd] *a*: **~ (with)** infesté(e) (de).
infidelity [ɪnfɪ'dɛlɪtɪ] *n* infidélité *f*.
in-fighting ['ɪnfaɪtɪŋ] *n* querelles *fpl* internes.
infiltrate ['ɪnfɪltreɪt] *vt* (*troops etc*) faire s'infiltrer; (*enemy line etc*) s'infiltrer dans // *vi* s'infiltrer.
infinite ['ɪnfɪnɪt] *a* infini(e).
infinitive [ɪn'fɪnɪtɪv] *n* infinitif *m*.
infinity [ɪn'fɪnɪtɪ] *n* infinité *f*; (*also MATH*) infini *m*.
infirm [ɪn'fəːm] *a* infirme.
infirmary [ɪn'fəːmərɪ] *n* hôpital *m*; (*in school, factory*) infirmerie *f*.
infirmity [ɪn'fəːmɪtɪ] *n* infirmité *f*.
inflame [ɪn'fleɪm] *vt* enflammer.
inflammable [ɪn'flæməbl] *a* inflammable.
inflammation [ɪnflə'meɪʃən] *n* inflammation *f*.
inflate [ɪn'fleɪt] *vt* (*tyre, balloon*) gonfler; (*fig*) grossir; gonfler; faire monter; **to ~ the currency** avoir recours à l'inflation;

~d a (style) enflé(e); (value) exagéré(e);
inflation [ɪn'fleɪʃən] n (ECON) inflation f.
inflexible [ɪn'flɛksɪbl] a inflexible, rigide.
inflict [ɪn'flɪkt] vt: **to ~ on** infliger à;
~ion [ɪn'flɪkʃən] n infliction f; affliction
f.
inflow ['ɪnfləʊ] n afflux m.
influence ['ɪnfluəns] n influence f // vt
influencer; **under the ~ of** sous l'effet
de; **under the ~ of drink** en état d'ébriété.
influential [ɪnflu'ɛnʃl] a influent(e).
influenza [ɪnflu'ɛnzə] n grippe f.
influx ['ɪnflʌks] n afflux m.
inform [ɪn'fɔ:m] vt: **to ~ sb (of)** informer
or avertir qn (de); **to ~ sb about**
renseigner qn sur, mettre qn au courant
de.
informal [ɪn'fɔ:ml] a (person, manner)
simple, sans façon; (visit, discussion)
dénué(e) de formalités; (announcement,
invitation) non-officiel(le); **'dress ~'**
'tenue de ville'; **~ity** [-'mælɪtɪ] n
simplicité f, absence f de cérémonie;
caractère non-officiel; **~ language** n
langage m de la conversation.
information [ɪnfə'meɪʃən] n information
f; renseignements mpl; (knowledge)
connaissances fpl; **a piece of ~** un
renseignement.
informative [ɪn'fɔ:mətɪv] a instructif(ive).
informer [ɪn'fɔ:mə*] n dénonciateur/-
trice; (also: **police ~**) indicateur/trice.
infra-red [ɪnfrə'rɛd] a infrarouge.
infrequent [ɪn'fri:kwənt] a peu
fréquent(e), rare.
infringe [ɪn'frɪndʒ] vt enfreindre // vi: **to
~ on** empiéter sur; **~ment** n: **~ment
(of)** infraction f (à).
infuriate [ɪn'fjʊərɪeɪt] vt mettre en fureur;
infuriating a exaspérant(e).
ingenious [ɪn'dʒi:njəs] a ingénieux(euse).
ingenuity [ɪndʒɪ'nju:ɪtɪ] n ingéniosité f.
ingenuous [ɪn'dʒɛnjuəs] a naïf(ïve),
ingénu(e).
ingot ['ɪŋgət] n lingot m.
ingrained [ɪn'greɪnd] a enraciné(e).
ingratiate [ɪn'greɪʃɪeɪt] vt: **to ~ o.s. with**
s'insinuer dans les bonnes grâces de, se
faire bien voir de.
ingratitude [ɪn'grætɪtju:d] n ingratitude f.
ingredient [ɪn'gri:dɪənt] n ingrédient m;
élément m.
ingrown ['ɪngrəʊn] a: **~ toenail** ougle
incarné.
inhabit [ɪn'hæbɪt] vt habiter.
inhabitant [ɪn'hæbɪtnt] n habitant/e.
inhale [ɪn'heɪl] vt inhaler; (perfume)
respirer // vi (in smoking) avaler la fumée.
inherent [ɪn'hɪərənt] a: **~ (in or to)**
inhérent(e) (à).
inherit [ɪn'hɛrɪt] vt hériter (de); **~ance** n
héritage m; **law of ~ance** n droit m de
la succession.
inhibit [ɪn'hɪbɪt] vt (PSYCH) inhiber; **to ~
sb from doing** empêcher or retenir qn de
faire; **~ing** a gênant(e); **~ion** [-'bɪʃən] n
inhibition f.
inhospitable [ɪnhɔs'pɪtəbl] a inhospita-
lier(ère).
inhuman [ɪn'hju:mən] a inhumain(e).

inimitable [ɪ'nɪmɪtəbl] a inimitable.
iniquity [ɪ'nɪkwɪtɪ] n iniquité f.
initial [ɪ'nɪʃl] a initial(e) // n initiale f //
vt parafer; **~s** npl initiales fpl; (as
signature) parafe m; **~ly** ad initialement,
au début.
initiate [ɪ'nɪʃɪeɪt] vt (start) entreprendre;
amorcer; lancer; (person) initier; **to ~ sb
into a secret** initier qn à un secret; **to
~ proceedings against sb** (LAW) intenter
une action à qn; **initiation** [-'eɪʃən] n (into
secret etc) initiation f.
initiative [ɪ'nɪʃətɪv] n initiative f.
inject [ɪn'dʒɛkt] vt (liquid) injecter;
(person) faire une piqûre à; **~ion**
[ɪn'dʒɛkʃən] n injection f, piqûre f.
injure [ɪn'dʒə*] vt blesser; (wrong) faire
du tort à; (damage: reputation etc)
compromettre.
injury ['ɪndʒərɪ] n blessure f; (wrong) tort
m; **~ time** n (SPORT) arrêts mpl de jeu.
injustice [ɪn'dʒʌstɪs] n injustice f.
ink [ɪŋk] n encre f.
inkling ['ɪŋklɪŋ] n soupçon m, vague idée
f.
inky ['ɪŋkɪ] a taché(e) d'encre.
inlaid ['ɪnleɪd] a incrusté(e); (table etc)
marqueté(e).
inland a ['ɪnlənd] intérieur(e) // ad
[ɪn'lænd] à l'intérieur, dans les terres; **I~
Revenue** n (Brit) fisc m, contributions
directes; **~ waterways** npl canaux mpl et
rivières fpl.
in-laws ['ɪnlɔ:z] npl beaux-parents mpl;
belle famille.
inlet ['ɪnlɛt] n (GEO) crique f; **~ pipe** n
(TECH) tuyau m d'arrivée.
inmate ['ɪnmeɪt] n (in prison) dêtenu/e; (in
asylum) interné/e.
inn [ɪn] n auberge f.
innate [ɪ'neɪt] a inné(e).
inner ['ɪnə*] a intérieur(e); **~ city** n centre
m de zone urbaine; **~ tube** n (of tyre)
chambre f à air.
innocence ['ɪnəsns] n innocence f.
innocent ['ɪnəsnt] a innocent(e).
innocuous [ɪ'nɔkjuəs] a inoffensif(ive).
innovation [ɪnəʊ'veɪʃən] n innovation f.
innuendo, ~es [ɪnju'ɛndəʊ] n
insinuation f, allusion (malveillante).
innumerable [ɪ'nju:mrəbl] a innombrable.
inoculation [ɪnɔkju'leɪʃən] n inoculation f.
inopportune [ɪn'ɔpətju:n] a inoppor-
tun(e).
inordinately [ɪ'nɔ:dɪnətlɪ] ad démesuré-
ment.
inorganic [ɪnɔ:'gænɪk] a inorganique.
in-patient ['ɪnpeɪʃənt] n malade
hospitalisé(e).
input ['ɪnput] n (ELEC) énergie f, puissance
f; (of machine) consommation f; (of
computer) information fournie.
inquest ['ɪnkwɛst] n enquête (criminelle).
inquire [ɪn'kwaɪə*] vi demander // vt
demander, s'informer de; **to ~ about** vt
fus s'informer de, se renseigner sur; **to ~
after** vt fus demander des nouvelles de;
to ~ into vt fus faire une enquête sur;
inquiring a (mind) curieux(euse),
investigateur(trice); **inquiry** n demande f
de renseignements; (LAW) enquête f,

investigation f; **inquiry office** n bureau m de renseignements.

inquisitive [ɪn'kwɪzɪtɪv] a curieux(euse).

inroad ['ɪnrəud] n incursion f.

insane [ɪn'seɪn] a fou(folle); (MED) aliéné(e).

insanitary [ɪn'sænɪtərɪ] a insalubre.

insanity [ɪn'sænɪtɪ] n folie f; (MED) aliénation (mentale).

insatiable [ɪn'seɪʃəbl] a insatiable.

inscribe [ɪn'skraɪb] vt inscrire; (book etc): **to ~ (to sb)** dédicacer (à qn).

inscription [ɪn'skrɪpʃən] n inscription f; dédicace f.

inscrutable [ɪn'skru:təbl] a impénétrable.

insect ['ɪnsɛkt] n insecte m; **~icide** [ɪn'sɛktɪsaɪd] n insecticide m.

insecure [ɪnsɪ'kjuə*] a peu solide; peu sûr(e); (person) anxieux (euse); **insecurity** n insécurité f.

insensible [ɪn'sɛnsɪbl] a insensible; (unconscious) sans connaissance.

insensitive [ɪn'sɛnsɪtɪv] a insensible.

inseparable [ɪn'sɛprəbl] a inséparable.

insert vt [ɪn'sə:t] insérer // n ['ɪnsə:t] insertion f; **~ion** [ɪn'sə:ʃən] n insertion f.

inshore [ɪn'ʃɔ:*] a côtier(ère) // ad près de la côte; vers la côte.

inside ['ɪn'saɪd] n intérieur m // a intérieur(e) // ad à l'intérieur, dedans // prep à l'intérieur de; (of time): **~ 10 minutes** en moins de 10 minutes; **~s** npl (col) intestins mpl; **~ forward** n (SPORT) intérieur m; **~ lane** n (AUT: in Britain) voie f de gauche; (know) à fond; **to turn ~ out** retourner.

insidious [ɪn'sɪdɪəs] a insidieux(euse).

insight ['ɪnsaɪt] n perspicacité f; (glimpse, idea) aperçu m.

insignificant [ɪnsɪg'nɪfɪknt] a insignifiant(e).

insincere [ɪnsɪn'sɪə*] a hypocrite; **insincerity** [-'sɛrɪtɪ] n manque m de sincérité, hypocrisie f.

insinuate [ɪn'sɪnjueɪt] vt insinuer; **insinuation** [-'eɪʃən] n insinuation f.

insipid [ɪn'sɪpɪd] a insipide, fade.

insist [ɪn'sɪst] vi insister; **to ~ on doing** insister pour faire; **to ~ that** insister pour que; (claim) maintenir or soutenir que; **~ence** n insistance f; **~ent** a insistant(e), pressant(e).

insolence ['ɪnsələns] n insolence f.

insolent ['ɪnsələnt] a insolent(e).

insoluble [ɪn'sɔljubl] a insoluble.

insolvent [ɪn'sɔlvənt] a insolvable; en faillite.

insomnia [ɪn'sɔmnɪə] n insomnie f.

inspect [ɪn'spɛkt] vt inspecter; (ticket) contrôler; **~ion** [ɪn'spɛkʃən] n inspection f; contrôle m; **~or** n inspecteur/trice; contrôleur/euse.

inspiration [ɪnspə'reɪʃən] n inspiration f.

inspire [ɪn'spaɪə*] vt inspirer; **inspiring** a inspirant(e).

instability [ɪnstə'bɪlɪtɪ] n instabilité f.

install [ɪn'stɔ:l] vt installer; **~ation** [ɪnstə'leɪʃən] n installation f.

instalment, installment (US) [ɪn'stɔ:lmənt] n acompte m, versement partiel; (of TV serial etc) épisode m.

instance ['ɪnstəns] n exemple m; **for ~** par exemple; **in many ~s** dans bien des cas.

instant ['ɪnstənt] n instant m // a immédiat(e); urgent(e); (coffee, food) instantané(e), en poudre; **the 10th ~** le 10 courant; **~ly** ad immédiatement, tout de suite.

instead [ɪn'stɛd] ad au lieu de cela; **~ of** au lieu de; **~ of sb** à la place de qn.

instep ['ɪnstɛp] n cou-de-pied m; (of shoe) cambrure f.

instigation [ɪnstɪ'geɪʃən] n instigation f.

instil [ɪn'stɪl] vt: **to ~ (into)** inculquer (à); (courage) insuffler (à).

instinct ['ɪnstɪŋkt] n instinct m.

instinctive [ɪn'stɪŋktɪv] a instinctif(ive); **~ly** ad instinctivement.

institute ['ɪnstɪtju:t] n institut m // vt instituer, établir; (inquiry) ouvrir; (proceedings) entamer.

institution [ɪnstɪ'tju:ʃən] n institution f; établissement m (scolaire); établissement m (psychiatrique).

instruct [ɪn'strʌkt] vt instruire, former; **to ~ sb in sth** enseigner qch à qn; **to ~ sb to do** charger qn or ordonner à qn de faire; **~ion** [ɪn'strʌkʃən] n instruction f; **~ions** npl directives fpl; **~ions (for use)** mode m d'emploi; **~ive** a instructif(ive); **~or** n professeur m; (for skiing, driving) moniteur m.

instrument ['ɪnstrumənt] n instrument m; **~al** [-'mɛntl] a (MUS) instrumental(e); **to be ~al in** contribuer à; **~alist** [-'mɛntəlɪst] n instrumentiste m/f; **~ panel** n tableau m de bord.

insubordinate [ɪnsə'bɔ:dɪnɪt] a insubordonné(e); **insubordination** [-'neɪʃən] n insubordination f.

insufferable [ɪn'sʌfrəbl] a insupportable.

insufficient [ɪnsə'fɪʃənt] a insuffisant(e); **~ly** ad insuffisamment.

insular ['ɪnsjulə*] a insulaire; (outlook) étroit(e); (person) aux vues étroites.

insulate ['ɪnsjuleɪt] vt isoler; (against sound) insonoriser; **insulating tape** n ruban isolant; **insulation** [-'leɪʃən] n isolation f; insonorisation f.

insulin ['ɪnsjulɪn] n insuline f.

insult n ['ɪnsʌlt] insulte f, affront m // vt [ɪn'sʌlt] insulter, faire un affront à; **~ing** a insultant(e), injurieux(euse).

insuperable [ɪn'sju:prəbl] a insurmontable.

insurance [ɪn'ʃuərəns] n assurance f; **fire/life ~** assurance-incendie/-vie; **~ agent** n agent m d'assurances; **~ policy** n police f d'assurance.

insure [ɪn'ʃuə*] vt assurer.

insurrection [ɪnsə'rɛkʃən] n insurrection f.

intact [ɪn'tækt] a intact(e).

intake ['ɪnteɪk] n (TECH) admission f; adduction f; (of food) consommation f; (SCOL): **an ~ of 200 a year** 200 admissions fpl par an.

intangible [ɪn'tændʒɪbl] a intangible; (assets) immatériel(le).

integral ['ɪntɪgrəl] a intégral(e); (part) intégrant(e).

integrate ['ɪntɪgreɪt] vt intégrer // vi s'intégrer.

integrity [ɪn'tɛgrɪtɪ] n intégrité f.

intellect ['ɪntəlɛkt] n intelligence f; ~ual [-'lɛktjuəl] a, n intellectuel(le).

intelligence [ɪn'tɛlɪdʒəns] n intelligence f; (MIL etc) informations fpl, renseignements mpl; I~ **Service** n services mpl de renseignements.

intelligent [ɪn'tɛlɪdʒənt] a intelligent(e); ~ly ad intelligemment.

intelligible [ɪn'tɛlɪdʒɪbl] a intelligible.

intemperate [ɪn'tɛmpərət] a immodéré(e); (drinking too much) adonné(e) à la boisson.

intend [ɪn'tɛnd] vt (gift etc): **to ~ sth for** destiner qch à; **to ~ to do** avoir l'intention de faire; ~ed a (insult) intentionnel(le); (journey) projeté(e); (effect) voulu(e).

intense [ɪn'tɛns] a intense; (person) véhément(e); ~ly ad intensément; profondément.

intensify [ɪn'tɛnsɪfaɪ] vt intensifier.

intensity [ɪn'tɛnsɪtɪ] n intensité f.

intensive [ɪn'tɛnsɪv] a intensif(ive); ~ care unit n service m de réanimation.

intent [ɪn'tɛnt] n intention f // a attentif(ive), absorbé(e); **to all ~s and purposes** en fait, pratiquement; **to be ~ on doing sth** être (bien) décidé à faire qch.

intention [ɪn'tɛnʃən] n intention f; ~al a intentionnel(le), délibéré(e).

intently [ɪn'tɛntlɪ] ad attentivement.

inter [ɪn'tə:*] vt enterrer.

interact [ɪntər'ækt] vi avoir une action réciproque; ~ion [-'ækʃən] n interaction f.

intercede [ɪntə'si:d] vi: **to ~ (with)** intercéder (auprès de).

intercept [ɪntə'sɛpt] vt intercepter; (person) arrêter au passage; ~ion [-'sɛpʃən] n interception f.

interchange n ['ɪntətʃeɪndʒ] (exchange) échange m; (on motorway) échangeur m // vt [ɪntə'tʃeɪndʒ] échanger; mettre à la place l'un(e) de l'autre; ~able a interchangeable.

intercom ['ɪntəkɔm] n interphone m.

interconnect [ɪntəkə'nɛkt] vi (rooms) communiquer.

intercourse ['ɪntəkɔ:s] n rapports mpl.

interest ['ɪntrɪst] n intérêt m; (COMM: stake, share) intérêts mpl // vt intéresser; ~ed a intéressé(e); **to be ~ed in** s'intéresser à; ~ing a intéressant(e).

interfere [ɪntə'fɪə*] vi: **to ~ in** (quarrel, other people's business) se mêler à; **to ~ with** (object) tripoter, toucher à; (plans) contrecarrer; (duty) être en conflit avec; **don't ~** mêlez-vous de vos affaires.

interference [ɪntə'fɪərəns] n (gen) intrusion f; (PHYSICS) interférence f; (RADIO, TV) parasites mpl.

interim ['ɪntərɪm] a provisoire; (post) intérimaire // n: **in the ~** dans l'intérim.

interior [ɪn'tɪərɪə*] n intérieur m // a intérieur(e).

interjection [ɪntə'dʒɛkʃən] n interjection f.

interlock [ɪntə'lɔk] vi s'enclencher // vt enclencher.

interloper ['ɪntələupə*] n intrus/e.

interlude ['ɪntəlu:d] n intervalle m; (THEATRE) intermède m.

intermarry [ɪntə'mærɪ] vi former des alliances entre familles (or tribus); former des unions consanguines.

intermediary [ɪntə'mi:dɪərɪ] n intermédiaire m/f.

intermediate [ɪntə'mi:dɪət] a intermédiaire; (SCOL: course, level) moyen(ne).

intermission [ɪntə'mɪʃən] n pause f; (THEATRE, CINEMA) entracte m.

intermittent [ɪntə'mɪtnt] a intermittent(e); ~ly ad par intermittence, par intervalles.

intern vt [ɪn'tə:n] interner // n ['ɪntə:n] (US) interne m/f.

internal [ɪn'tə:nl] a interne; (dispute, reform etc) intérieur(e); ~ly ad intérieurement; 'not to be taken ~ly' 'pour usage externe'; ~ **revenue** n (US) fisc m.

international [ɪntə'næʃənl] a international(e) // n (SPORT) international m.

internment [ɪn'tə:nmənt] n internement m.

interplay ['ɪntəpleɪ] n effet m réciproque, jeu m.

interpret [ɪn'tə:prɪt] vt interpréter // vi servir d'interprète; ~ation [-'teɪʃən] n interprétation f; ~er n interprète m/f; ~ing n (profession) interprétariat m.

interrelated [ɪntərɪ'leɪtɪd] a en corrélation, en rapport étroit.

interrogate [ɪn'tɛrəugeɪt] vt interroger; (suspect etc) soumettre à un interrogatoire; **interrogation** [-'geɪʃən] n interrogation f; interrogatoire m; **interrogative** [ɪntə'rɔgətɪv] a interrogateur(trice) // n (LING) interrogatif m; **interrogator** n interrogateur/trice.

interrupt [ɪntə'rʌpt] vt interrompre; ~ion [-'rʌpʃən] n interruption f.

intersect [ɪntə'sɛkt] vt couper, croiser // vi (roads) se croiser, se couper; ~ion [-'sɛkʃən] n intersection f; (of roads) croisement m.

intersperse [ɪntə'spə:s] vt: **to ~ with** parsemer de.

intertwine [ɪntə'twaɪn] vt entrelacer // vi s'entrelacer.

interval ['ɪntəvl] n intervalle m; (SCOL) récréation f; (THEATRE) entracte m; (SPORT) mi-temps f; **bright ~s** (in weather) éclaircies fpl; **at ~s** par intervalles.

intervene [ɪntə'vi:n] vi (time) s'écouler (entre-temps); (event) survenir; (person) intervenir; **intervention** [-'vɛnʃən] n intervention f.

interview ['ɪntəvju:] n (RADIO, TV etc) interview f; (for job) entrevue f // vt interviewer; avoir une entrevue avec; ~er n interviewer m.

intestate [ɪn'tɛsteɪt] a intestat.

intestinal [ɪn'tɛstaɪnl] a intestinal(e).

intestine [ɪn'tɛstɪn] n intestin m.

intimacy ['ɪntɪməsɪ] n intimité f.

intimate a ['ɪntɪmət] intime; (knowledge) approfondi(e) // vt ['ɪntɪmeɪt] suggérer, laisser entendre ; (announce) faire savoir ; ~ly ad intimement.

intimation [ɪntɪ'meɪʃən] n annonce f.

intimidate [ɪn'tɪmɪdeɪt] vt intimider ; **intimidation** [-'deɪʃən] n intimidation f.

into ['ɪntu] prep dans ; ~ **3 pieces/French** en 3 morceaux/français.

intolerable [ɪn'tɔlərəbl] a intolérable.

intolerance [ɪn'tɔlərns] n intolérance f.

intolerant [ɪn'tɔlərnt] a intolérant(e).

intonation [ɪntəu'neɪʃən] n intonation f.

intoxicate [ɪn'tɔksɪkeɪt] vt enivrer ; ~d a ivre ; **intoxication** [-'keɪʃən] n ivresse f.

intractable [ɪn'træktəbl] a (child, temper) indocile, insoumis(e) ; (problem) insoluble.

intransigent [ɪn'trænsɪdʒənt] a intransigeant(e).

intransitive [ɪn'trænsɪtɪv] a intransitif(ive).

intra-uterine [ɪntrə'juːtərɪn] a intra-utérin(e) ; ~ **device (I.U.D.)** n moyen de contraception intra-utérin.

intravenous [ɪntrə'viːnəs] a intraveineux(euse).

intrepid [ɪn'trepɪd] a intrépide.

intricacy ['ɪntrɪkəsɪ] n complexité f.

intricate ['ɪntrɪkət] a complexe, compliqué(e).

intrigue [ɪn'triːg] n intrigue f // vt intriguer ; **intriguing** a fascinant(e).

intrinsic [ɪn'trɪnsɪk] a intrinsèque.

introduce [ɪntrə'djuːs] vt introduire ; **to ~ sb (to sb)** présenter qn (à qn) ; **to ~ sb to** (pastime, technique) initier qn à ; **introduction** [-'dʌkʃən] n introduction f ; (of person) présentation f ; **introductory** a préliminaire, d'introduction.

introspective [ɪntrəu'spektɪv] a introspectif(ive).

introvert ['ɪntrəuvəːt] a,n introverti(e).

intrude [ɪn'truːd] vi (person) être importun(e) ; **to ~ on** or **into** s'immiscer dans ; **am I intruding?** est-ce que je vous dérange? ; ~**r** n intrus/e ; **intrusion** [-ʒən] n intrusion f ; **intrusive** a importun(e), gênant(e).

intuition [ɪntjuː'ɪʃən] n intuition f.

intuitive [ɪn'tjuːɪtɪv] a intuitif(ive).

inundate ['ɪnʌndeɪt] vt: **to ~ with** inonder de.

invade [ɪn'veɪd] vt envahir ; ~**r** n envahisseur m.

invalid n ['ɪnvəlɪd] malade m/f ; (with disability) invalide m/f // a [ɪn'vælɪd] (not valid) invalide, non valide ; ~**ate** [ɪn'vælɪdeɪt] vt invalider, annuler.

invaluable [ɪn'væljuəbl] a inestimable, inappréciable.

invariable [ɪn'vɛərɪəbl] a invariable ; (fig) immanquable.

invasion [ɪn'veɪʒən] n invasion f.

invective [ɪn'vektɪv] n invective f.

invent [ɪn'vent] vt inventer ; ~**ion** [ɪn'venʃən] n invention f ; ~**ive** a inventif(ive) ; ~**iveness** n esprit inventif or d'invention ; ~**or** n inventeur/trice.

inventory ['ɪnvəntrɪ] n inventaire m.

inverse [ɪn'vəːs] a inverse // n inverse m, contraire m ; ~**ly** ad inversement.

invert [ɪn'vəːt] vt intervertir ; (cup, object) retourner ; ~**ed commas** npl guillemets mpl.

invertebrate [ɪn'vəːtɪbrət] n invertébré m.

invest [ɪn'vest] vt investir // vi faire un investissement.

investigate [ɪn'vestɪgeɪt] vt étudier, examiner ; (crime) faire une enquête sur ; **investigation** [-'geɪʃən] n examen m ; (of crime) enquête f, investigation f ; **investigator** n investigateur/trice.

investiture [ɪn'vestɪtʃə*] n investiture f.

investment [ɪn'vestmənt] n investissement m, placement m.

investor [ɪn'vestə*] n épargnant/e ; actionnaire m/f.

inveterate [ɪn'vetərət] a invétéré(e).

invidious [ɪn'vɪdɪəs] a injuste ; (task) déplaisant(e).

invigorating [ɪn'vɪgəreɪtɪŋ] a vivifiant(e) ; stimulant(e).

invincible [ɪn'vɪnsɪbl] a invincible.

inviolate [ɪn'vaɪələt] a inviolé(e).

invisible [ɪn'vɪzɪbl] a invisible ; ~ **ink** n encre f sympathique ; ~ **mending** n stoppage m.

invitation [ɪnvɪ'teɪʃən] n invitation f.

invite [ɪn'vaɪt] vt inviter ; (opinions etc) demander ; (trouble) chercher ; **inviting** a engageant(e), attrayant(e) ; (gesture) encourageant(e).

invoice ['ɪnvɔɪs] n facture f // vt facturer.

invoke [ɪn'vəuk] vt invoquer.

involuntary [ɪn'vɔləntrɪ] a involontaire.

involve [ɪn'vɔlv] vt (entail) entraîner, nécessiter ; (associate): **to ~ sb (in)** impliquer qn (dans), mêler qn à ; faire participer qn (à) ; ~**d** a complexe ; **to feel ~d** se sentir concerné(e) ; ~**ment** n mise f en jeu ; implication f ; ~**ment (in)** participation f (à) ; rôle m (dans).

invulnerable [ɪn'vʌlnərəbl] a invulnérable.

inward ['ɪnwəd] a (movement) vers l'intérieur ; (thought, feeling) profond(e), intime ; ~**ly** ad (feel, think etc) secrètement, en son for intérieur ; ~**(s)** ad vers l'intérieur.

iodine ['aɪəudiːn] n iode m.

iota [aɪ'əutə] n (fig) brin m, grain m.

IOU n (abbr of I owe you) reconnaissance f de dette.

IQ n (abbr of intelligence quotient) Q.I. m (quotient intellectuel).

Iran [ɪ'rɑːn] n Iran m ; ~**ian** [ɪ'reɪnɪən] a iranien(ne) // n Iranien/ne ; (LING) iranien m.

Iraq [ɪ'rɑːk] n Irak m ; ~**i** a irakien(ne) // n Irakien/ne ; (LING) irakien m.

irascible [ɪ'ræsɪbl] a irascible.

irate [aɪ'reɪt] a courroucé(e).

Ireland ['aɪlənd] n Irlande f.

iris, ~**es** ['aɪrɪs, -ɪz] n iris m.

Irish ['aɪrɪʃ] a irlandais(e) // npl: **the ~** les Irlandais ; ~**man** n Irlandais m ; ~ **Sea** n mer f d'Irlande ; ~**woman** n Irlandaise f.

irk [əːk] vt ennuyer ; ~**some** a ennuyeux(euse).

iron ['aɪən] n fer m ; (for clothes) fer m à repasser // a de or en fer // vt (clothes) repasser ; ~**s** npl (chains) fers mpl, chaînes *fpl* ; **to ~ out** *vt* (*crease*) faire disparaître au fer ; (*fig*) aplanir ; faire disparaître ; **the ~ curtain** *n* le rideau de fer.

ironic(al) [aɪˈrɔnɪk(l)] *a* ironique.

ironing [ˈaɪənɪŋ] *n* repassage *m* ; **~ board** *n* planche *f* à repasser.

ironmonger [ˈaɪənˌmʌŋgə*] *n* quincailler *m* ; **~'s (shop)** *n* quincaillerie *f*.

iron ore [ˈaɪənˈɔ:*] *n* minerai *m* de fer.

ironworks [ˈaɪənwə:ks] *n* usine *f* sidérurgique.

irony [ˈaɪrənɪ] *n* ironie *f*.

irrational [ɪˈræʃənl] *a* irrationnel(le) ; déraisonnable ; qui manque de logique.

irreconcilable [ɪrɛkənˈsaɪləbl] *a* irréconciliable ; (*opinion*): **~ with** inconciliable avec.

irredeemable [ɪrɪˈdi:məbl] *a* (*COMM*) non remboursable.

irrefutable [ɪrɪˈfju:təbl] *a* irréfutable.

irregular [ɪˈregjulə*] *a* irrégulier(ère) ; **~ity** [-ˈlærɪtɪ] *n* irrégularité *f*.

irrelevance [ɪˈrɛləvəns] *n* manque *m* de rapport *or* d'à-propos.

irrelevant [ɪˈrɛləvənt] *a* sans rapport, hors de propos.

irreligious [ɪrɪˈlɪdʒəs] *a* irréligieux(euse).

irreparable [ɪˈrɛprəbl] *a* irréparable.

irreplaceable [ɪrɪˈpleɪsəbl] *a* irremplaçable.

irrepressible [ɪrɪˈprɛsəbl] *a* irrépressible.

irreproachable [ɪrɪˈprəutʃəbl] *a* irréprochable.

irresistible [ɪrɪˈzɪstɪbl] *a* irrésistible.

irresolute [ɪˈrɛzəlu:t] *a* irrésolu(e), indécis(e).

irrespective [ɪrɪˈspɛktɪv]: **~ of** *prep* sans tenir compte de.

irresponsible [ɪrɪˈspɔnsɪbl] *a* (*act*) irréfléchi(e) ; (*person*) qui n'a pas le sens des responsabilités.

irretrievable [ɪrɪˈtri:vəbl] *a* irréparable, irrémédiable.

irreverent [ɪˈrɛvərənt] *a* irrévérencieux(euse).

irrevocable [ɪˈrɛvəkəbl] *a* irrévocable.

irrigate [ˈɪrɪgeɪt] *vt* irriguer ; **irrigation** [-ˈgeɪʃən] *n* irrigation *f*.

irritable [ˈɪrɪtəbl] *a* irritable.

irritate [ˈɪrɪteɪt] *vt* irriter ; **irritation** [-ˈteɪʃən] *n* irritation *f*.

is [ɪz] *vb see* **be**.

Islam [ˈɪzlɑ:m] *n* Islam *m*.

island [ˈaɪlənd] *n* île *f* ; (*also*: **traffic ~**) refuge *m* (pour piétons) ; **~er** *n* habitant/e d'une île, insulaire *m/f*.

isle [aɪl] *n* île *f*.

isn't [ˈɪznt] = **is not**.

isolate [ˈaɪsəleɪt] *vt* isoler ; **~d** *a* isolé(e) ; **isolation** [-ˈleɪʃən] *n* isolement *m* ; **isolationism** [-ˈleɪʃənɪzm] *n* isolationnisme *m*.

isotope [ˈaɪsəutəup] *n* isotope *m*.

Israel [ˈɪzreɪl] *n* Israël *m* ; **~i** [ɪzˈreɪlɪ] *a* israélien(ne) // *n* Israélien/ne.

issue [ˈɪsju:] *n* question *f*, problème *m* ; (*outcome*) résultat *m*, issue *f* ; (*of banknotes etc*) émission *f* ; (*of newspaper etc*) numéro *m* ; (*offspring*) descendance *f* // *vt* (*rations, equipment*) distribuer ; (*orders*) donner ;

(*book*) faire paraître, publier ; (*banknotes, cheques, stamps*) émettre, mettre en circulation ; **at ~** en jeu, en cause.

isthmus [ˈɪsməs] *n* isthme *m*.

it [ɪt] *pronoun* (*subject*) il(elle) ; (*direct object*) le(la), l' ; (*indirect object*) lui ; (*impersonal*) il ; ce, cela, ça ; **~'s raining** il pleut ; **I've come from ~** j'en viens ; **it's on ~** c'est dessus ; **he's proud of ~** il en est fier ; **he agreed to ~** il y a consenti.

Italian [ɪˈtæljən] *a* italien(ne) // *n* Italien/ne ; (*LING*) italien *m*.

italic [ɪˈtælɪk] *a* italique ; **~s** *npl* italique *m*.

Italy [ˈɪtəlɪ] *n* Italie *f*.

itch [ɪtʃ] *n* démangeaison *f* // *vi* (*person*) éprouver des démangeaisons ; (*part of body*) démanger ; **I'm ~ing to do** l'envie me démange de faire ; **~ing** *n* démangeaison *f* ; **~y** *a* qui démange.

it'd [ˈɪtd] = **it would** ; **it had**.

item [ˈaɪtəm] *n* (*gen*) article *m* ; (*on agenda*) question *f*, point *m* ; (*in programme*) numéro *m* ; (*also*: **news ~**) nouvelle *f* ; **~ize** *vt* détailler, spécifier.

itinerant [ɪˈtɪnərənt] *a* itinérant(e) ; (*musician*) ambulant(e).

itinerary [aɪˈtɪnərərɪ] *n* itinéraire *m*.

it'll [ˈɪtl] = **it will**, **it shall**.

its [ɪts] *a* son(sa), ses *pl* // *pronoun* le(la) sien(ne), les siens(siennes).

it's [ɪts] = **it is** ; **it has**.

itself [ɪtˈsɛlf] *pronoun* (*emphatic*) lui-même(elle-même) ; (*reflexive*) se.

ITV *n abbr of Independent Television* (chaîne fonctionnant en concurrence avec la BBC).

I.U.D. *n abbr see* **intra-uterine**.

I've [aɪv] = **I have**.

ivory [ˈaɪvərɪ] *n* ivoire *m* ; **~ tower** *n* (*fig*) tour *f* d'ivoire.

ivy [ˈaɪvɪ] *n* lierre *m*.

J

jab [dʒæb] *vt*: **to ~ sth into** enfoncer *or* planter qch dans // *n* coup *m* ; (*MED*: *col*) piqûre *f*.

jabber [ˈdʒæbə*] *vt,vi* bredouiller, baragouiner.

jack [dʒæk] *n* (*AUT*) cric *m* ; (*BOWLS*) cochonnet *m* ; (*CARDS*) valet *m* ; **to ~ up** *vt* soulever (au cric).

jacket [ˈdʒækɪt] *n* veste *f*, veston *m* ; (*of boiler etc*) enveloppe *f* ; (*of book*) couverture *f*, jaquette *f* ; **potatoes in their ~s** pommes de terre en robe des champs.

jack-knife [ˈdʒæknaɪf] *n* couteau *m* de poche // *vi*: **the lorry ~d** la remorque (du camion) s'est mise en travers.

jackpot [ˈdʒækpɔt] *n* gros lot.

jade [dʒeɪd] *n* (*stone*) jade *m*.

jaded [ˈdʒeɪdɪd] *a* éreinté(e), fatigué(e).

jagged [ˈdʒægɪd] *a* dentelé(e).

jail [dʒeɪl] *n* prison *f* ; **~break** *n* évasion *f* ; **~er** *n* geôlier/ière.

jam [dʒæm] *n* confiture *f* ; (*of shoppers etc*) cohue *f* ; (*also*: **traffic ~**) embouteillage *m* // *vt* (*passage etc*) encombrer, obstruer ; (*mechanism, drawer etc*) bloquer, coincer ; (*RADIO*) brouiller // *vi* (*mechanism, sliding* *part*) se coincer, se bloquer ; (*gun*) s'enrayer ; **to ~ sth into** entasser *or* comprimer qch dans ; enfoncer qch dans.

Jamaica [dʒə'meɪkə] *n* Jamaïque *f.*

jangle ['dʒæŋgl] *vi* cliqueter.

janitor ['dʒænɪtə*] *n* (*caretaker*) huissier *m* ; concierge *m.*

January ['dʒænjuərɪ] *n* janvier *m.*

Japan [dʒə'pæn] *n* Japon *m* ; **~ese** [dʒæpə'niːz] *a* japonais(e) // *n*, *pl inv* Japonais/e ; (*LING*) japonais *m.*

jar [dʒɑː*] *n* (*glass*) pot *m*, bocal *m* // *vi* (*sound*) produire un son grinçant *or* discordant ; (*colours etc*) détonner, jurer // *vt* (*subject: shock*) ébranler, secouer.

jargon ['dʒɑːgən] *n* jargon *m.*

jasmin(e) ['dʒæzmɪn] *n* jasmin *m.*

jaundice ['dʒɔːndɪs] *n* jaunisse *f* ; **~d** *a* (*fig*) envieux(euse), désapprobateur(trice).

jaunt [dʒɔːnt] *n* balade *f* ; **~y** *a* enjoué(e) ; désinvolte.

javelin ['dʒævlɪn] *n* javelot *m.*

jaw [dʒɔː] *n* mâchoire *f.*

jaywalker ['dʒeɪwɔːkə*] *n* piéton indiscipliné.

jazz [dʒæz] *n* jazz *m* ; **to ~ up** *vt* animer, égayer ; **~ band** *n* orchestre *m or* groupe *m* de jazz ; **~y** *a* bariolé(e), tapageur(euse).

jealous ['dʒeləs] *a* jaloux(ouse) ; **~y** *n* jalousie *f.*

jeans [dʒiːnz] *npl* (blue-)jean *m.*

jeep [dʒiːp] *n* jeep *f.*

jeer [dʒɪə*] *vi* : **to ~** (**at**) huer ; se moquer cruellement (de), railler ; **~s** *npl* huées *fpl*, sarcasmes *mpl.*

jelly ['dʒelɪ] *n* gelée *f* ; **~fish** *n* méduse *f.*

jeopardize ['dʒepədaɪz] *vt* mettre en danger *or* péril.

jeopardy ['dʒepədɪ] *n* : **in ~** en danger *or* péril.

jerk [dʒəːk] *n* secousse *f* ; saccade *f* ; sursaut *m*, spasme *m* // *vt* donner une secousse à // *vi* (*vehicles*) cahoter.

jerkin ['dʒəːkɪn] *n* blouson *m.*

jerky ['dʒəːkɪ] *a* saccadé(e) ; cahotant(e).

jersey ['dʒəːzɪ] *n* tricot *m.*

jest [dʒest] *n* plaisanterie *f* ; **in ~** en plaisantant.

jet [dʒet] *n* (*gas, liquid*) jet *m* ; (*AUT*) gicleur *m* ; (*AVIAT*) avion *m* à réaction, jet *m* ; **~-black** *a* (d'un noir) de jais ; **~ engine** *n* moteur *m* à réaction.

jetsam ['dʒetsəm] *n* objets jetés à la mer (et rejetés sur la côte).

jettison ['dʒetɪsn] *vt* jeter par-dessus bord.

jetty ['dʒetɪ] *n* jetée *f*, digue *f.*

Jew [dʒuː] *n* Juif *m.*

jewel ['dʒuːəl] *n* bijou *m*, joyau *m* ; **~ler** *n* bijoutier/ère, joaillier *m* ; **~ler's (shop)** *n* bijouterie *f*, joaillerie *f* ; **~lery** *n* bijoux *mpl.*

Jewess ['dʒuːɪs] *n* Juive *f.*

Jewish ['dʒuːɪʃ] *a* juif(juive).

jib [dʒɪb] *n* (*NAUT*) foc *m* ; (*of crane*) flèche *f* // *vi* : **to ~** (**at**) renâcler *or* regimber (devant).

jibe [dʒaɪb] *n* sarcasme *m.*

jiffy ['dʒɪfɪ] *n* (*col*) : **in a ~** en un clin d'œil.

jigsaw ['dʒɪgsɔː] *n* (*also*: **~ puzzle**) puzzle *m.*

jilt [dʒɪlt] *vt* laisser tomber, plaquer.

jingle ['dʒɪŋgl] *n* (*advert*) couplet *m* publicitaire // *vi* cliqueter, tinter.

jinx [dʒɪŋks] *n* (*col*) (mauvais) sort.

jitters ['dʒɪtəz] *npl* (*col*) : **to get the ~** avoir la trouille *or* la frousse.

jiujitsu [dʒuː'dʒɪtsuː] *n* jiu-jitsu *m.*

job [dʒɔb] *n* travail *m* ; (*employment*) emploi *m*, poste *m*, place *f* ; **~bing** *a* (*workman*) à la tâche, à la journée ; **~less** *a* sans travail, au chômage.

jockey ['dʒɔkɪ] *n* jockey *m* // *vi* : **to ~ for position** manœuvrer pour être bien placé.

jocular ['dʒɔkjulə*] *a* jovial(e), enjoué(e) ; facétieux(euse).

jog [dʒɔg] *vt* secouer // *vi* : **to ~ along** cahoter ; trotter ; **to ~ sb's memory** rafraîchir la mémoire de qn.

join [dʒɔɪn] *vt* unir, assembler ; (*become member of*) s'inscrire à ; (*meet*) rejoindre, retrouver ; se joindre à // *vt* (*roads, rivers*) se rejoindre, se rencontrer // *n* raccord *m* ; **to ~ up** *vi* s'engager.

joiner ['dʒɔɪnə*] *n* menuisier *m* ; **~y** *n* menuiserie *f.*

joint [dʒɔɪnt] *n* (*TECH*) jointure *f* ; joint *m* ; (*ANAT*) articulation *f*, jointure ; (*CULIN*) rôti *m* ; (*col: place*) boîte *f* // *a* commun(e) ; **~ly** *ad* ensemble, en commun.

joist [dʒɔɪst] *n* solive *f.*

joke [dʒəuk] *n* plaisanterie *f* ; (*also*: **practical ~**) farce *f* // *vi* plaisanter ; **to play a ~ on** jouer un tour à, faire une farce à ; **~r** *n* plaisantin *m*, blagueur/euse ; (*CARDS*) joker *m.*

jollity ['dʒɔlɪtɪ] *n* réjouissances *fpl*, gaieté *f.*

jolly ['dʒɔlɪ] *a* gai(e), enjoué(e) // *ad* (*col*) rudement, drôlement.

jolt [dʒəult] *n* cahot *m*, secousse *f* // *vt* cahoter, secouer.

Jordan ['dʒɔːdən] *n* Jordanie *f.*

jostle ['dʒɔsl] *vt* bousculer, pousser // *vi* jouer des coudes.

jot [dʒɔt] *n* : **not one ~** pas un brin ; **to ~ down** *vt* inscrire rapidement, noter ; **~ter** *n* cahier *m* (de brouillon) ; bloc-notes *m.*

journal ['dʒəːnl] *n* journal *m* ; **~ese** [-'liːz] *n* (*pej*) style *m* journalistique ; **~ism** *n* journalisme *m* ; **~ist** *n* journaliste *m/f.*

journey ['dʒəːnɪ] *n* voyage *m* ; (*distance covered*) trajet *m.*

jowl [dʒaul] *n* mâchoire *f* (inférieure) ; bajoue *f.*

joy [dʒɔɪ] *n* joie *f* ; **~ful**, **~ous** *a* joyeux(euse) ; **~ ride** *n* virée *f* (*gén avec une voiture volée*).

J.P. *n abbr see* **justice.**

Jr, Jun., Junr *abbr of* **junior.**

jubilant ['dʒuːbɪlnt] *a* triomphant(e), réjoui(e).

jubilation [dʒuːbɪ'leɪʃən] *n* jubilation *f.*

jubilee ['dʒuːbɪliː] *n* jubilé *m.*

judge [dʒʌdʒ] *n* juge *m* // *vt* juger ; **judg(e)ment** *n* jugement *m* ; (*punishment*) châtiment *m* ; **in my judg(e)ment** à mon avis, selon mon opinion.

judicial [dʒuː'dɪʃl] *a* judiciaire ; (*fair*) impartial(e).

judicious [dʒuː'dɪʃəs] a judicieux(euse).
judo ['dʒuːdəu] n judo m.
jug [dʒʌg] n pot m, cruche f.
juggernaut ['dʒʌgənɔːt] n (huge truck) mastodonte m.
juggle ['dʒʌgl] vi jongler ; ~r n jongleur m.
Jugoslav ['juːgəu'slɑːv] a,n = **Yugoslav**.
juice [dʒuːs] n jus m.
juicy ['dʒuːsɪ] a juteux(euse).
jukebox ['dʒuːkbɔks] n juke-box m.
July [dʒuː'laɪ] n juillet m.
jumble ['dʒʌmbl] n fouillis m // vt (also: ~ **up**) mélanger, brouiller ; ~ **sale** n (Brit) vente f de charité.
jumbo ['dʒʌmbəu] a: ~ **jet** avion géant, gros porteur (à réaction).
jump [dʒʌmp] vi sauter, bondir ; (start) sursauter ; (increase) monter en flèche // vt sauter, franchir // n saut m, bond m ; sursaut m ; **to** ~ **the queue** passer avant son tour.
jumper ['dʒʌmpə*] n pull-over m.
jumpy ['dʒʌmpɪ] a nerveux(euse), agité(e).
junction ['dʒʌŋkʃən] n (of roads) carrefour m ; (of rails) embranchement n.
juncture ['dʒʌŋktʃə*] n: **at this** ~ à ce moment-là, sur ces entrefaites.
June [dʒuːn] n juin m.
jungle ['dʒʌŋgl] n jungle f.
junior ['dʒuːnɪə*] a, n: **he's** ~ **to me (by 2 years), he's my** ~ **(by 2 years)** il est mon cadet (de 2 ans), il est plus jeune que moi (de 2 ans) ; **he's** ~ **to me** (seniority) il est en dessous de moi (dans la hiérarchie), j'ai plus d'ancienneté que lui ; ~ **executive** n jeune cadre m ; ~ **minister** n ministre m sous tutelle ; ~ **partner** n associé(-adjoint) m ; ~ **school** n école f primaire, cours moyen ; ~ **sizes** npl (COMM) tailles fpl fillettes/garçonnets.
juniper ['dʒuːnɪpə*] n: ~ **berry** baie f de genièvre.
junk [dʒʌŋk] n (rubbish) bric-à-brac m inv ; (ship) jonque f ; ~**shop** n (boutique f de) brocanteur m.
junta ['dʒʌntə] n junte f.
jurisdiction [dʒuərɪs'dɪkʃən] n juridiction f.
jurisprudence [dʒuərɪs'pruːdəns] n jurisprudence f.
juror ['dʒuərə*] n juré m.
jury ['dʒuərɪ] n jury m ; ~**man** n = **juror**.
just [dʒʌst] a juste // ad: **he's** ~ **done it/left** il vient de le faire/partir ; ~ **as I expected** exactement or précisément comme je m'y attendais ; ~ **right/two o'clock** exactement or juste ce qu'il faut/deux heures ; ~ **as he was leaving** au moment or à l'instant précis où il partait ; ~ **before/enough/here** juste avant/assez/là ; **it's** ~ **me/a mistake** ce n'est que moi/(rien) qu'une erreur ; ~ **missed/caught** manqué/attrapé de justesse ; ~ **listen to this!** écoutez un peu ça!
justice ['dʒʌstɪs] n justice f ; **Lord Chief J**~ n premier président de la cour d'appel ; **J**~ **of the Peace (J.P.)** n juge m de paix.
justifiable [dʒʌstɪ'faɪəbl] a justifiable.

justifiably [dʒʌstɪ'faɪəblɪ] ad légitimement.
justification [dʒʌstɪfɪ'keɪʃən] n justification f.
justify ['dʒʌstɪfaɪ] vt justifier.
justly ['dʒʌstlɪ] ad avec raison, justement.
justness ['dʒʌstnɪs] n justesse f.
jut [dʒʌt] vi (also: ~ **out**) dépasser, faire saillie.
juvenile ['dʒuːvənaɪl] a juvénile ; (court, books) pour enfants // n adolescent/e.
juxtapose ['dʒʌkstəpəuz] vt juxtaposer.

K

kaleidoscope [kə'laɪdəskəup] n kaléidoscope m.
kangaroo [kæŋgə'ruː] n kangourou m.
keel [kiːl] n quille f ; **on an even** ~ (fig) à flot.
keen [kiːn] a (interest, desire) vif(vive) ; (eye, intelligence) pénétrant(e) ; (competition) vif, âpre ; (edge) effilé(e) ; (eager) plein(e) d'enthousiasme ; **to be** ~ **to do** or **on doing sth** désirer vivement faire qch, tenir beaucoup à faire qch ; **to be** ~ **on sth/sb** aimer beaucoup qch/qn ; ~**ness** n (eagerness) enthousiasme m ; ~**ness** to do vif désir de faire.
keep [kiːp] vb (pt,pp kept [kɛpt]) vt (retain, preserve) garder ; (hold back) retenir ; (a shop, the books, a diary) tenir ; (feed: one's family etc) entretenir, assurer la subsistance de ; (a promise) tenir ; (chickens, bees, pigs etc) élever // vi (of food) se conserver ; (remain: in a certain state or place) rester // n (of castle) donjon m ; (food etc): **enough for his** ~ assez pour (assurer) sa subsistance ; **to** ~ **doing sth** continuer à faire qch ; faire qch continuellement ; **to** ~ **sb from doing/sth from happening** empêcher qn de faire or que qn (ne) fasse/que qch (n')arrive ; **to** ~ **sb happy/a place tidy** faire que qn soit content/qu'un endroit reste propre ; **to** ~ **sth to o.s.** garder qch pour soi, tenir qch secret ; **to** ~ **sth (back) from sb** cacher qch à qn ; **to** ~ **time** (clock) être à l'heure, ne pas retarder ; **to** ~ **on** vi continuer ; **to** ~ **on doing** continuer à faire ; **to** ~ **out** vt empêcher d'entrer ; '~ **out**' 'défense d'entrer' ; **to** ~ **up** vi se maintenir // vt continuer, maintenir ; **to** ~ **up with** se maintenir au niveau de ; ~**er** n gardien/ne ; ~**ing** n (care) garde f ; **in** ~**ing with** à l'avenant de ; en accord avec ; ~**sake** n souvenir m.
keg [kɛg] n barrique f, tonnelet m.
kennel ['kɛnl] n niche f ; ~**s** npl chenil m.
Kenya ['kɛnjə] n Kenya m.
kept [kɛpt] pt,pp de **keep**.
kerb [kəːb] n bordure f du trottoir.
kernel ['kəːnl] n amande f ; (fig) noyau m.
kerosene ['kɛrəsiːn] n kérosène m.
ketchup ['kɛtʃəp] n ketchup m.
kettle ['kɛtl] n bouilloire f.
kettle drums ['kɛtldrʌmz] npl timbales fpl.
key [kiː] n (gen, MUS) clé f ; (of piano, typewriter) touche f // cpd (-)clé ; ~**board** n clavier m ; ~**hole** n trou m de la serrure ;

~**note** n (MUS) tonique f; (fig) note dominante; ~ **ring** n porte-clés m.

khaki ['ka:kɪ] a,n kaki (m).

kibbutz [kɪ'bu:ts] n kibboutz m.

kick [kɪk] vt donner un coup de pied à // vi (horse) ruer // n coup m de pied; (of rifle) recul m; (thrill): **he does it for** ~**s** il le fait parce que ça l'excite, il le fait pour le plaisir; **to** ~ **around** vi (col) traîner; **to** ~ **off** vi (SPORT) donner le coup d'envoi; ~**off** n (SPORT) coup m d'envoi.

kid [kɪd] n gamin/e, gosse m/f; (animal, leather) chevreau m // vi (col) plaisanter, blaguer.

kidnap ['kɪdnæp] vt enlever, kidnapper; ~**per** n ravisseur/euse; ~**ping** n enlèvement m.

kidney ['kɪdnɪ] n (ANAT) rein m; (CULIN) rognon m.

kill [kɪl] vt tuer; (fig) faire échouer; détruire; supprimer // n mise f à mort; ~**er** n tueur/euse; meurtrier/ère; ~**ing** n meurtre m; tuerie f, massacre m; (col): **to make a** ~**ing** se remplir les poches, réussir un beau coup // a (col) tordant(e).

kiln [kɪln] n four m.

kilo ['ki:ləʊ] n kilo m; ~**gram(me)** ['kɪləʊgræm] n kilogramme m; ~**metre**, ~**meter** (US) ['kɪləmi:tə*] n kilomètre m; ~**watt** ['kɪləʊwɔt] n kilowatt m.

kilt [kɪlt] n kilt m.

kimono [kɪ'məʊnəʊ] n kimono m.

kin [kɪn] n see **next**, **kith**.

kind [kaɪnd] a gentil(le), aimable // n sorte f, espèce f; (species) genre m; **in** ~ (COMM) en nature; (fig): **to repay sb in** ~ rendre la pareille à qn.

kindergarten ['kɪndəgɑ:tn] n jardin m d'enfants.

kind-hearted [kaɪnd'hɑ:tɪd] a bon (bonne).

kindle ['kɪndl] vt allumer, enflammer.

kindly ['kaɪndlɪ] a bienveillant(e), plein(e) de gentillesse // ad avec bonté; **will you** ~... auriez-vous la bonté or l'obligeance de...; **he didn't take it** ~ il l'a mal pris.

kindness ['kaɪndnɪs] n bonté f, gentillesse f.

kindred ['kɪndrɪd] a apparenté(e); ~ **spirit** n âme f sœur.

kinetic [kɪ'nɛtɪk] a cinétique.

king [kɪŋ] n roi m; ~**dom** n royaume m; ~**fisher** n martin-pêcheur m; ~**pin** n cheville ouvrière; ~**-size** a long format inv; format géant inv.

kink [kɪŋk] n (of rope) entortillement m.

kinky ['kɪŋkɪ] a (fig) excentrique; aux goûts spéciaux.

kiosk ['ki:ɔsk] n kiosque m; cabine f (téléphonique).

kipper ['kɪpə*] n hareng fumé et salé.

kiss [kɪs] n baiser m // vt embrasser; **to** ~ **(each other)** s'embrasser.

kit [kɪt] n équipement m, matériel m; (set of tools etc) trousse f; (for assembly) kit m; ~**bag** n sac m de voyage or de marin.

kitchen ['kɪtʃɪn] n cuisine f; ~ **garden** n jardin m potager; ~ **sink** n évier m; ~**ware** n vaisselle f; ustensiles mpl de cuisine.

kite [kaɪt] n (toy) cerf-volant m; (ZOOL) milan m.

kith [kɪθ] n: ~ **and kin** parents et amis mpl.

kitten ['kɪtn] n petit chat, chaton m.

kitty ['kɪtɪ] n (pool of money) cagnotte f.

kleptomaniac [klɛptəʊ'meɪnɪæk] n kleptomane m/f.

knack [næk] n: **to have the** ~ **(for doing)** avoir le coup (pour faire); **there's a** ~ il y a un coup à prendre or une combine.

knapsack ['næpsæk] n musette f.

knave [neɪv] n (CARDS) valet m.

knead [ni:d] vt pétrir.

knee [ni:] n genou m; ~**cap** n rotule f.

kneel [ni:l] vi (pt,pp **knelt** [nɛlt]) s'agenouiller.

knell [nɛl] n glas m.

knelt [nɛlt] pt,pp of **kneel**.

knew [nju:] pt of **know**.

knickers ['nɪkəz] npl culotte f (de femme).

knife, **knives** [naɪf, naɪvz] n couteau m // vt poignarder, frapper d'un coup de couteau.

knight [naɪt] n chevalier m; (CHESS) cavalier m; ~**hood** n chevalerie f; (title): **to get a** ~**hood** être fait chevalier.

knit [nɪt] vt tricoter; (fig): **to** ~ **together** unir // vi (broken bones) se ressouder; ~**ting** n tricot m; ~**ting machine** n machine f à tricoter; ~**ting needle** n aiguille f à tricoter; ~**wear** n tricots mpl, lainages mpl.

knives [naɪvz] npl of **knife**.

knob [nɔb] n bouton m; (fig): **a** ~ **of butter** une noix de beurre.

knock [nɔk] vt frapper; heurter; (fig: col) dénigrer // vi (engine) cogner; (at door etc): **to** ~ **at/on** frapper à/sur // n coup m; **to** ~ **down** vt renverser; **to** ~ **off** vi (col: finish) s'arrêter (de travailler); **to** ~ **out** vt assommer; (BOXING) mettre k.-o.; ~**er** n (on door) heurtoir m; ~**-kneed** a aux genoux cagneux; ~**out** n (BOXING) knock-out m, K.-O. m; ~**out competition** n compétition f avec épreuves éliminatoires.

knot [nɔt] n (gen) nœud m // vt nouer; ~**ty** a (fig) épineux(euse).

know [nəʊ] vt (pt **knew**, pp **known** [nju:, nəʊn]) savoir; (person, author, place) connaître; **to** ~ **that...** savoir que...; **to** ~ **how to do** savoir comment faire; ~**-how** n savoir-faire m, technique f, compétence f; ~**ing** a (look etc) entendu(e); ~**ingly** ad sciemment; d'un air entendu.

knowledge ['nɔlɪdʒ] n connaissance f; (learning) connaissances, savoir m; ~**able** a bien informé(e).

known [nəʊn] pp of **know**.

knuckle ['nʌkl] n articulation f (des phalanges), jointure f.

K.O. n (abbr of knockout) K.-O. m // vt mettre K.-O.

Koran [kɔ'rɑ:n] n Coran m.

kudos ['kju:dɔs] n gloire f, lauriers mpl.

kw abbr of **kilowatt(s)**.

L

l. abbr of **litre**.

lab [læb] n (abbr of **laboratory**) labo m.

label ['leɪbl] n étiquette f; (brand: of record) marque f // vt étiqueter; **to ~ sb a...** qualifier qn de... .

laboratory [lə'bɔrətəri] n laboratoire m.

laborious [lə'bɔːrɪəs] a laborieux(euse).

labour ['leɪbə*] n (task) travail m; (workmen) main-d'œuvre f; (MED) travail, accouchement m // vi: **to ~ (at)** travailler dur (à), peiner (sur); **in ~** (MED) en travail; **L~, the L~ party** le parti travailliste, les travaillistes mpl; **~ camp** n camp m de travaux forcés; **~ed** a lourd(e), laborieux(euse); **~er** n manœuvre m; (on farm) ouvrier m agricole; **~ force** n main-d'œuvre f; **~ pains** npl douleurs fpl de l'accouchement.

labyrinth ['læbɪrɪnθ] n labyrinthe m, dédale m.

lace [leɪs] n dentelle f; (of shoe etc) lacet m // vt (shoe) lacer.

lack [læk] n manque m // vt manquer de; **through** or **for ~ of** faute de, par manque de; **to be ~ing** manquer, faire défaut; **to be ~ing in** manquer de.

lackadaisical [lækə'deɪzɪkl] a nonchalant(e), indolent(e).

laconic [lə'kɔnɪk] a laconique.

lacquer ['lækə*] n laque f.

lad [læd] n garçon m, gars m.

ladder ['lædə*] n échelle f; (in tights) maille filée // vt, vi (tights) filer.

laden ['leɪdn] a: **~ (with)** chargé(e) (de).

ladle ['leɪdl] n louche f.

lady ['leɪdɪ] n dame f; dame (du monde); **L~ Smith** lady Smith; **the ladies' (toilets)** les toilettes fpl des dames; **~bird, ~bug** (US) n coccinelle f; **~-in-waiting** n dame f d'honneur; **~like** a distingué(e).

lag [læg] n = **time ~** // vi (also: **~ behind**) rester en arrière, traîner // vt (pipes) calorifuger.

lager ['lɑːgə*] n bière blonde.

lagging ['lægɪŋ] n enveloppe isolante, calorifuge m.

lagoon [lə'guːn] n lagune f.

laid [leɪd] pt, pp of **lay**.

lain [leɪn] pp of **lie**.

lair [lɛə*] n tanière f, gîte m.

laity ['leɪətɪ] n laïques mpl.

lake [leɪk] n lac m.

lamb [læm] n agneau m; **~ chop** n côtelette f d'agneau; **~skin** n (peau f d')agneau m; **~swool** n laine f d'agneau.

lame [leɪm] a boiteux(euse).

lament [lə'mɛnt] n lamentation f // vt pleurer, se lamenter sur; **~able** ['læməntəbl] a déplorable, lamentable.

laminated ['læmɪneɪtɪd] a laminé(e); (windscreen) (en verre) feuilleté.

lamp [læmp] n lampe f.

lampoon [læm'puːn] n pamphlet m.

lamp: ~post n réverbère m; **~shade** n abat-jour m inv.

lance [lɑːns] n lance f // vt (MED) inciser;

~ corporal n (soldat m de) première classe m.

lancet ['lɑːnsɪt] n bistouri m.

land [lænd] n (as opposed to sea) terre f (ferme); (country) pays m; (soil) terre; terrain m; (estate) terre(s), domaine(s) m(pl) // vi (from ship) débarquer; (AVIAT) atterrir; (fig: fall) (re)tomber // vt (obtain) décrocher; (passengers, goods) débarquer; **to ~ up** vi atterrir, (finir par) se retrouver; **~ed gentry** n propriétaires terriens or fonciers; **~ing** n débarquement m; atterrissage m; (of staircase) palier m; **~ing craft** n chaland m de débarquement; (in quay) débarcadère m, embarcadère m; **~ing stage** n débarcadère m, embarcadère m; **~ing strip** n piste f d'atterrissage; **~lady** n propriétaire f, logeuse f; **~locked** a entouré(e) de terre(s), sans accès à la mer; **~lord** n propriétaire m, logeur m; (of pub etc) patron m; **~lubber** n terrien/ne; **~mark** n (point m de) repère m; **~owner** n propriétaire foncier or terrien.

landscape ['lænskeɪp] n paysage m; **~d** a aménagé(e) (par un paysagiste).

landslide ['lændslaɪd] n (GEO) glissement m (de terrain); (fig: POL) raz-de-marée (électoral).

lane [leɪn] n (in country) chemin m; (in town) ruelle f; (AUT) voie f; file f; (in race) couloir m.

language ['læŋgwɪdʒ] n langue f; (way one speaks) langage m; **bad ~** grossièretés fpl, langage grossier.

languid ['læŋgwɪd] a languissant(e); langoureux(euse).

languish ['læŋgwɪʃ] vi languir.

lank [læŋk] a (hair) raide et terne.

lanky ['læŋkɪ] a grand(e) et maigre, efflanqué(e).

lantern ['læntn] n lanterne f.

lap [læp] n (of track) tour m (de piste); (of body): **in** or **on one's ~** sur les genoux // vt (also: **~ up**) laper // vi (waves) clapoter; **~dog** n chien m d'appartement.

lapel [lə'pɛl] n revers m.

Lapland ['læplænd] n Laponie f.

Lapp [læp] a lapon(ne) // n Lapon/ne; (LING) lapon m.

lapse [læps] n défaillance f // vi (LAW) cesser d'être en vigueur; se périmer; **to ~ into bad habits** prendre de mauvaises habitudes; **~ of time** laps de temps, intervalle m.

larceny ['lɑːsənɪ] n vol m.

lard [lɑːd] n saindoux m.

larder ['lɑːdə*] n garde-manger m inv.

large [lɑːdʒ] a grand(e); (person, animal) gros(grosse); **at ~** (free) en liberté; (generally) en général; pour la plupart; **~ly** ad en grande partie; **~-scale** a (map) à grande échelle; (fig) important(e).

lark [lɑːk] n (bird) alouette f; (joke) blague f, farce f; **to ~ about** vi faire l'idiot, rigoler.

larva, pl **larvae** ['lɑːvə, -iː] n larve f.

laryngitis [lærɪn'dʒaɪtɪs] n laryngite f.

larynx ['lærɪŋks] n larynx m.

lascivious [lə'sɪvɪəs] a lascif(ive).

laser ['leɪzə*] n laser m.

lash [læʃ] n coup m de fouet ; (gen: **eyelash**) cil m // vt fouetter ; (tie) attacher ; **to ~ out** vi: **to ~ out (at** or **against sb/sth)** attaquer violemment (qn/qch) ; **to ~ out (on sth)** (col: spend) se fendre (de qch).

lass [læs] n (jeune) fille f.

lasso [læ'su:] n lasso m // vt prendre au lasso.

last [lɑːst] a dernier(ère) // ad en dernier // vi durer ; **~ week** la semaine dernière ; **~ night** hier soir, la nuit dernière ; **at ~** enfin ; **~ but one** avant-dernier(ère) ; **~ing** a durable ; **~-minute** a de dernière minute.

latch [lætʃ] n loquet m ; **~key** n clé f (de la porte d'entrée).

late [leit] a (not on time) en retard ; (far on in day etc) dernier(ère) ; tardif(ive) ; (recent) récent(e), dernier ; (former) ancien(ne) ; (dead) défunt(e) // ad tard ; (behind time, schedule) en retard ; **of ~** dernièrement ; **in ~ May** vers la fin (du mois) de mai, fin mai ; **the ~ Mr X** feu M. X ; **~comer** n retardataire m/f ; **~ly** ad récemment ; **~ness** n (of person) retard m ; (of event) heure tardive.

latent ['leitnt] a latent(e).

later ['leitə*] a (date etc) ultérieur(e) ; (version etc) plus récent(e) // ad plus tard.

lateral ['lætərl] a latéral(e).

latest ['leitist] a tout(e) dernier(ère) ; **at the ~** au plus tard.

latex ['leitɛks] n latex m.

lath, **~s** [læθ, læðz] n latte f.

lathe [leið] n tour m ; **~ operator** n tourneur m (en usine).

lather ['lɑːðə*] n mousse f (de savon) // vt savonner // vi mousser.

Latin ['lætin] n latin m // a latin(e) ; **~ America** n Amérique latine ; **~-American** a d'Amérique latine.

latitude ['lætitjuːd] n latitude f.

latrine [lə'triːn] n latrines fpl.

latter ['lætə*] a deuxième, dernier(ère) // n: **the ~** ce dernier, celui-ci ; **~ly** ad dernièrement, récemment.

lattice ['lætis] n treillis m ; treillage m.

laudable ['lɔːdəbl] a louable.

laudatory ['lɔːdətri] a élogieux(euse).

laugh [lɑːf] n rire m // vi rire ; **to ~ at** vt fus se moquer de ; **to ~ off** vt écarter or rejeter par une plaisanterie or par une boutade ; **~able** a risible, ridicule ; **~ing** a (face) rieur(euse) ; **the ~ing stock of** la risée de ; **~ter** n rire m ; rires mpl.

launch [lɔːntʃ] n lancement m ; (boat) chaloupe f ; (also: **motor ~**) vedette f // vt (ship, rocket, plan) lancer ; **~ing** n lancement m ; **~(ing) pad** n rampe f de lancement.

launder ['lɔːndə*] vt blanchir.

launderette [lɔːn'drɛt] n laverie f (automatique).

laundry ['lɔːndri] n blanchisserie f ; (clothes) linge m ; **to do the ~** faire la lessive.

laureate ['lɔːriət] a see **poet**.

laurel ['lɔrl] n laurier m.

lava ['lɑːvə] n lave f.

lavatory ['lævətəri] n toilettes fpl.

lavender ['lævəndə*] n lavande f.

lavish ['læviʃ] a copieux(euse) ; somptueux(euse) ; (giving freely): **~ with** prodigue de // vt: **to ~ on sb/sth** (care) prodiguer à qn/qch ; (money) dépenser sans compter pour qn/qch.

law [lɔː] n loi f ; (science) droit m ; **~-abiding** a respectueux(euse) des lois ; **~ and order** n l'ordre public ; **~breaker** n personne f qui transgresse la loi ; **~ court** n tribunal m, cour f de justice ; **~ful** a légal(e) ; permis(e) ; **~fully** ad légalement ; **~less** a sans loi.

lawn [lɔːn] n pelouse f ; **~mower** n tondeuse f à gazon ; **~ tennis** [-'tɛnis] n tennis m.

law: ~ school n faculté f de droit ; **~ student** n étudiant/e en droit.

lawsuit ['lɔːsuːt] n procès m.

lawyer ['lɔːjə*] n (consultant, with company) juriste m ; (for sales, wills etc) ≈ notaire m ; (partner, in court) ≈ avocat m.

lax [læks] a relâché(e).

laxative ['læksətiv] n laxatif m.

laxity ['læksiti] n relâchement m.

lay [lei] pt of **lie** // a laïque ; profane // vt (pt, pp **laid** [leid]) poser, mettre ; (eggs) pondre ; (trap) tendre ; (plans) élaborer ; **to ~ the table** mettre la table ; **to ~ aside** or **by** vt mettre de côté ; **to ~ down** vt poser ; **to ~ down the law** faire la loi ; **to ~ off** vt (workers) licencier ; **to ~ on** vt (water, gas) mettre, installer ; (provide) fournir ; (paint) étaler ; **to ~ out** vt (design) dessiner, concevoir ; (display) disposer ; (spend) dépenser ; **to ~ up** vt (to store) amasser ; (car) remiser ; (ship) désarmer ; (subj: illness) forcer à s'aliter ; **~about** n fainéant/e // **~-by** n aire f de stationnement (sur le bas-côté).

layer ['leiə*] n couche f.

layette [lei'ɛt] n layette f.

layman ['leimən] n laïque m ; profane m.

layout ['leiaut] n disposition f, plan m, agencement m ; (PRESS) mise f en page.

laze [leiz] vi paresser.

laziness ['leizinis] n paresse f.

lazy ['leizi] a paresseux(euse).

lb. abbr of **pound** (weight).

lead [liːd] see also next headword ; n (front position) tête f ; (distance, time ahead) avance f ; (clue) piste f ; (in battery) raccord m ; (ELEC) fil m ; (for dog) laisse f ; (THEATRE) rôle principal m // vb (pt,pp **led** [lɛd]) vt mener, conduire ; (induce) amener ; (be leader of) être à la tête de ; (SPORT) être en tête de // vi mener, être en tête ; **to ~ to** mener à ; conduire à ; aboutir à ; **to ~ astray** vt détourner du droit chemin ; **to ~ away** vt emmener ; **to ~ back to** ramener à ; **to ~ on** vt (tease) faire marcher ; **to ~ on to** vt (induce) amener à ; **to ~ up to** conduire à.

lead [lɛd] see also previous headword ; n plomb m ; (in pencil) mine f ; **~en** a de or en plomb.

leader ['liːdə*] n chef m ; dirigeant/e, leader m ; (of newspaper) éditorial m ; **~ship** n direction f ; qualités fpl de chef.

leading ['liːdiŋ] a de premier plan ; principal(e) ; **~ lady** n (THEATRE) vedette

(féminine); ~ **light** n (person) vedette f,
sommité f; ~ **man** n (THEATRE) vedette
(masculine).

leaf, leaves [li:f, li:vz] n feuille f; (of table)
rallonge f.

leaflet ['li:flɪt] prospectus m, brochure f;
(POL, REL) tract m.

leafy ['li:fɪ] a feuillu(e).

league [li:g] n ligue f; (FOOTBALL)
championnat m; (measure) lieue f; **to be
in ~ with** avoir partie liée avec, être de
mèche avec.

leak [li:k] n (out, also fig) fuite f; (in)
infiltration f // vi (pipe, liquid etc) fuir;
(shoes) prendre l'eau // vt (liquid)
répandre; (information) divulguer; **to ~
out** vi fuir; être divulgué(e).

lean [li:n] a maigre // n (of meat) maigre
m // vb (pt,pp **leaned** or **leant** [lɛnt]) vt:
to ~ sth on appuyer qch sur // vi (slope)
pencher; (rest): **to ~ against** s'appuyer
contre; être appuyé(e) contre; **to ~ on**
s'appuyer sur; **to ~ back/forward** vi se
pencher en arrière/avant; **to ~ over** vi
se pencher // ~**ing** a penché(e) // n: ~**ing
(towards)** penchant m (pour); ~**-to** n
appentis m.

leap [li:p] n bond m, saut m // vi (pt,pp
leaped or **leapt** [lɛpt]) bondir, sauter;
~**frog** n jeu m de saute-mouton; ~
year n année f bissextile.

learn, pt,pp **learned** or **learnt** [lə:n, -t]
vt,vi apprendre; ~**ed** ['lə:nɪd] a érudit(e),
savant(e); ~**er** n débutant/e; ~**ing** n
savoir m.

lease [li:s] n bail m // vt louer à bail.

leash [li:ʃ] n laisse f.

least [li:st] ad le moins // a: **the ~ + noun**
le (la) plus petit(e), le (la) moindre;
(smallest amount of) le moins de; **the ~
+ adjective** le moins; **the ~ money** le
moins d'argent; **the ~ expensive** le
moins cher; **at ~** au moins; **not in the
~** pas le moins du monde.

leather ['lɛðə*] n cuir m // cpd en or de
cuir.

leave [li:v] vb (pt,pp **left** [lɛft]) vt laisser;
(go away from) quitter // vi partir, s'en
aller // n (time off) congé m; (MIL, also:
consent) permission f; **to be left** rester;
there's some milk left over il reste du
lait; **on ~** en permission; **to take one's
~ of** prendre congé de; **to ~ out** vt
oublier, omettre.

leaves [li:vz] npl of **leaf**.

Lebanon ['lɛbənən] n Liban.

lecherous ['lɛtʃərəs] a lubrique.

lectern ['lɛktə:n] n lutrin m, pupitre m.

lecture ['lɛktʃə*] n conférence f; (SCOL)
cours (magistral) // vi donner des cours;
enseigner; **to ~ on** faire un cours (or son
cours) sur.

lecturer ['lɛktʃərə*] n (speaker)
conférencier/ère; (at university)
professeur m (d'université), ≈ maître
assistant, ≈ maître de conférences;
assistant ~ n ≈ assistant/e; **senior ~**
n ≈ chargé/e d'enseignement.

led [lɛd] pt,pp of **lead**.

ledge [lɛdʒ] n (of window, on wall) rebord
m; (of mountain) saillie f, corniche f.

ledger ['lɛdʒə*] n registre m, grand livre.

lee [li:] n côté m sous le vent.

leech [li:tʃ] n sangsue f.

leek [li:k] n poireau m.

leer [lɪə*] vi: **to ~ at sb** regarder qn d'un
air mauvais or concupiscent, lorgner qn.

leeway ['li:weɪ] n (fig): **to make up ~**
rattraper son retard; **to have some ~**
avoir une certaine liberté d'action.

left [lɛft] pt,pp of **leave** // a gauche // ad
à gauche // n gauche f; **the L~** (POL) la
gauche; ~**-handed** a gaucher(ère); ~**-
hand side** n gauche f, côté m gauche; ~**-
luggage (office)** n consigne f; ~**-overs**
npl restes mpl; ~ **wing** n (MIL, SPORT) aile
f gauche; (POL) gauche f; ~**-wing** a (POL)
de gauche.

leg [lɛg] n jambe f; (of animal) patte f; (of
furniture) pied m; (CULIN: of chicken) cuisse
f; **lst/2nd ~** (SPORT) match m
aller/retour; (of journey) 1ère/2ème
étape; ~ **of lamb** (CULIN) gigot m
d'agneau.

legacy ['lɛgəsɪ] n héritage m, legs m.

legal ['li:gl] a légal(e); ~**ize** vt légaliser;
~**ly** ad légalement; ~ **tender** n monnaie
légale.

legation [lɪ'geɪʃən] n légation f.

legend ['lɛdʒənd] n légende f; ~**ary** a
légendaire.

-legged ['lɛgɪd] suffix: **two~** à deux pattes
(or jambes or pieds).

leggings ['lɛgɪŋz] npl jambières fpl,
guêtres fpl.

legibility [lɛdʒɪ'bɪlɪtɪ] n lisibilité f.

legible ['lɛdʒəbl] a lisible.

legibly ['lɛdʒəblɪ] ad lisiblement.

legion ['li:dʒən] n légion f.

legislate ['lɛdʒɪsleɪt] vi légiférer;
legislation [-'leɪʃən] n législation f;
legislative ['lɛdʒɪslətɪv] a législatif(ive);
legislator n législateur/trice; **legislature**
['lɛdʒɪslətʃə*] n corps législatif.

legitimacy [lɪ'dʒɪtɪməsɪ] n légitimité f.

legitimate [lɪ'dʒɪtɪmət] a légitime.

leg-room ['lɛgru:m] n place f pour les
jambes.

leisure ['lɛʒə*] n loisir m, temps m libre;
loisirs mpl; **at ~** (tout) à loisir; à tête
reposée; ~ **centre** n centre m de loisirs;
~**ly** a tranquille; fait(e) sans se presser.

lemon ['lɛmən] n citron m; ~**ade** n [-'neɪd]
limonade f; ~ **squeezer** n presse-citron
m inv.

lend, pt,pp **lent** [lɛnd, lɛnt] vt: **to ~ sth
(to sb)** prêter qch (à qn); ~**er** n
prêteur/euse; ~**ing library** n
bibliothèque f de prêt.

length [lɛŋθ] n longueur f; (section: of road,
pipe etc) morceau m, bout m; ~ **of time**
durée f; **at ~** (at last) enfin, à la fin;
(lengthily) longuement; ~**en** vt allonger,
prolonger // vi s'allonger; ~**ways** ad
dans le sens de la longueur, en long; ~**y**
a (très) long(longue).

leniency ['li:nɪənsɪ] n indulgence f,
clémence f.

lenient ['li:nɪənt] a indulgent(e),
clément(e); ~**ly** ad avec indulgence or
clémence.

lens [lɛnz] n lentille f; (of spectacles) verre m; (of camera) objectif m.

lent [lɛnt] pt,pp of **lend**.

Lent [lɛnt] n Carême m.

lentil [ˈlɛntl] n lentille f.

Leo [ˈliːəu] n le Lion; **to be** ~ être du Lion.

leopard [ˈlɛpəd] n léopard m.

leotard [ˈliːətɑːd] n collant m (de danseur etc).

leper [ˈlɛpə*] n lépreux/euse.

leprosy [ˈlɛprəsı] n lèpre f.

lesbian [ˈlɛzbıən] n lesbienne f.

less [lɛs] det moins de // pronoun, ad moins; ~ **than that/you** moins que cela/vous; ~ **than half** moins de la moitié; ~ **and** ~ de moins en moins; the ~ **he works...** moins il travaille... .

lessen [ˈlɛsn] vi diminuer, s'amoindrir, s'atténuer // vt diminuer, réduire, atténuer.

lesson [ˈlɛsn] n leçon f; **a maths** ~ une leçon or un cours de maths.

lest [lɛst] cj de peur de + infinitive, de peur que + sub.

let, pt,pp **let** [lɛt] vt laisser; (lease) louer; he ~ **me go** il m'a laissé partir; ~ **the water boil and...** faites bouillir l'eau et...; ~'**s go** allons-y; ~ **him come** qu'il vienne; '**to** ~' 'à louer'; **to** ~ **down** vt (lower) baisser; (dress) rallonger; (hair) défaire; (disappoint) décevoir; **to** ~ **go** vi lâcher prise // vt lâcher; **to** ~ **in** vt laisser entrer; (visitor etc) faire entrer; **to** ~ **off** vt laisser partir; (firework etc) faire partir; (smell etc) dégager; **to** ~ **out** vt laisser sortir; (dress) élargir; (scream) laisser échapper; **to** ~ **up** vi diminuer, s'arrêter.

lethal [ˈliːθl] a mortel(le), fatal(e).

lethargic [lɛˈθɑːdʒık] a léthargique.

lethargy [ˈlɛθədʒı] n léthargie f.

letter [ˈlɛtə*] n lettre f; ~**s** npl (LITERATURE) lettres; ~ **bomb** n lettre piégée; ~**box** n boîte f aux or à lettres; ~**ing** n lettres fpl; caractères mpl.

lettuce [ˈlɛtıs] n laitue f, salade f.

let-up [ˈlɛtʌp] n répit m, détente f.

leukaemia, leukemia (US) [luːˈkiːmıə] n leucémie f.

level [ˈlɛvl] a plat(e), plan(e), uni(e); horizontal(e) // n niveau m; (flat place) terrain plat; (also: **spirit** ~) niveau à bulle // vt niveler, aplanir; **to be** ~ **with** être au même niveau que; '**A**' ~**s** npl ≈ baccalauréat m; '**O**' ~**s** npl ≈ B.E.P.C.; **on the** ~ à l'horizontale; (fig: honest) régulier(ère); **to** ~ **off** or **out** vi (prices etc) se stabiliser; ~ **crossing** n passage m à niveau; ~**-headed** a équilibré(e).

lever [ˈliːvə*] n levier m // vt: **to** ~ **up/out** soulever/extraire au moyen d'un levier; ~**age** n: ~**age (on** or **with)** prise f (sur).

levity [ˈlɛvıtı] n manque m de sérieux, légèreté f.

levy [ˈlɛvı] n taxe f, impôt m // vt prélever, imposer; percevoir.

lewd [luːd] a obscène, lubrique.

liability [laıəˈbılətı] n responsabilité f; (handicap) handicap m; **liabilities** npl obligations fpl, engagements mpl; (on balance sheet) passif m.

liable [ˈlaıəbl] a (subject): ~ **to** sujet(te) à; passible de; (responsible): ~ **for** responsable (de); (likely): ~ **to do** susceptible de faire.

liaison [liːˈeızɔn] n liaison f.

liar [ˈlaıə*] n menteur/euse.

libel [ˈlaıbl] n écrit m diffamatoire; diffamation f // vt diffamer.

liberal [ˈlıbərl] a libéral(e); (generous): ~ **with** prodigue de, généreux(euse) avec.

liberate [ˈlıbəreıt] vt libérer; **liberation** [-ˈreıʃən] n libération f.

liberty [ˈlıbətı] n liberté f; **at** ~ **to do** libre de faire; **to take the** ~ **of** prendre la liberté de, se permettre de.

Libra [ˈliːbrə] n la Balance; **to be** ~ être de la Balance.

librarian [laıˈbrɛərıən] n bibliothécaire m/f.

library [ˈlaıbrərı] n bibliothèque f.

libretto [lıˈbrɛtəu] n livret m.

Libya [ˈlıbıə] n Lybie f; ~**n** a lybien(ne), de Lybie // n Lybien/ne.

lice [laıs] npl of **louse**.

licence, license (US) [ˈlaısns] n autorisation f, permis m; (COMM) licence f; (RADIO, TV) redevance f; (also: **driving** ~) permis m (de conduire); (excessive freedom) licence; ~ **plate** n plaque f minéralogique.

license [ˈlaısns] n (US) = **licence** // vt donner une licence à; ~**d** a (for alcohol) patenté(e) pour la vente des spiritueux, qui a une patente de débit de boissons.

licensee [laısənˈsiː] n (in a pub) patron/ne, gérant/e.

licentious [laıˈsɛnʃəs] a licentieux(euse).

lichen [ˈlaıkən] n lichen m.

lick [lık] vt lécher // n coup m de langue; **a** ~ **of paint** un petit coup de peinture.

licorice [ˈlıkərıs] n = **liquorice**.

lid [lıd] n couvercle m.

lido [ˈlaıdəu] n piscine f en plein air.

lie [laı] n mensonge m // vi mentir; (pt **lay**, pp **lain** [leı, leın]) (rest) être étendu(e) or allongé(e) or couché(e); (in grave) être enterré(e), reposer; (of object: be situated) se trouver, être; **to** ~ **low** (fig) se cacher, rester caché(e); **to** ~ **about** vi traîner; **to have a** ~**-down** s'allonger, se reposer; **to have a** ~**-in** faire la grasse matinée.

lieu [luː]: **in** ~ **of** prep au lieu de.

lieutenant [lɛfˈtɛnənt] n lieutenant m.

life, lives [laıf, laıvz] n vie f // cpd de vie; de la vie; à vie; ~ **assurance** n assurance-vie f; ~**belt** n bouée f de sauvetage; ~**boat** n canot m or chaloupe f de sauvetage; ~**buoy** n bouée f de sauvetage; ~**expectancy** n espérance f de vie; ~**guard** n surveillant m de baignade; ~**jacket** n gilet m or ceinture f de sauvetage; ~**less** a sans vie, inanimé(e); (dull) qui manque de vie or de vigueur; ~**like** a qui semble vrai(e) or vivant(e); ressemblant(e); ~**line** n corde f de sauvetage; ~**long** a de toute une vie, de toujours; ~ **preserver** n (US) gilet m or ceinture f de sauvetage; (Brit: col) matraque f; ~**-raft** n radeau m de sauvetage; ~**-saver** n surveillant m de baignade; ~ **sentence** n condamnation f à vie *or* à perpétuité ; **~-sized** *a* grandeur nature *inv* ; **~ span** *n* (durée *f* de) vie *f* ; **~ support system** *n* (MED) respirateur artificiel ; **~-time** *n*: **in his ~-time** de son vivant ; **in a ~-time** au cours d'une vie entière ; dans sa vie.

lift [lɪft] *vt* soulever, lever ; (*steal*) prendre, voler // *vi* (*fog*) se lever // *n* (*elevator*) ascenseur *m* ; **to give sb a ~** emmener *or* prendre qn en voiture ; **~-off** *n* décollage *m*.

ligament ['lɪgəmənt] *n* ligament *m*.

light [laɪt] *n* lumière *f* ; (*daylight*) lumière, jour *m* ; (*lamp*) lampe *f* ; (AUT: *traffic ~*, *rear ~*) feu *m* ; (: *headlamp*) phare *m* ; (*for cigarette etc*): **have you got a ~?** avez-vous du feu? // *vt* (*pt, pp* **lighted** *or* **lit** [lɪt]) (*candle, cigarette, fire*) allumer ; (*room*) éclairer // *a* (*room, colour*) clair(e) ; (*not heavy, also fig*) léger(ère) ; **to ~ up** *vi* s'allumer ; (*face*) s'éclairer // *vt* (*illuminate*) éclairer, illuminer ; **~ bulb** *n* ampoule *f* ; **~en** *vi* s'éclaircir // *vt* (*give light to*) éclairer ; (*make lighter*) éclaircir ; (*make less heavy*) alléger ; **~er** *n* (*also*: **cigarette ~**) briquet *m* ; (: *in car*) allume-cigare *m inv* ; (*boat*) péniche *f* ; **~-headed** *a* étourdi(e), écervelé(e) ; **~-hearted** *a* gai(e), joyeux(euse), enjoué(e) ; **~house** *n* phare *m* ; **~ing** *n* (*on road*) éclairage *m* ; (*in theatre*) éclairages ; **~ing-up time** *n* heure officielle de la tombée du jour ; **~ly** *ad* légèrement ; **~ meter** *n* (PHOT) photomètre *m*, cellule *f* ; **~ness** *n* clarté *f* ; (*in weight*) légèreté *f*.

lightning ['laɪtnɪŋ] *n* éclair *m*, foudre *f* ; **~ conductor** *n* paratonnerre *m*.

lightship ['laɪtʃɪp] *n* bateau-phare *m*.

lightweight ['laɪtweɪt] *a* (*suit*) léger(ère) ; (*boxer*) poids léger *inv*.

light year ['laɪtjɪə*] *n* année-lumière *f*.

lignite ['lɪgnaɪt] *n* lignite *m*.

like [laɪk] *vt* aimer (bien) // *prep* comme // *a* semblable, pareil(le) // *n*: **the ~** un(e) pareil(le) *or* semblable ; le(la) pareil(le) ; (*pej*) (d')autres du même genre *or* acabit ; **his ~s and dislikes** ses goûts *mpl or* préférences *fpl* ; **I would ~, I'd ~** je voudrais, j'aimerais ; **to be/look ~ sb/sth** ressembler à qn/qch ; **that's just ~ him** c'est bien de lui, ça lui ressemble ; **nothing ~...** rien de tel que... ; **~able** *a* sympathique, agréable.

likelihood ['laɪklɪhud] *n* probabilité *f*.

likely ['laɪklɪ] *a* probable ; plausible ; **he's ~ to leave** il va sûrement partir, il risque fort de partir.

like-minded [laɪk'maɪndɪd] *a* de même opinion.

liken ['laɪkən] *vt*: **to ~ sth to** comparer qch à.

likewise ['laɪkwaɪz] *ad* de même, pareillement.

liking ['laɪkɪŋ] *n*: **~ (for)** affection *f* (pour), penchant *m* (pour) ; goût *m* (pour).

lilac ['laɪlək] *n* lilas *m* // *a* lilas *inv*.

lilting ['lɪltɪŋ] *a* aux cadences mélodieuses ; chantant(e).

lily ['lɪlɪ] *n* lis *m* ; **~ of the valley** *n* muguet *m*.

limb [lɪm] *n* membre *m*.

limber ['lɪmbə*]: **to ~ up** *vi* se dégourdir, se mettre en train.

limbo ['lɪmbəu] *n*: **to be in ~** (*fig*) être tombé(e) dans l'oubli.

lime [laɪm] *n* (*tree*) tilleul *m* ; (*fruit*) lime *f* ; (GEO) chaux *f* ; **~ juice** *n* jus *m* de citron vert.

limelight ['laɪmlaɪt] *n*: **in the ~** (*fig*) en vedette, au premier plan.

limerick ['lɪmərɪk] *n* poème *m* humoristique (de 5 vers).

limestone ['laɪmstəun] *n* pierre *f* à chaux ; (GEO) calcaire *m*.

limit ['lɪmɪt] *n* limite *f* // *vt* limiter ; **~ation** [-'teɪʃən] *n* limitation *f*, restriction *f* ; **~ed** *a* limité(e), restreint(e) ; **~ed (liability) company (Ltd)** *n* ≈ société *f* anonyme (S.A.).

limousine ['lɪməzi:n] *n* limousine *f*.

limp [lɪmp] *n*: **to have a ~** boiter // *vi* boiter // *a* mou(molle).

limpet ['lɪmpɪt] *n* patelle *f* ; **like a ~** (*fig*) comme une ventouse.

line [laɪn] *n* (*gen*) ligne *f* ; (*rope*) corde *f* ; (*wire*) fil *m* ; (*of poem*) vers *m* ; (*row, series*) rangée *f* ; file *f*, queue *f* ; (COMM: *series of goods*) article(s) *m(pl)* // *vt* (: *of clothes*): **to ~ (with)** doubler (de) ; (*box*): **to ~ (with)** garnir *or* tapisser (de) ; (*subj: trees, crowd*) border ; **in his ~ of business** dans sa partie, dans son rayon ; **in ~ with** en accord avec ; **to ~ up** *vi* s'aligner, se mettre en rang(s) // *vt* aligner.

linear ['lɪnɪə*] *a* linéaire.

linen ['lɪnɪn] *n* linge *m* (de corps *or* de maison) ; (*cloth*) lin *m*.

liner ['laɪnə*] *n* paquebot *m* de ligne.

linesman ['laɪnzmən] *n* (TENNIS) juge *m* de ligne ; (FOOTBALL) juge de touche.

line-up ['laɪnʌp] *n* file *f* ; (SPORT) (composition *f* de l')équipe *f*.

linger ['lɪŋgə*] *vi* s'attarder ; traîner ; (*smell, tradition*) persister ; **~ing** *a* persistant(e) ; qui subsiste ; (*death*) lent(e).

lingo, ~es ['lɪŋgəu] *n* (*pej*) jargon *m*.

linguist ['lɪŋgwɪst] *n* linguiste *m/f* ; personne douée pour les langues ; **~ic** *a* linguistique ; **~ics** *n* linguistique *f*.

lining ['laɪnɪŋ] *n* doublure *f*.

link [lɪŋk] *n* (*of a chain*) maillon *m* ; (*connection*) lien *m*, rapport *m* // *vt* relier, lier, unir ; **~s** *npl* (terrain *m* de) golf *m* ; **to ~ up** *vt* relier // *vi* se rejoindre ; s'associer ; **~-up** *n* liaison *f*.

linoleum [lɪ'nəulɪəm] *n* linoléum *m*.

linseed oil ['lɪnsɪ:dɔɪl] *n* huile *f* de lin.

lint [lɪnt] *n* tissu ouaté (*pour pansements*).

lintel ['lɪntl] *n* linteau *m*.

lion ['laɪən] *n* lion *m* ; **~ cub** lionceau *m* ; **~ess** *n* lionne *f*.

lip [lɪp] *n* lèvre *f* ; (*of cup etc*) rebord *m* ; (*insolence*) insolences *fpl* ; **~read** *vi* lire sur les lèvres ; **to pay ~ service to sth** ne reconnaître le mérite de qch que pour la forme *or* qu'en paroles ; **~stick** *n* rouge *m* à lèvres.

liquefy ['lɪkwɪfaɪ] *vt* liquéfier.

liqueur [lɪ'kjuə*] *n* liqueur *f*.

liquid ['lɪkwɪd] *n* liquide *m* // *a* liquide ; **~ assets** *npl* liquidités *fpl*, disponibilités *fpl*.

liquidate ['lıkwıdeıt] vt liquider;
liquidation [-'deıʃən] n liquidation f;
liquidator n liquidateur m.
liquidize ['lıkwıdaız] vt (CULIN) passer au mixeur.
liquor ['lıkə*] n spiritueux m, alcool m.
liquorice ['lıkərıs] n réglisse m.
lisp [lısp] n zézaiement m.
list [lıst] n liste f; (of ship) inclinaison f // vt (write down) inscrire; faire la liste de; (enumerate) énumérer // vi (ship) gîter, donner de la bande.
listen ['lısn] vi écouter; **to ~ to** écouter; **~er** n auditeur/trice.
listless ['lıstlıs] a indolent(e), apathique; **~ly** ad indolence or apathie.
lit [lıt] pt,pp of **light**.
litany ['lıtənı] n litanie f.
literacy ['lıtərəsı] n degré m d'alphabétisation, fait m de savoir lire et écrire.
literal ['lıtərl] a littéral(e); (unimaginative) prosaïque, sans imagination; **~ly** ad littéralement.
literary ['lıtərərı] a littéraire.
literate ['lıtərət] a qui sait lire et écrire, instruit(e).
literature ['lıtərıtʃə*] n littérature f; (brochures etc) copie f publicitaire, prospectus mpl.
lithe [laıð] a agile, souple.
lithography [lı'θɔgrəfı] n lithographie f.
litigate ['lıtıgeıt] vt mettre en litige // vi plaider; **litigation** [-'geıʃən] n litige m; contentieux m.
litmus ['lıtməs] n: **~ paper** papier m de tournesol.
litre, liter (US) ['li:tə*] n litre m.
litter ['lıtə*] n (rubbish) détritus mpl, ordures fpl; (young animals) portée f // vt éparpiller; laisser des détritus dans // vi (ZOOL) mettre bas; **~ bin** n boîte f à ordures, poubelle f; **~ed with** jonché(e) de, couvert(e) de.
little ['lıtl] a (small) petit(e); (not much): **it's ~** c'est peu; **~ milk** peu de lait // ad peu; **a ~** un peu (de); **a ~ milk** un peu de lait; **~ by ~** petit à petit, peu à peu; **to make ~ of** faire peu de cas de.
liturgy ['lıtədʒı] n liturgie f.
live vi [lıv] vivre; (reside) vivre, habiter // a [laıv] (animal) vivant(e), en vie; (wire) sous tension; (broadcast) (transmis(e)) en direct; **to ~ down** vt faire oublier (avec le temps); **to ~ in** vi être logé(e) et nourri(e); être interne; **to ~ on** vt fus (food) vivre de // vi survivre, subsister; **to ~ up to** vt fus se montrer à la hauteur de.
livelihood ['laıvlıhud] n moyens mpl d'existence.
liveliness ['laıvlınəs] n vivacité f, entrain m.
lively ['laıvlı] a vif(vive), plein(e) d'entrain.
liver ['lıvə*] n (ANAT) foie m; (fig) grincheux(euse); **~ish** a qui a mal au foie, (fig) grincheux(euse).
livery ['lıvərı] n livrée f.
lives [laıvz] npl of **life**.
livestock ['laıvstɔk] n cheptel m, bétail m.
livid ['lıvıd] a livide, blafard(e); (furious) furieux(euse), furibond(e).

living ['lıvıŋ] a vivant(e), en vie // n: **to earn** or **make a ~** gagner sa vie; **~ room** n salle f de séjour; **~ standards** npl niveau m de vie; **~ wage** n salaire m permettant de vivre (décemment).
lizard ['lızəd] n lézard m.
llama ['lɑ:mə] n lama m.
load [ləud] n (weight) poids m; (thing carried) chargement m, charge f; (ELEC, TECH) charge // vt: **to ~** (with) (lorry, ship) charger (de); (gun, camera) charger (avec); **a ~ of, ~s of** (fig) un or des tas de, des masses de; **~ed** a (dice) pipé(e); (question, word) insidieux(euse); (col: rich) bourré(e) de fric; (: drunk) bourré.
loaf, loaves [ləuf, ləuvz] n pain m, miche f // vi (also: **~ about, ~ around**) fainéanter, traîner.
loam [ləum] n terreau m.
loan [ləun] n prêt m // vt prêter; **on ~** prêté(e), en prêt; **public ~** emprunt public.
loath [ləuθ] a: **to be ~ to do** répugner à faire.
loathe [ləuð] vt détester, avoir en horreur; **loathing** n dégoût m, répugnance f.
loaves [ləuvz] npl of **loaf**.
lobby ['lɔbı] n hall m, entrée f; (POL: pressure group) groupe m de pression, lobby m // vt faire pression sur.
lobe [ləub] n lobe m.
lobster ['lɔbstə*] n homard m.
local ['ləukl] a local(e) // n (pub) pub m or café m du coin; **the ~s** npl les gens mpl du pays or du coin; **~ call** n communication urbaine; **~ government** n administration locale or municipale.
locality [ləu'kælıtı] n région f, environs mpl; (position) lieu m.
locally ['ləukəlı] ad localement; dans les environs or la région.
locate [ləu'keıt] vt (find) trouver, repérer; (situate) situer.
location [ləu'keıʃən] n emplacement m; **on ~** (CINEMA) en extérieur.
loch [lɔx] n lac m, loch m.
lock [lɔk] n (of door, box) serrure f; (of canal) écluse f; (of hair) mèche f, boucle f // vt (with key) fermer à clé; (immobilize) bloquer // vi (door etc) fermer à clé; (wheels) se bloquer.
locker ['lɔkə*] n casier m.
locket ['lɔkıt] n médaillon m.
lockjaw ['lɔkdʒɔ:] n tétanos m.
locomotive [ləukə'məutıv] n locomotive f.
locust ['ləukəst] n locuste f, sauterelle f.
lodge [lɔdʒ] n pavillon m (de gardien); (FREEMASONRY) loge f // vi (person): **to ~ (with)** être logé(e) (chez), être en pension (chez) // vt (appeal etc) présenter; déposer; **to ~ a complaint** porter plainte; **to ~ (itself) in/between** se loger dans/entre; **~r** n locataire m/f; (with room and meals) pensionnaire m/f.
lodgings ['lɔdʒıŋz] npl chambre f; meublé m.
loft [lɔft] n grenier m.
lofty ['lɔftı] a élevé(e); (haughty) hautain(e).
log [lɔg] n (of wood) bûche f; (book) = **logbook**.

logarithm ['lɔgərɪðəm] *n* logarithme *m*.

logbook ['lɔgbuk] *n* (NAUT) livre *m* or journal *m* de bord ; (AVIAT) carnet *m* de vol ; (of lorry-driver) carnet de route ; (of events, movement of goods etc) registre *m* ; (of car) ≈ carte grise.

loggerheads ['lɔgəhɛdz] *npl*: at ~ (with) à couteaux tirés (avec).

logic ['lɔdʒɪk] *n* logique *f* ; ~al a logique ; ~ally ad logiquement.

logistics [lɔ'dʒɪstɪks] *n* logistique *f*.

loin [lɔɪn] *n* (CULIN) filet *m*, longe *f* ; ~s *npl* reins *mpl*.

loiter ['lɔɪtə*] *vi* s'attarder ; to ~ (about) traîner, musarder ; (pej) rôder.

loll [lɔl] *vi* (also: ~ about) se prélasser, fainéanter.

lollipop ['lɔlɪpɔp] *n* sucette *f* ; ~ man/lady *n* contractuel/le qui fait traverser la rue aux enfants.

London ['lʌndən] *n* Londres *m* ; ~er *n* Londonien/ne.

lone [ləun] *a* solitaire.

loneliness ['ləunlɪnɪs] *n* solitude *f*, isolement *m*.

lonely ['ləunlɪ] *a* seul(e) ; solitaire, isolé(e) ; to feel ~ se sentir seul.

loner ['ləunə*] *n* solitaire *m/f*.

long [lɔŋ] *a* long(longue) // *ad* longtemps // *vi*: to ~ for sth/to do avoir très envie de qch/de faire ; attendre qch avec impatience/impatience de faire ; he had ~ understood that... il avait compris depuis longtemps que... ; how ~ is this river/course? quelle est la longueur de ce fleuve/la durée de ce cours? ; 6 metres ~ (long) de 6 mètres ; 6 months ~ qui dure 6 mois, de 6 mois ; all night ~ toute la nuit ; ~ before longtemps avant ; before ~ (+ future) avant peu, dans peu de temps ; (+ past) peu de temps après ; at ~ last enfin ; no ~er, any ~er ne...plus ; ~-distance a (race) de fond ; (call) interurbain(e) ; ~-haired a (person) aux cheveux longs ; (animal) aux longs poils ; ~hand *n* écriture normale or courante ; ~ing *n* désir *m*, envie *f*, nostalgie *f* // a plein(e) d'envie or de nostalgie.

longitude ['lɔŋgɪtjuːd] *n* longitude *f*.

long: ~ **jump** *n* saut *m* en longueur ; ~-lost a perdu(e) depuis longtemps ; ~-playing a; ~-playing record (L.P.) *n* (disque *m*) 33 tours *m inv* ; ~-range a à longue portée ; ~-sighted a presbyte ; (fig) prévoyant(e) ; ~-standing a de longue date ; ~-suffering a empreint(e) d'une patience résignée ; extrêmement patient(e) ; ~-term a à long terme ; ~-wave *n* grandes ondes ; ~-winded a intarissable, interminable.

loo [luː] *n* (col) w.-c. *mpl*, petit coin.

loofah ['luːfə] *n* sorte d'éponge végétale.

look [luk] *vi* regarder ; (seem) sembler, paraître, avoir l'air ; (building etc): to ~ south/on to the sea donner au sud/sur la mer // *n* regard *m* ; (appearance) air *m*, allure *f*, aspect *m* ; ~s *npl* mine *f*, physique *m* ; beauté *f* ; to ~ like ressembler à ; it ~s like him on dirait que c'est lui ; to ~ after vt fus s'occuper de, prendre soin de ; garder, surveiller ; to ~ at vt fus regarder ; to ~ down on vt fus

(fig) regarder de haut, dédaigner ; to ~ for vt fus chercher ; to ~ forward to vt fus attendre avec impatience ; to ~ on vi regarder (en spectateur) ; to ~ out vi (beware): to ~ out (for) prendre garde (à), faire attention (à) ; to ~ out for vt fus être à la recherche de ; guetter ; to ~ to vt fus veiller à ; (rely on) compter sur ; to ~ up vi lever les yeux ; (improve) s'améliorer // vt (word) chercher ; (friend) passer voir ; to ~ up to vt fus avoir du respect pour ; ~-out *n* poste *m* de guet ; guetteur *m* ; to be on the ~-out (for) guetter.

loom [luːm] *n* métier *m* à tisser // *vi* surgir ; (fig) menacer, paraître imminent(e).

loop [luːp] *n* boucle *f* ; (contraceptive) stérilet *m* ; ~hole *n* porte *f* de sortie (fig), échappatoire *f*.

loose [luːs] *a* (knot, screw) desserré(e) ; (stone) branlant(e) ; (clothes) vague, ample, lâche ; (animal) en liberté, échappé(e) ; (life) dissolu(e) ; (morals, discipline) relâché(e) ; (thinking) peu rigoureux(euse), vague ; (translation) approximatif(ive) ; to be at a ~ end ne pas trop savoir quoi faire ; ~ly ad sans serrer ; approximativement ; ~n vt desserrer, relâcher, défaire.

loot [luːt] *n* butin *m* // vt piller ; ~ing *n* pillage *m*.

lop [lɔp] *n*: to ~ off vt couper, trancher.

lop-sided ['lɔp'saɪdɪd] a de travers, asymétrique.

lord [lɔːd] *n* seigneur *m* ; L~ Smith lord Smith ; the L~ le Seigneur ; the (House of) L~s la Chambre des Lords ; ~ly a noble, majestueux(euse) ; (arrogant) hautain(e) ; ~ship *n*: your L~ship Monsieur le comte (or le baron or le Juge).

lore [lɔː*] *n* tradition(s) *f(pl)*.

lorry ['lɔrɪ] *n* camion *m* ; ~ driver *n* camionneur *m*, routier *m*.

lose [luːz], *pt,pp* lost [luːz, lɔst] vt perdre ; (opportunity) manquer, perdre ; (pursuers) distancer, semer // vi perdre ; to ~ (time) (clock) retarder ; to be lost vi se perdre ; ~r *n* perdant/e.

loss [lɔs] *n* perte *f* ; to be at a ~ être perplexe or embarrassé(e) ; to be at a ~ to do se trouver incapable de faire.

lost [lɔst] *pt,pp of* lose // a perdu(e) ; ~ property *n* objets trouvés.

lot [lɔt] *n* (at auctions) lot *m* ; (destiny) sort *m*, destinée *f* ; the ~ le tout ; tous *mpl*, toutes *fpl* ; a ~ beaucoup ; a ~ of beaucoup de ; ~s of des tas de ; to draw ~s (for sth) tirer (qch) au sort.

lotion ['ləuʃən] *n* lotion *f*.

lottery ['lɔtərɪ] *n* loterie *f*.

loud [laud] *a* bruyant(e), sonore, fort(e) ; (gaudy) voyant(e), tapageur(euse) // ad (speak etc) fort ; ~hailer *n* porte-voix *m inv* ; ~ly ad fort, bruyamment ; ~speaker *n* haut-parleur *m*.

lounge [laundʒ] *n* salon *m* // *vi* se prélasser, paresser ; ~ suit *n* complet *m* ; 'tenue de ville'.

louse, *pl* lice [laus, laɪs] *n* pou *m*.

lousy ['lauzɪ] *a* (fig) infect(e), moche.

lout [laut] n rustre m, butor m.

lovable ['lʌvəbl] a très sympathique ; adorable.

love [lʌv] n amour m // vt aimer ; aimer beaucoup ; **to ~ to do** aimer beaucoup or adorer faire ; **to be in ~ with** être amoureux(euse) de ; **to make ~** faire l'amour ; **'15 ~'** (TENNIS) '15 à rien or zéro' ; **~ at first sight** le coup de foudre ; **~ affair** n liaison (amoureuse) ; **~ letter** n lettre f d'amour ; **~ life** n vie sentimentale.

lovely ['lʌvlɪ] a (très) joli(e) ; ravissant(e), charmant(e) ; agréable.

lover ['lʌvə*] n amant m ; (amateur): **a ~ of** un(e) ami(e) de ; un(e) amoureux(euse) de.

lovesong ['lʌvsɔŋ] n chanson f d'amour.

loving ['lʌvɪŋ] a affectueux(euse), tendre, aimant(e).

low [ləu] a bas(basse) // ad bas // n (METEOROLOGY) dépression f // vi (cow) mugir ; **to feel ~** se sentir déprimé(e) ; **he's very ~** (ill) il est bien bas or très affaibli ; **to turn (down) ~** vt baisser ; **~-cut** a (dress) décolleté(e) ; **~er** vt abaisser, baisser ; **~ly** a humble, modeste ; **~-lying** a à faible altitude ; **~-paid** a mal payé(e), aux salaires bas.

loyal ['lɔɪəl] a loyal(e), fidèle ; **~ty** n loyauté f, fidélité f.

lozenge ['lɔzɪndʒ] n (MED) pastille f ; (GEOM) losange m.

L.P. n abbr see **long-playing**.

L-plates ['ɛlpleɪts] npl plaques fpl d'apprenti conducteur.

Ltd abbr see **limited**.

lubricant ['lu:brɪkənt] n lubrifiant m.

lubricate ['lu:brɪkeɪt] vt lubrifier, graisser.

lucid ['lu:sɪd] a lucide ; **~ity** [-'sɪdɪtɪ] n lucidité f.

luck [lʌk] n chance f ; **bad ~** malchance f, malheur m ; **good ~!** bonne chance! **~ily** ad heureusement, par bonheur ; **~y** a (person) qui a de la chance ; (coincidence) heureux(euse) ; (number etc) qui porte bonheur.

lucrative ['lu:krətɪv] a lucratif(ive), rentable, qui rapporte.

ludicrous ['lu:dɪkrəs] a ridicule, absurde.

ludo ['lu:dəu] n jeu m des petits chevaux.

lug [lʌg] vt traîner, tirer.

luggage ['lʌgɪdʒ] n bagages mpl ; **~ rack** n (in train) porte-bagages m inv ; (: made of string) filet m à bagages ; (on car) galerie f.

lugubrious [lu'gu:brɪəs] a lugubre.

lukewarm ['lu:kwɔ:m] a tiède.

lull [lʌl] n accalmie f // vt (child) bercer ; (person, fear) apaiser, calmer.

lullaby ['lʌləbaɪ] n berceuse f.

lumbago [lʌm'beɪgəu] n lumbago m.

lumber ['lʌmbə*] n bric-à-brac m inv ; **~jack** n bûcheron m.

luminous ['lu:mɪnəs] a lumineux(euse).

lump [lʌmp] n morceau m ; (in sauce) grumeau m ; (swelling) grosseur f // vt (also: **~ together**) réunir, mettre en tas ; **a ~ sum** une somme globale or forfaitaire ; **~y** a (sauce) qui a des grumeaux.

lunacy ['lu:nəsɪ] n démence f, folie f.

lunar ['lu:nə*] a lunaire.

lunatic ['lu:nətɪk] n fou/folle, dément/e // a fou(folle), dément(e).

lunch [lʌntʃ] n déjeuner m ; **it is his ~ hour** c'est l'heure où il déjeune ; **it is ~time** c'est l'heure du déjeuner.

luncheon ['lʌntʃən] n déjeuner m ; **~ meat** n sorte de saucisson ; **~ voucher** n chèque-déjeuner m.

lung [lʌŋ] n poumon m ; **~ cancer** n cancer m du poumon.

lunge [lʌndʒ] vi (also: **~ forward**) faire un mouvement brusque en avant.

lupin ['lu:pɪn] n lupin m.

lurch [lə:tʃ] vi vaciller, tituber // n écart m brusque, embardée f.

lure [luə*] n appât m, leurre m // vt attirer or persuader par la ruse.

lurid ['luərɪd] a affreux(euse), atroce.

lurk [lə:k] vi se tapir, se cacher.

luscious ['lʌʃəs] a succulent(e) ; appétissant(e).

lush [lʌʃ] a luxuriant(e).

lust [lʌst] n luxure f ; lubricité f ; désir m ; (fig): **~ for** soif f de ; **to ~ after** vt fus convoiter, désirer ; **~ful** a lascif(ive).

lustre, luster (US) ['lʌstə*] n lustre m, brillant m.

lusty ['lʌstɪ] a vigoureux(euse), robuste.

lute [lu:t] n luth m.

Luxembourg ['lʌksəmbə:g] n Luxembourg m.

luxuriant [lʌg'zjuərɪənt] a luxuriant(e).

luxurious [lʌg'zjuərɪəs] a luxueux(euse).

luxury ['lʌkʃərɪ] n luxe m // cpd de luxe.

lying ['laɪɪŋ] n mensonge(s) m(pl).

lynch [lɪntʃ] vt lyncher.

lynx [lɪŋks] n lynx m inv.

lyre ['laɪə*] n lyre f.

lyric ['lɪrɪk] a lyrique ; **~s** npl (of song) paroles fpl ; **~al** a lyrique ; **~ism** ['lɪrɪsɪzəm] n lyrisme m.

M

m. abbr of **metre, mile, million**.

M.A. abbr see **master**.

mac [mæk] n imper(méable) m.

macaroni [mækə'rəunɪ] n macaronis mpl.

macaroon [mækə'ru:n] n macaron m.

mace [meɪs] n masse f ; (spice) macis m.

machine [mə'ʃi:n] n machine f // vt (dress etc) coudre à la machine ; **~ gun** n mitrailleuse f ; **~ry** n machinerie f, machines fpl ; (fig) mécanisme(s) m(pl) ; **~ tool** n machine-outil f ; **machinist** n machiniste m/f.

mackerel ['mækrl] n, pl inv maquereau m.

mackintosh ['mækɪntɔʃ] n imperméable m.

mad [mæd] a fou(folle) ; (foolish) insensé(e) ; (angry) furieux(euse).

madam ['mædəm] n madame f ; **yes ~** oui Madame.

madden ['mædn] vt exaspérer.

made [meɪd] pt, pp of **make** ; **~-to-measure** a fait(e) sur mesure.

madly ['mædlɪ] ad follement.

madman ['mædmən] n fou m, aliéné m.

madness ['mædnɪs] n folie f.

magazine [mægə'ziːn] n (PRESS) magazine m, revue f; (MIL: store) dépôt m, arsenal m; (of firearm) magasin m.

maggot ['mægət] n ver m, asticot m.

magic ['mædʒɪk] n magie f // a magique; ~al a magique; ~ian [mə'dʒɪʃən] n magicien/ne.

magistrate ['mædʒɪstreɪt] n magistrat m; juge m.

magnanimous [mæg'nænɪməs] a magnanime.

magnate ['mægneɪt] n magnat m.

magnesium [mæg'niːzɪəm] n magnésium m.

magnet ['mægnɪt] n aimant m; ~ic ['nɛtɪk] a magnétique; ~ism n magnétisme m.

magnification [mægnɪfɪ'keɪʃən] n grossissement m.

magnificence [mæg'nɪfɪsns] n magnificence f.

magnificent [mæg'nɪfɪsnt] a superbe, magnifique.

magnify ['mægnɪfaɪ] vt grossir; (sound) amplifier; ~ing glass n loupe f.

magnitude ['mægnɪtjuːd] n ampleur f.

magnolia [mæg'nəʊlɪə] n magnolia m.

magpie ['mægpaɪ] n pie f.

mahogany [mə'hɒgənɪ] n acajou m // cpd en (bois d')acajou.

maid [meɪd] n bonne f; old ~ (pej) vieille fille.

maiden ['meɪdn] n jeune fille f // a (aunt etc) non mariée; (speech, voyage) inaugural(e); ~ name n nom m de jeune fille.

mail [meɪl] n poste f; (letters) courrier m // vt envoyer (par la poste); ~box n (US) boîte f aux lettres; ~ing list n liste f d'adresses; ~-order n vente f or achat m par correspondance.

maim [meɪm] vt mutiler.

main [meɪn] a principal(e) // n (pipe) conduite principale, canalisation f; the ~s (ELEC) le secteur; in the ~ dans l'ensemble; ~land n continent m; ~stay n (fig) pilier m.

maintain [meɪn'teɪn] vt entretenir; (continue) maintenir, préserver; (affirm) soutenir; **maintenance** ['meɪntənəns] n entretien m.

maisonette [meɪzə'nɛt] n appartement m en duplex.

maize [meɪz] n maïs m.

majestic [mə'dʒɛstɪk] a majestueux(euse).

majesty ['mædʒɪstɪ] n majesté f.

major ['meɪdʒə*] n (MIL) commandant m // a important(e), principal(e); (MUS) majeur(e).

majority [mə'dʒɒrɪtɪ] n majorité f.

make [meɪk] vt (pt, pp made [meɪd]) faire; (manufacture) faire, fabriquer; (cause to be): to ~ sb sad etc rendre qn triste etc; (force): to ~ sb do sth obliger qn à faire qch, faire faire qch à qn; (equal): 2 and 2 ~ 4 2 et 2 font 4 // n fabrication f; (brand) marque f; to ~ do with se contenter de; se débrouiller avec; to ~ for vt fus (place) se diriger vers; to ~ out

vt (write out) écrire; (understand) comprendre; (see) distinguer; to ~ up vt (invent) inventer, imaginer; (parcel) faire // vi se réconcilier; (with cosmetics) se maquiller, se farder; to ~ up for vt fus compenser; racheter; ~-believe a feint(e), de fantaisie; ~r n fabricant m; ~shift a provisoire, improvisé(e); ~-up n maquillage m.

making ['meɪkɪŋ] n (fig): in the ~ en formation or gestation.

maladjusted [mælə'dʒʌstɪd] a inadapté(e).

malaise [mæ'leɪz] n malaise m.

malaria [mə'lɛərɪə] n malaria f, paludisme m.

Malay [mə'leɪ] a malais(e) // n (person) Malais/e; (language) malais m.

Malaysia [mə'leɪzɪə] n Malaisie f.

male [meɪl] n (BIOL, ELEC) mâle m // a (sex, attitude) masculine(e); mâle; (child etc) du sexe masculin; ~ and female students étudiants et étudiantes.

malevolence [mə'lɛvələns] n malveillance f.

malevolent [mə'lɛvələnt] a malveillant(e).

malfunction [mæl'fʌŋkʃən] n fonctionnement défectueux.

malice ['mælɪs] n méchanceté f, malveillance f; **malicious** [mə'lɪʃəs] a méchant(e), malveillant(e); (LAW) avec intention criminelle.

malign [mə'laɪn] vt diffamer, calomnier.

malignant [mə'lɪgnənt] a (MED) malin(igne).

malingerer [mə'lɪŋgərə*] n simulateur/trice.

malleable ['mælɪəbl] a malléable.

mallet ['mælɪt] n maillet m.

malnutrition [mælnjuː'trɪʃən] n malnutrition f.

malpractice [mæl'præktɪs] n faute professionnelle; négligence f.

malt [mɔːlt] n malt m // cpd (whisky) pur malt.

Malta ['mɔːltə] n Malte f; **Maltese** [-'tiːz] a maltais(e) // n, pl inv Maltais/e.

maltreat [mæl'triːt] vt maltraiter.

mammal ['mæml] n mammifère m.

mammoth ['mæməθ] n mammouth m // a géant(e), monstre.

man, pl **men** [mæn,mɛn] n homme m; (CHESS) pièce f; (DRAUGHTS) pion m // vt garnir d'hommes; servir, assurer le fonctionnement de; être de service à; **an old** ~ un vieillard.

manage ['mænɪdʒ] vi se débrouiller // vt (be in charge of) s'occuper de; gérer; to ~ to do se débrouiller pour faire; réussir à faire; ~able a maniable; faisable; ~ment n administration f, direction f; ~r n directeur m; administrateur m; (of hotel etc) gérant m; (of artist) impresario m; ~ress [-ə'rɛs] n directrice f; gérante f; ~rial [-ə'dʒɪərɪəl] a directorial(e); ~rial staff n cadres mpl; **managing** a: **managing director** directeur général.

mandarin ['mændərɪn] n (also: ~ orange) mandarine f; (person) mandarin m.

mandate ['mændeɪt] *n* mandat *m*.

mandatory ['mændətərɪ] *a* obligatoire ; (*powers etc*) mandataire.

mandolin(e) ['mændəlɪn] *n* mandoline *f*.

mane [meɪn] *n* crinière *f*.

maneuver [mə'nu:və*] *etc* (*US*) = **manoeuvre** *etc*.

manful ['mænful] *a* courageux(euse), vaillant(e).

manganese [mæŋgə'ni:z] *n* manganèse *m*.

mangle ['mæŋgl] *vt* déchiqueter ; mutiler // *n* essoreuse *f* ; calandre *f*.

mango, ∼es ['mæŋgəu] *n* mangue *f*.

mangrove ['mæŋgrəuv] *n* palétuvier *m*.

mangy ['meɪndʒɪ] *a* galeux(euse).

manhandle ['mænhændl] *vt* malmener.

manhole ['mænhəul] *n* trou *m* d'homme.

manhood ['mænhud] *n* âge *m* d'homme ; virilité *f*.

manhunt ['mænhʌnt] *n* chasse *f* à l'homme.

mania ['meɪnɪə] *n* manie *f* ; ∼c ['meɪnɪæk] *n* maniaque *m/f*.

manicure ['mænɪkjuə*] *n* manucure *f* // *vt* (*person*) faire les mains à ; ∼ set *n* trousse *f* à ongles.

manifest ['mænɪfɛst] *vt* manifester // *a* manifeste, évident(e) ; ∼ation [-'teɪʃən] *n* manifestation *f*.

manifesto [mænɪ'fɛstəu] *n* manifeste *m*.

manipulate [mə'nɪpjuleɪt] *vt* manipuler.

mankind [mæn'kaɪnd] *n* humanité *f*, genre humain.

manly ['mænlɪ] *a* viril(e) ; courageux(euse).

man-made ['mæn'meɪd] *a* artificiel(le).

manner ['mænə*] *n* manière *f*, façon *f* ; ∼s *npl* manières ; ∼ism *n* particularité *f* de langage (*or* de comportement), tic *m*.

manoeuvre, maneuver (*US*) [mə'nu:və*] *vt,vi* manœuvrer // *n* manœuvre *f*.

manor ['mænə*] *n* (*also:* ∼ house) manoir *m*.

manpower ['mænpauə*] *n* main-d'œuvre *f*.

manservant, *pl* **menservants** ['mænsə:vənt, 'mɛn-] *n* domestique *m*.

mansion ['mænʃən] *n* château *m*, manoir *m*.

manslaughter ['mænslɔ:tə*] *n* homicide *m* involontaire.

mantelpiece ['mæntlpi:s] *n* cheminée *f*.

mantle ['mæntl] *n* cape *f* ; (*fig*) manteau *m*.

manual ['mænjuəl] *a* manuel(le) // *n* manuel *m*.

manufacture [mænju'fæktʃə*] *vt* fabriquer // *n* fabrication *f* ; ∼r *n* fabricant *m*.

manure [mə'njuə*] *n* fumier *m* ; (*artificial*) engrais *m*.

manuscript ['mænjuskrɪpt] *n* manuscrit *m*.

many ['mɛnɪ] *det* beaucoup de, de nombreux(euses) // *pronoun* beaucoup, un grand nombre ; **a great** ∼ un grand nombre (de) ; ∼ **a...** bien des... , plus d'un(e)... .

map [mæp] *n* carte *f* // *vt* dresser la carte de ; **to ∼ out** *vt* tracer.

maple ['meɪpl] *n* érable *m*.

mar [mɑ:*] *vt* gâcher, gâter.

marathon ['mærəθən] *n* marathon *m*.

marauder [mə'rɔ:də*] *n* maraudeur/euse.

marble ['mɑ:bl] *n* marbre *m* ; (*toy*) bille *f* ; ∼s *n* (*game*) billes.

March [mɑ:tʃ] *n* mars *m*.

march [mɑ:tʃ] *vi* marcher au pas ; défiler // *n* marche *f* ; (*demonstration*) rallye *m* ; ∼-**past** *n* défilé *m*.

mare [mɛə*] *n* jument *f*.

margarine [mɑ:dʒə'ri:n] *n* margarine *f*.

margin ['mɑ:dʒɪn] *n* marge *f* ; ∼**al** *a* marginal(e).

marigold ['mærɪgəuld] *n* souci *m*.

marijuana [mærɪ'wɑ:nə] *n* marijuana *f*.

marina [mə'ri:nə] *n* marina *f*.

marine [mə'ri:n] *a* marin(e) // *n* fusilier marin ; (*US*) marine *m*.

marital ['mærɪtl] *a* matrimonial(e).

maritime ['mærɪtaɪm] *a* maritime.

marjoram ['mɑ:dʒərəm] *n* marjolaine *f*.

mark [mɑ:k] *n* marque *f* ; (*of skid etc*) trace *f* ; (*SCOL*) note *f* ; (*SPORT*) cible *f* ; (*currency*) mark *m* // *vt* marquer ; (*stain*) tacher ; (*SCOL*) noter ; corriger ; **to ∼ out** *vt* désigner ; ∼**ed** *a* marqué(e), net(te) ; ∼**er** *n* (*sign*) jalon *m* ; (*bookmark*) signet *m*.

market ['mɑ:kɪt] *n* marché *m* // *vt* (*COMM*) commercialiser ; ∼ **day** *n* jour *m* de marché ; ∼ **garden** *n* (*Brit*) jardin maraîcher ; ∼**ing** *n* marketing *m* ; ∼ **place** *n* place *f* du marché.

marksman ['mɑ:ksmən] *n* tireur *m* d'élite ; ∼**ship** *n* adresse *f* au tir.

marmalade ['mɑ:məleɪd] *n* confiture *f* d'oranges.

maroon [mə'ru:n] *vt* (*fig*): **to be ∼ed (in** *or* **at)** être bloqué(e) (à) // *a* bordeaux *inv*.

marquee [mɑ:'ki:] *n* chapiteau *m*.

marquess, marquis ['mɑ:kwɪs] *n* marquis *m*.

marriage ['mærɪdʒ] *n* mariage *m* ; ∼ **bureau** *n* agence matrimoniale.

married ['mærɪd] *a* marié(e) ; (*life, love*) conjugal(e).

marrow ['mærəu] *n* moelle *f* ; (*vegetable*) courge *f*.

marry ['mærɪ] *vt* épouser, se marier avec ; (*subj: father, priest etc*) marier // *vi* (*also:* **get married**) se marier.

Mars [mɑ:z] *n* (*planet*) Mars *f*.

marsh [mɑ:ʃ] *n* marais *m*, marécage *m*.

marshal ['mɑ:ʃl] *n* maréchal *m* ; (*US: fire, police*) ≈ capitaine *m* // *vt* rassembler ; ∼**ing yard** *n* gare *f* de triage.

marshy ['mɑ:ʃɪ] *a* marécageux(euse).

martial ['mɑ:ʃl] *a* martial(e) ; ∼ **law** *n* loi martiale.

Martian ['mɑ:ʃɪən] *n* Martien/ne.

martyr ['mɑ:tə*] *n* martyr/e // *vt* martyriser ; ∼**dom** *n* martyre *m*.

marvel ['mɑ:vl] *n* merveille *f* // *vi*: **to ∼ (at)** s'émerveiller (de) ; ∼**lous**, ∼**ous** (*US*) *a* merveilleux(euse).

Marxism ['mɑ:ksɪzəm] *n* marxisme *m*.

Marxist ['mɑːksɪst] *a,n* marxiste (*m/f*).
marzipan ['mɑːzɪpæn] *n* pâte *f* d'amandes.
mascara [mæs'kɑːrə] *n* mascara *m*.
mascot ['mæskət] *n* mascotte *f*.
masculine ['mæskjulɪn] *a* masculin(e) // *n* masculin *m*; **masculinity** [-'lɪnɪtɪ] *n* masculinité *f*.
mashed [mæʃt] *a*: ~ **potatoes** purée *f* de pommes de terre.
mask [mɑːsk] *n* masque *m* // *vt* masquer.
masochist ['mæsəukɪst] *n* masochiste *m/f*.
mason ['meɪsn] *n* (*also*: **stone**~) maçon *m*; (*also*: **free**~) franc-maçon *m*; ~**ic** [mə'sɔnɪk] *a* maçonnique; ~**ry** *n* maçonnerie *f*.
masquerade [mæskə'reɪd] *n* bal masqué; (*fig*) mascarade *f* // *vi*: **to** ~ **as** se faire passer pour.
mass [mæs] *n* multitude *f*, masse *f*; (*PHYSICS*) masse; (*REL*) messe *f* // *vi* se masser; **the** ~**es** les masses.
massacre ['mæsəkə*] *n* massacre *m* // *vt* massacrer.
massage ['mæsɑːʒ] *n* massage *m* // *vt* masser.
masseur [mæ'sɜː*] *n* masseur *m*; **masseuse** [-'sɜːz] *n* masseuse *f*.
massive ['mæsɪv] *a* énorme, massif(ive).
mass media ['mæs'miːdɪə] *npl* mass-media *mpl*.
mass-produce ['mæsprə'djuːs] *vt* fabriquer en série.
mast [mɑːst] *n* mât *m*.
master ['mɑːstə*] *n* maître *m*; (*in secondary school*) professeur *m*; (*title for boys*): **M**~ **X** Monsieur X // *vt* maîtriser; (*learn*) apprendre à fond; (*understand*) posséder parfaitement or à fond; **M**~'**s degree** *n* ≈ maîtrise *f*; ~ **key** *n* passe-partout *m* *inv*; ~**ly** *a* magistral(e); ~**mind** *n* esprit supérieur // *vt* diriger, être le cerveau de; **M**~ **of Arts/Science (M.A./M.Sc.)** *n* ≈ titulaire *m/f* d'une maîtrise (en lettres/science); **M**~ **of Arts/Science degree (M.A./M.Sc.)** *n* ≈ maîtrise *f*; ~**piece** *n* chef-d'œuvre *m*; ~ **plan** *n* stratégie *f* d'ensemble; ~ **stroke** *n* coup *m* de maître; ~**y** *n* maîtrise *f*; connaissance parfaite.
masturbate ['mæstəbeɪt] *vi* se masturber; **masturbation** [-'beɪʃən] *n* masturbation *f*.
mat [mæt] *n* petit tapis; (*also*: **door**~) paillasson *m* // *a* = **matt**.
match [mætʃ] *n* allumette *f*; (*game*) match *m*, partie *f*; (*fig*) égal/e; mariage *m*; parti *m* // *vt* assortir; (*go well with*) aller bien avec, s'assortir à; (*equal*) égaler, valoir // *vi* être assorti(e); **to be a good** ~ être bien assorti(e); **to** ~ **up** *vt* assortir; ~**box** *n* boîte *f* d'allumettes; ~**ing** *a* assorti(e); ~**less** *a* sans égal.
mate [meɪt] *n* camarade *m/f* de travail; (*col*) copain/copine; (*animal*) partenaire *m/f*, mâle/femelle; (*in merchant navy*) second *m* // *vi* s'accoupler // *vt* accoupler.
material [mə'tɪərɪəl] *n* (*substance*) matière *f*, matériau *m*; (*cloth*) tissu *m*, étoffe *f* // *a* matériel(le); (*important*) essentiel(le); ~**s** *npl* matériaux *mpl*; ~**istic** [-ə'lɪstɪk] *a*

materialiste; ~**ize** *vi* se matérialiser, se réaliser; ~**ly** *ad* matériellement.
maternal [mə'tɜːnl] *a* maternel(le).
maternity [mə'tɜːnɪtɪ] *n* maternité *f* // *cpd* de maternité, de grossesse; ~ **hospital** *n* maternité *f*.
matey ['meɪtɪ] *a* (*col*) copain-copain *inv*.
mathematical [mæθə'mætɪkl] *a* mathématique.
mathematician [mæθəmə'tɪʃən] *n* mathématicien/ne.
mathematics [mæθə'mætɪks] *n* mathématiques *fpl*.
maths [mæθs] *n* math(s) *fpl*.
matinée ['mætɪneɪ] *n* matinée *f*.
mating ['meɪtɪŋ] *n* accouplement *m*; ~ **call** *n* appel *m* du mâle; ~ **season** *n* saison *f* des amours.
matriarchal [meɪtrɪ'ɑːkl] *a* matriarcal(e).
matrices ['meɪtrɪsiːz] *npl* of **matrix**.
matriculation [mətrɪkju'leɪʃən] *n* inscription *f*.
matrimonial [mætrɪ'məunɪəl] *a* matrimonial(e), conjugal(e).
matrimony ['mætrɪmənɪ] *n* mariage *m*.
matrix, *pl* **matrices** ['meɪtrɪks, 'meɪtrɪsiːz] *n* matrice *f*.
matron ['meɪtrən] *n* (*in hospital*) infirmière-chef *f*; (*in school*) infirmière; ~**ly** *a* de matrone; imposant(e).
matt [mæt] *a* mat(e).
matted ['mætɪd] *a* emmêlé(e).
matter ['mætə*] *n* question *f*; (*PHYSICS*) matière *f*, substance *f*; (*content*) contenu *m*, fond *m*; (*MED*: *pus*) pus *m* // *vi* importer; **it doesn't** ~ cela n'a pas d'importance; (*I don't mind*) cela ne fait rien; **what's the** ~? qu'est-ce qu'il y a?, qu'est-ce qui ne va pas?; **no** ~ **what** quoiqu'il arrive; **that's another** ~ c'est une autre affaire; **as a** ~ **of course** tout naturellement; **as a** ~ **of fact** en fait; **it's a** ~ **of habit** c'est une question d'habitude; ~**-of-fact** *a* terre à terre, neutre.
matting ['mætɪŋ] *n* natte *f*.
mattress ['mætrɪs] *n* matelas *m*.
mature [mə'tjuə*] *a* mûr(e); (*cheese*) fait(e) // *vi* mûrir; se faire; **maturity** *n* maturité *f*.
maudlin ['mɔːdlɪn] *a* larmoyant(e).
maul [mɔːl] *vt* lacérer.
Mauritius [mə'rɪʃəs] *n* l'île *f* Maurice.
mausoleum [mɔːsə'lɪəm] *n* mausolée *m*.
mauve [məuv] *a* mauve.
mawkish ['mɔːkɪʃ] *a* mièvre; fade.
max. *abbr* of **maximum**.
maxim ['mæksɪm] *n* maxime *f*.
maxima ['mæksɪmə] *npl* of **maximum**.
maximum ['mæksɪməm] *a* maximum // *n* (*pl* **maxima** ['mæksɪmə]) maximum *m*.
May [meɪ] *n* mai *m*.
may [meɪ] *vi* (*conditional*: **might**) (*indicating possibility*): **he** ~ **come** il se peut qu'il vienne; (*be allowed to*): ~ **I smoke?** puis-je fumer?; (*wishes*): ~ **God bless you!** (que) Dieu vous bénisse!; **he might be there** il pourrait bien y être, il se pourrait qu'il y soit; **I might as well go** je ferais aussi bien d'y aller, autant y

aller ; **you might like to try** vous pourriez (peut-être) essayer.

maybe ['meɪbi:] *ad* peut-être ; ~ he'll... peut-être qu'il... .

mayday ['meɪdeɪ] *n* S.O.S. *m*.

May Day ['meɪdeɪ] *n* le Premier mai.

mayhem ['meɪhɛm] *n* grabuge *m*.

mayonnaise [meɪə'neɪz] *n* mayonnaise *f*.

mayor [mɛə*] *n* maire *m* ; ~ess *n* maire *m* ; épouse *f* du maire.

maypole ['meɪpəʊl] *n* mât enrubanné (*autour duquel on danse*).

maze [meɪz] *n* labyrinthe *m*, dédale *m*.

M.D. *abbr* = *Doctor of Medicine*.

me [mi:] *pronoun* me, m' + *vowel* ; (*stressed, after prep*) moi.

meadow ['mɛdəʊ] *n* prairie *f*, pré *m*.

meagre, **meager** (*US*) ['mi:gə*] *a* maigre.

meal [mi:l] *n* repas *m* ; (*flour*) farine *f* ; ~time *n* l'heure *f* du repas ; ~y-mouthed *a* mielleux(euse).

mean [mi:n] *a* (*with money*) avare, radin(e) ; (*unkind*) mesquin(e), méchant(e) ; (*average*) moyen(ne) // *vt* (*pt, pp* **meant** [mɛnt]) (*signify*) signifier, vouloir dire ; (*intend*): **to ~ to do** avoir l'intention de faire // *n* moyenne *f* ; ~s *npl* moyens *mpl* ; **by ~s of** par l'intermédiaire de ; au moyen de ; **by all ~s** je vous en prie ; **to be meant for** être destiné(e) à ; **what do you ~?** que voulez-vous dire?

meander [mɪ'ændə*] *vi* faire des méandres ; (*fig*) flâner.

meaning ['mi:nɪŋ] *n* signification *f*, sens *m* ; ~ful *a* significatif(ive) ; ~less *a* dénué(e) de sens.

meanness ['mi:nnɪs] *n* avarice *f* ; mesquinerie *f*.

meant [mɛnt] *pt, pp* of **mean**.

meantime ['mi:ntaɪm] *ad*, **meanwhile** ['mi:nwaɪl] *ad* (*also*: **in the ~**) pendant ce temps.

measles ['mi:zlz] *n* rougeole *f*.

measly ['mi:zlɪ] *a* (*col*) minable.

measurable ['mɛʒərəbl] *a* mesurable.

measure ['mɛʒə*] *vt, vi* mesurer // *n* mesure *f* ; (*ruler*) règle (graduée) ; ~d *a* mesuré(e) ; ~ments *npl* mesures *fpl* ; **chest/hip ~ment** tour *m* de poitrine/hanches.

meat [mi:t] *n* viande *f* ; ~ **pie** *n* pâté *m* en croûte ; ~y *a* qui a le goût de la viande ; (*fig*) substantiel(le).

Mecca ['mɛkə] *n* la Mecque.

mechanic [mɪ'kænɪk] *n* mécanicien *m* ; ~s *n* mécanique *f* // *npl* mécanisme *m* ; ~al *a* mécanique.

mechanism ['mɛkənɪzəm] *n* mécanisme *m*.

mechanization [mɛkənaɪ'zeɪʃən] *n* mécanisation *f*.

medal ['mɛdl] *n* médaille *f* ; ~lion [mɪ'dæljən] *n* médaillon *m* ; ~list, ~ist (*US*) *n* (*sport*) médaillé/e.

meddle ['mɛdl] *vi*: **to ~ in** se mêler de, s'occuper de ; **to ~ with** toucher à ; ~some *a* indiscret(ète).

media ['mi:dɪə] *npl* media *mpl*.

mediaeval [mɛdɪ'i:vl] *a* = **medieval**.

mediate ['mi:dɪeɪt] *vi* s'interposer ; servir d'intermédiaire ; **mediation** [-'eɪʃən] *n* médiation *f* ; **mediator** *n* médiateur/trice.

medical ['mɛdɪkl] *a* médical(e) ; ~ **student** *n* étudiant/e en médecine.

medicated ['mɛdɪkeɪtɪd] *a* traitant(e), médicamenteux(euse).

medicinal [mɛ'dɪsɪnl] *a* médicinal(e).

medicine ['mɛdsɪn] *n* médecine *f* ; (*drug*) médicament *m* ; ~ **chest** *n* pharmacie *f* (*murale ou portative*).

medieval [mɛdɪ'i:vl] *a* médiéval(e).

mediocre [mi:dɪ'əʊkə*] *a* médiocre ; **mediocrity** [-'ɔkrɪtɪ] *n* médiocrité *f*.

meditate ['mɛdɪteɪt] *vi*: **to ~ (on)** méditer (sur) ; **meditation** [-'teɪʃən] *n* méditation *f*.

Mediterranean [mɛdɪtə'reɪnɪən] *a* méditerranéen(ne) ; **the ~ (Sea)** la (mer) Méditerranée.

medium ['mi:dɪəm] *a* moyen(ne) // *n* (*pl* **media**: *means*) moyen *m* ; (*pl* **mediums**: *person*) médium *m* ; **the happy ~** le juste milieu.

medley ['mɛdlɪ] *n* mélange *m*.

meek [mi:k] *a* doux(douce), humble.

meet, *pt, pp* **met** [mi:t, mɛt] *vt* rencontrer ; (*by arrangement*) retrouver, rejoindre ; (*for the first time*) faire la connaissance de ; (*go and fetch*): **I'll ~ you at the station** j'irai te chercher à la gare ; (*fig*) faire face à ; satisfaire à ; se joindre à // *vi* se rencontrer ; se retrouver ; (*in session*) se réunir ; (*join: objects*) se joindre ; **to ~ with** *vt fus* rencontrer ; ~ing *n* rencontre *f* ; (*session: of club etc*) réunion *f* ; (*interview*) entrevue *f* ; **she's at a ~ing** (*comm*) elle est en conférence.

megaphone ['mɛgəfəʊn] *n* porte-voix *m inv*.

melancholy ['mɛlənkəlɪ] *n* mélancolie *f* // *a* mélancolique.

mellow ['mɛləʊ] *a* velouté(e), doux(douce) ; (*colour*) riche et profond(e) ; (*fruit*) mûr(e) // *vi* (*person*) s'adoucir.

melodious [mɪ'ləʊdɪəs] *a* mélodieux(euse).

melodrama ['mɛləʊdrɑ:mə] *n* mélodrame *m*.

melody ['mɛlədɪ] *n* mélodie *f*.

melon ['mɛlən] *n* melon *m*.

melt [mɛlt] *vi* fondre ; (*become soft*) s'amollir ; (*fig*) s'attendrir // *vt* faire fondre ; (*person*) attendrir ; **to ~ away** *vi* fondre complètement ; **to ~ down** *vt* fondre ; ~ing **point** *n* point *m* de fusion ; ~ing **pot** *n* (*fig*) creuset *m*.

member ['mɛmbə*] *n* membre *m* ; ~ **country/state** *n* pays *m*/état *m* membre ; **M~ of Parliament (M.P.)** député *m* ; ~ship *n* adhésion *f* ; statut *m* de membre ; (*nombre m de*) membres *mpl*, adhérents *mpl*.

membrane ['mɛmbreɪn] *n* membrane *f*.

memento [mə'mɛntəʊ] *n* souvenir *m*.

memo ['mɛməʊ] *n* note *f* (de service).

memoir ['mɛmwɑ:*] *n* mémoire *m*, étude *f* ; ~s *npl* mémoires *mpl*.

memorable ['mɛmərəbl] *a* mémorable.

memorandum, *pl* **memoranda** [mɛmə'rændəm, -də] *n* note *f* (de service) ; (*diplomacy*) mémorandum *m*.

memorial [mɪ'mɔːrɪəl] n mémorial m // a commémoratif(ive).

memorize ['mɛməraɪz] vt apprendre or retenir par cœur.

memory ['mɛmərɪ] n mémoire f; (recollection) souvenir m; **in ~ of** à la mémoire de.

men [mɛn] npl of **man**.

menace ['mɛnəs] n menace f // vt menacer; **menacing** a menaçant(e).

menagerie [mɪ'nædʒərɪ] n ménagerie f.

mend [mɛnd] vt réparer; (darn) raccommoder, repriser // n reprise f; **on the ~** en voie de guérison; **~ing** n raccommodages mpl.

menial ['miːnɪəl] a de domestique, inférieur(e); subalterne.

meningitis [mɛnɪn'dʒaɪtɪs] n méningite f.

menopause ['mɛnəupɔːz] n ménopause f.

menservants npl of **manservant**.

menstruate ['mɛnstrueɪt] vi avoir ses règles; **menstruation** [-'eɪʃən] n menstruation f.

mental ['mɛntl] a mental(e).

mentality [mɛn'tælɪtɪ] n mentalité f.

mention ['mɛnʃən] n mention f // vt mentionner, faire mention de; **don't ~ it!** je vous en prie, il n'y a pas de quoi!

menu ['mɛnjuː] n (set ~) menu m; (printed) carte f.

mercantile ['məːkəntaɪl] a marchand(e); (law) commercial(e).

mercenary ['məːsɪnərɪ] a mercantile // n mercenaire m.

merchandise ['məːtʃəndaɪz] n marchandises fpl.

merchant ['məːtʃənt] n négociant m, marchand m; **timber/wine ~** négociant en bois/vins, marchand de bois/vins; **~ bank** n banque f d'affaires; **~ navy** n marine marchande.

merciful ['məːsɪful] a miséricordieux(euse), clément(e).

merciless ['məːsɪlɪs] a impitoyable, sans pitié.

mercurial [məː'kjuərɪəl] a changeant(e); (lively) vif(vive).

mercury ['məːkjurɪ] n mercure m.

mercy ['məːsɪ] n pitié f, merci f; (REL) miséricorde f; **to have ~ on sb** avoir pitié de qn; **at the ~ of** à la merci de.

mere [mɪə*] a simple; **~ly** ad simplement, purement.

merge [məːdʒ] vt unir // vi se fondre; (COMM) fusionner; **~r** n (COMM) fusion f.

meridian [mə'rɪdɪən] n méridien m.

meringue [mə'ræŋ] n meringue f.

merit ['mɛrɪt] n mérite m, valeur f // vt mériter.

mermaid ['məːmeɪd] n sirène f.

merrily ['mɛrɪlɪ] ad joyeusement, gaiement.

merriment ['mɛrɪmənt] n gaieté f.

merry ['mɛrɪ] a gai(e); **~-go-round** n manège m.

mesh [mɛʃ] n maille f; filet m // vi (gears) s'engrener.

mesmerize ['mɛzməraɪz] vt hypnotiser; fasciner.

mess [mɛs] n désordre m, fouillis m, pagaille f; (MIL) mess m, cantine f; **to ~**

about vi (col) perdre son temps; **to ~ about with** vt fus (col) chambarder, tripoter; **to ~ up** vt salir; chambarder; gâcher.

message ['mɛsɪdʒ] n message m.

messenger ['mɛsɪndʒə*] n messager m.

messy ['mɛsɪ] a sale; en désordre.

met [mɛt] pt, pp of **meet**.

metabolism [mɛ'tæbəlɪzəm] n métabolisme m.

metal ['mɛtl] n métal m // vt empierrer; **~lic** [-'tælɪk] a métallique; **~lurgy** [-'tælədʒɪ] n métallurgie f.

metamorphosis, pl **phoses** [mɛtə'mɔːfəsɪs, -iːz] n métamorphose f.

metaphor ['mɛtəfə*] n métaphore f.

metaphysics [mɛtə'fɪzɪks] n métaphysique f.

mete [miːt]: **to ~ out** vt fus infliger.

meteor ['miːtɪə*] n météore m.

meteorological [miːtɪərə'lɒdʒɪkl] a météorologique.

meteorology [miːtɪə'rɒlədʒɪ] n météorologie f.

meter ['miːtə*] n (instrument) compteur m; (US) = **metre**.

method ['mɛθəd] n méthode f; **~ical** [mɪ'θɒdɪkl] a méthodique.

Methodist ['mɛθədɪst] a,n méthodiste (m/f).

methylated spirit ['mɛθɪleɪtɪd'spɪrɪt] n (also: **meths**) alcool m à brûler.

meticulous [mɛ'tɪkjuləs] a méticuleux(euse).

metre, meter (US) ['miːtə*] n mètre m.

metric ['mɛtrɪk] a métrique; **~al** a métrique; **~ation** [-'keɪʃən] n conversion f au système métrique.

metronome ['mɛtrənəum] n métronome m.

metropolis [mɪ'trɒpəlɪs] n métropole f.

mettle ['mɛtl] n courage m.

mew [mjuː] vi (cat) miauler.

mews [mjuːz] n: **~ cottage** maisonnette aménagée dans les anciennes écuries d'un hôtel particulier.

Mexican ['mɛksɪkən] a mexicain(e) // n Mexicain/e.

Mexico ['mɛksɪkəu] n Mexique m; **~ City** Mexico.

mezzanine ['mɛtsəniːn] n mezzanine f; (of shops, offices) entresol m.

miaow [miː'au] vi miauler.

mice [maɪs] npl of **mouse**.

microbe ['maɪkrəub] n microbe m.

microfilm ['maɪkrəufɪlm] n microfilm m // vt microfilmer.

microphone ['maɪkrəfəun] n microphone m.

microscope ['maɪkrəskəup] n microscope m; **microscopic** [-'skɒpɪk] a microscopique.

mid [mɪd] a: **~ May** la mi-mai; **~ afternoon** le milieu de l'après-midi; **in ~ air** en plein ciel; **~day** midi m.

middle ['mɪdl] n milieu m; (waist) ceinture f, taille f // a du milieu; d'un certain âge; **the M~ Ages** npl le moyen âge; **~-class** a ≈ bourgeois(e); **the ~ class(es)** ≈ les classes moyennes; **M~ East** n Proche-Orient m, Moyen-Orient m;

~**man** n intermédiaire m ; ~ **name** n deuxième nom m.

middling ['mɪdlɪŋ] a moyen(ne).

midge [mɪdʒ] n moucheron m.

midget ['mɪdʒɪt] n nain/e // a minuscule.

Midlands ['mɪdləndz] npl comtés du centre de l'Angleterre.

midnight ['mɪdnaɪt] n minuit m.

midriff ['mɪdrɪf] n estomac m, taille f.

midst [mɪdst] n: **in the ~ of** au milieu de.

midsummer [mɪd'sʌmə*] n milieu m de l'été.

midway [mɪd'weɪ] a, ad: **~ (between)** à mi-chemin (entre).

midweek [mɪd'wiːk] n milieu m de la semaine.

midwife, midwives ['mɪdwaɪf, -vz] n sage-femme f ; ~**ry** [-wɪfərɪ] n obstétrique f.

midwinter [mɪd'wɪntə*] n milieu m de l'hiver.

might [maɪt] vb see **may** // n puissance f, force f ; ~**y** a puissant(e) // ad (col) rudement.

migraine ['miːɡreɪn] n migraine f.

migrant ['maɪɡrənt] n (bird, animal) migrateur m ; (person) migrant/e ; nomade m/f // a migrateur(trice) ; migrant(e) ; nomade ; (worker) saisonnier(ère).

migrate [maɪ'ɡreɪt] vi émigrer ; **migration** [-'ɡreɪʃən] n migration f.

mike [maɪk] n (abbr of **microphone**) micro m.

mild [maɪld] a doux(douce) ; (reproach) léger(ère) ; (illness) bénin(bénigne) // n bière légère.

mildew ['mɪldjuː] n mildiou m.

mildly ['maɪldlɪ] ad doucement ; légèrement.

mildness ['maɪldnɪs] n douceur f.

mile [maɪl] n mil(l)e m (= 1609 m) ; ~**age** n distance f en milles, ≈ kilométrage m ; ~**ometer** n = **milometer** ; ~**stone** n borne f (fig) jalon m.

milieu ['miːljəː] n milieu m.

militant ['mɪlɪtnt] a,n militant(e).

military ['mɪlɪtərɪ] a militaire // n: **the ~** l'armée f, les militaires mpl.

militate ['mɪlɪteɪt] vi: **to ~ against** militer contre.

militia [mɪ'lɪʃə] n milice f.

milk [mɪlk] n lait m // vt (cow) traire ; (fig) dépouiller, plumer ; ~ **chocolate** n chocolat m au lait ; ~**ing** n traite f ; ~**man** n laitier m ; ~ **shake** n milk-shake m ; ~**y** a lacté(e) ; (colour) laiteux(euse) ; **M~y Way** n Voie lactée.

mill [mɪl] n moulin m ; (factory) usine f, fabrique f ; (spinning ~) filature f ; (flour ~) minoterie f // vt moudre, broyer // vi (also: ~ **about**) grouiller.

millennium, pl ~**s** or **millennia** [mɪ'lenɪəm, -'lenɪə] n millénaire m.

miller ['mɪlə*] n meunier m.

millet ['mɪlɪt] n millet m.

milli... ['mɪlɪ] prefix: ~**gram(me)** n milligramme m ; ~**litre** n millilitre m ; ~**metre** n millimètre m.

milliner ['mɪlɪnə*] n modiste f ; ~**y** n modes fpl.

million ['mɪljən] n million m ; ~**aire** n millionnaire m.

millstone ['mɪlstəun] n meule f.

millwheel ['mɪlwiːl] n roue f de moulin.

milometer [maɪ'lɒmɪtə*] n ≈ compteur m kilométrique.

mime [maɪm] n mime m // vt, vi mimer.

mimic ['mɪmɪk] n imitateur/trice // vt, vi imiter, contrefaire ; ~**ry** n imitation f ; (ZOOL) mimétisme m.

min. abbr of **minute(s)**, **minimum**.

minaret [mɪnə'ret] n minaret m.

mince [mɪns] vt hacher // vi (in walking) marcher à petits pas maniérés // n (CULIN) viande hachée, hachis m ; **he does not ~ (his) words** il ne mâche pas ses mots ; ~**meat** n hachis de fruits secs utilisés en pâtisserie ; ~ **pie** n sorte de tarte aux fruits secs ; ~**r** n hachoir m.

mincing ['mɪnsɪŋ] a affecté(e).

mind [maɪnd] n esprit m // vt (attend to, look after) s'occuper de ; (be careful) faire attention à ; (object to): **I don't ~ the noise** je ne crains pas le bruit, le bruit ne me dérange pas ; **do you ~ if ...?** est-ce que cela vous gêne si ...? ; **I don't ~** cela ne me dérange pas ; **it is on my ~** cela me préoccupe ; **to my ~** à mon avis or sens ; **to be out of one's ~** ne plus avoir toute sa raison ; **never ~** peu importe, ça ne fait rien ; **to keep sth in ~** ne pas oublier qch ; **to bear sth in ~** tenir compte de qch ; **to make up one's ~** se décider ; **'~ the step'** 'attention à la marche' ; **to have in ~** to do avoir l'intention de faire ; ~**ful** a: ~**ful of** attentif(ive) à, soucieux(euse) de ; ~**less** a irréfléchi(e).

mine [maɪn] pronoun le(la) mien(ne), pl les miens(miennes) // a: **this book is ~** ce livre est à moi // n mine f // vt (coal) extraire ; (ship, beach) miner ; ~ **detector** n détecteur m de mines ; ~**field** n champ m de mines ; ~**r** n mineur m.

mineral ['mɪnərəl] a minéral(e) // n minéral m ; ~**s** npl (soft drinks) boissons gazeuses (sucrées) ; ~**ogy** [-'rælədʒɪ] n minéralogie f ; ~ **water** n eau minérale.

minesweeper ['maɪnswiːpə*] n dragueur m de mines.

mingle ['mɪŋɡl] vt mêler, mélanger // vi: **to ~ with** se mêler à.

mingy ['mɪndʒɪ] a (col) radin(e).

miniature ['mɪnətʃə*] a (en) miniature // n miniature f.

minibus ['mɪnɪbʌs] n minibus m.

minicab ['mɪnɪkæb] n minitaxi m.

minim ['mɪnɪm] n (MUS) blanche f.

minima ['mɪnɪmə] npl of **minimum**.

minimal ['mɪnɪml] a minimal(e).

minimize ['mɪnɪmaɪz] vt minimiser.

minimum ['mɪnɪməm] n (pl: **minima** ['mɪnɪmə]) minimum m // a minimum.

mining ['maɪnɪŋ] n exploitation minière // a minier(ère) ; de mineurs.

minion ['mɪnjən] n (pej) laquais m ; favori/te.

miniskirt ['mɪnɪskəːt] n (POL) mini-jupe f.

minister ['mɪnɪstə*] n (POL) ministre m ; (REL) pasteur m ; ~**ial** [-'tɪərɪəl] a (POL) ministériel(le).

ministry ['mɪnɪstrɪ] *n* ministère *m* ; (REL): **to go into the ~** devenir pasteur.

mink [mɪŋk] *n* vison *m* ; **~ coat** *n* manteau *m* de vison.

minnow ['mɪnəu] *n* vairon *m*.

minor ['maɪnə*] *a* petit(e), de peu d'importance ; (MUS) mineur(e) // *n* (LAW) mineur/e.

minority [maɪ'nɔrɪtɪ] *n* minorité *f*.

minster ['mɪnstə*] *n* église abbatiale.

minstrel ['mɪnstrəl] *n* trouvère *m*, mènestrel *m*.

mint [mɪnt] *n* (plant) menthe *f* ; (sweet) bonbon *m* à la menthe // *vt* (coins) battre ; **the (Royal) M~** ≈ l'hôtel de la Monnaie ; **in ~ condition** à l'état de neuf ; **~ sauce** *n* sauce *f* à la menthe.

minuet [mɪnju'ɛt] *n* menuet *m*.

minus ['maɪnəs] *n* (also: **~ sign**) signe *m* moins // *prep* moins.

minute *a* [maɪ'nju:t] minuscule ; (detail) minutieux(euse) // *n* ['mɪnɪt] minute *f* ; (official record) procès-verbal *m*, compte rendu ; **~s** *npl* procès-verbal.

miracle ['mɪrəkl] *n* miracle *m* ; **miraculous** [mɪ'rækjuləs] *a* miraculeux(euse).

mirage ['mɪrɑːʒ] *n* mirage *m*.

mirror ['mɪrə*] *n* miroir *m*, glace *f* // *vt* refléter.

mirth [mə:θ] *n* gaieté *f*.

misadventure [mɪsəd'vɛntʃə*] *n* mésaventure *f* ; **death by ~** décès accidentel.

misanthropist [mɪ'zænθrəpɪst] *n* misanthrope *m/f*.

misapprehension ['mɪsæprɪ'hɛnʃən] *n* malentendu *m*, méprise *f*.

misappropriate [mɪsə'prəuprɪeɪt] *vt* détourner.

misbehave [mɪsbɪ'heɪv] *vi* se conduire mal ; **misbehaviour** *n* mauvaise conduite.

miscalculate [mɪs'kælkjuleɪt] *vt* mal calculer ; **miscalculation** [-'leɪʃən] *n* erreur *f* de calcul.

miscarriage ['mɪskærɪdʒ] *n* (MED) fausse couche ; **~ of justice** erreur *f* judiciaire.

miscellaneous [mɪsɪ'leɪnɪəs] *a* (items) divers(es) ; (selection) varié(e).

miscellany [mɪ'sɛlənɪ] *n* recueil *m*.

mischance [mɪs'tʃɑːns] *n* malchance *f*.

mischief ['mɪstʃɪf] *n* (naughtiness) sottises *fpl* ; (harm) mal *m*, dommage *m* ; (maliciousness) méchanceté *f* ; **mischievous** *a* (naughty) coquin(e), espiègle ; (harmful) méchant(e).

misconception [mɪskən'sɛpʃən] *n* idée fausse.

misconduct [mɪs'kɔndʌkt] *n* inconduite *f* ; **professional ~** faute professionnelle.

misconstrue [mɪskən'struː] *vt* mal interpréter.

miscount [mɪs'kaunt] *vt,vi* mal compter.

misdemeanour, misdemeanor (US) [mɪsdɪ'miːnə*] *n* écart *m* de conduite ; infraction *f*.

misdirect [mɪsdɪ'rɛkt] *vt* (person) mal renseigner ; (letter) mal adresser.

miser ['maɪzə*] *n* avare *m/f*.

miserable ['mɪzərəbl] *a* malheureux(euse) ; (wretched) misérable.

miserly ['maɪzəlɪ] *a* avare.

misery ['mɪzərɪ] *n* (unhappiness) tristesse *f* ; (pain) souffrances *fpl* ; (wretchedness) misère *f*.

misfire [mɪs'faɪə*] *vi* rater ; (car engine) avoir des ratés.

misfit ['mɪsfɪt] *n* (person) inadapté/e.

misfortune [mɪs'fɔːtʃən] *n* malchance *f*, malheur *m*.

misgiving(s) [mɪs'gɪvɪŋ(z)] *n(pl)* craintes *fpl*, soupçons *mpl*.

misguided [mɪs'gaɪdɪd] *a* malavisé(e).

mishandle [mɪs'hændl] *vt* (treat roughly) malmener ; (mismanage) mal s'y prendre pour faire or résoudre etc.

mishap ['mɪshæp] *n* mésaventure *f*.

mishear [mɪs'hɪə*] *vt irg* mal entendre.

misinform [mɪsɪn'fɔːm] *vt* mal renseigner.

misinterpret [mɪsɪn'tə:prɪt] *vt* mal interpréter ; **~ation** [-'teɪʃən] *n* interprétation erronée, contresens *m*.

misjudge [mɪs'dʒʌdʒ] *vt* méjuger, se méprendre sur le compte de.

mislay [mɪs'leɪ] *vt irg* égarer.

mislead [mɪs'liːd] *vt irg* induire en erreur ; **~ing** *a* trompeur(euse).

mismanage [mɪs'mænɪdʒ] *vt* mal gérer ; mal s'y prendre pour faire or résoudre etc ; **~ment** *n* mauvaise gestion.

misnomer [mɪs'nəumə*] *n* terme or qualificatif trompeur or peu approprié.

misogynist [mɪ'sɔdʒɪnɪst] *n* misogyne *m/f*.

misplace [mɪs'pleɪs] *vt* égarer.

misprint ['mɪsprɪnt] *n* faute *f* d'impression.

mispronounce [mɪsprə'nauns] *vt* mal prononcer.

misread [mɪs'riːd] *vt irg* mal lire.

misrepresent [mɪsreprɪ'zɛnt] *vt* présenter sous un faux jour.

miss [mɪs] *vt* (fail to get) manquer, rater ; (regret the absence of): **I ~ him/it** il/cela me manque // *vi* manquer // *n* (shot) coup manqué ; (fig): **that was a near ~** il s'en est fallu de peu ; **to ~ out** vt oublier.

Miss [mɪs] *n* Mademoiselle.

missal ['mɪsl] *n* missel *m*.

misshapen [mɪs'ʃeɪpən] *a* difforme.

missile ['mɪsaɪl] *n* (AVIAT) missile *m* ; (object thrown) projectile *m*.

missing ['mɪsɪŋ] *a* manquant(e) ; (after escape, disaster: person) disparu(e) ; **to go ~** disparaître.

mission ['mɪʃən] *n* mission *f* ; **~ary** *n* missionnaire *m/f*.

missive ['mɪsɪv] *n* missive *f*.

misspent ['mɪs'spɛnt] *a*: **his ~ youth** sa folle jeunesse.

mist [mɪst] *n* brume *f*, brouillard *m* // *vi* (also: **~ over, ~ up**) devenir brumeux(euse) ; (windows) s'embuer.

mistake [mɪs'teɪk] *n* erreur *f*, faute *f* // *vt* (irg: like **take**) mal comprendre ; se méprendre sur ; **to make a ~** se tromper, faire une erreur ; **to ~ for** prendre pour ; **~n** *a* (idea etc) erroné(e) ; **to be ~n** faire erreur, se tromper ; **~n identity** *n* erreur *f* d'identité.

mister ['mɪstə*] *n* (col) Monsieur *m* ; see **Mr**.

mistletoe ['mɪsltəu] n gui m.
mistook [mɪs'tuk] pt of **mistake**.
mistranslation [mɪstræns'leɪʃən] n erreur f de traduction, contresens m.
mistreat [mɪs'tri:t] vt maltraiter.
mistress ['mɪstrɪs] n (also: lover) maîtresse f; (in primary school) institutrice f; see **Mrs**.
mistrust [mɪs'trʌst] vt se méfier de.
misty ['mɪstɪ] a brumeux(euse).
misunderstand [mɪsʌndə'stænd] vt, vi irg mal comprendre; ~ing n méprise f, malentendu m.
misuse n [mɪs'ju:s] mauvais emploi; (of power) abus m // vt [mɪs'ju:z] mal employer; abuser de.
mitigate ['mɪtɪgeɪt] vt atténuer.
mitre, miter (US) ['maɪtə*] n mitre f; (CARPENTRY) onglet m.
mitt(en) ['mɪt(n)] n mitaine f; moufle f.
mix [mɪks] vt mélanger // vi se mélanger // n mélange m; dosage m; to ~ up vt mélanger; (confuse) confondre; ~ed a (assorted) assortis(ies); (school etc) mixte; ~ed grill n assortiment m de grillades; ~ed-up a (confused) désorienté(e), embrouillé(e); ~er n (for food) batteur m, mixeur m; (person): he is a good ~er il est très liant; ~ture n assortiment m, mélange m; (MED) préparation f; ~-up n confusion f.
moan [məun] n gémissement m // vi gémir; (col: complain): to ~ (about) se plaindre (de); ~ing n gémissements mpl.
moat [məut] n fossé m, douves fpl.
mob [mɔb] n foule f; (disorderly) cohue f; (pej): the ~ la populace // vt assaillir.
mobile ['məubaɪl] a mobile // n mobile m; ~ home n caravane f.
mobility [məu'bɪlɪtɪ] n mobilité f.
moccasin ['mɔkəsɪn] n mocassin m.
mock [mɔk] vt ridiculiser, se moquer de // a faux(fausse); ~ery n moquerie f, raillerie f; ~ing a moqueur(euse); ~ingbird n moqueur m; ~-up n maquette f.
mod [mɔd] a see **convenience**.
mode [məud] n mode m.
model ['mɔdl] n modèle m; (person: for fashion) mannequin m; (: for artist) modèle m // vt modeler // vi travailler comme mannequin // a (railway: toy) modèle réduit inv; (child, factory) modèle; to ~ clothes présenter des vêtements; ~ler, ~er (US) n modeleur m; (~ maker) maquettiste m/f; fabricant m de modèles réduits.
moderate a,n ['mɔdərət] a modéré(e) // n (POL) modéré/e // vb ['mɔdəreɪt] vi se modérer, se calmer // vt modérer; **moderation** [-'reɪʃən] n modération f, mesure f; **in moderation** à dose raisonnable, pris(e) or pratiqué(e) modérément.
modern ['mɔdən] a moderne; ~ize vt moderniser.
modest ['mɔdɪst] a modeste; ~y n modestie f.
modicum ['mɔdɪkəm] n: a ~ of un minimum de.

modification [mɔdɪfɪ'keɪʃən] n modification f.
modify ['mɔdɪfaɪ] vt modifier.
modulation [mɔdju'leɪʃən] n modulation f.
module ['mɔdju:l] n module m.
mohair ['məuhɛə*] n mohair m.
moist [mɔɪst] a humide, moite; ~en ['mɔɪsn] vt humecter, mouiller légèrement; ~ure ['mɔɪstʃə*] n humidité f; (on glass) buée f; ~urizer ['mɔɪstʃəraɪzə*] n produit hydratant.
molar ['məulə*] n molaire f.
molasses [məu'læsɪz] n mélasse f.
mold [məuld] n, vt (US) = **mould**.
mole [məul] n (animal) taupe f; (spot) grain m de beauté.
molecule ['mɔlɪkju:l] n molécule f.
molehill ['məulhɪl] n taupinière f.
molest [məu'lɛst] vt tracasser; molester.
mollusc ['mɔləsk] n mollusque m.
mollycoddle ['mɔlɪkɔdl] vt chouchouter, couver.
molt [məult] vi (US) = **moult**.
molten ['məultən] a fondu(e).
moment ['məumənt] n moment m, instant m; importance f; ~ary a momentané(e), passager(ère); ~ous [-'mɛntəs] a important(e), capital(e).
momentum [məu'mɛntəm] n élan m, vitesse acquise; **to gather** ~ prendre de la vitesse.
monarch ['mɔnək] n monarque m; ~ist n monarchiste m/f; ~y n monarchie f.
monastery ['mɔnəstərɪ] n monastère m.
monastic [mə'næstɪk] a monastique.
Monday ['mʌndɪ] n lundi m.
monetary ['mʌnɪtərɪ] a monétaire.
money ['mʌnɪ] n argent m; **to make** ~ gagner de l'argent; faire des bénéfices; rapporter; **danger** ~ prime f de risque; ~ed a riche; ~lender n prêteur/euse; ~ order n mandat m.
mongol ['mɔngəl] a,n (MED) mongolien(ne).
mongoose ['mɔngu:s] n mangouste f.
mongrel ['mʌngrəl] n (dog) bâtard m.
monitor ['mɔnɪtə*] n (SCOL) chef m de classe; (also: television ~) moniteur m // vt contrôler.
monk [mʌŋk] n moine m.
monkey ['mʌŋkɪ] n singe m; ~ nut n cacahuète f; ~ wrench n clé f à molette.
mono... ['mɔnəu] prefix: ~chrome a monochrome.
monocle ['mɔnəkl] n monocle m.
monogram ['mɔnəgræm] n monogramme m.
monologue ['mɔnəlɔg] n monologue m.
monopolize [mə'nɔpəlaɪz] vt monopoliser.
monopoly [mə'nɔpəlɪ] n monopole m.
monorail ['mɔnəureɪl] n monorail m.
monosyllabic [mɔnəusɪ'læbɪk] a monosyllabique; (person) laconique.
monotone ['mɔnətəun] n ton m (or voix f) monocorde.
monotonous [mə'nɔtənəs] a monotone.
monotony [mə'nɔtənɪ] n monotonie f.
monsoon [mɔn'su:n] n mousson f.
monster ['mɔnstə*] n monstre m.

monstrosity [mɔns'trɔsɪtɪ] n monstruosité f, atrocité f.

monstrous ['mɔnstrəs] a (huge) gigantesque; (atrocious) monstrueux(euse), atroce.

montage [mɔn'tɑːʒ] n montage m.

month [mʌnθ] n mois m; ~**ly** a mensuel(le) // ad mensuellement // n (magazine) mensuel m, publication mensuelle.

monument ['mɔnjumənt] n monument m; ~**al** [-'mɛntl] a monumental(e); ~**al mason** n marbrier m.

moo [muː] vi meugler, beugler.

mood [muːd] n humeur f, disposition f; **to be in a good/bad** ~ être de bonne/mauvaise humeur; **to be in the** ~ **for** être d'humeur à, avoir envie de; ~**y** a (variable) d'humeur changeante, lunatique; (sullen) morose, maussade.

moon [muːn] n lune f; ~**beam** n rayon m de lune; ~**light** n clair m de lune; ~**lit** a éclairé(e) par la lune.

moor [muə*] n lande f // vt (ship) amarrer // vi mouiller.

Moor [muə*] n Maure/Mauresque.

moorings ['muərɪŋz] npl (chains) amarres fpl; (place) mouillage m.

Moorish ['muərɪʃ] a maure (mauresque).

moorland ['muələnd] n lande f.

moose [muːs] n, pl inv élan m.

moot [muːt] vt soulever // a: ~ **point** point m discutable.

mop [mɔp] n balai m à laver // vt éponger, essuyer; **to** ~ **up** vt éponger; ~ **of hair** n tignasse f.

mope [məup] vi avoir le cafard, se morfondre.

moped ['məupɛd] n (Brit) cyclomoteur m.

moquette [mɔ'kɛt] n moquette f.

moral ['mɔrl] a moral(e) // n morale f; ~**s** npl moralité f.

morale [mɔ'rɑːl] n moral m.

morality [mə'rælɪtɪ] n moralité f.

morally ['mɔrəlɪ] ad moralement.

morass [mə'ræs] n marais m, marécage m.

morbid ['mɔːbɪd] a morbide.

more [mɔː*] det plus de, davantage de // ad plus; ~ **people** plus de gens; **I want** ~ j'en veux plus или davantage; ~ **dangerous** than plus dangereux que; ~ **or less** plus ou moins; ~ **than ever** plus que jamais.

moreover [mɔː'rəuvə*] ad de plus.

morgue [mɔːg] n morgue f.

moribund ['mɔrɪbʌnd] a moribond(e).

morning ['mɔːnɪŋ] n matin m; matinée f; **in the** ~ le matin; **7 o'clock in the** ~ 7 heures du matin; ~ **sickness** n nausées matinales.

Moroccan [mə'rɔkən] a marocain(e) // n Marocain/e.

Morocco [mə'rɔkəu] n Maroc m.

moron ['mɔːrɔn] n idiot/e, minus m/f; ~**ic** [mə'rɔnɪk] a idiot(e), imbécile.

morose [mə'rəus] a morose, maussade.

morphine ['mɔːfiːn] n morphine f.

Morse [mɔːs] n (also: ~ **code**) morse m.

morsel ['mɔːsl] n bouchée f.

mortal ['mɔːtl] a, n mortel(le); ~**ity** [-'tælɪtɪ] n mortalité f.

mortar ['mɔːtə*] n mortier m.

mortgage ['mɔːgɪdʒ] n hypothèque f; (loan) prêt m (или crédit m) hypothécaire // vt hypothéquer.

mortified ['mɔːtɪfaɪd] a mortifié(e).

mortuary ['mɔːtjuərɪ] n morgue f.

mosaic [məu'zeɪɪk] n mosaïque f.

Moscow ['mɔskəu] n Moscou.

Moslem ['mɔzləm] a, n = **Muslim**.

mosque [mɔsk] n mosquée f.

mosquito [mɔs'kiːtəu] , ~**es** n moustique m; ~ **net** n moustiquaire f.

moss [mɔs] n mousse f; ~**y** a moussu(e).

most [məust] det la plupart de; le plus de // pronoun la plupart // ad le plus; (very) très, extrêmement; **the** ~ (also: + adjective) le plus; ~ **fish** la plupart des poissons; ~ **of** la plus grande partie de; **I saw** ~ j'en ai vu la plupart; c'est moi qui en ai vu le plus; **at the** (very) ~ au plus; **to make the** ~ **of** profiter au maximum de; ~**ly** ad surtout, principalement.

MOT n (abbr of Ministry of Transport): **the** ~ (test) la visite technique (annuelle) obligatoire des véhicules à moteur.

motel [məu'tɛl] n motel m.

moth [mɔθ] n papillon m de nuit; mite f; ~**ball** n boule f de naphtaline; ~**-eaten** a mité(e).

mother ['mʌðə*] n mère f // vt (care for) dorloter; ~**hood** n maternité f; ~**-in-law** n belle-mère f; ~**ly** a maternel(le); ~**-of-pearl** n nacre f; ~**-to-be** n future maman; ~ **tongue** n langue maternelle.

mothproof ['mɔθpruːf] a traité(e) à l'antimite.

motif [məu'tiːf] n motif m.

motion ['məuʃən] n mouvement m; (gesture) geste m; (at meeting) motion f // vt, vi: **to** ~ (**to**) **sb to do** faire signe à qn de faire; ~**less** a immobile, sans mouvement; ~ **picture** n film m.

motivated ['məutɪveɪtɪd] a motivé(e).

motivation [məutɪ'veɪʃən] n motivation f.

motive ['məutɪv] n motif m, mobile m // a moteur(trice).

motley ['mɔtlɪ] a hétéroclite; bigarré(e), bariolé(e).

motor ['məutə*] n moteur m; (col: vehicle) auto f // a moteur(trice); ~**bike** n moto f; ~**boat** n bateau m à moteur; ~**car** n automobile f; ~**cycle** n vélomoteur m; ~**cyclist** n motocycliste m/f; ~**ing** n tourisme m automobile // a: ~**ing accident** n accident m de voiture; ~**ing holiday** n vacances fpl en voiture; ~**ist** n automobiliste m/f; ~ **oil** n huile f de graissage; ~ **racing** n course f automobile; ~ **scooter** n scooter m; ~ **vehicle** n véhicule m automobile; ~**way** n (Brit) autoroute f.

mottled ['mɔtld] a tacheté(e), marbré(e).

motto , ~**es** ['mɔtəu] n devise f.

mould, mold (US) [məuld] n moule m; (mildew) moisissure f // vt mouler, modeler; (fig) façonner; ~**er** vi (decay) moisir; ~**ing** n (in plaster) moulage m, moulure f; (in wood) moulure; ~y a moisi(e).

moult, molt (US) [məʊlt] vi muer.

mound [maʊnd] n monticule m, tertre m.

mount [maʊnt] n mont m, montagne f; (horse) monture f; (for jewel etc) monture // vt monter // vi (also: ~ up) s'élever, monter.

mountain ['maʊntɪn] n montagne f // cpd de (la) montagne; ~**eer** [-'nɪə*] n alpiniste m/f; ~**eering** [-'nɪərɪŋ] n alpinisme m; **to go ~eering** faire de l'alpinisme; ~**ous** a montagneux(euse); (very big) gigantesque; ~ **side** n flanc m or versant m de la montagne.

mourn [mɔːn] vt pleurer // vi: **to ~ (for)** se lamenter (sur); ~**er** n parent/e or ami/e du défunt; personne f en deuil or venue rendre hommage au défunt; ~**ful** a triste, lugubre; ~**ing** n deuil m // cpd (dress) de deuil; **in ~ing** en deuil.

mouse, pl **mice** [maʊs, maɪs] n souris f; ~**trap** n souricière f.

moustache [məs'tɑːʃ] n moustache(s) f(pl).

mousy ['maʊsɪ] a (person) effacé(e); (hair) d'un châtain terne.

mouth, ~**s** [maʊθ, -ðz] n bouche f; (of dog, cat) gueule f; (of river) embouchure f; (of bottle) goulot m; (opening) orifice m; ~**ful** n bouchée f; ~ **organ** n harmonica m; ~**piece** n (of musical instrument) embouchure f; (spokesman) porte-parole m inv; ~**wash** n bain m de bouche; ~**watering** a qui met l'eau à la bouche.

movable ['muːvəbl] a mobile.

move [muːv] n (movement) mouvement m; (in game) coup m; (: turn to play) tour m; (change of house) déménagement m // vt déplacer, bouger; (emotionally) émouvoir; (POL: resolution etc) proposer // vi (gen) bouger, remuer; (traffic) circuler; (also: ~ **house**) déménager; **to ~ towards** se diriger vers; **to ~ sb to do sth** pousser or inciter qn à faire qch; **to get a ~ on** se dépêcher, se remuer; **to ~ about** vi (fidget) remuer; (travel) voyager, se déplacer; **to ~ along** vi se pousser; **to ~ away** vi s'en aller, s'éloigner; **to ~ back** vi revenir, retourner; **to ~ forward** vi avancer // vt avancer; (people) faire avancer; **to ~ in** vi (to a house) emménager; **to ~ on** vi se remettre en route // vt (onlookers) faire circuler; **to ~ out** vi (of house) déménager; **to ~ up** vi avancer; (employee) avoir de l'avancement.

movement ['muːvmənt] n mouvement m.

movie ['muːvɪ] n film m; **the ~s** le cinéma; ~ **camera** n caméra f.

moving ['muːvɪŋ] a en mouvement; émouvant(e).

mow, pt **mowed,** pp **mowed** or **mown** [məʊ, -n] vt faucher; (lawn) tondre; **to ~ down** vt faucher; ~**er** n faucheur/euse.

M.P. n abbr see **member.**

m.p.g. abbr = miles per gallon (30 m.p.g. = 29.5 l. aux 100 km).

m.p.h. abbr = miles per hour (60 m.p.h. = 96 km/h).

Mr ['mɪstə*] n: ~ **X** Monsieur X, M. X.

Mrs ['mɪsɪz] n: ~ **X** Madame X, Mme X.

Ms [mɪz] n (= Miss or Mrs): ~ **X** ≈ Madame X, Mme X.

M.Sc. abbr see **master.**

much [mʌtʃ] det beaucoup de // ad, n or pronoun beaucoup; ~ **milk** beaucoup de lait; **how ~ is it?** combien est-ce que ça coûte?; **it's not ~** ce n'est pas beaucoup.

muck [mʌk] n (mud) boue f; (dirt) ordures fpl; **to ~ about** vi (col) faire l'imbécile; (waste time) traînasser; **to ~ up** vt (col: ruin) gâcher, esquinter; ~**y** a (dirty) boueux(euse), sale.

mucus ['mjuːkəs] n mucus m.

mud [mʌd] n boue f.

muddle ['mʌdl] n pagaille f; désordre m, fouillis m // vt (also: ~ **up**) brouiller, embrouiller; **to be in a ~** (person) ne plus savoir où l'on en est; **to get in a ~** (while explaining etc) s'embrouiller; **to ~ through** vi se débrouiller.

mud: ~**dy** a boueux(euse); ~ **flats** npl plage f de vase; ~**guard** n garde-boue m inv; ~**pack** n masque m de beauté; ~**slinging** n médisance f, dénigrement m.

muff [mʌf] n manchon m.

muffin ['mʌfɪn] n petit pain rond et plat.

muffle ['mʌfl] vt (sound) assourdir, étouffer; (against cold) emmitoufler; ~**d** a étouffé(e), voilé(e).

mufti ['mʌftɪ] n: **in ~** en civil.

mug [mʌg] n (cup) tasse f (sans soucoupe); (: for beer) chope f; (col: face) bouille f; (: fool) poire f // vt (assault) agresser; ~**ging** n agression f.

muggy ['mʌgɪ] a lourd(e), moite.

mulatto, ~**es** [mjuː'lætəʊ] n mulâtre/sse.

mule [mjuːl] n mule f.

mull [mʌl] : **to ~ over** vt réfléchir à, ruminer.

mulled [mʌld] a: ~ **wine** vin chaud.

multi... ['mʌltɪ] prefix multi...; ~**coloured,** ~**colored** (US) a multicolore.

multifarious [mʌltɪ'fɛərɪəs] a divers(es); varié(e).

multiple ['mʌltɪpl] a, n multiple (m); ~ **crash** n carambolage m; ~ **sclerosis** n sclérose f en plaques; ~ **store** n grand magasin (à succursales multiples).

multiplication [mʌltɪplɪ'keɪʃən] n multiplication f.

multiply ['mʌltɪplaɪ] vt multiplier // vi se multiplier.

multitude ['mʌltɪtjuːd] n multitude f.

mum [mʌm] n maman f // a: **to keep ~** ne pas souffler mot; ~'s **the word!** motus et bouche cousue!

mumble ['mʌmbl] vt, vi marmotter, marmonner.

mummy ['mʌmɪ] n (mother) maman f; (embalmed) momie f.

mumps [mʌmps] n oreillons mpl.

munch [mʌntʃ] vt, vi mâcher.

mundane [mʌn'deɪn] a banal(e), terre à terre inv.

municipal [mjuː'nɪsɪpl] a municipal(e); ~**ity** [-'pælɪtɪ] n municipalité f.

munitions [mjuː'nɪʃənz] npl munitions fpl.

mural ['mjʊərl] n peinture murale.

murder ['mɜːdə*] n meurtre m, assassinat m // vt assassiner; ~**er** n meurtrier m, assassin *m* ; **~ess** *n* meurtrière *f* ; **~ous** *a* meurtrier(ère).

murk [mə:k] *n* obscurité *f* ; **~y** *a* sombre, ténébreux(euse).

murmur ['mə:mə*] *n* murmure *m* // *vt, vi* murmurer.

muscle ['mʌsl] *n* muscle *m* ; **to ~ in** *vi* s'imposer, s'immiscer.

muscular ['mʌskjulə*] *a* musculaire ; (*person, arm*) musclé(e).

muse [mju:z] *vi* méditer, songer // *n* muse *f*.

museum [mju:'zɪəm] *n* musée *m*.

mushroom ['mʌʃrum] *n* champignon *m* // *vi* (*fig*) pousser comme un (*or* des) champignon(s).

mushy ['mʌʃɪ] *a* en bouillie ; (*pej*) à l'eau de rose.

music ['mju:zɪk] *n* musique *f* ; **~al** *a* musical(e) ; (*person*) musicien(ne) // *n* (*show*) comédie musicale ; **~al box** *n* boîte *f* à musique ; **~al instrument** *n* instrument *m* de musique ; **~ hall** *n* music-hall *m* ; **~ian** [-'zɪʃən] *n* musicien/ne ; **~ stand** *n* pupitre *m* à musique.

musket ['mʌskɪt] *n* mousquet *m*.

Muslim ['mʌzlɪm] *a, n* musulman(e).

muslin ['mʌzlɪn] *n* mousseline *f*.

musquash ['mʌskwɒʃ] *n* loutre *f*.

mussel ['mʌsl] *n* moule *f*.

must [mʌst] *auxiliary vb* (*obligation*): **I ~ do it** je dois le faire, il faut que je le fasse ; (*probability*): **he ~ be there by now** il doit y être maintenant, il y est probablement maintenant, **I ~ have made a mistake** j'ai dû me tromper // *n* nécessité *f*, impératif *m*.

mustard ['mʌstəd] *n* moutarde *f*.

muster ['mʌstə*] *vt* rassembler.

mustn't ['mʌsnt] = **must not**.

musty ['mʌstɪ] *a* qui sent le moisi *or* le renfermé.

mute [mju:t] *a,n* muet(te).

muted ['mju:tɪd] *a* assourdi(e) ; voilé(e) ; (*MUS*) en sourdine ; (: *trumpet*) bouché(e).

mutilate ['mju:tɪleɪt] *vt* mutiler ; **mutilation** [-'leɪʃən] *n* mutilation *f*.

mutinous ['mju:tɪnəs] *a* (*troops*) mutiné(e) ; (*attitude*) rebelle.

mutiny ['mju:tɪnɪ] *n* mutinerie *f* // *vi* se mutiner.

mutter ['mʌtə*] *vt,vi* marmonner, marmotter.

mutton ['mʌtn] *n* mouton *m*.

mutual ['mju:tʃuəl] *a* mutuel(le), réciproque ; **~ly** *ad* mutuellement, réciproquement.

muzzle ['mʌzl] *n* museau *m* ; (*protective device*) muselière *f* ; (*of gun*) gueule *f* // *vt* museler.

my [maɪ] *a* mon(ma), mes *pl*.

myopic [maɪ'ɒpɪk] *a* myope.

myself [maɪ'sɛlf] *pronoun* (*reflexive*) me ; (*emphatic*) moi-même ; (*after prep*) moi.

mysterious [mɪs'tɪərɪəs] *a* mystérieux(euse).

mystery ['mɪstərɪ] *n* mystère *m* ; **~ story** *n* roman *m* à suspense.

mystic ['mɪstɪk] *n* mystique *m/f* // *a* (*mysterious*) ésotérique ; **~al** *a* mystique.

mystify ['mɪstɪfaɪ] *vt* mystifier ; (*puzzle*) ébahir.

mystique [mɪs'ti:k] *n* mystique *f*.

myth [mɪθ] *n* mythe *m* ; **~ical** *a* mythique ; **~ological** [mɪθə'lɔdʒɪkl] *a* mythologique ; **~ology** [mɪ'θɔlədʒɪ] *n* mythologie *f*.

N

nab [næb] *vt* pincer, attraper.

nag [næg] *n* (*pej: horse*) canasson *m* // *vt* (*person*) être toujours après, reprendre sans arrêt ; **~ging** *a* (*doubt, pain*) persistant(e) // *n* remarques continuelles.

nail [neɪl] *n* (*human*) ongle *m* ; (*metal*) clou *m* // *vt* clouer ; **to ~ sb down to a date/price** contraindre qn à accepter *or* donner une date/un prix ; **~brush** *n* brosse *f* à ongles ; **~file** *n* lime *f* à ongles ; **~ polish** *n* vernis *m* à ongles ; **~ scissors** *npl* ciseaux *mpl* à ongles.

naïve [naɪ'i:v] *a* naïf(ïve).

naked ['neɪkɪd] *a* nu(e) ; **~ness** *n* nudité *f*.

name [neɪm] *n* nom *m* ; réputation *f* // *vt* nommer ; citer ; (*price, date*) fixer, donner ; **in the ~ of** au nom de ; **~-dropping** *n* mention *f* (pour se faire valoir) du nom de personnalités qu'on connaît (ou prétend connaître) ; **~less** *a* sans nom ; (*witness, contributor*) anonyme ; **~ly** *ad* à savoir ; **~sake** *n* homonyme *m*.

nanny ['nænɪ] *n* bonne *f* d'enfants ; **~ goat** *n* chèvre *f*.

nap [næp] *n* (*sleep*) (petit) somme ; **to be caught ~ping** être pris à l'improviste *or* en défaut.

napalm ['neɪpɑ:m] *n* napalm *m*.

nape [neɪp] *n*: **~ of the neck** nuque *f*.

napkin ['næpkɪn] *n* serviette *f* (de table) ; (*Brit: for baby*) couche *f* (*gen pl*).

nappy ['næpɪ] *n* couche *f* (*gen pl*).

narcissus, *pl* **narcissi** [nɑ:'sɪsəs, -saɪ] *n* narcisse *m*.

narcotic [nɑ:'kɔtɪk] *n* (*drug*) stupéfiant *m* ; (*MED*) narcotique *m*.

nark [nɑ:k] *vt* mettre en rogne.

narrate [nə'reɪt] *vt* raconter, narrer.

narrative ['nærətɪv] *n* récit *m* // *a* narratif(ïve).

narrator [nə'reɪtə*] *n* narrateur/trice.

narrow ['nærəu] *a* étroit(e) ; (*fig*) restreint(e), limité(e) // *vi* devenir plus étroit, se rétrécir ; **to have a ~ escape** l'échapper belle ; **to ~ sth down to** réduire qch à ; **~ gauge** *a* à voie étroite ; **~ly** *ad*: **he ~ly missed injury/the tree** il a failli se blesser/rentrer dans l'arbre ; **he only ~ly missed the target** il a manqué la cible de peu *or* de justesse ; **~-minded** *a* à l'esprit étroit, borné(e).

nasal ['neɪzl] *a* nasal(e).

nastily ['nɑ:stɪlɪ] *ad* (*say, act*) méchamment.

nastiness ['nɑ:stɪnɪs] *n* (*of remark*) méchanceté *f*.

nasty ['nɑ:stɪ] *a* (*person*) méchant(e) ; très désagréable ; (*smell*) dégoûtant(e) ; (*wound, situation*) mauvais(e), vilain(e) ; **it's a ~ business** c'est une sale affaire.

nation ['neɪʃən] *n* nation *f*.

national ['næʃənl] *a* national(e) // *n* (*abroad*) ressortissant/e ; (*when home*) national/e ; ~ **dress** *n* costume national ; ~**ism** *n* nationalisme *m* ; ~**ist** *a,n* nationaliste (*m/f*) ; ~**ity** [-'nælɪtɪ] *n* nationalité *f* ; ~**ization** [-aɪ'zeɪʃən] *n* nationalisation *f* ; ~**ize** *vt* nationaliser ; ~**ly** *ad* du point de vue national ; dans le pays entier ; ~ **park** *n* parc national.

nation-wide ['neɪʃənwaɪd] *a* s'étendant à l'ensemble du pays ; (*problem*) à l'échelle du pays entier // *ad* à travers *or* dans tout le pays.

native ['neɪtɪv] *n* habitant/e du pays, autochtone *m/f* ; (*in colonies*) indigène *m/f* // *a* du pays, indigène ; (*country*) natal(e) ; (*language*) maternel(le) ; (*ability*) inné(e) ; **a** ~ **of Russia** une personne originaire de Russie ; **a** ~ **speaker of French** une personne de langue maternelle française.

NATO ['neɪtəu] *n* (*abbr of North Atlantic Treaty Organization*) O.T.A.N.

natter ['nætə*] *vi* bavarder.

natural ['nætʃrəl] *a* naturel(le) ; ~ **gas** *n* gaz naturel ; ~**ist** *n* naturaliste *m/f* ; ~**ize** *vt* naturaliser ; (*plant*) acclimater ; ~**ly** *ad* naturellement ; ~**ness** *n* naturel *m*.

nature ['neɪtʃə*] *n* nature *f* ; **by** ~ par tempérament, de nature.

naught [nɔːt] *n* zéro *m*.

naughty ['nɔːtɪ] *a* (*child*) vilain(e), pas sage ; (*story, film*) polisson(ne).

nausea ['nɔːsɪə] *n* nausée *f* ; ~**te** ['nɔːsɪeɪt] *vt* écœurer, donner la nausée à.

nautical ['nɔːtɪkl] *a* nautique ; ~ **mile** *n* mille marin (= *1853 m*).

naval ['neɪvl] *a* naval(e) ; ~ **officer** *n* officier *m* de marine.

nave [neɪv] *n* nef *f*.

navel ['neɪvl] *n* nombril *m*.

navigable ['nævɪgəbl] *a* navigable.

navigate ['nævɪgeɪt] *vt* diriger, piloter // *vi* naviguer ; **navigation** [-'geɪʃən] *n* navigation *f* ; **navigator** *n* navigateur *m*.

navvy ['nævɪ] *n* terrassier *m*.

navy ['neɪvɪ] *n* marine *f* ; ~**-(blue)** *a* bleu marine *inv*.

neap [niːp] *n* (*also*: ~**tide**) mortes- eaux *fpl*.

near [nɪə*] *a* proche // *ad* près // *prep* (*also*: ~ **to**) près de // *vt* approcher de ; **to come** ~ *vi* s'approcher ; ~**ly** [nɪə'baɪ] *a* proche // *ad* tout près, à proximité ; **N**~ **East** *n* Proche-Orient *m* ; ~**er** *a* plus proche // *ad* plus près ; ~**ly** *ad* presque ; **I** ~**ly fell** j'ai failli tomber ; ~ **miss** *n* collision évitée de justesse ; (*when aiming*) coup manqué de peu *or* de justesse ; ~**ness** *n* proximité *f* ; ~**side** *n* (*AUT*: *right-hand drive*) côté *m* gauche ; ~**-sighted** *a* myope.

neat [niːt] *a* (*person, work*) soigné(e) ; (*room etc*) bien tenu(e) *or* rangé(e) ; (*solution, plan*) habile ; (*spirits*) pur(e) ; **I drink it** ~ je le bois sec *or* sans eau ; ~**ly** *ad* avec soin *or* ordre ; habilement.

nebulous ['nɛbjuləs] *a* nébuleux(euse).

necessarily ['nɛsɪsrɪlɪ] *ad* nécessairement.

necessary ['nɛsɪsrɪ] *a* nécessaire.

necessitate [nɪ'sɛsɪteɪt] *vt* nécessiter.

necessity [nɪ'sɛsɪtɪ] *n* nécessité *f* ; chose nécessaire *or* essentielle.

neck [nɛk] *n* cou *m* ; (*of horse, garment*) encolure *f* ; (*of bottle*) goulot *m* ; ~ **and** ~ à égalité.

necklace ['nɛklɪs] *n* collier *m*.

neckline ['nɛklaɪn] *n* encolure *f*.

necktie ['nɛktaɪ] *n* cravate *f*.

née [neɪ] *a*: ~ **Scott** née Scott.

need [niːd] *n* besoin *m* // *vt* avoir besoin de ; **to** ~ **to do** devoir faire ; avoir besoin de faire.

needle ['niːdl] *n* aiguille *f* // *vt* asticoter, tourmenter ; ~**cord** *n* velours *m* milleraies.

needless ['niːdlɪs] *a* inutile ; ~**ly** *ad* inutilement.

needlework ['niːdlwəːk] *n* (*activity*) travaux *mpl* d'aiguille ; (*object*) ouvrage *m*.

needy ['niːdɪ] *a* nécessiteux(euse) ; **in** ~ **circumstances** dans le besoin.

negation [nɪ'geɪʃən] *n* négation *f*.

negative ['nɛgətɪv] *n* (*PHOT, ELEC*) négatif *m* ; (*LING*) terme *m* de négation // *a* négatif(ive) ; **to answer in the** ~ répondre par la négative.

neglect [nɪ'glɛkt] *vt* négliger // *n* (*of person, duty, garden*) le fait de négliger ; (*state of*) ~ abandon *m*.

negligee ['nɛglɪʒeɪ] *n* déshabillé *m*.

negligence ['nɛglɪdʒəns] *n* négligence *f*.

negligent ['nɛglɪdʒənt] *a* négligent(e) ; ~**ly** *ad* par négligence ; (*offhandedly*) négligemment.

negligible ['nɛglɪdʒɪbl] *a* négligeable.

negotiable [nɪ'gəuʃɪəbl] *a* négociable.

negotiate [nɪ'gəuʃɪeɪt] *vi* négocier // *vt* (*COMM*) négocier ; (*obstacle*) franchir, négocier ; **negotiation** [-'eɪʃən] *n* négociation *f*, pourparlers *mpl* ; **negotiator** *n* négociateur/trice.

Negress ['niːgrɪs] *n* négresse *f*.

Negro ['niːgrəu] *a* (*gen*) noir(e) ; (*music, arts*) nègre, noir // *n* (*pl*: ~**es**) Noir/e.

neighbour, neighbor (*US*) ['neɪbə*] *n* voisin/e ; ~**hood** *n* quartier *m* ; voisinage *m* ; ~**ing** *a* voisin(e), avoisinant(e) ; ~**ly** *a* obligeant(e) ; (*relations*) de bon voisinage.

neither ['naɪðə*] *a*, *pronoun* aucun(e) (des deux), ni l'un(e) ni l'autre // *cj*: **I didn't move and** ~ **did Claude** je n'ai pas bougé, (et) Claude non plus ; ..., ~ **did I refuse** ..., (et *or* mais) je n'ai pas non plus refusé // *ad*: ~ **good nor bad** ni bon ni mauvais.

neo... ['niːəu] *prefix* néo-.

neon ['niːɔn] *n* néon *m* // *a*: ~ **light** *n* lampe *f* au néon ; ~ **sign** *n* enseigne (lumineuse) au néon.

nephew ['nɛvjuː] *n* neveu *m*.

nerve [nəːv] *n* nerf *m* ; (*fig*) sang-froid *m*, courage *m* ; aplomb *m*, toupet *m* ; **he gets on my** ~**s** il m'énerve ; ~**-racking** *a* éprouvant (pour les nerfs).

nervous ['nəːvəs] *a* nerveux(euse) ; inquiet(ète), plein(e) d'appréhension ; ~ **breakdown** *n* dépression nerveuse ; ~**ly** *ad* nerveusement ; ~**ness** *n* nervosité *f* ; inquiétude *f*, appréhension *f*.

nest [nɛst] *n* nid *m* ; ~ **of tables** *n* table *f* gigogne.

nestle ['nɛsl] *vi* se blottir.
net [nɛt] *n* filet *m* // *a* net(te); ~**ball** *n* netball *m*.
Netherlands ['nɛðələndz] *npl*: the ~ les Pays-Bas *mpl*.
nett [nɛt] *a* = **net**.
netting ['nɛtɪŋ] *n* (*for fence etc*) treillis *m*, grillage *m*.
nettle ['nɛtl] *n* ortie *f*.
network ['nɛtwə:k] *n* réseau *m*.
neurosis, *pl* **neuroses** [njuə'rəusɪs, -siːz] *n* névrose *f*.
neurotic [njuə'rɔtɪk] *a*, *n* névrosé(e).
neuter ['njuːtə*] *a*, *n* neutre (*m*) // *vt* (*cat etc*) châtrer, couper.
neutral ['njuːtrəl] *a* neutre // *n* (*AUT*) point mort; ~**ity** [-'trælɪtɪ] *n* neutralité *f*.
never ['nɛvə*] *ad* (ne ...) jamais; ~ **again** plus jamais; ~**-ending** *a* interminable; ~**theless** [nɛvəðə'lɛs] *ad* néanmoins, malgré tout.
new [njuː] *a* nouveau(nouvelle); (*brand new*) neuf(neuve); ~**born** *a* nouveau-né(e); ~**comer** ['njuːkʌmə*] *n* nouveau venu/nouvelle venue; ~**ly** *ad* nouvellement, récemment; ~ **moon** *n* nouvelle lune; ~**ness** *n* nouveauté *f*.
news [njuːz] *n* nouvelle(s) *f(pl)*; (*RADIO, TV*) informations *fpl*; **a piece of** ~ une nouvelle; ~ **agency** *n* agence *f* de presse; ~**agent** *n* marchand *m* de journaux; ~**flash** *n* flash *m* d'information; ~**letter** *n* bulletin *m*; ~**paper** *n* journal *m*; ~**reel** *n* actualités (filmées) *f*; ~ **stand** *n* kiosque *m* à journaux.
New Year ['njuː'jiə*] *n* Nouvel An; ~**'s Day** *n* le jour de l'An; ~**'s Eve** *n* la Saint-Sylvestre.
New Zealand [njuː'ziːlənd] *n* la Nouvelle-Zélande.
next [nɛkst] *a* (*seat, room*) voisin(e), d'à côté; (*meeting, bus stop*) suivant(e); prochain(e) // *ad* la fois suivante; la prochaine fois; (*afterwards*) ensuite; **when do we meet** ~? quand nous revoyons-nous?; ~ **door** *ad* à côté; ~**of-kin** *n* parent *m* le plus proche; ~ **time** *ad* la prochaine fois; ~ **to** *prep* à côté de; ~ **to nothing** presque rien.
N.H.S. *n abbr of* National Health Service.
nib [nɪb] *n* (*of pen*) (bec *m* de) plume *f*.
nibble ['nɪbl] *vt* grignoter.
nice [naɪs] *a* (*holiday, trip*) agréable; (*flat, picture*) joli(e); (*person*) gentil(le); (*distinction, point*) subtil(e); ~**-looking** *a* joli(e); ~**ly** *ad* agréablement; joliment; gentiment; subtilement.
niceties ['naɪsɪtɪz] *npl* subtilités *fpl*.
nick [nɪk] *n* encoche *f* // *vt* (*col*) faucher, piquer; **in the** ~ **of time** juste à temps.
nickel ['nɪkl] *n* nickel *m*; (*US*) pièce *f* de 5 cents.
nickname ['nɪkneɪm] *n* surnom *m* // *vt* surnommer.
nicotine ['nɪkətiːn] *n* nicotine *f*.
niece [niːs] *n* nièce *f*.
Nigeria [naɪ'dʒɪərɪə] *n* Nigéria *m or f*; ~**n** *a* nigérien(ne) // *n* Nigérien/ne.
niggardly ['nɪgədlɪ] *a* pingre.
niggling ['nɪglɪŋ] *a* tatillon(ne).

night [naɪt] *n* nuit *f*; (*evening*) soir *m*; **at** ~ la nuit; **by** ~ de nuit; ~**cap** *n* boisson prise avant le coucher; ~ **club** *n* boîte *f* de nuit; ~**dress** *n* chemise *f* de nuit; ~**fall** *n* tombée *f* de la nuit; ~**ie** ['naɪtɪ] *n* chemise *f* de nuit.
nightingale ['naɪtɪŋgeɪl] *n* rossignol *m*.
night life ['naɪtlaɪf] *n* vie *f* nocturne.
nightly ['naɪtlɪ] *a* de chaque nuit or soir; (*by night*) nocturne // *ad* chaque nuit or soir; nuitamment.
nightmare ['naɪtmɛə*] *n* cauchemar *m*.
night school ['naɪtskuːl] *n* cours *mpl* du soir.
night-time ['naɪttaɪm] *n* nuit *f*.
night watchman ['naɪt'wɔtʃmən] *n* veilleur de nuit *m*.
nil [nɪl] *n* rien *m*; (*SPORT*) zéro *m*.
nimble ['nɪmbl] *a* agile.
nine [naɪn] *num* neuf; ~**teen** *num* dix-neuf; ~**ty** *num* quatre-vingt-dix.
ninth [naɪnθ] *a* neuvième.
nip [nɪp] *vt* pincer // *n* pincement *m*.
nipple ['nɪpl] *n* (*ANAT*) mamelon *m*, bout *m* du sein.
nippy ['nɪpɪ] *a* (*person*) alerte, leste.
nitrogen ['naɪtrədʒən] *n* azote *m*.
no [nəu] *det* pas de, aucun(e) + *sg* // *ad*, *n* non (*m*); ~ **entry** défense d'entrer, entrée interdite; ~ **dogs** les chiens ne sont pas admis.
nobility [nəu'bɪlɪtɪ] *n* noblesse *f*.
noble ['nəubl] *a* noble; ~**man** *n* noble *m*; **nobly** *ad* noblement.
nobody ['nəubədɪ] *pronoun* personne (*with negative*).
nod [nɔd] *vi* faire un signe de (la) tête (*affirmatif ou amical*); (*sleep*) somnoler // *n* signe *m* de (la) tête; **to** ~ **off** *vi* s'assoupir.
noise [nɔɪz] *n* bruit *m*; ~**less** *a* silencieux(euse); **noisily** *ad* bruyamment; **noisy** *a* bruyant(e).
nomad ['nəumæd] *n* nomade *m/f*; ~**ic** [-'mædɪk] *a* nomade.
no man's land ['nəumænzlænd] *n* no man's land *m*.
nominal ['nɔmɪnl] *a* (*rent, fee*) symbolique; (*value*) nominal(e).
nominate ['nɔmɪneɪt] *vt* (*propose*) proposer; (*elect*) nommer.
nomination [nɔmɪ'neɪʃən] *n* nomination *f*.
nominee [nɔmɪ'niː] *n* candidat agréé; personne nommée.
non... [nɔn] *prefix* non-; ~**-alcoholic** *a* non-alcoolisé(e); ~**-breakable** *a* incassable; ~**-committal** ['nɔnkə'mɪtl] *a* évasif(ive); ~**descript** ['nɔndɪskrɪpt] *a* quelconque, indéfinissable.
none [nʌn] *pronoun* aucun(e); **he's** ~ **the worse for it** il ne s'en porte pas plus mal.
nonentity [nɔ'nɛntɪtɪ] *n* personne insignifiante.
non: ~**-fiction** *n* littérature *f* non-romanesque; ~**-flammable** *a* ininflammable.
nonplussed [nɔn'plʌst] *a* perplexe.
nonsense ['nɔnsəns] *n* absurdités *fpl*, idioties *fpl*.
non: ~**-smoker** *n* non-fumeur *m*; ~**stick** *a* qui n'attache pas; ~**-stop** *a*

direct(e), sans arrêt (or escale) // ad sans arrêt.

noodles ['nu:dlz] npl nouilles fpl.

nook [nuk] n: ~s and crannies recoins mpl.

noon [nu:n] n midi m.

no one ['nəʊwʌn] pronoun = **nobody**.

nor [nɔ:*] cj = **neither** // ad see **neither**.

norm [nɔ:m] n norme f.

normal ['nɔ:ml] a normal(e); ~ly ad normalement.

Normandy ['nɔ:məndɪ] n Normandie f.

north [nɔ:θ] n nord m // a du nord, nord (inv) // ad au or vers le nord; N~ **America** n Amérique f du Nord; ~-east n nord-est m; ~ern ['nɔ:ðən] a du nord, septentrional(e); N~ern **Ireland** n Irlande f du Nord; N~ **Pole** n pôle m Nord; N~ **Sea** n mer f du Nord; ~ward(s) ['nɔ:θwəd(z)] ad vers le nord; ~-west n nord-ouest m.

Norway ['nɔ:weɪ] n Norvège f.

Norwegian [nɔ:'wi:dʒən] a norvégien(ne) // n Norvégien/ne; (LING) norvégien m.

nose [nəʊz] n nez m; (fig) flair m; ~**bleed** n saignement m de nez; ~-**dive** n (descente f en) piqué m; ~y a curieux(euse).

nostalgia [nɔs'tældʒɪə] n nostalgie f; **nostalgic** a nostalgique.

nostril ['nɔstrɪl] n narine f; (of horse) naseau m.

nosy ['nəʊzɪ] a = **nosey**.

not [nɔt] ad (ne ...) pas; ~ at all pas du tout; you must ~ or mustn't do this tu ne dois pas faire ça; he isn't... il n'est pas... .

notable ['nəʊtəbl] a notable.

notably ['nəʊtəblɪ] ad en particulier.

notch [nɔtʃ] n encoche f.

note [nəʊt] n note f; (letter) mot m; (banknote) billet m // vt (also: ~ **down**) noter; (notice) constater; ~**book** n carnet m; ~-**case** n porte-feuille m; ~**d** ['nəʊtɪd] a réputé(e); ~**paper** n papier m à lettres.

nothing ['nʌθɪŋ] n rien m; ~ **new** rien de nouveau; **for** ~ (free) pour rien, gratuitement.

notice ['nəʊtɪs] n avis m; (of leaving) congé m // vt remarquer, s'apercevoir de; **to take** ~ **of** prêter attention à; **to bring sth to sb's** ~ porter qch à la connaissance de qn; **to avoid** ~ éviter de se faire remarquer; ~**able** a visible; ~ **board** n (Brit) panneau m d'affichage.

notify ['nəʊtɪfaɪ] vt: **to** ~ **sth to sb** notifier qch à qn; **to** ~ **sb of sth** avertir qn de qch.

notion ['nəʊʃən] n idée f; (concept) notion f.

notorious [nəʊ'tɔ:rɪəs] a notoire (souvent en mal).

notwithstanding [nɔtwɪθ'stændɪŋ] ad néanmoins // prep en dépit de.

nougat ['nu:gɑ:] n nougat m.

nought [nɔ:t] n zéro m.

noun [naʊn] n nom m.

nourish ['nʌrɪʃ] vt nourrir; ~**ing** a nourrissant(e); ~**ment** n nourriture f.

novel ['nɔvl] n roman m // a

nouveau(nouvelle), original(e); ~**ist** n romancier m; ~**ty** n nouveauté f.

November [nəʊ'vɛmbə*] n novembre m.

novice ['nɔvɪs] n novice m/f.

now [naʊ] ad maintenant; ~ **and then**, ~ **and again** de temps en temps; **from** ~ **on** dorénavant; ~**adays** ['nauədeɪz] ad de nos jours.

nowhere ['nəʊwɛə*] ad nulle part.

nozzle ['nɔzl] n (of hose) jet m, lance f.

nuance ['nju:ɑ:ns] n nuance f.

nuclear ['nju:klɪə*] a nucléaire.

nucleus, pl nuclei ['nju:klɪəs, 'nju:klɪaɪ] n noyau m.

nude [nju:d] a nu(e) // n (ART) nu m; **in the** ~ (tout(e)) nu(e).

nudge [nʌdʒ] vt donner un (petit) coup de coude à.

nudist ['nju:dɪst] n nudiste m/f.

nudity ['nju:dɪtɪ] n nudité f.

nuisance ['nju:sns] n: it's a ~ c'est (très) ennuyeux or gênant; he's a ~ il est assommant or casse-pieds.

null [nʌl] a: ~ **and void** nul(le) et non avenu(e); ~**ify** ['nʌlɪfaɪ] vt invalider.

numb [nʌm] a engourdi(e) // vt engourdir.

number ['nʌmbə*] n nombre m; (numeral) chiffre m; (of house, car, telephone, newspaper) numéro m // vt numéroter; (include) compter; **a** ~ **of** un certain nombre de; **the staff** ~**s 20** le nombre d'employés s'élève à or est de 20; ~ **plate** n plaque f minéralogique or d'immatriculation.

numbness ['nʌmnɪs] n engourdissement m.

numeral ['nju:mərəl] n chiffre m.

numerical [nju:'mɛrɪkl] a numérique.

numerous ['nju:mərəs] a nombreux(euse).

nun [nʌn] n religieuse f, sœur f.

nurse [nə:s] n infirmière f // vt (patient, cold) soigner; (hope) nourrir; ~(**maid**) n bonne f d'enfants.

nursery ['nə:sərɪ] n (room) nursery f; (institution) pouponnière f; (for plants) pépinière f; ~ **rhyme** n comptine f, chansonnette f pour enfants; ~ **school** n école maternelle; ~ **slope** n (SKI) piste f pour débutants.

nursing ['nə:sɪŋ] n (profession) profession f d'infirmière; ~ **home** n clinique f; maison f de convalescence.

nut [nʌt] n (of metal) écrou m; (fruit) noix f, noisette f, cacahuète f (terme générique en anglais); he's ~**s** (col) il est dingue; ~-**case** n (col) dingue m/f; ~-**crackers** npl casse-noix m inv, casse-noisette(s) m; ~-**meg** ['nʌtmɛg] n (noix f) muscade f.

nutrient ['nju:trɪənt] n substance nutritive.

nutrition [nju:'trɪʃən] n nutrition f, alimentation f.

nutritious [nju:'trɪʃəs] a nutritif(ive), nourrissant(e).

nutshell ['nʌtʃɛl] n coquille f de noix; **in a** ~ en un mot.

nylon ['naɪlɔn] n nylon m; ~**s** npl bas mpl nylon.

O

oaf [əʊf] n balourd m.

oak [əuk] n chêne m.

O.A.P. abbr see **old.**

oar [ɔ:*] n aviron m, rame f; ~sman/woman rameur/euse.

oasis, pl **oases** [əu'eisis, əu'eisi:z] n oasis f.

oath [əuθ] n serment m; (swear word) juron m; **to take the** ~ prêter serment; **on** ~ sous serment; assermenté(e).

oatmeal ['əutmi:l] n flocons mpl d'avoine.

oats [əuts] n avoine f.

obedience [ə'bi:diəns] n obéissance f; **in** ~ **to** conformément à.

obedient [ə'bi:diənt] a obéissant(e).

obelisk ['ɔbilisk] n obélisque m.

obesity [əu'bi:siti] n obésité f.

obey [ə'bei] vt obéir à; (instructions, regulations) se conformer à // vi obéir.

obituary [ə'bitjuəri] n nécrologie f.

object n ['ɔbdʒikt] objet m; (purpose) but m, objet m; (LING) complément m d'objet // vi [əb'dʒekt]: **to** ~ **to** (attitude) désapprouver; (proposal) protester contre, élever une objection contre; **I** ~! je proteste!; **he** ~**ed that** ... il a fait valoir or a objecté que ...; ~**ion** [əb'dʒekʃən] n objection f; (drawback) inconvénient m; **if you have no** ~**ion** si vous n'y voyez pas d'inconvénient; ~**ionable** [əb'dʒekʃənəbl] a très désagréable; choquant(e); ~**ive** n objectif m // a objectif(ive); ~**ivity** [ɔbdʒik'tiviti] n objectivité f; ~**or** n opposant/e.

obligation [ɔbli'geiʃən] n obligation f, devoir m; (debt) dette f (de reconnaissance).

obligatory [ə'bligətəri] a obligatoire.

oblige [ə'blaidʒ] vt (force): **to** ~ **sb to do** obliger or forcer qn à faire; (do a favour) rendre service à, obliger; **to be** ~**d to sb for sth** être obligé(e) à qn de qch; **obliging** a obligeant(e), serviable.

oblique [ə'bli:k] a oblique; (allusion) indirect(e).

obliterate [ə'blitəreit] vt effacer.

oblivion [ə'bliviən] n oubli m.

oblivious [ə'bliviəs] a: ~ **of** oublieux(euse) de.

oblong ['ɔblɔŋ] a oblong(ue) // n rectangle m.

obnoxious [əb'nɔkʃəs] a odieux (euse); (smell) nauséabond(e).

oboe ['əubəu] n hautbois m.

obscene [əb'si:n] a obscène.

obscenity [əb'seniti] n obscénité f.

obscure [əb'skjuə*] a obscur(e) // vt obscurcir; (hide: sun) cacher; **obscurity** n obscurité f.

obsequious [əb'si:kwiəs] a obséquieux(euse).

observable [əb'zə:vəbl] a observable; (appreciable) notable.

observance [əb'zə:vns] n observance f, observation f.

observant [əb'zə:vnt] a observateur(trice).

observation [ɔbzə'veiʃən] n observation f; (by police etc) surveillance f.

observatory [əb'zə:vətri] n observatoire m.

observe [əb'zə:v] vt observer; (remark) faire observer or remarquer; ~**r** n observateur/trice.

obsess [əb'ses] vt obséder; ~**ion** [əb'seʃən] n obsession f; ~**ive** a, obsédant(e).

obsolescence [ɔbsə'lesns] n vieillissement m; **built-in** or **planned** ~ (COMM) désuétude calculée.

obsolete ['ɔbsəli:t] a dépassé(e); démodé(e).

obstacle ['ɔbstəkl] n obstacle m; ~ **race** n course f d'obstacles.

obstetrics [ɔb'stetriks] n obstétrique f.

obstinacy ['ɔbstinəsi] n obstination f.

obstinate ['ɔbstinit] a obstiné(e); (pain, cold) persistant(e).

obstreperous [əb'strepərəs] a turbulent(e).

obstruct [əb'strʌkt] vt (block) boucher, obstruer; (halt) arrêter; (hinder) entraver; ~**ion** [əb'strʌkʃən] n obstruction f; obstacle m; ~**ive** a obstructionniste.

obtain [əb'tein] vt obtenir // vi avoir cours; ~**able** a qu'on peut obtenir.

obtrusive [əb'tru:siv] a (person) importun(e); (smell) pénétrant(e); (building etc) trop en évidence.

obtuse [əb'tju:s] a obtus(e).

obviate ['ɔbvieit] vt parer à, obvier à.

obvious ['ɔbviəs] a évident(e), manifeste; ~**ly** ad manifestement; bien sûr.

occasion [ə'keiʒən] n occasion f; (event) événement m // vt occasionner, causer; ~**al** a pris(e) or fait(e) etc de temps en temps; occasionnel(le); ~**al table** n table décorative.

occupation [ɔkju'peiʃən] n occupation f; (job) métier m, profession f; **unfit for** ~ (house) impropre à l'habitation; ~**al disease** n maladie f du travail; ~**al hazard** n risque m du métier.

occupier ['ɔkjupaiə*] n occupant/e.

occupy ['ɔkjupai] vt occuper; **to** ~ **o.s. with** or **by doing** s'occuper à faire.

occur [ə'kə:*] vi se produire; (difficulty, opportunity) se présenter; (phenomenon, error) se rencontrer; **to** ~ **to sb** venir à l'esprit de qn; ~**rence** n présence f, existence f; cas m, fait m.

ocean ['əuʃən] n océan m; ~**-going** a de haute mer; ~ **liner** n paquebot m.

ochre ['əukə*] n ocre f.

o'clock [ə'klɔk] ad: **it is 5** ~ il est 5 heures.

octagonal [ɔk'tægənl] a octogonal(e).

octane ['ɔktein] n octane m.

octave ['ɔktiv] n octave f.

October [ɔk'təubə*] n octobre m.

octopus ['ɔktəpəs] n pieuvre f.

odd [ɔd] a (strange) bizarre, curieux(euse); (number) impair(e); (left over) seul, en plus; (not of a set) dépareillé(e); **60-**~ 60 et quelques; **at** ~ **times** de temps en temps; **the** ~ **one out** l'exception f; ~**ity** n bizarrerie f; (person) excentrique m/f; ~**-job man** n homme m à tout faire; ~ **jobs** npl petits travaux divers; ~**ly** ad bizarrement, curieusement; ~**ments** npl (COMM) fins fpl de série; ~**s** npl (in betting) cote f; **the** ~**s are against his coming** il y a peu de chances qu'il vienne; **it**

makes no ~s cela n'a pas d'importance ;
at ~s en désaccord.

ode [əud] n ode f.

odious ['əudɪəs] a odieux(euse), détestable.

odour, odor (US) ['əudə*] n odeur f ;
~less a inodore.

of [ɔv, əv] prep de ; **a friend** ~ **ours** un
de nos amis ; **3** ~ **them went** 3 d'entre
eux y sont allés ; **the 5th** ~ **July** le 5 juillet ; **a boy** ~ **10** un garçon de 10 ans.

off [ɔf] a,ad (engine) coupé(e) ; (tap)
fermé(e) ; (food: bad) mauvais(e),
avancé(e) ; (milk) tourné(e) ; (absent)
absent(e) ; (cancelled) annulé(e) // prep
de ; sur ; **to be** ~ (to leave) partir, s'en
aller ; **to be** ~ **sick** être absent(e) pour
cause de maladie ; **a day** ~ un jour de
congé ; **to have an** ~ **day** n'être pas en
forme ; **he had his coat** ~ il avait enlevé
son manteau ; **the hook is** ~ le crochet
s'est détaché ; le crochet n'est pas mis ;
10% ~ (COMM) 10% de rabais ; **5 km** ~
(the road) à 5 km (de la route) ; ~ **the
coast** au large de la côte ; **a house** ~ **the
main road** une maison à l'écart de la
grand-route ; **I'm** ~ **meat** je ne mange
plus de viande ; je n'aime plus la viande ;
on the ~ **chance** à tout hasard.

offal ['ɔfl] n (CULIN) abats mpl.

offbeat ['ɔfbi:t] a excentrique.

off-colour ['ɔf'kʌlə*] a (ill) malade, mal
fichu(e).

offence, offense (US) [ə'fɛns] n (crime)
délit m, infraction f ; **to give** ~ **to** blesser, offenser ; **to take** ~ **at** se vexer de,
s'offenser de.

offend [ə'fɛnd] vt (person) offenser, blesser ; ~**er** n délinquant/e ; (against regulations) contrevenant/e.

offensive [ə'fɛnsɪv] a offensant(e),
choquant(e) ; (smell etc) très
déplaisant(e) ; (weapon) offensif(ive) // n
(MIL) offensive f.

offer ['ɔfə*] n offre f, proposition f // vt
offrir, proposer ; **'on** ~' (COMM) 'en promotion' ; ~**ing** n offrande f.

offhand [ɔf'hænd] a désinvolte // ad
spontanément.

office ['ɔfɪs] n (place) bureau m ; (position)
charge f, fonction f ; **to take** ~ entrer en
fonctions ; ~ **block** n immeuble m de
bureaux ; ~ **boy** n garçon m de bureau ;
~ **r** n (MIL etc) officier m ; (of organization)
membre m du bureau directeur ; (also:
police ~**r**) agent m (de police) ; ~ **work**
n travail m de bureau ; ~ **worker** n
employé/e de bureau.

official [ə'fɪʃl] a (authorized) officiel(le) //
n officiel m ; (civil servant) fonctionnaire
m/f ; employé/e ; ~**ly** ad officiellement.

officious [ə'fɪʃəs] a trop empressé(e).

offing ['ɔfɪŋ] n: **in the** ~ (fig) en perspective.

off: ~**-licence** n (Brit: shop) débit m de
vins et de spiritueux ; ~**-peak** a aux
heures creuses ; ~**-putting** a
rébarbatif(ive) ; rebutant(e), peu
engageant(e) ; ~**-season** a, ad hors-saison.

offset ['ɔfsɛt] vt irg (counteract) contrebalancer, compenser // n (also: ~
printing) offset m.

offshore [ɔf'ʃɔ:*] a (breeze) de terre ;
(island) proche du littoral ; (fishing)
côtier(ère).

offside ['ɔf'saɪd] a (SPORT) hors jeu // n
(AUT: with right-hand drive) côté droit.

offspring ['ɔfsprɪŋ] n progéniture f.

off: ~**-stage** ad dans les coulisses ; ~**-the-
cuff** ad au pied levé ; de chic ; ~**-the-peg**
ad en prêt-à-porter ; ~**-white** a blanc
cassé inv.

often ['ɔfn] ad souvent ; **as** ~ **as not** la
plupart du temps.

ogle ['əugl] vt lorgner.

oil [ɔɪl] n huile f ; (petroleum) pétrole m ;
(for central heating) mazout m // vt
(machine) graisser ; ~**can** n burette f de
graissage ; (for storing) bidon m à huile ;
~ **change** n vidange f ; ~**field** n gisement
m de pétrole ; ~**fired** a au mazout ; ~
level n niveau m d'huile ; ~ **painting** n
peinture f à l'huile ; ~ **refinery** n raffinerie
f de pétrole ; ~ **rig** n derrick m ; (at sea)
plate-forme pétrolière ; ~**skins** npl ciré m ;
~ **slick** n nappe f de mazout ; ~ **tanker**
n pétrolier m ; ~ **well** n puits m de pétrole ; ~**y** a huileux(euse) ; (food) gras(se).

ointment ['ɔɪntmənt] n onguent m.

O.K., okay ['əu'keɪ] excl d'accord! // a
bien ; en règle ; en bon état ; pas mal //
vt approuver, donner son accord à ; **is it**
~**?, are you** ~**?** ça va?

old [əuld] a vieux(vieille) ; (person) vieux,
âgé(e) ; (former) ancien(ne), vieux ; **how
are you?** quel âge avez-vous? ; **he's 10
years** ~ il a 10 ans, il est âgé de 10 ans ;
~ **age** n vieillesse f ; ~**age pensioner**
(O.A.P.) n retraité/e ; ~**er brother/sis-
ter** frère/sœur aîné(e) ; ~**-fashioned** a
démodé(e) ; (person) vieux jeu inv ; ~
people's home n maison f de retraite.

olive ['ɔlɪv] n (fruit) olive f ; (tree) olivier
m // a (also: ~**-green**) (vert) olive inv ;
~ **oil** n huile f d'olive.

Olympic [əu'lɪmpɪk] a olympique ; **the** ~
Games, the ~**s** les Jeux mpl olympiques.

omelet(te) ['ɔmlɪt] n omelette f ;
ham/cheese ~ omelette au
jambon/fromage.

omen ['əumən] n présage m.

ominous ['ɔmɪnəs] a menaçant(e),
inquiétant(e) ; (event) de mauvais augure.

omission [əu'mɪʃən] n omission f.

omit [əu'mɪt] vt omettre.

on [ɔn] prep sur // ad (machine) en marche ;
(light, radio) allumé(e) ; (tap) ouvert(e) ; **is
the meeting still** ~**?** est-ce que la réunion
a bien lieu? ; la réunion dure-t-elle
encore? ; **when is this film** ~**?** quand
passe or passe-t-on ce film? ; ~ **the train**
dans le train ; ~ **the wall** sur le or au mur ;
~ **television** à la télévision ; ~ **learning
this** en apprenant cela ; ~ **arrival** à
l'arrivée ; ~ **the left** à gauche ; ~ **Friday**
vendredi ; ~ **Fridays** le vendredi ; ~ **a week**
~ **Friday** vendredi en huit ; **to have one's
coat** ~ avoir (mis) son manteau ; **to walk**
etc ~ continuer à marcher etc ; **it's not**
~**!** pas question! ; ~ **and off** de temps à
autre.

once [wʌns] ad une fois ; (formerly) autrefois // cj une fois que ; **at** ~ tout de suite,
immédiatement ; (simultaneously) à la fois ;

all at ~ *ad* tout d'un coup ; ~ **a week** une fois par semaine ; ~ **more** encore une fois ; ~ **and for all** une fois pour toutes.

oncoming ['ɔnkʌmɪŋ] *a* (*traffic*) venant en sens inverse.

one [wʌn] *det, num* un(e) // *pronoun* un(e) ; (*impersonal*) on ; **this** ~ celui-ci/celle-ci ; **that** ~ celui-là/celle-là ; **the** ~ **book which...** l'unique livre que... ; ~ **by** un(e) par un(e) ; ~ **never knows** on ne sait jamais ; ~ **another** l'un(e) l'autre ; ~-**man** *a* (*business*) dirigé(e) *etc* par un seul homme ; ~-**man band** *n* homme-orchestre *m* ; ~**self** *pronoun* se ; (*after prep, also emphatic*) soi-même ; ~-**way** *a* (*street, traffic*) à sens unique.

ongoing ['ɔngəuɪŋ] *a* en cours ; suivi(e).

onion ['ʌnjən] *n* oignon *m*.

onlooker ['ɔnlukə*] *n* spectateur/trice.

only ['əunlɪ] *ad* seulement // *a* seul(e), unique // *cj* seulement, mais ; **an** ~ **child** un enfant unique ; **not** ~ non seulement ; **I** ~ **took one** j'en ai seulement pris un, je n'en ai pris qu'un.

onset ['ɔnsɛt] *n* début *m* ; (*of winter, old age*) approche *f*.

onshore ['ɔnʃɔ:*] *a* (*wind*) du large.

onslaught ['ɔnslɔ:t] *n* attaque *f*, assaut *m*.

onto ['ɔntu] *prep* = **on to**.

onus ['əunəs] *n* responsabilité *f*.

onward(s) ['ɔnwəd(z)] *ad* (*move*) en avant ; **from this time** ~ dorénavant.

onyx ['ɔnɪks] *n* onyx *m*.

ooze [u:z] *vi* suinter.

opacity [əu'pæsɪtɪ] *n* (*of substance*) opacité *f*.

opal ['əupl] *n* opale *f*.

opaque [əu'peɪk] *a* opaque.

OPEC [əupɛk] *n* (*abbr of Organization of petroleum exporting countries*) C.P.E.P. (*Organisation des pays exportateurs de pétrole*).

open ['əupn] *a* ouvert(e) ; (*car*) découvert(e) ; (*road, view*) dégagé(e) ; (*meeting*) public(ique) ; (*admiration*) manifeste ; (*question*) non résolu(e) ; (*enemy*) déclaré(e) // *vt* ouvrir // *vi* (*flower, eyes, door, debate*) s'ouvrir ; (*shop, bank, museum*) ouvrir ; (*book etc: commence*) commencer, débuter ; **to** ~ **on to** *vt fus* (*subj: room, door*) donner sur ; **to** ~ **out** *vt ouvrir* // *vi* s'ouvrir ; **to** ~ **up** *vt* ouvrir ; (*blocked road*) dégager // *vi* s'ouvrir ; **in the** ~ (**air**) en plein air ; ~-**air** *a* en plein air ; ~-**ing** *n* ouverture *f* ; (*opportunity*) occasion *f* ; débouché *m* ; (*job*) poste vacant ; ~-**ly** *ad* ouvertement ; ~-**minded** *a* à l'esprit ouvert ; ~-**necked** *a* à col ouvert ; ~ **sandwich** *n* canapé *m* ; **the** ~ **sea** *n* le large.

opera ['ɔpərə] *n* opéra *m* ; ~ **glasses** *npl* jumelles *fpl* de théâtre ; ~ **house** *n* opéra *m*.

operate ['ɔpəreɪt] *vt* (*machine*) faire marcher, faire fonctionner ; (*system*) pratiquer // *vi* fonctionner ; (*drug*) faire effet ; **to** ~ **on sb (for)** (MED) opérer qn (de).

operatic [ɔpə'rætɪk] *a* d'opéra.

operating ['ɔpəreɪtɪŋ] *a*: ~ **table/theatre** table *f*/salle *f* d'opération.

operation [ɔpə'reɪʃən] *n* opération *f* ; **to be in** ~ (*machine*) être en service ;

(*system*) être en vigueur ; ~**al** *a* opérationnel(le).

operative ['ɔpərətɪv] *a* (*measure*) en vigueur // *n* (*in factory*) ouvrier/ère.

operator ['ɔpəreɪtə*] *n* (*of machine*) opérateur/trice ; (TEL) téléphoniste *m/f*.

operetta [ɔpə'rɛtə] *n* opérette *f*.

opinion [ə'pɪnjən] *n* opinion *f*, avis *m* ; **in my** ~ à mon avis ; ~**ated** *a* aux idées bien arrêtées ; ~ **poll** *n* sondage *m* (d'opinion).

opium ['əupɪəm] *n* opium *m*.

opponent [ə'pəunənt] *n* adversaire *m/f*.

opportune ['ɔpətju:n] *a* opportun(e) ; **opportunist** [-'tju:nɪst] *n* opportuniste *m/f*.

opportunity [ɔpə'tju:nɪtɪ] *n* occasion *f* ; **to take the** ~ **of doing** profiter de l'occasion pour faire.

oppose [ə'pəuz] *vt* s'opposer à ; ~**d to a** opposé(e) à ; **as** ~**d to** par opposition à ; **opposing** *a* (*side*) opposé(e).

opposite ['ɔpəzɪt] *a* opposé(e) ; (*house etc*) d'en face // *ad* en face // *prep* en face de // *n* opposé *m*, contraire *m* ; (*of word*) contraire *m* ; '**see** ~ **page**' 'voir ci-contre' ; **his** ~ **number** son homologue *m/f*.

opposition [ɔpə'zɪʃən] *n* opposition *f*.

oppress [ə'prɛs] *vt* opprimer ; ~**ion** [ə'prɛʃən] *n* oppression *f* ; ~**ive** *a* oppressif(ive).

opt [ɔpt] *vi*: **to** ~ **for** opter pour ; **to** ~ **to do** choisir de faire ; **to** ~ **out of** choisir de quitter.

optical ['ɔptɪkl] *a* optique ; (*instrument*) d'optique.

optician [ɔp'tɪʃən] *n* opticien/ne.

optimism ['ɔptɪmɪzəm] *n* optimisme *m*.

optimist ['ɔptɪmɪst] *n* optimiste *m/f* ; ~**ic** [-'mɪstɪk] *a* optimiste.

optimum ['ɔptɪməm] *a* optimum.

option ['ɔpʃən] *n* choix *m*, option *f* ; (SCOL) matière *f* à option ; (COMM) option ; **to keep one's** ~**s open** (*fig*) ne pas s'engager ; ~**al** *a* facultatif(ive) ; (COMM) en option.

opulence ['ɔpjuləns] *n* opulence *f* ; ʳ⁻¹⁻¹dance *f*.

opulent ['ɔpjulənt] *a* opulent(e) ; abondant(e).

or [ɔ:*] *cj* ou ; (*with negative*): **he hasn't seen** ~ **heard anything** il n'a rien vu ni entendu ; ~ **else** sinon ; ou bien.

oracle ['ɔrəkl] *n* oracle *m*.

oral ['ɔ:rəl] *a* oral(e) // *n* oral *m*.

orange ['ɔrɪndʒ] *n* (*fruit*) orange *f* // *a* orange *inv*.

oration [ɔ:'reɪʃən] *n* discours solennel.

orator ['ɔrətə*] *n* orateur/trice.

oratorio [ɔrə'tɔ:rɪəu] *n* oratorio *m*.

orb [ɔ:b] *n* orbe *m*.

orbit ['ɔ:bɪt] *n* orbite *f* // *vt* décrire une or des orbite(s) autour de.

orchard ['ɔ:tʃəd] *n* verger *m*.

orchestra ['ɔ:kɪstrə] *n* orchestre *m* ; ~**l** [-'kɛstrəl] *a* orchestral(e) ; (*concert*) symphonique.

orchid ['ɔ:kɪd] *n* orchidée *f*.

ordain [ɔ:'deɪn] *vt* (REL) ordonner ; (*decide*) décréter.

ordeal [ɔ:'di:l] *n* épreuve *f*.

order ['ɔ:də*] *n* ordre *m* ; (COMM) commande *f* // *vt* ordonner ; (COMM) commander ; **in** ~ en ordre ; (*of document*) en

règle ; **in ~ of size** par ordre de grandeur ;
in ~ to do/that pour faire/que + *sub* ;
to ~ sb to do ordonner à qn de faire ;
the lower ~s (*pej*) les classes inférieures ;
~ form n bon *m* de commande ; **~ly** n
(*MIL*) ordonnance *f* // *a* (*room*) en ordre ;
(*mind*) méthodique ; (*person*) qui a de
l'ordre.

ordinal ['ɔ:dɪnl] *a* (*number*) ordinal(e).

ordinary ['ɔ:dnrɪ] *a* ordinaire, normal(e) ;
(*pej*) ordinaire, quelconque.

ordination [ɔ:dɪ'neɪʃən] *n* ordination *f*.

ordnance ['ɔ:dnəns] *n* (*MIL*: *unit*) service
m du matériel ; **O~ Survey map** *n* ≈
carte *f* d'État-major.

ore [ɔ:*] *n* minerai *m*.

organ ['ɔ:gən] *n* organe *m* ; (*MUS*) orgue *m*,
orgues *fpl* ; **~ic** [ɔ:'gænɪk] *a* organique.

organism ['ɔ:gənɪzəm] *n* organisme *m*.

organist ['ɔ:gənɪst] *n* organiste *m/f*.

organization [ɔ:gənaɪ'zeɪʃən] *n* organisation *f*.

organize ['ɔ:gənaɪz] *vt* organiser ; **~d labour** *n* main-d'œuvre syndiquée ; **~r** *n*
organisateur/trice.

orgasm ['ɔ:gæzəm] *n* orgasme *m*.

orgy ['ɔ:dʒɪ] *n* orgie *f*.

Orient ['ɔ:rɪənt] *n*: **the ~** l'Orient *m* ;
oriental [-'entl] *a* oriental(e) // *n*
Oriental/e.

orientate ['ɔ:rɪəntent] *vt* orienter.

orifice ['ɔrɪfɪs] *n* orifice *m*.

origin ['ɔrɪdʒɪn] *n* origine *f*.

original [ə'rɪdʒɪnl] *a* original(e) ; (*earliest*)
originel(le) // *n* original *m* ; **~ity** [-'nælɪtɪ]
n originalité *f* ; **~ly** *ad* (*at first*) à l'origine.

originate [ə'rɪdʒɪneɪt] *vi*: **to ~ from** être
originaire de ; (*suggestion*) provenir de ; **to
~ in** prendre naissance dans ; avoir son
origine dans ; **originator** *n* auteur *m*.

ornament ['ɔ:nəmənt] *n* ornement *m* ;
(*trinket*) bibelot *m* ; **~al** [-'mɛntl] *a*
décoratif(ive) ; (*garden*) d'agrément ;
~ation [-'teɪʃən] *n* ornementation *f*.

ornate [ɔ:'neɪt] *a* très orné(e).

ornithologist [ɔ:nɪ'θɔlədʒɪst] *n* ornithologue *m/f*.

ornithology [ɔ:nɪ'θɔlədʒɪ] *n* ornithologie *f*.

orphan ['ɔ:fn] *n* orphelin/e // *vt*: **to be
~ed** devenir orphelin ; **~age** *n* orphelinat
m.

orthodox ['ɔ:θədɔks] *a* orthodoxe.

orthopaedic, **orthopedic** (*US*)
[ɔ:θə'pi:dɪk] *a* orthopédique.

oscillate ['ɔsɪleɪt] *vi* osciller.

ostensible [ɔs'tɛnsɪbl] *a* prétendu(e) ;
apparent(e) ; **ostensibly** *ad* en apparence.

ostentation [ɔstɛn'teɪʃən] *n* ostentation *f*.

ostentatious [ɔstɛn'teɪʃəs] *a* préten-
tieux(euse) ; ostentatoire.

osteopath ['ɔstɪəpæθ] *n* ostéopathe *m/f*.

ostracize ['ɔstrəsaɪz] *vt* frapper
d'ostracisme.

ostrich ['ɔstrɪtʃ] *n* autruche *f*.

other ['ʌðə*] *a* autre ; **~ than** autrement
que ; à part ; **~wise** *ad,cj* autrement.

otter ['ɔtə*] *n* loutre *f*.

ought, *pt* **ought** [ɔ:t] *auxiliary vb*: **I ~ to
do it** je devrais le faire, il faudrait que je
le fasse ; **this ~ to have been corrected**

cela aurait dû être corrigé ; **he ~ to win**
il devrait gagner.

ounce [auns] *n* once *f* (= *28.35 g* ; *16 in
a pound*).

our ['auə*] *a* notre, *pl* nos ; **~s** *pronoun*
le(la) nôtre, les nôtres ; **~selves** *pronoun
pl* (*reflexive, after preposition*) nous ; (*emphatic*) nous-mêmes.

oust [aust] *vt* évincer.

out [aut] *ad* dehors ; (*published, not at home
etc*) sorti(e) ; (*light, fire*) éteint(e) ; **~ here**
ici ; **~ there** là-bas ; **he's ~** (*absent*), il
est sorti ; (*unconscious*) il est sans connaissance ; **to be ~ in one's calculations**
s'être trompé dans ses calculs ; **to
run/back** *etc* **~** sortir en courant/en
reculant *etc* ; **~ loud** *ad* à haute voix ; **~
of** (*outside*) en dehors de ; (*because of:
anger etc*) par ; (*from among*): **~ of 10** sur
10 ; (*without*): **~ of petrol** sans essence,
à court d'essence ; **made ~ of wood** en
or de bois ; **~ of order** (*machine*) en
panne ; (*TEL: line*) en dérangement ; **~-
of-the-way** écarté(e) ; (*fig*) insolite.

outback ['autbæk] *n* campagne isolée ; (*in
Australia*) intérieur *m*.

outboard ['autbɔ:d] *n*: **~ (motor)**
(moteur *m*) hors-bord *m*.

outbreak ['autbreɪk] *n* accès *m* ; début *m* ;
éruption *f*.

outbuilding ['autbɪldɪŋ] *n* dépendance *f*.

outburst ['autbə:st] *n* explosion *f*, accès
m.

outcast ['autkɑ:st] *n* exilé/e ; (*socially*)
paria *m*.

outclass [aut'klɑ:s] *vt* surclasser.

outcome ['autkʌm] *n* issue *f*, résultat *m*.

outcry ['autkraɪ] *n* tollé *m* (général).

outdated [aut'deɪtɪd] *a* démodé(e).

outdo [aut'du:] *vt irg* surpasser.

outdoor [aut'dɔ:*] *a* de or en plein air ;
~s *ad* dehors ; au grand air.

outer ['autə*] *a* extérieur(e) ; **~ space** *n*
espace *m* cosmique ; **~ suburbs** *npl*
grande banlieue.

outfit ['autfɪt] *n* équipement *m* ; (*clothes*)
tenue *f* ; **'~ter's'** 'confection pour
hommes'.

outgoings ['autgəuɪŋz] *npl* (*expenses*)
dépenses *fpl*.

outgrow [aut'grəu] *vt irg* (*clothes*) devenir
trop grand(e) pour.

outing ['autɪŋ] *n* sortie *f* ; excursion *f*.

outlandish [aut'lændɪʃ] *a* étrange.

outlaw ['autlɔ:] *n* hors-la-loi *m inv* // *vt*
(*person*) mettre hors la loi ; (*practice*) proscrire.

outlay ['autleɪ] *n* dépenses *fpl* ; (*investment*) mise *f* de fonds.

outlet ['autlɛt] *n* (*for liquid etc*) issue *f*,
sortie *f* ; (*for emotion*) exutoire *m* ; (*for
goods*) débouché *m* ; (*also*: **retail ~**) point
m de vente.

outline ['autlaɪn] *n* (*shape*) contour *m* ;
(*summary*) esquisse *f*, grandes lignes.

outlive [aut'lɪv] *vt* survivre à.

outlook ['autluk] *n* perspective *f*.

outlying ['autlaɪɪŋ] *a* écarté(e).

outmoded [aut'məudɪd] *a* démodé(e) ;
dépassé(e).

outnumber [aut'nʌmbə*] vt surpasser en nombre.

outpatient ['autpeɪʃənt] n malade m/f en consultation externe.

outpost ['autpəust] n avant-poste m.

output ['autput] n rendement m, production f.

outrage ['autreɪdʒ] n atrocité f, acte m de violence ; scandale m // vt outrager ; **~ous** [-'reɪdʒəs] a atroce ; scandaleux(euse).

outrider ['autraɪdə*] n (on motorcycle) motard m.

outright ad [aut'raɪt] complètement ; catégoriquement ; carrément ; sur le coup // a ['autraɪt] complet(ète) ; catégorique.

outset ['autsɛt] n début m.

outside [aut'saɪd] n extérieur m // a extérieur(e) // ad (au) dehors, à l'extérieur // prep hors de, à l'extérieur de ; **at the ~** (fig) au plus or maximum ; **~ lane** n (AUT: in Britain) voie f de droite ; **~-left/-right** (FOOTBALL) ailier gauche/droit ; **~r** n (in race etc) outsider m ; (stranger) étranger/ère.

outsize ['autsaɪz] a énorme ; (clothes) grande taille inv.

outskirts ['autskə:ts] npl faubourgs mpl.

outspoken [aut'spəukən] a très franc(he).

outstanding [aut'stændɪŋ] a remarquable, exceptionnel(le) ; (unfinished) en suspens ; en souffrance ; non réglé(e).

outstay [aut'steɪ] vt: **to ~ one's welcome** abuser de l'hospitalité de son hôte.

outstretched [aut'strɛtʃt] a (hand) tendu(e) ; (body) étendu(e).

outward ['autwəd] a (sign, appearances) extérieur(e) ; (journey) (d')aller ; **~ly** ad extérieurement ; en apparence.

outweigh [aut'weɪ] vt l'emporter sur.

outwit [aut'wɪt] vt se montrer plus malin que.

oval ['əuvl] a,n ovale (m).

ovary ['əuvəri] n ovaire m.

ovation [əu'veɪʃən] n ovation f.

oven ['ʌvn] n four m ; **~proof** a allant au four.

over ['əuvə*] ad (par-)dessus // a (or ad) (finished) fini(e), terminé(e) ; (too much) en plus // prep sur ; par-dessus ; (above) au-dessus de ; (on the other side of) de l'autre côté de ; (more than) plus de ; (during) pendant ; **~ here** ici ; **~ there** là-bas ; **all ~** (everywhere) partout ; (finished) fini(e) ; **~ and ~ (again)** à plusieurs reprises ; **~ and above** en plus de ; **to ask sb ~** inviter qn (à passer) ; **to go ~ to sb's** passer chez qn.

over... ['əuvə*] prefix: **~abundant** sur-abondant(e).

overact [əuvər'ækt] vi (THEATRE) outrer son rôle.

overall a,n ['əuvərɔ:l] a (length) total(e) ; (study) d'ensemble // n (Brit) blouse f // ad [əuvər'ɔ:l] dans l'ensemble, en général // **~s** npl bleus mpl (de travail).

overawe [əuvər'ɔ:] vt impressionner.

overbalance [əuvə'bæləns] vi basculer.

overbearing [əuvə'bɛərɪŋ] a impérieux(euse), autoritaire.

overboard ['əuvəbɔ:d] ad (NAUT) par-dessus bord.

overcast ['əuvəkɑ:st] a couvert(e).

overcharge [əuvə'tʃɑ:dʒ] vt: **to ~ sb for sth** faire payer qch trop cher à qn.

overcoat ['əuvəkəut] n pardessus m.

overcome [əuvə'kʌm] vt irg triompher de ; surmonter ; **to be ~ by** être saisi(e) de ; succomber à ; être victime de ; **~ with grief** accablé(e) de douleur.

overcrowded [əuvə'kraudɪd] a bondé(e).

overcrowding [əuvə'kraudɪŋ] n surpeuplement m ; (in bus) encombrement m.

overdo [əuvə'du:] vt irg exagérer ; (overcook) trop cuire.

overdose ['əuvədəus] n dose excessive.

overdraft ['əuvədrɑ:ft] n découvert m.

overdrawn [əuvə'drɔ:n] a (account) à découvert.

overdrive ['əuvədraɪv] n (AUT) (vitesse) surmultipliée f.

overdue [əuvə'dju:] a en retard ; (recognition) tardif(ive).

overestimate [əuvər'ɛstɪmeɪt] vt sur-estimer.

overexcited [əuvərɪk'saɪtɪd] a sur-excité(e).

overexertion [əuvərɪg'zə:ʃən] n sur-menage m (physique).

overexpose [əuvərɪk'spəuz] vt (PHOT) sur-exposer.

overflow vi [əuvə'fləu] déborder // n ['əuvəfləu] trop-plein m ; (also: **~ pipe**) tuyau m d'écoulement, trop-plein m.

overgrown [əuvə'grəun] a (garden) envahi(e) par la végétation.

overhaul vt [əuvə'hɔ:l] réviser // n ['əuvəhɔ:l] révision f.

overhead ad [əuvə'hɛd] au-dessus // a ['əuvəhɛd] aérien(ne) ; (lighting) vertical(e) ; **~s** npl frais généraux.

overhear [əuvə'hɪə*] vt irg entendre (par hasard).

overjoyed [əuvə'dʒɔɪd] a ravi(e), enchanté(e).

overland ['əuvəlænd] a, ad par voie de terre.

overlap vi [əuvə'læp] se chevaucher // n ['əuvəlæp] chevauchement m.

overleaf [əuvə'li:f] ad au verso.

overload [əuvə'ləud] vt surcharger.

overlook [əuvə'luk] vt (have view on) donner sur ; (miss) oublier, négliger ; (forgive) fermer les yeux sur.

overlord ['əuvəlɔ:d] n chef m suprême.

overnight [əuvə'naɪt] ad (happen) durant la nuit ; (fig) soudain // a d'une (or de) nuit ; soudain(e) ; **he stayed there ~** il y a passé la nuit ; **if you travel ~...** si tu fais le voyage de nuit... ; **he'll be away ~** il ne rentrera pas ce soir.

overpass ['əuvəpɑ:s] n pont autoroutier.

overpower [əuvə'pauə*] vt vaincre ; (fig) accabler ; **~ing** a irrésistible ; (heat, stench) suffocant(e).

overrate [əuvə'reɪt] vt surestimer.

overreact [əuvəri:'ækt] vi réagir de façon excessive.

override [əuvə'raɪd] vt (irg: like ride) (order, objection) passer outre à ; (decision)

annuler; **overriding** a prépondérant(e).
overrule [əuvə'ru:l] vt (decision) annuler;
(claim) rejeter.
overseas [əuvə'si:z] ad outre-mer;
(abroad) à l'étranger // a (trade) exté-
rieur(e); (visitor) étranger(ère).
overseer ['əuvəsiə*] n (in factory) contremaître m.
overshadow [əuvə'ʃædəu] vt (fig)
éclipser.
overshoot [əuvə'ʃu:t] vt irg dépasser.
oversight ['əuvəsait] n omission f, oubli
m.
oversimplify [əuvə'simplifai] vt simplifier à l'excès.
oversleep [əuvə'sli:p] vi irg se réveiller
(trop) tard.
overspill ['əuvəspil] n excédent m de
population.
overstate [əuvə'steit] vt exagérer;
~ment n exagération f.
overt [əu'və:t] a non dissimulé(e).
overtake [əuvə'teik] vt irg dépasser; (AUT)
dépasser, doubler; **overtaking** n (AUT)
dépassement m.
overthrow [əuvə'θrəu] vt irg (government)
renverser.
overtime ['əuvətaim] n heures fpl supplémentaires.
overtone ['əuvətəun] n (also: ~s) note f,
sous-entendus mpl.
overture ['əuvətʃuə*] n (MUS, fig)
ouverture f.
overturn [əuvə'tə:n] vt renverser // vi se
retourner.
overweight [əuvə'weit] a (person) trop
gros(se); (luggage) trop lourd(e).
overwhelm [əuvə'wɛlm] vt accabler;
submerger; écraser; ~ing a (victory,
defeat) écrasant(e); (desire) irrésistible.
overwork [əuvə'wə:k] n surmenage m //
vt surmener // vi se surmener.
overwrought [əuvə'rɔ:t] a excédé(e).
owe [əu] vt devoir; **to ~ sb sth, to ~**
sth to sb devoir qch à qn.
owing to ['əuiŋtu:] prep à cause de, en raison de.
owl [aul] n hibou m.
own [əun] vt posséder // a propre; **a room**
of my ~ une chambre à moi, ma propre
chambre; **to get one's ~ back** prendre
sa revanche; **on one's ~** tout(e) seul(e);
to ~ up vi avouer; **~er** n propriétaire
m/f; ~**ership** n possession f.
ox, pl **oxen** [ɔks, 'ɔksn] n bœuf m.
oxide ['ɔksaid] n oxyde m.
oxtail ['ɔksteil] n: ~ **soup** soupe f à la
queue de bœuf.
oxygen ['ɔksidʒən] n oxygène m; ~
mask/tent n masque m/tente f à oxygène.
oyster ['ɔistə*] n huître f.
oz. abbr of **ounce(s)**.
ozone ['əuzəun] n ozone m.

P

p [pi:] abbr of **penny, pence**.
p.a. abbr of **per annum**.
P.A. see **public, personal**.

pa [pɑ:] n (col) papa m.
pace [peis] n pas m; (speed) allure f;
vitesse f // vi: **to ~ up and down** faire
les cent pas; **to keep ~ with** aller à la
même vitesse que; (events) se tenir au
courant de; ~**maker** n (MED) stimulateur
m cardiaque.
pacification [pæsifi'keiʃən] n
pacification f.
pacific [pə'sifik] a pacifique // n: **the P~**
(Ocean) le Pacifique, l'océan m Pacifique.
pacifist ['pæsifist] n pacifiste m/f.
pacify ['pæsifai] vt pacifier; (soothe)
calmer.
pack [pæk] n paquet m; ballot m; (of
hounds) meute f; (of thieves etc) bande f;
(of cards) jeu m // vt (goods) empaqueter,
emballer; (in suitcase etc) emballer; (box)
remplir; (cram) entasser; (press down)
tasser; damer; **to ~ (one's bags)** faire
ses bagages; **to ~ one's case** faire sa
valise.
package ['pækidʒ] n paquet m; ballot m;
(also: ~ **deal**) marché global; forfait m;
~ **tour** n voyage organisé.
packet ['pækit] n paquet m.
pack ice ['pækais] n banquise f.
packing ['pækiŋ] n emballage m; ~ **case**
n caisse f (d'emballage).
pact [pækt] n pacte m; traité m.
pad [pæd] n bloc(-notes) m; (for inking)
tampon encreur; (col: flat) piaule f // vt
rembourrer; ~**ding** n rembourrage m;
(fig) délayage m.
paddle ['pædl] n (oar) pagaie f // vi
barboter, faire trempette; ~ **steamer** n
bateau m à aubes; **paddling pool** n petit
bassin.
paddock ['pædək] n enclos m; paddock
m.
paddy ['pædi] n: ~ **field** n rizière f.
padlock ['pædlɔk] n cadenas m // vt
cadenasser.
padre ['pɑ:dri] n aumônier m.
paediatrics, pediatrics (US)
[pi:di'ætriks] n pédiatrie f.
pagan ['peigən] a,n païen(ne).
page [peidʒ] n (of book) page f; (also: ~
boy) groom m, chasseur m; (at wedding)
garçon m d'honneur // vt (in hotel etc)
(faire) appeler.
pageant ['pædʒənt] n spectacle m
historique; grande cérémonie; ~**ry** n
apparat m, pompe f.
pagoda [pə'gəudə] n pagode f.
paid [peid] pt, pp of **pay** // a (work, official)
rémunéré(e); **to put ~ to** mettre fin à,
régler.
pail [peil] n seau m.
pain [pein] n douleur f; **to be in ~** souffrir,
avoir mal; **to have a ~ in** avoir mal à
or une douleur à or dans; **to take ~s to**
do se donner du mal pour faire; ~**ed** a
peiné(e), chagrin(e); ~**ful** a
douloureux(euse); difficile, pénible;
~**fully** ad (fig: very) terriblement; ~**killer**
n calmant m; ~**less** a indolore; ~**staking**
['peinzteikiŋ] a (person) soigneux(euse);
(work) soigné(e).
paint [peint] n peinture f // vt peindre;
(fig) dépeindre; **to ~ the door blue**

peindre la porte en bleu ; **to ~ in oils** faire de la peinture à l'huile ; **~brush** n pinceau m ; **~er** n peintre m ; **~ing** n peinture f ; (*picture*) tableau m ; **~-stripper** n décapant m.

pair [peə*] n (*of shoes, gloves etc*) paire f ; (*of people*) couple m ; duo m ; paire ; **~ of scissors** (paire de) ciseaux mpl ; **~ of trousers** pantalon m.

pajamas [pɪ'dʒɑːməz] npl (US) pyjama(s) m(pl).

Pakistan [puːkɪ'stɑːn] n Pakistan m ; **~i** a pakistanais(e) // n Pakistanais/e.

pal [pæl] n (col) copain/copine.

palace ['pæləs] n palais m.

palatable ['pælɪtəbl] a bon(bonne), agréable au goût.

palate ['pælɪt] n palais m.

palaver [pə'lɑːvə*] n palabres fpl or mpl ; histoire s f(pl).

pale [peɪl] a pâle ; **to grow ~** pâlir ; **~ blue** a bleu pâle inv ; **~ness** n pâleur f.

Palestine ['pælɪstaɪn] n Palestine f ; **Palestinian** [-'tɪnɪən] a palestinien(ne) // n Palestinien/ne.

palette ['pælɪt] n palette f.

palisade [pælɪ'seɪd] n palissade f.

pall [pɔːl] n (*of smoke*) voile m// vi: **to ~ (on)** devenir lassant (pour).

pallid ['pælɪd] a blême.

pally ['pælɪ] a (col) copain(copine).

palm [pɑːm] n (ANAT) paume f ; (*also: ~ tree*) palmier m ; (*leaf, symbol*) palme f // vt: **to ~ sth off on sb** (col) refiler qch à qn ; **~ist** n chiromancien/ne ; **P~ Sunday** n le dimanche des Rameaux.

palpable ['pælpəbl] a évident(e), manifeste.

palpitation [pælpɪ'teɪʃən] n palpitation s f(pl).

paltry ['pɔːltrɪ] a dérisoire ; piètre.

pamper ['pæmpə*] vt gâter, dorloter.

pamphlet ['pæmflət] n brochure f.

pan [pæn] n (*also: sauce~*) casserole f ; (*also: frying ~*) poêle f ; (*of lavatory*) cuvette f // vi (CINEMA) faire un panoramique.

panacea [pænə'sɪə] n panacée f.

Panama ['pænəmɑː] n Panama m ; **~ canal** n canal m de Panama.

pancake ['pænkeɪk] n crêpe f.

panda ['pændə] n panda m ; **~ car** n ≈ voiture f pie inv.

pandemonium [pændɪ'məunɪəm] n tohu-bohu m.

pander ['pændə*] vi: **to ~ to** flatter bassement ; obéir servilement à.

pane [peɪn] n carreau m (de fenêtre).

panel ['pænl] n (*of wood, cloth etc*) panneau m ; (RADIO, TV) panel m ; invités mpl, experts mpl ; **~ling, ~ing** (US) n boiseries fpl.

pang [pæŋ] n: **~s of remorse** pincements mpl de remords ; **~s of hunger/conscience** tiraillements mpl d'estomac/de la conscience.

panic ['pænɪk] n panique f, affolement m // vi s'affoler, paniquer ; **~ky** a (*person*) qui panique or s'affole facilement.

pannier ['pænɪə*] n (*on animal*) bât m ; (*on bicycle*) sacoche f.

panorama [pænə'rɑːmə] n panorama m ; **panoramic** a panoramique.

pansy ['pænzɪ] n (BOT) pensée f ; (col) tapette f, pédé m.

pant [pænt] vi haleter // n: see pants.

pantechnicon [pæn'tɛknɪkən] n (grand) camion de déménagement.

panther ['pænθə*] n panthère f.

panties ['pæntɪz] npl slip m, culotte f.

pantomime ['pæntəmaɪm] n spectacle m de Noël.

pantry ['pæntrɪ] n garde-manger m inv ; (*room*) office f or m.

pants [pænts] n (*woman's*) culotte f, slip m ; (*man's*) slip m, caleçon m ; (US: *trousers*) pantalon m.

papacy ['peɪpəsɪ] n papauté f.

papal ['peɪpəl] a papal(e), pontifical(e).

paper ['peɪpə*] n papier m ; (*also: wall~*) papier peint ; (*also: news~*) journal m ; (*study, article*) article m ; (*exam*) épreuve écrite // a en or de papier // vt tapisser (de papier peint) ; (identity) **~s** npl papiers (d'identité) ; **~back** n livre m de poche ; livre broché or non relié // a: **~back edition** édition brochée ; **~ bag** n sac m en papier ; **~ clip** n trombone m ; **~ hankie** n mouchoir m en papier ; **~ mill** n papeterie f ; **~weight** n presse-papiers m inv ; **~work** n paperasserie f.

papier-mâché ['pæpɪeɪ'mæʃeɪ] n papier mâché.

paprika ['pæprɪkə] n paprika m.

par [pɑː*] n pair m ; (GOLF) normale f du parcours ; **on a ~ with** à égalité avec, au même niveau que.

parable ['pærəbl] n parabole f (REL).

parabola [pə'ræbələ] n parabole f (MATH).

parachute ['pærəʃuːt] n parachute m // vi sauter en parachute ; **~ jump** n saut m en parachute.

parade [pə'reɪd] n défilé m ; (*inspection*) revue f ; (*street*) boulevard m // vt (fig) faire étalage de // vi défiler.

paradise ['pærədaɪs] n paradis m.

paradox ['pærədɔks] n paradoxe m ; **~ical** [-'dɔksɪkl] a paradoxal(e).

paraffin ['pærəfɪn] n: **~ (oil)** pétrole (lampant) ; **liquid ~** huile f de paraffine.

paragraph ['pærəgrɑːf] n paragraphe m.

parallel ['pærəlɛl] a parallèle ; (fig) analogue // n (*line*) parallèle f ; (fig, GEO) parallèle m.

paralysis [pə'rælɪsɪs] n paralysie f.

paralytic [pærə'lɪtɪk] a paralysé(e) ; paralysant(e).

paralyze ['pærəlaɪz] vt paralyser.

paramount ['pærəmaunt] a: **of ~ importance** de la plus haute or grande importance.

paranoia [pærə'nɔɪə] n paranoia f.

paraphernalia [pærəfə'neɪlɪə] n attirail m, affaires fpl.

paraphrase ['pærəfreɪz] vt paraphraser.

paraplegic [pærə'pliːdʒɪk] n paraplégique m/f.

parasite ['pærəsaɪt] n parasite m.

paratrooper ['pærətruːpə*] n parachutiste m (*soldat*).

parcel ['pɑːsl] n paquet m, colis m // vt

(also: ~ **up**) empaqueter; ~ **post** n service m de colis postaux.

parch [pɑːʃ] vt dessécher; **~ed** a (person) assoiffé(e).

parchment ['pɑːtʃmənt] n parchemin m.

pardon ['pɑːdn] n pardon m; grâce f // vt pardonner à; (LAW) gracier; **~!** pardon!; **~ me!** excusez-moi!; **I beg your ~!** pardon!, je suis désolé!; **I beg your ~?** pardon?

parent ['pɛərənt] n père m or mère f; **~s** npl parents mpl; **~al** [pə'rɛntl] a parental(e), des parents.

parenthesis, pl **parentheses** [pə'rɛnθisɪs, -siːz] n parenthèse f.

Paris ['pærɪs] n Paris.

parish ['pærɪʃ] n paroisse f; (civil) ≈ commune f // a paroissial(e); **~ioner** [pə'rɪʃənə*] n paroissien/ne.

Parisian [pə'rɪzɪən] a parisien(ne) // n Parisien/ne.

parity ['pærɪtɪ] n parité f.

park [pɑːk] n parc m, jardin public // vt garer // vi se garer; **~ing** n stationnement m; **~ing lot** n (US) parking m, parc m de stationnement; **~ing meter** n parcomètre m; **~ing place** n place f de stationnement.

parliament ['pɑːləmənt] n parlement m; **~ary** [-'mɛntərɪ] a parlementaire.

parlour, **parlor** (US) ['pɑːlə*] n salon m.

parochial [pə'rəukɪəl] a paroissial(e); (pej) à l'esprit de clocher.

parody ['pærədɪ] n parodie f.

parole [pə'rəul] n: **on ~** en liberté conditionnelle.

parquet ['pɑːkeɪ] n: **~ floor(ing)** parquet m.

parrot ['pærət] n perroquet m; **~ fashion** ad comme un perroquet.

parry ['pærɪ] vt esquiver, parer à.

parsimonious [pɑːsɪ'məunɪəs] a parcimonieux(euse).

parsley ['pɑːslɪ] n persil m.

parsnip ['pɑːsnɪp] n panais m.

parson ['pɑːsn] n ecclésiastique m; (Church of England) pasteur m.

part [pɑːt] n partie f; (of machine) pièce f; (THEATRE etc) rôle m; (MUS) voix f; partie // a partiel(le) // ad = **partly** // vt séparer // vi (people) se séparer; (roads) se diviser; **to take ~ in** participer à, prendre part à; **on his ~** de sa part; **for my ~** en ce qui me concerne; **for the most ~** en grande partie; dans la plupart des cas; **to ~ with** vt fus se séparer de; se défaire de; (take leave) quitter, prendre congé de; **in ~ exchange** en reprise.

partial ['pɑːʃl] a partiel(le); (unjust) partial(e); **to be ~ to** aimer, avoir un faible pour; **~ly** ad en partie, partiellement; partialement.

participate [pɑː'tɪsɪpeɪt] vi: **to ~ (in)** participer (à), prendre part (à); **participation** [-'peɪʃən] n participation f.

participle ['pɑːtɪsɪpl] n participe m.

particle ['pɑːtɪkl] n particule f.

particular [pə'tɪkjulə*] a particulier(ère); spécial(e); (detailed) détaillé(e); (fussy) difficile; méticuleux(euse); **~s** npl détails mpl; (information) renseignements mpl;

~ly ad particulièrement; en particulier.

parting ['pɑːtɪŋ] n séparation f; (in hair) raie f // a d'adieu.

partisan [pɑːtɪ'zæn] n partisan/e // a partisan(e); de parti.

partition [pɑː'tɪʃən] n (POL) partition f, division f; (wall) cloison f.

partly ['pɑːtlɪ] ad en partie, partiellement.

partner ['pɑːtnə*] n (COMM) associé/e; (SPORT) partenaire m/f; (at dance) cavalier/ère // vt être l'associé or le partenaire or le cavalier de; **~ship** n association f.

partridge ['pɑːtrɪdʒ] n perdrix f.

part-time ['pɑːt'taɪm] a,ad à mi-temps, à temps partiel.

party ['pɑːtɪ] n (POL) parti m; (team) équipe f; groupe m; (LAW) partie f; (celebration) réception f; soirée f; fête f.

pass [pɑːs] vt (time, object) passer; (place) passer devant; (car, friend) croiser; (exam) être reçu(e) à, réussir; (candidate) admettre; (overtake, surpass) dépasser; (approve) approuver, accepter // vi passer; (SCOL) être reçu(e) or admis(e), réussir // n (permit) laissez-passer m inv; carte f d'accès or d'abonnement; (in mountains) col m; (SPORT) passe f; (SCOL: also: ~ **mark**): **to get a ~** être reçu(e) (sans mention); **to ~ sth through a ring** etc (faire) passer qch dans un anneau etc; **could you ~ the vegetables round?** pourriez-vous faire passer les légumes?; **to ~ away** vi mourir; **to ~ by** vi passer // vt négliger; **to ~ for** passer pour; **to ~ out** vi s'évanouir; **~able** a (road) praticable; (work) acceptable.

passage ['pæsɪdʒ] n (also: ~**way**) couloir m; (gen, in book) passage m; (by boat) traversée f.

passenger ['pæsɪndʒə*] n passager/ère.

passer-by [pɑːsə'baɪ] n passant/e.

passing ['pɑːsɪŋ] a (fig) passager(ère); **in ~** en passant.

passion ['pæʃən] n passion f; amour m; **to have a ~ for sth** avoir la passion de qch; **~ate** a passionné(e).

passive ['pæsɪv] a (also LING) passif(ive).

Passover ['pɑːsəuvə*] n Pâque (juive).

passport ['pɑːspɔːt] n passeport m.

password ['pɑːswɜːd] n mot m de passe.

past [pɑːst] prep (further than) au delà de, plus loin que; après; (later than) après // a passé(e); (president etc) ancien(ne) // n passé m; **he's ~ forty** il a dépassé la quarantaine, il a plus de or passé quarante ans; **it's ~ midnight** il est plus de minuit, il est passé minuit; **for the ~ few/3 days** depuis quelques/3 jours; ces derniers/3 derniers jours; **to run ~** passer en courant; **he ran ~ me** il m'a dépassé en courant; il a passé devant moi en courant.

pasta ['pæstə] n pâtes fpl.

paste [peɪst] n (glue) colle f (de pâte); (jewellery) strass m; (CULIN) pâté m (à tartiner); pâte f // vt coller.

pastel ['pæstl] a pastel inv.

pasteurized ['pæstəraɪzd] a pasteurisé(e).

pastille ['pæstl] n pastille f.

pastime ['pɑːstaɪm] n passe-temps m inv, distraction f.

pastoral ['pɑ:stərl] a pastoral(e).

pastry ['peɪstrɪ] n pâte f ; (cake) pâtisserie f.

pasture ['pɑ:stʃə*] n pâturage m.

pasty n ['pæstɪ] petit pâté (en croûte) // a ['peɪstɪ] pâteux(euse) ; (complexion) terreux(euse).

pat [pæt] vt donner une petite tape à // n: **a ～ of butter** une noisette de beurre.

patch [pætʃ] n (of material) pièce f ; (spot) tache f ; (of land) parcelle f // vt (clothes) rapiécer ; **a bad ～** une période difficile ; **to ～ up** vt réparer ; **～work** n patchwork m ; **～y** a inégal(e).

pate [peɪt] n: **a bald ～** un crâne chauve or dégarni.

pâté ['pæteɪ] n pâté m, terrine f.

patent ['peɪtnt] n brevet m (d'invention) // vt faire breveter // a patent(e), manifeste ; **～ leather** n cuir verni ; **～ medicine** n spécialité f pharmaceutique.

paternal [pə'tə:nl] a paternel(le).

paternity [pə'tə:nɪtɪ] n paternité f.

path [pɑ:θ] n chemin m, sentier m ; allée f ; (of planet) course f ; (of missile) trajectoire f.

pathetic [pə'θɛtɪk] a (pitiful) pitoyable ; (very bad) lamentable, minable ; (moving) pathétique.

pathologist [pə'θɔlədʒɪst] n pathologiste m/f.

pathology [pə'θɔlədʒɪ] n pathologie f.

pathos ['peɪθɔs] n pathétique m.

pathway ['pɑ:θweɪ] n chemin m, sentier m.

patience ['peɪʃns] n patience f ; (CARDS) réussite f.

patient ['peɪʃnt] n patient/e ; malade m/f // a patient(e) // **～ly** ad patiemment.

patio ['pætɪəu] n patio m.

patriotic [pætrɪ'ɔtɪk] a patriotique ; (person) patriote.

patrol [pə'trəul] n patrouille f // vt patrouiller dans ; **～ car** n voiture f de police ; **～man** n (US) agent m de police.

patron ['peɪtrən] n (in shop) client/e ; (of charity) bienfaiteur/trice ; **～ of the arts** mécène m ; **～age** ['pætrənɪdʒ] n patronage m, appui m ; **～ize** ['pætrənaɪz] vt être (un) client or un habitué de ; (fig) traiter avec condescendance ; **～ saint** n saint(e) patron(ne).

patter ['pætə*] n crépitement m, tapotement m ; (sales talk) boniment m // vi crépiter, tapoter.

pattern ['pætən] n modèle m ; (SEWING) patron m ; (design) motif m ; (sample) échantillon m.

paunch [pɔ:ntʃ] n gros ventre, bedaine f.

pauper ['pɔ:pə*] n indigent/e ; **～'s grave** n fosse commune.

pause [pɔ:z] n pause f, arrêt m ; (MUS) silence m // vi faire une pause, s'arrêter.

pave [peɪv] vt paver, daller ; **to ～ the way for** ouvrir la voie à.

pavement ['peɪvmənt] n (Brit) trottoir m.

pavilion [pə'vɪlɪən] n pavillon m ; tente f.

paving ['peɪvɪŋ] n pavage m, dallage m ; **～ stone** n pavé m.

paw [pɔ:] n patte f // vt donner un coup de patte à ; (subj: person: pej) tripoter.

pawn [pɔ:n] n gage m ; (CHESS, also fig) pion m // vt mettre en gage ; **～broker** n prêteur m sur gages ; **～shop** n mont-de-piété m.

pay [peɪ] n salaire m ; paie f // vb (pt, pp paid) vt payer // vi payer ; (be profitable) être rentable ; **to ～ attention (to)** prêter attention (à) ; **to ～ back** vt rembourser ; **to ～ for** vt payer ; **to ～ in** vt verser ; **to ～ up** vt régler ; **～able** a payable ; **～ day** n jour m de paie ; **～ee** n bénéficiaire m/f ; **～ing** a payant(e) ; **～ment** n paiement m ; règlement m ; versement m ; **～ packet** n paie f ; **～roll** n registre m du personnel ; **～ slip** n bulletin m de paie.

p.c. abbr of **per cent**.

pea [pi:] n (petit) pois.

peace [pi:s] n paix f ; (calm) calme m, tranquillité f ; **～able** a paisible ; **～ful** a paisible, calme ; **～-keeping** n maintien m de la paix ; **～ offering** n gage m de réconciliation.

peach [pi:tʃ] n pêche f.

peacock ['pi:kɔk] n paon m.

peak [pi:k] n (mountain) pic m, cime f ; (fig: highest level) maximum m ; (: of career, fame) apogée m ; **～ period** n période f de pointe.

peal [pi:l] n (of bells) carillon m ; **～s of laughter** éclats mpl de rire.

peanut ['pi:nʌt] n arachide f, cacahuète f ; **～ butter** n beurre m de cacahuète.

pear [pɛə*] n poire f.

pearl [pə:l] n perle f.

peasant ['pɛznt] n paysan/ne.

peat [pi:t] n tourbe f.

pebble ['pɛbl] n galet m, caillou m.

peck [pɛk] vt (also: **～ at**) donner un coup de bec à ; (food) picorer // n coup m de bec ; (kiss) bécot m ; **～ing order** n ordre m des préséances ; **～ish** a (col): **I feel ～ish** je mangerais bien quelque chose, j'ai la dent.

peculiar [pɪ'kju:lɪə*] a étrange, bizarre, curieux(euse) ; particulier(ère) ; **～ to** particulier à ; **～ity** [pɪkju:lɪ'ærɪtɪ] n particularité f ; (oddity) bizarrerie f.

pecuniary [pɪ'kju:nɪərɪ] a pécuniaire.

pedal ['pɛdl] n pédale f // vi pédaler.

pedantic [pɪ'dæntɪk] a pédant(e).

peddle ['pɛdl] vt colporter.

pedestal ['pɛdəstl] n piédestal m.

pedestrian [pɪ'dɛstrɪən] n piéton m // a piétonnier(ère) ; (fig) prosaïque, terre à terre inv ; **～ crossing** n passage clouté m.

pediatrics [pi:dɪ'ætrɪks] n (US) = **paediatrics**.

pedigree ['pɛdɪgri:] n ascendance f ; (of animal) pedigree m // cpd (animal) de race.

peek [pi:k] vi jeter un coup d'œil (furtif).

peel [pi:l] n pelure f, épluchure f ; (of orange, lemon) écorce f // vt peler, éplucher // vi (paint etc) s'écailler ; (wallpaper) se décoller ; **～ings** npl pelures fpl, épluchures fpl.

peep [pi:p] n (look) coup d'œil furtif ; (sound) pépiement m // vi jeter un coup d'œil (furtif) ; **to ～ out** vi se montrer (furtivement) ; **～hole** n judas m.

peer [pɪə*] *vi*: **to ~ at** regarder attentivement, scruter // *n* (*noble*) pair *m*; (*equal*) pair *m*, égal/e; **~age** *n* pairie *f*; **~less** *n* incomparable, sans égal.

peeved [piːvd] *a* irrité(e), ennuyé(e).

peevish [ˈpiːvɪʃ] *a* grincheux(euse), maussade.

peg [pɛg] *n* cheville *f*; (*for coat etc*) patère *f*; (*also*: **clothes ~**) pince *f* à linge; **off the ~** *ad* en prêt-à-porter.

pejorative [pɪˈdʒɔrətɪv] *a* péjoratif(ive).

pekingese [piːkɪˈniːz] *n* pékinois *m*.

pelican [ˈpɛlɪkən] *n* pélican *m*.

pellet [ˈpɛlɪt] *n* boulette *f*; (*of lead*) plomb *m*.

pelmet [ˈpɛlmɪt] *n* cantonnière *f*; lambrequin *m*.

pelt [pɛlt] *vt*: **to ~ sb (with)** bombarder qn (de) // *vi* (*rain*) tomber à seaux // *n* peau *f*.

pelvis [ˈpɛlvɪs] *n* bassin *m*.

pen [pɛn] *n* (*for writing*) stylo *m*; (*for sheep*) parc *m*.

penal [ˈpiːnl] *a* pénal(e); **~ize** *vt* pénaliser; (*fig*) désavantager; **~ servitude** *n* travaux forcés.

penalty [ˈpɛnltɪ] *n* pénalité *f*; sanction *f*; (*fine*) amende *f*; (*SPORT*) pénalisation *f*; **~ (kick)** *n* (*FOOTBALL*) penalty *m*.

penance [ˈpɛnəns] *n* pénitence *f*.

pence [pɛns] *npl of* **penny**.

pencil [ˈpɛnsl] *n* crayon *m* // *vt*: **to ~ sth in** noter qch au crayon; **~ sharpener** *n* taille-crayon(s) *m* *inv*.

pendant [ˈpɛndnt] *n* pendentif *m*.

pending [ˈpɛndɪŋ] *prep* en attendant // *a* en suspens.

pendulum [ˈpɛndjuləm] *n* pendule *m*; (*of clock*) balancier *m*.

penetrate [ˈpɛnɪtreɪt] *vt* pénétrer dans; pénétrer; **penetrating** *a* pénétrant(e); **penetration** [-ˈtreɪʃən] *n* pénétration *f*.

penfriend [ˈpɛnfrɛnd] *n* correspondant/e.

penguin [ˈpɛŋgwɪn] *n* pingouin *m*.

penicillin [pɛnɪˈsɪlɪn] *n* pénicilline *f*.

peninsula [pəˈnɪnsjulə] *n* péninsule *f*.

penis [ˈpiːnɪs] *n* pénis *m*, verge *f*.

penitence [ˈpɛnɪtns] *n* repentir *m*.

penitent [ˈpɛnɪtnt] *a* repentant(e).

penitentiary [pɛnɪˈtɛnʃərɪ] *n* (*US*) prison *f*.

penknife [ˈpɛnnaɪf] *n* canif *m*.

pennant [ˈpɛnənt] *n* flamme *f*, banderole *f*.

penniless [ˈpɛnɪlɪs] *a* sans le sou.

penny, *pl* **pennies** *or* **pence** [ˈpɛnɪ, ˈpɛnɪz, pɛns] *n* penny *m* (*pl* pennies) (*new*: 100 in a pound; *old*: 12 in a shilling; on tend à employer 'pennies' ou 'two-pence piece' *etc* pour les pièces, 'pence' pour la valeur).

pension [ˈpɛnʃən] *n* retraite *f*; (*MIL*) pension *f*; **~able** *a* qui a droit à une retraite; **~er** *n* retraité/e; **~ fund** *n* caisse *f* de retraite.

pensive [ˈpɛnsɪv] *a* pensif(ive).

pentagon [ˈpɛntəgən] *n* pentagone *m*.

Pentecost [ˈpɛntɪkɔst] *n* Pentecôte *f*.

penthouse [ˈpɛnthaʊs] *n* appartement *m* (de luxe) en attique.

pent-up [ˈpɛntʌp] *a* (*feelings*) refoulé(e).

penultimate [pɛˈnʌltɪmət] *a* pénultième, avant-dernier(ère).

people [ˈpiːpl] *npl* gens *mpl*; personnes *fpl*; (*citizens*) peuple *m* // *n* (*nation, race*) peuple *m* // *vt* peupler; **4/several ~ came** 4/plusieurs personnes sont venues; **the room was full of ~** la salle était pleine de monde *or* de gens; **~ say that...** on dit *or* les gens disent que.

pep [pɛp] *n* (*col*) entrain *m*, dynamisme *m*; **to ~ up** *vt* remonter.

pepper [ˈpɛpə*] *n* poivre *m*; (*vegetable*) poivron *m* // *vt* poivrer; **~mint** *n* (*plant*) menthe poivrée; (*sweet*) pastille *f* de menthe.

peptalk [ˈpɛptɔːk] *n* (*col*) (petit) discours d'encouragement.

per [pə:*] *prep* par; **~ hour** (*miles etc*) à l'heure; (*fee*) (de) l'heure; **~ kilo** *etc* le kilo *etc*; **~ day/person** par jour/personne; **~ cent** pour cent; **~ annum** par an.

perceive [pəˈsiːv] *vt* percevoir; (*notice*) remarquer, s'apercevoir de.

percentage [pəˈsɛntɪdʒ] *n* pourcentage *m*.

perceptible [pəˈsɛptɪbl] *a* perceptible.

perception [pəˈsɛpʃən] *n* perception *f*; sensibilité *f*; perspicacité *f*.

perceptive [pəˈsɛptɪv] *a* pénétrant(e); perspicace.

perch [pə:tʃ] *n* (*fish*) perche *f*; (*for bird*) perchoir *m* // *vi* (se) percher.

percolator [ˈpə:kəleɪtə*] *n* percolateur *m*; cafetière *f* électrique.

percussion [pəˈkʌʃən] *n* percussion *f*.

peremptory [pəˈrɛmptərɪ] *a* péremptoire.

perennial [pəˈrɛnɪəl] *a* perpétuel(le); (*BOT*) vivace // *n* plante *f* vivace.

perfect *a,n* [ˈpə:fɪkt] *a* parfait(e) // *n* (*also*: **~ tense**) parfait *m* // *vt* [pəˈfɛkt] parfaire; mettre au point; **~ion** [-ˈfɛkʃən] *n* perfection *f*; **~ionist** *n* perfectionniste *m/f*; **~ly** *ad* parfaitement.

perforate [ˈpə:fəreɪt] *vt* perforer, percer; **perforation** [-ˈreɪʃən] *n* perforation *f*; (*line of holes*) pointillé *m*.

perform [pəˈfɔ:m] *vt* (*carry out*) exécuter, remplir; (*concert etc*) jouer, donner // *vi* jouer; **~ance** *n* représentation *f*, spectacle *m*; (*of an artist*) interprétation *f*; (*of player etc*) prestation *f*; (*of car, engine*) performance *f*; **~er** *n* artiste *m/f*; **~ing** *a* (*animal*) savant(e).

perfume [ˈpə:fju:m] *n* parfum *m* // *vt* parfumer.

perfunctory [pəˈfʌŋktərɪ] *a* négligent(e), pour la forme.

perhaps [pəˈhæps] *ad* peut-être; **~ he'll...** peut-être qu'il... .

peril [ˈpɛrɪl] *n* péril *m*; **~ous** *a* périlleux(euse).

perimeter [pəˈrɪmɪtə*] *n* périmètre *m*; **~ wall** *n* mur *m* d'enceinte.

period [ˈpɪərɪəd] *n* période *f*; (*HISTORY*) époque *f*; (*SCOL*) cours *m*; (*full stop*) point *m*; (*MED*) règles *fpl* // *a* (*costume, furniture*) d'époque; **~ic** [-ˈɔdɪk] *a* périodique; **~ical** [-ˈɔdɪkl] *a* périodique // *n* périodique *m*; **~ically** [-ˈɔdɪklɪ] *ad* périodiquement.

peripheral [pə'rıfərəl] a périphérique.

periphery [pə'rıfərı] n périphérie f.

periscope ['pərıskəup] n périscope m.

perish ['pərıʃ] vi périr, mourir ; (decay) se détériorer ; ~**able** a périssable ; ~**ing** a (col: cold) glacial(e).

perjure ['pə:dʒə*] vt: to ~ o.s. se parjurer ; **perjury** n (LAW: in court) faux témoignage ; (breach of oath) parjure m.

perk [pə:k] n avantage m, à-côté m ; to ~ up vi (cheer up) se ragaillardir ; ~**y** a (cheerful) guilleret(te), gai(e).

perm [pə:m] n (for hair) permanente f.

permanence ['pə:mənəns] n permanence f.

permanent ['pə:mənənt] a permanent(e) ; ~**ly** ad de façon permanente.

permeable ['pə:mıəbl] a perméable.

permeate ['pə:mıeıt] vi s'infiltrer // vt s'infiltrer dans ; pénétrer.

permissible [pə'mısıbl] a permis(e), acceptable.

permission [pə'mıʃən] n permission f, autorisation f.

permissive [pə'mısıv] a tolérant(e) ; **the** ~ **society** la société de tolérance.

permit n ['pə:mıt] permis m // vt [pə'mıt] permettre ; to ~ sb to do autoriser qn à faire, permettre à qn de faire.

permutation [pə:mju'teıʃən] n permutation f.

pernicious [pə:'nıʃəs] a pernicieux(euse), nocif(ive).

pernickety [pə'nıkıtı] a pointilleux(euse), tatillon(ne).

perpendicular [pə:pən'dıkjulə*] a,n perpendiculaire (f).

perpetrate ['pə:pıtreıt] vt perpétrer, commettre.

perpetual [pə'pɛtjuəl] a perpétuel(le).

perpetuate [pə'pɛtjueıt] vt perpétuer.

perpetuity [pə:pı'tju:ıtı] n: **in** ~ à perpétuité.

perplex [pə'plɛks] vt rendre perplexe ; (complicate) embrouiller.

persecute ['pə:sıkju:t] vt persécuter ; **persecution** [-'kju:ʃən] n persécution f.

persevere [pə:sı'vıə*] vi persévérer.

Persian ['pə:ʃən] a persan(e) // n (LING) persan m ; **the** (~) **Gulf** n le golfe Persique.

persist [pə'sıst] vi: to ~ (**in doing**) persister (à faire), s'obstiner (à faire) ; ~**ence** n persistance f, obstination f ; opiniâtreté f ; ~**ent** a persistant(e), tenace.

person ['pə:sn] n personne f ; ~**able** a de belle prestance, au physique attrayant ; ~**al** a personnel(le) ; individuel(le) ; ~**al assistant (P.A.)** n secrétaire privé/e ; ~**al call** (TEL) communication f avec préavis ; ~**ality** [-'nælıtı] n personnalité f ; ~**ally** ad personnellement ; ~**ify** [-'sɔnıfaı] vt personnifier.

personnel [pə:sə'nɛl] n personnel m ; ~ **manager** n chef m du personnel.

perspective [pə'spɛktıv] n perspective f.

perspex ['pə:spɛks] n sorte de plexiglas.

perspicacity [pə:spı'kæsıtı] n perspicacité f.

perspiration [pə:spı'reıʃən] n transpiration f.

perspire [pə'spaıə*] vi transpirer.

persuade [pə'sweıd] vt persuader.

persuasion [pə'sweıʒən] n persuasion f.

persuasive [pə'sweısıv] a persuasif(ive).

pert [pə:t] a (brisk) sec(sèche), brusque ; (bold) effronté(e), impertinent(e).

pertaining [pə:'teınıŋ]: ~ **to** prep relatif(ive) à.

pertinent ['pə:tınənt] a pertinent(e).

perturb [pə'tə:b] vt perturber ; inquiéter.

Peru [pə'ru:] n Pérou m.

perusal [pə'ru:zl] n lecture (attentive).

Peruvian [pə'ru:vjən] a péruvien(ne) // n Péruvien/ne.

pervade [pə'veıd] vt se répandre dans, envahir.

perverse [pə'və:s] a pervers(e) ; (stubborn) entêté(e), contrariant(e).

perversion [pə'və:ʃn] n perversion f.

perversity [pə'və:sıtı] n perversité f.

pervert n ['pə:və:t] perverti/e // vt [pə'və:t] pervertir.

pessimism ['pɛsımızəm] n pessimisme m.

pessimist ['pɛsımıst] n pessimiste m/f ; ~**ic** [-'mıstık] a pessimiste.

pest [pɛst] n animal m (or insecte m) nuisible ; (fig) fléau m.

pester ['pɛstə*] vt importuner, harceler.

pesticide ['pɛstısaıd] n pesticide m.

pestle ['pɛsl] n pilon m.

pet [pɛt] n animal familier ; (favourite) chouchou m // vt choyer // vi (col) se peloter ; ~ **lion** n lion apprivoisé.

petal ['pɛtl] n pétale m.

peter ['pi:tə*]: to ~ **out** vi s'épuiser ; s'affaiblir.

petite [pə'ti:t] a menu(e).

petition [pə'tıʃən] n pétition f // vt adresser une pétition à.

petrified ['pɛtrıfaıd] a (fig) mort(e) de peur.

petrify ['pɛtrıfaı] vt pétrifier.

petrol ['pɛtrəl] n (Brit) essence f ; ~ **engine** n moteur m à essence.

petroleum [pə'trəulıəm] n pétrole m.

petrol: ~ **pump** n (in car, at garage) pompe f à essence ; ~ **station** n station-service f ; ~ **tank** n réservoir m d'essence.

petticoat ['pɛtıkəut] n jupon m.

pettifogging ['pɛtıfɔgıŋ] a chicanier(ère).

pettiness ['pɛtınıs] n mesquinerie f.

petty ['pɛtı] a (mean) mesquin(e) ; (unimportant) insignifiant(e), sans importance ; ~ **cash** n menue monnaie ; ~ **officer** n second-maître m.

petulant ['pɛtjulənt] a irritable.

pew [pju:] n banc m (d'église).

pewter ['pju:tə*] n étain m.

phallic ['fælık] a phallique.

phantom ['fæntəm] n fantôme m ; (vision) fantasme m.

Pharaoh ['fɛərəu] n pharaon m.

pharmacist ['fɑ:məsıst] n pharmacien/ne.

pharmacy ['fɑ:məsı] n pharmacie f.

phase [feız] n phase f, période f // vt: to ~ **sth in/out** introduire/supprimer qch progressivement.

Ph.D. (abbr = Doctor of Philosophy) title ≈ Docteur m en Droit or Lettres etc // n ≈ doctorat m ; titulaire m d'un doctorat.

pheasant ['feznt] n faisan m.
phenomenon, pl **phenomena** [fə'nɔminən, -nə] n phénomène m.
phew [fju:] excl ouf!
phial ['faiəl] n fiole f.
philanderer [fi'lændərə*] n don Juan m.
philanthropic [filən'θrɔpik] a philanthropique.
philanthropist [fi'lænθrəpist] n philanthrope m/f.
philatelist [fi'lætəlist] n philatéliste m/f.
philately [fi'lætəli] n philatélie f.
Philippines ['filipi:nz] npl (also: Philippine Islands) Philippines fpl.
philosopher [fi'lɔsəfə*] n philosophe m.
philosophical [filə'sɔfikl] a philosophique.
philosophy [fi'lɔsəfi] n philosophie f.
phlegm [flɛm] n flegme m; **~atic** [flɛg'mætik] a flegmatique.
phobia ['fəubjə] n phobie f.
phone [fəun] n téléphone m // vt téléphoner; **to be on the ~** avoir le téléphone; (be calling) être au téléphone; **to ~ back** vt,vi rappeler.
phonetics [fə'nɛtiks] n phonétique f.
phoney ['fəuni] a faux(fausse), factice // n (person) charlatan m; fumiste m/f.
phonograph ['fəunəgra:f] n (US) électrophone m.
phony ['fəuni] a,n = **phoney.**
phosphate ['fɔsfeit] n phosphate m.
phosphorus ['fɔsfərəs] n phosphore m.
photo ['fəutəu] n photo f.
photo... ['fəutəu] prefix: **~copier** n machine à photocopier; **~copy** n photocopie f // vt photocopier; **~electric** a photoélectrique; **~genic** [-'dʒɛnik] a photogénique; **~graph** n photographie f // vt photographier; **~grapher** [fə'tɔgrəfə*] n photographe m/f; **~graphic** [-'græfik] a photographique; **~graphy** [fə'tɔgrəfi] n photographie f; **~stat** ['fəutəustæt] n photocopie f, photostat m.
phrase [freiz] n expression f; (LING) locution f // vt exprimer; **~book** n recueil m d'expressions (pour touristes).
physical ['fizikl] a physique; **~ly** ad physiquement.
physician [fi'ziʃən] n médecin m.
physicist ['fizisist] n physicien/ne.
physics ['fiziks] n physique f.
physiology [fizi'ɔlədʒi] n physiologie f.
physiotherapist [fiziəu'θɛrəpist] n kinésithérapeute m/f.
physiotherapy [fiziəu'θɛrəpi] n kinésithérapie f.
physique [fi'zi:k] n physique m; constitution f.
pianist ['pi:ənist] n pianiste m/f.
piano [pi'ænəu] n piano m.
piccolo ['pikələu] n piccolo m.
pick [pik] n (tool: also: **~axe**) pic m, pioche f // vt choisir; (gather) cueillir; **take your ~** faites votre choix; **the ~ of** le(la) meilleur(e) de; **to ~ a bone** ronger un os; **to ~ one's teeth** se curer les dents; **to ~ pockets** pratiquer le vol à la tire; **to ~ on** vt fus (person) harceler; **to ~ out** vt choisir; (distinguish)

distinguer; **to ~ up** vi (improve) remonter, s'améliorer // vt ramasser; (telephone) décrocher; (collect) passer prendre; (learn) apprendre; **to ~ up speed** prendre de la vitesse; **to ~ o.s. up** se relever.
picket ['pikit] n (in strike) gréviste m/f participant à un piquet de grève; piquet m de grève // vt mettre un piquet de grève devant; **~ line** n piquet m de grève.
pickle ['pikl] n (also: **~s**: as condiment) pickles mpl // vt conserver dans du vinaigre or dans de la saumure.
pick-me-up ['pikmi:ʌp] n remontant m.
pickpocket ['pikpɔkit] n pickpocket m.
pickup ['pikʌp] n (on record player) bras m pick-up; (small truck) pick-up m inv.
picnic ['piknik] n pique-nique m // vi pique-niquer; **~ker** n pique-niqueur/euse.
pictorial [pik'tɔ:riəl] a illustré(e).
picture ['piktʃə*] n image f; (painting) peinture f, tableau m; (photograph) photo(graphie) f; (drawing) dessin m; (film) film m // vt se représenter; (describe) dépeindre, représenter; **the ~s** le cinéma m; **~ book** n livre m d'images.
picturesque [piktʃə'rɛsk] a pittoresque.
picture window ['piktʃəwindəu] n baie vitrée, fenêtre f panoramique.
piddling ['pidliŋ] a (col) insignifiant(e).
pidgin ['pidʒin] a: **~ English** n pidgin m.
pie [pai] n tourte f; (of meat) pâté m en croûte.
piebald ['paibɔ:ld] a pie inv.
piece [pi:s] n morceau m; (of land) parcelle f; (item): **a ~ of furniture/advice** un meuble/conseil // vt: **to ~ together** rassembler; **in ~s** (broken) en morceaux, en miettes; (not yet assembled) en pièces détachées; **to take to ~s** démonter; **~meal** ad par bouts; **~work** n travail m aux pièces.
pier [piə*] n jetée f; (of bridge etc) pile f.
pierce [piəs] vt percer, transpercer.
piercing ['piəsiŋ] a (cry) perçant(e).
piety ['paiəti] n piété f.
piffling ['pifliŋ] a insignifiant(e).
pig [pig] n cochon m, porc m.
pigeon ['pidʒən] n pigeon m; **~hole** n casier m; **~-toed** a marchant les pieds en dedans.
piggy bank ['pigibæŋk] n tirelire f.
pigheaded ['pig'hɛdid] a entêté(e), têtu(e).
piglet ['piglit] n petit cochon, porcelet m.
pigment ['pigmənt] n pigment m; **~ation** [-'teiʃən] n pigmentation f.
pigmy ['pigmi] n = **pygmy.**
pigsty ['pigstai] n porcherie f.
pigtail ['pigteil] n natte f, tresse f.
pike [paik] n (spear) pique f; (fish) brochet m.
pilchard ['piltʃəd] n pilchard m (sorte de sardine).
pile [pail] n (pillar, of books) pile f; (heap) tas m; (of carpet) épaisseur f // vt (also: **~ up**) vt empiler, entasser // vi s'entasser.
piles [pailz] n hémorroïdes fpl.
pileup ['pailʌp] n (AUT) télescopage m, collision f en série.
pilfer ['pilfə*] vt chaparder; **~ing** n chapardage m.

pilgrim ['pɪlgrɪm] n pèlerin m; **~age** n pèlerinage m.

pill [pɪl] n pilule f; **the ~** la pilule.

pillage ['pɪlɪdʒ] vt piller.

pillar ['pɪlə*] n pilier m; **~ box** n (Brit) boîte f aux lettres.

pillion ['pɪljən] n (of motor cycle) siège m arrière; **to ride ~** être derrière; (on horse) être en croupe.

pillory ['pɪlərɪ] n pilori m // vt mettre au pilori.

pillow ['pɪləu] n oreiller m; **~case** n taie f d'oreiller.

pilot ['paɪlət] n pilote m // cpd (scheme etc) pilote, expérimental(e) // vt piloter; **~ boat** n bateau-pilote m; **~ light** n veilleuse f.

pimp [pɪmp] n souteneur m, maquereau m.

pimple ['pɪmpl] n bouton m, **pimply** a boutonneux(euse).

pin [pɪn] n épingle f; (TECH) cheville f // vt épingler; **~s and needles** fourmis fpl; **to ~ sb against/to** clouer qn contre/à; **to ~ sb down** (fig) obliger qn à répondre.

pinafore ['pɪnəfɔ:*] n tablier m; **~ dress** n robe-chasuble f.

pincers ['pɪnsəz] npl tenailles fpl.

pinch [pɪntʃ] n pincement m; (of salt etc) pincée f // vt pincer; (col: steal) piquer, chiper // vi (shoe) serrer; **at a ~** à la rigueur.

pincushion ['pɪnkuʃən] n pelote f à épingles.

pine [paɪn] n (also: **~ tree**) pin m // vi: **to ~ for** aspirer à, désirer ardemment; **to ~ away** vi dépérir.

pineapple ['paɪnæpl] n ananas m.

ping [pɪŋ] n (noise) tintement m; **~-pong** n ® ping-pong m ®.

pink [pɪŋk] a rose // n (colour) rose m; (BOT) œillet m, mignardise f.

pin money ['pɪnmʌnɪ] n argent m de poche.

pinnacle ['pɪnəkl] n pinacle m.

pinpoint ['pɪnpɔɪnt] n pointe f d'épingle // vt indiquer (avec précision).

pinstripe ['pɪnstraɪp] n rayure très fine.

pint [paɪnt] n pinte f (= 0.56 l).

pinup ['pɪnʌp] n pin-up f inv.

pioneer [paɪə'nɪə*] n explorateur/trice; (early settler) pionnier m; (fig) pionnier m, précurseur m.

pious ['paɪəs] a pieux(euse).

pip [pɪp] n (seed) pépin m; (time signal on radio) top m.

pipe [paɪp] n tuyau m, conduite f; (for smoking) pipe f; (MUS) pipeau m // vt amener par tuyau; **~s** npl (also: **bag~s**) cornemuse f; **to ~ down** vi (col) se taire; **~ dream** n chimère f, utopie f; **~line** n pipe-line m; **~r** n joueur/euse de pipeau (or de cornemuse); **~ tobacco** n tabac m pour la pipe.

piping ['paɪpɪŋ] ad: **~ hot** très chaud(e).

piquant ['pi:kənt] a piquant(e).

pique ['pi:k] n dépit m.

piracy ['paɪərəsɪ] n piraterie f.

pirate ['paɪərət] n pirate m; **~ radio** n radio f pirate.

pirouette [pɪru'ɛt] n pirouette f // vi faire une or des pirouette(s).

Pisces ['paɪsi:z] n les Poissons mpl; **to be ~** être des Poissons.

pistol ['pɪstl] n pistolet m.

piston ['pɪstən] n piston m.

pit [pɪt] n trou m, fosse f; (also: **coal ~**) puits m de mine; (also: **orchestra ~**) fosse f d'orchestre // vt: **to ~ sb against sb** opposer qn à qn; **~s** npl (AUT) aire f de service; **to ~ o.s. against** se mesurer à.

pitch [pɪtʃ] n (throw) lancement m; (MUS) ton m; (of voice) hauteur f; (SPORT) terrain m; (NAUT) tangage m; (tar) poix f // vt (throw) lancer // vi (fall) tomber; (NAUT) tanguer; **to ~ a tent** dresser une tente; **to be ~ed forward** être projeté en avant; **~-black** a noir(e) comme poix; **~ed battle** n bataille rangée.

pitcher ['pɪtʃə*] n cruche f.

pitchfork ['pɪtʃfɔ:k] n fourche f.

piteous ['pɪtɪəs] a pitoyable.

pitfall ['pɪtfɔ:l] n trappe f, piège m.

pith [pɪθ] n (of plant) moelle f; (of orange) intérieur m de l'écorce; (fig) essence f; vigueur f.

pithead ['pɪthɛd] n bouche f de puits.

pithy ['pɪθɪ] a piquant(e); vigoureux(euse).

pitiable ['pɪtɪəbl] a pitoyable.

pitiful ['pɪtɪful] a (touching) pitoyable; (contemptible) lamentable.

pitiless ['pɪtɪlɪs] a impitoyable.

pittance ['pɪtns] n salaire m de misère.

pity ['pɪtɪ] n pitié f // vt plaindre; **what a ~!** quel dommage!; **~ing** a compatissant(e).

pivot ['pɪvət] n pivot m // vi pivoter.

pixie ['pɪksɪ] n lutin m.

placard ['plækɑ:d] n affiche f.

placate [plə'keɪt] vt apaiser, calmer.

place [pleɪs] n endroit m, lieu m; (proper position, rank, seat) place f; (house) maison f, logement m; (home): **at/to his ~** chez lui // vt (object) placer, mettre; (identify) situer; reconnaître; **to take ~** avoir lieu; se passer; **to ~ an order** passer une commande; **to be ~d** (in race, exam) se placer; **out of ~** (not suitable) déplacé(e), inopportun(e); **in the first ~** d'abord, en premier; **~ mat** n set m de table.

placid ['plæsɪd] a placide; **~ity** [plə'sɪdɪtɪ] n placidité f.

plagiarism ['pleɪdʒjərɪzm] n plagiat m.

plagiarize ['pleɪdʒjəraɪz] vt plagier.

plague [pleɪg] n fléau m; (MED) peste f.

plaice [pleɪs] n, pl inv carrelet m.

plaid [plæd] n tissu écossais.

plain [pleɪn] a (clear) clair(e), évident(e); (simple) simple, ordinaire; (frank) franc(franche); (not handsome) quelconque, ordinaire; (cigarette) sans filtre; (without seasoning etc) nature inv; (in one colour) uni(e) // ad franchement, carrément // n plaine f; **in ~ clothes** (police) en civil; **~ly** ad clairement; (frankly) carrément, sans détours; **~ness** n simplicité f.

plaintiff ['pleɪntɪf] n plaignant/e.

plait [plæt] n tresse f, natte f // vt tresser, natter.

plan [plæn] n plan m; (scheme) projet m // vt (think in advance) projeter; (prepare) organiser // vi faire des projets ; **to ~ to do** projeter de faire.

plane [pleɪn] n (AVIAT) avion m ; (tree) platane m ; (tool) rabot m ; (ART, MATH etc) plan m // a plan(e), plat(e) // vt (with tool) raboter.

planet ['plænɪt] n planète f.

planetarium [plænɪ'teərɪəm] n planétarium m.

plank [plæŋk] n planche f ; (POL) point m d'un programme.

plankton ['plæŋktən] n plancton m.

planner ['plænə*] n planificateur/trice.

planning ['plænɪŋ] n planification f ; **family ~** planning familial.

plant [plɑːnt] n plante f ; (machinery) matériel m ; (factory) usine f // vt planter ; (colony) établir ; (bomb) déposer, poser.

plantation [plæn'teɪʃən] n plantation f.

plant pot [plɑːntpɔt] n pot m (de fleurs).

plaque [plæk] n plaque f.

plasma ['plæzmə] n plasma m.

plaster ['plɑːstə*] n plâtre m ; (also: **sticking ~**) pansement adhésif // vt plâtrer ; (cover): **to ~ with** couvrir de ; **in ~** (leg etc) dans le plâtre ; **~ed** a (col) soûl(e) ; **~er** n plâtrier m.

plastic ['plæstɪk] n plastique m // a (made of plastic) en plastique ; (flexible) plastique, malléable ; (art) plastique.

plasticine ['plæstɪsiːn] n ® pâte f à modeler.

plastic surgery ['plæstɪk'səːdʒərɪ] n chirurgie f esthétique.

plate [pleɪt] n (dish) assiette f ; (sheet of metal, PHOT) plaque f ; (in book) gravure f ; **gold/silver ~** (dishes) vaisselle f d'or/d'argent.

plateau, ~s or **~x** ['plætəu, -z] n plateau m.

plateful ['pleɪtful] n assiette f, assiettée f.

plate glass [pleɪt'glɑːs] n verre m (de vitrine).

platelayer ['pleɪtleɪə*] n (RAIL) poseur m de rails.

platform ['plætfɔːm] n (at meeting) tribune f ; (stage) estrade f ; (RAIL) quai m ; **~ ticket** n billet m de quai.

platinum ['plætɪnəm] n platine m.

platitude ['plætɪtjuːd] n platitude f, lieu commun.

platoon [plə'tuːn] n peloton m.

platter ['plætə*] n plat m.

plausible ['plɔːzɪbl] a plausible ; (person) convaincant(e).

play [pleɪ] n jeu m ; (THEATRE) pièce f (de théâtre) // vi (game) jouer à ; (team, opponent) jouer contre ; (instrument) jouer de ; (play, part, piece of music, note) jouer // vi jouer ; **to ~ down** vt minimiser ; **to ~ up** vi (cause trouble) faire des siennes ; **to ~act** vi jouer la comédie ; **~ed-out** a épuisé(e) ; **~er** n joueur/euse ; (THEATRE) acteur/trice ; (MUS) musicien/ne ; **~ful** a enjoué(e) ; **~goer** n amateur/trice de théâtre, habitué/e des théâtres ; **~ground** n cour f de récréation ; **~group** n garderie f ; **~ing card** n carte f à jouer ; **~ing field** n terrain m de sport ; **~mate** n camarade m/f, copain/copine ; **~-off** n (SPORT) belle f ; **~ on words** n jeu m de. mots ; **~pen**

n parc m (pour bébé) ; **~thing** n jouet m ; **~wright** n dramaturge m.

plea [pliː] n (request) appel m ; (excuse) excuse f ; (LAW) défense f.

plead [pliːd] vt plaider ; (give as excuse) invoquer // vi (LAW) plaider ; (beg): **to ~ with sb** implorer qn.

pleasant ['plɛznt] a agréable ; **~ly** ad agréablement ; **~ness** n (of person) amabilité f ; (of place) agrément m ; **~ry** n (joke) plaisanterie f ; **~ries** npl (polite remarks) civilités fpl.

please [pliːz] vt plaire à // vi (think fit): **do as you ~** faites comme il vous plaira ; **~!** s'il te (or vous) plaît ; **my bill, ~** l'addition, s'il vous plaît ; **~ yourself!** à ta (or votre) guise! ; **~d** a: **~d (with)** content(e) (de) ; **~d to meet you** enchanté (de faire votre connaissance) ; **pleasing** a plaisant(e), qui fait plaisir.

pleasurable ['plɛʒərəbl] a très agréable.

pleasure ['plɛʒə*] n plaisir m ; **'it's a ~'** 'je vous en prie' ; **~ steamer** n vapeur m de plaisance.

pleat [pliːt] n pli m.

plebiscite ['plɛbɪsɪt] n plébiscite m.

plebs [plɛbz] npl (pej) bas peuple.

plectrum ['plɛktrəm] n plectre m.

pledge [plɛdʒ] n gage m ; (promise) promesse f // vt engager ; promettre.

plentiful ['plɛntɪful] a abondant(e), copieux(euse).

plenty ['plɛntɪ] n abondance f ; **~ of** beaucoup de ; (bien) assez de.

pleurisy ['pluərɪsɪ] n pleurésie f.

pliable ['plaɪəbl] a flexible ; (person) malléable.

pliers ['plaɪəz] npl pinces fpl.

plight [plaɪt] n situation f critique.

plimsolls ['plɪmsəlz] npl (chaussures fpl) tennis fpl.

plinth [plɪnθ] n socle m.

plod [plɔd] vi avancer péniblement ; (fig) peiner ; **~der** n bûcheron/euse ; **~ding** a pesant(e).

plonk [plɔŋk] (col) n (wine) pinard m, piquette f // vt: **to ~ sth down** poser brusquement qch.

plot [plɔt] n complot m, conspiration f ; (of story, play) intrigue f ; (of land) lot m de terrain, lopin m // vt (mark out) pointer ; relever ; (conspire) comploter // vi comploter ; **~ter** n conspirateur/trice.

plough, plow (US) [plau] n charrue f // vt (earth) labourer ; **to ~ back** vt (COMM) réinvestir ; **to ~ through** vt fus (snow etc) avancer péniblement dans ; **~ing** n labourage m.

ploy [plɔɪ] n stratagème m.

pluck [plʌk] vt (fruit) cueillir ; (musical instrument) pincer ; (bird) plumer // n courage m, cran m ; **to ~ one's eyebrows** s'épiler les sourcils ; **to ~ up courage** prendre son courage à deux mains ; **~y** a courageux(euse).

plug [plʌg] n bouchon m, bonde f ; (ELEC) prise f de courant ; (AUT: also: **sparking ~**) bougie f // vt (hole) boucher ; (col: advertise) faire du battage pour, matraquer ; **to ~ in** vt (ELEC) brancher.

plum [plʌm] *n* (*fruit*) prune *f* // ~ **job** *n* (*col*) travail *m* en or.

plumb [plʌm] *a* vertical(e) // *n* plomb *m* // *ad* (*exactly*) en plein // *vt* sonder.

plumber ['plʌmə*] *n* plombier *m*.

plumbing ['plʌmɪŋ] *n* (*trade*) plomberie *f*; (*piping*) tuyauterie *f*.

plumbline ['plʌmlaɪn] *n* fil *m* à plomb.

plume [plu:m] *n* plume *f*, plumet *m*.

plummet ['plʌmɪt] *vi* plonger, dégringoler.

plump [plʌmp] *a* rondelet(te), dodu(e), bien en chair // *vt*: **to ~ sth (down) on** laisser tomber qch lourdement sur; **to ~ for** (*col: choose*) se décider pour.

plunder ['plʌndə*] *n* pillage *m* // *vt* piller.

plunge [plʌndʒ] *n* plongeon *m* // *vt* plonger // *vi* (*fall*) tomber, dégringoler; **to take the ~** se jeter à l'eau; **plunging** *a* (*neckline*) plongeant(e).

pluperfect [plu:'pə:fɪkt] *n* plus-que-parfait *m*.

plural ['pluərl] *a* pluriel(le) // *n* pluriel *m*.

plus [plʌs] *n* (*also:* ~ **sign**) signe *m* plus // *prep* plus; **ten/twenty ~** plus de dix/vingt; **it's a ~** c'est un atout; ~ **fours** *npl* pantalon *m* (de) golf.

plush [plʌʃ] *a* somptueux(euse) // *n* peluche *f*.

ply [plaɪ] *n* (*of wool*) fil *m*; (*of wood*) feuille *f*, épaisseur *f* // *vt* (*tool*) manier; (*a trade*) exercer // *vi* (*ship*) faire la navette; **three ~** (*wool*) *n* laine *f* trois fils; **to ~ sb with drink** donner continuellement à boire à qn; ~**wood** *n* contre-plaqué *m*.

P.M. *abbr see* **prime**.

p.m. *ad* (*abbr of post meridiem*) de l'après-midi.

pneumatic [njuː'mætɪk] *a* pneumatique.

pneumonia [njuː'məunɪə] *n* pneumonie *f*.

P.O. *abbr see* **post office**.

poach [pəutʃ] *vt* (*cook*) pocher; (*steal*) pêcher (*or* chasser) sans permis // *vi* braconner; ~**ed** *a* (*egg*) poché(e); ~**er** *n* braconnier *m*; ~**ing** *n* braconnage *m*.

pocket ['pɔkɪt] *n* poche *f* // *vt* empocher; **to be out of ~** en être de sa poche; ~**book** *n* (*wallet*) portefeuille *m*; (*notebook*) carnet *m*; ~ **knife** *n* canif *m*; ~ **money** *n* argent *m* de poche.

pockmarked ['pɔkmɑːkt] *a* (*face*) grêlé(e).

pod [pɔd] *n* cosse *f* // *vt* écosser.

podgy ['pɔdʒɪ] *a* rondelet(te).

poem ['pəuɪm] *n* poème *m*.

poet ['pəuɪt] *n* poète *m*; ~**ic** [-'ɛtɪk] *a* poétique; ~ **laureate** *n* poète lauréat (*nommé et appointé par la Cour royale*); ~**ry** *n* poésie *f*.

poignant ['pɔɪnjənt] *a* poignant(e); (*sharp*) vif(vive).

point [pɔɪnt] *n* (*tip*) pointe *f*; (*in time*) moment *m*; (*in space*) endroit *m*; (GEOM, SCOL, SPORT, *on scale*) point *m*; (*subject, idea*) point *m*, sujet *m*; (*also:* **decimal** ~): **2 ~ 3 (2.3)** 2 virgule 3 (2,3) // *vt* (*show*) indiquer; (*wall, window*) jointoyer; (*gun etc*): **to ~ sth at** braquer *or* diriger qch sur // *vi* montrer du doigt; ~**s** *npl* (AUT) vis platinées *f*; (RAIL) aiguillage *m*; **to make a ~** faire une remarque; **to make one's ~** se faire comprendre; **to get the ~** comprendre, saisir; **to come to the ~** en

venir au fait; **there's no ~ (in doing)** cela ne sert à rien (de faire); **good ~s** qualités *fpl*; **to ~ out** *vt* faire remarquer, souligner; **to ~ to** montrer du doigt; (*fig*) signaler; ~**-blank** *ad* (*also:* **at ~-blank range**) à bout portant; (*fig*) catégorique; ~**ed** *a* (*shape*) pointu(e); (*remark*) plein(e) de sous-entendus; ~**edly** *ad* d'une manière significative; ~**er** *n* (*stick*) baguette *f*; (*needle*) aiguille *f*; (*dog*) chien *m* d'arrêt; ~**less** *a* inutile, vain(e); ~ **of view** *n* point *m* de vue.

poise [pɔɪz] *n* (*balance*) équilibre *m*; (*of head, body*) port *m*; (*calmness*) calme *m* // *vt* placer en équilibre; **to be ~d for** (*fig*) être prêt à.

poison ['pɔɪzn] *n* poison *m* // *vt* empoisonner; ~**ing** *n* empoisonnement *m*; ~**ous** *a* (*snake*) venimeux(euse); (*substance etc*) vénéneux(euse).

poke [pəuk] *vt* (*fire*) tisonner; (*jab with finger, stick etc*) piquer; (*put*): **to ~ sth in(to)** fourrer *or* enfoncer qch dans // *n* (*to fire*) coup *m* de tisonnier; **to ~ about** *vi* fureter.

poker ['pəukə*] *n* tisonnier *m*; (CARDS) poker *m*; ~**-faced** *a* au visage impassible.

poky ['pəukɪ] *a* exigu(ë).

Poland ['pəuland] *n* Pologne *f*.

polar ['pəulə*] *a* polaire; ~ **bear** *n* ours blanc.

polarize ['pəuləraɪz] *vt* polariser.

pole [pəul] *n* (*of wood*) mât *m*, perche *f*; (ELEC) poteau *m*; (GEO) pôle *m*.

Pole [pəul] *n* Polonais/e.

polecat ['pəulkæt] *n* (US) putois *m*.

polemic [pɔ'lɛmɪk] *n* polémique *f*.

pole star ['pəulstɑː*] *n* étoile polaire *f*.

pole vault ['pəulvɔ:lt] *n* saut *m* à la perche.

police [pə'li:s] *n* police *f*; (*man: pl inv*) policier *m*, homme *m*; // *vt* maintenir l'ordre dans; ~ **car** *n* voiture *f* de police; ~**man** *n* agent *m* de police, policier *m*; ~ **record** *n* casier *m* judiciaire; ~ **state** *n* état policier; ~ **station** *n* commissariat *m* de police; ~**woman** *n* femme-agent *f*.

policy ['pɔlɪsɪ] *n* politique *f*; (*also:* **insurance** ~) police *f* (d'assurance).

polio ['pəulɪəu] *n* polio *f*.

Polish ['pəulɪʃ] *a* polonais(e) // *n* (LING) polonais *m*.

polish ['pɔlɪʃ] *n* (*for shoes*) cirage *m*; (*for floor*) cire *f*, encaustique *f*; (*for nails*) vernis *m*; (*shine*) éclat *m*, poli *m*; (*fig: refinement*) raffinement *m* // *vt* (*put polish on shoes, wood*) cirer; (*make shiny*) astiquer, faire briller; (*fig: improve*) perfectionner; **to ~ off** *vt* (*work*) expédier; (*food*) liquider; ~**ed** *a* (*fig*) raffiné(e).

polite [pə'laɪt] *a* poli(e); ~**ly** *ad* poliment; ~**ness** *n* politesse *f*.

politic ['pɔlɪtɪk] *a* diplomatique; ~**al** [pə'lɪtɪkl] *a* politique; ~**ian** [-'tɪʃən] *n* homme *m* politique, politicien *m*; ~**s** *npl* politique *f*.

polka ['pɔlkə] *n* polka *f*; ~ **dot** *n* pois *m*.

poll [pəul] *n* scrutin *m*, vote *m*; (*also:* **opinion** ~) sondage *m* (d'opinion) // *vt* obtenir.

pollen ['pɔlən] *n* pollen *m*; ~ **count** *n* taux *m* de pollen.

pollination [pɔlɪ'neɪʃən] n pollinisation f.
polling booth ['pəulɪŋbu:ð] n isoloir m.
polling day ['pəulɪŋdeɪ] n jour m des élections.
polling station ['pəulɪŋsteɪʃən] n bureau m de vote.
pollute [pə'lu:t] vt polluer.
pollution [pə'lu:ʃən] n pollution f.
polo ['pəuləu] n polo m ; ~-neck a à col roulé.
polyester [pɔlɪ'estə*] n polyester m.
polygamy [pə'lɪgəmɪ] n polygamie f.
Polynesia [pɔlɪ'ni:zɪə] n Polynésie f.
polytechnic [pɔlɪ'teknɪk] n (college) I.U.T. m, Institut m Universitaire de Technologie.
polythene ['pɔlɪθi:n] n polyéthylène m ; ~ bag n sac m en plastique.
pomegranate ['pɔmɪgrænɪt] n grenade f.
pommel ['pɔml] n pommeau m.
pomp [pɔmp] n pompe f, faste f, apparat m.
pompous ['pɔmpəs] a pompeux(euse).
pond [pɔnd] n étang m ; mare f.
ponder ['pɔndə*] vi réfléchir // vt considérer, peser ; ~ous a pesant(e), lourd(e).
pontiff ['pɔntɪf] n pontife m.
pontificate [pɔn'tɪfɪkeɪt] vi (fig) : to ~ (about) pontifier (sur).
pontoon [pɔn'tu:n] n ponton m.
pony ['pəunɪ] n poney m ; ~tail n queue f de cheval ; ~ trekking n randonnée f à cheval.
poodle ['pu:dl] n caniche m.
pooh-pooh [pu:'pu:] vt dédaigner.
pool [pu:l] n (of rain) flaque f ; (pond) mare f ; (artificial) bassin m ; (also: **swimming** ~) piscine f ; (sth shared) fonds commun ; (money at cards) cagnotte f ; (billiards) poule f // vt mettre en commun.
poor [puə*] a pauvre ; (mediocre) médiocre, faible, mauvais(e) // npl: **the** ~ les pauvres mpl ; ~**ly** ad pauvrement ; médiocrement // a souffrant(e), malade.
pop [pɔp] n (noise) bruit sec ; (MUS) musique f pop ; (US: col: father) papa m // vt (put) fourrer, mettre (rapidement) // vi éclater ; (cork) sauter ; **to** ~ **in** vi entrer en passant ; **to** ~ **out** vi sortir ; **to** ~ **up** vi apparaître, surgir ; ~ **concert** n concert m pop ; ~**corn** n pop-corn m.
pope [pəup] n pape m.
poplar ['pɔplə*] n peuplier m.
poplin ['pɔplɪn] n popeline f.
poppy ['pɔpɪ] n coquelicot m ; pavot m.
populace ['pɔpjuləs] n peuple m.
popular ['pɔpjulə*] a populaire ; (fashionable) à la mode ; ~**ity** [-'lærɪtɪ] n popularité f ; ~**ize** vt populariser ; (science) vulgariser.
populate ['pɔpjuleɪt] vt peupler.
population [pɔpju'leɪʃən] n population f.
populous ['pɔpjuləs] a populeux(euse).
porcelain ['pɔ:slɪn] n porcelaine f.
porch [pɔ:tʃ] n porche m.
porcupine ['pɔ:kjupaɪn] n porc-épic m.
pore [pɔ:*] n pore m // vi: to ~ **over** s'absorber dans, être plongé(e) dans.
pork [pɔ:k] n porc m.

pornographic [pɔ:nə'græfɪk] a pornographique.
pornography [pɔ:'nɔgrəfɪ] n pornographie f.
porous ['pɔ:rəs] a poreux(euse).
porpoise ['pɔ:pəs] n marsouin m.
porridge ['pɔrɪdʒ] n porridge m.
port [pɔ:t] n (harbour) port m ; (opening in ship) sabord m ; (NAUT: left side) bâbord m ; (wine) porto m ; **to** ~ (NAUT) à bâbord.
portable ['pɔ:təbl] a portatif(ive).
portal ['pɔ:tl] n portail m.
portcullis [pɔ:t'kʌlɪs] n herse f.
portend [pɔ:'tend] vt présager, annoncer.
portent ['pɔ:tent] n présage m.
porter ['pɔ:tə*] n (for luggage) porteur m ; (doorkeeper) gardien/ne, portier m.
porthole ['pɔ:thəul] n hublot m.
portico ['pɔ:tɪkəu] n portique m.
portion ['pɔ:ʃən] n portion f, part f.
portly ['pɔ:tlɪ] a corpulent(e).
portrait ['pɔ:treɪt] n portrait m.
portray [pɔ:'treɪ] vt faire le portrait de ; (in writing) dépeindre, représenter ; ~**al** n portrait m, représentation f.
Portugal ['pɔ:tjugl] n Portugal m.
Portuguese [pɔ:tju'gi:z] a portugais(e) // n, pl inv Portugais/e ; (LING) portugais m.
pose [pəuz] n pose f ; (pej) affectation f // vi poser ; (pretend): **to** ~ **as** se poser en // vt poser, créer ; ~**r** n question embarrassante.
posh [pɔʃ] a (col) chic inv.
position [pə'zɪʃən] n position f ; (job) situation f // vt mettre en place or en position.
positive ['pɔzɪtɪv] a positif(ive) ; (certain) sûr(e), certain(e) ; (definite) formel(le), catégorique ; indéniable, réel(le).
posse ['pɔsɪ] n (US) détachement m.
possess [pə'zes] vt posséder ; ~**ion** [pə'zeʃən] n possession f ; ~**ive** a possessif(ive) ; ~**ively** ad d'une façon possessive ; ~**or** n possesseur m.
possibility [pɔsɪ'bɪlɪtɪ] n possibilité f ; éventualité f.
possible ['pɔsɪbl] a possible ; **if** ~ si possible ; **as big as** ~ aussi gros que possible.
possibly ['pɔsɪblɪ] ad (perhaps) peut-être ; **if you** ~ **can** si cela vous est possible ; **I cannot** ~ **come** il m'est impossible de venir.
post [pəust] n poste f ; (collection) levée f ; (letters, delivery) courrier m ; (job, situation) poste m ; (pole) poteau m // vt (send by post, MIL) poster ; (appoint): **to** ~ **to** affecter à ; (notice) afficher ; ~**age** n affranchissement m ; ~**al** a postal(e) ; ~**al order** n mandat(-poste) m ; ~**box** n boîte f aux lettres ; ~**card** n carte postale.
postdate [pəust'deɪt] vt (cheque) postdater.
poster ['pəustə*] n affiche f.
poste restante [pəust'rɛstɑ:nt] n poste restante.
posterior [pɔs'tɪərɪə*] n (col) postérieur m, derrière m.
posterity [pɔs'terɪtɪ] n postérité f.
postgraduate ['pəust'grædjuət] n ≈ étudiant/e de troisième cycle.

posthumous ['pɔstjuməs] a posthume ; ~ly ad après la mort de l'auteur, à titre posthume.

postman ['pəustmən] n facteur m.

postmark ['pəustmɑːk] n cachet m (de la poste).

postmaster ['pəustmɑːstə*] n receveur m des postes.

post-mortem [pəust'mɔːtəm] n autopsie f.

post office ['pəustɔfɪs] n (building) poste f ; (organization) postes fpl ; ~ **box (P.O. box)** n boîte postale (B.P.).

postpone [pəs'pəun] vt remettre (à plus tard), reculer ; ~**ment** n ajournement m, renvoi m.

postscript ['pəustskrɪpt] n post-scriptum m.

postulate ['pɔstjuleɪt] vt postuler.

posture ['pɔstʃə*] n posture f, attitude f // vi poser.

postwar [pəust'wɔː*] a d'après-guerre.

posy ['pəuzɪ] n petit bouquet.

pot [pɔt] n (for cooking) marmite f, casserole f ; (for plants, jam) pot m ; (col: marijuana) herbe f // vt (plant) mettre en pot ; **to go to ~** aller à vau-l'eau.

potash ['pɔtæʃ] n potasse f.

potato, ~**es** [pə'teɪtəu] n pomme f de terre ; ~ **flour** n fécule f.

potency ['pəutnsɪ] n puissance f, force f ; (of drink) degré m d'alcool.

potent ['pəutnt] a puissant(e) ; (drink) fort(e), très alcoolisé(e).

potentate ['pəutnteɪt] n potentat m.

potential [pə'tɛnʃl] a potentiel(le) // n potentiel m ; ~**ly** ad en puissance.

pothole ['pɔthəul] n (in road) nid m de poule ; (underground) gouffre m, caverne f ; ~**r** n spéléologue m/f ; **potholing** n: **to go potholing** faire de la spéléologie.

potion ['pəuʃən] n potion f.

potluck [pɔt'lʌk] n: **to take ~** tenter sa chance.

potpourri [pəu'purɪ] n pot-pourri m.

potshot ['pɔtʃɔt] n: **to take ~s at** canarder.

potted ['pɔtɪd] a (food) en conserve ; (plant) en pot.

potter ['pɔtə*] n potier m // vt: **to ~ around, ~ about** bricoler ; ~**y** n poterie f.

potty ['pɔtɪ] a (col: mad) dingue // n (child's) pot m ; ~**-training** n apprentissage m de la propreté.

pouch [pautʃ] n (ZOOL) poche f ; (for tobacco) blague f.

pouf(fe) [puːf] n (stool) pouf m.

poultice ['pəultɪs] n cataplasme m.

poultry ['pəultrɪ] n volaille f ; ~ **farm** n élevage m de volaille.

pounce [pauns] vi: **to ~ (on)** bondir (sur), fondre sur // n bond m, attaque f.

pound [paund] n livre f (weight = 453g, 16 ounces ; money = 100 new pence, 20 shillings) ; (for dogs, cars) fourrière f // vt (beat) bourrer de coups, marteler ; (crush) piler, pulvériser ; (with guns) pilonner // vi (beat) battre violemment, taper ; ~ **sterling** n livre f sterling.

pour [pɔː*] vt verser // vi couler à flots ; (rain) pleuvoir à verse ; **to ~ away or off** vt vider ; **to ~ in** vi (people) affluer, se précipiter ; **to ~ out** vi (people) sortir en masse // vt vider ; déverser ; (serve: a drink) verser ; ~**ing** a: ~**ing rain** pluie torrentielle.

pout [paut] n moue f // vi faire la moue.

poverty ['pɔvətɪ] n pauvreté f, misère f ; ~**-stricken** a pauvre, déshérité(e).

powder ['paudə*] n poudre f // vt poudrer ; ~ **room** n toilettes fpl (pour dames) ; ~y a poudreux(euse).

power ['pauə*] n (strength) puissance f, force f ; (ability, POL: of party, leader) pouvoir m ; (MATH) puissance f ; (mental) facultés mentales ; (ELEC) courant m // vt faire marcher ; ~ **cut** n coupure f de courant ; ~**ed** a: ~**ed by** actionné(e) par, fonctionnant à, à puissant(e) ; ~**less** a impuissant(e) ; ~ **line** n ligne f électrique ; ~ **point** n prise f de courant ; ~ **station** n centrale f électrique.

powwow ['pauwau] n assemblée f.

pox [pɔks] n see **chicken.**

p.p. abbr (= per procurationem): ~ **J. Smith** pour M. J. Smith.

P.R. abbr of **public relations.**

practicability [præktɪkə'bɪlɪtɪ] n possibilité f de réalisation.

practicable ['præktɪkəbl] a (scheme) réalisable.

practical ['præktɪkl] a pratique ; ~ **joke** n farce f ; ~**ly** ad (almost) pratiquement.

practice ['præktɪs] n pratique f ; (of profession) exercice m ; (at football etc) entraînement m ; (business) cabinet m ; clientèle f // vt,vi (US) = **practise** ; **in** (in reality) en pratique ; **out of** ~ rouillé(e) ; **2 hours' piano** ~ 2 heures de travail or d'exercices au piano ; ~ **match** n match m d'entraînement.

practise, (US) **practice** ['præktɪs] vt (work at: piano, one's backhand etc) s'exercer à, travailler ; (train for: skiing, running etc) s'entraîner à ; (a sport, religion, method) pratiquer ; (profession) exercer // vi s'exercer, travailler ; (train) s'entraîner ; **to ~ for a match** s'entraîner pour un match ; **practising** a (Christian etc) pratiquant(e) ; (lawyer) en exercice.

practitioner [præk'tɪʃənə*] n praticien/ne.

pragmatic [præg'mætɪk] a pragmatique.

prairie ['prɛərɪ] n savane f ; (US): **the ~s** la Prairie.

praise [preɪz] n éloge(s) m(pl), louange(s) f(pl) // vt louer, faire l'éloge de ; ~**worthy** a digne de louanges.

pram [præm] n landau m, voiture f d'enfant.

prance [prɑːns] vi (horse) caracoler.

prank [præŋk] n farce f.

prattle ['prætl] vi jacasser.

prawn [prɔːn] n crevette f (rose).

pray [preɪ] vi prier.

prayer [prɛə*] n prière f ; ~ **book** n livre m de prières.

preach [priːtʃ] vt,vi prêcher ; **to ~ at sb** faire la morale à qn ; ~**er** n prédicateur m.

preamble [prɪ'æmbl] n préambule m.
prearranged [pri:ə'reɪndʒd] a organisé(e) or fixé(e) à l'avance.
precarious [prɪ'kɛərɪəs] a précaire.
precaution [prɪ'kɔ:ʃən] n précaution f; **~ary** a (measure) de précaution.
precede [prɪ'si:d] vt,vi précéder.
precedence ['prɛsɪdəns] n préséance f.
precedent ['prɛsɪdənt] n précédent m.
preceding [prɪ'si:dɪŋ] a qui précède (or précédait).
precept ['pri:sɛpt] n précepte m.
precinct ['pri:sɪŋkt] n (round cathedral) pourtour m, enceinte f; **pedestrian ~** n zone piétonnière; **shopping ~** n centre commerical.
precious ['prɛʃəs] a précieux(euse).
precipice ['prɛsɪpɪs] n précipice m.
precipitate a [prɪ'sɪpɪtɪt] (hasty) précipité(e) // vt [prɪ'sɪpɪteɪt] précipiter; **precipitation** [-'teɪʃən] n précipitation f.
precipitous [prɪ'sɪpɪtəs] a (steep) abrupt(e), à pic.
précis, pl **précis** ['preɪsi:, -z] n résumé m.
precise [prɪ'saɪs] a précis(e); **~ly** ad précisément.
preclude [prɪ'klu:d] vt exclure, empêcher; **to ~ sb from doing** empêcher qn de faire.
precocious [prɪ'kəʊʃəs] a précoce.
preconceived [pri:kən'si:vd] a (idea) préconçu(e).
precondition [pri:kən'dɪʃən] n condition f nécessaire.
precursor [pri:'kə:sə*] n précurseur m.
predator ['prɛdətə*] n prédateur m, rapace m; **~y** a rapace.
predecessor ['pri:dɪsɛsə*] n prédécesseur m.
predestination [pri:dɛstɪ'neɪʃən] n prédestination f.
predetermine [pri:dɪ'tə:mɪn] vt déterminer à l'avance.
predicament [prɪ'dɪkəmənt] n situation f difficile.
predicate ['prɛdɪkɪt] n (LING) prédicat m.
predict [prɪ'dɪkt] vt prédire; **~ion** [-'dɪkʃən] n prédiction f.
predominance [prɪ'dɒmɪnəns] n prédominance f.
predominant [prɪ'dɒmɪnənt] a prédominant(e); **~ly** ad en majeure partie; surtout.
predominate [prɪ'dɒmɪneɪt] vi prédominer.
pre-eminent [pri:'ɛmɪnənt] a prééminent(e).
pre-empt [pri:'ɛmt] vt acquérir par droit de préemption; (fig): **to ~ the issue** conclure avant même d'ouvrir les débats.
preen [pri:n] vt: **to ~ itself** (bird) se lisser les plumes; **to ~ o.s.** s'admirer.
prefab ['pri:fæb] n bâtiment préfabriqué.
prefabricated [pri:'fæbrɪkeɪtɪd] a préfabriqué(e).
preface ['prɛfəs] n préface f.
prefect ['pri:fɛkt] n (Brit: in school) élève chargé(e) de certaines fonctions de discipline; (in France) préfet m.
prefer [prɪ'fə:*] vt préférer; **~able** ['prɛfrəbl] a préférable; **~ably** ['prɛfrəblɪ]

ad de préférence; **~ence** ['prɛfrəns] n préférence f; **~ential** [prɛfə'rɛnʃəl] a préférentiel(le) **~ential treatment** traitement m de faveur.
prefix ['pri:fɪks] n préfixe m.
pregnancy ['prɛgnənsɪ] n grossesse f.
pregnant ['prɛgnənt] a enceinte af.
prehistoric ['pri:hɪs'tɔrɪk] a préhistorique.
prehistory [pri:'hɪstərɪ] n préhistoire f.
prejudge [pri:'dʒʌdʒ] vt préjuger de.
prejudice ['prɛdʒʊdɪs] n préjugé m; (harm) tort m, préjudice m // vt porter préjudice à; **~d** a (person) plein(e) de préjugés; (view) préconçu(e), partial(e).
prelate ['prɛlət] n prélat m.
preliminary [prɪ'lɪmɪnərɪ] a préliminaire; **preliminaries** npl préliminaires mpl.
prelude ['prɛlju:d] n prélude m.
premarital ['pri:'mærɪtl] a avant le mariage.
premature ['prɛmətʃuə*] a prématuré(e).
premeditated [pri:'mɛdɪteɪtɪd] a prémédité(e).
premeditation [pri:mɛdɪ'teɪʃən] n préméditation f.
premier ['prɛmɪə*] a premier(ère), capital(e), primordial(e) // n (POL) premier ministre.
première ['prɛmɪɛə*] n première f.
premise ['prɛmɪs] n prémisse f; **~s** npl locaux mpl; **on the ~s** sur les lieux; sur place.
premium ['pri:mɪəm] n prime f.
premonition [prɛmə'nɪʃən] n prémonition f.
preoccupation [pri:ɔkju'peɪʃən] n préoccupation f.
preoccupied [pri:'ɔkjupaɪd] a préoccupé(e).
prep [prɛp] n (SCOL: study) étude f; **~ school** n = **preparatory school.**
prepackaged [pri:'pækɪdʒd] a préempaqueté(e).
prepaid [pri:'peɪd] a payé(e) d'avance.
preparation [prɛpə'reɪʃən] n préparation f; **~s** npl (for trip, war) préparatifs mpl.
preparatory [prɪ'pærətərɪ] a préparatoire; **~ school** n école primaire privée.
prepare [prɪ'pɛə*] vt préparer // vi: **to ~ for** se préparer à; **~d for** preparé(e) à; **~d to** prêt(e) à.
preponderance [prɪ'pɒndərns] n prépondérance f.
preposition [prɛpə'zɪʃən] n préposition f.
preposterous [prɪ'pɒstərəs] a absurde.
prerequisite [pri:'rɛkwɪzɪt] n condition f préalable.
prerogative [prɪ'rɔgətɪv] n prérogative f.
presbyterian [prɛzbɪ'tɪərɪən] a,n presbytérien(ne).
presbytery ['prɛzbɪtərɪ] n presbytère m.
preschool ['pri:'sku:l] a préscolaire.
prescribe [prɪ'skraɪb] vt prescrire.
prescription [prɪ'skrɪpʃən] n prescription f; (MED) ordonnance f.
prescriptive [prɪ'skrɪptɪv] a normatif(ive).
presence ['prɛzns] n présence f; **~ of mind** n présence d'esprit.
present ['prɛznt] a présent(e) // n cadeau m; (also: **~ tense**) présent m // vt

[pri'zɛnt] présenter ; (give): **to ~ sb with sth** offrir qch à qn ; **at ~** en ce moment ; **~able** [pri'zɛntəbl] a présentable ; **~ation** [-'teiʃən] n présentation f ; (gift) cadeau m, présent m ; (ceremony) remise f du cadeau ; **~day** a contemporain(e), actuel(le) ; **~ly** ad (soon) tout à l'heure, bientôt ; (at present) en ce moment.

preservation [prezə'veiʃən] n préservation f, conservation f.

preservative [pri'zə:vətiv] n agent m de conservation.

preserve [pri'zə:v] vt (keep safe) préserver, protéger ; (maintain) conserver, garder ; (food) mettre en conserve // n (for game, fish) réserve f ; (often pl: jam) confiture f ; (: fruit) fruits mpl en conserve.

preside [pri'zaid] vi présider.

presidency ['prezidənsi] n présidence f.

president ['prezidənt] n président/e ; **~ial** ['dɛnʃl] a présidentiel(le).

press [prɛs] n (tool, machine, newspapers) presse f ; (for wine) pressoir m ; (crowd) cohue f, foule f // vt (push) appuyer sur ; (squeeze) presser, serrer ; (clothes: iron) repasser ; (pursue) talonner ; (insist): **to ~ sth on sb** presser qn d'accepter qch // vi appuyer, peser ; se presser ; **we are ~ed for time** le temps nous manque ; **to ~ for sth** faire pression pour obtenir qch ; **to ~ on** vi continuer ; **~ agency** n agence f de presse ; **~ conference** n conférence f de presse ; **~ cutting** n coupure f de presse ; **~-gang** n recruteurs de la marine (jusqu'au 19ème siècle) ; **~ing** a urgent(e), pressant(e) // n repassage m ; **~ stud** n bouton-pression m.

pressure ['prɛʃə*] n pression f ; (stress) tension f ; **~ cooker** n cocotte-minute f ; **~ gauge** n manomètre m ; **~ group** n groupe m de pression ; **pressurized** a pressurisé(e).

prestige [prɛs'ti:ʒ] n prestige m.

prestigious [prɛs'tidʒəs] a prestigieux(euse).

presumably [pri'zju:məbli] ad vraisemblablement.

presume [pri'zju:m] vt présumer, supposer ; **to ~ to do** (dare) se permettre de faire.

presumption [pri'zʌmpʃən] n supposition f, présomption f ; (boldness) audace f.

presumptuous [pri'zʌmpʃəs] a présomptueux(euse).

presuppose [pri:sə'pəuz] vt présupposer.

pretence, pretense (US) [pri'tɛns] n (claim) prétention f ; **to make a ~ of doing** faire semblant de faire ; **on the ~ of** sous le prétexte de.

pretend [pri'tɛnd] vt (feign) feindre, simuler // vi (feign) faire semblant ; (claim): **to ~ to sth** prétendre à qch ; **to ~ to do** faire semblant de faire.

pretense [pri'tɛns] n (US) = pretence.

pretentious [pri'tɛnʃəs] a prétentieux(euse).

preterite ['prɛtərit] n prétérite m.

pretext ['pri:tɛkst] n prétexte m.

pretty ['priti] a joli(e) // ad assez.

prevail [pri'veil] vi (win) l'emporter, prévaloir ; (be usual) avoir cours ; (persuade): **to ~ (up)on sb to do**

persuader qn de faire ; **~ing** a dominant(e).

prevalent ['prɛvələnt] a répandu(e), courant(e).

prevent [pri'vɛnt] vt: **to ~ (from doing)** empêcher (de faire) ; **~able** a évitable ; **~ative** a préventif(ive) ; **~ion** [-vɛnʃən] n prévention f ; **~ive** a préventif(ive).

preview ['pri:vju:] n (of film) avant-première f ; (fig) aperçu m.

previous ['pri:viəs] a précédent(e) ; antérieur(e) ; **~ to doing** avant de faire ; **~ly** ad précédemment, auparavant.

prewar [pri:'wɔ:*] a d'avant-guerre.

prey [prei] n proie f // vi: **to ~ on** s'attaquer à ; **it was ~ing on his mind** ça le rongeait or minait.

price [prais] n prix m // vt (goods) fixer le prix de ; tarifer ; **~less** a sans prix, inestimable ; **~ list** n liste f des prix, tarif m.

prick [prik] n piqûre f // vt piquer ; **to ~ up one's ears** dresser or tendre l'oreille.

prickle ['prikl] n (of plant) épine f ; (sensation) picotement m.

prickly ['prikli] a piquant(e), épineux(euse) ; (fig: person) irritable ; **~ heat** n fièvre f miliaire ; **~ pear** n figue f de Barbarie.

pride [praid] n orgueil m ; fierté f // vt: **to ~ o.s. on** se flatter de ; s'enorgueillir de.

priest [pri:st] n prêtre m ; **~ess** n prêtresse f ; **~hood** n prêtrise f, sacerdoce m.

prig [prig] n poseur/euse, fat m.

prim [prim] a collet monté inv, guindé(e).

primarily ['praimərili] ad principalement, essentiellement.

primary ['praiməri] a primaire ; (first in importance) premier(ère), primordial(e) ; **~ colour** n couleur fondamentale ; **~ school** n école primaire f.

primate n (REL) ['praimit] primat m ; (ZOOL) ['praimeit] primate m.

prime [praim] a primordial(e), fondamental(e) ; (excellent) excellent(e) // vt (gun, pump) amorcer ; (fig) mettre au courant ; **in the ~ of life** dans la fleur de l'âge ; **~ minister (P.M.)** n premier ministre ; **~r** n (book) premier livre, manuel m élémentaire ; (paint) apprêt m ; (of gun) amorce f.

primeval [prai'mi:vl] a primitif(ive).

primitive ['primitiv] a primitif(ive).

primrose ['primrəuz] n primevère f.

primus (stove) ['praiməs(stəuv)] n ® réchaud m de camping.

prince [prins] n prince m.

princess [prin'sɛs] n princesse f.

principal ['prinsipl] a principal(e) // n (headmaster) directeur m, principal m ; (money) capital m, principal m.

principality [prinsi'pæliti] n principauté f.

principally ['prinsipli] ad principalement.

principle ['prinsipl] n principe m.

print [print] n (mark) empreinte f ; (letters) caractères mpl ; (fabric) imprimé m ; (ART)

gravure f, estampe f; (*PHOT*) épreuve f //
vt imprimer; (*publish*) publier; (*write in
capitals*) écrire en majuscules; **out of ~**
épuisé(e); **~ed matter** n imprimés *mpl*;
~er n imprimeur m; **~ing** n impression
f; **~ing press** n presse f typographique;
~out n listage m.

prior ['praɪə*] a antérieur(e), précédent(e)
// n prieur m; **~ to doing** avant de faire.

priority [praɪˈɒrɪtɪ] n priorité f.

priory ['praɪərɪ] n prieuré m.

prise [praɪz] vt: **to ~ open** forcer.

prism ['prɪzəm] n prisme m.

prison ['prɪzn] n prison f; **~er** n
prisonnier/ère.

prissy ['prɪsɪ] a bégueule.

pristine ['prɪstiːn] a virginal(e).

privacy ['prɪvəsɪ] n intimité f, solitude f.

private ['praɪvɪt] a privé(e);
personnel(le); (*house, car, lesson*)
particulier(ère) // n soldat m de deuxième
classe; '**~**' (*on envelope*) 'personnelle'; **in
~** en privé; **~ eye** n détective privé; **~ly**
ad en privé; (*within oneself*)
intérieurement.

privet ['prɪvɪt] n troène m.

privilege ['prɪvɪlɪdʒ] n privilège m; **~d** a
privilégié(e).

privy ['prɪvɪ] a: **to be ~ to** être au courant
de; **P~ council** n conseil privé.

prize [praɪz] n prix m // a (*example, idiot*)
parfait(e); (*bull, novel*) primé(e) // vt
priser, faire grand cas de; **~ fight** n
combat professionnel; **~ giving** n
distribution f des prix; **~winner** n
gagnant/e.

pro [prəu] n (*SPORT*) professionnel/le; **the
~s and cons** le pour et le contre.

probability [prɒbəˈbɪlɪtɪ] n probabilité f.

probable ['prɒbəbl] a probable; **probably**
ad probablement.

probation [prəˈbeɪʃən] n (*in employment*)
essai m; (*LAW*) liberté surveillée; (*REL*)
noviciat m, probation f; **on ~** (*employee*)
à l'essai; (*LAW*) en liberté surveillée; **~ary**
a (*period*) d'essai.

probe [prəub] n (*MED, SPACE*) sonde f;
(*enquiry*) enquête f, investigation f // vt
sonder, explorer.

probity ['prəubɪtɪ] n probité f.

problem ['prɒbləm] n problème m; **~atic**
['-mætɪk] a problématique.

procedure [prəˈsiːdʒə*] n (*ADMIN, LAW*)
procédure f; (*method*) marche f à suivre,
façon f de procéder.

proceed [prəˈsiːd] vi (*go forward*) avancer;
(*go about it*) procéder; (*continue*): **to ~
(with)** continuer, poursuivre; **to ~ to**
aller à; passer à; **to ~ to do** se mettre
à faire; **~ing** n procédé m, façon d'agir
f; **~ings** npl mesures fpl; (*LAW*) poursuites
fpl; (*meeting*) réunion f, séance f; (*records*)
compte rendu; actes mpl; **~s** ['prəusiːdz]
npl produit m, recette f.

process ['prəusɛs] n processus m;
(*method*) procédé m // vt traiter; **~ed
cheese** fromage fondu; **in ~** en cours;
~ing n traitement m.

procession [prəˈsɛʃən] n défilé m, cortège
m; (*REL*) procession f.

proclaim [prəˈkleɪm] vt déclarer,
proclamer.

proclamation [prɒkləˈmeɪʃən] n
proclamation f.

proclivity [prəˈklɪvɪtɪ] n inclination f.

procrastination [prəukræstɪˈneɪʃən] n
procrastination f.

procreation [prəukrɪˈeɪʃən] n procréation
f.

procure [prəˈkjuə*] vt (*for o.s.*) se
procurer; (*for sb*) procurer.

prod [prɒd] vt pousser // n (*push, jab*) petit
coup, poussée f.

prodigal ['prɒdɪgl] a prodigue.

prodigious ['prəˈdɪdʒəs] a prodi-
gieux(euse).

prodigy ['prɒdɪdʒɪ] n prodige m.

produce n ['prɒdjuːs] (*AGR*) produits mpl
// vt [prəˈdjuːs] produire; (*to show*)
présenter; (*cause*) provoquer, causer;
(*THEATRE*) monter, mettre en scène; **~r** n
(*THEATRE*) metteur m en scène; (*AGR, CINEMA*)
producteur m.

product ['prɒdʌkt] n produit m.

production [prəˈdʌkʃən] n production f;
(*THEATRE*) mise f en scène; **~ line** n chaîne
f (de fabrication).

productive [prəˈdʌktɪv] a productif(ive).

productivity [prɒdʌkˈtɪvɪtɪ] n
productivité f.

profane [prəˈfeɪn] a sacrilège; (*lay*)
profane.

profess [prəˈfɛs] vt professer.

profession [prəˈfɛʃən] n profession f;
~al n (*SPORT*) professionnel/le // a
professionnel(le); (*work*) de
professionnel; **he's a ~al man** il exerce
une profession libérale; **~alism** n
professionnalisme m.

professor [prəˈfɛsə*] n professeur m
(*titulaire d'une chaire*).

proficiency [prəˈfɪʃənsɪ] n compétence f,
aptitude f.

proficient [prəˈfɪʃənt] a compétent(e),
capable.

profile ['prəufaɪl] n profil m.

profit ['prɒfɪt] n bénéfice m; profit m //
vi: **to ~ (by or from)** profiter (de);
~ability [-'bɪlɪtɪ] n rentabilité f; **~able** a
lucratif(ive), rentable.

profiteering [prɒfɪˈtɪərɪŋ] n (*pej*)
mercantilisme m.

profound [prəˈfaund] a profond(e).

profuse [prəˈfjuːs] a abondant(e); (*with
money*) prodigue; **~ly** ad en abondance,
profusion; **profusion** [-ˈfjuːʒən] n
profusion f, abondance f.

progeny ['prɒdʒɪnɪ] n progéniture f;
descendants mpl.

programme, program (*US*)
['prəugræm] n programme m; (*RADIO, TV*)
émission f // vt programmer;
programming, programing (*US*) n
programmation f.

progress n ['prəugrɛs] progrès m // vi
[prəˈgrɛs] progresser, avancer; **in ~** en
cours; **to make ~** progresser, faire des
progrès, être en progrès; **~ion** [-ˈgrɛʃən]
n progression f; **~ive** [-ˈgrɛsɪv] a
progressif(ive); (*person*) progressiste;
~ively [-ˈgrɛsɪvlɪ] ad progressivement.

prohibit [prə'hıbıt] vt interdire, défendre ; **to ~ sb from doing** défendre or interdire à qn de faire ; **~ion** [prəuı'bıʃən] n (US) prohibition f ; **~ive** a (price etc) prohibitif(ive).

project n ['prɔdʒɛkt] (plan) projet m, plan m ; (venture) opération f, entreprise f ; (gen SCOL: research) étude f, dossier m // vb [prə'dʒɛkt] vt projeter //. vi (stick out) faire saillie, s'avancer.

projectile [prə'dʒɛktaıl] n projectile m.

projection [prə'dʒɛkʃən] n projection f ; saillie f.

projector [prə'dʒɛktə*] n projecteur m.

proletarian [prəulı'tɛərıən] a prolétarien(ne) // n prolétaire m/f.

proletariat [prəulı'tɛərıət] n prolétariat m.

proliferate [prə'lıfəreıt] vi proliférer ; **proliferation** [-'reıʃən] n prolifération f.

prolific [prə'lıfık] a prolifique.

prologue ['prəulɔg] n prologue m.

prolong [prə'lɔŋ] vt prolonger.

prom [prɔm] n abbr of **promenade** ; (US: ball) bal m d'étudiants.

promenade [prɔmə'na:d] n (by sea) esplanade f, promenade f ; **~ concert** n concert m (de musique classique) ; **~ deck** n pont m promenade.

prominence ['prɔmınəns] n proéminence f ; importance f.

prominent ['prɔmınənt] a (standing out) proéminent(e) ; (important) important(e).

promiscuity [prɔmıs'kju:ıtı] n (sexual) légèreté f de mœurs.

promiscuous [prə'mıskjuəs] a (sexually) de mœurs légères.

promise ['prɔmıs] n promesse f // vt,vi promettre ; **promising** a prometteur(euse).

promontory ['prɔməntrı] n promontoire m.

promote [prə'məut] vt promouvoir ; (venture, event) organiser, mettre sur pied ; (new product) lancer ; **~r** n (of sporting event) organisateur/trice ; **promotion** [-'məuʃən] n promotion f.

prompt [prɔmpt] a rapide // ad (punctually) à l'heure // vt inciter ; provoquer ; (THEATRE) souffler (son rôle or ses répliques) à ; **to ~ sb to do** inciter or pousser qn à faire ; **~er** n (THEATRE) souffleur m ; **~ly** ad rapidement, sans délai ; ponctuellement ; **~ness** n rapidité f ; promptitude f ; ponctualité f.

promulgate ['prɔməlgeıt] vt promulguer.

prone [prəun] a (lying) couché(e) (face contre terre) ; **~ to** enclin(e) à.

prong [prɔŋ] n pointe f ; (of fork) dent f.

pronoun ['prəunaun] n pronom m.

pronounce [prə'nauns] vt prononcer // vi : **to ~ (up)on** se prononcer sur ; **~d** a (marked) prononcé(e) ; **~ment** n déclaration f.

pronunciation [prənʌnsı'eıʃən] n prononciation f.

proof [pru:f] n preuve f ; (test, of book, PHOT) épreuve f ; (of alcohol) degré m // a: **~ against** à l'épreuve de ; **to be 70° ~** ≈ titrer 40 degrés ; **~reader** n correcteur/trice (d'épreuves).

prop [prɔp] n support m, étai m // vt (also:

~ up) étayer, soutenir ; (lean): **to ~ sth against** appuyer qch contre or à.

propaganda [prɔpə'gændə] n propagande f.

propagation [prɔpə'geıʃən] n propagation f.

propel [prə'pɛl] vt propulser, faire avancer ; **~ler** n hélice f ; **~ling pencil** n porte-mine m inv.

propensity [prə'pɛnsıtı] n propension f.

proper ['prɔpə*] a (suited, right) approprié(e), bon(bonne) ; (seemly) correct(e), convenable ; (authentic) vrai(e), véritable ; (col: real) n + fini(e), vrai(e) ; **~ly** ad correctement, convenablement ; bel et bien ; **~ noun** n nom m propre.

property ['prɔpətı] n (things owned) biens mpl ; propriété(s) f(pl) ; immeuble m ; terres fpl, domaine m ; (CHEM etc: quality) propriété f ; **it's their ~** cela leur appartient, c'est leur propriété ; **~ owner** n propriétaire m.

prophecy ['prɔfısı] n prophétie f.

prophesy ['prɔfısaı] vt prédire // vi prophétiser.

prophet ['prɔfıt] n prophète m ; **~ic** [prə'fɛtık] a prophétique.

proportion [prə'pɔ:ʃən] n proportion f ; (share) part f ; partie f // vt proportionner ; **~al, ~ate** a proportionnel(le).

proposal [prə'pəuzl] n proposition f, offre f ; (plan) projet m ; (of marriage) demande f en mariage.

propose [prə'pəuz] vt proposer, suggérer // vi faire sa demande en mariage ; **to ~ to do** avoir l'intention de faire ; **~r** n (of motion etc) auteur m.

proposition [prɔpə'zıʃən] n proposition f.

propound [prə'paund] vt proposer, soumettre.

proprietary [prə'praıətərı] a de marque déposée.

proprietor [prə'praıətə*] n propriétaire m/f.

propulsion [prə'pʌlʃən] n propulsion f.

pro rata [prəu'ra:tə] ad au prorata.

prosaic [prəu'zeıık] a prosaïque.

prose [prəuz] n prose f ; (SCOL: translation) thème m.

prosecute ['prɔsıkju:t] vt poursuivre ; **prosecution** [-'kju:ʃən] n poursuites fpl judiciaires ; (accusing side) accusation f ; **prosecutor** n procureur m ; (also: **public ~**) ministère public.

prospect n ['prɔspɛkt] perspective f ; (hope) espoir m, chances fpl // vt,vi [prə'spɛkt] prospecter ; **~s** npl (for work etc) possibilités fpl d'avenir, débouchés mpl ; **prospecting** n prospection f ; **prospective** a (possible) éventuel(le) ; (certain) futur(e) ; **prospector** n prospecteur m.

prospectus [prə'spɛktəs] n prospectus m.

prosper ['prɔspə*] vi prospérer ; **~ity** [-'spɛrıtı] n prospérité f ; **~ous** a prospère.

prostitute ['prɔstıtju:t] n prostituée f.

prostrate ['prɔstreıt] a prosterné(e) ; (fig) prostré(e).

protagonist [prə'tægənıst] n protagoniste m.

protect [prə'tɛkt] *vt* protéger ; ~**ion** *n* protection *f* ; ~**ive** *a* protecteur(trice) ; ~**or** *n* protecteur/trice.

protégé ['prəutɛʒei] *n* protégé *m* ; ~**e** *n* protégée *f*.

protein ['prəuti:n] *n* protéine *f*.

protest ['prəutɛst] *n* protestation *f* // *vi* [prə'tɛst] protester.

Protestant ['prɔtistənt] *a,n* protestant(e).

protocol ['prəutəkɔl] *n* protocole *m*.

prototype ['prəutətaip] *n* prototype *m*.

protracted [prə'træktid] *a* prolongé(e).

protractor [prə'træktə*] *n* rapporteur *m*.

protrude [prə'tru:d] *vi* avancer, dépasser.

protuberance [prə'tju:bərəns] *n* protubérance *f*.

proud [praud] *a* fier(ère) ; (*pej*) orgueilleux(euse) ; ~**ly** *ad* fièrement.

prove [pru:v] *vt* prouver, démontrer // *vi*: **to ~ correct** *etc* s'avérer juste *etc* ; **to ~ o.s.** montrer ce dont on est capable ; **to ~ o.s./itself (to be) useful** *etc* se montrer *or* se révéler utile *etc*.

proverb ['prɔvə:b] *n* proverbe *m* ; ~**ial** [prə'və:biəl] *a* proverbial(e).

provide [prə'vaid] *vt* fournir ; **to ~ sb with sth** fournir qch à qn ; **to ~ for** *vt* (*person*) subvenir aux besoins de ; (*emergency*) prévoir ; ~**d (that)** *cj* à condition que + *sub*.

Providence ['prɔvidəns] *n* Providence *f*.

providing [prə'vaidiŋ] *cj* à condition que + *sub*.

province ['prɔvins] *n* province *f* ; **provincial** [prə'vinʃəl] *a* provincial(e).

provision [prə'viʒən] *n* (*supply*) provision *f* ; (*supplying*) fourniture *f* ; approvisionnement *m* ; (*stipulation*) disposition *f* ; ~**s** *npl* (*food*) provisions *fpl* ; ~**al** *a* provisoire ; ~**ally** *ad* provisoirement.

proviso [prə'vaizəu] *n* condition *f*.

provocation [prɔvə'keiʃən] *n* provocation *f*.

provocative [prə'vɔkətiv] *a* provocateur(trice), provocant(e).

provoke [prə'vəuk] *vt* provoquer ; inciter.

prow [prau] *n* proue *f*.

prowess ['prauis] *n* prouesse *f*.

prowl [praul] *vi* (*also*: ~ **about,** ~ **around**) rôder // *n*: **on the ~** à l'affût ; ~**er** *n* rôdeur/euse.

proximity [prɔk'simiti] *n* proximité *f*.

proxy ['prɔksi] *n* procuration *f* ; **by ~** par procuration.

prudence ['pru:dns] *n* prudence *f*.

prudent ['pru:dnt] *a* prudent(e).

prudish ['pru:diʃ] *a* prude, pudibond(e).

prune [pru:n] *n* pruneau *m* // *vt* élaguer.

pry [prai] *vi*: **to ~ into** fourrer son nez dans.

psalm [sɑ:m] *n* psaume *m*.

pseudo- ['sju:dəu] *prefix* pseudo- ; ~**nym** *n* pseudonyme *m*.

psyche ['saiki] *n* psychisme *m*.

psychiatric [saik'ætrik] *a* psychiatrique.

psychiatrist [sai'kaiətrist] *n* psychiatre *m/f*.

psychiatry [sai'kaiətri] *n* psychiatrie *f*.

psychic ['saikik] *a* (*also*: ~**al**) (méta)psychique ; (*person*) doué(e) de télépathie *or* d'un sixième sens.

psychoanalyse [saikəu'ænəlaiz] *vt* psychanalyser.

psychoanalysis, *pl* **lyses** [saikəuə'nælisis, -si:z] *n* psychanalyse *f*.

psychoanalyst [saikəu'ænəlist] *n* psychanalyste *m/f*.

psychological [saikə'lɔdʒikl] *a* psychologique.

psychologist [sai'kɔlədʒist] *n* psychologue *m/f*.

psychology [sai'kɔlədʒi] *n* psychologie *f*.

psychopath ['saikəupæθ] *n* psychopathe *m/f*.

psychosomatic ['saikəusə'mætik] *a* psychosomatique.

psychotic [sai'kɔtik] *a,n* psychotique (*m/f*).

P.T.O. *abbr* (= *please turn over*) T.S.V.P. (tournez s'il vous plaît).

pub [pʌb] *n* (*abbr of* **public house**) pub *m*.

puberty ['pju:bəti] *n* puberté *f*.

public ['pʌblik] *a* public(ique) // *n* public *m* ; **the general ~** le grand public ; ~ **address system (P.A.)** sonorisation *f* ; haut-parleurs *mpl*.

publican ['pʌblikən] *n* patron *m* de pub.

publication [pʌbli'keiʃən] *n* publication *f*.

public: ~ company *n* société *f* anonyme (*cotée en bourse*) ; ~ **convenience** *n* toilettes *fpl* ; ~ **house** *n* pub *m*.

publicity [pʌb'lisiti] *n* publicité *f*.

publicly ['pʌblikli] *ad* publiquement.

public: ~ opinion *n* opinion publique ; ~ **relations (PR)** *n* relations publiques ; ~ **school** *n* (*Brit*) école privée ; ~**-spirited** *a* qui fait preuve de civisme.

publish ['pʌbliʃ] *vt* publier ; ~**er** *n* éditeur *m* ; ~**ing** *n* (*industry*) édition *f* ; (*of a book*) publication *f*.

puce [pju:s] *a* puce.

puck [pʌk] *n* (*elf*) lutin *m* ; (*ICE HOCKEY*) palet *m*.

pucker ['pʌkə*] *vt* plisser.

pudding ['pudiŋ] *n* dessert *m*, entremets *m* ; (*sausage*) boudin *m*.

puddle ['pʌdl] *n* flaque *f* d'eau.

puerile ['pjuərail] *a* puéril(e).

puff [pʌf] *n* bouffée *f* ; (*also*: **powder ~**) houppette *f* // *vt*: **to ~ one's pipe** tirer sur sa pipe // *vi* sortir par bouffées ; (*pant*) haleter ; **to ~ out smoke** envoyer des bouffées de fumée ; ~**ed** *a* (*col*: *out of breath*) tout(e) essoufflé(e).

puffin ['pʌfin] *n* macareux *m*.

puff pastry ['pʌf'peistri] *n* pâte feuilletée.

puffy ['pʌfi] *a* bouffi(e), boursouflé(e).

pugnacious [pʌg'neiʃəs] *a* pugnace, batailleur(euse).

pull [pul] *n* (*tug*): **to give sth a ~** tirer sur qch ; (*fig*) influence *f* // *vt* tirer ; (*muscle*) se claquer // *vi* tirer ; **to ~ a face** faire une grimace ; **to ~ to pieces** mettre en morceaux ; **to ~ one's punches** ménager son adversaire ; **to ~ one's weight** y mettre du sien ; **to ~ o.s. together** se ressaisir ; **to ~ sb's leg** faire marcher qn ; **to ~ apart** *vt* séparer ; (*break*) mettre en pièces, démantibuler ; **to**

~ **down** vt baisser, abaisser; (house) démolir; (tree) abattre; **to ~ in** vi (AUT: at the kerb) se ranger; (RAIL) entrer en gare; **to ~ off** vt enlever, ôter; (deal etc) conclure; **to ~ out** vi démarrer, partir; se retirer; (AUT: come out of line) déboîter // vt sortir; arracher; (withdraw) retirer; **to ~ round** vi (unconscious person) revenir à soi; (sick person) se rétablir; **to ~ through** vi s'en sortir; **to ~ up** vi (stop) s'arrêter // vt remonter; (uproot) déraciner, arracher; (stop) arrêter.

pulley ['puli] n poulie f.

pull-in ['pulin] n (AUT) parking m.

pullover ['puləuvə*] n pull-over m, tricot m.

pulp [pʌlp] n (of fruit) pulpe f; (for paper) pâte f à papier.

pulpit ['pulpit] n chaire f.

pulsate [pʌl'seit] vi battre, palpiter; (music) vibrer.

pulse [pʌls] n (of blood) pouls m; (of heart) battement m; (of music, engine) vibrations fpl.

pulverize ['pʌlvəraiz] vt pulvériser.

puma ['pju:mə] n puma m.

pummel ['pʌml] vt rouer de coups.

pump [pʌmp] n pompe f; (shoe) escarpin m // vt pomper; (fig: col) faire parler; **to ~ up** gonfler.

pumpkin ['pʌmpkin] n potiron m, citrouille f.

pun [pʌn] n jeu m de mots, calembour m.

punch [pʌntʃ] n (blow) coup m de poing; (fig: force) vivacité f, mordant m; (tool) poinçon m; (drink) punch m // vt (hit): **to ~ sb/sth** donner un coup de poing à qn/sur qch; (make a hole) poinçonner, perforer; **to ~ a hole (in)** faire un trou (dans); **~-drunk** a sonné(e); **~-up** n (col) bagarre f.

punctual ['pʌŋktjuəl] a ponctuel(le); **~ity** [-'æliti] n ponctualité f.

punctuate ['pʌŋktjueit] vt ponctuer; **punctuation** [-'eiʃən] n ponctuation f.

puncture ['pʌŋktʃə*] n crevaison f // vt crever.

pundit ['pʌndit] n individu m qui pontifie, pontife m.

pungent ['pʌndʒənt] a piquant(e); (fig) mordant(e), caustique.

punish ['pʌniʃ] vt punir; **~able** a punissable; **~ment** n punition f, châtiment m.

punt [pʌnt] n (boat) bachot m; (FOOTBALL) coup m de volée.

punter ['pʌntə*] n (gambler) parieur/euse.

puny ['pju:ni] a chétif(ive).

pup [pʌp] n chiot m.

pupil ['pju:pl] n élève m/f.

puppet ['pʌpit] n marionnette f, pantin m.

puppy ['pʌpi] n chiot m, petit chien.

purchase ['pə:tʃis] n achat m // vt acheter; **~r** n acheteur/euse.

pure [pjuə*] a pur(e).

purée ['pjuərei] n purée f.

purge [pə:dʒ] n (MED) purge f; (POL) épuration f, purge // vt purger; (fig) épurer, purger.

purification [pjuərifi'keiʃən] n purification f.

purify ['pjuərifai] vt purifier, épurer.

purist ['pjuərist] n puriste m/f.

puritan ['pjuəritən] n puritain/e; **~ical** [-'tænikl] a puritain(e).

purity ['pjuəriti] n pureté f.

purl [pə:l] n maille f à l'envers // vt tricoter à l'envers.

purple ['pə:pl] a violet(te); cramoisi(e).

purport [pə:'pɔ:t] vi: **to ~ to be/do** prétendre être/faire.

purpose ['pə:pəs] n intention f, but m; **on ~** exprès; **~ful** a déterminé(e), résolu(e); **~ly** ad exprès.

purr [pə:*] n ronronnement m // vi ronronner.

purse [pə:s] n porte-monnaie m inv, bourse f // vt serrer, pincer.

purser ['pə:sə*] n (NAUT) commissaire m du bord.

pursue [pə'sju:] vt poursuivre; **~r** n pursuivant/e.

pursuit [pə'sju:t] n poursuite f; (occupation) occupation f, activité f; **scientific ~s** recherches fpl scientifiques.

purveyor [pə'veiə*] n fournisseur m.

pus [pʌs] n pus m.

push [puʃ] n poussée f; (effort) gros effort; (drive) énergie f // vt pousser; (button) appuyer sur; (thrust): **to ~ sth (into)** enfoncer qch (dans); (fig) mettre en avant, faire de la publicité pour // vi pousser; appuyer; **to ~ aside** vt écarter; **to ~ off** vi (col) filer, ficher le camp; **to ~ on** vi (continue) continuer; **to ~ over** vt renverser; **to ~ through** vt (measure) faire voter; **to ~ up** vt (total, prices) faire monter; **~chair** n poussette f; **~ing** a dynamique; **~over** n (col): it's a **~over** c'est un jeu d'enfant; **~y** a (pej) arriviste.

puss, pussy(-cat) [pus, 'pusi(kæt)] n minet m.

put, pt, pp **put** [put] vt mettre, poser, placer; (say) dire, exprimer; (a question) poser; (estimate) estimer; **to ~ about** vi (NAUT) virer de bord // vt (rumour) faire courir; **to ~ across** vt (ideas etc) communiquer; faire comprendre; **to ~ away** vt (store) ranger; **to ~ back** vt (replace) remettre, replacer; (postpone) remettre; (delay) retarder; **to ~ by** vt (money) mettre de côté, économiser; **to ~ down** vt (parcel etc) poser, déposer; (pay) verser; (in writing) mettre par écrit, inscrire; (suppress: revolt etc) réprimer, faire cesser; (attribute) attribuer; **to ~ forward** vt (ideas) avancer, proposer; (date) avancer; **to ~ in** vt (gas, electricity) installer; (application, complaint) soumettre; **to ~ off** vt (light etc) éteindre; (postpone) remettre à plus tard, ajourner; (discourage) dissuader; **to ~ on** vt (clothes, lipstick etc) mettre; (light etc) allumer; (play etc) monter; (food, meal) servir; (airs, weight) prendre; (brake) mettre; **to ~ on the brakes** freiner; **to ~ out** vt mettre dehors; (one's hand) tendre; (news, rumour) faire courir, répandre; (light etc) éteindre; (person: inconvenience) déranger, gêner; **to ~ up** vt (raise) lever, relever, remonter; (pin up) afficher; (hang) accrocher; (build) construire, ériger; (a tent) monter; (increase) augmenter;

(*accommodate*) loger ; **to ~ up with** *vt fus* supporter.

putrid ['pju:trɪd] *a* putride.

putt [pʌt] *vt* poter (la balle) // *n* coup roulé ; **~er** *n* (*GOLF*) putter *m* ; **~ing green** *n* green *m*.

putty ['pʌtɪ] *n* mastic *m*.

put-up ['putʌp] *a*: **~ job** *n* affaire montée.

puzzle ['pʌzl] *n* énigme *f*, mystère *m* ; (*jigsaw*) puzzle *m* ; (*also*: **crossword ~**) problème *m* de mots croisés // *vt* intriguer, rendre perplexe // *vi* se creuser la tête ; **puzzling** *a* déconcertant(e), inexplicable.

PVC *abbr of polyvinyl chloride.*

pygmy ['pɪgmɪ] *n* pygmée *m/f.*

pyjamas [pɪ'dʒɑːməz] *npl* pyjama *m.*

pylon ['paɪlən] *n* pylône *m.*

pyramid ['pɪrəmɪd] *n* pyramide *f.*

python ['paɪθən] *n* python *m.*

Q

quack [kwæk] *n* (*of duck*) coin-coin *m inv* ; (*pej: doctor*) charlatan *m.*

quad [kwɔd] *abbr of* **quadrangle, quadruplet.**

quadrangle ['kwɔdræŋgl] *n* (*MATH*) quadrilatère *m* ; (*courtyard: abbr:* **quad**) cour *f.*

quadruped ['kwɔdruped] *n* quadrupède *m.*

quadruple [kwɔ'drupl] *a,n* quadruple (*m*) // *vt, vi* quadrupler ; **~t** ['dru:plɪt] *n* quadruplé/e.

quagmire ['kwæɡmaɪə*] *n* bourbier *m.*

quail [kweɪl] *n* (*ZOOL*) caille *f.*

quaint [kweɪnt] *a* bizarre ; (*old-fashioned*) désuet(ète) ; au charme vieillot, pittoresque.

quake [kweɪk] *vi* trembler // *n abbr of* **earthquake.**

Quaker ['kweɪkə*] *n* quaker/esse.

qualification [kwɔlɪfɪ'keɪʃən] *n* (*degree etc*) diplôme *m* ; (*ability*) compétence *f*, qualification *f* ; (*limitation*) réserve *f*, restriction *f.*

qualified ['kwɔlɪfaɪd] *a* diplômé(e) ; (*able*) compétent(e), qualifié(e) ; (*limited*) conditionnel(le).

qualify ['kwɔlɪfaɪ] *vt* qualifier ; (*limit: statement*) apporter des réserves à // *vi*: **to ~ (as)** obtenir son diplôme (de) ; **to ~ (for)** remplir les conditions requises (pour) ; (*SPORT*) se qualifier (pour).

qualitative ['kwɔlɪtətɪv] *a* qualitatif(ive).

quality ['kwɔlɪtɪ] *n* qualité *f* // *cpd* de qualité ; **the ~ papers** la presse d'information.

qualm [kwɑːm] *n* doute *m* ; scrupule *m.*

quandary ['kwɔndrɪ] *n*: **in a ~** devant un dilemme, dans l'embarras.

quantitative ['kwɔntɪtətɪv] *a* quantitatif(ive).

quantity ['kwɔntɪtɪ] *n* quantité *f* ; **~ surveyor** *n* métreur *m* vérificateur.

quarantine ['kwɔrntɪːn] *n* quarantaine *f.*

quarrel ['kwɔrl] *n* querelle *f*, dispute *f* // *vi* se disputer, se quereller ; **~some** *a* querelleur(euse).

quarry ['kwɔrɪ] *n* (*for stone*) carrière *f* ;

(*animal*) proie *f*, gibier *m* // *vt* (*marble etc*) extraire.

quart [kwɔːt] *n* ≈ litre *m* (= *2 pints*).

quarter ['kwɔːtə*] *n* quart *m* ; (*of year*) trimestre *m* ; (*district*) quartier *m* // *vt* partager en quartiers or en quatre ; (*MIL*) caserner, cantonner ; **~s** *npl* logement *m* ; (*MIL*) quartiers *mpl*, cantonnement *m* ; **a ~ of an hour** un quart d'heure ; **~-deck** *n* (*NAUT*) plage *f* arrière ; **~ final** *n* quart *m* de finale ; **~ly** *a* trimestriel(le) // *ad* tous les trois mois ; **~master** *n* (*MIL*) intendant *m* militaire de troisième classe ; (*NAUT*) maître *m* de manœuvre.

quartet(te) [kwɔː'tɛt] *n* quatuor *m* ; (*jazz players*) quartette *m.*

quartz [kwɔːts] *n* quartz *m* ; **~ watch** *n* montre *f* à quartz.

quash [kwɔʃ] *vt* (*verdict*) annuler, casser.

quasi- ['kweɪzaɪ] *prefix* quasi- + *noun* ; quasi, presque + *adjective.*

quaver ['kweɪvə*] *n* (*MUS*) croche *f* // *vi* trembler.

quay [kiː] *n* (*also*: **~side**) quai *m.*

queasy ['kwiːzɪ] *a* (*stomach*) délicat(e) ; **to feel ~** avoir mal au cœur.

queen [kwiːn] *n* (*gen*) reine *f* ; (*CARDS etc*) dame *f* ; **~ mother** *n* reine mère *f.*

queer [kwɪə*] *a* étrange, curieux(euse) ; (*suspicious*) louche ; (*sick*): **I feel ~** je ne me sens pas bien // *n* (*col*) homosexuel *m.*

quell [kwɛl] *vt* réprimer, étouffer.

quench [kwɛntʃ] *vt* (*flames*) éteindre ; **to ~ one's thirst** se désaltérer.

query ['kwɪərɪ] *n* question *f* ; (*doubt*) doute *m* ; (*question mark*) point *m* d'interrogation // *vt* mettre en question or en doute.

quest [kwɛst] *n* recherche *f*, quête *f.*

question ['kwɛstʃən] *n* question *f* // *vt* (*person*) interroger ; (*plan, idea*) mettre en question or en doute ; **it's a ~ of doing** il s'agit de faire ; **there's some ~ of doing** il est question de faire ; **beyond ~** *ad* sans aucun doute ; **out of the ~** hors de question ; **~able** *a* discutable ; **~ing** *a* interrogateur(trice) // *n* interrogatoire *m* ; **~ mark** *n* point *m* d'interrogation.

questionnaire [kwɛstʃə'nɛə*] *n* questionnaire *m.*

queue [kjuː] *n* queue *f*, file *f* // *vi* faire la queue.

quibble ['kwɪbl] *vi* ergoter, chicaner.

quick [kwɪk] *a* rapide ; (*reply*) prompt(e), rapide ; (*mind*) vif(vive) // *ad* vite, rapidement // *n*: **cut to the ~** (*fig*) touché(e) au vif ; **be ~!** dépêche-toi! ; **~en** *vt* accélérer, presser ; (*rouse*) stimuler // *vi* s'accélérer, devenir plus rapide ; **~lime** *n* chaux vive ; **~ly** *ad* vite, rapidement ; **~ness** *n* rapidité *f* ; promptitude *f* ; vivacité *f* ; **~sand** *n* sables mouvants ; **~step** *n* (*dance*) fox-trot *m* ; **~-witted** *a* à l'esprit vif.

quid [kwɪd] *n*, *pl inv* (*Brit: col*) livre *f.*

quiet ['kwaɪət] *a* tranquille, calme ; (*ceremony, colour*) discret(ète) // *n* tranquillité *f*, calme *m* ; **keep ~!** tais-toi! ; **on the ~** en secret, en cachette ; **~en** (*also*: **~en down**) *vi* se calmer, s'apaiser // *vt* calmer, apaiser ; **~ly** *ad* tranquillement, calmement ;

discrètement; **~ness** n tranquillité f, calme m; silence m.
quill [kwɪl] n plume f (d'oie).
quilt [kwɪlt] n édredon m; **(continental) ~** n couverturé f édredon; **~ing** n ouatine f; molletonnage m.
quin [kwɪn] abbr of **quintuplet**.
quince [kwɪns] n coing m; (tree) cognassier m.
quinine [kwɪ'niːn] n quinine f.
quintet(te) [kwɪn'tet] n quintette m.
quintuplet [kwɪn'tjuːplɪt] n quintuplé(e).
quip [kwɪp] n remarque piquante or spirituelle, pointe f // vt: ... he **~ped** ... lança-t-il.
quirk [kwəːk] n bizarrerie f.
quit, pt, pp **quit** or **quitted** [kwɪt] vt quitter // vi (give up) abandonner, renoncer; (resign) démissionner; **to ~ doing** arrêter de faire; **notice to ~** congé m (signifié au locataire).
quite [kwaɪt] ad (rather) assez, plutôt; (entirely) complètement, tout à fait; **I ~ understand** je comprends très bien; **~ a few of them** un assez grand nombre d'entre eux; **~ (so)!** exactement!
quits [kwɪts] a: **~ (with)** quitte (envers).
quiver ['kwɪvə*] vi trembler, frémir // n (for arrows) carquois m.
quiz [kwɪz] n (game) jeu-concours m; test m de connaissances // vt interroger; **~zical** a narquois(e).
quoits [kwɔɪts] npl jeu m du palet.
quorum ['kwɔːrəm] n quorum m.
quota ['kwəʊtə] n quota m.
quotation [kwəʊ'teɪʃən] n citation f; (of shares etc) cote f, cours m; (estimate) devis m; **~ marks** npl guillemets mpl.
quote [kwəʊt] n citation f // vt (sentence) citer; (price) donner, fixer; (shares) coter // vi: **to ~ from** citer; **to ~ for a job** établir un devis pour des travaux.
quotient ['kwəʊʃənt] n quotient m.

R

rabbi ['ræbaɪ] n rabbin m.
rabbit ['ræbɪt] n lapin m; **~ hole** n terrier m (de lapin); **~ hutch** n clapier m.
rabble ['ræbl] n (pej) populace f.
rabid ['ræbɪd] a enragé(e).
rabies ['reɪbiːz] n rage f.
RAC n abbr of Royal Automobile Club.
raccoon [rə'kuːn] n raton m laveur.
race [reɪs] n race f; (competition, rush) course f // vt (person) faire la course avec; (horse) faire courir; (engine) emballer // vi courir; **~course** n champ m de courses; **~horse** n cheval m de course; **~ relations** npl rapports mpl entre les races; **~track** n piste f.
racial ['reɪʃl] a racial(e); **~ discrimination** n discrimination raciale; **~ism** n racisme m; **~ist** a, n raciste m/f.
racing ['reɪsɪŋ] n courses fpl; **~ car** n voiture f de course; **~ driver** n pilote m de course.
racist ['reɪsɪst] a,n (pej) raciste (m/f).
rack [ræk] n (also: **luggage ~**) filet m à bagages; (also: **roof ~**) galerie f // vt tourmenter; **magazine ~** n porte-revues

m inv; **shoe ~** n étagère f à chaussures; **toast ~** n porte-toast m.
racket ['rækɪt] n (for tennis) raquette f; (noise) tapage m; vacarme m; (swindle) escroquerie f; (organized crime) racket m.
racoon [rə'kuːn] n = **raccoon**.
racquet ['rækɪt] n raquette f.
racy ['reɪsɪ] a plein(e) de verve; osé(e).
radar ['reɪdɑː*] n radar m // cpd radar inv.
radiance ['reɪdɪəns] n éclat m, rayonnement m.
radiant ['reɪdɪənt] a rayonnant(e); (PHYSICS) radiant(e).
radiate ['reɪdɪeɪt] vt (heat) émettre, dégager // vi (lines) rayonner.
radiation [reɪdɪ'eɪʃən] n rayonnement m; (radioactive) radiation f.
radiator ['reɪdɪeɪtə*] n radiateur m; **~ cap** n bouchon m de radiateur.
radical ['rædɪkl] a radical(e).
radii ['reɪdɪaɪ] npl of **radius**.
radio ['reɪdɪəʊ] n radio f; **on the ~** à la radio; **~ station** station f de radio.
radio... ['reɪdɪəʊ] prefix: **~active** a radioactif(ive); **~activity** n radioactivité f; **~grapher** [-'ɔgrəfə*] n radiologue m/f (technicien); **~graphy** [-'ɔgrəfɪ] n radiographie f; **~logy** [-'ɔlədʒɪ] n radiologie f; **~therapist** n radiothérapeute m/f.
radish ['rædɪʃ] n radis m.
radium ['reɪdɪəm] n radium m.
radius, pl **radii** ['reɪdɪəs, -ɪaɪ] n rayon m; (ANAT) radius m.
raffia ['ræfɪə] n raphia m.
raffish ['ræfɪʃ] a dissolu(e); canaille.
raffle ['ræfl] n tombola f.
raft [rɑːft] n (also: **life ~**) radeau m; (logs) train m de flottage.
rafter ['rɑːftə*] n chevron m.
rag [ræg] n chiffon m; (pej: newspaper) feuille f, torchon m; (for charity) attractions organisées par les étudiants au profit d'œuvres de charité // vt chahuter, mettre en boîte; **~s** npl haillons mpl; **~-and-bone man** n chiffonnier m; **~bag** n (fig) ramassis m.
rage [reɪdʒ] n (fury) rage f, fureur f // vi (person) être fou(folle) de rage; (storm) faire rage, être déchaîné(e); **it's all the ~** cela fait fureur.
ragged ['rægɪd] a (edge) inégal(e), qui accroche; (cuff) effiloché(e); (appearance) déguenillé(e).
raid [reɪd] n (MIL) raid m; (criminal) hold-up m inv; (by police) descente f, rafle f // vt faire un raid sur or un hold-up dans or une descente dans; **~er** n malfaiteur m; (plane) bombardier m.
rail [reɪl] n (on stair) rampe f; (on bridge, balcony) balustrade f; (of ship) bastingage m; (for train) rail m; **~s** npl rails mpl, voie ferrée; **by ~** par chemin de fer; **~ing(s)** n(pl) grille f; **~road** n (US), **~way** n chemin m de fer; **~wayman** n cheminot m; **~way station** n gare f.
rain [reɪn] n pluie f // vi pleuvoir; **in the ~** sous la pluie; **~bow** n arc-en-ciel m; **~coat** n imperméable m; **~drop** n goutte f de pluie; **~fall** n chute f de pluie; (measurement) hauteur f des précipitations;

~**proof** a imperméable ; ~**storm** n pluie torrentielle ; ~**y** a pluvieux(euse).

raise [reɪz] n augmentation f // vt (lift) lever ; hausser ; (build) ériger ; (increase) augmenter ; (a protest, doubt) provoquer, causer ; (a question) soulever ; (cattle, family) élever ; (crop) faire pousser ; (army, funds) rassembler ; (loan) obtenir ; **to ~ one's voice** élever la voix.

raisin [ˈreɪzn] n raisin sec.

raj [rɑːdʒ] n empire m (aux Indes).

rajah [ˈrɑːdʒə] n radja(h) m.

rake [reɪk] n (tool) râteau m ; (person) débauché m // vt (garden) ratisser ; (fire) tisonner ; (with machine gun) balayer ; **to ~ through** (fig: search) fouiller (dans).

rakish [ˈreɪkɪʃ] a dissolu(e) ; cavalier(ère).

rally [ˈrælɪ] n (POL etc) meeting m, rassemblement m ; (AUT) rallye m ; (TENNIS) échange m // vt rassembler, rallier // vi se rallier ; (sick person) aller mieux ; (Stock Exchange) reprendre ; **to ~ round** vt fus se rallier à ; venir en aide à.

ram [ræm] n bélier m // vt enfoncer ; (soil) tasser ; (crash into) emboutir, percuter ; éperonner.

ramble [ˈræmbl] n randonnée f // vi (pej: also: ~ **on**) discourir, pérorer ; ~**r** n promeneur/euse, randonneur/euse ; (BOT) rosier grimpant ; **rambling** a (speech) décousu(e) ; (BOT) grimpant(e).

ramification [ræmɪfɪˈkeɪʃən] n ramification f.

ramp [ræmp] n (incline) rampe f ; dénivellation f ; (in garage) pont m.

rampage [ræmˈpeɪdʒ] n: **to be on the ~** se déchaîner // vi: **they went rampaging through the town** ils ont envahi les rues et ont tout saccagé sur leur passage.

rampant [ˈræmpənt] a (disease etc) qui sévit.

rampart [ˈræmpɑːt] n rempart m.

ramshackle [ˈræmʃækl] a (house) délabré(e) ; (car etc) déglingué(e).

ran [ræn] pt of **run**.

ranch [rɑːntʃ] n ranch m ; ~**er** n propriétaire m de ranch ; cowboy m.

rancid [ˈrænsɪd] a rance.

rancour, rancor (US) [ˈrænkə*] n rancune f.

random [ˈrændəm] a fait(e) or établi(e) au hasard // n: **at ~** au hasard.

randy [ˈrændɪ] a (col) excité(e) ; lubrique.

rang [ræŋ] pt of **ring**.

range [reɪndʒ] n (of mountains) chaîne f ; (of missile, voice) portée f ; (of products) choix m, gamme f ; (MIL: also: **shooting ~**) champ m de tir ; (also: **kitchen ~**) fourneau m (de cuisine) // vt (place) mettre en rang, placer ; (roam) parcourir // vi: **to ~ over** couvrir ; **to ~ from ... to** aller de ... à ; ~**r** n garde m forestier.

rank [ræŋk] n rang m ; (MIL) grade m ; (also: **taxi ~**) station f de taxis // vi: **to ~ among** compter or se classer parmi // a (qui sent) fort(e) ; extrême ; **the ~s** (MIL) la troupe ; **the ~ and file** (fig) la masse, la base.

rankle [ˈræŋkl] vi (insult) rester sur le cœur.

ransack [ˈrænsæk] vt fouiller (à fond) ; (plunder) piller.

ransom [ˈrænsəm] n rançon f ; **to hold sb to ~** (fig) exercer un chantage sur qn.

rant [rænt] vi fulminer ; ~**ing** n invectives fpl.

rap [ræp] n petit coup sec ; tape f // vt frapper sur or à ; taper sur.

rape [reɪp] n viol m // vt violer.

rapid [ˈræpɪd] a rapide ; ~**s** npl (GEO) rapides mpl ; ~**ity** [rəˈpɪdɪtɪ] n rapidité f.

rapist [ˈreɪpɪst] n auteur m d'un viol.

rapport [ræˈpɔː*] n entente f.

rapture [ˈræptʃə*] n extase f, ravissement m ; **to go into ~s over** s'extasier sur ; **rapturous** a extasié(e) ; frénétique.

rare [rɛə*] a rare ; (CULIN: steak) saignant(e).

rarebit [ˈrɛəbɪt] n see **Welsh**.

rarefied [ˈrɛərɪfaɪd] a (air, atmosphere) raréfié(e).

rarely [ˈrɛəlɪ] ad rarement.

rarity [ˈrɛərɪtɪ] n rareté f.

rascal [ˈrɑːskl] n vaurien m.

rash [ræʃ] a imprudent(e), irréfléchi(e) // n (MED) rougeur f, éruption f.

rasher [ˈræʃə*] n fine tranche (de lard).

rasp [rɑːsp] n (tool) lime f.

raspberry [ˈrɑːzbərɪ] n framboise f ; ~ **bush** n framboisier m.

rasping [ˈrɑːspɪŋ] a: ~ **noise** grincement m.

rat [ræt] n rat m.

ratable [ˈreɪtəbl] a = **rateable**.

ratchet [ˈrætʃɪt] n: ~ **wheel** roue f à rochet.

rate [reɪt] n (ratio) taux m, pourcentage m ; (speed) vitesse f, rythme m ; (price) tarif m // vt classer ; évaluer ; **to ~ sb/sth as** considérer qn/qch comme ; **to ~ sb/sth among** classer qn/qch parmi ; ~**s** npl (Brit) impôts locaux ; (fees) tarifs mpl ; ~**able value** n valeur locative imposable ; ~ **of exchange** n taux m or cours m du change ; ~ **of flow** n débit m ; ~**payer** n contribuable m/f (payant les impôts locaux).

rather [ˈrɑːðə*] ad plutôt ; **it's ~ expensive** c'est assez cher ; (too much) c'est un peu cher ; **I would** or **I'd ~ go** j'aimerais mieux or je préférerais partir ; **I had ~ go** il vaudrait mieux que je parte.

ratification [rætɪfɪˈkeɪʃən] n ratification f.

ratify [ˈrætɪfaɪ] vt ratifier.

rating [ˈreɪtɪŋ] n classement m ; cote f ; (NAUT: category) classe f ; (: sailor) matelot m.

ratio [ˈreɪʃɪəu] n proportion f ; **in the ~ of 100 to 1** dans la proportion de 100 contre 1.

ration [ˈræʃən] n (gen pl) ration(s) f(pl) // vt rationner.

rational [ˈræʃənl] a raisonnable, sensé(e) ; (solution, reasoning) logique ; (MED) lucide ; ~**e** [-ˈnɑːl] n raisonnement m ; justification f ; ~**ize** vt rationaliser ; (conduct) essayer d'expliquer or de motiver ; ~**ly** ad raisonnablement ; logiquement.

rationing [ˈræʃnɪŋ] n rationnement m.

rat poison [ˈrætpɔɪzn] n mort-aux-rats f inv.

rat race ['rætreɪs] *n* foire *f* d'empoigne.

rattle ['rætl] *n* cliquetis *m*; (*louder*) bruit *m* de ferraille; (*object: of baby*) hochet *m*; (: *of sports fan*) crécelle *f* // *vi* cliqueter; faire un bruit de ferraille *or* du bruit // *vt* agiter (bruyamment); **~snake** *n* serpent *m* à sonnettes.

raucous ['rɔːkəs] *a* rauque; **~ly** *ad* d'une voix rauque.

ravage ['rævɪdʒ] *vt* ravager; **~s** *npl* ravages *mpl*.

rave [reɪv] *vi* (*in anger*) s'emporter; (*with enthusiasm*) s'extasier; (MED) délirer.

raven ['reɪvən] *n* corbeau *m*.

ravenous ['rævənəs] *a* affamé(e).

ravine [rə'viːn] *n* ravin *m*.

raving ['reɪvɪŋ] *a*: **~ lunatic** *n* fou furieux/folle furieuse.

ravioli [rævɪ'əʊlɪ] *n* ravioli *mpl*.

ravish ['rævɪʃ] *vt* ravir; **~ing** *a* enchanteur(eresse).

raw [rɔː] *a* (*uncooked*) cru(e); (*not processed*) brut(e); (*sore*) à vif, irrité(e); (*inexperienced*) inexpérimenté(e); **~ material** *n* matière première.

ray [reɪ] *n* rayon *m*; **~ of hope** *n* lueur *f* d'espoir.

rayon ['reɪɔn] *n* rayonne *f*.

raze [reɪz] *vt* raser, détruire.

razor ['reɪzə*] *n* rasoir *m*; **~ blade** *n* lame *f* de rasoir.

Rd *abbr of* **road**.

re [riː] *prep* concernant.

reach [riːtʃ] *n* portée *f*, atteinte *f*; (*of river etc*) étendue *f* // *vt* atteindre; parvenir à // *vi* s'étendre; **out of/within ~** (*object*) hors de/à portée; **within easy ~ (of)** (*place*) à proximité (de), proche (de); **to ~ out** *vi*: **to ~ out for** allonger le bras pour prendre.

react [riː'ækt] *vi* réagir; **~ion** [-'ækʃən] *n* réaction *f*; **~ionary** [-'ækʃənrɪ] *a,n* réactionnaire (*m/f*).

reactor [riː'æktə*] *n* réacteur *m*.

read, *pt,pp* **read** [riːd, rɛd] *vi* lire // *vt* lire; (*understand*) comprendre, interpréter; (*study*) étudier; (*subj: instrument etc*) indiquer, marquer; **to ~ out** *vt* lire à haute voix; **~able** *a* facile ou agréable à lire; **~er** *n* lecteur/trice; (*book*) livre *m* de lecture; (*at university*) maître *m* de conférences; **~ership** *n* (*of paper etc*) nombre *m* de lecteurs *mpl*.

readily ['rɛdɪlɪ] *ad* volontiers, avec empressement; (*easily*) facilement.

readiness ['rɛdɪnɪs] *n* empressement *m*; **in ~** (*prepared*) prêt(e).

reading ['riːdɪŋ] *n* lecture *f*; (*understanding*) interprétation *f*; (*on instrument*) indications *fpl*; **~ lamp** *n* lampe *f* de bureau; **~ room** *n* salle *f* de lecture.

readjust [riːə'dʒʌst] *vt* rajuster; (*instrument*) régler de nouveau // *vi* (*person*): **to ~ (to)** se réadapter (à).

ready ['rɛdɪ] *a* prêt(e); (*willing*) prêt, disposé(e); (*quick*) prompt(e); (*available*) disponible // *ad*: **~-cooked** tout(e) cuit(e) (d'avance) // *n*: **at the ~** (MIL) prêt à faire feu; (*fig*) tout(e) prêt(e); **~ cash** *n* (argent *m*) liquide *m*; **~-made** *a* tout(e) fait(e); **~-mix** *n* (*for cakes etc*) préparation *f* en

sachet; **~ reckoner** *n* barème *m*; **~-to-wear** *a* en prêt-à-porter.

real [rɪəl] *a* réel(le); véritable; **in ~ terms** dans la réalité; **~ estate** *n* biens fonciers *or* immobiliers; **~ism** *n* (*also* ART) réalisme *m*; **~ist** *n* réaliste *m/f*; **~istic** [-'lɪstɪk] *a* réaliste.

reality [riː'ælɪtɪ] *n* réalité *f*; **in ~** en réalité, en fait.

realization [rɪəlaɪ'zeɪʃən] *n* prise *f* de conscience; réalisation *f*.

realize ['rɪəlaɪz] *vt* (*understand*) se rendre compte de; (*a project*, COMM: *asset*) réaliser.

really ['rɪəlɪ] *ad* vraiment.

realm [rɛlm] *n* royaume *m*.

ream [riːm] *n* rame *f* (*de papier*).

reap [riːp] *vt* moissonner; (*fig*) récolter; **~er** *n* (*machine*) moissonneuse *f*.

reappear [riːə'pɪə*] *vi* réapparaître, reparaître; **~ance** *n* réapparition *f*.

reapply [riːə'plaɪ] *vi*: **to ~ for** faire une nouvelle demande d'emploi concernant; reposer sa candidature à.

rear [rɪə*] *a* de derrière, arrière *inv*; (AUT: *wheel etc*) arrière // *n* arrière *m*, derrière *m* // *vt* (*cattle, family*) élever // *vi* (*also:* **~ up**) (*animal*) se cabrer; **~-engined** *a* (AUT) avec moteur à l'arrière; **~guard** *n* arrière-garde *f*.

rearm [riː'ɑːm] *vt, vi* réarmer; **~ament** *n* réarmement *m*.

rearrange [riːə'reɪndʒ] *vt* réarranger.

rear-view ['rɪəvjuː] *a*: **~ mirror** *n* (AUT) rétroviseur *m*.

reason ['riːzn] *n* raison *f* // *vi*: **to ~ with sb** raisonner qn, faire entendre raison à qn; **to have ~ to think** avoir lieu de penser; **it stands to ~ that** il va sans dire que; **~able** *a* raisonnable; (*not bad*) acceptable; **~ably** *ad* raisonnablement; **one can ~ably assume that ...** on est fondé à *or* il est permis de supposer que ...; **~ed** *a* (*argument*) raisonné(e); **~ing** *n* raisonnement *m*.

reassemble [riːə'sɛmbl] *vt* rassembler; (*machine*) remonter.

reassert [riːə'səːt] *vt* réaffirmer.

reassure [riːə'ʃuə*] *vt* rassurer; **to ~ sb of** donner à qn l'assurance répétée que; **reassuring** *a* rassurant(e).

reawakening [riːə'weɪknɪŋ] *n* réveil *m*.

rebate ['riːbeɪt] *n* (*on product*) rabais *m*; (*on tax etc*) dégrèvement *m*; (*repayment*) remboursement *m*.

rebel *n* ['rɛbl] rebelle *m/f* // *vi* [rɪ'bɛl] se rebeller, se révolter; **~lion** *n* rébellion *f*, révolte *f*; **~lious** *a* rebelle.

rebirth [riː'bəːθ] *n* renaissance *f*.

rebound *vi* [rɪ'baʊnd] (*ball*) rebondir; (*bullet*) ricocher // *n* ['riːbaʊnd] rebond *m*; ricochet *m*.

rebuff [rɪ'bʌf] *n* rebuffade *f* // *vt* repousser.

rebuild [riː'bɪld] *vt irg* reconstruire.

rebuke [rɪ'bjuːk] *n* réprimande *f*, reproche *m* // *vt* réprimander.

rebut [rɪ'bʌt] *vt* réfuter; **~tal** *n* réfutation *f*.

recall [rɪ'kɔːl] *vt* rappeler; (*remember*) se rappeler, se souvenir de // *n* rappel *m*; **beyond ~** *a* irrévocable.

recant [rɪ'kænt] *vi* se rétracter ; (*REL*) abjurer.

recap ['riːkæp] *n* récapitulation *f* // *vt, vi* récapituler.

recapture [riː'kæptʃə*] *vt* reprendre ; (*atmosphere*) recréer.

recede [rɪ'siːd] *vi* s'éloigner ; reculer ; redescendre ; **receding** *a* (*forehead, chin*) fuyant(e) ; **receding hairline** *n* front dégarni.

receipt [rɪ'siːt] *n* (*document*) reçu *m* ; (*for parcel etc*) accusé *m* de réception ; (*act of receiving*) réception *f* ; **~s** *npl* (*COMM*) recettes *fpl*.

receive [rɪ'siːv] *vt* recevoir ; (*guest*) recevoir, accueillir.

receiver [rɪ'siːvə*] *n* (*TEL*) récepteur *m*, combiné *m* ; (*of stolen goods*) receleur *m* ; (*COMM*) administrateur *m* judiciaire.

recent ['riːsnt] *a* récent(e) ; **~ly** *ad* récemment ; **as ~ly as** pas plus tard que.

receptacle [rɪ'sɛptɪkl] *n* récipient *m*.

reception [rɪ'sɛpʃən] *n* réception *f* ; (*welcome*) accueil *m*, réception ; **~ desk** *n* réception ; **~ist** *n* réceptionniste *m/f*.

receptive [rɪ'sɛptɪv] *a* réceptif(ive).

recess [rɪ'sɛs] *n* (*in room*) renfoncement *m* ; (*for bed*) alcôve *f* ; (*secret place*) recoin *m* ; (*POL etc: holiday*) vacances *fpl*.

recharge [riː'tʃɑːdʒ] *vt* (*battery*) recharger.

recipe ['rɛsɪpɪ] *n* recette *f*.

recipient [rɪ'sɪpɪənt] *n* bénéficiaire *m/f* ; (*of letter*) destinataire *m/f*.

reciprocal [rɪ'sɪprəkl] *a* réciproque.

reciprocate [rɪ'sɪprəkeɪt] *vt* retourner, offrir en retour.

recital [rɪ'saɪtl] *n* récital *m*.

recite [rɪ'saɪt] *vt* (*poem*) réciter ; (*complaints etc*) énumérer.

reckless ['rɛkləs] *a* (*driver etc*) imprudent(e) ; (*spender etc*) insouciant(e) ; **~ly** *ad* imprudemment ; avec insouciance.

reckon ['rɛkən] *vt* (*count*) calculer, compter ; (*consider*) considérer, estimer ; (*think*): **I ~ that ...** je pense que ... ; **to ~ on** *vt fus* compter sur, s'attendre à ; **~ing** *n* compte *m*, calcul *m* ; estimation *f* ; **the day of ~ing** le jour du Jugement.

reclaim [rɪ'kleɪm] *vt* (*land*) amender ; (*: from sea*) assécher ; (*: from forest*) défricher ; (*demand back*) réclamer (le remboursement or la restitution de) ; **reclamation** [rɛklə'meɪʃən] *n* amendement *m* ; assèchement *m* ; défrichement *m*.

recline [rɪ'klaɪn] *vi* être allongé(e) *or* étendu(e) ; **reclining** *a* (*seat*) à dossier réglable.

recluse [rɪ'kluːs] *n* reclus/e, ermite *m*.

recognition [rɛkəg'nɪʃən] *n* reconnaissance *f* ; **to gain ~** être reconnu(e) ; **transformed beyond ~** méconnaissable.

recognizable ['rɛkəgnaɪzəbl] *a*: **~ (by)** reconnaissable (à).

recognize ['rɛkəgnaɪz] *vt*: **to ~ (by/as)** reconnaître (à/comme étant).

recoil [rɪ'kɔɪl] *vi* (*gun*) reculer ; (*spring*) se détendre ; (*person*): **to ~ (from)** reculer (devant) // *n* recul *m* ; détente *f*.

recollect [rɛkə'lɛkt] *vt* se rappeler, se souvenir de ; **~ion** [-'lɛkʃən] *n* souvenir *m*.

recommend [rɛkə'mɛnd] *vt* recommander ; **~ation** [-'deɪʃən] *n* recommandation *f*.

recompense ['rɛkəmpɛns] *vt* récompenser ; (*compensate*) dédommager.

reconcilable ['rɛkənsaɪləbl] *a* (*ideas*) conciliable.

reconcile ['rɛkənsaɪl] *vt* (*two people*) réconcilier ; (*two facts*) concilier, accorder ; **to ~ o.s. to** se résigner à ; **reconciliation** [-sɪlɪ'eɪʃən] *n* réconciliation *f* ; conciliation *f*.

recondition [riːkən'dɪʃən] *vt* remettre à neuf ; réviser entièrement.

reconnaissance [rɪ'kɔnɪsns] *n* (*MIL*) reconnaissance *f*.

reconnoitre, reconnoiter (*US*) [rɛkə'nɔɪtə*] (*MIL*) *vt* reconnaître // *vi* faire une reconnaissance.

reconsider [riːkən'sɪdə*] *vt* reconsidérer.

reconstitute [riː'kɔnstɪtjuːt] *vt* reconstituer.

reconstruct [riːkən'strʌkt] *vt* (*building*) reconstruire ; (*crime*) reconstituer ; **~ion** [-kʃən] *n* reconstruction *f* ; reconstitution *f*.

record *n* ['rɛkɔːd] rapport *m*, récit *m* ; (*of meeting etc*) procès-verbal *m* ; (*register*) registre *m* ; (*file*) dossier *m* ; (*also: police ~*) casier *m* judiciaire ; (*MUS: disc*) disque *m* ; (*SPORT*) record *m* // *vt* [rɪ'kɔːd] (*set down*) noter ; (*relate*) rapporter ; (*MUS: song etc*) enregistrer ; **in ~ time** dans un temps record *inv* ; **to keep a ~ of** noter ; **off the ~** *a* officieux(euse) ; **to keep the ~ straight** (*fig*) mettre les choses au point ; **~ card** *n* (*in file*) fiche *f* ; **~er** *n* (*LAW*) avocat nommé à la fonction de juge ; (*MUS*) flûte *f* à bec ; **~-holder** *n* (*SPORT*) détenteur/trice du record ; **~ing** *n* (*MUS*) enregistrement *m* ; **~ library** *n* discothèque *f* ; **~ player** *n* électrophone *m*.

recount [rɪ'kaunt] *vt* raconter.

re-count *n* ['riːkaunt] (*POL: of votes*) pointage *m* // *vt* [riː'kaunt] recompter.

recoup [rɪ'kuːp] *vt*: **to ~ one's losses** récupérer ce qu'on a perdu, se refaire.

recourse [rɪ'kɔːs] *n* recours *m* ; expédient *m* ; **to have ~ to** recourir à, avoir recours à.

recover [rɪ'kʌvə*] *vt* récupérer // *vi* (*from illness*) se rétablir ; (*from shock*) se remettre ; (*country*) se redresser.

re-cover [riː'kʌvə*] *vt* (*chair etc*) recouvrir.

recovery [rɪ'kʌvərɪ] *n* récupération *f* ; rétablissement *m* ; redressement *m*.

recreate [riːkrɪ'eɪt] *vt* recréer.

recreation [rɛkrɪ'eɪʃən] *n* récréation *f* ; détente *f* ; **~al** *a* pour la détente, récréatif(ive).

recrimination [rɪkrɪmɪ'neɪʃən] *n* récrimination *f*.

recruit [rɪ'kruːt] *n* recrue *f* // *vt* recruter ; **~ing office** *n* bureau *m* de recrutement ; **~ment** *n* recrutement *m*.

rectangle ['rɛktæŋgl] *n* rectangle *m* ; **rectangular** [-'tæŋgjulə*] *a* rectangulaire.

rectify ['rɛktɪfaɪ] *vt* (*error*) rectifier, corriger ; (*omission*) réparer.

rector ['rɛktə*] *n* (*REL*) pasteur *m* ; **rectory** *n* presbytère *m*.

recuperate [rɪ'kju:pəreɪt] vi récupérer ; (from illness) se rétablir.

recur [rɪ'kə:*] vi se reproduire ; (idea, opportunity) se retrouver ; (symptoms) réapparaître ; ~**rence** n répétition f ; réapparition f ~**rent** a périodique, fréquent(e) ; ~**ring** a (MATH) périodique.

red [rɛd] n rouge m ; (POL: pej) rouge m/f // a rouge ; **in the** ~ (account) à découvert ; (business) en déficit ; ~ **carpet treatment** n réception f en grande pompe ; **R~ Cross** n Croix-Rouge f ; ~ **currant** n groseille f (rouge) ; ~**den** vt,vi rougir ; ~**dish** a rougeâtre ; (hair) plutôt roux(rousse).

redecorate [ri:'dɛkəreɪt] vt refaire à neuf, repeindre et retapisser ; **redecoration** [-'reɪʃən] n remise f à neuf.

redeem [rɪ'di:m] vt (debt) rembourser ; (sth in pawn) dégager ; (fig, also REL) racheter ; ~**ing** a (feature) qui sauve, qui rachète (le reste).

redeploy [ri:dɪ'plɔɪ] vt (resources) réorganiser.

red-haired [rɛd'hɛəd] a roux(rousse).

red-handed [rɛd'hændɪd] a: **to be caught** ~ être pris(e) en flagrant délit or la main dans le sac.

redhead ['rɛdhɛd] n roux/rousse.

red herring ['rɛd'hɛrɪŋ] n (fig) diversion f, fausse piste.

red-hot [rɛd'hɔt] a chauffé(e) au rouge, brûlant(e).

redirect [ri:daɪ'rɛkt] vt (mail) faire suivre.

redistribute [ri:dɪ'strɪbju:t] vt redistribuer.

red-letter day ['rɛdlɛtə'deɪ] n grand jour, jour mémorable.

red light ['rɛd'laɪt] n: **to go through a** ~ (AUT) brûler un feu rouge ; **red-light district** n quartier réservé.

redness ['rɛdnɪs] n rougeur f ; (of hair) rousseur f.

redo [ri:'du:] vt irg refaire.

redolent ['rɛdəulnt] a: ~ **of** qui sent ; (fig) qui évoque.

redouble [ri:'dʌbl] vt: **to** ~ **one's efforts** redoubler d'efforts.

redress [rɪ'drɛs] n réparation f.

red tape ['rɛd'teɪp] n (fig) paperasserie f (administrative).

reduce [rɪ'dju:s] vt réduire ; (lower) abaisser ; '~ **speed now**' (AUT) 'ralentir' ; **at a** ~**d price** (of goods) au rabais, en solde ; (of ticket etc) à prix réduit ; **reduction** [rɪ'dʌkʃən] n réduction f ; (of price) baisse f ; (discount) rabais m ; réduction.

redundancy [rɪ'dʌndənsɪ] n licenciement m, mise f au chômage.

redundant [rɪ'dʌndnt] a (worker) mis(e) au chômage, licencié(e) ; (detail, object) superflu(e) ; **to make** ~ licencier, mettre au chômage.

reed [ri:d] n (BOT) roseau m ; (MUS: of clarinet etc) anche f.

reef [ri:f] n (at sea) récif m, écueil m.

reek [ri:k] vi: **to** ~ (**of**) puer, empester.

reel [ri:l] n bobine f ; (TECH) dévidoir m ; (FISHING) moulinet m ; (CINEMA) bande f // vt (TECH) bobiner ; (also: ~ **up**) enrouler // vi (sway) chanceler.

re-election [ri:ɪ'lɛkʃən] n réélection f.

re-engage [ri:ɪn'geɪdʒ] vt (worker) réembaucher.

re-enter [ri:'ɛntə*] vt rentrer dans ; **re-entry** n rentrée f.

ref [rɛf] n (col: abbr of referee) arbitre m.

refectory [rɪ'fɛktərɪ] n réfectoire m.

refer [rɪ'fə:*] vt: **to** ~ **sb** (or sth) **to** (dispute, decision) soumettre qch à ; (inquirer: for information) adresser or envoyer qn à ; (reader: to text) renvoyer qn à ; **to** ~ **to** vt fus (allude to) parler de, faire allusion à ; (apply to) s'appliquer à ; (consult) se reporter à ; ~**ring to your letter** (COMM) en réponse à votre lettre.

referee [rɛfə'ri:] n arbitre m ; (for job application) répondant/e // vt arbitrer.

reference ['rɛfrəns] n référence f, renvoi m ; (mention) allusion f, mention f ; (for job application: letter) références ; lettre f de recommandation ; (: person) répondant/e ; **with** ~ **to** ce qui concerne ; (COMM: in letter) me référant à ; **'please quote this** ~' (COMM) 'prière de rappeler cette référence' ; ~ **book** n ouvrage m de référence.

referendum, pl referenda [rɛfə'rɛndəm, -də] n référendum m.

refill vt [ri:'fɪl] remplir à nouveau ; (pen, lighter etc) recharger // n ['ri:fɪl] (for pen etc) recharge f.

refine [rɪ'faɪn] vt (sugar, oil) raffiner ; (taste) affiner ; ~**d** a (person, taste) raffiné(e) ; ~**ment** n (of person) raffinement m ; ~**ry** n raffinerie f.

reflect [rɪ'flɛkt] vt (light, image) réfléchir, refléter ; (fig) refléter // vi (think) réfléchir, méditer ; **to** ~ **on** vt fus (discredit) porter atteinte à, faire tort à ; ~**ion** [-'flɛkʃən] n réflexion f ; (image) reflet m ; (criticism): ~**ion on** critique f de ; atteinte f à ; **on** ~**ion** réflexion faite ; ~**or** n (also AUT) réflecteur m.

reflex ['ri:flɛks] a, n réflexe (m) ; ~**ive** [rɪ'flɛksɪv] a (LING) réfléchi(e).

reform [rɪ'fɔ:m] n réforme f // vt réformer ; **the R~ation** [rɛfə'meɪʃən] n la Réforme ; ~**ed** a amendé(e), assagi(e) ; ~**er** n réformateur/trice.

refrain [rɪ'freɪn] vi: **to** ~ **from doing** s'abstenir de faire // n refrain m.

refresh [rɪ'frɛʃ] vt rafraîchir ; (subj: food) redonner des forces à ; (: sleep) reposer ; ~**er course** n cours m de recyclage ; ~**ment room** n buffet m ; ~**ments** npl rafraîchissements mpl.

refrigeration [rɪfrɪdʒə'reɪʃən] n réfrigération f.

refrigerator [rɪ'frɪdʒəreɪtə*] n réfrigérateur m, frigidaire m.

refuel [ri:'fjuəl] vt ravitailler en carburant // vi se ravitailler en carburant.

refuge ['rɛfju:dʒ] n refuge m ; **to take** ~ **in** se réfugier dans.

refugee [rɛfju'dʒi:] n réfugié/e.

refund n ['ri:fʌnd] remboursement m // vt [rɪ'fʌnd] rembourser.

refurbish [ri:'fə:bɪʃ] vt remettre à neuf.

refurnish [ri:'fə:nɪʃ] vt remeubler.

refusal [rɪ'fju:zəl] n refus m.

refuse n ['rɛfjuːs] ordures fpl, détritus mpl // vt, vi [rɪ'fjuːz] refuser ; ~ **collection** n ramassage m d'ordures ; ~ **collector** n éboueur m.

refute [rɪ'fjuːt] vt réfuter.

regain [rɪ'geɪn] vt regagner ; retrouver.

regal ['riːgl] a royal(e) ; ~**ia** [rɪ'geɪlɪə] n insignes mpl de la royauté.

regard [rɪ'gɑːd] n respect m, estime f, considération f // vt considérer ; **to give one's** ~**s to** faire ses amitiés à ; '**with kindest** ~**s**' 'bien amicalement' ; ~**ing, as** ~**s, with** ~ **to** en ce qui concerne ; ~**less** ad quand même ; ~**less of** sans se soucier de.

regatta [rɪ'gætə] n régate f.

regency ['riːdʒənsɪ] n régence f.

regent ['riːdʒənt] n régent/e.

régime [reɪ'ʒiːm] n régime m.

regiment ['rɛdʒɪmənt] n régiment m ; ~**al** [-'mɛntl] a d'un or du régiment ; ~**ation** [-'teɪʃən] n réglementation excessive.

region ['riːdʒən] n région f ; **in the** ~ **of** (fig) aux alentours de ; ~**al** a régional(e) ; ~**al development** n aménagement m du territoire.

register ['rɛdʒɪstə*] n registre m ; (also: **electoral** ~) liste électorale // vt enregistrer, inscrire ; (birth) déclarer ; (vehicle) immatriculer ; (luggage) enregistrer ; (letter) envoyer en recommandé ; (subj: instrument) marquer // vi se faire inscrire ; (at hotel) signer le registre ; (make impression) être (bien) compris(e) ; ~**ed** a (design) déposé(e) ; (letter) recommandé(e).

registrar ['rɛdʒɪstrɑː*] n officier m de l'état civil ; secrétaire (général).

registration [rɛdʒɪs'treɪʃən] n (act) enregistrement m ; inscription f ; (AUT: also: ~ **number**) numéro m d'immatriculation.

registry ['rɛdʒɪstrɪ] n bureau m de l'enregistrement ; ~ **office** n bureau m de l'état civil ; **to get married in a** ~ **office** ≈ se marier à la mairie.

regret [rɪ'grɛt] n regret m // vt regretter ; **to** ~ **that** regretter que + sub ; ~**fully** ad à or avec regret ; ~**table** a regrettable.

regroup [riː'gruːp] vt regrouper // vi se regrouper.

regular ['rɛgjulə*] a régulier(ère) ; (usual) habituel(le), normal(e) ; (soldier) de métier ; (COMM: size) ordinaire // n (client etc) habitué/e ; ~**ity** [-'lærɪtɪ] n régularité f ; ~**ly** ad régulièrement.

regulate ['rɛgjuleɪt] vt régler ; **regulation** [-'leɪʃən] n (rule) règlement m ; (adjustment) réglage m // cpd réglementaire.

rehabilitation ['riːhəbɪlɪ'teɪʃən] n (of offender) réhabilitation f ; (of disabled) rééducation f, réadaptation f.

rehash [riː'hæʃ] vt (col) remanier.

rehearsal [rɪ'hɜːsəl] n répétition f.

rehearse [rɪ'hɜːs] vt répéter.

reign [reɪn] n règne m // vi régner ; ~**ing** a (monarch) régnant(e) ; (champion) actuel(le).

reimburse [riːɪm'bɜːs] vt rembourser.

rein [reɪn] n (for horse) rêne f.

reincarnation [riːɪnkɑː'neɪʃən] n réincarnation f.

reindeer ['reɪndɪə*] n (pl inv) renne m.

reinforce [riːɪn'fɔːs] vt renforcer ; ~**d concrete** n béton armé ; ~**ment** n (action) renforcement m ; ~**ments** npl (MIL) renfort(s) m(pl).

reinstate [riːɪn'steɪt] vt rétablir, réintégrer.

reissue [riː'ɪʃjuː] vt (book) rééditer ; (film) ressortir.

reiterate [riː'ɪtəreɪt] vt réitérer, répéter.

reject n ['riːdʒɛkt] (COMM) article m de rebut // vt [rɪ'dʒɛkt] refuser ; (COMM: goods) mettre au rebut ; (idea) rejeter ; ~**ion** [rɪ'dʒɛkʃən] n rejet m, refus m.

rejoice [rɪ'dʒɔɪs] vi: **to** ~ (**at** or **over**) se réjouir (de).

rejuvenate [rɪ'dʒuːvəneɪt] vt rajeunir.

rekindle [riː'kɪndl] vt rallumer ; (fig) raviver.

relapse [rɪ'læps] n (MED) rechute f.

relate [rɪ'leɪt] vt (tell) raconter ; (connect) établir un rapport entre ; ~**d** a apparenté(e) ; ~**d to** apparenté à ; **relating: relating to** prep concernant.

relation [rɪ'leɪʃən] n (person) parent/e ; (link) rapport m, lien m ; ~**ship** n rapport m, lien m ; (personal ties) relations fpl, rapports ; (also: **family** ~**ship**) lien m de parenté ; (affair) liaison f.

relative ['rɛlətɪv] n parent/e // a relatif(ive) ; (respective) respectif(ive) ; **all her** ~**s** toute sa famille ; ~**ly** ad relativement.

relax [rɪ'læks] vi se relâcher ; (person: unwind) se détendre // vt relâcher ; (mind, person) détendre ; ~**ation** [riːlæk'seɪʃən] n relâchement m ; détente f ; (entertainment) distraction f ; ~**ed** a relâché(e) ; détendu(e) ; ~**ing** a délassant(e).

relay ['riːleɪ] n (SPORT) course f de relais // vt (message) retransmettre, relayer.

release [rɪ'liːs] n (from prison, obligation) libération f ; (of gas etc) émission f ; (of film etc) sortie f ; (record) disque m ; (device) déclencheur m // vt (prisoner) libérer ; (book, film) sortir ; (report, news) rendre public, publier ; (gas etc) émettre, dégager ; (free: from wreckage etc) dégager ; (TECH: catch, spring etc) déclencher ; (let go) relâcher ; lâcher ; desserrer ; **to** ~ **one's grip** or **hold** lâcher prise ; **to** ~ **the clutch** (AUT) débrayer.

relegate ['rɛləgeɪt] vt reléguer.

relent [rɪ'lɛnt] vi se laisser fléchir ; ~**less** a implacable.

relevance ['rɛləvəns] n pertinence f ; ~ **of sth to sth** rapport m entre qch et qch.

relevant ['rɛləvənt] a approprié(e) ; (fact) significatif(ive) ; (information) utile, pertinent(e) ; ~ **to** ayant rapport à, approprié à.

reliability [rɪlaɪə'bɪlɪtɪ] n sérieux m ; solidité f.

reliable [rɪ'laɪəbl] a (person, firm) sérieux(euse) ; (method) sûr(e) ; (machine) solide ; **reliably** ad: **to be reliably informed** savoir de source sûre.

reliance [rɪ'laɪəns] n: ~ (**on**) confiance f (en) ; besoin m de, dépendance f (de).

relic ['rɛlɪk] n (REL) relique f ; (of the past) vestige m.

relief [rɪ'liːf] n (from pain, anxiety) soulagement m ; (help, supplies) secours m(pl) ; (of *guard*) relève *f*; (ART, GEO) relief *m*; ~ **road** *n* route *f* de délestage; ~ **valve** *n* soupape *f* de sûreté.

relieve [rɪ'liːv] *vt* (*pain, patient*) soulager; (*bring help*) secourir; (*take over from: gen*) relayer; (: *guard*) relever; **to** ~ **sb of sth** débarrasser qn de qch.

religion [rɪ'lɪdʒən] *n* religion *f*; **religious** *a* religieux(euse); (*book*) de piété.

reline [riː'laɪn] *vt* (*brakes*) refaire la garniture de.

relinquish [rɪ'lɪŋkwɪʃ] *vt* abandonner; (*plan, habit*) renoncer à.

relish ['rɛlɪʃ] *n* (CULIN) condiment *m*; (*enjoyment*) délectation *f* // *vt* (*food etc*) savourer; **to** ~ **doing** se délecter à faire.

relive [riː'lɪv] *vt* revivre.

reload [riː'ləud] *vt* recharger.

reluctance [rɪ'lʌktəns] *n* répugnance *f*.

reluctant [rɪ'lʌktənt] *a* peu disposé(e), qui hésite; ~**ly** *ad* à contrecœur, sans enthousiasme.

rely [rɪ'laɪ] : **to** ~ **on** *vt fus* compter sur; (*be dependent*) dépendre de.

remain [rɪ'meɪn] *vi* rester; ~**der** *n* reste *m*; (COMM) fin *f* de série; ~**ing** *a* qui reste; ~**s** *npl* restes *mpl*.

remand [rɪ'mɑːnd] *n*: **on** ~ en détention préventive // *vt*: **to** ~ **in custody** écrouer; renvoyer en détention provisoire; ~ **home** *n* maison *f* d'arrêt.

remark [rɪ'mɑːk] *n* remarque *f*, observation *f* // *vt* (*faire*) remarquer, dire; (*notice*) remarquer; ~**able** *a* remarquable.

remarry [riː'mærɪ] *vt* se remarier.

remedial [rɪ'miːdɪəl] *a* (*tuition, classes*) de rattrapage.

remedy ['rɛmədɪ] *n*: ~ (**for**) remède *m* (*contre or* à) // *vt* remédier à.

remember [rɪ'mɛmbə*] *vt* se rappeler, se souvenir de; ~ **me to** (*in letter*) rappelez-moi au bon souvenir de; **remembrance** *n* souvenir *m*; mémoire *f*.

remind [rɪ'maɪnd] *vt*: **to** ~ **sb of sth** rappeler qch à qn; **to** ~ **sb to do** faire penser à qn à faire, rappeler à qn qu'il doit faire; ~**er** *n* rappel *m*; (*note etc*) pense-bête *m*.

reminisce [rɛmɪ'nɪs] *vi*: **to** ~ (**about**) évoquer ses souvenirs (de).

reminiscences [rɛmɪ'nɪsnsɪz] *npl* réminiscences *fpl*, souvenirs *mpl*.

reminiscent [rɛmɪ'nɪsnt] *a*: ~ **of** qui rappelle, qui fait penser à.

remission [rɪ'mɪʃən] *n* rémission *f*; (*of debt, sentence*) remise *f*; (*of fee*) exemption *f*.

remit [rɪ'mɪt] *vt* (*send: money*) envoyer; ~**tance** *n* envoi *m*, paiement *m*.

remnant ['rɛmnənt] *n* reste *m*, restant *m*; ~**s** *npl* (COMM) coupons *mpl*; fins *fpl* de série.

remorse [rɪ'mɔːs] *n* remords *m*; ~**ful** *a* plein(e) de remords; ~**less** *a* (*fig*) impitoyable.

remote [rɪ'məut] *a* éloigné(e), lointain(e); (*person*) distant(e); ~ **control** *n* télécommande *f*; ~**ly** *ad* au loin; (*slightly*) très vaguement; ~**ness** *n* éloignement *m*.

remould ['riːməuld] *n* (*tyre*) pneu rechapé.

removable [rɪ'muːvəbl] *a* (*detachable*) amovible.

removal [rɪ'muːvəl] *n* (*taking away*) enlèvement *m*; suppression *f*; (*from house*) déménagement *m*; (*from office: sacking*) renvoi *m*; (MED) ablation *f*; ~ **man** *n* déménageur *m*; ~ **van** *n* camion *m* de déménagement.

remove [rɪ'muːv] *vt* enlever, retirer; (*employee*) renvoyer; (*stain*) faire partir; (*doubt, abuse*) supprimer; ~**r** (*for paint*) décapant *m*; (*for varnish*) dissolvant *m*; ~**rs** *npl* (*company*) entreprise *f* de déménagement.

remuneration [rɪmjuːnə'reɪʃən] *n* rémunération *f*.

rename [riː'neɪm] *vt* rebaptiser.

rend, *pt, pp* **rent** [rɛnd, rɛnt] *vt* déchirer.

render ['rɛndə*] *vt* rendre; (CULIN: *fat*) clarifier; ~**ing** *n* (MUS *etc*) interprétation *f*.

rendez-vous ['rɔndɪvuː] *n* rendez-vous *m* *inv* // *vi* opérer une jonction, se rejoindre.

renegade ['rɛnɪgeɪd] *n* rénégat/e.

renew [rɪ'njuː] *vt* renouveler; (*negotiations*) reprendre; (*acquaintance*) renouer; ~**al** *n* renouvellement *m*; reprise *f*.

renounce [rɪ'nauns] *vt* renoncer à; (*disown*) renier.

renovate ['rɛnəveɪt] *vt* rénover; (*art work*) restaurer; **renovation** [-'veɪʃən] *n* rénovation *f*; restauration *f*.

renown [rɪ'naun] *n* renommée *f*; ~**ed** *a* renommé(e).

rent [rɛnt] *pt, pp of* **rend** // *n* loyer *m* // *vt* louer; ~**al** *n* (*for television, car*) (prix *m* de) location *f*.

renunciation [rɪnʌnsɪ'eɪʃən] *n* renonciation *f*; (*self-denial*) renoncement *m*.

reopen [riː'əupən] *vt* rouvrir; ~**ing** *n* réouverture *f*.

reorder [riː'ɔːdə*] *vt* commander de nouveau; (*rearrange*) réorganiser.

reorganize [riː'ɔːgənaɪz] *vt* réorganiser.

rep [rɛp] *n* (COMM: *abbr of* **representative**) représentant *m* (de commerce); (THEATRE: *abbr of* **repertory**) théâtre *m* de répertoire.

repair [rɪ'pɛə*] *n* réparation *f* // *vt* réparer; **in good/bad** ~ en bon/mauvais état; ~ **kit** *n* trousse *f* de réparations; ~ **man** *n* réparateur *m*; ~ **shop** *n* (AUT *etc*) atelier *m* de réparations.

repartee [rɛpɑː'tiː] *n* repartie *f*.

repay [riː'peɪ] *vt irg* (*money, creditor*) rembourser; (*sb's efforts*) récompenser; ~**ment** *n* remboursement *m*; récompense *f*.

repeal [rɪ'piːl] *n* (*of law*) abrogation *f*; (*of sentence*) annulation *f* // *vt* abroger; annuler.

repeat [rɪ'piːt] *n* (RADIO, TV) reprise *f* // *vt* répéter; (*pattern*) reproduire; (*promise, attack, also* COMM: *order*) renouveler; (SCOL: *a class*) redoubler; ~**edly** *ad* souvent, à plusieurs reprises.

repel [rɪ'pɛl] *vt* (*lit, fig*) repousser; ~**lent** *a* repoussant(e) // *n*: **insect** ~**lent** insectifuge *m*; **moth** ~**lent** produit *m* antimite(s).

repent [rɪ'pɛnt] *vi*: **to** ~ (**of**) se repentir (de); ~**ance** *n* repentir *m*.

repercussion [riːpə'kʌʃən] *n* (*consequence*) répercussion *f*.

repertoire ['rɛpətwɑ:*] n répertoire m.

repertory ['rɛpətəri] n (also: ~ theatre) théâtre m de répertoire.

repetition [rɛpı'tıʃən] n répétition f; (of promise, COMM: order etc) renouvellement m.

repetitive [rı'pɛtıtıv] a (movement, work) répétitif(ive); (speech) plein(e) de redites.

replace [rı'pleıs] vt (put back) remettre, replacer; (take the place of) remplacer; (TEL:) '~ the receiver' 'raccrochez'; ~ment n remplacement m; remplacement m; (person) remplaçant/e; ~ment part n pièce f de rechange.

replenish [rı'plɛnıʃ] vt (glass) remplir (de nouveau); (stock etc) réapprovisionner.

replete [rı'pli:t] a rempli(e); (well-fed) rassasié(e).

replica ['rɛplıkə] n réplique f, copie exacte.

reply [rı'plaı] n réponse f // vi répondre.

report [rı'pɔ:t] n rapport m; (PRESS etc) reportage m; (also: school ~) bulletin m (scolaire); (of gun) détonation f // vt rapporter, faire un compte rendu de; (PRESS etc) faire un reportage sur; (bring to notice: occurrence) signaler; (: person) dénoncer // vi (make a report) faire un rapport (or un reportage); (present o.s.): to ~ (to sb) se présenter (chez qn); it is ~ed that on dit or annonce que; ~ed speech n (LING) discours indirect; ~er n reporter m.

reprehensible [rɛprı'hɛnsıbl] a répréhensible.

represent [rɛprı'zɛnt] vt représenter; (explain): to ~ to sb that expliquer à qn que; ~ation [-'teıʃən] n représentation f; ~ations npl (protest) démarche f; ~ative n représentant/e; (US: POL) député m // a représentatif(ive), caractéristique.

repress [rı'prɛs] vt réprimer; ~ion [-'prɛʃən] n répression f; ~ive a répressif(ive).

reprieve [rı'pri:v] n (LAW) grâce f; (fig) sursis m, délai m // vt gracier; accorder un sursis or un délai à.

reprimand ['rɛprımɑ:nd] n réprimande f // vt réprimander.

reprint n ['ri:prınt] réimpression f // vt [ri:'prınt] réimprimer.

reprisal [rı'praızl] n représailles fpl.

reproach [rı'prəutʃ] n reproche m // vt: to ~ sb with sth reprocher qch à qn; beyond ~ irréprochable; ~ful a de reproche.

reproduce [ri:prə'dju:s] vt reproduire // vi se reproduire; **reproduction** [-'dʌkʃən] n reproduction f; **reproductive** [-'dʌktıv] a reproducteur(trice).

reprove [rı'pru:v] vt (action) réprouver; (person): to ~ (for) blâmer (de); **reproving** a réprobateur(trice).

reptile ['rɛptaıl] n reptile m.

republic [rı'pʌblık] n république f; ~an a,n républicain(e).

repudiate [rı'pju:dıeıt] vt (wife, accusation) répudier; (friend) renier.

repugnant [rı'pʌgnənt] a répugnant(e).

repulse [rı'pʌls] vt repousser.

repulsion [rı'pʌlʃən] n répulsion f.

repulsive [rı'pʌlsıv] a repoussant(e), répulsif(ive).

reputable ['rɛpjutəbl] a de bonne réputation; (occupation) honorable.

reputation [rɛpju'teıʃən] n réputation f; to have a ~ for être réputé(e) pour.

repute [rı'pju:t] n (bonne) réputation; ~d a réputé(e); ~dly ad d'après ce qu'on dit.

request [rı'kwɛst] n demande f; (formal) requête f // vt: to ~ (of or from sb) demander (à qn); ~ stop n (for bus) arrêt facultatif.

requiem ['rɛkwıəm] n requiem m.

require [rı'kwaıə*] vt (need: subj: person) avoir besoin de; (: thing, situation) demander; (want) vouloir; exiger; (order) obliger; ~d a requis(e), voulu(e); if ~d s'il le faut; ~ment n exigence f; besoin m; condition requise.

requisite ['rɛkwızıt] n chose nécessaire // a requis(e), nécessaire; **toilet** ~s accessoires mpl de toilette.

requisition [rɛkwı'zıʃən] n: ~ (for) demande f (de) // vt (MIL) réquisitionner.

reroute [ri:'ru:t] vt (train etc) dérouter.

resale ['ri:'seıl] n revente f.

rescind [rı'sınd] vt annuler; (law) abroger; (judgment) rescinder.

rescue ['rɛskju:] n sauvetage m; (help) secours mpl // vt sauver; ~ party n équipe f de sauvetage; ~r n sauveteur m.

research [rı'sə:tʃ] n recherche(s) f(pl) // vt faire des recherches sur; ~er n chercheur/euse; ~ work n recherches fpl; ~ worker n chercheur/euse.

resell [ri:'sɛl] vt irg revendre.

resemblance [rı'zɛmbləns] n ressemblance f.

resemble [rı'zɛmbl] vt ressembler à.

resent [rı'zɛnt] vt éprouver du ressentiment de, être contrarié(e) par; ~ful a irrité(e), plein(e) de ressentiment; ~ment n ressentiment m.

reservation [rɛzə'veıʃən] n (booking) réservation f; (doubt) réserve f; (protected area) réserve; (on road: also: central ~) bande f médiane; to make a ~ (in an hotel/a restaurant/a plane) réserver or retenir une chambre/une table/une place.

reserve [rı'zə:v] n réserve f; (SPORT) remplaçant/e // vt (seats etc) réserver, retenir; ~s npl (MIL) réservistes mpl; in ~ en réserve; ~d a réservé(e); **reservist** n (MIL) réserviste m.

reservoir ['rɛzəvwɑ:*] n réservoir m.

reshape [ri:'ʃeıp] vt (policy) réorganiser.

reshuffle [ri:'ʃʌfl] n: **Cabinet** ~ (POL) remaniement ministériel.

reside [rı'zaıd] vi résider.

residence ['rɛzıdəns] n résidence f; ~ permit n permis m de séjour.

resident ['rɛzıdənt] n résident/e // a résidant(e).

residential [rɛzı'dɛnʃəl] a de résidence; (area) résidentiel(le).

residue ['rɛzıdju:] n reste m; (CHEM, PHYSICS) résidu m.

resign [rı'zaın] vt (one's post) se démettre de // vi démissionner; to ~ o.s. to (endure) se résigner à; ~ation [rɛzıg'neıʃən] n démission f; résignation f; ~ed a résigné(e).

resilience [rɪ'zɪlɪəns] n (of material) élasticité f; (of person) ressort m.

resilient [rɪ'zɪlɪənt] a (person) qui réagit, qui a du ressort.

resin ['rɛzɪn] n résine f.

resist [rɪ'zɪst] vt résister à; ~ance n résistance f.

resolute ['rɛzəluːt] a résolu(e).

resolution [rɛzə'luːʃən] n résolution f.

resolve [rɪ'zɔlv] n résolution f // vt (decide): to ~ to do résoudre or décider de faire; (problem) résoudre; ~d a résolu(e).

resonant ['rɛzənənt] a résonnant(e).

resort [rɪ'zɔːt] n (town) station f; (recourse) recours m // vi: to ~ to avoir recours à; in the last ~ en dernier ressort.

resound [rɪ'zaund] vi: to ~ (with) retentir (de); ~ing a retentissant(e).

resource [rɪ'sɔːs] n ressource f; ~s npl ressources; ~ful a plein(e) de ressource, débrouillard(e); ~fulness n ressource f.

respect [rɪs'pɛkt] n respect m // vt respecter; with ~ to en ce qui concerne; in ~ of sous le rapport de, quant à; in this ~ sous ce rapport, à cet égard; ~ability [-ə'bɪlɪtɪ] n respectabilité f; ~able a respectable; ~ful a respectueux(euse).

respective [rɪs'pɛktɪv] a respectif(ive); ~ly ad respectivement.

respiration [rɛspɪ'reɪʃən] n respiration f.

respirator ['rɛspɪreɪtə*] n respirateur m.

respiratory [rɛs'pɪrətərɪ] a respiratoire.

respite ['rɛspaɪt] n répit m.

resplendent [rɪs'plɛndənt] a resplendissant(e).

respond [rɪs'pɔnd] vi répondre; (to treatment) réagir.

response [rɪs'pɔns] n réponse f; (to treatment) réaction f.

responsibility [rɪspɔnsɪ'bɪlɪtɪ] n responsabilité f.

responsible [rɪs'pɔnsɪbl] a (liable): ~ (for) responsable (de); (character) digne de confiance; (job) qui comporte des responsabilités; **responsibly** ad avec sérieux.

responsive [rɪs'pɔnsɪv] a qui n'est pas réservé(e) or indifférent(e).

rest [rɛst] n repos m; (stop) arrêt m, pause f; (MUS) silence m; (support) support m, appui m; (remainder) reste m, restant m // vi se reposer; (be supported): to ~ on appuyer or reposer sur; (remain) rester // vt (lean): to ~ sth on/against appuyer qch sur/contre; the ~ of them les autres; it ~s with him to c'est à lui de.

restart [riː'stɑːt] vt (engine) remettre en marche; (work) reprendre.

restaurant ['rɛstərɔŋ] n restaurant m; ~ car n wagon-restaurant m.

rest cure ['rɛstkjuə*] n cure f de repos.

restful ['rɛstful] a reposant(e).

rest home ['rɛsthəum] n maison f de repos.

restitution [rɛstɪ'tjuːʃən] n (act) restitution f; (reparation) réparation f.

restive ['rɛstɪv] a agité(e), impatient(e); (horse) rétif(ive).

restless ['rɛstlɪs] a agité(e); ~ly ad avec agitation.

restock [riː'stɔk] vt réapprovisionner.

restoration [rɛstə'reɪʃən] n restauration f; restitution f.

restore [rɪ'stɔː*] vt (building) restaurer; (sth stolen) restituer; (peace, health) rétablir.

restrain [rɪs'treɪn] vt (feeling) contenir; (person): to ~ (from doing) retenir (de faire); ~ed a (style) sobre; (manner) mesuré(e); ~t n (restriction) contrainte f; (moderation) retenue f; (of style) sobriété f.

restrict [rɪs'trɪkt] vt restreindre, limiter; ~ed area n (AUT) zone f à vitesse limitée; ~ion [-kʃən] n restriction f, limitation f; ~ive a restrictif(ive).

rest room ['rɛstrum] n (US) toilettes fpl.

result [rɪ'zʌlt] n résultat m // vi: to ~ in aboutir à, se terminer par.

resume [rɪ'zjuːm] vt, vi (work, journey) reprendre.

resumption [rɪ'zʌmpʃən] n reprise f.

resurgence [rɪ'səːdʒəns] n réapparition f.

resurrection [rɛzə'rɛkʃən] n résurrection f.

resuscitate [rɪ'sʌsɪteɪt] vt (MED) réanimer; **resuscitation** [-'teɪʃn] n réanimation f.

retail ['riːteɪl] n (vente f au) détail m // cpd de or au détail // vt vendre au détail; ~ n détaillant/e; ~ price n prix m de détail.

retain [rɪ'teɪn] vt (keep) garder, conserver; (employ) engager; ~er n (servant) serviteur m; (fee) acompte m, provision f.

retaliate [rɪ'tælɪeɪt] vi: to ~ (against) se venger (de); to ~ (on sb) rendre la pareille (à qn); **retaliation** [-'eɪʃən] n représailles fpl, vengeance f.

retarded [rɪ'tɑːdɪd] a retardé(e).

retch [rɛtʃ] vi avoir des haut-le-coeur.

retentive [rɪ'tɛntɪv] a: ~ memory excellente mémoire.

rethink ['riː'θɪŋk] vt repenser.

reticence ['rɛtɪsns] n réticence f.

reticent ['rɛtɪsnt] a réticent(e).

retina ['rɛtɪnə] n rétine f.

retinue ['rɛtɪnjuː] n suite f, cortège m.

retire [rɪ'taɪə*] vi (give up work) prendre sa retraite; (withdraw) se retirer, partir; (go to bed) (aller) se coucher; ~d a (person) retraité(e); ~ment n retraite f; **retiring** a (person) réservé(e); **retiring age** n âge m de la retraite.

retort [rɪ'tɔːt] n (reply) riposte f; (container) cornue f // vi riposter.

retrace [riː'treɪs] vt reconstituer; to ~ one's steps revenir sur ses pas.

retract [rɪ'trækt] vt (statement, claws) rétracter; (undercarriage, aerial) rentrer, escamoter // vi se rétracter; rentrer; ~able a escamotable.

retrain [riː'treɪn] vt (worker) recycler; ~ing n recyclage m.

retread [riː'trɛd] vt (AUT: tyre) rechaper.

retreat [rɪ'triːt] n retraite f // vi battre en retraite; (flood) reculer.

retrial [riː'traɪəl] n nouveau procès.

retribution [rɛtrɪ'bjuːʃən] n châtiment m.
retrieval [rɪ'triːvəl] n récupération f; réparation f; recherche f et extraction f.
retrieve [rɪ'triːv] vt (sth lost) récupérer; (situation, honour) sauver; (error, loss) réparer; (COMPUTERS) rechercher; ~r n chien m d'arrêt.
retrospect ['rɛtrəspɛkt] n: **in** ~ rétrospectivement, après coup; ~**ive** [-'spɛktɪv] a (law) rétroactif(ive).
return [rɪ'təːn] n (going or coming back) retour m; (of sth stolen etc) restitution f; (recompense) récompense f; (FINANCE: from land, shares) rapport m; (report) relevé m, rapport // cpd (journey) de retour; (ticket) aller et retour; (match) retour // vi (person etc: come back) revenir; (: go back) retourner // vt (bring back; bring back) rapporter; (send back) renvoyer; (put back) remettre; (POL: candidate) élire; ~**s** npl (COMM) recettes fpl; bénéfices mpl; **many happy** ~**s (of the day)!** bon anniversaire!; ~**able** a (bottle etc) consigné(e).
reunion [riː'juːnɪən] n réunion f.
reunite [riːjuː'naɪt] vt réunir.
rev [rɛv] n (abbr of **revolution**: AUT) tour m // vb (also: ~ **up**) vt emballer // vi s'emballer.
revamp ['riː'væmp] vt (house) retaper; (firm) réorganiser.
reveal [rɪ'viːl] vt (make known) révéler; (display) laisser voir; ~**ing** a révélateur(trice); (dress) au décolleté généreux or suggestif.
reveille [rɪ'vælɪ] n (MIL) réveil m.
revel ['rɛvl] vi: **to** ~ **in sth/in doing** se délecter de qch/à faire.
revelation [rɛvə'leɪʃən] n révélation f.
reveller ['rɛvlə*] n fêtard m.
revelry ['rɛvlrɪ] n festivités fpl.
revenge [rɪ'vɛndʒ] n vengeance f; (in game etc) revanche f // vt venger; **to take** ~ se venger; ~**ful** a vengeur(eresse); vindicatif(ive).
revenue ['rɛvənjuː] n revenu m.
reverberate [rɪ'vəːbəreɪt] vi (sound) retentir, se répercuter; (light) se réverbérer; **reverberation** [-'reɪʃən] n répercussion f; réverbération f.
revere [rɪ'vɪə*] vt vénérer, révérer.
reverence ['rɛvərəns] n vénération f, révérence f.
reverent ['rɛvərənt] a respectueux(euse).
reverie ['rɛvərɪ] n rêverie f.
reversal [rɪ'vəːsl] n (of opinion) revirement m.
reverse [rɪ'vəːs] n contraire m, opposé m; (back) dos m, envers m; (AUT: also: ~ **gear**) marche f arrière // a (order, direction) opposé(e), inverse // vt (turn) renverser, retourner; (change) renverser, changer complètement; (LAW: judgment) réformer // vi (AUT) faire marche arrière//; ~**d charge call** n (TEL) communication f en PCV.
reversion [rɪ'vəːʃən] n retour m.
revert [rɪ'vəːt] vi: **to** ~ **to** revenir à, retourner à.
review [rɪ'vjuː] n revue f; (of book, film) critique f // vt passer en revue; faire la critique de; ~**er** n critique m.

revise [rɪ'vaɪz] vt (manuscript) revoir, corriger; (opinion) réviser, modifier; (study: subject, notes) réviser; **revision** [rɪ'vɪʒən] n révision f.
revitalize [riː'vaɪtəlaɪz] vt revitaliser.
revival [rɪ'vaɪvl] n reprise f; rétablissement m; (of faith) renouveau m.
revive [rɪ'vaɪv] vt (person) ranimer; (custom) rétablir; (hope, courage) redonner; (play, fashion) reprendre // vi (person) reprendre connaissance; (hope) renaître; (activity) reprendre.
revoke [rɪ'vauk] vt révoquer; (promise, decision) revenir sur.
revolt [rɪ'vault] n révolte f // vi se révolter, se rebeller; ~**ing** a dégoûtant(e).
revolution [rɛvə'luːʃən] n révolution f; (of wheel etc) tour m, révolution; ~**ary** a, n révolutionnaire (m/f); **rev(olution) counter** n compte-tours m inv; ~**ize** vt révolutionner.
revolve [rɪ'vɔlv] vi tourner.
revolver [rɪ'vɔlvə*] n revolver m.
revolving [rɪ'vɔlvɪŋ] a (chair) pivotant(e); (light) tournant(e); ~ **door** n (porte f à) tambour m.
revue [rɪ'vjuː] n (THEATRE) revue f.
revulsion [rɪ'vʌlʃən] n dégoût m, répugnance f.
reward [rɪ'wɔːd] n récompense f // vt: **to** ~ **(for)** récompenser (de); ~**ing** a (fig) qui (en) vaut la peine.
rewind [riː'waɪnd] vt irg (watch) remonter; (ribbon etc) réembobiner.
rewire [riː'waɪə*] vt (house) refaire l'installation électrique de.
reword [riː'wəːd] vt formuler or exprimer différemment.
rewrite [riː'raɪt] vt irg récrire.
rhapsody ['ræpsədɪ] n (MUS) rhapsodie f; (fig) éloge délirant.
rhetoric ['rɛtərɪk] n rhétorique f; ~**al** [rɪ'tɔrɪkl] a rhétorique.
rheumatic [ruː'mætɪk] a rhumatismal(e).
rheumatism ['ruːmətɪzəm] n rhumatisme m.
Rhine [raɪn] n: **the** ~ le Rhin.
rhinoceros [raɪ'nɔsərəs] n rhinocéros m.
Rhodesia [rəʊ'diːʒə] n Rhodésie f; ~**n** a rhodésien(ne) // n Rhodésien/ne.
rhododendron [rəʊdə'dɛndrn] n rhododendron m.
Rhone [rəʊn] n: **the** ~ le Rhône.
rhubarb ['ruːbɑːb] n rhubarbe f.
rhyme [raɪm] n rime f; (verse) vers mpl.
rhythm ['rɪðm] n rythme m; ~**ic(al)** a rythmique; ~**ically** ad avec rythme.
rib [rɪb] n (ANAT) côte f // vt (mock) taquiner.
ribald ['rɪbəld] a paillard(e).
ribbed [rɪbd] a (knitting) à côtes; (shell) strié(e).
ribbon ['rɪbən] n ruban m; **in** ~**s** (torn) en lambeaux.
rice [raɪs] n riz m; ~**field** n rizière f; ~ **pudding** n riz m au lait.
rich [rɪtʃ] a riche; (gift, clothes) somptueux(euse); **the** ~ les riches mpl; ~**es** npl richesses fpl; ~**ness** n richesse f.
rickets ['rɪkɪts] n rachitisme m.

rickety ['rɪkɪtɪ] a branlant(e).

rickshaw ['rɪkʃɔ:] n pousse(-pousse) m inv.

ricochet ['rɪkəʃeɪ] n ricochet m // vi ricocher.

rid, pt, pp rid [rɪd] vt: to ~ sb of débarrasser qn de; to get ~ of se débarrasser de; good riddance! bon débarras!

ridden ['rɪdn] pp of ride.

riddle ['rɪdl] n (puzzle) énigme f // vt: to be ~d with être criblé(e) de.

ride [raɪd] n promenade f, tour m; (distance covered) trajet m // vb (pt rode, pp ridden [raud, 'rɪdn]) vi (as sport) monter (à cheval), faire du cheval; (go somewhere: on horse, bicycle) aller (à cheval or bicyclette etc); (journey: on bicycle, motor cycle, bus) rouler // vt (a certain horse) monter; (distance) parcourir, faire; we rode all day/all the way nous sommes restés toute la journée en selle/avons fait tout le chemin en selle or à cheval; to ~ a horse/bicycle/camel monter à cheval/à bicyclette/à dos de chameau; to ~ at anchor (NAUT) être à l'ancre; horse/car ~ promenade or tour à cheval/en voiture; to take sb for a ~ (fig) faire marcher qn; rouler qn; ~r n cavalier/ère; (in race) jockey m; (on bicycle) cycliste m/f; (on motorcycle) motocycliste m/f; (in document) annexe f, clause additionnelle.

ridge [rɪdʒ] n (of hill) faîte m; (of roof, mountain) arête f; (on object) strie f.

ridicule ['rɪdɪkju:l] n ridicule m; dérision f // vt ridiculiser, tourner en dérision.

ridiculous [rɪ'dɪkjuləs] a ridicule.

riding ['raɪdɪŋ] n équitation f; ~ school n manège m, école f d'équitation.

rife [raɪf] a répandu(e); ~ with abondant(e) en.

riffraff ['rɪfræf] n racaille f.

rifle ['raɪfl] n fusil m (à canon rayé) // vt vider, dévaliser; ~ range n champ m de tir; (indoor) stand m de tir.

rift [rɪft] n fente f, fissure f; (fig: disagreement) désaccord m.

rig [rɪg] n (also: oil ~: on land) derrick m; (: at sea) plate-forme pétrolière f // vt (election etc) truquer; to ~ out vt habiller; (pej) fringuer, attifer; to ~ up vt arranger, faire avec des moyens de fortune; ~ging n (NAUT) gréement m.

right [raɪt] a (true) juste, exact(e); (correctly chosen: answer, road etc) bon(bonne); (suitable) approprié(e), convenable; (just) juste, équitable; (morally good) bien inv; (not left) droit(e) // n (title, claim) droit m; (not left) droite f // ad (answer) correctement; (not on the left) à droite // vt redresser // excl bon! ; to be ~ (person) avoir raison; (answer) être juste or correct(e); ~ now en ce moment même; tout de suite; ~ against the wall tout contre le mur; ~ ahead tout droit; droit devant; ~ in the middle en plein milieu; ~ away immédiatement; by ~s en toute justice; on the ~ à droite; ~ angle n angle droit; ~eous ['raɪtʃəs] a droit(e), vertueux(euse); (anger) justifié(e); ~eousness ['raɪtʃəsnɪs] n droiture f, vertu f; ~ful a (heir) légitime;

~fully ad à juste titre, légitimement; ~handed a (person) droitier(ère); ~hand man n bras droit (fig); the ~hand side le côté droit; ~ly ad bien, correctement; (with reason) à juste titre; ~minded a sensé(e), sain(e) d'esprit; ~ of way n droit m de passage; (AUT) priorité f; ~wing n (MIL, SPORT) aile droite; (POL) droite f; ~wing a (POL) de droite.

rigid ['rɪdʒɪd] a rigide; (principle) strict(e); ~ity [rɪ'dʒɪdɪtɪ] n rigidité f; ~ly ad rigidement; (behave) inflexiblement.

rigmarole ['rɪgmərəul] n galimatias m; comédie f.

rigor mortis ['rɪgə'mɔ:tɪs] n rigidité f cadavérique.

rigorous ['rɪgərəs] a rigoureux (euse); ~ly ad rigoureusement.

rigour, rigor (US) ['rɪgə*] n rigueur f.

rig-out ['rɪgaut] n (col) tenue f.

rile [raɪl] vt agacer.

rim [rɪm] n bord m; (of spectacles) monture f; (of wheel) jante f; ~less a (spectacles) à monture invisible; ~med a bordé(e); janté(e).

rind [raɪnd] n (of bacon) couenne f; (of lemon etc) écorce f.

ring [rɪŋ] n anneau m; (on finger) bague f; (also: wedding ~) alliance f; (for napkin) rond m; (of people, objects) cercle m; (of spies) réseau m; (of smoke etc) rond; (arena) piste f, arène f; (for boxing) ring m; (sound of bell) sonnerie f; (telephone call) coup m de téléphone // vb (pt rang, pp rung [ræŋ, rʌŋ]) vi (person, bell) sonner; (also: ~ out: voice, words) retentir; (TEL) téléphoner // vt (TEL: also: ~ up) téléphoner à; to ~ the bell sonner; to ~ back vt, vi (TEL) rappeler; to ~ off vi (TEL) raccrocher; ~ binder n classeur m à anneaux; ~leader n (of gang) chef m, meneur m.

ringlets ['rɪŋlɪts] npl anglaises fpl.

ring road ['rɪŋrəud] n route f de ceinture.

rink [rɪŋk] n (also: ice ~) patinoire f.

rinse [rɪns] n rinçage m // vt rincer.

riot ['raɪət] n émeute f, bagarres fpl // vi faire une émeute, manifester avec violence; a ~ of colours une débauche or orgie de couleurs; to run ~ se déchaîner; ~er n émeutier/ère, manifestant/e; ~ous a tapageur(euse); tordant(e); ~ously funny tordant(e).

rip [rɪp] n déchirure f // vt déchirer // vi se déchirer; ~cord n poignée f d'ouverture.

ripe [raɪp] a (fruit) mûr(e); (cheese) fait(e); ~n vt mûrir // vi mûrir; se faire; ~ness n maturité f.

riposte [rɪ'pɒst] n riposte f.

ripple ['rɪpl] n ride f, ondulation f; égrènement m, cascade f // vi se rider, onduler // vt rider, faire onduler.

rise [raɪz] n (slope) côte f, pente f; (hill) élévation f; (increase: in wages) augmentation f; (: in prices, temperature) hausse f, augmentation; (fig: to power etc) essor m, ascension f // vi (pt rose, pp risen [raɪz, 'rɪzn]) s'élever, monter; (prices) augmenter, monter; (waters, river) monter; (sun, wind, person: from chair, bed) se lever; (also: ~ up: rebel) se révolter;

se rebeller; **to give ~ to** donner lieu à; **to ~ to the occasion** se montrer à la hauteur.

risk [rɪsk] n risque m; danger m // vt risquer; **to take** or **run the ~ of doing** courir le risque de faire; **at ~** en danger; **at one's own ~** à ses risques et périls; **~y** a risqué(e).

risqué ['riːskeɪ] a (joke) risqué(e).

rissole ['rɪsəul] n croquette f.

rite [raɪt] n rite m.

ritual ['rɪtjuəl] a rituel(le) // n rituel m.

rival ['raɪvl] n rival/e; (in business) concurrent/e // a rival(e); qui fait concurrence // vt être en concurrence avec; **to ~ sb/sth in** rivaliser avec qn/qch de; **~ry** n rivalité f; concurrence f.

river ['rɪvə*] n rivière f; (major, also fig) fleuve m; **~bank** n rive f, berge f; **~bed** n lit m (de rivière or de fleuve); **~side** n bord m de la rivière or du fleuve // cpd (port, traffic) fluvial(e).

rivet ['rɪvɪt] n rivet m // vt riveter; (fig) river, fixer.

Riviera [rɪvɪ'ɛərə] n: **the (French) ~** la Côte d'Azur.

RN abbr of Royal Navy.

road [rəud] n route f; (small) chemin m; (in town) rue f; (fig) chemin, voie f; '**~ up**' 'attention travaux'; **~block** n barrage routier; **~hog** n chauffard m; **~map** n carte routière; **~side** n bord m de la route, bas-côté m // cpd (situé(e) etc) au bord de la route; **~sign** n panneau m de signalisation; **~ user** n usager m de la route; **~way** n chaussée f; **~worthy** a en bon état de marche.

roam [rəum] vi errer, vagabonder // vt parcourir, errer par.

roar [rɔː*] n rugissement m; (of crowd) hurlements mpl; (of vehicle, thunder, storm) grondement m // vi rugir; hurler; gronder; **to ~ with laughter** éclater de rire; **a ~ing fire** une belle flambée; **to do a ~ing trade** faire des affaires d'or.

roast [rəust] n rôti m // vt (meat) (faire) rôtir.

rob [rɔb] vt (person) voler; (bank) dévaliser; **to ~ sb of sth** voler or dérober qch à qn; (fig: deprive) priver qn de qch; **~ber** n bandit m, voleur m; **~bery** n vol m.

robe [rəub] n (for ceremony etc) robe f; (also: **bath ~**) peignoir m // vt revêtir (d'une robe).

robin ['rɔbɪn] n rouge-gorge m.

robot ['rəubɔt] n robot m.

robust [rəu'bʌst] a robuste; (material, appetite) solide.

rock [rɔk] n (substance) roche f, roc m; (boulder) rocher m; roche; (sweet) ≈ sucre m d'orge // vt (swing gently: cradle) balancer; (: child) bercer; (shake) ébranler, secouer // vi (se) balancer; être ébranlé(e) or secoué(e); **on the ~s** (drink) avec des glaçons; (ship) sur les écueils; (marriage etc) en train de craquer; **to ~ the boat** (fig) jouer les trouble-fête; **~-bottom** a (fig) niveau le plus bas; **~ery** n (jardin m de) rocaille f.

rocket ['rɔkɪt] n fusée f; (MIL) fusée f, roquette f.

rock face ['rɔkfeɪs] n paroi rocheuse.

rock fall ['rɔkfɔːl] n chute f de pierres.

rocking chair ['rɔkɪŋtʃɛə*] n fauteuil m à bascule.

rocking horse ['rɔkɪŋhɔːs] n cheval m à bascule.

rocky ['rɔkɪ] a (hill) rocheux(euse); (path) rocailleux(euse); (unsteady: table) branlant(e).

rod [rɔd] n (metallic) tringle f; (TECH) tige f; (wooden) baguette f; (also: **fishing ~**) canne f à pêche.

rode [rəud] pt of **ride**.

rodent ['rəudnt] n rongeur m.

rodeo ['rəudɪəu] n rodéo m.

roe [rəu] n (species: also: **~ deer**) chevreuil m; (of fish) œufs mpl de poisson; **soft ~** laitance f; **~ deer** n chevreuil m; chevreuil femelle.

rogue [rəug] n coquin/e; **roguish** a coquin(e).

role [rəul] n rôle m.

roll [rəul] n rouleau m; (of banknotes) liasse f; (also: **bread ~**) petit pain; (register) liste f; (sound: of drums etc) roulement m; (movement: of ship) roulis m // vt rouler; (also: **~ up: string**) enrouler // (also: **~ out: pastry**) étendre au rouleau // vi rouler; (wheel) tourner; (sway: person) se balancer; **to ~ by** vi (time) s'écouler, passer; **to ~ in** vi (mail, cash) affluer; **to ~ over** vi se retourner; **to ~ up** vi (col: arrive) arriver, s'amener // vt (carpet) rouler; **~ call** n appel m; **~ed gold** n plaqué or inv; **~er** n rouleau m; (wheel) roulette f; **~er skates** npl patins mpl à roulettes.

rollicking ['rɔlɪkɪŋ] a bruyant(e) et joyeux(euse); (play) bouffon(ne); **to have a ~ time** s'amuser follement.

rolling ['rəulɪŋ] a (landscape) onduleux(euse); **~ pin** n rouleau m à pâtisserie; **~ stock** n (RAIL) matériel roulant.

roll-on-roll-off ['rəulɔn'rəulɔf] a (ferry) transroulier(ère).

roly-poly ['rəulɪ'pəulɪ] n (CULIN) roulé m à la confiture.

Roman ['rəumən] a romain(e) // n Romain/e; **~ Catholic** a, n catholique (m/f).

romance [rə'mæns] n histoire f (or film m or aventure f) romanesque; (charm) poésie f; (love affair) idylle f // vi enjoliver (à plaisir), exagérer.

Romanesque [rəumə'nɛsk] a roman(e).

Romania [rəu'meɪnɪə] n Roumanie f; **~n** a roumain(e) // n Roumain/e.

romantic [rə'mæntɪk] a romantique; sentimental(e).

romanticism [rə'mæntɪsɪzəm] n romantisme m.

romp [rɔmp] n jeux bruyants // vi (also: **~ about**) s'ébattre, jouer bruyamment.

rompers ['rɔmpəz] npl barboteuse f.

rondo ['rɔndəu] n (MUS) rondeau m.

roof [ruːf] n toit m; (of tunnel, cave) plafond m // vt couvrir (d'un toit); **the ~ of the mouth** la voûte du palais; **~ garden** n toit-terrasse m; **~ing** n toiture f; **~ rack** n (AUT) galerie f.

rook [ruk] n (bird) freux m; (CHESS) tour f // vt (cheat) rouler, escroquer.

room [ru:m] n (in house) pièce f; (also: **bed~**) chambre f (à coucher); (in school etc) salle f; (space) place f; **~s** npl (lodging) meublé m; **'~s to let'** 'chambres à louer'; **~ing house** n (US) maison f de rapport; **~mate** n camarade m/f de chambre; **~ service** n service m des chambres (dans un hôtel); **~y** a spacieux(euse); (garment) ample.

roost [ru:st] n juchoir m // vi se jucher.

rooster ['ru:stə*] n coq m.

root [ru:t] n (BOT, MATH) racine f; (fig: of problem) origine f, fond m // vt (plant, belief) enraciner; **to ~ about** vi (fig) fouiller; **to ~ for** vt fus applaudir; **to ~ out** vt extirper.

rope [rəup] n corde f; (NAUT) cordage m // vt (box) corder; (climbers) encorder; **to sb in** (fig) embringuer qn; **to know the ~s** (fig) être au courant, connaître les ficelles; **~ ladder** n échelle f de corde.

rosary ['rəuzərɪ] n chapelet m; rosaire m.

rose [rəuz] pt of **rise** // n rose f; (also: **~bush**) rosier m; (on watering can) pomme f // a rose.

rosé ['rəuzeɪ] n rosé m.

rose: ~bed n massif m de rosiers; **~bud** n bouton m de rose; **~bush** n rosier m.

rosemary ['rəuzmərɪ] n romarin m.

rosette [rəu'zɛt] n rosette f; (larger) cocarde f.

roster ['rɔstə*] n: **duty ~** tableau m de service.

rostrum ['rɔstrəm] n tribune f (pour un orateur etc).

rosy ['rəuzɪ] a rose; **a ~ future** un bel avenir.

rot [rɔt] n (decay) pourriture f; (fig: pej) idioties fpl, baliverness fpl // vt, vi pourrir.

rota ['rəutə] n liste f, tableau m de service; **on a ~ basis** par roulement.

rotary ['rəutərɪ] a rotatif(ive).

rotate [rəu'teɪt] vt (revolve) faire tourner; (change round: crops) alterner; (:jobs) faire à tour de rôle // vi (revolve) tourner; **rotating** a (movement) tournant(e); **rotation** [-'teɪʃən] n rotation f; **in rotation** à tour de rôle.

rotor ['rəutə*] n rotor m.

rotten ['rɔtn] a (decayed) pourri(e); (dishonest) corrompu(e); (col: bad) mauvais(e), moche; **to feel ~** (ill) être mal fichu(e).

rotting ['rɔtɪŋ] a pourrissant(e).

rotund [rəu'tʌnd] a rondelet(te), arrondi(e).

rouble, ruble (US) ['ru:bl] n rouble m.

rouge [ru:ʒ] n rouge m (à joues).

rough [rʌf] a (cloth, skin) rêche, rugueux(euse); (terrain) accidenté(e); (path) rocailleux(euse); (voice) rauque, rude; (person, manner: coarse) rude, fruste; (: violent) brutal(e); (district, weather) mauvais(e); (plan) ébauché(e); (guess) approximatif(ive) // n (GOLF) rough m; (person) voyou m; **to ~ it** vivre à la dure; **to play ~** jouer avec brutalité; **to sleep ~** coucher à la dure; **to feel ~** être mal fichu(e); **to ~ out** vt (draft)

ébaucher; **~en** vt (a surface) rendre rude ou rugueux(euse); **~ justice** n justice f sommaire; **~ly** ad (handle) rudement, brutalement; (make) grossièrement; (approximately) à peu près, en gros; **~ness** n rugosité f; rudesse f; brutalité f; **~ work** n (at school etc) brouillon m.

roulette [ru:'lɛt] n roulette f.

Roumania [ru:'meɪnɪə] n = **Romania**.

round [raund] a rond(e) // n rond m, cercle m; (of toast) tranche f; (duty: of policeman, milkman etc) tournée f; (: of doctor) visites fpl; (game: of cards, in competition) partie f; (BOXING) round m; (of talks) série f // vt (corner) tourner; (bend) prendre; (cape) doubler // prep autour de // ad: **right ~, all ~** tout autour; **the long way ~** (par) le chemin le plus long; **all the year ~** toute l'année; **it's just ~ the corner** c'est juste après le coin; (fig) c'est tout près; **to go ~** faire le tour or un détour; **to go ~ to sb's (house)** aller chez qn; **to go ~ an obstacle** contourner un obstacle; **go ~ the back** passe par derrière; **to go ~ a house** visiter une maison, faire le tour d'une maison; **to go the ~s** (disease, story) circuler; **to ~ off** vt (speech etc) terminer; **to ~ up** vt rassembler; (criminals) effectuer une rafle de; (prices) arrondir (au chiffre supérieur); **~about** n (AUT) rond-point m (à sens giratoire); (at fair) manège m (de chevaux de bois) // a (route, means) détourné(e); **~ of ammunition** n cartouche f; **~ of applause** n ban m, applaudissements mpl; **~ of drinks** n tournée f; **~ of sandwiches** n sandwich m; **~ed** a arrondi(e); (style) harmonieux(euse); **~ly** ad (fig) tout net, carrément; **~-shouldered** a au dos rond; **~sman** n livreur m; **~ trip** n (voyage m) aller et retour m; **~up** n rassemblement m; (of criminals) rafle f.

rouse [rauz] vt (wake up) réveiller; (stir up) susciter; provoquer; éveiller; **rousing** a (welcome) enthousiaste.

rout [raut] n (MIL) déroute f // vt mettre en déroute.

route [ru:t] n itinéraire m; (of bus) parcours m; (of trade, shipping) route f; **'all ~s'** (AUT) 'toutes directions'; **~ map** n (for journey) croquis m d'itinéraire; (for trains etc) carte f du réseau.

routine [ru:'ti:n] a (work) ordinaire, courant(e); (procedure) d'usage // n (pej) routine f; (THEATRE) numéro m; **daily ~** occupations journalières.

roving ['rəuvɪŋ] a (life) vagabond(e); **~ reporter** n reporter volant.

row [rəu] n (line) rangée f; (of people, seats, KNITTING) rang m; (behind one another: of cars, people) file f // vi (in boat) ramer; (as sport) faire de l'aviron // vt (boat) faire aller à la rame or à l'aviron; **in a ~** (fig) d'affilée.

row [rau] n (noise) vacarme m; (dispute) dispute f, querelle f; (scolding) réprimande f, savon m // vi se disputer, se quereller.

rowdiness ['raudɪnɪs] n tapage m, chahut m; (fighting) bagarre f.

rowdy ['raudɪ] a chahuteur(euse); bagarreur(euse) // n voyou m.

rowing ['rəuɪŋ] n canotage m; (as sport) aviron m; ~ **boat** n canot m (à rames).

rowlock ['rɔlək] n dame f de nage, tolet m.

royal ['rɔɪəl] a royal(e); ~**ist** a, n royaliste (m/f).

royalty ['rɔɪəltɪ] n (royal persons) (membres mpl de la) famille royale; (payment: to author) droits mpl d'auteur; (: to inventor) royalties fpl.

r.p.m. abbr (AUT: = revs per minute) tr/mn (tours/minute).

R.S.P.C.A. n (abbr of Royal Society for the Prevention of Cruelty to Animals), ≈ S.P.A..

R.S.V.P. abbr (= répondez s'il vous plaît) R.S.V.P.

Rt Hon. abbr (= Right Honourable) titre donné aux députés de la Chambre des communes.

rub [rʌb] n (with cloth) coup m de chiffon or de torchon; (on person) friction f // vt frotter; frictionner; **to** ~ **sb up the wrong way** prendre qn à rebrousse-poil; **to** ~ **off** vi partir; **to** ~ **off on** déteindre sur.

rubber ['rʌbə*] n caoutchouc m; (Brit: eraser) gomme f (à effacer); ~ **band** n élastique m; ~ **plant** n caoutchouc m (plante verte); ~ **stamp** n tampon m; ~-**stamp** vt (fig) approuver sans discussion; ~**y** a caoutchouteux(euse).

rubbish ['rʌbɪʃ] n (from household) ordures fpl; (fig:pej) choses fpl sans valeur; camelote f; bêtises fpl, idioties fpl; ~ **bin** n boîte f à ordures, poubelle f; ~ **dump** n (in town) décharge publique, dépotoir m.

rubble ['rʌbl] n décombres mpl; (smaller) gravats mpl.

ruble ['ru:bl] n (US) = **rouble**.

ruby ['ru:bɪ] n rubis m.

rucksack ['rʌksæk] n sac m à dos.

ructions ['rʌkʃənz] npl grabuge m.

rudder ['rʌdə*] n gouvernail m.

ruddy ['rʌdɪ] a (face) coloré(e); (sky) rougeoyant(e); (col: damned) sacré(e), fichu(e).

rude [ru:d] a (impolite: person) impoli(e); (: word, manners) grossier(ère); (shocking) indécent(e), inconvenant(e); ~**ly** ad impoliment; grossièrement; ~**ness** n impolitesse f; grossièreté f.

rudiment ['ru:dɪmənt] n rudiment m; ~**ary** [-'mentərɪ] a rudimentaire.

rueful ['ru:ful] a triste.

ruff [rʌf] n fraise f, collerette f.

ruffian ['rʌfɪən] n brute f, voyou m.

ruffle ['rʌfl] vt (hair) ébouriffer; (clothes) chiffonner; (water) agiter; (fig: person) émouvoir, faire perdre son flegme à.

rug [rʌg] n petit tapis; (for knees) couverture f.

rugby ['rʌgbɪ] n (also: ~ **football**) rugby m.

rugged ['rʌgɪd] a (landscape) accidenté(e); (tree bark) rugueux(euse); (features, kindness, character) rude; (determination) farouche.

rugger ['rʌgə*] n (col) rugby m.

ruin ['ru:ɪn] n ruine f // vt ruiner; (spoil: clothes) abîmer; ~**s** npl ruine(s); ~**ation** [-'neɪʃən] n ruine f; ~**ous** a ruineux(euse).

rule [ru:l] n règle f; (regulation) règlement m; (government) autorité f, gouvernement m // vt (country) gouverner; (person) dominer; (decide) décider; (draw: lines) tirer à la règle // vi commander; décider; (LAW) statuer; **as a** ~ normalement, en règle générale; ~**d** a (paper) réglé(e); ~**r** n (sovereign) souverain/e; (leader) chef m (d'État); (for measuring) règle f; **ruling** a (party) au pouvoir; (class) dirigeant(e) // n (LAW) décision f.

rum [rʌm] n rhum m // a (col) bizarre.

Rumania [ru:'meɪnɪə] n = **Romania**.

rumble ['rʌmbl] n grondement m; gargouillement m // vi gronder; (stomach, pipe) gargouiller.

rummage ['rʌmɪdʒ] vi fouiller.

rumour, rumor (US) ['ru:mə*] n rumeur f, bruit m (qui court) // vt: **it is** ~**ed that** le bruit court que.

rump [rʌmp] n (of animal) croupe f; ~**steak** n rumsteck m.

rumpus ['rʌmpəs] n (col) tapage m, chahut m; (quarrel) prise f de bec.

run [rʌn] n (pas m de) course f; (outing) tour m or promenade f (en voiture); parcours m, trajet m; (series) suite f, série f; (THEATRE) série de représentations; (SKI) piste f // vb (pt ran, pp run [ræn, rʌn]) vt (operate: business) diriger; (: competition, course) organiser; (: hotel, house) tenir; (force through: rope, pipe): **to** ~ **sth through** faire passer qch à travers; (to pass: hand, finger): **to** ~ **sth over** promener or passer qch sur; (water, bath) faire couler // vi courir; (pass: road etc) passer; (work: machine, factory) marcher; (bus, train: operate) être en service; (: travel) circuler; (continue: play) se jouer; (: contract) être valide; (slide: drawer etc) glisser; (flow: river, bath) couler; (colours, washing) déteindre; (in election) être candidat, se présenter; **there was a** ~ **on** (meat, tickets) les gens se sont rués sur; **to break into a** ~ se mettre à courir; **in the long** ~ à longue échéance; à la longue, en fin de compte; **in the short** ~ à brève échéance, à court terme; **on the** ~ en fuite; **I'll** ~ **you to the station** je vais vous emmener or conduire à la gare; **to** ~ **a risk** courir un risque; **to** ~ **about** vi (children) courir çà et là; **to** ~ **across** vt fus (find) trouver par hasard; **to** ~ **away** vi s'enfuir; **to** ~ **down** vi (clock) s'arrêter (faute d'avoir été remonté) // vt (AUT) renverser; (criticize) critiquer, dénigrer; **to be** ~ **down** être fatigué(e) or à plat; **to** ~ **off** vi s'enfuir; **to** ~ **out** vi (person) sortir en courant; (liquid) couler; (lease) expirer; (money) être épuisé(e); **to** ~ **out of** vt fus se trouver à court de; **to** ~ **over** vt sep (AUT) écraser // vt fus (revise) revoir, reprendre; **to** ~ **through** vt fus (instructions) reprendre, revoir; **to** ~ **up** vt (debt) laisser accumuler; **to** ~ **up against** (difficulties) se heurter à; ~**away** a (horse) emballé(e); (truck) fou(folle); (inflation) galopant(e).

rung [rʌŋ] pp of **ring** // n (of ladder) barreau m.

runner ['rʌnə*] n (in race: person) coureur/euse; (: horse) partant m; (on sledge) patin m; (on curtain) suspendeur *m*; (*for drawer etc*) coulisseau *m*; (*carpet: in hall etc*) chemin *m*; ~ **bean** *n* (BOT) haricot *m* (à rames); ~**-up** *n* second/e.

running ['rʌnɪŋ] *n* course *f*; direction *f*; organisation *f*; marche *f*, fonctionnement *m* // *a* (*water*) courant(e); (*commentary*) suivi(e); **6 days** ~ 6 jours de suite.

runny ['rʌnɪ] *a* qui coule.

run-of-the-mill ['rʌnəvðə'mɪl] *a* ordinaire, banal(e).

runt [rʌnt] *n* (*also: pej*) avorton *m*.

run-through ['rʌnθruː] *n* répétition *f*, essai *m*.

runway ['rʌnweɪ] *n* (AVIAT) piste *f* (d'envol *ou* d'atterrissage).

rupee [ruː'piː] *n* roupie *f*.

rupture ['rʌptʃə*] *n* (MED) hernie *f* // *vt*: **to ~ o.s.** se donner une hernie.

rural ['ruərl] *a* rural(e).

ruse [ruːz] *n* ruse *f*.

rush [rʌʃ] *n* course précipitée; (*of crowd*) ruée *f*, bousculade *f*; (*hurry*) hâte *f*, bousculade; (*current*) flot *m* // *vt* transporter *or* envoyer d'urgence; (*attack: town etc*) prendre d'assaut; (*col: overcharge*) estamper; faire payer // *vi* se précipiter; **don't ~ me!** laissez-moi le temps de souffler!; ~**es** *npl* (BOT) jonc *m*; ~ **hour** *n* heures *fpl* de pointe *or* d'affluence.

rusk [rʌsk] *n* biscotte *f*.

Russia ['rʌʃə] *n* Russie *f*; ~**n** *a* russe // *n* Russe *m/f*; (LING) russe *m*.

rust [rʌst] *n* rouille *f* // *vi* rouiller.

rustic ['rʌstɪk] *a* rustique // *n* (*pej*) rustaud/e.

rustle ['rʌsl] *vi* bruire, produire un bruissement // *vt* (*paper*) froisser; (*US: cattle*) voler.

rustproof ['rʌstpruːf] *a* inoxydable; ~**ing** *n* traitement *m* antirouille.

rusty ['rʌstɪ] *a* rouillé(e).

rut [rʌt] *n* ornière *f*; (ZOOL) rut *m*.

ruthless ['ruːθlɪs] *a* sans pitié, impitoyable; ~**ness** *n* dureté *f*, cruauté *f*.

rye [raɪ] *n* seigle *m*; ~ **bread** *n* pain *m* de seigle.

S

sabbath ['sæbəθ] *n* sabbat *m*.

sabbatical [sə'bætɪkl] *a*: ~ **year** *n* année *f* sabbatique.

sabotage ['sæbətɑːʒ] *n* sabotage *m* // *vt* saboter.

saccharin(e) ['sækərɪn] *n* saccharine *f*.

sack [sæk] *n* (*bag*) sac *m* // *vt* (*dismiss*) renvoyer, mettre à la porte; (*plunder*) piller, mettre à sac; **to get the ~** être renvoyé *or* mis à la porte; **a ~ful of** (*plein*) sac de; ~**ing** *n* toile *f* à sac; renvoi *m*.

sacrament ['sækrəmənt] *n* sacrement *m*.

sacred ['seɪkrɪd] *a* sacré(e).

sacrifice ['sækrɪfaɪs] *n* sacrifice *m* // *vt* sacrifier.

sacrilege ['sækrɪlɪdʒ] *n* sacrilège *m*.

sacrosanct ['sækrəusæŋkt] *a* sacro-saint(e).

sad [sæd] *a* (*unhappy*) triste; (*deplorable*) triste, fâcheux(euse); ~**den** *vt* attrister, affliger.

saddle ['sædl] *n* selle *f* // *vt* (*horse*) seller; **to be ~d with sth** (*col*) avoir qch sur les bras; ~**bag** *n* sacoche *f*.

sadism ['seɪdɪzm] *n* sadisme *m*; **sadist** *n* sadique *m/f*; **sadistic** [sə'dɪstɪk] *a* sadique.

sadly ['sædlɪ] *ad* tristement; fâcheusement.

sadness ['sædnɪs] *n* tristesse *f*.

safari [sə'fɑːrɪ] *n* safari *m*.

safe [seɪf] *a* (*out of danger*) hors de danger, en sécurité; (*not dangerous*) sans danger; (*cautious*) prudent(e); (*sure: bet etc*) assuré(e) // *n* coffre-fort *m*; ~ **from** à l'abri de; ~ **and sound** sain(e) et sauf(sauve); (**just**) **to be on the ~ side** pour plus de sûreté, par précaution; ~**guard** *n* sauvegarde *f*, protection *f* // *vt* sauvegarder, protéger; ~**keeping** *n* bonne garde; ~**ly** *ad* sans danger, sans risque; (*without mishap*) sans accident.

safety ['seɪftɪ] *n* sécurité *f*; ~ **belt** *n* ceinture *f* de sécurité; ~ **curtain** *n* rideau *m* de fer; ~ **first!** la sécurité d'abord!; ~ **pin** *n* épingle *f* de sûreté *or* de nourrice.

saffron ['sæfrən] *n* safran *m*.

sag [sæg] *vi* s'affaisser, fléchir; pendre.

sage [seɪdʒ] *n* (*herb*) sauge *f*; (*man*) sage *m*.

Sagittarius [sædʒɪ'tɛərɪəs] *n* le Sagittaire; **to be** ~ être du Sagittaire.

sago ['seɪɡəu] *n* sagou *m*.

said [sɛd] *pt, pp* of **say**.

sail [seɪl] *n* (*on boat*) voile *f*; (*trip*): **to go for a** ~ faire un tour en bateau // *vt* (*boat*) manœuvrer, piloter // *vi* (*travel: ship*) avancer, naviguer; (: *passenger*) aller *or* se rendre (en bateau); (*set off*) partir, prendre la mer; (SPORT) faire de la voile; **they ~ed into Le Havre** ils sont entrés dans le port du Havre; **to ~ through** *vi, vt fus* (*fig*) réussir haut la main; ~**boat** *n* (US) bateau *m* à voiles, voilier *m*; ~**ing** *n* (SPORT) voile *f*; **to go ~ing** faire de la voile; ~**ing boat** *n* bateau *m* à voiles, voilier *m*; ~**ing ship** *n* grand voilier; ~**or** *n* marin *m*, matelot *m*.

saint [seɪnt] *n* saint/e; ~**ly** *a* saint(e), plein(e) de bonté.

sake [seɪk] *n*: **for the ~ of** pour (l'amour de), dans l'intérêt de; par égard pour; **for pity's ~** par pitié.

salad ['sæləd] *n* salade *f*; ~ **bowl** *n* saladier *m*; ~ **cream** *n* (sorte *f* de) mayonnaise *f*; ~ **dressing** *n* vinaigrette *f*; ~ **oil** *n* huile *f* de table.

salaried ['sælərɪd] *a* (*staff*) salarié(e), qui touche un traitement.

salary ['sælərɪ] *n* salaire *m*, traitement *m*.

sale [seɪl] *n* vente *f*; (*at reduced prices*) soldes *mpl*; **'for ~'** 'à vendre'; **on ~** en vente; **on ~ or return** vendu(e) avec faculté de retour; ~**room** *n* salle *f* des ventes; ~**sman** *n* vendeur *m*; (*representative*) représentant *m* de commerce; ~**smanship** *n* art *m* de la vente; ~**swoman** *n* vendeuse *f*.

salient ['seɪlɪənt] *a* saillant(e).

saliva [sə'laɪvə] *n* salive *f*.

sallow ['sæləu] *a* cireux(euse).

salmon ['sæmən] *n, pl inv* saumon *m*; ~ **trout** *n* truite saumonée.

saloon [sə'lu:n] n (US) bar m; (AUT) berline f; (ship's lounge) salon m.

salt [sɔlt] n sel m // vt saler // cpd de sel; (CULIN) salé(e); ~ **cellar** n salière f; ~**-free** a sans sel; ~**y** a salé.

salutary ['sæljutərɪ] a salutaire.

salute [sə'lu:t] n salut m // vt saluer.

salvage ['sælvɪdʒ] n (saving) sauvetage m; (things saved) biens sauvés or récupérés // vt sauver, récupérer.

salvation [sæl'veɪʃən] n salut m; **S— Army** n Armée f du Salut.

salver ['sælvə*] n plateau m de métal.

salvo ['sælvəu] n salve f.

same [seɪm] a même // pronoun: **the** ~ le(la) même, les mêmes; **the** ~ **book as** le même livre que; **all** or **just the** ~ tout de même, quand même; **to do the** ~ faire de même, en faire autant; **to do the** ~ **as sb** faire comme qn; **the** ~ **again!** (in bar etc) la même chose!

sample ['sɑ:mpl] n échantillon m; (MED) prélèvement m // vt (food, wine) goûter.

sanatoria [sænə'tɔ:rɪəm, -rɪə] n sanatorium m.

sanctify ['sæŋktɪfaɪ] vt sanctifier.

sanctimonious [sæŋktɪ'məunɪəs] a moralisateur(trice).

sanction ['sæŋkʃən] n sanction f // vt cautionner, sanctionner.

sanctity ['sæŋktɪtɪ] n sainteté f, caractère sacré.

sanctuary ['sæŋktjuərɪ] n (holy place) sanctuaire m; (refuge) asile m; (for wild life) réserve f.

sand [sænd] n sable m // vt sabler; ~**s** npl plage f (de sable).

sandal ['sændl] n sandale f.

sandbag ['sændbæg] n sac m de sable.

sandcastle ['sændkɑ:sl] n château m de sable.

sand dune ['sænddju:n] n dune f de sable.

sandpaper ['sændpeɪpə*] n papier m de verre.

sandpit ['sændpɪt] n (for children) tas m de sable.

sandstone ['sændstəun] n grès m.

sandwich ['sændwɪtʃ] n sandwich m // vt (also: ~ **in**) intercaler; ~**ed between** pris en sandwich entre; **cheese/ham** ~ sandwich au fromage/jambon; ~ **course** n cours m de formation professionnelle.

sandy ['sændɪ] a sablonneux(euse); (colour) sable inv, blond roux inv.

sane [seɪn] a (person) sain(e) d'esprit; (outlook) sensé(e), sain(e).

sang [sæŋ] pt of **sing**.

sanguine ['sæŋgwɪn] a optimiste.

sanitarium [sænɪ'tɛərɪəm, -rɪə] n (US) = **sanatorium**.

sanitary ['sænɪtərɪ] a (system, arrangements) sanitaire; (clean) hygiénique; ~ **towel**, ~ **napkin** (US) n serviette f hygiénique.

sanitation [sænɪ'teɪʃən] n (in house) installations fpl sanitaires; (in town) système m sanitaire.

sanity ['sænɪtɪ] n santé mentale; (common sense) bon sens.

sank [sæŋk] pt of **sink**.

Santa Claus [sæntə'klɔ:z] n le Père Noël.

sap [sæp] n (of plants) sève f // vt (strength) saper, miner.

sapling ['sæplɪŋ] n jeune arbre m.

sapphire ['sæfaɪə*] n saphir m.

sarcasm ['sɑ:kæzm] n sarcasme m, raillerie f.

sarcastic [sɑ:'kæstɪk] a sarcastique.

sarcophagus, pl sarcophagi [sɑ:'kɔfəgəs, -gaɪ] n sarcophage m.

sardine [sɑ:'di:n] n sardine f.

Sardinia [sɑ:'dɪnɪə] n Sardaigne f.

sardonic [sɑ:'dɔnɪk] a sardonique.

sartorial [sɑ:'tɔ:rɪəl] a vestimentaire.

sash [sæʃ] n écharpe f; ~ **window** n fenêtre f à guillotine.

sat [sæt] pt,pp of **sit**.

satanic [sə'tænɪk] a satanique, démoniaque.

satchel ['sætʃl] n cartable m.

satellite ['sætəlaɪt] a, n satellite (m).

satin ['sætɪn] n satin m // a en or de satin, satiné(e).

satire ['sætaɪə*] n satire f; **satirical** [sə'tɪrɪkl] a satirique; **satirize** ['sætɪraɪz] vt faire la satire de, satiriser.

satisfaction [sætɪs'fækʃən] n satisfaction f.

satisfactory [sætɪs'fæktərɪ] a satisfaisant(e).

satisfy ['sætɪsfaɪ] vt satisfaire, contenter; (convince) convaincre, persuader; ~**ing** a satisfaisant(e).

saturate ['sætʃəreɪt] vt: **to** ~ **(with)** saturer (de); **saturation** [-'reɪʃən] n saturation f.

Saturday ['sætədɪ] n samedi m.

sauce [sɔ:s] n sauce f; ~**pan** n casserole f.

saucer ['sɔ:sə*] n soucoupe f.

saucy ['sɔ:sɪ] a impertinent(e).

sauna ['sɔ:nə] n sauna m.

saunter ['sɔ:ntə*] vi: **to** ~ **to** aller en flânant or se balader jusqu'à.

sausage ['sɔsɪdʒ] n saucisse f; ~ **roll** n friand m.

savage ['sævɪdʒ] a (cruel, fierce) brutal(e), féroce; (primitive) primitif(ive), sauvage // n sauvage m/f // vt attaquer férocement; ~**ry** n sauvagerie f, brutalité f, férocité f.

save [seɪv] vt (person, belongings) sauver; (money) mettre de côté, économiser; (time) (faire) gagner; (food) garder; (avoid: trouble) éviter // vi (also: ~ **up**) mettre de l'argent de côté // n (SPORT) arrêt m (du ballon) // prep sauf, à l'exception de.

saving ['seɪvɪŋ] n économie f // a: **the** ~ **grace of** ce qui rachète; ~**s** npl économies fpl; ~**s bank** n caisse f d'épargne.

saviour ['seɪvjə*] n sauveur m.

savour, savor (US) ['seɪvə*] n saveur f, goût m // vt savourer; ~**y** a savoureux(euse); (dish: not sweet) salé(e).

savvy ['sævɪ] n (col) jugeote f.

saw [sɔ:] pt of **see** // n (tool) scie f // vt (pt **sawed**, pp **sawed** or **sawn** [sɔ:n]) scier; ~**dust** n sciure f; ~**mill** n scierie f.

saxophone ['sæksəfəun] n saxophone m.

say [seɪ] n: **to have one's** ~ dire ce qu'on a à dire; **to have a** ~ avoir voix au chapitre // vt (pt, pp **said** [sɛd]) dire; **could you** ~ **that again?** pourriez-vous répéter ceci?; **that is to** ~ c'est-à-dire; **to** ~ **nothing of** sans compter; ~ **that** ... mettons or disons que ...; **that goes without** ~**ing** cela va sans dire, cela va de soi; ~**ing** n dicton m, proverbe m.

scab [skæb] n croûte f; (pej) jaune m; ~**by** a croûteux(euse).

scaffold ['skæfəuld] n échafaud m; ~**ing** n échafaudage m.

scald [skɔ:ld] n brûlure f // vt ébouillanter; ~**ing** a (hot) brûlant(e), bouillant(e).

scale [skeɪl] n (of fish) écaille f; (MUS) gamme f; (of ruler, thermometer etc) graduation f, échelle (graduée) f; (of salaries, fees etc) barème m; (of map, also size, extent) échelle f // vt (mountain) escalader; (fish) écailler; ~**s** npl balance f, (larger) bascule f; **on a large** ~ sur une grande échelle, en grand; ~ **drawing** n dessin m à l'échelle; ~ **model** n modèle m à l'échelle; **small-**~ **model** modèle réduit.

scallop ['skɔləp] n coquille f Saint-Jacques.

scalp [skælp] n cuir chevelu // vt scalper.

scalpel ['skælpl] n scalpel m.

scamp [skæmp] vt bâcler.

scamper ['skæmpə*] vi: **to** ~ **away,** ~ **off** détaler.

scan [skæn] vt scruter, examiner; (glance at quickly) parcourir; (poetry) scander; (TV, RADAR) balayer.

scandal ['skændl] n scandale m; (gossip) ragots mpl; ~**ize** vt scandaliser, indigner; ~**ous** a scandaleux(euse).

Scandinavia [skændɪ'neɪvɪə] n Scandinavie f; ~**n** a scandinave // n Scandinave m/f.

scant [skænt] a insuffisant(e); ~**y** a peu abondant(e), insuffisant(e), maigre.

scapegoat ['skeɪpgəut] n bouc m émissaire.

scar [skɑ:] n cicatrice f // vt laisser une cicatrice or une marque à.

scarce [skɛəs] a rare, peu abondant(e); ~**ly** ad à peine, presque pas; **scarcity** n rareté f, manque m, pénurie f.

scare [skɛə*] n peur f; panique f // vt effrayer, faire peur à; **to** ~ **sb stiff** faire une peur bleue à qn; **bomb** ~ alerte f à la bombe; ~**crow** n épouvantail m; ~**d** a: **to be** ~**d** avoir peur; ~**monger** n alarmiste m/f.

scarf, scarves [skɑ:f, skɑ:vz] n (long) écharpe f; (square) foulard m.

scarlet ['skɑ:lɪt] a écarlate; ~ **fever** n scarlatine f.

scarves [skɑ:vz] npl of **scarf**.

scary ['skɛərɪ] a (col) qui fiche la frousse.

scathing ['skeɪðɪŋ] a cinglant(e), acerbe.

scatter ['skætə*] vt éparpiller, répandre; (crowd) disperser // vi se disperser; ~**brained** a écervelé(e), étourdi(e); ~**ed** a épars(e), dispersé(e).

scatty ['skætɪ] a (col) loufoque.

scavenger ['skævəndʒə*] n éboueur m.

scene [si:n] n (THEATRE, fig etc) scène f; (of crime, accident) lieu(x) m(pl), endroit m; (sight, view) spectacle m, vue f; **to appear on the** ~ faire son apparition; ~**ry** n (THEATRE) décor(s) m(pl); (landscape) paysage m; **scenic** a scénique; offrant de beaux paysages or panoramas.

scent [sɛnt] n parfum m, odeur f; (fig: track) piste f; (sense of smell) odorat m // vt parfumer; (smell, also fig) flairer.

sceptic, skeptic (US) ['skɛptɪk] n sceptique m/f; ~**al** a sceptique; ~**ism** ['skɛptɪsɪzm] n scepticisme m.

sceptre, scepter (US) ['sɛptə*] n sceptre m.

schedule ['ʃɛdju:l] n programme m, plan m; (of trains) horaire m; (of prices etc) barème m, tarif m // vt prévoir; **as** ~**d** comme prévu; **on** ~ à l'heure (prévue); à la date prévue; **to be ahead of/behind** ~ avoir de l'avance/du retard.

scheme [ski:m] n plan m, projet m; (method) procédé m; (dishonest plan, plot) complot m, combine f; (arrangement) arrangement m, classification f // vt,vi comploter, manigancer; **scheming** a rusé(e), intrigant(e) // n manigances fpl, intrigues fpl.

schism ['skɪzm] n schisme m.

schizophrenic [skɪtsə'frɛnɪk] a schizophrène.

scholar ['skɔlə*] n érudit/e; ~**ly** a érudit(e), savant(e); ~**ship** n érudition f; (grant) bourse f (d'études).

school [sku:l] n (gen) école f; (in university) faculté f; (secondary school) collège m, lycée m // cpd scolaire // vt (animal) dresser; ~**book** n livre m scolaire or de classe; ~**boy** n écolier m; collégien m, lycéen m; ~**days** npl années fpl de scolarité; ~**girl** n écolière f; collégienne f, lycéenne f; ~**ing** n instruction f, études fpl; ~**-leaving age** n âge m de fin de scolarité; ~**master** n (primary) instituteur m; (secondary) professeur m; ~**mistress** n institutrice f; professeur m; ~**report** n bulletin m (scolaire); ~**room** n (salle f de) classe f; ~**teacher** n instituteur/trice; professeur m.

schooner ['sku:nə*] n (ship) schooner m, goélette f; (glass) grand verre (à xérès).

sciatica [saɪ'ætɪkə] n sciatique f.

science ['saɪəns] n science f; ~ **fiction** n science-fiction f; **scientific** [-'tɪfɪk] a scientifique; **scientist** n scientifique m/f; (eminent) savant m.

scintillating ['sɪntɪleɪtɪŋ] a scintillant(e), étincelant(e).

scissors ['sɪzəz] npl ciseaux mpl; **a pair of** ~ une paire de ciseaux.

sclerosis [sklɪ'rəusɪs] n sclérose f.

scoff [skɔf] vt (col: eat) avaler, bouffer // vi: **to** ~ **(at)** (mock) se moquer (de).

scold [skəuld] vt gronder, attraper, réprimander.

scone [skɔn] n sorte de petit pain rond au lait.

scoop [sku:p] n pelle f (à main); (for ice cream) boule f à glace; (PRESS) reportage exclusif or à sensation; **to** ~ **out** vt évider, creuser; **to** ~ **up** vt ramasser.

scooter ['sku:tə*] n (motor cycle) scooter m; (toy) trottinette f.

scope [skəup] *n* (*capacity: of plan, under-taking*) portée *f*, envergure *f*; (: *of person*) compétence *f*, capacités *fpl*; (*opportunity*) possibilités *fpl*; **within the ~ of** dans les limites de.

scorch [skɔːtʃ] *vt* (*clothes*) brûler (légère-ment), roussir; (*earth, grass*) dessécher, brûler; **~ed earth policy** *n* politique *f* de la terre brûlée; **~er** *n* (*col: hot day*) journée *f* torride; **~ing** *a* torride, brûlant(e).

score [skɔː*] *n* score *m*, décompte *m* des points; (*MUS*) partition *f*; (*twenty*) vingt // *vt* (*goal, point*) marquer; (*success*) rempor-ter // *vi* marquer des points; (*FOOTBALL*) marquer un but; (*keep score*) compter les points; **on that ~** sur ce chapitre, à cet égard; **to ~ well/6 out of 10** obtenir un bon résultat/6 sur 10; **~board** *n* tableau *m*; **~card** *n* (*SPORT*) carton *m*; feuille *f* de marque; **~r** *n* auteur *m* du but; marqueur *m* de buts; (*keeping score*) marqueur *m*.

scorn [skɔːn] *n* mépris *m*, dédain *m* // *vt* mépriser, dédaigner; **~ful** *a* méprisant(e), dédaigneux(euse).

Scorpio ['skɔːpɪəu] *n* le Scorpion; **to be ~** être du Scorpion.

scorpion ['skɔːpɪən] *n* scorpion *m*.

Scot [skɔt] *n* Écossais/e.

scotch [skɔtʃ] *vt* faire échouer; enrayer; étouffer; **S~** *n* whisky *m*, scotch *m*.

scot-free ['skɔt'friː] *a* sans être puni(e); sans payer.

Scotland ['skɔtlənd] *n* Écosse *f*.

Scots [skɔts] *a* écossais(e); **~man/woman** Écossais/e.

Scottish ['skɔtɪʃ] *a* écossais(e).

scoundrel ['skaundrl] *n* vaurien *m*; (*child*) coquin *m*.

scour ['skauə*] *vt* (*clean*) récurer; frotter; décaper; (*search*) battre, parcourir; **~er** *n* tampon abrasif *or* à récurer.

scourge [skəːdʒ] *n* fléau *m*.

scout [skaut] *n* (*MIL*) éclaireur *m*; (*also:* **boy ~**) scout *m*; **to ~ around** explorer, chercher.

scowl [skaul] *vi* se renfrogner, avoir l'air maussade; **to ~ at** regarder de travers.

scraggy ['skrægɪ] *a* décharné(e), ef-flanqué(e), famélique.

scram [skræm] *vi* (*col*) ficher le camp.

scramble ['skræmbl] *n* bousculade *f*, ruée *f* // *vi* avancer tant bien que mal (à quatre pattes *or* en grimpant); **to ~ for** se bous-culer *or* se disputer pour (avoir); **~d eggs** *npl* œufs brouillés.

scrap [skræp] *n* bout *m*, morceau *m*; (*fight*) bagarre *f*; (*also:* **~ iron**) ferraille *f* // *vt* jeter, mettre au rebut; (*fig*) aban-donner, laisser tomber; **~s** *npl* (*waste*) dé-chets *mpl*; **~book** *n* album *m*.

scrape [skreɪp] *vt,vi* gratter, racler // *n*: **to get into a ~** s'attirer des ennuis; **~r** *n* grattoir *m*, racloir *m*.

scrap: **~ heap** *n* tas *m* de ferraille; (*fig*): **on the ~ heap** au rancart *or* rebut; **~ merchant** *n* marchand *m* de ferraille; **~ paper** *n* papier *m* brouillon; **~py** *a* fragmentaire, décousu(e).

scratch [skrætʃ] *n* égratignure *f*, rayure *f*; éraflure *f*; (*from claw*) coup *m* de griffe // *a*: **~ team** *n* équipe de fortune *or* im-provisé(e) // *vt* (*record*) rayer; (*paint etc*) érafler; (*with claw, nail*) griffer // *vi* (*se*) gratter; **to start from ~** partir de zéro; **to be up to ~** être à la hauteur.

scrawl [skrɔːl] *n* gribouillage *m* // *vi* gribouiller.

scrawny ['skrɔːnɪ] *a* décharné(e).

scream [skriːm] *n* cri perçant, hurlement *m* // *vi* crier, hurler; **to be a ~** être im-payable.

scree [skriː] *n* éboulis *m*.

screech [skriːtʃ] *n* cri strident, hurlement *m*; (*of tyres, brakes*) crissement *m*, grince-ment *m* // *vi* hurler; crisser, grincer.

screen [skriːn] *n* écran *m*, paravent *m*; (*CINEMA, TV*) écran *m*; (*fig*) écran, rideau *m* // *vt* masquer, cacher; (*from the wind etc*) abriter, protéger; (*film*) projeter; (*book*) porter à l'écran; (*candidates etc*) filtrer; **~ing** *n* (*MED*) test *m* (*or* tests) de dépistage.

screw [skruː] *n* vis *f*; (*propeller*) hélice *f* // *vt* visser; **to have one's head ~ed on** avoir la tête sur les épaules; **~driver** *n* tournevis *m*; **~y** *a* (*col*) dingue, cinglé(e).

scribble ['skrɪbl] *n* gribouillage *m* // *vt* gribouiller, griffonner.

scribe [skraɪb] *n* scribe *m*.

script [skrɪpt] *n* (*CINEMA etc*) scénario *m*, texte *m*; (*in exam*) copie *f*.

Scripture ['skrɪptʃə*] *n* Écriture Sainte.

scriptwriter ['skrɪptraɪtə*] *n* scénariste *m/f*, dialoguiste *m/f*.

scroll [skrəul] *n* rouleau *m*.

scrounge [skraundʒ] *vt* (*col*): **to ~ sth (off** *or* **from sb)** se faire payer qch (par qn), emprunter qch (à qn) // *vi*: **to ~ on sb** vivre aux crochets de qn; **~r** *n* para-site *m*.

scrub [skrʌb] *n* (*clean*) nettoyage *m* (à la brosse); (*land*) broussailles *fpl* // *vt* (*floor*) nettoyer à la brosse; (*pan*) récurer; (*wash-ing*) frotter; (*reject*) annuler.

scruff [skrʌf] *n*: **by the ~ of the neck** par la peau du cou.

scruffy ['skrʌfɪ] *a* débraillé(e).

scrum(mage) ['skrʌm(ɪdʒ)] *n* mêlée *f*.

scruple ['skruːpl] *n* scrupule *m*.

scrupulous ['skruːpjuləs] *a* scrupu-leux(euse).

scrutinize ['skruːtɪnaɪz] *vt* scruter, examiner minutieusement.

scrutiny ['skruːtɪnɪ] *n* examen minutieux.

scuff [skʌf] *vt* érafler.

scuffle ['skʌfl] *n* échauffourée *f*, rixe *f*.

scull [skʌl] *n* aviron *m*.

scullery ['skʌlərɪ] *n* arrière-cuisine *f*.

sculptor ['skʌlptə*] *n* sculpteur *m*.

sculpture ['skʌlptʃə*] *n* sculpture *f*.

scum [skʌm] *n* écume *f*, mousse *f*; (*pej: people*) rebut *m*, lie *f*.

scurrilous ['skʌrɪləs] *a* haineux(euse), virulent(e); calomnieux(euse).

scurry ['skʌrɪ] *vi* filer à toute allure.

scurvy ['skəːvɪ] *n* scorbut *m*.

scuttle ['skʌtl] *n* (*NAUT*) écoutille *f*; (*also:* **coal ~**) seau *m* (à charbon) // *vt* (*ship*) saborder // *vi* (*scamper*): **to ~ away, ~ off** détaler.

scythe [saɪð] *n* faux *f*.

sea [siː] *n* mer *f* // *cpd* marin(e), de (la) mer, maritime; **on the ~** (*boat*) en mer;

(*town*) au bord de la mer ; **to be all at ~** (*fig*) nager complètement ; **~ bird** n oiseau m de mer ; **~board** n côte f ; **~ breeze** n brise f de mer ; **~farer** n marin m ; **~food** n fruits mpl de mer ; **~ front** n bord m de mer ; **~going** a (*ship*) de haute mer ; **~gull** n mouette f.

seal [si:l] n (*animal*) phoque m ; (*stamp*) sceau m, cachet m ; (*impression*) cachet, estampille f // vt sceller ; (*envelope*) coller ; (: *with seal*) cacheter.

sea level ['si:lɛvl] n niveau m de la mer.

sealing wax ['si:lɪŋwæks] n cire f à cacheter.

sea lion ['si:laɪən] n lion m de mer.

seam [si:m] n couture f ; (*of coal*) veine f, filon m.

seaman ['si:mən] n marin m.

seamless ['si:mlɪs] a sans couture(s).

seamy ['si:mɪ] a louche, mal famé(e).

seance ['seɪɔns] n séance f de spiritisme.

seaplane ['si:pleɪn] n hydravion m.

seaport ['si:pɔ:t] n port m de mer.

search [sə:tʃ] n (*for person, thing*) recherche(s) f(pl) ; (*of drawer, pockets*) fouille f ; (*LAW: at sb's home*) perquisition f // vt fouiller ; (*examine*) examiner minutieusement ; scruter // vi: **to ~ for** chercher ; **to ~ through** vt fus fouiller ; **in ~ of** à la recherche de ; **~ing** a pénétrant(e) ; minutieux(euse) ; **~light** n projecteur m ; **~ party** n expédition f de secours ; **~ warrant** n mandat m de perquisition.

seashore ['si:ʃɔ:*] n rivage m, plage f, bord m de (la) mer.

seasick ['si:sɪk] a qui a le mal de mer.

seaside ['si:saɪd] n bord m de la mer ; **~ resort** n station f balnéaire.

season ['si:zn] n saison f // vt assaisonner, relever ; **~al** a saisonnier(ère) ; **~ing** n assaisonnement m ; **~ ticket** n carte f d'abonnement.

seat [si:t] n siège m ; (*in bus, train: place*) place f ; (*PARLIAMENT*) siège ; (*buttocks*) postérieur m ; (*of trousers*) fond m // vt faire asseoir, placer ; (*have room for*) avoir des places assises pour, pouvoir accueillir ; **~ belt** n ceinture f de sécurité ; **~ing room** n places assises.

sea water ['si:wɔ:tə*] n eau f de mer.

seaweed ['si:wi:d] n algues fpl.

seaworthy ['si:wə:ðɪ] a en état de naviguer.

sec. abbr of **second(s)**.

secede [sɪ'si:d] vi faire sécession.

secluded [sɪ'klu:dɪd] a retiré(e), à l'écart.

seclusion [sɪ'klu:ʒən] n solitude f.

second ['sɛkənd] num deuxième, second(e) // ad (*in race etc*) en seconde position ; (*RAIL*) en seconde // n (*unit of time*) seconde f ; (*in series, position*) deuxième m/f, second/e ; (*SCOL*) ≈ licence f avec mention bien or assez bien ; (*AUT: also: ~ gear*) seconde f ; (*COMM: imperfect*) article m de second choix // vt (*motion*) appuyer ; **~ary** a secondaire ; **~ary school** n collège m, lycée m ; **~ class** a de deuxième classe ; **~er** n personne f qui appuie une motion ; **~hand** d'occasion ; **de seconde main** ; **~ hand** (*on clock*) trot-

teuse f ; **~ly** ad deuxièmement ; **~ment** [sɪ'kɔndmənt] n détachement m ; **~-rate** a de deuxième ordre, de qualité inférieure ; **~ thoughts** npl doutes mpl ; **on ~ thoughts** à la réflexion.

secrecy ['si:krəsɪ] n secret m ; **in ~** en secret, dans le secret.

secret ['si:krɪt] a secret(ète) // n secret m.

secretarial [sɛkrɪ'tɛərɪəl] a de secrétaire, de secrétariat.

secretariat [sɛkrɪ'tɛərɪət] n secrétariat m.

secretary ['sɛkrətərɪ] n secrétaire m/f ; (*COMM*) secrétaire général ; **S~ of State (for)** (*Brit*: *POL*) ministre m (de).

secretive ['si:krətɪv] a réservé(e) ; (*pej*) cachottier(ère), dissimulé(e).

sect [sɛkt] n secte f ; **~arian** [-'tɛərɪən] a sectaire.

section ['sɛkʃən] n coupe f, section f ; (*department*) section ; (*COMM*) rayon m ; (*of document*) section, article m, paragraphe m // vt sectionner ; **~al** a (*drawing*) en coupe.

sector ['sɛktə*] n secteur m.

secular ['sɛkjulə*] a profane ; laïque ; séculier(ère).

secure [sɪ'kjuə*] a (*free from anxiety*) sans inquiétude, sécurisé(e) ; (*firmly fixed*) solide, bien attaché(e) (or fermé(e) etc) ; (*in safe place*) en lieu sûr, en sûreté // vt (*fix*) fixer, attacher ; (*get*) obtenir, se procurer.

security [sɪ'kjurɪtɪ] n sécurité f ; mesures fpl de sécurité ; (*for loan*) caution f, garantie f.

sedate [sɪ'deɪt] a calme ; posé(e) // vt donner des sédatifs à.

sedation [sɪ'deɪʃən] n (*MED*) sédation f.

sedative ['sɛdɪtɪv] n calmant m, sédatif m.

sedentary ['sɛdntrɪ] a sédentaire.

sediment ['sɛdɪmənt] n sédiment m, dépôt m.

seduce [sɪ'dju:s] vt (*gen*) séduire ; **seduction** [-'dʌkʃən] n séduction f ; **seductive** [-'dʌktɪv] a séduisant(e), séducteur(trice).

see [si:] vb (pt **saw**, pp **seen** [sɔ:, si:n]) vt (*gen*) voir ; (*accompany*): **to ~ sb to the door** reconduire or raccompagner qn jusqu'à la porte // vi voir // n évêché m ; **to ~ that** (*ensure*) veiller à (ce que + sub, faire en sorte que + sub, s'assurer que ; **to ~ off** vt accompagner (à la gare or à l'aéroport etc) ; **to ~ through** vt mener à bonne fin // vt fus voir clair dans ; **to ~ to** vt fus s'occuper de, se charger de ; **~ you!** au revoir!, à bientôt!

seed [si:d] n graine f ; (*fig*) germe m ; (*TENNIS*) tête f de série ; **to go to ~** monter en graine ; (*fig*) se laisser aller ; **~ling** n jeune plant m, semis m ; **~y** a (*shabby*) minable, miteux(euse).

seeing ['si:ɪŋ] cj: **~ (that)** vu que, étant donné que.

seek, pt,pp **sought** [si:k, sɔ:t] vt chercher, rechercher.

seem [si:m] vi sembler, paraître ; **there seems to be ...** il semble qu'il y a ... ; on dirait qu'il y a ... ; **~ingly** ad apparemment.

seen [si:n] pp of **see**.

seep [si:p] vi suinter, filtrer.

seer ['sɪə*] n prophète/prophétesse, voyant/e.

seersucker ['sɪəsʌkə*] n cloqué m, étoffe cloquée.

seesaw ['si:sɔ:] n (jeu m de) bascule f.

seethe [si:ð] vi être en effervescence ; **to ~ with anger** bouillir de colère.

see-through ['si:θru:] a transparent(e).

segment ['sɛgmənt] n segment m.

segregate ['sɛgrɪgeɪt] vt séparer, isoler ; **segregation** [-'geɪʃən] n ségrégation f.

seismic ['saɪzmɪk] a sismique.

seize [si:z] vt (grasp) saisir, attraper ; (take possession of) s'emparer de ; (LAW) saisir ; **to ~ (up)on** vt fus saisir, sauter sur ; **to ~ up** vi (TECH) se gripper.

seizure ['si:ʒə*] n (MED) crise f, attaque f ; (LAW) saisie f.

seldom ['sɛldəm] ad rarement.

select [sɪ'lɛkt] a choisi(e), d'élite ; select inv // vt sélectionner, choisir ; **~ion** [-'lɛkʃən] n sélection f, choix m ; **~ive** a sélectif(ive) ; (school) à recrutement sélectif ; **~or** n (person) sélection-neur/euse ; (TECH) sélecteur m.

self [sɛlf] n (pl selves [sɛlvz]): **the ~** le moi inv // prefix auto- ; **~-adhesive** a auto-collant(e) ; **~-assertive** a autoritaire ; **~-assured** a sûr(e) de soi, plein(e) d'assurance ; **~-catering** a avec cuisine, où l'on peut faire sa cuisine ; **~-centred** a égocentrique ; **~-coloured** a uni(e) ; **~-confidence** n confiance f en soi ; **~-conscious** a timide, qui manque d'assurance ; **~-contained** a (flat) avec entrée particulière, indépendant(e) ; **~-control** n maîtrise f de soi ; **~-defeating** a qui a un effet contraire à l'effet recherché ; **~-defence** n légitime défense f ; **~-discipline** n discipline personnelle ; **~-employed** a qui travaille à son compte ; **~-evident** a évident(e), qui va de soi ; **~-explanatory** a qui se passe d'explication ; **~-indulgent** a qui ne se refuse rien ; **~-interest** n intérêt personnel ; **~-ish** a égoïste ; **~-ishness** n égoïsme m ; **~-lessly** ad sans penser à soi ; **~-pity** n apitoiement m sur soi-même ; **~-portrait** n autoportrait m ; **~-possessed** a assuré(e) ; **~-preservation** n instinct m de conservation ; **~-reliant** a indépendant(e) ; **~-respect** n respect m de soi, amour-propre m ; **~-respecting** a qui se respecte ; **~-righteous** a satisfait(e) de soi, pharisaïque ; **~-sacrifice** n abnégation f ; **~-satisfied** a content(e) de soi, suffisant(e) ; **~-seal** a (envelope) auto-collant(e) ; **~-service** n libre-service m, self-service m ; **~-sufficient** a indépen-dant(e) ; **~-supporting** a financièrement indépendant(e) ; **~-taught** a autodidacte.

sell, pt,pp **sold** [sɛl, səuld] vt vendre // vi se vendre ; **to ~ at** or **for 10F** se vendre 10F ; **to ~ off** vt liquider ; **~er** n vendeur/euse, marchand/e ; **~ing price** n prix m de vente.

sellotape ['sɛləuteɪp] n ® papier collant, scotch m ®.

sellout ['sɛlaut] n trahison f, capitulation f ; (of tickets): **it was a ~** tous les billets ont été vendus.

selves [sɛlvz] npl of **self**.

semantic [sɪ'mæntɪk] a sémantique ; **~s** n sémantique f.

semaphore ['sɛməfɔ:*] n signaux mpl à bras ; (RAIL) sèmaphore m.

semen ['si:mən] n sperme m.

semi ['sɛmɪ] prefix semi-, demi- ; à demi, à moitié ; **~breve** ronde f ; **~circle** n demi-cercle m ; **~colon** n point-virgule m ; **~conscious** a à demi conscient(e) ; **~detached (house)** n maison jumelée or jumelle ; **~final** n demi-finale f.

seminar ['sɛminɑ:*] n séminaire m.

semiquaver ['sɛmɪkweɪvə*] n double croche f.

semiskilled ['sɛmɪ'skɪld] a: **~ worker** n ouvrier/ère spécialisé/e.

semitone ['sɛmɪtəun] n (MUS) demi-ton m.

semolina [sɛmə'li:nə] n semoule f.

senate ['sɛnɪt] n sénat m ; **senator** n sénateur m.

send, pt,pp **sent** [sɛnd, sɛnt] vt envoyer ; **to ~ sb to Coventry** mettre qn en quarantaine ; **to ~ away** vt (letter, goods) envoyer, expédier ; **to ~ away for** vt fus commander par correspondance ; **to ~ back** vt renvoyer ; **to ~ for** vt fus envoyer chercher ; faire venir ; **to ~ off** vt (goods) envoyer, expédier ; (SPORT: player) expulser or renvoyer du terrain ; **to ~ out** vt (invitation) envoyer (par la poste) ; **to ~ up** vt (person, price) faire monter ; (parody) mettre en boîte, parodier ; (blow up) faire sauter ; **~er** n expéditeur/trice ; **~-off** n: **a good ~-off** des adieux chaleureux.

senile ['si:naɪl] a sénile.

senility [sɪ'nɪlɪtɪ] n sénilité f.

senior ['si:nɪə*] a (older) aîné(e), plus âgé(e) ; (of higher rank) supérieur(e) // n aîné/e ; (in service) personne f qui a plus d'ancienneté ; **~ity** [-'ɔrɪtɪ] n priorité f d'âge, ancienneté f.

sensation [sɛn'seɪʃən] n sensation f ; **to create a ~** faire sensation ; **~al** a qui fait sensation ; (marvellous) sensationnel(le).

sense [sɛns] n sens m ; (feeling) sentiment m ; (meaning) signification f ; (wisdom) bon sens // vt sentir, pressentir ; **it makes ~** c'est logique ; **~s** npl raison f ; **~less** a insensé(e), stupide ; (unconscious) sans connaissance ; **anyone in his ~s** tout homme sensé.

sensibility [sɛnsɪ'bɪlɪtɪ] n sensibilité f ; **sensibilities** npl susceptibilité f.

sensible ['sɛnsɪbl] a sensé(e), raisonnable ; sage ; pratique.

sensitive ['sɛnsɪtɪv] a: **~ (to)** sensible (à) ; **sensitivity** [-'tɪvɪtɪ] n sensibilité f.

sensual ['sɛnsjuəl] a sensuel(le).

sensuous ['sɛnsjuəs] a voluptueux(euse), sensuel(le).

sent [sɛnt] pt,pp of **send**.

sentence ['sɛntns] n (LING) phrase f ; (LAW: judgment) condamnation f, sentence f ; (: punishment) peine f // vt: **to ~ sb to death/to 5 years** condamner qn à mort/à 5 ans.

sentiment ['sɛntɪmənt] n sentiment m ; (opinion) opinion f, avis m ; **~al** [-'mɛntl] a sentimental(e) ; **~ality** [-'tælɪtɪ] n sentimentalité f, sensiblerie f.

sentry ['sɛntrɪ] n sentinelle f, factionnaire m.

separable ['sɛprəbl] a séparable.

separate a ['sɛprɪt] séparé(e), indépendant(e), différent(e) // vb ['sɛpəreɪt] vt séparer // vi se séparer; **—ly** ad séparément; **—s** npl (clothes) coordonnés mpl; **separation** [-'reɪʃən] n séparation f.

September [sɛp'tɛmbə*] n septembre m.

septic ['sɛptɪk] a septique; (wound) infecté(e).

sequel ['si:kwl] n conséquence f; séquelles fpl; (of story) suite f.

sequence ['si:kwəns] n ordre m, suite f; **— of tenses** concordance f des temps.

sequin ['si:kwɪn] n paillette f.

serenade [sɛrə'neɪd] n sérénade f // vt donner une sérénade à.

serene [sɪ'ri:n] a serein(e), calme, paisible; **serenity** [sə'rɛnɪtɪ] n sérénité f, calme m.

sergeant ['sɑ:dʒənt] n sergent m; (POLICE) brigadier m.

serial ['sɪərɪəl] n feuilleton m // a (number) de série; **—ize** vt publier (or adapter) en feuilleton.

series ['sɪərɪs] n série f; (PUBLISHING) collection f.

serious ['sɪərɪəs] a sérieux(euse), réfléchi(e); grave; **—ly** ad sérieusement, gravement; **—ness** n sérieux m, gravité f.

sermon ['sə:mən] n sermon m.

serrated [sɪ'reɪtɪd] a en dents de scie.

serum ['sɪərəm] n sérum m.

servant ['sə:vənt] n domestique m/f; (fig) serviteur/servante.

serve [sə:v] vt (employer etc) servir, être au service de; (purpose) servir à; (customer, food, meal) servir; (apprenticeship) faire, accomplir; (prison term) faire; purger // vi (also TENNIS) servir; (be useful): **to — as/for/to do** servir de/à/faire // n (TENNIS) service m; **it —s him right** c'est bien fait pour lui; **to — out, — up** vt (food) servir.

service ['sə:vɪs] n (gen) service m; (AUT: maintenance) révision f // vt (car, washing machine) réviser; **the S—s** les forces armées; **to be of — to sb, to do sb a —** rendre service à qn; **to put one's car in for (a) —** donner sa voiture à réviser; **dinner — n** service m de table; **—able** a pratique, commode; **— area n** (on motorway) aire f de services; **—man n** militaire m; **— station n** station-service f.

serviette [sə:vɪ'ɛt] n serviette f (de table).

servile ['sə:vaɪl] a servile.

session ['sɛʃən] n (sitting) séance f; (SCOL) année f scolaire (or universitaire); **to be in — siéger, être en session or en séance**.

set [sɛt] n série f, assortiment m; (of tools etc) jeu m; (RADIO, TV) poste m; (TENNIS) set m; (group of people) cercle m, milieu m; (CINEMA) plateau m; (THEATRE: stage) scène f; (: scenery) décor m; (MATH) ensemble m; (HAIRDRESSING) mise f en plis // a (fixed) fixe, déterminé(e); (ready) prêt(e) // vb (pt, pp set) (place) mettre, poser, placer; (fix) fixer; (adjust) régler; (decide: rules etc) fixer, choisir; (TYP) composer // vi (sun) se coucher; (jam, jelly, concrete) prendre; **to be — on doing**

être résolu à faire; **to be (dead) — against** être (totalement) opposé à; **to — (to music)** mettre en musique; **to — on fire** mettre le feu à; **to — free** libérer; **to — sth going** déclencher qch; **to — sail** partir, prendre la mer; **to — about** vt fus (task) entreprendre, se mettre à; **to — aside** vt mettre de côté; **to — back** vt (in time): **to — back (by)** retarder (de); **to — off** vi se mettre en route, partir // vt (bomb) faire exploser; (cause to start) déclencher; (show up well) mettre en valeur, faire valoir; **to — out** vi: **to — out to do** entreprendre de; avoir pour but or intention de // vt (arrange) disposer; (state) présenter, exposer; **to — up** vt (organization) fonder, constituer; (record) établir; (monument) ériger; **to — up shop** (fig) s'établir, s'installer; **—back** n (hitch) revers m, contretemps m.

settee [sɛ'ti:] n canapé m.

setting ['sɛtɪŋ] n cadre m; (of jewel) monture f.

settle ['sɛtl] vt (argument, matter) régler; (problem) résoudre; (MED: calm) calmer // vi (bird, dust etc) se poser; (sediment) se déposer; (also: — down) s'installer, se fixer, se calmer; se ranger; **to — to sth** se mettre sérieusement à qch; **to — for sth** accepter qch, se contenter de qch; **to — in** vi s'installer; **to — on sth** opter or se décider pour qch; **to — up with sb** régler (ce que l'on doit à) qn; **—ment n** (payment) règlement m; (agreement) accord m; (colony) colonie f; (village etc) établissement m; hameau m; **—r n** colon m.

setup ['sɛtʌp] n (arrangement) manière f dont les choses sont organisées; (situation) situation f, allure f des choses.

seven ['sɛvn] num sept; **—teen** num dix-sept; **—th** num septième; **—ty** num soixante-dix.

sever ['sɛvə*] vt couper, trancher; (relations) rompre.

several ['sɛvərl] a,pronoun plusieurs (m/fpl); **— of us** plusieurs d'entre nous.

severance ['sɛvərəns] n (of relations) rupture f; **— pay** n indemnité f de licenciement.

severe [sɪ'vɪə*] a sévère, strict(e); (serious) grave, sérieux(euse); (hard) rigoureux(euse), dur(e); (plain) sévère, austère; **severity** [sɪ'vɛrɪtɪ] n sévérité f; gravité f; rigueur f.

sew [səu], pt sewed, pp sewn [səu, səud, səun] vt,vi coudre; **to — up** vt (re)coudre; **it is all sewn up** (fig) c'est dans le sac or dans la poche.

sewage ['su:ɪdʒ] n vidange(s) f(pl).

sewer ['su:ə*] n égout m.

sewing ['səuɪŋ] n couture f; **— machine** n machine f à coudre.

sewn [səun] pp of sew.

sex [sɛks] n sexe m; **to have — with** avoir des rapports (sexuels) avec; **— act n** acte sexuel.

sextet [sɛks'tɛt] n sextuor m.

sexual ['sɛksjuəl] a sexuel(le).

sexy ['sɛksɪ] a sexy inv.

shabby ['ʃæbɪ] a miteux(euse); (behaviour) mesquin(e), méprisable.

shack [ʃæk] n cabane f, hutte f.
shackles ['ʃæklz] npl chaînes fpl, entraves fpl.
shade [ʃeɪd] n ombre f; (for lamp) abat-jour m inv; (of colour) nuance f, ton m; (small quantity): a ~ of un soupçon de / vt abriter du soleil, ombrager; **in the ~** à l'ombre; **a ~ smaller** un tout petit peu plus petit.
shadow ['ʃædəu] n ombre f / vt (follow) filer; ~ **cabinet** n (POL) cabinet parallèle formé par le parti qui n'est pas au pouvoir; ~**y** a ombragé(e); (dim) vague, indistinct(e).
shady ['ʃeɪdɪ] a ombragé(e); (fig: dishonest) louche, véreux(euse).
shaft [ʃɑːft] n (of arrow, spear) hampe f; (AUT, TECH) arbre m; (of mine) puits m; (of lift) cage f; (of light) rayon m, trait m.
shaggy ['ʃægɪ] a hirsute; en broussaille.
shake [ʃeɪk] vb (pt shook, pp shaken [ʃuk, 'ʃeɪkn]) vt secouer; (bottle, cocktail) agiter; (house, confidence) ébranler // vi trembler // n secousse f; **to ~ hands with sb** serrer la main à qn; **to ~ off** vt secouer; (fig) se débarrasser de; **to ~ up** vt secouer; ~**-up** n grand remaniement; **shaky** a (hand, voice) tremblant(e); (building) branlant(e), peu solide.
shale [ʃeɪl] n schiste argileux.
shall [ʃæl] auxiliary vb: **I ~ go** j'irai.
shallot [ʃə'lɔt] n échalote f.
shallow ['ʃæləu] a peu profond(e); (fig) superficiel(le), qui manque de profondeur.
sham [ʃæm] n frime f; (jewellery, furniture) imitation f // a feint(e), simulé(e) // vt feindre, simuler.
shambles ['ʃæmblz] n confusion f, pagaïe f, fouillis m.
shame [ʃeɪm] n honte f // vt faire honte à; **it is a ~ (that/to do)** c'est dommage (que + sub/de faire); **what a ~!** quel dommage!; ~**faced** a honteux(euse), penaud(e); ~**ful** a honteux(euse), scandaleux(euse); ~**less** a éhonté(e), effronté(e); (immodest) impudique.
shampoo [ʃæm'puː] n shampooing m // vt faire un shampooing à.
shamrock ['ʃæmrɔk] n trèfle m (emblème national de l'Irlande).
shandy ['ʃændɪ] n bière panachée.
shan't [ʃɑːnt] = **shall not**.
shanty ['ʃæntɪ] n cabane f, baraque f; ~**town** n bidonville m.
shape [ʃeɪp] n forme f // vt façonner, modeler; (statement) formuler; (sb's ideas) former; (sb's life) déterminer // vi (also: ~ **up**) (events) prendre tournure; (person) faire des progrès, s'en sortir; **to take ~** prendre forme or tournure; -**shaped** suffix: **heart-shaped** en forme de cœur; ~**less** a informe, sans forme; ~**ly** a bien proportionné(e), beau(belle).
share [ʃɛə*] n (thing received, contribution) part f; (COMM) action f // vt partager; (have in common) avoir en commun; **to ~ out (among or between)** partager (entre); ~**holder** n actionnaire m/f.
shark [ʃɑːk] n requin m.
sharp [ʃɑːp] a (razor, knife) tranchant(e), bien aiguisé(e); (point) aigu(guë); (nose,

chin) pointu(e); (outline) net(te); (cold, pain) vif(vive); (MUS) dièse; (voice) coupant(e); (person: quick-witted) vif(vive), éveillé(e); (: unscrupulous) malhonnête // n (MUS) dièse m // ad: **at 2 o'clock** à 2 heures pile or tapantes; **look ~!** dépêche-toi!; ~**en** vt aiguiser; (pencil) tailler; (fig) aviver; ~**ener** n (also: **pencil ~ener**) taille-crayon(s) m inv; (also: **knife ~ener**) aiguisoir m; ~**-eyed** a à qui rien n'échappe; ~**-witted** a à l'esprit vif, malin(igne).
shatter ['ʃætə*] vt fracasser, briser, faire voler en éclats; (fig: upset) bouleverser; (: ruin) briser, ruiner // vi voler en éclats, se briser, se fracasser.
shave [ʃeɪv] vt raser // vi se raser // n: **to have a ~** se raser; ~**n** a (head) rasé(e); ~**r** n (also: **electric ~**) rasoir m électrique.
shaving ['ʃeɪvɪŋ] n (action) rasage m; ~**s** npl (of wood etc) copeaux mpl; ~ **brush** n blaireau m; ~ **cream** n crème f à raser; ~ **soap** n savon m à barbe.
shawl [ʃɔːl] n châle m.
she [ʃiː] pronoun elle // cpd: ~- femelle; ~**-cat** n chatte f; ~**-elephant** n éléphant m femelle; NB: for ships, countries follow the gender of your translation.
sheaf, sheaves [ʃiːf, ʃiːvz] n gerbe f.
shear [ʃɪə*] vt (pt ~ed, pp ~ed or shorn [ʃɔːn]) (sheep) tondre; **to ~ off** vt tondre; (branch) élaguer; ~**s** npl (for hedge) cisaille(s) f(pl).
sheath [ʃiːθ] n gaine f, fourreau m, étui m; (contraceptive) préservatif m; ~**e** [ʃiːð] vt gainer; (sword) rengainer.
sheaves [ʃiːvz] npl of **sheaf**.
shed [ʃɛd] n remise f, resserre f // vt (pt,pp **shed**) (leaves, fur etc) perdre; (tears) verser, répandre.
she'd [ʃiːd] = **she had**; **she would**.
sheep [ʃiːp] n, pl inv mouton m; ~**dog** n chien m de berger; ~**ish** a penaud(e), timide; ~**skin** n peau f de mouton.
sheer [ʃɪə*] a (utter) pur(e), pur et simple; (steep) à pic, abrupt(e); (almost transparent) extrêmement fin(e) // ad à pic, abruptement.
sheet [ʃiːt] n (on bed) drap m; (of paper) feuille f; (of glass, metal) feuille, plaque f; ~ **lightning** n éclair m en nappe(s); ~ **metal** n tôle f.
sheik(h) [ʃeɪk] n cheik m.
shelf, shelves [ʃɛlf, ʃɛlvz] n étagère f, rayon m; **set of shelves** rayonnage m.
shell [ʃɛl] n (on beach) coquillage m; (of egg, nut etc) coquille f; (explosive) obus m; (of building) carcasse f // vt (peas) écosser; (crab, prawn etc) décortiquer; (MIL) bombarder (d'obus).
she'll [ʃiːl] = **she will**; **she shall**.
shellfish ['ʃɛlfɪʃ] n, pl inv (crab etc) crustacé m; (scallop etc) coquillage m; (pl: as food) crustacés m, coquillages.
shelter ['ʃɛltə*] n abri m, refuge m // vt abriter, protéger; (give lodging to) donner asile à // vi s'abriter, se mettre à l'abri; ~**ed** a (life) retiré(e), à l'abri des soucis; (spot) abrité(e).
shelve [ʃɛlv] vt (fig) mettre en suspens or en sommeil; ~**s** npl of **shelf**.

shepherd ['ʃɛpəd] n berger m // vt (guide) guider, escorter; ~ess n bergère f; ~'s pie n ≈ hachis m Parmentier.

sheriff ['ʃɛrɪf] n shérif m.

sherry ['ʃɛrɪ] n xérès m, sherry m.

she's [ʃiːz] = she is; she has.

shield [ʃiːld] n bouclier m // vt: to ~ (from) protéger (de or contre).

shift [ʃɪft] n (change) changement m; (of workers) équipe f, poste m // vt déplacer, changer de place; (remove) enlever // vi changer de place, bouger; ~ work n travail m en équipe or par relais or par roulement; ~y a sournois(e); (eyes) fuyant(e).

shilling ['ʃɪlɪŋ] n shilling m (= 12 old pence; 20 in a pound).

shilly-shally ['ʃɪlɪʃælɪ] vi tergiverser, atermoyer.

shimmer ['ʃɪmə*] n miroitement m, chatoiement m // vi miroiter, chatoyer.

shin [ʃɪn] n tibia m.

shine [ʃaɪn] n éclat m, brillant m // vb (pt,pp shone [ʃɔn]) vi briller // vt faire briller or reluire; (torch): to ~ sth on braquer qch sur.

shingle ['ʃɪŋgl] n (on beach) galets mpl; (on roof) bardeau m; ~s n (MED) zona m.

shiny ['ʃaɪnɪ] a brillant(e).

ship [ʃɪp] n bateau m; (large) navire m // vt transporter (par mer); (send) expédier (par mer); (load) charger, embarquer; ~building n construction navale; ~ canal n canal m maritime or de navigation; ~ment n cargaison f; ~per n affréteur m, expéditeur m; ~ping n (ships) navires mpl; (traffic) navigation f; ~shape a en ordre impeccable; ~wreck n épave f; (event) naufrage m; ~yard n chantier naval.

shire ['ʃaɪə*] n comté m.

shirk [ʃəːk] vt esquiver, se dérober à.

shirt [ʃəːt] n (man's) chemise f; in ~ sleeves en bras de chemise; ~y a (col) de mauvais poil.

shiver ['ʃɪvə*] n frisson m // vi frissonner.

shoal [ʃəul] n (of fish) banc m.

shock [ʃɔk] n (impact) choc m, heurt m; (ELEC) secousse f; (emotional) choc, secousse f // vt (MED) commotion f, choc // vt choquer, scandaliser; bouleverser; ~ absorber n amortisseur m; ~ing a choquant(e), scandaleux(euse); épouvantable; révoltant(e); ~proof a anti-choc inv.

shod [ʃɔd] pt,pp of shoe; well-~ a bien chaussé(e).

shoddy ['ʃɔdɪ] a de mauvaise qualité, mal fait(e).

shoe [ʃuː] n chaussure f, soulier m; (also: horse~) fer m à cheval // vt (pt,pp shod [ʃɔd]) (horse) ferrer; ~brush n brosse f à chaussures; ~horn n chausse-pied m; ~lace n lacet m (de soulier); ~ polish n cirage m; ~shop n magasin m de chaussures; ~tree n embauchoir m.

shone [ʃɔn] pt,pp of shine.

shook [ʃuk] pt of shake.

shoot [ʃuːt] n (on branch, seedling) pousse f // vb (pt,pp shot [ʃɔt]) vt (game) chasser; tirer; abattre; (person) blesser (or tuer) d'un coup de fusil (or de revolver); (execute) fusiller; (film) tourner // vi (with gun, bow): to ~ (at) tirer (sur); (FOOTBALL) shooter, tirer; to ~ down vt (plane) abattre; to ~ in/out vi entrer/sortir comme une flèche; to ~ up vi (fig) monter en flèche; ~ing n (shots) coups mpl de feu, fusillade f; (HUNTING) chasse f; ~ing range n stand m de tir; ~ing star n étoile filante.

shop [ʃɔp] n magasin m; (workshop) atelier m // vi (also: go ~) faire ses courses or ses achats; ~ assistant n vendeur/euse; ~ floor n ateliers mpl; (fig) ouvriers mpl; ~keeper n marchand/e, commerçant/e; ~lifter n voleur/euse à l'étalage; ~lifting n vol m à l'étalage; ~per n personne f qui fait ses courses, acheteur/euse; ~ping n (goods) achats mpl, provisions fpl; ~ping bag n sac m (à provisions); ~ping centre, ~ping center (US) n centre commercial; ~-soiled a défraîchi(e), qui a fait la vitrine; ~ steward n (INDUSTRY) délégué/e syndical(e); ~ window n vitrine f.

shore [ʃɔː*] n (of sea, lake) rivage m, rive f // vt: to ~ (up) étayer.

shorn [ʃɔːn] pp of shear; ~ of dépouillé(e) de.

short [ʃɔːt] a (not long) court(e); (soon finished) court, bref(brève); (person, step) petit(e); (curt) brusque, sec(sèche); (insufficient) insuffisant(e) // n (also: ~ film) court métrage; (a pair of) ~s un short; to be ~ of sth être à court de or manquer de qch; I'm 3 ~ il m'en manque 3; in ~ bref; in brief; ~ of doing à moins de faire; everything ~ of tout sauf; it is ~ for c'est l'abréviation or le diminutif de; to cut ~ (speech, visit) abréger, écourter; (person) couper la parole à; to fall ~ of ne pas être à la hauteur de; to stop ~ s'arrêter net; to stop ~ of ne pas aller jusqu'à; ~age n manque m, pénurie f; ~bread n ≈ sablé m; ~-circuit n court-circuit m // vt court-circuiter // vi se mettre en court-circuit; ~coming n défaut m; ~(crust) pastry pâte brisée; ~cut n raccourci m; ~en vt raccourcir; (text, visit) abréger; ~ening n (CULIN) matière grasse; ~hand n sténo(graphie) f; ~hand typist n sténodactylo m/f; ~list n (for job) liste f des candidats sélectionnés; ~-lived a de courte durée; ~ly ad bientôt, sous peu; ~ness n brièveté f; ~-sighted a myope; (fig) qui manque de clairvoyance; ~ story n nouvelle f; ~-tempered a qui s'emporte facilement; ~-term a (effect) à court terme; ~-wave n (RADIO) ondes courtes.

shot [ʃɔt] pt,pp of shoot // n coup m (de feu); (person) tireur m; (try) coup, essai m; (injection) piqûre f; (PHOT) photo f; like a ~ comme une flèche; (very readily) sans hésiter; ~gun n fusil m de chasse.

should [ʃud] auxiliary vb: I ~ go now je devrais partir maintenant; he ~ be there now il devrait être arrivé maintenant; I ~ go if I were you si j'étais vous j'irais; I ~ like to j'aimerais bien, volontiers.

shoulder ['ʃəuldə*] n épaule f; (of road): hard ~ accotement m // vt (fig) endosser, se charger de; ~ bag n sac m à bandoulière; ~ **blade** n omoplate f; ~ **strap** n bretelle f.

shouldn't ['ʃudnt] = should not.

shout [ʃaut] n cri m // vt crier // vi crier, pousser des cris; **to give sb a** ~ appeler qn; **to** ~ **down** vt huer; ~**ing** n cris mpl.

shove [ʃʌv] vt pousser; (col: put): **to** ~ **sth in** fourrer or ficher qch dans; **to** ~ **off** vi (NAUT) pousser au large; (fig: col) ficher le camp.

shovel ['ʃʌvl] n pelle f // vt pelleter, enlever (or enfourner) à la pelle.

show [ʃəu] n (of emotion) manifestation f, démonstration f; (semblance) semblant m, apparence f; (exhibition) exposition f, salon m; (THEATRE) spectacle m, représentation f; (CINEMA) séance f // vb (pt ~**ed**, pp **shown** [ʃəun]) vt montrer; (courage etc) faire preuve de, manifester; (exhibit) exposer // vi se voir, être visible; **to** ~ **sb in** faire entrer qn; **to** ~ **off** vi (pej) crâner // vt (display) faire valoir; (pej) faire étalage de; **to** ~ **sb out** reconduire (or jusqu'à la porte); **to** ~ **up** vi (stand out) ressortir; (col: turn up) se montrer // vt démontrer; (unmask) démasquer, dénoncer; ~ **business** n le monde du spectacle; ~**down** n épreuve f de force.

shower ['ʃauə*] n (rain) averse f, (of stones etc) pluie f, grêle f; (also: ~**bath**) douche f // vi prendre une douche, se doucher // vt: **to** ~ **sb with** (gifts etc) combler qn de; (abuse etc) accabler qn de; (missiles) bombarder qn de; ~**proof** a imperméable; ~**y** a (weather) pluvieux(euse).

showground ['ʃəugraund] n champ m de foire.

showing ['ʃəuiŋ] n (of film) projection f.

show jumping ['ʃəudʒʌmpiŋ] n concours m hippique.

showmanship ['ʃəumənʃip] n art m de la mise en scène.

shown [ʃəun] pp of **show**.

show-off ['ʃəuɔf] n (col: person) crâneur/euse, m'as-tu-vu/e.

showpiece ['ʃəupi:s] n (of exhibition etc) joyau m, clou m.

showroom ['ʃəurum] n magasin m or salle f d'exposition.

shrank [ʃræŋk] pt of **shrink**.

shrapnel ['ʃræpnl] n éclats mpl d'obus.

shred [ʃred] n (gen pl) lambeau m, petit morceau // vt mettre en lambeaux, déchirer; (CULIN) râper; couper en lanières.

shrewd [ʃru:d] a astucieux(euse), perspicace; ~**ness** n perspicacité f.

shriek [ʃri:k] n cri perçant or aigu, hurlement m // vt,vi hurler, crier.

shrift [ʃrift] n: **to give sb short** ~ expédier qn sans ménagements.

shrill [ʃril] a perçant(e), aigu(guë), strident(e).

shrimp [ʃrimp] n crevette grise.

shrine [ʃrain] n châsse f; (place) lieu m de pèlerinage.

shrink, pt **shrank**, pp **shrunk** [ʃriŋk, ʃræŋk, ʃrʌŋk] vi rétrécir; (fig) se réduire; se contracter // vt (wool) (faire) rétrécir // n (col: pej) psychanalyste; ~**age** n rétrécissement m.

shrivel ['ʃrivl] (also: ~ **up**) vt ratatiner, flétrir // vi se ratatiner, se flétrir.

shroud [ʃraud] n linceul m // vt: ~**ed in mystery** enveloppé(e) de mystère.

Shrove Tuesday ['ʃrəuv'tju:zdi] n (le) Mardi gras.

shrub [ʃrʌb] n arbuste m; ~**bery** n massif m d'arbustes.

shrug [ʃrʌg] n haussement m d'épaules // vt,vi: **to** ~ **(one's shoulders)** hausser les épaules; **to** ~ **off** vt faire fi de.

shrunk [ʃrʌŋk] pp of **shrink**; ~**en** a ratatiné(e).

shudder ['ʃʌdə*] n frisson m, frémissement m // vi frissonner, frémir.

shuffle ['ʃʌfl] vt (cards) battre; **to** ~ **(one's feet)** traîner les pieds.

shun [ʃʌn] vt éviter, fuir.

shunt [ʃʌnt] vt (RAIL: direct) aiguiller; (: divert) détourner // vi: **to** ~ **(to and fro)** faire la navette; ~**ing** n (RAIL) triage m.

shush [ʃuʃ] excl chut!

shut, pt, pp **shut** [ʃʌt] vt fermer // vi (se) fermer; **to** ~ **down** vt, vi fermer définitivement; **to** ~ **off** vt couper, arrêter; **to** ~ **up** vi (col: keep quiet) se taire // vt (close) fermer; (silence) faire taire; ~**ter** n volet m; (PHOT) obturateur m.

shuttle ['ʃʌtl] n navette f; (also: ~ **service**) (service m de) navette f.

shuttlecock ['ʃʌtlkɔk] n volant m (de badminton).

shy [ʃai] a timide; **to fight** ~ of se dérober devant; ~**ness** n timidité f.

Siamese [saiə'mi:z] a: ~ **cat** chat siamois.

Sicily ['sisili] n Sicile f.

sick [sik] a (ill) malade; (vomiting): **to be** ~ vomir; (humour) noir(e), macabre; **to feel** ~ avoir envie de vomir, avoir mal au cœur; **to be** ~ **of** (fig) en avoir assez de; ~ **bay** n infirmerie f; ~**en** vt écœurer; ~**ening** a (fig) écœurant(e), révoltant(e), répugnant(e).

sickle ['sikl] n faucille f.

sick: ~ **leave** n congé m de maladie; ~**ly** a maladif(ive), souffreteux(euse); (causing nausea) écœurant(e); ~**ness** n maladie f; (vomiting) vomissement(s) m(pl); ~ **pay** n indemnité f de maladie.

side [said] n côté m; (of lake, road) bord m // cpd (door, entrance) latéral(e) // vi: **to** ~ **with sb** prendre le parti de qn, se ranger du côté de qn; **by the** ~ **of** au bord de; **by** ~ **by** ~ côte à côte; **from all** ~**s** de tous côtés; **to take** ~**s (with)** prendre parti (pour); ~**board** n buffet m; ~**boards**, ~**burns** npl (whiskers) pattes fpl; ~ **effect** n (MED) effet m secondaire; ~**light** n (AUT) veilleuse f; ~**line** n (SPORT) (ligne f de) touche f; (fig) activité f secondaire; ~**long** a oblique, de coin; ~ **road** n petite route, route transversale; ~**saddle** ad en amazone; ~ **show** n attraction f; ~**track** vt (fig) faire dévier de son sujet; ~**walk** n (US) trottoir m; ~**ways** ad de côté.

siding ['saidiŋ] n (RAIL) voie f de garage.

sidle ['saidl] vi: **to** ~ **up (to)** s'approcher furtivement (de).

siege [si:dʒ] n siège m.

sieve [sɪv] n tamis m, passoire f // vt tamiser, passer (au tamis).

sift [sɪft] vt passer au tamis or au crible; (fig) passer au crible.

sigh [saɪ] n soupir m // vi soupirer, pousser un soupir.

sight [saɪt] n (faculty) vue f; (spectacle) spectacle m; (on gun) mire f // vt apercevoir; **in** ~ visible; (fig) en vue; **out of** ~ hors de vue; **~-seeing** n tourisme m; **to go ~seeing** faire du tourisme; **~-seer** n touriste m/f.

sign [saɪn] n (gen) signe m; (with hand etc) signe, geste m; (notice) panneau m, écriteau m // vt signer; **to** ~ **in/out** signer le registre (en arrivant/partant); **to** ~ **up** (MIL) vt engager // vi s'engager.

signal ['sɪgnl] n signal m // vi (person) faire signe à; (message) communiquer par signaux.

signature ['sɪgnətʃə*] n signature f; ~ **tune** n indicatif musical.

signet ring ['sɪgnætrɪŋ] n chevalière f.

significance [sɪg'nɪfɪkəns] n signification f; importance f.

significant [sɪg'nɪfɪkənt] a significatif(ive); (important) important(e), considérable.

signify ['sɪgnɪfaɪ] vt signifier.

sign language ['saɪnlæŋgwɪdʒ] n langage m par signes.

signpost ['saɪnpəust] n poteau indicateur.

silence ['saɪlns] n silence m // vt faire taire, réduire au silence; **~r** n (on gun, AUT) silencieux m.

silent ['saɪlnt] a silencieux(euse); (film) muet(te); **~ly** ad silencieusement.

silhouette [sɪlu:'et] n silhouette f // vt: **~d against** se profilant sur, se découpant contre.

silicon chip ['sɪlɪkən'tʃɪp] n plaquette f de silicium.

silk [sɪlk] n soie f // cpd de or en soie; **~y** a soyeux(euse).

silly ['sɪlɪ] a stupide, sot(te), bête.

silt [sɪlt] n vase f; limon m.

silver ['sɪlvə*] n argent m; (money) monnaie f (en pièces d'argent); (also: **~ware**) argenterie f // cpd d'argent, en argent; **~ paper** n papier m d'argent or d'étain; **~-plated** a plaqué(e) argent; **~smith** n orfèvre m/f; **~y** a argenté(e).

similar ['sɪmɪlə*] a: **~ to** (to) semblable (à); **~ity** [-'lærɪtɪ] n ressemblance f, similarité f; **~ly** ad de la même façon, de même.

simile ['sɪmɪlɪ] n comparaison f.

simmer ['sɪmə*] vi cuire à feu doux, mijoter.

simple ['sɪmpl] a simple; **~-minded** a simplet(te), simple d'esprit; **simplicity** [-'plɪsɪtɪ] n simplicité f; **simplification** [-keɪʃən] n simplification f; **simplify** ['sɪmplɪfaɪ] vt simplifier; **simply** ad simplement; avec simplicité.

simulate ['sɪmjuleɪt] vt simuler, feindre; **simulation** [-'leɪʃən] n simulation f.

simultaneous [sɪməl'teɪnɪəs] a simultané(e); **~ly** ad simultanément.

sin [sɪn] n péché m // vi pécher.

since [sɪns] ad, prep depuis // cj (time) depuis que; (because) puisque, étant

donné que, comme; ~ **then** depuis ce moment-là.

sincere [sɪn'sɪə*] a sincère; **sincerity** [-'serɪtɪ] n sincérité f.

sine [saɪn] n (MATH) sinus m.

sinew ['sɪnju:] n tendon m; **~s** npl muscles mpl.

sinful ['sɪnful] a coupable.

sing, pt **sang**, pp **sung** [sɪŋ, sæŋ, sʌŋ] vt, vi chanter.

singe [sɪndʒ] vt brûler légèrement; (clothes) roussir.

singer ['sɪŋə*] n chanteur/euse.

singing ['sɪŋɪŋ] n chant m.

single ['sɪŋgl] a seul(e), unique; (unmarried) célibataire; (not double) simple // n (also: ~ **ticket**) aller m (simple); (record) 45 tours m; **~s** npl (TENNIS) simple m; **to** ~ **out** vt choisir; distinguer; **~ bed** n lit à une place; **~-breasted** a droit(e); **in** ~ **file** en file indienne; **~-handed** ad tout(e) seul(e), sans (aucune) aide; **~-minded** a résolu(e), tenace; ~ **room** n chambre f à un lit or pour une personne.

singlet ['sɪŋglɪt] n tricot m de corps.

singly ['sɪŋglɪ] ad séparément.

singular ['sɪŋgjulə*] a singulier(ère), étrange; remarquable; (LING) (au) singulier, du singulier // n (LING) singulier m; **~ly** ad singulièrement; remarquablement; étrangement.

sinister ['sɪnɪstə*] a sinistre.

sink [sɪŋk] n évier m // vb (pt **sank**, pp **sunk** [sæŋk, sʌŋk]) vt (ship) (faire) couler, faire sombrer; (foundations) creuser; (piles etc): **to** ~ **sth into** enfoncer qch dans // vi couler, sombrer; (ground etc) s'affaisser; **to** ~ **in** vi s'enfoncer, pénétrer; **a ~ing feeling** un serrement de cœur.

sinner ['sɪnə*] n pécheur/eresse.

Sino- ['saɪnəu] prefix sino-.

sinuous ['sɪnjuəs] a sinueux(euse).

sinus ['saɪnəs] n (ANAT) sinus m inv.

sip [sɪp] n petite gorgée // vt boire à petites gorgées.

siphon ['saɪfən] n siphon m; **to** ~ **off** vt siphonner.

sir [sə*] n monsieur m; **S~ John Smith** sir John Smith; **yes** ~ oui Monsieur.

siren ['saɪərn] n sirène f.

sirloin ['sə:lɔɪn] n aloyau m.

sirocco [sɪ'rɔkəu] n sirocco m.

sissy ['sɪsɪ] n (col: coward) poule mouillée.

sister ['sɪstə*] n sœur f; (nun) religieuse f, (bonne) sœur; (nurse) infirmière f en chef; **~-in-law** n belle-sœur f.

sit, pt, pp **sat** [sɪt, sæt] vi s'asseoir; (assembly) être en séance, siéger; (for painter) poser // vt (exam) passer, se présenter à; **to** ~ **tight** ne pas bouger; **to** ~ **down** vi s'asseoir; **to** ~ **up** vi s'asseoir; (not go to bed) rester debout, ne pas se coucher.

sitcom ['sɪtkɔm] n (abbr of situation comedy) comédie f de situation.

site [saɪt] n emplacement m, site m; (also: **building** ~) chantier m // vt placer.

sit-in ['sɪtɪn] n (demonstration) sit-in m inv, occupation f de locaux.

siting ['saɪtɪŋ] n (location) emplacement m.
sitter ['sɪtə] n (for painter) modèle m.
sitting ['sɪtɪŋ] n (of assembly etc) séance f; (in canteen) service m; ~ **room** n salon m.
situated ['sɪtjueɪtd] a situé(e).
situation [sɪtjuˈeɪʃən] n situation f; '~s vacant/wanted' 'offres/demandes d'emploi'.
six [sɪks] num six; ~**teen** num seize; ~**th** a sixième; ~**ty** num soixante.
size [saɪz] n taille f; dimensions fpl; (of clothing) taille; (of shoes) pointure f; (glue) colle f; **to ~ up** vt juger, jauger; ~**able** a assez grand(e) or gros(se); assez important(e).
sizzle ['sɪzl] vi grésiller.
skate [skeɪt] n patin m; (fish: pl inv) raie f // vi patiner; ~**board** n skateboard m, planche f à roulettes; ~**r** n patineur/euse; **skating** n patinage m; **skating rink** n patinoire f.
skeleton ['skɛlɪtn] n squelette m; (outline) schéma m; ~ **staff** n effectifs réduits.
skeptic ['skɛptɪk] n (US) = **sceptic**.
sketch [skɛtʃ] n (drawing) croquis m, esquisse f; (THEATRE) sketch m, saynète f // vt esquisser, faire un croquis or une esquisse de; ~ **book** n carnet m à dessin; ~ **pad** n bloc m à dessin; ~**y** a incomplet(ète), fragmentaire.
skew [skju:] n: **on the** ~ de travers, en biais.
skewer ['skju:ə*] n brochette f.
ski [ski:] n ski m // vi skier, faire du ski; ~ **boot** n chaussure f de ski.
skid [skɪd] n dérapage m // vi déraper; ~**mark** n trace f de dérapage.
skier ['ski:ə*] n skieur/euse.
skiing ['ski:ɪŋ] n ski m.
ski jump ['ski:dʒʌmp] n saut m à skis.
skilful ['skɪlful] a habile, adroit(e).
ski lift ['ski:lɪft] n remonte-pente m inv.
skill [skɪl] n habileté f, adresse f, talent m; ~**ed** a habile, adroit(e); (worker) qualifié(e).
skim [skɪm] vt (milk) écrémer; (soup) écumer; (glide over) raser, effleurer // vi: **to ~ through** (fig) parcourir.
skimp [skɪmp] vt (work) bâcler, faire à la va-vite; (cloth etc) lésiner sur; ~**y** a étriqué(e); maigre.
skin [skɪn] n peau f // vt (fruit etc) éplucher; (animal) écorcher; ~**deep** a superficiel(le); ~ **diving** n plongée sous-marine; ~ **graft** n greffe f de peau; ~**ny** a maigre, maigrichon(ne); ~ **test** n cuti(-réaction) f; ~**tight** a (dress etc) collant(e), ajusté(e).
skip [skɪp] n petit bond or saut m; (container) benne f // vi gambader, sautiller; (with rope) sauter à la corde // vt (pass over) sauter.
ski pants ['ski:pænts] npl fuseau m (de ski).
skipper ['skɪpə*] n (NAUT. SPORT) capitaine m // vt (boat) commander; (team) être le chef de.
skipping rope ['skɪpɪŋrəup] n corde f à sauter.

skirmish ['skə:mɪʃ] n escarmouche f, accrochage m.
skirt [skə:t] n jupe f // vt longer, contourner; ~**ing board** n plinthe f.
skit [skɪt] n sketch m satirique.
ski tow ['ski:təu] n = **ski lift**.
skittle ['skɪtl] n quille f; ~**s** n (game) (jeu m de) quilles.
skive [skaɪv] (Brit) vi (col) tirer au flanc.
skulk [skʌlk] vi rôder furtivement.
skull [skʌl] n crâne m.
skunk [skʌŋk] n mouffette f; (fur) sconse m.
sky [skaɪ] n ciel m; ~**-blue** a bleu ciel inv; ~**light** n lucarne f; ~**scraper** n gratte-ciel m inv.
slab [slæb] n plaque f; dalle f.
slack [slæk] a (loose) lâche, desserré(e); (slow) stagnant(e); (careless) négligent(e), peu sérieux(euse) or conscencieux(euse) // n (in rope etc) mou m; ~**s** npl pantalon m; ~**en** (also: ~**en off**) vi ralentir, diminuer; (in one's work, attention) se relâcher // vt relâcher.
slag [slæg] n scories fpl; ~ **heap** n crassier m.
slam [slæm] vt (door) (faire) claquer; (throw) jeter violemment, flanquer; (criticize) éreinter, démolir // vi claquer.
slander ['slɑ:ndə*] n calomnie f; diffamation f // vt calomnier; diffamer; ~**ous** a calomnieux(euse); diffamatoire.
slang [slæŋ] n argot m.
slant [slɑ:nt] n inclinaison f; (fig) angle m, point m de vue; ~**ed** a tendancieux(euse); ~**ing** a en pente, incliné(e); couché(e).
slap [slæp] n claque f, gifle f; tape f // vt donner une claque or une gifle or une tape à // ad (directly) tout droit, en plein; ~**dash** a fait(e) sans soin or à la va-vite; ~**stick** n (comedy) grosse farce, style m tarte à la crème; a ~**-up meal** un repas extra or fameux.
slash [slæʃ] vt entailler, taillader; (fig: prices) casser.
slate [sleɪt] n ardoise f // vt (fig: criticize) éreinter, démolir.
slaughter ['slɔ:tə*] n carnage m, massacre m // vt (animal) abattre; (people) massacrer; ~**house** n abattoir m.
Slav [slɑ:v] a slave.
slave [sleɪv] n esclave m/f // vi (also: ~ **away**) trimer, travailler comme un forçat; ~**ry** n esclavage m.
Slavic ['slævɪk] a slave.
slavish ['sleɪvɪʃ] a servile.
Slavonic [sləˈvɔnɪk] a slave.
sleazy ['sli:zɪ] a miteux(euse), minable.
sledge [slɛdʒ] n luge f; ~**hammer** n marteau m de forgeron.
sleek [sli:k] a (hair, fur) brillant(e), luisant(e); (car, boat) aux lignes pures or élégantes.
sleep [sli:p] n sommeil m // vi (pt, pp **slept** [slɛpt]) dormir; (spend night) dormir, coucher; **to go to** ~ s'endormir; **to** ~ **in** vi (lie late) faire la grasse matinée; (oversleep) se réveiller trop tard; ~**er** n (person) dormeur/euse; (RAIL: on track) traverse f; (: train) train m de voitures-lits; ~**ily** ad d'un air endormi; ~**ing** a

qui dort, endormi(e) ; ~ing bag n sac m de couchage ; ~ing car n wagon-lits m, voiture-lits f ; ~ing pill n somnifère m ; ~lessness n insomnie f ; a ~less night une nuit blanche ; ~walker n somnambule m/f ; ~y a qui a envie de dormir ; (fig) endormi(e).

sleet [sli:t] n neige fondue.

sleeve [sli:v] n manche f ; ~less a (garment) sans manches.

sleigh [sleɪ] n traîneau m.

sleight [slaɪt] n: ~ of hand tour m de passe-passe.

slender ['slɛndə*] a svelte, mince ; faible, ténu(e).

slept [slɛpt] pt,pp of **sleep**.

slice [slaɪs] n tranche f ; (round) rondelle f // vt couper en tranches (or en rondelles).

slick [slɪk] a brillant(e) en apparence ; mielleux(euse) // n (also: oil ~) nappe f de pétrole, marée noire.

slid [slɪd] pt,pp of **slide**.

slide [slaɪd] n (in playground) toboggan m ; (PHOT) diapositive f ; (also: hair ~) barrette f ; (in prices) chute f, baisse f // vb (pt,pp **slid** [slɪd]) vt (faire) glisser // vi glisser ; ~ rule n règle f à calcul ; **sliding** a (door) coulissant(e) ; **sliding scale** n échelle f mobile.

slight [slaɪt] a (slim) mince, menu(e) ; (frail) frêle ; (trivial) faible, insignifiant(e) ; (small) petit(e), léger(ère) (before n) // n offense f, affront m // vt (offend) blesser, offenser ; **the ~est** le (or la) moindre ; **not in the ~est** pas le moins du monde, pas du tout ; ~ly ad légèrement, un peu.

slim [slɪm] a mince // vi maigrir, suivre un régime amaigrissant.

slime [slaɪm] n vase f ; substance visqueuse ; **slimy** a visqueux(euse), gluant(e).

sling [slɪŋ] n (MED) écharpe f // vt (pt,pp **slung** [slʌŋ]) lancer, jeter.

slip [slɪp] n faux pas ; (mistake) erreur f, étourderie f ; bévue f ; (underskirt) combinaison f ; (of paper) petite feuille, fiche f // vt (slide) glisser // vi (slide) glisser ; (move smoothly): **to ~ into/out of** se glisser or se faufiler dans/hors de ; (decline) baisser ; **to give sb the ~** fausser compagnie à qn ; **a ~ of the tongue** un lapsus ; **to ~ away** vi s'esquiver ; **to ~ in** vt glisser ; **to ~ out** vi sortir ; ~**ped disc** n déplacement m de vertèbres.

slipper ['slɪpə*] n pantoufle f.

slippery ['slɪpərɪ] a glissant(e) ; insaisissable.

slip road ['slɪprəud] n (to motorway) bretelle f d'accès.

slipshod ['slɪpʃɔd] a négligé(e), peu soigné(e).

slip-up ['slɪpʌp] n bévue f.

slipway ['slɪpweɪ] n cale f (de construction or de lancement).

slit [slɪt] n fente f ; (cut) incision f ; (tear) déchirure f // vt (pt,pp **slit**) fendre ; couper ; inciser ; déchirer.

slither ['slɪðə*] vi glisser, déraper.

slob [slɔb] n (col) rustaud m.

slog [slɔg] n gros effort ; tâche fastidieuse // vi travailler très dur.

slogan ['sləugən] n slogan m.

slop [slɔp] vi (also: ~ over) se renverser ; déborder // vt répandre ; renverser.

slope [sləup] n pente f, côte f ; (side of mountain) versant m ; (slant) inclinaison f // vi: **to ~ down** être or descendre en pente ; **to ~ up** monter ; **sloping** a en pente, incliné(e) ; (handwriting) penché(e).

sloppy ['slɔpɪ] a (work) peu soigné(e), bâclé(e) ; (appearance) négligé(e), débraillé(e) ; (film etc) sentimental(e).

slot [slɔt] n fente f // vt: **to ~ into** encastrer or insérer dans ; ~ **machine** n distributeur m (automatique), machine f à sous.

slouch [slautʃ] vi avoir le dos rond, être voûté(e).

slovenly ['slʌvənlɪ] a sale, débraillé(e), négligé(e).

slow [sləu] a lent(e) ; (watch): **to be ~** retarder // ad lentement // vt,vi (also: ~ **down, ~ up**) ralentir ; ' ~ ' (road sign) 'ralentir' ; ~ly ad lentement ; **in ~ motion** au ralenti ; ~ness n lenteur f.

sludge [slʌdʒ] n boue f.

slug [slʌg] n limace f ; (bullet) balle f ; ~gish a mou(molle), lent(e).

sluice [slu:s] n vanne f ; écluse f.

slum [slʌm] n taudis m.

slumber ['slʌmbə*] n sommeil m.

slump [slʌmp] n baisse soudaine, effondrement m ; crise f // vi s'effondrer, s'affaisser.

slung [slʌŋ] pt,pp of **sling**.

slur [slə:*] n bredouillement m ; (smear): ~ **(on)** atteinte f (à) ; insinuation f (contre) ; (MUS) liaison f // vt mal articuler ; **to be a ~ on** porter atteinte à.

slush [slʌʃ] n neige fondue ; ~y a (snow) fondu(e) ; (street) couvert(e) de neige fondue ; (fig) sentimental(e).

slut [slʌt] n souillon f.

sly [slaɪ] a rusé(e) ; sournois(e) ; **on the ~** en cachette.

smack [smæk] n (slap) tape f ; (on face) gifle f // vt donner une tape à ; gifler ; (child) donner la fessée à // vi: **to ~ of** avoir des relents de, sentir ; **to ~ one's lips** se lécher les babines.

small [smɔ:l] a petit(e) ; ~ **ads** npl petites annonces ; ~**holder** n petit cultivateur ; **in the ~ hours** au petit matin ; ~**ish** a plutôt or assez petit ; ~**pox** n variole f ; ~ **talk** n menus propos.

smarmy ['smɑ:mɪ] a (col) flagorneur(euse), lécheur(euse).

smart [smɑ:t] a élégant(e), chic inv ; (clever) intelligent(e), astucieux(euse), futé(e) ; (quick) rapide, vif(vive), prompt(e) // vi faire mal, brûler ; **to ~en up** vi devenir plus élégant(e), se faire beau(belle) // vt rendre plus élégant(e).

smash [smæʃ] n (also: ~-up) collision f, accident m // vt casser, briser, fracasser ; (opponent) écraser ; (hopes) ruiner, détruire ; (SPORT: record) pulvériser // vi se briser, se fracasser ; s'écraser ; ~ing a (col) formidable.

smattering ['smætərɪŋ] n: **a ~ of** quelques notions de.

smear [smɪə*] *n* tache *f*, salissure *f*; trace *f*; (MED) frottis *m* // *vt* enduire; (*fig*) porter atteinte à.

smell [smɛl] *n* odeur *f*; (*sense*) odorat *m* // *vb* (*pt,pp* **smelt** *or* **smelled** [smɛlt, smɛld]) *vt* sentir // *vi* (*food etc*): **to ~ (of)** sentir; (*pej*) sentir mauvais; **~y** *a* qui sent mauvais, malodorant(e).

smile [smaɪl] *n* sourire *m* // *vi* sourire; **smiling** *a* souriant(e).

smirk [smə:k] *n* petit sourire suffisant *or* affecté.

smith [smɪθ] *n* maréchal-ferrant *m*; forgeron *m*; **~y** *n* forge *f*.

smitten ['smɪtn] *a*: **~ with** pris(e) de; frappé(e) de.

smock [smɔk] *n* blouse *f*, sarrau *m*.

smog [smɔg] *n* brouillard mêlé de fumée.

smoke [sməuk] *n* fumée *f* // *vt*, *vi* fumer; **to have a ~** fumer une cigarette; **~d a** (*bacon, glass*) fumé(e); **~r** *n* (*person*) fumeur/euse; (RAIL) wagon *m* fumeurs; **smoking** *n*: '**no smoking**' (*sign*) 'défense de fumer'; **smoking room** *n* fumoir *m*; **smoky** *a* enfumé(e); (*surface*) noirci(e) par la fumée.

smolder ['sməuldə*] *vi* (US) = **smoulder**.

smooth [smu:ð] *a* lisse; (*sauce*) onctueux(euse); (*flavour, whisky*) moelleux(euse); (*movement*) régulier(ère), sans à-coups *or* heurts; (*person*) doucereux(euse), mielleux(euse) // *vt* lisser, défroisser; (*also*: **~ out**) (*creases, difficulties*) faire disparaître.

smother ['smʌðə*] *vt* étouffer.

smoulder ['sməuldə*] *vi* couver.

smudge [smʌdʒ] *n* tache *f*, bavure *f* // *vt* salir, maculer.

smug [smʌg] *a* suffisant(e), content(e) de soi.

smuggle ['smʌgl] *vt* passer en contrebande *or* en fraude; **~r** *n* contrebandier/ère; **smuggling** *n* contrebande *f*.

smutty ['smʌtɪ] *a* (*fig*) grossier(ère), obscène.

snack [snæk] *n* casse-croûte *m inv*; **~ bar** *n* snack(-bar) *m*.

snag [snæg] *n* inconvénient *m*, difficulté *f*.

snail [sneɪl] *n* escargot *m*.

snake [sneɪk] *n* serpent *m*.

snap [snæp] *n* (*sound*) claquement *m*, bruit sec; (*photograph*) photo *f*, instantané *m*; (*game*) sorte *f* de jeu de bataille // *a* subit(e); fait(e) sans réfléchir // *vt* faire claquer; (*break*) casser net; (*photograph*) prendre un instantané de // *vi* se casser net *or* avec un bruit sec; **to ~ open/shut** s'ouvrir/se refermer brusquement; **to ~ at** *vt fus* (*subj*: *dog*) essayer de mordre; **to ~ off** *vt* (*break*) casser net; **to ~ up** *vt* sauter sur, saisir; **~ fastener** *n* bouton-pression *m*; **~py** *a* prompt(e); **~shot** *n* photo *f*, instantané *m*.

snare [snɛə*] *n* piège *m* // *vt* attraper, prendre au piège.

snarl [snɑ:l] *n* grondement *m* *or* grognement *m* féroce // *vi* gronder.

snatch [snætʃ] *n* (*fig*) vol *m*; (*small amount*): **~es of** des fragments *mpl or*

bribes *fpl* de // *vt* saisir (*d'un geste vif*); (*steal*) voler.

sneak [sni:k] *vi*: **to ~ in/out** entrer/sortir furtivement *or* à la dérobée; **~y** *a* sournois(e).

sneer [snɪə*] *n* ricanement *m* // *vi* ricaner, sourire d'un air sarcastique.

sneeze [sni:z] *n* éternuement *m* // *vi* éternuer.

snide [snaɪd] *a* sarcastique, narquois(e).

sniff [snɪf] *n* reniflement *m* // *vi* renifler // *vt* renifler, flairer.

snigger ['snɪgə*] *n* ricanement *m*; rire moqueur // *vi* ricaner; pouffer de rire.

snip [snɪp] *n* petit bout; (*bargain*) (bonne) occasion *or* affaire // *vt* couper.

sniper ['snaɪpə*] *n* (*marksman*) tireur embusqué.

snippet ['snɪpɪt] *n* bribes *fpl*.

snivelling ['snɪvlɪŋ] *a* (*whimpering*) larmoyant(e), pleurnicheur(euse).

snob [snɔb] *n* snob *m/f*; **~bery** *n* snobisme *m*; **~bish** *a* snob *inv*.

snooker ['snu:kə*] *n* sorte de jeu de billard.

snoop ['snu:p] *vi*: **to ~ on sb** espionner qn.

snooty ['snu:tɪ] *a* snob *inv*, prétentieux(euse).

snooze [snu:z] *n* petit somme // *vi* faire un petit somme.

snore [snɔ:*] *vi* ronfler; **snoring** *n* ronflement(s) *m(pl)*.

snorkel ['snɔ:kl] *n* (*of swimmer*) tuba *m*.

snort [snɔ:t] *n* grognement *m* // *vi* grogner; (*horse*) renâcler.

snotty ['snɔtɪ] *a* morveux(euse).

snout [snaut] *n* museau *m*.

snow [snəu] *n* neige *f* // *vi* neiger; **~ball** *n* boule *f* de neige; **~bound** *a* enneigé(e), bloqué(e) par la neige; **~drift** *n* congère *f*; **~drop** *n* perce-neige *m*; **~fall** *n* chute *f* de neige; **~flake** *n* flocon *m* de neige; **~man** *n* bonhomme *m* de neige; **~plough, ~plow** (US) *n* chasse-neige *m inv*; **~storm** *n* tempête *f* de neige.

snub [snʌb] *vt* repousser, snober // *n* rebuffade *f*; **~-nosed** *a* au nez retroussé.

snuff [snʌf] *n* tabac *m* à priser.

snug [snʌg] *a* douillet(te), confortable.

so [səu] *ad* (*degree*) si, tellement; (*manner: thus*) ainsi, de cette façon // *cj* donc, par conséquent; **~ as to do** afin de *or* pour faire; **~ that** (*purpose*) afin de + *infinitive*, pour que *or* afin que + *sub*; (*result*) si bien que, de (telle) sorte que; **~ do I, ~ am I** *etc* moi *etc* aussi; **if ~** si oui; **I hope ~** je l'espère; **10 or ~** 10 à peu près *or* environ; **~ far** jusqu'ici, jusqu'à maintenant; (*in past*) jusque-là; **~ long!** à bientôt!, au revoir!; **~ many** tant de; **~ much** *ad* tant // *det* tant de; **~ and ~ n** un tel(une telle).

soak [səuk] *vt* faire *or* laisser tremper // *vi* tremper; **to be ~ed through** être trempé jusqu'aux os; **to ~ in** *vi* pénétrer, être absorbé(e); **to ~ up** *vt* absorber.

soap [səup] *n* savon *m*; **~flakes** *npl* paillettes *fpl* de savon; **~ powder** *n* lessive *f*, détergent *m*; **~y** *a* savonneux(euse).

soar [sɔ:*] vi monter (en flèche), s'élancer.
sob [sɔb] n sanglot m // vi sangloter.
sober ['səubə*] a qui n'est pas (or plus) ivre ; (sedate) sérieux(euse), sensé(e) ; (moderate) mesuré(e) ; (colour, style) sobre, discret(ète) ; **to ~ up** vt dégriser // vi se dégriser.
Soc. abbr of **society**.
so-called ['səu'kɔ:ld] a soi-disant inv.
soccer ['sɔkə*] n football m.
sociable ['səuʃəbl] a sociable.
social ['səuʃl] a social(e) // n (petite) fête ; **~ club** n amicale f, foyer m ; **~ism** n socialisme m ; **~ist** a,n socialiste (m/f) ; **~ly** ad socialement, en société / ; **~ science** n sciences humaines ; **~ security** n aide sociale ; **~ welfare** n sécurité sociale ; **~ work** n assistance sociale ; **~ worker** n assistant/e social/e.
society [sə'saiəti] n société f ; (club) société, association f ; (also: **high ~**) (haute) société, grand monde.
sociological [səusiə'lɔdʒikl] a sociologique.
sociologist [səusi'ɔlədʒist] n sociologue m/f.
sociology [səusi'ɔlədʒi] n sociologie f.
sock [sɔk] n chaussette f // vt (hit) flanquer un coup à.
socket ['sɔkit] n cavité f ; (ELEC: also: **wall ~**) prise f de courant ; (: for light bulb) douille f.
sod [sɔd] n (of earth) motte f ; (col!) con m (!) ; salaud m (!).
soda ['səudə] n (CHEM) soude f ; (also: **~ water**) eau f de Seltz.
sodden ['sɔdn] a trempé(e) ; détrempé(e).
sodium ['səudiəm] n sodium m.
sofa ['səufə] n sofa m, canapé m.
soft [sɔft] a (not rough) doux/(douce) ; (not hard) doux ; mou/(molle) ; (not loud) doux, léger(ère) ; (kind) doux, gentil(le) ; (weak) indulgent(e) ; (stupid) stupide, débile ; **~ drink** n boisson non alcoolisée ; **~en** ['sɔfn] vt (r)amollir ; adoucir ; atténuer // vi se ramollir ; s'adoucir ; s'atténuer ; **~hearted** a au cœur tendre ; **~ly** ad doucement ; gentiment ; **~ness** n douceur f ; **~ware** n logiciel m, software m.
soggy ['sɔgi] a trempé(e) ; détrempé(e).
soil [sɔil] n (earth) sol m, terre f // vt salir ; (fig) souiller ; **~ed** a sale ; (COMM) défraîchi(e).
solar ['səulə*] a solaire.
sold [səuld] pt,pp of **sell** ; **~ out** a (COMM) épuisé(e).
solder ['səuldə*] vt souder (au fil à souder) // n soudure f.
soldier ['səuldʒə*] n soldat m, militaire m.
sole [səul] n (of foot) plante f ; (of shoe) semelle f ; (fish: pl inv) sole f // a seul(e), unique ; **~ly** ad seulement, uniquement.
solemn ['sɔləm] a solennel(le) ; sérieux(euse), grave.
solicitor [sə'lisitə*] n (for wills etc) ≈ notaire m ; (in court) ≈ avocat m.
solid ['sɔlid] a (not hollow) plein(e), compact(e), massif(ive) ; (strong, sound, reliable, not liquid) solide ; (meal) consistant(e), substantiel(le) // n solide m.

solidarity [sɔli'dæriti] n solidarité f.
solidify [sə'lidifai] vi se solidifier // vt solidifier.
solidity [sə'liditi] n solidité f.
soliloquy [sə'liləkwi] n monologue m.
solitaire [sɔli'tɛə*] n (game, gem) solitaire m.
solitary ['sɔlitəri] a solitaire ; **~ confinement** n (LAW) isolement m.
solitude ['sɔlitju:d] n solitude f.
solo ['səuləu] n solo m ; **~ist** n soliste m/f.
solstice ['sɔlstis] n solstice m.
soluble ['sɔljubl] a soluble.
solution [sə'lu:ʃən] n solution f.
solve [sɔlv] vt résoudre.
solvent ['sɔlvənt] a (COMM) solvable // n (CHEM) (dis)solvant m.
sombre, somber (US) ['sɔmbə*] a sombre, morne.
some [sʌm] det (a few) quelques ; (certain) certains(certaines) ; (a certain number or amount) see phrases below ; (unspecified) un(e)... (quelconque) / : **~** (quelconque) ou quelqu'un ; **~** uns(unes) ; un peu // ad : **~ 10 people** quelque 10 personnes, 10 personnes environ ; **~ children came** des enfants sont venus ; **have ~ tea/ice-cream/water** prends du thé/de la glace/de l'eau ; **there's ~ milk in the fridge** il y a un peu de lait ou du lait dans le frigo ; **~ (of it) was left** il en est resté un peu ; **I've got ~** (i.e. books etc) j'en ai (quelques uns) ; (i.e. milk, money etc) j'en ai (un peu) ; **~body** pronoun quelqu'un ; **~ day** ad un de ces jours, un jour ou l'autre ; **~how** ad d'une façon ou d'une autre ; (for some reason) pour une raison ou une autre ; **~one pronoun = somebody** ; **~place** ad (US) = **somewhere**.
somersault ['sʌməsɔ:lt] n culbute f, saut périlleux // vi faire la culbute or un saut périlleux ; (car) faire un tonneau.
something ['sʌmθiŋ] pronoun quelque chose m ; **~ interesting** quelque chose d'intéressant.
sometime ['sʌmtaim] ad (in future) un de ces jours, un jour ou l'autre ; (in past): **~ last month** au cours du mois dernier.
sometimes ['sʌmtaimz] ad quelquefois, parfois.
somewhat ['sʌmwɔt] ad quelque peu, un peu.
somewhere ['sʌmwɛə*] ad quelque part.
son [sʌn] n fils m.
sonata [sə'nɑ:tə] n sonate f.
song [sɔŋ] n chanson f ; **~book** n chansonnier m ; **~writer** n auteur-compositeur m.
sonic ['sɔnik] a (boom) supersonique.
son-in-law ['sʌninlɔ:] n gendre m, beau-fils m.
sonnet ['sɔnit] n sonnet m.
sonny ['sʌni] n (col) fiston m.
soon [su:n] ad bientôt ; (early) tôt ; **~ afterwards** peu après ; see also **as** ; **~er** ad (time) plus tôt ; (preference): **I would ~er do** j'aimerais autant or je préférerais faire ; **~er or later** tôt ou tard.
soot [sut] n suie f.

soothe [su:ð] *vt* calmer, apaiser.

sop [sɔp] *n*: **that's only a ~** c'est pour nous (*or* les *etc*) amadouer.

sophisticated [sə'fıstıkeıtıd] *a* raffiné(e) ; sophistiqué(e) ; hautement perfectionné(e), très complexe.

sophomore ['sɔfəmɔ:*] *n* (*US*) étudiant/e de seconde année.

soporific [sɔpə'rıfık] *a* soporifique // *n* somnifère *m*.

sopping ['sɔpıŋ] *a* (*also*: ~ **wet**) tout(e) trempé(e).

soppy ['sɔpı] *a* (*pej*) sentimental(e).

soprano [sə'prɑ:nəu] *n* (*voice*) soprano *m* ; (*singer*) soprano *m/f*.

sorcerer ['sɔ:sərə*] *n* sorcier *m*.

sordid ['sɔ:dıd] *a* sordide.

sore [sɔ:*] *a* (*painful*) douloureux(euse), sensible ; (*offended*) contrarié(e), vexé(e) // *n* plaie *f* ; **~ly** *ad* (*tempted*) fortement.

sorrel ['sɔrəl] *n* oseille *f*.

sorrow ['sɔrəu] *n* peine *f*, chagrin *m* ; **~ful** *a* triste.

sorry ['sɔrı] *a* désolé(e) ; (*condition, excuse*) triste, déplorable ; **~!** pardon!, excusez-moi! ; **to feel ~ for sb** plaindre qn.

sort [sɔ:t] *n* genre *m*, espèce *f*, sorte *f* // *vt* (*also*: ~ **out**: *papers*) trier ; classer ; ranger ; (: *letters etc*) trier ; (: *problems*) résoudre, régler ; **~ing office** *n* bureau *m* de tri.

SOS *n* (*abbr of save our souls*) S.O.S. *m*.

so-so ['səusəu] *ad* comme ci comme ça.

soufflé ['su:fleı] *n* soufflé *m*.

sought [sɔ:t] *pt,pp of* **seek**.

soul [səul] *n* âme *f* ; **~-destroying** *a* démoralisant(e) ; **~ful** *a* plein(e) de sentiment ; **~less** *a* sans cœur, inhumain(e).

sound [saund] *a* (*healthy*) en bonne santé, sain(e) ; (*safe, not damaged*) solide, en bon état ; (*reliable, not superficial*) sérieux(euse), solide ; (*sensible*) sensé(e) // *ad*: **~ asleep** dormant d'un profond sommeil // *n* (*noise*) son *m* ; bruit *m* ; (*GEO*) détroit *m*, bras *m* de mer // *vt* (*alarm*) sonner ; (*also*: ~ **out**: *opinions*) sonder // *vi* sonner, retentir ; (*fig*: *seem*) sembler (être) ; **to ~ one's horn** (*AUT*) actionner son avertisseur ; **to ~ like** ressembler à ; **~ barrier** *n* mur *m* du son ; **~ effects** *npl* bruitage *m* ; **~ing** *n* (*NAUT etc*) sondage *m* ; **~ly** *ad* (*sleep*) profondément ; (*beat*) complètement, à plate couture ; **~proof** *vt* insonoriser // *a* insonorisé(e) ; **~track** *n* (*of film*) bande *f* sonore.

soup [su:p] *n* soupe *f*, potage *m* ; **in the ~** (*fig*) dans le pétrin ; **~ course** *n* potage *m* ; **~spoon** *n* cuiller *f* à soupe.

sour ['sauə*] *a* aigre, acide ; (*milk*) tourné(e), aigre ; (*fig*) acerbe, aigre ; revêche ; **it's ~ grapes** c'est du dépit.

source [sɔ:s] *n* source *f*.

south [sauθ] *n* sud *m* // *a* sud *inv*, du sud // *ad* au sud, vers le sud ; **S~ Africa** *n* Afrique *f* du Sud ; **S~ African** *a* sud-africain(e) // *n* Sud-Africain/e ; **S~ America** *n* Amérique *f* du Sud ; **S~ American** *a* sud-américain(e) // *n* Sud-Américain/e ; **~-east** *n* sud-est *m* ; **~erly** ['sʌðəlı] *a* du sud ; au sud ; **~ern** ['sʌðən] *a* (du) sud ; méridional(e) ; exposé(e) au

sud ; **S~ Pole** *n* Pôle *m* Sud ; **~ward(s)** *ad* vers le sud ; **~-west** *n* sud-ouest *m*.

souvenir [su:və'nıə*] *n* souvenir *m* (*objet*).

sovereign ['sɔvrın] *a,n* souverain(e) ; **~ty** *n* souveraineté *f*.

soviet ['səuvıət] *a* soviétique ; **the S~ Union** l'Union *f* soviétique.

sow *n* [sau] truie *f* // *vt* [səu] (*pt* **~ed**, *pp* **sown** [saun]) semer.

soy [sɔı] *n* (*also*: ~ **sauce**) sauce *f* de soja.

soya bean ['sɔıəbi:n] *n* graine *f* de soja.

spa [spɑ:] *n* (*spring*) source minérale ; (*town*) station thermale.

space [speıs] *n* (*gen*) espace *m* ; (*room*) place *f* ; espace ; (*length of time*) laps *m* de temps // *cpd* spatial(e) // *vt* (*also*: ~ **out**) espacer ; **~craft** *n* engin spatial ; **~man/woman** *n* astronaute *m/f* ; cosmonaute *m/f* ; **spacing** *n* espacement *m* ; **single/double spacing** interligne *m* simple/double.

spacious ['speıʃəs] *a* spacieux(euse), grand(e).

spade [speıd] *n* (*tool*) bêche *f*, pelle *f* ; (*child's*) pelle ; **~s** *npl* (*CARDS*) pique *m* ; **~work** *n* (*fig*) gros *m* du travail.

spaghetti [spə'getı] *n* spaghetti *mpl*.

Spain [speın] *n* Espagne *f*.

span [spæn] *pt of* **spin** // *n* (*of bird, plane*) envergure *f* ; (*of arch*) portée *f* ; (*in time*) espace *m* de temps, durée *f* // *vt* enjamber, franchir ; (*fig*) couvrir, embrasser.

Spaniard ['spænjəd] *n* Espagnol/e.

spaniel ['spænjəl] *n* épagneul *m*.

Spanish ['spænıʃ] *a* espagnol(e), d'Espagne // *n* (*LING*) espagnol *m*.

spank [spæŋk] *vt* donner une fessée à.

spanner ['spænə*] *n* clé *f* (de mécanicien).

spare [speə*] *a* de réserve, de rechange ; (*surplus*) de *or* en trop, de reste // *n* (*part*) pièce *f* de rechange, pièce détachée // *vt* (*do without*) se passer de ; (*afford to give*) donner, accorder, passer ; (*refrain from hurting*) épargner ; (*refrain from using*) ménager ; **to ~** (*surplus*) en surplus, de trop ; **~ part** *n* pièce *f* de rechange, pièce détachée ; **~ time** *n* moments *mpl* de loisir.

sparing ['spεərıŋ] *a* modéré(e), restreint(e) ; **~ of** chiche de ; **~ly** *ad* avec modération.

spark [spɑ:k] *n* étincelle *f* ; (*fig*) étincelle, lueur *f* ; **~(ing) plug** *n* bougie *f*.

sparkle ['spɑ:kl] *n* scintillement *m*, étincellement *m*, éclat *m* // *vi* étinceler, scintiller ; (*bubble*) pétiller ; **sparkling** *a* étincelant(e), scintillant(e) ; (*wine*) mousseux (euse), pétillant(e).

sparrow ['spærəu] *n* moineau *m*.

sparse [spɑ:s] *a* clairsemé(e).

spasm ['spæzəm] *n* (*MED*) spasme *m* ; (*fig*) accès *m* ; **~odic** [-'mɔdık] *a* spasmodique ; (*fig*) intermittent(e).

spastic ['spæstık] *n* handicapé/e moteur.

spat [spæt] *pt,pp of* **spit**.

spate [speıt] *n* (*fig*): **~ of** avalanche *f* or torrent *m* de ; **in ~** (*river*) en crue.

spatter ['spætə*] *n* éclaboussure(s) *f(pl)* // *vt* éclabousser // *vi* gicler.

spatula ['spætjulə] *n* spatule *f*.

spawn [spɔ:n] *vt* pondre // *vi* frayer // *n* frai *m*.

speak, *pt* **spoke,** *pp* **spoken** [spi:k, spəʊk, spəʊkn] *vt* (*language*) parler; (*truth*) dire // *vi* parler; (*make a speech*) prendre la parole; **to ~ to sb/of or about sth** parler à qn/de qch; **it ~s for itself** c'est évident; **~ up!** parle plus fort!; **~er** *n* (*in public*) orateur *m*; (*also:* loud~er) haut-parleur *m*; (*POL*): **the S~er** *le président de la chambre des Communes*; **to be on ~ing terms** se parler.

spear [spɪə*] *n* lance *f* // *vt* transpercer.

spec [spɛk] *n* (*col*): **on ~** à tout hasard.

special ['spɛʃl] *a* spécial(e); **take ~ care** soyez particulièrement prudents; **today's ~** (*at restaurant*) le menu; **~ist** *n* spécialiste *m/f*; **~ity** [spɛʃɪ'ælɪtɪ] *n* spécialité *f*; **~ize** *vi* **to ~ize (in)** se spécialiser (dans); **~ly** *ad* spécialement, particulièrement.

species ['spi:ʃi:z] *n* espèce *f*.

specific [spə'sɪfɪk] *a* précis(e); particulier(ère); (*BOT, CHEM etc*) spécifique; **~ally** *ad* expressément, explicitement; **~ation** [spɛsɪfɪ'keɪʃn] *n* spécification *f*; stipulation *f*.

specify ['spɛsɪfaɪ] *vt* spécifier, préciser.

specimen ['spɛsɪmən] *n* spécimen *m*, échantillon *m*; (*MED*) prélèvement *m*.

speck [spɛk] *n* petite tache, petit point; (*particle*) grain *m*.

speckled ['spɛkld] *a* tacheté(e), moucheté(e).

specs [spɛks] *npl* (*col*) lunettes *fpl*.

spectacle ['spɛktəkl] *n* spectacle *m*; **~s** *npl* lunettes *fpl*; **spectacular** [-'tækjulə*] *a* spectaculaire // *n* (*CINEMA etc*) superproduction *f*.

spectator [spɛk'teɪtə*] *n* spectateur/trice.

spectra ['spɛktrə] *npl of* **spectrum**.

spectre, specter (*US*) ['spɛktə*] *n* spectre *m*, fantôme *m*.

spectrum, *pl* **spectra** ['spɛktrəm, -rə] *n* spectre *m*; (*fig*) gamme *f*.

speculate ['spɛkjuleɪt] *vi* spéculer; (*try to guess*): **to ~ about** s'interroger sur; **speculation** [-'leɪʃən] *n* spéculation *f*; conjectures *fpl*; **speculative** *a* spéculatif(ive).

speech [spi:tʃ] *n* (*faculty*) parole *f*; (*talk*) discours *m*, allocution *f*; (*manner of speaking*) façon *f* de parler, langage *m*; (*enunciation*) élocution *f*; **~ day** *n* (*SCOL*) distribution *f* des prix; **~less** *a* muet(te); **~ therapy** *n* orthophonie *f*.

speed [spi:d] *n* vitesse *f*; (*promptness*) rapidité *f*; **at full or top ~** à toute vitesse *or* allure; **to ~ up** *vi* aller plus vite, accélérer // *vt* accélérer; **~boat** *n* vedette *f*; hors-bord *m inv*; **~ily** *ad* rapidement, promptement; **~ing** *n* (*AUT*) excès *m* de vitesse; **~ limit** *n* limitation *f* de vitesse, vitesse maximale permise; **~ometer** [spɪ'dɔmɪtə*] *n* compteur *m* (de vitesse); **~way** *n* (*SPORT*) piste *f* de vitesse pour motos; **~y** *a* rapide, prompt(e).

speleologist ['spɛlɪ'ɔlədʒɪst] *n* spéléologue *m/f*.

spell [spɛl] *n* (*also:* **magic ~**) sortilège *m*, charme *m*; (*period of time*) (courte) période // *vt* (*pt,pp* **spelt** *or* **~ed** [spɛlt, spɛld]) (*in writing*) écrire, orthographier; (*aloud*) épeler; (*fig*) signifier; **to cast a ~ on sb**

jeter un sort à qn; **he can't ~** il fait des fautes d'orthographe; **~bound** *a* envoûté(e), subjugué(e); **~ing** *n* orthographe *f*.

spelt [spɛlt] *pt,pp of* **spell**.

spend, *pt,pp* **spent** [spɛnd, spɛnt] *vt* (*money*) dépenser; (*time, life*) passer; consacrer; **~ing money** *n* argent *m* de poche; **~thrift** *n* dépensier/ère.

spent [spɛnt] *pt,pp of* **spend** // *a* (*patience*) épuisé(e), à bout.

sperm [spə:m] *n* spermatozoïde *m*; (*semen*) sperme *m*; **~ whale** *n* cachalot *m*.

spew [spju:] *vt* vomir.

sphere [sfɪə*] *n* sphère *f*; (*fig*) sphère, domaine *m*; **spherical** ['sfɛrɪkl] *a* sphérique.

sphinx [sfɪŋks] *n* sphinx *m*.

spice [spaɪs] *n* épice *f* // *vt* épicer.

spick-and-span ['spɪkən'spæn] *a* impeccable.

spicy ['spaɪsɪ] *a* épicé(e), relevé(e); (*fig*) piquant(e).

spider ['spaɪdə*] *n* araignée *f*.

spiel [spi:l] *n* laïus *m inv*.

spike [spaɪk] *n* pointe *f*.

spill, *pt,pp* **spilt** *or* **~ed** [spɪl, -t, -d] *vt* renverser; répandre // *vi* se répandre.

spin [spɪn] *n* (*revolution of wheel*) tour *m*; (*AVIAT*) (chute *f* en) vrille *f*; (*trip in car*) petit tour, balade *f* // *vb* (*pt* **spun, span,** *pp* **spun** [spʌn, spæn]) *vt* (*wool etc*) filer; (*wheel*) faire tourner // *vi* tourner, tournoyer; **to ~ a yarn** débiter une longue histoire; **to ~ a coin** jouer à pile ou face; **to ~ out** *vt* faire durer.

spinach ['spɪnɪtʃ] *n* épinard *m*; (*as food*) épinards.

spinal ['spaɪnl] *a* vertébral(e), spinal(e); **~ cord** *n* moelle épinière.

spindly ['spɪndlɪ] *a* grêle, filiforme.

spin-drier [spɪn'draɪə*] *n* essoreuse *f*.

spine [spaɪn] *n* colonne vertébrale; (*thorn*) épine *f*, piquant *m*; **~less** *a* invertébré(e); (*fig*) mou(molle), sans caractère.

spinner ['spɪnə*] *n* (*of thread*) fileur/euse.

spinning ['spɪnɪŋ] *n* (*of thread*) filage *m*; (*by machine*) filature *f*; **~ top** *n* toupie *f*; **~ wheel** *n* rouet *m*.

spinster ['spɪnstə*] *n* célibataire *f*; vieille fille.

spiral ['spaɪərl] *n* spirale *f* // *a* en spirale // *vi* (*fig*) monter en flèche; **~ staircase** *n* escalier *m* en colimaçon.

spire ['spaɪə*] *n* flèche *f*, aiguille *f*.

spirit ['spɪrɪt] *n* (*soul*) esprit *m*, âme *f*; (*ghost*) esprit, revenant *m*; (*mood*) esprit, état *m* d'esprit; (*courage*) courage *m*, énergie *f*; **~s** *npl* (*drink*) spiritueux *mpl*, alcool *m*; **in good ~s** de bonne humeur; **in low ~s** démoralisé(e); **~ed** *a* vif(vive), fougueux(euse), plein(e) d'allant; **~ level** *n* niveau *m* à bulle.

spiritual ['spɪrɪtjuəl] *a* spirituel(le); religieux(euse) // *n* (*also:* **Negro ~**) spiritual *m*; **~ism** *n* spiritisme *m*.

spit [spɪt] *n* (*for roasting*) broche *f* // *vi* (*pt, pp* **spat** [spæt]) cracher; (*sound*) crépiter.

spite [spait] *n* rancune *f*, dépit *m* // *vt* contrarier, vexer; **in ~ of** en dépit de, malgré; **~ful** *a* malveillant(e), rancunier(ère).

spitroast ['spit'rəust] *vt* faire rôtir à la broche.

spittle ['spitl] *n* salive *f*; bave *f*; crachat *m*.

spiv [spiv] *n* (*col*) chevalier *m* d'industrie, aigrefin *m*.

splash [splæʃ] *n* éclaboussement *m*; (*sound*) plouf; (*of colour*) tache *f* // *vt* éclabousser; *vi* (*also:* ~ **about**) barboter, patauger.

splay [splei] *a*: **~-footed** marchant les pieds en dehors.

spleen [spli:n] *n* (ANAT) rate *f*.

splendid ['splendid] *a* splendide, superbe, magnifique.

splendour, splendor (*US*) ['splendə*] *n* splendeur *f*, magnificence *f*.

splice [splais] *vt* épisser.

splint [splint] *n* attelle *f*, éclisse *f*.

splinter ['splintə*] *n* (*wood*) écharde *f*; (*metal*) éclat *m* // *vi* se fragmenter.

split [split] *n* fente *f*, déchirure *f*; (*fig: POL*) scission *f* // *vb* (*pt, pp* **split**) *vt* fendre, déchirer; (*party*) diviser; (*work, profits*) partager, répartir // (*divide*) se diviser; **to ~ up** *vi* (*couple*) se séparer, rompre; (*meeting*) se disperser; **~ting headache** *n* mal *m* de tête atroce.

splutter ['splʌtə*] *vi* bafouiller; postillonner.

spoil, *pt,pp* **spoilt** *or* **~ed** [spɔil, -t, -d] *vt* (*damage*) abîmer; (*mar*) gâcher; (*child*) gâter; **~s** *npl* butin *m*; **~sport** *n* trouble-fête *m*, rabat-joie *m*.

spoke [spəuk] *pt* of **speak** // *n* rayon *m*.

spoken ['spəukn] *pp* of **speak**.

spokesman ['spəuksmən] *n* porteparole *m inv*.

sponge [spʌndʒ] *n* éponge *f* // *vt* éponger // *vi*: **to ~ on** vivre aux crochets de; **~ bag** *n* sac *m* de toilette; **~ cake** *n* ≈ gâteau *m* de Savoie; **~r** *n* (*pej*) parasite *m*; **spongy** *a* spongieux(euse).

sponsor ['spɔnsə*] *n* (RADIO, TV) personne *f* (or organisme *m*) qui assure le patronage // *vt* patronner; parrainer; **~ship** *n* patronage *m*; parrainage *m*.

spontaneity [spɔntə'neɪɪtɪ] *n* spontanéité *f*.

spontaneous [spɔn'teiniəs] *a* spontané(e).

spooky ['spu:kɪ] *a* qui donne la chair de poule.

spool [spu:l] *n* bobine *f*.

spoon [spu:n] *n* cuiller *f*; **~-feed** *vt* nourrir à la cuiller; (*fig*) mâcher le travail à; **~ful** *n* cuillerée *f*.

sporadic [spə'rædɪk] *a* sporadique.

sport [spɔ:t] *n* sport *m*; (*person*) chic type/chic fille // *vt* arborer; **~ing** *a* sportif(ive); **to give sb a ~ing chance** donner sa chance à qn; **~s car** *n* voiture *f* de sport; **~s jacket** *n* veste *f* de sport; **~sman** *n* sportif *m*; **~smanship** *n* esprit sportif, sportivité *f*; **~s page** *n* page *f* des sports; **~swear** *n* vêtements *mpl* de sport; **~swoman** *n* sportive *f*; **~y** *a* sportif(ive).

spot [spɔt] *n* tache *f*; (*dot: on pattern*) pois *m*; (*pimple*) bouton *m*; (*place*) endroit *m*, coin *m*; (*small amount*): **a ~ of** un peu de // *vt* (*notice*) apercevoir, repérer; **on the ~** sur place, sur les lieux; **to come out in ~s** se couvrir de boutons, avoir une éruption de boutons; **~ check** *n* sondage *m*, vérification ponctuelle; **~less** *a* immaculé(e); **~light** *n* projecteur *m*; (AUT) phare *m* auxiliaire; **~ted** *a* tacheté(e), moucheté(e); à pois; **~ted with** tacheté(e) de; **~ty** *a* (*face*) boutonneux(euse).

spouse [spauz] *n* époux/épouse.

spout [spaut] *n* (*of jug*) bec *m*; (*of liquid*) jet *m* // *vi* jaillir.

sprain [sprein] *n* entorse *f*, foulure *f* // *vt*: **to ~ one's ankle** se fouler *or* se tordre la cheville.

sprang [spræŋ] *pt* of **spring**.

sprawl [sprɔ:l] *vi* s'étaler.

spray [sprei] *n* jet *m* (en fines gouttelettes); (*container*) vaporisateur *m*, bombe *f*; (*of flowers*) petit bouquet // *vt* vaporiser, pulvériser; (*crops*) traiter.

spread [spred] *n* propagation *f*; (*distribution*) répartition *f*; (CULIN) pâte *f* à tartiner // *vb* (*pt,pp* **spread**) *vt* étendre, étaler; répandre; propager // *vi* s'étendre; se répandre; se propager.

spree [spri:] *n*: **to go on a ~** faire la fête.

sprig [sprig] *n* rameau *m*.

sprightly ['spraitli] *a* alerte.

spring [spriŋ] *n* (*leap*) bond *m*, saut *m*; (*coiled metal*) ressort *m*; (*season*) printemps *m*; (*of water*) source *f* // *vi* (*pt* **sprang**, *pp* **sprung** [spræŋ, sprʌŋ]) bondir, sauter; **to ~ from** provenir de; **to ~ up** *vi* (*problem*) se présenter, surgir; **~board** *n* tremplin *m*; **~-clean** *n* (*also:* **~-cleaning**) grand nettoyage de printemps; **~time** *n* printemps *m*; **~y** *a* élastique, souple.

sprinkle ['spriŋkl] *vt* (*pour*) répandre; verser; **to ~ water** *etc* **on**, **~ with water** *etc* asperger d'eau *etc*; **to ~ sugar** *etc* **on**, **~ with sugar** *etc* saupoudrer de sucre *etc*; **~d with** (*fig*) parsemé(e) de.

sprint [sprint] *n* sprint *m* // *vi* sprinter; **~er** *n* sprinteur/euse.

sprite [sprait] *n* lutin *m*.

sprout [spraut] *vi* germer, pousser; (**Brussels**) **~s** *npl* choux *mpl* de Bruxelles.

spruce [spru:s] *n* épicéa *m* // *a* net(te), pimpant(e).

sprung [sprʌŋ] *pp* of **spring**.

spry [sprai] *a* alerte, vif(vive).

spud [spʌd] *n* (*col: potato*) patate *f*.

spun [spʌn] *pt, pp* of **spin**.

spur [spə:*] *n* éperon *m*; (*fig*) aiguillon *m* // *vt* (*also:* ~ **on**) éperonner; aiguillonner; **on the ~ of the moment** sous l'impulsion du moment.

spurious ['spjuəriəs] *a* faux(fausse).

spurn [spə:n] *vt* repousser avec mépris.

spurt [spə:t] *n* jet *m*; (*of energy*) sursaut *m* // *vi* jaillir, gicler.

spy [spai] *n* espion/ne // *vi*: **to ~ on** espionner, épier // *vt* (*see*) apercevoir; **~ing** *n* espionnage *m*.

sq. (MATH), **Sq.** (in address) abbr of **square**.

squabble ['skwɔbl] n querelle f, chamaillerie f // vi se chamailler.

squad [skwɔd] n (MIL, POLICE) escouade f, groupe m; (FOOTBALL) contingent m.

squadron ['skwɔdrn] n (MIL) escadron m; (AVIAT, NAUT) escadrille f.

squalid ['skwɔlɪd] a sordide, ignoble.

squall [skwɔ:l] n rafale f, bourrasque f.

squalor ['skwɔlə*] n conditions fpl sordides.

squander ['skwɔndə*] vt gaspiller, dilapider.

square [skwɛə*] n carré m; (in town) place f; (instrument) équerre f // a carré(e); (honest) honnête, régulier(ère); (col: ideas, tastes) vieux jeu inv, qui retarde // vt (arrange) régler; arranger; (MATH) élever au carré // vi (agree) cadrer, s'accorder; **all** – quitte; à égalité; **a** – **meal** un repas convenable; **2 metres** – (de) 2 mètres sur 2; **1** – **metre** 1 mètre carré; **–ly** ad carrément.

squash [skwɔʃ] n (drink): **lemon/orange** – citronnade f/ orangeade f; (SPORT) squash m // vt écraser.

squat [skwɔt] a petit(e) et épais(se), ramassé(e) // vi s'accroupir; **–ter** n squatter m.

squawk [skwɔ:k] vi pousser un or des gloussement(s).

squeak [skwi:k] n grincement m; petit cri // vi grincer, crier.

squeal [skwi:l] vi pousser un or des cri(s) aigu(s) or perçant(s).

squeamish ['skwi:mɪʃ] a facilement dégoûté(e); facilement scandalisé(e).

squeeze [skwi:z] n pression f; restrictions fpl de crédit // vt presser; (hand, arm) serrer; **to** – **out** vt exprimer; (fig) soutirer.

squelch [skwɛltʃ] vi faire un bruit de succion; patauger.

squib [skwɪb] n pétard m.

squid [skwɪd] n calmar m.

squint [skwɪnt] vi loucher // n: **he has a** – il louche, il souffre de strabisme.

squire ['skwaɪə*] n propriétaire terrien.

squirm [skwə:m] vi se tortiller.

squirrel ['skwɪrəl] n écureuil m.

squirt [skwə:t] n jet m // vi jaillir, gicler.

Sr abbr of **senior**.

St abbr of **saint**, **street**.

stab [stæb] n (with knife etc) coup m (de couteau etc); (col: try): **to have a** – **at (doing) sth** s'essayer à (faire) qch // vt poignarder.

stability [stə'bɪlɪtɪ] n stabilité f.

stabilize ['steɪbəlaɪz] vt stabiliser; **–r** n stabilisateur m.

stable ['steɪbl] n écurie f // a stable.

stack [stæk] n tas m, pile f // vt empiler, entasser.

stadium ['steɪdɪəm] n stade m.

staff [stɑ:f] n (work force) personnel m; (: SCOL) professeurs mpl; (: servants) domestiques mpl; (MIL) état-major m; (stick) perche f, bâton m // vt pourvoir en personnel.

stag [stæg] n cerf m.

stage [steɪdʒ] n scène f; (profession): **the** – le théâtre; (point) étape f, stade m; (platform) estrade f // vt (play) monter, mettre en scène; (demonstration) organiser; (fig: perform: recovery etc) effectuer; **in** – **s** par étapes, par degrés; **–coach** n diligence f; – **door** n entrée f des artistes; – **fright** n trac m; – **manager** n régisseur m.

stagger ['stægə*] vi chanceler, tituber // vt (person) stupéfier; bouleverser; (hours, holidays) étaler, échelonner; **–ing** a (amazing) stupéfiant(e), renversant(e).

stagnant ['stægnənt] a stagnant(e).

stagnate [stæg'neɪt] vi stagner, croupir.

stag party ['stægpɑ:tɪ] n enterrement m de vie de garçon.

staid [steɪd] a posé(e), rassis(e).

stain [steɪn] n tache f; (colouring) colorant m // vt tacher; (wood) teindre; **–ed glass window** n vitrail m; **–less** a (steel) inoxydable; – **remover** n détachant m.

stair [stɛə*] n (step) marche f; **–s** npl escalier m; **on the** – **s** dans l'escalier; **–case**, **–way** n escalier m.

stake [steɪk] n pieu m, poteau m; (BETTING) enjeu m // vt risquer, jouer; **to be at** – être en jeu.

stalactite ['stæləktaɪt] n stalactite f.

stalagmite ['stæləgmaɪt] n stalagmite m.

stale [steɪl] a (bread) rassis(e); (beer) éventé(e); (smell) de renfermé.

stalemate ['steɪlmeɪt] n pat m; (fig) impasse f.

stalk [stɔ:k] n tige f // vt traquer // vi marcher avec raideur.

stall [stɔ:l] n éventaire m, étal m; (in stable) stalle f // vt (AUT) caler // vi (AUT) caler; (fig) essayer de gagner du temps; **–s** npl (in cinema, theatre) orchestre m.

stalwart ['stɔ:lwət] n partisan m fidèle.

stamina ['stæmɪnə] n vigueur f, endurance f.

stammer ['stæmə*] n bégaiement m // vi bégayer.

stamp [stæmp] n timbre m; (mark, also fig) empreinte f; (on document) cachet m // vi taper du pied // vt tamponner, estamper; (letter) timbrer; – **album** n album m de timbres(-poste); – **collecting** n philatélie f.

stampede [stæm'pi:d] n ruée f.

stance [stæns] n position f.

stand [stænd] n (position) position f; (structure) guéridon m; support m; (COMM) étalage m, stand m; (SPORT) tribune f // vb (pt,pp stood [stud]) vi être or se tenir (debout); (rise) se lever, se mettre debout; (be placed) se trouver // vt (place) mettre, poser; (tolerate, withstand) supporter; **to make a** – prendre position; **to** – **for parliament** se présenter aux élections (comme candidat à la députation); **it** – **s to reason** c'est logique; cela va de soi; **to** – **by** vi (be ready) se tenir prêt // vt fus (opinion) s'en tenir à; **to** – **for** vt fus (defend) défendre, être pour; (signify) représenter, signifier; (tolerate) supporter, tolérer; **to** – **in for** vt fus remplacer; **to** – **out** vi (be prominent) ressortir; **to** – **up** vi (rise) se lever, se mettre debout; **to** – **up for** vt *fus* défendre ; **to ~ up to** *vt fus* tenir tête à, résister à.

standard ['stændəd] *n* niveau voulu ; *(flag)* étendard *m // a (size etc)* ordinaire, normal(e) ; courant(e) ; **~s** *npl (morals)* morale *f*, principes *mpl* ; **~ization** [-'zeɪʃən] *n* standardisation *f* ; **~ize** *vt* standardiser ; **~ lamp** *n* lampadaire *m* ; **~ of living** *n* niveau *m* de vie.

stand-by ['stændbaɪ] *n* remplaçant/e ; **~ ticket** *n (AVIAT)* billet *m* sans garantie.

stand-in ['stændɪn] *n* remplaçant/e ; *(CINEMA)* doublure *f*.

standing ['stændɪŋ] *a* debout *inv // n* réputation *f*, rang *m*, standing *m* ; **of many years' ~** qui dure or existe depuis longtemps ; **~ committee** *n* commission permanente ; **~ order** *n (at bank)* virement *m* automatique, prélèvement *m* bancaire ; **~ orders** *npl (MIL)* règlement *m* ; **~ room** places *fpl* debout.

stand-offish ['stænd'ɔfɪʃ] *a* distant(e), froid(e).

standpoint ['stændpɔɪnt] *n* point *m* de vue.

standstill ['stændstɪl] *n*: **at a ~** à l'arrêt ; *(fig)* au point mort ; **to come to a ~** s'immobiliser, s'arrêter.

stank [stæŋk] *pt of* **stink.**

stanza ['stænzə] *n* strophe *f* ; couplet *m.*

staple ['steɪpl] *n (for papers)* agrafe *f // a (food etc)* de base, principal(e) *// vt* agrafer ; **~r** *n* agrafeuse *f.*

star [stɑ:*] *n* étoile *f* ; *(celebrity)* vedette *f // vi*: **to ~ (in)** être la vedette (de) *// vt (CINEMA)* avoir pour vedette.

starboard ['stɑ:bəd] *n* tribord *m* ; **to ~** à tribord.

starch [stɑ:tʃ] *n* amidon *m* ; **~ed** *a (collar)* amidonné(e), empesé(e) ; **~y** *a* riche en féculents ; *(person)* guindé(e).

stardom ['stɑ:dəm] *n* célébrité *f.*

stare [stɛə*] *n* regard *m* fixe *// vt*: **to ~ at** regarder fixement.

starfish ['stɑ:fɪʃ] *n* étoile *f* de mer.

stark [stɑ:k] *a (bleak)* désolé(e), morne *// ad*: **~ naked** complètement nu(e).

starlight ['stɑ:laɪt] *n*: **by ~** à la lumière des étoiles.

starling ['stɑ:lɪŋ] *n* étourneau *m.*

starlit ['stɑ:lɪt] *a* étoilé(e) ; illuminé(e) par les étoiles.

starry ['stɑ:rɪ] *a* étoilé(e) ; **~-eyed** *a (innocent)* ingénu(e).

start [stɑ:t] *n* commencement *m*, début *m* ; *(of race)* départ *m* ; *(sudden movement)* sursaut *m // vt* commencer *// vi* partir, se mettre en route ; *(jump)* sursauter ; **to ~ doing sth** se mettre à faire qch ; **to ~ off** *vi* commencer ; *(leave)* partir ; **to ~ up** *vi* commencer ; *(car)* démarrer *// vt* déclencher ; *(car)* mettre en marche ; **~er** *n (AUT)* démarreur *m* ; *(SPORT: official)* starter *m* ; *(: runner, horse)* partant *m* ; *(CULIN)* entrée *f* ; **~ing handle** *n* manivelle *f* ; **~ing point** *n* point *m* de départ.

startle ['stɑ:tl] *vt* faire sursauter ; donner un choc à ; **startling** *a* surprenant(e), saisissant(e).

starvation [stɑ:'veɪʃən] *n* faim *f*, famine *f* ; **to die of ~** mourir de faim or d'inanition.

starve [stɑ:v] *vi* mourir de faim ; être affamé(e) *// vt* affamer ; **I'm starving** je meurs de faim.

state [steɪt] *n* état *m // vt* déclarer, affirmer ; formuler ; **the S~s** les États-Unis *mpl* ; **to be in a ~** être dans tous ses états ; **~ control** *n* contrôle *m* de l'État ; **~d** *a* fixé(e), prescrit(e) ; **~ly** *a* majestueux(euse), imposant(e) ; **~ment** *n* déclaration *f* ; *(LAW)* déposition *f* ; **~ secret** *n* secret *m* d'État ; **~sman** *n* homme *m* d'État.

static ['stætɪk] *n (RADIO)* parasites *mpl // a* statique ; **~ electricity** *n* électricité *f* statique.

station ['steɪʃən] *n* gare *f* ; poste *m* *(militaire or de police etc)* ; *(rank)* condition *f*, rang *m // vt* placer, poster.

stationary ['steɪʃnərɪ] *a* à l'arrêt, immobile.

stationer ['steɪʃənə*] *n* papetier/ère ; **~'s (shop)** *n* papeterie *f* ; **~y** *n* papier *m* à lettres, petit matériel de bureau.

station master ['steɪʃənmɑ:stə*] *n (RAIL)* chef *m* de gare.

station wagon ['steɪʃənwægən] *n (US)* break *m.*

statistic [stə'tɪstɪk] *n* statistique *f* ; **~s** *npl (science)* statistique *f* ; **~al** *a* statistique.

statue ['stætju:] *n* statue *f* ; **statuesque** [-'ɛsk] *a* sculptural(e).

stature ['stætʃə*] *n* stature *f* ; *(fig)* envergure *f.*

status ['steɪtəs] *n* position *f*, situation *f* ; prestige *m* ; statut *m* ; **the ~ quo** le statu quo ; **~ symbol** *n* marque *f* de standing, signe extérieur de richesse.

statute ['stætju:t] *n* loi *f* ; **~s** *npl (of club etc)* statuts *mpl* ; **statutory** *a* statutaire, prévu(e) par un article de loi.

staunch [stɔ:ntʃ] *a* sûr(e), loyal(e).

stave [steɪv] *n (MUS)* portée *f // vt*: **to ~ off** *(attack)* parer ; *(threat)* conjurer.

stay [steɪ] *n (period of time)* séjour *m // vi* rester ; *(reside)* loger ; *(spend some time)* séjourner ; **to ~ put** ne pas bouger ; **to ~ with friends** loger chez des amis ; **to ~ the night** passer la nuit ; **to ~ behind** *vi* rester en arrière ; **to ~ in** *vi (at home)* rester à la maison ; **to ~ on** *vi* rester ; **to ~ out** *vi (of house)* ne pas rentrer ; **to ~ up** *vi (at night)* ne pas se coucher.

STD *n (abbr of Subscriber Trunk Dialling)* l'automatique *m.*

steadfast ['stɛdfɑ:st] *a* ferme, résolu(e).

steadily ['stɛdɪlɪ] *ad* progressivement ; sans arrêt ; *(walk)* d'un pas ferme.

steady ['stɛdɪ] *a* stable, solide, ferme ; *(regular)* constant(e), régulier(ère) ; *(person)* calme, pondéré(e) *// vt* stabiliser ; assujettir ; calmer ; **to ~ oneself** reprendre son aplomb.

steak [steɪk] *n (meat)* bifteck *m*, steak *m* ; *(fish)* tranche *f* ; **~house** *n* ≈ grill-room *m.*

steal, *pt* **stole**, *pp* **stolen** [sti:l, stəul, 'stəuln] *vt,vi* voler.

stealth [stɛlθ] *n*: **by ~** furtivement ; **~y** *a* furtif(ive).

steam [sti:m] *n* vapeur *f // vt* passer à la vapeur ; *(CULIN)* cuire à la vapeur *// vi* fumer ; *(ship)*: **to ~ along** filer ; **~ engine**

n locomotive *f* à vapeur ; ～**er** *n* (bateau *m* à) vapeur *m* ; ～**roller** *n* rouleau compresseur ; ～**y** *a* embué(e), humide.

steed [sti:d] *n* coursier *m*.

steel [sti:l] *n* acier *m* // *cpd* d'acier ; ～**works** *n* aciérie *f*.

steep [sti:p] *a* raide, escarpé(e) ; (*price*) très élevée(e), excessif(ive) // *vt* (faire) tremper.

steeple ['sti:pl] *n* clocher *m* ; ～**chase** *n* steeple(-chase) *m* ; ～**jack** *n* réparateur *m* de clochers et de hautes cheminées.

steeply ['sti:plɪ] *ad* en pente raide.

steer [stɪə*] *n* bœuf *m* // *vt* diriger, gouverner ; guider // *vi* tenir le gouvernail ; ～**ing** *n* (*AUT*) conduite *f* ; ～**ing column** *n* colonne *f* de direction ; ～**ing wheel** *n* volant *m*.

stellar ['stɛlə*] *a* stellaire.

stem [stɛm] *n* tige *f* ; queue *f* ; (*NAUT*) avant *m*, proue *f* // *vt* contenir, endiguer, juguler ; **to** ～ **from** *vt fus* provenir de, découler de.

stench [stɛntʃ] *n* puanteur *f*.

stencil ['stɛnsl] *n* stencil *m* ; pochoir *m* // *vt* polycopier.

step [stɛp] *n* pas *m* ; (*stair*) marche *f* ; (*action*) mesure *f*, disposition *f* // *vi*: **to** ～ **forward** avancer un pas en avant, avancer ; ～**s** *npl* = **stepladder** ; **to** ～ **down** *vi* (*fig*) se retirer, se désister ; **to** ～ **off** *vt fus* descendre de ; **to** ～ **over** *vt fus* marcher sur ; **to** ～ **up** *vt* augmenter ; intensifier ; ～**brother** *n* demi-frère *m* ; ～**child** *n* beau-fils/belle-fille ; ～**father** *n* beau-père *m* ; ～**ladder** *n* escabeau *m* ; ～**mother** *n* belle-mère *f* ; **stepping stone** *n* pierre *f* de gué ; (*fig*) tremplin *m* ; ～**sister** *n* demi-sœur *f*.

stereo ['stɛrɪəu] *n* (*system*) stéréo *f* ; (*record player*) chaîne *f* stéréo // *a* (*also*: ～**phonic**) *a* stéréophonique.

stereotype ['stɪərɪətaɪp] *n* stéréotype *m* // *vt* stéréotyper.

sterile ['stɛraɪl] *a* stérile ; **sterility** [-'rɪlɪtɪ] *n* stérilité *f* ; **sterilization** [-'zeɪʃən] *n* stérilisation *f* ; **sterilize** ['stɛrɪlaɪz] *vt* stériliser.

sterling ['stə:lɪŋ] *a* sterling *inv* ; (*silver*) de bon aloi, fin(e) ; (*fig*) à toute épreuve, excellent(e) ; ～ **area** *n* zone *f* sterling *inv*.

stern [stə:n] *a* sévère // *n* (*NAUT*) arrière *m*, poupe *f*.

stethoscope ['stɛθəskəup] *n* stéthoscope *m*.

stevedore ['sti:vədɔ:*] *n* docker *m*, débardeur *m*.

stew [stju:] *n* ragoût *m* // *vt*, *vi* cuire à la casserole ; ～**ed tea** thé trop infusé.

steward ['stju:əd] *n* (*AVIAT*, *NAUT*, *RAIL*) steward *m* ; (*in club etc*) intendant *m* ; ～**ess** *n* hôtesse *f*.

stick [stɪk] *n* bâton *m* ; morceau *m* // *vb* (*pt*, *pp* **stuck** [stʌk]) *vt* (*glue*) coller ; (*thrust*): **to** ～ **sth into** piquer or planter or enfoncer qch dans ; (*col*: *put*) mettre, fourrer ; (*col*: *tolerate*) supporter // *vi* se planter ; tenir ; (*remain*) rester ; **to** ～ **out**, **to** ～ **up** *vi* dépasser, sortir ; **to** ～ **up for** *vt fus* défendre ; ～**er** *n* auto-collant *m*.

stickleback ['stɪklbæk] *n* épinoche *f*.

stickler ['stɪklə*] *n*: **to be a** ～ **for** être pointilleux(euse) sur.

sticky ['stɪkɪ] *a* poisseux(euse) ; (*label*) adhésif(ive).

stiff [stɪf] *a* raide ; rigide ; dur(e) ; (*difficult*) difficile, ardu(e) ; (*cold*) froid(e), distant(e) ; (*strong*, *high*) fort(e), élevé(e) ; ～**en** *vt* raidir, renforcer // *vi* se raidir ; se durcir ; ～ **neck** *n* torticolis *m* ; ～**ness** *n* raideur *f*.

stifle ['staɪfl] *vt* étouffer, réprimer ; **stifling** *a* (*heat*) suffocant(e).

stigma, *pl* (*BOT*, *MED*, *REL*) ～**ta**, (*fig*) ～**s** ['stɪgmə, stɪg'mɑ:tə] *n* stigmate *m*.

stile [staɪl] *n* échalier *m*.

stiletto [stɪ'lɛtəu] *n* (*also*: ～ **heel**) talon *m* aiguille.

still [stɪl] *a* immobile ; calme, tranquille // *ad* (*up to this time*) encore, toujours ; (*even*) encore ; (*nonetheless*) quand même, tout de même ; ～**born** *a* mort-né(e) ; ～ **life** *n* nature morte.

stilt [stɪlt] *n* échasse *f* ; (*pile*) pilotis *m*.

stilted ['stɪltɪd] *a* guindé(e), emprunté(e).

stimulant ['stɪmjulənt] *n* stimulant *m*.

stimulate ['stɪmjuleɪt] *vt* stimuler ; **stimulating** *a* stimulant(e) ; **stimulation** [-'leɪʃən] *n* stimulation *f*.

stimulus, *pl* **stimuli** ['stɪmjuləs, 'stɪmjulaɪ] *n* stimulant *m* ; (*BIOL*, *PSYCH*) stimulus *m*.

sting [stɪŋ] *n* piqûre *f* ; (*organ*) dard *m* // *vt* (*pt*,*pp* **stung** [stʌŋ]) piquer.

stingy ['stɪndʒɪ] *a* avare, pingre, chiche.

stink [stɪŋk] *n* puanteur *f* // *vi* (*pt* **stank**, *pp* **stunk** [stæŋk, stʌŋk]) puer, empester ; ～**er** *n* (*col*) vacherie *f* ; dégueulasse *m/f* ; ～**ing** *a* (*col*): **a** ～**ing**... un(e) vache de..., un(e) foutu(e)... .

stint [stɪnt] *n* part *f* de travail // *vi*: **to** ～ **on** lésiner sur, être chiche de.

stipend ['staɪpɛnd] *n* (*of vicar etc*) traitement *m*.

stipulate ['stɪpjuleɪt] *vt* stipuler ; **stipulation** [-'leɪʃən] *n* stipulation *f*, condition *f*.

stir [stə:*] *n* agitation *f*, sensation *f* // *vt* remuer // *vi* remuer, bouger ; **to** ～ **up** *vt* exciter ; ～**ring** *a* excitant(e) ; émouvant(e).

stirrup ['stɪrəp] *n* étrier *m*.

stitch [stɪtʃ] *n* (*SEWING*) point *m* ; (*KNITTING*) maille *f* ; (*MED*) point de suture ; (*pain*) point de côté // *vt* coudre, piquer ; suturer.

stoat [stəut] *n* hermine *f* (*avec son pelage d'été*).

stock [stɔk] *n* réserve *f*, provision *f* ; (*COMM*) stock *m* ; (*AGR*) cheptel *m*, bétail *m* ; (*CULIN*) bouillon *m* ; (*FINANCE*) valeurs *fpl*, titres *mpl* // *a* (*fig*: *reply etc*) courant(e) ; classique // *vt* (*have in stock*) avoir, vendre ; **well-**～**ed** bien approvisionné(e) or fourni(e) ; **to take** ～ (*fig*) faire le point ; **to** ～ **up** *vt* remplir, garnir // *vi*: **to** ～ **up (with)** s'approvisionner en.

stockade [stɔ'keɪd] *n* palissade *f*.

stockbroker ['stɔkbrəukə*] *n* agent *m* de change.

stock exchange ['stɔkɪkstʃeɪndʒ] *n* Bourse *f* (des valeurs).

stocking ['stɔkɪŋ] *n* bas *m*.

stockist ['stɔkɪst] n stockiste m.
stock market ['stɔkmɑːkɪt] n Bourse f, marché financier.
stock phrase ['stɔkfreɪz] n cliché m.
stockpile ['stɔkpaɪl] n stock m, réserve f // vt stocker, accumuler.
stocktaking ['stɔkteɪkɪŋ] n (COMM) inventaire m.
stocky ['stɔkɪ] a trapu(e), râblé(e).
stodgy ['stɔdʒɪ] a bourratif(ive), lourd(e).
stoic ['stəuɪk] n stoïque m/f; ~al a stoïque.
stoke [stəuk] vt garnir, entretenir; chauffer; ~r n chauffeur m.
stole [stəul] pt of **steal** // n étole f.
stolen ['stəuln] pp of **steal**.
stolid ['stɔlɪd] a impassible, flegmatique.
stomach ['stʌmək] n estomac m; (abdomen) ventre m // vt supporter, digérer; ~ ache n mal m à l'estomac or au ventre.
stone [stəun] n pierre f; (pebble) caillou m, galet m; (in fruit) noyau m; (MED) calcul m; (weight) mesure de poids = 6.348 kg.; 14 pounds // cpd de or en pierre // vt dénoyauter; ~-cold a complètement froid(e); ~-deaf a sourd(e) comme un pot; ~-mason n tailleur m de pierre(s); ~work n maçonnerie f; **stony** n pierreux(euse), rocailleux(euse).
stood [stud] pt,pp of **stand**.
stool [stuːl] n tabouret m.
stoop [stuːp] vi (also: have a ~) être voûté(e); (bend) se baisser, se courber.
stop [stɔp] n arrêt m; halte f; (in punctuation) point m // vt arrêter; (break off) interrompre; (also: **put a ~ to**) mettre fin à // vi s'arrêter; (rain, noise etc) cesser, s'arrêter; **to ~ doing sth** cesser or arrêter de faire qch; **to ~ dead** vi s'arrêter net; **to ~ off** vi faire une courte halte; **to ~ up** vt (hole) boucher; ~**lights** npl (AUT) signaux mpl de stop, feux mpl arrière; ~**over** n halte f, (AVIAT) escale f.
stoppage ['stɔpɪdʒ] n arrêt m; (of pay) retenue f; (strike) arrêt de travail.
stopper ['stɔpə*] n bouchon m.
stop-press ['stɔp'pres] n nouvelles fpl de dernière heure.
stopwatch ['stɔpwɔtʃ] n chronomètre m.
storage ['stɔːrɪdʒ] n emmagasinage m; (COMPUTERS) mise f en mémoire or réserve.
store [stɔː*] n provision f, réserve f; (depot) entrepôt m; (large shop) grand magasin m // vt emmagasiner; **to ~ up** vt mettre en réserve, emmagasiner; ~**room** n réserve f, magasin m.
storey, story (US) ['stɔːrɪ] n étage m.
stork [stɔːk] n cigogne f.
storm [stɔːm] n orage m, tempête f; ouragan m // vi (fig) fulminer // vt prendre d'assaut; ~ **cloud** n nuage m d'orage; ~**y** a orageux(euse).
story, story ['stɔːrɪ] n histoire f; récit m; (US) = **storey**; ~**book** n livre m d'histoires or de contes; ~**teller** n conteur/euse.
stout [staut] a solide; (brave) intrépide; (fat) gros(se), corpulent(e) // n bière brune.
stove [stəuv] n (for cooking) fourneau m; (: small) réchaud m; (for heating) poêle m.

stow [stəu] vt ranger; cacher; ~**away** n passager/ère clandestin(e).
straddle ['strædl] vt enjamber, être à cheval sur.
strafe [strɑːf] vt mitrailler.
straggle ['strægl] vi être (or marcher) en désordre; ~**d along the coast** disséminé(e) tout au long de la côte; ~**r** n traînard/e; **straggling, straggly** a (hair) en désordre.
straight [streɪt] a droit(e); (frank) honnête, franc(he) // ad (tout) droit; (drink) sec, sans eau // n: **the** ~ la ligne droite; **to put or get** ~ mettre de l'ordre dans; ~ **away**, ~**off** (at once) tout de suite; ~ **off**, ~ **out** sans hésiter; ~**en** vt (also: ~**en out**) redresser; ~**forward** a simple; honnête, direct(e).
strain [streɪn] n (TECH) tension f; pression f; (physical) effort m; (mental) tension (nerveuse); (MED) entorse f; (streak, trace) tendance f; élément m // vt tendre fortement; mettre à l'épreuve; (filter) passer, filtrer // vi peiner, fournir un gros effort; ~**s** npl (MUS) accords mpl, accents mpl; ~**ed** a (laugh etc) forcé(e), contraint(e); (relations) tendu(e); ~**er** n passoire f.
strait [streɪt] n (GEO) détroit m; ~ **jacket** n camisole f de force; ~**-laced** a collet monté inv.
strand [strænd] n (of thread) fil m, brin m // vt (boat) échouer; ~**ed** a en rade, en plan.
strange [streɪndʒ] a (not known) inconnu(e); (odd) étrange, bizarre; ~**ly** ad étrangement, bizarrement; ~**r** n inconnu/e; étranger/ère.
strangle ['stræŋgl] vt étrangler; ~**hold** n (fig) emprise totale, mainmise f; **strangulation** [-'leɪʃən] n strangulation f.
strap [stræp] n lanière f, courroie f, sangle f; (of slip, dress) bretelle f // vt attacher (avec une courroie etc); (child etc) administrer une correction à.
strapping ['stræpɪŋ] a bien découplé(e), costaud(e).
strata ['strɑːtə] npl of **stratum**.
stratagem ['strætɪdʒəm] n stratagème m.
strategic [strə'tiːdʒɪk] a stratégique.
strategist ['strætɪdʒɪst] n stratège m.
strategy ['strætɪdʒɪ] n stratégie f.
stratosphere ['strætəsfɪə*] n stratosphère f.
stratum, pl strata ['strɑːtəm, 'strɑːtə] n strate f, couche f.
straw [strɔː] n paille f.
strawberry ['strɔːbərɪ] n fraise f; (plant) fraisier m.
stray [streɪ] a (animal) perdu(e), errant(e) // vi s'égarer; ~ **bullet** n balle perdue.
streak [striːk] n raie f, bande f, filet m; (fig: of madness etc): **a ~ of** une or des tendance(s) à // vt zébrer, strier // vi: **to ~ past** passer à toute allure; ~**y** a zébré(e), strié(e); ~**y bacon** n ≈ lard m (maigre).
stream [striːm] n ruisseau m; courant m, flot m; (of people) défilé m ininterrompu, flot // vt (SCOL) répartir par niveau // vi

ruisseler; to ~ in/out entrer/sortir à flots.

streamer ['stri:mə*] n serpentin m, banderole f.

streamlined ['stri:mlaɪnd] a (AVIAT) fuselé(e), profilé(e); (AUT) aérodynamique; (fig) rationalisée(e).

street [stri:t] n rue f; ~car n (US) tramway m; ~ lamp n réverbère m.

strength [strɛŋθ] n force f; (of girder, knot etc) solidité f; ~en vt fortifier; renforcer; consolider.

strenuous ['strɛnjuəs] a vigoureux(euse), énergique; (tiring) ardu(e), fatigant(e).

stress [strɛs] n (force, pressure) pression f; (mental strain) tension (nerveuse); (accent) accent m // vt insister sur, souligner.

stretch [strɛtʃ] n (of sand etc) étendue f // vi s'étirer; (extend): to ~ to/as far as s'étendre jusqu'à // vt tendre, étirer; (spread) étendre; (fig) pousser (au maximum); at a ~ sans discontinuer, sans interruption; to ~ a muscle se distendre un muscle; to ~ out vi s'étendre // vt (arm etc) allonger, tendre; (to spread) étendre; to ~ out for something allonger la main pour prendre qch.

stretcher ['strɛtʃə*] n brancard m, civière f.

strewn [stru:n] a: ~ with jonché(e) de.

stricken ['strɪkən] a très éprouvé(e); dévasté(e); ~ with frappé(e) or atteint(e) de.

strict [strɪkt] a strict(e); ~ly ad strictement; ~ness n sévérité f.

stride [straɪd] n grand pas, enjambée f // vi (pt strode, pp stridden [strəud, 'strɪdn]) marcher à grands pas.

strident ['straɪdnt] a strident(e).

strife [straɪf] n conflit m, dissensions fpl.

strike [straɪk] n grève f; (of oil etc) découverte f; (attack) raid m // vb (pt,pp struck [strʌk]) vt frapper; (oil etc) trouver, découvrir // vi faire grève; (attack) attaquer; (clock) sonner; to ~ a match frotter une allumette; to ~ down vt (fig) terrasser; to ~ out vt rayer; to ~ up vt (MUS) se mettre à jouer; to ~ up a friendship with se lier d'amitié avec; ~breaker n briseur m de grève; ~r n gréviste m/f; (SPORT) buteur m; striking a frappant(e), saisissant(e).

string [strɪŋ] n ficelle f, fil m; (row) rang m; chapelet m; file f; (MUS) corde f // vt (pt,pp strung [strʌŋ]): to ~ out échelonner; the ~s npl (MUS) les instruments mpl à corde; ~ bean n haricot vert; ~(ed) instrument n (MUS) instrument m à cordes.

stringent ['strɪndʒənt] a rigoureux(euse); (need) impérieux(euse).

strip [strɪp] n bande f // vt déshabiller; dégarnir, dépouiller; (also: ~ down: machine) démonter // vi se déshabiller; ~ cartoon n bande dessinée.

stripe [straɪp] n raie f, rayure f; ~d a rayé(e), à rayures.

strip light ['strɪplaɪt] n (tube m au) néon m.

stripper ['strɪpə*] n strip-teaseuse f.

striptease ['strɪpti:z] n strip-tease m.

strive, pt **strove,** pp **striven** [straɪv, strəuv, 'strɪvn] vi: to ~ to do s'efforcer de faire.

strode [strəud] pt of stride.

stroke [strəuk] n coup m; (MED) attaque f; (caress) caresse f // vt caresser; at a ~ d'un (seul) coup; on the ~ of 5 à 5 heures sonnantes; a 2-~ engine un moteur à 2 temps.

stroll [strəul] n petite promenade // vi flâner, se promener nonchalamment.

strong [strɒŋ] a fort(e); vigoureux(euse); solide; vif(vive); they are 50 ~ ils sont au nombre de 50; ~hold n bastion m; ~ly ad fortement, avec force; vigoureusement; solidement; ~room n chambre forte.

strove [strəuv] pt of strive.

struck [strʌk] pt,pp of strike.

structural ['strʌktʃərəl] a structural(e); (CONSTR) de construction; affectant les parties portantes; ~ly ad du point de vue de la construction.

structure ['strʌktʃə*] n structure f; (building) construction f; édifice m.

struggle ['strʌgl] n lutte f // vi lutter, se battre.

strum [strʌm] vt (guitar) gratter de.

strung [strʌŋ] pt,pp of string.

strut [strʌt] n étai m, support m // vi se pavaner.

stub [stʌb] n bout m; (of ticket etc) talon m; to ~ out vt écraser.

stubble ['stʌbl] n chaume m; (on chin) barbe f de plusieurs jours.

stubborn ['stʌbən] a têtu(e), obstiné(e), opiniâtre.

stubby ['stʌbɪ] a trapu(e); gros(se) et court(e).

stuck [stʌk] pt,pp of stick // a (jammed) bloqué(e), coincé(e); ~-up a prétentieux(euse).

stud [stʌd] n clou m (à grosse tête); bouton m de col; (of horses) écurie f, haras m; (also: ~ horse) étalon m // vt (fig): ~ded with parsemé(e) or criblé(e) de.

student ['stju:dənt] n étudiant/e // cpd estudiantin(e); universitaire; d'étudiant.

studied ['stʌdɪd] a étudié(e), calculé(e).

studio ['stju:dɪəu] n studio m, atelier m.

studious ['stju:dɪəs] a studieux(euse), appliqué(e); (studied) étudié(e); ~ly ad (carefully) soigneusement.

study ['stʌdɪ] n étude f; (room) bureau m // vt étudier; examiner // vi étudier, faire ses études.

stuff [stʌf] n chose(s) f(pl), truc m; affaires fpl; (substance) substance f // vt rembourrer; (CULIN) farcir; ~ing n bourre f, rembourrage m; (CULIN) farce f; ~y a (room) mal ventilé(e) or aéré(e); (ideas) vieux jeu inv.

stumble ['stʌmbl] vi trébucher; to ~ across (fig) tomber sur; stumbling block n pierre f d'achoppement.

stump [stʌmp] n souche f; (of limb) moignon m // vt: to be ~ed sécher, ne pas savoir que répondre.

stun [stʌn] vt étourdir; abasourdir.

stung [stʌŋ] *pt, pp of* **sting**.

stunk [stʌŋk] *pp of* **stink**.

stunning ['stʌnɪŋ] *a* étourdissant(e), stupéfiant(e).

stunt [stʌnt] *n* tour *m* de force ; truc *m* publicitaire ; (*AVIAT*) acrobatie *f* // *vt* retarder, arrêter ; ~**ed** *a* rabougri(e) ; ~**man** *n* cascadeur *m*.

stupefy ['stju:pɪfaɪ] *vt* étourdir ; abrutir ; (*fig*) stupéfier.

stupendous [stju:'pɛndəs] *a* prodigieux(euse), fantastique.

stupid ['stju:pɪd] *a* stupide, bête ; ~**ity** ['pɪdɪtɪ] *n* stupidité *f*, bêtise *f* ; ~**ly** *ad* stupidement, bêtement.

stupor ['stju:pə*] *n* stupeur *f*.

sturdy ['stə:dʒɪ] *a* robuste, vigoureux(euse) ; solide.

sturgeon ['stə:dʒən] *n* esturgeon *m*.

stutter ['stʌtə*] *n* bégaiement *m* // *vi* bégayer.

sty [staɪ] *n* (*of pigs*) porcherie *f*.

stye [staɪ] *n* (*MED*) orgelet *m*.

style [staɪl] *n* style *m* ; (*distinction*) allure *f*, cachet *m*, style *m* ; **stylish** *a* élégant(e), chic *inv*.

stylized ['staɪlaɪzd] *a* stylisé(e).

stylus ['staɪləs] *n* (*of record player*) pointe *f* de lecture.

suave [swɑ:v] *a* doucereux(euse), onctueux(euse).

sub... [sʌb] *prefix* sous-..., sous- ; **subconscious** *a* subconscient(e) // *n* subconscient *m* ; **subdivide** *vt* subdiviser ; **subdivision** *n* subdivision *f*.

subdue [səb'dju:] *vt* subjuguer, soumettre ; ~**d** *a* contenu(e), atténué(e) ; (*light*) tamisé(e) ; (*person*) qui a perdu de son entrain.

subject *n* ['sʌbdʒɪkt] sujet *m* ; (*SCOL*) matière *f* // *vt* [səb'dʒɛkt]: **to** ~ **to** soumettre à ; exposer à ; **to be** ~ **to** (*law*) être soumis(e) à ; (*disease*) être sujet(te) à ; ~**ion** ['dʒɛkʃən] soumission *f*, sujétion *f* ; ~**ive** *a* subjectif(ive) ; (*LING*) sujet(te) ; ~ **matter** *n* sujet *m* ; contenu *m*.

sub judice [sʌb'dju:dɪsɪ] *a* devant les tribunaux.

subjunctive [səb'dʒʌŋktɪv] *a* subjonctif(ive) // *n* subjonctif *m*.

sublet [sʌb'lɛt] *vt* sous-louer.

sublime [sə'blaɪm] *a* sublime.

submachine gun ['sʌbmə'ʃi:ngʌn] *n* fusil-mitrailleur *m*.

submarine [sʌbmə'ri:n] *n* sous-marin *m*.

submerge [səb'mə:dʒ] *vt* submerger ; immerger // *vi* plonger.

submission [səb'mɪʃən] *n* soumission *f*.

submissive [səb'mɪsɪv] *a* soumis(e).

submit [səb'mɪt] *vt* soumettre // *vi* se soumettre.

subordinate [sə'bɔ:dɪnət] *a,n* subordonné(e).

subpoena [səb'pi:nə] (*LAW*) *n* citation *f*, assignation *f* // *vt* citer *or* assigner (à comparaître).

subscribe [səb'skraɪb] *vi* cotiser ; **to** ~ **to** (*opinion, fund*) souscrire à ; (*newspaper*) s'abonner à ; être abonné(e) à ; ~**r** *n* (*to periodical, telephone*) abonné/e.

subscription [səb'skrɪpʃən] *n* souscription *f* ; abonnement *m*.

subsequent ['sʌbsɪkwənt] *a* ultérieur(e), suivant(e) ; consécutif(ive) ; ~**ly** *ad* par la suite.

subside [səb'saɪd] *vi* s'affaisser ; (*flood*) baisser ; (*wind*) tomber ; ~**nce** ['saɪdns] *n* affaissement *m*.

subsidiary [səb'sɪdɪərɪ] *a* subsidiaire, accessoire // *n* filiale *f*.

subsidize ['sʌbsɪdaɪz] *vt* subventionner.

subsidy ['sʌbsɪdɪ] *n* subvention *f*.

subsistence [səb'sɪstəns] *n* existence *f*, subsistance *f*.

substance ['sʌbstəns] *n* substance *f* ; (*fig*) essentiel *m* ; **a man of** ~ un homme jouissant d'une certaine fortune.

substandard [sʌb'stændəd] *a* de qualité inférieure.

substantial [səb'stænʃl] *a* substantiel(le) ; (*fig*) important(e) ; ~**ly** *ad* considérablement ; en grande partie.

substantiate [səb'stænʃɪeɪt] *vt* étayer, fournir des preuves à l'appui de.

substitute ['sʌbstɪtju:t] *n* (*person*) remplaçant/e ; (*thing*) succédané *m* // *vt*: **to** ~ **sth/sb for** substituer qch/qn à, remplacer par qch/qn ; **substitution** ['tju:ʃən] *n* substitution *f*.

subterfuge ['sʌbtəfju:dʒ] *n* subterfuge *m*.

subterranean [sʌbtə'reɪnɪən] *a* souterrain(e).

subtitle ['sʌbtaɪtl] *n* (*CINEMA*) sous-titre *m*.

subtle ['sʌtl] *a* subtil(e) ; ~**ty** *n* subtilité *f*.

subtract [səb'trækt] *vt* soustraire, retrancher ; ~**ion** ['trækʃən] *n* soustraction *f*.

subtropical [sʌb'trɒpɪkl] *a* subtropical(e).

suburb ['sʌbə:b] *n* faubourg *m* ; **the** ~**s** la banlieue ; ~**an** [sə'bə:bən] *a* de banlieue, suburbain(e).

subvention [səb'vɛnʃən] *n* (*US: subsidy*) subvention *f*.

subversive [səb'və:sɪv] *a* subversif(ive).

subway ['sʌbweɪ] *n* (*US*) métro *m* ; (*Brit*) passage souterrain.

sub-zero [sʌb'zɪərəu] *a* au-dessous de zéro.

succeed [sək'si:d] *vi* réussir ; avoir du succès // *vt* succéder à ; **to** ~ **in doing** réussir à faire ; ~**ing** *a* (*following*) suivant(e).

success [sək'sɛs] *n* succès *m* ; réussite *f* ; ~**ful** *a* (*venture*) couronné(e) de succès ; **to be** ~**ful (in doing)** réussir (à faire) ; ~**fully** *ad* avec succès.

succession [sək'sɛʃən] *n* succession *f*.

successive [sək'sɛsɪv] *a* successif(ive) ; consécutif(ive).

successor [sək'sɛsə*] *n* successeur *m*.

succinct [sək'sɪŋkt] *a* succinct(e), bref(brève).

succulent ['sʌkjulənt] *a* succulent(e).

succumb [sə'kʌm] *vi* succomber.

such [sʌtʃ] *a, det* tel(telle) ; (*of that kind*): ~ **a book** un livre de ce genre ou pareil, un tel livre ; ~ **books** des livres de ce genre ou pareils, de tels livres ; (*so much*): ~ **courage** un tel courage ; ~ **a long trip** un si long voyage ; ~ **good books** de si bons livres ; ~ **a long trip that** un voyage si or tellement long que ; ~ **a lot of** tellement or tant de ; **making** ~ **a noise that** faisant un tel bruit que or tellement de bruit que ; ~ **as** (like) tel(telle) que, comme ; **a noise** ~ **as** to un bruit de nature à ; **as** ~ ad en tant que tel(telle), à proprement parler ; ~**-and-**~ det tel(telle) ou tel(telle).

suck [sʌk] vt sucer ; (breast, bottle) téter ; ~**er** n (BOT, ZOOL, TECH) ventouse f ; (col) naïf/ive, poire f.

suckle ['sʌkl] vt allaiter.

suction ['sʌkʃən] n succion f.

sudden ['sʌdn] a soudain(e), subit(e) ; **all of a** ~ soudain, tout à coup ; ~**ly** ad brusquement, tout à coup, soudain.

suds [sʌdz] npl eau savonneuse.

sue [su:] vt poursuivre en justice, intenter un procès à.

suede [sweid] n daim m, cuir suédé // cpd de daim.

suet ['suit] n graisse f de rognon or de bœuf.

Suez Canal ['su:izkə'næl] n canal m de Suez.

suffer ['sʌfə*] vt souffrir, subir ; (bear) tolérer, supporter // vi souffrir ; ~**er** n malade m/f ; victime m/f ; ~**ing** n souffrance(s) f(pl).

suffice [sə'fais] vi suffire.

sufficient [sə'fiʃənt] a suffisant(e) ; ~ **money** suffisamment d'argent ; ~**ly** ad suffisamment, assez.

suffix ['sʌfiks] n suffixe m.

suffocate ['sʌfəkeit] vi suffoquer ; étouffer ; **suffocation** ['keiʃən] n suffocation f ; (MED) asphyxie f.

sugar ['ʃugə*] n sucre m // vt sucrer ; ~ **beet** n betterave sucrière ; ~ **cane** n canne f à sucre ; ~**y** a sucré(e).

suggest [sə'dʒest] vt suggérer, proposer ; dénoter ; ~**ion** ['dʒestʃən] n suggestion f ; ~**ive** a suggestif(ive).

suicidal [sui'saidl] a suicidaire.

suicide ['suisaid] n suicide m.

suit [su:t] n (man's) costume m, complet m ; (woman's) tailleur m, ensemble m ; (CARDS) couleur f // vt aller à ; convenir à ; (adapt): **to** ~ **sth to** adapter or approprier qch à ; ~**able** a qui convient ; approprié(e) ; ~**ably** ad comme il se doit (or se devait etc), convenablement.

suitcase ['su:tkeis] n valise f.

suite [swi:t] n (of rooms, also MUS) suite f ; (furniture): **bedroom/dining room** ~ (ensemble m de) chambre f à coucher/salle f à manger.

sulfur ['sʌlfə*] etc (US) = **sulphur** etc.

sulk [sʌlk] vi bouder ; ~**y** a boudeur(euse), maussade.

sullen ['sʌlən] a renfrogné(e), maussade ; morne.

sulphur, sulfur (US) ['sʌlfə*] n soufre m ; ~**ic** ['fjuərik] a: ~**ic acid** acide m sulfurique.

sultan ['sʌltən] n sultan m.

sultana [sʌl'tɑ:nə] n (fruit) raisin sec de Smyrne.

sultry ['sʌltri] a étouffant(e).

sum [sʌm] n somme f ; (SCOL etc) calcul m ; f ; **to** ~ **up** vt, vi résumer.

summarize ['sʌməraiz] vt résumer.

summary ['sʌməri] n résumé m // a (justice) sommaire.

summer ['sʌmə*] n été m // cpd d'été, estival(e) ; ~**house** n (in garden) pavillon m ; ~**time** n (season) été m ; ~ **time** n (by clock) heure f d'été.

summit ['sʌmit] n sommet m ; ~ (**conference**) n (conférence f au) sommet m.

summon ['sʌmən] vt appeler, convoquer ; **to** ~ **up** vt rassembler, faire appel à ; ~**s** n citation f, assignation f // vt citer, assigner.

sump [sʌmp] n (AUT) carter m.

sumptuous ['sʌmptjuəs] a somptueux(euse).

sun [sʌn] n soleil m ; **in the** ~ au soleil ; ~**bathe** vi prendre un bain de soleil ; ~**burnt** a bronzé(e), hâlé(e) ; (painfully) brûlé(e) par le soleil ; ~ **cream** n crème f (anti-)solaire.

Sunday ['sʌndi] n dimanche m.

sundial ['sʌndaiəl] n cadran m solaire.

sundry ['sʌndri] a divers(e), différent(e) ; **all and** ~ tout le monde, n'importe qui ; **sundries** npl articles divers.

sunflower ['sʌnflauə*] n tournesol m.

sung [sʌŋ] pp of **sing**.

sunglasses ['sʌnglɑ:siz] npl lunettes fpl de soleil.

sunk [sʌŋk] pp of **sink** ; ~**en** a submergé(e) ; creux(euse).

sun: ~**light** n (lumière f du) soleil m ; ~**lit** a ensoleillé(e) ; ~**ny** a ensoleillé(e) ; (fig) épanoui(e), radieux(euse) ; ~**rise** n lever m du soleil ; ~**set** n coucher m du soleil ; ~**shade** n (over table) parasol m ; ~**shine** n (lumière f du) soleil m ; ~**spot** n tache f solaire ; ~**stroke** n insolation f, coup m de soleil ; ~**tan** n bronzage m ; ~**tan oil** n huile f solaire ; ~**trap** n coin très ensoleillé.

super ['su:pə*] a (col) formidable.

superannuation [su:pərænju'eiʃən] n cotisations fpl pour la pension.

superb [su:'pə:b] a superbe, magnifique.

supercilious [su:pə'siliəs] a hautain(e), dédaigneux(euse).

superficial [su:pə'fiʃəl] a superficiel(le) ; ~**ly** ad superficiellement.

superfluous [su:'pə:fluəs] a superflu(e).

superhuman [su:pə'hju:mən] a surhumain(e).

superimpose ['su:pərim'pəuz] vt superposer.

superintendent [su:pərin'tendənt] n directeur/trice ; (POLICE) ≈ commissaire m.

superior [su'piəriə*] a, n supérieur(e) ; ~**ity** ['ɔriti] n supériorité f.

superlative [su'pə:lətiv] a sans pareil(le), suprême // n (LING) superlatif m.

superman ['su:pəmæn] n surhomme m.

supermarket ['su:pəmɑ:kit] n supermarché m.

supernatural [su:pə'nætʃərəl] a surnaturel(le).

superpower ['su:pəpauə*] n (POL) grande puissance.

supersede [su:pə'si:d] vt remplacer, supplanter.

supersonic ['su:pə'sɒnɪk] a supersonique.
superstition [su:pə'stɪʃən] n superstition f.
superstitious [su:pə'stɪʃəs] a superstitieux(euse).
supertanker ['su:pətæŋkə*] n pétrolier géant, superpétrolier m.
supervise ['su:pəvaɪz] vt surveiller ; diriger ; **supervision** [-'vɪʒən] n surveillance f ; contrôle m ; **supervisor** n surveillant/e ; (in shop) chef m de rayon ; **supervisory** a de surveillance.
supper ['sʌpə*] n dîner m ; (late) souper m.
supple ['sʌpl] a souple.
supplement n ['sʌplɪmənt] supplément m // vt [sʌplɪ'mɛnt] ajouter à, compléter ; **~ary** [-'mɛntərɪ] a supplémentaire.
supplier [sə'plaɪə*] n fournisseur m.
supply [sə'plaɪ] vt (provide) fournir ; (equip): **to ~ (with)** approvisionner or ravitailler (en); fournir (en); alimenter (en) // n provision f, réserve f; (supplying) approvisionnement m ; (TECH) alimentation f // cpd (teacher etc) suppléant(e); **supplies** npl (food) vivres mpl; (MIL) substances fpl; **~ and demand** l'offre f et la demande.
support [sə'pɔ:t] n (moral, financial etc) soutien m, appui m; (TECH) support m, soutien // vt soutenir, supporter; (financially) subvenir aux besoins de; (uphold) être pour, être partisan de, appuyer; (endure) supporter, tolérer; **~er** n (POL etc) partisan/e; (SPORT) supporter m.
suppose [sə'pəuz] vt, vi supposer; imaginer; **to be ~d to do** être censé(e) faire; **~dly** [sə'pəuzɪdlɪ] ad soi-disant; **supposing** cj si, à supposer que + sub; **supposition** [sʌpə'zɪʃən] n supposition f, hypothèse f.
suppress [sə'prɛs] vt réprimer; supprimer; étouffer; refouler; **~ion** [sə'prɛʃən] n suppression f, répression f; **~or** n (ELEC etc) dispositif m antiparasite.
supremacy [su'prɛməsɪ] n suprématie f.
supreme [su'pri:m] a suprême.
surcharge ['sə:tʃɑ:dʒ] n surcharge f; (extra tax) surtaxe f.
sure [ʃuə*] a (gen) sûr(e); (definite, convinced) sûr(e), certain(e); **~!** (of course) bien sûr!; **~ enough** effectivement; **to make ~ of** s'assurer de; vérifier; **~-footed** a au pied sûr; **~ly** ad sûrement; certainement.
surety ['ʃuərətɪ] n caution f.
surf [sə:f] n ressac m.
surface ['sə:fɪs] n surface f // vt (road) poser le revêtement de // vi remonter à la surface; faire surface; **~ mail** n courrier m par voie de terre (or maritime).
surfboard ['sə:fbɔ:d] n planche f de surf.
surfeit ['sə:fɪt] n: **a ~ of** un excès de; une indigestion de.
surfing ['sə:fɪŋ] n surf m.
surge [sə:dʒ] n vague f, montée f // vi déferler.
surgeon ['sə:dʒən] n chirurgien m.
surgery ['sə:dʒərɪ] n chirurgie f; (room) cabinet m (de consultation); **to undergo**

~ être opéré(e); **~ hours** npl heures fpl de consultation.
surgical ['sə:dʒɪkl] a chirurgical(e); **~ spirit** n alcool m à 90s.
surly ['sə:lɪ] a revêche, maussade.
surmise [sə:'maɪz] vt présumer, conjecturer.
surmount [sə:'maunt] vt surmonter.
surname ['sə:neɪm] n nom m de famille.
surpass [sə:'pɑ:s] vt surpasser, dépasser.
surplus ['sə:pləs] n surplus m, excédent m // a en surplus, de trop.
surprise [sə'praɪz] n (gen) surprise f; (astonishment) étonnement m // vt surprendre; étonner; **surprising** a surprenant(e), étonnant(e).
surrealist [sə'rɪəlɪst] a surréaliste.
surrender [sə'rɛndə*] n reddition f, capitulation f // vi se rendre, capituler.
surreptitious [sʌrəp'tɪʃəs] a subreptice, furtif(ive).
surround [sə'raund] vt entourer; (MIL etc) encercler; **~ing** a environnant(e); **~ings** npl environs mpl, alentours mpl.
surveillance [sə:'veɪləns] n surveillance f.
survey n ['sə:veɪ] enquête f, étude f; (in housebuying etc) inspection f, (rapport m d')expertise f; (of land) levé m // vt [sə:'veɪ] passer en revue; enquêter sur; inspecter; **~ing** n (of land) arpentage m; **~or** n expert m; (arpenteur m) géomètre m.
survival [sə'vaɪvl] n survie f; (relic) vestige m.
survive [sə'vaɪv] vi survivre; (custom etc) subsister // vt survivre à, réchapper de; (person) survivre à; **survivor** n survivant/e.
susceptible [sə'sɛptəbl] a: **~ (to)** sensible (à); (disease) prédisposé(e) (à).
suspect a, n ['sʌspɛkt] suspect(e) // vt [səs'pɛkt] soupçonner, suspecter.
suspend [səs'pɛnd] vt suspendre; **~ed sentence** n condamnation f avec sursis; **~er belt** n porte-jarretelles m inv; **~ers** npl jarretelles fpl; (US) bretelles fpl.
suspense [səs'pɛns] n attente f; (in film etc) suspense m.
suspension [səs'pɛnʃən] n (gen AUT) suspension f; (of driving licence) retrait m provisoire; **~ bridge** n pont suspendu.
suspicion [səs'pɪʃən] n soupçon(s) m(pl).
suspicious [səs'pɪʃəs] a (suspecting) soupçonneux(euse), méfiant(e); (causing suspicion) suspect(e).
sustain [səs'teɪn] vt supporter; soutenir; corroborer; (suffer) subir; recevoir; **~ed** a (effort) soutenu(e), prolongé(e).
sustenance ['sʌstɪnəns] n nourriture f; moyens mpl de subsistance.
swab [swɒb] n (MED) tampon m; prélèvement m.
swagger ['swægə*] vi plastronner, parader.
swallow ['swɒləu] n (bird) hirondelle f; (of food etc) gorgée f // vt avaler; (fig) gober; **to ~ up** vt engloutir.
swam [swæm] pt of **swim**.
swamp [swɒmp] n marais m, marécage m // vt submerger; **~y** a marécageux(euse).

swan [swɔn] *n* cygne *m*.

swap [swɔp] *n* échange *m*, troc *m* // *vt*: **to ~ (for)** échanger (contre), troquer (contre).

swarm [swɔ:m] *n* essaim *m* // *vi* fourmiller, grouiller.

swarthy ['swɔ:ðɪ] *a* basané(e), bistré(e).

swastika ['swɔstɪkə] *n* croix gammée.

swat [swɔt] *vt* écraser.

sway [sweɪ] *vi* se balancer, osciller; tanguer // *vt* (*influence*) influencer.

swear, *pt* **swore**, *pp* **sworn** [swɛə*, swɔ:*, swɔ:n] *vi* jurer; **to ~ to sth** jurer de qch; **~word** *n* gros mot, juron *m*.

sweat [swɛt] *n* sueur *f*, transpiration *f* // *vi* suer; **in a ~** en sueur.

sweater ['swɛtə*] *n* tricot *m*, pull *m*.

sweaty ['swɛtɪ] *a* en sueur, moite *or* mouillé(e) de sueur.

swede [swi:d] *n* rutabaga *m*.

Swede [swi:d] *n* Suédois/e.

Sweden ['swi:dn] *n* Suède *f*.

Swedish ['swi:dɪʃ] *a* suédois(e) // *n* (LING) suédois *m*.

sweep [swi:p] *n* coup *m* de balai; (*curve*) grande courbe; (*range*) champ *m*; (*also:* **chimney ~**) ramoneur *m* // *vb* (*pt, pp* **swept** [swɛpt]) *vt* balayer // *vi* avancer majestueusement *or* rapidement; s'élancer; s'étendre; **to ~ away** *vt* balayer; entraîner; emporter; **to ~ past** *vi* passer majestueusement *or* rapidement; **to ~ up** *vt, vi* balayer; **~ing** *a* (*gesture*) large; circulaire; **a ~ing statement** une généralisation hâtive.

sweet [swi:t] *n* dessert *m*; (*candy*) bonbon *m* // *a* doux(douce); (*not savoury*) sucré(e); (*fresh*) frais(fraîche), pur(e); (*fig*) agréable, doux; gentil(le); mignon(ne); **~bread** *n* ris *m* de veau; **~corn** *n* maïs sucré; **~en** *vt* sucrer; adoucir; **~heart** *n* amoureux/euse; **~ly** *ad* gentiment; mélodieusement; **~ness** *n* goût sucré; douceur *f*; **~pea** *n* pois *m* de senteur; **to have a ~ tooth** aimer les sucreries.

swell [swɛl] *n* (*of sea*) houle *f* // *a* (*col: excellent*) chouette // *vb* (*pt* **~ed**, *pp* **swollen**, **~ed** ['swəulən]) *vt* augmenter; grossir // *vi* grossir, augmenter; (*sound*) s'enfler; (MED) enfler; **~ing** *n* (MED) enflure *f*; grosseur *f*.

sweltering ['swɛltərɪŋ] *a* étouffant(e), oppressant(e).

swept [swɛpt] *pt,pp of* **sweep.**

swerve [swə:v] *vi* faire une embardée *or* un écart; dévier.

swift [swɪft] *n* (*bird*) martinet *m* // *a* rapide, prompt(e); **~ness** *n* rapidité *f*.

swig [swɪg] *n* (*col: drink*) lampée *f*.

swill [swɪl] *n* pâtée *f* // *vt* (*also:* **~ out, ~ down**) laver à grande eau.

swim [swɪm] *n*: **to go for a ~** aller nager *or* se baigner // *vb* (*pt* **swam**, *pp* **swum** [swæm, swʌm]) *vi* nager; (SPORT) faire de la natation; (*head, room*) tourner // *vt* traverser (à la nage); faire (à la nage); **~mer** *n* nageur/euse; **~ming** *n* nage *f*, natation *f*; **~ming baths** *npl* piscine *f*; **~ming cap** *n* bonnet *m* de bain; **~ming costume** *n* maillot *m* (de bain); **~ming**

pool *n* piscine *f*; **~suit** *n* maillot *m* (de bain).

swindle ['swɪndl] *n* escroquerie *f* // *vt* escroquer; **~r** *n* escroc *m*.

swine [swaɪn] *n, pl inv* pourceau *m*, porc *m*; (*col!*) salaud *m* (!).

swing [swɪŋ] *n* balançoire *f*; (*movement*) balancement *m*, oscillations *fpl*; (MUS) swing *m*; rythme *m* // *vb* (*pt, pp* **swung** [swʌŋ]) *vt* balancer, faire osciller; (*also:* **~ round**) tourner, faire virer // *vi* se balancer, osciller; (*also:* **~ round**) virer, tourner; **to be in full ~** battre son plein; **~ bridge** *n* pont tournant; **~ door** *n* porte battante.

swingeing ['swɪndʒɪŋ] *a* écrasant(e); considérable.

swinging ['swɪŋɪŋ] *a* rythmé(e); entraînant(e).

swipe [swaɪp] *n* grand coup; gifle *f* // *vt* (*hit*) frapper à toute volée; gifler; (*col: steal*) piquer.

swirl [swə:l] *n* tourbillon *m* // *vi* tourbillonner, tournoyer.

swish [swɪʃ] *a* (*col: smart*) rupin(e) // *vi* siffler.

Swiss [swɪs] *a* suisse // *n, pl inv* Suisse/esse; **~ German** *a* suisse-allemand(e).

switch [swɪtʃ] *n* (*for light, radio etc*) bouton *m*; (*change*) changement *m*, revirement *m* // *vt* (*change*) changer; intervertir; **to ~ off** *vt* éteindre; (*engine*) arrêter; **to ~ on** *vt* allumer; (*engine, machine*) mettre en marche; **~back** *n* montagnes *fpl* russes; **~board** *n* (TEL.) standard *m*; **~board operator** standardiste *m/f*.

Switzerland ['swɪtsələnd] *n* Suisse *f*.

swivel ['swɪvl] *vi* (*also:* **~ round**) pivoter, tourner.

swollen ['swəulən] *pp of* **swell** // *a* (*ankle etc*) enflé(e).

swoon [swu:n] *vi* se pâmer.

swoop [swu:p] *n* (*by police etc*) rafle *f*, descente *f* // *vi* (*also:* **~ down**) descendre en piqué, piquer.

swop [swɔp] *n, vt* = **swap.**

sword [sɔ:d] *n* épée *f*; **~fish** *n* espadon *m*.

swore [swɔ:*] *pt of* **swear.**

sworn [swɔ:n] *pp of* **swear.**

swot [swɔt] *vt, vi* bûcher, potasser.

swum [swʌm] *pp of* **swim.**

swung [swʌŋ] *pt, pp of* **swing.**

sycamore ['sɪkəmɔ:*] *n* sycomore *m*.

sycophantic [sɪkə'fæntɪk] *a* flagorneur(euse).

syllable ['sɪləbl] *n* syllabe *f*.

syllabus ['sɪləbəs] *n* programme *m*.

symbol ['sɪmbl] *n* symbole *m*; **~ic(al)** [-'bɔlɪk(l)] *a* symbolique; **~ism** *n* symbolisme *m*; **~ize** *vt* symboliser.

symmetrical [sɪ'mɛtrɪkl] *a* symétrique.

symmetry ['sɪmɪtrɪ] *n* symétrie *f*.

sympathetic [sɪmpə'θɛtɪk] *a* compatissant(e); bienveillant(e), compréhensif(ive); **~ towards** bien disposé(e) envers; **~ally** *ad* avec compassion (*or* bienveillance).

sympathize ['sɪmpəθaɪz] *vi*: **to ~ with**

sb plaindre qn ; s'associer à la douleur de qn ; **~r** n (POL) sympathisant/e.

sympathy ['sɪmpəθɪ] n compassion f; **in ~ with** en accord avec ; (strike) en or par solidarité avec ; **with our deepest ~** en vous priant d'accepter nos sincères condoléances.

symphonic [sɪm'fɒnɪk] a symphonique.

symphony ['sɪmfənɪ] n symphonie f; **~ orchestra** n orchestre m symphonique.

symposium [sɪm'pəuzɪəm] n symposium m.

symptom ['sɪmptəm] n symptôme m; indice m; **~atic** [-'mætɪk] a symptomatique.

synagogue ['sɪnəgɒg] n synagogue f.

synchromesh [sɪŋkrəu'mɛʃ] n synchronisation f.

synchronize ['sɪŋkrənaɪz] vt synchroniser // vi: **to ~ with** se produire en même temps que.

syncopated ['sɪŋkəpeɪtɪd] a syncopé(e).

syndicate ['sɪndɪkɪt] n syndicat m, coopérative f.

syndrome ['sɪndrəum] n syndrome m.

synonym ['sɪnənɪm] n synonyme m; **~ous** [sɪ'nɒnɪməs] a: **~ous (with)** synonyme (de).

synopsis, pl **synopses** [sɪ'nɒpsɪs, -si:z] n résumé m, synopsis m or f.

syntax ['sɪntæks] n syntaxe f.

synthesis, pl **syntheses** ['sɪnθəsɪs, -si:z] n synthèse f.

synthetic [sɪn'θɛtɪk] a synthétique ; **~s** npl textiles artificiels.

syphilis ['sɪfɪlɪs] n syphilis f.

syphon ['saɪfən] n, vb = **siphon**.

Syria ['sɪrɪə] n Syrie f; **~n** a syrien(ne) // n Syrien/ne.

syringe [sɪ'rɪndʒ] n seringue f.

syrup ['sɪrəp] n sirop m; (also: **golden ~**) mélasse raffinée ; **~y** a sirupeux(euse).

system ['sɪstəm] n système m; (order) méthode f; (ANAT) organisme m; **~atic** [-'mætɪk] a systématique ; méthodique ; **~s analyst** n analyste-programmeur m/f.

T

ta [tɑ:] excl (Brit: col) merci!

tab [tæb] n (loop on coat etc) attache f; (label) étiquette f; **to keep ~s on** (fig) surveiller.

tabby ['tæbɪ] n (also: **~ cat**) chat/te tigré(e).

tabernacle ['tæbənækl] n tabernacle m.

table ['teɪbl] n table f // vt (motion etc) présenter ; **to lay** or **set the ~** mettre le couvert or la table ; **~ of contents** n table f des matières ; **~cloth** n nappe f; **~ d'hôte** [tɑ:bl'dəut] a (meal) à prix fixe ; **~lamp** n lampe f décorative ; **~mat** n (for plate) napperon m, set m; (for hot dish) dessous-de-plat m inv ; **~ salt** n sel fin or de table ; **~spoon** n cuiller f de service ; (also: **~spoonful**: as measurement) cuillerée f à soupe.

tablet ['tæblɪt] n (MED) comprimé m; (: for sucking) pastille f; (for writing) bloc m; (of stone) plaque f.

table: **~ tennis** n ping-pong m, tennis m de table ; **~ wine** n vin m de table.

taboo [tə'bu:] a, n tabou (m).

tabulate ['tæbjuleɪt] vt (data, figures) mettre sous forme de table(s) ; **tabulator** n tabulateur m.

tacit ['tæsɪt] a tacite.

taciturn ['tæsɪtə:n] a taciturne.

tack [tæk] n (nail) petit clou ; (stitch) point m de bâti ; (NAUT) bord m, bordée f // vt clouer ; bâtir // vi tirer un or des bord(s) ; **to change ~** virer de bord ; **on the wrong ~** (fig) sur la mauvaise voie.

tackle ['tækl] n matériel m, équipement m; (for lifting) appareil m de levage ; (RUGBY) plaquage m // vt (difficulty) s'attaquer à ; (RUGBY) plaquer.

tacky ['tækɪ] a collant(e) ; pas sec(sèche).

tact [tækt] n tact m; **~ful** a plein(e) de tact ; **~fully** ad avec tact.

tactical ['tæktɪkl] a tactique ; **~ error** n erreur f de tactique.

tactics ['tæktɪks] n,npl tactique f.

tactless ['tæktlɪs] a qui manque de tact ; **~ly** ad sans tact.

tadpole ['tædpəul] n têtard m.

taffy ['tæfɪ] n (US) (bonbon m au) caramel m.

tag [tæg] n étiquette f; **to ~ along** vi suivre.

tail [teɪl] n queue f; (of shirt) pan m // vt (follow) suivre, filer ; **~s** (on coin) (le côté) pile ; **to ~ away, ~ off** vi (in size, quality etc) baisser peu à peu ; **~back** n bouchon m; **~ coat** n habit m; **~ end** n bout m, fin f; **~gate** n hayon m (arrière).

tailor ['teɪlə*] n tailleur m (artisan) ; **~ing** n (cut) coupe f; **~-made** a fait(e) sur mesure ; (fig) conçu(e) spécialement.

tailwind ['teɪlwɪnd] n vent m arrière inv.

tainted ['teɪntɪd] a (food) gâté(e) ; (water, air) infecté(e) ; (fig) souillé(e).

take, pt **took,** pp **taken** [teɪk, tuk, 'teɪkn] vt prendre ; (gain: prize) remporter ; (require: effort, courage) demander ; (tolerate) accepter, supporter ; (hold: passengers etc) contenir ; (accompany) emmener, accompagner ; (bring, carry) apporter, emporter ; (exam) passer, se présenter à ; **to ~ sth from** (drawer etc) prendre qch dans ; (person) prendre qch à ; **I ~ it that** je suppose que ; **to ~ for a walk** (child, dog) emmener promener ; **to ~ after** vt fus ressembler à ; **to ~ apart** vt démonter ; **to ~ away** vt emporter ; enlever ; **to ~ back** vt (return) rendre, rapporter ; (one's words) retirer ; **to ~ down** vt (building) démolir ; (letter etc) prendre, écrire ; **to ~ in** vt (deceive) tromper, rouler ; (understand) comprendre, saisir ; (include) couvrir, inclure ; (lodger) prendre ; **to ~ off** vi (AVIAT) décoller // vt (remove) enlever ; (imitate) imiter, pasticher ; **to ~ on** vt (work) accepter, se charger de ; (employee) prendre, embaucher ; (opponent) accepter de se battre contre ; **to ~ out** vt sortir ; (remove) enlever ; (licence) prendre, se procurer ; **to ~ sth out of** enlever qch de ; prendre qch dans ; **to ~ over** vt (business) reprendre // vi: **to ~ over from sb** prendre la relève de qn ; **to ~ to** vt fus (person) se prendre d'amitié pour ; (activity) prendre goût à ; **to ~ up** vt (one's story, a dress) reprendre ; (occupy: time, space) prendre, occuper ; (engage in: hobby etc) se mettre à ; **~away** a (food) à emporter ; **~-home pay** n salaire net ; **~off** n (AVIAT) décollage m ; **~over** n (COMM) rachat m ; **~over bid** n offre publique d'achat.

takings ['teɪkɪŋz] npl (COMM) recette f.

talc [tælk] n (also: **~um powder**) talc m.

tale [teɪl] n (story) conte m, histoire f ; (account) récit m ; (pej) histoire.

talent ['tælnt] n talent m, don m ; **~ed** a doué(e), plein(e) de talent.

talk [tɔːk] n propos mpl ; (gossip) racontars mpl (pej) ; (conversation) discussion f ; (interview) entretien m ; (a speech) causerie f, exposé m // vi (chatter) bavarder ; **to ~ about** parler de ; (converse) s'entretenir or parler de ; **to ~ sb out of/into doing** persuader qn de ne pas faire/de faire ; **to ~ shop** parler métier or affaires ; **to ~ over** vt examiner, discuter ; **~ative** a bavard(e) ; **~er** n causeur/euse ; (pej) bavard/e.

tall [tɔːl] a (person) grand(e) ; (building, tree) haut(e) ; **to be 6 feet ~** ≈ mesurer 1 mètre 80 ; **~boy** n grande commode ; **~ness** n grande taille ; hauteur f ; **~ story** n histoire f invraisemblable.

tally ['tælɪ] n compte m // vi: **to ~ (with)** correspondre (à).

tambourine [tæmbə'riːn] n tambourin m.

tame [teɪm] a apprivoisé(e) ; (fig: story, style) insipide.

tamper ['tæmpə*] vi: **to ~ with** toucher à (en cachette ou sans permission).

tampon ['tæmpən] n tampon m hygiénique or périodique.

tan [tæn] n (also: **sun~**) bronzage m // vt,vi bronzer, brunir // a (colour) brun roux inv.

tandem ['tændəm] n tandem m.

tang [tæŋ] n odeur (or saveur) piquante.

tangent ['tændʒənt] n (MATH) tangente f.

tangerine [tændʒə'riːn] n mandarine f.

tangible ['tændʒəbl] a tangible.

tangle ['tæŋgl] n enchevêtrement m // vt enchevêtrer ; **to get in(to) a ~** s'emmêler.

tango ['tæŋgəu] n tango m.

tank [tæŋk] n réservoir m ; (for processing) cuve f ; (for fish) aquarium m ; (MIL) char m d'assaut, tank m.

tankard ['tæŋkəd] n chope f.

tanker ['tæŋkə*] n (ship) pétrolier m, tanker m ; (truck) camion-citerne m.

tanned [tænd] a (skin) bronzé(e).

tantalizing ['tæntəlaɪzɪŋ] a (smell) extrêmement appétissant(e) ; (offer) terriblement tentant(e).

tantamount ['tæntəmaunt] a: **~ to** qui équivaut à.

tantrum ['tæntrəm] n accès m de colère.

tap [tæp] n (on sink etc) robinet m ; (gentle blow) petite tape // vt frapper or taper légèrement ; (resources) exploiter, utiliser ; **~-dancing** n claquettes fpl.

tape [teɪp] n ruban m ; (also: **magnetic ~**) bande f (magnétique) // vt (record) enregistrer (sur bande) ; **~ measure** n mètre m à ruban.

taper ['teɪpə*] n cierge m // vi s'effiler.

tape recorder ['teɪprɪkɔːdə*] n magnétophone m.

tapered ['teɪpəd], **tapering** ['teɪpərɪŋ] a fuselé(e), effilé(e).

tapestry ['tæpɪstrɪ] n tapisserie f.

tapioca [tæpɪ'əukə] n tapioca m.

tappet ['tæpɪt] n (AUT) poussoir m (de soupape).

tar [tɑː] n goudron m.

tarantula [tə'ræntjulə] n tarentule f.

tardy ['tɑːdɪ] a tardif(ive).

target ['tɑːgɪt] n cible f ; (fig: objective) objectif m ; **~ practice** n exercices mpl de tir (à la cible).

tariff ['tærɪf] n (COMM) tarif m ; (taxes) tarif douanier.

tarmac ['tɑːmæk] n macadam m ; (AVIAT) aire f d'envol // vt goudronner.

tarnish ['tɑːnɪʃ] vt ternir.

tarpaulin [tɑː'pɔːlɪn] n bâche goudronnée.

tarragon ['tærəgən] n estragon m.

tart [tɑːt] n (CULIN) tarte f ; (col: pej: woman) poule f // a (flavour) âpre, aigrelet(te).

tartan ['tɑːtn] n tartan m // a à écossais(e).

tartar ['tɑːtə*] n (on teeth) tartre m ; **~ sauce** n sauce f tartare.

task [tɑːsk] n tâche f ; **to take to ~** prendre à partie ; **~ force** n (MIL, POLICE) détachement spécial.

Tasmania [tæz'meɪnɪə] n Tasmanie f.

tassel ['tæsl] n gland m ; pompon m.

taste [teɪst] n goût m ; (fig: glimpse, idea) idée f, aperçu m // vt goûter // vi: **to ~ of** (fish etc) avoir le or un goût de ; **it ~s like fish** ça a un or le goût de poisson, on dirait du poisson ; **what does it ~ like?** quel goût ça a? ; **you can ~ the garlic (in it)** on sent bien l'ail ; **can I have a ~ of this wine?** puis-je goûter un peu de ce vin? ; **to have a ~ of sth** goûter (à) qch ; **to have a ~ for sth** aimer qch, avoir un penchant pour qch ; **~ful** a de bon goût ; **~fully** ad avec goût ; **~less** a (food) qui n'a aucun goût ; (remark) de mauvais goût ; **tasty** a savoureux(euse), délicieux(euse).

tattered ['tætəd] a see **tatters**.

tatters ['tætəz] mpl: **in ~** (also: **tattered**) en lambeaux.

tattoo [tə'tuː] n tatouage m ; (spectacle) parade f militaire // vt tatouer.

tatty ['tætɪ] a (col) défraîchi(e), en piteux état.

taught [tɔːt] pt,pp of **teach**.

taunt [tɔːnt] n raillerie f // vt railler.

Taurus ['tɔːrəs] n le Taureau ; **to be ~** être du Taureau.

taut [tɔːt] a tendu(e).

tavern ['tævən] n taverne f.

tawdry ['tɔːdrɪ] a (d'un mauvais goût) criard.

tawny ['tɔːnɪ] a fauve (couleur).

tax [tæks] n (on goods etc) taxe f ; (on income) impôts mpl, contributions fpl // vt taxer ; imposer ; (fig: strain: patience etc) mettre à l'épreuve ; **~ation** [-'seɪʃən] n taxation f ; impôts mpl, contributions fpl ; **~ avoidance** n évasion fiscale ; **~ collector** n percepteur m ; **~ evasion** n fraude fiscale; ~ exile n personne qui s'expatrie pour fuir une fiscalité excessive; ~-free a exempt(e) d'impôts.

taxi ['tæksɪ] n taxi m // vi (AVIAT) rouler (lentement) au sol.

taxidermist ['tæksɪdə:mɪst] n empailleur/euse (d'animaux).

taxi: ~ driver n chauffeur m de taxi; ~ rank, ~ stand n station f de taxis.

tax: ~ payer n contribuable m/f; ~ return n déclaration f d'impôts or de revenus.

TB abbr of tuberculosis.

tea [ti:] n thé m; (snack: for children) goûter m; high ~ collation combinant goûter et dîner; ~ bag n sachet m de thé; ~ break n pause-thé f; ~cake n petit pain brioché.

teach, pt, pp taught [ti:tʃ, tɔ:t] vt: to ~ sb sth, ~ sth to sb apprendre qch à qn; (in school etc) enseigner qch à qn // vi enseigner; ~er n (in secondary school) professeur m; (in primary school) instituteur/trice; ~ing n enseignement m; ~ing staff n enseignants mpl.

tea cosy ['ti:kəuzɪ] n couvre-théière m.

teacup ['ti:kʌp] n tasse f à thé.

teak [ti:k] n teck m // a en or de teck.

tea leaves ['ti:li:vz] npl feuilles fpl de thé.

team [ti:m] n équipe f; (of animals) attelage m; ~ games/work jeux mpl/travail m d'équipe.

tea party ['ti:pɑ:tɪ] n thé m (réception).

teapot ['ti:pɔt] n théière f.

tear n [tɛə*] déchirure f; [tɪə*] larme f // vb [tɛə*] (pt tore, pp torn [tɔ:*, tɔ:n]) vt déchirer // vi se déchirer; in ~s en larmes; to burst into ~s fondre en larmes; to ~ along vi (rush) aller à toute vitesse; ~ful a larmoyant(e); ~ gas n gaz m lacrymogène.

tearoom ['ti:ru:m] n salon m de thé.

tease [ti:z] n taquin/e // vt taquiner; (unkindly) tourmenter.

tea set n service m à thé.

teashop ['ti:ʃɔp] n pâtisserie-salon de thé f.

teaspoon ['ti:spu:n] n petite cuiller; (also: ~ful: as measurement) ≈ cuillerée f à café.

tea strainer ['ti:streɪnə*] n passoire f (à thé).

teat [ti:t] n tétine f.

teatime ['ti:taɪm] n l'heure f du thé.

tea towel ['ti:tauəl] n torchon m (à vaisselle).

tea urn ['ti:ə:n] n fontaine f à thé.

technical ['tɛknɪkl] a technique; ~ity [-'kælɪtɪ] n technicité f; (detail) détail m technique; ~ly ad techniquement.

technician [tɛk'nɪʃn] n technicien/ne.

technique [tɛk'ni:k] n technique f.

technological [tɛknə'lɔdʒɪkl] a technologique.

technologist [tɛk'nɔlədʒɪst] n technologue m/f.

technology [tɛk'nɔlədʒɪ] n technologie f.

teddy (bear) ['tɛdɪ(bɛə*)] n ours m (en peluche).

tedious ['ti:dɪəs] a fastidieux(euse).

tedium ['ti:dɪəm] n ennui m.

tee [ti:] n (GOLF) tee m.

teem [ti:m] vi grouiller, abonder; to ~ with grouiller de; it is ~ing (with rain) il pleut à torrents.

teenage ['ti:neɪdʒ] a (fashions etc) pour jeunes, pour adolescents; ~r n jeune m/f, adolescent/e.

teens [ti:nz] npl: to be in one's ~ être adolescent(e).

tee-shirt ['ti:ʃə:t] n = T-shirt.

teeter ['ti:tə*] vi chanceler, vaciller.

teeth [ti:θ] npl of tooth.

teethe [ti:ð] vi percer ses dents.

teething ['ti:ðɪr] a: ~ ring n anneau m (pour bébé qui perce ses dents); ~ troubles npl (fig) difficultés initiales.

teetotal ['ti:'təutl] a (person) qui ne boit jamais d'alcool.

telecommunications ['tɛlɪkəmju:nɪ'keɪʃənz] n télécommunications fpl.

telegram ['tɛlɪgræm] n télégramme m.

telegraph ['tɛlɪgrɑ:f] n télégraphe m; ~ic [-'græfɪk] a télégraphique; ~ pole n poteau m télégraphique.

telepathic [tɛlɪ'pæθɪk] a télépathique.

telepathy [tə'lɛpəθɪ] n télépathie f.

telephone ['tɛlɪfəun] n téléphone m // vt (person) téléphoner à; (message) téléphoner; ~ booth, ~ box n cabine f téléphonique; ~ call n coup m de téléphone, appel m téléphonique; communication f téléphonique; ~ directory n annuaire m (du téléphone); ~ exchange n central m (téléphonique); ~ number n numéro m de téléphone; ~ operator téléphoniste m/f, standardiste m/f; telephonist [tə'lɛfənɪst] n téléphoniste m/f.

telephoto ['tɛlɪ'fəutəu] a: ~ lens n téléobjectif m.

teleprinter ['tɛlɪprɪntə*] n téléscripteur m.

telescope ['tɛlɪskəup] n télescope m // vi télescoper; telescopic [-'skɔpɪk] a télescopique.

televiewer ['tɛlɪvju:ə*] n téléspectateur/trice.

televise ['tɛlɪvaɪz] vt téléviser.

television ['tɛlɪvɪʒən] n télévision f; ~ programme n émission f de télévision; ~ set n poste m de télévision.

tell, pt, pp told [tɛl, təuld] vt dire; (relate: story) raconter; (distinguish): to ~ sth from distinguer qch de // vi (have effect) se faire sentir, se voir; to ~ sb to do dire à qn de faire; to ~ on vt fus (inform against) dénoncer, rapporter contre; to ~ off vt réprimander, gronder; ~er n (in bank) caissier/ère; ~ing a (remark, detail) révélateur(trice); ~tale a (sign) éloquent(e), révélateur(trice) // n (CONSTR) témoin m.

telly ['tɛlɪ] n (col: abbr of television) télé f.

temerity [tə'mɛrɪtɪ] n témérité f.

temp [tɛmp] n (abbr of temporary) (secrétaire f) intérimaire f.

temper ['tɛmpə*] n (nature) caractère m; (mood) humeur f; (fit of anger) colère f // vt (moderate) tempérer, adoucir; to be in a ~ être en colère; to lose one's ~ se mettre en colère.

temperament ['temprəmənt] *n* (*nature*) tempérament *m*; ~**al** [-'mentl] *a* capricieux(euse).

temperance ['tempərns] *n* modération *f*; (*in drinking*) tempérance *f*.

temperate ['temprət] *a* modéré(e); (*climate*) tempéré(e).

temperature ['temprətʃə*] *n* température *f*; **to have** *or* **run a** ~ avoir de la fièvre; ~ **chart** *n* (*MED*) feuille *f* de température.

tempered ['tempəd] *a* (*steel*) trempé(e).

tempest ['tempist] *n* tempête *f*.

tempi ['tempi:] *npl of* **tempo.**

template ['templit] *n* patron *m*.

temple ['templ] *n* (*building*) temple *m*; (*ANAT*) tempe *f*.

tempo, ~**s** *or* **tempi** ['tempəu, 'tempi:] *n* tempo *m*; (*fig*: *of life etc*) rythme *m*.

temporal ['tempərl] *a* temporel(le).

temporarily ['tempərərili] *ad* temporairement; provisoirement.

temporary ['tempərəri] *a* temporaire, provisoire; (*job, worker*) temporaire; ~ **secretary** *n* (secrétaire *f*) intérimaire *f*.

temporize ['tempəraiz] *vi* atermoyer; transiger.

tempt [tempt] *vt* tenter; **to** ~ **sb into doing** induire qn à faire; ~**ation** [-'teiʃən] *n* tentation *f*; ~**ing** *a* tentant(e).

ten [ten] *num* dix.

tenable ['tenəbl] *a* défendable.

tenacious [tə'neiʃəs] *a* tenace.

tenacity [tə'næsiti] *n* ténacité *f*.

tenancy ['tenənsi] *n* location *f*; état *m* de locataire.

tenant ['tenənt] *n* locataire *m/f*.

tend [tend] *vt* s'occuper de // *vi*: **to** ~ **to do** avoir tendance à faire; (*colour*): **to** ~ **to** tirer sur.

tendency ['tendənsi] *n* tendance *f*.

tender ['tendə*] *a* tendre; (*delicate*) délicat(e); (*sore*) sensible; (*affectionate*) tendre, doux(douce) // *n* (*COMM*: *offer*) soumission *f*; (*money*): **legal** ~ cours légal // *vt* offrir; ~**ize** *vt* (*CULIN*) attendrir; ~**ly** *ad* tendrement; ~**ness** *n* tendresse *f*; (*of meat*) tendreté *f*.

tendon ['tendən] *n* tendon *m*.

tenement ['tenəmənt] *n* immeuble *m* (de rapport).

tenet ['tenət] *n* principe *m*.

tennis ['tenis] *n* tennis *m*; ~ **ball** *n* balle *f* de tennis; ~ **court** *n* (court *m* de) tennis; ~ **racket** *n* raquette *f* de tennis.

tenor ['tenə*] *n* (*MUS*) ténor *m*; (*of speech etc*) sens général.

tense [tens] *a* tendu(e); (*person*) tendu, crispé(e) // *a* (*LING*) temps *m*; ~**ness** *n* tension *f*.

tension ['tenʃən] *n* tension *f*.

tent [tent] *n* tente *f*.

tentacle ['tentəkl] *n* tentacule *m*.

tentative ['tentətiv] *a* timide, hésitant(e); (*conclusion*) provisoire.

tenterhooks ['tentəhuks] *npl*: **on** ~ sur des charbons ardents.

tenth [tenθ] *num* dixième.

tent: ~ **peg** *n* piquet *m* de tente; ~ **pole** *n* montant *m* de tente.

tenuous ['tenjuəs] *a* ténu(e).

tenure ['tenjuə*] *n* (*of property*) bail *m*; (*of job*) période *f* de jouissance; statut *m* de titulaire.

tepid ['tepid] *a* tiède.

term [tə:m] *n* (*limit*) terme *m*; (*word*) terme, mot *m*; (*SCOL*) trimestre *m*; (*LAW*) session *f* // *vt* appeler; ~**s** *npl* (*conditions*) conditions *fpl*; (*COMM*) tarif *m*; ~ **of imprisonment** peine *f* de prison; **in the short/long** ~ à court/long terme; **'easy** ~**s'** (*COMM*) 'facilités de paiement'; **to be on good** ~**s with** bien s'entendre avec, être en bons termes avec; **to come to** ~**s with** (*person*) arriver à un accord avec; (*problem*) faire face à.

terminal ['tə:minl] *a* terminal(e); (*disease*) dans sa phase terminale // *n* (*ELEC*) borne *f*; (*for oil, ore etc*) terminal *m*; (*also*: **air** ~) aérogare *f*; (*also*: **coach** ~) gare routière.

terminate ['tə:mineit] *vt* mettre fin à // *vi*: **to** ~ **in** finir en *or* par.

termination [tə:mi'neiʃən] *n* fin *f*; (*of contract*) résiliation *f*; ~ **of pregnancy** *n* (*MED*) interruption *f* de grossesse.

termini ['tə:minai] *npl of* **terminus.**

terminology [tə:mi'nɔlədʒi] *n* terminologie *f*.

terminus, *pl* **termini** ['tə:minəs, 'tə:minai] *n* terminus *m inv*.

termite ['tə:mait] *n* termite *m*.

terrace ['terəs] *n* terrasse *f*; (*row of houses*) rangée *f* de maisons (*attenantes les unes aux autres*); **the** ~**s** (*SPORT*) les gradins *mpl*; ~**d** *a* (*garden*) en terrasses.

terracotta ['terə'kɔtə] *n* terre cuite.

terrain [te'rein] *n* terrain *m* (*sol*).

terrible ['teribl] *a* terrible, atroce; (*weather, work*) affreux(euse), épouvantable; **terribly** *ad* terriblement; (*very badly*) affreusement mal.

terrier ['teriə*] *n* terrier *m* (*chien*).

terrific [tə'rifik] *a* fantastique, incroyable, terrible; (*wonderful*) formidable, sensationnel(le).

terrify ['terifai] *vt* terrifier.

territorial [teri'tɔ:riəl] *a* territorial(e).

territory ['teritəri] *n* territoire *m*.

terror ['terə*] *n* terreur *f*; ~**ism** *n* terrorisme *m*; ~**ist** *n* terroriste *m/f*; ~**ize** *vt* terroriser.

terse [tə:s] *a* (*style*) concis(e); (*reply*) laconique.

test [test] *n* (*trial, check*) essai *m*; (: *of goods in factory*) contrôle *m*; (*of courage etc*) épreuve *f*; (*MED*) examens *mpl*; (*CHEM*) analyses *fpl*; (*exam: of intelligence etc*) test *m* (d'aptitude); (: *in school*) interrogation *f* de contrôle; (*also*: **driving** ~) (*examen du*) permis *m* de conduire // *vt* essayer; contrôler; mettre à l'épreuve; examiner; analyser; tester; faire subir une interrogation (de contrôle) à.

testament ['testəmənt] *n* testament *m*; **the Old/New T**~ l'Ancien/le Nouveau Testament.

test: ~ **case** *n* (*LAW, fig*) affaire-test *f*; ~ **flight** *n* vol *m* d'essai.

testicle ['testikl] *n* testicule *m*.

testify ['tɛstɪfaɪ] vi (LAW) témoigner,
déposer.

testimonial [tɛstɪ'məʊnɪəl] n (reference)
recommandation f; (gift) témoignage m
d'estime.

testimony ['tɛstɪmənɪ] n (LAW)
témoignage m, déposition f.

test: ~ match n (CRICKET, RUGBY) match
international; ~ paper n (SCOL)
interrogation écrite; ~ pilot n pilote m
d'essai; ~ tube n éprouvette f.

testy ['tɛstɪ] a irritable.

tetanus ['tɛtənəs] n tétanos m.

tether ['tɛðə*] vt attacher // n: at the end
of one's ~ à bout (de patience).

text [tɛkst] n texte m; ~book n manuel
m.

textile ['tɛkstaɪl] n textile m.

texture ['tɛkstʃə*] n texture f; (of skin,
paper etc) grain m.

Thai [taɪ] a thaïlandais(e) // n
Thaïlandais/e; (LING) thaï m; ~land n
Thaïlande f.

Thames [tɛmz] n: the ~ la Tamise.

than [ðæn, ðən] cj que; (with numerals):
more ~ 10/once plus de 10/d'une fois;
I have more/less ~ you j'en ai
plus/moins que toi; she has more apples
~ pears elle a plus de pommes que de
poires.

thank [θæŋk] vt remercier, dire merci à;
~ you (very much) merci (beaucoup);
~s npl remerciements mpl // excl merci!;
~s to prep grâce à; ~ful a: ~ful (for)
reconnaissant(e) (de); ~less a ingrat(e);
T~sgiving (Day) n jour m d'action de
grâce.

that [ðæt, ðət] cj que // det ce(cet + vowel
or h mute), f cette; (not 'this'): ~ book
ce livre-là // pronoun ce; (not 'this one')
cela, ça; (the one) celui(celle); (relative:
subject) qui; (: object) que, prep +
lequel(laquelle); (with time): on the day
~ he came le jour où il est venu // ad:
~ high aussi haut; si haut; it's about ~
high c'est à peu près de cette hauteur;
~ one celui-là(celle-là); what's ~? qu'est-
ce que c'est?; who's ~? qui est-ce?; is
~ you? c'est toi?; ~'s what he said c'est
or voilà ce qu'il a dit; ~ is... c'est-à-dire...,
à savoir...; all ~ tout cela, tout ça; I can't
work ~ much je ne peux pas travailler
autant que cela.

thatched [θætʃt] a (roof) de chaume; ~
cottage n chaumière f.

thaw [θɔ:] n dégel m // vi (ice) fondre;
(food) dégeler // vt (food) (faire) dégeler;
it's ~ing (weather) il dégèle.

the [ðiː, ðə] det le, f la, (l' + vowel or h
mute), pl les;(NB: à + le(s) = au(x); de +
le = du; de + les = des).

theatre, theater (US) ['θɪətə*] n théâtre
m; ~goer n habitué/e du théâtre.

theatrical [θɪ'ætrɪkl] a théâtral(e); ~
company n troupe f de théâtre.

theft [θɛft] n vol m (larcin).

their [ðɛə*] a leur, pl leurs; ~s pronoun
le(la) leur, les leurs; it is ~s c'est à eux;
a friend of ~s un de leurs amis.

them [ðɛm, ðəm] pronoun (direct) les;
(indirect) leur; (stressed, after prep)

eux(elles); I see ~ je les vois; give ~
the book donne-leur le livre.

theme [θiːm] n thème m; ~ song n
chanson principale.

themselves [ðəm'sɛlvz] pl pronoun (reflexive) se; (emphatic) eux-
mêmes(elles-mêmes); between ~ entre
eux(elles).

then [ðɛn] ad (at that time) alors, à ce
moment-là; (next) puis, ensuite; (and also)
et puis // cj (therefore) alors, dans ce cas
// a: the ~ president le président d'alors
or de l'époque; from ~ on dès lors.

theologian [θɪə'ləʊdʒən] n théologien/ne.

theological [θɪə'lɒdʒɪkl] a théologique.

theology [θɪ'ɒlədʒɪ] n théologie f.

theorem ['θɪərəm] n théorème m.

theoretical [θɪə'rɛtɪkl] a théorique.

theorize ['θɪəraɪz] vi élaborer une théorie;
(pej) faire des théories.

theory ['θɪərɪ] n théorie f.

therapeutic(al) [θɛrə'pjuːtɪk(l)] a
thérapeutique.

therapist ['θɛrəpɪst] n thérapeute m/f.

therapy ['θɛrəpɪ] n thérapie f.

there [ðɛə*] ad là, là-bas; ~, ~! allons,
allons!; it's ~ c'est là; he went ~ il y
est allé; ~ is, ~ are il y a; ~ he is le
voilà; ~ has been il y a eu; on/in ~
là-dessus/ -dedans; to go ~ and back
faire l'aller et retour; ~abouts ad (place)
par là, près de là; (amount) environ, à peu
près; ~after ad par la suite; ~fore ad
donc, par conséquent; ~'s = ~ is; ~
has.

thermal ['θɜːml] a thermique.

thermometer [θə'mɒmɪtə*] n thermomètre m.

thermonuclear ['θɜːməʊ'njuːklɪə*] a
thermonucléaire.

Thermos ['θɜːməs] n ® (also: ~ flask)
thermos m or f inv ®.

thermostat ['θɜːməʊstæt] n thermostat m.

thesaurus [θɪ'sɔːrəs] n dictionnaire m
synonymique.

these [ðiːz] pl pronoun ceux-ci(celles-ci) //
pl det ces; (not 'those'): ~ books ces livres-
ci.

thesis ['θiːsɪs, θiːsiːz] pl theses n thèse
f.

they [ðeɪ] pl pronoun ils(elles); (stressed)
eux(elles); ~ say that... (it is said that)
on dit que...; ~'d = they had; they
would; ~'ll = they shall; they will;
~'re = they are; ~'ve = they have.

thick [θɪk] a épais(se); (crowd) dense;
(stupid) bête, borné(e) // n: in the ~ of
au beau milieu de, en plein cœur de; it's
20 cm ~ ça a 20 cm d'épaisseur; ~en
vi s'épaissir // vt (sauce etc) épaissir;
~ness n épaisseur f; ~set a trapu(e),
costaud(e); ~skinned a (fig) peu sensible.

thief, thieves [θiːf, θiːvz] n voleur/euse.

thieving ['θiːvɪŋ] n vol m (larcin).

thigh [θaɪ] n cuisse f; ~bone n fémur m.

thimble ['θɪmbl] n dé m (à coudre).

thin [θɪn] a mince; (person) maigre; (soup)
peu épais(se); (hair, crowd) clairsemé(e);
(fog) léger(ère) // vt (hair) éclaircir; to ~
(down) (sauce, paint) délayer.

thing [θɪŋ] n chose f; (object) objet m; (contraption) truc m; ~s npl (belongings) affaires fpl; **for one** ~ d'abord; **the best** ~ **would be** to le mieux serait de; **how are** ~**s?** comment ça va?

think, pt, pp **thought** [θɪŋk, θɔːt] vi penser, réfléchir // vt penser, croire; (imagine) s'imaginer; **to** ~ **of** penser à; **what did you** ~ **of them?** qu'as-tu pensé d'eux?; **to** ~ **about sth/sb** penser à qch/qn; **I'll** ~ **about it** je vais y réfléchir; **to** ~ **of doing** avoir l'idée de faire; **I** ~ **so** je crois or pense que oui; **to** ~ **well of** avoir une haute opinion de; **to** ~ **over** vt bien réfléchir à; **to** ~ **up** vt inventer, trouver.

thinly ['θɪnlɪ] ad (cut) en tranches fines; (spread) en couche mince.

thinness ['θɪnnɪs] n minceur f; maigreur f.

third [θɜːd] num troisième // n troisième m/f; (fraction) tiers m; (SCOL: degree) ≈ licence f avec mention passable; **a** ~ **of** le tiers de; ~**ly** ad troisièmement; ~ **party insurance** n assurance f au tiers; ~**-rate** a de qualité médiocre; **the T**~ **World** n le Tiers-Monde.

thirst [θɜːst] n soif f; ~**y** a (person) qui a soif, assoiffé(e).

thirteen [θɜː'tiːn] num treize.

thirty ['θɜːtɪ] num trente.

this [ðɪs] det ce(cet + vowel or h mute), f cette; (not 'that'): ~ **book** ce livre-ci // pronoun ce; ceci; (not 'that one') celui-ci(celle-ci); ~ **is what he said** voici ce qu'il a dit.

thistle ['θɪsl] n chardon m.

thong [θɒŋ] n lanière f.

thorn [θɔːn] n épine f; ~ **bush** n buisson m d'épines; ~**y** a épineux(euse).

thorough ['θʌrə] a (search) minutieux(euse); (knowledge, research) approfondi(e); (work) conscien-cieux(euse); (cleaning) à fond; ~**bred** n (horse) pur-sang m inv; ~**fare** n rue f; 'no ~**fare**' 'passage interdit'; ~**ly** ad minu-tieusement; en profondeur; à fond; **he** ~**ly agreed** il était tout à fait d'accord.

those [ðəuz] pl pronoun ceux-là(celles-là) // pl det ces; (not 'these'): ~ **books** ces livres-là.

though [ðəu] cj bien que + sub, quoique + sub // ad pourtant.

thought [θɔːt] pt, pp of **think** // n pensée f; (opinion) avis m; (intention) intention f; ~**ful** a pensif(ive); réfléchi(e); (considerate) prévenant(e); ~**less** a étourdi(e); qui manque de considération.

thousand ['θauzənd] num mille; ~**th** num millième; **one** ~ mille; ~**s of** des milliers de.

thrash [θræʃ] vt rouer de coups; donner une correction à; (defeat) battre à plate couture; **to** ~ **about** vi se débattre; **to** ~ **out** vt débattre de.

thread [θrɛd] n fil m; (of screw) pas m, filetage m; (of needle) enfiler; **to** ~ **one's way between** se faufiler entre; ~**bare** a râpé(e), élimé(e).

threat [θrɛt] n menace f; ~**en** vi (storm) menacer // vt: **to** ~**en sb with sth/to do** menacer qn de qch/de faire.

three [θriː] num trois (m inv); ~**-dimensional** a à trois dimensions; (film) en relief; ~**fold** ad: **to increase** ~**fold** tripler; ~**-piece suit** n complet m (avec gilet); ~**-piece suite** n salon m comprenant un canapé et deux fauteuils assortis; ~**-ply** a (wood) à trois épaisseurs; (wool) trois fils inv; ~**-wheeler** n (car) voiture f à trois roues.

thresh [θrɛʃ] vt (AGR) battre; ~**ing machine** n batteuse f.

threshold ['θrɛʃhəuld] n seuil m.

threw [θruː] pt of **throw**.

thrift [θrɪft] n économie f; ~**y** a économe.

thrill [θrɪl] n frisson m, émotion f // vi tressaillir, frissonner // vt (audience) électriser; **to be** ~**ed** (with gift etc) être ravi; ~**er** n film m (or roman m or pièce f) à suspense.

thrive, pt **thrived**, **throve** pp **thrived**, **thriven** [θraɪv, θrəuv, 'θrɪvn] vi pousser or se développer bien; (business) prospérer; **he** ~**s on it** cela lui réussit; **thriving** a vigoureux(euse); prospère.

throat [θrəut] n gorge f; **to have a sore** ~ avoir mal à la gorge.

throb [θrɒb] n (of heart) pulsation f; (of engine) vibration f; (of pain) élancement m // vi (heart) palpiter; (engine) vibrer; (pain) lanciner; (wound) causer des élancements.

throes [θrəuz] npl: **in the** ~ **of** au beau milieu de; en proie à; **in the** ~ **of death** à l'agonie.

thrombosis [θrɒm'bəusɪs] n thrombose f.

throne [θrəun] n trône m.

throttle ['θrɒtl] n (AUT) accélérateur m // vt étrangler.

through [θruː] prep à travers; (time) pendant, durant; (by means of) par, par l'intermédiaire de; (owing to) à cause de // a (ticket, train, passage) direct(e) // ad à travers; **to put sb** ~ **to sb** (TEL) passer qn à qn; **to be** ~ (TEL) avoir la communication; (have finished) avoir fini; 'no ~ **way**' 'impasse'; ~**out** prep (place) partout dans; (time) durant tout(e) le(la) // ad partout.

throve [θrəuv] pt of **thrive**.

throw [θrəu] n jet m; (SPORT) lancer m // vt (pt **threw**, pp **thrown** [θruː, θrəun]) lancer, jeter; (SPORT) lancer; (rider) désarçonner; (fig) déconcerter; (pottery) tourner; **to** ~ **a party** donner une réception; **to** ~ **away** vt jeter; **to** ~ **off** vt se débarrasser de; **to** ~ **out** vt jeter dehors; (reject) rejeter; **to** ~ **up** vi vomir; ~**away** a à jeter; ~**-in** n (SPORT) remise f en jeu.

thru [θruː] prep, a, ad (US) = **through**.

thrush [θrʌʃ] n grive f.

thrust [θrʌst] n (TECH) poussée f // vt (pt, pp **thrust**) pousser brusquement; (push in) enfoncer; ~**ing** a dynamique; (fig) qui se met trop en avant.

thud [θʌd] n bruit sourd.

thug [θʌg] n voyou m.

thumb [θʌm] n (ANAT) pouce m // vt (book) feuilleter; **to** ~ **a lift** faire de l'auto-stop, arrêter une voiture; ~ **index** n répertoire m (à onglets); ~**nail** n ongle m du pouce; ~**tack** n (US) punaise f (clou).

thump [θʌmp] *n* grand coup ; (*sound*) bruit sourd // *vt* cogner sur // *vi* cogner, frapper.

thunder ['θʌndə*] *n* tonnerre *m* // *vi* tonner ; (*train etc*): **to ~ past** passer dans un grondement *or* un bruit de tonnerre ; **~clap** *n* coup *m* de tonnerre ; **~ous** *a* étourdissant(e) ; **~storm** *n* orage *m* ; **~struck** *a* (*fig*) abasourdi(e) ; **~y** *a* orageux(euse).

Thursday ['θə:zdı] *n* jeudi *m*.

thus [ðʌs] *ad* ainsi.

thwart [θwɔ:t] *vt* contrecarrer.

thyme [taım] *n* thym *m*.

thyroid ['θaırɔıd] *n* thyroïde *f*.

tiara [tı'ɑ:rə] *n* (*woman's*) diadème *m*.

tic [tık] *n* tic (nerveux).

tick [tık] *n* (*sound: of clock*) tic-tac *m* ; (*mark*) coche *f* ; (*ZOOL*) tique *f* ; (*col*): **in a ~** dans un instant // *vi* faire tic-tac // *vt* cocher ; **to ~ off** cocher ; (*person*) réprimander, attraper.

ticket ['tıkıt] *n* billet *m* ; (*for bus, tube*) ticket *m* ; (*in shop: on goods*) étiquette *f* ; (: *from cash register*) reçu *m*, ticket ; (*for library*) carte *f* ; **~ collector** *n* contrôleur/euse ; **~ holder** *n* personne munie d'un billet ; **~ office** *n* guichet *m*, bureau *m* de vente des billets.

tickle ['tıkl] *n* chatouillement *m* // *vt* chatouiller ; (*fig*) plaire à ; faire rire ; **ticklish** *a* chatouilleux(euse).

tidal ['taıdl] *a* à marée ; **~ wave** *n* raz-de-marée *m inv*.

tiddlywinks ['tıdlıwıŋks] *n* jeu *m* de puce.

tide [taıd] *n* marée *f* ; (*fig: of events*) cours *m* // *vt*: **to ~ sb over** dépanner qn.

tidily ['taıdılı] *ad* avec soin, soigneusement.

tidiness ['taıdınıs] *n* bon ordre ; goût *m* de l'ordre.

tidy ['taıdı] *a* (*room*) bien rangé(e) ; (*dress, work*) net(nette), soigné(e) ; (*person*) ordonné(e), qui a de l'ordre // *vt* (*also: ~ up*) ranger ; **to ~ o.s. up** s'arranger.

tie [taı] *n* (*string etc*) cordon *m* ; (*also: neck~*) cravate *f* ; (*fig: link*) lien *m* ; (*SPORT: draw*) égalité *f* de points ; match nul // *vt* (*parcel*) attacher ; (*ribbon*) nouer // *vi* (*SPORT*) faire match nul ; finir à égalité de points ; **'black/white ~' 'smoking/habit de rigueur'** ; **to ~ sth in a bow** faire un nœud à *or* avec qch ; **to ~ a knot in sth** faire un nœud à qch ; **to ~ down** *vt* attacher ; (*fig*): **to ~ sb down to** contraindre qn à accepter, fixer à qn ; **to ~ up** *vt* (*parcel*) ficeler ; (*dog, boat*) attacher ; (*arrangements*) conclure ; **to be ~d up** (*busy*) être pris or occupé.

tier [tıə*] *n* gradin *m* ; (*of cake*) étage *m*.

tiff [tıf] *n* petite querelle.

tiger ['taıgə*] *n* tigre *m*.

tight [taıt] *a* (*rope*) tendu(e), raide ; (*clothes*) étroit(e), très juste ; (*budget, programme, bend*) serré(e) ; (*control*) strict(e), sévère ; (*col: drunk*) ivre, rond(e) // *ad* (*squeeze*) très fort ; (*shut*) à bloc, hermétiquement ; **~s** *npl* collant *m* ; **~en** *vt* (*rope*) tendre ; (*screw*) resserrer ; (*control*) renforcer // *vi* se tendre, se resserrer ; **~-fisted** *a* avare ; **~ly** *ad* (*grasp*) bien, très fort ; **~-rope** *n* corde *f* raide.

tile [taıl] *n* (*on roof*) tuile *f* ; (*on wall or floor*) carreau *m* ; **~d** *a* en tuiles ; carrelé(e).

till [tıl] *n* caisse (enregistreuse) // *vt* (*land*) cultiver // *prep, cj* = **until**.

tiller ['tılə*] *n* (*NAUT*) barre *f* (du gouvernail).

tilt [tılt] *vt* pencher, incliner // *vi* pencher, être incliné(e).

timber ['tımbə*] *n* (*material*) bois *m* de construction ; (*trees*) arbres *mpl*.

time [taım] *n* temps *m* ; (*epoch: often pl*) époque *f*, temps ; (*by clock*) heure *f* ; (*moment*) moment *m* ; (*occasion, also* MATH) fois *f* ; (*MUS*) mesure *f* // *vt* (*race*) chronométrer ; (*programme*) minuter ; (*remark etc*) choisir le moment de ; **a long ~** un long moment, longtemps ; **for the ~ being** pour le moment ; **from ~ to ~** de temps en temps ; **in ~** (*soon enough*) à temps ; (*after some time*) avec le temps, à la longue ; (*MUS*) en mesure ; **in a week's ~** dans une semaine ; **on ~** à l'heure ; **5 ~s 5** 5 fois 5 ; **what ~ is it?** quelle heure est-il? ; **to have a good ~** bien s'amuser ; **~'s up!** c'est l'heure! ; **I've no ~ for it** (*fig*) cela m'agace ; **~ bomb** *n* bombe *f* à retardement ; **~keeper** *n* (*SPORT*) chronomètre *m* ; **~ lag** *n* décalage *m* ; (*in travel*) décalage *m* horaire ; **~less** *a* éternel(le) ; **~ limit** *n* limite *f* de temps, délai *m* ; **~ly** *a* opportun(e) ; **~ off** *n* temps *m* libre ; **~r** *n* (*in kitchen*) compte-minutes *m inv* ; **~-saving** *a* qui fait gagner du temps ; **~ switch** *n* minuteur *m* ; (*for lighting*) minuterie *f* ; **~table** *n* (*RAIL*) (indicateur *m*) horaire *m* ; (*SCOL*) emploi *m* du temps ; **~ zone** *n* fuseau *m* horaire.

timid ['tımıd] *a* timide ; (*easily scared*) peureux(euse).

timing ['taımıŋ] *n* minutage *m* ; chronométrage *m* ; **the ~ of his resignation** le moment choisi pour sa démission ; **~ device** *n* mécanisme *m* de retardement.

timpani ['tımpənı] *npl* timbales *fpl*.

tin [tın] *n* étain *m* ; (*also: ~ plate*) fer-blanc *m* ; (*can*) boîte *f* (de conserve) ; (*for baking*) moule *m* (à gâteau) ; **~ foil** *n* papier *m* d'étain.

tinge [tındʒ] *n* nuance *f* // *vt*: **~d with** teinté(e) de.

tingle ['tıŋgl] *n* picotement *m* ; frisson *m* // *vi* picoter.

tinker ['tıŋkə*] *n* rétameur ambulant ; (*gipsy*) romanichel *m* ; **to ~ with** *vt* bricoler, rafistoler.

tinkle ['tıŋkl] *vi* tinter // *n* (*col*): **to give sb a ~** passer un coup de fil à qn.

tinned [tınd] *a* (*food*) en boîte, en conserve.

tinny ['tını] *a* métallique.

tin opener ['tınəupnə*] *n* ouvre-boîte(s) *m*.

tinsel ['tınsl] *n* guirlandes *fpl* de Noël (argentées).

tint [tınt] *n* teinte *f* ; (*for hair*) shampooing colorant.

tiny ['taını] *a* minuscule.

tip [tıp] *n* (*end*) bout *m* ; (*protective: on umbrella etc*) embout *m* ; (*gratuity*) pourboire *m* ; (*for coal*) terril *m* ; (*for rubbish*) décharge *f* ; (*advice*) tuyau *m* // *vt* (*waiter*) donner un pourboire à ; (*tilt*) incliner ; (*overturn: also: ~ over*) renverser ; (empty: also: ~ out) dèverser ; ~-off n (hint) tuyau m ; ~ped a (cigarette) (à bout) filtre inv ; steel-~ped à bout métallique, à embout de métal.

tipple ['tɪpl] vi picoler // n: **to have a ~** boire un petit coup.

tipsy ['tɪpsɪ] a un peu ivre, émèché(e).

tiptoe ['tɪptəʊ] n: **on ~** sur la pointe des pieds.

tiptop ['tɪp'tɔp] a: **in ~ condition** en excellent état.

tire ['taɪə*] n (US) = tyre // vt fatiguer // vi se fatiguer ; (~d a fatigué(e)) ; **to be ~d of** en avoir assez de, être las(lasse) de ; **~dness** n fatigue f ; **~less** a infatigable, inlassable ; **~some** a ennuyeux(euse) ; **tiring** a fatigant(e).

tissue ['tɪʃu:] n tissu m ; (paper handkerchief) mouchoir m en papier, kleenex m ® ; ~ **paper** n papier m de soie.

tit [tɪt] n (bird) mésange f ; **to give ~ for tat** rendre coup pour coup.

titanium [tɪ'teɪnɪəm] n titane m.

titbit ['tɪtbɪt] n (food) friandise f ; (news) potin m.

titillate ['tɪtɪleɪt] vt titiller, exciter.

titivate ['tɪtɪveɪt] vt pomponner.

title ['taɪtl] n titre m ; ~ **deed** n (LAW) titre (constitutif) de propriété ; ~ **role** n rôle principal.

titter ['tɪtə*] vi rire (bêtement).

tittle-tattle ['tɪtltætl] n bavardages mpl.

titular ['tɪtjʊlə*] a (in name only) nominal(e).

tizzy ['tɪzɪ] n: **to be in a ~** être dans tous ses états.

to [tu:, tə] prep à ; (towards) vers ; envers ; **give it ~ me** donne-le-moi ; **the key ~ the front door** la clé de la porte d'entrée ; **the main thing is ~ ...** l'important est de... ; **to go ~ France/Portugal** aller en France/au Portugal ; **I went ~ Claude's** je suis allé chez Claude ; **to go ~ town/school** aller en ville/à l'école ; **pull/push the door ~** tire/pousse la porte ; **to go ~ and fro** aller et venir.

toad [təʊd] n crapaud m ; ~**stool** n champignon (vénéneux) ; ~**y** vi flatter bassement.

toast [təʊst] n (CULIN) pain grillé, toast m ; (drink, speech) toast // vt (CULIN) faire griller ; (drink to) porter un toast à ; **a piece** or **slice of ~** un toast ; ~**er** n grille-pain m inv ; ~**master** n animateur m pour réceptions ; ~**rack** n porte-toast m.

tobacco [tə'bækəʊ] n tabac m ; ~**nist** n marchand/e de tabac ; ~**nist's (shop)** n (bureau m de) tabac m.

toboggan [tə'bɔgən] n toboggan m ; (child's) luge f.

today [tə'deɪ] ad,n (also fig) aujourd'hui (m).

toddler ['tɔdlə*] n enfant m/f qui commence à marcher, bambin m.

toddy ['tɔdɪ] n grog m.

to-do [tə'du:] n (fuss) histoire f, affaire f.

toe [təʊ] n doigt m de pied, orteil m ; (of shoe) bout m ; **to ~ the line** (fig) obéir, se conformer ; ~**hold** n prise f ; ~**nail** n ongle m de l'orteil.

toffee ['tɔfɪ] n caramel m ; ~ **apple** n pomme caramélisée.

toga ['təʊgə] n toge f.

together [tə'geðə*] ad ensemble ; (at same time) en même temps ; ~ **with** prep avec ; ~**ness** n camaraderie f ; intimité f.

toil [tɔɪl] n dur travail, labeur m // vi travailler dur ; peiner.

toilet ['tɔɪlət] n (lavatory) toilettes fpl, cabinets mpl // cpd (bag, soap etc) de toilette ; ~ **bowl** n cuvette f des W.-C. ; ~ **paper** n papier m hygiénique ; ~**ries** npl articles mpl de toilette ; ~ **roll** n rouleau m de papier hygiénique ; ~ **water** n eau f de toilette.

token ['təʊkən] n (sign) marque f, témoignage m ; (voucher) bon m, coupon m ; **book/record** ~ n chèque-livre/disque m.

told [təʊld] pt, pp of **tell.**

tolerable ['tɔlərəbl] a (bearable) tolérable ; (fairly good) passable.

tolerance ['tɔlərns] n (also: TECH) tolérance f.

tolerant ['tɔlərnt] a: ~ **(of)** tolérant(e) (à l'égard de).

tolerate ['tɔləreɪt] vt supporter ; (MED, TECH) tolérer ; **toleration** [-'reɪʃən] n tolérance f.

toll [təʊl] n (tax, charge) péage m // vi (bell) sonner ; **the accident ~ on the roads** le nombre des victimes de la route ; ~**bridge** n pont m à péage.

tomato, ~**es** [tə'mɑ:təʊ] n tomate f.

tomb [tu:m] n tombe f.

tombola [tɔm'bəʊlə] n tombola f.

tomboy ['tɔmbɔɪ] n garçon manqué.

tombstone ['tu:mstəʊn] n pierre tombale.

tomcat ['tɔmkæt] n matou m.

tomorrow [tə'mɔrəʊ] ad,n (also fig) demain (m) ; **the day after** ~ après-demain ; ~ **morning** demain matin.

ton [tʌn] n tonne f (= 1016 kg ; 20 cwt) ; (NAUT: also: **register** ~) tonneau m (= 2.83 cu.m ; 100 cu. ft) ; ~**s of** (col) des tas de.

tonal ['təʊnl] a tonal(e).

tone [təʊn] n ton m ; (of radio) tonalité f // vi s'harmoniser ; **to ~ down** vt (colour, criticism) adoucir ; (sound) baisser ; **to ~ up** vt (muscles) tonifier ; ~-**deaf** a qui n'a pas d'oreille.

tongs [tɔŋz] npl pinces fpl ; (for coal) pincettes fpl ; (for hair) fer m à friser.

tongue [tʌŋ] n langue f ; ~ **in cheek** ad ironiquement ; ~-**tied** a (fig) muet(te) ; ~-**twister** n phrase f très difficile à prononcer.

tonic ['tɔnɪk] n (MED) tonique m ; (MUS) tonique f ; (also: ~ **water**) tonic m.

tonight [tə'naɪt] ad, n cette nuit ; (this evening) ce soir.

tonnage ['tʌnɪdʒ] n (NAUT) tonnage m.

tonne [tʌn] n (metric ton) tonne f.

tonsil ['tɔnsl] n amygdale f ; ~**litis** [-'laɪtɪs] n amygdalite f.

too [tu:] ad (excessively) trop ; (also) aussi ; ~ **much** ad trop // det trop de ; ~ **many** det trop de ; ~ **bad!** tant pis!

took [tʊk] pt of **take.**

tool [tu:l] n outil m // vt travailler,

ouvrager ; ~ **box/kit** n boîte f/trousse f
à outils.

toot [tu:t] n coup m de sifflet (or de klaxon)
// vi siffler ; (with car-horn) klaxonner.

tooth [tu:θ, ti:θ] n (ANAT, TECH)
dent f ; **~ache** n mal m de dents ; **~brush**
n brosse f à dents ; **~paste** n (pâte f)
dentifrice m ; **~pick** n cure-dent m ; **~
powder** n poudre f dentifrice.

top [tɔp] n (of mountain, head) sommet m ;
(of page, ladder) haut m ; (of box, cupboard,
table) dessus m ; (lid: of box, jar) couvercle
m ; (: of bottle) bouchon m ; (toy) toupie
f // a du haut ; (in rank) premier(ère) ;
(best) meilleur(e) // vt (exceed) dépasser ;
(be first in) être en tête de ; **on ~ of** sur ;
(in addition to) en plus de ; **from ~ to toe**
de la tête aux pieds ; **at the ~ of the list**
en tête de liste ; **to ~ up** vt remplir ;
~coat n pardessus m ; **~ floor** n dernier
étage ; **~ hat** n haut-de-forme m ; **~-
heavy** a (object) trop lourd(e) du haut.

topic [ˈtɔpɪk] n sujet m, thème m ; **~al** a
d'actualité.

top: **~less** a (bather etc) aux seins nus ;
~less swimsuit n monokini m ; **~-level**
a (talks) à l'échelon le plus élevé ; **~most**
a le(la) plus haut(e).

topple [ˈtɔpl] vt renverser, faire tomber //
vi basculer ; tomber.

topsy-turvy [ˈtɔp sɪˈtɜːvɪ] a,ad sens
dessus-dessous.

torch [tɔ:tʃ] n torche f ; (electric) lampe f
de poche.

tore [tɔ:*] pt of **tear**.

torment n [ˈtɔ:mɛnt] tourment m // vt
[tɔ:ˈmɛnt] tourmenter ; (fig: annoy) agacer.

torn [tɔ:n] pp of **tear** // a: **~ between**
(fig) tiraillé(e) entre.

tornado, **~es** [tɔ:ˈneɪdəu] n tornade f.

torpedo, **~es** [tɔ:ˈpi:dəu] n torpille f.

torpor [ˈtɔ:pə*] n torpeur f.

torque [tɔ:k] n couple m de torsion.

torrent [ˈtɔrnt] n torrent m ; **~ial** [-ˈrɛnʃl]
a torrentiel(le).

torso [ˈtɔ:səu] n torse m.

tortoise [ˈtɔ:təs] n tortue f ; **~shell**
[ˈtɔ:təʃɛl] a en écaille.

tortuous [ˈtɔ:tjuəs] a tortueux(euse).

torture [ˈtɔ:tʃə*] n torture f // vt torturer.

Tory [ˈtɔ:rɪ] a tory (pl tories),
conservateur(trice) // n tory m/f,
conservateur/trice.

toss [tɔs] vt lancer, jeter ; (pancake) faire
sauter ; (head) rejeter en arrière ; **to ~ a
coin** jouer à pile ou face ; **to ~ up for
sth** jouer qch à pile ou face ; **to ~ and
turn** (in bed) se tourner et se retourner.

tot [tɔt] n (drink) petit verre ; (child)
bambin m.

total [ˈtəutl] a total(e) // n total m // vt
(add up) faire le total de, totaliser ; (amount
to) s'élever à.

totalitarian [təutælɪˈtɛərɪən] a totalitaire.

totality [təuˈtælɪtɪ] n totalité f.

totem pole [ˈtəutəmpəul] n mât m
totémique.

totter [ˈtɔtə*] vi chanceler.

touch [tʌtʃ] n contact m, toucher m ;
(sense, also skill: of pianist etc) toucher ;
(fig: note, also: FOOTBALL) touche f // vt

(gen) toucher ; (tamper with) toucher à ; **a
~ of** (fig) un petit peu de ; une touche de ;
in ~ with en contact or rapport avec ; **to
get in ~ with** prendre contact avec ; **to
lose ~** (friends) se perdre de vue ; **to ~
on** vt fus (topic) effleurer, toucher ; **to ~
up** vt (paint) retoucher ; **~-and-go** a
incertain(e) ; **it was ~-and-go whether
we did it** nous avons failli ne pas le faire ;
~down n atterrissage m ; (on sea)
amerrissage m ; **~ed** a touché(e) ; (col)
cinglé(e) ; **~ing** a touchant(e),
attendrissant(e) ; **~line** n (SPORT) (ligne f
de) touche f ; **~y** a (person) susceptible.

tough [tʌf] a dur(e) ; (resistant)
résistant(e), solide ; (meat) dur, coriace //
n (gangster etc) dur m ; **~ luck!** pas de
chance! ; tant pis! ; **~en** vt rendre plus
dur(e) (or plus résistant(e) or plus solide) ;
~ness n dureté f ; résistance f ; solidité f.

toupee [ˈtu:peɪ] n postiche m.

tour [ˈtuə*] n voyage m ; (also: **package
~**) voyage organisé ; (of town, museum)
tour m, visite f ; (by artist) tournée f //
vt visiter ; **~ing** n voyages mpl
touristiques, tourisme m.

tourism [ˈtuərɪzm] n tourisme m.

tourist [ˈtuərɪst] n touriste m/f // ad
(travel) en classe touriste // cpd
touristique ; **~ office** n syndicat m
d'initiative.

tournament [ˈtuənəmənt] n tournoi m.

tour operator [ˈtuərˈɔpəreɪtə*] n organisateur m de voyages.

tousled [ˈtauzld] a (hair) ébouriffé(e).

tout [taut] vi: **to ~** for essayer de
raccrocher, racoler ; **to ~ sth (around)**
essayer de placer or (re)vendre qch.

tow [təu] vt remorquer ; **'on ~'** (AUT)
'véhicule en remorque'.

toward(s) [təˈwɔ:d(z)] prep vers ; (of
attitude) envers, à l'égard de ; (of purpose)
pour.

towel [ˈtauəl] n serviette f (de toilette) ;
(also: **tea ~**) torchon m ; **~ling** n (fabric)
tissu-éponge m ; **~ rail** n porte-serviettes
m inv.

tower [ˈtauə*] n tour f ; **~ block** n tour
f (d'habitation) ; **~ing** a très haut(e),
imposant(e).

towline [ˈtəulaɪn] n (câble m de) remorque
f.

town [taun] n ville f ; **to go to ~** aller
en ville ; (fig) y mettre le paquet ; **~ clerk**
n ≈ secrétaire m/f de mairie ; **~ council**
n conseil municipal ; **~ hall** n ≈ mairie
f ; **~ planner** n urbaniste m/f ; **~
planning** n urbanisme m.

towpath [ˈtəupɑ:θ] n (chemin m de)
halage m.

towrope [ˈtəurəup] n (câble m de)
remorque f.

toxic [ˈtɔksɪk] a toxique.

toy [tɔɪ] n jouet m ; **to ~ with** vt fus jouer
avec ; (idea) caresser ; **~shop** m magasin
m de jouets.

trace [treɪs] n trace f // vt (draw) tracer,
dessiner ; (follow) suivre la trace de ;
(locate) retrouver ; **without ~** (disappear)
sans laisser de traces.

track [træk] n (mark) trace f ; (path: gen)
chemin m, piste f ; (: of bullet etc)

trajectoire f; (: of suspect, animal) piste ; (RAIL) voie ferrée, rails mpl; (on tape, SPORT) piste // vt suivre la trace or la piste de ; **to keep ~ of** suivre ; **to ~ down** vt (prey) trouver et capturer ; (sth lost) finir par retrouver ; **~ed** a (AUT) à chenille ; **~er dog** n chien policier ; **~suit** n survêtement m.

tract [trækt] n (GEO) étendue f, zone f; (pamphlet) tract m; **respiratory ~** (ANAT) système m respiratoire.

tractor ['træktə*] n tracteur m.

trade [treɪd] n commerce m; (skill, job) métier m // vi faire du commerce ; **to ~ with/in** faire du commerce avec/le commerce de ; **to ~ in** vt (old car etc) faire reprendre ; **~-in** (value) n reprise f; **~mark** n marque f de fabrique ; **~name** n marque déposée ; **~r** n commerçant/e, négociant/e ; **~sman** n (shopkeeper) commerçant ; **~ union** n syndicat m; **~ unionist** n syndicaliste m/f; **trading** n affaires fpl, commerce m; **trading estate** n zone industrielle ; **trading stamp** n timbre-prime m.

tradition [trə'dɪʃən] n tradition f; **~s** npl coutumes fpl, traditions ; **~al** a traditionnel(le).

traffic ['træfɪk] n trafic m; (cars) circulation f // vi: **to ~ in** (pej: liquor, drugs) faire le trafic de ; **~ circle** n (US) rond-point m; **~ jam** n embouteillage m; **~ lights** npl feux mpl (de signalisation) ; **~ sign** n panneau m de signalisation ; **~ warden** n contractuel/le.

tragedy ['trædʒədɪ] n tragédie f.

tragic ['trædʒɪk] a tragique.

trail [treɪl] n (tracks) trace f, piste f; (path) chemin m, piste ; (of smoke etc) traînée f // vt traîner, tirer ; (follow) suivre // vi traîner ; **to ~ behind** vi traîner, être à la traîne ; **~er** n (AUT) remorque f; (US) caravane f; (CINEMA) court métrage de lancement ; **~ing plant** n plante rampante.

train [treɪn] n train m; (in underground) rame f; (of dress) traîne f // vt (apprentice, doctor etc) former ; (sportsman) entraîner ; (dog) dresser ; (memory) exercer ; (point: gun etc): **to ~ sth on** braquer qch sur // vi recevoir sa formation ; s'entraîner ; **one's ~ of thought** le fil de sa pensée ; **~ed** a qualifié(e), qui a reçu une formation ; dressé(e) ; **~ee** [treɪ'ni:] n stagiaire m/f; (in trade) apprenti/e ; **~er** n (SPORT) entraîneur/euse ; (of dogs etc) dresseur/euse ; **~ing** n formation f; entraînement m; dressage m; **in ~ing** (SPORT) à l'entraînement ; (fit) en forme ; **~ing college** n école professionnelle ; (for teachers) ≈ école normale.

traipse [treɪps] vi (se) traîner, déambuler.

trait [treɪt] n trait m (de caractère).

traitor ['treɪtə*] n traître m.

tram [træm] n (also: **~car**) tram(way) m; **~line** n ligne f de tram(way).

tramp [træmp] n (person) vagabond/e, clochard/e // vi marcher d'un pas lourd // vt (walk through: town, streets) parcourir à pied.

trample ['træmpl] vt: **to ~ (underfoot)** piétiner ; (fig) bafouer.

trampoline ['træmpəli:n] n trampolino m.

trance [trɑ:ns] n transe f; (MED) catalepsie f.

tranquil ['træŋkwɪl] a tranquille ; **~lity** n tranquillité f; **~lizer** n (MED) tranquillisant m.

transact [træn'zækt] vt (business) traiter ; **~ion** [-'zækʃən] n transaction f; **~ions** npl (minutes) actes mpl.

transatlantic ['trænzət'læntɪk] a transatlantique.

transcend [træn'sɛnd] vt transcender ; (excel over) surpasser.

transcript ['trænskrɪpt] n transcription f (texte) ; **~ion** [-'skrɪpʃən] n transcription.

transept ['trænsɛpt] n transept m.

transfer n ['trænsfə*] (gen, also SPORT) transfert m; (POL: of power) passation f; (picture, design) décalcomanie f; (: stick-on) autocollant m // vt [træns'fə:*] transférer ; passer ; décalquer ; **to ~ the charges** (TEL) téléphoner en P.C.V. ; **~able** [-'fə:rəbl] a transmissible, transférable ; **'not ~able' 'personnel'**.

transform [træns'fɔ:m] vt transformer ; **~ation** [-'meɪʃən] n transformation f; **~er** n (ELEC) transformateur m.

transfusion [træns'fju:ʒən] n transfusion f.

transient ['trænzɪənt] a transitoire, éphémère.

transistor [træn'zɪstə*] n (ELEC. also: **~ radio**) transistor m.

transit ['trænzɪt] n: **in ~** en transit ; **~ lounge** n salle f de transit.

transition [træn'zɪʃən] n transition f; **~al** a transitoire.

transitive ['trænzɪtɪv] a (LING) transitif(ive).

transitory ['trænzɪtərɪ] a transitoire.

translate [trænz'leɪt] vt traduire ; **translation** [-'leɪʃən] n traduction f; (SCOL: as opposed to prose) version f; **translator** n traducteur/trice.

transmission [trænz'mɪʃən] n transmission f.

transmit [trænz'mɪt] vt transmettre ; (RADIO, TV) émettre ; **~ter** n émetteur m.

transparency [træns'pɛərnsɪ] n (PHOT) diapositive f.

transparent [træns'pærnt] a transparent(e).

transplant vt [træns'plɑ:nt] transplanter ; (seedlings) repiquer // n ['trænsplɑ:nt] (MED) transplantation f.

transport n ['trænspɔ:t] transport m // vt [træns'pɔ:t] transporter ; **~ation** [-'teɪʃən] n (moyen m de) transport m; (of prisoners) transportation f; **~ café** n ≈ restaurant m de routiers.

transverse ['trænzvə:s] a transversal(e).

transvestite [trænz'vɛstaɪt] n travesti/e.

trap [træp] n (snare, trick) piège m; (carriage) cabriolet m // vt prendre au piège ; (immobilize) bloquer ; (jam) coincer ; **to shut one's ~** (col) la fermer ; **~ door** n trappe f.

trapeze [trə'pi:z] n trapèze m.

trapper ['træpə*] n trappeur m.

trappings ['træpɪŋz] npl ornements mpl; attributs mpl.

trash [træʃ] n (pej: goods) camelote f; (: nonsense) sottises fpl; ~ **can** n (US) boîte f à ordures.

trauma [ˈtrɔːmə] n traumatisme m; ~**tic** [-ˈmætɪk] a traumatisant(e).

travel [ˈtrævl] n voyage(s) m(pl) // vi voyager; (move) aller, se déplacer // vt (distance) parcourir; ~ **agent's** n agence f de voyages; ~**ler**, ~**er** (US) n voyageur/euse; ~**ler's cheque** n chèque m de voyage; ~**ling**, ~**ing** (US) n voyage(s) m(pl) // cpd (bag, clock) de voyage; (expenses) de déplacement; ~ **sickness** n mal(pl) de la route (or de mer or de l'air).

traverse [ˈtrævəs] vt traverser.

travesty [ˈtrævəstɪ] n parodie f.

trawler [ˈtrɔːlə*] n chalutier m.

tray [treɪ] n (for carrying) plateau m; (on desk) corbeille f.

treacherous [ˈtrɛtʃərəs] a traître(sse).

treachery [ˈtrɛtʃərɪ] n traîtrise f.

treacle [ˈtriːkl] n mélasse f.

tread [trɛd] n pas m; (sound) bruit m de pas; (of tyre) chape f, bande f de roulement // vi (pt **trod**, pp **trodden** [trɔd, ˈtrɔdn]) marcher; to ~ **on** vt fus marcher sur.

treason [ˈtriːzn] n trahison f.

treasure [ˈtrɛʒə*] n trésor m // vt (value) tenir beaucoup à; (store) conserver précieusement; ~ **hunt** n chasse f au trésor.

treasurer [ˈtrɛʒərə*] n trésorier/ère.

treasury [ˈtrɛʒərɪ] n trésorerie f; **the T~** (POL) le ministère des Finances.

treat [triːt] n petit cadeau, petite surprise // vt traiter; **it was a** ~ ça m'a (or nous a etc) vraiment fait plaisir; **to** ~ **sb to sth** offrir qch à qn.

treatise [ˈtriːtɪz] n traité m (ouvrage).

treatment [ˈtriːtmənt] n traitement m.

treaty [ˈtriːtɪ] n traité m.

treble [ˈtrɛbl] a triple // n (MUS) soprano m // vt, vi tripler; ~ **clef** n clé f de sol.

tree [triː] n arbre m; ~**lined** a bordé(e) d'arbres; ~**top** n cime f d'un arbre; ~ **trunk** n tronc m d'arbre.

trek [trɛk] n voyage m; randonnée f; (tiring walk) tirée f // vi (as holiday) faire de la randonnée.

trellis [ˈtrɛlɪs] n treillis m, treillage m.

tremble [ˈtrɛmbl] vi trembler; (machine) vibrer; **trembling** tremblement m; vibrations fpl // a tremblant(e); vibrant(e).

tremendous [trɪˈmɛndəs] a (enormous) énorme, fantastique; (excellent) formidable.

tremor [ˈtrɛmə*] n tremblement m; (also: **earth** ~) secousse f sismique.

trench [trɛntʃ] n tranchée f.

trend [trɛnd] n (tendency) tendance f; (of events) cours m; (fashion) mode f; ~**y** a (idea) dans le vent; (clothes) dernier cri inv.

trepidation [trɛpɪˈdeɪʃən] n vive agitation.

trespass [ˈtrɛspəs] vi: **to** ~ **on** s'introduire sans permission dans; (fig) empiéter sur; **'no** ~**ing'** 'propriété privée', 'défense d'entrer'.

tress [trɛs] n boucle f de cheveux.

trestle [ˈtrɛsl] n tréteau m; ~ **table** n table f à tréteaux.

trial [ˈtraɪəl] n (LAW) procès m, jugement m; (test: of machine etc) essai m; (hardship) épreuve f; (worry) souci m; **to be on** ~ passer en jugement; **by** ~ **and error** par tâtonnements.

triangle [ˈtraɪæŋgl] n (MATH, MUS) triangle m; **triangular** [-ˈæŋgjulə*] a triangulaire.

tribal [ˈtraɪbəl] a tribal(e).

tribe [traɪb] n tribu f; ~**sman** n membre m de la tribu.

tribulation [trɪbjuˈleɪʃən] n tribulation f, malheur m.

tribunal [traɪˈbjuːnl] n tribunal m.

tributary [ˈtrɪbjuːtərɪ] n (river) affluent m.

tribute [ˈtrɪbjuːt] n tribut m, hommage m; **to pay** ~ **to** rendre hommage à.

trice [traɪs] n: **in a** ~ en un clin d'œil.

trick [trɪk] n ruse f; (clever act) astuce f; (joke) tour m; (CARDS) levée f // vt attraper, rouler; **to play a** ~ **on sb** jouer un tour à qn; ~**ery** n ruse f.

trickle [ˈtrɪkl] n (of water etc) filet m // vi couler en un filet or goutte à goutte; **to** ~ **in/out** (people) entrer/sortir par petits groupes.

tricky [ˈtrɪkɪ] a difficile, délicat(e).

tricycle [ˈtraɪsɪkl] n tricycle m.

trifle [ˈtraɪfl] n bagatelle f; (CULIN) ≈ diplomate m // ad: **a** ~ **long** un peu long; **trifling** a insignifiant(e).

trigger [ˈtrɪgə*] n (of gun) gâchette f; **to** ~ **off** vt déclencher.

trigonometry [trɪgəˈnɔmətrɪ] n trigonométrie f.

trilby [ˈtrɪlbɪ] n (chapeau m en) feutre m.

trim [trɪm] a net(te); (house, garden) bien tenu(e); (figure) svelte // n (haircut etc) légère coupe; (embellishment) finitions fpl; (on car) garnitures fpl // vt couper légèrement; (decorate): **to** ~ **(with)** décorer (de); (NAUT: a sail) gréer; ~**mings** npl décorations fpl; (extras: gen CULIN) garniture f.

Trinity [ˈtrɪnɪtɪ] n: **the** ~ la Trinité.

trinket [ˈtrɪŋkɪt] n bibelot m; (piece of jewellery) colifichet m.

trio [ˈtriːəu] n trio m.

trip [trɪp] n voyage m; (excursion) excursion f; (stumble) faux pas // vi faire un faux pas, trébucher; (go lightly) marcher d'un pas léger; **on a** ~ en voyage; **to** ~ **up** vi trébucher // vt faire un croc-en-jambe à.

tripe [traɪp] n (CULIN) tripes fpl; (pej: rubbish) idioties fpl.

triple [ˈtrɪpl] a triple.

triplets [ˈtrɪplɪts] npl triplés/ées.

triplicate [ˈtrɪplɪkət] n: **in** ~ en trois exemplaires.

tripod [ˈtraɪpɔd] n trépied m.

tripper [ˈtrɪpə*] n touriste m/f; excursionniste m/f.

trite [traɪt] a banal(e).

triumph [ˈtraɪʌmf] n triomphe m // vi: **to** ~ **(over)** triompher (de); ~**al** [-ˈʌmfl] a triomphal(e); ~**ant** [-ˈʌmfənt] a triomphant(e).

trivia [ˈtrɪvɪə] npl futilités fpl.

trivial [ˈtrɪvɪəl] a insignifiant(e); (commonplace) banal(e); ~**ity** [-ˈælɪtɪ] n caractère insignifiant; banalité f.

trod [trɔd] *pt of* **tread** ; **~den** *pp of* **tread**.
trolley ['trɔlɪ] *n* chariot *m* ; **~ bus** *n* trolleybus *m*.
trollop ['trɔləp] *n* prostituée *f*.
trombone [trɔm'bəʊn] *n* trombone *m*.
troop [tru:p] *n* bande *f*, groupe *m* ; **~s** *npl* (MIL) troupes *fpl* ; (: *men*) hommes *mpl*, soldats *mpl* ; **to ~ in/out** *vi* entrer/sortir en groupe ; **~er** *n* (MIL) soldat *m* de cavalerie ; **~ing the colour** (*ceremony*) le salut au drapeau ; **~ship** *n* (navire *m* de) transport *m*.
trophy ['trəʊfɪ] *n* trophée *m*.
tropic ['trɔpɪk] *n* tropique *m* ; **in the ~s** sous les tropiques ; **T~ of Cancer/Capricorn** *n* tropique du Cancer/Capricorne ; **~al** *a* tropical(e).
trot [trɔt] *n* trot *m* // *vi* trotter ; **on the ~** (*fig*: *col*) d'affilée.
trouble ['trʌbl] *n* difficulté(s) *f(pl)*, problème(s) *m(pl)* ; (*worry*) ennuis *mpl*, soucis *mpl* ; (*bother*, *effort*) peine *f* ; (POL) conflits *mpl*, troubles *mpl* ; (MED): **stomach** *etc* **~** troubles gastriques *etc* // *vt* déranger, gêner ; (*worry*) inquiéter // *vi*: **to ~ to do** prendre la peine de faire ; **~s** *npl* (POL *etc*) troubles *mpl* ; **to be in ~** avoir des ennuis ; (*ship*, *climber etc*) être en difficulté ; **to go to the ~ of doing** se donner le mal de faire ; **it's no ~!** je vous en prie! ; **what's the ~?** qu'est-ce qui ne va pas? ; **~d** *a* (*person*) inquiet(ète) ; (*epoch*, *life*) agité(e) ; **~-free** *a* sans problèmes *or* ennuis ; **~maker** *n* élément perturbateur, fauteur *m* de troubles ; **~shooter** *n* (*in conflict*) conciliateur *m* ; **~some** *a* ennuyeux(euse), gênant(e).
trough [trɔf] *n* (*also*: **drinking ~**) abreuvoir *m* ; (*also*: **feeding ~**) auge *f* ; (*channel*) chenal *m* ; **~ of low pressure** *n* (GEO) dépression *f*.
trounce [traʊns] *vt* (*defeat*) battre à plates coutures.
troupe [tru:p] *n* troupe *f*.
trousers ['traʊzəz] *npl* pantalon *m* ; **short ~** *npl* culottes courtes.
trousseau, *pl* **~x** *or* **~s** ['tru:səʊ, -z] *n* trousseau *m*.
trout [traʊt] *n*, *pl inv* truite *f*.
trowel ['traʊəl] *n* truelle *f*.
truant ['truənt] *n*: **to play ~** faire l'école buissonnière.
truce [tru:s] *n* trêve *f*.
truck [trʌk] *n* camion *m* ; (RAIL) wagon *m* à plate-forme ; (*for luggage*) chariot *m* (à bagages) ; **~ driver** *n* camionneur *m* ; **~ farm** *n* (US) jardin maraîcher.
truculent ['trʌkjʊlənt] *a* agressif(ive).
trudge [trʌdʒ] *vi* marcher lourdement, se traîner.
true [tru:] *a* vrai(e) ; (*accurate*) exact(e) ; (*genuine*) vrai, véritable ; (*faithful*) fidèle.
truffle [trʌfl] *n* truffe *f*.
truly ['tru:lɪ] *ad* vraiment, réellement ; (*truthfully*) sans mentir ; (*faithfully*) fidèlement ; **'yours ~'** (*in letter*) 'je vous prie d'agréer l'expression de mes sentiments respectueux.'
trump [trʌmp] *n* atout *m* ; **~ed-up** *a* inventé(e) (de toutes pièces).

trumpet ['trʌmpɪt] *n* trompette *f* ; (*player*) trompettiste *m/f*.
truncated [trʌŋ'keɪtɪd] *a* tronqué(e).
truncheon ['trʌntʃən] *n* bâton *m* (d'agent de police) ; matraque *f*.
trundle ['trʌndl] *vt*, *vi*: **to ~ along** rouler bruyamment.
trunk [trʌŋk] *n* (*of tree*, *person*) tronc *m* ; (*of elephant*) trompe *f* ; (*case*) malle *f* ; **~s** *npl* caleçon *m* ; (*also*: **swimming ~s**) maillot *m or* slip *m* de bain ; **~ call** *n* (TEL) communication interurbaine ; **~ road** ≈ route nationale.
truss [trʌs] *n* (MED) bandage *m* herniaire ; **to ~ (up)** *vt* (CULIN) brider.
trust [trʌst] *n* confiance *f* ; (LAW) fidéicommis *m* ; (COMM) trust *m* // (*rely on*) avoir confiance en ; (*entrust*): **to ~ sth to sb** confier qch à qn ; **~ed** *a* en qui l'on a confiance ; **~ee** [trʌs'ti:] *n* (LAW) fidéicommissaire *m/f* ; (*also*: *of school etc*) administrateur/trice ; **~ful**, **~ing** *a* confiant(e) ; **~worthy** *a* digne de confiance ; **~y** *a* fidèle.
truth, **~s** [tru:θ, tru:ðz] *n* vérité *f* ; **~ful** *a* (*person*) qui dit la vérité ; (*description*) exact(e), vrai(e) ; (*also*: sincèrement, sans mentir ; **~fulness** *n* véracité *f*.
try [traɪ] *n* essai *m*, tentative *f* ; (RUGBY) essai *m* // *vt* (LAW) juger ; (*test*: *sth new*) essayer, tester ; (*strain*) éprouver // *vi* essayer ; **to ~ to do** essayer de faire ; (*seek*) chercher à faire ; **to ~ on** *vt* (*clothes*) essayer ; **to ~ it on** (*fig*) tenter le coup, bluffer ; **to ~ out** *vt* essayer, mettre à l'essai ; **~ing** *a* pénible.
tsar [zɑ:*] *n* tsar *m*.
T-shirt ['ti:ʃə:t] *n* tee-shirt *m*.
T-square ['ti:skwɛə*] *n* équerre *f* en T.
tub [tʌb] *n* cuve *f* ; baquet *m* ; (*bath*) baignoire *f*.
tuba ['tju:bə] *n* tuba *m*.
tubby ['tʌbɪ] *a* rondelet(te).
tube [tju:b] *n* tube *m* ; (*underground*) métro *m* ; (*for tyre*) chambre *f* à air.
tuberculosis [tjubə:kju'ləʊsɪs] *n* tuberculose *f*.
tube station ['tju:bsteɪʃən] *n* station *f* de métro.
tubing ['tju:bɪŋ] *n* tubes *mpl* ; **a piece of ~** un tube.
tubular ['tju:bjʊlə*] *a* tubulaire.
TUC *n* (*abbr of* Trades Union Congress) confédération *f* des syndicats britanniques.
tuck [tʌk] *n* (SEWING) pli *m*, rempli *m* // *vt* (*put*) mettre ; **to ~ away** *vt* cacher, ranger ; **to ~ in** *vt* rentrer ; (*child*) border // *vi* (*eat*) manger de bon appétit ; attaquer le repas ; **to ~ up** *vt* (*child*) border ; **~ shop** *n* boutique *f* à provisions (*dans une école*).
Tuesday ['tju:zdɪ] *n* mardi *m*.
tuft [tʌft] *n* touffe *f*.
tug [tʌg] *n* (*ship*) remorqueur *m* // *vt* tirer (*sur*) ; **~-of-war** *n* lutte *f* à la corde.
tuition [tju:'ɪʃən] *n* leçons *fpl*.
tulip ['tju:lɪp] *n* tulipe *f*.
tumble ['tʌmbl] *n* (*fall*) chute *f*, culbute *f* // *vi* tomber, dégringoler ; (*with somersault*) faire une *or* des culbute(s) // *vt* renverser, faire tomber ; **~down** *a*

délabré(e) ; ~ **dryer** n séchoir m (à linge) à air chaud.

tumbler ['tʌmblə*] n verre (droit), gobelet m ; acrobate m/f.

tummy ['tʌmɪ] n (col) ventre m.

tumour ['tju:mə*] n tumeur f.

tumult ['tju:mʌlt] n tumulte m ; ~**uous** [-'mʌltjuəs] a tumultueux(euse).

tuna ['tju:nə] n, pl inv (also: ~ **fish**) thon m.

tune [tju:n] n (melody) air m // vt (MUS) accorder ; (RADIO, TV, AUT) régler, mettre au point ; **to be in/out of** ~ (instrument) être accordé/désaccordé ; (singer) chanter juste/faux ; **to be in/out of** ~ **with** (fig) être en accord/désaccord avec ; **to** ~ **in (to)** (RADIO, TV) se mettre à l'écoute (de) ; **to** ~ **up** vi (musician) accorder son instrument ; ~**ful** a mélodieux(euse) ; ~**r** n (radio set) radio-préamplificateur m ; **piano** ~**r** accordeur de pianos ; ~**r amplifier** n radio-ampli m.

tungsten ['tʌŋstn] n tungstène m.

tunic ['tju:nɪk] n tunique f.

tuning ['tju:nɪŋ] n réglage m ; ~ **fork** n diapason m.

Tunisia [tju:'nɪzɪə] n Tunisie f ; ~**n** a tunisien(ne) // n Tunisien/ne.

tunnel ['tʌnl] n tunnel m ; (in mine) galerie f // vi creuser un tunnel (or une galerie).

tunny ['tʌnɪ] n thon m.

turban ['tə:bən] n turban m.

turbid ['tə:bɪd] a boueux(euse).

turbine ['tə:baɪn] n turbine f.

turbojet ['tə:bəu'dʒɛt] n turboréacteur m.

turbot ['tə:bət] n, pl inv turbot m.

turbulence ['tə:bjuləns] n (AVIAT) turbulence f.

turbulent ['tə:bjulənt] a turbulent(e) ; (sea) agité(e).

tureen [tə'ri:n] n soupière f.

turf [tə:f] n gazon m ; (clod) motte f (de gazon) // vt gazonner ; **the T~** n (le) turf, les courses fpl ; **to** ~ **out** vt (col) jeter ; jeter dehors.

turgid ['tə:dʒɪd] a (speech) pompeux(euse).

Turk [tə:k] n Turc/Turque.

turkey ['tə:kɪ] n dindon m, dinde f.

Turkey ['tə:kɪ] n Turquie f.

Turkish ['tə:kɪʃ] a turc(turque) // n (LING) turc m ; ~ **bath** n bain turc ; ~ **delight** n loukoum m.

turmoil ['tə:mɔɪl] n trouble m, bouleversement m.

turn [tə:n] n tour m ; (in road) tournant m ; (tendency: of mind, events) tournure f ; (performance) numéro m ; (MED) crise f, attaque f // vt tourner ; (collar, steak) retourner ; (milk) faire tourner ; (change): **to** ~ **sth into** changer qch en // vi tourner ; (person: look back) se (re)tourner ; (reverse direction) faire demi-tour ; (change) changer ; (become) devenir ; **to** ~ **into** se changer en ; **a good** ~ un service ; **a bad** ~ un mauvais tour ; **it gave me quite a** ~ ça m'a fait un coup ; **'no left** ~**'** (AUT) 'défense de tourner à gauche' ; **it's your** ~ c'est (à) votre tour ; **in** ~ à son tour ; **à tour de rôle** ; **to take** ~**s** se relayer ; **to take** ~**s at** faire à tour de rôle ; **to** ~ **about** vi faire demi-tour ;

faire un demi-tour ; **to** ~ **away** vi se détourner, tourner la tête ; **to** ~ **back** vi revenir, faire demi-tour ; **to** ~ **down** vt (refuse) rejeter, refuser ; (reduce) baisser ; (fold) rabattre ; **to** ~ **in** vi (col: go to bed) aller se coucher // vt (fold) rentrer ; **to** ~ **off** vi (from road) tourner // vt (light, radio etc) éteindre ; (engine) arrêter ; **to** ~ **on** vt (light, radio etc) allumer ; (engine) mettre en marche ; **to** ~ **out** vt (light, gas) éteindre // vi: **to** ~ **out to be...** s'avérer..., se révéler... ; **to** ~ **up** (person) arriver, se pointer ; (lost object) être retrouvé(e) // vt (collar) remonter ; (increase: sound, volume etc) mettre plus fort ; ~**around** n volte-face f ; ~**ed-up** a (nose) retroussé(e) ; ~**ing** n (in road) tournant m ; ~**ing circle** n rayon m de braquage ; ~**ing point** n (fig) tournant m, moment décisif.

turnip ['tə:nɪp] n navet m.

turnout ['tə:naut] n (nombre m de personnes dans l') assistance f.

turnover ['tə:nəuvə*] n (COMM: amount of money) chiffre m d'affaires ; (: of goods) roulement m ; (CULIN) sorte de chausson.

turnpike ['tə:npaɪk] n (US) autoroute f à péage.

turnstile ['tə:nstaɪl] n tourniquet m (d'entrée).

turntable ['tə:nteɪbl] n (on record player) platine f.

turn-up ['tə:nʌp] n (on trousers) revers m.

turpentine ['tə:pəntam] n (also: **turps**) (essence f de) térébenthine f.

turquoise ['tə:kwɔɪz] n (stone) turquoise f // a turquoise inv.

turret ['tʌrɪt] n tourelle f.

turtle ['tə:tl] n tortue marine ; ~**neck (sweater)** n pullover m à col montant.

tusk [tʌsk] n défense f.

tussle ['tʌsl] n bagarre f, mêlée f.

tutor ['tju:tə*] n (in college) directeur/trice d'études ; (private teacher) précepteur/-trice ; ~**ial** [-'tɔ:rɪəl] n (SCOL) (séance f de) travaux mpl pratiques.

tuxedo [tʌk'si:dəu] n (US) smoking m.

T.V. [ti:'vi:] n (abbr of television) télé f.

twaddle ['twɔdl] n balivernes fpl.

twang [twæŋ] n (of instrument) son vibrant ; (of voice) ton nasillard // vi vibrer // vt (guitar) pincer les cordes de.

tweed [twi:d] n tweed m.

tweezers ['twi:zəz] npl pince f à épiler.

twelfth [twɛlfθ] num douzième ; **T~ Night** n la fête des Rois.

twelve [twɛlv] num douze ; **at** ~ à midi ; (midnight) à minuit.

twentieth ['twɛntɪɪθ] num vingtième.

twenty ['twɛntɪ] num vingt.

twerp [twə:p] n (col) imbécile m/f.

twice [twaɪs] ad deux fois ; ~ **as much** deux fois plus.

twig [twɪg] n brindille f // vt, vi (col) piger.

twilight ['twaɪlaɪt] n crépuscule m.

twill [twɪl] n serge m.

twin [twɪn] a,n jumeau(elle) // vt jumeler.

twine [twaɪn] n ficelle f // vi (plant) s'enrouler ; (road) serpenter.

twinge [twɪndʒ] n (of pain) élancement m ; (of conscience) remords m.

twinkle ['twɪŋkl] n scintillement m; pétillement m // vi scintiller; (eyes) pétiller.
twin town [twɪn'taun] n ville jumelée.
twirl [twəːl] n tournoiement m // vt faire tournoyer // vi tournoyer.
twist [twɪst] n torsion f, tour m; (in wire, flex) tortillon m; (in story) coup m de théâtre // vt tordre; (weave) entortiller; (roll around) enrouler; (fig) déformer // vi s'entortiller; s'enrouler; (road) serpenter.
twit [twɪt] n (col) crétin/e.
twitch [twɪtʃ] n saccade f; (nervous) tic m // vi se convulser; avoir un tic.
two [tuː] num deux; **to put ~ and ~ together** (fig) faire le rapport; **~-door** a (AUT) à deux portes; **~-faced** a (pej: person) faux(fausse); **~fold** ad: **to increase ~fold** doubler; **~-piece (suit)** n (costume m) deux-pièces m inv; **~-piece (swimsuit)** n (maillot m de bain) deux-pièces m inv; **~-seater** n (plane) (avion m) biplace m; (car) voiture f à deux places; **~some** n (people) couple m; **~-way** a (traffic) dans les deux sens.
tycoon [taɪˈkuːn] n: **(business) ~** gros homme d'affaires.
type [taɪp] n (category) genre m, espèce f; (model) modèle m; (example) type m; (TYP) type, caractère m // vt (letter etc) taper (à la machine); **~-cast** a (actor) condamné(e) à toujours jouer le même rôle; **~script** n texte dactylographié; **~writer** n machine f à écrire; **~written** a dactylographié(e).
typhoid ['taɪfɔɪd] n typhoïde f.
typhoon [taɪˈfuːn] n typhon m.
typhus ['taɪfəs] n typhus m.
typical ['tɪpɪkl] a typique, caractéristique.
typify ['tɪpɪfaɪ] vt être caractéristique de.
typing ['taɪpɪŋ] n dactylo(graphie) f; **~ error** n faute f de frappe; **~ paper** n papier m machine.
typist ['taɪpɪst] n dactylo m/f.
tyranny ['tɪrənɪ] n tyrannie f.
tyrant ['taɪərnt] n tyran m.
tyre, tire (US) ['taɪə*] n pneu m; **~ pressure** n pression f (de gonflage).
tzar [zɑː*] n = **tsar**.

U

U-bend ['juːˈbɛnd] n (AUT) coude m, virage m en épingle à cheveux; (in pipe) coude.
ubiquitous [juːˈbɪkwɪtəs] a doué(e) d'ubiquité, omniprésent(e).
udder ['ʌdə*] n pis m, mamelle f.
UFO ['juːfəu] n abbr of unidentified flying object) O.V.N.I. (objet volant non identifié).
ugh [əːh] excl pouah!
ugliness ['ʌglɪnɪs] n laideur f.
ugly ['ʌglɪ] a laid(e), vilain(e); (fig) répugnant(e).
UHF abbr of ultra-high frequency.
UHT (abbr of ultra-heat treated): **~ milk** n lait upérisé or longue conservation.
U.K. n abbr see **united**.
ulcer ['ʌlsə*] n ulcère m; (also: **mouth ~**) aphte f.
Ulster ['ʌlstə*] n Ulster m.

ulterior [ʌlˈtɪərɪə*] a ultérieur(e); **~ motive** n arrière-pensée f.
ultimate ['ʌltɪmət] a ultime, dernier(e); (authority) suprême; **~ly** ad en fin de compte; finalement; par la suite.
ultimatum [ʌltɪˈmeɪtəm] n ultimatum m.
ultraviolet ['ʌltrəˈvaɪəlɪt] a ultraviolet(te).
umbilical [ʌmbɪˈlaɪkl] a: **~ cord** cordon ombilical.
umbrage ['ʌmbrɪdʒ] n: **to take ~** prendre ombrage, se froisser.
umbrella [ʌmˈbrɛlə] n parapluie m; (fig): **under the ~ of** sous les auspices de; chapeauté(e) par.
umpire ['ʌmpaɪə*] n arbitre m // vt arbitrer.
umpteen [ʌmpˈtiːn] a je ne sais combien de; **for the ~th time** pour la nième fois.
UN, UNO abbr see **united**.
unabashed [ʌnəˈbæʃt] a nullement intimidé(e).
unabated [ʌnəˈbeɪtɪd] a non diminué(e).
unable [ʌnˈeɪbl] a: **to be ~** to ne (pas) pouvoir, être dans l'impossibilité de; être incapable de.
unaccompanied [ʌnəˈkʌmpənɪd] a (child, lady) non accompagné(e).
unaccountably [ʌnəˈkauntəblɪ] ad inexplicablement.
unaccustomed [ʌnəˈkʌstəmd] a inaccoutumé(e), inhabituel(le); **to be ~ to** sth ne pas avoir l'habitude de qch.
unadulterated [ʌnəˈdʌltəreɪtɪd] a pur(e), naturel(le).
unaided [ʌnˈeɪdɪd] a sans aide, tout(e) seul(e).
unanimity [juːnəˈnɪmɪtɪ] n unanimité f.
unanimous [juːˈnænɪməs] a unanime; **~ly** ad à l'unanimité.
unashamed [ʌnəˈʃeɪmd] a sans honte; impudent(e).
unassuming [ʌnəˈsjuːmɪŋ] a modeste, sans prétentions.
unattached [ʌnəˈtætʃt] a libre, sans attaches.
unattended [ʌnəˈtɛndɪd] a (car, child, luggage) sans surveillance.
unattractive [ʌnəˈtræktɪv] a peu attrayant(e).
unauthorized [ʌnˈɔːθəraɪzd] a non autorisé(e), sans autorisation.
unavoidable [ʌnəˈvɔɪdəbl] a inévitable.
unaware [ʌnəˈwɛə*] a: **to be ~ of** ignorer, ne pas savoir, être inconscient(e) de; **~s** ad à l'improviste, au dépourvu.
unbalanced [ʌnˈbælənst] a déséquilibré(e).
unbearable [ʌnˈbɛərəbl] a insupportable.
unbeatable [ʌnˈbiːtəbl] a imbattable.
unbeaten [ʌnˈbiːtn] a invaincu(e).
unbecoming [ʌnbɪˈkʌmɪŋ] a malséant(e), inconvenant(e).
unbeknown(st) [ʌnbɪˈnəun(st)] ad: **~ to** à l'insu de.
unbelief [ʌnbɪˈliːf] n incrédulité f.
unbelievable [ʌnbɪˈliːvəbl] a incroyable.
unbend [ʌnˈbɛnd] vb (irg) vi se détendre // vt (wire) redresser, détordre.
unbounded [ʌnˈbaundɪd] a sans bornes, illimité(e).

unbreakable [ʌn'breɪkəbl] a incassable.
unbridled [ʌn'braɪdld] a débridé(e), déchaîné(e).
unbroken [ʌn'brəukən] a intact(e); continu(e).
unburden [ʌn'bə:dn] vt: **to ~ o.s.** s'épancher, se livrer.
unbutton [ʌn'bʌtn] vt déboutonner.
uncalled-for [ʌn'kɔ:ldfɔ:*] a déplacé(e), injustifié(e).
uncanny [ʌn'kænɪ] a étrange, troublant(e).
unceasing [ʌn'si:sɪŋ] a incessant(e), continu(e).
uncertain [ʌn'sə:tn] a incertain(e); mal assuré(e); **~ty** n incertitude f, doutes mpl.
unchanged [ʌn'tʃeɪndʒd] a inchangé(e).
uncharitable [ʌn'tʃærɪtəbl] a peu charitable.
uncharted [ʌn'tʃɑ:tɪd] a inexploré(e).
unchecked [ʌn'tʃɛkt] a non réprimé(e).
uncle ['ʌŋkl] n oncle m.
uncomfortable [ʌn'kʌmfətəbl] a inconfortable; (uneasy) mal à l'aise, gêné(e); désagréable.
uncommon [ʌn'kɔmən] a rare, singulier(ère), peu commun(e).
uncompromising [ʌn'kɔmprəmaɪzɪŋ] a intransigeant(e), inflexible.
unconditional [ʌnkən'dɪʃənl] a sans conditions.
uncongenial [ʌnkən'dʒi:nɪəl] a peu agréable.
unconscious [ʌn'kɔnʃəs] a sans connaissance, évanoui(e); (unaware) inconscient(e) // n: **the ~** l'inconscient m; **~ly** ad inconsciemment.
uncontrollable [ʌnkən'trəuləbl] a irrépressible; indiscipliné(e).
uncork [ʌn'kɔ:k] vt déboucher.
uncouth [ʌn'ku:θ] a grossier(ère), fruste.
uncover [ʌn'kʌvə*] vt découvrir.
unctuous ['ʌŋktjuəs] a onctueux(euse), mielleux(euse).
undaunted [ʌn'dɔ:ntɪd] a non intimidé(e), inébranlable.
undecided [ʌndɪ'saɪdd] a indécis(e), irrésolu(e).
undeniable [ʌndɪ'naɪəbl] a indéniable, incontestable.
under ['ʌndə*] prep sous; (less than) (de) moins de; au-dessous de; (according to) selon, en vertu de // ad au-dessous; en dessous; **from ~ sth** de dessous or de sous qch; **~ there** là-dessous; **~ repair** en (cours de) réparation.
under... ['ʌndə*] prefix sous-; **~-age** a qui n'a pas l'âge réglementaire; **~carriage**, **~cart** n train m d'atterrissage; **~clothes** npl sous-vêtements mpl; (women's only) dessous mpl; **~coat** n (paint) couche f de fond; **~cover** a secret(ète), clandestin(e); **~current** n courant sous-jacent; **~cut** n (CULIN) (morceau m de) filet m // vt irg vendre moins cher que; **~developed** a sous-développé(e); **~dog** n opprimé m; **~done** a (CULIN) saignant(e); (pej) pas assez cuit(e); **~estimate** vt sous-estimer, mésestimer; **~exposed** a (PHOT) sous-exposé(e); **~fed** a sous-alimenté(e); **~foot** ad sous les pieds; **~go** vt irg subir; (treatment) suivre; **~graduate** n

étudiant/e (qui prépare la licence); **~ground** n métro m; (POL) clandestinité f; **~growth** n broussailles fpl, sous-bois m; **~hand(ed)** a (fig) sournois(e), en dessous; **~lie** vt irg être à la base de; **~line** vt souligner; **~ling** ['ʌndəlɪŋ] n (pej) sous-fifre m, subalterne m; **~mine** vt saper, miner; **~neath** [ʌndə'ni:θ] ad (en) dessous // prep sous, au-dessous de; **~paid** a sous-payé(e); **~pants** npl (Brit) caleçon m, slip m; **~pass** n passage souterrain; (on motorway) passage inférieur; **~play** vt minimiser; **~price** vt vendre à un prix trop bas; **~privileged** a défavorisé(e), économiquement faible; **~rate** vt sous-estimer, mésestimer; **~shirt** n (US) tricot m de corps; **~shorts** npl (US) caleçon m, slip m; **~side** n dessous m; **~skirt** n jupon m.
understand [ʌndə'stænd] vb (irg: like stand) vt, vi comprendre; **I ~ that...** je me suis laissé dire que...; je crois comprendre que...; **~able** a compréhensible; **~ing** a compréhensif(ive) // n compréhension f; (agreement) accord m.
understatement [ʌndə'steɪtmənt] n: that's an **~** c'est (bien) peu dire, le terme est faible.
understood [ʌndə'stud] pt, pp of **understand** // a entendu(e); (implied) sous-entendu(e).
understudy ['ʌndəstʌdɪ] n doublure f.
undertake [ʌndə'teɪk] vt irg entreprendre; se charger de.
undertaker ['ʌndəteɪkə*] n entrepreneur m des pompes funèbres, croque-mort m.
undertaking [ʌndə'teɪkɪŋ] n entreprise f; (promise) promesse f.
underwater [ʌndə'wɔ:tə*] ad sous l'eau // a sous-marin(e).
underwear ['ʌndəwɛə*] n sous-vêtements mpl; (women's only) dessous mpl.
underweight [ʌndə'weɪt] a d'un poids insuffisant; (person) (trop) maigre.
underworld ['ʌndəwə:ld] n (of crime) milieu m, pègre f.
underwriter ['ʌndəraɪtə*] n (INSURANCE) souscripteur m.
undesirable [ʌndɪ'zaɪərəbl] a peu souhaitable; indésirable.
undies ['ʌndɪz] npl (col) dessous mpl, lingerie f.
undisputed [ʌndɪ'spju:tɪd] a incontesté(e).
undistinguished [ʌndɪs'tɪŋgwɪʃt] a médiocre, quelconque.
undo [ʌn'du:] vt irg défaire; **~ing** n ruine f, perte f.
undoubted [ʌn'dautɪd] a indubitable, certain(e); **~ly** ad sans aucun doute.
undress [ʌn'drɛs] vi se déshabiller.
undue [ʌn'dju:] a indu(e), excessif(ive).
undulating ['ʌndjuleɪtɪŋ] a ondoyant(e), onduleux(euse).
unduly [ʌn'dju:lɪ] ad trop, excessivement.
unearth [ʌn'ə:θ] vt déterrer; (fig) dénicher.
unearthly [ʌn'ə:θlɪ] a surnaturel(le); (hour) indu(e), impossible.
uneasy [ʌn'i:zɪ] a mal à l'aise, gêné(e); (worried) inquiet(ète).

uneconomic(al) ['ʌniːkə'nɔmɪk(l)] a peu économique ; peu rentable.

uneducated [ʌn'ɛdjukeɪtɪd] a sans éducation.

unemployed [ʌnɪm'plɔɪd] a sans travail, en chômage // n: **the ~** les chômeurs mpl.

unemployment [ʌnɪm'plɔɪmənt] n chômage m.

unending [ʌn'ɛndɪŋ] a interminable.

unenviable [ʌn'ɛnvɪəbl] a peu enviable.

unerring [ʌn'ə:rɪŋ] a infaillible, sûr(e).

uneven [ʌn'iːvn] a inégal(e) ; irrégulier(ère).

unexpected [ʌnɪk'spɛktɪd] a inattendu(e), imprévu(e).

unexploded [ʌnɪk'spləʊdɪd] a non explosé(e) or éclaté(e).

unfailing [ʌn'feɪlɪŋ] a inépuisable ; infaillible.

unfair [ʌn'fɛə*] a: **~ (to)** injuste (envers) ; **~ly** ad injustement.

unfaithful [ʌn'feɪθful] a infidèle.

unfamiliar [ʌnfə'mɪlɪə*] a étrange, inconnu(e).

unfasten [ʌn'fɑːsn] vt défaire ; détacher.

unfathomable [ʌn'fæðəməbl] a insondable.

unfavourable, unfavorable (US) [ʌn'feɪvərəbl] a défavorable.

unfeeling [ʌn'fiːlɪŋ] a insensible, dur(e).

unfinished [ʌn'fɪnɪʃt] a inachevé(e).

unfit [ʌn'fɪt] a en mauvaise santé ; pas en forme ; (incompetent): **~ (for)** impropre (à) ; (work, service) inapte (à).

unflagging [ʌn'flægɪŋ] a infatigable, inlassable.

unflappable [ʌn'flæpəbl] a imperturbable.

unflinching [ʌn'flɪntʃɪŋ] a stoïque.

unfold [ʌn'fəʊld] vt déplier ; (fig) révéler, exposer // vi se dérouler.

unforeseen [ʌnfɔː'siːn] a imprévu(e).

unforgivable [ʌnfə'gɪvəbl] a impardonnable.

unfortunate [ʌn'fɔːtʃnət] a malheureux-(euse) ; (event, remark) malencontreux-(euse) ; **~ly** ad malheureusement.

unfounded [ʌn'faʊndɪd] a sans fondement.

unfriendly [ʌn'frɛndlɪ] a froid(e), inamical(e).

unfurnished [ʌn'fɜːnɪʃt] a non meublé(e).

ungainly [ʌn'geɪnlɪ] a gauche, dégingandé(e).

ungodly [ʌn'gɔdlɪ] a impie ; **at an ~ hour** à une heure indue.

unguarded [ʌn'gɑːdɪd] a: **~ moment** n moment m d'inattention.

unhappiness [ʌn'hæpɪnɪs] n tristesse f, peine f.

unhappy [ʌn'hæpɪ] a triste, malheureux(euse) ; **~ with** (arrangements etc) mécontent(e) de, peu satisfait(e) de.

unharmed [ʌn'hɑːmd] a indemne, sain(e) et sauf(sauve).

unhealthy [ʌn'hɛlθɪ] a (gen) malsain(e) ; (person) maladif(ive).

unheard-of [ʌn'hə:dɔv] a inouï(e), sans précédent.

unhook [ʌn'hʊk] vt décrocher ; dégrafer.

unhurt [ʌn'hə:t] a indemne, sain(e) et sauf(sauve).

unicorn ['juːnɪkɔːn] n licorne f.

unidentified [ʌnaɪ'dɛntɪfaɪd] a non identifié(e).

uniform ['juːnɪfɔːm] n uniforme m // a uniforme ; **~ity** [-'fɔːmɪtɪ] n uniformité f.

unify ['juːnɪfaɪ] vt unifier.

unilateral [juːnɪ'lætərəl] a unilatéral(e).

unimaginable [ʌnɪ'mædʒɪnəbl] a inimaginable, inconcevable.

unimpaired [ʌnɪm'pɛəd] a intact(e).

uninhibited [ʌnɪn'hɪbɪtɪd] a sans inhibitions ; sans retenue.

unintentional [ʌnɪn'tɛnʃənəl] a involontaire.

union ['juːnjən] n union f; (also: **trade ~**) syndicat m // cpd du syndicat, syndical(e) ; **U~ Jack** n drapeau du Royaume-Uni.

unique [juːˈniːk] a unique.

unison ['juːnɪsn] n: **in ~** à l'unisson, en chœur.

unit ['juːnɪt] n unité f; (section: of furniture etc) élément m, bloc m ; (team, squad) groupe m, service m.

unite [juːˈnaɪt] vt unir // vi s'unir ; **~d** uni(e) ; unifié(e) ; (efforts) conjugué(e) ; **U~d Kingdom (U.K.)** n Royaume-Uni m ; **U~d Nations (Organization) (UN, UNO)** n (Organisation f des) Nations unies (O.N.U.) ; **U~d States (of America) (US, USA)** n États-Unis mpl.

unit trust ['juːnɪttrʌst] n (Brit) société f d'investissement.

unity ['juːnɪtɪ] n unité f.

universal [juːnɪ'vəːsl] a universel(le).

universe ['juːnɪvəːs] n univers m.

university [juːnɪ'vəːsɪtɪ] n université f.

unjust [ʌn'dʒʌst] a injuste.

unkempt [ʌn'kɛmpt] a mal tenu(e), débraillé(e) ; mal peigné(e).

unkind [ʌn'kaɪnd] a peu gentil(le), méchant(e).

unknown [ʌn'nəʊn] a inconnu(e).

unladen [ʌn'leɪdn] a (ship, weight) à vide.

unlawful [ʌn'lɔːful] a illégal(e).

unleash [ʌn'liːʃ] vt détacher ; (fig) déchaîner, déclencher.

unleavened [ʌn'lɛvnd] a sans levain.

unless [ʌn'lɛs] cj: **~ he leaves** à moins qu'il (ne) parte ; **~ we leave** à moins de partir, à moins que nous (ne) partions ; **~ otherwise stated** sauf indication contraire.

unlicensed [ʌn'laɪsənst] a non patenté(e) pour la vente des spiritueux.

unlike [ʌn'laɪk] a dissemblable, différent(e) // prep à la différence de, contrairement à.

unlikely [ʌn'laɪklɪ] a improbable ; invraisemblable.

unlimited [ʌn'lɪmɪtɪd] a illimité(e).

unload [ʌn'ləʊd] vt décharger.

unlock [ʌn'lɔk] vt ouvrir.

unlucky [ʌn'lʌkɪ] a malchanceux(euse) ; (object, number) qui porte malheur.

unmannerly [ʌn'mænəlɪ] a mal élevé(e), impoli(e).

unmarried [ʌnˈmærɪd] *a* célibataire.
unmask [ʌnˈmɑːsk] *vt* démasquer.
unmistakable [ʌnmɪsˈteɪkəbl] *a* indubitable; qu'on ne peut pas ne pas reconnaître.
unmitigated [ʌnˈmɪtɪgeɪtɪd] *a* non mitigé(e), absolu(e), pur(e).
unnatural [ʌnˈnætʃrəl] *a* non naturel(le); contre nature.
unnecessary [ʌnˈnɛsəsərɪ] *a* inutile, superflu(e).
unnerve [ʌnˈnəːv] *vt* faire perdre son sang-froid à.
UNO [juːˈnəu] *n see* **united**.
unobtainable [ʌnəbˈteɪnəbl] *a* (*TEL*) impossible à obtenir.
unoccupied [ʌnˈɔkjupaɪd] *a* (*seat etc*) libre.
unofficial [ʌnəˈfɪʃl] *a* non officiel(le); (*strike*) ≈ non sanctionné(e) par la centrale.
unorthodox [ʌnˈɔːθədɔks] *a* peu orthodoxe.
unpack [ʌnˈpæk] *vi* défaire sa valise, déballer ses affaires.
unpalatable [ʌnˈpælətəbl] *a* (*truth*) désagréable (à entendre).
unparalleled [ʌnˈpærəleld] *a* incomparable, sans égal.
unpleasant [ʌnˈplɛznt] *a* déplaisant(e), désagréable.
unplug [ʌnˈplʌg] *vt* débrancher.
unpopular [ʌnˈpɔpjulə*] *a* impopulaire.
unprecedented [ʌnˈprɛsɪdəntɪd] *a* sans précédent.
unpredictable [ʌnprɪˈdɪktəbl] *a* imprévisible.
unprepossessing [ʌnpriːpəˈzɛsɪŋ] *a* peu avenant(e).
unpretentious [ʌnprɪˈtɛnʃəs] *a* sans prétention(s).
unqualified [ʌnˈkwɔlɪfaɪd] *a* (*teacher*) non diplômé(e), sans titres; (*success*) sans réserve, total(e).
unravel [ʌnˈrævl] *vt* démêler.
unreal [ʌnˈrɪəl] *a* irréel(le).
unreasonable [ʌnˈriːznəbl] *a* qui n'est pas raisonnable.
unrelated [ʌnrɪˈleɪtɪd] *a* sans rapport; sans lien de parenté.
unrelenting [ʌnrɪˈlɛntɪŋ] *a* implacable; acharné(e).
unreliable [ʌnrɪˈlaɪəbl] *a* sur qui (*or* quoi) on ne peut pas compter, peu fiable.
unrelieved [ʌnrɪˈliːvd] *a* (*monotony*) constant(e), uniforme.
unremitting [ʌnrɪˈmɪtɪŋ] *a* inlassable, infatigable, acharné(e).
unrepeatable [ʌnrɪˈpiːtəbl] *a* (*offer*) unique, exceptionnel(le).
unrepentant [ʌnrɪˈpɛntənt] *a* impénitent(e).
unrest [ʌnˈrɛst] *n* agitation *f*, troubles *mpl*.
unroll [ʌnˈrəul] *vt* dérouler.
unruly [ʌnˈruːlɪ] *a* indiscipliné(e).
unsafe [ʌnˈseɪf] *a* dangereux(euse), hasardeux(euse).
unsaid [ʌnˈsɛd] *a*: **to leave sth** ~ passer qch sous silence.

unsatisfactory [ˈʌnsætɪsˈfæktərɪ] *a* qui laisse à désirer.
unsavoury, unsavory (*US*) [ʌnˈseɪvərɪ] *a* (*fig*) peu recommandable, répugnant(e).
unscathed [ʌnˈskeɪðd] *a* indemne.
unscrew [ʌnˈskruː] *vt* dévisser.
unscrupulous [ʌnˈskruːpjuləs] *a* sans scrupules, indélicat(e).
unseemly [ʌnˈsiːmlɪ] *a* inconvenant(e).
unsettled [ʌnˈsɛtld] *a* perturbé(e); instable; incertain(e).
unshaven [ʌnˈʃeɪvn] *a* non *or* mal rasé(e).
unsightly [ʌnˈsaɪtlɪ] *a* disgracieux(euse), laid(e).
unskilled [ʌnˈskɪld] *a*: ~ **worker** *n* manœuvre *m*.
unsophisticated [ʌnsəˈfɪstɪkeɪtɪd] *a* simple, naturel(le).
unspeakable [ʌnˈspiːkəbl] *a* indicible; (*bad*) innommable.
unsteady [ʌnˈstɛdɪ] *a* mal assuré(e), chancelant(e), instable.
unstuck [ʌnˈstʌk] *a*: **to come** ~ se décoller; (*fig*) faire fiasco.
unsuccessful [ʌnsəkˈsɛsful] *a* (*attempt*) infructueux(euse); (*writer, proposal*) qui n'a pas de succès; (*marriage*) malheureux(euse), qui ne réussit pas; **to be** ~ (*in attempting sth*) ne pas réussir; ne pas avoir de succès; (*application*) ne pas être retenu(e); ~**ly** *ad* en vain.
unsuitable [ʌnˈsuːtəbl] *a* qui ne convient pas, peu approprié(e); inopportun(e).
unsuspecting [ʌnsəˈspɛktɪŋ] *a* qui ne se méfie pas.
unswerving [ʌnˈswəːvɪŋ] *a* inébranlable.
untangle [ʌnˈtæŋgl] *vt* démêler, débrouiller.
untapped [ʌnˈtæpt] *a* (*resources*) inexploité(e).
unthinkable [ʌnˈθɪŋkəbl] *a* impensable, inconcevable.
untidy [ʌnˈtaɪdɪ] *a* (*room*) en désordre; (*appearance*) désordonné(e), débraillé(e); (*person*) sans ordre, désordonné; débraillé; (*work*) peu soigné(e).
untie [ʌnˈtaɪ] *vt* (*knot, parcel*) défaire; (*prisoner, dog*) détacher.
until [ənˈtɪl] *prep* jusqu'à; (*after negative*) avant // *cj* jusqu'à ce que + *sub*, en attendant que + *sub*; (*in past, after negative*) avant que + *sub*; ~ **then** jusque-là.
untimely [ʌnˈtaɪmlɪ] *a* inopportun(e); (*death*) prématuré(e).
untold [ʌnˈtəuld] *a* incalculable; indescriptible.
untoward [ʌntəˈwɔːd] *a* fâcheux (euse), malencontreux(euse).
untranslatable [ʌntrænzˈleɪtəbl] *a* intraduisible.
unused [ʌnˈjuːzd] *a* neuf(neuve).
unusual [ʌnˈjuːʒuəl] *a* insolite, exceptionnel(le), rare.
unveil [ʌnˈveɪl] *vt* dévoiler.
unwavering [ʌnˈweɪvərɪŋ] *a* inébranlable.
unwell [ʌnˈwɛl] *a* indisposé(e), souffrant(e).
unwieldy [ʌnˈwiːldɪ] *a* difficile à manier.
unwilling [ʌnˈwɪlɪŋ] *a*: **to be** ~ **to do** ne pas vouloir faire; ~**ly** *ad* à contrecœur, contre son gré.

unwind [ʌn'waind] *vb* (*irg*) *vt* dérouler // *vi* (*relax*) se détendre.
unwitting [ʌn'witiŋ] *a* involontaire.
unworthy [ʌn'wə:ði] *a* indigne.
unwrap [ʌn'ræp] *vt* défaire; ouvrir.
unwritten [ʌn'ritn] *a* (*agreement*) tacite.
up [ʌp] *prep*: **to go/be ~** sth monter/être sur qch // *ad* en haut; en l'air; **~ there** là-haut; **~ above** au-dessus; **~ to** jusqu'à; **to be ~** (*out of bed*) être levé(e), être debout *inv*; **it is ~ to you** c'est à vous de décider, ça ne tient qu'à vous; **what is he ~ to?** qu'est-ce qu'il peut bien faire?; **he is not ~ to it** il n'en est pas capable; **~-and-coming** *a* plein d'avenir *or* de promesses; **~s and downs** *npl* (*fig*) hauts *mpl* et bas *mpl*.
upbringing ['ʌpbriŋiŋ] *n* éducation *f*.
update [ʌp'deit] *vt* mettre à jour.
upend [ʌp'ɛnd] *vt* mettre debout.
upgrade [ʌp'greid] *vt* promouvoir; (*job*) revaloriser.
upheaval [ʌp'hi:vl] *n* bouleversement *m*; branle-bas *m*; crise *f*.
uphill [ʌp'hil] *a* qui monte; (*fig: task*) difficile, pénible // *ad*: **to go ~** monter.
uphold [ʌp'həuld] *vt* *irg* maintenir; soutenir.
upholstery [ʌp'həulstəri] *n* rembourrage *m*; (*of car*) garniture *f*.
upkeep ['ʌpki:p] *n* entretien *m*.
upon [ə'pɔn] *prep* sur.
upper ['ʌpə*] *a* supérieur(e); du dessus // *n* (*of shoe*) empeigne *f*; **the ~ class** ≈ la haute bourgeoisie; **~-class** *a* ≈ bourgeois(e); **~most** *a* le(la) plus haut(e); en dessus.
upright ['ʌprait] *a* droit(e); vertical(e); (*fig*) droit, honnête // *n* montant *m*.
uprising ['ʌpraiziŋ] *n* soulèvement *m*, insurrection *f*.
uproar ['ʌprɔ:*] *n* tumulte *m*, vacarme *m*.
uproot [ʌp'ru:t] *vt* déraciner.
upset *n* ['ʌpsɛt] dérangement *m* // *vt* [ʌp'sɛt] (*irg: like* **set**) (*glass etc*) renverser; (*plan*) déranger; (*person: offend*) contrarier; (: *grieve*) faire de la peine à; bouleverser // *a* [ʌp'sɛt] contrarié(e); peiné(e); (*stomach*) détraqué(e), dérangé(e).
upshot ['ʌpʃɔt] *n* résultat *m*.
upside ['ʌpsaid]: **~-down** *ad* à l'envers.
upstairs [ʌp'stɛəz] *ad* en haut // *a* (*room*) du dessus, d'en haut // *n*: **there's no ~** il n'y a pas d'étage.
upstart ['ʌpstɑ:t] *n* parvenu/e.
upstream [ʌp'stri:m] *ad* en amont.
uptake ['ʌpteik] *n*: **he is quick/slow on the ~** il comprend vite/est lent à comprendre.
up-to-date ['ʌptə'deit] *a* moderne; très récent(e).
upturn ['ʌptə:n] *n* (*in luck*) retournement *m*.
upward ['ʌpwəd] *a* ascendant(e); vers le haut; **~(s)** *ad* vers le haut; **and ~(s)** et plus, et au-dessus.
uranium [juə'reiniəm] *n* uranium *m*.
urban ['ə:bən] *a* urbain(e).
urbane [ə:'bein] *a* urbain(e), courtois(e).

urchin ['ə:tʃin] *n* gosse *m*, garnement *m*; **sea ~** *n* oursin *m*.
urge [ə:dʒ] *n* besoin *m*; envie *f*; forte envie, désir *m* // *vt*: **to ~ sb to do** exhorter qn à faire, pousser qn à faire; recommander vivement à qn de faire; **to ~ on** *vt* aiguillonner, talonner.
urgency ['ə:dʒənsi] *n* urgence *f*; (*of tone*) insistance *f*.
urgent ['ə:dʒənt] *a* urgent(e); **~ly** *ad* d'urgence, sans délai.
urinal ['juərinl] *n* urinoir *m*.
urinate ['juərineit] *vi* uriner.
urn [ə:n] *n* urne *f*; (*also*: **tea ~**) fontaine *f* à thé.
us [ʌs] *pronoun* nous.
US, USA *n abbr see* **united**.
usage ['ju:zidʒ] *n* usage *m*.
use *n* [ju:s] emploi *m*, utilisation *f*; usage *m* // *vt* [ju:z] se servir de, utiliser, employer; **she ~d to do it** elle le faisait (autrefois), elle avait coutume de le faire; **in ~** en usage; **out of ~** hors d'usage; **it's no ~** ça ne sert à rien; **to have the ~ of** avoir l'usage de; **to be ~d to** avoir l'habitude de, être habitué(e) à; **to ~ up** *vt* finir, épuiser; consommer; **~d** *a* (*car*) d'occasion; **~ful** *a* utile; **~fulness** *n* utilité *f*; **~less** *a* inutile; **~r** *n* utilisateur/trice, usager *m*.
usher ['ʌʃə*] *n* placeur *m*; **~ette** [-'rɛt] *n* (*in cinema*) ouvreuse *f*.
USSR *n*: **the ~** l'URSS *f*.
usual ['ju:ʒuəl] *a* habituel(le); **as ~** comme d'habitude; **~ly** *ad* d'habitude, d'ordinaire.
usurer ['ju:ʒərə*] *n* usurier/ère.
usurp [ju:'zə:p] *vt* usurper.
utensil [ju:'tɛnsl] *n* ustensile *m*.
uterus ['ju:tərəs] *n* utérus *m*.
utilitarian [ju:tili'tɛəriən] *a* utilitaire.
utility [ju:'tiliti] *n* utilité *f*; (*also*: **public ~**) service public.
utilization [ju:tilai'zeiʃn] *n* utilisation *f*.
utilize ['ju:tilaiz] *vt* utiliser; exploiter.
utmost ['ʌtməust] *a* extrême, le(la) plus grand(e) // *n*: **to do one's ~** faire tout son possible.
utter ['ʌtə*] *a* total(e), complet(ète) // *vt* prononcer, proférer; émettre; **~ance** *n* paroles *fpl*; **~ly** *ad* complètement, totalement.
U-turn ['ju:'tə:n] *n* demi-tour *m*.

V

v. *abbr of* **verse**, **versus**, **volt**; (*abbr of* **vide**) voir.
vacancy ['veikənsi] *n* (*job*) poste vacant; (*room*) chambre *f* disponible; **'no vacancies'** 'complet'.
vacant ['veikənt] *a* (*post*) vacant(e); (*seat etc*) libre, disponible; (*expression*) distrait(e).
vacate [və'keit] *vt* quitter.
vacation [və'keiʃən] *n* vacances *fpl*; **~ course** *n* cours *mpl* de vacances.
vaccinate ['væksineit] *vt* vacciner; **vaccination** [-'neiʃən] *n* vaccination *f*.
vaccine ['væksi:n] *n* vaccin *m*.

vacuum ['vækjum] n vide m; **~ cleaner** n aspirateur m; **~ flask** n bouteille f thermos ℞.

vagary ['veɪgərɪ] n caprice m.

vagina [və'dʒaɪnə] n vagin m.

vagrant ['veɪgrnt] n vagabond/e, mendiant/e.

vague [veɪg] a vague, imprécis(e); (blurred: photo, memory) flou(e); **~ly** ad vaguement.

vain [veɪn] a (useless) vain(e); (conceited) vaniteux(euse); **in ~** en vain.

valance ['væləns] n (of bed) tour m de lit.

valentine ['væləntaɪn] n (also: **~ card**) carte f de la Saint-Valentin.

valeting ['vælɪtɪŋ] a: **~ service** n pressing m.

valiant ['vælɪənt] a vaillant(e), courageux(euse).

valid ['vælɪd] a valide, valable; (excuse) valable; **~ity** [-'lɪdɪtɪ] n validité f.

valise [və'liːz] n sac m de voyage.

valley ['vælɪ] n vallée f.

valuable ['væljuəbl] a (jewel) de grande valeur; (time) précieux (euse); **~s** npl objets mpl de valeur.

valuation [vælju'eɪʃən] n évaluation f, expertise f.

value ['væljuː] n valeur f // vt (fix price) évaluer, expertiser; (cherish) tenir à; **~ added tax (VAT)** n taxe f à la valeur ajoutée (T.V.A.); **~d** a (appreciated) estimé(e); **~r** n expert m (en estimations).

valve [vælv] n (in machine) soupape f; (on tyre) valve f; (in radio) lampe f.

van [væn] n (AUT) camionnette f; (RAIL) fourgon m.

vandal ['vændl] n vandale m/f; **~ism** n vandalisme m; **~ize** vt saccager.

vanguard ['vængɑːd] n avant-garde m.

vanilla [və'nɪlə] n vanille f // cpd (ice cream) à la vanille.

vanish ['vænɪʃ] vi disparaître.

vanity ['vænɪtɪ] n vanité f; **~ case** n sac m de toilette.

vantage ['vɑːntɪdʒ] n: **~ point** bonne position.

vapour, vapor (US) ['veɪpə*] n vapeur f; (on window) buée f.

variable ['vɛərɪəbl] a variable; (mood) changeant(e).

variance ['vɛərɪəns] n: **to be at ~ (with)** être en désaccord (avec); (facts) être en contradiction (avec).

variant ['vɛərɪənt] n variante f.

variation [vɛərɪ'eɪʃən] n variation f; (in opinion) changement m.

varicose ['værɪkəus] a: **~ veins** npl varices fpl.

varied ['vɛərɪd] a varié(e), divers(e).

variety [və'raɪətɪ] n variété f; (quantity) nombre m, quantité f; **~ show** n (spectacle m de) variétés fpl.

various ['vɛərɪəs] a divers(e), différent(e); (several) divers, plusieurs.

varnish ['vɑːnɪʃ] n vernis m // vt vernir.

vary ['vɛərɪ] vt, vi varier, changer; **~ing** a variable.

vase [vɑːz] n vase m.

vast [vɑːst] a vaste, immense; (amount,

success) énorme; **~ly** ad infiniment, extrêmement; **~ness** n immensité f.

vat [væt] n cuve f.

VAT [væt] n abbr see **value**.

Vatican ['vætɪkən] n: **the ~** le Vatican.

vault [vɔːlt] n (of roof) voûte f; (tomb) caveau m; (in bank) salle f des coffres; chambre forte; (jump) saut m // vt (also: **~ over**) sauter (d'un bond).

vaunted ['vɔːntɪd] a: **much-~** tant célèbre(e).

VD n abbr see **venereal**.

veal [viːl] n veau m.

veer [vɪə*] vi tourner, virer.

vegetable ['vɛdʒtəbl] n légume m // a végétal(e); **~ garden** n potager m.

vegetarian [vɛdʒɪ'tɛərɪən] a, n végétarien(ne).

vegetate ['vɛdʒɪteɪt] vi végéter.

vegetation [vɛdʒɪ'teɪʃən] n végétation f.

vehemence ['viːɪməns] n véhémence f, violence f.

vehicle ['viːɪkl] n véhicule m.

vehicular [vɪ'hɪkjulə*] a: **'no ~ traffic'** 'interdit à tout véhicule'.

veil [veɪl] n voile m // vt voiler.

vein [veɪn] n veine f; (on leaf) nervure f; (fig: mood) esprit m.

velocity [vɪ'lɔsɪtɪ] n vélocité f.

velvet ['vɛlvɪt] n velours m.

vending machine ['vɛndɪŋməʃiːn] n distributeur m automatique.

vendor ['vɛndə*] n vendeur/euse.

veneer [və'nɪə*] n placage m de bois; (fig) vernis m.

venerable ['vɛnərəbl] a vénérable.

venereal [vɪ'nɪərɪəl] a: **~ disease (VD)** n maladie vénérienne.

Venetian [vɪ'niːʃən] a: **~ blind** n store vénitien.

Venezuela [vɛnɛ'zweɪlə] n Venezuela m; **~n** a vénézuélien(ne) // n Vénézuélien(ne).

vengeance ['vɛndʒəns] n vengeance f; **with a ~** (fig) vraiment, pour de bon.

venison ['vɛnɪsn] n venaison f.

venom ['vɛnəm] n venin m; **~ous** a venimeux(euse).

vent [vɛnt] n orifice m, conduit m; (in dress, jacket) fente f // vt (fig: one's feelings) donner libre cours à.

ventilate ['vɛntɪleɪt] vt (room) ventiler, aérer; **ventilation** [-'leɪʃən] n ventilation f, aération f; **ventilator** n ventilateur m.

ventriloquist [vɛn'trɪləkwɪst] n ventriloque m/f.

venture ['vɛntʃə*] n entreprise f // vt risquer, hasarder // vi s'aventurer, se risquer.

venue ['vɛnjuː] n lieu m de rendez-vous or rencontre; (SPORT) lieu de la rencontre.

veranda(h) [və'rændə] n véranda f.

verb [vəːb] n verbe m; **~al** a verbal(e); (translation) littéral(e).

verbatim [vəː'beɪtɪm] a, ad mot pour mot.

verbose [vəː'bəus] a verbeux(euse).

verdict ['vəːdɪkt] n verdict m.

verge [vəːdʒ] n bord m; **'soft ~s'** 'accotements non stabilisés'; **on the ~ of doing** sur le point de faire; **to ~ on** vt fus approcher de.

verger ['vɜːdʒə*] n (RÉL) bedeau m.

verification [vɛrɪfɪ'keɪʃən] n vérification f.

verify ['vɛrɪfaɪ] vt vérifier.

vermin ['vɜːmɪn] npl animaux mpl nuisibles ; (insects) vermine f.

vermouth ['vɜːməθ] n vermouth m.

vernacular [və'nækjulə*] n langue f vernaculaire, dialecte m.

versatile ['vɜːsətaɪl] a (person) aux talents variés ; (machine, tool etc) aux usages variés ; aux applications variées.

verse [vɜːs] n vers mpl ; (stanza) strophe f ; (in bible) verset m.

versed [vɜːst] a: (well-)~ in versé(e) dans.

version ['vɜːʃən] n version f.

versus ['vɜːsəs] prep contre.

vertebra, pl ~e ['vɜːtɪbrə, -briː] n vertèbre f.

vertebrate ['vɜːtɪbrɪt] n vertébré m.

vertical ['vɜːtɪkl] a vertical(e) // n verticale f ; ~ly ad verticalement.

vertigo ['vɜːtɪgəu] n vertige m.

verve [vɜːv] n brio m ; enthousiasme m.

very ['vɛrɪ] ad très // a: the ~ book which le livre même que ; at the ~ end tout à la fin ; the ~ last le tout dernier ; at the ~ least au moins ; ~ much beaucoup.

vespers ['vɛspəz] npl vêpres fpl.

vessel ['vɛsl] n (ANAT, NAUT) vaisseau m ; (container) récipient m.

vest [vɛst] n tricot m de corps ; (US: waistcoat) gilet m // vt: to ~ sb with sth, to ~ sth in sb investir qn de qch ; ~ed interests npl (COMM) droits acquis.

vestibule ['vɛstɪbjuːl] n vestibule m.

vestige ['vɛstɪdʒ] n vestige m.

vestry ['vɛstrɪ] n sacristie f.

vet [vɛt] n (abbr of veterinary surgeon) vétérinaire m/f // vt examiner minutieusement ; (text) revoir.

veteran ['vɛtərn] n vétéran m ; (also: war ~) ancien combattant ; ~ car n voiture f d'époque.

veterinary ['vɛtrɪnərɪ] a vétérinaire ; ~ surgeon n vétérinaire m/f.

veto ['viːtəu] n, pl ~es veto m // vt opposer son veto à.

vex [vɛks] vt fâcher, contrarier ; ~ed a (question) controversé(e).

VHF abbr of very high frequency.

via ['vaɪə] prep par, via.

viable ['vaɪəbl] a viable.

viaduct ['vaɪədʌkt] n viaduc m.

vibrate [vaɪ'breɪt] vi: to ~ (with) vibrer (de) ; (resound) retentir (de) ; **vibration** [-'breɪʃən] n vibration f.

vicar ['vɪkə*] n pasteur m (de l'Église anglicane) ; ~age n presbytère m.

vice [vaɪs] n (evil) vice m ; (TECH) étau m.

vice- [vaɪs] prefix vice- ; ~chairman n vice-président/e.

vice squad ['vaɪskwɔd] n ≈ brigade mondaine.

vice versa ['vaɪsɪ'vɜːsə] ad vice versa.

vicinity [vɪ'sɪnɪtɪ] n environs mpl, alentours mpl.

vicious ['vɪʃəs] a (remark) cruel(le), méchant(e) ; (blow) brutal(e) ; ~ness n méchanceté f, cruauté f ; brutalité f.

vicissitudes [vɪ'sɪsɪtjuːdz] npl vicissitudes fpl.

victim ['vɪktɪm] n victime f ; ~ization [-'zeɪʃən] n brimades fpl ; représailles fpl ; ~ize vt brimer ; exercer des représailles sur.

victor ['vɪktə*] n vainqueur m.

Victorian [vɪk'tɔːrɪən] a victorien(ne).

victorious [vɪk'tɔːrɪəs] a victorieux(euse).

victory ['vɪktərɪ] n victoire f.

video ['vɪdɪəu] cpd vidéo inv ; ~ (-tape) recorder n magnétoscope m.

vie [vaɪ] vi: to ~ with lutter avec, rivaliser avec.

Vienna [vɪ'ɛnə] n Vienne.

view [vjuː] n vue f ; (opinion) avis m, vue // vt (situation) considérer ; (house) visiter ; on ~ (in museum etc) exposé(e) ; in my ~ à mon avis ; in ~ of the fact that étant donné que ; to have in ~ avoir en vue ; ~er n (viewfinder) viseur m ; (small projector) visionneuse f ; (TV) téléspectateur/trice ; ~finder n viseur m ; ~point n point m de vue.

vigil ['vɪdʒɪl] n veille f ; ~ance n vigilance f ; ~ance committee n comité m d'autodéfense ; ~ant a vigilant(e).

vigorous ['vɪgərəs] a vigoureux(euse).

vigour, vigor (US) ['vɪgə*] n vigueur f.

vile [vaɪl] a (action) vil(e) ; (smell) abominable ; (temper) massacrant(e).

vilify ['vɪlɪfaɪ] vt calomnier.

villa ['vɪlə] n villa f.

village ['vɪlɪdʒ] n village m ; ~r n villageois/e.

villain ['vɪlən] n (scoundrel) scélérat m ; (criminal) bandit m ; (in novel etc) traître m.

vindicate ['vɪndɪkeɪt] vt défendre avec succès ; justifier.

vindictive [vɪn'dɪktɪv] a vindicatif(ive), rancunier(ère).

vine [vaɪn] n vigne f ; (climbing plant) plante grimpante ; ~ grower n viticulteur m.

vinegar ['vɪnɪgə*] n vinaigre m.

vineyard ['vɪnjɑːd] n vignoble m.

vintage ['vɪntɪdʒ] n (year) année f, millésime m ; ~ wine n vin m de grand cru.

vinyl ['vaɪnl] n vinyle m.

viola [vɪ'əulə] n alto m.

violate ['vaɪəleɪt] vt violer ; **violation** [-'leɪʃən] n violation f.

violence ['vaɪələns] n violence f ; (POL etc) incidents violents.

violent ['vaɪələnt] a violent(e) ; ~ly ad violemment ; extrêmement.

violet ['vaɪələt] a (colour) violet(te) // n (plant) violette f.

violin [vaɪə'lɪn] n violon m ; ~ist n violoniste m/f.

VIP n (abbr of very important person) V.I.P. m.

viper ['vaɪpə*] n vipère f.

virgin ['vɜːdʒɪn] n vierge f // a vierge ; she is a ~ elle est vierge ; the Blessed V~

la Sainte Vierge ; ~ity [-'dʒɪnɪtɪ] n virginité f.

Virgo ['vɜ:gəʊ] n la Vierge ; **to be** ~ être de la Vierge.

virile ['vɪraɪl] a viril(e).

virility [vɪ'rɪlɪtɪ] n virilité f.

virtually ['vɜ:tjʊəlɪ] ad (almost) pratiquement.

virtue ['vɜ:tju:] n vertu f ; (advantage) mérite m, avantage m ; **by** ~ **of** par le fait de.

virtuoso [vɜ:tjʊ'əʊzəʊ] n virtuose m/f.

virtuous ['vɜ:tjʊəs] a vertueux(euse).

virulent ['vɪrʊlənt] a virulent(e).

virus ['vaɪərəs] n virus m.

visa ['vi:zə] n visa m.

vis-à-vis [vi:zə'vi:] prep vis-à-vis de.

viscount ['vaɪkaʊnt] n vicomte m.

visibility [vɪzɪ'bɪlɪtɪ] n visibilité f.

visible ['vɪzəbl] a visible ; **visibly** ad visiblement.

vision ['vɪʒən] n (sight) vue f, vision f ; (foresight, in dream) vision ; ~ary n visionnaire m/f.

visit ['vɪzɪt] n visite f ; (stay) séjour m // vt (person) rendre visite à ; (place) visiter ; ~ing card n carte f de visite ; ~ing professor n ≈ professeur associé ; ~or n visiteur/euse ; (in hotel) client/e ; ~ors' book n livre m d'or ; (in hotel) registre m.

visor ['vaɪzə*] n visière f.

vista ['vɪstə] n vue f, perspective f.

visual ['vɪzjʊəl] a visuel(le) ; (nerve) optique ; ~ **aid** n support visuel (pour l'enseignement).

visualize ['vɪzjʊəlaɪz] vt se représenter ; (foresee) prévoir.

vital ['vaɪtl] a vital(e) ; ~ity [-'tælɪtɪ] n vitalité f ; ~ly ad extrêmement ; ~ **statistics** npl (fig) mensurations fpl.

vitamin ['vɪtəmɪn] n vitamine f.

vitiate ['vɪʃɪeɪt] vt vicier.

vivacious [vɪ'veɪʃəs] a animé(e), qui a de la vivacité.

vivacity [vɪ'væsɪtɪ] n vivacité f.

vivid ['vɪvɪd] a (account) frappant(e) ; (light, imagination) vif(vive) ; ~ly ad (describe) d'une manière vivante ; (remember) de façon précise.

vivisection [vɪvɪ'sɛkʃən] n vivisection f.

V-neck ['vi:nɛk] n décolleté m en V.

vocabulary [vəʊ'kæbjʊlərɪ] n vocabulaire m.

vocal ['vəʊkl] a (MUS) vocal(e) ; (communication) verbal(e) ; (noisy) bruyant(e) ; ~ **chords** npl cordes vocales ; ~**ist** n chanteur/euse.

vocation [vəʊ'keɪʃən] n vocation f ; ~**al** a professionnel(le).

vociferous [və'sɪfərəs] a bruyant(e).

vodka ['vɔdkə] n vodka f.

vogue [vəʊg] n mode f ; (popularity) vogue f.

voice [vɔɪs] n voix f ; (opinion) avis m // vt (opinion) exprimer, formuler.

void [vɔɪd] n vide m // a : ~ **of** vide de, dépourvu(e) de.

voile [vɔɪl] n voile m (tissu).

volatile ['vɔlətaɪl] a volatil(e) ; (fig) versatile.

volcanic [vɔl'kænɪk] a volcanique.

volcano, ~**es** [vɔl'keɪnəʊ] n volcan m.

volition [və'lɪʃən] n : **of one's own** ~ de son propre gré.

volley ['vɔlɪ] n (of gunfire) salve f ; (of stones etc) pluie f, volée f ; (TENNIS etc) volée f ; ~**ball** n volley(-ball) m.

volt [vəʊlt] n volt m ; ~**age** n tension f, voltage m.

voluble ['vɔljʊbl] a volubile.

volume ['vɔlju:m] n volume m ; ~ **control** n (RADIO, TV) bouton m de réglage du volume.

voluntarily ['vɔləntrɪlɪ] ad volontairement ; bénévolement.

voluntary ['vɔləntərɪ] a volontaire ; (unpaid) bénévole.

volunteer [vɔlən'tɪə*] n volontaire m/f // vi (MIL) s'engager comme volontaire ; **to** ~ **to do** se proposer pour faire.

voluptuous [və'lʌptjʊəs] a voluptueux(euse).

vomit ['vɔmɪt] n vomissure f // vt, vi vomir.

vote [vəʊt] n vote m, suffrage m ; (cast) voix f, vote ; (franchise) droit m de vote // vt (bill) voter ; (chairman) élire // vi voter ; ~ **of censure** n motion f de censure ; ~ **of thanks** n discours m de remerciement ; ~**r** n électeur/trice ; **voting** n scrutin m.

vouch [vaʊtʃ] : **to** ~ **for** vt se porter garant de.

voucher ['vaʊtʃə*] n (for meal, petrol) bon m ; (receipt) reçu m.

vow [vaʊ] n vœu m, serment m // vi jurer.

vowel ['vaʊəl] n voyelle f.

voyage ['vɔɪɪdʒ] n voyage m par mer, traversée f.

vulgar ['vʌlgə*] a vulgaire ; ~**ity** [-'gærɪtɪ] n vulgarité f.

vulnerability [vʌlnərə'bɪlɪtɪ] n vulnérabilité f.

vulnerable ['vʌlnərəbl] a vulnérable.

vulture ['vʌltʃə*] n vautour m.

W

wad [wɔd] n (of cotton wool, paper) tampon m ; (of banknotes etc) liasse f.

wade [weɪd] vi : **to** ~ **through** marcher dans, patauger dans // vt passer à gué.

wafer ['weɪfə*] n (CULIN) gaufrette f ; (REL) pain m d'hostie f.

waffle ['wɔfl] n (CULIN) gaufre f ; (col) rabâchage m ; remplissage m // vi parler pour ne rien dire ; faire du remplissage.

waft [wɔft] vt porter // vi flotter.

wag [wæg] vt agiter, remuer // vi remuer.

wage [weɪdʒ] n salaire m, paye f // vt : **to** ~ **war** faire la guerre ; ~**s** npl salaire, paye ; ~ **claim** n demande f d'augmentation de salaire ; ~ **earner** n salarié/e ; (breadwinner) soutien m de famille ; ~ **freeze** n blocage m des salaires.

wager ['weɪdʒə*] n pari m.

waggle ['wægl] vt, vi remuer.

wag(g)on ['wægən] n (horse-drawn) chariot m ; (truck) camion m ; (RAIL) wagon m (de marchandises).

wail [weɪl] n gémissement m ; (of siren) hurlement m // vi gémir ; hurler.

waist [weist] *n* taille *f*, ceinture *f*; ~**coat** *n* gilet *m*; ~**line** *n* (tour *m* de) taille *f*.
wait [weit] *n* attente *f* // *vi* attendre; **to lie in** ~ **for** guetter; **I can't** ~ **to** (*fig*) je meurs d'envie de; **to** ~ **behind** *vi* rester (à attendre); **to** ~ **for** attendre; **to** ~ **on** *vt fus* servir; ~**er** *n* garçon *m* (de café), serveur *m*; **'no** ~**ing'** (*AUT*) 'stationnement interdit'; ~**ing list** *n* liste *f* d'attente; ~**ing room** *n* salle *f* d'attente; ~**ress** *n* serveuse *f*.
waive [weiv] *vt* renoncer à, abandonner.
wake [weik] *vb* (*pt* **woke**, ~**d**, *pp* **woken**, ~**d**) [wauk, 'waukn] *vt* (*also*: ~ **up**) réveiller // *vi* (*also*: ~ **up**) se réveiller // *n* (*for dead person*) veillée *f* mortuaire; (*NAUT*) sillage *m*; ~ *n* *vt*, *vi* = **wake**.
Wales [weilz] *n* pays *m* de Galles.
walk [wɔ:k] *n* promenade *f*; (*short*) petit tour; (*gait*) démarche *f*; (*pace*): **at a quick** ~ d'un pas rapide; (*path*) chemin *m*; (*in park etc*) allée *f* // *vi* marcher; (*for pleasure, exercise*) se promener // *vt* (*distance*) faire à pied; (*dog*) promener; **10 minutes'** ~ **from** à 10 minutes de marche de; **from all** ~**s of life** de toutes conditions sociales; ~**er** *n* (*person*) marcheur/euse; ~**ie-talkie** [wɔ:ki'tɔ:ki] *n* talkie-walkie *m*; ~**ing** *n* marche *f* à pied; ~**ing holiday** *n* vacances passées à faire de la randonnée; ~**ing shoes** *npl* chaussures *fpl* de marche; ~**ing stick** *n* canne *f*; ~**out** *n* (*of workers*) grève-surprise *f*; ~**over** *n* (*col*) victoire *f* or examen *m* etc facile; ~**way** *n* promenade *f*.
wall [wɔ:l] *n* mur *m*; (*of tunnel, cave*) paroi *m*; ~ **cupboard** *n* placard mural; ~**ed** *a* (*city*) fortifié(e).
wallet ['wɔlit] *n* portefeuille *m*.
wallflower ['wɔ:lflauə*] *n* giroflée *f*; **to be a** ~ (*fig*) faire tapisserie.
wallop ['wɔləp] *vt* (*col*) taper sur, cogner.
wallow ['wɔləu] *vi* se vautrer.
wallpaper ['wɔ:lpeipə*] *n* papier peint.
walnut ['wɔ:lnʌt] *n* noix *f*; (*tree*) noyer *m*.
walrus ['wɔ:lrəs] *pl* ~ *or* ~**es** *n* morse *m*.
waltz [wɔ:lts] *n* valse *f* // *vi* valser.
wan [wɔn] *a* pâle; triste.
wand [wɔnd] *n* (*also*: **magic** ~) baguette *f* (magique).
wander ['wɔndə*] *vi* (*person*) errer, aller sans but; (*thoughts*) vagabonder; (*river*) serpenter; ~**er** *n* vagabond/e.
wane [wein] *vi* (*moon*) décroître; (*reputation*) décliner.
wangle ['wæŋgl] *vt* (*col*) se débrouiller pour avoir; carotter.
want [wɔnt] *vt* vouloir; (*need*) avoir besoin de; (*lack*) manquer de // *n*: **for** ~ **of** par manque de, faute de; ~**s** *npl* (*needs*) besoins *mpl*; **to** ~ **to do** vouloir faire; **to** ~ **sb to do** vouloir que qn fasse; **to be found** ~**ing** ne pas être à la hauteur.
wanton ['wɔntn] *a* capricieux(euse); dévergondé(e).
war [wɔ:*] *n* guerre *f*; **to go to** ~ se mettre en guerre.
ward [wɔ:d] *n* (*in hospital*) salle *f*; (*POL*) section électorale; (*LAW: child*) pupille *m/f*; **to** ~ **off** *vt* parer, éviter.

warden ['wɔ:dn] *n* (*of institution*) directeur/trice; (*of park, game reserve*) gardien/ne; (*also*: **traffic** ~) contractuel/le.
warder ['wɔ:də*] *n* gardien *m* de prison.
wardrobe ['wɔ:drəub] *n* (*cupboard*) armoire *f*; (*clothes*) garde-robe *f*; (*THEATRE*) costumes *mpl*.
warehouse ['wεəhaus] *n* entrepôt *m*.
wares [wεəz] *npl* marchandises *fpl*.
warfare ['wɔ:fεə*] *n* guerre *f*.
warhead ['wɔ:hεd] *n* (*MIL*) ogive *f*.
warily ['wεərili] *ad* avec prudence, avec précaution.
warlike ['wɔ:laik] *a* guerrier(ère).
warm [wɔ:m] *a* chaud(e); (*thanks, welcome, applause*) chaleureux(euse); **it's** ~ il fait chaud; **I'm** ~ j'ai chaud; **to** ~ **up** *vi* (*person, room*) se réchauffer; (*water*) chauffer; (*athlete, discussion*) s'échauffer // *vt* réchauffer; chauffer; (*engine*) faire chauffer; ~**hearted** *a* affectueux(euse); ~**ly** *ad* chaudement; vivement; chaleureusement; ~**th** *n* chaleur *f*.
warn [wɔ:n] *vt* avertir, prévenir; ~**ing** *n* avertissement *m*; (*notice*) avis *m*; ~**ing light** *n* avertisseur lumineux.
warp [wɔ:p] *vi* travailler, se voiler // *vt* voiler; (*fig*) pervertir.
warrant ['wɔrnt] *n* (*guarantee*) garantie *f*; (*LAW: to arrest*) mandat *m* d'arrêt; (*: to search*) mandat de perquisition.
warranty ['wɔrənti] *n* garantie *f*.
warrior ['wɔriə*] *n* guerrier/ère.
warship ['wɔ:ʃip] *n* navire *m* de guerre.
wart [wɔ:t] *n* verrue *f*.
wartime ['wɔ:taim] *n*: **in** ~ en temps de guerre.
wary ['wεəri] *a* prudent(e).
was [wɔz] *pt of* **be**.
wash [wɔʃ] *vt* laver // *vi* se laver // *n* (*paint*) badigeon *m*; (*washing programme*) lavage *m*; (*of ship*) sillage *m*; **to give sth a** ~ laver qch; **to have a** ~ se laver, faire sa toilette; **to** ~ **away** *vt* (*stain*) enlever au lavage; (*subj: river etc*) emporter; **to** ~ **down** *vt* laver; laver à grande eau; **to** ~ **off** *vi* partir au lavage; **to** ~ **up** *vi* faire la vaisselle; ~**able** *a* lavable; ~**basin** *n* lavabo *m*; ~**er** *n* (*TECH*) rondelle *f*, joint *m*; ~**ing** *n* (*linen etc*) lessive *f*; ~**ing machine** *n* machine *f* à laver; ~**ing powder** *n* lessive *f* (en poudre); ~**ing-up** *n* vaisselle *f*; ~**out** *n* (*col*) désastre *m*; ~**room** *n* toilettes *fpl*.
wasn't ['wɔznt] = **was not**.
wasp [wɔsp] *n* guêpe *f*.
wastage ['weistidʒ] *n* gaspillage *m*; (*in manufacturing, transport etc*) déchet *m*.
waste [weist] *n* gaspillage *m*; (*of time*) perte *f*; (*rubbish*) déchets *mpl*; (*also*: **household** ~) ordures *fpl* // *a* (*material*) de rebut; (*heat*) perdu(e); (*food*) inutilisé(e); (*land*) inculte; // *vt* gaspiller; (*time, opportunity*) perdre; ~**s** *npl* étendue *f* désertique; **to** ~ **away** *vi* dépérir; ~**bin** *n* corbeille *f* à papier; (*in kitchen*) boîte *f* à ordures; ~ **disposal unit** *n* broyeur *m* d'ordures; ~**ful** *a* gaspilleur(euse); (*process*) peu économique; ~ **ground** *n* terrain *m* vague; ~**paper basket** *n* corbeille *f* à papier.

watch [wɔtʃ] n montre f; (act of watching) surveillance f; guet m; (guard: MIL) sentinelle f; (: NAUT) homme m de quart; (NAUT: spell of duty) quart m // vt (look at) observer; (: match, programme) regarder; (spy on, guard) surveiller; (be careful of) faire attention à // vi regarder; (keep guard) monter la garde; **to ~ out** vi faire attention; **~ dog** n chien m de garde; **~ful** a attentif(ive), vigilant(e); **~maker** n horloger/ère; **~man** n gardien m; (also: **night ~man**) veilleur m de nuit; **~ strap** n bracelet m de montre.

water ['wɔ:tə*] n eau f // vt (plant) arroser; **in British ~s** dans les eaux territoriales Britanniques; **to ~ down** vt (milk) couper d'eau; (fig: story) édulcorer; **~ closet** n w.-c. mpl, waters mpl; **~colour** n aquarelle f; **~colours** npl couleurs fpl pour aquarelle; **~cress** n cresson m (de fontaine); **~fall** n chute f d'eau; **~ hole** n mare f; **~ ice** n sorbet m; **~ing can** n arrosoir m; **~ level** n niveau m de l'eau; (of flood) niveau m des eaux; **~ lily** n nénuphar m; **~logged** a détrempé(e); imbibé(e) d'eau; **~line** n (NAUT) ligne f de flottaison; **~ main** n canalisation f d'eau; **~mark** n (on paper) filigrane m; **~melon** n pastèque f; **~polo** n water-polo m; **~proof** a imperméable; **~shed** n (GEO) ligne f de partage des eaux; (fig) moment m critique, point décisif; **~-skiing** n ski m nautique; **~ softener** n adoucisseur m d'eau; **~ tank** n réservoir m d'eau; **~tight** a étanche; **~ works** npl station f hydraulique; **~y** a (colour) délavé(e); (coffee) trop faible.

watt [wɔt] n watt m.

wave [weɪv] n vague f; (of hand) geste m, signe m; (RADIO) onde f; (in hair) ondulation f // vi faire signe de la main; (flag) flotter au vent // vt (handkerchief) agiter; (stick) brandir; (hair) onduler; **~length** n longueur f d'ondes.

waver ['weɪvə*] vi vaciller; (voice) trembler; (person) hésiter.

wavy ['weɪvɪ] a ondulé(e); onduleux(euse).

wax [wæks] n cire f; (for skis) fart m // vt cirer; (car) lustrer // vi (moon) croître; **~en** a cireux(euse); **~works** npl personnages mpl de cire; musée m de cire.

way [weɪ] n chemin m, voie f; (path, access) passage m; (distance) distance f; (direction) chemin m, direction f; (manner) façon f, manière f; (habit) habitude f, façon f; (condition) état m; **which ~?** this ~ par où or de quel côté? — par ici; **to be on one's ~** être en route; **to be in the ~** bloquer le passage; (fig) gêner; **to go out of one's ~ to do** (fig) se donner du mal pour faire; **in a ~** d'un côté; **in some ~s** à certains égards; d'un côté; **in the ~ of** en fait de, comme; **'~ in'** 'entrée'; **'~ out'** 'sortie'; **the ~ back** le chemin du retour; **this ~ and that** par-ci par-là; **'give ~'** (AUT) 'cédez la priorité'.

waylay [weɪ'leɪ] vt irg attaquer; (fig) I got waylaid quelqu'un m'a accroché.

wayward ['weɪwəd] a capricieux(euse), entêté(e).

W.C. ['dʌblju'si:] n w.-c. mpl, waters mpl.

we [wi:] pl pronoun nous.

weak [wi:k] a faible; (health) fragile; (beam etc) peu solide; **~en** vi faiblir // vt affaiblir; **~ling** n gringalet m; faible m/f; **~ness** n faiblesse f; (fault) point m faible.

wealth [wɛlθ] n (money, resources) richesse(s) f(pl); (of details) profusion f; **~y** a riche.

wean [wi:n] vt sevrer.

weapon ['wɛpən] n arme f.

wear [wɛə*] n (use) usage m; (deterioration through use) usure f; (clothing): **sports/baby~** vêtements mpl de sport/pour bébés // vt (pt wore, pp worn [wɔ:*, wɔ:n]) (clothes) porter; mettre; (beard etc) avoir; (damage: through use) user // vi (last) faire de l'usage; (rub etc through) s'user; **town/evening ~** n tenue f de ville/de soirée; **~ and tear** n usure f; **to ~ away** vt user, ronger // vi s'user, être rongé(e); **to ~ down** vt user; (strength) épuiser; **to ~ off** vi disparaître; **to ~ on** vi se poursuivre; passer; **to ~ out** vt user; (person, strength) épuiser.

wearily ['wɪərɪlɪ] ad avec lassitude.

weariness ['wɪərɪnɪs] n épuisement m, lassitude f.

weary ['wɪərɪ] a (tired) épuisé(e); (dispirited) las(lasse); abattu(e) // vt lasser // vi: **to ~ of** se lasser de.

weasel ['wi:zl] n (ZOOL) belette f.

weather ['wɛðə*] n temps m // vt (wood) faire mûrir; (tempest, crisis) essuyer, être pris(e) dans; survivre à, tenir le coup durant; **~-beaten** a (person) hâlé(e); (building) dégradé(e) par les intempéries; **~ cock** n girouette f; **~ forecast** n prévisions fpl météorologiques, météo f; **~ vane** n = **~ cock.**

weave [wi:v], pt **wove**, pp **woven** [wi:v, wəuv, 'wəuvn] vt (cloth) tisser; (basket) tresser; **~r** n tisserand/e; **weaving** n tissage m.

web [wɛb] n (of spider) toile f; (on foot) palmure f; (fabric, also fig) tissu m; **~bed** a (foot) palmé(e); **~bing** n (on chair) sangles fpl.

wed [wɛd] vt (pt, pp **wedded**) épouser // n: **the newly-~s** les jeunes mariés.

we'd [wi:d] = **we had, we would.**

wedded ['wɛdɪd] pt,pp of **wed.**

wedding ['wɛdɪŋ] n mariage m; **silver/golden ~** n noces fpl d'argent/d'or; **~ day** n jour m du mariage; **~ dress** n robe f de mariage; **~ present** n cadeau m de mariage; **~ ring** n alliance f.

wedge [wɛdʒ] n (of wood etc) coin m; (under door etc) cale f; (of cake) part f // vt (fix) caler; (push) enfoncer, coincer; **~-heeled shoes** npl chaussures fpl à semelles compensées.

wedlock ['wɛdlɔk] n (union f du) mariage m.

Wednesday ['wɛdnzdɪ] n mercredi m.

wee [wi:] a (Scottish) petit(e); tout(e) petit(e).

weed [wi:d] n mauvaise herbe // vt désherber; **~-killer** n désherbant m.

week [wi:k] n semaine f; **~day** n jour m de semaine; (COMM) jour ouvrable; **~end** n week-end m; **~ly** ad une fois par semaine, chaque semaine // a,n hebdomadaire (m).

weep, pt, pp **wept** [wi:p, wɛpt] vi (person) pleurer; ~**ing willow** n saule pleureur.

weigh [weɪ] vt,vi peser; **to** ~ **anchor** lever l'ancre; **to** ~ **down** vt (branch) faire plier; (fig: with worry) accabler; **to** ~ **up** vt examiner; ~**bridge** n pont-bascule m.

weight [weɪt] n poids m; **sold by** ~ vendu(e) au poids; ~**lessness** n apesanteur f; ~ **lifter** n haltérophile m; ~**y** a lourd(e).

weir [wɪə*] n barrage m.

weird [wɪəd] a bizarre; (eerie) surnaturel(le).

welcome ['wɛlkəm] a bienvenu(e) // n accueil m // vt accueillir; (also: **bid** ~) souhaiter la bienvenue à; (be glad of) se réjouir de; **to be** ~ être le(la) bienvenu(e); **welcoming** a accueillant(e); (speech) d'accueil.

weld [wɛld] n soudure f // vt souder; ~**er** n (person) soudeur m; ~**ing** n soudure f (autogène).

welfare ['wɛlfɛə*] n bien-être m; ~ **state** n État-providence m; ~ **work** n travail social.

well [wɛl] n puits m // ad bien // a: **to be** ~ aller bien // excl eh bien!; bon!; enfin!; ~ **done!** bravo!; **get** ~ **soon!** remets-toi vite!; **to do** ~ **in sth** bien réussir en or dans qch.

we'll [wi:l] = **we will**, **we shall**.

well: ~**-behaved** a sage, obéissant(e); ~**-being** n bien-être m; ~**-built** a (building) bien construit(e); (person) bien bâti(e); ~**-developed** a (girl) bien fait(e); ~**-earned** a (rest) bien mérité(e); ~**-groomed** a très soigné(e) de sa personne; ~**-heeled** a (col: wealthy) fortuné(e), riche.

wellingtons ['wɛlɪŋtənz] npl (also: **wellington boots**) bottes fpl de caoutchouc.

well: ~**-known** a (person) bien connu(e); ~**-meaning** a bien intentionné(e); ~**-off** a aisé(e), assez riche; ~**-read** a cultivé(e); ~**-to-do** a aisé(e), assez riche; ~**-wisher** n: **scores of** ~**-wishers had gathered** de nombreux amis et admirateurs s'étaient rassemblés; **letters from** ~**-wishers** des lettres d'encouragement.

Welsh [wɛlʃ] a gallois(e) // n (LING) gallois m; ~**man/woman** n Gallois/e; ~ **rarebit** n croûte f au fromage.

went [wɛnt] pt of **go**.

wept [wɛpt] pt, pp of **weep**.

were [wə:*] pt of **be**.

we're [wɪə*] = **we are**.

weren't [wə:nt] = **were not**.

west [wɛst] n ouest m // a ouest inv, de or à l'ouest // ad à or vers l'ouest; **the W**~ n l'Occident m, l'Ouest m; **the W**~ **Country** n le sud-ouest de l'Angleterre; ~**erly** a (situation) à l'ouest; (wind) d'ouest; ~**ern** a occidental(e), de or à l'ouest // n (CINEMA) western m; **W**~ **Germany** n Allemagne f de l'Ouest; **W**~ **Indies** npl Antilles fpl; ~**ward(s)** ad vers l'ouest.

wet [wɛt] a mouillé(e); (damp) humide; (soaked) trempé(e); (rainy) pluvieux-(euse); **to get** ~ se mouiller; ~ **blanket** n (fig) rabat-joie m inv; ~**ness** n humidité f; '~ **paint**' 'attention peinture fraîche'; ~ **suit** n combinaison f de plongée.

we've [wi:v] = **we have**.

whack [wæk] vt donner un grand coup à; ~**ed** a (col: tired) crevé(e).

whale [weɪl] n (ZOOL) baleine f.

wharf, wharves [wɔ:f, wɔ:vz] n quai m.

what [wɔt] excl quoi!, comment! // det quel(le) // pronoun (interrogative) que, prep + quoi; (relative, indirect: object) ce que; (: subject) ce qui; ~ **are you doing?** que fais-tu?, qu'est-ce que tu fais?; ~ **has happened?** que s'est-il passé?, qu'est-ce qui s'est passé?; ~**'s in there?** qu'y a-t-il là-dedans?, qu'est-ce qu'il y a là-dedans?; **I saw** ~ **you did/is on the table** j'ai vu ce que vous avez fait/ce qui est sur la table; ~ **a mess!** quel désordre!; ~ **is it called?** comment est-ce que ça s'appelle?; ~ **about doing ...?** et si on faisait ...?; ~ **about me?** et moi?; ~**ever** det: ~**ever book** quel que soit le livre que (or qui) soit + sub; n'importe quel livre // pronoun: **do** ~**ever is necessary/you want** faites (tout) ce qui est nécessaire/(tout) ce que vous voulez; ~**ever happens** quoi qu'il arrive; **no reason** ~**ever or** ~**soever** pas la moindre raison.

wheat [wi:t] n blé m, froment m.

wheel [wi:l] n roue f; (AUT: also: **steering** ~) volant m; (NAUT) gouvernail m // vt pousser, rouler // vi (also: ~ **round**) tourner; ~**barrow** n brouette f; ~**chair** n fauteuil roulant.

wheeze [wi:z] n respiration bruyante (d'asthmatique) // vi respirer bruyamment.

when [wɛn] ad quand // cj quand, lorsque; (whereas) alors que; **on the day** ~ **I met him** le jour où je l'ai rencontré; ~**ever** ad quand donc // cj quand; (every time that) chaque fois que.

where [wɛə*] ad,cj où; **this is** ~ c'est là que; ~**abouts** ad où donc // n: **sb's** ~**abouts** l'endroit où se trouve qn; ~**as** cj alors que; ~**ver** [-'ɛvə*] ad où donc // cj où que + sub.

whet [wɛt] vt aiguiser.

whether ['wɛðə*] cj si; **I don't know** ~ **to accept or not** je ne sais pas si je dois accepter ou non; **it's doubtful** ~ il est peu probable que; ~ **you go or not** que vous y alliez ou non.

which [wɪtʃ] det (interrogative) quel(le), pl quels(quelles); ~ **one of you?** lequel(laquelle) d'entre vous?; **tell me** ~ **one you want** dis-moi lequel tu veux or celui que tu veux // pronoun (interrogative) lequel(laquelle), pl lesquels (lesquelles); (indirect) celui(celle) qui (or que); (relative: subject) qui; (: object) que, prep + lequel(laquelle) (NB: à + lequel = auquel; de + lequel = duquel); **I don't mind** ~ peu importe lequel; **the apple** ~ **you ate/**~ **is on the table** la pomme que vous avez mangée/qui est sur la table; **the chair on** ~ la chaise sur laquelle; **the book of** ~ le livre dont or duquel; **he said he knew,** ~ **is true/I feared** il a dit qu'il le savait, ce qui est vrai/ce que je craignais ; **after ~** après quoi ; **in ~ case** auquel cas ; **~ever** det: **take ~ever book you prefer** prenez le livre que vous préférez, peu importe lequel ; **~ever book you take** quel que soit le livre que vous preniez ; **~ever way you** de quelque façon que vous + sub.

whiff [wɪf] n bouffée f.

while [waɪl] n moment m // cj pendant que ; (as long as) tant que ; (whereas) alors que ; bien que + sub ; **for a ~** pendant quelque temps.

whim [wɪm] n caprice m.

whimper ['wɪmpə*] n geignement m // vi geindre.

whimsical ['wɪmzɪkl] a (person) capricieux(euse) ; (look) étrange.

whine [waɪn] n gémissement m // vi gémir, geindre ; pleurnicher.

whip [wɪp] n fouet m ; (for riding) cravache f ; (Brit: POL: person) chef m de file (assurant la discipline dans son groupe parlementaire) // vt fouetter ; (snatch) enlever (or sortir) brusquement ; **~ped cream** n crème fouettée ; **~-round** n collecte f.

whirl [wə:l] n tourbillon m // vt faire tourbillonner ; faire tournoyer // vi tourbillonner ; **~pool** n tourbillon m ; **~wind** n tornade f.

whirr [wə:*] vi bruire ; ronronner ; vrombir.

whisk [wɪsk] n (CULIN) fouet m // vt fouetter, battre ; **to ~ sb away or off** emmener qn rapidement.

whisker ['wɪskə*] n: **~s** (of animal) moustaches fpl ; (of man) favoris mpl.

whisky, whiskey (Irlande, US) ['wɪskɪ] n whisky m.

whisper ['wɪspə*] n chuchotement m ; (fig: of leaves) bruissement m ; (rumour) rumeur f // vt,vi chuchoter.

whist [wɪst] n whist m.

whistle ['wɪsl] n (sound) sifflement m ; (object) sifflet m // vi siffler.

white [waɪt] a blanc(blanche) ; (with fear) blême // n blanc m ; (person) blanc/blanche ; **~bait** n blanchaille f ; **~collar worker** n employé/e de bureau ; **~ elephant** n (fig) objet dispendieux et superflu ; **~ lie** n pieux mensonge ; **~ness** n blancheur f ; **~ paper** n (POL) livre blanc ; **~wash** n (paint) lait m de chaux // vt blanchir à la chaux ; (fig) blanchir.

whiting ['waɪtɪŋ] n, pl inv (fish) merlan m.

Whitsun ['wɪtsn] n la Pentecôte.

whittle ['wɪtl] vt: **to ~ away, ~ down** (costs) réduire, rogner.

whizz [wɪz] vi aller (or passer) à toute vitesse ; **~ kid** n (col) petit prodige.

WHO n (abbr of World Health Organization) O.M.S. f (Organisation mondiale de la Santé).

who [hu:] pronoun qui ; **~dunit** [hu:'dʌnɪt] n (col) roman policier ; **~ever** pronoun: **~ever finds it** celui(celle) qui le trouve, (qui que ce soit), quiconque le trouve ; **ask ~ever you like** demandez à qui vous voulez ; **~ever he marries** qui que ce soit or quelle que soit la personne qu'il épouse ; **~ever told you that?** qui a bien pu vous dire ça?, qui donc vous a dit ça?

whole [həul] a (complete) entier(ère), tout(e) ; (not broken) intact(e), complet(ète) // n (total) totalité f ; (sth not broken) tout m ; **the ~ of the time** tout le temps ; **the ~ of the town** la ville tout entière ; **on the ~, as a ~** dans l'ensemble ; **~hearted** a sans réserve(s), sincère ; **~sale** n (vente f en) gros m // a de gros ; (destruction) systématique ; **~saler** n grossiste m/f ; **~some** a sain(e) ; (advice) salutaire ; **wholly** ad entièrement, tout à fait.

whom [hu:m] pronoun que, prep + qui (check syntax of French verb used) ; (interrogative) qui.

whooping cough ['hu:pɪŋkɔf] n coqueluche f.

whopping ['wɔpɪŋ] a (col: big) énorme.

whore [hɔ:*] n (col: pej) putain f.

whose [hu:z] det: **~ book is this?** à qui est ce livre? ; **~ pencil have you taken?** à qui est le crayon que vous avez pris?, c'est le crayon de qui que vous avez pris? ; **the man ~ son you rescued** l'homme dont or qui vous avez sauvé le fils ; **the girl ~ sister you were speaking to** la fille à la sœur de qui or laquelle vous parliez // pronoun: **~ is this?** à qui est ceci? ; **I know ~ it is** je sais à qui c'est.

Who's Who ['hu:z'hu:] n ≈ Bottin Mondain.

why [waɪ] ad pourquoi // excl eh bien!, tiens! ; **the reason ~** la raison pour laquelle ; **~ever** ad pourquoi donc, mais pourquoi.

wick [wɪk] n mèche f (de bougie).

wicked ['wɪkɪd] a mauvais(e), méchant(e) ; inique ; cruel(le) ; (mischievous) malicieux(euse).

wicker ['wɪkə*] n osier m ; (also: **~work**) vannerie f.

wicket ['wɪkɪt] n (CRICKET) guichet m ; espace compris entre les deux guichets.

wide [waɪd] a large ; (region, knowledge) vaste, très étendu(e) ; (choice) grand(e) // ad: **to open ~** ouvrir tout grand ; **to shoot ~** tirer à côté ; **~-angle lens** n objectif m grand-angulaire ; **~-awake** a bien éveillé(e) ; **~ly** ad (different) radicalement ; (spaced) sur une grande étendue ; (believed) généralement ; **~n** vt élargir ; **~ness** n largeur f ; **~ open** a grand(e) ouvert(e) ; **~spread** a (belief etc) très répandu(e).

widow ['wɪdəu] n veuve f ; **~ed** a (qui est devenu(e)) veuf(veuve) ; **~er** n veuf m.

width [wɪdθ] n largeur f.

wield [wi:ld] vt (sword) manier ; (power) exercer.

wife, wives [waɪf, waɪvz] n femme (mariée), épouse f.

wig [wɪg] n perruque f.

wiggle ['wɪgl] vt agiter remuer // vi (loose screw etc) branler ; (worm) se tortiller.

wild [waɪld] a sauvage ; (sea) déchaîné(e) ; (idea, life) fou(folle) ; extravagant(e) ; **~s** npl régions fpl sauvages ; **~erness** ['wɪldənɪs] n désert m, région f sauvage ; **~-goose chase** n (fig) fausse piste ; **~ life** n faune f ; **~ly** ad (applaud) frénétiquement ; (hit, guess) au hasard ; (happy) follement.

wilful ['wɪlful] a (person) obstiné(e); (action) délibéré(e); (crime) prémédité(e).

will [wɪl] auxiliary vb: he ~ come il viendra // vt (pt, pp ~ed): to ~ sb to do souhaiter ardemment que qn fasse; he ~ed himself to go on par un suprême effort de volonté, il continua // n volonté f; testament m; ~ing a de bonne volonté, serviable; he's ~ing to do it il est disposé à le faire, il veut bien le faire; ~ingly ad volontiers; ~ingness n bonne volonté.

willow ['wɪləu] n saule m.

will power ['wɪlpauə*] n volonté f.

wilt [wɪlt] vi dépérir.

wily ['waɪlɪ] a rusé(e).

win [wɪn] n (in sports etc) victoire f // vb (pt, pp won [wʌn]) vt (battle, money) gagner; (prize) remporter; (popularity) acquérir // vi gagner; to ~ over, ~ round vt gagner, se concilier.

wince [wɪns] n tressaillement m // vi tressaillir.

winch [wɪntʃ] n treuil m.

wind [wɪnd] (also MED) vent m // vb [waɪnd] (pt, pp wound [waund]) vt enrouler; (wrap) envelopper; (clock, toy) remonter; (take breath away) [wɪnd] couper le souffle à // vi (road, river) serpenter; the ~(s) (MUS) les instruments mpl à vent; to ~ up vt (clock) remonter; (debate) terminer, clôturer; ~break n brise-vent m inv; ~fall n coup m de chance; ~ing a (road) sinueux(euse); (staircase) tournant(e); ~ instrument n (MUS) instrument m à vent; ~mill n moulin m à vent.

window ['wɪndəu] n fenêtre f; (in car, train, also: ~ pane) vitre f; (in shop etc) vitrine f; ~ box n jardinière f; ~ cleaner n (person) laveur/euse de vitres; ~ frame n châssis m de fenêtre; ~ ledge n rebord m de la fenêtre; ~ pane n vitre f, carreau m; ~sill n (inside) appui m de la fenêtre; (outside) rebord m de la fenêtre.

windpipe ['wɪndpaɪp] n gosier m.

windscreen, **windshield** (US) ['wɪndskri:n, 'wɪndʃi:ld] n pare-brise m inv; ~ washer n lave-glace m inv; ~ wiper n essuie-glace m inv.

windswept ['wɪndswɛpt] a balayé(e) par le vent.

windy ['wɪndɪ] a venté(e), venteux(euse); it's ~ il y a du vent.

wine [waɪn] n vin m; ~ cellar n cave f à vins; ~ glass n verre m à vin; ~ list n carte f des vins; ~ merchant n marchand de vins; ~ tasting n dégustation f (de vins); ~ waiter n sommelier m.

wing [wɪŋ] n aile f; (in air force) groupe m d'escadrilles; ~s npl (THEATRE) coulisses fpl; ~er n (SPORT) ailier m.

wink [wɪŋk] n clin m d'œil // vi faire un clin d'œil; (blink) cligner des yeux.

winner ['wɪnə*] n gagnant/e.

winning ['wɪnɪŋ] a (team) gagnant(e); (goal) décisif(ive); ~s npl gains mpl; ~ post n poteau m d'arrivée.

winter ['wɪntə*] n hiver m // vi hiverner; ~ sports npl sports mpl d'hiver.

wintry ['wɪntrɪ] a hivernal(e).

wipe [waɪp] n coup m de torchon (or de chiffon or d'éponge) // vt essuyer; to ~ off vt essuyer; to ~ out vt (debt) régler; (memory) oublier; (destroy) anéantir; to ~ up vt essuyer.

wire ['waɪə*] n fil m (de fer); (ELEC) fil électrique; (TEL) télégramme m // vt (fence) grillager; (house) faire l'installation électrique de; (also: ~ up) brancher; ~ brush n brosse f métallique.

wireless ['waɪəlɪs] n télégraphie f sans fil; (set) T.S.F. f.

wiry ['waɪərɪ] a noueux(euse), nerveux(euse).

wisdom ['wɪzdəm] n sagesse f; (of action) prudence f; ~ tooth n dent f de sagesse.

wise [waɪz] a sage, prudent(e), judicieux(euse).

...wise [waɪz] suffix: time~ en ce qui concerne le temps, question temps.

wisecrack ['waɪzkræk] n sarcasme m.

wish [wɪʃ] n (desire, desire) souhait m, vœu m // vt souhaiter, désirer, vouloir; best ~es (on birthday etc) meilleurs vœux; with best ~es (in letter) bien amicalement; give her my best ~es faites-lui mes amitiés; to ~ sb goodbye dire au revoir à qn; he ~ed me well il me souhaitait de réussir; to ~ to do/sb to do désirer or vouloir faire/que qn fasse; to ~ for souhaiter; it's ~ful thinking c'est prendre ses désirs pour des réalités.

wisp [wɪsp] n fine mèche (de cheveux); (of smoke) mince volute f; a ~ of straw un fétu de paille.

wistful ['wɪstful] a mélancolique.

wit [wɪt] n (gen pl) intelligence f, esprit m; présence f d'esprit; (wittiness) esprit; (person) homme/femme d'esprit; to be at one's ~s' end (fig) ne plus savoir que faire; to ~ ad à savoir.

witch [wɪtʃ] n sorcière f; ~craft n sorcellerie f.

with [wɪð, wɪθ] prep avec; red ~ anger rouge de colère; the man ~ the grey hat l'homme au chapeau gris; to be ~ it (fig) être dans le vent; I am ~ you (I understand) je vous suis.

withdraw [wɪθ'drɔ:] vb (irg) vt retirer // vi se retirer; (go back on promise) se rétracter; ~al n retrait m; (MED) état m de manque.

wither ['wɪðə*] vi se faner; ~ed a fané(e), flétri(e); (limb) atrophié(e).

withhold [wɪθ'həuld] vt irg (money) retenir; (decision) remettre; (permission): to ~ (from) refuser (à); (information): to ~ (from) cacher (à).

within [wɪð'ɪn] prep à l'intérieur de // ad à l'intérieur; ~ sight of en vue de; ~ a mile of à moins d'un mille de; ~ the week avant la fin de la semaine.

without [wɪð'aut] prep sans.

withstand [wɪθ'stænd] vt irg résister à.

witness ['wɪtnɪs] n (person) témoin m; (evidence) témoignage m // vt (event) être témoin de; (document) attester l'authenticité de; to bear ~ to sth témoigner de qch; ~ box, ~ stand (US) n barre f des témoins.

witticism ['wɪtɪsɪzm] *n* mot *m* d'esprit.
witty ['wɪtɪ] *a* spirituel(le), plein(e)
d'esprit.
wives [waɪvz] *npl of* **wife**.
wizard ['wɪzəd] *n* magicien *m*.
wk *abbr of* **week**.
wobble ['wɒbl] *vi* trembler; (*chair*)
branler.
woe [wəu] *n* malheur *m*.
woke [wəuk] *pt of* **wake**; **~n** *pp of* **wake**.
wolf, wolves [wulf, wulvz] *n* loup *m*.
woman, pl women ['wumən, 'wɪmɪn] *n*
femme *f*; **~ doctor** *n* femme *f* médecin;
~ly a féminin(e); **~ teacher** *n* professeur
m femme *f*.
womb [wu:m] *n* (ANAT) utérus *m*.
women ['wɪmɪn] *npl of* **woman**.
won [wʌn] *pt,pp of* **win**.
wonder ['wʌndə*] *n* merveille *f*, miracle
m; (*feeling*) émerveillement *m* // *vi*: **to ~**
whether se demander si; **to ~ at**
s'étonner de; s'émerveiller de; **to ~**
about songer à; **it's no ~ that** il n'est
pas étonnant que + *sub*; **~ful** a
merveilleux(euse); (*feeling*)
merveilleusement *m*; (+ *adjective*)
merveilleusement; (+ *vb*) à merveille.
wonky ['wɒŋkɪ] *a* (*col*) qui ne va *or* ne
marche pas très bien.
won't [wəunt] = **will not**.
woo [wu:] *vt* (*woman*) faire la cour à.
wood [wud] *n* (*timber, forest*) bois *m*; **~-**
carving *n* sculpture *f* en *or* sur bois; **~ed**
a boisé(e); **~en** a en bois; (*fig*) raide;
inexpressif(ive); **~pecker** *n* pic *m*
(*oiseau*); **~wind** *n* (MUS) bois *m*; **the**
~wind (MUS) les bois; **~work** *n*
menuiserie *f*; **~worm** *n* ver *m* du bois.
wool [wul] *n* laine *f*; **to pull the ~ over**
sb's eyes (*fig*) en faire accroire à qn;
~len, **~en** (US) a de laine; (*industry*)
lainier(ère); **~lens** *npl* lainages *mpl*; **~ly**,
~y (US) a laineux(euse); (*fig: ideas*)
confus(e).
word [wə:d] *n* mot *m*; (*spoken*) mot, parole
f; (*promise*) parole; (*news*) nouvelles *fpl* //
vt rédiger, formuler; **in other ~s** en
d'autres termes; **to break/keep one's ~**
manquer à/tenir sa parole; **I'll take your**
~ for it je vous crois sur parole; **to send**
~ of prévenir de; **~ing** *n* termes *mpl*,
langage *m*; **~y** a verbeux(euse).
wore [wɔ:*] *pt of* **wear**.
work [wə:k] *n* travail *m*; (ART, LITERATURE)
œuvre *f* // *vi* travailler; (*mechanism*)
marcher, fonctionner; (*plan etc*) marcher;
(*medicine*) faire son effet // *vt* (*clay, wood*
etc) travailler; (*mine etc*) exploiter;
(*machine*) faire marcher *or* fonctionner; **to**
be out of ~ être au chômage; **~s** *n*
(*factory*) usine *f* // *npl* (*of clock, machine*)
mécanisme *m*; **Minister/Ministry of**
W~s ministre *m*/ministère *m* des
Travaux publics; **to ~** se défaire,
se desserrer; **to ~ on** *vt fus* travailler à;
(*principle*) se baser sur; **to ~ out** *vi* (*plans*
etc) marcher // *vt* (*problem*) résoudre;
(*plan*) élaborer; **it ~s out at £100** ça fait
100 livres; **to get ~ed up** se mettre dans
tous ses états; **~able** a (*solution*)
réalisable; **~er** *n* travailleur/euse,
ouvrier/ère; **~ing class** *n* classe
ouvrière; **~ing-class** a ouvrier(ère);

~ing man *n* travailleur *m*; **in ~ing order**
en état de marche; **~man** *n* ouvrier *m*;
~manship *n* métier *m*, habileté *f*; facture
f; **~shop** *n* atelier *m*; **~-to-rule** *n* grève
f du zèle.
world [wə:ld] *n* monde *m* // *cpd*
(*champion*) du monde; (*power, war*)
mondial(e); **to think the ~ of sb** (*fig*) ne
jurer que par qn; **out of this ~** a
extraordinaire; **~ly** a de ce monde; **~-**
wide a universel(le).
worm [wə:m] *n* ver *m*.
worn [wɔ:n] *pp of* **wear** // a usé(e); **~-**
out a (*object*) complètement usé(e);
(*person*) épuisé(e).
worried ['wʌrɪd] a inquiet(ète).
worrier ['wʌrɪə*] *n* inquiet/ète.
worry ['wʌrɪ] *n* souci *m* // *vt* inquiéter //
vi s'inquiéter, se faire du souci; **~ing** a
inquiétant(e).
worse [wə:s] a pire, plus mauvais(e) //
ad plus mal // *n* pire *m*; **a change for**
the ~ une détérioration; **~n** *vt,vi*
empirer; **~ off** a moins à l'aise
financièrement; (*fig*): **you'll be ~ off this**
way ça ira moins bien de cette façon.
worship ['wə:ʃɪp] *n* culte *m* // *vt* (*God*)
rendre un culte à; (*person*) adorer; **Your**
W~ (*to mayor*) Monsieur le Maire; (*to*
judge) Monsieur le Juge; **~per** *n*
adorateur/trice; (*in church*) fidèle *m/f*.
worst [wə:st] a le(la) pire, le(la) plus
mauvais(e) // *ad* le plus mal // *n* pire *m*;
at ~ au pis aller.
worsted ['wustɪd] *n*: (**wool**) **~** laine
peignée.
worth [wə:θ] *n* valeur *f* // a: **to be ~**
valoir; **it's ~** it cela en vaut la peine; **50**
pence ~ of apples (pour) 50 pence de
pommes; **~less** a qui ne vaut rien;
~while a (*activity*) qui en vaut la peine;
(*cause*) louable; **a ~while book** un livre
qui vaut la peine d'être lu.
worthy [wə:ðɪ] a (*person*) digne; (*motive*)
louable; **~ of** digne de.
would [wud] *auxiliary vb*: **she ~ come** elle
viendrait; **he ~ have come** il serait venu;
~ you like a biscuit? voulez-vous *or*
voudriez-vous un biscuit?; **he ~ go there**
on Mondays il y allait le lundi; **~-be** a
(*pej*) soi-disant.
wound *vb* [waund] *pt, pp of* **wind** // *n,vt*
[wu:nd] *n* blessure *f* // *vt* blesser; **~ed**
in the leg blessé à la jambe.
wove [wəuv] *pt of* **weave**; **~n** *pp of*
weave.
wrangle ['ræŋgl] *n* dispute *f* // *vi* se
disputer.
wrap [ræp] *n* (*stole*) écharpe *f*; (*cape*)
pèlerine *f* // *vt* (*also*: **~ up**) envelopper;
~per *n* (*of book*) couverture *f*; **~ping**
paper *n* papier *m* d'emballage; (*for gift*)
papier cadeau.
wrath [rɔθ] *n* courroux *m*.
wreath, ~s [ri:θ, ri:ðz] *n* couronne *f*.
wreck [rɛk] *n* (*sea disaster*) naufrage *m*;
(*ship*) épave *f*; (*pej: person*) loque humaine
// *vt* démolir; (*ship*) provoquer le
naufrage de; (*fig*) briser, ruiner; **~age** *n*
débris *mpl*; (*of building*) décombres *mpl*;
(*of ship*) épave *f*.

wren [rɛn] *n* (ZOOL) roitelet *m*.

wrench [rɛntʃ] *n* (TECH) clé *f* (à écrous); (*tug*) violent mouvement de torsion; (*fig*) arrachement *m* // *vt* tirer violemment sur, tordre; **to ~ sth from** arracher qch (violemment) à *or* de.

wrestle [ˈrɛsl] *vi:* **to ~ (with sb)** lutter (avec qn); **to ~ with** (*fig*) se débattre avec, lutter contre; **~r** *n* lutteur/euse; **wrestling** *n* lutte *f*; (*also:* **all-in wrestling**) catch *m*; **wrestling match** *n* rencontre *f* de lutte (*or* de catch).

wretched [ˈrɛtʃɪd] *a* misérable; (*col*) maudit(e).

wriggle [ˈrɪgl] *n* tortillement *m* // *vi* se tortiller.

wring, *pt, pp* **wrung** [rɪŋ, rʌŋ] *vt* tordre; (*wet clothes*) essorer; (*fig*): **to ~ sth out of** arracher qch à.

wrinkle [ˈrɪŋkl] *n* (*on skin*) ride *f*; (*on paper etc*) pli *m* // *vt* rider, plisser // *vi* se plisser.

wrist [rɪst] *n* poignet *m*; **~ watch** *n* montre-bracelet *f*.

writ [rɪt] *n* acte *m* judiciaire; **to issue a ~ against sb** assigner qn en justice.

write, *pt* **wrote**, *pp* **written** [raɪt, rəʊt, ˈrɪtn] *vt,vi* écrire; **to ~ down** *vt* noter; (*put in writing*) mettre par écrit; **to ~ off** *vt* (*debt*) passer aux profits et pertes; (*depreciate*) amortir; **to ~ out** *vt* écrire; (*copy*) recopier; **to ~ up** *vt* rédiger; **~-off** *n* perte totale; **the car is a ~-off** la voiture est bonne pour la casse; **~r** *n* auteur *m*, écrivain *m*.

writhe [raɪð] *vi* se tordre.

writing [ˈraɪtɪŋ] *n* écriture *f*; (*of author*) œuvres *fpl*; **in ~** par écrit; **~ paper** *n* papier *m* à lettres.

written [ˈrɪtn] *pp. of* **write**.

wrong [rɔŋ] *a* faux(fausse); (*incorrectly chosen: number, road etc*) mauvais(e); (*not suitable*) qui ne convient pas; (*wicked*) mal; (*unfair*) injuste // *ad* faux // *n* tort *m* // *vt* faire du tort à, léser; **you are ~ to do it** tu as tort de le faire; **you are ~ about that, you've got it ~** tu te trompes; **to be in the ~** avoir tort; **what's ~?** qu'est-ce qui ne va pas?; **to go ~** (*person*) se tromper; (*plan*) mal tourner; (*machine*) tomber en panne; **~ful** a injustifié(e); **~ly** ad à tort; **~ side** *n* (*of cloth*) envers *m*.

wrote [rəʊt] *pt of* **write**.

wrought [rɔːt] *a:* **~ iron** fer forgé.

wrung [rʌŋ] *pt, pp of* **wring**.

wry [raɪ] *a* désabusé(e).

wt. *abbr of* **weight**.

X Y Z

Xmas [ˈɛksməs] *n abbr of* **Christmas**.

X-ray [ɛksˈreɪ] *n* rayon *m* X; (*photograph*) radio(graphie) *f* // *vt* radiographier.

xylophone [ˈzaɪləfəʊn] *n* xylophone *m*.

yacht [jɔt] *n* yacht *m*; voilier *m*; **~ing** *n* yachting *m*, navigation *f* de plaisance; **~sman** *n* yacht(s)man *m*.

Yank [jæŋk] *n* (*pej*) Amerloque *m/f*.

yap [jæp] *vi* (*dog*) japper.

yard [jɑːd] *n* (*of house etc*) cour *f*;

(*measure*) yard *m* (= 914 *mm*; 3 *feet*); **~stick** *n* (*fig*) mesure *f*, critère *m*.

yarn [jɑːn] *n* fil *m*; (*tale*) longue histoire.

yawn [jɔːn] *n* bâillement *m* // *vi* bâiller; **~ing** *a* (*gap*) béant(e).

yd. *abbr of* **yard(s)**.

year [jɪə*] *n* an *m*, année *f*; **every ~** tous les ans, chaque année; **to be 8 ~s old** avoir 8 ans; **~ly** *a* annuel(le) // *ad* annuellement.

yearn [jəːn] *vi:* **to ~ for sth/to do** aspirer à qch/à faire, languir après qch; **~ing** *n* désir ardent, envie *f*.

yeast [jiːst] *n* levure *f*.

yell [jɛl] *n* hurlement *m*, cri *m* // *vi* hurler.

yellow [ˈjɛləʊ] *a,n* jaune (*m*); **~ fever** *n* fièvre *f* jaune.

yelp [jɛlp] *n* jappement *m*; glapissement *m* // *vi* japper; glapir.

yeoman [ˈjəʊmən] *n:* **Y~ of the Guard** hallebardier *m* de la garde royale.

yes [jɛs] *ad* oui; (*answering negative question*) si // *n* oui *m*.

yesterday [ˈjɛstədɪ] *ad,n* hier (*m*).

yet [jɛt] *ad* encore; déjà // *cj* pourtant, néanmoins; **it is not finished ~** ce n'est pas encore fini *or* toujours pas fini; **must you go just ~?** dois-tu déjà partir?; **the best ~** le meilleur jusqu'ici *or* jusque-là; **as ~** jusqu'ici, encore; **a few days ~** encore quelques jours.

yew [juː] *n* if *m*.

Yiddish [ˈjɪdɪʃ] *n* yiddish *m*.

yield [jiːld] *n* production *f*, rendement *m*; rapport *m* // *vt* produire, rendre, rapporter; (*surrender*) céder // *vi* céder.

yodel [ˈjəʊdl] *vi* faire des tyroliennes, jodler.

yoga [ˈjəʊgə] *n* yoga *m*.

yog(h)ourt, yog(h)urt [ˈjəʊgət] *n* yaourt *m*.

yoke [jəʊk] *n* joug *m*.

yolk [jəʊk] *n* jaune *m* (d'œuf).

yonder [ˈjɔndə*] *ad* là(-bas).

you [juː] *pronoun* tu; (*polite form*) vous; (*pl*) vous; (*complement*) te,t' + *vowel*; vous; (*stressed*) toi; vous; (*one*): **fresh air does ~ good** l'air frais fait du bien; **~ never know** on ne sait jamais.

you'd [juːd] = **you had**; **you would**.

you'll [juːl] = **you will**; **you shall**.

young [jʌŋ] *a* jeune // *npl* (*of animal*) petits *mpl*; (*people*): **the ~** les jeunes, la jeunesse; **~ish** *a* assez jeune; **~ster** *n* jeune *m* (garçon *m*); (*child*) enfant *m/f*.

your [jɔː*] *a* ton(ta), *pl* tes; votre, *pl* vos.

you're [juə*] = **you are**.

yours [jɔːz] *pronoun* le(la) tien(ne), les tiens(tiennes); le(la) vôtre, les vôtres; **is it ~?** c'est à toi (*or* à vous?); **yours sincerely/faithfully** je vous prie d'agréer l'expression de mes sentiments les meilleurs/mes sentiments respectueux *or* dévoués.

yourself [jɔːˈsɛlf] *pronoun* (*reflexive*) te; vous; (*after prep*) toi; vous; (*emphatic*) toi-même; vous-même; **yourselves** *pl pronoun* vous; (*emphatic*) vous mêmes.

youth [juːθ] *n* jeunesse *f*; (*young man: pl* **~s** [juːðz]) jeune homme *m*; **~ful** *a* jeune ; de jeunesse ; juvénile ; ~ **hostel** n auberge f de jeunesse.

you've [juːv] = you have.

Yugoslav ['juːgəu'slɑːv] a yougoslave // n Yougoslave m/f.

Yugoslavia   ['juːgəu'slaːvɪə]   n Yougoslavie f.

Yule [juːl]: ~ **log** n bûche f de Noël.

zany ['zeɪnɪ] a farfelu(e), loufoque.

zeal [ziːl] n zèle m, ferveur f; empressement m; ~**ous** ['zɛləs] a zélé(e) ; empressé(e).

zebra ['ziːbrə] n zèbre m ; ~ **crossing** n passage m pour piétons.

zenith ['zɛnɪθ] n zénith m.

zero ['zɪərəu] n zéro m ; ~ **hour** n l'heure f H.

zest [zɛst] n entrain m, élan m ; zeste m.

zigzag ['zɪgzæg] n zigzag m // vi

zigzaguer, faire des zigzags.

zinc [zɪŋk] n zinc m.

Zionism ['zaɪənɪzm] n sionisme m.

zip [zɪp] n (also: ~ **fastener**, ~**per**) fermeture f éclair ® // vt (also: ~ **up**) fermer avec une fermeture éclair ®.

zither ['zɪðə*] n cithare f.

zodiac ['zəudɪæk] n zodiaque m.

zombie ['zɔmbɪ] n (fig): like a ~ l'air complètement dans les vapes, avec l'air d'un mort vivant.

zone [zəun] n zone f; (subdivision of town) secteur m.

zoo [zuː] n zoo m.

zoological [zuə'lɔdʒɪkl] a zoologique.

zoologist [zuː'ɔlədʒɪst] n zoologiste m/f.

zoology [zuː'ɔlədʒɪ] n zoologie f.

zoom [zuːm] vi: to ~ **past** passer en trombe ; ~ **lens** n zoom m, objectif m à focale variable.

acquérir *1* acquérant *2* acquis *3* acquiers, acquérons, acquièrent *4* acquérais *5* acquerrai *7* acquière

ALLER *1* allant *2* allé *3* vais, vas, va, allons, allez, vont *4* allais *5* irai *6* irais *7* aille

asseoir *1* asseyant *2* assis *3* assieds, asseyons, asseyez, asseyent *4* asseyais *5* assiérai *7* asseye

atteindre *1* atteignant *2* atteint *3* atteins, atteignons *4* atteignais *7* atteigne

AVOIR *1* ayant *2* eu *3* ai, as, a, avons, avez, ont *4* avais *5* aurai *6* aurais *7* aie, aies, ait, ayons, ayez, aient

battre *1* battant *2* battu *3* bats, bat, battons *4* battais *7* batte

boire *1* buvant *2* bu *3* bois, buvons, boivent *4* buvais *7* boive

bouillir *1* bouillant *2* bouilli *3* bous, bouillons *4* bouillais *7* bouille

conclure *1* concluant *2* conclu *3* conclus, concluons *4* concluais *7* conclue

conduire *1* conduisant *2* conduit *3* conduis, conduisons *4* conduisais *7* conduise

connaître *1* connaissant *2* connu *3* connais, connaît, connaissons *4* connaissais *7* connaisse

coudre *1* cousant *2* cousu *3* couds, cousons, cousez, cousent *4* cousais *7* couse

courir *1* courant *2* couru *3* cours, courons *4* courais *5* courrai *7* coure

couvrir *1* couvrant *2* couvert *3* couvre, couvrons *4* couvrais *7* couvre

craindre *1* craignant *2* craint *3* crains, craignons *4* craignais *7* craigne

croire *1* croyant *2* cru *3* crois, croyons, croient *4* croyais *7* croie

croître *1* croissant *2* crû, crue, crus, crues *3* croîs, croissons *4* croissais *7* croisse

cueillir *1* cueillant *2* cueilli *3* cueille, cueillons *4* cueillais *5* cueillerai *7* cueille

devoir *1* devant *2* dû, due, dus, dues

3 dois, devons, doivent *4* devais *5* devrai *7* doive

dire *1* disant *2* dit *3* dis, disons, dites, disent *4* disais *7* dise

dormir *1* dormant *2* dormi *3* dors, dormons *4* dormais *7* dorme

écrire *1* écrivant *2* écrit *3* écris, écrivons *4* écrivais *7* écrive

ÊTRE *1* étant *2* été *3* suis, es, est, sommes, êtes, sont *4* étais *5* serai *6* serais *7* sois, sois, soit, soyons, soyez, soient

FAIRE *1* faisant *2* fait *3* fais, fais, fait, faisons, faites, font *4* faisais *5* ferai *6* ferais *7* fasse

falloir *2* fallu *3* faut *4* fallait *5* faudra *7* faille

FINIR *1* finissant *2* fini *3* finis, finis, finit, finissons, finissez, finissent *4* finissais *5* finirai *6* finirais *7* finisse

fuir *1* fuyant *2* fui *3* fuis, fuyons, fuient *4* fuyais *7* fuie

joindre *1* joignant *2* joint *3* joins, joignons *4* joignais *7* joigne

lire *1* lisant *2* lu *3* lis, lisons *4* lisais *7* lise

luire *1* luisant *2* lui *3* luis, luisons *4* luisais *7* luise

maudire *1* maudissant *2* maudit *3* maudis, maudissons *4* maudissait *7* maudisse

mentir *1* mentant *2* menti *3* mens, mentons *4* mentais *7* mente

mettre *1* mettant *2* mis *3* mets, mettons *4* mettais *7* mette

mourir *1* mourant *2* mort *3* meurs, mourons, meurent *4* mourais *5* mourrai *7* meure

naître *1* naissant *2* né *3* nais, nait, naissons *4* naissais *7* naisse

offrir *1* offrant *2* offert *3* offre, offrons *4* offrais *7* offre

PARLER *1* parlant *2* parlé *3* parle, parles, parle, parlons, parlez, parlent *4* parlais, parlais, parlait, parlions, parliez, parlaient *5* parlerai, parleras, parlera, parlerons, parlerez, parleront *6* parlerais, parlerais, parlerait, parlerions, parleriez, parleraient *7*

parle, parles, parle, parlions, parliez, parlent *impératif* **parle! parlez!**

partir *1* partant *2* parti *3* pars, partons *4* partais *7* parte

plaire *1* plaisant *2* plu *3* plais, plaît, plaisons *4* plaisais *7* plaise

pleuvoir *1* pleuvant *2* plu *3* pleut, pleuvent *4* pleuvait *5* pleuvra *7* pleuve

pourvoir *1* pourvoyant *2* pourvu *3* pourvois, pourvoyons, pourvoient *4* pourvoyais *7* pourvoie

pouvoir *1* pouvant *2* pu *3* peux, peut, pouvons, peuvent *4* pouvais *5* pourrai *7* puisse

prendre *1* prenant *2* pris *3* prends, prenons, prennent *4* prenais *7* prenne

prévoir *like voir* *5* prévoirai

RECEVOIR *1* recevant *2* reçu *3* reçois, reçois, reçoit, recevons, recevez, reçoivent *4* recevais *5* recevrai *6* recevrais *7* reçoive

RENDRE *1* rendant *2* rendu *3* rends, rends, rend, rendons, rendez, rendent *4* rendais *5* rendrai *6* rendrais *7* rende

résoudre *1* résolvant *2* résolu *3* résous, résolvons *4* résolvais *7* résolve

rire *1* riant *2* ri *3* ris, rions, *4* riais *7* rie

savoir *1* sachant *2* su *3* sais, savons, savent *4* savais *5* saurai *7* sache *impératif* sache, sachons, sachez

servir *1* servant *2* servi *3* sers, servons *4* servais *7* serve

sortir *1* sortant *2* sorti *3* sors, sortons *4* sortais *7* sorte

souffrir *1* souffrant *2* souffert *3* souffre, souffrons *4* souffrais *7* souffre

suffire *1* suffisant *2* suffi *3* suffis, suffisons *4* suffisais *7* suffise

suivre *1* suivant *2* suivi *3* suis, suivons *4* suivais *7* suive

taire *1* taisant *2* tu *3* tais, taisons *4* taisais *7* taise

tenir *1* tenant *2* tenu *3* tiens, tenons, tiennent *4* tenais *5* tiendrai *7* tienne

vaincre *1* vainquant *2* vaincu *3* vaincs, vainc, vainquons *4* vainquais *7* vainque

valoir *1* valant *2* valu *3* vaux, vaut, valons *4* valais *5* vaudrai *7* vaille

venir *1* venant *2* venu *3* viens, venons, viennent *4* venais *5* viendrai *7* vienne

vivre *1* vivant *2* vécu *3* vis, vivons *4* vivais *7* vive

voir *1* voyant *2* vu *3* vois, voyons, voient *4* voyais *5* verrai *7* voie

vouloir *1* voulant *2* voulu *3* veux, veut, voulons, veulent *4* voulais *5* voudrai *7* veuille *impératif* veuillez.

LES NOMBRES

NUMBERS

un (une)/premier(ère)	1er 1 1st	one/first
deux/deuxième	2ème 2 2nd	two/second
trois/troisième	3ème 3 3rd	three/third
quatre/quatrième	4ème 4 4th	four/fourth
cinq/cinquième	5ème 5 5th	five/fifth
six/sixième	6	six/sixth
sept/septième	7	seven/seventh
huit/huitième	8	eight/eighth
neuf/neuvième	9	nine/ninth
dix/dixième	10	ten/tenth
onze/onzième	11	eleven/eleventh
douze/douzième	12	twelve/twelfth
treize/treizième	13	thirteen/thirteenth
quatorze	14	fourteen
quinze	15	fifteen
seize	16	sixteen
dix-sept	17	seventeen
dix-huit	18	eighteen
dix-neuf	19	nineteen
vingt/vingtième	20	twenty/twentieth
vingt et un/vingt-et-unième	21	twenty-one/twenty-first
vingt-deux/vingt-deuxième	22	twenty-two/twenty-second
trente/trentième	30	thirty/thirtieth
quarante	40	forty
cinquante	50	fifty
soixante	60	sixty
soixante-dix	70	seventy
soixante et onze	71	seventy-one
soixante-douze	72	seventy-two
quatre-vingts	80	eighty
quatre-vingt-un	81	eighty-one
quatre-vingt-dix	90	ninety
quatre-vingt-onze	91	ninety-one
cent/centième	100	a hundred, one hundred/hundredth
cent un/cent-unième	101	a hundred and one/hundred-and-first
trois cents	300	three hundred
trois cent un	301	three hundred and one
mille/millième	1,000	a thousand, one thousand/thousandth
cinq mille	5,000	five thousand
un million/millionième	1,000,000	a million, one million/millionth

il arrive le 7 (mai)	he's coming on the 7th (of May)
il habite au 7	he lives at number 7
au chapitre/à la page sept	chapter/page seven
il habite au 7ème (étage)	he lives on the 7th floor
il est arrivé le 7ème	he came (in) 7th
une part d'un septième	a share of one seventh

L'HEURE

THE TIME

quelle heure est-il? *c'est* or *il est* *à quelle heure?* *à*		*what time is it?* *it's* ou *it is* *(at) what time?* *at*
minuit	**00.00**	midnight
une heure (du matin)	**01.00**	one (o'clock) (a.m. *ou* in the morning), 1 a.m.
une heure dix	**01.10**	ten past one
une heure et quart, une heure quinze	**01.15**	a quarter past one, one fifteen
une heure et demie, une heure trente	**01.30**	half past one, one thirty
deux heures moins (le) quart, une heure quarante-cinq	**01.45**	a quarter to two, one forty-five
deux heures moins dix, une heure cinquante	**01.50**	ten to two, one fifty
midi, douze heures	**12.00**	twelve (o'clock), midday, noon
une heure (de l'après-midi), treize heures	**13.00**	one (o'clock) (p.m. *ou* in the afternoon)
sept heures (du soir), dix-neuf heures	**19.00**	seven (o'clock) (p.m. *ou* at night)